FILM REVIEW ANNUAL

1996
Films of 1995

FILM
REVIEW
ANNUAL

1996

Films of 1995

Film Review Publications
JEROME S. OZER, PUBLISHER

Editor: Jerome S. Ozer
Associate Editor: Richard Zlotowitz
Assistant Editor: Genant B. Sheridan

ISBN 0-89198-149-7
ISSN 0737-9080

Manufactured in the United States of America

Jerome S. Ozer, Publisher
340 Tenafly Road
Englewood, NJ 07631

PN
1995
.F465
1996

TABLE OF CONTENTS

PREFACE

FILM REVIEWS 1

INDEX 1594

PREFACE

The FILM REVIEW ANNUAL provides, in a convenient format, a single reference volume covering important reviews—*in their entirety*—of full-length films released in major markets in the United States during the course of the year.

The format of the FILM REVIEW ANNUAL has been kept as clear and simple as possible. Films are reviewed in alphabetical order by title. Following each film title, we provide production information, cast and crew listings, the running time, and the MPAA rating. The reviews for each film are arranged alphabetically by publication. Each review is identified by the name of the publication, the date of the review, the page number, and the name of the reviewer. After the last review of a film, there is an *Also reviewed* section which lists other publications in which the film was reviewed. Because of restrictions in obtaining permission, we were unable to include reviews from certain publications. However, we felt that users of the FILM REVIEW ANNUAL should have help in gaining access to those reviews. Therefore, we included the *Also reviewed* section.

At the end of the FILM REVIEW ANNUAL, we provided full listings of the major film awards, including the nominees as well as the winners.

There are eight Indexes in the FILM REVIEW ANNUAL: Cast, Producers, Directors, Screenwriters, Cinematographers, Editors, Music, and Production Crew.

We have not attempted to force a single editorial style upon the reviews for the sake of achieving consistency. The reader will readily recognize that some reviews were written under deadline pressure and that others were prepared in a more leisurely and reflective style. Some reviews were written to help the moviegoer determine whether or not to see the film. Other reviews assumed the reader had already seen the film and was interested in getting another point of view. We believe this diversity of purposes and styles is one of the major strengths of the FILM REVIEW ANNUAL.

Because of our respect for the integrity of the writers' styles, we made changes from the original only where absolutely necessary. These changes were confined to typographical errors in the original review and errors in the spelling of names. When the reviewer made a reference to another film, we inserted the name of that film. Otherwise the reviews remain as written. British spelling used in English publications has been kept.

We have tried to make the FILM REVIEW ANNUAL pleasurable to read as well as useful for scholars and students of film, communications, social and cultural history, sociology, and also for film enthusiasts. We, the editors, would appreciate your suggestions about how we might make subsequent editions of the FILM REVIEW ANNUAL even more useful.

FILM REVIEWS

ACE VENTURA: WHEN NATURE CALLS

A Warner Bros. release of a Morgan Creek production. *Executive Producer:* Gary Barber. *Producer:* James G. Robinson. *Director:* Steve Oedekerk. *Screenplay:* Steve Oedekerk. *Director of Photography:* Donald E. Thorin. *Editor:* Malcolm Campbell and Paul Cichocki. *Music:* Robert Folk. *Music Editor:* Jeff Carson and J.J. George. *Sound:* Brian Paccassi, Stacy F. Brownrigg, David Husby and (music) Dennis Sands. *Sound Editor:* Michael Hilkene. *Casting:* Ferne Cassel. *Production Designer:* Stephen J. Lineweaver. *Art Director:* Christopher A. Nowak. *Set Designer:* Jef B. Adams, Jr., Adele Plauche, and Andrew Menzies. *Set Decorator:* Derek R. Hill. *Special Effects:* Mike Vezina. *Visual Effects:* April Lawrence. *Costumes:* Elsa Zamparelli. *Make-up:* Sheryl Leigh Ptak. *Stunt Coordinator:* Rick Barker and J.J. Makaro. *Running time:* 105 minutes. *MPAA Rating:* PG-13.

CAST: Jim Carrey (Ace Ventura); Ian McNeice (Fulton Greenwall); Simon Callow (Vincent Cadby); Maynard Eziashi (Ouda); Bob Gunton (Burton Quinn); Sophie Okonedo (The Princess); Tommy Davidson (Tiny Warrior); Adewalé (Hitu); Danny D. Daniels (Wachootoo Witch Doctor); Sam Motoana Phillips (Wachootoo Chief); Ramon Standifer (Wachati Chief); Andrew Steel (Mick Katie); Bruce Spence (Gahjii); Thomas Grunke (Derrick McCane); Arsenio "Sonny" Trinidad (Ashram Monk); Kristen Norton (Pompous Woman); Michael Reid MacKay (Skinny Husband); Kayla Allen (Airplane Stewardess); Ken Kirzinger (Helicopter Pilot); Dev Kennedy (Dad Tourist); Patti Tippo (Mom Tourist); Sabrinah Christie (Girl Tourist); Warren Sroka (Boy Tourist).

LOS ANGELES TIMES, 11/10/95, Calendar/p. 1, Kenneth Turan

A perpetual motion machine. When a film makes money, it's a foregone conclusion that its star will be rolled over into another one just like the other one.

So here comes Jim Carrey, hero of "Ace Ventura: Pet Detective," complete with his jet-stream pompadour and Hawaiian shirts, back trying to make the world safe for animals and amusing for that audience segment that likes its humor keyed to bodily functions.

Since making that first "Ace," Carrey has had an impressive string of hits, including "The Mask," "Dumb and Dumber" and "Batman Forever," and it's inevitable that his trademark demented persona does not feel quite as fresh here as it has on previous occasions.

Yet, there is also little doubt that when it comes to extreme physical humor, Carrey is remarkably gifted, a throwback to the vintage antics of Jerry Lewis or even the slapstick gang of silent comedy. Capable of twisting his face into wind-tunnel contortions and thrusting his body into outrageous situations, he is the new model wild and crazy guy, out of control and loving it.

And those who venture into "When Nature Calls" will find at least a few moments of amusement, most of them impossible to describe because they are so dependent on Carrey's out-there physicality. Try to imagine him conscientiously spitting up dinner far a baby bird and carefully wiping off its beak, or straining to escape from the rear-end of a stealth rhino. It's dumb and dumber, but it's also hard not to laugh at.

Most of "When Nature Calls," however, is so flat it's hard to stay awake. Written and directed by Steve Oedekerk, an old stand-up pal of Carrey's making his feature debut, the film has the hit-and-miss quality of a weak stand-up act, with a rapid fire delivery attempting to make up for the lack of consistent humor.

"Nature's" opening sequence, however, is a gem. A clever parody of the Sylvester Stallone-starring "Cliffhanger," it has Ace inching up a mountain in a daring attempt to rescue a raccoon stranded after a plane crash, a climb that comes to a bad end when a buckle gives way and the raccoon plummets to its demise.

Broken in spirit by this tragedy, Ace retreats to a Tibetan monastery to repair his soul. He's found there by Fulton Greenwall (Ian McNeice), who entices him out with an African assignment. Find a sacred animal and prevent a war between a pair of neighboring tribes, the Wachatis and the Wachootoos.

As those two names make obvious, this is very much a cartoon Africa, an out-of-date caricature of the continent complete with a nasty British counsel (Simon Callow) and comic-opera natives in elaborate costumes. In fact, the film's entire plot would be completely at home as a vehicle for Abbott and Costello.

Carrey is generally funny as he comes to grips with the fact that the missing sacred animal is a great white bat, the one kind of animal ("a filthy flying weasel") that is his weakness. Still, it is difficult not to agree with a tribal princess (Sophie Okonedo) when she tells Ace, "You make me smile, yet I am troubled."

Because if almost anything that Carrey does is at least a little bit funny, not enough effort is put into making sure that his material is always as good as it could be. And, given that his comic persona is not exactly cerebral, making a smart film with Carrey as its star could be quite a challenge. Even for Ace Ventura.

NEW YORK POST, 11/10/95, p. 43, Thelma Adams

"Ace Ventura: When Nature Calls" won't let Jim Carrey fans down.

In the follow-up to the mammoth hit "Ace Ventura: Pet Detective," a silly riff on the absurd occupation of a detective who recovers lost pets, Carrey takes his newfound clout and moolah all the way to Africa. The sequel's key is location, location, location.

"When Nature Calls" starts off with a cliffhanger—a poke in the ribs to Sylvester Stallone's over-produced actioners. High in the Himalayas, Ventura loses a raccoon in a daring rescue attempt. The tragedy sends the pet detective to an ashram, where he becomes Zen Ventura (a halo of white butterflies zipping around his head).

When colonial cliché Fulton Greenwall (Ian McNeice) presses the detective back into service, Ventura's fellow monks are ecstatic to see him go. He's as annoying to them as he is to us—and that's the joke. We're laughing at Ventura, not with Jim Carrey, the butt of the jest, gets the last laugh, pocketing our money. He has learned one lesson from the Zen masters: a rude belly laugh can be spiritually cleansing.

On to Africa! At the bequest of British consul Vincent Cadby (sensitive to critics, are we ?), played by Merchant/Ivory regular Simon Callow (look what success can buy!), Ventura must find a sacred animal in order to keep two tribes of African natives from mutual annihilation.

The animal turns out to be a great white bat. Despite Ventura's affinity for animals—the delinquent Dr. Doolittle is both a politically correct animal activist and an offensive rude boy—he draws the line at bats. "Filthy flying weasel," is how Ventura describes the winged beast before following a trail of guano, red herrings and incidental virgins to the movie's conclusion.

With a glossy, bouncy jollity, "When Nature Calls" dishes up jungle movie cliches at a frenetic pace. Writer/director Steve Oedekerk provides Carrey with ample opportunities to bounce off the frame in a series of set pieces: The natives test his manhood (he's found wanting but funny), the colonials test his patience and he rides to the rescue on an ostrich.

Like Ventura's hairstyle, which rises seven inches above his scalp, Carrey is over-the-top.

The elastic comic has become the poster boy for the dumbing down of America. His Ventura character—basically 5-year-old boy on crystal meth with a teen's testosterone—is firmly in touch with the nation's inner child.

As Ace would say, "Spank you very much."

NEWSDAY, 11/10/95, Part II/p. B7, Jack Mathews

Jim Carrey's wildly over-the-top physical comedy is an acquired taste and I'm afraid I've acquired it. Didn't want to, couldn't help it.

It started, of course, with "Ace Venture: Pet Detective," a film I avoided seeing until its office receipts surpassed the gross national product of the Balkan states. Critics, whose task it is to define their movie experiences, found Carrey's animated narcissism and flatulent, adolescent vulgarity unworthy of viewing even by the animals in the movie. And audiences, having to answer to no one, howled like baboons.

That was just last year, before "The Mask" and "Dumb and Dumber" completed Carrey's meteoric rise to superstardom, before his turn as the Riddler in this summer's "Batman 3" guaranteed that tired series another episode or two. And now, with indecent haste, he returns in the first sequel to "Ace Ventura," part two bearing the subtitle "When Nature Calls."

My determination not to laugh at Carrey in this particularly juvenile role lasted only a few seconds into the opening scene, when he pauses while scaling a vertical rock mountain and regurgitates a meal directly into the beak of a begging baby bird. It's a gesture that is totally unexpected, a little disgusting, physically weird and amiably nutty all at the same time, sort of like Carrey himself.

"When Nature Calls," made without the burden of having to sell Carrey's shtick, is a much better movie. Writer-director Steve Oedekerk, a standup comedian who has known Carrey since they were both honing their acts at improv clubs in Los Angeles, created the thinnest pretext of a story, just enough to get Carrey into a strange world and cut loose with 90 minutes worth of physical comedy.

Unlike so many comedy sequels which attempt to duplicate the original's success by repeating its jokes, "When Nature Calls" flies off into a completely different environment. Oedekerk and Carrey know the terrain, and buoyed by the acceptance of Carrey's style of visual puns and non sequiturs, turn this exotic setting into his playground stage.

The movie opens in the Himalayas with a parody of the opening sequence of the Sylvester Stallone thriller "Cliffhanger." You remember Stallone being traumatized by the loss of a friend he was trying to save while the friend was dangling from a wire over a river gorge? Well, Ace is trying to rescue a raccoon, and his failure sends him into a meditative funk in a Buddhist temple in Tibet.

It is there that an emissary for a British consul in Africa finds Ace and hires him to locate a sacred white bat upon whose fate rests the fate of the Bonai Province. Don't ask. The purpose is to get Ace on a case, and to drive everyone a little nuts in the process. Putting up with him in the jungle are the consul general (Simon Callow), a snob with ulterior motives for hiring him, his avuncular emissary (Ian McNeice), and the various leaders, warriors and princesses of the tribes he encounters.

Critics, myself included, have been quick to compare Carrey to Jerry Lewis and predict great things for him in France. But there is a hipness and audience awareness behind Carrey's cartoon facade that makes him far more enjoyable. He's going to have to add some moves if he doesn't want his luck to run out (Lewis was still sticking straws in his nose the last time I saw him in a movie), but for now, Carrey seems to be drawing only aces.

SIGHT AND SOUND, 1/96, p. 34, Leslie Felperin

After tragically failing to save a racoon during a dangerous mountain rescue Ace Ventura, a detective who finds lost or stolen animals, enrolls in an ashram. He is persuaded to take on a new case on behalf of the British Consul General, Vincent Cadby in the African province of Bonai. Ace must find the sacred animal of the Wachati tribe, a Great White Bat, so that it may be given as a dowry when the Wachati Chief's daughter weds the head warrior of the Wachootoo tribe. If the bat is not recovered, a war will break out between the two tribes.

After enjoying the hospitality of the Wachati, whose food and economy centres on the use of bat guano, Ace and his trusty sidekick monkey, Spike, come to suspect that safari park officer Burton Quinn is involved in the sacred bat's abduction. However, under Ace's absurd torture, Quinn confesses that, though he tried to steal the bat, somebody else had beaten him to it.

Someone tries to immobilise Ace with one of the poisoned darts common to the Wachootoo tribe. Ace, Spike, and their Wachati guide Ouda confront the Wachootoo, but after battling the Wachootoo's head warrior and losing, Ace realises that the earlier darts were fakes. He traces these to two Australian hunters who have stolen the sacred bat, but he is thwarted in his attempt to recover the stolen chiropteran. After astrally projecting his spirit to the ashram to ask his guru for advice, Ace realises that it was Cadby who ordered the theft of the bat in order to provoke a war between the two tribes and wrest control of the profitable guano economy. Ace confronts Cadby who confesses. When the Consul tries to seize Ace, he summons all the beasts of the jungle and in the ensuing melee caused by the stampede, Ace restores the bat in time to avert the tribal war. While trying to escape Cadby is besieged by a Silverback Gorilla on heat. The wedding goes ahead, but both tribes set upon Ace when it is discovered that he has deflowered the Wachati princess.

There was something instantly appealing about Jim Carrey when he made his debut as a star in *Ace Ventura Pet Detective*. While many comedians have been likened to Jerry Lewis, in Carrey's case the comparison is justified: like Lewis he is graceful and elastic of frame, blessed with near-perfect comic timing, and excels at making slightly repulsive *schlemiels* oddly likeable. But context is all, and just as Lewis' goofball persona was most engaging when contrasted with Dean Martin's oily *roué*, Carrey's aggressively manic qualities are best tempered by animal foils. This is why the first *Ace Ventura* film grew on one so quickly—how could one fail to like a man, no matter how rubbery and obnoxious, who likes animals that much?

In almost every film since then, Carrey has been paired with a bestial companion, and so what is disappointing about *Ace Ventura When Nature Calls* is its curious paucity of animals. The first *Ace Ventura* film opened strikingly with Ace rescuing a little dog from a thief and was a *tour de force* of slapstick mixed with sweetness. This film gets off to a similar start by having a fetching racoon die heartbreakingly in a parody of *Cliffhanger*. However, from there on in animals are relegated to only minor cameo roles—as is the case with a bat who should be centrally important but whose main function is really just to provide an opportunity for a serious of intertextual jokes about *Batman*. So much alone in the spotlight, Carrey stands out as a cruel, slightly arrogant figure with his pelvis athrust and his cocky smile full of bared gums and smarm. There's been a streak of cruelty in all Carrey's characters so far, and here, torturing a man by scraping his cutlery on a plate, there's less of a sense of soft-heartedness to offset the sadism. Perhaps his fees were so high that not enough money was left over for animal wranglers, or maybe he just doesn't want to be upstaged anymore. It tells you a lot that the film's best gag has Ace being 'born' out of a plastic rhinoceros (long story, don't ask). Hollywood's a cruel, man-eat-dog kind of town.

Ace Ventura When Nature Calls is clearly aimed at pre-pubescent teenage boys and those who might share this age group's sense of humour and interests. For this constituency, Ace is a heroic better self, attractive to girls but still reliant on masturbation, fond of monster-tyred off-road vehicles, and brave enough to insult guests at a fancy party by sticking glacé cherries in his nose, like a tall child staying up past his bedtime. Studded *Naked Gun*-like with mini movie spoofs (including *Deliverance, King Solomon's Mines,* and all of Carrey's previous vehicles) the film is no less and no more than a battery of precision tooled gags (my favourite is Ace, always the big kid at heart, insisting on sending his Slinky down the huge flight of steps that descend from the mountaintop ashram). Director Steve Oedekerk, whose first film this is, keeps his star centered in every shot, cuts away constantly during other people's dialogue to Ace's antic grimaces and pranks, and oversees the editing so that things nip nimbly along. A star-vehicle right down to the last molecule of its celluloid, the rest of the cast are given few funny lines or much to work with. Only the appropriately oleaginous Simon Callow (whose character's name, Vincent Cadby, sounds like a dig at that of *The New York Times* film critic's, Vincent Canby) stand out from the herd of supporting humans.

When Nature Calls has not a shred of compunction about stereotyping African tribespeople, but then given that it's dealing in comedy as broad as a elephant's backside, why should it? Nevertheless, given what is going on in Nigeria and Rwanda at the moment, having the British Consul conspiring to steal natural resources by starting a tribal war is unintentionally a trifle tasteless. But then, who would be naive enough to expect a Jim Carrey film to be tasteful?

TIME, 11/27/95, p. 92, Richard Corliss

The weekend before last, moviegoers spent $37.8 million to see the new Jim Carey comedy, *Ace Ventura: When Nature Calls*—more money than the combined take of Nos. 2 through 20 on the box-office list. Few films have achieved such instant dominance, and certainly none so awful as this sequel, about the pet detective's trip to Africa to find a precious white bat and prevent a war between two backward tribes. Nearly the best one can say of *Ace 2* is that it's blithely, ceaselessly racist.

In *The Mask, Dumb & Dumber* and *Batman Forever*, the star created a maniacally precise comic style. Here—well, he works hard. In the 105 minutes of *Ace 2*, Carrey rides an ostrich; feeds an eaglet mouth to mouth; emerges from the anus of a mechanical rhino; makes his eyebrows move like kooky caterpillars; bends over and utters the Tarzan cry through his rear; sneezes on, spits at and blows paper wads into the faces of various African men; and sings *Chitty Chitty Bang Bang* several times more than is absolutely necessary.

This review is not the cry of a prude. Frankly, we don't care if a joke's funny as long as it's dirty. But in switching writer-directors, from the first film's Tom Shadyac to Steve Oedekerk, Carrey lost a clever farceur and got what Ace would call a la-*hoo*-za-*her* (loser). The star plays more than ever to himself; the cast stands around starched and embarrassed, like white-tie judges at a wet-T shirt contest. Wearying, stupefying, dumber than dumb, *When Nature Calls* would be a career ender for Carrey—except that a zillion people have seen it. Stop this, folks. It'll only encourage him.

VILLAGE VOICE, 11/21/95, Film Special/p. 22, Gary Dauphin

Jim Carrey was discovered on *In Living Color*, a rubber-limbed white guy goofing through the wilds of black television, so there's a certain perverse symmetry to his *Ace Ventura* sequel being set in a fictional African country ("Nibia" to be exact). The plot follows the franchise's established pet-detective trajectory: Lured out of retirement in a Zen monastery (Ace retreats there after the film's high point, a snafued raccoon-rescue shot just like the opening of *Cliffhanger*), our stone-freak hero makes the trip to Nibia to find a kidnapped bat sacred to two warring tribes, this on the eve of a peacemaking wedding. The film's "native humor" is as old as Bud and Lou's *Africa Screams*, only shifted a few degrees here by more recent comedy (lifting for instance, the *In Living Color* skit where a "friendly" native deliberately mistranslates an "I come in peace" speech). Ace solves the case of course, talking out his butt and hawking monster loogies along the road to uncovering a European plot to seize the natives only natural resource (bat guano), and even gets to bed down the native princess (discreetly offscreen, naturally).

Such details out of the way, the only two questions worth asking then are "is it funnier" and "is it racist?" The two are actually related for me in that I have a problem getting upset by anything this stupid. Carrey is still very funny to watch, but by this point his shtick has settled into pure mechanics, his movie-mad riffs (*Star Trek! Night of the Hunter! Marathon Man! Trading Places! The Mask!*) often only as interesting as watching someone recite a cable schedule while doing back flips. Contrary to popular belief, what Carrey does with his voice and body requires constant physical control, and control is precisely what this film sorely lacks. Whether this is because Carrey's guaranteed $20 million makes him a difficult man to say no to, or because fictional Africa is where white guys go to get loose, I really can't say. Eitherway, it's no surfin' safari.

Also reviewed in:
CHICAGO TRIBUNE, 11/10/95, Friday/p. C, Michael Wilmington
NEW YORK TIMES, 11/10/95, p. C8, Janet Maslin
VARIETY, 11/13-19/95, p. 53, Leonard Klady
WASHINGTON POST, 11/10/95, p. F6, Rita Kempley
WASHINGTON POST, 11/10/95, Weekend/p. 45, John F. Kelly

ACROSS THE SEA OF TIME

A Sony Pictures Classics release of a Columbia Pictures and Sony New Technologies presentation. *Executive Producer:* Andrew Gellis. *Producer:* Stephen Low. *Director:* Stephen Low. *Screenplay:* Andrew Gellis. *Director of Photography:* Andrew Kitzanuk. *Editor:* James Lahti. *Music:* John Barry. *Sound:* Peter Thillaye. *Casting:* Avy Kaufman. *Production Designer:* Charley Beal. *Costumes:* Cynthia Flynt. *Running time:* 53 minutes. *MPAA Rating:* G.

CAST: Peter Reznik (Tomas); John McDonough (Freighter Chief); Avi Hoffman (Seaman/Bow); Victor Steinbach (Seaman/Pilot); Peter Boyden (Con Ed Worker); Philip Levy (Hot Dog Vendor); Nick Muglia (Policeman); Abby Lewis (Julia Minton); Matt Malloy (Wall Street Businessman); Luigi Petrozza (Pizza Pie Man); Bernard Ferstenberg (Pickle Vendor); Robert Buckley (Socialite); Donald Trump (Himself); Patrick Flynn (Bartender).

LOS ANGELES TIMES, 7/3/96, Calendar/p. 1, Kevin Thomas

"Across the Sea of Time," in Imax 3-D, imagines a young Russian stowaway (Peter Reznik) landing in New York in hopes of finding family members. All he has is a clutch of Stereopticon photos taken in the early 20th century by a relative who included them in copious, platitudinous letters home to his parents. Although adults will see this tale, written by executive producer Andrew Gellis, as the obvious contrivance it is, the boy and his adventures in Manhattan will offer wide and thrilling identification for youngsters.

Still, adults won't complain too much considering the awesome visual experience of "Across the Sea of Time." An Imax veteran, director Stephen Low knows how to make best use of the medium's immense scale and depth and how to incorporate 3-D into the process to approach a near-virtual-reality experience. In the 51-minute film's opening sequence, we're instantly made to feel that we're right there in the dingy hold of a Russian freighter with Reznik's intrepid 11-year-old Tomas.

The use of vintage black-and-white Stereopticon slides is inspired and heightens our sense of what it would be like to be thrust into the midst of turn-of-the-century Lower East Side's bustling Hester Street and, in a remarkable sequence, what it was like to be excavating for the subway system. Throughout, Low matches vintage Stereopticon views with contemporary ones. Most vistas are startlingly different, but a few are remarkably unchanged.

Not surprisingly, views of the subway system are followed by a breathtaking present-day ride on a subway train. Of course, Low takes on a Coney Island roller-coaster ride so dizzying you might have to look away. And wouldn't you know that Tomas' attempt to match sky lines takes him to the top of a skyscraper so that he might peer down to the street far, far below? Essentially, "Across the Sea of Time" is a glorious travelogue framed by the thinnest and most sentimental of stories, but most everybody is likely to go along with it.

Although assuredly a crowd-pleaser, Ben Burtt's 40-minute "Special Effects" plays like a promo for George Lucas' Industrial Light & Magic, which is preparing the "Star Wars Trilogy Special Edition" to mark the 20th birthday of the original "Star Wars" next year.

There's a nod to past accomplishments, all the way back to Georges Méliès' "A Trip to the Moon" (1902) and an elaborate re-creation of the downfall of King Kong (in San Francisco instead of Manhattan).

The emphasis, however, is strongly on the present and the upcoming: e.g., the intricate staging of an alien attack on the White House in "Independence Day" and Shaquille O'Neal's appearing to bicycle through the sky in "Kazaam." Although the sheer scale and depth of the Imax image naturally intensifies everything on its immense screen, "Special Effects" in itself doesn't seem to make much special use of the Imax format.

Special effects have become so technical that there's not much sense of fun-spoiling secrets being given away, although we do learn that "Independence Day's" spaceships, 3 miles wide and larger, could in reality probably be squeezed into a two-car garage.

Unintentionally, however, "Special Effects" makes us think about the zillions upon zillions of dollars being spent to make images of death and destruction look ever more convincing and spectacular. And when it deals with Animatronics, we discover that a docile zoo elephant was studied meticulously by experts to create a scary elephant stampede for the recent "Jumanji." It's enough to make you glad that Imax in 3-D is a full year away in Exposition Park.

NEW YORK POST, 10/21/95, p. 17, Bill Hoffmann

I'll start off with the good news about "Across the Sea of Time."

Back, at the turn of the century, cameramen experimented with a revolutionary new process called three-dimensional photography.

The early 3D black-and-white snapshots that resulted were the rage for a few years before going the way of the Edsel and being all but forgotten.

Thankfully, director Stephen Low has dusted off dozens of the prints shot in New York City around 1916 and shows them off on the huge IMAX screen.

Magnified hundreds of times their original size, these breathtaking pictures take on a magical life of their own—treating us to some never-before-seen views of a Big Apple long past.

There are magnificent shots of workers dangerously dangling from partly constructed skyscrapers; grime-covered diggers building a subway tunnel; formally dressed strollers in Central Park; thousands of bathers cramming the beach at Coney Island; and poignant street scenes on the Lower East Side.

The director contrasts these old stills with striking new footage of 1990s New York in full-color 3D glory.

Much is gimmicky: a dizzying ride on the Cyclone, kicking chorus girls and flames dancing into your lap.

But the tricks are offset by some truly striking aerial shots that prove what a true architectural miracle our fair city really is.

The bad news is that the filmmakers didn't trust the source material enough to just leave it be as a straight documentary.

Instead they've added a dumb, syrupy plot in which a 11-year-old Russian boy travels to Manhattan to track down the family of his ancestors who emigrated to America 100 years earlier.

The boy (Peter Reznik) uses a box of 3D slides his long-dead father supposedly took 80 years earlier to aid in his search. It's a threadbare plot that's annoying, unnecessary and unfortunately impossible to ignore.

Still, anybody who loves this city—and even those who only tolerate it—should rush to see "Across the Sea of Time" for its unique and awe-inspiring view of the world's greatest metropolis.

NEWSDAY, 10/23/95, Part II/p. B7, Joseph Gelmis

At the precise moment that Billy Joel's mellow voice began flooding Sony's cavernous Imax Theater with his "I'm in a New York State of Mind," the singer and his pubescent daughter were beginning a slow single-file, trek through an immense gauntlet of hundreds of seats uninterrupted by aisles.

The tune was part, of a taped medley of New York-themed songs played on the theater's speakers before a preview screening of "Across the Sea of Time." The sound stopped father and daughter in their tracks. The slim, dark-haired girl turned and looked wide-eyed at her dad for a long moment. Then they grinned at each other and continued on to seats in the center of the theater, the best place from which to view the colossal 80-foot-high, 100-foot-wide screen. Several songs later, the houselights dimmed, everyone donned a 3-D headset and the show began.

Watching "Across the Sea of Time," it soon became obvious that the Long Islander who composed and recorded the most famous I Love New York ballad in decades and his daughter were not just celebrities invited to the preview but the target audience as well. The movie, a tribute to the Big Apple whose central character is an 11-year-old boy, is designed to be especially appealing to schoolchildren, tourists and people who love the city.

"Across the Sea of Time" may also be for you, if you're in the mood for a change from conventional multiplex fare. It's a unique spectacle that uses 21st-Century technology to illuminate the Imperial City's past and to immerse us viscerally in offfbeat approaches to its current sights and sounds.

Imax is, quite simply, the Rolls-Royce of film exhibition. Its film frame is 10 times the size of a standard 35-mm. frame, and its rock-steady projection system produces moviedom's biggest and most detailed picture. Its surround-sound system perfectly reproduces what the filmmaker intended you to hear. And it's worth a trip to Manhattan's state-of-the-art Sony Imax theater just to experience what is arguably the coolest illusion of three dimensions yet achieved by a Hollywood-commissioned movie. The amazing 3-D effect is created by liquid-crystal display glasses whose right and left lenses are alternately opened and shut at high speed by wireless signals from twin projectors.

Director Stephen Low and writer-producer Andrew Gellis artfully mix sensory thrills—knock-your-socks-off helicopter footage of Manhattan's canyons, a high-velocity trip through subway tunnels and a dizzying Coney Island roller-coaster ride—with poignant historical stereo photographs of arriving immigrants, teeming city streets, and the first skyscrapers and subways under construction. The old photos were originally seen with wooden stereoptican viewers. The filmmakers evoke potent emotional resonance by juxtaposing them with contemporary footage of the city's icons. New York, the de facto star of "Across the Sea of Time," is haunted by its past (a feeling subtly augmented by sounds fed directly to the viewer's ears via supplemental stereo speakers in the 3-D headset).

The narrative that connects the tour of New York past and present is, essentially, a fairy tale. A Russian boy stows away on a freighter, jumps ship in the harbor, climbs ashore on Ellis Island, takes a ferry to Manhattan, spends two days wandering around searching for relatives. He carries with him a stereoptican and letters written home by an immigrant great-uncle between 1901 and 1916. The boy's odyssey is meant to remind us that New York has always been a city of immigrants.

VILLAGE VOICE, 10/24/95, p. 86, Gary Dauphin

Across the Sea of Time is the new Sony IMAX 3-D extravaganza. It tells the story of a young Russian boy in New York alone and in search of long-lost relatives, his only map a collection of turn-of-the-century stereoscope images of the city and its immigrants sent back by his great uncle. Using this slight premise and its treasure trove of found materials, *Across* creates a fluid portrait of the city. Familiar images are suddenly made new by the 3-D effects; crowded street scenes find latter-day echoes in sweeping contemporary vistas. The sights might be a bit touristy, but they reminded me of the physical grandeur of a hometown I have been seeing mostly from subway level lately.

Also reviewed in:
NEW YORK TIMES, 10/20/95, p. C8, Janet Maslin
VARIETY, 10/30-11/5/95, p. 72, Godfrey Cheshire

ADDICTION, THE

An October Films release. *Executive Producer:* Russell Simmons and Preston Holmes. *Producer:* Denis Hann and Fernando Sulichin. *Director:* Abel Ferrara. *Screenplay:* Nicholas St. John. *Director of Photography:* Ken Kelsch. *Editor:* Mayin Lo. *Music:* Joe Delia. *Production Designer:* Charles Lagola. *Costumes:* Melinda Eshelman. *Running time:* 84 minutes. *MPAA Rating:* Not Rated.

CAST: Robert Castle (Narrator); Lili Taylor (Kathleen Conklin); Edie Falco (Jean); Annabella Sciorra (Casanova); Michael Fella (Cop); Paul Calderon (Professor); Louis A. Katz (Doctor); Leroy Johnson and Fred Williams (Homeless Victims); Avron Coleman (Cellist); Fredro Starr (Black); Jamel "RedRum" Simmons (Black's Friend); Kathryn Erbe (Anthropology Student); Lisa Casillo (Mary); Frank Aquilino (Delivery Man); Christopher Walken (Peina); Nicholas Decegli (Cabby); Michael Imperioli (Missionary); Jay Julien (Dean); Chuck Jeffries (Bartender); Ed Conna (Waiter); Nancy Ellen Anzalone (Dress Victim); Heather Bracken (Nurse); Robert Castle (Priest).

LOS ANGELES TIMES, 10/6/95, Calendar/p. 8, Kevin Thomas

[The following review by Kevin Thomas appeared in a slightly different form in
NEWSDAY, 10/4/95, Part II/p. B7.]

"The Addiction" is unlike any vampire picture you've ever seen—but then it was directed by Abel Ferrara, poet of urban violence, from a script by Nicholas St. John so imaginative that it gets away with being as intellectual as it is visceral.

Wisely, Ferrara shot it in harsh, high-contrast black and white, for at moments it's such a blood bath that seeing it in color would be inconceivable. For Lili Taylor, that most distinctive of actresses—at once vulnerable and nervy—it affords an amazingly rich, ambitious role.

Taylor plays Kathleen, a New York University grad student in philosophy soon to receive her doctorate. We meet her as she's watching a slide show presentation of the My Lai massacre, a horror she regards as a matter of collective U.S. guilt, not just that of Lt. William Calley and his men.

As Kathleen walks home to her East Village basement apartment, a woman in an elegant evening gown (Annabella Sciorra) approaches her, greets her in a friendly manner and, with shocking swiftness, yanks her down a dark staircase and bites her in the neck. After much sickness, diagnosed as anemia, Kathleen realizes she has in fact become a vampire with a thirst for blood that will not be denied.

The gist of this jolting film is how Kathleen's new state alters forever her view of the universe. What she discovers is that evil is the most addictive drug of all. The film suggests that unless we recognize the capacity for evil within ourselves and resist it with all our might, and that unless we all take responsibility for the evil in the world, there will be no way of stopping its remorseless spread.

Although Ferrara dares to be intellectual in a manner virtually unique in commercial American cinema, he nevertheless doesn't forget how to entertain in the gory, bravura manner associated with him. Although it undeniably helps, you don't have to know your Heidegger from Hamburger Helper to enjoy "The Addiction" as a grisly yet unusual thriller of the supernatural.

Alternately lovely and ravaged-looking, Taylor carries the picture capably with an assist from Christopher Walken as a brutally tough-minded vampire far more experienced than she—"Eternity is a long time, get used to it" is his terse advice—and from Edie Falco as her friend and fellow student Jean, who has a cool, rational detachment that Kathleen now sees as obtuse.

"The Addiction" is no more for the faint of heart than any other film directed by Ferrara, whose concern for redemption increases with each new picture. It's tough, gritty, darkly humorous—and made with the hard-edged, get-on-with-it spirit and aura of danger that characterizes so much of Manhattan itself.

NEW YORK POST, 10/4/95, p. 35, Thelma Adams

"Look sin in the face and tell it to go," a thirsty vampire challenges her quaking victim. Meet Kathleen (Lili Taylor), philosophy student and recently-converted fang-hound.

In Abel Ferrara's latest movie, "The Addiction," vampires walk the streets of lower Manhattan, the physical manifestation of society's lust for blood and violence. Shot largely on location in and around New York University, the silken black-and-white photography gives an otherworldly glow to familiar pizza hang-outs, cafes and alleyways.

Ferrara's bloodsuckers are the sons and daughters of Friedrich Nietszche; this must be the only movie to boast a soundtrack that ranges from rap to a cut written by the German philosopher himself. In one scene, Kathleen stares into the bathroom mirror where she casts no reflection. What could be a more perfect or darkly funny example of Jean-Paul Sartre's "Being and Nothingness"?

The undead are also "living" proof that evil exists. As in Ferrara's "Bad Lieutenant," the movie has a strong Catholic dimension: God and the devil battle for lost souls on New York sidewalks. In Ferrara's vision, the devil is a mugger and God, at first, appears to be a jaded policeman.

For Ferrara and his long-time collaborator, screen-writer Nicholas St. John, vampirism is also a metaphor for substance abuse. Kathleen begins as a grad student who expresses moral outrage—at such historical atrocities as My Lai—but she is frozen in academic life, completely untried.

One dark night Kathleen is returning to her basement digs to chip away at her Ph.D. thesis when Casanova (Annabella Sciorra, cast against type) accosts her. Given the same choice, she later offers her victims to "just say no" to the dark side, Kathleen succumbs with barely a whimper. Casanova turns Kathleen on to the other side.

Before long, the shy grad student becomes a jugular junkie. She roams the streets, preying on the homeless, young black men, taxi drivers, lonely students—any stray sheep she can separate from the crowd. Drinking blood temporarily solves the mind-body problem, clarifying her mind, strengthening her body, creating a link between her philosophical theories and her actions.

The petite Taylor ("Short Cuts") brings a quiet intensity to a role tailor-made to her strengths as an actress. She has the capacity to project intelligence, emotional turmoil, fragility and strength, using a soft, smoky voice that commands the audience to lean forward to listen carefully.

And like the ghoul she plays, Taylor has the capacity to transform herself; she goes from a frumpy frail half-hidden in her own uncombed hair to a luminous presence whose beauty spills out of dark eyes and spreads over strong cheekbones to a sensuous mouth.

Taylor's addict enters the inevitable spiral. "We drink to escape our alcoholism," she says. Is there a 12-step program for bloodsuckers?

On her way to a climactic, crunchy feeding frenzy that redefines academic in-fighting, Kathy encounters bitemaster Peina. Played by Christopher Walken with a muted ferocity well-matched to Taylor, Peina is another intellectual ghoul. He suggests Kathleen read William Burroughs' "Naked Lunch," a bible of addiction lit, mentoring the philosophy student before sucking her dry.

Sciorra's seductive Casanova has a more direct approach to living the undead life: "We do evil because we are evil." Within those words are the seeds of Kathleen's salvation. Ferrara and St. John put a new twist on a genre that seems as undead as its subjects. They give the vampire an alternative to the inevitable stake-in-the-heart or burning sunlight: the healing power of re-demption.

VILLAGE VOICE, 10/10/95, p. 69, J. Hoberman

What is Abel Ferrara's addiction? Is he strung out on the realness of sleaze or the beauty of illu-sion? Or the idea that all is vanity, if not nothingness? To be innocent in Ferrara's world is to become necessarily corrupt; to fall from grace is to be eligible for the ritual of redemption.

It's a pity Ferrara didn't direct the would-be morality play, *Showgirls*. This guy actually believes in suffering. He really seems to think there's such thing as mortal sin, lying in wait ... just around the corner. Thus, returning home from class one night, a dogged dweeb of a philosophy grad student named Kathleen Conklin (Lili Taylor) is accosted by a smiling babe in evening clothes (Annabella Sciorra). Casanova, as the cast list identifies this glamorous figure, flicks away her cigarette and drags helpless Kathleen into an alley.

There, shrouded in a voluptuous mantilla of lacy shadows, she feasts on Kathleen's neck: Yo, *The Addiction*.

The season's second black-and-white, Lower Manhattan-set revisionist vampire saga, Ferrara's rap-scored, typically ferocious opus is daringly sybaritic—a deliberately underlit movie of hissed whispers and police sirens, as stylized as vintage noir. Sumptuously shot in and around NYU's Washington Square campus, with Bleecker Street as a conveniently nearby drug-addled combat zone, *The Addiction* establishes an acute, at times lacerating, tension between visual pleasure and narrative scuzz. The movie ponders the mystery of existence by reveling in splatterific materialism—noisy ERs and bloody bandages, the messy minutiae of urban vampirism. You might call it a vision.

Like Michael Almereyda's more gently sardonic *Nadja*, *The Addiction* is founded on a bravura female performance. Lili Taylor's sunken eyes and bony, masklike face have made her an icon of recent independent movies—here she seems close to the living dead.

Soon after the initial attack, her onmi-sexual character is dressing in black, wearing shades to class, and gazing hungrily at other women—although her first foray into vampirism consists of using a syringe to remove blood from a sleeping vagrant. Soon, she's haunting the school library as though it were a graveyard and luring smugly fashionable professors back to her lair: "It's the violence of my will against theirs."

No less caught between art and exploitation than Ferrara's infernal masterpiece, *Bad Lieutenant*, *The Addiction* is an equally oppressive meditation on the nature of evil. Ferrara rushes in where angels fear to tread, flashing images of My Lai, the Holocaust and Bosnia amid Kathleen's studies to suggest our pitiful lives on a mound of corpses. With its many hospital scenes, *The Addiction* is typically overt in evoking the spector of AIDS: "Am I gonna get sick now?" whimpers the anthropology student Kathleen has managed to seduce. But, in its globalized view of life as an insatiable hunger for blood, evil, or whatever gets you through the night, it's even more a junkie's manifesto. Looking for her angry fix, Kathleen's angel-headed hipster staggers through the negro streets at dawn. To ward off a bloodsucker in this universe, you need not brandish a crucifix, but only just say *No!* as if you mean it.

Fashionable? I don't think so. This is one vampire flick that insists on blaming the victim, while Nicholas St. John's script is nothing if not ridiculously heady. In the literary set piece, Kathleen picks up a mysterious stranger (Christopher Walken) who stops the movie dead by complaining that her breath "smells like shit" and inquiring if she's read *Naked Lunch*. He bites her (offscreen), then spends the rest of their night together holding forth on the power of *his* will to control *his* addiction, boasting, "I'm almost human."

Is *The Addiction* intentionally funny! (Abel and Nicky are surely acquainted with the old *Mad* magazine credo, "humor in a jugular vein.") Kathleen punctuates the torrent of frenzied babble with which she's transfixed a bewildered colleague by yanking a tooth out of her own mouth: "See? I'm rotting inside but I'm not dying." The movie might almost have been made to short-circuit the irony-contaminated Houston Street audience described in the *Voice* several weeks back. Moving between academia and the "real world" of Bleecker Street, *The Addiction* juxtaposes staged and newsreel horror, sinister histrionics and philosophical jargon. Kathleen quotes Feuerbach to one victim, debates the nature of collective guilt with another. The dialogue is awash in solenm aphorisms: "We drink to escape the fact we're alcoholics." Ferrara and St. John have pioneered a new sort of camp: Everything is equally grim, bloody, stylish, lurid and absurd.

Arguing throughout that "we do evil because we are evil," *The Addiction* ends by raising the possibility of redemption. I was less convinced of that salvation than of Ferrara's faith that one might find God in the sort of pre-porn 42nd Street triple bill that conflated atrocity footage from *Night and Fog* with Tod Brownings *Freaks* and *Olga's House of Shame*—a cautionary triptych in a Cine Urinal cathedral.

Also reviewed in:
CHICAGO TRIBUNE, 10/30/95, Tempo/p. 5, Michael Wilmington
NATION, 10/23/95, p. 480, Stuart Klawans
NEW YORK TIMES, 10/4/95, p. C16, Caryn James
VARIETY, 2/6-12/95, p. 73, Todd McCarthy
WASHINGTON POST, 10/27/95, p. D1, Hal Hinson
WASHINGTON POST, 10/27/95, Weekend/p. 48, Desson Howe

AMAZING PANDA ADVENTURE, THE

A Warner Bros. release of a Lee Rich/Gary Foster production. *Executive Producer:* Gabriella Martinelli. *Producer:* Lee Rich, John Wilcox, Gary Foster, and Dylan Sellers. *Director:* Christopher Cain. *Screenplay:* Jeff Rothberg and Laurice Elehwany. *Story:* John Wilcox and Steven Alldredge. *Director of Photography:* Jack N. Green. *Editor:* Jack Hofstra. *Music:* William Ross. *Sound:* Andy Wiskes. *Casting:* Marion Dougherty. *Production Designer:* John Willett. *Art Director:* Willie Heslup. *Set Decorator:* Doug Carnegie and Clive Thomasson. *Costumes:* Marjorie Chan. *Panda Effects:* Rick Baker. *Stunt Coordinator:* Mickey Gilbert. *Running time:* 93 minutes. *MPAA Rating:* PG.

CAST: Stephen Lang (Michael); Ryan Slater (Ryan); Yi Ding (Ling); Huang Fei (Chu).

LOS ANGELES TIMES, 8/28/95, Calendar/p. 6, Kevin Thomas

"The Amazing Panda Adventure" is a lively family entertainment in which two very capable young actors, Ryan Slater and Yi Ding, plus an irresistible panda cub, sustain pretty well some continuity glitches and credibility-straining moments. Its wilderness locations in China's Himalayan mountain highlands are also a real plus.

(The film, which opened Friday, was not screened in advance for critics by Warner Bros.)

Sturdy, poised Slater—yes, he's Christian's brother—plays a 10-year-old reluctantly going off to spend spring vacation with his workaholic, neglectful father (Stephen Lang), a naturalist specializing in the conservation of the beloved but highly endangered giant pandas at a reserve, which the Chinese government threatens to shut down imminently unless at least one baby panda turns up. A mother and child do surface, but the mother is wounded in a trap while Slater and the pretty Yi (who's helpfully fluent in English) find themselves on the run, the cub in tow, with the poachers in pursuit.

Writers Jeff Rothberg and Laurice Elehwany establish a credible relationship between the youngsters while piling on all the usual adventure movie incidents—the crumbling rope-and-plank bridge, the tumble into the rapids and over a waterfall and some literal cliffhanging. Director Christopher Cain moves the film fast enough to paper over a certain aura of contrivance and over-familiarity in all these exploits. Rick Baker and the Cinovation Studios crew's panda effects are absolutely undetectable, matching the actual animals perfectly.

Ironically, by the finish, Slater has scarcely spent any time, quality or otherwise, with his father, but at least he's gotten his attention at last—and an invitation to come back in the summer.

Playing with it is "Carrotblanca," a new Looney Tunes cartoon spoof of "Casablanca" in which Bugs Bunny takes the Humphrey Bogart role.

NEW YORK POST, 8/26/95, p. 15, Bill Hoffmann

The most amazing thing about "The Amazing Panda Adventure" is that Warner Brothers has given it such little publicity and didn't even have enough faith in the film to screen it for critics.

That's a shame because as the summer comes to an end and the big-budget, effects-filled blockbusters fade away, "The Amazing Panda Adventure" comes as a welcome finale—a perfect family film.

It's got almost non-stop action, breathtaking scenery at the edge of the Himalayas in China, two likeable kids in constant danger—and of course, those marvelous, scene-stealing pandas.

The story begins as 10-year-old Nintendo-freak Ryan Tyler (Ryan Slater) leaves the comforts of his divorced mother's home to visit his father, who runs a nature preserve for giant pandas in rural China.

"Don't eat anything with eyeballs in it," mom warns.

Ryan's father, Michael (Stephen Lang) is Dysfunctional Dad No. 1—totally absorbed his fight to save the endangered creatures and hardly giving his son the time of day.

But that attitude quickly changes when gun-toting poachers trap a mother panda, swipe its baby—spurring Ryan and Ling, (Yi Ding) an ultra-serious Chinese girl his age, to give chase and get lost in the wilderness.

Soon they're dodging bullets, falling through rickety old bridges, zipping down whitewater rapids and scaling unstable cliffs.

The action sequences are quite exciting and rely on good old fashioned derring-do with nary a high-priced special effect in sight.

The kids learn some valuable lessons along the way. Ryan's "Ugly American" personality is tempered when he's forced to learn about a different culture and (yuk!) eat monkey brains and slugs.

And Ling learns to lighten up and have a little, fun—yikes, could it be that Ryan's Americanizing her?

The pair even have their first anatomy lesson when they have to strip naked to get rid of bloodsucking leeches.

"I've seen plenty of naked women before—I have cable TV," Ryan cracks.

At the end of it all, Ryan and his dad are closer than ever and the little panda is saved. It is all a bit heavy-handed and the moral that pandas are the cure to the world's ills is a bit too much.

But that's quibbling. "The Amazing Panda Adventure" has a very big heart and it's by far the best family movie of the season. It would be a shame to miss it.

On the same program is a new Looney Tune called "Carrotblanca," with Bugs Bunny, Daffy Duck, Sylvester and other cartoon staples parodying the famed Humphrey Bogart movie.

Sad to say, the dialogue is dull, the action mediocre and all of characters seem to have been cleaned up for the politically correct '90s. What's sorely needed is more violence, risque lines and on-the-edge behavior—just like in the old days. PC cartoons are no fun.

Also reviewed in:
CHICAGO TRIBUNE, 8/27/95, Tempo/p. 7, Mark Caro
NEW YORK TIMES, 8/26/95, p. 15, Stephen Holden
VARIETY, 8/28-9/3/95, p. 66, Daniel M. Kimmel
WASHINGTON POST, 8/28/95, p. D7, Rita Kempley

AMERICAN PRESIDENT, THE

A Castle Rock Entertainment and Universal Pictures release of a Wildwood Enterprises Inc. production. *Executive Producer:* Charles Newirth and Jeffrey Stott. *Producer:* Rob Reiner. *Director:* Rob Reiner. *Screenplay:* Aaron Sorkin. *Director of Photography:* John Seale. *Editor:* Robert Leighton. *Music:* Marc Shaiman. *Music Editor:* Scott Stambler. *Sound:* Robert Eber and (music) Dennis Sands. *Sound Editor:* Robert Grieve. *Casting:* Jane Jenkins and Janet Hirshenson. *Production Designer:* Lilly Kilvert. *Art Director:* John Warnke. *Set Designer:* Nick Navarro, Louis Montejano, Eric Orbom, and Alan S. Kaye. *Set Decorator:* Karen O'Hara. *Set Dresser:* Katherine Lucas, Patrick Cassidy, Tommy Samona, Quentin Schierenberg, James Marchwick, and Tristan P. Bourne. *Special Effects:* Clay Pinney. *Visual Effects:* Ken Ralston. *Costumes:* Gloria Gresham. *Make-up:* Daniel C. Striepeke. *Make-up (Michael Douglas):* Tom Lucas. *Make-up (Annette Bening):* Valli O'Reilly. *Running time:* 115 minutes. *MPAA Rating:* PG-13.

CAST: Michael Douglas (Andrew Shepherd); Annette Bening (Sydney Ellen Wade); Martin Sheen (A.J. MacInerney); Michael J. Fox (Lewis Rothschild); Anna Deavere Smith (Robin McCall); Samantha Mathis (Janie Basdin); Shawna Waldron (Lucy Shepherd); David Paymer (Leon Kodak); Anne Haney (Mrs. Chapil); Richard Dreyfuss (Senator Bob Rumson); Nina Siemaszko (Beth Wade); Wendie Malick (Susan Sloan); Beau Billingslea (Agent Cooper); Gail Strickland (Esther MacInerney); Joshua Malina (David); Clement Von Franckenstein (President D'Astier); Efrat Lavie (Madame D'Astier); John Mahoney (Leo Solomon); Taylor Nichols (Stu); John Mahon (Chairman of the Joint Chiefs); Tom Dahlgren (Defense Secretary); Ralph Meyering, Jr. (General); Kurt A. Boesen (Security Advisor); Joseph Latimore, Darryl Alan Reed, and Andrew Steel (Secret Service Agents); Jordan Lund (Carl); Richard F. McGonagle, Frank Cavestani, and Richard Stahl (Rumson Staffers); Alice Kushida (Carol); Renee Phillips (Lisa); Beans Morocco (Doorkeeper); Kathryn Ish (Education Secretary); Kamilah Martin (Flower Girl); Augie Blunt (Groundskeeper); Thom Barry (Guard); Steven Gonzalez (Hud Secretary); Gabriel Jarret (Jeff); Karen Maruyama (Leo's Secretary); Nancy Kandal (Leslie); George Murdock (Congressman); Bernie McInerney (Congressmn Millman); Jack Gilroy (Congressman Pennybaker); Matthew Saks (Congressional Staffer); Googy Gress (Gil); Ron Canada (Reporter Lloyd); Brian Pietro and Rick Garcia (Reporters); Aaron Sorkin (Aide in Bar); Kymberly S. Newberry (Sally); Greg Poland (Mark); Leslie Rae Bega (White House Staffer Laura); Jennifer Crystal (White House Staffer Maria); Arthur Senzy (Deputy); Nick Troth, Jorge Noa, and Maud Winchester (White House Aides); Jeffrey Anderson (T.V. News Anchorman); Suzanne Michaels (T.V. News Anchorwoman); Mark Thompson (Kenneth Michaels); David Drew Gallagher (New Guy); Todd Odom (Uniformed Secret Service Agent); Michael G. Alexander (Color Guard Officer).

CHRISTIAN SCIENCE MONITOR, 11/17/95, p.12, David Sterritt

Rob Reiner's new comedy, "The American President," comes from a long line of movie romances in political settings. Earnest political men and feisty political women work out complicated issues of love and statesmanship in time for a happy Hollywood ending.

Frank Capra was the master of this formula, with pictures like "State of the Union" and "Mr. Smith Goes to Washington," and Reiner's movie pays tribute to him in one of the opening scenes—specifically naming "Mr. Smith Goes to Washington," which clearly inspired "The American President. "

The new picture may not become a Capraesque hit, if only because it's not cynical enough about power to suit many of today's moviegoers. But it has good performances and snappy dialogue, and in the end it dares to take a stand on real political issues—which makes it a rarity in today's timid movie world,

The aptly named hero is Andrew Shepherd, a well-meaning but somewhat wishy-washy chief executive (sound familiar?) who wants to make America great. He believes that endless dealmaking is the only way to succeed.

Since he's a widower, his personal life is on the lonely side. But this changes when he meets the attractive lobbyist of a powerful environmental group. Their professional acquaintance becomes a love affair, and soon all America knows the president's got a girlfriend. This gives new ammunition to his political enemies and makes him rethink his attitudes toward principle and commitment.

In style, "The American President" is an old-fashioned Hollywood entertainment, and not a bad one at that—full of movie stars Michael Douglas and Annette Bening making eyes at each other while velvety music swells in the background. When even the gofers are played by major talents like Martin Sheen and Michael J. Fox, you know the picture wants to give its audience an enjoyable ride.

Also on hand are Anna Deveare Smith as the White House press secretary, David Paymer as a pollster appropriately called Kodak, the up-and-coming Samantha Mathis as a presidential aide, and Richard Dreyfuss as an opposition senator with a mile-wide nasty streak. The quickly paced screenplay is by Aaron Sorkin, who collaborated with Reiner on "A Few Good Men" three years ago, and John Seale did the good-looking cinematography.

Looking beyond the big-studio touches, what gives substance to "The American President" is its willingness to raise its voice on a few controversies that most commercial filmmakers wouldn't touch with the proverbial 10-foot pole. At one point, the hero actually promotes the American Civil Liberties Union, defends the right of protesters to burn American flags, and calls on his right-wing enemies to debate real issues instead of whining about phony character charges all the time.

Whether or not you agree with these positions, it's refreshing to see a movie that dares to speak their names. "The American President" isn't great cinema, but it has a foot in the real world, and that's more than I can say about most of the frivolities now passing for entertainment at the local multiplex.

LOS ANGELES TIMES, 11/17/95, Calendar/p. 1, Kenneth Turan

Leader of the free world or not, President Andrew Shepherd (Michael Douglas) has to follow the rules like anyone else, and the rules of a romantic comedy like "The American President" insist that he and lobbyist Sydney Ellen Wade (Annette Bening) meet cute if they are to meet at all.

So the President just happens to tiptoe into a White House meeting right at the point where Wade is laying into him as "the chief executive of Fantasyland." Gosh, is she embarrassed and, gosh again, doesn't the President think she's awfully cute when she gets mad?

A return to mass-appeal form by director Rob Reiner after the fiasco of "North," "The American President" deals with the pressing question of whether a man can run the country and give flowers to a woman at the same time. As a lightly amusing sentimental fantasy, "President" is genial and entertaining if not notably inspired. But its most interesting aspect turns out to be fantasies of another kind, pipe dreams about the American political system and where it could theoretically be headed.

Just having Douglas and Bening starring in this fluffy comedy brings a touch of unreality to the proceedings, for both actors have been most impressive in distinctly hardball roles: Douglas most notably in "Wall Street" and Bening in "The Grifters." In "American President," they spend much of their time beaming at each other and glowing a lot, which adds a distinct level of play-acting to the proceedings.

Not that President Shepherd can't be tough when he needs to be. According to Aaron Sorkin's script, he is a pragmatic, hands-on chief executive who believes in "fighting the fights we can win" and is not averse to wheeling and dealing. Partly because he is a stoic widower raising a 12-year-old daughter, the President's approval ratings are high enough for him to feel confident of getting a crime bill through Congress, albeit one that is not as tough on handguns as top domestic adviser Lewis Rothschild (a sparkling Michael J. Fox) would like.

The President is also not sure how tough an environmental bill he can get passed, which worries a tree-hugger organization called the Global Defense Council, They're the ones who hire Sydney Wade, Syd to her friends, a powerhouse lobbyist from the great state of Virginia who is charged with changing all that.

Much of what "The American President" details about the Syd-Andy relationship is visible a good ways down the road, including machinations by the opposition's Sen. Rumson (Richard Dreyfuss), a Bob Dole clone who is itching to do some character assassination.

And though the President keeps insisting to his advisers after the relationship becomes public that "there is no Sydney issue," it should not come as a surprise that the liaison threatens to compromise her professional credibility or that the President's political ambitions will at some point conflict with his personal commitments.

While all this tends to sound rather serious, "The American President" is in general determinedly comic in tone, helped by a level of solid professionalism that starts with Douglas and Bening, who work hard at their roles though they are not ideally cast.

More interesting, though not necessarily more engaging, than the film's pro forma romantic games is "The American President's" political context. The filmmakers spent a good deal of time in the Clinton White House and some of the actors, like Fox, have admitted to basing their characterizations on real-life counterparts, and the entire venture is so intent on conjuring up the spirit of Frank Capra, director of "Mr. Smith Goes to Washington," that there is even some dialogue about his work.

Capra's films on government were often fantasy riffs on how Americans would like their political system to operate, and it is interesting to see this film follow in its footsteps. Here is a White House filled with totally competent, dedicated, even idealistic folks and presided over by a paragon of virtues who is a nice guy and a great parent in addition to being a peerless chief executive. One look at the front page of any daily newspaper shows that today's reality is somewhat different.

But Reiner and writer Sorkin have gone even further—they've put a distinctly liberal spin on this dream White House. They've created a President who believes in the Democratic Party dream and isn't afraid to speak up about it, who can passionately defend the ACLU and gun control and still have the great majority of the country on his side. Exactly how much of a fantasy is that? Tune in next November to find out.

NEW YORK, 11/20/95, p. 84, David Denby

On the same night that I attended a screening of *The American President*, a new romantic comedy set in the White House, I happened to watch an edition of ABC's *Night Line* in which a number of journalists and historians discussed President Clinton's habit of agonizing over his policies in public. They concluded that the president cannot hold his tongue; that he somehow expects to pick up points from the electorate for his public soul-searching. In any case, the kind of candor that might be endearing or admirable in an ordinary mortal is embarrassing—even infuriating—in the most powerful man on earth. Rob Reiner's *The American President* is a snappy commercial entertainment before anything else, but it's also a kind of convoluted message from Hollywood liberals to Bill Clinton: Stiffen up; you have nothing to lose but your negative poll numbers. Andrew Shepherd (Michael Douglas) is a Democrat and a centrist liberal, highly intelligent but with a tendency to waffle. Shepherd has a general "character" issue hanging over him. (Or so the movie says.) He also has a 12-year-old daughter. In other words, he's very much like Clinton—except that he's a widower. President Shepherd falls for a liberal environmental lobbyist, Sydney Ellen Wade (Annette Bening), and immediately his principal political opponent, a family-values blowhard (Richard Dreyfuss), denounces him as an immoral man. The suspense builds. Will the president stick with his girl? Will he sell out the environmentalists in order to get his crime bill passed?

The American President, was concocted by the same pair—writer Aaron Sorkin, director Rob Reiner—who made *A Few Good Men*, and like that movie, it is highly professional but also synthetically plotted and glib. The very idea of romance in the Oval Office is movie-ish in a kind of cloying old-Hollywood way. Yet any movie set in that place (*Seven Days in May, Fail-Safe, Dave*, etc.) has something going for it—our curiosity about how power works in a democracy, how the president leads or fails to lead. Sorkin and Reiner offer us a president who is apparently superb at the executive part of his job. Andrew Shepherd rushes through meetings with the Joint Chiefs at breakneck speed yet still takes time to mourn some innocent Libyans killed in an American air strike; he listens to criticism from his staff, only to cut it off when it goes too far. Trailed by this group of aides, who attend to him as if he were simultaneously God and a sickly hospital patient who needed constant injections, he sweeps from room to room of the White House, receiving advice and help, dispatching people on errands, doing the job on his feet. As he faces his many constituencies, he's like a large, lonely fish passing through many schools of smaller fish, each with its own interests, speed, and destination.

As the big tuna, Michael Douglas gives an entertaining and self-assured star performance. Douglas is not beating up on Korean-Americans this time, or fending off ravenous women; he doesn't have to carry the burdens of an embattled white male. He is *the* white male. His chin-up cockiness has at last found an appropriate outlet, and when he gets angry, the emotion has weight. Martin Sheen, twinkling sagely as the president's old friend and closest adviser, and the mighty Anna Deavere Smith, furrowing her brow as White House press secretary, do well enough in mock-serious roles, though Michael J. Fox, as a Stephanopoulos-type young policy adviser, carries whippersnapper audacity to the point of foolishness. The brash Fox wouldn't last a day in my administration.

The joke of the movie is that the most powerful man in the world doesn't enjoy the prerogatives of an ordinary man—the freedom to call a woman on the phone and send her flowers without the whole country going into a tizzy. After suffering delays that no teenager would put up with, the president finally makes his romantic intentions known to Sydney, and she is pleased but flustered, and pulls away. If only her dilemma were of some interest! There follow many scenes of narrative fumbling as Sydney tries to decide whether her sense of her own dignity will allow her to go to bed with the head of the Free World. *The American President* is a clear descendant of those old Hollywood movies in which kings or princesses long to cast off the robes of state and snuggle like commoners. Real-life kings, of course, do quite a bit of common snuggling, and some presidents have, too. But the media have turned royal romance into a bed of nails: They can't so much as smile at each other without the press going apoplectic.

The filmmakers refer to Frank Capra once or twice, and they seem to be trying for soulful Capraesque fable. The trouble is, you can't do Capra by calculation. Either you have something like his warmth and charm naturally or you don't, and Sorkin and Reiner are too knowing. They give us a love affair so strained and overdefined that it's not much of a love affair at all. After creating an aura of power and pomp, with all the presidential symbols in place (much is made of the White House china), the filmmakers can't easily shift into intimate banter and spontaneity. That's part of the point, of course: what woman can afford not to laugh at the president's jokes? But it's not a point that does much for romance. *The American President* suffers from unintentional irony: After all the nervous buildup—Sydney's principles, the president's anxiety about sex after long abstinence—what Shepherd and Sydney finally say and do seems anti-climactic and banal. The awkwardness even extends to Annette Bening, who was so devastating as a bad girl in *The Grifters* and *Bugsy*. As she works up the externals of a high-powered professional woman, Bening flutters about like a leaf in a storm. We see her acting and reacting, shifting gears and putting on brakes, and she never quite settles down and becomes a person. Not only does Andrew Shepherd rush her off her feet; Rob Reiner does, too. In fact, Reiner never quite finds the rhythm of his story; he's too paralyzed by awe of the presidency to liberate the material from self-consciousness. He's made a skillful commercial movie that is fatally lacking in magic.

And there's a big hole: Andrew Shepherd doesn't seem to have a character problem at all. As far as we can see, he's extremely decisive, and no more or less devious than any other president. The filmmakers have created a false issue, which they resolve in the standard way: The president makes a Big Speech, thereby saving his own honor and the honor of his job. Dry-eyed as we are at Shepherd's grandstanding, we may wish that the intelligent but vacillating Bill Clinton could make a speech like it. *The American President* isn't much of a romantic comedy, but as an example of liberal longing for a strong president, it's a fascinating show.

NEW YORK POST, 11/17/95, p. 49, Michael Medved

Republicans (as exemplified by snickering pompous Senate *Minority* Leader Richard Dreyfuss) are all mean-spirited, conspiratorial, embittered old men, given to dastardly deeds like attacking the president's girlfriend on TV as a "whore."

The Democrats, on the other hand, are all good-looking, witty and well-dressed idealists, devoted parents, loyal friends and tireless public servants equipped with ready one-liners and above-average dancing skills.

Welcome to Rob Reiner's Washington, a place with all the moral complexity and subtle shadings of Hopalong Cassidy's Wild West. As a work of political melodrama, "The American President" (produced and directed by Reiner) is so childish and partisan that it's amazing that the romance that co-exists alongside the preaching manages to work as well as it does.

The energy in this love story arises almost entirely from the two stars, who are both perfectly cast. Michael Douglas plays a former history professor elected president of the United States shortly after losing his wife to cancer. Three years later, while confidently facing a campaign for re-election, the popular chief executive suddenly seems to realize he's a lonely widower.

A contrived, cloyingly cute meeting introduces him to environmental lobbyist Annette Bening—she's in the White House talking with chief of staff Martin Sheen when the president tiptoes in unannounced and overhears her angry and contemptuous words about his waffling on the issue of global warming.

This unique politician enjoys such a secure sense of himself that he's instinctively drawn to her feisty spirit and invites her into a private chat in the Oval Office. The movie then earns several good laughs when the Leader of the Free World trying to do ordinary "guy" things like calling for a first date or ordering flowers.

On their initial evening out, Douglas asks Bening to escort him to a state dinner for the president of France—a beautifully staged sequence with magical echoes of Cinderella and Prince Charming.

The problem in the movie is the context it establishes for their developing relationship. According to the movie, the president begins dropping precipitously in the polls as soon as the public learns that he has a love interest. In actuality, America (which has proven notably forgiving concerning even alleged *extramarital* peccadilloes by the current incumbent) would probably love it if a widower president suddenly found romance.

Moreover, the movie inexplicably avoids the slightest mention of the "M-word" (marriage)—with neither the president nor his worried aides (including Sheen, Michael J. Fox, David Paymer and Anna Deavere Smith) ever entertaining the idea of engagement to a woman the chief executive says he "loves deeply"—even though the popular prospect of a White House wedding would undoubtedly enhance his popularity.

Screenwriter Aaron ("A Few Good Men") Sorkin provides a few telling moments and funny lines, such as the president's nervous insistence to Bening, just before they go to bed together for the first time, that even though he may be the Most Powerful Man in the World, she shouldn't expect anything too extraordinary.

When it comes to *public* affairs, however, the movie has a distinctly dated quality, making clear its origins long before the electoral earthquake of 1994.

According to the movie, the two biggest issues on the national agenda are legislation to curb assault weapons and another bill to reduce auto emissions; discussions of these crusades, and the president's ringing defense of the ACLU, have as much cutting edge currency in today's Washington as debates on the Rural Electrification Project.

Despite moments of humor and charm, "The American President" proves that filmmaker Reiner (whose previous credits include the likable love stories "When Harry Met Sally ..." and "The Princess Bride") knows a good deal more about romance than he does about politics.

NEWSDAY, 11/17/95, Part II/p. B2, Jack Mathews

Anyone uncomfortable with the image of America as a Hollywood monarchy may be put off, as I certainly am, by Rob Reiner's trite romantic drama and sure holiday hit "The American President."

While serving up a leader who is a liberal's fantasy, a common-sense humanitarian simultaneously supporting gun control, environmental protection and the ACLU, Reiner and screenwriter Aaron Sorkin turn his office into a throne room, and the American people into his subjects. There are so many scenes of sycophancy and ring-kissing in this tale about a widowed president and his lobbyist girlfriend, you'd think it was the Pope who was dating.

OK, OK, don't take it so seriously. It is just an old-fashioned Hollywood star vehicle, with Michael Douglas as the morally sterling chief executive, and slinky Annette Bening as the lobbyist with the legs. Hollywood has taken us into the White House many times before, and introduced us to a wide variety of presidential personalities. The republic can survive another.

The problem for me is that Reiner, who took his crew into the taxpayers' capital and talked the current taxpayers' president into debriefing him on White House procedure, is trying to elevate the adolescent fatuousness of his love story by propping it up with the presidential seal. And, at the same time, he's trumped up a president so accustomed to power and its exigencies that he seems to have been fashioned more on the life of former agent king Michael Ovitz—whose ring one may assume Reiner has had occasion to kiss—than on Bill Clinton.

Other than his immediate crew—chief of staff Martin Sheen, press secretary Anna Deavere Smith, public pulse-taker David Paymer, and George Stephanopoulos lookalike Michael J. Fox—the only people Andrew Shepherd encounters are mortal political enemies or folks whose knees buckle under the pressure of being in his presence.

That includes Bening's Sydney Ellen Wade, a powerful Washington lawyer hired by an environmental group to hold the president's feet to the fire over pending air pollution legislation. You'd imagine a person in her position having steeled herself against the seductions of power, but she's reduced to a babbling school girl when Shepherd invites her over for some home-cooked meat loaf and starts field-testing her at state dinners for the potential role of First Lady.

The hooey doesn't really begin, however, until word leaks out of the president's new romance, and Sen. Bob Rumson (Richard Dreyfuss), the mean, Phil Gramm-like pit bull on the right, declares Sydney the "First Mistress" and dishes some dirt to the media about her having once appeared at a flag-burning political rally.

That a president's love interest could hurt him politically has recent historical precedent; just last year, Bill Clinton's health care plan, with wife Hillary's name attached, sank faster than a deck chair on the Titanic. But this is ridiculous. In a few short weeks after meeting a beautiful, smart, elegant woman who dazzles dignitaries from around the world, President Shepherd's approval ratings have dropped from 60-plus percentage points to about 40, and his administration, with all of its idealism and good intentions, is on the ropes. Maybe if he was seeing Harvey Fierstein ... not Annette Bening.

There is some admirable verisimilitude to the White House setting. I know this from having got the lay of the land in the infinitely superior "Dave" a couple of years ago. The Oval Office, the halls, the executive quarters, the Cabinet Room; they're all pretty much on target. And there is a lot of colorful detail, the way the president's schedule is constantly spilling over, or how his staff whips into action to solve unexpected problems, that seems absolutely true.

But the overriding impression is that "The American President" is pure Hollywood political fantasy, a view of the country's top office as a temporary kingdom, just like the top jobs at the studios, where a good man—a man who, say, supports increased funding for the arts—can lead his people out of the dark *and* have a little fun.

Hear, hear!

NEWSWEEK, 11/20/95, p. 91, Jack Kroll

OK, General Powell, if we can't have you, we've got Michael Douglas. In *The American President*, Douglas is the latest fantasy prexy to be served up by Hollywood, that home-shopping network for alternate universes. Recently it gave us Kevin Kline as Dave, a presidential look-alike, who was dragooned to sit in for the Boss. Just plain Dave turned out to be a helluva chief executive; he ran the country much better than the real guy, who was ... gulp ... a *philanderer*. Douglas plays a real prez, Andrew Shepherd, just as nice as Dave, even though he's a politician. I mean, get that name—he's our good shepherd, right? No philanderooski for Andy; he's a widower who makes meat loaf for his adorable young daughter (Shawna Waldron) and has approval ratings as high as his ideals.

Those ideals include a commitment to gun control, backing the American Civil Liberties Union and a fierce advocacy of environmental issues. While backing same, he encounters Sydney Ellen Wade (Annette Bening), an environmental lobbyist. Get *that* name: masculine steel, feminine velvet, the whole package. Andy falls, but he doesn't skulk around the White House, using the Secret Service as pimps with beepers. He's right out front, dropping in to buy roses from an astonished florist, dancing with Syd at an astonished state dinner, driving his own astonished car on a date.

Despite his upfrontness, Andy's morals are attacked (it's an election year) by his adversary, right-wing Sen. Robert Rumson (Richard Dreyfuss). How about *that* Dickensian name—

screenwriter Aaron Sorkin is good with these Post-it labels. Rumson's attacks cause those approval ratings to fall, to the horror of Andy's staff, including top aide Martin Sheen, press secretary Anna Deavere Smith, adviser Michael J. Fox. (Yes, Fox is little and cute, just like you know who.) But Andy is steadfast despite the dropping numbers, despite the inevitable flare-up with Syd. Does virtue triumph—plus gun control, the ACLU and the environment? Would a shopping network sell you a defective president?

All this is good fun—some of which is anticipating the pained reaction from conservative Hollywood-hasslers. Director Rob Reiner has a fine smooth touch, Douglas is charismatic, Bening is scrumptious—you want to put all these dream politicos in a doggy bag and take them home. To *our* home, the White House.

SIGHT AND SOUND, 1/96, p. 36, John Wrathall

With a 63 percent approval rating in the polls in election year, President Andrew Shepherd is preparing two controversial pieces of legislation—an Energy Bill and a Crime Bill—in the hope that by the time of his State of the Union address he can secure enough votes in Congress to pass them. A widower, Shepherd is attracted to Sydney Ellen Wade, the new lobbyist hired by an environmental pressure group, and asks her out. His subsequent attempts to court her, however, are discouraged by the White House staff, impeded by his official duties and criticised in the press.

As rival Presidential candidate Bob Rumson uses Shepherd's intimate relationship with a lobbyist as the basis for an attack on his character, the President's approval rating starts to slide, particularly when Rumson uncovers an old photograph of Sydney burning an American flag. But Shepherd insists his private life should not become a political issue and refuses to respond to Rumson's attacks. As State of the Union approaches, Sydney's lobbying has secured the votes necessary to pass the Energy Bill with stringent controls on fossil fuel emissions. But Shepherd, realising he no longer has enough support in Congress, decides to dilute the Energy Bill in order to secure crucial votes he needs to pass the Crime Bill.

When the news breaks, Sydney is fired from her job, and breaks off the affair. Shepherd makes an unscheduled appearance at a White House press briefing to announce that he has decided to scrap the Crime Bill, which is unworkable because of its lack of controls on assault weapons, and give his full support to the Energy Bill. At the same time he launches a blistering attack on Rumson for his slurs on Sydney's character, even going so far as to defend an American citizen's right to burn the flag. Sydney, having seen the speech on television, rushes to the White House to be reunited with Shepherd before he goes to deliver his State of the Union address where he is greeted with a standing ovation.

"This is my first time at the White House," says Sydney when she arrives at the gate for her first briefing with the President's staff. "I'm trying to savour the Capraesque quality." That, of course, is exactly what Rob Reiner is after too, (he even hired one Frank Capra III as his Assistant Director); but whereas Capra's Mr Smith was a regular guy catapulted into a unique situation when he went to Washington, Andrew Shepherd—in a reversal that provides this very funny film with its best situations—is a unique guy (leader of the free world) trying to behave like a regular Mr Smith.

Compared to the neuroses keeping apart Reiner's previous set of star-crossed lovers in *When Harry Met Sally*, the problems faced by the President in his efforts to date Sydney are indeed extreme. For a start, when he even tries to make a phone call for himself, everyone—even Sydney—assumes it's a prank. An unmarried President dating someone is the closest Americans can come to a royal courtship of their own, and Reiner and his screenwriter Aaron Sorkin (commissioned by the director following their collaboration on *A Few Good Men*) cleverly play off Sydney's confusion about whether she is involved with a man or an institution. Screen couples who are unapologetically middle-aged, intelligent and highly articulate are a rarity in Hollywood these days (it's no coincidence that Reiner also slips us a clip of Tracy and Hepburn in *Adam's Rib*), and Annette Bening and Michael Douglas respond to the challenge admirably. Bening, rising from the ashes of Warren Beatty's *Love Affair* displays a sort of twinkly dynamism that no other actress in Hollywood can quite match, while Michael Douglas, relishing the chance to play a decent, unflawed character for once, manages to seem both lovable and Presidential. Equally inspired is the casting of the supporting roles, with three stars of former decades—Martin Sheen,

Michael J. Fox and Richard Dreyfuss—miraculously rescued from career doldrums and reinvented as, respectively, Shepherd's pragmatic Chief of Staff, his George Stephanopoulos-like Chief Domestic Advisor, and the ferocious rival Rumson.

While the White House detail (achieved with the full co-operation of President Clinton, who would have been well advised to have Sorkin write him a few speeches while he was at it) is fascinating, and the countdown to the State of the Union address provides the required dramatic momentum, the film's politics are more ambiguous. Despite Shepherd's nostalgia for a pre-mass media age when a man in a wheelchair could be elected President, the film actually seems to bear out the observations of the cynics, John Mahoney's veteran environmental campaigner (who tells us "Politics is perception") and Dreyfuss's Rumson ("Voters only care about character"). When we're sent out on a high after Shepherd's final *tour de force* at the press briefing, it's not because we know he's right to scrap the Crime Bill (the gun control issue has hardly been addressed), but because he is at last seen to be acting in a powerful, Presidential way (his pay-off line, significantly, is: "I *am* the President"), Shepherd's last-minute decision to go all out for the Energy Bill, meanwhile suggests that perhaps Rumson was right all along, and that the President *has* allowed his policies to be unduly influenced by his personal life.

TIME, 11/20/95, p. 117, Richard Corliss

The take-charge lobbyist is scolding White House officials about the president of the United States. "Your boss," she says, "is the Chief Executive of Fantasyland!" In *The American President*, this speech is mainly a meet-cute device—a way to put lobbyist Sydney Wade (Annette Bening) on a collision course with President Andrew Shepherd (Michael Douglas) before they become friends, lovers and the stuff of tabloid scandal. But the line is also a clue to the politics of this witty romantic comedy, written by Aaron Sorkin (*A Few Good Men*) and directed by Rob Reiner (*When Harry Met Sally ...*). It's a liberal fantasy—a vision of the President as a good man who can coax the national consensus just slightly leftward—that is as anachronistic as it is seductive.

Think of Bill Clinton on his best day: charming, committed, goof-free. Think of him, in other words, as Hollywood's liberals did during the 1992 campaign. Now the twist: imagine a Clinton presidency if Hillary had died a few years before the election. He's been in office a while and enjoys high approval ratings. His likely opponent for re-election is the leader of the Senate Republicans—a crabby Kansan named Bob (played by Richard Dreyfuss as if he were a geyser about to gush right-wing bile). On the domestic front, the President has two things to care for: a daughter about Chelsea's age and a man-size libido. He's behaved himself but, in his budding desire for Sydney, hopes the nation might not mind if the President goes on a date.

As bustling and impassioned as the best Sturges and Capra movies, this one captures both the purposeful edginess of Administration Pooh-Bahs (Martin Sheen, Michael J. Fox, David Paymer and Samantha Mathis—nice jobs, all) and the isolation of the President. You understand why the ultimate lonely guy might make a late-night call to Annette Bening, or Ben Wattenberg. Bening emits too many anguished giggles but is ultimately winning. And Douglas, with his instinct for touchy material that pays off, sells his big speech—a ringing defense of the environment *and* the A.C.L.U.—so persuasively it might even play in Limbaugh Land.

Aaaaaah, maybe not. This *American President* exists in an alternate universe from the one the real Bill Clinton must inhabit. The movie offers nostalgia for a time that might have been—say, 1938.

VILLAGE VOICE, 11/21/95, Film Special/p. 20, J. Hoberman

Scarcely less generic than its title, *The American President* is a movie that dares to ask the question: Is the Leader of the Free World free to date!

The personal is the political in this Rob Reiner opus, produced with the utmost veneration. *The American President* may be a comedy but it is the opposite of satire. The opening credits recall Ronald Reagan's 1984 TV spots: stately music, Old Glory, the Constitution, dissolves from images of JFK to FDR to George Washington. The trappings of theocracy coalesce in the image of the White House—and then, in a stunning act of lèse majesté, a cut to Michael Douglas purposefully striding through the corridors of power.

The American President was originally written for Robert Redford, although unfortunately it hasn't been sufficiently slimed down to accommodate the Douglas persona. Summoning up all the dignity he can muster, jutting out his jaw and tucking in his butt, Douglas appears as President Andrew Shepherd. The leader of the flock is an ex-professor baby-boom Democrat with a 12-year-old daughter and no military service who, narrowly elected, now enjoys a 63 per cent rating despite his being—or, perhaps, because he is—a pragmatic waffler. As he tells his Stephanopoulos-like aide (Michael J. Fox): "We gotta fight the fights we can win." So pardon the repulsive spectacle of Douglas's triumphalist strut. He embodies a svelter, more popular, sitcom-perfect Clinton, lacking only the old ball-and-chain.

Hillary provides the movie's structuring absence. Douglas plays a lonely widower who instantly falls for Annette Bening, the fast-talking hired gun the environmental lobby has engaged to improve the administration's stand on auto-emission standards. No sooner does Bening visit the White House than the smitten Douglas lures her into the Oval Office and, using his powers of persuasion make a flirtatious offer: "If you can get 24 votes, I'll get you the last 10." (Lucky, for him, she doesn't pull a Paula Jones.) After conferring with his adviser Martin Sheen, Douglas decides to ask Bening out. "Just be yourself," his daughter advises him, adding that he should compliment her shoes. "Women like that."

Escorted by Douglas to a state banquet for the snooty French president, Bening breaks the ice with her vivacious and apparently unique command of a foreign language. Suddenly, she's in the center of the room—waltzing, alone on the dance floor with the most powerful man in the world to a lush arrangement of the geriatric Rogers and Hammerstein pulse-pounder "I Have Dreamed" (taken, appropriately enough, from *The King and I*). The room spins, the glamorous dignitaries are of one mind in pondering the identity of this mysterious Cinderella. The next morning Bening has her picture plastered across the front page of *The Washington Times*, although rather than rejoicing in this unprecedented access, her irate boss complains; "I hired a pit bull, not a prom queen."

As the woman who finally landed Warren Beatty, Bening brings at least as much credibility to her role as Douglas does to his. Given the emphasis on menus, power perks, and dress-up, *The American President* is an anachronistic example of what used to be called women's magazine fiction, including ads: *I dreamed I danced with the President in my Maidenform bra*. No sooner does Douglas overcome Bening's resistance to a cozy "meat-loaf night" chez Douglas than Reiner cuts to the presidential whirlybird lofting by the Washington monument. Their first kiss interrupted by the Secret Service bringing word of a breaking international crisis, the affair is basically a dizzy whirl of requited Oedipal love: the fireplace at Camp David, Christmas at the White House, roses from the Rose Garden ...

Douglas's trademark sex-agony is here discreetly verbal; the snake in this Eden is a Republican senator, Richard Dreyfuss, The minority [sic] leader, this silver-haired smoothy from (heh-heh) Kansas is running for president on family values and a bizarrely incumbent slogan, "The pride is back." Dreyfuss sniffs out Bening and begins referring to her as "the First Mistress." (Do past indiscretions include a stint as a Vegas lap dancer! No such luck.) Emergency staff meetings in the presidential boudoir! The "girlfriend factor" ignites some unspecified "character question." The message spreads by talk-radio drums. The presidents popularity drops 8 per cent over-night and then goes in to free fall.

At this point *The American President* is designed to turn from Bening's fantasy to ours. "They want leadership," Fox sagely points out. Do tell. Although the movie was shot last winter, the filmmakers clearly did not factor the Brave Newt World of Republican Nation into their entertainment equation. The suspense of politicking the presidents program or the fantasy of sweet-talking Congress are quaintly obsolete. Even stranger, the movie fails to understand the implications of putting a politician in bed with a lobbyist. All you need is love—tailoring one's position to placate a lover is presented as a greater profile in courage than making policy by focus group.

The American President makes the point several times that perception, in politics, rules reality. Douglas even suggests that someone like Ronald Reagan (prudently unnamed) hypnotized the American people. The movie's wittiest touch is casting David Gergen as Dreyfuss's media crony, but, of course, *The American President* is a thoroughly mediated experience. "I'm trying to savor the Capra-esque quality," Bening says the first time she visits the White House. (Because this is "America," the guard knows just what she means.) Reiner even hired Frank Capra III as his first A.D. Still, if *The American President* resembles any Capra fantasy it's the turgid 1948 Tracy-Hepburn vehicle, *State of the Union*, in which a Wendell Wilkie-like presidential candidate patches up his marriage by courageously returning to his (wife's) authentic values.

State of the Union has been credited with bucking up a demoralized Harry Truman. (It also provided Reagan with a career one-liner.) *The American President* will be lucky if it inspires Bill Clinton to forego a single Dove bar. As comedy, no less than camp, the movie inspires little more than rote chuckles. It's too smugly mush-brained to be funny and may even be too snuggly mush-hearted to sell.

Also reviewed in:
CHICAGO TRIBUNE, 11/17/95, Friday/p. C, Michael Wilmington
NEW YORK TIMES, 11/17/95, p. C8, Janet Maslin
NEW YORKER, 11/20/95, p. 116, Terrence Rafferty
VARIETY, 11/6-12/95, p. 71, Todd McCarthy
WASHINGTON POST, 11/17/95, p. F1, Rita Kempley
WASHINGTON POST, 11/17/95, Weekend/p. 44, Desson Howe

ANGUS

A New Line Cinema release of an Atlas Entertainment/BBC/Syalis/Tele München/Quality Entertainment in association with Turner Pictures. *Executive Producer:* Robert Cavallo, Gary Levinsohn, and Susan B. Landau. *Producer:* Dawn Steel and Charles Roven. *Director:* Patrick Read Johnson. *Screenplay:* Jill Gordon. *Based on a short story by:* Chris Crutcher. *Director of Photography:* Alexander Grusynski. *Editor:* Janice Hampton. *Music:* David Russo. *Music Editor:* Charles Martin Inouye. *Choreographer:* Vincent Paterson. *Sound:* Ann Scibelli and (music) Frank Wolfe. *Sound Editor:* Catherine M. Speakman and Larry Mann. *Casting:* Ronnie Yeskel. *Production Designer:* Larry Miller. *Art Director:* Jeff Knipp. *Set Designer:* Theodore Sharps. *Set Decorator:* Cloudia. *Set Dresser:* James Barrows, David Leon McCardle, Joseph Genna, Ruben Santaella and Norman Skinner. *Special Effects:* T. "Brooklyn" Bellisimo. *Costumes:* Jill Ohanneson. *Make-up:* Michael "Mic" Tomasino. *Make-up: (George C. Scott):* Del Acevedo. *Stunt Coordinator:* Richard Butler. *Running time:* 91 minutes. *MPAA Rating:* PG.

CAST: Perry Anzilotti (Tuxedo Salesman); Kathy Bates (Meg); Robert Curtis-Brown (Alexander); Kevin Connolly (Andy); Tony Denman (Kid); Yvette Freeman (Science Teacher); Salim Grant (Mike); Epatha Harris (Ellen); Steven Hartman (Rick, Age 11); Robin Lynn Heath (Jody Cole); Grant Hoover (Angus, Age 8); Evan Kaufman (Alex Immergluch); James Keane (Coach); Irvin Kershner (Mr. Stoff); Michael McLeod (Rick, Age 8); Wesley Mann (Mr. Kessler); Rita Moreno (Madame Rulenska); Monty O'Grady (Minister); Chris Owen (Troy Wedberg); Bob Pepper (Wedding Photographer); Tanner Lee Prairie (Rick, Age 5); Lawrence Pressman (Principal Metcalf); Lindsay Price (Recycling Girl); Christopher Ragsdale (Boy Playing Football); Bethany Richards (Melissa, Age 11); Ariana Richards (Melissa Lefevre); Cameron Royds (Baby Angus); George C. Scott (Ivan); Aaron Siefers (Angus, Age 11); Charlie Talbert (Angus Bethune); Eric E. Thomas, II (Kid at Birthday Party); Anna Thomson (April Thomas); James Van Der Beek (Rick Sanford); Bryan Warloe (Troy, Age 8); Michael Wesley (Angus, Age 5).

LOS ANGELES TIMES, 9/15/95, Calendar/p. 10, Kevin Thomas

"Angus" takes us right smack back into the hell that was high school for all of us who didn't fit in for one reason or another. It's a journey made many times over in the movies, but this film, although uneven, has an uncommon honesty and a beguiling young actor, Charlie Talbert, in the title role. Angus describes himself accurately as "a fat guy who's good at science"—and therefore, the guy least likely to rake an impression on the prettiest, most popular girl in school (Ariana Richards).

Since this is a movie, after all, and ostensibly a comedy as well, we suspect Angus is going to get his chance. Yet its makers don't dodge the reality that no matter how much resilience hefty kids can develop, it doesn't mean they're really going to go off into the sunset with a boyfriend or girlfriend of spectacular good looks.

Although an asset on the football team, Angus is subjected to constant ridicule and has but one friend, the slight but enthusiastic Troy (Chris Owen), whose ears stick beyond what is considered socially acceptable at their small-town Midwestern school. It would seem that Angus and Troy have hunkered down pretty well, having taught themselves to roll—sometimes literally—with the punches. But then Angus is the victim of a prank, which finds him elected king of the freshman prom. Encouraged by his tart grandfather (George C. Scott), Angus gradually realizes that there might be some kind of inner victory for him if he dares to attend. What's more, Richards' lovely Melissa has been chosen queen of the prom.

Jill Gordon's script from a short story by Chris Crutcher illuminates Angus and his relationship to his grandfather and to his staunch, earthy mother (Kathy Bates, perfectly cast), but needs to have shed more light on Angus' key tormentor, the school's handsomest, most popular youth—and, inevitably, Melissa's boyfriend—Rick (James Van Der Beek). Decrying Angus as "not normal," Rick is actually obsessed by him, cruel to him—and even worse to Troy—to a degree that's downright pathological.

It's not difficult for director Patrick Read Johnson to make Rick's behavior believable, but a simple abhorrence of those who are different and therefore vulnerable doesn't satisfactorily explain the ferocity of Rick's contempt.

Also, the film defies credibility in having a beautiful, youngish blonde (Anna Thomson) fall hard for the grandfather; we never see them together, yet their relationship is supposed to give hope and inspiration to Angus. "Angus" furthermore never raises the possibility and value of dieting, and it rather surprisingly downplays the value of Angus' opportunity to transfer to a magnet school.

On the whole, however, the pluses of nicely observed, well-played characters—including a funny cameo by Rita Moreno as Angus' dance teacher—and an important theme help offset these drawbacks in what is otherwise an appealing film.

NEW YORK POST, 9/15/95, p. 42, Larry Worth

Zzzzz.

That's the best line given to George C. Scott in "Angus," starring as a feisty grandfather who falls asleep in mid-sentence. It's also the sound audiences will make right after the opening credits.

That's no fault of the great Scott. He tries hard to bring dignity and spirit to a thankless role. But being forced to recite Jill Gordon's puerile dialogue could bring even Gen. Patton to his knees.

Worse, Scott is playing second banana to a group of talentless teen stars—make that alleged stars—featured in this tired tale of an overweight schoolboy trying to fit in with his peers.

Yes, it's more of "Little Giants," "The Sandlot" and every other underdog-beats-the-odds movie, ad nauseam. And like its forebears, it stinks like last week's garbage.

The hero, titular Angus (Charlie Talbert), is perceived as a loser since his waistline reflects enough Twinkies to satisfy the entire senior class. He hangs out with a nerdy outcast (Chris Owen), lusts after the prettiest girl in school (Ariana "Jurassic Park" Richards) and is tormented by her handsome jock boyfriend (James Van Der Beek). Deja vu, anyone?

However, director Patrick Read Johnson wants to have it both ways. For instance, audiences are meant to laugh as the bully runs Angus' huge underpants up the flagpole. Then audiences are meant to tear up over Angus' humiliation. And despite Johnson's heavy-handedness, audiences are meant not to retch.

Actually, compassion comes from Kathy Bates' brief bits as Angus' distraught mom, another veteran in the war against heft. But a cameo by Academy Award winner Rita Moreno is as out of place as the heavy metal score.

Accordingly, like its bovine namesake, "Angus" is as big and dumb as they come.

NEWSDAY, 9/15/95, Part II/p. B7, John Anderson

News flash: Kids are pathologically cruel. Fat boys get picked on. Social success in high school has more to do with looks and personality than with the inner man. Cute girls don't date geeks.

If you didn't already know all this, "Angus" will be quite a revelation. If you did, it will likely be a torturous exercise in the obvious.

The story certainly has a ring to it, though it lacks the "Carrie"-style ending one might begin hoping for. Angus Bethune (Charlie Talbert) possesses a physique as large and soft as his disposition; he excels in science, is an unstoppable defensive lineman on the J.V. team and is constantly on the receiving end of life's swift punt in the shorts. All his life, he's been in love with Melissa Lefevre (Ariana Richards of "Jurassic Park"), with whom he's never even spoken.

She, of course, is the steady girlfriend of Rick Sanford (James Van Der Beek), the golden boy/quarterback who's made it his life's work to torment Angus—and who thinks it amusing to rig the school election for king and queen of the winter dance, pairing Melissa and Angus for the latter's ultimate humiliation.

There is, unfortunately, no carnage, no infernal retribution, no overturned cars or demonic possession. Just a lesson in individuality that is presented as a celebration of self, but that's too exaggerated in its gestures to come off as much but a cartoon.

For all the good intentions, director Patrick Read Johnson goes through a lot of teen-movie motions, and even though Angus is someone you root for, his weight is too often part of the gag. Almost every time Melissa appears, she's shot in slo-mo; grievous bodily injury is used for comedic effect. And when Angus' beloved grandfather Ivan (George C. Scott) drops dead on his own wedding day, it's not just overdue—he's been marked for death since the opening credits—it provides the opportunity for some really heavy-handed symbolism: Angus goes to see Ivan's old chess partner in the park to break the news, and wordlessly topples the white king on the board. A tender moment, during which it's tough not to chortle.

The young performers are uniformly good, though. Talbert plays the older Angus (Michael Wesley and Aaron Siefers play the younger versions) with just the right amount of self-pity and pathos. Van Der Beek is appropriately loathsome as Rick. Kathy Bates has a slim role as Angus' mom, a truck driver nicknamed Bruiser who tempts Angus with Haagen-Dazs when he's depressed (a strangely incongruous scene suggesting that perhaps genetic obesity isn't the problem here).

Ariana Richards, who was quite good as the imperiled girl in "Jurassic Park," has a pretty thankless role as Angus' dream girl. Even though she's oblivious to his pain, it doesn't matter in these kinds of stories, where the self-involvement of the hero is infectious.

SIGHT AND SOUND, 4/96, p. 36, Claire Monk

Good at science and a heavyweight asset to his school football team, lumbering teenager Angus Bethune is none the less a figure of fun among his high school peers and so he applies to a more academic school. In the meantime he is constantly taunted by star quarterback Rick Sanford and invisible to Melissa Lefevre—a cheerleader who is also Rick's girlfriend. Support comes from Angus' nerdy, undersized best friend Troy and his family: widowed truck-driver mum Meg and 72-year-old grandfather Ivan who (to Meg's disapproval) is soon to marry April, a blonde 30 years his junior.

Rick and his clique rig the votes for the school's freshman winter ball so that Angus is elected King of the Ball with Melissa his Queen. Angus faces an impossible decision: should he refuse to go and miss his one chance to get close to Melissa, or be brave enough to risk the humiliation? Troy and Ivan take steps to build his confidence for the big moment: Troy videos him practising dance moves with an inflatable doll, and Ivan books him a lesson with Madame Rulenska, a professional dance instructor. Realising that Angus is taking the challenge seriously, Rick bullies Troy into handing over the dancing video.

Angus' interview for the new school falls on the same day as the ball. He gains strength from sharing Ivan's pre-wedding nerves—but when Ivan dies before the ceremony, he decides to withdraw from the ball. Putting all his energy into his experiment, he astounds the interviewer with the "Bethune theory"—namely that in every 'normal' system there is an aberration which, if strong enough, will cause the system itself to change.

Going to the ball after all, Angus discovers that Melissa is as nervous as he is. Rick plays the video of Angus and the doll but his prank repels Melissa. Impressed by his courage she continues to dance with Angus—until Rick punches him to the floor. Challenging Rick on behalf of the majority of students who don't fit Rick's idea of 'normal', Angus announces that, although he has won a place at the new school, he means to stay put and be himself. Rick is suspended for the assault and Angus is delighted when Melissa asks him to walk her home.

At first glance a conventional Hollywood teen product, *Angus* was in fact made in America with the aid of European co-production money, including some from the BBC. The unusual nature of this funding arrangement has its analogy in the quirky qualities of the film itself. Shot in Minnesota—the heart of the Midwest, but also, with the strong Scandinavian roots of many of its inhabitants, not the conventional America of the movies—*Angus* depicts an unhip, everyday adolescent world, light years away from the rich Beverly Hills teens of the recent satire *Clueless*. *Angus* is likeable precisely because of the distance between its good-hearted but unslushy humanitarian comedy and the slick satire of the undeniably pleasurable *Clueless*. This gap is not reducible to *Angus'* identification with a teenage social underdog. Where *Clueless* defines success as acceptance by the teenage social elite, *Angus* argues that resistance to homogeneity causes the system to accommodate difference.

Although the plot is in the triumph-against-the-odds tradition, this is no simplistic anthem to American individualism. *Angus'* cry from the heart is a collective one: "There are 400 kids in the hall, and *none* of them are normal!" says the hero during his final showdown with Rick. The point about Angus is that he is an accidental outsider. He just wants to be allowed to get on with being himself—"a fat kid who's good at science and fair at football," as he puts it—without being bullied, belittled or harassed. Angus' contribution is overlooked primarily because of his fatness. Early in the film, Angus is shown winning a football match for his high school team, the Huskies, by means of his sheer bulk—an opposing player collides with Angus so forcefully that the ball shoots into the sky—but it is Rick, who catches it, and who is treated as the hero. Even Angus' teachers are complicit: his female science teacher is more interested in praising Rick's sporting achievement than in paying attention to the experiment that Angus is trying to demonstrate.

Unusually, *Angus* resists this tyranny of physical perfection even in its casting. It's not just that the intimidatingly bulky Angus and his carrot-haired, jug-eared *ET*-like sidekick Troy (so tiny that when Rick suspends him from a coat hanger in a school locker his feet dangle a foot above the floor) are lacking in looks. Even Rick and Melissa—ostensibly the peak of Hollywood blonde physical perfection—project an amorphous blandness which is deeply unattractive. The film's success in engaging us in its hero's predicament owes much to its experienced comedy director Patrick Read Johnson (*Martians!!!*, *Spaced Invaders*, *Speed Racer*, *Baby's Day Out*) and also to the bathetic humour of Jill Gordon's script. Angus' step-by-step metamorphosis transforms him merely "from a large, pathetic virgin into a large, pathetic virgin with a new look." Angus and Troy's relationship to the language of adolescence is not one of ownership but of exclusion: "Yeah, I'm a babe magnet," Angus retorts sourly in response to some ego-bolstering faint praise from Troy.

In the sense that its concerns lie outside brand-conscious teen materialism, *Angus* could be described as nostalgic. That the film gets away with championing equality of opportunity without slipping into sentimentality says much about the way the characters are performed: George C. Scott has a complex warmth as Angus' dogged chess-playing grandfather. Kathy Bates makes a vivid arm-wrestling, truck-driving mum as Meg, although she is given disappointingly little to do as the film progresses. As Angus, 16-year-old Charlie Talbert—reputedly discovered by the director in a Wendy's queue in Illinois—is more than a match for his co-stars in this, his sensitive, funny and unaffected movie debut.

VILLAGE VOICE, 9/26/95, p. 75, Georgia Brown

There're no Jews in *Angus*, at least that I noticed, but like *Unstrung Heroes*, the angst-ridden *Angus*—leans heavily on a parents death for old fashioned schmaltz. Technically here it's the death of a father surrogate, a boy's maternal grandfather (poor George C. Scott). "My father died in childbirth," reports Angus (Charlie Talbert), and so he, Mom (Kathy Bates), and Gramps are a family.

Some people think *Angus* is about cows—the bovine answer to *Babe*—but no, Angus is a real live boy, albeit one who wears husky sizes. The movie is an after-school special for fat kids, or whatever the preferred euphemism (Angus calls himself "fat"). The comedy's heavily hammered home moral is that since everyone is different society ought to honor, not stifle, diversity.

The movie's climax takes place at a class dance where, as a cruel joke, Angus has been voted King. Here, I was praying for a *Carrie*-type denouement, the bucket of blood, etc. Fat chance.

Also reviewed in:
CHICAGO TRIBUNE, 9/15/95, Friday/p. H, Michael Wilmington
NEW YORK TIMES, 9/15/95, p. C16, Janet Maslin
VARIETY, 9/18-24/95, p. 94, Godfrey Cheshire
WASHINGTON POST, 9/15/95, p. D4, Rita Kempley

APOLLO 13

A Universal Pictures release of an Imagine Entertainment presentation. *Executive Producer:* Todd Hallowell. *Producer:* Brian Grazer. *Director:* Ron Howard. *Screenplay:* William Broyles, Jr., and Al Reinert. *Based on the book "Lost Moon" by:* Jim Lovell and Jeffrey Kluger. *Director of Photography:* Dean Cundey. *Editor:* Mike Hill and Dan Hanley. *Music:* James Horner. *Music Editor:* Jim Hendriksen and Thomas Drescher. *Sound:* David Macmillan and (music) Shawn Murphy. *Sound Editor:* Stephen Hunter Flick. *Casting:* Jane Jenkins and Janet Hirshenson. *Production Designer:* Michael Corenblith. *Set Designer:* Joseph A. Hodges and Lori Rowbotham. *Art Director:* David J. Bomba and Bruce Alan Miller. *Set Decorator:* Merideth Boswell. *Set Dresser:* Lisa K. Sessions. *Special Effects:* Matt Sweeney. *Costumes:* Rita Ryak. *Make-up:* Daniel Striepeke. *Stunt Coordinator:* Mickey Gilbert and Jim Halty. *Running time:* 135 minutes. *MPAA Rating:* PG.

CAST: Tom Hanks (Jim Lovell); Bill Paxton (Fred Haise); Kevin Bacon (Jack Swigert); Gary Sinise (Ken Mattingly); Ed Harris (Gene Kranz); Kathleen Quinlan (Marilyn Lovell); Mary Kate Schellhardt (Barbara Lovell); Emily Ann Lloyd (Susan Lovell); Miko Hughes (Jeffrey Lovell); Max Elliott Slade (Jay Lovell); Jean Speegle Howard (Blanch Lovell); Tracy Reiner (Mary Haise); David Andrews (Pete Conrad); Michelle Little (Jane Conrad); Chris Ellis (Deke Slayton); Joe Spano (NASA Director); Xander Berkeley (Henry Hurt); Marc McClure (Glynn Lunney); Ben Marley (John Young); Clint Howard (EECOM White); Loren Dean (EECOM Arthur); Tom Wood (EECOM Gold); Googy Gress (RETRO White); Patrick Mickler (RETRO Gold); Ray McKinnon (FIDO White); Max Grodenchik (FIDO Gold); Christian Clemenson (Dr. Chuck); Brett Cullen (CAPCOM 1); Ned Vaughn (CAPCOM 2); Andy Milder (GUIDO White); Geoffrey Blake (GUIDO Gold); Wayne Duvall (LEM Controller White); Jim Meskimen (TELMU White); Joseph Culp (TELMU Gold); John Short (INCO White); Ben Bode (INCO Gold); Todd Louiso (FAO White); Gabriel Jarret (GNC White); Christopher John Fields (Booster White); Kenneth White (Grumman Rep); Jim Ritz (Ted); Andrew Lipschultz (Launch Director); Mark Wheeler (Neil Armstrong); Larry Williams (Buzz Aldrin); Endre Hules (Guenter Wendt); Karen Martin (Tracey); Maureen Hanley (Woman); Meadow Williams (Kim); Walter Von Huene (Technician); Brian Markinson and Steve Rankin (Pad Rats); Austin O'Brien (Whiz Kid); Louisa Marie (Whiz Kid Mom); Thom Barry (Orderly); Arthur Senzy, Carl Gabriel Yorke, and Ryan Holihan (SIM Techs); Rance Howard (Reverend); J.J. Chaback (Neighbor); Todd Hallowell (Noisy Civilian); Matthew Goodall (Stephen Haise); Taylor Goodall (Fred Haise, Jr.); Misty Dickinson (Margaret Haise); Roger Corman (Congressman); Lee Anne Matusek and Mark D. Newman (Loud Reporters); Mark McKeel (Suit Room Assistant); Patty Raya (Patty); Jack Conley and Jeffrey S. Kluger (Science Reporters); Bruce Wright, Ivan Allen, and Jon Bruno (Anchors); Reed Rudy (Roger Chaffee); Steve Bernie (Virgil Grissom); Steven Ruge (Edward White).

CHRISTIAN SCIENCE MONITOR, 6/30/95, p. 12, David Sterritt

"Apollo 13" is well over two hours long, and when I realized there weren't going to be any surprises, I passed the time by recalling earlier movies with outer-space themes—pictures that do have surprises, marking milestones in the development of rocket-powered cinema.

One such moment in "2001: A Space Odyssey," when the movie cuts from a bone wielded by a primitive humanoid to a spacecraft designed by 21st century scientists, indicating that both are tools inspired by the same basic impulse toward mastery and progress.

Another is in "Star Wars," when Han Solo jump-starts the balky Millennium Falcon by whopping the control panel with his hand, suggesting that space-age technology isn't so mysterious or intimidating after all.

Yet another is in "E.T. the Extra-Terrestrial," when Elliott's bicycle suddenly soars into the sky, demonstrating that science-fiction subject matter and fairytale plot twists can go hand in hand when feel-good entertainment is the filmmaker's only goal.

Alas, there are no such surprises in "Apollo 13," one of this season's most conspicuous bids for a high-tech superhit. To be fair, the movie is reigned in by its fact-based narrative, which prevents director Ron Howard and his collaborators from letting their imaginations soar as they might have in a purely fictional setting. For the same reason, the picture will disappoint people looking for megadoses of suspense, since the outcome of the story—everyone back on Earth, safe and sound—is a given from the start.

What compensates for this predictable plot is the professionalism with which it's told, turning a minor piece of 1970s history into an engaging yarn with equal quantities of special-effects wizardry and human feeling.

The events of "Apollo 13" come from the eponymous NASA mission launched in 1970, intended to land another team of Americans on the moon about eight months after Neil Armstrong and company inaugurated the era of lunar exploration.

Preparation for the flight was marred by significant glitches, including the last-minute replacement of a crew member for health reasons. But nothing prepared the astronauts for the calamity that hit right after liftoff: A string of minor accidents caused an oxygen tank to explode, disabling the command module and putting the three crew members in deadly danger. Reluctantly giving up hope of a moon landing, they turned their attention to getting back home in one piece, supported by the talented yet increasingly anxious experts at Mission Control in Houston.

Dramatic as they sound when outlined in a few phrases, these events don't automatically add up to sure-fire screen material, largely because American interest in space travel has dropped off drastically since pre-Apollo days. This had already begun when Apollo 13 started its journey, as the movie itself shows. Not much press showed up at Cape Kennedy for the launch, and the crew's inflight telecasts were ignored by TV networks.

Today, many still regard space voyages as dull, mechanical procedures—an accurate perception, if one believes an expert like Tom Wolfe, who shows in "The Right Stuff" how the astronauts' own training was designed to turn their flights into routines as predictable as the drills they practiced in their simulators. No wonder modern science-fictioneers like Steven Spielberg take care to spice up their space-oriented stories with the fantastical trappings of an "E.T." or the mystical overtones of a "Close Encounters of the Third Kind," using nonscience ingredients to prevent technology-based tales from seeming as dry as moon dust.

Howard's solution to this problem is a major dose of human-interest drama revolving around the personal lives of the astronauts. The first part of the picture is strictly earthbound, as module commander Jim Lovell reassures his nervous wife, rookie astronaut Jack Swigert hops into the mission with little warm-up time, and grounded pilot Ken Mattingly copes with disappointment at being dropped from the expedition. Minor characters like Lovell's apprehensive kids take on more importance as the story unfolds, and even his cranky, old mother makes a few appearances for comic relief.

While none of this is very original, it works reasonably well thanks to a smartly chosen cast. Tom Hanks makes a welcome change in his recent image, trading Gumpian goofiness for Lovell's controlled intelligence. Kevin Bacon and Bill Paxton make strong contributions as Swigert and crewmate Fred Haise, respectively, and Gary Sinise is solid if not inspired as the astronaut they had to leave behind. Ed Harris lends a hint of his patented weirdness as the Mission Control chief, and Kathleen Quinlan is richly believable as Lovell's spouse. Their efforts help "Apollo

13" function as efficiently as the mission itself was supposed to—by the numbers, but with enough guts and gumption to make the ride worthwhile.

After seeing the picture, I polled a few friends who were young adults (like me) when the real-life ordeal took place, and found that they (like me) barely remember the incident and paid little attention at the time—contrary to the movie's insistence that all America was huddled over TV sets and radios from the moment the mishap became known. I now join my once-apathetic friends, all of whom like the movie fairly well, in thanking Howard for letting me relive a historical moment that I didn't bother to live when it happened. "Apollo 13" is no trendsetter like "2001" or "E.T.," but it's a good enough adventure while it lasts.

FILMS IN REVIEW, 9-10/95, p. 54, Andy Pawelczak

First *Crimson Tide*, followed by *Apollo 13*. The submarine movie and the space flight movie inevitably have things in common: both take place in alien elements, invite a mise-en-scene of claustrophobia, and place men in tense situations working against the clock. The spacecraft in *Apollo 13*, the tale of NASA's ill-fated flight to the moon in 1970, is named *Odyssey*, which was appropriate in a sense NASA never imagined. Homer's epic poem is not really about a journey of exploration—it's about Odysseus's homesickness and long voyage back to Ithaca. *Apollo 13* is about just such a journey home and the Odyssean resourcefulness of the astronauts and the Mission Control crew when one piece of technology after another fails and the ship is almost marooned in space. The picture has a higher energy quotient than *Crimson Tide* but ultimately succumbs, contra the movie's theme and the best intentions of all involved, to the doldrums of the technological drama which all but submerges the human factor.

Home in the movie is represented by the classic house in the suburbs and a close-knit community of family and friends. Ron Howard, the director, doesn't overload the picture with period detail but enough is sketched in to suggest the ever-widening fracture of the family in the late sixties—a teenage girl's hysteria over the breakup of the Beatles, a father's slight irritation over a son's lengthening hair. Still, the family here is the mythical haven in a heartless world of the fifties and Jim Lovell (Tom Hanks), the commander of Apollo 13, is the ideal paterfamilias-sensitive father, tender husband, loyal comrade and friend. At one point he stares out the spacecraft window at the earth and Howard cuts to a shot of his wife (Kathleen Quinlan) looking up at the sky, and we know that the gravitational pull of home will bring this starman back to earth.

In the movie's central scenes, Howard crosscuts between the astronauts in their cramped, crippled command module and the frantic activity of the Mission Control crew in Houston. As one disaster after another afflicts the ship—an explosion, depletion of oxygen, a buildup of carbon dioxide, loss of electrical power—the astronauts are reduced to the basic existential human condition (for that spacecraft bouncing in the void, read planet earth) with nothing to rely on but their wits and their comrades back in Houston. The problem with all of this is that the drama in the ship isn't all that compelling. The astronauts are too passive—all they really have to do is keep their heads, endure and carry out the directions of the whiz-kids at Mission Control—and their interpersonal relations are minimal. Lovell and Fred Haise (Bill Paxton), the two family men, distrust the newcomer to the crew, swinging bachelor Jack Swigert (Kevin Bacon), who has to prove himself in the course of the crisis. And that's about it.

The drama back at Mission Control has slightly more voltage as scientists improvise ingenious solutions to the various technical problems and Ken Mattingly (Gary Sinise), a disappointed astronaut slated for the flight but left behind after his exposure to measles, demonstrates the right stuff by devising a method to conserve the ship's electrical power. As Flight Director Gene Kranz, Ed Harris exudes male authority, barking out orders in a manner reminiscent of Tommy Lee Jones in *The Fugitive*.

Reportedly, President Clinton liked this picture and it's not hard to understand why. The movie celebrates American pragmatism and patriotism and the myth of the nuclear family, and in Tom Hanks' Lovell it has a hero for our time—a stolid, straight-arrow family man who still vibrates to the siren call of the frontier. Perhaps Clinton also responded to the film's take on the media. Initially the networks refuse to carry the Apollo 13 launch because space flight has become routine, but once the astronauts are endangered, Lovell's wife, his Penelope, is besieged, not by suitors but by TV newsmen. Clinton, often snubbed by the networks, must have recognized something of his own experience here.

LOS ANGELES TIMES, 6/30/95, Calendar/p. 1, Kenneth Turan

Apollo 13 (the mission, not the movie) was the space flight no one cared about. Men had been sent to the moon before and presumably would be again. When its trio of astronauts transmitted television pictures back to Earth, the networks couldn't be bothered to broadcast them live. But, two days-plus into the journey, a handful of words changed everything.

"OK, Houston, we've had a problem," astronaut Jim Lovell radioed to Mission Control, and with that sentence the most attenuated emergency in manned space flight history began: three men in a dying ship 200,000 miles from home needing to survive for 100 hours to preserve any chance of returning. It almost sounds like an entry in the captain's log of the Starship Enterprise.

The story of that struggle involves as much courage and skill as anything the space program offered. Reading both "Lost Moon," Lovell and Jeffrey Kluger's book about that benighted flight, and "A Man on the Moon," Andrew Chaikin's excellent examination of the entire Apollo project, underlines why, as Chaikin relates, President Richard M. Nixon resisted pressure to cancel the Apollo series: "The moon program held magic for Nixon for one reason: He liked heroes ... It was good for the nation, Nixon believed, to have heroes."

"Apollo 13," directed by Ron Howard from a script by William Broyles Jr. and Al Reinert based on Lovell's book, is certainly a movie of which the late President would have approved. There is no revisionism here, none of the kind of bemused tweaking Tom Wolfe gave the space program in "The Right Stuff." This film is wall-to-wall with straight-arrow, manly types like Lovell, inevitably played by Tom Hanks, who are such wholesome heroes that it's something of a shock to remember that all this took place in 1970, not the 1950s of "Father Knows Best."

Ron Howard, the master of Opie-Vision, is certainly well-suited to the kind of sentimental, middle-of-the-road filmmaking of which "Apollo 13" is the epitome. And because the material to a certain extent cries out for this kind of worshipful treatment, the picture stands as Howard's most impressive to date. As noted, genuine courage was involved, and Howard is effective at putting the tension and bravery of that mission on screen.

But "Apollo 13" can't leave well enough alone. Self-conscious about its heroism with portrayals that lean toward the glib and the professionally uplifting, the film milks our sympathies too readily to be emotionally convincing. And its tendency to mimic attitudes of bravery rather than effectively convey them allows a certain hollowness to sink into the inspirational moments.

Before they get lost in space, "Apollo 13" introduces us to the astronauts here on planet Earth. Lovell, with three previous flights, 572 hours and almost 7 million space miles on his résumé, is crew commander and pure great guy, devoted in equal parts to wife Marilyn (Kathleen Quinlan), his family and getting to walk on the moon. Although no heavy lifting is involved in the acting department, only someone of Hanks' presence and charisma could make this character believable and involving.

Lovell's two partners on Apollo 13 are supposed to be Fred Haise (Bill Paxton) and Ken Mattingly (Gary Sinise), but at the last moment Mattingly gets exposed to German measles and much against his will is replaced by Jack Swigert (Kevin Bacon), a bachelor astronaut who seems to believe that dating different women is within his rights as an American.

The key operative in Mission Control in Houston is flight director Gene Kranz (an excellent performance by Ed Harris). Despite an uncharacteristic belief in the wearing of a lucky vest, Kranz is even more buttoned-down and no-nonsense than the astronauts, qualities that turn out to be much in demand.

For, during the eighth hour of the third day in space, things begin to go seriously wrong. A routine stirring of the liquid oxygen tanks triggers an electrical short and then a major explosion. Not only does the planned landing on the moon have to be scrubbed, but several daunting problems (buildup of carbon dioxide gas in the cabin, a lack of power, question marks about the engines) have to be overcome if the three men have even a hope of making it back to Earth.

Although "Apollo 13" is so jargon heavy it can be unclear exactly what is happening in space, the scramble both in Houston and on board ship to bring everyone back alive is well done and easily the most effective part of the movie. Helped by a completely convincing physical re-creation and Howard's willingness to be straight ahead with his directing, the film's derring-do aspects have the advantage of showing the men simply being heroic as opposed to acting like heroes.

But some of the power of this impressive story is undercut by "Apollo 13's" macho overlay. This is a quintessential guy movie, filled with tough talk, cigarette smoke and no end of significant man-to-man looks. What it resembles most is a war movie without a human enemy, a kind of "combat-lite" where heroism and camaraderie can be displayed without the messiness of blowing anybody away.

This kind of subtle hyping of reality is the film's most persistent problem. "Apollo 13" leads you to believe the men never slept during their ordeal, when in fact they did, albeit badly. It presents a scene of dramatic bickering on board that apparently did not occur. And it shows us corny bad omen scenes like Marilyn Lovell losing her wedding ring in the shower that feel inescapably phony.

Blessed with a great story, which they mostly tell rather well, the filmmakers don't seem to totally trust it and end up creating, in a phrase used to describe the mission itself, "a successful failure." They're so intent on never letting us forget how brave and noble these people were they allow an unnecessary sense of phoniness to intrude on the proceedings. Engrossing though it is, "Apollo 13" feels more like a venerated relic than the realistic tribute it wants badly to be.

NEW STATESMAN & SOCIETY, 9/22/95, p. 29, Jonathan Romney

A few weeks ago, Channel 4 screened the infamous "Roswell" footage—grainy black-and-white film that purported to show an autopsy performed on a genuine extra-terrestrial. There was a time when the media would have been in a frenzy over even the possibility that there might be evidence of life elsewhere in the universe. These days, however, such cosmic imponderables seem like a quaint side-platter of *National Enquirer* fodder; and even if the High Plenipotentiary of Alpha Centauri had landed this week in Trafalgar Square with a full cadre of purple people-eaters, the event would have had less tabloid space than Prince Wills's schooldays or the launch of the latest cable porn channel.

The success of Ron Howard's *Apollo 13*—it has so far taken $200 million worldwide—is less to do with our fascination with space than with a collective nostalgia for a time when space was fascinating. We can most of us remember a time when the infinite seemed infinite—before Neil Armstrong's walk on the moon, before the famous photo of the glowing earth had become a money-spinner for Athena Posters. *Close Encounters, ET*, and *Star Wars*—and the political appropriation of that term—had yet to domesticate the idea of space, or bring the alien uncanny into the realm of suburban kitsch.

It's commonly accepted that space ceased to be transcendental the moment that Armstrong took his one giant leap for the recyclable soundbite. *Apollo 13*, with some degree of regret, shows space travel as being firmly on a human footing. Its nicest touch is that Armstrong and Buzz Aldrin appear in a very domestic light—they're brought in as jovial neighbours to distract Jim Lovell's old mom from the Apollo 13 crisis. It reminds you that, although they always seemed destined for demi-god status, in the cosmic icon stakes they somehow ended up lagging somewhere behind Yuri Gagarin and Laika the dog.

Apollo 13 is an account of human bravery so everyday and pragmatic it's altogether banal. It's a story of failure snatched from the jaws of defeat—a story in which nothing *really* happens. Jim Lovell, Fred Haise and Jack Swigert (Tom Hanks, Kevin Bacon, Bill Paxton) set out for the moon in 1970, ran into problems *en route*, and made a perilous return to earth, missing the moon entirely. It would be a wonderful basis for allegorical farce; there is indeed a degree of bitter humour, largely directed at the blasé media of the time, who refused to cover the mission until it became a life-and-death nail-biter.

But by and large, the film is played straight, with one eye on the human factor—the brave boys and the hugely undercharacterised little ladies at home—and another on spectacle and authenticity. The filmmakers had unprecedented access to Nasa facilities and advice in a deal that has handsomely paid back the budget-beleaguered space agency in good PR.

Curiously, gripping as it is, *Apollo 13* is a non-drama. It's a suspense story whose outcome we already know, so its appeal lies entirely in putting us through the events for ourselves. (In fact, John Sturges' *Marooned*, a fiction film that did have the benefit of unknown outcome, and which anticipated the Apollo incident, suffered from being released just as it was happening.) What appeals is the inexorability of it all—the sense that there only can be one outcome, and that it will be good. At one point in the rescue attempt, Mission Control boss Gene Kranz (Ed Harris) manfully declares, "Failure is not an option." One hell of a catchphrase, this was recently quoted: with approval by Bill Clinton.

Apollo 13 nevertheless functions quite adequately as a theme-park experience that lets you feel what it might be like to be marooned in space with no certainty of returning. Theme-park simulation has been desperately overworked as a paradigm for the spectacle movie of the 1990s, but it's peculiarly applicable here. The heroes are actually saved from death by a feat of imaginative projection on the part of their colleague Ken Mattingly (Gary Sinise), who spends his time locked in a flight simulator trying to figure out what he'd do in their position. Watching the film, it could be us in that simulator. When the astronauts are saved, there's no catharsis, surprise or moral payoff—simply the feeling we'd have if we were stepping out of a fun capsule at Universal City. We heave a sign of relief and head for the cold drinks stand.

Since American politicians are always looking to appropriate pop culture images to illustrate their own ideal of national spirit, it's no surprise that *Apollo 13*'s simple-guy-can-do premise has been endorsed both by Clinton and Newt Gingrich. It speaks of America's current crisis of self-image that the tale stirring the nation is not triumphalist, as the Apollo 13 story might have been, but a real piece of muddling through pragmatism in the face of confusion—reassurance for a nation with a sense of siege culture.

What's missing, curiously, is a sense of what the astronauts have left behind on earth, and what they hope to return to. The 1970 we see is never real, but as much a simulation as the journey itself. Howard gives us not a feeling of a real past, but period effect—history denoted by hideous wallpaper and bouffant hairdos, the sort of kitsch stylistic nudge Hollywood uses to denote what it thinks of as more innocent times. But the sense of what 1970 might have felt like to live in—other than a joke about the Beatles break-up—is largely absent. Space is something we can handle, but the past really is *terra incognita*.

NEW YORK, 7/10/95, p. 51, David Denby

As three astronauts lie in a cramped command module, ready to take off for the moon, technicians tread on their shoulders, jamming the men into place. Later, somewhere between Florida and the lunar seas, the module's power and filtering systems break down, and the men, freezing, gaze at their steamy breath with disgust: They are poisoning themselves with the carbon dioxide they exhale from their own lungs. You have to love the weird details in *Apollo 13*. Just like ancient explorers ravaged by weather and fatigue, the astronauts on this 1970 moon shot are forced to withstand bizarre physical humiliations. Director Ron Howard and his longtime collaborator, producer Brian Grazer, took a considerable risk and decided to do the picture straight. They must have figured that a moon shot that almost ended in disaster was quite dramatic enough; the story didn't have to be pumped. And they were right. *Apollo 13* follows the three astronauts through preparation, launch, the amazing weightless hours on the way to the moon, and then the accidents and the bumpy, cold, and terrifying ride home. Contained and realistic as it is, the movie nevertheless works up terrific excitement.

The sick joke of *Apollo 13* is that no one was much interested until things went awry. Neil Armstrong had walked on the moon the previous summer, and the public took a blasé attitude toward a new attempt. When the commander of the flight, Jim Lovell (Tom Hanks), beamed a live feed of the spaceship back to Earth, not one of the broadcast networks picked it up. Lovell, a space-flight veteran, comes off as a very straight guy with a touch of poetic fancy underneath. Tom Hanks, in the great American heroic style of no sweat, makes him a man so sure of himself that he can afford to be relaxed. Bill Paxton, as Fred Haise, and Kevin Bacon, as Jack Swigert, aren't as charismatic as one would ideally want, but charisma is not the point of this movie.

Apollo 13 might be called an answer to *The Right Stuff*. These were not swaggering romantic adventurers, the movie says, but lifetime military men, with the fierce codes and tightly controlled demeanor typical of their tribe. They did what they were told, and were very loyal to one another. It's the team that is heroic. During the flight of *Apollo 13*, the vaunted technology that had already taken men to the moon blows up like a toy spacecraft pushed too hard. As one failure causes another, the flock of nervous, white-shirted flight controllers back in Houston, each one wired into a particular part of *Apollo*'s misbehavior, begin to go nuts. Their honor is at stake. This community of macho techies (led by a taut, hostile Ed Harris) breaks its collective neck trying to bring the men back. The movie is very straight, very square stuff, but stirring and satisfying. There are weaknesses: Lovell has a prescient wife (Kathleen Quinlan) who suffers through premonitory dreams and drops her wedding ring down the shower drain—she's a walking foreshadow of trouble. Some of the family scenes are awfully bland. But when the module is going crazy, turning red-hot as it enters the Earth's atmosphere, you're with the three men, and you are scared.

NEW YORK POST, 6/30/95, p. 31, Michael Medved

The underlying irony of "Apollo 13" is that a lunar mission that went disastrously wrong should now provide the basis for a film in which everything goes miraculously right.

Like any successful space shot, the picture soars past the bounds of gravity with deceptively effortless ease—making it possible to ignore the difficulties and complexities of such a hugely ambitious enterprise.

Tom Hanks plays Jim Lovell, commander of the purportedly anti-climatic 1970 expedition that followed Apollo 11, Neil Armstrong's historic first lunar landing, and Apollo 12 by a mere eight months.

This original Apollo 13 mission might have done little to enrich our knowledge of the moon's surface, but it certainly advanced the cause of old-fashioned superstition. Talking to the press prior to liftoff, the astronauts (as portrayed in the film) laughingly dismissed all questions about "Unlucky 13," but before long these concerns seemed eerily appropriate.

On the way to the moon Lovell and his colleagues, Fred Haise and Jack Swigert (Bill Paxton and Kevin Bacon), suffered a midnight explosion that severely crippled their spacecraft. With barely enough power or oxygen left to make the emergency journey back to Earth, the astronauts faced the distinctly unpleasant prospect of becoming the first humans ever interred in a permanently orbiting coffin.

Meanwhile, back in Houston, NASA's Mission Control struggled to improvise some solution. As flight director Gene Kranz (fiercely well-played by Ed Harris) told his desperate crew, "Failure is not an option."

Fortunately, they received resourceful assistance from astronaut Ken Mattingly (Gary Sinise) who had been scrubbed from the ill-fated mission at the last moment and knew the capacities of the Apollo 13 craft better than anyone else.

In the hands of director Ron Howard, this story emerges as the summer's most thrilling movie adventure—despite the fact that everyone already knows the outcome. (The tight, skillful script is based on Lovell's book, "Lost Moon").

Unlike some of his previous films (notably "Backdraft"), Howard never allows breathtaking special effects (like the shattering force of liftoff or the uncannily re-created scenes of weightlessness) to overwhelm the human dimensions of the drama.

Hanks provides the heroic focus of that drama with a portrait of decency, decisiveness and resolute courage in the face of unimaginable adversity. His understated perfect-pitch performance is every bit as remarkable in its own quiet way as his more showy Oscar-outings in "Philadelphia" and "Forrest Gump."

Kathleen Quinlan plays his adoring, worried wife with similar balance and conviction—never crossing the line into melodrama or hysteria.

One of the themes of the film is the way the astronauts depended on hundreds of anonymous but dedicated technicians in Mission Control; and by the same token, the success of this film involved the brilliant efforts of countless "little people" at every phase of production.

The period details offer particular pleasure—even showing slide rules (remember them?) employed to facilitate all-important calculations by Apollo's Houston handlers.

Much of the discussion of the film will center around the chance for a Tom Hanks "three-peat" as Best Actor at the next Oscar ceremonies. Though 1995 is still too young for definitive predictions, there's little doubt he'd make a deserving nominee, and that the film itself will merit consideration as Best Picture of the year.

NEWSDAY, 6/30/95, Part II/p. B2, Jack Mathews

When John Kennedy upped the ante of the Cold War Space Race by telling a 1961 joint session of Congress that America should dedicate itself to punching a round-trip ticket to the moon by the end of that decade, it seemed an impossibly ambitious goal. Nonetheless, we pulled it off, with one small step and a giant leap, and by 1970, Americans had become so complacent about space travel, the three television networks didn't even bother to pick up NASA's live feed from the crew of the moon-bound Apollo 13.

But they would soon wish they had. By ignoring Apollo 13 Commander Jim Lovell's calm tour of the command module and the attached lunar landing craft, they missed the first act of what was to become the most hair-raising human drama of the Space Age, and fodder 25 years later for Ron Howard's extraordinary "Apollo 13," the best movie ever made about the U.S. space program.

Turning complicated technical detail to his advantage, Howard puts us in the cramped quarters of the Apollo 13 with Lovell (Tom Hanks), pilot Jack Swigert (Kevin Bacon) and navigator Fred Haise (Bill Paxton) and let's us count the ways they almost became the first Americans to die in space, and why, with the heroic efforts of their colleagues in Houston, they didn't.

Ten minutes after Lovell signed off from that April 13, 1970, broadcast, which was seen only by NASA employees and the astronauts' families, an explosion crippled Apollo 13, scrubbing the moon mission, and hurling its three-member crew farther and farther into space, with rapidly depleting supplies of oxygen and electrical power, and with no flight plan for pulling a U and rushing home.

The Apollo 13 accident is nothing compared to the Apollo 1 and Challenger disasters that killed a total of 10, but those events were over in seconds. The fate of the Apollo 13 crew was in doubt for 3½ days!

During that period, the crew had to steer the limping spacecraft manually around the moon and back to Earth, jury-rig carbon monoxide filters to save themselves from suffocating, and help Houston help them stretch their oxygen and battery power to twice their intended service.

Howard, working with an accurately and superbly detailed script by former journalists William Broyles Jr. and Al Reinert, tells the story in straightforward chronological time, providing a leisurely paced introduction of the characters—the crew members, their families, the operational leaders at NASA—who will fill out the foreground of the drama.

The hardware and the special effects work on "Apollo 13" is staggering. Without borrowing a frame of film from NASA, the movie gives us spectacular shots of lift-off, space flight, and re-entry. And rather than attempt to simulate weightlessness in a studio, they went to the trouble of building sets of the space craft inside NASA's KC-135 training plane, which achieves zero gravity, in 25-second bursts, by flying in a high-altitude arc.

To get the weightless footage they needed for the film, the cast and crew had to go through that arc more than 600 times.

But the real key to the film's success is Howard's effort to make us feel both what the astronauts were going through, and what their families and their colleagues were going through. Getting those men back safely from space was NASA's greatest achievement, showing not only how much brainpower it could rally to a crisis, but how much greater they valued lives than missions.

The performances are all solid, anchored by the reliable Tom Hanks, who could end up with his third Oscar nomination in as many years. But there's also fine work by Bacon, as the pilot who joined the crew as a last-minute replacement, by Gary Sinise, as the pilot left behind, and Ed Harris, the dapper flight director who had to direct the ad-libbed rescue operation.

Howard is not a flashy stylist, which is a tremendous plus on this movie. To see how a director's self-conscious vision can turn space history into a cartoon, rent Philip Kaufman's "The Right Stuff." The sentimentality that has undermined many of Howard's films shows up occasionally, particularly in a series of contrived comic relief scenes involving Jim Lovell's mother (played by Ron Howard's mother). But it is not excessive, and the emotional release that comes with Apollo 13's return is going to be hard to top as the year's most exhilarating movie moment.

NEWSWEEK, 7/3/95, p. 55, Jack Kroll

Apollo 13 recounts the final episode of a true epic trilogy. First came the tragedy of Apollo 1 that took the lives of three astronauts, then the triumph of Apollo 11, in which Neil Armstrong walked on the moon, and finally the human drama of Apollo 13, the most amazing rescue operation of all time. By sticking resolutely to the facts, the movie builds tremendous suspense, even though most people will know how it came out. The tension lies in the myriad details of the flight, details that reveal the character of the astronauts and the innumerable people on the ground, all of whom make up a marvelous human community interacting at a pitch of intelligence and passionate efficiency.

The movie beautifully captures the crescendo of desperate problems that starts when an oxygen tank explodes, turning the mission into a race for survival in a deteriorating spacecraft hurtling amid cosmic forces. The screenplay by William Broyles Jr. and Al Reinert (with an uncredited polish by John Sayles), the direction by Ron Howard, the performances of a superb cast, the technical magic (especially the reality of the weightless sequences) all work together with gripping effect. The movie takes just one major liberty with the facts, inventing a tense confrontation among astronauts Jim Lovell (Tom Hanks) Fred Haise (Bill Paxton) and Jack Swigert (Kevin Bacon), who had been a late replacement for Ken Mattingly (Gary Sinise).

This unneeded Hollywood touch doesn't spoil the integrity of an exciting and moving film. It's also sad, an elegy for a union of vision and can-do that seems almost prehistoric. Hanks establishes an American model of brains, dreams and decency. And Ed Harris turns flight director Gene Kranz, controlling and mediating a flood of ideas and solutions into a figure that goes beyond mission control. He's a prototype—for an ideal president to handle the spaceship of state.

SIGHT AND SOUND, 9/95, p. 42, Lizzie Francke

1969. Astronauts Jim Lovell, Fred Haise and Ken Mattingly train for Apollo 13, the next mission in the US space programme. Lovell, who wants to walk on the moon before he retires, promises his wife Marilyn that this will be his last mission. 1970. With a week to go to the launch, Mattingly is withdrawn after being exposed to measles, and replaced by one of the back-up crew, Jack Swigert. The launch goes smoothly, but the media have lost interest in the programme. As they cruise towards their destination, Swigert is asked to make a routine stirring of the oxygen tanks and one of them explodes in the service module, causing the space-craft to lose power as well as the precious gas. The moon landing is now cancelled—the priority is to bring the crew back safely to Earth.

The crew are forced to move up from the command module into the lunar module and to cut down on facilities. Mattingly is brought in to Mission Control to work out how to restart the computer for re-entry using the minimum power necessary. Tensions run high, the temperature drops in the command module, and Haise develops a fever. Carbon dioxide levels reach a dangerously high level, though Mission Control come up with a solution just in time. Swigert has calculated that they are slightly off-track for re-entry. He is proved right and Lovell and Haise have to re-align the craft using the earth as a fixed point target.

Finally, a re-powering procedure is devised and communicated to the crew. Swigert has to pilot the craft manually to line it up for the return. When the lunar module is finally discarded with the main body, the crew see the full extent of the damage. There may be a high risk of the craft burning up when it enters the earth's atmosphere. As they re-enter, they lose radio contact for longer than expected. For a moment, they seem lost to the world, but then the capsule is seen parachuting to splash-down. The astronauts are safely returned.

As the film *Apollo 13* launches, a voice-over (which we swiftly realise belongs to Tom Hanks as Jim Lovell) explains the NASA programme, stating that it was inspired by JFK and cold war politics. Apart from these brief comments, and a later mention that the Beatles have just broken up, global history is eschewed while the film covers the six-day story of three men who were nearly lost in space: James Lovell, Fred Haise and Jack Swigert. One reason why the Apollo mission was such a government priority was as a distraction from the Vietnam war. This political context is conspicuously disregarded here. Instead, director Ron Howard shows us a bright and cheerful America, blooming with vibrant flower prints and grooving to Jimi Hendrix and James

Brown. Only the comment about the Beatles indicates that the 60s dream is about to turn sour. Dubbed a 'successful failure', Apollo 13 smoothed over cracks evident in the space programme by becoming a major story—a moment of triumph—just when the media's interest was beginning to flag.

A more astute film-maker might have teased out the ironies and contradictions of an event that, in retrospect, seems to signal the downbeat and fearful mood of the new decade. There is an eerie glimmer of this when the crew's battery-depleted tape recorder floats weightlessly about blaring a run-down version of 'Blue Moon', but otherwise the film fails to convey a real sense of terror. Indeed, it has about as much atmosphere as the moon itself. Nor is it improved by James Horner's soundtrack, which is like some space sampler wavering between allusions to the *Aliens* (which Horner also composed) and the angelic chorus schmaltz of *E. T.* There is little sense of the claustrophobia and dramatic tension needed to render the incident as an adventure story.

Instead, Ron Howard tells a story of courage in which the crew and Mission Control pull together to work the problem through (much in the way that the firemen do in Howard's *Backdraft* or the family members in his *Parenthood*. No doubt science buffs will be happy that the audience are kept abreast of the technical side of the operation in the same way that *ER* keeps its medical details straight. Concentrate hard and one might even learn how to make a carbon dioxide extractor out of bits of tubing and odd socks.

Meanwhile, the characters have no time for mutiny or questioning the wisdom of superior officers back at the base. Instead, we are shown a moment in which the establishment gets it right. Unlike Philip Kaufman's perceptive study of the Mercury Project in *The Right Stuff*, Howard's film does not care to comment that the Apollo spacemen were as good as specimens in a rather risky experiment run by balding boffins, given things to do that could just as easily be done by remote control—a fact which would have given more dramatic weight to the accident that forced the astronauts to truly take some control. Howard may have cast Ed Harris, who played John Glenn in the Kaufman film, to play Mission Control leader Gene Kranz, but otherwise *Apollo 13* hardly measures up to the earlier film's dazzling adaptation of Tom Wolfe's wry critique.

Ultimately, there is something very chipper about *Apollo 13*, as if it wants to be a homage to the all-American spirit—the real Right Stuff. Cut-aways to Lovell's teenage son stoically watching the news reports with his classmates at a military academy seem to symbolise this. He is undoubtedly his father's son, for Lovell, along with Haise and Swigert, are brave men with few visible flaws. Tensions might run high in the capsule as Haise lashes out at Swigert and blames him for their predicament, but they are swiftly abated with a few calm words from Lovell. While Lovell's ambitions of becoming one of the few to walk on the moon are dashed, in the end he pulls off a feat more remarkable. Such a clean-cut crew makes for bland heroes. It is a problem endemic to films based on true life events which are honoured rather than interrogated. This is no *Quiz Show*. Only the skirt-chasing Swigert has any roguish appeal—particularly with Kevin Bacon in the role, who proved to be such a mean villain in *The River Wild*. Meanwhile, Hanks' Lovell is as solid, and as about as intriguing, as a chunk of moon rock. But his is a performance in keeping with *Apollo 13*, which makes all the right moves but lacks inspiration.

TIME, 7/3/95, p. 51, Richard Corliss

The typical adventure movie is a big, gaudy lie. It says life is a battle of one man, armed with only wit and grit, against a hostile universe. This romantic, existential notion does a disservice to the way most people live and work. We aren't solo flyers or secret agents. We are a squadron of team players dependent on our colleagues and increasingly on our machines to get us through our jobs. Often, because of those machines or those colleagues—or ourselves—we fail. And sometimes the bravest thing we can do is react quickly, boldly, gracefully to the failures and compromises we face every day. Getting along, getting by it's a big subject the movies hardly ever touch.

The 17 Apollo moon missions, from 1967 to 1972, provided cubic tons of melodrama, from the explosion of the Apollo 1 test module that killed three astronauts to Neil Armstrong's buoyant lunar stroll from Apollo 11. The apogee of American know-how and teamwork, the program could, at the flick of a wrong switch, careen from triumph to tragedy. In this job, success meant you forged the ultimate frontier; failure meant you died with the whole world watching.

The Apollo 13 mission—launched at 13:13 military time on an April afternoon in 1970—carried the threat of death in its oxygen tanks. They exploded on April 13, imperiling both the mission and the lives of astronauts Jim Lovell, Fred Haise and Jack Swigert. Commander Lovell, history's greatest traveler with almost 7 million miles on his Gemini and Apollo odometers, had dreamed of walking on the moon. Now he and his companions would be lucky to walk again on the earth. In an anxious four days, they would learn how to pilot a wounded, runaway craft; they would assemble an air purifier using homely artifacts found in any space module; and they would hope against hope that the guys back in Houston knew how to improvise against chaos.

Apollo 13, based on Lovell's memoir of the mission, chronicles those hairy days and salutes the men who worked to keep a disappointment from becoming a catastrophe. Ron Howard's film pays tribute to the signal and endangered American virtues of individual ingenuity and team spirit. "It gives credit where a great amount of credit has been forgotten," says Tom Hanks, the exemplary Hollywood star and former astro-nut teen who realized a dream of his own by playing Lovell. "Launching men into space is a fantastic undertaking, which very few people today seem to appreciate. It's ironic that we made a movie about a mission that was a 'failure,' because it's probably the best celebration of what NASA did."

A throwback to classic Hollywood pictures about men in groups—notably Howard Hawks' gruff flyboy panegyrics *Dawn Patrol, Only Angels Have Wings* and *Air Force*—the new film is also a splendid display of old-fashioned realistic special effects, which convince viewers not that they are in a cartoon but that they are inside a real rocket with real people who really might die. The result is that rare Hollywood achievement, an adventure of the intelligent spirit. From lift-off to splashdown, *Apollo 13* gives one hell of a ride.

In *Cocoon, Gung Ho, Parenthood, Backdraft* and *The Paper*, Howard splashed his vision on a huge canvas and peopled it with a sprawling cast. His problem was that in pushing a zillion buttons on the plot console, he often pushed too hard. Perhaps fearful of losing his audience, Howard would let his films get shrill or dewy. In *Apollo 13*, though, he has only a few dips into bathos (a too-cute child's face here, a dotty grandma there). Mostly, he makes viewers partners, trusting them to keep track of all the techno-talk, to take on faith what they don't immediately grasp.

Led by Ed Harris as flight director Gene Kranz and Gary Sinise as Ken Mattingly, who was scrubbed from the mission two days before launch, the grunts of Mission Control are efficient and almost faceless, a Greek chorus busily computing solutions. The astronauts' wives, notably Marilyn Lovell (lustrous Kathleen Quinlan), cope sensibly with despair. Lovell's partners in jeopardy (Bill Paxton as Haise, Kevin Bacon as Swigert) keep things cool, especially when they nearly freeze in their icy cabin. And Hanks provides the anchor. His Lovell—as strong, faithful and emotionally straightforward as Forrest Gump—carries the story like a precious oxygen backpack. His resourcefulness gives Lovell strength; his gift for conveying worry gives the film its humanity and a purchase on ordinary-Joe heroism.

In '60s newspapers and magazines, the Apollo astronauts were portrayed as heroes in the old mold: God-fearin', jut-jawed, steely-eyed missilemen, gazing into the skies they would soon conquer. These brainy jocks with their laconic C.B. chatter and their diplomas from M.I.T., Princeton, Caltech and Harvard were icons of stability in a most fractious decade. Americans looked across the Pacific and saw defeat. They looked at their campuses and saw revolt; at their inner cities and saw flames. For inspiration there was nowhere to look but up.

But what was there to see inside the techie Trekkies of Apollo? They seemed defiantly bland: all sinew, not much soul. They were the country-club Republican answer to '60s radicals. Instead of growing beards and dropping out, they kept their haircuts short and their rebellion in check. The most privileged among them played golf on the moon.

Which helps explain why, by Apollo 13—just the third moonwalk flight, nine months after the *Eagle* had landed—Americans were already sated with their star-cruising stars. Jim Lovell's little TV show on the third night of the mission, intended for the whole country's viewing pleasure, was not carried by the networks; it was a rerun of a rerun. Fly me to the moon? Yawn—no thanks. A vicarious lunar trip was now no more exciting than a seaside vacation with the kids.

All right, then. Imagine a minivan towing a small boat to the beach. The minivan is *Odyssey*, Apollo 13's command module (named after the Stanley Kubrick film about a man lost and transformed in space); the boat is *Aquarius*, the lunar module (after the song from *Hair*, Broadway's hymn to hippie insurrection). Now imagine that, on a nowhere stretch of road, your van just about blows up. How do you get home?

In essence, that was Apollo 13's problem. After the explosion, *Aquarius* became a lifeboat; in it the astronauts would try sailing home on the gravitational breezes of the moon and the earth. To steer their vessel, they would refute the argument that astronauts were not so much pilots as passengers or cargo—they had to navigate using the sun and the earth as a compass. And with doom dogging their flight, newsfolk and viewers finally paid attention. Imminent death is great for ratings.

Today it may be the recipe for hero making in the new conservative style. Here, after all, was a team that actually fulfilled its contract with America. The Apollo gang got a man on the moon in one urgent decade. Then they worked even more impressively to bring three men back safely from the beyond. William Broyles Jr., the former editor of *Texas Monthly* and *Newsweek*, and creator of the TV series *China Beach*, who wrote *Apollo 13*'s script with Al Reinert, spells out the family values: "In these cynical times, when exploitation of violence in movies is the norm, it was great to make a movie about real, ordinary people who do extraordinary things."

As any producer or key grip can attest, the making of a big movie can seem more complex and fraught with peril than any missile launch. The miracle of *Apollo 13* is that for a relatively spare $52 million, Howard and his team got it right. They knew what they wanted—and what they didn't. They were not aiming for the wild mix of comedy and rapture in the ultimate astronaut movie, *The Right Stuff* (1983); that, says Harris, "was about the space program as a p.r. phenomenon, whereas *Apollo 13* is about men fulfilling a duty." They didn't want a stratospheric disaster movie like the whiny *Marooned*, a 1969 annoyance about a fatal mission and a dead commander (named Jim!), or a paranoid thriller like 1978's zippy *Capricorn One*. The astronauts had felt burned by some of the space soap operas. "Listen," Lovell told Howard, "Just tell our story as it happened, and you'll have a thrilling movie."

Howard's goal was meticulous realism, in everything from the arc of emotion to the gizmos on the module dashboards. "There must be more than 400 controls, switches, circuit breakers, buttons and lights in the spacecraft," says Dave Scott, the film's technical adviser, who as commander of Apollo 15 was the seventh man to walk on the moon. "I spent about three months looking at them all and found just one little, insignificant thing wrong: the color of a small scribe on a window."

"It was like cramming for an exam," says Harris of the film's preproduction. Hanks calls himself "the most annoying person around" as a stickler for following procedure. He pored over the air-to-ground transcripts of the Apollo 13 flight to make sure he got the nomenclature down solid. "Most people," he says, "think a spacecraft moves like the *Millennium Falcon* as it zooms by the Death Star at light speed to defeat Darth Vader. We did this film in the real physical universe. It not only gave us more credence as filmmakers and actors, but it should help the movie become more involving for audiences." The hyper-real special effects were provided by James Cameron's Digital Domain unit, with Cameron (director of *The Terminator* and *True Lies*) serving as an uncredited consultant. Remarkably, not one frame of film was lifted from documentaries or NASA footage. All effects were created from scratch.

To achieve the effect of weightlessness in the space capsule, the *Apollo* team used NASA's KC-135, a converted Boeing 707 jet with an open cargo bay that climbs 30,000 ft. and then arcs into a dive, creating a 23-sec. period of weightlessness. The crew shot about four hours of weightlessness footage, which required more than 500 topsy-turvy takes—97 in one day. Says Lovell: "The actors playing astronauts actually spent more time in the zero-gravity plane than any real astronaut ever did."

The weightlessness took a while to master. "There were times when we'd finish shooting a scene, and I had no idea which way I was going to fall," says Hanks. But soon he learned to love defying gravity. "It's not a sensation you can liken to anything else," he says dreamily. "It's not floating like Superman but kind of floating like an angel."

Apollo 13 has a trace of this mooniness, the mystical nostalgia that seized most of the astronauts who got there and back. This cosmic optimism, the movie suggests, is one of the reasons for spending billions of dollars on the Apollo program: something wonderful is out there.

And something silly. When Howard toured NASA, he learned that the visitors' favorite question was: How do you pee in space? "Well," he decided, "that means we'll have to show it in the movie." So they do. Adds Hanks: "Maybe in the sequel we'll show how they go doo-doo."
Spoken like a steely-eyed missile man.

VILLAGE VOICE, 7/4/95, p. 54, Amy Taubin

Only 12 years separate Philip Kaufman's sprawling *The Right Stuff* from Ron Howard's straight 'n' narrow *Apollo 13*, but they seem to have come from different planets. And although Howard goes out of his way to connect to the right stuff by casting Ed Harris, so complicated as John Glenn in the earlier film, as *Apollo 13*'s tight-jawed flight-director Gene Kranz, the strategy only points up how devoid of characters this new film is. Remember the inchoate sense of betrayal eating away at Harris's photo-op grin as he watches a stripper tip her pasties skyward during a political fundraiser held in NASA's honor? Well there are no moments like that here, especially not from Harris's Kranz, who, when informed by a NASA nerd that the Apollo 13 crew might die in space hisses, "Not on my watch." As if the possibility of Americans dying anywhere—as they were, in fact, doing at that very moment in Vietnam—was outside his sphere of reality.

I wasn't that much of a fan of *The Right Stuff*, which was basically a John Ford western that pitted heroic cowboy-pilot loners against the slime of big government—the military-industrial complex. (I remember being particularly pissed at Sam Shepard's romanticized Chuck Yeager). But, at least, it had the courage of its libertarian contradictions. More to the point, it placed NASA in a historical context. *Apollo 13,* on the other hand, is so totally vacuumed of politics and history that a stray reference to "President Nixon" is totally disorienting. If *Forrest Gump* was right-wing revisionist history, then *Apollo 13* represses history entirely. In the lingo of the times, this is really a spaced-out movie. So this summer, Tom Hanks is Jim Lovell, flight commander of the Apollo 13, dubbed by NASA "the successful failure." Designed to transport its crew of three to the moon, where they would walk in Neil Armstrong's footsteps, the Apollo 13 was forced to abort its mission when it was disabled by an explosion in its oxygen supply. The problem for the three astronauts and the NASA ground control team boiled down to figuring out how to get the men back to earth using less energy than it would take to run the average vacuum cleaner. After the umpteenth round of number crunching, *Apollo 13* reads like nothing so much as a metaphor for the heroics of balancing the budget. Basically a boyz-'n'-their-toyz picture (What is it that men find so thrilling about rocket launchings? Just kidding) crossed with a disaster picture, *Apollo 13* is so totally predictable that one could be forgiven for wishing that everyone would die, if only to relieve the boredom. Which doesn't mean that some viewers (including yours truly) won't find themselves with sweaty palms at crucial moments. We're so programmed by the Hollywood machine (its form, not its content) that even when the machine is as crudely deployed as it is here (*Apollo 13* uses so many small crane shots that it feels like the whole film is written in bold type), it can still flip our switches to auto-pilot. Given that the astronauts, their wives, and all the folk at mission control are one happy family (minor frictions notwithstanding), the only villain of the piece is, you guessed it, the media—specifically network TV. "How come it's only when they're in trouble that you're interested?" demands Lovell's long suffering wife (Kathleen Quinlan) of the NASA public relations guy, who wants her to allow TV news cameras on her front lawn. "It's more dramatic," he answers with a shrug. And how many times can Hollywood run this pot'n' kettle routine? It's not as if Howard and Hanks and producer Brian Grazer were falling all over themselves to make a movie about a mission where nothing out of the ordinary happened.

The leading actors—Hanks, Harris, Kevin Bacon, Bill Paxton, and Gary Sinise—are all fine, and that goes double for Sinise. Hanks, our best loved misty-eyed star, gets close to tears when he realizes he'll never walk on the moon and then again when he realizes how much he just wants to go home. There's nothing like a ghost in the machine to turn a bad case of arrested development into a real family man.

Also reviewed in:
CHICAGO TRIBUNE, 6/30/95, Friday/p. C, Michael Wilmington
NEW REPUBLIC, 7/31/95, p. 26, Stanley Kauffmann

NEW YORK TIMES, 6/30/95, p. C1, Janet Maslin
NEW YORKER, 7/10/95, p. 79, Terrence Rafferty
VARIETY, 6/26-7/9/95, p. 78, Todd McCarthy
WASHINGTON POST, 6/30/95, p. D1, Rita Kempley
WASHINGTON POST, 6/30/95, Weekend/p. 42, Joe Brown

ARABIAN KNIGHT

A Miramax Films release of an Allied Filmmakers presentation. *Executive Director:* Jake Eberts. *Producer:* Imogen Sutton and Richard Williams. *Director:* Richard Williams. *Screenplay:* Richard Williams. *Director of Photography:* John Leatherbarrow. *Editor:* Peter Bond. *Music:* Robert Folk. *Master Animator:* Ken Harris. *Art Director:* Roy Naisbitt. *Special Effects:* John M. Cousen. *Character Animation:* Neil Boyle and Tim Watts. *Background:* Paul Dilworth and Errol Le Cain. *Color Model:* Barbara McCormack. *Paint & Trace:* Maggie Brown. *Head Tracer:* Katherine McDonald. *Running time:* 81 minutes. *MPAA Rating:* G.

VOICES: Vincent Price (Zigzag); Matthew Broderick (Tack, the Cobbler); Jennifer Beals (Princess Yum Yum); Eric Bogosian (Phido); Toni Collette (Nurse & Witch); Jonathan Winters (Thief); Clive Revill (King Nod); Kevin Dorsey (Mighty One-Eye); Stanley Baxter (Gofer & Slap); Kenneth Williams (Goblet & Tickle); Clinton Sunberg (Dying Soldier); Windsor Davies (Roofless); Frederick Shaw (Goolie); Thick Wilson (Sergeant Hook); Eddie Byme (Hoof).

LOS ANGELES TIMES, 8/28/95, Calendar/p. 7, Kevin Thomas

"Arabian Knight" is a charmer for children but is a bit too simple a tale to hold adult attention. However, parents who go with their kids cannot fail to be blown away by the sheer beauty and sophistication of the film's fanciful, exotic design. Among those lending their voices to fine effect are Matthew Broderick, Jennifer Beals, the late Vincent Price, Jonathan Winters and Clive Revill.

You can believe that Oscar-winning writer-director-animator Richard Williams spent decades on this project; you can also believe that this is not quite the version of the film that Williams, the man who gave life to Roger Rabbit, wanted us to see, since he left the project before it was completed, apparently over the usual "creative differences." (Miramax did not screen the film in advance for critics.)

Possibly, Williams intended more story. As it is, it's about how a feckless but persistent Thief (Winters) and a young cobbler, Tack (Broderick), are swept up in an adventure in which they and Baghdad's beautiful but heretofore bored Princess Yum Yum (Beals) strive to retrieve the three golden balls that protect the city-kingdom from evil.

Their adversaries are Zigzag (Price), the wicked grand vizier to the king (Revill) and a thundering horde of one-eyed warriors.

Along the way there's considerable incident, some wit and humor and some pleasant songs. The vocal talents are first-rate, with a special nod to the late Price, who gives his inimitable sly, sinister twists to such phrases as "Have no fear/Your grand vizier is here."

The characters are gracefully drawn with a light touch, but the big news is the film's extraordinary backgrounds. Williams took his inspiration from the paradoxical paintings of M.C. Escher, which results in all manner of visual trickery and forced perspective to give "Arabian Knight" its unique effect. Williams' key team-art director Roy Naisbett, the late master animator Ken Harris (one of Bugs Bunny's creators)—and background stylist Errol Le Cain have called it "2½ dimensions."

They also came up with the most intricate and detailed of Rube Goldberg-like weapons and devices. As background stylist, Le Cain took as his inspiration exquisite Persian miniatures, emulating their fairy-tale look with meticulous fidelity. If "Arabian Knight", is less than enchanting an entertainment for an adult, it certainly *looks* enchanting.

NEW YORK POST, 8/26/95, p. 16, Thelma Adams

Chalk up Princess Yum Yum as another victim of cartoon-feminism. On the way to scoring her "Arabian Knight," the animated gumdrop voiced by Jennifer Beals must first sing a painful p.c. anthem.

Despite a busty body built for harem pleasures, Yum Yum whines for empowerment: "There's a mind in the body of this pretty miss ... [she] has a point of view that must be expressed."

Gone are the simple days of my Malibu Barbie. At least we knew where she was coming from. Now a doll to drool over has to be both beautiful and defiant, a mistress of mixed messages.

I don't expect anyone to be able to explain to me why the delicious Yum Yum has a nude bath scene in Miramax Family Films first adventure in toon town. Despite being a labor of love from Oscar-winner Richard Williams, the creator of the wonderful animation in "Who Framed Roger Rabbit," this fable of old Bagdad has all the charm of Saddam Hussein.

The villainous sorcerer Zigzag (voiced by Vincent Price and as blue as Aladdin) has his eye on Yum Yum (who wouldn't?). Yum craves a schlubby cobbler (Matthew Broderick). When King Nod (Clive Revill) won't give his only daughter (harems aren't producing like they used to) to the Zigzag, the wizard betrays the kingdom to their mortal enemy, the army of the one-eyed monster.

Those expecting the toon pyrotechnics of "Roger Rabbit" will be sorely disappointed. At best, the Arabian motif lends itself to attractive abstract backgrounds and the characters play cat-and-mouse in a world M.C. Escher inspired. But, for the most part, "Arabian Knight" seems stuck in a time warp, returning to the roguish simplicity of TVs Fractured Fairy Tales or cannibalizing "Fantasia."

The greatest pleasure to be squeezed from "Arabian Knight" is the voice of the late, great Price. Close your eyes and think of the "Pit and the Pendulum."

A more dubious pleasure is that there are only four songs in this semi-musical. Beals and Broderick sing a duet—"Am I Feeling Love?"—that is sure to inspire children's fidgets and sudden desperate pleas for a trip to the loo.

Also reviewed in:
CHICAGO TRIBUNE, 8/31/95, Tempo/p. 26, Michael Wilmington
NEW YORK TIMES, 8/26/95, p. 11, Caryn James
VARIETY, 8/28-9/3/95, p. 65, Leonard Klady
WASHINGTON POST, 8/26/95, p. D3, Hal Hinson

ARIZONA DREAM

Kit Parker Films release of a Constellation UGC Hachette Premiere film with participation of Ministère de la Culture et de la Communicaton. *Executive Producer:* Paul R. Gurian. *Producer:* Claudie Ossard and Yves Marmion. *Director:* Emir Kusturica. *Screenplay:* David Atkins. *Director of Photography:* Vilko Filac. *Editor:* Andrija Zafranovic. *Music:* Goran Bregovic. *Sound:* Jim Steube. *Sound Editor:* Gerard Hardy. *Casting:* Pennie Du Pont. *Production Designer:* Miljen Kljakovic. *Art Director:* Jan Pascale. *Set Decorator:* Jan Pascale and Elaine O'Donnell. *Set Dresser:* Erik Polczwartek, Christie Addis, Francine Byrne, Heidi Baumgarten, Deborah Finn, and Thomas Conway. *Special Effects:* Gregory C. Landerer and Kenny Estes. *Costumes:* Jill M. Ohanneson. *Make-up:* Patti York, Charles Balazs, and Cheryl Voss. *Stunt Coordinator:* Everett L. Creach. *Running time:* 142 minutes. *MPAA Rating:* Not Rated.

CAST: Johnny Depp (Axel Blackmar); Jerry Lewis (Leo Sweetie); Faye Dunaway (Elaine); Lili Taylor (Grace); Paulina Porizkova (Millie); Vincent Gallo (Paul); Candyce Mason (Blanche); Alexia Rane (Angie); Polly Noonan (Betty); Ann Schulman (Carla); Michael J. Pollard (Fabian); Patricia O'Grady (MC/Announcer); James R. Wilson (Lawyer); Eric Polczwartek (Man with Door); Kim Keo (Mechanical Doll); Sal Jenco (Man at the Phone); James P. Marshall (Boatman); Vincent Tockton (Eskimo Man).

LOS ANGELES TIMES, 7/11/95, Calendar/p. 3, Kevin Thomas

"Arizona Dream" is the quintessential Nuart movie. It's a dazzling, daring slice of cockamamie tragicomic Americana envisioned with magic realism by a major, distinctive European filmmaker, the former Yugoslavia's Emir Kusturica. He also directed the Oscar-nominated "When Father Was Away on Business" and "Underground," which took the Palme d'Or at Cannes this year.

It has an iconic cast that only a film buff could come up with—Johnny Depp, Faye Dunaway, Jerry Lewis, Lili Taylor and Vincent Gallo, plus Paulina Porizkova and Michael J. Pollard. The Nuart, of course, is showing it in its lengthy yet rewarding 142-minute director's cut. Written by David Atkins, a student of Kusturica at Columbia University, "Arizona Dream" is a kind of cross between Gus Van Sant and Robert Altman. As determinedly hip as it is, however, it most likely will cut as deep five years from now as it does today.

It opens with an extended Eskimo sequence—the meaning of which will eventually become clear—that turns out to be a dream of Depp's Axel Blackmar. At 23, Axel has found contentment both living in Manhattan, "where you can see everybody and nobody can see you," and counting fish for New York's Department of Fish and Game. When he's summoned back to his hometown in Arizona, where his Uncle Leo (Lewis), the local Cadillac dealer, is marrying his "little Polish cupcake" (Porizkova) and wants Axel to be his best man.

In an instant, the likable, laid-back Axel is caught up in a caldron of other people's guilt and dreams. There is a strong bond of love between Axel and Leo—Depp interacts with Lewis as warmly as he did with Marlon Brando in "Don Juan de Marco"—but Leo cannot forgive himself for having been the driver of a car in which Axel's parents were killed in an accident six years earlier.

Leo fears that Axel will end up a bum, and he wants to make a Cadillac salesman out of him. Gallo plays Paul, one of Leo's employees, who's supposed to show Axel the ropes. Paul has a dream, too, of becoming an actor, he can recite the dialogue of "Raging Bull" and comes up with the most confounding impression of Cary Grant running from the crop-duster in "North by Northwest."

Just as he's bending to his loving uncle's will, Axel becomes swiftly entangled with Dunaway's manic-depressive Elaine Stalker and her oppressed stepdaughter, Grace (Taylor). It seems Elaine fatally shot her husband—the circumstances aren't too clear—but she and Grace at times blame each other.

In any event, Grace has ended up inheriting the state's third-largest copper mine, and the two women—bonded more by love and loneliness than hatred—live in a vast Victorian ranch house outside town. Initially, Axel is more beguiled by the glamorous, sexy Elaine and her dream of building a flying machine á la the Wright Brothers than by Grace, who talks about suicide and hopes for reincarnation as a turtle.

Working from what must be a most ambitious screenplay, Kusturica lays on the eccentricities and extravagant behavior of his people thick, pushing them to caricature, then providing them with surprising dimension. In Elaine, Dunaway in particular has found one of her most challenging roles as an extremely mercurial, outrageous woman with an image of a crazed nymphomaniac whose vulnerability and longing actually expresses an acute perception.

Of course, Lewis is funny, but he also gives a serious, endearing performance of one of the most normal men he has ever played. Taylor is at her best as a young woman in need of discovering her own identity. Depp yet again reveals his unique ability to be the seductive yet compassionate idealist, discovering strength in tenderness. Although not quite in the center of action, Gallo nonetheless as a sure-fire scene-stealer. Porizkova and Pollard (as a nerdy would-be customer Leo gives the brushoff) score in brief appearances.

Amid a maelstrom of emotion and calamitous action, Kusturica manages to suggest not merely Axel's need to pursue his own dream—that's clear enough—but to evoke a sense of the ultimate isolation of us all and to jolt us with juxtapositions of comedy and tragedy, and of life and death themselves.

NEW STATESMAN & SOCIETY, 6/30/95, p. 33, Jonathan Romney

There are few notions in cinema mythology quite as appealing as the *film maudit*—the damned film that somehow, through hubris or bad timing, ends up heroically underachieving. It's the sort of film one loves to speculate about, but in most cases could happily live without actually seeing. In most cases, such films don't get released—or if they do, not until well past their sell-by date where no one's interested any more. A recent example is Gus Van Sant's misbegotten *Even Cowgirls Get the Blues*, which finally reached Britain after a year's worth of bad reputation and recutting.

One *film maudit* that has survived its birth traumas is Emir Kusturica's *Arizona Dream*. Having won this year's Palme d'Or at Cannes with his unruly epic of Yugoslavian history, *Underground*—itself something of a *film maudit*, allegedly cut down from eight hours to three in time for the Festival—the Sarajevo-born director is a headline name again, which should ensure that *Arizona Dream* does at last get an audience. (And besides, it stars Johnny Depp.) But *Arizona Dream* looked for a while like the over-reaching folly that would ruin Kusturica's career after his acclaimed picaresque saga *Time of the Gypsies*. A US/French co-production starring Depp, Faye Dunaway and Jerry Lewis, *Arizona Dream* stirred up all the suspicions that often greet a European director's first foray into Americana. After a stormy production process, *Arizona Dream* screened in Cannes in 1992—its release here now looks like an afterthought.

You can see why *Arizona Dream* was universally greeted with dropped jaws. It's a two-hour magic-realist shaggy dog story set in Arizona and Alaska involving Inuit trappers and car salesmen, mariachi bands and flying fish, and it makes no concessions to common sense. It's portentous, at times sluggish to the point of somnolence, utterly self-indulgent and entertains the worst kind of romantic fantasies about *amour fou*, artistry and the death wish. Yet it's absolutely riveting: it works entirely on its own terms and no recognisable others. It may not be in the same league as *Time of the Gypsies*, but then it's not in the same universe either—that film, sprawling as it was, was a conventionally finished statement, but this is a fragmentary set of half thought-out speculations, and therefore all the more fun to disentangle. It's also far more interesting than *Underground*, which though heartfelt, looked like three hours of circus jollity with a devastating ending tacked on to remind us that it had a serious point to make about the fate of an ex-nation.

Originally a script presented to Kusturica by his Columbia student David Atkins, *Arizona Dream* floats as blithely and seemingly aimlessly as the mystical flying fish (an arrow tooth halibut, according to the subtitles) that wafts gnomically through it. The fish is caught by an Inuit who returns home and blows up its stomach into a balloon. The balloon drifts off until it reaches New York, where it wakes Axel (Depp), who counts fish and has a particular interest in their dreams. He meets his cousin Paul (Vincent Gallo), a narcissist convinced he's the new De Niro, who whisks him off to Arizona for the wedding of the car salesman uncle, Leo (Lewis). Reluctantly working in Leo's showroom, Axel falls for Elaine (Dunaway), an overpowering *femme fatale* who has a tempestuous relationship with her daughter Grace (Lili Taylor). At that point, the film retreats for the duration to Elaine's desert ranch, where Axel helps her to build the flying machine of her dreams—and what seemed to be proceeding nicely as a small-town screwball comedy suddenly subsides into a doomy, claustrophobic Tennessee Williams-esque mood, peppered with a touch of airborne slapstick.

Like the fish and the flying machine, *Arizona Dream* seems genuinely to have no idea where it's going. This, although it spends practically no time at all on the open road, is what makes the film, in a peculiar way, a sort of road movie. All that's important is the ride, how ever slow and however stationary it seems, and the incidental (sometimes apparently accidental) marvels witnessed *en route*. You can list the film's pleasures like roadside oddities that flash by: a row of cars slacked like tombstones; a litter of puppies in a deserted car showroom; an ambulance that floats off towards the moon; Paul's inept re-enactment of the crop-dusting scene from *North By Northwest*; a Vietnamese pot-bellied pig that appears out of nowhere like a satanic visitation; wildly incongruous snatches of what may have started as a coherent Iggy Pop soundtrack.

The characters themselves come off like fabulous monsters in a prehistoric landscape. Leo, "the last dinosaur who smells of cheap cologne", is Jerry Lewis in the enormously sad heavyweight mode he displayed in Scorsese's *The King of Comedy*—a weary, unctuous presence, leaden but still possessed, as if by a demonic tic, by flashes of his youthful nerdy self that emerge in the extraordinary symphony of facial gestures he fires off at his bride in an early scene. Lili Taylor, who was so good in *Short Cuts*, builds her character entirely around a facial routine—a defiant, ironic little twitch of the mouth. And Vincent Gallo's charming cretin Paul somehow keeps the film anchored to reality throughout—he's the one character who doesn't get to levitate at any point. *Arizona Dream* may come across as a display of freaks and wonders, but then it's a freakish wonder itself, beyond being good or bad. You'll probably hate it. But you should see it anyway, because it's such a wild and wonderful anomaly—the sort of film a fish might have dreamed of.

NEW YORK POST, 6/7/95, p. 30, Thelma Adams

Sometimes, a director's cut is just a longer movie.

Between winning a Palme d'Or—the, top prize—at Cannes in 1985 for "When Father Was Away on Business" and another last month for "Underground," director Emir Kusturica went through a long period of being known as Emir who?

It was during this period that Kusturica made "Arizona Dream." The 1992 dark, hallucinogenic comedy went straight to video in a shortened 120-minute version.

Starting today, the Film Forum offers audiences the 142-minute directors cut. With a magnetic cast (Johnny Depp, Faye Dunaway, Jerry Lewis and Lili Taylor) and an award-winning director, you figure this must be a hidden treasure—until you see it for yourself.

The film's overheated exploration of the American dream naintains a loopy stride for the first hour before falling apart. But the actors struggle to be believable even after the script hangs them out to dry.

Dark-haired, mop-top Depp plays Axel, a dreamy, latter-day Tom Jones. One of Depp's acting strengths is his ability to connect with and draw out the talents of others (Martin Landau was right to tip his hat to Depp for the older actor's "Ed Wood" Oscar.) Depp plays it straight for Jerry Lewis. The comedian, as Axel's Uncle Leo, chews into another crotchety father figure role. Appearing in pink cowboy boots, a pink tuxedo jacket and boxers in his first scene, Lewis is the king of angry comics, stamping down ugliness with an oily smile.

After Axel dallies in coping with his familial obligations (to sell Caddies with Uncle Leo or not to sell Caddies, that is the American question), he stares down his sexual identity. The boy toy falls in with two women on the other side of sanity. Oversexed Elaine (a glowing Faye Dunaway) and her angry accordion-playing stepdaughter Grace (Lili Taylor)—a two-headed beast of desire—bounce Axel between them.

The movie has some wildly entertaining scenes: Lewis teaches Depp how to be sexy by making fish lips, the blind leading the sighted; Taylor attempts suicide by hanging—from panty hose—an act that is more uplifting than somber; Depp does a wacky chicken impression.

And there is the bit when Axel's pal Paul (Vincent Gallo), an aspiring actor, auditions at a dinner theater. His piece? The crop-dusting scene in "North By Northwest." Paul, as Cary Grant, looks nervously at the sky and then tosses himself prone on the stage—again and again. Paul gets the hook—and has no idea why.

But there is only so much whimsy a person can stomach—and tolerance wanes in the second hour. Desperate for an ending, the plot starts to convulse. Suddenly, characters are playing Russian roulette, the sky is cracking open with apocalyptic thunder and the saga surges towards a climax of rain-drenched desire under the elms. And, look, there's a mariachi band!

You know when you check the time on a character's watch as she dangles from a roof that the movie is way too long.

NEWSDAY, 6/7/95, Part II/p. B9, John Anderson

The much-honored Emir Kusturica, who won the Palme d'Or at Cannes this year for "Underground" (and for "When Father Was Away on Business" a decade earlier), presents "Arizona Dream" as exactly that. Although ostensibly located in the state of the same name, it's a place populated by people you recognize, doing things you don't; events, or their shadows, recur without pattern or purpose; conscious reality is slippery as a fish. And, like a persistent dream, you simply can't take your eyes off it.

Indulgently long and gleefully nutty, "Arizona Dream" opens appropriately—with an Inuit hunter rescuing his dogs from a hole in the ice, being rescued himself by those same dogs and awakening in his igloo to make love to his wife. What does this mean? We get disjointed explanations from Axel Blackmar, who's having this particular dream and is played by Johnny Depp (taking Gilbert Grape a few steps further).

A fish-counter for the New York Department of Fish and Game, Axel loves the city (because "you can see everybody, but no one can see you"). So when his Cadillac-dealing uncle Leo (Jerry Lewis) sends his chief salesman Paul (the talented Vincent Gallo) to bring Axel back to Arizona so he can be best man at Leo's marriage to Millie (Paulina Porizkova), Axel resists. But after passing out from drink in Paul's convertible on Broadway, he wakes up in Paul's convertible at Leo's house in Arizona, and finds a life that is half auto sales, half Electra-inspired nightmare.

The rich vein of humor in "Arizona Dreams" can be credited to both Jerry Lewis, from whom we expect laughs, and Faye Dunaway, from whom we don't. Dunaway plays Elaine Stalker, the glamorous widow who's at psychological war with her husband's disturbed daughter Grace (Lili Taylor), as full-tilt wacko; she's fun to watch and knows it. Lewis' Leo Sweetie, on the other hand, is restrained—sweetly menacing with just a bit of the bellhop. And so continues the artistic rehabilitation of Jerry Lewis. Kusturica's film is an elegy to wish fulfillment and a poetically rendered piece of cinema that invokes deeply-felt memory while at the same time coasting along on an intentionally harebrained plot (by Kusturica and David Atkins) and some of the more eccentric performances of some decidedly eccentric careers. The movie, which should find itself a nice comfortable cult audience in its run at Film Forum, hardly deserved its so-far byzantine fate: Warner Bros. abandoned the 1992 film after test-screening a two-hour version, and a shortened video was released. Film Forum is showing the full 142 minutes. It's worth every second, as it turns out, even if it will be best appreciated by filmgoers who are themselves a bit cracked.

SIGHT AND SOUND, 7/95, p. 39, Geoffrey Macnab

Returning home to his igloo after a sleigh accident, an Eskimo blows up a fish's stomach like a balloon and gives it to his young son to play with. The balloon floats across the atmosphere, eventually bursting in New York, next to Axel Blackmar, who is asleep on the back of a fish truck. Axel works for the New York Department of Fish and Game, counting fish. His cousin Paul, a struggling actor, arrives in town and cajoles him into going to Arizona for his uncle Leo's wedding. Leo, a Cadillac salesman, feels responsible for Axel; he was driving in the crash which killed Axel's parents. Now he wants to help the young man by taking him on in the family firm.

One afternoon, Elaine, a glamorous, middle-aged woman, and her stepdaughter Grace, pay a visit to the car showroom. Axel takes a shine to Elaine. A few days later, he and Paul are invited to her place in the country for dinner. Elaine shot her husband, a tin magnate, a few years before, and Grace has never forgiven her. Mother and stepdaughter bicker throughout the meal, even as Paul caresses Elaine's legs under the table. Grace finally leaves the dinner party and makes an unsuccessful suicide attempt.

Elaine and Axel become lovers. She tells him she always wanted to fly. He resolves to stay with her and help her build an aeroplane. At first, none of the machines can get off the ground, and Grace keeps destroying the equipment. Leo and Paul disapprove of the affair, and try to prise Axel away from Elaine; she scares them off with a gun. Relations between Grace and Elaine continue to deteriorate. Axel decides that he must kill one or other of them to save both from misery. With this in mind, he breaks into Grace's room. When his nerve fails, she grabs the pistol and invites him to play Russian roulette; both survive the ordeal.

At a local talent night, Paul startles the locals with an interpretation of the crop-dusting sequence in *North by Northwest*. Halfway through the evening, Axel hears that Leo has taken some pills and collapsed. On the way to hospital, Leo dies. After making the funeral arrangements, Axel returns to the homestead. He and Elaine have a bitter argument, but are eventually reconciled. They plan to go to Alaska, but Elaine can't decide whether she wants to take the train or fly. Paul, Grace and Axel celebrate Elaine's birthday with a lavish party. Presented with a brand new plane, she gleefully jumps in and takes off. Watching her from the roof of the house, Axel and Grace share an illicit kiss. That evening, the four play blind man's buff in the rain, and Grace releases her pet turtles. She and Axel conspire to elope together. In the night, Grace heads out into the storm and shoots herself. Axel returns to town alone, and falls asleep in Leo's derelict showroom. He dreams he is in Alaska with his uncle; the two catch a fish with eyes on both sides of the head, a good omen. The fish flies away into the distance.

A testament to its European director's bewildered fascination with the vast open spaces, small towns and seething cities of modern-day America, *Arizona Dream* occupies familiar iconographic territory. Cadillacs abound, there are frequent references to old Hollywood movies, the picture even has its own crop of bona fide stars, all of them playing recognisable variations on their usual roles. Johnny Depp is the visionary delinquent who refuses to accept the strictures of the adult world. Faye Dunaway, in best *Mommie Dearest* mode, is the imperious but vulnerable older woman he falls in love with. And, perhaps most provocatively, Jerry Lewis, as Uncle Leo, combines elements of his old comic persona with a touching portrayal of middle-American man-in-crisis. Like John Updike's Harry Angstrom in the novel *Rabbit at Rest*, Leo is an elderly car dealer whose physical decline is mirrored by that of the industry he works in.

Kusturica was presented with the script by one of his students at Columbia University. There is nothing particularly new in the themes it broaches, and it comes as no surprise to discover the original title was *American Dreamers*. However, in the Serb director's hands, the material undergoes a startling metamorphosis, taking on the opaque, dreamlike quality of an old European fable. He manages to defamiliarise even the most humdrum aspects of American life. Conventional symbols, automobiles, guns and the like, are juxtaposed with flying fish and baby turtles. Even capitalism is made poetic: Leo doesn't merely want to make money—his ambition is to stack Cadillacs "high as the moon".

The opening sequences, in the frozen limits of Alaska, are reminiscent of *Nanook of the North*, but from here we float into contemporary New York, before heading out to the rugged West. We seem to slip across epochs. Leo's car lot looks like a relic from the 1950s. Elaine's homestead has all the trimmings of a nineteenth-century country house, and Faye Dunaway dresses as if she is playing Hedda Gabler. At certain points, characters levitate for no very discernible reason. The film is by turns infuriating and inspiring: it has a random, haphazard quality utterly at odds with most American cinema.

Apparently, Kusturica experienced all sorts of spats with the French financiers. When they complained about the form it was taking, he simply walked off the set and refused to come back until they allowed him to do things in his own wilful perverse way. The version which is finally reaching Britain looks as if it may well have been tampered with (Iggy Pop is mentioned in the press release cast list as 'Man with Pumpkin', but doesn't seem to put in an appearance). Yet *Arizona Dream* remains overlong, and often meanders purposelessly. Chunks of *Raging Bull, North by Northwest* and *The Godfather Part II* are quoted at various key points in the story. Vincent Gallo watches them, speaks along with the characters as if he is uttering a sacred catechism, and offers a splendid imitation of Cary Grant running away from the crop-dusting plane, but these sequences only serve to highlight how lacking in suspense, narrative momentum and meaningful dialogue *Arizona Dream* itself is. Still, its vices are its virtues: the film isn't straitjacketed by genre or convention, and can amble off in whichever direction it pleases.

Like Depp and Dunaway, who spend much of their time attempting to build primitive aeroplanes in the backyard, Kusturica feels free to experiment. If some of his gambits don't come off, he needn't worry: he knows he'll be airborne soon. For audiences, too, this work-in-process ought ultimately to prove rewarding, even if it is full of hideously improvised scenes, where he simply seems to have turned the camera on and left the actors to their own devices. *Arizona Dream*'s many moments of outrageous virtuosity more than compensate. It is as bizarre and original a film as any European has ever made about America.

VILLAGE VOICE, 6/13/95, p. 54, Amy Taubin

I first saw *Smoke* at the Berlin Film Festival where the audience embraced it as a quintessential American art movie—something like Jarmusch-does-Brooklyn. Nothing confirms Jarmusch's importance to American independent film more than the fact that not only does the anally restrained *Smoke* bear his influence, but so does a film that, otherwise, is its polar opposite—Emir Kusturica's hysterically expressionist *Arizona Dream*. There's a scene early in *Arizona Dream* of Johnny Depp and Vincent Gallo arguing in a bar that, except for the restless camera movement, is pure Jarmusch.

Re-edited and dumped directly onto video by Warners, *Arizona Dream* is finally getting an American theatrical release. The print that's being shown at the Film Forum is billed as "the director's cut."

A darling of the Cannes Film Festival, where he's just collected his second Palme d'Or for *Underground*, Kusturica is kind of a Bosnian Norman Mailer. His films mix inspired, bravura passages with utter bombast. *Arizona Dream* opens with a brilliant emotional roller-coaster ride—an Eskimo boy's anxiety dream about how his father is all but lost under the ice floes only to be miraculously rescued by a resourceful sled dog. At that point, I thought I was watching one of the great films of all time. Once the scene shifts to Arizona, however, it's pretty much over.

Kusturica is not the first European director to be wooed by Hollywood only to discover himself in a work situation so infuriating that it finds its way onto film as a contempt for all things American. When he's not willfully misreading the American psyche, he's imposing his own obsessions on his characters, so much so that half the time it seems like we're watching some Middle Eastern melodrama from which the subtitles have been inadvertently omitted.

Flamboyant though they are, Kusturica's best films (*Time of the Gypsies, When Father Was Away on Business*) have a grounding in social realism that's altogether lacking in *Arizona Dream*. The putative plot involves two fragmented, dysfunctional families. Depp plays a wildlife conservation worker (he specializes in fish) who's persuaded by his friend (Gallo) to return to Arizona to attend the wedding of his beloved car-dealer uncle (Jerry Lewis) from whom he's been estranged.

Lewis makes a notable entrance wearing a pink tuxedo jacket, pink and white snakeskin cowboy boots, and little else. Depp however loses interest in his uncle when he meets a homicidal widow (Faye Dunaway) who's mad about flying machines and her suicidal daughter (Lili Taylor) who's inherited all her father's money and dreams of being reincarnated as a turtle. Depp beds both mother and daughter—is this incest or merely symbiosis?

Given the circumstances, it's no surprise that Lewis is slightly embarassing to watch and Dunaway much more so. Depp's light touch stands him in good stead, although his moment-by-moment reactions never add up to a character. What's amazing is that Taylor and Gallo are flat-out terrific. Taylor plays a young woman who'd literally rather die than turn into her mother but can't keep her from influencing her every gesture and word. Taylor, who bears no resemblance to Dunaway, somehow manages to suggest that the metamorphosis is imminent.

As an aspiring actor who idolizes De Niro and Pacino, Gallo gets to play a scene that will have film buffs rolling in the aisles. For his turn in a local talent show, Gallo reenacts, with great exactitude, Cary Grant's every move in the crop-dusting scene from *North by Northwest*—looking repeatedly at his watch, standing frozen in terror, hurling himself face down on the ground, leaping to his feet, and so on, over and over again Kusturica intercuts Gallo's "performance" with clips from the Hitchcock film. It's a fabulous send-up of film acting—it shows that doing next to nothing can be transformed, through editing, into a fight to the death. Chaotic and overwrought, *Arizona Dream* nevertheless delivers scenes no one should miss.

Also reviewed in:
CHICAGO TRIBUNE, 1/6/95, Friday/p. L, Michael Wilmington
NEW YORK TIMES, 6/7/95, p. C11, Janet Maslin
VARIETY, 1/4/93, p. 67, Lisa Nesselson

ART FOR TEACHERS OF CHILDREN

A Zeitgeist Films release. *Director:* Jennifer Montgomery. *Screenplay:* Jennifer Montgomery. *Director of Photography:* Jennifer Montgomery. *Editor:* Jennifer Montgomery. *Sound:* Crosby McCloy. *Running time:* 82 minutes. *MPAA Rating:* Not Rated.

CAST: Caitlin Grace McDonnell (Jennifer); Duncan Hannah (John); Coles Burroughs (Molly); Bryan Keane (Counselor); Jennifer Williams (Alex).

NEW YORK POST, 8/2/95, p. 35, Thelma Adams

"Do you want me to leave my shirt on?" nubile 14-year-old Jennifer (Caitlin Grace McDonnell) asks the man behind the still camera in Jennifer Montgomery's "Art For Teachers of Children."

John (Duncan Hannah) Jennifer's father confessor, photography tutor, boarding school counselor and a married man twice her age—coolly encourages his subject to follow her instincts.

Off comes the shirt. Seated in a wild field, topless, Jennifer, in granny glasses, scowl and long, hippie hair, teeters on the border of sensuality and awkwardness, the adolescence poster child. The moment is all the more engrossing because of our heightened awareness of the young actress posing semi-nude for our pleasure/pursuit of art.

Simultaneously, since the character, like the director, is named Jennifer, and is intended to be an autobiographical figure, we both identify with the girl and see the scene from a distance, staring out over the passage of time. We sympathize with the young girl who feels invisible in the adult world until John makes her visible through the camera's lens as an object of desire. We can also see John through her adolescent eyes: his preppie good looks, his comforting voice, his willingness to listen.

Again, the mature director intrudes and we, the audience, the adults, see another side to John: his weakness, his desire to be a guru among children rather than being a man among his peers, his irresponsible use of his position of authority. While sharing erotic art photography with Jennifer, John says with a whispery-voiced intimacy aimed with deadly, if off-hand, accuracy at the boarding school virgin: "Did you know Weston slept with all his models."

Inspired by her real-life affair with noted photographer (and alleged child pornographer) Jock Sturges in the mid-70s, Montgomery makes a carefully considered directorial debut that is probing, funny, erotically charged and provocative. Using black-and-white photography, she explores the shades of gray in the art of seduction between teachers and students.

When it comes to the mutual flirtation between Jennifer and John, Montgomery delivers a Lolita's eye view that shifts between the sensual and the downright embarrassing quality of memories of early sexual exploits.

Jennifer comes on to John, proclaiming her desire to cast off her virginity during one in a series of confidential (and school-sanctioned) conferences with her mentor in his campus study. John's initial protest that he "can't act on these feelings" lasts a laughable half a day. Their initial coupling—in John's darkroom—is both brusquely erotic and disturbing. He zips up with a functional, "it'll feel better next time."

The relationship between adviser and student teaches Jennifer the definition of "clandestine." It also quickly becomes clear that John has much to lose in pursuing a liaison with a minor (his wife, his job). Is the relationship consensual? Yes. Is it in the best interests of the minor? No. Montgomery resists seeing the affair as a clear-cut instance of abuse. Her sympathetic, if controversial, perspective examines the shifting power dynamics between two mismatched lovers. If, in hindsight, the director paints John as a cad, she won't go so far as to label the man who ushered in her sexual awakening a pervert.

VILLAGE VOICE, 8/8/95, p. 43, Georgia Brown

As Godard once put it, "Revenger and reporter begin with the same letter." Jennifer Montgomery's *Art for Teachers of Children* is a wicked act of revenge. (I'm using wicked as in "a wicked curve ball," meaning dazzling, skillful, and effective.) Close in impulse to documentary, the film is a fictional re-creation of Montgomery's affair, beginning when she was 14, with photographer Jock Sturges, beginning when he was 28, married, and her dorm adviser in a New England boarding school. (Sturges's name is never mentioned in the film but Montgomery openly uses his name in interviews. Sturges was unavailable for comment.) That the film is a true story, and the filmmaker's own story, makes an enormous difference in how we view this deliberately raw yet artful movie. How we view anything—a glowing, pristine photo of a naked prepubescent girl, say—is one of the film's provocative subjects.

Montgomery's report and inquiry has been made 20 years later, but it's not a victim's blurt to the world ("He ruined my life"). In essence, Montgomery chooses to fight art with art: hers, blunt, unglamorous, sometimes deliberately corny, even tacky; his, luminous, poetic, formal. Anyone who sees the film will look at Sturges's photos in a new light, as it were.

Basically, the only two characters here are Jennifer (Caitlin Grace McDonnell, who, by the way, is a recent college graduate, not a 14-year-old) and her teacher, John (Duncan Hannah) . The Jennifer depicted here is hardly what one thinks of as Sturges's type: sleek, thin, almost androgynous child beauties who frankly, proudly, expose their bodies to the world. She hides her face behind hair and glasses and slumps to conceal her ripening, slightly chubby figure. It's Jennifer's first year at the ivy-covered prep school: "A terrible mistake had been made, I was not ready to leave home." (The intermittent voiceover text is read by Montgomery.) Lonely, she begins hanging out with John, her dorm counselor, a strange man some kids find creepy for the way he observes, perhaps spies on them. In retrospect, Montgomery calls him "an aristocratic hippie." Sometimes he and his wife invite her to join them for dinner.

John's passion for photographing students ("He performed an important service: We needed to know that we existed") leads Jennifer to value him as a connoisseur of the adolescent body. She's not at all at home in hers, so that notice from him comes as validation and encouragement. He leads her on by setting up rivalries with her friend Molly, for example, whom he's helping work through what he's diagnosed as a childhood molestation. (It's no surprise that Molly's therapy involves sex with him.)

And Jennifer pursues John, eventually proposing he relieve her of her virginity. Not one to shirk a challenge, he complies, after sharing his worries about jail, where he could be raped. By now she's his model, although there's no sense that she turns into a swan. Weston slept with all of his models, he informs her, "he said it was an essential part of the process."

It's the oldest of subjects: this call women heed to act as models, muses, stars, subjects. To be cast in his drama, seen by his eyes, and thus to lead surrogate lives. Later in their relation-ship—he's asked to leave the school, but she manages to visit him often—Jennifer finds some badly scratched Stieglitz negatives, some of them photos of O'Keeffe. (Like Bluebeard, John has forbidden her to open the box where they're stored.) John's explanation is that a "greedy" O'Keeffe destroyed the negatives to raise the value of the prints; besides, he adds, she was jealous of her younger self.

This is hardly a subtle portrait of John. In Hannah's calculatedly wooden performance, he comes off as a pretentious fool, a cold man of no substantial talent. I'm not sure it would hurt to make him more formidable. Sturges may be a bore (who else would title a collection *Radiant Identities*, but his work has reached a certain level of critical respectability as well as commercial success—much of this triggered by the FBI's clumsy attempt to prosecute him (they couldn't convince a grand jury). In *Art for Teachers*, the FBI sleuth who comes to interview Montgomery is a dotty Clouseau-type, and she gets points from art-colony colleagues for mocking him.

In the afterword to Sturges's 1994 *Radiant Identities*—large-format photos of naked nymphets on uncrowded beaches—critic A.D. Coleman raises the matter of consent. He notes with awe that each young subject signs a contract giving permission for each separate use of a photo (each time their page is drooled over?), and that parents sign, too. As if in answer, *Art for Teachers* opens with a reading of a generic contract—endless relinquishments of claims and rights, ending on the forlorn word *forever*—over a clutch of softcore photos of young girls. Implicitly, Montgomery raises the question of what a child's consent means. And what a parent's consent is worth.

It's interesting to read Coleman's apologia after seeing *Art for Teachers*. Chalking up Sturges's little girl fixation to a quest for "what a Jungian would call his own feminine aspect," Coleman considers these girls' very nakedness their knowing stares and long-term cooperation, to be proof that the photographer has "no designs on them, no ulterior motives." "Had the integrity of his intentions not been palpable," Coleman goes on, "Sturges could never have evoked this degree of openness. ... There's not an ounce of malice in these pictures, nor greed, nor treachery. Clearly the photographer believed, and persuaded his subjects that their fragile truths were not only safe with him but in no danger from the world." Childhood is fleeting, art is long?

After *Art for Teachers*, what are we supposed to make of the *Identities* photo of Sturges's wife and collaborator, Maia, body-to-body with a naked teenage girl? Or the fact that Sturges's favorite model here, the lithesome, prepubescent Misty Dawn, is photographed both in northern California and at the French nudist colony where Sturges hangs out each summer? Does he take her along so as not to miss the "moment of passage," as Coleman neatly puts it? Prurient of me to ask?

Also reviewed in:
CHICAGO TRIBUNE, 10/27/95, Tempo/p. 2, Michael Wilmington
NEW YORK TIMES, 8/2/95, p. C16, Janet Maslin
VARIETY, 3/27-4/2/95, p. 76, Godfrey Cheshire

ASSASSINS

A Warner Bros. release of a Silver Pictures production in association with Donner/Shuler-Donner Productions. *Executive Producer:* Lauren Shuler-Donner and Dino De Laurentiis. *Producer:* Richard Donner, Joel Silver, Bruce Evans, Raynold Gideon, Andrew Lazar, and Jim van Wyck. *Director:* Richard Donner. *Screenplay:* Andy Wachowski, Larry Wachowski, and Brian Helgeland. *Story:* Andy Wachowski and Larry Wachowski. *Director of Photography:* Vilmos Zsigmond. *Editor:* Richard Marks. *Music:* Mark Mancina. *Music Editor:* Zigmund Gron. *Sound:* Petur Hliddal and (music) Alan Meyerson and Steve Kempster. *Sound Editor:* Robert G. Henderson. *Casting:* Marion Dougherty. *Production Designer:* Tom Sanders. *Art Director:* Daniel T. Dorrance. *Set Designer:* Alan Manzer, Gilbert Wong, Chad Griffin, and Noelle King. *Set Decorator:* Lisa Dean. *Special Effects:* Jon Belyeu and Rafael Perez. *Costumes:* Elizabeth McBride. *Make-up:* Lee Harman. *Stunt Coordinator:* Conrad Palmisano and Dick Hancock. *Running time:* 135 minutes. *MPAA Rating:* R.

CAST: Sylvester Stallone (Robert Rath); Antonio Banderas (Miguel Bain); Julianne Moore (Electra); Anatoly Davydov (Nicolai); Muse Watson (Ketcham); Stephen Kahan (Alan Branch); Kelly Rowan (Jennifer); Reed Diamond (Bob); Kai Wulff (Remy); Kerry Skalsky, James Douglas Haskins, and David Shark (Buyers); Edward J. Rosen (Cemetery Caretaker); Christina Orchid (Dowager); Bruce R. Orchid, Anibal O. Lleras, and Michael DeCourcey (Cabbies); James Louis Oliver (Customs Officer); Sue Carolyn Wise (Obnoxious Woman); Ron Ben Jarrett (Maintenance Man); Marian Collier (Pet Shop Lady); Dave Young (Male Guard); Ragna Sigrum (Female Guard); Mark Woodford (Room Service Waiter); Marta Labatut and Choco Orta (Cemetery Women); Ivonne Piazza (Bank Teller); Angel Vazquez (Bank Official); Axel Anderson (Bank President); David Dollase and Jim Graham (Bodyguards); Wally Dalton (Priest); Paul Tuerpe, John Procaccino, and Merissa E. Williams (Reporters); Juan Manuel Lebron (Puerto Rican Cafe Waiter); Eddie Bellaflorres (Fruit Vendor); Thomas Helgeland (Soloist); James W. Gavin (Police Helicopter Pilot); Scott Stuber (Parking Attendant); Richard Blum (Watcher); Eric Sather (Cab Customer); Wally Gudgell (Upset Passenger); J. Mills Goodloe (Newlywed Man); Peter Sebastian Lackaff (Singer); John Lamar (Money Hungry Man); Robert Sanders (Monorail Driver); Rhonda J. Osborne (Police Dispatcher); Christina Herrera (Pro Choice Woman); Carry Sanchez (Bank Receptionist); Frankie R. Jimenez, Jr. (Towel Boy); Jeff King (Helicopter Pilot).

LOS ANGELES TIMES 10/6/95, Calendar/p. 1, Jack Mathews

[The following review by Jack Mathews appeared in a slightly different form in **NEWSDAY, 10/6/95, Part II/p. B2.]**

For those of you who choked on laughter when Sylvester Stallone stood in the middle of a futuristic street in "Judge Dredd," dressed in a Halloween outfit from Acme Plastics and bellowed to the skies, "I yam the law!," some good news. Stallone barely raises his voice in Richard Donner's "Assassins" and darned if his character isn't actually engaging.

That doesn't mean he is more real than Judge Dredd, or any of the others in the actor's gallery of action heroes. But he's definitely more pleasant, more interesting, less intense. In most of his films, Stallone plays every scene like a thoroughbred racing for the wire, threatening to blow a main artery with every heartbeat.

Here, he plays Robert Rath—the finest free-lance hitman on the CIA vendor list—as if he were Rambo on Prozac. He kills, but without taking his shirt off, or taking any particular moral satisfaction from it. In fact, he would be retiring as the world's preeminent assassin right now if there weren't this new kid on the block, a wild Spaniard named Miguel Bain (Antonio Banderas) who keeps showing up at Rath's jobs and beating him to the kill.

"Assassins" is a contemporary, high-tech Western, with these two gun slingers—one with a conscience, one without—heading for the inevitable showdown. The plot, which brings the two men and another CIA operative (Julianne Moore) from the Pacific Northwest to the Caribbean, has something to do with a computer disk, espionage, and post-Cold War betrayal, but it exists solely as a stage for the collisions between its stars.

The screenplay, by the brothers Andy and Larry Wachowski with a polish by Brian Helgeland ("The Nightmare on Elm Street IV), doesn't measure up on any score to producer Joel Silver's description—"suspenseful, romantic and intelligent"—and it is far too thin to justify its two hour and 15-minute running time. But Donner's low-key, almost leisurely pace and some surprisingly effective chemistry between its two male stars make it a better show than most in the action genre.

In a way, the dueling egos of Rath and Bain reflect the relationship between Stallone and Banderas. Stallone has been one of the hottest international action stars for nearly two decades; Banderas, currently in the midst of the biggest PR launch afforded a Spaniard in this country since Julio Iglesias, is the cocky newcomer. And Banderas has a clear grasp of what makes an action star shine.

In both "Desperado" and "Assassins," Banderas is sort of a lovable maniac, an icy killer with fiery passion and a perceptible, Mel Gibson-like awareness of the manure he's spreading. By the end of the improbable trail of bodies leading Bain to Rath, Banderas has become an irresistible adversary. This is not a good week to admire cold-blooded killers, but by the end of the improbable trail of bodies leading Bain to Rath, Banderas has become an irresistible adversary.

Comparisons to Gibson may stick. Banderas has the same combination of looks, sex appeal and physical athleticism, plus the knack for spontaneous nuttiness that Gibson made his signature in the three Donner-directed "Lethal Weapon" movies. Even as an irredeemable sociopath, there's something heroic about Bain in "Assassins," and this performance—more than the one in "Desperado"—figures to cover all his publicity bills.

But as the old dog trying to protect his territory against the indiscriminate spray of the upstart, Stallone holds his own very well. He seems to have learned that counterplay is the best play when competing with a charming scenery-chewer like Banderas, and the quiet, professional calm he keeps as Rath suits him.

Moore, playing a surveillance whiz recruited as Rath's partner, has a few good moments of reluctant action, but her Electra is an otherwise routine love interest, and Stallone—for all his experience and newfound sensitivity—is asked to stretch too far when the old assassin starts getting sentimental.

NEW YORK POST, 10/6/95, p. 45, Michael Medved

When it comes to reviewing new releases produced by action specialist Joel Silver ("Die Hard," "Lethal Weapon," "Demolition Man") it hardly makes sense to employ the same aesthetic standards one night apply to "Remains of the Day."

Potential patrons for Silver's movies don't want to know if they're getting great art; they just need a basic evaluation of the hero, the villain, the action scenes and the girl. In each of these particulars, "Assassins" shines. To break it down to its predictable component parts:

1. THE HERO: Sylvester Stallone plays Robert Rath, a master assassin formerly trained by the CIA, now working for private contractors, who wants to perform "one last job" so he can abandon the brutal world in which he functions (sound familiar?). Stallone makes as much of this hackneyed role as any actor possibly could, performing with convincing world-weariness and impressive dignity, avoiding the hammy excesses of so many of his recent parts ("Judge Dredd," "The Specialist").

2. THE VILLAIN: Antonio Banderas is an up-and-coming young assassin who's determined to knock off Robert Rath so he can establish himself as the world's new "Number One." He is simply sensational, providing an even more electrifying performance than he delivered in "Desperado," giving pulsing life to a jittery, brilliant, sexy deadly dangerous and utterly charming nutcase—perhaps the most fascinating bad guy to turn up in any film so far this year.

3. THE ACTION SCENES: Richard Donner ("Superman" and all the "Lethal Weapon" films) is an acknowledged master at choreographing violence in a simultaneously witty and exciting style and here he's at the top of his form. Aided immeasurably by the spectacularly rich three dimensional cinematography of Vilmos Zsigmond ("Close Encounters of the Third Kind," "The Deer Hunter"), he creates a few expertly-edited chase scenes that may be remembered as classics—including a sequence in which the dueling assassins are trapped together in the same

cab, and an elaborate climax in which the rivals stake out one another around the delivery of $20 million at a Caribbean bank. Throughout the film, Donner provides plenty of excitement and menace without the slightest hint of gratuitous gore.

4. THE GIRL: Julianne Moore is one of those amazing actresses who can do absolutely anything—last year, even playing some memorable Chekhov (in "Vanya on 42nd St.") which must count as a far cry from "Assassins." Here, she's just about perfect as a lonely, cat-fancying computer and surveillance expert in Seattle who's making a fortune in industrial espionage, until Stallone is hired to rub her out—and Banderas gets the same assignment, determined to liquidate Stallone in the process. Naturally, Moore gravitates to Stallone as her only chance for survival and their surprisingly chaste interaction (featuring only one brief kiss) nevertheless generates memorable chemistry.

The plot (by the first time screenwriters—and brothers—Larry and Andy Wachowski) doesn't make a great deal of sense but at least it seems occasionally plausible as it unfolds in this film's appropriately breathless pace. "Assassins" may not provide any sense of lingering edification or uplift, but for those who can enjoy a mindless shoot-em-up, it does deliver killer entertainment. In other words, it's not pure gold, but it is solid Silver.

SIGHT AND SOUND, 12/95, p. 39, Nick James

A disenchanted contract killer, Robert Rath, receives a commission to assassinate an FBI witness at a funeral. He is about to take aim when his victim is shot by another hitman. Rath engages his rival in a gun battle which leads to the latter's arrest but then the rival gets away. Rath 'borrows' a yellow cab and picks him up. The killer soon realises who Rath is and introduces himself as Miguel Bain. He too was commissioned by the same employer. They fight and Bain makes his escape.

The next contract involves some Dutchmen trying to purchase software from an anonymous source. Rath must eliminate the buyers and the source and recover the software disk. Rath follows the Dutch to a hotel where the source, Electra, has hired two rooms connected by an air duct. While Rath is zoning in on Electra's base room, Bain bursts into the other just as the information the Dutch are seeking is being transferred and kills them all. Electra deletes the files before the transfer is complete, then Rath detains her. After a gun battle with Bain they escape. Electra then slips away from Rath.

Rath and Bain separately track Electra to her apartment. Two tenants are lulled before an explosion blows Bain out of window unharmed. Rath and Electra then agree to become partners and offer Rath's boss the disk for one million dollars. An exchange takes place but the money is booby trapped and Electra has held back the real disk. She and Rath renegotiate for vastly more money to be deposited in a Caribbean bank. Rath realises that Bain will be called in to get him so he devises a plan based on Bain knowing that Rath once had to shoot his best friend, Nicolai, from a hotel window opposite the same Caribbean bank. Sure that Bain will try and duplicate that killing, Rath hopes to remain inside the bank while Bain goes mad with impatience. When Bain finally quits the hotel, Electra must grab his rifle. The plan goes well except that the hotel is now a ruin and Electra falls through the floor before she can reach the rifle. In the final fight, Rath's boss turns out to be Nicolai, and Nicolai and Bain finally die.

Assassins starts with a black and white flashback to hitman Robert Rath's assassination of his best friend Nicolai and then several shots of a big clock, leading one to expect what this film never delivers: a genuine sense of keen suspense and *noir* fatalism. Director Richard Donner has proved he is an expert constructor of buddy-buddy action thrillers with the *Lethal Weapon* series, but in those films he had two nicely contrasted but equally powerful screen presences in Mel Gibson and Danny Glover. Here Donner's two male leads do not survive the comparison with their predecessors, and their weakness contributes to a general lack of engagement. Stallone can be a deeply etched physical presence on screen, even in the sombre half-light that bathes *Assassins'* opening scenes, but as soon as his eyelids flicker with cognition he becomes faint. As hit-man-with-a-heart Robert Rath, a man who metaphorically bleeds with his victims, who mixes empathy with his endgame, he looks drowsy on the job and golf-gear cuddly when at home behind his powerbook. Donner establishes Rath's career angst with shots of drizzle on a windowpane, the muted blues and greys of his reflection merging in a bruisy smear, but you never feel that he's doomed to anything more infernal than a lifetime of mild ennui.

The contrast with his young rival Miguel Bain couldn't be more artificial or extreme. Antonio Banderas seems particularly keen here to expunge all memory of other stereotypical mad dog killer Latinos with a teeth-baring, eye-rolling performance that is nevertheless unmistakably reminiscent of Maradona at the US World Cup finals. Whether in a Pacific downpour or the swelter of a Caribbean afternoon, Banderas is constantly in a sweat. As a marksman he's ruined from the start, you feel, because his fringe keeps flopping on the eyepiece. The third major character is, however, played by someone with stage credentials. Julianne Moore's hacker Electra, a redhaired cat lover (and implied manhater) with plenty of techno-suss looks like her second bid after *Nine Months* to compete with Meg Ryan as a light comedian (with added reach and gravitas). But she can make little impact on a film whose defining action is the firing of pinpoint accurate weapons with your eyes shut. After seeing her wasted here, anyone who also saw her brilliant performance in *Uncle Vanya on 42nd Street* might wish that American lotteries were as dedicated to the "elitist" theatre as the UK's National Lottery.

Structurally *Assassins* is simple: two set-piece shootings (one a prologue in which Rath allows an ex-colleague he's been ordered to kill to commit suicide) followed by three separate stalk-and-chase sequences before the final, long climactic scene around which the film was clearly built. Each of these constituent parts is briskly and efficiently rendered by Donner, unhampered as he is by complications of motive beyond the simple one of protecting the disk/Macguffin. Only the chillingly casual deaths of Moore's tenants disrupt the flow from one inanity to another.

Rath's final plan—leaving Bain to sit all day waiting in the ruined hotel for Rath to emerge from the bank into his sights—should be a major suspense finale. It is not dissimilar in formal terms to the climax of John Frankenheimer's *The Manchurian Candidate*. The lone killer is in position and the stage is set for his victim. All we can do is wait and watch the big clock ticking. The difference is that in *Assassins* there is no sense of a larger community who might get involved, who might catch a stray bullet, or even discover the assassin before he gets to work. We remain hermetically within a nonsensical triangle that gets squared rather perfunctorily when Rath's old Russian buddy Nicolai proves not to be dead.

VILLAGE VOICE, 10/17/95, p. 47, J. Hoberman

Assassins, Sylvester Stallone's latest payday, has its own tortuous end-of-an-era quality. In the curious logic of this morally muscle-bound Joel Silver production, directed by hack supremo Richard Donner, Sly plays a lovable hit man—although he's supposedly the best in the world, the entire movie is cleverly designed so that he never actually kills anybody. Is murder then a metaphor for acting! A giggling Antonio Banderas appears as the Stallone fan who wants to supplant the master as No. 1.

Banderas's campy performance—full of matador pirouettes and Bruce Lee whoops—is *Assassins*'s sole sign of life. To fully appreciate *Strange Days*, sit through *Assassins*'s first. The only thing more lugubrious than *Assassins* pointless helicopter tracking shots and slack stuntman escapes, its *Lethal Weapon*-style liberal T-shirt slogans, tedious Internet conversations, and feeble attempt at paranoid gun posturing (John Woo via Quentin Tarantino), is the spectacle of Sly in lumbering doofus mode. He eats a banana while pondering the message of cyberspace, then barge in on a "tense" scene like Kramer skidding into Seinfeld's apartment.

Julianne Moore, on hand as a ditzy hacker and quasi-love-interest, at one point calls Stallone "the enemy of fun." Indeed, the star is so chivalrous he never even comes close to insinuating his tongue down Moore's throat, (Is he afraid to catch whatever it was she had in *Safe*?) The only genuine thing in this movie is the Stallone characters desire to retire. You don't have to be a Santa Claus of the subconscious to see someone begging to be put out of his misery.

Also reviewed in:
CHICAGO TRIBUNE, 10/6/95, Friday/p. D, Michael Wilmington
NEW YORK TIMES, 10/6/95, p. C3, Janet Maslin
VARIETY, 10/2-8/95, p. 39, Todd McCarthy
WASHINGTON POST, 10/6/95, p. B7, Hal Hinson

AUGUSTIN

A Kino International release of a Sepia/Cinea coproduction with the participation of the French National Center of Cinematography. *Producer:* Philippe Jacquier and Brigitte Faure. *Director:* Anne Fontaine. *Screenplay (French with English subtitles):* Anne Fontaine. *Director of Photography:* Jean-Marie Dreujou. *Editor:* Sylvie Gadmer. *Sound:* François de Morant and Jean-Pierre Laforce. *Running time:* 61 minutes. *MPAA Rating:* Not Rated.

CAST: Jean-Chretien Sibertin-Blanc (Augustin); Stephanie Zhang (Caroline); Guy Casabonne (Cyril Cachones); Nora Habib (Shula); Claude Pecher (Monsieur Poirier); James Lord (Hotel Guest); Jacqueline Vimpierre (Madame Batavoine); Rahim Mazioud (Hotel Manager); Rene Boulet (Monsieur Liviescu); Thierry Lhermitte (Himself).

NEW YORK POST, 10/11/95, p. 34, Thelma Adams

I saw the French comedy "Augustin" at Lincoln Center's Alice Tully Hall surrounded by Frenchmen. Their gales of laughter dwarfed my occasional smiles. I spent more time wondering what these Gauls were laughing at than laughing myself.

Anne Fontaine's modest comedy had its American premiere Monday at the New York Film Festival and opens today at the Lincoln Plaza.

Fontaine, in her second feature, cast her brother, Jean-Chretien Sibertin-Blanc, in the title role. Augustin works as an insurance claims adjuster by morning, freeing the rest of his day to pursue his dream: acting.

Writer/director Fontaine builds the short film—61 minutes—on a series of long scenes that showcase Augustin's quirks in the face of an almost death-defying normalcy. "Augustin" is a comedy of small lives.

The beauty of Fontaine's film is that, despite Augustin's somewhat grand dreams, small is beautiful—and safe—for this Parisian schlemiel. "I have years and years of peace ahead of me," he says.

Augustin's ambition as an actor is as modest as the film. He'd like to play action roles, perhaps a truck driver, but he's no method actor: "Feelings, I don't like feelings," he tells a baffled casting agent who is considering him for a bit part as a jealous room service waiter.

On the way to the film's climax—a mildly amusing audition sequence with popular French actor Thierry Lhermitte—Augustin researches the room service role with the commitment of a De Niro. While observing workers at a four-star hotel, the would-be actor has a 10-minute flirtation with a charming Chinese chambermaid (Stephanie Zhang) that leads nowhere.

The film's irony is that Augustin's audition leads somewhere. It is just the actor's earnestness and bag of nervous tics that charms Lhermitte.

The French Tom Hanks might be the more successful actor, but he doesn't take his craft anywhere near as seriously as the amateur Augustin. With his ambition within reach, will the claims adjuster abandon his amateur status in exchange for a shot at the big time?

Sibertin-Blanc endows his dreamer with a deadpan innocence. His Augustin is an eccentric precisely because he finds life's little pleasures and difficulties so satisfying. He leaves the bigger picture—and the bigger laughs—to others. It wasn't until the final scene, when a hefty white bunny upstages Sibertin-Blanc, that I finally laughed.

NEWSDAY, 10/11/95, Part II/p. B7, Jack Mathews

"Be careful what you wish for ..." might be the theme of Portuguese-French director Anne Fontaine's whimsical, one-hour-long "Augustin," if it weren't for the fact that its title character is so devoted to his dreams he's not about to let reality put them at risk.

Augustin, played by Fontaine's brother Jean-Chretien Sibertin-Blanc, is a shy, part-time claims processor in a Paris insurance agency who fancies a career tor himself as a serious movie actor, not realizing that what few acting jobs come his way—that insecticide commercial, that role as a Portuguese cod thief—are due to his naturally zany presence. He may be a rank amateur, but his combination of earnestness and nervous mannerisms make him an irresistible comic figure.

When we first meet Augustin, in a casting agent's office where he is babbling on proudly about his minuscule triumphs, we wonder why the agent is talking to him at all. He doesn't know the first thing about the auditioning process, having shown up with a batch of snapshots and passport photos instead of 8-by-10 glossies, and with absolutely no sense of his limitations.

Still, the casting agent sees something useful in his personality, and quickly sets him up to read for a role in a movie with French star Thierry Lhermitte,. The part is that of a room service waiter in a swank Paris hotel who confronts a guest he discovers has been sleeping with his chambermaid wife. That the scene is meant as comic farce is apparent to everyone but Augustin, who researches the role with the dedication of a method actor.

Sibertin-Blanc and Lhermitte, the bemused straight man to Augustin's crazily self-conscious audition, are the only professional actors in the film, which Fontaine more or less dedicates to those legions of people who hold down mundane jobs while dreaming of stardom. The amateur actors, who were not told what to expect from Sibertin-Blanc, add to the naturalism of the film, and there is a particularly nice scene between him and the hotel chambermaid (Stephanie Zhang) hired to play a ... hotel chambermaid.

"Augustin," part of a comedy double-bill featured this week in the New York Film Festival, has been on the festival circuit since winning a prize at Cannes two years ago, and gets its first commercial opening today at the Lincoln Plaza Cinema. At 61 minutes, it barely qualifies as a feature film, and the story is the slightest wisp of an idea.

But it does introduce to American audiences an actor who may be a fixture in French comedy for years to come.

VILLAGE VOICE, 10/17/95, p. 52, Leslie Camhi

In the States, it's been called a 'UFO', or 'Unidentified Filmic Object,' director Anne Fontaine told me bemusedly as we discussed the strange fate of *Augustin*, her second feature. One hour long and made on a shoestring, it's become a surprise hit in Paris and at film festivals. *Augustin* follows the exploits of an impassive, part-Portuguese insurance clerk with a terrible stutter who dreams of acting while working in a large Parisian company. "I wanted to create a borderline persona," she says, "someone comically burlesque but also very true-to-life." The result is this obsessive portrait of an obsessional character, whose skewed delusions of grandeur are touchingly close to those of Everyman. Its humor is odd and unfamiliar—there's little funny dialogue and few pratfalls. Yet, like Augustin himself, the film impresses with the sheer peculiarity and weird dignity of its vision.

Fontaine, whose anodyne good looks belie her single-minded intensity, became an actor almost by accident. She began as an actress, but found that the mostly "normal" roles she got didn't interest her. So at age 25 she quit and, while working as a salesgirl, began writing the script that became her first feature.

Though she's now a professional, the world of amateurs continues to fascinate her. "Almost all the clerks who appear in *Augustin* are employed in a real insurance company. People who work in offices often dream of being artists. In fact, there are only two actors in my film: Thierry L'Hermitte (the French equivalent of Kevin Costner), and Jean-Chretien Sibertin-Blanc, our antihero and star."

Sibertin-Blanc, known primarily for his work in theater, also happens to be the director's younger brother. Fontaine insists that his work as an actor, rather than any fraternal (or fratricidal) feelings, inspired her to create this role for him. Yet there's certainly something Oedipal in her camera's fixation on his megalomaniacal and self-enclosed character.

Does she plan to use him again?

"Not immediately. But Albert Cheung, a filmmaker who describes himself as a kind of Chinese Woody Allen, has proposed that we collaborate on a sequel, to be called *Augustin in Hong Kong*. In it, Augustin will travel to Hong Kong and try to learn Kung Fu in order to get parts in movies there. It's a project that's still waiting in the wings."

Also reviewed in:
NEW YORK TIMES, 10/9/95, p. C15, Janet Maslin
VARIETY, 6/5-11/95, p. 38, Lisa Nesselson

WASHINGTON POST, 1/5/96, p. F6, Hal Hinson
WASHINGTON POST, 1/5/96, Weekend/p. 32, Desson Howe

AWFULLY BIG ADVENTURE, AN

A Fine Line Features release of a Portman/Wolfhound production with the participation of British Screen and in association with BBC Films. *Executive Producer:* John Kelleher, Mark Shivas, and John Sivers. *Producer:* Hilary Heath and Philip Hinchcliffe. *Director:* Mike Newell. *Screenplay:* Charles Wood. *Based on the novel by:* Beryl Bainbridge. *Director of Photography:* Dick Pope. *Editor:* Jon Gregory. *Music:* Richard Hartley. *Sound:* Peter Sutton and (music) Phil Chapman. *Sound Editor:* Sue Baker. *Casting:* Susie Figgis. *Production Designer:* Mark Geraghty. *Art Director:* Dave Wilson. *Costumes:* Joan Bergin. *Make-up:* Ann Buchanan. *Stunt Coordinator:* Martin Grace. *Running time:* 113 minutes. *MPAA Rating:* R.

CAST: Alan Rickman (P.L. O'Hara); Hugh Grant (Meredith Potter); Georgina Cates (Stella); Alun Armstrong (Uncle Vernon); Peter Firth (Bunny); Prunella Scales (Rose); Rita Tushingham (Aunt Lily); Alan Cox (Geoffrey); Edward Petherbridge (Richard St. Ives); Nicola Pagett (Dotty Blundell); Carol Drinkwater (Dawn Allenby); Clive Merrison (Desmond Fairchild); Gerard McSorley (George); Ruth McCabe (Grace Bird); James Frain (John Harbour); Pat Laftan (Mr. Harcourt); Patti Love (Mary Deare); Hilary Reynolds (Babs Osbourne); Tom Hickey (Freddie Reynalde); Robbie Doolin (Reporter); Brendan Conroy (Disley); Johnny Murphy (One Eye); Peter O'Farrell (Long John Silver); Agnes Bernelle (Mrs. Ackerly); Larry Murphy (Inspector); Vicky Curtis (Ellen); Brian McGrath (Vicar); Padraig O'Raghallaigh (GPO Clerk); Nick Grennell (Actor); Willie Smith (Empire Stage Manager); Katy O'Donnell (Young Stella); Kate O'Malley (Baby Stella); Horace Hessey and Betty Casey (Singers); Paddy Casey (Pianist).

LOS ANGELES TIMES, 7/21/95, Calendar/p. 2, Peter Rainer

Movies about a life in the theater, no matter how hollowly that life is portrayed, almost always end up as valentines. And, for people who love backstage backbiting and Master Thespian antics, the genre is irresistible.

"An Awfully Big Adventure," based on the Beryl Bainbridge novel, has its share of life-in-the-theater shenanigans, and some of them are flavorful. Set in 1947 in Liverpool, it's about stage-struck 16-year-old Stella (Georgina Cates), who becomes an assistant stage manager for a theater company run by the imperially effete Meredith Potter (Hugh Grant). The troupe is scheduled to put on three plays in six weeks, including "Peter Pan," and the movie itself is a kind of "Peter Pan" in reverse. Without being terribly worldly, Stella enters into a world that wises her up fast. She's ripe for the learning, which includes sexual learning.

Director Mike Newell and screenwriter Charles Wood give Stella's sentimental education a decidedly unsentimental cast. Though the film captures a little of the knockabout frivolity of low-grade theater life, it plays up the sordidness, "An Awfully Big Adventure" is a valentine etched in acid.

Newell, who last directed the overrated high-brow slapstick "Four Weddings and a Funeral," goes in for a more somber mood here. Too somber, actually. What he shows us is so dank that we can't see how a girl's genuine love of the theater could force itself through all this gloom. Stella is a bit of a plaything with the troupe; and she's a bit of a plaything with the filmmakers, too.

Cates is believable in the role and, at times, as in her scenes with the troupe's Captain Hook (Alan Rickman), she's more than that. But Stella's yearning for Potter is too bedewed for someone so cagey.

As Grant plays him, Potter, who is vicious with his boyfriends in the troupe, carries on like a cross between Alastair Sim and Dame Edna. Grant tries to turn his patented flibbertigibbet charm into something acrid. He overdoes both the charm and the acridness.

The best reason to see the film is for Rickman's withering portrait of a moody rotter. He's such a stunning actor that, even though he turns up in the film more than halfway through, he immediately makes it his. He gives the film—or at least his role—a tragic dimension. And, in so doing, he justifies a life in the theater.

NEW YORK POST, 7/21/95, p. 40, Michael Medved

"An Awfully Big Adventure" is an awfully big bore.

That's too bad, because it means that only a tiny fraction of those who've watched Hugh Grant's embarrassing Bozo bit in "Nine Months"—or viewed his eyelash-fluttering apologetics on innumerable talk shows—will get to see his sharp and skillful performance in this film.

Grant plays Meredith Potter, director of a struggling theater troupe in the grim and devastated city of Liverpool in the years following World War II. He's a sneering aesthete with nicotine-stained fingers and a monocle who can't quite believe that an actor of his genius and sophistication has been stranded in a second-rate provincial company comprised in equal measure of has-beens and never-weres.

He takes out his frustrations with consistent cruelty to his colleagues—especially to those young and aspiring thespians, both male and female, who feel drawn to his creepy charisma.

The story unfolds from the point of view of one of those admirers: a tremblingly intense teen-ager named Stella (Georgina Cates), who takes a job as assistant stage manager at this threadbare repertory theater. Abandoned by her mother years before, she lives in a crowded flat with her aunt and uncle and views the stage as the only escape from her horribly humdrum existence.

While she nurses a burning crush on the Hugh Grant character, she's ultimately seduced by another member of the troupe, and one of Grant's old rivals—a weary stage veteran (Alan Rickman) who shows up to perform one of his theatrical specialties, as Captain Hook in "Peter Pan."

Rickman is, as usual, absolutely riveting, while Grant infuses his character's every tic and twitch with a demonic and destructive intensity that offers an impressive contrast to the nice-guy tweediness of his normal fumbling-Freddie persona.

Mike Newell—Grant's gifted director in "Four Weddings and a Funeral" and the creator of 1992's most perishable film, "Enchanted April"—has drawn similarly vivid performances from the rest of his fine cast, but it's not enough to rescue a script that has both the form and flavor of stale pudding.

Based on an autobiographical novel by Beryl Bainbridge, the movie does a fine job of portraying the black circumstances of the actors' lives. But after more than an hour of this indus-trial-strength depression, you begin to feel as trapped and hopeless as they are. Meanwhile, the only plot element worth mentioning involves a lurid, National Enquirer twist near the end of the picture that's so jaw-dropping and manipulative that it feels as if it came from a different film altogether—or perhaps even from a Harlequin romance.

The gritty, slice-of-life tone and this outrageously melodramatic story line not only pull the picture in different directions but actually break it apart. By the end of the film, director Newell seems to be straining for an epic sense of doom and grandeur, but his earnest and well-acted movie remains merely dreary, rather than memorably tragic.

NEWSDAY, 7/21/95, Part II/p. B2, Jack Mathews

If Mike Newell's "An Awfully Big Adventure" had opened before its star, Hugh Grant, was arrested at the intersection of Hollywood and Divine last month, people smitten by his "Four Weddings and a Funeral" charms might not have been so shocked. The character he plays in "Big Adventure" is a supercilious, degenerate creep.

In fact, the same may be said of the movie, a sour black comedy about the coming of age of a spirited and vulnerable teenage girl (Georgina Cates) who takes a job as a gofer for a post-World War II Liverpool theater company. Adapted from Beryl Bainbridge's novel, "Big Adventure" taps into the uniquely black mood of the Brits in the years immediately after the war, when the exhilaration of peace was tempered by so many years of shellings, disorientation and destruction.

That mood does not travel well into late 20th-Century America, especially when the central character is—by our increasingly enlightened view of what constitutes abuse—a child. Cates'

Stella is a 16-year-old virgin, full of energy, spirit, curiosity and ambition, and eager to enter an adult world that she is spectacularly unprepared to handle. It would be hard enough for her to protect herself in an accounting office; joining a repertory company is like doing a swan dive into a shark tank.

The chief predator in this tank is Meredith Potter (Grant), the self-obsessed manager-director whose passion for the theater is matched by a passion for seducing and destroying the young people who come in—specifically the young boys, a predilection noticeable to everyone except Stella, who falls instantly in love with him.

Blaming her inexperience for Potter's lack of interest in her, Stella seeks a sexual mentor in the middle-aged P.L. O'Hara (Alan Rickman), a vagabond actor playing Captain Hook in the company's rushed production of "Peter Pan." O'Hara, after a moment of noble reluctance, takes the assignment, and attempts to teach her enough about the broader issues of life for her to avoid the trap being set for her by Potter.

If this sounds like tawdry soap opera, it sure is. And I haven't even hinted at the melodramatic twist that Fine Line Features formally asked critics not to reveal. I'll just say that the last-act revelation is not worth the wait—not as a resolution to the story, and certainly not as entertainment. It turns "Big Adventure" into a psychological shaggy dog story.

Casting Grant as the vicious Potter and Rickman as O'Hara, a decent man with a troubled past, is a nice casting switch. No one is better at playing villains than Rickman, and Grant's stammering charms have made him—recent events notwithstanding—Hollywood's new heartthrob. Only Rickman has the range to pull it off, however. While Grant attempts to get by with an assortment of adopted mannerisms, Rickman suggests depths to O'Hara that go far beyond what was written into the part.

But it's a limited role for Rickman, who doesn't show up until midway through the movie, and we have to rely on the newcomer Cates to get us there. Cates, playing a character very reminiscent of the "Georgy Girl" role that made young and plump Lynn Redgrave a star, is by far the best thing about "An Awfully Big Adventure." It's no small trick to be insightful and innocent at the same time, and though the accomplishment is blunted by the overall wretchedness of the movie, we can assume there will better days ahead for her.

SIGHT AND SOUND, 4/95, p. 38, Philip Kemp

Liverpool. 1941: nine-year-old Stella Bradshaw stands clapping with delight at the spectacle of a nighttime air-raid. Her Uncle Vernon drags her into a shelter. Liverpool, 1947: with misgivings, Vernon and his wife Lily arrange for Stella to have an audition at the Playhouse theatre. Unimpressed by her prepared speech but amused by her pretentions, the company's director Meredith Potter and his stage manager Bunny take her on as an unpaid assistant stage manager. Stella phones her absent mother, Renee, to report her success.

Besotted by Meredith, Stella learns to her dismay that he has a lover, Hilary, in London. She is befriended by George, the set designer, but resented by her fellow ASM, Geoffrey, who makes a clumsy pass at her. Watchful but naive, she misreads much of what she sees, failing to realise that actress Dawn Allenby is nursing a hopeless passion for leading man Richard St Ives, or that Geoffrey, briefly seduced by Meredith, has been thrown over for juvenile lead John Harbour. To her delight, she is cast in a minor role in *Caesar and Cleopatra*.

After Dawn, drunk and hysterical, is dismissed from the company, Stella inadvertently causes St Ives, playing Caesar, to trip and break his leg. The play's run is terminated and the next production, *Peter Pan*, in which St Ives was to play Hook, is in jeopardy. Rose Lipman, the company manager, sends for her ex-lover P. L. O'Hara, a famous Hook and one-time member of the company. The first night, with O'Hara as Hook and Stella manipulating a torch and mirror to represent Tinkerbell, is a triumph. At the celebratory party O'Hara dances with Stella, then takes her back to his digs and beds her.

The affair continues, although Stella is still obsessed with Meredith. A football match is arranged with another troupe who are putting on *Treasure Island*. Acting as referee Meredith humiliates Geoffrey, who punches his nose. O'Hara warns Meredith against his treatment of Geoffrey, but Meredith retorts that O'Hara is having sex with a minor. Stella, devastated to learn that Hilary is a man, walks out on O'Hara; seeking her at her house, he sees a picture of Renee and realises that Stella is his daughter. Rushing to the docks where he last saw Renee he slips and drowns. Meredith goes on in his place as Hook. To report all this to her mother, Stella phones the speaking clock—whose voice Renee recorded before she vanished for good.

Mike Newell's film, and the Beryl Bainbridge novel on which it is based, borrows not only its title but many of its themes from JM Barrie's *Peter Pan* that most disquieting of children's classics. Absent mothers, incestuous father figures doubling as oppressive villains, the lure of fantasy and the betrayal of innocence are reflected and distorted in the tawdry, precarious world of post-war provincial rep. "The whole play's about innocence, not exploitation," says P.L. O'Hara, reproaching Meredith for his treatment of Geoffrey, but he's wrong: Barrie's play, like Newell's film, is about both. In the final scene Meredith (who has taken over the role of Captain Hook after O'Hara's death) stands on stage announcing "'This my hour of triumph." The hero-as-villain has been supplanted by the villain-as-villain, and between them innocence has lost out.

It is death, in *Peter Pan*'s line, that "will be an awfully big adventure". The tone of the film, haunted as it is by death and loss, is far darker than that of Newell's most recent work, recalling that before he diverged into feyness (*Into the West*) and self-conscious charm (*Four Weddings and a Funeral, Enchanted April*) he made his name with his biopic of Ruth Ellis, *Dance with a Stranger*. With its drab, claustrophic settings, vivid period sense and insight into the clash of social conventions, *Adventure* is closer in mood and texture to *Dance with a Stranger* than anything else Newell has directed since.

What it lacks, unfortunately, is the earlier film's narrative lucidity. Bainbridge's novel isn't long but it is rich in detail; perhaps in an attempt to recreate that richness, or with the aim of refracting events through Stella's uncomprehending gaze, the story now and then lapses into incoherence. Key characters are perfunctorily introduced and several crucial plot points are so fudged that they're unlikely to make sense to anyone who hasn't read the book. *An Awfully Big Adventure* had a long, troubled genesis (the BBC, for whom it was originally being produced, withdrew its commitment eight weeks before pre-production); it may be that during that period the film's makers got so close to their material they overlooked the needs of audiences coming to it cold.

Yet, despite the confusion, *Adventure* boasts some superb ensemble acting, with especially fine performances from Peter Firth, pink and spongy as the wretchedly put-upon Bunny, and Georgina Cates with her scrubbed face, avidly courting corruption ("I'm beginning to get the hang of fucking," she informs the nonplussed O'Hara). And Hugh Grant, a downturned rictus of contempt clamped on his face, plays Meredith with such relish as to suggest that his true *métier* may not be lovable ditherers, but fastidious villains in the Claude Rains mode.

Above all, there's the atmosphere. Liverpool having been disastrously modernised, most of the film was shot in Dublin which, as Newell rather tactlessly observes, "has a real smell of times past". Even so, he took full advantage of it, and much of the film seems permeated with a dank, evocative effluvium compounded of greasepaint, damp digs and overcooked stodge. As a story the film falters, but as a recreation of a lost milieu it's exact. *An Awfully Big Adventure*, it is safe to bet, won't come within miles of the headlong success of *Four Weddings and a Funeral*, but for all its flaws it's the more intriguing film.

VILLAGE VOICE, 8/1/95, p. 46, Jeff Taubin

Mike Newell's follow-up to his smarmy smash-success, *Four Weddings and a Funeral*, is a febrile, haunting, girl's coming-of-age story. An oedipal tragicomedy of errors set in the late 1940s in a tacky English theater company whose fall-back hit is *Peter Pan, An Awfully Big Adventure* is a cyclical tale of loss and discovery.

A former Voice music editor once explained why he thought *Four Weddings* was so terrific. "It's all about us," he said, us being 30-year-old males, edging toward the terrifying abyss of marital commitment. Well then, I love *An Awfully Big Adventure* because it's all about me (the adolescent me I still cherish), and, unlike the former music editor, I don't see myself onscreen very often. Decide who *you* are and buy your ticket accordingly, remembering, of course, that one-to-one identification is not the only pleasure of movies.

Newell first showed his talent for digging into the past and for twisting social history with sexual obsession in 1985's *Dance with a Stranger*. *An Awfully Big Adventure* is tougher and fresher, perhaps because the central character is less easily categorized than were the noir-ish types played by Rupert Everett and Miranda Richardson in the earlier film.

Faithfully adapted from Beryl Bainbridge's semi-autobiographical novel of the same name, *An Awfully Big Adventure* focuses on Stella (Georgina Cates), a 16-year-old aspiring actress who's hired as an apprentice by a Liverpool repertory company, less for her talent than for her naivete—she seems eminently exploitable. Abandoned in infancy by her single mother, Stella was raised by her aunt and uncle in a rancid flat with peeling wallpaper and matted carpets. The loss of her mother and the trauma of the Blitz have made her a little mad. She seems literal-minded but, in fact, she lives in a fantasy. She hasn't a clue how to read other people, which leaves her free to see only what she wants to.

Thus, she falls madly in love with the company's manipulative and self-loathing artistic director Meredith Potter (Hugh Grant), a rather inappropriate object of desire, being 20 years older than she and gay to boot. Her infatuation with Potter blinds her to the more direct sexual appeal of P. L. O'Hara (Alan Rickman), who arrives just in time to save the season by re-creating his legendary performance as Captain Hook. O'Hara, however, is an even more unsuitable lover than Potter would have been, and not just because he's old enough to be her father.

An Awfully Big Adventure is not couched in the first person. Nevertheless, Newell gives us access to Stella's subjectivity, putting us inside her skin at crucial moments as she begins to distinguish eroticism from romantic yearning, neither of them a satisfying substitute for the lost maternal bond. As Stella, Georgina Cates gives a nuanced, multilayered performance, managing to be at the same moment blockheaded and clear-sighted, clumsy and radiant, vulnerable and self-determined. The film is hers for the taking and she runs away with it.

That's not to say, that she doesn't get marvelous support from Grant, Rickman, and in smaller roles Rita Tushingham, Prunella Scales, and Alun Armstrong. Grant has the courage to make himself look despicable and disgusting (he plays one scene with vomit dribbling from his mouth) and, as a result, is more winning here than he was during his round of televised mea culpas, to say nothing of his toothy turn in *Nine Months*.

Rickman, the smart woman's romantic hero, enters late in the film, on a motorcycle wearing goggles and an aviator scarf. Newell shoots him from below for maximum phallic effect. His is the most emotionally demanding, and also, the most underwritten part. In *Peter Pan*, he who plays Hook must also play Mr. Darling, which means that O'Hara stands for both the good and the bad father. Rickman is both tender and frightening. He could easily have overpowered the film (and in a way I wish he had) but he keeps himself in check until the very end. Obsessed with the past, O'Hara trips on the present, causing havoc all around.

An Awfully Big Adventure hovers between memory and desire, fantasy and gritty realism. A torn dirty slipper can be a sign both of the world Stella is desperate to escape and of the anguish of her loss. In matters of the psyche, ambivalence is all.

Also reviewed in:
CHICAGO TRIBUNE, 9/22/95, Friday/p. J, Michael Wilmington
NEW REPUBLIC, 8/21 & 28/95, p. 31, Stanley Kauffmann
NEW YORK TIMES, 7/21/95, p. C8, Janet Maslin
VARIETY, 1/30-2/5/95, p. 48, Todd McCarthy
WASHINGTON POST, 9/15/95, p. D7, Rita Kempley
WASHINGTON POST, 9/15/95, Weekend/p. 44, Desson Howe

BAB EL-OUED CITY

A Jane Balfour Films release of a Les Matins Films/Flashback Audiovisuel/La Sept Cinema/Z.D.F./Thelma Film A.G. co-production. *Executive Producer:* Jacques Bidou, Jean-Pierre Gallepe and Yacine Djadi. *Producer:* Jacques Bidou and Jean-Pierre Gallepe. *Director:* Merzak Allouache. *Screenplay (Arabic and French with English subtitles):* Merzak Allouache. *Director of Photography:* Jean-Jacques Mrejen. *Editor:* Marie Colonna. *Music:* Rachid Bahri. *Running time:* 90 minutes. *MPAA Rating:* Not Rated.

CAST: Hassan Abdou (Boualem); Nadia Kaci (Yamina); Mohamed Ourdache (Said); Mourad Khen (Rachid); Mabrouk Ait Amara (Mabrouk); Nadia Samir (Ouradya); Ahmed Benaissa (The Iman).

NEW YORK POST, 6/14/95, p. 36, Larry Worth

Not that long ago, the city of Algiers conjured up images of the blue Mediterranean, exotic dancers and the Casbah's romance.

Fast-forward to the present and it's a pretty scary picture, effectively portrayed in "Bab el-Oued City"—a fictional but never far-from-the-truth look at life in the once-fabulous and now-fallen locale.

In the working-class section of town (known as the titular Bab el-Oued City), poverty has produced a black marketeer's haven which concerns—and ultimately engulfs—the half-dozen protagonists. In addition, Islamic fundamentalists have secured a foothold, creating still more tension and unrest.

The plot is set in motion by the theft of a community loudspeaker, an act with far-reaching repercussions for the handsome young thief, never mind the ravishing woman he loves and her revenge-obsessed extremist brother.

However, the screenplay proves somewhat muddled, with the various subplots taking too long to coalesce. Thankfully, Merzak Allouache's direction is light years ahead of his writing.

Using a cast of non-professionals, he invokes the universality of simple dreams: a woman seeking a job rather than marriage, a baker's labors to make the perfect croissant, a man whose goal is returning to his homeland.

While fusing such tales, Allouache nicely captures a time and place where violent political and religious, clashes are an everyday occurrence. When love even manages to emerge, it's a stolen embrace in a graveyard—a far cry from Pepe LeMoko's "Come with me to the Casbah" come-on.

Accordingly, ambience emerges as the film's strongest feature, and the main reason to visit "Bab el-Oued City."

NEWSDAY, 6/14/95, Part II/p. B8, John Anderson

Shoot a feature film in a country where religious/political conflict has taken 10,000 to 30,000 lives since 1992? It has advantages. For director Merzak Allouache, a filmmaker of great courage or pure insanity, it imbued his "Bab el-Oued City," which he filmed in Algiers in 1993, with the unmistakable odor of death—of people, of a city, and of self-determination and liberty worldwide.

So it should. Allouache's movie is a prophecy—much like Gabriel Garcia Marquez' "Chronicle of a Death Foretold," there is a feeling that doom has already befallen his world and we are watching everything in flashback. Which in a sense we are—our introduction to the story is through a woman narrating a letter to a man who has abandoned both the city and the woman to the runaway forces of Islamic fundamentalism. While the effect here is more confusing than forbidding—it takes a long time to make certain who's who—Allouache succeeds in convincing us that his characters, and the world, are careering through the squalid streets of Algiers toward religious thuggery and perdition.

Set just after the Algiers riots of 1988—which were sparked by a widening gulf of economic opportunity there and which led to the rise of fundamentalist influence nationwide—"Bab el-Oued City" embodies its conflict in two diametrically opposed characters: Said (Mohammed Ourdache)—self-appointed enforcer of public morality, who wears mascara to make his eyes look fiercer and has an unsavory association with some unsavory black marketeers—and Boualem (Hassan Abdou), a baker's assistant who works all night and whose sleep is interrupted by the incessant drone of fundamentalists, who have dotted the city with loudspeakers.

Said wants to be the Imam someday—"God willing"—and is brutally protective of his sister, Yamina (Nadia Kaci). It is she whom we've seen writing the letter, to Boualem, with whom she's become romantically involved, Boualem, in a rage, has cut the wires to the speaker on his roof, enraging Said and his gang, who ruthlessly search for the sinner.

Allouache isn't attacking Islam per se (of course, neither was Salman Rushdie): His Imam (Ahmed Benaissa) advises Said against violence, but Said has his own agenda. And so does everyone else in Algiers: There's a lusty market for forbidden goods, old people wax nostalgic about the days of revelry and contraband, but no one ever challenges the moralizers, which is Allouache's very pertinent and very pressing point.

VILLAGE VOICE, 6/20/95, p. 48, Amy Taubin

Made under circumstances that make the budgetary restrictions of *Two Girls* seem cushy, Merzak Allouache's *Bab el-Oued City* was shot on location in Algiers in 1993 when the campaign of Islamic fundamentalist violence was well underway. Allouache take's a neorealist approach using the actual streetlife to flesh out his bare-bones drama. Boualem, a young Muslim who yearns for a freer life, tears down a loudspeaker that blares fundamentalist propaganda day and night. Said, the leader of a group of right-wing thugs, vows to destroy the culprit. To complicate matters emotionally, as well as politically, Boualem is in love with Said's sister, who, like all women, is treated as a prisoner by the fundamentalist regime.

The circular form of the narrative emphasizes the constriction of a society ill which almost everyone dreams of escaping across the Mediterranean to Marseilles. Allouache goes round and round over the same ground but seldom penetrates the surface. Potentially complicated characters—the female, former Marxist revolutionary, now a delusioned alcoholic; the French-born Arab who viciously plays both ends against the middle—are never developed. *Bab el-Oued City* is finally more compelling to think about after the fact than to actually sit through. And, given the rise of the American fundamentalist right, the film is particularly resonant at this moment. The religious rationale for a brutish will to power is longer oceans away.

Also reviewed in:
CHICAGO TRIBUNE, 6/8/95, Tempo/p. 11, Michael Wilmington
NEW YORK TIMES, 6/14/95, p. C22, Stephen Holden
VARIETY, 5/30-6/5/94, p. 42, Deborah Young

BABE

A Universal Pictures release of a Kennedy Miller film. *Producer:* George Miller, Doug Mitchell, and Bill Miller. *Director:* Chris Noonan. *Screenplay:* George Miller and Chris Noonan. *Based on the novel by:* Dick King-Smith. *Director of Photography:* Andrew Lesnie. *Editor:* Marcus D'Arcy and Jay Friedkin. *Music:* Nigel Westlake. *Sound:* Ben Osmo and (music) Robin Gray. *Sound Editor:* Wayne Pashley. *Casting:* Liz Mullinar Casting and Valerie McCaffrey. *Production Designer:* Roger Ford. *Art Director:* Colin Gibson. *Set Decorator:* Kerrie Brown. *Animatronic Characters:* Jim Henson's Creature Shop. *Animation:* Sylvia Wong and Nancy Kato. *Special Effects:* Dave Roberts. *Animal Trainer:* Karl Lewis Miller. *Costumes:* Roger Ford. *Make-up:* Carolyn Tyrer. *Running time:* 91 minutes. *MPAA Rating:* G.

CAST: Christine Cavanaugh (Babe); Miriam Margolyes (Fly); Danny Mann (Ferdinand); Hugo Weaving (Rex); Miriam Flynn (Maa); Russie Taylor (Cat); Evelyn Krape (Old Ewe); Michael Edward-Stevens (Horse); Charles Bartlett (Cow); Paul Livingston (Rooster); Roscoe Lee Browne (Narrator); James Cromwell (Farmer Hoggett); Magda Szubanski (Esme Hoggett); Zoe Burton (Daughter); Paul Goddard (Son-in-law); Wade Hayward (Grandson); Britany Byrnes (Granddaughter); Mary Acres (Valda); Janet Foye, Pamela Hawken, and Karen Gough (Country Women); David Webb (The Vet); Marshall Napier (Chairman of Judges); Hec Macmillan and Ken Gregory (Lion's Club Men); Nicholas Lidstone (Sheep Rustler); Trevor Read and Nicholas Blake (Electrical Linesmen); Matthew Long (Sheepdog Trial Officer); John Doyle and Mike Harris (TV Commentators).

FILMS IN REVIEW, 11-12/95, p. 98, Edward Summer

If I had words to make a review for you,
I'd give you some praise golden and true.
I would make this film last for all time.
Then fill the night deep in re-runs ...

Babe has Astonishment, Wisdom, Humor, Talking Ducks, Pigs, Sheep, Dogs, Evil Thieves, Puppies, Poetry, Love, Dancing, Tears, Wonders, and Singing Mice. What more can a movie possibly have?

What more can be said?
See it.

LOS ANGELES TIMES, 8/4/95, Calendar/p. 1, Kenneth Turan

In this age of hype, over-hype and still more hype, what is sweeter than a genuine sleeper, a captivating film that dares to arrive without advance notice? "Babe," guilelessly trotting in on little pig's feet, is just such an unanticipated treat.

Its success is unlikely on every level. Its porker-of-destiny story line about a young pig that wants to be a sheep dog does not inspire confidence, its elaborate mixture of live action, animatronics and computer graphics sounds unwieldy and still photos don't do justice to its strengths.

But "Babe" turns out to be that rare movie that completely fulfills its admittedly modest aims. Coming at the end of a string of bloated summer movies, its gleeful Grinch-proof antics define irresistible, making you wish that words like *charming* and *enchanting* hadn't been overused on a slew of less likable films.

The film's special effects, which serve the story rather than call attention to themselves, are beautifully effective. Although considerable meticulous work has gone into the picture, including 18 months of preproduction, six months of shooting (with 48 fast-growing piglets used for the title character) and a year of post-production, the result is always carefree and light on its feet.

What all the effects have created is a curious sheep farm situated somewhere between enchantment and reality, Its nominal bosses are the taciturn Farmer Hoggett (James Cromwell) and his well-rounded wife (Magda Szubanski), but the creatures with the most engaging personalities are the farm animals, which, thanks to all that effects magic, move their lips and speak English when the Hoggetts are conveniently not around.

Babe, the runt of a litter of Large White Yorkshire pigs, almost doesn't get to the farm at all. But when Farmer Hoggett eyes him at a county fair, narrator Roscoe Lee Browne records "a faint sense of common destiny" passing between them, and soon Babe is on the yard.

Young as he is, Babe (voiced by Christine Cavanaugh) is ill at ease at first, but Fly, a border collie, takes him on as a surrogate son. Fly's mate Rex runs the farmyard, laying down the law to the animals and reminding them never to depart from "the way things are."

Next on the agenda is meeting the neighborhood characters, which include such animal crackers as the venerable Maa (Miriam Flynn), the crankiest sheep in captivity, and Ferdinand (Danny Mann), a conniving, fast-talking goose who believes his eccentric behavior will save him from the Christmas table, a fate that, he tragically moans, "eats away at the soul."

Given these pals, it's not surprising that Babe gets it into his head that he wants to herd sheep. Fly tries to give him standard dog advice about showing them who's boss, but Babe, a free spirit who refuses to accept others' definitions of whom he should be, has his own ideas. And watching this Little Pig That Could persevere on his own path is more satisfying than the cynical might imagine.

Babe's story is told in a way that consciously echoes silent films, with iris closes and title cards marking off the individual segments. It also has off-the-wall elements, like a trio of tiny field mice who can be heard singing both "Blue Moon" and the toreador aria from Bizet's "Carmen." And, with phrases like "This is a tale about an unprejudiced heart," the film retains the literary quality of its source material.

That would be "The Sheep-Pig," written by Dick King-Smith, the prolific author of children's books. Australian producer-director George Miller ("Mad Max," "Lorenzo's Oil") came across the book and determined to turn it into a film. He co-wrote the script with fellow Australian Chris Noonan, whose reputation is in documentaries and television, and, staying on as co-producer, hired Noonan, in his major feature debut, to direct.

With its smooth melding of real and artificial creatures and its interesting voice choices (Hugo Weaving of "The Adventures of Priscilla, Queen of the Desert" does Rex and "The Age of Innocence's" Miriam Margolyes is Fly), "Babe" makes its broadly defined but exactly performed characters completely convincing. If only people would be more like these animals, the world, though hardly saner, would certainly be a lot more fun.

NEW STATESMAN & SOCIETY, 12/15-29/95, p. 55, Jonathan Romney

The first thing all young children learn on opening their copy of *My First Ladybird Primer* is what horses, pigs and geese look like, which always struck me as a little bizarre. Unless they happen to live on some idyllic rural estate, and regularly have goats tripping in through the nursery window, getting the hang of their farmyard beasts isn't an immediate priority for most children, who'd be better off learning to recognize more practical objects first of all—this is a can-opener, this is a tax form, this is a telephone and this is the number for Childline.

In fact, that may be what's happening these days. A recent report suggested that a once unimaginably high percentage of British city children had no idea what certain rural animals looked like, had never seen a horse, were convinced that mice hatched from eggs, and so forth. For them, the new film *Babe* may come as a useful primer in country lore, while for children who know their geese and chickens like old household gods, the film will seem a very pantheon of these beasts given their most heroic, glorified status. Never were pigs so very piggy as in *Babe*, never did the quintessence of duck so flourish on the screen.

Most children's animal films play it by the rules, perpetuating common preconceptions of how animals should behave. This, Jane and John, is a dog. A dog rounds up sheep. This, children, is a piggie and it lies around going oink oink and getting nice and fat for Sophie Grigson's chopping board. And this is a cow, and, well, frankly, the cows have been rolling their eyes and frothing at the mouth lately, and are best avoided for the time being.

But in Chris Noonan's film, things ain't that simple. This is the first time I've seen the nature or nurture debate applied to the animal realm in a film. Produced in Australia by George Miller, who made the *Mad Max* films—make of that what you will—*Babe* is set in idyllic countryside, a hyper-kitsch imagining of Enid Blyton England, all rolling hedgerows and skies candy-coloured in orange and yellow. It's actually the world seen through the ingenuous eyes of a little piglet who hasn't yet realised what a cruel world he's landed in. Plucked from a horrific slaughterhouse and won in a raffle by the dour Farmer Hoggett, the winsome little bundle of pinkness is fated for the festive table.

By now, you may be retching and wondering whether there's a good revival of *Straw Dogs* on this Christmas. But *Babe* is one of the three films in history that you can call charming and mean it as a compliment. It looks extraordinary, photographed with extravagant style by Andrew Lesnie; it does technical things that you can hardly imagine being achievable; it tells a winning story; and, foremost in any *NSS* readers checklist, it, er, well, it raises important Questions Around Identity, if you must know.

What happens is that the melancholy porker is adopted by the farmer's sheepdogs, but finds that he doesn't have any active role in the barnyard. What he really wants to do is join in and round up the sheep like his adoptive mum and dad. Rebelling against the role that animal and human societies have in store for him, he sets his heart on becoming a sheepdog too, and has to negotiate the codes of animal and human protocol in order to get his wish. He nearly makes Farmer Hoggett look a fool, causes a terrible rift between his dog foster parents, and draws the derision of the sheep, who just won't cooperate. But he bravely battles the status quo in a way that my chime with any child that's beginning to ask questions about its own social conditioning. Your infant son will see this and realise he doesn't really have to be a train driver when he grows up; if he'd rather be a sheepdog, well and fine, as long as he doesn't bring fleas into the house.

The piglet really is remarkably fetching, even though, for reasons presumably to do with international sales, it does speak with the voice of a little girl from Sacramento. Most of the animals' voices are American, including a duck that sounds remarkably like Joe Pesci, and an old ewe that speaks with the tobaccoey twang of Granny in *The Beverly Hillbillies*. The idea of talking animals is something that takes some getting used to, especially if you've tried long and hard to forget Johnny Morris' ventriloquism on *Animal Magic*. After a while, you get use to the fact that the animals are talking; but what remains of surpassing fascination is the fact that they are moving their lips at all. Much of the film is predicated on the digital jiggery-pokery of those butter ads in which cows do an Andrews Sisters routine; there are also a lot of animatronics effects, some more obvious than others. But on the whole, the animals are real, and they behave like real animals—or like real animals do when they've been trained to act in films. (The pigs, of which there were several, were trained for ten weeks each from the age of two weeks old by a man called Karl Miller; on stage at the London Film Festival, he seemed a a perfectly nice man, and no one got eaten after filming, so everything seems quite in order.) But it's the lip movements, mostly digitally painted in as far as I can make out, that are extraordinary. You'll believe sheep can laugh.

NEW YORK POST, 8/4/95, p. 37, Michael Medved

It may sound absurd to suggest that the year's most enjoyable film so far is a funny little fable about a plucky pig, but don't dismiss the notion until you've actually seen the absurdly beautiful "Babe."

This altogether admirable Australian import is so witty, so sophisticated, so touching, so wildly inventive and so gorgeously crafted that it's a joy to watch from the first frame to the last.

The story, based on a fanciful tale by children's novelist Dick King-Smith, centers on a baby pig who's orphaned when his mother's hauled away to a pork packing plant. Through an odd combination of circumstances, he's adopted by the kindly but taciturn Farmer Hoggett (splendidly played by the craggy James Cromwell), and settles into the regimented life of the Hoggett homestead.

Making friends, in particular with a family of hard-working border collies, Babe aspires to emulate their lofty status on the farm, but finds it difficult to herd the sheep the way the barking and biting canines do.

Instead, Babe manages to persuade the herd to do his will through courtesy and reason, so successfully that Farmer Hoggett enters him into a big annual competition to choose the nation's top sheep dog (a contest in which our hero would definitely be rated as an under-pig).

What makes this simple story so captivating on screen is the uncanny characterization of each of these critters, who deliver their lines while moving mouths and changing expressions with the help of animatronic doubles devised by Jim Henson's Creature Shop.

These effects bring to life a duck who thinks he's a rooster (and persuades Babe to steal the alarm clock that forced him out of his daily job rousing the farm), a horse who puts Mr. Ed to shame, a conniving cat who scares Babe concerning his fate as food, a band of singing mice, and a whole herd of cantankerous sheep.

The picture is produced and co-written by George Miller, best-known for "Mad Max" movies (which bear no earthly resemblance to this one), and directed by a gifted documentarian, Chris Noonan. The cinematography (by the previously little known Andrew Lesnie) surely deserves an Oscar nomination for bringing a luscious storybook glow to every scene, and the infectious musical score by Nigel Westlake, (memorably adapting themes from the Saint-Saens "Organ Symphony") helps immeasurably in supporting the film's big emotional moments.

The movie's message, of triumphant non-conformity, with Babe bravely defying his pre-ordained role on the farm, comes across with surprising force, as does the welcome notion that you can achieve more with courtesy than with aggression and intimidation.

In a year already conspicuous for splendid family films (including "The Indian in the Cupboard," "A Little Princess," and, in its own way, "Apollo 13"), "Babe" might be just the pick of the litter.

After 91 minutes of enchantment, in fact, I grew so affectionate and sympathetic toward this porcine protagonist that I will readily confess that I have never in my life felt so glad I keep kosher.

NEWSDAY, 8/4/95, Part II/p. B5, Jonathan Mandell

Pigs are big in the movies these days. This is not a comment on this week's corporate acquisitions or this summer's bloated budgets or this era's star salaries, though certainly the pig is an appropriate metaphor for all that.

But insatiable greed is not all that the pig symbolizes to the culture, judging from the several pig-centered movies in the past couple of years, the most recent of which was "Gordy," by the creators of "Green Acres." Most of these films invest the pig with innocence or simplicity, contrasting it with the guilt or duplicity of humans.

Now comes "Babe," which, as sweet and droll as it is, is so full of moral instruction and obvious allegory it's like "Animal Farm" with a happy ending. This is one profound pig movie.

Filmed in Australia, "Babe" has much in common with "Gordy": The animals are real, not cartoon characters, and they speak in English to one another, moving their mouths (or beaks or snouts) in a generally persuasive way. Both movies begin with a voice-over narration that makes it clear this will be a fable for young children. They both also show the title character crying for a mother who is taken away by evil meat-packers. But, unlike "Gordy," "Babe" makes the wise decision to stay on the farm, and make the animals the lead characters (and the more animated actors). This is a movie in which Christmas is a time of terror, because of Christmas dinner.

Babe is befriended, nearly adopted, by Fly, the farm's female sheepdog. (Fly's irritatingly wise and maternal voice is that of Miriam Margolyes, an Oscar-nominated actress; Babe's predictably cute voice is by Christine Cavanaugh). Fly explains to Babe the rules of the farm: The dogs and cats are allowed in the house; the pig must stay outdoors. Only the dogs can go out with the farmer, whom the animals call the Boss, to help round up the sheep; "the pig's proper place" is at the trough. Ferdinand the duck reveals a darker side to the hierarchy; unless Babe makes himself useful on the farm, Ferdinand tells him, he is going to be killed and eaten. That's why Ferdinand himself tries each morning to crow like a rooster; he is trying to avoid his destiny as duck l'orange. Indeed, in one of the most charming sequences in the film, a frantic Ferdinand enlists Babe to sneak into the house and steal the farmer's new alarm clock, so that the new technology will not make his job (and his life) obsolete.

"The only way you'll find happiness," a cow warns Babe, "is to face that the way things are, are the way things are." But Babe becomes determined to find a purpose in life and escape his fate. He fights hard to gain the Boss' notice and get promoted to sheepdog. He is so successful that the farmer enrolls him in the National Sheep Dog Association's annual competition.

"Babe" is as quaint as old clockwork: Each scene is introduced by a title card, and then by three mice acting like a squeaky Greek chorus. It is also grim and stiff, with ominous music and dark sets streaked with the dusty yellow of life's harsh sun. But this is not just an old-fashioned fairy tale. The messages are as up-to-date as the farmer's fax machine.

NEWSWEEK, 8/14/95, p. 73, Jack Kroll

The babe in *Babe* is a pig. Relax, ladies, I haven't turned into Howard Stern: Babe is a *real* pig. Well, a real *talking* pig. All creatures talk in this Australian movie. It's a fable based on a children's book by British author Dick King-Smith, and it has a surprising charm. Your kiddie of course won't say, "Mom, this has a surprising charm." But he/she might squeal with delight, Babe, the porktagonist, is won in a raffle by farmer Hoggett (James Cromwell). Hoggett is otherwise hogless, so Babe bonds with Fly, the beautiful border collie. Fly and her spouse Rex are ace sheepherders, so Babe decides he, too, can be a sheep dog. Hoggett enters Babe in a sheepherding competition, confounding the officials and embarrassing his sweet dumpling of a wife, Esme (Magda Szubanski). The dogs are bred to herd by intimidation and fear, but Babe's method is to politely ask them to obey. Will Babe's revolutionary technique succeed? Can animals transcend their genetic destiny? (Ferdinand the wise-guy duck gets into trouble when he tries to avoid his orange-sauced future by pretending to be a rooster.) "Babe" is an ancient genre, the beast story updated with animatronics, computerized effects and voice-dubbing by some good actors, including Miriam Margolyes, an Oscar nominee for "The Age of Innocence," Director Chris Noonan is clearly having fun; he even uses Brechtian intertitles and a Greek chorus, or eek chorus, of mice. "Babe" is a loining experience.

SIGHT AND SOUND, 12/95, p. 40, Philip Kemp

Babe an orphaned pig, is won as a prize at a fair by farmer Arthur Hoggett. On Hoggett's farm, Babe is adopted by the sheepdog Fly and brought up with her puppies, despite the warnings of Fly's mate Rex that this is contrary to the order of things. He is also befriended by Maa, an elderly sheep, and Ferdinand, an eccentric duck. Hoggett becomes attached to Babe, though his wife sees the piglet as a promising Christmas dinner.

After Fly's pups are sold off, she treats the piglet like a surrogate child. At Christmas, Hoggett finds an excuse not to kill Babe, and duck is served instead. Ferdinand prudently quits the farm. Catching sheep rustlers at work, Babe raises the alarm. Hoggett, impressed with Babe's sagacity, invites the pig to try sheep-herding, much to Rex's disgust. At first Babe tries to intimidate the sheep, but when he asks them politely, they co-operate.

Rex, furious at this betrayal, attacks Fly, wounding her paw, and bites Hoggett when he intervenes. Hoggett has Rex sedated, and with both dogs disabled comes to rely on Babe for help with the sheep. When wild dogs attack the herd Babe sees them off, but not before Maa is killed; thinking Babe responsible, Hoggett is about to shoot the pig when he learns the truth. In Mrs Hoggett's absence, Hoggett takes Babe into the house and trains him for the forthcoming sheepdog trials.

At the trials Hoggett and Babe are greeted with indignation by the judges and derision by the crowd, while the trial sheep ignore the pig. Dashing back to the farm, Rex persuades the sheep to give him a secret password that ensures the co-operation of all their kind. Armed with this, Babe gives a flawless performance, and he and Hoggett achieve a 100 per cent score.

The hero is a loveable pink piglet. A motherly sheepdog, a wacky duck, a cuddly litter of puppies and a mouse trio who sing in squeaky voices fill out the supporting cast. The message—that all species deserve to be treated with respect—is unimpeachable. Thus anyone with a low cuteness threshold might feel inclined to give *Babe* the widest possible berth. This would be a mistake, since the film is funny, engaging and almost entirely uncloying. To make a good children's film in a cynical age like ours is a tough assignment: you need to believe in your story wholeheartedly enough to carry the kids with you, while keeping your treatment sufficiently tongue-in-cheek to divert the adults. It's no easy trick but, barring the odd uneasy moment, *Babe* carries it off with aplomb.

Babe is an Australian production, and this kind of balancing act may be one that Australians, with their idiosyncratic mix of Old World cynicism and New World optimism, are peculiarly well suited to handle. Baz Luhrmann's 1992 smash hit, *Strictly Ballroom* shares with *Babe* a do-your-own-thing theme and blithely predictable storyline. It also contrives to take itself seriously, so that we care about the characters and want to see them triumph, and to send itself up rotten. *Babe* lacks the earlier film's high-camp pizzazz but partakes of something of the same delight in stylised, highly coloured storytelling.

And like Luhrmann's film, *Babe* deals with rebellion, but safe rebellion, contained within a system. Babe may revolt against Rex's doctrine of "the way things are" and do things that aren't 'right' for pigs—entering the house, herding sheep—but it's all ultimately for the sake of "the boss", Farmer Hoggett. If herding sheep by polite request is better than barking and biting, the sheep still end up getting herded. From this angle, rather unexpectedly, Babe can be seen to overlap with a much more trenchant farmyard fable, *Animal Farm*.

Babe is also lively, likeable, and sends you out of the cinema grinning and humming the theme tune. This, like most of the score, derives from, nineteenth-century French classical music: Faure, Bizet, Delibes and in particular the finale of Saint-Saens' 'Organ' Symphony, which at one stage metamorphoses into a fairly yucky little ditty entitled 'If I Had Words'. (Saint-Saens, an ultra-respectable figure who suppressed his own *Carnaval des Animaux* on the grounds of frivolity, would no doubt have been horrified.) Elsewhere, though, the music's sheer brio carries all before it. Technically *Babe*'s a *tour de force*; it's often difficult to know whether you're watching puppetry, animation, animatronics, or an artful meshing of all three. And as for the ideology, well, from a film that advocates being nice to sheep, what would you expect but woolly liberalism?

TIME, 8/21/95, p. 69, Richard Schickel

He's brave and bright, good-natured and ambitious, naive and vulnerable. All in all, he's probably the most winsome orphan to appear on the screen since Freddie Bartholomew impersonated David Copperfield 60 years ago. To be sure, Babe is a piglet, but hey, these days you take goodness where you can find it—and resolutely deny whatever snooty qualms anthropomorphism raises in you.

His tale is simple. Farmer Hoggett wins Babe in a raffle, then leaves him to fend for himself in the barnyard. A motherly sheep dog adopts him, a fatherly sheep dog growls dubiously at him, and a kooky duck gets him in trouble. But Babe wins respect, animal and human, when he drives off some sheep poachers, in the process gaining his first sense of vocation: he'd like to herd sheep himself. The dogs think he's too nice a guy for that line of work. But the sheep, tired of being nipped and woofed at, take a shine to him because Babe speaks politely to them and treats them with respect. He's sort of a liberal humanist on trotters, capable even of the odd, soulful thought about mortality, and a welcome addition to a public life largely given over these days to swinishness of a less exemplary kind.

One would like to think that *Babe*'s surprise success at the box office is a tribute to the good cheer with which its eponymous hero reminds us of our better selves. But it also has the enchantment of an extended magical illusion—91 minutes of wondering how they did it. Mostly, it would seem, with a lot of patience. Producer and co-writer George Miller (of the Mad Max films) bought Dick King-Smith's children's story, on which the movie is based, nearly a decade ago. Co-writer and director Chris Noonan worked six years to bring it to the screen. The $25 million production seamlessly blends computer-graphic images (mostly of the creatures talking), animatronic doubles (for the facial expressions real creatures couldn't do) and live action supplied by 800 oinking, barking, baaing animals. "It had the logistical difficulty of a big action movie," says Miller, who claims his intimately scaled film is the biggest, most complicated Australian production ever.

He and Noonan credit much of its success to veteran animal trainer Karl Lewis Miller—"a genius," the director says, at bringing out the character of his charges. Miller and his staff raised 60 pigs by hand to gain their trust. It took 26 weeks to educate the first batch, by which time they had outgrown their optimal cuteness; the training was eventually shortened to 13 weeks. In all, 48 pigs appeared onscreen as Babe.

"You don't train a pig like you do a dog," says Miller. "You can train them to sit, but not by command." Still, the animals' ability to hit their marks never failed to amaze Noonan. His set, he says, "worked musically, rather than chaotically." Adds producer Miller: "We never once got jaded. As in all good allegories, you get a lot of bang for your buck." Now, it seems, he and his colleagues are going to be rewarded with a lot of bucks because they refused to bang audiences over the head with their effects, their moral or their own cleverness. It may have been complex to make, but their fable shines with the classic virtues of the form—surface simplicity, seductive imagery, gently instructive resonances.

VILLAGE VOICE, 8/8/95, p. 55, Michael Musto

Babe—not to be confused with John Goodman as *the* Babe—tells us that a pig can be a dog if he wants to. But can a pig be a movie star? Still in doubt, folks.

In the film's emphatically anthropomorphic world, the little porkers are lovably oppressed creatures who *have* to develop some extraordinary skill or they'll quickly become Baco Bits. That our porcine hero inexplicably speaks perfect English apparently isn't deemed enough of an achievement, nor is the fact that his mouth moves flawlessly in synch, which apparently wasn't the case with *Gordy*, the *last* blockbuster Hollywood film starring a pig (do I smell a trend?).

But *Babe* has even bigger mudcakes to roll. As the loosely constructed plot has it, the piglet is won by a weird farmer, who naturally plans to turn him into some form of festive, if artery-clogging, entree. But the crafty little oinker finds a spiritual mom in a dog named Fly—are you following me?—and even attains a purpose beyond pork chops when he emerges as the most polite yet effective sheep dog ever. He's the world's first sheep *pig*! Too bad the ramifications of Babe's putting real sheep dogs out of work are never addressed. And his journey to this career apotheosis is enacted with such storybook earnestness that the occasional loopy touches—the three mice who chirpily introduce the chapters—become a little *too* welcome.

It's all lovingly done—there are gorgeous close-ups of the sheep that even the Michelle Pfeiffers of the world might envy. But once past the admirably unexploitive tone and the novel cuteness of the animatronic wizardry, you tend to focus on the comments from the kids in the audience ("Mom, could cats eat pigs?") and to start wondering if any of the creatures is named Ewe Grant.

Also reviewed in:
CHICAGO TRIBUNE, 8/4/95, Friday/p. H, Gary Dretzka
NEW YORK TIMES, 8/4/95, p. C3, Stephen Holden
NEW YORKER, 9/4/95, p. 99, Terrence Rafferty
VARIETY, 7/24-30/95, p. 70, Leonard Klady
WASHINGTON POST, 8/4/95, p. D1, Rita Kempley
WASHINGTON POST, 8/4/95, Weekend/p. 38, Desson Howe

BABYSITTER, THE

A Spelling Films International release. *Producer:* Kevin J. Messick and Steve Perry. *Director:* Guy Ferland. *Screenplay:* Guy Ferland. *Based on a story by:* Robert Coover. *Director of Photography:* Rick Bota. *Editor:* Jim Prior. *Music:* Loek Dikker. *Running time:* 90 minutes. *MPAA Rating:* R.

CAST: Alicia Silverstone (Baby Sitter); J.T. Walsh (Harry Tucker); Lee Garlington (Dolly Tucker); Nicky Katt (Mark); Jeremy London (Jack); George Segal (Bill); Lois Chiles (Bernice).

NEW YORK POST, 11/15/95, p. 45, Larry Worth

Its becoming trendy for movies to go directly to cable or video, then be "rediscovered" on the big screen. But not every film is another "Red Rock West" or "The Last Seduction," as evidenced by "The Babysitter."

Indeed, the latest production to travel a circuitous route to theaters may have less to do with quality than with its hotter-than-hot star, Alicia Silverstone.

The nymph who found fame last summer in "Clueless" had previously starred in this flawed yet diverting look at hypocrisy and lust among the middle class.

In a 180-degree spin from her materialistic Valley girl, Silverstone plays a sensible bright high schooler who's barely aware of her blonde good looks, or the daydreams she inspires.

The list of panting admirers included her nice-guy boyfriend, his nasty ex-buddy, the 10 year-old she's tending and the kid's bloated, fiftysomething father, all of whom indulge in lengthy babysitter reveries. Heck, when Silverstone cuddles an infant, one expects to see the newborn's nursing fantasies.

But the more effective sequences are when writer/director Guy Ferland zeroes in on the matronly wife/mother who hires the titular babysitter. After squeezing into a too-tight black cocktail dress, she entertains her own delusions of being desirous at a neighborhood bash.

As played to perfection by Lee Garlington, the scenes are a bittersweet blend of humor and poignance, with fully-realized turns from J.T. Walsh's lecherous hubby, and George Segal and Lois Chiles as beautifully aging hosts.

Since the fetching Silverstone proves competent—ably abetted by Jeremy London as her football hero beau and Nicky Katt's troublemaking bully—the acting can't be faulted. Unfortunately, the same isn't true of Ferland's lethargic pacing or a dramatic denouement that seems to belong to another movie.

Still, "The Babysitter" earns credit for being more than kid stuff—even if the mixed results seem better suited to video.

NEW YORK, 11/20/95, p. 85. David Denby

For reasons too complicated to explain, *The Babysitter*, an interestingly dark new film with Alicia Silverstone—the young actress with the great big kisser who starred in *Clueless*—is heading straight into video. Only the invaluable, enterprising Film Forum has managed to grab the picture (for an open-ended run beginning November 15). *The Babysitter*, based on an old Robert Coover story and directed by young Guy Ferland, a protégé of Joel Schumacher (not a fact I would advertise), is about a beautiful teenager (Silverstone) in an unnamed suburban town, a level-headed, responsible girl who causes sexual fantasies in a variety of men—the 10-year-old boy she's taking care of; her sodden middle-aged employer (J.T. Walsh), who's at odds with his wife; her seemingly sweet-natured boyfriend (Jeremy London), who can't get her into bed; and his envious, no-good friend (Nicky Katt). At first, the movie seems a kind of malicious comedy of male illusion, with each man triumphing in his head and getting nowhere in life. Shot in dreamy flesh tones, the picture moves back and forth between these heated imaginings and everyday reality, where Silverstone, with her big hair, downward-curving mouth, and huge eyes, presides in utter calm, entirely unaware of the thickening web of lust gathering around her. But after a while, the joke turns sinister. The fantasies get wilder and more violent, and the men, convinced they can actually get away with the stuff they dream about, begin to act in increasingly idiotic and dangerous ways. Ferland shoots the movie as a suburban horror film: Everything is smooth and beautiful, but the currents of dismay and self-disgust grow almost unbearable. I'm not entirely pleased with the violent climax, which seems forced and over the top, but the layered portrait of male sexual stupidity—a gift handed down from generation to generation—could not have been more acidly drawn by the most radical of feminists.

VILLAGE VOICE, 11/21/95, Film Special/p. 22, Georgia Brown

Film Forum's resourceful Karen Cooper has rescued Guy Ferland's *The Babysitter* from a straight-to-video sentence. This worthy-of-release black comedy, starring the delicious Alicia Silverstone, is benefiting from *Clueless*'s huge (deserved) success.

Working from Robert Coover's ferocious short story is something of a risk since Coover's lurid series of violation fantasies never call on some grounded reality for comfort. Ferland tames the beast by plumping up characters, choosing between parallel universes, and carefully sticking to a plot we can all agree on. Even so, he communicates the message that flawless young bodies are potent hallucinogens.

One bright day, Little Red Riding Hood (the babysitter) sets off on her appointed rounds. It's sunny California and she's a California girl—blithely complacent as to her perfection. Like a skilled private dick or a would-be predator, the camera keeps its prey—all long legs and long swinging hair—in sight. Her studious looking boyfriend, Jack (Jeremy London, Jason's twin), rides by with his eye on her. A rougher-looking boy/man in black leather, Mark (Nicky Katt), approaches but is rebuffed. Hot for another shot, revenge maybe, Mark goes to work on Jack.

The babysitter arrives at her employers; the caricatured Tuckers (J.T. Walsh and Lee Garlington): he's a paunchy lech; she's in a panic about age. They have a boy, a girl, and a baby. The boy, too, has designs on the babysitter, who can seem, depending on who's perceiving her at the moment, either virginal, slutty, or a simple object for abuse. An ordinary domestic situation quickly takes on aspects of a horror story. Perhaps Ferland should've played this *more* for horror, because despite the injected fantasies, the movie pulls its punches, moving merely to an underwhelming accident.

Also reviewed in:
NEW YORK TIMES, 11/15/95, p. C16, Janet Maslin

BABY-SITTERS CLUB, THE

A Columbia Pictures and Beacon Pictures release of a Scholastic production. *Executive Producer:* Martin Keltz, Deborah Forte, Marc Abraham, Thomas A. Bliss, and Armyan Bernstein. *Producer:* Jane Startz and Peter O. Almond. *Director:* Melanie Mayron. *Screenplay:* Dalene Young. *Based on the book series by:* Ann M. Martin. *Director of Photography:* Willy Kurant. *Editor:* Christopher Greenbury. *Music:* David Michael Frank. *Music Editor:* Virginia Ellsworth. *Choreographer:* Gui Andrisano. *Sound:* David Ronne and (music) Gary Lux. *Sound Editor:* Darren Paskal and Ben Wilkins. *Casting:* Mary Artz and Barbara Cohen. *Production Designer:* Larry Fulton. *Art Director:* Charles Collum. *Set Designer:* Daniel Bradford and Keith Cunningham. *Set Decorator:* Douglas Mowat. *Set Dresser:* Cynthia C. Rebman. *Special Effects:* Josh Hakian. *Costumes:* Susie DeSanto. *Make-up:* Kathryn Kelly. *Stunt Coordinator:* Patrick Romano. *Running time:* 85 minutes. *MPAA Rating:* PG.

CAST: Schuyler Fisk (Kristy); Bre Blair (Stacey); Rachel Leigh Cook (Mary Anne); Larisa Oleynik (Dawn); Tricia Joe (Claudia); Stacey Linn Ramsower (Mallory); Zelda Harris (Jessi); Vanessa Zima (Rosie Wilder); Christian Oliver (Luca); Brooke Adams (Elizabeth Thomas Brewer); Bruce Davison (Watson); Jessica Needham (Karen); Ellen Burstyn (Mrs. Haberman); Asher Metchik (Jackie Rodowsky); Austin O'Brien (Logan Bruno); Marla Sokoloff (Cokie Mason); Ashlee Turner (Bebe); Natanya Ross (Grace); Katie Earle (Nina Marshall); Scarlett

Pomers (Suzi Barrett); Kyla Pratt (Becca); Anne Costner (Anne); Lily Costner (Lily); David Quittman (Buddy Barrett); Jonah Bliss (Nicky); Josh Berman (Ricky); Emmy Yu (Emmy/Camper); E.J. De La Peña (Jonas); Madison Fisk (Beth); Cleo Brock-Abraham (Cleo); Lance O'Reilly (Matt); Bridget Kate Geraghty (Vanessa); Erica Hess (Margie Klinger); Samantha Alanis (Charlotte Johannson); Aaron Metchik (Alan); Peter Horton (Patrick); Jeffrey Quittman (Jamie Newton); Colleen Camp (Maureen McGill); Teddy Dale (David Michael); Robin Swid (Brookes); Richard Guiton (Mark); Peter Gregory (Bouncer); Candy Trabucco (Cabbie); Harris Yulin (Harold); Aixa Clemente (Louise); Nancy Mette (Sheila).

LOS ANGELES TIMES, 8/18/95, Calendar/p. 8, Kevin Thomas

Movies don't get much more beguiling than "The Baby-Sitters Club," which takes us into the leafy, affluent community of Stoneybrook, Conn., to spend a crucial summer with seven lovely adolescent girls who've decided to expand their baby-sitting business into a summer camp for the local children.

Adapted gracefully by Dalene Young from Ann M. Martin's phenomenally popular book series, the film marks an uncommonly promising feature directorial debut by former "thirtysomething" star Melanie Mayron. It also introduces us to at least two dozen entirely appealing and talented young actors, ably supported by veterans Ellen Burstyn, Peter Horton, Brooke Adams and Bruce Davison.

Of course, the girls dream of making some money—why, they figure that if they make enough to buy a car they could all be driving it in another five years! The underlying, unstated reason for the venture is that they sense the need to reinforce their bonds just as they're approaching the threshold of adulthood. By the time summer's over, however, those bonds will be severely tested.

That's because Horton's Patrick, father of club president Kristy (Schuyler Fisk), has unexpectedly turned up, living in his camper on the outskirts of town. Although Kristy hasn't seen her father since she was 6 and has received exactly two cards since, she's thrilled to see him. Horton, in a splendid portrayal, reminds us why "charming" and "ne'er-do-well" so often go together.

Clearly, Patrick hungers for the love of the daughter he's so shamefully neglected—and believes, at the moment he says it, that he's got "a real shot as a job as a sportswriter" at the local paper. Until he gets it, however, he's got prepared to face his former wife (Adams) and her husband (Davison), who live in an imposing traditional-style home.

As the weeks and days roll by, Patrick gives no thought to the increasing and cruel pressure he's placed upon his young daughter, taught to be open and honest with friends and relatives, by taking up so much of her time yet requiring her to keep his presence secret.

On a less intense level, Kristy's dilemma is counterpoised with that of fellow baby-sitter Stacey (Bre Blair), a raving beauty of 13 intent on passing for 16 for the handsome visiting Swiss, 17-year-old Luca (Christian Oliver).

Kristy and Stacey do more growing up in the course of the summer than they could ever have anticipated. The patrician, staunch Fisk, in her screen debut, is such an intelligent, poised actress of great promise in her own right that you feel you're somehow taking away from her achievement by revealing that she is the daughter of Sissy Spacek and her husband, director Jack Fisk.

All of the young actresses—and a couple of young actors too—are impressive. They include Rachel Leigh Cook as the brunette beauty Mary Anne, Kristy's sole confidante, who also experiences the strain of her friend's secret; Larisa Oleynik's Dawn, who most resents Mary Anne's loyalty to Kristy; Tricia Joe as Claudia, struggling to pass an all-important biology exam; Stacey Lynn Ramsower as Mallory, the budding novelist of the group; and Zelda Harris as Jessi, an aspiring dancer.

Burstyn adds a brisk note as a neighbor to the club's campsite whose crankiness masks loneliness, and Adams and Davison are effective as loving parents rightly concerned with Kristy's increasing moodiness and unreliability.

To be sure, there's plenty of humor to offset serious matters, and Mayron reveals both terrific rapport with youngsters and ability in maintaining a gentle flow to material that is inherently episodic when there are so many characters' stories to tell.

Photographed gorgeously by Godard and Welles alumnus Willy Kurant in irresistibly idyllic locales, "The Baby-Sitters Club" is a beautiful film that possesses the power to enchant all ages. It's worth noting that the film admirably casts an African American and an Asian American among the club members without any fuss whatsoever, but then subtlety is a hallmark of this fine film.

NEW YORK POST, 8/18/95, p. 39, Michael Medved

Since the series began in 1986, the 201 books chronicling the adventures of "The Baby-Sitters Club" have sold some 125 million copies through a cunning combination of stubbornly old-fashioned and touchy, topical elements.

On the one hand, the likable 12- and 13-year-old girls who comprise the club inhabit a pleasant Norman Rockwellish suburb known as Stoneybrook, Conn., and a plucky, unified "Hey, kids, let's put on a show!" attitude toward all the challenges they face. On the other hand, author Ann Martin spices her books with frequent references to divorce, dysfunction, disease and other dilemmas of modern life to give the stories a more contemporary edge.

The movie that brings the "BSC" to the big screen for the first time tries for the same balancing act between the timeless and the trendy, but achieves only mixed success.

The darker, more disturbing aspects of the story come across more powerfully than the film's contrived moments of innocence and playfulness, gradually overwhelming (and undermining) the picture's insistently sunny tone.

The story begins when Kristy, tomboyish leader of the gang, comes up with an inspired scheme for the summer months. Since the club's seven members have already combined their talents in a successful baby-sitting business, Kristy (played by Sissy Spacek's unmistakably talented daughter, Schuyler Fisk, in her movie debut) suggests that they expand their operations to offer regular customers a summer camp for little kids.

This backyard enterprise at first arouses consternation from a grumpy neighbor (Ellen Burstyn), who inevitably turns out to have a heart of gold, but the girls also face more substantive difficulties.

Thirteen-year-old Stacey (played by 15-year-old Bre Blair, who looks like a twentysomething supermodel) begins hanging out with an older boy from Switzerland (Christian Oliver) without telling him the truth about her age, or her diabetes.

Kristy, meanwhile, finds her summer disrupted when her divorced dad (Peter Horton) re-enters her life after a five-year gap, insisting she say nothing to her mother or her friends about the fact that he's back in town living in his van, talking fecklessly of getting work as a sportswriter.

First-time director Melanie Mayron gets solid performances from all in her large cast, drawing especially touching work from Horton, her one-time co-star on TVs "thirtysomething." As Cokie, the snooty sworn enemy of all members of the Baby-sitters Club, Marla Sokoloff goes over the top, but will draw laughs from young moviegoers. (My 6- and 8-year-old daughters both thoroughly enjoyed the film.)

Parents, however, may not be laughing at several sequences showing deep-kissing, attempts at club-hopping in Manhattan, and budding romance among pre-teens. Swooning over "dreamy" boys works against the movie's underlying (and very refreshing) emphasis on self-reliance and powerful friendship among its female protagonists.

Meanwhile, the parents on screen (nearly all of them divorced) are shown for the most part as irrelevant and unenlightened. Despite its attempts at social responsibility and wholesomeness, "The Baby-Sitters Club" ends up conveying the all-too familiar Hollywood theme that kids know best.

NEWSDAY, 8/18/95, Part II/p. B2, John Anderson

Welcome to "twelvesomething," where strife is what you make it, the suburbs are an emotional obstacle course and there's money to be made—but where friends, of course, always come first.

"We're not just a club, we're friends ... best friends." So say the members of "The Baby-Sitters Club," which for all its adolescent anxiety is a bright and fairly entertaining comedy about preteen girls, for preteen girls, especially those who haven't yet developed the misguided notion that boys know everything. Or anything. Directed by Melanie ("thirtysomething") Mayron and featuring her TV co-star Peter Horton as a failed father, the film is structured along a number of dramatic threads that coalesce with sitcom-like patness but, oddly enough, also a large degree of emotional honesty.

Based on the very successful series of books by Ann M. Martin, the movie centers on Kristy (Schuyler Fisk), the overalls-wearing president of the Baby-Sitters Club, a cartel of caregivers in the verdant burg of Stoneybrook, Conn. Kristy, who founded the club, comes up with a plan for a summer camp for little kids. The profits, she says, should be enormous. But just as it's getting started, her prodigal father (Horton) reappears, swearing Kristy to secrecy: He's in line for a sports-columnist job at a local paper and wants to make sure he's got it before letting Kristy's remarried mother (Brooke Adams) know he's back in town. Wanting to spend time with him—and unable to tell what's up—Kristy neglects her duties to the camp and endangers her friendships with the other members.

They include the sophisticated, New York-born Stacey (Bre Blair); the very pretty, very serious Mary Anne (Rachael Leigh Cook); the environmentally concerned Dawn (Larisa Oleynik), and the less well-defined Claudia (Tricia Joe), Mallory (Stacey Linn Ramsower) and Jessi (Zelda Harris). All have their mini-crises, including Claudia's upcoming science exam, which Kristy has *not* been helping her study for; Stacey's May-July romance with a handsome Swiss student (Christian Oliver), and Dawn's problematic relationship with Mrs. Haberman (Ellen Burstyn), a nice woman who wants peace and quiet but instead has found a kids' summer camp in the yard next door.

The relationships are all warm and fuzzy, as is the entire movie. Except for Kristy's father, who's put her in an impossible position (and for no particular reason is a journalist, Hollywood's favorite whipping boy), parents are fairly invisible. It's the kids who are important, and that's one reason "The Baby-Sitters Club" will probably do very well with kids.

VILLAGE VOICE, 8/22/95, p. 52, Amy Taubin

If I had a daughter, I'd be happy to take her to see *Babe* as many times as she wanted, but I'd hope once more enough for the *The Baby-Sitters Club*, although I doubt it would be. But the film doesn't need a crossover audience—it probably doesn't matter that males of all ages and adults of both sexes will find it a bit bland. Preteen girls who are devoted to Ann Martin's *Baby-Sitters Club* book series (there are over 200 titles in print and more than 125 million copies have been sold) will thrill to be seeing their favorite characters on the big screen, despite a certain liveliness having been lost in the translation.

The Baby-Sitters Club is special in that it provides a workplace setting in which the girls take on the problems and pleasures of preadolescence. It's a kind of training camp for progressive, female entrepreneurs who learn early that cooperation and trust are more effective and fun than competition (or just punking out). And in fact, the series's success is the best proof of the efficacy of its ideas.

The central character is Kristy, who organizes several of her friends into a club that provides baby-sitting services for their affluent Connecticut suburban community. Schuyler Fisk, the remarkably unaffected 12-year-old actor who plays Kristy, carries most of the film on her tomboy shoulders, and she does just fine. Kristy's biggest emotional problem is that she's lost her Dad. Her parents were divorced when she was six and her mother has remarried a nice, dependable, rich man who's everything Kristy's real dad isn't.

In the film, Kristy's real dad (played with whirlwind romanticism by Peter Horton) makes a surprise reappearance, claiming he's come back for good—provided that he lands a sportswriting gig at the local newspaper. He asks Kristy not to tell anyone, not even her mother, that he's in town until he knows for sure he has the job. Thus the main conflict revolves around the lies one tells for love and how they can alienate you from the people who support and want the best for you. Preoccupied with her father, Kristy nearly lets the BSC go down the drain. Impulsive and evasive, this is the kind of dad who leaves his daughter with major Oedipal problems that years on the couch can't resolve. In the safe world of *The Baby-Sitters Club*, however, Kristy gets to have her heartbreak, learn from it, and go forward eagerly into adolescence.

Except for Kristy, the other members of the BSC are sketchily handled. Followers of the books will be able to project their special knowledge onto the screen, but I had trouble enough keeping track of who was who. The film also makes a misguided effort to be color-blind in a way that the books aren't. Thus Jessi, whose situation as the only African American girl in the BSC—and indeed in her grammar-school class—gives her a unique perspective, is limited in the film to doing pirouettes in the corner of the screen. (All the more a pity since she's played by *Crooklyn* star Zelda Harris). Melanie Mayron's direction is more conventional than the material warrants, although she succeeds in making her young actors comfortable in front of the camera. In the end, comfort just isn't enough. What *The Baby-Sitters Club* lacks is a sense of daring.

Also reviewed in:
CHICAGO TRIBUNE, 8/18/95, Friday/p. F, Michael Wilmington
NEW YORK TIMES, 8/18/95, p. C6, Caryn James
VARIETY, 8/14-20/94, p. 55, Leonard Klady
WASHINGTON POST, 8/18/95, Weekend/p. 44, Eve Zibart
WASHINGTON POST, 8/19/95, p. C1, Hal Hinson

BAD BOYS

A Columbia Pictures release. *Executive Producer:* Bruce S. Pustin and Lucas Foster. *Producer:* Don Simpson and Jerry Bruckheimer. *Director:* Michael Bay. *Screenplay:* Michael Barrie, Jim Mulholland, and Doug Richardson. *Story:* George Gallo. *Director of Photography:* Howard Atherton. *Editor:* Christian Wagner. *Music:* Mark Mancina. *Music Editor:* Curtis Roush. *Sound:* Peter J. Devlin and (music) Alan Meyerson. *Sound Editor:* Robert Henderson. *Casting:* Francine Maisler and Lynn Kressel. *Production Designer:* John Vallone. *Art Director:* Peter Politanoff. *Set Decorator:* Kate Sullivan. *Set Dresser:* Mark Dane. *Special Effects:* Richard Lee Jones. *Costumes:* Bobbie Read. *Make-up:* Jeni Lee Dinkel. *Make-up (Martin Lawrence and Will Smith):* Laini Thompson. *Stunt Coordinator:* Ken Bates. *Running time:* 126 minutes. *MPAA Rating:* R.

CAST: Lisa Boyle (Girl Decoy); Michael Taliferro (Carjacker); Emmanuel Xuereb (Eddie Dominguez); Tcheky Karyo (Fouchet); Marc Macaulay (Noah Trafficante); Ralph Gonzalez (Kuni); Vic Manni (Ferguson); Frank John Hughes (Casper); Mike Kirton (Andy); Martin Lawrence (Marcus Burnett); Will Smith (Mike Lowrey); Will Knickerbocker (Officer Bill O'Fee); Theresa Randle (Theresa Burnett); Tiffany Samuels (Megan Burnett); Cory Hodges (James Burnett); Scott Cumberbatch (Quincy Burnett); Anna Thomson (Francine); Joey Romano and Sam Ayers (Detectives); Joe Pantoliano (Captain Howard); Marg Helgenberger (Alison Sinclair); Nestor Serrano (Detective Sanchez); Julio Oscar Mechoso (Detective Ruiz); Michael Imperioli (Jojo); Karen Alexander (Max Logan); Fawn Reed (Woman at Boxing Gym); Heather Davis (Lois Fields); Téa Leoni (Julie Mott); Saverio Guerra (Chet the Doorman); Maureen Gallagher (Yvette); Juan Cejas (Ether Van Driver); Ed Amatrudo (Ether Van Boss); Jimmy Franzo (Club Bartender); Tony Bolano (Drunk Guy at Urinal); Shaun Toub (Store Clerk); Marty McSorley and Norman Max Maxwell (Henchmen); Kevin Corrigan (Elliot); Buddy Bolton (Wally); Stan Miller (News Anchor); Dug Jones (Man); John Spider Salley (Hacker "Fletcher"); Dana Mark (Police Technician); Mario Ernesto Sanchez (Drug Buyer).

LOS ANGELES TIMES, 4/7/95, Calendar/p. 1, Kenneth Turan

Given how much good "Bad Boys" is going to do for Martin Lawrence's feature career, it's a pity the film couldn't do any more for itself.

Seeing Lawrence, the star of TV's "Martin," prove himself as a potent comic force on the big screen is reminiscent of watching Eddie Murphy ignite in "48HRS." And co-star Will Smith, though his role is less flashy, makes his usual strong impact as well.

Though audiences will leave theaters with an increased appreciation of this pair's talents, they will also leave pondering the perennial Hollywood question: How come so little of interest could be found for performers who are capable of so much more?

Produced by Don Simpson and Jerry Bruckheimer ("Beverly Hills Cop," "Top Gun"), "Bad Boys" is, not surprisingly, a high-concept cops-and-robbers film with a role-reversal plot that could, if necessary, be made to fit on the head of a pin.

Marcus Burnett (Lawrence) and Mike Lowrey (Smith) are odd-couple partners on the Miami police force. Marcus is an untidy family man, devoted to his wife and three kids, while Mike is a moneyed playboy who lives in a pristine penthouse and has more girlfriends than Coral Gables has grains of sand.

Enter Fouchet (French actor Tcheky Karyo), one of those criminal geniuses whose European accent is irrefutable proof of ruthlessness and acuity. He undertakes a smooth heist of $100 million in heroin which, embarrassingly enough, happened to be under lock and key in police headquarters. Naturally, Marcus and Mike get the job of getting it back. "Just do what you do," their captain tells them helpfully, "only faster."

The team's only lead is (surprise) an attractive young woman named Julie Mott (Tea Leoni). For reasons too silly to relate, she comes to believe that Marcus is Mike and Mike is Marcus. And since the captain believes the investigation would suffer irreparable harm if she were told the truth, happily married Marcus has to pretend he is the womanizer and Mike has to hang out with his partner's wife and kids.

Flimsy as this premise is, both actors find the humor in it, though Smith, who made a strong impression in "Six Degrees of Separation," gets the smaller share of the laughs. Partly this is because his character is conceived of primarily as the straight man and partly because it's hard to be funnier than Martin Lawrence.

As those who made it through his scabrous concert film, "You So Crazy," can testify, Lawrence is a treat to watch whether his language is tame or otherwise. "Bad Boys" doesn't give him the kinds of bravura scenes Murphy got in "48HRS.," but even in smaller moments, like having difficulty with the speed bag at a boxing gym or getting queasy when corpses are around, he doesn't have to do anything special to make you smile.

What makes Lawrence and Smith's success notable is that they do what they do without much help, either from their co-stars (though Theresa Randle as Marcus' wife is effective as always), the film's more-is-less crew of writers (script by Michael Barrie and Jim Mulholland and Doug Richardson, story by George Gallo) or even first-time director Michael Bay.

A boy-wonder commercial-maker, Bay has not made use of the wit that characterized his award-winning Aaron Burr/Got Milk spot. He and cinematographer Howard Atherton have given "Bad Boys" a slick look, but instead of cleverness he's served up standard-issue explosions, heroines who wear nothing but short skirts, and interminable noisy bickering between Mike and Marcus.

So while "Bad Boys" is unremarkable, you might want to write Martin Lawrence's name down for future reference. Maybe by the time his next film comes around, someone in the business will have figured out a better way to utilize his ability.

NEW STATEMAN & SOCIETY, 6/16/95, p. 33, Jonathan Romney

[*Bad Boys* was reviewed jointly with *Jefferson in Paris*; see Romney's review of that film.]

NEW YORK POST, 4/7/95, p. 45, Thelma Adams

"Bad Boys" is a bullets-and-banter action pic.

Two black Miami cops, Martin Lawrence and Will Smith (TVs "Martin" and "The Fresh Prince of Bel Air") execute a career-making drug bust. Then high-tech fiends steal the evidence: $100 million in heroin. The narcs must get back the drugs and keep the sole witness to a related murder, Tea Leoni (the pride of Fox TV's short-lived "Flying Blind"), under wraps.

The jug-eared, mobile-faced Lawrence and the buff Smith have the comic timing down. They toss off barbs and shoot off rounds as a married partner who isn't getting any sex from wife Theresa Randle and a smooth trust funder who's getting more than his share, ("Married life is easy," Smith tells Lawrence. "You only have one woman to satisfy.")

The tartly talented Leoni shows off her knees in a series of fly-girl minis, but adds a hip twist to the woman-in-peril role, Both Randle and Tcheky Karyo ("La Femme Nikita"), the criminal mastermind behind the heroin heist, are underused.

The real stars here are that big-budget, big-brawn producing team of the spend, spend, spend '80s, Don Simpson and Jerry Bruckheimer. Remember "Top Gun," "Beverly Hills Cop" and "Days of Thunder"?

From the title—the stick-in-your-head anthem of TVs "Cops"—on down, we're deep in formula country. But if you like your "Miami Vice" mixed with "48HRS." "Starsky and Hutch," "Scarface" (the remake), and "Passenger 57," then "Bad Boys" is bad in a good way.

Director Michael Bay, a rock video and advertising wunderkind doing the feature thing for the first time, has a thing for chilly blues and smoke machines.

With careening shots and whiplash cuts, Bay occasionally tosses action sequences into the cinematic blender until they're one big, senseless blur. But, hey, bad boys will be bad boys and when the substance is pretty much the stuff of '80s TV, we can deal with excesses of style.

NEWSDAY, 4/7/95, Part II/p. B2, Gene Seymour

For the most part, "Bad Boys" clicks along with enough breezy humor and stylish energy to make you resent the explosions, car chases and gunfights for ruining the nice-and-easy buzz established by co-stars Martin Lawrence and Will Smith. As odd-couple Miami detectives, they offer ample proof in this ground-breaking black-buddy-shoot'em-up that they're ready to ditch their respective sitcoms and move on to bigger things.

Lawrence is Marcus Burnett, married, volatile and a bit of a slob. Smith is Mike Lowrey, single, silky and immaculate to a fault. As with most mismatched pairs, they work spectacularly well together, being the most effective members of a special narcotics strike force. But if they don't find several kilos of heroin swiped from a police locker by a ruthless drug dealer (Tcheky Karyo), their unit may get shut down.

One of Mike's ex-girlfriends runs into the dealer's gang and is shot dead in plain sight of her roommate (Tea Leoni), who, in turn, becomes a target. She calls the cops, but the only one she'll speak to is Mike, who's not around. Marcus takes her call and is forced to assume Mike's identity so the witness isn't lost. Thus the short-fused family man has to Be Like Mike while the sexy playboy moves into Marcus' home to protect his wife (Theresa Randle) and three kids.

The actors make this contrivance even cuter than it looks on paper. Lawrence sometimes overdoes the mugging, but he's a strong big-screen presence. So is Smith, who has enough dry wit and cool magnetism at his disposal to play James Bond, if 007 were African-American. Their scenes together have a laid-back charm and as you'd expect from culture heroes of the hip-hop generation) hilarious word-play.

Leoni and Randle bring beguiling vigor to their otherwise thankless roles. First-time director Michael Bay is an award-winning veteran of commercials and videos. So it's not surprising to see how handy he is with visual composition and pacing. His exteriors of Miami strike just the right balance of grit and glitz.

Things hum along just fine before every expendable actor and machine is sacrificed to a climactic firestorm so noisy and near-apocalyptic that it's amazing that Miami was left intact. It's as if someone at the helm (probably producers Don Simpson and Jerry Bruckheimer, the manly men behind "Top Gun" and "Beverly Hills Cop") suddenly realized, "Hey! Yo! This thing is targeted for young males! We gotta blow more stuff up!" Don't get me wrong. I like explosions as much as the next manly man. But, at least in this instance, I like the other stuff better.

SIGHT AND SOUND, 7/95, p. 40, Nick James

Porsche-driving bachelor Mike Lowrey and his married buddy Marcus Burnett are black Narcotics cops in Miami. When one million dollars worth of heroin captured in evidence is stolen from their station-house, Mike asks his friend Max Logan, a high-class hooker, to look out for any new big spenders in town. Lois Fields, a madame, puts her on to Eddie Dominguez, who turns out to be a former cop and the driver for the robbery gang. Max persuades her friend Julie to go with her. While Max is partying with Eddie, who has helped himself to one of the dope packages from the robbery, Julie goes to the bathroom. On her return, she sees the robbery gang—led by the crazed Fouchet—shoot Eddie and Max. Julie escapes via the roof.

Wanting revenge, Mike goes to find Lois, but she's already dead. Meanwhile Marcus is trying to access Dominguez's old cop file on the computer. His boss Captain Howard gets a call from Julie, saying she will only talk to Mike. At Howard's insistence, Marcus pretends to be Mike.

He goes to Julie's apartment but she is suspicious. Only when Fouchet's hoods arrive does she agree to go along, taking her two dogs with her. As 'Mike', Marcus brings her to Mike's apartment.

That night Marcus's wife Theresa locks him out of their bedroom, but Howard orders Marcus to continue the deception. After Julie identifies Fouchet's henchman Noah from mug-shots, Marcus and Mike visit Noah's favourite haunt, Club Hell. Julie follows, armed with one of Mike's guns, and tries to shoot Fouchet but misses. Mike, Marcus and Julie then make their getaway in a truck full of ether. Noah pursues them onto a road under repair where Mike unloads the barrels of ether and sets them aflame, killing Noah. A helicopter television news crew films the result.

Two of Fouchet's men are arrested outside Marcus' home and give up Fouchet's name. Mike, Marcus and Julie are spotted watching Fouchet's boat, and are followed back to Mike's apartment building. During a gun battle in the lobby, the gang kidnap Julie. Marcus persuades a computer hacker felon to access Dominguez's file and the cops discover that their receptionist is his former lover. She gives Mike a car phone number which they track to an airport hangar where a major drug deal is about to occur. Mike, Marcus and two Latino colleagues attack the heavily protected site, rescuing Julie, blowing up the drugs, a huge cash payoff and a private jet before pursuing Fouchet to his doom in a final car chase across the airfield.

Those who regard a director's credit as the most crucial piece of information about a film will be interested to know that the promotional credits sheet for *Bad Boys* contains no reference to the director at all. He is credited on the film print itself, fleetingly, but even there the actual authorship of *Bad Boys* is clearly denied him. For this is a Don Simpson and Jerry Bruckheimer film, branded by the production duo who defined a certain kind of 80s action movie with *Top Gun* and *Beverly Hills Cop*, as well as a particular image of the bodybuilt, Tao-reading Hollywood production exec who was perpetually 'ready to go'.

That might be the first question that an audience asks of an action movie: is it ready to go? The immediate answer for *Bad Boys* is undoubtedly yes. All of the gunfights, car chases and explosions that one would expect are there, unobtrusively directed by Michael Bay in the requisite rock-video style and edited as much for punch and easy laughs as ever. They were also there when the duo came a cropper with the hugely expensive car racing flop *Days of Thunder*. *Bad Boys* is more like *Beverly Hills Cop*, and so it relies for its main strength on the ideological double-whammy of slick African-American humour and a near-fetishistic reverence for destructive mayhem, as if the two go naturally together.

The plot simply requires us to dip into the lifestyles on view and to enjoy the almost Shakespearean cuckoldry humour while waiting for the next burst of gunfire. Both the action heroics and the sexual banter are well managed by Will Smith (of *Fresh Prince of Bel Air* fame) and Martin Lawrence (star of the spoof US talkshow *Martin* and host of *Russell Simmons' Def Comedy Jam*). They work in a similar but sufficiently different vein to that of the *Lethal Weapon* pairing Mel Gibson and Danny Glover but in a more subtle key than Eddie Murphy's. The obvious contrast between Smith's character, Mike Lowrey, a smoothie with a private income and a beautiful apartment, and Lawrence's character Marcus, a working-class married man with a suspicious wife, is nicely shaded by their role-reversal when Marcus has to pretend to be Mike. Obsessed as it is with male sexual performance, their patter is often edgy and tense. Some of this tension cannot resolve itself because the affect-free white girl Julie Mott who comes between them isn't allowed to have a meaningful or physical relationship with either of them. She is the object of frustration for both of them, yet she remains somehow unattainable. Clearly, American mainstream action movies are still not ready to go on miscegenation any more than they were in the days of *Beverly Hills Cop*.

On the other hand the vigilante cop ethics required of the Hollywood action hero might nowadays be more palatably expressed by black characters than white as there's not much chance of these cops moonlighting with the militia. It is also refreshing that the villain is French rather than English with Tcheky Karyo reprising his more psychotic moments from *Nikita*. Otherwise *Bad Boys* is as nasty, thrilling, sexist, sexy, dumb, sharp and reprehensible as you want it to be—any number of qualifying adjectives will do because the experience it provides is so infuriatingly, enjoyably and successfully all-encompassing an entertainment.

VILLAGE VOICE, 4/18/95, p. 62, Gary Dauphin

Martin Lawrence and Will Smith may be playing a pair of Miami narcs in *Bad Boys*, but they're still Martin and Will to me. This is what you'd call a happy-to-mixed blessing: At this moment Martin is so relentlessly good at what he does (i.e., playing the very funny "Martin") that stepping into a goofy cop named "Marcus Burnett" requires no more than a stand-up comic's face change. And despite the undercurrent of bass in his voice, Will Smith's shoulders are still a bit too narrow to carry more than a gun-toting spin to the Fresh Prince. But then that's exactly as it should be. From the opening skit wherein they outwit a pair of car-jackers by bickering about the french fry Martin has dropped in Will's otherwise spotless Porsche, *Bad Boys* is about two familiarly funny guys playing at cops and robbers.

Ostensibly concerned with $100 million of stolen heroin, *Bad Boys* is mostly an excuse for Martin to grouse about stuff like how married life is synonymous with infrequent sex ("You know I'm a better cop when I get it in the morning," he tells his wife) with Will, his slick straight man. After it's been lifted in properly high-tech style by a properly continental bad guy named Fouchet (Tcheky Karyo, last seen predicting the future in *Nostradamus*), the heroin's trail leads to a comely reluctant witness (Téa Leoni making the best of a role that might otherwise have been defined by her miniskirts). Protecting said witness involves the usual action-movie tangles such as dodging Fouchet's bullets, as well as a surprisingly effective prince and pauper switch between Will and Martin.

Given little more than those Glocks, that Porsche, and each other to work with, Will and Martin still manage to fit comfortably into producers Don Simpson and Jerry Bruckheimer's by-the-numbers mixture of *Beverly Hills Cop* funny and *Die Hard* body count. First-time director Michael Bay came up in advertising, so *Bad Boys* hard sells its principals via big guns, nice clothes, and loud scoring, the crisp action sequences playing out against smoothly "Miami Vice" backdrops. Bay also understands the difference between Martin-funny and Will-funny. Scenes only end when Martin decides they're done, Will looking deadpan while Martin mumbles a bit maniacally in the aural background. *Bad Boys* curiously enough allows Will and Martin to kick a much greater number of white than black asses, but I imagine this has more to do with the ass-kicking prerogatives of Hollywood stardom than any racial politics. Will and Martin are as good, and as comforting, as Eddie Murphy was in his prime, which means that no matter how many white boys go down, the most race-conscious moment in *Bad Boys* involves a Porsche, albeit a black one.

Also reviewed in:
CHICAGO TRIBUNE, 4/7/95, Friday/p. M, Michael Wilmington
NEW YORK TIMES, 4/7/95, p. C10, Caryn James
VARIETY, 4/3-9/95, p. 141, Todd McCarthy
WASHINGTON POST, 4/7/95, p. D6, Rita Kempley
WASHINGTON POST, 4/7/95, Weekend/p. 44, Desson Howe

BAD COMPANY

A Touchstone Pictures release. *Producer:* Amedeo Ursini and Jeffrey Chernov. *Director:* Damian Harris. *Screenplay:* Ross Thomas. *Director of Photography:* Jack N. Green. *Editor:* Stuart Pappé. *Music:* Carter Burwell. *Music Editor:* Adam Smalley. *Sound:* Larry Sutton, (music) Michael Farrow and Scott Ansell. *Sound Editor:* David Kneupper and Glenn T. Morgan. *Casting:* Deborah Aquila. *Production Designer:* Andrew McAlpine. *Art Director:* William Heslup. *Set Decorator:* Elizabeth Wilcox. *Set Dresser:* Matt Reddy. *Special Effects:* Randy Shymkiw. *Costumes:* Richard Shissler and Charles De Caro. *Make-up:* Victoria Down. *Make-up (Laurence Fishburne):* Bernadine M. Anderson. *Make-up (Ellen Barkin):* Desne Holland. *Stunt Coordinator:* Ernie Jackson. *Running time:* 108 minutes. *MPAA Rating:* R.

CAST: Ellen Barkin (Margaret Wells); Laurence Fishburne (Nelson Crowe); Frank Langella (Vic Grimes); Michael Beach (Tod Stapp); Gia Carides (Julie Ames); David Ogden Stiers (Judge Beach); Daniel Hugh Kelly (Les Goodwin); Spalding Gray (Walter Curl); James Hong (Bobby Birdsong); Tegan West (Al); Fred Henderson (John Cartwain); Michelle Beaudoin

(Wanda); Sherry Bie (Mrs. Beach); Alan Robertson (Phil); L. Harvey Gold (Doctor); Alan C. Peterson (Cleaners Clerk); Larry Musser (Detective Harrison); Brian Drummond (Ed the Doorman); Sook Yin Lee (Waitress); Marcus Youssef (Concierge); Nicholas Lea (Jake); Jill Teed (Jane).

LOS ANGELES TIMES, 1/20/95, Calendar/p. 20, Peter Rainer

Now that the Cold War is over, expect an ever-increasing lava flow of movies about renegade/free-lance/disgruntled ex-or ex-ex-CIA agents. These folks have to do *something* to keep active—at least until the next Hot War cools—and, if "Bad Company" is any indicator, that activity involves mucho industrial espionage. This makes sense: Corporate infighting has always been blood sport anyway, so why not hire your very own private cadre of crooks to tip the balance?

In "Bad Company," former CIA operative Nelson Crowe (Laurence Fishburne) inserts himself into the nefarious Grimes Organization, a boutique of spies bunkered in Seattle and headed by Victor Grimes (Frank Langella) and Margaret Wells (Ellen Barkin). The Organization specializes in Fortune 500 companies, with an emphasis on blackmail and other sordid sundries. Not long after Crowe joins up, the double and triple and quadruple crosses begin. "Bad Company" is enjoyably nasty—everybody in it is a bad guy.

Mystery novelist Ross Thomas wrote the script, and it's just preposterous enough to make you think it could really happen. (The ring of truth in spy movies is their implausibility.) Thomas understands the entertainment value in watching a tankful of barracuda and the director, Damian Harris, lights the film as if we were peering into an aquarium. The predators move in and out of the shallows—it's like watching underwater *noir*.

The shiny awfulness of Crowe and Grimes and Margaret is amusing even when the film teeters on the verge of unintentional camp (which is often). Langella's purry depravity is a great match for Barkin's voracious funk. Her Maggie likes her men medium rare. Fishburne plays Crowe as a brilliant blank—his IQ is 141, just about twice Forrest Gump's. (Smart is bad.)

When he and Maggie go at each other, it's a race to see who will devour the other first. (At times they seem to be aiming for simultaneous extinction.) Then there's the supporting cast of craven CEOs and judges and bully-boys and intelligence creeps, well-played by the likes of Spalding Gray, David Ogden Stiers, and Michael Beach.

It's not always easy to follow the action but the confusion seems built into the helter-skelter design. In "Bad Company" everyone, including the audience, is in the dark. Our pleasure lies not in piecing together the puzzle but in dodging the pieces.

NEW YORK, 2/13/95, p. 101, David Denby

Rather than read to the children, I escaped the house last week, shouting, "Bye! I've got to see that Guatemalan documentary," and headed for the local sixplex, where, hoping for a swank, nasty thriller, I settled in at *Bad Company*, which is definitely not about Guatemala. Alas, I got to enjoy my night of liberty very little. *Bad Company*, which was written by Ross Thomas and directed by someone named Damian Harris, is about CIA agents, rogue CIA agents, and ex-CIA agents, and it's the kind of naively sinister movie in which the sleek and vicious characters come very close to one another and say quietly and with great distinctness, "You're going to feel more pain than you ever have in your life." If I'm not mistaken, Ellen Barkin, coming in even closer, also uttered the words (to Frank Langella) "I don't want to fish. I want to fuck." The integrity of the movie, I believe, will not be seriously compromised if I tell you that they did both. *Bad Company* is too dreary to qualify as enjoyable trash. It remains to be said, however, that Spalding Gray, too mischievous to go straight, plays a wealthy corporate head as a neurasthenic whiner in pajamas who needs a good slap across the kisser now and then. Some of the other people on the set should have been treated the same way.

NEW YORK POST, 1/20/95, p. 43, Michael Medved

What are writers of Cold War thrillers supposed to do with themselves now that the Cold War is over?

One possible activity is to speculate on what all those wily Cold War intelligence operatives are supposed to do with themselves now that the Cold War is over.

Veteran novelist Ross Thomas pursues such speculation in "Bad Company," his first original screenplay, in which he suggests that former CIA spooks have recently turned to the lucrative business of industrial espionage. This premise follows the lead of an article he wrote for the Los Angeles Times, reporting that hundreds of suddenly unemployed intelligence agents now sell their specialized services to unscrupulous businessmen to spy, bribe, and intimidate the competition.

In "Bad Company," Laurence Fishburne plays one such CIA veteran, who makes his way to Seattle to go to work in a high-tech espionage company informally known as "The Tool Shed." This outfit is led by the suave, amoral Frank Langella and his "ice queen" assistant, Ellen Barkin.

They assign Fishburne to bribe a Supreme Court justice (David Ogden Stiers) to protect a corrupt corporation. Fishburne pursues his errand with ruthless efficiency, never letting on that he's secretly cooperating with his former CIA handlers in their efforts to infiltrate and dominate the private sector "Tool Shed."

Meanwhile, the inevitable attraction between Fishburne and Barkin leads them to conclude that they might take over the company themselves—if only they can get rid of the all-powerful Langella.

This intricate plot contains more than enough betrayals and surprises to keep the audience interested. and all the actors give flashy, effective performances. Barkin is especially well-cast in her hard-as-nails role, looking tough, world-weary and searingly sexy, rather than conventionally glamorous. She generates considerable heat in her interaction with Fishburne, capably impersonating passion and ecstasy in some of the most detailed (but fully clothed) sex scenes this side of "Disclosure."

The problem is that some of the campy, wised-up dialogue that Ross Thomas sticks in the mouths of his characters sometimes gets in the way of his story. It doesn't help that they deliver these zinger lines with smirks or sneers, as if they're far wittier than they actually are.

British director Damian Harris (who previously did the disappointing Goldie Hawn thriller "Deceived") also goes over the top trying to show off his "artistic" style, telling this gritty little story with the sort of gaudy color and melodramatic camera moves that you'd normally associate with some epic spectacle.

It's true that the amazing interiors (designed by Andrew McAlpine, who also worked with Jane Campion on "The Piano") are consistently lush and gorgeous, but these eye-catching rooms often upstage the people who inhabit them. In short, Harris takes a redoubtable film noir plot and blows it up like some puffy float in the Thanksgiving Day Parade.

He ought to remember; "To do it right, you work up close."

NEWSDAY, 1/20/95, Part II/p. B2, Jack Mathews

Ever wonder what happened to all the highly trained assassins, spies and political agitators in the CIA who were laid off at the end of the cold war? Well, as fantasized in Damian Harris' slick and empty "Bad Company," they've gone the way of other ex-government workers, into the private sector where a person gifted at subversion, backbiting and betrayal can become employee of the month.

"Bad Company," written by veteran mystery author Ross Thomas, is enough to make you pine for the good old days of the Red Scare, when there was something at stake and a moral point of view. This is a movie about evil feeding on itself, about the further corrupting of the already corrupt, and there isn't an honest moment—let alone an honest character—in the entire story.

There is some fun in the performances of Laurence Fishburne and Ellen Barkin as a pair of sexually overheated operatives scheming between the sheets to take over Frank Langella's Seattle-based espionage boutique. The company, the Grimes Organization, has a clientele of Fortune 500 companies for whom it bribes judges, blackmails rivals and commits an occasional murder. Fishburne is Nelson Crowe, an agent trying to work his way out of the CIA doghouse (an Iranian general has accused him of pocketing bribe money) by infiltrating the Grimes Organization and turning it into an unofficial branch of the agency. Barkin is Margaret Wells, the predatory Grimes executive who seduces Crowe and enlists his help in killing the boss so they can run the company themselves. Talk about a hostile takeover!

There was the potential for a good tongue-in-cheek comedy here. What *are* trained government subversives to do in the peacetime aftermarket? But except for a very funny performance by Spalding Gray as a fey CEO fretting over an imminent State Supreme Court decision, "Bad Company" is shot and played as a straightforward thriller, with everyone sublimely unaware that the story has zero credibility and the audience has no emotional investment in the outcome.

Fishburne and Barkin, two highly attractive and sexually charged stars, do get it on, but their most graphic sex scene will be remembered less for its interracial daring than for its noise level. If all CIA agents make love this loudly, it's a wonder anybody in Washington gets any sleep.

VILLAGE VOICE, 1/31/95, p. 55, Beth Coleman

Bad Company slows down the fast pace of capital espionage with a slow glance around the post-postindustrial office of the Grimes Organization (the best 10 minutes are all about architecture). There, designer-dressed employees—government trained in blackmail, subterfuge, and murder—walk about trying to pick each other up or stab each other in the back. Same difference, apparently.

Based on the large-scale CIA layoffs of 10 years ago, *Company* gives Laurence Fishburne another stab at secret agency as Nelson Crowe, former federal spy entering the private sector. Just whom he's working for becomes the question, when double agent changes to double-double agent, until we realize it's for himself. *Deep Cover* at least gave him the hilarious Jeff Goldblum to lighten the Fish gloom. This time, he's locked with a humorless Ellen Barkin in the conspiratorial kiss. These are mean people, so directly heartless they should be scared, not inured. Where's the flying gunfire, the speeding bus, or, if the filmmakers are going to take their time, the characters? Respect, however, to Frank Langella as Vic Grimes and Spalding Gray as a simpering millionaire for understanding theatricality and making us laugh.

If we could see the heart blood of ethical behavior, a regard for life and love, dripping out of this ripe Mod Squad, then the story of Crowe's destruction might matter. What we get is Fishburne in sunglasses, playing it cool to the point of no pulse. He didn't find the body, he is the body. And cringingly—booty looks like just another detail in the working man's day—Barkin acts like she's loading a gun or doing push-ups.

It's easy enough to imagine Fishburne digging the script with its to absurdity race-blind policy, in speech if not motion. (Gays are the low man in this discrete spy world, but *Company* has one nice switch up there.) Secret agent Crowe is a dull role anyone, any hunk guy in Hollywood, could have played—hooray for equal time. As a movie about interior design and the movement of dollars into property, *Bad Company* has good taste.

Also reviewed in:
CHICAGO TRIBUNE, 1/20/95, Friday/p. J, Michael Wilmington
NEW YORK TIMES, 1/20/95, p. C21, Stephen Holden
VARIETY, 1/23-29/95, p. 70, Godfrey Cheshire
WASHINGTON POST, 1/20/95, p. D6, Hal Hinson
WASHINGTON POST, 1/20/95, Weekend/p. 36, Desson Howe

BALLET

A Zipporah Films release. *Producer:* Frederick Wiseman. *Director:* Frederick Wiseman. *Director of Photography:* John Davey. *Editor:* Frederick Wiseman. *Running time:* 170 minutes. *MPAA Rating:* Not Rated.

WITH: Agnes de Mille, Irina Kolpakova, David Richardson, and Michael Somes (Choreographers/Ballet Masters); Alessandra Ferri, Cynthia Harvey, Susan Jaffe, Christine Dunham, Julio Bocca, and Wes Chapman (Principal Dancers).

NEW YORK POST, 3/22/95, p. 34, Larry Worth

Watching people dance on tip-toe has always been an acquired taste. Sadly, Frederick Wiseman's new documentary, "Ballet," does nothing to expand that audience.

The man who earned renown with "Titicut Follies"—his harrowing cinematic trip inside a state prison for the criminally insane—and then lensed projects on hospitals, the welfare system and much more has altered tacks with his study of the American Ballet Theater.

The change of pace is fine, but his cutting edge is nowhere in evidence, The result: Wiseman-lite.

More than half of the three-hour running time unfolds in the studio as troupe members practice—under tough taskmasters—for a European tour. Just when the steps have been turned into a perfectly fluid movement comes the shout, "and again."

So, what gives performers their endless drive? And how do they handle that hothouse choreography? For that matter, do male ballet stars still fit a gay stereotype? Don't hold your breath waiting for answers; the interviews are fluff.

And as the director demonstrated in last year's "High School II," his editing abilities have waned over the years, proven here as the tour moves from Athens to Copenhagen. Coverage of a command performance in either city would have been sufficient; having both is excessive.

Wiseman redeems himself with fleeting behind-the-scenes looks at late choreographer Agnes de Mille—who, along with everyone else in the film, is never identified—and the ABT's no-nonsense financial manager. Both emerge as fascinating characters.

Further, Wiseman's photograph of the breathtakingly lovely dances preserves all their delicacy, beauty, grace and style. That's no small feat.

Accordingly, ballet fans will find plenty to revel in. But for Wiseman fans, the documentary master still falls a bit flat.

NEWSDAY, 3/22/95, Part II/p. B11, Janice Berman

Documentary filmmaker Frederick Wiseman achieved virtual immortality by training his camera on such unglamorous institutions as mental hospitals ("Titicut Follies"), the army ("Basic Training") and education ("High School.")

"Ballet" is a whole new dance.

In this new documentary, he doesn't look to right wrongs, or uncover dramatic evidence of suffering in a place where no such thing has been anticipated. Rather, Wiseman takes American Ballet Theater, an institution whose very name conjures up images of drama and glamor, and makes it look everyday. He turns his color camera on the company both at home at 890 Broadway and on tour, showing us dancers stretching their improbably hyperextended bodies, struggling via physical therapy to stay ahead of their injuries, having costume fittings with people poking and pulling at their tights.

But even Wiseman is incapable of reducing "Ballet" to drudgery. What is behind all the work is pursuit of an art form. The very plainness of Wiseman's documentary style emphasizes the commitment to that pursuit.

The sequences of the company performing are as straightforward as the rest of the film. They are unenhanced and unadorned, but the beauty comes through, and I believe Wiseman planned it that way.

Wiseman never narrates or opinionates; still, he knows what is interesting about the company. He doesn't, for instance, show us 30 minutes of the repetitive exercises that are part of every ballet dancer's daily routine. What could be more interesting than Jane Hermann, the company's director when the film was shot in 1993, reaming out someone at the Metropolitan Opera House for selling her company down the river? Or scenes of the late choreographer Agnes de Mille, seated in a wheelchair as she creates what will be her final ballet, "The Other"?

Dance is in the details. Michael Somes (who has also died since this film was made) is seen coaching four dancers for the revival of Frederick Ashton's "Symphonic Variations," describing exactly how big the space should be between the dancers' bent legs.

But dance also is about matters less concrete, and Wiseman gives time to those details as well. Irina Kolpakova coaches Susan Jaffe in "La Bayadere," speaking not about her feet, but her head. "At the start of the variation, you talk with yourself only," Kolpakova says, a note of quiet urgency in her voice as she adds, "Susan, think about this. It's very difficult, but it's a higher level."

We return to rehearsals over and over again, watching "The Other" as it grows, watching two ballerinas—Christine Dunham and Jaffe—rehearse the same solo, seeing the differences. We glimpse dancers between rehearsals, napping, lining up their toe shoes, reading, giggling. And finally we go on the road to Greece.

There are no glimpses of dancers' personal lives, although we do watch a few civilian moments—the dancers shaking their booties at a taverna and visiting Tivoli Gardens when the company goes to Copenhagen. But when they return to the theater, it's the same story as in New York: rehearse and perform and try not to get hurt. And along the way, as in the final sequence where Julio Bocca and Alessandra Ferri do a duet from "Romeo and Juliet," create moments of magic.

The stunning artistry is there, but at the same time, Wiseman's microphone reveals that Ferri and Rocca are panting from exertion. As usual, the master documentarian lets nobody get away with anything.

VILLAGE VOICE, 3/28/95, p. 66, Tobi Tobias

The link between Frederick Wisemen's signature film, *Titicut Follies*, and his latest effort, *Ballet?* Both seek to reveal a complex and compelling subculture. But where *Titicut Follies* was gritty, searing—probing a madhouse so horrific that even its ostensibly sane custodians seemed demonically crazed—*Ballet*, culled from three months of tracking American Ballet Theatre, is oddly sanitized. Only once during its peaceable 170 minutes (in fabulous color) does someone get expletive-hurling angry; no one in this huge, precarious, finalists-only institution is seen to be sad or exhausted; no one even sweats.

Wiseman uses his familiar epic-documentary technique here, stacking up evidence without overt commentary such as voiceover narration. Of course, this objectivity is an illusion. Editorializing necessarily occurs at every stage—the selection of what to shoot, what to use, and how to organize the material. Wiseman also cheats on his own rules, inserting verbal information and manipulating the viewer's emotions through interviews recorded as if they were merely part of an artist's daily round.

The beehive that is ABT is catalogued exhaustively, from administrative affairs to dancers' endless cycle of warm-up class, rehearsal, makeup and costuming, performance, physical therapy, downtime, and playtime (this last picturesquely on an Aegean beach and in Tivoli, Copenhagen's fabled amusement park). The detail is painstaking and dutiful. It lacks spontaneity and it doesn't quite add up dramatically. Wiseman does capture the claustrophobia of the company's clinically serviceable studios in New York and the monotony of the dancer's life. Just barely—when the rehearsing company spontaneously cheers the miraculously light, precise execution of a solo—he touches on the ecstasy of achieving superhuman power and grace that makes the boredom and insularity tolerable.

The film boasts two memorable scenes. In one, the former Kirov ballerina Irina Kolpokova urges "expression" on a young American star who, typical of her nation and generation, has made her mark largely through brilliance in the legs and feet. Demonstrating, Kolpokova rushes toward the imagined object of her passion, utterly impetuous and vulnerable, then elucidates eloquence in the upper body, seemingly guiding herself by the relationship of her cheekbones to the light. The other noteworthy sequence, well-nigh Shakespearean in its humanity, has the late Agnes de Mille being asked by an interviewer why she persists in choreographing despite her advanced age and grave physical incapacity. De Mille, easily the heroine of this show, considers the question and responds with feisty, devastating directness: "Stubbornness." Pause. "Probably ego." Longer pause, then: "What else *should* I do?"

Also reviewed in:
NEW YORK TIMES, 3/22/95, p. C13, Caryn James
VARIETY, 3/27-4/2/95, p. 76, Godfrey Cheshire

BALLOT MEASURE 9

A Zeitgeist Films release of an Oregon Tape Project production. *Executive Producer:* David Meieran. *Producer:* Heather MacDonald. *Director:* Heather MacDonald. *Director of Photography:* Ellen Hansen. *Editor:* Heather MacDonald and B.B. Jorissen. *Music:* Julian Dylan Russell, Sunny McHale Skyedancer, and Linda and the Family Values. *Running time:* 72 minutes. *MPAA Rating:* Not rated.

WITH: Donna Red Wing; Kathleen Saadat; Scott Seibert; Jim Self; Elise Self; Cindy Paterson; Ann Sweet; Tom Potter; Lon Mabon; Bonnie Mabon; Scott Lively; Oren Camenish.

LOS ANGELES TIMES, 7/14/95, Calendar/p. 10, Kevin Thomas

Heather MacDonald's "Ballot Measure 9"—a comprehensive incisive documentary on the emotion-charged campaign surrounding the 1992 Oregon anti-gay measure—is all the more chilling because of its methodical, cool approach.

Wisely, MacDonald not only lets gay activists have their say but also allows Lon Mabon, chairman of the Oregon Citizen's Alliance, and numerous associates and supporters, to express their profoundly negative view of gays and lesbians. Many will recall how the vote went, but so skillful is MacDonald that she actually generates suspense as to its outcome.

"Ballot Measure 9" is a truly frightening film. It shows how a group of well-organized members of the extreme religious right used the Bible's condemnation of homosexuality as a license to indulge in vicious, no-holds barred rabble-rousing.

A lesbian points out that the Bible was used in the same way to oppress African Americans and women, but clearly these religious fundamentalists are the last to consider the implications of extensive biblical scholarship arguing that the Bible's homophobic passages are apocryphal.

In any event, we're shown the OCA using timeless "big lie" tactics, hurling specious statistics and depicting gays and lesbians as the most depraved minions of Satan imaginable. It raised homophobia in Oregon to a life-endangering level during the campaign.

The OCA is especially adept at exploiting the right-wing buzz phrases "special rights" and "family values" against gays and lesbians. At the same time the OCA's media offensive united the state's gays and lesbians as never before, and they fought back in a manner that invited the general public to perceive the merger civil and constitutional rights issues. As a young high school student asks an OCA panel: "Who's next?"

Through MacDonald's interplay of interviews with representatives of both sides, a lot of blunt truths emerge as the campaign grows increasingly bitter.

"Ballot Measure 9" makes painfully clear just how widespread ignorance of homosexuality is. As one lesbian remarks, it's as if the OCA believed everybody was born heterosexual, but that gays and lesbians chose to be "wicked." We see that those who believe that sexual orientation is a matter of choice also believe that gays and lesbians are somehow able to "recruit" youngsters to their "cause," a fear greatly heightened in the age of AIDS.

MacDonald reveals the OCA painting most gays as child molesters in the face of decades of scientific research that indicates otherwise; that more young adults, the majority presumably the parents of young children, than older people were in favor of Ballot 9 suggests just how potent the OCA message is.

"Ballot Measure 9" is a stirring, deeply troubling account of what combatants on both sides would agree is a first round in what is rapidly becoming a nationwide human rights struggle, one sure to figure in next year's presidential campaign.

NEW YORK POST, 6/21/95, p. 36, Thelma Adams

It can't happen here—or can it?

Heather MacDonald's suspenseful documentary "Ballot Measure 9" crisply demonstrates that the war over gay rights rages on. Her subject is a 1992 Oregon anti-gay initiative sponsored by the Oregon Citizen's Alliance (OCA).

Ballot Measure 9 lumped homosexuality with pedophilia, sadism and masochism, calling it "abnormal, wrong, unnatural, and perverse." Not only did the amendment, which eventually was defeated at the polls, move to end anti-discrimination protection for gays, it proposed curtailing the civil rights and equal protection under the law of Oregon's homosexuals. This was a law intent on running Heather and her two mommies out of the Beaver State.

The documentary, which shared the audience award at this year's Sundance Film Festival and opens today at Film Forum, takes a pro-gay stance without being dogmatic. What separates this film from the pack is the way it delivers a slice of the contemporary American culture wars by concentrating on a specific regional struggle. What the OCA's Lon Mabon describes as a "battle between good and evil" becomes a life-or-death fight in Oregon's once-sleepy gay community. The movie's scariest element is that, as the OCA and gay activists fought for the hearts and minds of Oregon voters, violence against homosexuals rose to unprecedented heights. Although it tends to make the OCA leaders look like snake-oil salesmen, the movie does give voice to the fears and prejudices of the "family values" pack.

MacDonald's cool, straightforward style never distracts from this chilling real-life story. Says mild-mannered Scott Seibert, gay activist and former Marine, "Oregon is a beautiful state. I truly believe if it can happen in Oregon, it can happen anywhere."

NEWSDAY, 6/21/95, Part II/p. 89, Jack Mathews

In the midst of the acrimony in Heather MacDonald's "Ballot Measure 9," a solidly crafted documentary chronicling the 1992 campaign to legalize discrimination against homosexuals in Oregon, there is a gentle confrontation between a lesbian woman and an elderly man trying to convince her that God can show her the way to a better life.

"I'm very happy with my life," the woman says.

"Well, there's your problem," he answers.

It would be hard to find a simpler declaration of the issues that prompted Ballot Measure 9, fomented months of heated debate and caused anti-gay crime to jump four-fold in a state once regarded as a model of political moderation. There is the sinking feeling on the religious right that mainstream America is beginning to accept behavior the Bible calls an abomination and that laws protecting the rights of homosexuals are tantamount to an endorsement of that lifestyle.

Figuring something had to be done to reverse the tide of acceptance, a born-again Christian named Lon Mabon, taking inspiration from Patrick Buchanan's declaration of cultural war at the '92 Republican Convention, crafted and promoted a referendum asking Oregon voters to compel government agencies and schools to recognize homosexuality as "abnormal, wrong, unnatural and perverse," and to treat it as such.

Mabon, being a little perverse himself, hooked his campaign to a few spectacular lies—equating homosexuality with pedophilia and sadomasochism, labeling discrimination laws as "special rights" for gays—and whipped up a statewide froth of homophobia.

The referendum ultimately failed, 57 to 43 percent, but the 14 percent margin of reason could hardly be taken as a victory by gay activists. All they accomplished, one of their leaders rightly concluded on election night, was to "hold on" to rights most Americans take for granted. And Mabon's Oregon Citizens Alliance, bolstered strong support and the passage of a similar referendum in Colorado that year, has since engineered local anti-gay laws in 21 of Oregon's 36 counties.

"Ballot Measure 9" is splendid advocacy journalism. MacDonald is obviously on the side of the "No on 9" campaign, and as ignorant, mean-spirited or misguided as the ballot proponents appear, they are given ample opportunity to state their case. Some of the pro-9ers, like the old man lecturing the lesbian, seem genuinely concerned for the fate of souls. But most are driven by the rank emotions of repulsion and fear.

In listening to these angry, frightened people, two thoughts kept occurring to me. One, how similar homophobia is to anti-Communist hysteria (they're trying to recruit our children!). And two, how wonderful it would be if there were a magic pill, like Prozac, that would short-circuit the mental wiring compelling so many people to dwell on what others may be doing behind closed doors.

Also reviewed in:
NEW REPUBLIC, 7/10/95, p. 24, Stanley Kauffmann
NEW YORK TIMES, 6/21/95, p. C15, Janet Maslin
VARIETY, 1/30-2/5/95, p. 50, Emanuel Levy

BALTO

A Universal Pictures and Amblin Entertainment release. *Executive Producer:* Steven Spielberg, Kathleen Kennedy, and Bonne Radford. *Producer:* Steve Hickner. *Director:* Simon Wells. *Screenplay:* Cliff Ruby, Elana Lesser, David Steven Cohen, and Roger S.H. Schulman. *Story:* Cliff Ruby and Elana Lesser. *Director of Photography (Live Action):* Jan Richter-Friis. *Editor:* Nick Fletcher and Slim Evan-Jones. *Music:* James Horner. *Music Editor:* Jim Henrikson. *Sound:* Tom Paul, Steve Rogers and (music) Shawn Murphy. *Sound Editor:* Louis L. Edemann and Charles L. Campbell. *Live Action Casting:* Ellen Parks. *Production Designer:* Hans Bacher. *Animation Production:* Colin J. Alexander. *Character Designer:* Carlos Grangel, Nicolas Marlet, and Patrick Maté. *Set Dresser:* Danny Goldfield. *Costumes:* Ellen Lutter. *Make-up:* Tracy Warbin. *Running time:* 74 minutes. *MPAA Rating:* G.

ANIMATED VOICES: Kevin Bacon (Balto); Bob Hoskins (Boris); Bridget Fonda (Jenna); Jim Cummings (Steele); Phil Collins (Muk and Luk); Jack Angel (Nikki); Danny Mann (Kaltag); Robbie Rist (Star); Juliette Brewer (Rosy); Sandra Searles Dickinson (Sylvie/Dixie/Rosy's Mother); Donald Sinden (Doc); William Roberts (Rosy's Father); Garrick Hagon (Telegraph Operator); Bill Bailey (Butcher); Mike McShane, Miriam Margolyes, Austin Tichenor, Reed Martin, and Adam Long (Extra Voices);

LIVE ACTION: Miriam Margolyes (Grandma Rosy); Lola Bates-Campbell (Granddaughter).

LOS ANGELES TIMES, 12/22/95, Calendar/p. F14, David Kronke

In "Balto," a goose makes a pun about a "wild goose chase," a mutt routinely bonks a dopey dog on the head with a paw balled up like a fist and roly-poly polar bears coo and giggle like precocious infants.

This, the filmmakers tell us with straight faces, is "based on a true story."

On "Balto's" poster and in print ads, the words "based on a true story" seem to be part of the film's title. (Remember how Disney tried to separate itself from historical fact with "Pocahontas"?) Universal is truly touting the movie's potential educational aspect, hoping that the history lesson, however dubious, will induce dutiful parents to drag children to the nearest multiplex. That may be its only selling point; the entertainment value is slight.

"Balto," an animated adventure about a heroic dog leading a sled team through treacherous Alaskan terrain to bring a vaccine for diptheria to a stricken community, is bookended by a live-action sequence that further underscores its "true story." A horribly made-up Miriam Margolyes (but then, how many other animated films even need a makeup artist?) schleps through Central Park in arch of a statue commemorating "The Sled Dog." Why the fuss, her granddaughter reasonably wonders; Margolyes begins a reverie that disconcertingly calls into question her grasp on reality by becoming a cartoon flashback.

From there, the film takes far too long in setting up its premise—that lovable Balto (voiced by Kevin Bacon) is the town outcast, only because he's part wolf; that Steele (Jim Cummings) is a dirt-bag dog posing as a hero, and that only the virtuous husky Jenna (Bridget Fonda) can divine the truth about both of them. The diptheria epidemic breaks, and Balto, though clearly the fastest animal in the territory, is barred from the team.

Obviously, however, he does end up leading the supporting canines on the fur-raising adventure. At that point, "Balto" picks up a bit, turning into something of a cartoon version of the French '50s classic "The Wages of Fear," only without the nihilism or the suspense.

This much is true: In 1925, a dog names Balto did lead a sled team during part of the mission (the route they took is now the one used for the Iditarod dog race). But the human sled-driver (here consigned to little more than skulking about in silhouette) and the other dogs did some work too. No records exist suggesting the dogs spoke among one another.

Even as voiced by Bacon, Balto doesn't have the sort of charisma to get kids to truly root for him. Bob Hoskins, as the goose, works far too hard at whimsy to be whimsical, while Cummings is one-dimensionally villainous. Only Fonda has the necessary light touch here.

Outside a couple of action sequences (an avalanche and a speedy jaunt through a cavern quickly dropping all its stalactites) the animation is merely competent, a consistent problem for non-Disney animated features. A bear-fighting sequence seems suspiciously cribbed from "The Fox and the Hound." Design is in general uninspired—none of the characters would make a particularly lovable plush toy, which seems to be the criterion for these things nowadays.

My own dog was annoyed by the film's depiction of distrust toward Balto solely because of his lupine background; she yelped, "How can America ever move forward until it gets over its prejudice toward wolf-like dogs?" That last sentence, of course, was "based on a true story."

NEW YORK POST, 12/22/95, p. 51, Michael Medved

In the winter of 1925 the frontier village of Nome, Alaska, experienced a diphtheria epidemic that threatened scores of children unless life-giving antitoxin could reach them on time. Blizzard conditions made the settlement inaccessible by sea or by air, and trains could bring the desperately needed medicine no closer than the rail head at Nenana—some 600 miles away.

The only hope involved teams of sled dogs, battling rough ice, treacherous waters and howling winds as art of the much-publicized "Great Race of Mercy." Finally, at 5:30 a.m. on Feb. 2, a tireless dog named Balto led his team into the stricken town and became an overnight national hero. A statue in Central Park commemorates Balto's achievement, as does the famous Iditarod dog sled race every year in Alaska.

Now there's also a handsome new movie to tell the story, courtesy of Steven Spielberg's Amblin Entertainment. Purists may protest that the cartoon characters come across as cute rather than heroic, or that the movie spends more time on silly subplots than on gripping history, but "Balto" is still a classy animated adventure that will thrill kids and entertain their parents.

In his version of the tale, we first meet Balto (the voice of Kevin Bacon) as a "half-breed" outcast, part dog and part wolf, living by his wits on the snowy streets of Nome. When this dashing scamp falls for a purebred husky hussy (the voice of Bridget Fonda) who's the pampered pet of a local family, the movie unmistakably recalls "Lady and the Tramp"—and this well-groomed beauty "Jenna" is indeed the sweetest, sexiest pooch since that beloved cocker spaniel.

As the little girl in Jenna's family falls ill with diphtheria, Balto wants to impress his lady love by doing his part to haul the needed medicine to town, but his efforts are blocked at every turn by the snarling bully Steele (the voice of Jim Cummings), local champ of dog sled racing, who wants to hog all the glory to himself.

As underdog in this melodrama, Balto gets encouragement from friends of other species, including twin polar bears (the voice of Phil Collins) and a comical Russian snow goose ("I was so scared I got people bumps!") played with an authentic-sounding accent by Bob Hoskins. (In fact, Hoskins is far more convincing here than is his embarrassing turn as J. Edgar Hoover in "Nixon.")

While it's true that the animation isn't at the level of Disney's best, it still glows and glistens with fluid professionalism, offering atmospheric views of vast arctic landscapes. Sequences involving a huge, rumbling avalanche and an eerily beautiful ice cave are especially well-drawn and effectively choreographed, while James Horner (who also did the superior score for "Land Before Time") provides appropriately stirring background music.

The movie begins and ends with brief, touching live-action sequences showing an elderly, lady (Miriam Margolyes) taking her granddaughter to see the Balto statue in Central Park, and this film version of "Balto" provides a similarly appropriate destination for a family outing.

If you've got restless kids over winter vacation, and you've already seen "Toy Story" three times (or don't want to risk lifelong nightmares with "Jumanji"), then this likable mutt deserves a chance.

NEWSDAY, 12/22/95, Part II/p. B3, John Anderson

Co-opting history, or goodness, has never hurt Steven Spielberg. Not as much as it hurts, his films, anyway. In "Balto," which is the work of his Amblimation animation studio, we get a fact-based story with a host of noble notions and right-thinking gestures that would have been twice as good if it had been half as righteous—and a quarter more original.

To say "Balto" is fine for kids sounds like a dismissal and is, in the general scheme of things. But young audiences don't have much to choose from (how many dozens of times can you see "Toy Story"?). And they probably won't be as familiar, or as taken aback, by the stock characters and situations found in this paint-by-numbers adventure story, which sublimates its own true tale for the sake of mediocre cartoon making.

"Balto" doesn't answer the very question it raises in its live-action opening sequence (and which, coincidentally, was also raised in "Six Degrees of Separation"). Namely, why is there a memorial to a sled dog on the east side of Central Park?

We get the story of the dog—Balto, who led the team bringing anti-toxin to the diphtheria-stricken children of Nome, Alaska, in 1925, and was lionized (so to speak); the route he took is apparently the same course used in the modern-day Iditarod. But why Central Park? All I could find out was that the Balto Memorial Committee commissioned the Brooklyn-born animal sculptor Frederick G.R. Roth to execute the statue, which won a national Academy of Design prize in 1925. Except that Balto didn't die until 1933. So who knows?

In actuality, Balto and his colleagues spent the years immediately after their mercy mission in a kind of sideshow, from which they were rescued—just as they had saved the Nome children—by a fund-raising drive among school kids that landed them in the Cleveland Zoo.

Nowhere was there an indication that Balto was half wolf, however, which is the angle that supplies the human-interest (or canine-interest) side of "Balto." When we meet the shaggy hero (voice of Kevin Bacon), he is an outcast in Nome, whose people distrust him and whose favorite, leading dog, Steele (voice of Jim Cummings), mocks him for his mixed blood. This is, from the beginning, a racial parable, and unless you're in the middle of a blizzard yourself, it's easy to see where things are going.

We get enough central-casting characters to stock a '30s Warner Bros. gangster film: Boris (Bob Hoskins) a Russian goose; Dixie, a dizzy Gloria Grahame-ish dog/flirt; Muk and Luk (Phil Collins), two polar bears who can't swim and one of whom has a British accent; Steele's trio of sycophantic flunkie dogs, one of whom sounds like Sheldon Leonard, and Jenna (Bridget Fonda), the beautiful she-dog (I can't bring myself to call her a bitch) who completes the Popeye-Olive-Bluto configuration with Steele and Balto.

The animation is fine, even if it lacks the poetry of the better Disney films. The problem is basically the hackneyed storyline—Balto is kept down, framed for lowlife acts by Steele, who turns out to be a real cur. Balto, meanwhile, triumphs by coming to terms with his own wolfishness, which gets him through the arduous sled drive and gets the life-saving serum to the children. I don't mean to be cold, but if creativity were Dog Chow, these hounds would be starving.

SIGHT AND SOUND, 4/96, p. 37, Karen Krizanovitch

A present-day grandmother, her granddaughter and a Husky puppy search New York's central park for a memorial statue ...

1925. Outside Nome, Alaska, a talented but nasty sled dog, Steele, cheats to win a race for the best sled team. In town, Balto, half-wolf half-dog, frolics with Boris the goose until Steele parades into town. Nearby, a little girl named Rosy is given a wooden sled for Jenna, her bitch, who is adored by both Balto and Steele. Balto shows Jenna some broken bottles under the hospital which shine like the Aurora Borealis. Jenna is impressed but more concerned about Rosy who is sick in the hospital above them. Steele and his evil gang of dogs taunt Balto about his mixed heritage. He retreats to an abandoned boat with Boris and the polar bears Muk and Luk who try to cheer him.

Nome's children are stricken with diphtheria. The local sled-maker fashions wooden coffins. The anti-toxin supply is exhausted and the townsfolk send the fastest dog sled team to the town of Nenana for more. Balto, the best dog for the job, is not enlisted because he is half-wolf and cannot be trusted. Steele gets lost returning from Nenana. The sled's driver is knocked cold.

Through dog-telegraph, Balto hears of their plight and goes to help. He is attacked by a bear. Jenna saves him but is injured and goes back to Nome with Boris and the polar bears.

Balto finds Steele, who attacks him. Balto remains passive and Steele falls off a cliff but lives. Steele returns to town and spreads lies about Balto. While the townspeople worry and wait, Balto and the team, having braved many dangers, lose their way. Balto meets a white wolf whose howl reminds him that "a dog cannot make this journey alone. But maybe a wolf can." Seeing an Aurora Borealis signal from Jenna, Balto returns to town. He wins the townspeople's affection and Jenna's Steele is revealed as a liar.

The grandmother searching for the statue turns out to be Rosy and the memorial, a commemoration to that 1925 heroic journey.

In Fred Schepisi's *Six Degrees of Separation*. Will Smith stands near a dog statue in New York's Central Park. *Balto* begins and ends with that same statue and explains why it is there. A dog named Balto really did come into Nome, Alaska, at 5.30 a.m. on February 2, 1925. He was lead dog of a sled team which covered the last 53-mile leg in a 674-mile round trip through blizzard conditions to bring the anti-toxin to town. Other relay teams, however, contributed to the trip's success as well as to its world record time of five and a half days. Although Balto's natural instincts reportedly saved the sled and the medicine from falling into the Topkok River, it was 'musher' Gunnar Kaasen who retrieved the anti-toxin when it tumbled from the sled, not his lead dog.

Kaasen, Balto and the other dogs toured America, saw the statue erected in Central Park and starred in the movie of their adventure *Balto's Race to Nome*. As interest waned, Balto and his canine peers were sold off to a sideshow. In 1927, a businessman raised $2,000 to move them to the Cleveland Zoo where Balto died in 1933 at the age of 11. Whether or not he was half-wolf isn't clear. However, with such a storyline, *Balto* is fully loaded to be a perfect animated feature for the 90s. It is as politically correct as *Pocahontas*. Human characters are as peripheral as they are in *Toy Story*. Balto battles Steele, the elements and his own insecurity to win acceptance, love and self-esteem, so he's a talking animal on a mission, similar to the hero of *Babe*.

The sum of *Balto*, however, is less than these parts. The talented Kevin Bacon voices Balto at a distance. He denies the hero-hound any depth or charisma, so Balto wins the day by being simple-minded rather than noble. Jenna, too, is personality-free. Bridget Fonda's pastel voice subtracts from this near-empty role as the love interest. It's the secondary characters who carry the picture. Steele is voiced with confidence by Jim Cummings, Phil Collins is amusing as the voice of the two eccentrically-sketched polar bears, Muk and Luk. The goose Boris, voiced by Bob Hoskins, is as close as *Balto* comes to Disneyesque wit and he is the most developed character.

Technically, *Balto* boasts the use of Softimage, a particle animation system similar to that used to produce the bubbles in *Crimson Tide* and which is responsible for the impressive variety of snow and ice textures displayed here. When the ice breaks under Balto's weight during the bear fight, the effect is astonishing. But one has to dig for such instances as these and there are only a handful of them—rare flashes of what *Balto* should have been. Ignoring moments of incongruity—how did the dogs get the comatose musher tucked and tied back onto the sled?—*Balto* is never allowed to be dynamic. Simon Wells, co-director of Amblin's *An American Tail: Fievel Goes West*, and supervising animator of *Who Framed Roger Rabbit* fails to capitalise on dramatic moments, being more confident with the 'touchy-feely' aspects of the story than with the macho adventure antics. The dangerous scenes are played too safe; the remainder wallow in their own sentiment.

Balto gives little indication that Amblimation can match the technical or storytelling skill of the Disney studio. Its style is retro, reminiscent of the Hanna-Barbara 60s television show *Scooby Doo*. Only young children will find *Balto* enthralling. Without catchy tunes, snappy lines, great animation or enough strong characters, *Balto* comes across as just another animated feature film striving for a bite of the family film market pie.

Also reviewed in:
CHICAGO TRIBUNE, 12/22/95, Friday/p. J, Mark Caro
NEW YORK TIMES, 12/22/95, p. C16, Stephen Holden
VARIETY, 1/1-7/96, p. 83, Brian Lowry

WASHINGTON POST, 12/22/95, p. C7, Rita Kempley
WASHINGTON POST, 12/22/95, Weekend/p. 43, Kevin McManus

BANDIT QUEEN

An Arrow release of a Film Four International and Kaleidoscope production. *Producer:* Sundeep Singh Bedi. *Director:* Shekhar Kapur. *Screenplay (Hindi with English subtitles):* Mala Sen. *Director of Photography:* Ashok Mehta. *Editor:* Renu Saluja. *Music:* Nusrat Fateh Ali Khan. *Music Director:* M. Arshad. *Sound:* Robert Taylor. *Sound Editor:* Tim Lewiston. *Casting:* Tigmanshu Dhulia. *Production Designer:* Eve Mavrakis. *Art Director:* Ashok Bhagat. *Set Dresser:* Sujata Sharma. *Costumes:* Dolly Ahluwalia. *Make-up:* Edwin Williams and Mohd Iqbal Sheikh. *Stunt Coordinator:* Alan Amin. *Running time:* 119 minutes. *MPAA Rating:* Not Rated.

CAST: Seema Biswas (Phoolan Devi); Nirmal Pandey (Vikram Mallah); Manjoj Bajpai (Man Singh); Rajesh Vivek (Mustaquim); Raghuvir Yadav (Madho); Govind Namdeo (Sriram); Saurabh Shukla (Kailash); Aditya Srivastava (Puttilal); Agesh Markam (Mad Woman); Anirudh Agarwal (Babu Guijar); Anupan Shyam (Ganshyam); Ajai Rohilla and Surendra Kora (Behmai Men); Ashok Bulani (D.S.P.); Ashok Sharma (Ashokchand Servant); Avinash Nemade (Doctor); Deepak Chibber (S.P. Bhind); Deepak Soni (Miandad); Dilip Raghuvanshi (Commander Yadav); Gajraj Rao (Ashokchand); G.B. Dixit (Ala Singer); Girish Solanki (Tarika's Partner); Guddi (Munni); Gyan Shivpuri (Phool Singh); Harish (Tarika); Hemant Mishra (Policeman); Hemnat Pandey (Ashokchand's Friend); Jeetendra Shastri (Bharat); Kanla Bhatt (Rukhmani, Age 11); K.D. Segan (A.D.C.); Khunni Lal Maina (Pundit); Mahesh Chandra (Chief Minister); Malabai Sonwani (Mother-in-Law); Mandakini Goswami (Kailash's Wife); Pallavi Bharti (Little Girl); Paritosh Sand (Devendra Singh); Ram Charan Nirmalker (Devideen); Ranjit Chaudhry (Shiv Narain); Raj Kumar Kamle (Thakur Gang); Ravi Sangde (Messenger); Savitri Raekwar (Moola); Sitaram Panchal (Lalaram); Sunil Gaekwad (Rattan Chand); Sunita Bhatt (Little Phoolan); Uma Vaish (Rukhmani); Vijay Shulka (Ashokchand's Friend).

LOS ANGELES TIMES, 6/30/95, Calendar/p. 20, Kevin Thomas

Phoolan Devi, released earlier this year after 11 years' imprisonment, has said of the hotly controversial Indian film "Bandit Queen" that it "should be called a work of imagination and not my real life story."

That's good advice because regardless of how close it is—or isn't—to the facts, this explosive picture is as potent in projecting its myth of the outlaw hero as "Butch Cassidy and the Sundance Kid" or "The Adventures of Robin Hood." Director Shekhar Kapur and writer Mala Sen have bonded dynamic adventure and romance and fiery social protest together with an "electrifying" effectiveness. "Bandit Queen" is an astonishing, over-powering piece of rabble-rousing, consciousness-raising, epic-scale filmmaking that unquestionably breaks ground in the Indian cinema in brutal candor if not theme.

Kapur and Sen place Devi at the worst possible conjunction of caste and gender. A member of the lowly Mallah caste of fishermen and their families in the state of Uttar Pradesh, she is traded by her father to a man 20 years her senior in exchange for a bicycle and a cow. She has in effect been sold into slavery and is promptly raped by her husband. From the start, however, young Phoolan (played as a child by Sunita Bhatt) displays a proud resistance to her fate.

Yet in running away from her husband, Devi rapidly discovers that now she has no status to protect her from rape by many men, in particular the higher-caste Thakurs. A woman of lesser spirit and strength surely would have died or been driven mad by such incessant brutality and public humiliation, but Devi (now played by Seema Biswas) survives, propelled inevitably into an outlaw gang. Its leader is shot to death by the handsome, enlightened Vikram Mallah (Nirmal

Pandey) while raping Devi; in no time Devi and Mallah are an Indian Bonnie and Clyde with Robin Hood instincts.

There's no doubt about it: Shekhar Kapur is a terrific storyteller, a highly visceral powerhouse filmmaker who can depict terrible brutality with an unflinching yet not exploitative gaze. The systematic, repetitive degradation of a woman that we witness is altogether convincing, as is Devi's endurance.

What we have to take on faith is that Devi and her gang were not mere bandits, that there was a romantic, tender quality to her relationships with the men she loves and that she possessed a nobility of purpose in calling attention to the doubly oppressive plight of low-caste Indian women.

Kapur's Devi, however, is shown to be unapologetically vengeful on a very large scale, which the real Devi has protested vehemently. In any event, Biswas gives us an often terrified but ultimately enduring Phoolan of awe-inspiring strength.

Wherever the truth lies, "Bandit Queen" on its own terms succeeds as a galvanic, eye-popping experience whose pain, vigor and passion is as richly expressed in Nusrat Fateh Ali Khan's mesmerizing score as in cinematographer Ashok Mehta's indelible images. One Indian columnist got carried away and proclaimed "Bandit Queen" the greatest Indian film ever made, but surely the many candidates for that honor fall among the films of Satyajit Ray, whose final—and radically different—picture, "The Stranger," by coincidence also opens today.

NEW YORK POST, 6/30/95, p. 36, Thelma Adams

Phoolan Devi's father sold the 11-year old girl to a much older man for a cow and a rusty bike. "A daughter is always a burden and ours is no beauty," says the father of the future "Bandit Queen." Thus begins Shekhar Kapur's blistering, fact-based, fast-paced action-adventure about a little girl born in the late 1950s who grew up to become one of India's most legendary outlaws. Banned in India and repudiated by the real Phoolan Devi, who is alive and well and running for political office in India, "Bandit Queen" is the moving story of an individual who made her own way in a strictly hierarchical society—but at a huge price. As a female and low-caste member, Devi was born on the bottom rung, born to be stepped on. When faced with her new husband, the flat-chested young Phoolan (Sunita Bhatt), defiantly announces, "I'll deal with the bastard." It will be a long time before she does: on Phoolan's chilling wedding night, her husband molests the pre-pubescent girl. A child's screams are heard; a mother-in-law turns away.

Phoolan leaves her husband and finds society offers her no protection. Back in her own village, an upper-caste Thakur attempts to rape her, but it is Phoolan who is banished. Thrown into jail when she tries to return home, guards rape and beat her. Later, a bandit leader, paid by the Thakurs, kidnaps and brutally takes Phoolan.

Shunned by society, Phoolan (played as an adult by Seema Biswas) slowly develop a relationship with a handsome bandit after Vikram Mallah (Nirmal Pandey) murders her most recent rapist. The movie takes a welcome detour into outlaw romance. Vikram is the first man ever to show her mercy. Phoolan is grateful as well as astonished at her own capacity for love and sex. Later Phoolan asks Vikram: "What was I born of? An act of love or violence?"

Vikram and Phoolan experience a Bonnie and Clyde heyday in which they live as near-equals, stealing by day, snuggling by night. This short-lived period ends when Vikram's upper-caste boss, Sriram (Govind Namdeo) gets out of jail. Sriram teaches Phoolan a lesson by instigating a marathon gang rape. Rarely have the simple words "three days later" across a screen been so freighted.

Battered, humiliated, but not beaten, Phoolan retreats to her native ravines to create a new gang and plot vengeance. Vikram's advice guides her: "Kill one and they hang you; kill 20 and you're famous."

As the bandit queen, Biswas commands the screen without romanticizing the heroine. Short, sturdy and plain, there is nothing coy in this ferocious performance. Phoolan is a woman who does not offer false smiles, but when she expresses true happiness it transforms her face into a thing of beauty.

I left the theater with the blood pounding in my ears, blown away by the violence, rage and righteous anger of a little girl who always knew she was worth more than a rusty bike and a cow—and wasn't content to suffer in silence like so many others.

NEWSDAY, 6/30/95, Part II/p. B7, John Anderson

The real Phoolan Devi—who may or may not be the same woman depicted in the Near-Eastern western "Bandit Queen"—initially condemned Shekhar Kapur's film as a fabrication. She has since relented, perhaps because she saw the film, or because someone suggested that no one with Devi's alleged political aspirations has ever been depicted on film more sympathetically or gloriously—not even Bill Clinton.

For all this, Devi's is the ugliest of tales. Played by the alternately ferocious/heartbreaking Seema Biswas, Phoolan spends a great deal of time being raped, beaten, humiliated and betrayed; she is a low-caste woman with an attitude and, as such, bears a triple burden in the Indian society of the '70s. Sold by her parents—for a cow and a bicycle—to be the 11-year-old bride of a child-rapist, she runs away from him, is accused of harlotry by the upper-caste Thakurs clan of her village, and is banished. Arrested for nothing and raped by her jailers, she is bailed out by Thakurs who want to rape her again, then kidnaped at their behest by bandits who do rape her again, at which point her one protector, Vikram (Nirmal Pandey), shoots the assailant, and he and Phoolan become partners in crime.

Time is short for the lovers in cahoots: Vikram is killed by the Thakur leader Sriram (Govind Namdeo), who has Phoolan gang-raped for three days and then paraded naked before townspeople, who do nothing. From this point, her vengeance is boundless.

In spite of its feminist fire and frank portrayal of Devi's sexual debasement—the film has had plenty of trouble from India's censors, for plenty of reasons—"Bandit Queen" is a fairly old-fashioned film. It's a Hollywoodized revenge tale. When she massacres 30 Thakurs at a wedding for harboring Sriram, the viewer is exhilarated. Even the assembling of her bandit image is promotional. When she finally dons her red headband, it's as if Batman had just put on his cape. Kapur's sequencing is confused at times, and certain subtleties of Indian society may be elusive, but there's a real nervous energy to the film—not just in the slo-mo slaughter and endangered babies, but in the moments of thoughtfulness. Generally, Kapur delivers the action in overheated, frantic fashion, but the momentum has less to do with the actual facts of the story than with Kapur's sense of outrage at the filthy secrets of Indian society.

"Kill one, and they'll hang you," Vikram tells her. "Kill twenty, and you're famous." They'll even beg you to surrender, he says, which is exactly what happened: Devi gave herself up before 10,000 cheering supporters, under terms dictated by her and honored by the government. "Bandit Queen" enjoys the same kind of anomaly: justified homicide on a massive scale, by a woman who became the hero of millions by acting like a man.

SIGHT AND SOUND, 2/95, p. 40, Philip Kemp

In a village in Uttar Pradesh, eleven-year-old Phoolan Devi is married against her will to the 30-year-old Puttilal. He takes her home, where he beats and eventually rapes her. She runs away to her family, who reluctantly accept her back. When she rejects the advances of the village headman's son, a member of the higher-caste Thakur clan, she is accused of leading him on. Banished from the village, she goes to live with her cousin Kailash, but his wife grows jealous and throws her out. Back in her village Phoolan is falsely accused of theft, and raped in jail by the police. The Thakurs arrange to have her kidnapped by local bandit chief Gujjar, who brutalises and repeatedly rapes her.

Vikram, Gujjar's young right-hand man, protests against this behaviour, and when Gujjar takes no notice shoots him dead. Though of low caste Vikram assumes command, and Phoolan becomes a fully-fledged bandit fighting alongside her comrades. The gang's fortunes prosper, and she and Vikram become lovers. The bandits' original leaders, the Thakur brothers Sriram and Lalaram, are let out of jail and resume command. Vikram is mysteriously shot, and Phoolan takes him to a doctor in the city. On his recovery they visit her family; her father tells her to go to her husband. Phoolan does so, and beats Puttilal almost to death.

Phoolan and Vikram rejoin the bandits, but Vikram is shot dead. Sriram has Phoolan tied up and raped by the gang, then takes her to the village of Behmai and publicly strips her naked. She takes refuge with Kailash who introduces her to Man Singh, a member of a mainly Muslim bandit force led by Mustaquim. With Mustaquim's backing, Phoolan forms her own gang with Man Singh. They launch a daring raid on the town of Jangrajpur, and Phoolan becomes famous as the

Bandit Queen. Told that Sriram and Lalaram are attending a wedding at Behmai she attacks the village, but the brothers escape. In their place she has 24 Thakur men massacred. The state authorities, alarmed at her reputation, launch a massive campaign against her, and through information supplied by Sriram most of her followers are lulled. Phoolan and Man Singh, evade capture, but in 1983 she surrenders on her own terms before a cheering crowd. End titles tell us she was released ten years later.

Simply on the ground of sexual outspokeness, *Bandit Queen* was guaranteed to raise a furor in its native country. When even on-screen kissing is taboo, to show nakedness and graphically enacted rape amounts to a deliberate challenge, and the film's producers can hardly have been surprised when it was banned. But the Delhi government's outraged response, one suspects, was due less to offended propriety than to the exposure of an India as far from the tourist-board image of timeless wisdom and harmony as can be imagined. *Bandit Queen* depicts a callous, caste-ridden and brutally sexist society where beating and rape—in or out of marriage—is the normal lot of lower caste women Phoolan's story is unusual only in that she resists. At one point, as the two Thakur bandit leaders negotiate their release from jail, we see in the background a woman being viciously slapped around by a group of police. No one else in the scene even glances at her; the spectacle is clearly too commonplace to be noticed.

Part of the film's strength lies its rejection of received images of India, There is nothing of the hippie-dream but equally nothing of the Oxfamposter version: life in these Uttar Pradesh villages may be hard, but nobody's starving. Religion scarcely figures (except that Phoolan gets better treatment from Muslim bandits than from Hindus, as they're indifferent to caste), nor does scenic beauty: most of the action is set in the barren ravines around the river Chambal, a terrain devoid of charm or grandeur. Relentlessly and single-mindedly *Bandit Queen* homes in on its central story—supposedly based on Phoolan's own memoirs, dictated in jail, though she herself now denounces it as a distortion (in particular she claims her struggle had nothing to do with caste, and that she wasn't present at the Behmai massacre).

But whatever its fidelity to the truth, the film exerts a shattering force—all the more so for its occasional rough edges. Some of the earlier scenes suffer from ragged pacing, and a few performances lack focus—though not that of Seema Biswas, who plays Phoolan with searing intensity and a tangible sense of anger. There are gaps in the narrative: it's never explained how Phoolan, out of water and ammunition, with all her followers killed except one, still has clout enough to dictate her own terms of surrender. These imperfections scarcely detract from the film's key quality, a headlong indignation whose impact might well be softened by a more polished production.

Not that *Bandit Queen* is technically crude: the camerawork is agile and at times—as in the gang rape sequence—tellingly oblique, and Nusrat Fateh Ali Khan contributes a subtle, classically-based score. But there's a harsh immediacy of texture that matches the subject matter, never letting us distance ourselves from the atrocities. At a time when screen violence is becoming increasingly stylised, from the choreographed shoot-outs of John Woo to the comic-book splatter of Tarantino, Kapur takes us right back to the basic article: stupid, sickeningly repetitive violence that bludgeons and degrades. We're even denied the easy comfort of retribution; Phoolan's victims are the wretched Puttilal and two dozen villagers of the wrong caste, while the chief villains Sriram and Lalaram escape her vengeance. Yet despite all this, *Bandit Queen* is far from depressing, thanks to the sheer resilience of its heroine. Too bad her fellow-countrywomen may never get the chance to see it.

TIME, 8/14/95, p. 67, Richard Corliss

Rape victim. Marauder. Murderer. Superstar! Phoolan Devi, an outcast Hindu woman, became a folk hero as head of a band of outlaws preying on India's corrupt elite. Part Joan of Arc, part Ma Barker, on Feb. 14, 1981, she staged her own St. Valentine's Day massacre, leading the slaughter of 22 villagers she suspected of aiding her enemies. Yet her surrender, in 1983, was on her own terms, to the cheers of 10,000 supporters. On her release from prison last year, three political parties asked her to run for office.

Bandit Queen, written by Mala Sen and directed by Shekhar Kapur, is a vibrant, instructive document with a fierce star performance by Seema Biswas. The film has an Indian heart but a Hollywood pulse; it moves with the fevered outrage of an Oliver Stone melodrama—*Natural Born*

Killers—meets *Heaven and Earth*. Most Indian movies are either humid musical fables or languid art films in the Satyajit Ray mold. *Bandit Queen* is neither. It is an assaultive experience, blistering with ripe obscenities, the frontal nudity of its star and three stark scenes in which Phoolan is raped—enough to have the film banned 10 times over in a country where a bare shoulder can send the censors frothing.

Bandit Queen was indeed banned. But Kapur believes that the censors, who demanded 25 significant cuts, have another agenda: "To them the film's most offensive aspect is its depiction of the caste system. To expose this hierarchy of inequality is the worst sin I've committed."

Devi, who sued to stop a Toronto Film Festival screening of *Bandit Queen*, has since settled with the producers and, says Kapur, "now stands by the film." But the Indian government would not grant her a passport to attend the U.S. premiere. American filmgoers can see an exciting movie that brings Devi's story to life with passion but without passing judgment. In India, though, a venal game is being played: the upper-class guardians of public morality who once defamed this low-caste rebel are now ensuring that *Bandit Queen* remains an untouchable.

VILLAGE VOICE, 7/4/95, 59, Gary Dauphin

Shekhar Kapur's epically minded tale of rape, outlawry, and political redemption in the north of modern-day India is a flawed but emotionally grueling two hours, its main arc being "bandit queen" Phoolan Devi's enraged survival in the face of escalating rounds of abuse and loss. Devi was sold into matrimonial slavery at the age of 11 (for a sickly cow and a rusted bicycle), and by the time she was in her early twenties, she had risen to the status of folk heroine, the vengeful "Goddess of Flowers" who robbed and killed her social betters and tormentors, and whose eventual surrender to police was a media event attended by politicians and 10,000 lumpen devotees.

Played initially by child actress Sunita Bhatt, Phoolan is a smallish girl with an explosively foul mouth who starts paying the heavy price that seems to be exacted from self-minded Indian women. Young Phoolan is raped by her husband, and the scene's length is more horrific than its visuals, the camera lingering on Phoolan's crying face while the back of her husband's obscenity-muttering head creeps in and out of the frame below. Torturous rape scenes provide *Bandit Queen* with its metaphor for Devi's life, a cycle of abuse involving the police, the upper-caste scions of her village, and various "bad" bandit leaders (Kapur's direction goes embarrassingly arty in some of these sequences, with slo-mo and languorous pans appearing out of nowhere). Finally Phoolan takes to the exile of banditry in the dry, scarred countryside between village outposts. There she falls in with a group of thieves and highwaymen, finding brief oases of safety among them and even love with a kindly bandit leader.

As a "true" story with significant implications in India (the real-life Devi is out of prison and considering a political career), *Bandit Queen* hinges on the actress playing the adult Phoolan. Seema Biswas embodies the title role with a fortitude that verges on the superhuman, conveying all the horror of Devi's situation yet still able to suggest the character's ample reserves of rage, intelligence, and playfulness. Despite the numerous and explicitly depicted rapes, Biswas also manages to carry two love scenes. The more wrenching is a fitful and awkward kiss, a conflicted Devi striking out reflexively whenever her lover tries to respond or touch her arm.

Bandit Queen's script is billed as being adapted from Devi's jailhouse notebooks as well as interviews with her, which if true turns *Bandit Queen* into a confession of guilt (with mitigating circumstances) to charges to which she'd earlier pled innocent. Before the film could be released in India, Devi denounced it as an exploitative fiction. More recently, she denounced her denunciation, saying her husband engineered her protests in order to enrich himself. The ugly irony of course is that given the numerous (albeit more physical) examples of exploitation in the movie, the legend of the "Bandit Queen" is one that Phoolan Devi seems fated to continually re-enact.

Also reviewed in:
CHICAGO TRIBUNE, 7/14/95, p. F, Michael Wilmington
NEW REPUBLIC, 7/10/95, p. 24, Stanley Kauffmann
NEW YORK TIMES, 3/18/95, p.18, Stephen Holden
VARIETY, 6/6-12/94, p. 36, Derek Elley

WASHINGTON POST, 6/28/95, p. C1, Rita Kempley
WASHINGTON POST, 6/30/95, Weekend/p. 42, Desson Howe

BAR GIRLS

An Orion Pictures release of a Lavender Hill Mob production. *Producer:* Lauran Hoffman and Marita Giovanni. *Director:* Marita Giovanni. *Screenplay (based her stage play):* Lauran Hoffman. *Director of Photography:* Michael Ferris. *Editor:* Carter Dehaven. *Music:* Lenny Meyers. *Sound:* Jessie Bender. *Art Director:* Darryl Fong and Keith Brunsmann. *Set Decorator:* Lia Niskanen and Andrew Rosen. *Costumes:* Houston Sams. *Running time:* 95 minutes. *MPAA Rating:* R.

CAST: Nancy Allison Wolfe (Loretta); Liza D'Agostino (Rachel); Camila Griggs (J.R.); Michael Harris (Noah); Justine Slater (Veronica); Paula Sorge (Tracy); Cece Tsou (Sandy); Lisa Parker (Annie).

LOS ANGELES TIMES, 4/7/95, Calendar/p. 6, Kevin Thomas

Nancy Allison Wolfe, a seasoned New York stage actress, lends a formidable presence to "Bar Girls," a lively lesbian romantic comedy. Not conventionally beautiful but striking looking with a resemblance to Golden Era screen star Ann Dvorak, Wolfe has the energy, passion and temperament that enables her to hold together this endearing but minor film, adapted by Lauran Hoffman from her own play and directed by Marita Giovanni.

Few of the other actresses in the movie possess the talent and skill of Wolfe—and none has such a meaty part, so Wolfe's contribution is crucial. She's Loretta, co-writer of a TV cartoon series, whose brash, confident manner belies her vulnerability in her search for love. She seeks it, as do all the other women in the film, in an L.A. lesbian bar, where one evening she zeros in on an aspiring actress, Rachel (Liza D'Agostino, also a confident player), who looks so much like Rae Dawn Chong you check the credits to make sure she isn't.

It's the familiar instance of everything happening so quickly that these women have to go through a rough period of painful reappraisal to discover if they truly love each other. "Bar Girls" hasn't the style, the quirky individuality or the assured ensemble portrayals of last year's "Go Fish," but it does have a number of great-looking, smartly dressed women in contrast to the women of the earlier film, most of whom seemed to take their fashion tips from Ethan Hawke.

"Bar Girls" touches upon the struggle lesbians have in mainstreaming their lifestyle—e.g., Loretta's fight to get a lesbian character in her cartoon series rings all too true. It also suggests that in coping with the vicissitudes of romance, gays and straights are pretty much alike.

"Bar Girls" has a proud feminist spirit without being heavy-handed, and there's a nice bantering, supportive quality in the relationship Loretta has with her male writing partner (played by Michael Harris with a light, easy touch). "Bar Girls" is breezy and upbeat but also takes emotions seriously.

NEW YORK POST, 4/7/95, p. 47, Larry Worth

"Bar Girls" has about as much appeal as flat beer and stale pretzels.

Like "Go Fish," it's yet another look at lesbians in the '90s—out, and proud of it. But unlike "Go Fish," it has none of the rich, emotional complexities, three-dimensional characters and an interesting storyline.

Under first-time director Marita Giovanni, hardly a moment rings true. For that matter, even the titular bar seems artificial. It looks more antiseptic then a dentist's office, and about as much fun.

Nonetheless, the eight women who serve as supposed heroines find no shortage of romance and heartbreak within the smokeless ambience. Chief among them is Loretta, an insecure cartoon show writer who's always searching for her Cinderella.

Enter struggling actress Rachel, a woman who would do any glass slipper proud. But a happy ending isn't around the corner. More in the manner of "The Young and the Restless," the usual barriers—and requisite catfights—will delay the lovers' final swoon into the sunset.

The introduction of a half-dozen sub-plots does nothing to increase viewers' interest—not when characters are as cliched as the wise-cracking barkeep, a butch cop, and the straight women yearning to be "one of the girls."

By ignoring the Los Angeles setting, Giovanni keeps the production as stagey as the play from which it originated. Further, screenwriter Lauran Hoffman" (who based the story on her own experiences) tries—and fails—to be a gay Woody Allen, relying on one-liners instead of dialogue.

Principal actresses Nancy Allison Wolfe, Liza D'Agostino and, in a smaller role, Chastity Bono, complement the amateurish feel with time-wasting histrionics.

Though the production tries hard to be hip—and earns points for tasteful sex scenes—"Bar Girls" could drive quality-seeking filmgoers to drink.

NEWSDAY, 4/7/95, Part II/p. B7, John Anderson

A romantic comedy, about lesbians that features a cameo by Chastity Bono needs o other reason to exist. Which is good news, and bad news.

There's something cynical and opportunistic about movies like "Bar Girls," a clumsy first feature by Marita Giovanni, adapted by Lauran Hoffman from her play. There's a hungry market out there for gay-themed films particularly among lesbians, and the number that have achieved something meaningful has been small—Rose Troche's "Go Fish," in fact, being the only recent one that comes to mind.

The conclusion one draws—and it's not much of a reach—is that filmmakers get lazy when they know they have a built-in audience. (Hello, Hollywood?)

"Bar Girls" has a certain sassiness about it, and may have been a sincere attempt to portray lesbian life in an honest, comedic way. It just doesn't work well most of the time, despite a few good gags, mostly because of the script and the direction. The cast is generally good, and should probably be assembled again for a movie with a better, firmer foundation.

At the center of this one is Loretta (Nancy Allison Wolfe), the brassy creator—with her partner Noah (Michael Harris) of "Heavy Myrtle"—of the first animated cartoon superhero who gets her period and may or may not come out of the closet. In her off-hours, Loretta leads a rather busy romantic life centered at Girl Bar, a rowdy joint inhabited by a wide lineup of enthusiastic lesbians.

Loretta has been involved with the flaky Annie (Lisa Parker), but once she sees Rachel (Liza D'Agostino) she thinks she's found true love; so does Rachel, who upon moving in with Loretta insists on total monogamy—a tough thing to maintain, given the musical chairs being played at Girl Bar, and the predatory eye that J.R. (Camilla Griggs), a policewoman-to-be, keeps giving Rachel.

This soap opera seesaws between the flippant and the serious, derailing itself with abandon. Why are Loretta and Rachel, whose appeal lies in their hipness, so timid and demure when approaching each other? It doesn't make sense, nor does the jokiness—particularly on the part of Loretta—that undoes the film's more serious moments.

People will go to see "Bar Girls," and should, since box-office returns are the only accepted evidence that there's an audience for lesbian movies and lesbian characters. Outside of making a political statement, however, there are few other reasons to see it.

VILLAGE VOICE, 4/18/95, p. 60, Lisa Kennedy

Last year, one of the old hands who invented the thumb system of film criticism said that what was really important about that year's lesbian film, Go Fish, was that it was The First. Which, of course, wasn't entirely true. It was the first the way the guy in "Like a Virgin" feels like the first. It was so good, it wiped a particular slate clean, raised the level of expectation, etc. If you accept that analogy, then the new girl film in town—Marita Giovanni's Bar Girls—feels like a relapse, a so-so night out, maybe even a mistake. Not that this small but underambitious girl-gets-loses-gets-girl movie doesn't have some moments; especially enjoyable was the odd couple pairing of Southern bull Tracy with Valley femme Veronica. But then I'm a fool for the familiar—a foolishness this film is banking on.

There are a few things that have nothing to do with sexuality working against the success of *Bar Girls*. First, there is its staginess: the screenplay by Lauran Hoffman is an adaptation of her original play; *Bar Girls* is also the film debut of stage director Giovanni. While this shouldn't damn a film to a sort of anticinematic hell, it does underscore what kind of finesse is required to make something dialogue-driven into a fluid motion picture. Indeed, there are times where the chattiness of its leads, Loretta (Nancy Allison Wolfe) and Rachel (Liza D'Agostino), reaches a *My Tequila with Andrea* stasis. This, too, would be okay if the talktalktalk weren't so absurdly earnest, even as it attempts irony. Here's the gist of one exchange: "Are you getting cold feet already?" "Maybe. Cold feet but a warm heart. Let's see if we can keep it that way." I dunno, but I think we deserve better than this. That's the sort of line some gal uses at a girl bar when she imagines she's in a movie—preferably a '30s romantic comedy. This could sound clever, I suppose, sweet, even, if you had been drinking all night, but here it's a clinker. And if *Bar Girls* has some audience beyond us image-deprived lesbians, this type of heh-heh insiderism will only get the film so far.

If there's one thing that's really annoying about us team players, it's the way we've started to believe that our lives are in themselves dramatic, as if we really are different, as if we don't have to do the work of imagining good stories and executing them well. In *Bar Girls*, one night owl walks into the dive and says, as we all do from time to time, "I've come to a point in my life where drama is a real turnoff," Yes, I wanted to say, but not in my moviegoing life.

Also reviewed in:
CHICAGO TRIBUNE, 4/7/95, Friday/p. L, John Petrakis
NEW YORK TIMES, 4/7/95, p. C10, Stephen Holden
VARIETY, 10/3-9/94, p. 63, Emanuel Levy
WASHINGTON POST, 4/7/95, p. D9, Hal Hinson

BASKETBALL DIARIES, THE

A New Line Cinema release of an Island Pictures presentation of a Liz Heller production. *Executive Producer:* Chris Blackwell and Dan Genetti. *Producer:* Liz Heller and John Bard Manulis. *Director:* Scott Kalvert. *Screenplay:* Bryan Goluboff. *Based on the novel by:* Jim Carroll. *Director of Photography:* David Phillips. *Editor:* Dana Congdon. *Music:* Graeme Revell. *Music Editor:* Joshua Wingett. *Sound:* William Sarokin and (music) Dan Wallin. *Casting:* Avy Kaufman. *Production Designer:* Christopher Nowak. *Set Decorator:* Harriet Zucker. *Set Dresser:* Jerry Kadar and Jacqueline Arnot. *Special Effects:* Steve Kirshoff. *Costumes:* David C. Robinson. *Make-up:* Diane Hammond. *Stunt Coordinator:* Edgard Mourino. *Running time:* 102 minutes. *MPAA Rating:* R.

CAST: Leonardo DiCaprio (Jim Carroll); Lorraine Bracco (Jim's Mother); Marilyn Sokol (Chanting Woman); James Madio (Pedro); Patrick McGaw (Neutron); Mark Wahlberg (Mickey); Roy Cooper (Father McNulty); Vinnie Pastore (Construction Worker); Bruno Kirby (Swifty); Jimmy Papiris (Iggy); Nick Gaetani (Referee #1); Alexander Gaberman (Bobo); Ben Jorgensen (Tommy); Josh Mostel (Counterman); Juliette Lewis (Diane Moody); Michael Imperioli (Bobby); Akiko Ashley (Stripper); Ernie Hudson (Reggie); Manny Alfaro (Manny); Cynthia Daniel (Winkie); Brittany Daniel (Blinkie); Eric Betts (Drug Dealer); Joyce R. Korbin (Mugging Victim); Barton Heyman (Confessional Priest); Lawrence Barth (Referee #2); Gary Iorio (Policeman); Toby Huss (Kenny); James Dennis Carroll (Frankie Pinewater); William Webb (Juju Johnson); John Vennema (Mr. Rubin); Michael Rapaport (Skinhead); Doc Dougherty (Policeman); John Hoyt (Billy the Bartender); Manny Siverio (Pino).

LOS ANGELES TIMES, 4/21/95, Calendar/p. 8, Kenneth Turan

"The Basketball Diaries" is a lose-lose proposition. Although it masquerades as a cautionary tale about the horrors of heroin, this epic of teen-age *Angst* is more accurately seen as a reverential wallow in the gutter of self-absorption.

When it's not boring you with its spittle-encrusted delineation of the agonies of addiction, "Basketball Diaries" is romanticizing the ultimate effects of drug use. It is an accomplishment of sorts to be repellent and glamorizing at the same time, but it is the only accomplishment to which this unfortunate film can lay claim.

"Diaries" is based on poet Jim Carroll's celebrated memoir of the same name, a cult favorite ever since it was first published in 1978. But its connection to that book is surprisingly weak.

For one thing, Bryan Goluboff's smug script lacks the book's gleeful flashes of self-deprecating humor. And, although they all profess to love the original to pieces, the filmmakers were clearly frightened by its episodic nature: It is supposed to be a diary, after all. So an artificial plot has been concocted to link everything together, fictitious characters created, the time frame pushed awkwardly forward to the present day, and the whole thing turned into a movie that might as well be called "Punks on Parade."

Jim Carroll (Leonardo DiCaprio) is head of this motley crew, the coolest of the dudes who play basketball for New York's St. Vitus Cardinals, "the hottest Catholic high school team in the city." The rest of the gang includes the arrogant Mickey (Mark Wahlberg, a.k.a. Marky Mark), the serious Neutron (Patrick McGaw) and the undersized hanger-on Pedro (James Madio).

When they're not fending off the advice of Swifty (Bruno Kirby), their clueless coach, the guys are the Four Mouseketeers of petty crime. They sniff glue, moon tourists on the Circle Line cruise and give a hard time to a neighborhood junkie-hooker (played, inevitably, by Juliette Lewis).

Then the gang discovers harder drugs, first cocaine and pills and later heroin. Soon they are mugging old ladies, crying, sniveling and getting so sick they can barely stand. It's even more tedious than it sounds.

While Jim Carroll's book has no interest in any kind of conventional ending, happy or otherwise, the film is not so fussy. So after watching the young man suffer, we get to witness his inevitable (i.e. commercial) redemption. Carroll, nicely dressed with a beatific "I've been there look" on his face and words like "know this" on his lips, is sadder but oh so much wiser at the close.

While first-time director Scott Kalvert (yet another stylish refugee from music videos) may not know it, what a resolution like that does is equate heroin addiction to a really scary amusement park ride. Yeah, it's hairy for a while, but you're OK in the end and you've got a really cool experience to tell your friends about. If they're still alive. It's sad to see as talented an actor as Leonardo DiCaprio taking part in this charade. The basic truth he brings to almost all his roles is in conflict with the film's essential bogusness, its willingness to place Carroll in Christ-like poses and turn him into a suffering saint of pubescent rebellion. Because they lack context and connection, DiCaprio's torments-of-the-damned exertions come across as miming, not acting, hardly something of which anyone can be proud.

NEW YORK, 5/8/95, p. 68, David Denby

Jim Carroll's *The Basketball Diaries*, allegedly a chronicle of Carroll's life in New York from ages 13 to 16, has sold well since it was published in 1978, when Carroll was 28, and it's not hard to see why. A teen basketball star, Trinity dropout, drug addict, and eventual underground poet and rock performer, Carroll filled his diary with bravado, good times, and heroic bad times—feats of 14-year-old sexual performance and monumentally self-destructive bouts of drug consumption—all of it written in a sub-Kerouac patter ("We beat some dopey private school chicks I know for ten beans pawning off a bag of dill weed from momma's spice cabinet as grass and talked this spade dealer into letting us light $2 for two sixers," etc.). To my ears, the diary feels like an expertly contrived record of fantasy: The boy—or man—who wrote that sentence may never have told the truth about anything in his life, but he understands a thing or two about prose rhythm. He understands teen self-dramatization too. Carroll successfully captures a defiant mood of extreme narcissism—the mood in which an adult world composed of phonies and corrupt homosexuals attempts to sully the purity of a 15-year-old heroin addict. Carroll wants us to think of his younger self as Holden Caulfield with balls—and veins.

However dubious its authenticity, Carroll's book might have served as the basis for an interesting movie. Fifteen-year-old boys do have a kind of magic: They may never again be as spontaneous or as loyal to one another. But *The Basketball Diaries* is so slovenly and inaccurate it seems an even worse fake than the book. Leonardo DiCaprio is a very talented actor, but as Carroll, he doesn't move like a teenage athlete. Nor does DiCaprio's cocky smile suggest much connection to the meaninglessly hostile and self-destructive acts perpetrated by young Jim. We never really find out why this boy is so alienated; the, movie just presents him as a fully formed dark angel, which means that DiCaprio's performance is both strained and unsupported.

The movie was shot in New York, but most of the time we can't tell where we are; Scott Kalvert, the director, demonstrates no feeling for the street. The parochial school that Jim attends appears to have only a single teacher, a sadistic priest played by a granite-jawed actor out of Victorian melodrama. One of Jim's friends on his supposedly terrific basketball team is played by the diminutive Mark Wahlberg (a.k.a. Marky Mark), who, with his overdeveloped wrestler's torso, doesn't look like he could jump more than an inch or two off the floor. The gorgeous rich twins who so obligingly sleep with the hero and his friend seem like glazed morons out of a porno movie. And so on.

Kalvert is yet another graduate of music videos with little sense of how to build a sequence. He creates a swirl of overcharged visual moods, but many of the sequences trail off into nowhere, and he lays the dolorous drug scenes one on top of another, linking the episodes with excerpts from Carroll's diaries. The basic form of the movie is false and undramatic, since the audience knows perfectly well that the hero, however messed up, will live to compose his book. The movie ends with Jim emerging from six months on Rikers Island and receiving the applause of a rapt Off Broadway-theater audience as he recites his diary. *The Basketball Diaries*—in any version—is a pathetically egocentric conception.

NEW YORK POST, 4/21/95, p. 48, Michael Medved

Leonardo DiCaprio is one of the more accomplished actors of his generation, as amply demonstrated by his spectacular work in "This Boy's Life" and "What's Eating Gilbert Grape," and even in his scene-stealing supporting role in "The Quick and the Dead."

In "The Basketball Diaries," DiCaprio turns in yet another ferociously fine performance—once again playing a defiant, long-suffering survivor—but it's not enough to help the movie itself survive its own structural weaknesses.

Adapted from Jim Carroll's raw, uncompromising autobiography, the picture follows the protagonist's horrifying descent from high school basketball star to hopeless street junkie.

Based on Carroll's own diaries as a teen-ager, the book takes you so deep into the author's tormented soul that his self-destructive behavior seems inevitable, driven by its own hellish logic.

In the film, you're watching the character from outside, rather than viewing the world through his eyes, so his behavior seems far more arbitrary. We occasionally see DiCaprio scribbling in crumpled notebooks, and hear a few sentences of colorful diary entries, but it's not nearly enough to create sympathy for a character whose behavior is utterly despicable even before he's crippled by cocaine and heroin addiction.

When we meet Carroll and his best friends (effectively played by Mark Wahlberg, Patrick McGaw and James Madio) they're part of the hottest Catholic high school basketball team in New York City.

Beyond victory on the court, they arrange to steal valuables from an opposing team's lockers during a game and savagely beat these competitors when they ask for their property back.

Carroll's only redeeming characteristic is his concern for a former teammate (Michael Imperioli), who's confined to a hospital bed where he's dying of leukemia.

Director Scott Kalvert a veteran of music videos who here makes his feature-film debut makes the life of a homeless addict, vicious mugger and car thief terrifyingly immediate and real.

The film has a fragrant sense of place—including a sequence in which Mark Wahlberg (a.k.a. Marky Mark) and his posse strip down to their Calvins and dive off sheer cliffs into the fetid Harlem River.

The sense of time is another matter—Carroll's 1960s diaries have been uneasily transposed to the current day and so at times the mood seems decidedly anachronistic.

For some reason, the movie also avoids all but the vaguest hints of Carroll's ultimate redemption as a legendary coffee house poet and musician. Had the filmmakers chosen to depict that transformation, it might have given their picture the dramatic focus it lacks, and provided some point or purpose to the degradation it so vividly (and indulgently) conveys.

NEWSDAY, 4/21/95, Part II/p. B5, Gene Seymour

It's a measure of Leonardo DiCaprio's huge potential for stardom that not even an abject misfire like "The Basketball Dairies" will hobble his trajectory. If anything, DiCaprio's ultra-wired performance as hoopster-poet-junkie Jim Carroll proves he's got the goods to rise so high above even the most ill-conceived material that he almost redeems it. Almost.

Not even DiCaprio's inspired emotion-riffing can save this adaptation of Carroll's autobiographical sketches of his on-the-edge Manhattan adolescence, first published in book form in 1978. Director Scott Kalvert, a rock-video veteran, doesn't make clear just when this story takes place. The references to Wilt Chamberlain seem to fix it 20, 30 years before. But 42nd Street is shown in its present, transitional state with post-modern poetry on the theater marquees. So if it *is* now, where's the crack? Or the AIDS from all the dirty needles being passed around?

Time-warp is just one of the many problems with this film, which doesn't resemble the original "Diaries" so much as it recalls some of those turgid cautionary melodramas made in the '50s about what happens when a good boy goes bad from drugs. Here, it's more like a bad boy getting worse since Jim and his fellow members of a sweet-shooting Catholic high school basketball team are seen from the start as swaggering sociopaths who not only whip their competitors on the court, but rip off the contents of their lockers.

DiCaprio's Jim carries a golden glow of Higher Destiny because of the poetry he scribbles intensely in his composition book. His buddies, Neutron (Patrick McGaw), Pedro (James Madio) and Mickey ("Marky" Mark Wahlberg), like living on the edge as much as he does. But when hard drugs become standard equipment for their never-ending party, it messes up their once-pristine timing on the court. All but Neutron quit school to take their chances on the streets.

From there, it's one long, dreary descent into hell as Jim becomes just another junkie stealing and hustling every way he can for a taste. Only the intervention of a saintly-cool friend (Ernie Hudson) briefly obstructs Jim's freefall to oblivion.

Hudson deserves better than this embarrassingly cliched role. So do Lorraine Bracco and Bruno Kirby, as, respectively, Jim's long-suffering mom and his wormy coach. Wahlberg plays his sidekick's role at a strident, goofy pitch. DiCaprio's hair-trigger intensity is the only thing that keeps the misshaped pieces of this film from sagging or breaking off. In the end, the movie even drags him down.

The only time it takes flight is when the real Jim Carroll appears in a cameo role of a veteran junkie waxing rhapsodic about the "ritual" of cooking and preparing the dose. This scene offers the kind of jolting lyricism that made the original "Diaries" a cultural phenomenon. But given how hard it is to imagine Carroll's rueful, elegiac vision of street life going mainstream in this age of Just-Say-No, one wonders why anyone bothered dragging it to the big screen in the first place.

SIGHT AND SOUND, 12/95, p. 41, Ben Thompson

Jim Carroll is one of a gang of unruly teenagers in New York. His mother struggles to keep him under control. Subjected to savage corporal punishment by the brutal Father McNulty at his Catholic school, his rebellious spirit is not subdued. Jim and his friends run off to smoke cigarettes, sniff cleaning fluid and cause mayhem on ferries.

A diary allows Jim to give rein to the more sensitive side of his nature, but most of his time is taken up with getting into trouble. Only basketball offers him and his friends a chance to excel. Coached by the kindly and sympathetic Swifty, they are heading for glory in the high school championships. Unable to share in this prospect is Bobo, one of the gang, who has fallen victim to leukaemia. In a bid to raise his spirits, Jim sneaks him out of hospital and takes him to a strip show on 42nd Street, but this only makes Bobo more unhappy.

Even basketball games become an opportunity for thieving and violence, and Jim and the dangerous Mickey become involved with drugs. Bobo's death and Jim's discovery that Swifty's interest in him was sexually motivated push him further down the road to delinquency. Only his older black friend Reggie Porter, with whom he plays one-on-one street basketball, can offer him any form of guidance. Reggie can do nothing to stop Jim being expelled from school and thrown out of his house by his despairing mother. But when he finds Jim freezing to death on the street, having sunk into an abyss of junkiedom and prostitution, he saves his life.

With Reggie's help, Jim goes cold turkey, but he is not strong enough to stay off heroin. He robs his friend and descends back into a life of crime. Pedro, one of his gang-mates, is caught by the police during a bungled shop-robbery, and Mickey also goes to prison for killing a drug dealer. Jim goes back to his mother for help but she calls the police to take him away. He serves three months on Ryker's Island. An audience breaks into applause as it turns out he is reading from his now celebrated diary.

Jim Carroll's torrid autobiographical saga of New York street adolescence has taken a long time to get to the screen, and as if to emphasise this fact, Scott Kalvert's film seems to be set in an unspecified anytime. In opting to play up the timelessness of their story the film's producers have unwittingly exacerbated a serious flaw within *The Basketball Diaries*. What was new and shocking in Jim Carroli's work in the 60s and 70s has since become the stuff of cliché. The street-smart kid's descent into crime and heroin addiction is now too familiar a story, and there is just nothing in this film to distinguish it.

Time has not been especially kind to Carroll's homely poeticisms: "I tried making friends with God by inviting him to my house to watch the World Series ... He never showed." And the supposed intimacy of the diary format—the self-important young Jim's "Suffice to say"s and "Know this"s—is irritating. Carroll himself (who makes a cameo appearance as a heroin enthusiast, and also acted as consultant) can hardly be blamed for the adolescent aspects of the original diaries, as he wrote them between the ages of 13 and 16, but it is a pity that the film also adopts such a whining self-justificatory mien.

By all accounts, Leonardo DiCaprio is much happier with the dark, depressing performance he gives here than he was with his breezy comic turn in Sam Raimi's *The Quick and the Dead*. There is something disturbing about this misjudgement. It is not that DiCaprio does anything wrong—he can clearly chew the doormat with the best of them, and no-one could accuse this film of making getting off heroin look easy—it's the fact that he felt the need to make it at all. The list of actors for whom this script was previously developed includes Matt Dillon (who eventually starred in the vastly superior *Drugstore Cowboy*), Eric Stoltz and the late River Phoenix. It is depressing that Phoenix's tragically premature demise does not seem to have diminished the allure of junkie-chic for the actor best qualified to succeed him at the top of the Hollywood charisma tree.

DiCaprio does a fine job early on of conveying Carroll's aspiration to a "presence like a panther, not presence like a chimp". And first time director Kalvert (who cut his teeth on rap videos and *The Fresh Prince of Bel Air*) brings a healthy snap to scenes of boyish high spirits, daredevil cliff dives into the Hudson river, and homoerotic on-court bonding. But once the junk kicks in, the fun stops. Which may well be how things happen in real life, but—as with paint taking a long time to dry—that does not necessarily make it something anyone would want to pay to watch.

VILLAGE VOICE, 4/25/95, p. 52, Georgia Brown

A lesser '60s phenom, [the reference is to *Crumb*; see Brown's review] Jim Carroll's *The Basketball Diaries*—parts of which were published in *The Paris Review*—has been made into a movie so lame, so compromised, it's enough to send this reviewer back into hibernation. Just sitting through it took yogic will power.

Whatever the virtues of Carroll's slender confessions—vivid voice, distinctive New York scene—they sure aren't present in the movie, directed in clueless music video style by Scott Kalvert and adapted with no charm whatsoever by Bryan Goluboff. The result is an advertisement for the latest beautiful boy, Leonardo DiCaprio, and his fading sidekick here, Marky Mark. Having forsaken any pretense to period ambience (the diaries, although they weren't published as a book until 1978, take place in the mid '60s), everything about this adaptation rings false. Carroll's elegy for youth and promise here becomes a dopey cautionary tale with not one but two uplifting endings.

Jim (DiCaprio) is a Catholic school basketball hotshot. He has two pals on the team (the muscled one is Marky) and another who's the team mascot. The four pals do kids' things like jump from a cliff into the Hudson after mooning the Circle Line. Sniffing glue turns to pills and then heroin. Jim and two of the others wind up hardcore junkies and thieves; one goes straight. Unbilled, Juliette Lewis toddles in and out with smeared lipstick. Jim's downtrodden single mom

(Lorraine Bracco) kicks him out. Thereupon he's picked out of the snow by one of his schoolyard one-on-one buddies (Ernie Hudson), a saintly older African American who guides him through the obligatory rough detox. Definitely not in the book.

No doubt to the relief of Trinity High School, the author's scholarship stint at that institution is deleted from the film. Here's another omission: In the diaries Carroll writes lyrically of a blow job he hustles, but the movie's Jim, sunk so low, grits his teeth in anguish. Let's not give anybody any wrong ideas.

Also reviewed in:
CHICAGO TRIBUNE, 4/21/95, Friday/p. J, John Petrakis
NEW YORK TIMES, 4/21/95, p. C12, Janet Maslin
VARIETY, 2/6-12/95, p. 74, Todd McCarthy
WASHINGTON POST, 4/21/95, p. D1, Hal Hinson
WASHINGTON POST, 4/21/95, Weekend/p. 44, Joe Brown

BATMAN FOREVER

A Warner Bros. release. *Executive Producer:* Benjamin Melniker and Michael E. Uslan. *Producer:* Tim Burton and Peter MacGregor Scott. *Director:* Joel Schumacher. *Screenplay:* Lee Batchler, Janet Scott Batchler, and Akiva Goldsman. *Story:* Lee Batchler and Janet Scott Batchler. *Based on the Batman characters by:* Bob Kane. *Director of Photography:* Stephen Goldblatt. *Editor:* Dennis Virkler. *Music:* Elliot Goldenthal. *Music Editor:* Christopher Brooks. *Sound:* Petur Hliddal and (music) Steve McLaughlin and Joel Iwataki. *Sound Editor:* John Leveque and Bruce Stambler. *Casting:* Mali Finn. *Production Designer:* Barbara Ling. *Art Director:* Chris Burian-Mohr and Joseph P. Lucky. *Set Designer:* James Bayliss, John Berger, Sean Haworth, Peter J. Kelly, Gene Nollman, Brad Ricker, and Patricia Klawonn. *Set Decorator:* Cricket Rowland. *Set Dresser:* David Ronan. *Special Effects:* Tommy Fisher. *Visual Effects:* John Dykstra. *Costumes:* Bob Ringwood and Ingrid Ferrin. *Make-up:* Ve Neill. *Make-up (Special Effects):* Rick Baker. *Stunt Coordinator:* Conrad Palmisano and Jeff Gibson. *Running time:* 121 minutes. *MPAA Rating:* PG-13.

CAST: Val Kilmer (Batman/Bruce Wayne); Tommy Lee Jones (Harvey Two-Face/Harvey Dent); Jim Carrey (Riddler/Edward Nygma); Nicole Kidman (Dr. Chase Meridian); Chris O'Donnell (Robin/Dick Grayson); Michael Gough (Alfred Pennyworth); Pat Hingle (Commissioner Gordon); Drew Barrymore (Sugar); Debi Mazar (Spice); Elizabeth Sanders (Gossip Gerty); Rene Auberjonois (Dr. Burton); Joe Grifasi (Bank Guard); Philip Moon and Jessica Tuck (Newscasters); Dennis Paladino (Crime Boss Moroni); Kimberly Scott (Margaret); Michael Paul Chan (Executive); Jon Favreau (Assistant); Greg Lauren (Aide); Ramsey Ellis (Young Bruce Wayne); Michael Scranton (Thomas Wayne); Eileen Seeley (Martha Wayne); David U. Hodges (Shooter); Jack Betts (Fisherman); Tim Jackson (Municipal Police Guard); Daniel Reichert (Ringmaster); Glory Fioramonti (Mom Grayson); Larry A. Lee (Dad Grayson); Bruce Roberts (Handsome Reporter); George Wallace (Mayor); Bob Zmuda (Electronic Store Owner); Rebecca Budig (Teenage Girl); Don "The Dragon" Wilson (Gang Leader); Sydney D. Minckler (Teen Gang Member); Gary Kasper (Pilot); Amanda Trees (Paparazzi Reporter); Andrea Fletcher (Reporter); Ria Coyne (Socialite); Jed Curtis (Chubby Businessman); William Mesnik (Bald Guy); Marga Gomez (Journalist); Kelly Vaughn (Showgirl); John Fink (Deputy).

CHRISTIAN SCIENCE MONITOR, 6/16/95, p. 12, David Sterritt

Batman is back, bringing along a new director, a new star, and a giant boatload of the same old hype.

Brandishing their bat-themed toys, T-shirts, and fast-food tie-ins, movie fans everywhere are wondering if filmmaker Joel Schumacher has steered the Batman juggernaut as capably as Tim

Burton, who directed the first two pictures in the series. They wonder whether handsome Val Kilmer can portray the Caped Crusader as seductively as moody Michael Keaton, another series veteran who decided to sit this one out.

The answer to both questions is clear before "Batman Forever" has ripped through its first few action scenes. Fueled by the critical and commercial success of its first two entries, the "Batman" series has become a perpetual-motion machine that's perfectly capable of running itself with a minimum of human intervention.

Stargazers may quibble over the relative merits of Kilmer's sweet smile vs. Keaton's limpid eyes, and auteurists may debate the visual effectiveness of Schumacher-style pyrotechnics vs. Burton-bred surrealism. At its core, though, "Batman Forever" is a corporate product with no more heart or soul than the action figures it's designed to market.

The oddball novelty of the first "Batman" and the dreamlike weirdness of "Batman Returns" have given way to ever-more-outlandish variations on a formula-driven theme. They deliver all the thrills and guffaws a Batman buff could ask for, but even fans may feel oddly unsatisfied once the commotion has faded from the screen.

Which is a pity, since "Batman Forever" makes occasional gestures toward interesting commentary on the present-day society that produces this sort of entertainment. The movie's most impressive villain, the Riddler, is a techno-wonk who's invented a new kind of television. It's designed to pipe images directly into people's heads—and to poke around inside those heads, as well, hunting for information the Riddler can use for his own gain.

This could be a cleverly chosen metaphor for pop culture's power to exploit our all-too-willing imaginations, but the joke gets exploded by the fact that "Batman Forever" isn't exactly high culture itself. The movie shows TV-watchers literally transfixed by the Riddler's insidious invention, and invites us to laugh at their stupidity, as if gawking at "Batman Forever" made us superior to all those other goons. (Thanks for the compliment, but it's hard to swallow.)

In another mildly ambitious move, the screenplay takes a whack at pop psychology, spinning a subplot about Batman's effort to dredge up repressed memories of his unhappy childhood, and suggesting that criminals like the Riddler and Two-Face were also shaped by traumatic past events.

Typically, though, the movie supplies our introspective hero with a gorgeous shrink (Nicole Kidman) who's clearly more interested in his handsome features than his troubled psyche.

But what's to complain about here? Spectacle is the main point of the movie—it's no accident that a key scene takes place at a circus—and as with the earlier pictures in the series, the best segments find Batman playing second fiddle to gimmicks, gizmos, and bad guys vastly more captivating than he is.

It's insane fun watching Jim Carrey and Tommy Lee Jones bounce off each other, even if they can't outdo Jack Nicholson as the Joker or Danny DeVito as the Penguin, their most uproarious predecessors in this wacko parade (Carrey wins the competition by a mile incidentally; maybe Jones used up his Three Stooges shtick in "Natural Born Killers" last year.)

In more subdued roles Chris O'Donnell makes a serviceable Robin and Michael Gough is still great as Alfred, the perfect butler.

Equally important are Barbara Ling's production design, making Gotham City a three-ring circus in itself, and Dennis Virkler's speed-of-light editing. Stephen Goldblatt did the dark-toned cinematography, and Elliott Goldenthal composed the atmospheric score.

Professionals all, they and other artisans have crafted "Batman Forever" into a monument of high-tech frivolity that'll keep your eyes popping, your head reeling, your spine tingling. And your mind spinning with the realization that such nonstop amazement will soon become the least amazing thing you ever saw.

LOS ANGELES TIMES, 6/16/95, Calendar/p. 1, Kenneth Turan

"Batman Forever" is not a film for the ages, but it will do for right now. If nameless dark forces compel a visit to a summer blockbuster, this loud and boisterous comic book confidential is serviceable enough to satisfy.

Did someone say loud? Jammed with massive explosions that are more jarring than exciting, "Batman" is also one of the season's noisiest efforts. If action directors took a pledge to detonate one less blast per picture and converted the money saved into a school lunch program, their core audience would be much better served.

Loudness is a drawback in the film's villains as well. Continuing an unfortunate trend that began with Jack Nicholson as the Joker in the first "Batman," the evil-doers of the moment—Tommy Lee Jones as Two-Face and Jim Carrey as the Riddler—are tirelessly over the top: This won't be a problem for the 14-year-olds in the audience, but older folks may find themselves begging for a little modulation.

Although all that noise will help draw the crowds, the surprise of this "Batman" is that the story's quiet moments (yes, it has them) are its most effective and its often neglected heroes turn out to be the most entertaining characters on screen.

To start at the top, Val Kilmer, a late-inning replacement for Michael Keaton, brings his ice-cold "Top Gun" persona to the dual role of caped crime-fighter and billionaire businessman Bruce Wayne and the fit is perfect. With steely eyes, inflectionless speech and a Zen-like calm, Kilmer is adept at both the heroic and the humorous aspects of his conflicted personality.

Just how conflicted is what Dr. Chase Meridian, a criminal psychologist specializing in multiple personalities, is keen to find out. Definitely on a roll after her performance in "To Die For" (slated to open in the fall after premiering at Cannes), Nicole Kidman brings a noticeable erotic charge to the proceedings as well as a fine sense of comic tuning.

The rapport between her and Kilmer is excellent and leads to memorable scenes of tongue-in-cheek bantering. "I read your work, insightful," he tells her, "naive but insightful." "I'm flattered," she replies. "It's not every girl who makes it onto a super-hero's night table". A later conversation, which ends with him advising her to "try firemen" if she's into men in leather, "there's less to take off," is a small jewel of ribald innuendo.

Equally effective are the scenes involving Chris O'Donnell as Dick Grayson, a circus aerialist whom tragedy turns into Robin, the caped one's comrade-in-arms. Whether it's doing martial arts moves with his laundry or breezily calling Wayne's venerable butler Alfred (Michael Gough) "Al," O'Donnell gives his character the kind of presence that is becoming this young actor's trademark.

Working as much like a circus ringmaster as a director, Joel Schumacher has brought several critical qualities to the mix, starting with much more of a pop culture sensibility and a sense of fun than Tim Burton, who directed the first two pictures, and he has a stylish visual sensibility as well.

In collaboration with production designer Barbara Ling and her crew, Schumacher has kept the series' dark and monumental look (the legacy of Frank Miller's brilliant graphic novel "Batman: The Dark Knight Returns") and, as advertised, lightened the project's overall tone. In his hands, even the kinky S&M hoods and facial ornaments the bad guys wear seem surprisingly innocent.

And, like an experienced ringmaster, Schumacher and Oscar-nominated editor Dennis Virkler ("The Hunt for Red October," "The Fugitive") excel at keeping things moving. None of the film's several elements are allowed to be on the screen for too long, which, where Two-Face and the Riddler are concerned, is certainly a good thing.

For it takes little time for this pair to become tedious. With Jones, a gifted actor with no noticeable sense of humor, the problem is simply one of miscasting. With Carrey, one of the funniest of comic performers, it's more that no one thought it was necessary to tone him down. When his character asks at one point, "Was that over the top? I can never tell," it's a sad rather than a funny moment.

Though "Batman Forever" has three credited screenwriters (Lee Batchler & Janet Scott Batchler and Akiva Goldsman, who worked with Schumacher on "The Client"), it is difficult at times to remember that it even has a plot. Basically, Two-Face and the Riddler are obsessed with accumulating money and power and eliminating Batman, while he, in addition to fending them off and fighting crime, has to decide how much he dares bring Dr. Chase and Robin into his double life. Just a typical interlude in the super-hero business.

Given its nearly $80-million budget and the accompanying need to appeal to as wide an audience as possible, the kind of mixed bag "Batman Forever" presents is inevitable. Egregious villains and excessive explosions are the trade-off for the film's more genuinely playful moments, and of the three "Batman," films, this one makes that price most worth paying.

NEW STATESMAN & SOCIETY, 7/14/95, p. 32, Jonathan Romney

Bad as it was, *The Flintstones* did have one saving grace—it wasn't afflicted by the psychologising New-Age sensibility that's creeping into Hollywood these days. We'll never know how close we might have been to seeing Fred and Barney stalk off into the petrified forest with their drums and brontosaurus bones to contact the caveman within, *Stone John* style.

It's become increasingly common for most mainstream films—particularly ones aimed at family audiences—to have a therapeutic factor built into the narrative. This can be as straightforward as having a psychiatrist character explain those underpinnings of the plot that we might have had more fun figuring out for ourselves: like the shrink in *The Mask* who lectures the shape-changing hero on masks as instruments of wish-fulfilment.

But it's more and more common for the cathartic resolution of the drama to be elaborated into extensive textbook exercises in family therapy. Family melodrama has always been an effective device for attracting parents to otherwise innocuous children's films; the narrative of estrangement and reconciliation provides a certain educational appeal, giving children a sneak preview of the burdens of adulthood.

Melodrama has now been supplemented by a more programmatic catharsis, through the language of psychotherapy. I became aware of this new film rhetoric when reading one of those books which reveal the ten key points for writing screenplays-that-sell. One of its recommendations was to give a screenplay an "embracing" ending, "embracing" being synonymous for the new three "Rs" of Hollywood screenplay—reconciliation, reunion and redemption.

The most successful therapy movie so far is *Mrs. Doubtfire*. It may have been conceived as a rollicking excuse for pantomime—dame jollity, but in the new Hollywood, laughs have to be dignified by a moral lesson and an emotional purging. By the end of the film, Robin Williams' arrested-adolescent daddy has made proper contact with his children, and learned to be a good father and mother, by strapping on comic breasts. The fact that he isn't reunited with his wife is part of Hollywood's new therapeutic realism; the film offers its viewers reassuring help in reconciling themselves to the end of the nuclear family. It's not so much a movie as a communal counselling session.

Robin Williams, of course, is Hollywood's specialist at coming to terms with the Child Within—something even a therapist needs to do (see his glutinising of Oliver Sacks in *Awakenings*). He was literally the Child Within in Spielberg's *Hook*, in which he played Peter Pan, grown up and estranged from the memory of childhood.

Now therapy gets thrown in as a commonplace. In *Batman Forever*, Batman/Bruce Wayne falls for a psychiatrist who's fascinated by his duality; she's obviously done her homework and read all those "Dark Side of the Superhero" articles inspired by the first Tim Burton *Batman*. Here, Batman—a brooding, prisoner of his adult repression—not only defeats the child-like villains, Id-ridden kids Two Face and Riddler, but comes to terms with his primal trauma, the killing of his parents. Among origin myths in the comics pantheon, this moment has something like the status of Oedipus' roadside tussle with his dad. *Batman Forever* culminates in Bruce Wayne remembering the image he came to fixate on fetishistically—a bat looming up out of the dark. And *voilà*, the emotional block is lifted.

Batman's exorcism may be a little desultory; *Casper* goes the whole clinical hog. Not content to be just another flash SFX movie for kids, *Casper* has aspirations, to heal. The pretext is the notion that ghosts are human spirits with unfinished business on earth—ie, that haven't completed their therapy before dying. Bill Pullman plays a ghost therapist, who doesn't exorcise phantoms so much as encourage them to exorcise their own phantoms. His daughter Kat is in denial over her mother's death, and Casper himself—a blob of marshmallow ectoplasm so twee he makes ET look like the Alien—suffering from prolonged babyhood, having died before reaching adolescence. By the end, everyone has benefited—Casper has learned to mourn his own family; Kat is ushered into adolescence by doing a slow dance with Casper's mortal incarnation; and Pullman has become a better father by completing his mourning for his wife, and conquering his over-protective anxiety about Kat's burgeoning sexuality.

This could have been designed expressly as a kids' film for a new generation aware of all the hitherto-unpublicised new strains of family trauma that *Oprah* has revealed to us. It can't be long before sexually abusive parents become legitimate plot commonplaces in Hollywood's children films. *Casper* is a prime example of Hollywood's current predilection for films as all-in redemptiveness packages, a ghastly refinement of its perennial fixation on the feel-good factor. Bill Forsyth's ill-fated *Being Human*, just out on video, illustrates this. The last story in this portmanteau has Robin Williams again playing a father estranged from his children. He takes them to the beach to bond, and everything is angled towards catharsis with swelling strings. But Forsyth, committed to the downbeat, rebels against it; it's clear that whatever bonding takes place, the father will go back to his isolated life. When Forsyth met the studio executives, they were outraged that a dad didn't immediately hug his kids; in order to get the film made, he wrote in a hug, as ambivalently sour as he could get away with. "The $20-million-dollar hug," as he's called it. I'd say he got away lightly.

NEW YORK, 7/10/95, p. 50, David Denby

Neither the overwhelming commercial success nor the overwhelming awfulness of *Batman Forever* should come as a surprise to anyone. Ever since Steven Spielberg's *Jaws* opened all over the country in the summer of 1975 and the audience, like complaisant angels, woke up and sang—you had to see it that first weekend or you died a little bit—the studios have been testing and learning. *Jaws* was a very good movie, but more than a few executives quickly understood that when it came to creating media frenzy, art was hardly a requirement. With *Batman Forever*, the process of transforming moviemaking into merchandising reaches its apotheosis. The picture is not only kid stuff in the worst sense of the phrase—jangled, repetitive, obvious, and emotionally empty—but quite *intentionally* all these things. The mess we see on the screen both feeds the hunger of the youngest media generation for constant stimulation and reinforces the new, alarming indifference to story logic and ordinary character development. I don't mean to be derisive about that audience: I'm talking about our children. Myself, I was exhausted after an hour of this hyperbolic nonsense.

Whatever one's misgivings about Tim Burton's work in *Batman* and *Batman Returns*, it had spirit and style, a mordant theatricality. Burton appropriated the exaggerated perspectives, the doomy colors and stiff, lurid sentiment of comic books, but he knew well enough that without spatial clarity and coherence, beauty becomes impossible. Burton let us see things: the different levels of the city, Batman gently falling through the air, the heart-stopping memory of an old catastrophe. Burton's work has a sinister, taunting elegance. The new director, Joel Schumacher (*Falling Down, The Client*), provides as many kicks as Burton, but without poetry or even ordinary continuity, Schumacher mashes things together. As I watched, I kept asking, Where *are* we? It's impossible to say. You can't tell how the different parts of Gotham City fit together, or where the heroes and villains are in relation to one another, or even where the characters are in relation to one another *within* scenes. Schumacher puts the camera right on top of the action, and during the fights, limbs whirl and bodies fly about in a wild spaghetti-toss of movement. The story is introduced in garbled spasms and indifferently developed. Batman rescues people and beats up villains, but he now seems less a hero than a fake, since nothing he does is convincing. He's not anguished any- more; he's just a gloomy avenger, a stud without sex. The hauntedness is gone. When Schumacher recapitulates the death of Batman's parents, he does it coldly, distantly, without deepening it in any way. He and screenwriters—Lee Batchler, Janet Scott Batchler, and Akiva Goldsman create villains who exist only as outre visual concepts that scream a lot. The women in the movie, including Nicole Kidman, who's supposed to be a doctor, breathe all over the men as if they had nothing better to do. In this regression from irony to square overstatement, the actors do their worst. Val Kilmer, the new Batman, must have received testosterone shots; his voice has fallen lower than a prize bull's. He mutters his lines in a trance that is meant to signify melancholia but that comes out as macho sludge. Chris O'Donnell, as Robin, survives because he projects decency in whatever he does, but Tommy Lee Jones betrays his coolly precise talent with a convulsively unfunny performance identical to the one he gave in *Natural Born Killers*. Jim Carrey's exciting performance as the Riddler is physically demonic in a way that Jack Nicholson and Danny DeVito could never be. Carrey does intricate, snaky things with his long-waisted body that evoke, of all things, the photographs of Nijinsky as the faun. But Schumacher overdraws on Carrey. The great comic seethes, taunts, and spins until he begins to seem like some ghastly showbiz creep who won't stop.

After a while, my attention went dead, and I could have been watching from the other side of the grave. Schumacher may be trying for a comic-book style, but whatever the affinity of the two forms, a movie can never be a comic book (Burton—and Warren Beatty in *Dick Tracy*—turned comic-book style into new movie styles). In a film, things keep moving; therefore, a director should stage the action intelligibly or even beautifully. Aesthetic order allows us to see things and to enjoy them. It's embarrassing to speak in these basic terms, and probably useless. Watching *Batman Forever*, I had the uncanny sensation that Schumacher had never wanted to make his movie, that he had purposely skipped a stage and gone directly to the trailer. What we see are the highlights, strung out to two hours, of a movie only alluded to.

The gimmick of cartoon and comic-book movies has now been thoroughly exhausted. There's nothing liberating, hip, or campy about *Batman Forever*. And its huge success could mean that the struggle to get children to sit through a fully developed narrative may be lost forever. Time Warner, I believe, really is depraved, though not in the sense that Senator Bob Dole meant. Warner Bros. is depraved because it wants to kill movies and replace them with sheer selling. Of course, so do all the other studios, if only they could figure out how.

NEW YORK POST, 6/16/95, p. 33, Michael Medved

Despite the participation of a new star, new director, new sidekick (Chris O'Donnell as Robin) and new villains, the most remarkable aspect of "Batman Forever" is how closely the feelings it generates resemble the experience of watching its predecessors.

That's good news for the many fans who adored the previous offerings, but bad news for cranky curmudgeons like me—since I disliked the first "Batman" and passionately hated "Batman Returns."

To be sure, this new adventure does make some attempts to provide a kinder, gentler Batman: The capable script features a more coherent plot and lightens the proceedings with frequent touches of humor. Val Kilmer is not only more physically imposing than Michael Keaton but he comes across as a much nicer guy; less the tormented existential hero, and more the shy, kind-hearted billionaire-next-door who just happens to dress up in black rubber and zoom around Gotham City at midnight.

Both Tommy Lee Jones as Two-Face and Jim Carry as The Riddler manage to duplicate Jack Nicholson's triumph in the first film, using outrageous intensity to enliven grotesque characterizations and to upstage even their own astonishing makeup.

In Jones' case, this is a notable achievement indeed, since the entire left side of his head has been horribly and convincingly disfigured to reflect the effects of an acid attack years before. As for Carry, he plays a brilliant but slighted employee of Bruce Wayne's company and gets to repeat the nerd-to-dervish transformation he portrayed so well in "The Mask"—donning yet another green mask in his Riddler guise.

Nicole Kidman, meanwhile, is a formidably glamorous asset as the police psychologist who's so obsessed with Batman that she's initially indifferent to the advances of Bruce Wayne. This unique romantic triangle (involving, after all, only two characters) gives our hero a richer, warmer love life than he's been allowed before.

Director Joel Schumacher ("Flatliners," "The Client") got his start in movies as a costume designer and art director, and the sets and costumes (including the anatomically-detailed bat suits) are as spectacular as you'd expect. In place of the expressionistic gloom favored by Tim Burton (who served this time as co-producer), Schumacher's added splashes of comic-book color to open up Gotham City with overwhelming art deco buildings and huge, fascistic sculptures—as if the Third Reich's Albert Speer had somehow redesigned 1930s Manhattan.

With its lavish resources (even squandering Drew Barrymore in a tiny, decorative part), this Rube Goldberg cinematic contraption whirs and stutters efficiently enough, but I must confess that it left me mildly depressed rather than entertained.

Part of the problem is, that brutal echoes of real-life crime—Bruce Wayne's parents (in flashback) gunned down in random violence, or Robin's family wiped out in a terrorist-style incident—co-exist uncomfortably with attempts to trivialize evil as mugging cartoon villains.

It's now harder than ever to view a chaotic, decadent, crime-ridden metropolis as a diverting, fun-filled place to spend two hours of your time: Even with somewhat brighter hues in the filmmaker's palette, Gotham City remains a claustrophobic nightmare and the phrase "Batman Forever" still sounds like a grim life sentence.

NEWSDAY, 6/16/95, Part II/p. B2, Jack Mathews

Riddle me this, Bat fan. What was dark is light, what was hip is flip, what was old is new, what was one is two. What am I, and will you still love me; tomorrow?

The answer to the riddle, of course, is "Batman Forever," Joel Schumacher's playful addition to the "Batman" movie series, and given its gloriously over-drawn sets, a brand new wardrobe of mesomorphic Bat suits, the introduction of the feisty sidekick Robin, and the inspired casting of Jim Carrey as the Riddler, what's not to love?

Serious fans of the forebodingly dark Batman books and movies may be put off by the strained campiness of the third episode, but for those of us who never quite understood the appeal of a humorless billionaire who identifies with bats and nurtures a conquering hero complex, the irreverence is welcomed.

That is not to say Schumacher has made a better movie. Tim Burton, who directed the first two films, is a brilliant visual stylist, and those first two films were extraordinary for their design and atmosphere. Schumacher ("The Client," "Falling Down") is a solid craftsman, and "Batman Forever" is certainly no embarrassment to the series. But there is a noticeable drop in the quality of the images. The least you expect from a superhero fantasy, with a price tag of $80 million, is to be dazzled by the illusions, and that rarely happens.

Still, this is a more entertaining episode, featuring a new and improved Batman. Val Kilmer, who took over for a disgruntled Michael ("This role is not big enough for me!") Keaton, is a taller and more imposing figure, especially in bat suits that appear to have been molded from the form of Mr. Universe, and—note the irony—this is the most time we have yet spent with the character. Both sides of him.

Bruce Wayne-Batman is still brooding over the double-murder of his parents that we learned about in the first film, and his nightmares are compounded by his chance encounter with Dick Grayson-Robin (Chris O'Donnell), a trapeze artist whose parents suffered the same fate. Plus, he's being constantly reminded of his troubled psyche by the luscious psychologist Chase Meridian (Nicole Kidman), a multiple personality expert too in love with both Batman and Bruce Wayne to notice they're the same guy.

Beyond the romance, Batman has to deal with Two-Face (Tommy Lee Jones), a former DA determined to avenge the acid bath he claims Batman gave him, and the Riddler, a demented scientist who has invented a machine that allows him to drain off the collective brain power of Gotham. It takes half the movie for the Riddler and Two-Face to join forces, and for Batman to accept Robin as his partner, and the rest is non-stop action.

The movie ends with the image of Batman and Robin, capes billowing, running directly at the camera, promising a full partnership in the event of a "Batman 4," and we can only hope. Kilmer, with equal measures of cool and vulnerability, and O'Donnell, playing Robin as an irrepressible daredevil, are a terrific team. And I wouldn't mind seeing Chase Meridian return as Mrs. Batman, which is left a possibility. Kidman is a knock-out.

Most of the talk, however, will be over the performances of Jim Carrey and Tommy Lee Jones, both so over-the-top, they can give you a headache. Carrey can get away with over-acting. That's what he does! And his physical humor is perfectly suited to his crazed character.

Jones, however, is not a natural clown, and it's painful watching him try to hold the screen with Carrey. Two-Face is essentially a sight gag, a guy who dresses his deformed half in gawdy decadence and his normal half in spiffy business attire, and it's not a strong enough sight gag to warrant all the jokey riffs done on it, and it leaves Jones with nothing to do but wail about what a cruel, cruel world it is. For actors and villains.

NEWSWEEK, 6/26/95, p. 54, Jack Kroll

In the summer movie sweepstakes "Batman Forever" is a sure blockbuster. And the presence of Jim Carrey is bound to add a few blocks: Holy Catching a Star at the Pivotal Nanosecond of his Popularity! But this third installment may not find as much favor with Batulectuals as the previous two, which were saturated with director Tim Burton's own surreal, brooding sensibility.

New director Joel Schumacher ("The Client," "Falling Down") had a mission to lighten up the series. Well, he has and he hasn't.

The movie (script credit to Lee Batchler & Janet Scott Batchler and Akiva Goldsman) does have somewhat more lilt and levity, much of it due to Carrey as the Riddler. But there's still plenty of murk, physical and metaphysical, and more psychobabble about Bruce Wayne's obsessions and repressions. The new hero, Val Kilmer, is younger, sexier, less cerebral than Michael Keaton but lacks Keaton's undercurrent of complexity. When this Batman meets up with Nicole Kidman as brilliant, gorgeous psychologist Chase Meridian, the two banter like sparring libidos. HE: You trying to get under my cape? SHE: A girl can't live by psychoses alone. HE: It's the car. Chicks love the car. SHE (*inspecting Batsuit*): Mmmmmmm, black rubber.

This is fun, but it's no big change: there was similar byplay between Keaton and Michelle Pfeiffer's Catwoman in "Batman Returns." The new film brings in Robin, Batman's original sidekick. This Batyouth, whose presence in the comics generated heavy-handed comment about homosexual fantasy, didn't appear in the first two movies. Is it too cynical to speculate that he's been disinterred with the increasingly coveted gay audience in mind? Chris O'Donnell as Robin sports a close-cropped head, long sideburns and an earring. Chew on that, you pop-culture iconographers!

It's Batman's evil adversaries that are crucial, and here the movie badly lets down Tommy Lee Jones as Two-Face, the acid-scarred archfiend. Unlike Jack Nicholson's Joker in the first "Batman," Jones has little to do but cackle insanely and endlessly flip a coin, his method for determining his victims' fate. Too much cackle-and-flip gets awfully wearing. Carrey's Riddler is another story. This character effloresces from computer nerd to baroque superwacko, out to revenge himself for billionaire Wayne's refusal to fund his machine that manipulates people's brain waves. Carrey gets full range for his ability to turn psychopathology into a manic ballet. His high-tech mad scientist cavorts like a nut Nijinsky and twirls his cane like a cheerleader from hell.

"Batman Forever" needs the radioactive Carrey; much of the film is heavy and clunky. Batman's hand-to-hand combats take place in muffling darkness; you can barely see the kung or the fu. In his rooftop flights you get a murky leap, a whooshing fall and a closeup of a hook clanking onto something. John Dykstra's special effects are grandiloquent without being thrilling. The design elements are more successful. Barbara Ling's Gotham City is a kitsch fantasia of actual New York, evoking a lost utopian vision that peaked in the 1939 World's Fair. Bob Ringwood has sexed up the Batsuit, Schwarzeneggering the musculature, adding nipples; there's even a close-up of a black-clad tush.

Burton's Batflicks were flawed visions, but they were visions, using comics conventions to express contemporary chaos and anxiety. "Batman Forever" is slicker, more domesticated. Dr. Meridian may have seduced Bruce Wayne right out of superheroism: "I choose to be cured," he tells her. This is a scary prospect. Can Bruce be Batman without his neuroses? Can there be a feel-good Dark Knight, clobbering evil with the smile of a well-integrated personality? Stay batty, Bruce.

SIGHT AND SOUND, 8/95, p. 40, Manohla Dargis

Harvey Two-Face, a former District Attorney, had one side of his face disfigured by a courtroom mishap and blames Batman. Two-Face tosses a security guard out of a skyscraper window in Gotham City, but Batman thwarts this attempt to trap him.

Batman is the alter ego of Bruce Wayne, owner of Wayne Enterprises, which employs a scientist named Edward Nygma. Wayne is approached by Nygma to consider a device that hijacks human brain waves and channels them into the mind of the device's wearer. Wayne rejects the invention as inhumane. Clandestinely, Nygma tests the machine on his reluctant manager and accidentally upends his own sanity. He returns home, a place plastered with photos of Bruce Wayne, and resolves to exact revenge on his former employer.

Wayne meets and falls for a beautiful criminal psychologist, Dr Chase Meridian, whose main pursuit is Batman, Meridian accompanies Wayne to a glittering circus event. A family of aerialists, the Graysons, are entertaining the crowd when Two-Face arrives, threatening to blow up the circus. Wayne fights the thugs, and the Graysons join in. Two-Face causes three of the Graysons to fall to their deaths. The remaining member, Dick, removes the bomb. He is put under Wayne's guardianship. The young aerialist bonds with Wayne's faithful butler, Alfred, and soon stumbles into the Batcave. After a clandestine spin in the Batmobile, Dick confronts Wayne and insists they become partners. Wayne/Batman refuses.

Nygma assumes a super-criminal identity as the Riddler and approaches Two-Face with a plan to uncover Batman's identity. As E. Nygma, an urbane entrepreneur closely modelled on Wayne, he sells a version of his device to thousands of customers. Among the invited guests at his launch party for the device are Wayne and Meridian, The Riddler's scheme is to submit each guest to his invention and from their brain waves determine who is Batman, Two-Face grows impatient with the scheme, however, and brings in the heavy artillery, only to be scuppered by Batman with Dick's help.

The Riddler figures out that Wayne is Batman. With Two-Face, he invades Wayne's mansion, destroys the Batcave and kidnaps Meridian. Grayson adopts the identity of Robin and Batman agrees that they become partners. The two home in on the villains and save the day.

Director Joel Schumacher—auteur of such disposable classics as *The Lost Boys* and *Flatliners*—doesn't traffic in the same grim whimsy as Tim Burton, the original visionary behind this popular franchise, but when it comes to camp values his *Batman Forever* far exceeds the first and second instalments. It's a fusion of old-school Hollywood spectaculars, Kenneth Anger-inflected fetishism, and all the hardware studio money can buy.

A pouty Val Kilmer plays the billionaire depressive who undergoes a radical personality change once he slips on his form-enhancing rubber suit (one version features nipples that virtually snap to attention). Less opaque than Michael Keaton, his predecessor in the role, Kilmer essays a more sensual and benevolent creature of the night, his lips occasionally curling into an actual smile. Yet, although more accessible, Kilmer's Batman is no more distinct a character. He is still closer to a smudged sketch than bone and gristle.

This decidedly prettier Batman is in keeping with a general mellowing. The second movie,—directed, like the first, by Burton—frightened away profitable product tie-in deals; somehow the whip-wielding Catwoman, psychotic Penguin, and too dark knight didn't fit tidily enough on hamburger wrappers. Enter Schumacher, a talent for hire who's never dived too deep, even in his Dystopia Lite fantasy of Los Angeles, *Falling Down*. This most unlikely of action directors (best remembered for his great witty scripts for *Car Wash* and *D.C. Cab*) steers the third Batman movie into safer, more lucrative waters. Yet he's also engineered the most gaudily camp spectacle to hit screens since *Wigstock: The Movie*.

Crammed with provocative quips and not-so-*double entendres, Batman Forever* proves how mainstream camp has become—so much so that most critics have side-stepped the issue. Maybe it's because the camp impulse has been so fully absorbed into the popular stream? Why else ignore the wisecrack about biker bars? Or the Riddler's fixation on Bruce Wayne? Or the outrageous attention to male genitalia both in costume and visual cues? When Robin first emerges in his vermilion costume, Batman not only gives him a studied looking-over, he stops to fix his gaze on his comrade's bright red package.

Given that in *Batman Forever*, the text is all about subtext, it's no surprise that no real story emerges. Batman chases Two-Face, the Riddler chases Batman, Dr Meridian chases Bruce Wayne, and so on. It's all a lot of bat-and-mouse. While tangy repartee helps to fill the cavernous void, it's really too bad that Schumacher has no feel for action. The post-production design is fabulous—neon greens and fuchsia push through the shadows, the costumes wouldn't look out of place at a Vegas cotillion, and the Riddler's secret weapon looks exactly like an enormous Deco blender—but Schumacher's *mise en scène* is as cluttered as a rummage sale, his direction as inert as a panel strip.

The one intriguing narrative glimmer in *Batman Forever* is how certain male power brokers lead very divided lives, squiring beautiful women in public (Nicole Kidman as Dr Meridian) while in private they swing with the boys—in this case a surprisingly game Chris O'Donnell as Robin, a turbo-charged Jim Carrey as the Riddler, and Tommy Lee Jones doing yet another of his psychotics. Although Jones' Two-Face is the only character whose two-dimensionality is telegraphed by his name (and his neatly cleaved face), he's not the only one endowed with a split personality. It's no wonder. After all, the story of the double life is one that Hollywood knows full well, on screen and off, confidentially or not.

TIME, 6/26/95, p. 79, Richard Corliss

Every movie, it now seems, is a sequel of every other movie. Writers pick over the carcasses of hit films and try to extract the golden elements for their own projects. Why, it's *Die Hard* in a minivan, or *Pretty Woman* but with Lassie and Beethoven, or *Terms of Endearment* only she gets the Ebola virus. It's filming by numbers—last year's box-office grosses. The uniform look and feel of recent films suggest that the mad scientists in *A Clockwork Orange* had it wrong. You don't make a viewer a zombie by force-feeding him scenes of sex and violence. You do it by making every movie a dull retread, in a Möbius strip of mediocrity.

In this dumbed-down universe, the prospect of *Batman Forever* gave some hope. The series' first two films, directed by Tim Burton, were the top summer hits of 1989 and 1992; *Batman Returns* was also a wonderful film. Joel Schumacher, director of *Forever*, hasn't Burton's creepy poetic vibes, but in *The Client* he showed real storytelling talent. He also wanted to give the series a fresh look, with a new Batman—Val Kilmer for Michael Keaton—in a new costume and car, both retooled in fine Corinthian leather. Even Gotham gets a make-over.

The only thing Schumacher and his scrupulous craftsfolk forgot to give the movie was life—the energizing spirit of wit and passion that makes scenes work and characters breathe. The script, by Lee Batchler, Janet Scott Batchler and Akiva Goldsman, settles for the stale pose of antiheroic dialogue and TV sitcom irony. Barbara Ling's sumptuous production design is mainly a reminder of better, quirkier films (*Blade Runner, The Hudsucker Proxy*). The special effects aces have created a big destruct-o-fest, with explosions all over Gotham, yet the film is pizazz deficient. A series of set pieces with no forward momentum, *Batman Forever* drags laboriously, as if the Batmobile were being towed away with the emergency brake still on. The picture leaves thick black skid marks.

The plot? Umm, we've forgotten it—probably a threat to Gotham by some bad people—but we know there was a lot of it. Lots of characters too. Robin (Chris O'Donnell) joins the series, which undercuts Batman's heroic loneliness. Nicole Kidman, as the requisite love interest, is little more than a party decoration. And two villains are too many. Tommy Lee Jones as Two-Face and Jim Carrey as the Riddler have dueling star turns, with Carrey winning, of course; he can torture the most innocent banalities, like a simple "Well, yes," into delirious comedy. At the end he's still there, potentially available for a fourth *Batman*.

And so the cycle continues. Maybe someone will bring vitality to the next film. This one just gives viewers a deeper case of the been-there, seen-that blues.

Also reviewed in:
CHICAGO TRIBUNE, 6/16/95, Friday/p. C, Michael Wilmington
NEW REPUBLIC, 7/17 & 24/95, p. 35, Stanley Kauffmann
NEW YORK TIMES, 6/16/95, p. C1, Janet Maslin
NEW YORKER, 7/10/95, p. 80, Terrence Rafferty
VARIETY, 6/19-25/95, p. 77, Lisa Nesselson
WASHINGTON POST, 6/16/95, p. F1, Hal Hinson
WASHINGTON POST, 6/16/95, Weekend/p. 45, Desson Howe

BEFORE THE RAIN

A Gramercy Pictures release of an Aim Productions/Noe Productions/Vardar Film coproduction with the participation of British Screen and the European Coproduction Fund (UK) in association with PolyGram Audiovisuel and the Ministry of Culture for the Republic of Macedonia. *Producer:* Judy Counihan, Cedomir Kolar, Sam Taylor, and Cat Villiers. *Director:* Milcho Manchevski. *Screenplay (Macedonian, Albanian and English with English subtitles):* Milcho Manchevski. *Director of Photography:* Manuel Teran. *Editor:* Nicolas Gaster. *Music:* "Anastasia," Zlatko Origjanski, Zoran Spasovski, Goran Trajkovski, and Dragan Dautovski. *Sound:* Aidan Hobbs. *Sound Editor:* Peter Baldock. *Casting:* Moni Damevski and Liora Reich. *Production Designer:* Sharon Lamofsky and David Munns. *Set Dresser:* Pance Minov and Nicole

Albert. *Special Effects:* Valentin Lozey. *Costumes:* Caroline Harris and Sue Yelland. *Make-up:* Morag Ross and Joan Hills. *Stunt Coordinator:* Parvan Parvnov and Rob Woodruff. *Running time:* 116 minutes. *MPAA Rating:* Not Rated.

CAST: Katrin Cartlidge (Anne); Rade Serbedzija (Aleksandar); Gregoire Colin (Kiril); Labina Mitevska (Zamira); Jay Villiers (Nick); Silvija Stojanovska (Hana); Phyllida Law (Anne's Mother); Josif Josifovski (Father Marko); Kiril Ristoski (Father Damjan); Petar Mircevski (Zdrave); Ljupco Bresliski (Mitre); Igor Madzirov (Stojan); Ilko Stefanovski (Bojan); Suzana Kirandziska (Neda); Katerina Kocevska (Kate); Vladimir Endrovski (Trajce); Abdurahman Salja (Zekir); Vladimir Jacev (Alija); Peter Needham (Maitre d'); Rob Woodruff (Waiter in Flight); Aleksander Mikic (Atanas); Meto Jovanoski (Dr. Saso); Cveto Mareski (Boy with Gun); Boris Delcevski (Petre); Dejan Velkov (Mate); Mladen Krstevski (Trifun); Dzemail Maksut (Kuzman); Mile Jovanovski (Priest Singing at Funeral); Milica Stojanova (Aunt Cveta); Kiril Psaltirov (Mome); Metodi Psaltirov (Tome); Blagoja Spirkovski-Dzumerko (Gang Leader); Sando Monev (Blagoj); Atila Klince (Sefer); Arben Kastrati (Ramiz); Danny Newman (Ian); Gabrielle Hamilton (Woman in Cab); Moni Damevski (George); Ljupco Todrovski (Kizo); Melissa Wilkes (Retarded Child); Joe Gould (Redhead Waiter); Goran (Himself); Nino Levi (Mailman); Lence Delova (Bossy Clerk); Jordan Vitanov (Policeman).

CHRISTIAN SCIENCE MONITOR, 3/1/95, p. 12, David Sterritt

Lands far from Hollywood are sending films to American theaters, and while the movies vary in quality—as art, as entertainment, and as statements on contemporary issues—their presence allows a refreshing change from commercial cinema as usual.

"Before the Rain" comes to American screens with film-festival credentials, having earned major prizes at the Venice filmfest a few months ago. It's in the current Academy Awards race, as Macedonia's entry for best foreign-language film. Milcho Manchevski, who directed the picture from his own screenplay, is a Macedonian native who returned there for this project after launching his career with American films and videos. Part of it was also feted in London, where its central episode takes place.

Divided into three distinct but related segments, "Before the Rain" begins with a story called "Words," set in a Macedonian monastery, where a young monk confronts disorienting new challenges when an Albanian woman is found hiding in his room. The second tale, "Faces," centers on a journalist who's caught between an interesting British husband and a Macedonian lover disturbed by accounts of violence in his homeland. The third story, "Pictures," shows his return to Macedonia, where ethnic strife leads to a tragic climax.

The fragmentation of "Before the Rain" echoes the fragmentation of Macedonia itself, a tense area of the unstable Balkan region. This metaphorical use of narrative structure is interesting to observe, but it doesn't go very deep in terms of analysis or insight. And unfortunately the film never progresses much beyond this level.

To be sure, Manchevski arrives at some clever ideas in tying all three stories together, and some of the acting—most vividly that of Rade Serbedzija as the combat photographer who returns to his Macedonian village—is reasonably forceful.

But most of the characters are two-dimensional embodiments of commonplace attitudes, and few of the narrative developments gather much momentum.

The movie's overall impact is no more memorable than its last plot maneuver, a heavily symbolic rainfall that we've been waiting for since the opening credits. It's sincere but simplistic, stirring less emotion than the picture's important subject deserves.

CINEASTE, Vol. XXI No. 3, p. 44, Andrew Horton

Inside an ancient Orthodox monastery covered with elaborate pre-Renaissance frescoes of biblical scenes, a simple Mass is in progress attended by a small group of monks. Outside in a stunning mountain landscape under a sky that threatens rain, young boys play war with two turtles, calling them "ninja turtles," as they cast real bullets into a burning circle of sticks they have set up. From inside the monastery again, the thunder of exploding bullets sounds like the shooting they have all been afraid would start in their once-peaceful corner of the Balkans.

This seemingly incongruous clash of ancient and contemporary, spiritual and extremely physical, humorous and deadly serious, radiates throughout Milcho Manchevski's debut feature, *Before the Rain*. This British, French, and Macedonian coproduction, despite its shortcomings, is a stunning first film. Nominated for a 1994 Oscar as Best Foreign Film, it is, by far, the most important movie to appear from the war-torn Balkan republics that once constituted Yugoslavia since the current war began in 1991. Moreover, it is a film worthy of discussion as a 'border crossing' text that negotiates both the demands of commercial cinema and a cinema of personal vision.

Before the Rain is centered in the newly established republic of Macedonia, which used to be part of the former Yugoslavia. It is difficult to imagine a more beautiful and yet more conflict-torn area of the world, beginning with its name. The United Nations recognizes it as "the former Yugoslavian Republic of Macedonia" pending an agreement with neighboring states, particularly Greece, regarding borders. The Greeks, on the other hand, object to the state being called Macedonia without a qualifying adjective, such as "Slavic" or "Northern," as the name might otherwise imply designs on the Greek province of Macedonia. Political leaders in Macedonia, in fact, have stated that large parts of Bulgaria and Greece are unredeemed homelands.

The potential for a Bosnia-like situation is real. The population of some two million is comprised of from fifty to seventy percent Orthodox Slavs who want to call themselves Macedonians, twenty to thirty percent Albanians who are Moslem, and ten to twenty-five percent Serbs, Gypsies, Greeks, Vlachs, Bulgarians, and Turks of varied religious and linguistic preferences. Just how large each group is remains a matter of dispute since there is no reliable census. In some places the minorities are clustered but more often the villages are mixed like raisins in a cookie. Further complicating the ethnic mix is that there are secessionist tendencies among Albanian Macedonians to make common cause with Albanians in Kosovo and possibly fuse with Albania proper.

Clearly, few film critics in this country or elsewhere could be expected to be knowledgeable about these and numerous other political realities out of which Manchevski's film has grown. Manchevski appears aware of this difficulty, since he has stated the tale is, and is not, a story from Macedonia. When examining *Before the Rain*, therefore, we should consider the 'universal' and 'Western' influences on his film as well as the distinctly 'Balkan' aspects.

As Manchevski has explained (see interview in this issue), he did not set out to make a docudrama, shot in a realistic or *cinéma-vérité* style, reflecting the current Yugoslav war. *Before the Rain* takes a very different route. In its highly stylized cinematography, its haunting musical soundtrack (mixing lyrical elements of Macedonian music with more contemporary strands), its circular narrative, its careful cultivation of telling thematic and symbolic motifs (headed, naturally, by the sense of impending 'rain'), and in its doubling of moments throughout the tale (including the mirage-like appearance and disappearance of women to male protagonists), the film transports us into its own world. In concept and structure, *Before the Rain* owes an immediate debt, as Manchevski acknowledges, to Aleksandar Petrovic's 1965 Yugoslav film, *Three (Tri)*. Viewing death during World War II from three perspectives—persecutor, victim, and savior—Petrovic distanced his tales stylistically from any conventional 'war film' (especially Yugoslav partisan film) formulas so that we focus on the more universal implications of each narrative.

Manchevski has done much the same. But, unlike Petrovic, who was exploring a war that had ended twenty years before, Manchevski has shaped a film about a war which currently surrounds his native Macedonia, but which has yet to burst full force upon the hauntingly beautiful landscape.

No simple description of this triptych narrative—divided into sections labeled "Words," "Faces," and "Pictures"—can do justice to the complexity of his tale. For Western audiences, however, the film is accessible as an unusual and intense love story between two very different couples. The first tale explores the innocent love of a young monk, Kiril (played with striking simplicity by Gregoire Colin, the star of Agnieska Holland's *Olivier, Olivier*), for a shorn-headed young Albanian village girl, Zamira (Labina Mitevska), accused of being a "whore." At the end of this segment, she loses her life when she runs after Kiril to join him, not caring that her relatives have warned her not to go to him. She dies for love ("He loves me," she tells her angry grandfather before being shot) and, more particularly, for a young Macedonian monk who is presumably a virgin and who had not spoken for two years as part of a religious vow of silence.

The second love story, and part two of the narrative, is set in London and follows the relationship between an unhappily married English photo editor, Anne (Katrin Cartlidge), and a Pulitzer Prize winning Macedonian photographer, Aleksandar (Rade Serbedzija). This, too, ends tragically as Anne's husband is randomly shot to death in a bizarre London restaurant murder spree, while Anne is delivering three messages to him—she is pregnant with their child, she wants a divorce, and she still loves him.

Part three, though second in terms of chronology, 'wraps' the tale by intertwining both romances. Aleksandar's death is the direct result of his love for an old flame, an Albanian woman who happens to be Zamira's mother, while he, we learn early in the film, is Kiril's uncle.

"The circle is not round," we are told throughout the film, underlining both theme and structure. But while such a nonchronological approach immediately brings *Pulp Fiction* to mind, in Manchevski's hands the effects are byzantine and Balkan more than they are postmodern. While Manchevski has been quick to say that this tale could happen in many other places (in part two, Aleksandar catalogs world disaster areas ranging from Northern Ireland to Somalia), the evocation of the byzantine Balkan reality in the opening section (the monastery) suggests much of that culture which is so little studied and even less understood in the West. *Before the Rain* thus draws upon Manchevski's familiarity with his native land as well as his personal vision of the tale he wishes to tell.

We can now enter the realm of the political. Jean-Luc Godard once said that it is not important to make political films. It is more important to make films politically. Films that quite clearly announce their political agenda, such as Costa Gavras's Z (1969), are 'political.' But Godard is speaking about something less direct in filmmaking: the act of constructing a film so that it engages the audience in a dialog about issues raised in the film without 'preaching' a simple doctrine or course of action to the audience. On this level, *Before the Rain* emerges as a film made politically.

Manchevski refuses easy answers or even a clear sense of cause and effect in his film. Yet some patterns become clear. The deaths we witness in the Macedonian sections (parts one and three) are caused by Albanians shooting Albanians and by Orthodox Macedonians shooting one of their own. Thus, on one level, Manchevski has turned the focus of the conflict away from ethnic hatred and, as in Greek tragedy, has implied that the ultimate violence is that between family members.

Finally, the concept that "The circle is not round" suggests that all is not futile, on a personal, cultural, or political level. If the circle were round, the seemingly senseless cycle of violence, prejudice, fear, and hatred born of centuries of strife, would be endless. But Manchevski's film is about individuals who 'take sides' and do so, in each case, "against war," as Anne comments in part two. The potential for change still exists despite the heavy sense of tragedy evoked within the narrative(s). The long discussions that I have observed viewers engaged in after the three screenings I have attended, further suggest that, in Godard's deepest meaning of 'political,' Manchevski has succeeded in making viewers go beyond his 'beautiful cinematography' to seriously engage the tough issues raised by the film.

The elegance of his film, which a number of critics have singled out, seems to be a fascinating combination of Manchevski's American and Balkan influences. A graduate of an American film school with years of successful work for MTV and commercials, Manchevski has learned his craft well in terms of how to create compelling images combined with powerful music and how to create a sense of urgency in each scene. These are all skills, of course, we particularly associate with classical American cinema. Nevertheless, in terms of subject matter, location, and dislocation of traditional narrative modes, Manchevski also draws on other non-Hollywood traditions.

The film has some rough edges, to be sure. Despite the intellectual and emotional 'logic' in the nonlinear narrative presented, too many unanswered questions and unsolved riddles persist. The result is that many viewers are left more confused than provoked. Likewise, the numerous 'borrowings' from other films call so much attention to themselves that they at times threaten to derail the focus and unity of the film's narrative. Clear allusions are made to the work of Sergei Eisenstein, Andrei Tarkovsky, John Ford, and George Roy Hill (as Aleksandar rides a bike around his native village, he whistles the tune to "Raindrops Keep Falling On My Head," much in the style of Paul Newman's bicycle ride during the same song in *Butch Cassidy and the Sundance Kid*.

Perhaps surprisingly to many, *Before the Rain* has been one of the most critically acclaimed films—American or foreign—to date in 1995, including rave reviews from *Entertainment Weekly* and Siskel & Ebert. Some critics of the film, however, feel that Manchevski has at times unnecessarily reduced, for more simplistic artistic effects, areas of political and ethnic turmoil which do have specific and coherent claims. The character of Aleksandar, the bearded, soul-suffering photographer who says he "has killed," feels too much like the stereotype of the tortured artist. Such critics have also argued that Manchevski appears more interested in the esthetics of politics and suffering than in offering any 'hope' or solution to the crisis in Macedonia. There is substance to such criticism, but we should remember that this is a debut film made by someone who has been away from his homeland for over ten years.

In part, such criticisms reflect the particular political persuasions of each critic. What is ultimately more important in *Before the Rain* is that Manchevski manages to go beyond the Evening News and CNN to spotlight the fact that hatred and intolerance themselves are the most dangerous viruses of our times—as the recent Oklahoma City bombing and the renewed Croatian-Serbian fighting make clear. And this, for a young director in a first film, is an accomplishment worth noting.

LOS ANGELES TIMES, 2/24/95, Calendar/p. 1, Peter Rainer

The ancient beauty of the Macedonian landscape in "Before the Rain" is a heartbreaking contrast to the violence within its borders. The expanses—the pure, limitless vistas and star-clustered night skies—are like fairy-tale enclosures for a tale of fratricidal horror. Even though the film deals with the current Balkan crises the landscape keeps drawing you back in time. The ongoing wars, we are made to feel, are as ancient as the terrain.

Writer-director Milcho Manchevski is astute in letting the landscape figure so massively in his movie. It gives "Before the Rain" a gravity beyond the scope of his script, which is often weighted down with obvious eye-for-an-eye ironies. Manchevski, who was born in Macedonia but has spent most of his professional career working in America on rock videos, has a swift, hokey sense of melodrama and a memory bank crammed with bits from old movies. "Before the Rain"—which is one of the five films nominated this year for a best foreign Oscar—is not an example of untutored amateur folk art. It's a slick piece of work redeemed by a sense of outrage that keeps heating up the shiny, gliding imagery.

The film is divided into three parts. In the first, "Words," Kiril (Gregoire Colin), a Greek Orthodox monk who has taken a vow of silence, shelters an Albanian girl (Labina Mitevska) in a 12th-Century monastery. When a band of armed Macedonian revengers come looking for her—she is supposed to have killed their brother—Kiril, smitten, takes off with her. They run into her Albanian clan, who, literally, have their own ax to grind.

In "Faces," the second part, the scene shifts abruptly to London, where Anne (Katrin Cartlidge) who works in a photo agency, is pulled between her conflicting feelings for her estranged husband—a doting, dour Brit (Jay Villiers)—and her lover, Aleksandar (Rade Serbedzija), a Pulitzer Prize-winning photographer who is disgusted by his recent tour of duty in Serbia and wants to return home after 16 years to Macedonia.

Aleksandar returns to his family in Part III, "Pictures," in which the story, in a roundabout piece of experimentalism, comes full circle. Aleksandar wants to drop out of the horrors he's witnessed—and recorded—but he finds his native village inflamed with the same horror. Families split apart from within. The Christian villagers and their Muslim Albanian neighbors skirmish and shoot each other. In the film's best scene, Aleksandar walks into the Albanian settlement to visit an old girlfriend. The entire sequence has a hair-trigger volatility.

Manchevski isn't fatalistic, exactly, but it's clear he's condemning the people of both sides for the troubles, and not the politicians or the U.N. "peacekeepers." Besides, the war's lines of demarcation can no longer be contained. The violence in Macedonia erupts into a London restaurant. "Before the Rain" is about the *interconnectedness* of the horror.

The movie has such a rich subject that Manchevski's slickness sometimes seems like a cheapening. The Macedonians, especially in the first part, speak in a kind of elevated pseudo-biblical dialect that makes them seem like stentorian waxworks. Although the culture shock of seeing these brigands wearing Adidas sneakers and listening to rap is real, Manchevski overplays his hand. Would Aleksandar, tootling around on a bicycle back home, really sing out loud "Raindrops Keep Falling on My Head," mimicking the sequence with Paul Newman in "Butch Cassidy and the Sundance Kid"?

Rade Serbedzija is a powerful presence—he played to great acclaim Oedipus Rex and Richard III on the Yugoslavian stage—but his role here is romanticized and hero-worshippy. He's like Rick in "Casablanca," only with a lot more facial hair. The camera dotes on moody fatalism, while swoony women garland his torso with kisses and he takes deep drags on his cigarette. (As a demonstration of the depths of his anguish, he starts smoking again when he returns home.) Aleksandar has seen too much of war and, by the end of the movie, we've seen too much of Aleksandar.

But the tragic conflict in which he figures remains in the memory. How could it not?

NEW STATESMAN & SOCIETY, 8/11/95, p. 33, Jonathan Romney

The time you feel most churlish as a film critic is when you're reviewing political films. One way or another, they're always found wanting. If a film about a political issue or current affair or, to put it more loosely, the *real*, tackles its subject head on, then it seems guilty of naive faith in cinema's ability to describe the real, and by describing, to intervene in it. And invariably you end up unpicking that naiveté as a form of cynicism, and take issue with the way such films construct their version of the real by adjusting facts. Witness the impassioned but forensic debates that recently surrounded *In the Name of the Father* and *Ladybird, Ladybird.* Conversely, if a film attempts to invoke issues in a more coded form, we tend to accuse it of skirting its subject as if it dared not name it, of using it merely as atmosphere. The real ends up looking like trimming, simply a pretext for poetics.

I'm talking about fiction films, of course, because it's in fiction that we remain uncertain about film's capacity to address the real at all. Most of us, willy-nilly, still adhere to the idea of cinema as a realist medium, but at the same time we tend to be troubled if cinema gives us more than a certain degree of the real, if it exceeds its traditional brief—which is to provide entertainment, a commodity we prefer to bracket away from reality. It's only with documentaries that we can ignore such qualms, easily forgetting that documentary is a form of fiction too.

Milcho Manchevski's *Before the Rain* is very much caught up in this anxiety about what reportage can and fiction can't do. It's the second type of film mentioned above, the sort that frustrates because it attempts to touch you through allusions and images. At the same time, as such films often do, it betrays a lack of self-confidence by opting for images that's too explicit, that too shrilly demands to be read.

Set in London and Macedonia, and officially a British-French-Macedonian co-production, *Before the Rain* is an intriguing conceit. It comes in three parts, each of which, thanks to Möbius strip chronology and recurring images, cancels out the other two. In part one, a young monk, vowed to silence, gives shelter to an Albanian girl hunted for murder. When her presence is discovered he's kicked out of the monastery, and the young pair leave together. He hopes they can find refuge with his uncle, a photographer in London, but they are soon intercepted. In part two, a London photo editor (Katrin Cartlidge) looks at photos of the monk before meeting her lover Aleksandar (Rade Serbedzija), a Macedonian photographer. A dinner with her husband is then interrupted by a mysterious gun attack. Finally, Aleksandar returns home to find his family at war with the Albanian Muslims, who used to be their friends: he defends the girl from part one and the story loops round on itself.

This paradoxical chronology owes less to *Pulp Fiction* than to Borges, or to the fabulist realism of Serbian novelist Milorad Pavic. But the poetry can be too lush to swallow. A moon straight out of *ET* hangs over a velvety sky as monks proceed across the horizon; Cartlidge is enigmatically present at a funeral in part one.

But sometimes it's too obvious, too intent on giving us a shock, to an effect that is not always clear. An early image shows children playing cruel games with bullets, fire and tortoises—*Ninja Turtles.* It's powerful, but what does it tell us—that violence is an import from western culture? That it's an affliction of modernity? Or just something innate to children, and that war is a childish pursuit?

It need not matter that such images should not be clear, except that their vagueness jars with the sense, elsewhere, that we are being told something important that needs to be understood. An old priest tells Kiril, "Time never dies. The circle is not round." What goes around comes around, I suppose, but the unevenness of the tripartite structure prevents the film from being rounded off too neatly. It's true that a film can happily accommodate different visual and discursive styles: witness Todd Haynes' playful *Poison*, a fine example of an elusive political film which encourages you to form connections for yourself.

Manchevski, however, simply gives us different levels of cliché. The most suggestive part is the first, because it largely restricts itself to visual language. Despite the bludgeoning ending and the aestheticising of the landscape, it makes a neat poetic vignette. But part three is too explicitly a bitter return: Manchevski is intent on telling us what sort of conflict is going on, what its roots are, and how hard it will be to end it. The London sequence is the worst. It seeks to demonstrate that we can never escape the consequences of war, no matter how distant it seems. But what we get is an embarrassing piece of Hampstead marital melodrama that turns into Peckinpah.

The clichés come home to roost. Aleksandar, we learn, has not only seen violence but caused it; a soldier has killed for his camera's benefit. What brings the whole edifice crashing down is the fact that he's won a Pulitzer. If it weren't for that cliché of macho integrity, Aleksandar's gruff bravado might be believable. As it is, by part three, he looks like a joke on the Hemingwayesque seeker of truth—flak-jacketed Oliver Stone extra.

It's a dead giveaway of the film's anxieties. *Before the Rain* is embarrassed by its own poetry. It wants us to feel awe at the timeless mystery of peace, but feels bound to give us photographic evidence of everything that disrupts it—a UN tank, a Coca-Cola sign, a series of photos of shootings. That's what really makes the film so hard to watch; it's fantasy wish that soft poetry could have the realistic hard currency of Pulitzer material.

NEW YORK, 3/13/95, p. 62, David Denby

Before the Rain, a film from tiny, landlocked Macedonia, has both poetic immediacy and a frightening premonitory force. Writer-director Milcho Manchevski has lived in New York for years, making commercials and music videos, but he was born in Macedonia (part of the former Yugoslavia), and this movie—his first feature—represents his dark view of the way his homeland is going. *Before the Rain* is an anguished portrait of a country on the verge of civil war. As a movie experience, however, the picture is almost completely elating. Manchevski, 35, has superb visual skills; he also has the unforced volatility that marks a natural-born director.

Manchevski tells three interconnected stories. The first and third are set in a mountain village in Macedonia, the middle one in London, and all three are seething with the Christian-Muslim hatreds that tore apart Bosnia and Herzegovina. As in *Pulp Fiction*, the stories are placed out of sequence chronologically, and the movie ends by recapitulating its beginning. What goes around comes around—in this case, violence, paranoia, and the destruction of the elementary bonds that hold communities together. In the mountain village, people one can only call moral cretins, armed for the first time in their lives, shoot off guns as if they were toys. But sane and intelligent men and women are caught up in the struggle as well. Neighbors who have gotten along for years are now at one another's throats.

The first story is set in a monastery high in the mountains, where a slender, handsome young monk (Gregoire Colin) with wide-open eyes and a trusting face—a boy happy in his piety—walks into his room and discovers a frightened girl. Shorn and bruised, she looks like a hungry animal; the two face each other silently, in the dark, each reacting to the other's tiniest movements with a start. The next morning, Christian militia from a nearby village turn up, looking for the girl: She is both a Muslim and an Albanian (there is a sizable Albanian minority in Macedonia), and they call her "whore" and insist she killed a member of their family.

Up to that point, the episode has a fairy-tale look to it: Unnaturally bright stars and a huge painted moon hang over the monastery; the monks are massively bearded, quiet, and dignified; and the boy and girl, with their odd, mutual wariness, seem like matched partners in a fable. Avoiding the militia, they are expelled from the monastery, and they walk out into the golden mountains like Adam and Eve. For a moment, we hope they are entering paradise, not leaving it, but that illusion dies quickly. In all, the surreal clarity of the night scenes and the sun-baked splendor of the day are reminiscent of the crystalline, aching purity of the images in the Taviani brothers' masterpiece *The Night of the Shooting Stars*. As in so many of the Taviani movies, extreme delicacy and the most violent brutality exist side by side.

In the London section, Anne (Katrin Cartlidge, from Mike Leigh's *Naked*), another hurt, wary woman, works in a news-photo agency; her lover is the agency's star combat photographer, Aleksandar, a Macedonian. The photographer is played by the formidable Yugoslavian actor Rade

Serbedzija, a bearded, shaggy, full-bodied man who looks like he's been around. Aleksandar has known war and violence, and he's disgusted by his own role in recording it. Serbedzija gives the character inunense sexual authority and a restless, antic humor, as if Aleksandar were past making sense of the world and wanted only to amuse himself. Returning from assignment in Bosnia, Aleksandar quits and tries to take Anne home to Macedonia with him. In a remarkable scene between these two in a taxi, Manchevski jumps from emotional peak to peak, exposing the tangled feelings of two highly complex people at a moment of crisis. The sequence leaves one exhausted. When Anne refuses to go with Aleksandar, she stumbles into violence in London. The terror is spreading everywhere.

There is another virtuoso sequence, at the beginning of the third section. Aleksandar returns home—and home, of course, is the same mountain village that the Albanian girl and the militia are from. As the globe-straddling photographer—his name is clearly meant to echo that other Macedonian's, Alexander the Great—enters the village, eager to make contact with his friends, fragments of the Balkan pathology flash before him: children with guns, ruined houses that spill their insides, stares of blank-faced hostility. Aleksandar is cavalier and flamboyant, but he also thinks he can restore rationality by evoking the roots that they all share. The villagers have their detailed, furious grievances, however, and the civilized man has nothing to offer but his own sense of how life should go. When a director allows his hero to represent his own conscience, there's always a danger of self-love, but Serbedzija is such a lionlike, charismatic actor—Kris Kristofferson with ferocious eyes—that he effortlessly carries the burden of rage and grief.

Not all the loose ends are tied up, and Manchevski indulges in a few fancy touches, but the movie is a triumph; the oddities of structure pay off. It takes us a while to realize that parts two and three take place before the first story, but by the end we sense that the skewed chronology makes a point the same device could not make in the sardonic and mocking *Pulp Fiction* that in these ethnic and religious struggles, violence is always in the air, that murder in such situations doesn't have to follow logically (as in a chronological story), that there is no beginning or end when both sides conceive of themselves as victims. *Before the Rain* is an expression of sorrow for a war that hasn't yet begun.

NEW YORK POST, 2/24/95, p. 44, Michael Medved

Rugged, passionate, lyrical, haunting and wildly, improbably poetic, "Before the Rain" is one of the most memorable motion pictures we're likely to see this year. It's also the only film from Macedonia ever nominated for an Academy Award (as Best Foreign Language Picture).

Now, if you haven't been paying close attention to the past output of the Macedonian film industry, don't blame yourself: Macedonia (formerly one of six component republics of the old Yugoslavia) has been an independent country only since 1993.

Like its bloodied Balkan neighbors, the new nation faces the prospect of wrenching ethnic violence, and that threat provides the focus for this film. As writer-director Milcho Manchevski explains his title: "'Before the Rain' refers to the feeling of heavy expectation, when the skies are pregnant with the possibility of an outburst, when the people are silent, waiting for a tragedy and cleansing."

That sense of tragedy and cleansing unfolds here in three seemingly disconnected stories.

The first tale focuses on a young monk (French star Gregoire Colin of "Olivier Olivier") in a 12th-century monastery in the mountains of Macedonia. He ultimately breaks his vow of silence to protect a mysterious, teen-aged Albanian from the heavily armed nationalist thugs who are pursuing her.

In the second story, a photo editor in London (Kartrin Cartlidge) must choose between her devoted but colorless husband and her passionate, unpredictable lover—a Pulitzer Prize-winning war photographer (Rade Serbedzija) from Macedonia.

In the final section of the film, that photographer returns home for the first time in many years and journeys to the remote, picturesque village of his childhood, where conflict between Eastern Orthodox Macedonians and their Moslem Albanian neigbors has changed life beyond recognition.

The photographer attempts to reconnect with a Moslem woman who was his first love, only to find himself forced into a dangerous mission to rescue her headstrong daughter.

The jagged pieces of this narrative puzzle finally come together with devastating impact in the last moments of the film, revealing the hidden connections that all along tied the separate stories together. Meanwhile, a wealth of breathtakingly beautiful images—highlighting the craggy, desolate, almost lunar landscape of Macedonia—carry the audience forward with hypnotic force.

The powerful Balkan-flavored musical score (by a composer identified only as "Anastasia") adds immeasurably to the dramatic impact, and will leave many viewers clamoring for the sound-track album.

Leading man Rade Serbedzija (who plays the photographer) is already well-known in the former Yugoslavia and he combines star power and dramatic subtlety to such a degree that he should become a major figure in the world's cinema.

As for writer-director Milcho Manchevski, he left Macedonia after high school and since then has been living in the United States, working on commercials, experimental shorts, and music videos. "Before the Rain" represents his astonishingly accomplished feature film debut—and a stunning step forward for the struggling Macedonian film industry.

Rather than turning out new fodder for MTV, Manchevski has answered the highest artistic calling: indelibly inscribing the drama of his faraway homeland in the collective imagination of humanity.

NEW STATESMAN & SOCIETY, 8/11/95, p. 33, Jonathan Romney

The time you feel most churlish as a film critic is when you're reviewing political films. One way or another, they're always found wanting. If a film about a political issue or current affair or, to put it more loosely, the *real*, tackles its subject head on, then it seems guilty of naive faith in cinema's ability to describe the real, and by describing, to intervene in it. And invariably you end up unpicking that naiveté as a form of cynicism, and take issue with the way such films construct their version of the real by adjusting facts. Witness the impassioned but forensic debates that recently surrounded *In the Name of the Father* and *Ladybird, Ladybird*. Conversely, if a film attempts to invoke issues in a more coded form, we tend to accuse it of skirting its subject as if it dared not name it, of using it merely as atmosphere. The real ends up looking like trimming, simply a pretext for poetics.

I'm talking about fiction films, of course, because it's in fiction that we remain uncertain about film's capacity to address the real at all. Most of us, willy-nilly, still adhere to the idea of cinema as a realist medium, but at the same time we tend to be troubled if cinema gives us more than a certain degree of the real, if it exceeds its traditional brief—which is to provide entertainment, a commodity we prefer to bracket away from reality. It's only with documentaries that we can ignore such qualms, easily forgetting that documentary is a form of fiction too.

Milcho Manchevski's *Before the Rain* is very much caught up in this anxiety about what reportage can and fiction can't do. It's the second type of film mentioned above, the sort that frustrates because it attempts to touch you through allusions and images. At the same time, as such films often do, it betrays a lack of self-confidence by opting for images that's too explicit, that too shrilly demands to be read.

Set in London and Macedonia, and officially a British-French-Macedonian co-production, *Before the Rain* is an intriguing conceit. It comes in three parts, each of which, thanks to Möbius strip chronology and recurring images, cancels out the other two. In part one, a young monk, vowed to silence, gives shelter to an Albanian girl hunted for murder. When her presence is discovered he's kicked out of the monastery, and the young pair leave together. He hopes they can find refuge with his uncle, a photographer in London, but they are soon intercepted. In part two, a London photo editor (Katrin Cartlidge) looks at photos of the monk before meeting her lover Aleksandar (Rade Serbedzija), a Macedonian photographer. A dinner with her husband is then interrupted by a mysterious gun attack. Finally, Aleksandar returns home to find his family at war with the Albanian Muslims, who used to be their friends: he defends the girl from part one and the story loops round on itself.

This paradoxical chronology owes less to *Pulp Fiction* than to Borges, or to the fabulist realism of Serbian novelist Milorad Pavic. But the poetry can be too lush to swallow. A moon straight out of *ET* hangs over a velvety sky as monks proceed across the horizon; Cartlidge is enigmatically present at a funeral in part one.

But sometimes it's too obvious, too intent on giving us a shock, to an effect that is not always clear. An early image shows children playing cruel games with bullets, fire and tortoises—*Ninja Turtles*. It's powerful, but what does it tell us—that violence is an import from western culture?

That it's an affliction of modernity? Or just something innate to children, and that war is a childish pursuit?

It need not matter that such images should not be clear, except that their vagueness jars with the sense, elsewhere, that we are being told something important that needs to be understood. An old priest tells Kiril, "Time never dies. The circle is not round." What goes around comes around, I suppose, but the unevenness of the tripartite structure prevents the film from being rounded off too neatly. It's true that a film can happily accommodate different visual and discursive styles: witness Todd Haynes' playful *Poison*, a fine example of an elusive political film which encourages you to form connections for yourself.

Manchevski, however, simply gives us different levels of cliché. The most suggestive part is the first, because it largely restricts itself to visual language. Despite the bludgeoning ending and the aestheticising of the landscape, it makes a neat poetic vignette. But part three is too explicitly a bitter return: Manchevski is intent on telling us what sort of conflict is going on, what its roots are, and how hard it will be to end it. The London sequence is the worst. It seeks to demonstrate that we can never escape the consequences of war, no matter how distant it seems. But what we get is an embarrassing piece of Hampstead marital melodrama that turns into Peckinpah.

The clichés come home to roost. Aleksandar, we learn, has not only seen violence but caused it; a soldier has killed for his camera's benefit. What brings the whole edifice crashing down is the fact that he's won a Pulitzer. If it weren't for that cliché of macho integrity, Aleksandar's gruff bravado might be believable. As it is, by part three, he looks like a joke on the Hemingwayesque seeker of truth—flak-jacketed Oliver Stone extra.

It's a dead giveaway of the film's anxieties. *Before the Rain* is embarrassed by its own poetry. It wants us to feel awe at the timeless mystery of peace, but feels bound to give us photographic evidence of everything that disrupts it—a UN tank, a Coca-Cola sign, a series of photos of shootings. That's what really makes the film so hard to watch; it's fantasy wish that soft poetry could have the realistic hard currency of Pulitzer material.

NEWSDAY, 2/24/95, Part II/p. B2, Jack Mathews

"The circle is not round," which is another way of saying history doesn't have to repeat itself, is the rercurring theme of writer-director Milcho Manchevski's Oscar-nominated "Before the Rain," a parable about ethnic hatred that explains, by example, the strife ripping apart the people of the former Yugoslavia.

The specific setting of Manchevski's story is Macedonia, where he was raised, and which is the only liberated republic of Yugoslavia not to havc begun some sort of ethnic bloodletting. But the elements are all there, and though UN troops have so far kept a lid on the tension between various factions, "Before the Rain" has the ominous feel of prophecy.

Manchevski, who went to film school in the United States and lives in New York, is asking a lot of viewers who don't have a working knowledge of the social and political history of the area. His Byzantine plot, which interconnects the lives of Macedonians, Albanians and a couple of Londoners, plays tricks with time, digresses from its own narrative, and keeps you trying to sort out who's who, where they're going, and where they've been.

It's a brilliantly intricate weave, a deliberate riddle designed to dramatize the conundrum of the imperfect circle. But once the circle is completed, the confusion seems to vanish, and you're left with a clear and profoundly sad understanding of the ways people there are allowing the past to destroy their future.

"Before the Rain" is told in three distinct parts, labeled "Words," "Faces," and "Pictures." The first story tells of the relationship between an Albanian Muslim girl (Labina Mitevska) and the Greek Orthodox monk (Gregoire Colin) who is banished from his monastery after giving her refuge from a band of armed Macedonians.

The second story makes a jolting departure from the spectacular Maccdonian hillsides to busy London, where a successful photo agent (Katrin Cartlidge) is trying to choose between two men, her solidly dependable husband (Jay Villiers) and the Macedonian freelance photographer with whom she's been having an affair.

In part three, we follow that photographer, Aleksandar (Rade Serbedzija, in a hauntingly fine performance), back to Macedonia, to his childhood village where he hopes to numb the senseless ethnic slaughter he had seen while covering the war in Bosnia. He's fed up with the brutality, and his own part in it (a soldier pulled a prisoner out of line and executed him after Aleksandar complained he wasn't getting any good photos), but there is no escape. His own family, he discovers, is at war with the neighboring Albanians—among them, his former girlfriend.

Each of these stories ends with a jolting tragedy, and only after the third one, do we learn how the events and characters are linked. On one level, the film is simply a teasing mind puzzle. But its real business is to drive home the madness and futility of ethnic hatred, and explain its apparent inevitability.

"Before the Rain" is a showcase debut for Manchevski, whose bicultural experiences are evident in the film's hybrid American-Eastern European style. Shot on location in Macedonia and London, it has the look of a slick Hollywood production, yet makes no effort to shorten or simplify its complex issues. There is no good guy-bad guy motif; in fact, our confusion in sorting out the rival groups is part of the film's design. No point in taking sides. Manchevski is saying, because the Muslim-Christian conflict in the former Balkan States is ancient tribalism, not contemporary politics.

Manchevski isn't providing any answers, or much hope. He's just peeling away the layers of international propaganda to get at the core of a problem that will never be resolved through diplomacy. It is only after everyone has become as fed up with a warring life-style as Alekssandar that the old wounds will finally heal.

Until then, the circle is round.

SIGHT AND SOUND, 5/95, p. 38, Lizzie Francke

'Words'—Macedonia. Kiril, a young monk, shelters Zamira, a young Albanian Muslim girl who is on the run from a bandit gang headed by Mitre. Mitre and his men turn up at the monastery and, unable to find Zamira, they set up camp outside. When Kiril and Zamira, now lovers, escape, they run into her family who force her to stay with them, dismissing Kiril. Zamira tries to follow him but is shot down by her brother.

'Faces'—London. Anne, a picture editor at a photo agency, is told she is pregnant. She must now decide whether to return to her estranged husband, Nick, or leave him for her lover, Aleksandar, a Pulitzer prize-winning photographer who left his native Macedonia years ago. Aleksandar has decided to return home and wants her to accompany him. She hesitates and he leaves without her. Anne meets Nick at a restaurant to tell him about the pregnancy and ask for a divorce. A dispute between a foreign visitor (possibly Macedonian) and a waiter ends with the visitor being thrown out but, moments later, he returns and guns down staff and guests. Anne survives but finds Nick dead amongst the debris.

'Pictures'—Macedonia. Aleksandar arrives in his old village. First to greet him is one of Mitre's young brigands. Anne tries to contact him by phone from London. Aleksandar visits his childhood sweetheart, Hana, a Muslim. For this he is treated with contempt by the Christian villagers. When one of Aleksandar's cousins is found murdered, they kidnap Hana's daughter Zamira. Hana visits Aleksandar in the night and pleads with him to protect Zamira. He intervenes in the dispute, but escorting Zamira away, is shot dead by one of his cousins. Anne arrives just in time to witness his murder. Zamira flees towards the local monastery.

A triptych of stories that fold into one another, *Before the Rain*'s manifest theme is "the vicious circle of violence". In part one, 'Words', there is a glimpse of Anne as she arrives to witness the shooting of Aleksander. In part two, 'Faces', she examines a photograph that intimates the same event.

Manchevski (here making his feature debut) is clearly interested in such elliptical and fragmentary moments, but his imagery suggests a more obvious approach. In the Orthodox Monastery's church the camera lingers on medieval paintings depicting atrocities, emphasising that there has always been bloodlust in the name of religion. In the 'Faces' section, radio bulletins report a bomb explosion in Oxford Street as a preface to the restaurant massacre, ensuring that the audience understands that violence is never far away, even in peaceful countries.

This London section is a rusty link in the chain, as if Manchevski arrived in Britain only to have his creative judgement affected by the general malaise afflicting many recent British films. Dialogue is stilted, characterisation and acting unconvincing—even the crisp and alluring visual style that marks the Macedonian sequences is absent. London cannot offer the honey-gold colours of the Macedonian landscape, but more might have been made of the city's grey and rainy texture than monotonous indifference.

The crude contrast between the two locations heightens the impression of Macedonia as a faraway mythical place—a glossy postcard landscape with peasants wielding Uzis rather than riding donkeys. If pictorial otherworldliness was Manchevski's intention, then it is at odds with the film's implicit foregrounding of the exoticising process. In making the central character a war photographer, Manchevski begs familiar questions about the way images of war are aestheticised and the reporter's complicity in that process. Yet Aleksandar, with his long grey locks and nonchalant swagger, is presented as a daredevil romantic hero, whose machobravado echoes that of his war-mongering cousins. Thus a shorthand debate never develops beyond a few perfunctory jottings.

Written all over the film (whether or not the director is aware of it) is a revealing essay on gender and war. There is a certain instability around the women characters: they appear as phantoms in the dreams of both Kiril and Aleksandar. Anne is a spectral witness to the carnage in London and Macedonia—her white dress just waiting to be stained red. Zamira appears and disappears with catlike stealth; she is accused of killing a shepherd while he was tending his sheep—a very feline crime. Called "slut" and "whore" by the male members of her family, she is also accused of starting the conflict. What then, do we make of a particularly explosive moment when a cat is shot to pieces? In a film full of loaded symbolism, this is perhaps the most telling image of all.

TIME, 3/20/95, p. 71, Richard Schickel

In an ancient hilltop monastery in Macedonia, a young monk named Kiril (Gregoire Colin of *Olivier, Olivier*) finds a frightened girl (Labina Mitevska) hiding in his cell. She is, we learn, the victim of ethnic hatred, and once her enemies track her down, the peace of this retreat is violently, permanently shattered.

In a London restaurant Anne (Katrin Cartlidge of *Naked*) and her estranged husband meet to discuss their problems. Their conversation is interrupted by a loud argument between a waiter and a customer. The customer leaves, then returns and sprays the room with shots, killing the husband, among others.

A famous photographer, Aleksandar (played by a fine actor of the former Yugoslavia, Rade Serbedzija), who has become famous and burned-out taking pictures of war and its victims, returns to his native Macedonian village seeking peace. What he finds instead are Christians and Muslims feuding bitterly. He is at last caught in the kind of deadly cross fire he had managed to elude elsewhere.

These lives and deaths are ultimately linked in writer-director Milcho Manchevski's intricately structured *Before the Rain*, an Academy Award nominee for Best Foreign Film. Anne and Aleksandar are lovers—that is why her marriage is in trouble—while the refugee hiding in the monastery is the daughter of Aleksandar's former lover. Even when the connections between characters are not that intimate, they sometimes know one another by sight, because commerce and communications keep shrinking the world. War zones nowadays have area codes, and the vision of a terrorist with a Kalashnikov in one hand and a cellular phone in the other, talking to some faraway co-conspirator (or maybe his mother), is not farfetched. Manchevski makes this point almost surrealistically: his peasant gunmen go about their bloody business clad in Nikes and other American-made sports gear.

But wardrobe merely hints at a larger linkage that Manchevski, a young Macedonian filmmaker who somehow ended up at Southern Illinois University and moved on to music videos, wants to make. It is put simply by a doctor who is a minor character in his film: "War is a virus," meaning that, in an era of ethnic and religious conflict, the disease can be carried everywhere by impassioned terrorists and can infect anyone—in this case the young priest, the isolated Anne (who works as a photo editor, coolly studying images of violence) or even the seemingly well-inoculated Aleksandar, who has seen and recorded most of the horrors of our time yet remains physically unscathed.

Telling his story in three movements (*Words, Faces* and *Pictures*), Manchevski deliberately blurs group identities. You have to strain to understand what ideals the people in this film are willing to die for (and, more to the point, kill for). One's idea of God as opposed to another's?

The heritage of one's blood as opposed to that of someone else's? As we lean in to catch their garbled, often hysterical self-justifications, we also catch a larger point—that none of these principles is worth a single human life.

It can be argued that when the blame for tragedies like those afflicting the former Yugoslavia is generalized, or attributed to cosmic forces, individuals who may be guilty of terrible crimes escape just condemnation.

But even if Manchevski is eliding this point, his eerily beautiful film constantly reminds us that there is an irresistible fascination, an absurd and terrible beauty, in the violence of our times. Properly framed—aestheticized—by someone like Aleksandar (or Manchevski), meaningless death can be transformed into "meaningful" art, imprinting a nanosecond of hollow pity and empty terror on busy, distant lives. Maybe it's just a viral side effect, but the irony is stunning. And in its allusive, elliptical way, so is this movie.

VILLAGE VOICE, 1/28/95, p. 63, J. Hoberman

The collapse of European Communism, it would seem, augured the period of pre-Millennial wonders. Mashing its nose against the original Bon Marché window, last week's Russian release, *Window to Paris*, burlesqued the impossible desire for a magical road from post-Soviet underdevelopment hell to late-Capitalist consumer heaven. *Window to Paris* prays for Paradise Now; the so-called End of History weighs a bit more heavily on Milcho Manchevski's slick and brooding *Before the Rain*.

The first feature made in the newly independent (and for the moment still peaceable) post--Yugoslavian state of Macedonia, *Before the Rain* seemingly came out of nowhere to win the Golden Lion at last September's Venice Film Festival. In fact, the 35-year-old, Macedonian-born, American-educated, New York-based Manchevski is a well-established director of music videos and TV commercials, and *Before the Rain* is a solemnly accomplished movie with high-gloss production values. Designated pull quote: exotic yet reassuring, (The cast is international and nearly a third of the minimal dialogue is spoken in English.)

Moving from the ruins of the former Yugoslavia to the capital of the old British empire and back again, the movie's quasi-circular narrative loops pleasingly over and around itself. In the first of its three discrete sections, titled "Words," a young Macedonian monk, Kiril (Gregoire Colin, the returned son in Agnieszka Holland's *Olivier, Olivier*), who has taken a vow of silence, finds an Albanian Muslim girl, perhaps a terrorist, hiding in his room. As the film makes repeatedly clear, there are no sanctuaries. The postcard-picturesque monastery is invaded by Macedonian nationalists and Kiril is expelled.

The film's central section, "Faces," provides a shock cut from the ancient Macedonian hills to the London studio of a fashionable, abundantly concerned art director, Anne (Katrin Cartlidge, who played *Naked*'s masochistic punkette). Her work table is cluttered with Balkan atrocity pictures. Nor is this the only trace of former Yugoslavia embedded in her life. Anne discovers she's pregnant by the Pulitzer Prize-winning Macedonian war photographer Aleksandar—a shaggy, stereotypically morose, wild and crazy old goat (Rade Serbedzija).

In the movie's final third, "Pictures," Aleksandar returns to his childhood village—discovering that the house is a complete wreck and the town a near war zone policed by gun-toting teenagers of various nationalities. A madman artist in England, Aleksandar is a confused tourist here. Despite the ethnic tensions, he crosses over into the Albanian quarter to visit an old flame, with mixed results—defeated, despite his best intentions, by the lethal provincialism he presumably fled.

Before the Rain's mystical global ambience, in which each episode includes a brief—not always corporeal—visitation from one of the others, suggests the rise of Oscar-nominee Krysztof Kieslowski as the model post-Communist. East European filmmaker. But unlike the sardonic Pole, humorless Manchevski (also nominated) earnestly wants us to Bosnify our perceptions. *Before the Rain*'s most horrific incident is pointedly set in a chic London restaurant where inexplicable Balkan nationalists grandly expand their dispute to encompass a room full of oblivious, champagne-swilling diners, some at cusp moments in their lives. The scene is powerfully absurd, if not exactly laughable. (What's sobering is the inadvertent reminder of Western cine-nihilism—the situation would be the comic highlight of a Quentin Tarantino film.)

Portentous, borderline lugubrious, *Before the Rain* is at once effectively coarse and disconcertingly glamorous. Manchevski's magic realism is largely apolitical. Still, this is a film of charged atmospherics and spooky, cumulative effects. A new specter is haunting Europe—the specter of tribalism.

Also reviewed in:
CHICAGO TRIBUNE, 3/10/95, Friday/p. G1, Michael Wilmington
NEW REPUBLIC, 3/27/95, p. 28, Stanley Kauffmann
NEW YORK TIMES, 2/24/95, p. C3, Janet Maslin
NEW YORKER, 3/13/95, p. 109, Anthony Lane
VARIETY, 9/12-18/94, p. 43, Deborah Young
WASHINGTON POST, 3/10/95, p. C7, Rita Kempley
WASHINGTON POST, 3/10/95, Weekend/p. 36, Desson Howe

BEFORE SUNRISE

A Castle Rock Entertainment release of a Detour Film production in association with F.I.L.M.H.A.U.S., Wien. *Executive Producer:* John Sloss. *Producer:* Anne Walker-McBay. *Director:* Richard Linklater. *Screenplay:* Richard Linklater and Kim Krizan. *Director of Photography:* Lee Daniel. *Editor:* Sandra Adair. *Music:* Arlene Fishbach. *Sound:* Thomas Szabolcs. *Sound Editor:* Tom Hammond. *Casting:* Judy Henderson and Alycia Aumuller. *Production Designer:* Florian Reichmann. *Costumes:* Florentina Welley. *Make-up:* Karen Dunst. *Running time:* 100 minutes. *MPAA Rating:* R.

CAST: Ethan Hawke (Jesse); Julie Delpy (Celine); Andrea Eckert (Wife on Train); Hanno Pöschl (Husband on Train); Karl Bruckschwaiger and Tex Rubinowitz (Guys on Bridge); Erni Mangold (Palm Reader); Dominik Castell (Street Poet); Haymon Maria Buttinger (Bartender); Harold Waiglein (Guitarist in Club); Bilge Jeschim (Belly Dancer); Kurti (Percussionist); Barbara Klebel and Wolfgang Staribacher (Musicians on Boat); Wolfgang Glüxam (Harpsicord Player).

CHRISTIAN SCIENCE MONITOR, 1/27/95, p. 14, David Sterritt

"Before Sunrise" marks an interesting new step for Richard Linklater, a young filmmaker with a lot of talent and an admirable desire to avoid the usual youth-movie formulas.

His first two pictures, "Slacker" and "Dazed and Confused," were offbeat visits to the world of adolescence. The characters of "Before Sunrise" are a little older and wiser, and equally important—as is Linklater himself.

He hasn't yet reached full maturity as an artist, and there are moments in the new movie when he strains to grow up in a hurry, decking the story with highbrow touches that seem more showy than profound. But it's refreshing to find a young filmmaker who wants to be highbrow in the first place, and who possesses the boldness to do his growing up in public.

Each of Linklater's previous pictures focuses on a large group of characters, following their interactions over the course of a single day. "Slacker" is the more innovative of the two, constantly moving from one narrative line to another in a sort of cinematic relay race. "Dazed and Confused" harks back to the "American Graffiti" tradition, showing how a bustling crowd of teenagers relate to one another at a period of transition in their lives.

"Before Sunrise" keeps the compact time structure Linklater favors—very proper and classical, recalling ancient Greek drama—but drastically cuts the number of people with significant roles in the story.

There are only two: Jesse, an American about to return home after a European sojourn, and Celine, a French student he meets by chance on a train. They strike up a conversation, discover many interests and feelings in common, and decide to spend a day and night wandering through Vienna before Jesse boards his plane to cross the Atlantic.

This being a movie, it goes without saying that they fall more goofily in love with every passing hour. What's surprising about the picture is the extravagant amount of time it spends on the long meandering conversations that preoccupy the romantic couple.

There's nothing deep about their ideas, their emotions, or their use of language—this is Linklater territory, not Eric Rohmer or Jean-Luc Godard—but there's nothing cheap or cheesy here, either.

The youngsters discuss love, death, and other Big Issues of the human condition, as well as their hopes, dreams, and experiences. We listen with alternating interest, boredom, and affection. Then their day is over, and there's nothing left to learn except whether they'll decide to meet again and turn their brief infatuation into a long-term commitment.

As this description indicates, "Before Sunrise" is both modest and ambitious—modest in its minimalist plot and short list of characters, yet ambitious in its willingness to stretch these into the stuff of a full-length film.

What attracts me most about the movie is the importance it gives to the act of sharing one's life through language, at a time when most filmmakers are less interested in words than in whatever slam-bang action they can dream up. "Before Sunrise" isn't an intellectual movie, but it's a literate one, and that's cause for celebration even when the screenplay falls short of its aspirations and slides into mere talkiness.

Many key ingredients of "Before Sunrise" clearly stem from Linklater's wish to make the movie appealing beyond the teen audience he courted in his earlier work. Setting the tale mostly in Vienna, punctuating it with classical music, giving Jesse and Celine college educations and a taste for books—all these decisions announce Linklater's determination to seem adult and sophisticated, although his maneuvers would work better if they weren't so numerous and conspicuous.

Moviegoers who enjoy European cinema will also spot a wide range of film-related references. One is the heroine's name, which pays tribute to Jacques Rivette's great "Celine and Julie Go Boating" as well as Louis-Ferdinand Celine, the controversial French author. Another is an episode that salutes Michelangelo Antonioni's classic "Eclipse" by revisiting various locations of the story after the characters have departed from them.

Nods to Robert Bresson's expressive "Four Nights of a Dreamer" appear to be present, too, and it's possible the title refers to F.W. Murnau's silent masterpiece "Sunrise," about an unhappy couple whose marriage heals when they spend a day in the city. There's nothing wrong with allusions like these, but one can't help feeling they diminish the film by calling attention to far greater achievements.

Ethan Hawke and Julie Delpy are ideal choices to play the young lovers, and the small supporting cast does well with the minor characters who wander into the story now and then—most memorably a pair of amateur Austrian actors who have a brief chat with Jesse and Celine, in a scene suggesting that "Slacker"-style cameos are still what Linklater does best.

Kim Krizan co-wrote the screenplay, and Lee Daniel did the fine-looking cinematography.

LOS ANGELES TIMES, 1/27/95, Calendar/p. 6, Peter Rainer

Ethan Hawke and Julie Delpy are in practically every frame of "Before Sunrise," so it's a good thing they're so engaging.

In the end, they never become much *more* than engaging, but the characters' deeply-felt shallowness has its own youthful ardor. As Jesse and Celine, who meet on a train crossing central Europe and spend a long day and night together in Vienna before separating—she to Paris, he to America—the actors play out a string of feints and gambits and mini-seductions.

Director Richard Linklater, who co-wrote the script with Kim Krizan, understands how these two vagabonds are consumed, pleasurably, by self-consciousness. He captures the tentative thrill of chance encounters.

There's nothing much to the movie, except for the amiability of the actors and the layers of feeling Linklater provides, but that's just almost enough. Superficially "Before Sunrise" resembles a Sandra Dee/Tab Hunter-style vehicle—two swoony lovebirds backdropped by a beautiful city.

But Linklater is trying for a winsome, melancholy mood, with a lit-crit twist, and he throws in references to Eric Rohmer, Antonioni, "The Third Man," and even Joyce's "Ulysses." (The entire film takes place in 24 hours, and the date the two agree to meet again is Bloomsday.) And yet the film never seems pretentious—maybe because it's so attractively aware of its own pretensions.

But Linklater, whose two previous films were "Slacker" and "Dazed and Confused," is still young enough to connect up with Jesse and Celine. He follows them around as they play off each other and, after awhile, they become less exotic, more familiar to us.

Too familiar, perhaps. Celine, alluring and shaggy-maned and oblique, resembles many of the women one sees in French films (though she smiles more than most French actresses). She's playing up her ah-sweet-mystery-of-life Frenchiness for Jesse, but she's also a companionable cipher. That's what turns Jesse on about her—she's approachable and yet illusory. And Celine is attracted to Jesse's scruffy rambunctiousness—his *American-ness*.

So "Before Sunrise" is, in some ways, a romantic comedy about the erotic appeal of nationality. But Linklater doesn't provide much context for the comedy; he doesn't really fill in the lives of Jesse and Celine, apart from their time together. There's an unreality to their confab that is both enticing (because it rings true) and annoying (because it maroons them from their social situation).

"Before Sunrise" would be better if Linklater had been more—dare I say it?—ambitious. A film-maker like Jean-Luc Godard in "Breathless" could show us a Frenchman and an American ex-patriate woman and somehow bring an entire dispossessed generation to life. Linklater opts for smaller, cozier pleasures.

"Before Sunrise" has the virtues of its limitations—it's *enjoyably* minor—but Linklater is so intuitively gifted that the film looks like a classy form of slumming. It's an attempt to make a mainstream youth movie with a bit more feeling and mysteriousness than most, and, in this, it succeeds. But what price success?

NEW YORK, 2/6/95, p. 58, David Denby

The earnestness of intellectual youth—the style that's usually called sophomoric—is a very tender affair, and if you value it at all, you probably value it a great deal. In Richard Linklater's lovely romantic comedy *Before Sunrise*, a young American, Jesse (Ethan Hawke), and a French student, Celine (Julie Delpy), meet on a train and spend a night in Vienna talking about the droopy subjects—parents, boredom, love affairs, death—that self-serious young people always talk about. *Before Sunrise* is charming and often funny and sweet; this meeting of privileged soul mates has a grave delicacy, evoking Eric Rohmer at times, but with a softer, warmer American hopefulness. Linklater earlier made two goofy, intermittently inspired movies about apathetic American kids, *Slacker* and *Dazed and Confused*. But he has now passed beyond hip drollery into something less guarded and ironic. Will he pay for it? A willfully vulnerable movie like *Before Sunrise* enters our derisive culture like a dolphin plunging into a tank filled with sharks.

The beautiful and brilliant Celine at first seems too fast for Jesse; she threatens to see right through him. But Jesse hangs in there. He has a slightly scattered poetic sense of life; he's very bright but unformed, a nineties Holden Caufield, not as well educated as Celine, not as sophisticated. Luckily for him—it's the break of a lifetime—his boyishness appeals to her. Rather than continue home to Paris, she gets off the train with him in Vienna. They agree to part the next morning (broke, Jesse has a return flight home), but for a day and a night, they're in a foreign city, unable to speak to most of the natives. Sticking together becomes an adventure that could lead anywhere. They go to clubs and bars, meet the street people (and hustlers), stroll the imperial boulevards and intimate little alleys where a lone harpsichordist plays Bach or a Middle Eastern belly dancer entertains a few people. *Before Sunrise* is so pleasing, in part, because the situation is artificial and movieish (will they become lovers? will they see each other again?) yet close to something many Americans have done—spent a wandering night in a foreign city, blissfully removed from American violence and banality. Celine and Jesse say awkwardly candid things that one might have said oneself at 23. For anyone over 40, listening to them talk is an experience of nostalgia without regret. That tender moment of self-importance is a good moment to get past.

Before Sunrise doesn't have the edged playfulness and spontaneity of Godard's lyrical movies about smart sixties kids, *Band of Outsiders* and *Masculine-Feminine*. Godard was the great movie modernist, mixing tropes out of old American movies with contemporary fads in a glancingly poetic, allusive style. Linklater, who worked with the writer-actress Kim Krizan on the script, is closer to Rohmer, who is more literal and methodical than Godard. And like Rohmer, Linklater brings a gentle romantic flare to the material. The casting of the leads is surprisingly effective. Ethan Hawke has a soft touch of mustache and beard, like a suburban Galahad, and Julie Delpy, pale and slender, with golden hair, has the atavistic beauty of a princess in a tower. Too pretty and soft-featured to be typical of contemporary youth, they seem slightly out of this world, like figures in a storybook about courtly love.

Since they come from different countries, Jesse and Celine don't share the usual pop-culture references and knowingness; they *have* to talk about their feelings, their fears, and so on. The actors sustain a lilting intimacy. Hawke turns out to be a soulful, likable New York actor with a heavy burden of rue. And Delpy, born in France but educated in the United States, is here liberated from the cryogenic sleep imposed on her by the Polish director Kieslowski, who turned her into a freezing, tormenting bitch in *White*. Awakened, she becomes a vibrant and funny woman with a touch of intellectual sternness.

Such recent romantic comedies from Hollywood as *I Love Trouble, I.Q.*, and *Speechless* have left audiences cold, and that's because the movies *were* cold—mechanical retreads of formulas that no longer work. Writers and directors don't seem to realize that you can't do screwball comedy when you no longer have the social forms and manners that gave rise to those conventions in the first place. Linklater depends on artifice, too, but he knows how to redeem it. My heart sank when Jesse, desperate to make contact, asked Celine, "What was your first sexual experience?" But Linklater holds the camera on the two actors in a Viennese trolley through a long-lasting shot, and they have to work out the scene moment by moment, with all the hesitations, embarrassments, withdrawals, and tentative advances of an actual encounter. The playing is sincere enough to absolve the device of slickness. Jesse, it turns out, is a bit sheepish, intensely aware of himself as a half-equipped American trying to pick up a brainy French girl. He's got nothing to offer but his looks, his restlessness, his readiness—but then, the same is mostly true for her. Linklater is even more generous to these two than he was to the layabout potheads and solipsists in his earlier films; his young characters are all *waiting*. They haven't been pulled into careers yet; they don't have political passions or even a strong sense of rebellion, and they know that they are faintly comical.

"You have to go through the same old shit anyway," Celine says, and that's the point of the movie. Even if you have nothing to rebel against, it's still hard to become a human being and not (the eternal worry of intelligent youth) part of the machine. Hence the soulfulness, untested by experience—soulfulness that, in this case, is a form of grace.

NEW YORK POST, 1/27/95, p. 52, Michael Medved

A greasy-haired American traveler with a leather jacket and a goatee meets a gorgeous French girl on the train. She's supposed to ride on to Paris (where she's studying at the Sorbonne), but he persuades her to get off with him in Vienna so they can wander the picturesque streets till dawn the next morning, when he'll catch the plane taking him back to the States.

It sounds like a shallow adolescent fantasy—or, at least, a Grunge Generation version of "An Affair to Remember"—but cult director Richard Linklater ("Slacker," "Dazed and Confused") manages to confound all expectations.

In contrast to his much-discussed (and somewhat overrated) previous films, which presented an abundance of characters in slick, smug sketches, he here lavishes artistry and intelligence on portraying just two people in remarkable depth. As a result, "Before Sunrise" becomes one of the most audacious and moving cinematic romances of recent years.

Much of the credit goes to the two supremely talented leads, Ethan Hawke and Julie Delpy.

Hawke plays basically the same sulky-poet part he played in "Reality Bites," but this time the script gives him enough intellectual substance so that his moodiness seems endearing rather than affected.

Delpy, the 23-year-old actress previously best known for her roles in "Europa Europa" and "White," projects the sort of warmth and vulnerability that make her spectacular beauty more accessible than intimidating.

Both performers handle their rambling, non-stop conversation with a maximum of freshness and energy; smart talk fills the movie, and it's fascinating for its own sake, in addition to the way it reveals the quickly evolving relationship between the characters.

They manage to discuss just about all the big subjects in the course of their 14 hours together, covering death and sex and faith and fate and Georges Seurat and fortune tellers and Quaker weddings; at times, the movie feels like "My Dinner With Andre" with a poignant romantic edge.

Even the most quotable lines ("Sometimes I think feminism was really invented by men so they could fool around more") emerge with such natural flair that they call attention to the characters rather than to the clever screen writing (by Linklater in collaboration with actress and belly dancer Kim Krizan).

Besides Delpy and Hawke, the only other notable character in the film is the city of Vienna, displayed in all its splendor, and captured with the character and conviction that Hollywood usually lacks in its air-brushed, glossy views of European grandeur.

The plot poses only two significant questions: will the two characters make love to each other before he leaves, and will they resolve to see each other again? Both questions receive somewhat unexpected answers, creating an ending that is both achingly ambiguous but profoundly satisfying.

In short, there's every reason to see this movie, and even an incentive to recommend it to your friends.

If enough people see "Before Sunrise" it's possible Linklater could be persuaded to do a sequel, and these are characters you care about so deeply that it's only natural to want to see them again.

NEWSDAY, 1/27/95, Part II/p. B2, Jack Mathews

A young American man and a young French woman are strangers on a train, bound from Budapest to Paris. Celine (Julie Delpy) is on her way home from a visit with her grandmother; Jesse (Ethan Hawke) is going to get off in Vienna and fly back to the United States from there in the morning.

They meet, they talk, they click. They get off the train together in Vienna and spend the entire night walking the streets, talking, eating, talking, holding hands, talking, making love, talking, talking, talking. It's as if they were auditioning for one of those talkathons, by French director Eric Rohmer.

But "Before Sunrise" is an American movie made by a Texan named Richard Linklater, and for unhurried romantics who appreciate the seductive nature of communications, and have the patience for a movie with more continuous dialogue than C-SPAN, it's the sweet surprise of the young year. Linklater, who set his first two films—"Slacker" and "Dazed and Confused"—in Austin, Texas, where he lives, has dramatically expanded his world view in "Before Sunrise," without abandoning his previous themes. The 33-year-old filmmaker is fascinated by the randomness of life, the ways in which people occupying the same space either connect with or ignore each other, and by the importance we place on the moment at hand.

In the minuscule-budgeted "Slacker," we met dozens of unrelated people criss-crossing on the streets of Austin, most of them filled with ideas and nearly all devoid of direction. "Dazed and Confused" dropped us into the midst of a group of 1976 high school students trying to make the most of a time they know they'll look back on with exaggerated fondness.

The characters in "Before Sunrise" are full of ideas, too, and they are driven by whims of the moment. And all three films are set within a 24-hour time period. But Linklater's focus is far sharper here, and his tone less cynical. He's telling a common romantic adventure story, one that most people who've traveled alone have either experienced or fantasized.

When Jesse pitches his night-in-Vienna idea to Celine, he asks her to look ahead 10 years, to when she's married and bored and thinking back on her missed adventures, and challenges her not to let this one get away. It's a timeless line, of course, and she knows it. She also knows he may be right and, with nothing to lose but some sleep, agrees to go along.

What follows is an amazingly authentic evolution of characters and ideas. The key to writing good screen dialogue is making unnatural conversation sound natural, and Linklater and cowriter Kim Krizan make nearly every line ring true. Whether Jesse and Celine are grilling each other about their sex lives, their childhoods, or their developing philosophies on life, it feels as if we're eavesdropping on strangers.

That is not to say their conversation is totally honest. They are two young people trying to have a relationship on what is in fact a first date, and they're on their best behavior, measuring, their words, withholding criticism, determined not to let their differences destroy the mood or the adventure.

And as the night wears on, the differences loom ever larger. Jesse is sort of a suspended adolescent, one of Linklater's slackers, and his glib patter often descends into airhead crap.

Hawke plays the character with great charm, but it isn't hard to understand why the old girlfriend Jesse came to Europe to see has found other interests.

Celine is another matter. She's both more spiritual and more grounded than Jesse, and there is more light in the upstairs windows. And Delpy, an actress who just seems to exude intelligence and good humor, makes her all the more adorable.

You watch this relationship develop with the same anxiety you'd have in their situation. The objective for both Jesse and Celine is to construct a pleasant memory, but it's a fragile task. Do they kiss? Do they make love? Do they vow to see each other again? Those simple quandaries provide all the emotional action, and with gorgeous, historical Vienna as a backdrop, the answers build a memory we can all take home.

NEWSWEEK, 2/6/95, p. 58, Jeff Giles

Jesse (Ethan Hawke) is an American headed to Vienna, and Celine (Julie Delpy) is a French student bound for Paris. Don't hate them because they're beautiful. In Richard Linklater's luminous little romance, *Before Sunrise*, the pair bond in the lounge car on a train from Budapest. Then, in a come-on of surpassing sweetness, Jesse begs Celine to come check out Vienna, where he has a night to kill before flying home. ("If I turn out to be some kind of psycho, you can get on the next train.") So Jesse and Celine stroll around Vienna, playing pinball, kissing on that Ferris wheel from "The Third Man" and exchanging deep and semideep thoughts about sex, death and cable-access TV. You'd think this wouldn't add up to much. But Hawke, who does a sunny variation on the armchair philosopher he played in "Reality Bites," has a great unwashed charm, and Delpy is just magnificent: she's gorgeous, she's moody and she swears in two languages. Late at night, Jesse and Celine lie in the grass and wonder if they'll ever meet again. It's a nice scene—unapologetically tender and not encased in all that god-awful Gen-X irony.

Linklater, who co-wrote "Sunrise" with Kim Krizan, debuted with the independent movie "Slacker." Since then, he's made deals with big studios, but he remains a conscientious objector, refusing to kowtow to Hollywood's idea of dramatic tension. "Sunrise" is an audaciously talky movie, and it plays out in something approximating real time. We go to the movies to escape real time, of course. But that may be this movie's true contribution: that it picks up the ordinary moment, dusts it off and hands it back to you.

SIGHT AND SOUND, 4/95, p. 39, John Wrathall

Jesse, a young American travelling round Europe, and Céline, a French student, fall into conversation on the train between Budapest and Vienna. When the train reaches Vienna, Jesse, who is getting off there to catch a flight back to America the following morning, persuades Céline to come with him so they can continue talking while wandering about the city.

On a bridge, they briefly encounter two Austrian actors who invite them to a play about a cow. On a tram, Jesse suggests a question and answer session so that he and Céline can learn more about each other. In a record shop, Céline plays Jesse a folk record in the listening booth. They visit the Friedhof der Namenlosen, where bodies washed up on the banks of the Danube are buried. Riding on the Ferris Wheel in the Prater amusement park at sunset, they kiss. At an outdoor cafe, Céline has her palm read by an old woman, but Jesse is sceptical about her predictions. Walking by the river, they are stopped by a homeless man who writes a poem for them in return for money.

At a nightclub, they discuss previous relationships over a game of pinball. In another cafe, they play a role-playing game, each pretending to ring up their best friend so that they can discuss their feelings about the other. On a restaurant boat on the Danube they agree not to meet again in the future: they will just enjoy this one night together. At another bar, Jesse, out of money, persuades the barman to give them a bottle of wine; they drink it in the park under the full moon.

Céline tells Jesse she doesn't want to have sex with him now that they are never going to see each other again. At dawn, they hear a man playing the harpsichord and dance in the street. They realise that they forgot to go to the play. As Céline is about to catch her train, they decide to meet at the same place in six months' time. Jesse gets the bus to the airport. Céline, sitting alone on the train, falls asleep.

Like Whit Stillman's *Barcelona, Before Sunrise* was backed by Castle Rock, and the two films also share their basic premise: young Americans broaden their minds through encounters with European women in European cities. In fact, the preppy American overheard in *Before Sunrise* complaining about the decadence of European culture as exemplified by poor service in cafés could have strayed in from a Stillman film. On a more general level, though, the two films seem to symbolise a return to European cinema amongst a new generation of American film-makers (Linklater joins Hal Hartley, *Little Odessa's* James Gray, and at least in terms of his ongoing Godard fixation, Quentin Tarantino).

With its young lovers who talk at length about whether they'll go to bed together, but never actually do, *Before Sunrise* recalls Eric Rohmer, while naming the two characters Céline and Jesse is surely a nod to Jacques Rivette. By Rohmer's standards, Céline and Jesse's marathon conversation may lack philosophical rigour, but it does touch upon a comprehensive range of half-baked twentysomething concerns of the 90s. On the subject of reincarnation, for instance, Jesse wonders how there are enough souls to go round if there are more people alive now than ever before. Meanwhile Céline, the daughter of a 1968 radical turned successful architect, worries that the media are trying to control our minds, and thinks feminism was invented by men so they could sleep around more.

Ideas like these could have come straight out of *Slacker*, but the humour in *Before Sunrise* is much less wild and flaky; working with a co-writer, Kim Krizan (who acted in both *Slacker* and *Dazed and Confused*), Linklater has risen to the challenge of creating whole characters rather than walk-on mouthpieces for wacky opinions. With a cast of two as opposed to the large, free-wheeling ensembles of his first two films—and classical music on the soundtrack—instead of grunge or 70s oldies—*Before Sunrise* clearly marks a conscious departure for the director. Yet his underlying interests remain the same; when Jesse first meets Céline on the train, he tells her his idea for a programme for cable access television—a year-long series of 365 24-hour real-time video diaries of ordinary people. What he wants to capture, he explains, is "the poetry of everyday life". Later he finds a soulmate in the riverside poet who offers to write a poem for them using any word they choose—who even manages to make something of Céline's suggestion, "milkshake".

This is where the film's charm lies, in the balance Linklater strikes between poetry and the everyday. The *Brief Encounter* scenario and some of the situations (the first kiss on the Ferris wheel, drinking wine in the park under a full moon) may be conventionally romantic, but his lovers are refreshingly cynical about love (which, for Jesse, is just "an escape for two people who don't know how to be alone"). Perhaps uniquely for an American film, *Before Sunrise* is about people who are attracted to each other's minds rather than simply by looks or that elusive movie concept, "chemistry". As with Rivette's *Céline and Julie Go Boating*, there's also a sense that Céline and Jesse exist to fuel each other's imaginary lives. Linklater's interest in alternative realities, brilliantly encapsulated by the speech he delivers himself in *Slacker*, is echoed when Jesse first persuades Céline to get off the train, arguing that it will save her from looking back wistfully on missed opportunities in 20 years' time when her marriage has grown boring. Later in the evening they return to the subject of what they would both be doing if Céline hadn't got off the train (a reminder, perhaps, of Kieslowski's *Blind Chance*, which presents three alternative lives for the hero depending on whether or not he catches a train), while the final shot, of Céline falling asleep on the train, raises the possibility that she may have dreamed the whole thing.

In a conversation piece such as this, much inevitably depends on the actors, and Ethan Hawke and Julie Delpy both respond to the looseness of Linklater's approach with their most engaging performances to date. Hawke's reactions are very subtle—his expressions in the record shop booth, when Céline subjects him to a fey folk song by Kath Bloom, encapsulate the feelings of a thousand boyfriends forced to listen to their girlfriends' Tracey Thorn albums. The often po-faced Delpy, meanwhile, reveals a relaxed comic touch, particularly when imitating the California dude Jesse pretends to ring up.

Despite the considerable charm of the actors, however, *Before Sunrise* ultimately stretches itself a little too thin. It's disappointing that the characters never interact with the city; Vienna—like Austin, Texas—certainly has a thriving cafe culture, but beyond that any other European capital would have done as well. With no conflict to keep Céline and Jesse apart beyond their own whimsical decision never to meet again, the conversation/walk/conversation format does get repetitive. But that only makes the film that much more convincing as an evocation of the first, tentative steps in any relationship, and of the aimless wandering in European cities that is now a youthful rite of passage for the English and American middle classes.

TIME, 1/30/95, p. 88, Richard Corliss

Can anything be more annoying than the prattle of an insensitive guy trying to impress a woman? Yes: the prattle of a *sensitive* guy. Surely you've overheard this banter in parks and restaurants. The fellow pontificates on the mystery of love, quotes from the Lake poets, shares the most fragile intimacies. And lurking inside his earnestness is this tacit question: "So—now that I've proved what a refined soul I am—can we have sex?"

In Richard Linklater's *Before Sunrise*, two young people meet on a train, strike up a conversation and, for the rest of the movie, never stop talking. Jesse (Ethan Hawke) is American, Celine (Julie Delpy) is French, and the setting is Vienna on a sweet June night. But the chat is universal. Jesse and Celine while, and wile, away the night declaiming every cool thing they ever heard, every reeeeeally deep notion that ever crossed their minds. He: "Love is the escape for two people who don't know how to be alone." She: "If there's a God in the world, it's not in you, or me, but in the space in between … in trying to connect." He: "Everyone's been having this conversation forever." She: "And nobody's come up with the answer."

Neither has Linklater. His *Slacker* and *Dazed and Confused* had huge casts, rambling narratives and a notion of film as a grab bag of blasé attitude and barroom philosophizing. It's all very '90s. *Before Sunrise*, on the other hand, seems instantly dated. This two-character talkfest, a kind of Eric Rohmer meets Harry meets Sally, wins points for daring to be a love story—how defiantly unhip is that?—and is presumably meant as sensitivity training for 20-year-olds, But in reaching for winsome charm, the film falls flat. This meeting of bright minds often plays like desperate showing-off.

Still, it may have some future utility. In olden days, as a token of his romantic seriousness, a gent used to give his lady a copy of Kahlil Gibran's profoundly woozy *The Prophet*. Perhaps the gift of a videocassette of *Before Sunrise* will offer a similar opportunity for '90s fellows too clever to announce that they're on the make.

VILLAGE VOICE, 1/31/95, p. 50, Georgia Brown

Richard Linklater's ploy, his sly grace, is in underdevelopment—suppressing individuality and accenting the generic and generational until they become the essence of cool. In *Before Sunrise*, his sweet, sentimental journey to the end of the night, Linklater might as well—as he did literally in *Slacker*—cut the heads off his protagonists. Call them A Girl and A Boy.

American boy, French girl: Jesse (Ethan Hawke) meet Celine (Julie Delpy). With his wispy, faux-grown-up goatee and slightly piggy eyes, Jesse comes off as the original dumb American—no language to speak of, or with. To make him comfortable, the beautiful, blond Celine immediately rips off her veil of Gallic *profondeur* by speaking his language.

The two meet on a train gliding toward Vienna. (Even the pace of the train and the landscape, the gentle hills and dales and lazy rivers, spell out Linklater's avoidance of drama.) Across the aisle from the girl, who's pretending to read, a middle-aged couple starts up a quarrel in abrasive German. The fight isn't translated, presumably because it merely evokes couples closeted too long—i.e., parents. (So far in his work, Linklater has relegated people with jobs and "responsibilities" to a shadowy background.) It's the last thing the girl wants to be near, so she moves, taking a place across from the quiet young man with a book of his own. They compare props: her edition of Bataille's *Mme. Edwarda* versus the most repulsive actor's autobiography ever written, Klaus Kinski's. Such fancy reading matter is close to being the movie's last quirky or offbeat detail.

Since *Before Sunrise* turns out to be a twentysomething *An Affair to Remember*, it's interesting that men in both pictures use a grandmother as bait. Here, Jesse describes a childhood vision of his granny's spirit (in a garden hose's rainbow), and Celine is moved to disembark with him in Vienna. He's catching a plane home in the morning and has no money left for a hotel, which leaves them one night to wander a strange city and bare their souls.

In the baroque and sinister city where Freud charted the underside and the evil Harry Lime dissolved into the sewers, the couple's perfectly banal conversation begins. Parodying the therapeutic interview, Jesse invites Celine to recall her "first sexual feelings for another person." She answers something about a boy in school. Here, Linklater's technique is less free association (*Slacker*'s cunning *ronde*) than simple interruption. No train of thought that can't be broken; everything broached, nothing pursued. *Slacker* hippety-hopped from speaker to speaker; *Sunrise* stays with the same couple while their conversation flits from subject to subject.

(Let's have no comparisons with Rohmer where the dialogue really does matter. Here, you could dub in wholly different dialogue, yet still have essentially the same movie.)

Typical of the movie's quiet charm is a scene where the two crowd into a record store's tiny listening booth. The camera trains on Jesse's face as he alternately steals looks at Celine and then looks away so she can look. For Celine's inspection, he nervously composes a series of expressions—concentration, private amusement, faraway, dreamy detachment.

First dates offer new life. It's this familiar, reasonable hope that our personalities will be appreciated when seen by a stranger that Linklater catches so beautifully. And when the self feels trust and support, the outside world conspires to bless it. Each chance encounter—with a palm reader, a poet, a bartender—reinforces the sense of magic. In a harsh light—easily supplied if you're not with the program—these incidents look silly, or at best, mundane. (At the end, Linklater lets that harsh morning sun shine in.) An early encounter with a pair of Viennese slackers is by far the film's funniest bit. A way of seeing this: Linklater includes these clowns to show what sort of Jarmusch-type comedy he could've made if he'd wanted to.

The film's attitude toward Jesse in particular may seem more tender than the character deserves. Or perhaps Linklater and cowriter Kim Krizan haven't given Hawke enough intelligence. This all-accepting, wide-net strategy may account for some wildly disparate views of *Before Sunrise*. Two twentyish young men accompanying me to a screening hated the movie (one to the point of contempt), adding that they could imagine "girls" going crazy for it. True to form, a colleague's 15-year-old daughter loved it. Older adults like me may be more tolerant of the shallow presentation of "deep" subjects. My main impression: What a wonderful *idea* for a movie!

Also reviewed in:
CHICAGO TRIBUNE, 1/27/95, Friday/p. C, Michael Wilmington
NEW YORK TIMES, 1/27/95, p. C8, Janet Maslin
NEW YORKER, 1/30/95, p. 93, Anthony Lane
VARIETY, 1/23-29/95, p. 71, Todd McCarthy
WASHINGTON POST, 1/27/95, p. C7, Hal Hinson
WASHINGTON POST, 1/27/95, Weekend/p. 36, Desson Howe

BELLE DE JOUR

A Miramax Zoë and Martin Scorsese re-release of a Paris Film Five/Five Films production. Producer: Robert Hakim and Raymond Hakim. Director: Luis Buñuel. Screenplay (French with English subtitles): Jean-Claude Carriere and Luis Buñuel. Adapted from the novel by: Joseph Kessel. Director of Photography: Sacha Vierny. Editor: Louisette Hautecoeur. Sound: Rene Longuet. Art Director: Pierre Lary. Set Designer: Robert Clavel. Costumes: Helene Nourry. Costumes (Catherine Deneuve): Yves Saint Laurent. Make-up: Janine Jarreau. Running time: 100 minutes. MPAA Rating: R.

CAST: Catherine Deneuve (Severine Serizy); Jean Sorel (Pierre Serizy); Genevieve Page (Mm. Anais); Michel Piccoli (Henri Husson); Macha Meril (Renee); Francisco Rabal (Hyppolite); Pierre Clementi (Marcel); Georges Marchal (Le Duc); Francoise Fabian (Charlotte); Marie Latour (Mathilde); Francis Blanche (M. Adolphe); Muni (Pallas); Iska Khan (Customer).

FILMS IN REVIEW, 11-12/95, p. 98, Harry Pearson Jr.

I find it ironic that not one of our major critics writing about *Belle de Jour* bothered to point out that the film element used for the re-issue prints was in such poor shape. And that it looks as if Miramax worked some technological jiggerypook on that element which creates artifacts that look suspiciously like those found on high definition video. For much of the first half of the movie, every time there is a horizontal pan, solid vertical lines break up and fragment. The colors themselves have acquired a yellowish cast not present in the original, a coloration that makes the film look cheesy: part of the cool style of *Belle* derives from the purity and coolness of director Luis Buñuel's color schemes (this was his first color film) with their alabaster whites and scarlet reds. Not so in the re-issue. And worse, the sound—evidently digitized—becomes harsh every time the conversations pass a simple forte, which they often do, given the live room acoustics Buñuel uses with particular frequency in the whorehouse scenes. One would expect Martin Scorsese to have addressed these problems in sponsoring the film's re-appearance: one could not accuse him of the kind of visual illiteracy rampant in today's debased state of film criticism. Perhaps *Belle* will look, and sound, better on laserdisc (if we're lucky and get a better element, and if Criterion's talented Maria Palazzola gets to do the transfer).

One more questionable feature of the re-issue (and I do not remember whether this was true of the original) lies in the decision to italicize the subtitles during the fantasy sequences. For the French, and for the audiences who originally saw it, there was no telling where Catherine Deneuve's fantasies began and ended, although it seems to me that today's American audiences might be more sophisticated about sadomasochistic fantasies than they were back in 1967. However, based upon the critical readings of the reissue, I would tend to doubt it, for no one seems to have either understood, or much less gotten, the point.

The movie begins, appropriately enough, with one of Deneuve's fantasies: she and her mild-mannered (young doctor) husband are out in the countryside riding, in a carriage no less, driven by two coachmen. The husband decides to punish her for being cold and sexually unresponsive. He orders the coachmen to tie her to a tree, whip, and sexually molest her. (It's clear she enjoys this and the scene is played so artificially that we know we're either seeing a good movie or a half-baked fantasy.) Back in real time, we soon enough see that the husband has not a notion in his head about what she "requires" of him. He just gets nicer and nicer, while she gets colder and colder. He is not, in a word, playing Daddy to her daughter. In the end, she will have symbolically castrated him so that he becomes sonny to her as Mother, and thus, in the final shots, the carriage drives by empty, and we know her fantasies have been fulfilled. The insight here, and how subtle and shrewd it is on Buñuel's part, is that we get even with the nice guys by punishing them if they don't abuse us in the way we require or expect.

In between, Deneuve goes to work, afternoons, in an upscale brothel, where her fantasies can be, more often than not, let out. All of this portrayed in the coolest and most aristocratic style imaginable, so the picture is never pornographic, and not even erotic. Indeed, we watch it in bemused detachment, which is the intended effect. Even when she finally, in the course of "business," meets her fantasy man, a sulky (and, by the way, quite gay looking) young gangster, we are soon enough shown his rotten teeth in such closeup that he effectively becomes de-eroticized as well. He becomes obsessed with her, but she is adamant about not leaving her husband, just as she is adamant about being at home for him evenings. The gangster Marcel, played by Pierre Clementi, shortly follows her home, since she is not at all attentive (deliberately?) about being followed. And brings matters to a most unpleasant outcome for himself and the husband, but not for Deneuve, who finally has her way with the real and unconquerable object of her fixation, her husband. And that's all there is to that.

I suppose what makes this film so fascinating to watch—at least once, or at 28-year intervals—is the contrast between the pulpy subject matter and the classically cool style with which Buñuel has told the tale. I confess I was as much interested in how my perception of it had changed from then to now as I was in the film itself—then I was fascinated by Oriental man with the "thing" in the little box and I didn't understand the ending one whit. Now, Buñuel's vision makes sense to me, perhaps because I am more acquainted with the small cruelties we inflict on the people we care deeply about (or vice versa), and the larger ones on those we love most. But, I wonder, as I do about virtually all of this director's films, do such insights a masterpiece make? Or just a most arresting curio from an offbeat corner of film history?

NEW YORK, 7/17/95, p. 48, David Denby

I'm not usually very good at remembering details from movies seen long, long ago, but for years, images and moods from *Belle de Jour*—Luis Buñuel's 1967 masterpiece, now triumphantly revived at the Paris Theater—kept appearing unbidden in my thoughts. Seeing the movie again, I quickly discovered why: *Belle de Jour* is simply and beautifully shot by a director who clears out the muck and clutter of conventional filmmaking. Buñuel never wastes a shot or chooses an unnecessary angle; he refuses to overstate or even underline an emotion; he avoids music altogether, except for the rapid, rhythmic ringing of bells, the maddening bells attached to that horse-drawn carriage that appears again and again in the erotic daydreams of the beautiful Séverine (Catherine Deneuve). Where is the carriage going? It is the vehicle of Séverine's desire. With absolute precision, and also much insolent mockery, Buñuel and his co-scenarist Jean-Claude Carriere tell the story of this Parisian *haute bourgeoise* who loves her handsome and thoughtful husband (Jean Sorel) but remains unresponsive to his rather tentative caresses. Her face a blank, Séverine lies in bed dreaming of violation at the hands of coachmen, and finally takes a job at a high-class bordello, where she makes herself available, after many hesitations, to a variety of extremely strange men. Séverine is there from only two to five in the afternoon; hence her name, Belle de Jour.

Enacted onscreen, the content of Séverine's daydreams may verge on the pornographic, but Buñuel shoots them in a style that is anything but voluptuous. Indeed, the limpid beauty of the images is extraordinarily chaste, and that is the source of the movie's wit. *Belle de Jour* is less a psychological exploration or an erotic turn-on than a triumph of surrealist mischief-making. After all, this is the same anarchist director who, in 1930, incited riots with his hilarious and orgiastic lousing up of church and family in *L'Age d'Or*. Buñuel never softened or wavered in his aesthetic contempt for the bourgeoisie. *Belle de Jour* is a chic and arrogant joke whose real malice is directed against moviegoers who demand pedestrian psychological motivations and routine narrative logic. But don't worry: Buñuel's naughty sense of play is irresistible.

Séverine exists amid fantasies, dreams, and sinister actualities, and if she doesn't always know where she is, we're not absolutely certain, either. Nor are we meant to be. The fastidious glamour of the puzzlements is infinitely suggestive, starting with the beauty of Catherine Deneuve, then 24 and literally a living doll, both in her Yves Saint Laurent clothes and in her frequent dishabille. Amazingly slender, with breasts locked into a punishingly tight brassiere, Deneuve has skin so pale it appears to have been buffed with wax. (Maybe it was the image of Catherine Deneuve working in a whorehouse that made the film so hard to forget.) Deneuve's too-perfect perfection is surely intentional, though not everyone seems to get the joke. At the film's opening in 1967, the critic at *Le Monde* wrote that "one can't believe that such bad dreams could go on inside Catherine Deneuve's pretty head," a line that quickly achieved high distinction in the pantheon of critical idiocy. Deneuve, as her deadpan performance suggests, knew what she was doing, even if the critic didn't. In Séverine's dreams, the whips leave no marks; and when mud is flung into her face, fresh makeup appears to have been applied to Deneuve's features between the shots. Though frequently violated, she is never mussed, which is precisely the point. Buñuel mixes elegantly perverse Freudian gags with mordant contempt for the self-loving prudence of the French. An actress whose beauty was less than perfect—an actress suggesting experience, like Jeanne Moreau—couldn't possibly have been as funny in the role.

What's amusing about *Belle de Jour*, becomes a lot clearer if you recall that a few years later, in 1972, Buñuel made *The Discreet Charm of the Bourgeoisie*, in which a group of wealthy and powerful men and women are repeatedly frustrated in their desire to settle down and eat dinner together. Buñuel loves making fun of the rituals through which the bourgeoisie expresses its *amour-propre*. In the bordello, Séverine falls in love, but she is not—as sentimental therapeutic critics would have it—"liberated" by her adventures. When things get a little rough, she retreats to her sumptuous apartment.

Many things have changed in the film world since 1967, and one is that feminist consciousness would now make such a scenario very difficult to film in any style. But before *Belle de Jour* itself gets pelted with mud, let me point out that Séverine doesn't want to be beaten. She tells the young gangster (Pierre Clementi) she meets at the brothel—a brutal dandy who becomes her lover—that she will walk out on him if he hits her, and there is no reason not to believe her. No, she wants to fantasize about violation, which is a very different thing (outlaw fantasy of one sort or another being all but universal). What interests Buñuel is not aberrant psychology in itself but the comic potential of masochistic fantasy controlled by bourgeois pragmatism.

Séverine may be treated with a degree of hostile objectivity, but then so is everyone else in the movie. Séverine's passive husband really is a bit of a ninny, so relentlessly considerate that he unwittingly sends Séverine back to Paris and her lover just when, at last, she's beginning to respond to him. Their friend, a cynical voluptuary played by the gloating Michel Piccoli, arrives at the bordello seeking exotic pleasures but is first heard to ask if the central heating is working well. I agree with those critics who have described *Belle de Jour* as "a comedy of manners." A famous gynecologist addressed by the whores as "Professor" demands that the props and dialogue of his perversion be arranged in exactly the same way every visit. The paraphernalia of dirty ritual is so funny for Buñuel because it is so essentially conservative.

Does Séverine "really" take part in profane rites at the chateau of a perverse duke? Over the years, much ink has been spilled over the question of which sequences are imaginary, which real, but arguing the issue too closely may be one way of letting the movie make a fool of you. In *Belle de Jour*, the different levels of representation flow together and finally merge: Buñuel shoots fantasy very plainly while turning reality into fable. The point is that Surrealism carries us to an extremity at which that particular distinction (reality versus fantasy) no longer much matters. *Belle de Jour* is not a humanist work. As psychology, it doesn't quite parse; its morality is outrageous, and the ending is both baffling and cruel. When Buñuel extends tenderness to Séverine, he does so because her most flagrantly weird dreams are so perfectly composed they make you laugh. I remembered *Belle de Jour* so clearly because the imagery is pure—stripped of junk, and also of cloying sentiment and "psychology." What remains is not only very beautiful but also about the coolest comedy ever made.

NEW YORK POST, 7/3/95, p. 26, Michael Medved

The much-heralded re-release of "Belle de Jour" serves to remind us of the excitement that used to surround new cinematic arrivals from Paris at a time when the very phrase "French movie" carried racy connotations.

This acclaimed piece of oddball erotica went out of circulation 10 years after its 1967 debut, and it's been unavailable (in any format) for the better part of two decades.

Now "Belle de Jour" is with us once again, at the Paris Theater, as a co-presentation by Martin Scorsese and the new Miramax Zoe division, which is dedicated to promoting French cinema in America.

The provocative plot derives from a 1928 novel by Joseph Kessel, as adapted by director Luis Buñuel, the Spanish surrealist whose ironic fantasies had been affronting conventional sensibilities since the 1920s.

Catherine Deneuve plays a bored doctor's wife in Paris who shares no sex life with her adoring, handsome husband (Jean Sorel). While fending off his affectionate advances, she's tormented by dreams of degradation—with her husband ordering two coachmen to rape her in punishment for unnamed crimes, or pelting her with mud and animal waste while she's tied to a post.

She's also troubled by gossip about a friend from her social circle who earns extra money at a brothel. Drawn by curiosity, Deneuve wanders into a discreet establishment and soon goes to work as Belle de Jour, ministering to a variety of eccentric patrons, but returning every afternoon · at 5 to her perfect, proper home.

Eventually, one of her regular customers, a hot-blooded hood (Pierre Clementi) with conspicuously imperfect hygiene, becomes obsessed with her and threatens to shatter the wall that has neatly divided the two halves of her double life.

This role helped catapult the then-23-year-old Deneuve to international stardom; no other actress could have projected so intriguingly the twin aspects of her role as both ice princess and whore. Even the film's most ardent admirers, however, describe this character as "enigmatic," which is another way of saying we have no real clue as to what is going on with her.

Buñuel shoots his heroine almost entirely from a distance, avoiding close-ups, and Deneuve also seems to act at arm's length from her audience—providing an alluring but aloof surface, rather than insights of emotion.

Today the film plays more like a dark comedy than a psycho-sexual shocker, as Buñuel artfully fudges the line between fantasy and reality.

It's also striking how little nudity and sexual specificity this once infamous picture displays—Deneuve is never totally naked, and the movie's controversial couplings, while vaguely suggesting all sorts of decadent excesses, never actually show anything more than kissing.

Like other cinematic classics, the picture achieves a timeless, almost other-worldly quality; its haunting scenes are no more dated than the imperishably elegant Yves Saint Laurent wardrobe that Deneuve so handsomely displays.

Sadly enough, the one aspect of the film that most inescapably identifies it as an artifact of another era is the fact that its brothel escapades unfold without a single reference (or the slightest fear) concerning sexually transmitted diseases.

NEWSDAY, 6/30/95, Part II/p. B7, Jack Mathews

When Luis Buñuel's "Belle de Jour" was released in the United States in 1968, audiences liked it more than the critics. At least, the number of people who bought tickets to it was out of proportion to the number of critics actually recommending it.

To the many reviewers who found it tawdry, the plot read like the wish list of Larry Flynt. A frigid housewife (the beautiful Catherine Deneuve) who dreams of being whipped, raped and humiliated, finds sexual gratification as a day-time hooker in a Paris brothel, a job that brings her in contact with clients with interests in feet, necrophilia, sado-masochism and whatever one Japanese gentleman was carrying around in his suitcase.

Today, "Belle de Jour" is generally acknowledged to be a classic, a visionary piece of social analysis about the unrest of a generation of women about to declare its independence. Who knew? We just went to see it because we heard it was outrageously wicked and irreverent, and a must-see for anyone wanting a front seat for the social revolution.

Seeing it 28 years later, "Belle de Jour" (it's being re-released by Miramax Films) seems both restrained and as provocative as ever. Compared to the miles of flesh and hours of simulated sex we've since seen exhibited and performed by major stars on the screen, not a lot is shown. Panties and bra for Deneuve, that's about it. Buñuel was a master of suggestion anyway, so we didn't need to see people up to no good to know they were up to it.

On the other hand, Deneuve's emotionally disconnected Severine is a character we are better able to understand now, perhaps better than Buñuel and his screenwriter Jean-Claude Carriere understood her then.

"Belle de Jour" begins and ends ambiguously, as fantasies overlap reality, intermesh and seemingly become one and the same. The narrative thread running through it is Severine's relationship with a dangerously obsessive client (Pierre Clementi) who, when she attempts to withdraw, follows her home and attempts to kill her husband (Jean Sorel).

Make of it what you will. Buñuel, working at a time when filmmakers didn't have to give everything away, gave nothing away. At its most obvious, it is a tease on bourgeois morality, and at its most suggestive, it is a glimpse into the collectively wounded psyche of women who have spent a few millenia too many serving the egos and desires of men.

Either way, the 1967 film is the most provocative one you're likely to find at a theater in the summer of '95.

VILLAGE VOICE, 7/4/95, p. 49, Georgia Brown

Is it deep or is it empty? Art or a trick on the masses? In the '60s, mystification was the cinematic rage, perfect dinner party fodder in a better dinner party age. Art house hits tantalized with dreamy enigmas. Antonioni's *L'Avventura* may be said to have kicked off this "new vague" and his *Blow Up* gave it a boost; Resnais's ravishing *Last Year at Marienbad* provided a good deal of discussion; Fellini can be said to have had a hand in the stew. The decadent rich, alienated bourgeoisie, emotionally stunted intelligentsia—these were the natural born killers of yesterday. Not that the films themselves were meretricious—a position Pauline Kael argues charmingly in "The Come-Dressed-as-the-Sick-Soul-of-Europe Parties"—it's just that they were *popular*. Buffs got pissed off.

In 1967, *Belle de Jour*'s elegant coach jingled ever so slowly down that stately lane and through the stillness of an alley of trees. Perhaps Buñuel was the last of the grand riddlers. His tongue-in chic comedy of manners centered on a beautiful, frigid married woman, Severine (Catherine Deneuve), who daydreams degradation and ravishment by coachmen, and may or may not work the afternoon shift—2 'til 5—in a homey Paris brothel ("Belle de Jour" is her *nom de travail*.) Does she or doesn't she glide through the chateau naked under a black veil? Might the whole plot—this is the radical position—take place in Severine's head? And by the way, what's inside the Japanese client's little box?

The mysterious box—containing some exotic pet or sex toy that frightens the other girls but yields bliss to our Belle de Jour—is particularly Buñuelian: paraphernalia of some exotic ritual, like the chalice and wafer, which also make an appearance here. Catholicism and Surrealism, Buñuel said, were his two great influences. The magical and the deadpan.

Before the aforementioned coach moves out of the opening frame, a modern train whistle sounds and an ordinary automobile appears in the distance. This combination of mundane and exotic is also Buñuelian. More intriguing than the grand shocks are certain well-placed, equally enigmatic, everyday details.

At some point we deduce that the coach bells signal Severine's fantasies—scenes with whips or slung dung—yet nothing in the film feels quite "normal." Severine's husband, Pierre (Jean Sorel), a handsome young doctor out of a soap, a talking Ken doll, is elaborately gentle and understanding when his wife shoos him from her bed. Pierre comes off as a figment of a stimulated wife's imagination.

Stylewise, women in *Belle de Jour* dress in the '60s' anti-hippie mode, the one popularized by Jackie K.: the bubble hairdo, Chanel-type suits, shiny patent pumps. (Shoes are particularly important to the fetishist Buñuel.) Just seeing Severine walk the boulevards in her tiny pillbox and mock-military coat is slightly hilarious. Her little beige dress has epaulets, too. An urge rises in the spectator to violate something so timid and immaculate. It's an urge Severine herself seems to feel, and one shared by a couple of her friends, Macha Meril, Godard's straying married woman, plays one; the other is an especially wooden Michel Piccoli. Piccoli's Husson is the sort of evil-oriented "gentleman" whose metier is corruption of the innocent.

Characters in *Belle de Jour* all seem semi-parodies figures out of previous fictions. The gangsters who turn up midway through are out of Melville—at least the elder one is. The younger, Marcel, played by the always weird and campy Pierre Clementi, has metal front teeth and a sword sheathed in his cane. The first time we see Marcel it's on the Champs-Elysees and someone is hawking "New York Herald Tribune"; the last time we see him he's gunned down in the middle of a side street à la *Breathless*.

I can't say that *Belle de Jour* is particularly moving or sexually stimulating. Like Deneuve herself, it's cool and neat, but it's also something of a put-on, a spoof. Buñuel succeeds in making a haunting film without greatly engaging the emotions. Martin Scorsese, who is re-releasing the film with Miramax, came up with precisely the right adjectives: "perverse, hilarious, and poetic." In a time when everything in movies is supposed to be spelled out for the nitwits among us, it's nice to find a film whispering, Hush now ... don't explain.

Also reviewed in:
CHICAGO TRIBUNE,7/14/95, Friday/p. C, Michael Wilmington
NEW YORK TIMES, 4/11/68, p. 51, Renata Adler
WASHINGTON POST, 7/14/95, p. D6, Rita Kempley

BETRAYAL

A Charon Film/Channel 4 Television/Swedish Film Institute/Swedish Television/National Film Board of Denmark/Nordic Film & TV Fund production. *Producer:* Fredrick von Krusenstjerna. *Director:* Fredrick von Krusenstjerna. *Director of Photography:* Jan Roed. *Editor:* Niels Pagh Andersen. *Running time:* 58 minutes. *MPAA Rating:* Not Rated.

WITH: Bjorn Cederberg (Interviewer); John Hurt (Narrator).

NEW YORK POST, 12/13/96, p. 42, Larry Worth

[*Betrayal* was reviewed jointly with *In the Name of the Emperor*: see Worth's review of that film.]

Also reviewed in:
NEW YORK TIMES, 12/13/95, p. C19, Stephen Holden
VARIETY, 7/11-17/94, p. 43, Lisa Nesselson

BETTY BOOP CONFIDENTIAL

11 short cartoons by Max Fleischer's studio. *Animator:* Max Fleischer and Dave Fleischer. *Running time:* 90 minutes. *MPAA Rating:* Not Rated.

NEWSDAY, 5/12/95, Part II/p. B7, Gene Seymour

Growing up, I often wondered why Betty Boop "Talkartoons" weren't shown on TV kiddie shows as often as, say, the Popeye the Sailor shorts that were also made in the 1930s by Max and Dave Fleischer. Not that it mattered all that much to me. Being a small boy, I was more into Popeye's swift, Spinach-driven retribution than Betty's coy, come-hither promise of hootchie-coo (or whatever).

With more enlightened eyes, I've figured out why the Boop toons rarely made the daily after-school rotation. Someone must have figured out that these cute little cartoons really were wiggy, sometimes scary lightshows from the subconscious. Granted, there's enough winsomeness on the surface of these shorts to beguile most toddlers. But it takes a grownup to appreciate the Fleischers' lush surrealism and funky suggestiveness.

In "Betty Boop Confidential," the Film Forum has pieced together 11 Depression-era cartoon shorts with the kind of care and intelligence one finds in a prestigious museum exhibit. The Fleischer brothers, who made these films on Broadway, deserve no less. Before Warner Bros. and Tex Avery usurped their rowdy mantle, Max and Dave truly were what one critic called the "anti-Disneys."

Not even crazy ol' Tex could match the raunch in "Boop-Oop-a-Doop," the 1932 short in which scantily clad, bareback-riding Betty is sexually harassed by a carnival ringmaster so grabby that even his handlebar mustache has fingers. Our heroine is duskier and almost topless in "Betty Boop's Bamboo Isle," made that same year, in which she does a fierce hula. If you listen carefully, one of the South Sea natives utters "Shalom aleichem!" as a tribal greeting.

As that offhand gag demonstrates, the folks who worked at the Fleischer studios were hep jokesters in the fast-talking vaudeville tradition. Based on Broadway, they were able to call on the services of stage stars such as Lillian Roth and Ethel Merman, who are shown in live-action performances in the studio's sing-along cartoons. Merman's number is "You Try Somebody Else," a dirge about "open marriage." One would have expected the Fleischers to have had mad fun with the song's literal meaning. Instead, they frame the tune with a typically antic prison melee.

The program would be worthwhile even if it only showed the unforgettable "Snow White" (1933), in which Cab Calloway's song-and-dance to "St James Infirmary" is rotoscoped with Koko the Clown's transforming figure. There are also color films such as "Dancing on the Moon" (1935) and "Poor Cinderella" (1934), which, like the black-and-white shorts, are restored to crisp vitality by the UCLA Film Archives.

VILLAGE VOICE, 5/16/95, p. 47, J. Hoberman

No less than the Angels of Light's *don't dream it, be it* credo, the guiding principle of the great Fleischer brothers "Talkartoons" is that anything can mutate into anything else. In one brief passage in the 1933 masterpiece *Snow White*, Koko the Clown is successively transformed into Cab Calloway, a strutting ghost, a gold piece, and a self-drinking bottle of booze. Elsewhere, Betty Boop's trademark garter serves as a mock funeral wreath.

An irreverent spritz of hot jazz and cheesecake, vintage Fleischers are crazy amalgams of Times Square, Coney Island, the Cotton Club, the Lower East Side, and Sigmund Freud's *Interpretation of Dreams*. In *Swing You Sinner* (1930), an army of singing and dancing tombstones chase a cuddly little cat straight to Hell. The tenement setting of the 1932 *Any Rags*, complete with a pair of faux Disney mice smooching in the garbage, showcases Betty's full-fledged debut, halter-top repeatedly slipping to reveal her brassiere. A duskier, topless Boop wriggles the hula in the same year's *Betty Boop's Bamboo Isle*. (Because this is a Fleischer cartoon, Hawaiian natives greet Betty's canine boyfriend Bimbo with a garbled "sholom aleichem.")

Every generation deserves an opportunity to reexperience the Fleischers—and there's no better opportunity than these pristine 35mm prints. It's appropriate that this surreal hi-de-ho would be showing under the same roof as *Crumb*. Widely telecast during the 1950s, vintage Fleischers were an influence on underground cartoonists, as well as overground filmmakers like Tim Burton, not to mention the Cockettes (who, at one point in *Pickup's Tricks*, mass on stage to drone "Minnie the Moocher").

Meta-vaudeville that it is, *Betty Boop Confidential* includes a pair of 1932 "Screen Song" animations, each featuring an interpolated performance by one of La Boop's real-life, fellow New Yorker kewpie doll cousins—vivacious Lillian Roth in the ickily visceral *Down Among the Sugar Cane* and the more piercing Ethel Merman in the anything-for-a-laff *You Try Somebody Else*. (In one gag, a bunch of funny animal cops put down a jailbreak by machine-gunning a gaggle of funny animal convicts in the prison yard.) Where rival Walt Disney strove to create empathy, the Fleischers specialized in pure sensation. Disney cartoons are tightly plotted and painstakingly rendered; the best Fleischers are free-associative successions of barely connected gags.

Still, the Fleischers intermittently attempted to do Disney—particularly when working in color. Best attempt is the 1935 *Dancing on the Moon* (quoted to excellent effect in Michael Almereyda's pixel-feature *Another Girl Another Planet*). On the other hand, the 1934 Boop vehicle *Poor Cinderella* is mediocre animation but hilarious Disney travesty, tasteless rather than coy. The absence of narrative suspense here only heightens the Fleischer attractions: Betty's striptease transformation, Cupid's use of a sledgehammer, a big toe that develops a face.

Also reviewed in:
CHICAGO TRIBUNE, 6/16/95, Friday/p. I, Michael Wilmington
NEW YORK TIMES, 5/12/95, p. C18, Caryn James
WASHINGTON POST, 6/17/95, p. C2, Richard Harrington

BEYOND RANGOON

A Castle Rock Entertainment release of a Pleskow/Spikings production. *Executive Producer:* Sean Ryerson. *Producer:* Barry Spikings, Eric Pleskow, and John Boorman. *Director:* John Boorman. *Screenplay:* Alex Lasker and Bill Rubenstein. *Director of Photography:* John Seale. *Editor:* Ron Davis. *Music:* Hans Zimmer. *Music Editor:* Adam Smalley. *Sound:* Gary Wilkins and (music) Paul Hulme. *Sound Editor:* Ian Fuller. *Casting:* Mary Gail Artz and Barbara Cohen. *Production Designer:* Anthony Pratt. *Art Director:* Errol Kelly. *Set Decorator:* Eddie Fowlie. *Special Effects:* John Evans. *Costumes:* Deborah La Gorce Kramer. *Make-up:* Felicity Bowring. *Stunt Coordinator:* William Ong. *Running time:* 99 minutes. *MPAA Rating:* R.

CAST: Patricia Arquette (Laura Bowman); U Aung Ko (Himself); Frances McDormand (Andy); Spalding Gray (Jeremy Watt); Tiarra Jacquelina (Desk Clerk); Kuswadinath Bujang (Colonel); Victor Slezak (Mr. Scott); Jit Murad (Sein Htoo); Tiara Jacquelina (San San); Ye Myint (Zaw Win); Cho Cho Myint (Zabai); Johnny Cheah (Min Han); Haji Mohd Rajoli (Karen Father); Azmi Hassan (Older Karen Boy); Ahmad Fithi (Younger Karen Boy); Adele Lutz (Aung San Suu Kyi); Mohd Wan Nazri (Check Point Soldier #1 at Train); Zaidi Omar (Check Point Officer at Train); Roslee Mansor (Check Point Officer #2 at Train); Michael Pickells (Laura's Husband); Enzo Rossi (Laura's Son); Ridzuan Hashim (Officer Min); Samko (Birdman); Ramona Sanchez-Waggoner (Woman Tourist); Norlela Ismail (Young Woman, Sula); Nyak Osman (Village Headman); Yusof Abdul Hamid (River Trader); Lutang Anyie (Karen Leader); Ali Fiji (Fuel Vendor); Dion Abu Baker (Rapist); Yeoh Keat Chye (Black Beret Major); Johari Ismail (Black Beret Sergeant); Rashidi Mohd (Secret Police Officer); William Saw (Bandana Man); Anna Howard (Australian Doctor); Manisah Mandin (Aung Ko's Daughter); Charley

Boorman (Photographer); Hani Mohsin Hanafi (Young Monk/Soldier); Ismail Din (Burmese Official); Jamaludin Rejab (Cig Soldier #1); Aung (Cig soldier #2); Peter Win (Aung Ko's Helper); John Mindy (Burmese Soldier); U Kyaw Win (Sule Aide/Buddha Monk); Gael d' Oliviera (French Boy); Pascale d' Oliviera (French Mother); Gilles d' Oliviera (French Father); Asmi Wahab (Sula Commander); Albert Thaw (Sule Officer); Mansell Rivers-Bland (Hotel Guest); Siti Abdullah (Village Woman); Satish Chand Bhandari (Aung Ko's Friend).

CHRISTIAN SCIENCE MONITOR, 6/7/95, p. 14, David Sterritt

"Beyond Rangoon," an epic directed by John Boorman was heralded by Variety, the entertainment trade paper, as the [Cannes] festival's most keenly anticipated studio release. Showing an American woman's escape from murderous armed forces during Burma's student democracy movement in 1988, the movie turns out to be strong on action and ambition, but weak on everything else.

Not that any civilized person could argue with its indictment of Burma's military dictatorship. But the filmmakers have subordinated their message to such an over-the-top string of chase scenes, suspense episodes, and hide-in-the-jungle heroics that the seriousness of their purpose is nearly lost during much of the story.

Defending this strategy, one could use Moore's argument that commercial movies based on time-tested formulas are an effective way of promoting political awareness among the public; but I doubt whether movies as hyperactive and superficial as "Beyond Rangoon" are likely to encourage thinking of any real depth, duration, or adventurousness.

On the level of sheer craft, there's much to admire in John Seale's color-filled cinematography, and much to howl at in Patricia Arquette's numbingly flat readings of the screenplay's equally flat dialogue. In all, this movie was directed by the klutzy Boorman of "The Emerald Forest" and "Zardoz," not the agile Boorman who made "Hope and Glory" and "Exorcist II: The Heretic" so memorable.

I have profound admiration for the life and work of Aung San Suu Kyi, the Burmese dissident whose activities (movingly acknowledged in the film) have brought her a Nobel Peace Prize and a long spell of house arrest in her own country; yet under the movie's stupefying spell, I left the festival auditorium not contemplating her greatness but dreaming up alternative titles inspired by better films on similar subjects. "The Year of Living Tediously" is one that came to mind.

FILMS IN REVIEW, 11-12/95, p. 99, Andy Pawelczak

Beyond Rangoon takes place in Burma during the political repression in 1988 when the military dictatorship began cracking down on the democracy movement. Aung San Suu Kyi, the movement's leader and a Nobel Peace Prize winner, spent six years under house arrest during which time she studied Buddhism. When she was finally released this past year, her first act in freedom was to announce a policy of national reconciliation with her military tormentors. John Boorman's movie isn't about her (she appears in one brief scene, played by an actress) but it borrows some of her aura and spiritual authority. Boorman has always been interested in myth and the vicissitudes of the spirit. In his most successful film, *Deliverance*, he delivered the requisite action movie thrills while telling an archetypal story of initiatory ordeal and rebirth, and in *Excalibur* he went right to the mythic source itself, the Arthurian legends. In *Beyond Rangoon* he's back in the fairy-tale forest, this time the Burmese jungle, in a film that is part political thriller in the manner of Costa-Gavras, part chase movie, and part spiritual odyssey.

Laura Bowman (Patricia Arquette) is a young doctor on a tour of Southeast Asia trying to recover from the murder of her husband and child during a robbery. We first see her looking at a huge stone Buddha as her off-screen voice says nothing stirs in her and she's stone herself. She's a doctor who can't stand the sight of blood and who has lost any sense of purpose in life; as played by Arquette, she seems stunned, out-of-focus, washed away by grief. She's also astonishingly naive about the political realities that prevail in three-quarters of the world. At one point she expostulates that she can't understand how the Burmese government can kill its own citizens.

These early scenes of the movie, establishing Laura's disengagement from life, are hobbled by a schematic script and wooden dialogue, and Arquette's Laura is so innocent and childlike that you get impatient with her—such naivete is almost criminal. The script simplifies the Burmese political situation into a basic good guys versus bad guys scenario, and Boorman all but puts a halo around the young student adherents of the democracy movement. As filmed here, they belong to the same tribe as the saintly Sandinistas in Roger Spottiswoode's *Under Fire* and the Salvadoran revolutionaries in Oliver Stone's *Salvador*. Once Laura goes beyond Rangoon—in the film's mythic scheme this means into the liminal world of initiation and rebirth—things pick up as she gets involved with the democracy movement and helps an elderly professor (U Aung Ko) escape military thugs. Much of the second half of the movie features Arquette hacking her way through the jungle and running with the out-thrust-jaw intensity of Sigourney Weaver.

The banalities of *Beyond Rangoon*'s script are partially redeemed by the conviction of its performances—in the movie's second half, both Arquette and U Aung Ko bring a sense of mission to their roles—and Boorman's mise-en-scene. His rendering of a confrontation between students and trigger-happy soldiers captures the feeling of panic, helplessness, and aloneness-in-the-midst-of-a-crowd you get in a street demonstration gone bad, and a shot of students pleading for America's help is a surprising reminder that this country is still viewed as a moral exemplar by the rest of the world. And the shots of the Burmese landscape dotted with omni-present stone Buddhas are more than mere pictorialism. Those Buddhas are concrete representations of Laura's spiritual regeneration. Boorman doesn't push his Buddhism (he's not another faddish Hollywood Buddhist) but it subtly pervades the whole movie and almost lofts it into another dimension. *Beyond Rangoon* isn't the great movie some critics have called it, but for its moral seriousness and its sense of a world in pain and turmoil beyond these sheltered shores, it deserves at least a one-hand clap.

Note: *Beyond Rangoon* is aided immeasurably by a big screen. Boorman is preeminently a visual filmmaker, and in the second half of the movie, particularly, there are long passages with almost no dialogue that will inevitably lose some of their impact in the boxy, cramped confines of a video screen.

LOS ANGELES TIMES, 8/25/95, Calendar/p. 1, Kenneth Turan

Director John Boorman has a strong personal connection to Myanmar, starting with his father's presence there during World War I, when this isolated Asian country was still known as Burma. Concerned about the current military regime's stifling of political life, he in part made "Beyond Rangoon" to expose that brutal situation to the kind of international audience motion pictures can ensure.

If "Beyond Rangoon's" intentions are laudable, the film itself is not. And this despite the fact that Boorman, here working with director of photography John Seale, shows once again that he is a compelling visual craftsman whose strong filmmaking sense is something for others to envy.

But when the focus goes from the pictorial to the dramatic, "Beyond Rangoon" proves to be something of a devil's bargain. In attempting to make its politics palatable as entertainment, the film has grafted them onto a boatload of Hollywood implausibilities whose excesses cripple believability. Inspired by terribly real events, "Rangoon" is unable to consistently re-create a persuasive reality on screen.

Part of the problem lies with the heroine, Laura Bowman (Patricia Arquette), a young American doctor who is visiting Burma with her sister Andy (Frances McDormand) in 1988. Still in mourning for her husband and their child, murdered by an intruder, she looks on the country's stone monuments only to feel "I was stone myself." Obviously, she is ready for something completely different and that is what she gets.

Hearing a commotion outside her Rangoon hotel room, Laura sneaks out to investigate and stumbles upon a massive political demonstration for the real-life Aung San Suu Kyi (played by Adele Lutz), the leader of the country's democracy movement. With strength of personality alone, Aung San Suu Kyi personally defuses a potential massacre by armed soldiers. Understandably, Laura is impressed.

Back at her hotel, in the next of numerous contrivances in Alex Lasker & Bill Rubenstein's script, Laura discovers that her passport has been stolen, which means she'll have to stay in the country for a day after her group leaves. "Don't do anything dumb," are her sister's parting words. She must have had a peek at the script.

Killing time in a local market, Laura meets a kindly elderly guide named U Aung Ko (played by an actor of the same name). Though tourists are not allowed outside Rangoon, on a whim she decides to accompany him on a visit to an outlying monastery. Then their car breaks down and they are forced to stay the night with some of U Aung Ko's young friends, who tell her that he is a former university professor who lost his job and was imprisoned for opposing the regime.

Like a thirsty sponge, audience surrogate Laura soaks up all kinds of information about the country's political situation.

The next day, everything comes to a convenient boil. The army opens fire on civilians in Rangoon, martial law is declared, the airport closed, and tourist Laura finds herself having to transport a seriously wounded U Aung Ko to a conveniently distant hospital.

This Saturday matinee part of "Beyond Rangoon," rife with unlikely situations and overdone peril, including the threat of rape, is the film's weakest link. Not helping things is Arquette, apparently cast after Michelle Pfeiffer pulled out. Though the actress is awfully game, crawling through mud and hacking through jungle, her Laura comes off as strident and devoid of sense, a difficult character to feel anything for once the impossibilities of the plot are thrown into the mix.

As mentioned, "Rangoon's" surface (the film was shot in Malaysia) is beautiful, and Boorman is especially adept at staging large-scale scenes of political confrontation. But even though the rush of current events (the real Aung San Suu Kyi was recently freed after years of military house arrest) has given this film and added relevance, it's still not as persuasive as its reality deserves.

NEW YORK, 9/4/95, p. 46, David Denby

John Boorman's *Beyond Rangoon* is a true heartbreaker, a failed great film, noble in intention and theme, often exciting, almost always beautiful, but finally—it kills me to say so—banal, an infuriating epic with a large soul and the mind of a fortune cookie.

Who is John Boorman? A major filmmaker without quite a major career. Boorman directs intermittently—twelve films in 30 years—but almost everything he's done has been notable (or exasperating) in some way. Born in 1933, a Brit of mixed Dutch, Irish, and Scottish background, Boorman came to international prominence back in 1967 with the stunningly nasty crime picture *Point Blank*, starring Lee Marvin and Angie Dickinson and featuring some of the sharpest, funniest scenes of the sixties. He later solidified his reputation with the survival thriller *Deliverance*. But then, alas, Boorman took himself off and communed with the Blarney Stone, or became reincarnated as Merlin, or something like that, and entered a wild and woolly period in which he made a string of visually extravagant and generally preposterous movies. There was the awful, druggy *Zardoz* and the unbelievable *Exorcist II: The Heretic*, and also *Excalibur*. Here was a filmmaker with a strong feeling for atmosphere, a genius for staging complex action scenes, a love of exotic locations and soul-testing stories—and a tin ear. Boorman has a frequently indulged taste for ornate and secondhand profundities. Later he recovered his good sense with *The Emerald Forest* and *Hope and Glory*, his award-winning autobiographical memoir of the London blitz. You certainly could never count this guy out: He's one of the few directors of international reputation who matter.

One of Boorman's favorite themes is Western man (and now woman) let loose in the wilderness, facing strangeness and violence in a test of courage that becomes, by the end, a journey of self-recognition. It's a Conradian theme without Conrad's pessimism. *Beyond Rangoon* is set in Burma, that proud, cut-off unknown, a country devoted more to spirituality than to automobiles and TV sets. (Run by a military dictatorship, Burma—now, officially, Myanmar—has long refused ties with much of the Communist and the capitalist worlds.) When we first see the young American widow Laura Bowman (Patricia Arquette), she's riding a tour boat up a river, staring at nothing, her body slack, her mouth half open in boredom. The year is 1988, and Laura is as passive as a reclining Buddha. The only thing alive in her is her nightmares: She dreams repeatedly of her husband and little boy, whom she discovered at home, both mysteriously murdered. Around her, the jungle is thick and dark, with golden-roofed pagodas gleaming in the sun. Later, she stares at monks in ocher robes sitting in rows and chanting, and she thinks they are numbing themselves to the pain of life just as she is. Boorman, at his best, creates spiritual moods physically: an unhappy woman, surrounded by a hot, slow-moving country. Laura, a doctor who has stopped practicing, has taken Burma into herself, for good and for ill; she just doesn't know it yet.

Back in Rangoon, Laura wanders out of her hotel room at night and walks smack into a political demonstration. Soldiers from the military dictatorship, armed to the teeth, face the students of the pro-democracy movement and their extraordinary leader, Aung San Suu Kyi (played by actress and costume designer Adele Lutz), who calmly walks past the uniformed thugs pointing rifles at her. Stretching time slightly, Boorman makes the encounter magical: The slender smiling woman, extremely beautiful and preternaturally calm, embodies sheer will, which astonishes Laura, who has lost hers. Later, Laura hooks up with a charming old gent, U Aung Ko, a former professor thrown out of work by the military and reduced to shepherding tourists around the country in a huge, ancient, crumbling Chevrolet—a sort of Third World limo, which, like all such cars in the movies, tends to fall apart at exactly the most dangerous moments. When the military cracks down, the professor and some former students devoted to him take care of Laura, and she's forced, almost painfully, to realize that there's something larger in the world than her own sorrows.

It is, of course, the story of an awakening, And God knows we're impatient to see Laura connect to something, because Patricia Arquette is a very trying actress. She's strong-looking in a thickwaisted way that is not, at the moment, the approved (i.e., Sharon Stone) physique among actresses. Which is fine, but there's also something sluggish and thoughtless about her that makes one want to give her a kick. The way the role is written, it takes forever for Laura to realize the simple fact that she's in a country undergoing a state of siege, with panic and slaughter all around her, and Arquette's blank stare doesn't help. Being out of it is one thing; being stupid is another, and we suffer chagrin for her stupidity (Boorman allows us to get too far ahead of her). With her petulant voice, Arquette brings a touch of American commonness and naiveté to the part, which would be interesting if she knew how to use it—how to transcend it. But she can't. You don't believe, for instance, that this woman could ever have been a doctor: She doesn't suggest the physical authority or mental concentration needed for the job.

Laura flees the military with the professor (played by a refugee whose real name is also U Aung Ko), and Boorman, changing tempo, stages a series of terrifying and entirely convincing escapes. In the jungle and in the towns and along the rivers, military men kill with impunity (CNN is not watching Burma), and people run out of the way or keep their heads down. Neither the professor nor Laura is a warrior. They have to scramble, beg for assistance, hide, and steal, and we know that however local the circumstances, we are watching the classic twentieth-century experience of war, in which ordinary people are hounded remorselessly from one place to another. Boorman keeps the camera moving, but in action sequences, he's a classicist: no jump-cutting or convenient elisions; you can see exactly how desperate people get from water to land, from jungle to bridge. Laura breaks into a village where everyone is hiding and steals some medicine, and Arquette, fully energized now, has her best moments: As a soldier tries to rape her, a wild-animal desperation comes out in her eyes and thrusting jaw. Boorman's touch is perfect in these scenes, and back in Rangoon, he outdoes himself: Escaping some soldiers, Laura, the professor, and a group of pro-democracy students rush through a large, roofed bazaar, the camera rushing with them, and as they emerge from the other side of the building, they run into a violent confrontation between ranks of soldiers and demonstrators. Halted, the group around Laura surges forward and back, seething and undulating like the waves at the mouth of an ocean cave. The sequence has the frenzied dynamism of some legendary set piece from the heroic age of the Soviet cinema.

And yet, despite many superb sequences, the movie lets us down. *Beyond Rangoon*, written by Bill Rubenstein and Alex Lasker (they also co-produced), lacks writerly idiosyncrasy—detail and humor and human complication. The material has been shaped, rather too obviously, as a story of redemption. A woman lost in sorrow must learn to care; she must be reconnected to life; a Western individualist must learn to accept an Asian ethos of mutual responsibility. *Beyond Rangoon* turns upbeat in a conventional way (the last sequence is pure, corrupt Old Hollywood). And it's a little dull: For long stretches, Laura and the old man take care of each other, and the sequences, however generous morally, come out as emotionally complacent and predictable. Redeemed from self-absorption, Laura still isn't an interesting person.

Beyond Rangoon needed, perhaps, less goodness and a little sexual interest—a James Woods type snapping at Laura's dragging heels, or something else to break up the high-minded moralism. Every time they open their mouths, the two principals talk nonsense. "I am going to arrange to get you asylum. Wait here," Laura screams at the professor, which, coming in the middle of a mob scene, is an absurd remark. And the professor offers Buddhist pearls like "Suffering is the one promise life always keeps. If happiness comes, it is a gift that is precious." U Aung Ko has great dignity, but with his white hair and his sententiousness, amid his overall placidity, he's too much a cable-TV swami, a wisdom figure with a long Hollywood lineage behind him. In *Beyond Rangoon*, Boorman fails to match the raging physicality of the production with a dramatic intelligence of equal strength.

NEW YORK POST, 8/25/95, p. 35, Michael Medved

One of the most wonderful features of the best films of director John Boorman ("Deliverance," "Excalibur," "The Emerald Forest") is that they are so hard to classify or predict.

The one element they most obviously have in common, though, is a wide-eyed sense of wonder—a characteristic conveyed most memorably of all in "Hope and Glory", Boorman's bittersweet masterpiece about his boyhood memories of wartime London during the blitz.

His latest effort, "Beyond Rangoon," provides that same thrill of discovery as he once again takes both characters (and audience) on a journey to previously exotic and inaccessible corners of reality.

Patricia Arquette plays an American doctor trying to recover from the senseless murder of her husband and son. With her sister (Frances McDormand) she goes on a tightly organized art tour of Asia, arriving in Burma in 1988 in the midst of political turmoil in the capital city of Rangoon.

Wandering away from her hotel one restless, steamy night, she witnesses a massive demonstration led by the courageous, beautiful pacifist leader Aung San Suu Kyi (Adele Lutz)—the real-life Nobel Peace Prize winner subsequently held for six years under house arrest (and released only two months ago) by the nation's repressive military regime.

In the midst of the night's confusion. Arquette somehow loses her passport, and is thus unable to leave Burma with the rest of her tour group. While waiting for help from the U.S. Embassy, she's approached by a kindly old man who offers her a tour of the scenic countryside around in his battered American car.

It turns out, of course, that this gray-haired gentleman is no ordinary tour guide; he is a former professor and prominent dissident (played by a real-life Burmese expatriate dissident named U Aung Ko in a deeply affecting movie debut) who is sought by troops in the midst of a nationwide crackdown.

When Arquette impulsively acts to protect him from arrest, the movie smoothly shifts gears to become an edge-of-your-seat tale of escape and survival easily as spell-binding as "Deliverance" or "Emerald Forest."

Arquette is splendidly suited for her role, projecting a sturdy, almost monumental vitality as she gradually lets go of her personal pain to share in the larger agony of Burma.

The script (which Boorman co-wrote) is full of well-crafted, thought-provoking lines ("Suffering is the one promise life always keeps"), but it's the visual poetry of cinematographer John Seale ("Rainman," "Witness," "Gorillas in the Mist") that makes the deepest impression. Nearby Malaysia provides a credible stand-in for the Burmese locations, with a stunning array of sunsets, jungles and swiftly flowing rivers.

In one sense, "Beyond Rangoon" is structured like a contrived political-message movie that is too obviously indebted to "The Killing Fields"—with its initially indifferent American drawn into the agony of a remote Asian culture through the agency of heartfelt friendship with a decent, heroic local.

In the hands of John Boorman, however, this potentially tired and tendentious skeleton is fleshed out with such immediacy, conviction and gorgeous imagery that it becomes a truly epic adventure.

NEWSDAY, 8/25/95, Part II/p. B4, Jack Mathews

With the exception of "Hope and Glory," his brilliant autobiographical account of a young boy's perspective on the London Blitz, English director John Boorman's best films have followed the adventures of men in quest of identity or spiritual purpose. "Deliverance" and "Excalibur" are the prime examples.

Unfortunately, the same can be said of Boorman's most notable failures—"Exorcist II" and "The Emerald Forest" spring to mind—and though "Beyond Rangoon" has the temerity to follow a woman's quest, it definitely falls into the second category.

Patricia Arquette, in a role originally conceived as a star vehicle for Meg Ryan, plays Laura Bowman, a young medical doctor who, in a profound depression following the murders of her husband and child back home, is on a long excursion in Southeast Asia. It's intended as a journey of healing by the sister traveling with her, but it's merely marking time for Laura who allows nothing to penetrate her veil of grief.

That is, until they reach Rangoon, the capital of politically unstable Burma. The year is 1988, and Laura and her sister Andy (Frances McDormand) arrive there with a travel group that has to leave the next day because of potential confrontations between protesters and the Burmese military. Laura alone is left behind, because (a) she loses her passport, (b) she doesn't care whether she lives or dies and (c) she feels a strong surge of empathy while watching protest leader Aung San Suu Kyi gently part a sea of armed soldiers during a protest march.

To this point, Boorman and his screenwriters are really on to something. They've taken as their setting a citizen uprising that cost thousands of lives at the hands of the military government, an event that went shamefully unnoticed by the outside world, and they link that slaughter to the one that brings Laura Bowman to Burma.

With great dramatic economy, they personalize an entire country's suffering, and give purpose to Laura's life. Like Aung San Suu Kyi, who in real life was awarded the Nobel Peace Prize for her attempts to stop the killing in Burma, Laura realizes that resisting acts of inhumanity is reason enough to go on living.

But what follows is the most wretched sort of Hollywood melodrama, with Laura out front, as a sort of Lawrence of Burma, hacking her way through the humid jungle, joining up with a spiritually wise elder (U Aung Ko), a band of young fugitive, protesters and, finally, a large group of refugees that she leads through the jungle toward safety in Thailand, dodging mortar shells and machine-gun fire all the way.

Much of the action is staged with "Bridge on the River Kwai" verve and firepower, but the events themselves go beyond adventure cliché into the realm of insult. Forget the good doctor's gender. Rare as the Hollywood heroine is these days, the idea of an outraged Westerner dropping in on a revolution in a tropical jungle and taking charge is fertilizer stacked higher than Mt. Everest. It's been done successfully before—the Yank in foreign wars was sort of a staple of the '30s and '40s in Hollywood—but we expect a little more authenticity from political drama these days, and to hang cartoon action on a tragedy of such recent vintage is truly tacky.

Arquette throws herself into the role, and is very effective in the early going, allowing us to glimpse through her enigmatic stare the confused and tortured person inside, and she looks athletic enough to handle some of Laura's feats. You can only imagine how bad this movie would have been with frothy Meg Ryan in the role (there aren't many opportunities for those benignly blinding smiles).

Still, it's a lost cause. The exploits of the white doc in the troubled Third World would be comic-book stuff no matter who played the role, or whether it was written for a man or a woman.

SIGHT AND SOUND, 7/95, p. 41, Trevor Johnston

Burma, August 1988. Traumatised by the death of her husband and infant son in a domestic assault, American doctor Laura Bowman has taken her sister Andy's advice and joined her on a sightseeing tour of South-East Asia. Unable at first to blank out such painful recent events, Laura's curiosity at the demonstration outside her Rangoon hotel room window one night leads her through the city streets to witness pro-democracy leader Aung San Suu Kyi fearlessly confronting a phalanx of armed soldiers, part of the ruling military junta's brutal regime of repression. On her return to her hotel however, the discovery of the loss of her passport forces her to stay behind alone in Rangoon to sort out a replacement.

After her initial visit to the US embassy, she's accosted in the street by U Aung Ko, a self-proclaimed 'unofficial' guide. After bribing a checkpoint guard, they're soon driving in the country, where U Aung's car breaks down and they're given shelter by a group of former student activists who reveal that U Aung was dismissed from a university professorship for helping the cause. The next day, news of an army massacre of pro-democracy protesters in Rangoon causes them to leave their cover and head for the Thai border. En route, Laura rescues U Aung from being shot by a suspicious soldier, whereupon the two make off by car with the soldiers giving chase. Eventually they escape via the river, but at the cost of a bad chest wound to U Aung.

Persuading a bamboo-seller to take them down river, Laura obtains medicines during a brief stop, though she has to shoot a soldier to do so. Operating on U Aung on the raft, she saves his life, but he repays the favour by spiriting her away from the Burmese military surrounding the US embassy in Rangoon. While ruthless government troops mow down groups of pro-democracy supporters, Laura and U Aung tag along with a group of students hoping to reach the safety of Thailand. Breaking through a military checkpoint, they head through the jungle on foot and reach the haven of an anti-government guerrilla camp, from which, under heavy shelling from state troops which occasions much loss of life and serious injury, Laura and U Aung both make it over the river into safe territory. Arriving in a refugee camp on the Thai side of the border, Laura immediately pitches in to help the Red Cross medical team.

There's a certain industry shorthand that describes as a 'fish out of water' any film that throws its protagonist into unfamiliar territory to dramatic and/or comic effect. It's a narrative form that John Boorman has turned to time and again (in, for example, *Hell in the Pacific*, *Deliverance* and *The Emerald Forest*). The set of tensions between man and nature/Westerner and wilderness enacted in *Beyond Rangoon* are rich in psychological and eco-political resonance beyond their basic narrative-building potential—the action drama is both an interior journey and a plea for environmental/human rights awareness. At the same time, Boorman, the maker of *Excalibur*, brings a mythological aura to these trials of fortitude, where the test set for the individual exists outside of normal social circumstances and seems designed to test the very fibre of her humanity at some essential level. (In his most recent work, *Hope and Glory* and the ill-received *Where the Heart Is* we find the quotidian domestic world turned upside-down.)

That *Beyond Rangoon* seeks to take all this on board, while adding, for the first time in its director's career, a specific political imperative in its platform for the plight of Burma's pro-democracy movement and its housebound Nobel Prize-winning leader Aung San Suu Kyi, is certainly evidence of Boorman's ambition. Yet on this occasion, the conventional mechanisms of the film's chase-thriller narrative leave little room to indulge its roster of weighty aspirations, and the result is a sketchy, over-reaching piece that's at its best when delivering basic suspense setpieces. Shooting on location, with Malaysia standing in for Burma, John Seale's camera is all too eager to cut its way through the jungle undergrowth or plunge into the local rivers, matching Patricia Arquette's plucky heroine step for step as her vacationing American doctor finds herself by the side of a former political dissident on the run from the country's trigger-happy military.

Unsurprisingly, from a director who's probed the Amazon basin and crossed the Appalachians in his time, the film's potent sense of place is its strongest suit, although slightly dissipated from time to time by some awkward process work (post-production tinkering or logistical exigencies?). If Patricia Arquette proves herself equal to the *physical* demands of the role, her success in dealing with Laura Bowman's growing commitment to fight injustice and her concomitant recovery from the traumatic loss of her husband and child in a fatal attack on her home in the US is a good deal more qualified.

In this respect, Alex Lasker and Bill Rubenstein's script doesn't give her much of a chance. It's as if the bathetic lessons of *The Killing Fields* had entirely passed them by. Spalding Gray's casting as the befuddled tour guide here seems no accident, while Hans Zimmer's pan-pipe-heavy score seems a self-conscious steal from Ennio Morricone's work on that other Puttnam/Joffe épic *The Mission*. The use of an ongoing national tragedy in South-East Asia as the backdrop to the personal development of one messed-up Westerner seems counter-productive at best, somewhat dubious at worst, dwarfing the human drama while it trivialises the political one.

Of course, it's difficult to argue against the positive aspects in the film if it brings the courage of Aung San Suu Kyi to a wider audience. However, the film seems simply unable to bridge the chasm between the very real sacrifices made by her and her supporters and the scriptwriters' contrivances that have disposed of the heroine's family and put her through any number of hair-raising scrapes. While the very notion of the troubled Westerner finding spiritual balm in the mystic East comes over as the usual well-meaning cliché, it's equally disappointing that a film which offers such compassion for the Burmese people should treat its Burmese characters (martial automata on the one hand, courageous freedom fighters on the other, and nothing in-between) as ciphers.

With its intermittently nerve-wracking action highlights, including a well-mounted finale in which Patricia Arquette and her pals in the resistance cross the river into safe Thailand under heavy army shelling, *Beyond Rangoon* has the air of Boorman bidding to reach the box office after the dull thud of *Where the Heart Is*. Approached as an empty-headed actioner, it's partially successful, but when so much more has obviously been intended (and achieved in Boorman's previous work) one wonders where this perennial cinematic adventurer has left to go. Boorman is a director to write off at your peril, but now in his sixties his travelling days must surely be numbered and the spectre of Werner Herzog must be there to remind him that the visionary who spends too much time in the wilderness might just leave his career there on a permanent basis.

TIME, 9/4/95, p. 72, Richard Corliss

Dr. Laura Bowman seems in a perpetual Burma daze. In 1988 Laura (Patricia Arquette), the heroine of *Beyond Rangoon*, is with a group of tourists who want to get out of Burma before the thugs who run the place start killing everyone. But Laura has not recovered from a personal trauma back home, and when her group leaves she just ... stays there. It's a pretty region—like the Mekong Delta in the mid-'60s. Now if only she can find an escort. Why, here's an amiable native (U Aung Ko). "Hello," he says, in effect "I'm an illegal guide in a military dictatorship, and I'd like to plop you into a genocidal civil war." "Hello," she visually replies, "I'm a shell-shocked ninny. Let's go."

The history of Myanmar, as Burma is now called, resonates with melodrama and tragedy. The heroic battle of Aung San Suu Kyi, a Nobel Peace Prize winner for her nonviolent resistance against the ruling junta, is surely worth a movie. But in Hollywood the problems of one little country—or one big country with little brown people—don't amount to a hill of unsold scripts. The Burmese must have a Caucasian mediator, Laura, whose sufferings illuminate those of the locals.

Director John Boorman, an artist-adventurer with an eye for pictorial rapture and social turmoil, brought this sort of scenario alive in *The Emerald Forest*. Not so here, where he lapses into banal visual stereotyping: the rebels are thin, winsome, saintly, while the nasty soldiers have bad skin and potbellies.

Cast at the last minute (after Meg Ryan left to make another American-twit-abroad epic, *French Kiss*), Arquette can do little but whine and pine in an impossible role. And the film simply forfeits belief with its notion that Laura, who stumbles through Burma like a girl in a monster movie after she's seen the giant ants, is a physician. She hardly seems smart enough to be a patient.

VILLAGE VOICE, 8/29/95, p. 51, Georgia Brown

In his sixties now, John Boorman keeps plugging away at worthy themes. His message is that there are more things in this world than are dreamt of by Western consciousness. Like Boorman's *The Emerald Forest, Beyond Rangoon* is a fairly didactic political adventure, once again with an urgent subject: political repression in Burma, or, as it's currently called, Myanmar.

Here, an American woman's happy American life has been upset by what's commonly billed as "senseless tragedy." Laura Bowman, M.D. (Patricia Arquette), loses husband and child as a result of "random violence."

In a bird's-eye flashback, we watch her arrive home to find the house ransacked and her husband and young son laid out on the floor—not even in one another's arms—with their throats slit, ("All my pretty ones ..."?) Months later, in an attempt at therapeutic diversion, her sister, Andy (Frances McDormand), also a physician, persuades Laura to join her on an Asian tour.

We meet the sisters in Yangon formerly Rangoon, where they're barely speaking. Laura is listless, unengaged by the sights; Andy claims the trip was a mistake. The fussy tour guide (Spalding Gray, playing an ugly American out of his own *Swimming to Cambodia*) can't conceal his impatience.

What pulls Laura out of her grief is witnessing a midnight protest march led by a beatific Aung San Suu Kyi (Adele Lutz), the pacifist opposition leader. (While under house arrest Aung San Suu Kyi won the Nobel Peace Prize. She was released last month.) Here she faces down soldiers' rifles and passes untouched through their ranks. Laura returns to the hotel elated. In the process, however, she's lost her passport—the American's ticket to safe conduct—and must stay behind just as the government declares martial law. (McDormand and Gray disappear from the movie before you can say Myanmar.)

Having already lost everything, Laura barely consents to live, and therefore is invulnerable. She turns down an invitation from a young American diplomat—life as she's known it—for the company of a self-proclaimed "guide," a white-haired gentleman she meets in the market. U Aung Ko (the character takes the actor's name, though production notes stress that the story is not his own) turns out to be a revered professor barred from teaching for his prodemocracy activities. He takes Laura into the interior (everything here corresponds to a mythic or spiritual journey), where, from several dissidents, she hears stories of murder and torture as horrific as hers. Symbolically, she sheds drenched Western clothes for the local wrapped skirt and vomits some held-in anger. Still wrapped in herself, however, she puts her hosts in danger: Trying to return her to safety, one student is killed and the professor wounded. She accrues obligations.

Tragedy, the movie proposes, is many people's way of life. "I was brought up to believe that if I were good I would be happy," Laura tells Aung Ko. "We were brought up," he counters, "believing that suffering is the only thing that life can promise."

Although the recent release of Aung San Suu Kyi made the front page for a couple of days, Burma's plight has barely earned mention in the U.S. press. "In case you haven't noticed, this country is a military dictatorship," hisses Spalding Gray's professor-tour guide. He notices but is content merely to regard the country's art. The murderous crackdown of '88—which Laura finds herself in the midst of—wasn't documented because the media were expelled. A single photographer (played by Boorman's son Charley) takes and smuggles out photos. The movie obliquely suggests that American diplomats supported the dictatorship.

The movie's actors are limited. U Aung Ko is tentative and Patricia Arquette seems to move through most of the movie with one desperate expression on her face. Boorman compensates by showing Laura running a good deal (there're some impressive traveling shots), so that you exit the theater out of breath. I was also quite moved. The title, *Beyond Rangoon*, I take to mean that such countries are centers from which suffering radiates.

Also reviewed in:
CHICAGO TRIBUNE, 8/25/95, Friday/p. C, Michael Wilmington
NATION, 9/18/95, p. 291, Stuart Klawans
NEW REPUBLIC, 9/18 & 25/95, p. 38, Stanley Kauffmann
NEW YORK TIMES, 8/25/95, p. C3, Caryn James
NEW YORKER, 8/21-28, p. 132, Terrence Rafferty
VARIETY, 5/22-28/95, p. 93, Todd McCarthy
WASHINGTON POST, 8/25/95, p. D6, Hal Hinson

BIG GREEN, THE

A Walt Disney Pictures release in association with Caravan Pictures. *Executive Producer:* Dennis Bishop. *Producer:* Roger Birnbaum. *Director:* Holly Goldberg Sloan. *Screenplay:* Holly Goldberg Sloan. *Director of Photography:* Ralf Bode. *Editor:* John F. Link. *Music:* Randy Edelman. *Music Editor:* John LaSalandra. *Sound:* Robert Allan Wald and (music) Dennis Sands. *Casting:* Rick Montgomery and Dan Parada. *Production Designer:* Evelyn Sakash. *Art Director:* Harry Darrow. *Set Decorator:* Helen Britten. *Set Dresser:* Tom Christopher, Patricia Dillon, Christopher Haynes, Bryant Jackson, Coco Rost, Kenneth R. Rector, and E. Colleen Saro. *Special Effects:* Randy E. Moore. *Costumes:* Rondi Hillstrom Davis. *Make-up:* Carla Palmer. *Stunt Coordinator:* Jeff Dashnaw and Russell Towery. *Running time:* 100 minutes. *MPAA Rating:* PG.

CAST: Steve Guttenberg (Tom Palmer); Olivia d'Abo (Anna Montgomery); Jay O. Sanders (Jay Huffer); John Terry (Edwin V. Douglas); Chauncey Leopardi (Evan Schiff); Patrick Renna (Larry Musgrove); Billy L. Sullivan (Jeffrey Luttrell); Yareli Arizmendi (Marbelly Morales); Bug Hall (Newt Shaw); Jessie Robertson (Kate Douglas); Anthony Esquivel (Juan Morales);

Jordan Brower (Nick Anderssen); Hayley Kolb (Sophia Convertino); Haley Miller (Polly Neilson); Ashley Welch (Lou Gates); Ariel Welch (Sue Gates); Jimmy Higa (Tak Yamato); Gil Glasgow (Cookie Musgrove); Libby Villari (Brenda Neilson); Louanne Stephens (Bomma Cole); John Bourg (Jay Huffer, Jr.); Tyler Bishop (Knight #2); Casey Lee (Knight #3); Milt Oberman (Referee); Nik Hagler (Chief Bishop); Stephen Parr (Stadium Announcer).

LOS ANGELES TIMES, 9/29/95, Calendar/p. 4, John Anderson

[The following review by John Anderson appeared in a slightly different form in **NEWSDAY, 9/29/95, Part II/p. B4.]**

Anna Montgomery (Olivia d'Abo), the nicest thing Britain's done for Texas since deciding not to colonize it, explains to her skeptical and seriously attitudinal students that there are four important factors to the game of soccer: fitness, technique, tactics and game psychology. They respond by staring, slackjawed.

What she might have added, perkily, is that there are four important factors to making an inspirational sports movie like "The Big Green":

1. Organization of misfits.
2. Humiliating defeat.
3. Development of skills and team camaraderie.
4. Glorious victory/revenge over team that perpetrated No. 2.

Throw in one kid who has both a big secret and the best athletic skills and what you have, in essence, is a puckless "Mighty Ducks." Which is not necessarily bad, just necessarily derivative and a little tedious, unless you're 6; as a 12-year-old consultant whispered to me during the last few moments of this movie, "Why don't they stop it now? We know what's gonna happen." Yeah, but that's the point. Why tamper with a game plan that works?

And it does, to a large degree, although freshman director/writer Holly Goldberg Sloan is certainly plowing old ground. The kids are an endearing group—particularly Larry (Patrick Renna of "The Sandlot") and Newt (Bug Hall of "The Little Rascals")—even if they're stuck in the depressed Texas town of Elma, where "nothing ever happens." But Anna happens, captivating both the kids and the unshaven, quasi-blockheaded Sheriff Tom Palmer (Steve Guttenberg), whom she persuades to help her organize a town soccer team, on the field once known as "the big green."

The opening game between the Big Green and the Knights, who are coached by the insufferably arrogant Jay Huffer (Jay O. Sanders), is a debacle. But things get better after Juan Morales (Anthony Esquivel), a real player, joins the team. The problem is, Juan's mother is nervous about something. Will Juan make the big game? Will the Big Green snatch victory from the jaws of defeat? Will Newt make the winning shot on goal? If you don't know the answer, you haven't been to the movies in a while.

NEW YORK POST, 9/29/95, p. 43, Michael Medved

"The Mighty Ducks" meets "Hoosiers"—on a soccer field.

That's the Hollywood "high concept" behind "The Big Green," an amiably exploitative family movie that seeks to capitalize on the soaring U.S. popularity of a sport that has already enrolled more than 2 million kids in youth soccer leagues.

The Disney company is obviously counting on this built-in audience to fuel the box-office performance of this predictable but pleasant tale of down-hearted small-town losers miraculously transformed into unstoppable champions.

The magic begins when a new teacher arrives in the dusty, dreary, down-at-the-heels hamlet of Elma, Texas. She's a spectacularly spunky British import who's part of some unexplained exchange program and who comes across like an ultra-athletic version of Mary Poppins.

As played by Olivia d'Abo, who bathes the screen with her own honey-thick glow of sweetness and sex appeal, it's hard not to root for this character in her efforts to inspire her impoverished students by introducing them to the game she loves—soccer.

Registering her reluctant warriors in a league based in the nearby city of Austin, d'Abo proceeds to whip her team into shape. The squad includes the usual collection of misfits—an overweight goalie (Patrick Renna of "The Sandlot"); a sullen sufferer (Jessie Robertson) with an alcoholic single dad; and a potential star player (Anthony Esquivel) who's afraid to participate because he and his mother are illegal immigrants from El Salvador.

There's also the town's deputy sheriff (Steve Guttenberg), who helps organize the team because he's sweet on d'Abo. Guttenberg's surprisingly effective and utterly charming in the good ol' boy role as a former high school football hero who once enjoyed regional glory on the long abandoned local field known as "The Big Green"—which now provides the underdog soccer team with its name.

On the way to the inevitable championship game, the movie takes several gratuitous detours in the name of political correctness, Hollywood style. When the British teacher tells her charges, "America is a place where you can be anything you want to be," one of them shoots back, that was before Reagonomics, ma'am." The film also makes a point of assembling its heroic team almost entirely of girls and boys who are members of ethnic minorities (black, Hispanic, Vietnamese) while all of the overconfident, bad-guy squads they oppose are entirely white and exclusively male.

The movie also falls into the trap of many another sports movie, broadcasting the dubious message that athletic success instantly solves all life's problems, from strained parental relationships to dismal academic performance.

The entire film, in fact, is little more than a collection of comforting cliches. But debuting director Holly Goldberg Sloan (who previously wrote the breezie comedies "Angels in the Outfield" and "Made in America") handles the potentially tired material with good humor and sunny self-assurance.

She also keeps in constant touch with the kids in the audience. For instance, adults may not be particularly amused when an arrogant opposing coach (Jay O. Sanders) is forced to kiss the Big Green's mascot goat, but youngsters will most likely howl with delight.

Also reviewed in:
CHICAGO TRIBUNE, 9/29/95, Friday/p. J, John Petrakis
NEW YORK TIMES, 9/29/95, p. C6, Stephen Holden
VARIETY, 10/2-8/95, p. 40, Joe Leydon
WASHINGTON POST, 9/29/95, p. F7, William F. Powers

BILLY MADISON

A Universal Pictures release. *Executive Producer:* Fitch Cady. *Producer:* Robert Simonds. *Director:* Tamra Davis. *Screenplay:* Tim Herlihy and Adam Sandler. *Director of Photography:* Victor Hammer. *Editor:* Jeffrey Wolf. *Music:* Randy Edelman. *Music Editor:* John LaSalandra and Sally Boldt. *Choreographer:* Clarence Ford. *Sound:* Allan Byer and (music) Dennis Sands and Elton Ahi. *Sound Editor:* Jerry Ross and Kimberly A. Harris. *Casting:* Jaki Brown-Karman, Todd Thaler, and Deirdre Bowen. *Production Designer:* Perry Blake. *Art Director:* Gordon Barnes. *Set Decorator:* Enrico Campana. *Set Dresser:* Bill Johnson and Ernesto Camera. *Special Effects:* Jordan Craig. *Costumes:* Marie-Bylvie Deveau. *Make-up:* Edelgarde K. Pfluegl. *Stunt Coordinator:* Ted Hanlan. *Running time:* 88 minutes. *MPAA Rating:* PG-13.

CAST: Adam Sandler (Billy Madison); Darren McGavin (Brian Madison); Bridgette Wilson (Veronica); Bradley Whitford (Eric Gordon); Josh Mostel (Max Anderson); Norm MacDonald (Frank); Mark Beltzman (Jack); Larry Hankin (Carl Alphonse); Theresa Merritt (Juanita); Dina Platias (Miss Lippy); Hrant Alianak (Pete); Vincent Marino (Cook); Jack Mather (Clemens); Christopher Kelk (Janitor); Marc Donato (Nodding 1st Grader); Keith Cole and Chris Mei (Penguin); Conor Devitt (O'Doyle, Grade 1); Jared Durand (Scotty, Grade 1); Jessica Nakamura (Tricia, Grade 1); Helen Hughes (2nd Grade Teacher); Jacelyn Holmes (2nd Grader); Claire Cellucci (Attractive Lady); Shane Farberman (Clown); Al Maini (Chauffeur);

Jared Cook (Ernie, Grade 3); Christian Matheson (O'Doyle, Grade 3); Kyle Bailey (Kyle); Vernon Chapman (Butler); Mandy Watts (Maid); Austin Pool (Dan, Grade 3); Gladys O'Connor (Tour Guide); Marcia Bennett (4th Grade Teacher); Diane Douglas (Nurse); Tim Herlihy and Frank Nakashima (Architects); Joyce Gordon (Lunch Lady); Jordan Lerner-Ellis and Daniel Lerner-Ellis (Potheads); Robert Smigel (Mr. Oblaski); Melissa Korzenko (Nancy Connors); Colin Smith (O'Doyle, Grade 9); Jeff Moser (Paul); Amos Crawley (Rod); Tex Konig and Eduardo Gomez (Crazy Persons); Tanya Grout (Eric's Secretary); Benjamin Barrett and Matthew Ferguson (Tenth Graders); Sean Lett (O'Doyle, Grade 12); Stacey Wheal (Jennifer, Grade 3); Shanna Bresee (Susan, Grade 3); Michael Ayoub (Drama Teacher); Lawrence Nakamura (Lawn Guy); Gino Veltri (Rock Singer); James Downey (Principal); Bob Rodgers (Mr. O'Doyle); Margo Wladyka (Mrs. O'Doyle); Allison Robinson (Newswoman); Marcel Jean Gilles (Haitian Gardener); Suzanna Shebib (High School Girl); Kevin Leroy and Kelly Childerhose (Jet Skiers); Ken Shires (Fire-Eater).

LOS ANGELES TIMES, 2/11/95, Calendar/p. 2, Peter Rainer

"Billy Madison" looks as if it were made to fill the void left by Pee-wee Herman. We never needed Pee-wee more.

Adam Sandler plays Billy Madison, a spoiled rich nudnik who stands to inherit the family business from his hotel tycoon father (Darren McGavin)—except Madison Sr. seems to think his jerky scion isn't up to it. For one thing, the only reason he graduated public school is because his father paid off the teachers. So, unless Billy can repeat grades 1 through 12 in 24 weeks, the business will revert to the business' scuzzball vice president (Brad Whitford).

Repeating public school as an adult is a well-worn movie fantasy and "Billy Madison" rings no new changes. Director Tamra Davis and screenwriters Sandler and Tim Herlihy scatter the bad jokes like fertilizer. Nothing sprouts. As a comic actor, Sandler has a bad habit of thinking he's funnier than we do—although he's not aiming very high here. He's trying to be the King of the Peepee and Doodoo jokes. Worse, he isn't.

Actors such as Norm MacDonald and Josh Mostel takes turns trying to blow up this bladder but a whoopee cushion without air can't make a funny sound.

NEW YORK POST, 2/11/95, p. 16, Larry Worth

"Saturday Night Live" has been in a crash-and-burn mode for years. The fact that Adam Sandler is now among its top stars is one reason why.

Simply put, Sandler is comedians' answer to the Peter Principle. He's a staggeringly untalented waste of space. He makes Jerry Lewis' gooniest efforts look positively Chaplinesque.

In "Billy Madison," he plays a spoiled, rich twentysomething who must return to school—graduating each grade in two weeks—if he's to take over his father's hotel business.

That means Billy has to play Gulliver to successive classes of Lilliputians: He sits at a child's desk, uses the "little boy" urinal and is tested on story hour. So far, so funny?

Hedging bets, the plot later incorporates a dopey love story, lines from "The Godfather, Part II," a parody of big-budget musicals, a rip-off of "Harvey" (Billy keeps seeing an 8-foot penguin that's invisible to everyone else) that's invisible and the high-pitched voices of Sandler's "Cajun Man," "Opera Man" and "Canteen Boy."

Who thinks up this junk? Well, anyone who's watched the downward spiral of "Saturday Night Live" won't be surprised that Sandler and fellow "SNL" staffer Tim Herlihy share dumb-and-dumber screenplay honors.

Condolence cards should be sent to co-stars Darren McGavin, Josh Mostel and Bridgette Wilson for having to play off Sandler's amateurish antics and Tamra "CB4" Davis' moronic direction.

In a tale ostensibly about the educational experience, it's embarrassingly clear that Sandler and company have a lot to learn.

NEWSDAY, 2/13/95, Part II/p. B9, John Anderson.

Adam Sandler follows in a long and illustrious/notorious tradition that includes Darwin, trench warfare, Auschwitz, J. Robert Oppenheimer and Beavis and Butthead. He may be the final phenomenon of the late 20th Century with the power to make us question the very meaning of life. And then to question whether questioning is worth the effort.

What does Adam Sandler mean? If "Billy Madison" is any indication, what he means is that humor, talent, purpose and worldview are unnecessary, and in fact may be handicaps, in the creation of mainstream entertainment. His existence in our cultural consciousness implies intellectual sloth of previously unimagined proportions. His presence on the big screen is more proof of Hollywood's utter contempt for its audiences. And his budget—since there are highly paid, presumably intelligent but evidently godless people determining these things—indicates that people will not only attend this movie but may even tell their friends to do the same. If someone does this, he or she is not your friend.

"BM" contains elements of "Arthur" and "Harvey"—the ambitiously alcoholic Billy is pursued by a giant penguin only he can see—as well as the long-forgotten "Miss Tatlock's Millions" (1948), in which John Lund has to act like an idiot to help heiress Wanda Hendrix. Here, the idiot has to act like a scholar: Threatened with disinheritance by his tycoon father (Darren McGavin) who wants to turn corporate control over to the scheming Eric Gordon (Bradley Whitford), the ill-educated Billy offers to repeat elementary and high school—two weeks per grade—and by doing so win his father's wealth and affection. At this point, you begin counting the grades, and hope he skips a few.

Along the way, he encounters the gorgeous Veronica (Bridgette Wilson), who is his third-grade teacher and for no good reason changes her opinion of Billy from loathing to love (probably because he's such a debonair bon vivant). The under-utilized Josh Mostel is a principal with a secret and a yen for Billy, something he shares with Billy's maid, Juanita (Theresa Merritt), whose purpose here is to make lewd suggestions to Billy and erode the good name of domestics everywhere.

Sandler's previous films include "Mixed Nuts" and "Airheads," which at least had Steve Buscemi to redeem it. "Billy Madison" is pure Sandler, i.e. infantile. Unlike Beavis & Butthead, which also is essentially about nothing, "Billy" can't even be true to itself: If the point of Sandler's humor is a nihilistic disregard for social structure, moral values and self-respect, then why should his character go to such an extent to win his father's fortune? An answer, of course, would require thought, something anathema to either "Billy Madison" or its star.

SIGHT AND SOUND, 4/96, p. 38, Leslie Felperin

Spoilt 27-year-old ne'er-do-well Billy Madison spends his days drinking with his friends by his billionaire father Brian's poolside. Disgusted with his son's indolence, Brian decides to leave the management of his business to Eric, his obsequious lackey. Billy, whose high school diploma was acquired by bribery and cheating, vows to prove himself by working his way through each grade of primary and secondary school every two weeks. If he passes without cheating, his father promises to leave him the business.

Finding the rigours of academic life difficult at first, Billy soon advances through the grades at the agreed rate. After each completion, he throws a huge party for all his friends and schoolmates. He makes many new prepubescent friends and falls in love with Veronica, his third grade teacher. Veronica scorns him at first, but is soon won round, and they start dating.

In high school, Billy is victimised by bullies. Feeling guilty for having done the same thing, Billy apologises to a nerdy former schoolmate, who crosses Billy off a list of people he plans to kill. Eric schemes to discredit Billy by blackmailing his elementary school principal, Max, into falsely claiming that Billy cheated. Billy's name is eventually cleared, but he challenges Eric to a final academic decathlon to prove who is the more worthy inheritor. The final contest degenerates into a mêlée, where Eric reveals his true nature and is shot in the ass by the nerd to whom Billy apologised. At his graduation, Billy decides he will go to college before taking over of the family company.

Taking its inspiration from the recent crop of films featuring stupid protagonists (*Forrest Gump, Dumb & Dumber*) and a slightly older cycle concerned with grown men amongst schoolchildren (*Big, Kindergarden Cop*) *Billy Madison* is as derivative a compound as the dross left over from a particularly noxious junior school chemistry experiment. The aforementioned movies all have something to recommend them, be it slick production values, superb slapstick, emotional resonance, or at the very least a charismatic star presence. The only thing that recommends *Billy*

Madison, apart from its director Tamra Davis, who made the interesting indie movie *Guncrazy*, is Steve Buscemi in an uncredited cameo as a psychotic nerd turned serial killer.

The weakest link in this chain of mediocrity is the film's star and coscreenwriter Adam Sandler, a former member of the ever-declining American skit comedy show *Saturday Night Live*. Sandler is blandly handsome in a way that comedians seem to need to be now in order to be popular (think of *Seinfeld* or *Friends*), yet he has poor comic timing, little grace, and hardly any acting ability. He can't even occupy what precious little of the equally dislikable character of Billy there is. Throughout the film he slips into a poor parody of a southern cracker, recalling the character "Cajun Man" for which he was best known on *SNL*.

Moments of absurd nonsense—a man in a penguin suit, a lame parody of a musical comedy number—are included in a desperate effort to emulate the wacky atmosphere of *Wayne's World*. These only serve to remind us how ridiculous the film's basic premise is—if Billy wants to prove how responsible he can be to his father, why doesn't he just get a job? One supposes he goes back to primary school because that is where the film-makers expect to find their audience. Thus the film is infantile in the most derogatory sense, streaked with a cruelty that would only appeal to the kind of class bullies it superficially attempts to decry.

Also reviewed in:
CHICAGO TRIBUNE, 2/12/95, Tempo/p. 6, John Petrakis
NEW YORK TIMES, 2/11/95, p. 16, Janet Maslin
VARIETY, 2/13-19/95, p. 48, Brian Lowry
WASHINGTON POST, 2/11/95, p. D3, Rita Kempley

BLACK IS ... BLACK AIN'T

A Tara Releasing release of a California Newsreel production. *Producer:* Marlon T. Riggs. *Director:* Marlon T. Riggs. *Director of Photography:* Robert Shepard. *Editor:* Bob Paris and Christine Badgley. *Music:* Mary Watkins. *Sound:* Sekou Shepard. *Running time:* 87 minutes. *MPAA Rating:* Not Rated.

WITH: Angela Davis; Bill T. Jones; bell hooks; Barbara Smith; Maulana Karenga; Essex Hemphill; Michele Wallace; Cornel West.

LOS ANGELES TIMES, 5/19/95, Calendar/p. 16, Kevin Thomas

The late documentarian Marlon Riggs' altogether remarkable 86-minute "Black Is ... Black Ain't" is a final testament from an important, groundbreaking filmmaker dying of AIDS. Riggs—who died in April, 1994, at 36—attempts a definition of blackness as broad as possible as a way to plead for inclusiveness among African Americans, calling for a banishment of divisive distinctions based on skin color, class, gender, sexual orientation and religion.

It is a wide-ranging work celebrating diversity and filled with warmth and humor, in which Riggs sought the views of many people, famous and otherwise. It is also a loving chronicle of Riggs' family, rooted in Louisiana, and a harrowing diary of his day-to-day battle against AIDS.

As in previous Riggs' films, most notably the controversial "Tongues Untied," "Black Is ... Black Ain't" is gracefully structured, incorporating performance arts, especially dance.

NEW YORK POST, 10/11/95, p. 34, Larry Worth

Little Black Sambo, Mandingo, Uncle Tom, Aunt Jemima and all other African-American stereotypes can rest in peace. Filmmaker Marlon Riggs—who speaks out as both a black man and a gay man—lays them to rest once and for all in the fascinating "Black Is ... Black Ain't."

Through an eclectic mix of poetry, music, dance and interviews, Riggs' semi-documentary explores countless aspects of the black consciousness, ranging from history and religion to appearance, language and self-definition.

Using speakers such as Angela Davis, Bill T. Jones and bell hooks, the emphasis shifts constantly, and fascinates consistently. One minute, audiences are listening to a daughter heartbreakingly recall her mother being thrown out of the house; the next blacks debate their assimilation into white culture. It's soup to nuts, and all the more involving for its lack of segues and stream-of-consciousness style.

Riggs, whose previous film "Tongues Untied" brought Jesse Helms' wrath to PBS' door, also incorporates his own struggle against AIDS into the scenario. Adding bittersweet resonance is the fact that Riggs died before the film's completion. (Co-workers completed the production and dedicated it in his memory.)

He zeroes in on every facet of prejudice, as when Davis notes that "a black African was once the worst thing to be called," or Louis Farrahkan refers to "the damned deceitful games women play," and Ice Cube assures that "true niggers ain't faggots."

But Riggs never falls into the trap of overdoing on homophobia. Instead, it becomes one more ingredient in Big Mama's gumbo, the making of which provides a framing device—and launching pad—for yet more anecdotes.

What gradually emerges is that there's no such thing as a collective black reality, a concept which should be—but still isn't—a given. Riggs' attempts to change all that—even on his deathbed—makes "Black Is ... Black Ain't" an engaging, thought-provoking argument for tolerance and diversity.

VILLAGE VOICE, 10/24/95, p. 76, Lisa Kennedy

Before his death Riggs had a dream. In it Harriet Tubman guided a boat to the banks of a river and shuttled the director to the other side. Beyond the undeniable grace of the dream, this vision provides *Black Is ... Black Ain't* with one of its most beautiful recurring images: a river flowing, undulating really, beneath superimposed clips of dancers stepping furiously or portraits of Malcom and Sojourner and Marcus Garvey.

On-screen these flags of faces are a little dizzying, but then so is the scope of *Black Is ... Black Ain't*. Too generous to be called an interrogation and often too playful in spirit to be a meditation, this 87-minute documentary, completed after the directors death from AIDS in April 1994, is, as Riggs put it, a gumbo.

The film stews on the question of black identity: Whose is it anyway? is it male and straight? Is there such a thing as not black enough? Or too black? And because Riggs was not particularly worried about too many chefs, he enlists Angela Davis, Michele Wallace, bell hooks, Cornel West, as well as Barbara Smith, Bill T. Jones, Essex Hemphill, and a cast as numerous as there are types of black folk, to enrich the mix.

It is a personal and a communal sojourn; it is evangelical and celebratory. While Riggs may be evenhanded, his film is not without a profoundly ethical point of view: Blackness should be humane. Black ain't homophobic and it ain't misogynist. One of the film's most powerful moments arrives as it alternates bell hooks's retelling of the night her father threw her mother out of the house with a clip of Louis Farrakhan's hawk-in-a-chicken-yard bit justifying Mike Tyson's appetites.

Blown up from video to a 16mm print, *Black Is ... Black Ain't* isn't always pretty—though Riggs running buck-naked in the Louisiana woods has a lyrical, life-affirming power. And though it's not long, it eludes its end at least three times. But then, closure and limits are precisely what Riggs, and now his film, fight against.

Also reviewed in:
NATION, 11/6/95, p. 552, Stuart Klawans
NEW YORK TIMES, 10/11/95, p. C18, Stephen Holden
VARIETY, 2/13-19/95, p. 51, Emanuel Levy
WASHINGTON POST, 8/18/95, p. G6, Rita Kompley

BLESSING

A Starr Valley Films release. *Executive Producer:* Christopher A. Cuddihy. *Producer:* Melissa Powell and Paul Zehrer. *Director:* Paul Zehrer. *Screenplay:* Paul Zehrer. *Director of Photography:* Stephen Kazmierski. *Editor:* Andrew Morreale and Paul Zehrer. *Music:* Joseph S. DeBeasi. *Sound:* Derek Felska. *Casting:* Shiela Jaffe, Georgianne Walker, and Cassandra Han. *Production Designer:* Steve Rosenzweig. *Costumes:* Janie Bryant. *Running time:* 94 minutes. *MPAA Rating:* Not Rated.

CAST: Melora Griffis (Randi); Carlin Glynn (Arlene); Guy Griffis (Jack); Clovis Siemon (Clovis); Garreth Williams (Lyle); Randy Sue Latimer (Fran); Tom Carey (Snuff); Frank Taylor (Early).

NEW YORK POST, 4/12/95, p. 34, Bill Hoffmann

For Randi, the young heroine of "Blessing," there is a hell on earth and it's the dreary dairy farm in rural Wisconsin where she works and lives with her family.

At 23, Randi's dreams of leaving the place where she milks cows in the morning and clerks at the Star Valley General Store afternoons have reached the boiling point.

Her alcoholic father, Jack, is a bitter, broken-down farmer who rants about the fact his eldest son abandoned home for the Navy and raves about the terrible state of life.

Her mom, Arlene, is an overweight, pill-popping wreck who tries her best to keep the family together.

Randi's only shining star, the only thing keeping her tied to home is her kid brother, Clovis, a blonde-haired, 10-year-old angel who sadly watches his dysfunctional family from the sidelines.

It's this heartbreaking setup that provides fine dramatic punch to writer-director Paul Zehrer's powerful tale of the American heartland in turmoil.

Griffis' Randi is an attractive, intelligent woman with virtually no way out of a quickly worsening situation—until a free-spirited milk truck driver who dabbles in astrology offers her the chance for freedom.

Whether she'll have the guts to take that chance or throw it away because of her love of Clovis and the guilt she feels toward her downtrodden mother provide the film's edgy, crackling tension.

The film's unsettling mood is greatly enhanced by the fine cinematography of Stephen Kazmierski, who sepia-like colors make us feel the desperation and dampness of the stark landscape.

Further, the ensemble cast shines, particularly Melora Griffis and Carlin Glynn.

There are a few problems. Zehrer's liberal use of the F-word by several of the characters rings false. He seems to be using the profanity for shock value, but all it really does is make the actors appear as if they're reading from the script.

Also, after 90 minutes of angst and teeth-grinding, the film's somewhat pat ending may leave viewers a bit unsatisfied.

But all in all, this is one hell of a debut for Zehrer. He's a name to watch and "Blessing" is a film to see. Its truths and realities are things not easily forgotten.

NEWSDAY, 4/12/95, Part II/p. B9, John Anderson

The famous line at the end of Akira Kurosawa's "Seven Samurai" is a benediction to farmers. "they have their earth," says a departing warrior, "but we have nowhere." In Paul Zehrer's "Blessing," which is as deromanticized a vision of agriculture as has ever been filmed, the farmers have their earth, and it equals nowhere.

Not to stress the reference, "Blessing" also is about warfare, the kind that goes on within the four walls of a home, in this case among the four members of a family under siege by itself. As a metaphor for America it's more than apt, but the story has enough inevitable blind tragedy to make it resonate in surprisingly classical ways.

Which is not to say "Blessing" works all the time. The acting is occasionally maudlin and the situations forced. But we know the characters. Randi (Melora Griffis) is a restless young woman, wanting the money promised by her parents for staying and working, and wanting to move on. Her pre-adolescent brother, Clovis (Clovis Siemon)—who's used as blackmail to keep Randi down on the farm—is her confidant, makeup artist ("Be still," he says, and adjusts her face with a finger) and heartbreak.

The parents, Jack (Guy Griffis, father of Melora) and Arlene (Carlin Glynn), suggest what it might have been like if King Lear married Mary Tyrone: He's a hard-drinking, self-destructive tyrant who's already chased off one son, the unseen Tommy; she's a frustrated woman in denial whose hope lies in contests and lotteries and who thinks that Jack, when he climbs the silo with a rifle over his back (and isn't *that* a significant bit of Americana), is flirting with the "floozy" next door. Their deep-seated resentments, compounded by the agonizingly slow death of their dairy farm—and family—take increasingly manic turns. The children, of course, do more than their share of the suffering.

Zehrer, making his directing debut, is good with the story but better with the land: The universe of "Blessing" looks sandblasted and secondhand (cinematographer Stephen Kazmierski's palette is well-intentioned gray). There are no cosmetics, and the relentless mud—which is everywhere—sucks at the feet and the soul.

Randi is trying to save hers, of course, and thinks salvation has arrived via Lyle (Gareth Williams), the nice guy who picks up the milk and does personal horoscopes for people on his laptop. Lyle's not exactly a prize catch: He has a wife and child he's left behind in the East, and his aspirations are strictly astrological. But Randi is desperate, and torn between responsibility and a need to see the ocean. Clovis, symbol of doom that he is, wants to be a farmer; when he and Randi walk the fields and pull up rocks, Clovis fills the resulting holes with seed corn.

Much of "Blessing's" strength lies in such details. The farm family dining on boxed macaroni and cheese, for instance. Or the small intrusions of the non-farm world—a Walkman, marijuana, a baseball cap worn backward, heavy-metal music, Paul Harvey on the radio—that make the farm seem even more like a prison, one in which the bars are wrought of familial love.

VILLAGE VOICE, 4/18/95, p. 63, Jason Vincz

Somewhere in the hilly cornfields of Pennsyltucky, young Randi is trying to find herself. Sadly, that self is not on the family dairy farm where she's stranded. As days drift by, she milks the cows, ignores her father (the strong, silent, abusive type), and endures the commingled stench of cow dung and the grill where she works. Her mother, who lives in faith that the lotto and her stars will align someday, feeds Randi stale reminiscences and bland platitudes with every plate of macaroni'n'slop.

Ecch. What's not to leave?

For starters, Randi loves her lil' brother Clovis, who'll get stuck with all the chores if she leaves. She's also not sure if drifter-divorcee-astrologer-milkman Lyle is the right RV out of town. So we wait and wait, while scene after scene of her life fades to black.

First-time director Paul Zehrer's sense of basic, average Midwesternness is impeccable, and Stephen Kazmierski's slow and lovely photography evokes a corn-fed Sven Nykvist. And while Melora Griffis and Gareth Williams feel genuine as Randi and Lyle, much of their dialogue staggers around on built-in stilts. The bouncing, haphazard discussions of cows, whales, and stars sound like an earnest, pot-smoking intellectual's idea of the Simple Man's Poetry.

"Nothing happens beautifully" might be an accurate assessment of farm life, but it's a difficult premise for a film.

Also reviewed in:
NEW YORK TIMES, 4/12/95, p. C21, Stephen Holden
VARIETY, 1/24-30/94, p. 64, Todd McCarthy

BLUE IN THE FACE

A Miramax Films release of a Peter Newman/Interal Production film in association with NDF/Euro Space. *Executive Producer:* Harvey Keitel, Bob Weinstein, and Harvey Weinstein. *Producer:* Greg Johnson, Peter Newman, and Diana Phillips. *Director:* Wayne Wang and Paul

Auster. *Screenplay (in collaboration with the actors):* Wayne Wang and Paul Auster. *Director of Photography:* Adam Holender. *Editor:* Christopher Tellefsen. *Music:* John Lurie, Calvin Weston, and Billy Martin. *Music Editor:* Todd Kason, Pat Mullens, and Steve Borne. *Choreographer:* Linda Talcott. *Sound:* Drew Kunin and John Hirst. *Sound Editor:* Robert Hein. *Casting:* Heidi Levitt. *Production Designer:* Kalina Ivanov. *Set Decorator:* Karen Wiesel and Diane Lederman. *Costumes:* Claudia Brown. *Make-up:* Patricia Regan. *Running time:* 90 minutes. *MPAA Rating:* R.

CAST: Harvey Keitel (Auggie Wren); Roseanne (Dot); Michael J. Fox (Peter); Lily Tomlin (Derelict); Mel Gorham (Violet); Jared Harris (Jimmy Rose); Giancarlo Esposito (Tommy); Victor Argo (Vinnie); Madonna (Singing Telegram Girl); Keith David (Jackie Robinson); Mira Sorvino (Blonde Woman).

LOS ANGELES TIMES, 10/13/95, Calendar/p. 8, Kevin Thomas

Harvey Keitel, director Wayne Wang and writer Paul Auster had such fun making "Smoke" they got their producers to go along with a second film, "Blue in the Face," in which Keitel returns as Auggie Wren, proprietor of the Brooklyn Cigar Co. Several other characters from the first film return, too.

If you enjoyed "Smoke" you'll most likely want to see "Blue in the Face," which has considerable charm and humor, but to avoid being a bit let down it's important to view it as a companion film rather than a sequel.

That's because the two are different kinds of films and offer different rewards. Whereas "Smoke" has a plot to move it along, "Blue in the Face" has none, and the only question—a large one, for sure—is whether Auggie's boss Vinnie (Victor Argo) is going to go through with selling the place. "Tobacco's out, wheat germ's in," Vinnie says with a shrug, triggering a speech by Auggie that is the heart of the film as to how the corner cigar store "helps keep the neighborhood together."

Indeed, "Blue in the Face" is above all a Valentine to Brooklyn, a salute to a glorious past epitomized by the Brooklyn Dodgers and Ebbets Field and a resilient, though edgy, present. Essentially, it's the background of "Smoke" moved to the fore, composed of all the colorful people who drop by the store and punctuated by person-on-the-street interviews attesting to the sturdy character of Brooklynites and a series of locals reeling off statistics—"98 nationalities, 720 murders in a year."

This time Wang and Auster co-directed, and they "created situations" in collaboration with the actors, which sounds mighty like improvisation. That's always a risky approach, of course, with an inherent hit-or-miss factor. Luckily, there are more hits than misses, and wisely, Wang and Auster proceed as if the whole undertaking were a lark, moving right along with considerable bounce. Adam Holender's fresh, airy camera work and a vibrant electric score also add vitality to an all-talk film.

Among the visitors to the Brooklyn cigar store are independent filmmakers Jim Jarmusch, who's come to share a final cigarette with Augie while extolling the pleasures of smoking; Roseanne, as Vinnie's bored wife, determined to take off for Las Vegas with or without her spouse; Madonna, as a singing/dancing telegram girl, RuPaul, who leads a street dance; an amusingly wry Lou Reed, who admits a love for a town he's been trying to get away from for 35 years; Mira Sorvino, victim of a purse-snatcher; Lily Tomlin, in a sly disguise; returnee Giancarlo Esposito, as a neighborhood guy subjected to a bizarre interview by a weird Michael J. Fox; and Malik Yoba as an especially imaginative and funny neighborhood guy.

Also returning from "Smoke" are Mel Gorham, this time overly strident as Auggie's girlfriend; Jared Harris as Auggie's sweetly dim assistant; and Stephen Gevedon and Jose Zuniga, who hang out at Brooklyn Cigar. John Lurie and his group are around for musical interludes. Yoba and Argo make the strongest impressions.

Holding everything together is Keitel as the warm corner-store philosopher, who leaves us wishing we had an Auggie Wren in our own neighborhood.

NEW YORK POST, 10/13/95, p. 45, Thelma Adams

Wayne Wang and Paul Auster's "Blue in the Face—an improvational companion piece to last summer's "Smoke"—is as much a novelty item as the inflatable mermaids that greet visitors stepping off the "F" train at Coney Island.

Made in three days in Brooklyn's Windsor Terrace after "Smoke" was in the can, this chatty comedy is at its best a love letter to Brooklyn.

The rough-and-tumble, low-budget movie exalts the borough that still mourns the Dodgers' exodus after 40 years. Brooklyn is a raucous state of mind, a place where people continue to smoke against all odds and packet warnings to the contrary, an ethnic melting pot where locals yell and laugh with their mouths full and slap each other and tell endless stories.

"Blue in the Face" works best at its most heartfelt, when the camera holds a real storyteller within its gaze and lets him rip. Rocker Lou Reed leans against the counter of the Brooklyn Cigar Company and riffs on New York, a city that he claims he's been trying to leave for 35 years. "But," the shopworn singer confesses to the camera in conversational poetry, "I get scared in Sweden."

Director Jim ("Mystery Train") Jarmusch turns up in Brooklyn to smoke his last Lucky Strike with Auggie Wren (Harvey Keitel reprises his role as the cigar store manager). Jarmusch improvises with ease, doing the cigar store hang while Keitel plays straight man. Facing the end of a long-time addiction, Jarmusch laments: "Coffee and cigarettes: that's the breakfast of champions."

Like Reed, Jarmusch is someone you'd like to hang out with in a dusty cigar store nestled in a neighborhood that time forgot, just a healthy spit away from a beer at Farrell's bar. Keitel makes an amiable host, an able listener who can pull out a good story like a good cigar and make it last.

What gives the project directed in tandem by Wang ("The Joy Luck Club") and novelist Auster, its hip cachet is the list of featured players. Roseanne screeches as an angry housewife (what's new except the big hair?), Madonna delivers a singing telegram, Lily Tomlin putters as a Belgian waffle-loving bum, a second cousin to Cousin It, and Michael J. Fox intrudes as a manic yuppie who might have just escaped from the mental ward at nearby Methodist Hospital.

It's just this parade of phonies slumming in shaggytown that tramples on what would otherwise be a refreshing romance with Manhattan's better half. The misplaced stars are like the false notes in a love letter, the phrases that reveal that this love isn't the real thing, but a faked effort, a token of a cheesy love affair.

NEWSDAY, 10/13/95, Part II/p. B6, John Anderson

That much of "Blue in the Face" doesn't work—not the way a standard movie does, anyway—is perhaps the strongest point in its favor. In the oft-described "collaborative art" of cinema, spontaneity is not only rare, it can be disastrous. Not, however, in "Blue in the Face."

A loosely structured but playful film and an offshoot of Wayne Wang's "Smoke," "Blue" grew out of improvisations for the earlier movie, which were done to give the actors background for their characters. Harvey Keitel apparently suggested that the filmmakers—including "Smoke's" writer, Paul Auster—make another film, which would pick up where the improvisations left off. The cast clearly didn't want to let go of the characters.

The action—if you can call it that, given the abundance of talk implied by the title—revolves around the same Brooklyn cigar shop that was the focus of "Smoke." The manager, Auggie (Keitel), remains the moral ballast for a fractured gang of misfits, hustlers and losers: the "OTB guys" (Giancarlo Esposito, Jose Zuniga and Stephen Gevedon), the demented, homeless "Belgian Waffle Man" (Lily Tomlin in drag) and a suspicious schmoozer who may be a cult recruiter (Michael J. Fox, whose scene with Esposito is the film's funniest). What happens, without giving away too much, is the interpersonal exchanges of people who might not have a lot in common, but because they inhabit the same borough, come into daily contact. And still manage to surprise each other.

Some performances, naturally, come off better than others. Fox and Esposito are good, as is relative newcomer Mel Gorham, who as Auggie's girlfriend provides the most brazen bits of improv. Keitel is warm and sober; he lends gravity to the scenes he has with Jim Jarmuseh, who embarks on some wryly amusing cerebral ramblings. Roseanne, as the unhappy wife of Victor Argo, seems uncomfortable; Madonna, delivering a singing telegram, should be.

Lou Reed acts as a kind of emcee, philosophizing behind a counter. His reminiscences are mirrored by real Brooklynites, who are interviewed about real Brooklyn.

One needn't see "Smoke" to get "Blue in the Face"; it isn't a sequel, a prequel or a parody. It is just spontaneous acting—Auster and Wang reportedly created loose mini-story structures for the actors to work within. It's exciting cinema because, like the OTB guys, it takes some chances.

SIGHT AND SOUND, 5/96, p. 50, Chris Darke

Brooklyn, the present. Auggie Wren is standing outside his tobacconist's, the Brooklyn Cigar Company, with his assistant Jimmy Rose, the so-called OTB men (Off-Track Betting) and his new girlfriend Violet who is reminding him of the time and date of her brother's performance with his band. A young woman walks by and has her handbag snatched by a young black kid. Auggie catches the boy and returns the bag. He is about to call the police when the woman decides she doesn't wish to press charges. She and Auggie argue ferociously until Auggie takes her bag and hands it to the kid who runs off with it.

Auggie is visited in the store by several local characters who each relate their feelings about such topics as living in Brooklyn and smoking. Dot, the wife of the shop's owner, Vinnie, complains about her husband's unwillingness to take her to Las Vegas. A young hustler attempts to sell watches to Auggie and the OTB men. He berates Tommy for being a black man who hangs out with white guys. Meanwhile, local residents talk and reel off statistics about their lives in Brooklyn and documentary footage gives a history of the now-departed Brooklyn Dodgers.

Vinnie tells Auggie he is considering selling the shop. Auggie attempts to persuade him that the shop is important to the community. The ghost of baseball star Jackie Robinson visits Vinnie and makes him think again. Dot returns, even more frustrated than before. She tries to seduce Auggie into accompanying her to Vegas. When Auggie refuses, Dot takes money from the till. Vinnie appears, makes up with Dot, and they go to Vegas. Auggie and Violet have an argument when he cries off from seeing her brother's band.

Auggie and the OTB men are visited by a sharp-suited guy with a strong Spanish accent, selling Cuban cigars. They soon realise that this is the same guy who tried to sell them watches. A singing telegram girl delivers a raunchy message which explains that Vinnie has decided not to sell the store. A crowd gather outside and impromptu dancing starts up. Nine months later Auggie and Violet have a baby named Jackie .

A deliberately ramshackle assembly of sketches interspersed with celebrity cameos, and with musical and documentary interludes, *Blue in the Face* is the handrolled companion to the luxury-length pleasures of Wayne Wang and Paul Auster's *Smoke*. It takes the soaplike format of *Smoke* and develops it into a kind of hip *Cheers*, with that sitcom's bar-room banter replaced by the over-the-counter culture of 'The Brooklyn Cigar Company'. Using six days shooting added to *Smoke*'s production schedule, the strategy for *Blue in the Face* was that each scene should last no longer than a ten minute reel of stock, with one take for rehearsal and another for real. The emphasis is thus on improvisation with Auggie Wren as the corner MC presiding over a festival of Brooklyn street talk, and the OTB men, who lurk in the background of *Smoke*, brought to the fore from their former role as an earthy in-store Greek Chorus.

The cameos are among the movie's principal pleasures. Roseanne is all shrewish with frustration as Dot, Vinnie's love-hungry, Vegas-aspiring wife. As Tommy's schoolfriend Pete, a former high-flier now plainly in a parallel universe, Michael J. Fox is an unsettling presence, his low-key madness hinted at in the way he gnaws at the neck of his Snapple bottle. Lou Reed's drollery as The Man with the Unusual Glasses just about overcomes the comedy of his magnificently awful perm, while Jim Jarmusch makes a charmingly witty wannabe ex-smoker of Bob, delivering nice takes on cinematic smoking. The principle of these cameos—the famous face being more recognisably itself when thinly disguised in a walk-on part—has a strange effect on the main performers. While the cameos range from straightforward to-camera recitation to unrecognizable masquerade (Lily Tomlin in shabby drag as a derelict) the performers who were in *Smoke* here appear to be almost quoting their previous roles, holding them at a distance from the development demanded by the more conventional narrative structure of that film.

If *Blue in the Face* appears a bit cameo-happy, its improvised nature is nevertheless in keeping with the film's celebration of 'Planet Brooklyn' in all its street-level, historical and mythical diversity. So we get archive footage of the great days of the Brooklyn Dodgers and the sad day of the demolition of their stadium—as well as the mythical presence of star-player and local hero Jackie Robinson. When the ghost of Jackie appears to Vinnie in the cigar store—a scene combining whimsical fantasy and nostalgic remembrance—the visitation bears heavily on Vinnie's later decision to retain the store in the name of community. While *Smoke* treats the theme of community in terms of emotional kinship, a function of family and friends, *Blue in the Face* approaches it from the point-of-view of the actual locality. Auggie's store is an urban oasis where a sense of civic belonging is forged, but it also speaks of the endangered hangout, a reminder that the space of the modern city has to be made up of smaller places, built to a human scale in order to be inhabitable.

Blue in the Face makes the most of its metropolitan setting, grounding itself in local statistics and precise map-locations, as well as providing video-reportage on real-life inhabitants. Any city dweller will have seen plastic bags caught in the branches of trees. This fascinating and troubling detail of city life features here in video footage of a local white-collar guy's vendetta against what he describes as these "little flags of chaos". If this seems a bit cute set down on paper, it makes perfect sense in terms of the movie's insistence on the significance of local detail within the bigger urban picture. The 'tough love' sentimentality that somewhat blunted the edges of *Smoke* is here replaced by a devotion to home turf and a clearer focus on racial politics, with the character of The Rapper being the catalyst for confronting and parodying racial absolutism. That these scenes should feature impromptu song routines gives the movie a nicely distanced effect and the question of racial authenticity is handled with effective comedy. *Blue in the Face* is a good-natured enjoyably baggy monster. Maybe some enterprising television producer will buy up the format for the first smoke-opera to be sponsored by Schimmelpenincks.

VILLAGE VOICE, 10/24/95, p. 76, Georgia Brown

The day I was to see *Blue in the Face* I found myself traveling the IRT to my old subway stop of 20-odd years, Grand Army Plaza. Brooklyn boy Norman Mailer was on the car as far as Clark Street; in age, honor, and wealth, he still takes the train. A girl from elsewhere, I remain enamored not only of Brooklyn-born men and Brooklyn public transportation but Brooklyn public schools, its central park and library, as well as those fascinating, far-flung neighborhoods. No one, for instance, really saw *Rocky IV* unless she saw it in Bay Ridge: As soon as Adrian shows her face (advising Rocky not to fight again), hundreds of male viewers rose up calling on Rocky to deck her.

A similar awe of, affection for, and desire to be included in Brooklyn's cozy community informs Wayne Wang and Paul Auster's *Blue in the Face*, a reportedly impromptu spin-off of the filmmakers' previous Brooklyn-based collaboration, *Smoke* (which I confess I have not seen). Jangly and raucous, *Blue*—or, should I say, *In the Face?*—is not my Brooklyn, and probably not anyone's. It's a visitor's *hommage*, a nostalgic take on the Brooklyn mystique, or, as someone calls it "Brooklyn attitude." Reminiscent of *Jungle Fever*'s candy store sections, *Blue* is greatly indebted to authentic sons of Brooklyn, Spike Lee and Woody Allen (both hugely indebted to France's New Wave).

A celebration of idle but colorful talk, *Blue in the Face*, moves in predictable collagist fashion between on-the-street interviews, talking-head monologues, and ensemble routines inside the Brooklyn Cigar Company, Auggie Wren (a bemused Harvey Keitel), proprietor. Store regulars are Jimmy (Jared Harris), the store's not-so-swift sweeper-upper, and the "OTB guys" (Jose Zuniga, Stephen Gevedon, and Giancarlo Espisito); two frequent visitors are a garrulous con man (Malik Yoba) and Auggie's feverish girlfriend (Mel Gorham doing Rosie Perez). Bit appearances are also made by Salt Lake City's Roseanne, Akron's Jim Jarmusch, Atlanta's RuPaul, and two ladies from Detroit: a pouty Madonna delivers a singing telegram and Lily Tomlin turns up in homeless drag. Then there's a wired Michael J. Fox—one sinister Canadian out of Michael Moore's *Canadian Bacon*.

The talent, in other words, is imported, and mostly from downtown Manhattan. Even Keitel—Brighton Beach to Nobu—is now synonymous with "the city," as Brooklynites refer to it. When Lou Reed drones on whimsically about New York—"I think the only reason I live in

New York is that I know my way around New York"—that's not Brooklyn's wild side he's talking about walking on. Even the savvy Auster, best known for his *New York Trilogy*, has resided in gentrified Park Slope maybe 10 years, and his principal audience lives in Paris. Like many of us, however, Auster and Wang obviously have fallen under Brooklyn's spell.

The movie's nostalgia-infused narrative grows out of absentee owner's announcement that he's selling the shop, a money-based decision that gets linked with Walter O'Malley's treachery towards Dodger fans—the betrayal that provided a generation of men with their first and most vivid heartbreak. *Field of Dreams*-style, *Blue* brings back Jackie Robinson (Keith David) to remind Billy that certain pacts should never be broken. Whether the movie convinces us that this cigar shop rates such a comparison is another matter.

There are real pleasures here: Jarmusch's cool Jarmuschy riff on his last smoke and Ian Frazier's dissertation on freeing unsightly plastic bags from tree branches are two. Thankfully, the movie's shriller passages can be counterbalanced by a glance at Keitel's bemused, sexy (in a Brooklyn way) mug.

Also reviewed in:
CHICAGO TRIBUNE, 10/20/95, Friday/p. C, Michael Wilmington
NEW REPUBLIC, 11/6/95, p. 30, Stanley Kauffmann
NEW YORK TIMES, 10/13/95, p. C26, Janet Maslin
NEW YORKER, 10/23/95, p. 98, Terrence Rafferty
VARIETY, 2/20-26/95, p. 76, David Stratton
WASHINGTON POST, 10/20/95, p. D6, Hal Hinson

BLUE VILLA, THE

A Nomad Films release of a Nomad Films production in association with Euripide Productions/La Sept Cinema/CAB Productions/RTBF with participation of Canal Plus, Investimage 4, CNC. *Producer:* Jacque de Clercq. *Director:* Alain Robbe-Grillet and Dimitri de Clercq. *Screenplay (French with English subtitles):* Alain Robbe-Grillet. *Director of Photography:* Hans Meier. *Editor:* France Duez. *Music:* Nikos Kypourgos. *Sound:* Francois Musy. *Art Director:* Alain Chennaux. *Costumes:* Bernadette Corstens. *Running time:* 100 minutes. *MPAA Rating:* Not Rated.

CAST: Fred Ward (Frank); Arielle Dombasle (Sarah-la-Blonde); Charles Tordjman (Edouard Nordmann); Sandrine Le Berre (Senta); Dimitri Poulikakos (Thieu); Christian Maillet (The Father); Muriel Jacobs (Kim); Michalis Maniatis (Mars).

NEW YORK POST, 9/14/95, p. 48, Thelma Adams

If life is a screenplay, who is writing your part?
In "The Blue Villa," the story unfolds as a tug-of-war between competing narrators.
A solitary sailor arrives on a teardrop of a Greek island to the bars of Richard Wagner's "The Flying Dutchman." Has Frank (a nearly silent Fred Ward) come to mourn his dead love, Senta (Sandrine Le Berre)? Or has he returned to the crime scene where he murdered her in cahoots with her lecherous stepfather (Charles Tordjman)? Or is Frank a phantom, a flying Dutchman carrying out a mythical quest to be redeemed by the love of a true woman?
All three possibilities converge as the story is alternately shaped by Senta's stepfather (who is trying to absolve himself in a screenplay he is dictating), the police inspector who is trying to unravel the mystery of Senta's death, and Senta's real father, who arrives on the island to tidy up the tale.
Up at the Blue Villa, a surprisingly trendy brothel and gambling house stuck on this craggy backwater, Sarah-la-Blonde (Eric Rohmer regular Arielle Domabasle) is singing her own siren song—and she's singing it to a young woman in a tower who resembles Senta.

The mystery, co-directed by the 73-year-old Alain Robbe-Grillet (who wrote Alain Resnais' "Last Year at Marienbad") and his apprentice Dimitri de Clercq, was based on a Robbe-Grillet script. It unfolds like a game of intellectual "Clue."

Amid seductive imagery that ranges from the realistic to the fantastic, from rustic location shots of Hyrdra off the Greek coast to evil-eyed ghost ships looming in the harbor, the crux of the story still boils down to: Was it Colonel Mustard in the library with the rope or Miss Scarlet in the kitchen with the knife?

The scenes at the brothel, with their loopy Orientalism, baffling Chinese men playing mah-jongg (the scrambling of the tiles is a sound that, the screenwriter claims, "drives men to madness") and morsels of lesbian love, reduce to cheesy titillation. They are part of a labored cinematic shell-game that fails to cover for a hollowness beneath the narrative jockeying.

When a story doesn't strike to the heart, who cares how many figures had a hand in shaping it?

SIGHT AND SOUND, 12/96, p. 38, Jonathan Romney

A mysterious ship with blood-red sails approaches a remote island, and Nordmann, a writer, begins to dictate on tape the screenplay of a film ... It is set on an island haunted by the myth of a vanished sailor, Frank, who is possibly dead, having killed his girlfriend and fled to sea. It is said that the sailor will return to commit his crime again. Thieu, the island's police chief, comes to tell Nordmann that Frank has returned, and confiscates his tape for possible information. It seems that Frank's victim was Nordmann's daughter, Senta; but Thieu argues that Senta was actually Nordmann's stepdaughter, and that the writer killed her himself. At the police station, Thieu narrates his own version of events.

At the island's gambling-house cum brothel, the Blue Villa. Senta is apparently alive under the name Lotus Blossom, locked up by the Villa's madame Sarah-la-Blonde. On the mainland, Sarah is seen in flashback approaching Nordmann, newly arrived from Indochina with Senta. In the present, Frank, who is wandering the island, retrieves pictures he has taken of Nordmann killing Senta; he confronts Nordmann and accuses him of the murder. One night, Nordmann is haunted by the vision of Frank's ship, and strays into a Chinese town; returning home, he sees Senta's photo seeping blood, then a vision of Senta herself.

On the mainland, Sarah has a rendezvous with a bald man who is working on a film script, apparently rewriting Nordmann's text. The bald man, apparently the Villa's owner, is Senta's real father; he and Sarah have faked Senta's death in a plot against Nordmann. Senta confronts Frank at the tomb where they are supposedly buried together; she tells him they are both ghosts. After a run-in with Frank at the barber's, Nordmann runs home to find that Thieu is placing him under house arrest. Nordmann dictates various theories of who is behind the whole plot—possibly the brothel-keeper Mars, or Thieu—but rejects the theory of a 'real father'. Meanwhile, Senta's father is rewriting the script, and changing its ending. Confronted by Senta, Nordmann escapes in a rickshaw, while Frank and Senta erase his tape. Trying to leave the island, he falls into the sea, his death narrated by Senta's father. The next morning, Frank and Senta sail away past his floating body, as the script begins again.

The Blue Villa was filmed on the Greek island of Hydra, and the narrative is as hydra-headed as you'd expect from Alain Robbe-Grillet, the one-time 'pope' of the *nouveau roman*. Characteristically, this is a shaggy-dog story in which the characters compose and de-compose their own stories, in which place and identity remain indeterminate, in which we are never certain who is narrating, who is real or imaginary, alive, dead or a ghost. All tenses here are interchangeable; past, present and a sort of phantom conditional. But about one tense, there can be no doubt: according to a review of the film in *Cahiers du cinéma*, this is an example of a cinema "with no future."

In other words, this is a dead end, a predicament of which the film is not unaware: this is, after all, a circular narrative set on an island. But if it lacks a future, the film is perhaps too laden with its own prehistory, that is, with Robbe-Grillet's own track record as an austere but playful avant-gardist. The cross-references between his written and filmed works have, over the years, made up a fenced-off textual landscape dotted with signposts for specialist exegetes; few film-makers—except perhaps for Peter Greenaway, for whom all roads lead back to *Last Year at Marienbad*—have so assiduously spotted their work with self-reference. Most telling is a copy on

Nordmann's desk of Robbe-Grillet's most recent autobiographical volume *Les Derniers Jours de Corinthe,* suggesting that Nordmann, extravagantly bearded like the author, is another of the many Robbe-Grillet doubles that appear throughout his work, or at least that he is an avid Robbe-Grillet reader, perhaps even plagiarist.

The synopsis above is, of course, provisional, one of many possible readings that suggest themselves—although it's surprising how easily this film yields a sort of closure, as the lovers are redeemed and the perverse tyrant-author defeated. But as usual this fiction is explicable not in traditional narrative terms of cause, effect and psychology, but as an effect of combinational strategies—as figured in the perpetual shuffle and realignment of pieces in the mahjong game. Here, however, it's hard even to determine who is the author of this text. For the first time, Robbe-Grillet has co-directed and co-scripted, with Dimitri de Clercq, son of the film's producer, and the film seems to play out an allegory of its own multiple paternity. At different points, Thieu, Mars, Sarah and Senta's father, a beefy figure who looks every inch like a movie producer) are posited as alternative creators of the text which Nordmann is dictating.

But the narrative core of the film is presented as autonomous and free-floating—an 'immortal story' similar to the one in Welles' film (the lighting effects and island more than suggest a degree of homage). The story used here is the legend of the Flying Dutchman, and embodied in its image of eternal return is the circularity characteristic of Robbe-Grillet's fictions: the sense that the investigation of a crime precedes, even begets the crime itself.

The Blue Villa also features the eternal return of some elements that have seen their day, among them a touristic exoticism more than tinged with colonialism; it is hard to know how much irony can be read into the delicate postcard photography of the island, some of which would not be out of place in *Il postino.* The Chinese population of this ostensibly Greek island are headed by the group of silent mahjong players, stereotypically sinister presences who play no part in the narrative but are called on to supply a chorus of ominous gazes. Also typical of Robbe-Griller are the swanky, and here somewhat jokey, sapphic *tableaux vivants,* played up with a certain grande dame fruitiness by Arielle Dombasle, an arthouse diva always game for self-parody. Sandrine Le Berre's squeakily camp Senta puts a surreal edge on the virgin-whore archetype, but the role does rather remind you that Robbe-Grillet's least creditable work was a series of captions for the Lolita-phile kitsch of photographer David Hamilton.

At a time when even the more adventurous European art-house films adhere to conventional narrative, there's pleasure in being reminded of a history of alternative fiction-making that has somewhat been left dangling. There are other pleasures here: a remarkable visual lushness, especially in the hyper-theatrical lighting, and an extraordinary attention to sound, notably the Buñuelian incongruity of the war sounds that flare up to obscure an exposition of the plot. There's also the comic sight of Fred Ward drifting in a grizzled stupor, with practically no lines to speak, lending his presence as a spur to international sales.

But, these pleasures apart, *The Blue Villa* feels like a game that's been played too many times before and has become too schematic. Besides, we're now familiar with such multi-layered, paradoxical narrative from the way it has been assimilated by more mainstream film-making (most recently, in the pop self-reflexivity of Tom DiCillo's *Living in Oblivion*), and above all from the work of Dennis Potter, who always yoked his rivalrous narrative hypotheses to the figure of the writer caught between his text and his psyche. Robbe-Grillet offers a purer version of that same tension—there is no psyche, only texts in discord—but this now seems like a game that can play itself, an ornamental conceit that doesn't particularly call for the viewer's participation.

Also reviewed in:
CHICAGO TRIBUNE, 1/5/96, Friday/p. F, Michael Wilmington
NEW YORK TIMES, 9/14/95, p. C17, Stephen Holden
VARIETY, 3/13-19/95, p. 54, Derek Elley

BORN TO BE WILD

A Warner Bros. release in association with Fuji Entertainment of an Outlaw production. *Executive Producer:* Brian Reilly. *Producer:* Robert Newmyer and Jeffrey Silver. *Director:* John Gray. *Screenplay:* John Bunzel and Paul Young. *Based on a story by:* Paul Young. *Director of Photography:* Donald M. Morgan. *Editor:* Maryann Brandon. *Music:* Mark Snow. *Sound:* John Patrick Pritchett. *Casting:* Debi Manwiller. *Production Designer:* Roy Forge Smith. *Art Director:* Gilbert Wong. *Set Decorator:* Jan Pascale. *Animatronic Effects:* Tony Gardner. *Costumes:* Ingrid Ferrin. *Make-up:* Katharina Hirsch-Smith. *Running time:* 98 minutes. *MPAA Rating:* PG.

CAST: Wil Horneff (Rick Heller); Helen Shaver (Margaret Heller); Peter Boyle (Gus Charmley); Jean Marie Barnwell (Lacey Carr); John C. McGinley (Max Carr); Marvin J. McIntyre (Bob).

LOS ANGELES TIMES, 4/3/95, Calendar/p. 5, Kevin Thomas

It's a shame that the makers of "Born to Be Wild" went to such great lengths to create an absolutely convincing gorilla via technical wizardry only to waste their efforts on such a trite, predictable comedy-adventure. Both Katie the Gorilla—the creation of special animatronics effects expert Tony Gardner and young Wil Horneff, who are the film's endearing stars, and its serious animal-rights theme, deserve much better.

Horneff's Rick is a troubled 14-year-old who bonds with Katie, who has learned to sign from Rick's mother, a UC Berkeley behavioral scientist. John Bunzel and Paul Young's script misfires quickly when we learn that the proprietor of a local indoor flea market (Peter Boyle, pure Simon Legree) is the true owner of Katie and now reclaims his property, her caged predecessor on his premises having died of despair.

It defies credibility that the University of California would enter such an arrangement in the first place, that it doesn't have funds to purchase Katie outright (even in these admittedly straitened times), and that it wouldn't resort to the media to plead its case on Katie's behalf.

At any rate, this turn of events allows Rick to denounce his single mother for failing both to fight for her marriage and for Katie—and then to take flight with Katie for the Canadian border, where he hopes to get help from John C. McGinley's eccentric Vietnam War draft resister.

Nothing that happens along the way is in the least bit inspired, and director John Gray wastes no opportunity to emphasize the obvious, which is further underlined by Mark Snow's loud, syrupy score, dousing the film like fudge on a sundae. This is an awfully dull picture to be called "Born to Be Wild."

NEW YORK POST, 4/1/95, p. 15, Michael Medved

"Born to Be Wild" is the latest version of a classic romance: Troubled boy meets captive animal. Boy bonds with beast. Boy dares all to help beast return to nature ...

Call it "Free Willy with Bananas," since the caged critter this time is a gorilla. She's learned human sign language through a sympathetic scientist and single mother (Helen Shaver) whose rebellious 14-year-old son (Wil Horneff is punished with the assignment of cleaning out animal cages at mom's lab.

There, he develops an intense friendship with Katie the gorilla and feels heartbroken where she's reclaimed by her original owner (Peter Boyle), who mistreats her as a tourist attraction at his grungy flea market. Naturally, our teen-aged hero won't stand for that, and so springs the gorilla from captivity and hits the road with her in a mad dash for the Canadian border—and freedom.

The long chase that follows is filled with the sort of silly slapstick that kids enjoy (a police car crashing into a tank of liquefied manure, etc.) and young viewers will also feel less bothered than their parents by the fact that Katie never looks especially convincing. The producers say they ruled out using a real gorilla because of the risks involving an endangered species, so instead we spent the entire movie with some guy in a gorilla suit "outfitted with radio-controlled facial elements."

The filmmakers feel so proud of these emotional expressions that they show them off in nearly every scene, and as a result the animatronic gorilla seems to shamelessly overact.

His co-star Will Horneff, however, is far more effective—an appealing and unaffected screen presence who brings surprising emotion and infectious energy to his role. He has an aw-shucks all-American quality that adds to this movie's sometimes uncomfortable echoes of "Huck Finn":

with the two fugitives heading north for freedom, and even enjoying a brief idyll aboard a raft on a lazy river.

Of course, offering up a boy and his gorilla as a latter-day equivalent of Huck and Jim is, to say the least, racially insensitive; to make matters worse, when Katie testifies in a climactic (and unintentionally hilarious) courtroom scene, it's an African-American in a loose-fitting African print shirt who translates her sign language to the court.

Now, if they could only find someone to translate the testimony of that crucial canine eyewitness in the Simpson trial ...

NEWSDAY, 4/3/95, Part II/p. B9, Jack Mathews

The "boy-and-his-dog" story is one of the oldest chestnuts in Hollywood, but when Warner Bros. put a topical ecological spin on it with "Free Willy" two years ago, it found a way to make the genre seem both sentimental and educational. If you really love animals, kids, respect their nature.

"Free Willy," actually about a boy's attempts to set free a performing killer whale from his cramped marine aquarium pool, found a wide receptive audience, prompting Warner Bros. to produce not only the inevitable sequel ("Free Willy 2: The Adventure Home" arrives this summer), but a couple of other movies with identical themes and different wild animals. The irresistible Chinese panda is the object of a boy's affection in the upcoming "The Little Panda," and our first cousin, the ape, is getting the treatment in the current "Born to Be Wild."

"Born to Be Wild" is a shameless copy of "Free Willy," duplicating most of its themes and story elements and repeating virtually every one of its Greenpeace slogans. A gorilla named Katie was taken by humans from the wild when she was young, and as an adult, finds herself in a cramped cage on public view in some sleazy San Francisco entrepreneur's flea market.

Along comes an alienated adolescent boy, abandoned by the father he loved, and the two bond instantly. Soon, Rick (Wil Horneff) is plotting to help Katie escape and return to nature, even if it's just across the border into Canada.

Because of Katie's facial expressions, her puppy dog personality and her ability to speak in sign language, the interaction between child and beast here is vastly more familiar. If your kids suffered some anxiety separation at the end of "Free Willy," this one could break their hearts.

I'm not sure why Warner Bros. decided "Born to Be Wild" was unfit to show in advance to critics. It's corny and farfetched, more slapstick comedy than adventure, but in a market shy on family fare, it's a pleasant enough diversion. Horneff, first seen in "The Sandlot," is an engaging young actor, and ably supported by veterans Helen Shaver and Peter Boyle in the standard-issue roles of concerned mother and despicable villain.

Katie herself is little more than a costume party ape, a short, agile person cavorting around in shag carpeting. But after watching her and Rick wrestle, have paint and water fights, and team up to outsmart the villains and authorities chasing them, your kids are going to forget all about this return-them-to-nature stuff, and put apes on their Christmas lists.

Also reviewed in:
NEW YORK TIMES, 4/1/95, p. 13, Stephen Holden
VARIETY, 4/3-9/95, p. 142, Emanuel Levy
WASHINGTON POST, 4/3/95, p. D7, Rita Kempley

BOYS ON THE SIDE

A Warner Bros. release of a Le Studio Canal+/Regency Enterprises/Alcor Films presentation of a New Regency/Hera production. *Executive Producer:* Don Roos and Patricia Karlan. *Producer:* Arnon Milchan, Steven Reuther, and Herbert Ross. *Director:* Herbert Ross. *Screenplay:* Don Roos. *Director of Photography:* Donald E. Thorin. *Editor:* Michael R. Miller. *Music:* David Newman. *Music Editor:* Tom Kramer and Sally Boldt. *Sound:* Jim Webb and (music) Bobby Fernandez. *Sound Editor:* John Nutt. *Casting:* Hank McCann. *Production Designer:* Ken Adam.

Art Director: William F. O'Brien. *Set Designer:* James Bayliss, Jann K. Engel, and Stephen Berger. *Set Decorator:* Rick Simpson. *Set Dresser:* Christopher Hayes, Gary Kudroff, John A. Scott III, Luigi S. Mugavero. *Special Effects:* Dale L. Martin and Conrad Brink. *Costumes:* Gloria Gresham. *Make-up:* Michael Germain and Fern Buchner. *Stunt Coordinator:* Phil Neilson. *Running time:* 115 minutes. *MPAA Rating:* R.

CAST: Whoopi Goldberg (Jane DeLuca); Mary-Louise Parker (Robin Nickerson); Drew Barrymore (Holly); Matthew McConaughey (Abe Lincoln); James Remar (Alex); Billy Wirth (Nick); Anita Gillette (Elaine); Dennis Boutsikaris (Massarelli); Estelle Parsons (Louise); Amy Aquino (Anna); Stan Egi (Henry); Stephen Gevedon (Johnny Figgis); Amy Ray and Emily Saliers (Indigo Girls); Jude Ciccolella (Jerry); Gede Watanabe (Steve); Jonathan Seda (Pete); Mimi Toro (Carrie); Lori Alan (Girl with Attitude); Mary Ann McGarry (Dr. Newbauer); Michael Storm (Tommy); Danielle Shuman (Young Robin); Julian Neil (Nightclub Owner); Niecy Nash (Woman at Diner); Ted Zerkowski (Drug Buyer); Jill Klein (Waitress); Marnie Crossen (Nurse); Aaron Lustig (Judge); Terri White (Guard); George Georgiadis (Cab Driver); Cheryl A. Kelly (Hotel Clerk); Adria Contreras (Mary Todd, Age 5 months); Malika Edwards (Mary Todd, Age 10 months); Pablo Espinosa and Kevin La PrEsle (New Mexico Police); John F. Manfredonia (Obstetrician); Sjames Shuffield (Gynecologist); Thomas Kevin Danaher and Richard Loewll McDole (Tuscon Police); Don Hewitt and Andy Duppin (Tow Truck Drivers).

LOS ANGELES TIMES, 2/3/95, Calendar/p. 1, Peter Rainer

By all rights "Boys on the Side" should be a howler. It has the kind of high-low concept that sounds like a parody of a post-"Thelma & Louise" bond-a-thon—and, at times, the film *plays* like a parody.

Whoopi Goldberg is Jane DeLuca, a lesbian and struggling club singer: Mary-Louise Parker is Robin Nickerson, a prim, gravely ill real-estate agent: Drew Barrymore's Holly is a little love dumpling on the run from her abusive boyfriend. The film is about how they form a kind of family, so family values-'90s-style-get a boost.

"Boys on the Side" gives *everything* a boost: feminism and traditionalism, sex and abstinence, the straight-arrow and the squiggly. It's so shamelessly obliging that just about every audience of whatever stripe will find something to like in it at least some of the time. It's a confoundingly enjoyable movie because, by all rights, it should be terrible.

The characters and situations are as sudsy and manipulative as any daytime soaper. Worse, the film dabbles in high-mindedness. But the three women are so spirited and funny—so emotionally keyed into all the hearts and flowers—that they give the movie their own kind of truth. It's a performers truth. These actresses get so far inside the joys of character acting that they transcend their material. They turn all those suds into bubble bath.

Jane and Robin hook up for the first time at the beginning of the film by ride-sharing a trip from New York to L.A. Jane has been recently dumped by a girlfriend, and her career playing second-rate East Village gigs is going nowhere. Robin wants to retrace a family trip to San Diego she made as a girl with her mother and baby brother. En route, in Pittsburgh, they end up taking along Holly, a friend of Jane's, after Holly clonks her drug-dealing scumball boyfriend with a baseball bat and ties him up with tape.

Until the women decide to settle down in Tucson, the film putters along agreeably on the road. They are all so different from each other that, of course, they become soul mates. There's a terrific hokey scene early on when Jane and Robin (who doesn't suspect Jane's sexual orientation) end up watching "The Way We Were" on television and the director, Herbert Ross, just keeps the camera on their faces: Jane's is aghast, Robin's is tear-streaked.

Ross, and his screenwriter Don Roos, work in a number of other movie references, including "An Officer and a Gentleman" and—natch—"Thelma & Louise." The filmmakers are trying for instant classic status by shoving these clips into view. (Given the shamelessness of the production it's surprising Ross didn't work in his "Turning Point," too.)

But movies don't get to be classics by association, and this sort of stuff comes across as pandering. So do the frequent sops to the sobbier sectors of the audience: the finale makes the closing sections of "Terms of Endearment" look ascetic. The soundtrack is mostly composed of tracks from hit female vocalists, ranging from Annie Lennox to Melissa Etheridge, and it's the kind of high-concept idea that also comes across as pandering. It's sisterhood as marketing ploy.

Still, it's surprisingly easy to bypass everything that's wrong with this movie because the actresses are so right. Parker has the bone-white pallor and rigorous whittled politeness of a superannuated debutante queen. She's played this sort of role before—in "Fried Green Tomatoes"—but by now she's a whiz at it. When Jane coaxes her into blurting out an obscenity, she flushes with excitement. She's tickled by her naughtiness.

Barrymore; usually cast as a bad-girl, stretches here. She plays a delicate innocent who can't help attracting a swarm of men wherever she goes. With her big lipstick smile and cutesy-poo blonde locks, Holly is like a Generation X flapper. When she takes up with a super-square police officer in Tucson named Abe Lincoln (Matthew McConaughey), Barrymore lets us see the squareness in Holly too—and it's just as radiant as her flippiness.

Goldberg holds everything together. It's a remarkably un-showy performance—perhaps her best. Her role is conceived rather coarsely, as a kind of lesbian earth-mother, but she deepens it by going against the grain. Jane is no feminist standard-bearer; even at her sassiest there's a deep well of longing in her eyes. When she sits down alone at the piano and sings a bluesy version of a song by the Carpenters, the moment seems genuine. Jane has the ability to transform pop suds into something heartfelt. So does Goldberg.

And so, ultimately, does "Boys on the Side."

NEW YORK, 2/27/93, p. 111, David Denby

Whoopi Goldberg, a rhythm-and-blues singer without a job, and Mary-Louise Parker, a real-estate agent fleeing personal troubles, leave New York in a minivan, heading west, and pick up along the way Drew Barrymore, a lovable, boycrazy ninny. For a while, Herbert Ross's *Boys on the Side* is almost as exhilaratingly funny as *Thelma & Louise*. But then the three arrive in Tucson, and the movie sinks into a bog—endless scenes about AIDS (an international tragedy but virtually unusable as movie material), endless prim lectures about female-bonding. Since when did friendship among women become such a solemn institution? (No, I don't like it any better when the friends are men.) Parker is wonderful, and Drew Barrymore's innocently dirty-minded style is beginning to jell. But Whoopi Goldberg does not triumph in the unplayable role of a lesbian who mothers everybody and never gets laid. When will this talented woman actually do something in the movies?

NEW YORK POST, 2/3/95, p. 37, Michael Medved

The characters in "Boys on the Side" seem to have emerged from some diabolical Frankenstein's laboratory where white-jacketed screenwriters scientifically assemble politically correct victims.

There's the lonely black lesbian (Whoopi Goldberg), the battered, pregnant, single-mother-to-be (Drew Barrymore), and the uptight, white bread, suffering-in-secret AIDS patient (Mary-Louise Parker).

Goldberg's a frustrated club singer who wants to make a fresh start by moving from New York to LA; she answers an ad and ends up sharing a ride to the coast with Parker, who's making a nostalgic last trip to her childhood home in San Diego.

Along the way, they call on Goldberg's old friend Drew Barrymore in Pittsburgh. This visit lasts just long enough for the three fun-loving femmes to unwittingly murder Barrymore's abusive, coke dealing boyfriend while in the process of defending themselves from his brutal assaults.

As fast as you can say "Thelma and Louise", they're transformed into merry fugitives, and even though these women don't drive off a cliff, their movie very quickly does.

Once Parker's new friends learn of her tragic condition, they settle into a ridiculously perfect Tucson adobe (with no hint how they pay for it) where they also await the birth of Barrymore's baby.

Before long a too-good-to-be-true, straight arrow cop (solidly played by Matthew McConaughey of "Dazed and Confused") turns up as suitor for this pregnant free spirit, raising the possibility that his amorous attentions may turn up any number of guilty secrets.

Barrymore gives joyous life to her ditzy character, she is, in fact, perfectly cast as an airhead. Goldberg, meanwhile, is reliably effective as the sort of wisecracking, cynical survivor she could play in her sleep. The revelation is Parker—lending dignity, humor and a genuinely affecting delicacy to her role.

No amount of capable acting, however, can save this wretchedly maudlin and manipulative script (by Don Roos who previously wrote "Love Field"). There's even an altogether arbitrary and formulaic falling out among the principal characters near the end of the picture so they can all come together with the resounding declaration, "You are my family! And I love you!"

Veteran director Herb Ross has previously created some memorable movies about female friendship ("The Turning Point" and "Steel Magnolias") but those scripts, as sentimental as they were, focused on creating characters rather than touching hot button social issues. Here, the people in the movie seem to inhabit the pages of some pamphlet rather than anything resembling real life. Heavy-handed touches—like a long, shadowy shot of an empty wheelchair to mourn a character's death—hardly help.

The inane title, by the way, comes from a line delivered by Parker's suburban mom (Estelle Parsons) who condemns today's women for "treating men like side dishes, that you stick a fork in from time to time." The problem with the picture isn't the side dishes, however,—it's the female main courses who offer scant nourishment, and no taste, leaving "Boys on the Side" as a tearjerker without tears; and a road picture that goes nowhere.

NEWSDAY, 2/3/95, Part II/p. B2, Jack Mathews

The overworked comic scenes, one terribly inappropriate joke, and some lamentably contrived attempts at sentiment show up like foot-high speed bumps in Herbert Ross' "Boys on the Side." But the terrific performances of Whoopi Goldberg, Mary-Louise Parker, and—no kidding—Drew Barrymore lift it above its shaky writing and make this journey into female bonding worthwhile.

Comparisons to "Thelma and Louise," "Steel Magnolias," and "Fried Green Tomatoes" are inevitable, since "Boys" wouldn't have been made had those earlier movies not found a sizable audience. None of these films is going to go down as landmarks of feminism in Hollywood, but they are least testing the imagination of the old boy network.

Like "Thelma and Louise," "Boys" is propelled by a murder committed in self-defense. It occurs in Pittsburgh, where Jane (Goldberg), an out-of-work New York musician with a salty tongue, and Robin (Parker), an uptight real-estate agent with whom she's ride-sharing across country, stop to pick up Jane's friend Holly (Barrymore). They happen to show up just as Holly is being smacked around by her drug-dealing boyfriend, and in the chaos that ensues, one of them gives the thug a fatal whack with a baseball bat.

That sequence is one of the film's problems. Its tone jumps back and forth between almost slapstick comedy and graphic violence, neither of which is in Ross' comfort zone. He's far more sure-handed with the urbane comedy of Neil Simon (he's directed five Simon scripts, including "The Goodbye Girl" and "California Suite") and "Boys" really doesn't begin to take shape until the three women have settled down in Tucson, Ariz., where the action focuses specifically on the relationships between the three women.

They could not be more different. Jane is a monogamous lesbian whose recent breakup with a longtime lover has left her wounded and vulnerable. Robin is an unliberated square, trying to relive some romanticized memories by retracing a cross-country road trip she took with her family years earlier. Holly is a promiscuous innocent, finding love in all the wrong places, and cheerfully pregnant with a baby whose father is anybody's guess.

There is a wealth of humor in these relationships, and a wealth of bathos. Like "Steel Magnolias," which Ross directed, "Boys" ultimately turns on the grave illness of one of its central characters. That tragedy is the catalyst that brings the three women back together, sorts out the emotional conflicts that separated them, and strengthens their bond. Since the disease in question is AIDS, revealed less than halfway through the movie, you await the inevitable Hollywood death-bed scene with more than the usual dread.

Ross handles that melodrama with a measure of restraint, but his attempt to relieve the tension with a contrived joke about a nickname for a woman's genitalia is going to be hard to top as the year's most ill-timed gag. Still, those looking for a good cry won't be disappointed. These characters are so well-developed, and played, that you hurt for them despite the mawkish sentimentality.

Goldberg has never had a role better suited to both her edgy humor and the strength of her personality, and Don Roos' script, flawed in other ways, gives her an array of hilarious off-hand lines. Robin takes some getting used to, but it's not Parker's fault. Her character is a cartoon figure in the early going, and it is not until the influence she and Jane have on each other begins to take effect that she becomes a real person.

As for Barrymore, it's sort of a revelation to find her so thoroughly engaging. After playing a string of teenage sluts, she does an amazing turnaround, and is completely convincing as a young woman whose open sexuality actually underscores her innocence. Holly is less a bimbo than a diamond in the rough.

The men, as the title implies, are the ornamental objects of "Boys on the Side," and that's fair enough. Besides, the only potential love story here is the one Jane hopes to have with Robin. That romance may not go where most people will hope it does, but to acknowledge lesbian desire at all—an element of "Fried Green Tomatoes" that was cowardly abandoned between the book and the movie—Hollywood is showing some sign of growing up.

NEWSWEEK, 2/20/95, p. 72, Karen Schoemer

Like a lot of women out there, Jane (Whoopi Goldberg), Robin (Mary-Louise Parker) and Holly (Drew Barrymore) really want to be Thelma and Louise. They know their lives are dull and confining, so they hit the road in search of liberation, bags packed with the requisite cute sunglasses, soul tunes and toenail polish. "Boys on the Side" owes such a debt to "Thelma & Louise" that it includes a subplot about an unintentional murder the cops will never believe was self-defense; when Whoopi says, "I am not going over a cliff for you two," it's straight homage. Whoopi approaches her role of feisty, lovelorn blues singer with unusual understatement, while Parker is quite solid as a repressed real-estate agent with a dark secret. Barrymore just seems adorable. But director Herbert Ross ("The Goodbye Girl," "Steel Magnolias") is too old-school Hollywood to take the risks "Boys on the Side" needs. Once the film devolves into teary hospital scenes and courtroom shtik, you might pine for Thelma and Louise's daring road to oblivion.

SIGHT AND SOUND, 5/95, p. 39, Leslie Felperin

Disappointed with life in New York, club singer/musician Jane DeLuca answers Robin Nickerson's advertisement for a woman to help her drive across country. Robin is white, heterosexual and likes The Carpenters whereas Jane is black, a lesbian, and likes Janis Joplin. She is hesitant about Robin's offer, but succumbs when her own car is towed away.

In Pittsburgh, the women visit Holly, an old friend of Jane's. When Holly's boyfriend Nick, a drug dealer, beats her up the women persuade her to come with them. To keep Nick from stopping her, Holly knocks him out with a baseball bat, ties him up, and photographs the two of them together for a laugh. After she leaves, Nick, reaching for the phone, falls over and further injures his head; subsequently he dies of concussion. On the road, the three women begin to bond. The pregnant Holly learns of Nick's death, Robin discovers that Jane is gay, and Jane finds out that Robin has Aids when she collapses from pneumonia in Tucson, Arizona.

Three months later, the three women have settled in a communal house in Tucson. Jane plays in a band at a local gay bar, Holly is dating a cop named Abraham Lincoln, and Robin's health is better. Jane and Robin fall out when Jane discloses Robin's health problems to someone else, so Jane moves out. Robin's prim mother comes to visit and is shocked by the company her daughter keeps. Meanwhile, Holly confesses to Abe about her involvement in Nick's death and he turns her in to the police. She goes on trial in Pittsburgh, and the photo she took is used in evidence against her. Jane gives testimony, but the District Attorney discredits her by revealing her sexuality.

When all seems lost, Robin shows up, and her testimony secures Holly a light sentence. Robin's health promptly deteriorates. She is taken to hospital, where her mother proves surprisingly supportive. Holly gives birth, and eventually rejoins Abe in Tucson. Sometime later, all assemble for a party back in Arizona. The camera pans around the full room as Jane sings to a now emaciated and wheelchair-bound Robin. When the camera makes a second circuit of the now empty room, the wheelchair is empty.

Boys on the Side is the cinematic equivalent of a spanokopita: a flakey pastry package, tasty but mostly hot air, wrapped around a cheesy, spinachy, 'good for you' mix of issues. Just as suburban cocktail parties have forsaken cheddar and pineapple on a stick for faintly exotic appetisers like spanokopita, so has Hollywood tarted up the menu for that old box-office war horse, the 'woman's movie'. The usual diet of adultery, ungrateful progeny, and steel shoulder pads just won't do anymore. As *Boys on the Side* demonstrates, you now have to have Aids, lesbians, and female bonding in cars to really impress the guests.

This film certainly lays on a big spread. Like a peripatetic hostess, it flits ceaselessly from guest to guest. Each character's back story is sketched in enough to make them sympathetic. Even Robin's harridan mother's emotional constipation is explained by a fatal-disease-felled son and a first husband who committed suicide as a result. One begins to expect the assorted nurses and waiters in the background to come forward any minute with their child abuse traumas and back problems.

Actors relish this sort of thing, and the leads give strong, well-rounded, Oscar-friendly performances. Mary Louise Parker is a touch studied, but frequently endearing as the tragedy queen of the piece. The scene in which she battles a lifetime's inhibition in order to enunciate the word "cunt" is touching in its comic elegance. Whoopi Goldberg, egging her on, hasn't had a part this good in years. She even manages a fair pastiche of Nina Simone's off-key warble in her rendition of Roy Orbison's 'You Got It'. Finally, Drew Barrymore draws in the boyfriends (or girlfriends), making the film a date-movie, as well as one to take your mother to. Barrymore is seldom called upon to do more than look irresistibly sexy, which she manages even when pregnant and wearing a hideous hippie smock.

Herbert Ross handles the ensemble well and doesn't try anything too flashy. He thus cements his reputation as the George Cukor of our times, having been the man in charge of such earlier all-girl weep fests such *The Turning Point* and *Steel Magnolias*. He is, however, overindulgent with the screenplay—the film heaves with emotionally-charged scenes of characters revealing their feelings. But then that's the essence of the women's film genre—no pain, no gain. *Boys on the Side* celebrates not only female friendship but outright love between women. Yet, despite the presence of several gay characters, their sex lives are never actually shown. New queer cinema buffs will be disgusted with the film's cowardice—it is rather frustrating that after all those cow eyes at each other Robin and Jane never get to have sex—but then this film preaches quietly to the conventional, not the converted.

VILLAGE VOICE, 2/14/95, p. 49, Hoberman

Herbert Ross's *Boys on the Side* is a feminist buddy flick cum weepie that has odd trio Whoopi Goldberg, Drew Barrymore, and Mary-Louise Parker driving cross-country and, with the help of the car radio, bonding for life.

Each woman has a soon-revealed sexual secret (surely by now you know that Goldberg is a hetero-attracted lesbian, Barrymore unmarried and pregnant, and Parker HIV-positive). Despite these vicissitudes and a trajectory taking the women from New York to Pittsburgh to Tucson and beyond, *Boys on the Side* is closer in mood to *How to Marry a Millionaire* (directed by Jean Negulesco, a sort of Herbert Ross of the '50s) than it is to *On the Road*: Chastely raunchy Goldberg and prissy Parker switch off between Betty Grable and Lauren Bacall with bouncy bimbo Drew Barrymore in the Marilyn Monroe role.

There's a guy who gets killed, but that drama more or less dissolves soon after the trio arrives in Tucson—a paradise of multicultural tolerance and family values, populated by a company of Mexican dancers, the Indigo Girls, and a cop named Abraham Lincoln. As Mary-Louise is liberated by having to say the word *cunt*, so Whoopi-cast again as a professional singer, despite a condition that, in keeping with the film's spirit, can be termed "musically challenged"—learns to dig the Carpenters. (The same, in a sense, is true for the director. The movie's first five minutes employ the expletive *fuck* more times than in the entire Ross oeuvre, although he doesn't have to be taught to appreciate the pathos of "Close to You.")

Boys on the Side was written, directed, and 80 per cent produced by men, which may be why, although it aspires to the mythic stature of *Thelma & Louise*, the movies it quotes are *The Way*

We Were and *An Officer and a Gentleman.* Thus armed, *Boys on the Side* sets out to plumb every emotion every woman has ever had since the dawn of time—mostly in the person of Parker, who, albeit bracketed by two cold-blooded hambones, manages to turn the movie into an all-purpose screen test. Quickly pegged by Goldberg as "the whitest woman on the face of the earth," Parker is soon pulling faces, choking back tears, flaunting her turned-up nose, batting her spaniel eyes, playing drunk, enacting hot sex, and running through characterizations from Elvis to Camille.

Just about the only experience denied these plucky women is marriage to a wooden tiki doll. Nevertheless, thanks to Matthew McConaughey, who plays Barrymore's straight-arrow swain as Forrest Gump with a dick, Drew comes close.

Also reviewed in:
CHICAGO TRIBUNE, 2/3/95, Friday/p. C1, Michael Wilmington
NEW REPUBLIC, 3/6/95, p. 30, Stanley Kauffmann
NEW YORK TIMES, 2/3/95, p. C3, Janet Maslin
VARIETY, 1/23-29/95, p. 70, Brian Lowry
WASHINGTON POST, 2/3/95, p. D6, Rita Kempley
WASHINGTON POST, 2/3/95, Weekend/p. 36, Desson Howe

BRADY BUNCH MOVIE, THE

A Paramount Pictures release. *Executive Producer:* Alan Ladd, Jr. *Producer:* Sherwood Schwartz, Lloyd J. Schwartz, and David Kirkpatrick. *Director:* Betty Thomas. *Screenplay:* Laurice Elehwany, Rick Copp, Bonnie Turner, and Terry Turner. *Based on characters created by:* Sherwood Schwartz. *Director of Photography:* Mac Ahlberg. *Editor:* Peter Teschner. *Music:* Guy Moon. *Music Editor:* Danny Garde. *Choreographer:* Margaret T. Hickey-Perez. *Sound:* Russell Williams II. *Sound Editor:* John Benson. *Casting:* Deborah Aquila and Jane Shannon. *Production Designer:* Steven Jordan. *Art Director:* William J. Durrell, Jr. and Nanci B. Roberts. *Set Decorator:* Lynn Wolverton-Parker. *Set Dresser:* Jim Labarge, Stacy Doran, David A. Schoenbrun, and Scott Huke. *Special Effects:* Peter Albiez and Terry W. King. *Costumes:* Rosanna Norton. *Make-up:* Alan "Doc" Friedman and Dina Defazio. *Stunt Coordinator:* Pat Romano. *Running time:* 95 minutes. *MPAA Rating:* PG-13.

CAST: Shelley Long (Carol Brady); Gary Cole (Mike Brady); Christopher Daniel Barnes (Greg Brady); Christine Taylor (Marcia Brady); Paul Sutera (Peter Brady); Jennifer Elise Cox (Jan Brady); Jesse Lee (Bobby Brady); Olivia Hack (Cindy Brady); Henriette Mantel (Alice); David Graf (Sam); Jack Noseworthy (Eric); Megan Ward (Donna); Jean Smart (Mrs. Dittmeyer); Michael McKean (Mr. Dittmeyer); Moriah Snyder (Missy); Alanna Ubach (Noreen); Shane Conrad (Doug); Marissa Ribisi (Holly); R.D. Robb (Charlie); Steven Gilborn (Mr. Phillips); Alexander Pourtash (Mr. Amir); Keone Young (Mr. Watanabe); James Avery (Mr. Yeager); Yolanda Snowball (Mrs. Yeager); Robert Rothwell (Mr. Simmons); Elisa Pensler Gabrielli (Miss Lynley); David Proval (Electrician); Arnold Turner (Officer Axelrod); Darion Basco (Eddie); Gaura Vani Buchwald (Leon); Shannah Laumeister (Molly); David Leisure (Jason); Archie Hahn (Mr. Swanson); Barry Williams (Music Producer); Beverly Archer (Mrs. Whitfield); Tammy Townsend (Danielle); Patrick Thomas O'Brien (Auctioneer); RuPaul (Mrs. Cummings); Ann B. Davis (Trucker); Eric Nies (Hip MC); Davy Jones, Micky Dolenz, and Peter Tork (Themselves); Tully Jensen (Model); Jennifer Blanc (Valley Girl); Julie Payne (Mrs. Simmons); Tamara Mello (Stacy); Christopher Knight (Coach); Selma Archerd (Neighbor); James Randall White (Limo Driver); Lisa Sutton (Hooker); Dan Lipe and John R. Fors (Angry Neighbors); Kim Hasse (Student).

LOS ANGELES TIMES, 2/17/95, Calendar/p. 1, Kenneth Turan

Starting out as six single-parent children in search of a TV family, the Brady Bunch have turned into a multi-media conglomerate of daunting proportions.

Besides that original ABC series about the dad with three boys who married the mom with three girls, there has been an animated show, a pair of TV movies, two sequel series, numerous Brady books and even a successful stage production ("The Real Life Brady Bunch"). So is anyone surprised that "The Brady Bunch Movie" is now insisting on attention?

Though many have no doubt made the attempt, it doesn't require someone with a doctorate to analyze the reasons for the success of this resilient show. The Bradys were "Father Knows Best" for the 1970s, giving the children of divorce a fantasy family to focus on. And the fact that the Bradys' collective problems were so feeble they couldn't make the waiting list for "My So-Called Life" somehow added to their appeal.

Given all this, and how close the original shows are to self-parody, the creators of "The Brady Bunch Movie" have made a crafty decision. They've transplanted unreasonable facsimiles of the utopian Bradys to today's borderline dystopian Los Angeles and tried to figure out how they'd survive. The results, though hardly epochal, are more successfully silly than non-Brady fans will expect.

The San Fernando Valley, the Bunch's home base, has changed a lot in 25 years, but you'd never know that from the Bradys. Still the family that twinkles with sitcom perkiness, they remain blissful and oblivious to modernity, stuck like a stereo needle in the potent grooves of the '70s.

Architect father Mike (Gary Cole) continues to dress in the wide collars and impossible colors of those times, while wife Carol (Shelley Long) is still reading "Jonathan Livingston Seagull," helping long-suffering maid Alice (Henriette Mantel) with the shopping, and somehow finding time to organize sack races and family trips to Sears.

Not that the neighbors aren't doing things somewhat differently. Mr. Dittmeyer (Michael McKean) is a grasping Realtor who wants the Bradys to sell their house so he can turn the neighborhood into a mini-mall, and Mrs. Dittmeyer (Jean Smart) spends all of her time recovering from hangovers and trying to seduce those growing Brady boys.

Westdale High is different, too. When Greg (Christopher Daniel Barnes) says, "Hey there, groovy chick," people call him "dangerously retro," and the thoughts Marcia (Christine Taylor) arouses in pal Noreen (Alanna Ubach) go way past friendly.

What the film's bunch of screenwriters (Laurice Elehwany & Rick Copp and Bonnie Turner & Terry Turner of "Wayne's World") have done is ratchet those familiar Brady character traits up a notch, making what was implicit explicit. So sister Jan (Jennifer Elise Cox) is so jealous of Marcia she starts to hear "Exorcist"-type voices in her head, and Mike's fatherly advice becomes so convoluted you really believe it when the kids say, "I never thought of it that way."

Directed by TV veteran Betty Thomas, this "Brady Bunch" is structured like a nearsighted Mr. Magoo cartoon, with the family, continually careening toward near-disaster (mainly in the form of a property tax debt of $20,000), only to miraculously right itself in typical fashion at the last minute.

Though familiarity with the original show is not necessary to be diverted, the film has worked hard to capture the aura of its predecessors. The sets were constructed from the show's original blueprints and dressed with vintage props, and four of the old gang (most notably Florence Henderson and Ann B. Davis) make cameo appearances.

And not only does the new cast look uncannily like the original Bunch, the ensemble acting is uniformly right as well. "The Brady Bunch Movie" is never more than lightly amusing, but then neither was the TV show. And if all goes well, perhaps we'll next see the Bradys beamed up to the deck of the Starship Enterprise. That's about the only frontier they've neglected to explore.

NEW STATESMAN & SOCIETY, 6/9/95, p. 33, Jonathan Romney

The Brady Bunch Movie is the ultimate in-joke film—so "in" that it's just as well its humour is entirely transparent, or else no one in Britain would get it at all. Of all the TV-obsessed baby-boomers I've quizzed, only two admit to having seen the long-running programme it's based on, and even they weren't entirely sure they weren't getting it mixed up with *The Partridge Family*. I wouldn't swear that it was ever shown in Britain at all, but in the United States, the series—about two nice families merged into one even nicer unit— is legendary for its unremittingly bright-eyed vision of the world. A participant on *Oprah*, bemoaning the break-up of her family, once lamented, "I was in *The Brady Bunch*—then, one day, they cancelled the series." After a good deal of head-scratching, I realised she was speaking figuratively. You can't quite see anyone standing up on *Kilroy* and representing themselves as a regular in *Crossroads*.

The Brady Brunch may mean next to nothing here, but the principle of its spoofing in Betty Thomas' film is so simple that all you have to do is pretend they're the Partridges, and you've got the rudiments. The Bradies, however, come in their own patina of scandal—the show's peachy-keen optimism was clouded by the death from Aids of the actor who played Dad, while Mom turned out in real life to have had an affair with one of the sons. The *BBM*—for the sake of brevity—is a sneaky little enterprise. It sniggers coyly at the idea that we could ever have believed in the Bradies' factitious wholesomeness, but it also surreptitiously yearns for their values, if not their dress sense. It's aimed fairly at the generation of kitsch-fixated irony junkies who bought The Carpenters tribute LP featuring Sonic Youth; but it also has its eye on the type of person who'd leap up on *Oprah* and say, "You know what? We need the Bradies right now!" The *BBM* is actually quite funny, simply because the concept is so no-nonsense. The idea is that the world has changed but the Bradies haven't. LA is a depressed, corrupt hell, ridden with drugs, violence and sexual deviance—oh, sure, and what a gentle bucolic haven it must have been in the early 1970s. None of the Bradies is any older: they're all as naive and sunny-natured as they were 20 years ago, and they're wearing exactly the same clothes. The daughters all have Breck blonde tresses and wear white knee socks. Dad (Gary Cole) dispenses endless moral homilies, and Mom just grins winsomely and says pretty much nothing—which makes this one of the more tolerable films to feature Shelley Long.

The Bradies inhabit an invisible bubble that separates them from the rest of the world, hence the film's sharpest (in fact, only) stylistic touch: while everything else is shot in the glossy naturalism of the standard US comedy, whatever happens within the Bradies' garden walls is framed in the flat compositions of TV sitcom, complete with garish saturated colour and flipped screens.

Inexplicably, the Bradies do function in the world; they simply don't chime with it. The last family on the block to still buy red meat, they don't know what's going on outside their bubble: they don't realise their neighbour is a villainous speculator; Dad can't see his architectural designs are schlocky beyond the wildest dreams of Las Vegas post-modernism; and sex is another world entirely.

Here, of course, the film has to play fast-and-loose with its central gag. It can't decide whether to make the Bradies impeccably, impossibly innocent or play to the scandal factor and lay on the conventional weirdness-behind-the-picket-fence intimations of repression and perversion; so it does a bit of both. The family maid's coy relationship with the local butcher is spiced up when she starts sneaking around in racy undies; perennial virgin Marcia ("harder to get into than a Pearl Jam concert") fends off tentative passes from her adoring dyke friend; and the youngest son, the class Safety Monitor, innocently parades around in an "SM" armband. All these are versions of the film's central joke: that the Bradies *are* the joke, but they don't get it.

The film is pretty funny, as one-joke films go. But it only works if you're prepared to see the Bradies as village idiots, to be equally mocked and embraced: as holy fools do, they're supposed to make the hostile world itself look more foolish. That effect works only because everyone else *overestimates* them: Marcia's hip classmates misread her as a "retro-wannabe": they don't realise she's just a sitcom character. But this doesn't quite have the satiric thrust of Tony Hancock's inept artist in *The Rebel* being mistaken for a neo-primitive. The Bradies are only funny because they're one-dimensional in a two-dimensional world.

Oddly enough, this tale of unimaginably nice people is actually a variation on a much better TV spin-off about unimagillably nasty people. The Bradies bear the same cordoned-off relationship to the world as the Addams family, but with the Addamses, the stakes are higher. The Bradies demonstrate only that innocence is untenable and bad taste to boot. The Addamses are far more complex, at once subverting the canons of good behaviour and proving infinitely more agreeable than the normal people who surround them; in all their ghoulish European decadence, the Addamses invariably turn out to embody family values that would warm any Southern fundamentalist's heart. Still, *The Brady Bunch Movie* proves how serviceable the "Weird Folks Next Door" genre can be, and you have endless fun thinking up our own variations—serial killers, Aum cultists, absinthe drinkers, you name it. Having just snored through the tasteful amours of

Lytton Strachey in the forth coming *Carrington*, I couldn't help thinking how much jollier *The Bloomsbury Bunch Movie* would have been.

NEW YORK POST, 2/17/95, p. 39, Michael Medved

"The Brady Bunch Movie" slavishly recycles every element of the beloved old TV series except its innocence—and the "The Brady Bunch" without innocence is as pointless as "I Love Lucy" without laughs.

Why bother to revisit such sweet, simplistic material when it's placed in a leering, gratuitously off-color context that makes it inappropriate for the small-fry audience that's always represented the show's core constituency?

Despite the movie's questionable elements for kids, parents might still get a nostalgic kick out of its energetic, well-chosen cast. Shelley Long plays the "lovely lady" who combines her three blonde daughters with the three grinning sons of architect Mike Brady (Gary Cole) to form the most celebrated blended family in the history of civilization.

In the movie version, the kids face many of the same crises their TV predecessors confronted more than 20 years before. Pretty teen-aged Marcia (Christine Taylor) comes to the chilling realization that she's made a date with two different boys for the same Friday night; middle child Jan (Jennifer Elise Cox) frets that her popular big sister is soaking up all the world's attention, and Greg (Christopher Daniel Barnes) resolves to lead his younger siblings in a "far-out" performance at a talent show to win the $20,000 they need to save the family home.

These familiar stories play themselves out alongside the movie's central conceit: the Bradys now live in the year 1995, but in age, attitude and (most disastrously) polyester grooming, they are exactly as they appeared in the '70s. In a sense, this curious time warp reflects the spirit of the original show, which ran between 1969 and 1974. No one could honestly describe this period of Vietnam, Watergate—and Archie Bunker—as an era of carefree simplicity, and even at the time the Bradys' chirpy, Wonderbread perfection seemed endearingly anachronistic.

The original show, however, and the wildly successful stage adaptation, "The Real Live Brady Bunch," had the good sense to play it straight: the Bradys are more amusing without all of this movie's sniggering reminders as to how out-of-it they are. It's simply not necessary to give Marcia a lesbian best friend or for the family's alcoholic neighbor (Jean Smart) to lecherously urge the two oldest Brady boys to come next door to help her make a sandwich.

Sherwood Schwartz, who created the TV series, draws a co-producer credit for the film and brings back Florence Henderson, Ann B. Davis and other original cast members for amusing cameos. He also lavishes attention on every detail of the family's bell-bottoms and leisure suits, together with the avocado-and-peach interiors of their home, reminding us that the '70s spawned some of the most appalling fashions .

Speaking of appalling, Schwartz also created the TV series "Gilligan's Island" and is currently producing "Gilligan's Island—The Movie." One can only hope that this time he'll stick to the spirit of the original, without adding unnecessary elements of "The Blue Lagoon"—or "Lord of the Flies."

NEWSDAY, 2/17/95, Part II/p. B2, John Anderson

It's definitely far out. But is it groovy? "The Brady Bunch Movie," which opens about 25 years after the first episode hit the airwaves, treats the now-cherished TV sitcom the way it always asked to be treated: as an antiseptic, asexual goof in which the ideals of suburban America were taken to a near-nightmarish extreme. You might call it "Revenge on the Nerds," or "Newt Faces of '95."

It's not an approach that has to be funny, though. The show, which has never gone off the air, evidently touches some kind of nerve. As this newspaper's television editor and a Brady authority, Andy Edelstein, wrote in FanFare last Sunday, for post-boomer generations, "The Brady Bunch" represents the kind of family life that epidemic divorce and disillusion rendered nonexistent. Never mind that such domestic bliss hardly existed anyway, except onscreen. What the movie does is make fun of that imagined ideal.

So the smartest thing director Betty Thomas did was incorporate real Brady faces, which not only inspire gasps of recognition but make the joke a shared one. Original cast members Barry

Williams and Christopher Knight have cameos, as does Ann B. Davis, the original Alice, who pushes the inside-joking even farther as a trucker named Schultzy—the name of her character in the long-ago comedy "Love That Bob." And while Shelley Long, as Carol Brady, has perfected the ominous perkiness of echt TV mom Florence Henderson, the real thing makes an uncredited cameo, just to scare the hell out of you.

The story is a goulash of "Brady" plots—middle child Jan (Jennifer Elise Cox) is neurotically jealous of Marcia (Christine Taylor); Greg (Christopher Daniel Barnes) wants to be rock star Johnny Bravo; Bobby (Jesse Lee) is an overzelaous safety patroller. The cast is consistently funny, but it also bears an eerie resemblance to the original; Gary Cole's spoof of the late Robert Reed and his platitude-spewing Mike Brady borders on brutal.

The thematic gag is that the real Los Angeles of 1995 exists just beyond the Brady's Astroturfed backyard, its runway-size driveway and stockade fence. Reality barges in via the next-door neighbor Dittmeyer (Michael McKean), a developer who wants to build a residential mall in the neighborhood, but to whom the Bradys won't sell (in another inside gag, his boozy, lascivious wife is played by Jean Smart, the good girl of "Designing Women"). The crisis arrives via a property tax bill for $20,000—the Bradys, apparently, haven't paid their taxes since the TV show went to reruns in 1974. The kids then make several ludicrous attempts to raise the money.

Most of jokes in "The Brady Bunch Movie" aren't supposed to be funny, but because they're straight out of a '70s sitcom sensibility, we laugh—because we laughed at it once. The clothes, the hairdos, the groovy lingo are atrocious—but they were part of the culture. The nice thing about "The Brady Bunch Movie" is that while laughing at the Bradys we laugh at ourselves, and it doesn't hurt that much.

SIGHT AND SOUND, 6/95, p. 38, Ingrid Randoja

Los Angeles, 1995. The city is a loud, violent mess, but for the Bradys—architect Dad Mike, homemaker mom Carol, and their six kids. Greg, Marcia, Peter, Jan, Bobby and Cindy—it's still 1975. Little Cindy visits next door neighbour and amoral real estate agent Mr Dittmeyer to retrieve lost mail. As the Bradys are the only family on the street who won't sell their home to make way for a mini-mall, Dittmeyer holds onto a $20,000 property tax bill in the hopes they will be forced out. The kids, dressed in double-knit vests and polyester, go off to school. Greg decides to become a rock star to woo a girl. Marcia swoons when superjock Doug asks her to the school dance, but is oblivious to the love signals being sent her way by her lesbian best friend Noreen. Hearing devilish voices, insecure about her new glasses and obsessively jealous of Marcia, Jan visits the jaded school counsellor who tells her to establish her own identity.

Meanwhile, Mike's gas station-style designs aren't selling and he's given three chances to land a client. Dittmeyer informs Mike that he must come up with the money for the taxes in a few days or the house will be auctioned off. Cindy overhears, and the kids have a meeting in which Jan suggests they enter the school talent contest, which offers a $20,000 cash prize. The kids balk, but a few days later after they've failed to make any money, Marcia suggests the talent show option and the kids agree.

An outraged Jan runs away and is picked up by a woman trucker who uses the CB radio to inform the worried family that Jan is safe and sound. The next day the kids enter the contest as a sequinned singing group, win, and rush back home just in time to pay the taxes and convince the neighbours not to sell. They go inside where Grandma Brady is waiting. She ignores Jan but hugs Marcia, thereby sending Jan into a psychotic rage. Grandma slaps Jan, she feels better, and then Cindy starts hearing voices.

When it was announced that Hollywood was going to bring television's *The Brady Bunch* to the big screen there were loud rumblings that it would be a colossal commercial bomb to match *The Coneheads* or *The Beverly Hillbillies*, especially as *The Brady Bunch*'s audience is a very specific one. Since it originally aired in North America between 1969 and 1971—and then enjoyed constant re-runs throughout the 70s and early 80s—this cheesy sitcom never really appealed to the then-teenage Baby Boom generation, and had petered out before the kitsch-savvy 'Generation X' could claim it as their own. It's the in-between generation, those who watched the show as impatient, yearning pre-teens, who embraced a show which was considered out of date even when originally broadcast.

Those with an encyclopedic knowledge of the show will really appreciate *The Brady Bunch Movie* because the screenwriting team has sewn together bits and pieces from over a dozen episodes. True fans will notice touches such as the kitchen blackboard with the words "porkchops and applesauce" written on it, which refers to an episode in which Peter repeats that saying in an annoying Humphrey Bogart voice. Is that funny? No, not really, but it makes fans feel at home, as if they are looking at a favourite family album. Non-fans will have more trouble with the film. Relying on horrific 70s fashions and campy wholesome behaviour to produce more general laughter is risky, so the film-makers finds a neat escape route in having the alien-like family rub against modern-day society.

Allowing the boy-crazy Marcia a lesbian best friend is one of the screenplay's more effective twists. The scene in which Noreen, wide-eyed and frozen with desire, shares Marcia's bed during a sleep-over is hilarious. Turning Jan into a schizophrenic is also an inspired move, while the brief glimpse of the old maid housekeeper, Alice, in a dominatrix outfit is downright subversive. *The Brady Bunch Movie* is at its best when giving its fish-out-of-water premise a mean edge. Yet there isn't enough nastiness in this movie. The film-makers pull back when they should be charging ahead, seemingly afraid of alienating their audience.

Since the less-compelling bulk of *The Brady Bunch Movie* is made up of corny sitcom jokes, producers Sherwood Schwartz and his son Lloyd must share part of the blame, as they were also at the controls of the original television show. Barry Williams (the original Greg) in his book *Growing Up Brady* quotes a remark by Robert Reed (the original Mike): "Sherwood Schwartz was absolutely the worst writer working in television. But that all changed when suddenly there showed up one writer who was even worse. It was Lloyd." So the late Reed underscores a constant problem with television translated into cinema: poor writing. *The Flintstones, The Beverly Hillbillies* and *The Addams Family* movies have all faltered because they can't get around the basic narrative problem of how to create a two hour story for characters who previously existed in a 22 minute universe.

What works best in *The Brady Bunch Movie* are the performances from the younger cast members. Particularly outstanding is Christine Taylor as Marcia, who fine-tunes vacuous, hair-brushing vanity into an art form. But it's Jennifer Elise Cox who steals the film as Jan. Her moments of Linda Blair-meets-Sybil psychosis show the makings of a fine comedic actress. Even the often-maligned Shelley Long turns in a top notch, albeit small, performance as a carbon copy of the blandly daffy Henderson. There are also fun cameos from RuPaul as the school guidance counsellor, Barry Williams as a record executive, Florence Henderson (the original Carol Brady) as Grandma Brady, and the original Alice (Ann B. Davis) as the helpful trucker.

TIME, 3/6/95, p. 100, Richard Schickel

Whole lot of stupidity going on at the movies these day's which is not altogether unusual. What's different is that dumbness is so often a film's subject, not merely the prime cause of its being made. *Forrest Gump* is poised to win a bunch of Oscars for sweetly celebrating an imbecile, and Jim Carrey stands on the brink of superstardom for satirizing a certain type of idiocy—the kind that actually thinks it's smart—in *Dumb and Dumber*. A couple of weeks ago, *Billy Madison*, the story of a rich moron forced to repeat all the grades (1 through 12) he had flunked, and one of the most execrable movies ever made, was No. 1 at the box office. Last week a comedy about a dim American family, *The Brady Bunch Movie*, succeeded *Billy* at the top of the charts.

Quivers of alarm in all the best places! First the bellowing inanity of talk radio, then the meanest political season anyone can remember and now this goofball assault on the higher sensibility. Are we confronting the death of civilization as we know it? Maybe yes, maybe no. But before you choose door No. 1, here are three simple, ultimately consoling exercises to try.

1) Count backward on your fingers, letting each stand for a month. Stop around 15 or 16, and then recall which movie was about to gross an astonishing $100 million back then. That's right, folks, it was *Wayne's World*. Now calculate how long it takes for the competition to crank up hit imitations. Oh, something like 15 to 16 months. All movie trends begin in the yearning hearts of producers who missed the first boat.

2) Remember the Three Stooges, Abbott and Costello, Inspector Clouseau and Jerry Lewis when he was still willing to cross his eyes and gibber simultaneously. A little historical-

perspective music, maestro, if you please: everybody has always laughed—and always will—at dumb and childish behavior. It makes us feel better when we remember all the times we've acted dumb and childish. And the *Billy Madison* aside, it's infinitely preferable to so-called wit that deteriorates into *Ready to Wear* snottiness.

3) Go see *The Brady Bunch Movie*. Its largest aim, of course, is to encourage aging boomers to nostalgize over the television programs that warped their childhood. But Sherwood Schwartz, who created the show back in 1969 (and also contributed *Gilligan's Island* to American thought and culture), is no dope. He has encouraged a legion of producers and writers (and one quick-witted director, Betty Thomas) to another kind of warping—time warping. They've moved the Bradys—lock, stock and retro-moderne suburban home—into the 1990s and invited them to confront the world of carjackings, alternative life-styles and grunge with their serene, antique innocence.

Thanks, no, is their response. Dad (Gary Cole) is still reading *Jonathan Livingston Seagull*. Mom (Shelley Long) confidently orders 20 lbs. of red meat for a family feast; cholesterol is no more part of her world view than Beavis and Butthead are. The eldest daughter Marcia (Christine Taylor), who still ties up the bathroom every morning giving her long blond hair the 3,000 daily brushstrokes she deems necessary to maintain its luster, is outraged by an attempt at a French kiss ("I thought you were from Nebraska," she tells the boy) and sweetly oblivious to her best pal's lesbian longings. Her younger sister Jan (Jennifer Elise Cox) is, by Brady standards, more troubled. What's the problem, inquires the guidance counselor who's seen it all—suicidal thoughts, bulimia, pregnancy? Nope, sibling rivalry and the justifiable fear that her glasses make her look nerdy.

The implicit acknowledgement that the Bunch always was out of it (on TV Vietnam never left its muddy footprints on their AstroTurf yard) is good self-satire. More important, the Bradys represent the manners and morals idealized by conservatives. But in fin-de-siècle America they just look silly, and this movie suggests (probably unintentionally) that we have to find new ways and words to express our best impulses. If dumbness is a large part of our problem, then *The Brady Bunch Movie* is a small (and oddly cheery) part of its solution.

VILLAGE VOICE, 2/28/95, p. 74, Beth Coleman

When you're a Brady, living in a '70s sitcom world, the hard realities of modern-day suburban Los Angeles just float by: drive-by means food pickup, car-jack is something with which to fix a flat, and groovy chick is a respectful title. With a screenplay by *Wayne's World* and *Dream On* graduates, directed by a *Hill Street Blues*, and produced by Sherwood Schwartz of *The Brady Bunch Movie* and *Gilligan's Island* millions, *The Brady Bunch Movie* might have been good parody—self-serious TV of the '80s rubbing up against the flibbertigibbet of the early '70s—if it didn't suck.

It's the story of a lovely lady, who was bringing up three very lovely girls, and a man named Brady, busy with three boys of his own. Except in *Brady Bunch*, the movie, we see the kids function in an expanded, accelerated universe. At school, with those flawless complexions and dispositions, they are the most freakish instead of the most popular. Sex shows up in duh-joke style, where a lesson learned in a near date-rape situation becomes the bud for a new romance. Shelley Long plays good-witch Carol to Michael McKean's villainous real estate broker next door, the rift between the neighbors representing the break between all that is '70s, family valued, and sunshine day, with everything dirty, multicultured, and current. The time warp is the joke. In this particular episode, a back property tax is due or the house will be auctioned. Kids and parents scramble generationally to raise the scratch, realizing, in the nick of time, that they have to work together to save *la casa familiar*.

Although the costuming is *Pee-wee's Playhouse* perfect absurdist and the Brady home an artifact of California dreamin', Los Angeles 1995 rattles and radicalizes the bunch. But in their differentiation of the Bradys from the rest of the world, the moviemakers mistake sitcom sensibility for Christian-cult values—they aren't the Osmonds for pity's sake! Once the sight gags are over, which are not without their puerile pleasures (Marcia is uncanny), the movie becomes the uninterrupted, redemptive *Brady Bunch* that was never meant to be. Bad TV—larger, longer than you'd ever dreamed.

Also reviewed in:
CHICAGO TRIBUNE, 2/17/95, Friday/p. J, Michael Wilmington
NEW YORK TIMES, 2/17/95, p. C1, Janet Maslin
VARIETY, 2/20-26/95, p. 73, Leonard Klady
WASHINGTON POST, 2/17/95, p. F1, Rita Kempley
WASHINGTON POST, 2/17/95, Weekend/p. 42, Joe Brown

BRAVEHEART

A Paramount Pictures release of an Icon Productions/Ladd Company production. *Executive Producer:* Stephen McEveety. *Producer:* Mel Gibson, Alan Ladd, Jr., and Bruce Davey. *Director:* Mel Gibson. *Screenplay:* Randall Wallace. *Director of Photography:* John Toll. *Editor:* Steven Rosenblum. *Music:* James Horner. *Music Editor:* Jim Henrikson. *Sound:* Brian Simmons and (music): Shawn Murphy. *Casting:* Patsy Pollock. *Production Designer:* Tom Sanders. *Art Director:* Dan Dorrance. *Set Decorator:* Peter Howitt. *Special Effects:* Nick Allder. *Costumes:* Charles Knode. *Make-up:* Peter Frampton. *Stunt Coordinator:* Simon Crane and Mic Rodgers. *Running time:* 179 minutes. *MPAA Rating:* R.

CAST: Mel Gibson (William Wallace); Sophie Marceau (Princess Isabelle); Patrrick McGoohan (Longshanks, King Edward I); Catherine McCormack (Murron); Brendan Gleeson (Hamish); James Cosmo (Campbell); David O'Hara (Stephen); Alun Armstrong (Mornay); Angus MacFadyen (Robert the Bruce); Ian Bannen (Leper); Peter Hanly (Prince Edward); James Robinson (Young William); Sean Lawlor (Malcolm Wallace); Sandy Nelson (John Wallace); Sean McGinley (MacClannough); Alan Tall (Elder Stewart); Andrew Weir (Young Hamish); Gerda Stevenson (Mother MacClannough); Ralph Riach and Robert Paterson (Priests); Mhairi Calvey (Young Murron); Brian Cox (Argyle Wallace); Stephen Billington (Phillip); Barry McGovern (King's Advisor); John Kavanagh (Craig); Tommy Flanagan (Morrison); Julie Austin (Mrs. Morrison); Alex Norton (Bride's Father); Jeanne Bett (Toothless Girl); Rupert Vansittart (Lord Bottoms); Michael Byrne (Smythe); Malcolm Tierney (Magistrate); William Masson (Corporal); Dean Lopata (Madbaker/Flagman); Tam White (MacGregor); Donal Gibson (Stewart); Jeanne Marine (Nicolette); Martin Dunne (Lord Dolecroft); Fred Chiverton (Leper's Caretaker); Jimmy Chisholm (Faudron); David O'Hara (Stephen); John Murtagh (Lochlan); David McKay (Young Soldier); Peter Mullan (Veteran); Martin Murphy (Lord Talmadge); Gerard McSorley (Cheltham); Bernard Horsfall (Balliol); Richard Leaf (Governor of York); Daniel Coli (York Captain); Niall O'Brien (English General); Liam Carney (Sean); Bill Murdoch (Villager); Phil Kelly (Farmer); Martin Dempsey and Jimmy Keogh (Drinkers); Joe Savino (Chief Assassin); David Gant (Royal Magistrate); Mal Whyte (Jailor); Paul Tucker (English Commander).

LOS ANGELES TIMES, 5/24/95, Calendar/p. 1, Peter Rainer

In "Braveheart," Mel Gibson plays 13th Century Scottish freedom fighter William Wallace, and, boy, is his heart ever brave. So are his eyes, his mane, his pecs, his knuckles. But he's not just brave—he's smart too. As the young William's father tells the boy just before the British slaughter him, "It's our wits that make us men."

At close to three hours, "Braveheart" is a great big chunk of brogues and pillaging and whooping. Gibson, who also directed, is priming us for an epic experience—"Spartacus" in kilts. As a filmmaker, he lacks the epic gift, but the movie, scripted by Randall (no relation) Wallace, works on a fairly basic level as a hiss-the-English medieval Western. Gibson's calisthenic efforts are clunky but they're not boring, at least not until the film moves into battle overkill in the third hour and the soundtrack turns into one big *aaarrgh*.

Wallace, who leads a rebellion against the tyrannical English King Edward the Longshanks (Patrick McGoohan) after his wife (Catherine McCormack) is tragically sundered, is a celebrated Scottish hero about whom very little that isn't legendary is known.

Gibson plunges straight into the folklore. Just before the battle of Stirling, where his men are hopelessly outnumbered against the British, Wallace rouses his troops with a speech that plays like a Classics Illustrated version of the St. Crispin's Day speech from Shakespeare's "Henry V."

Once he gets the fighting spirit early on, Wallace never lightens up, not even when he's knocking around with his shaggy Wild Bunch of fellow liberators—the burly porcine Hamish (Brendan Gleeson), the Irish hothead Stephen (David O'Hara) and the old warrior Campbell (James Cosmo), who yanks arrows out of his chest with his bare hands and then laughs lustily. These guys aren't just medieval: They're practically Cro-Magnon.

Even though Wallace practically keens with a love for freedom, the real reason the Scots whoop and war in this film appears to be less than transcendent. With all the horrors inflicted by the English, the film portrays the Scots as perpetually ready-to-rumble, even among their own clans. Freedom is a guy thing. (In a recent New Yorker, a Ziegler cartoon depicts a clan of warring Scots with the caption, "Has it ever occurred to anyone that if we stopped wearing these damned skirts we wouldn't have to march off to defend our manhood every five minutes?")

With such a bunch, it would be a feat to hold up the English as much worse than anybody else. But Gibson has his ace in the hole: Patrick McGoohan is in possession of perhaps the most villainous enunciation in the history of acting. (Who can forget the way he ripped into the word *scanners* in "Scanners"?)

In actual history, King Edward came up with the idea of Parliament—no mean feat—but here he's a lizardly terror. And he's given a gay son, Prince Edward (Peter Hanly), who is depicted as such a mincing recidivist caricature that, when his father cautions him that he may one day become king, you half expect him to add, "or ... queen?"

Gibson realizes he needs a love interest to soften up his Wide World of War so he periodically works in kissy pastoral interludes involving Wallace's wife and, later, Princess Isabelle (Sophie Marceau), the daughter of the French king who is married to the prince but who hankers for the fiery Scot. The ruffian impresses her at their first powwow by speaking to her in French, then in Latin. When they clasp against sylvan settings, her fiery long tresses are twinned with his. Gibson's longhaired look not only outdoes Liam Neeson in "Rob Roy," it even trumps Brad Pitt in "Legends of the Fall." (Did the title of that film refer to Pitt's mane?)

The battle scenes are more impressive than the love scenes. From a commercial standpoint, Gibson may be wondering, particularly with his female fans: If they come to see me, will they stay for the beheadings? The skirmishes are well-staged. The rain of British arrows upon the Scots has an obscene horror—shot high into the air, they dart down deep into flesh. The Scots' ingenious use of 14-foot sharpened poles at Stirling is a ringing endorsement of the wits-that-make-us-men stuff.

But Gibson, as a director, doesn't go beyond the good guys/bad guys war plan. For the battle scenes to be great, they would have to show us how the Scots, especially when they pushed into York, were also driven into frenzies of inhumanity. The film never tries to confuse our loyalties or question the strategies of our hero or bring home the all-embracing soul-destroying horrors of war for *all* sides. "Braveheart" may be rip-roaring, but it isn't all that brave.

NEW YORK, 6/5/95, p. 48, David Denby

What in the name of Saint Andrew causes movie moguls in America, Britain, and Australia to imagine that the world is waiting for not one but two epics about British-Scottish strife in ages past? Only a few weeks ago, we had *Rob Roy*, with Liam Neeson exposing his knees and making tender, manful love to Jessica Lange out there in the damp, and now there's *Braveheart*, with Mel Gibson in shoulder-length hair, waving his enormous broadsword and leading the commoners back in the thirteenth century against the unspeakable English tyrant King Edward I. *Braveheart*, which Gibson directed himself, is stirring in a workmanlike, square-jawed way; but as troops gather, arrows fly, and bodies fall, I found myself, as I did at *Rob Roy*, wondering why I was watching it. Like many Americans, I am sometimes baffled by sectarian and nationalist claims. Cannot the noble Scots live within Great Britain? New Yorkers live within the United States, and we have far less in common with the rest of America than a citizen of Glasgow does with one of

London. When Mel Gibson tells us at the end that after much sacrifice, and many battles, Scotland received her independence from England in 1328, a little voice inside me said, "Yes, and was folded into Great Britain a few hundred years later." What are we rooting for? The cause of Scottish nationalism does not, in 1995, stir many people outside Scotland, and perhaps not everyone in Scotland. Hollywood has always loved freedom and hated tyranny as long as those abstractions possess as little current political relevance as possible. I don't, for instance, see anyone making an epic about the Bosnian Muslims, whose freedoms will have shrunk a little further by the time you finish this review.

Compared with *Rob Roy,* which was directed by Michael Caton-Jones, *Braveheart* has a relatively simple plot; it also has more action and violence. The accents are easier to understand, and the mists do not drift, ever so slowly, into the glens. *Rob Roy,* which attempted to sum up an entire culture, at times tried one's patience—though in compensation one received the acting of John Hurt and Tim Roth, who shook their ruffles and wigs at each other in ornate, mock-Shakespearean insults. English actors are made for that sort of upper-class bitchery and theatricality, and both Roth and Hurt indulged themselves to the hilt.

The American-born, Australian-raised Mel Gibson is a plainer sort of fellow. In *Braveheart,* he has made a lusty, crowd-pleasing movie, the kind of movie in which one man shows his affection for another by knocking him down. William Wallace (Gibson) returns home to Scotland after long wanderings, intending to live in peace. But he's provoked: Scotland has no king, and the English nobility and their hirelings are sullying Scottish womanhood. William falls in love with a village girl, Murron (Catherine McCormack), who looks come-hitherish in her dun-colored but body-clinging burlap. The storybook romance that follows, in glittering photographic clichés, is accompanied by rather too much of James Horner's music, with its tender flute solos (can't some movie composer give the oboe a chance?). Standing naked in an icy grove, their breath frosting in the night air, the couple consummate their union, thereby depriving an English lord of his "right" to deflower the bride on her wedding night. Soon Murron gets her throat cut, and all hell breaks loose.

Which feels familiar. One quickly recalls that Liam Neeson in *Rob Roy* was also roused to action, in part, by violence perpetrated against his wife. In the old days, Hollywood dissolved political and economic issues into easily grasped moral issues; now it dissolves them into easily grasped sexual issues. A man's possession of his wife may not be tampered with. Patriarchal energies set both movies into motion, but in *Braveheart* this drive has an ugly side that Gibson should be ashamed of. King Edward's son (Peter Hanly), who will inherit the English throne, is a gentle, gawky homosexual who makes eyes at a young courtier. The prince is loathed by his father, and Gibson allows us to identify with the king's contempt. I don't blame Patrick Mc-Goohan, who plays the king and uses his thorn-dry voice for a variety of hostile and ironic effects; McGoohan is often amusing. But when the king throws his son's lover out the window—which we're supposed to find funny (the scene is staged for comic shock)—Gibson's direction collapses into simple gay-baiting.

Some man of peace! Who is Gibson kidding? As an actor, Mel Gibson has always been hot to trot. He's happiest when scampering about, jumping from one place to another on his springy legs. Gibson, even more than usually bulked up for the occasion, is not tall, but he's a real spark plug. He's always specialized in macho-lite heroics, but this time he's playing a leader—a man whom other men follow into battle. Since much of the Wallace material is legendary (the main source appears to be a balladeer known as Blind Harry), Gibson and screenwriter Randall Wallace (an American) invent freely. This Wallace turns a Scottish military weakness into defiance, luring the overconfident English into strategic battle errors. Larking about in front of his troops, Gibson seems split between obeying his usual instinct to hit the emotions off-center and his new desire to assume the hero's mantle. But you can't be a hipster and the tribune of your people at the same time, and it isn't until Gibson gets his voice up into a solid roar that the performance begins to make sense. In the large-scale battle scenes, Gibson the director does decent work. He's obviously had a look at Sergei Elsenstein's *Alexander Nevsky,* at Welles's *Chimes at Midnight,* and at both Olivier's and Branagh's versions of *Henry V,* and he's assimilated ideas from all of them and added his own rowdy touches (the Scots mooning the English heavy armor). I can't escape the feeling, however, that Monty Python has already parodied this movie. The battles are heavy on the old H&H (hacking and hewing), with much gouging, slashing, and lopping as well, such that nary a limb remains attached to its trunk by the end. Why are we being worked up by this furious violence? *Henry V* has poetry, *Nevsky* the music of Prokofiev. There's no point to *Braveheart*, however, unless you're a hacking-and-hewing aficionado. At the end, we have to sit through an interminable scene in which the hero, captured by the English, is choked, racked, and disemboweled. Gibson puts us in the peculiar position of longing for him to die. *Braveheart* overstays its welcome. It's an epic looking not only for a point but an exit line.

NEW YORK POST, 5/24/95, p. 33, Michael Medved

For all its heroic hacking and slicing, employing and impressive array of swords and battle axes, "Braveheart" should have found one extra blade to chop the movie itself down to manageable size.

With a running time of 2 hours and 50 minutes, the picture is easily an hour too long, and that's a shame since "Braveheart" at its best—especially in its breathtaking battle sequences—is very good indeed.

Mel Gibson demonstrates that he is not only a formidable actor (in a remarkably demanding role?) but also a resourceful, accomplished director who rises to the challenge of a vastly more ambitious project than his one previous film (the intense and effective "The Man Without a Face"). He infuses every frame of this new movie with obvious love for the material, but that devotion ultimately works against him; he seems unwilling to let go of even those big chunks of the film that don't work at all.

The first half-hour, for instance, is slow, stodgy and ill-considered. Gibson tries to establish motivation for his main character (the legendary 13th-century Scottish rebel William Wallace) by showing the future freedom fighter as a boy, reacting to the death of his father at the hands of the hated English, and then as a peace-loving young man, viewing the attempted rape and brutal mistreatment of his fiancee (newcomer Catherine McCormack) by occupying English troops.

It's all terribly pat and predictable, with the perfume-commercial-style romantic interludes thrown in as a sop to all of Mel's female fans who might otherwise be put off by a film that concentrates on armed conflict. Gibson also looks too old and grizzled to be playing this sort of innocent kid, especially opposite the appropriately sweet-faced and earthy McCormack.

When his character changes, however, and becomes a ferocious and fiery avenger, Gibson is just right, conveying a fascinating combination of idealism and viciousness. The battle scenes quickly kick the movie into high gear, with spectacular staging that seems at the same time historically responsible and utterly thrilling—no easy combination to bring off. You'd have to go all the way back to 1938 and Eisentein's masterpiece "Alexander Nevsky" to find comparably stirring recreations of medieval warfare.

Political machinations are also well-sketched, with Patrick McGoohan riveting as the cruel, competent English monarch Edward I, and Angus MacFadyen (in a memorable movie debut) as future Scottish sovereign Robert the Bruce. Kilted patriots may not like the way that this national hero is presented in the movie (emphasizing his tormented betrayal of William Wallace) but it does make for absorbing drama.

Similarly absorbing is the movie's brutal, horrifying (and historically accurate) conclusion—so well-filmed—that it will stay with you for weeks after you leave the theater.

Unfortunately, even such powerful moments are marred by yet another insipid romantic interlude—this one laughably suggesting a one-night stand between the ferocious Wallace and the pampered Princess of Wales (Sophie Marceau), daughter-in-law of his arch-enemy, King Edward.

"Braveheart" is indeed a brave attempt for Mel Gibson, but it ultimately displays more heart than smarts.

NEWSDAY, 5/24/95, Part II/p. B3, Gene Seymour

"Braveheart" looks, feels and sounds like the classic it strives mightily to be, but isn't. Not quite.

Still, in orchestrating its raw energy, evocative beauty and senses-shattering violence to compelling emotional peaks, Mel Gibson shows he's got the goods to be as powerful a force in the director's chair as he is at the box office. Even with its lapses in characterization and pace, "Braveheart" is illuminated by a fierce, headlong obsession matching that of its renegade hero, William Wallace, the medieval Scot who fought British tyranny.

As played by Gibson, Wallace is a diamond in the rough who, though well-schooled in the ways of war and the world, wants little more than to settle on his family's farmland and marry the heartbreakingly beautiful peasant girl (Catherine McCormack) he's loved since childhood.

He's picked a bad time to seek a peaceful life in Scotland, which, in the late 13th Century, is under brutal occupation by the forces of King Edward I (Patrick McGoohan), known to the people squirming under his mailed fist as "Longshanks." Wallace, who saw his family and many of his friends slaughtered by the occupation, declares all-out war after his bride is killed for striking a British soldier trying to rape her.

The king isn't impressed at first by this wild insurgent and his ragtag forces. He thinks otherwise after Wallace's cunning, stunning display of strategic might at Stirling. Gibson's reconstruction of this historic battle and many others scattered throughout make up the greater glory of "Braveheart." There's a near-ecstatic charge in these graphic sequences matching the best of Akira Kurosawa and Sam Peckinpah, the Stanley Kubrick who directed "Spartacus" and "Paths of Glory" as well as the Orson Welles, who directed "Chimes at Midnight." They're tremendously exciting—and not for the faint-hearted.

Gibson's touch is less assured in the interpersonal area. Granted, you don't come to a movie like this expecting deftly drawn, intimate human relations. ("Rob Roy," the season's other men-in-kilts swashbuckler, handled such matters with smart and lusty aplomb.) But the subplot involving Longshanks' ineffectual son (Peter Hanly) and hot-blooded daughter-in-law (Sophie Marceau) comes across as shallow as Prince Edward himself, whose pronounced sissiness verges dangerously close to stereotype.

Still, the performers are a pleasure to watch. It's especially nice to see McGoohan, all flashing blue eyes and imperious rage, inhabiting as vividly malevolent a character as Edward I. (Memo to fans of McGoohan's classic TV series, "The Prisoner": If you're still wondering who Number One was, this leonine Longshanks bears a strong resemblance to your worst fears.)

Wallace's motley band of warriors includes Brendan Gleeson, James Cosmo and David O'Hara, who's a hoot as a mad Irish recruit. Angus MacFadyen treads perhaps too carefully through the ambivalent nature of Wallace's sometime ally, Robert the Bruce. However sketchily designed, the men's parts come off more substantially than those of Marceau and McCormack, who enchant, despite their underdeveloped characters.

But face it. No one matches Mel's magnetism. Without strain or ostentation, Gibson puts everything he knows about pure film acting into his portrayal of Wallace, who's got the stolid cool of "Mad Max," the manic-bemused gleam of "Lethal Weapon's" Riggs and a brooding intensity worthy of his much-underrated "Hamlet".

For the first two of its nearly three hours, "Braveheart" carries you along with such surging momentum that you barely notice how long it is. Lethargy sets in after Wallace's last major battle. Intrigue then more or less drags the story to its grand—and inevitable—finale. But by then, you know you've been through a movie that, while falling short of greatness, has greatness in it.

NEWSWEEK, 5/29/95, p. 60, Jack Kroll

Shopping for a hero this week? Featured in the summer hero department are Mel Gibson and Bruce Willis. You want a hero with long romantic hair? Mel's your man in *Braveheart* as William Wallace, the 13th-century Scot who fired up the rebellion against English rule. Don't dig those medieval dreadlocks? Take scruffy-scalped Bruce in *Die Hard With a Vengeance*, third in the hard-dying series about detective John McClane. You prefer a hero who'd rather love than fight? That's Wallace, who starts killing people only after the English do something awful to his angelic wife, Murron (Catherine McCormack). With McClane, all that gooey stuff is off-screen; he's separated from his wife, so he can get right down to battling the terrorist gang that invades New York led by the fiendishly clever Simon (Jeremy Irons).

Summer heroes run up the body count. Wallace and his no-tech medieval guys outscore McClane and the high-tech moderns. With spears, swords, lances, axes, arrows, burning pitch, the Scots and English hack, pierce, disembowel, decapitate, and torch one another in the biggest, bloodiest battle scenes in years. In "Die Hard WAV," there's one measly guy sliced in half, but there are lots of sophisticated bombs planted all over New York: in a department store, a public school, the subway, the Federal Reserve Bank vaults, where the terrorists are after $140 billion in gold.

Heroes need worthy adversaries. Randall Wallace's screenplay provides a historical one: England's King Edward I, known as Longshanks (Patrick McGoohan). His monomaniacal fury (he tosses his effete son's friend out the castle window) is scarier than Teutonic terrorist Simon's smirky plotting in "Die Hard WAV." Heroes also need sidekicks, and here "Die Hard" wins big. The Hamishes and Campbells in "Braveheart" don't match "Die Hard's" Zeus Carver, the owner of a Harlem appliance store who becomes Bruce's reluctant buddy. Zeus, the inspiration of screenwriter Jonathan Hensleigh, is played by the brilliant Samuel L. Jackson (Oscar nominee for "Pulp Fiction") with wit and relish.

Wallace is a real person; McClane is a comic-strip figure. "Braveheart" is a huge historical epic directed by Gibson with a well-balanced blend of romantic and documentary styles. "Die Hard WAV" is a ludicrous, impossible story, another whiplashing ride through the world of amazing stunts and special effects, directed by action specialist John McTiernan. But both are hero-driven movies. In "Braveheart" the injustices of history, the horror of flesh-ripping war, are simply the setting for Gibson's valiant Wallace, going after the bad guys. In "Die Hard WAV," the silliness of the story recedes before the titanic reality of New York, defended by a human Mighty Mouse.

"Braveheart" is an impressive achievement, Gibson's honorable shot at a big, resonant paean to freedom, like "Spartacus." But it's too long at nearly three hours; there's too much repeating of treacheries and battles. "Die Hard WAV" lacks the freshness of its two predecessors: we've had it with gassy police psychiatrists and supersmart terrorists. But somehow its sheer ridiculous manic energy is more fun than "Braveheart's" blood-drenched piety. Both movies romanticize violence: the real Wallace and his Scots were patriots, but were not above stripping the skin of their foes for trophies. And "Die Hard WAV" reflects the explosive madness of our time. As for the heroes, Gibson has a masculine sweetness that balances his physical dynamism. Willis is an engaging urban everyman; he looks like your plumber who can't believe that the john has just exploded all over him. Willis is the action version of Buster Keaton or Harold Lloyd, the guy caught in a Rube Goldberg world that's become a minefield. Mel and Bruce should get together before they're too old to bounce.

SIGHT AND SOUND, 9/95, p. 45, Colin McArthur

Scotland at the end of the thirteen century. The royal succession is in dispute; King Edward I of England presses his claim to feudal overlordship of the Scottish lands and crown. Orphaned in the resistance, the child William Wallace, of gentle but not noble birth, is spirited out of Scotland by his uncle. Returning as a man, he finds English garrisons throughout southern Scotland. Wallace marries his childhood friend, Murron, and when she is abused and murdered by English soldiers, he slays her murderers. He becomes the focus of resistance against the English and, while the Scots nobles hold aloof, leads a ragged army to victory at the battle of Stirling Bridge. Manoeuvring for position among themselves and against Edward, the Scots nobles knight Wallace and dub him Guardian of Scotland.

When Wallace begins to sack northern English towns, Edward sends Isabelle—a French princess married to his effete, homosexual son—to seek a truce. Much taken with Wallace, she warns him of Edward's treachery. The Scots nobles, among them Robert the Bruce, pledge support, but at the battle of Falkirk they quit the field with their cavalry, leaving Wallace's infantry exposed. Wallace is aghast to find the Bruce riding in the ranks of the English. However, the Bruce is a reluctant English ally and helps Wallace to escape. Once more Edward sends Isabelle to treat with Wallace and this time they become lovers. Wallace wreaks vengeance on many of those Scots nobles who fled the field at Falkirk but he is betrayed, taken to London and, despite the intercession of Isabelle, brutally executed.

Some years later the Bruce, having finally come out against the English, invokes Wallace's name on the field of Bannockburn and proceeds to the victory which will establish the independence of Scotland.

1995 is being widely canvassed as Scotland's cinematic *annus mirabilis*. Two home-nurtured projects, *Shallow Grave* and *Rob Roy* have been critical and commercial successes and if, at the last moment, *Braveheart* was lured from Scotland to the Republic of Ireland by tax concessions and the promise of the Irish Army as extras, it nevertheless is seen to add to the cinematic profile of Scotland and to give work to Scottish actors. All of this does, indeed, mark a victory for those Scottish film interests and institutions which have sought to create a "Hollywood on the Clyde" against those Cassandra voices (the present writer's included) which have argued for a more diverse, low-budget Scottish cinema interrogating, among other things, the way Scotland is represented on screen.

There are several regressive discourses within which Scotland is represented, the most distasteful being Tartanry (doubly so in 1995/6 when the 250th anniversary of the 1745 uprising and the battle of Culloden are being commemorated). This is the discourse within which *Rob Roy* was constructed and the reason it has been so enthusiastically promoted by the Scottish Tourist Board. Tartanry vestigially informs *Braveheart* (a nocturnal burial scene is clearly based on an *Illustrated London News* print of Queen Victoria at Balmoral), but it has been constructed mainly within quite another discourse which might be called Dark Ageism.

Certainty about how to represent historical periods recedes the further back you go. The convention is that late Victorians are stiff and hypocritical at home and languidly supercilious in the colonial setting; early Victorians jolly and Dickensian; and eighteenth century figures sexually rumbustious. Prior to that, however, things begin to mist over and certain 'Dark Ages' tropes predominate: darkness; religiosity and/or mysticism; grinding poverty and filth; physical deformity; and, above all, unspeakable cruelty. These are the dominant tropes of *Braveheart*, although its simple-mindedness also owes something to Errol Flynn's star vehicle *The Adventures of Robin Hood*, even to the extent of giving William Wallace a Little John-type companion.

This cinematic Dark Ageism can be tracked through Alexander Korda's *The Private Life of Henry VIII* (Charles Laughton's messy eating is a key trope); Carl Dreyer's *Day of Wrath*; Ingmar Bergman's *The Seventh Seal* and *The Virgin Spring*; and Richard Fleischer's *The Vikings*; the cinematic adaptation of Umberto Eco's novel *The Name of the Rose*. This discourse informs the *mise en scène* of *Braveheart*, particularly the battle scenes which are all gore, pierced eyes and genitals, cloven skulls, severed limbs and high-pitched screams. It is present too in the morbid explicitness of Wallace's execution and the malignant leprosy of the Bruce's father. The obverse of this explicit unpleasantness is a cloying sentimentality which pervades the film as a whole, but is particularly evident in Wallace's relationships with Murron and Isabelle, both in the words spoken and the way the scenes are photographed.

The ideological project of *Braveheart* is to valorise both Wallace and the Bruce as Scottish national heroes. This is done in the crudest possible way. The complexity of the medieval Scottish social formation—with thirteen claimants to the throne only a few of which were based on the recognisably modern notion of primogeniture—would tax the skills of a trained historian. Predictably the issue is posed in *Braveheart* (set five hundred years before the concept of nationalism was articulated) as "freedom" for the Scottish people. It is part of *Braveheart's* vulgarity that it cannot begin to signify how a thirteenth century consciousness might differ from a modern one.

The only feudal concept the film offers is *jus primae noctis*, the lord's right of sexual access on the first night of a tenant's marriage. Interestingly, the rejection of sexual violation fuel's *Rob Roy's* resistance too, as though this is the only kind of motivation a modern audience could grasp. *Braveheart's* incapacity to signify the melange of personal ambitions, familial ties and feudal obligations which motivated historical figures such as Robert the Bruce seriously affects the narrative, rendering the characters' motivations quite simply incomprehensible and making the Bruce, in particular, seem weak and credulous despite the film's attempts to heroise him. The valorising of Wallace and the Bruce is, in fact, a modern restatement of that 'invention of tradition' which has been active since the second half of the nineteenth century and is the key cultural strategy of nationalism. In the nineteenth century this process constructed Wallace as the Scottish hero *par excellence* and statues were raised to him in Scotland and throughout the Scottish Diaspora. Who knows, perhaps director and star, Mel Gibson, was inspired by the statue of Wallace raised at Ballarat in 1889. Certainly, if his film has any appeal to Scots it will be to the most regressively xenophobic among us.

TIME, 5/29/95, p. 66, Richard Schickel

You'd think the market for movies about scottish freedom fighters of yore would be relatively inelastic. Once a decade ought to fill such need as we have for tallish tales about brawny, if disheveled, folk heroes rallying the clans against the English interlopers. But here comes Mel Gibson's *Braveheart*, recounting the revolutionary doings of myth-enshrouded William Wallace in the 13th century, while *Rob Roy*, featuring Liam Neeson as the legendary 17th century freedom fighter, is still in the theaters. One has to suspect that this curious coincidence is inspired less by a sudden Hollywood interest in the murkier realms of British history than by an irresistible temptation to get a couple of cute guys into kilts—and common business sense be damned.

The aesthetic of the male knee being a matter far too subtle for a mere movie reviewer to contemplate, he is left with broader, possibly less relevant, judgments to pass. Chief among them is this: *Braveheart* is too much, too late. Gibson, who directs himself in Randall Wallace's screenplay, starts with certain disadvantages vis-à-vis *Rob Roy*: Sir Walter Scott never wrote a novel about William Wallace, and no one named a cocktail after him either. Got a real name-recognition problem here. Got a real length problem too. *Braveheart* runs almost three hours, and though it's full of incident, including several big and expertly staged battle sequences, it really doesn't have enough on its mind to sustain our full attention over that span. Freedom, Wallace keeps telling everyone, is a good thing, worth dying for. Tyranny, on the other hand, is a bad thing. It leads to rape and pillage, and besides, its soldiers always march in straight lines, which is stupid.

But we know all that; it's what historical movies have taught us over the years. What you need in this situation is world-class villainy, somebody full of wicked surprise to break up the banalities. This *Braveheart* lacks, though not for want of trying by Patrick McGoohan. As the English King, Edward Longshanks, he sneers realpolitik as well as George Sanders, Basil Rathbone or Henry Kissinger ever did. But he's not around as much as he should be—especially compared with Tim Roth's evil Energizer Bunny, who powers *Rob Roy* with his capering snottiness.

The other problem with *Braveheart* is its unhappy ending. After all that time, you want and expect evil to be confounded. What you get instead is the hero being tortured to death. The suspense is this: Will he crack, cry out in pain, thus robbing posterity of an inspiring example of masochism—sorry, heroism? Come on. That's Mel Gibson the wild horses are trying to pull apart. Of course he's going to die stoically. Everybody knows that a non-blubbering clause is standard in all movie stars' contracts. Too bad there isn't one banning self-indulgence when they direct.

VILLAGE VOICE, 5/30/95, p. 60, Gary Dauphin

As the second kilt-fest of the year, *Braveheart* could easily be processed in terms of a Scotsman mini-trend (with *Rob Roy*), or a Euro-history movie trend (with *Queen Margot* and *The Madness of King George*), but considering how often this overlong movie skirts outright tedium, insipid medieval hagiography, and continental-accented pomposity, the best spin to put on it might be that Mel Gibson has inadvertently made the world's most monumental drag movie. Of course, kilts aren't really women's clothing and *Braveheart* is ostensibly about the 13th-century Scottish rebellion led by one William Wallace (Gibson) against the minions of the English king Edward I, a/k/a "Longshanks" (played by Patrick McGoohan with the sadistic good humor usually reserved for Brit villains in sci-fi movies). It's just that unless you throw *Braveheart* into the recent cycle of mainstream movies about men in women's clothing, it starts to really drag after a while, amounting to little more than three hours of rigorously declaimed speeches and gratuitous slow-mo broken up by some pretty cool fight scenes.

In *Braveheart*, as in the history books, the Scottish people are oppressed and taxed by their southern neighbors, their women in constant danger of being raped (especially on wedding nights), until William Wallace returns from a pilgrimage to show that guys in skirts don't have to be wimps. *Braveheart* occasionally delivers on the more traditional pleasures such a scenario allows for: The Scottish Highlands provide a consistently beautiful backdrop, the potentates and nobles are as devious as the peasants are dirty, and *Braveheart*'s restaging of important (if you're Scottish) battles at Stirling and Falkirk are something to behold—chaotic, bloody, and rousing. Gibson himself does his usual megastar acting job—equal parts funny, earnest, and virile—but his direction would rate more appreciative kudos if it wasn't so dependent on slooowwiiing things down to make every scene that much more poetic or dramatic. History provides two love interests for William—one a childhood sweetheart, the other Isabelle, Princess of Wales (Sophie Marceau)—and *Braveheart* goes out of its way to provide the audience with an Olde English example of the love that dare not speak its name. The film's longest running "joke" is

Longshanks's gay weakling of a son Prince Edward, who is much more interested in dressing in fine silks with a male chum than he is in producing an heir with his wife Isabelle. The mere sight of Prince Edward sent one preview audience into titters, up to and including the scene where Longshanks pushes Edward's boyfriend out of a tower for no other reason than that he's there and he's gay (yuck, yuck). For all of its clichéd prattle about honor and freedom, the movie pushes the homosexual-panic button much more vigorously than any other, making *Braveheart* more about Gibson's idea of manhood than it is about the man he's playing.

Also reviewed in:
CHICAGO TRIBUNE, 5/24/95, Tempo/p. 1, Michael Wilmington
NEW YORK TIMES, 5/24/95, p. C15, Caryn James
NEW YORKER, 6/5/95, p. 94, Anthony Lane
VARIETY, 5/22-28/95, p. 91, Brian Lowry
WASHINGTON POST, 5/24/95, p. C1, Hal Hinson
WASHINGTON POST, 5/26/95, Weekend/p. 42, Desson Howe

BRIAN WILSON: I JUST WASN'T MADE FOR THESE TIMES

A Palomar Pictures release in association with Cro-Magnon Films. *Executive Producer:* Anne-Marie Mackay and Jonathon Ker. *Producer:* Don Was, Larry Shapiro, David Passick, and Ken Kushnick. *Director:* Don Was. *Director of Photography:* Wyatt Troll. *Editor:* Helen Lowe. *Sound:* Bob Dreebin, Gary Gossett, and Mike Fredriksz. *Art Director:* Justin Bailey. *Running time:* 69 minutes. MPAA Rating: Not Rated.

WITH: Brian Wilson; Tom Petty; Lindsey Buckingham; Thurston Moore; David Crosby; Graham Nash; Linda Ronstadt.

LOS ANGELES TIMES, 8/26/95, Calendar/p. 17, Steve Hochman

If Brian Wilson's life were a song, it would be in "In My Room," with its frightened melancholy, not "Fun Fun Fun." That's been well-chronicled over the years in books, interviews and histories recounting Wilson's uneasy life and struggles to keep his head above the surf, metaphorically speaking.

So what new can we expect from "Brian Wilson: I Just Wasn't Made for These Times," an affectionate film portrait of the Beach Boy at middle age? Plenty, it turns out—not shocking revelations, though such episodes as brutal beatings by his father are recounted. Rather, here are the subtle shadings of a figure who for the past 35 years has been lauded and laughed at in equal measure.

The first-time direction by Don Was, a Grammy-winning musician and producer who has worked with Bonnie Raitt, the Rolling Stones and many others, uses rich black and white, literally and figuratively, to look into the shadows and contrasts of Wilson's life. The mix of Wilson's own anecdotes with those of his family, colleagues and such star acolytes as Tom Petty, Linda Ronstadt, David Crosby and Graham Nash, support the common image of him as a musical savant, a childlike genius.

But it's presented with a personal touch that goes a long way toward explaining the drive that has kept Wilson going all these years, through mental illness and familial infighting as much as through his creative triumphs. The latter are recapped with footage of recording sessions featuring Wilson reinterpreting some of his classic songs.

Most revealing and affecting, aside from comments from Wilson himself, are matter-of-fact observations from his mother, Audrey, and Beach Boy brother Carl, who sound as if they themselves are just finally coming to grips with what life has been like for their kin.

The moment that symbolically ties it all together: the three of them sitting around a piano and harmonizing for the first time since Eisenhower was in the White House. It's a touchingly unguarded scene that marks this bittersweet film.

NEW YORK POST, 8/16/95, p. 33, Bill Hoffmann

As a raving mad Beach Boys fan, I go wild when "Good Vibrations" and "Fun, Fun, Fun" come blasting over the radio.

Nothing conjures up the easy-going days of summer and youth better than the cool, catchy ditties of Brian Wilson, creator of the band's famed "California sound."

But listening to the sublime surfing anthems, it's hard not to ponder the band's personal tragedies: particularly Wilson's well publicized mental breakdown, a collapse the band never truly recovered from.

Wilson's phenomenal success as a musical teen prodigy, his crippling depression and slow recovery are chronicled with dignity and compassion in "Brian Wilson: I Just Wasn't Made For These Times," a short and fascinating documentary by record producer Don Was.

Wilson's demon's struck in the late '60s as he tried to break from the band's surf music image with an avant-garde project called "Smile."

But the band balked, the project was scrapped and a depressed Wilson turned to drugs, built a huge sandbox in his house and refused to leave his bed for several years.

He recovered after intensive therapy, although to watch and listen to him now isn't always easy. Something still seems off.

Regardless, Wilson remains a musical wunderkind and is seen here belting out new versions of his old hits with a passion that makes them more thrilling than the originals.

On "Do It Again," Wilson's daughters, Wendy and Carney, who have their own success in the group Wilson Phillips, join in. It's a wonderful moment.

Oddly, Was ignores the controversial work of Brian's longtime therapist, Eugene Landy, who was ousted by the Wilson family, who saw him as an evil Svengali out to control Brian's finances and music.

There's also no reference to the tragic death of the Beach Boys' drummer, Dennis Wilson. Surely the loss of his kid brother must have some effect on Brian's psyche.

Was' portrait is too short and seems incomplete. Still, what's there is quite moving and assures us that Brian Wilson is a survivor—and that's very good news.

NEWSDAY, 8/16/95, Part II/p., B7, John Anderson

"Scary" is one of the adjectives used to describe the subject of "Brian Wilson: I Just Wasn't Made for These Times," and it's apt. This isn't because Wilson's brutal upbringing and drug abuse have left him visibly damaged, or because his mind seems to take the occasional 12-bar rest away from reality. It's because of the music.

And it's the music that's the message of this affectionate tribute by director Don Was—the celebrated record producer for Bonnie Raitt, the Rolling Stones and his own Was (Not Was)—who tries to establish what made the Beach Boys so special. "It's not just surfin' music," says John Cale. No, but saying what it *is*, exactly, isn't so easy. Was tries to nail it down.

As the title implies, what he finds at the source of all that surf and car music—which evolved into the multilayered complexities of the landmark "Pet Sounds"—is Brian Wilson, who out of compulsion, reclusiveness and emotional instability created some of the lushest pop harmony music ever heard. What makes his body of work so intriguing as well as beautiful is that it relies on both musical sophistication and lyrical innocence. (Linda Ronstadt, apparently interviewed during her "Canciones De Mi Padre" tour in an incongruous mariachi outfit, offers the most articulate explanation of early Beach Boys music, as jewel-like expressions of adolescent self-absorption.)

More lasting of course, is what Wilson did with vocal harmonies, chord changes and the recording studio. The job of explaining all that is left to the musicologists—who do it well—and to other performers, such as David Crosby and Graham Nash, two old harmonizers themselves, who are more gushing than informative but who know what makes for pop genius. "How do you do that?" Nash wonders about certain Beach Boy records. "You do it by sitting for hours at a piano," Crosby answers, "with that being your major thing in life." Wilson's social handicaps, in short, were a musical gift.

In his efforts to get at the sounds, Was makes short shrift of the life, but it's probably not his fault. Except for Carl Wilson, no other Beach Boy appears in the film, presumably because of grudges held (and Brian's other brother Dennis drowned years ago). Eugene Landy, Wilson's onetime therapist and apparent Svengali, receives only passing mention. Both the person and domestic crimes of Murray Wilson, the Wilson boys' martinet of a father, are described, if not dwelled upon (although no mention is made of Brian Wilson's deafness in one ear, the reported result of a childhood blow from Murray). The regret in the face of Audree Wilson, the boys' mother, says it all. "He's sort of how he used to be," she says of Brian, not close to believing it.

The film, in lovely black and white, includes some sparkling studio sequences of Wilson performing music new and old, and testimony from well-known musicians regarding Wilson's genius. Tom Petty even compares Wilson's accomplishments to Beethoven's. By the time he does, you may be willing to buy it, too.

VILLAGE VOICE, 8/22/95, p. 54, Ann Powers

It's possible to fall into Brian Wilson's life story and never come back, just as he tumbled, wide-eyed and speechless, into the water-blue depths of his own pet sounds. The question *What Happened to Brian*? can mean a lot of different things. What happened to this stocky suburban guy that made him crazy, a famous recluse who lived in a sandbox like some ever-regressing child? Before that, what made him one of contemporary music's most committed innovators, transforming an unusually constrictive artistic base—the three-minute, radio-friendly pop song—into cosmic territory, trying anything that shouldn't work by the rules of melody and harmony and coming up with mind-boggling subtleties of sound? What made him a prodigy to begin with, although he'd never had a music lesson in his life and worked in relative isolation? And at the very beginning, when Brian Wilson started inventing the world that eventually swallowed him, what happened to make him dream about the beach, of a place so ideal and ephemeral that it at once embodied and sorrowfully revealed the impossibility of every American dream?

And so on. Hyperbole accrues around Brian Wilson; he's a legendary shipwreck, and people just want to keep excavating him. There have been novels, lawsuits, biographies, gossip, reams of rock criticism, a tribute album. Blown away by emotional trauma and drugs both illegal and prescribed, hidden in his famous weird ranch near the beach, Wilson himself remained in a decades-long fog punctuated by very few outings, and then he'd seem somnambulant or brainwashed.

But now that's over. In Don Was's compassionate new biopic *I Just Wasn't Made for These Times*, Brian Wilson pulls himself out of the dunes and tells what he knows (or at least what can say) about himself. The focus is on what happened to make Wilson such a great composer and musician—not a surprising slant, considering Was's own status as a blockbuster pop-album producer. *I Just Wasn't Made* has the whimsical flavor of an artist experimenting in another medium, but doing so to illuminate his own field. There's not a lot of fancy cinema here, mostly just artily framed head shots, with a few archival clips and a generous amount of VH-1-video-style studio performance thrown in to substantiate the talk. Keeping the music at the center, Was cuts through the muck of Wilson's tragedy to uncover the basic reason why most of us care, anyway: the magic of the Beach Boys' songs only enhanced now that their structural secrets are revealed.

The most instructive portions of the film involve Wilson and others showing how a sound is made: music professor Daniel Harrison sitting at a piano and demonstrating the chord changes in "The Warmth of the Sun"; shift to Brian discussing how the song was composed the night John F. Kennedy was assassinated—and singing a snippet to remind us of the melody's devastating melancholy. Soon, the film jumps to David Crosby, another harmony addict, riffing about how the Beach Boys' major sevenths and minor-ninth chords confounded everyone else on the rock scene. These varied approaches to a seemingly limited text—an innocent ballad about a boy who recovers from a breakup by contemplating the waves—present it as a kind of magic crystal, already rich with meanings, and able to contain more.

Was has edited his interviews artfully, using only the barest bones of narration, letting the anecdotes build. Enough detail is given to certain songs to elucidate their structure, and to particular moments in Wilson's career, such as his encounter with the musicians of Phil Spector's Gold Star studios, to show why they mattered. Intricate explanations alternate with brief insights; it's fun to hear musicians like Tom Petty and Lindsey Buckingham offer praise in specific, musical terms, instead of the usual empty paeans of awards ceremonies and history-of-rock does. It's also a pleasure to discover that Wilson-heads come in all stripes. Sonic Youth's Thurston Moore, for example, discusses *Pet Sounds* as a punk album. "The cover is really creepy looking," he says, justifying how it fit in with his Velvets and Voidoids discs. "These guys with these sheep." They're goats, actually, but the point's still made.

I Just Wasn't Made's emphasis on Wilson as composer doesn't mean that Was overlooks Wilson as nutcase. A good amount of biographical information is provided, mostly in the service of explaining Wilson's artistic ups and downs. "He's a people pleaser," says Wilson's mother, who's a rather sad presence throughout, at the film's onset. "I understand that because I'm the same way." That said, Wilson's story proceeds as a tale of extreme, defensive introversion interrupted by the unavoidable forces of family and the outside world. No mention is made of brother Dennis's own tragic life and death; the influence of Dr. Eugene Landy, the psychologist who ruled Wilson's life for much of the '80s, is only alluded to. Scandal only signifies if it helps define Wilson's art. Abuse at the hands of his father accounted for his early retreat into music, Wilson says; his ex-wife, Marilyn, relates how disappointment in their relationship contributed to the sadness of "Caroline No." And what ultimately devastated Wilson, Was asserts (as many have before), was his group's failure to complete the great, lost *Smile*. After that loss Marilyn says, "I don't think Brian ever came back."

Was's film means to bring Brian back, as a revered artist who's not merely considered a genius freak but respected as a brilliant composer and still-vital musical presence. He's damaged, that can't be denied; he slurs his words, occasionally forgets himself, discusses his estrangement from his family with hope but trepidation. For a man who looks like a worn-out linebacker or Vietnam vet, he's disarmingly feckless. But Was pulls a smart move by just letting Wilson be. A very large portion of the film is simply devoted to showing him sing and play, and letting him talk about his life. The music—mostly new versions of Beach Boys classics, and a few newer songs, performed with an accomplished and respectful studio band—rarely hits the perfection of the originals, but as Brian sings them in his wrinkled, middle-aged voice, they breathe anew.

Was's project is ultimately a tribute, and although it does much to further the understanding of Brian Wilson's musical gift and personal sorrows, it can't help but be incomplete. But it may just be that Brian Wilson's story is just too difficult for anyone to tell completely, filled as it is with the kind of devastation that average people aren't supposed to encounter, but regularly do. There's a scene in *I Just Wasn't Made*, in which Wilson, his brother Carl, and his mother Audree harmonize shakily on "In My Room." You can feel the absences—the drowned Dennis, the feared father Murray. This was the ultimate song about being alone. And as the family sings there, missing each other's notes, each of them still is.

Also reviewed in:
NEW YORK TIMES, 8/16/95, p. C11, Janet Maslin
NEW YORKER, 9/4/95, p. 101, Terrence Rafferty
VARIETY, 1/30-2/5/95, p. 46, Emanuel Levy
WASHINGTON POST, 8/26/95, p. D1, Richard Harrington
WASHINGTON POST, 11/17/95, Weekend/p. 45, Desson Howe

BRIDGES OF MADISON COUNTY, THE

A Warner Bros. release of an Amblin/Malpaso production. *Producer:* Clint Eastwood and Kathleen Kennedy. *Director:* Clint Eastwood. *Screenplay:* Richard LaGravenese. *Based on the novel by:* Robert James Waller. *Director of Photography:* Jack N. Green. *Editor:* Joel Cox. *Music:* Lennie Niehaus. *Music Editor:* Donald Harris. *Sound:* Willie D. Burton and (music): Bobby Fernandez. *Sound Editor:* Alan Robert Murray and Bub Asman. *Casting:* Ellen Chenoweth. *Production Designer:* Jeanine Oppewall. *Art Director:* William Arnold. *Set Decorator:* Jay Hart. *Special Effects:* Steve Riley. *Costumes:* Coleen Kelsall. *Make-up:* Mike Hancock. *Running time:* 135 minutes. *MPAA Rating:* PG-13.

CAST: Clint Eastwood (Robert Kincaid); Meryl Streep (Francesca Johnson); Annie Corley (Carolyn Johnson); Victor Slezak (Michael Johnson); Jim Haynie (Richard); Sarah Kathryn Schmitt (Young Carolyn); Christopher Kroon (Young Michael); Phylis Lyons (Betty); Debra Monk (Madge); Richard Lage (Lawyer); Michelle Benes (Lucy Redfield); Alison Wiegert and Brandon Bobst (Children); Pearl Faessler (Wife); R.E. "Stick" Faessler (Husband); Tania Mishler and Billie McKabb (Waitresses); Art Breese (Cashier); Lana Schwab (Saleswoman); Larry Loury (UPS Driver).

CHRISTIAN SCIENCE MONITOR, 6/2/95, p. 12, Frank Scheck

The film version of "the Bridges of Madison County" needed someone like the reliable Clint Eastwood, who brings it instant credibility.

Robert James Waller's novel is firmly ensconced in the national consciousness since its debut, maintaining a permanent place on the bestseller lists. Despite widespread critical derision, millions of readers have adored it.

What most of the reviewers had a problem with was Waller's florid dialogue, which at its worst resembled the turgid excesses of Harlequin romance novels.

Eastwood's no-nonsense direction and Richard LaGravenese's screenplay have jettisoned the book's excesses, and what remains, personified by Eastwood and his co-star Meryl Streep, is a love story: It revolves around a four-day extramarital affair between Francesca, a repressed Italian housewife in Iowa and Robert Kincaid, the dashing photographer on assignment to shoot the covered bridges of the area for National Geographic. What made the book, and now the film, resonate is its appeal to anyone who has felt that there was a passionate side to them lying dormant.

Eastwood, who has discovered new resources within himself as he has aged, and Streep, who brings her formidable technique to the role, create a mature romantic duo who serve as an antidote to the usual Hollywood obsession with nubile babes and vapid hunks. At one point in their lengthy conversational courtship, Streep casually puts a hand on Eastwood's shoulder as she is speaking on the phone. It is the first physical contact between the two, and the moment carries more of a romantic charge than an explicit love scene would.

Like the book, the film is structured as a lengthy flashback, detailing the events of Robert and Francesca's affair, as told in the form of a journal that Francesca's children discover after her death. The scenes involving the grownup children, both immersed in unhappy marriages, have a stilted quality that weighs the film down. The ending, in which both of the children resolve to work harder on their own relationships (their mother chose to stay in the marriage), is merely perfunctory.

But other aspects of the film work spectacularly well. Jack N. Green's cinematography, for instance, captures the rustic beauty of Madison County, Iowa (the film was shot entirely on location).

Eastwood and Streep, polar opposites when it comes to screen personas and acting techniques, blend beautifully. If anything, these differences only create a more meaningful love story between their characters.

Streep, who gained weight and dyed her hair brown for the role, delivers yet another expert accent, capturing every emotional nuance of Francesca. And Eastwood gives a relaxed, marvelously open performance that is one of the best he's ever done.

At one point, Kincaid tells Francesca that there are people who will never find what the two of them have found, and that some don't even think it exists. No doubt, those types of people will be immune to the charms of the film in any incarnation.

But cynics will have to step over the rest of the audience, who have been reduced to puddles, on the way out of the theater.

FILMS IN REVIEW, 9-10/95, p. 54, Andy Pawelczak

Right off, I have to confess that I haven't read Robert James Waller's *The Bridges of Madison County*. Life is short, there's a lot to read and I begrudged even the few hours it would have taken to read Waller's platitudinous ode to love. Of course, seeing the movie was a different order of business—the combination of Meryl Streep and Clint Eastwood in an Eastwood directed weepie was too tantalizing to pass up. By now I'm not giving anything away to say that the novel tells the story of a four-day affair between a frustrated farmer's wife and a romantic drifter that ends with her renunciation of the man in favor of husband and family. The burning question was—how would Eastwood treat this ancient, soggy material? We now have the answer—intelligently, tastefully, perhaps too much so, and without excessive reverence for the best selling novel.

Eastwood and his scriptwriter, Richard LaGravenese, have turned Waller's novel into a well made drama consisting of a series of scenes, each with a clear beginning, middle and end. Some of these scenes go on too long (particularly those in the movie's framing device in which the wife's grown children discover her journal after her death), and the movie has four endings, each upping the sentimental ante, but still the picture at its best gives the satisfactions of good, clean carpentry, which is appropriate given the Andrew Wyeth/Edward Hopper provenance of Eastwood's visuals. In one shot that somehow works against all the odds, Streep stands on a porch alone and opens her robe to the night wind and moonlight, and it's like one of those mysterious Hopper paintings that suggest a whole history of longing and loneliness.

Eastwood's best idea was to give the movie to Streep, who as Francesca, the farmer's wife, is allowed to show for the first time in years her range and depth as an actress. When we first see Francesca, she's with her husband and two children who are on their way to a four-day visit to the state fair, Without overdoing it—it's all a matter of a few aborted gestures and an almost extinguished light in the eyes—Streep suggests Francesca's melancholy, restlessness and human complexity. Francesca is no country bumpkin—she reads Yeats, listens to blues (Eastwood's soundtrack includes some great songs by Johnny Hartman and Dinah Washington) and dreams of the greater world beyond her little patch of Iowa. When Robert Kincaid (Eastwood), a photographer for *The National Geographic* on assignment to photograph Madison County's covered bridges, stops at the farm to ask directions, you can see some unused part of her kick into life as she jokes with Robert and offers to take him to a bridge. Not much happens in the movie—there are a few dinners in the farmhouse, some love-making (with blessed little nudity), a night at a jazz club, Francesca's dawning realization that she loves Robert and her painful renunciation at the end—but Streep brings such reserves of emotion and intelligence to the role that she makes Francesca into a woman who could glean more experience and wisdom from a walk to the corner than the average person would get from a trip around the world.

And of course that's the movie's message—it's better to stay home and cultivate inwardness than to wander through life. It's a conflict that's played out in a lot of American movies—particularly *noirs* and Westerns—and in fact *Bridges* is a kind of sensitivized, New Age Western. Eastwood brings his own iconic valence to the movie—his Robert is a modern day high plains drifter with a camera instead of a gun. It was shrewd of Waller to make Robert a photographer, a perennial tourist on the surface of life's panorama, and it was shrewder yet of Eastwood to make him ever so slightly reminiscent of the promiscuous D.J. in the Eastwood-directed *Play Misty For Me*. At first, Robert could almost be mistaken for a predatory male on the prowl, the hero of one of those old farmer's daughter jokes. Of course, ultimately he's a sublimely sensitive New Male, and by the end he even learns what it means to be a committed artist, thanks to the wound he suffers from his love for Francesca. And we learn the meaning of those bridges—far from the pyramids, far from the Ganges, they're repositories of the humbler but no less deep mysteries of love, both domesticated and undomesticated.

LOS ANGELES TIMES, 6/2/95, Calendar/p. 1, Kenneth Turan

Clint Eastwood, Meryl Streep and Richard LaGravenese have pooled their resources and turned "The Bridges of Madison County," a literary sow's ear if ever there was one, into a surprisingly serviceable cotton purse. This is so unexpected an accomplishment that no one is likely to care they haven't gotten all the way to silk.

Few books have been subjected to so much critical opprobrium, or shrugged it off so casually, as Robert James Waller's slender story of a passionate four-day affair between a careworn Iowa housewife and a charismatic National Geographic photographer. Written in a grotesque style that goes well beyond self-parody, this pumped-up Harlequin novel has spent a prosperous three years on hardcover bestseller lists and isn't about to leave.

Yet any book that sells that many copies, no matter how mawkish, has to have a core that connects with an audience, and screenwriter LaGravenese ought to get the Croix de Guerre for doing battle with Waller's fatuous prose and paring "Bridges" down to its most appealing fantasy romance essence.

LaGravenese, who is having a remarkable summer with "A Little Princess" already out and Diane Keaton's "Unstrung Heroes" on the way, has understood that the worst of "Bridges" is not in its dialogue but in the silent musings that occupy its characters' minds. By keeping those thoughts unspoken, by allowing the camera to show instead of having words tell, much has been accomplished.

Unfortunately the least successful aspect of the movie "Bridges" is a newly added extended framing device that opens the proceedings. Set in the present, it introduces Francesa Johnson's two children, Caroline (Annie Corley) and Michael (Victor Slezak), arriving at a worn Iowa farmhouse after their mother's death to deal with her estate.

Both children are shocked, *shocked*, to hear that Francesa wants to be cremated with her ashes scattered over Roseman Bridge, a landmark in the area. And as they discover the even more disturbing letters and journals that detail her secret life, their obtuse comments about "some damn perverted photographer" and the generally careless, pro forma way these sequences have been put together, lead to fears for the worst.

But once "Bridges" flashes back to 1965, everything settles down. Here is Francesca (Streep), looking forward to the quiet that will result when husband Richard (Jim Haynie) and their already bratty kids take off for the Illinois state fair with a prize steer. A chance, she thinks, to spend four days as a lady of leisure with only her dog for company.

But not long after the family leaves, a man pulls up in an artistically battered pickup. It's Robert Kincaid (Eastwood), a photographer for National Geographic on assignment to photograph Madison County's celebrated covered bridges. Could she direct him to Roseman Bridge? With little else to do, Francesa impulsively decides to take him there personally.

Soon they are sharing confidences, as he tells her of his wanderings around the world in search of just the right light and she of her Italian upbringing and a life as a war bride and farm wife that "isn't what I dreamed of as a girl." Once they begin quoting Yeats to each other, the kind of romance that mostly appears on books with Fabio on the cover can't help but follow.

Especially after his Oscar for "Unforgiven," Clint Eastwood's bona fides as a filmmaker are not in question but the Man With No Name is still an unlikely choice for "Bridges," for what 50 years ago would've been called a classic women's picture. But Eastwood's sturdy utilitarianism, the spareness and efficiency that characterize his style, are actually what this kind of material, which is susceptible to being as overheated as Waller's prose, most needs.

You can, however, have too much of a good thing, and one of "Bridges'" persistent problems is that it is more genteel, restrained and reverential than it ought to be.

At 2 hours and 15 minutes, it takes more time to watch than the 171-page book takes to read, and though no one will be expecting a sequel to "Speed," a little more pace would have helped.

Balancing this weakness, however, is a performance of exceptional strength by Streep. Though it is easy to mock her love of accents (she gives herself a slight Italian one though the book does not), it remains true that when she is right, as she is here, she has the magic of believability about her.

She makes Francesca more real than she ever was on the page, and watching her build the character, being alternately nervous, flustered, comic and filled with yearning, underlines how lucky the film is to have her as one of its stars.

And, more unexpected, she and Eastwood turn out to have considerable rapport on screen, and are easily believable in the genteel love scenes that make up the most anticipated part of the movie. Partly because they come from different poles of acting—he being the prototypical intuitive actor, she the brilliantly schooled technician—they have an opposites-attract quality, like the captain of the football team suddenly taking an interest in the smartest girl in the class. Without the distraction of the soft-core thoughts that litter the book, their chemistry is quite enjoyable, at least up to a point.

For the final problem that besets "The Bridges of Madison County," the problem that no amount of talent can make go away, is that Robert Kincaid is about as real a person as Little Lord Fauntleroy, a wish-fulfillment cartoon of masculinity whose success as a fantasy figure led directly to the book's enormous financial success but creates believability problems when transferred to the screen.

It's worse in Waller's version, where Kincaid is variously described as "a half-man, half-some-thing-else creature" and "not of this earth" and is such a paragon he even shuts the screen door gently. LaGravenese's script and Eastwood's ability to play Kincaid completely without affect help soften this, but we are still left with a Sensitive New Age Guy who talks about "embracing the mystery" and has not a single rough edge to hang onto. Always saying and doing the right thing at the right time, Kincaid is a snore as a character, and a snore is the last thing this excessively modulated movie really needs.

NEW YORK, 6/12/95, p. 56, David Denby

It's a commonplace of film criticism that movies, for all their narrative and emotional fluency, can never quite capture the fine-grained idiosyncrasy, the texture of feeling and perception, of a writer's vision. But what if the words and the vision are neither Edith Wharton's nor Ernest Hemingway's but Robert James Waller's? Could anyone with sense want the equivalent of Waller's words on film? Almost three years on the *Times* best-seller list, *The Bridges of Madison County* has sold roughly 5.5 million copies and become this decade's publishing phenom—a great read for nonreaders, or at any rate for readers not likely to become peevish or worse when Waller writes of a woman's postcoital state that "with her face buried in [her lover's] neck and her skin against his, she could smell rivers and woodsmoke, could hear steaming trains chuffing out of winter stations in long-ago nighttimes, could see travelers in black robes moving steadily along frozen rivers and through summer meadows, beating their way toward the end of things. " Thank God the camera cannot capture that kind of sex. And who but the tone-deaf or camp-hungry would long to hear the lover's proposal: "Come travel with me, Francesca. ... We'll make love in desert sand and drink brandy on balconies in Mombasa, watching dhows from Arabia run up their sails in the first wind of morning"? Who'd sit still through Francesca's extraordinary refusal: "Don't you see, I love you so much that I cannot think of restraining you for a moment. To do that would be to kill the wild, magnificent animal that is you, and the power would die with it"?

Well, the power has not quite died, but it has been transformed into plainer English and something recognizably human. *The Bridges of Madison County* isn't my kind of movie—it's too solemn by half—but it's not bad. Clint Eastwood, who directed the movie and starred in it with Meryl Streep, has displayed considerable literary taste—he's jettisoned most of Waller's prose—as well as gallantry and sense. Not that he and screenwriter Richard La Gravenese have changed the basic fantasy: A handsome stranger (Eastwood), a photographer for the *National Geographic*, still drifts into Iowa farm country in 1965 to take pictures of covered bridges; he still asks directions from a lovelorn farm wife (Streep) and winds up staying for four days while her family is away; and the two still have a passionate affair that lasts, if only in memory, forever. The book is somber, majestical-mystical trash—a genteel bodice-ripper—crossed with a midsixties *Cosmo* story of ecstasy with an overpowering male. And the movie follows the same emotional progression: Loneliness ... immediate attraction ... flowers ... dancing ... bliss ... and then ... renunciation. The creators of both book and movie have taken careful measure of American prurience and hypocrisy: The reader and the moviegoer get to experience not only the pleasures of erotic awakening but also the pleasure of virtue.

Yet Eastwood and LaGravenese have handled dishonest material as straightforwardly as one could have hoped. They've dropped Waller's mystic rant, the indecent poetry, the talk of the hero as a "shaman." There's nothing in the movie remotely as swoony as Waller's infatuation with the hero's "hard" body. The part of Robert Kincaid is modestly written, and Eastwood plays him modestly, too, receding into the movie as far as he can while shifting the emotional weight decisively to Francesca, the Italian woman who married an American soldier and found herself stranded among good, dull people in the American Midwest—and the extraordinary good luck to get herself played by Meryl Streep.

Her hair a nondescript parcel brown (or so it seems at first), a little stocky, often shy—no one has ever noticed her—Streep's Francesca stands in her kitchen, at a table with a yellow Formica top. She's as rooted as a turnip. Like every heroine of this kind of fiction, Francesca must overcome her physical hesitations and take the perilous plunge. But if the scheme is banal, the emotions of doubt, fear, and lust, perceived truly enough, are certainly not, and Meryl Streep's acting, which at times has seemed overcalculated, is here so liquid that the character and the situations are absolved of the embarrassment of drabness. Streep clings to the kitchen yet finally breaks away, look by look, gesture by gesture. This is her most sensually appealing role—the years and the extra pounds have given her an irresistible strength. By speaking the lines in slightly halting English, dropping words here and there but then suddenly lunging at a phrase, she creates something musical, a touch of strangeness, and Eastwood keeps the strangeness at the center of the movie, which is framed by Streep reading a journal discovered years after the event by her children. That slight Italian accent has been shaped for longing and regret.

As *Unforgiven* and *A Perfect World* demonstrated, Clint Eastwood has developed into our last classical director, the last to try to make movies the way John Ford did. He builds emotions slowly and carefully rather than jamming things together, MTV-style, with a few frantic, discontinuous scenes. Setting up the physical space of the farm, the land around it, the roads and bridges, he does nothing visually inspired, but he does let you know that the land is there. *Bridges* is a decent piece of moviemaking—it substitutes solid, unexciting prose for Waller's overripe drivel.

Eastwood offers classical filmmaking and classical sex—sober, romantic, exalted. Sixty-four when the movie was shot, a rugged, weathered man, he's more believable than Waller's aboriginal stud but still a modern ideal. A modern ideal knows that women want to be transported, but they also want respect and choice. So this primal man, who is supposed to be a law unto himself—a completely independent spirit—responds to Francesca's sexual mood precisely when she's most ready for him. He couldn't be more attentive and practiced if he were a queen's consort. How odd that a famous action star should play this role! Ordinary expository lines sound bodiless when spoken in Eastwood's light, hoarse voice, and when he's contradicted or criticized, he has that awkward, wounded-wolf look; he lacks range. He's not a great actor, but in this movie he's a real gent. And as a director, he delivers the goods: He makes a romantic fantasy that works for women. Both as director and actor, he seems to be making love to every woman in the audience.

NEW YORK POST, 6/2/95, p. 45, Michael Medved

The film version of "The Bridges of Madison County" as a far richer, far stronger piece of work than the wildly popular novel that inspired it—but that hardly makes it a good movie.

Out of respect for the 8 million readers who paid good money to buy the incomparably insipid book, director Clint Eastwood has borrowed altogether too much of author Robert James Waller's stilted dialogue and his mendacious, manipulative plot.

As a result, this long, ambitious, handsomely photographed film—despite noble and heartfelt performances by Eastwood himself and co-star Meryl Streep—still plays like self-parody. After all, not even Dirty Harry can fire off lines like "This kind of certainty comes but once, no matter how many lifetimes you live" with a straight face.

By now, every reader of "Doonesbury's" strikingly apt spoof knows the stark plot. It's the sultry summer of 1965, and farm wife Francesca Johnson (Streep) has four days on her own while her husband and two children take a prize steer to the state fair.

Then a macho, free-spirit photographer from National Geographic (repeatedly described as "The Last Cowboy" in the book) drives up her dusty lane to ask for directions to one of the local bridges he's supposed to shoot.

Of course, it's Clint Eastwood, and while his die hard fans may long for him to squint at the horizon and say, "Go ahead. Make my four days," he actually does nothing of the kind. Instead, he delivers "sensitive" lines like "Francesca, do you think that what happened to us just happens to anyone? ... We're hardly two separate people now.

Despite such overripe romanticism, Eastwood and Streep are a joy to watch together and their long, talky scenes are intermittently intriguing. Both principals are more believable and complex than their counterparts in the novel, and the Robert Kincaid/Eastwood character gains hugely in terms of audience sympathy and vulnerability.

Director Eastwood wisely avoided staging the decathlon of lovemaking described by Waller in the book; the movie shows lots of deep kissing, but nothing more. The film is also enriched by a much firmer sense of time and place, with all its scenes lyrically shot on location in the real life Madison County, Iowa. The fundamental problem is that there's not enough tension or surprise to keep this pretty, petty contraption sputtering along for two-and-a-half hours.

Screenwriter Richard LaGravenese ("The Fisher King", "The Ref") begins the picture with Francesca's grown children reading her will, and learning of her long ago affair with a man (also deceased) who she never saw for the last 22 years of his life. In other words, the story's outcome is entirely clear before the picture even gets started. There's also an unmistakably pernicious tinge to the middle-aged fantasy that this material purveys: the notion that four days of sizzling, adulterous sex with a stranger can actually strengthen a fading marriage and provide enough thrills to last a lifetime. In reality, those thrills aren't even sufficient to sustain an overlong and over-earnest motion picture for a couple of hours.

NEWSDAY, 6/2/95, Part II/p. B2, John Anderson

When the handsome, hard Robert Kincaid pulls into Francesca Johnson's driveway on a sweaty summer's day in 1965, moths fly, but not sparks.

Francesca may be Italian, she may be a war bride, but her sensuality has been hog-tied by 15 years of lifeless marriage; she can't just slip out of her corn-fed Iowa insulation. Instead, she tries to explain to Kincaid how to get to Roseman bridge, the place he needs to photograph. And then she tries again. Inevitably, reluctantly—and generously, given that her family is away and she cherishes the privacy—she offers to take him there. And thus begins the great love affair of her life.

Anyone familiar with Robert James Waller's slim but enormously popular novel, "The Bridges of Madison County," knows this isn't how it happens. No, in the book, Francesca is in Robert's truck before the flies have dried on the windshield. The implication—or rather, your presumption, since there's little else to go on—is that life in Iowa is so suffocatingly drab that a hard (Waller uses the word about a dozen times; I've used it twice), handsome, rugged individualist like Kincaid—artist, poet, love magician—would be too much temptation for a suppressed '60s hausfrau not to instantly risk everything for the chance to clean his lens cap.

Believable? Only to those eager to believe—and, given that "Bridges" has sold 5.7 million copies, there evidently are plenty of eager believers.

Things are different in Clint Eastwood's "The Bridges of Madison County," where action is pondered, motivations are clearer and the story is fleshed out almost as fully as Meryl Streep's Anna Magnani figure. The result is a movie far better than its source material.

Still, Eastwood's not working with much. Stripped of Waller's New Age platitudes—Richard LaGravenese's inventive script is weakest when it quotes directly from the book—this is "Back Street" on the farm, except she's married, not him. Francesca and Robert will make love—movies seldom build up to the sex act anymore the way this one does—and they will part. It's sad, yes. In Eastwood's version, at least, it sort of makes sense.

What doesn't is how LaGravenese and Eastwood have structured the story—as a memoir, spinning back from Francesca's death in 1989. Her children, Michael (Victor Slezak) and Caroline (Annie Corley) receive their mother's personal effects, including a letter that immediately reveals her affair with Kincaid.

The attention given the children, to whom the film returns regularly and whose own marital problems add considerable resonance to Francesca's, is not a bad idea. But what little suspense there was in the book—and there wasn't much—has been eliminated. There's all that pre-coital momentum, sure, but we're forced to rely on the performances for what ever tension exists.

Fortunately for Eastwood, he has Meryl Streep, who is right where she belongs: Out of the rubber raft and into another accent. Her Francesca isn't just believable. She's lovable and passionate and intelligent and right. Streep takes the novel's character—who is far less remarkable—and imbues her with a fatalistic sense of romance, and the erotic abandon of a woman who's been watching her own soul wither in a small-minded midwestern purgatory.

The best thing Eastwood can do as Robert Kincaid is get out of her way—which he does, even to the point of making Kincaid less noble than he is in the book, more pleading and, as he gets drawn to Francesca, almost ineffectual.

Some novels are destined to be movies because they contain inherently cinematic qualities, others because they've sold too many copies not to be filmed. "Bridges," of course, "is of the latter sort. I can't imagine people not being bored by it all; during one earnest exchange between Robert and Francesca, I watched a fly crawl across the back of a dining room chair. And then I watched it crawl back again. Still, Eastwood couldn't pass up this film, and not just for the money; having turned 65 on Wednesday, how many more times can he play the love hunk (he looks great, of course, so who knows)? And how many heartthrob parts are written as 52-year-old men? And who else could play it?

But he shows, once again, on his 18th film as director, what a smart filmmaker he is, and what an intellect. It's really Meryl Streep's movie, but Eastwood has the good sense, and good fortune, to be her director.

NEWSWEEK, 6/5/95, p. 74, Jack Kroll

Gagged on the book, liked the movie. That will be the experience of many who see Clint Eastwood's *The Bridges of Madison County*. Director-star Eastwood and his collaborators have done a fascinating cleanup job on Robert James Waller's stupefyingly successful best seller. The novella about a four-day romance between a fortyish Iowa farm wife and a fiftyish photographer hit the dream buttons of baby boomers just when their dreams were running down. The book was a hermaphroditic fantasy; if you were a man, you could be Robert Kincaid, a guy who could induce orgasm in a redwood tree. If you were a woman, you could be Francesca Johnson, whose 96 hours with RK is the only brush with ecstasy in her life.

The book was an amazing farrago of sub-Hemingway macho and New Age moon dust. What Eastwood, costar Meryl Streep and screenwriter Richard LaGravenese have done is to bring a semblance of emotional reality to the story. As a result the movie "Bridges" has much more poignancy than the book. From their first meeting, when Kincaid jolts up to her farmhouse in his pickup, asking directions to the famous Iowa covered bridges he's shooting for National Geographic magazine, the juice flows between Eastwood and Streep. Francesca's a quietly resigned woman who came from her native Italy to be the wife of Richard, a decent but unexciting man (Jim Haynie). Robert's divorced, a loner who buries his emotional dissatisfaction in his solid photographic craftsmanship.

In the book Waller makes him a poet of the camera who "was after art for art's sake." But in the movie Robert modestly tells Francesca: "I'm no artist." Waller's Robert said stuff like "I am the highway and a peregrine and all the sails that ever went to sea." Most of that gas has been siphoned out of the movie, except for an occasional emission when Eastwood is forced to say lines like "I embrace the mystery." But the erotic tension that develops between Eastwood and Streep is a believable force that rises out of myriad beautifully observed details. Streep slaps her cheeks when she feels herself drawn to him. The self-punishing gesture is somehow European; it goes with her perfect vestigial Italian accent, worn down to a musical nuance in the alien corn of Iowa. Eastwood's eloquent squint works as well with a camera as it has with a gun.

Eastwood and Streep—it seemed an unlikely pairing, but they work together with a sensual dignity that develops real heat and power. You can feel their desire reviving long-suppressed dreams. Soaking in her bathtub, she looks up at the shower head, still dripping from his recent use. It's sexier than all the pervasive Hollywood bimbolatry. And where Waller wallows in Robert's mystic maleness, the film wisely lets Francesca, at one point, angrily accuse him of macho complacency: "You get to be a voyeur, hermit and lover ... You're a hypocrite and a phony."

The movie's one uncertain device is its framing of the story in flashback, when Francesca's son (Victor Slezak) and daughter (Annie Corley) find their mother's diaries after her death 22 years after her four ecstatic days. Their recurrent appearances interrupt the story's momentum. And the effect of learning about their mother's affair on their own marital problems lends a taint of glib psychotherapy to a story that should stand on its own romantic feet.

Those feet might have slipped badly without the strength of Streep and Eastwood, just as Tom Hanks gave touching integrity to Forrest Gump. Gumpism was a fantasy of redemption: the mildly retarded Forrest was a kind of holy fool, whose insertion into our recent history canceled its corruptions and restored our innocence. Wallerism is the fantasy of erotic transcendence—four days to redeem a lifetime of conformity. The tremendous success of both fantasies doesn't say much for our current sense of reality. But Streep and Eastwood seduce you into believing the fantasy. As one of Hemingway's heroes said, isn't it pretty to think so?

SIGHT AND SOUND, 9/95, p. 46, Leslie Felperin

Madison County, Iowa. Brother and sister Carolyn and Michael Johnson are puzzled by their deceased mother, Francesca's, strange request to be cremated and have her ashes sprinkled from the Roseman covered bridge nearby, instead of being buried next to her dead husband, Richard. Instructions lead them to her notebooks, and they learn the story of what happened to her back in 1965 ...

1965. Francesca sees off Carolyn and Michael, then in their teens, and her husband, Richard, as they leave for the State Fair. Soon after their departure, a photographer named Robert Kincaid, on an assignment for *National Geographic* to photograph the covered bridges of Madison County, pulls up in his truck and asks for directions to the Roseman Bridge. Francesca shows him the way and invites him back to her house for dinner. She invites him back again the next night, they dance in the kitchen, and soon retire for a passionate night of lovemaking. Robert asks Francesca to run away with him. However, Francesca refuses to leave, knowing that the scandal would ruin her family's life and leave her eventually feeling embittered. Robert understands and leaves her on the fourth day of their time together, before her family returns home.

Over the years, Francesca takes out a subscription to *National Geographic*, receives a love letter from Robert, and thinks of him always. When Richard finally dies and the children are grown, she tries to contact Robert, only to find that he died some years ago and left everything to her. His lawyers send her his personal effects, including a book of photographs he made entitled *Four Days* which is dedicated to "F". The lawyer's letter explains that he had himself cremated and the ashes sprinkled from the Roseman Bridge ...

After reading the notebooks , Michael and Carolyn go to the Roseman covered Bridge and sprinkle Francesca's ashes into the wind.

The Bridges of Madison County is that rarity, a film that is infinitely better than the original book on which it was based. Having slogged through Robert James Waller's appallingly-written but slim volume, I can only conjecture that the book's runaway success is attributable to the old-fashioned fantasy it embodies. Its pitch is that people in Middle American small towns are capable of enormous passions and that it is noble to forsake those passions to go on living in hellish little Hicksvilles. This must be a generational thing because I don't get it, yet, at the screening I attended, many audience members over the age of 50 seemed to be in tears.

Many of the corniest bits are directly translated from Waller, such as the romantic hero Robert Kincaid's kiss-off line, delivered with uncharacteristic moistness by writer-director Clint Eastwood, "This kind of certainty comes but once in a lifetime." Screenwriter Richard LaGravenese, who also wrote *The Fisher King*, has wisely pruned and snipped out the most embarrassing Wallerisms (my favourite being "I am the highway and a peregrine and all the sails that ever went to sea," uttered during sex no less) and sneaked in some funny lines, such as the heroine's daughter Carolyn's lament: "In between bake sales I find out my mother was Anais Nin."

In spite of the mawkishness at its heart, the film's clean, technical efficiency makes it rather enjoyable. Eastwood is a highly competent director, although occasionally a dull one. Here, he shows that he knows the mechanics of romance and how to generate a *frisson* from the juxtaposition of mundanity with intense, cloaked passion. Such an intensity can only be effectively conveyed with judicious close-ups of very good actors, and, blessed with Meryl Streep on top form (looking very sexy in frumpy dresses) as Carolyn's mother Francesca, Eastwood is able to generate top class tear-jerking material. Knowing his own limitations as an actor, Eastwood, perhaps over-generously, lets Streep carry the picture, lighting her beautifully inside darkened bridges, framing her in compositions filched from Edward Hopper's country paintings. Detail is sensuous and domestic, suggesting that Eastwood is mellowing and perhaps more in touch with his 'feminine side' than usual.

There is a beautifully executed scene close to the end, only partly based on Waller, where Francesca sees Robert standing in the rain staring at her while she waits in the truck for her husband to come back from the shops. The rain is particularly convenient since Eastwood is not one of the great on-screen weepers, but in this instance he looks miserable and soggy with despair. Streep's distressed and repressed mannerisms which, hitherto accompanied by her obligatory perfect accent, had seemed over-polished, are spot-on in this sequence, especially when she watches him pulling away in his truck. With this Brief (momentary) Encounter, I forgave most of the risible schmaltz that had preceded it. If the film had ended there it would have been almost worthy of David Lean, but tied to Waller's original story, it bumbles on disappointingly for some time to its vapid conclusion.

TIME, 6/5/95, p. 64, Richard Corliss

Lit crits, those old prunes, scratched their high foreheads at the success of Robert James Waller's *The Bridges of Madison County*. This tale of middle-age passion—in which a roving photographer, Robert Kincaid, has a volcanic three-day affair with Francesca Johnson, an Italian woman who has lived for 20 years as an Iowa farm wife—was filled with clichés masquerading as erotic eruptions. But Waller knows the secret of romance novels. He writes the way people feel and think when they are first in love—as if every emotion had the force of God's creation, as if such shivers had never been experienced or expressed before. *Madison County* was like the affair it describes: a brief skinny-dip in the warm lake of nostalgia.

In one sense, Clint Eastwood's film version was doomed before it started, for the book's readers had played the movie version in their heads, cast the roles, lived the love scenes. Also, today's films have a sophisticated language for the depiction of violence but become tongue tied when the subject is serious eroticism. Told from Francesca's point of view, the book runs its words over Robert's body as if they were the fingers or lips of a new lover. He is hard, an animal, physical and spiritual. Her orgasms are liberating, exhausting visits to a land where he is king, ("Robert," she exclaims in postcoital awe, "you're so powerful, it's frightening!") In the age of facetiousness, could any director film this without giggling? Would any actor dare display himself as such a paragon of pagan love?

Not Eastwood, he is the most reticent of directors—where the book ogles, the film discreetly observes—and, here, the courtliest of stars. The movie has a scene in which Francesca watches Robert wash himself. But Clint would never let the camera play over his body. For, as director, would he be anything but protective of Streep's corporal mortality. The two stars are past miming youth's sleek exertions. Why do it now? They didn't do it then.

What's left is a brooding romantic fantasy. As scripted by Richard LaGravenese (*The Fisher King*), the *Madison County* movie has a slightly riper theme than the book's. It is about the anticipation and consequences of passion—the slow dance of appraisal, of waiting to make a move that won't be rejected, of debating what to do when the erotic heat matures into love light. What is the effect of an affair on a woman who has been faithful to her husband, and on a rootless man who only now realizes he needs the one woman he can have but not hold?

These are issues worth considering at length and leisure. Eastwood does; he is a man who likes to take his time. The picture clocks in at 2¼ hours—a span in which anyone who got past 10th grade could read the book, linger over favorite passages and smoke a reflective cigarette afterward. Part of this time is wasted on a framing story about the affair's impact decades later on Francesca's grown children. The rest is lavished on the warming of two stars and styles as they reach accommodation.

Eastwood behaves; Streep acts. He relaxes into a role; she wills her self into it, like a woman determined to make a dress two sizes too small look stunning on her. This time she tries on a southern Italian accent, with the weary, knowing lilt of an Anna Magnani. Soon she is Francesca—or some rarefied version of her—aching but not expecting to find someone who can tap her gift for love. Before she commits to the affair, you understand her tension, her indecision. In a medley of bold and subtle gestures, Streep tells Francesca's plaintive story. Through the actress's effort and her director's generosity, this book about an irresistible man becomes a movie about a remarkable woman. *Madison County* is Eastwood's gift to women: to Francesca, to all the girls he's loved before—and to Streep, who alchemizes literary mawkishness into intelligent movie passion.

VILLAGE VOICE, 6/13/95, p. 58, Gary Indiana

Offering Clint Eastwood as the sensitive *National Geographic* photographer and Meryl Streep as the Italian woman married to a farmer who's off at the state fair, *Bridges* follows the dull four-day arc of Robert James Waller's wildly popular novel. Four days is just enough time for a deep and unforgettable love to develop between two very special people, who part, in the end, for the sake of preserving a perfect memory and sparing Francesca's nice though boring family the trauma of a local scandal.

This story, which takes place in 1965, is bracketed by some portentous narrative garnish set in the present, when the recently deceased Francesca's grown-up son and daughter come home to sort through her belongings, discovering a three-volume journal, addressed to them, telling the story of those four fateful days. Why it should take up three whole volumes is a puzzle, unless Francesca shared her contemporary Robbe-Grillet's mania for minute description. Daughter Caroline, who's thinking about divorce, is beguiled and moved by the secret depths of her mother's heart; son Michael, a more conventional soul, prudishly resists the tsunami of emotional revelation with a great deal of wincing and nattering as Caroline reads the journal aloud. Such is the power of Francesca and Robert's love, however, that Michael too succumbs to its bittersweet wisdom, after a few belts of whiskey have loosened him up, confessing that he's cheated on his own wife thousands of times in his dreams.

An unintended effect of this flashback structure is that one comes to expect the two siblings, inspired by mom's romance in the faraway past, to fall into bed with each other at the end of the film: they just don't establish that brother-sister thing firmly enough at the outset, and they would look nice together. As for Francesca and Robert, the main item, their affair is perfectly paced, and even hits some moving peaks, but is constantly undercut by the spectacle of two brilliant actors manufacturing a silk purse from a sow's ear. This is pure romance, unencumbered by conflict: by the time Francesca has to decide whether or not to run off with Robert, we already know she didn't, so the drama consists entirely in seeing what happens between them over four days—and, frankly, *Last Tango in Paris* it isn't. It's sweet as a marzipan frog, and only the consummate skill of the leads rescues the viewer from insulin shock. One constantly expects the whole thing to unravel in some painfully trite way; there's just enough unhappiness built into the plot to keep it from doing so. In its broader implications the film *is* horribly banal, reaffirming the inevitability if not the joys of family values, though it's a pleasure to watch two nice people commit in an American movie commit adultery without the wrath of God descending on them.

Streep gets off to a shaky start, unable to decide if she's Anna Magnani or some hotel chambermaid she once noticed in Venice, but she quickly becomes, as usual, completely believable, here as a woman who wished for a different life than the one she ended up with. It's just as well that she doesn't articulate what sort of life she wishes she had—it's enough of a job to incarnate one cliché without piling another one on. Eastwood refashions the fatuous autobiographical hero of Waller's rotten novel into Clint Eastwood, an infinitely more interesting and attractive figure. Whenever Kincaid has a speech about Life or his Artistic Obsession, we get an unpleasant whiff of what scriptwriter Richard LaGravenese had to slice off the original material. An early, truncated anecdote about Kincaid's encounter with an ape makes us grateful for his general laconicism.

Also reviewed in:
CHICAGO TRIBUNE, 6/2/95, Friday/p. C, Michael Wilmington
NEW REPUBLIC, 7/3/95, p. 26, Stanley Kauffmann
NEW YORK TIMES, 6/2/95, p. C4, Janet Maslin
NEW YORKER, 6/19/95, p. 97, Anthony Lane
VARIETY, 5/22-28/95, p. 91, Todd McCarthy
WASHINGTON POST, 6/2/95, p. D1, Rita Kempley
WASHINGTON POST, 6/2/95, Weekend/p. 57, Desson Howe

BROKEN HARVEST

A Kit Parker Films release of a Destiny Films production. *Producer:* Jerry O'Callaghan. *Director:* Maurice O'Callaghan. *Screenplay:* Maurice O'Callaghan and Kate O'Callaghan. *Based upon a story "The Shilling" by:* Maurice O'Callaghan. *Director of Photography:* Jack Conroy. *Editor:* J. Patrick Duffner. *Music:* Patrick Cassidy. *Sound:* Trevor O'Connor and Liam Saurin. *Production Designer:* Alan Gallett. *Set Designer:* Laura Bowe. *Costumes:* Maeve Paterson. *Running time:* 98 minutes. *MPAA Rating:* Not Rated.

CAST: Colin Lane (Arthur O'Leary); Marian Quinn (Catherine O'Leary); Niall O'Brien (Josie McCarthy); Darren McHugh (Jimmy O'Leary); Joy Florish (Mary Finnegan); Joe Jeffers (Willie Hogan); Pete O'Reilly (Adult Jimmy); Michael Crowley (Adult Willie).

NEW YORK POST, 10/6/95, p. 50, Larry Worth

It's said that patience is a virtue. It's also a necessity, at least for viewers of "Broken Harvest."

This look at 70 years of Irish history is as divided as the country: The first half is ponderous and amateurish; but the remainder features a compelling romance and surprisingly poignant finale. Go figure.

Writer/director Maurice O'Callaghan finally gets his act together by jumping from half-baked lessons about Ireland's Civil War to a romantic triangle rooted in love of the land, long-forgotten trysts and the inevitability of tragedy.

It all segues into a emotionally rich denouement about the consequences of living in the past, meanwhile driving home the film's cumulative impact.

But in keeping with the production's Jekyll/Hyde nature, the acting proves inconsistent. Colin Lane and Niall O'Brien expertly portray bitterly stubborn rivals, but Marian Quinn (Aidan's sister) is annoyingly stiff as the object of their affection.

So, much like the metaphor-laden scene that gives the film its title, "Broken Harvest" makes audiences sort through the chaff to get to the wheat.

VILLAGE VOICE, 10/17/95, p. 56, Michael Atkinson

Making an interesting, complex or profound movie about the Irish troubles must be as difficult as mating pandas in captivity. *Cal* and *In the Name of the Father* got the melancholy and angst right, but still assaulted the nostrils with sanctimony. If romantic nationalism doesn't muddle it up, it seems, blind moralism will. A tiny-budgeted sermon on war, what is it good for, *Broken Harvest* is Irish from bow to stern, and clumsily appropriates mainstream formulas, as many poor nations with underdeveloped film cultures do. Set in the '50s, 30 years after the Civil War, the movie centers on young Jimmy O'Leary (Darren McHugh), who couldn't give a peat wedge about politics, his grouchy, gun-polishing Republican Dad (Colin Lane), and a neighbor (Niall O'Brien), who quit the Civil War sick of bloodshed and who's still living it down. There are the small matters of a theft, a romantic triangle, a make-or-break wheat harvest, and a bank looking to foreclose on the farm. Predictably, the war haunts everyone and taints everything.

The homilies of *Broken Harvest* would be only insufferable if the film weren't so amateurishly acted, written, and photographed. No sides are taken, and the largest questions go unanswered—as in, how can movies like this be released when remarkable work like *Les Amonts du Pont Neuf, Nouvelle Vogue, Rouge, Bullet in the Head, Cobra Verde*, etc., cannot?

Also reviewed in:
NEW REPUBLIC, 10/16/95, p. 38, Stanley Kauffmann
NEW YORK TIMES, 10/6/95, p. C14, Stephen Holden
VARIETY, 8/15-21/94, p. 44, Derck Elloy

BROKEN JOURNEY, THE

A Filmhaus Releasing and C.E.G. Worldwide release of a National Film Development Corp. Of India/Doordashan production. *Producer:* Sandip Ray. *Director:* Sandip Ray. *Screenplay:* Satyajit Ray. *Story:* Satyajit Ray. *Director of Photography:* Barun Raha. *Editor:* Dulal Dutt. *Music:* Sandip Ray. *Sound:* Sujit Sarkar. *Production Designer:* Ashoke Bose. *Running time:* 82 minutes. *MPAA Rating:* Not Rated.

CAST: Soumitra Chatterjee (Dr. Sengupta); Sadhu Meher (Jatin Kundu); Subhalakshmi Munshi (Manashi); Debotosh Ghosh (Haladhar); WITH: Bina; Minakshi Goswami; Masood Akhtar; Pallavi Roy; Bimal Deb; Subendu Chatterjee; Lily Chakraborty; Soven Lahiri; Ashish Mukherji.

LOS ANGELES TIMES, 10/4/95, Calendar/p. 2, Kevin Thomas

When India's great filmmaker Satyajit Ray was stricken with heart disease, he became all too aware that only the rich could afford good medical care for even the simplest treatments. As he recuperated, he determined to address this problem and commenced writing a script, "The Broken Journey," that he believed would be "his best and most important film yet."

Just a few weeks before the February, 1992, start of production, Ray was again hospitalized and decided that his director-son Sandip, who had worked with his father since he was a child, would direct the exteriors under his supervision. But Ray would never leave the hospital alive, dying on April 13 at age 70. Exactly a year later Sandip would begin directing the film himself—and honoring his fathers legacy with a stunning picture that has the impact of Satyajit's finest efforts.

Understandably and forgivably, it begins a bit statically, a bit self-consciously and not just a little didactically. But very soon Sandip Ray's confidence grows and the inherent cumulative power of the material takes over. Soumitra Chatterjee, a veteran actor of understated strength, stars as Dr. Nihar Sengupta, a self-absorbed, middle-aged Calcutta high-society physician whose social consciousness goes no further than commenting on the irony that widespread failure of family planning is occurring at the same time life spans are increasing.

Sengupta takes off for Jamshedpur, less than a day's drive, to stay overnight with an old friend he hasn't seen in a decade and, the next day to address the local Rotary Club on medical advances of the past two decades. Along the way, when his luxury car has a flat tire, he discovers lying in a field a peasant, Haladhar (Debotosh Ghosh), near death from pneumonia.

Satyajit Ray's wisdom gleams in allowing the transforming effect of this encounter upon the doctor to sink into him in stages. Only when he actually witnesses Haladhar being beaten by brooms and his chest stomped on by the local witch doctor does he at last assert himself and take over the treatment of the desperately ill man.

What Sengupta discovers in Haladhar's village is that he's stumbled into antiquity—there's no electricity, no government health center and no phone closer than a half-hour drive. He also meets Haladhar's pretty daughter Manashi (Subhalakshmi Munshi), who is 17, about the same age as his own daughter. Manashi has lost her mother to malaria and her husband to a snakebite.

Whereas Sengupta's own daughter, in her mother's words, has become rude and indifferent: Manashi exudes a quiet strength, resigned to being ill-fated and calmly going about caring for her father, the local drunk, and her younger brother.

By now Sengupta has recalled his Hippocratic oath, yet an ever-inspired Satyajit Ray has come up with a couple of twists and turns to elicit a devastating finish, beautifully timed and staged by Sandip, who also shares his father's gifts with actors and the composition of spare, eloquent film scores. Intimate and leisurely, "The Broken Journey" is small in scale but universal in its timeliness, with implications that apply to the United States—Los Angeles in particular—with just as much force as to India.

NEWSDAY, 5/19/95, Part II/p. B5, John Anderson

Like tea after a banquet, Satyajit Ray's final two films—"The Stranger" and "The Broken Journey"—give modest closure to one of the brilliant careers in world cinema.

The great Indian director, who died three years ago, made films that were often parables, small tales with large scope. Early in his career, beginning with the splendid "Pather Panchali" and the other films in the "Apu trilogy," his work also possessed a signature visual poetry, and took subtle note of the relationship between humans and their environment. Both. "The Stranger" and "The Broken Journey" are almost perversely flat in style, as if the filmmaker wanted to get beyond the incidentals of beauty—which they do, although both films also make profound visual statements about how people fit in the world, or don't.

"The Stranger," Ray's last directorial effort, is about stiff, ungenerous people in a stiff, ungenerous and artificial environment. It's an archetypal story of modern life: A well-to-do couple, Anila (Mamata Shankar) and her husband, Sudhindra (Deepanker De), get a letter, allegedly from her uncle, who left home when Anila was a child and of whom she has no memory. Regretting the imposition, he asks whether he might be their guest for a few days and avail himself of "traditional Indian hospitality."

The husband is immediately suspicious, but it's not just wariness, or concern for Anila's welfare. Ray doesn't paint chromatically, and Sudhindra's reluctance to play host is also about his reluctance to be inconvenienced. The extent to which he'll go to "expose" the urbane and entertaining Uncle Manmohan (Utpal Dutt), and the chagrin both he and Anila feel at the end of the film, make "The Stranger" both quaint and resonant.

Loss of basic values is also at the heart of "The Broken Journey," which was scripted by Ray but directed by his son, Sandip. In it, a society doctor (Soumitra Chatterjee), en route from Calcutta to a medical convention, encounters a dying peasant villager with no access to proper medical care. The doctor gets involved with both the man and his daughter (Subhalakshmi Munshi), whose nobility and sense of duty are in sharp contrast to his own spoiled child. The experience evokes the impulses that made him a physician in the first place, which both shame him and renew his sense of self.

Simple stories, shot in intentionally unglamorous fashion. But the sense of high morality is there, as is the use of film for moral instruction. Which itself is not a bad postscript to a brilliant career.

Also reviewed in:
NEW REPUBLIC, 6/19/95, p. 31, Stanley Kauffmann
NEW YORK TIMES, 5/19/95, p. C16, Stephen Holden
VARIETY, 5/9-15/94, p. 78, Dennis Harvey

BROTHER MINISTER: THE ASSASSINATION OF MALCOLM X

An X-ceptional Productions release in accociation with Illuminati Entertainment Group Inc. and Why Productions Inc. *Executive Producer:* Lewis Kesten. *Producer:* Jack Baxter. *Director:* Jack Baxter and Jefri Aalmuhammed. *Screenplay:* Jack Baxter and Jefri Aalmuhammed. *Director of Photography:* Robert Haggins. *Editor:* Mitchell Kress. *Music:* Richie Havens and Frank Herrero. *Running time:* 120 minutes. *MPAA Rating:* Not Rated.

WITH: Roscoe Lee Browne (Narrator); Peter Bailey; John Henry Clarke; James Fox; Khalil Islam (aka Thomas 15x Johnson); William Kunstler; Jack Newfield; Percy Sutton; Bill Tatum.

NEW YORK POST, 1/11/95, p. 36, Bill Hoffmann

Incendiary controversy has followed "Brother Minister: The Assassination of Malcolm X" every step of the way from its conception to its commercial debut here today.

Last year, when Post columnist Jack Newfield revealed the movie contained a fiery speech by Nation of Islam leader Louis Farrakhan in which he talked about Malcolm X as a "traitor," a firestorm erupted.

The film's director, Jack Baxter, received death threats frightening enough to prompt him to hire bodyguards.

Newfield himself was subsequently sued for $4.4 million by the Nation of Islam for a related Malcolm X story he wrote.

And now, the movie has finally crawled up out of the innuendo, the smears, the anger, to surface at the 57th Street Playhouse, a venue more at home with the likes of heartthrob Mel Gibson and filmmakers like Spielberg.

The verdict: It's brilliant and will stand as a definitive document in the understanding of one of the most monumental events in black history.

The charismatic black leader was shot dead at Harlem's Audubon Ballroom on Feb. 21, 1965. One of his bodyguards and two other men were convicted and imprisoned for the crime.

But the question lingered: Who was really behind the shooting?

Using interviews with key members of Malcolm's inner circle, fascinating documentary footage and rare photos, Baxter slowly, carefully shows us the possible complicity of several agencies including the FBI and the NYPD.

He also probes the secret origin of the Nation of Islam and its political and religious legacy in America.

Of particular interest are the speeches and impromptu press conferences by Malcolm X, seen here for the first time in years.

With the assuredness of a dogged gumshoe, the director shows us that many of the real facts behind the Malcolm X assassination have been hidden on a grand scale for years.

I won't tell you the various conclusions the film reaches, because like a good detective novel, "Brother Minister" has got plenty of surprises.

NEWSDAY, 1/11/95, Part II/p. B9, John Anderson

Why did Malcolm X refuse to allow a search at the doors of the Audubon Ballroom on that fateful Sunday afternoon? It may be the one question for which "Brother Minister: The Assassination of Malcolm X" doesn't have a solid answer, although it makes a pretty good case for premeditated martyrdom.

It also makes a better than pretty good case that the murder of Malcolm was one of those rare moments of solidarity—if not outright cooperation—between the FBI and a black organization. Required viewing for anyone interested in race relations, religious fundamentalism, the perversion of democracy or the history, period, of the United States, "Brother Minister" attempts to strip away the 30 years' worth of obfuscation and smoke screens that surround Malcolm X's assassination, implicating the FBI, the Nation of Islam and to a large degree, Louis Farrakhan.

It's a documentary that gets to introduce itself with was first shown in February of last year. We get a feverish, TV news-derived summation of the uproar that occurred when the taped Farrakhan speech was shown here—where he claims that "we dealt with [Malcolm] like a nation deals with their traitors"—first came to light. There is the Gabe Pressman interview with Betty Shabazz, Malcolm's widow, who said that, yes, she thought Farrakhan had been a party to the plot because it had been "a badge of honor ... everybody talked about it." But it isn't until the very end of the film, when the rest of the story has been told and the speech is repeated, that its full impact is felt.

The film does tend to bog down in the middle, just because there's just so much information, and so many witnesses whom director Jack Baxter is trying to weave together. There's Gene Roberts, the police plant who was among Malcolm's bodyguards on the day he died, recounting the aftermath and who was where. Thomas 15X Johnson, who spent 10 years in prison for the shooting but was almost certainly innocent, is candid about the sentiment felt by Nation of Islam members toward Malcolm. A number of sources say that on Feb. 21, 1965—the day Malcolm was killed—Farrakhan was in Newark Mosque No. 25, the same mosque to which all the convicted killers belonged. Farrakhan himself confirms this, placing himself there as well in a 1990 speech at Malcolm X College in Chicago.

This is circumstantial, of course, as is much of Baxter's case. But each piece of evidence tends to attain more gravity as the total swells. And together with several indisputable facts make for a volatile whole: Malcolm was the subject of an orchestrated disinformation campaign by the Nation of Islam after he revealed that Nation leader Elijah Muhammad had fathered a number of children with his young secretaries. And his all-but-announced plans to work with the Rev. Martin Luther King Jr. had to be, as someone puts it, "J. Edgar Hoover's worst nightmare."

"Brother" uses actual film footage as well as dramatizations of the shooting and subsequent chaos, still photographs and many, many talking heads—who, besides being remarkably candid, can't slow the film down much because it has a momentum of its own. According to Benjamin 2X Karim, who was on the Audubon podium, "Malcolm always said, 'Everything happens on time'"—except this movie, perhaps, which is overdue.

VILLAGE VOICE, 1/17/95, p. 52, Gary Dauphin

Another meditation on the perils of choosing mentors and disciples, *Brother Minister: The Assassination of Malcolm X* arrives with press buzz about its "startling" new information on the Audubon Ballroom shooting in February 1965. Visually, *Brother Minister* is standard doc-exposé fare, filling its two hours with talking-head recollections, reenactments, oodles of found footage and internal NYPD memorandums. Unfolding along the spaghetti-like spine of a way too leisurely editing scheme, *Brother Minister* does occasionally contract like a noose around the neck of its targets, making buckshot suggestions that the FBI killed Malcolm, that the Nation killed Malcolm, that Louis Farrakhan killed Malcolm, that the CIA killed Malcolm, that the men convicted of killing Malcolm killed Malcolm—only to then contradict itself on all counts with subsequent talking heads.

While all this definitely has an intriguing *In Search* feel to it, *Brother Minister* can't help but come off as well meaning but sloppy. Besides the fact that there really is no new information here (PBS's *American Experience* did a better overview in less time), *Brother* goes and squanders the one lead it does have that's worth pursuing: Louis Farrakhan's presence at a Newark mosque (the assassins' alleged base of operations) on the day of the shooting. The filmmakers bury it in a meandering haze of interviews, with the authoritative word going to William Kunstler (whose ubiquity in radical-left reminiscences, while certainly well deserved, is starting to bug me for some reason). Along with Kunstler, Elijah Mohammed's son W. Deen makes an appearance, with little to add that doesn't serve the greater glory of his own nation of Islam splinter group; former Organization of Afro-American Unity member Gene Roberts spends long moments on screen looking haunted. Roberts was the NYPD Bureau of Special Services infiltrator who leapt onstage at the Audubon to administer mouth-to-mouth, and whatever secrets he's been keeping all these long years stay secrets in *Brother Minister*, hovering in plain view about the corners of his eyes but never uttered.

Also reviewed in:
NEW YORK TIMES, 1/11/95, p. C16, Janet Maslin
VARIETY, 8/8-14/94, p. 75, Emanuel Levy
WASHINGTON POST, 2/17/95, p. F1, Alona Wartofsky

BROTHERS McMULLEN, THE

A Fox Searchlight Pictures release. *Executive Producer:* Edward J. Burns, Ted Hope, and James Schamus. *Producer:* Edward Burns and Dick Fisher. *Director:* Edward Burns. *Screenplay:* Edward Burns. *Director of Photography:* Dick Fisher. *Editor:* Dick Fisher. *Music:* Seamus Egan. *Sound:* Mario Porporino, Mike Marson, Andrew Yarme, and Stefan Springman. *Sound Editor:* Steve Borne. *Running time:* 97 minutes. *MPAA Rating:* R.

CAST: Shari Albert (Susan); Maxine Bahns (Audrey); Catharine Bolz (Mrs. McMullen); Connie Britton (Molly); Edward Burns (Barry); Peter Johansen (Marty); Jennifer Jostyn (Leslie); Mike McGlone (Patrick); Elizabeth P. McKay (Ann); Jack Mulcahy (Jack).

LOS ANGELES TIMES, 8/9/95, Calendar/p. 1, Kenneth Turan

"The Brothers McMullen" is ragged but right. Made on the run in little time for almost no money, it has the kind of life and spirit that often goes away when budgets go up. While other films struggle for their effects, "Brothers" simply lives and breathes, thoroughly likable from beginning to end.

Written, directed by and starring 26-year-old Edward Burns and costing less than $25,000, this casual, conversational film arrives laden with distinction. It won the Grand Jury Prize, the top honor at this year's Sundance Film Festival, and ended up the first picture to be distributed by Fox's new Searchlight Pictures division. But it's best seen without the burden of expectation, but rather with the open heart of someone amenable to falling in love.

The vagaries of the heart is what "Brothers" is about, as well as the related questions of commitment, fidelity and the demands and benefits of family. Burns' native wit keeps things loose and natural, as does the pleasure at being exposed to an unexplored setting for romance, the Irish Catholic suburbs of Long Island.

Though they don't always go to church, the three McMullen brothers are both supported and comically tortured by their Catholicism, by the need they feel to varying degrees to reconcile their lives to their religion. Burns, who shot the film in his parents' house "out on the island," has an intimate knowledge of this unexpected milieu and casually but firmly hooks us into caring about these people and their concerns.

The three good-looking McMullen brothers are in their 20s, and, with their abusive father dead and their mother's departure for Ireland to rejoin an old sweetheart, they have only each other to turn to as they puzzle out how to relate to the women they're involved with.

Though their personalities and personal situations are different, the brothers are united by a shared unreadiness to commit to one-woman romance. The idea of being "a real guy with a real life" is initially too frightening for any of them to contemplate for too long.

This applies even to Jack (Jack Mulcahy), the oldest of he brothers and the only one with both a real job (as a high school coach) and a wife. But when the beautiful Molly (Connie Britton) starts talking about children, Jack gets nervous and enviously eyes brother Barry's hedonistic lifestyle and his wild date, Ann (Elizabeth P. McKay).

An affable rogue who is teasingly known in the family as Mr. Hotshot Noncommittal, Barry (played by writer-director Burns) is a would-be screenwriter with a wicked tongue and a firm belief that no one should ever get married.

"Your wife," he reasons, "is the last woman you'll see completely naked and be allowed to touch. It's something to think about." Both irresponsible and irresistible, he is proud of never having been in love and considers himself an expert in the art of breaking up. Which is what he thinks his younger brother, Patrick (Mike McGlone), should be doing as soon as possible.

Though not as entertaining as Barry or as solid as Jack, Patrick has an earnest commitment to the Catholic religion that makes him the moral center of the family. Although they jokingly call him "altar boy," it is to Patrick, just out of college, that the others come when their worries about what constitutes "a big-time sin" threaten to get out of hand. And it is much to the picture's credit that Patrick's devoutness is presented in an affectionate, appealing light.

Deeply enough involved with his intense Jewish girlfriend Susan (Shari Albert) that she at least is considering marriage, Patrick is unconvinced. Not because he doesn't believe in the institution, but rather that he's romantically obsessed with finding his "true soul mate" and doesn't want to take the big step until he is sure who that is.

A lack of funds on both their parts moves Patrick and Barry back into their old rooms in the attic of what is now Jack's house, and that change in living conditions ends up bringing new women into their lives, Patrick starts to notice Leslie (Jennifer Jostyn), a fetching neighborhood girl he used to admire in high school, and Barry, on a desperate apartment-hunting mission in Manhattan, finds himself outsmarted by the self-reliant Audrey (Maxine Bahns), an actress who is resistant to his practiced charms.

Though its "Will love find a way?" plot is cheerful and diverting, it's the characters that make "The Brothers McMullen" the success it is. Writer-director Burns has a gift for amusing and profane dialogue for the affable way people, especially brothers, needle each other. And he is especially fortunate in his cast, which mixes professional and non-professional actors and makes his characters sweetly realistic.

And though he did it partly for economic reasons, Burns' decision to cast himself as Barry was the choice that puts "The Brothers McMullen" over the top: He, no surprise, understands the character exactly, and his way with the script's blasphemous banter keeps the picture from getting somber.

Burns, who is only 26, told the audience after the film's initial Sundance screening that he first got into acting in college because "I didn't want theater majors in black turtlenecks to come in and bash my scripts." Rarely has artistic paranoia paid off so quickly and so well.

NEW YORK POST, 8/9/95, p. 31, Michael Medved

"The Brothers McMullen," winner of the grand jury prize at this year's Sundance Festival, is the sort of audacious, underdog moviemaking that's easy to over-praise.

It uses appealing altogether unknown actors to create a gallery of earthy characters who are deployed in (mostly) believable situations.

The film even throws up a few serious questions about true love and burdens of Irish Catholic guilt, handling this material like an apprentice juggler who's delighted merely to get all the balls in the air at once.

If young Edward Burns, the movie's writer/director and star, never gets around to answering those Big Questions, and lets the juggler's balls come thudding to earth long before the end of the picture, it seems churlish to complain.

After all, how much can you reasonably expect from a no-budget effort shot by amateurs on available weekends during which the filmmaker's mother fed cast and crew with her famous corned beef and cabbage?

You can almost smell those meals on the set as you watch the film, and it shamelessly trades on this salt-of-the-earth family flavor.

The principal characters are three Long Island brothers who are temporarily living together in the house their parents left them after the death of their father (fondly recalled as "our favorite wife-beating child-abusing alcoholic"), and their mother's return to Dublin to join the man she should have married some 35 years before.

Oldest son Jack (Jack Mulcahy) is a well-fed high school football coach who's been married for five years to the sweet, sexy colleen of his dreams (Connie Britton). He's never been tempted to cheat on his wife, until a sexual predator (Elizabeth P. McKay), who briefly went out with middle brother Barry, begins setting elaborate traps to lure big brother into an affair.

Meanwhile, Barry himself (diffidently played by filmmaker Burns) is an aspiring writer who instantly runs from any woman who starts talking commitment, until he crosses paths with a sassy model, Audrey (Maxine Bahns), who manages to turn his head.

The youngest brother, Patrick (superbly played by Mike McGlone) recently finished college and is awkwardly involved with Susan (Shari Albert)—an insultingly stereotypical "Jewish princess" who wants to give her boyfriend a job in the shmatta business, so long as Patrick agrees to convert.

This is a problem, because Patrick, alone among McMullens, takes his Catholicism seriously, and feels horrified when suddenly pregnant Susan considers an abortion.

The plot offers neither profundities nor surprises, but sustains our attention by skillfully shifting its focus among the brothers.

The frequent references to Catholicism are so heavy-handed and superficial ("You can't be Catholic and have a healthy sex life") that they seem to have been inserted to give the movie an aura of seriousness it doesn't really deserve; the family name of these brothers is definitely "McMullen," not Karamazov.

In contrast to its incoherent philosophizing, the picture is at its best in portraying the passionate bonding of the brothers. We may not end up valuing them as much as they treasure one another, but these boys do provide an evenings worth of entertaining company.

NEWSDAY, 8/9/95, Part II/p. B7, Jack Mathews

Long Island native Edward Burns's "The Brothers McMullen" is this year's "Clerks," which was last year's "El Mariachi," which was some other year's "Hollywood Shuffle." They're low-budget films so much better than the home movies they resemble that agents and critics are agog, major careers are launched and you are asked to shell out the full price of a ticket to see what the fuss is all about.

What the fuss is usually about is how much a talented young filmmaker can do with pocket change (Burns' family ponied up the initial $28,000 budget), borrowed equipment and actors working on deferred salaries. Just as reviewers are guilty of being overly critical of a profligate clinker like "Waterworld" ("They spent $180 million for *that*?"), we tend to over-appraise the little gems that pop out at a festival like Sundance, where "The Brothers McMullen" copped a major prize last winter.

The movie, a very savvy take on the romantic entanglements of three Irish-Catholic brothers on Long Island, has already earned its 27-year-old writer, director, co-producer and co-star a major studio assignment, and he clearly deserves the opportunity. But go to "The Brothers McMullen" expecting a big deal, and you'll be disappointed.

The brothers McMullen of the Irish-Catholic Burns' informed imagination are oldest brother Jack (Jack Mulcahy), whose 5-year-old marriage is threatened by his impetuous affair with an aggressive female friend; youngest brother Patrick (Mike McGlone), a recent college grad whose relationship with a Jewish-American princess is giving him a double dose of Catholic guilt (thou shalt not have premarital sex, but if thou must, keep it in the faith); and Barry (Burns), a likable but self-absorbed bachelor unwilling to commit to anything other than his stubborn determination to become a filmmaker.

We join the brothers as they're burying their abusive alcoholic father and saying goodbye to their mom, who's returning to her native Ireland to marry the childhood sweetheart she says she should have married 35 years before. Add to this sense of abandonment enough Catholic guilt to sink the Good Ship Lollipop, and you have three confused men in a world that's about three steps ahead of them.

Burns has a fine ear for dialogue, particularly in those scenes of casual banter between the close-knit but highly individual brothers, and he's gotten fine performances from a cast that includes both amateur and professional actors. Mulcahy and McGlone both have film and stage experience, and with the surprisingly strong presence of Burns, who has never acted before, they make for a very convincing brood.

The five actresses playing the brothers' love interests (two each for Jack and Patrick, one for Barry) have little to do in this boys' tale, but Connie Britton, a young New York stage actress making her film debut, is a standout as Jack's rock-solid wife.

It's too soon to proclaim Burns a wunderkind. He has made a movie very specific to his own experiences, and the earnestness of the work overcomes some awkward staging and over-long conversations. Still, at what could be a 6,000th the price, it's a better movie than "Waterworld." There ought to be a message in that for somebody.

NEWSWEEK, 8/14/95, p. 73, Jeff Giles

There are many clues that Ed Burns's *The Brothers McMullen* is a homegrown production. For instance, the movie was largely filmed in his parents' house on New York's Long Island, and the credits list his mother as the caterer. When Burns, 27, sent a rough cut of the movie to film festivals and distribution companies, they spoke as if in unison. "It was rejected by Telluride, Toronto, New York," he says. "Even the Hamptons' f--king film festival rejected us." And the studios? "Miramax rejected us. New Line. Everyone. No one wanted to have anything to do with us. We were the friggin' underdog of the underdogs."

Finally, Fox Searchlight Pictures, a new division of Twentieth Century Fox, advanced Burns enough money to get "McMullen" in shape for the only festival smart enough to have him: Sundance. The movie won top prize, and this month it's Searchlight's inaugural release. "McMullen" is a funny, beguiling and neurotic picture about three Irish-American brothers foundering in the choppy waters of romantic commitment. After the death of their alcoholic father, Patrick (Mike McGlone) and Barry (Burns) crash with Jack (Jack Mulcahy) and his wife, Molly (Connie Britton), and the three men try to talk each other through various crises of faith and fidelity, though each brother is more screwed up than the last. Mulcahy was in "Porky's"—"He played the guy with the crooked penis," says Burns—but virtually everyone else is a newcomer and some of the acting is clunky. Still, Burns makes a great, raspy-voiced cad. McGlone is a hilarious, Roman Catholic Woody Allen. And Britton's shrewd and earthy betrayed wife is a ground wire for the whole fluttering movie.

Burns grew up on Long Island, the son of a New York City police sergeant. He didn't have the grades or the money for film school, so he shot "McMullen" while lugging lights and fetching coffee for "Entertainment Tonight." He couldn't pay his cast or crew. He auditioned actors in "E.T.'s" offices and clandestinely borrowed their vans, their editing facilities, their sound engineers, a cameraman and all of their interns. Burns filmed in Central Park and lower Manhattan without permits. When stopped by police, he dropped his father's name.

Burns made "McMullen" for about $16,000, though it took Fox Searchlight's $500,000 to pay back salaries and get the film ready for theaters. The director's second feature will follow a retired fireman and his sons, one of them (to be played by Burns) a cabdriver who marries a passenger hours after picking her up. His dream movie is a "Godfather"-size epic about Irish-American cops, but he knows that's a long way off. Fortunately, Burns is still riding on the high of recent coups, like introducing his mother to Robert Redford at a Sundance party last winter. "He took off his hat and he said, 'Oh, Mrs. Burns, you should be very proud of your son'," he remembers. "And then he gives her a friggin' hug and a kiss! You could see her melting in his arms." The underdogs are having their day.

SIGHT AND SOUND, 12/95, p. 41, Geoffrey Macnab

Long Island, New York. At the funeral of her husband. Mrs. McMullen announces that she is heading to Ireland for a reunion with her lover from 30 years before. Her three grown sons are to be left to fend for themselves; Patrick and Barry move in with their elder brother, Jack, and his wife, Molly, while they try to sort out their lives. Barry, an aspiring scriptwriter, wants to live in downtown Manhattan. But the only place he can afford is rented from under his nose by Audrey, a model who tells him she is married. Patrick debates splitting up with his Jewish girlfriend, Susan. Jack, although devoted to his wife, is tempted to start an affair with Ann, a single woman who makes a pass at him during his wife's 30th birthday party.

Barry bumps into Audrey again, and asks her out. He learns she is not married and is soon smitten with her. Patrick is given the boot by Susan. He begins to spend time with Leslie, an Irish-American girl. She tells him that, as soon as she can, she is going to buy a car and take off for California. Jack starts the affair with Ann. Susan tells Patrick that she is pregnant. A staunch Catholic, he believes he must marry her. Barry, on the verge of selling his first script, warns Audrey that he can't commit himself to a long-term relationship. She threatens to leave town. Molly learns about Jack's infidelity and confronts him.

Patrick is all set to move in with Susan (who has had a miscarriage) and to begin working for her father. At the last minute, he realises he can't go through with it. Instead, he borrows money from Jack so he can help Leslie buy her car and joins her on a trip out west. Jack and Molly vow to make a new start in their marriage. Barry manages to track Audrey down just before she leaves New York. At first, he still won't make a commitment. But when she heads off, he runs after her. The two embrace, stopping the traffic.

Winner of this year's Grand Jury Prize at the Sundance Festival. *The Brothers McMullen* is a rarity: a low budget, independent film, set in a working class area of New York, that owes more to Nora Ephron than to Martin Scorsese. No guns, drugs, spats in pool halls, ethnic tensions or money troubles disturb the prevailing mood of tranquillity. The only worries facing the three brothers here are their tortuous love lives and occasionally strained relations with each other. Debut director Edward Burns creates a charmed, self-enclosed world reminiscent of the one depicted in Whit Stillman's equally talkative *Metropolitan*. However, whereas Stillman's film took place in the rarefied upper-reaches of Manhattan, this romantic comedy unfolds in the less than romantic location of Long Island, a blue collar corner of America, famous in recent years for the Amy Fisher scandal, and for very little else. ("Writers live in Manhattan," aspiring author Barry McMullen [played by Burns] is told by his agent, "Joey Buttafuocos live in Long Island.")

Not that Burns does much to bring his Irish-American neighbourhood to life or to contrast it with other, more familiar, New York localities. There are occasional sorties uptown; one or two sequences set in the park, the street or the subways but, on the whole, the movie stays indoors. This is both an aesthetic and an economic decision: by concentrating on characters and their emotions, close-ups and dialogue, rather than aiming for any big cinematic set-pieces. Burns was able to make the film on a pittance. (It was shot mainly at weekends over a period of eight months.) He was also able to make it easily accessible to a mass audience. Its soft-centred narrative ends on as mawkish a note as any mainstream Hollywood melodrama.

Whatever debates *The Brothers McMullen* provokes about the shifting, ever more intimate relations between independent film makers and the studios they once defined themselves against, this is certainly an assured, likable debut. It captures brilliantly the irritable intimacy between the three adult brothers forced to share a house. From the early sequence, in which they embark on an absurdly earnest discussion about the relationship between JFK and Marilyn Monroe, to their last scene together, in which Patrick prepares to head to California with his new girlfriend, the trio show an easy, comic rapport. They all have different philosophies toward life, and are wont to give each other plenty of pompous, unsolicited advice. Burns expertly weaves the three different strands of the narrative together. As a tyro filmmaker, he may not offer much in terms of formal innovation, but his film is seamlessly edited and boasts some cracking one-liners, most of them delivered in throwaway, deadpan fashion. There are occasional sequences, especially those involving guilt-stricken Catholic Patrick, in which interior monologues are used to heighten the comic effect. There are also some poignant moments in which Burns captures a telling glance or a gesture, for instance Molly, baffled by her husband's infidelity, or Susan, finally realising that Patrick is going to leave her.

Burns could easily be accused of a certain auteurial narcissism: after all, he writes, produces, directs, edits, stars ... and gets the girl. His character, Barry, charismatic but insufferably arrogant, is the least sympathetic of the brothers. The saccharine finale, which sees him reunited with Audrey, is shot like a Pepsi commercial. At this point, the film loses its fizz and irony. Still, the acutely observed dialogue, fresh performances and general freewheeling charm of everything that has gone before ensure that even such a cornball ending is just about palatable.

TIME, 8/28/95, p. 69, Richard Corliss

[*The Brothers McMullen* was reviewed jointly with *The Usual Suspects*, see Corliss' review of that film.]

VILLAGE VOICE, 8/15/95, p. 41, Georgia Brown

Whatever minuscule figure is being quoted as the budget of Edward Burns's *The Brothers McMullen*, it looks like they spent half of that. "Grainy" is putting it politely. Nonetheless this amiable, good-hearted family comedy won Sundance's Grand Jury Prize. It's not what I might vote for but I can see its wholesome appeal.

Burns's movie is set in an Irish-Catholic enclave of Queens, or Long Island (I can't say I know the difference)—the sort of all-white neighborhood where houses nestle cheek to jowl and the stars and stripes droop protectively over the front steps. One house with flag belongs to the eldest of the three McMullen brothers. The family's surrogate patriarch, Jack (Jack Mulcahy), is 33, a high school coach married to the lively, pretty Molly, (Connie Britton). She's ready to have kids now, he clings to boyhood. For the moment, however, the house is full since Jack's two younger brothers, Barry (played by the film's writer and director), and Patrick (Mike McGlone), have moved in for an indefinite stay. Although they set New Year's for their departure date, before you know it, Palm Sunday and Lent have rolled around.

Five years ago, the brothers' father died, at which time Mom departed hastily for Ireland (from grave site to airport), where she'd left her true love a lifetime before. "Don't make the mistake I did," she warns her sons as she takes off. Each of the boys grapples with the legacy of their parent's unhappy marriage. Jack backs into an affair. Barry, budding screenwriter and director, scorns love and commitment, even when he meets his obvious match, Audrey (Maxine Bahns). The youngest, Patrick, a serious Catholic, is breaking up with the favorite daughter of a garment district king. I'm struggling not to say Jewish princess, though this is what the movie makes of Susan (Shari Albert). The biggest laugh at the screening I went to came when Susan suggests Patrick convert and he blurts out, "*Become a JEW?!*"

Neatly interweaving its three stories, Burns's film follows each brother into the Manhattan that Queens kids would most like to know—Central Park and the West Village. If Jack is something of a lug, and Barry more than a bit smug, the youngest, Patrick, is easily the most winning (McGlone is the best actor of the three) as he finds a spunky Catholic girl almost next door.

Also reviewed in:
CHICAGO TRIBUNE, 8/18/95, Friday/p. C, Michael Wilmington
NEW YORK TIMES, 8/9/95, p. C9, Janet Maslin
VARIETY, 1/30-2/5/95, p. 47, Todd McCarthy

WASHINGTON POST, 8/18/95, p. G1, Rita Kempley
WASHINGTON POST, 8/18/95, Weekend/p. 42, Desson Howe

BULLETPROOF HEART

A Keystone Films release in association with Worldvision Enterprises. *Executive Producer:* Robert Sigman, Gary Delfiner, and Michael Strange. *Producer:* Robert Vince and William Vince. *Director:* Mark Malone. *Screenplay:* Gordon Melbourne. *Story:* Mark Malone. *Director of Photography:* Tobias Schliessler. *Editor:* Robin Russell. *Music:* Graeme Coleman. *Sound:* David Husby and (music) Greg Reely. *Sound Editor:* Richard Baumgarter and Issac "Skud" Strozberg. *Casting:* Abra Edelman, Elisa Goodman, Marcia Shulman, and Katie Eland. *Production Designer:* Lynne Stopkewich. *Art Director:* Eric McNab. *Set Decorator:* Elizabeth Patrick. *Set Dresser:* Steph Watts, Geoff Hoare, and Jason B. Landels. *Special Effects:* Michael S. Vincent. *Costumes:* Maxyne Baker. *Make-up:* Pamela M. Athayde and Suzanne Willet. *Stunt Coordinator:* Marc Akerstream. *Running time:* 100 minutes. *MPAA Rating:* R.

CAST: Anthony LaPaglia (Mick); Mimi Rogers (Fiona); Matt Craven (Archie); Peter Boyle (George); Monika Schnarre (Laura); Joseph Maher (Dr. Alstricht); Mark Acheson (Hellbig); Philip Hayes (FBI Agent); Christopher Mark Pinhey and Claudio de Victor (Partygoers); Justine Priestly (Masseuse).

LOS ANGELES TIMES, 3/3/95, Calendar/p. 10, Peter Rainer

In the press notes for "Bulletproof Heart," starring Anthony LaPaglia and Mimi Rogers, director Mark Malone describes how he conceived a movie about a hit man who seems to have stepped out of a Camus novel.

For one thing, Malone read a lot of Camus novels. He also "read an article about organized crime in New York that said many mobsters have stopped hiring psychopaths to do their killings for them. It seems that they have found them too unmanageable and unpleasant. Some of the men who arrange Mob killings now seek out nihilists instead."

Nihilist hit men: Doesn't this sound like the premise for a great, early Woody Allen comedy? Imagine organized crime figures raiding the university philosophy departments for talent. Would the rationalists run New Jersey? Would the pragmatists take over Chicago?

Malone is aware of the comic possibilities in the premise but he keeps a lid on them. He and his Screenwriter, Gordon Melbourne, "and his gifted cinematographer, Tobias Schliessler, are far more interested in making a moody, blues piece of neo-noir fatalism. It's low-rent, single-room-occupancy Camus. What makes it compelling is that the filmmakers and the actors are completely absorbed by the fatalism, they're entranced by it. And so, miraculously, "Bulletproof Heart" never comes across as a gag, a joke. It wins you over.

The French will love it.

LaPaglia's Nick is very good at his killing job but he's grown numb. When we first see him, with a call girl, he seems more interested in murdering her than dallying with her. Mick isn't a bad guy, exactly, he's just caught up in the wrong line of work. He's a hit man because he's good at it—nothing personal.

But, of course, it gets personal. When George (Peter Boyle), a mobster and frequent client, pressures Mick into agreeing to hit George's ex-girlfriend Fiona (Mimi Rogers), Mick ends up falling for her.

The early scenes between Mick and Fiona are edgy, kinky duets. Fiona knows why Mick is visiting at her apartment; she *welcomes* the opportunity to shuffle off her mortal coil. This is what makes "Bulletproof Heart" an existential double-whammy: Fiona seeks her own obliteration. And Mick, who is used to having his victims offer some resistance, is flummoxed by Fiona's fatalism. She's even more nihilistic than *he* is, and it spooks him.

LaPaglia is very good at showing how Mick is pulled into Fiona's web of misery. He's never met anyone like her and he's touched by her—he wants to reclaim her. But she's too much for him; she's also smart enough to understand that Mick the control freak needs to be overwhelmed. (They have a sex scene early on that really clarifies their temperaments; it's a great example of how explicit sex in a movie can be anything *but* gratuitous.) By the time they're eating take-out Chinese food in a mortuary, while Mick's trigger-happy aide Archie (the gifted Matt Craven) practices looking mean in a rear-view mirror, "Bulletproof Heart" has become deeply loco.

But no more so than most film noirs. In that genre, the more darkly nutty the better. And the better the vamp, the better the piece. Rogers is deeply upsetting as Fiona; it's easy to see how she could cause a hardened hit man to unflex. Rogers in recent years has become an extraordinarily subtle and intuitive actress and she gets to give a full-fledged performance in "Bulletproof Heart"—reason enough to see it. She gives the film a genuinely troubling core that overrides all the artsy-fartsy fatalism.

NEW YORK POST, 4/7/95, p. 44, Larry Worth

Like a spider spinning its web, first-time director Mark Malone weaves simple plot threads into a network of alluring filaments, and practically redefines film noir in the process.

The result—"Bulletproof Heart"—may be the '90s answer to "Body Heat."

But instead of the deliciously bitchy banter between sultry minx Kathleen Turner and dumb hunk William Hurt the dynamic has evolved and blurred. When Mimi Rogers and Anthony LaPaglia command the screen, it's hard to tell who's the victim of the sexually-laced game-playing.

Taking place over one action filled night from New York City to New Jersey docks, it's an evening when secret pasts, macho ethics, long-buried passions and the art of murder are the featured players.

The scene is set when world-weary hitman Mick (La Paglia) comes home from a hard day of killing and a mobster pal (Peter Boyle) pressures him into another assignment: knock off a beautiful woman (Rogers) by dawn before she can turn informer.

There's a hitch, more than a willing target, Fiona embraces the thought of death. But like Medusa's benign twin, she has a history of melting iron-clad hearts, and continuing her tortured existence in the bargain.

Sure enough, as Mick and his sad-sack sidekick (Matt Craven) accompany Fiona from a wild bash to a desolate graveyard, then a chillingly empty warehouse, a fissure in Mick's armor draws all the players into a hellacious vortex. But amidst the unpredictable twists, one certainty emerges: No one's getting out unscathed.

Though Gordon Melbourne's script could have been tightened, Malone knows how to entice. Through flashbacks and tight cross-cuts, he leads audiences on a breathless race to the finale. And complementing a growing number of films to place a scene after the end credits, the coda here is a real haunter.

But none of it would ignite without the energies of LaPaglia and Rogers. Both display a jaw-dropping range of emotions, capped by a graphic sexual encounter that's guaranteed to raise temperatures to the boiling point.

Unexpected comic turns from Peter Boyle, Matt Craven, Joseph Maher and fetching newcomer Monika Schnarre—along with Tobias Schliessler's moody photography—guarantee that "Bulletproof Heart" keeps thumping to a gloriously twisted beat.

NEWSDAY, 4/7/95, Part II/p. B7, John Anderson

Yes, yes, yes, everything these days is about sex or violence, which is exactly what makes Mark Malone's "Bulletproof Heart" so novel. It's about sex *and* violence. Doesn't that make you happy?

It should, actually, because besides being an intelligent, darkly funny film—one in the irreverent New Noir tradition of John Dahl's "Red Rock West" and "The Last Seduction," and Steven Soderbergh's upcoming "Underneath"—it makes pungent observations about power, libido and disillusion without getting in its own way. It may, in fact, be more cerebral than atmospheric, less able to intimidate than to probe the reasons why it might, but Malone's debut feature is confident enough to inhabit a genre without relying on conventions. Which isn't bad for a director's debut feature.

That the entire film is a black joke, and fails to rise above it, is where Malone falters. He's made an adult (as in un-stoopid) film, at the center of which is an alienated hit man (there's another kind?) in the midst of a career crisis. Like many a successful small businessman and independent contractor, Mick (Anthony LaPaglia) is good at what he does, but his passion is spent in his work. Sex and work have merged in his mind; when his associate, George (a dryly funny Peter Boyle), sends him a beautiful call girl (Monika Schnarre) as a gift, Mick considers stabbing her in the heart. He's lost his zest for anything but murder; he's lustless in the dust. A dealer in death, he's wondering if life has any meaning.

This is not hysterically funny, but how serious can you take it? The sensitive hit man has been done (by Jack Nicholson, among others) and the identity crisis of a hired assassin isn't of particular urgency, not to me at least. Luckily, LaPaglia, whose charisma is a delicate thing anyway, is just about perfectly cast: His Mick is a study in mannered cool, a man who knows what a man's gotta do, and who, when he finds he can't do it, questions his whole existence. In addition, LaPaglia has the unique ability to shrink in stature right before our eyes, as he does when he meets the glamorous and beguiling Fiona (Mimi Rogers).

Mick's persona is overripe and deliberate, but Fiona—Rogers is particularly confident and alluring, wields a refined kind of disdain. She's used her seductive gifts to cheat George out of a great deal of money, and must be dealt with. The problem for Mick is that she wants to die. Or seems to. What Fiona is about—and how well this remains a secret during the course of the film—will depend on the cynicism of the individual viewer. Mick is enticed by her nonchalance, though. And after she takes him to bed and dominates him, his goose is cooked.

Malone uses air the way Dahl does, suspending his characters in a kind of spatial as well as moral limbo; there is both warm light and a chilly cast over all we see. There is a strong sense of duty, of course—there always is in hit man movies—although Mick's allegiance changes during the film, as does he. Morality is malleable, but so is the film noir genre, and Malone, like Dahl, seems to know how to bend it to his will.

SIGHT AND SOUND, 6/95, p. 47, Nick James

In New York, an FBI officer inspects a hotel room before ushering in Mr Hellbig, an injured witness under his protection. After the officer has left, a hitman, Mick, emerges from the wardrobe and murders Hellbig.

Part of Mick's reward is a visit from a hooker, Laura, but she fails to excite him and they are interrupted by Archie, a trainee hitman who has come to apologise for fouling up a previous attempt on Hellbig's life. Archie wants another chance to work with Mick, but he refuses. George, who commissioned the hit, arrives and attacks Archie on sight, but Mick intervenes and Archie escapes. George has come to offer Mick another job. A woman downtown, Fiona, is in serious debt with the mob and they want her whacked, but there's a twist: she wants it to happen herself for medical reasons. George warns Mick to be careful because "men go soft around her".

Archie pleads with Mick for a second chance to prove himself. Mick finally concedes, but when they arrive at Fiona's apartment block, he makes Archie wait downstairs. At Fiona's swanky apartment, an art crowd party is beginning to wind down. Mick learns that Fiona is incurably ill. As the guests leave, he helps Fiona's drunk psychoanalyst Dr Alstricht into the lift where he falls asleep. Fiona then seduces Mick. She ties him to her bed and slaps him hard. He finds the pain a welcome stimulation and has his first satisfying sex in several years. They leave and get into Mick's car with Archie.

While Mick is ringing George to question the necessity of the hit, Archie begins to describe to Fiona how he messed up the first attempt on Hellbig's life. This anecdote, shown in flashback, is told intermittently throughout the night. It ends with Archie unable to shoot Hellbig at the crucial moment. Meanwhile, Mick meets with George to explain his reluctance to kill Fiona, but George insists on him carrying through with it. Later, while walking through Idlewood cemetary, Fiona eludes Mick. He finds her lying inside a tomb, in extreme pain and apparently out of her mind. Leaving her in the car with Archie, Mick returns to her apartment block and interrogates Dr Albricht, who confirms that she is suffering from an incurable and painful disease that threatens her sanity.

Fiona returns to consciousness and she, Mick and Archie reach the appointed execution site, a warehouse in New Jersey, in the early hours. Mick seats Fiona in a chair with her back to the river but he can't bring himself to pull the trigger despite her weary pleading. George arrives and during a lengthy squabble between him and Mick outside, Archie comes to believe that Mick has left him alone with Fiona as a test. With her encouragement, Archie finally summons the will to shoot her through the head. As dawn breaks, Mick sits on the riverbank cradling Fiona's limp body in his arms.

Debut director Mark Malone is a self-confessed, self-concious resurrector of *film noir* and *Killer* is steeped in admiration of its lowlife milieu and its central theme, the transcendent and fateful power of obsessive passion. His tragic plot's all-in-one-night structure, punctuated by Archie's recollections of his failed hit, and preceded by Mick's completion of the job, is realised with an assured sense of dramatic weight and timing, although it errs somewhat on the portentous side. The central idea of a victim who wants to die and a killer who has fallen for her and doesn't want to carry out his commission works well, although it's stretched almost to breaking point by the time Mimi Rogers' Fiona finally hits the deck. The film also looks as moody and bruised as a good *noir* should, with deeply etched shadows and muted colours.

Strangely though, all the care that Malone has taken with the film's look and in getting committed performances from his small ensemble cast seems to impede the film's dramatic flow. It's hard to tell whether this is because the attention to gesture and *mise en scène* is excessive to the point of mannerism, or because he and his male actors are so keen to let us know how well they're doing. Whatever the reason, its not just the men whose appearance seems to shout: "look at me, I'm the new Bobby De Niro"; the cars, the clothes, even the ice-cream cones seem to be saying, "Are you talking to me?".

An atmosphere of smug criminal camaraderie is to some extent an inevitable byproduct of Mick's impotent narcissism (Anthony LaPaglia exudes a steely self-regard even after his bewildered character has supposedly "gone soft" on Fiona). But Matt Craven's jumpy, jerky wannabe Archie and Peter Boyle in the part that Peter Boyle always gets to play—the older and wiser wise guy, George—compound a feeling that everyone is practising their ad-libs before auditioning for Martin Scorsese's *Casino*. Malone's one serious weakness in his handling of *Killer* is that he allows the buzz his cast get from playing wise guys to show beyond the limits of their characters.

Fortunately, *Killer* has one central impeccable performance that never skips a beat. The part of Fiona gives Mimi Rogers a welcome break from playing so many walk-on mothers (in *Far From Home* and *Monkey Trouble* to name but two), and she proves with her best effort since *Someone to Watch Over Me* that she is perhaps the most sorely under-rated actress among many in Hollywood. Fiona's wild behaviour swings could so easily have been rendered in terms of a *Fatal Attraction*-style, monstrous, unknowable other. Instead, Rogers makes a poignant terrified victim out of a cipher-like role, and turns what could have been an extravagant exercise in wiseguy kitsch into an intriguing near-miss.

VILLAGE VOICE, 4/11/95, p. 64, Henry Beck

"I'm burnt out; there's something wrong with my brain," says weary hit man Mick (Anthony LaPaglia) to his boss George (Peter Boyle). Even though George recommends a therapist when Mick begins spouting depressing oddities like "What is the meaning of meaning?" he nevertheless wants Mick to whack socialite Fiona. Played by Mimi Rogers, Fiona has a penchant for staggering around cemeteries in Lauren Bacall drag, looking like a slightly cadaverous Candy Clark. The catch is, Fiona has engineered George into hiring Mick to kill her. Like Ole Andreson in Hemingway's *The Killers*, she waits calmly for the iceman to come and deliver her from a spiritual and psychological malaise that causes her to whimper, fall limp, and stare off into space like a zombie. She is evidently beyond the reach of all pharmacology but the .38 caliber variety.

So terribly disaffected is Mick that he allows himself to be wheedled into taking the job, which violates all his professional protocols, and whined into taking along the ratlike Archie (Matt Craven), who has already demonstrated his unreliability in tight spots (Archie claims his cowardice is caused by a magnesium deficiency). Mick even allows his intended victim to tie him up and smack him around—a bout of s/m-lite that gives him his first erection in years. Needless to say, he falls in love, rekindles his spirit, and loses his nerve.

While it sounds like this kind of low-key goodfellas stuff might be funny, there are few laughs here and those are mostly unintentional. In the past couple of decades there have been some decent efforts of this kind, most notably the vastly underrated *Hard Contract* (1969), starring

James Coburn and Lee Remick, but *Bulletproof Heart* is like a bad episode of *Tales From the Crypt* minus the horrific punch line—a tale of whackers, whackees, and the just plain whacked out.

Also reviewed in:
CHICAGO TRIBUNE, 7/21/95, Friday/p. C, Michael Wilmington
NEW YORK TIMES, 4/7/95, p. C5, Janet Maslin
VARIETY, 5/30-6/5/94, p. 47, Emanuel Levy
WASHINGTON POST, 5/20/95, p. H3, Hal Hinson

BURNT BY THE SUN

A Sony Pictures Classics release of a Studio Trite/Camera One coproduction with the participation of Canal+ and the Russian Ministry for Cinema. *Executive Producer:* Leonid Vereshchagin, Jean-Louis Piel, and Vladimir Sedov. *Producer:* Nikita Mikhalkov and Michel Seydoux. *Director:* Nikita Mikhalkov. *Screenplay (Russian with English subtitles):* Nikita Mikhalkov and Roustam Ibragimbekov. *Based on a story by:* Nikita Mikhalkov. *Director of Photography:* Vilen Kaliuta. *Editor:* Enzo Meniconi. *Music:* Edouard Artemiev. *Music Editor:* Minna Blank. *Sound:* Vincent Arnardi and Thierry Lebon. *Sound Editor:* Jean Umansky and Andre Rigaut. *Casting:* Tamara Odintsova. *Art Director:* Vladimir Aronin and Aleksandr Samulekin. *Costumes:* Natalia Ivanova. *Make-up:* Larisa Avidiushko. *Running time:* 134 minutes. MPAA *Rating:* R.

CAST: Nikita Mikhalkov (Sergei Petrovitch Kotov); Oleg Menchikov (Dimitri/Mitya); Ingeborga Dapkunaite (Maroussia); Nadia Mikhalkov (Nadia); Andre Umansky (Philippe); Viacheslav Tikhonov (Vsevolod Konstantinovitch); Svetlana Kriuchkova (Mokhova); Vladimir Ilyin (Kirik); Alla Kazanskaia (Lidiia Stepanovna); Nina Arkhipova (Elena Mikhailovna); Avangard Leontiev (Driver); Inna Ulianova (Olga Nikolaevna); Liubov Rudneva (Liuba); Vladimir Riabov (NKVD Officer); Vladimir Belousov and Aleksei Polatilov (NKVD Men); Evgenii Mironov (Lieutenant).

CINEASTE, Vol. XXI, No. 4, 1995, p. 43, Louise Menashe

One of the murkier chapters in the history of the Soviet security services relates to their activity among 'White' émigré groups, especially in the two decades after the 1917 Revolution. The capitals of Central and Western Europe pulsated with the anti-Red politics of the émigrés in those days, and Moscow riddled them with agents, often recruited from among the émigrés themselves. Decisions to turn coat were not easy, and often complex in motivation. Some of the émigrés had a change of heart about the Soviet regime and were willing to work for it; others, ardent patriots, placed Russia above their politics, even if it was now Soviet Russia. Then there were others who simply wanted to get back to the motherland, and were willing to contract with the devil to realize that wish, which may have meant agreeing to assist in the "liquidation," as a Politburo directive put it in 1923, of "especially dangerous enemies of the Soviet regime."

One of the most scandalous of such cases centered on Sergei Efron, husband of the great lyric poet, Marina Tsvetaeva. Efron fought for the Whites during the Civil War, made his way out of Russia, and eventually settled in Paris, writing and editing, and even working as an extra in French films to make ends meet. But politics was his passion—politics and Russia. His political sympathies flip-flopped, and he was active in trying to reconcile the émigrés to the Soviet regime, encouraging a back-to-Russia movement. His own attempts to return were denied by Moscow. Perhaps he was already an agent and this was part of his cover! Perhaps he was forced to do a little dirty work in exchange for permission to get back! We don't know. What is known is that in a celebrated Swiss trial for the murder of Ignaz Reiss, a former Soviet agent and defector, Efron was named as a Moscow operative, something long suspected by the émigrés. (He was also implicated in the murder of one of Trotsky's sons.) Efron promptly disappeared, and turned up in Russia living in a government dacha outside of Moscow. Later, he disappeared again, this time for good, probably into the dungeons of the Lubyanka.

There is wonderful dramatic and psychological material embedded in this sordid stuff, and not just for the historian. Parts of this story are depicted in Nikita Mikhalkov's engrossing *Burnt by the Sun*, winner of the 1994 Oscar for Best Foreign Film.

Mikhalkov is a resourceful and prolific filmmaker. Not all of his films have been shown here, but those that have reveal an ability to reach Western audiences shared by few modern Soviet and post-Soviet directors. He gets magnificent performances from his actors, often in virtuosic ensemble efforts. His films look good; they are painted in rich colors, and his camera and editing are always lively. He is a romantic and a Slavophile who dotes on sentiment, and his vivid characters inhabit melodramatic scenarios frequently drawn from Russian literary sources. *A Slave of Love* (1976), *Unfinished Piece for Player Piano* (1977), *Oblomov* (1980), *Dark Eyes* (1987), and *Close to Eden* (1992) display a talent for successfully uniting very 'Russian' themes with the conventions of global cinema.

In *Burnt by the Sun* Mikhalkov gets very Russian indeed; he manages, mostly successfully, but sometimes irritatingly, to fold Chekhov into the terror-ridden atmosphere of the Stalinist 1930s. The result is a compelling historical melodrama, but one quite reckless with clichés. Deadly Russian Roulette? Yes, the film begins with such a sequence. The beloved bathhouse? That's next. Indolent gentry hanging about the dacha? The mix of humor and pathos—the laughter through tears? A Gogolesque touch or two—a poor lost truck driver wandering around in circles? Yes, it's all there. It would all be shameless were it not redeemed by the film's powerful emotional crosscurrents of an unusual love triangle tinged by sinister purpose, and—especially—by a terrifically explosive denouement layered with psycho-political complexity. And this is Russian, too: everyone gets it in the end; there are crimes and everyone is punished.

The monstrous evil of Stalinism, 'burning' even those who worshipped its radiance, certainly comes through in the film. (Mikhalkov quotes a popular tango of the day, "Burnt by the Sun," throughout the film to make this bitterly ironic point.) But some of the details may be lost on the Western viewer. Mitya, the returned émigré, played brilliantly with a combination of charm and menace by Oleg Menshikov, is modeled on the Efron-like émigrés described above. Through a series of devices, sometimes very strained, amid the Chekhovian goings-on at the beach, or in the richly populated dacha, we are fed bits of information letting us know that after fighting against the Bolsheviks and surviving the Civil War, he emigrated to Paris where he knocked about, sometimes earning money from his musical and dancing talent. At one point he tells someone that he works for the NKVD (the Stalinist predecessor of the KGB), a jest of course.

Of course it's not a jest. Mitya was recruited to finger White officers in Paris for the NKVD. His reward—he is allowed to return to Russia. More, he is asked to supervise the quiet arrest of a Bolshevik Civil War hero, Colonel Sergei Kotov, at his country dacha. Remember, this is 1936, the high season of Stalin's terror, when even revered party, state, and military officials were mowed down by the security apparatus. Contrary to what many viewers concluded from the documentary-like title cards at the end of the film, Kotov was not a historical figure, but, like Mitya-Efron, a historically-based composite evoking the military of many larger-than-life Soviet military heroes victimized by Stalin's murderous paranoia. (One example: the dashing and innovative Marshal Mikhail Tukhachevsky, Civil War hero and Deputy Commissar of Defense—arrested, tried, convicted *in camera* on trumped-up charges, and executed in 1937.)

In the film, Mitya and Kotov are no strangers. Cunningly, the Mikhalkov-Ibragimbekov screenplay has them doubly connected. Mitya was recruited to the NKVD by Kotov. More important, Kotov is now married to Maroussia, Mitya's former lover back in the days of the sweet life among the gentry-intelligentsia before the Revolution. It so happens that Kotov's arrest will take place in the very dacha that was the site of Mitya and Maroussia's happiest hours in their former lives. The film filters these script contrivances through an evocative overall mood (behind the jocularity, we know something terrible is in the offing), and through superb acting. Some of the best comes from Ingeborga Dapkunaite who creates a wholly believable Maroussia—slender, handsome, quietly expressive, at once seductive and girlish, and very vulnerable. She is at the center of the strange choreography played out in the course of one sunny day that pits Mitya on his ominous mission against the older Kotov, who not only knows what the younger man is up to, but is suspicious that he has rekindled Maroussia's affection. There are some effective touches conveying Maroussia's inner anxiety over Mitya's mysterious reappearance—not very subtle, but effective, in the Mikhalkov cinematic style. When Mitya asks her for water to drink, the camera comes in close to show how she overfills the glass, dazed, letting the tap run on and on. When Mitya chronicles his life in the form of a puppet fable for Nadya, the Kotov's six-year-old daughter, again the camera dwells on the tea cup in Maroussia s trembling hands.

Nadya is played by Mikhalkov's own daughter (remember how he brought her on stage to accept his Oscar!), and Mikhalkov himself plays Colonel Kotov, a decision I think a casting mistake. Mikhalkov is a supremely gifted actor, sensuous and louche, a kind of Russian Jack Nicholson—his part as the footloose oil field worker in the epic film, *Siberiade*, directed by his brother, Andrei Konchalovsky, is a good example of his skill. Mikhalkov has said that he gave himself the part of Kotov only because he was determined to cast his daughter as Nadya, and he wanted her to be comfortable. She is not the problem; he is. She does very well as an engagingly precocious wiseacre who is immediately won over by the charming Mitya (another source of tension between him and Kotov.) She is all the more poignant since we know that, like all relatives of 'enemies of the people,' young and old, she too will be a victim of the Stalin machine. But Mikhalkov's considerable talents work against the story here; he is too full of himself, somehow too overwhelming a performing presence for our comfort. He and his daughter show off too much. Yes, the bigger the Soviet hero he is, the harder he will fall. But there are, in Mikhalkov's rendition, several notches more glamor than the gruffness needed to realize a big Soviet hero.

There is something else about Mikhalkov-Kotov that skews the political moral of the story, or masks its complexity. Our sympathies go out to him when—in the best scene of the film—he is brutally bludgeoned by NKVD thugs in the back seat of their black limousine. This, after he expresses his cocksure certainty that a simple telephone call to the private number of his good friend Stalin will clear up this mistake. "If only Stalin knew," was often the last desperate cry of Stalin's victims before they got a bullet in the back of the head. Kotov's bloody face grabs our attention more than the extraordinary reaction of Mitya to the gruesome spectacle. He sits coolly in his elegant whites, to Kotov's left, and looks away, through the car window, in supreme indifference to the Colonel's ugly fate, almost as if he is bored. *What a monster.*

But there is a more subtle meaning in that look, one which disburses moral responsibility for the violence a little less one-sidedly. It is this: You, Kotov, served the Bolsheviks willingly, and helped put them in power; this whole system which now devours you is of your own making. What did you expect! I, Mitya, had my life shattered by you, in the deepest personal, not just political, sense; because of you and your bloody Bolsheviks, what hurts most came to pass—I was, as he tells Maroussia, "obliterated" from her memory. I assisted in this crime against you to get one last look at the world taken away from me. Pardon me, Colonel, if I look away; I can't pity you.

Paradoxically, Mikhalkov's own sympathies as a Russian nationalist and monarchist (this despite his belonging to the old Soviet cultural elite) probably lean to Mitya, but his own powerful presence in the film tilts reactions in favor of Kotov. The film could also have done without two dubious devices, one the periodic appearance in and out of doors, of a moving fireball; the other, a large portrait of Stalin hanging from a hot-air balloon rising suddenly from the countryside. (Mockingly, Mitya salutes it.) Both devices are flat; they might have worked better to convey the surrealistic atmosphere of the times if some very special effects were available to the filmmakers. As it is, the times and the story told here are, in themselves, surrealistic and nightmarish enough.

FILMS IN REVIEW, 7-8/95, p. 54, Eva H. Kissin

Burnt By The Sun recalls one of those small, painted Russian boxes from Pahlav—brilliant in color and detail—and intense enough to suggest something much larger than its limited surface.

The setting of this Russian film is a fine old country house right out of Turgenev—white gauze curtains filling out like sails with the summer breeze. The dacha is of course surrounded by the inevitable white birches and inhabited by excitable and frequently manic characters.

The head of the household is a retired army colonel with his young wife and daughter. The writer and director of the film, Nikita Mikhalkov (*Dark Eyes* and *Slave of Love*), plays the Colonel with proper force of a Soviet hero. Ingeborga Dapkunaite is a fine sensual young wife, and Nadia Mikhalkov, the director's own child, steals the film with her absolute innocence and essential charm. Her particular smile remains in the mind's eye long after the credits disappear. In fact, all of the acting is exuberant with peasant vitality and a bohemian edge.

The film deals with a young man, a former lover of the Colonel's beautiful wife, who returns from the West to find her married and a mother. The jealousy between the passionate young man (excellently played by Oleg Menchikov,) and the aging Colonel create the surface story. The larger tale behind the romance is political, the Revolution, with its power plays and effect on the lives of the people. It suggests their original enthusiasm and eventual disillusion. We see it symbolically as a golden sun warming and burning the great Russian land mass and its people.

All of this material is quite personal to Mikhalkov, himself a retired Soviet hero, whose revolutionary ideals were eventually modified by the realities of communism under Stalin.

The film is really splendid on all counts and more than merits its many awards. Nadia also steals the show when her father brings her along to collect his Oscar. She deserved it.

LOS ANGELES TIMES, 4/21/95, Calendar/p. 12, Kenneth Turan

Overlooked and overshadowed since its Cannes debut one year ago, the luminous Russian film "Burnt by the Sun" is about to get the attention it has always deserved.

Directed by Nikita Mikhalkov, "Burnt" took the Grand Jury Prize at Cannes, the runner-up to the Palme d'Or, but when Quentin Tarantino's rambunctious "Pulp Fiction" grabbed the top spot, nobody could be bothered to care about second place.

Among the five nominees for best foreign-language film, "Burnt," the only one yet to appear in theaters, was the least known and easiest to ignore. Yet, as the academy recognized by voting it the Oscar, it's the best of the group, a rich and subtle drama, both delicate and powerful, a classically accomplished piece of emotional, character-driven filmmaking.

Mikhalkov, who also co-wrote the film and co-stars with his 6-year-old daughter Nadia, is best known ("Dark Eyes," "A Slave of Love," "Oblomov" and the masterful "An Unfinished Piece for Player Piano") for his ability to re-create Russia's past and his affinity for the empathetic world of Anton Chekhov.

What makes "Burnt by the Sun," set in 1936, so impressive is the way it uses a Chekhovian sensibility to investigate one of the most horrific periods in modern Russian history, the years of Stalinist terror in which the Soviet system devoured its most promising believers with a ferocity that is beyond understanding.

"Burnt" takes place almost entirely on a long, languid summer day at a country house outside of Moscow, filled with the usual Russian collection of eccentric relatives, servants and hangers-on. With their fine china, linens and elaborate meals, these people live much as they did before the revolution, Bolsheviks or no Bolsheviks. Excesses have not touched them, but implicit in the film's uneasy stillness is the sense that that innocence is about to end.

Undisputed master here is virile, mustachioed Col. Sergei Kotov (Mikhalkov). A benevolent hero of the Civil War, a friend of Stalin and Gorky so celebrated in his own right that his mere presence can stop maneuvering tanks in their tracks, the magnetic, immensely likable Kotov relishes his influence as well as his beautiful young wife, Maroussia (Ingeborga Dapkunaite), and their 6-year-old pixie daughter Nadia (Nadia Mikhalkov).

On this particular Sunday, just before lunch, a stranger arrives. At least, with his outlandish disguise, that's what he appears to be. But Maroussia sees beneath the subterfuge and recognizes the handsome Dimitri, familiarly known as Mitia (Oleg Menchikov), an old family friend who no one has seen for eight years.

A jaunty dancer, piano player and storyteller, Mitia brings a giddy intensity to this sleepy afternoon and soon captivates little Nadia. But Maroussia is flustered by his sudden appearance because Mitia was her lover when he left. And Kotov is thrown off balance by the tension of Mitia's ambiguous presence, by the air of unspoken agendas he offhandedly carries with him.

Overhanging all of this is a sadness no one can quite put a finger on, a foreknowledge of the doom both Stalin and World War II have stored up for this entire generation. This is discreetly symbolized by the plight of a lost truck driver, unable to figure out where he's headed and the metaphoric appearance of the disturbing, destructive fireball that echoes the film's title.

What "Burnt by the Sun" does best is elegantly intertwine the personal and political themes of love, trust and betrayal. In addition to an assured evocation of the period, Mikhalkov has taken enormous care with the acuteness of his characterizations, and the entire cast responds with heartbreaking performances.

At 2 hours and 8 minutes, "Burnt by the Sun" is considerably shorter than it was at Cannes, but nothing of importance has been lost.

NEW STATESMAN & SOCIETY, 8/18/95, p. 29, Jonathan Romney

Writing about *Before the Rain* last week, I complained about the way that political films often tend to fall into one of two traps—either their imagery is too direct, or it's not direct enough. Nikita Mikhalkov's *Burnt by the Sun* is a good example of a film that succeeds by using extremely explicit images in a context where, for much of the time, you wouldn't realise you were watching a political film at all.

Mikhalkov's film is set in the Russian countryside in the summer of 1936, and the image it contains is of a balloon rising over a field, gradually revealing the banner it's trailing—a huge portrait of Stalin. It's as incongruous a sign as the airborne statue of Christ in Fellini's *La Dolce Vita*, and works to much the same effect—an ideological icon that we're used to regarding as abstract is suddenly brought to overbearing, concrete life. You couldn't quite call it a surreal image, though—that would be to deny its straightforward political content, the message that even here, miles from nowhere, Stalin's presence literally hangs over everything.

By standards of cinematic good taste, it's too big an image—at once flamboyantly vulgar and far too obvious. Yet it makes sense that the gargantuan iconography of Stalinism should give rise to film images that are overblown. Besides, the image can be taken quite literally: this is just the sort of advertising that the regime used, and a fairly restrained example at that.

It's not easy for Stalinism's excess to be represented with subtlety, and Mikhalkov responds, at the start of this film, by doing away with subtlety altogether. The rural idyll of *Burnt by the Sun* kicks off with a flourish of absurdist bombast. Sergei Kotov, a Bolshevik military hero, is the subject of his own local personality cult. When tanks are about to roll through the cornfields, the farm workers call on him to intervene, and the tanks stop at his command. Looking at his muscular physique, no-nonsense grey crop and bristling moustaches, the impressed soldiery clearly see him as their own local Uncle Joe. He's played by Mikhalkov himself with an only partly ironic degree of self-aggrandisement. Few actor-directors have ever given themselves so much avuncular dignity on screen.

But for the most part, the film isn't a political satire at all—at least, it feigns to impress us that it isn't. Mikhalkov stages his drama as a bucolic interlude, far away from the wintry urban grimness that opens the film. The Kotovs Sergei, his young wife Maroussia (Ingeborga Dapkunaite) and six-year-old daughter Nadia—enjoy a gentle existence on a dacha. The corn sways, the bees hum and the atmosphere would seem Chekhovian if everyone weren't so happy. In fact, the sunlit laziness seems more like a homage to (or parodic tilt at?) the mood of *A Nest of Gentlefolk*, the 1969 Turgenev adaptation made by Mikhalkov's brother Andrei Konchalovsky. (At Cannes last year, *Burnt by the Sun* was competing against Konchalovsky's *Ryaba My Chicken*, a rougher and more anarchic film about contemporary rural Russia; you can't help seeing the two films as fraternal swipes at each other.)

When the idyll is interrupted, the tone is initially farcical. Everyone's lying by the river, taking the sun in their Edwardian-looking swimsuits, and it all looks like a retro-Soviet exercise in Cinema of Conviviality—when suddenly a no-nonsense, *Dad's Army*-like civil defence detachment arrives to corral everyone into testing gas masks. Most of the time, the satire seems only too mild: like Kotov telling his daughter that the Soviets are working for the future to keep people's feet soft. But there's often an uncomfortable twist in the background. Throughout the bathing scene, the camera keeps returning to a stray shard of glass that someone's soft foot is bound to step on at any moment.

When the outside world arrives, it's in the shape of Mitya (Oleg Menchikov), a smooth urban charmer already seen in the opening sequence playing the tormented romantic hero. What's on his mind, other than the seduction of Maroussia, an old flame? The answer, when it comes, is rather obvious, but still distressing. While we're waiting, Mikhalkov does his best to distract us, as casually and as mystifyingly as possible. Mitya tells Nadia a coded version of his life as a fairy-tale about "*latim*"—and while we're listening, a mysterious fireball floats through the house and out again. We're never sure what the fireball means, but its irreducibly weird presence throws us off kilter, and softens us up for the finale. The state heavies who preside over Kotov's fate, two sweaty men guzzling sandwiches, are a textbook example of the "banality of evil", as encountered in countless Russian fictions, where it's usually defined as *pohlost*, a transcendental naffness. But, because their appearance is so out of place in Kotov's cosy heroic world, it comes as a genuine shock.

Burnt by the Sun is a bizarre film that works on so many clashing registers that you're never quite sure how to take it. It's what is meant by comical-historical-pastoral. But it's so effective because it leaves you as disoriented as its characters. The Russian title literally means, "The people exhausted by the Sun", and exhaustion seems to be Mikhalkov's technique here. He gives us too much—too charming, too burlesque, and finally too cruel. He lets it all pass over us like a mystifying heat-haze, then tells us what's really going on. It becomes an unnerving parable about the way that even history's most obvious strokes can take us by surprise, leave us placidly bedazzled until it's too late.

NEW YORK, 5/1/95, p. 64, David Denby

There's too much sunshine in *Burnt by the Sun*, the new film by Russian director Nikita Mikhalkov (*A Slave of Love, Oblomov, Dark Eyes*). Or so I thought at first: The refulgent golden rays pour in everywhere, irradiating wheat fields and streaming through the trees surrounding a lovely old dacha. Mikhalkov has long been addicted to brilliant natural light and summer-afternoon scenes of gorgeous excess. In his films, ripeness, literally, is all. He feasts on his enchanted moments, as if everyone in his country of short summers got only one chance to be happy or sad. Mikhalkov, who just won the Oscar, is a highly theatrical director, and some of his symbolic effects announce themselves as rudely as a missile parade through Red Square. In *Burnt by the Sun*, there is actually a melancholy character who plays Russian roulette with a loaded pistol. And as if the sunshine weren't enough, little sun meteors run like Tinkerbell through the background of scenes and then fly out the window.

But if some directors have a talent for the obvious, Mikhalkov has a genius for it. *Burnt by the Sun* is an extremely powerful work. By the end of the movie, Mikhalkov's usual mood of bittersweet sentiment has reached an unnerving pitch of anguish. He doesn't need those mini-fireballs. We get the point—this time the sunshine is dangerous and blinding.

Burnt by the Sun is set in 1936, at the beginning of the Great Terror, the last possible moment in which anyone not an idiot or a scoundrel might have believed in the Soviet revolution. Somewhere outside Moscow, in the country near the wheat fields, Colonel Kotov, a true believer and bristling revolutionary patriot, lives with his young wife, Maroussia (Ingeborga Dapkunaite), the daughter of a famous musician. At Maroussia's dacha, a Chekhovian house party appears to be in full swing. Elderly relatives have gathered for the summer, and also friends, hangers-on, a longtime servant—in all, a gracious remnant of the old bourgeois prerevolutionary culture. Kotov, the untouchable revolutionary hero, protects them. A formidable, barrel-chested man, fiftyish, with beautiful eyes and a fine mustache, he is played by Mikhalkov himself, who has been made up (intentionally, I am sure) to look like a more handsome version of Stalin. Kotov, the people's hero, with his beautiful young wife, is a happy egotist who finds it easy to be benevolent. He romps with his little daughter, played by Mikhalkov's own child, Nadia, who was so appealing on Oscar night. By bringing the wistful landowners and aesthetes of *The Cherry Orchard* and *Uncle Vanya* nearly 40 years forward, deep into the Communist period, Mikhalkov emphasizes the fragility of a certain kind of human richness. Kotov, it turns out, can't protect them; he can't even protect himself. All they've got is their sunshine, which blinds them to the vipers everywhere.

Mikhalkov works with Fellini-like exuberance shading into menace. Little groups of fanatics—children mobilized by the state—march about the countryside chanting and holding aloft pictures of Stalin. Civil-defense officials show up at a river bank where people are lolling in the sun and absurdly insist that everyone put on a gas mask; eventually, a heavyset, distracted woman, masked, gets carried out on a stretcher, which is not a bad metaphor for the country itself. In all, one gets the impression that the Soviet Union of the thirties was supremely equipped to defeat fascism but to do nothing else.

The abundant theatricality—the festive, noisy performances, the general air of physical delight—drives the story forward, but there are nasty surprises hidden in the jokes, a sense of dismay under the lilting tone. Mitya (Oleg Menchikov), Maroussia's old lover, mysteriously away for ten years, enters with a flourish of laughter and music. He sings, dances, plays the piano; he's an actor, a genius, a great seducer—as much a part of the old culture as the rest of them. At first, the young Mitya, handsome and dark, with a knifelike slenderness, seems to be there to fight the burly, middle-aged Kotov for Maroussia's love. But a much more sinister game is afoot. In the person of Menchikov, Mitya has a Dostoevskian intensity—he could be someone out of *The Possessed*. A jumble of aggression and masochism, he has been destroyed by the Communist state and then put back together as a charmer suited for betrayal. He is now a member of the secret police. Exactly what Mitya is doing there is the first mystery; the greater mystery is why he's doing it. And Mikhalkov's answer is convoluted and fascinating in a way only possible within the tormented history of the Soviet Union. Mitya carries out the betrayal of the revolution in the name of the revolution.

There's too much sunshine; and Mitya plays the piano a little too violently. By the end, however, Mikhalkov's excess makes perfect sense. The careless abundance of life, spilling over the edges, is about to come to an end. *Burnt by the Sun* conveys the desperation of a culture trying to feel good in the face of a past so dreadful that it renders the future almost unimaginable.

NEW YORK POST, 4/21/95, p. 50, Thelma Adams

The year is 1936. A Sunday in the Russian countryside. An old friend returns to the family estate, changing the lives of all concerned forever.

Gliding from social comedy to tragedy in a Chekhovian manner, Nikita Mikhalkov's "Burnt by the Sun" mounts a criticism of Stalin couched in the most intimate of family dramas.

The film won the Oscar last month in the most heated competition: best foreign-language film. Mikhalkov confessed to the press that had he thought "Before the Rain" would win. He was wrong.

There is little wrong with "Burnt by the Sun," a near-perfect film that wears its few flaws like beautiful ornaments.

Mikhalkov ("Dark Eyes") directs and stars as Col. Kotov. This aging but vigorous hero of the Bolshevik revolution shares a dacha with his young wife, Maroussia (Ingeborga Dapkunaite); 6-year-old daughter, Nadia (played by the director's real-life daughter, Nadia); and his wife's artistic family and friends.

Dimitri (Oleg Menchikov) breaks into this circle unbidden one bright summer day, a holiday for Stalin's balloons and airships. The favorite pupil of Maroussia's late father, a music teacher, "Mitia" was also her first love.

The tension between the two men flares, The handsome Mitya is more at home with Maroussia's family than Kotov can ever be. Mitya plays the piano, dances and jokes his way into their hearts, pursuing Maroussia and charming Nadia ("Call me Uncle Mitya.").

What appears at first glance like a lover's triangle gradually deepens like a shadow crossing a lawn in late afternoon. There is something sinister about Mitya, something which Mikhalkov teases out in little details that, taken alone, seem benign: the musician takes Kotov's chair by the dinner table; he doesn't warn the barefooted Kotov that a broken bottle is hidden in the grass nearby; he bangs out the Can Can on the piano while raffishly wearing a gas mask that smothers his features and makes him look like a monster in stylish clothes.

Mitya charms us along with Maroussia and Nadia: his quick, vaguely sad smile; his dark, familiar eyes beneath black bangs; his hunger that passes as vulnerability; his easy intimacy. We are seduced by this master charmer so that any warning bells ring like a distant alarm muffled by pillows.

Mitya has returned with an agenda. Is it strictly romantic?

"Burnt by the Sun" refers to a popular song and, symbolically, to the sunblindness of the Russian revolution and the politics and purges that followed. Far from being a political tract, Mikhalkov anchors the movie in the emotional life of its characters. Nikita and Nadia Mikhalkov display an incredible intimacy that shows the deep, often physical, father-daughter bond (a tie that some may consider suspect given current child abuse concerns).

In a rowboat lazily floating on a green river by the green banks beneath the noonday sun, father and daughter commune:

You've no idea how good I feel with you," says Nadia.

"With you everything is calm ..." says Kotov.

"Can we drift like this for all our lives?" she asks.

Mikhalkov condenses the powerful pleasures of summer, of warmth, of intimacy, of family connection in a single afternoon—and, then tears it apart in one fell swoop. There's no more heartbreakingly beautiful movie this year.

NEWSDAY, 4/21/95, Part II/p. B5, Jack Mathews

When I learned that Russian director Nikita Mikhalkov had trimmed 15 minutes from the version of "Burnt by the Sun" that won the runner-up prize at last year's Cannes Film Festival and this year's Oscar for Best Foreign Language Film, I was hoping he had eliminated the symbolic fireball that floats into a key dialogue scene to underscore its meaning.

That's the kind of device Oliver Stone uses to make sure the audience gets his message, and Mikhalkov did not need it. As complex as the issues underpinning the story, "Burnt by the Sun" is so deftly developed and so completely involving, that you soon find yourself being carried along—to recreate another symbolic image from the film—as if on a boat drifting downriver toward some uncertain destination.

The fireball did survive the cuts, unfortunately, but that is the only flaw in an otherwise staggering personal achievement. Mikhalkov is the writer, director, producer and star of a film that combines in an intricate tapestry the elements of romance, tragedy, history, and sociopolitical essay.

Evoking the mood of Jean Renoir and the character analysis of Chekhov, Mikhalkov takes us back to 1936 Soviet Russia, into the lives of the Bolshevik Revolution hero Sergei Kotov (Mikhalkov), his wife, Maroussia (Ingeborga Dapkunaite), 6-year-old Nadia (played by Mikhalkov's own daughter), and various relatives and friends spending one sunny day at Sergei's country home. The scene virtually Rockwellian, a portrait of simple people enjoying each other's company, nearly oblivious to the purge mentality of Stalinism sweeping the country.

Then an old friend arrives, and the day is transformed in ever-increasing layers from joy to impending tragedy. Dimitri (Oleg Menchikov), we quickly learn, was Maroussia's lover before going off to war, leaving her so despondent she attempted suicide. And having met him in the opening scene in Paris, we know he has come back with an assignment from the Stalin secret police so grave he nearly took his own life rather than accept it.

There are many things going on beneath the bucolic surface of this day in the country, and they all have to do with the religious faith the Soviet people placed in their socialist-cum-totalitarian government, which at that moment was decimating them like a runaway virus. No one was safe from the purge that sent millions of innocent people to their deaths or to labor camps, not even loyal Red Army veterans like Sergei.

Mikhalkov cast himself well as Sergei, a physically imposing man with a gentle spirit and an expressive face. And by casting his own precocious and photogenic daughter, he not only scored big points at home but gave his crucial father-daughter scenes a naturalness and warmth that informs the entire movie. In a beautifully shot boat sequence, which has Sergei passing along some philosophy to Nadia, the love that passes between them is palpable.

All of the performances are strong, but Oleg Menchikov overcame the toughest challenge, having to play Dimitri as a man barely able to contain his depression and bitterness beneath the outward appearance of a clown. He is two people throughout, the jovial uncle to Nadia, a clear threat to Sergei, and he has an unsettling presence on both the family and the audience.

The fireball and the movie's title, taken from a Russian folk song beloved by Nadia, have to do with the misplaced loyalties and subsequent betrayals that followed the Russian Revolution. By focussing tightly on one effected family for one day, Mikhalkov shows how about 300 million people surrendered their freedom to a bad idea.

SIGHT AND SOUND, 8/95, p. 41, Geoffrey Macnab

A hot summer in the Russian countryside, 1936. Comrade Kotov, renowned Soviet military hero, is relaxing in the bath house with his young wife, Marusia, and his six-year old daughter, Nadia. A farmer disturbs him, begging him to come quickly to the wheat fields. Russian tanks have turned up, seemingly under orders to destroy the peasants' harvest. Kotov intervenes. The soldiers defer to his authority and withdraw.

An eccentric old man turns up at the Kotovs' country house. The family are at first alarmed, but soon realise this is Dmitrii, Marusia's childhood sweetheart, in outlandish disguise. He had vanished ten years earlier in mysterious circumstances, and Marusia, heartbroken, had attempted suicide. The family now give him a warm welcome. Only Kotov is suspicious.

Later that day, while bathing at a nearby river, Dmitrii manages to waylay Marusia. It seems he is keen to rekindle their old romance. Kotov, who has taken Nadia out in a rowing boat, arrives back at the shore and sees that they, and everybody else, have disappeared. Jealous, he doesn't realise they've all been press ganged into taking part in an exercise to test the efficiency of gas masks.

At the house, Dmitrii is playing the piano and entertaining everyone with his clowning. He tells Nadia a sad, allegorical story which is clearly about himself and why he had to leave. Kotov and Marusia argue, but are reconciled, and end up making love. Kotov tells Marusia that Dmitrii is a coward.

Dmitrii finally reveals the reason for his visit to Kotov. He is a former White Russian, now working for the Secret Police. Kotov is to be arrested and taken to Moscow. That evening, a car draws up with three heavies inside. Kotov goes willingly, sure that he will be able to iron matters out. He hasn't told his family why he is making the trip. It's only when he argues with one of the heavies and is brutally beaten up that he realises how serious his predicament is. Captions reveal that he was tried as a traitor and executed, and that his reputation was 'rehabilitated' posthumously in the 1950s. Dmitrii is shown lying in his bath, having slit his wrists.

Burnt by the Sun is set, very specifically, in the mid 1930s, in the Russia of the show trials and of Stalin's reign of political terror. Mikhalkov opens the film in predictably stark fashion: a young man (later we learn it is Dmitrii, the White Russian coerced into working for the Secret Police) empties his pistol of all but one of the bullets, and prepares to play Russian roulette.

But the world the director proceeds to evoke is as far removed from the conventional Stalinist landscape as it is possible to imagine. Action is set in the countryside. Characters dress in white jackets and blazers, dance impromptu can-cans, eat fulsome lunches, and lounge by the river. Uncle Joe is far away, although we're reminded of him by photographs, uniforms and absurd balloon displays in his honour. This may be the era of Proletkult and Socialist Realism, but that doesn't stop the sun from shining and families from going about their business in the ways they always did. Changes in routine at the dacha are often only cosmetic: for instance, Comrade Kotov and his household no longer play croquet or tennis in the afternoon (bourgeois games) but have turned to football instead. In every other particular, this could be the countryside idealised by Turgenev or Chekhov.

"It's the aroma, the taste of life that has vanished for good," one of the Kotovs' elderly relatives observes in a fit of reactionary pique when he realises that he's about to be forced to take part in a ridiculous exercise to test gas masks. His complaints are belied by the timeless beauty of the landscapes. The wheat fields, skies, forests and rivers create a mood of such universal benevolence it seems unthinkable that any harm can befall the characters.

Mikhalkov has described the film as, "The tragedy of a man blinded by the sun." In an early scene, Comrade Sergei Petrovich Kotov (played with swaggering braggadocio by the director himself shoos off the Red Army tanks which have turned up to destroy the peasants' wheat fields. There's a deceptive sense that all that is needed to keep political reality at bay is bluster and optimism. But gradually, as the narrative unfolds, it becomes apparent that this particular country house idyll is never quite as innocent as it seems. Sinister little motifs hint at its darker underside. These range from the trivial (a green shard of broken glass beside the river which one or other of the barefoot characters will inevitably end up standing on) to the apocalyptic: fireballs flash across the screen at regular intervals, as if intimating disasters to come.

The plot, at first, seems to hinge on a love affair which may or may not be rekindled. Marusia, Kotov's beautiful young wife, meets up again with her sweetheart from a decade before. It's a stock 'romantic triangle,' with the older husband jealous of his handsome young rival, Dmitrii, suspicious of his wife, and unsure what passed between them all those years ago. Even on this familiar level, the film is beautifully handled. Marusia's confused emotions are hinted at by telling cutaways which show her fingers distractedly tapping a tea-cup or picture her pouring herself a glass of water and failing to notice that it is already overflowing. Kotov's insecurity is signalled by the way he hangs back at the edge of the room or retires on his own to the lunch table when Dmitrii takes centre stage with his clowning.

Mikhalkov's screenplay offers four very different perspectives on the same events. Nadia, the six-year-old child, is trusting and ingenuous, and utterly oblivious to the conspiracies going on around her. Marusia, likewise, seems unaware of the real reason for Dmitrii's visit. It is kept as a secret between him and Kotov. They alone know that the dacha is not the self-enclosed, charmed little world it appears: their lives have all been moulded in one way or another by social and political necessity. The film ends on a shockingly brutal note, with the spectre of Stalin finally unleashed. (To celebrate the latest of the great dictator's triumphs, workers deep in the woods have built a balloon to raise his image high in the sky. A huge poster of his face looks out over the sundrenched countryside as the film's final tragic heist takes place.)

Burnt by the Sun, garlanded at the Oscars and at last year's Cannes Festival, manages the unlikely feat of combining warm-hearted, summer-in-the-country style romantic comedy with stark insights into how the Stalin Terror disfigured relationships and destroyed families. Mikhalkov refuses to judge his characters or the system which formed them: he neither waxes nostalgic for some long lost, pre-revolutionary Arcadia or lapses into crude polemic about the 'evils' of the Soviet state, and his film is all the richer for it.

TIME, 5/8/95, p. 88, Richard Schickel

The dacha in the country outside Moscow, the self-absorbed extended family living there oblivious to events in the outside world, the visitor whose energy and mystery stir this nest of gentlefolk—*Burnt by the Sun* has the air of something Chekhov or Turgenev might have imagined.

Might have imagined, that is, if he had lived in the age of Stalin. For the year is 1936, and the central figure of Nikita Mikhalkov's marvelous film, which won this year's Oscar for Best Foreign Film, is an old Bolshevik at terrible risk, Sergei Kotov (played by the director himself). Lost in contentment with his radiant young wife and adorable child, he does not see that, far from protecting him, his stature as a beloved hero of the revolution is precisely what makes him a threat to paranoid tyranny. He knows their visitor, Dimitri, works for the secret police but worries only that this handsome, charming man, his wife's lover, may reawaken buried emotions.

But that's not Dimitri's mission. His job is to extract Sergei from his happiness quietly, without alarming anyone, and politely conduct him to prison, humiliation, death. This Sergei does not know until it is too late. And neither do we. Like him, we are disarmed by the sweetness of this life, so richly detailed by Mikhalkov. The genius of his film lies in his refusal to foreshadow, for it makes the outcome more chilling. This is how evil often comes to us, masked in geniality, on a day when the sun is shining, the music playing. And the way Sergei clings to his ordinariness even as he's carried off, trying to preserve it for his family to the end, is unbearably poignant.

VILLAGE VOICE, 4/25/95, p. 47, J. Hoberman

History is as history does: the Oscar awarded Nikita Mikhalkov's *Burnt by the Sun* confirms the supremely well-connected Mikhalkov's international status, even as "Russia's best known and most successful film director" (per *The New York Times*) stakes out a xenophobic position on the former Soviet Union's ideological new frontier.

Scion of a remarkable family, Mikhalkov is more complex a man than he is a filmmaker. *Burnt by the Sun* is simultaneously glib and resonant, heartfelt and sleazy—collapsing Soviet history into a bloody domestic quarrel while conflating nostalgia for the prerevolutionary gentry with the onset of Stalinist terror. As a further complication, the movie is a psychodrama in which the 50-year-old director casts himself as an indulgent father (named for his own), a Bolshevik war hero, and a political martyr heedlessly enjoying his last day of freedom.

Mikhalkov plays Kotov as a monument. Rousted from his rustic steambath to protect the neighboring potato fields from mysterious war games, he bristles with unconvincingly lovable strut and bluster. For much of the movie, Kotov is jovially overbearing, a two-fisted pussycat surrounded by comic servants and clownish in-laws. His dacha seems the dowry of his slim, pretty wife. She's half his age but even that isn't young enough: Kotov spends more time nuzzling their winsome daughter Nadia, played by Mikhalkov's own six-year-old Nadia. The movie's perfect moment—from his point of view—comes when the child hugs him and croons, "I adore you."

Burnt by the Sun isn't the first Mikhalkov movie to feature one of his children. In 1979, Mikhalkov began filming an annual interview with his then six-year-old daughter Anna, asking her what she loved, hated, feared, and wanted most. (By age seven, Anna figured out a response for the last question—namely "to give good answers.") As Anna's childhood corresponded with the deterioration of Soviet leadership and then the Soviet Union, so *Anna: 6-18* became a documentary of political adaptation. At eight, the girl wept for Brezhnev; at nine, she mourned Andropov; and, at 10, acknowledged, red-eyed, the death of Chernenko: "There are no joys today."

Anna's ability to internalize the current line continued beyond perestroika; so does her dad's. Given his survivor background, Mikhalkov knows first-hand the cost of accommodation. Still, *Burnt by the Sun* dramatizes Soviet political terror as a combination of natural disaster and Oedipal struggle. The movie is set during the summer of 1936, precisely the time of the first Moscow show trial. (If Comrade Kotov has any thoughts about Zinoviev, Kamenev, and the 12 co-conspirators who confessed to the assassination of Leningrad Party boss Kirov, he keeps them to himself.) Signs of mobilization are everywhere. The irony, of course, is that danger strikes from another direction. Kotov's eden is infiltrated by his wife's sardonic childhood sweetheart Mitya, who arrives in the first of several disguises and cannily plays the fool. (In one scene, Kotov comes upon his wife's family dancing a mad cancan while Mitya, in gas mask, plays the piano.)

Albeit opening at a hectic pace, *Burnt by the Sun* soon bogs down. Nearly 20 minutes have been cut since the movie's premiere last year at Cannes, but the spectacle of Kotov's deceptive idyll is overly languorous. Mikhalkov charms himself and his daughter more than he does the audience—the veteran soldier's jolly self-assertion yielding to pathos and finally mawkish gallantry as the afternoon wears on. The battle between the sentimental old hero and his cynical young rival insures an abundance of self-pity. *Burnt by the Sun* takes its title from the new lyrics Mikhalkov has given the popular Russian tango repeated throughout. If popular songs have a particular significance in his oeuvre—*An Unfinished Piece for Player Piano* and *Dark Eyes* take them for titles—it may be because his father, Sergei Mikhalkov, cowrote the hymn that replaced the "Internationale" as the Soviet anthem in 1943. (Did this paternity leave its mark? The protagonist of *Close to Eden* has the score for another patriotic ballad tattooed on his back.) Sergei Mikhalkov was a man for all seasons. He wrote anti-cosmopolitan plays during the High Stalinist period and, as head of the Writer's Union, attacked Andrei Tarkovsky's first movie during the Khrushchev thaw. As late as 1986, the "permanent secretary" authored a report entitled *The Task of the Party is the Task of Literature*, and linked Gorbachev-era rock bands to AIDS, prostitution, drugs, and treason. He currently serves on a committee to write a new anthem to replace his last one. Neither a dissident nor a party member, and no less politically adept than his father, Nikita Mikhalkov began his career as an actor and established a subsequent reputation for vulgar Chekhovian comedies of pre-Soviet life with *A Slave of Love* (1977), *Unfinished Piece for Player Piano* (1977), and *Oblomov* (1980)—the latter reversing the traditional Marxist critique to present its indolent hero as a generous embodiment of the Russian folk. After two unsuccessful contemporary films, the director, who actively supported the old leadership when the Filmmaker's Union underwent perestroika in 1986, went to Italy to make the kitsch snorefest *Dark Eyes* (1987), then ventured to Inner Mongolia for the more compelling *Close to Eden* (1991), Oscar nominees both. "Contemporary Soviet cinema is obsessed with being 'anti,'" the director said then. "It produces nothing but films against drugs, films against prostitution, against Stalin, etc. It's a cinema primarily of social issues which tries to imitate a Western model and court the West's approval."

Bankrolled by a French producer, *Close to Eden* proved more allegorically "anti" than most contemporary Russian cinema, advocating a return to the steppe while identifying modernity with TV, condoms, and Sylvester Stallone. Moreover, in winning the Gold Lion at Venice, it actually garnered greater Western approval. So, too, *Burnt by the Sun*. *Anna: 6-18*'s inadvertent exercise in Russo-patriarchy is here perfected, as is its celebration of denial.

Although *Burnt by the Sun* was shot just outside Moscow, during the summer and autumn of 1993, the only crisis to which Mikhalkov alludes in his press-notes interview has to do with bad weather. Nevertheless, production coincided exactly with the power struggle between Yeltsin and Mikhalkov's friend, Vice President Rutskoi, leading to Yeltsin's abolition of the parliament,

Rutskoi's abortive countercoup, the ensuing state of emergency, and the election during which nationalist buffoon Vladimir Zhirinovsky won a plurality.

Mikhalkov's older brother, Andrei Konchalovsky, is also a filmmaker of note. But where Konchalovsky made his anti-Stalinist movie, *The Inner Circle*, as a brutal, self-implicating comedy about Stalin's projectionist, Mikhalkov vagues out on half truths and bad faith. A bogus epilogue factualizes the fictional family even as the filmmaker's interviews suggest that the story is his own: "I lived it. It was my childhood." A monarchist who considers all governments since 1917 to be illegitimate, Mikhalkov now traces his lineage to Catherine the Great—burned, or is it basking, in the sun?

Also reviewed in:
CHICAGO TRIBUNE, 5/19/95, Friday/p. M, Michael Wilmington
NEW REPUBLIC, 5/8/95, p. 27, Stanley Kauffmann
NEW YORK TIMES, 4/21/95, p. C6, Caryn James
NEW YORKER, 5/8/95, p. 92, Anthony Lane
VARIETY, 5/30-6/5/94, p. 42, Steven Gaydos
WASHINGTON POST, 5/19/95, p. D1, William F. Powers
WASHINGTON POST, 5/19/95, Weekend/p. 57, Desson Howe

BUSHWHACKED

A Twentieth Century Fox release. *Executive Producer:* Daniel Stern. *Producer:* Charles B. Wessler and Paul Schiff. *Director:* Greg Beeman. *Screenplay:* John Jordan, Danny Byers, Tommy Swerdlow, and Michael Goldberg. *Story:* John Jordan and Danny Byers. *Director of Photography:* Theo Van de Sande. *Editor:* Ross Albert. *Music:* Bill Conti. *Music Editor:* Jeff Carson. *Sound:* Tim Cooney and (music): Lee DeCarlo. *Sound Editor:* Don Hall. *Casting:* Linda Lowy and John Brace. *Production Designer:* Mark W. Mansbridge and Sandy Veneziano. *Art Director:* Bruce Crone. *Set Designer:* Randy D. Wilkins. *Set Decorator:* Joe Mitchell. *Set Dresser:* Mike Driscoll. *Special Effects:* John Richardson. *Costumes:* Mary Zophres. *Make-up:* Angela Moos. *Stunt Coordinator:* Freddie Hice. *Running time:* 90 minutes. *MPAA Rating:* PG-13.

CAST: Daniel Stern (Max Grabelski); Jon Polito (Agent Palmer); Brad Sullivan (Jack Erickson); Ann Dowd (Mrs. Patterson); Anthony Heald (Bragdon); Tom Wood (Agent McMurrey); Blake Bashoff (Gordy); Corey Carrier (Ralph); Michael Galeota (Dana); Max Goldblatt (Barnhill); Ari Greenberg (Fishman); Janna Michaels (Kelsey Jordan); Natalie West (Mrs. Fishman); Michael P. Byrne (Mr. Fishman); Michael O'Neill (Jon Jordan); Jane Morris (Beth Jordan); Christopher Curry (Trooper); Kenneth Johnson (State Patrolman); Robert Donley (Proprietor); Sue Kwon (TV Newscaster); Reed Clark Means (Kid); Harley Kelsey (Forest Ranger); Cesarina Vaughn (Business Woman); Cory Buck (Tricycle Kid); Theodor Scott Owens (Business Man).

LOS ANGELES TIMES, 8/4/95, Calendar/p. 12, Kevin Thomas

"Bushwhacked": That's what you're likely to feel very early on in this strained, way, way over-the-top comedy-thriller in which its star, Daniel Stern, as the film's executive producer, gives himself free rein to mug and show off to increasingly numbing and tedious effect.

Stern, so often terrific, casts himself as a numskull deliveryman framed for murder who winds up deep in a forest, mistaken for a Scout leader and charged with taking six youngsters on a mountain-climbing expedition while dodging the bad guys.

Director Greg Beeman and a team of four writers make no pretense at establishing even minimal credibility. For openers, how is it that an otherwise seemingly responsible mother (Ann Dowd) turns over her son and five other children to a clearly rattled guy whose mountain-climbing outfit includes loafers and a leather jacket?

Once the plot is cranked into motion the filmmakers reach deep into the movies' ancient bag of suspense tricks, including having Stern and the youngsters cross a flimsy bridge spanning a crevice, thrown into the roiling rapids and hanging onto cliffs—devices familiar from the time of D.W. Griffith. These gimmicks can still be amusing, but Stern's incessant manic abrasiveness takes all the fun out of them.

Whereas Stern here is shamelessly self-indulgent, his young co-stars—Blake Bashoff, Corey Carrier, Ari Greenberg, Max Goldblatt, Michael Galeota and Janna Michaels—are bright, game and likable. Brad Sullivan scores some laughs as the unflappable actual Scout leader. There are always films that can be recommended for children that would not engage adults, but in the case of "Bushwhacked," young audiences deserve lots better.

NEW YORK POST, 8/4/95, p. 46, Thelma Adams

Would someone please explain a family movie to me?

"Bushwhacked" should fit the mold. It's a routine slapstick, fish-outta-water comedy. Daniel ("Home Alone") Stern plays an urban delivery dork who witnesses a murder and finds himself accused of the crime. He heads for the hills and hides out as a Ranger Scout master leading a cuddly bunch of kids on a wilderness hike.

But where does five boys pulling out their "lizards" and giving G-man Palmer (Jon Polito) a golden shower fit with the notion of family fun?

And what about the know-it-all, scaredy-cat Fishman's (Ari Greenberg) undescended-testicle joke?

And when it comes to that classic set piece—the adult explaining the birds and bees to a rapt audience of confused pre-teens—"Bushwhacked" stalks the vulgar trail. Using a pair of Ken and Barbie dolls as a visual aid, Stern performs a little demo. He calls out, "Work it, mama, work it," in a feverish voice, and then the camera cuts to Ken, stripped down to boxer shorts, smoking a cigarette.

The fugitive's nature lesson left the kids—and me—open-mouthed and dumb-founded.

"Bushwhacked" is on surer ground during the antic action sequences. Stern and his bratpack subdue a grizzly, cross a ravine on a rope bridge, ride the rapids, have a close encounter with a beehive and hang off the unyielding face of a mountain with Stallone's strength. The faux scout master survives on the luck of pure idiocy, and the kids save the day with previously unknown shrewdness and pluck.

Stern's performance starts out manic and spirals upward like a toddler on a sugar rush. It's a version of the unsavory schlemiel he molded in "Home Alone" and its sequel. His eyebrows arch as if taped to his hairline, his jaw is permanently, slack, his blue eyes glow out of the putty of his face with an ironic sincerity. It's a one-note samba that begs for a pair of stooges to modulate it.

NEWSDAY, 8/4/95, Part II/p. B7, John Anderson

"Don't do anything stupid," the boss tells Max Grabelski (Daniel Stern). "Try and stop me!" Max answers.

And that, in a nutshell (and we do mean nut), is the trajectory of "Bushwhacked," an unguided missile of mirth that crash-lands long before reaching the vicinity of wit. As the self-deluded hipster Max—whom we first see doing a wannabe-Travolta strut to the strains of "Staying Alive"—Stern is framed for murder and takes to the hills. Literally. What someone should have told the star/executive producer is that when you run through the woods howling with your mouth wide open, it usually means a healthy helping of flies.

Max (did he have to be an idiot with a *Polish* name?) is on the lam from some frantic parents, a corrupt FBI agent (Jon Polito) and Erickson, the veteran Scout leader he's impersonating (Brad Sullivan), the kind of guy who shaves with a bowie knife while driving a Land Rover over a washboard road. Max—in leather, chains and Italian loafers—is assumed by his troop of six wood naifs to be a rugged outdoorsman. But he doesn't know a sheepshank from sheep-dip. Hilarity ensues.

Stern, of the elastic face and extremely likable personality, is simply out of control here; what director Greg Beeman does, basically, is get out of his way. His antics do distract, however, from a profoundly awful script, which has four writers and no jokes. There's a sequence with a grizzly bear and an unconscious Max that gets a few laughs.

The kids (Blake Bashoff, Corey Carrier, Michael Galeota, Max Goldblatt, Ari Greenberg and Janna Michaels) are cute. The mountains are lovely. But the story is a torturous series of unlikelihoods unredeemed by humor. Stern runs amok, as if in the vague hope that hysterics will salvage a movie skidding down a slope. But there's no hope.

We've seen much better things from Stern ("Breaking Away," "Diner," "City Slickers" and his directorial debut, "Rookie of the Year"), so perhaps he should reassess, now that he has his development deal with Fox. Because "Bushwhacked" is nobody's idea of a day at the beach.

Also reviewed in:
CHICAGO TRIBUNE, 8/4/95, Friday/p. L, Michael Wilmington
NEW YORK TIMES, 8/4/95, p. C19, Caryn James
VARIETY, 7/31-8/6/95, p. 36, Leonard Klady
WASHINGTON POST, 8/4/95, p. D6, Rita Kempley

BUSINESS AFFAIR, A

A Castle Hill Productions release of a Film and General Productions/Osby Films/Connexion Films coproduction with financial asssistance from Eurimages Fund of the Council of Europe/The European Co-production Fund/Canal+/Podeve/Sofiarpe 2. *Executive Producer:* Martha Wansbrough and Willi Baer. *Producer:* Xavier Larere, Clive Parsons, and Davina Belling. *Director:* Charlotte Brandstrom. *Screenplay:* William Stadiem. *Story (Inspired by the books "Tears Before Bedtime" and "Weep No More" by:* Barbara Skelton): William Stadiem and Charlotte Brandstrom. *Director of Photography:* Willy Kurant. *Editor:* Laurence Mery-Clark. *Music:* Didier Vasseur. *Sound:* Chris Munro. *Sound Editor:* Rodney Glenn. *Casting:* Simone Reynolds. *Production Designer:* Sophie Becher. *Art Director:* Kave Naylor. *Costumes:* Tom Rand. *Make-up:* Morag Ross. *Running time:* 101 minutes. *MPAA Rating:* Not Rated.

CAST: Christopher Walken (Vanni Corso); Carole Bouquet (Kate); Jonathan Pryce (Alec); Sheila Hancock (Judith); Anna Manahan (Bianca); Fernando Guillen Guervo (Angel); Tom Wilkinson (Bob); Marisa Benlloch (Carmen); Paul Bentall (Drunken Man); Bhasker (Jaboul); Roger Brierly (Barrister); Allan Corduner and Marian McLoughlin (Dinner Guests); Miguel de Angel (Spanish Taxi Driver); Christopher Driscoll (Policeman); Beth Goddard and Fergus O'Donnell (Students); Richard Hampton (Doctor); Togo Igawa (Japanese Golfer); Susan Kyd (Fawn); Annabel Leventon (Literary Guest); Patti Love (Prostitute); Simon McBurney (Salesman); Usha Patel and Natalie Sherman (Indian Women); Geraldine Somerville (Saleswoman); William Stadiem (William King); Robert Swann (Maitre d'); Peter van Dissel (Boat Guest); Jerome Willis (Moderator); Alfonso Galan (Bullfighter).

LOS ANGELES TIMES, 12/8/95, Calendar/p. 8, Jack Mathews

It is something of an irony that films with feminist appeal are accused of being either too soft or too shrill, compromising or overbearing, too political or not political enough. Sometimes, a movie is just a movie.

Charlotte Brandstrom's "A Business Affair" is a romantic comedy with a very distinct feminist bent. It's the story of a London department store floor model (French actress Carole Bouquet) who outgrows her temperamental author husband (Jonathan Pryce), begins an affair with his aggressively flamboyant American publisher (Christopher Walken) and outgrows him too.

The movie was an audience pleaser on last year's festival circuit. Yet, the early buzz in the industry was that Brandstrom had sold her gender out, portraying her heroine not as the inherently strong-willed woman upon whom she is based, but as a beautiful ditz who comes by her independence almost by accident.

A "Business Affair" is a minor movie event, to be sure, and Brandstrom had some trouble blending the film's comedic and dramatic elements. But it is at this wonderfully entertaining, and better than most of what's been passing for women's movies from Hollywood recently.

William Stadiem's screenplay is based ever-so-loosely on the really 1950s love triangle involving married British writers Barbara Skelton and Cyril Connolly, and Connolly's publisher George Weidenfeld. Skelton, a woman of independent means and spirit, married and divorced both men, as fellow British literati cocked their eyes on the sidelines, and now—in her 70s—can look back on them as just two on a long list of lovers that includes such diverse fellows as King Farouk and New Yorker cartoonist Charles Addams.

The true story may have made a more political movie. Certainly, Skelton was more the model of a liberated woman in the '50s than Bouquet's Kate Swallow is in the '90s. But it is Kate's growth, and the increasingly heavy blows she delivers to her men's egos, that give the film its steady comic pace.

Bouquet's expansive personality is limited by the role, at least until Kate herself becomes a best-selling author and begins to believe in her own worth, and Pryce, as the morbidly serious author Alec Bolton, is such a sour pill it's hard to imagine him having a companion of any sort.

Walken got the best of the roles, for sure, and has a high time with it. Vanni Corso is an outlandish caricature of an American hustler, a publisher with undeveloped literary tastes but an uncanny sense of marketing. If his father could sell pizza in Harlem, he explains to Kate, he ought to be able to sell culture in Europe, and he does.

But as time goes by, after he has stolen his client's wife and been chastened by the ensuing scandal, he seems to shrink in direct proportion to Kate's growth, and it's a nice bit of comedy acting. Walken, who has made a career of playing weird psychos, doesn't get many opportunities to play conventional movie characters, and it's clear from this that it is our loss.

SIGHT AND SOUND, 6/94, p. 43, Geoffrey Macnab

British author Alec Bolton signs up with a brash American publisher, Vanni, who has promised to make his fortune. Alec, however, is suffering from writer's block. As he struggles with his new book, his wife Kate, an unemployed model, works on a novel of her own. Alec tells her it is hopeless. Nonetheless, she sends the novel to Vanni. He immediately recognises its potential and agrees to publish it. Vanni and Kate start an affair.

Alec, cuckolded and furious, reneges on his agreement with Vanni. Kate, torn between the competing attentions of the two men, flies off to Spain for a secret holiday. Both Alec and Vanni pursue her. Alec hires a handsome matador to pretend to be a suitor and to take Kate's mind off the American. But the scheme backfires, and Kate ends up returning to London with Vanni, whom she subsequently marries.

The literary world is horrified by these incestuous conspiracies, the critics savage Kate's novel and Vanni's business suffers. Kate soon discovers Vanni is just as egotistical a husband as Alec had been. He also seems threatened by her writing and wants her to stay at home and look after the house. Matters worsen when his Italian mother, who disapproves of everything about her, moves in. Alec, meanwhile, has overcome his writer's block and completed a bestseller.

Kate leaves Vanni, moves into a bedsit, and finishes her second novel. She sends this off on spec and soon finds a publisher. The book proves to be a terrific success. Alec turns up at a signing in a London bookshop and tells her how impressed he is by her writing. The couple take a walk and end up kissing in Trafalgar Square. Eventually, Kate disappears into the crowd, telling him not to call her. If they ever get back together, it will have to be on her terms.

At least in sartorial terms, A Business Affair is a smart comedy: Christopher Walken's suits were made in Savile Row while Carole Bouquet, who goes through more than 50 changes of costume in the course of the film, borrowed most of her clothes from Chanel. Thematically, too, the film hints at sophistication. Set in the rarefied world of London publishing, it abounds in book launches and dinner parties where characters indulge in all sorts of high-faluting discussions about literature, love and money.

Unfortunately, though, no amount of high-culture dressing can conceal the threadbare nature of the script. For all its literary chatter and musings on the nature of creativity, this is essentially a whimsical love-triangle saga with the production values of a mineral water commercial. A European coproduction, it lacks any sense of national identity, instead offering tourist-eye views of Britain and Spain. Locations range from the Ritz Hotel and Trafalgar Square to bullfights and Spanish carnivals, and sometimes verge on the eccentric (it's not clear, for instance, why Bolton the reclusive author, should want to live above the Ann Summers sex shop in Wardour Street).

Charlotte Brandstrom has a reputation as an 'actors' director; but the performances she elicits here from her leads are largely disappointing. Pryce and Walken are both associated with intense, brooding drama. Neither has ever shown much aptitude for light comedy. "Do not expect Vanni to be a psychopath or manic oddball just because he's played by Christopher Walken," the production notes warn us, but this is precisely what we do expect, and, at least initially, the American actor doesn't let us down. Even if he is supposed to be more buffoon than mafioso, he manages to mix icy charm and bristling menace in the usual measures. However, while he is trying to play the publisher as an urbane, sophisticated anglophile, and perhaps to parody some of his own previous work in the process, the script continually pushes him toward broad slapstick. Jonathan Pryce also struggles in his one-dimensional role as the 'great writer'. His character is so earnest, and so given to sententious, egotistical utterances, that he soon forfeits any sympathy. Caught between these two cardboard suitors is Carole Bouquet as Kate, who wants her independence as a woman and a writer—in fact, wants the right to earn as much money and behave as self-indulgently as the men in her life. Hers is a cheerful, if slightly bland, performance, but she can hardly be blamed for the saccharine nature of the material.

Producer Clive Parsons claims he sees the film as following in the tradition of *A Touch of Class*, but it often seems even more old-fashioned than that. If anything, it harks back to all those vapid, slightly risque Mayfair comedies the British used to make in the 30s, where the manners and milieu were blithely assumed to compensate for any shortcomings in terms of narrative or character development. Aiming to be light-hearted and clever, it ends up merely smug and routine.

VILLAGE VOICE, 11/7/95, p. 72, Christian Finnegan

A *Business Affair* is that rarest of films, simultaneously boring and infuriating. Ostensibly a story about an intelligent woman coming into her own, this British film is actually a long-winded paean to codependency. That respectable actors like Jonathan Pryce and Christopher Walken find themselves aboard this sinking ship is indeed unfortunate.

Based on the memoirs of British novelist Barbara Skelton, the film stops French actress Carole Bouquet as Kate Swallow, a department store model with literary aspirations. Unfortunately, her egotistical husband Alec (Pryce), himself on esteemed novelist, is none too encouraging. Undernourished both emotionally and sexually, Kate is swept away by Alec's ruthless publisher, Vanni Corso (Walken), the archetypal brash American. In the end, she stumbles over something resembling self-respect and forges out on her own. She, of course, becomes a wildly successful novelist.

Though he can't help but occasionally slip into creepy mode, Walken does display a good degree of comic facility, but is never able to elevate the character above a nouveau riche stereotype. And while Pryce, too, tries valiantly to liven things up, the scripts for his Infiniti car commercials are far better than the schlock he's given here. Bouquet, the star of many fine French films, is thoroughly unengaging here. Her Kate shows so little emotional depth that it's a mystery why anyone's fighting over her in the first place.

Also reviewed in:
NEW REPUBLIC, 12/4/95, p. 27, Stanley Kauffmann
NEW YORK TIMES, 11/3/95, p. C8, Janet Maslin

BYE BYE, LOVE

A Twentieth Century Fox release of a UBU production. *Producer:* Gary David Goldberg, Brad Hall, and Sam Weisman. *Director:* Sam Weisman. *Screenplay:* Gary David Goldberg and Brad Hall. *Director of Photography:* Kenneth Zunder. *Editor:* Roger Bondelli. *Music:* J.A.C. Redford. *Music Editor:* Michael T. Ryan. *Sound:* David Kelson and (music): John Vigran. *Sound Editor:* Robert L. Sephton. *Casting:* Janet Gilmore. *Production Designer:* Linda DeScenna. *Art Director:* Greg Papalia. *Set Designer:* Antoinette J. Gordon. *Set Dresser:* Donn Piller, Mark Boucher, and Sam Anderson. *Special Effects:* Burt Dalton. *Costumes:* Linda Bass.

Make-up: Steve Abrums. *Stunt Coordinator:* James M. Halty. *Running time:* 107 minutes.
MPAA Rating: PG-13.

CAST: Matthew Modine (Dave); Randy Quaid (Vic); Paul Reiser (Donny); Janeane Garofalo (Lucille); Amy Brenneman (Susan); Eliza Dushku (Emma); Ed Flanders (Walter); Maria Pitillo (Kim); Lindsay Crouse (Grace); Ross Malinger (Ben); Johnny Whitworth (Max); Wendell Pierce (Hector); Cameron Boyd (Jed); Mae Whitman (Michele); Jayne Brook (Claire); Dana Wheeler-Nicholson (Heidi); Amber Benson (Meg); Rob Reiner (Dr. Townsend); Pamela Dillman (Sheila); Brad Hall (Phil); Danny Masterson (Mikey); James Arone (Waiter in Italian Restaurant); Karlie M. Gavino Brown and Kirstie R. Gavino Brown (Lindsay); Marguerite Weisman (Sarah); Max Ryan Ornstein (Ring Bearer at Wedding); Dean Williams (Wedding Photographer); Caroline Lagerfelt (Mother #1 at McDonald's); Christopher Curry (Dad #1 at McDonald's); Daniel Weisman (Boy at McDonald's); Stephanie Shroyer (Mother #2 at McDonald's); Michael Bofshever (Dad #2 at McDonalds); Christina Massari (Girl at McDonald's); Brian Frank (Screener); Shang Forbes (Engineer); T.K. Meehan (T-Ball Coach); Mina Kolb (Dorothy); Geoffrey Woodhall (Gerald); Michael Spound (Mike); Joe Basile (Father #1 Dad's Day Out); Dennis Bowen (Father #2 Dad's Day Out); Donald Bishop (Grandfather); Kate Williamson (Grandmother); Nicholas Davey (Heidi's Son); Justin Garms (Sheila's Son); Lauren Kopit (Sheila's Daughter); Jack Black (D.J. at Party); Keaton Simons (Party Dude); Juney Smith (Security Guard).

LOS ANGELES TIMES, 3/17/95, Calendar/p. 6, Kevin Thomas

With Matthew Modine, Randy Quaid and Paul Reiser as a trio of divorced dads, "Bye Bye, Love" sounds promising as a serious comedy, but its writers, Gary David Goldberg and Brad Hall, and director, Sam Weisman, betray their TV origins at every turn. Each time they convey the lingering pain of divorce for adults and children alike, they put a comedy spin on it. Too often the film's raft of characters seems to behave like puppets rather than actual people. Pretty soon you feel as manipulated as they seem to be, with the result that "Bye Bye, Love" gets progressively grimmer, increasingly removed from those moments that suggest what it might have been.

Modine, Reiser and Quaid are pals who gather every Saturday morning at a McDonald's, "neutral territory" where they pick up their kids for the weekend from their ex-wives. Modine is an incessant playboy, Reiser a deeply wounded man still carrying a torch for his wife and having trouble communicating with his indifferent 14-year-old daughter, and Quaid is an angry guy still battling his ex. It's never spelled out, however, what really caused Reiser and Quaid and their wives to split up.

Although Reiser gets a chance to work up some sympathy for his divorcé and suggest some dimension to him, all three men, no fault of the fine actors portraying them, grow tiresome in their self-pity. As a result, some of the peripheral people are more likely to engage your attention.

Janeane Garofalo is hilarious as Quaid's date from hell, an incessant kvetch justifying her outrageous behavior in the name of women's liberation. Rob Reiner, too, is pretty funny as an overbearing radio therapist, spouting clichés about the emotional fallout from divorce. Amid all the *Sturm und Drang*, you can be grateful for Johnny Whitworth and the late Ed Flanders, nice normal types, co-workers at that McDonald's, who strike up a father-and-son relationship. One thing none of these people need worry about is money: They all live in the Pasadena area in grand, elegantly decorated old homes, most of them classics of the Craftsman style.

NEW YORK, 3/27/95, p. 86, David Denby

Several key scenes in *Bye Bye, Love* were shot at McDonald's—not just any McDonald's but the huge "production store" where the chain's commercials are made. This should give you some idea of what the director, Sam Weisman, considers an original "look." The movie is about three ordinary guys (Matthew Modine, Randy Quaid, Paul Reiser), all divorced fathers, who don't understand their own feelings or anyone else's, and it's been made in the assumption that the men are exactly like you and me. Well, they aren't; they've been bleached. They live in a suburban nowhere section of Los Angeles, and they have no work they care about. *Bye, Bye Love* is set on a busy weekend in which the men take custody of their kids, and all their problems with children, wives, and other women come to a head. Cutting back and forth among the three, Weisman gets some decent comic momentum going near the end—for a scene or two, the movie lifts itself out of sitcom ordinariness. The highlight: Janeane Garofalo (of *Saturday Night Live*) shows up for a blind date with Quaid and gives a fresh performance as a neurotic so convinced men will find fault with her that she can't even bring herself to order dinner.

NEW YORK POST, 3/17/95, p. 39, Michael Medved

Just as you might expect for a movie that begins and ends under the Golden Arches of McDonald's, there's a certain fast-food, assembly-line aroma surrounding "Bye Bye, Love."

It's as if the studio honchos got together and said, "Hey, divorced dads are the hot topic of the moment (after the huge success of "Mrs. Doubtfire" and "The Santa Clause"), so let's serve up three new sensitive sufferers, together with Coke and fries.

The result is a sitcom set-up all the way. That's the bad news. The good is that producer/co-writer Gary David Goldberg (creator of TV's "Family Ties" and "Brooklyn Bridge" really knows how to make such material come to life. Thanks to deft writing and superior performances, "Bye Bye, Love" turns out to be consistently engaging and, at points, unexpectedly touching.

Randy Quaid, Paul Reiser and Matthew Modine play three best friends who only get to see their children on the weekends. Each Friday afternoon, they gather at the neutral territory of a suburban McDonald's to participate in the weekly ritual of "kid exchange" with their ex-wives.

The movie follows one eventful 48-hour period as they use these precious moments to re-connect with their confused offspring; at the same time, they fumble over meat-loaf recipes and make some feckless stabs at a social life.

Quaid, for instance, is a cynical driver-training instructor who's only gone out three times in the last year (on one occasion with his cousin), but now feels ready to try a blind date—who turns out to be the outrageously obnoxious (and thoroughly hilarious) Janeane Garofalo (of "Saturday Night Live").

Modine, on the other hand, has a pretty, much-younger girlfriend (Maria Pitillo, who makes an appealing California airhead) but can't control his roving eyes—the same problem that broke up his marriage with Amy Brenneman (of "NYPD Blue").

Meanwhile, Reiser feels himself uncomfortably attracted to Brenneman (the wounded ex-wife of his best friend) while trying to win acceptance from his own 14-year-old daughter (Eliza Dushku), who prefers her slick new stepfather to her embarrassingly emotional dad.

Reiser, Brenneman and, especially, Quaid are all excellent—portraying their divorce-survivors as stunned, numbed, walking wounded, and making their pain exquisitely real. Modine is less impressive, in part because his role gives him little to do other than farcically juggle the various women in his life.

Rob Reiner turns up in a small but crucial part as a pompous psychologist whose insufferable radio rants provide an accompaniment to all the weekend's activities—in much the same way that the voice of Wolfman Jack unified the diverse characters and adventures in "American Graffiti."

Reiner nags his listeners to "grow up" and angrily blames them for their broken marriages; the main characters, and the movie itself, take the opposite view; that divorce is a force of nature that's nobody's fault, as unstoppable and unpredictable as an earthquake.

"That's just the way it is," they repeatedly intone, to heart-broken kids and one another. It's a point of view that lets everyone off the hook, and facilitates a silly, tacked-on, feel-good epilogue.

True to its fast-food roots, "Bye Bye, Love" is tasty, even salty at times, though never particularly nourishing.

NEWSDAY, 3/17/95, Part II/p. B2, Jack Mathews

A lot of TV sitcom talent went into Sam Weisman's divorced dads comedy "Bye Bye, Love," and the story often suffers from its facile superficiality and meandering narrative. But if you'd just like to celebrate spring with some good laughs, it's funnier than the replacement Mets.

This is about the happiest face you can put on divorce, in America. There's no abuse, no deadbeat dads, no unloved children, no lovers trying to climb out bedroom windows with their pants around their ankles. And though it strains a couple of muscles trying to comment on the psychological fallout from broken families, you'll find more sociology in "Mrs. Doubtfire."

That's good, because there's not a lot to learn about life from three regular guys from a middle class white suburban neighborhood whose biggest crises are getting back in the dating game and juggling their child visitation and work schedules. It's as if we're revisiting the boys from "Diner," after they've gotten married, had children, been divorced, and are now hanging out at McDonald's, having learned nothing about women.

The group even includes one of the cast members from "Diner," Paul Reiser, now the star of TV's hit "Mad About You." Reiser plays Donny, a wounded romantic who is still in love with his wife and full of hope, even though she is now happily married to someone else. Reiser's deadpan comic style is an acquired taste, and I'm still working on it, but he gives Donny a born-to-be-a-husband earnestness that contrasts nicely with the angry cynicism of Vic (Randy Quaid) and the sexual adolescence of Dave (Matthew Modine).

Weisman, co-writers Gary David Goldberg and Brad Hall, and some of the principal crew members are all alumni of the TV series "Brooklyn Bridge," and I'll be surprised if a sitcom isn't spun from "Bye Bye, Love." There is no particular story being told, it just moves in and out of the lives of the three divorced buddies, makes jokes about their situations, and moves on.

You can look at it as three episodes interwoven. In one, the incorrigibly unfaithful Dave gets himself into a jam with his girlfriend by inviting the single mothers of his children's friends to drop by whenever they're in the mood for company. In another, Vic, so fed up with women that he's had only two dates in the last three years, ventures out on a blind date with an eccentric feminist (Janeane Garofalo). And in the third, Donny has to make peace with the teenage daughter (Eliza Dushku) embittered by her parents' divorce.

Filling out the background of these stories is an irritating 48-hour marathon divorce special being hosted by Rob Reiner (another sitcom grad) on radio station KGAB.

"Bye Bye, Love" becomes temporarily insufferable when it takes itself seriously, particularly in the sentimental sequences between Reiser and Dushku, and some of the physical comedy, which might work fine on the tube, is embarrassingly awkward on the big screen. Still, Goldberg and Hall have written some hilarious dialogue. Weisman times them with near perfection, and the odd casting of the three principals produces an interesting mix of styles.

SIGHT AND SOUND, 6/95, p. 39, Geoffrey Macnab

Los Angeles, a Friday evening. Dave, Donny and Vic, three firm friends who also happen to be divorced fathers, wait in a burger restaurant to pick up their kids for the weekend. One by one, their former wives turn up with the children in tow.

Each father has a different idea of how to spend the weekend. Dave is keen that his two young children should get to know and like his current girlfriend. Donny wants to cook a special celebratory meal to mark his adolescent daughter Emma's high school graduation. Vic simply takes his kids home to watch their favourite videos. All the while, whenever the fathers turn on the radio, they hear the admonishing tones of Dr Townsend, a pompous media psychiatrist who presents a show called 'Divorce In The 90s.'

Come Saturday morning, Dave flirts with various softball mums, most of whom are also divorced, as they watch their children play. Donny attends Emma's high school graduation party, but is cold-shouldered by both his daughter and her new stepfather. Vic is furious with his ex-wife's bedraggled, layabout boyfriend. He sneaks round to his old house to destroy the verandah that he himself built so that the boyfriend cannot use it.

Saturday evening. Dave's dinner with his girlfriend and the kids turns into a nightmare when the kids refuse to eat his girlfriend's food and two of the softball mums turn up unannounced. Donny's daughter runs out on him, gets drunk at a party, steals a car, and eventually gets stuck up a tree outside her old house. Donny almost starts an affair with Dave's ex-wife, Susan, but learns about his daughter's predicament, rescues her and is reconciled with her. Vic goes for a disastrous blind date with a woman called Lucille, attempts to assault Dr Townsend live on air, but instead is invited to be a special guest on the show. There's a brief postscript in which we learn that the three old friends sorted out their domestic imbroglios. Vic married Lucille, Donny married Susan, Dave married his girlfriend, and they all lived happily ever after.

Three divorced fathers anxiously trying to sort out their lives: it sounds like the kind of subject that might provide the starting point for a John Cassavetes film. It scarcely seems like material for light comedy. Divorce, after all, is the new American epidemic: Dr Townsend (Rob Reiner) the radio DJ whose show provides a sort of running commentary to the main action in *Bye Bye, Love*, bombards us with statistics underlining the fact. "It isn't for better or worse," he complains, "it's until somebody feels they want more space. If you want more space, buy a ranch in Colorado."

However, his jeremiads are belied by the film, which soon turns into a paean to family values. (Marriages may come unstuck but families never do, seems to be the message.) Given the setting, the mood could hardly be otherwise: the picture opens and closes in a McDonalds, and is shot in the same garishly cheerful way as the average Big Mac commercial. Young and old alike are catered for. There are plentiful images of kids playing softball and munching popcorn. There is even a mawkish, tagged-on sub-plot about the relationship between an elderly man, employed to fry up the hamburgers as part of the McDonalds "Adopt a Geezer" programme, and the mixed-up adolescent who teaches him the tricks of the trade.

All the upbeat imagery begs the question: where's the beef? If, as Townsend announces with typical mock flippancy, "divorced Americans are the most unhappy people in the world with the possible exception of married Scandinavians," why does *Bye Bye, Love* make them all look so cheerful? Director Sam Weisman claims that he sees his characters as the middle-aged descendants of the heroes of *American Graffiti*, but there is none of the detail or local colour that distinguished George Lucas's film: Vic, Dave and Donny live in an anodyne patch of suburbia where the outer world never seems to intrude. The film broaches all sorts of issues, but lacks the gumption to follow up on any of them. When one of the ex-wives complains that she could never get her husband to love her as much as he did his two friends, it seems as if the film-makers are attempting at least a mild critique of buddydom, but this is not the case. Dave may be a womaniser, Donny may be consumed with regret over the breakup of his marriage, but all the characters are presented as such genial, well-adjusted sorts that it beggars belief that they have marital problems at all. Divorce here isn't presented as any kind of social malaise, but is used as a comic motor: it's a device to confront the characters with the kind of domestic problems faced by Tom Selleck and co. in *Three Men and a Baby*. In other words, the men may have to do a little housework now and again. Only Randy Quaid, in scowling form as Donny, does anything to puncture the prevailing mood. In a scene which seems all too clearly pilfered from Altman's *Short Cuts*, he sets about his ex-wife's verandah with a chain-saw. As he rips a family photograph out of its frame, simply because he isn't in it, he hints at much darker emotions than the film is prepared to confront. It's typical of the way the movie pulls its punches that when he finally gets round to assaulting Dr Townsend live on air, he stops trying to throttle him as soon as he is offered a chance to broadcast his own thoughts. Dave's problems with his new girlfriend and the rift between Donny and his daughter are smoothed over in an equally glib fashion as the film-makers graft on a conventionally happy ending. In its own genial, enervating way, *Bye Bye, Love* makes for pleasant enough comedy. The film-makers have a background in television, with credits which range from *Moonlighting* and *LA Law* to *Lou Grant* and *Family Ties*. They very capably fashion a movie which nods politely in the direction of social problems without actually addressing them. There is plenty of crisp, witty dialogue. The acting, too, is perfectly efficient. After *Birdy* and *Equinox*, it's a surprise to see Matthew Modine take on such an undemanding role, but he, like his co-stars Quaid and Paul Reiser offers a neat, personable performance. But the bland, unchallenging view of family life offered by the movie is never credible for an instant.

VILLAGE VOICE, 3/28/95, p. 68, Christian Finnegan

It's no big secret that, in many cases, a divorced father is more an entertainment director than a nurturer to his children. Those cherished every-other weekends often consist of little more than Disney movies and trips to the zoo. Balanced with the intricacies of dating and the struggle to coexist peacefully with an ex-wife, single-fatherdom is no easy job. And that's the premise of *Bye Bye, Love* which charts one weekend in the lives of three guys and their respective kids.

Boasting a cast of about 10 semi-names, *Bye Bye, Love* covers all the bases; while Paul Reiser pines after his remarried ex, Randy Quaid wages war against his. Matthew Modine plays the resident Casanova, simultaneously trying to warm the kids up to his new love interest while scouting attractive mommies at his son's soccer practice. The loosely structured plot is tied together by the musings of an obnoxious radio therapist, played (quite obnoxiously) by Rob Reiner. Other subplots, of which there are many, include a horrific blind date (featuring current *SNL* martyr Janeane Garofalo) and a *Sassy*-esque McDonald's worker with family problems we couldn't care less about.

It's strange that Hollywood hasn't more thoroughly plundered this frontier of American family life. There might be a sizable market for a movie that took a humorous, insightful look at the travails of the single dad; something not quite as embittered as *Kramer vs Kramer*, but not so puerile as *Mrs. Doubtfire*. In *Bye Bye, Love* there are understated, idiosyncratic moments that capture the collective befuddlement associated with post-divorce protocol, but these are repeatedly bookended by ones of such utter idiocy that any genuine poignancy is rendered DOA. Don't blame the cast, which, excluding the pack of faceless brats and teenage twits, acquits itself well. It's director Sam Weisman and writers Gary David Goldberg and Brad Hall who ultimately ruin things with schmaltzy, "insert emotion here" underscoring and cheap sitcom payoffs.

No one should feel worse about the results than the folks at McDonald's, who appear to have bankrolled the entire project (in the film, Mickey D's is a suburban oasis where everyone is beautiful and polite). Since the movie inexplicably avoids fast-food jokes, I'll refrain from equating it with a Big Mac. But I tell you, it isn't easy.

Also reviewed in:
NEW YORK TIMES, 3/17/95, p. C16, Stephen Holden
VARIETY, 3/13-19/95, p. 49, Leonard Klady
WASHINGTON POST, 3/17/95, p. B7, Hal Hinson
WASHINGTON POST, 3/17/95, Weekend/p. 35, Desson Howe

CANADIAN BACON

A Gramercy Pictures release of a Polygram Filmed Entertainment presentation in association with Propaganda Films of a David Brown/Maverick Picture Co. *Executive Producer:* Freddy DeMann and Sigurjon Sighvatsson. *Producer:* David Brown, Ron Rotholz, and Michael Moore. *Director:* Michael Moore. *Screenplay:* Michael Moore. *Director of Photography:* Haskell Wexler. *Editor:* Wendey Stanzler and Michael Berenbaum. *Music:* Elmer Bernstein and Peter Bernstein. *Music Editor:* Nicholas Meyers and Lori Slovka. *Sound:* Douglas Ganton. *Sound Editor:* Paul B. Clay. *Casting:* Lynn Kressell. *Production Designer:* Carol Spier. *Art Director:* Tamara Deverell. *Set Decorator:* Carol Lavoie. *Special Effects:* Bob Hall and Arthur Langevin. *Costumes:* Kathleen Glynn. *Make-up:* Katherine Southern. *Stunt Coordinator:* Branko Racki. *Running time:* 110 minutes. *MPAA Rating:* PG.

CAST: Alan Alda (President of the United States); John Candy (Bud B. Boomer); Rhea Perlman (Deputy Honey); Kevin Pollak (Stu Smiley); Rip Torn (General Dick Panzer); Kevin J. O'Connor (Roy Boy); Bill Nunn (Kabral); G.D. Spradlin (R.J. Hacker); Steven Wright (Niagara Mountie); James Belushi (Charles Jackal); Brad Sullivan (Gus); Stanley Anderson (Edwin S. Simon); Richard Council (Russian President); Michael Copeman (Panzer's Aide); Bruce Hunter (President's Aide); Beth Amos (Ruthie); Jack Mather (Pops); Kenner Ames (Mountie Sergeant); Roger Dunn (Mountie Major); Natalie Rose (Toronto Kid); Michael Woods (State Trooper #1); Matt Cooke (State Trooper #2); Barbara Schroeder (Newswoman); Tara Meyer (Candy Stripper #1); Fab Filippo (Candy Striper #2); Carlton Watson (Clarence Thomason); Stan Coles (Secretary of State); Adrian Hough (Russian Aide); Bryan Armstrong (Auctioneer); Kelsey Binder Moore (Ice Cream Girl #1); Leah Binder Moore (Ice Cream Girl #2); Wally Bolland (Special Ops Soldier); Marcos Parilo (Omega Force Leader); Jim Czarnecki (Snake); Tony Proffer (Dell); Ben Hamper (Redneck Guy #1); Michael Moore (Redneck Guy #2); Linda Genovesi (Polite Canadian Woman); Sheila Gray (Voice of Hacker Hellstorm); Dana Brooks (Paulette Kalin).

CHRISTIAN SCIENCE MONITOR, 6/7/95, p. 14, David Sterritt

A movie that's definitely headed for American theaters [from the Cannes Film Festival] is "Canadian Bacon" written and directed by Michael Moore, whose "Roger & Me" was a popular documentary about Moore's effort to confront the head of General Motors with the disastrous results of factory closings in a Michigan city.

Moore turns to fiction in "Canadian Bacon," which tells the sardonic story of a Niagara Falls sheriff caught in a war between the United States and Canada, sparked by an American president who needs a new enemy now that the Soviet Union no longer presents an "evil empire" to US citizens. Much of the film recalls "The Mouse That Roared," the Peter Sellers comedy about a tiny country at war with American forces, and the last portion—about a missile-defense system that's out of human control—is clearly influenced by the all-time classic of cold-war comedy, "Dr. Strangelove, or, How I Learned to Stop Worrying and Love the Bomb."

Starring the late John Candy, with Alan Alda and Rhea Perlman backing him up, "Canadian Bacon" is awfully silly, peppering its serious messages—about the dangers of nationalism, the power of the military-industrial complex, and the way politicians manipulate the public—with generous amounts of slapstick humor, exaggerated images, and dopey dialogue. While this undercuts the movie's thoughtful impulses, it plays into Moore's strategy of making a political film that won't just provide tea-time talk for intellectuals, but will stir up thought about complex issues while attracting broad-based audiences in malls and multiplexes.

It remains to be seen whether Moore's approach will usher in a new era of political filmmaking, or turn audiences off by appearing inflammatory, contradictory, or patronizing.

Response among critics has been unenthusiastic so far, but perhaps the festival's high-toned "Un Certain Regard" series was not the best testing ground for such a deliberately undignified romp. It will be interesting to see how "Canadian Bacon" plays with the general public.

LOS ANGELES TIMES, 9/22/95, Calendar/p. 12, John Anderson

[The following review by John Anderson appeared in a slightly different form in NEWSDAY, 11/22/95, Part II/p. B19.]

Michael Moore is a sniper whose main talent is taking potshots at conservatives, corporations and the constipated policies of the U.S. government. In "Roger & Me," his acclaimed documentary about trying to interview General Motors CEO Roger Smith, he had a gimmick that took care of itself, allowing him to crack wise and sardonic about the pathetic and/or arrogant people his film was about.

But what worked for him in "Roger & Me" is what deep-sixes "Canadian Bacon," his first feature, John Candy's last, and a film whose one big joke—a beleaguered U.S. President promoting a cold war with Canada—is worn out before the film is half over. There are funny bits, sure—Steven Wright's Canadian Mountie is pretty hilarious, and Rip Torn's Strangelove-esque Gen. Panzer is one of the film's few consistent elements—but Moore can't make a straight comedy and not be fully engaged. Like Roger Smith, he needs to show his commitment, even though it's a no-win situation: In order to be really funny, "Canadian Bacon", would have to be more serious. And that's not what he's aiming for.

Candy plays Bud Boomer, a Niagara County, N.Y., sheriff who spends much of his day fishing for laid-off, suicidal defense-plant workers at the foot of the falls. His sidekick, Honey (Rhea Perlman), is psychotic; his buddies Roy Boy and Kabral (Kevin J. O'Connor and Bill Nunn) are thickheaded and unemployed. The plant, owned by R.J. Hacker (G.D. Spradlin), has become the victim of the pro-peace policies of a President (Alan Alda) whose approval ratings are on a slide; he needs a war in order to give people jobs and keep his own. With most of the world's major villains dead or imprisoned, the President's only national security adviser, Stu Smiley (Kevin Pollack)—who is also in Hacker's pocket—suggests Canada. The smear campaign is under way.

Despite the big names involved—the producers are David Brown ("A Few Good Men," "The Player") and Madonna's Maverick Picture Co., the music is by Elmer Bernstein, and the cinematography is by Haskell Wexler—"Canadian Bacon" looks like it was made for about a buck-and-a-half. Moore seems to have overlooked the fact that while in a documentary you are handed a world with which to work, in a feature film you have to create one. He doesn't need special effects and a massive budget, but he does need to convince people that when an American President makes a personal appearance, there's usually a crowd.

Moore does make some caustic points about Desert Storm and this country's fixation on war and the military. But it's somewhat ironic that his main position—that Americans will swallow anything that's handed to them—is unlikely to extend to this movie.

NEW YORK POST, 9/22/95, p. 45, Michael Medved

In his first feature film comedy, writer/director Michael Moore (known for his cheeky documentary "Roger and Me" and the irreverent magazine show "TV Nation") dares to ask a terrifying question: How many dumb jokes about Canada and snow can an audience stand before it begins howling in rage and disgust?

Moore provides the answer in "Canadian Bacon," a painfully unfunny concoction that recycles every stale gag you've ever heard about Mounties, hockey players, bad beer and worse weather.

Allegedly inspired by Moore's horror at the fact that America turned so readily against the previously little-known nation of Iraq during the Gulf war, the plot of "Canadian Bacon" involves an ineffectual American president (Alan Alda) who needs to focus attention on a foreign enemy in order to distract the people from dire domestic difficulties. "I wonder if we couldn't mix it up a little bit like we did in the good old days." Alda pleads with the Russian leader at a summit conference.

The man from Moscow won't go along, but a slick White House assistant (Kevin Pollak) comes up with a better idea: he'll help the president by poisoning public opinion against the harmless Canadians, who "walk among us undetected, passing as Americans."

The late John Candy plays a deputy sheriff in Niagara Falls who is stirred by the presidential propaganda into enlisting unemployed defense workers and a fellow officer (Rhea Perlman) in a freelance invasion of Canada. When a munitions magnate unleashes his doomsday machine in the midst of the chaos, the world comes to the brink of thermonuclear destruction—and the movie gets perilously close to a shameless rip-off of "Dr. Strangelove," complete with a general played by Rip Torn in perhaps the worst performance of his career.

All the acting is, in fact, terrible: as if each member of this talented cast merely performed his overdone bit in front of a mirror, rather than connecting in any way with co-stars or story.

Slow moving and stilted at all times, "Canadian Bacon" is full of fat and grease, with no comic meat worth mentioning.

SIGHT AND SOUND, 10/95, p. 44, Lizzie Francke

With the cold war now over, the US President's popularity is flagging so his National Security Advisor Stu Smiley, the Joint Chiefs of Staff, and General Dick Panzer suggest a little skirmish abroad to deflect attention. They decide to pick on Canada and put into motion a subtle anti-Canadian campaign.

Meanwhile in Niagara, on the US/Canadian border, Bud Boomer, the Sheriff of Niagara Falls, and his deputies, Honey and Roy Boy, are having a hard time. Their former place of employment, ammunition manufacturer Hacker Dynamics, has closed down and recession grips the town. When R.J. Hacker hears of the anti-Canada campaign, he meets up with Smiley to suggest that they need arms as well as words. A CIA man masquerading as a Canadian attempts to blow up the ammunitions plant, but is caught by Boomer and his company. Later Boomer, Honey and Boy decide to mount a raid on Canada, planning to dump a pile of litter there. Almost apprehended by a Mountie, they flee back to the US, but leave Honey behind. It is presumed that she has been taken hostage by the Mounties, though in fact she has escaped.

Boomer and Boy return to Canada where they infiltrate a power plant and close it down. The Canadian Prime Minister contacts the US President to protest the action. The President decides that Boomer is a liability and sends the Omega Force to track him down. Meanwhile, Boomer goes to Toronto in pursuit of Honey, while Hacker, backed by Smiley, programmes a missile launch aimed at Canada. Arriving in Toronto, Honey makes her way to the tower followed by Boomer and the Omega Force. Hacker has installed an explosives device in the tower, but Honey manages to prevent it from going off. With the crisis over, she and Boomer return to the US.

Michael Moore made his name with his politically acerbic and punchy documentary *Roger and Me*. A rare example of a successful non-fictional theatrical release it chronicled the demise of his home town of Flint, Michigan after General Motors closed down their plant there. Now in his first fictional feature film, he turns his attention to America's imperialist appetite. According to the press notes, he conceived the idea for *Canadian Bacon* after the United States' Operation Desert Storm invasion of Iraq. The concept for this post-Cold-War satire has a levity to it: America has to kick someone's ass so why not pick on Canada.

It is the anti-Canada jokes that give the film its zing—as if the whole point is to play on the famous Canadian inferiority complex. After all, as one character puts it, what have the Canadians given us but metric systems and Neil Young? "They walk among us undetected—look at William Shatner, Michael J. Fox, Michael Myers," says another propagandist (the ultimate joke being that star John Candy was a Canadian). Meanwhile the drinking of Molson beer and the playing of ice-hockey are banned as un-American activities. It starts out as a delightfully ludicrous idea, although some of the references might not translate well outside North America. Dan Aykroyd (another Canadian) plays a highway patrolman who flags Boomer down only to point out that the graffiti on his van should be in both French as well as English. One has to know that Canada is famous for its cleanliness to get some of the jokes—Toronto is described as being like the notoriously dull New York State capital Albany, "only cleaner".

Soon, however, the comedy begins to wear pretty thin. The presence, in cameo roles of Ackroyd, along with Jim Belushi and Steve Wright reminds one that *Canadian Bacon* is really no more than an over-extended sketch for *Saturday Night Live*—or even its Canadian counterpart *SCTV*, of which Candy was a founding member. Once the audience gets the point about the US Government's—and arms manufacturers'—need for an enemy, there is little else to focus on. Moore has proved he's able to pace his documentary work, whether for *Roger and Me* or his alternative news show *Michael Moor's TV Nation*, but there is nothing lean about *Canadian Bacon*.

VILLAGE VOICE, 9/26/95, p. 75, Georgia Brown

All those who think Canada is funny raise your hands. Michael Moore does, but that's because he's from Michigan. Having spent several formative years in Moore's state, I really giggled at his long-canned spoof, *Canadian Bacon*. At least at the Canada stuff. American unemployment—Moore's old standby (you remember *Roger & Me*)—is less funny. American foreign policy, well, that part is truly grim.

As before, Moore begins with the layoffs. When Hacker Dynamics, a munitions manufacturer in Niagara Falls, New York, shuts down its plant (for want of a national enemy), laid-off workers begin jumping into the falls. Local law enforcers are offered incentive bonuses: $25 for preventing a jump, $50 for retrieving the body. "Jump! Jump!" yell craftily positioned Sheriff Bud Boomer (John Candy) and his scruffy deputy, Honey (Rhea Perlman). On recognizing the would-be jumper as a fellow dimwit, Roy Boy (Kevin J. O'Connor), the two officers insist he accompany them to an auction of Hacker weaponry. Here, the battered Roy Boy wins a war toy. Coincidentally, the buffoonish first-term president (Alan Alda as a giddy, peaceable George Bush) is scheduled to speak.

At its weakest, *Canadian Bacon* comes off as a poor man's *Dr. Strangelove*, which it shamelessly draws on. (The movie's very poverty, though, its contempt for production values, will endear it to some.) Presidential aides—the battle-crazed General Dick Panzer (Rip Torn) and the smarmy, pragmatic Stu Smiley (Kevin Pollak)—cast about for possible antagonists, "a little *tension*," to boost the Chiefs ratings. Once Smiley settles on Canada the situation quickly escalates to a nuclear countdown.

But back to Canada. The essence of the Canada joke is that it's all so tidy, pleasant, and well-run up there. Having benefitted from state-subsidized college, health care, transportation, and condoms, Canadians are literate, clean, healthy, and polite in contrast to the slovenly, warlike primitives to their south. When Boomer and pals (they're joined by Bill Nunn's Kabral) conduct a guerrilla raid onto Canadian soil, they cross the border ... hee, hee ... to litter.

Canada jokes, it gradually seeps through, are America jokes. As Boomer boasts to an unarmed Mountie (Steven Wright): "I'm your worst nightmare: A citizen with the right to bear arms."

Paradoxically, the movie conveys a subtle affection for these idiots. It's not their fault they were born here.

Moore has said that he was trying to make a political movie that could play the malls, whereas in fact his film has had a hard enough time even getting into a New York art house. (*Bacon* can't even be called John Candy's last movie.) The satire's essentials, however, are fresh enough. How many Canada jokes have you heard in the last seven years!

Also reviewed in:
NEW YORK TIMES, 9/22/95, p. C20, Stephen Holden
VARIETY, 5/29-6/4/95, p. 54, Leonard Klady
WASHINGTON POST, 9/22/95, p. D6, William F. Powers

CANDYMAN: FAREWELL TO THE FLESH

A Gramercy Pictures release of a Polygram Filmed Entertainment presentation of a Propaganda Films production. *Executive Producer:* Clive Barker. *Producer:* Sigurjon Sighvatsson and Gregg D. Fienberg. *Director:* Bill Condon. *Screenplay:* Rand Ravich and Mark Kruger. *Director of Photography:* Tobias Schliessler. *Editor:* Virginia Katz. *Music:* Philip Glass. *Music Editor:* Lori Eschler. *Sound:* Walter Hoylman. *Sound Editor:* Jon Johnson. *Casting:* Carol Lewis. *Production Designer:* Barry Robison. *Art Director:* Dawn Snyder Stebler. *Set Designer:* Robert Goldstein and Stephanie J. Gordon. *Set Decorator:* Suzette Sheets. *Set Dresser:* Teusa Koiwai. *Special Effects:* John Hartigan. *Costumes:* Bruce Finlayson. *Make-up:* Sheri P. Short. *Stunt Coordinator:* William Washington. *Running time:* 99 minutes. *MPAA Rating:* R.

CAST: Tony Todd (Candyman); Caroline Barclay (Caroline Sullivan); Michael Bergeron (Coleman Tarrant); Brianna Blanchard (Young Caroline); Clotiel Bordeltier (Liz); Russell Buchanan (Voice of Kingfish); Nate Bynum (Reporter #2); Sandy Byrd (Woman #2 in Bookstore); Eric Cadora (Man in Bookstore); Timothy Carhart (Paul McKeever); Veronica Cartwright (Octavia); Carl N. Ciafalio (Bartender); Matt Clark (Thibideaux); Michael Culkin (Phillip Purcell); Stephen Dunn (Thug #2); Daniel Dupont (Reporter #1); David Gianopoulos (Det. Ray Levesque); Glen Gomez (Kingfish); Steven Hartman (Young Boy); Fay Hauser (Pam Carver); Margaret Howell (Clara); Ralph Joseph (Mr. Jeffries); Erin Labranche (Little Girl Doctor); Carl Leblanc (Little Boy King); George Lemore (Drew); Maria Mason (Befuddled Teacher); Joshua Gibran Mayweather (Matthew); Monica L. Monica (Reporter #3); Brian Joseph Moore (Thug #1); Bill Nunn (Reverend Ellis); William O'Leary (Ethan Tarrant); Randy Oglesby (Heyward Sullivan); Steve Picerni (Police Guard); Eric Pierson (Ben the Busboy); Terrence Rosemore (Suspicious Man at Matthew's House); Kelly Rowan (Annie Tarrant); Amy Ryder (Hostile Woman at Cabrini Green); Patricia Sansone (Woman #2 at Bookstore); Hunt Scarritt (Scraggly Vagrant); Carol Sutton (Angry Woman at Matthew's House).

LOS ANGELES TIMES, 3/20/95, Calendar/p. 2, Kevin Thomas

"Candyman: Farewell to the Flesh," like the 1992 "Candyman," overflows with blood and guts, drowning a potent metaphor for African American rage and oppression. Those who saw the original film will recall that the supernatural figure of its title, summoned by repeating his nickname five times while peering into a mirror, materialized in Chicago's Cabrini-Green housing project, already the site of so much crime and poverty.

The Candyman was Daniel Robitaille, son of a Louisiana slave, an artist of such talent that an aristocratic landowner had him paint a portrait of his daughter Caroline. The two fell in love, and Robitaille was punished by having his right hand lopped off and his head and chest smeared with honey to attract a swarm of bees—hence his new moniker. As he lay dying, however, Caroline, manages to hold up her hand-mirror to his face, thus preserving his soul and allowing him to return from the dead to seek vengeance, his missing hand replaced with a scythe. You have the feeling that the Candyman will be lurking around as long as there's racial injustice.

This time Candyman (again Tony Todd) has turned up on home turf, New Orleans, for Mardi Gras, which marks the beginning of Lent, a "farewell to the flesh." He's intent upon slaughtering Caroline's descendants but doesn't reckon with Caroline's spunky great-great-granddaughter (Kelly Rowan).

As before, the film has been adapted from a story by the film's executive producer, horror-meister Clive Barker. Visually, "Candyman 2" dazzles, with ace cinematographer Tobias Schliessler, editor Virginia Katz and a top-notch special effects crew creating a film noirish New Orleans—always the most picturesque of locales—but also churning up gallons of gore.

Once again, Philip Glass composes one of his insistent scores—and again the effect is pretentious, considering the circumstances, Director Bill Condon has a sense of style but a heavy hand with actors—you can all but hear them telling themselves to hit their marks and punch out their lines. Still, Rowan is game, Todd again a figure of sinister dignity—this time the Candyman is allowed more pathos—and veteran Matt Clark shines in supporting role as a dabbler in the occult.

As before, however, grisly wretched excess spoils the show.

NEW YORK POST, 3/18/95, p. 17, Bill Hoffmann

March is not turning out to be a good month for horror movies.

Two weeks ago, I told you about an abysmal piece of dreck called "The Mangler"—about a killer laundry machine.

Now comes "Candyman: Farewell to the Flesh," an equally moronic, by-the-numbers fright fest about a killer from the 19th century out to wreak havoc in New Orleans during Mardi Gras.

This hokey movie relies on two tired gimmicks to try to scare us.

First, every few minutes a hand or a face pops out of nowhere to frighten our heroine—accompanied by a loud noise. This is a cheap trick and it works more than it should.

Second, there's loads of gore, a concept which is not scary but which will have you squirming in disgust.

Even then, how many times can you watch somebody get run through, then gutted from the crotch all the way up to the neck?

This is the second of two outings for the Candyman, which is the nickname of a young black painter who in the 1890s was brutally tortured and murdered by a Southern mob after he got a rich white man's daughter pregnant. (In lovingly disgusting detail, they chop off one of his hands, cover him with honey and let bees attack him).

In present-day Louisiana, a young teacher (Kelly Rowan) begins having nightmares about the Candyman legend, only to find out it was her great-grandmother who was the Candyman's lover. And now that ghostly legend is back for revenge.

I didn't see the first "Candyman," but this sequel appears to be just more of the same as the killer (Tony Todd) appears before various victims, calmly curses them in a deep voice (generously helped by an electronic resonator), then uses a hooked arm to mutilate them.

You know the movie's in trouble when it occasionally cuts away to the Mardi Gras parade and some of the costumes of the revelers seem creepier than the Candyman himself.

Why can't we just remember "Candyman" as that insipid but cute song Sammy Davis Jr, used to sing?

NEWSDAY, 3/18/95, Part II/p. B5, John Anderson

Marry Catholic imagery to pagan ritual and what do you get? Santeria, Mardi Gras or "Candyman: Farewell to the Flesh." Given the choice, we'll take animal sacrifice and a hangover.

But for fans of the original "Candyman"—and there must be some, or they wouldn't have made a sequel—prepare for the same amount of incongruity and gore, but prepare to make certain reality adjustments. There's the locale, for one thing. Although the original was set in the Cabrini housing project in Chicago—because that's where Candyman's ashes were buried—we are now in New Orleans, where his grave will be discovered late in the film (you can't worry about these things, just go with the flow).

There are also the religious and anthropological pretentions that pepper the movie, all of which are callous appropriations. When it opens, the Crescent City is on the verge of Lent—which adds faux spiritual overtones to an overwrought, pedestrian story—and schoolteacher Annie Tarrant (Markie Post look-alike Kelly Rowan) is being sucked into the Candyman myth: Say his name fives time in the mirror and he'll appear, hook-handed and bloodthirsty. Well, her father did and died, and now her brother (William O'Leary) has been implicated in a rash of gruesome eviscerations. In order to assure her young students that Candyman doesn't exist, she repeats his name five times in a schoolroom mirror. Uh-oh.

In the first film, Candyman was established as one of those archetypal modern myths that grow out of some societal fear. The fear here, clearly, is of black males: For the first 30 minutes of the movie, suspense is established by having the principal characters jump every time an African-American face appears. There's also a distinct racial friction established between the virtue of the blond heroine and the licentious abandon of the Mardi Gras revelers. And there's the demonization of the Candyman—who in the 1890s, according to the story, was horribly murdered by the father of the white woman he'd impregnated. In the afterlife, however, he's strictly from hell. There's a lame attempt to explain all this, but any potential damage has been done.

What damage? This film is after a youth audience, and its use of the black male as an object of fear seems malignant. There are far better things to do than watch "Candyman," a horror film that's not only shoddily made but has no conscience, please find one.

SIGHT AND SOUND, 12/95, p. 42, Kim Newman

In New Orleans, Philip Purcell, an anthropologist, gives a lecture on the subject of the Candyman, a hook-handed boogeyman of urban legend who allegedly committed a string of murders in Chicago officially ascribed to academic Helen Lyle. Purcell is challenged by Ethan Tarrant, a young man who blames him for the death of his father and who once invoked Candyman on Purcell's advice. Purcell defiantly recites the monster's name five times while looking into a mirror the regulation method of summoning Candyman, and is killed by the spirit Ethan Tarrant is arrested for the murder, to the shame of his mother Octavia.

Ethan's sister Annie, a teacher, is disturbed because Matthew, one of her pupils, is drawing pictures of Candyman. During Mardi Gras, the spook manifests himself in the real world and slaughters in turn Annie's husband Paul McKeever, Ethan, Octavia and magical goods dealer Honore Thibideaux. Annie follows Matthew to the derelict mansion that once belonged to her family and is confronted by Candyman, who reveals that in life he was Daniel Robitaille, a black artist who dared love a white woman. Robitaille was murdered by a mob who hacked off his hand and covered him in honey so he would be stung by bees. Annie is Robitaille's great-great-grand daughter and Candyman sees her as the reincarnation of his lost love. Rejecting the monster, Annie shatters the hand mirror which gives him his power and he is banished from reality.

Bernard Rose's *Candyman*, adapted form Clive Barker's short story 'The Forbidden', remains perhaps the best attempt at translating Barker's distinctive tone to the cinema. It was also the most commercially successful of all Barker-related films. However, in the 90s, there is no such thing as a one-off horror hit and so this is not merely an attempt to come up with a sequel to Rose's *Candyman* but a twisting of the premise into the blueprint for a potential money-spinning franchise along the lines of the *Nightmare on Elm Street* or *Hellraiser* series.

Tony Todd's dignified, hollow-voiced, hook-handed urban legend is here promoted to *Fangoria* cover-boy status in the hope that he can take a place in the monster pantheon between Freddy Krueger and *Hellraiser*'s Pinhead, which means the film has to be entirely structured around his appearances. *Candyman*, by contrast, was actually about Helen Lyle, played in the original by Virginia Madsen, a character who is barely mentioned here and sorely missed. The power of the monster was in his elusiveness, which the sequel fritters away as he turns up every ten minutes to stick his hook into yet more disposable supporting stooges.

Even worse is the feebleness of the central thread. Faced with the need to come up with a plot that focuses on Candyman rather than a potential victim, screenwriters Rand Ravich and Mark Kruger have resorted to the most ancient and tiresome cliché of the genre: the monster's search for the reincarnation of his lost love (used in *The Mummy, Blacula* and *Bram Stoker's Dracula*). It was all very well the first time round to recount one possible origin for Candyman, but it's quite another to use a prosaic enactment of his martyrdom (complete with cackling, honey-pouring rednecks) in lieu of a climax for this picture.

Bill Condon, screenwriter of the underrated *Strange Behavior* and *Strange Invaders*, made a directing debut with *Sister, Sister*, an effective Southern gothic with *Baby Jane*-level performances from Judith Ivey and Jennifer Jason Leigh. This assignment is perhaps an attempt to gain a solid commercial credit before proceeding to more personal work: the dilapidated Southern mansion and plantation flashbacks are tangential spin-offs from *Sister, Sister* but hardly make much of an impression. Given the subtitle ('Carnival' means 'Farewell to the Flesh', loosely), the Mardi Gras setting is surprisingly throwaway, though there is a running DJ commentary for all the world like *Reservoir Dogs* without the song rights clearances.

A few decent performers (Bill Nunn, Matt Clark, Veronica Cartwright) are underused while Kelly Rowan, last seen as the heroine of *The Gate*, isn't up to the femme role. Tony Todd, whose character never seems to wonder whether or not murdering his beloved's entire family will endear him to her, reacts to the star turn spotlight by exercising rather too much ham.

Also reviewed in:
NEW YORK TIMES, 3/18/95, p. 18, Caryn James
VARIETY, 3/20-26/95, p. 49, Leonard Klady
WASHINGTON POST, 3/17/95, p. B7, Richard Harrington

CARMEN MIRANDA: BANANAS IS MY BUSINESS

An International Cinema Inc. release of an International Cinema production in assocciation with the Corporation for Public Broadcasting Channel 4, and the National Latino Communications Center. *Producer:* David Meyer and Helena Solberg. *Director:* Helena Solberg. *Director of Photography:* Tomasz Magierski. *Narrative: (English and Portuguese with English subtitles).* *Editor:* David Meyer and Amanda Zinoman. *Sound:* Mario Garcia and Firmino Antunes. *Sound Editor:* Marlena Grzaslewicz. *Running time:* 90 minutes. *MPAA Rating:* Not Rated.

INTERVIEWS WITH: Maria José Oueiroz Miranda; Aurora Miranda; Mario Cunha; Caribé da Rocha; Laurindo Almeida; Synval Silva; Aloysio de Oliveira; Estela Romero; Cássio Barsante; Jorginho Guinle; Raul Smandek; Ivan Jack; Cesar Romero; Alice Faye; Rita Moreno.

REENACTMENTS WITH: Cynthia Adler (Luella Hopper); Erick Barreto (Carmen Miranda, fantasy sequences); Leticia Monte (Carmen Miranda, teen-ager).

CINEASTE, Vol. XXII, No. 1, 1996, p. 41, Dennis West & Joan M. West

Actress-singer Carmen Miranda, the Brazilian Bombshell in tutti-frutti headdress and platform shoes, was well known to American movie audiences of the Forties and early Fifties as a sort of generic Latina from somewhere down 'souse of the border.' The titles of Miranda's first three U.S. films say it best—*Down Argentine Way, That Night in Rio,* and *Weekend in Havana*—all for 20th Century-Fox in 1940-41. In these and other musical comedies, Miranda was not the romantic lead since her aggressive sexuality and volatile demeanor were apparently deemed culturally inappropriate for Hollywood's heroes. The flamboyant, ever-gesturing Miranda served as a plot complication for the romantic leads and provided exotic entertainment as, with midriff bared and hips gyrating, she would samba and sashay her way through musical numbers in Portuguese and her own uniquely fractured English—completely unhindered by the fruits hanging from her hat and elsewhere on her carnivalesque costumes. Miranda was launched in the U.S. as an appealing 'good neighbor' during the era of the economically and militarily important Good Neighbor Policy. For Americans the Brazilian star would always remain a gaudy, clownish, self-mocking, excitable, sexually attractive but nonthreatening tropical 'Other'—as bright and 'tropical' as the bananas she wore.

Hollywood did not create the Carmen Miranda persona; she herself had developed it in Brazil before ever setting a platform shoe in the U.S. Miranda, who was born in 1909, had enjoyed a remarkably rapid and productive career in Brazil as a radio star, recording artist, film actress, and entertainer. Over 300 successful records, five movies, and nine South American tours attest to her early popularity and tremendous appeal in Latin America. But Miranda became problematic for Brazilians when she moved to Hollywood, where she was one of the highest paid women in America—and the omnipresent pop icon of Brazil in the eyes of U.S. audiences. Today Miranda represents the greatest myth in Brazilian show business—there is even a museum dedicated to her and her costumes in Rio—but she remains a controversial figure for many Brazilians. Did her willing collaboration as a 'good neighbor' make her the compliant tool of U.S. cultural imperialism? Or did her long-sustained U.S. success reflect favorably on Brazil by proving the originality of her art as well as her ability to achieve fame and money in the Colossus to the North?

Carmen Miranda: Bananas Is My Business is an unusual part-fiction part-documentary feature that innovatively and generally successfully interrelates two complementary film exercises or essays. In one exercise, the Brazilian-born and -raised director-narrator Helena Solberg creates a multifaceted documentary portrait of the workaholic Brazilian superstar. To develop her portrait, Solberg draws on a wealth of wide-ranging materials: home-movie footage of the entertainer relaxing; clips from Hollywood production numbers and Miranda's single extant Brazilian film; actuality footage of crowds of admirers mourning their recently deceased idol in the streets of Rio in 1955; still photos, re-creations; and a final image of Carmen as she tapes a number for the Jimmy Durante television show the night of her death. This documentary portrait is further developed by a gallery of knowledgeable interviewees including Brazilian journalists and musicians; a Portuguese cousin; contemporary Hollywood stars such as Cesar Romero and Alice Faye; Miranda's first lover, a Brazilian rowing champion; Miranda's actress/singer sister Aurora; and a friend and lover who knew the star intimately as a member of her backup band. Solberg's voice-over narration guides viewers through this rich and smoothly edited material.

Carmen Miranda as documentary portrait works best as a sensitive introduction to the Brazilian Bombshell for those unfamiliar with her life and work. More knowledgeable viewers will note gaps in Solberg's rendition of this life story: for example, the star's longed-for pregnancy, at age thirty-nine, ended in a miscarriage; an obsession with the appearance of her nose led her to a quack plastic surgeon who nearly killed her; and in 1946 a widely publicized no-panties photo of Miranda created a scandal that soured her relationship with 20th Century-Fox. *Bananas Is My Business*, then, does not add significant new dimensions to our understanding of the star; and, indeed, the film leaves unanswered key questions about the historical figure.

But *Carmen Miranda* is less important as documentary portrait; it is above all an intriguing and highly original exercise in the understanding of cultural and other identities. In exploring the transformation of Maria do Carmo da Cunha, the Portuguese-born daughter of a humble immigrant family, into Carmen Miranda, 'The Lady in the Tutti-Frutti Hat' and the internationally acclaimed icon of Brazil, Solberg turns her film into a provocative meditation on what it means to be Brazilian. The director prefaces her film with a brief re-creation of Miranda's early death from a heart attack at age forty-six. The final image of this prologue, a broken mirror clutched in the singer's hand, appropriately reflects the nature of the investigation Solberg is about to undertake. The shattering mirror marks the moment in time when Miranda's image became forever fixed. The mosaic of shards left in the frame suggests equally the multiplicity of images the star reflected back to each idiosyncratic viewer and the multifaceted approach that Solberg will bring to her subject.

The first few sequences after the opening credits introduce the three characters whose intertwined cultural identities the filmmaker will explore. There is Carmen Miranda the celebrity, surrounded by the gorgeous Technicolor bananas of Hollywood, made famous by her international fans, and mourned by thousands of her fellow Brazilians upon her death. There is Helena Solberg herself, shown in black-and-white photos as a child, an adoring young fan whose parents prevented her attending the star's funeral because it was "better to stay at home when the poor people filled the streets." Joining the superstar and the director-narrator is the third character, Brazil, their mutual country. Brazil is portrayed in a dual guise: as the tropical, exotic, and pop-ular international tourist destination of a Technicolor travelogue and as the land of opportunity glimpsed across the ocean by many humble Portuguese immigrants—such as Carmen's family—seeking a better life.

This dual portrayal of Brazil serves Solberg as a point of departure for her essay on identities. At the end of the film's introductory segment, the director wonders in voice-over what gets lost when seeing through foreign eyes and if this has something to do with what happened to Carmen. Taking Brazil as an example, she has already suggested a partial answer to her query, as well as revealed her particular critical stance: persons on the outside—foreigners—see differently from those on the inside. In Solberg's film, however, the eyes looking at Carmen Miranda are not foreign; and they clearly aspire to observe their subject through many lenses—nationality, memory, photographic images, race, class, gender, music, costume.

Solberg convincingly demonstrates that when seen through eyes tinged by nationality the vision of Carmen Miranda (and by extension, that of Brazil) becomes variously transformed, depending on the observer's idiosyncracies. Carmen's Portuguese cousin looks upon her as "not Brazilian," as the immigrant who found success and even married in the New World, but who remains fundamentally European by blood and birth. The Brazilians, Solberg implies, are divided in their attitudes along lines of class and race. The 'people' adored the singer-actress as a beloved-exponent and ambassador of (their) Brazilian culture, the Europeanized elite accused the entertainer of becoming Americanized after her first trip to the U.S. Was this, at least in part, an excuse for having denied the African-Brazilian heritage inherent in the music Carmen sang and danced and in the costume that had made her famous! Did this cold shoulder indicate that many of her snobbish compatriots saw her as *too* 'Brazilian,' too 'native!'

North Americans superimposed on the Brazilian singer their myths and dreams of an exotic, mysterious, Latin 'South.' The Kingdom of Hollywood saw Miranda in terms of sex appeal, exoticism, glamor, and especially dollar signs. Clearly, what gets lost here, amidst so many egocentrically nationalistic perceptions, is the individual herself. Solberg uses memories of Carmen's relatives, friends, lovers, and colleagues not only to offer the viewer details of her professional career, but more significantly to remind the audience that a human being existed behind the star facade. These eyes are prejudiced, too, by their relationship to Miranda; but at least they hint at the human being—charming, vivacious, generous, responsible, hard-working—and offer U.S. audiences a previously unfamiliar vision of what the singer was in her own country before going to Hollywood. A note of sadness nonetheless tinges these interviews as various individuals recount the pressures on Miranda's career that made it increasingly less feasible for her to either abandon or change the image that she had brought with her from Brazil. A former lover remarks that he feared he was becoming "Mr. Carmen Miranda"; the film shows that, in effect, Carmen herself was overwhelmed by the tutti-frutti hat.

Elements of class and race played roles in this transformation from woman to icon. Carmen successfully appropriated a costume and music that originated ethnically within African-Brazilian culture. When she added lyrics of a nationalistic bent to the borrowed rhythms, the cultural associations tied to the image lost even more of their specific ethnic identity; and image and woman both began shifting to a point where they would be defined, especially when seen through foreign eyes, as representative of the entire Brazilian populace.

Solberg raises two gendered issues. Sympathetically allying her own identity as a female to that of her fellow countrywoman, the director remembers as a young woman admiring Miranda's ability to navigate successfully in an essentially masculine artistic milieu. The singer, then, provided the young Helena with a strong role model vis-à-vis the sexist society they both lived in. The very existence of this film as a cinematic essay on identities bears witness to the impact that the Carmen Miranda image had on the director. Solberg also raises the issue of victimization. How much control *did* the star exert over her career choices; and to what extent was she exploited by men like Brazil's Populist-nationalist president Getúlio Vargas, Broadway impresario Lee Shubert, Hollywood producer Darryl Zanuck, and her American husband David Sebastian!

The film presents evidence on both sides of this issue, but the question remains unanswered. This may be due in part to the fact that, in spite of the many and varied images that Solberg offers of Carmen Miranda, through photos as well as memories, they remain glimpses from the outside. Only twice do viewers come close to feeling that they are hearing or seeing Carmen Miranda the woman and not Carmen Miranda the phenomenon. Yet even these instances, which come from private moments in her life—the photo dedication to her first beau and the snippet of home movie showing her dancing with friends—give one the impression of having been in some manner 'staged' because someone or a camera was watching. Carmen Miranda never really speaks off the record and 'off-camera.' There are only suggestive echoes in some of the song lyrics of what she must have been thinking.

The stylized Bahiana costume that became Carmen's performing trademark inspires some of the film's richest commentary on how identity is created and assigned and on what happened to Carmen Miranda. As Solberg demonstrates, the costume eventually becomes an icon itself. The woman originally wearing it disappears, and the clothing is appropriated by various groups as a means of conferring identity on certain others. Many Brazilians, for instance, perceive the fruit-basket headgear as emblematic of African-Bahian culture, while Americans identify it as simply Brazilian; and Europeans are likely to understand it broadly as an image of the Americas, i.e., the New World.

The costume has even usurped the gender and personality of Miranda, and thus possesses the power to confer an exotic, flamboyant, caricatured, and fetishized femininity on males, as the clips of Miranda spoofers Milton Berle, Mickey Rooney, and Bob Hope prove. The film offers a unique twist along this line, one that recognizes a certain international development of the Miranda image, and that is the costume's popularity among transvestite groups: the color re-creation scenes in the film are acted by Carmen Miranda impersonator Erick Barreto, whose performance rings eerily authentic.

Unfortunately, one serious flaw mars this exploration of identity issues. Some of the dream/fantasy sequences (e.g., Carmen returning to Portugal) show imaginative inspiration, but their purpose and meaning remain simply too ambiguous in terms of the principal themes examined in the film. Another fantasy re-creation, Carmen travelling in a plane, is superfluous.

By the end of these two interwoven cinematic essays, neither viewer nor filmmaker ever quite manages to reach the personal and private core of the human being behind the Carmen Miranda image in spite of the richly detailed portrait that is sketched. We do, however, come to appreciate how cultural identities may be forged through the complex dialog among expectations, perceptions, and reality itself. Solberg ends Carmen Miranda on a note of both personal and national reconciliation. She suggests that many of her compatriots (her mother and composer Heitor Villa-Lobos included) now accept Carmen Miranda (the individual and the image) as authentically Brazilian. In this acceptance they have come to terms with the citizen many believed had betrayed her country; and—perhaps influenced by foreign perceptions—they have embraced ethnic dimensions of their own cultural heritage that they may have once shunned. Perhaps in making this film Helena Solberg herself has discovered, if not exactly what lay behind the Carmen Miranda mask, at least why visions of tutti-frutti hats lurk in the eyes of Americans when they hear the word 'Brazil.'

NEW YORK POST, 7/5/95, p. 30, Thelma Adams

In such movies as "Down Argentine Way" and "Springtime in the Rockies", Brazilian bombshell Carmen Miranda leaps from the screen like a 3-D image leaving co-stars behind in her Technicolor wake. With her fruit salad hats and belly-baring Bahia-meets-Broadway costumes, she was earthy, ebullient, always in motion, never coy.

Miranda, nee Maria do Carmo da Cunha, was born in Portugal, not Brazil, in 1909. Transplanted to Rio as a toddler, Miranda grew up to be a symbol of Brazil, achieving stardom as a singer in her adopted country. In 1939, Lee Shubert "discovered" Carmen and imported the singer to Broadway. She was an instant hit in "The Streets of Paris" and the following year found her mugging for the camera in "Down Argentine Way."

On one level, the documentary "Carmen Miranda: Bananas is My Business," which opens today at the Film Forum, is a star-is-born saga: a poor little girl rich in talent, family and friends grows up to be a fabulous, wealthy star unmoored from the very things that made her who she was. In 1945, Miranda was the highest paid woman in Hollywood. A decade later, she was dead of a heart attack at 46.

Using film clips, archival footage, family photos and interviews with Cesar Romero, Alice Faye, Rita Moreno, Miranda's sister, ex-boyfriend, and Brazilian musicians, director Helena Solberg ("From the Ashes ... Nicaragua Today") begins to mount portrait of an under-appreciated, and long-neglected star.

But Solberg has no desire to create a conventional portrait but struggles to place Miranda in the pantheon of victimhood. Narrating chunks of the movie in the drone of the self-obsessed, the director inserts her personal search for the identity of Carmen Miranda as Latina role-model—a role model Solberg asserts was coopted by the Hollywood machine and twisted into a stereotype of Latin culture.

While the director's desire to make a more personal statement about Miranda is understandable, it's an artistic misstep. Solberg's bland musings—and embarrassing dramatic recreations performed by a second-rate Miranda impersonator—cannot upstage Miranda, the consummate performer whose charisma cannot be bounded by cries of "stereotype" or "Yankee cultural imperialism." Solberg's theories appear leaden when compared to the vibrant, complex images of Miranda that refuse to be pigeon-holed.

Miranda could have remained in Brazil, performing in a context that might have allowed her more leeway to grow as an artist, and adopt more than just the trademark tutti-frutti hat. Instead, she rode to Hollywood stardom on a potent Brazilian bombshell image that brushed against self-parody and landed gleefully close to camp.

Like stars from Judy Garland to Marilyn Monroe, there was a cost for this level of ambition and public exposure, a whistling hole at the center of the individual that swallowed the performer up before her time.

VILLAGE VOICE, 7/4/95, p. 50, Amy Taubin

At last, a fabulous summer movie. Helena Solberg's *Bananas Is My Business* probes the icon that was and is Carmen Miranda, threading a point of view that is both analytic and empathetic through a dazzling array of film clips, recordings, radio broadcasts, newsreel footage, and interviews with friends, relatives, and artistic collaborators. Sure, it's just a documentary, but as *Hoop Dreams* and *Crumb* has shown, they can be as audience friendly as fiction features—and *Bananas Is My Business* is the most ingratiating of the bunch. There aren't many films that can send one out of the theater feeling sad, angry, and like dancing.

For women of Solberg's generation, which is roughly my own, our childhood memory of Carmen Miranda is tied up with our relationship to our mothers. Solberg begins her narration by recalling that her mother refused to let her go to the funeral of Brazil's greatest pop star: "People like my parents always thought that when poor people filled the streets, for whatever reason, it was better to stay at home."

Like "The Lady in the Tutti-Frutti Hat," Solberg was brought up in Brazil but made her filmmaking career in the U.S. Although there's both a class and a generational difference between the filmmaker and her subject, they share the experience of being caught between the two Americas.

Solberg follows Carmen Miranda's life chronologically: her birth in 1909 in Portugal (the Brazilian bombshell carried a Portuguese passport her whole life); her girlhood in Brazil; her discovery at age 20 by RCA Victor (her test demo became a hit record); her reign as Brazil's leading samba singer and movie star during the '30s; her first American success in Lee Shubert's revue *The Streets of Paris* (she was credited with rescuing Broadway from the competition of the World's Fair); her disastrous return to Brazil where she was jeered for having been Americanized, thus selling out herself and her culture; her wartime stint in Hollywood as the emblem of the U.S.'s Good Neighbor Policy (in 1945, she was the highest paid woman in the U.S.); her break with 20th Century Fox and her failed attempt to remake her image. From here it's all downhill. She made a disastrous marriage to a sycophantic, wife-beating producer. On her brief return to Brazil, in the throes of a nervous breakdown she was given shock treatment; she died a few months later in Hollywood of a heart attack at age 46.

Like Elvis, Miranda became a star by giving a white face to black music. Although almost all of her Brazilian films have been lost, the fragments that Solberg managed to unearth, and, of course, the early recordings reveal her as a samba singer and dancer of extraordinary subtlety, fluidity, and wit. In 1939, she adopted the costume—the turban, lacy blouse, and arm bangles—of the Baiana, the black women who sell food on the streets of Bahia. She was performing in Baiana costume when Lee Shubert first saw her, although it's doubtful that he distinguished, anymore than would her U.S. audience, the Afro-Brazilian signifiers from the overall "Latina" package.

"When Carmen arrived in New York, she already was not the Carmen we knew," says Solberg in voice-over. Fresh off the boat, Miranda proclaimed to an enthralled press that she only knew 100 words of English—among them "men, men, men" and "money, money, money." From today's vantage point, the resemblance to the Material Girl is staggering. Clips from this period show a Miranda who feels increasingly in control of her image, an entertainer who aims to please. The generosity of her early performing persona is displaced onto costume, her excess fetishized in the fruit-laden headdresses that dwarfed her body and soul.

Although Miranda was complicit in her own fetishization, her talents, as Solberg observes, "were used by many to many different ends." During the period when she was 20th Century Fox's leading box office attraction, she was said to have had Darryl Zanuck wrapped around her finger, yet he never allowed her to deviate from the image of the Brazilian Bombshell. She was patronized for her foreignness. Her sexuality was famed through comedy. She got the laughs and the blonds got the wedding rings.

If Madonna has disguised the limitations of her musical talents through repackagings, Miranda's enormous talent atrophied with repetition. In the Fox film clips here, we can see her initial exuberance become edged in doubt as she realizes on some level that she's being treated with contempt. Her mode of fighting back was to add a defiant layer of mockery on top of the mockery the films already made of her. The Brazilians disowned her for parodying her own culture; they didn't realize that what she was parodying was the travesty Hollywood had made of her identity and of theirs.

Solberg assembled a dozen of the people who knew Miranda best to speak about her talent and its destruction. The film was made in the nick of time. Most of Miranda's contemporaries are well into their eighties and a few of them—like the great samba singer and composer Synval Silva—have since died. To flesh out the clips and interviews, Solberg invents fantasy sequences in which the drag performer Erick Barreto incarnates the star who herself inspired a mini-camp industry.

In *Bananas Is My Business*, a good director handles a great subject. But Solberg doesn't shy away from her own subjectivity; as a result the film pricks one's own, becoming, as Solberg puts it, "a tale of reconciliation between Carmen and ourselves."

Also reviewed in:
NEW YORK TIMES, 7/5/95, p. C11, Stephen Holden
VARIETY, 7/10-16/95, p. 36, Godfrey Cheshire
WASHINGTON POST, 8/25/95, p. D6, Ken Ringle

CARRINGTON

A Gramercy Pictures release of a Polygram Filmed Entertainment presentation of a Freeway/Shedlo production in association with Cinea & Orsons and Le Studio Canal+. *Executive Producer:* Francis Boespflug, Philippe Carcassonne, and Fabienne Vonier. *Producer:* Ronald Shedlo and John McGrath. *Director:* Christopher Hampton. *Screenplay:* Christopher Hampton. *Based on the book "Lytton Strachey" by:* Michael Holroyd. *Director of Photography:* Denis Lenoir. *Editor:* George Akers. *Music:* Michael Nyman. *Choreographer:* Stuart Hopps. *Sound:* Peter Lindsay. *Sound Editor:* Dennis McTaggart. *Casting:* Fothergill & Lunn Casting. *Production Designer:* Caroline Amies. *Art Director:* Frank Walsh. *Costumes:* Penny Rose. *Make-up:* Chrissie Beveridge. *Running time:* 123 minutes. *MPAA Rating:* Not Rated.

CAST: Emma Thompson (Carrington); Jonathan Pryce (Lytton Strachey); Steven Waddington (Ralph Partridge); Samuel West (Gerald Brenan); Rufus Sewell (Mark Gertler); Penelope Wilton (Lady Ottoline Morrell); Janet McTeer (Vanessa Bell); Peter Blythe (Phillip Morrell); Jeremy Northam (Beacus Penrose); Alex Kingston (Frances Partridge); Sebastian Harcombe (Roger Senhouse); Richard Clifford (Clive Bell); David Ryall (Mayor); Stephen Boxer (Military Rep); Annabel Mullion (Mary Hutchinson); Gary Turner (Duncan Grant); Georgiana Dacombe (Marjorie Gertler); Helen Blatch (Nurse); Neville Phillips (Court Usher); Christopher Birch

(Dr. Starkey Smith); Daniel Betts (Porter); Simon Bye (Fly Driver); Marzio Idoni (Gondolier).

FILMS IN REVIEW, 1-2/96, p. 59, Barbara Cramer

It took almost 20 years for *Carrington* to reach the screen, but it was worth the wait. What a classy, genteel masterwork. Nurtured over these past decades by Oscar-winner Christopher Hampton (for his *Dangerous Liaisons* screenplay) the writer, also making his directorial debut, has keenly adapted "Lytton Strachey," Michael Holroyd's landmark profile of one of the linchpins of Britain's famed Bloomsbury Group.

So, to begin, the film's title is a misnomer. It is Strachey, the homosexual essayist and irreverent literary critic ("Eminent Victorians"), who is the centerpiece here and not Dora Carrington. Till now, the world might little note nor long remember the artistic endeavors of this obscure, mid-1920's English painter—quite talented, actually—and the titular heroine of this faintly precious, but thoroughly rewarding film bio. Played by Emma Thompson with her usual (and seemingly effortless) skill, her role as the shy, sexually indeterminate Carrington, Strachey's longtime companion, is really secondary to the virtuoso, gender-bending performance of Jonathan Pryce, who won Best Actor at 1995's Cannes Film Festival for his luminous portrayal.

The trim Welshman—probably as well known for his sophisticated TV pitches for the Infiniti as he is for his long list of stage and screen roles (he was the original Engineer in "Miss Saigon" and is currently filming *Evita* opposite Madonna)—is barely recognizable. Looking fey and frail, hidden behind prim spectacles, and a burly tweed coat—every bit like a schoolmarm with whiskers—his Strachey emerges as a most unlikely love object for the much younger Carrington.

Indeed, they are an odd couple. During their first meeting at a country estate, her androgynous mien immediately enlists his lecherous gaze. Understandably, with her bobbed pageboy haircut and scrubbed face, she's mistaken for a male. It's a short-lived comedy of errors, soon rectified, and their ensuing relationship evolves into 17 years of intense mutual devotion.

At 22, *Carrington* (she hated her first name) was 15 years his junior. Unlike Strachey, sex was never one of her prime predilections, and Hampton's script is rather unclear here as to whether their relationship was platonic or not.

Regardless, any shared intimacies with the gay literary gadfly persisted through her marriage and affairs with other men who became his lovers as well.

Theirs was a *La Ronde*, as told with crisp, clipped British accents. Such was the nature of Bloomsbury, the post-World War I circle of upper-class writers and artists (including Leonard and Virginia Woolf, Woolf's sister Vanessa Bell and husband Clive, E. M. Forster, and economist John Maynard Keynes among others), who extolled the many virtues of socialism and free speech, along with the vices of free love—lots of free love.

Those happy few, that band of brothers, iconoclasts all, typified a milieu that fostered both intellectual creativity and curiosity, and no matter how perverse, was geared to furthering a personal sense of "honesty." Accomplished, intellectual, and unconventional, they were the hippies of their day, with a bohemian lifestyle that embraced amour in all its possible permutations and combinations. Within their set, departures from Victorian-Edwardian norms were routinely accepted sans recriminations, with *ménage à trois* and *quatres* the rule rather than exception.

The film recounts those indulgences, though without the blur of groping bodies usually found nowadays on screen. Rather, Hampton's direction sensitively captures the couple, almost chastely coupling with others who move in and out of their lives over the years.

First, there's painter Rufus Sewell (Mark Gertler), a young hunk whose advances Ms. Carrington fends off. Ralph Partridge (Steven Waddington), the man she marries is next, though Strachey wants the dense but dashing war hero for himself, and the three set up housekeeping together. A few years later, she liaises with Gerald Brenan (Samuel West), her husband's best friend, and he joins their expanding household. To this group add Ralph's mistress and Strachey's varied male conquests. After a while, one loses count.

One affecting sequence finds Carrington standing outside her country home, poignantly staring into the windows, observing the pairing off of the lovers inside. In her adoring, almost childlike worship of Strachey, her reality is made quite clear: even unrequited, her commitment to him is total. Throughout her life, she can find no satisfaction with any other man.

Carrington spans the years from 1915 until Strachey's death in 1932. ("If this is dying, I don't think much of it.") Just before, he admits he always wanted to marry her, and as the bereaved artist is soon to write: "I find it virtually impossible to think that every day of my life, he will be away."

As might be expected, the ending is not upbeat. Yet this film, beautifully photographed by Denis Lenoir (*Monsieur Hire*) with precise set design and costumes by Caroline Amies (*In the Name of the Father*) and Penny Rose (*Shadowlands*), respectively, graphically, and with humor, captures moments that advance insight into an era long past. One other noteworthy facet is Michael Nyman's sweepingly romantic score. The talented composer—he created the music for Jane Campion's *The Piano*—once again confirms his genius.

Hampton's witty script is liberally sprinkled with Strachey's aphorisms, making this period piece deliciously enchanting. After all, he was master of the bon mots that literally blanket the dialogue, e.g., "people in love should never live together. They'll drive each other insane"; "there are times when I feel like I'm in a farce by Molière"; or, during World War I, on his learning German, "a most disagreeable language." "Why?" asks Carrington. "Suppose they win?" Strachey responds.

Withal, a most enjoyable, beautifully acted movie that rivals Merchant-Ivory at their best.

LOS ANGELES TIMES, 11/10/95, Calendar/p. 17, Kenneth Turan

How many kinds of romantic experience really exist, how many strange and unruly paths can the human heart stumble on in its search for happiness? For Lytton Strachey, his life with Dora Carrington gave evidence of "a great deal of a great many kinds of love." Thoughtful, dense with emotion, preeminently human, "Carrington" explores that intimate but maddening affair of the heart and reveals a thicket of conflicted passions seldom encountered on the screen.

Both Strachey, a celebrated writer whose 1918 "Eminent Victorians" revolutionized the modern writing of biography, and Carrington, a talented artist who shared his life from 1915 to 1932, were members of England's Bloomsbury group, a loose collection of like-minded creative souls. But neither knowledge of nor familiarity with Bloomsbury is necessary to appreciate this empathetic story of a quite unlikely pairing.

The only film to win two major awards at this year's Cannes Film Festival, including a special jury prize, "Carrington" stars Emma Thompson and Jonathan Pryce and is the directing debut of writer Christopher Hampton, who won an Oscar for the "Dangerous Liaisons" screenplay and a best book of a musical Tony for "Sunset Boulevard."

Hampton wrote the script here as well, a situation his director persona was surely grateful for. Well-stocked with engaging conversation and displaying a keen and caring eye for human foibles, Hampton's screenplay focuses not on the mechanics of Bloomsbury but on the peculiar conundrum of this singular relationship, which caused Carrington to feelingly write to Strachey, "no one will ever know the utter happiness of our life together."

Why wouldn't anyone know? Firstly because Strachey was a homosexual who found women's bodies "subtly offensive," while Carrington, after a somewhat asexual start, was passionately heterosexual. Though they lived together for more than a decade, neither had any intention of remaining celibate, and what "Carrington" particularly investigates is what happens when sexual drives and emotional needs are at cross-purposes.

The comprises Carrington and Strachey made, the pain their conflicting sexual entanglements caused each other, are all shown, underlining why Michael Holroyd, whose magisterial Strachey biography is the basis of Hampton's script, wrote that the couple's "amatory gyrations produced a tragi-comedy of intensely felt emotions."

Yet, and this is the story's fascination, the film equally emphasizes the deep connection these two had for each other, what Carrington called "the very big and devastating love" they shared. Though the sands of their various sexual relationships kept shifting, their care for each other was the one constant in their lives, a port they could always return to when the storms outside got too rough.

Essential in re-creating all this emotion are the film's pair of stars. Jonathan Pryce, best known for starring in "Miss Saigon" on stage, gives a superb performance, theatrical in the best sense, as the biting, trenchant Strachey, a precise and imposing figure capable of putting a malignant twist on even harmless phrases like "Oh, I see."

When he won the best actor award at Cannes, Pryce said that he probably had more fun playing Strachey's life than the man did living it, and that energy is always obvious. Exactly looking the part down to Strachey's famous standoffish beard, Pryce conveys the right combination of hauteur and tentativeness in a part bristling with direct quotations from Strachey's acerbic writings, like his thought that "idealists are so much trouble. You can never convince them there's no such thing as the ideal."

Because her title role is less flashy, it is possible to ignore how critical Emma Thompson is in all this. Her Carrington is a pulled together, centered performance, the solid counterpoint to Pryce's necessary flamboyance. With her evident sincerity and the ability to express shades of feeling without words, Thompson has the presence capable of making Carrington's considerable emotional gyrations sympathetic at all times.

Certainly the pair's initial encounter, at a country weekend at Vanessa Bell's house, was less than promising. Strachey at first mistakes her for a boy, tries to kiss her anyway, only to be told icily "would you mind not." Carrington is so irked she sneaks into Strachey's bedroom in the early morning, intent on cutting off his beard, but, in a delicate reverse twist on the Samson story, finds to her surprise that her feelings prevent her from doing so.

Thrown together a good deal because she is trying to flee from the attentions of painter Mark Gertler (an overwrought Rufus Sewell), Carrington and Strachey find, to their surprise as much as that of their friends, that they are ideal companions. They even move in together in a country mill at Tidmarsh, Berkshire, to Gertler's great horror. "He's a disgusting person," he fumes at Carrington, who calmly replies, "You always have to put up with something."

Over the course of their years together, what Carrington and Strachey most have to put up with is each other's taste in lovers. Perhaps the most curious situation the film details involves Ralph Partridge (Steven Waddington), a handsome blockhead who falls carnally for Carrington at the same time that Strachey falls platonically for him. "Ladies in love with buggers, and buggers in love with womanizers, and the price of coal going up too," Strachey wrote to Carrington with typical wit. "Where will it all end?"

Helped by Michael Nyman's energetic score and strategic use of Schubert's String Quintet in C, "Carrington" provides the kind of rich and thoughtful pleasures not, often encountered. Its story of a love that could not fit into conventional boundaries is as intelligent and idiosyncratic as the performances that give it life.

NEW YORK, 12/4/95, p. 129, David Denby

I expect that very few people in America now read Lytton Strachey, the author of *Eminent Victorians* and the man who perhaps more than anyone else created the twentieth-century perception of the Victorians as morally overbearing and hypocritical. But even those unfamiliar with Strachey's biographies may be fascinated by Jonathan Pryce's impersonation of him in *Carrington*. Pryce creates what might be called the charisma of diffidence—he is largely silent and hardly asserts himself, yet every word is memorable. Tall, with unending arms and immense flapping hands, a Russian monk's beard hiding as much face as possible, this Strachey is an improbable, unbeautiful figure, a fussy, awkward intellectual wraith. In the pantheon of homosexual wits, Strachey, I suppose, stands halfway between Oscar Wilde and Joe Orton: The style is mandarin camp, with a touch of obscenity. The twittering remarks, emerging from long silences, are often very funny. And Pryce pulls together the contraries in this man and makes him a plausible human being, both selfish and kindly, remote and loving.

However unresponsive physically, Strachey inspired an extraordinary loyalty in the young painter Dora Carrington, who set up house with him in 1918 and lived with him in platonic bliss until his death in 1932. As the subservient Carrington, Emma Thompson, clumping about in shapeless, drab clothes, stares a great deal; Thompson, normally so sure, seems unable to decide whether Carrington was a noble free spirit or a self-sacrificing booby. She plays her both ways at once, and at times, she comes close to embarrassing us. As much as Pryce's performance is all of a piece, hers is all fragments. The movie also makes a largely unsuccessful attempt to straighten out the complicated erotic arrangements (both Strachey and Carrington had numerous lovers, sometimes sharing the same man), and such minor Bloomsbury figures as Ralph Partridge and Gerald Brenan hang around for a while, passing in and out of various beds, and disappear.

Christopher Hampton, who wrote the screenplay (from Michael Holroyd's biography) and also assumed the director's chair when experienced directors stayed away from the project, wants mainly to celebrate the originality and placid beauty of the long Carrington-Strachey relationship. The movie features scene after scene of the two of them sitting outdoors in near silence, Strachey folded into a chair, reading a slender volume, Carrington sprawled at his feet with her sketch pad. We may be unclear much of the time about where the money for the lovely country houses comes from, or what either wanted from the other except peace and quiet, but it looks like an awfully nice life.

NEW YORK POST, 11/10/95, p. 49, Thelma Adams

"If this is dying. I don't think much of it," biographer Lytton Strachey pronounces on his deathbed in "Carrington." Wit-starved audiences will drink in his every bon mot, turned to perfection by Infiniti pitchman Jonathan Pryce.

Pryce earned the best-actor award at the 1995 Cannes Film Festival for his arch yet aching portrayal of Strachey. The author, a footnote in English literary history was a member of the Bloomsbury group that included novelist Virginia Woolf and economist John Maynard Keynes.

Buried under a holly bush of a beard, Pryce's Strachey is the sickly child grown up into a fragile but intellectually charged adulthood. A mama's boy and homosexual, Strachey reveled in the Bohemian life in the early 20th century, most often from behind a pen or reclining on a divan with his legs covered by an afghan (if "Carrington" is to be believed).

Why call this movie "Carrington"? While Christopher Hampton drew on Michael Holyroyd's biography of Strachey, the writer/director claims to have shifted the focus onto the lesser-known painter Dora Carrington (Emma Thompson).

Carrington rakishly dropped the dreary Dora and was Strachey's constant companion from the mid-teens until his 1932 death. The heart of Hampton's drama is the profound, if frustrating, love affair between the straight artist and the gay writer.

This romance explores the divide between lust and love, celebrating an unconventional alternative to man and wife with '60s-era fervor.

Wrapped in frumpy cardigans, Thompson's Carrington sports a Prince Valiant bob and a pigeon-toed stance. The British actress ("Much Ado About Nothing") does not deliver her usual charismatic performance, partly because the part is sadly underwritten.

The painter left Hampton without witticisms to cut and paste into his script. She remains opaque and no match for Strachey. Her adoration of the gay author, exposed with such abject servility as "I'm your pen wiper, use me," begins to cloy.

Carrington depends on production design to externalize the artist's inner life. The homes she keeps for Strachey are an artful jumble of lavender walls and pink ceilings, painted bathtubs and mock-naive murals. You know when you are catalog-shopping the array of mismatched mugs and plates displayed in the buffet that something is missing in the foreground.

Hampton, the man responsible for the script of the abysmal "Total Eclipse," another tour of torrid literary tangles past, makes a similar dramatic misstep here, although "Carrington" is by far the better film.

The filmmaker knows a steamy scholarly story when he sees it. But he doesn't shape the material to maximize his blending of high art and pop culture kitsch, After establishing an unusual relationship, he proceeds chronologically from one uninteresting lover of Carrington's to another, stretching out the story far beyond anything profound he has to say about his leads.

The painter Carrington is a maze of complexity compared to the depiction of her husband and many lovers, played by Steven Waddington, Rufus Sewell, Samuel West and Jeremy Northam. With straight males like these—bland, jealous, shallow and brutish—it's no wonder Carrington bonded with Strachey.

The sexual calisthenics between Thompson and her many partners are explicit but unerotic. Poor Emma gamely sweats and pants, her breasts squeezed against bed or board, but where is her passion? Hampton undercuts his ambitious drama of complex human relationships by reducing "Carrington" to an episode of "BBC Blue."

NEWSDAY, 11/10/95, Part II/p. B2, John Anderson

"No one will ever know the utter happiness of our life together," Dora Carrington wrote of Lytton Strachey, shortly after his death and just before hers. Unfortunately, she was quite right. For all the style and ardor of Christopher Hampton's "Carrington," it is the essence of their love—which also happens to be the subject of the film—that proves elusive. What was it that made Carrington (Emma Thompson) the straight painter and Strachey (Jonathan Pryce) the gay writer, so crucial to each other? What made their love so strong, so vital—so important that it became the topic of a major motion picture? What about it, exactly, produced such "utter happiness"? We never really know—although, to Hampton's credit perhaps, we'd like to.

Love is eternal, and evanescent, and when you've decided to make a film about an unorthodox relationship—one that endured 17 years and a number of intermediary liaisons—it's best if you get to the point. Yes, Carrington and Strachey were unconventional—even though, as members of the Bloomsbury group (Strachey was its sun, Carrington a minor moon), bohemianism was required. Thanks to their association with Bloomsbury's single genius, Virginia Woolf, they and other subordinate groupies have become romantic figures in a romantic era. But Hampton isn't interested in the group; Woolf never appears, and her sister, Vanessa Bell (Janet McTeer), is seen only fleetingly. Hampton prefers to put Carrington and Strachey at center stage, presumably because their love transcended conformity and resisted biology. And then he fails to give it a pulse.

What adds to this problem, paradoxically, is also the movie's principal asset: Jonathan Pryce, who as the imperiously tart and charming Lytton Strachey, often considers Carrington with a querulous eye: What, he seems to ask, is she going on about? Pryce gives a glorious performance, fully realized and fully possessed. From the moment he gets off the train to Vanessa's, presumes someone will carry his bags and immediately strikes up an intimate conversation with whatever young man is around, he captivates. World War I is raging, and Lytton's scene before the conscription board, where he is a committed and comic conscientious objector, is wonderful. Incidentally, you'd never know it was Pryce if you didn't know it was Pryce—which may not be the essence of a great performance but is a heck of a start.

Thompson, conversely, fills the eye with tics and slouches, wide-eyed fretfulness and slack-jawed dismay, striving hard where Pryce merely acts. To some degree, of course, this is the part as written: Carrington cares more; she has to. For his part, Strachey's insouciance says he's more ready for it all to end, and soon, which may be the product of being homosexual in an age ... well, any age thus far.

The film is divided into chapters, all with dates ("1915: Lytton and Carrington" stages their meeting at Vanessa's, where Strachey inexplicably mistakes the hippy Emma Thompson for a young boy) and some with the names of the other players in their small circle of love and lust. "1916-1918: Gertler" chronicles the randy pursuit by Mark Gertler (Rufus Sewell) of Carrington, who isn't having any. When Mark enlists Carrington's new confidant, Strachey, as his aide-de-seduction, it leads to a kind of ad-hoc Committee to Deflower Dora, featuring Lady Ottoline Morrell (Penelope Wilton) and her brother Phillip (Peter Blythe), and eventually introduces Carrington to painful, insensitive heterosexual acts that Hampton clearly finds abominable, or boring.

No, Carrington wants Strachey, even though it's impossible; their attempts at "the physical" are failures. Her own hormones do cry out and, are relieved: first with Ralph Partridge (Steven Waddington), an Adonisian dullard whom Strachey and Carrington find equally attractive; Hampton doesn't exactly ignore the three-way attraction, but Partridge apparently slept with both of them, and it's left unsaid. Hampton does give us the marriage of Ralph and Dora, though, which she entered presumably so Strachey would have more reason to stick around. Later, Carrington beds Ralph's best friend, Gerald Brenan (Samuel West), and then forgets him.

Sexual ambiguity was nothing to the Bloomsburians: Strachey nearly married Virginia Woolf in 1909, and Woolf had a much-celebrated affair later on with Vita Sackville-West. Merrily they all did roll around. It is, however, Hampton's fixation: Dora, for all her supposed standing as an artist, leads a life devoid of art. Outside of a few scenes at her easel, which provides an excuse to place the characters on the English countryside, she is reduced almost to an appendage of Lytton's. What was it that made her so fascinating? Was it her slavish devotion? Plenty of relationships have been based on as little. But they aren't particularly cinematic.

NEWSWEEK, 11/20/95, p. 91, David Ansen

No screenwriter could possibly have invented the love story at the heart of *Carrington*, Christopher Hampton's fascinating, moving depiction of the bond between painter Dora Carrington (Emma Thompson) and Bloomsbury giant Lytton Strachey (Jonathan Pryce). Their rule-breaking relationship—mostly platonic, but allowing each to have many other lovers—defies the easy psychologizing and tidy dramaturgy that most movies rely on. And that's why it's a great, fresh subject: in its best scenes, "Carrington" takes us to places of the heart we haven't been, exploring Strachey's credo that there are "a great deal of a great many kinds of love."

Sickly, eccentric, acerbic and homosexual, Strachey is taken with Carrington at first sight—he thinks the androgynous girl is a boy. She falls in love with him at an equally odd moment: about to clip the sleeping Lytton's beard with scissors to punish him for making a pass at her, she's overcome with a passion that will determine the rest of their lives.

Writer-director Hampton, using Michael Holroyd's superb biography of Strachey as his bible, has only two hours in which to condense one of the more byzantine bohemian arrangements in history. Carrington (she hated her first name) had many suitors: first the Jewish Painter Mark Gertler (Rufus Sewell), driven half mad by her refusal to sleep with him. She then marries the athletic ex-soldier Ralph Partridge (Steven Waddington)—as much to please Lytton, who also adores him—and lives with both men in a happy *ménage à trois*. Soon she takes her husband's best friend, the writer Gerald Brenan (Samuel West), as her lover. Later she, Partridge and Strachey complicate matters with further affairs (the key omission is Carrington's liaisons with other women).

What could have become a sniggering sex farce is instead a grave yet deliciously witty portrait of two inseparable but independent souls. With so much erotic turf to cover, it's almost inevitable that the later affairs are sketched in perfunctorily. "Carrington" bites off more than it can chew, but it succeeds where it counts, in illuminating Lytton and Carrington's singular passion.

Strachey, the bitchily brilliant author of "Eminent Victorians," wasn't an easy man to like, and Pryce honors his prickliness. It's an astonishing performance that captures both the fussiness and the diffident courage of the man. Needless to say, he has the best lines—Strachey's own words. Pryce doesn't try to warm his character's cold edges, and yet by the end we understand why this improbable love object—next to whom all the other men seem like puppies—warrants Carrington's adoration.

Thompson strips herself down to a simpler, bolder mode to play a woman at once submissive and willful, who found her strength living in one man's shadow while forcing her other lovers to bend to her rules. It's the more mysterious, difficult role, and Thompson, finding Carrington's ungainly grace, makes her poignantly believable. This is Hampton's impressive debut as a director; he tells his story with a tactful English reserve that allows deep feelings to find their own way to the surface. He's given a great assist from Michael Nyman's score. His music is beautiful, discordant and hauntingly sad, much like "Carrington" itself.

SIGHT AND SOUND, 9/95, p. 46, Geoffrey Macnab

Winter, southern England, 1915. Writer Lytton Strachey arrives at the country house of artist Vanessa Bell and her husband. He notices an unusual, boyish-looking character frolicking in the garden. This turns out to be a young artist, Dora Carrington.

As they walk along the clifftops, Strachey attempts to kiss Carrington. She is repulsed, and later retaliates by creeping into his room by dead of night with a pair of scissors to cut off his beard. She decides against it, and the two become fast friends. Mark Gertler, another painter, is obsessed with Carrington and determined to sleep with her. She eventually consents, but not before she has declared her love for Strachey, who is gay. She and Strachey set up house in the country. Carrington takes a lover, a handsome young soldier named Reginald Partridge. Strachey falls for Partridge, suggests he change his name to Ralph and invites him to move in. Carrington, fearful that Strachey wouldn't consent to live with her alone, marries Partridge.

She starts an affair with Partridge's best friend, Gerald Brenan. Partridge, far from a faithful husband himself, is bitter. Carrington cares little about either man's jealousy. It is Strachey she loves. Strachey's book, *Eminent Victorians*, is published to enormous acclaim. With the proceeds, he buys a bigger house, and also starts an affair with a much younger man. Partridge leaves

Carrington for another woman but Carrington is still happy to live with Strachey. He helps her cope with an unwanted pregnancy and she consoles him when his love affair breaks up.

In 1932, Strachey falls ill. Carrington becomes his devoted nurse. One day, when he's lying in bed, seemingly talking in his sleep, he confesses that he loved Carrington all along and bitterly regrets not marrying her. Shortly afterwards, he dies. Carrington decides she can't bear life without him and commits suicide with a shotgun.

Although inspired by Michael Holroyd's celebrated biography of Lytton Strachey, Carrington makes no attempt to portray Strachey's world in full. Its main concern is his relationship with Dora Carrington, and events are seen as much from her perspective as from his. The narrowness of focus is one of the film's strengths. Despite occasional glimpses of such sacred cows of the Bloomsbury Group as Duncan Grant, Lady Ottoline Morrell and Vanessa Bell, there is little wallowing in nostalgia, and a merciful absence of dialogue of the "How do you do I'm Maynard Keynes" variety. Carrington and Strachey's rejection of aristocratic high-jinks is spelled out early on, both by their caustic reaction to one of Lady Ottoline's hearty mid-war garden parties and by their decision to retreat from London's fashionable salons to the countryside.

Visually, we're in the realm of heritage cinema: country houses, gardens and pictorial English landscapes are foregrounded; costume and production design are intricately detailed. Hampton opts for a literary structure. The film opens with a lengthy intertitle and unfolds as a series of chapters. Much of the dialogue and voice-over narration is taken from Carrington and Strachey's diaries, and from the letters they exchanged. There's occasionally something a little arch about Strachey's gnomic one-liners on such subjects as semen, death or posterity. (Jonathan Pryce claims to have based the voice for the character on a mix of Malcolm Muggeridge and Ned Sherrin, and speaks in clipped, high-pitched tones.) However, despite the literary-heritage trappings that come with the territory, Hampton never loses sight of the love affair at the core of the story.

"His knees," Carrington once replied when asked what attracted her to Strachey. Theirs was certainly a very unlikely romance. He was a sagacious, owl-like man of letters, a confirmed homosexual who rarely displayed any feeling, while she was an impulsive young artist. On the surface, this seems like another of those quintessentially English liaisons of the sort celebrated in such recent pictures as The Remains of the Day and Shadowlands. (Presumably, the success of those films enabled Carrington, which was written in the mid 1970s, finally to be made.)

But there is much more comedy here than either James Ivory or Richard Attenborough were able to bring to their stiff-upper-lipped weepies. Strachey's beard as much as his knees is the key to the romance. Not long after the they first meet, Carrington creeps into his room by dead of night, intending to cut it off as a prank. He wakes up just before she begins to snip, looks into her eyes, and she is mesmerised. As a couple, they're altogether too eccentric to fit comfortably into the stereotype of emotionally repressed lovers.

Strachey is, almost by definition, odd, but, compared to the other examples of English masculinity on display, he seems a paragon of commonsense. Hampton takes great pleasure in satirising the behaviour of the various boyfriends who flit through Carrington's life. There's Mark Gertler, the East End painter (played by Rufus Sewell in manic groove) who comes across as a ridiculous caricature of the conventional romantic artist; there's her husband, 'Ralph' Partridge, an upright, unimaginative Englishman with all the conversational ability of the average "Norwegian dentist;" and there's her lover, Gerald Brenan, an intense, D. H. Lawrence-type who wants to run away with her to Spain.

Most of the action takes place in rooms or gardens. There are few big set-pieces. Hampton, roped in to direct his own script when Mike Newell withdrew from the project at the last minute, avoids Merchant Ivory-style grandeur. He places as much emphasis on looks and glances between the characters, on Michael Nyman's score and on Denis Lenoir's lighting, as on his own dialogue. In one telling scene, an excluded Carrington stands outside at dusk, looking in at the windows of the house as the various couples (Strachey with his new boyfriend, Partridge with his new mistress) prepare for bed. Hampton also has an eye for detail: after Strachey's death, Carrington is shown burning his possessions, and there's a little close-up of his round spectacles on the fire.

Ultimately, Carrington relies on its two central performances. Both are mannered—given the quiddities of the characters they're playing, they could hardly be otherwise. Pryce, pipe-smoking, swathed in tweed and with that extraordinary beard, may strike an irritating note with his affected diction, but shows such precision of gesture and such gentleness that he manages to make what easily could have been a caricature immensely moving. Emma Thompson is hardly a natural androgyne, but she too is effective, capturing both Carrington's fiery non-conformism and her vulnerability, her bafflement at her own all-consuming obsession with a man she has next to nothing in common with. Wipe off the high culture gloss and period sheen, and the film emerges as a delicately observed, very affecting melodrama.

TIME, 11/13/95, p. 118, Richard Schickel

Is it the good turtle soup or only the mock? Or to put the question more directly, Is the lengthy, unconsummated love affair between Dora Carrington (Emma Thompson) and Lytton Strachey (Jonathan Pryce) one of the great tragic romances of our century or just another of those neurotic dithers the Bloomsbury crowd was always working themselves into?

Christopher Hampton, the playwright who wrote and directed *Carrington*, obviously believes it was the former. Yet his account of the relationship between the half-forgotten painter and the homosexual who turned biography into a modernist art form is distant and gingerly, respectful and respectable. Reason tells us that there must have been something more needy and smothering in her nature, something more grasping and careless in his, than Hampton shows us. After all, Dora did marry a handsome youth not because she was smitten with him but because Lytton was. Yet their ménage à trois is presented blandly, and her forays in search of sexual satisfaction have little dramatic consequence. Mostly this is a movie in which people take soulful country strolls or wait expectantly for Lytton to lob a withering epigram.

Pryce is awfully good at this, and his hard, gleaming performance as Strachey—a physically frail, morally strong man who never asks for sympathy but somehow elicits it—almost redeems the film. Thompson, however, keeps undoing it. Hers is a commonsensical presence, and try as she may, she cannot catch the fever of hopeless love. Or the suicidal despair to which Carrington eventually came. You want her—and the movie—to rattle the teacups with rage. But they never do.

VILLAGE VOICE, 11/14/95, p. 90, Georgia Brown

The man who looks like a bearded stork pokes his head out the train window. Although it's clearly not winter, he sports a wool hat as well—as a muffler coiled nooselike around his neck. Coyly, this fabled creature, never known to lift his own bag, appraises the loitering cabbies, setting on a fresh-faced lad with a whip. It's on this visit to Vanessa and Clive's that Lytton Strachey (Jonathan Pryce) will be introduced to (Dora) Carrington (Emma Thompson). Or so Christopher Hampton's Carrington would have it. In fact "the Strache," as the foremost prince of Bloomsbuggery was fondly known, first encountered Carrington at Virginia and Leonard's, but that locale would not have provided the occasion for the following:

Lytton, examining three young figures on the lawn: "Vanessa, who on earth is that ravishing boy!"

Vanessa, archly: "I take it you're not referring to either of my sons!"

No, the object of scrutiny is the fetchingly awkward Carrington, a young painter whose thick hair has been chopped Buster Brown-style to reveal the nape of the neck. (Virginia Woolf, who kept her bun, liked to call the hair rebels "cropheads.") Thompson wittily impersonates Carrington by pitching forward on pigeon toes, letting her jaw hang slack, and furrowing her brow as if she has only the vaguest grasp of the language. Such ingenuiousness captivates Lytton who, once she expresses a fervent desire to be a man, tries vainly to kiss her. That night, she creeps into his bedroom intending to cut off his beard. "To punish you," she whispers. (True story, apparently.)

Thus the pair's lifelong intimacy begins. She needs to minister; he to be ministered unto. The old patriarchy under the guise of new bohemianism. She would create perfect environments for him to nurture his talents. By not desiring her, he would always remind her that she was not a boy.

The first third of *Carrington*—the amusing part—relies heavily on Pryce-less views of Queen Lytton: Lytton knitting, Lytton jumping at the sound of a cork's pop ("Can you imagine what the *war* must be like!"), Lytton elaborately blowing up a large rubber hemorrhoid cushion before seating himself on it (he's been called to defend his conscientious-objector status to a military tribunal). Crossing his legs: "I'm a martyr to piles."

Then there are the wry pronouncements. "When it comes to a creature with a cunt, I'm infinitely *disorienté*." "I'm a perfectly respectable buffer of modest means. This is before *Eminent Victorians* gives him adequate means. (Having only read about Strachey, imagine my surprise, on taking down *Queen Victoria*, to discover a perfectly ordinary writer of popular bios.)

At Cannes, this Fussy Man portrayal earned Pryce a Best Actor prize. Seeing the film a second time, I'm more impressed by Thompson's Carrington—eclipsed, as she subject was in life, because speech is not her thing. Once the tale turns painful, and it does, Hampton seems loath to put off the audience by actually representing anguish, although he can just bring himself to suggest certain occasions for it. (The death scenes, accompanied by Michael Nyman's grating score, are quite clumsy.) Conveniently, Hampton omits the fact that Ralph Partridge (played here by Steven Waddington)—whom Carrington marries to keep Lytton on the premises—slept with Lytton, too, or that Partridge had several affairs before Carrington fell for his friend Gerald Brenan (here, Samuel West). In this version Partridge is firmly hetero and doting. The movie stays at the level of quaint.

Mark Gertler (Carrington's jealous boyfriend), fuming: "He's a disgusting pervert!" Carrington (subdued monotone) "You always have to put up with something."

For some reason, Hampton denies in publicity interviews that his protagonists belong to Bloomsbury, but they do, of course, and so do their ethics and aesthetics. Like Vanessa Bell's and Duncan Grant's, Carrington's decorative art—nude-strewn murals, fancy fireplaces—is directly derived from Roger Fry. And it's the continuing appeal of that cozy coterie which will attract audiences to this gay '90s *La Cage aux Folles*.

Also reviewed in:
CHICAGO TRIBUNE, 11/17/95, Friday/p. H, Michael Wilmington
NEW REPUBLIC, 12/4/95, p. 26, Stanley Kauffmann
NEW YORK TIMES, 10/13/95, p. C1, Janet Maslin
NEW YORKER, 11/27/95, p. 106, Anthony Lane
VARIETY, 5/22-28/95, p. 95, Derek Elley
WASHINGTON POST, 11/17/95, p. F7, Rita Kempley
WASHINGTON POST, 11/17/95, Weekend/p. 44, Desson Howe

CASINO

A Universal Pictures and Syalis D.A. & Legende Enterprises release of a De Fina/Cappa production. *Producer:* Barbara De Fina. *Director:* Martin Scorsese. *Screenplay:* Nicholas Pileggi and Martin Scorsese. *Based on the novel by:* Nicholas Pileggi. *Director of Photography:* Robert Richardson. *Editor:* Thelma Schoonmaker. *Music Consultant:* Robbie Robertson *Music Editor:* Bobby Mackston. *Sound:* Charles M. Wilborn. *Sound Editor:* Skip Lievsay. *Casting:* Ellen Lewis. *Production Designer:* Dante Ferretti. *Art Director:* Jack G. Taylor, Jr. *Set Designer:* Steven Schwartz and Daniel Ross. *Set Decorator:* Rick Simpson. *Set Dresser:* Omar Abderrahman, Angelo Moreno, Seyton Pooley, John A. Scott III, and David Snodgrass. *Special Effects:* Paul Lombardi. *Costumes:* Rita Ryack and John Dunn. *Make-up:* Jo-Anne Smith-Ojeil. *Make-up (Robert De Niro):* Ilona Herman. *Make-up (Joe Pesci):* James Sarzotti. *Make-up (Sharon Stone):* Tricia Sawyer. *Stunt Coordinator:* Doug Coleman and Daniel W. Barringer. *Running time:* 170 minutes. *MPAA Rating:* R.

CAST: Robert De Niro (Sam "Ace" Rothstein); Sharon Stone (Ginger McKenna); Joe Pesci (Nicky Santoro); James Woods (Lester Diamond); Don Rickles (Billy Sherbert); Alan King (Andy Stone); Kevin Pollak (Phillip Green); L.Q. Jones (Pat Webb); Dick Smothers (Senator); Frank Vincent (Frank Marino); John Bloom (Don Ward); Pasquale Cajano (Remo Gaggi); Melissa Prophet (Jennifer Santoro); Bill Allison (John Nance); Vinny Vella (Artie Piscano); Oscar Goodman (Himself); Catherine Scorsese (Piscano's Mother); Phillip Suriano (Dominick

Santoro); Erika Von Tagen (Older Amy); Frankie Avalon (Himself); Steve Allen (Himself); Jayne Meadows (Herself); Jerry Vale (Himself); Joseph Rigano (Vincent Borelli); Gene Ruffini (Vinny Forlano); Dominick Grieco (Americo Capelli); Richad Amalfitano and Richard F. Strafella (Casino Executives); Casper Molee and David Leavitt (Counters); Peter Conti (Arthur Capp); Catherine T. Scorsese (Piscano's Daughter); Steve Vignari (Beeper); Rick Crachy (Chastised Dealer); Larry E. Nadler (Lucky Larry); Paul Herman (Gambler in Phone Booth); Salvatore Petrillo (Old Man Capo); Joey De Pinto (Stabbed Gambler); Heidi Keller (Blonde at Bar); Millicent Sheridan (Senator's Hooker); Nobu Matsuhisa (Ichikawa); Toru Nagai (Ichikawa's Associate); Barbara Spanjers (Ticket Agent); Dom Angelo (Craps Dealer); Joe Molinaro (Shift Manager); Ali Pirouzkar (High Roller); Frankie Allison (Craps Dealer); Jeff Scott Anderson (Parking Valet); Jennifer M. Abbott (Cashier); Frank Washko, Jr. (Parking Valet); Christian A. Azzinaro (Little Nicky, 7 yrs.); Robert C. Tetzlaff (Customs Agent); Anthony Russell (Bookie); Carol Wilson (Classroom Nun); Joe Lacoco (Detective Bob Johnson); John Manca (Wiseguy Eddy); Ronald Maccone (Wiseguy Jerry); Buck Stephens (Credit Clerk); Joseph Reidy (Winner); Joe La Due (Signaler); Fred Smith, Sonny D'Angelo, and Greg Anderson (Security Guards); Stuart Nisbet (L.A. Banker); Tommy DeVito (Crooked Poker Dealer); Frank Adonis (Rocky); Joseph Bono (Moosh); Craig Vincent (Cowboy); Daniel P. Conte (Doctor Dan); Paul Dottore (Slim); Richard T. Smith (Security Guard/Cowboy); David Rose (David); Jonathan Kraft (Jonathan); Michael McKensie Pratt (Showgirls Stage Manager); Patti James, Ruth Gillis, and Carol Cardwell (Country Club Women); Dean Casper (Elderly Man); Nan Brennan, Karyn Amalfitano, and C.C. Carr (Wives); Davvid Varriale (Flirting Executive); Carol Krolick (Slapping Woman); Frank Regich (Slapped Man); Herb Schwartz (Maitre d'); Max Raven (Bernie Blue); Clem Caserta (Sal Fusco); Jed Mills (Jack Hardy); Janet Denti (Receptionist); Cameron Milzer (Secretary); Leain Vashon (Bellman); Jim Morgan Williams (Pit Boss); Brian Le Baron (Valet Parker); Mortiki Yerushalmi (Jewelry Store Owner); Mufid M. Khoury and Khosrow Abrishami (Jeweler Fences); Richard Riehle (Charlie Clark); Mike Maines and Bobby Hitt (Cops in Restaurant); Shellee Renee (Showgirl in Parking Lot); Alfred Nittoli (Chastised Gambler); Carl Ciarfalio (Tony Dogs); Jack R. Orend (Baker); Linda Perri (Ace's Secretary); Ffolliotte Le Coque (Anna Scott); J. Charles Thompson (Judge); Michael Paskevich, Mike Weatherford, and Eric Randall (Reporters at Airport); Gwen Castaldi (Business Week Reporter); Brian Reddy and Roy Conrad (Board Investigators); Mike Bradley and Dave Courvouisier (TV Newsmen); George Comando (Piscano's Brother-in-Law); Andy Jarrell (Commissioner Bales); Robert Sidell and Tyde Kierney (Control Board Members); Paige Novodor (Female Newscaster); Claudia Haro (Trudy/Announcer); Sasha Semenoff (Orchestra Leader); Gil Dova (Juggler); George w. Allf (FBI Agent); Madeline Parquegte (Woman Black Jack Dealer); Gino Bertin (Maitre'd); Mitch Kolpan and Csaba Maczala (Detectives); Peter Sugden (Lip Reader); Rudy Guerrero (Maitre'd at Disco); Randy Sutton and Jeff Corbin (Cops at Ace's House); Sly Smith, Joe Anastasi, F. Marcus Casper, Richard Wagner and David Arcerio (FBI Agents); Jeffrey Azzinaro (Nicky Jr., 10 yrs.); Carrie Cipollini (Piscano's Wife); Loren Stevens and Gary C. Rainey (Agents, Piscano Raid); Haven Earle Haley (Judge); Sam Wilson (Ambulance Driver); Michael Toney (Fat Sally).

CHRISTIAN SCIENCE MONITOR, 11/24/95, p. 12, David Sterritt

"Casino" hits the screen with dazzling credentials. It's directed by Martin Scorsese, regarded by many as the most gifted American filmmaker of his generation. He wrote the screenplay with Nicholas Pileggi, who also inspired "GoodFellas," one of Scorsese's most inventive pictures.

And as they used to say in Hollywood, whatta cast! Robert De Niro continues the long Scorsese partnership that ranges from "Mean Streets" and "Taxi Driver" through "GoodFellas" and beyond. Sharon Stone gives her most fully realized screen performance to date. Joe Pesci revives the lowdown intensity that makes him unique among today's actors. Smaller roles are filled to perfection by talents as different as Alan King, James Woods, and the inimitable Don Rickles.

It would be regrettable if all these gifted folks poured their abilities into a picture that promoted gambling, especially in the current American climate, when governments and criminals seem equally eager to snatch the money of people who haven't learned the odds are always against them. "Casino" fills the screen with glitz-and-glitter gambling joints, but the story is full of warnings about who profits from them—namely, the shady characters who set them up for precisely that purpose—and if you miss the point, De Niro's narration makes it perfectly plain that only insiders stand a chance of avoiding empty pockets in the end.

De Niro's character also illustrates this lesson. His name is Sam "Ace" Rothstein, and he's the newly installed chief of a major Las Vegas casino. Since it's unlikely his checkered past would allow him to obtain a license, he runs the place in secret, publicly presenting himself as a second-rank administrator. The film chronicles his rise to power, his marriage to a beautiful but deeply troubled drug abuser, and his relationships with underworld types like Lester Diamond, his wife's former lover, and Nicky Santoro, a childhood friend with a penchant for dangerous behavior.

As pure filmmaking, "Casino" is as brilliant as anything Scorsese has done in years. His camera swoops, pans, glides, cuts, and Steadicams its way through immaculately designed sets and atmospherically chosen locations, charging the story with a visual energy that's downright exhilarating at times.

Meanwhile the sound track bubbles—with golden oldies—many from the '50s, although the story takes place mainly in the '70s—that will have spectators tapping their toes when they aren't busy ducking the graphic violence that punctuates the action.

For all the excitement of its sounds and images, though, the brilliance of "Casino" is ultimately as cool and superficial as the jewels one of its crooked characters likes to steal. The episodic story never picks up a full head of steam, and if you've seen the very similar "GoodFellas" you'll find more nostalgia than novelty here, especially when Pesci's unstable character was on the screen. Stone's excellent acting is undercut by the fact that her character has little to do but intoxicate herself and stagger around. And no other woman in this male-dominated movie gets to do even that much.

The production values of "Casino" are consistently superb, thanks to cinematographer Robert Richardson—best known for several Oliver Stone movies—and a list of top-notch technical wizards including editor Thelma Schoonmaker, designer Dante Ferretti, and the team of Elaine and Saul Bass, who designed the eye-enticing credits.

You couldn't ask for more creative or energetic contributions. What you could request, especially from an epic with a three-hour running time, is a more original story with a deeper set of values on its mind.

FILM QUARTERLY, Spring 1996, p. 43, Karen Jaehne

Just as Warren Beatty's *Bugsy* said more about Hollywood than Las Vegas, so the recent spate of Vegas-bashing films reveal Hollywood's need to displace its self-loathing. British director Mike Figgis's *Leaving Las Vegas* exploited dead-end assumptions as a substitute for plotline, while Dutch director Paul Verhoeven's *Showgirls* managed to be both lurid and plastic. Of course, Americans wrote both these scripts, but the most interesting things about Las Vegas managed to escape them for the same reason they escaped Nicholas Pileggi, whose script for *Casino* was based on his own book, *Casino: Love and Honor in Las Vegas*. Las Vegas has a life of its own. It's not that different from most single-industry cities in America. Detroit, D.C., L.A., and L.V., to name but a few, are obsessed with themselves and able to become the obsession of others.

Martin Scorsese's *Casino* is a vile twist on "Nostalgia ain't what it used to be." Formally structured as a memoir of the rise and fall of bookie Sam "Ace" Rothstein (Robert De Niro), the movie looks back at an artless if not innocent world. In the city's golden era, blood and money flowed like water through the Nevada desert; hot-blooded gangsters ran casinos; and racketeering was the blood sport of kings. Once, guys like Anthony "Tony the Ant" Spilotro, reconstructed here as Nicky Santoro (Joe Pesci), could shake down Vegas like a monkey in a coconut tree and put a bullet through a recalcitrant mug before you could say "blackjack." The film tries to shock us with an inferno of mogul mania, mobster mayhem, and meretricious modernity. The narration sentimentalizes the past as we hear the cynical voice-over of Ace Rothstein, who's an amalgam of San Diego bookie/retired casino boss Allen Glick and an actual undesirable of the casino crowd, Frank "Lefty" Rosenthal (both of whom chatted at length with Pileggi for his book). The movie's shell game is this: Ace is sent to manage a mob property; his old buddy Nicky shows up as an enthusiastic enforcer; Ace marries a Vegas hooker, and the three of them form a wobbly triangle. Along the way we discover the strange world of gaming casinos, which is presented as too bizarre for any meaningful connection to be made between the cheap melodrama of Vegas and the minimalist degeneracy of state-run lotteries.

De Niro (who never really leaves the actor behind to arrive at the character of Ace), has been a notorious bookie and now takes his job of running the Tangiers—a casino on The Strip loosely modeled on the Sands—too seriously. He's proud of his club and only a hair's breadth from corporate. The first half hour of the film is devoted to the mechanics of a casino: the counting room, the chutes rattling with coins, the savvy placement of tables and machines, the various types of gamblers, and the hierarchy from dealer through pit boss to the "eye in the sky" that watches everything. The clever braiding of information and zero-degree drama in this introduction leads us to accept Ace in a positive role as hands-on C.E.O.

Woven through the tapestry of this enterprise is a thumbnail sketch of Ginger (Sharon Stone). Stone's flawless physique makes her a vertiginously high-class hooker, a perfection of plasticity she effectively undercuts with the edgy insecurity of the gambler who knows there's nothing left to lose but self-respect. She and Ace "meet cute" as he watches her confront a gambling mate, demand her cut of the winnings, then toss chips into the air like confetti. This does not get her thrown out of the club, as it would anyone else, because Ace is smitten. As a slo-mo bottle-blonde in sequins and fuck-me heels, she is the ideal Vegas trophy. But a wife? In the love-at-first-sight phase, Ginger's accomplishment seems to be knowing how to grease the palms of bell captains, parking lot attendants, etc., which shows that "she knew how to take care of people." But Ginger's not a nurse, she's a prostitute. As a bad wife and mother in the third act, her harlotry spices up nasty marital rows. (Ginger's idea of parenting is to tie her daughter to the bed while she goes bar-hopping with Nicky.) Has Ace forgotten what he knew about Ginger before he married her?

Angry at her bad habits, Ace welches on the deal he cut with her—a pioneering prenuptial that promised Ginger a horde of jewelry. The plot goes overboard, however, when Ace adds a boy scout's pledge to take care of Ginger financially for the rest of her life, no matter what happens. We have no reason to believe either of these hustlers could hear that without a guffaw. What's more, Ace is dumb enough to give her the only key to a safe deposit box with some $2 million in it—ransom money, in case he's kidnapped or something. You don't need a keno card to tell you Ginger will wind up treating him like any other john. Besides, it's Scorsesan doctrine: women cannot be booked.

The plot would be as short as a Vegas winning streak were it not for Ace's pal Nicky, a sadistic goon who's intent on becoming boss. Seventies-Vegas, Nicky wistfully reminisces, "was the last time street guys like us were given anything that valuable." But Nicky doesn't enjoy rolling in money nearly as much as bathing in blood. He will crash and burn, but not before screwing Ginger and his own best buddy. Ace will be redeemed by his paternal love for his daughter Amy at the end of a narration that takes us from an opening scene of him being blown up in his car to a closing where he miraculously escapes from that same conflagration.

I object to this mess—as a film critic and as a Nevada native with family ties to neon. I grew up in the 1960s watching the gaming business, an industry so lucrative that Nevada has no state income taxes. *Godfather II* is much better than *Casino* at explaining how an East Coast mob eyed the Nevada terrain and fled from the Feds. That the guys upon whom this story is based had to report and carry profits to a Kansas deli says more about them than about the neon desert.

The Nevada State Gaming Commission is a powerful body unafraid to wield its authority, which is not to say it's not corrupt. Power corrupts, but the loss of power corrupts even more, which is part of the unacknowledged background of *Casino*. The film is no more typical as a business history of gambling than *The Great Train Robbery* is of the banking industry's shipping of legal tender. The State Gaming Commission may exercise benevolent neglect at times; it may be as much on the take as any corrupt corporation you may care to name, but it's not a round-up of dumb cowpokes, which these East Coast cineastes (gambling with other people's money in the movie biz) would have you believe. "Every guy in cowboy boots," whines Ace, "is either a County Commissioner or related to one."

One scene that does strike an honest chord has a commissioner warning Ace that this territory does not belong to Ace's kind; the Nevadans own and run it—this because Ace won't hire back an incompetent nephew of a local politician. On the heels of Ace's sudden escalation of standards comes an official inquiry into his lack of a gaming license. Ace was initially worried about passing the scrutiny of the Gaming Commission, but his pals tell him not to worry: the commission can be so slow as never to get to his application. But now things speed up, and Ace's license is denied. So is the bad guy the bookie or the regulators? The truth is that the Gaming

Commission prefers to play by its own rules, even when it gets frog-walked into playing dice with wiseguys. Some casino owners are more difficult than others; perhaps that's why the Gaming Commission cottoned on to the corporations that Scorsese finds so much less admirable than bozos beating each other into pulp with baseball bats. At least corporate lawyers can cut a deal everybody can live with, the operative word being live.

Scorsese has got the decade wrong (the age he describes was more 1950s/1960s); the ethos wrong (the conflict between local yokels and the crumbs in the casinos is far more complex); and his cardinal rule of casinos dead wrong. Contrary to Ace's claim, savvy casino owners are not intent on taking back all the money. The maxim of the industry is the title of casino-pioneer Harold Smith's autobiography: *You Gotta Send Out Winners to Get Players*. Sufficient bucks flow in to let 10 percent flow back out (some will debate that figure as only 3 percent; there are sufficient casinos to allow such a range, but no house wants a reputation of nobody ever winning).

The gaming industry may incite the prurient instincts of people who think like gangsters, and they may not want to see it as a massively regulated business with a healthy profit margin even when run legally. When filtered through Scorsese's lens, it's the law, not the mobster, who's the bad guy. Yet underlying this film is a puritanical distrust of gaming and disdain of the nouveau riche types that it breeds. Scorsese wants to show how a reasonably disciplined casino boss like Ace (who is a Jew beset by an unspoken anti-Semitism that Scorsese won't address) can be brought down. But this character would have screwed up dealing second-hand cars because he's stuck in the mistake of constructing an ideal of middle-class life with a material girl and a maniac best friend. His fatal flaw lies not in his discipline but in the one area where he briefly abandons it.

To be sure, few movies are made about honest men, and during the long hour of the second act, I credited Scorsese with finding the paradox in a Vegas casino making an honest man out of a bookie like Ace. He says things like, "Here I was celebrated as a solid citizen for things that'd get me thrown in jail back home." What Scorsese and production designer Dante Ferretti do get right is the ambience of the sprawling, air-conditioned, pool-studded, wall-to-wall carpeted luxury available to the haves in Las Vegas. And the Tangiers puts up a good show as a casino. The sound track is awash with the sassy brass of lounge bands fused with the jangle of the slots, the clink of bourbon and ice, the call of dealers, and delirious shrieks of odds-beaters. The music track is cleverly compiled out of the funk and jive of anxious entertainers droning songs about luck—not the Sahara's Showroom headliners like Tony Bennett and Frank Sinatra. This dayless, nightless eternity of the hopeful gambler is so well documented that, in conjunction with the lessons on casino operations, it could play on PBS.

There remain, however, the long sequences of pointless violence that have been turning Scorsese's films into genre pieces with pretensions. To get back to the mean streets, Scorsese detours through the air-conditioned antechambers of vice in Vegas. As he has moved up in the world, so have his dramatis personae, and he has them spouting the clichés of wealth as only the wealthy can: "It can't buy me love." On this principle he ricochets through an illogical plot, exclaiming over the overt skimming in a casino as if he'd never known that comparable evil exists at the local Bijou, where cinema owners work their nut like a sponge and have only fairly recently been forced to the accountability of computerized ticketing.

The sensationalism built into Ginger's disintegration or Nicky's demanding blow-jobs are threadbare thrills to compensate for weak plot. Actually, Scorsese's inaccuracies about the gaming industry are just a byproduct of his need to reinvent the slasher movie for the art audience. *Casino* has gangsters who start as old men munching salami in the back of a deli and end up blasting or blasted full of holes. It revels in a Scorsese staple—a gangland mentality disguised as masculine virtue among men with a vision so narrow they cannot contemplate anything larger than being together. That's the outer limits of social organization in their world, glued together by dim-witted loyalty. It recalls *Mean Streets* just before the characters start dying, when the boys in the bar laugh at each other over the line "Balls, said the queen, if I had them I'd be king." Such is the wannabe tragedy in *Casino*. Ace and Nicky and Ginger—they're good as long as they pull together, but once separated, they gotta die. In Scorsese's world, nobody gets to be king.

FILMS IN REVIEW, 1-2/96, p. 60, Andy Pawelczak

Casino, Martin Scorsese's three-hour long slice of Americana based on Nicholas Pileggi's book, opens with a car explosion. In the succeeding credits, a body free-falls through flames that turn into an abstract pattern reminiscent of stained glass windows which in turn become the neon lights of Vegas as Bach's "St. Matthew's Passion" plays on the soundtrack. Purifying fires or the fires of hell? Once the narrative begins, the sacerdotal theme is carried on as Ace Rothstein (Robert De Niro), a mob-connected casino director, tells us in a voiceover that for guys like him Vegas is a paradise, a place that washes away your sins. Like some of the defining works of American art—*Citizen Kane, The Great Gatsby*—*Casino* is a tale of paradise lost and a mordant examination of the state religion of the almighty buck. Scorsese gives his own genre-subverting spin to the familiar story and a half-concealed subtext that links the picture to such movies as *Raging Bull* and *New York, New York* and the result is a complex, often dizzying film.

Invention and improvisation takes place in front of the movieola just as much as it does on the set. Cutting a camera movement in four may prove more effective than keeping it as a shot ... To direct means to scheme, and one says of a scheme that it is well or badly mounted. "
— Godard:
The movie has a loose, meandering plot that will put some people off, though in the end all the pieces click into place. The first third is a pseudo-documentary with explanatory voice-over about the esoteric mechanics of Vegas, a schemer's paradise. It's Meliès (fantasy) plus Lumière (realism), a documentary about a fantasy world. The movie is constructed like a slot machine with a succession of rapid-fire micro-thrills. The editing is brisk, the early scenes are all short, and the continuous rock soundtrack contributes to the general sensory overload. Scorsese uses the Rolling Stones' "Satisfaction" twice in the course of the movie and of course it fits right in with the theme—Vegas as the apotheosis of American consumerism which is founded on the principle of endless seduction without satisfaction, all adding up to the square root of a negative number, the entropic realm of the purely imaginary. The mixed response the film has drawn from critics and audiences alike has something to do with how form mirrors content here—the picture's nervous, edgy rhythm never lets up and we don't get the cathartic payoff we expect from Hollywood movies, unless you count the death's-head finale, tempered by an ambiguous hint of redemption, as a catharsis.

As Ace Rothstein, De Niro, dressed in sports jackets ranging in color from canary yellow to cardinal red, is a tightly-wound anti-hero. Ace is a whiz-kid gambler who is given the directorship of a casino by the mob. For Ace, gambling is a science and he runs the casino with a fanatical eye for detail. He's as obsessive-compulsive on the floor of the casino as legendary director Erich von Stroheim was on a movie set, and in some ways *Casino* can be read as an allegory about Hollywood with Ace/De Niro as a director besieged by greedy money-men and hangers-on. Ace's fall from grace comes when he stubbornly insists on firing an incompetent employee who happens to be related to the State Gaming Commissioner and as a result is refused a license to operate in Vegas. It's a classic case of gangster hubris.

Scorsese's characteristic themes emerge in the triangle between Ace, his wife Ginger (Sharon Stone), and Nicky (Joe Pesci), a mob enforcer who moves out to Vegas to live off the fat of the land. As Ginger, a Vegas hustler, Stone gives her best performance to date; she's the perfect blond, lacquered embodiment of Vegas' meretricious glamor. Ace falls hard for her but with his eyes wide open. When he proposes, he says he's basing his life on a long shot, and Scorsese comments wittily on their relationship by, at one point, playing the Stones' "Heart of Stone" on the soundtrack as they smooch—with its pun on Stone's name, it's the kind of touch that gives the movie a vertiginous feeling. The marriage quickly degenerates into the adversarial standoff of Liza Minnelli and De Niro in *New York, New York* as the irredeemable Ginger boozes and cokes it up and her pimp ex-boyfriend (played with manic brilliance by James Woods) lurks in the background.

The real emotional center of the movie rests in the relationship between Ace and Nicky. In a typical Scorsese male agon, they compete for who is going to be the king of Vegas. For Nicky, Vegas is the Old West where anything goes; Scorsese underlines the parallel with a brief two-gun shootout in a bar that's shot like a scene in a classic Western. Nicky terrorizes his way into Vegas and opens a celebrity-patronized restaurant resembling a small-scale version of Ace's casino, and when he gets involved with Ginger it's clear that his motivation comes from the fact that she belongs to Ace. As Nicky, Pesci does a replay of his role in *GoodFellas*—he's an unpredictable, motor-mouthed, frightening killer—but he gives the movie a furious blind drive it wouldn't have without him.

"If one had to pin down a somewhat excessive taste for death in the American cinema, I would suggest that it lies in the fear of repose ... "

— *Godard*

In an interview, Scorsese admitted that in some ways *Casino* is a reprise of *GoodFellas*, though he pointed out that John Ford repeated himself in the "Cavalry Trilogy" and Hitchcock made the same film throughout his career. He could have mentioned Howard Hawks who made all but identical films in *Rio Bravo* and *El Dorado*. *Casino* does cover some of the same territory as *GoodFellas*, but its emblematic use of Vegas gives it added resonance, and the picture is a visual and aural tour de force. Of all the American directors, Scorsese has always been the biggest risk-taker, the joker in the deck, as unpredictable and driven as the characters Pesci plays for him. In the current Tarantino-besotted atmosphere, he continues to be the man younger directors have to measure themselves against, his real-life drama as a director an ironic replay of the competitive dramas in his movies. He's practically a one-man New Wave, and he's still moving—he recently announced that his next film will be about the Dalai Lama. From Vegas to the Himalayas, without stopping.

FILMS IN REVIEW, 3-4/96, p. 56, Victoria Alexander

When I walk into a casino I can smell the sweet, welcoming fragrances. I inhale deeply, taking advantage of the pumped-in oxygen the Casinos provide. I haven't caught The (gambling) Virus yet, probably because to me everyone looks like they're spending long hours there killing time rather than making a killing. It doesn't seem to be a fun place to work either—someone is always looking over an employee's shoulder. Everybody watches everything.

It was quite an experience seeing Martin Scorsese's *Casino* at its sole venue in Las Vegas—The Gold Coast Hotel and Casino. And oddly embarrassing, since Robert De Niro's opening voice-over remarks let us know that anyone who plans on gambling in Vegas is a fool. As De Niro's character, casino manager Sam Rothstein puts it, no one ever wins but the casino. But we sat smug: the parking was free, our movie ticket cost $4.00 before six o'clock, and later we'd be able to enjoy The Gold Coast's live band, free country-western lessons and drinks for 50¢.

As for the film, director and co-screenwriter Martin Scorsese gives us an insider's tour of the world of gangsters, this time spotlighting the fascinating era when organized crime families of the Midwest came to Las Vegas in the 70's and early 80's. This is a tailor-made project for Scorsese, teaming him again with Nicholas Pileggi, editor Thelma Schoonmaker, producer (and ex-wife) Barbara De Fina, and stars De Niro and Joe Pesci.

De Niro plays the sanctimonious Rothstein, obsessed with strict decorum as he oversees the daily activities of the mob-owned casino. Nothing else matters to him until he meets chip hustler/part-time hooker Ginger McKenna (Sharon Stone). The critics have hailed Stone's performance, bestowing on her—like knighthood—the title of Actress. Stone's career leapt forward to sex goddess status by way of *Basic Instinct* after many years of straight-to-video dues. Yet, Stone's sex scenes with co-star Michael Douglas were nearly eclipsed by her character's complex sexuality, showcased by a lesbian relationship. Stone gave a fascinating performance: she understood the sexual dynamics inherent in her female audience. What woman wouldn't enjoy the chance to turn down a sexual advance from Sharon Stone? Herein lies Stone's wide appeal and it is rumored to be mined again in the upcoming remake of *Diabolique*, with Isabelle Adjani the object of Stone's attention.

In *Casino*, Stone is the woman who weakens the stoic Rothstein and comes between him and his boyhood friend, Nicky Santoro (Pesci). Rothstein patiently endures Ginger's drunkenness, perpetual infidelity, and commitment to a former lover, played with sleazy perfection by James Woods. We sympathize with the long-suffering Rothstein, who has to negotiate with Ginger for a marriage and family. Stone richly deserves praise for this role and plays it with wonderful abandon. Ginger has absolutely no redeeming virtues. She's even a bad mother, tying her young daughter to a bed so she can go out with Santoro. Rarely do movie stars allow themselves to portray a character who doesn't even have a valid reason for being bad.

Nicholas Pileggi's book, *Casino: Love and Honor in Las Vegas*, is about the lives of Frank "Lefty" Rosenthal, one of the most powerful and influential men in Las Vegas in the 1970's, wife Geri McGee, and notorious hit man Anthony "The Ant" Spilotro. The movie shadows the lives of these three with the exactness to detail Scorsese is adept at. There is so much information cleverly relayed through the small details, e.g., Rothstein sitting in his office in boxer shorts, only putting on his perfectly pressed pants when receiving a visitor. Could there be a better way to depict an anal-retentive, Type A control freak? Again, Pesci plays a ruthless hit man but this time gives his character a peculiar Brooklyn/Chicago accent and a dangerous, but likeable, personality. He's much older than the real Spilotro was—they all are by a decade at least, but it really doesn't matter.

Pileggi based his book largely on the first-hand account of Rosenthal, though Geri's friends accused Rosenthal of being abusive to her and an indiscreet, bold womanizer. Geri died a few days after Rosenthal divorced her at the age of 46 from alcohol and drugs. Rosenthal read the handwriting on the wall after the car bombing attempt on his life and retired from Las Vegas. He now helps run a nightclub in Boca Raton. Three years later, Spilotro and his brother were found in shallow graves, beaten to death. Pileggi probably had no trouble getting Scorsese interested in this colorful story. It has everything that fascinates the director: gangsters, the 70's, and lots of violence. New for Scorsese though, the story has a woman as a central figure and she's Scorsese-proof: destructive, violent, and a player.

Scorsese's brilliance as a filmmaker and storyteller is evident though I was troubled by the first part of the film, largely devoted to the actors walking through scenes narrated by De Niro and Pesci (apparently from the grave). There had to be one "decent" person in the film so De Niro's character was turned into a straight-arrow Las Vegas mobster. I asked Las Vegas journalist George Knapp about Rosenthal and Spilotro. Knapp had narrated an acclaimed television documentary, "Mob on the Run," which originally aired eight years ago, and knew both Rosenthal and Spilotro personally. "Rosenthal fancied himself a ladies man, had a reputation for fooling around, always had an entourage, and demanded a lot of attention. And still does." said Knapp. "He's an insufferable blowhard." Knapp spoke to Rosenthal six months ago about the pending film. Still an egomaniac, Rosenthal had hoped to play himself and didn't think De Niro could do it. "He'll try," Rosenthal told Knapp. Spilotro was remembered more kindly. "He was always a perfect gentlemen, would send over drinks, very polite and kept a low-key profile. There may have been different sides to him, but he was careful in public." Knapp recalled.

Why is Rosenthal now speaking out against *Casino* in interviews? Apparently, Las Vegas insiders say the real reason Rosenthal didn't have any "hands on" involvement in the film was that his old associates preferred he stay out of town.

LOS ANGELES TIMES, 11/22/95, Calendar/p. 1, Kenneth Turan

"Casino," the story of how the mob won and lost Las Vegas, proves two points so conclusively you can take them, so to speak, to the bank. One is that Martin Scorsese is a master filmmaker, so skilled in the manipulation of imagery he might be the most proficient of active American directors. The other is that despite his dazzling ability, Scorsese is finding it increasingly difficult to make his personal obsessions accessible to an audience.

Based on the fascinating nonfiction book by Nicholas Pileggi (who co-wrote the script with the director), "Casino," at three hours and change in length, is clearly meant to be a major statement, a film whose dark vision of a society driven to disaster by money, violence and pride is supposed to echo in the American consciousness like "The Godfather."

For Scorsese, "Casino" is familiar territory in a number of ways. It stars two of his trademark actors, Robert De Niro and Joe Pesci, as boyhood friends Sam (Ace) Rothstein and Nicky Santoro, who end up controlling Las Vegas before a rivalry for Ace's wife, Ginger McKenna (Sharon Stone), ruins the party.

It is also a return to the hard-guy life the director loves to chronicle, the specifically Italian American milieu of "GoodFellas" and "Mean Streets." Plus it continues Scorsese's deeper fasci nation with volcanic men inevitably exploding into deadly violence that encompasses films as diverse as "Taxi Driver," "Raging Bull" and "Cape Fear."

In "Casino," however, that attraction feels increasingly like the working out of a private fantasy in a language only the director can appreciate. Despite Scorsese's great skill, he makes too few emotional connections to persuade us to see things the way he does. So instead of being operatic and cathartic, this film ends up exhausting and claustrophobic.

"Casino," the film, has an intrinsic interest because it is a fictional reworking of the remarkable true story Pileggi tells in his book, which details the rise and fall of the real-life models for the trio of lead characters: gambler and Stardust Hotel honcho Frank (Lefty) Rosenthal, his wife, Geri, and the explosive Anthony (Tony the Ant) Spilotro, a man so violent, said an acquaintance, "he dared you to murder him."

"Casino" opens promisingly, as Scorsese sets the scene for the drama to come with a spectacularly cinematic three-quarters of an hour that introduces his protagonists, details how the casino system operates and outlines their position in it. Using elaborate tracking shots, montages, flashbacks within flashbacks and two competing voiceovers (one from Ace and the other from Nicky) that continue throughout the film, Scorsese conveys a great amount of information in an intense, concise, breathtaking way.

Ace Rothstein (De Niro) is a gambler of legendary skill who even checks wind velocities (for their effect on field goal attempts) before betting on football games. The mob in the Midwest calls Ace the Golden Jew and in the early 1970s sends him out to Las Vegas to manage its newly acquired Tangiers Hotel and Casino. An unflappable perfectionist who cares how well-distributed the berries are in blueberry muffins and dresses in coordinated pastels (one outfit even matches his bottle of Mylanta), Ace loves Vegas because "it's like a morality carwash," a place where a gambler and bookmaker like himself could be transformed into a solid citizen.

At the Tangiers, as Mickey & Sylvia's "Love Is Strange" plays on the soundtrack ("Casino's" taste in music is impeccable), Ace trades glances with the glamorous Ginger McKenna (Stone) and that is that. Even though he knows at once that she's a hustler and an operator and soon finds out that she doesn't love him and is obsessed with sleazy ex-boyfriend Lester Diamond (James Woods), marriage is just a matter of time.

Also headed to Las Vegas is Nicky Santoro (Pesci), sent by the bosses in the Midwest to make sure that nothing interferes with Ace's ability to make money. A professional thief and thoroughgoing psychopath, Nicky soon sees his way clear to becoming the town's de facto boss, though his penchant for violence conflicts with Ace's desire for respectability. And when Ace and Ginger start their predictable decline, Nicky inevitably gets involved.

It is the worsening of that marriage, never more than a fiscal union, that hijacks this film. As Ace and Ginger scream and beat on each other, as she turns to drugs and alcohol and he becomes more paranoid and inflexible, "Casino," as if transfixed, follows their every move, losing momentum and wandering down a repetitive path where few will want to follow.

"Casino" also gets increasingly violent as it goes on. Much of the violence comes from Nicky, who turns simple tools like a pen and a vise into murderous weapons, but, especially at the film's finale, several other people get into the act, administering a series of stomach-turning beatings. The question is not whether the violence is accurate, which it seems to be, but whether making audiences cringe is enough of a reason to include it.

One of the ironies of "Casino" is that even though Scorsese is interested in the story's wider implications, he focuses so much energy on that unsavory romantic triangle that he and the film lose sight of the larger issues. It would be worth knowing, for instance, that in real life the model for Ace's character ended up controlling four casinos for the mob, but if the film does mention that, it's easy to miss.

None of this is the fault of the actors, all of whom, from supporting players like Woods, Don Rickles and Alan King, to the stars, perform faultlessly. Since both De Niro and Pesci, skilled as they are, essentially reprise previous work, the film does the most for Stone, who displays star quality and a feral intensity that is the equal of what the boys are putting down.

Frustrating as it is to see such a skilled filmmaker working on material with so little intrinsic interest, as long as auteur directors remain absolute rulers little can be done about it. It's the current Hollywood system, and as visitors to Las Vegas inevitably find out, the system can be awfully tough to beat.

NEW YORK, 11/27/95, p. 81, David Denby

Late every night at the great Tangiers Hotel in Las Vegas, the true point of running a casino becomes clear for anyone in the know. All day long, Sam "Ace" Rothstein (Robert De Niro), the hero of Martin Scorsese's new gangster film, *Casino*, applies his genius to a very simple problem: how to squeeze more money out of the greatest moneymaking machine ever invented. The mob has bought the hotel and set up Sam, a longtime mob bookie and gambler, as boss. A cautious and vigilant man—he wants only to be an honest crook—Sam thinks that all he has to do is increase profits and everything will be fine. The reckoning comes nightly: A stolid-looking gent with a small suitcase enters the casino's sacred inner temple, the "count room," and, in full view of hotel employees, shovels a portion of the evening's take into his suitcase. He then flies to Kansas City, where he delivers the "skim" to some white-haired elders, solemn as bishops, who sit in the back of a meat-and-produce store. To disappoint these geriatric gentlemen is to invite death. Sam may be a businessman at heart, but he depends on these ancient mafiosi, and in Las Vegas he depends on the muscle of his old friend Nicky Santoro (Joe Pesci), who frightens away other gangsters and in general serves as enforcer of the casino's good health. Nicky protects Sam; that is, he protects the skim. If Sam thinks he can control everything through calculation, Nicky, who regularly commits robbery and murder, thinks he can control everything through force. *Casino* is the story of the downfall of these two men and the eclipse of the old gangster-run Vegas that they embody. The movie means to be a sorrowful epic: These two street guys had control of everything, and they blew it. But the critical question is, how important an issue is either man's illusion, or either man's fall? Do we care about either guy?

Casino turns out to be an odd case in the Scorsese canon, an extraordinary production that outstrips the dramatic and human interest of the material. The movie begins with a car-bomb explosion and a man falling through flames, accompanied by a magnificent choral excerpt from Bach's "Matthauspassion BMV," all of which suggests a work of great tragic weight. But *Casino* is not a movie that wounds us, as Scorsese's early *Mean Streets* did. Nor is it an exuberant expose of the voluptuous enchantments of crime, like *GoodFellas*. When the movie opens, Sam and Nicky are already in their forties and well established—hardened, efficient men with nothing unresolved, ambivalent, or soulful in their characters (as there was in the characters of Scorsese's earlier gangsters). With these two at its center, *Casino* never develops much in the way of emotion or even ordinary human interest. The two men and the beautiful Vegas hustler Ginger (Sharon Stone), whom they both get involved with, are limited, obsessive people—monomaniacs, trapped in the prison of unending obsession.

Nicholas Pileggi, author of *Wiseguy* (and a *New York* contributing editor), spent five years researching mob activities in Las Vegas for a book. Pileggi and Scorsese then sifted through the material and pulled out the central narrative of this film. The movie fictionalized the characters; Pileggi tells the story straight, with real names, in his recently published *Casino*. As in *GoodFellas* (the movie made from *Wiseguy*), Pileggi's reportorial skills and his feeling for the antlike industriousness and everyday quality of criminal behavior feeds Scorsese's longtime obsession with hoods and operators. Sam and Nicky take turns narrating, and as they talk, we see the action. "Follow the money," Deep Throat told Woodward and Bernstein, and Scorsese seems to be operating on the same principle. The money originates, of course, in gamblers' pockets, but Scorsese's camera (Robert Richardson did the alert cinematography) catches the flow into the hands of dealers and croupiers, all of whom are watched by pit bosses, who in turn are watched by managers, who are watched by still other watchers, stationed above—on and on, in an endless daisy chain of surveillance and mutual distrust, until the money, which has been protected at every stage, winds up in the count room, only to be skimmed by the mob.

A serious business! De Niro, with his iron stare, walks through the casino without a smile or a flicker of enjoyment, followed by a grim Don Rickles (looking more lizardlike than ever). Throughout its three-hour length, *Casino* is rich in chicanery and Vegas lore—the way big winners are kept at the tables, even by means of such scams as "canceled" airline flights until, at last, they begin to lose; the way cheaters are detected, punished (i.e., mutilated), and thrown out. At its best, the movie is like a dramatized circuit diagram: You can see the nodal points, where the money changes hands.

Sharon Stone, tall as a Viking princess, enters the movie in glittering clothes and moves around fast. With Scorsese directing her, she's a real actress, liquid, even volatile. It's not her fault that

Ginger never makes much sense. Sam falls in love with her, and lavishes money and jewels on her, but Ginger never loves Sam; she loves a sleazy pimp from her earlier life, a leech named Lester (James Woods). The trouble is, Pileggi and Scorsese fail to make her emotional dependency on the pathetic Lester at all plausible. After a few years, Ginger, drinking hard, fades away from Sam, and their relationship collapses into endless scenes of Scorsesian rancor—at which point the movie collapses, too. Why are we watching scene after scene of marital discord and bickering? It's not as if these two had a great love that failed. This screwed-up marriage might have worked as a mock fable, a comic ballad of perverse devotion—Ginger gets everything from her husband but still loves her moth-eaten pimp. (It's almost a country-and-western song.) But done realistically and exhaustively, as it is here, the relationship is about as interesting as that of an unknown couple screaming through a hotel wall. Sam's relationship with the vicious and ungovernable Nicky disintegrates, too, but since Sam never seemed to like Nicky much—how can you like a psychopath?—we're not wrenched by their split. As Nicky, Joe Pesci seems to be showing off how vicious he can be. Snarling and glaring at everyone, he gives an effectively hateful performance, but without the staggering verbal inventiveness that made a similar character in *GoodFellas* so much scary fun.

What Scorsese has done earlier—discovering the lyrical, even operatic possibilities of gangster life—he can't or won't do this time. *Casino* is a little remote: When the men narrate, we don't enter into complicity with them; they're just two tough guys giving us information. Scorsese, as always, does violence with a charge of sadism and shock—the men work on each other with hammer, vise, and baseball bat—but the overall coldness of the conception seeps into the viewer's mood. Pileggi and Scorsese have made an honest movie about crime as a normally sordid business, and they've paid a price for it. That body grandly flying through the air in the opening sequence has landed with a silent thud.

NEW YORK POST, 11/22/95, p. 47, Michael Medved

Near the end of Martin Scorsese's "Casino," a half-dozen mob enforcers graphically beat two characters to death with baseball bats. The scene lasts several minutes, artfully re-creating the crushing of skulls, the breaking of limbs, the gradual, horrifying transformation of terrified faces into bloody, featureless masks. The sequence might well stand as a summary of the entire film, which mercilessly bludgeons its stunned audience for nearly three hours.

The key difference between the assault on these characters and Scorsese's assault on his audience is that at least the crime bosses seemed to have some purpose in mind for their attack.

The film, by contrast, wanders aimlessly for what seems like an eternity across a desert landscape populated exclusively by vicious, cold-hearted creeps. Of course, this meandering tale of Vegas and the mob is supposed to be a vast metaphor (yawn!) for the corruptions of capitalism or, as Nicholas Pileggi (who wrote the non-fiction book released simultaneously with the film and collaborated on the script with Scorsese) baldly declares: "It's the story of the American Dream."

The chief dreamer is a brilliant bookie from the Midwest named Sam ("Ace") Rothstein (Robert De Niro) who comes out to Nevada in 1973 to run a casino for his connections back home. He justifies his nickname ("The Golden Jew") by doubling the take for his bosses, but his "paradise on earth" is soon sullied by the arrival of boyhood chum Joe Pesci.

As a conniving psychotic with a short fuse, Pesci gets essentially the same role he played (more effectively) in the previous Scorsese-Pileggi collaboration, "GoodFellas." Meanwhile, De Niro falls in love with a gorgeous, amoral hustler (a surprisingly effective Sharon Stone), who secretly maintains contact with her longtime pimp, a drug addict and all-around sleazeball played by (who else?) James Woods.

Moments of love and happiness between De Niro and Stone lack all warmth and conviction so that the inevitable collapse of their relationship carries little emotional weight. There are also problems with the static, tautly-controlled nature of De Niro's performance, with no visible disintegration or other personality changes such as the Ray Liotta character underwent in "GoodFellas."

Instead Scorsese here delivers great gobs of pseudo-literary narration ("Las Vegas ... it's like a morality car wash. It does for us what Lourdes does for cripples ...") delivered by both De Niro and Pesci. There's also wall-to-wall, with more than 40 (count 'em!) songs from the '70s operatically underscoring every scene and constituting a supremely annoying distraction.

No one can doubt Scorsese's unmatched virtuosity as a filmmaker, and every few minutes the film does manage some new visual dazzlement. Startling camera angles, inventive editing or telling details of production design cannot, however, overcome the chill and emptiness at the heart of the story. The film's only energy comes from its periodic bursts of gruesome violence, with graphic views of a spurting jugular vein after an attack with a ballpoint pen, or a mobster's already bloodied head slowly squashed inside an industrial vice.

The random assemblage of such moments, no matter how expertly staged, can't be squeezed into sublime cinematic satisfaction. Scorsese's "Casino' offers plenty of flash and noise and glitz, but remains a prodigious waste of talent and a sucker bet.

NEWSDAY, 11/22/95, Part II/p. B4, Jack Mathews

There is no way of avoiding direct comparisons, so let's cut to the chase and declare "Casino," the 15th feature in Martin Scorsese's brilliant career and his third in a direct line of mob movies, "GoodFellas" Lite.

That is not the same as saying it is bad.

In my Scorsese scorebook, "Casino" ranks behind his four masterpieces—"Raging Bull," "Taxi Driver," "Mean Streets" and "GoodFellas"—and nothing else. And if the same film appeared with any other director's name, it would be a sensation. It is a visually spectacular recreation of Las Vegas in the preconvention, pre-Circus Circus '60s and '70s; it contains eye-opening details on how the mob ran the city and raped the golden goose, and features at least one stunning performance, from (cross my legs and hope to die) Sharon Stone.

But the Scorsese name promises something more than a rehashed "GoodFellas" in Vegas. And for all the A-list talent involved—co-screenwriter Nicholas Pileggi, upon whose book-in-progress "Casino" was based, and Scorsese troupers Robert De Niro and Joe Pesci—"Casino" at times resembles a Vegas Night Party in Queens.

De Niro's snappy-dressing, cool-headed Tangiers casino boss Ace Rothstein is Jewish and more ambitious but otherwise indistinguishable from Irish Jimmy Conway in "GoodFellas," Pesci, as Ace's treacherous pal Nicky Santoro, gives a virtual repeat of his Oscar-winning temper tantrums in "GoodFellas." And good as she is as Ace's self-destructive wife Ginger, Stone is playing out the same emotional string that won a second "GoodFellas" Oscar for Lorraine Bracco five years ago.

The primary story elements of "Casino" are factual. Rothstein is based on a Midwest mob bookie named Lefty Rosenthal, who was set up in Vegas with illegal teamsters pension money and became one of the city's most recognized figures—a hobnobber with politicos and performers, a country club member, and eventually, a television personality.

The Santoro character is Ace's best friend, and enforcer. But over the years in Vegas, their contrasting interests—Ace wants nothing more than a certain respectability, Nicky wants to run the whole industry—lead them into a conflict that not only, destroys their friendship, but brings ruin to the mob and to half of their political allies in the city.

"Casino" is at its best during the opening 40 minutes when, in almost documentary style, Scorsese introduces us to the mob's Las Vegas, and to the characters who will dominate the film's three-hour running time. The story, again with familiar echoes from "GoodFellas," is narrated by the mobsters themselves. Somewhere in that opening, we see De Niro climbing into his Cadillac and apparently being blown to bits, then we hear his voice, as from the grave, promising to tell us about the decade leading up to the moment of the explosion.

The film does come full circle, and by then, we know very well why someone would want Ace dead, and who that someone might be. But it is a long and windy road. There's no reason for "Casino" to dawdle three hours. Points are belabored, characters overstay their welcome, and Scorsese devotes far too many minutes trying to relate the human side of Ace.

Like most of De Niro's characters, Ace has no sympathetic core. He's a wanter, and has the force of personality and power to get what he wants. But there is a moral absence about him that makes Ginger, the decorous and savvy casino call girl that he cajoles into marrying him, far more appealing.

Stone is a perfect physical fit for Ginger, a woman who looks fabulous, knows what every man in the room is thinking about her, and knows how to use them to her advantage. But that's the woman Ace meets. After they're married, have a child, and she tires of his jealous tyranny, she begins a descent into self-abuse that is startling for Stone's raw portrayal of it.

If "Casino" doesn't resonate with audiences in the way "GoodFellas" did, it will be because Scorsese is revisiting old themes, and because Las Vegas is such an artificial setting. Yeah, it's there, and the mob was there, and all these things happened. But in a town whose appeal and image are deliberately superficial, it is hard to get beneath the neon clamor and feel anything genuine.

There is, throughout Ginger's and Ace's and Nicky's ordeal, the modifying reminder that in those days, people who went to Vegas—as gamblers, mobsters, or hookers—went with their eyes open and ready to roll the dice, and pretty much got what they deserved.

NEWSWEEK, 11/27/95, p. 86, David Ansen

Martin Scorsese's "Casino" is concieved on a grand scale, as a gangster's paradise lost. Paradise was Las Vegas in the 1970s, a Wild West town ruled by the mob, where guys from the street like "Ace" Rothstein (Robert De Niro) and Nicky Santoro (Joe Pesci) could reign in gaudy splendor as long as the skim money from the casinos kept flowing back to the mob bosses in Kansas City. In an unholy alliance with the corrupt local politicians and the Teamsters, the mob had Vegas in its fist. But it all came crashing down, the sinners expelled from their goldleaf Eden, the Mafia casinos replaced by the new corporate-owned, junk-bond-financed pleasure palaces of the '80s and '90s.

Pride goeth before the fall, in the testament according to Scorsese and writer Nicholas Pileggi. Their ambitious epic wants to be both a definitive anthropological chronicle of the inner workings of Mafia-run Vegas and a personal tragedy. In the story of the overreaching Rothstein and Santoro—childhood friends who would end up pitted against each other in a battle to control the town—we're meant to see a fall of Shakespearean proportions. Naturally, there's an Eve in this garden of nouveau-riche delights—the gold-digging, coke-snorting hustler Ginger (Sharon Stone), who marries the casino-running Rothstein and betrays him with the vicious, trigger-happy Santoro.

As anthropology, "Casino" is fascinating. You get an insider's view of the gaming hall: the hierarchy of surveillance; how to detect a blackjack cheat; what you can get for greasing the palm of a parking attendant; how a great bookmaker sets the odds. And as a demonstration of Scorsese's stylistic finesse, it's dazzling. Everything about the production is first class: the camera work, the cutting, the perfect vulgarity of Dante Ferretti's sumptuous sets, and a dead-on selection of source music that includes Dinah Washington, Louis Prima, the Rolling Stones and Georges Delerue's plangent theme from the Godard film "Contempt."

But the human drama at the heart of this movie is stillborn. As hard as Scorsese tries to elevate Ace and Nicky and Ginger into a triangle of mythic dimensions, they remain small and mean; their dreams don't resonate. Scorsese and Pileggi assert their themes, but they haven't found a way to dramatize them. At the start, Scorsese pours Bach's St. Matthew Passion over the sight of Rothstein exploding in a car bombing: but in the three hours he takes to flash back and tell Rothstein's story, he doesn't earn the grandiosity. The mooks in "Mean Streets" were penny ante next to these hoods, but Scorsese got inside their souls, and they mattered to us. In "GoodFellas," written by Pileggi, there was more irony, but you could still feel Scorsese's passionate connection. Here what you feel is emotional distance.

It doesn't help that he's been to this wiseguy well once too often. The sense of discovery, and the shock value, are gone. We know how well Pesci can play a peppy, conscienceless killer, but after his savage turn in "GoodFellas," do we really need an encore? De Niro faces a different problem: "Ace" Rothstein, a former bookie and gambling expert, has the soul of an accountant. For all DeNiro's weight, there's no way he can make this guy a tragic figure, and it seems a little screwy to try. There's not much pathos to be had from his infatuation with the money-grubbing Ginger, when we know from the get-go it can only end in grief. It's a love story with no love in it. Stone—tough, tortured and slinkily manipulative—is terrific. It's not the actors' fault that no one is able to break through the film's gorgeous but chilly surface. You watch "Casino" with respect and appreciation, reveling in as documentary sense of detail. Filled with brilliant journalism, "Casino" leaves you hungry for drama.

SIGHT AND SOUND, 3/96, p. 39, Jonathan Romney

1983. Sam 'Ace' Rothstein triggers a bomb planted in his car. Ten years earlier: Sam, a master bookie, is entrusted by the mob with overseeing the Tangiers casino. His role is to oversee what is on the surface a legitimate operation designed to take the maximum of money for the mob, through a system by which cash is discreetly skimmed from the counting room and flown to the mob's base in Kansas City. The casino is nominally run by puppet chairman Phillip Green. Ace has no license to run a casino, but he can evade detection by constantly changing his job title. Ace makes a great success of the Tangiers, with his ambition, managerial flair, and total understanding of gaming.

Ace falls in love with Ginger McKenna, a hooker who hustles the gambling tables. She becomes his mistress, but is still emotionally attached to her former lover, pimp Lester Diamond. Ace persuades Ginger to marry him, promising that whatever happens she will be taken care of for life. He places two million dollars—intended as security in case of kidnapping—in a Los Angeles bank and entrusts her with the only key. To give Ace extra protection, the mob assigns to Vegas his old acquaintance Nicky Santoro, a volatile and violent mobster. Nicky begins to run his own racket in town, sending the bosses regular payoffs. When his misdemeanours get him blacklisted from every casino in town, Nicky sets up a new operation with his brother Dominick, and begins a reign of terror.

Ginger asks Ace for $25,000, but will not tell him why. With Nicky's help, Ace tracks her to a rendezvous with Lester, who he then has beaten up. After sacking an inept employee, Ace receives a visit from the man's brother-in-law, local commissioner Pat Webb, who threatens him with the Gaming Control Board. In a newspaper interview, Ace appears to portray himself as the true boss of the Tangiers; the Board, launches an investigation.

1980: at Ace's Board hearing, he is refused a license by a senator in league with Webb. The bosses want Ace to lie low, but instead he makes himself conspicuous by hosting an in-house television show. His relations with Nicky are deteriorating. Ginger, increasingly turning to drink and drugs, wants to divorce him and to keep her money and jewels, but Ace refuses. She takes their daughter Amy to LA, planning to run off with Lester. Nicky intervenes, and she returns, but things get worse between her and Ace. She goes to see Nicky, hoping he can help get her jewellery back; they start an affair. Meanwhile, Kansas boss Remo Gaggi suspects that all is not well in Vegas; Nicky's gang, high on coke, are getting sloppy.

Ace and Ginger have a showdown and she leaves, managing to get to the bank and take his two million dollars. By now the FBI have enough information to arrest the mob network and have the Tangiers shut down. To cover their tracks, the bosses order a whole series of killings. Ginger dies of an overdose in LA. Sam's car is bombed by Nicky. However, Ace reveals that, fortuitously, he survived the blast. The bosses have the Santoro brothers killed. With the old regime gone, Las Vegas itself changes; the Tangiers is destroyed and business corporations transform the casinos to resemble theme parks. In San Diego, an ageing Ace, back where he started as a successful bookie, looks back on the old days.

Casino is the flashiest, most superficial film Martin Scorsese has ever made—which is to say, it serves its theme brilliantly. It portrays a place that is Hollywood's counterpart as an archetypal American city. Artificially situated in mid-desert, Las Vegas is a construction of flashing, seductive surfaces that conceal a tawdry machinery, in this case quite literally the 'factory' underneath the Tangiers that processes the banknotes and coins relieved in bulk from its customers. The city itself is also a machine which drains human interiority. Some critics have complained that the characters in *Casino* are two-dimensional, but this flatness is essential to the film's logic. These people move in a world that obliges them to be simply embodiments of desire, appetite-driven cogs in the Vegas machine. Ace inherits his paradise at the cost of 18-hour working days, and consequently has no time to be a 'person'.

Casino appears at first glance to be a traditional Hollywood tale of conflicting passions: greed, lust, jealousy. But it's more about the way that such drives are obliged to accommodate themselves to social protocol. Ace's appetite for power is legitimate as long as it supports the smooth running of the Tangiers; but when his pride in stewardship takes on a megalomaniac aspect, it then becomes too conspicuously a fully fledged desire, and all hell breaks loose.

To discuss the human motivation in Casino is to get hold of the film from one corner only. This prodigal film invites a proliferation of readings—in terms of character, of visual style, of narrative construction of gaming theory, of Scorsesean religious-ethical debate, and of cinema itself. Among other things *Casino* is an allegorical account of the dangerous seductiveness of Hollywood cinema, another strident mechanism for harvesting dollars. It constantly dazzles with visual, auditory and thematic stimuli, beginning with the opening credits with their mesmerically shifting lights and flames. The film's non-stop flash can blind us to its underlying complexity; if we simply fall for its *son et lumière* appeal, then we might easily dismiss *Casino* as a restatement of *GoodFellas*, as yet another of Marty's guided tours of the world of bad guys in bad suits.

The similarity with *GoodFellas* is at times uncomfortably close—Joe Pesci's variant on that film's psychotic hood takes some adjusting to—but Scorsese invites the comparison by collaborating again with co-writer Nicholas Pileggi, again casting Pesci and De Niro, and again using a relentless pop soundtrack. In fact, this is very much a companion piece; where *GoodFellas* was the tale of a tyro's ascent, Casino begins with its central figure as a 'made man', an angel (Nicky calls Ace "The Golden Jew"), and prepares us for his Luciferian plummet. Because we know we're in familiar territory, Scorsese can let us find our own way around without having to take us narratively by the hand.

Perversely, Scorsese encourages us to explore his Vegas by telling us too much. At the start, a construction of densely explanatory voice-overs from Ace and Nicky, fast cutting and characteristically complex Steadicam shots tells us all we need to know about the Tangiers and its workings. From the start we anticipate a story of big-time razzmatazz and melodrama. Yet Scorsese immediately tells us the bottom line at its most prosaic—hard, dull cash, placed in the hands of hard dull men. We understand that immediately, but we don't yet understand the workings of the floor, or of the city and its inhabitants. What we can obscurely apprehend, though, is a general structure, the game's basic rules—and we have to get the hang of it as we watch.

It isn't made easy for us. Scorsese, Pileggi and Thelma Schoonmaker—whose editing here goes beyond the fluidity of *The Age of Innocence*—give us a complex chronology, layered from two main voice-over narrations, flashbacks and sideswipes with apparently extraneous anecdotes. The visuals also flout coherence, taking in slow-motion, subtitling, freeze-frames, impossible 'trick' points of view (a remarkable shot from inside a cocaine tube), and glaringly self-conscious close-ups of dice, tumbling gems, all the insignia of conspicuous consumption. *Casino* plays with a language of celebratory vulgarity, as befits a town like Las Vegas; but it also has moments of remarkable subtlety. When Nicky violently attacks a man in a bar, his status as a would-be Wild West desperado is prefigured by cigarette fumes drifting over his face like gunsmoke. On his wedding night, Ace, overhearing a tearful Ginger talking to his rival Lester, is framed in a doorway with motes of dust drifting in a beam behind him; the dust portends both the ephemerality of the marriage, and the cocaine that will be her downfall.

Ginger, as we might expect in a Scorsese film, is *Casino*'s blind spot; we are told less about her than about Ace and Nicky, and she is never the narrator. She is first seen turning 'tricks', in both the gaming and prostitution senses; clearly, she is as skilled and as driven an operator as Ace himself. But he sees her instead as the random factor personified. Admired by Ace in the act of anarchically tossing chips in the air, she embodies the side of Vegas that is opposite to his control-mania: she is pure expenditure. His taming her is partly an attempt to level the stakes, to control a symbolic threat to his ordered domain. Also, he is fascinated with the possibility of his own downfall.

We are aware from the start of the irony in this marriage; just before Ace's car explodes, he tells us, "When you love someone, you've got to trust them—you've got to give them the key to everything that's yours." He does this literally, tempting fate by giving her the key to his emergency bank stash. But the theme of trust is tied in with a larger debate about ethical responsibility. In contrast to Nicky's instinctive savagery, Ace adopts a facade of corporate and civic respectability. For him, the casino represents a chance to be legit in every sense. "For guys like me," he explains, "Las Vegas is like washing away your sins ... a morality car wash." Ace may be Jewish, a tolerated outsider in the Italian mob world, but *Casino* is as Catholic as any of Scorsese's films; and Vegas is as autonomous a city state as the Vatican.

Ace prides himself on running a "square joint" immune to the chicanery of his enemies and of his own employers; one factor in his downfall is that he won't collude with the corrupt local official Webb. But built into the running of the Tangiers is a system of institutionalised mistrust, the chain of security surveillance (ironically doubled in the FBI's own surveillance of the mob).

Ace is the hundred-eyed Argus who sees all, ever attentive to the signs by which cheats reveal themselves and earn brutal punishments by ice-pick and cattle-prod. But he is only part of a chain—officials on the gaming floor watch each other and all are watched by the surveillance camera, "the eye in the sky."

This suggests not only the panoptic eye of God, but also the eye of the filmmaker and ultimately of the viewer, who is offered all the information needed to get an overall view of the story. Nicky's voice-over tells us that "nobody knew all the details," but by the end, we stand a chance of knowing it all—as much as Ace, Nicky, the mob and the FBI put together. Apart from its one major sleight of hand concerning the car bomb, *Casino* doesn't deceive or short-change us. It deals us all the cards we need, but leaves it to our narrative skills to combine them into the hand that completes the game.

TIME, 11/27/95, p. 93, Richard Schickel

Sam Rothstein (Robert De Niro) favors sports jackets in blinding solids—sometimes in the primary hues, sometimes in less-than-subtle pastels. These he color-coordinates with silky haberdashery and alligator loafers dyed to match. But underneath his sight-gag plumage lives a gray, watchful, calculating spirit. He's a professional gambler, always looking for an edge. Or, once the Mob makes him manager of a Las Vegas casino in the 1970s, the preternaturally alert defender of its edge over the assembled suckers.

He is not, however, what you'd call a people person. And therein lies the downfall it takes *Casino* (or should we call it *GoodFellas Go West?*) three hours to record. Until it's too late, Sam is entirely too tolerant of his lifelong buddy Nicky Santoro (Joe Pesci), a cheerful psychopath who is more trouble than he's worth. Sam also falls into distracting obsession with Ginger McKenna (Sharon Stone), and that's not good for him or for business either. She's a hustler whose excessive interest in furs and jewels would warn off a more worldly man. As would the fact that she leaves their wedding banquet to make a tearful call to the sleazy lover (James Woods) whom she never fully abandons.

The film is based on material Nicholas Pileggi gathered for a nonfiction book that has just been published, and the screenplay he wrote with director Martin Scorsese is at its best in its reportorial passages. If you want to know just how the Mafia skimmed the profits from its Las Vegas operation, or how not-so-wise-guys tried to scam it, *Casino* is instructive in an almost documentary way. But Scorsese, one of the cinema's great stylists, has evolved a manner for his film—a compound of mini-dissolves, jump cuts, freeze frames and optical effects—that is anything but documentary. It is a kind of objective correlative for the way Sam keeps an eye on things—roving distantly, then boring in on whatever looks suspicious—and if it is sometimes distancing, it is equally often brilliant.

What Scorsese and Pileggi have not evolved is an attitude toward their material that is equally riveting. Mostly they romanticize the Vegas that was, before the corporations moved in to Disneyfy and democratize gambling. In the good old days, they say in their voice-over narration (of which there is far too much), the place was to wiseguys what "Lourdes was to hunchbacks and cripples," a holy ground where organized crime was free to practice its amoral rites and where that miracle cure for the terminally outcast—sudden, improbable wealth—was always a real possibility. There's something a little too easy in this conceit, although there's good black comedy in it too—especially in the notion that it is the tragic flaw of hubris that eventually robs Sam and Nicky of their place in paradise. The former, apparently unaware of Bugsy Siegel's fate, aspires to celebrity-mobster status; the latter ratchets up his murder rate to crime-spree levels; both fatally attract the attention of the law and their own godfathers back home, who naturally prefer quieter business methods.

So long as *Casino* stays focused on the excesses—of language, of violence, of ambition—in the life-styles of the rich and infamous, it remains a smart, knowing, if often repetitive, spectacle. But in its last hour, as it concentrates more and more on Ginger's increasingly desperate and degrading attempts to escape Sam's smothering affections, the film winds neurotically in on itself. And neither the controlled rage of De Niro's playing nor the entrapped ferocity of Stone's, as she breaks definitively with her sex-symbol past, can prevent the film—and its audience—from sinking into a been-here, seen-that mood.

VILLAGE VOICE, 11/28/95, p. 59, J. Hoberman

Is it dumb luck that the season has brought three would-be down-and-dirty paeans to Las Vegas! *Showgirls, Leaving Las Vegas,* and *Casino* all went into production at more or less the moment when, led by the refurbished MGM Grand Hotel, the world's most notorious wide-open town successfully reinvented itself as the new Orlando—a family-oriented theme-park resort.

God bless America. Pols may squawk about our unravelling moral fabric, but the sometime crime of gambling has been reborn as an essential source of tax revenue and a billion-dollar form of mass entertainment. This is not to say that Hollywood's Vegas doesn't make a spectacle of sin. *Showgirls* and *Leaving Las Vegas* are, each in their own way, meditations on the perils of self-indulgence. *Casino,* directed by Martin Scorsese from Nicholas Pileggi's book, is more centered on the sin of self-pity.

Scorsese is far too talented to achieve Paul Verhoeven's transcendent vulgarity. Nevertheless, *Casino* starts out hustling. The first hour is posh and polished—a Saturday Night of gaudy long-shots, choreographed crowd scenes, and sensational expository montages. The wheel spins, the little oranges, lemons, and cherries whirl before your eyes, but the game is fixed—there's never any payoff. The movie ceases to resonate. It becomes as hollow as *Showgirl'*s head.

Like *GoodFellas* but to far lesser effect, *Casino* sets itself up as the tale of America's decline. Would that it were. Narrated in flashback, the movie is a priori nostalgic. *Casino* dreams of a lost Golden Age that—thanks to coke, paranoia, duplicitous women, and bottom-line-conscious executives—goes kerflooey. The belle epoque is not, as one might imagine, the Ratpack reign of the late '50s and early '60s. *Casino* more suggestively spans the decade 1973-83 (or *Mean Streets* through *The King of Comedy*).

Midwestern bookmaker Sam "Ace" Rothstein (Robert De Niro) is hired to run the Tangiers casino because he knows how to "bet like a fucking brain surgeon." On the one hand, the Tangiers is a cash cow to be milked by a bunch of Kansas City mobsters. On the other, it's Ace's work of art—his "paradise on earth,"—the last time street guys like us were ever given something that valuable." Us includes Ace's childhood friend Nicky Santoro (Joe Pesci). Some guys, as Woody Guthrie wrote, rob you with a fountain pen. Others, like Nicky, use it to stab you in the throat. Nicky's smiling little maniac has all the big erotic scenes—bludgeoning one cohort with a telephone handset, putting another wiseguy's head in a vice—while romance is personified by Ginger McKenna (Sharon Stone), the high-class hooker Ace mistakenly marries.

Embellished with religious imagery that has as much to do with *2001* as Roman Catholicism, *Casino* is a Scorsese epic. But the movie has neither *New York, New York'*s dark, crazy brashness nor *The Age of Innocence'*s nuance. The mode is iconic—big cars, suburban spreads, scenes opening with a mega close-up of some lounge crooner's silver pompadour—but the mood is secondhand. Whole sequences (the recurring image of the toad-faced bosses croaking baroque ep-ithets and chowing down on mama's meatballs, not to mention Pesci's entire performance) seem recovered from *GoodFellas'*s cutting room floor.

Casino is a movie about gambling that never takes a risk. However impressively edited, it's remarkably static, the narrative propelled mainly by Ace and Nicky's tag-team voiceover and a wall-to-wall music track that mixes Dino and Muddy Waters, doowop and c&w, Betty Calter and Louis Prima to ever-diminishing effect. Ace is described as "flamboyant" but the liveliest thing about De Niro is his color-coordinated pink wardrobe. (However awful the actor was in *Cape Fear*, at least he gave a performance. Here, he seems to be wondering whether to have his sushi flown in from Matsuhisa or Nobu.) Dully kvetching for most of the movie as if auditioning for Woody Allen, De Niro abruptly shifts gears at the end to quote Al Pacino's Michael Corleone. Pesci pitches his tent in this vacuum—his monotonous posturing all but wears a hole through the screen.

By the time Ace and Nicky have serious disagreements and Ginger succumbs to pills-and-booze (Stone's general competence here disintegrating), the movie has sunk into a tedium deeper than De Niro's depression. "Today it looks like Disneyland," whines Ace of the new Las Vegas. (And vice versa: That Luxor sphinx is a dead ringer for Disney's Hollywood Pictures logo.) *Casino* is a vision of Scorsese in hell.

Also reviewed in:
CHICAGO TRIBUNE, 11/22/95, Tempo/p. 1, Michael Wilmington
NATION, 12/18/96, p. 804, Stuart Klawans
NEW REPUBLIC, 12/25/95, p. 26, Stanley Kauffmann
NEW YORK TIMES, 11/22/95, p. C9, Janet Maslin
NEW YORKER, 12/4/95, p. 118, Terrence Rafferty
VARIETY, 11/20-26/95, p. 47, Todd McCarthy
WASHINGTON POST, 11/22/95, p. B1, Hal Hinson
WASHINGTON POST, 11/24/95, Weekend/p. 54, Desson Howe

CASPER

A Universal Pictures release of an Amblin Entertainment production in association with The Harvey Entertainment Company. *Executive Producer:* Steven Spielberg, Gerald R. Molen, and Jeffrey A. Montgomery. *Producer:* Colin Wilson. Director: Brad Silberling. *Screenplay:* Sherri Stoner and Deanna Oliver. *Based on the character "Casper The Friendly Ghost" created by:* Joseph Oriolo. *Story:* Seymour Reit and Joseph Oriolo. *Director of Photography:* Dean Cundey. *Editor:* Michael Kahn. *Music:* James Horner. *Music Editor:* Jim Henrikson. *Choreographer:* Adam Shankman. *Animation:* Eric Armstrong and Phil Nibbelink. *Sound:* Charlie Wilborn and (music) Shawn Murphy. *Casting:* Nancy Nayor. *Production Designer:* Leslie Dilley. *Art Director:* Ed Verreaux and Daniel Maltese. *Set Designer:* Antoinette J. Gordon, Josh Lusby, Gary A. Lee, and Gene Nollmann. *Set Decorator:* Rosemary Brandenburg. *Set Dresser:* Jim Meehan, Edward J. Protiva, Jonathan Bobbitt, and Eric Ramirez. *Special Effects:* Michael Lantieri. *Costumes:* Rosanna Norton. *Make-up:* Christina Smith. *Stunt Coordinator:* Gary Hymes. *Running time:* 95 minutes. *MPAA Rating:* PG.

CAST: Chauncey Leopardi (Nicky); Spencer Vrooman (Andreas); Malachi Pearson (Casper); Cathy Moriarty (Carrigan); Eric Idle (Dibs); Ben Stein (Rugg); Don Novello (Father Guido Sarducci); Mr. Rogers (Himself); Terry Murphy (Herself); Bill Pullman (Dr. Harvey); Christina Ricci (Kat); Ernestine Mercer (Woman Being Interviewed); Douglas J. O. Bruckner (Voice of Reporter); Joe Nipote (Stretch); Joe Alaskey (Stinkie); Brad Garrett (Fatso); Rodney Dangerfield (Himself); John Kassir (Voice of The Crypt Keeper); Garette Ratliff Henson (Vic); Jessica Wesson (Amber); Wesley Thompson (Mr. Curtis); Michael Dubrow (Student #1); J.J. Anderson (Student #2); Jess Harnell (Voice of Arnold); Michael McCarty (Drunk in Bar); Micah Winkelspecht (Student); Mike Simmrin (Phantom); Amy Brenneman (Amelia); Devon Sawa (Casper on Screen).

LOS ANGELES TIMES, 5/26/95, Calendar/p. 1, Peter Rainer

Casper the Friendly Ghost is awfully friendly in "Casper" and more's the pity. He's so adorable that he might as well be the Pillsbury Dough Boy, with whom he shares more than a passing resemblance here.

The problem with Casper has always been his goodness. It's much easier—and more fun—to get behind a cartoon villain. (Dramatically speaking, this applies to humans, too.) Goodness easily devolves into sappiness, and, in "Casper," the Friendly One is upstaged from the start by his three goofball uncles, Stinkie, Stretch and Fatso. This trio rules the roost at Maine's Whipstaff Manor, a dilapidated spread bequeathed to a short-changed heiress (Cathy Moriarty) who wants the place de-ghosted so she and her weak-kneed assistant (Eric Idle) can root around for the buried treasure rumored within.

She hires Dr. Harvey (Bill Pullman), a "ghost therapist," who arrives with his skeptical daughter Kat (Christina Ricci) in tow. Dr. Harvey dabbles with unsettled specters: it's his unacknowledged way of trying to contact his dead wife, who is deeply missed. When he settles into Whipstaff, he doesn't really expect anything spooky. He's not really much of a believer either. (At best, he believes, ghosts are ghosts because they "lack resolution.") But pretty soon he's getting tweaked and clonked by the uncles, while Kat gets chummy with Casper.

Just about the only imaginative things about "Casper" are the digitized Amblin/Industrial Light & Magic effects involving the ghosts and a few fun-ride scenes with a mini-roller coaster inside the mansion. And even these are more cheesy than transporting. The emotional core of the movie is chilly; the effects surround a void. Kat's loneliness has no emotional resonance. Ditto Casper's. And, unlike Kat, Casper, try as he might, can't even remember his early childhood. (At times the film threatens to become a weird kiddie recovered-memory scenario.)

Director Brad Silberling and screenwriters Sherri Stoner and Deanna Oliver can't figure out how to play a lot of this material. They pour on the sentiment and then they pour on the dopiness. They work in celebrity cameos by—who else?—ghostbuster Dan Aykroyd, and by Mel Gibson, Rodney Dangerfield and others. They provide a twinge of funniness with a bit by Father Guido Sarducci (Don Novello). But most of the time the film wavers and falters on its woozy way. The ghosts in this movie aren't the only ones who lack resolution. So do the filmmakers.

Ricci was such a mock-sinister delight in the "Addams Family" movies that her mellowing here, once she hooks up with Casper, is a letdown. She's charming and she can act, but it would a mistake if this powerhouse comic actress segued into conventional ingenue roles. Pullman looks dazed, as if he wasn't sure where the ghosts were supposed to be in his scenes. (It might be funny if someone were to film one of these actors-vs.-special-effects jobs minus the effects.) Children in the low-to mid-single-digit-age bracket may not mind the movie's bumbling tackiness but, then again, "Casper" is just the beginning of a vast marketing blitz. You can't avoid the blitz—not unless you live in a convent—but you can duck the movie.

NEW STATESMAN & SOCIETY, 7/14/95, p. 32, Jonathan Romney

[*Casper* was reviewed jointly with *Batman Forever*; see Romney's review of that film.]

NEW YORK POST, 5/26/95, p. 37, Michael Medved

We associate numerous virtues and faults with movies produced or directed by Steven Spielberg: They can be inspiring, kitschy, spectacularly cinematic or heavy-handed. But the one thing Spielberg movies are—never, ever supposed to be is boring.

Never, that is, till now.

"Casper" isn't the worst movie ever associated with the Spielberg name (he is one of three executive producers), but it is easily the dullest, despite attempts by the screenwriters (TV scribes Sherri Stoner and Deanna Oliver) to fill up the emptiness with a frenetic and absurdly convoluted plot. Even Spielberg's famous flops, "1941" and "Batteries Not Included," featured more energy and forward momentum.

The story begins when the greedy Cathy Moriarty ties to tear down an abandoned mansion she's inherited in order to locate the treasure reputedly hidden on its premises.

Unfortunately for her, the ghosts who haunt the place chase away all demolition workers she hires, so she sends for self-styled "ghost therapist" (Bill Pullman) to try to placate the pesky poltergeists.

This spook-shrink is actually hoping to contact the spirit of his own dear, departed wife (Amy Brenneman) so he moves into the haunted house with his 12-year-old daughter (Christina Ricci, who inhabited another creepy mansion in the two "Addams Family" movies).

In her new home, the girl quickly befriends Casper, whose sweet disposition stands in stark contrast to the nastiness of his three ghostly uncles, Stretch, Stinkie and Fatso. These spectral Stooges torment Pullman (and us) with bad slapstick, while Casper shows the daughter hidden chambers in the old house—including a lab housing a machine developed long ago by his inventor dad that can bring ghosts back from the spirit world and give them new life as flesh-and-blood citizens.

All this is much too dark and complex for young viewers targeted by this film. At times, the brooding meditations on the after-life begin to sound as if Shirley MacLaine has served as an uncredited spiritual adviser to the film. "What's it like to die?" Christina Ricci asks her new pal, Casper, "Like bein born. Only backward," he helpfully replies. "

If this sort of Hollywood zen seems out of place in a kiddie movie, the story's sexual subtext is even more inappropriate. Casper falls in love with his new "fleshie" friend and snuggles next to her in bed. Later the amiable apparition briefly takes human form as a 12-year-old "hunk," complete with blow-dried 'do and pouty lips, and engages in deep, passionate kisses with the pre-teen object of his affections. This ghost in other words, is more than just friendly.

The computer-based animation that brings Casper and his obnoxious uncles to the screen is so smooth that you quickly forget about the dazzling technical wizardry and accept it as part of the story—which is bad news since the story is such a mess.

Despite world-class special effects and a few funny gags involving surprise celebrity cameos, "Casper" doesn't stand a ghost of a chance of living up to its hype. It is a pale imitation of what entertainment ought to be.

NEWSDAY, 5/26/95, Part II/p. B2, Gene Seymour

The people who brought Casper the Friendly Ghost to feature films did at least one thing right: they merged the dewy-eyed sweetness of his animated cartoon persona with the heads-up pluck of his comic-book incarnation to fashion as satisfying a family film hero as you'll find anywhere beyond "A Little Princess" herself. If only "Casper" the movie had even a little of that other movie's captivating charm and bright wisdom. What it has instead is the overamped awkwardness of middle schoolers on a sugar rush.

It also has, of course, great special effects. Casper and his three notorious uncles—Stretch, Stinky and Fatso (whom some of you may remember as the Ghostly Trio)—are rendered with care and conviction by the computer-generating wizards at Industrial Light and Magic, who make you believe, if not in ghosts per se, at least in glowing ectoplasms that zip through walls. The spooks' see-through bodies carry just about all the imagination "Casper" has to offer.

What's left is a second-rate rehash of "Beetlejuice" and "The Addams Family," complete with a scary old Maine mansion that Casper and his uncles call home. At the movie's start, the house, called Whipstaff Manor, is inherited by shrewish Carrigan Crittenden (Cathy Moriarty), who believes there's valuable treasure lurking within its dilapidated walls. With weasely aide (Eric Idle) in tow, she tries to collect this hypothetical loot. Casper's uncles, who detest "fleshies," are in the way—and aren't budging.

Not even Father Guido Sarducci or Ghostbuster Dan Aykroyd, making cameo appearances, can purge Whipstaff Manor of its spectral tenants. But Carrigan obtains the services of Dr. James Harvey (Bill Pullman), a shrink who's become a traveling "ghost therapist" partly in grief over the loss of his wife. Carrigan hires Harvey to "counsel" the ghosts into moving on to the afterlife. Harvey's skeptical 12-year-old daughter, Kat (Christina Ricci), doesn't care what happens as long as she and her dad can stay in one place long enough for her to make even one friend.

Casper, naturally, thinks Kat's a soulmate. After some initial (and understandable) qualms, Kat agrees. But she'd still rather have a flesh-and-blood boyfriend and, toward that end, arranges to stage a Halloween party for her class at Whipstaff. As party time approaches, the Ghostly Trio makes off with Kat's dad while the Greedy Duo close in on the treasure.

This cluttered, hackneyed plot has more gratuitous quirks than a mechanical rollercoaster-cum-grooming aid that carries Kat to an underground laboratory where Casper finds the means to bring himself back to life.

The whole enterprise would be little more than a glorified video game if it weren't for Ricci's captivating presence and Pullman's heroic realization of yet another thankless role.

SIGHT AND SOUND, 8/95, p. 43, Nick James

Obsessively greedy heiress Carrigan Crittenden inherits an old mansion, Whipstaff Manor, in Friendship, Maine. Rumoured to conceal a hidden treasure, Whipstaff is haunted by three malevolent spirits, Stretch, Stinkie and Fatso, and their friendly nephew Casper. An exorcism and an attempt to demolish the house having failed, Carrigan is secretly influenced by Casper to contact Dr James Harvey, a widower who offers therapy for ghosts as a cover for his attempt to get back in touch with his dead wife, Amelia.

Dr Harvey and his adolescent daughter Kat move in and, while Harvey battles with the three uncles, Kat is befriended by Casper. Kat attends the local school where her notorious address makes an immediate impression and is voted the perfect location for the school Halloween party. Casper and Kat investigate the attic where Kat discovers toys that belonged to Casper when he was alive thereby triggering his dormant memory. They find a trackway that leads to a secret basement where Casper's father once experimented to bring his son back from the dead. Carrigan watches them and sees a safe in the basement for which no one knows the combination. Realising the potential of Casper's partner's machine, she decides to become a ghost herself by driving off a cliff. Meanwhile, Casper's uncles have grown so fond of Dr Harvey, that they consider killing him to make him a full-time gang member. He pre-empts them by drunkenly stumbling into a trench and dying.

The ghostly Carrigan enters the safe and emerges with a treasure chest. In getting her hands on both the machine and the treasure chest, however, she has resolved all her earthly desires and is thus claimed by the Afterlife before she can return back to corporeality. The treasure chest contains nothing but Casper's old baseball glove. Realising that Dr Harvey has become a ghost, Casper surrenders his last chance of life in favour of Dr Harvey. His reward, brought to him by the angelic form of Amelia, is to be granted a brief return to life until 10pm to attend Kat's party. When he becomes a ghost again on the dancefloor, Kat's guests flee into the night.

In the 60s and 70s, the first boom period for Marvel and DC comics in the UK, Casper the friendly ghost remained a largely esoteric figure known from ads in other DC comics, but not distributed here. Even then, it was clear that he was specific to an American suburban lifestyle that seemed rather too preachy-keen and saccharine to succeed with Britain's post war offspring, raised as it was on me The Bash Street Kids and the British version of Dennis the Menace.

Casper's suburbia is now the focus of American nostalgia for a supposedly more morally upright era which nurtured optimism and innocence. It's a mood which this film version half-heartedly tries to recreate by making Casper a simpering animated balloon-head too cute even for Happy Days and through its nudgingly-titled setting, Friendship, Maine. The film's plot, however, seems to accept that recreating post-war innocence is impossible, and substitutes instead a modern parable of irresolvable grief that bubbles beneath the hysteria of the slapstick humour and the special effects.

In his longing for his dead wife, Amelia, Dr Harvey seeks out representatives of the Afterlife. Those he finds—Casper's mischievous uncles Stretch, Stinkie and Fatso—soon become the reprobate male boozing companions he might have been given in a less supernaturally-bent film. His rootless recent life with his daughter, Kat, in which she was moved from school to school, provides them with the motivation that justifies their move into Whipstaff Manor: Kat's need for friendship and a home. Although Dr Harvey is eventually granted his wished-for audience with Amelia's ghost, seeing Kat through adolescence never seems like a convincing consolation for Amelia's absence. He remains a doleful single parent, with ghosts his only trusted companions.

At first, Casper, the benign bump, is like the imaginary friends that many younger children create for themselves, an unpredictable and exasperating companion. Soon, however, he is an adolescent boy-substitute, who turns winsome flesh for a last waltz with Kat before permanent wispiness engulfs him. It's a transformation that crosses the line between two potential audiences—children and adolescents—(both of which the film wants to appeal to) and demonstrates the identity crisis besetting so many films that might or might not be for either audience.

Thus Casper has to be everything for Kat, from silly putty pal to candy floss lover, because this rather bleak film leaves her with nothing else. Having reconciled the ghosts of Whipstaff to human company, Kat and her father can have the children from Kat's school in for a party. But the schoolchildren's only function is to act as cheerleaders for the young love between Kat and Casper until the moment when Casper reverts to insubstantiality and clears the room with a "Boo". Kat, like her father, is left in a remote home with only tame ghosts for company, while the tame ghost of pleasant suburbia recedes back down the hill with the other children. Kat may have found the permanent friend and home which she desired but her and her father's bereavement remains a solid reality compared to the chimaera of community. Against this sombre psychological backdrop, the frantic antics of Casper and his uncles to amuse and annoy are neither sufficiently sinister nor cheering enough to stand out.

TIME, 6/12/95, p. 68, Richard Corliss

Amid the lastest hoo-haha and brouhaha about toxic culture, a media maven is led to wonder: Has Bob Dole ever read his kids a fairy tale? Or sung a nursery rhyme? Or seen a classic Disney cartoon? In Hansel and Gretel, Jack and Jill, Bambi and Dumbo, the obsessive themes are death and dismemberment. These graphic horror stories tell toddlers that life is a dark forest where parents get killed and kids get eaten. As purveyors of Dole's "nightmares of depravity," Warner Bros. ain't a patch on the Grimm Bros.

In its cheerful, knowing way, the hit movie *Casper* mines this same dark soil. On its face, it is a high-gloss update of the "friendly ghost" who starred in 55 cartoons between 1946 and 1959, a long-running comic book and a short-lived 1979 TV series. Director Brad Silberling mixes rude slapstick for the kids with pop-culture cues for their parents, including gag cameos by Clint Eastwood, Mel Gibson and *Ghostbusters'* Dan Aykroyd. The movie even has its own theme-park ride, a kind of human car wash. All jolly enough. But in its haunted heart, *Casper* is another invitation to kids to flirt with the idea of being dead.

The film, written by Sherri Stoner and Deanna Oliver, has the cartoons' familiar plot: Casper searches for a friend and finds one in Kat (Christina Ricci), a lonely girl now in residence at sepulchral Whipstaff Manor. Among the contenders for possession of this dark old house, which looks like a tyrant's wedding cake that has started to melt, are a venal heiress (the ripely funny Cathy Moriarty) and her sidekick (Eric Idle); Casper's uncles, three ectoplasmic boors named Stretch, Fatso and Stinkie; and Kat's klutzy dad (crinkly Bill Pullman).

Here's where the *Liebestod* kicks in. Still grieving for his late wife, Dad has become a "therapist to the dead," vowing to ease their turmoil so they can rest in peace. The sensible Kat is automatically spooky because she is played by Ricci, the *Addams Family* daughter. With her wide eyes and genius-size forehead, Ricci now officially assumes the mantle of death-driven teen that Winona Ryder once wore so becomingly. She is Casper's perfect human soul mate.

In the expert computer animation by Dennis Muren and his fellow effects wizards at ILM, Casper is cute and pudgy—a Pillsbury ghost boy. Yet he is also a dead child speaking from an unquiet grave. Poaching on her father's turf, Kat serves as Casper's therapist and helps him remember his life and early death. "What's it like to die?" Kat asks eagerly, and Casper replies, "Like being born—only backwards." Before long, Kat is forced to decide who lives and who dies—her father or her new best friend!

This is the primal theme—trying to bring the dead back to life—that has pre-occupied *Casper*'s executive producer, Steven Spielberg, in *E.T.* and *Poltergeist, Always* and *Jurassic Park.* The new film is sprightly enough to conceal its subtext from censorious politicians. But children, who dwell in fear at least as much as in innocence, may get the message: that it would be cool, bitchin', totally awesome to join the Dead Kids Society.

VILLAGE VOICE, 6/6/95, p. 56, Jeff Salamon

A specter is haunting Hollywood—the specter of computer-generated animation. Twenty-eight trillion bytes of computer-generated animation, in the case of Brad Silberling's *Casper*, which is 28 trillion bytes more than Joe Oriolo required a half century ago to create the charming little dead baby who inspired this Steven Spielberg production. *Lifelike* is the word Universal Pictures uses to describe this Casper, and while that seems appropriate for a character who's, after all, not really alive, *lifeless* is the adjective that more readily comes to mind.

Though Casper's Pinocchio-like attempt to reclaim fleshy status is the plot device that drives this movie, he functions best not as a character, but as a metaphor for something else that Spielberg would like to resurrect: the '80s spectacle. Back in that pre-*Jurassic* era, giants like Spielberg and George Lucas strode the earth, churning out special effects epics that resonated with the Reaganite vision of America walking tall. In our more malaissic era, such movies still rake in the box office, but they evoke no sense of moment, only a desperate sense of compensatory gigantism.

Casper wears its '80s ambitions on its sleeve: Mel and Clint show up in live-action cameos (as does Dan Aykroyd, in ghostbuster regalia), *Beetlejuice* echoes run amok, the hapless parent/wise child dichotomy remains unchanged from the days of *E.T.*, and the haunted-house set looks like it sprang from Tim Burton's sketchbook. Casper himself resembles the towering Pillsbury Doughboy of *Ghostbusters*, only scaled down for this decade of lowered expectations. Yet one expectation remains undiminished: that technology will give us bigger and better (and, need I add, louder) movies. Like *Jurassic Park, Casper* is a film for people who thought the shark was the most interesting character in *Jaws*.

Though the movie therefore wastes the talents of Bill Pullman, Cathy Moriarty, and Eric Idle, in Christina Ricci *Casper*'s producers managed to stumble onto a genuinely compelling biological presence. It's difficult to find a word to describe this teenager that doesn't seem inappropriate coming from a 30-year-old man, so I'll settle for *appealing* as long as we all understand that I'm hedging. Unfortunately, Ricci isn't the point of the movie; Casper's struggle to convince her that he's a suitable soulmate is. But a Cyrano plot only works if Cyrano is deserving, and Casper isn't. He's nothing more than a computer-generated poltergeist by way of Keane, and Ricci is, well, life itself. By film's end the two of them have discovered a machine that can grant mortal status to the friendliest ghost you know. But technology proves far more capable of resurrecting Casper from the dead than of bringing *Casper* to life.

Also reviewed in:
CHICAGO TRIBUNE, 5/26/95, Friday/p. C, Michael Wilmington
NEW YORK TIMES, 5/26/95, p. C16, Caryn James
VARIETY, 5/22-28/95, p. 92, Brian Lowry
WASHINGTON POST, 5/26/95, p. F7, Rita Kempley
WASHINGTON POST, 5/26/95, Weekend/p. 42, Desson Howe

CHRONICLE OF THE WARSAW GHETTO UPRISING ACCORDING TO MAREK EDELMAN

A Documentary and Features Polish Film production. *Director:* Jolanta Dylewska. *Screenplay (Polish with English subtitles):* Jolanta Dylewska. *Director of Photography:* Jolanta Dylewska. *Editor:* Wanda Zeman. *Music:* Arthur Brauner. *Sound:* Piotr Strzelecki. *Special Effects:* Ryzsard Kujawski. *Running time:* 72 minutes. *MPAA Rating:* Not Rated.

WITH: Marek Edelman; Adina Blady-Szwajgier

NEW YORK POST, 8/30/95, p. 42, Larry Worth

In the wake of internationally-acclaimed Holocaust epics like "Shoah" and "Schindler's List," why should audiences want to take in more of the same?

The answer can be summed up in 10 words: "Chronicle of the Warsaw Ghetto Uprising According to Marek Edelman."

Granted, it's not on a level with the monumental creations of Claude Lanzmann or—to a lesser degree—Steven Spielberg. But it contains enough heart-wrenching footage and thought-provoking comments to invite—if not demand—viewers' attention.

Director Jolanta Dylewska spends much of the production with the camera focused squarely on the sad-eyed visage of Polish cardiologist Marek Edelman, once a prominent member of the Jewish underground operation who saved hundreds from the World War II death camps.

In a clear, somewhat world-weary voice, Edelman recounts the tortuous days and harrowing nights in the Warsaw Ghetto as German stormtroopers closed in on a people who refused to accept defeat.

The stories of heroism and perseverance can't fail to move, but it's Edelman's asides that linger longest. His recollection of looking through a hole in a burning house to see a merry-go-round in the free world beyond is the ultimate irony.

"When something doesn't concern us, we don't see it," he says in explaining the revelers' indifference.

Similarly, he defines a triumph for his comrades as a clash in which no one was killed or sent to camp. Mighty victories indeed.

Director Dylewska breaks up Edelman's reveries with footage lensed by Nazis in the ghetto from 1940 to '43. Haunting shots of children left by the wayside or elderly citizens being strong-armed by SS officers are accompanied by a somber score or—more effective still—a frighteningly stark silence.

Dylewska errs only in taking too much for granted. A narrative structure could have put some moments in a clearer context, thus enhancing their power. In particular, two sequences with Adina Blady-Szwajgier—who symbolizes those who fought outside the ghetto don't really flow within the effort's unique framework.

But at 72 minutes, the film remains a passionate, eloquent reminder that there can never be enough productions on the Holocaust, at least when they contain as much heart, soul and insight as Edelman's "Chronicle."

VILLAGE VOICE, 9/5/95, p. 61, Georgia Brown

Remember *Schindler's List*? Remember what was said then? Jeffrey Katzenberg predicted that Spielberg's movie would rid the world of evil: "Whenever that little green monster is lurking somewhere, this movie is going to press it down again ... I think it will bring peace on earth, good will to men. Enough of the right people will see it that it will actually set the course of world affairs." Yes, I've noticed how the planet's problems have evaporated. "Steven is a national treasure," Katzenberg went on. "I'm breakin' my neck lookin' up at this guy." Now that he and Spielberg (and Geffen) rule Dreamworks together, the angle of vision must be less of a strain.

That was less than two years ago, and the collective memory is fickle. Think of *JFK*, four years old and practically a laughingstock. Reviewers can only hope that the issues in which their effusions appeared have quietly been filched from the archives. Even Norman Mailer has now determined that Oswald did it alone—a far cry from the stance he took at *The Nation*'s Carnegie Hall Stone-in. I'm saying that time may likewise turn *Schindler's* into something less than a sanctified Holocaust text.

Quick, when you think *Schindler's List*, what's the first image that comes to mind! I'm betting it's the soft, white torso of Ralph Fiennes as he fondles his rifle between potshots from his balcony. Or maybe it would be the lordly profile of Liam Neeson playing the taller-than-all, swashbuckling Schindler. The Crackow and Plaszow Jews, though, what do you remember of them! The frightened housemaid in the wet slip! Ben Kingsley's moist-eyed accountant! The elusive girl in the red coat (á la *Don't Look Now*)? The wealthy couple chagrined to find themselves sharing ghetto quarters with the icky Orthodox? (That was a good one!) Let's not forget the adorable tyke who hides in the latrine and escapes detection. So tiny, so resourceful!

This munchkin, shuddering in the corner, chest deep in shit, was a big hit. Stanley Kauffmann saw the kid's "ordure-streaked" face as an image that might take a place alongside the famous Nazi photo of the Warsaw boy with hands raised. (Bergman used this photo in *Persona*, where I would say it didn't belong. Ophüls used it at the end of *Memory of Justice*, where it did.) For me, this cute tyke saving himself summons up all that was false—sentimental as well as factually wrong—about *Schindler's List*.

Spielberg played some of the movie for cuteness with Goeth and Schindler as adult and the Jews as children. In this sense, the film sees from the Nazi perspective since Jews had no choice but to be slavishly obedient in their presence. Whenever Spielberg showed Jews in their own milieu (rarely), he seemed unable to make them complex, strong, suffering adults. Take the scene toward the end when the war is over and the freed Schindler Jews are resting along a road. A Russian soldier rides up and asks if he can do anything for them. One of the number, one of the film's familiar character actors, pipes up, "We could use some food!" The cadence and timing of that response, the man's comic demeanor, give the scene a Disneyish feel. Maybe this is what Katzenberg, then being praised for revitalizing Disney's animation department responded to.

More modest, somber, and quietly devasting is Jolanta Dylewska's *Chronicle of the Uprising in the Warsaw Ghetto According to Marek Edelman*, now opening at Film Forum, after three showings during the 1993 Human Rights Watch Film Festival. (I put the film on my top 10 that year.) As its tide indicates, *Chronicle* films Edelman—and in two brief instances; another witness, Adina Blady-Szwajgier—narrating the ghetto's fall. Since this event has already been described from several points of view, Edelman says simply, "Everyone tells about himself, and I will tell about myself." Dylewska supplements his account with footage shot by the Nazis in and around the ghetto.

Chronicle is mercifully spare. No biographical information clutters it; there's no furrowed-brow interrogator. It's not reported that Edelman, once he escaped the ghetto, hid until the Uprising of 1944 in an apartment on the Aryan side, unable to leave the premises. After the war, unlike most survivors who immigrated to Israel or the U.S., Edelman stayed on in Poland and practiced as a cardiologist.

In his unembellished but riveting narrative, Edelman paints himself matter-of-factly as one of a group still alive in the ghetto on April 18, 1943, and determined to defend themselves. Realistically, there could've been little hope of winning, given a limited supply of weapons and ammunition as well as man power. In the end, some survivors were sent to death camps and a handful, Edelman among them, escaped through the sewers. That any particular individual survived is an aberration.

In *Schindler's List*, a fairly large group of Jews survives the extermination machine—an event so out of the ordinary it rates as a miracle. In a literal sense, Edelman's may be a survivors story, but in the real sense it's a story of extermination. He tells of heroic fighters, women as well as men, who died and how they died. No angel of mercy, no figure-on-horseback intervenes.

Since accounts of the Warsaw Ghetto uprising are available elsewhere and books can provide more detail than Edelman's eloquent but succinct tale, *Chronicle* is more memorable for its presentation of archival footage—films taken by Nazi cameramen and, until recently, tucked away in Warsaw archives. Dylewska manipulates this footage, slowing it down, focusing in on certain details in certain frames, repeating these in tense rhythmic ways. Dates are vague and people unidentified; sometimes the drama is that of a facial expression. In the sense that Germans operated the cameras, we're seeing through their eyes.

Some 1940 footage shows families transporting belongings in carts and by foot, perhaps moving into the ghetto (although the laws dictated that Jews were to arrive without possessions). Children file down the street with chairs on their heads like a spiky caterpillar. A body lies in the street and people step around it. (This might be a typhus victim.) In one of the few openly dramatic sequences, a Nazi soldier worries an old woman's head with his crop. First, Dylewska focuses on the soldier's expression, then on the woman's kerchiefed head as it's pushed from side to side. We see a man in a hat crying. We see a father walking with three children, all dressed in plaid. Dylewska searches out the man's eyes, which dart in the opposite direction. Two of the children look into the camera. The elder child reacts protectively toward the youngest. Dylewska zeroes in on the little one's face.

There's no mystery about the fate of these children. Here toddlers try to hold on to adults' hands, try to keep up. Grips are already being broken. In some cases there being loaded onto trucks. A little boys fist goes to his eye. Slowing the footage may give the momentary illusion of suspending time, but the film's central purpose is more to respect, and inspect, the record. Dylewska does with her camera what the spectator wants to do with such evidence: search, magnify, hold on.

Also reviewed in:
NEW YORK TIMES, 8/30/95, p. C9, Stephen Holden
VARIETY, 6/6-12/94, p. 44, Paul Lenti

CIRCLE OF FRIENDS

A Savoy Pictures release in association with Rank Film Distributors of a Price Entertainment/Lantana production with the assistance of Bord ScannánnahÉireann/The Irish Film Board. *Executive Producer:* Terence Clegg and Rod Stoneman. *Producer:* Arlene Sellers, Alex Winitsky, and Frank Price. *Director:* Pat O'Connor. *Screenplay:* Andrew Davies. *Based on the novel by:* Maeve Binchy. *Director of Photography:* Ken MacMillan. *Editor:* John Jympson. *Music:* Michael Kamen. *Music Editor:* Dina Eaton and Christopher Brooks. *Sound:* Brian Simmons and (music) Stephen P. McLaughlin. *Sound Editor:* Peter Pennell. *Casting:* Mary Selway and Simone Ireland. *Production Designer:* Jim Clay. *Art Director:* Chris Seagers. *Set Decorator:* Judy Farr. *Costumes:* Anushia Nierdazik. *Make-up:* Dorka Neieradzik. *Stunt Coordinator:* Martin Grace. *Running time:* 112 minutes. *MPAA Rating:* PG-13.

CAST: Chris O'Donnell (Jack); Minnie Driver (Benny); Geraldine O'Rawe (Eve); Saffron Burrows (Nan); Alan Cumming (Sean); Colin Firth (Simon Westward); Aidan Gillen (Aidan); Mick Lally (Dan Hogan); Britta Smith (Mrs. Hogan); John Kavanagh (Brian Mahon); Ruth McCabe (Emily Mahon); Ciaran Hinds (Professor Flynn); Tony Doyle (Dr. Foley); Marie Mullen (Mrs. Foley); Marie Conmee (Mrs. Healy); Gerry Walsh (Mr. Flood); Sean McGinley (Mr. Duggan); Tom Hickey (Professor Maclure); Seamus Forde (Parish Priest); Ingrid Graigie (Celia Westward); Major Lambert (Major Westward); Pauline Delany (Big House Maid); Jason Barry (Nasey Mahon); Edward Manning (Paul Mahon); Phil Kelly (Hibernian Waiter); Gwynne McElveen (Rosemary); Marguerite Drea (Sheila); Stephen Rooney (Bill Dunne); Cathy Belton (Moaning Girl); Elizabeth Keller (Sobbing Girl); Tanya Cawley (Rugby Girl); Niamh O'Byrne (Dancing Girl); Dervla O'Farrell (Benny, 10 Years Old); Pamela Cardillo (Nan, 10 Years Old); Louise Maher (Eve, 10 Years Old); Karen O'Neill (1st Little Girl); Elaine Dunphy (2nd Little Girl); Emma Lannon (3rd Little Girl); Margaret O'Neill (1st Nun); Maureen Lyster (2nd Nun); Eliza Dear (3rd Nun); Brendan Conroy (Priest).

LOS ANGELES TIMES, 3/15/95, Calendar/p. 5, Peter Rainer

"Circle of Friends," set mostly in 1957, is about the coming age of three best friends—Irish schoolgirls from the small town of Knockglen who go on to attend college in Dublin. It's sweet and winsome and a little pat, done with just enough feeling to lift it out of its class. The tang and rumpus of Irish conviviality come across without a lot of blarney. The Irish eyes in "Circle of Friends" are smiling—not grinning.

Bernadette (Minnie Driver), or, as she is called, "Benny"—she narrates the film—is a "plain Jane" who retains the frizzy, self-absorbed look of a grade school *savant*. She's a winning combination of wide-eyed and down-to-earth. Her best friend, Eve (Geraldine O'Rawe), is as excited as Benny is about ditching the small-town life with its petty tyrannies and repressions. Their movement to Dublin is dramatized as both a sexual and an intellectual awakening: They spend most of the movie tugging at the confines of their Catholic upbringing.

Nan (Saffron Burrows), the third friend from grade school, is glamorous and ambitious. While Benny has her eye set on the school's rugby star Jack (Chris O'Donnell), Nan is after more seasoned game: Simon (Colin Firth), a upper-crust layabout who doesn't, at first, suspect her meager upbringing.

Directed by Pat O'Connor and scripted by Andrew Davies from the Maeve Binchy novel, "Circle of Friends" doesn't overextend its passion. Although the movie reputedly has more sexual content than the novel, it's still a rather chaste and lulling sexuality. The filmmakers don't get into the overpowering rush of feelings that these girls, particularly Benny and Nan, must have been experiencing.

O'Connor doesn't try to draw us inside their whirligig tensions or make us see the world the way they might have seen it. O'Connor is primarily an actor's director, not a visual stylist, and he's content to let his performers work up their own little universes for us.

Since the performers are so appealing, the film stays involving. The scenes between Benny and Jack have a babes-in-the-woods sweetness. Even the fact that both O'Donnell and Driver are struggling with their Irish accents gives their confabs a sweetness. (Only O'Rawe among the leads is Irish.)

Even though the filmmakers are attempting rather too strenuously to make this story "timeless," one of its chief charms is the way it fits into a particular time and place—Ireland in the late '50s.

The despicable people in this movie's universe are small-time innocents as well, like Sean (Alan Cumming), the weaselly would-be heir to Benny's father's business, who makes Eddie Haskell seem like Mr. Sincerity. The most powerful scene in the movie comes when Sean drops his comic conniver act and moves to ravish Benny—it's as if beneath Sean's worminess was a rattlesnake.

"Circle of Friends" needs more of those chordal shifts; it needs to be more startling about the ways in which people are torn up by their emotions. But it's satisfying anyway.

NEW YORK POST, 3/15/95, p. 32, Thelma Adams

"There's a lot to be said for these big, soft girls," Jack's father tells his son (sweet-cheeked Chris O'Donnell from "Scent of a Woman").

Benny (Minnie Driver) is such a colleen, the plain Jane among three former convent girls who form a "Circle of Friends."

Director Pat ("Cal") O'Connor's sweet, slight adaptation of Maeve Binchy's coming-of-age novel follows the little women through their first year at a Dublin university circa 1957. According to formula, it's a period of virginity lost, wisdom found.

Driver brings a square-faced sparkle and a pleasant solidity to Benny. She's the rare common-sense, coming-of-age heroine who has a solid identity—but Benny still needs to find her place in the world, to separate what she wants for herself from her parents' plans for her future.

Would that the whole movie had been as rare as Benny!

"Circle of Friends," adapted by Andrew Davies, succumbs to too many rites-of-passage cliches.

When Benny falls for Jack, she blows on a bus window and traces a heart in the fog. Smarmy Sean (Alan Cumming) takes Benny on a date and there's the obligatory boy-puts-arm-around-shoulder-and-gets-fresh scene. Premed Jack faints over his first cadaver. Benny's friend Nan (Saffron Burrows) vomits; she must be pregnant.

The movie revives during occasional dark patches. Sean goes to extreme lengths to secure Benny; girls betray girls and break the "Circle of Friends."

But no sooner does Benny's journey to adulthood get rough and stormy—and interesting—than it gets smoothed over with pat answers. When it comes to rites of passage, "Circle of Friends" is the movie.

NEWSDAY, 3/15/95, Part II/p. B9, Jack Mathews

The year is 1957, the setting is lush, green Ireland, the music is imported rock and roll, the subject is young love, and the mood is strictly sentimental.

Pat O'Connor's adaptation of author Maeve Binchy's novel about the romantic adventures of three Irish girlfriends during their first year in college, takes us back to the pre-pill, pre-sexual revolution era, to a Catholic culture where threat of damnation was making its last stand against the forces of temptation.

O'Connor, who's been on a prolonged sophomore slump since his fine 1984 debut film "Cal," has returned to his Irish heritage, and though "Circle of Friends" slogs through some pretty thick melodrama, it is an act of redemption for the director.

And just in time for St. Patrick's Day.

After introducing the three teenagers in an unnecessary prologue and leisurely paced first act, O'Connor narrows his focus to Benny (Minnie Driver), a haberdasher's daughter who falls in love with the handsome star (Chris O'Donnell) of her university rugby team. And to her great surprise, since she compares her appearance to that of whales, rhinos and heifers, finds him falling in love with her.

Benny's friends are Eve (Geraldine O'Rawe), an orphan raised by nuns, and Nan (Saffron Burrows), a sculptured beauty determined to escape her impoverished background by seducing her way into a wealthy Protestant family through its philandering heir, Simon Westward (Colin Firth).

Nan's desperation, along with a cartoonishly developed subplot about a local geek's tireless pursuit of Benny, leads to some dreadful plot contortions, but the film's buoyant spirit—largely owing to Driver's energetic, honest performance—makes it all worthwhile.

Benny is a big girl—tall, hefty and buxomy—but she's hardly unattractive. She has a wonderfully expressive face, an irresistible curiosity, and a disposition that radiates warmth right off the screen. "Circle of Friends" is her story, that of a vulnerable romantic reaching maturity through an obstacle course of passion, moral crises, disappointment and tragedy.

Andrew Davies' screenplay simplifies some of the novel's issues, and opts for a patly contrived Hollywood ending over Binchy's more reasoned conclusion. But it does a very good job of evoking the sexual tension and dilemmas facing the characters. Benny, Eve and Nan are not only struggling for independence from their backgrounds, but at the same time, are being tugged in opposite directions by growing desire and lingering Catholic guilt.

Is a young woman's body to be like her soul, a "garden for Jesus," a priest asks during a Sunday sermon that seems to speak directly to them, or a "vessel for sin?"

Garden or vessel, it's never been an easy choice. And it's made more difficult for Benny and Eve (Nan has other plans for her garden) by the lectures of their anthropology professor, who titillates his virginal students with tales of the unrestricted sexual practices of teenagers in healthy tribal cultures.

Against such news, damnation was no match for temptation.

SIGHT AND SOUND, 5/95, p. 41, Ben Thompson

Ireland, the early 50s. Three young girlfriends, Nan, Eve, and Benny, are confirmed together in the small village of Knockglen. Shortly after, Nan and her family move away. In the autumn of 1957, Eve and Benny are delighted to bump into her again, enrolling at college in Dublin. Nan is more worldly-wise than her old friends. Eve, an orphan, has been raised by nuns, while Benny must get the bus home every night to her parents, who are hell-bent on marrying her off to the repulsive Sean, who works in her father's drapery business.

Nan introduces Benny to college rugby star Jack Foley. She swiftly falls for the handsome medical student, and after an anxious evening observing him at a dance, she finds that her feelings are reciprocated. Eve and her new boyfriend Aidan do up the cottage where Eve's parents once lived and have a party. Exacerbated by college lectures about primitive tribes in which the sexes mingle freely, the young women's carnal inclinations rub up against the strictures of Catholicism. Nan uses the cottage for illicit assignations with Simon, a local Protestant landlord. Benny falls out with her parents over her dislike of Sean, but when her father dies of a heart attack, she is forced to stay away from college and work in his shop.

Nan discovers she is pregnant, and is horrified when Simon tells her she is not rich enough for him to marry. She takes advantage of a drunken Jack's separation from Benny to seduce him, and then convinces him that he is responsible for her condition and must marry her. Regretfully but honourably, he agrees, breaking Benny's heart. At Nan's insistence, the unhappy couple attend another party at Eve's cottage. Eve confronts Nan with her suspicions that she had been using the cottage with Simon, and Nan turns away and puts her arm through a window. Only prompt action by Jack saves her life, and also allays his doubts that medicine is the career for him. Sean tries to force his attentions on Benny, but she shrugs him off. In the struggle she comes upon the stash of money he had embezzled from her father's business. Nan having run away to England, Benny agrees to let Jack woo her again, and eventually becomes a successful writer.

Maeve Binchy apparently advises regular readers, curious as to how this film will compare to the novel *Circle of Friends* on which Andrew Davies' screenplay is based, to "be prepared for the sex!" Regular cinemagoers, unfamiliar with the improving tone of Ms Binchy's literary oeuvre, might equally well be warned to look out for the chastity.

This is not to say that the female principals of this warm-hearted if somewhat rudimentary rites-of-passage saga are wholly devoid of feistiness, just that in the end the principle is very much one of virtue rewarded. Caught in the middle of an awkward triangle—college lectures on the sexual freedom of primitive tribes, stern words from the papist pulpit, and enrapturing cinematic visions of Marlon Brando and Eva Marie Saint in *On the Waterfront*—our heroine's determination to do the right thing ultimately earns her the right to pre-marital gratification: "Bless me father, for I have sinned".

Circle of Friends has what is technically termed a *Stand By Me* structure: the narrator sets the tone—"Eve was an orphan, raised by the nuns, but you know that only made her special"—then wanders off to the newsagents to buy a packet of crisps, returning just in time for the denouement to confirm that he or she has now become a successful writer. Minnie Driver handles this tricky assignment with considerable aplomb as the well-meaning and resourceful Benny, managing to convey a real sense of innocence with no concomitant dimness of wit.

There is nothing innocent about the single-mindedness with which this film is directed at the international market. Barely a line of dialogue goes by without a shifting backdrop of bustling period street-scene, a babbling brook or a misty hillside, while Michael Kamen's score wears its shamrock on its sleeve with almost comical commitment. The screenplay has its fair share of tourist board Irishry too: the breathless giggling of trios of brash young Irish women is becoming something of a cinematic cliché post Roddy Doyle, and I'm not sure how convincing everybody saying "altogether" at the end of every sentence is as a signifier of Gaelic warmth.

More worrying and in view of director Pat O'Connor's pedigree (he made the well-received Troubles drama *Cal*), quite surprising, is the fact that only one of the six main roles is played by an Irish actor. The accents of the ethno-tourists are not bad to the inexpert ear, and a bravura performance from a surely Hollywood-bound Alan Cumming as the lizard-like Sean all but steals the show. But accepting that the casting of doe-eyed American Chris O'Donnell in the male lead was probably vital for the film's financing and chances of a proper US distribution it would have been a nice touch to compensate with a young Irishman replacing Colin Firth as the uptight Anglo.

TIME, 3/27/95, p. 73, Richard Schickel

Repression, as everyone knows, makes for bad sex. But it does wonders for romance, obliging the yearning heart to make wondrous imaginative leaps mostly unduplicable when you're tangled in the reality of rumpled sheets. It follows, therefore, that Ireland in the 1950s, a place where condoms were illegal and priests braying the glories of continence were everywhere, was probably the world capital of romance.

The confusions it could impose on you if you were young, fresh from an upcountry village and suddenly exposed to the subversive stimulations of Trinity College, Dublin, are the subject of the ingratiating, clearheaded coming-of-age comedy that director Pat O'Connor and writer Andrew Davies have fashioned from Maeve Binchy's novel *Circle of Friends*. It revolves around three convent-educated girls: Eve (Geraldine O'Rawe), cautiously quirky; Nan (Saffion Burrows); incautiously ambitious, whose effort to seduce her way into the Protestant gentry brings her to near tragedy; and, at the center of the circle, Benny, large, plain, smart and, in Minnie Driver's performance, utterly luminous.

A shopkeeper's daughter, forced by her parents to return home every night lest she be lost to the moral ambiguities of college life, she is lusted after by her father's at first comically creepy, then dangerous clerk (Alan Cumming) and truly loved by, of all people, the cutest, nicest guy on campus (Chris O'Donnell). It shouldn't work, this romance between the ruffled duckling and the swan prince, but it does. To him she's beautiful, no matter how ungainly she thinks she is. And Benny sees beyond Jack's good looks to the insecure and awkward boy beneath the façade. Their sweet, determined, gently understated struggle for fulfillment in a superstitiously conservative society makes this densely, deftly packed movie a quiet joy to behold.

VILLAGE VOICE, 3/21/95, p. 58, Ben Greenman

Short, sweet, and moving despite its formulaic construction, Pat O'Conner's *Circle of Friends* traces the coming-of-age of three girls in late-'50s Ireland. There's Eve, the fierce-willed orphan raised by nuns; Nan, the beauty with a killing lack of good judgment; and Benny (Minnie Driver), short for Bernadette, the sturdiest side of the triangle. Benny is a bit of an ugly duckling, but blessed with self-possession, a good sense of humor, and a loving family. "I was an only child," she says, "but my mother fed me as if I were two."

Based on the novel by Maeve Binchy, the film follows the three girls as they begin studies at the University of Ireland. Quicker than you can say "love at first sight," Benny falls for Jack (Chris O'Donnell), a handsome pre-med. They become soulmates, experts in the art of easy talk. There are obstacles, of course—most notably Sean (Alan Cumming), the creepy clerk who ogles Benny. But even creeps can't ruin the mysterious joys of sexual awakening. Even the academic scenes conspire in this naive carnality—in Basic Latin, the students read about the Trobriander Islanders, a people who allow their adolescents "unfettered sexual experimentation."

Young love and ambivalent virginity are well-worn themes, but Andrew Davies's screenplay is refreshingly sharp when it needs to be. With the exception of the St. Patrick's Day release date, there's a happy lack of hokey local color in the film—no leprechauns appear to Benny in her dreams, and the actors restrain themselves from slathering Gaelic inflection all over their dialogue. Religious and class differences maintain quiet but powerful presences.

The understatement doesn't last. Nan embarks on an ill-fated affair with a local landowner, tragedy strikes Benny's family and separates her from Jack. While this turn toward melodrama doesn't hurt the principals to any great degree, it has the unfortunate effect of thrusting forth the film's antagonists, especially Sean—a supreme weasel whose smirky evildoing draws more on Pee-Wee Herman than Uriah Heep. When he finally slinks out of the picture, *Circle of Friends* regains its equilibrium and affirms its central questions—Can true love triumph? Does the dream ennoble the dreamer? Is there any such thing as a second chance? Utter predictability, finally, is the film's strongest virtue.

Also reviewed in:
CHICAGO TRIBUNE, 3/24/95, Friday/p. K, John Petrakis
NEW REPUBLIC, 4/10/95, p. 30, Stanley Kauffmann
NEW YORK TIMES, 3/15/95, p. C14, Janet Maslin
VARIETY, 3/13-19/95, p. 51, Emanuel Levy
WASHINGTON POST, 3/24/95, p. C7, Hal Hinson
WASHINGTON POST, 3/24/95, Weekend/p. 42, Desson Howe

CITY OF LOST CHILDREN, THE

A Sony Pictures Classics release of a Claudie Ossard Productions/Constellation Productions/Lumiere/Studio Canal+/France 3 Cinéma/Elias Querejeta/Télé Münchin production in association with Centre National de la Cinématographie/Cofimage 4/Cofimage 5/Studio Image. *Producer:* Claudie Ossard. *Director:* Jean-Pierre Jeunet and Marc Caro. *Screenplay (French with English subtitles):* Gilles Adrien, Jean-Pierre Jeunet, and Marc Caro. *Director of Photography:* Darius Khondji. *Editor:* Hervé Schneid. *Music:* Angelo Badalamenti. *Sound:* Pierre Excoffier and Gerard Hardy. *Casting:* Pierre-Jacques Benichou. *Set Designer:* Jean Rabasse. *Set Decorator:* Aline Bonetto. *Special Effects:* Yves Domenjoud, Jean-Baptiste Bonetto, Olivier Gleyze, and Jean-Christophe Spadaccini. *Costumes:* Jean-Paul Gaultier. *Make-up:* Nathalie Tissier. *Stunt Coordinator:* Patrick Cauerlier. *Running time:* 112 minutes. *MPAA Rating:* R.

CAST: Ron Perlman (One); Daniel Emilfork (Krank); Joseph Lucien (Denree); Judith Vittet (Miette); Dominique Pinon (The Clones/The Diver); Mireille Mosse (Miss Bismuth); Jean-Claude Dreyfus (Marcello, the Flea-Tamer); Genevieve Brunet and Odile Mallet (The Octopus); Jean-Louis Trintignant (Irvin's Voice); Serge Merlin (Cyclops Leader); François Hadji-Lazaro (The Killer, Cyclops); Rufus (The Peeler); Ticky Holgado (The Ex-Acrobat); Dominique Bettenfeld (Bogdan); Lotfi Yahyajedidi (Melchior); Thierry Gibault (Brutus); Marc Caro (Brother Ange-Joseph); Mapi Galan (Lune); Briac Barthélémy (Bottle); Alexis Pivot (Tadpole); Leo Rubion (Jeannot); Pierre Quentin-Faesch (Pipo); Frankie Pain (The Barmaid); Guillaume Billod-Morel (First Child); Ham-Chau Luong (The Tattoo Artist); Hong-Mai Thomas (The Tattoo Artist's Wife); Daniel Adric (A Cyclops); Enrique Villanueva (The Spaniard); Chris Huerta (Father Christmas); Lorella Cravotta (Woman at her Window); René Marquant (Captain); Bezak (Helmsman); Dominique Chevallier (Tied-up Guard); René Pivot (Glazier); Michel Smolianoff (Awake Tramp); Christophe Salengro and Eric Houzelot (Soldiers); Lili Cognard (Winner); Raphaele Bouchard (Miette, age 15); Babeth Etienne (Miette, age 37); Rachel Boulenger (Miette, age 43); Nane Germon (Miette, age 82); Buster Verbraeken (Krank, age 4); Jérémie Freund (Krank, age 12); Joris Geneste (Krank, age 36); Michel Motu (Krank, age 45).

LOS ANGELES TIMES, 12/22/95, Calendar/p. 6, Kevin Thomas

"The City of Lost Children" is a stunningly surreal fantasy, a fable of longing and danger, of heroic deeds and bravery, set in a brilliantly realized world of its own. It is one of the most audacious, original films of the year.

Not even the weirdness of its greatly gifted French creators Jean-Pierre Jeunet and Marc Caro's 1991 "Delicatessen," a comic post-apocalyptic nightmare in which meat-eaters prey upon each other while vegetarians form an underground resistance movement, prepares you for this new film of theirs, at once more ambitious yet also more easily accessible and involving than their earlier effort.

Perched on pilings in the sea outside a port is an amazing and sinister laboratory/aerie of a distraught scientist named Krank (Daniel Emilfork, he of narrow face and beak-like nose, familiar from countless films) who is rapidly aging because he lacks the capacity to dream. He and his cohorts represent the family at its most dysfunctional.

Attended by the diminutive Miss Bismuth (Mireille Mosse), challenged constantly by the philosopher Irvin (a disembodied brain voiced by Jean-Louis Trintignant) and served by six Clones (Dominique Pinon)—one of whom is convinced that he's the original—and an army (the Cyclops), Krank directs the systematic kidnapping of the children on the nearby harbor. Once in Krank's clutches they're strapped down, their heads encased in some sort of infernal device that allows Krank to invade his little captives' dreams and make them his own.

When the adorable toddler Denrée (Joseph Lucien) falls into Krank's clutches, his adoptive brother, a gentle giant named One (Ron Perlman), a street carnival strongman, goes into action, aided by 9-year-old Miette (Judith Vittet), a beautiful, intrepid leader of a gang of orphans.

Jeunet and Caro, who conceived the film 14 years ago, in effect spun a fairy tale celebrating the sacredness of the imagination and the importance of preserving a child's capacity to dream, as One and Miette embark on a series of astonishing adventures and encounters—such as one in a vast gallery filled with blind men hoping they'll be selected to be fitted out with an intricate optical device that allows them to become Cyclops.

A simple, ancient saga of the hero battling evil in order to rescue an innocent captive unfolds within an astounding universe, one conceived as a darkly quaint yet arbitrary mechanism in the manner of many of the animated films of Eastern Europe.

In "The City of Lost Children," allegory melds Jules Verne with "Oliver Twist," for Miette and her pals are in the thrall of the Fagin-like Octopus, the collective name for a pair of comically nasty, aging, sharp-featured Siamese-twin sisters (Genevieve Brunet, Odile Mallet) whose primitive orphanage allows them to turn their charges into little thieves. At the same time the film, set in the late '20s or early '30s, has something of the look of "20,000 Leagues Under the Sea" with Krank's lab and its wizardly devices possessed of a distinctly Victorian design. The harbor town, in turn, is a red-bricked arched maze that could have been designed by M.C. Escher.

For all the eerie grandeur of this film with its battery of special effects, intricate design (by Caro and Jean Rabasse, true visionaries), Jean-Paul Gaultier costumes and richly atmospheric score by Angelo Badalamenti, Caro and Jeunet never allow its unique dazzle to overwhelm its people. For they are no less creators of their own universe than they are storytellers who inspire the finest, most beautifully shaded performances from their distinctive actors.

As captivating as Perlman and the children are, their bizarre adversaries, who are not so much figures of evil as they are objects of pity, also hold our attention, with Krank recalling "Nosferatu's" epicene Dracula in all his tormented loneliness. So awe-inspiring is "The City of Lost Children" that in describing it you are in danger of forgetting to mention how very funny it so often is.

NEW YORK POST, 12/15/95, p. 52, Thelma Adams

My favorite character in the grotesque fairy tale "The City of Lost Children" is nicknamed "The Octopus." She's a pair of Siamese-twin school marms who run a grotty school for theft among urchins in a squalid harbor town.

The bit in which The Octopus sautes zucchini, one twin stirring, the other tasting, the first responding with a splash of oil—all the while talking conspiratorially among her selves—is priceless.

Directors Jean-Pierre Jeunet and Marc Caro ("Delicatessen") serve up such dark jokes with frenzied appetite. "The City of Lost Children" so evokes the visual riots of Terry Gilliam ("Brazil" and "Time Bandits") that it borders on homage.

The opening sequence sets a devilishly delicious tone. It's a gleaming vision of Santa Claus coming down the fireplace as if seen from inside a souvenir Christmas paperweight. This child's Yule dream of Santa's entry is quickly complicated: another Santa appears and then another and then another. The once-robust St. Nicks start to look wheezy, tired, puffy and hungry. Threatening, they fill the room, peopling an adult nightmare.

We are witnessing a stolen vision. Mad scientist Krank (Daniel Emilfork) cannot dream. This failure has aged him prematurely; with a self-made apparatus, he steals kids' dreams to stave off death. But the bitter man transforms their dreams into nightmares.

When Krank abducts Denree, the scientist brings the toddler's adopted brother, sideshow strongman One (Ron Perlman) down upon his head. The gentle giant enlists streetwise sharpy Miette (pre-teen vixen Judith Vittet) in his quest to free his baby brother.

The pair might meld brains and brawn, but the overt Humbert-and-Lolita chemistry between One and Miette is among the movie's queasier elements.

Add to this mixture six Clones and a deep-sea diver (all played by "Deli" star Dominique Pinon), a midget, a lethal flea circus, a sect of fanatical Cyclops and Irwin, a disembodied brain that speaks with the voice of famed French actor Jean-Louis Trintignant ("The Conformist").

The movie crumbles under its own weight. The convoluted plot doesn't satisfy. Grimm's dark tales spoke to generations of kids and parents because the stories were in touch with the human psyche. "The City of Lost Children" becomes increasingly out of touch as it progresses. The spectacle swallows the narrative and transforms the dream into its own nightmare: the city of the lost audience.

NEWSDAY, 12/15/95, Part II/p. B7, John Anderson

What if Walt Disney had taken the fairy tales he lifted and run in the opposite direction—away from the clover and fuzzy "aminals" and into the primal dark of archetypal fable? It might have looked something like "The City of Lost Children," which is live action but boasts the liquid freedom of animation. And the creative use of fear.

Owing something to Terry Gilliam's twisted vision and a lot to their own, Marc Caro and Jean-Pierre Jeunet creators of 1991's memorably lurid "Delicatessen"—have created a wasted world of industrial ruins and makeshift mechanisms that look post apocalyptic, or just post-hygiene. What it also looks like is vaguely recognizable—like the freaks of Tod Browning, or their counterparts among the misshapen playthings of "Toy Story" what we see are the right parts in the wrong place. Which is both fascinating and chilling.

But "The City of Lost Children"—a title that sounds far too somber for this movie—is also very funny, both visually and in the way it tells its tale, which in the retelling isn't quite that funny at all.

A malignant scientist named Krank (Daniel Emilfork) is aging prematurely because he cannot dream. So he sends his crew of Cyclops—blind cult members who see through elaborate optical devices worn over one sightless eye—to steal children so he can steal their dreams. In his lab, he is assisted by the diminutive Miss Bismuth (Mireille Mosse), a brain named Irvin (voice of Jean-Louis Trintignant) who is kept in a fish tank and six Clones (the rubberfaced Dominique Pinon).

The children of the squalid harbor town—a place both futuristic and Dickensian—loathe adults. None is cared for and all are exploited, either by Krank, the Cyclops or by the Octopus (Genevieve Brunet, Odile Mallet), Siamese twins who act like a two-headed Fagin (without the warmth). When One (Ron Perlman) a circus strongman, loses his baby brother Denree (Joseph Lucien) to Krank's henchmen, he gets no help from the kids, who are led by the beautiful and street-tough Miette (Judith Vittet). But they soften, realizing that One is nothing but a big kid, and is the only adult in sight who's been caring for a child in the first place.

Miette and One, the brain and the muscle, join up and, in the course of trying to free the children from Krank's reign of dream-terror, share something that looks like love. And it all seems right. Caro and Jeunet are working in a very delicate place of their own nimble creation, but it not only works, it's enchanting.

Many of the sets and shots are simply startling, as are several of the devices that run throughout the film: The fleas of circus owner Marcello (Jean-Claude Dreyfus), a master who arms his insects with venom-loaded headgear that turns ordinary people into homicidal maniacs (one scene, in which a Cyclops hooks his own eyepiece into the headgear of his victim so the latter can watch his own murder, is almost identical to a scene in "Strange Days," which may not be significant but seems worth noting). And the elaborate, Rube Goldberg-style means by which certain things are accomplished—the retrieving of a key, the saving of a life—are ingenious and hilarious.

It took Caro and Jeunet years to put this film together and it was worth it. Imaginative, moving and a combination of the novel and the primal, "The City of Lost Children" is a classic to be.

SIGHT AND SOUND, 9/95, p. 48, Tony Rayns

A dank and decrepit port has seen a spate of child kidnappings by members of The Cyclops, an apocalyptic sect of blind people who see through single artificial eyes. Sideshow strongman One takes the hungry three-year-old orphan Denrée as his adopted brother just before the child is kidnapped and whisked off to a rig in the heavily mined sea, base of the powercrazed Krank, who lacks the ability to dream and tries to steal dreams from the kidnapped children. (Krank provides the sect with artificial eyes in return for the children.) Krank uses the dream machines devised by his former colleague Irvin—who survives only as a disembodied brain in a tank and is prone to migraines—but cannot understand why the children yield him nothing but nightmares. He is consoled by his servant Miss Bismuth, who commands a team of six identical clones.

Determined to rescue Denrée. One tries to enlist the help of the gang of street kids controlled by the twin sisters Zette and Line (known as The Octopus) and eventually teams up with the feisty nine-year-old Miette. Captured and sentenced to death by The Cyclops, one is rescued by retired freak show manager Marcello (whose help has been enlisted by his former employees The Octopus), but Miette apparently drowns in the harbour. She is in fact saved by a mysterious diver, an amnesiac scavenger living in an air-tight underwater chamber, who returns to the city—where she finds One drowning his sorrows over her death in a bar. The diver meanwhile retrieves from the sea one of Denrée's bottled dreams, which has been smuggled off the rig at Irvin's instigation; the dream reawakens the diver's memory (he recalls that he was once Krank's partner, and the man from whom the servants were cloned) and then wafts around the port, alerting Miette and others to Denrée's plight.

Escaping a fiendish plan by The Octopus to turn them against each other, one and Miette row out to the rig, avoiding the mines with the aid of a map found tattooed on the skull of a Vietnamese tattooist. At the same time, the diver sets out for the rig across the sea bed. Krank is about to vamp the entire contents of Denrée's brain when One/Miette and the diver launch parallel attacks on the rig. Miss Bismuth is harpooned and the clones scatter in confusion. Irvin tells Miette that she can save Denrée only by entering his dream, which she does—almost succumbing to Krank's malign influence in the process. Krank dies in his own machine as everyone else evacuates the rig—except for the diver, who has dynamited the entire structure and tied himself to its girders. He decides he would rather escape after all, but a seagull settles on the plunger, setting off a huge explosion. Safe on a boat in the arms of One and Miette, the well-fed Denrée gives a satisfied burp.

Jeunet and Caro go digital. The images in *The City of Lost Children* are vastly more elaborate (and expensive) than those in *Delicatessen* and crowded with high-tech visual effects, but rooted in the same MTV aesthetic: all surface dazzle, no space for depth or resonance. This is a cinema without after-images, engineered for maximum instant gratification.

As a "dark fairy tale for all ages", the movie is a non-starter compared with films like *Gremlins* and the first *Nightmare on Elm Street*. Its postmodern insistence on recycled images and ideas and its obsession with the freakish and grotesque at the expense of any immediate reality rob it of true emotional impact. It misunderstands the nature of fairy tales as comprehensively as *Desperate Remedies* misunderstood the nature of melodrama, ending up a camp shadow of the film it would like to be. As an extended music video, though, it's not too bad. The concept is David Lynch meets Wes Craven, with Dickens and Mervyn Peake as the fashionably retro matchmakers; the visuals run the gamut from fascinating fascism (the 'religious' ceremonies of the Cyclops sect) to interactive games (point-of-view shots through the eyes of a leaping poisoned flea). The occasional image even approaches the level of poetic fantasy routinely achieved by Georges Méliès nearly a century ago.

But the plot, for all its density, quickly becomes a drag. Lacking the analytical underpinnings which put *The Company of Wolves* into the interesting failure category, The *City of Lost Children* spends nearly two hours trying to scale its own peak of technical ingenuity, coming up with 'spectacular' visuals (six identical clones in one frame, images which distort as if printed on melting plastic) whose only real tension arises from the need to out-do the preceding visuals. It soon becomes apparent that the profusion of characters and narrative threads is a camouflage for the shortage of engaging dramatic ideas. The movie is full of scenes like the attempted seduction of one by a blowsy hooker in a waterfront bar which would pass muster as referential motifs in a music video but lack even the most basic attempts to bring them to life as drama. And the generally low level of humour does little to rescue viewer morale.

There is the odd compensation to reward those kept awake by Angelo Badalamenti's over-lush score. Judith Vittet makes a spirited debut as Miette, suggesting that she has a future beyond vacuous special-effects movies. Jean-Paul Gaultier's costumes are functionally witty; it was a particularly smart idea to dress the ugly sisters Zette and Line like the famous Berlin transvestite Charlotte von Mahlsdorf. And the climactic battle between Krank and Miette for the mind of Denrée is as well-imagined as anything in the Elm Street series: Krank is morphed back to his handsome youth and infancy while Miette morphs to old age in a dance of time that has an authentic oneiric charge. Mostly, though, this is one strictly for overgrown boys who get a kick out of digital visual effects.

VILLAGE VOICE, 12/19/95, p. 76, Georgia Brown

A river of tears is nothing compared to the impressive chain reaction set off by a single teardrop in *The City of Lost Children,* Canne's opening nighter and a wild, loopy, Gilliam-esqe ride. Too quirky for its own good, in fact, *City* was quickly dismissed while French audiences and press swooned over the more gritty *La Haine* (which could have been called *The Suburb of Lost Children).*

A gadget-laden, F/X, sci-fairy tale created by *Delicatessen* duo Jean-Pierre Jeunet and Marc Caro (Jeunet is billed as director, Caro as artistic director), *City of Lost Children* is so extravagantly cluttered, so packed to the portholes, it's hard to sort out, or even see, what's there. Under the overload, however, it has some perfectly lovely elements—especially the odd couple relationship between a baffled lug known as One (Ron Perlman) and a startlingly beautiful, tough cookie nymphet, Miette (Judith Vittet). The movie manages to put the nine-year-old Miette and One under the covers together, to articulate their love (including Miette's transparent desire), and yet not to be prurient.

The best thing about the movie is its interest in saving the children. A kind of futuristic (or is it Dickensian?) *Peter Pan,* the movie is set in a gloomy port where bands of orphans fend off exploitation, and a mad scientist, Krank (Daniel Emilfork)—a version of Hook—kidnaps children, importing them to his floating lab in order to capture their dreams. Growing old fast because he's lost the capacity to dream, Krank has developed a machine to tap into a child's sleep. Each time he tries, though, the kid's dream turns into a nightmare. Krank is assisted by an officious dwarf (Mireille Mosse) and six squabbling clones (all played, with digital enhancement, by Dominique Pinon) and is heckled by a pickled brain (voice by Jean-Louis Trintignant).

The pure-hearted strong man, One, gets involved when his *petit frere,* Denree, is captured; Mietteis searching for missing confederates. Between the two and their goal stand several other monsters, including a gang of cyclopes and some sinister Siamese twins (Genevieve Brunet and Odile Mallet). Distinguishing the film also are its jerky but lyric narrative rhythms; these are enhanced by Angelo Badalamenti's lush and spooky score.

Something that doesn't make me happy; several prolonged shots of toddlers looking frightened to death and sobbing violently. This actually made the screening audience laugh! You would think a movie about saving children would want to attach the disclaimer: "In the making of this film, no child shed a tear."

Also reviewed in:
CHICAGO TRIBUNE, 12/15/95, Friday/p. L, Michael Wilmington
NEW YORK TIMES, 12/15/95, p. C34, Stephen Holden
VARIETY, 5/22-28/95, p. 93, Derek Elley
WASHINGTON POST, 2/9/96, p. F7, Rita Kempley
WASHINGTON POST, 2/9/96, Weekend/p. 38, Desson Howe

CITY UNPLUGGED

A Filmhaus release of a Film Zolffo production in association with Upstream Pictures/Film Teknik/EXITfilm. *Executive Producer:* Ilkka Järvilaturi. *Producer:* Lasse Saarinen. *Director:*

Ilkka Järvilaturi. *Screenplay (Estonian with English subtitles):* Paul Kolsby. *Based on an idea by:* Ilkka Järvilaturi and Paul Kolsby. *Director of Photography:* Rein Kotov. *Editor:* Christopher Tellefsen. *Music:* Mader. *Music Editor:* Christopher Tellesen. *Sound:* J. Sergio Väntänen. *Sound Editor:* J. Sergio Väntänen, Olli Parnanen, Kyösti Vantanen, and Olli Huhtanen. *Production Designer:* Toomas Hörak. *Special Effects:* Heikki Takkinen. *Costumes:* Mare Raidma. *Make-up:* Ly Kärner. *Running time:* 99 minutes. *MPAA Rating:* Not Rated.

CAST: Ivo Uukkivi (Toivo); Milena Gulbe (Maria); Monika Mäger (Terje); Enn Klooren (Mihhail "Misha"); Väinö Laes (Andres); Peeter Oja (Dmitri, Mihhail's Son); Juri Järvet (Anton); Villem Indrikson (Officer Kallas); Andres Raag (Kallas' Colleague); Gerardo Contreras (Doctor); Martin Tulmin (Baby); Kadri Kilvet, Salme Poopuu, and Ulvi Kreitsmann (Nurses); Kristel Kärner (Pregnant Woman); Aleksander Kortava and Raivo Tamm (Men); Tönu Kark (Koni "Stub"); Stepan Maurits (Koni's Colleague); Ain Lutsepp (Ernst, Tobacco Factory Worker); Vladimir Laptev (Priest); Vladimir Laptev, Jr. (Priest's Son); Anna-Liisa Lehtmets (Priest's Daughter); Saime Reek (Grocery Shop Owner); Kristel Leesmend (Shop Assistant); Raivo Tamm (Man); Dajan Ahmetov (Gangster); Ants Vain (Toivo's Superior); Aarne Leet (Aarne, Guard); Leida Paju (Cleaner); Paul Laasik (Edgar Luks); Aado Hermlin (Shot Policeman); Jaan Tatte (Peeter, Anton's Son-in-Law); Carmen Tabor (Diana); Marlo Tamme (Peeter and Diana's Child); Enn Nömmik (Gold Car Driver); Jüri Vlassov and Mihkel Smeljanski (Folk Dancers); Elina Aasa (Fiddler); Leigarid (Folk Dance Band); Tarmo Kruusimäe and Kristian Müller (Hooligans in Grocery Story); Kerstin Raidma (Hooligan in Wine Shop); Igor Põldma (Mihhail's Bodyguard); Tooms Tatrik (Anton's Bodyguard); Tarmo Mannard (Drunken Russian Soldier); Enn Pauk (Man on Tram); Dieg Mihhailov (Crane Operator); Toomas Tamme (Taxi Driver); Toomas Hussar (Driver); Mati Talvik (Bank President); Rein Lind (Politician on TV); Aare Kasemaa (Politician at Eesti Bank); Külli Palmsaar (TV Director).

NEW YORK POST, 6/23/95, p. 39, Bill Hoffmann

"City Unplugged" is a taut, involving little thriller that proves American mobsters have nothing up on the cold, calculating organized crime syndicates of the former Soviet Union.

The film is set in the tiny Baltic nation of Estonia, which between the two world wars amassed a national treasury of $900 million in gold, which leaders hid in a Paris bank on the eve of World War II. Fifty years later, after the nation its independence from the Soviet Union, the gold bullion is being returned home to the National Bank of Estonia in Tallinn.

That's the plan anyway, because a band of Russian mobsters has hatched a plot to steal the bullion, melt it and recast it into gold cigarettes to be sold.

Into this scheme is recruited a mild-mannered electric plant worker named Toivo (Ivo Uukkivi) who is hired to shut down Tallinn's power for a few hours so the gold can be grabbed.

Toivo is not the bad-guy type—he's doing it strictly for the cash to make a better life for his soon-to-be-born baby.

But just as Toivo begins dismantling the power plant, he learns that his wife (Milena Gulbe) has given birth to a premature infant, who needs an electric-powered incubator to survive.

Toivo suddenly finds himself in a dash-to-the-death race to mess up the mob's plan and restore power to save his child.

Part of the film's power is found in its portrayal of the mob as a group of ruthless, power-mad men struggling to keep their evil empire alive despite the changing social and political climates in Estonia.

These guys are tough. They actually brand each other to signify the passing of the leadership torch and taunt, torture and murder without blinking an eye.

Rein Kotov's stark black-and-white photography (which turns to color at the end) adds to the threateningly desperate atmosphere.

Screenwriter Paul Kolsby has a sharp eye for detail in chronicling every day Estonian life and provides many jolting touches such as the old lady shopkeeper who single-handedly dispatches two young punks who try to hold her up.

"City Unplugged" doesn't have the polish of "GoodFellas" or the grandeur of "The Godfather," but on its own terms, its a whole lot tougher.

NEWSDAY, 6/23/95, Part II/p. B6, John Anderson

Somewhere within the former Eastern Bloc, there may be a Baltic Jim Carrey, cutting up with post-Communist abandon. But it's unlikely. What constitutes humor in, say, Estonia, is something far more fatalistic, far more rooted in a resigned acceptance of the fact that life stinks—and is, therefore, hilarious.

It's just speculation, of course, but that dark outlook may be the result of years under the Soviet yoke. Which would explain both the rogue strain of optimism infecting "City Unplugged"—formerly titled "Darkness at Tallinn," and the first independent Estonian film released in the United States—and its sense of payback. A caper film and an absurdist take on the gangster genre, "City" involves the heist of Estonia's immense gold reserve—amassed during its 11 years of independence between the world wars—by, of course, Russians.

Written by an American (Paul Kolsby), directed by an Americanized Finn (Ilkka Jarvilaturi), and a U.S.-Finnish-Estonian co-production, the film pays homage to American gangster movies (as did "Reservoir Dogs," and there are similarities here), as well as to "The Producers," while maintaining its own unmodulated tone of cosmic dread. As the unwieldy scheme gets under way—it takes some time to figure out just what's up, but the stolen gold is to be processed through a cigarette factory and shipped out of the country—we see that Russians can't pull off a robbery any better than they could run a Union of Soviet Socialist Republics. So they compensate with brutality for what they lack in competence.

To succeed at all, the mobsters—who include the ancient and lethal Anton (Juri Jarvis, of Andre Tarkovsky's "Solaris")—are relying on Toivo (Ivo Uukivi), a young electrician who is feverishly rewiring the city's circuits to effect a total blackout, unaware of the nature of the crime. He needs the money—like ignorance, a common enough excuse—because his wife, Maria (Milena Gulbe), is pregnant. But when she goes into premature labor and delivers just as Toivo cuts the lights, she and the baby are both endangered making Toivo complicit not just in the economic death of his country but in the physical death of his family.

Toivo will come to the rescue, but the messages about personal responsibility and the interconnections within society are strong—when the hospital's backup diesel generators fail to go on, and an aggrieved doctor complains, a nurse asks, "Your new car, sir, it runs on diesel ...?" And even the gangsters' families are ruined by their greed. "City Unplugged," for all its dry, morbid hilarity, is more than funny. It's a statement about community—emotional communism, perhaps, although Estonians may not find that label so very funny.

SIGHT AND SOUND, 10/94, p. 53, Julian Graffy

1991. After finally regaining its independence, Estonia awaits the return of $970 million in gold, secreted in a Paris bank during the half century of Soviet rule. The people are assured that prosperity lies ahead. But Mihhail, the new boss of the local mob, has other plans, which involve getting Toivo, a young electrician at the local power plant, to black out the city on the night of the gold's delivery, thus securing the darkness in Tallinn necessary for the plot's success. Toivo's heavily pregnant wife Maria has persuaded him that his cut will ensure a better life for their child. While Toivo works to disable the plant, the gang begin to fight among themselves, and Maria goes into premature labour. A young girl, Terje, rushes to the plant to get Toivo, only to be told by Dmitri, Mihhail's son, that he has died in an explosion. Terje takes the grief-stricken Maria to hospital and she struggles to give birth while her husband, a gun at his head, rewires the electricity circuits, and the gold arrives, greeted by a patriotic crowd.

Andres, a gang member bothered by scruple, kills no-good Dmitri and tells Toivo of his lies to Terje. In the raid on the bank a guard, Peeter, the son-in-law of former gang boss Anton, is killed. The baby boy is born but the mother is losing consciousness. The electricity failure plunges the hospital too into darkness, threatening both their lives. The gang melt down the gold at a commandeered cigarette factory and package it up as Tallinn cigarettes. In the pitch black streets, Toivo meets Terje and together they return to the plant to try to switch the electricity back on and save his family. Toivo kills Andres and captures Mihhail but Mihhail takes Terrje hostage. In a shoot-out in the port Anton shoots Mihhail. At the hospital, Toivo finds his son crying and his wife dead, but his tears fall on her face and she opens her eye.

Darkness and light are at the heart of Ilkka Järvilaturi's second feature—physically so, as the monochrome photography of the first half of the film gives way first to an extended sequence of blackness, and then to colour as light is returned to Tallinn. The moral implications of these chromatics are easy to fathom. In preparing for the heist the gang buy up all possible sources of light, including even the church candles. When an almost apocalyptic darkness falls upon the city, young Estonians take to looting. *Darkness in Tallinn* is a crime movie that makes effective use of its setting, though we see little of the ancient capital's picturesque beauty the Estonian folk singers in the cobbled streets are perplexed and marginal figures here, irrelevant to the drama unfolding around them.

The film's sense of place emerges rather through its acute and pervasive sense that the new country is undergoing a moral challenge, a challenge delineated not only on the grand scale of politics and history—the credits unfold against newsreels of Estonia's recent past, the national anthem greets the arrival of the bullion—but more pressingly in the minor decisions of individual lives, where no small sin passes unnoticed. Almost the first action of brutal Dmitri is to crush a young girl's treasured drink can, and it is a sure path from there to perdition. The equally callous Stub smashes the gold watch a young man has inherited from his grandfather. His fate will be to be fried beneath an upturned pot of molten gold. Another gang member, Andres, asks whether a killer can enter the kingdom of heaven.

But *Darkness in Tallinn* is not weighed down by its serious concerns, and it works extremely effectively as a compelling and densely plotted heist movie, with the three stories, the delivery of the gold, the delivery of the child and the extinguishing of the light satisfyingly intercut. Järvilaturi has a nice eye for incidental detail—young people on stilts roam the streets ordering people to "Smile!", a radio offers "more hits, less talk from Estonia"—and the film is sometimes darkly humorous in a way reminiscent of its director's older compatriot, Aki Kaurismäki.

Above all, though, like Kaurismäki's *Ariel* and like Järvilaturi's much praised debut *Homebound, Darkness in Tallinn* looks at its characters through the prism of their (secure, corrupted, aspired to) family relationships. The gang's new "godfather", Mihhail is, in his own words, "merciless" when the old boss, Anton, wants him to spare his son-in-law, Peeter. Mihhail himself is tempted into recklessness by the shock of the retributive death of his own son, Dmitri. When Anton's daughter Diana abuses and abandons him after he has failed to prevent her husband's death, he (Juri Järvet, who played Snaut in Tarkovsky's *Solaris* and another patriarch brought to nemesis, Kozintsev's *Lear)* shoots Mihhail dead. (In this film the worst of the criminals have Russian names; the innocent, and those open to the call to repent, are Estonians.) Diana, Peeter and their child are a (Russian-Estonian) family who even in death can resist the force of evil—both son-in-law and daughter cast Anton, the "demon-tempter" to the ground—and in this they offer an example to the film's wavering central family, Toivo, Maria and their infant son.

If Maria's miraculous "resurrection" at the end of the film takes it beyond the verisimilitude it has hitherto espoused, it echoes an earlier scene at the electricity plant when Toivo himself had seemed to die of an electric shock, and the threatened death of their son in his incubator. It is also consistent with the film's allegorical agenda (in which they figure as an earthly, sinful "holy family" for Estonia), with its (optimistic) insistence that love and faith (a voice had told Toivo that both he and his wife would see this baby) can redeem, and conquer the forces of darkness.

VILLAGE VOICE, 6/27/95, p. 49, Georgia Brown

City Unplugged—formerly titled *Darkness in Tallinn*—is a stylish heist pic written by an American, directed by a Finn, and set in the newly independent Republic of Estonia. The premise: A cache of gold sent during World War II to Paris for safekeeping is finally being returned to the country. Demonstrating a slimy but characteristic lack of civic-mindedness, the Russian mafia intends to hijack the gold for their own ends. The thugs commandeer a nearby cigarette factory where the shipment will be melted down and packaged as cigarettes. To facilitate their ends, they've hired a local electrician, Toivo (Ivo Uukkivi), who will plunge Tallinn into darkness at the crucial moment.

City Unplugged has been compared to *Reservoir Dogs*, no doubt because the gang leaders dub themselves Fire, Earth, and Air (or Smoke, as Air prefers to be called)—though by this token the comparison should be to *The Taking of Pelham One Two Three,* which is where Tarantino lifted *his* little naming game from (without even changing the names). Plotwise, *City Unplugged* is closer to Roger Avary's *Killing Zoe* in that Toivo the electrician, the savvy technician brought in from outside like Eric Stoltz's Zed, is the film's central character and more or less the movie's sole decent adult male.

Toivo accepts the job only after being persuaded by his pregnant wife, Maria (Milena Gulbe), who wants money for their baby. When Toivo objects that "We used to live by ideals," Maria scoffs with true post-Communist cynicism, "Ideals? Those were dreams." The couple is guarded over by a resourceful street urchin, Terje, an adolescent tomboy in a baseball cap. This part becomes a bit precious.

Smartly directed by Ilkka Jarvilaturi, the film is shot mostly in noirish black-and-white, with many fancy camera angles, and is stitched into quick, elliptical scenes. Writer Paul Kolsby supplies a more humanistic dialogue than is the norm in such pictures. When a gangster brags, "I've got God," flashing a medallion, Toivo replies, "That's not God, that's jewelry." God, of course, is on Toivo's side. In this and other matters (I won't spoil the ending), the film differs from the standard American brand thriller. This must be why it took three years for this classy little picture to win a U.S. release.

Also reviewed in:
NEW YORK TIMES, 6/23/95, p. C12, Stephen Holden
VARIETY, 10/25/93, p. 83, David Stratton

CLEAN, SHAVEN

A DSM III Films Inc. production. *Executive Producer:* J. Dixon Byrne. *Producer:* Lodge H. Kerrigan. *Director:* Lodge H. Kerrigan. *Screenplay:* Lodge H. Kerrigan. *Director of Photography:* Teodoro Maniaci. *Music:* Hahn Rowe. *Editor:* Jay Rabinowitz and Megan Agosto. *Sound:* John Kelsey and Matthew Perry. *Sound Editor:* Tony Martinez. *Production Designer:* Tania Ferrier. *Set Dresser:* Jose Claudio. *Make-up (Special):* Rob Benevides *Running time:* 80 minutes. *MPAA Rating:* Not Rated.

CAST: Peter Greene (Peter Winter); Robert Albert (Jack McNally); Jennifer MacDonald (Nicole Frayne); Megan Owen (Mrs. Winter); Molly Castelloe (Melinda Frayne); J. Dixon Byrne (Dr. Michaels); Alice Levitt (Girl with Ball); Jill Chamberlain (Teenager at Motel); Agathe Leclerc (Murdered Girl); Roget Joly (Police Photographer); Rene Beaudin (Boy on Bicycle); Eliot Rockett (Man on Ladder); Lee Kayman (Bartender); Peter Lucas (Drunk); Rob Benevides (Robber); Angela Vibert and Karen MacDonald (Girls in Rain); Ismael Ramirez (Psychotic Derelict); Marty Clinis and Ruth Gottheimer (Library Patrons); June Kelly (Librarian); Grace Vibert (Schoolteacher); James Hance (Man in Adoption Agency); Marti Wilkerson (Adoption Agent); Michael Benson and Eliot Rockett (Men in Jeep); Cathleen Biro and Harlan Hamilton (Drunks).

NEW YORK POST, 4/14/95, p. 41, Thelma Adams

What's it like to be schizophrenic? Hopefully, the closest you'll ever come to knowing the answer is viewing Lodge Kerrigan's disorienting debut, "Clean, Shaven."

The central plot is simple: schizophrenic Peter Winter (Peter Greene) returns to his hometown to visit his daughter. Nicole (Jennifer MacDonald) has been put up for adoption. Meanwhile, someone is killing Nicole look-alikes. Detective Jack McNally (Robert Albert) connects the dots.

Kerrigan approaches his subject with a harrowing you-are-there technique. He uses experimental techniques to place the viewer deep inside Winter's insanity. Trees blowing in the wind become threatening mammoths; scenery passed by in the blur of a man whose thoughts are speeding out of control.

Since aural hallucinations are a common symptom of the mental disorder, the soundtrack is a demonic symphony of crackling electrical wires, police sirens, flags snapping threateningly in the breeze and paranoid talk radio programs.

At one point, we see a little girl outside Winter's stolen car. He exits the car. A child screams. There is a thud.

The camera doesn't reveal events outside the car. Winter gets back behind the wheel and drives away. Robbed of the rational establishing shot, we lose our anchor and share in the driver's disturbed reality,

Among the most difficult sequences—and there are many—is the bathroom scene that gives the movie its title. Greene's grooming is nearly unwatchable. He showers, scraping his skin with steel wool. He shaves, leaving red trails. He cuts his hair—and scalp—with pointed scissors.

While Winter's clearly a clinical case, this scene gives the visit to his mother's house that follows an added sting. "You still aren't taking care of yourself," the elderly woman nags her son.

"Clean, Shaven" is not a movie intent on shocking for shock's sake. It uses unsettling visual techniques to create an emotional intensity. Caught up in the movie, I reached a state of hypersensitivity. Even the detective catching his hand on a splinter made me whimper.

Greene, the tall, skeletal, fair-haired, blue-eyed star of "Laws of Gravity," an East Coast Peter Weller, never displays a false moment.

He bears the tragedy of an intelligent man who suddenly snapped. He grasps at the shards of sanity that come his way in an existence hurtling towards the abyss. When the movie strays from Greene, particularly when it follows the detective or slips into a gratuitous barroom shoot-out, it's less effective.

"Clean, Shaven" premiered at the Telluride Film Festival in 1993, and played Sundance, Cannes and New Directors/ New Films in 1994. Now it's filtered down to the Quad Cinema in the West Village. It's the most disturbing movie you'll see this year—if you dare to watch it.

NEWSDAY, 4/14/95, Part II/p. B5, John Anderson

What, precisely, defines horror in a horror film? Is it carnage, death, grossly inflated overhead? If it were that simple, Sylvester Stallone would be Bela Lugosi. No. It has more to do with the nearness of the abyss. How unsure our footing is. How close to the edge a director can escort us.

By the end of "Clean, Shaven"—first-time director Lodge Kerrigan's guided tour of the schizophrenic mind—we've seen self-mutilation and paranoid terror and fairly floated over the dark hole of madness. The first real horror film to hit the screens in years—at least since "Henry: Portrait of a Serial Killer"—"Clean, Shaven" suspends its audience on twin wires of meaning and misperception, its pitifully insane protagonist embodying both terror and pathos. In a deft melding of the sane and the disturbed, it may not make you question your own balance of mind, but it will at least undo your ability to distinguish reality from illusion on a movie screen.

"Clean, Shaven" is a short story, about a mentally ill man named Peter Winter (Peter Greene of "Laws of Gravity") on a search for his motherless daughter Nicole (Jennifer MacDonald); during his institutionalization, Nicole has been given up for adoption—and by his own mother (Megan Owen). While Peter hunts Nicole, a detective named McNally (Robert Albert) hunts Peter; a child has been brutally beaten to death, and though the connection to Peter is tenuous, McNally certainly thinks *he* knows who did it.

Kerrigan is a cinematographer himself, and Teodoro Maniaci's camera work on "Clean, Shaven" imparts the near-to-panicked look the movie needs. It's the sound of the film, however, that imparts much of its creepy quality. Combined with Greene's fully realized portrayal of a man fighting madness, the sound forces us to share his terror.

Yes, Peter is terrified—of the people who stare at him in their own terror, of not finding his daughter, of the static-radio voices that scream inside his head. Often, there are sounds only he and we can hear. But not always. Kerrigan keeps us off balance, by allowing us to see through Peter's eyes, and by not being obvious.

Two scenes in particular are noteworthy for what they say about Peter, and about Kerrigan's purposes: When we first see Peter outside the institution—there are several previous glimpses of him fetal-positioned and trembling in his cell—a little girl bounces a ball off his car. He gets out and we hear screams and the sound either of a ball bouncing or of someone being pummeled. But when Peter gets back in his car and drives away, he passes a man in a nearby garage who stares at him impassively—something he'd be unlikely to do had he just witnessed a murder.

The second scene involves Peter in a public library, searching through adoption books for traces of Nicole. The voices increase in volume; Peter pounds his head against the shelves in an effort to stop them, and the entire scene reaches a crescendo—just as Kerrigan cuts the voices off. He then pulls back to reveal Peter as seen by the other people in the library, who can't hear the voices and can't possibly share his horror. We, however, can.

"Clean, Shaven" is not an easy film to watch; several scenes can only be described as excruciating, although the violence they contain is committed by Peter against himself. There are also scenes of the murdered girl's body that will cause some revulsion, but help explain McNally's single-minded pursuit of Peter. All in all, Kerrigan has produced a film of visceral as well as intellectual power, one that will remain in the mind of the viewer in much the same way as one of Peter's persecuting voices.

SIGHT AND SOUND, 2/95, p. 42, Philip Kemp

Peter Winter, a schizophrenic just out of an institution, goes in search of his young daughter Nicole. After the death of his wife and during his incarceration, Peter's mother Gladys had sent the child for adoption. Nicole now lives with Melinda Frayne, who works on a fishing boat on the Atlantic coastline, in Canada. Peter stops off at a motel, where he cuts his face and body with a razor. The next day he continues to his mother's house; she receives him without warmth.

Peter is being trailed by detective Jack McNally, who suspects him of being a killer. The mutilated body of a young girl is found near the motel where Peter stayed, and there are bloodstains in the room he occupied. Peter visits a library and looks up books on gifted children; his unbalanced behaviour alarms the librarian, who later reports it to McNally.

When Melinda and Nicole visit Gladys, Peter is watching the house and follows them home. Approaching Nicole, playing by herself in the garden, he reveals himself as her father and takes her to the beach. On the deserted shore he tries to explain his torment to her. McNally shows up; thinking Peter is harming the child, he shoots him dead. Later McNally broods in a bar, while Nicole tries to contact her father on the boat's radio.

The above synopsis, being linear and explicit, misrepresents *Clean, Shaven*. Plot elements in Lodge Kerrigan's film are conveyed piecemeal and obliquely, mostly through the turmoil of interference that clogs Peter Winter's mind. Few films have succeeded so convincingly in putting us inside a schizophrenic's head, making us feel what it's like to be battered and wrenched by a jumble of uncontrollable impulses. More than once Winter turns on his car radio but we can scarcely hear it, drowned out as it is by the angry voices, harsh metallic noises and buzz of static in his brain, tuned in to a whole world of pitiless aggression. The visuals are equally abrupt and fragmented, strewn with bleak, near-monochrome images of concrete and rusted metal. It's like a jigsaw puzzle where all the pieces have jagged edges and none of them fit.

What makes the film even more disturbing is that while adopting the *Fugitive*-style formula of innocent man hunted by relentless cop, it never allows us the comforting certainty that Winter really is innocent. Early on, as he sits in his car, a ball bounces against the windscreen; a young girl peers worriedly in; and Winter gets out. The camera holds on the empty car while on the soundtrack we hear a child's screams. A savage beating for a trivial offence—or more of Winter's tormented aural memories? No way of telling, any more than we know whether he killed the girl found near the motel. McNally's viewpoint is no guide, since he's almost as unbalanced as his quarry. Their actions often run parallel and in the end, as if by transference, the detective's mind is invaded by the same noises that plagued Winter.

Clean, Shaven might seem mannered but for the tortured intensity of Peter Greene in the central role—a performance all the more impressive given that the film had to be shot over a period of two years. Greene frighteningly creates the sense of a man hounded by unendurable self-loathing, unable even to face the gaze of mirrors (which he tapes over, smashes or turns to the wall) and careering helplessly towards destruction. "If I could just slow down a little bit," he wistfully tells Nicole, "I could come up with a solution." Instead he takes out his agony on inanimate objects, himself and—perhaps—other people, and in one near-unwatchable scene prises off one of his fingernails with a knife and gouges around in the wound.

Occasionally we get a hint of a certain skewed reasoning behind Winter's behaviour. He was an abnormally gifted, solitary child, his mother tells McNally (a pattern Winter is alarmed to see repeating in his daughter), and his self-mutilation stems from believing he has a radio receiver in his head and a transmitter in his finger. But so effectively are we drawn into his fractured world that these attempts at explanation feel like an intrusion, a muting of the film's inarticulate howl. This apart, the strength of Kerrigan's first feature lies in its refusal to compromise, to make things easy or pleasant for the viewer; as such, it's a stark riposte to the string of recent Hollywood movies depicting the mentally damaged as founts of simple wisdom.

VILLAGE VOICE, 4/18/95, p. 60, J. Hoberman

Not for the squeamish, *Clean, Shaven* is a portrait of a peripatetic schizophrenic who may or may not be a serial child murderer. A half dozen years ago, *Henry: Portrait of a Serial Killer* established itself at the outer limits of American Gothic; *Clean, Shaven* is its more cerebral successor as study of antisocial pathology and purveyor of cinematic pain.

Produced, written, and directed by 31-year-old New York-based cinematographer Lodge Kerrigan, this crisp, cryptic first feature was shot hand-to-mouth over a two-year period on a remote island off New Brunswick. Kerrigan spent another year editing the film, which had its world premiere at the 1993 Telluride Film Festival, went on to win the Silver Hugo for best first feature in Chicago, garnered notoriety at Sundance after a viewer passed out during one particularly harrowing scene, was included in last year's "New Directors" series, was shown at Cannes, and most recently awarded Swatch's $20,000 prize for the independent "Filmmaker To Watch." The film's delay in finding a distributor may be related to the fact that even favorable reviews have described it as "unbearable," "agonizing," and "excruciating."

Like *Henry*, *Clean, Shaven* spends most of its time contemplating the protagonist's behavior; unlike Henry, however, Lodge's *isolato* is communicating terminal weirdness from the moment he appears. Employing perhaps three lines of dialogue in its first 20 minutes, *Clean, Shaven* opens with Peter (Peter Greene) cowering in his room, assailed by a virtuoso mix of industrial noise and muttering voices. Assailed by flashbacks, Peter plasters tabloid newspapers over his car windows and cruises around the bleak landscape, a sinister bundle in his back seat and a rifle hidden in his trunk. (That this nutmobile is never stopped may be taken for proof that we don't yet live in a police state.)

Someone has murdered and mutilated a child; Peter is pursued by a grim investigator even as Peter carries out his own mysterious quest, visiting his mother and stalking a child. Kerrigan presents Peter's case with a stunning absence of glamour. The mode is studied, cool, fragmented. The ambience is predicated on the antihero's tormented blandness—a remarkable performance by Peter Greene, who appeared to entirely different effect as the small-time Brooklyn hustler in Nick Gomez's *Laws of Gravity* and the rapist cop in *Pulp Fiction*. Panicked yet blank, Peter checks into a motel, turns the mirror to the wall, showers, shaves his body hair, and then gouges a wound in his scalp, trying to stop the voices in his skull.

Clean, Shaven is all the more a horror film in that its world seems to parallel Peter's. Kerrigan opens a scene with a megaclose-up of a knife slicing a tomato—heightening the existential horror of the sandwich being fashioned with the brain-piercing whistle of a tea kettle coming to boil. No sooner does the detective shadowing Peter wander into a bar than the place is robbed by another bare-chested lunatic. And the film's eerie ending suggests that Peter's deranged legacy will live on.

Also reviewed in:
CHICAGO TRIBUNE, 3/31/95, Friday/p. J, Michael Wilmington
NEW YORK TIMES, 4/14/95, p. C5, Janet Maslin
VARIETY, 9/27/93, p. 38, Todd McCarthy

CLOCKERS

A Universal Pictures release of a 40 Acres and a Mule Filmworks production. *Executive Producer:* Rosalie Swedlin and Monty Ross. *Producer:* Martin Scorsese, Spike Lee, and Jon Kilik. *Director:* Spike Lee. *Screenplay:* Richard Price and Spike Lee. *Based on the novel by:* Richard Price. *Director of Photography:* Malik Hassan Sayeed. *Editor:* Sam Pollard. *Music:* Terence Blanchard. *Music Editor:* Alex Steyermark. *Sound:* Tod Maitland. *Sound Editor:* Skip Lievsay. *Casting:* Robi Reed-Humes. *Production Designer:* Andrew McAlpine. *Art Director:* Tom Warren. *Set Decorator:* Debra Schutt. *Set Dresser:* Peter J. Von Bartheld, William Butler, Anthony Baldasare, Daniel Kenney, Raymond Murphy, Mark Simon, and Mitch Towse. *Special Effects:* Steve Kirshoff. *Costumes:* Ruth Carter. *Make-up:* Diane Hammond. *Stunt Coordinator:* Jeff Ward. *Running time:* 129 minutes. *MPAA Rating:* R.

CAST: Harvey Keitel (Rocco Klein); John Turturro (Larry Mazilli); Delroy Lindo (Rodney); Mekhi Phifer (Strike); Isaiah Washington (Victor); Keith David (Andre the Giant); Pee Wee Love (Tyrone); Regina Taylor (Iris Jeeter); Tom Byrd (Errol Barnes); Sticky Fingaz (Scientific); Fredro (Go); E.O. Nolasco (Horace); Lawrence B. Adisa (Stan); Hassan Johnson (Skills); Frances Foster (Gloria); Michael Imperioli (Jo-Jo); Lisa Arrindell Anderson (Sharon); Paul Calderon (Jesus at Hambones); Brendan Kelly (Big Chief); Mike Starr (Thumper); Graham Brown (Mr. Herman Brown); Steve White (Darryl Adams); Spike Lee (Chucky); Shawn McLean (Solo); Arthur Nascarella (Bartucci); Harry Lennix (Bill Walker); Bray Poor (Detective #1); Craig McNulty (Detective #2); Christopher Wynkoop (Detective #3); Paul Schulze (Detective #4); Donald Stephenson (Detective #5); John Fletcher (Al the Medic); J.C. Mackenzie (Frank the Medic); David Evanson (Smart Mike); Norman Matlock (Reverend Paul); Isaac Fowler (Charles); Leonard Thomas (Onion the Bar Patron); Maurice Sneed (Davis the Bartender); Calvin Hart (Guarrd #1); Ginny Yang (Kiki); Michael Badalucco (Cop #1); Ricky Aiello (Cop #2); Scot Anthony Robinson (Earl); Richard Ziman (Moe); David Batiste (T); Mar'qus Sample (Ivan); Mar'rece Sample (Mark); Ron Brice (Dead Man Begging); Ken Garito (Louie); Anthony Nocerino (Teen #1); Brian Konowal (Teen #2); Michael McGruther (Teen #3); Carlo Vogel (Teen #4); Harvey Williams ("Pick Me Up" Kid); Michael Cullen (Narc #1); Tim Kelleher (Narc #2); Skipp Sudduth (Narc #3); Larry Mullane (Larry the Narc); Patrick Ferraro (Bike Cop #1); L.B. Williams (Bike Cop #2); Jeff Ward (Bike Cop #3); Ronda Fowler (Bomb Girl); Hal Sherman (Forensics Officer); Marc Webster (EMS Technician); James Saxenmeyer (EMS Attendant #1); Paul Dubois (EMS Attendant #2); Jordan Brown (EMS Attendant #3); Michael Marchetta (Corrections Officer #1); Joanna Gardner (Corrections Officer #2); Mark Howard (Baby Recruit #1); Michael Shepherd (Baby Recruit #2); Gerald King (Baby Recruit #3); Ronta Davis (Baby Recruit #4); Lord Kayson (T's Crewmember #1); Orran Farmer (T's Crewmember #2); Wayne Muhammad (Fruit of Islam Vendor); Martin Jaffe (Street Vendor); Freddie Velez (Pedro the Security Guard).

CHRISTIAN SCIENCE MONITOR, 9/13/95, p. 13, David Sterritt

"Clockers" marks an important step in the career of Spike Lee, easily the most gifted and controversial African-American filmmaker of his generation.

Based on Richard Price's streetwise novel, the film plunges into the violent world of urban drug dealers, a rigidly defined hierarchy with high-powered suppliers at the top and no-power dealers at the bottom. The main character is Strike, a hard-working teenager whose energetic mind and almost puritanical habits would probably bring middle-class success if he lived in a more civilized environment.

Instead, Strike is a clocker, forever racing against an imaginary two-minute clock as he peddles cocaine to inner-city addicts and suburban thrill-seekers while dodging jaded cops, turf-conscious rivals, and assorted psychopaths who happen to live in the neighborhood.

Similar terrain has been explored in earlier pictures by black filmmakers, such as John Singleton's thoughtful "Boyz N the Hood" and Mario Van Peebles's flashy "New Jack City," two of the most widely seen examples. Most of Lee's movies are also steeped in African-American city life, but he has generally steered away from hands-on contact with the awful realities that surge through "Clockers" from beginning to end.

This one-step-removed stance was appropriate for movies like "She's Gotta Have It," a spunky romantic comedy, and "School Daze," about racial tensions on an all-black college campus. But it got Lee in trouble when he made "Do the Right Thing," a brilliant study of black-white relations in a working-class Brooklyn neighborhood. Many critics rightly applauded this film's stylized approach to issues that might have stirred more emotion than thought if treated more bluntly. But others blasted it for glossing over the everyday challenges of inner-city poverty. One reviewer accused it of making a strife-loaded ghetto look like Sesame Street.

Lee responded to these criticisms through some of his later films—particularly "Jungle Fever," a story of black-white romance that also showed a middle-class black man's gradual realization that he can neither avoid nor deny the drug-spawned horrors that have invaded his neighborhood and even his family.

FILMS IN REVIEW, 11-12/95, p. 100, Andy Pawelczak

Several times in the course of *Clockers*, Spike Lee's neo-thriller, the camera momentarily grazes a billboard showing a gun accompanied by the written legend "No More Packing." Who is it directed to? Kids in the audience who might be tempted by the ready availability and spurious phallic potency of guns? Adults who want their entertainment with a pre-digested message? Lee has always been a message filmmaker, though in *Do the Right Thing* the message was complicated by Danny Aiello's appealing humanity as the racist pizza man. In *Clockers*, the message—guns are bad, drugs are bad, father-figures and mothers are good—looms so large that it makes the drama seem almost an afterthought.

Richard Price's novel, on which he based his screenplay, is a linguistic tour de force. Price captures the vocabulary and cadences of street argot and its funny, imaginative naming mania, e.g., Buddha Hat, Andre the Giant. The teenage hero's name, Strike, suggests both the verb "to strike" and the strike in baseball—three of them and you're out. And Strike, a clocker (the novel's term for a street-level drug dealer), is on his way out. Tormented by a bleeding ulcer, he's caught between the police, who suspect him of a murder to which his brother has confessed, and his drug supplier who fears Strike might expose his role in the killing. Both novel and film follow him as he's buffeted between these opposing forces and searches for a way out.

In the novel, Price gets deep inside the skin and brain of the anomic, despairing Strike, but the film stays strictly on the surface and Mekhi Phifer doesn't have enough presence to make the role resonate. His Strike is a cipher at the center of the film; passive and bewildered, he stumbles, clutching at his stomach, from one episode to the next as we wait for him to do something. Inevitably, a secondary character begins to occupy center stage, and this precipitates a whole new set of problems. In the book, Rocco Klein is a burnt-out homicide cop who, in his own way, is as rudderless as Strike. We see him at home with his mismatched wife, drinking with his partner, and helplessly ensnared in celebrity worship of a Hollywood actor who is doing research for a cop movie. Convinced that Strike's brother, Victor (played in the movie by Isaiah Washington), is covering up for him, Rocco embarks on a quixotic quest to prove Victor innocent and salvage his life—it's Rocco's last chance to do something real, to give his life meaning. But the movie so flattens the character—in an interview, Lee said he wasn't interested in "white, middle-aged angst"—that we don't understand his motivation in getting so involved with the two brothers. As Rocco, Harvey Keitel is oddly listless, even at those moments when he should be most obsessive and energized.

The film's most compelling presence is Delroy Lindo as Rodney, the drug supplier. Rodney is a false father figure to his worshipful teenage acolytes, a point that Lee establishes early on with a closeup of Strike staring at Rodney with longing and love. With his lined, weathered face and easy, insinuating manner, Lindo lets us see both Rodney's manna-charged charisma and under-lying corruption and menace. In the supporting cast, John Turturro, as Rocco's partner on the homicide squad, proves that a strong actor can make his presence felt even in a role that is no more than a sketch. In the novel, the Turturro character owns a liquor store on the same street as Rodney's grocery store, and the two men have a kind of wary businessmen's chumminess; it's one more aspect of the symbiosis between cops and bad guys in the ghetto, but the point is lost in Lee's evisceration of the book.

With *Clockers*, Spike Lee has gone back to his brash, in-your-face *Do the Right Thing* style. At its best, the movie is the visual equivalent of rap, with rap's virtues and limitations; what it lacks in subtlety it makes up for in flamboyance and rawness. Lee gets the buzz of the streets with overlapping dialogue and hyperactive visuals that often contain more information than you can immediately process, and the overall film has an appropriately claustrophobic feeling. What's missing is the seamless continuum of Mafia and drug dealers and cops and clockers, who are the exploited proletarians at the bottom of the drug hierarchy. Price's novel emphasizes, in the classic Naturalist manner, the determining power of environment. Lee chooses to stress something else: the horrors of fratricidal, inner-city violence and the regenerative powers of the family. Fair enough, but after the opening illustrational montage of mutilated corpses, filmed in garish color, the film doesn't have anywhere to go.

LOS ANGELES TIMES, 9/13/95, Calendar/p. 1, Kenneth Turan

Playing under the opening credits, a series of stark images sets the mood for "Clockers," the disturbing movie Spike Lee has made from Richard Price's best-selling novel. These careful re-creations of crime scene photos of drug-related homicides show young black men sprawled in cars, tossed face down in dumpsters, motionless on sidewalks. Though not as horrific as the real thing, the pictures are grim enough to convey the message the rest of "Clockers" underlines: Don't even think about getting comfortable while this movie is on the screen.

"Clockers," Lee's eighth feature in nine years, demonstrates how accomplished a filmmaker he has become, securely in control of plot, actors and imagery. And because it is so much the film he wanted to make, "Clockers" illustrates another, less audience-friendly aspect of Lee's technique that is not always noticed, his particular combination of emotional distance and moral instruction.

Although other directors tend to make films because they want to tell stories or explore character, neither of these purposes feels paramount with Lee. He directs, or so it seems, to make points and deliver messages, and he has turned Price's novel into a cold, angry, unsettling motion picture about a cold, pitiless world.

Lee doesn't really want us to root too hard for anyone, even Strike, "Clockers'" young protagonist (effectively played by newcomer Mekhi Phifer). Getting viewers to bond to any one personality is too easy an out to his way of thinking. Lee is not after empathetic hearts who bleed for the deserving poor, he wants us to look at the larger picture and realize how deep the problem is, how much society has to change before any of us are allowed the luxury of getting off the hook through personal caring.

Strike, known to his mother and no one else as Ronald Dunham, is the nearly 20-year-old head of a crew of youthful dealers who sit on the benches outside a public housing project in Brooklyn (changed from the novel's New Jersey setting) and do nothing but dispense crack cocaine.

So conscientious he's developed stomach problems (which he sporadically treats with doses of a convenience store chocolate drink), Strike has become a particular favorite of his boss, Rodney Little (Delroy Lindo), a neighborhood Fagin who both cares about his kids and coldly exploits their willingness to sell crack, "the world's greatest product."

Quite literally losing the stomach for his work, hassled by the local police and a housing authority cop nicknamed Andre the Giant (Keith David), Strike is desperate to "get off the benches." So when Rodney talks one night about a drug rival named Darryl Adams and how grateful he would be if the guy were gone, Strike understands. After a quick stop at a neighborhood bar, where he runs into his hard-working, family man older brother Victor (Isaiah Washington), Strike heads out armed and dangerous.

Though we don't see it on screen, Darryl Adams is murdered that night, but to the surprise of everyone in the neighborhood, straight-arrow Victor, of all people, almost immediately confesses to the crime. He is, of course, arrested, but no one who knows anything thinks he did it, including homicide detective Larry Mazilli (John Turturro) and his especially unbelieving partner Rocco Klein (Harvey Keitel).

A cop for just about as long as Strike has been alive, Klein views the kid simply as "a known scumbag." And the longer he investigates Victor's personal history, the less likely he thinks it is that the older Dunham pulled the trigger. Convinced that the brothers are pulling some kind of scam on him, he takes Victor's confession as a deep personal affront and begins to put so much pressure on Strike that the young man's world threatens to unravel one strand at a time.

Though Lee has shifted the novel's focus from Rocco to Strike, what "Clockers" is particularly interested in is illustrating these two universes in collision, the dark spectacle of cynical, casually racist cops who joke about death battling both physically and psychologically with the kids who are inevitably the victims of violence.

What this brooding, unsettling film (written by Price and Lee) does most successfully is re-create the desperation and hopelessness of Strike's life on the benches and off it, forcefully showing how trapped he is between competing antagonists who care about no agenda but their own.

Even though Strike is allowed a few human touches, like his love of trains and his mentoring of a younger neighborhood kid named Tyrone (Pee Wee Love), the portrait of a pitiless society and the film's fierce frontal attacks on drugs ("You are selling your own people death") and shootings ("This ain't no TV violence, real guns kill") have a more lasting impact than any personal story.

Helping make these points is as strong a cast as Lee has yet worked with. As antagonists who confront each other through Strike, both Keitel and especially Lee veteran Delroy Lindo give strong and chilling performances. Also remarkable is Tom Byrd as Errol Barnes, Rodney's heroin-addicted, AIDS-ravaged enforcer, yet another in Lee's gallery of terrifying victims of drugs.

What problems "Clockers" has stem from Lee's lack of interest in story for its own sake. He encourages cinematographer Malik Hassan Sayeed to indulge in distracting camera tricks and doesn't seem to care that the dialogue in a critical scenes is difficult to understand or that the film's ending has a hollow feeling. Because, whether anyone likes it or not, whatever happens to Strike does not compel him as much as the enduring factors that put the young man on the benches in the first place.

NEW YORK, 9/18/95, p. 72, David Denby

The word *nigger* sounds uniquely ugly in the mouth of a white person, so ugly that it has been widely replaced in the media with the absurd locution *n-word*—a euphemism that implies our nerves are now so raw, we cannot bear to hear the word spoken even when clearly surrounded by quotation marks. Yet a word that is unspeakable for whites is spoken by many African-Americans all the time, in the streets, in rap music, in movies and novels, and spoken with varying shades of contempt and affection. The word is alive with rage and disgust and sometimes pride in ways that CNN and the New York *Times* can't begin to deal with.

In Spike Lee's jaggedly powerful new film, *Clockers*, blacks use "nigger" as a taunt, an insult, a warning, a compliment. The movie is about a black inner-city community tearing itself apart—about people who are all tangled up, with emotions working against themselves. *Clockers* opens with a series of still shots of murdered African-Americans lying in the street, the bodies, punctured and ripped, surrounded by congealed and darkened blood. Spike Lee intercuts the stills with wall murals on the theme of urban violence. We get the point: The rest of the movie may be a story, a fiction, but people are dying in the streets every day. Later in *Clockers*, the Brooklyn homicide detectives Rocco Klein (Harvey Keitel) and Larry Mazilli (John Turturro) examine a dead African-American man lying in his own blood, just like the men in the pictures. They jeer at the corpse, making obscene jokes. Rotten jokes are the only means they have of distancing themselves from the stench and muck of spilling dead bodies. As the scene goes on, it is clear the men are expressing their disgust at death. The entire movie is an expression of disgust at death. *Clockers* is a crime picture in which a Brooklyn community is living in crime, fighting it, losing to it, and abhorring it, and dying from it.

Richard Price wrote the first version of the script, which is based on his 1992 novel of the same title, and Spike Lee rewrote Price's version. Because the movie took a few years to produce, it now seems to combine two different periods—the late-eighties peak of the crack madness, which produced a degree of carnage in American cities perhaps without equal in the history of the advanced industrial countries; and the Giuliani era of greater police vigilance, with its nonstop surveillance of drug dealers. In *Clockers*, the black street kids and the black and white Brooklyn cops are all over one another. They "do business," sharing the peculiar coarse intimacy, the loyalties and betrayals, of people living in crime. The many scenes of harassment and interrogation, the streams of vituperation and tirade are all written and played with a poetic vitality seen before only in Martin Scorsese's movies. (Scorsese, at one point set to direct the movie, stayed on the project as producer.) Harvey Keitel, polite but relentless, like Dostoyevsky's implacable detective in *Crime and Punishment*, is subdued for most of the picture, but when he finally opens up, screaming at a suspect in front of a police station, the rhythm of his speech becomes hypnotic. *Clockers* is grim stuff, but much of it is so vivid and deeply felt that it's also highly engaging.

Strike (Mekhi Phifer), perhaps 20 years old, commands the top slat of a bench in front of the projects in Brooklyn somewhere, running his crew of clockers (bottom-rung street dealers, who work around the clock). These young men aren't violent—they sit around all day talking and slapping palms and planting dope in garbage cans for buyers—yet their trade is killing everyone around them. Strike is the smartest of the bunch; he's also, like so many Richard Price heroes, a worrier, a young man trying to keep his business together while dousing his bleeding ulcer with a *Yoo-hoo*-like soda called *Moo*. His pain, like Billy Budd's stutter, seems intended as a gesture of absolution, even grace. Strike is trapped, and his insides are telling him to get out.

He works as a lieutenant for the neighborhood crime boss, Rodney Little, who, in the person of the great actor Delroy Lindo (West Indian Archie in *Malcolm X*), is an exceptionally complex and frightening man. Lindo has a deep, caressing voice and the gift of intimacy; you want to trust his leathery good nature. Rodney runs his operation out of a pleasantly ramshackle corner store where half the fatherless young boys in the projects hang out for entertainment and instruction. In other words, the most paternal man around is a murderer and drug dealer—a bitter irony in a movie that never strays far from irony. Rodney gives the young boys good, serious advice; his stone-killer partner also gives good advice: *Stay away from this shit, save your money, think of the long term.* The killers warn the young ones against crime and pull them into it at the same time, just by being more exciting than anyone else. Rodney tries to seduce Strike into murdering someone by saying "You're my son" and promising him bigger turf. When Rodney's enemy winds up dead, we don't know who did it—Strike or his exceptionally virtuous brother, Victor (Isaiah Washington), who may be going crazy from the burden of always being good. The movie charges through a few tense weeks in which the ruthlessly intelligent Rocco puts the squeeze on Strike, and his world implodes.

Richard Price's mesmerizing novel was filled with operational detail—the cutting of the drugs, the division of the crack into "bottles," and so on. Spike Lee's adaptation is less factual, more emotional; Lee is concerned less with Strike's spiritual condition than with the survival of the entire community. Malik Sayeed's cinematography is rough and dark-hued, with an almost tabloid angriness in the scenes of violence. As always, Spike Lee jumps around a lot, telling his story in hot flashes, and at times *Clockers* is difficult to follow. But I will not complain yet again that Spike Lee can't tell a story straight; it turns out not to matter much in *Clockers*. Unlike, say, *Jungle Fever*, this movie has a center—not, perhaps, an entirely coherent story but a fully realized world. The young mother (Regina Taylor) who comes storming out of her project apartment and furiously attacks Strike and his crew, the huge black cop (Keith David) who slaps Strike around, even the white cops who harangue Strike in sheer disgust, are all part of a community living through the extinction of its children.

Clockers is not a cool movie; it's an anguished movie. Spike Lee sets himself against a black culture that's grown all too accepting of young men lying dead in the street. The rap artists whom the kids quote may not be "selling" violence, but they're getting off on it, glorying in the danger and excitement. A young boy watches a virtual-reality enactment of a kid like himself plugging someone—and later does just that. For Spike Lee, it's all a long, sorry distance from bebop and Stevie Wonder. *Clockers* is didactic: The reiterated message of the movie, which even turns up on billboards, is "No more packing"—no more guns. But *Clockers* is perhaps the most loose-limbed didactic movie ever made. At one point, Delroy Lindo delivers an extraordinary, arialike speech in praise of crack cocaine, the drug that is making him rich, and the devil himself couldn't have said it better, with more richly ambiguous tonalities. *Clockers* doesn't turn away from anything.

NEW YORK POST, 9/13/95, p. 33, Michael Medved

"Clockers" is the eighth film from the acclaimed and controversial Spike Lee, and it represents a huge, leap forward in his career.

Each of his previous pictures combined unmistakable flashes of energy and brilliance with a self-destructive tendency toward student-film showboating. Lee can be the most intrusive of major directors, willfully upstaging his actors and story lines to call attention to his own stylistic indulgence and inventiveness. At times, it's difficult to hear his characters talking to one another because of the deafening whirr of the director grinding his ax.

But in "Clockers," Lee gets out of the way of the material and presents his more mature and satisfying motion picture. Except for distracting and gratuitous cameo appearances at both the beginning and end of his film (as if to say, "Hey, look here, everybody, it's still me. Spike!"), he's created a passionate and altogether persuasive piece of work that should convince even die-hard skeptics of his prodigious gifts.

The plot pivots around police detective Rocco Klein (Harvey Keitel), a world-weary but compassionate Italian-Jewish hybrid who's been working homicide so long he can smell a fake confession when it's offered to him.

It makes no sense that a hard-working, church-going family man like Victor Dunham (the utterly sympathetic Isaiah Washington), who toils at two jobs to support his beautiful wife and two adorable children, would impulsively empty a revolver into a small-time Brooklyn hood at a fast-food restaurant. Klein suspects that Victor's confession represents a misguided attempt to protect his irresponsible teen-aged brother, Strike (Mekhi Phifer).

Strike is a "clocker"—a low-level drug dealer who works the projects around the clock—and henchman to smooth but ferocious neighborhood crime boss and candy store owner Rod (the always imposing Delroy Lindo).

Each of these characters emerges with overwhelming vitality, thanks to universally superb performances by Lee's exceptionally well-chosen cast. Mekhi Phifer, a 19-year-old newcomer chosen at an open-casting call from over 1,000 candidates, is especially effective. His character—coughing blood, battling an ulcer, focusing his dreams on an odd obsession with trains—is both despicable and endearing, an unsentimentalized inner-city anti-hero whose fate (and soul) hang in the balance through the course of the picture.

Based on the critically praised 600-page novel by screenwriter ("Sea of Love," "The Color of Money") Richard Price (who also co-wrote this script with Lee) "Clockers" teems with compelling characters balancing its vividly rendered cops and criminals with an array of decent, self-respecting citizens who rage against the creeps and crack dealers who make life in the projects a nightmare.

The opening credits unfold over a series of truly horrifying full-color stills that stunningly re-create crime-scene photographs of drug-related murders.

Despite such lurid depictions of violence, and a resolution of the central mystery that may seem just a mite smug and contrived, "Clockers" soars through its splendid acting and lyrical camera work (by first-time cinematographer Malik Sayeed), transforming urban squalor into the stuff of high tragedy.

NEWSDAY, 9/13/95, Part II/p. B2, Jack Mathews

The early word on Spike Lee's adaptation of "Clockers," Richard Price's best-seller about the relationships between white cops and black drug dealers in the inner city, was that the movie was playing better with those who hadn't read the book than with those who had.

That is a typical response. Fans of novels rarely find the condensed and altered screen dramatizations as rich or as involving as the original work. In this instance, however, Lee has done much more than condense and alter; he has absorbed the gritty story and its racial politics, fermented them in his own bitter juices, and concocted something equally potent, but clearly more his than Price's.

Superficially, both the book and the film are genre pieces, urban dramas pitting hardened, authoritarian police against the ghetto's lethal drug culture, in a war over abstract middle-class values that seem as distant from the scene as the Emerald City or Shangri-la. In fact, most films of the type count on the audience to represent those values, and for the threats against them to generate the real tension.

"Clockers" is not so clear-cut. The central conflict is fairly conventional, and very much the product of liberal white fantasy. A young drug dealer named Strike (newcomer Mekhi Phifer), living in the Brooklyn projects, is caught between the powers of his conscience and of his environment, and a cynical, inherently decent white detective, Rocco Klein (Harvey Keitel), is there ultimately to help him make the right turn.

But Lee, who rewrote Price's screenplay, has turned the main plot—solving the murder of a drug informer—into a subplot. He's shifted the emphasis from Rocco to Strike, the point of view from white to black, and taken as his central theme the internal battle between blacks trying to claw their way up from the ghetto and the drug lords trying to hold them down.

"If God invented anything better than crack, he's kept it for himself," says Rodney (Delroy Lindo), the local drug boss who serves as Strike's mentor, father figure and oppressor.

Strike is one of Rodney's "clockers," low-end street dealers who work all hours handling the walk-up business from junkies and white out-of-towners. He doesn't use the products himself (addicts, Rodney assures him, are terrible salesmen); instead, he calms his stressed stomach with constant sips of chocolate soda, a therapy that fails miserably after Rodney orders him to make a kill.

Whether Strike carries out the order is a mystery to the final moments, and secondary to the fact that he is horrified by the thought of committing murder. From the provocative crime-scene photos of murdered black men and women lying in pools of blood during the opening credits, the matter-of-factness of drug-related death in the projects is palpable.

"Another stain on the sidewalk," is how the police glibly refer to the daily killings. When one white cop says, "They ought to blow these projects up," another says, "Why bother? They kill themselves anyway."

Lee is determined to get beyond that broad-stroke cynicism and make us think about what's really going on inside, where people with higher ideals are held down by the twin tyrannies of drugs and poverty. The supporting characters—a child enchanted by the clockers, his furious mother (Regina Taylor, in the film's strongest performance), the good black cop (Keith David), Strike's conciliatory but secretly enraged brother (Isaiah Washington), their tormented mother—may be a little too patly representative of the cross-section. But they are so well drawn, and convincingly portrayed, that their viewpoints and emotions overwhelm the relatively mundane elements of plot and resonate far more strongly than those of the main characters.

Lindo, who played West Indian Archie in Lee's "Malcolm X," is a terrific villain as the vicious charmer Rodney, but it's a character we've seen many times. And though Keitel is always interesting to watch, he too is in a familiar role, that of the proverbial white cop who can't leave it alone on the eve of retirement. John Turturro, playing Rocco's downsized (from the book) sidekick Mazilli, barely registers at all.

Lee's penchant for stylistic experimentation and Oliver Stone-size moral lecturing are, as usual, more distracting than insightful, and the deliberate use of grainy photography for certain scenes does more to draw attention to itself than to create the intended sense of dramatic urgency. Still, "Clockers" is a powerful piece of filmmaking, at times as compelling and unsettling as "Do the Right Thing," whose core issue—the cause and effect of racism and rage—it shares.

Lee's eight movies are the work of a gifted but perplexingly uneven filmmaker, capable of following a biographical masterwork ("Malcolm X") with an autobiographical clinker ("Crooklyn"). At the same time, however, he has pioneered the new wave of social-conscious black film and continues to be the most forceful voice among that group.

NEWSWEEK, 9/25/95, p. 92, David Ansen

In the Brooklyn housing project that is the setting of Spike Lee's grimly passionate *Clockers,* the 19-year-old Strike (Mekhi Phifer) conducts his business—selling crack—from a park bench, taking swigs of chocolate Yoo-Hoo to soothe his raging ulcer, a byproduct of his high-risk trade. Strike has a lot to worry about, and his ulcer won't get better before his tale is told. The cops, led by Det. Rocco Klein (Harvey Keitel), periodically swoop down on the projects, subjecting Strike to humiliating strip searches. Ten-year-old Tyrone (Pee Wee Love) has become enamored of the dealer's swagger, outraging both his upright mother and Andre (Keith David), the gigantic neighbor cop who threatens to break Strike's bones if he gets this good kid into trouble.

Even worse, Strike's Fagin-like mentor, Rodney (Delroy Lindo), wants him to ice a dealer named Darryl. Strike's never killed a man, but it will lead to a promotion, a chance to get off the benches into a more secure side of the business.

Darryl ends up dead, but did Strike do it? Rocco Klein thinks so, even though another man has confessed—Strike's model-citizen brother Victor (Isaiah Washington), a decent family man holding down two jobs in an effort to work his way out of the projects. Klein's gut tells him Victor is covering for his brother—and he sets out to get his man.

The outlines of the story come straight from Richard Price's densely researched and highly praised novel "Clockers" (slang for dealers who'll work round the clock). But Lee, who rewrote Price's screenplay, has altered the tale to address his own concerns. From the ghastly snapshots under the opening credits—crime-scene photos of young, black male corpses—to the background glimpses of violent videogames and music clips glamorizing gunpacking rappers, Lee announces his furious protest at the culture of violence that has decimated the black urban community. There are moments when Lee's didactic impulse gets the better of him—he literally enshrines his message, Stop Packing, on a billboard. But more often the filmmaker adroitly uses his anger to fuel his storytelling, catching the viewer in a taut web of conflicting and painful emotions.

This is the first Lee movie based on someone else's novel, and it feels different. His usual stop-start rhythms are less pronounced here; the dramatic pressure builds in a straighter line. The look is grittier (he's got an impressive new cinematographer, Malik Hassan Sayeed) and though there are still obtrusive stylistic flourishes, he's more willing to settle into the characters and let them dictate the flow of the story.

Where Price split the novel equally between Strike and Rocco, Lee puts the young drug dealer at center stage. Phifer had no acting experience before this role, but his charisma makes up for his lack of technique. You find yourself both despising Strike's blindly amoral opportunism and pulling for his survival. Keitel is extraordinary at capturing Rocco's ambiguous mixture of cynicism and idealism, professionalism and self-delusion. And Lindo's smooth, reasonableness. He's the kind of guy who warns his dealers never to touch the product he's happy to sell. It's only when he thinks Strike has crossed him that we get a terrifying glimpse of his viciousness.

"Clockers" may be Lee's strongest film since "Do the Right Thing," but he runs into trouble at the end when he tries to tie up all his threads in neat bows. Though this isn't a murder mystery, the killer's motivation is far too murky, and his ultimate fate raises more questions than it answers. In Lee's understandable eagerness to let a few rays of hope shine, the polemicist trips up the dramatist—movie conventions replace honest observation. But the passion of this raw, mournful urban epic remains, in spite of the false moves. You won't find it easy to shake.

SIGHT AND SOUND, 10/95, p. 45, Amy Taubin

In a drug-ridden Brooklyn housing project, Strike is a 16-year-old-clocker (lowest level drug dealer). Troubled by ulcers so severe they cause him to spit blood, he is nevertheless the favourite of Rodney Little, the local crack kingpin. Rodney asks Strike to prove his loyalty by killing Darryl, a young pusher that Rodney claims has been cheating him.

Strike heads for Ahab's, a fast food joint where Darryl does his dealing. Trying to work up his nerve, he goes to the bar next door where he meets his older brother Victor, a model African-American citizen. Strike babbles some story about how Darryl deserves to die because he beat up a 14-year-old girl. When Victor says that he might know someone who could kill Darryl, Strike realises that his brother is drunk and splits. A short while later, someone pumps four bullets into Darryl.

The next day, Victor turns himself in, claiming he killed Darryl in self-defence. Veteran homicide detective Rocco Klein thinks Victor is protecting Strike. Rocco begins pursuing Strike with a vengeance. For Strike, Rocco is one too many among the people—narcotics cops, his mother, local black cop Andre and bright, idolising 12-year-old Tyrone—who hassle him on a daily basis. Rocco arrests Rodney, suggesting that it's Strike who ratted on him. Strike realises he'd better get out of town. While packing his gear, he realises his gun is missing. He gives Victor's wife the money for Victor's bail but Strike's mother refuses to make peace with him.

Errol, a stone killer in the last stages of Aids dementia and Rudy's right hand man, comes gunning for Strike. Tyrone sees him before Strike does, pulls out the gun he's 'borrowed' from Strike and shoots Errol dead. At the police station, Andre begs Rocco to help Tyrone get off with a minimum sentence. He then beats up Strike for getting Tyrone involved. Strike barely makes it back to his car when he spots Rodney coming after him. He takes refuge in the police station where Rocco presses him to confess to murdering Darryl. Suddenly, Strike's mother appears and tells Rocco that Victor came home that night acting crazy and that his story is true. Strike is set free but, finding his car has been trashed by Rodney, he leaves on a train heading west.

Adapted from the Richard Price novel of the same name, Spike Lee's *Clockers* is about black-on-black violence. Lee shifts the focus from Price's central character Rocco Klein (a middle-aged white cop having an identity crisis) to Strike, the African-American teenage crack dealer who makes what he believes is a rational choice—to earn his living selling a product people want even though it kills them—and finds himself torn apart by the violence of the drug world and the unexpected revolt of his own conscience. The film shows that there are no positive choices for black men born into the underclass. Attempting to live an upstanding life, Strike's brother Victor is also driven crazy.

Clockers opens with a title sequence that's bravura even for Lee. The camera travels over a succession of grisly police photos of murder scenes—black male bodies torn apart by bullets. Behind a yellow police tape, crowds of black faces watch a nightly spectacle of bloodletting that's both too immediate and too removed to be comprehensible. At once didactic and operatic, this opening positions us for the film that follows. What's most startling about *Clockers* is its intimacy. Lee puts us inside the skin of a kid who seems morally reprehensible at the outset, making the agony of his experience inescapable.

Lee's choice of camera placement and movement has never been more brilliant. The camera's erratic rhythms and circular patterns articulate the extreme confinement of Strike's world and his panicky sense of being held in a vice. Similarly, the narrative, though dense with incident, seems to turn in on itself, covering the same ground over and over again. Everything in Strike's world—the repetitive riffs of rap music, the claustrophobic space of video games, his fetishised electric trains that circle a single track even as they testify to the existence of unknown and distant places—reinforces the feeling of confinement.

Given everything that comes before it, the final sequence—Strike's face pressed against the train window as it crosses a desert landscape that must seem to him as vast and charged with possibility as outer space—is, for a moment, wildly liberating. But Lee undercuts this feeling with a cutaway to one of Strike's crew, lying dead in a pool of blood on the concrete platform where we first saw Strike. Already the crowd is gathering around the corpse. Strike has escaped but he carries his past with him. Given what we know of American society today, why would we think there's a place for him that's different from where he's been?

In terms of form and content easily Lee's riskiest and most accomplished film to date, *Clockers* is not without its flaws. In focusing so much on Strike, Lee makes the other characters one-dimensional. Newcomer Mekhi Phifer makes an amazing Strike, so much like an ordinary kid it's hard to remember that he's acting. Yet such extraordinary actors as Isaiah Washington, Delroy Lindo, Harvey Keitel and John Turturro are strait-jacketed by the script and direction.

Lee encourages cinematographer Malik Sayeed to extend the experiments with the cutting together of various types of film stock begun by Arthur Jaffa in Lee's *Crooklyn*. Sometimes this method yields expressive results, as in the flashback sequences which have the texture of over-saturated 16mm Kodachrome. Just as often, the effect is purely decorative, as in the burn-up look of the police interrogation's scenes which seem borrowed from Oliver Stone's *J.F.K.*

The director's most serious mistake, however, is to toy with a whodunnit structure until the climactic and hopelessly stagy interrogation of Strike by Rocco reveals the truth about Darryl's death. Viewers who have read the novel will know that Strike is not a murderer (Price puts that issue to rest early on in his narrative) but newcomers will be led down paths that are irrelevant, if not downright destructive, to the sense of subjectivity that Lee wants to convey.

With the mystery out of the way, the film seems infinitely more powerful on the second viewing, and even more so on the third. Desolate, hallucinatory and fearlessly heartfelt it is the 'hood movie to end all 'hood movies. In its violence, there is neither glamour, nor pleasure, nor release.

TIME, 9/18/95, p. 108, Richard Schickel

Strike (Mekhi Phifer) works long hours, enjoys the unswerving loyalty of his admiring employees and conducts his small, prospering business with ruthless efficiency. Aside from a persistent, insoluble public relations problem—certain elements in the community despise him—he is a model of the entrepreneurial spirit that we like to believe made America great, and at 19 he has the ulcer to prove it. Strike is a crack dealer monopolizing the trade in a Brooklyn, New York, housing project.

Rocco Klein (Harvey Keitel) is a homicide detective whose cynicism energizes rather than wearies him. He'll match his street smarts against any neighborhood punk's, and he's convinced that Strike must have murdered a rival drug dealer. The only other logical suspect is the kid's older brother Victor (Isaiah Washington), but that makes no sense; the man is working two jobs to support a wife and two kids, trying to engineer a respectable rise in the world.

They are wonderfully well-matched antagonists, Strike and Rocco. The former is wary, sullen and perhaps more ambivalent about his work than he dares to admit. The latter is bustling, voluble and perhaps more sympathetic toward Strike—with everyone trying to survive in this milieu—than he cares to admit. *Clockers* is careful not to overexplain these figures. Director Spike Lee, who shares screenplay credit with novelist Richard Price, lets Phifer (in his first film role) and Keitel (in his umpty-umpth) find the characters, which they do with unimprovable unpredictability.

But the film is more than a murder mystery and more than a study in character conflict. At its best, it is an intense and complex portrait of an urban landscape on which the movies' gaze has not often fallen. Yes, this housing project is home to a feckless delinquent population. But it is also home to middle-class black families struggling to preserve their values and save their children from drugs, crime and despair.

The confrontations between these people—among them, an angry mom and a tough housing cop—and Strike's clockers (so called because pushers work around the clock) are some of the film's most potent and haunting scenes. Indeed, it's almost as if the director has taken his cue from them instead of the other way around. For there is a force and focus in Lee's world an absence of intellectual posturing and a willingness to let his material speak for itself that he has not achieved before.

Speak? Well, not exactly. His people howl and mumble, wisecrack and menace, muse and abuse—a lot of the time obscenely. But never idly. The language of *Clockers* is finally transformative, turning what might have been no more than a slice of mean-streets realism into a sort of rap opera, in which pained recitative prepares the way for anguished (and curiously moving) arias.

But it's an opera without a tragic ending. The sense of doom that begins gathering from the very first moments is suddenly, not quite persuasively, blown away in its final ones. This is not a movie imposition. It's pretty much the conclusion Price chose for his novel. Perhaps understandably. There is a human need to temper misery with mercy. And as we emerge from this exigent movie, we have some reason to be grateful for this last-minute softening of its spirit.

VILLAGE VOICE, 9/19/95, p. 71, Georgia Brown

Once upon a time the luscious Nola Darling entertained three suitors, the better to weigh their virtues, sift their shortcomings, and make her choice. And so we were introduced, in simplest terms, to Spike Lee's dialectical narrative—plot development by argument and opposing voices. As the unsuitable suitors bickered over Nola's svelte torso, so would teachers and tempters dicker over the souls of Lee's future protagonists, just as, outside the frame, critics and constituencies proceeded to tear at Lee's own puny limbs. (White liberals aside, have you read Amiri Baraka's Lee-lashng!) By now you would think even the most nervous of Nellies could relay, recognizing that Lee's arguments are ever evolving, subject to amplification, emendation, further study, as well as life lessons.

But no. Pre-release rumors swirling around *Clockers*—adapted from Richard Price's popular, and in some quarters sacrosanct, novel—suggest that once more Spike will get it from all sides. (He's quite right he can't win.) With the stench of Mark Fuhrman in the air, Lee, as well as

Price, is being charged with being far too romantically enamored of white law enforcers. On the other hand, fans of, and perhaps the author of, said novel, may be lamenting that Scorsese and De Niro didn't finish their own *Clockers* as projected.

From my one viewing (not enough to sort out several plot details, much less the score), *Clockers* seems the most simply moving of Lee's films, heartbreakingly beautiful, brave, and socially important. I watched much of it through tears.

Clockers starts off with some of the dead who knew Brooklyn: gruesome (simulated) homicide close-ups. Black male corpses. "POLICE LINE DO NOT CROSS," advises the yellower-than-yellow tape, this print message juxtaposed a few beats later, Godard-style, with the dire tabloid headline "TOY GUN REAL BULLETS," this next to the school photo of the kid whose funeral it was.

Here, Lee's trademark "wake-up call," the workday alarm clock signaling "It's time, folks, time," translates into what you and I know as Yoo-Hoo (though the film doesn't use the brand name)—the milky soda Ronnie "Strike" Dunham (Mekhi Phifer) slugs to soothe his raging ulcer. (It's about as efficacious as voodoo.) Rising like the morning sun (and morning son) over the Gowanus projects, Strike strides forth like a gleaming Apollo, his shaved pate ordering the "slovenly wilderness" around like Wallace Stevens's jar in Tennessee. Pressed robin's-egg overalls make him look fresh as a daisy. Clean as a whistle but going about a filthy business. (Strike's gut functions like a conscience.)

Like Lee, Strike is a workaholic, but like *Mo' Better*'s Bleek and *Fever*'s Flipper as well as the those semicute slackers Mars and Mookie, Strike suffers from working for the Man. The difference being that this Man, Rodney Little (*Crooklyn*'s jazzman dad, Delroy Lindo) is black and his trade is crack cocaine. African American economic self-reliance (Lee's longtime theme and project) perverted. Strike is a "clocker," one of Rodney's soldiers—"my rod and staff," Rodney dubs him—and expendable. (Seeing that Little was Malcolm's pre-conversion name, does this make even Rodney redeemable?) Assigned to shoot a rival to the boss's cause, Strike risks not only his own future but, through a set of coincidences, that of his straight-arrow brother Victor (a soulful Isaiah Washington).

Clean as a whistle, I said, but Strike's whistle sends off a lonesome sound. The boss's pleasure is neither rap nor movies nor Saturday-morning cartoons; he has an old-fashioned passion for choo-choo trains, a hobby that makes for a rapturous ending. (Those overalls come to have a secret connotation.)

As for the dialectic, if the corrupting voices (bad fathers) here are Rodney and the twisted, Virus-addled Errol (Tom Byrd), on the other side of the scale sit the saintly Victor and homicide detective Rocco Klein (Harvey Keitel playing a very, very good lieutenant in a superbly modulated performance). Whereas the morose, rueful Klein is the lyric heart of Price's novel, the movie slightly reduces his status, or at least his playing time, though it doesn't moderate his goodness. Another voice vying for attention is that of the 12-year-old Tyrone, surrogate for Strike's younger, uncommitted self.

From pizza man Sal to Paulie and Angie from Bensonhurst, Lee's white characters have been complex and sympathetic, but this hardly makes it easier to believe in this angel on the force. Klein's jokey partner Larry Mazilli (John Turturro) is not so bad either. These guys' only vice is tossing candy wrappers out their wagon's window. You may prefer to take Rocco Klein as one more of Lee's lessons in behavior modification: Here, says the teacher, is how representatives of the law ought to behave.

Clockers is virtually female-free, a fact that suits me fine. Whenever Lee turns to family, the noise level gets to me. I'm not talking about dialogue-music overlapping but abrasive, abusive bickering and compulsive cruelty towards intimates. Presented as a black *Who's Afraid of Virginia Woolf*, this would be one thing, but Lee seems to accept that this is the way families are. In *Crooklyn*, a glorious project was spoiled, rendered unbearable, by the pitch of a mother's hysteria and the family's casual rudeness toward one another. It was no mean feat to turn Alfre Woodard into a one-note shrew whose death comes practically as a blessing—at least as a respite. The sources of this woman's pain and bitterness were never addressed; meanwhile, her shirking, self-absorbed husband was credited with grace for staying calm. I call him some sort of sadist. (The Mookie-Tina relation in *Do the Right Thing* contains the same dynamics. At least Rosie Perez's character directs her wrath where it belongs, onto Mookie instead of their child.) Fathers and sons make for a more mournful, dignified focus.

Despite Price's 599 pages, Lee has no trouble paring down. There's less compulsion here than in his former films to fill the frame, float by sundry minor characters, cram in every last message to the people. There's less of the doofy stuff, too, though happily there s some of this—as when Rocco is reflected in Strike's eyeball ("I want to see what you see!"), or when Rocco's talking head tracks Tyrone on his bike like his superego.

Shot by 26-year-old Malik Sayeed in moody black-black shadows with a nervous, shifty grain, *Clockers* is more bluesy, more noirish, than the Ernest Dickerson-era Lee. Some may call this Spike's first genre film but it's too personal and eccentric for that. Tender and generous, and surprisingly nonviolent given the subject, it's clearly meant to help real people through hard places. How many movies can you say that about!

Actually, you could say it about Francisco J. Lombardi's *No Mercy (Sin compasión)*, a deeply felt quasi-Bressonian update of *Crime and Punishment* set in Lima, Peru. Ramón (the handsome Diego Bertie), an intense, febrile philosophy student, is extraordinarily bothered by the fate of poverty—his own, and, more altruistically, that of Sonia (Adriana Davila), a young neighbor driven into prostitution by an alcoholic father. Why, Ramón ponders, should his shrewish landlady spend his rent on dresses and shoe's when families are starving! Why not kill someone so useless?

A question many have pondered, but Ramón, as Dostoyevsky readers know, acts. The murder itself is shocking, with the violence understated (most of it takes place offscreen) yet surprisingly real. A shrewd kindly detective on the case (Jorge Chiarella) plays cat and mouse with Ramón, even after a befuddled gardener confesses to the crime. (There are several intriguing parallels with *Clockers* here.) Meanwhile, Ramón and Sonia become lovers, and she tries to evade the clutches of Velaochaga, her wealthy former employer. A child-molester, Velaochaga's another creep who deserves to be killed, although Ramón is not obliged to carry out the deed. Then there is the matter of religion, Sonia's solace and mainstay, an institution Ramón-the-intellectual rejects, even as its consolations rub off on him. (The narrative is framed as Ramón's informal confession to a priest.)

Although not that many street killers are philosophy students, several leaders of violent movements, as well as some heads of violent states, have been. Whereas Lombardi's serious film raises issues about the rationalization of killing in the name of justice, it might be more exciting to witness a debate between Ramón and the Peruvian equivalent of Rodney Little.

VILLAGE VOICE, 9/19/95, p. 71, Amy Taubin

Bleak, hallucinatory, and fearlessly heartfelt, *Clockers* is precisely what its director Spike Lee said he wanted it to be: "the hood movie to end all hood movies." In its bloodletting, there is neither glamour, pleasure, nor release.

Adapted from Richard Price's novel of the same name, the film is about black-on-black violence. Lee focuses much less than Price did on Rocco Klein, a middle-aged white cop having an identity crisis. Instead, the story belongs to Strike, an African American teenage crack dealer who makes what he believes is a rational choice—to earn his living selling a product so desirable that people die for it—and finds himself torn apart by the brutality of the drug world and the unexpected revolt of his own conscience.

The film reveals Strike's confusion, desperation, and vulnerability. The camera that dogs his heels also puts us inside his skin, making the agony of his existence inescapable. *Clockers* shows the humanity of a kid who could easily be written off as morally reprehensible. Almost all the characters in the film—black or white, good or bad—wish Strike would just disappear, or worse. *Clockers* insists that we, who are complicit in his plight, give him the attention he deserves.

Strike is a clocker (a low-level drug dealer), trying to rise in a profession he literally has no stomach for. Troubled by ulcers so severe they cause him to spit up blood when he's under pressure (which is all the time), he nevertheless is the favorite of Rodney Little, the local crack kingpin. Rodney asks Strike to prove his loyalty by killing Darryl, a young pusher who, Rodney claims, has been cheating him.

When Darryl turns up dead, Victor, Strike's older brother, confesses to shooting him in self-defense. Rocco, who's in charge of the case, believes that Victor is covering for his brother and pursues Strike relentlessly. He sees Victor, who works two jobs to provide for his family, as a model African American—as Abel to Strike's Cain. Rocco, who's just your average racist—

nowhere near the Mark Fuhrman league—is obsessed with proving the truth of his master narrative.

Clockers opens with a title sequence that's bravura, even for Lee. The camera travels over a succession of grisly police Polaroids of murder scenes—young black bodies torn apart by bullets. Behind a yellow police tape, crowds of black faces watch the bloody spectacle that's both too immediate and too removed to be comprehensible. At once didactic and operatic, this opening readies us for the film.

Radically expressionistic, *Clockers* projects the inner life of its protagonist onto mise-en-scène and narrative. When we first see Strike, he's crossing a concrete circular platform at the center of the courtyard of the Brooklyn housing project where he commands his operation. The courtyard is both stage and prison—an inversion of Foucault's panopticon. Trapped within it, Strike is under constant surveillance, vulnerable to aggressors who enter from all sides: the police; his boss Rodney; his mother who watches him from her window; the residents of the housing project who despise him for dealing death to their children; Andre, the black cop who's known Strike from infancy and is outraged that Strike is teaching Tyrone, a bright 12-year-old the drug-dealing routines he learned from Rodney. *Clockers* is as much about fathers and sons as it is about brothers.

Lee's choice of camera placement and movement has never been more brilliant. The camera's erratic rhythms and circular patterns articulate the extreme confinement of Strike's world and his panicky sense of being held in a vise. Similarly, the narrative though dense with incident seems to turn in on itself, covering the same ground over and over again. Everything in Strike's world—the repetitive rhythmic hooks of rap music, the claustrophic space of video games, his fetishized electric trains that circle a single track even as they testify to the existence of unknown and distant places—reinforces the feeling of confinement.

The architecture of the film allows only a single instance of release—a lateral tracking shot from a train window as it crosses the desert southwest. Given where we've been, the landscape seems as vast and charged with possibility as outer space. But Lee undermines the moment with a cutaway to one of Strike's crew, lying dead in a pool of blood on the concrete platform where we first saw Strike. The implication is that although no one can escape the past, one is responsible for the choices one makes—even when circumstances make choice all but impossible.

Easily Lee's riskiest and most accomplished film (in terms of both form and content), *Clockers* is not without flaws. By focusing so relentlessly on Strike, the other characters are made one-dimensional. Lee found an amazing Strike in newcomer Mekhi Phifer who seems so much like an ordinary kid it's hard to remember he's performing. But such fine actors as Isaiah Washington, Delroy Lindo, Keith David, Regina Taylor, Harvey Keitel, and John Turturro are somewhat straitjacketed by the script and direction. In particular, Washington, who manages to convey in half a dozen short scenes something of Victor's pressure-cooked experience, deserves a film of his own.

Lee allows cinematographer Malik Sayeed to extend the experiments with cutting together various types of film stock that Arthur Jafa began in *Crooklyn*. Sometimes this method yields expressive results, as in the flashback sequences which have the texture of over-saturated 16mm Kodachrome. (The reds and blues are straight out of *Scorpio Rising*.) Just as often, the effect is largely decorative, as in the burnt-up silvery look of the police interrogation scenes, which seem borrowed from *JFK*.

By pushing the expressive possibilities of filmmaking beyond the conventions of realism—almost into the terrain of avant-garde film—Lee heightens both intimacy and spectacle. The hallucinatory quality of the image is expressive of Strike's psyche and of the insane position in which he finds himself—having to live like a tough guy when he's barely out of childhood. The film even has a bogeyman: Errol, Rodney's henchman who's in the final stages of AIDS dementia, becomes, even more than Rocco, Strike's nemesis.

The radical form also makes us aware of our position as spectators, fascinated, like the neighborhood folk in the opening credit sequence, by violent death and bodies that bleed. Lee refuses to indulge that fascination. Instead, he shoves his distrust of popular culture, and indeed, of narrative itself in our face. There's a moment when Rocco tries to shape a young boy's confession so that he'll get off with the lightest possible sentence. It's Rocco's finest hour, and yet, it's sullied by his belief in himself as an omniscient narrator.

If Rocco isn't aware of how events are transformed by narration (and the position of the narrator), Lee is. By allowing the contradictions of his position to leak into the film (compared to Strike, Spike has had a privileged life from birth), Lee intensifies the inside/outside dynamic that's crucial to the film's meaning. Obviously, there are degrees of being an insider, and Lee's identification has more to do with race than class. *Clockers* is first of all about agency—the agency that Lee demands for African Americans despite the prison of racist society. It also speaks to the necessity of taking responsibility for the other who is never less than part of oneself.

Also reviewed in:
CHICAGO TRIBUNE, 9/13/95, Tempo/p. 1, Michael Wilmington
NATION, 10/9/95, p. 399, Stuart Klawans
NEW REPUBLIC, 10/2/95, p. 38, Stanley Kauffmann
NEW YORK TIMES, 9/13/95, p. C11, Janet Maslin
NEW YORKER, 9/18/95, p. 107, Anthony Lane
VARIETY, 9/4-10/95, p. 73, Todd McCarthy
WASHINGTON POST, 9/13/95, p. B1, Hal Hinson
WASHINGTON POST, 9/15/95, Weekend/p. 44, Kevin McManus

CLUELESS

A Paramount Pictures release. *Producer:* Scott Rudin and Robert Lawrence. *Director:* Amy Heckerling. *Director of Photography:* Bill Pope. *Editor:* Debra Chiate. *Music:* David Kitay. *Music Editor:* Danny Garde. *Choreographer:* Mary Ann Kellogg. *Sound:* David Ronne and (music) John Richards. *Sound Editor:* Uncle J. Kamen. *Casting:* Marcia S. Ross. *Production Designer:* Steven Jordan. *Art Director:* William Hiney. *Set Decorator:* Amy Wells. *Set Dresser:* James LaBarge, Wendy Murray, Ken Abraham, and Mark Kusy. *Costumes:* Mona May. *Make-up:* Alan "Doc" Friedman. *Stunt Coordinator:* Patrick Romano. *Running time:* 113 minutes. *MPAA Rating:* PG-13.

CAST: Alicia Silverstone (Cher); Stacey Dash (Dionne); Brittany Murphy (Tai); Paul Rudd (Josh); Donald Faison (Murray); Elisa Donovan (Amber); Breckin Meyer (Travis); Jeremy Sisto (Elton); Dan Hedaya (Mel Hamilton); Aida Linares (Lucy); Wallace Shawn (Mr. Wendell Hall); Twink Caplan (Miss Toby Geist); Justin Walker (Christian); Sabastian Rashidi (Paroudasm); Herb Hall (Principal); Julie Brown (Ms. Stoeger); Susan Mohun (Heather); Nicole Bilderback (Summer); Ron Orbach (DMV Tester); Sean Holland (Lawrence); Roger Kabler (College Guy); Jace Alexander (Robber); Josh Lozoff (Logan); Carl Gottlieb (Priest); Joseph D. Reitman (Student); Anthony Beninati (Bartendar).

LOS ANGELES TIMES, 7/19/95, Calendar/p. 1, Kenneth Turan

To hear almost-16 Cher Horowitz tell it, "I actually have a way normal life." True, her mom died during "routine liposuction," but she now lives happily with her fierce litigator father ("He gets paid $500 an hour to fight with people") in great Beverly Hills style. "Isn't my house classic?" she enthuses. "Its columns date back to 1972."

Effervescent, unflappable, supremely pleased with herself, Cher (delightfully played by the much-publicized Alicia Silverstone) is the comic centerpiece of "Clueless," a wickedly funny teen-age farce from writer-director Amy Heckerling that, like its heroine, turns out to have more to it than anyone could anticipate.

Heckerling, of course, has been to high school before. In 1982, she directed Sean Penn and Phoebe Cates in the hip "Fast Times at Ridgemont High." "Clueless" is as clever and amusing, and this time Heckerling has the advantage of a heroine even Jane Austen could love. In fact, she had a hand in creating her.

For though Paramount is not exactly basing its ad campaign around the fact, "Clueless" is a shrewd modern reworking of some of the themes and plot lines of Austen's beloved "Emma," another story of a self-confident, socially prominent young woman who was surprised to find out how much she had to learn.

That connection points out the unexpected smartness of "Clueless," which may be about high school but depends on familiarity with Billie Holiday and "Hamlet" for its laughs. Put together with verve and style, "Clueless" is a sweet-natured satire of L.A.'s over-pampered youth that gets more fun out of high school than most people had attending it.

Named, like her best friend Dionne (Stacey Dash), after "great singers of the past who now do infomercials," Cher is absolutely the most popular girl at Bronson Alcott (Beverly Hills High under another name). Convinced that "looking for a boyfriend in high school is as useless as searching for meaning in a Pauly Shore movie," Cher is also a self-assured virgin who blithely explains "you see how picky I am about my shoes, and they only go on my feet."

Still, even for Cher, life does present problems. Like her serious ex-stepbrother Josh (Paul Rudd), a future environmental lawyer who wears Amnesty International T-shirts, listens to "complaint rock" and takes pleasure in observing the superficiality of Cher's life while helping her dad (Dan Hedaya) with some legal chores.

Even though it makes extensive use of voice-over, always a dicey choice, "Clueless'" script is a treat. And because Heckerling knows just where the jokes are, her direction is dead-on as well, with every actor in the extensive cast both understanding and responding admirably to the material.

Responding best of all is Silverstone, who gives a performance as flawless as Cher's complexion. Cher can sound off-putting and manipulative, but Silverstone emphasizes her good-hearted guilelessness until we have no choice but to embrace her, maxed-out credit cards and all.

NEW STATESMAN & SOCIETY, 10/20/95, p. 35, Jonathan Romney

The "high art-low art" debate tends not to raise its dreary head much in film circles because, thank God, it is largely thought to be irrelevant. Even the most devout worshipper at the art-house shrine will usually prove to be cheerfully catholic, and readily talk of Carl Dreyer and Russ Meyer in the same breath. The last time the argument had much publicity, however, it centred on whether the film critic's role was to wax eloquent about Terence Davies' zen-like contemplation of his carpet, or to celebrate the way-excellent Weltanschauung of *Wayne's World*. Pointless debate, of course: you have to do both. Last week, I grappled with Davies' "numinous avatars" (ouch): this week, West Coast teen argot in *Clueless*. It's a fantastic life.

The general consensus among, ahem, serious critics is that you wade through so many trashy films, that it comes as a breath of fresh air to see and (optionally) write about the occasional Davies or Kieslowski or Rivette. However, after spending most weeks umming and ahhing about "quality" films that you respect rather than enjoy, or mainstream films that you neither respect nor enjoy, it's genuinely exciting to find a film that reminds you of the pleasures of disposable trash. Pardon the snobbery of this phrase, and let me define my terms. By "disposable trash" I don't mean the sort of tripe that's thrown together with maximum budget and explosions, and minimal wit, and which usually features Tommy Lee Jones gamely slumming as the villain to earn the keep on his ranch. I don't mean the brain-rotting *Mondo Rosso* so-bad-it's-good school of one-legged turkeys; elevating those to cult adulation seems to me like queueing to gawp at carnival freaks (although, having said that, let me recommend *Species* with all urgency—it makes *Congo* look like Cocteau).

No, the disposable trash I'm talking about is the sort of film that's put together with the aim of chalking up maybe two weeks at the top of the US box-office charts, shifting a few thousand bags of popcorn to a junior drive-in audience, and being quickly and decently forgotten. It's a rare film that does that successfully, but here's one put together with the clean, functional good humour of a Whigfield single. *Clueless* is a teen comedy by Amy Heckerling, who knows something about disposable, having directed *Look Who's Talking*. It's done the job of making its hitherto little-known lead, 18-year-old Alicia Silverstone, into a name worth a $10m contract. And it does what *Wayne's World* did—make a whole style of teen-speak briefly hip among posy film aesthetes who a few years ago would never have dreamed of exclaiming "Excellent!" or, in this case, "As if!"

The good thing about this brittle comedy of amorous manners set among Beverly Hills youth are: (a) it's a lot more fun than the Eric Rohmer equivalent would be, and (b) the press kit comes with a handy glossary explaining terms like "audi", "jeepin", and "monet" (the latter means, "looks fine from a distance, but really a mess up close"—and you thought high culture didn't come into it). Five minutes into the film, of course, even the most recondite terms become perfectly transparent (although if I hadn't already checked my crib-sheet, I might have had trouble figuring "Baldwins" and "Bettys"). But the fact that they supply it signifies something rather laudable about the film: the makers know that a couple of years from now, the idiom will have faded completely and none of this will mean anything, just as Bill and Ted already look like elders of some arcane bygone sect. *Clueless* will be completely baffling to future generations, by which I mean the kids who will be around when the film comes out on video.

Clueless does, however, have a certain degree of timelessness, a built-in mechanism to ensure its chances of survival. That is to say, it's basically a John Hughes teen movie ten years on. The basic elements are the same—a feisty heroine who falls for the wrong guy, a class clown, a sympathetic teacher or two, copping off (or not) with the school dreamboat at some awful party, and one or two pointed lessons in life. Plus some ropey forgotten English pop band given a second chance on the sound track; then it was the Psychedelic Furs, now stand up General Public. Alicia Silverstone, though, is a sight wittier, more barbed and better at funny voices than Molly Ringwald, and if she can avoid making the same mistakes (like working with Jean-Luc Godard), her future is assured.

And if you're still wondering why *Clueless* should demand your attention as much as the current Marguerite Duras season at the Everyman, I should point out that the plot is nothing other than a thinly disguised reworking of Jane Austen's *Emma*. That opens up new perspectives: if we're used to Shakespeare in modern dress—Macbeth in the executive wash room, Titus Andronicus down the pie shop—why can't we have literary classics done the same way, instead of having to endure BBC 2's customary round of swirling flounces and furbelows? They should take a leaf out of Heckerling's high-school yearbook for their next Austen adaptation and take *Mansfield Park* to Grange Hill. As if!

NEW YORK, 8/7/95, p. 71, David Denby

Cher (Alicia Silverstone), who lives with her father in a Beverly Hills mansion, picks out her clothes by computer and drives to her high school in a white Jeep, where she walks in state across the sunny school courtyard, shrugging off the grubby boys who launch themselves into her path ("As *if!*" she cries indignantly). With her big shoulders, big hair, big mouth, a friend on her arm, she's so preposterously majestic that you can't find it in your heart to dislike her, especially since she doesn't have a mean bone in her body. Amy Heckerling's terrific comedy *Clueless* is a worthy successor to her *Fast Times at Ridgemont High* (1982), which, in memory, stands out from the *Porky's* era of teen exploitation like a diamond glistening in trash. In *Clueless*, Heckerling affectionately joshes the fab life of a Rodeo Drive princess, creating a look, a code of manners, and a hilarious jargon that enclose Cher and her friends in their own boutique of pastel-pink self-consciousness. The movie goes like a shot, with narration pulling the sequences together, but you won't have trouble seeing everything—Heckerling doesn't go in for flashcutting and mess. A teen party is people having a good time, not a saturnalia. The resplendent Miss Silverstone, 18, late of those ubiquitous Aerosmith videos on MTV, appears to be some sort of deluxe found object; she is very funny and entirely likable. Her Cher doesn't know the name of anything, and she has an unfortunate experience explaining policy on Haitian immigration to her class, but she reminds me of Judy Holliday's blonde ditzes from 40 years ago: The more she babbles, the shrewder she seems. The surprise of her character in *Clueless*—which is based, amazingly, on Jane Austen's *Emma*—is that she's more interested in looking great and in being nice to other people than she is in her own happiness. Is there a catch somewhere? How can virtue be encased in an ethos of consumerist narcissism? But Heckerling loves Cher and her friends: Their posing conceals a small gift of poetry. By the end, we're won over by the comedy of goodness. By contrast, the nastiness of a "smart" teen movie like *Heathers* seems like a failure of imagination.

NEW YORK POST, 7/19/95, p. 35, Michael Medved

The fluffy promotional campaign for "Clueless" leaves the public clueless on just how smart and sophisticated this surprising comedy turns out to be. Teen-agers will flock to see it, of course, but parents may appreciate it even more—as a breezy guide to a youth culture (and language) that seems increasingly incomprehensible. As if!

Writer-director Amy Heckerling first explored such territory 13 years ago with her fondly remembered debut movie, "Fast Times at Ridgemont High."

Both pictures use infectious humor and a gifted young cast to highlight the simultaneously trendy and timeless aspects of the contemporary high school experience.

This new movie, however, is lighter and brighter—without the undercurrent of pain and melodrama that slowed "Fast Times." Here, even a mugging is played basically for laughs.

"Clueless" further differs from "Fast Times" in making no attempt to show a cross section of typical teenagers; the characters this time attend fictional Bronson Alcott High School in Beverly Hills, and they are all patently pampered.

At the pinnacle of this privileged pack stands Cher (Alicia Silverstone), with her perfect hair, perfect wardrobe, and perfect wheels—even though she's not yet 16.

She lives in a pillared mansion with her lawyer father (Dan Hedaya), retaining few memories of her mother who, Cher informs us, died in "a tragic accident during a routine liposuction."

The stunning Stacey Dash plays Cher's best friend Dionne ("We're both named after great singers of the past who now do infomercials," Cher helpfully explains) and together they face all life's great challenges—like finding appropriate accessories for their wardrobes, or persuading debate teacher Wallace Shawn to raise their grades.

They also work together to provide a fashion makeover (and arrange a friend) for a frumpy transfer student (Brittany Murphy) Cher takes under her wing.

"It's like that long book they made us read in ninth grade, Cher sighs. "Tis a far, far better thing, like when you do stuff for other people."

Silverstone, the 18 year-old star whose angelic face and supple body graced three Aerosmith music videos, combines undeniable glamour with masterful comic timing. Against all odds, she makes Cher likable; despite her narcissism, this character is genuinely good-hearted, as demonstrated by her solicitous concern for her brusque, workaholic father.

We even come to care about her romantic frustrations ("Looking for a worthwhile boy in high school is like looking for meaning in a Pauly Shore movie"), especially with her bickering ex-stepbrother (Paul Rudd), a freshman at UCLA who reads Nietzsche and affects a goatee.

Cher is so appealing, in fact, and so (relatively) reasoned in her sexual attitudes, that it seems a shame when director Heckerling shows her indulging marijuana with the crowd at a wild party.

Sure, it might be realistic, but would the film have somehow lost its edge (or earned even one dime less at the box office) without this implied sanction for a habit that no parent wants to encourage? Perhaps the best way to assimilate this unnecessary scene is to assume that the stylish heroine, like other leaders of our time, might have smoked the weed, but didn't, after all, inhale.

NEWSDAY, 7/19/95, Part II/p. B7, Jack Mathews

Bob Dole and Bill Clinton, those strange bedfellows of the Family Values Movement, ought to love Amy Heckerling's "Clueless," even though, some of its teenagers acknowledge being sexually active and the kids smoking dope in one party scene appear to inhale. Because at the center of it all is Cher Horowitz (Alicia Silverstone), a going-on-16 dream teen who loves her father, helps her friends, is kind to animals and is saving her virginity for the man she will someday love.

"Clueless," a fresh-faced send-up of the privileged world of "Beverly Hills, 90210," is great fun, if you can stand the nonstop adolescent jargon. Paramount has included a glossary of "Clueless" blab in its press materials, 45 words and phrases that punctuate the coded language of the film's small circle of friends. It is sort of the Windows '95 version of the Dudespeak in Heckerling's 1982 hit "Fast Times at Ridgemont High."

"Fast Times" was Heckerling's first film, and since then she has kept herself busy mostly with the lucrative "Look Who's Talking" franchise. With "Clueless," she returns to high school, in an excessively affluent 'burb that looks just like Beverly Hills, and introduces us to Cher, her best friend, Dionne (Stacey Dash), and Tai (Brittany Murphy), a grunge transfer from New York whom Cher and Dionne decide to make over in their own Saks Fifth Avenue image.

Cluelessness is relative in this story. Cher, who like Dionne was named after a great singer of the past who now does infomercials, thinks Tai is clueless because she doesn't dress the dress or talk the talk of Bronson Alcott High. Tai doesn't even know whom to date, at least to Cher's thinking, so the boy—Mr. Wrong, it turns out—is chosen for her. As events unfold, Cher begins to realize it is she who is clueless, about life, love and her own feelings.

If the storyline sounds vaguely familiar to you English lit majors, it comes directly from Jane Austen's 1815 novel "Emma," about a self-assured young woman of upper British society who rediscovers herself while trying to mold another woman's life. Heckerling has taken that concept, and the vagaries of upper-class snobbery, and given it a deliciously dizzy contemporary spin.

Heckerling has written some wonderfully sharp dialogue, with some cultural references (one to Billie Holiday, for instance) that will shoot right over the heads of teenagers and tickle their parents. But it is the marvelous deadpan performance of Silverstone, the sultry teenage vixen from "The Crush," that keeps "Clueless" from wearing out its welcome. You can only take so much beaming airheadedness, and with a cast made up entirely of caricatures, there is not enough context to engage the audience emotionally.

Silverstone has been getting the superstar-is-born treatment by the entertainment press, and "Clueless" should make it a reality. But as she did with her ensemble cast for "Fast Times," which launched the careers of Sean Penn and Jennifer Jason Leigh, Heckerling showcases a couple of other young actors we're likely to see many times again.

Stacey Dash is a stunning beauty, and Justin Walker, making his screen debut, is very funny as Christian, the outsider whose aggressive machismo conceals his true sexual-orientation from no one other than the naïve and infatuated Cher. That these two would end up shopping together tells it all.

NEWSWEEK, 7/24/95, p. 52, John Leland

In the summer's most compelling movie about teenagers, the passage through adolescence is a perilous haul. This is not the Hollywood idyll of Ozzie and Harriet. Family structures have broken down, parents and adults are either absent or irrelevant. The kids thrash about in a sea of pop cultural junk, cobbling lives out of casual sex and even more casual drug use. Moral issues are whatever. A drawn handgun is just a bad way to end an already bad night.

The movie is "Clueless," the Mentos-fresh comedy from Amy Heckerling, who directed the teen classic "Fast Times at Ridgemont High." Set in a snooty Los Angeles high school—I think you know which ZIP code—"Clueless" draws adolescence as a meaningless but zesty quest to get baked, get busy and get over—preferably in a form-fitting Azzedine Alaia dress. In Larry Clark's "Kids," which also opens this week, the teenagers stagger beneath a similar hormonal storm, but to much different effect. Shot in a neutral, documentary style, and released without a rating—the MPAA deemed it a commercially damaging NC-17—"Kids" tracks a day in the life of some New York skate kids as they also mindlessly troll for sex and drugs. "Clueless" is loosely based on Jane Austen's novel "Emma"; "Kids" evolved from Clark's graphic photos of street kids in Tulsa, Okla., and New York shooting up, copulating and toying with guns. Otherwise, really, they're a lot alike.

"Clueless" is largely a long roll of shiny gift wrap for Alicia Silverstone, the 18-year-old siren whose pedigree includes roles in three Aerosmith videos. She doesn't so much come of age during the film as ripen. As Cher, the most popular girl in Bronson Alcott High, she is beautiful, pampered, savvy and owns a lot of daring plaid ensembles. Her life, as she says in the breezy opening voice-over, is "like a Noxzema commercial *or what*." She seems to be the only girl in school not undergoing cosmetic surgery (this movie never met a nose-job joke it didn't like). She has the comfort of her own moral code. "It is one thing to spark up a doobie and get laced at parties," she waxes, "but it is quite another to be fried all day." And her pout could melt a Carvel Cookie Puss. But still, all is not perfect for Cher. She lost her mother to a fluke accident during a routine liposuction. Her best friend, Dionne—"We were both named after great singers of the past who now do infomercials," she says—refers to Cher as "hymenally challenged." Worse, as another girl tosses at her, in the film's coldest cut, "You're a virgin who can't drive." And though she meddles selflessly in the romantic affairs of others, Cher herself is strangely without a boyfriend. Somehow, you just know, by the third act she will find a way out of this existential heck.

Like "Kids," "Clueless" proceeds without killjoy grown-ups or antagonists: no Officer Krupke, no Jim Backus in an apron. Adolescence itself is the menace to be subdued. These are teen films modeled after disaster movies. An evil essence descends on the citizenry, leaving havoc and occasional plot devices in its wake. (Evidently the baby boomers making teen movies these days, in the interest of being modern, have abandoned the quaint notion of parental responsibility.) Heckerling captures her characters' squirmings with affection and wonder. She has a sharp ear for slang. The multiracial teens talk a careless mixture of Valley-speak and hip-hop argot. The African-American kids drop Yiddish; the princesses talk Compton. When Silverstone, all saucer eyes and infectious comic twinkle, declares a round of junk food "dope," it is a Benetton moment.

"Kids," Clark's directorial debut, offers no such tender moments. "I wanted to show what it was really like to be a teenager," says Clark, who made the film after hanging out with skateboard kids in New York's Washington Square Park. "The hormones are raging. You have an intense appetite for sex and violence ... These Hollywood movies about teenagers aren't realistic at all." The film opens on Telly (Leo Fitzpatrick), the "virgin surgeon," locked in an oceanic kiss with a girl barely out of puberty. (The actors, nonprofessionals, were at the time both 17; they're younger and more breakable than the kids we usually see enacting this scene.) Telly is awkward but cocky, a half-man with a speech impediment. Surrounded by her stuffed animals, he coaxes the girl out of her virginity. After she has cried her way through his spasms, he deposits a puddle of spittle on her dining-room table, bolts outside and describes the encounter in cold detail to his friend. "Virgins," he says, "I love 'em. No diseases ... No skank ... Just pure pleasure."

This is the world of "Kids": relentless predation, callous disregard and no real joy. There is also a lot of pot, and an occasional hit of something stronger. It is a boy's world; the girls here function mostly as ill-used toys. "They want you to be so kind, so gentle," says one boy. "Like you give a f--- or something." Clark and screenwriter Harmony Korine, 21, evoke this world with vivid verisimilitude and a discomforting reluctance to pass judgment. It just is. At its most convincing, the film starkly captures the closeness between sexy teen swagger—the pretense of brutality—and the real thing. In "Kids," as in his photos, Clark unflinchingly accepts both.

There's not much driving the plot: Telly wants to find the next virgin; Jennie (Chloe Sevigny), who discovers that he has given her the AIDS virus, wants to tell him before he beds someone else. Along the way there's an extraordinarily brutal spontaneous group assault and a listless rape. But these are all awkward filmic devices, and they feel artificially imposed to squeeze a narrative out of static summer boredom. Boredom doesn't make a movie; it makes a photograph, and Clark's photos tell tougher, better stories than his film. Bluntly powerful in its imagery, and milieu, "Kids" stumbles when it tries to shape itself into a feature film.

So why does all the underlying business—the mundane pursuit of heterosexual bunny-hopping and a good buzz—make such sugary froth in "Clueless" and feel like the end of the world in "Kids"? The difference lies in part in Clark's grittier tone, but also in ways the films cast adolescence. In "Clueless," as in most teen movies, adolescence is a hump to get over; when these kids talk about makeovers, malls or drugs, they're really talking about rites of deliverance. In "Kids," the reckless pursuits of sex and highs aren't metaphors for more elevated goals—they're what life is all about. Without glorifying it, Clark shows a romantic respect for this life, and for the dangerous boys who live in it. In his work, "Kids" included, adolescence is more than an inconvenient obstacle in the arc of life: it is the raw nut. The film's most unsettling scene shows four boys of about 11 or 12 sitting shirtless on a couch, smoking pot and talking the talk of the older kids. In this disaster movie, the disaster isn't capped at the end, it's spreading its domain.

SIGHT AND SOUND, 10/95, p. 46, Amanda Lipman

Cher Hamilton is a smart, motherless 15-year-old from Beverly Hills who looks after her wealthy lawyer father Mel. Josh, the serious, politically-minded son of one of Mel's ex wives, turns up and raises Cher's hackles. When some of her term grades are too low, she sweet-talks all her teachers into raising them except for Mr Hall, the debating teacher, so she concocts a plan to make him fall in love with another teacher. As a result, everyone gets higher grades and Cher is the most popular girl in the school.

Her next project is to transform Tai, a "clueless"uncool, new girl—into a fashionable Beverly Hills acolyte. Cher attempts to match her up with Elton, the most desirable boy in school, but to Cher's surprise, Elton proclaims his passion for her rather than Tai. When she rebuffs him, he throws her out of his car leaving her to be mugged. She calls Josh who comes to pick her up.

Another new arrival at school, Christian, seems to be the man of Cher's dreams, but turns out to be gay. Tai is fast taking Cher's place as the most popular girl in school. Cher becomes despondent about this and her own lack of perception about men. She argues with Tai, who has fallen for Josh, and realises that she is in love with Josh herself. To win him she sets about bettering herself by helping her father and volunteering for charity work. When she makes a bad mistake in her father's work, she thinks her incompetence has lost her Josh but he declares his love for her instead. At the wedding of the two teachers, she catches the bride's bouquet.

"Clueless", meaning uncool, lost, or out of touch with what is happening, is part of the very particular lingo of Beverly Hills teenagers. The exclusivity of its meaning highlights how Beverly Hills makes an apt setting for a contemporary version of Jane Austen's *Emma*, and how a rich, superficial teenager makes a remarkably apposite heroine. Both early nineteenth-century Surrey and upper-class Los Angeles are small societies with pretensions to greatness, teeming with strict mores and ludicrous social niceties. The film contains a plethora of humorous details which echo the lady novelist's refined but stringent satire, such as Cher's nonchalant comment that her mother died during a routine liposuction procedure.

The handsome, clever, and rich heroine of Jane Austen's novel is transformed into a pretty, knowing, rich 15-year-old, who makes up for what she lacks in academic intelligence with impressive powers of persuasion and her unerring sense of her own rightness. Cher is completely tuned into her specific culture. It is one with its own language, fashions, cars and television programmes, one obsessed with shopping. If Cher has a bad day, she shops. If she needs to think up a plot, she shops. Even during her most philosophical and miserable monologue about her life, she breaks off to wonder about a dress she spots in a shop window. Cher's world is unashamedly narrow. Asked to debate on whether or not to allow Haitian immigrants sanctuary in the United States, she talks about her father's birthday party. She has no interest in current affairs and thinks Bosnia is in the Middle East. However, although she only knows *Hamlet* through the Mel Gibson film, she can outquote Josh's pseudo-intellectual girlfriend.

Her strong sense of morality is purely pragmatic. She disapproves of dope smoking except at parties because it makes you dress badly and hang around with losers. Though she may be "hymenally challenged", or a virgin, it is only because she is saving herself for the right man. Yet while she is dismissive of most people in her school she is no snob, and is horrified by Elton's assertion that his father's standing makes him too good for Tai.

This version of 90s Californian materialism has a tang of a conservatism that is both intriguing and repellent. Intriguing because quaintly credible as it is, it is far from the teenage portraits usually presented to us on screen, and repellent because this lifestyle celebrates emptiness. This apes perfectly the portrait of young women spending their time doing nothing in the original novel. Cher's friend Dionne quips accurately that make-overs give Cher "a sense of control in a world of chaos".

Perhaps in the spirit of feminism, Cher is treated with a little more tenderness than her predecessor, Emma, while the equivalent to Mr Knightley, Josh, is less wholly perfect than the novel's hero. She is shocked (not satisfied as Emma was after the novel's equivalent incident) when silly Tai, trying to impress her new friends, publicly rebuffs her former friend Travis, the dopey but sweet skateboarder. Meanwhile, Josh, the Nietzsche-reading existentialist "nerd", is clever enough to see through Cher but is also naive enough to get excited about the prospect of Markie Mark opening some environmental event.

Aside from the nod to feminism, the novel is updated in two other ways. Cher has a best friend, the equally well turned out, equally pretty and rich Dionne (also named after a popstar who now appears on infomercials, as Cher blithely puts it) who happens to be black. Black people here are not consigned to South Central LA; and Cher's status is not a white prerogative. Frank Churchill, the man on whom Emma decides to bestow her own lofty attentions in Austen's book, here becomes Christian, a James Dean/Luke Perry-type, who turns out to be gay.

As a satirical moral tale, showing how the society in which a self-satisfied young woman establishes herself can rebound on her and teach her a few lessons, *Clueless* unfolds deftly. It is always difficult to infuse real emotion into satire without making it grossly sentimental, and this opts instead for chirpily affectionate moments. No one can really be expected to believe that Cher is going to change her ways because she loves Josh. The point is that she has learnt that she is not quite who she thought she was.

This is essentially a one-joke movie, but it is an enjoyably witty one, packed with vignettes of middle-class teenage lifestyles without resorting too much to video-style musical interludes. It may not have the laidback feel of *Dazed and Confused* or the sharpness of *Heathers* but it has its own perkily scripted realism and enough unmoralistic affection to keep us clued in to the follies of its heroine.

TIME, 7/31/95, p. 65, Richard Corliss

In moments of stress, Alicia Silverstone has the adorable and quite marketable habit of squinting—as if trying to read a TelePrompTer or possibly hatch a thought. This makes the 18-year-old actress the ideal vessel for *Clueless*, an enjoyable movie that says a lot about the needs of Americans, and not just teens, in the mid-'90s. The tale has Cher (Silverstone), a popular high-schooler in Beverly Hills, toiling as a matchmaker, as her father's confidant, as a makeover adviser to a clumsy friend (Brittany Murphy) and as her stepbrother's nemesis. All this echoes the plot of a certain Jane Austen novel. But the touchstone of *Clueless* is less *Emma* than Hammacher Schlemmer. The movie is about conspicuous consumption: wanting, having and wearing, in style. And in LA.

Clueless has another ancestor in *Heathers*, the most influential unseen film of the past 10 years. *Heathers* made the mistake of treating the peer success of blond teenage girls satirically. Amy Heckerling, the writer-director of *Clueless*, is cannier than that. An able architect of loosey-goosey comedy (she directed *Fast Times at Ridgemont High* and the *Look Who's Talking* films), Heckerling wants the viewer to like these girls even as she pokes fun at them. The toughest intellectual challenge for Cher and her friends may be deciphering the Thomas Guidemap of Los Angeles streets, but they have an ease and a good nature that ultimately, if at times strenuously, endear.

Paying to see *Clueless* is not really mandatory. You can learn most of the jokes by surfing the TV and newspaper reviews and get a hint of Silverstone's blithe luster by watching MTV's relentless promotions. Taking this Cliffs Notes route, moreover, saves you from sitting through several slow stretches of plot sludge. During these scenes, *Clueless* has the feel of some mild sitcom purring in a far corner of the living room. You don't watch it so much as notice it, from time to time, in a genial miasma.

As if that matters. No one lately has said a good movie must also be a good film. This one is best taken as a thing of bits and pieces, attitude and gestures. It's like a restaurant where you go for the food and go back for the atmosphere. Or for the waitress. Silverstone is a giddy delight, a beguiling performer and an icon for her generation. Catch *Clueless* quickly, though: in the MTV era, a generation lasts about a nanosecond.

VILLAGE VOICE, 8/1/95, p. 50, Stan Dauphin

MTV has been running an in-house promo that does double duty as a stealth ad for *Clueless*: music-vid sex-pot Alicia Silverstone and her BAP buddy Stacey Dash sit in a sunny restaurant contemplating the caloric implications of croutons. The scene doesn't appear in the film, making it an MTV-specific adjunct to a movie that's already a feature-length frame enlargement of Music Television.

Clueless is also an update of Jane Austen's *Emma* set to a "Top-20 Countdown" friendly soundtrack. Cher and Dionne (Silverstone and Dash) spend most of their days in pursuit of matchmaking and good deeds, their most sustained "project" being the makeover of a new girl with stoner sensibilties. *Emma* might have cast a long shadow during the writing of *Clueless*, and the subplots about tending to other people's affairs while your own are a shambles do provide most of its comedy, but the debt may be something that strikes you as clever only after the fact.

What does strike you up front is *Clueless*'s MTV look, which shifts from skateboarding alternative to basement party to teen catwalk stylings in an eyeblink, all that ostensibly housed in an upper-tax-bracket high school and orbiting Cher thanks to her late adolescent charm and good looks. Writer-director Amy Heckerling is good at keeping her mainstream kids from looking like fashion victims and thus gets the most of Silverstone's teeny bopper sex appeal, recasting her crooked smile as irony and letting Cher narrate the film in tones that range from teenaged innocence to compulsive-shopper-neurotic.

Clueless's answer to the style-versus-substance thing is that the question is moot compared to the intricacies of being a nice person, which is why this is a comfortably light comedy instead of something more overbearing. Heckerling has crafted an adult fantasy about hypothetical kids in an MTV-ordered universe, but it's also a summer movie aimed at kids who'd like to dress like Dionne, Cher, et al. someday, if not exactly live by their code of ethics. Having made *Fast Times at Ridgemont High* and set one of the many passing tones for teens in the '80s, Heckerling must know that she's indulging in an exercise in planned obsolescence here, this even as she reaches back to Austen for inspiration.

Also reviewed in:
CHICAGO TRIBUNE, 7/19/95, Tempo/p. 22, John Petrakis
NEW YORK TIMES, 7/19/95, p. C9, Janet Maslin
VARIETY, 7/17-23/95, p. 50, Brian Lowry
WASHINGTON POST, 7/19/95, p. D1, Hal Hinson
WASHINGTON POST, 7/21/95, Weekend/p. 38, Joe Brown

CONGO

A Paramount Pictures release of a Kennedy/Marshall production. *Executive Producer:* Frank Yablans. *Producer:* Kathleen Kennedy and Sam Mercer. *Director:* Frank Marshall. *Screenplay:* John Patrick Shanley. *Based on the novel by:* Michael Crichton. *Director of Photography:* Allen Daviau. *Editor:* Anne V. Coates. *Music:* Jerry Goldsmith. *Music Editor:* Kenneth Hall and Darrell Hall. *Choreographer:* Adam Shankman. *Choreographer (Gorilla):* Peter Elliott. *Sound:* Ronald Judkins and (music) Bruce Botnick. *Sound Editor:* Wylie Stateman and Gregg Baxter. *Casting:* Mike Fenton and Allison Cowitt. *Production Designer:* J. Michael Riva. *Art Director:* Richard Holland. *Set Designer:* Charles Daboub, Gary Diamond, Robert Fechtman, Dawn Snyder, Sally Thornton, and Darrell L. Wight. *Set Decorator:* Lisa Fischer. *Set Dresser:* Roger Knight, Taylor H. Black, Robert Gray, and Hope M. Parrish. *Special Effects:* Michael Lantieri. *Visual Effects:* Scott Farrar. *Gorilla Animatronics:* Star Winston. *Costumes:* Marilyn Matthews. *Make-up:* Christina Smith. *Make-up (Special):* Matthew W. Mungle and John E. Jackson. *Stunt Coordinator:* M. James Arnett. *Stunt Coordinator (Aerial):* Jeff Habberstad. *Running time:* 109 minutes. *MPAA Rating:* PG-13.

CAST: Dylan Walsh (Peter Elliot); Laura Linney (Dr. Karen Ross); Ernie Hudson (Monroe Kelly); Tim Curry (Herkermer Homolka); Grant Heslov (Richard); Joe Don Baker (R.B. Travis); Lorene Hoh (Amy) and Misty Rosas (Amy); Mary Ellen Trainor (Moira); Stuart Pankin (Boyd); Carolyn Seymour (Eleanor Romy); Romy Rosemont (Eleanor Romy's Assistant); James Karen (College President); Bill Pugin (William); Lawrence T. Wrentz (Arliss Wender); Robert Almodovar (Rudy); Kathleen Connors (Sally); Joel Weiss (Travicom Employee); John Hawkes (Bob Driscol); Peter Jason (Mr. Janus); Jimmy Buffett (727 Pilot); James R. Paradise and William John Murphy (Transport Workers); Thom Barry (Samahani); Ayo Ade Jugbe (African Airport Guard); Kahara Muhoro (Roadblock Soldier); Kevin Grevioux (Hospital Officer/Roadblock Officer); M. Darnell Suttles (Hospital Interrogator); Michael Chinyamurindi (Claude); Willie Amakye (Lead Porter); Jackson Gitonga and Andrew Kamuyu (Mizumu Tribesman); Fidel Bateke (Witch Doctor); Shayna Fox (Amy's Voice); Bruce Campbell (Charles Travis); Taylor Nichols (Jeffery Weems); Adewale (Kahega).

LOS ANGELES TIMES, 6/9/95, Calendar/p. 1, Kenneth Turan

Michael Crichton writes suspense thrillers. Quite successful suspense thrillers that get turned into even more successful movies. At least up to now.

For the makers of "Congo" see things differently. They view Crichton, if this maladroit effort is to be believed, as the creator of jokey adventure farces that generate as much tension as an America's Cup race on a calm day. There have been worse ideas around town, but not many.

Given the success of "Jurassic Park" and "Disclosure," it is difficult to work up sympathy for the prolific Crichton, but the mishmash that director Frank Marshall, screenwriter John Patrick Shanley and the rest of the "Congo" company have made of his work makes you want to reach out in commiseration.

Not only have bothersome plot changes been made, but the entire tone of the book has been transformed from tension to tongue-in-cheek with dismal results. Even the waning episodes of "Ramar of the Jungle" seem like models of dramatic construction compared to what is visible here.

The clumsiness of the effort notwithstanding, it's not difficult to see what "Congo" had in mind, for both director Marshall and his producing partner Kathleen Kennedy worked with Steven Spielberg on "Raiders of the Lost Ark" and the two subsequent Indiana Jones pictures.

Not satisfied with Crichton's combination of "King Kong," "King Solomon's Mines" and trendy science (the book lists more than 60 titles in its "References" section), they've tried to combine action with humor a la Indy with uniformly wretched results.

Once it gets sorted out, "Congo's" core plot involves several characters with diverse motives who end up on the same charter plane to Africa's heart, the Congo region:

● Karen Ross (Laura Linney) of communications giant TraviCom is searching—who knows why—for flawless blue diamonds as well as her ex-fiancé, the son of surly boss R.B. Travis (Joe Don Baker), mysteriously lost on a similar mission.

● Peter Elliot (Dylan Walsh), a gentle, tree-hugging primatologist who feels so guilty about having taught a gorilla named Amy to talk that he has decided to return the creature to her jungle home.

● Herkermer Homolka (the reliable Tim Curry), a self-described Romanian humanitarian who is in reality an adventurer searching for the lost city of Zinj, the site of King Solomon's fabled diamond mines.

Under the guidance of Monroe Kelly (Ernie Hudson), who, in a typically feeble line of dialogue explains, "I'm your great white hunter, though I happen to be black," this group is fated to encounter a bunch of apes with bad attitudes that place their plans and their lives in considerable jeopardy.

Summarized this way, "Congo" sounds acceptable because it doesn't indicate how flabby the film's execution is. Screenwriter Shanley, a well-known playwright and an Oscar winner for "Moonstruck," must have dozed through the creation of this one, filled as it is with soggy retorts and plot points that range from preposterous to plainly incomprehensible.

Not much better are "Congo's" numerous performing apes, which, despite the best efforts of makeup and visual effects master Stan Winston, are transparently people in state-of-the-art monkey suits. And once the nasty gorillas that have been hinted at since the film's opening moments finally appear, they come off more like bad-tempered Pomeranians than worthy successors to King Kong.

Every once in a while, "Congo" remembers it's supposed to be exciting and shovels some off-putting violence onto the screen, like having a character hit by a tossed eyeball. And the film rarely misses an opportunity to treat Africa and Africans in an insulting and clichéd manner. It's yet another baffling element in a more than usual disappointing film.

NEW STATESMAN & SOCIETY, 7/7/95, p. 33, Jonathan Romney

It's easy to see why *Ed Wood* fired filmgoers' imaginations (except, that is, at the US box office—but we're hypothesising the Ideal Film-Goer, who's too busy staying in reading the views to actually visit a multiplex).

When it comes to bad films, the fact is that they don't make them like that any more, not like Edward D Wood did. Anyone working on the contemporary equivalent of Wood's budgets would only ever get to make films destined for the low end of the festival circuit or for straight-to-video limbo, where few are watching and fewer could care less. As for finding a cast-iron plonker at your local MGM, in these days of test screenings, demographics and terror of the next

Waterworld, it's rare that any studio would get the chance to be so enthusiastically brainless. These days, they make them naff or dull or unimaginative, but upper-case Stupid never.

Ah, but there's always *Congo*. To be honest, it isn't madcap-awful like the Wood canon; it's more like the wooden-headed dullard B-pics that used to get programmed at Golden Turkeys all-nighters. Films like *The Brain from Planet Arous, Robot Monster, Cat Women on the Moon*, in which square-jawed, slow-talking heroes pitted their wits against balsawood sets and cheap by-the-yard dialogue. With *Congo* you can only assume that everyone involved had a hangover at the time. The funniest thing about it is that it recently went to No 1 in the States, the week when everyone was off-guard waiting for *Batman Forever*. It's based on a novel by Michael Crichton, who since *Jurassic Park* has seen all his still-unfilmed properties snapped up with barrel-scraping frenzy, which must make him the E M Forster of the airport novel.

On paper, *Congo* looks like *Jurassic Park* with bananas— another African ape-terror movie in the wake of *Outbreak*, which featured the best film poster ever: the letters "DUSTIN HOFFMAN" over a picture of a screeching Capuchin monkey (is there no limit to the man's virtuosity, you marvelled). This is a sci-fi update of the Rider Haggard ripping-yarn genre set in Darkest Africa, which is what they used to call it before *The Lion King*. The director is Frank Marshall, formerly Steven Spielberg's production sidekick, who made the creditable horror comedy *Arachnophobia* and the stranded-in-the-Andes plane crash saga *Alive!* (aka *Honey I Ate the Crew*). it tries to be a little bit different, a little bit politically correct, but in that respect it's like a slow fourth-former trying to catch up with its smarter big sisters and brothers. It takes a bunch of stars you've never heard of—Dylan Walsh, Laura Linney, Ernie Hudson—and puts them in vaguely mould-breaking roles. Linney is a scientist, but she's also square-jawed, slow-talking, fearless and a crack shot; while the chap, Walsh, is gentle with gorillas and gets nervous under fire. Hudson is the dashing chap with the safari suit and David Niven accent, except that he's black.

Even so, that doesn't mean we don't get excruciating run-ins with unruly natives. There's a talcum-powdered phantom tribe who do a run-through of the dance routines that got cut from *I Walked With a Zombie*, and an African militia man clearly modelled on John Bird's Idi Amin impersonation of the early 1970s. "This is pure Kafka," complains one of our heroes. "Who's Kafka!" snaps the troublesome khaki johnny, "Tell me!"

Congo is written by John Patrick Shanley, who scripted *Moonstruck* and directed a venturesome but much-hated Tom Hanks flop, *Joe Versus the Volcano*. I can only assume he was taking the piss, or that this was the result of a private bet with Joe Eszterhas, to see which one could write the biggest tosh for the biggest dosh. Let *Congo*'s finest lines be carved in stone. "I don't have a price—I'm not a pound of sugar, I'm a paleontologist"—"We're returning her to the jungle from whence she came"—"Don't perpetuate the King Kong myth"— and the ever-dependable "Shit! Let's get out of here while we still can!" But no one quite does their lines like Tim Curry, as the comic bad-egg in a safari suit. He is Herkermer Homolka, a "Romanian philanthropist" and "free from the chains of Ceaucescu". There's a line you can really chew on. If I were a *Rocky Horror* fan, I'd be very upset to see how much he now resembles Jeremy Beadle.

The plot is that a bunch of stout types are in search of the Lost City of Zinj, where a pure blue diamond and a few mutilated missing Americans can be found. The team are accompanied by Any, a gorilla who has been taught to speak, and who has had her photo on the cover of *Life* sniffing gently at a little yellow flower—a lesson to us all, I think. Amy speaks by waving her arms, while a computer produces sentences like "Hi! I'm Amy!" All this technology for a Barbie doll with body hair and long arms. When Walsh is menaced by the guardians of Zinj, a gang of mean, pie-eyed apes with silver hair, it's Amy who saves the day by leaping into the fray and yelping, "Ugly gorillas! Ugly! Go away!" And they do.

If you want to see a cracking good City of Apes adventure, may I recommend the recent live action *Rudyard Kipling's Jungle Book* from Disney, which should be on video by now. But if you want to see *Scooby Doo on Safari*, look no further. I have recently seen *Casper, Batman Forever, First Knight* and a whole load of big-budget products that looked as if they were put together by brilliant technicians who'd planned it all with algorithms. *Congo* is the work of people who had the finest resources of Industrial Light and Magic in hand, and still couldn't figure out which button to press. I tell you, it's made my year.

NEW YORK POST, 6/9/95, p. 39, Michael Medved

Everyone's expecting that Kevin Costner's "Waterworld" will emerge as the summer's most embarrassing big-studio bomb. But in terms of incoherent idiocy, this upcoming release would have to go a long way to top "Congo."

At least the creators of this ludicrous lunacy (longtime Spielberg associates Frank Marshall and Kathleen Kennedy, who here served as director and producer) haven't skimped on ambition: They serve up four different (and disconnected) dumb movies for the price of one.

First and foremost there's an old-fashioned sentimental love story about a boy and his gorilla.

A Berkeley primatologist (Dylan Walsh) has trained his research specimen, Amy, to communicate with sign language, but unlike the creature in the silly Michael Crichton novel that inspired the film, the movie Amy isn't satisfied with flashing fingers.

She's been hooked up to an elaborate virtual reality glove that transforms her gestures onto a girlish cutesie-pie voice endlessly declaring, "Amy good gorilla!" or "Amy loves Peter!"

It doesn't help that the animal expressing these tender sentiments is actually an athletic little guy in a gorilla suit who only occasionally resembles an actual ape.

In any event, Amy and master travel to Africa to return the homesick hominid to her mountain habitat, but they're accompanied by an odd collection of characters with different agendas who each seem to be functioning in some unrelated movie.

There is, for instance, the glamorous former CIA agent (Laura Linney) now employed by an evil corporation which wants her to go into the jungle to retrieve rare diamonds that will help develop a powerful new laser gun.

Then there's the Rumanian adventurer (Tim Curry) who's convinced that the talking gorilla's impressionistic paintings (!) prove that the artist can lead him to the "lost city of Zinj" and—you guessed it—King Solomon's mines.

As if this weren't enough, we also get an aerial battle involving the Zaire Air Force, exploding volcanoes, earthquakes, a treasure trove of Egyptian hieroglyphics, hordes of politically incorrect natives chanting "ooga-booga!" and even a hippo attack directly inspired by the Jungle Cruise at Disneyland.

This cinematic thrill ride, however, isn't much fun because the gee-whiz sense of playfulness and wonder that enlivened Spielberg adventures from "Indiana Jones" to "Jurassic Park" has been replaced by an atmosphere of cynical nastiness—screenwriter John Patrick ("Moonstruck") Shanley tried to pen a high-camp hoot, but director Marshall never seems to be in on the joke, with special effects too technically impressive (and too bloody) to treat these monkey shines as comedy.

Only Tim Curry, among the cast of embarrassingly earnest actors, manages to cut loose and enjoy himself, with his ridiculous accent and eye-rolling delivery of lines like "It is the city of Zinj that I have looked for all my life!" and "The myth of the killer ape is true!!!"

The movie takes forever to finally reveal the mystery of these "killer apes" and the big payoff is a wretched anti-climax.

Instead of the awesome, supernatural horror we've been promised from the beginning, all we get is a few more guys in moth-eaten monkey suits—a painfully disappointing version of "Gorillas in the Mess."

NEWSDAY, 6/9/95, Part II/p. B2, Jack Mathews

A decade before he wrote "Jurassic Park," novelist, screenwriter, occasional director and non-practicing physician Michael Crichton combined his passions for fiction and science in his big ape adventure, "Congo." And now, thanks to the book and screen successes of his dinosaurs, here come the gorillas.

They should have stayed on the shelf.

"Congo," adapted from the book by John Patrick Shanley ("Moonstruck") and directed by Frank Marshall ("Arachnophobia"), is shlock on a $50 million budget, the movie Ed Wood might have made had he lived and won the Powerball lottery. It features a talking ape with the personality of Gidget, a high-tech heroine who can kick butt *and* set up a satellite transmission dish, a Romanian con-man with an accent that makes Bela Lugosi sound like a network anchor, and a rowdy band of flesh-eating, mutant gorillas.

Plus ... *plus!* ... a hidden city, the vault to King Solomon's mines, and a volcano that is about to blow its cork!

"Congo" makes "Jurassic Park" look like a documentary.

This is really Hollywood at its most vulnerable. "Congo," written in 1980 and optioned throughout the interim, is one of the prolifically glib Crichton's most overheated ideas, and a foreboding gamble for its financiers. Its canvas is large and expensive, there are no major stars and the plot is unbearably stupid. But after "Jurassic Park," somebody—Paramount, it turns out—had to make it.

Besides the reflexive popularity of the book, revived as a post-"Jurassic Park" bestseller, the movie came with the comforting name of Frank Marshall, a co-founder and producer at Steven Spielberg's Amblin Entertainment. With his first two directing jobs, "Arachnophobia" and "Alive," Marshall demonstrated a strong visual sense for action, and he clearly knows what it takes to give an adventure film that "Spielberg look." But a bad act is a bad act, no matter how grand the stage.

All the Crichton elements that made "Jurassic Park" go—unmanageable beasts, tension between technology and nature, the moral conflict brought on by entrepreneurial greed—have their antecedents in "Congo." The Lost City of Zinj, where mutant gorillas stand guard over King Solomon's Mines, isn't exactly a theme park, but as the setting for the film's cartoon climax, it serves the same purpose.

It is Zinj, in the thick of the jungle and in the shadow of a percolating volcano, where all of the principle characters end up. The primatologist (Dylan Walsh) returning his homesick ape, Amy (created by special-effects wiz Stan Winston), to the wilds. The high-tech maven (Laura Linney) searching for her missing boyfriend and the diamond that, when affixed to a laser gun, will make her ambitious boss (Joe Don Baker) the most powerful communications magnate on Earth. The wisecracking African guide (Ernie Hudson). And the Romanian tongue twister Herkermer Homolka (Tim Curry) at his campiest.

NEWSWEEK, 6/19/95, p. 76, Jack Kroll

"Congo" is basically the old African ooga-mooga movie brought into the P.C. high-tech age. Instead of a bunch of white guys (and a girl) hunting ivory or seeking King Solomon's mines, you have a bunch of white guys (and a girl) seeking ... well, actually they are seeking King Solomon's mines. At least one of them is. He's Herkermer Homolka (Tim Curry), a Romanian hustler who lusts after Sol's diamonds. Karen Ross (Laura Linney) also is looking for rare gems, as components for her company's satellite communications. And Peter Elliot (Dylan Walsh), a primatologist, is returning his pet project, Amy the talking gorilla, to her jungle home.

So, Herk and Karen and Peter and Amy—consider the possibilities. Which writer John Patrick Shanley ("Moonstruck"), adapting Michael Crichton's 1980 best seller, does, along with the director-producer team Frank Marshall and Kathleen Kennedy, longtime colleagues of Steven Spielberg's. Crichton-Spielberg-Kennedy did "Jurassic Park," the King Solomon's mine of movies. "Congo" is not in that league. Behind the computers, the satellites, the lasers and the special effects that make the volcano erupt and the lost city of Zinj get lost again, lurk all the African clichés. The old headhunters are now bribe-taking wise guys in the uniforms of authoritarian regimes. A giant hippo attacks the expedition's raft, just like the brontosaurus in "King Kong." The leech that latches onto Peter's genitalia is a postmodernizing of the leeches chomping on Humphrey Bogart in "The African Queen."

As the expedition hacks its way deep into the heart of schlockness, the fun is almost all technical. Tarzan's cute screechy chimp is replaced by the much cuter Amy, who has been taught sign language and wears a computerized glove that converts her signs into a synthesized voice. Amy is played by a performer wearing an ape suit, while off-screen technicians control her facial expressions through the electronic puppetry called animatronics, the work of the wizardly Stan Winston.

All the techno-wizardry pays limited thrill dividends. Despite the agreeable ensemble (notably "Ghostbusters's" Ernie Hudson as a takeoff on the classic white hunter) the movie suffers from the lack of a hero figure, an Indiana Jones. The real star is Amy. See her belt back a martini. Watch her cuddle with nerdy Peter, in the movie's strongest emotional relationship. Gasp as the simian teeny-bopper single-handedly stops a horde of bloodthirsty mutant gray gorillas from dismantling Peter. At the end, after Amy sadly toddles off into the bush, Peter mistily sniffs a flower she's given him. This bodes no good for the budding romance between Peter and Karen. You know the old song: "Once in love with Amy, always in love with Amy."

SIGHT AND SOUND, 8/95, p. 44, Philip Kemp

Charles Travis, leading an expedition to a remote region of the Congo around the volcanic Mt Mukenko, reports back via satellite to his father R.B. Travis, boss of Travicom, that they have located the rare blue diamond needed to fuel Travicom's latest project, an ultra-powerful laser gun. Moments afterwards, Travis and his safari party are massacred by savage apelike beasts. R.B. Travis tells Project Supervisor Dr Karen Ross, Charles' ex-fiancee, to make her way to the Congo and find out what happened.

At Berkeley, primatologist Peter Elliot publicly displays Amy, a young mountain gorilla he has taught to 'speak' via signing technology. In the audience is Herkermer Homolka, a mysterious Romanian who offers a finance Peter's expedition to return Amy to her own kind, in the hope she can teach them human speech. At the airport, Karen manages to gatecrash Peter's group by coming up with ample funds when Homolka's credit gives out.

The party arrives in the Congo to find a civil war in progress. With the help of their guide, Monroe Kelly, and bribe, handed out by Karen, they negotiate roadblocks and escape military detention before boarding a plane for the Zairean border. The plane is shot down by rockets, but everyone parachutes to safety and the expedition continues on foot. Approaching the Burunzu region whence Charles Travis last transmitted they are guided by members of the Uzumi tribe to Bob Driscol, sole survivor of Travis' expedition, who dies of fear at the sight of Amy.

The safari reaches Mt Mukenko where they find the ruins of the lost city of Zinj, fabled source of King Solomon's diamonds, which Homolka has long been seeking. But the mines prove to be guarded by lethal grey gorillas, specially bred for savagery by Solomon's guards. Homolka, avidly gathering gems, is killed by the gorillas and the others retreat into the mines where soon only Karen, Peter and Monroe survive. Peter, about to be killed by the gorillas, is saved by Amy. As the volcano erupts the four make the their escape, but Amy elects to stay with a family of normal gorillas. Karen contacts R.B. Travis, but realising he cares only for the diamond and not for his son, uses the laser to destroy his satellite. Peter, Karen and Monroe leave on a hot-air balloon previously sent by Travis, and Karen throws the blue diamond away.

Ex Africa semper aliquid novi, remarked Pliny; there's always something new coming out of Africa. He might have changed his mind if he'd seen *Congo*. Killer apes, lost cities in the jungle, military uprisings, foreign-accented diamond-hunters, volcanoes, witch doctors—Frank Marshall's film recycles almost every corny cliché of African-adventure movies from the past 60 years, even daring to rope in that haggard old standby, King Solomon's Mines. Several elements seem to have strayed in from Marshall's previous films: the plane-crash/survival story from the Andean cannibal film *Alive* and the fated jungle expedition that likewise opened *Arachnaphobia*. *Congo* comes closer to the latter film in its candidly far-fetched plot, but totally misses *Arachnaphobia*'s tension or its malicious wit.

In its favour, though, it also lacks the heavy-handed didacticism of recent Crichton-based films with their solemn warnings against genetic meddling, Japanese expansionism or sexual PC. If the original novel (which I've not read) contained a moral, it certainly hasn't survived the transition to screen. Just as well, really, since anything as substantial as an idea would have looked sadly out of place in such a shamelessly inane confection. *Congo*, indeed, is several decades behind its time: with its cardboard characters, slapdash motivation and one-damn-thing-after-another plot, it should have found its true home chopped into 12 episodes and spread across Saturday matinees.

The usual jibe with a film like this is to say the best acting comes from the animatronic animals. In fact the apes are strangely unconvincing, given the involvement of the great effectsmeister Stan Winston, though they're certainly no worse than the nominal leads, Dylan Walsh and Laura Linney. With Joe Don Baker wasted on a role that lets him do nothing but rant, the film is stolen by Ernie Hudson's sardonic guide and an outrageous turn from Tim Curry sporting a 'Romanian' accent which veers wildly from Moscow to Barcelona. And *Congo*, for all its vacuity, does score one cherishable moment. Deep in the heart of the jungle, trying to comfort Amy, Peter starts crooning *California Dreamin'* to her—then looks up in surprise as every member of the safari, American and African alike, word-perfectly joins in.

VILLAGE VOICE, 6/20/95, p. 54, Gary Dauphin

Taken from the Michael Crichton novel of the same name and basically doing for the already suspect genre of jungle action/adventure flicks what *Disclosure* did for sexual harassment (i.e., induce tepid distraction in the viewer), *Congo* has the odd distinction of being much more silly and boring than it is offensive, a small favor if there ever was one. *Congo* is set in Central Africa and its plot follow's an ever-expanding group of searchers as they hike into the heart of Crichtonian darkness after various grail. There's sensitive primatologist Peter Elliot (Dylan Walsh), who is trying to return Amy, his computer-assisted talking gorilla, to her natural habitat. (Amy is played for maximum cutes by a puppet/guy in a gorilla suit.) There's a Romanian con man named Herkermer Homolka (Tim Curry, cheerfully sinister as a ridiculously accented chewer of vine-covered scenery), who joins Peter and Amy in order to fortune hunt for King Solomon's mines, a/k/a "The Lost City of Zinj." And then there's Karen Ross (Laura Linney), an ex-CIA agent currently employed by TraviCom, a stateside communications conglomerate. Sent to the Congo by TraviCom's CEO in search of her ex-fiance and some laser enhancing diamonds ("the future of telecommunications"), Karen commandeers Peter et al's cash-poor expedition. In the process she not only provides the party with the hardware needed to keep a handful of them alive until the final credits, but also gives *Congo* the technophilic window dressing that any Crichton adaptation requires.

The film's thin science-fiction veneer is no match for the laws of the jungle, though. *Congo's* head porter might go out with all the grit of a Colonial Marine from Aliens, but go out he does (his anonymous fellows are distinguished from the screaming natives of a Tarzan flick by virtue of being able to sing Beach Boy's tunes while pottering). *Congo's* other talking puppet is Monroe Kelly, the party's roguishly dapper guide. Since Kelly is black (Ernie Hudson doing a role Crichton had written white), his calculatedly racist riffs about banana republics and cannibal rebels are magically transformed into little more than ritual P.C.-bashing. *Congo's* ad blitz makes much of an "unknown species" of killer ape, but the film's real surprise is how zipless that whole angle turns out to be. Director Frank Marshall stages a random hippo attack with more energy than is contained in the killer ape encounters, and the beauties themselves look like angry midget stragglers from the hominid sequence in *2001*. Amy the talking ape may only know 650 words, but by the time she says "Bad gorillas!" about a half dozen times in *Congo's* last reel, no truer words will have been spoken.

Also reviewed in:
CHICAGO TRIBUNE, 6/9/95, Friday/p. C, Michael Wilmington
NEW YORK TIMES, 6/9/95, p. C, Janet Maslin
VARIETY, 6/12-18/95, p. 59, Brian Lowry
WASHINGTON POST, 6/9/95, p. B1, Hal Hinson
WASHINGTON POST, 6/9/95, Weekend/p. 42, Desson Howe

CONGRESS OF PENGUINS, THE

An Ariane Film AG release. *Director:* Hans-Ulrich Schlumpf. *Screenplay (German with English subtitles):* Franz Hohler and Hans-Ulrich Schlumpf. *Director of Photography:* Pio Corradi, Patrick Lindenmaier, and Luc Jacquet. *Editor:* Feekliechti. *Running time:* 90 minutes. *MPAA Rating:* Not Rated.

NEW YORK POST, 1/4/95, p. 31, Thelma Adams

Penguin Little, Penguin Little, the sky is falling!

In "The Congress of Penguins," Hans-Ulrich Schlumpf takes us on a fantastic voyage to Antarctica led by a self-flagellating environmental dreamer.

Part documentary, part fiction, "The Congress of Penguins" includes rapturous nature photography fit for the Discovery Channel. There are snowswept vistas, sculptural ice formations, rolling seas under gunmetal skies. Schlumpf and crew make the rusty detritus of an abandoned whaling station assume the power of somber poetry.

Irrepressible penguins star. God must have had a sense of humor to create such playful animals. They zip onto the ice, warm their young between their feet, and flap their flippers, communicating in a language unintelligible to humans. Unintelligible, that is, except to the dream-narrator.

In the fanciful narrative, a citydweller falls asleep and dreams of Antarctica. A lone parka-wearing figure on a plain of ice, the dreamer encounters a penguin gathering. He instantly anthropomorphizes the birds: They are a congress with a message of protest to convey. They are angry at man's environmental transgressions; on his knees before the assembled fowl, the dreamer begs for forgiveness.

The film wanders away from the dreamscape to examine an abandoned whaling town where live penguins were occasionally used to fuel blubber-burning ovens. It sails aboard the ship "Polarstern" and trudges across the frozen tundra to a remote science station. As we watch scientists test global warming, water quality or the ozone layer, an ironic turn occurs: the men and women seem less human than the penguins.

The doc-dreamscape circles back to the penguin rave where the kneeling narrator continues to project his own environmental doom and despair onto the frolicking creatures. He claims they look disturbed; to me, they seemed like people waiting for a bus on a cold day.

In the narrator's eyes, the fowl chastise him for man's destructiveness, and then, having imagined their feelings out of thin ice, he says somberly, "I understood how they felt." When I watched God's little butlers, they seemed to be telling Schlumpf to lighten up, to play. "Chill out." said the penguins. I understood.

NEWSDAY, 1/4/95, Part II/p. B2, John Anderson

Some people have responded to the worldwide environmental crisis by denying there's a crisis. Others have been caught on the horns of a nagging question: Does Homo sapiens actually have a purpose on the planet, other than destroying it? The record, after all, suggests the Species Who Came to Dinner, and set the house on fire.

Are we carpetbaggers in our own world? It's tough not feeling like an intruder after watching "Congress of Penguins," an extraordinary Swiss documentary-cum-dreamscape that indicts not just humankind for its environmental crimes but also contemporary researchers—who impose themselves on the last pristine environment on Earth in order to study signs of creeping human influence. Even when the film is paying tepid tribute to these scientists, their very presence is portrayed as a pollutant, and nothing if not ironic.

This is not your standard wildlife film—for one thing, the viewer is not perched atop some paternal, Disney-style food chain. We're being chastised, and by penguins. The unnamed narrator is in a dream, which carries him to a congress—of emperor, king, adélie and gentoo penguins—the purpose of which is an indictment of man and the formulation of a message that will be carried back by the narrator. The narrator, a veritable blank slate, is then introduced to a history of crimes against the birds, their world, and ends up asking for absolution. It is not granted.

In a way, this is a Holocaust film. Found footage of the Norwegian whaling factory at Grytviken, dating to 1930, resembles outtakes from Alain Resnais' Auschwitz film "Night and Fog," except the victims are birds. If this seems presumptuous, perhaps that's the point: That man presumes the natural world to be at his disposal, to the point that live, blubber-rich penguins were burned in the ovens at Grytviken when other fuel was scarce.

The found footage is perhaps the most absorbing part of "Congress": Men are shown tormenting seals and penguins for sport, and reducing an enormous whale, through the factory process, to a spine and a tail. While the slaughter proceeds, a narrator recites a litany of products and uses that result from the whale, including "nitroglycerine for whale harpoons"—a line delivered straight-faced—and "whale steaks for the connoisseur," a menu item we hear just as the last mangled bit of meat goes over the conveyor.

The naturally comic posture of the penguins—who are not the focus of the film exactly, more like its Greek chorus—becomes resigned and mournful. The beauty of their ice blue world is made more majestic by its muteness. For a lifeless climate—it is a desert, after all—it certainly seems to be alive. And as captured by cinematographers Pio Corradi, Patrick Lindenmaier and Luc Jacquet, the beauty of the place is not just esthetically potent but purposeful; the icebergs become mesas, and the terrain resembles Monument Valley as portrayed by John Ford, with all the accompanying ambiguity (although I can't identify it, some of the music, credited here to Rachmaninoff, Saint-Saëns and Brunn Spoerri, recalls that of "Days of Heaven," another film in which a spectacular landscape and a tawdry humanity were in direct contrast).

Following the environmental researchers around their ship as it plies the vast Antarctic seas, our narrator is unseen and ineffectual. He can't influence what he sees, or even seek atonement for the crimes of his species. As such, he and his film take on an absurdist quality. And so do people in general, juxtaposed against the nobility of the penguins, who merely turn their back on us, their message having been delivered. "Congress of Penguins" isn't strident, although it easily could have been. It is, however, very beautiful and very sad.

VILLAGE VOICE, 1/10/95, p. 48, Georgia Brown

Those snappy little tuxes, all that pluck: Penguins always look buoyant. Up they waddle to the top of the slide, then down they slip ... splash! Hey, they make us happy; they must be happy, too.

In his often ravishing polemic *The Congress of Penguins*, Swiss filmmaker Hans-Ulrich Schlumpf projects a very different mind-set onto penguins. They may feel about us the way Jews feel about Nazis. This, anyway, is his fiction, the initial tack of his ecological meditation, as he reviews with great sorrow some of the atrocities visited on penguins. In whaling operations, butchers threw live penguins on the flames to keep their fires burning. The species' pristine Antarctica home is blighted by noisy man-made work stations, while the notorious hole in the ozone layer is destroying life-sustaining organisms.

Schlumpf's tantalizing reverie begins in an anonymous industrial city: No images, just the sounds of traffic, then the voice-over of our nameless, faceless narrator complaining about noise and smog. He has difficulty sleeping, but at some point drops off, only to wake in a land of ice and snow. At first, he's frightened at the vast white expanse, his own insignificance. Then, in the distance—and these shots are truly spectacular—he spies a line of penguins walking in his direction. As they come nearer, he waits with trepidation, thinking they're coming for him, but they pass him by.

Unlike those diminutive birds we're used to seeing in zoos, emperor penguins are at least three feet high and colorful. At the top of their white "shirts," where the tie would be, there's a vivid radish-gold stain-like bleeding rust or the last seconds of a sunset. An orange Nike-type emblem is set toward the back of their heads, and their long, curved beaks glow the same color. As they file past, occasionally one will flop to his or her belly and begin to glide along horizontally, short flippers churning.

Schlumpf's spectacle of penguins is marvelous, but his narration often verges on the ridiculous. The narrator considers himself chosen by the penguins as their interpreter. Their shrieks, he decides, sound like the word *Grytviken*, a South Georgia whaling village, where we now go by boat. Schlumpf's tour of Grytviken's deserted buildings and rusted machinery is somewhat reminiscent of Resnais's visit to Auschwitz in *Night and Fog*. Here, the victims were whales, penguins, seals, and other sea creatures.

At the town's collapsed movie theater—KINO 1930, reads the sign on the facade—the narrator wonders what movies might have played here. "*Moby Dick? The Gold Rush?*" We're shown grisly archival footage of Grytviken in its prime. Smug, imbecilic-looking men mug for the camera while poking viciously at seals and penguins and stealing birds' eggs. We witness some of the whale butchery. In a redundant exercise, the narrator imagines himself a whale, still conscious, dragged into the slaughterhouse. The script persists in this sort of annoying didacticism when the images themselves are powerful and sufficient. The narrator makes a production of begging the penguins' forgiveness while pleading innocence, "I'm not like those men! It wasn't me! When I buy soap I ask if it's made of whale blubber."

The Congress of Penguins isn't really about penguins. I wish it were. I wish Schlumpf had furnished more hard facts about their habits and life cycles and had skipped the moralizing. It's not even clear why the penguins assemble here for the so-called "congress." Later, it appears that the trek may be a cyclic return to a "brooding ground." (Nice pun.) We watch as infants emerge from eggs hatched under the upright adults. When the fluffy gray babies are old enough, they sit out on the parents' feet, as if on a front porch. Two adults face each other, gabbing—comparing notes?—while down below their offspring conduct their own colloquy.

As the documentary skips off to introduce scientists at work in the Antarctic, the penguins seem something of a ruse. Too much of the film takes place on a ship, the Polarstern out of Bremenhaven, watching intent crew gather and analyze data. Here, the fiction of the dream grows truly cumbersome. The narrator can't be seen by the researchers as he asks, "Do you know what we dream about?" and, one by one, the scientists look solemnly into the camera. "Do the penguins dream about us?" (It's always a mistake for a lesser film to remind the viewer of Chris Marker's travel journals with their heart-stopping lyric intelligence.)

The Congress of Penguins has a great and pressing subject—the destruction of the earth—but it's mucked up with corny narration and superfluous sermonizing. If only Schlumpf had let the penguins speak for themselves. Go, but take earplugs.

Also reviewed in:
NEW YORK TIMES, 1/4/95, p. C9, Stephen Holden

CONVENT, THE

A Strand Releasing presentation of a Madragoa Filmes/Gemini Films/La Sept-Cinema coproduction with the participation of Instituto Português da Arte Cinematográfica e Audiovisual, Secretaria de Estado da Cultura, and Canal Plus. *Producer:* Paulo Branco. *Director:* Manoel de Oliveira. *Screenplay (English, Portuguese, and French with English subtitles):* Manoel de Oliveira. *Based on a original idea by:* Agustina Bessa-Luís. *Director of Photography:* Mário Barroso. *Editor:* Manoel de Oliveira and Valerie Loiseleux. Music: Sofia Gubaidulina. *Sound:* Jean-Paul Mugel. *Production Designer:* Zé Branco and Ana Vaz da Silva. *Costumes:* Isabel Branco. *Running time:* 90 minutes. *MPAA Rating:* Not Rated.

CAST: Catherine Deneuve (Hélène); John Malkovich (Michael); Luís Miguel Cintra (Baltar); Leonor Silveira (Piedade); Duarte D'Almeida (Baltazar); Heloísa Miranda (Berta); Gilberto Gonçalves (Pescador).

LOS ANGELES TIMES, 12/1/95, Calendar/p. 12, Kevin Thomas

Manoel de Oliveira's "The Convent" is a sly, beautiful enigma of a movie, a reflection upon the eternal mystery of life itself. It's a film full of portents, cryptic asides, insinuations and warnings, all of which may mean something—or nothing at all.

In any event, it is the first international venture by the often outrageous, ever-idiosyncratic 87-year-old Portuguese maestro who began his career in the silent era and, as a matinee idol, starred in Portugal's first talkie in 1933. There is an elegant, contemplative quality to the film that is the mark of a filmmaker of long and distinguished experience. Ironically, "The Convent" is almost certainly the first Oliveira film to receive a U.S. release, his previous work showing up only at festivals.

A Paris-based scholar (John Malkovich) and his beautiful French wife (Catherine Deneuve) arrive at the ancient convent of Arrabida in Portugal where he hopes to find in its library documents that will prove that Shakespeare was in fact a Spanish Jew named Jacques Perez who fled Spain for Portugal during the Inquisition, settling finally in Florence.

What actor could state this outlandish thesis with a straight face better than Malkovich? Or so convincingly suggest that he really believes his research to be more important than, of all women, Deneuve? As for her somewhat bored wife, she feels a connection with the place. Could she come to embody some ancient goddess? Who better than Deneuve for that?

The couple is greeted by the convent's guardian (Luis Miguel Cintra), a man of reptilian charm who resembles Bela Lugosi in appearance and demeanor. He goes on about the monks who lived in a starkly primitive style in nearby caves and about a chapel dedicated to the worship of Lucifer. In residence there's an elderly professor (Duarte D'Almeida) who takes a rather skeptical view of the convent's legends yet spends much time with the housekeeper (Heloisa Miranda), a Tarot card devotee.

There's considerable philosophical debating between the scholar and the guardian, with the second constantly referring to Faust. Indeed, the exquisite young woman (Leonor Silveira) who is to be the scholar's research assistant could easily stand for Goethe's Marguerite. Or maybe the visitors have simply stumbled upon a bunch of satanists or a coven of witches.

"The Convent" is suffused with an amusing quality of tentativeness, which Oliveira sustains with the ease of a veteran tightrope walker. Essential to the unsettling mood he creates is the dramatic, edgy score composed by Sofia Gubaidulina and incorporating portions of Stravinsky's "The Rake's Progress" and Toshiro Mayuzumi's "Prelude for a String Quartet." For all its intimations of evil and even danger, this most graceful of fables can in the end be taken as a simple tale of a couple who needed to get away for awhile to a place that's actually lots more charming than sinister so as to get their marriage back on track.

NEW YORK POST, 12/8/95, p. 50, Thelma Adams

The locations are gorgeous.

Catherine Deneuve has a flair with a scarf.

It's comforting to know that John Malkovich can't pull off *every* very role.

In "The Convent," which played at this year's New York Film Festival and opens today at the Quad, octogenarian Portuguese director Manoel de Oliveira pairs a pinch-faced Malkovich and a puffy Deneuve as an American professor and his French wife. The two are hardly George Burns and Gracie Allen, but it must be the definition of failed humor when you wish someone had warned you a movie was a comedy before you entered the theater. Comedy doesn't travel well.

Michael (Malkovich) arrives at a remote Portuguese convent to research his thesis that Shakespeare was a Sephardic Jew. This interesting claim serves as a pretext for Oliveira ("The Satin Slipper") to schlep his international cast to home turf. We get no further information on this tantalizing theory—nor does it function to illuminate the battle between good and evil at the movie's core.

How Michael snared Helene (Deneuve) might provide the subject of a prequel. Here, their marriage appears to be an emotional desert. They are only in tandem when sharing the front seat of a car. He is preoccupied by his ambitions; she pouts at the neglect.

Helene's only solace seems to be tossing on another fabulous sweater set which Michael refuses to notice. But Baltar (Luis Miguel Cintra), the convent's guardian, recognizes her charms. Baltar throws willowy archivist Piedade (Leonor Silveira) Michael's way so that he can scoop up Helene for himself.

Helene's flirtation with Baltar makes as little sense as her marriage to Michael. The dark-haired local with the devilish laugh looks as if he should be hosting a late-night TV fright show—hardly the match for the sophisticated professor's wife.

"The Convent" takes an unmagical, mystical turn when it begins to suggest that the vaguely fanged Baltar has a direct line to Mr. Darkness himself. But it could be that this demi-demon has hooked a bigger fish than he intended. Helene is not all that she seems—is she Helen of Troy or the devil in blue cashmere?

Between the unintentional laughter and the clunky quotations from Goethe's "Faust," which serves as a Michelin's Guide for the moral territory to be covered, "The Convent" is tough to sit through.

NEWSDAY, 12/8/95, Part II/p. B7, John Anderson

Cardinal sins have become au courant. Odder still, they provide a link between Brad Pitt and the fabled Portuguese director Manoel de Oliveira: in "Seven," the sins were so bold they provided not just the plot but the title. Unsurprisingly, in de Oliveira's "The Convent," they are much less conspicuous, almost covert, as understated as the Devil himself.

De Oliveira's films—at 87, he has produced 12 features over the last 23 years—are studies in visual gravity and languorous pacing. Like Antonioni, he is far less interested in narrative entertainment than in creating a disturbed and disturbing universe. He exerts such control over his actors, his sets and what is portrayed on screen that you often feel you are being taken somewhere, rather than told something.

These qualities are present in "The Convent," but, for de Oliveira at least, the storyline is virtually mainstream: Michael Padovic (John Malkovich) and his wife Helene (Catherine Deneuve), arrive at an ancient Portuguese monastery in search of some papers Michael hopes will prove his academic thesis: that Shakespeare was a Spanish Jew. He believes the proof lies within the crumbling walls. What he finds is pride, greed, lust, wrath and envy.

The guardian of the place is an off-kilter character named Baltar (Luis Miguel Cintra), who takes an immediate and lustful interest in Helene; he provides, as a diversion, Piedade (Leonor Silveira) as Michael's research assistant. Desire doesn't exactly run rampant through the old mission—the director doesn't work quite that way—but evil is definitely afoot.

The gravity of de Oliveira's imagery is in concert with the slow pace of his film: Each frame seems to contain destiny within it, and the individual pictures, always perfectly composed, are both mirrors and eternities. It is difficult to look away.

Like any director, though, de Oliveira can lapse into the obvious. "Look at it, the whole world at your feet," Baltar crows to Michael, echoing Christ's temptation by Satan. Piedade reads to Michael from Goethe's "Faust." Helene contains obvious parallels to that earlier Helen, as well as to the serpent himself. But while relying on archetypes to make his story, the director seems to create an archetype of his own: "The Convent" has the look and feel of something biblically primal.

If there's a flawed aspect to the film, it's in the casting: Malkovich is too arch and mannered for the beautiful Deneuve, who looks as if evil would succumb to her.

VILLAGE VOICE, 12/12/95, p. 67, J. Hoberman

Closing in on 90, Portugal's Manoel de Oliveira may be the last working director to have begun his career in silent movies. Even more amazing, de Oliveira has completed over half of his 17 films since 1980—the year he made his New York debut among the relative teenagers of "New Directors/New Films."

De Oliveira may have contrived the longest swan song in the history of movies, but he is known here almost entirely due to the institutional support of the Museum of Modern Art, the New York Film Festival, and, particularly, Fabiano Canosa's late, lamented film program at the Public Theater. Still, wonders never cease—de Oliveira's latest, *The Convent*, not only has an American distributor but is even opening at a commercial movie house.

That *The Convent* is arriving in time for Christmas has less to do with its adroit metaphysical vaudeville than in being de Oliveira's first (at least partially) English-language movie, as well as his first to feature international stars, namely Catherine Deneuve and John Malkovich. A trim 90 minutes, marginally more bankable than most of his oeuvre, this elegant, enigmatic movie is no less characterized by the director's acerbic sense of humor—a distinctive blend of the antic and the portentous. Like many of de Oliveira's autumnal works, it seems both a distillation and a parody of European high culture.

An American professor (Malkovich) and his chic French wife, Hélène (Deneuve), mismatched and unhappily married, are touring Iberia looking for evidence that will enable the work-obsessed academic to prove his thesis that William Shakespeare was of Spanish-Jewish origin. The quest leads them to an ancient Portuguese convent administered by the theatrically sinister; black-clad Baltar (Luis Miguel Cintra, who might be auditioning for the Portuguese version of the 1930 *Dracula*).

Isolated in the woods (yet convenient to the sea), the convent is itself a sort of Shakespearean set. It's as though the place were under a spell—coming to life just for its foreign visitors. The guests are favored with a tour of sacred sites that have long since been pillaged by vandals: "Look," their none-too-reverent guide carols at the entrance to one cave, "Nothing!" Nevertheless, the convent has a library from which the professor will, per Baltar's promise, extract "wisdom comparable only to the knowledge of God." That knowledge is made as explicit as it will ever be in the person of the ascetically beautiful archivist (Leonor Silveira the sloe-eyed Emma Bovary of de Oliveira's *Valley of Abraham*), who suddenly materializes among the dark, dusty books.

The Convent's premise, reminiscent of vintage Antonioni in its haute bourgeoise angst, is more than weird enough for Malkovich—his purse-lipped affect fits right in—particularly as it is larded with baroque theology and is rendered all the more oddball for its theatrical bits of business and the sort of aggressively modernistic score that might have been used to accompany a '50s production of *Oedipus Rex*. Even before the characters start quoting Goethe, it's clear that *The Convent* is some sort of a Faust story. But who is selling souls and who is buying! The avid, sleazy Baltar all but flaunts his cloven hoofs when he takes the professor to the edge of a precipice to show him the world at his feet and suggest that the American's discovery will make him immortal.

Sex in *The Convent* is basically a case of not-quite not-quite hanky panky. "I wish you weren't so pure," the professor complains to the apparently chaste librarian. "It's cruel." "Cruel!" is her dreamy response. As with more than one Iberian saint, erotic tension fuels the mystical ecstasy—or is it vice versa? What's most impressive about de Oliveira's sly comedy is how he contrives to render the medieval contemporary—although the notion of a world populated by devils and angels is increasingly less exotic as we slouch toward the millenium.

Is the librarian a fallen angel? Is the American professor an innocent abroad? Repeated references to Helen of Troy underscore the point that this possible Faust has long since made his pact with the devil—or at least he is already married to the lovely Hélène. In any case, the unfailingly gracious, uncannily preserved Hélène is hardly naive. "I love hearing you talk like a Witch," Baltar cackles after one of their little walks in the woods.

Also reviewed in:
NEW YORK TIMES, 12/8/95, p. C12, Stephen Holden
VARIETY, 5/29-6/4/95, p. 57, Deborah Young

COPYCAT

A Warner Bros. release of a Regency Enterprises presentation of an Arnon Milchan production. *Executive Producer:* Michael Nathanson and John Fiedler. *Producer:* Arnon Milchan and Mark Tarlov. *Director:* Jon Amiel. *Screenplay:* Ann Biderman and David Madsen. *Director of Photography:* Laszlo Kovacs. *Editor:* Alan Heim and Jim Clark. *Music:* Christopher Young. *Music Editor:* Thomas Milano. *Sound:* Chris Newman and (music) Bobby Fernandez and Larry Mah. *Sound Editor:* Eddy Joseph. *Casting:* Billy Hopkins, Suzanne Smith, and Kerry Barden. *Production Designer:* Jim Clay. *Art Director:* Chris Seagers. *Set Decorator:* Catherine Davis. *Special Effects:* R. Bruce Steinheimer. *Costumes:* Claudia Brown. *Make-up:* Stephen Dupuis. *Stunt Coordinator:* Tim A. Davison and John C. Meier. *Running time:* 124 minutes. *MPAA Rating:* R.

CAST: Sigourney Weaver (Helen Hudson); Holly Hunter (M.J. Monahan); Dermot Mulroney (Ruben Goetz); William McNamara (Peter Foley); Harry Connick, Jr. (Daryll Lee Cullum); J.E. Freeman (Lieutenant Quinn); Will Patton (Nicoletti); John Rothman (Andy); Shannon O'Hurley (Susan Schiffer); Bob Green (Pachulski); Tony Haney (Kerby); Danny Kovacs (Kostas); Tahmus Rounds (Landis); Scott De Venney and Terry Brown (Cops); David Michael Silverman (Mike); Diane Amos (Gigi); Richard Conti (Harvey); Nick Scoggin (Conrad); Bert Kinyon (Burt); Dennis Richmond (KXBU Anchorman); Rob Nilsson (SWAT Commander); Kenny Kwong (Chinese Kid); Charles Branklyn (Doc); Kelly De Martino (Festival Girl); Rebecca Jane Klinger (Peter's Wife); Corie Henninger and Arlon G. Greene (Joggers); Bill Bonham (Photographer); Kathleen Stefano (Peter's Mother); Chris Beale (Tech Guy); Hansford Prince (Fred); Don West (Attorney); Jay Jacobus (Judge); John Charles Morris (Young Peter); Keith Phillips (Felix Mendoza); Johnetta Shearer and Eleva Singleton (Paramedics); Ron Kaell (Mac); Kelvin Han Yee (Chinese Detective); James Cunningham (Hal); Victor Talmadge (Head Waiter); Brian Russell (Coroner's Man); Damon Lawner (Festival Dude); Russ Christoff

(Commissioner Petrillo); Doug Morrision (SWAT); Edith Bryson (Landlady); Jeni Chau (Michelle); William Oates (Man in Corrider); Lee Kopp (Haircut Man); Thomas J. Fieweger (Bodger the Cop); Floyd Gale Holland (L. Bottemy); Anthony Moore (Uniformed Policeman); Stuart W. Yee (Thug); Vincenetta Gunn (Screaming Woman); David Ferguson (Dock Onlooker); Gena Bingham (Victim in Car at Gas Station).

FILMS IN REVIEW, 1-2/96, p. 61, Victoria Alexander

Serial killers are society's supernatural demon beings, but with a perverse twist. They function daily among and with us, yet, when they act, are outside any laws governing their behavior. We are told there are 30 to 50 serial killers operating right now in the U.S., each finding scores of nameless victims. The randomness of their crimes only increases our terror of them. Since the serial killer's appetite always increases, the thrill and pleasure must be overwhelmingly potent—and impossible to give up.

Why did the bogeyman live in my basement and not next door? *Just because.*

Copycat is an exciting and suspenseful film. Sigourney Weaver plays a psychologist who's stalked by a serial killer re-enacting infamous murders. A near fatal victim of a serial killer herself, she is agoraphobic, suffers from anxiety attacks, and guzzles brandy all day long. Holly Hunter, still whiny-voiced and still short, plays a homicide detective who demands Weaver's help. You'd think the wealthy psychologist would increase her personal security and hire a beefy bodyguard instead of standing in front of her open windows in the dark (as all intended movie victims seem to enjoy doing). It's creepy how she keeps the dress she was tortured and nearly killed in. Being a target again seems to re-energize Weaver's character. Instead of careening head first into a complete mental breakdown, she becomes less neurotic and more focused. It straightens her out and gives her life purpose. I would have liked to see Weaver go from almost looney to completely nuts. She's good at playing freaked-out women—her post-anorexic physique and taut drawn face are tailor-made for screaming fits.

Who didn't think Harry Connick, Jr. could play a serial killer? He's been wildly praised for this portrayal. Why I bet he could have auditioned in a tuxedo and still have gotten the part. Quite possibly, learning to play the piano was his salvation.

LOS ANGELES TIMES, 10/27/95, Calendar/p. 1, Kenneth Turan

Every age, it's often said, gets the entertainment it deserves, and no one living in today's America can doubt that we're experiencing an era of near-paranoid obsession with crime and personal safety.

We double-lock our doors, purchase whatever security systems we can afford, insist on more prisons and demand three-strikes-and-you're-out legislation because we're worried sick about courts being too soft on those who would harm us.

But though terrified of real-life violence, we paradoxically can't seem to stay away from it on screen. We pay the market price to have our most fearful fantasies confirmed, to see vivid visualizations of our worst nightmare, the more vivid the better. And, Lord help us, we call that fun.

Which is all by way of saying that America seems to have gone serial killer mad. "Seven," a grotesque examination of a perverse criminal mind, was No. 1 at the nation's box office for four weeks running, and now, joining in the plague, comes "Copycat," which features not one but two serial killers for devotees to choose from.

Though "Copycat" is not as across-the-board repulsive as "Seven," this is not for lack of trying, as director Jon Amiel and writers Ann Biderman and David Madsen have loaded the film with terrorized women and graphic close-ups of tortured female corpses.

But, by having Sigourney Weaver and Holly Hunter play the maniacs' feisty antagonists, the filmmakers seem to believe that they've made a significant feminist statement, the movie's two hours-plus of almost continual sadistic abuse of women notwithstanding. Even in an industry known for self-delusion, that is quite a feat.

Weaver is introduced first as Helen Hudson, a criminal psychologist who is the world's leading authority on the serial killer breed. Some of that knowledge apparently comes firsthand: Hudson is almost immediately attacked, tormented and trussed up like a Christmas goose ripe for killing by cretinous psychopath Daryll Lee Cullum (Harry Connick Jr.).

Though Cullum is captured, that attack, not surprisingly, so traumatizes Hudson that she becomes a prisoner in her swank San Francisco apartment. But she still has a rooting interest in the serial killer game, and enjoys anonymously second-guessing the doltish police when a new mass murderer makes an appearance.

Trying to solve the murders is Police Detective M.J. Monahan (Hunter), the standard-issue "one pushy broad" kind of tough cop with a cute young guy (Dermot Mulroney) for a partner. Monahan finds out about Hudson and makes her a part of the investigative team. Together, in a same-sex riff on Hitchcock's "Rear Window," they form a Ms. Inside and Ms. Outside combination, attempting to double-team the wacko of the moment.

That wacko turns out to be a fan of the imprisoned Daryll Lee. More than that, he idolizes all the great serial killers of the recent past. Kind of like an Elvis impersonator with a will to kill, he's a conscious duplicator of the work of twisted legends such as the Boston Strangler and Son of Sam.

A fair amount of this creepy film is told through the eyes of the maniac, as we watch him calmly stalking victims or cheerfully attacking them. Like most of the world's serial killers, he has a thing for Hudson ("I'm their pin-up girl," she explains to M.J. in a typically fake-glib line of dialogue) and he's soon simultaneously stalking her while running through his regular list of victims.

The most interesting questions "Copycat" raises have little to do with this unfortunate script or its predictable ending. Are roles for talented actresses so limited that they're eager to appear in such unsavory, exploitative films? Or does someone like Weaver, with a master's degree from the Yale School of Drama, really think that being bound, gagged and humiliated not once but twice like an outtake from a bondage video is what fine acting is all about?

A bigger, probably unanswerable question, is why audiences embrace this kind of material with such avidity. Are we so jaded, our lives so overloaded with sensation, that we need something as excessive as "Copycat" or "Seven" to arouse our interest? Why is getting a rise out of audiences by any means necessary something to boast about? And when did watching people being graphically tortured become America's favorite form of theatrical entertainment?

And isn't it also possible that these films are making viewers unrealistically fearful for their personal safety and thus having a pernicious influence on public policy? And isn't it becoming increasingly true, to quote Lt. Col. David Grossman's "On Killing," a recent study on how soldiers act in battle, that "we are reaching that stage of desensitization at which the inflicting of pain and suffering has become a source of entertainment: vicarious pleasure rather than revulsion. We are learning to kill, and we are learning to like it."

Though pornography has always been a difficult concept to define satisfactorily, one way it has been traditionally looked at is as a one-step-beyond phenomenon, showing us things either sexual or violent that go one step beyond what society normally tolerates. In that context, "Copycat" seems pornographically intent on pushing the envelope of what is acceptable for thrillers on screen. If the trend continues it is not at all pleasant to contemplate where everything will end.

NEW STATESMAN & SOCIETY, 5/3/96, p. 35, Jonathan Romney

The press kit for *Copycat* requests that reviews should not reveal the film's ending or the killer's identity. I suppose, grudgingly, I must cooperate, although I would argue with the with the terms. As with most recent Hollywood whodunits, the killer does not have much of an identity, but is a sort of generic lurker tailored to fit the drama. For once, however, the fact that everything seems to have been assembled piece by piece from a genre kit is no disadvantage, for *Copycat* is an incisive commentary on serial killer cinema, and a ruthless nailbiter into the bargain.

Director Jon Amiel and writers Ann Biderman and David Madsen hit a strange note between novelty and familiarity. The plot is routine: there is a killer behind bars and one at large; a tough, astute female cop (an engagingly wry Holly Hunter) not unlike Jodie Foster's FBI agent in *The Silence of the Lambs;* and a cerebral expert, Helen Hudson (Sigourney Weaver), who, again like

Foster, has her own demons. It would be easy to dismiss all this as state formula, especially with Weaver's persona as tough, thinking battler remaining intact from *Alien*. But from the initial hair raising suspense routine, which is left dangling for us to worry over, the familiarity is used brilliantly.

Copycat is about repetition. The killer gets his kicks from reproducing, with slavish accuracy, the techniques of famous precursors, from the Boston Strangler to Jeffrey Dahmer. You wonder how distant a horror has to be before it becomes legitimate thriller material. Dahmer's exploits seem too recent to figure as a smart plot twist. A British film referring to the Wests would surely seem nightmarishly close to the knuckle.

Copycat could exist only in a climate in which serial killing enjoys a peculiar media status. It preoccupies the western imagination as the ultimate horror of urban life, yet is domesticated by saturation coverage in the hard media or in semi-fictionalising movies-of-the-week.

Exploitative as it is, *Copycat* makes an enterprising attempt to read through this fascination. It highlights the way we fictionalise killing by using its own copycatting to parallel the killer's. It is peppered with allusions to *Psycho*, *The Silence of the Lambs*, and Brian De Palma, especially *Dressed to Kill*. This should make for a stifling, genre bound archness, but it is more adroit than that.

Copycat suggests that our relative immunity to the horror of killing derives from our tendency to see it in the same luridly ureal terms as the movies which mythify it: it actually works against genre.

It might seem a modish device to have the killer send Hudson his repellent artwork by Internet, but when we see him playing with a victim's image on screen, it comes across as a comment on the film's own manipulation of images.

The Net bears on another modish metaphor: viral contagion. The urge to kill seems to communicate itself virally, through the media: Hudson's murderous arch-nemesis (crooner Harry Connick Jr) is the author of a best-selling memoir, *My Life With a Knife*.

He boasts of being like Jesus; his unholy word spreads through a publicity virus. As the copycat killer points out: "More books have been written about Jack the Ripper than Abraham Lincoln. It's a sick world, isn't it?"

Copycat is a riposte to *The Silence of the Lambs*, the film that did most to make the serial killer a folk hero. For all its slickness, *Copycat* aims from the outset to deglamorise the killer myth. Hudson lectures a classroom of regular students, and reveals its average "cute guys" as statistically standard killer material. There is a paranoid edge to the film's focus on apparent normality, but such an argument engages the intelligence rather more than the reassuring satanic stereotype of Hannibal Lecter.

The film's conservative thrust is to suggest that we have become too interested in slaughter and should perhaps have a moratorium on depicting it fictionally.

Perversely, it does so by using some of the more explicit postmortem imagery that we have seen on screen, along with more glamorous images that push genre gloss to an anxious extreme.

This exhaustive repertoire of killer lure and commonplaces makes it seem that in future there will simply be no ground left to cover. *Copycat* looks like the serial-killer film to end them all, and that, in its brilliant and contradictory way, might be exactly what it aspires to do.

NEW YORK POST, 10/27/95, p. 43, Thelma Adams

"More books have been written about Jack the Ripper than Abe Lincoln," the "Copycat" killer tells one of his intended victims. Ted Bundy, Jeffrey Dahmer and David Berkowitz got more than their 15 minutes of fame—and the fiend in Jon Amiel's thriller wants to carve his name into the flesh of history.

In "Copycat," there are damsels in distress and dames in charge. Dr. Helen Hudson (Sigourney Weaver) wants desperately to escape from the former category into the latter. A self-described "muse of serial killers," the good doctor has bought her swanky condo on the San Francisco Bay with her best sellers on mass murderers. After a close encounter with psychopath Darryl Lee Cullum (musician Harry Connick Jr.), Hudson is switch-hitting brandy and tranquilizers, afraid to leave her personal biosphere.

Meanwhile, there's a new boy in town killing and killing again. Homicide detective M.J. Monahan (Holly Hunter) will do anything to get her man—except shoot to kill. M.J. hooks up with Hudson. The doc provides the cop with crucial information while unintentionally baiting the trap.

The two actresses play well together. Weaver does her high-IQ, high-wire act. With her slinky negligees and charcoal circles beneath dark, watchful eyes, she has become the diva of the elegant, intelligent neurotic, the class act of the post-nervous breakdown set.

Hunter plays Monahan quietly, an emotional woman who learned a "just the facts, please" attitude from watching "Dragnet" as a kid. She isn't just a little gal with bangs and a glossy ponytail and a badge; she's a smart cookie who uses her little-girl looks, her little voice, to move through the police hierarchy and always get her man.

What makes the dynamic between M.J. and Hudson interesting is that they both call each other on their B.S. They see through the masks each has put up to protect themselves and there's nothing delicate about the way they verbally rip them down.

But while the two women are bonding, a murderer is imitating the serial killer all-stars on the streets of San Francisco, a Son of Sam here and a Dahmer there. As Hudson's nemesis, Connick shows he's not afraid to go grunge, acting largely, but not inappropriately, with a set of bad teeth and a zeal that would suit Jim Varney's evil twin in "Ernest Goes to Jail."

Amiel ("Sommersby") slickly ushers the plot along, alternating between shots of gruesome corpses (but easy on the torture in progress) and those "don't open that closet" moments that invite audience participation. Ann Biderman and David Madsen's script gives character its due en route to an ending that's no "Copycat" cop-out—although they're a little too reliant on the cliche of patrolman ineptitude.

"Copycat" is a glossy, gory story that will have dates all over America clutching their companion's arms and crying out to Weaver to "leave the apartment, *now*" while pleading with Hunter to "shoot to kill."

NEWSDAY, 10/27/95, Part II/p. B2, Jack Mathews

Serial killers are the scariest and most loathsome creatures lurking in the shadows of American life, human vermin to be flushed out and eradicated with all haste. But for Hollywood, they are natural resources, their twisted minds and foul deeds providing a steady flow of inspiration to writers in that most enduring of all genres, the suspense thriller.

More than anything else, serial killers make for model movie villains, and for Jon Amiel's "Copycat," writers Ann Biderman and David Madsen have come up with one of the most inspired. Their killer is a homicidal performance artist, an ingenious fruitcake who makes detailed studies of the work of such famous serial killers as Son of Sam, the Hillside Strangler, and Ted Bundy, and re-enacts their crimes.

It is up to San Francisco homicide detectives Holly Hunter and Dermot Mulroney, with the reluctant help of retired criminal psychologist Sigourney Weaver, to connect the dots between the killer's victims, whose deaths mimic those from the historical cases, and try to catch him before he completes his program.

"Copycat" is the smartest and most gripping thriller since "The Silence of the Lambs," with which it bears some similarities. Both films are driven by intuitive heroines, and in both instances, the audience knows the killer's identity long before the police. The movies are cat-and-mouse games where our identification with the mouse is heightened by our awareness of what the damn cat's up to.

Finally, both movies benefit from their strong female casting. Jodie Foster won an Oscar for her work in "Silence," and though "Copycat" is not likely to generate that kind of enthusiasm, Hunter and Weaver are terrific, as well.

From the jarring opening sequence, which begins with Weaver's Helen Hudson giving a lecture on serial killers and ends with her being attacked by one (Harry Connick Jr.), "Copycat" announces itself as a thriller with brains. I don't know if the lecture, or any of the serial killer psychology that follows, is valid, but it all meets the test of screen plausibility. There is an authentic creepiness to the material that raises the emotional stakes far beyond that of routine Hollywood potboilers.

The story picks up 13 months after that lecture and assault, which leaves Hudson alcoholic and agoraphobic, self-imprisoned in her Sausalito loft, with only her gay assistant (John Rothman), a bank of computers and some Internet e-mail buddies to link her to the outside world. But she can't help following a rash of random murders being reported in the news, analyzing them, and offering anonymous tips to the police that they bear the unmistakable stamps of a serial killer.

After being traced and recruited as a consultant by homicide cops M.J. Monahan (Hunter) and Ruben Goetz (Mulroney), Hudson begins to piece together the puzzle and figure out that the serial killer is not only mimicking some of the century's most notorious murders, but in a pattern that inevitably leads right back to her.

Hunter and Weaver play wonderfully off each other. Though circumstances make allies of them, this is in no way a buddy movie. Monahan is a pragmatic, no-nonsense cop using the psychologist's expertise—against her supervisor's orders—as an investigative tool. And Hudson cooperates because she is still compulsive about serial killers, and vaguely aware that the case may free her from her own demons.

"Copycat" gets a little carried away in depicting its killer as a gleeful, premeditated sadist, there are some lapses in logic as police keep being distracted for plot convenience, and a completely unnecessary subplot about Hunter's relationship with an ex-lover (Will Patton) on the force. But compared to the mundane nature, of most Hollywood thrillers, exemplified by the current hit "Seven," it's an intelligent and enthralling surprise.

NEWSWEEK, 11/6/95, p. 86, David Ansen

Are serial killers the great performance artists of our era? You might think so judging from the reverence Hollywood has bestowed on these fashionable cinematic villains. In "Silence of the Lambs," "Seven" and now the slickly scarifying *Copycat*, serial killers have become artists of depravity, painting their masterpieces in blood (it used to be mad scientists who were evil's elite). Their appeal, dramatically, is in their twisted parody which requires an adversary—part Sherlock Holmes, part Sigmund Freud—who can break the code of their demented logic.

"Copycat's" adversary is a good one: she's Dr. Helen Hudson (Sigourney Weaver), a criminal psychologist whose expertise in serial killers has, in her embittered words, made her their pinup girl. Also their victim. Having barely escaped death at the hands of one psycho (Harry Connick Jr., surprisingly well cast), she's become an agoraphobic wreck, afraid to leave her swank San Francisco apartment.

But now a desperate homicide detective (Holly Hunter) needs her incomparable insights to stop the city's latest sicko—who, it turns out, also wants to finish the job on Dr. Hudson his predecessor bungled.

The unraveled shrink quickly cottons to the fact that this brilliant wacko is a copycat serial killer—he imitates the modus operandi of such famous predecessors as the Boston Strangler, the Hillside Strangler and the Son of Sam. This allows the screenwriters, Ann Biderman and David Madsen (with an uncredited assist from Jay Presson Allen) to let the real-life criminals dictate the scenario: it's a kind of serial killers' greatest-hits anthology, covered by our fictional fiend.

Fortunately, director Jon Amiel has chosen to play this for glossy Hollywood thrills, not grisly verisimilitude. "Copycat" is satisfyingly tense, but the disgusto factor is balanced by its obvious theatricality—neatly captured in the contrasting performances of Weaver and Hunter, the one playing neurotic standard poodle to the other's tightly wound terrier. Instead of the usual romance, "Copycat" tries for something subtler—an unresolved flirtation both women have with Hunter's handsome young partner (Dermot Mulroney), further complicated by the jealousy of another detective (Will Patton) who once had an affair with Hunter. It doesn't really come off—you want either more or less than what the script gives—but you can appreciate the attempt.

The eclectic Amiel, whose credits range from "The Singing Detective" to "Tune In Tomorrow" to "Sommersby," knows how to wring suspense. And he gets better dramatic use out of computers than most recent movies have (check out the unthrilling "Assassins" to see how not to use them). The killer, a techno-whiz, communicates with the housebound Dr. Hudson via PC, and when he sends her a message—fleshed out with vivid computer graphics—teasing her with the sight of his next chosen victim, the moment is genuinely chilling. For anyone who likes to stoke adrenaline with anxiety, "Copycat" delivers the goods.

SIGHT AND SOUND, 5/96, p. 51, Lizzie Francke

Helen Hudson, an expert criminal psychologist, is giving a lecture on serial killers at the University of California at Berkeley. Afterwards, she is attacked by Daryll Lee Cullum, one of her subjects, and forced to witness the murder of a policeman. This experience brings on an acute and prolonged case of agoraphobia and she becomes a recluse. Her assistant Andy and her computer provide her only contact with the outside world.

Some 13 months later, a serial killer is at large in the city. Detective M.J. Monahan and her side-kick Ruben Goetz are working on the case. Hudson contacts Monahan who decides to take her offer of advice. Monahan then invites her to work on the case but she declines. An intruder gets into Hudson's apartment and police protection is arranged. Hudson points out that the killer is copying the same pattern as the Boston Strangler. Later, she receives an ominous message through the Internet. Goetz offers to stay with her. In another part of the city, a young man, Peter Foley, prepares his latest victim. Her body is found the following day. Now Foley is imitating the Hillside Strangler. Hudson realises that he is reenacting famous serial killer cases and that she has become part of his plan.

Monahan's boss is not happy about involving Hudson. It becomes apparent that Foley is communicating with Cullum, who is now in jail. Hudson is persuaded to talk to Cullum via computer link and he gives her an important lead. Before Monahan and Goetz have a chance to follow it up, Goetz is shot dead in an unrelated incident. Hudson receives a call from Foley and realises that he was at her lecture at Berkeley. Meanwhile Foley, who has been chatting-up Andy at a nightclub murders him. The following night, he abducts Hudson. Andy's companion at the club identifies Foley in a photograph. The police turn up at Foley's house only to see it go up in flames. Meanwhile Foley has taken Hudson to the Berkeley lecture hall and he reconstructs the scene from 13 months ago. Monahan is invited to join them. After a particularly nasty showdown, which forces Hudson to face her agoraphobia and escape onto the roof of the lecture hall, Foley is shot dead by Monahan.

Scripted by newcomers Ann Biderman and David Madsen and directed with some flair by Jon Amiel as a follow-up to *Sommersby, Copycat* has an ingenious premise. Its serial killer is reconstructing a history of infamous cases from the Boston Strangler to Ted Bundy to the movie's fictional Daryll Lee Cullum. It could be argued that *Copycat* is just as much about the wave of serial killer movies as about the murders—not because it quotes from any directly, but rather because it explores familiar themes with a feminist perspective. There is also some historical poignancy to the film's backdrop, San Francisco's twenty-fifth anniversary celebrations of the 'summer of love', a period of immense liberating change.

With *Copycat*'s two female investigative protagonists venturing into uneasy territory and the once-assured Hudson being forced to overcome fears that have incapacitated her, it is obvious that *The Silence of the Lambs* was a point of departure for Amiel. Following convention, law-breaker and law-maker become confused categories from which the two women have to extricate themselves. Hudson describes herself as the serial killer's muse, the "dead pin-up girl". After the Berkeley lecture incident, she is deemed, by default, a cop killer by the police-chief. Consequently Monahan must defy her boss in order to work with Hudson.

The casting of Holly Hunter and Sigourney Weaver in these roles is pivotal to the film, enhancing its status as an instant post-feminist classic. While the role of Monahan couldn't be more different for Hunter than her mute migrant Ada in *The Piano*, her two characters share the same steely resolve. Similarly, Weaver is forever Ripley—the viewer is somehow safe in the knowledge that she is immune from the dangers that threaten, however sadistic. And they are pretty sadistic. She is strung up in a mock hanging and subjected to a bed filled with ants. She realises that someone is in her apartment because her red dress has been laid out on the bed. Indeed, her vast, dark and baroquely decorated apartment is full of eerie opportunities—the joke being that this gothic space has been recreated in a high tech glass and steel apartment block in which Amiel deftly explores the dramatic possibilities of Hudson's agoraphobia.

At first Hudson and Monahan are victim-identified with cross-cuts between the two women examining photos of the dead girls. But as they stealthily turn the tables, the film builds up to a victorious climax. The euphoric final battle on the lecture hall rooftop, though, is won more by

Hudson's outburst of delirious laughter than by Monahan's gun. In that moment a whole range of fears are exorcised.

TIME, 11/13/95, p. 120, Richard Corliss

Serial killers don't deserve much sympathy, but jeez, can't we leave them alone for a while? There aren't all that many multiple maniacs in the forensic literature—not nearly so many, it seems, as in the new movies. To judge from Hollywood's fall fad, folks can't go to bed or step into a shower or visit a ladies' room without bumping into an evil genius who has exotic plans for kitchen cutlery. With *Seven, Never Talk to Strangers* and now *Copycat*, serial-killer thrillers are as thick and windy as Republican candidates in New Hampshire.

Copycat, directed by Jon Amiel (*The Singing Detective, Sommersby*), means to be a Greatest Hits album of atrocities. Its murderer has eyes to replicate the artistry of such superstar psychos as Son of Sam, Jeffrey Dahmer, the Boston and Hillside Stranglers—that crowd. His pursuer is a crazy cop (Holly Hunter). His nemesis is a psychologist (Sigourney Weaver) who studies the serial killer's mentality. And his hero is a recently arrested multiple murderer (cleverly played by saloon crooner Harry Connick Jr, as if he were a more deranged cousin of Jim Varney's goony Ernest character).

Screenwriters Ann Biderman and David Madsen are copycats too, primarily of Thomas Harris' terrific novels *Red Dragon* and *The Silence of the Lambs*. *Copycat* is also faithful to other melodramatic conventions. The sympathetic gay friend will be killed. The brilliant schemer will go implausibly stupid at the climax. And the filmmakers will forget what Harris knows: that there is great horror and pathos inside these creatures. A sick mind is a terrible thing to waste.

VILLAGE VOICE, 11/7/95, p. 67, J. Hoberman

"That's what this whole movie is about, a catharsis for the American nobody," says Arthur cagily about his project. Lets hope he isn't predicting the response to Jon Amiel's *Copycat*, which, generically slick rather than creepily stylized, introduces our jaded selves to the prospect of a postmodern serial killer.

Strange days in rerun city: As *The November Men* recapitulates the Kennedy assassination, so the modus operandi of the so-called Copycat Killer re-creates the greatest hits of the Boston Strangler, Son of Sam, Jeffrey Dahmer, et al. His stage is Dirty Harry's hometown of San Francisco and, to add to *Copycat*'s second-hand flavor, there even seems to be some sort of gratuitous anniversary Be-In in Golden Gate Park. Sigourney Weaver dusts off her action heroine persona to play a pop serialkillerologist who is unable to leave her high-tech penthouse, so traumatized is she by a run-in with one of her subjects (Harry Connick Jr. grinning, for the movie's single shivery moment like a satanic Alfred E. Newman amid a lecture hall full of attentive students).

The parallel lives might remind some of *Silence of the Lambs*. Connick is jailed and so, in a sense, is Weaver as, tended by a gay housekeeper and surrounded by flickering screen savers, she ponders the police investigation run by that spunky little critter Holly Hunter. Weaver suffers from agoraphobia but *Copycat* has no such problem going to the marketplace. Not only does the movie smarmily traffic in serial-killer name recognition and wax-museum recreations of actual grisly murders, but director Amiel at one point gooses a succession of lurid, color corpse-photos with a pseudo-religious chorale.

Inexplicably anointed by *Variety* as the buzzy successor to recent No. 1 hits *Seven* and *Get Shorty*, *Copycat* takes an amorphously written scenario and subjects it to sloppy direction. Still, Weaver—an actress remarkably devoid of vanity—brings a bitter, drawn intensity to her role, particularly when dealing with Hunter's impossibly mannered face-scrunching "wee inspector." Given their lack of chemistry and negative female bonding, the movie's greatest mystery may be the absence of a role for Whoopi Goldberg.

Also reviewed in:
CHICAGO TRIBUNE, 10/27/95, Friday/p. C, Michael Wilmington
NATION, 11/27/95, p. 683, Stuart Klawans

NEW YORK TIMES, 10/27/95, p. C10, Janet Maslin
NEW YORKER, 11/13/95, p. 130, Anthony Lane
VARIETY, 10/16-22/95, p. 93, Todd McCarthy
WASHINGTON POST, 10/27/95, p. D7, Rita Kempley

CORMORANT, THE

A BBC Worldwide Americas release of a Holmes Associates production for BBC Wales. *Executive Producer:* Andrew Holmes, Mark Shivas, and Ruth Caleb. *Producer:* Ruth Kenley-Letts. *Director:* Peter Markham. *Screenplay:* Peter Ransley. *Based on the novel by:* Stephen Gregory. *Director of Photography:* Ashley Rowe. *Editor:* Tim Kruydenberg. *Music:* John Lunn. *Sound:* Tim Ricketts and Richard Dyer. *Sound Editor:* Paul Jeffries. *Production Designer:* Ray Price. *Costumes:* Jakki Winfield. *Make-up:* Marina Monios. *Stunt Coordinator:* Gareth Milne. *Cormorant Handlers:* Tony Durkin and Lloyd Buck. *Running time:* 90 minutes. *MPAA Rating:* Not Rated.

CAST: Ralph Fiennes (John); Helen Schlesinger (Mary); Thomas Williams (Tom); Buddug Morgan (Jenny); Derek Hutchinson (Dave); Karl Francis (Uncle Ian); Dyfan Roberts (Glyn); Mici Plwm (Brian); Ray Gravell (Michael); Stewart Jones (Aled Owen); Gwilym Evans (Young John).

NEW YORK POST, 4/14/95, p. 40, Larry Worth

Love triangles, don't come much odder than man, woman and bird. But that doesn't keep "The Cormorant" from soaring to the kind of delirious highs achieved by Alfred Hitchcock.

Thirty-two years have passed since the master of suspense let a flock of winged terrors peck at Tippi Hedren, Suzanne Pleshette and Jessica Tandy. So the time seems ripe for more feathered friends to go amok.

Actually, director Peter Markham shot "The Cormorant" for BBC Television two years ago. And as anyone who attended last fall's Public Theater series on BBC dramas knows, it features a pre-"Schindler's List" Ralph Fiennes as a hero with divided loyalties.

He plays John Talbot, a pensive writer who moves to Northern Wales with wife and adorable toddler when his Uncle Ian wills him a cottage in Snowdonia. But there's a catch: the family must live with the uncle's pet cormorant—a diving bird with a long, hooked beak, webbed toes and a very bad attitude.

The creature, dubbed Archie, is no sooner out of its crate than the exasperated wife dubs it evil incarnate. Depending on the moment, the bird appears to be part vulture, part pelican or—as when stretching its mammoth wings before a fire—full-fledged phoenix.

But Archie has a mesmerizing effect on John. Or maybe it's just the associations with Audubon-loving Uncle Ian, who—as revealed through a series of flashbacks—left an unforgettable impression on his young nephew.

For that matter, the grown-up John could swear that he keeps glimpsing Uncle Ian's ghost around town and on the beach.

Screenwriter Peter Ransley lets the mysterious tale develop nicely, though the sense of growing dread escalates to an anti-climactic showdown. Much of the excitement comes via imaginative photography, ranging from bird's-eye views of potential victims to dazzling—and harrowing—underwater footage.

First-time director Markham also earns points for his depiction of the near mythical cormorant, making it alternately inspire fear, smiles and—believe it or not—sexual tension.

In the acting department, Fiennes holds his own against a certain scene-stealing co-star, as well as the gorgeous scenery. He's perfect at conveying the complexities of an average man under duress—as opposed to a maniacal Nazi or puffed-up quiz-show contestant. Helen Schlesinger and Karl Francis are fine complements.

But top honors still go to Markham. His seemingly endless resources make "The Cormorant" as creepy, captivating and bewitching as the beady-eyed center of attention.

NEWSDAY, 4/14/95, Part II/p. B5, John Anderson

John Talbot (Ralph Fiennes) is a writer, one who decries the rise of spiritual faddism in a secular world. "We have lost religion," he writes, "but instead of an Age of Reason we have one of unreason." He's an unlikely candidate for possession, especially by a streamlined, web-footed, fish-sucking scavenger. But John is to learn very quickly that one man's cormorant is another man's albatross.

A cormorant is a seabird, a predator and a rather homely example of ornithological evolution. "The Cormorant," on the other hand, is a moody and sometimes goofy psychological thriller directed by Peter Markham that does exactly what serious thrillers should do—it restrains itself from explaining too much. Hard facts, after all, aren't always as effective as doubt in persuading one that the improbable is happening. And "The Cormorant" never lets us know for sure what's actually occurred.

What we do know is that John and wife Mary (Helen Schlesinger) have inherited a house in Wales from John's uncle, and moved in with their infant son, Tom (Thomas Williams). They find, to their dismay, that the will has a rider, a winged one: the uncle's pet cormorant, a bad-tempered creature whose presence unnerves Mary. There's little, they can do, save abandon their new home. "You've inherited the bird and the house comes with it," a lawyer explains, "not the other way around."

Markham creates a nice air of menace around the bird, shooting him in quick cuts and then contrasting the frenetic results with lingering close-ups of the beautiful Tom, whose innocence seems like ripe fruit ready to be picked, or plucked. The threat posed by the bird is always a bit absurd, though, given Archie's natural gracelessness; he's a water fowl, after all, and ungainly on land. John becomes increasingly fascinated, even obsessed, with him, and begins seeing his dead Uncle Ian (Karl Francis) on the streets around town. John's sanity, in short, starts taking flight.

Birds, like circus clowns, are both inherently joyous and rich in potential malevolence. Hitchcock proved this; Markham does also, if not so deftly. But this is a sturdy little suspense film, with a quirky style and a good Ralph Fiennes, even if it doesn't hint at anything Poe hadn't already told us about man and bird.

SIGHT AND SOUND, 5/93, p. 62, Geoff Brown

John Talbot, a writer, moves with his wife Mary and young son Tom to a remote house in Snowdonia, inherited from his uncle Ian along with the uncle's pet cormorant. When he tries to get rid of the unmanageable bird, Ian's solicitor reveals that by the terms of the will they may lose the house if the bird is not cared for. John calls the cormorant Archie (though it turns out to be female), takes it for exercise tied to a rope, and makes less and less progress with his writing. After the bird kills their cat, Mary insists on taking Tom away for two weeks, leaving John to, in her words, "sort it out".

John tries to kill the bird with an axe, but fails. He releases it, but it returns, and his obsession with Archie grows. He also becomes haunted by childhood memories of Uncle Ian, supposedly found dead in a boat with the cormorant, his eyes pecked out. John buys the bird a new cage, and lets it catch fish in the cold December sea, where the bird's cunning almost causes him to drown. When Mary returns a day earlier than planned, she finds Archie in their bedroom and the house in disarray.

After Tom wanders into the bird's unlocked cage at night, Mary and son take off again. John grows increasingly drunk and disoriented, but on Mary's return lunges at the bird in a frenzied and fatal attack. Mary wants the body burned, to prove to Tom that the bird is no more. A burning log from the bonfire lands on the house, but John wants the house and its memories consumed. Tom clutches a charred feather as it falls through the air.

At the height of the turmoil in *The Cormorant*, with his home, marriage and sanity near collapse, the hero sits at his computer, tapping out his recipe for a "painted devil": "Take some uneasy indefinable feelings, add a large quantity of stress, mix with alcohol and simmer in firelight." In adapting Stephen Gregory's novel, director Peter Markham follows the recipe as best he can, given the cramped confines of a *Screen Two* film and the nature of the devil under review: an amalgam of four sea birds trained and manipulated by the BBC Nature Unit. Alas, the recipe does not stretch far.

Things bode ill as soon as the cormorant lands on the screen. We get a point-of-view shot from inside the crate, coupled with ominous growls from the soundtrack synthesizer. Markham's summonings of "uneasy indefinable feelings" become more ambitious as the story advances and the cormorant runs riot, but they never grow much more persuasive.

The large quantity of stress is the lot of Mary, John's wife, who sees the reality of the bird's behaviour and its effect on their home life where John sees only dark enchantment. She seems blind, however, to her weak-willed husband's growing obsession; and Helen Schlesinger's bleating performance only exacerbates audience annoyance.

Alcohol is the preserve of John, the bookish husband increasingly drawn into the cormorant's vicious world. Fresh from scowling on the Yorkshire moors in *Wuthering Heights*, Fiennes wears the stubble, slurred speech and hollowed eyes like a seasoned pro; though the childhood memories of Uncle Ian, styled in pale slow-motion, give the most garbled reasons for his disturbed psyche.

Firelight? There are flickering flames inside the dark house, but Ashley Rowe's photography only comes into its own once hero and bird take the air and water on the bleak Welsh coast. In one respect at least *The Cormorant* casts an authentic chill, with its picture of a closed, often hostile Welsh community. In other ways, the novel has made a dull, unedifying TV drama: it's never much fun seeing irritating characters get what they deserve.

Also reviewed in:
NEW YORK TIMES, 4/14/95, p. C18, Caryn James

COUNTRY LIFE

A Miramax Films release of an Australian Film Finance Corporation presentation of a Dalton Films production. *Producer:* Robin Dalton. *Director:* Michael Blakemore. *Screenplay:* Michael Blakemore. *Suggested by "Uncle Vanya" by:* Anton Chekhov. *Director of Photography:* Stephen Windon. *Editor:* Nicholas Beauman. *Music:* Peter Best. *Sound:* Ben Osmo, Phil Judd, and (music) David Hemming. *Casting:* Alison Barrett. *Production Designer:* Laurence Eastwood. *Set Decorator:* Donna Brown. *Set Dresser:* Dimity Huntington and Ken Muggleston. *Costumes:* Wendy Chuck. *Make-up:* Lesley Rouvray. *Running time:* 107 minutes. *MPAA Rating:* PG-13.

CAST: Sam Neill (Max Askey); Greta Scacchi (Deborah Voysey); John Hargreaves (Jack Dickens); Kerry Fox (Sally Voysey); Michael Blakemore (Alexander Voysey); Googie Withers (Hannah); Maurie Fields (Fred Livingstone); Robyn Cruze (Maud Dickens); Ron Blanchard (Wally); Patricia Kennedy (Maud Dickens); Bryan Marshall (Mr. Pettinger); Tony Barry and Terry Brady (Loggers); Tom Long (Billy Livingstone); Rob Steele (James); Ian Bliss (David Archdale); Colin Taylor (Mr. Wilson); Ian Cockburn (Mr. Archdale); Reg Cribb (Vicar); Derani Scarr (Woman in Crowd); Owen Buik (Stationhand).

LOS ANGELES TIMES, 7/28/95, Calendar/p. 2, Kenneth Turan

It has been a good year for Anton Chekov, so much so that if he were still alive he could probably acquire a development deal and even his own parking space on any lot in town.

"Uncle Vanya," one of the Russian playwright's classic works, has been the subject of two recent but very different productions. Louis Malle and Andre Gregory's brilliant "Vanya on 42nd Street" appeared late last year to uniformly rapturous reviews, and now comes "Country Life," which is more like variations on a "Vanya" theme than a full-dress reinterpretation.

Written by, directed and starring Michael Blakemore, "Country Life" had the interesting concept of transposing Chekov to the Australian outback, the desolate New South Wales territory to be specific, and somewhat modernizing the time frame to 1919, just after the conclusion of the First World War.

Ever resilient, the play survives the change of scenery, but many of Blakemore's other choices are not so successful. He has decided to use this most nuanced writer's work as the skeleton on which to construct a broad, buffoonish farce. Everything is cruder and coarser and that is not necessarily an improvement.

Returning home after 25 years in England, 22 of them spent as the theater critic for the London Standard, is the fussy Alexander (Blakemore). While he has been occupied with higher things, the family sheep farm has been managed by Sally (Kerry Fox), Alexander's daughter by his late first wife, and Uncle Jack (John Hargreaves), that poor woman's brother.

And Alexander is not returning alone. In addition to his all-important sinus drops, he is bringing with him Deborah (Greta Scacchi), his stunning new wife. Though the sheep don't seem to notice, everyone else in the neighborhood does, and what with Alexander's insistence on eating fashionably later and his wife's come-hither looks, life on the farm is very far from normal.

Especially disconcerted are Uncle Jack, once a local dandy but now mainly notable for a very red face, and Dr. Max (Sam Neill).

Though he too drinks too much, this pacifist doctor who believes in helping the aborigines and not raping the land has no trouble attracting Deborah's attention.

Australia-born Blakemore, who did the regrettably little-seen "Privates on Parade," made his directing reputation in the London theater. He has acquitted himself honorably enough here, helped by solid acting, especially from the versatile Kerry Fox ("An Angel at My Table," "Shallow Grave").

But though some of the changes Blakemore's made (the incorporation of World War I and the addition of more obvious sexuality) are interesting, making things cruder across the board is not a winning idea. An extended scene of drunkenness by a hired man is hell to sit through, and dialogue like "When was the last time you called me Booboo" are not an improvement on the original. All in all, if Chekhov is on your mind, renting "Vanya on 42nd" is a much better way to go.

NEW STATESMAN & SOCIETY, 7/21/95, p. 35, Jonathan Romney

Little mother, little father, let us drink—to Anton Chekhov, the most abused playwright in the English theatre. It has been his fate finally to pass into history as the true begetter of the school of Merchant and Ivory, of the cinema of suavity, excess leisure and crisp white linen. The Englishness of Chekhov is a peculiar effect accumulated over generations of languidly paced, overdressed stage productions with their dapper, melancholy Trigorins and grand dame Arkadinas swanking it up in genteel Chichester Festival style.

Such was Chekhov's brilliance as a satirist of a moribund Russian social class that his plays lend themselves all too effectively to cultural translation. All the signs of everyday Russianness that seem so glaring in English—all the freshly boiled samovars, and old Osip sleeping on the stove—come across on the British stage as a taste for the exotic, no more "foreign" than Shakespeare's Padua. Chekhov has become as domesticated a part of the repertoire as that other not altogether English dramatist who wrote The Importance of Being Earnest.

The latest film version of Chekhov is Michael Blakemore's Country Life, which, by his estimate, comprises the outline and about a third of Uncle Vanya. Although much more traditional as a film, it's rather more interesting than Louis Malle's well-intentioned but studious Vanya on 42nd Street, which was simply a workshop staging of the play in a bombed-out-off-Broadway basement. Malle didn't make much of the interplay between the rehearsed play and the real world of the actors: it was as if he was giving himself a break from cinema in favour of some sort of quintessential, pared-down theatre. But the low-lit close-ups and long takes came across as deadly claustrophobic and oppressively thespian.

As a theatre director, Blakemore clearly sees the cinema as a bit of a break, and although his approach to the screen is highly traditional, he seems to be having fun. This quasi-Vanya succeeds because it plays on the acquired Englishness of Chekhov, and uses the shape of the play to make a commentary on Australian-British relations.

In this version, set after the first world war, the homecoming professor becomes a posturing hack of a London theatre critic, played by Blakemore himself with all the high ham of the actor-manager. He's Robert Morley as the Pom Who Came to Dinner, a wine snob pontificating about his "reliable straightforward claret", and exclaiming" Del-phiniums! " with the haughty horror of a goatee'd Edith Evans. The good-hearted doctor becomes Sam Neill's genial but weary Askey, who's accused of being a Bolshevik for his scepticism about Britain and the Great War. Sonya becomes Sally (Kerry Fox), who rolls her sleeves up and gets on with the sheep-shearing, and recommends planting some hardy Kangaroo's Paw to brighten up the faded English rose arbour—cue a heavy-handed coda of indigenous flora. There are a few too many such obvious revisionist touches to make this a 1990s film—Askey seems to be the outback's first signed-up Green, tut-tutting at Uncle Jack's (Vanya's) parrot shooting, and giving a lecture on restoring the land that carries its contemporary hindsight a little too heavily. A couple of references to his empathy with Aboriginals seems a little tokenistic in this respect.

There's nothing mould-breaking a bout the style of the film, which has all the usual costume commonplaces. There's Greta Scacchi in big hats, quizzically pert and throwing too many arched-eyebrow doubletakes for comfort. There are steam trains and steam kettles, and a ferocious old Irish cook who seems to be imported directly from *Upstairs Downstairs*. Visually the film takes Australian cinema back two decades, to the time when Peter Weir and Gillian Armstrong were forging a briefly illustrious national genre of net-curtain drama.

But, given the setting's scope for dusty languor, the pace comes as a nice surprise. *Country Life* is done almost as end-of-the-pier farce with screeching cockatoos, dropped trousers, risque remarks about rock cakes, and mating kangaroos. There's a touch of John Duigan's misbegotten *Sirens* about it—tender British sensibilities running aground of brisk outback ways—but without that film's idiot Lawrentian bullishness.

Old-fashioned and gamey in a very Ealing manner, *Country Life* restores a style of Chekhov that has generally been sidelined since Stanislavsky introduced the "official" line of torpid melancholy. Blakemore goes for the boisterous, but when the farce breaks, Kerry Fox, who discreetly underplays it most of the time, rises to the fore. Few players are so good at registering embarrassment and excess energy that hasn't found its goal.

There's no getting round Peter Best's misbegotten score, dripping in phoney lyricism; the tone is perfectly pitched throughout. The linens actually get mucky, and the house, with its clutter of faded Edwardiana, is a very tangible pile but not remotely haunted by end-of-empire nostalgia; in fact, we end the film rather looking forward to a refurbishing a bit more hopeful than Chekhov promises. It's the consummate Sunday afternoon film: genteelly larky and even featuring Googie Withers, but surprisingly compelling. Blakemore's last fiction feature, back in 1982, was an adaptation of Peter Nichols' *Privates on Parade*, the play which provided a template for *It Ain't Half Hot, Mum*. Oddly enough, he's not that far off in *Country Life*, and it's all to Chekhov's benefit.

NEW YORK POST, 7/28/95, p. 40, Thelma Adams

If you want peace, make for a nunnery. Don't expect "Country Life" to provide a respite from worldly cares.

In Michael Blakemore's adaptation of Anton Chekhov's "Uncle Vanya"—transposed to the wilds of Australia between the wars—lives of quiet desperation can be led down under just as easily as they were in old Russia.

Alkie Uncle Jack (John Hargreaves) manages the ramshackle family estate, falling into midlife with literary ambitions unrealized and amorous ties unknotted. His niece Sally (Kerry Fox of "Shallow Grave") is the family ox, the backbone of what's left of the estate. A plain Jane, Sally moons over the idealistic local doctor, Max Askey (Sam "Jurassic Park" Neill), but dares not declare her love. The dashing doctor drinks to drown some unspeakable hole in his heart.

All is quietly desperate on the Far Western front until the arrival of Sally's long-absent father, Alexander (Michael Blakemore). After 20 years of living it up in London as a theater critic and man about town, the gouty, demanding gent returns to the family farm with a new wife, the much younger Deborah (Greta "The Player" Scacchi).

The classic structure of Vanya works its magic here. The arrival of the old man and his young bride bring all the family tensions to the fore. Both Jack and Max fall hard for the self-involved English beauty, leaving Sally out in the cold.

The mediocre legend-in-his-own-mind Alexander is one of those "idea men" who leave all the work to others and expect the world to take care of them; both Jack and Sally must confront a world where their destiny is to drone on in the service of lesser mortals.

Australian-born Blakemore has made a name for himself from the West End to Broadway as the director of "City of Angels" and "Noises Off," among others. He plays the country mice versus the city mice theme as a contrast between the new world and the old, between England and its rebellious stepchild. Despite the New South Wales locations, Blakemore's approach to Chekhov is very much grounded in England.

There is a certain "Masterpiece Theater" charm in the crisp corset-and-waistcoat costuming and crackerjack cast. Neill and Scacchi spark—the lustiness of the Australian outback raising the ample skirts of straight-laced old England. Fox, Hargreaves and Blakemore all hit their marks, although there is a blurring of individual conflicts as if smaller key scenes that revealed individual characters might have been clipped in favor of a brisker running time.

Unlike last year's fabulous "Vanya on 42nd Street," a masterpiece of pared down staging that jettisoned all the bells and whistles in order to distill the play into its most affecting elements of bitter laughter and tears, "Country Life," is a more middle-of-the-road production with modest laughs and gently tugged heartstrings.

NEWSDAY, 7/28/95, Part II/p. B5, John Anderson

Australia, like America before it, suffers from an inferiority complex rooted in the fact that it isn't England. It's a culturally crippling condition, but several recent films from down under—"Hotel Sorrento" among them—have dealt bluntly with the infectious Anglophilia that keeps Australians apologizing for Australia.

In Michael Blakemore's "Country Life," which is more than loosely based on Chekhov's "Uncle Vanya," they even apologize for the weather. It is 1919 on the New South Wales frontier, and Alexander Voysey (Blakemore), the local success, has returned to the family sheep ranch after 20 years in England as a theater critic. The ranch has been turned upside down in anticipation of this stuffed shirt, who suffers from a sinus condition, chronic pomposity and the damaged ego of an old man with a young wife—Deborah (Greta Scacchi), a woman who turns heads wherever she goes but especially on the parched ranch. He's immune to any guilt concerning the daughter he abandoned two decades earlier—Sally (Kerry Fox), who's run the ranch with her late mother's brother, Jack Dickens (John Hargreaves). He certainly doesn't notice that Sally is in love with the slightly boozy doctor, Max Askey (Sam Neill), or that Askey has developed a light in his eye for Deborah.

Alexander disrupts the already imbalanced universe of the ranch, and as such that's standard "Vanya"—a play with distinctly memorable characters and timeless anxieties that seem particularly current now (see Louis Malle's "Vanya on 42nd Street"). But along with the standard Chekhovian concerns of discontent, ennui, lust, fear of aging and civic responsibility, Blakemore has added nationalism, of a modest Australian variety. Nothing is good enough for Alexander—the weather's intolerable, dinner's too early, dinner's too boring, there's no decent wine, the English garden's gone to seed, the house is a mess—but the fact that Jack and Sally feel bad about these things is their fault, Blakemore says, because they've bought into the belief that British is better.

The situation is comic when confined to the house, but gets more serious when it travels. While making a presentation in a local hall, Askey criticizes the recently concluded war, one in which he sees Australia as having sacrificed its young men for England. This prompts several young vets to break up the place and punch out Askey. But clearly he's right: These people went to war for an idea, but one that wasn't theirs.

Back at the ranch, Deborah is registering discomfort at the goings-on, while reveling in the attention. Sally's pining, Alexander's whining, Jack is irate: Alexander, whom he's been supporting for years, is a fraud, he says. As per Chekhov's plot-line, Deborah and Sally get over their initial dislike for each other, and Deborah promises to find out Askey's feelings toward Sally. His feelings, of course, are made clear, and he and Deborah have an interrupted tryst in the barn (a particularly not-Chekhovian moment). When Alexander suggests selling the ranch, Jack starts shooting.

Considering the fact that Blakemore adapted the play strictly to his own devices, there's a surprising staginess about "Country Life," at least in the way the characters enter the story and leave it. The film begins with Askey's losing a patient—the shroud might be symbolic of England—then declining payment from the man's co-workers, accepting their whiskey and riding toward the ranch. But once he gets there, we get a hard dose of drawing-room comedy: Hannah the dictatorial housekeeper (Googie Withers), Jack's mother Maud (Robyn Cruze) and Wally (Ron

Blanchard) might have entered with their character descriptions on placards. But they settle in, and the film takes on a comfortable feeling of discontent.

Neill and Scacchi are good, if underutilized. Kerry Fox—who has been seen here recently in "Shallow Grave," and before that in "Angel at My Table" and "Last Days of Chez Nous"—is a chameleon and just about perfect as Sally, a woman resigned to her homeliness and loneliness. She's ably abetted by John Hargreaves, who supplies the antidote to Blakemore's own cool, slightly preposterous performance as Alexander, who represents "civilization" in a hostile world where idleness is no virtue.

SIGHT AND SOUND, 7/95, p. 43, Robert Yates

Canterbury, an Australian sheep station just after the First World War. Alexander returns home form London with a beautiful wife, Deborah, having left 22 years earlier to make his name as a theatre critic. His brother-in-law Jack and his daughter Sally have been taking care of the land. Alexander disrupts the household by insisting on doing things his way. Both Jack and the local doctor, Max, are attracted to Deborah. Sally is in love with Max. The women attend a lecture by Max on progressive farming which is disrupted when Max is accused being a friend of the Aborigines and a pacifist.

While Max takes Deborah out for a walk, Jack rifles through Alexander's room, and discovers the poor quality of his writing. Jack becomes obsessed by Deborah, and wants to save her from Alexander. In order to ease the tension between the two women, Deborah promises to find out if Max loves Sally. In the stables, Max shows more interest in Deborah and the two are about to have sex when they are interrupted. Alexander calls a family meeting about his plans to sell Canterbury. Disturbed by a glimpse of Max and Deborah embracing, Jack is angered by the suggestion, runs for a rifle and starts firing at Alexander. He misses, and is talked out of taking his own life by Max.

Alexander and Deborah decide to leave. An uneasy truce is established between Jack and Alexander, as Jack promises to keep sending him money from the land. Max says he won't return for months. Alone again, Jack and Sally determine to carry on their lives as before.

In the opening credits, we read that *Country Life* was "suggested by *Uncle Vanya*". This seems something of an understatement since the film's characters correspond directly to those in Chekhov's play and follow the actions and fortunes of their equivalents directly. Why didn't writer/director Blakemore simply set *Uncle Vanya* in Australia after the First World War since, after all, we are used to far more radical transpositions of such frequently-performed works? But Blakemore has done something different. His narrative strategy might be compared to that behind Jane Smiley's Pulitzer Prize-winning novel, *A Thousand Acres* where a new story justifies itself and, as if only by coincidence, turns out to be a reworking of *King Lear*.

Those working with a canonical piece often insist on its universality. This point was well illustrated by a recent film, Louis Malle's *Vanya on 42nd Street*. That film's conceit—a group of present-day actors rehearsing in their civvies—suggests that the relationships' dynamic transcends the turn-of-the-century Russian countryside setting. Blakemore is keen to do something different. He needs the looseness a "suggested by" credit offers because he is less interested in universals than in specific points about Australia's relationship with Britain, with his characters becoming emblems.

Alexander is the Australian infected by Englishness. He is prissy, snobbish, idle. Worse, he is a fraud, claiming a talent he does not have, having spent his time in London living off profits from the Australian land. Max is his opposite in many ways, a practical and hardworking doctor. He looks into the future, not nostalgically into the past: he is the new Australian, keen to be free of ties to the "mother country". Running parallel to these divisions, and possibly resulting from them, are contrasting sensual matters. While Alexander finds it difficult to meet his marital duties and is uninterested in nature, Max is the picture of virility, at home in the wild land. Deborah, bored with her husband, is taken by the sight of Max's buttocks as he bathes in the kitchen. The sight suggests that perhaps Sam Neill thought he was given the wrong part in *The Piano* and is keen to show he can match Harvey Keitel in the bare *derrière* department.

During the past few years, Australian and New Zealand cinema has dwelt on this repression/liberation dualism. Considering such a cultural legacy it's an obvious topic, but it's one that has produced ludicrous results. In John Duigan's *Sirens* an uptight English pair, played by Tara Fitzgerald and Hugh Grant, was subjected to family of freethinking Aussies (including Sam Neill). That film ought to have killed off for good the symbolic potential of snakes in the bush. But no, *Country Life* sees Max taking Deborah into the country, past a snake, and introducing her to a couple of kangaroos having sex.

Flora also serves symbolic service: Canterbury's English rose garden has withered. Sally proposes in its place a garden of hardy native flowers. While Deborah is the English rose, Sally is herself something of a hardy native. Somewhat bizarrely, Deborah also becomes the "sleek English fox come to gobble up native wildlife". Sonya in *Vanya*—here, Deborah—is always a difficult role. The men project their fantasies onto her, and the character is often silent. In *Vanya on 42nd Street* Julianne Moore managed to suggest that the silence was the result of a decision to keep her own counsel; Scacchi's Deborah just appears to have nothing to say.

VILLAGE VOICE, 8/1/95, p. 41, Jeff Brown

Plays are often constructed around a disruptive visit—a device you could quickly get your fill of by regularly attending the current MOMA series, *Screen Plays: From Broadway to Hollywood, 1920-1966.* (Personally: this would be my idea of movie hell.)

Longtime stage director Michael Blakemore bases his *Country Life* on *Uncle Vanya*, which Chekhov subtitled "Scenes From Country Life in Four Acts," its well-known plot revolving around the visit of an insensitive city couple to their needy "country cousins." Blakemore stipulates that the Chekhov source is primarily "inspiration," adding that in keeping with the times he has tried for "a funnier and probably coarser story." He locates his adaptation on a sheep farm in his own native Australia—a frontier country in 1919—with the elegant but boorish visitors coming from "civilized" England.

The pair who come to dinner, lunch, and breakfast (and find all the meals wanting) are Alexander (Blakemore), a retired drama critic currently in the process of writing his memoirs, and his much younger, very decorative wife, Deborah (Greta Scacchi). Alexander is the long-ago absconded father of Sally (Kerry Fox, even plainer than she was in *Angels at My Table*), a young woman rancher immediately intimidated by her hypercritical father as well as his seductive wife. Instantly smitten by Deborah are Sally's silly but blunt Uncle Jack (John Hargreaves) and the ironic Dr. Max (Sam Neill), the country physician whom Sally has always had a crush on.

The moral dice, of course, are loaded on the side of the country mice. Jack may be a fool and a drunk, but unlike his brother-in-law Alex, he works hard—hard enough to support Alex and raise Alex's daughter. When Alex arrives at the tiny New South Wales station, he not only doesn't recognize Sally, but doesn't care to. He immediately demands that his hosts alter their habits and schedules to suit his and criticizes their routines. There's no subtlety or suspense as to what a fraud Alex is. The only two questions here: How far will his bored, dolled-up wife go with the doctor, and how long will poor Sally persist in her pathetic illusions?

Neill is his usual amiable, yet sexy self as Max, physician to the aborigines as well as a leftist-environmentalist (he's denounced as a Bolshevik for suggesting that Australians might not have sent their boys to die for King and *that* country). Max is quite upfront, and openly lusty, in his pursuit of the repressed Deborah. There's no sense that he loves or wishes to marry her; he just would like to get her alone in the bush or the barn. Meanwhile Alex, who's in his sixties and troubled by impotence ("The Lord giveth ..." Dr. Max advises), tries to feel up a teenage servant girl.

In the Hollywood version, Sally, a secret beauty, would wipe the sheep dung off her face, let down her hair, and be recognized by the prince (Dr. Max) as his true mate. To his credit Blakemore resists and Fox bravely remains pudgy-looking and somewhat pathetic throughout (in contrast to the chic, edgy doctor she was in *Shallow Grave*). Casting himself as he fatuous father, Blakemore—native son returned to direct the natives in a film—possibly intends the performance to be confessional or apologetic. *Country Life* comes across less a study in character than an ode to the country itself, putting itself on the side of native things, the local flora and fauna. A glimpse of kangaroos fucking sums up Australia's crude life force.

Also reviewed in:
CHICAGO TRIBUNE, 8/4/95, Friday/p. K, Johanna Steinmetz

NEW REPUBLIC, 9/11/95, p. 26, Stanley Kauffmann
NEW YORK TIMES, 7/28/95, p. C5, Caryn James
VARIETY, 8/8-14/94, p. 75, David Stratton
WASHINGTON POST, 8/4/95, p. D2, Hal Hinson

COW, THE

A Czech Television release. *Producer:* Helena Sykorova and Karel Skorpik. *Director:* Karel Kachyna. *Screenplay (Czech with English subtitles):* Karel Kachyna and Karel Cabradek. *Based on the novel by:* Jan Prochazka. *Director of Photography:* Petr Hohjda. *Editor:* Jan Svoboda. *Music:* Petr Hapka. *Sound:* Jaroslav Novak. *Production Designer:* Jiri Zavrel. *Costumes:* Jana Smetanova. *Running time:* 94 minutes. *MPAA Rating:* Not rated.

CAST: Radek Holub (Adam); Alena Mihulova (Rosa); Valerie Zawadska; Viktorie Knotkova; Antonin Molcik; Zenek Dusek.

NEWSDAY, 2/22/95, Part II/p. B11, John Anderson

The velvet revolution may have demolished the infrastructure of Czech filmmaking, but it helped resurrect such masters as Karel Kachyna, who in "The Cow" has produced a story of such utter simplicity and visual poetry that it becomes its own archetype.

"The Cow" tells the tale of Adam (Radek Holub), an antisocial bumpkin whose ailing mother has had the cruel timing to die just as he's sold their cow to buy her morphine. In flashbacks of sepia and gold, we see her as a woman of high times and low repute and, through the young Adam's eyes, as an object of revulsion and love; her painted face is a garish advertisement for his emotional pain, and her breast is his pillow.

"The Cow" isn't about child abuse, though, or about the politics of Adam's plight, or his abandonment by God, or the economics of his universe. It's about the constant effort needed to overcome one's own history, and the struggle that mere living requires.

Adam works like a dog at the local quarry—Kachyna makes us feel the dust and the water when he bathes in a stream—and in his off hours, builds a field. Carrying buckets of dirt from a local riverbank to his hillside home, whose location itself is an exercise in blind optimism, his task is almost Sisyphean, and an exercise in faith. This is an Adam who's building his own Garden.

He needs an Eve, though, and she arrives with all her possessions in tow: Roza (Alena Mihulova) is a local woman with a reputation as low as Mom's, and Adam repels her insistent advances. One night, after work, he arrives home to find his clothes laundered, his food cooked, his house clean. He flies into a rage, and rapes her. But the next morning, out of guilt or lust or need, he decides he wants Roza to stay. Which she's happy to do.

This would be high melodrama as well as a rather offensive sexual scenario if Adam and Roza weren't clinging to each other with such desperation. The survival of each misfit depends on the other, the desperation turns to love, they build a life and—uh-oh—make plans. Always, the petty world intrudes. And tragedy looms.

At no time, however, does bathos intrude on "The Cow"—indelicately, perhaps, Kachyna makes the point that it's the female of any species on whom the fate of the world turns. And he tailors the rhythm of his film to his characters. From its methodical opening moments through the exhilarated tempo that accompanies Adam and Roza's temporary happiness, "The Cow" is like a comet's tail of emotion. And somewhere in its arc, it manages to become the very qualities it purports to be about.

VILLAGE VOICE, 2/28/95, p. 63, J. Hoberman

Another treatment [The reference is to *Before the Rain*; see Hoberman's review of that film.] of peasant passion in the primordial heart of Europe, veteran Czech director Karel Kachyna's *The Cow* is set somewhere in the Carpathians in a ramshackle settlement of "forgotten cottages belonging to forgotten people."

The Cow was made for Czech TV and, as modest as its title suggests, begins like a fairy tale with the youthful Adam—lanky and rawboned, perhaps a simpleton—leading his sick mother's cow down the mountain path to market. Instead of a handful of magic beans, however, Adam sells the cow for morphine; his mother, an unmarried former prostitute, is apparently dying of syphilis.

Soon, the bereft Adam takes a punishing job in a nearby rock quarry where the roar of the machinery underscores his sepia memories of childhood misfortune. His solitude is broken with the unwelcome arrival of Rosa, the town butcher's flirtatious, far from straitlaced housemaid. As in *Before the Rain*, human relations in the European outback tend toward the blunt and brutish. One dark and stormy night, Adam finds Rosa crouched in the straw; he impulsively beats and rapes her, then decides she can move in. (Thereafter they sleep in adjoining boxes.)

In the world of *The Cow,* seeing someone smashed to a bloody pulp is obviously conducive to creature sympathy. Sometime later, Adam's response to Rosa's seeming infidelity results in his getting his teeth kicked in at the local tavern. She's moved by his plight to return to his cottage and yoke herself, mule-like, to his fate-working together in the quarry, painfully carrying up a barrel of soil for a future garden plot each time they return to their mountain aerie.

Kachyna is best known here for his long-banned *nomenklatura* satire, *The Ear.* (Made in 1970, it surfaced at Cannes 20 years later and was subsequently shown at the Public.) More conventional but equally adroit in its vision of lumpen peasantry, *The Cow* seems Kachyna's belated tribute to his late guru—the charismatic, sometime Central Committee member and working-class hero Jan Procházka; it was Procházka who provided the film's premise before his death in 1971, although one wonders whether his script would have been as devoid of what used to be called social significance.

Accompanied throughout by a refrain of plaintive pan-piping, *The Cow* is part paean to earthy pleasures, part horrified appreciation of backbreaking labor, and part bemused revelation of quaint hillbilly folkways: Adam and Rosa struggle and scheme to buy a new cow and, after bringing it to stud, gravely retire to the local church to light candies and pray; Adam and his neighbor get falling-down roaring drunk but can sober up in a nanosecond when called upon to birth a calf.

The Cow makes a virtue of such abruptness. A brief, sweet interlude ends with Rosa's own pregnancy. Once more, Adam has to sell the cow in order to buy medicine. Impressively fatalistic, albeit in a fashion more resigned than *Before the Rain* to senseless existence, *The Cow* takes a late leap into post-Communist metaphor to suggest the resilience of life in the absence of happiness.

Also reviewed in:
CHICAGO TRIBUNE, 7/14/95, Friday/p. J, Michael Wilmington
NEW YORK TIMES, 2/22/95, p. C18, Stephen Holden
VARIETY, 5/9-15/94, p. 78, Dennis Harvey

CRIMSON TIDE

A Buena Vista release of a Hollywood Pictures presentation. *Executive Producer:* Bill Unger, Lucas Foster, and Mike Moder. *Producer:* Don Simpson and Jerry Bruckheimer. *Director:* Tony Scott. *Screenplay:* Michael Schiffer. *Story:* Michael Schiffer and Richard P. Henrick. *Director of Photography:* Dariusz Wolski. *Editor:* Chris Lebenzon. *Music:* Hans Zimmer. *Music Editor:* Bob Badami and Will Kaplan. *Sound:* William B. Kaplan and (music) Jay Rifkin. *Casting:* Victoria Thomas. *Production Designer:* Michael White. *Art Director:* Donald B. Woodruff, James J. Murakami, and Dianne Wager. *Set Designer:* Richard Lawrence and Nick Navarro. *Set Decorator:* Mickey S. Michaels. *Special Effects:* Alfred A. DiSarro, Jr. *Costumes:* George L. Little. *Make-up:* Ellen Wong. *Make-up (Denzel Washington):* Edna M. Sheen. *Stunt Coordinator:* Steve Picerni. *Running time:* 113 minutes. *MPAA Rating:* R.

CAST: Denzel Washington (Hunter); Gene Hackman (Ramsey); Matt Craven (Zimmer); George Dzundza (Cob); Viggo Mortensen (Weps); James Gandolfini (Lt. Bobby Dougherty);

Rocky Carroll (Lt. Westergaurd); Jaime P. Gomez (Ood Mahoney); Michael Milhoan (Hunsicker); Scott Burkholder (TSO Billy Linkletter); Danny Nucci (Danny Rivetti); Lillo Brancato, Jr. (Russell Vossler); Eric Bruskotter (Bennefield); Rick Schroder (Lt. Paul Hellerman); Steve Zahn (William Barnes); Marcello Thedford (Lawson); R.J. Knoll (Marty Sotille); Billy Devlin (Navigator); Matt Barry (Planesman); Christopher Birt (Helmsman); Jim Boyce (Diving Officer); Jacob Vargas (Sonarman #2); Kai Lennox (Sonarman #3); Michael Weatherred (Radioman #1); Tommy Bush (Admiral Williams); Earl Billings (Rick Marichek); Mark Christopher Lawrence (Head Cook Rono); Michael Chieffo (Chief Kline); Ashley Smock (Guard #1); James Lesure (Guard #2); Trevor St. John (Launcher); Dennis Garber (Fire Control Technician); Vanessa Bell Calloway (Julia Hunter); Brenden Jefferson (Luke); Ashley Calloway (Robin); Daniel Von Bargen (Vladimir Radchenko); Richard Valeriani (Richard Valeriani); Warren Olney (Anchorman); Rad Daly (Lt. Comdr. Nelson); Sean O'Bryan (Phone Talker #1); Victor Togunde (Sailor With Oba); Troy A. Cephers (Sailor #1); Armand Watson (Seaman Davis); Brent Michael Goldberg (Phone Talker #2); Scott Grimes (Petty Officer Hilaire); Ryan Phillippe (Seaman Grattam); Dale Andre Lee Everett (Firing Key Runner); Angela Tortu (Ramsey Aide); Ronald Ramessar (Westergaurd Dad); Robin Faraday (Westergaurd Mom); Bob Stone (Bob the Magician); Henry Mortensen (Henry Ince); Chris Ellis (Additional Magician).

CHRISTIAN SCIENCE MONITOR, 5/15/95, p. 14, David Sterritt

Like many politicians, Hollywood has been discombobulated by the end of the cold war, which provided a set of social and political certainties that allowed filmmakers to bypass original thought where international intrigue was concerned. Not surprisingly, two of moviedom's most successful producers—the unstoppable Don Simpson and Jerry Bruckheimer, purveyors of "Top Gun" and "Beverly Hills Cop," among other hits—have figured out a way to fill this gap.

"Crimson Tide," their latest action-adventure epic, begins with a TV reporter telling us that a nasty Russian insurgent has seized a bunch of nuclear weapons aimed at international targets, and is threatening to kick off Armageddon if anyone interferes with his revolution.

This way the picture can scare us with the menace of Russian missiles, just as movies did in the bad old days when Mutual Assured Destruction was policy in East and West alike. But at the same time, it can hold out the possibility that new-style Russians, more benign than their communist forebears, will defuse the revolutionary's scheme and bring us all to a happy ending.

Fiendishly clever, those California capitalists, managing to have their cold war and deny it, too. In the end, though, all this stuff about missiles and warheads is just a "McGuffin," as Alfred Hitchcock used to call such things—a gimmick that sets the story in motion, after which nobody gives a hoot about it, including the audience.

What's really on everyone's mind in "Crimson Tide" is the fascinating tension between its two main characters, submarine commanders who provide a few additional McGuffins of their own: frictions between white and black, age and youth, authority and flexibility.

These may not sound like McGuffins, but like the missile-menace that launches the movie's plot, they're important and complicated matters that the filmmakers exploit in the most superficial way, building oodles of suspense while giving hardly a thought to what should be their main interest—how private psychology shapes public action in the world of high-tech military might.

Such is the power of high-tech military entertainment, however, that this utter lack of depth doesn't prevent "Crimson Tide" from being great fun on its own shallow terms.

The most obvious key to its success is a pair of expert performances that give it a firm center of gravity even when the plot occasionally runs out of steam.

Gene Hackman plays the older of the two protagonists, Ramsey, a crusty submarine skipper who's honed his skills and hardened his sensibilities through decades of hands-on work. Denzel Washington plays his younger counterpart, Hunter, a new executive officer who's slim on experience but has all the book-learning that places like Annapolis and Harvard could give him.

More character-driven than the average war-related movie, "Crimson Tide" lets these guys work up their simmering antagonisms one step at a time, a process that takes up the first half of the movie. There's even a bit of subtlety involved, especially in the area of race.

Color is hardly mentioned—just a couple of jokey references near the end—but it's clearly a factor in the story's development, and the whole notion of Washington's character as a "new breed" of top officer carries unstated racial connotations.

Subtlety gets scuttled when hostilities break into the open, throwing Ramsey and Hunter into unrestrained conflict and turning their sub, the Alabama, into two camps of sharply divided loyalists even as it hovers dangerously near its Russian adversary.

The crew scurries around with rifles and pistols at one point, threatening to make the picture a "Shootout at the OK Submarine" with a watery grave for the losers.

This mixture of war-movie characters and western-style action takes on a tinge of surrealism from the look of the Alabama itself, full of weird lights and blinking gizmos that recall the Starship Enterprise—mentioned in the dialogue, in case we miss the similarities—more than the grimly metallic subs of more old-fashioned pictures. The hokeyness is charming at moments; seen from outside, the Alabama looks like a toy you'd get in a cereal box and play with in the bathtub.

Written by Michael Schiffer and Richard P. Henrick, the screenplay of "Crimson Tide" rings truer than its title, which suggests a lipstick shade rather than an adventure yarn. Washington's dialogue allows him to ingratiate himself without clamoring for our affection, and Hackman gets at least one potentially classic line to say; "We're here to preserve democracy," he reminds his overly independent subordinate, "not to practice it."

The movie doesn't practice democracy, either, focusing almost entirely on officers at the expense of crewmen who might have been just as interesting to know.

As for females, women seeking role models will have to make do with a glimpse of Hunter's wife before the Alabama hits the open sea.

Most noteworthy in the supporting cast is George Dzundza, always dependable when a touch of anguished uncertainty is called for. The picture was directed by Tony Scott, auteur of such motley projects as "Days of Thunder" and the recent "True Romance" not to mention "Top Gun," one of several Simpson-Bruckheimer collaborations.

"Crimson Tide" is his most respectable offering to date. Here's hoping it starts a trend in his career.

FILMS IN REVIEW, 9-10/95, p. 55, Andy Pawelczak

Some notes on submarine warfare: blips on the radar screen, signifying a prowling enemy sub, are likely to appear and mysteriously disappear but don't be fooled—they'll be back, on the attack; in the event of damage to the sub, it sometimes becomes necessary to seal off part of the ship, often resulting in the sacrifice of a small number of men for the survival of the others and the mission itself. I learned this, and more, from watching such submarine movies as *Run Silent, Run Deep*, *The Hunt for Red October* and the German-made *Das Boot* which proved that the pleasures of the genre have nothing to do with what side you're on and everything to do with the claustrophobic fear of premature entombment. *Crimson Tide*, the latest reincarnation of the sub movie as directed by Tony Scott (*Top Gun, True Romance*), has a few moments of underwater terror but it's fatally handicapped by a weak plot, pallid characterizations and a too familiar handling of the genre's conventions.

By now it's a cliche to say that in this post-Cold War era, movies like *Crimson Tide* are thrillers in search of an adversary. Last year's *True Lies* gave us demonized, comic book Arab terrorists while *Clear and Present Danger* fell back on Colombian drug cartels. *Crimson Tide* solves the problem by resurrecting the old reliable Russians, this time in the form of right-wing rebels who seize a nuclear base and threaten to bomb the US if the Americans intervene in Chechnya, thus giving the movie a specious, right-out-of-the-headlines credibility. The *U.S.S. Alabama* is sent out into the Pacific with orders to be prepared to nuke the Russian base, and what suspense the movie has focuses on the conflict between the sub's captain, Ramsey (Gene Hackman), a gung-ho type more than ready to ignite a nuclear holocaust, and his more cool-headed executive officer, Hunter (Denzel Washington).

Hackman does his usual professional job as the cigar-chomping, macho, authoritarian Ramsey who in his private moments listens to Beethoven and Schubert. He doesn't go as far out on a semi-parodistic limb as Jack Nicholson did, to terrific effect, in a similar role in *A Few Good Men*, but his Ramsey is the classic Bad Father you love to hate and the movie is most alive when

Hackman is on the screen, a fact the filmmakers seem to acknowledge in a curiously muted, valedictory ending that celebrates Ramsey's obsolete, heroic machismo.

As the executive officer Hunter, Denzel Washington is saddled with a terminal good-guy blandness. The battle lines between the two men are drawn early on when Ramsey, in tried-and-true old-boy fashion, baits the intellectual, peace-loving Hunter into an argument about the justification for war. Later, when the conflict breaks out into the open, Ramsey asserts—in the film's single best line—that their job is to defend democracy, not practice it. Ultimately, the two men come down to a predictable mano-a-mano confrontation when Hunter takes over the ship to prevent Ramsey from launching its missiles without a clear directive from the White House.

Tony Scott's direction doesn't add much excitement to the pedestrian script which keeps playing out the central conflict over and over again without any real development. There are a few mildly evocative shots of narrow sub corridors and eerily lit rooms pulsating with high-tech blips and bleeps, but most of the movie is so deficient in adrenaline that Scott keeps pumping it up with Hans Zimmer's bombastic, pseudo-heroic soundtrack. The exterior shots of the sub under water don't help—it looks suspiciously like a toy in a bathtub.

LOS ANGELES TIMES, 5/12/95, Calendar/p. 1, Kenneth Turan

Don't plan on getting much sleep after seeing "Crimson Tide." It's not just that the tension, tangible enough to be eaten off a plate, is capable of squeezing out your every last breath. It's that a troubling dilemma has been placed at the heart of a crackling good piece of popular entertainment.

And if ever a picture crackled, "Crimson Tide" fits the description. Crisp as the creases in its Naval officers' uniforms, this tale of seething conflicts aboard an American submarine on the eve of nuclear war is strictly by-the-numbers, but hardly ever are traditional elements executed with such panache.

Wedding a shrewd concept and a lean script to on-the-nose acting and direction, "Crimson Tide" is one of the rare times when a whole mess of commercial elements are thrown together and everything works out for the best.

Though high testosterone boy-toy films like "Crimson Tide" (especially those produced, as this one is, by Don Simpson and Jerry Bruckheimer) usually are oblivious to things like convincing writing and classy acting, this one is not, and is capped by taut performances by stars Denzel Washington and Gene Hackman and a brisk job of direction by Tony Scott.

Washington plays Lt. Cmdr. Ron Hunter, an impressively educated submarine officer first glimpsed wearing a silly hat at his daughter's birthday party. Those moments of frivolity, however, are fated not to last, as a TV news broadcast details a world in terrible crisis.

The rebellion in Chechnya has led to a civil war in Russia, and ultranationalist rebels led by one Vladimir Radchenko are attempting to capture nuclear-tipped ICBMs and threatening to use them on the United States if they succeed. "Is it as bad as it looks?" Hunter's pal Weps (Viggo Mortensen) asks. You know it is.

Hunter's assignment is with Capt. Frank Ramsey, commander of the Trident submarine USS Alabama (hence the movie's name), modestly described as "the most lethal killing machine ever devised." Persuasively played by Hackman, Ramsey is one of those tougher than tough commanders that movies specialize in, in love only with the Navy and his dog, a No. 1 who believes that aboard ship "we're here to preserve democracy, not practice it."

The relationship between these two is the fissionable core of "Crimson Tide" and one of several places where the spare Michael Schiffer script, with well-publicized additions by the impressive trio of Quentin Tarantino, Robert Towne and Steve Zaillian ("These three guys could punch up 'Hamlet,'" Schiffer told the New York Times), makes its expertise felt.

Right from their initial meeting, the best kind of movie tension, a combination of distaste and respect, bubbles up between the captain and his executive officer. Ramsey, a seat-of-the-pants combat veteran, distrusts Hunter's book learning while the younger man, though irked at being continually needled, comes to understand that the captain really does care for his men.

Obviously energizing each other in a sweet display of complementary acting, both Hackman and Washington, helped by expert supporting performances by Mortensen, the veteran George Dzundza and several others, bring their antagonism to life.

Aside from convincingly delineating character, "Crimson Tide's" script gradually builds the tension from small incidents like a fire in the galley and the unwelcome attentions of a Russian Akula class submarine until the ultimate in crises inevitably arrives.

That would be the news, transmitted via EAM, or Emergency Action Message, that those pesky rebels have captured both the ICBMs and their launch codes and are getting ready to blast the free world. The Alabama is commanded to attack the Russian bases with its own nuclear arms before it's too late. Then, as if any more tension were needed, another EAM comes in that just might countermand that order to strike, but mechanical problems break off the transmission before the message is completed.

So the dilemma, which causes Ramsey and Hunter to lock horns for a final nail-biting confrontation, is this: Do you take the time to confirm the attack message and risk having the entire United States blown away during the delay, or do you fire without confirmation and perhaps start an unprovoked nuclear war?

Helping make all this chillingly plausible is the great sense of verisimilitude "Crimson Tide" creates, both verbal and visual, including the convincing use of jargon ("zero bubble, commence hovering" is one of the more lyrical bits), the story help of sub authority Richard P. Henrick, and a combination of production design, art direction, lighting and cinematography that makes the inside of the Alabama look and feel compellingly real.

Though Tony Scott has always had the reputation of being a shooter, a director who can be counted on to make his footage look terrific, none of his other films—and that includes mindless successes like "Top Gun"—have even come close to what he has accomplished here.

Confident as ever with the visuals, Scott has added an expertness at moving plot along and a facility with actors that is both welcome and new. Whether it's a fluke or the harbinger of wonders to come, "Crimson Tide" serves as a reminder of what Hollywood professionalism can accomplish when it stays on its best behavior.

NEW STATESMAN & SOCIETY, 11/3/95, p. 32, Jonathan Romney

To state the obvious first: *Crimson Tide* is a submarine movie and therefore entirely about penises. The *USS Alabama* and its Russian counterpart surge through the depths in a way that can only be called priapic, discharging manfully streamlined torpedoes at each other. When the US craft strikes a leak, it doesn't so much sink as detumesce. Just to drive the point home, fearless captain Gene Hackman—never without a correspondingly thrusting cigar close at hand—retorts when he's told that the enemy craft is loading: "You don't put on a condom unless you're gonna fuck."

There was a time, decades ago, when it was possible to imagine that film-makers didn't know what they were really dealing with when they played with boats and planes, and that it was the job of the discreet Freudian to explain it all gently to them. These days, Hollywood scriptwriters probably attend weekend seminars on "Penile Innuendo within the Three-Act Structure". Director Tony Scott certainly knows the score: he made *Top Gun*, probably the most explicitly phallic war movie ever made, until now. Last year, Quentin Tarantino had a cameo role in a comedy called *Sleep With Me* in which he expounded feverishly on *Top Gun*'s homoerotic subtext. That must have appealed to Scott, who, having already filmed Tarantino's *True Romance*, has now enlisted the *wunderkind* for an uncredited rewrite on *Crimson Tide*.

The screenplay is actually credited to Michael Schiffer, although what strikes one are the single lines that seem to reveal the Tarantino touch. Watching *Crimson Tide* in a cinema is an extraordinary experience—at certain points, a thunderous wave of nudging can be felt passing round the stalls. The lines jump out—a reference to *Star Trek* here, the *Silver Surfer* there, a busful of navy men chatting about Hardy Kruger films. Maybe these bits are all Schiffer originals, but the effect is pure Tarantino. The audience wants to ask, does anything exist outside cinema?

In *Crimson Tide*, this is a pertinent question because the film's central issue is nothing less than the fate of the world. The plot is simple; a US sub goes to war against the enemy Nuclear firepower is evenly matched. gung-ho Captain Ramsey (Hackman) wants to blast the other side out of the water, knowing that the result will mean world destruction; his second-in-command, Lt Hunter (Denzel Washington), would rather be circumspect and await instructions. It's not that complex a plot option: either the world will end or it won't. What's interesting is not the outcome, but the amount of scowling and jaw-clenching our men have to do to reach it.

What's also interesting is that *Crimson Tide* is an almost indecently eager welcome home to the cold war movie; the bad guys for the first time in ages turn out to be Russian. The end of the Soviet Union was an uncomfortable day for Hollywood, which was suddenly obliged to think up convincing new international villains. If it wasn't Alan Rickman in a vague German accent, the Arabs were the safest bet, calculated to set middle America hissing and flinging popcorn at the screen. However, that option seems to have been soured for the foreseeable future: first, by the exceptionally racist portrayal of Arabs in James Cameron's *True Lies*; and, second, by the embarrassing haste with which the US media jumped the gun by hypothesising Arab perpetrators in the Oklahoma bombing.

How reassuring it must be, then, once again to have for your villain a crazed Russian warhawk. It is a bit of cobbled-together topicality calculated to offend no one: knock up an extremist Vladimir Zhirinovsky figure, make him some sort of maverick off on his own track, replace the sinister Red Army with a sinister rebel faction of the Red Army, and it's business as usual. The film takes self-conscious pains early on to make it known that dusting down the Red Peril genre is absolutely its primary concern. "I hope you enjoyed the peace," Hackman tells his men, "because as of now we're back in business."

Crimson Tide is a very effective nail-biter and compellingly tackles the defining limitation of the submarine genre—the fact that sub films can't show us much more than a bunch of men cooped up in claustrophobic proximity with the odd periscope popping up, and cramped, visually austere sets rocking from time to time. Perhaps directors take on sub movies for the same reason that theatre people do Racine; for the challenge of the constraints. Scott gives us a few choice moments of underwater action, without copping out of the sub movie's more ascetic formal requirements. But *Crimson Tide* is very much about talk, as befits an Oedipal dream: the best clashes between Ramsey and Hunter take place at the dinner table, father and rebellious older son quietly but furiously squaring off in front of the younger brothers, the other officers.

What you remember of *Crimson Tide* in fact is not the action but the words—the one-off lines like Ramsey on cigars ("I don't trust air I can't see"); the left-field routines like the 11th hour exchange about the Lippizaner horses, and the pop culture riffs—Hunter encouraging one of his men with a bit of *Star Trek* lore. In one way, *Crimson Tide* is an encouraging sign; it seems to signal the advent of the primarily verbal action movie, in which words speak louder than flying glass. But neither the words nor the action finally add up to that much; *Crimson Tide* is one step away from being the courtroom drama that it forms the back-story to. When they make that film, let's hope Quentin's around to give the judge some good innuendo about gavels.

NEW YORK, 5/15/95, p. 62, David Denby

Despite a ferocious atmosphere of hype—thudding soundtrack, torrential rains, red and blue lights playing across the faces of the actors—Tony Scott's new movie, *Crimson Tide*, is an absorbing and at times thrilling entertainment. Once again, Scott uses the cheap techniques of intensification that he learned as a director of commercials and then perfected in such films as *Top Gun*. But this time, Scott and producers Don Simpson and Jerry Bruckheimer are not selling Tom Cruise's smooth flesh and gleaming teeth. *Crimson Tide*, in other words, is a largely serious action movie with two grown-up actors, Gene Hackman and Denzel Washington, going at full tilt. It's the story of a mutiny set at a time of international crisis. In Russia, a fascist dissident modeled after Vladimir Zhirinovsky has broken with the regime, taking a part of the army and some nuclear missiles with him, and threatens to launch the weapons against America. The U.S.S. *Alabama*, a nuclear sub with ballistic missiles, is sent out for a possible preemptive strike. The heart of the movie is a series of remarkable struggles between the captain (Hackman), who wants to launch the strike without getting confirmation of his orders, and his executive officer (Washington), who refuses to give his formal assent. It's reassuring, I suppose, to discover that a nuclear holocaust cannot be set off without the agreement of at least two men.

The material shrewdly recapitulates the scheme of such earlier pictures as *Mutiny on the Bounty* and *The Caine Mutiny*. In all three movies, a career officer who is both a martinet and the hardworking soul of the Navy arouses the indignation of a smart, educated, and humane junior officer, who leads a mutiny against the aging dictator. The great Hackman dominates the first part of the movie, defining the character's quirks with that rich, private sense of amusement he always draws on. His Captain Ramsey is an extremely intelligent but limited man, jealous of his absolute powers, alert to the tiniest failures of deference in his officers; Washington's Executive Officer Ramsey, properly cautious but prideful, knows how to torment him—out of vanity at first, and then out of an overwhelming sense of necessity.

Much of Michael Schiffer's screenplay is literate and revealing, and I found myself fascinated by the minutiae of launching a nuclear strike—the elaborate protocol of codes, keys, arming devices, authorization and assent, the clipped yet bizarrely formal language—all of which makes mistakes or irrational acts unlikely. (Though not entirely impossible, if *Crimson Tide* is anywhere near accurate.) If only the restless Scott would not pump up the movie when he doesn't have to! He sends men running across catwalks or fighting one another or hitting punching bags. We seem to be trapped inside a New York health club. But still, this is Tony Scott's best work to date. The confrontations between the two men are tremendous set pieces of acting and directing, and Scott stages the mutiny itself with crisp attention to physical detail. The summer season is upon us: At least it begins with a strong, heavy blow to the midsection.

NEW YORK POST, 5/12/95, p. 35, Michael Medved

In "Crimson Tide," the fate of the human race hangs in the balance during a drawn-out confrontation between two unforgettable characters who represent contrasting styles of machismo.

Gene Hackman plays the captain of the nuclear sub Alabama; he's a lonely cigar-chomping, foul-mouthed, swaggering, Schubert-loving combat veteran who is both earthy and eccentric, accompanied everywhere by his beloved Jack Russell terrier.

Denzel Washington is his new executive officer—a silky smooth, Harvard-trained family man whose flawless self-control masks an iron will every bit as implacable as his commander's.

In the hands of two of the best actors in the business—who seem to savor every moment of their on-screen interaction—these characters do indeed come across as the proverbial irresistible force and immovable object, and thanks to a clever script by Michael Schiffer ("Colors," "Lean on Me") their collision course is exhilarating to watch.

The film begins with the all-too-plausible premise that a rogue ultra-nationalist in Russia (obviously modeled on the mad, bad Vladimir Zhirinovsky) leads a rebel faction of the army in taking over the Siberian missile base. As loyalist troops struggle to reassert control, he threatens to blow up America with nuclear warheads.

The U.S. president then dispatches Hackman's awesomely-equipped submarine to hit first, if necessary. (We're asked to believe that the decision makers will have exactly one hour's warning between the time the Russian missiles are fueled and armed and their deadly launch against American targets.)

Hackman gets the order to strike, and he prepares his own nuclear missiles; but then new instructions been coming through, only to be interrupted by transmission problems. The skipper insists on going through with the original order, but Washington refuses to back him until they can read the later dispatches.

They ultimately struggle for control of the ship—and for the fate of civilization,

This battle works because both characters are altogether justified in their positions—and both are portrayed as hugely sympathetic.

Director Tony Scott and producers Don Simpson and Jerry Bruckhelmer previously collaborated on "Top Gun," and once again they've combined admiration for dedicated military personalities with fascination with their elaborate equipment.

"Crimson Tide" functions like a training cruise, introducing audiences to a wealth of compelling details about nuclear submarines; I have no idea if those technical particulars are authentic, but at the end of the film you do feel like a battle-hardened old salt.

Of course, there are too many crises—fires, torpedoes, gun battles, equipment malfunctions—that run right down to the final second, but that seems to be an inevitable aspect of submarine movies. At least the filmmakers show a sense of humor on the subject—as they begin their fateful cruise, the sailors quiz each other on "Run Silent, Run Deep" and "The Enemy Below."

Here, the miniatures and techno wizardry are solid but never spectacular. In fact, they're really not needed—two incomparable special effects named Hackman and Washington are enough to power even the most overloaded sub through dangerous waters.

NEWSDAY, 5/12/95, Part II/p. B2, Jack Mathews

For people who become even slightly claustrophobic while watching movies contained in tight spaces (and I get it bad), submarine adventures operate at a high level of tension when things are going well! When the sub is disabled, sinking, or trying to dodge torpedoes or depth charges, it's nearly unbearable.

Those elements are just for openers in Tony Scott's "Crimson Tide." Besides sweating it out in a metal tube 1,000 feet beneath the sea, the crew members of the nuclear sub Alabama are racing the clock to either stop or start World War III and their commander and first officer are fighting like Captain Bligh and Fletcher Christian.

Hello summer!

Yes, the season of high-test(osterone) action films gets off to an early start this year, and it ought to be a jump-start. "Crimson Tide" is such a crafty piece of filmmaking—a perfect blend of hand-held camerawork, sound effects, and foreboding choral music—that it seems to grab your seat and shake it progressively harder from beginning to end.

The story, inspired by the continuing threat of right-wing hawks in post-Soviet Russia, has a breakaway rebel force taking over a nuclear missile base and threatening to attack the United States if the rebels' own government doesn't turn over power to them. The Alabama is hurling toward the Russian coast, dodging torpedoes from a pesky Russian sub, with orders to launch a preemptive strike against the base.

One other little problem. A torpedo blast knocks out the Alabama's communications system, right in the midst of a presidential message that may be ordering them to abort the mission. Do they launch on schedule, insuring a nuclear war, as Capt. Ramsey (Gene Hackman) insists, or wait until communications are restored, as Lt. Cmdr. Hunter (Denzel Washington) wants, and risk leaving America exposed?

Similarities to "Fail-Safe" and "Dr. Strangelove," the two 1964 films about nuclear brinksmanship, are inescapable, as are the parallels between the captains and first officers on the Alabama and the Bounty. Bligh and Ramsey are old salts rooted in the past, believing in the absolute power of a ship's captain. Christian and Hunter represent, four centuries apart, a new generation of leaders, more sensitive to the consequences of their actions, more apt to question authority.

"We're here to protect democracy, not to practice it," Ramsey barks at Hunter, as their relationship teeters on the brink of its own nuclear war.

"Crimson Tide" doesn't seem to be anything more than a strained Hollywood hypothesis, as we'll probably hear from Naval commanders on the talk-show circuit in the coming weeks. I know nothing about nuclear submarines, but it is a stretch to believe nuclear war can hang on a communication system that falls apart like a transistor radio.

But that is a thought, and thoughts have no place in the summer season. "Crimson Tide" is pure visceral entertainment, and its two stars know exactly how to play it. Hackman, snarling through his cigar smoke, is a great thundering bully, driven by equal measures of patriotism, military zeal and egomania. There is a good man beneath the crust, but the crust is thick.

Washington brings a cool to the Harvard-educated Hunter that is the perfect counterpoint to his captain's quick-tempered aggressiveness, and represents at least the ideal leader in the nuclear age.

The personality conflict, and the tests of loyalty it places on the other officers as it moves toward inevitable mutiny, heightens the tension that is inherent to films operating in such tight quarters. "Crimson Tide" doesn't match the claustrophobic panic created by Wolfgang Petersen's "Das Boot," the best sub movie ever made, but it's enough to get your heart racing and into shape for summer.

SIGHT AND SOUND, 12/95, p. 43, John Wrathall

When a Russian "ultra-nationalist" rebel seizes a missile base, the submarine USS Alabama is sent to Russian waters to forestall a threatened nuclear strike. Once in position, the Alabama receives an EAM (Emergency Action Message) ordering a pre-emptive nuclear attack against the rebels, who are fuelling their missiles, which means they will be ready to launch in an hour. But when the Alabama takes evasive action from the torpedoes of a rebel submarine, radio contact is broken, and a second EAM comes through incomplete. Navy veteran Captain Ramsey decides they must obey the last complete order received, and launch their missiles. His new, Harvard-educated XO (executive officer), Hunter, disagrees, demanding that they try to restore radio contact before risking starting World War Three on a false alarm. When Ramsey insists on proceeding, Hunter, with the support of 'Cob' (the Chief Of Bridge), relieves him of his command and has him locked in his state room.

Hunter fights off a second attack by the rebel submarine, sinking it, but not before the *Alabama* has been hit, flooding the "bilge bays" and damaging the radio. Meanwhile loyal officers, including Hunter's best friend 'Weps' (the Weapons Officer), free Ramsey and take over the 'con' (control room) at gunpoint, locking up Hunter in the officer's mess. As Ramsey prepares again to launch the missiles, Hunter escapes and, over the intercom, persuades Weps to delay the launch while radio operator Vossler tries to fix the radio. Then Hunter and his allies arm themselves and try to secure the bridge. The ensuing Mexican standoff is only resolved when, minutes before the rebel missiles will be fuelled and ready, the radio is fixed and the second EAM received in full: the rebels have surrendered and the launch must be terminated. At the court martial back at Pearl Harbor, Ramsey announces his early retirement and recommends that Hunter should be given his command.

Nine years ago producers Don Simpson and Jerry Bruckheimer and director Tony Scott took us to the brink of World War Three in their paean to US Navy fighter pilots, *Top Gun*. This time the trio have put another branch of the Navy in the spotlight and—significantly—without the co-operation of the US Department of Defense, who took exception to the film's portrayal of a mutiny at sea.

But *Crimson Tide* is not just *Top Gun* underwater: it's a tribute to the producers' skill that they can keep the style of their product so distinctive while also keeping up with the times. Russians, of course, still make handy villains: all it takes is a topical reference to Chechnya and a Zhirinovsky-like "ultra-nationalist". In a more definite break with the warmongering, Cold War rhetoric of *Top Gun*, though, it is the avoidance of war—the realisation that the *Alabama* doesn't have to attack—that provides the film's climax. *Crimson Tide* harks back instead to the nuclear scare movies of the mid-60s. The basic situation of the irrevocable "emergency action message" echoes *Fail Safe* and *Dr. Strangelove*, while the opposition of a black liberal and a hard-bitten white Naval veteran recalls the confrontation of Sidney Poitier and Richard Widmark in *Strangelove* producer James B. Harris's excellent *The Bedford Incident*.

With an eye on the box office, *Crimson Tide* has also taken on board the lessons of two of last year's surprise action hits. Though the screenplay is credited to Michael Schiffer, it was extensively rewritten, at Scott's insistence, by Quentin Tarantino (who worked with Scott on *True Romance*). As a result, the characters keep breaking off from the business in hand to engage in hip exchanges about *Star Trek*, the *Silver Surfer* and, in a post-modern flourish, the relative merits of other submarine movies such as *Run Silent, Run Deep* and *The Enemy Below*. In true Tarantino style, the film also climaxes with a Mexican stand-off. (Uncredited rewrites were also contributed by Robert Towne and Steve Zaillian, and one of the film's incidental pleasures is playing spot the screenwriter; an early discussion between Ramsey and Hunter about different interpretation's of Clausewitz's theory of war, for instance, can safely be attributed to Towne.)

Crimson Tide's structure, meanwhile, owes a debt to *Speed*, which proved that the fail-safe way to keep a 90s audience gripped is to cram a preposterous succession of races against the clock into a real-time frame. *Crimson Tide* pivots around a relentless series of countdowns. The *Alabama* almost sinks to "hold crush depth" at 1,850 feet below sea level. The 15-minute missile launch preparation, for which it must rise of 150 feet, is set in operation (twice). It also awaits the impact of enemy torpedoes, retreats to 1,000 yards from the rebel submarine so that its own torpedoes have time to arm themselves etc. etc.—all within the outer concentric countdown of the hour from when the rebels start fuelling their missiles to when they attain "launch capacity".

For all its manful efforts to keep up with the latest developments in Russian politics and Hollywood story structure, *Crimson Tide* still bears the unmistakable stamp of Simpson, Bruckheimer and Scott, not only from *Top Gun* but also from their intervening collaborations, *Beverly Hills Cop II* and *Days of Thunder*. The obsession with jargon has reached a new apogee here: even the characters' names are Naval jargon ("Weps" equals Weapons Officer, "Cob" equals Chief Of Bridge). With its non-stop litany of EAMs and DEFCON 25, as regulation computer print-out captions across the screen keep us tuned to "Zulu time" (Greenwich Mean, apparently), *Crimson Tide* is in fact a film about military jargon; after all, the central conflict between Ramsey and Hunter revolves around their differing interpretations of Navy regulations.

Equally distinctive is Tony Scott's shooting style: tilted, tight-cropped telephoto close-ups, backlighting and clouds of diffusion smoke. Scott can make anything look glamorous; in fact, he seems incapable of making anything look unglamorous, even Ramsey's Jack Russell cocking its leg. About to take the *Alabama* below the waves, Ramsey bids a fond farewell to the golden smog floating above the ocean with the quip, "I don't trust air you can't see,"—words which should be enscribed on Tony Scott's gravestone.

In *Crimson Tide*, Scott takes his visual stylisation even further than usual. To differentiate the various areas of the submarine in which the action unfolds, Scott colour-codes them, an excuse to bathe the actors in floods of gorgeous primary colours; at times, with sailors stripped to their singlets, *Crimson Tide* could almost be mistaken for Fassbinder's hymn to a very different branch of nautical life, *Querelle*. Meanwhile, with Ramsey and Hunter's verbal duels focusing on the size of their cigars and the relative merits of black and white stallions, the homoerotic subtext seems to be rising, if not quite to the surface, at least to missile-launch depth. Bearing in mind Tarantino's contribution, it's hard to believe that anyone involved with *Crimson Tide* could be unaware of his celebrated, Pauline Kael-inspired deconstruction of *Top Gun*'s gay undercurrent in the film *Sleep With Me*. Which begs the question: Are they doing it deliberately? That would surely be the ultimate sign that those high priests of 80s machismo, Simpson, Bruckheimer and Scott, were willing to adapt themselves to the spirit of the 90s.

TIME, 5/15/95, p. 72, Richard Corliss

The Russians are back! The Russians are back! writers of international thrillers, on page or screen, must have whooped for joy when Vladimir Zhirinovsky began spouting his virulent nationalism. What if this character got his finger on the nuclear button? Why, we'd have a right-wing update of the old red menace. So here, lighting a flame under Cold War II, is *Crimson Tide*, a burly, chatty melodrama about the imminence of annihilation. On a U.S. nuclear submarine, only two men—grizzled old Captain Ramsey (Gene Hackman) and his starchy second-in-command, Lieut. Commander Ron Hunter (Denzel Washington)— have the power to trigger the apocalypse or, just maybe, prevent it.

Prevent war? Forget that! This is an action movie, isn't it? And as Clausewitz might have said, action movies are a continuation of war by other means. The genre demands that stuff blow up real good. But the most physical *Crimson Tide* gets is when the villain punches the hero in the face, twice—without getting punched back. And in a bizarre climax, the good guy and the bad guy sit down and talk for three minutes while waiting for somebody else to tell them what to do.

We soon learn that the Russian sub plot is a red herring. The real cold war is being waged between these two American officers. The real explosive device is inside Captain Ramsey's wayward head. And the film's real theme is executive stress. It's a charged debate among middle-management types agonizing over fuzzily transmitted orders from their boss, who happens to be the President of the U.S.

As devised by writers Michael Schiffer and Richard P. Henrick (with a script polish by Quentin Tarantino), *Crimson Tide* is an old-fashioned mutiny movie—on the U.S.S. *Alabama* instead of the *Bounty* or the *Caine*. Actually, this is a three-mutiny movie: commanders change faster than Italian Prime Ministers. This king-of-the-hill game gives Hackman, Washington and their cohort the chance to run around the submarine with guns and purposeful scowls. The milling is underscored with a heavy bass line that will leave moviegoers' butts tingling; and it is shot with lots of low-angle close-ups of manly jawlines, as if every sailor were posing to be sculpted onto Mount Rushmore. When in doubt, director Tony Scott (*Top Gun, Days of Thunder*) lets loose a spray of water, sparks and sweat—the signature flourish of this Helmut Newton of movie machismo.

Washington does nicely playing the company man as '90s hero, an African American who has learned when to speak up and when to shut up in the white world. Perhaps the actor has learned too well; he simmers handsomely but rarely displays the informed rage he showed in *A Soldier's Story* and *Glory*. In his box-office hits (*Philadelphia, The Pelican Brief*), Washington cedes the fiercer emotions to his co-stars. No surprise, then, that Hackman, as a Bobby Knight-style sociopath, gets all the high notes and good lines ("We're here to preserve democracy, not practice it"). If the performance consists largely of Hackman briskly massaging his scalp every few minutes, that's his way of suggesting that Ramsey is trying to soothe or stir the demons inside.

Both stars give *Tide* a pedigree and, despite any critic's cavils, a safe shot at being the year's first big hit. Not a *Red October*: a *Crimson* summer.

VILLAGE VOICE, 5/16/95, p. 52, Georgia Brown

Here's my scenario: Somebody—producers Don Simpson and Jerry Bruckheimer, perhaps—said, Okay, time to bring back *The Hunt for Red October* only crossed this time with *A Few Good Men*. They toss around names of quality hack directors. Tony Scott? Perfecto! At a later point, somebody must've yawned and suggested calling in Tarantino to sprinkle Silver Surfer allusions as well as what-I'm-going-to-stick-up-your-butt cracks. (Reputedly, Tarantino was the movie's unbilled script doctor. Either that or he's been ripped off.) Behold, *Crimson Tide*.

Actually, I like sub movies. They offer a nice correlative for the bottled-up personality. Tons of pressure building up, controlled panic in a confined space, the enemy cruising silently all around, ominous blips on the sonar screen. No matter how solid the craft, there's always a big leak, the infinite sea pouring in. And a free fall into the cold, crushing depths. One thing missing: nobody peers out periscopes anymore.

For a not-so-implausible premise, writer Michael Schiffer has blithely resuscitated the Red menace. A Zhirinovsky type, supported by a rebel faction of the military, threatens a coup, and since he may have his thumb on the nuclear button, the U.S. poises itself for a preemptive strike. When Lieutenant Commander Ron Hunter (Denzel Washington) gets the call from Naval Headquarters, he's home celebrating his daughter's birthday (note that *Red October* opened with Alec Baldwin's CIA analyst and *his* daughter). Our hero has human ties. On the other hand, Captain Frank Ramsey (Gene Hackman), Hunter's senior officer, relies on contradictory phallic props, a huge cigar and a small dog. Improbably, Ramsey appoints Hunter his second in command. That the restrained, gentlemanly Hunter (Annapolis, Harvard) is African American adds a bit of spice. How much shit will he take?

Virtually everything fits familiar patterns. Like Jack Nicholson in *A Few Good Men* (or Henry Fonda in *Fort Apache*), Ramsey is the crude, crafty, potentially mad, aging warrior in a system that's shifted from under him. "We're here to preserve democracy, not practice it," he barks when openly contradicted, Indeed, *Crimson Tide* floats on anachronisms. The debate over nuclear warfare is presented as if taking place for the first time, And once more the world's fate hangs on a lowly techie frantically trying to fix the ship's radio. Why don't they fax?

In the first half of the film a driving rain (on shore) and a kitchen fire (on board) provide most of the drama, but the last half crackles as one doomsday countdown spawns another, mutinies breed mutinies, and the sub begins to resemble the Death Star with its oedipal pyrotechnics and troop movements. I caught the spirit and even came up with a blurb: *Crimson Tide* makes claustrophobics of us all.

Also reviewed in:
CHICAGO TRIBUNE, 5/12/95, Friday/p. C, Michael Wilmington
NEW YORK TIMES, 5/12/95, p. C1, Janet Maslin
NEW YORKER, 5/15/95, p. 94, Terrence Rafferty
VARIETY, 5/8-14/95, p. 65, Todd McCarthy
WASHINGTON POST, 5/12/95, p. B1, Rita Kempley
WASHINGTON POST, 5/12/95, Weekend/p. 48, Desson Howe

CROSSING GUARD, THE

A Miramax Films release. *Executive Producer:* Bob Weinstein, Harvey Weinstein, and Richard Gladstein. *Producer:* Sean Penn and David S. Hamburger. *Director:* Sean Penn. *Screenplay:* Sean Penn. *Director of Photography:* Vilmos Zsigmond. *Editor:* Jay Cassidy. *Music:* Jack

Nitzsche. *Music Editor:* Richard Whitfield. *Choreographer:* Russell Clark. *Sound:* Thomas Causey. *Sound Editor:* Per Hallberg. *Casting:* Don Phillips. *Production Designer:* Michael Haller. *Art Director:* Helen Gene Nichols. *Set Decorator:* Derek R. Hill. *Special Effects:* Eddie E. Surkin. *Costumes:* Jill Ohanneson. *Make-up:* Stephen Abrums. *Make-up (Anjelica Huston):* Hallie D'Amore. *Stunt Coordinator:* Chuck Waters. *Running time:* 117 minutes. *MPAA Rating:* R.

CAST: Jack Nicholson (Freddy Gale); David Morse (John Booth); Anjelica Huston (Mary); Robin Wright (JoJo); Piper Laurie (Helen Booth); Richard Bradford (Stuart Booth); Priscilla Barnes (Verna); David Baerwald (Peter); Robbie Robertson (Roger); John Savage (Bobby); Kari Wuhrer (Mia); Jennifer Leigh Warren (Jennifer); Kellita Smith (Tanya); Richard Sarafian (Sunny Ventura); Bobby Cooper (Coop); Jeff Morris (Silas); Buddy Anderson (Buddy); Edward L. Katz (Eddie); Joe Viterelli (Joe at Bar); Eileen Ryan (Woman in Shop); Ryo Ishabashi (Jefferey); Dennis Fanning (Cop #1); Lisa Crawford (Cop #2); Jay Koiwai (Asian Man); Elizabeth Gilliam (Little Asian Girl); Michael Ryan and Matthew Ryan (Twin Boys); Penny Allen (Woman on Bus); Nicky Blair (Himself); Gene Kirkwood (Swinger); Jason Kristofer (Bus Passenger #1); Randy Meadoff (Bus Passengers Mother); Leo Penn (Hank); Michael Abelar (Bum); Daysi Moreno (Freddy's Chicana); Erin Dignam (Peter's Guest #1); Jeremiah Wayne Birkett (Jefferey's Boyfriend); Hadda Brooks (Piano Player); Ruby McKoy (Deputy Sheriff); Hanna Newmaster (Little Girl); William Dignam (The Crossing Guard).

LOS ANGELES TIMES, 11/15/95, Calendar/p. 1, Kenneth Turan

Sean Penn brings the same visceral intensity and raw emotionality to writing and directing as he does to acting, and while that may sound like a good thing, it finally isn't. "The Crossing Guard," Penn's second film behind the camera, is a troubling, troublesome movie whose makeshift structure cannot contain the powerful flood of passions that he and his cast have poured into it.

When he works as an actor, Penn's performance is tempered and adjusted (Penn would probably say diluted) by the input of the writer and director. But as a filmmaker, Penn has allowed no one to modulate his vision. As a result, this study of naked obsession, while showing evidence of considerable talent, has been allowed to go past its mark. Despite a determination to explore extremes of emotion, "The Crossing Guard" will leave most viewers cold.

As with "The Indian Runner," his first film, Penn is most impressive with actors, here convincing Jack Nicholson and Anjelica Huston to give themselves over completely to his vision while creating a brooding, claustrophobic mood on screen. Working with cinematographer Vilmos Zsigmond, Penn favors the kind of filmmaking that wants to claw for the essence of behavior, that attempts to drag audiences inside its characters' pain.

And there is a lot of it to be dragged into, for "The Crossing Guard" is one of those movies in which nobody even thinks of having a nice day. Artful cross-cutting introduces us to three people who are dealing, six years after the fact, with the death of a small girl in a drunk driving accident.

Freddy Gale (Nicholson), the girl's now-divorced father, has turned into an alcoholic wastrel who hangs out in strip clubs and neglects his small jewelry store. His ex-wife Mary (Huston) has sought solace in support groups and taken their two remaining children into a new marriage with the saner Roger (Robbie Robertson). And John Booth (David Morse), the man who drove the car, has spent all those years in prison.

But now the day Freddy has obsessively marked on his calendar is here. John Booth is being released from prison and Freddy, whose existence is anchored to nothing but thoughts of revenge, announces to Mary his determination to fulfill his life's purpose and kill his daughter's murderer.

While this scenario lacks nothing as a premise, problems arise in how Penn has worked it out. Consistently troubling is a kind of arbitrariness that taints both the script and the casting. Freddy, for instance, does track John Booth down but inexplicably gives him a three-day reprieve, which makes things at once more dramatic but less plausible.

And the way Booth is envisioned, capped by the casting of Morse, is also off. Though Morse is a capable actor, Booth is too much the gentle, saintly giant, too fine and sensitive a presence, to seem other than a hollow construct. And, fascinated by the possibilities of contrasting Freddy's boozing and wenching to Booth's philosophical discussions with sensitive artist JoJo (Robin Wright) about the nature of guilt, Penn has not noticed how schematic it all is.

In terms of dialogue, Penn's script is similarly lacking, his characters tending to say things that are either pompous or ponderous, Though Penn clearly sees himself as too much of a personal artist to consider it, he is one filmmaker who would truly be well served by collaborating with a writer.

Another problem, one common to performers moving behind the camera, is that "The Crossing Guard" is rich with extraneous, indulgent actor's moments that would earn this film the Actors Studio Seal of Approval (if there were such a thing) but in practical terms add little while unnecessarily encumbering the action.

Given all that, it is a mark of Penn's strengths as a director that he is able to get strong and emotional performances out of both Huston and Nicholson without much of a script to help them. Looking convincingly bleary-eyed and believably self-destructive, Nicholson is as impressive as he's been in years as a man who has willfully turned his own life into hell on Earth.

But good as they are, these performances are lonely arias that never coalesce into an ensemble. Investing emotion in banal situations is not likely to pay off, and for all the ostentatious naked agony on display, no one in this film feels particularly human. While Sean Penn embarked on "The Crossing Guard" because its story means a great deal to him, the finished film has not been able to noticeably broaden that audience.

NEW YORK POST, 11/15/95, p. 45, Michael Medved

Sean Penn's "The Crossing Guard" is not only grim, pretentious, wretchedly written and indulgently directed, it is also exquisitely boring. It's safe to say that this movie won't do much business at the box office, but it could work wonders for the sale of popcorn to restless moviegoers who will find it difficult to remain in their seats for the duration of the picture.

This is, essentially, a vanity project filled with pointless, portentous pauses and meaningless montages that seem self-consciously designed to impress us at every turn with the filmmaker's gaseous artistic aspirations.

It's easy to imagine how writer-director Sean Penn persuaded Robin Wright to appear in this maudlin muddle, (he's the father of their children, after all), but it's far more difficult to understand why so many other major talents agreed to participate.

Jack Nicholson brings his usual edge-of-madness intensity to the role of the main character, an alcoholic jeweler in downtown L.A. who seems to spend all his time, day and night, boozing in a seedy, dimly-lit strip joint.

He's mourning the loss of his 5-year-old daughter, killed six years before by a hit-and-run drunken driver (named John Booth in an incoherent allusion to Lincoln's assassin). As the movie begins, that driver (David Morse) is about to be released from prison (where a flashback shows him permanently scarring his face, by banging his head against the bars), and Nicholson goes to visit his ex-wife, (a somnolent Anjelica Huston) in her neat suburban home to tell her he intends to win revenge by shooting the killer of their beloved child.

Theoretically, this might be an interesting set-up for a movie, but for the next two hours nothing happens. We know Nicholson is serious about murdering the now-repentant Booth, but his long delay in following this climactic confrontation isn't quite as fascinating as the hesitation of Hamlet.

Nicholson gets drunk a lot and takes strippers to his apartment, though he's too soused to do anything with them. Meanwhile, ex-con Morse goes home to live with his parents (Piper Laurie and Richard Bradford), gets a job on a fishing boat and begins an enigmatic relationship with a moody artist played by Robin Wright.

Sample (Sean Penn-scripted dialogue—He: "What is guilt? Define it." She: "You wanna dance?" The screenplay's idea of poetry and insight is the insertion of the F-word in nearly every line of dialogue from every (male and female) character, which here conveys a sense of mannered phoniness rather the desired realism.

Morse (who previously starred in Penn's similarly moody and overdone filmmaking debut, "Indian Runner") gives a sensitive and thoughtful performance but his impressive work is undermined by Penn's deadly pacing and constantly intrusive direction.

The fine cinematography by Vilmos Zsigmond is also wasted on loads of sequences showing Nicholson in slow motion, staggering endless through downtown crowds; additional slow-motion elements are, in fact, the last thing this staggering, sluggish movie needs.

SIGHT AND SOUND, 9/96, p. 37, Trevor Johnston

John Booth is about to be released from prison, having served five years for causing a young girl's death in a drunk-driving incident. Both her parents are still coping with the loss: Mary attends a group therapy session, while Freddy, a jeweler, numbs the pain with drink, beds the exotic dancers in a club he frequents and crosses the days off until Booth hits the streets again. As John is welcomed home by his parents, Helen and Stuart, Freddy visits Mary, now living with their surviving two children and her second husband, Roger, to reveal the "great news" of Booth's release and reaffirm his determination to kill him. As tempers rise, Mary reminds him that nothing will bring their daughter Emily back and that he has never visited her grave.

Freddy makes his first assassination attempt at John Booth's trailer, but he's forgotten to load the gun, and offers him a further three days to live. John meets an artist, JoJo, at a party thrown by friends in honour of his release. The next evening, while a drunken Freddy winds up in a Mexican whorehouse, John and JoJo have a tender sexual encounter, before he alienates her by wallowing in guilt about the child's death. The following day, John returns to JoJo's apartment but feels shut out by her evasiveness.

As Freddy's excessive drink and philandering bring him to the point of breakdown, he summons Mary to a cafe in the early hours, where he responds to her accusation of selfish emotional withdrawal by storming out. Having run to evade the cops who pulled him up on a drunk driving charge, Freddy arrives at Booth's trailer, where his target is also armed with a rifle but neither of them can quite pull the trigger. After an extended chase, during which Freddy wounds Booth, the latter manages to draw his would-be killer to the graveyard where his child is buried. With the grave in front of them, the two men reach a reconciliation as dawn breaks.

"A crossing guard takes people who, through either immaturity or blindness, cannot find their way safely across the street on their own," is how writer-director Sean Penn explains the central metaphor in *The Crossing Guard*, his second feature. The presence of a school's elderly road safety patrolman in one fleeting slow-motion travelling shot marks a moment of thematic emphasis in a story where a child's death in an alcohol-related auto accident is the cause of prolonged emotional anguish. Unfortunately, this conceit seems trowelled on top of the drama rather than fully integrated within it, just as in *The Indian Runner*, Penn's 1991 scripting and directing debut, the Native American messenger who 'becomes' his message is meant to elucidate a post-Vietnam story of rivalry between two blue-collar brothers. In both cases Penn's investment in his material is put over with such commitment that the point has already been made. It's a measure of his inexperience that he pushes things harder than he needs to.

Overstatement is rife. Slow motion becomes less effective when deployed with such abandon. Street scenes, shot from the middle-distance and overlaid with rock music of the sincerest kind, try to implicate the viewer in the grungy universalities of the metropolitan grind. Extreme close-ups on Jack Nicholson's ravaged features, in the role of the child's distraught father, long to penetrate the self-destructive stumblings of a man at the end of his tether. The first shot we see is of a dancer daubing herself with flames, before cutting to Freddy Gale (Nicholson) and then the soon-to-be-released prisoner John Booth (David Morse). Penn's engagement is palpable, but the manner in which he uses the sleazy strip-club background is unflatteringly redolent of John Cassavetes' *The Killing of a Chinese Bookie* (1976). Cassavetes put his faith in an improvised screenplay without recourse to formal interventionism; Penn the director has a tendency to get in the way of Penn the writer, with his emotional analysis, so hung up is he on replicating the free-wheeling insouciance of the best American movies from the early 70s.

As an actor in, say, *Dead Man Walking*, Penn shows that surface tics are only a facade for the ferment going on beneath them. As a director, though, he allows his cast a method indulgence that sometimes blurs the focus on the very real pain the film seeks to address. (Robin Wright, as John Booth's artist girlfriend, JoJo, has one of those awful scenes where characters channel their inarticulacy into dancing.) Yet, in confronting head-on the unending anger, frustration and self-laceration engendered by the senseless loss of a child, *The Crossing Guard* is never pat. Penn's sincere understanding of the extent of the emotional carnage is actually the core of his over-egged aesthetic. Freddy seems locked in his own existential hell of debauchery and revenge fantasy; his ex-wife Mary (Anjelica Huston) walks on eggshells into a new life but not without a deeper cost, and John Booth, convicted of the manslaughter of five-year-old Emily, seems to feel unease at the way prison has allowed him to come to terms with himself. Just how do you confront all that on mere celluloid? Can the tasteful restraint of a Sidney Lumet, or the degree-zero bland-out of TV-movie intimacy, for instance, really do justice to the extremes of experience negotiated within these frames?

Hopefully Penn will continue to look for the answer to those questions. *The Crossing Guard* gives us the most honourable Jack Nicholson performance this decade (scintillating in its sharp turns of viciousness, although the younger Nicholson would have nailed the character more completely) and a devastating contribution from Anjelica Huston. Penn is a genuine film-maker, and if his promise matures into accomplishment in the way that *The Crossing Guard*'s brute courage often suggests, the future of a personal American cinema may not be as dark as it sometimes seems.

VILLAGE VOICE, 11/21/95, Film Special/p. 20, J. Hoberman

As *The American President* revels in bonafide American bullshit [see Hoberman's review], so *The Crossing Guard* bursts with bogus American realness. Writer-director Sean Penn's long-germinating second feature is doubly overwrought—combining Cassavetes-style actor indulgence with Cimino-esque visual bombast. The movie tricks itself out with showy close-ups, dissolve based montage sequences, double ex-postures, and interpolated slow-motion that's further retarded by the torturous throat-clearing that precedes every scene.

A fearful heaviness oppresses the brain. Once upon a time, a hit-and-run drunk driver killed a seven-year-old girl, destroying the marriage of her distraught parents (Jack Nicholson and Anjelica Huston). Six years later, the driver (bearish David Morse) is released from prison and the child's father, a bitter jeweler with a heart of frozen sleaze, prepares to wreak vengeance. Bursting into Morse's trailer, only to have his gun jam, Nicholson gives Morse three days of grace. In the ensuing juxtaposition of guilt and grief, Penn stages the jeweler's tawdry date with two topless dancers against the ex-con's tender, life-affirming, level-gazed tryst with a hippie chick of serious wisdom and sexual healing (the execrable Robin Wright). One humps, the other gumps.

The movie's only irony is that the character most resistant to therapy provides the actor who plays him all manner of psychodrama. The emotional scene in which Nicholson reminisces with his ex is overcome with subtext, as is the sub—*Five Easy Pieces* crowd-pleaser in which he demolishes a bitchy customer. Nicholson does whatever it takes to keep the movie alive. He tilts, he swivels, he dances a soft-shoe with a stripper to "On the Good Ship Lollipop." He even cries—twice. Top that, Bob Dole.

Also reviewed in:
CHICAGO TRIBUNE, 12/1/95, Friday/p. C, Michael Wilmington
NEW YORK TIMES, 11/15/95, p. C15, Janet Maslin
VARIETY, 9/11-17/95, p. 104, David Rooney
WASHINGTON POST, 12/1/95, p. F1, Hal Hinson
WASHINGTON POST, 12/1/95, Weekend/p. 48, Desson Howe

CRUDE OASIS, THE

A Miramax Films release of a Bluestone Films production. *Producer:* Alex Graves. *Director:* Alex Graves. *Screenplay:* Alex Graves. *Director of Photography:* Steven Quale. *Editor:* Alex Graves. *Music:* Steven Bramson. *Sound:* Peter Rea. *Art Director:* Tom Mittlestadt. *Set Decorator:* Jennifer Carra. *Running time:* 80 minutes. *MPAA Rating:* R.

CAST: Jennifer Taylor (Karen Webb); Aaron Shields (Harley Underwood); Robert Peterson (Jim Webb); Mussef Sibay (Earp); Lynn Bieler (Stone); Roberta Eaton (Cheri); Kirk Kinsinger (Radio Voice).

LOS ANGELES TIMES, 7/7/95, Calendar/p. 16, Peter Rainer

"The Crude Oasis" takes a long time getting to where it wants to go. Since we're generally way ahead of it anyway, this is a problem.

Karen Webb (Jennifer Taylor) lives in a Kansas nowheresville with a blank husband (Robert Peterson) who disappears every night. Suicidal, plagued by recurring bad dreams, she encounters a gas station attendant (Aaron Shields) who is the mysterious star of those dreams. Instead of attempting to end it all, she secretly follows the guy on his nightly rounds at an out-of-the-way bar.

Alex Graves, the first-time writer-director, made this feature in two weeks for about $25,000. He's trying for a rural noir with Southern Gothic vibes, and it's not an easy meld. (Steve Kloves, the writer-director of "Flesh and Bone" a few years back, *almost* most did it.)

The actors mostly seem to be in a fog and the snail's pace doesn't make you want to find out if they'll pull out of it. There's a good lovemaking scene back-dropped by a prairie lightning storm that indicates Graves might one day make a good florid movie if he keeps his eyes open and his head clear.

NEW YORK POST, 7/7/95, p. 41, Thelma Adams

"The Crude Oasis" might have made a respectable calling card for University of Southern California film grad Alex Graves. It might not please audiences, but the producer/ writer/director demonstrates he can move actors from Point A to Point B, create atmosphere and tell most of a story on a shoestring budget.

Unfortunately, Miramax Films is releasing it to theaters at the height of the summer. Sounds like a dump to me.

Set in a dreary Kansas of the mind, three characters lead a prairie dog's life in the shadow of an oil refinery. In the ominous silence between thunderstorms, they form a love triangle after which, of course, *no one will ever be the same.*

The once-pretty Karen Webb (Jennifer Taylor), a mad housewife of the two-car-garage set, waits nervously in the trough between nervous breakdowns. She's not even practical enough to manage her own suicide.

Karen's oil exec hubby (played with wormy zeal by Robert Peterson) trundles off to work each morning in suit, tie and shiny new car. At night, the balding, pointy-chinned spouse—a Dagwood/Dennis Hopper—slips off the Serta sleeper for a mysterious rendezvous.

Alone, terrified by the endless nodding of the oil derrick outside her window, Karen dreams of a dangerous drifter with greasy hair and a pointy devil's beard. He turns out to be local as gas jockey and trailer trash Harley Underwood (Aaron Shields), a prairie slacker with an uncanny knack for predicting the weather.

Graves manages to make everything ominous: from the rising and falling of the electric garage door opener and the image of Karen vacuuming a white rug in white pumps to the relatively harmless roadside tavern called the Crude Oasis. On the radio, storms are always in the forecast.

Metaphorically, the crude oasis seems to be the moment of sexual bliss Harley shares with Karen in the emotional desert that is her marriage.

The big bang occurs after an arresting series of images in which Graves simply aims his camera at the horizon as the Kansas clouds do their thing in a spectacular meteorological display. The director holds this scene too long (cool image, huh? huh?). He follows it with an overwrought, straight-from-daytime-soaps sex scene. Caught in the headlights of Harley's pickup, drenched by the rain machines, we can see every rain drop play in the drifter's scraggly beard, every flaw in the housewife's chin.

An obligatory paranoid subplot about oil leaks and coverups at the local refinery never gets tied up—and we never get tied up in the lives of these vague characters sleepwalking through an American Gothic nightmare. When it was over, I sighed with relief and thought, "We're not in Kansas anymore, Toto."

NEWSDAY, 7/10/95, Part II/p. B11, Gene Seymour

"The Crude Oasis" is an appropriate title for this film, the cinematic equivalent of a pond overstuffed with red herrings.

Granted, it's a *scenic* little pond that writer-director Alex Graves has set up—with its big-sky landscapes, its tricky visual insinuations, its ornate, rain-soaked love scene.

For all its excesses, the film leaves little doubt that Graves, one of the many fine products of the University of Southern California film school, can make an atmospheric movie. Trouble is, there's no story here to speak of.

Well, actually, there may be pieces of several stories strewn throughout this extended nightmare of Karen Webb (Jennifer Taylor), the high-strung wife of an oil executive (Robert Peterson). Karen, who's just recently recovered from a nervous breakdown, keeps having these strange dreams in which a goateed young man wearing a silver cross is coming toward her through a windswept stream.

Each night, she wakes up, startled, from her dream. And each night, her husband is missing from their bed. He tells her that problems with oil runoff into a nearby river are calling him into the company at odd hours. She thinks, Yeah, right.

Adding to Karen's brushfire of anxieties are radio reports of a missing woman, presumed dead, with emotional problems similar to her own. Karen attempts suicide in her two-car garage, but finds there's not enough gas to finish the job. So she drives to a local station, where she finds ... her Dream Guy, so to speak, working the pump.

His name's Harley Underwood (Aaron Shields), and neither she nor we know quite what to make of him at first. She follows him from the station on a long night's crawl that takes them both, at one point, to this roadside tavern called the Crude Oasis, which, like much of the film, looks a lot more forbidding than it actually is.

Graves gooses our expectations at every step, freighting every sequence with menace and portent. He's obviously bright enough to know what buttons to push. When he clears away the red herrings, he delivers an altogether unexpected resolution that could have been genuinely moving. But after so much elaborate tickling, the emotional payoff is so relatively slight that you feel a bit like you're at the receiving end of a clever but not-very-funny practical joke.

VILLAGE VOICE, 7/11/95, p. 54, Gary Dauphin

Writer-director Alex Graves certainly knows the script for up-and-coming film-school grads. Shot in two weeks for a paltry $25,000, his *The Crude Oasis* is an occasionally decent freshman effort that works best when viewed as a Miramax-distributed calling card, which means its true milieu is the festival or private screening, preferably held for the folks in the film biz who finance sophomore efforts.

Aggressively atmospheric in that demonstrative way common to better-financed film-school projects (Look, Mom! Foley editors!), *Oasis* follows housewife Karen Webb (onetime *Edge of Night* regular Jennifer Taylor) as a series of increasingly portentous omens appear on her previously empty Kansas horizon. Caught in a childless and (according to the film) therefore loveless marriage, Karen is the type of woman you'd expect to find ghosting the edges of a Todd Haynes flick: Wracked with nightmares, by day she wanders blankly around her house in white heels while the pistons of oil rigs pump monotonously in the background. The overall texture of Karen's world comes from such backdrops, boiling down to a combination of sterile midwestern visuals (stark shots of the Kansas landscape predominate) and intrusive ambient noise (Graves is also credited as *Oasis*'s sound designer, which might explain the constant sounds of car wheels on gravel, AM radio, department store Muzak, and so on).

Karen's rail of a husband (Robert Peterson) disappears for long stretches on a nightly basis, leaving Karen to wrestle with dreams of a mystery man who walks out of a nearby river in affectedly eerie slo-mo. If it looks at first as if these visions are scaring the living daylights out of Karen, her tossing and turning soon takes on a decidedly less Stephen King cast when she starts rising out of her empty marital bed to stare out at those rigs, pumping, pumping, pumping. Taylor's Karen has a kind of Dana Delany-on-expired-antidepressants thing going: Morose and just-plain-not-getting-any, she decides to end it all, but runs out of gas during an attempted suicide via carbon monoxide poisoning. Venturing out to the filling station in her house dress, Karen discovers that Harley (Aaron Shields, playing the local nozzle jockey) is none other than the man from her dreams, and from there she spends the rest of the film following him around on various errands, business that eventually comes to involve her husband, the town dive (called "The Crude Oasis") and Harley's trailer of the lonely Kansas prairie.

An already lethargic film, *Oasis* expands precious energy lobbing plotline possibilities at the audience, the director testing the waters with a number of moods and genres that suggest future film projects more than they enliven the one at hand. Is Karen's husband having an affair? Who is the "missing woman" the newscasts on Karen's car radio keep updating her about? And what's that Harley is trying to pull out of the river? Graves has enough on the ball to answer some of these questions with quietly neat twists (his closing image of Karen is a surprising breath of fresh air), but *The Crude Oasis* ends up a solid résumé builder and little more. Graves may thank Spike Lee, Richard Linklater, Gregg Araki, and Roberto Rodriguez for their inspiration in the film's earnest closing credits, but *El Mariachi* or *Slacker* it ain't.

Also reviewed in:
CHICAGO TRIBUNE, 7/7/95, Friday/p. K, John Petrakis
NEW YORK TIMES, 7/7/95, p. C10, Stephen Holden
VARIETY, 7/10-16/95, p. 35, Godfrey Cheshire
WASHINGTON POST, 7/8/95, p. F3, Rita Kempley

CRY, THE BELOVED COUNTRY

A Miramax Films release of a Distant Horizon production in association with Alpine Films and Videovision Entertainment. *Executive Producer:* Harry Allan Towers, Sudhir Pragjee, and Sanjeev Singh. *Producer:* Anant Singh. *Director:* Darrell James Roodt. *Screenplay:* Ronald Harwood. *Based on the novel by:* Alan Paton. *Director of Photography:* Paul Gilpin. *Editor:* David Heitner. *Music:* John Barry. *Music Editor:* Clif Kohlweck. *Sound:* Richard Sprawson and (music) Shawn Murphy. *Casting:* Marina Van Tonder. *Production Designer:* David Barkham. *Art Director:* Roland Hunter. *Set Dresser:* Emelia Roux. *Costumes:* Ruy Filipe. *Make-up (James Earl Jones):* Gabriella Molnar. *Make-up (Richard Harris):* Colin Polson. *Stunt Coordinator:* Gavin Mey. *Running time:* 108 minutes. *MPAA Rating:* PG-13.

CAST: Tsholofelo Wechoemang (Child); Richard Harris (James Jarvis); James Earl Jones (Rev. Stephen Kumalo); Dolly Rathebe (Mrs. Kumalo); Ramolao Makhene (Mpanza); Jack Robinson (Ian Jarvis); Jennifer Steyn (Mary Jarvis); Patrick Ndlovu (Man 1); Darlington Michaels (Man 2); King Twala (Man 3); Somizi Mhlongo (Young Thief); Sam Ngakane (Mafolo); Vusi Kunene (Theophilus Msimangu); John Whiteley (Father Vincent); Lillian Dube (Mrs. Lithebe); Temise Times (Shebeen Queen); Tiny Masilo (Brothel Singer); Babes Jazz Band (Jazz Band); Dambisa Kente (Gertrude Kumalo); Fats Bookholane and George Phologane (Brothel Men); Morena Sefatsa (Nephew); Charles S. Dutton (John Kumalo); Sydney Chama (Dubula); Moses Rakharebe (Tomlinson); Ron Smerczak (Captain van Jaarsveld); Tobias Sikwayo (Thomas); Anne Curteis (Mrs. Jarvis); Abigail Kubeka (Mrs. Mkize); Jerry Mofokeng (Hlabeni, Taxi Driver); Grace Mahlaba (Nurse); Ian Roberts (Evans); Leleti Khumalo (Katie); Jonathan Rands (Glyn Henderson); Shirley Johnston (Barbara Henderson); Ben Kruger (Police Officer 1); Dan

Robbertse (Police Officer 2);   Eric Miyeni (Absalom Kumalo);   Patrick Shai (Robert Ndela);   Robert Whithead (Carmichael);   David Clatworthy (Clerk of the Court);   Themba Ndaba (Matthew Kumalo);   Louis Seboko (Johannes Pafuri);   Graham Armitage (Judge);   Greg Latter (Prosecutor);   Thomas Hall (Court Usher);   Chris Steyn (Warder 1);   Antonio Rodrigues (Warder 2);   Stuart Monthieth (Warder 3);   Alfred D. Nokwe (Old Man);   Lorraine Nyathikazi (Apron Woman);   David Phetoe (Black Priest).

CHRISTIAN SCIENCE MONITOR, 12/15/95, p. 12, David Sterritt

In one of the most resounding political developments of recent years, institutionalized racism has been overthrown in South Africa after four decades of oppressive rule. But like the Holocaust and other 20th-century traumas, the apartheid system must continue to be remembered and pondered by those who suffered through it.

Therefore it's fitting that the first major film produced under South Africa's new regime is "Cry, the Beloved Country," based on an Alan Paton novel written in the 1940s as a passionate protest against racial inequality. Finding the story as resonant as ever in the post-apartheid era, a team of South African filmmakers has brought it to the screen in an interpretation that's as noteworthy for its intelligence and emotional force as for its powerful stand against racism and repression.

The main character is Kumalo (played by James Earl Jones), a black Anglican priest in a Zulu mountain village. Although he and his wife have tried to raise their family in a wise and constructive way, their son Absalom has moved to Johannesburg and fallen in with dubious company.

Visiting the city to rescue his sister from difficulties of her own, Kumalo discovers that Absalom is being held for the murder of a white man—and not just any white man, but one known for liberal views and a staunch hatred of apartheid.

Kumalo tries desperately to help Absalom, but everything works against him, and the young man is sentenced to death. Returning home, Kumalo receives comfort from an unexpected source—the murdered man's father (Richard Harris), a longtime apartheid supporter who has been enlightened by the moral strength of his deceased son's views.

As directed by Darrell James Roodt, a noted South African filmmaker, "Cry the Beloved Country" is a slow and sometimes ungainly tale that makes few concessions to current box-office fashions. Its idiosyncrasies are outweighed, however by the sense of quiet dignity that runs below the picture's deceptively still surface.

Equally important are the thematic threads that run through the movie. Chief among these is a clear-eyed opposition not only to apartheid, but also to all systems that divide people and bestow arbitrary power on one group over another. Also present is a recognition of the evils attached to capital punishment, seen here as a violent and vindictive tool devoid of moral or practical justification. And it's refreshing to see the strength Kumalo receives from active dedication to his religious ideas.

Written by Ronald Harwood and produced by Anant Singh, two of Roodt's fellow South Africans, the movie is being released in American theaters by Miramax Films, which has mobilized an impressive roster of supporters on its behalf. The premiere screening in New York was introduced by Hillary Rodham Clinton, who praised its commitment to human rights, and followed with a speech by South African President Nelson Mandela, who called it a "monument to the future," stressing its value not as a record of the past but as a pointer to progress.

With its humane view of social and personal hardships, and its reminder that religion can contribute to political growth in ways neither mean-spirited nor narrow-minded, the movie has much to teach American audiences as well as their South African counterparts.

LOS ANGELES TIMES, 12/15/95, Calendar/p. 18, Kevin Thomas

For a lot of Americans, Zoltan Korda's 1951 film of South African novelist Alan Paton's "Cry, the Beloved Country" served as an unforgettable introduction to the evils of apartheid, and had inescapable application to the still heavily segregated United States of the early '50s.

The makers of the handsome, period-perfect new version of Paton's novel, which also became the basis of the stage and film musical "Lost in the Stars," seem to understand that they cannot hope for the impact of revelation of the original film.

Yet there are understandable reasons for a remake at this time, and the new "Cry, the Beloved Country" confers a mythic, tragic dimension to South Africa's brutal past while evoking a spiritual dimension in pointing to a future of racial equality and harmony.

What director Darrell James Roodt (a South African) and screenwriter Ronald Harwood (an Englishman born in Cape Town) have done is to stage the Johannesburg odyssey of rural black minister Stephen Kumalo as an enactment of a familiar kind of ritual—one akin to a Nativity play in which everyone's demeanor and behavior is formal and symbolic and in which everything that occurs has the quality of inevitability.

It may well have been the best approach to a story written in 1946—during, incidentally, a brief period of postwar hope for a changing South Africa that was dashed when already crushing de facto segregation became official South African government policy in 1948.

With his towering presence and deep voice, James Earl Jones is perfectly cast as Kumalo, who reluctantly leaves the beautiful countryside for the big city he has never seen to visit his sister (Dambisa Kente), reportedly desperately ill but in reality driven to prostitution.

Meanwhile, his younger brother John (Charles S. Dutton) has lost faith in Christianity and has become a civil rights leader organizing a bus boycott. The pastor now decides to search for his estranged son Absalom (Eric Miyeni), only to catch up with him in prison, where he has been arrested for shooting to death a white man during a robbery attempt. Absalom, who admits to the shooting, insists it was accidental, a response to overwhelming fear.

In a stunning coincidence of double irony, the victim turns out not only to have been a dedicated activist on behalf of blacks but also the son of the pastor's neighbor, a rich Afrikaans farmer, James Jarvis (Richard Harris), a firm but not virulent segregationist.

All of this unfolds eloquently, with both Jones and Harris depicting two men no less strong for revealing vulnerability. The gaunt Harris, so good at showing grief beneath pride, is asked to portray a man who undergoes a profound change of heart, enabling him to accept rather than reject his late son's views and to form a bond with the similarly bereft pastor that transcends racial barriers. Harris is quite capable of this but deserves more screen time to keep this transformation from seeming so abrupt.

The film's key relationship, however, is between the pastor and the vibrant young Johannesburg priest (Vusi Kunene, who brings a vital spark to a somber film) who befriends him, broadening the older man's understanding in the process.

In bringing "Cry, the Beloved Country" to the screen in such a resolutely traditional style at this point in South Africa's history, it was probably impossible to avoid a certain feeling of self-consciousness, even self-importance. These qualities unfortunately are reinforced by John Barry's soaring old-fashioned score, the kind that immediately evokes all those old screen epics glorifying the British empire. Fortunately, in image and structure Roodt and Harwood go for a steadfast simplicity that builds to a beautiful moment of rekindled faith for the grieving Rev. Kumalo that lifts "Cry, the Beloved Country" to a climactic moment of redemption.

NEW YORK POST, 12/15/95, p. 52, Michael Medved

The new film version of Alan Paton's 1946 novel "Cry, the Beloved Country" boasts the same virtues as its excellent musical score by John ("Out of Africa") Barry—it is sweeping, slow, weighty, lyrical, and full of throbbing bass notes.

James Earl Jones plays Stephen Kumalo, a simple, kindly pastor in a back country village in the picturesque mountains of South Africa. His story begins when he makes his first trip to the bustling city of Johannesburg to redeem his sister (who's fallen into drunkenness and prostitution) and to try to make contact with his son (Eric Miyeni), who's gone to work in the mines but then disappeared.

In his quest, Kumalo expects little help from his long-lost brother (Charles S. Dutton) who's become a prominent activist in the black nationalist movement—and a non-believer. "How can he have the truth on his side—without God?" the pastor asks.

From the beginning, Kumalo's journey has a hellish dimension, but he receives shelter and assistance from a fellow Anglican priest (the superb South African actor Vusi Kunene), who insists, "I am a cynical and selfish man. But God put his hands on me."

Together, the two clerics search for Kumalo's missing son, who's made his way from reform school to impregnating a good-hearted young woman out of wedlock.

Finally, they learn that the unfortunate young man is now implicated in the pointless murder of a white idealist who had dedicated his life to helping native Africans in their struggle for justice.

Coincidentally, this victim was the only son of the wealthiest landowner of Kumalo's district (Richard Harris), who has also come to Johannesburg. After a chance encounter, the pastor begs forgiveness from the neighbor he scarcely knows—recognizing that they are both shattered fathers, bound grief.

Previous adaptations of this classic tale appeared in 1951 (with young Sidney Poitier in a supporting role) and in 1974, as "Lost in the Stars," with distracting Broadway songs by Kurt Weill and Maxwell Anderson. Both earlier treatments emphasized political dimensions of the story, hoping to mobilize world opinion against apartheid, but now, with apartheid a thing of the past, the latest movie focuses on personal, intimate aspects of the story.

As a result, the white farmer, brilliantly played by Harris in some of the subtlest, most intense work of his flamboyant career, emerges with more complexity and compassion than he ever has before. It is Jones, however, who dominates the movie, with an altogether noble (and Oscar-worthy) performance as a man of rocklike, unshakable faith, creating, against all odds, a figure every bit as compelling as the characterization in Paton's novel.

Thirty-two-year-old director Darrell James Roodt—who previously made the disappointing anti-apartheid message movie "Sarafina!"—here makes full use of the authentic South African landscape, providing stunning vistas of the craggy, lush green mountains around Kumalo's home.

The filmmaker takes his time, letting the force of the history build gradually, and at times his work does seem self-consciously impressed with itself. But the amazing thing about "Cry, the Beloved Country" is how often this poetic film manages to live up to its own lofty ambitions.

NEWSDAY, 12/15/95, Part II/p. B3, John Anderson

Every now and then—no, more like once in a blue moon—a film comes along that makes you doubt your own cynicism. I have to admit that while watching Darrell James Roodt's "Cry, the Beloved Country," I was put off by the earnestness of both the script and the performances of its stars, Richard Harris and James Earl Jones. Everything about it said noble, which is usually a bad sign.

By the end of the film, I was asking myself: What's so bad about noble? What's my problem with earnest?

My problem is that experience has taught us that a film so righteously intent on saying something good about humanity usually falters, and what we learn about humanity is its inability to make films that accept, goodness as a reality. The accomplishment of "Cry, the Beloved Country" is that it leaves you believing it believes in itself. And you, in turn, believe in it.

Based on the 1946 novel by Alan Paton, which has been required reading in high school lit classes for three generations, director Roodt's film is the first version shot in South Africa (it was filmed once before in 1951 with Sidney Poitier; the book-based Kurt Weill-Maxwell Anderson musical "Lost in the Stars" was made in 1974). Producer Anant Singh bought the rights to the novel five years ago, but was so intent on filming in the land where the book was born that he waited until apartheid was abolished and democracy installed. So there's an implied sense of closure about the whole production.

The story itself is simple and, were redemption not its point, would seem tragically Greek. Stephen Kumalo (James Earl Jones), a poor pastor from the Zulu countryside, receives a letter and knows it can portend no good. It prompts him to leave for the city, where members of his family—including his son Absalom (Eric Miyeni) have gone before him. What he finds is a sister, Gertrude (Dambisa Kente), who has turned to prostitution; a brother, John (Charles S. Dutton), who has turned to political activism and away from God; and a son who has turned to crime: Absalom has been to jail, has impregnated a young girl (Leleti Khumalo) out of wedlock and, now, is suspected of the murder of the liberal son of a wealthy white reactionary, James Jarvis (Richard Harris).

Roodt is no visionary. He miscalculates in spending so much time on Kumalo's search for his son, which meanders through Johannesburg to no real purpose. Father and son will be reunited—Kumalo finds him frightened, claiming the shooting was accidental—and Kumalo will come face to face with the father of his son's victim. But while the director flounders visually—the South African landscapes are gorgeous, but that's not his doing—he does know enough to get out of the way of his two old pros.

In his portrayal of Jarvis, Richard Harris reminds us how he got to be Richard Harris. His control is extraordinary, as is his daring: There are scenes of grief—Jarvis first learning of his son's death, for instance—where a lesser actor would crack and a lesser director would bail out. But Roodt lingers on Harris, and Harris pays him back for the confidence.

Jones is not, you may want to remember, just the voice of CNN or Darth Vader, or a monument, but an actor of considerable depth. As Kumalo, he carries the world on his back and his heart on his sleeve. You become thoroughly convinced that this is a man whose soul, although sorely tested and scourged, is too great to break.

"Cry, the Beloved Country" is a spiritual film that doesn't ask very much of you except to let down your guard. The payback is well worth turning vulnerable for two hours.

VILLAGE VOICE, 12/19/95, p. 82, Gary Dauphin

There's a stifling seriousness to *Cry, the Beloved Country*, that chokes life out of it even as the film preaches the gospel of secular rebirth. Not only the big screen version of Alan Paton's 47-year-old novel, *Cry* is also the first major motion picture to come out of the country since Nelson Mandela's election. Endorsed by the black President as a "monument to the future," *Cry* the movie founders under the weight of such burdens, its wide release—friendly mixture of slick sentimentality and world-beat visual spice an ill-chosen foundation for the emotions it hopes to evoke.

Directed by Darrell James Roodt with the same smoothly manipulative touch he brought to his other S.A. uplift film *Sarafina!*, *Cry* tells a simple enough story. Two fathers (James Earl Jones and Richard Harris) are brought together when the black son murders the white son, the older men having previously known one another with only the nodding familiarity you'd expect to find between a black rural minister and a white landowner in 1940s South Africa. This setup had room for subtlety and nuance in the novel, but here it devolves into rote tearjerking. Jones settles into the bent attitude of addled martyrdom common to depictions of the black and old. While Harris rings false at every turn. Given such performances, the characters' inevitable accommodation doesn't convey Paton's sense of the goodness in people, but instead illustrates how anger wanes with age.

Also reviewed in:
CHICAGO TRIBUNE, 12/20/95, Tempo/p. 3, John Petrakis
NEW YORK TIMES, 12/15/95, p. C27, Stephen Holden
VARIETY, 9/25-10/1/95, p. 94, Leonard Klady
WASHINGTON POST, 12/20/95, p. C6, Hal Hinson
WASHINGTON POST, 12/22/95, Weekend/p. 43, Desson Howe

CURE, THE

A Universal Pictures and Island Pictures release. *Executive Producer:* Todd Baker and Bill Borden. *Producer:* Mark Burg and Eric Eisner. *Director:* Peter Horton. *Screenplay:* Robert Kuhn. *Director of Photography:* Andrew Dintenfass. *Editor:* Anthony Sherin. *Music:* Dave Grusin. *Music Editor:* Scott Grusin. *Sound:* Matthew Quast. *Sound Editor:* Anthony J. Miceli. *Casting:* Mali Finn. *Production Designer:* Armin Ganz. *Art Director:* Troy Sizemore. *Set Decorator:* Claire Bowin. *Set Dresser:* Jason Wolf. *Special Effects:* Paul Murphy. *Costumes:* Louise Frogley. *Make-up:* Darcy Knight. *Stunt Coordinator:* Steve Davison. *Running time:* 95 minutes. *MPAA Rating:* PG-13.

CAST: Brad Renfro (Erik); Aeryk Egan (Tyler); Delphine French (Tyler's Girlfriend); Andrew Broder (Tyler's Buddy); Jeremy Howard (Tyler's Buddy #2); Joseph Mazzello (Dexter); Annabella Sciorra (Linda); Diana Scarwid (Gail); Rosemary Corman (Elderly Woman in Street);

T. Mychael Rambo (Garbage Man #1); David Alan Smith (Garbage Man #2); Delia Jurek (Angry Woman); Fran Korba (Elderly Woman in Market); John Lynch (Skipper #1); John Beasley (Skipper #2); Raymond Nelson (Skipper #3); Scott Stockton (Skipper #4); Dale Handevidt (Skipper #5); Nicky Katt (Pony); Craig Gierl (Jim); Renée Humphrey (Angle); Laurie A. Sinclair (Cheryl); Stephen D'Ambrose (Bus Station Clerk); Shirley Venard (Nurse Snyder); Mary McCusker (Nurse Murphy); Bruce Davison (Dr. Stevens); Peter Moore (Male Nurse); Rodney W. England (Final Doctor); Bill Schoppert (Funeral Director); Samantha Lemole (Funeral Attendant).

LOS ANGELES TIMES, 4/21/95, Calendar/p. 7, Kevin Thomas

"The Cure," a well-acted heart-tugger about two 11-year-old boys, one of whom has AIDS, works as a drama on friendship and its challenges, but has too many loose ends, too much that hasn't been thoroughly thought out. Where many films fall apart toward the finish, "The Cure" gets into gear at last but too late to redeem earlier flaws.

It opens with a vexing vagueness that undercuts all that follows. We don't know where its charming small-town setting is supposed to be; the end credits tell us we've been in Stillwater, Minn. For reasons we never learn, a single mother, Linda (Annabella Sciorra) has just moved there with her son Dexter (Joseph Mazzello). Apparently, their next-door neighbors, a bitter divorcée Gail (Diana Scarwid) and her son Erik (Brad Renfro) are seemingly also fairly recent arrivals; we don't know why Gail, a real estate broker, has picked out this obscure community either. We never learn what happened to Dexter's father.

Apparently, Erik is sufficiently unhappy and new in town that he hasn't made any friends. He bluntly tells Dexter across the fence that having a "faggot" for a neighbor is not going to help matters for him. When Dexter replies he got AIDS via a blood transfusion, Erik accepts him with a credibility-defying rapidity.

Shortly thereafter, the boys are beset by bullies, also slurring Erik. Erik stands up for Dexter but later admits that he doesn't understand how he could associate with "homos" during his hospital stays. Intentionally or not, writer Robert Kuhn lets stand a distinction between straights and gays infected with the AIDS virus when he might better have suggested that all people with AIDS, regardless of sexual orientation, are worthy of compassion.

Dexter and Erik are exceptionally bright and articulate lads, as is usual for "sensitive" Hollywood films, so it is difficult to accept that they'd try to run away to New Orleans, where Erik's father lives and where a man with a purported cure for AIDS also lives.

They've read about him in a supermarket tabloid and told Linda, who responds with tactful skepticism, suggesting that Dexter discuss the matter with his doctor.

It's therefore all the harder to believe they'd actually take off—especially with only $40 and a limited supply of medicine for Dexter.

Despite all these flaws, actor Peter Horton, in his feature directing debut, does elicit beautifully drawn and sustained portrayals from his young actors and also from Sciorra, whose mother—gallant, tough-minded, loving yet vulnerable—is perhaps the film's most fully realized individual, even though we don't know as much about her as we could.

As for Scarwid, this fine actress is stuck with yet another thankless role, this time as a nasty, ignorant wino. Bruce Davison appears briefly but effectively as Dexter's staunch physician.

All told, "The Cure" plays more like a movie made for TV than the big screen.

NEW YORK POST, 4/21/95, p. 49, Michael Medved

Two lonely 11-year-old-boys strike up a friendship over the fence that separates their backyards in a small town in Minnesota.

They're normal, all-American kids who spend their time in such uplifting pursuits as burning, impaling and hanging their plastic toy soldiers.

The only extraordinary aspect to their relationship is the fact that one of them is dying of AIDS (from a blood transfusion), and is therefore shunned and taunted by most of his classmates.

When the two lads read a tabloid headline about a new cure for the disease allegedly developed by a doctor in New Orleans, they decide to run away from home and head down the mighty Mississippi in pursuit of this forlorn hope.

That's the heart-tugging setup for "The Cure," which turns out to be far more moving and satisfying than we have any right to expect thanks to the superbly sensitive directing by Peter Horton (best known from his acting role in TVs "thirtysomething") in his big-screen filmmaking debut.

Horton not only captures the green, placid beauty of summertime mid-America with an almost elegiac eloquence, but draws complex emotions from even the most minor scenes and relationships in the script.

The most intriguing of those relationships involves the frail but intrepid AIDS kid (brilliantly played by Joseph Mazello of "Jurassic Park," "Shadowlands" and "The River Wild") and his adoring single mother, Annabella Sciorra.

Her career-best performance allows us to feel not only her heroic character's emotions but also, in an extraordinary achievement of acting alchemy, to virtually read her thoughts as she struggles with an impossible situation.

Given their status as new arrivals in town, Sciorra naturally welcomes her son's blossoming friendship with the broad-shouldered, impetuous kid next door.

Brad Renfro, who made his movie debut as the title character in "The Client," is even better here, playing a troubled but good-hearted boy who seems endearing in even his most lunkheaded excesses—like forcing his sick pal to drink experimental tea brewed from various leaves they harvest from the woods in hopes of discovering some miraculous potion.

Though blessed with robust health, Renfro's character bears the burden of an embittered, hard-drinking divorcee of a mother (played by Diana Scarwid in yet another of the film's perfectly pitched performances) who wants to stop her son from associating with what she considers their potentially infectious neighbors.

With all these nicely sketched nuances, the picture never needed its big, credibility-stretching downriver adventure on a Huckleberry Finn-style raft.

This episode also seems to justify (and even glorify) outright theft from some tattooed, twentysomething drifters who help the boys with a ride on their cabin cruiser.

The film also suffers from a thick-as-molasses film score by Dave Grusin that tries to tell you how you're supposed to be reacting to nearly every scene—and often gets it wrong, by undermining the fundamental truth of acting.

Nevertheless, the emotional impact is cumulative and considerable, so a box of a kleenex is required equipment at the theater. There is, of course, no real "Cure" for the tragedy the movie describes, but the sort of friendship the two boys enjoy, and the heartfelt filmmaking that brings it to life on screen, certainly helps to ease the pain.

NEWSDAY, 4/21/95, Part II/p. B7, John Anderson

Gail (Diana Scarwid) is semi-alcoholic, and semi-absentee. If she were around more—and more sober when she was around—she'd know that her son Erik (Brad Renfo has become best friends with Dexter (Joseph Mazello), the dreaded "AIDS kid" next door; that Dexter's mother, Linda (Annabella Sciorra), has practically adopted Erik; that Linda is everything Gail is not, and that Gail herself is something of a dope about AIDS, and kids, and her stalled-out life.

But "The Cure" isn't about Gail, who goes to work every day, drowns her sorrows in zinfandel every night and embodies most of the preconceptions and biases middle America harbors toward people with AIDS. Everyone besides Erik shuns Dexter in their suffocated little town. And the only reason Erik and Dexter hook up is that they're both outcasts—Dexter for obvious reasons, Erik because his attitude and Louisiana accent mark him as odd in Minnesota.

Otherwise, they're quite different: Dexter is bright and wry, Erik duller and prone to bluntness. "My grandma says you're going to hell," Erik tells Dexter, who replies cheerily that Grandma must be a genius.

That Grandma works in a Kmart becomes a recurring joke in "The Cure." Which is cheap. If you're making a movie that's supposed to be a plea for understanding, why be snobbish about who works where? And why not hint at the real, hand-to-mouth existence endured by a single parent of a child with AIDS? Because you'd have a box-office debacle. That's why both Linda and Gail live in rambling homes in a pasteurized suburb and don't have real money worries or, for that matter, real lives. This makes for comfortable viewing, but it isn't about AIDS.

The best way to watch "The Cure" is as a young-buddy movie in which the two principals have only a passing acquaintance with intelligence. The movie's centerpiece is an extended trip along the Mississippi toward New Orleans, where Erik and Dexter think a doctor has found a cure for AIDS; they read it in a supermarket tabloid. They get in trouble with some low-life characters, including one young woman named Angel (Renee Humphrey) whose tattoo reads "Angle." This is more white-trash bashing, of course, and a way to let the audience feel superior, in a movie about a disease about which none of us can feel very superior or confident or immune.

SIGHT AND SOUND, 8/96, p. 47, Vicky Allan

Stillwater, Minnesota, the beginning of the school holidays. Ever since Dexter, a boy who caught Aids from a blood transfusion, moved in next door, neighbourhood tough Erik has been teased by local kids. Yet he befriends Dexter and, when they pass a gang who shout "faggot", he stands up to them, initiating a supermarket trolley chase. Erik's mother, Gail, warns her son to avoid their neighhour, but Erik nevertheless accepts Dexter's invitation to dinner to meet his mother, Linda.

To help Dexter find the cure for Aids, Erik experiments with candy, which the two boys eat in sickening quantities. Then, he urges Dexter to try leaf tea. A story on the cover of the *National Examiner* claims that a Dr. Fishburne in New Orleans has found a cure. Realising the spuriousness of the article, Linda refuses to take the boys to see him. Erik and Dexter pursue their leaf experiments further—with devastating results: Dexter is poisoned. When Linda comes round to Erik's to find out which plant Dexter has eaten, Gail realises that the two boys have been seeing each other.

Dexter recovers, but Gail, determined that the boys will never see each other again, is planning to send Erik to summer camp. Instead, Erik runs away to New Orleans, persuading Dexter to go with him. They build a raft and follow their local stream down to the Mississippi hoping to reach New Orleans. They hitch a lift on a motor boat owned by two young men, Pony and Jim. But the men take two women on board and moor up for a couple of days.

Running out of medicine, Dexter begins to feel ill. He gets scared in the night, so Erik gives him his baseball boot for security. When Pony and Jim refuse to move on, Erik steals back the money he paid them and he and Dexter set off hitch-hiking by road. Pony and Jim catch up with them and chase them for the money. Dexter slits his hand, threatening, "My blood is like poison," and the two men run away. Erik then takes Dexter home to his mother. Dexter is taken into hospital; Erik visits him and, eventually, Dexter dies. At the funeral Erik places his baseball boot in the coffin, then he takes one of Dexter's shoes and sends it floating downstream.

This latest film to tackle the Aids tragedy has the summer holiday adventures of two 11-year-old boys as its unexpected framework. More a rites-of-passage drama than a disease movie, *The Cure* (thirtysomething actor and sometime director Peter Horton's feature debut) merely touches on Aids issues of prejudice and misinformation, saving its energies for its core concern: childhood friendship. The film charts the blossoming buddy-dom between a local tough boy, Erik, and his quirky HIV + neighbour, Derek, who is beginning to suffer from Aids-related symptoms. In the tradition of Mark Twain's novels, *Huckleberry Finn* and *Tom Sawyer*, *The Cure*, comes complete with river adventures, life lessons and poignant illustrations of morality.

With a plot that could so easily have plunged into TV-movie sentimentality, *The Cure* relies heavily on its two child stars for credibility. Playing Erik, the rebel who matures from burning dolls hair and vandalising school seats into semi-adult responsibility, Brad Renfro is something of a mini-James Dean. Like River Phoenix in *Stand By Me*, he is all guts and instinct and he plays Erik as a boy of reckless bravado. He made his name as the wild-child witness caught in the middle of *The Client*. By contrast, the performance of Joseph Mazzello—aready a veteran, having been in *Jurassic Park, Shadowlands* and *The River Wild* as Dexter is one of low-key and unlaboured sensitivity. The two are an ideal 'odd couple' in the same mould as Dustin Hoffman and Jon Voight in *Midnight Cowboy* or Tom Cruise and Hoffman in *Rain Man*. Without their rapport, *The Cure* would collapse under the weight of its middle-American backdrop of public bigotry and misunderstanding. Unfortunately, the only other character of any depth is Dexter's mother, Linda, played with patient stoicism by Annabella Sciorra. She, Erik and Dexter are surrounded by stereotypes. Erik has an 'evil' alcoholic mother, Gail, who warns him to stay clear of Dexter; the local kids call Erik "faggot" and his father—in keeping with the fashion for single-parents in such Hollywood movies as *E.T.* and *The Client*—is a voice at the end of a telephone line.

There is a moment when the boys' search for a cure, after experiments with herbal potions in their leafy Stillwater back-gardens, is taken out into the wide world as they embark on a journey to find the crank Doctor Fishburne in New Orleans. At this point *The Cure* shifts from a bright soap opera domesticity reminiscent of *The Wonder Years* and *thirtysomething* to action sequences. The film then becomes a boys' own adventure, complete with boats, knives, girls, chases and stolen money. Bewilderingly incongruous as they seem, these adventures form the real core of the film. The boys' quest for the unattainable cure is the transformative element in their lives, the process through which Erik comes to terms with his own limitations and accepts responsibility, and through which Dexter faces the inevitability of his death.

The Cure is a straightforward first feature for Horton, modest in its attempts to deal with social issues, but dedicated to its conjuring of childhood nostalgia. Ex-stand-up comedian Robert Kuhn's script is saved from over-sentimentality by his insistence on burnout in the face of adversity, as when Dexter dies while performing a gag. There are many such bittersweet moments, not least Erik's final act of placing the baseball boot in Dexter's coffin. By creating a sunny, world, where Dexter dies in sexual innocence and Erik experiences first grief, Horton and Kuhn have hitched Aids to a high-sentiment formula, but at least they've done it with delicacy.

Also reviewed in:
CHICAGO TRIBUNE, 4/21/95, Friday/p. M, Michael Wilmington
NEW YORK TIMES, 4/21/95, p. C12, Stephen Holden
VARIETY, 4/17-23/95, p. 36, Leonard Klady
WASHINGTON POST, 4/21/95, p. D1, Megan Rosenfeld

CUTTHROAT ISLAND

An MGM release of a Mario Kassar presentation of a Carolco/Forge production in association with Laurence Mark Productions and Beckner/Gorman Productions. *Executive Producer:* Mario Kassar. *Producer:* Joel B. Michaels, Laurence Mark, Renny Harlin, and James Gorman. *Director:* Renny Harlin. *Screenplay:* Robert King and Marc Norman. *Story:* Michael Frost Beckner, James Gorman, Bruce A. Evans and Raynold Gideon. *Director of Photography:* Peter Levy. *Editor:* Frank J. Urioste and Ralph E. Winters. *Music:* John Debney. *Music Editor:* Tom Carlson. *Sound:* Ivan Sharrock. *Sound Editor:* Michael Wilhoit. *Casting:* Mindy Marin. *Production Designer:* Norman Garwood. *Art Director:* Roger Cain and Keith Pain. *Set Decorator:* Maggie Gray. *Special Effects:* Allen Hall. *Costumes:* Enrico Sabbatini. *Make-up:* Paul Engelen. *Make-up (Geena Davis):* Ben Nye, Jr. *Stunt Coordinator:* Vic Armstrong. *Running time:* 123 minutes. *MPAA Rating:* PG-13.

CAST: Geena Davis (Morgan); Matthew Modine (Shaw); Frank Langella (Dawg); Maury Chaykin (John Reed); Patrick Malahide (Ainslee); Stan Shaw (Glasspoole); Rex Linn (Mr. Blair); Paul Dillon (Snelgrave); Chris Masterson (Bowen); Jimmie F. Skaggs (Scully); Harris Yulin (Black Harry); Carl Chase (Bishop); Peter Geeves (Fiddler Pirate); Angus Wright (Captain Trotter); Ken Bones (Toussant); Mary Pegler (Mandy Rickets); Mary Peach and Lucinda Aurel (Ladies); Thomas Lockyer (Lieutenant); Roger Booth (Auctioneer); George Murcell (Mordachai Fingers); Simon Atherton (Bartender); Dickey Beer (Executioner); Christopher Halliday (Hastings); Chris Johnston (Helmsman); Richard Leaf (Snake the Lookout); Tam White (Fleming); Rupert Vansittart (Captain Perkins).

LOS ANGELES TIMES, 12/22/95, Calendar/p. 1, Kenneth Turan

[*The following review by Kenneth Turan appeared in a slightly different form in* NEWSDAY, 12/22/95, Part II/p. B11.]

It shouldn't be surprising that movie stars are not immune from big-screen dreams of their own, but who would have guessed that Geena Davis harbored a secret desire to be Errol Flynn?

Yet here she is in "Cutthroat Island," sword-fighting, head-butting, groin-kicking and leaping around with a knife in her mouth. As Morgan Adams, "the notorious lady pirate" and scourge of the 17th-Century Caribbean, Davis seems to be having quite a good time, even if she does have to say lines like "Dawg will pay for this, I swear."

But though audiences may be pleased that Davis is enjoying herself, the more pertinent question is what's in it for the rest of us, and the answer is not encouraging. Stitched together by six writers and directed by Renny Harlin, "Cutthroat Island" is a bloated, jokey production whose motto, no doubt tattooed on the back of some poor assistant director's neck, could well be, "When in doubt, blow something up."

Costing untold millions of dollars, "Cutthroat" is filled with elaborate stunts and fiery explosions. Hordes of carpenters, welders, sand blasters and other minions combined to create enough on-screen chaos to topple the government of a banana republic. Full-sized ships, impressive waves, thousands of costumes accurate down to the shoelaces, anything and everything an unreasonable amount of money could buy has been pressed into service here.

But what no one seems to have remembered is that the great buccaneer movies, from Douglas Fairbanks Sr. in "The Black Pirate," to Flynn in "Captain Blood," to Burt Lancaster in "The Crimson Pirate," managed to forge a human connection between the audience and the action, something that this production has no idea how to do.

It's tempting but probably wrong to fault Harlin, Davis' husband, for this lack. One peek at his filmography, which includes "Cliffhanger" and "Die Hard 2," shows that his reputation as a shooter, someone who just wants to put the action on the screen, is well-founded. Let the overpaid writers worry about the dialogue and characterization; I'm busy setting up my Technocrane.

What those writers have come up with is a weary rehash of every pirate movie under the sun, complete with uninspired "take him away and hang him" dialogue and all manner of venerable brigand paraphernalia, including guys with peg legs, guys with tattoos, and a passel of cute monkey tricks.

Davis' Morgan Adams is the daughter of Black Harry and the granddaughter of a rather devilish pirate who captured and hid an enormous treasure and then divided the map showing the way among his three sons. Not only is Morgan eager to collect the pieces, so is Morgan's notorious uncle Dawg (Frank Langella), a particularly ruthless brigand with a blade serrated like a Sizzler steak knife.

Dragooned into service as a non-threatening leading man who wouldn't overshadow Davis is Matthew Modine, who after "Wind" should have known better than to take any part that took him near the water. He plays Will Shaw, a cheeky thief and liar who Morgan buys at a slave market a purchase she, though perhaps not the rest of us, eventually considers money well spent.

As for Davis, it's enough to say that she did not become a star by taking on roles that require her to throw as many punches as Jake LaMotta. If this picture gets her Errol Flynn obsession out of her system, we'll all be better off.

NEW YORK POST, 12/22/95, p. 50, Michael Medved

A secret map of buried treasure. Weathered skulls guarding gold doubloons. Furious sword play, storms at sea, shipwrecks, desert islands, tropical romance ...

"Cutthroat Island" recyles all the elements of traditional pirate movies, with one essential innovation: the dashing captain this time is a female. You know that she's supposed to be making some powerful feminist statement because she repeatedly assaults her male opponents in the groin with broad swords, clubs, torches, daggers, knees, feet and even cannon balls.

Geena Davis plays the 17th century swashbucklerette, but despite her thigh-high boots and piratical pout, there's something imperishably genial and sweet-natured about her, so that her director (and husband), Renny Harlin goes overboard trying to make her look tough and mean.

Again and again, she comes crashing to earth from great heights, and even survives a bullet in her hip (which is later graphically removed).

The script (a flimsy excuse tenuously linking spectacular action scenes) shows Davis inheriting her affirmative-action command from her pirate papa (Harris Yulin) who, just before he dies, tells of the fabled treasure of Cutthroat Island.

To translate the Latin on a mysterious map, she buys a sly, educated slave (Matthew Modine) at auction in Jamaica, but he's soon scheming to get the gold for himself.

She must also do battle with evil uncle (a splendidly effective Frank Langella), a black-hearted brigand with his own ship who's determined to claim the treasure as his own.

The ships and sets and costumes and stunts and lavish locations (Thailand and Malta) are all stunning—with director Harlin indulging the same special skill at world-class explosions he displayed in "Die Hard 2."

Human elements are far less satisfying, with the miscast Modine (a last-minute replacement for Michael Douglas) far too whiny and slimy to develop any romantic chemistry with Davis. The only authentic love this movie displays is for ancient cliches, which are indeed effectively freshened in this shamelessly silly but undeniably energetic exercise.

SIGHT AND SOUND, 4/96, p. 41, Leslie Felperin

Jamaica 1668. Morgan Adams, the daughter of the respected pirate, Black Harry Adams, races to save her father from being forced to walk the plank by his brother Dawg. Though she rescues her father, he is mortally wounded in the escape. Black Harry's dying bequest to Morgan is his scalp on which is tattooed a third of a map to CutThroat Island where the treasure of a Spanish galleon is buried. Morgan's other uncle, Mordachai Fingers, has another third of the map, and Dawg the final third. After being elected captain of Black Harry's ship, Morgan and her closest shipmates resolve to find a slave who speaks Latin and can thus help them decipher the map. Disguising themselves as gentry in Port Royal they purchase the slave William Shaw, a self-proclaimed doctor and convicted thief. Morgan's identity is discovered by the Governor's troops; she and her friends narrowly escape capture. They visit Mordachai at Spitalfields Harbour where they are discovered by Dawg and his brigands; they escape, this time with Mordachai's map and an idea of what the code signifies.

On their way to Crooked Man Keys, Morgan and Shaw share a romantic moment and then quarrel. A mutinous crew, led by a man in Dawg's pay, set Shaw, Morgan and a few men loyal to her adrift in a boat. During a storm Shaw is washed overboard. Morgan and her men come ashore at CutThroat Island where they find Shaw, who has one of the pieces of the map. Morgan and Shaw discover the treasure in a hidden cave, but, while looking for help to carry it out, Shaw is tricked by a treacherous crewmate and taken prisoner by the combined forces of Dawg and the Governor. Morgan returns to her ship, quells the mutineers and pursues the treasure now aboard Dawg's ship. After a long battle with cannons and cutlasses, Shaw and Morgan contrive to blow up Dawg's ship and save the treasure. Aboard her ship, all vote to divide the spoils and set sail for further adventures.

Having helped to sink Carolco, the company that bankrolled it, with its exorbitant costs, *CutThroat Island* washes up on these shores at last, trailing the flotsam of poor reviews and poorer box-office receipts in its wake. A hoary pastiche of pirate movies of old, tricked out in cast-off clichés (inscrutable maps, monkey sidekicks, quicksand) and groaning under the strain of being driven so hard (breathless chases, an endless final battle), it is a sorry hulk of a film.

CutThroat Island deserves a place on every young producers' induction syllabus as an exemplar of how much a film with seemingly everything going for it can go badly wrong. Renny Harlin earned a credible reputation as an action director after *Die Hard 2* and the gripping *Cliffhanger*. He's good at explosions and orchestrating huge set pieces, but he seems to lack the knack for storytelling or character development. So we have speedy action sequences at regular 10 minute intervals (some nicely done, such as the pursuit of Morgan and Shaw on a coach through Port Royale), but we are burdened with an overriding feeling of indifference as to who is caught or slain. After the third chase even the director seems to be nodding off, repeating certain choreographed moves in the fight scenes, beating out the same incessant rhythm as before.

Geena Davis and Matthew Modine are charismatic and competent leads, recognisable but not too over-exposed. Yet each turns in here the worst performance of their respective careers. Davis is somnolent for the most part, her usually expressive face drained of all emotion. Presumably she was trying to look commanding and authoritative as a woman pirate should. Instead, she looks exhausted, as if all she really wants is a long holiday in a cooler clime away from all this buccaneering.

Modine, mugging away with boyish smiles and half-hearted roguish gestures, seems equally lost. His most convincing moment comes when pleading desperately for rescue from a quicksand pit. Given the role he's stuck with, he hardly needs to delve deep into the Method for this. A crew of unimaginatively drawn supporting pirates and characters comes and goes, bad continuity visiting unexplained catastrophes on them (one man seems to lose an eye between scenes). Life is obviously cheap on the open seas, but editing is expensive.

This is a film that wants to sell itself to everyone but whose cost is too high at every turn. As an action film, it offers authentic sets and gunpowder aplenty—but who wants gunpowder when one can see more exciting gadgets (and better film craft) in any other blockbuster. At the same time, *CutThroat Island* is not a heritage film either, despite its vogueish revisionism (it has a proto-feminist heroine and a happy multiracial crew), since it is too riddled with anachronisms. One minor character is planning to "use all this nautical stuff to write a best-selling book". You expect a little historical distortion in movies, but this is too much. No one thought in those terms about books in 1668 or ever used such language—that's pure hack writing.

Pre-publicity suggests that *CutThroat Island* may be marketed as a children's film, it's handlers apparently resigned to thinking it may only be 'good enough' for kids. With its considerable quota of gore (a human scalp, lots of stab wounds, a nasty bullet retrieval from a conscious patient) it fails even as this. It has none of the creepy sense of menace of Alexander Mackendrick's *A High Wind in Jamaica*. The only hope now for Carolco's creditors to recoup their losses is that it finds an audience in the international market among prepubescent teenagers with a taste for shallow swashbucklers but who don't know the genre too well.

Also reviewed in:
CHICAGO TRIBUNE, 12/22/95, Friday/p. C, Michael Wilmington
NEW YORK TIMES, 12/22/95, p. C1, Janet Maslin
VARIETY, 1/1-7/96, p. 82, Todd McCarthy
WASHINGTON POST, 12/22/95, p. C6, Rita Kempley

DANCER, THE

Lincoln Center "Dancers on Film" series.   *Producer:* Lisbet Gabrielsson and Gerd Edwards. *Director:* Donya Feuer.   *Screenplay (Swedish with English subtitles):* Donya Feuer.   *Director of Photography:* Gunnar Kallstrom.   *Editor:* Kerstin Eriksdotter.   *Running time:* 100 minutes. *MPAA Rating:* Not Rated.

WITH: Katja Bjorner; Anneli Alhanko; Erland Josephson; Valentina Savina; Aleksandr Khmelnitski.

NEW YORK POST, 12/1/95, p. 47, Thelma Adams

Rarely has a film so nimbly articulated the relationship between art and craft as "The Dancer."

Donya Feuer's engaging documentary, singles out Swedish ballerina Katja Bjorner. Spanning the years 1987-92, the film captures Bjorner's leap from 13-year-old student to principal ballerina at Amsterdam's Het Nationale Ballet.

In the taut opening montage, the filmmaker intercuts pale dancers' feet warming up in rehearsal with sure-fingered, brownskinned hands molding ballet shoes. The shoemaking craft parallels the creation of the ballet dancer's primary instrument—the feet.

The opening introduces Feuer's thesis: hard work, skill and talent form the foundation of a dancer's art; the ballerina erupts out of a spiritual jump that transcends the sum of her technique.

American-born Feuer began her career as a Martha Graham dancer and has since frequently collaborated with director Ingmar Bergman. She enriches this portrait of a young dancer by introducing Bergman repertory actor Erland Josephson.

The canny dialogue between Josephson and Bjorner, actor and dancer, generalizes the concerns of the artist. In the older man's inquiry, we see his envy of the spark of the dancer just discovering her talent, as well as the mature artist's continued search for a deeper understanding of his craft. He suggests that the ballerina, unfettered by words, experiences more joy and can accomplish greater pure expression than the actor.

Feuer's meditation on art and craft is as meticulous and carefully phrased as Bjorner's dancing—and as much of a joy to watch.

Also reviewed in:
NEW YORK TIMES, 12/1/95, p. C10, Anna Kisselgoff

DANGEROUS MINDS

A Hollywood Pictures release of a Don Simpson/Jerry Bruckheimer production in association with Via Rosa Productions. *Executive Producer:* Sandra Rabins and Lucas Foster. *Producer:* Don Simpson and Jerry Bruckheimer. *Director:* John N. Smith. *Screenplay:* Ronald Bass. *Based on the book "My Posse Don't Do Homework"* by: LouAnne Johnson. *Director of Photography:* Pierre Letarte. *Editor:* Tom Rolf. *Music:* Kathy Nelson. *Music Editor:* Bob Badami. *Sound:* David Ronne. *Sound Editor:* John Stacy. *Casting:* Bonnie Timmermann. *Production Designer:* Donald Graham Burt. *Art Director:* Nancy Patton. *Set Designer:* Philip Toolin. *Set Decorator:* Catherine Mann. *Set Dresser:* Carol Decarr. *Special Efects:* Darrell D. Pritchett. *Costumes:* Bobbie Read. *Make-up:* Marietta Carter Narcisse. *Make-up (Michelle Pfeiffer):* Ronnie Specter. *Running time:* 94 minutes. *MPAA Rating:* R.

CAST: Michelle Pfeiffer (LouAnne Johnson); George Dzundza (Hal Griffith); Courtney B. Vance (Mr. George Grandey); Robin Bartlett (Ms. Carla Nichols); Beatrice Winde (Mary Benton); John Neville (Waiter); Lorraine Toussaint (Irene Roberts); Renoly Santiago (Raul Sanchero); Wade Dominguez (Emilio Ramirez); Bruklin Harris (Callie Roberts); Marcello Thedford (Cornelius Bates); Roberto Alvarez (Gusmaro Rivera); Richard Grant (Durrell Benton); Marisela Gonzales (Angela); Toni Nichelle Buzhardt (Nikki); Norris Young (Kareem); Rahman Ibraheem (Big "G"); Desire Galvez (Taiwana); Wilson Limpo (Roderick); Raymond Grant (Lionel Benton); Veronica Robles (Stephanie); Michael Archuleta (Oso); Deshanda Carter (Tanyekia); Ebony Jerido (Deanne); Brandi Younger (Grip); Asia Minor (Pam); Karina Arroyave (Josy); Paula Garces (Alvina); Ivan Sergei (Huero); Mark Prince Edwards (P.J.); Ismael Archuleta (Lalo); Skye Bassett (Jody); Gaura Buchwald (Warlock); Cynthia Avila (Mrs. Sanchero); Roman J. Cisneros (Mr. Sanchero); Camille Winbush (Tyeisha Roberts); Al Israel (Mr. Santiego); Brian Anthony (Joey); Jason Gutman (Adam); Lara Spotts (Dianna); Danny Strong (Student); Boris Vaks (Student); Irene Olga Lopez (Woman in School Office); Jeff Feringa (Librarian #1); Sarah Marshall (Librarian #2); Freeze-Luv (Security Guard).

LOS ANGELES TIMES, 8/11/95, Calendar/p. 1, Kenneth Turan

While films are admired for making fantasy real, some manage a reverse, unwanted kind of alchemy, turning involving reality into meaningless piffle. It is that kind of regrettable transformation that "Dangerous Minds" achieves.

This Michelle Pfeiffer-starring film started with a nonfiction book, "My Posse Don't Do Homework," by LouAnne Johnson, a former Marine lieutenant who left the Corps and signed up to teach English at a high school in Belmont in Northern California. But what happened to Johnson and what the film describes turn out to have the most superficial relationship, and the movie's version of things is by no means the more interesting.

As "Dangerous Minds" relates, those kids were hardly promising students. Bright but unschooled, with few social or academic skills, they were, as one character calls them, "the rejects from hell." When Johnson walks into the classroom for the first time, the loud and unruly bunch alternates between ignoring her, calling her "white bread" and yelling like bleacher bums.

Johnson's problem is several-fold. She has to first get this group's attention, then their, respect and then actually teach them something. All without experiencing the nervous breakdowns that foiled those who came before her. "You lose your sense of humor," advises fellow teacher and old pal Hal Griffith (George Dzunda), "and it's over."

Even in this brief synopsis, the appeal of Johnson's story stands out. Unfortunately for the moviemakers, her book was a series of loosely connected vignettes, not a conventional narrative with a plotted arc and a dramatic ending. To make it into a film, a story would have to be constructed around Johnson's character. And unfortunately for filmgoers, the tale screenwriter Ronald Bass came up with, and the way director John N. Smith tells it, is stereotypical, predictable and simplified to the point of meaninglessness.

The first thing Johnson does is assertively trade on her experience with Marine hand-to-hand combat. Then, with promises of trips to amusement parks and the more immediate bribe of free candy bars, she gets her class interested in poetry, starting with Bob Dylan and connecting him to Dylan Thomas. Finally, she begins to make home visits, proving to her charges that she truly cares about their lives.

Though these events sound acceptable when summarized, on screen none of it, with the exception of Pfeiffer's performance, seems even vaguely real. This is especially true of the film's excessively melodramatic climactic events, a bogus tragedy that does not occur in the book and has contrived written all over it.

With kids as unconvincing as troubled toughs as Leo Gorcey and the Bowery Boys were in their day, even the picture's everyday classroom situations can't manage to appear realistic. And Canadian director Smith whose "The Boys of St. Vincent" was a deserved success at festivals and on cable (legal problems prevent it from getting a domestic theatrical release), has settled for an emotional tone that is distressingly reminiscent of "Welcome Back, Kotter."

Given how few the opportunities are for women to carry a motion picture, and with the chance to be a positive role model thrown into the bargain, it's not surprising to find Pfeiffer starring in "Dangerous Minds," and she is as believable as the film allows her to be. But if this trivialization of involving subject matter is the best a star of her considerable abilities can latch onto, today's actresses have it worse than we've imagined.

NEW YORK POST, 8/11/95, p. 43, Michael Medved

At the beginning of "Dangerous Minds," a veteran teacher played by George Dzundza informs his new colleague that the only way to take control of her class is to somehow get the, kids' attention.

Are we really supposed to believe that someone who looks like Michelle Pfeiffer would find it hard to get attention—in the classroom or anywhere else?

That's part of the problem with this well-intentioned, consistently well-acted film—the star is too damnably, distractingly beautiful for the role. We're busy admiring her perfect bone structure or the elegant shape of her ears when were supposed to be impressed by her grit and spunk.

The way that she's lit and photographed (by Canadian director John N. Smith, who previously created the acclaimed telefilm "The Boys of St. Vincent") only adds to the difficulty. Despite attempts to disguise her star quality in baggy sweaters and ill-fitting plain-Jane dresses, Pfeiffer still looks otherworldly and angelic—giving her character an aura of superhuman power and perfection that the script never intended.

That script (by Oscar-winner Ron Bass of "Rainman") is based on the memoir "My Posse Don't Do Homework" by LouAnne Johnson, a former Marine Corps officer who, following a painful divorce, got a job teaching "at risk" students in northern California.

For the most part, this picture follows the familiar path of every "inspired teacher" movie you've ever seen, where the dedicated instructor breaks through the cynicism of hopeless youngsters by showing deep caring and commitment, then proceeds to transform young lives.

In "Dangerous Minds," this predictable process generates more energy than expected due to authentic, intense and altogether impressive performances by a cast of untried young actors recruited to play the kids in Pfeiffer's classroom.

Unfortunately, these extraordinary kids come across far more vividly and believably than their teacher does. In contrast to Edward James Olmos' growlingly effective fury in "Stand and

Deliver," you can't imagine Pfeiffer inspiring anyone with lines like, "The mind is like a muscle. And if you want it to be really powerful, you gotta work it out!"

Meanwhile, her character's chief educational innovations—treating her entire class to a day at an amusement park in order to bond with them, or rewarding students for academic performance with candlelight dinner in the town's most expensive restaurant—might tax the resources of most real-life teachers.

At least the script has the courage to show that bribery and Pfeiffer's focus on the immortal words of Bob Dylan as the way to introduce literary greatness don't necessarily work miracles with all the kids.

The movie enjoys its most moving moment conveying the heartbreak associated with the main character's failures. But it immediately undermines these honest elements with an appallingly sentimental scene full of tearful declarations of love and appreciation where one of the fine young actors is actually forced to tell her teacher "you are our light."

The phony and overly familiar feel of this finale suggests a verdict on all of "Dangerous Minds" that echoes one of America's most familiar educational slogans: Our Time Is A Terrible Thing To Waste.

NEWSDAY, 8/11/95, Part II/p. B2, Jack Mathews

The idealistic, determined high school teacher who faces and wins over a class full of insecure and usually rude underachievers in an urban public high school is sort of the Hamlet of Hollywood. So rich, so dramatic, so full of conflict and resolution, an actor can hardly resist, even if it has been done in every possible hue.

The teacher-and-the-tough-class theme, of course, is played out for real every day in schools around the country, and whether it's dramatized in 1955 ("Blackboard Jungle"), 1967 ("Up the Down Staircase"), 1989 ("Lean on Me") or today, in director John N. Smith's "Dangerous Minds," the moral is never outdated. Children need both love and knowledge, and without the first it's hard to impart the second.

Whether the story can be told in a fresh and engaging way is another question. Michelle Pfeiffer acts up a storm and cries a river as the earnest LouAnne Johnson in "Dangerous Minds," but the story is so predictably charted, absent either surprises or revelations, that the audience has nothing to do but admire Pfeiffer's effort and the author's good intentions.

What distinguishes LouAnne Johnson's experience in California is her unique background. She spent eight years in the Marines before becoming a teacher, and it is the adaptation of her military training to the classroom that turns the class around. After being ignored and humiliated by the students on her first day on the job, Pfeiffer's LouAnne returns with a new resolve and, with a couple of graphic demonstrations in the technique of karate, earns their respect.

That happens in the first 20 minutes of the movie. LouAnne has a few nagging problems hanging over her head. Her principal (Courtney B. Vance) is a rigid disciplinarian who won't abide her eccentric approach, even if it works. Her smartest and most supportive student (Bruklin Harris) is pregnant, and about to be transferred to an alternative school: And the boy she's worked hardest to change (Wade Dominguez) is having to defend his honor against a gun-toting crack peddler. But the main dramatic question—can she do the job?—is answered in a flash.

If Pfeiffer portraying an ex-Marine is a stretch for her, it's a colossal leap for the audience. When she says she was a Marine, it sounds like a joke, and when she assumes the karate stance, you expect the macho student in front of her to keel over, in laughter. There's not much to work with if your premise has been obliterated in the casting.

Better she did "Hamlet."

SIGHT AND SOUND, 1/96, p. 37, Lizzie Francke

Recently divorced ex-US Marine, LouAnne Johnson gets a job as a supply teacher at the school where her friend Hal teaches, working with kids with special educational needs. At first put off by the disruptive class, she decides to meet the challenge. She junks the approved reading curriculum in favour of poetry, and bribes her students to pay attention with karate demonstrations and promises of trips to an amusement park. One of her charges, Emilio, proves to be particularly troublesome. One day she breaks up a fight between Emilio and two other boys. When the kids are suspended, she goes to visit their families to offer support. She is hauled up by the headmaster for her unusual teaching techniques.

Undeterred, she offers to buy dinner for the kid who solves a literary puzzle that she sets. Three win and she takes a special interest in all of them. When one girl, Callie, tells her that she is going to drop out because she is pregnant, LouAnne pleads with her and the authorities to continue her education. Meanwhile, Emilio has been given a death threat by a boy from a rival gang. LouAnne offers to shelter him while also advising him to tell the authorities. Emilio goes to see the head teacher who turns him away for not knocking on his door. Later Emilio is stabbed to death. Upset and disillusioned, LouAnne resigns. Her class mount a protest and she changes her mind.

Ostensibly, the biggest surprise about *Dangerous Minds* is the producing credit. This is the third major film in the last 12 months from Don Simpson and Jerry Bruckheimer, a considerable revival in their careers after the hiatus of the last few years following the commercial disaster of their Tom Cruise vehicle *Days of Thunder*. This true life story—based on the experiences of one LouAnne Johnson, who chronicled her experiences of teaching an 'at-risk' class in *My Posse Don't Do Homework*—hardly has the same testosterone punch as Simpson and Bruckheimer's recent titles, *Crimson Tide* and *Bad Boys*, or such previous successes as *Top Gun* and *Beverly Hills Cop II*.

Nevertheless, given the anonymous direction of John N. Smith (a Canadian of some experience whose work has yet to show theatrically here), if one wanted to argue for the producer as auteur, then a tenuous case could be made for *Flashdance* as a precursor to *Dangerous Minds*. Both films follow 'triumph against the odds' trajectories with ordinary female heroines. Jennifer Beals' blue-collar welder/wannabe dancer is similar to Michelle Pfeiffer's ex-marine divorcee who wants to reinvent herself as a teacher (watch Pfeiffer's streetwise make-over swapping frowzy tweeds and lacy shirt for racy leather jacket and jeans). Crucially, in each film the women take 'on their challenges with hefty doses of warmhearted optimism. Bearing the music-driven *Flashdance* in mind, one also suspects that Simpson and Bruckheimer had their eye on the MTV market with the film benefiting from a gutsy rap score by Wendy and Lisa and plenty of pop promo crossover marketing possibilities. Certainly the opening sequence, shot in a grainy monochrome and featuring disaffected looking black and white kids in a run-down, graffiti-scrawled 'hood is very much a promo cliche. This is gritty urban social realism filtered through a Hollywood sensibility.

As such *Dangerous Minds* is also indebted to *Blackboard Jungle*, which has a similar storyline. And there is something admirable about the intentions of films which set out to investigate the sorry state of education for the dispossessed of America—specifically, here, Hispanic and Afro-American kids. In this respect, it is very much a hippie (or is it Clintonesque?) kind of film, haunted by the failure of the 60s dream. LouAnne uses Bob Dylan's lyrics to inspire kids from socially disadvantaged backgrounds, whose learning 'difficulties' only stem from their frustrations, The stock types are all there: the dangerously good-looking toughie gang member Emilio (Wade Dominguez) who attempts to put a machismo spell on his teacher; the bright, quietly spoken Callie (Bruldin Harris), whose pregnancy jeopardises her education; the cheeky-chappie Raul (Renoly Santiago). All too recognisable, these cliches have their counter-part in real-life statistics. All the more important then is the film's obvious message that with care and attention they all have the potential to bloom.

What is revealing is just how far the film has to stretch the imagination to believe in this fantasy of equality in education. (Meanwhile one can believe in Pfeiffer as a teacher about as much as one could believe in her ugly-duckling low-rent diner waitress in *Frankie and Johnny*.) Apart from Pfeiffer's inability to convince as a teacher, anyone who has ever taught professionally will find much else to scoff at. LouAnne has an ever-full private purse out of which she subsidises her charges' educational needs, whether with the copious photocopies that she hands out or with fiscally damaging treats (day trips for the class *en masse*, swanky dinners for teachers' pets). From this perspective, the ' feelgood factor' in *Dangerous Minds* curdles as it is milked.

VILLAGE VOICE, 8/22/95, p. 52, Amy Taubin

Worse than colorblind, *Dangerous Minds* is an old-fashioned white missionary movie brought to you by *Top Gun* producers Don Simpson and Jerry Bruckheimer and helmed in TV non-style by John N. Smith, who showed a similar lack of directorial talent in the overrated *Boys of St.*

Vincent. Formerly titled *My Posse Don't Do Homework*, it stars Michelle Pfeiffer as an ex-Marine and newly hired high school teacher assigned to a "special-ed section" where the students are described as very bright but lacking in learning skills—in other words, they're black and Hispanic. Told that the most important thing is to capture her students' attention, Pfeiffer starts by showing them karate moves and then throws out the standard reading text, substituting those grandfathers of rap, Bob Dylan and Dylan Thomas. And what do you know, pretty soon she has every one of them eating out of her hand (sometimes literally, since rewards for scholastic achievement involve trips to the amusement park and dinners in expensive restaurants).

In *Dangerous Minds*, it's the black adults (the bureaucratic principal, the bigoted mom) who make problems for black kids, and it's the dedicated white teachers who have their best interests at heart. The film makes a big deal about how teachers are underpaid. Pfeiffer, however, seems to have to teach only one class for one period each day. Which, for $23,500, isn't such a bad gig.

In fact, *Dangerous Minds* is, in all ways, so removed from reality, that it's not worth getting upset about. "It's not a film—it's a series of cues for the soundtrack album," said a screenwriter friend. Note however, that Bob Dylan is not included on the album, which features Coolio, Wendy & Lisa, and other rap artists. The least Pfeiffer could have done is test her lit crit smarts on *The Chronic*.

Also reviewed in:
CHICAGO TRIBUNE, 8/11/95, Friday/p. H, Michael Wilmington
NEW YORK TIMES, 8/11/95, p. C3, Janet Maslin
NEW YORKER, 8/21-28/95, p. 132, Terrence Rafferty
VARIETY, 8/14-20/95, p. 55, Todd McCarthy
WASHINGTON POST, 8/11/95, p. F1, Rita Kempley
WASHINGTON POST, 8/11/95, Weekend/p. 39, Kevin McManns

DARKER SIDE OF BLACK, THE

A Black Audio Film Collective/Normal Films production, in association with BBC-TV and the Arts Council of Great Britain. *Producer:* David Lawson and Lena Gopual. *Director:* Isaac Julien. *Screenplay:* Isaac Julien. *Director of Photography:* Arthur Jaffa and David Scott. *Editor:* Joy Chamberlain. *Music:* Trevor Mathison. *Sound:* Trevor Mathison. *Running time:* 55 minutes. *MPAA Rating:* Not Rated.

WITH: Ice Cube; Chuck D; Buju Banton; Brand Nubian; Michael Franti; Trisha Rose; Michael Manley; Monie Love; Shabba Ranks; Cornel West.

NEW YORK POST, 1/6/95, p. 43, Larry Worth

Over the last few years, documentaries like "Silver Lake" "Living Proof" and Derek Jarman's "Blue" have delivered hard-hitting, thought-provoking examinations of the AIDS crisis. Accordingly, filmmakers must work that much harder to find innovative ways to address the subject.

Example A: HIV-positive director Gregg Bordowitz's "Fast Trip, Long Drop" has the best intentions, but it borders on the redundant. Speeches like "I am no longer a person with AIDS ... I am AIDS"—never mind reflections with his parents about coming out are sincere, but awfully familiar.

More interesting is Bordowitz's black humor, evidenced when depicting himself as the guest on a new talk show, "Thriving With AIDS," hosted by a ghoulishly cheery scandalmonger. Bordowitz also integrates black-and-white footage, of daredevils' stunts—assumedly to draw parallels with others who've tempted fate.

The varying moods don't always jell, but "Fast Trip, Long Drop" at least remains focused on its subject. Which is more than "The Darker Side of Black" can claim.

To call Isaac Julien's Jamaica-based documentary disjointed is an understatement. It begins as a damning look at the link between hip-hop music and gun use, with talking heads ranging from Jamaica's former prime minister to Public Enemy's Chuck D.

Then it's on to Jamaica's raging homophobia (born from Bible-spouting singers as well as fear of AIDS), before tackling island music's anti-omen sentiments. Someone asks: Is it all due to inhabitants internalizing the violence of slavery? God knows you couldn't prove it from this conglomeration of half-thoughts.

The bottom line: AIDS documentaries won't get a bad name from this mediocre double-feature, but neither will it do much to advance the cause.

NEWSDAY, 1/6/95, Part II/p. B7, John Anderson

Outside of their gay themes, there probably aren't two documentaries more stylistically at odds than Isaac Julien's "Darker Side of Black" and Gregg Bordowitz' "Fast Trip, Long Drop." As such, of course, it makes perfect sense to show them together, as Cinema Village will be doing for the next two weeks.

The film by Julien, a gay, black Londoner whose films have included the rowdy "Young Soul Rebels" and "Black and White in Color," is a profoundly troubling and highly successful investigation of the roots of gun love and homophobia in the music cultures of hip-hop, dancehall and whatever remains of reggae.

Drawing a kind of Bermuda triangle with London, Greenwich Village and Jamaica—the source of those musical styles, Julien posits—he examines the bloodlust seemingly endorsed by such performers as Ice Cube, the virulent gay-bashing espoused by Shabba Ranks and Buju Banton, the effect of this on the gay communities in all three locales, and, far more ambitiously, he considers how the violent legacy of slavery just might be what makes the black community an incubator for such destructive, divisive attitudes.

Julien makes effective use of rap videos and his own audacious devices ... one recurring beach scene shows white hands holding a Bible, beside shackled black legs being buried in the sand. All the same, it's a talking heads picture, albeit with a difference: The heads, shot in highly stylized fashion, are really saying something. That they're saying what Julien wants to say is a foregone conclusion, I suppose, but the quality of thought is fascinating.

Academics like Cornel West and Trish Rose, former Jamaican Prime Minister Michael Manley, Chuck D. of Public Enemy and Michael Franti of the Disposable Heroes of Hiphoprisy, all offer deeply felt and thoughtful analyses of the nihilism that infects black culture, especially young black culture. Conversely, Ice Cube rationalizes black-on-black crime as the unavoidable result of being American, and Shabba Ranks falls back on the Bible to defend his suggestion that gays be crucified.

Video-maker Gregg Bordowitz was diagnosed HIV positive in 1988 and decided to chronicle his battle with the illness. The result is "Fast Trip, Long Drop," a collage of self-inquiry, farce, archival film and newsreel footage combined into what is in the end a too-personal treatment of the AIDS crisis.

Some of the comic bits work well—Bob Huff, who plays several roles, skewers the media neglect of the plague. But his sendup of AIDS-activist and writer Larry Kramer—as Harry Blamer, ranting and self-absorbed—is mirrored far too closely by Bordowitz himself as Alter Allesman, a talk-show guest who, I have to assume, is meant to personify self-realization among the infected population.

Although Bordowitz' pain is real, as he says himself, "What's unique about my pain is that it's mine." Had he made it ours, "Fast Trip, Long Drop" would be a far more affecting film.

Also reviewed in:
NEW YORK TIMES, 1/6/95, p. C6, Stephen Holden
VARIETY, 5/2-8/94, p. 91, David Rooney

DAY THE SUN TURNED COLD, THE

A Kino International release of a Pineast Pictures Ltd. production. *Executive Producer:* Ann Hui. *Producer:* Yim Ho. *Director:* Yim Ho. *Screenplay (Mandarin with English subtitles):* Wang Xing Dong and Wang Zhe Bin. *Director of Photography:* Hou Yong. *Editor:* Wong Yee-shun, Zhou Ying Wu, and Yun Jiang Chun. *Music:* Otomo Yoshihide. *Sound:* Zhang Wen. *Art Director:* Gong Ming Hui. *Set Decorator:* Yu Zhen Xue, Guo Wu Long, and Huang Chang Chun. *Special Effects:* Go Wen Tai. *Costumes:* Zhang Shu Fang. *Make-up:* Ji Wei Hua. *Running time:* 99 minutes. *MPAA Rating:* Not Rated.

CAST: Siqin Gowa (Pu Fengying, the Mother); Tuo Zhong Hua (Guan Jin, the Son); Ma Jing Wu (Guan Shichang, the Father); Wu'ai Zi (Liu Dagui, the Lover); Shu Zi'ong (Young Guan Jian); Li Hu (Chen, the Police Captain); Zhao Na Na (Niuniu); Zhang Xue (Young Niuniu); Wei Pang (Young Qing); Song Yu (Qing); Chu Lin (Momo); Lu Qi Feng (Teacher Zhang); Ming Yi (Auntie Guo); Li Wen Fu (Factory Foreman); Yuan Xiao Jun (The Guard); Zhao Nai Xun (The Old Uncle); Wu Gui Lin (Uncle Guan).

LOS ANGELES TIMES, 2/9/96, Calendar/p. 8, Kevin Thomas

The hard lot of women is a persistent, concern in Asian cinema, where women frequently emerge as symbols of endurance.

The heroine of Yim Ho's "The Day the Sun Turned Cold" is seemingly like countless others; an illiterate, hard-working bean-curd peddler (Siqin Gowa) making the best of an unhappy marriage to the severe principal (Ma Jing Wu) of the school in their remote village in Northern China. Her life brightens a bit, when a woodsman (Wai Zhi) rescues the woman and her 14-year old son in a snowstorm and begins helping her sell her bean curd.

From the start, however, Yim makes it clear we're in for something different, for he opens his film with the son, now a young man living in a big city—a laborer by day and a criminal law student by night—entering a police station. In a crisis of conscience, he reports that he suspects his mother, who married the woodsman after her husband's death, of murdering his father. Because this young man, Guan Jin (Tuo Zhong Hua) can so easily demonstrate his solid citizenship, a veteran police captain (Li Hu) concludes that he must investigate the death, which occurred 10 years earlier.

The result is a complex and compelling mystery in an unlikely setting. Through a series of plot twists and turns, the mother emerges as a staunch, free-thinking woman, now long married to a nice guy who is devoted to her. It's no wonder that Guan Jin's brother and sister deeply resent the scandal he has stirred up with his accusations.

Yim does a terrific job of keeping us guessing about whether the woman is guilty and whether her current husband was involved. Then there's the entire question of Guan Jin's motivation: Is his accusation strictly an act of conscience on his part—he does owe his success to his father's strictness in relation to his studies—or is there an unacknowledged, long-brewing Oedipal rage driving him? Can he—or we—ever know for certain?

"The Day the Sun Turned Cold" is a handsome film, greatly enhanced by Yoshihide Otomo's plaintive score. It's also an instance of splendid ensemble acting, but it's rightly dominated by Siqin, a round-faced, stocky woman who is a formidable actress, best known for her portrayal of another beleagured wife and mother in Xie Fei's equally impressive "Woman From the Lake of Scented Souls."

NEW YORK POST, 4/28/95, p. 42, Thelma Adams

"The Day the Sun Turned Cold" sparked a letter-writing campaign when it opened in China. Half the responses supported Guan Jin (Tuo Zhong Hua) for accusing his mother (Siqin Gaowa) of murder. The other half insisted that, even if his mother was guilty of killing his father 10 years earlier, it was a betrayal to report mom to the authorities.

Part thriller, part rural family drama, Yim Ho's movie turns on the love/hate relationship between a son and his mother. It premiered last month at New Directors/New Films" at the Museum of Modern Art.

Guan is a hard-working, humorless adult. The day his father died of a mysterious illness changed his personality forever. Before, he was his mother's pet, a joyful irresponsible monkey. Afterward, as his mother began life with a new husband and a new family, Guan became an awkward and unwelcome reminder of his father.

After a decade's passage, his father's death still torments Guan. His mother had means, opportunity and motive—her affair with a local woodsman was common knowledge to everyone but his father. One day, Guan enters a police station in a distant city and tells all. Even the chain-smoking detective encourages the serious young worker to let sleeping dogs lie.

"How'd you get to hate [your mother] so?" the detective asks.

"I love her very much," Guan says, but he persists.

Guan and the detective travel to the boy's home village. Based on an actual case, the movie flashes back to the events that led up to the alleged murder. Writer/director Yim ("Red Dust") sketches life on the chilly tundra with calligraphic simplicity. It's an existence so barren that the mother's fateful grasping for joy in a closed society almost seems justifiable. Almost.

Mongolian actress Siqin ("Woman From the Lake of Scented Souls") makes no attempt to play for cheap sympathy. She portrays a stocky, hard-working, passionate woman with a peasant's cunning. Unhappy in her marriage to a rigid school principal who constantly reminds her of the difference in their status, she heaps all her pent up emotion on her eldest son, Guan—until she falls for the woodsman's ax.

Like Hamlet, who must overcome his terror of his father's ghost and confront his mother and her lover with their terrible crime, Guan is a man torn in two by split loyalties. His most beautiful childhood memory is not one of domestic bliss, but a sleigh ride across the chilly landscape where he shared sweet potatoes with his mother and her lover.

"Raise a son and you bring up resentment," says the mother in a home truth typical of the movie.

Yim slowly unravels the puzzle of the past, but it's the impossibility of the present that is memorable and lends the movie its edge. The truth might bring justice, but it doesn't set the son free. By avenging his father, Guan closes one wound and opens another.

NEWSDAY, 4/28/95, Part II/p. B7, Jack Mathews

The Oedipus complex gets even more complex in Chinese director Yim Ho's "The Day the Sun Turned Cold," a deftly told psychological mystery story about a young man whose childhood jealousies and suspicions lead him 10 years later to accuse his mother of murder.

Shot in the stark, wintry tundra of northern China, "The Day the Sun Turned Cold" opens with 24-year-old Guan Jin (Tuo Zhong Hua) walking into a police station, and disrupting the investigation of a recent murder by insisting they look into the death of his father a decade earlier. Jin has more theory to offer than evidence, but as he tells his story—proclaiming at the outset that his mother, whom he still loves, is the killer—the detective becomes more and more intrigued.

On the surface, it's a very simple story that Jin tells—of how his mother scandalized the family by beginning an affair with a young woodsman, and then poisoned her husband so she'd be free to marry him. But with his delicate and precise use of flashbacks, Ho turns Jin's story inward, so that we understand exactly *why* he wants his mother punished long before we find out if she actually deserves it.

The Oedipal connection is immediately evident. Jin's mother (Siqin Gowa), a gentle, loving woman who does backbreaking work producing bean curd for her children to sell in the village, is the spirited young Jin's sanctuary from his severe, abusive father. And his love for her gives her comfort from the same source of cruelty.

But when his mother and the woodsman (Wai Zhi) start sneaking around in the bean mill, his jealousy turns to rage, then spite, and finally—after his father suffers a series of convulsions—into blunt suspicion. The events lead Jin into an uneasy alliance with his deteriorating father, and his hostility toward the woodsman after his father's death gets him sent away to live with relatives and stew over his heartbreak for the next 10 years.

Ho plays the mystery element convincingly close to the vest. The more we know of the family's history, the less certain we are of anyone's actions, and the ending delivers a couple of genuine surprises. But it is the probing of the tortured Jin's ambivalence about his mother, and Ho's crafty, neatly paced storytelling, that make "The Day the Sun Turned Cold" such a compelling and eventually draining emotional experience.

SIGHT AND SOUND, 11/96, p. 47, Mark Sinker

China. A 24-year-old welder, Guan Jian, enters a small urban police station to turn in his mother, Pu Fengying, for murdering his father, Guan Shichang, up in the northeastern village where the family lived ten years before. The sceptical Police Captain reluctantly takes up the case. He listens as Jian recalls the events in question.

A flashback begins: Fengying makes bean curd, which her three children sell, while Guan Shichang is a teacher. The marriage is unhappy. At 14, Jian is a bad pupil, and his father beats him mercilessly; when his mother intervenes, she is beaten too. In a fierce storm, Jian and Fengying are thrown off their cart and into a deep snowdrift. A woodsman, Liu Dagui, saves their lives. Guan tells him he's always welcome in their house.

Jian and Guan learn—through gossip and what Jian sees—that Fengying and Liu are having an affair. Guan confronts and beats her, but she persuades him to wait until they've eaten before confronting Liu: at the meal, Guan suffers a terrible seizure. Some days later, Jian sees Fengying put powder into a meal he refuses to let the children share. Fengying dies in agony. Guan dies in agony. Fengying then marries Liu: Jian, furious, disrupts the wedding sled-cavalcade. Later, he takes a letter of complaint to the local courthouse, but the official can't read his handwriting. On his return, Fengying is back: she'd argued with Liu and he'd hit her. Jian throws his accusation on the fire. Next day, Jian and Fengying's sled is ambushed by thugs who chase Jian off and take Fengying away. Jian then left the village for ten years. Having laid out his story, he returns home with the Captain: the family are delighted to see him, but his mother refuses to say anything when he confronts her. The Village Elders permit the digging up of Guan's body. They find arsenic, but not at unusual levels. Jian, mortified, begs his mother's forgiveness. He also makes up with Liu: but then a flashback proves that Liu and Fengying *did* poison Guan. Further forensic examination finds rat poison in Guan's body. Fengying tries to take all the blame, but when the arrest is made, Liu tries to take it all: both are then charged, tried, convicted and sentenced to death. Visiting Fengying in her cell, Jian tells her to appeal; she hardly speaks to him, but as he leaves, she gives him a jumper she's knitted for him. Once outside the prison, he throws it away.

"How did you get to hate your mother?" the Captain asks Jian. Confused, he replies that on the contrary, he loves her. The basic dynamic of this prize-winning but emotionally relentless film may be intended to be every son-mother relationship anywhere: as boy becomes man, his triumph will be her defeat (albeit with every conflict here hugely magnified by an unresolved and mysterious death). Hong Kong born director Yim Ho who's been making award-winning television and movies since the late 70s, including the acclaimed 1990 film *Red Dust (Gungun Hongchen)*—says he wished to take this true story and make it universal: but the ineluctable unfolding of doom and familial implosion aren't what we lock onto. Instead the real revelation in *The Day the Sun Turned Cold* is the non-universality of Yim Ho's portrait of this extensive but unfamiliar society, mainland peasant China in the 80s and 90s, a society touched but hardly transformed by the social forces and changes of the modern age.

So for example, crowding round Guan's sickbed, his fellow teachers—mostly women—joke about how marriage for women means being beaten, and how this is in the end a good thing. Of Fengying they ask, "What's this Western garbage about divorce? Doesn't she care about *face?*" And it's fascinating—if unsettling—to be caught up in a story where the police in a totalitarian state are just the same bone-weary professionals ravelling some hateful domestic crime that we can see on British television: if no law officer in this film is ever less than rigorous about the law, we catch from many of them an edge of disgust towards Jian, the son who reports his own mother (Jian seems to have taken his inspiration as an informant from the West, specifically a French paperback cataloguing the great murders of the century).

Greatly focused by the often-claustrophobic camerawork, a sense of rage spirals up like sub-zero breath-mist from every character, from the taciturn Captain, to the gossiping teachers, to the other two children (the sister has only two long speeches, both in essence outbursts against Jian for bringing shame on them, and rendering her unmarriable), to Fengying with her desperate, clumsy and disastrous grab at new happiness. And then there's dead Guan and his vicious physical temper and bruised demeanour, a defeated, unbelieving look his son has by the end inherited.

That this rage is everywhere shared some might call universal: none of us can escape the attentions of the Furies. Yet none of the characters is dislikeable. For example, the Captain first meets Liu when he pitches in to help get the police-car unstuck from a hole in a track across a vast, frozen lake. Nevertheless, there is almost no respite from the elements in question, no gallows burnout even. By contrast, in a western policier, the hurt of betrayal within families is so endlessly parlayed against the routine charm of 'ordinary' life that it's now both the subject and the sales-pitch: we watch David Jason in *A Touch of Frost* for his banter, not crime's terrors.

To represent, as Yim Ho does, a community's life as so seamlessly unvaried is a choice others will call political perhaps as an attack on the failure of the Red Chinese way to deliver utopia here on Earth; that this family aren't free to achieve a decent life. In the end, however, the details that remain are less social than sensory: the steamy smokiness that attends the making of bean curd; the sudden bright colours and squalling music of village ceremonial, when the children dress up and walk around on little stilts; the look of a Chinese child's copybook complete with painstaking but incompetent Mandarin calligraphy; the bizarre dissociation of the shabby little rural disco, with its Canto-pop cherub and flashing lights; the dreary corridors and outlook of the prison; the mournful and unending blue glare of the permafrost. And even when all the stories have already been told, there's always what the camera's really for: pointing your eyes at things you never thought to see. The storm scene, astounding in its sudden violence, recalls nothing so much as silent Hollywood cinema: the capture on film of real actors in realtime peril, struggling against the inhuman ferocity of the elements, like little Lillian Gish in 1920, lying on an ice-floe hurtling towards the rapids and certain death in *Way Down East*.

VILLAGE VOICE, 5/2/95, p. 50, Georgia Brown

From the chill plains of northeast China comes a spooky tale of family violence. Yim Ho's *The Day the Sun Turned Cold* is based on a true event: A young man initiates an inquiry into his father's death, naming his mother as the murderer. The impassive Guan Jin (Tuo Zhonghua) may have Hamlet's motive and task but he's neither audacious nor indecisive nor wily. He's also not a prince but a lowly welder. A vindictive enigma, Jin acts in ways that often left this viewer perplexed. In the end, I couldn't decide whether his depressed distance stood at the heart of the movie's weakness or its haunting appeal.

One day Jin drops into a district police station to make his charge. The on-duty detective is skeptical. The crime—if such it was—took place 10 years before. Recently Jin read a French book about a housewife who laced her husband's hot milk with arsenic; it brought back the night his mother (Siqin Gowa, the *Woman From the Lake of Scented Souls*) sprinkled powder into his father's dinner and his father (Ma Jing Wu) took ill and died. Not exactly recovered memory: the kid had tried to report the mother the year after his father's death, only to be rebuffed.

Detective: "How'd you get to hate her so much?"

Jin: "I don't … I love her."

Told mostly in flashback, Yim's film focuses on the son's partial, opaque view of his parents' marriage, his father's death and his mother's posting "with such dexterity to incestuous sheets." Of the mother's point of view, we get only glimpses, though her son's memory contains ameliorating or exculpatory materials. When his father is beating him, she throws her body over his. She first meets the man who becomes her lover (Wai Zhi) when she's risked her life to save her son, and the woodcutter pulls them both from a deadly snowdrift. That she sees the man as a savior from the rest of her misery isn't surprising. Yet after her remarriage she abandons her children, leaving Jin, as the eldest, in charge. Whether he's avenging his father so much as he's punishing his mother isn't clear. One thing is certain: He hasn't a clue either.

What's Yim Ho's perspective? I can't say I'm surer. Intentionally or not, he's created a troubling, perhaps unforgettable melodrama. The Oedipus story has been told so many times, it's refreshing to find a new version.

Also reviewed in:
NEW REPUBLIC, 5/8/95, p. 26, Stanley Kauffmann

NEW YORK TIMES, 4/1/95, p. 14, Caryn James
VARIETY, 10/24-30/94, p. 68, Ken Eisner
WASHINGTON POST, 7/1/95, p. C2, William F. Powers

DEAD BEAT

A Northern Arts Releasing release. *Executive Producer:* Anant Singh. *Producer:* George Moffly. *Director:* Adam Dubov. *Screenplay:* Janice Shapiro and Adam Dubov. *Director of Photography:* Nancy Schreiber. *Editor:* Lorraine Salk. *Music:* Anton Sanko. *Sound:* Ed White. *Casting:* Johanna Ray. *Production Designer:* Vincent Jefferds. *Art Director:* Lauren Sharfman. *Costumes:* Alexis Scott. *Running time:* 92 minutes. *MPAA Rating:* R.

CAST: Bruce Ramsey (Kit); Balthazar Getty (Rudy); Natasha Gregson Wagner (Kirsten); Meredith Salenger (Donna); Deborah Harry (Mrs. Kurtz); Sara Gilbert (Martha); Max Perlich (Jimmie); Alex Cox (English Teacher).

NEW YORK POST, 10/13/95, p. 51, Bill Hoffmann

Teen angst and '60s kitsch are alive and well in Adam Dubov's "Dead Beat," a laid-back black comedy with a lot more style than substance.

The scene is Albuquerque, N.M., in 1965 and all of the cheesy fashions, bizarre color clashes and god-awful architecture of the era are in full evidence.

Kit (Bruce Ramsey) is the local heartthrob who is psychologically tied to wallflower Martha (Sara Gilbert of "Roseanne"), but he's head-over-heels for rich girl Kirsten (Natasha Gregson Wagner).

Beyond their zest in making out at the drive-in and haunting the local burger joint, these kids are bored. So bored, that Kit, Martha and another chum go off and commit murder for kicks.

The question is: When and where will violence erupt again?

It's a dramatic point that nearly carries "Dead Beat" through a bit of "Blue Velvet" territory. But in the long-run, it's David Lynch Lite.

There's very little plot and the characters amble along with little purpose. Some of the dialogue is quite good, but when the cast—particularly Kit—spouts off about the meaning and pointlessness of life, the film badly sputters.

Luckily, the energetic players throw themselves into their roles—particularly Wagner, the stunning daughter of Natalie Wood.

Rock fans should note that Blondie's Deborah Harry has a small part as a housewife.

"Dead Beat" ultimately fails because it really doesn't have a point, But it does score as a cool period piece.

VILLAGE VOICE, 10/17/95, p. 56, Abby McGanney Nolan

A straight-to-video release that goes straight to hell after its credit sequence, *Dead Beat* is set in oh-so-faux Albuquerque 1965 (the kitschy sets and clothes are a welcome distraction). It follows the local high school idol, Kit Dobbs (Bruce Ramsey), an Elvis holdout in the Beatles era, as he searches for someone who will take him "to the outer limits." Enter rich, rebellious Kirsten (Natasha Gregson Wagner, daughter of Natalie Wood), a wild girl without a decent line of dialogue. Balthazar Getty, doing some sort of Charlie Sheen-Corey Feldman imitation, presides over this tale of mad love as the narrator.

Dead Beat's actors are forced to overact and camp it up. The script, by director Dubov and Janice Shapiro, is painfully aimless: with a few dream sequences and flashbacks added just for show. Why such actors as Max Perlich, Sara Gilbert, and Debbie Harry bothered is a mystery.

Also reviewed in:
NEW YORK TIMES, 10/13/95, p. C10, Stephen Holden
VARIETY, 5/23-29/94, p. 59, David Rooney

DEAD FUNNY

An A-Pix Entertainment release of an Avondale Pictures/Movie Screen Entertainment presentation. *Executive Producer:* Paul L. Newman, James M. Gould, Robert Baruc, and David Marlow. *Producer:* Richard Abramowitz and David Hannay. *Director:* John Feldman. *Screenplay:* John Feldman and Cindy Oswin. *Director of Photography:* Todd Crockett. *Editor:* Einar Westerlund. *Music:* Sheila Silver. *Sound:* Melanie Johnson. *Casting:* Susan Shopmaker. *Production Designer:* Mike Shaw. *Costumes:* Sara Slotnick. *Running time:* 96 minutes. *MPAA Rating:* R.

CAST: Elizabeth Peña (Vivian Saunders); Andrew McCarthy (Reggie Barker); Paige Turco (Louise); Blanche Baker (Barbara); Allison Janney (Jennifer); Adelle Lutz (Maria); Lisa Jane Persky (Sarah); Michael Mantell (Harold).

NEW YORK POST, 8/25/95, p. 44, Larry Worth

An hour into "Dead Funny," its lead character exclaims, "I'm in a real mess." Truer words were never spoken.

Writer/director John Feldman has fashioned a production that's part murder mystery, part romantic comedy, part domestic drama and total disaster.

It begins when Vivian, the supposedly lovable screwball heroine, walks into her apartment and finds her boyfriend, Reggie, dead on the kitchen table with a machete through his chest. She simply shrugs and goes to the bathroom.

As Vivian flashes back to their courtship, viewers learn that the pair always played practical jokes. But once discovering that Reggie is coffin-ready, Vivian still postpones calling the police. And that's where credibility—and any chance for the film's success evaporates.

Feldman simply devises a series of dim excuses—visits from Viv's closest gal pal, nosy neighbors, a women's support group (which doubles as a stab at parody)—to give the non-story a respectable running time.

He also borrows bits from celebrated relationship films—like the wear-your-food scene from "9½ Weeks"—to flesh out the principals. He'd have accomplished far more if he'd penned at least five minutes of coherent dialogue.

Not helping is an embarrassing performance from Andrew McCarthy as the late lamented Reggie. Sporting a goatee, ponytail and a series of wide-eyed stares, he tries hard to leave his bratpacker days behind. A return to acting class would be a more useful step.

Then there's Elizabeth Peña as his scatterbrained lover. She's a case study in affected mannerisms, nervous tics and pathetic prat-falls. In her first leading lady role, it's increasingly clear that Pena should give thought to waitressing.

But supporting cast members Blanche Baker, Lisa Jane Persky and Paige Turco showcase new levels of histrionics. If bad acting were a crime, they'd be on Death Row.

Those failings—and countless others—ensure that "Dead Funny" is no laughing matter.

NEWSDAY, 8/25/95, Part II/p. B7, John Anderson

Having dragged a body around through two "Weekends at Bernie's," former brat-packer Andrew McCarthy now gets to play one. In "Dead Funny,"which is an anatomy of a murder, McCarthy is the anatomy.

Is this a step up? Not exactly. During the flashbacks, McCarthy is more charming than he's probably ever been, but when deceased, he's a distraction. Having discovered Reggie (McCarthy) pinned by a samurai sword to the kitchen table of their West Side apartment, his girlfriend Viv (Elizabeth Pena) spends the rest of the movie trying to figure out what happened. But she never does anything about him. So, like a sinkful of dirty dishes, he's always there in the back of your mind, something untidy and undone.

And let's face it, it's a strictly weird situation. Director-writer John Feldman—who gave us the quirky, noirish "Alligator Eyes" of 1990—wants us to believe that Viv hesitates to call the police because she'd immediately become the prime suspect: Their history as a couple, as we see through Viv's occasionally hallucinogenic flashbacks, was peppered with rough sex and practical jokes; their constant disagreements are common knowledge to their friends. But it's a pretty flimsy thread on which to hang a tale, especially one that sets up the one-joke scenario immediately and then relies, situation-comedy style, on a resulting series of mishaps and misunderstandings.

Urban romances are never depicted the way romances are in, say, Madison County. City love is unstable, like nitroglycerin. Consequently, each romance is an exercise in Sisyphean hopefulness. Or dopefulness. In the case of Viv and Reggie, of course, one of them's already dead. So how do you accept Feldman's attempts to paint their past as destiny? It's tough.

Visually, the film is unobtrusively stylish, and Feldman is sure-handed about keeping the camera and characters moving with purpose—which is good considering the number of friends and acquaintances traipsing through Viv's apartment-cum-morgue. They include Louise (Paige Turco), who tells Viv they're going to get to the bottom of things—"things" being a magnum of champagne. With the cockeyed Louise in her bedroom, Viv also has to cope with her women's support group—including the anxious, child-befuddled Sarah (Lisa Jane Persky)—whose weekly meeting she's forgotten entirely. Why did Viv schedule a group session in her home on the night of her and Reggie's anniversary? We cannot say. But the poignancy mounts.

"Dead Funny" isn't, really. It's a sad story, thanks to all those misunderstandings, and it's also a practical joke. You realize that, as weird as the setup is, it's going to get weirder. And when it does, there's the accompanying sensation of having been skewered.

VILLAGE VOICE, 8/29/95, p. 62, Gary Dauphin

If scaring the bejeezus out of each other is how you and your significant other like to say, "I love you," then the two of you will probably enjoy *Dead Funny*. Judging from the postjoke sex life of Viv and Reggie (Elizabeth Peña and Andrew McCarthy), the shtick must have its merits. The two youngish New Yorkers with disparate incomes stage elaborate pranks, but when Viv comes home one day to find Reggie pinned to the kitchen table by a samurai sword and she thinks he's just up to the usual tricks, a quick kiss reveals otherwise. Viv must piece together events before the cops can pin them on her.

Dead Funny is writer-director John Feldman's second indie feature (after *Alligator Eyes*), but it has a first-film feel to it; his cleverness as a writer often outpaces his visual skills. Peña charms her way through a role assembled mostly out of flashbacks and reactions, while McCarthy has little trouble delivering convincing gotcha's. As a supporting cast of drop-ins starts to appear at Viv's door (including her entire "women's support group"), *Dead Funny* gets strong and steady infusions of new blood, but the line between comic dread and boredom has already been stretched thin. Like many films by new directors, *Dead Funny*'s most resonant image is its last. It's a strikingly simple moment, almost worth the price of admission, but the punch line is so long in coming that rigor mortis has set in.

Also reviewed in:
NEW YORK TIMES, 8/25/95, p. C14, Stephen Holden
VARIETY, 5/29-6/4/95, p. 61, Ken Eisner
WASHINGTON POST, 7/21/95, p. C7, Hal Hinson

DEAD MAN WALKING

A Polygram Filmed Entertainment release of a Working Title/Havoc production. *Executive Producer:* Tim Bevan and Eric Fellner. *Producer:* Jon Kilik, Tim Robbins, and Rudd Simmons. *Director:* Tim Robbins. *Screenplay:* Tim Robbins. *Based on the book "Dead Man Walking" by:* Sister Helen Prejean. *Director of Photography:* Roger A. Deakins. *Editor:* Lisa Zeno Churgin. *Music:* David Robbins. *Music Editor:* Patrick Mullins. *Sound:* Tod A. Maitland. *Sound Editor:* Dan Sable. *Casting:* Douglas Aibel. *Production Designer:* Richard Hoover. *Art Director:* Tom Warren. *Set Decorator:* Laurie Friedman. *Set Dresser:* Larry Amanuel, Harvey Goldberg, Eric M. Metzger, and Henry Kaplan. *Costumes:* Renee Ehrlich Kalfus. *Make-up:* Michael Bigger. *Make-up (Susan Sarandon):* Marilyn Carbone. *Running time:* 120 minutes. *MPAA Rating:* R.

CAST: Susan Sarandon (Sister Helen Prejean); Sean Penn (Matthew Poncelet); Robert Prosky (Hilton Barber); Raymond J. Barry (Earl Delacroix); R. Lee Ermey (Clyde Percy); Celia Weston (Mary Beth Percy); Lois Smith (Helen's Mother); Scott Wilson (Chaplain Farley); Roberta Maxwell (Lucille Poncelet); Margo Martindale (Sister Colleen); Barton Heyman (Captain Beliveau); Steve Boles (Sgt. Neal Trapp); Nesbitt Blaisdell (Warden Hartman); Ray Aranha (Luis Montoya); Larry Pine (Guy Gilardi); Gil Robbins (Bishop Norwich); Kevin Cooney (Governor Benedict); Clancy Brown (State Trooper); Adele Robbins (Nurse); Michael Cullen (Carl Vitello); Peterr Sarsgaard (Walter Delacroix); Missy Yager (Hope Percy); Jenny Krochmal (Emily Percy); Jack Black (Craig Poncelet); Jon Abrahams (Sonny Poncelet); Arthur Bridgers (Troy Poncelet); Steve Carlisle (Helen's Brother); Helen Hester (Helen's Sister); Eva Amurri (9-Year Old Helen); Jack Henry Robbins (Opossum Kid #1); Gary "Buddy" Boe (Opossum Kid #2); Amy Long (Opossum Kid #3); Dennis F. Neal (Henry); Molly Bryant (Nellie); Pamela Garmon (Mirabeau); Adrian Colon (Reporter); John D. Wilmot (Supporter); Margaret Lane (Reporter #1); Sally Ann Roberts (Reporter #2); Alec Gifford (Reporter #3); John Hurlbutt (Reporter #4); Mike Longman (News Anchor); Pete Burris (Parent #1); Joan Glover (Parent #2); Florrie Hathorn (Parent #3); Lenore Banks (Parent #4); Idella Cassamier (Idella); Marlon Horton (Herbie); Kenitra Singleton (Kenitra); Palmer Jackson (Palmer); Johnathan Thomas (Johnathan); Walter Breaux, Jr. (Guard #1); Scott Sowers (Guard #2); Cortez Nance, Jr. (Guard #3); Adam Nelson (Guard #4); Dalvin Ford (Guard #5); Derek Steeley (Guard #6); Jeremy Knaster (Guard #7); Mary Robbins (Aide to Governor Benedict); Miles Guthrie Robbins (Boy in Church).

CHRISTIAN SCIENCE MONITOR, 12/29/95, p. 13, David Sterritt

Is the holiday season a felicitous time to release "Dead Man Walking," a movie so serious and sober that it makes pictures like "Restoration" and "Richard III" look positively playful?

I thought it was a miscalculation at first, but on second thought I've decided the idea has plenty of merit. True enough, one main character is a convicted killer on death row; and the movie reenacts his awful crime in brutal detail, leaving no doubt as to the wickedness of the criminal and the anguish he's wrought on his victim and her family.

But the other protagonist is a Roman Catholic nun who befriends him, assists him in appealing his sentence, and helps him prepare for possible punishment. She believes in her Christian calling with all her heart, and stands by her conviction that the least among us—even those despised by society for what seem unchallengeable reasons—are still God's children, deserving of compassion in their hours of need.

Since this is a profoundly Christian message, its appearance just after Christmas seems more than justified, even if it isn't likely to win the box-office competition with "Toy Story" and other light entertainments.

"Dead Man Walking" may also signal a new willingness by some filmmakers to take on meaningful subjects that churn up thought instead of pacifying it with fluff.

"Cry, the Beloved Country" is another late-year release that engages with difficult issues (including the death penalty) via a compelling narrative and dignified performances. Based on the respected Alan Paton novel, this film also has a deeply religious person as a main character—an Anglican priest in South Africa during apartheid—and demonstrates that Christian ideas can enter the social arena in ways that are neither as mean-spirited nor as narrow-minded as some being touted in American politics.

Other new movies deal with hefty topics as well. "Nixon" asks audiences to ponder historical, geopolitical, and constitutional issues for more than three hours of chronologically complex storytelling. "Twelve Monkeys" brings ecological safety and animal-rights activism into its wild tale about a time-traveling mission. Even the misconceived "White Man's Burden" has weighty things on its mind as it explores racial antagonism in a hypothetical United States where color roles are reversed.

None of these movies is likely to lure many viewers from the romances ("Sabrina") and comedies ("Jumanji") and melodramas ("Heat") and sequels ("Father of the Bride Part II") that studios hope will make their fortunes this season. But it's refreshing to see that social and political topics are not entirely absent from multiplex screens as the decade passes its midpoint.

Equally heartening is the willingness of some writers and directors to abandon the knee-jerk happy endings that have perennially fueled and falsified Hollywood pictures. Viewers of the superbly acted "Georgia" or the vividly filmed "Leaving Las Vegas" will find no last minute panaceas to smooth over the sadly self-destructive behaviors these films harrowingly depict.

No current film is more somber and single-minded than "Dead Man Walking," based on a book by Sister Helen Prejean, who wrote about her own experiences with a Louisiana convict. The movie stars Susan Sarandon as a nun who had never dreamed of visiting death row until she was contacted by a man living there.

Their acquaintance begins when the prisoner (Sean Penn) writes a letter begging for help. Approaching the situation with understandable caution, she listens to the condemned man's story—he admits he was present at the murders but claims his partner did all the killing—and agrees to lend a hand in the appeals process. Their relationship grows more complex as they get to know each other better and as it becomes more probable that he'll undergo the lethal injection they both dread.

It's noteworthy that "Dead Man Walking" was written and directed by Tim Robbins, whose previous picture was the political comedy "Bob Roberts," and that it stars Penn, another celebrity whose film making projects lean toward thoughtful treatments of substantial subjects.

The movie is often preachy and self-conscious, especially in long dialogue scenes, where Robbins's inexpert scriptwriting makes people talk at instead of with each other. Yet the picture's solid assets enable it to soar: above such problems, both intellectually and emotionally. Chief among these assets is Robbins's boldness in telling such a story—resounding with empathy for the misguided and unpriviledged, bristling with anger at capital punishment—at a time when Hollywood rarely takes on political topics.

This said, it must be added that the clear political views of "Dead Man Walking" do not make it a one-sided polemic. Indeed, the movie works hard to make its death-row inmate the creepiest criminal since Hannibal Lector stalked the screen—not just a thug, but a bigot and hate-monger.

Robbins takes two big risks in calling for understanding and sympathy toward such an incorrigible character. One is that he'll turn off audiences from the start, harming the story's ability to engage hearts as well as minds. The other is that moviegoers will miss what I take to be the movie's point—a negative stance toward capital punishment—and will instead find execution a perfectly fitting fate for a hugely unlikable villain. This is how some people interpret Krzysztof Kieslowski's recent Polish drama "A Short Film About Killing," which shows a murder and an execution as comparably evil in their dehumanizing violence.

What makes "Dead Man Walking" one of the year's most encouraging screen events, however, is precisely its insistence on carrying compassionate convictions to their logical extreme, challenging viewers to consider perspectives on crime and punishment—including the Christian mandate to love one's enemy—that aren't heard very often these days.

All involved in the picture should be proud of it. This includes not only Robbins and his stars, Sarandon and Penn, but also the fine supporting players (including Robert Prosky, R. Lee Ermey, and Scott Wilson) and the films many able technicians, mostly cinematographer Roger Deakins.

CINEASTE, Vol. XXII No. 2, p. 42, Christy Rodgers

Social melodramas like Tim Robbins's *Dead Man Walking* have an interesting niche in the vast array of product manufactured by Hollywood studios. The Hollywood style, of course, was perfected to create films which were seamlessly escapist. Rather than examining actual human life, they at best lift the viewer out of it entirely, into the static realm of modern myth, or at least provide a mindless distraction from it for an hour or two. Accordingly, few Hollywood pictures have featured complex, unresolved issues or characters who resemble unidealized human beings.

The social melodrama, or 'message movie,' strays from this norm in one respect. Historically these films have served to tell the story of a social conflict or political idea: like the legal fight against religious bigotry in *Inherit the Wind,* or against institutionalized American racism in various films, from *To Kill a Mockingbird* to *Mississippi Burning*. In so doing they violate the Hollywood norm by dealing directly with disturbing social realities, instead of serving to distract the viewer from them. Interestingly, these movies are overwhelmingly liberal in their political ideology, and while they counter the norm they are frequently celebrated by Hollywood after the fact, generally achieving critical success and often awards from the industry itself.

This apparent contradiction is easier to understand when one looks more closely at the films themselves. Almost without exception good and evil are clearly identified within them. Good is the enlightened liberal ideology and the characters who represent it, evil the reactionary narrow-mindedness of bigotry, fear, opportunism, and greed. Irony and ambiguity are just as excluded here as they are from the most frivolous 'pure' entertainment. The social melodrama ends with a clear triumph of good, and however exhausting or conditional that victory is personalized through an unremitting focus on the actions and motivations of individual characters (usually played by stars), so that the social evil presented comes to lose its systemic quality. Instead, it is located in the actions of the 'bad' characters. When these individuals are converted or disposed of, the evil—injustice, oppression, prejudice—is neutralized.

The result is that, while espousing unquestionably noble ideals, most Hollywood social melodramas do not threaten or challenge viewers, or even make us think very much. They assuage the conscience of the industry without upsetting the status quo. In general, they do not lead us to an understanding of the real root causes of social ills. If they did so, they would definitely not produce the sense of comfort which ensures the commercial success upon which the industry depends.

Dead Man Walking, a film treatment of Sister Helen Prejean's book on her work with death row inmates in Louisiana, sits squarely, if somewhat uneasily, within the confines of this Hollywood tradition. Tim Robbins is a film industry liberal known for his integrity in support of left-liberal causes. His earlier *Bob Roberts* was a sometimes deft, sometimes awkward satire of the rise of the New Right in America. Like Prejean's book, Robbins's movie sets out to show us how the death penalty works, not as an abstract legality, but by presenting its effect on families and inmates. It has been championed by some critics as a dramatic story, not a 'tract,' about capital punishment. But the inevitable conclusion, drawn somewhat crudely in the film's closing sequences, is that state-sponsored killing and individual murder are morally equal and equally wrong.

The problem is not, as some critics would have it, with the message itself, nor in the concept of political art or political entertainment. Just about anywhere else in the world, directors (one thinks of Costa Gavras, Jean-Luc Godard, or Ousmane Sembène) have made successful, entertaining, and accomplished films with expressly political themes, some of which have even been accepted by less politically sophisticated American audiences. The problem is simply that the Hollywood style—with its big stars, big performances, and big drama—guts the political message and thus the real power of the film.

There are ways in which Robbins, who also wrote the screenplay, is obviously trying to create a more-than-normal challenge for the commercial film viewer. One of his two main characters, Matthew Poncelet (Sean Penn), the convict facing execution, is clearly meant to be an anti-hero—he's a racist punk, and he's guilty of the crime for which he's on death row. He's supposed to subvert our expectations for a hero on whom we can pin our fantasies. And if audiences come away questioning his execution, theoretically, it's a challenge to their conventional wisdom about the death penalty (which over sixty percent of the American people apparently support).

The movie's early scenes avoid sensationalized storytelling and formulaic characterizations. The two principals, Prejean (Susan Sarandon) and Poncelet, are introduced in such a way that they emerge almost casually from their vividly-shot Southern surroundings. Robbins takes care not to romanticize Poncelet's prison life or Prejean's life and work in the slums of New Orleans. He doesn't spend too much time depicting these aspects of their lives, either, which might have been interesting. What is most revealing about the real Helen Prejean's work is precisely that the injustice it documents is not exceptional and is rarely dramatic in the conventional sense. It is incorporated into the fabric of daily life, happening to otherwise unremarkable people; it is not something happening apart.

In any case, the understated tone is not sustained. The irony of *Dead Man Walking* is that both its finest elements, including a remarkable performance by Sean Penn, and its worst, most maudlin ones, serve in the end to undercut its effect either as polemic, or as an alternative to hidebound Hollywood melodrama. Ultimately, the larger context—the reason, one supposes, for telling this story in the first place—is lost. It is backgrounded until it disappears entirely as the emotional energy of the film zeroes in (you can count the increasing number of tight close-ups) on the psychodrama between the characters portrayed by Penn and Sarandon.

Of the two, Sean Penn is both better served by the script and maintains a more sophisticated sense of his character throughout. His performance, as the quintessential loser who gradually comes to an awareness of himself and his place in the world through the process of fighting against his own death, is so controlled, so translucent, so sure-footed, that it's easy to see how he walks off with the picture. And whether or not it dilutes the movie's political impact, one of the things Robbins unquestionably does right is to let his actor do his thing. It's as if the physical restrictions of the role—his hands shackled, Penn can't move around or gesticulate in his scenes, he's seldom more than a disembodied head and shoulders on screen—create an actor's challenge to which he rises fully, deepening the intensity and conviction of his portrayal.

As if the formulaic call of melodrama were irresistible, however, Poncelet's march toward death becomes not only a referendum on capital punishment, but also a quest for his individual soul. He is forced to have a tearful epiphany at the hour of his death, to repent his crimes, ask forgiveness of his victims' parents, and acknowledge himself, confusingly, as a 'victim'—as if crime and punishment, repentance and salvation were some sort of recovery program. The emotional pitch is jacked to its highest and most rating as Poncelet is ponderously reconstructed as a Christ-figure in his last moments, strapped to the cruciform death table, arms outstretched, then exposed to face the hostile witnesses in the observation chamber, while Prejean alone sobs and mourns him. The details may be authentic, but the tone is all wrong. If these final scenes had been played with the subdued disquiet, and disembodied sense of routine of a real execution, their effect on an audience might have been revelatory.

Only at this transformed point does Robbins allow Poncelet to be presented as a spokesman against state-sponsored killing. Which begs the question: had the character gone snarling and unrepentant to his death, cursing his victims' families to his last breath, would the death penalty be less wrong? Or would the story merely be less acceptable?

Finally, shots of his surgically sterile execution are intercut with scenes from the bloody killings in which he participated. This sequence is awkward, because it seems to exist for no other reason than to drive home the point that execution equals murder. It has no connection to the journey to personal redemption Robbins has just established for his character, or, in fact, anything else that's been going on during the movie's last half hour.

Susan Sarandon, as Prejean, Poncelet's spiritual counselor and foil, has a difficult task which proves impossible as the movie succumbs to the melodramatic formula. She starts out fine, consistently underplaying her scenes. The difficult task is to make her character's combination of innocence, savvy, and integrity believable, and at first this formidable actress succeeds. But then scene after scene forces us to focus on her tear-stained face as she tries to offer Christ-like love to both Poncelet and his victims' embittered, enraged families. The real Helen Prejean tells a number of stories, and her authorial voice is balanced and self-effacing. The polemical force of her work comes from the relentless accumulation of detail. It is her very plainness, her matter-of-factness, which would lead an audience to believe in the reality of the events she experiences. But in the movie she becomes an icon, loaded with all the weight of the moral rightness of the liberal cause. By the end, dramatically whispering from the Bible as emotive music thunders on the soundtrack during Poncelet's last walk, Sarandon's Prejean is laughable, drowned in the piety she represents. The fact that the real Prejean describes a scene exactly like this in its details but nothing like it in its self-serving emotionalism is significant. Robbins's desire to make this story 'real' expressly depends on Prejean's character, but it breaks down with his inflated conception of her.

Another irritating tendency which DMW shares with the traditional message movie, is to isolate the political message in speeches or conversations rather than consistently and effectively using the structural language of films, its visual power, which has far more symbolic resonance for the viewer. In this movie, as in many others, there is a courtroom scene where the issue is put on trial, and the audience, standing in for the jury, is addressed directly. At a clemency hearing, a lawyer for Poncelet graphically describes the process of death by lethal injection. The scene is such an obvious frame that it has no internal force, much less coherence. What purpose would such a speech serve in the banal procedural events of a real hearing? Another scene has Poncelet remarking, "Ain't no rich men on death row." In social terms, this, not Matthew's character, is the real heart of the matter. But for all we know from Dead Man Walking, he could be the only man on death row. As his is the only story told, or even suggested, the statement simply hangs in the air, stripped of context, then disappears. While it may have everything to do with justice or the lack of it in America, it has nothing to do with the emotional power, or lack of it, in *Dead Man Walking.*

There are some strong vignettes in the prison scenes: the blandness of the prison officials and forced denial of prison workers Prejean encounters are captured with sensitivity and verisimilitude. Throughout the film, however, such individual moments come to feel 'placed.' At the same time there's no sense that the overall selection and progression of scenes is strengthening its argument. It's as if you can hear the mental calculations of industry moguls wondering how they can hold onto even a percentage of the American movie-going public which only turns out in major numbers for *Terminator* or *Jurassic Park.* The answer: Give them, if you must, a 'human story,' not—horrors—a political story. If it has to make a point, make sure no one is overly threatened by it. Give it an uplifting ending.

Tim Robbins may not have wanted to tell this story Hollywood's way, but in the end, it's as though he can't help himself. He never develops a style of storytelling that can really illuminate a systemic evil like capital punishment, in which actually the heart of the story is dehumanization and the intertwining strands of social responsibility and complicity, which are its real threat. Instead, he resorts to standard emotional string-pulling. Where the imagination of an artist wavers, there is neither life nor art, and thus a film, though it may contain powerful elements, as this one does, is ultimately inert.

All that said, I must add that time after time, something in me is touched by movies like *Dead Man Walking,* even while I am feeling cheated by their final inadequacy. Melodrama is an elaborate framework of sentiment, like a rococo facade, which actually serves to conceal rather than illuminate a grain of human or social truth. Anyone still awake under the barrage of spectacle our society produces as cultural soporific is forced to hunt desperately through the maze of images for that grain of truth. Seeing its reflection in some passing moment of popular culture is sadly stirring, but it is not enough.

FILMS IN REVIEW, 3-4/96, p. 58, Leon Friedman

Dead Man Walking is a film about the experiences of Sister Helen Prejean, a Louisiana nun who, as part of her ministry to the poverty stricken in New Orleans, began visiting death row inmates. She eventually becomes a spiritual adviser to the convicts facing execution. "I will be the face of Christ for you," she tells her first confidant, as her face provides a loving image of consolation for them in their last moments. Prejean wrote a book about her experiences in 1991, the title of which was appropriated for the movie. ("Dead Man Walking" is the shouted announcement that guards make as they walk a condemned prisoner to the place of execution.) Susan Sarandon read the book when she was in Louisiana shooting *The Client* and gave it to her significant other, Tim Robbins, who bought the rights, wrote the screenplay, and directed the film.

In the interests of complete disclosure, I should mention that I served as Sister Helen's lawyer in the negotiations with Tim Robbins' company. I was referred to her by her literary agent with whom I share other clients. I consider myself a close friend of Sister Helen as well, since we work together on anti-death penalty efforts.

I first became aware of Sister Helen when I saw her on a television program, talking about her ministry to condemned murderers. "How can you spend so much time and effort helping these monsters who have committed such despicable, outrageous acts and who deserve the punishment they are getting?" the program's interviewer asked. Sister Helen stared straight at the interviewer and in a strong, even voice responded: "A man is more than the worst thing he has ever done."

The profound truth inherent in that remark really struck me. I always felt the worst part of the death penalty was the dehumanizing effect it had on everyone connected with it—we must take a human life in order to show what a monstrous act murder is. Reverence for life is the only message that can truly reflect society's proper attitude toward crime. Furthermore, Sister Helen's remark epitomized the philosophies of all religions i.e., everyone retains a spark of God, and all can be redeemed. It is the function of all religious believers to help inspire that redemption. Can we, as a society, really kill anyone who possesses that spark?

I immediately bought Sister Helen's book and discovered that she had spent much time studying and contemplating the implications of the death penalty. (Her inspiration was provided by Albert

Camus, whose *Reflections on the Guillotine* remains the most thoughtful book about the subject.) Sister Helen's calling to comfort condemned killers had most certainly arisen from true principle and conviction. The book is a careful, thorough, and profound study of the horrors, contradictions, and arbitrary application of the death penalty in America. It also exposes the moral void attached to the ultimate punishment.

The character depicted by Susan Sarandon in *Dead Man Walking* is not the same Sister Helen who wrote the book. One example may suffice to show the difference. In the movie, Sister Helen visits the Percys, parents of one of the killer's victims, in an effort to comfort them. They ask how she can "set with that scum?" referring to Matthew Poncelot (Sean Penn) who has killed their daughter. Susan Sarandon responds, in a stumbling, hesitant voice saying, "Mr. Percy, I've never done this before. I'm trying—I'm just trying to follow the example of Jesus, who said every person is worth more than their worst act." Sarandon's tentative, unsure nun is not the confident, articulate, principled scholar who wrote the book.

Sarandon's Sister Helen is confronted by the victim's parents, prison guards, a governor who refuses to grant clemency, and the prison chaplain who can't understand her merciful efforts. Instead of arguing with each about the futility, horrors, and inconsistencies of the death penalty, which the real Sister Helen would surely have done, Sarandon excuses herself by explaining that it's the first time she has ever visited anyone on death row, and she has been trying to get the condemned man to express his remorse; she was doing it because "he asked me."

But for all my disappointment at the somewhat belittling portrayal of the real Sister Helen, the character portrayed by Sarandon does have integrity and appeal. And the movie as a whole is one of the most thought-provoking films that Hollywood has produced in years. Tim Robbins has decided to de-intellectualize Sister Helen and focus completely on her generosity of spirit and sense of mercy. Though she never confronts or debates those opposing her on an intellectual level, she remains steadfast in her determination to save the condemned man's soul.

In the film, Sister Helen is attempting to comfort a condemned murderer, Poncelot, played by Sean Penn in one of the most remarkable performances of the last decade. He writes to her, she meets him and tries to break through his arrogance to reach the human feelings of confusion, loneliness, and fear that are being denied and covered up as he faces his execution,

The scenes between Sarandon and Penn as they fence with each other through bars or a reflecting plastic screen, as his defenses slip and his need for her surfaces, her religious love reaching and changing him, are among the most genuine and moving ever seen on a movie screen.

The two of them move together, inexorably to the gas chamber. There will be no escape, no discovery of exonerating evidence, no final grant of clemency, no concluding sexual embrace. The most that we can hope for, and the highest gift that Sister Helen can bestow on Poncelot, is to have him reveal that one ounce of humanity he must have—he confesses his involvement, expresses his remorse, and seeks forgiveness from the parents of the victims before the poison courses through his veins.

The actors' performances are amazing. Sean Penn must play a character who himself is play-acting. When Sister Helen first meets him, Poncelot is full of bravado, a macho, Southern redneck, making sexual advances to the nun, denying his guilt, excusing his actions while brazenly challenging the state to do its worst. Sister Helen refuses to be diverted by his racist comments, instead reaching for his soul. Sarandon's character has the strength of her religious beliefs. She knows that she has a mission to accomplish, and her firmness and spirit will not be denied.

The evenhandedness of the film has struck a chord with most critics. Although Robbins and Sarandon's liberal views are well-known, the film does not shrink from showing the horror of the crime and the anguish of the victims' families. But the humanity of Sister Helen's character shines through, and we reject the death penalty for precisely the religious reasons that drive her actions. Even friends of Sister Helen, who know how much more complex she really is, can accept and admire this depiction.

LOS ANGELES TIMES, 12/29/95, Calendar/p. 1, Kenneth Turan

It is happenstance as much as anything else that gets Sister Helen Prejean (Susan Sarandon) to death row. On impulse she answers a letter from an inmate at the Louisiana State Penitentiary at

Angola and now she's in the chaplin's office, listening politely as he tells her that condemned prisoners are without exception manipulative and barbaric. "Do you know," he asks her evenly, "what you're getting into?"

She doesn't, of course, but more to the point, neither do we. For "Dead Man Walking," written and directed by Tim Robbins from Sister Prejean's highly praised book on her death row experiences, is neither easy nor conventional. Unusual in both its subject matter and its approach, this film guides us on a pair of intertwined paths American movies rarely venture down.

Taking the death penalty as its subject, "Dead Man Walking" is first of all an example of the cinema of ideas. Robbins, an accomplished actor whose directorial debut was the political satire "Bob Roberts," is a careful and forceful filmmaker whose movies have something to say. His thrust here is not so much polemical as exploratory: He wants to examine capital punishment with as much dispassion as possible, trusting the power of events to engage us without the aid of over-dramatization.

But because Sister Prejean is its protagonist, "Dead Man Walking" has another aim as well. Her involvement with convicted murderer Matthew Poncelet (Sean Penn) has to do with saving his soul, with allowing him to take responsibility for his acts so he can die in peace and grace. So, with something like the austere gravity more usually associated with the films of French director Robert Bresson, "Dead Man" takes us along on the reluctant, difficult, essentially spiritual journey these two unlikely people make together.

For this kind of straight-ahead movie to work, the acting must be strong without even a breath of theatricality, and in Penn and Sarandon, "Dead Man Walking" has performers capable of making that happen.

Though it's hardly a stretch for Penn to be playing a bad boy, he brings a renewed conviction and a skewered intensity to this part that makes his performance fresh and overpowering. Everything about Poncelet is unsettling and slightly off-center, from his helmet-like lacquered pompadour to the disturbing restraint with which he talks. Cold around the eyes and as mesmerizing as a snake, Poncelet is disturbing as only hard-core evil can be, yet Penn also has the ability to make the character's emotional turmoil believable.

Since complete goodness is harder to make convincing on screen than unblinking evil, Sarandon's part is by definition more challenging. Though her portrayal finally breaks through and gives the film much of its power, it is not as clear-cut or straightforward a success as Penn's work is.

Easy and secure in her belief, with a resilient smile and an unflappable temperament, Sister Helen works at Hope House in a particularly hopeless corner of New Orleans. When she answers Poncelet's letter, goes to meet him on death row and helps interest attorney Hilton Barber (Robert Prosky) in his appeal, she sees her aim of saving a human life as simple and self-evident.

It doesn't remain that way for long. Though Poncelet (a composite of two real-life inmates) maintains his innocence, Sister Helen is disturbed by the horrific nature of the crime he and an associate were convicted of, the brutal murder of a pair of teenage lovers. She is disgusted by his unalloyed prejudice, and finds that as her involvement with his case gets into the papers, her friends and family are increasingly unsympathetic to what she's doing. "A full heart," her mother warns her, "shouldn't follow an empty head."

In fact, "Dead Man Walking" is weakest in not expanding on Sister Helen's reasons for persevering with a case that is causing difficulty with almost everyone close to her. She simply shrugs, smiles and soldiers on, which, combined with Robbins' occasional coldness as a director, makes her seem not as believably human as she needs to be.

One thing that is explored in provocative detail is the strongest jolt Sister Helen receives, the hostility of the murder victims' parents. Their agony at a wound that can never be healed, their challenge to the sister to comfort them as well as the condemned man, are compassionately explored, and their emotional stories are likely to tear up audiences as much as they do Sister Helen.

But though one of the parents tells the sister she must choose sides, she can't have it both ways, Sister Helen disagrees. She is determined to minister to the parents if they'll let her, but also to be Poncelet's designated spiritual advisor, to be with him in the final week before his execution, trying to break through his reserve and save him. While "Dead Man's" conclusion has its doubtful moments, by the time it arrives Sarandon has demonstrated the strength and resolve of Sister Prejean, the sheer forcefulness of her will to goodness.

Though it is not hard to guess which side Robbins is on in all of this, "Dead Man Walking" is not an anti-capital punishment pamphlet. By giving a full hearing to several aspects of this complex issue, the director wants audiences to do what the sister does, to see both Poncelet and the parents as people first and symbols second, to find the human places in this acrimonious and often impersonal debate.

NEW STATESMAN & SOCIETY, 3/22/96, p. 33, Lizzie Francke

At the beginning of *Dead Man Walking* comment is passed on the attire of the central character, Sister Helen Prejean. The nun explains that habits are no longer obligatory—the directive being for modest but distinctive clothing. And modest but distinctive are words one could use to describe this movie adaptation of the real-life experiences of Sister Helen, the New Orleans-based nun who, in the early 1980s, took the unusual and consequently much commented on step of becoming the spiritual adviser to a convicted killer, Matthew Poncelet, in the days before his execution.

It is a powerful story that has already been thoughtfully told—Prejean wrote a book of the same title, while recently the BBC broadcast a documentary directed by Liesl Evans in its *Everyman* slot. One might balk at the Hollywoodisation of it as big stars go sincere. But that is not the case here. Actor turned director/writer/producer Tim Robbins and actress Susan Sarandon (the two are a couple) have a long-standing reputation for their left-wing political involvement off-screen while on screen they have been circumspect about the roles they have played. In a good old-fashioned liberal sense, it would seem that film to them can be a campaigning tool. Robbins' debut movie as a director, *Bob Roberts*, bore this out in rather elementary fashion—the spoof documentary about a folk-singer turned proto-fascist presidential candidate that attempted to tackle the legacy of the 1960s while urging its audience to partake in the democratic process lacked the subtlety of successful satire. But with his second feature, Robbins is more assured.

Dead Man Walking is a no-frills account that avoids heavy-handed cinematic tricks, relying rather on the conviction of the performances from Sarandon as Sister Helen and Sean Penn as Poncelet, as well as the supporting cast. As such, the film's stylistic simplicity belies its complex moral—and spiritual—dimension. This is not just a one-line message movie about the iniquities of capital punishment—but rather a quiet meditation on the terrible conflicting feelings that might erupt after a violent crime. When I first watched the film a couple of weeks ago, it seemed, however, to be something that had a particular purpose, not so much here but in the US, where the death sentence is on the statute books of 38 states. But as I write, *Dead Man Walking* has accrued a more dreadful resonance: watching the film again the day after hearing about the Dunblane massacre put into sharp focus questions about forgiveness and retribution, and what kind of strength it might require for relatives and friends of the victims to humanise the perpetrator of such heinous crimes comes.

Poncelet, who was found guilty of murdering and mutilating a teenage couple while they were courting in the woods, is deemed by a hell-fire preacher on the radio to be the evil scum of the earth. Meanwhile, in a state that has just introduced death by lethal injection to replace electrocution, another commentator airs his views: "Call me sentimental, but I'd rather see him fry" (injection, we are told, is just as painful: the peaceful-looking faces belie internal torture). In Bible-belt country, the Catholic Sister Helen struggles against a very particular creed. Living in a New Orleans housing project where "March for the homeless" posters adorn her walls, her work in the community is inspired by a belief in a God who went among the poor and social outcasts, rallying their cause. For every fiery biblical text quoted to her from "an eye for an eye" through to "those who live by the sword must die by the sword", she has her own more compassionate reading. But clearly, the subject rocks her. It is not presented as a glib matter of quote for quote. Beyond the theological debates, however, the film clearly makes the social comment that "you're not going to find many rich people on death row"; rather impoverished black men and white trash felons like Poncelet.

But true to Sister Prejean's own difficult journey, Robbins does not allow us to draw conclusions easily. Poncelet is certainly not presented as a likeable type. With his pompadour quiff and little goatee beard, Penn characterises him as someone who first comes across as a cocky and arrogant lad, instantly seizing the opportunity, as he takes a drag on his cigarette, to assert to his new visitor "I didn't kill nobody", while even trying to hit on her. Interviewed on

TV, Poncelet does himself no favours as he espouses the crass rhetoric of the white supremacy movement. But gradually Prejean sees through his smoke screen to come face to face with someone who is not evil, but a flawed and frightened individual who was brought up on hate. In the culture that lives by the sword, there will, sadly, be those who brandish it.

Meanwhile, Prejean meets with the parents or the dead boy and girl and attempts to accommodate her own beliefs with their lacerating grief and despair. It is the film's one documentary-style moment as, seated on the sofa, Mr and Mrs Percy (R Lee Ermey and Celia Weston) recount the night their daughter died. And as with documentary, it is the little casual details that fire the emotions—here Mrs Percy's regret that the last words to her daughter were about her skirt hem coming undone. *Dead Man Walking*'s success does not rest in its Oscar nominations, or box office grosses or good reviews, but on audiences leaving the cinema turning over such unbearable moments in the same considered way as this most distinctive and inspirational of characters, Prejean.

NEW YORK, 1/8/96, p. 47, David Denby

Dandified goatee and full, rich head of hair; tattoos and prison-house rant; a rapid, furtive way of speaking, as if designed to conceal meaning—a few minutes of Sean Penn's performance in *Dead Man Walking*, and you know that he's got the role of the Louisiana death-row inmate Matthew Poncelet down right. Penn, narrowing his eyes, looks more like the photographs of actual criminals than any Hollywood actor I can think of. He defines "shifty"; he's mean, cut off, mocking. His Poncelet tries to bully and seduce a nun, Sister Helen Prejean (Susan Sarandon), who takes an interest in his case; and when she proves to be tougher than he thought, he slowly opens up to her, seeking friendship and finally someone to confess to. *Dead Man Walking*, directed by Tim Robbins, and based on a book by the actual Helen Prejean, is the story of Matthew Poncelet's redemption and death.

The movie leaves me a little nonplussed. For long stretches, I admired Robbins's steady, sober decency and his willingness to look painful facts in the face. Poncelet has been convicted of murdering two teenagers, and as Sister Helen defends him, she takes abuse from the parents of the dead kids. Robbins observes the parents' rage neutrally, evenly, without turning them into vengeful hysterics. Unadorned, her voice low and steady, Sarandon gives a solid (though unexciting) performance as a woman determined to take risks and break through to one of God's more unsavory creatures.

But at the end, as nun and murderer reach out to each other in the death chamber, I began to get queasy. I don't question Sister Helen's commitment. But I can't help noticing that she seems to be doing ever so much more for herself than she is for Matthew Poncelet; and I can't help wondering if his death does not conveniently bring to an end (and on a very high-minded note) an attraction that would have proved troublesome in the extreme. The movie's high-mindedness goes askew. The filmmakers blow the case they are plainly making against capital punishment. The implication is that Poncelet shouldn't be executed because he has accepted God and may become a good man. But if you are truly against capital punishment, you're against executing the redeemed and the unredeemed alike. Robbins wants to horrify us, and he shows the execution in detail; the final scene mixes exaltation and death-pornography in a combination that left me almost ill. Matthew Poncelet, spread out like Jesus, goes to Heaven before our eyes. But in my religion, you see, dead men don't walk. They just die. The problem is to make something of yourself in life.

NEW YORK POST, 12/29/95, p. 37, Thelma Adams

Restraint is not what I'd expect when Tim Robbins and Susan Sarandon (who met and meshed romantically on the set of "Bull Durham") team up for a movie about capital punishment.

With "Dead Man Walking," the pair pull off an emotionally complex, intelligent, balanced movie. They resist the easy path to the catharsis in the shadow of the gallows that is the signature of death row dramas.

The title refers to a convict's final steps to the execution chamber. His fate sealed, he's the walking dead. Sister Helen Prejean picked this phrase for the title of her non-fiction book about Louisiana death row inmate's and their victims' families.

Robbins adapted Prejean's book and directed Sarandon in the pivotal role of Sister Helen. Only Robbins would have the guts to show us Sarandon deglamorized without make-up, she's still beautiful but she's carrying some freight. Her big eyes dominate her face, but it's a face with flesh pockets, an early-morning, late-night face.

Sarandon's Sister Helen is no singing nun. She makes mistakes, gets in over her head, jokes and laughs. She has faith in God but not in her own infallibility. Sarandon guides the viewer in a confident performance that's wide and deep and made to seem as easy as her soft Southern accent.

"Dead Man Walking" opens with an unusual home movie. The hand-held footage of the day Helen took her vows play like wedding footage. She married Christ with all the joy of a blushing bride coupled with a "today I become a woman" solemnity. These fleeting scenes remind us that Helen wasn't always a nun. She grew up like we did, listening to rock 'n' roll and eating Twinkies. The narrative shorthand humanizes Helen.

Helen lives in the projects where she does social service work. It is only when she becomes the pen pal of a a of convicted killer Matthew Poncelet (Sean Penn), that the sister stumbles into the center of the capital punishment storm.

In the same low-key way that Robbins deglamorizes Sarandon, he resists romanticizing Poncelet. Convicted in a lover's lane double-murder of two teens—and the rape of the girl—Poncelet maintains his innocence. Unrepentant, he blames his partner who, through the ministrations of a better lawyer, does not share his seat on death row.

While Poncelet gains sympathy with his complaint "ain't nobody with money on death row"—and brings in a sharp intake of breath in this, the year of our O.J.—he quickly loses it. He comes on to Helen sexually and makes racist remarks. In one indelible moment at the climax of a series of flashbacks to the crime, brilliantly played by Penn, we see the criminal's feral wildness.

The exchanges between Penn and Sarandon forms the drama's core. The actress serves as a foil for the felon's flamboyance. Penn's blue-eyed redneck has a Charles Manson intensity—but he's also a young man who will die before he has matured, a kid whose mouth runs ahead of his brains to his own detriment.

Penn rings these changes without saying, Look at me, I'm Penn in the pen. One of his most affecting scenes frames the familiar banter he carries on with his younger brothers when they visit him just hours before his death. Like Helen, like his victims, Poncelet has a mother who loves him, was the subject of baby pictures, has a role in the family hierarchy that no one else can fill.

The victims' parents provide the third point of the triangle that gives "Dead Man Talking" its balance. They yank Sister Helen away from her ritual ministrations to Poncelet and rage: what about us, what about our children, what about our loss? Like the pleas of Ronald Goldman's father earlier this year, they ask where is our justice?

Whatever your opinion on the death penalty, "Dead Man Waking" offers a stimulating dialogue and one hell of a good drama. See it with someone you love—to argue with.

NEWSDAY, 12/28/95, Part II/p. B2, Jack Mathews

Where do you stand on the issue of capital punishment?

Do you believe every human being has value, regardless of what that person does, and that the state commits murder every time it executes someone? Do you believe that executing killers hastens the healing of the victims' families and deters others from committing the crime?

Where you stand is a fair predictor of how you'll respond to Tim Robbins' "Dead Man Walking," a death-row drama based on the experiences of New Orleans nun Sister Helen Prejean in her work as a spiritual counselor to Louisiana inmates facing execution. Though the film's political message is clearly anti-capital punishment, Robbins has created such an effective illusion of fairness—showing us the pain of the victims' families as well as the brutality of the crimes—that people in favor of the death penalty will have no reason to change their minds.

In adapting his script, Robbins made a composite character of two men of widely differing temperaments whom Prejean had counseled before their deaths. One man was a pure sociopath, feeling no remorse for his crime; the other was overwhelmed with fear and guilt. The film's Matthew Poncelet (Sean Penn), a low-life punk and Aryan Supremacist, runs the entire spectrum of emotion from cold-hearted denial to sobbing repentance, and it is the performance of Penn's career.

In fact, Penn and Susan Sarandon, who plays Prejean, do extraordinary work with two of the year's most difficult acting assignments. Except for one scene, on the afternoon of Poncelet's scheduled execution when she and his family are allowed to share a room with him, Sarandon and Penn act out the evolving, dynamic relationship of their characters with a partition between them.

It is a strange and powerful relationship, a deeply spiritual woman struggling through her own inexperience and emotions to save the soul of a man who has committed unspeakable acts. It's a salvage job she cannot pull off until he has acknowledged his sins and asked for redemption; and getting him to that point is the dramatic arc of the story.

Robbins, in a bold move likely to sabotage his own agenda, shows us just how brutal Poncelet's acts were, through recurring flashbacks that re-enact the evening he and a friend, high on alcohol and drugs, surprised a pair of teenage lovers in the woods and executed them after raping the girl.

Robbins craftily intercuts the last moments of the murders with the execution of Poncelet, showing us just what an-eye-for-an-eye justice looks like. The cold, clinical execution, a lethal injection done on a virtual proscenium before an audience comprising the victims' parents, reporters, prison officials and Prejean, is indeed a ghastly sight. But compared to the images from the woods, the prison event isn't the gut-wrencher it's intended to be, and I expect Poncelet's death will evoke cheers in some theaters.

It is not cheered in that witness room. The victims' families, whose pain and anger we get to know through Prejean's efforts to console them throughout the story, seem more drained than ever afterward, and we are left with the sense that the execution they demanded has cost them some of their own humanity.

That is Robbins' view, and presumably Prejean's, and it's an honest one. Whether it will persuade others, however, remains to be seen. In his attempts to avoid overloading his argument, by balancing it with the feelings of injured and righteous people on the other side, Robbins has debated himself to a draw.

NEWSWEEK, 1/8/96, p. 69, David Ansen

Sister Helen Prejean (Susan Sarandon) is a nun who works in a New Orleans housing project. Matthew Poncelet (Sean Penn) is a tattooed convict facing execution for the murder of two teenage lovers. About all they have in common, quips the nervous Sister Helen when she first encounters this unsavory killer, is that "we both live with the poor."

In writer-director Tim Robbins's *Dead Man Walking*, the nun and the murderer are forced into a kind of spiritual intimacy. Hoping to escape his death sentence, Poncelet writes Sister Helen for help—to find him a lawyer for his appeal, and then to become his spiritual adviser. The man she encounters is a slimy, racist, arrogant low-life who insists he didn't kill anyone. And as the good sister becomes obsessed with reaching this scumbag's soul, she finds herself alienating others. The black kids she works with at Hope House wonder why she's cozying up to a white supremacist; the grieving parents of Poncelet's victims despise her for giving comfort to the enemy.

"Dead Man Walking" is no simple diatribe against capital punishment. Robbins, through this story based on Sister Prejean's book about her death-row experiences, is asking us to consider what it means to take a human life. What's admirable about his approach is his refusal to stack the deck: he neither turns his condemned man into a misunderstood martyr nor short-shrifts the pain of the victims' families. He sustains his balancing act to the dreadful climax, when he crosscuts between Poncelet's execution by lethal injection and the brutal murders he committed.

It's a strong film, made stronger by two terrific performances. Penn's acting has ruthless honesty. Because his meanness can chill us so deeply, his terror in the face of death—and his last grasp at redemption—move us the more deeply. Sarandon's challenge is even harder: playing saintliness is a tough act—but there's no sanctimony in her performance. Sister Helen is not always sure of herself; there's a touching naivete, and a toughness, to her faith. She's always leaning forward toward Poncelet, nose upturned, wide eyed, her radar attuned to any glimmer of virtue this repellent man might possess.

"Dead Man Walking" is a powerful and intelligent piece of work, yet there's something impersonal about Robbins's approach, a hint of the medicinal. You yearn for an encounter that isn't locked into the interrogatory form of a social worker's visit. And in one great scene you get it: when Poncelet, let out of his cell, pays his final visit with his family. The awkward small talk, the crazy attempt to normalize an unbearable moment, the pointless cheeriness are brilliantly observed. It could be any strained family gathering, except the prodigal son is chained to his chair, and no one is allowed to hug him goodbye.

SIGHT AND SOUND, 4/96, p. 43, Philip Kemp

Sister Helen Prejean, a Catholic nun doing social work in a poor district of New Orleans, receives a letter from Matthew Poncelet, a prisoner on Death Row. She replies, and he asks her to visit him. Poncelet, she learns, was convicted of brutally killing a teenage couple, Walter Delacroix and Hope Percy, and of raping Hope before killing her. Despite being warned by the prison chaplain that she's out of her depth, Helen goes ahead and sees Matthew. Claiming he's innocent, he tells her the killings were the work of his companion Carl Vitello. Though unconvinced and finding Matthew in many ways repellent, Helen agrees to support his appeal for a pardon.

Helen engages a lawyer, Hilton Barber, to represent Matthew at the Pardon Board hearing, and persuades Lucille Poncelet, Matthew's mother, to attend. At the hearing Helen meets the victims' parents, Earl Delacroix and Clyde and Mary Beth Percy, who reproach her for not having contacted them. Matthew's appeal is turned down, and the execution set for one week hence. Helen agrees to become his spiritual adviser until his death, though her resolve is shaken when he makes racist, neo-nazi remarks in a television interview.

Helen visits the parents of Matthew's victims. Earl Delacroix, whose marriage is breaking up, receives her courteously, but the Percys order her out on learning that she is still, as they see it, "on Matthew's side". In her meetings with Matthew, Helen urges him to acknowledge his part in the killings, though he pins his hopes on taking a lie-detector test. An appeal to the Governor gets nowhere, and the test proves inconclusive. On the day of the execution, Matthew says goodbye to his mother and brothers before confessing to Helen that he killed Walter. In the death chamber he asks forgiveness of Earl and the Percys, who are watching, and fixes his gaze on Helen as he dies. After his funeral, Helen and Earl kneel side by side in a church.

Dead Man Walking could so easily have been utterly dire. A death-row killer brought to last-minute repentance by the love of a Catholic nun suggests at best yet another back-and-forth debate on the death penalty, and at worst great washes of gooey moral uplift. Instead Tim Robbins' film rejects polemic and sentimentality, and delivers something far more moving and, given a subject like this, far more difficult to achieve: emotional honesty. He's immeasurably helped by two outstanding central performances: Sarandon has never been better (which is saying a lot), and Sean Penn gives by far his finest performance to date.

And they in turn draw sustenance from the intelligence of Robbins' script and the integrity of his direction.

As a writer and a director, Robbins values ambiguity. In his first film, Bob Roberts, he could well have made his rightist singer-politician a sneering villain or redneck, a bogeyman to laugh at and dismiss. But by daring to let him be witty, personable, even persuasive, the film turned him into a much scarier individual. Similarly, Matthew Poncelet is neither a pathetic victim of society nor a repellent monster, though he has aspects of both. Just as we register what seems like an expected point—absentee, alcoholic father—Matthew tells a story of getting plastered with his old man at age 12, and tells it as a cherished memory. His dealings with his mother and brothers are warm and jokey: this is no poor deprived kid who "never had no love".

In its structure, the film winds itself ever tighter around the key central relationship. Initially, Helen is repelled by Matthew's cocky callousness, while he sees in her a sucker to be used and exploited. Helen herself is no burnished icon of goodness; though never sanctimonious, there's an unconscious arrogance behind her diffidence (as Earl Delacroix shocks her by pointing out). As they gradually narrow the emotional gap, acknowledging their respective fears and weaknesses, the dynamic between them is visually defined by the space dividing them and what's in it.

To begin with, they're separated by a fine-mesh grille, on which Roger Deakins' camera varies focus, sometimes making it an opaque barrier, at others near-transparent. Later they're divided by clear perspex, later again by wide-set bars, until the intervening space clears and Helen can at last touch Matthew, her hand grasping his shoulder in the final death walk. Here too, in lighting and set design, the film discards prison-movie cliché: this jail is no shadowy gothic hell-hole, but institutional, dull, almost cosy in its drab way. The horror comes in the obscene clinical minutiae of the killing process: the straps and plastic tubes, the needle and the calibrated phials.

One or two details strain credulity but they are trivial matters beside the way the film builds, steadily and inexorably, to a climax of shattering intensity. Right to the end, Robbins plays scrupulously fair, never letting us forget what Matthew did, repeatedly cutting from execution back to killings, juxtaposing the unforgivable cruelty of his death with the no less unforgivable brutality of his crime. Against these images of violence can be set nothing except Sarandon's Helen singing the hymn 'Be not afraid' in a cracked, tuneless voice, and offering herself as "the face of love" for Matthew to see as he dies. Given a more meretricious film (or an actress with less grasp of emotional nuance), this could be intolerably cloying. It's a measure of Robbins' achievement that moments like these create a genuine sense of consolation, fragile but profoundly moving.

TIME, 1/8/96, p. 69, Richard Schickel

The achievement of *Dead Man Walking* is quite a simple one: at its end you don't know where Tim Robbins, its writer-director, stands on the issue of capital punishment. Considering that there is no more tendentious topic available to a filmmaker, Robbins' restraint, his determination to explore the moral and psychological nuances of the relationship that develops between Matthew Poncelet (Sean Penn), a man condemned to death for his participation in a heinous crime, and Sister Helen Prejean (Susan Sarandon), who becomes his spiritual counselor in his final months, is exemplary.

And in a way surprising, since Robbins and Sarandon, a real-life couple, are not known for their shyness in expressing outraged opinions on controversial subjects. Here, however, working from a free adaptation of an autobiographical book by Sister Prejean, they have chosen to pursue a matter too subtle for sloganeering: the faint possibility that evil and goodness can find a way of speaking to one another, the dim hope that the former can be in some sense redeemed, the latter in some sense educated.

Cases don't come any harder than Poncelet's. His drifting life reaches its nadir when, with another man, he commits a lovers' lane rape and double murder, steadfastly (and unpersuasively) insisting that he did not commit the killings. There is about him an inchoate rage tempered, if that's the word we want, by self-pity and a certain raw intelligence, which has led him to jailhouse lawyering and several stays of execution. It is largely the latter quality, and the challenging seductiveness of his manner, that leads Sister Helen to see in him the possibilities of redemption.

Cases don't come any gentler than hers. She is a woman of solid middle-class background. If anything, she has been more mysteriously called to a life caring for the marginal than Poncelet has been to his life of darkness. All we really know about her is that her moral courage is matched by her moral acuity. She opens herself up not just to the condemned man but also to the families of his victims, thereby squaring the movie's moral drama. Whatever she may think about the brutal finality of capital punishment, she cannot deny the anguish of these victims, the brutal finalities that a terrible crime has imposed on them.

Sister Helen can find only limited possibilities for mercy in this situation. Perhaps if Poncelet can be persuaded to admit his full complicity in the crime, he will find some peace, some honor, in his final moments. Perhaps if he does so, the victims' families will find a closure more consoling than revenge.

It is a measure of this movie's integrity that it offers no reprieve more melodramatically satisfying than this. It is a measure of its complexity—and of the forces Penn and Sarandon have held in reserve during their hypnotic struggle for his soul—that its final moments leave us awash in emotion. How hard it is to achieve even modest states of grace in this world. How patiently we must work to achieve them. How easy, absent a Sister Helen, it is to miss them entirely.

VILLAGE VOICE, 1/2/96, p. 45, J. Hoberman

Dead Man Walking could easily have been dead on arrival and writer-director Tim Robbins de-serves credit for tackling what just might be the least popular cause in Clinton's

America—opposition to the death penalty. Inspired by incidents in the 1993 nonfiction bestseller by Sister Helen Prejean (and casting a new light on Robbins's own prison performance in *The Shawshank Redemption*), the movie pivots on the death row relationship between a socially progressive New Orleans nun (Susan Sarandon) and the condemned killer of a teenage couple (Sean Penn).

From the perspective of the nun, the movie is a test of faith. Less radiant than confused, Sarandon's Sister Helen assumes the thankless task of serving as Penn's spiritual adviser, exuding a thoughtful nobility while ceding center screen. Penn makes up for Sarandon's lack of makeup—playing the killer as a showboat cavalier with a mustache and goatee, as well as a lacquered pompadour so pulled up it could be a wig. But if his character is all bravado it's a facade constructed to be broken down. Steely-eyed and diffident, Penn manages to appear vulnerable without being likable—particularly in a powerfully awkward farewell scene with his mother and brothers. (It's a pity he didn't cast himself in the role of the ex-con in *The Crossing Guard*.)

Given its tough subject matter (and a defensive nod toward comparative victimology notwithstanding), *Dead Man Walking* is not nearly as self-congratulatory as it might have been. Although the exposition is fragmented by flashbacks showing increasingly more of the crime, all narrative coyness is abandoned once Robbins gets down to the nuts-and-bolts reality of state-sanctioned murder. As such, *Dead Man Walking* is one of the least compromised Hollywood dramas of recent years—although it's a bit soft compared to Krzysztof Kieslowski's 1989 *A Short Film About Killing*, the most unflinching treatment of capital crime and punishment I've ever seen.

Also reviewed in:
CHICAGO TRIBUNE, 1/12/96, Friday/p. C, Michael Wilmington
NATION, 2/5/96, p. 35, Stuart Klawans
NEW REPUBLIC, 2/5/96, p. 26, Stanley Kauffmann
NEW YORK TIMES, 12/29/95, p. C1, Janet Maslin
NEW YORKER, 1/8/96, p. 68, Terrence Rafferty
VARIETY, 12/18-31/95, p. 66, Emanuel Levy
WASHINGTON POST, 1/12/96, p. D1, Hal Hinson
WASHINGTON POST, 1/12/96, Weekend/p. 32, Desson Howe

DEAD PRESIDENTS

A Hollywood Pictures release in association with Caravan Pictures of an Underworld Entertainment production. *Executive Producer:* Darryl Porter. *Producer:* Albert Hughes and Allen Hughes. *Director:* Albert Hughes and Allen Hughes. *Screenplay:* Michael Henry Brown. *Story:* Allen Hughes and Albert Hughes. *Suggested by the story "Specialist No. 4 Hayward T. 'The Kid' Kirkland"* *by:* Wallace Terry. *Director of Photography:* Lisa Rinzler. *Editor:* Dan Lebental. *Music:* Danny Elfman. *Music Editor:* E. Gedney Webb. *Sound:* Frank Stettner and (music) Robert Fernandez and Dennis Sands. *Casting:* Risa Bramon Garcia and Mary Vernieu. *Production Designer:* David Brisbin. *Art Director:* Kenneth A. Hardy. *Set Decorator:* Karin Wiesel. *Set Dresser:* Anne Wenniger. *Costumes:* Paul A. Simmons. *Make-up:* Ellie Winslow. *Stunt Coordinator:* Jeff Ward. *Running time:* 120 minutes. *MPAA Rating:* R.

CAST: Larenz Tate (Anthony Curtis); Keith David (Kirby); Chris Tucker (Skip); Freddy Rodriguez (Jose); Rose Jackson (Juanita Benson); N'Bushe Wright (Delilah Benson); Alvaletah Guess (Mrs. Benson); James Pickens, Jr. (Mr. Curtis); Jenifer Lewis (Mrs. Curtis); Clifton Powell (Cutty); Elizabeth Rodriguez (Marisol); Terrence Howard (Cowboy); Ryan Williams (Young Revolutionary); Larry McCoy (Nicky); Rodney Winfield (Mrs. Warren); Cheryl

Freeman (Mrs. Barton); Sticky Fingaz (Martin); Bokeem Woodbine (Cleon); David Barry Gray (DeVaughn); Michael Imperioli (D'Ambrosio); Jaimz Woolvett (Lt. Dugan); Quynh Phann (Skivvie Girl #1); Clifton Gonzalez Gonzalez (Betancourt); Jean Claude La Marre (Ramsuer); Daniel Kruse (Corporal Rob); Robert Smith (Helicopter Pilot); Bernard Telsey (Protester #1); Rik Colitti (Cabbie); Heather B. (Peaches); Carlton Wilborn (Spyder); Frank Albanese (Mr. Gianetti); Monti Sharp (Officer Brown); Tony Sirico (Officer Spinelli); Robert Lupone (Attorney Salvatore Rizzo); Joelle Hernandez (Juanita's Child, Sarah); Tim Zay (Protester #2); Charles E. Lesene (Numbers Taker); Cuc Dinh (Madame Minh); Yen Chin Grow (Skivvie Girl #2).

CHRISTIAN SCIENCE MONITOR, 10/13/95, p. 12, David Sterritt

"Dead Presidents" comes from the Hughes Brothers, the young black filmmakers who burst into prominence with "Menace II Society" two years ago. They are now achieving a rare measure of acclaim by having their new picture bow at the New York Film Festival before opening in theaters.

Again their subject is the difficulty of living, loving, and surviving in the mean streets of an African-American ghetto. But this time they broaden their canvas and deepen their analysis by pursuing an angle that few movies have explored: the relationship between inner-city violence and military indoctrination, which can be just as deadly even though it's sanctioned by society and promoted as a pathway to a respectable career.

The story begins in the late 1960s, as young Anthony ponders the options available to him as a young black man from a South Bronx neighborhood. He gets no shortage of advice from friends and relatives—his parents, who hope he'll go to college; his girlfriend, who wishes he'd stay with her; and his mentor, a local thug who urges him to stick around the 'hood to see what criminal opportunities come along.

Bypassing all of them, Anthony joins the Marines and heads for Vietnam, where his thick-skinned attitudes help him stay alive longer than many of his fellow soldiers. Returning to New York in the early '70s, he finds his circumstances somewhat changed, but the basic facts of life are the same as ever. Jobs are scarce, finances are low, and the future looks as uninviting as the present.

The only major difference is that he's now a seasoned fighter, stalker and killer courtesy of the Marine Corps training and a lot of practice in the Vietnam jungle. Driven by need and tempted by greed, he joins a scheme to steal a truckload of outdated cash—the "dead presidents" of the title, worn-out bills on their way to a Treasury incinerator.

Much of "Dead Presidents" plays like a regular inner-city melodrama. Aspects of the story recall such pictures as "Boyz N the Hood" and "New Jack City," and the plot culminates in a holdup and chase scene that combines effective suspense with more violence than the filmmakers need to make their point.

What gives the film unusual interest is its probing of the link between Anthony's experiences and the environments that shape them: his poor Bronx community burdened with harsh social realities, and the battlefields of Vietnam overflowing with mayhem.

While the movie doesn't try to equate these very different places and situations, it shows how inseparable they become in Anthony's evolving consciousness: He returns home and tries to establish a decent life on the strength of his record as a brave young man who risked his life for his country—only to discover that the community at large couldn't care less, but expects him to lead the same hand-to-mouth existence that would have been his lot if he'd never left home.

At its most thoughtful moments, "Dead Presidents" poses a question so troubling that Hollywood normally steers away from it. What are the rewards for a person who starts off playing by society's rules but finds the game skewed by racial, economic, and cultural handicaps? The movie offers no easy answers, but deserves credit for raising the issue loudly and clearly.

Larenz Tate, who made his debut in "Menace II Society" gives the picture a solid center of gravity as the troubled main character. Skillful support comes from Keith David as his low-life mentor, Rose Jackson and N'Bushe Wright as his girlfriend and her politically active sister, and Chris Tucker and Freddy Rodriguez as his best friends. Michael Henry Brown wrote the uneven but powerful screenplay. Lisa Rinzler did the crisp cinematography.

LOS ANGELES TIMES, 10/4/95, Calendar/p. 1, Kenneth Turan

Coming after Spike Lee's "Clockers" and Carl Franklin's "Devil in a Blue Dress," the Hughes brothers' "Dead Presidents" is the third significant work by an African American filmmaker to be released by a major studio within the last month. And though twins Allen and Albert Hughes are the youngest of the group, it is their film that is the most ambitious, the most unsettling and often the most powerful.

"Dead Presidents" (a slang term for paper money) is a film that is both expected and surprising, familiar and yet somehow different. Made with fluid skill and a passion for storytelling, its tale of how the Vietnam War and American society affect a black Marine remains accessible while confounding expectations. Set largely in a single neighborhood in the Bronx, this is an occasionally awkward film that still manages an epic feeling, one that has the ambition to tell a larger story through one individual's experience.

Given the critical and box-office success of their first effort, "Menace II Society," made when they were but 20 years old, it was inevitable that the Hughes brothers would be given carte blanche for their next project. But instead of the self-indulgence that usually results from this kind of free ticket, "Dead Presidents" is a film of unexpected heft and scope.

By focusing on just four or five years in the life of young Anthony Curtis (Larenz Tate), "Dead Presidents" (written by Michael Henry Brown of HBO's "Laurel Avenue") echoes the experience of a generation of men whose lives were distorted by Vietnam. And though there is as much violence as viewers of "Menace II" would expect, the film's strong comments on American society are made with restraint and noticeable lack of stereotyping, and are the more telling for it.

Though the northeast Bronx has become a symbol of urban wretchedness, when "Presidents" opens in 1968 (with a deliberately Andy Hardyesque scene of Anthony delivering milk) it was a multiracial area of tidy one-family houses. Anthony himself is a high school senior with a serious girlfriend named Juanita (Rose Jackson) but no definite plans for the future.

Responsible enough to work as a numbers runner for a pool hall owner named Kirby (another striking performance by "Clockers'" Keith David), he has difficulty focusing on a direction for his life. Because both Kirby, who lost part of a leg in Korea, and his own father are veterans, he opts to join the Marines and take his chances in Vietnam, where neighborhood pals Skip (Chris Tucker) and Jose (Freddy Rodriguez) soon join him.

Life in the combat zone takes up only 15 or 20 minutes of "Dead Presidents'" screen time, but it's long enough to demonstrate why soldiering in that charnel house with comrades like the psychotic Cleon (Bokeem Woodbine), who prefers severed heads as souvenirs, puts a permanent mark on him. "No bad habits," he laconically tells his mother when he gets back to the Bronx, "except a little killing. For my country, of course."

His country, it turns out, does not return the favor. Drugs have become a force in the neighborhood but even worse, the jobs are disappearing, and what happened to Anthony overseas clouds all his relationships, especially that with girlfriend Juanita, who gave birth to his daughter while he was gone. All Anthony wants to do is to get over, to survive, and when an opportunity presents itself that is outside the law, his choice is inevitable.

Perhaps the most impressive aspect of "Dead Presidents'" story is its refusal to indulge in stereotyping. Unlikely, even unsavory characters like a pimp named Cutty (strongly played by Clifton Powell) turn out to have provocative things to say. Though the feeling of despair that hovers around Anthony is inescapable, the film does without convenient villains to blame it on. The few white people that manage to penetrate into Anthony's world are more figures of indifference or even assistance than of malice.

What "Dead Presidents" is implicitly saying is that the fault lies with powerful but unseen forces of society-wide racism and indifference. Racial issues hover at the periphery, just outside of Anthony's consciousness for most of the film. His pal Skip says Vietnam "is not our war"; he finds a pamphlet saying the same thing on a bloody battlefield. By the time Anthony reacquaints himself with Juanita's radical sister Delilah (N'Bushe Wright) and begins to have a handle on the nature of the problem, it is too late.

Actor Larenz Tate galvanized "Menace II" with his performance as the thoughtlessly homicidal O-Dog, and his work here is equally impressive. While playing one or the other of Anthony's personalities would not be difficult, Tate is convincing both as the dreamy prewar innocent and the haunted Vietnam veteran. By making Anthony's terrible change believable, Tate gives the Hughes brothers' work an intimate, human quality it might not otherwise have,

"Dead Presidents" is marred by such sins of youth as the occasional awkward or obvious sequence and moments of excess. But working with their "Menace II" cinematographer Lisa Rinzler, the Hughes brothers manage visual nods to Martin Scorsese and Sergio Leone while making the material completely their own. By taking a step back and looking at the world that came before, they've taken a major step ahead in their own filmmaking careers.

NEW YORK POST, 10/4/95, p. 36, Thelma Adams

Albert and Allen Hughes ("Menace II Society") know how to give their audiences a rush.

In a breathless sequence in the fraternal twins' latest movie, "Dead Presidents," Anthony Curtis (Larenz Tate) runs through a series of Bronx backyards to escape the wrath of his girlfriend's mother.

One minute, Curtis is kissing Juanita (Rose Jackson) and his virginity goodbye, the next he's vaulting chain-link fences, beset by dogs and neighbors. Without missing a beat, the 18-year-old is racing through Vietnamese jungles, hip deep in muck and carnage.

The moment is shrewd and super-charged. Before the run, the movie had a tough-but-tender, young-black-man-coming-of-age in the '60s feeling. The Hughes brothers play the couple's fumbled first sexual encounter for laughs, with the boy as the bewildered love object.

After the run, Curtis has his boots planted in "Platoon" territory. The laughs are darker now, shuffled between unspeakable atrocities and intimate moments of soldiers, black and white, bonded by fear and a shared mission.

While Curtis is bombarded by the idea that this isn't his war, it's a white man's war, he briefly finds a sense of purpose in the Marines. It might be hell, but he finds an outlet for his abilities. Amid the destruction, he walks like a man.

The rush of the running sequence represents both what works and what doesn't in this good-hearted film. Despite half a dozen pungent moments and an appealing cast that includes Keith David as Curtis' streetwise mentor and Bokeem Woodbine as a whacked-out preacher's son, "Dead Presidents" rushes through a series of shorter movies.

Coming-of-age comedy collides with war story feeds into Vietnam-vet-coming-home saga and hits the wall in an adrenaline-pumped caper finale. It's up to the audience to connect the dots. Working in tandem with screenwriter Michael Henry Brown (cable's "Laurel Avenue"), the Hughes brothers don't have the control or the distance on their subject to communicate the total picture.

As the movie layers on scene after scene, Curtis becomes increasingly vague. The veteran returns to a shattered Bronx where Juanita has been raising their love child. His domestic life doesn't gel: Curtis connects with his daughter, gets Juanita pregnant again, but he appears just as bewildered by adult love as he was on that fateful graduation night spent in Juanita's arms. Is this a failing of character, a result of Vietnam or the fact that, upon returning home, he cannot get a job and the respect that comes with it?

Intent on jump-starting his civilian life, Curtis, the good Marine beaten down by the war at home, masterminds a plot to shanghai a shipment of dead presidents—slang for cash. The Hughes brothers direct the sequence with enormous energy and an edgy humor on the brink of despair.

But there's one unavoidable problem: is Curtis' pilgrim's progress from good boy to armed robber supposed to be a tragedy? If it is, the Hughes are more adept at planting explosives than tending character motivations. If it isn't, then why should we care what happens to this son of the Bronx?

NEWSDAY, 10/4/95, Part II/p. B3, John Anderson

Burning money is a pretty good way of getting people's attention, and the Hughes brothers—Albert and Allen, makers of the incendiary "Menace II Society"—know how to get people's attention. They also know how to make movies.

They certainly know how to provoke. "Dead Presidents"—whose opening credit sequence pictures Lincolns, Grants, Washingtons and even Benjamin Franklins going up in flames—is a tragedy in three acts, each of which possesses its own distinct atmosphere and quotient of dread, and each of which is an indictment of societal turpitude. It is not entirely serious, however. The violence is always a little too mischievous, and the nervous energy that infects the entire film has a vaguely absurdist quality to it.

It hangs together, though, in a way that makes its two-hour running time feel like a profoundly deliberate heartbeat.

Larenz Tate is not just the star of the film; he is its map and its soul. As Anthony Curtis—who transmutates from a good-natured Bronx numbers runner to a lethal military tool in Vietnam to a despondent statistic in a country that doesn't need him anymore—he's far closer to the sweetly daffy character he played in "The Inkwell" than to the murderous O-Dog of "Menace II Society." But the crushed naïveté he brings to the role is what makes him so endearing, and disturbing. In his journey from petty crime to government-sanctioned murder to the ill-planned heist that is the film's final movement, he embodies the national trauma that was the war and is the streets.

Although it has a conscience, the film doesn't jam us up with sociology. It's an entertainment, and its characters and screenplay—by Michael Henry Brown—are built for speed, not comfort. Keith David gives a commanding performance as Kirby, the Faginesque hustler and strong-arm man who becomes Anthony's surrogate father (his real father, played by James Pickens Jr., is a sphinx). As with Delroy Lindos' character in "Clockers," Kirby's power and business acumen—which includes the occasional thumping of deadbeats—is irresistible to a kid who never sees strength displayed in any other way. And their relationship is part of an ongoing nightmare.

Each of the three parts of Anthony's story life gets a different treatment. The first, a sunny, coming-of-age tale set in the Bronx, sets up Anthony with his friends Skippy (Chris Tucker, who's very good) and Jose (Freddy Rodriguez), as well as with Juanita (Rose Jackson), who will have his baby while he's in Vietnam. The wartime chapter shifts the film into the land of "Apocalypse Now," where the battle scenes may lack verisimilitude but the sense of blind madness feels quite correct. Anthony's return home—to an altered landscape of closed options, street revolution and dead ends—is straight street drama. It includes his troubled reunion with Juanita, his humiliation at the hands of her ex-lover—the menacing Cutty (Clifton Powell)—and his loss of job, face and future. The heist itself may be pure mayhem, but it's also inevitable.

Much of "Dead Presidents"—street slang for money, which is the root of all Anthony's problems—is alarming, particularly the Hughes brothers' penchant for grisly violence and its gory results. It isn't gratuitous exactly; what Anthony sees, and does, is not science fiction. But the directors have their fun: Anthony, returning to the Bronx from Vietnam, gets a job with a butcher (Seymour Cassel), which provides for plenty of 'Nam-evoking visuals. But for all their posturing, the Hughes brothers are among the most promising of the promising young filmmakers, full of electricity and fire and an ability to make us think while we think we're being entertained.

SIGHT AND SOUND, 9/96, p. 38, Chris Darke

North East Bronx, 1968. Anthony Curtis, an 18-year old black man, and his friends Skip and José debate whether to go to college or serve in Vietnam. Spring, 1969. Anthony is running numbers for Kirby, a pool hall owner. Cowboy, a hustler, challenges Anthony to a frame but when Anthony wins, Cowboy scars his face. Graduation night, 1969. Skippy, José and Anthony have been called up. After sex at her parents' home, Anthony's girl Juanita asks him if he will marry her when he comes back from Vietnam.

Vietnam, April 1971. Anthony and Skip are pinned down under enemy fire. After a napalm strike, squad leader Dugan commands them to investigate the enemy position. One of their number, Cleon, hacks off the head of a dead Vietcong as a lucky souvenir. At base camp, Anthony tells Skippy that Juanita's given birth to a daughter. On the next mission, Cleon is forced to bury the putrefying head. Dugan is killed in an ambush. Six months later, Skippy is sent home.

North East Bronx, 1973. Anthony finds Skippy addicted to heroin. Anthony visits Juanita and her daughter Sarah. Later that night, Juanita chats to a local gangster, Cutty. Five months later, Juanita is pregnant and Anthony is drinking heavily and working in a poorly, paid job. Anthony, Kirby and José plan a heist on a bank van. Anthony finds Cutty leaving Juanita's flat but Cutty knocks him down the stairs. Anthony and Juanita have a row and he walks out. Anthony visits a Black Power meeting where Juanita's sister Delilah is speaking. They go for a drink and he tells her about the heist. The group, now including Delilah, plans the job. Anthony recruits Cleon, now a preacher.

On the day of the heist, Anthony and José wait for the lorry to load, Delilah hides in a bin opposite, Cleon and Skip keep look-out, and Kirby mans the getaway car. A passing policeman questions Cleon and overhears shots as the robbery begins. Cleon shoots the cop, Joss blows up the van and Delilah is shot dead. José is chased and killed by police. At Christmas time, Anthony distributes free toys to the local children. Cleon is giving away dollar bills at his church. Anthony sees Cleon being arrested. Skip is found dead of an overdose. Anthony and Kirby are about to flee to Mexico when they are pinned down by the police. Later, Anthony is sentenced to 15 years to life.

In its own way, *Dead Presidents* is a heritage picture, a wannabe revisionist-historical epic, tooled in a post-modern style which follows the gangster film templates of *GoodFellas* and Once *Once Upon a Time in America*. Spanning the years between 1968 to 1973, the film takes in the Vietnam War, Black Power and the ghettoisation of the Bronx. The protagonist Anthony's trajectory from naive street kid through hardened soldier to desperate gangster is true to the genre, but the ambition of the film's historical scope is not helped by its frantic, pop-video style. Typical of this is its treatment of the Vietnam war. *Dead Presidents* wants to unpack the complexities of Black urban Americans fighting in a "white man's war", yet it too often depicts the war in a visual shorthand straight from *Apocalypse Now*.

Directed by the Hughes Brothers who made *Menace II Society*, *Dead Presidents* demonstrates that they know their audience's genre predilections and how to combine them—gangster film meets war film meets buddy movie using the visual *lingua franca* of American youth culture. But as a way of doing justice to story, characters and the underlying theme of the ever-diminishing opportunities for urban African-Americans (and to a Black History perspective) this aesthetic reveals itself as too glib and impoverished.

This is shown most clearly by the straightforward lifting of moments and motifs from other films. While visual quotation is always part of the ritual of genre, here it is unmotivated, simply there. So we have a Lynchian cigarette end, shot in lovingly extreme close-up, smouldering like a fuse; a series of *Apocalypse Now*-style superimpositions during protagonist Anthony's dark combat-zone night of the soul; and standard issue Scorsesian camera pirouettes through Kirby's pool hall. These borrowings sit on the film rather than feel as if they're embedded in it; they're no means flashy but by no means fundamental.

The same is true of the film's use of transitions. The opening sections feel the most authentic. Shot in nostalgic autumnal hues they melt together through a series of slow fades-to-black. The shift to Vietnam is handled with what seems like a bravura cinematic solution: hiding out in Juanita's back garden, Anthony flees across neighbouring fences and yards until a match cut moves Anthony's flight straight into the smoke and turmoil of a platoon mission. It is a sudden, startling and meaningful moment on several levels, and sets up the pace for the rest of the film. Yet, at the same time, this transition tells us that Vietnam is swiftly to be galloped through, with sickeningly graphic violence decorating the route. Everything prior to and including Vietnam functions only to lead up to the closure and narrative pay-off of the robbery of the 'dead presidents' (dollar bills). The heist is too clearly signalled as doomed to fail from the moment when Delilah and Cleon are recruited. It is also handled in a clumsy fumble of cutting that drains it of vital tension.

Revisionist genre films such as this take on myth and history simultaneously. While pulling back from the generic terrain of recent black gangster movies such as *Menace II Society*, *Dead Presidents* sets out to provide a history lesson, but style again jeopardises the laudable intention. Films as disparate as *GoodFellas* and *Forrest Gump* demonstrate that such an undertaking is an excellent excuse to utilise period styles and exploit a 'Best of ...' soundtrack. But where *GoodFellas* was inspired in its choice and application of music, *Dead Presidents'* admittedly enjoyable music and accurate clothes do nothing to thicken, complicate or even counterpoint the plot.

The final image of Anthony being bussed to jail to serve a life-sentence should feel tragic but it doesn't. He's too stolid and straightforward a character to carry the full weight of the story. His circumstances trap him but the bright kid on his bicycle doesn't become the reckless armed robber with anything near the degree of bitter opportunism that might have made his transformation moving. In this respect Anthony's progress might be read as a fable about the path of least resistance being the one most likely to lead to a dead end. We don't even discover what happens to his mentor, Kirby, a major character well rounded by Keith David to represent 'hood resourcefulness and surrogate fatherliness. This relationship alone could have made an entire film, but with its rap-video stylistic leanings and its ambitious but problematic relationship to the history it recounts, *Dead Presidents* comes across instead as merely a perfect post-modern movie, which doesn't mean it's a good film.

VILLAGE VOICE, 10/10/95, p. 74, Georgia Brown

Love the title. *Dead Presidents*. I know it means bills with their engraved superstars, but what first jumps to mind is JFK, Johnson, Nixon, *all* the dead presidents. Whatever, Albert and Allen Hughes's ambitious, deadly serious follow-up to *Menace II Society* links cash and slaughter, contemporary street violence and Vietnam in a do-it-all epic that in scope resembles John Woo's *Bullet in the Head*—three kids from the 'hood go to 'Nam and come back changed utterly. The Hugheses' gritty period realism, however, is nothing like Woo's soulful pop.

When we meet *Dead Presidents*'s coming-of-age hero, Anthony Curtis (Larenz Tate), it's 1968 and he's a sweet, hardworking kid from the South Bronx, a high school senior who rises before dawn to make door-to-door rounds with a milk truck. Two buddies, scattered Skip (Chris Tucker) and hyper Jose (Freddy Rodriguez doing John Leguizamo), tag along for the ride; he leaves milk at the home of his girlfriend, Juanita (Rose Jackson), where he's waylaid by her serious sister Delilah (N'bushe Wright). Nice neighborhood, clean job, good people. The swinging '60s seem not to have hit this area of town, where somber, brown-based tints seem more '40s or '50s. Anyway, long time ago.

Shades of things to come, Anthony already has one foot in the straight world the other in the underworld. After school—or is it during?—he runs numbers for Kirby (Keith David), an older, marginally wiser figure who conducts a rough trade from his pool hall's back room. Occasionally, Anthony muses about college (the route taken by his elder brother), though there's no hint of the academic in his or his friends' conversations. Various details like this come off as obligatory. A couple of dinner table conversations seem meant to dispose of, or explain, the family: cheery, well-meaning mom; intellectual, slightly bitter brother; withdrawn, pent-up, breadwinning pop.

Making a film that attempts to take us from there to here, the Hughes brothers and screenwriter Michael Henry Brown seem to have begun with a thesis about Vietnam causing what could mildly be termed the deterioration of quality of American life. After the inflammatory *Menace*, perhaps the filmmakers felt the need to follow up with socio-historical analysis. Loaded with cinematic flash and grisly detail, *Dead Presidents* tries to do much that, paradoxically, the film is most exciting in small, intimate moments, such as the charmingly awkward first sex between Anthony and Juanita (it's after the prom and she's wearing falsies).

The big intervening event—in Anthony's life, in the movie itself—is Vietnam. A mini-*Platoon*, replete with gore and grotesquery, sits in the middle of the movie like a decomposing body part. In one fluid editing move, Anthony vaulting backyard fences (he's fleeing Juanita's mom, who's nearly caught him in Juanita's bed) becomes Anthony in camouflage stalking, and being stalked by, Vietcong. In Vietnam, old friend Skippy turns up and so does another Bronx boy, Cleon (Bokeem Woodbine), a preacher's son who whacks off an enemy soldier's head and carries it around in his rucksack for luck. By the time Anthony, still in uniform, taxis back to the Bronx, he finds a new world: Juanita and their daughter in thrall to a nasty pimp, Delilah spouting Power to the people, and Skippy, supported by veteran disability checks, nodding out on a street corner.

In Walter Mosley's *Devil in a Blue Dress*, World War II vet Easy Rawlins reflects often on the blood and death he witnessed in the war, and especially his killing of a blue-eyed man with his bare hands, but he also notes that casual killing is nothing new in the old neighborhood: "Back in Texas, Fifth Ward, Houston, men would kill over a dime wager or a rash word. And it was always the evil ones that would kill the good or the stupid."

If *Menace* dealt with evil, *Presidents* might be said to deal with the good and the stupid. To support Juanita and the baby girl born while he was away, Anthony takes a job in a butcher shop (good for shock cuts featuring animal body parts), but when the place closes due to hard times, he starts thinking in terms of a big score. Heretofore, bills have floated through the picture, but the focus on cold cash intensifies as Anthony and friends conspire in a poorly planned armored car holdup. The end of the movie seems to side with Anthony (he takes his cue from Mookie in

Do the Right Thing) as he lashes out at a society that doesn't honor his prior service. It's a hard conclusion to swallow.

Given that Larenz Tate is almost unrecognizable from the hyped psycho he played in *Menace*, I tend to think he must be a talented actor. Something else must be wrong because I never feel strongly for Anthony or his plight. This affable, personable young man never rises above a generic, representative type, so his going off the track is still a mystery.

Also reviewed in:
CHICAGO TRIBUNE, 10/4/95, Tempo/p. 1, Michael Wilmington
NATION, 11/6/95, p. 552, Stuart Klawans
NEW YORK TIMES, 9/29/95, p. C28, Caryn James
VARIETY, 10/2-8/95, p. 39, Todd McCarthy
WASHINGTON POST, 10/4/95, p. B1, Hal Hinson
WASHINGTON POST, 10/6/95, Weekend/p. 44, Desson Howe

DEAR BABE

A Stratton Films release of a Stratton Films production. *Producer:* Rosanne Ehrlich and David Wilson. *Director:* Rosanne Ehrlich. *Screenplay:* Rosanne Ehrlich. *Director of Photography:* Greg Andrake. *Sound:* Den Sarjeant. *Running time:* 82 minutes. *MPAA Rating:* Not Rated.

CAST: Hazel Siegelbaum (Mike's Wife); Paul Siegelbaum (His Son); Fred Blau (His Brother-In-Law); Dean Coleman (Narrator).

VILLAGE VOICE, 10/31/95, p. 76, Leslie Camhi

During World War II, Mike Siegelbaum, a 25-year-old army private (now deceased), wrote his wife Hazel every day, from basic training in Ft. Riley, Kansas to his march across France and Germany. His daughter has combined the text of these letters with archival footage of army life and occupied Europe, as well as interviews with (among others) her 84-year-old mother. *Dear Babe* is a simple testament to a seemingly innocent era, when the enemy was still before us.

At first, Mike's a fresh-faced army enthusiast; his patriotism makes him a willing apprentice to the art of killing. Soon, though, he comes to hate the army's mindless hierarchy, its "stupidity, cruelty, and arrogance." He writes continually of his great pleasure at receiving photographs of his wife and two daughters; he dreams obsessively of returning home.

Yet it's striking how little of his experience the letters actually reveal to her; he's wary of the army censor but clearly his internal controls are also working overtime. So he writes about rations but leaves out the horror of war. His battalion is among the first to enter Ohrdruf, a German concentration camp for political deportees, but Hazel says he only wrote her that "it smelled badly"; in the newspaper she read about the stacks of cadavers and emaciated prisoners there. Instead, he goes on enthusiastically about a day's leave in liberated Paris, where he yearns to take in Heifetz and Picasso. Such contradictions lend this story of every soldier a certain fascination, though the flat restraint of Ehrlich's filmmaking does little to mine her material; it's undoubtedly difficult to turn a truly analytic eye on your parents' heroic love.

Also reviewed in:
NEW YORK TIMES, 10/28/95, p. 18, Caryn James
VARIETY, 3/13-19/95, p. 52, Emanuel Levy

DESPERADO

A Columbia Pictures release of a Los Hooligans production. *Producer:* Bill Borden and Robert Rodriguez. *Director:* Robert Rodriguez. *Screenplay:* Robert Rodriguez. *Director of Photography:* Guillermo Navarro. *Editor:* Robert Rodriguez. *Music:* Los Lobos. *Music Editor:* Michael Connell. *Sound:* Mark Ulano. *Sound Editor:* Dean Beville. *Casting:* Reuben Cannon. *Production Designer:* Cecilia Montiel. *Art Director:* Felipe Fernandez del Paso. *Set Dresser:* Eduardo Lopez. *Special Effects:* Bob Shelley. *Costumes:* Graciela Mazón. *Make-up:* Ermahn Ospina. *Stunt Coordinator:* Steve M. Davison. *Running time:* 106 minutes. *MPAA Rating:* R.

CAST: Antonio Banderas (El Mariachi); Salma Hayek (Carolina); Joaquim de Almeida (Bucho); Cheech Marin (Short Bartender); Steve Buscemi (Buscemi); Carlos Gomez (Right Hand); Quentin Tarantino (Pick-up Guy); Tito Larriva (Tavo); Angel Aviles (Zamira); Danny Trejo (Navajas); Abraham Verduzco (Nino); Carlos Gallardo (Campa); Albert Michel, Jr. (Quino); David Alvarado (Buddy); Angela Lanza (Tourist Girl); Mike Moroff (Shrug); Robert Arevalo (Opponent); Gerardo Moscoso (Priest); Peter Marquardt (Moco); Consuelo Gomez (Domino); Jaime De Hoyos (Bigoton); Christos (Himself); Richie Gaona (Case Opener); Mark Dalton and Tommy Nix (Fighting Barflies); Patricia Vonne (Bar Girl); Elizabeth Rodriguez (Mariachi Fan).

FILMS IN REVIEW, 11-12/95, p. 101, Andy Pawelczak

In the pre-credits sequence of *Desperado*, director/writer Robert Rodriguez's sequel to his low-budget *El Mariachi*, Steve Buscemi (who played in *Reservoir Dogs* and the recent *Living in Oblivion)* nonchalantly ambles into the meanest, seediest bar this side of Akim Tamiroff's establishment in *Touch of Evil* and turns in what is already a vintage Buscemi performance—eccentric, slyly comic, full of shrugs and side-long eye-balling. Buscemi, along with a few other actors such as Harvey Keitel and John Turturro, is part of what has almost become an independents' stock company, and his appearance in a movie signals a hip New York theater crowd sensibility at work. But *Desperado* is a big-budget studio film with a patented star (Antonio Banderas), and aims at the teenage action movie crowd as well as the downtown film aficionado set. It has some funny moments, but in the end it feels like an exercise in finding out how many different ways you can stage a shoot-out and still hold the audience's attention.

The movie's plot is a simple framework on which Rodriguez hangs his comic riffs and big set-piece gunfights, the most spectacular of which includes a nose-to-nose confrontation on top of a bar. The Mariachi, a guitar-playing drifter, has returned to town to avenge his girlfriend's murder which took place at the end of the first movie. As played by Banderas, he's a teenager's romantic fantasy. Dressed in black with a scorpion emblazoned on the back of his jacket, he's part rock star, part cowboy loner, part angel of death—all-in-all the most shrewdly packaged combination of teen eros and thanatos since Brandon Lee in *The Crow*. When he dresses for a shoot-out, he's like a priest ritualistically donning his vestments. Unlike the previous film's hero, who was an innocent mistaken for someone else, this Mariachi is a self-conscious, romantically tortured high priest of violence. Banderas plays the role partly straight and partly for hip giggles. In between the numerous action scenes, he exchanges wry comic banter with his bookstore-owning girlfriend (played by the vacantly beautiful Salma Hayek) and his friend, Buscemi.

The film's supporting cast includes the now iconic Quentin Tarantino (whose appearance caused a stir in the audience) in a brief role in which he delivers an endless joke about a human waste product, Joaquim de Almeida as a murderous drug baron, and Cheech Marin as a low-down bartender with a face that looks like it came from the barroom floor. Rodriguez has assembled a rogue's gallery of faces for the barroom scenes—each one of these characters could do a star-turn on *America's Most Wanted*. They're stereotypical Mexican banditos, the sort politically incorrect Hollywood used to churn out without a qualm, this time played for neo-campy laughs.

Made for $7000, *El Mariachi* was almost a home movie, and Rodriguez, constrained by the low-budget, had to improvise to achieve his effects; the result had the freshness, lack of pretension, and originality of early Godard. The film's style mirrored its impoverished Mexican setting, and the acting was appropriately unpolished. In comparison, *Desperado*, brought in at seven million, feels like a study in conspicuous consumption; a big scene at the end involving a rocket launcher is emblematic of the whole picture. Rodriguez hasn't lost his directorial flair. The film is practically a catalogue of tricky camera work, with the expressionistic use of color adding visual energy. Rodriguez maintains the slippery tone that slides back and forth between parody and Sergio Leone-like pop myth-making. But none of it adds up to much. It's as dazzling and empty as MTV.

LOS ANGELES TIMES, 8/25/95, Calendar/p. 1, Kenneth Turan

The story behind "El Mariachi," Robert Rodriguez's first film, is the kind of Hollywood tale Hollywood likes to tell. A young movie-struck writer-director takes $7,000 earned as a medical research subject and makes a picture he thinks might sell in the Spanish-language video market. Instead, it captivates agents and executives, gets a major-studio release and earns Rodriguez the chance to work with better actors and a considerably bigger budget.

The question on industry minds after "El Mariachi," namely what could this filmmaker accomplish with increased financing, turns out to be more interesting than the answer. For what Rodriguez has essentially done in "Desperado" is make a slicker, more expensive copy of what came before. And what looked promising for $7,000 looks tiresome for a whole lot more.

Seeing "Desperado" makes obvious what was only implicit in the fuss over "El Mariachi." What the suits saw in Rodriguez was not necessarily the next Orson Welles but, rather, someone with a clear facility for action, the one genre that can be counted on to sell tickets worldwide.

And, true to form, "Desperado" is a weakly comic splatter movie oversupplied with jokey, cartoonish violence. According to the press notes, more than 8,000 rounds of ammunition and six gallons of blood got expended during the shooting, and "Desperado" may be the first film where one of the assistant directors found it useful to keep separate lists labeled "Killed to Date," "To Be Killed Today" and "Yet to Be Killed."

Though he is no John Woo, Rodriguez, who co-produced and edited in addition to writing and directing, is better than average at blowing things up. But if you're not a fan of huge explosions, oversized weapons and people getting sliced and diced in all kinds of ways, "Desperado" doesn't have a lot more to offer.

Whatever wit the film does have is expended in its opening sequence, as an amusing Steve Buscemi wanders into a lowlife-laden bar in a Mexican border town with a story to tell. Just one town over, in a bar just like this one, he witnessed a blood bath engineered by a mysterious stranger who carried an impressive arsenal in his guitar case.

That character, held over from the first movie, is El Mariachi, a riff on the spaghetti Western concept of the mysterious man with no name. Played here by the handsome, magnetic Antonio Banderas (the one good thing studio money did buy), El Mariachi is a loner on a mission, looking for the sinister drug dealer named Bucho (Joaquim de Almeida) he holds responsible for his beloved's death.

Other than orchestrating occasions for violence, Rodriguez also manages to work in cameos for friends, including Cheech Marin and Quentin Tarantino, who plays an ill-starred hit man. And there is, of course, time for a brief romance between El Mariachi and the attractive Carolina (Mexican star Salma Hayek), who runs a book store cafe in a town where nobody reads. That's about as sensible as "Desperado" gets.

Despite the anticipation Rodriguez's new feature has aroused, all that really needs to be said is "he came, he saw, he did it again." Or, as El Mariachi himself puts it: "It's easier to pull the trigger than play guitar. It's easier to destroy than create."

NEW YORK POST, 8/25/95, p. 41, Thelma Adams

Antonio Banderas is the next Valentino.

With "Desperado," the smoldering Spanish star of "Philadelphia" proves he can carry a movie (and carry it he must). Action hero Banderas is a sexual weapon, taking deadly aim at women's hearts as a two fisted shootist.

Like Sharon Stone in "The Quick and the Dead," Banderas pulls off the ornery gunslinger with a chestful of pain with surface slickness, working tight pants and terrific hair for all they're worth.

"Desperado" is the revenge fantasy sequel to Mexican director Robert Rodriguez's micro-budgeted "El Mariachi." At the dark conclusion of the cult shoot'em-up, the guitar player sees his girlfriend killed in cold blood and catches a bullet with his chord hand. Banderas assumes the title role, living out a bittersweet ballad as he singlemindedly sets out to destroy Bucho (Joaquim de Almeida), the drug lord responsible for snuffing his two loves.

The movie has a bright start. Steve ("Living in Oblivion") Buscemi, the low-rent Peter Lorre, walks into a dingy bar south of the border. Cheech Marin pours swill beneath a tell-tale sign: "The client is always wrong." As the mariachis unlikely best friend, Buscemi cracks wise and writer/director Rodriguez sets the tone for over-the-top entertainment that doesn't take itself seriously.

The coolness unlimited roll call continues as Mr. Pulp Fiction, Quentin Tarantino, steps in for a scene and a celluloid benediction of his young colleague. (The two worked together on the upcoming omnibus feature "Four Rooms.") Tarantino, looking like a candidate ripe for Overactors Anonymous, stretches a bar joke about urination beyond legal limits, and then, mercifully, has his brains splattered across the set.

A balletic barroom brawl follows, Hong Kong style. Banderas takes on the dirty dozen denizens of the cantina with enough firepower to secure Grenada.

It's a climactic scene with only one problem: The movie is only halfway over. All the firepower to come seems like skips in a broken record.

To ease the pain of "El Mariachi's" increasing hollowness, Banderas stirs up real heat with Mexican actress Salma Hayek. The guitar player and the curvy bookstore owner make love with the same over-the-top energy as the fight scenes. Their brown manes duke it out on the pillow, or anywhere else their heads happen to be, as Rodriguez gets creative with sexual positioning and cuts away to a moment as tender as channel surfing past the Playboy Channel.

Gunplay interrupts the swordplay. Thankful, the rich Los Lobos soundtrack distracts from the splash of the bloodbath.

"It's easier to pull the trigger than play the guitar," confesses the mariachi. "It's easier to destroy than to create." For the talented Rodriguez, the second time around it's easier to blow things up than to compose a movie as intense and soulful as a mariachi ballad.

NEWSDAY, 8/25/95, Part II/p. B2, John Anderson

Sit back. Let the Antonio Banderas experience wash over you like a hot Mexican wind. Surrender to his power. Revel in his eyes, wish upon his lips. Drink him in, savor him. Like tequila. Like love ...

Am I serious? As a sawed-off shotgun. You gotta go with the flow with "Desperado." Otherwise, you might let all the remodeled movie clichés, postmodernist posturing and smugly encyclopedic filmfreak attitude get to you. You'll become irritated. You'll start calling it "Revenge of El Nerdos."

And "Desperado," for all its cocky, clublike atmosphere, is too much pure fun to waste time worrying about attitude. Robert Rodriguez, who wrote, directed and produced the 1992 film festival favorite "El Mariachi" (for an alleged $7,000) has, for a lot more money, taken the same basic theme and turned it into one of the better action (emphasis on action) flicks of the '90s. It's total hooey, of course; everything is either parody or homage, nothing is to be taken seriously, and when Rodriguez does get serious—his characters make anti-violence and anti-drug statements that are completely correct, completely inappropriate to the tone of the film and hence completely unconvincing—it just shows he's lost temporary control of his material. That's OK. Bodies will be flying through the air shortly.

Banderas is the unnamed Mariachi, a character who in the previous film was an itinerant musician who stumbled into the murderous path of a drug cartel. The mobsters killed his girlfriend and shot him through the hand. Now his repertoire is strictly revenge. And his guitar case is full of guns.

The movie starts off, fittingly enough, with a bang. A stranger named Buscemi (Steve Buscemi) enters a filthy dive and begins regaling the filthy bartender (Cheech Marin) with the story of a huge killer who wiped out the patrons of another dive over a deal gone bad. The patrons of *this* particular establishment have been waiting for such a man; their boss, Bucho (Joaquim de Almeida of "A Clear and Present Danger") is the one the Mariachi is after. The customers' seething evil combined with Buscemi's off-handed, downtown delivery make for a delightfully ridiculous situation and starts the movie on the right track, which is burlesque.

The action is there, too—at least at the beginning. What we see, as Buscemi narrates the bar battle he's seen, is one gloriously overblown gunfight, with hurtling victims and dizzying quantities of lead. And blood. Rodriguez shows a keen sense—and sense of humor—in handling violent action; it's safe to say he's seen more than one John Woo movie. His only problem is not knowing when to pull back. If the violence is a joke, which it seems to be, then the Mariachi shouldn't blow a guy's head off in cold-blooded vengeance. It seems, well, serious. We don't want serious.

Banderas knows this. And when it comes to Banderas, so does director Rodriguez. The way he shoots his star so emphasizes the actor's dark good looks that we have to laugh (or maybe moan) at just how good-looking he is—and how blatantly exploitative Rodgriguez is being; there are some slow-motion sequences where Banderas is so pouty and haughty and frozen in space that he reminds me of Stephanie Seymour in one of those over-posed Victoria's Secrets layouts. Banderas is, of course, *muy macho*, but this flaunting of the actor is another way the director winks at his audience. So, for that matter, is Quentin Tarantino's cameo, in which he comes into Marin's bar, tells a joke and blows the punchline. He also gets shot, which some people may find funny.

Behind every great Mariachi is a good woman, and in this case she owns a bookstore. Carolina (Salma Hayek), who has some tenuous ties to Bucho, nurses the wounded Mariachi back to health and helps him fight evil. Banderas and Hayek may be the best-looking couple that has ever handled automatic weapons, and Rodriguez should be applauded for giving the Mexican actress such a part. She, in turn, should be credited for being so funny, and Banderas deserves praise for being a good sport. For all its distracting clique-iness, "Desperado" delivers.

SIGHT AND SOUND, 2/96, p. 38, John Wrathall

In a small town in Mexico, Buscemi enters the Tarasco Bar and tells the bartender about a massacre he has just witnessed at the hands of a man with a guitar case full of weapons who is searching for someone called Bucho. Meanwhile, in his room, El Mariachi awakes from a dream/flashback in which Bucho's underling Moco kills his girlfriend and then shoots him through the hand. Buscemi arrives and tells Mariachi he has delivered his message. Mariachi goes to the Tarasco, and in the ensuing bloodbath kills everyone there—except for one man who follows him outside and is about to kill him when a passing woman, Carolina, warns Mariachi. Mariachi kills the man, but is shot in the arm. Carolina takes him back to her café-cum-bookshop and removes the bullet.

Meanwhile Bucho, realising Mariachi is in town, sends his gang out from his hacienda fortress with orders to kill any stranger on the streets. Mariachi goes to church, where he meets Buscemi. As they leave they are attacked by Navajas, who has been sent to kill Mariachi by Bucho's Colombian associates. Navajas kills Buscemi, but as he is about to finish off Mariachi, he is shot by Bucho's gang, who do not recognise him. Mariachi takes refuge at the bookshop, where Carolina patches him up again and hides him when Bucho comes round: it turns out that Bucho uses the bookshop as a drop-off point for his drug deliveries.

When Bucho has left, Mariachi and Carolina make love in her bedroom, but are interrupted when Bucho's men return. As they escape over the rooftops, Mariachi has a clear shot at Bucho, but lowers his gun when he recognises him. Mariachi calls for assistance from his fellow mariachis, Quino and Campa. They arrive and help him in a gun battle with Bucho's men, in which they both die. Mariachi and Carolina go to the hacienda for a final showdown, but Bucho recognises Mariachi as his long-lost brother and says he will let him go as long as he can kill Carolina for betraying him. Instead, Mariachi shoots Bucho. Driving away with Carolina, Mariachi throws away his guitar case, then comes back to pick it up, "just in case".

Like Sam Raimi after *The Evil Dead*, Robert Rodriguez has been rewarded for *El Mariachi*—his allegedly $7,000 underground debut which went on to enjoy enormous box-office success—with a chance to make the same film again only on an infinitely larger budget. Originally entitled *Return of the Mariachi*, *Desperado* repeats many of the first film's situations: the bar shootouts; the glamorous bar/café-owner who shelters the hero before turning out to be in the pay of his enemy; the erotically charged wound-dressing; and, of course, the repeated gag about what's in the hero's guitar case. *Desperado*'s Mariachi is clearly the same character from the original film—he remembers the first film's climax, which provides the motivation for his revenge. But at the same time, slightly confusingly, he is played by a new actor, Antonio Banderas, while the first film's star (and producer), Carlos Gallardo, now plays the Mariachi's friend Campa.

However much it retreads old ground, though, *Desperado* is still a definite advance on *El Mariachi*, not least in the quality of the cinematography (the only one of his many functions that Rodriguez has relinquished here). Still low by American standards ($6 million), the budget has allowed Rodriguez to stage wonderfully preposterous action sequences which consciously try to out-Woo John Woo in terms of balletic extravagance.

The money has also bought the services of Antonio Banderas, here given his first solo lead in an American movie, and now surely set to be that rarity, a bankable Latin star in Hollywood. Unlike any home-grown US action star, Banderas combines matinee idol looks, physical threat and the sort of dancer's grace which Rodriguez's choreography requires; on two magnificent occasions in *Desperado*, Banderas climbs up on to the bar midfight and practically vogues his way down it. Again, his only rival for sheer charisma in an action movie is Woo's actor-muse, Chow Yun Fat.

Rodriguez has much in common with his friend and *Four Rooms* collaborator Quentin Tarantino: lavish blood-letting, death as a throwaway joke, an interest in stories within stories—as in the wry opening anecdote related by Steve Buscemi, whose very presence is a Tarantino tribute. Unlike Tarantino, however, Rodriguez also makes adventurous use of the camera; he still edits his films himself, which gives him a total control over the rhythm and movement of his images. If anything, he needs to learn a little restraint: the first half hour of *Desperado* is so breathtaking that Rodriguez has nothing left to throw at us by the final showdown, which can't help but seem an anti-climax. But where he does show admirable restraint is in his use of Tarantino the actor, limiting him to one set-piece funny story before blowing his head off—and one great line: when the carnage—in the bar below catches Tarantino's eye on a closed-circuit television screen, he squints at it before asking, "Is that going on right now?"

TIME, 8/28/95, p. 69, Richard Corliss

[*Desperado* was reviewed jointly with *The Usual Suspects*; see Corliss' review of that film.]

VILLAGE VOICE, 8/29/95, p. 56, Amy Taubin

What is it that Robert Rodriguez's *Desperado* has that the collected works of John Woo do not? A score by Los Lobos featuring the Latin Playboys for one thing and Antonio Banderas for two or three things more (no insult to Woo's great star Chow Yun-Fat intended).

Rodriguez's follow-up to his no-budget debut feature *El Mariachi* (made for $7000, it was polished up by Columbia for a lot more) is either a remake or a sequel; the narrative is so nonexistent that it's hard to tell. A guitar player turned gunfighter, El Mariachi (Banderas) comes to a small Mexican town seeking revenge on Bucho (Joaquim de Almeida), the drug honcho who's responsible for killing his lover. Bucho sics his henchmen on El Mariachi, who blows them all away. When Rodriguez runs out of variations on how one man, albeit armed with some heavy-duty firepower, can dispose of three, or six, or 12 equally well-armed opponents at one go, he lets his hero and villain meet face to face. The outcome is overdetermined, to say the least,

What *Desperado* lacks in plot and character, it almost compensates for in style. The film is fabulous to look at—as classy as a *Vogue*-goes-to-the-Barrio fashion spread. The colors are sun-bleached and burnished at the same time. No Southwest-boutique peach and aqua, but weathered green, dirt brown, and, what else, dried-blood red.

Desperado is also an editing tour de force, a marvel of comic timing, a festival of sight gags. When it comes to hyperbolic, parodic violence, Rodriguez has absorbed the lessons of the masters Sergio Leone and the aforementioned John Woo. But *Desperado* is completely lacking in the allegorical underpinning that make Leone's spaghetti westerns or Woo's *The Killer* so absorbing. Nor does Rodriguez have the enthusiasm for the intricacies of storytelling that distinguishes his buddy Quentin Tarantino. It's a riot for the first hour, and almost a bore for the rest. If Rodriguez didn't have Banderas to turn up the heat, the film would be a disaster. (But the fact is that he does have Banderas and he's going to direct him in *Zorro*, the next remake extravaganza from Amblin Entertainment.)

Neither does it help the picture's shape that all the best cameos are in the first half. *Desperado* opens with a monologue by a bleary-eyed, scummy-toothed Steve Buscemi that's both precision-tooled and over-the-top. Destined to become a video classic in itself (Columbia has been using it as a promo-tape for the film), it's proof of how editing and music can enhance an actor's timing. Rodriguez does equally well by Tarantino, who shows up a little later to deliver a piss'n'dick joke and then to tiptoe through a shit-coated latrine on the way to meet his maker. It's the least self-conscious Tarantino's ever been on camera and the first time his head looks neither too big nor too small but just right for his Gummi bear body.

As for the love interest played by Salma Hayek, she has little more to do than sashay around in some nifty midriff-baring outfits (her mismatched red and black shoes may spark a 10-minute fashion trend) and look simultaneously unfazed and overwhelmed by Banderas, whether he's fingering her flesh or she's picking bullets out of his. *Desperado* is awash in crimson fluid—it spurts, it splatters, it gushes. And if no one literally bathes in blood, someone does mop the floor with it.

But *Desperado* is nothing if not a ballet for Banderas, who proves himself not only an action hero but also that rare combination, a romantic comedian. "When I want to seduce a woman, I make her laugh because when she laughs, she's helpless," says Marceau, the poacher in Jean Renoir's *Rules of the Game*. Marceau, the disenfranchised French peasant of the '30s, looked as scuzzy, however, as everyone does today in *Desperado*—except Banderas, who learned to maintain his poise, good manners, and excellent grooming in numerous Pedro Almodóvar films (and in an ambience far more campy than anything Rodriguez could envision).

Banderas is that fusion of opposites that signals a great star. He seems part Brando, part Cary Grant; and he has the ambisexuality that was essential to both. He's both reserved and infinitely receptive—less passive than potentially active. He's the "Latin Lover" that Brando could only fantasize being. But he's more goofy and less tormented than Brando. Comedy is his way of maneuvering through the opposition, and his timing is as easy and impeccable as Grant's.

Unlike certain American actors (Jeff Bridges comes immediately to mind), Banderas isn't resistant to being an object of desire. He wears his sexuality openly, suggesting straightforwardness rather than perversity. In *Desperado*, Rodriguez lights him for his vital points—eyes, mouth, hands, the feline curvature of his spine. He has the bee-stung upper lip of the moment. Val Kilmer, John Malkovich, and Christopher Walken have it too. On them, it reads as spoiled; on Banderas, it's a sign of sweetness. And no male actor, except Clint, can look as magnetic on a poster as Banderas.

In the Almodóvar films (*Law of Desire, Matador, Tie Me Up! Tie Me down!*), Banderas was indistinguishable from a dozen other European male actors. In America, his identity began to change. He appeared at once more exotic but less foreign. Forget the boredom of *The Mambo Kings*, in *Philadelphia* he stole Tom Hanks's deathbed scene out from under him and in *Interview With the Vampire*, he had to be hustled off screen as fast as possible, lest he show up, by contrast, the SoCal callowness of Tom Cruise and Brad Pitt.

But in *Desperado*, directed by the Tex-Mex Rodriguez, Banderas seems rather SoCal himself, part of a new brand of multi-culti SoCal that's primed for a Hollywood gone global as never before. There have always been Latin lovers in Hollywood (and the danger for Banderas is that his flair for comedy could turn self-parodic, that he could become the Gilbert Roland or Carmen Miranda of '90s—*Zorro*, the rock and roll bandit). The difference now is that Latin is a very U.S. thing to be. Or almost. Banderas may be exactly on the moment. Only history will tell.

As for Rodriguez, he's almost everything the industry hopes its farm team (the indie film sector) will deliver. He can make a great-looking, mindless action film for a 30th of the cost of *Waterworld*. He has an ear for music and an eye for casting actors. He's a workaholic: in addition to *Desperado*, *Roadracers*, a film he directed for Showtime, will be in theaters this year along with *Four Rooms*, the anthology film to which he contributed. And he's currently in production with *From Dusk Till Dawn*, a Tarantino-scripted vampire movie, to be followed by *Zorro*. Rodriguez's only drawback is his aversion to narrative. Provided it isn't ideological, Tarantino probably will cure him of it. And if he doesn't, Spielberg will.

Also reviewed in:
CHICAGO TRIBUNE, 8/25/95, Friday/p. C, Michael Wilmington
NEW YORK TIMES, 8/25/95, p. C6, Janet Maslin
NEW YORKER, 9/18/95, p. 94, Anthony Lane
VARIETY, 5/20-6/4/95, p. 53, Todd McCarthy
WASHINGTON POST, 8/25/95, p. D1, Rita Kempley
WASHINGTON POST, 8/25/95, Weekend/p. 44, Desson Howe

DESTINY TURNS ON THE RADIO

A Savoy Pictures release of a Rysher Entertainment presentation. *Executive Producer:* Keith Samples and Peter Martin Nelson. *Producer:* Gloria Zimmerman. *Director:* Jack Baran. *Screenplay:* Robert Ramsey and Matthew Stone. *Director of Photography:* James Carter. *Editor:* Raul Davalos. *Music:* Steve Soles. *Music Editor:* Jacqueline Tager. *Sound:* Steuart P. Pierce. *Sound Editor:* Richard Yawn. *Casting:* Nicole Arbusto and Joy Dickson. *Production Designer:* Jean-Philippe Carp. *Art Director:* Easton Michael Smith and Dominic Wymark. *Set Decorator:* Lisa R. Deutsch. *Set Dresser:* Don G. Smith. *Special Effects:* David Wayne. *Costumes:* Beverly Klein. *Make-up:* Julie Purcell. *Stunt Coordinator:* Webster Whinery. *Running time:* 102 minutes. *MPAA Rating:* R.

CAST: James Le Gros (Thoreau); Dylan McDermott (Julian); Quentin Tarantino (Destiny); Nancy Travis (Lucille); James Belushi (Tuerto); Janet Carroll (Escabel); David Cross (Ralph Dellaposa); Richard Edson (Gage); Bobcat Goldthwait (Mr. Smith); Barry "Shabaka" Henley (Dravec); Lisa Jane Persky (Katrina); Sarah Trigger (Francine); Tracey Walter (Pappy); Allen Garfield (Vinnie Vidivici); Ralph Brannen (Henchman #1); Robert Sparks (Henchman #2); Gorden Michaels (Motorist); Che Lujan (Jose); Michael O'Connell (Stage Manager); Michael Matthys (Lighting Technician).

LOS ANGELES TIMES, 4/28/95, Calendar/p. 12, Peter Rainer

The film is called "Destiny Turns on the Radio," but after a few minutes you may wish it were called "Projectionist Turns Off the Movie."

The only rationale for this smug, facetious mess—which was developed at the Sundance Institute—is to provide a how-to guide on how *not* to make a good movie. (Or maybe it's an anti-fund-raiser for the Sundance Institute.) The director, Jack Baran, has worked as a music supervisor and executive producer for filmmakers such as s Jim McBride and Barbet Schroeder, but his arty pretentiousness is all his own. Or maybe it belongs jointly to his screenwriters, Robert Ramsey and Matthew Stone. They've cooked up a metaphysical snore fest that manages to strand an entire platoon of attractive performers in an oasis of pseudo-hip pseudo-cool.

Dylan McDermott plays Julian, an escaped convict who is rescued in the Nevada desert by a mysterious dude, Johnny Destiny (Quentin Tarantino), driving a Plymouth Roadrunner convertible. In Vegas, hoping to recover his lost loot, he hooks up with his partner in crime, Harry Thoreau (James Le Gros), the great-great-grandson of the "Walden" guy, and seeks out an old flame (Nancy Travis) who is now living with a casino mogul (Jim Belushi) who entertains her by doing camp impressions of Elvis in "Viva Las Vegas" (a much, much better movie, incidentally, than "Destiny").

Along the way performers such as Bobcat Goldthwait, Richard Edson, Tracey Walter and Allen Garfield turn up, mostly to no advantage. (Garfield plays a big shot named Vinnie Vidivici—har, har.) Tarantino breezes through periodically issuing gnomic pronouncements—he's Destiny, you see.

The low-budget, independently made "Destiny" isn't awful in the ways that most big-budget studio movies are. It's clear everybody involved wasn't trying to make standard Hollywood pap. But the results are so stultifyingly vacuous that pap would have been a godsend.

NEW YORK POST, 4/28/95, p. 43, Thelma Adams

The "Pulp Fiction" director stars as Johnny Destiny, a smug, motto-slinging mystery man in the quirky ensemble comedy "Destiny Turns on the Radio." Destiny rises out of a cracked swimming pool at the Marilyn Motel in Las Vegas to shape the fates of two unlikely thieves, Julian (Dylan McDermott) and Thoreau (James Le Gros), and Lucille (Nancy Travis), a luscious lounge singer. Along the way, Destiny touches James Belushi and Bobcat Goldthwait.

In kitsch overdrive, the candy-colored comedy tries, very hard to be hip, and the strain shows. Tarantino would be better off sticking to small parts in movies he directs rather than thrusting his over-sized chin into the deep end, but watching such talents as Mulroney, Le Gros and Travis desperately tread water, ever conscious that the camera is only a few feet away, was like visiting friends trapped in a horrible high school play. I felt embarrassed for them.

It's not that "Destiny Turns on the Radio" is horrible: it's just all window dressing and no soul, all set up and no delivery. It's "Blue Velvet" without Dennis Hopper, "Twin Peaks" without the dwarf, "Viva Las Vegas" without Ann-Margret and Elvis. Directed by newcomer Jack Baran, with a script by Robert Ramsey and Matthew Stone, "Destiny" is arch and overblown without the writing or the wisdom to back it up. It's so self-referential it hurts; it plays like a bad movie within a movie.

In the end we discover that the ultra-cool Johnny Destiny has risen out of the primordial chlorine to remind this winning but ragtag band of no-accounts of a simple, un-hip theme straight out of Robert Frost: consider the road not taken. I have a feeling it's a philosophy that hits home for the stars of "Destiny"—they probably wish they had taken other movie projects. On the other hand, this comedy was probably a lot more fun to make than it is to watch.

NEWSDAY, 4/28/95, Part II/p. B5, Jonathan Mandell

After "Pulp Fiction" started making trunksful of money, people asked aloud whether filmmaker Quentin Tarantino would bring to life a tinsel-town's worth of imitators. They wondered what the new movies would be like: would they borrow "Pulp Fiction's" structural innovation or its hip/camp style, it's pop culture references or just its over-the-top violence?

The first such movie has now come to theaters, it is called "Destiny Turns on The Radio"—a title as meaningless as the rest of the movie—and though there are some obvious pop culture references, some mild violence, and a strained, derivative effort at appearing hip and innovative, what the movie borrows above all from Quentin Tarantino is Quentin Tarantino.

Tarantino plays a character named Johnny Destiny, a god with great powers who has made a trunkful of money disappear. (Think of this movie as a Hollywood allegory.)

We first see him in the desert, driving a 1969 Plymouth Roadrunner convertible, complete with hubcap that says "Road Runner," straight at an escaped convict named Julian (Dylan McDermott).

But Destiny, who wears a ruffled red tuxedo shirt, does not run Julian over; he gives him a ride to nearby Las Vegas.

Julian goes to the Marilyn Motel, which features a neon sign of the blonde star of "Bus Stop" and "Some Like It Hot." Indeed, each motel room is named for a Monroe movie. It was in "The Misfits," that Julian last saw his love, the Vegas singer Lucille (Nancy Travis).

Instead of Lucille, Julian meets his old partner, the motel's new proprietor, Thoreau (James Le Gros), with whom he robbed a bank three years ago. Thoreau has two pieces of bad news. First, Julian's gal Lucille is with another man, casino boss James Belushi.

"This is, this is truly offensive," Julian replies, and he smashes up a few things.

Then there is the second piece of bad news. "I spent three long years in prison dreaming about the money," Julian interrupts. "Don't tell me it's gone."

"It's gone."

"What do you mean, gone?"

"I mean, gone. As in, away."

During a lightning storm shortly after the heist, as Thoreau explains (and we see in flashback), Destiny emerged naked from the motel pool, there was a flash and swirl of light, and then he disappeared, and so did the stacks of stolen cash, which were in the trunk of their car. It was during just such a freakish (i.e. Destiny-inspired) electrical storm, we learn later, that Julian was able to escape from jail.

To say that the rest of "Destiny Turns on the Radio" is Julian's efforts to win back his girl and his loot is to bestow on the film a coherence that it does not come close to possessing. Endless, often witless, this film did not need to be so hopeless. Tarantino could have helped in at least two ways. He could have rewritten the script. And he could have refused the role of Johnny Destiny. Get hip, Quentin. Quit acting. You and Sam Shepard do not have the same destiny.

SIGHT AND SOUND, 7/95, p. 45, Nick James

Julian Goddard has busted out of prison. He is picked up on the road by the fast-talking, enigmatic Johnny Destiny who drives a Plymouth Roadrunner similar to that driven by Julian's partner Thoreau for a robbery three years before. Destiny drops him in Las Vegas at the Marilyn hotel where Thoreau is working. Julian wants his money and his girl, Lucille. Thoreau tells him that Lucille is now Tuerto's girl and that the money was stolen by a man who is clearly Johnny Destiny. They recall how, on the night of the robbery, they were about to make their getaway when Julian insisted on going to fined Lucille and was arrested. Thoreau tells Julian how Johnny Destiny emerged magically out of the motel pool during an electrical storm and zapped Thoreau unconscious. When he woke up, his money and car were gone.

Lucille wants out of Vegas and into a singing career, but she is pregnant. Her manager Ralph has set up a performance for music biz mogul Vinnie Vidivici. She spots Julian from Tuerto's office on the security video. They meet and she tells him that she disappeared on the night of the robbery because she couldn't see any future in being on the run. Destiny makes a deal with Thoreau in return for repairing the crack in the pool and refilling it, Thoreau will get the car and the money back.

Julian persuades Lucille to sleep with him but Tuerto catches them at it. Julian and Lucille get away, evading the police and Tuerto's hoods. The two decide to get married but after the ceremony Tuerto's men kidnap Lucille and return her to the casino. She tells Tuerto that she loves Julian and he fires her, but the police insist that her evening performance should go ahead as bait for the capture of Julian. Lucille goes on stage and gives the performance of her life. Vinnie raves about her, but she decides to make her get away with Julian.

Julian, Lucille and Thoreau gather at the motel where the pool has an unearthly glow to it. Destiny arrives and tells them that the pool offers all the directions your life could have taken if you'd made different decisions, then he jumps in. The cops come and, rather than surrender, Julian and Lucille dive in. Thoreau throws in his money bag and the cops give up through lack of evidence. Thoreau, however, had switched bags, and he leaves Vegas a rich man.

Although it might be seen as another piece of film associated with Quentin Tarantino, *Destiny Turns on the Radio* is of an older tradition. Like Tom DiCillo's *Johnny Suede* (to name one of many) it is an arch exercise in the recycling of favourite iconography (in this case 50s roadside Americana with a smidgen of 70s Vegas kitsch) in the tranquilised B-movie format that so often passes for serious artistry in the American independent film ever since the inimitable success of Jim Jarmusch. The film's pulp heart—made of sassy dialogue, cheesy characters and an amoral mayhem of mixed motivation—is buried so deep by an ironic distance of tone and performance that it barely pulses.

Director Jack Baran places a heavy burden on his cast, requiring them to regurgitate feedbags of cornball dialogue in longish, static takes (sample: "I've been rolling snake eyes ever since you left"). Action is provided either by the non-stop shoulder-heaving wiggle of Tarantino as Destiny—too embarassed, at a guess, to stand still for the excruciating lines he's given—or by the deliberately undermined stunting of Dylan McDermott as Julian, such as his skidding arrival at the motel on a motorbike (staged rather than slapstick-clumsy). McDermott's particular stiff quality may well be blow to standard macho characterisation, but he comes across like a fashion model trying to act tough without chipping his fingernails.

If it's all part of the same joke that Nancy Travis as Lucille is neither a particularly steamy presence nor a halfway competent chanteuse, or that Johnny Destiny is about as charismatic as a church deacon in shades, or that Julian looks more like he's been touring Morocco than spending three years in jail, then it is a peculiarly slim one, lost on anyone who hasn't long ago OD'd on repeated viewings of such so-bad-it's-good films as Edgar G. Ulmer's *Detour*. If, however, Baran was trying for something more convincing, then he is not a good judge of when a performer is giving their best. Many of his cast members have done well in other films—including Travis, Le Gros and Tarantino—but none of them is more than perfunctory here.

The plot's melding of mild sci-fi and cod-*noir* cries out for a psychological spin on the characters such as that found in the stories of Jim Thompson. Thompson's characters are just as often tools of fate but they strive against it, generating a delirious sense of panic and desperation. The dominant mood in *Destiny* is rather one of fatalism, leaving Johnny Destiny (the character, the symbol and perhaps even the actor himself with all the cards in his favour and no-one trying to kick his chair over.

VILLAGE VOICE, 5/9/95, p. 78, Ed Morales

The first thing you need to know is that Quentin Tarantino is nowhere near as obnoxious as he is in the trailer or in *Pulp Fiction* (he doesn't say *nigger* even once). With his exaggerated chin and whispery, Method Ventriloquist delivery, he's coy, understated, and not too nerdy. His Johnny Destiny, a kind of supernatural "god with a small g" created by the sum total of the gambling karma in Las Vegas, is a metaphor for the whole Tarantino phenomenon.

The debut directorial effort by *Kiss of Death* producer Jack Baran, *Destiny Turns on the Radio* is a bizarre romantic comedy twist on grunge noir (*Repo Man, Guncrazy*), replete with goofy caricatures by the usual suspects. The Vegas setting is the film's crucial grounding, provoking garish bursts of color, and providing the characters with their greedy, lusty motivations. Julian Goddard (Dylan McDermott), an escaped convict looking for stolen loot and his old squeeze Lucille, is picked up hitchhiking by Mr. Destiny, who drives the ultimate car, a '69 Plymouth Roadrunner. "This town has unlimited possibilities," he portends, dropping Goddard at the Marilyn Motel, a flophouse run by Thoreau (James Le Gros), Goddard's erstwhile partner. The flash of Marilyn's cheesy neon sign presages the psychedelic L.A. magical realist fun to come.

There's a pretty amusing triangle here as well. While Goddard was in prison, lounge singer Lucille (Nancy Travis) took up with Tuerto (James Belushi), sending McDermott into over-the-top jealous rages, while Belushi is surprisingly charming as a cranky, horny hotelier. But Travis almost steals the film from its overdetermined, crude humor, fretting and pouting her way through the testosterone storm toward the climactic sequence. In a barebacked polka-dot dress, she delivers a gratifyingly cheesy portrayal of the wholesome 'ho. The moral of the story? "It's beyond one man's power to stem the tide of chaos," says Thoreau, which might explain the weak *Thelma & Louise* homage that sends the film hurtling into the abyss.

Also reviewed in:
CHICAGO TRIBUNE, 4/28/95, Friday/p. H, Michael Wilmington
NEW YORK TIMES, 4/28/95, p. C8, Janet Maslin
VARIETY, 5/1-7/95, p. 37, Todd McCarthy
WASHINGTON POST, 4/29/95, p. D3, Hal Hinson

DEVIL IN A BLUE DRESS

A TriStar Pictures release of a Clinica Estetico and Mundy Lane Entertainment production. *Executive Producer:* Jonathan Demme and Edward Saxon. *Producer:* Jesse Beaton and Gary Goetzman. *Director:* Carl Franklin. *Screenplay:* Carl Franklin. *Based on the novel by:* Walter Mosley. *Director of Photography:* Tak Fujimoto. *Editor:* Carole Kravetz. *Music:* Elmer Bernstein. *Music Editor:* Alex Gibson and Kathy Durning. *Choreographer:* Tony Selznick and Russell Clark. *Sound:* Ken Segal and (music) Dan Wallin. *Sound Editor:* Robert Grieve. *Casting:* Victoria Thomas. *Production Designer:* Gary Frutkoff. *Art Director:* Dan Webster. *Set Designer:* Lauren Polizzi and Cheryl Smith. *Set Decorator:* Kathryn Peters. *Set Dresser:* Cheryle A. Grace, Alan Baptiste, Mark Little, Joel Osborne, and Greg Sanger. *Special Effects:* Tom Ward. *Costumes:* Sharen Davis. *Make-up:* Edna Sheen. *Stunt Coordinator:* Tony Brubaker. *Running time:* 102 minutes. *MPAA Rating:* R.

CAST: Denzel Washington (Easy Rawlins); Tom Sizemore (Dewitt Albright); Jennifer Beals (Daphne Monet); Don Cheadle (Mouse); Maury Chaykin (Matthew Terell); Terry Kinney (Todd Carter); Mel Winkler (Joppy); Albert Hall (Odell); Lisa Nicole Carson (Coretta James); Jernard Burks (Dupree Brouchard); David Wolos-Fonteno (Junior Fornay); John Roselius (Mason); Beau Starr (Miller); Steven Randazzo (Benny Giacomo); Scott Lincoln (Richard McGee); L. Scott Caldwell (Hattie Parsons); Barry Shabaka Henley (Woodcutter); Nicky Corello (Shariff); Kenny Endoso (Manny); Joseph Latimore (Frank Green); Renee Humphrey (Barbara); Robert J. Knoll (Herman); Kai Lennox (Football); Poppy Montgomery (Barbara's Sister); Brendan Kelly (Terell's Chauffeur); Peggy Rea (Carter's Secretary); Vinny Argiro (Baxter); Deborah Lacey (Sophie); Brazylia Kotere (Neighborhood Woman); Jeris Lee Poindexter (Alphonso Jenkins); Frank Davis (Butcher); Matt Barry (Cop in Car); Mark Cotone (Cop in Station); Brian O'Neal (John's Band/Singer); G. Smokey Campbell (Nightclub Owner); Alan Craig Schwartz (Johnny); Steve Sekely (Abe); J.D. Smith (Pool Hall Owner); Nigel Gibbs (Bootlegger).

CINEASTE, Vol. XXII, No. 1, 1996, p. 38, Ed Guerro

One of the few charms of director Carl Franklin's *Devil in a Blue Dress*, adapted by him from Walter Mosley's hit novel, is his insightful rendering of the post-WWII, black world in Los Angeles, before the civil rights movement and the ensuing social upheaval of integration. Although L.A. in 1948 is clearly Raymond Chandler's turf, and both Mosley and Franklin pay ample homage to him, this *noir* journey is definitely viewed through the prism of the black experience. Moving from the heart of black L.A., starting with Central Avenue, its smoky bars, soul food restaurants and juke joints, and then out of the ghetto into the 'white only' canyons, beaches, and mansions of L.A.'s elite, part-time detective Easy Rawlins (Denzel Washington) tracks the whereabouts of a mystery lady, Daphne Monet (Jennifer Beals), who occasionally strays from the white world for the forbidden pleasures of soul food, jazz, and "dark meat." True to *noir* style Easy pursues the enigmatic Daphne Monet through a convoluted intrigue, coming across various shady characters, colorful social types, spontaneous murders, and corpses left as appropriate markers at turning points in the plot.

Yet, for reasons both obvious and veiled, *Devil in a Blue Dress* cannot be considered a typical Hollywood *noir* period piece. The cars and fashions look right, the music fits, and Washington (the cinematic heir of Sidney Poitier) plays the part with that sense of dignified reserve reflecting the social outlook and personal decorum of those black vets just returned from World War II, with high expectations of things changing in America. Rather, what Franklin has achieved here is a *funky noir* style, as only black people could have imagined and honed it in the fiction of Richard Wright, Chester Himes, Donald Goines, or in the films of Blaxploitation and the contemporary gangsta poetics of Snoop Doggy Dogg and Coolio. This funkier side of *noir* reveals itself in the subtle ironies and shadings of *Devil's* detailed cultural gestures, its racial ironies, sketches, and impressions of the black world. For instance, instead of the cheap suit favored by the typical *noir* detective, Easy Rawlins mostly wears the casual clothes of a laid-off aircraft worker, a windbreaker with the company logo on the pocket, over a sleeveless T-shirt with slacks. Just as the cheap suit marks the social distance between the white private eye and his wealthy clientele, Rawlins's attire signifies his black, working-class status and powerlessness relative to the forces he's up against.

With mortgage payments due on his modest West Side house and no prospects of a steady job in sight, Easy Rawlins is an ordinary brother trying to unravel a mystery while being acutely aware that he's meddling in the corrupt business of powerful, contending, white forces—the city government's ruling elite, the police department, and organized crime. Denzel Washington well understands the psychology and appeal of Easy Rawlins, a black man painfully squeezed by every conceivable power relation and economic circumstance. He plays Rawlins with social vulnerability and caution mixed with a persistent toughness that gradually builds into a cunning, assertive rage against injustice as the narrative evolves. "They thought I was some kinda new fool ... and I guess I was," Easy says, recognizing the duplicity and danger of his situation.

Devil's funky noir mood is greatly enhanced by the exceptional performance of Don Cheadle as Rawlins's homicidal sidekick, Mouse, who comes up from Texas to assist on the case, sporting a smile with a gold-capped tooth, wearing a rakish derby, and packing two handguns. Cheadle rightly interprets Mouse as pathologically violent, a man whose reckless edginess is both funny and scary. Mouse is the kind of guy who can kill on very little notice, or on no notice at all, as he almost does when, after a night of drinking, he points a cocked automatic at Rawlins, to prove that his psychotic impulses are sincere and include even his good buddies. This is the complex beauty of Don Cheadle's Mouse, who, on the surface, projects a down-home, blues persona that masks a tightly wound, stone-cold killer underneath. Carl Franklin adroitly directs Easy and Mouse in psychological counterpoint. Easy reasons and strategizes while Mouse packs the heat. They form the perfect complementary, dramatic pair, with Mouse violently acting out Easy's repressed or dissembled rage.

A quality supporting cast does much to provide additional nuances in *Devil*'s energy and style. Unfortunately, except for brief periods like Blaxploitation or the start of the Nineties black film wave, African-American actors still find too few roles and vehicles to really open up and consistently show their stuff. Consequently, one often sees thoroughly brilliant performers in relatively minor parts, gracing many black-directed or black-focused films with fresh faces and superb performances at all levels of a production. Jerard Burks and Lisa Nicole Carson, for example, bring the exactly the right touch of black vernacular to their roles as Easy's working-class friends Dupree and Coretta, as does Mel Winkler as the double-crossing saloon-keeper, Joppy. The only flat performance belongs to Jennifer Beals as Daphne Monet. Beals seems to play too close to the standard *noir* vamp, without looking deeply enough into the tense doubleness and marginality of the character.

Mouse's homicidal nature and Rawlins's righteous, simmering anger are implicitly contrasted with the more impersonal and systematic violence of the Establishment. Murders occur everywhere, and while the thugs come in all sizes and colors, *Devil in a Blue Dress* makes it clear that they're all running errands for L.A.'s wealthy political elite. The outstanding Tom Sizemore, playing Albright, the seedy white gangster who initially hires Rawlins to find Daphne Monet, has for good reason been Hollywood's pick for major heavy in a number of recent films. When he moves to gouge out Easy's eyes, the threat is uncomfortably convincing. The routine insults and violence the police inflict on Rawlins, including a cop punching him during interrogation, is directed by Franklin with a world-weary sense of realism. The scene shows the detailed touch of someone who is familiar with the workings of authoritarian racism. In an uncanny moment paralleling real-life events occurring outside the theater, the cops threaten to plant evidence on Rawlins if he doesn't cooperate, thus framing him for the string of ongoing murders. Easy's encounters with the L.A.P.D. subtly underscore defense claims in the O.J case, as well as evoke the Rodney King beating. That Franklin understands the banal, routine nature of violence, cruelty, and death is one of his distinctive traits as a director. In an eerie scene alluding to his crime masterpiece, *One False Move* (1992), in which drug criminals snort coke while ignoring a man slowly suffocating with a plastic bag over his head, Easy and Mouse nonchalantly watch the gangster Albright slowly expire after the film's climactic shootout.

The principal, tangled mystery of *Devil in a Blue Dress* is, in part, reflected in a nagging question: how could a film based on a hit novel, directed by an outstanding journeyman, a film uniformly praised by the critics, and featuring the star power of Denzel Washington, be such a dismal flop with the moviegoing audience! One possible answer to the mystery of *Devil* at the box office involves the answer to the central mystery of the film's narrative. The key to both mysteries is found in the multiple expressions of that enduring social construct, the great American obsession and catastrophe: *race*. The persistent irony driving all of Mosley's novels, and certainly Franklin s film, is the way that Easy Rawlins's double consciousness as a black man empowers him as an occasional private eye. The fact that he's on this case at all is because he's black and can move and detect things in those circles and that world forever closed to whites. The ultimate joke of *Devil* is that double consciousness facilitates double vision. Easy can see deeply into both the black and white worlds and find out not only what powerful whites want to know, hut also what they don't want to know, or at least what they want to deny or hide.

As the mystery of the narrative unravels, we find out that the elusive Daphne Monet is engaged to one of the city's leading mayoral candidates, Todd Carter (Terry Kinney). In an attempt to protect herself in a counterblackmail scheme, Daphne disappears into the black world where Rawlins finds her. Then, in a spectacular gunfight, he rescues her from the gangsters who originally retained him. At this point the mystery of the *Devil in a Blue Dress* is revealed: Daphne

Muse is not white at all, but a 'tragic mulatto,' as stereotypes go, passing for white. Miscegenation being the potent, socially charged act that it was in 1948 (and still is), Daphne's planned marriage into one of the city's elite families can definitely never happen. In a final act of double consciousness confirming his true powers as a black private eye, Easy Rawlins functions as go-between, negotiating the breakup of the miscegenous liaison. For his trouble, Easy receives a generous settlement for himself, Mouse, and Daphne, as the rich white man, Todd Carter, retreats back across the color line into his own world, telling Easy that the police will no longer "bother" him. All is happily resolved as *noir* turns into a bright L.A. morning, the foreboding ghetto into the black community.

As for the other mystery, when one considers the role of *race* in the film's demise, what happened off the screen is not much of a mystery at all. *Devil in a Blue Dress*, like *Strange Days*, had the great misfortune to be released at the moment of the O.J. verdict, and that was the kiss of death at the box office. The film did not cross over. Racial divisions and tensions throughout the country were running as high as they have ever run, and angry, post-O.J.-trial whites were in no mood for a tour of L.A.'s black world, 1948 or otherwise. In addition, *Devil* did not attract the youth audience, black or white, which accounts for much of the black film market. Although the appeal of the 'hood-homeboy-action flick has basically played out, and black cinema's audience seems ready for experimentation with genre conventions and narratives, young filmgoers clearly didn't make the leap to recognizing this excellent filmic translation of a brilliant novel. This is to some extent the result of contemporary youth's focus on electronic rather than print culture. But it is also related to the difference in social visions between now and 1948, between an inherent contemporary pessimism, as opposed to the optimism of post-World War II America. *Devil in a Blue Dress* ends on exactly the right historical note, with Easy the homeowner walking down the sunny street of his modest community, waving at friendly neighbors, as superficial order and separation between the races, for the moment at least, have been restored.

FILMS IN REVIEW, 1-2/96, p. 62, Andy Pawelczak

Based on the first of writer Walter Mosley's series of mysteries, *Devil in a Blue Dress* is atmospherically rich and undernourished in practically everything else, with the cardinal exception of Denzel Washington's performance as Easy Rawlins, an average Joe drafted into becoming a private detective when he loses his airplane factory job. The film takes place in Los Angeles in the late forties, and the director, Carl Franklin, recreates that mythologically loaded time and place in brilliant primary colors. The picture induces déjà vu—it's like a dream of film noir; we've been here before, but we've never seen the landscape quite from this angle, that of a black man struggling to hang onto his piece of the American dream.

Devil's McGuffin is unusually slight and the revelations and resolution are correspondingly anti-climactic. Easy is hired to find a rich white man's missing girlfriend who harbors a predilection for "colored men." As in the classics of the private eye genre, the search will take Easy into all the strata of L.A. society from the fortified mansions of well-heeled poobahs to smoky after-hours clubs. There's a sly, mordant joke here; the implication is that only a black man can negotiate the other America, a black America all but invisible to dominant white society. The plot involves the usual reversals and betrayals, all competently laid out but none of it very exciting. It's the details that make this movie worth seeing.

Easy's house, for example. Early on, Easy is described as "one of the few colored people to own his own house," and Easy takes on the detective job in order to keep up his mortgage payments. It's just a little tract house with a plot of grass, but Washington makes Easy's house-pride palpable and deeply touching—he makes home-ownership into a spiritual birthright. You can't help but think of the current condition of south-central L.A. where the American dream for African-Americans has collided with racist cops and economic injustice.

As Easy, Denzel Washington comes into his own as a sexy, charismatic leading man with all the presence and laid-back gravity of a Robert Mitchum. His Easy is an Everyman who just wants to tend his garden but keeps getting drawn into the undergrowth of crime and political corruption. In the picture's violent scenes, Washington quietly captures Easy's deep humanity; even the death of an enemy leaves him bereft and stricken. He also reveals a gift for comedy in a scene where the normally self-contained Easy is utterly undone by lust for a teasing, sexy woman.

In the movie's supporting cast, Tom Sizemore is very good as a pudgy, seemingly genial thug who turns out to have a scary, sadistic streak. As the missing white girl, the eponymous devil in a blue dress, Jennifer Beals leaves you wondering what all the fuss is about. She's so bland that even her flirtatious scenes with Washington lack sizzle. Don Cheadle as Mouse, Easy's trigger-happy, homburg-wearing friend from Texas, adds comic energy to the film, though a flashback recounting Mouse's earlier adventures will be all but incomprehensible to anyone who hasn't read the novel.

Carl Franklin's previous film, *One False Move*, was a low-budget noir that ended up being surprisingly moving. *Devil* doesn't have a comparable emotional impact—it's hampered by the P.I. conventions of Mosley's novel—but it's distinguished by Franklin's fluid camera work and graceful way with a story. *Devil* doesn't strong-arm you with its racial theme, but it's there in the casual racist remarks of peripheral characters and the business-as-usual brutality of two porcine cops. And a montage of Easy looking for a gangster in various venues is a textbook illustration of how the right combination of music—in this case, Thelonius Monk's "Round About Midnight"—and visual rhythms can make even a simple narrative transition into something large and thrilling.

LOS ANGELES TIMES, 9/29/95, Calendar/p. 1, Kenneth Turan

Hard-boiled fiction is a been-around genre about done-that individuals, so the pleasant air of newness and excitement that "Devil in a Blue Dress" gives off isn't due to its familiar find-the-girl plot. Rather it's the film's glowing visual qualities, a striking performance by Denzel Washington and the elegant control Carl Franklin has over it all that create the most exotic crime entertainment of the season.

There's an irony about "Devil's" exoticism, because its setting isn't some remote overseas locale but right here in Los Angeles, the circa 1948 streets surrounding a vibrant Central Avenue. It says quite a bit about the nature of Hollywood and the history of American race relations that that time and place are as remote as Burkina Faso as far as mainstream movie audiences are concerned.

For writer-director Franklin, adapting the first of Walter Mosley's popular series of Ezekiel (Easy) Rawlins detective novels for a major studio also had its exotic aspects. Franklin's last film was the acclaimed and accomplished low-budget thriller "One False Move," and carrying off the transition to larger budgets without the loss of creative edge could have presented a problem.

Instead, "Devil in a Blue Dress" turns out to be a major accomplishment, a fluid, persuasive piece of movie-making graced with the considerable visual sophistication of Tak Fujimoto, executive producer Jonathan Demme's favorite cinematographer. Starting with its mood-setting credit sequence—a slow pan over a gorgeous Archibald Motley Jr. painting of "Bronzeville at Night" while a T-Bone Walker blues plays on the soundtrack—this is a film in smooth control of its ways and means.

Also in complete charge of his resources is Denzel Washington, who establishes himself once again as a superb leading man. Coolly handsome, able to project a sly humor and a measurable sexuality as well as dignity and strength, Washington can also play confused uncertainty when the story demands it. And no one since Marlon Brando's "A Streetcar Named Desire" days has looked better in a tight T-shirt.

Washington also has the sensitivity to play Easy Rawlins as a man of his era, a 1940s Negro who must of necessity leaven his heroic qualities with the kind of circumspect behavior demanded by those more overtly racist times, when it was risky for black men to venture north of Wilshire Boulevard at night and even the Ambassador Hotel was segregated by color.

"Devil" opens with Easy in trouble. Fired from his job in a defense plant, he has an overdue house payment and a lack of prospects. Then a bartender introduces him to the mysterious Dewitt Albright (Tom Sizemore), whose living consists of "doing favors for friends." He asks Easy to help him find a white woman named Daphne Monet (Jennifer Beals), the fiancee of one of the city's most powerful men, who fancies jazz and likes to hang out around Central Avenue. It sounds too easy, which, of course, it is.

With its frequent twists and references to corruption at the highest levels of Los Angeles' power elite, "Devil" owes a good deal to Robert Towne's script for Roman Polanski's classic "Chinatown."' To no one's surprise but his own, Easy is soon in way over his head in the usual world of murder, blackmail and betrayal, where all his attempts to do the right thing only get him into more and more trouble.

Fortunately for Easy, Mouse, a pal from his past who would truly as soon kill someone as look at them, shows up and helps out. Played with a picture-stealing bravado by Don Cheadle, Mouse is a more comic character here than in Mosley's book, but that change, like the others Franklin has made to the novel, turns out to be an audience-friendly alteration.

Though "Devil's" plot is a standard one, the same is not true of its setting. Production designer Gary Frutkoff and his team have superbly re-created not only Central Avenue (which was shot on an appropriately dressed section of downtown's Main Street) but the interiors of loud bars, smoky jazz clubs and all the rest of Rawlins' milieu. To watch this film is to feel like a privileged visitor in an unfamiliar world that ought to be gone but, "Brigadoon"-like, unexpectedly lives again.

Making "Devil's" world worth visiting is the way Carl Franklin presents it. It's a brutal place, but Franklin, as "One False Move" showed, knows how to make onscreen violence effective without overdoing things. It is also rife with prejudice, and Franklin refuses to shortchange that while insisting on his characters' dignity and humanity. If there were more films like this, to lean on Raymond Chandler one more time, movie houses would be safer places to visit without becoming too dull to be worth the trip.

NEW YORK, 10/2/95, p. 82, David Denby

In Carl Franklin's wonderful *Devil in a Blue Dress*, bodies grappling with one another fall to the floor with the thud and heft of palpable flesh. Working with the great cinematographer Tak Fujimoto, Franklin (*One False Move*) has achieved a ripely tactile visual style for this retro-*noir* drama, set in black Los Angeles in 1948. Walter Mosley adapted his own novel, the first in the popular "Easy Rawlins" series, and Denzel Washington stars as the up-from-Texas machinist who gets laid off after the war and is then drawn into a frighteningly complicated maze of desire and corruption. As Easy moves around the city, everything has superb density and weight—the beautiful, rounded old cars, the seductive California daylight, the smoke of a crowded nightclub and lilt of a woman's aroused laughter.

As in the Dashiell Hammett and Raymond Chandler classics on which this book and movie are based, dirty doings in high places lead to many acts of violence and betrayal below. But Mosley and Franklin have invested an old genre with fresh feeling. The familiar mood of voluptuous paranoia is enhanced and made more explicit by the shift to a black man's point of view. Easy lives in a racially segregated America, and without hysteria or exaggeration, Franklin puts us in his place. Tom Sizemore's vicious white gangster, friendly one minute, antagonistic the next, epitomizes the treacherousness of the terrain for Easy: The tolerance of whites can be withdrawn at any minute and for any reason. For once, in *noir*, paranoia is a matter not of style but of survival. People try to use Easy—cops, white gangsters, other blacks—and he struggles to hold on not just to the truth (like all *noir* heroes) but also to his dignity. Franklin, as *One False Move* amply illustrated, is a wonderful director of actors. Denzel Washington conveys just the right measure of necessary deference and implacable male pride.

Tom Sizemore is terrifying, and Don Cheadle does a frighteningly funny turn as a completely amoral little man who finds it easier to kill someone than to talk to him. The only disappointment is Jennifer Beals, who, as the femme fatale, lacks the glittering insolence of Jane Greer or any of the luscious good bad girls of the forties. Without a strong performance from Beals, *Devil* becomes a labyrinth without a center, an obsession without an object. But see this beautifully made movie, an important step in what looks like a major directorial career.

NEW YORK POST, 9/29/95, p. 49, Michael Medved

A beautiful woman with a shocking, guilty secret; a lonely investigator who gets more deeply drawn into the mystery than he ever intends; powerful politicos and businessmen whose dark manipulations shape the twisted, turbulent (and lovingly re-created world of long ago Los Angeles ...

Yes, it's "Chinatown," but it's also "Devil in a Blue Dress" which offers many of the same satisfactions as Roman Polanski's moody classic along with something extra. The added element here is a focus on L.A.'s vibrant black community in the years immediately following World War II when the now-forgotten neighborhood around Central Avenue flourished as a center of African-American culture and vitality that rivaled the older establishment in Harlem.

Director Carl Franklin (whose stylish, low-budget debut "One False Move" earned appropriate acclaim) brings this lost world to the screen with gorgeous detail, letting us savor its colors (mostly rich earth tones), flavors, smells and sweats. This background is, in fact, so rich that it makes up for occasional lapses in pacing of the convoluted and confusing plot.

The action centers on Ezekiel ("Easy") Rawlins, the mellow, reliably humane hero created by Walter Mosley in his 1990 novel "Devil in a Blue Dress," and who since appeared in three more popular mysteries. His adventures begin in 1948 when Easy (flawlessly played by Denzel Washington in a role that will inspire Oscar talk) runs into a patch of bad luck.

He's a decorated veteran who's moved from his native Texas to L.A and bought himself a neat little home on the G.I. Bill. But when he's fired from his job as an aircraft mechanic, he can't make payments and fears that he'll lose his new stake in the American dream.

He's therefore an easy mark for Dewitt Albright (played with suitable menace by Tom Sizemore), who offers $100 for Easy to locate a missing socialite (Jennifer Beals) who's engaged to the leading mayoral candidate, but has also displayed a dangerous taste for violent black gangsters.

The quest for this mysterious, seductive figure (whose blue dress indeed glows and vibrates against the film's otherwise muted palette) uncovers a web of intrigue, blackmail and murder that leads Easy to summon his old Texas friend, Mouse (Don Cheadle, in a high-voltage, scene-stealing effort), a cheerfully murderous, trigger-happy tough guy who takes infectious joy from friendship and brutality.

These characters are so vivid that it clearly matters that the contrived storyline leads to a big and supposedly devastating revelation that seems oddly anti-climactic. Atmosphere is more important than logic, as the movie's elegiac mood evokes a caring, hopeful community vastly different from todays blighted inner cities.

Visual seductions reinforce an intoxicating soundtrack featuring T-Bone Walker, Jimmy Witherspoon and other actual participant in the 1940s Central Avenue scene. Like the best jazz, "Devil in a Blue Dress" weaves together jagged and seemingly spontaneous elements in a surprising intricate and moving tapestry.

NEWSDAY, 9/29/95, Part II/p. B2, Jack Mathews

Carl Franklin's critically praised but little-seen 1992 film, "One False Move," was sort of a trumpet roll for a major new talent in American film, and with the sleekly evocative and deliciously entertaining "Devil in a Blue Dress," he's arrived.

Adapted from the first of Walter Mosley's Easy Rawlins novels, "Devil" is film noir of a very special sort. It takes us back, with perfectly designed sets and decorated streets, to post-World War II Los Angeles, where so many movies from the genre's heyday were set. But Franklin shows us an area—black South Central L.A.—rarely seen on film as anything other than a hothouse of drugs, gangs and violence.

There was a time, during and immediately after the war, when South Central Los Angeles represented the American Dream to blacks who migrated there for jobs in the area's booming aircraft industry, and then the American Disappointment, as they became the first to lose their jobs when the boom ended.

Mosley created Ezekiel (Easy) Rawlins, played to perfection in the film by Denzel Washington, as a fictional representative of the young blacks caught in that collapsing economy.

Easy is a war veteran and unemployed airplane mechanic who becomes a detective out of financial need.

Desperate to make the payments on his house, a tidy bungalow in a spanking new neighborhood, Easy takes on the dubious job of tracking a mysterious white woman named Daphne Monet (Jennifer Beals), whom he's been told has a predilection for "jazz, pig's feet and dark meat," and he is quickly up to his ears in murder, blackmail and political scandal.

The plot complications of "Devil" aren't particularly compelling, especially when it begins to beg comparisons to Roman Polanski's "Chinatown." The similarities between the two films are unmistakable, and a mistake. It seems almost foolhardy to remind people of a movie that cannot be topped.

But that's a minor distraction. "Devil" is so rich in texture, and fresh in approach, it blows away everything else in the current rash of films noir.

Though the story pivots on an interracial romance, Franklin does no overt commentary on the class issues. But they are there, underpinning every scene, whether in the smoky, bebop clubs where Easy's friends hang out, and where the always blue-clad Daphne has been sighted; in his own neighborhood, where he tries to refresh his senses, or in the white community and its estates, where the case takes him.

Franklin's script faithfully adapts most of Mosley's characters and much of his sharp, Chandleresque dialogue. Beals doesn't quite possess the femme fatale qualities attributed to Daphne, but elsewhere the casting is flawless. Tom Sizemore is a genuine menace as the underworld thug who plays the devil to Easy's Faust, and Don Cheadle is a scream as Mouse, Rawlins' pint-sized but lethally quick-tempered sidekick.

There is plenty of traditional action fare; knuckle sandwiches and hot bullets are specials of the house. But violence doesn't come naturally to Easy, who reacts to his predicaments—at least until he warms to the job—much as any working stiff would, with confusion, fear and a strong urge to run like hell.

Washington, who has the physical presence and charisma to keep Easy employed on screen for a long time, plays the character with a deft mix of gallows humor and passion.

Easy knows exactly who he is and what he's faced with; he's a guy with meager opportunities, modest middle-class ambitions and enormous vitality at a time when the energy and high spirits of the postwar era were being sapped.

There were a lot of men in Easy's predicament in South Central Los Angeles, and probably none who retrained themselves as private eyes. But it's a noble fantasy.

NEWSWEEK, 10/2/95, p. 85, David Ansen

Film noir style was born in Los Angeles in the '40s—think "Double Indemnity" and "The Big Sleep"—and the images have proven so indelible that it's now hard to think of that city, in that time, separate from the shadow-streaked look of Hollywood thrillers. Now, in Carl Franklin's *Devil in a Blue Dress*—based on Walter Mosley's Easy Rawlins mystery—we're back in 1948 L.A., but as you settle into the familiar pleasures of its noir plot, you realize you're in a part of town Hollywood has neglected to show. It's Central Avenue, the hub of postwar black L.A., a vital, jazz-and-blues-infused community brought to vivid life by Franklin, production designer Gary Frutkoff and cinematographer Tak Fujimoto.

The evocation of that vanished world is alone worth the price of admission. But this classically built genre movie has plenty else to offer, not least of which is Franklin's solid, measured craftsmanship. He is not one to impose the hyperrhythms and shock tactics of the '90s on his period tale: when, in a striking scene, a bad guy dies, the camera, along with the heroes, hovers over his death throes with respect.

Denzel Washington is Easy, a war veteran who's lost his job and worries about losing his cherished house. So he accepts $100 from a shady, well-connected white man (Tom Sizemore) to find a missing woman named Daphne Monet (Jennifer Beals), the fiance of a rich mayoral candidate. It seems she has a fondness for the company of Negroes, a dangerous taste in the segregated city. Suffice it to say this seemingly simple job will drag Easy into a maze of trouble—murders, frame-ups and political corruption on the highest levels. To get out of this mess, he'll call in Mouse (the scene-stealing Don Cheadle), his trigger-happy crony from Houston. One of the surprises of Franklin's adaptation is how much comic juice he gets out of a character who seemed flat-out scary in print.

The acting ensemble shines. Lisa Nicole Carson stands out as the ill-fated Coretta, a lusty woman who riotously enjoys her one-night fling with Easy. There's a wonderful scene in which Washington and Cheadle get Coretta's boyfriend Odell (Albert Hall) passing-out drunk: you feel that the characters have been living upside each other for years. Washington, a subtle actor and natural-born movie star, understands that Easy himself is a kind of actor, forced to adjust his style depending on whether he's functioning in the white world or his own. But he's a little more noble than Mosley's Easy. You féel a tension in his performance, as if the matinee idol were restraining the actor from fully cutting loose.

As good as this movie is, it never quite achieves the startling sense of discovery that Franklin's terrific low-budget "One False Move" did. That burst the seams of its genre, and this one is content to stay contained within its conventions. What stays with you finally is not the mystery's byzantine twists and turns, which are fun but don't resonate very deeply. It's the time, the place, the palpable feel of community.

SIGHT AND SOUND, 1/96, p. 38, Manohla Dargis

At a black-only bar in Los Angeles, 1948, the owner Joppy introduces a white man, Dewitt Albright, to one Easy Rawlins, a black laid-off aircraft worker. Albright offers him $100 to help him locate a white woman called Daphne Monet. The fiancée of mayoral candidate Todd Carter, Daphne is known to enjoy the company of black men. At an after hours joint, Easy makes enquiries, and talks to his friends Odell and Dupree. The latter's girl, Coretta James, knows Daphne, and asks Easy to help her take the drunk Dupree home. In return for sex, she tells Easy that Daphne is living with black gangster Frank Green.

Carter pulls out of the election. Easy is taken down town by police detectives who beat him and tell him Coretta was murdered shortly after Easy left her. He is released, only to be offered a lift by another candidate for mayor, Matthew Terell. Later, Daphne calls Easy and summons him to the Ambassador Hotel. She wants Easy to drive her to a remote house where they find a man named Richard McGee, murdered. Daphne flees the scene leaving Easy behind.

Albright and two thugs threaten Easy and then offer him more money to find Daphne and Green. Easy summons his old friend Mouse, a stone killer from Houston. Easy visits Carter who denies all knowledge of Albright but offers Easy $1,000 to track down Daphne. Easy is then attacked by Frank Green but is saved by Mouse. The cops come to arrest Easy but they agree to give him more time to solve Coretta's murder. Easy and Mouse visit Junior, the bouncer at the after hours club. He tells them he delivered a letter from McGee to Daphne through Coretta. At Dupree's house they find the letter, which contains pictures of Terell having sex with young children.

Daphne is waiting for Easy at his house. She confesses that Frank Green is her brother and that she has been 'passing for white'. Terell has used this to force Carter out of the election—the pictures are the counter-blackmail. Albright and his thugs arrive and kidnap Daphne without getting the pictures. Easy and Mouse force Albright's likely whereabouts from Joppy. At a remote house in Malibu, they kill Albright and his men and Mouse chokes Joppy. They take Daphne to see Carter, but he refuses to agree to marry her. Carter tells Easy that the police will now leave him alone.

Even as Carl Franklin's *Devil in a Blue Dress* opens in Britain, its presence in the United States has all but evaporated—the critically acclaimed film has earned only $15 million in six weeks. *Devil* isn't the only film to go belly up last autumn (*Strange Days* and *Assassins* are two other big-ticket flops), but in some ways its failure is the most alarming, indicating as it does Hollywood's failure to sell to mainstream America a black film that defies both stereotype and expectation.

Written and directed by the well-respected Franklin, based on a novel by one of the most lauded of modern American detective writers, with one of the industry's hottest stars at its fore, *Devil in a Blue Dress* is a movie that should not have failed. The film racked up reams of glowing reviews and seemed to have a lock on the very best in publicity. Still, there were signs of weakness in the print and television campaigns. One could blame it on O.J. (one LA movie reviewer announced that, post-O.J., white people were too angry to get behind *Strange Days* and its message of racial unity) or just maybe blame it on an industry that one hundred years after its launch still can't escape the Jim Crow logic of separate-but-equal in movies as in life.

Close to the end of the film, Easy Rawlins, a former aircraft worker who's gotten tangled up in mystery and murder runs up a dark staircase, clutching his stomach. Hurt, exhausted and driven by a purpose not yet fully understood, Easy is going to see his old friend Joppy, who may or may not have done him a great wrong. The camera waits for him, picking him out from the shadows. The scene is familiar, a blurred memory from a dozen *films noirs*: the hero, maybe Robert Mitchum, maybe Burt Lancaster, races upstairs. He's wounded and terminally alone.

Except that, this time, the scene is shaded differently; this time the man stumbling towards his destiny is played by Denzel Washington.

Based on the sensationally popular novel by Walter Mosley, *Devil in a Blue Dress* is Franklin's follow-up to *One False Move*, his deceptively simple, brutally-felt genre-bender. Both films are crime stories in which violence is less a matter of guts and gunplay than of human passions and the American calamity known as race. Set in post-second World War LA, *Devil* reaches beyond the co-ordinates of story and genre. Although it plays its hand against a pulp tradition that reaches from Raymond Chandler to Chester Himes, the existential crises upon which it twists and turns are rooted in history.

Like a lot of classic *noir, Devil in a Blue Dress* opens while the sun is still shining. The camera prowls through a busy Central Avenue afternoon and into Joppy's bar, stopping on Easy, sitting alone at a table. Easy is out of work, and recently fired from a good job. Still, there's a drink on his table. As for the room, it's a study in brown—not the sepia of nostalgia but a dirty yellow through years of nicotine and casual neglect. There are other men in the bar but they're just silhouettes, gone soft in the fading light. Then a white man walks in, and Easy's world collapses.

At the core of *Devil in a Blue Dress*, is a mystery and a couple of murders. Easy has seen death before as a GI in Europe but there's a different kind of death that walks in with the white man, Dewitt Albright. It has to do with the soul, and what it means to put yourself up on the auction block. Because she's known to stray into the company of black men, Albright figures on Easy to search Daphne out ("she likes jazz, pig's feet and dark meat, know what I mean?" The pay is $100, more than enough to take care of Easy's mortgage.

Easy eventually finds Daphne but only after he's been plunged into political, racial and sexual intrigue. The central mystery, which works fine in the novel, doesn't make sense in the film because of the curiously misjudged casting of Jennifer Beals as Daphne. The mistake, however, is not a ruinous one. All it proves is that Franklin's heart lies less with the specificity of *film noir* and detective fiction than in the ways he can use them. Franklin's adaptation is faster and leaner than Mosley's book. It knows how to hit the funny notes as well as the hardboiled. Its surprises aren't in empty cigarette packages and dribbles of blood but in unfathomables like love and hate and the way a man called Mouse can be Easy's oldest friend and still turn a gun on him. Don Cheadle's Mouse is the single biggest shock in the film. Compact, with lustrous ebony skin and a gold cap that catches light, Cheadle enters laughing, maybe because he knows he's about to steal home. Washington may never have been as good as he is here but he pales significantly next to his friend.

Such characters and concerns are new to the American screen but for all of its convolutions, the first half of *Devil* holds to a deliberate, occasionally slow pace with few fluctuations in tone—it's easy does it. When the pace picks up, the body count does too: rage floods the scene then drops to a savage whisper. The first devil that Easy meets is a corpulent creep with a pet baby boy. The second wears a sky blue dress; the third a crisp fedora and a neatly pressed suit and then there's the devil who stares back when things go sour, and the one who comes up from Texas with two cocked guns and a swallowing grin—a Southern Gothic gone north to remind Easy where he's come from. "They thought I was some kind of new fool," says Easy at one point of his voice over, "and I guess I was." For better and sometimes worse, Easy has left Joppy's bar for good. He's put the *noir* back into *film noir* and crossed over into the world; there's no turning back.

TIME, 10/2/95, p. 72, Richard Schickel

Easy Rawlins is a private citizen, not strictly speaking a private eye. He is also a black man. But these two significant—and dramatically potent—differences aside, novelist Walter Mosley's creation is the truest heir we have yet had to Raymond Chandler's immortal Philip Marlowe. And writer-director Carl Franklin s cool, expert adaptation of *Devil in a Blue Dress*, Mosley's first novel, evokes the spirit of '40s film noir more effectively than any movie since *Chinatown*.

This is not just a matter of recapturing the look of postwar Los Angeles or making an attractive figure of a smart, righteous loner. It requires as well a taste for labyrinthine plotting (and a confidence that the audience will pay close attention to it despite the lack of car chases and explosions); a gift for bizarre, boldly stated characterizations (often enough hinting at several kinks); and, most important, a nose for social nuance.

Mosley, like Chandler, sets seemingly simple task for his hero—in this instance, Easy (Denzel Washington) is hired to find a young woman (Jennifer Beals), mistress to a wealthy candidate for mayor, who has gone missing—but one that will lead him eventually from lowlife bars and jazz clubs to the mansions of the rich and respectable. Who are then revealed to be the source of all civic corruption. Precisely because Easy is black and an unlicensed investigator, his journey through the social strata is much more perilous than Marlowe's ever was. In Los Angeles 50 years ago a "Negro" risked his life (or anyway a nasty beating) if he was found in a white neighborhood or in the company of a white woman. And the cops, of course, could be counted on to treat him with brutal contempt (perhaps the only American tradition that has survived intact to this day).

There are other, subtler differences between Easy and his predecessor. He owns a trim little house (complete with worrisome mortgage), yearns for the settled life and narrates his adventures in a style that avoids the lush metaphors Chandler favored. He even has a sidekick, Mouse (Don Cheadle), a genial psychopath in a bowler hat, comically eager to rub out anyone who crosses his path, whether he deserves it or not. He's a scene stealer, but so is everyone else Easy encounters: the nervously sexy Beals, a brutal-funny fixer with ambiguous loyalties (Tom Sizemore), an epicene politician (Maury Chaykin). But Washington, like the character he plays, knows how to roll with their punches. Reserved but agile, wary but thrusting when he needs to be, he gracefully reanimates a lost American archetype, the lonely lower-class male absorbing more cigarette smoke, bourbon whiskey and nasty beatings than is entirely healthy, as he pursues miscreants and moral imperatives down mean, palm-lined streets.

VILLAGE VOICE, 10/3/95, p. 80, Georgia Brown

You can locate Walter Mosleys bluesy Easy Rawlins books in the mystery novel section, but they're even better read as odes to African American suffering. For Caucasians like me, they're also American history lessons and urban studies texts. Like any 19th-century British novelist—Jane Austen for instance—Mosley writes about property, status, and economic forces shaping individual fortunes. *Devil in a Blue Dress*, set in 1948 L.A., tells us, among other things, that the American city has long been a system of zones that many cross each day at their peril. Call them neighborhoods when you wish to sound friendly.

Carl Franklin director of 1992's superb *One False Move* and one of the smartest men to get a word in edgewise with Charlie Rose, adapts *Devil* (writing the screenplay as well as directing) with finesse and comprehension and with no weakness for cheap, or even expensive, sensationalism. No false moves, I'd say. In more ways than one, *Devil* is *Chinatown* with soul.

Ezekiel "Easy" Rawlins (Denzel Washington) is a war vet from Houston who's come to L.A. following the dream. "California was like heaven for the Southern Negro," writes Mosley.

"People told stories of how you could eat fruit right off the trees and get enough work to retire some day." Easy found a job at Champion Aircraft and bought a fine little house with a yard and its own fruit trees. This house he loves like a woman, and, judging from the femmes fatale he meets in the course of *Devil*, it's less trouble (though Franklin inserts a neighborhood crazy who chops at people's fruit trees). But now our man of property is fired by his (white) boss—and stands to forfeit on his mortgage. When Joppy, an ex-boxer who owns his own bar, introduces Easy to the shady Dewitt Albright (Tom Sizemore), Easy is receptive to the white man's business proposition. (Book and movie are constructed as a series of life-threatening encounters with white men.)

"I've got a West Side baby, she lives way across town ...," sings T-Bone Walker over the titles. Easy's job is to locate Daphne Monet (Jennifer Beals), a lady who lives, it seems, all over town. Daphne is a border-crosser. Leers Albright: "She likes jazz, pigs' feet, dark meat, know what I mean!" What Easy doesn't know is that Daphne's crosstown bus travels two directions. Moreover, her relationships with the highest of the cities politicos, including two candidates for mayor, will make his quest especially perilous. In *Chinatown*, Jack Nicholson's shamus stuck his nose into sleazy city business and look what happened to it.

Devil is true to classic noir in setting the viewer, like the hero, down in strange territory: Much of the time something is happening and we don't know what it is. Except for Easy's own golden-hued family neighborhood, greater LA. is a beautiful but threatening network. Hollywood canyons are dark and deep, Santa Monica's pier is a place a man might get dumped off of at night. When trouble invades Easy's precious home ground, he calls on an old buddy from Houston, Mouse (the very funny Don Cheadle), a skinny guy with gold teeth and a talent for roughness.

More edgy than easy, Washington brings along his sweet face and exhibits good manners, but basically he comes off as a damaged, angst-ridden man—alert suspicious, and a chronic loner. As with Marlowe, beautiful women flirt with Easy when they want things, but he's wary enough to keep a distance. Franklin has excised the book's hot sex scene between Easy and Daphne (as he's altered several other major details), as if to say, Easy is too repressed for that. The first time we see Beals's Daphne (and we see very little of her for one reason or another), she wears a dressing gown the color of a gas flame. The flare delineates her deadliness, but basically she's not a rounded character here. It's part of the movie's mystery that Daphne is out of reach.

Race is the main event in Mosley, and so it is here. "Step out your door in the morning, you already in trouble," could be etched on every colored person's threshold. As well as most people, Easy knows the value of a shade tree and a porch chair, but it isn't just his role in this genre that prevents him from enjoying them.

Also reviewed in:
CHICAGO TRIBUNE, 9/29/95, Friday/p. C, Michael Wilmington
NATION, 10/23/95, p. 480, Stuart Klawans
NEW REPUBLIC, 10/30/95, p. 34, Stanley Kauffmann
NEW YORK TIMES, 9/29/95, p. C8, Janet Maslin
NEW YORKER, 10/2/95, p. 104, Terrence Rafferty
VARIETY, 9/18-24/95, p. 93, Todd McCarthy
WASHINGTON POST, 9/29/95, p. F1, Hal Hinson
WASHINGTON POST, 9/29/95, Weekend/p. 44, Desson Howe

DIE HARD WITH A VENGEANCE

A Twentieth Century Fox release in association with Cinergi. *Executive Producer:* Andrew G. Vajna, Buzz Feitshans, and Robert Lawrence. *Producer:* John McTiernan and Michael Tadross. *Director:* John McTiernan. *Screenplay:* Jonathan Hensleigh. *Based on certain original characters by:* Roderick Thorpe. *Director of Photography:* Peter Menzies. *Editor:* John Wright. *Music:* Michael Kamen. *Music Editor:* Eric Reasoner. *Sound:* Dennis Maitland, Sr. and (music) Steve McLaughlin and Joe Iwataki. *Sound Editor:* Mark Mangini. *Casting:* Pat McCorkle. *Production Designer:* Jackson DeGovia. *Art Director:* John R. Jensen and Woods Mackintosh. *Set Designer:* Bob Shaw, Kyung W. Chang and Peter Rogness. *Set Decorator:* Leslie Bloom. *Special Effects:* Phil Cory and Conrad F. Brink. *Visual Effects:* John E. Sullivan. *Costumes:* Joseph G. Aulisi. *Make-up:* Marilyn Peoples. *Make-up (Bruce Willis):* Cristina Bartolucci. *Make-up (Jeremy Irons):* Linda deVetta. *Stunt Coordinator:* Terry J. Leonard and Terry Jackson. *Running time:* 112 minutes. *MPAA Rating:* R.

CAST: Bruce Willis (John McClane); Jeremy Irons (Simon); Samuel L. Jackson (Zeus); Graham Greene (Joe Lambert); Colleen Camp (Connie Kowalski); Larry Bryggman (Arthur Cobb); Anthony Peck (Ricky Walsh); Nick Wyman (Targo); Sam Phillips (Katya); Kevin Chamberlin (Charles Weiss); Sharon Washington (Officer Jane); Stephen Pearlman (Dr. Schiller); Michael Alexander Jackson (Dexter); Aldis Hodge (Raymond); Mischa Hausserman (Mischa); Edwin Hodge (Dexter's Friend); Rob Sedgwick (Rolf); Tony Halme (Roman); Bill Christ (Ivan); Anthony Thomas (Gang Member #1); Glenn Herman (Gang Member #2); Kent Faulcon (Gang Member #3); Akili Prince (Gang Member #4); Ardie Fuqua (Gang Member #5); Mike Jefferson (Gang Member #6); Frank Andre Ware (Gang Member #7); Michael Lee Merrins (Van Driver); Birdie M. Hale (Harlem Woman); Daryl Edwards (Livery Driver); Barbara Hipkiss (Phone Woman); Aasif Mandvi (Arab Cabbie); Bill Kux (Business Guy, Taxi); Scott Nicholson (Transit Cop); Ralph Buckley (Businessman, Station); Charles Dumas (Cross); Michael Cristofer (Jarvis); Phyllis Yvonne Stickney (Wanda Shepard); J.R. Horne (Sgt. John Turley); Michael Tadross (Greek Deli Proprietor); Elvis Duran (Radio D.J.); John McTiernan,

Sr. (Fisherman); Greg A. Skoric (Kurt); Sven Toorvald (Karl); Todd A. Langenfeld (Berndt); Timothy Adams (Gunther); John C. Vennema (Felix Little); Gerrit Vooren (Nils); Willis Sparks (Klaus); Tony Travis (Marshal #1); Danny Dutton (Marshal #2); James Saito (Korean Propreitor); Patrick Dorriello (Kid #1); Victor Rojas (Kid #2); Jeffrey Dreisbach (Yuppie Stockbroker); Joe Zaloom (Jerry Parks); John Doman (Foreman); Patricia Mauceri (Miss Thomas); Franchelle Stewart Dorn (Principal Martinez); Kharisma (Little Tina); Gerry Becker (Larry Griffith); Richard Council (Otto); John Robert Tillotson (Second Broker); Ray Arahna (Janitor); Phil Theis (Erik); Flip (Subway Man); Dory Binyon (Reporter); David Vitt (Kid at Gas Station); John Glenn Hoyt (Federal Reserve Guard #1); Bray Poor (Federal Reserve Guard #2); David P. Martin (Federal Reserve Guard #3); Shari-Lyn Safir (Secretary); Ivan Skoric (Villian); Faisal Hassan (FBI Agent); Richard Russell Ramos (FBI Chief); Angela Amato (Cop #1); Richard V. Allen (Chief Allen); Shirley J. Hatcher (Cop #2); James Patrick Whalen, Sr. (Fat Larry Lumis); Paul Simon (Man in Precint); Carl Brewer (Helicopter Villain).

LOS ANGELES TIMES, 5/19/95, Calendar/p. 1, Peter Rainer

The kabooms start early in "Die Hard With a Vengeance." Before we've had a chance to ease into our seats we're treated to a rock-the-Dolby explosion in New York's Bonwit Teller department store.

And the explosions—or the threat of explosions—just keep on coming. This third installment of the "Die Hard" series, starring Bruce Willis as the heroically beleaguered police officer John McClane, is a grand-scale demolition derby—a demolition derby on steroids. It throws the audience into a state of heightened, exhilarated queasiness.

The trigger for all the kapowie is a cat-and-mouse game between McClane and a malevolent genius—is there any other kind in these films?—who goes by the name Simon (Jeremy Irons). Simon, who has mastered the art of snooty, untraceable phone calls to the N.Y.P.D, and who bears a king-size, unexplained animus toward McClane, likes to play Simon Says.

The police play along because they have no other way of averting more bombings. And so McClane, on the skids with the police, separated from his wife, hung over, is delivered up for Simon's delectation.

Simon's first little game sends McClane into a life-threatening situation in Harlem, where he ends up uneasily allied with a shopkeeper, Zeus Carver (Samuel L. Jackson), who regards all white skin as a red flag. For most of the movie, Simon sends these two on a series of beat-the-clock escapades all over New York.

The "Die Hard" series was never exactly big on nuance, but this new installment relentlessly zeros in on sensation. It's almost sadistically single-minded. Did Simon also direct it?

John McTiernan (who directed the first "Die Hard") and screenwriter Jonathan Hensleigh keep throwing conflagrations at us. They stage a chase scene through Central Park and another across 90 rush-hour blocks that, strictly from the point of view of crowd-control logistics, are marvels.

In the popular imagination, it would be difficult to make New York seem any more horrific than it already is, but the filmmakers succeed. They deliver up a New York where everything is in hair-trigger peril: the subways, the buildings, the crowds.

There's a double message for us in all these high jinks. The people who made the film are out to top not only the other two "Die Hard" movies but also every other film like it—including, most recently, "Speed."

Their "generosity" is a form of drubbing. Are we supposed to be elevated by the idea that supposedly the only way we can be entertained by an action thriller these days is by having it pounded into our DNA?

Even McClane's usual squiggles of wiseacre throwaway dialogue are mostly lost in the din. (This is the kind of film where everyone in the audience is always leaning over to ask, "What did he just say?")

The big set pieces don't build, really, they just pile up. The filmmakers throw in everything, even a children-in-peril ploy, just in case we thought one of our favorite disasters was being neglected. No doubt a lot of people in the audience will be thinking of Oklahoma City during "Die Hard With a Vengeance," but it's too flagrantly over-the-top to be truly disturbing in a real-world way. The subtext never becomes the text.

And what is the text? It's an essay in adrenaline rush all done up in spray-painted graffiti and cartoon doodles. Willis and Jackson, as adept and entertaining as they often are, spend most of the movie huffing and puffing. They barely keep pace with the effects.

Screenwriter Hensleigh also worked on the "Indiana Jones" TV series, and he seems to have transposed a lot of Lucasland thrills intact into the bowels of New York. (There's an underground aqueduct flooding scene that Indie will be sorry he missed out on.) The film's spirit isn't very Indiana Jones-ish, though. The Saturday-matinee feeling is uglified by all the pounding squalor. As McClane and Zeus press on in pursuit, they turn into blood-streaked speed demons. Tattered, they wear their welts like the latest fashion.

Speaking of fashion, why is it that terrorists in the movies always dress in the best threads? Simon, once we get to see the man behind the voice, is buffed and spiffy. He's dressed for success.

Jeremy Irons gives Simon a maniacal elegance that occasionally lifts him into the realm of the best James Bond movie meanies. Simon enjoys how *irrational* the rational can be. He's a nut-brained respite from the McClane/Zeus shenanigans, which resemble the "Roadrunner" crossed with "Lethal Weapon."

Their brothers-under-the-skin badinage seems engineered for a new pairing, a new series—"Lethal Die Hard" perhaps? When Zeus scores McClane for being white, there's no explosiveness behind it. It's just shtick.

Still, it's nice that *something* in this movie doesn't explode.

NEW YORK, 5/29/95, p. 52, David Denby

We suffer, in this country, from an increasing sense of unreality. It didn't require an actual event in Oklahoma City to make me feel greenish and depressed about watching *Die Hard With a Vengeance,* another $75 million movie about a mad bomber. My mood takes a swan dive at the beginning of every summer season, though I admit I found pleasure, last year, in *Speed,* a movie that extended and embellished a small number of physical possibilities with the disciplined virtuosity of a great silent comedy. But the latest *Die Hard* is a mess, a shapeless, nonsensical exploding thing, with Bruce Willis trying to stop a fiendish bomber from terrorizing New York, and getting mangled and bloodied along the way. Covered with gore, Willis takes punishment in a blown-up subway car, a turned-over automobile, a tunnel filled with rushing water, the hold of a ship, and so on. The hero's function here is merely to endure; he gets mashed so often the movie turns into a weird, sick joke—James Bond as Jason the unkillable. In fact, *Die Hard* stops making any kind of sense after about an hour. The movie leaves Manhattan, which had given it a nominal unity, heads for the bridges, and becomes nothing more than one generic disconnected thrill after another. (As recently as three weeks ago, the filmmakers were still trying to reshoot a sequence of a car jumping off the Brooklyn-Queens Expressway—the scene never made it into the movie.) Watching *Die Hard,* and knowing that however ridiculous the movie may be, the media will promote it into a huge hit, because it's big, it's happening, and there's nothing else out there but *Crimson Tide,* one begins to think the country may be suffering a nervous breakdown. Oklahoma City doesn't make *Die Hard with a Vengeance* into a bad movie, but it certainly makes it a preposterous one.

Bruce has a sidekick this time—Samuel L. Jackson as a touchy black man with a good, honest soul beneath his rage. Jackson, as always, gives a forceful performance, and grounds the movie in whatever reality it has, but he doesn't have much to work with. Anyone can see that he's there to bring in the black audience and possibly a bit of *Pulp Fiction* cachet, as well as to provide the all-male buddy-buddy movie's obligatory equivalent of a romantic quarrel. Like *True Lies,* this monster movie is pasted together from bits and pieces that have worked before in other contexts. Jeremy Irons, as the bomber, manages to be everywhere at once, just like the villains of last year's mad-bomber movies (*Speed, Blown Away*), and he makes threats in the form of elaborate riddles that require the hero to run all over town—as if terrorists excelled at organizing scavenger hunts at camp. As always, goodness is straightforward and evil is effete, intellectual, and baroque. Willis's Lieutenant John McClane is a tough Irish prole who sweats and bleeds, and Irons, literate, witty, and ironic, plays a blond East German—a generic Nazi. (In pop-cult junkland, a German accent remains a sign of vileness a half-century after V-E Day.)

The movie uses New York as an obstacle course, which is not the same thing as using it well. In the best sequence, a subway car, uprooted by bombs, goes skidding across a platform, a scene that re-creates the terrifying dynamic of unbound physical force. But a lot of the action sequences feel fragmentary and fake. The director, John McTiernan (who made the original, much better *Die Hard*), stages a savage, tearing taxi ride across the lawns and rocks of Central Park but keeps the camera so close in, and the shots so brief, that one can't get much sense of what's actually happening. A shoot-out inside an elevator turns out to be unstageable. Photographed from very close, even routine movements will seem eruptive, and editing can cover all sorts of gaps. The unreality of the thrills, combined with their pointlessness as narrative, adds to one's sense of unease. We never see any blood except on Willis, who wears it proudly, as makeup. The explosions are just for fun. But who's supposed to be having fun? I love action movies but explosions do nothing for me. I really don't get their appeal. When an ersatz Bonwit Teller blows up, early in the movie, the scene looks exactly like what it is—a staged stunt. Movie bombers use advanced technology and play complicated mind-bending games. But all it takes to wreak actual havoc is a couple of guys filling a rented truck with fertilizer and fuel oil. In this country, fear and an exhilarated fascination with weapons and technology grow together like evil twins. The big summer movies only add to the dissociation, to the growing sense of panic.

NEW YORK POST, 5/19/95, p. 33, Michael Medved

No one expects sensitive artistic statements from "Die Hard With a Vengeance." The only real question concerning this heavily-hyped kick-off to Hollywood's summer silly season is how well it stacks up against its two hugely successful predecessors in the "Die Hard" series.

In that regard, there's both good news and bad news.

The good news is that the stunts and special effects are more spectacular than ever, with half a dozen elaborately staged set pieces that will provoke gasping audiences to erupt into spontaneous applause.

The bad news, however, involves such inconveniently essential movie elements as story line and characterization, and these shortcomings are serious enough to overwhelm all the showy explosions and slick chase scenes.

Set in New York City, the plot begins quite literally with a bang as a terrorist mastermind blows up a department store in order to grab the attention of the NYPD, not mention the movie audience.

In phone calls to the cops, a German-accented fiend known as "Simon" promises more deadly bombings unless officer John McClane (Bruce Willis) plays the game of "Simon Says" and goes through a series of tests and humiliations.

In the first of these, his life is saved by a Harlem shopkeeper played by Samuel L. Jackson, and for some reason (never explained) the mad bomber spends the rest of the movie including this stranger in his playful but deadly challenges.

It turns out that the evil genius behind these games (Jeremy Irons) is the younger brother of the psycho (Alan Rickman) that Willis dispatched in the first "Die Hard." Yes, revenge is part of his motivation, but he also wants to distract the authorities so he can pull off a preposterously improbable heist, assisted by scores of muscular bad guys about whom we know nothing at all, other than the fact that they speak German and scowl a lot.

Irons himself seems to be having a grand time; he looks great with spikey blond hair and captures the same combination of world weary elegance and sociopathic menace that "brother" Rickman brought to the first film.

Irons' suave sadism, however, altogether overshadows the Willis character, in part because McClane's motivation never adds up here. He's not fighting to protect his wife (who's mentioned but never seen) nor is he trapped in some desperate situation in an enclosed space where he's forced into heroics against his will.

This time, Willis chases his adversaries all over greater New York (and beyond) like a standard issue Dudley Do-Right, trying to foil crime and bring evil-doers to justice. The only echo of his previously cynical, gritty persona comes from constant complaints about hangovers and headaches and his frequent requests for aspirin.

Despite script weaknesses, director John McTiernan (who also teamed with Willis on the original "Die Hard") definitely gives the audience its money's worth in terms of violent and overblown excess, aided considerably by a booming, screeching, teeth-rattling soundtrack that will test any theater's speaker system.

All in all, it's one of the noisiest, most frenetic movies ever made. Trouble is, it's full of sound and fury, signifying nothing—and leaves the audience craving its own bottle of aspirin.

NEWSDAY, 5/19/95, Part II/p. B2, John Anderson

Massive explosions don't seem as gleefully entertaining as they one did; watching the infrastructure come apart doesn't pack quite the same joyously liberating punch. But the cosmic implications of bad timing aren't something we're either inclined, or entitled, to address here: If you feel you have to forgive Bruce Willis for Oklahoma City before you can enjoy "Die Hard With a Vengeance," then you should probably stay at home.

But making moral pronouncements about action movies at this stage of the game isn't just posturing, it's self-defeating: "Die Hard With a Vengeance" is state-of-the-art action/thriller/comedy, a movie fast-paced and funny enough to earn forgiveness for most of its sins—of logic, physics, geography—as well as for being a big, beefy cartoon that flaunts its flaws like tattoos. It's not so pure, but it is entertainment.

"Die Hard WAV" features the same aging juvenile delinquent—New York City Det. John McClane—played by the same actor—Bruce Willis—in much the same way as in the first two films: Willis' specialty is self-deprecating smugness, which should be oxymoronic but instead is endearing. And although separated from his wife (thus sparing us Bonnie Bedelia) he *is* in partnership with Samuel L. Jackson, as the quick-witted but bigoted Zeus, a Harlem electrician who will progress from being a reluctant participant in the war against terrorism to a crime-fighting, helicopter-riding hero with a bullet in his leg (one of those conceits you have to forgive).

McClane is progressing, too, caught up in the natural metamorphosis that overcomes heros in Hollywood series: They start out being lionized for what they're not and end up being humiliated for what they are. McClane, in this case, is hung over, bad-tempered, on suspension and the pet target of an unseen terrorist named Simon (Jeremy Irons), who introduces himself to New York by blowing Bonwit Teller to bits. To appease Simon, McClane has to stand on a Harlem street corner in his underwear with a race-baiting sign around his neck, which attracts a gang of summer-heated, beer-swilling thugs (one of the films more dubious moments) and the good services of Zeus—the beginning of a beautiful, and fractious, friendship.

Having saved Los Angeles from Alan Rickman and Dulles Airport from William Sadler, McClane now has to rescue his hometown from Irons, who, like Rickman, is an Englishman in a German accent, and, like Sadler, is totally ruthless. Almost. By blowing up Bonwit's—in a scene full of verisimilitude and hurtling trucks—he's picked a target that is, in real life, already defunct. This shows a certain care in demolition on the part of director John McTiernan; bombing Bloomie's would only increase the odds of a copy-cat crime. But let's face it: The film has opened with the sound of the Lovin' Spoonful rather than Tupac Shakur, so it's a big softie at heart, a blockbuster with boomers on its mind.

There's a wild drive through Central Park as McClane and Zeus try to catch a bomb-laden No. 3 train. There's a spectacular explosion at the Wall Street station when the bomb goes off. There's a traffic jam at Columbus Circle that brings the action to such an abrupt halt you can feel yourself being held captive by an aromatic cab driver billowing El Producto and blasting Howard Stern. And there's a queasy sense of insecurity engendered by the fragile quality of New York's bridges and tunnels. Even so, the city looks pretty good—even as McTiernan uses its idiosyncrasies to maximum effect.

The film's first act, as it were, is better than what follows. Irons is an unseen villain, his voice nettling the police with nursery rhymes and riddles, is better than Irons in person. When he does appear, and starts pulling the heist that preoccupies most of the film, the whole production takes a step down. This isn't Irons' fault, really—he's 90 percent English decadent, 10 percent von Bulow. It's just that "Die Hard" reverts at this point to formula, and McTiernan has to rely on adornments rather than a novel structure to keep his audience entertained. Which he does. Of course, whether explosions and violence are the best way of being entertained is another question—and not necessarily one McTiernan has to answer.

NEWSWEEK, 5/29/95, p. 60, Jack Kroll

[*Die Hard with a Vengeance* was reviewed with *Braveheart*; see Kroll's review of that film.]

SIGHT AND SOUND, 8/95, p. 45, José Arroyo

Summer in New York City. Bonwit Teller's, the department store on 5th Avenue, blows up. The police receive a phone call from someone playing a deadly game of Simon Says. He demands to speak to John McClane. McClane is separated from his wife Holly, on suspension from the police, and hungover. Simon orders McClane to the corner of 138th and Amsterdam or there will be another big bang. In Harlem, Zeus, a proprietor of an electronics store, sees McClane wearing a sandwich-board stating 'I hate niggers'. A gang of black youths is standing nearby. Zeus goes to confront McClane but ends up saving him.

Simon is not happy. He makes Zeus accompany McClane on the next part of the game. They have to answer a phone on 72nd and Broadway or another bomb will blow up. The pair make it only to be given a half hour to answer a phone at the Wall Street Subway station. This occasions a car chase through Central Park. Zeus arrives first but the phone is busy. He harasses a man into hanging up only to have a policeman draw a gun on him. He finally answers the phone but Simon realises that McClane is not there and detonates the bomb. McClane is in the train, finds the bomb in the nick of time and throws it away but the detonation derails the subway car. McClane is then met by government agents who identify Simon as Peter Gruber, whose brother, Hans, McClane threw off a skyscraper in Los Angeles.

Simon tells the police that there is a bomb in one of New York's 446 primary schools that will detonate at 3pm. While the city's resources are channelled into finding the bomb, Simon robs the Federal Reserve Bank of New York of 140 billion dollars in gold. McClane and Zeus figure this out only to arrive after the loot has gone. In pursuit of another riddle, Zeus goes to Yankee Stadium where Simon's assassins decide not to kill him because McClane isn't there. Meanwhile, McClane tracks Simon's truck convoy through the tunnels of an aqueduct. McClane and Zeus reunite on the highway when McClane is spewed out of a water tunnel. They follow the villains on to a ship. Simon captures Zeus and forces McClane's surrender. They are tied to a huge bomb. Back in New York City, the police find the bomb in the school that Zeus' nephews attend. Zeus and McClane extricate themselves and at the Canadian border destroy Simon's helicopter. The bomb in the school proves fake. John McLane lives to call his wife.

After a touristy montage of New York summer scenes which lasts barely through the credits, *Die Hard with a Vengeance* opens with an unexpectedly prompt bang as Bonwit Teller's blows up. From those first few minutes, the film delivers the delights promised by the big-budget action genre—spectacular stunts, thrilling car chases, big explosions, suspenseful shoot-'em-ups—all depicted with the best production values money can buy. There is more of all of this than in any of the previous *Die Hard* films, and most of it is bigger, but not better.

There are several reasons though why *Die Hard with a Vengeance* is a disappointment. The major one is that the film is barely recognisable as a sequel. If the title, the name of the hero and that of the villain were changed, there could be little to connect it to the previous *Die Hard* films. The central concept of these was 'lone cop fighting to free loved ones from an enclosed space in which they are held for ransom by a greedy madman'. Here, however, John McClane has a sidekick, Samuel L. Jackson's Zeus; his loved ones are not in danger (albeit by the end of the film, Zeus' are); and the plot takes us not only through most of New York but also practically into Canada. These changes are fundamental. They don't affect genre expectations but they do deny the audience the pleasures generally expected from sequels.

I miss the recurring supporting cast of the previous two films—William Atherton, Sheila McCarthy and particularly Bonnie Bedelia. This is not only because this hyperactive film could have used the calm and understated emotionality Bedelia brought to the role of Holly. It was only after watching *Die Hard with a Vengeance* that I realised how important Holly was to the very structure of the films. Her role in the *Die Hard* films is analogous to that of women in the Western. She represents order, stability, family. McClane's attempt to save her is an attempt to overturn the moral and social chaos imposed by the villain. She not only symbolises the utopian value the hero attempts to restore but also provides the moral context for the hero's derring-do. It is because he fights for her, for what she represents, that he is allowed to kill. Because of her, we are allowed to see McClane express love, anxiety, fear—emotions whose expression is denied the villain. Holly is both the motivation for the hero's extraordinary deeds and the source of the melodrama.

Die Hard with a Vengeance makes no attempt to replace the moral and emotional context for bangs and bloodshed which Holly previously provided. Perhaps this is why it seems such a cynical thrill machine, particularly in light of the Oklahoma bombing—too many deaths and too little emotional residue. The film falls short in other areas as well: the script has as many happy coincidences (McClane being spewed out of the tunnel as Zeus happens to drive past) as plot holes (several aspects of the end are still not clear to me); the editing is often clumsy (the alternation between Zeus and McClane and Zeus' kids at the end); and the extensive use of hand-held camera is an enervating addition to the film's general frenzy. It is as if McTiernan hasn't quite shaken off *The Last Action Hero*. Whenever his direction attempts more, it produces a kind of nervous elephantiasis.

What saves *Die Hard with a Vengeance* from the charmlessness of *Last Action Hero* is the actors. With the exception of Jeremy Irons—who hasn't quite figured out when to add camp relish to an inflection and when to simply throw a line away—the cast is excellent. Genre is often not considered when evaluating acting. But different genres call for different styles of performance. Action requires actors who can read lines and move their bodies with equal nonchalance and breezy agility. Willis is so superb at this I even forgive him for looking slightly less hunky in his vest than he usually does. The banter between Jackson and Willis, witty exchanges on questions of race and power, is perhaps the best thing about the film.

Good acting however is not essential to action cinema. Good action is. *Die Hard with a Vengeance* delivers more than the bare essentials. The scene where water gets released in the underground tunnel is imaginative and exciting. The revelation of the slogan McClane is wearing in Harlem and the revelation that a man has been chopped in half later in the film both demonstrate visual wit. The stunts throughout are spectacular. Yet the film's pace is too furious. The action scenes don't achieve the effects they should because the director hasn't allowed for the breather necessary to set them up properly. A better pace would have generated a bigger payoff.

Speed, last Summer's hit action film, is a measure of how *Die Hard with a Vengeance* falls short. Jan De Bont, the director of *Speed* and cinematographer of *Die Hard*, seems to have absorbed more from his collaboration with McTiernan on *Die Hard* than McTiernan himself. *Speed* is not only the better action film, it is arguably a better film than *Die Hard with a Vengeance*.

TIME, 5/29/95, p. 60, Richard Corliss

Some movies ought to be reviewed not by critics but by the Bureau of Alcohol, Tobacco and Firearms. Watching *Die Hard with a Vengeance*, third in the series that pits New York City cop John McClane (Bruce Willis) against a wily, chatty nut case with a fondness for TNT, the viewer simply suspends belief and coolly appraises the things that go boom. Say, wasn't that a nicely staged Wall Street explosion? My, that runaway subway train crashed onto the platform with a certain vigorous verismo. Oh, look—more actors playing dead people! So little wit is expended on the dialogue and so much on the imagination of disaster that you may as well sit back and enjoy the jolting ride.

Having seen concepts for sequels pre-empted by *Under Siege* (*Die Hard* on a destroyer) and *Speed* (*Die Hard* on a bus), director John McTiernan and writer Jonathan Hensleigh turned the tables and appropriated a device sure to be used in this summer's *Batman Forever*. Like the Riddler, *Vengeance's* evil genius (Jeremy Irons) taunts the hero with word games, history quizzes and math problems—riddles, see? This keeps the plot clock ticking as McClane and a good-hearted black racist (Samuel L. Jackson) dash around Manhattan at Irons' bidding.

Whereas the first two *Die Hard* films made smart use of their enclosed locations, this one devolves into a skittish travelogue that ends up in Canada. Still, Willis' aggrieved burliness is always persuasive, and red-meat lovers will have an agreeably volatile two hours of fantasy—if, that is, they can keep one word out of their minds: militia. A scary scenario on that subject is doubtless being drafted for next summer's macho blockbuster.

VILLAGE VOICE, 5/30/95, p. 47, J. Hoberman

Announcing itself as the ultimate New York City slam dance, *Die Hard With a Vengeance* opens with a blast of "Summer in the City," a moshpit montage of sweaty Midtown, and then, in panoramic long shot ... a department store casually blowing up in your face.

That opening salvo should, by now, have gotten the movie some negative attention. (Well before the premiere, 20th Century Fox had the stars on TV doing damage control.) But the barn door has long since been blown away. If this latest installment of the *Die Hard* saga was inspired by the 1993 World Trade Center bombing, it's also possible that the original *Die Hard*—in which Bruce Willis's NYPD street cop McLane battled international terrorists in an L.A. skyscraper—may have contributed to the WTC scenario.

Still, like Oklahoma City and the recent terror attacks in the New York and Tokyo subways, *Die Hard With a Vengeance* is a post-WTC production—which is why it's hard to laugh (even with a vengeance) at the various bomb jokes, especially when the resident (or rather, resident alien) urban terrorist, Simon (Jeremy Irons), threatens to blow up a public school full of kids. Oklahoma City has definitely taken some of the fun out of the situation. (Of course, if Fox had released *Die Hard With a Vengeance* before April 19, Clinton could have used it as a pretext to attack Rupert Murdoch.)

Die Hard With a Vengeance has its share of free-floating social metaphors. The bad guys are a para-military bunch of crypto-Nazi German skinhead thugs and Simon uses talk radio to panic the population. Despite the requisite anti-FBI scene, *Vengeance* lacks the anti-bureaucratic edge of *Die Hard* and *Die Hard 2*—although the Rambotic premise remains that one man can do it, almost alone, even with a monstrous hangover.

For the most part, the movie is played as a total grudge match in which Simon spends the movie's first and best 45 minutes running McClane all over our hostage-ized city in much the way that, two dozen years ago, Zodiac tortured Dirty Harry. The mood is a bit more jocular. Clint never had to position himself on West 138 Street in boxer shorts and a sandwich sign reading "I Hate Niggers." The setup enables Willis to be rescued by (and eventually bond with) Samuel L. Jackson, playing a testy black nationalist with even more attitude than McClane.

The buddies absorb much punishment—by the end of the movie they're slimy with blood—but the money scenes are mainly vehicular. In the most impressive, McClane requisitions a cab, then runs a light and makes like the taxi has four-wheel drive by plowing off the road in Central Park (posited in the movie as a short cut to Wall Street), barreling through Columbus Circle behind the ambulance he's conned into running interference in order to catch up with, and jump atop, the moving subway on which Simon has planted yet another bomb. When the station does explode, you get a sense of how the movie views us. A vapid bunch of popcorn-chomping spectators are shown watching from their office tower: cool.

New Yorkers will remember that *Die Hard With a Vengeance* tied up a considerable portion of Manhattan real estate last summer—which is perhaps why the city appears here as an unfathomable terrain of crazed natives and hassled unflappable cops. Strictly as a local, I appreciated the scene where McClane drives through Water Tunnel 3 as well as the shoot out and bumper car crash on the Saw Mill River Parkway. (But why is it raining in Westchester and sunny in the Bronx?)

A comedy whose best sight gag involves a body blown in half, *Die Hard With a Vengeance* aspires to be *Speed* with crowds. Unfortunately, it lacks consistent velocity. The Steadicam immediacy of director John McTiernan's hectic, bruising style gives the sensation of being trapped in a speeding taxi that repeatedly stops short. McClane's recurring complaint—"I've had a bad fucking headache all day"—is contagious.

Basically, *Die Hard With a Vengeance* is lumpen James Bond (*Goldfinger* without Pussy Galore). McClane always shoots first and never loses his bad attitude—nor gets back his wife—but his bon mots aren't even wisecracks, just bellicose insults. Although the movie's most emotionally satisfying moments are those in which McClane liberates a car phone from a Wall Street yuppie or blows away five or six neo-Nazis at outrageously close quarters, *Die Hard* is basically a fantasy of oral aggression where the bloody, unbowed hero can stop the villain in his tracks with a brusque, "Hey, dick-head."

Also reviewed in:
CHICAGO TRIBUNE, 5/19/95, Friday/p. C, Michael Wilmington
NEW YORK TIMES, 5/18/95, p. C6, Caryn James
NEW YORKER, 5/29/95, p. 91, Terrence Rafferty
VARIETY, 5/22-28/95, p. 92, Brian Lowry
WASHINGTON POST, 5/19/95, p. D7, Rita Kempley
WASHINGTON POST, 5/19/95, Weekend/p. 57, Desson Howe

DIRTY MONEY

A Bruce/Deane Productions release. *Producer:* James Bruce. *Director:* James Bruce. *Screenplay:* Frederick Deane. *Director of Photography:* Christian Faber, Rick DiGregorio, and Michael Meyers. *Editor:* James Bruce and Robert Barrere. *Music:* Paul Barrere and Bill Payne. *Sound:* Rick Scheexnayder and Vladimir Tukan. *Costumes:* Alexandra Welker. *Running time:* 82 minutes. *MPAA Rating:* Not Rated.

WITH: Frederick Deane; Timothy Patrick Cavanaugh; Bill Yeager; Charmagne Eckert; David Jean Thomas; Dagmar Stansora; Delaune Michel; Jorge "Maromero" Paez.

NEW YORK POST, 5/12/95, p. 43, Bill Hoffmann

"Dirty Money," an ambitious action thriller made on a shoestring budget, works with one of the oldest plots in moviemaking: An innocent man is on the run from the cops, who think he's a coldblooded killer, and from the real murderers, who are out to silence him.

Isn't it time to put this well-worn premise in Hollywood heaven? Maybe. But director James Bruce dusts it off one more time and injects it with fresh, invigorating juice thanks to an energetic cast, fast-moving script and first-class editing job.

Frederick Deane plays Sam Reed, a good Samaritan who unwittingly stops to help two brothers whose car has stalled in downtown Los Angeles after a stickup.

The pair hold him up, steal his wallet and car and later show up at his house and blow away his wife.

The cops think Reed is the coldblooded culprit. Meanwhile, the bad guys believe Reed has absconded with their stolen loot and the chase is on.

The two crooks, played like an evil Laurel and Hardy by Timothy Patrick Cavanaugh and Bill Yeager, dog Reed through Southern California, following him all the way into Mexico, wounding him with a bullet to the gut.

The setting turns to super-sleazy Tijuana, its streets lined with bars, hookers and every other kind of vice you can imagine. Oddly, It's here where the film—steel-cold and Godless thus far—finds a high moral ground.

Reed is befriended by a kind woman (Dagmar Stansora) who happens to be an acrobat with a low-rent traveling circus.

Recuperating in a trailer with circus freaks and street urchins looking after him, Reed learns from this bizarre menagerie that life, while very, very cheap, is still worth living.

With his new-found hope, Reed dives head first into the inevitable wham-bam finale laced with blood, guts and revenge.

No, it's not original. Yes, it's derivative. But "Dirty Money" flows with a low-budget energy that's hard to resist.

You can almost sense the cast and crew, just one step ahead of the bill collectors, acting and producing their little hearts out. Timothy Patrick Cavanaugh may be a little too Quentin Tarantinoish for my taste, but it's a minor point.

Director Bruce uses the seedy atmosphere of the Mexican border town to distinct advantage. Even when holes in the plot surface, and they do every now and then, Bruce is already on to the next scene, so we don't really notice or care that much.

And isn't that the way most movies, even those with 10 times the budget, do it?

NEWSDAY, 5/12/95, Part II/p. B8, Jonathan Mandell

Though the setup of "Dirty Money" bears some resemblance to the O.J. Simpson case, it winds up unintentionally evoking President Bill Clinton's State of the Union address.

Sam Reed (Frederick Deane) is a man from Los Angeles who the cops think killed his wife. But he is innocent. For most of the movie, he is chased from L.A. to San Diego and then to Mexico by the police—actually by just two cops, a black male veteran and a young blond female rookie—and by the real killer, Frank, along with Frank's side-kick Tommy.

Frank has long, greasy hair, a five-day stubble, a big-shouldered, double-breasted jacket and a floral-print shirt open to show the gold chain around his hairy chest; in other words, he is the villain. He is given to such profundities as "A man's wallet is his life," when he isn't cursing people out and then killing them. This same actor (Timothy Patrick Cavanaugh) has appeared in similar thankless roles on TV shows like "Santa Barbara," and "America's Most Wanted." This makes sense, since almost everything about "'Dirty Money" plays like a too-long episode of an especially dull, cheap and empty-headed action-adventure series—from the annoying, fake-suspense score of plucks and pings to the implausible or impenetrable plot twists to the pretty-boy mannequin school of acting.

Deane, who wrote "Dirty Money" apparently as a vehicle for his own stardom, seems to be driving it under the influence; he acts as if in a lithium haze.

What separates "Dirty Money" from bad television is only its profanity and its violence, which are excessive, dopey and dull, and which bring to mind the part of Clinton's address where he urged the entertainment industry to "understand the damage that comes from the incessant, repetitive, mindless violence and irresponsible conduct that permeates our media all the time." That damage must surely be compounded when the mindless repetition isn't even exciting.

VILLAGE VOICE, 5/9/95, p. 78, Tom Kertes

You can't take your eyes off the gritty, black-and-white, opening scene: an icily efficient payroll robbery as seen through the eye of the security camera, ending in a vicious murder. Suddenly, the film morphs into color, but you remain safely within noir territory nonetheless: every character lacks the slightest semblance of humanity, loot is the lone thing that matters. In *Dirty Money*'s unclean world, there are no good guys in sight.

Then, out of nowhere, one emerges, and boy, is he sorry; a simple act of kindness toward strangers sets off a chain of events that lead this pristine innocent into a cruel web. Both the gangsters and the cops want him dead.

This plot, which fairly reeks of *The 39 Steps*, cries out for the delicate Hitchcockian touch—and, amazingly, director James Bruce manages a faithful tribute-cum-imitation of the master on a $50,000 budget. Bruce has got Hitch's ambiance down pat: the murky doings inevitably leading to fatal misunderstandings, the all-powerful pull of one's own destiny, the seedy locales where that destiny unfolds. Bruce even has some comparable set pieces: a pick-up-the-loot scene in a darkened park, is particularly well done, with the jumpy, handheld camera confidently creating an aura of anxiety and chaos.

Does any of this sound like one of the more far-fetched episodes on *America's Most Wanted*? It should: the screenplay is based exactly on such an event. Not so coincidentally, Bruce has directed 25 segments of that hit show, and was in fact forced to shoot *Money* on hurried weekend breaks from his *Wanted* duties. In spite of some amateurish acting—well, they didn't get paid the film is one of the best of the recent neo-noirs.

Also reviewed in:
CHICAGO TRIBUNE, 10/13/95, Friday/p. L, Michael Wilmington
NEW YORK TIMES, 5/12/95, p. C10, Stephen Holden
VARIETY, 9/5-11/94, p. 56, Daniel M. Kimmel

DR. JEKYLL AND MS. HYDE

A Savoy Pictures release in association with Rank Film Distributors of a Rastar/Leider-Shapiro production. *Executive Producer:* John Morrissey. *Producer:* Robert Shapiro and Jerry Leider. *Director:* David Price. *Screenplay:* Tim John, Oliver Butcher, William Davies, and William Osborne. *Story:* David Price. *Suggested by the novel "The Strange Case of Dr. Jekyll & Mr. Hyde"* by: Robert Louis Stevenson. *Director of Photography:* Tom Priestley. *Editor:* Tony Lombardo. *Music:* Mark McKenzie. *Music Editor:* Dick Bernstein, John Finklea, and Jim Young. *Sound:* David Lewis Yewdall. *Sound Editor:* David Lewis Yewdall. *Casting:* Mike Fenton and Allison Cowitt. *Production Designer:* Gregory Melton. *Art Director:* Guy Lalande. *Set Decorator:* Francine Danis, Paul Hotte, Michéle Nolet, and Ginette Robitaille. *Costumes:* Molly Maginnis. *Make-up:* Diane Simard. *Special Make-up Effects:* Kevin Yagher. *Stunt Coordinator:* Minor Mustain. *Running time:* 95 minutes. *MPAA Rating:* PG-13.

CAST: Sean Young (Helen Hyde); Tim Daly (Richard Jacks); Lysette Anthony (Sarah Carver); Stephen Tobolowsky (Oliver Mintz); Harvey Fierstein (Yves DuBois); Thea Vidale (Valerie); Jeremy Piven (Pete); Polly Bergen (Mrs. Unterveldt); Stephen Shellen (Larry); Sheena Larkin (Mrs. Mintz); John Franklyn-Robbins (Professor Manning); Aron Tager (Lawyer); Jane Connell (Aunt Agatha); Julie Cobb (DuBois' Psychiatrist); Kim Morgan Greene (Paparazzi Lady/Party Lady); Victor Knight (Bill); Mark Camacho (Waiter); Robert Wuhl (Man with Lighter); Susan Trustman (Cocktail Party Woman); Manon Deschenes (Gorgeous Female Model); Jean-Claude Page (Gorrgeous Male Model); Maria Stanton (Dress Admirer 1 & 2); Donna Barnes (Young Woman); Rachel Bertrand (Pneumatic Young Woman); Herb Goldstein (Nose #1); Michael Rudder (Nose #2); Susan Glover (Nose #3); Kate Asner (Female Admirer); Lizz Larson (Carson); Mike Hodge (Eagleton); Stephane Lefebvre (Bus Boy); Don Jordan (Driver); Donna Sarrasin (Mintz's Secretary).

LOS ANGELES TIMES, 8/25/95, Calendar/p. 6, David Kronke

In the laughless and lifeless "Dr. Jekyll and Ms. Hyde," Tim Daly plays Richard Jacks, a scientist at a perfume company whose career is in a downward spiral when he inherits some papers written by his great-grandfather, Dr. Henry Jekyll. Yes, *that* Dr. Jekyll.

Jacks messes around with his ancestor's infamous formula, and before you can say, "'Young Frankenstein' did all this much more cleverly," he's morphing into Helen Hyde, who is—if you haven't figured it out already—a woman.

That's what passes for comic invention here. Getting Sean Young to ostensibly parody her quixotic media image by playing Hyde, who exploits her feminine wiles to claw her way over Jacks and up the corporate ladder, might have been funny six or seven years ago when that reputation was fresh on people's minds.

Directed by David Price, who has a couple of barely released horror sequels on his résumé, and credited to four writers who usually labor as script doctors (script Physicians, heal thine own screenplay!), "Dr. Jekyll and Ms. Hyde" is a smirky, uninspired work that treats all its characters as one-dimensional dopes. Plotting is both illogical and predictable—Jacks' and Hyde's transformations occur at the most inconvenient times—and paste-and-stitch editing, working in tandem with klutzy voice-over narration, can't mask the fact that many scenes have been drastically altered or jettisoned altogether. For example, Robert Wuhl turns up in the finale, without any explanation of who his character is or why he's there.

Already, the sexist humor here is as dated as the drug humor in "Jekyll and Hyde ... Together Again," the similarly hapless 1982 cinematic parody of the Robert Louis Stevenson yarn. Before Helen barters her sex appeal for company muscle, she's embraced by various characters as being "alive" and "her own person"—for doing what? Shopping, mainly.

Unsurprisingly, no one's heart seems to be into this. Some of the cast (such as Young) barely put forth any effort, while those who do try (such as Daly) only embarrass themselves with their broad, reaching performances. Unlike the tormented Hyde of lore, there's nothing redeeming in this movie struggling to get out.

NEW YORK POST, 8/25/95, p. 46, Michael Medved

At least they got one thing right: It's entirely appropriate that "Dr. Jekyll and Ms. Hyde" should take place in a perfume company since the entire movie smells.

Tim Daly (of TV's "Wings") plays a researcher named Richard Jacks who works in a Manhattan fragrance factory. Jacks happens to be the great-grandson of the ill-fated Dr. Jekyll. When he inherits the lab books of his notorious ancestor, he begins fooling around with the old formula to isolate man's dark side and inevitably tests it on himself. The result is his shocking transformation into "Helen Hyde" (Sean Young)—who is amoral, dangerous and, worst of all, a wretchedly incompetent actress. She delivers all her lines as if she were reading cue cards she's never seen before and invests her role as an unstoppable seductress with all the sexual magnetism of a throw pillow.

Ms. Hyde introduces herself in the perfume company as Richard's assistant and proceeds to undermine his position and to entice his bosses (Stephen Tobolowsky and Harvey Fierstein) so that when he resumes his nice guy, male persona he's in deep ambergris.

His alter-ego also threatens his relationship with his adoring fiancee (radiant Lysette Anthony, the only member of the cast who doesn't embarrass herself) until his girlfriend agrees to help him get rid of Ms. Hyde.

The many transformation scenes feature subpar special effects as breasts suddenly sprout on Daly's chest to the accompaniment of reverberant "Boinnnggg!!!" sound effects. The entire project is pitched at this level of maturity and misogyny, as if the film were the work of giggly 12-year-old boys who grew up in homes without sisters.

NEWSDAY, 8/25/95, Part II/p. B4, Jack Mathews

Robert Louis Stevenson's classic 1886 novel "Strange Case of Dr. Jekyll and Mr. Hyde" has kept filmmakers busy since the new storytelling medium was invented. Its moral conflict—the fight between good and evil inside each of us—is of timeless relevance and, as externalized fantasy, of universal appeal.

It's been done as serious drama, the best in class being the 1931 version starring Spencer Tracy, and as pop-culture comedy (Jerry Lewis' best film, "The Nutty Professor"). It's also been used to explore genetic guilt ("The Son of ..." "The Daughter of ...") racism ("Dr. Black and Mr. Hyde," who is white) and sexual transcendance ("Dr. Jekyll and Sister Hyde").

The subject of that last film, which was made in England in 1971, is particularly ripe for the '90s, when many men are taking the Women's Movement as a threat to their power both at home and at the office, and it gets a really ripe going-over in David Price's adolescent "Dr. Jekyll and Ms. Hyde."

In this updating, Tim Daly plays Richard Jacks, the great-grandson of Dr. Jekyll and a young chemist who, after inheriting Jekyll's journals, finds the "unstable gene" in the original formula, calms it down with a massive dose of estrogen, swallows the brew and then has breasts break out on his chest in the middle of a job interview.

Sean Young is the alter-ego who takes over after each transformation, and she's got her eyes on the prize, using her guile to seduce Jacks' boss (Stephen Tobolowsky), his gay colleague (Harvey Fierstein) and even his fiance (Lysette Anthony) in an attempt to take over his job, his life and his body.

There are some very funny scenes, and some nifty special effects, accompanying the Jekyll-Hyde makeovers. For Price, however, whose previous films were sequels to bad horror movies, what's worth doing once is worth doing over and over, and a man can only explore his suddenly vacant crotch so many times before penis panic gives you a case of exit envy.

When the humor is not being vulgar, it's being cruel. In a pathetically lame subplot, Ms. Hyde repels the sexual advances of Jacks' lab buddy Pete (Jeremy Piven) by getting him to slap sulphuric acid on his face (he thinks it's an aphrodisiac) and electrocuting him with a car battery. Yes, he bounces up each time, begging for more, but it's the basest form of slapstick.

I would love to see what somebody like Woody Allen, who can turn pop culture and intellectual insight into delirious whimsy, would do with this premise. It's a perfect opportunity for sophisticated satire about gender politics, and particularly about male ego and insecurity, the lynchpins of Allen's career.

Even in this genitals-obsessed knockoff, the notion holds some interest to the end. But it's an opportunity clearly missed.

SIGHT AND SOUND, 12/95, p. 44, Kim Newman

New York. Dr Richard Jacks, a dissatisfied scientist working at a perfume company, strains his relationship with his live-in fiancée Sarah Carver by working all night on his own research. When his great uncle dies, Richard is left the effects of an ancestor, Dr Henry Jekyll, and he comes to the conclusion that Jekyll's famous dual-personality formula could be used for good if the aggression-producing ingredients were replaced with oestrogen, tempering the Hyde personality with womanly virtues. Richard takes the formula and immediately changes into a woman. He adopts the name Helen Hyde, and impresses Richard's male co-worker, Pete Walston, his boss Oliver Mintz and even the firm's gay *perfumier*, Yves DuBois.

When Richard returns, he discovers Helen has advised Sarah to move out. Helen, who takes over for ever-lengthening periods, maims Pete and seduces both Oliver and Yves, foiling Richard's attempts to make her look bad. Richard convinces Sarah of his predicament by showing her a videotape of the transformation and cooks up an antidote which must be injected into Helen within 45 minutes of the next, possibly permanent, transformation.

Richard changes and Helen escapes from Sarah to a party where the firm are launching Indulge, a perfume Richard has created but which Helen is taking credit for. Sarah jabs Helen with the cure and Richard reappears, justifying his strange dress by saying he has been trying to live like a woman while working on the perfume project. Oliver, humiliated, allows Richard lab facilities to do his own work, and Richard and Sarah marry.

No doubt coincidentally, this film combines elements of two Hammer Films' reworkings of Robert Louis Stevenson's story *Dr Jekyll and Mr. Hyde: The Ugly Duckling*, in which Bernard Bresslaw as a meek descendent of the original Jekyll becomes a hulking teddy boy, and *Dr Jekyll and Sister Hyde*, in which prissy Ralph Bates transforms into homicidally kittenish Martine Beswicke. There are a few overtones also of the soon-to-be-remade *The Nutty Professor* and the nearly forgotten *Dr. Heckyl and Mr. Hype*, and a sex-change wrinkle that has been exploited not only by *Sister Hyde* but also by the hardcore porno film *Oversexed*. This would hardly win points for the originality of its concept then, even if it were not a glossily garish comedy confection full of embarrassed performers straining in inappropriate underwear for cheap laughs.

Some kind of a peak in excruciation is reached by a running gag in which Harvey Fierstein is agonised to be suddenly attracted to a woman and relieved that Helen turns out to be Richard. But the film is littered with embarrassingly ham-fisted farce. Tim Daly, the only member of the *Diner* cast who hasn't gone on to be a star, finds himself in inexplicable situations, mostly naked but sometimes in female underwear, as his co-workers and fiancée gawp at him. *Dr. Jekyll and Ms. Hyde* was originally intended as a reteaming of Jim Carrey and Sean Young, stars of *Ace Ventura Pet Detective*, but Carrey's departure for the big pay-day stratosphere has left an opening Daly can hardly be blamed for failing to fill. After all, it is hard to imagine Carrey would have allowed Young all the fun scenes and saved only the humiliating 'straight' sequences for himself.

David F. Price, who has previously directed only straight-to-video sequels (*Son of Darkness: To Die For II, Children of the Corn II: The Final Sacrifice*), tries for a hectic, perverse feel and at least has the benefit of bitch diva Young. It's a more misogynist film than *Sister Hyde*, and Young a less ambiguous figure than Beswicke, who was at once a seductress and Jack the Ripper. Evidently, there has been a great deal of post-production pruning, reshooting and rearranging. Typical of the film's refusal to think things through is the moment when Richard inherits both Dr Jekyll's notes and a signed first edition of the Stevenson novel and assumes he can make more money with the notes.

Also reviewed in:
NEW YORK TIMES, 8/25/95, p. C17, Janet Maslin
VARIETY, 8/28-9/3/95, p. 66, Leonard Klady

DOLORES CLAIBORNE

A Castle Rock Entertainment release. *Producer:* Taylor Hackford and Charles Mulvehill. *Director:* Taylor Hackford. *Screenplay:* Tony Gilroy. *Based on the novel by:* Stephen King. *Director of Photography:* Gabriel Beristain. *Editor:* Mark Warner. *Music:* Danny Elfman. *Music Editor:* Curt Sobel. *Sound:* Glen Gauthier and (music) Shawn Murphy. *Sound Editor:* David E. Stone. *Casting:* Nancy Klopper. *Production Designer:* Bruno Rubeo. *Art Director:* Dan Yarhi. *Set Decorator:* Steve Shewchuk. *Set Dresser:* David Hopkins, Lorne Armstrong, Robert Grani, and Dan Owens. *Special Effects:* Ted Ross. *Costumes:* Shay Cunliffe. *Make-up:* Luigi Rocchetti. *Stunt Coordinator:* Gary Davis. *Running time:* 131 minutes. *MPAA Rating:* R.

CAST: Kathy Bates (Dolores Claiborne); Jennifer Jason Leigh (Selena St. George); Judy Parfitt (Vera Donovan); Christopher Plummer (Detective John Mackey); David Strathairn (Joe St. George); Eric Bogosian (Peter); John C. Reilly (Constable Frank Stamshaw); Ellen Muth (Young Selena); Bob Gunton (Mr. Pease); Roy Cooper (Magistrate); Wayne Robson (Sammy Marchant); Ruth Marshall (Secretary); Weldon Allen (Bartender); Tom Gallant (Searcher); Kelly Burnett (Jack Donovan); Matt Appleby and Thomas Skinner (Kids on Street); Vernon Steele (Ferry Vendor); Taffara Jessica (Young Selena, Age 5); Stella Murray (Young Selena, Age 5); Susan Lane (Crying Girl); Frank Adamson and Ed Rubin (Detective Supervisors); Sandy MacDonald (Sheriff); Dean Eilertson (Moving Man).

LOS ANGELES TIMES, 3/24/95, Calendar/p. 4, Kenneth Turan

Like a frightening situation from one of the man's own novels, no power on Earth can apparently stop the zombielike progression of Stephen King books to the screen. Page turners usually make for engrossing films, but with King it's been largely downhill since Brian De Palma did the electric "Carrie" in 1976. "Dolores Claiborne" is the latest King novel to make the transition, and it makes you wonder who would have bothered if the author's first name had been Irving.

And considerable bother has certainly gone into "Dolores." If nothing else, the cast and crew trekked up to wintry Nova Scotia, which apparently looks more like King's beloved Maine than Maine itself, and the usual infinite pains were taken with things like furnishings, makeup and accents.

More than that, there are occasional bursts of notable work here. Director Taylor Hackford brings an appropriate level of pulpy energy to the telling, and star Kathy Bates, who won a best actress Oscar for her performance in "Misery," a previous King adaptation, gives a better performance than the film deserves as the grumpy and possibly homicidal title character.

In fact, most things here are better than this film deserves. While it is difficult to tell without reading the original novel how much screenwriter Tony Gilroy had to work with, even with an assist from William Goldman (who is given a "consultant" credit near end of the closing titles) all that has been produced is a bewildering hodgepodge of diverse and disconnected elements.

Though mostly set on fictional Little Tall Island, "Dolores" begins with a brief foray into Manhattan to introduce one of its protagonists. Celebrated magazine journalist Selena St. George (Jennifer Jason Leigh) is playfully sparring with slimy editor (Eric Bogosian) when an attention-getting fax comes in. It seems wealthy socialite Vera Donovan has died back home in Maine, and who is suspected of murder but Vera's longtime housekeeper and Selena's esstranged mother, Dolores Claiborne (Bates).

High-strung Selena, who likes pills almost as much as she likes Scotch, has not been in contact with her mother for 15 years, but home she comes in a real snit, looking like the Night of the Living Dead version of Holly Golightly. She snarls at Maine State Police Detective John Mackey (Christopher Plummer) and moves back into the old family dump with her sullen parent in tow.

Since not much happens on Little Tall Island, Dolores has ample time to contemplate the extended series of visions that conveniently recapitulate the family history. It's here that we meet husband Joe St. George (David Strathairn), Selena's father, an abusive hellhound who does everything but drool and foam at the mouth. Joe is no longer around, and persistent detective

Mackey has thought for years that Dolores is the reason why, which makes him extra curious about exactly what happened to Vera (British actress Judy Parfitt), who was almost as horrific a companion as Joe.

As a peevish, non-maternal mom, Kathy Bates gives a performance you have to admire. Her Dolores is meant to be very much the down-home character, given to salty curses and bawdy phraseology.

But with the usually reliable Leigh showing the effects of playing a tense journalist for the third time in a row (after "The Hudsucker Proxy" and "Mrs. Parker and the Vicious Circle"), Bates and the film are hampered by the lack of sufficiently strong performances to work off of.

More of a problem is that "Dolores Claiborne" is never quite sure what kind of a film it means to be. The plot centers on suspicious deaths, but doesn't manage to be more than sporadically thrilling, and a bogus climactic courtroom scene only adds to the disarray.

NEW YORK, 4/3/95, p. 58, David Denby

Kathy Bates has a round, beefy face and heavy legs, and a voice that can flick meanly across the surface of her lines. Her star status is a triumph of personality and skill. In her latest vehicle, *Dolores Claiborne*, the thirty-first Stephen King text-cum-movie, she plays a widow who lives on an island off the Maine coast—Dolores, the island bitch, the one kids throw stones at. Dolores is believed to have murdered her vicious, alcoholic husband years earlier, and now she's in trouble again, suspected this time of doing away with the wealthy old termagant (Judy Parfitt) she took care of for years. In the midst of all these swirling suspicions, Bates has a fascinating neutrality. Angry without malice, she suggests the reserve and patience of people New Yorkers rarely see: Americans from small towns or trailer parks, conventional in all outward appearance but powerfully individual inside.

Bates might have had a triumph in *Dolores Claiborne* if the director, Taylor Hackford, had not cut up her performance into so many pieces. The picture is one of those buried-secrets things in which every present action causes one of the characters to have a Profound Memory, which we then see at laborious length, past and present linking up in a structure of reverberant cliché. Stephen King has been churning out this stuff for a long time, and Hackford revels in the cheap movieishness of dreadful material. Hackford isn't imaginative enough for poetic horror; he goes for luridness and clangorous music. A few scenes between Bates and Judy Parfitt's tough old woman have a startling candor, but the heart of the movie is mother and daughter talking things over, and as Dolores's daughter, a hardbitten New York journalist, Jennifer Jason Leigh is lethally bad, all tics and slit-eyed misery. Jason Leigh is a virtuoso of discordant effects, but there isn't a fresh emotion in this performance; and when she works with Kathy Bates, she looks mannered and overwrought—an ambitious killjoy.

NEW YORK POST, 3/24/95, p. 45, Michael Medved

At the beginning of "Dolores Claiborne," the postman doesn't even ring once, let alone twice, before he inadvertently walks in on a terrifying scene while delivering the mail to the richest citizen on a rugged island off the coast of Maine.

There, lying in a bloody heap at the bottom of her stairway, is elderly socialite Vera Donovan (Judy Parfitt). Standing over her, about to club the dying woman with a rolling pin, is Vera's long-suffering, longtime maid, Dolores Claiborne (Kathy Bates).

Inevitably, Dolores is suspected of first-degree murder—especially since the demise of her imperious employer doesn't mark the first time she's been implicated in an untimely death.

Twenty years before, her abusive, alcoholic husband (played by David Strathairn in chilling flashbacks) died in an incident officially ruled an accident, but the police detective assigned to that case (Christopher Plummer) never believed Dolores was innocent.

Now he's back, more determined than ever to prove that the earthy, hard-working woman is a murderer.

To increase the pressure on his suspect, Plummer contacts her daughter in New York, and that resentful child, a hard-drinking, depressive magazine writer (played with smoldering conviction by Jennifer Jason Leigh) returns home for the first time in more than a decade.

In the course of the movie, Dolores finds it even more difficult to explain herself to her cynical daughter than she does to clarify her situation with the police.

Director Taylor Hackford ("An Officer and a Gentleman" and the underrated "Everybody's All-American") handles this material with such artistry and intensity that the film achieves far more emotional impact than you'd expect from its somewhat contrived plot (based on a best-selling novel by Stephen King) and convoluted structure.

When he answers the ultimate mystery in the story by flashing back to a confrontation between Dolores and her late husband in the midst of a much-heralded solar eclipse on the island, it could easily have been hokey, but Hackford uses understated effects and admirable restraint in making the scene seem natural and logical.

He is, of course, immensely aided by his outstanding cast. Kathy Bates delivers an even more finely nuanced and fully realized performance than her Oscar-winning work in "Misery" (based, coincidentally, on another Stephen King novel).

In crucial supporting roles, British actress Judy Parfitt, David Strathairn and Christopher Plummer are spectacularly effective: Plummer, in particular, drives the entire plot with the energy he brings to bear as the heroine's crafty, implacable, fearsomely effective police detective foe.

"Sometimes being a bitch is all a woman has to hang on to," Dolores emphatically declares and we know it's supposed to be a key lesson of the film because that line is repeated three different times.

The problem is that the point she's making is muddled by plot twists that allow the film to fudge on whether the need to "be a bitch" includes an amoral right to commit murder in certain circumstances.

Thanks to these equivocations, "Dolores Claiborne" may fall short as an issues-based melodrama, but it remains a uniquely spellbinding piece of cinematic storytelling.

NEWSDAY, 3/24/95, Part II/p. B2, Jack Mathews

Finding a role big enough for Kathy Bates is no easy task, and I'm not talking about her weight. She's an actress with as big a talent as Meryl Streep's, and if she were as svelte as Streep, she would be competing for the same parts.

But if life is unfair for large women in our general culture, it is punishing in Hollywood, and Bates hasn't had a role of any great substance since playing the psychopathic fan of a romance novelist in the film adaptation of Stephen King's "Misery." Or, at least she hadn't until she got the call to star in yet another adaptation of a King novel, "Dolores Claiborne."

Directed by Taylor Hackford ("Against All Odds"), "Dolores Claiborne" takes us into a totally different area of suspense from "Misery." This is a sort of torn-from-the-headlines story that blends elements of domestic abuse, police harassment, suppressed memory—and questions of justifiable homicide into a taut psychological mystery.

Within all that, Bates turns in a performance rich enough to qualify as a character study of a woman trapped in a vicious domestic cycle, but determined to create an escape route for her daughter.

Hackford, known more for slickness than subtlety, has managed to work both into this film. The story covers 20 years in the lives of Dolores, her daughter, Selena (played as an adult by Jennifer Jason Leigh), and others in the small coastal Maine village where Dolores has spent her life.

The film divides itself into two specific time periods, when Dolores was trying to protect the 13-year-old Selena (Ellen Muth) from her alcoholic husband (David Strathairn), and 20 years later, when Selena—now a hot-dog reporter with a New York-based national magazine—returns home to try to learn why her mother is suspected of murdering her employer.

This is as intricately plotted a story as "Misery" was simple, but Hackford, working with a very clever script by Tony Gilroy, has turned its complications into an advantage. "Dolores" is a beautifully edited movie, craftily cutting back and forth and in and around the two time zones. There are two mysteries in one. Did Dolores' husband and her employer both die in accidental falls, or did she push them? The movie answers both questions in great dramatic detail.

The front story, of the uneasy relationship between Dolores and her daughter, and her confrontations with the tough local cop (Christopher Plummer) convinced of her guilt, moves chronologically forward, but from there we are constantly leaping back in time, from a few days ago, to 20 years ago, and a few days before that. The flashbacks, far from being confusing, give the film a momentum that doesn't slow down until it reaches an ending that isn't quite as satisfying as it should be.

I don't know whether to blame King or Gilroy, but Dolores' colorful dialogue seems impossibly glib at times ("I'm going to kick you in the ass so hard, you'll look like a hunchback," she tells one person who's crossed her). But she is a fascinating character, tormented and hopeful at the same time, and it is Bates' most complete film performance.

Leigh, who does get the kinds of roles that would not be offered to Bates, gives another strong performance as a writer (her third in a row, after "Dorothy Parker and the Vicious Circle" and "The Hudsucker Proxy") who is driven by demons she doesn't know she has. Selena has scars on her neck and on her soul, and how they got there is part of the mystery.

SIGHT AND SOUND, 9/95, p. 49, Lizzie Francke

Tall Island, Maine. Elderly Vera Donovan is found dead and her live-in housekeeper Dolores Claiborne is suspected of the murder and arrested. Dolores' daughter, Selena St George, a young, New York-based journalist, returns to her home town to investigate. Years ago, Dolores was accused and acquitted of murdering her husband, Joe. Selena believes her mother is guilty of both murders and confronts her, but Dolores maintains her innocence. Dolores is let out on bail and returns to her old home with Selena, who reluctantly agrees to stay with her. Through flashbacks, Joe is shown to have been an alcoholic who beat his wife. Dolores had originally started working for Vera to save up money so that she could escape with Selena.

At Vera's house to collect Dolores' things, Selena and Dolores are confronted by Detective Mackey, who worked on Dolores' previous murder case. He reveals that Vera left everything in her will to Dolores, which provides a possible motive for the murder. However, a flashback reveals that Vera fell accidentally and refused Dolores' attempts to help her. In the past, Joe had become increasingly violent in his attacks on Dolores and he abused Selena, who has blocked the memory. When Dolores discovered the abuse, she made haste with her plans to leave Tall Island but discovered that Joe had embezzled her savings. Under all the strain, she broke down in front of Vera who proved sympathetic to her case and suggested getting rid of Joe. Dolores then killed him while the rest of the town was celebrating an eclipse of the sun, making the murder look like an accident.

In the present, Selena decides to leave Tall Island. Listening to a tape Dolores made that explains the past, Selena at last begins to remember what happened to her as a child and turns back. She arrives just as Dolores' case comes up, gives evidence and pleads for the case to be dismissed. Dolores' innocence is established.

"Sometimes being a bitch is the only thing that a woman can hold onto," is the oft-repeated line in *Dolores Claiborne*. Bette Davis might well have spat such a sentiment as Rosa in King Vidor's *Beyond the Forest*, a sister under the prickly skin to murder suspect Dolores Claiborne. Indeed, this Taylor Hackford adaptation of Stephen King's psychological thriller seems to be harking back to the excessive splendours of films by Vidor and John Stahl (director of the original films *Magnificent Obsession* and *Imitation of Life* later remade by Douglas Sirk).

This is most obvious in the scenes around the killing of Dolores' husband Joe that takes place while Tall Island—the kind of lost resort that most girls would want to get out of—prepares for the sun's total eclipse. It's an apocalyptic moment when the sun is briefly snuffed out and the sky bleeds deepest crimson as Dolores leads the despicable Joe to his well deserved fate. This is as gory a moment as this particular Stephen King can offer. Horror here is of a kind that festers away unseen while three generations of women deal with abusive men (Dolores' supposed victim Vera also disposed of her philandering husband.) Yet here the revenge of the abused—which has recently become a soap opera staple (think of the Jordaches in *Brookside*)—is given a euphoric twist, and depicted as a cathartic act of exorcism.

With its concertina flashback structure bleeding between the present and several different points in the past, the film is fairly unconcerned about whether Dolores committed the crimes. It would rather come to some understanding of her along with Selena and Vera. The film is more about the cracking of their polished carapaces, the understanding of a seemingly unsympathetic trio. In this respect Hackford has got the cast just right with Kathy Bates, Jennifer Jason Leigh and Judy Parfitt all acting out roles which are in themselves carefully constructed acts.

Particularly apt here is Jennifer Jason Leigh's tendency towards an aloof interiority in her performance. As Selena, she is a woman bound in on herself who can only be read by her gestures, such as the constant application of handcream (her mother, we learn, has rough skinned mitts), while Dolores can only find out about her daughter's present life by looking through her luggage. Consequently, the twists in *Dolores Claiborne* are provided when the women of Tall Island let their characters slip: for example, when the cold and haughty Vera, dictating elaborate rules and regulations about the shining of the silver and the starching of the linen, softens to the distraught Dolores' dilemma. Similarly, one begins to see beyond Dolores' bufoonish, grouchy persona and discern the pain, as she bustles around muttering such idiotic catchphrases as "cheese and crackers".

Certainly to begin with, Kathy Bates' Dolores shares the same howdy-doody hick mannerisms as the character Annie Wilkes she played in *Misery*. With Bates cast in the title role, *Dolores Claiborne* draws overt comparisons between its heroine and the psychotic, frumpy nurse of the earlier film, thus playing on the audience's expectations. There is even the obligatory in-joke as Dolores cleans Vera's collection of porcelain porkers, reminding us of Annie Wilkes' favorite pets. Sows. Bitches. Women: it's a familiar King theme. But *Dolores Claiborne* is like a revisionist take on his earlier themes, as though he wants to spell out quite overtly what might make the women monstrous.

Carrie and *Misery* (both the books and the film adaptations) allow for feminist against-the-grain readings, but here the film is quite clearly inviting a feminist interpretation. "It's a depressingly masculine world that we live in," declares Vera, as if we need clarification after witnessing Joe's savage bouts. Dolores castigates the bank for allowing her husband to draw on the savings account that she opened: "It's because I am a woman, isn't it?" And it's because it is a man's, man's world Dolores has to be so devilishly sneaky. Meanwhile, Selena is the disbelieving daughter who like Detective Mackey believes in her mother's guilt. Hers is a voyage of conversion, as she finally sees what has been bleached out and eclipsed in her memory over the years. Indeed, *Dolores Claiborne* sheds new light on just what a bitch might be.

TIME, 3/27/95, p. 73, Richard Schickel

At no point in *Dolores Claiborne* is its eponymous protagonist tied to a railroad track or strapped down in the path of a rapidly impending train or buzz saw. And a good thing too, for this adaptation of Stephen King's best seller (does he write anything else?) also lacks a hero, or indeed any remotely admirable masculine figure, eager to race to her rescue.

These omissions are not careless. King is a storyteller who boldly uses the most primitive and melodramatic forms to explore very basic emotional issues, and this is his fantasia on feminist themes. Dolores (Kathy Bates) in some ways resembles the heroine of a gaslit theatrical enterprise of the 19th century. She is haunted by an ancient crime, stands falsely accused of a new one and is bedeviled by a policeman (Christopher Plummer) who could give *Les Miserables'* Inspector Javert lessons in sneering implacability.

But she is also a tough-minded, coarse-tongued woman who is supporting herself by taking care of Mrs. Donovan (Judy Parfitt), a rich-bitch invalid, and mourning her estrangement from Selena, her deeply disturbed daughter Jennifer Jason Leigh). Precisely because of the absence of decent men in her life, Dolores is obliged to combine traditional masculine and feminine roles in one surprising, ultimately endearing persona.

And the villain? Why, he's as broadly written (by Tony Gilroy) and played (by David Strathairn) as anyone who ever twirled a wickedly waxed moustache. A drunk and a wife beater, Joe St. George is Dolores' husband and Selena's father—so suspiciously sweet with the latter that we know long before we're told that he lusted unnaturally for her when she was a child and is the source of her repressed memories—and more than deserves the bad end Dolores arranges for him.

But that's only half the story, for King is never niggardly when it comes to plotting. Working us toward the fairly easy verdict of justifiable homicide in Joe's death, King must also relieve us of our rather trumped-up suspicions about Dolores' role in the death of Mrs. Donovan and arrange a just reward for the years of misery Dolores has endured.

Sometimes it seems the point of this exercise is simply to complicate—mainly by arbitrarily withholding vital information—what is, in its emotional essence, a not very complicated matter.

But the sensible formality of Taylor Hackford's direction has the effect of cooling the film's narrative frenzies and helping the actors dig some simple, truthful stuff out of the hubbub. There is something great souled in Bates' work, which is at once sweet and fierce, hesitant and determined. She seems always to be surprising herself with her actions, brushing aside the calculations of the story with the sheer force of her humanity.

VILLAGE VOICE, 4/4/95, p. 58, Henry Cabot Beck

"It's a depressingly masculine world we live in," says Vera Donovan, haute bitch in this skewed Stephen King mini-version of *The Women*. Vera's death in the opening moments tears open old psychic wounds and an unresolved murder case.

This is really a classical woman's picture, but there is no romance, no Ralph Bellamy or Melvyn Douglas waiting in the wings. As a mystery, the movie is all revelation and flashback, but *Dolores Claiborne* is no more about solving puzzles than *Marnie* was about a kleptomaniac with a dye job who liked to ride horses.

Kathy Bates plays Dolores with astonishing clarity, aging over 20 years in a film that moves from the Technicolor past to the gray present with a frighteningly hallucinatory grace. She has the ability to be physically off-putting and sympathetic in equal measure. Jennifer Jason Leigh brings to daughter Selena St. George, an *Esquire* feature writer, equal portions of her two prior literary turns, the type A Lois Lane scribe from *Hudsucker Proxy* and the besotted Dorothy Parker. Selena is a damaged daddy's girl, locked from the age of 13 in a limbo of adolescent fury and tortured denial, forever mourning her Everyslob father (David Strathairn), whom we know to be an alcoholic wife beater (and worse).

But the linchpin of the film is Judy Parfitt's superb Vera, who plays the control-freak den mother to this bitches brew. It is she who offers these prefeminist gems: "Husbands die every day, Dolores. An accident can be an unhappy woman's best friend," and "Sometimes being a bitch is all a woman has to hold on to." That dowagers might bond over murders is an unexpected delight, not seen since *Arsenic and Old Lace*; it's as though Thelma and Louise retired to open a B&B.

Taylor Hackford has crafted a powerful film, rife with penny-ante clichés, but, like the best of Stephen King's books, all the stronger for it. There are surreal moments that recall Hitchcock's most delirious psychological experiments in *Spellbound, Marnie,* and *Vertigo,* but with less hysteria and greater insight. A few men may squirm a bit in their seats, but in *Dolores Claiborne,* all is fair in love and murder.

Also reviewed in:
CHICAGO TRIBUNE, 3/24/95, Friday/p. C, Michael Wilmington
NEW REPUBLIC, 4/17/95, p. 34, Stanley Kauffmann
NEW YORK TIMES, 3/24/95, p. C14, Janet Maslin
NEW YORKER, 4/1/95, p. 93, Terrence Rafferty
VARIETY, 3/20-26/95, p. 48, Brian Lowry
WASHINGTON POST, 3/24/95, Weekend/p. 42, Desson Howe
WASHINGTON POST, 3/25/95, p. C1, Hal Hinson

DON JUAN DEMARCO

A New Line Productions release of an American Zoetrope production. *Executive Producer:* Ruth Vitale and Michael De Luca. *Producer:* Francis Ford Coppola, Fred Fuchs, and Patrick Palmer. *Director:* Jeremy Leven. *Screenplay:* Jeremy Leven. *The character of Don Juan is based in part on "Don Juan" by:* Lord Byron. *Director of Photography:* Ralf Bode. *Editor:* Tony Gibbs. *Music:* Michael Kamen. *Music Editor:* Christopher Brooks and Zigmund Gron. *Sound:* Richard Lightstone and (music) Stephen Mclaughlin. *Sound Editor:* Dane A. Davis. *Casting:* Lynn Kressel. *Production Designer:* Sharon Seymour. *Art Director:* Jeff Knipp. *Set Designer:* Lori Rowbotham and Theodore Sharps. *Set Decorator:* Maggie Martin. *Set Dresser:* McPherson O. Downs. *Special Effects:* James Fredburg. *Costumes:* Kirsten Everberg. *Make-up:* Ron

Berkeley. *Make-up (Marlon Brando):* Phillip Rhodes; *Make-up (Johnny Depp):* Patty York; *Stunt Coordinator:* Victor Paul. *Running time:* 97 minutes. *MPAA Rating:* PG-13.

CAST: Marlon Brando (Jack Mickler); Johnny Depp (Don Juan DeMarco); Faye Dunaway (Marilyn Mickler); Geraldine Pailhas (Dona Ana); Bob Dishy (Dr. Paul Showalter); Rachel Ticotin (Dona Inez); Talisa Soto (Dona Julia); Marita Geraghty (Woman in Restaurant); Richard Sarafian (Detective Sy Tobias); Tresa Hughes (Grandmother DeMarco); Stephen Singer (Dr. Bill Dunsmore); Franc Luz (Don Antonio); Carmen Argenziano (Don Alfonzo); Jo Champa (Sultana Gulbeyaz); Esther Scott (Nurse Alvira); Nada Despotovich (Nurse Gloria); Gilbert Lewis (Judge Ryland); "Tiny" Lister, Jr. (Rocco Compton); Tom Mardirosian (Baba the Eunuch); Al Corley (Woman's Date); Nick La Tour (Nicholas the Doorman); Bill Capizzi (Sultan); Patricia Mauceri (Dona Querida); Cliff Weissman (Delivery Man #1); Michael Malota (Young Don Juan); Renee Sicignano (Flower Girl); Trevor Long (Waiter); Sanjay (Auctioneer); Diane Lee (Night Duty Nurse); Joni Kramer (Nurse #1); Shirlee Reed (Nurse #2); Ken Gutstein (Doctor #1); Adriana Jardini (Social Worker); Robert Polanco Rodriguez (Priest); Roberta Danza, Bridget Mariano, and Christine Wolfe (Nuns); Jose Hernandez (Bandleader); Selena Perez (Singer).

LOS ANGELES TIMES, 4/7/95, Calendar/p. 1, Peter Rainer

In "Don Juan DeMarco," a young masked man (Johnny Depp) effortlessly seduces a wide-eyed woman he picks up in a swank restaurant and then, proclaiming his sadness at the loss of his one true love, prepares to jump from a billboard to his death.

The police call in veteran psychiatrist Jack Mickler (Marlon Brando) to talk the boy down. Jack hospitalizes him and becomes his therapist. In record time, a bond is formed. Jack may start out by humoring this self-proclaimed Don Juan, but he quickly gets pulled into the boy's fantasy life. After a while he's not even sure it *is* a fantasy.

What we have here is another variation on "Equus"—it's a movie about the drudgery of normality and the romanticism of the deluded. Jack is decent and caring, but he's burnt-out by the unfeeling bureaucracies of his profession. He disdains the medications that his supervisor (Bob Dishy) tries to force on Don Juan; he buys time—10 days—to allow the boy to persuade him he really *is* the masked lover, before his colleagues take over.

Writer-director Jeremy Leven—who has never directed a movie before but has worked as a screenwriter, novelist and clinical psychologist—buys into the boy's fantasy, too. He makes Don Juan a genuine romantic: The nurses swoon all over him and the flashbacks to his purported childhood and young manhood in Mexico are photographed in a syrupy gauze.

In his sort-of Castilian accent, Don Juan may refer seductively to a conquest as a "wooooman"—like George Hamilton in "Zorro the Gay Blade"—but there's no camp in his come-ons.

We're meant to take him not as a deluded boy in torment but as a liberating spirit—a holy innocent. The movie isn't about Don Juan's self-realization but about Jack's—and, by extension, ours as well. Leven wants us to embrace our fantasies and ditch humdrum normality. As Jack says to his by-the-book colleagues, "We've surrendered to the momentum of mediocrity." (But can we surrender to the mediocrity of this movie?)

In "Don Juan DeMarco," the young lover is given just enough of a sordid background to make us sympathize with his need to create a new and perfumed life for himself. But mostly he exists apart from any background, real or imagined. He's the romantic as exotic—he devotes himself to women as a humble servant of *amore.*

It's a measure of Leven's infatuation that, in his movie, the Don Juan myth is prettified. No rake he. This Don Juan doesn't exploit women, he's God's gift to them. He's a love teacher, and he inspires Jack to romance his own yearning-to-be-loved wife (Faye Dunaway). For us, that's a plus: The chummy amorousness between Brando and Dunaway is one of the film's bright spots.

Actually, Brando is pretty sunny all the way through. He's not really extending himself much here, and Leven doesn't always protect his actor from unflattering angles. But Brando has a wizardly way of dumping on the role—exposing its dubiousness—and yet having fun with it anyway. He enjoys acting—or at least he enjoys the flippancy of it. (It has been years since

Brando has tested himself in a movie; he must not want to.) And his scenes with Depp are curious, tricky little duets: The old pro and the young turk team up.

Depp is rather sweet in portraying Don Juan's self-delusions, but his performance is hampered by the role. With women, Don Juan is not allowed to show any conflicting emotions; he's not in conflict with himself either. We don't get to see the kind of hurt and isolation that this delusional boy would experience, and that's an injustice to what he's really going through. (The film argues that medication would destroy him.) His pain is not an issue in the movie because it denies he *has* any.

For the film to work, we'd have to be in denial, too, and it's just not magical enough for that.

NEW STATESMAN & SOCIETY, 5/19/95, p. 33, Lizzie Francke

Jeremy Leven's *Don Juan DeMarco* may not have been written for Marlon Brando, but his presence in the movie anchors the featherweight conceit and gives it a semblance of substance to contemplate.

When he first appears on the screen, he is being hoisted up alongside a vast billboard, as if to advertise his own larger than life place in the film, proclaiming that Brando is still every inch the Hollywood giant (though one who is framed for the most part of the film from the waist upwards).

But then, he is a monument not only to a particular period of cinema history when there was a madness for the Method, but also to a particular manifestation of masculinity, from the pouting and dangerous Stanley Kowalski in his muscle licking white T-shirt in *A Streetcar Names Desire* (1951), to the demented Colonel Kurtz who sits Buddha-like at the dank heart of *Apocalypse Now* (1976). It is no coincidence that in his first film, *The Men* (1950), Brando played a war-veteran paraplegic who is as much emotionally broken as anything else. The actor carries these raw images around with him—men exploding and imploding in the era where the hero was on his way to be certified dead.

In the rare film appearances that he has made in recent years, his classic corpus of work has become something for him to toy with as though he wants to make light of the turmoil. In the off kilter comedy *The Freshman* (1990) he spoofs it up as the mobster who makes an offer that a penniless NYU film student cannot refuse. Meanwhile, said student finds that his studies take a funny turn when *The Godfather* is made a set text. Brando delights in the knowingness of the film, his bloody paterfamilias Don Corleone transformed into a comic *schtick*. In *Don Juan DeMarco* there's a not dissimilar frisson, though here it doesn't play on any one particular role in Brando's past canon, rather it arises because the more disturbing aspects of his screen persona are so conspicuously absent.

The film casts Brando as the twinkly eyed Dr Mickler, a psychiatrist who is counting the ten days until his retirement. But, as with many a cop film, there is always time for that one last case that is destined to change a career. In this instance, it is a young man (Johnny Depp), bought into Mickler's hospital after attempting suicide, who claims to be the legendary Latin lover "Don Juan De Marco", the best and most beautiful of them all. Ostensibly it seems like a common enough diagnosis of delusional behaviour complete with the requisite rich accent and elegant fancy dress of billowing white silk shirt unbuttoned down to the tanned and toned waist, flowing locks and pencil thin moustache. But as Mickler starts working with his new patient, it becomes clear that things are not so simple. For the young man insists he really is Don Juan, while demanding of the doctor why he himself persists with "this fantasy that you are some Dr Mickler".

Transference would not seem to be more troubled. For Mickler becomes quite intrigued with the patient, as he tells of his gilded childhood on a lush Mexican plantation, his first amorous encounter with his voluptuous tutor, the flight from an enraged husband, the consequent two-year sojourn in a harem somewhere in Arabia ... This boy is faithful to the text, and while he might well just be a kid from New Jersey, he knows how to spin a tale. And, of course, like many a movie before from *Spellbound* to *Awakenings*, it becomes apparent that it is the doctor, not the patient, who is about to undergo a cure. For, enchanted by his imaginative young charge, Mickler feels a need to freshen up his own life and gracefully woos his wife Marilyn (Faye Dunaway) all over again. Cue giggling afternoon trysts with bowls of popcorn.

Don Juan DeMarco might be about reminding audiences that it was Brando who was once one the most beautiful and the best, while now that award has gone to Depp. But it does so by scrubbing the memory clean of Brando's persona's more shadowy and difficult associations. Forget the scummy chauvinism of *Last Tango in Paris*, this film turns back nostalgically to an era when tangos could be conceived to be about two entwined people slinking their way across shiny parquet flooring: it's the lighting here that's buttery rather than anything else. Indeed, the images of manhood that Leven is attempting to conjure up belong to another cinematic age. Think of such masked lovers as Rudolph Valentino, Douglas Fairbanks and Errol Flynn, for whom women would just swoon for a delicate kiss.

Indeed, swooning is mostly what the women do in this film, that or thundering off in fits of pique only to be chased by the ardent lover boy. Only Faye Dunaway is allowed to be something more than just a smouldering presence, but even she knows that this film could not be about her. A romantic comedy in the full sense of the word romance, it is a paean to some fanciful ideas of "chivalry". That the audience, unlike Mickler, might have problems in allowing the Don Juan manqué to indulge in his amorous fantasies is never given a question, nor are his adventures given the satirical edge that at least Byron could root for. We are meant to be swept off our feet by the sweetness of it and giddily delight in Depp's dapper charms, as the film yearns for a time when gentlemen could be gentlemen before the likes of Brando came along to rough things up.

NEW YORK POST, 4/7/95, p. 37, Thelma Adams

"No woman has ever left my arms unsatisfied," Johnny Depp says with a fruity Castilian accent in the title role of "Don Juan DeMarco."

Wearing a cape, leather pants, a red velvet vest with silver buttons and more eyeliner that his conquests, this latter-day Latin lover revives romance in one fell swoop.

Depp, knock on "Ed Wood," has created a second memorable character whose delusion is another form of grandeur.

Beneath Don Juan's swagger, Depp reveals an irresistible, underlying sweetness. The movie begins with Don Juan's last conquest before attempting a broken-hearted suicide. In a ripe moment, he seals the artful seduction of a beautiful woman with a kiss between her knuckles.

For Don Juan, "Every woman is a mystery to be solved."

The suicide attempt is a clumsy mechanism to unite Don Juan and Jack Mickler (Marlon Brando), a therapist on the verge of retirement. (First-time director Jeremy Leven, who wrote the screenplay, also happens to be a clinical psychologist.)

And so to the question everyone's asking. How's Brando? Well, larger than life.

The audience gasped when the camera caught the great actor from behind and revealed a backside as big as a fridge. With his golden fright wig and "Godfather" mumbles, at times Brando looks like Rod Steiger imitating Brando.

Brando's Mickler is a man who's lost his passion. In a series of therapy sessions, Don Juan tells his life story, Scheherazade style. The doctor-patient relationship switches.

Mickler becomes less concerned with curing a young man's delusion that he's the world's greatest lover than with reconnecting with the lover in himself.

Once Brando warms up, the two actors, rebels behind the scenes but professionals on cue, seem to be having a lark together. Mickler regains his ardor, much to the surprise of his wife (Faye Dunaway). Dunaway and Brando share some lovely bedroom scenes.

Marital relations performed after teeth are flossed and books are set aside with the places carefully marked give way to a playfulness and mutual appreciation that promises a retirement that might just be golden even if it's not exactly restful.

From "Disclosure" to "Erotica," theaters are filled with overheated movies about sex: no blouse remains unbuttoned; no limb unturned. It's amazing how few American films are about genuine passion.

"Don Juan DeMarco," an astonishingly fresh erotic comedy, revels in a passion so pure it's contagious.

NEWSDAY, 4/7/95, Part II/p. B5, Jack Mathews

Among the many enchantingly sensuous stories told by a young mental patient to his psychiatrist in "Don Juan DeMarco" is one about his childhood memory of seeing a woman standing at an open window one moonlit night, and noticing how her underwear followed and caressed the curves of her body, as if "on a cushion of air."

It was then, at age 10, said Don Juan, that "I learned how a woman is to be touched."

Don Juan DeMarco, who may or may not be a delusional schizophrenic from Queens, is an obsessed romantic who loves women—*all* women—and knows how to tell them. With flowers, with poetry and with the confidence of a lover who can say, without fear of contradiction, "no woman has ever left my arms unsatisfied."

Writer-director Jeremy Leven, a novelist who once made his living as a clinical psychologist, has pulled off a minor miracle in turning what might have been insufferable schmaltz into a "Field of Dreams" for romantics devoted to the oldest sport of all. And he was able to pull it off largely due to the charms and interplay of his two stars—Johnny Depp, as Don Juan, and Marlon Brando, as the psychiatrist Jack Mickler.

Brando, in his first leading role since the 1980 "The Formula," is physically huge, massive, so large that Leven and the gamely self-deprecating star chose to make a joke about his weight the moment he first appears, so we can all laugh about it and get on with the story.

And it is a wonderful story, a romantic fable about a modern-day Don Juan who prowls the finer restaurants in New York wearing a cape, and mask, sweeping women off their feet, and into bed, with his poetic wiles and seductive Castilian voice. He has made love to more than 1,000 appreciative women, he assures us, and been rejected only once—by his true love, which is what causes him to threaten suicide in the opening moments, and to end up under Mickler's care at a mental hospital.

It is there, during a 10-day evaluation, that Don Juan begins to regale the psychiatrist with fantastic tales of romantic conquest, stories of such compelling passion that Mickler, previously burned out and on the brink of retirement, is moved to try some of these techniques at home. Mickler's friskiness around his wife (a disarming Faye Dunaway) sounds fatal in a romantic comedy, and looks wretched in the trailers. But Brando gives Mickler a personality to match his girth, and I don't think he has ever been more engagingly playful for the camera.

Depp, working with some of the most colorfully romantic dialogue written in Hollywood's post-romantic era, reads it with an irresistible sincerity. Lines that Errol Flynn would have delivered with a wink and an air of romantic arrogance, Depp delivers with profound conviction. When he describes looking into the eyes of the woman he loves and seeing his unborn children there, you know this is the guy to team up with for a night on the town.

Though some attempt is made to show Don Juan's delusions as an elaborate rejection of a tragic life, Leven doesn't let the film touch ground, let alone become melancholy. It is really a celebration of the ideals of romance and seduction, and you either surrender to it, or die a slow death.

I say, go with someone you love, surrender, and take notes.

NEWSWEEK, 4/24/95, p. 64, Jeff Giles

When Esquire told Johnny Depp he had to take his shirt off for the current photo, he said, "Who do you think I am, Brad Pitt?" Well, he's not, and thank God. Depp has done a magnificent job of playing against type. He's avoided the heartthrob posing you'd expect from a guy who has been engaged to half of Hollywood, and specialized in childlike outsiders and eccentrics. His latest is the title character in Jeremy Leven's sweet but listless *Don Juan De Marco*, a nice guy from Queens, N.Y., who wears a cape and mask and insists he's the world's greatest lover. At the outset, Depp's suicidal, broken-hearted Don Juan is admitted to a state hospital and assigned to a burned-out psychiatrist, Dr. Jack Mickler (Marlon Brando). Soon, he's got every nurse's heart aflutter, and he's assuring his shrink, "You are a great lover like myself, even though you may have lost your way—and your accent." Depp attacks his role with relish, stamping his boot heels and recounting improbable erotic adventures in a wonderful Castilian lisp. Unfortunately, Depp's the only one flying over this cuckoo's nest. Brando does a kindly, avuncular turn—his affection for Depp is palpable on screen—but it's a perfunctory performance. (He'll probably continue to make movies, but will he ever act again?) Faye Dunaway makes even less of an impression as Mickler's joyless wife. All this is disappointing, as is the movie's plodding pace. Still, "Don Juan" is so goodhearted it's hard to begrudge it much. In the end, Dr. and Mrs. Mickler do a tango on the beach. The movie just loves love. How could you hate it?

SIGHT AND SOUND, 6/95, p. 41, Philip Kemp

A caped and masked young man who calls himself Don Juan DeMarco enters the Hotel Madrid in New York. Noticing an attractive redheaded woman stood up by her date, he seduces her. This done, he climbs a high hoarding and seems to be about to commit suicide. The police summon a top psychiatrist, Dr Jack Mickler, who by entering into Don Juan's fantasy coaxes the young man down. Juan is committed for ten days to the Woodhaven State Hospital where Mickler works. Since Mickler is about to retire, his boss Dr Paul Showalter overrides his protests and assigns a younger man, Bill Dunsmore, to the case. But Dunsmore, utterly flummoxed by Juan, soon hands him back to Mickler.

Juan tells Mickler his life story: he was born in a remote Mexican village where his father, an Italian-American dance champion called Antonio DeMarco, met and married the beautiful ranchera Doña Inez. At the age of 16, Juan is seduced by his tutor Doña Julia, wife of the much older Don Alfonzo. In revenge, Alfonzo claims to be Inez's lover. Antonio challenges him to a duel and is mortally wounded; Juan snatches up the rapier and kills Alfonzo. Inez, before entering a convent, sends Juan to Cadiz, but the ship diverts to an Arab sultanate where Juan is sold into slavery. The Sultana takes him as her lover, and during his leisure hours he diverts himself with the other 1500 women of the harem. Discovery threatens and Juan escapes on a ship, which is wrecked. Washed up on the island of Eros he meets the lovely and innocent Anna, but their idyll ends when she learns of his previous worldly experience. In despair at losing her, Juan had intended suicide.

Despite his scepticism, Mickler finds himself increasingly drawn into Juan's fantasy and refuses to prescribe medication for him. He also begins to take a more romantic attitude to his own becalmed marriage, to the delighted surprise of his wife Marilyn. The hospital has meanwhile located Juan's grandmother, who tells Mickler that the boy was born in Queens (NY), and raised in Phoenix, Arizona, where his father, Tony DeMarco, died in a car crash. Anna is really a centrefold model, Chelsea Stoker, with whom Juan is now obsessed though he has never met her. Mickler is further confused by the arrival of Doña Inez, wearing a nun's habit, who confirms her son's original story.

With the ten-day committal nearly up and Mickler's retirement imminent, Showalter plans to have Juan committed long-term by a judge, given medication and entrusted to Dr Dunsmore. But at the hearing Juan shows up out of costume and gives a story similar to his grandmother's version of events. The judge discharges him, ignoring Showalter's protests. Mickler, Marilyn and Juan fly together to the island of Eros, where they find Anna waiting for her lover.

The end credits of *Don Juan DeMarco* unexpectedly carry an acknowledgement to Lord Byron—unexpected not so much because copyright lapsed long ago on the mad bad lord's literary estate, but because the preceding story seems but scantily influenced by his sardonic, satiric epic poem. (Nor, despite Mozart on the soundtrack, is there any whiff of sulphur; this Don Giovanni's conquests are wholly beneficent.) The film's true antecedents lie in classic Hollywood-Hispanic swashbucklers like *The Mark of Zorro*, all capes and swordplay and florid dialogue, to whose conventions the fantasy sequences of *Don Juan DeMarco* pay explicit homage.

In doing so, it hits the problem that confronts all latter-day attempts to revisit the swashbuckler: how do you spoof something that was spoofing itself in the first place? Director Jeremy Leven's film never seems certain how deeply its tongue should be kept in its cheek—not so much because its tone varies, but because it doesn't. Whether operating in fantasy or reality mode the dialogue remains relentlessly over-the-top. This works well enough in the harem episode, played openly for laughs ("You have brought my manhood alive and made it sing," Juan tells the amorous Sultana. "It sings?" she responds incredulously), or when the two worlds collide, with Juan playing out seduction routines in modern-day New York complete with cape, mask and Speedy Gonzales accent. But the same bombast spills over into the exchanges between Mickler and his wife. "What happened," he inquires, "to the celestial fires that used to light our way?"

This could be taken to indicate that Juan's romanticism is enriching Mickler's dry, prosaic life, but instead it feels more like a calculated attempt to create high camp. (Hence perhaps the casting of Faye Dunaway, something of a camp icon ever since her portrayal of Joan Crawford in *Mommie Dearest*—although in this she gives her most relaxed and likeable performance for years.) It also allows the film to sidestep the issue it initially raised, the conflict between the two levels of reality—and along the way loses a potentially more interesting plotline, in which Mickler would have to deal with the knowledge that Juan has seduced his wife.

But where Leven's film winds up, intentionally or not, is in the cycle of 'loony chic' movies running parallel to the 'dumb chic' strand currently obsessing Hollywood. 'Dumb chic' (*Forrest Gump*) says the stupid are healthier and clearer-sighted than all those pointy-head intellectuals; 'loony chic' (*Rain Man, Regarding Henry, Mr Jones*) says that the mentally disturbed are founts of wisdom and integrity who can put the rest of us back in touch with our true selves. (Of recent mainstream Hollywood movies, only Peter Weir's underrated *Fearless* has had the courage to buck this trend.) In conforming to the pattern, *Don Juan DeMarco* reduces one of the great myths of Overreaching to a trite little feelgood parable. Let's hope nobody lends Jeremy Leven a copy of *Faust*.

VILLAGE VOICE, 4/18/95, p. 60, Ben Greenman

With a patchy Castilian accent and a patchier goatee, Johnny Depp struggles valiantly to animate the tiresome *Don Juan DeMarco*. A few days after his 21st birthday, Depp's title character—a young man in modern-day New York who believes that he is the famed Spanish lover—dresses in a cape and mask and climbs to the catwalk of a billboard, where he announces that he will end his life. The Don is talked down from his perch by Dr. Jack Mickler (Marlon Brando), a shrink who has long since lost his joie de vivre.

After he rescues the despondent swashbuckler, Mickler decides to take on the case as his swan song. Under psychoanalysis, Don Juan sticks to his swords, insisting that he is none other than the fictional character. His tales are mostly borrowings from Byron's early 19th-century romance, but they have an erotic and exotic charm, and Mickler soon finds himself entranced by the young man's imagination. Don Juan's delusions rekindle Mickler's own flagging spirits. Don Juan's lavish descriptions reawaken Mickler to life's sensual pleasures. Don Juan's psychosexual fantasies resharpen Mickler's professional acumen and even recharge his libido. Get the point? If not, *Don Juan DeMarco* will be happy to hammer it home for you again and again.

Following his ingratiating turn as inept auteur Ed Wood, Depp continues to show impressive versatility as a leading man. But no measure of charisma can hone this dull blade of a movie. In his directorial debut, Jeremy Leven, who also wrote the screenplay, has a workmanlike sense of whimsy, but his dialogue and camera work are so static they verge on the sadistic. The torpor contaminates the cast—Brando looks more beached than washed-up; Faye Dunaway is wasted as Mickler's wife; and some of the minor performances are so empty they're unwatchable (although there's a spirited but brief musical interlude featuring Selena, the tragically murdered Tejano queen). Each new scene brings another reason for complaint, from a hackneyed subplot about a male nurse to Mickler's entry-level Freudian reading of Don Juan's delusions. But in the name of mercy, it's perhaps best to paraphrase Byron—"Bad writers, bad roles, bad moving pictures,/ On which I cannot pause to make my strictures."

Also reviewed in:
CHICAGO TRIBUNE, 4/7/95, Friday/p. N, Michael Wilmington
NEW REPUBLIC, 5/1/95, p. 29, Stanley Kauffmann
NEW YORK TIMES, 4/7/95, p. C16, Janet Maslin
NEW YORKER, 4/10/95, p. 103, Anthony Lane
VARIETY, 3/27-4/2/95, p. 75, Emanuel Levy
WASHINGTON POST, 4/7/95, p. D1, Hal Hinson
WASHINGTON POST, 4/7/95, Weekend/p. 44, Desson Howe

DOOM GENERATION, THE

A Trimark Pictures release of a Union Générale Cinématographie/The Teen Angst Movie Company production in association with with Desperate Pictures/Blurco/Why Not Productions. *Executive Producer:* Nicole Arbib, Pascal Caucheteux, and Gregoire Sorlat. *Producer:* Andrea

Sperling and Gregg Araki. *Director:* Gregg Araki. *Screenplay:* Gregg Araki. *Director of Photography:* Jim Fealy. *Editor:* Gregg Araki. *Music:* Peter M. Coquillard. *Music Editor:* Dave Yamamoto. *Sound:* Mark Deren. *Casting:* Joseph Middleton. *Production Designer:* Therese DePrez. *Art Director:* Michael Krantz. *Set Decorator:* Jennifer Gentile. *Special Effects:* Kevin Hudson. *Costumes:* Catherine Cooper-Thoman. *Make-up:* Jason Rail. *Running time:* 90 minutes. *MPAA Rating:* Not Rated.

CAST: James Duval (Jordan White); Rose McGowan (Amy Blue); Johnathon Schaech (Xavier Red,'X'); Cress Williams (Peanut); Skinny Puppy (Gang of Goons); Dustin Nguyen (Quickiemart Clerk); Margaret Cho (Clerk's Wife); Lauren Tewes and Christopher Knight (TV Anchor Couple); Nicky Katt (Carnoburger Cashier); Johanna West (Carnoburger Co-Worker); Perry Farrell (Stop 'n' Go Clerk); Amanda Hearse (Barmaid); Parker Posey (Brandl); Salvator Xuereb (Biker); Heidi Fleiss (Liquor Store Clerk); Don Galloway (FBI Man); Dewey Weber (George); Khristofor Rossianov (Dan); Paul Fow (Pat).

LOS ANGELES TIMES, 10/27/95, Calendar/p. 6, Kevin Thomas

With four features in the past six years, Gregg Araki has established himself as one of America's most gifted and provocative filmmakers, chronicling the lives of young people sometimes uncertain of their sexual orientation, most always unsure of what to do with their lives.

"Totally F***ed Up" tackled teen suicide head-on and, before that, "The Living End" found two very different HIV-positive young men working out a relationship while on the road.

In each of these films Araki was ahead of the pack. But "The Doom Generation" finds him for the first time following it. It has Araki's edge and energy, his terse mastery of the visual, his deadpan humor and despair, and his ability to inspire go-for-broke portrayals—all to the accompaniment of a dynamite, bleak, driving score featuring a slough of numbers from the best current groups.

But Araki's distinctive, no-holds-barred personality cannot mask its over-familiarity or compensate for its overwhelming violence. "The Doom Generation" plays like a low-budget "Natural Born Killers"—and that is not intended as a compliment.

Against a collage of pop art landscapes (Jim Fealy is Araki's formidable cinematographer), a teen-age couple—foul-mouthed, sarcastic Amy (Rose McGowan) and dim, sweet-natured Jordan (James Duval)—hit the road. There they take lots of drugs and cross paths with virile, insinuating, dominating Xavier (Johnathon Schaech), who swiftly seduces Amy and commences moving in on Jordan as well.

What ensues is the usual odyssey of cheap motels, fast-food joints, convenience stores—each site marked by portentous slogans. Petty and not-so-petty crime ensues, but the evolving *ménage à trois* is on a collision course with society's darkest, most intolerant forces of sexual violence.

Araki takes us to an authentically scary place, but he's traveled over a road that we've been over too many times before to make a point that has also been made, before, although perhaps not quite so terrifyingly. "The Doom Generation" leaves you feeling that he can't get back to his "no-budget" style fast enough.

NEW YORK POST, 10/25/95, p. 40, Thelma Adams

Gregg Araki's "The Doom Generation" is an obscene Generation X-cess, rockin' road movie that is largely unquotable in a family paper. WARNING: this film may be hazardous to your mental health. If decapitations, castrations, lewd sex and Encino make you squeamish, STOP READING NOW.

Still with me? In the past, I have found Araki's low-budget, L.A. grunge movies to have a glutton-for-punishment appeal that escapes me. The nihilism of this writer/director/producer/editor is writ large in his titles: "Totally F**ked Up" started the trilogy that continues with "Doom" and will end with "Nowhere."

Araki's first bigger-budget movie is as dark as ever, but the humor is so wicked and sharp and over-the-top that it pulled me back every time I wanted to look away from the screen. The gags provide a counterpoint to such typical Araki teen laments as Amy's deadpan: "I think sometimes this city is sucking away at my soul."

Amy Blue (bold and confident young actress Rose McGowan) is a Valley dominatrix who lashes her tongue like a whip while speeding through the night on crystal meth. She and her teenage boy toy, the gentle Jordan White (Araki regular James Duval has the dopey charm of the young Keanu Reeves), are partying in a drive-in when trouble literally lands on their dashboard.

Sex-and-violence swinger Xavier Red (Johnathon Schaech) gets thrown into the teens-playing-tough lives of Amy and Jordan by chain-wielding thugs. From that moment on, the two kids step out of rebel wannabe status and collide with the continually escalating violence that this demon attracts.

For most of the movie, Araki uses violence archly: these are the spurting limbs and bloody stumps of splatter movies, of Monty Python. A decapitation of an Asian man in a mini-mart happens under the sign: "shoplifters will be executed." When the disembodied head continues to talk from the floor of the mart, surrounded by exploded hot dogs radiant with mustard, ketchup and relish, the audience is clued in: This is only a movie, this is only a movie.

After the mini-mart murder, the trio takes it on the lam. Alongside running jokes where all tabs add up to $6.66, close encounters with cameo performers (Heidi Fleiss, Amanda Bearse and Parker Posey) and more far-out scenes of violence, Amy and Jordan and X navigate towards a sexual threesome.

Araki directs highly-charged sex scenes among beautiful people that have the appearance of naturalism. During a bathtub romp, Jordan bloodies his nose on the tile; at a delicate moment among the three players, Amy has to get up and urinate. The characters maintain intimacy even while performing porn gymnastics.

What keeps the film together—and makes the ending more shocking—is that for all the visual splash, the sight gags and blood geysers and steamy sex scenes, the relationship between Amy and Jordan retains a loony sweetness,

Jordan is never anything less than a teenaged boy gaga in love. Amy's bruised vixen goes from talking tough to acting tough in a moment of horrifying violence, simultaneously losing Jordan and shedding whatever innocence she was so hell-bent on concealing with pouts and profanity.

NEWSDAY, 10/25/95, Part II/p. B9, John Anderson

At a time when every wannabe bad boy with a borrowed Brooklyn attitude and four feet of film stock is trying to make the definitive teenage-wasteland epic, Gregg Araki has shown them how it's done. "The Doom Generation" isn't just sex, nachos and bad news. In its eagerly outrageous way, it defines the void of innocence into which Americans are birthed.

Araki's fifth film—and his first since the sad and angry "Totally F***ed Up"—"Doom" is happily offensive, and to almost everyone: The gross-out moments are so over-the-top they're hilarious as well as disgusting, while remaining consistent with the film's sense of moral alienation. Not just alienation, though. The way the three main characters ping-pong between ruthless cynicism and awkward politeness just shows how they have no moral moorings at all.

The film features the startling Rose McGowan as Amy, a foul-mouthed, ivory-complexioned, Louise Brooks-lookalike whose first word in the film is _____ and who, eyeing the riotous party around her, declares, "This place is so boring, I wish someone would burn it to the ground." She's serious. So she and Jordan (James Duval) head off for some intra-vehicular copulation.

Under the mournful eyes of a bleeding Jesus—who recalls, in his kitsch-of-death manner, the wobbly Christs in "A Clockwork Orange"—their coupling is interrupted by Xavier (Johnathon Schaech), dubbed X by Jordan. X supplies the missing piece of their unholy trinity: The demon to Jordan's angel, and the supercharger for Amy's 400-hp libido. Together, they embark on a road trip to die for.

It's tempting to paste "Doom Generation" with film-smart labels—"Clueless" on battery acid! A post-MTV "Jules and Jim"!—but Araki himself tosses off film quotes as cavalierly as he does the pop detritus of his threesome's vapid culture: There are cameos by Lauren ("Loveboat") Tewes, Christopher ("Brady Bunch") Knight, Perry Farrell, Heidi Fleiss and "Party Girl's" Parker Posey, all of which is cute, but tangential. What works in the film are the characters, whose existence is defined best by their small circle—which, of course, is destroyed by the loathing of the excluded.

"There's no place for us in this world," Amy tells Jordan, who is a sort of existential divinity with a learning disability. "Don't you think sex is totally strange," he asks Amy, who responds that yes, it's like eating spaghetti. Jordan doesn't get it, and neither do we. Somehow, however, it makes a kind of sense, like the Nazi-inspired killer at the end of the film who screams at Jordan, "Don't ever talk about my mother!!!" No, some things are sacred. As Gregg Araki knows, the hard part is figuring out what they are.

SIGHT AND SOUND, 6/96, p. 37, Geoffrey Macnab

Jordan White and Amy Blue are two bored Los Angeles teenagers. One evening, after a party, they're attempting to have sex in the back of a car when there's a brawl in front of them. Handsome young drifter, Xavier Red, wounded in the fight, jumps in beside them and tells them to drive away. Amy takes an immediate dislike to Xavier. She drops him off by the side of the road. Amy and Jordan stop a short distance away at a local Quickie Mart to get something to eat. When they're unable to pay, the Korean store trains a shotgun on them. Xavier suddenly appears and jumps him. There's a struggle and the Korean's head is blown off. The trio hole up in a motel. Jordan and Amy have sex in the bath. Later that night, Xavier seduces Amy. They're having sex in the car when a lovesick burger store attendant turns up with a gun, threatening to kill Amy. Xavier wrestles with him and shoots off his arm.

As they wind their way across America, the three have various other bizarre and bloody encounters with barmaids, liquorstore clerks and fast food salesmen. Between times, they stop off in gaudy roadside motels. Television shows monitor their progress. The FBI ponder how to deal with them. In one small town, they set up bed for the night in a huge shed. They're all having sex together when they're interrupted by a group of crazed rednecks, brandishing the American flag. These naked neo-Nazis accuse Jordan and Xavier of being faggots, rape Amy, and murder Jordan by emasculating him with a pair of scissors. Amy escapes her bonds, grabs a gun, and shoots her captors. Xavier and Amy are last seen heading off down the open road.

Early on in *The Doom Generation,* there is a grotesque but comic little incident which sums up the picture's expressionist, cartoon-style approach to violence in a nutshell: after a scuffle in a quickie-mart, a Korean clerk's head is blown off. It somersaults through the air in slow motion, and lands on a tray of half-eaten fast food. Relish is seen oozing from its mouth. The three narcissistic slacker heroes react to the event with typical Californian cool, as if decapitations were a daily event. Nothing fazes them. Nothing much, outside of sex, food and music, intrigues them very much either.

Writer/director Gregg Araki claims that he likes making films about teenagers because "there's something monumental and heightened about their hormone-mad lives—like they get a zit and the world ends; they live and die ten times a day." What is most striking about these heroes, though, is their world-weariness, the sense that they've seen it all before. Only when they accidentally run over a dog on the highway do they show the slightest flicker of emotion. "Do you ever wonder what life means?" dreamy adolescent Jordan Blue (James Duval) asks from time to time. His question is barely heeded. This is a road movie, but it isn't one with any kind of existential undertow. Nor, despite frequent cut-aways to absurd television news shows, does it seem especially concerned with making satirical points about violence and the media. The America it depicts, a surreal expanse of fast-food outlets, bars and derelict cars, is too kitsch to bear easy comparison with the landscapes of *Natural Born Killers*. If anything, it recalls the hyper-animated world of Jim Carrey.

This is Araki's fifth feature, but his first with a significant budget. Much of the $1 million he was given by his French backers seems to have gone on production and costume design; on the absurd uniforms which the various burger and liquor store attendants wear, and on the gaudy backdrops. The three leads are named after colors. (By calling them White, Blue and Red, Araki may even be having a little joke at the expense of Kieslowski's Trilogy, as well as Tarantino's bank heist gang in *Reservoir Dogs.* Casting seems to follow the John Waters principle: there are several clean-cut faces from American sitcoms lurking in the minor roles and there's even a part for real-life Hollywood Madame, Heidi Fleiss.

The various motel rooms where the three teenage runaways hole up are decorated like bordellos, all chequered wallpaper and fluorescent light. Dialogue, too, is stylised: Araki takes Californian "surfer" speak and pushes it to extremes. Amy Blue (Rose McGowan), who is made up to look like Louise Brooks' nymphet teenage sister, rattles out her invective in breathless, but sardonic fashion. "God, when will you take a reality pill?" she yawns when Xavier Red (Johnathon

Schaech) spins her an outlandish yarn about killing a traffic cop. Jordan comes up with more cryptic remarks. "I feel like a gerbil smothered in Richard Gere's butt-hole," is a typically gnomic one-liner.

The sex sequences are frenetic and played for laughs, all humping and pumping. Gregg Araki has labelled *The Doom Generation* as his "first hetrosexual movie." He suggests that it's a "straight movie for gay people" in the way that *Philadelphia* and *Longtime Companion* were "gay films for straight people." However, there's a clear sense that the relationship which most interests him is the one between Jordan and Xavier. They're the ones who are in each others' arms just before the bloody finale. It sometimes seems that Amy Blue is just along for the ride. Whenever she makes love too one of the boys, the other is sure to be watching from the sidelines.

It's a moot point whether the increased budget helps or hinders Ariki. His last effort, *Totally F***d Up*, had a tough, anarchic energy in keeping with the way it was shot. (It used camcorders as well as 16mm to tell the stories of six different characters.) *The Doom Generation,* by contrast, is all surface 35mm gloss. The fervour here is displaced into the narrative. As if to counter the relative conservatism of the shooting style, Araki packs the soundtrack with hardcore indie music, and lays on the sex and violence with a trowel. Much of the comedy comes from the sheer hyperbolic zest with which he tackles the material. At one moment, during a bar room brawl, Xavier is stabbed in the genitals. Blood sports out in profusion. But the scene is wilfully exaggerated. We know he can't really be hurt.

It's this sense that nothing is for real that makes the film's denouement disquieting. With the sudden arrival of a gang of fascist homophobes, the mood of fey surrealism is shattered. The sequence certainly satirises gung-ho patriotism (the rednecks rape and murder to the accompaniment of 'The Land Of The Free And The Brave') but is so wantonly gruesome that it seems utterly out of keeping with the comic book-style antics that have preceded it. This time, the dead stay dead. It's no wonder that even Xavier and Amy, sole survivors of the massacre, look a little chastened as they drive off into the sunset, munching nachos. Audiences are likely to be similarly disorientated by Araki's shock tactics.

VILLAGE VOICE, 10/31/95, p. 80, Amy Taubin

An ancient trend that defies extinction, the romance of nihilism has inspired three idiosyncratic current releases—Abel Ferrara's *The Addiction*, Mike Figgis's *Leaving Las Vegas*, and Gregg Araki's *The Doom Generation*—all guaranteed to induce anxiety attacks in 12-step types. If the first two could be characterized as postbeat, *Doom Generation* is SoCal postpunk with a vengeance, and—despite an opening title calculated to coax guffaws from the cognoscenti ("A Heterosexual Movie by Gregg Araki")—as queer as anything in the director's oeuvre.

Jordan White (James Duval) and Amy Blue (Rose McGowan), a teenage odd couple (he's a dumber, limper Keanu; she's a Valley update on Lydia Lunch) are making out and waxing philosophical in her car, when suddenly Xavier Red (Jonathon Schaech) lands on the windshield causing a seismic shifting of gears in their womblike world. X, as he prefers to be called, is an onmisexual drifter right out of Tennessee Williams. "You're like a life support system for a cock," says the ever-eloquent Amy.

Amy and X go for each other's jugulars in way that inevitably leads to fucking and sucking, although it's obvious that, for X, Amy is merely his conduit to Jordan. When X blasts off the head of an Asian grocery store owner who's threatening Jordan and Amy with an assault rifle, the three take it on the lam into the heart of AmeriKa.

Splatterrific in the extreme, *Doom Generation* marries gross bodily injury (decapitation, castration) to food fights. Severed from his body, the head of the Asian grocery store owner flies across the counter and lands in the relish and onions. While blood from the spurting artery in the neck stump covers the horrified onlookers, the head spews epithets mixed with green vomit.

If there's an underlying metaphor in *Doom Generation*, it's bulimia. The starving Jordan is continually scarfing down and belching up junk food while Amy, who's speeding, lives on Diet Coke. So too, Araki's filmmaking aesthetic involves an endless consuming and regurgitating of a mass culture that he clearly loathes (shrimp balls, Doritos, TV news, plastic nativity scenes, billboards promising the Rapture, genre movies, guns, teenspeak, racial and sexual stereotypes, you name it, it's there). There's no satisfaction to be found in *Doom Generation*. But not content to allow his aimless characters to pursue their own paths to self-destruction—or to something less dramatic—Araki drags in, from right field, a couple of skinheads armed with the flag and a nasty pair of garden shears, and gives them free rein to act out his worst queer nightmare on the hapless threesome.

This final temper tantrum aside, *Doom Generation* is a terrifically crafted film. Araki makes the leap from no-budget to low-budget filmmaking with grace and humor. If the world of the film is a delayed adolescent version of Grand Guignol, Araki's direction is sophisticated to a fault. A pastiche of Godard, George Kuchar, Tennessee Williams, and Nine Inch Nails, *Doom Generation* moves so assuredly its 82 minutes feel like 40. Araki combines Godardian widescreen close-ups and primary colors with punkzine language to arrive at something like Fox TV gone delirious.

That said, I still prefer Araki's lyrical, heartfelt, and genuinely transgressive *The Living End* to the campy second-guessing and one-upmanship of *Doom Generation*. Araki has more contempt than pity for these characters—that's clear from the slap-dash script in which everyone's jokes are inter-changeable.

Still the actors cope quite well. Rose McGowan's red lipped, Louise Brooks-coiffed Amy is rude and resilient; James Duval's Jordan teeters touchingly between stupidity and innocence; and Johnathon Schaech's X is as narcissistic an object of desire as anyone could possibly want. Among the cameos: fast talkers Parker Posey and Heidi Fleiss.

Also reviewed in:
CHICAGO TRIBUNE, 11/10/95, Friday/p. G, John Petrakis
NATION, 11/27/95, p. 684, Stuart Klawans
NEW YORK TIMES, 10/25/95, p. C14, Janet Maslin
VARIETY, 2/6-12/95, p. 73, Emanuel Levy
WASHINGTON POST, 11/10/95, p. F7, Hal Hinson
WASHINGTON POST, 11/10/95, Weekend/p. 45, Desson Howe

DOUBLE HAPPINESS

A Fine Line Features release of a First Generation Films Inc./New Views Films production. *Producer:* Steve Hegyes and Rose Lam Waddell. *Director:* Mina Shum. *Screenplay (English and Cantonese with English subtitles):* Mina Shum. *Director of Photography:* Peter Wunstorf. *Editor:* Alison Grace. *Music:* Shadowy Men on a Shadowy Planet. *Casting:* Ann Anderson and Carmen Ruiz-Laza. *Production Designer:* Michael Bjornson. *Art Director:* Candice Dickens and Jill Haras. *Set Decorator:* Francois Milly. *Costumes:* Cynthia Summers. *Running time:* 87 minutes. *MPAA Rating:* PG-13.

CAST: Sandra Oh (Jade Li); Alannah Ong (Mom Li); Stephen Chang (Dad Li); Frances You (Pearl Li); Johnny Mah (Andrew Chau); Callum Rennie (Mark); Donald Fong (Sau Wan Chin); Claudette Carracedo (Lisa Chan); Barbara Tse (Mrs. Mar); Nathan Fong (Robert Chu); Lesley Ewen (Carmen); So Yee Shum (Auntie Bing); Greg Chan (Uncle Bing).

LOS ANGELES TIMES, 7/28/95, Calendar/p. 6, Kevin Thomas

Korean Canadian actress Sandra Oh lights up the screen in "Double Happiness," Mina Shum's lively, astringent, semi-autobiographical comedy about the travails of asserting one's independence within an ultra-conservative Asian emigré family. In Oh's quizzical, quicksilver personality Shum has found a perfect match for her own mercurial style, and the result is a first feature of much charm and painful truths.

Shum begins on a light note as she acquaints us with Oh's Jade Li, the 22-year-old elder daughter of Chinese parents (Alannah Ong, Stephen Chang) who came from Hong Kong to settle in Vancouver. Jade seems irrepressible at first, initially laughing off matchmaking attempts from her parents and a go-between, her employer at a costume rental company. She also fends off less-than encouraging parental remarks on her struggle to become an actress.

Ever so gradually, however Shum tightens the screws, getting serious without losing her sense of humor. As the pressure upon Jade to marry increases we come to realize how schizoid Jade's existence really is. When she deftly changes a C to an A to give her younger sister Pearl (Frances You) a straight-A report card to present her father, Jade is actually marking the beginning of revealing how much of her life is a lie.

Outside home she's freewheeling, liberated and ambitious, yet when she returns she finds herself reverting to the dutiful traditional Chinese daughter role with her parents, most especially to her ultra-strict father.

Jade's know-it-all father may surprise us by unbending enough to lip-sync "MacArthur Park" in a convivial moment, but it increasingly becomes clear that he is fully prepared to break his daughter's spirit while believing unquestioningly that he's doing it for her own good. Truly, Jade is in deep conflict: She loves and respects her parents, doesn't want to hurt them for the world, yet desperately wants to live her own life and knows full well just how high the price could be for trying to do so.

Shum deserves high marks for both fairness and subtlety in her most satisfying, beautifully acted and crafted film. Jade's parents really are loving, do want the best for her and are rightly concerned about their daughter's chances of successfully pursuing a career as an actress. Besides, the young lawyer (Andrew Chau) they're eager to have her marry is exceptionally handsome and polished.

By the same token, Shum speaks volumes simply by following up the father's brief recollection of living in a house full of servants as a child in pre-revolutionary China with a later glimpse of him returning home in his security guard's uniform. "Double Happiness" brims with such telling details and sly touches, and it finally belongs to Sandra Oh, who by the time the film is over, has emerged as an actress as formidable as she is funny.

NEW YORK POST, 7/28/95, p. 39, Thelma Adams

"Double Happiness" star Sandra Oh is about as likely to get a best-actress nomination as the video vixen of "Clueless," Alicia Silverstone. Neither actress plays deaf, dumb or blind or cribs an accent from Anna Magnani, but both offer fresh portraits of young women who actually drive the plot, rather than waiting to be rescued at the side of the celluloid road.

Oh won a Canadian Genie award (the equivalent of an Oscar) for her role as a spunky first-generation Chinese-Canadian. Jade, a 22-year-old aspiring actress, is at a crossroads. Either she can marry a nice Chinese boy of her parents' choosing and start cooking up dishes like "Double Happiness," or she can please herself, pursue a career and play the field.

"We didn't come here so you could completely ruin your life, we came here to give you opportunities," says Jade's authoritarian papa (Stephen Chang).

The irony is that it's just those opportunities that those opportunities that erode the tightknit family. Too much choice doesn't always lead to a double helping of happiness.

For most of the movie Jade leads a double life, trying to be both dutiful daughter and modern woman. After a one-night-stand with Mark (Callum Rennie), she tries to resist the genuine attraction of this white grad student who is too adorable for words: blue eyes hidden beneath Elvis Costello glasses, bleeding heart socked away under argyle sweaters. He'd walk the earth for Jade in his saddle shoes.

Jade is aware that the consequences for pursuing this romance are potentially severe. Her elder brother Winston has left the family fold and been disowned by her father, cut out of the family photos. (It wasn't so long ago that orthodox Jewish families sat shiva—went through formal mourning—for children who married gentiles.)

Writer/director Mina Shum presents these issues with a sure and light touch. She has a strong, humorous voice that speaks directly to the audience. Watching "Double Happiness"—winner of the jury prize at the 1994 Turino (Italy) Film Festival—is like sharing a couch with a best friend on a summer night, eating ice cream and trading family stories.

Shum achieves something in her feature debut that's always hard to pull off: she switches gears from warm humor to sudden heartbreak with an apparent effortlessness that confirms the underlying art.

"Double Happiness" will no doubt be compared to Ang Lee's father-knows-best trilogy "The Wedding Banquet" et al.) The Hong Kong-born, Canadian-bred Shum expresses sympathy for a father figure who has become all the more rigid since he has been uprooted from a society where his own father was "always sure and always right."

Not surprisingly, Shum's loyalties are with the women in the family. They face a difficult choice: achieve what joy you can within the family through indirection or sacrifice the security of the family circle for a risky venture into the mainstream. Daughters might not always know best, but they are the future.

NEWSDAY, 7/28/95, Part II/p. B5, John Anderson

The title might sound like one of those shrimp-and-chicken dishes available for takeout, but the intent of "Double Happiness" is the irony born of paradox: pleasing the Old World parents while succeeding in the New, when neither aim is reconcilable with the other and you don't know who you are anyway.

Chinese-Canadian filmmaker Mina Shum's debut is a confident, often funny film that takes the standard assimilation comedy a few steps further than farce. Jade Li (Sandra Oh) is an aspiring actress whose parents (Stephen Chang and Alannah Ong) dismiss her dream as a whim. They keep hoping she'll marry a "nice Chinese boy." Change the ethnicity and the story doesn't change very much: It's about matchmaking and disapproval, of both individuals and the society the parents naïvely thought was supposed to provide financial opportunity without cultural trauma. The parents are always dismayed, the children always caught in the middle.

But Jade—played with a great deal of charm by the screen-wise Sandra Oh—has also chosen a profession that puts every importance on looks. And that, for her, is something as inescapable as familial guilt. When she auditions for a bit part, they ask her for an accent. "Parisian?" she quips. The director doesn't think that's funny. "I want them to remember they are Chinese," her father says of Jade and her sister, Pearl (Frances You). There's never a chance they'll forget.

The Asian-American conundrum has been explored recently, and well, by other directors, such as Ang Lee, who also take a seriocomic view of the entire tradition-meets-liberty problem. But Shum uses ethnic characters in her own particular way. Jade and Pearl take an affectionately jaundiced view of their dotty elders, although their father is an impenetrable wall of tradition and regret. Jade isn't above using her own ethnicity when it suits her—when Mark (Callum Rennie) tries to strike up a conversation outside a nightclub, she demurely laughs into her hand, pretending not to speak English in the hope he'll go away. He won't and they become lovers, and that in itself—Mark being white—adds to Jade's multilayered crisis.

The director has both a keen eye for color and a smart sense of how to use it; her palette is vibrant and corresponds in wonderful ways to the rhythm and texture of the story. And even though the film slows down considerably in the second half, just as the narrative darkens a bit, she isn't afraid to be playful, or take chances. The opening scene, in which the audience meets the family at dinner—from the point of view of a rotating lazy susan—might have been just cute, but it works as both visual mischief and a symbol of the family members' conflicting orbits. Jade's several fantasy sequences, in which she becomes Joan of Arc or Blanche Dubois (with Pearl's voice interrupting the soliloquy by calling her sister to dinner), might have seemed trite but instead deliver the bitter with the sweet: All actors may try to become someone else, but few as talented as Jade have the visible minority hurdle to jump, or the double unhappiness of blinkered parents and blinkered casting directors.

VILLAGE VOICE, 8/1/95, p. 41, Jeff Brown

If the ethnic family drama has driven 20th-century American narrative, from *Long Day's Journey* to *Portnoy* to *The Godfather*, Asians have relatively recently, so to speak, gotten on the boat. Once again, children of immigrants fight strict, protective, culturally suspicious parents for small plots of autonomy. (This, while homegrown children flounder in a guidance vacuum.) In the case of Chinese parents versus America, the foremost culture of obedience meets the foremost culture of self-fulfillment.

Mina Shum's wry coming-of-age picture. *Double Happiness*, was filmed in Canada—it looks to be Vancouver—but could take place anywhere in the U.S. Jade (Sandra Oh) is the second child, eldest daughter, in the Li family, and at 22 she's now considered old enough to date—i.e., ready for a sanctioned union with a Chinese man of prospects. Her elder brother Winston, present only in a photo—a photo hidden under the bed, yet has become a family ghost, having disappeared into the wilder world of white people. (Shum keeps Winston's whereabouts and precise fate tantalizingly vague.) "You'll become like Winston!" is the curse held up to the girls.

You too can become a nonperson, disowned and dishonored. Same old message: Be grateful. We've sacrificed so much that you could come here and have so many advantages.

Double Happiness (the title is the Chinese character for marriage) is fairly clumsy movie-making; I'm thinking particularly of cutesy pseudo-Godardian set pieces and a camera supposedly attached to the dinner table's lazy Susan. But the movie calms down from its manic opening and begins to grow on you. So does its protagonist. Oh's chameleon-like Jade (who looks older than 22) writhes in post-adolescent indecision, alternating between cool sophisticate, wiseass tomboy, petulant schoolgirl, and desperate sexpot. Who shall I be now'? (Here's someone you could call a bit slutty, a bit nutty and mean it as a compliment.) Like the movie itself, she's normally gawky, though in a pinch—and when it counts —entirely poised.

An actress without roles, Jade auditions for what's available to Asians. She has a bit part as a waitress, she tries out as a newscaster (oops, they wanted a Filipino), while pining for a challenging role: "Something I have to gain weight for." When she dresses up for a date arranged by her parents, she complains she looks like Connie Chung. (The hair.) Sometimes she clearly enjoys Connie Chung mode. When a club doorman relegates her to a previously nonexistent line and she's joined by a fellow nerd, she mimes a sort of geisha modesty. But once she and the guy, Mark (Callum Rennie), start talking, she erupts in apparently long-suppressed heat, goes to his place and more or less rips off his clothes. Mark, I should add, is a white boy.

Dad (Stephen Chang) and Mom (Alannah Ong) are horrified that she's stayed out all night though they think she's been at her girlfriend's. Even bringing home Dad's favorite buns (red bean) doesn't work. He's particularly enraged because an old friend is coming from Hong Kong and he wishes to impress him with the family's unwavering rectitude and success. (They've a story made up about Winston.) The genial "Uncle" (Donald Fong) who shows up is actually far more tolerant than Mom and Dad.

Double Happiness is small, occasionally coy, but mostly smart, resourceful, and peppy. To Shum's credit, there are no villains here. She's especially effective in conveying Jade's love for her parents (a double-edged knife) as well as the need to escape managed care. Even to a DAR WASP like me, this story seems painfully familiar.

Also reviewed in:
NATION, 8/28-9/4/95, p. 216, Stuart Klawans
NEW YORK TIMES, 7/28/95, p. C10, Janet Maslin
VARIETY, 9/19-25/94, p. 79, Leonard Klady
WASHINGTON POST, 8/11/95, p. F6, Rita Kempley

DRACULA: DEAD AND LOVING IT

A Castle Rock Entertainment release of a Brooksfilms production. *Executive Producer:* Peter Schindler. *Producer:* Mel Brooks. *Director:* Mel Brooks. *Screenplay:* Mel Brooks, Rudy De Luca, and Steve Haberman. *Story:* Rudy De Luca and Steve Haberman. *Based on characters created by:* Bram Stoker. *Director of Photography:* Michael D. O'Shea. *Editor:* Adam Weiss. *Music:* Hummie Mann. *Music Editor:* Chris Ledesma. *Choreographer:* Alan Johnson. *Sound:* Michael Reale, David Cunningham and David Marquette and (music) Rick Riccio. *Sound Editor:* Gregory M. Gerlich and Gary S. Gerlich. *Casting:* Lindsay D. Chag and Bill Shepard. *Production Designer:* Roy Forge Smith. *Art Director:* Bruce Robert Hill. *Set Designer:* Joseph G. Pacelli, Jr. *Set Decorator:* Jan Pascale. *Set Dresser:* Deborah Harman, Tim Bowen, Chris Gutierrez, and Gary H. Rizzo. *Special Effects:* Richard Ratliff. *Visual Effects:* Mike Shea. *Costumes:* Dodie Shepard. *Make-up:* Todd A. McIntosh and Alan "Doc" Friedman. *Stunt Coordinator:* Gary Combs. *Running time:* 90 minutes. *MPAA Rating:* PG-13.

CAST: Leslie Nielsen (Dracula); Peter MacNicol (Renfield); Steven Weber (Harker); Amy Yasbeck (Mina); Lysette Anthony (Lucy); Harvey Korman (Dr. Seward); Mel Brooks (Professor Van Helsing); Mark Blankfield (Martin); Megan Cavanagh (Essie); Clive Revill (Sykes); Chuck McCann (Innkeeper); Avery Schreiber and Cherie Franklin (Peasant Couple in Coach); Ezio Greggio (Coach Driver); Leslie Sachs (Usherette); Matthew Porretta (Handsome

Lieutenant at Ball); Rudy De Luca (Guard); Jennifer Crystal (Nurse); Darla Haun (Brunette Vampire); Karen Roe (Blond Vampire); Charlie Callas (Man in Straight Jacket); Phillip Connery (Ship Captain); Tony Griffin, Casey King, and Nick Rempel (Crewmen); Zale Kessler (Orchestra Leader); Lisa Cordray (Hat Check Girl); Cindy Marshall-Day and Benjamin Livingston (Young Lovers at Picnic); Gregg Binkley (Woodbridge); Anne Bancroft (Gypsy Woman).

LOS ANGELES TIMES, 12/22/95, Calendar/p. 4, David Kronke

Not to venture forth some sort of radical idea, but aren't comedies supposed to have jokes? Mel Brooks' "Dracula: Dead and Loving It" has its share of misfired gags, to be sure, but what's truly surprising is how little anyone is trying here—there are great, arid stretches of this film in which there aren't even any bad jokes to not laugh at.

Brooks, who wrote the script with Rudy De Luca and Steve Haberman, remains for some reason faithful to the original story, which may bog him down some—all the plot points seem to get in the way of the potential for humor. Perhaps Brooks' gravest error is not realizing that the ultimate vampire movie parody was made just three years ago—it was called "Bram Stoker's Dracula." Compared to that orgy of overkill, Brooks' little trifle is downright tame.

Quickly: Dracula (Leslie Nielsen) comes to London; his mad minion Renfield (Peter MacNicol) is placed in an asylum; Dracula attacks Lucy (Lysette Anthony) and Dr. Seward (Harvey Korman) is disturbed enough to bring in Van Helsing (Brooks), who figures the whole thing out and has the simp Harker (Steven Weber) save Lucy by killing her (in a rare scene that at least gets your attention, he strikes a gusher). Dracula then sets his sights on Harker's fiancée and Seward's daughter Mina (Amy Yasbeck).

And honestly, the movie is no funnier than the above description. All Brooks and his conspirators seem to be able to muster up is a handful of pratfalls and jokes about the actors, bad accents. His direction is clumsily stagey to the point of playing like a high school talent revue. And Brooks apparently harbors an affinity for the Hammer Films of the '60s—the sets and special effects are breathtakingly cheesy.

Nielsen, who presumably did this of his own free will, is frightfully stiff as the Count. MacNicol is clearly the guy trying the hardest here, which means he has a couple of amusing moments but when his shtick doesn't work it's really deadly. Brooks himself earns a chuckle or two as Van Helsing, but Korman, Weber and the rest of the cast simply go through the motions and try not to grimace too much on-screen.

Hard to believe, but it has been 21 years since Brooks' classic "Young Frankenstein." And you can feel every one of those years pass during "Dracula: Dead and Loving It."

NEW YORK POST, 12/22/95, p. 54, Michael Medved

You know a comedy's in deep trouble when it begins repeating stupid gags that were never that funny in the first place.

That's the case with Mel Brooks' disappointing dreary "Dracula: Dead and Loving It," which uses the tired old bit about a shadow out-of-synch with its owner some four different times.

It also pads its running time by giving us two different drawn-out, boring and supposedly sultry dance numbers (both a tango and a czardas) between Count Dracula (Leslie Nielsen) and his latest victim, Mina (Amy Yasbeck).

Director and co-writer Brooks resorts to such time-wasting tactics because he obviously and embarrassingly runs out of ideas before his film is even one third finished. That's a special shame, since he's working with a fine cast and his spoof begins with energy and promise.

As the nervous British solicitor Renfield (Peter MacNicol, in an amusingly manic and over-the-top performance) visits Dracula in his castle, Nielsen echoes one of the count's most famous lines with a perfectly calibrated Lugosi accent. "Children of the night ..." he smilingly intones, "What a mess they make!" and then proceeds to slip on some gooey bat guano and to execute an expert pratfall down the stone stairway.

After this dramatic entrance, you expect to see Dracula as a benign and bumbling bloodsucker—with Nielsen portraying the killer count as the same sort of clueless klutz he played so endearingly in the "Naked Gun" movies.

Alas, Brooks has other ideas, making his main character needlessly mean and formidable and deadly and undermining the fun of the movie. In one especially unpleasant scene, Dracula's arch-enemy Professor Van Helsing (played by Brooks himself with a music hall German accent) joins romantic hero Jonathan Harker (Steven Weber of TVs "Wings") in driving a stake through the heart of one of the count's vampirized victims (Lysette Anthony).

Several times they pound the stake, and on each occasion a huge gusher of blood covers everything on screen with the sticky red liquid. "This is ghastly!" Harker declares, and the audience will no doubt agree with him. Equally ghastly is the fate of Amy Yasbeck and Lysette Anthony, two talented and radiantly beautiful actresses who are utterly wasted in their witless roles as two-dimensional Drac snacks.

Part of the problem is that Brooks displays no discernible affection for the films he is spoofing, especially since many scenes (showing group sex with girlish ghouls or an aged Dracula's oddly shaped white hair piece) are inspired not by campy classics but by Francis Ford Coppola's dreadful 1992 box-office bonanza.

By contrast, Brooks' brilliant "Young Frankenstein", with its gorgeously antique black-and-white, worked wonderfully because its creator so obviously loved the old films he simultaneously satirized and honored.

It would be unreasonable to expect this new picture to rise to that level of inspiration, but at least one could hope for the occasional chuckles of "Robin Hood: Men in Tights"—chuckles which this dead-on-arrival dud pointedly fails to deliver.

Instead, this is the sort of pain-in-the-neck project that will lead some frustrated audience members to demand their money back. As Dracula himself might declared "Exhausted comic geniuses ... what a mess they make!"

NEWSDAY, 12/22/95, Part II/p. B11, Jonathan Mandell

Does the world need another vampire movie? Does it need another vampire parody? Can a vampire parody really exist anymore now that we have the movie starring Tom Cruise?

I ask these questions as a way of making this review long enough to fill the space they've given me, because I don't have much to say about "Dracula: Dead and Loving It," except that it's a typical Mel Brooks movie, only not as funny.

Actually, there are plenty of funny moments in it. It's also not totally typical. What this Brooks film has that the others don't are the silly faces and inventive pratfalls of Leslie Nielsen, the klutzy cop of the "Naked Gun" series, who plays Count Dracula as—will this surprise you?—a klutz.

This vampire slips on bat excrement, falls off the ceiling and dreams of no longer living as a nocturnal being; he walks out in the middle of a sunny day and joins picnickers on a lawn, eating a leg of their chicken and drinking a glass of their wine, until he notices that his arms have started to smoke because of the sunlight. Suddenly we see him waking up in his coffin in a sweat. "A day-mare," he says.

Leslie Nielsen has some silly props—a hat that looks like a wig belonging to the B-52s—and a few especially effective special effects: He sweeps his cape before him and transforms into a little bat, with a tiny Leslie Nielsen face. He then attempts to fly into the boudoir of a sexy conquest but smashes into her window face first.

There are other characters: a couple of voluptuous vampirettes, Ann Bancroft in a cameo as a gypsy who likes to twiddle with the loose skin of her neck so that she'll trill more ominously, and some other townspeople who react in fear and amazement when a stranger tells them, "I'm scheduled to meet Count Dracula."

"Dracula?" says one in horror.

"Dracula?" says another.

"Scheduled?" says a third, in the same tone of horror.

Harvey Korman is a doctor who likes to prescribe an enema for any problem. Peter MacNicol, the legal counsel on "Chicago Hope," here plays a British lawyer who is hypnotized into becoming the count's slave and develops a taste for eating bugs. Brooks himself is professor Van Helsing, famed vampire hunter, who likes to gross out his medical students and who tells the young, dumb suitor played by Steven Weber that he must drive a stake through the heart of a woman the count has turned into one of the undead. Weber resists, Brooks insists, and the resulting geyser is probably the funniest scene in the movie. I say probably because I didn't see the whole movie: Dracula put me to sleep; too much of it was dead, and I wasn't loving it.

SIGHT AND SOUND, 10/96, p. 39, Ben Backley

Transylvania, 1893. Property broker Renfield travels to Count Dracula's mountaintop castle. After concluding the Count's purchase of Carfax Abbey in England, he retires to his bedroom to sleep. During the night he is disturbed by Dracula's undead virgin brides, but the Count persuades Renfield that he's been dreaming. He hypnotises the Englishman, turning him into his slave. They depart immediately by ship to England.

Once on dry land, Dracula infiltrates London high society. He befriends his next door neighbour Dr Seward, the head of a psychiatric asylum. At the opera Dr Seward introduces Dracula to his ward Lucy, his daughter Mina, and her fiancé Jonathan Harker. The Count soon bewitches Lucy before departing abruptly. Meanwhile, Renfield is cast into a cell at Dr Seward's asylum. Later that night, as Lucy lies in bed, Dracula transforms himself into a bat and bites her. Lucy falls desperately ill, confounding all the doctors, and forcing her guardian to employ the services of Dr Van Helsing, a doctor and expert on the supernatural. Van Helsing concludes that she has been infected by a vampire. He tries to protect her from future attack, but Dracula lures her from her bed to drain her blood once more, and she dies.

After the funeral, Lucy rises from the dead, and kills a guard. Van Helsing and Harker are forced to drive a stake through her heart. Van Helsing, suspicious that either Dracula or Renfield is a vampire, arranges a ball at which Dracula is exposed because he has no reflection in a mirror, but he escapes with Mina. Renfield inadvertently leads Seward, Harker, and Van Helsing right to the Dracula's secret lair before he gets a chance to plunge his fangs into Mina's neck. Using a cross and a wooden stake as weapons, they struggle with the Count who is forced to transform into a bat. He is destroyed by light that Renfield accidentally lets in through the roof.

Mel Brooks has been lampooning Hollywood's back-catalogue since long before *National Lampoon* started making films. Some of his targets have included Hitchcock, the Western, 30s and 40s musicals. This adherence to one genre per parodic film creates stronger narrative foundations than the multi-referenced patchworks found in the *Airplane!* and *Naked Gun* films. Casting Leslie Nielson as Dracula could be read as an attempt to bridge these two approaches, but unfortunately Nielson is such an icon of the *Airplane!* style that he swamps *Dracula Dead and Loving It* with his presence.

Nonetheless, Brooks' regular team of actors takes a crack at the Bram Stoker/Coppola version of the myth with a familiar gusto: Avery Schreiber plays a Middle European peasant as he often does, Harvey Korman here does a difficult Nigel Bruce impression, and Brooks slots in his own wife, Ann Bancroft, for a cameo as a gypsy woman, tugging her own throat to get the wobbly horror voice right. The result was no doubt intended to be a companion piece to *Young Frankenstein*, but apart from a handful of genuinely funny set pieces (generally involving Brooks himself) it falls woefully short of the mark.

Some of the problems lie in the decision to base the bulk of the comedy on aping English reserve. Stoker dealt with the tensions between Dracula's rampant sexuality and its absence in the British temperament metaphorically. The spoof doesn't need to concern itself with such subtleties. There are a whole host of *No Sex Please—I'm British*-style puns that work for a while, but then gently wear out after excessive use. As he watches two semi-clad vampire-virgins pressing themselves against the phallic woodwork, all Renfield can offer them is "My God! What are you doing to the furniture?" In the sight-gag department there is slightly more success, with Dracula transforming into a bat with Nielson's distinctive face and white hair attached to it. There's another tasty moment as Dracula dances with Mina. A huge mirror is unveiled showing Mina being flung around the bathroom with her partner nowhere to be seen, a feat of special effects that's a far cry from the old wire and cloak techniques, but still not up to current standards.

These gags can work but the one liner's and visual tricks need to be the comic equivalent of mayflies, and here too many uncomfortable spaces and occasionally embarrassed silences creep in. Brooks cut his comic teeth in television, writing quick-fire sketches for the *Sid Caesar Show* with his pals Woody Allen and Neil Simon. Since then he has shown a talent for sticking the skits on to a solid narrative base, with the best of the resulting films (such as *The Producers* and *Blazing Saddles*) creating a huge following for his old-fashioned humour. By coming unstuck in taking on Dracula he's in good company. Polanski tried it with *Dance of the Vampires,* (otherwise known as *The Fearless Vampire Killers or Pardon me, But Your Teeth are in My Neck:*), Clive Donner with *Vampira,* and most recently Wes Craven with the Eddie Murphy vehicle *Vampire in Brooklyn,* all with less than barnstorming success.

VILLAGE VOICE, 1/2/96, p. 52, Georgia Brown

The ads joke that in *Dracula: Dead and Loving It* Mel Brooks has created his most "biting" satire yet. Ha. It's also billed as "the companion piece to *Young Frankenstein.*" I say, not at all in the same vein! I don't even know what that subtitle "Dead and Loving It" is supposed to mean. There's certainly a lot of dead time here, but nobodys going to love it. A bloodless Brooks supplies very few of his trademark taste-defying gags. Instead, he relies much too heavily on the stumbling and bumbling of his star, Leslie Nielsen, and the frantic mugging of Peter MacNicol.

The movie starts off with the silly solicitor, Renfield (MacNicol), on his way for an appointment with Count Dracula. He's duly warned by the cringing townspeople—including a gypsy played by Anne Bancroft—but persists going alone, at night. At the castle, he meets our clutzy, silver-maned count (Nielsen essentially doing Naked Gums), as well as several props from former *Draculas,* like the sticky cobweb from Tod Browning's 1931 version and Gary Oldman's wig.

Without much of a fuss, Renfield becomes Dracula's abject slave, and the count shifts his residence to London. There he preys on the two bosomy daughters of Dr. Seward (Harvey Korman), director of the mental asylum where Renfield is incarcerated. One daughter, Mina (Amy Yasbeck), is engaged to the vapid Jonathan Harker (Steven Weber). When sister Lucy (Lysette Anthony) seduces, or is seduced by, Dracula, vampire expert Professor Van Helsing (Brooks) is called in.

Van Helsing asks Seward to check his library for vampire texts: "Do you have Nosferatu!" Answer (to Chiquita banana tune): "Yes, we have Nosferatu, we have Nosferatu *today.*" Quick, drive a stake through its heart!

Also reviewed in:
CHICAGO TRIBUNE, 12/22/95, Friday/p. H, Michael Wilmington
NEW YORK TIMES, 12/22/95, p. C35, Janet Maslin
VARIETY, 12/18-31/95 p. 67, Joe Leydon
WASHINGTON POST, 12/22/95, p. C6, Hal Hinson

DREAMING OF RITA

A First Run Features release of a FilmLance Int'l. Production for the Swedish Film Institute/Sveriges Television TV2/Film Teknik/Svensk Filmindustri/Finnish Film Foundation/Nordic Film & TV-Fund. *Producer:* Börje Hansson. *Director:* Jon Lindström. *Screenplay (Swedish with English subtitles):* Rita Holst and Jon Lindström. *Director of Photography:* Kjell Lagerros. *Set Designer:* Staffan Erstam. *Running time:* 108 minutes. *MPAA Rating:* Not Rated.

CAST: Per Oscarsson (Bob); Marika Lagercrantz (Rita); Philip Zanden (Steff); Yaba Holst (Sandra); Patrik Ersgard (Erik XIV); Lise Ringheim (Sabine).

NEW YORK POST, 5/12/95, p. 42, Thelma Adams

Brooklyn-born Rita Hayworth, Orson Welles' "The Lady From Shanghai," fuels the fantasies of an aging cinematographer playing his last reel in Jon Lindstrom's Swedish film "Dreaming of Rita."

Bob (Per Oscarsson), a white-haired, skinny Santa, mourns his wife's death. Drowning in sorrow, he seems destined to follow her to the grave. Unfinished business tugs at his heart: 30 years before, he fell for a Dane who revered Hayworth. Bob has pined for a faux-Gilda named Sabine ever since.

What would have happened if Bob had left his pregnant wife for Sabine? After a serious stroke, Bob heads for Copenhagen to answer that question and rediscover his bliss. His redheaded beauty of a daughter, Rita (Marika Lagercrantz), pursues.

Under the guise of daughterly duty, Rita flees an unsatisfactory bourgeois marriage. Her slick-haired yuppie husband refuses to help Rita care for their baby son, while their teen-aged daughter wryly comments from the sidelines.

Bob and Rita wind up together on the road, pursuing the old man's pipe dream and rediscovering each other in a comedy about the amorous road not taken. Along the way, Rita collides with a Zen computer hacker who might just be the love of her life. Bob's dilemma gains resonance: Rita must determine if she should abandon her family for a chance encounter that might just be the real thing.

"Dreaming of Rita" is a rare slice of Swedish whimsy. In an off-beat recurring joke, the nursing Rita wets the front of her blouse, an aching reminder of her separation from her son. A baby pacifier falling on a corpse frames the movie, a quirky image of rebirth.

The warm-hearted movie weighs fantasies against realities and endorses mixing the two. Even Hayworth couldn't have lived up to Bob's dreams. Born Margarita Carmen Cansino, Ginger Rogers' cousin didn't become a star until after a name change and a tricky bit of electrolysis raised her hairline and her glamour quotient. But facts should never keep an old man from "Dreaming of Rita."

NEWSDAY, 5/12/95, Part II/p. B7, John Anderson

The great cosmic yuppie joke—on women—is that for all their increased liberation and opportunity, they still get stuck with the kids. Put another way: In order not to be Mom, you have to work twice as hard.

In Jon Lindstrom's smartly cynical "Dreaming of Rita," the ethereal and seriously over-obligated Rita (Marika Lagercrantz) is handling the usual domestic disorder—plus a new baby (Adam Blannings) who's cranky, an insensitive husband, Steff (Philip Zanden), who's work-obsessed, a snotty older daughter named Sandra (Yaba Holst) who's just so *beyond* it all, and a father, Bob (Per Oscarsson), who's a little bit crazy over the recent death of his wife. When he also has a stroke, Rita's ready to snap. And when Bob flees his hospital in search of an old love named Sabine (Lise Ringheim), Rita dumps the baby with Steff and hits the road with him.

It takes everyone a long time to get anywhere, but Lindstrom makes it a smoothly entertaining trip. He's wading into a nest of unruly themes here—including family, familial guilt, infidelity and the importance of babies versus breadwinning. And he's certainly on Rita's side; he makes Steff suffer, and it's fun to watch. But nobody's a villain. They're just insensitive, and apt to take advantage of the person in their life who can't bring herself not to do everything.

Rita is just one of two title characters. The other is Rita Hayworth, whom we see in musical footage from "Gilda" and after whom Bob named his daughter—as a memory of his time with Sabine. Part of Rita's on-the-road education involves coming to terms with Bob's early infidelity, and the fact that he harbored these romantic dreams of Sabine all those years her mother was alive. What she has to do is see her parent as a person, flawed and sexual—something Sandra will have to deal with as well.

The other part of Rita's instruction comes via the self-dubbed Erik XIV (Patrik Ersgard), a Nick Cage look-alike and ne'er-do-well who helps her out and falls in love with her. It's a situation rife with absurdity: Rita, lactating like mad—she carries her electric breast pump with her everywhere she goes—just as she's becoming reacquainted with herself as a sensual being. Not the most serendipitous set of circumstances, but as Lindstrom might say, such is life.

Lindstrom stages a number of the chase sequences in the manner of a cheese-ball spy thriller, which clashes nicely with the quietly lovely Rita, her pursuers, her admirers and the rather pedestrian family life that's driving her to distraction. She's something of an original. And despite a tendency to be a bit long-winded, so is this film.

VILLAGE VOICE, 5/23/95, Film Special/p. 30, Georgia Brown

In Jon Lindström's snappy Swedish road movie *Dreaming of Rita*, a father names his only child after a lover's resemblance to Rita Hayworth. Yet, 30-some-odd years later, he seems never to have fallen for his own beautiful redheaded daughter, Rita (the lovely Marika Lagercrantz). As if to replicate this neglect, Rita marries a man, Steff (Philip Zanden), who takes her for granted while she stays home tending their baby. A crisis in their marriage is set off when Rita's long-suffering mother dies and her ailing father (Per Oscarsson) suddenly takes off for Copenhagen, hoping to take up with his old flame, the sultry *Gilda*-smitten Sabine. Fearing for his health, Rita takes off after him, reluctantly leaving the baby with her husband.

Lindström has a nice grasp of a mother's dependence on her infant. (Personally, I would describe it as two years carrying around a package that grows heavier and heavier but can't be opened or put down.) Rita and Steff's son Adam sleeps in a wicker cradle that swings over their bed. A cute Scandinavian contrivance and one that gives the sense of a precarious weight dangling over the marriage. When Rita leaves Adam, her breasts ache and milk leaks down her blouse. For his part, Steff tries to involve the couple's older daughter in child care, but she's savvy enough not to let Dad turn her into Mom.

On the road, Rita meets up with the dreamy-looking Erik (Patrik Ersgard), who helps her pump her breasts. He also lends a sympathetic hand with Gramps. Whereas Steff markets computer-security systems, Erik is a confirmed hacker. Steff has always prided himself as holding the line against both hackers and slackers, but Erik has silvery blue eyes, the better to see Rita's beauty. Once he gets wind of the existence of Rita's admiring hitchhiker, Steff—now in hot pursuit with both kids—begins to view his wife with new eyes.

Dreaming of Rita dreams on a little too long. Its predictability didn't bother me, but the film lets down once the mysterious Sabine is located, and, more crucially, it finally fails to elucidate the lovely, harried Rita herself. Although she's at the center, she's almost as much a cipher at the end as at the beginning. Yet this amiable romantic comedy is much fresher than feeble Hollywood fare—a happy dating movie for once or future married.

Also reviewed in:
CHICAGO TRIBUNE, 8/25/95, Tempo/p. 3, Michael Wilmington
NEW REPUBLIC, 6/12/95, p. 32, Stanley Kauffmann
NEW YORK TIMES, 5/12/95, p. C20, Stephen Holden
VARIETY, 1/25/93, p. 134, Gunnar Rehlin

ECLIPSE

A Strand Releasing release of a Fire Dog Films/Medienvertrieb production with the participation of Telefilm Canada/Ontario Film Development Corporation/National Film Board of Canada/P.S. Production Services Ltd and The Canada Council: Media Arts in co-production with Liason of Independent Filmmakers of Toronto (LIFT). *Executive Producer:* Wolfram Tichy. *Producer:* Camelia Frieberg and Jeremy Podeswa. *Director:* Jeremy Podeswa. *Screenplay:* Jeremy Podeswa. *Director of Photography:* Miroslaw Baszak. *Editor:* Susan Maggi. *Music:* Ernie Tollar. *Sound:* David Horton. *Sound Editor:* Jane Tattersall. *Art Director:* Tamara Deverell. *Set Decorator:* Michael McShane. *Set Dresser:* Patrick Lefebvre and Denis A. Mildner. *Costumes:* Aline Gilmore. *Make-up:* Sylvain Gournoyer. *Running time:* 95 minutes. *MPAA Rating:* Not Rated.

CAST: Von Flores (Henry); John Gilbert (Brian); Pascale Montpetit (Sylvie); Manuel Aranguiz (Gabriel); Maria Del Mar (Sarah); Greg Ellwand (Norman); Matthew Ferguson (Angelo); Earl Pastko (Michael); Daniel MacIvor (Jim); Kirsten Johnson (Carlotta); Ian Orr (Professor); Rosalind Kerr (Brian's Wife); Dylan Stukator-McMahon (Sarah's Baby); Tracy Wright (Souvenir Shop Clerk); Michael McMurtry (Record Store Clerk); Scott Wilson (Tattoo Guy); Yan Cui (Eclipse Scientist); Greg Mandziuk (TV Newscaster).

LOS ANGELES TIMES, 10/13/95, Calendar/p. 14, Kevin Thomas

Jeremy Podeswa's sleek, stylized "Eclipse" is a film of surprises. Set in Toronto eight or nine days before a solar eclipse, it starts out as a contemporary "La Ronde" covering the spectrum of sexual orientation—straight, gay and bi.

Initially, the moon and the sun crossing paths as a symbol of individuals engaging in a brief sexual encounter like ships passing in the night seems a bit schematic, just as the initial interludes seem somewhat arbitrary and even improbable, as if Podeswa is asking us to believe that every time one person meets another, they swiftly proceed to sex.

Maybe it's an instance of a first-time feature director making a movie that gets better as it goes along, but the encounters do, in fact, gain in substance as the film progresses. It proves to be a work of accumulative emotional impact and meaning by the time it reaches that climactic eclipse, a sequence of dramatic power evoking a sense of the spiritual and of the mystery and danger of the universe.

Like Max Ophuls' "La Ronde," itself an adaptation of Arthur Schnitzler's 1897 "Reigen," "Eclipse" is composed of vignettes in which one lover moves on to the next, who in turn moves on to another until the last lover connects with the first, thus completing a circle.

A French Canadian housekeeper (Pascale Montpetit), recently arrived in Toronto from a small town in Quebec, is insolent and contemptuous of her middle-aged employer (John Gilbert) when she submits to the advances he's paying extra for. But when she encounters a warm, affable Central American (Manuel Aranguiz) at a language school, they make love tenderly after she confesses to an abusive past he cannot understand because of the language barrier.

Similarly, an androgynous-looking teen-ager (Matthew Ferguson, last seen in Denys Arcand's "Love and Human Remains") confidently seduces a married man (Greg Ellwand) only to find himself hurt and vulnerable after an encounter with a dismissive artist (Earl Pastko) interested only in casual sex.

Beautifully crafted and well-acted, "Eclipse" is sensual rather than erotic and always discreet. Podeswa appreciates physical beauty, but what interests him is emotion rather than lust, and an individual's place in the world.

NEW YORK POST, 11/17/95, p. 48, Bill Hoffmann

Canada is producing many fine independent films these days and the latest example is "Eclipse," an ambitious, sex-drenched movie with an intriguing style.

Writer/director Jeremy Podeswa has jammed enough quirky characters into 95 minutes to fill a soap opera for an entire season, and "Eclipse" is more a series of vignettes than a complete movie. Still, it has much going for it.

The premise is that an upcoming solar eclipse has turned 10 Toronto residents from various backgrounds into horny little devils who launch into a frenzied game of musical beds:

Middle-aged Brian picks up Asian hustler Henry for alley-way sex then zips home for a quickie with his housekeeper Sylvie, who goes off and makes with Gabriel, who in turn does the horizontal mambo with his lawyer's wife, Sarah.

Sarah and her husband, Norman, go at it—but Norman has other things on his mind, picking up an androgynous teen named Angelo for some fast nooky in a hotel room. Angelo turns around and does it with avant-garde artist Michael, who goes off and has a fling in the woods with his best friend, Jim.

Jim meets mindless Madonna-wannabe Carlotta, who jumps his bones in the men's room of a disco. Carlotta then goes home with Henry. Remember Henry? The Asian guy who started the whole thing? Whew!

Of note are two superb performances: As Sylvie, Pascale Montpetit projects more eroticism with a single glance than do a stable of porno stars in a hardcore film.

And Kirsten Johnson gives a brutally honest performance as Carlotta, the aimless, spaced-out club girl who lives for the moment—scrounging for drinks and hopping idly from bed to bed with strangers. Johnson is so good, I'm sure Hollywood will be calling.

As good as the actors are, though, their scenes come and go too quickly to really make the picture click as a whole. I wish Podeswa had allowed his characters a little more breathing room.

NEWSDAY, 11/17/95, Part II/p. B5, John Anderson

In ancient cultures—which apparently include Canada—the solar eclipse has been linked to fertility, mortality, dragons eating the sun and general lunacy. In Jeremy Podeswa's sensuous and occasionally languid "Eclipse," it provides the spark for a series of human phenomenon, interconnected sexual encounters and desperate passion.

The archipelago of fractured relationships and interrupted longing that Podeswa creates is interesting, but less so than the characters themselves: There is Henry (Von Flores), a gay hustler picked up by the well-to-do Brian (John Gilbert) for some guilt-racked, back-alley sex. We follow Brian home where he has more sex with his Quebecois maid Sylvie (Pascale Montpetit), who goes on to couple with the South American émigré Gabriel (Manuel Aranguiz), who has spontaneous sexual combustion with the Venezuelan Sarah (Maria Del Mar), whose husband, Norman (Greg Ellwand), has a hotel rendezvous with the angel-faced Angelo (Matthew Ferguson), who makes love to the artist Michael (Earl Pastko), who's driven to reignite his relationship with the actor Jim (Daniel MacIvor). Henry reappears eventually, in bed with a woman/social nightmare named Carlotta (Kirsten Johnson).

Their various libidinous collisions are presumably the result of the imminent eclipse, a phenomenon that can be emotional, terrifying and provocative—and provides a stark reminder of our mortality. Podeswa seems to feel (probably rightly) that the first thing on the human mind when it confronts death is copulation. His characters behave accordingly.

But these are not just randy bodies seeking heat. Unlike most film meditations on modern romance and anxiety, the sex here comes first, then the revealing self-examinations: Sylvie tells Gabriel of her sexual exploitation from the age of 12; Jim breaks into post-coital tears at having reunited with Michael; Angelo provides sophomoric but gives consoling advice to Norman about why he isn't really cheating on his wife ("you need a doctor *and* a dentist").

The music, by Ernie Tollar, provides an exotic, Semitic tonality to the urban sexscape Podeswa mounts, in various monotonal and black-and-white imagery, as well as color—but only when we look through Angelo's camcorder. As he walks around Toronto, recording the hordes of visiting eclipse watchers, Angelo captures one skywatcher who describes the coming attraction as a "reversal of nature." What we have in "Eclipse" is more a distillation of nature, the essence of human sexuality gone astronomical.

SIGHT AND SOUND, 7/95, p. 46, Claire Monk

In the two weeks leading up to an eclipse of the sun over Toronto, Canada—a countdown marked by media overkill, and recorded on camcorder by a precocious teenager, Angelo, for a school project—ten men and women of diverse ages and backgrounds (including Angelo) become part of a chain of sexual encounters.

Brian, a repressed, married, middle-aged businessman, has anxious backstreet sex with Henry, a young southeast Asian hustler. On another day, Henry snatches sex with his indifferent and contemptuous housekeeper Sylvie, a French-speaking Québécoise recently arrived in Toronto. At the language centre where Sylvie learns English, she meets Gabriel, a Central American refugee. Her pity for him unleashes desire and she initiates lovemaking.

Crying at the sight of his scars, she pours out memories—in French—of her unhappy adolescent promiscuity with her brothers and their friends, none of which he can understand. Gabriel visits Sarah, the beautiful upper-class Venezuelan wife of his Canadian immigration lawyer, and they resume a passionate affair. However his awareness that this bourgeois "bored housewife" would never be available to him in his own country makes him hostile, and they part.

The affair exacerbates Sarah's doubts about her relationship with her husband, Norman, and his bland reassurances fail to satisfy her. A day later the nervous, guilt-ridden Norman has his first-ever gay sexual encounter—with Angelo, the beautiful teenager who is videoing the run-up to the eclipse. Angelo drops in on Michael, a jaded and promiscuous artist with whom he once had sex. Though tritely fascinated by Angelo's beauty, recording it on endless polaroids, Michael rejects him after sex. Michael visits his best friend Jim, once briefly his lover. After cynically dissecting the failings of their past sexual relationship, Michael manipulates Jim into making love; but afterwards Jim, secretly in love with Michael, weeps, knowing that the encounter meant nothing to Michael.

Jim seeks solace in a gay club where, to his horror, he is accosted by Carlotta, a loud young woman whose unstoppable talk and tall stories are a front for desperation. Pursued by her into the orgiastic dark of the men's toilets he reluctantly gives in to her physical advances. Next morning—on the day of the eclipse—Carlotta wakes up with Henry. Although they are strangers and remember nothing of the night before, they make tentative, tender social contact, but she rejects his offer of a coffee and leaves. Rushing to the window, Henry sees the eclipse begin. As it darkens the city, each of the ten characters watches it in profound isolation—ending with Brian, who suffers a heart attack in his car.

Sharing a producer with Atom Egoyan's *Exotica*, featuring actors previously seen in Egoyan's *The Adjuster*, Denys Arcand's *Love and Human Remains* and (en masse) in David Wellington's *I Love a Man in Uniform*, and directed by the one-time publicist of David Cronenberg's *Dead Ringers*, *Eclipse*'s preoccupations—postmortem disengagement, alienated human relations, the sexuality of manipulation and its technology (video)—seem a little overdetermined. While the claim that its affinities with Egoyan's "cinema of disappointment" (a label which could equally well be applied to a broader set of Canadian films from Arcand's 1986 *Decline of the American Empire* onwards) has some substance, the sensation of watching a me-too movie is at times hard to shake off. Nevertheless, this cross-pollination has given the recent Canadian cinema much of its energy, and a first feature which succeeds (where *Love and Human Remains* failed) in bringing eloquence, subtlety and burnout to themes of urban impersonality and casual sex can't be so lightly dismissed.

Eclipse's subject is not sex in itself (pleasure and release are virtually absent from its couplings) so much as sexuality as it functions socially: sex as an expression—and exposer—of power, control, anxiety, self-image, joyless drives and unfulfilled (perhaps unfulfillable) needs. Layers of ambiguous analogy are embedded in the imagery of the eclipse: a professor Angelo interviews for his video project intones that "A world without light is a reminder of how precarious our existence really is". What the director Podeswa brings to this material is a self-deflating quality. Ironic parallels between the thrill/risk/disappointment of gazing at this natural wonder (looking at the eclipse unprotected can cause blindness) and the thrill/risk/disappointment of a sexual encounter are established early on when the camera lingers on a poster ad for sunglasses whose slogan—"Be smart, be safe: protect your eyes"—hijacks the language of safe sex campaigns to simultaneously exploit both the eclipse and fears about it.

Eclipse has a structural simplicity which works to its advantage when focusing on the finer nuances of trysts between characters who are strangers to one another as much as they are to us. The hustler Henry learns Brian's name not because Brian volunteers it but from a document he idly picks up in Brian's car. Brian, in turn, fails to understand (or ignores) his housekeeper Sylvie's pointed statements that sex between them is, for her, a necessary financial transaction. (When he asks "Do you find me attractive?" she replies: "Yeah, you're great—your cheques never bounce".)

By contrast, the tender pathos of Sylvie's encounter with Gabriel and the unexpected liberation Norman experiences with the promiscuous, noncommittal but emotionally generous Angelo, suggest that true intimacy may be snatched in the unlikeliest of collisions. The characters with the least economic and political power strive most to make contact with others; conversely, Brian and Michael, seemingly with the greatest power to define and gratify their sexual desires, are shown to be the least capable of intimacy, pleasure or reciprocation. For Michael in particular, the exercise of control whether by cataloguing his past conquests in a photographic installation entitled *Memento Mori*, freezing Angelo's "perfect" beauty on endless Polaroids or seducing Jim in order to reject him—is a joyless end in itself.

Shot in colour-tinted black-and-white (itself a distancing device), these unerotic sequences subject not the bodies of the participants to scrutiny but their faces: tense, repressed, indifferent, briefly released—but most often with a tantalising unreadability. Even at their moments of greatest intimacy, Podeswa's characters conceal more than they give away. These crisp duochrome encounters are intercut viewed with extracts, in grainy camcorder colour, from the video Angelo is supposed to be making. The twist is that the interviews he conducts with experts, astronomers, tourists and local traders frenziedly cashing in on eclipse fever—from a woman selling eclipse sweatshirts and beer glasses to a record-shop employee explaining that sales of *Don't Let the Sun*

Go Down On Me and *Total Eclipse of the Heart* are soaring—are in fact documentary footage shot in Baja California, Mexico at the time of the seven-minute solar eclipse of July 1991.

The resulting blurring of fact and fiction is by far *Eclipse*'s most appealing aspect—mainly because it drags the film away from clinical postmodern disengagement in the direction of the kind of larger-than-life social satire practised by Arcand in his better movies (notably *Jesus of Montreal*) and, in another context, by *TV Nation's* Michael Moore. The would-be profound pronouncements of the international eclipse experts are surreally banal beyond fictional invention ("It's like a reversal of nature," drivels one), and a party of Japanese eclipse enthusiasts are nonplussed when asked to describe what it is they have travelled halfway round the world to see. "I don't know—just day turned to night, I guess," one replies. Podeswa achieves his avowed goal of portraying his fictional human relationships with a complex, contradictory realism absent from most films; but he succeeds equally well in showing just how unreal late 20th-century reality can be.

VILLAGE VOICE, 11/21/95, Film Special/p. 24, Michael Atkinson

Story is in short demand as well [the reference is to *Rhythm Thief*] in the Canadian *La Ronde* reincarnation *Eclipse*, wherein a daisy chain of more or less abortive sexual encounters lead up to, for no discernible reason, a major solar eclipse. Like anyone who has endured 1993's *Chain of Desire*, I hoped that this sort of cheaply conceived, dubious portrait of the oversexed body politic was an endangered breed. But it's a cinch to make, like toast. Director Jeremy Podeswa makes sure all of the sketchily draw urbanites, from whore to business man to Latin refugee to club wastrel, have obligatory revealing monologues and lurking pathologies. Toronto is little more than a series of hotel rooms, studios, and nightclubs. The form itself is a hellish strain on credibility and patience—each of the 10 characters has sex twice with two different partners (often strangers) in 24 hours just so the chain will continue, and the sex itself is constantly interruptus to give them occasion for a little social intercourse. And whereas Ophüls's *La Ronde*, the template for so much circularly constructed flummery since, was primarily farcical, Podeswa's film is as grave as war footage.

Adroitly shot in a variety of grains, monochromes, and stocks, *Eclipse* pours on the portents, though I can't imagine why anyone would wonder where and when the liaisons come full circle. You get the sense that if Harrison's budgets grew, so would his ideas; Podeswa's limits, however, hardly seem merely financial.

Also reviewed in:
NEW YORK TIMES, 11/17/95, p. C12, Janet Maslin
VARIETY, 9/19-25/94, p. 79, Brendan Kelly

ENGLISHMAN WHO WENT UP A HILL, BUT CAME DOWN A MOUNTAIN, THE

A Miramax Films release of a Parallax Pictures production. *Executive Producer:* Sally Hibbin, Robert Jones, Bob Weinstein, and Harvey Weinstein. *Director:* Christopher Monger. *Producer:* Sarah Curtis. *Screenplay:* Christopher Monger. *Director of Photography:* Vernon Layton. *Editor:* David Martin. *Music:* Stephen Endelman. *Music Editor:* Todd Kasow. *Sound:* George Richards and (music) James P. Nichols. *Sound Editor:* Rusty Coppleman. *Casting:* Michelle Guish. *Production Designer:* Charles Garrard. *Art Director:* Chris Lowe. *Special Effects:* First Effects. *Costumes:* Janty Yates. *Make-up:* Kezia De Winne. *Running time:* 99 minutes. *MPAA Rating:* PG.

CAST: Hugh Grant (Reginald Anson); Tara Fitzgerald (Betty of Cardiff); Colm Meaney (Morgan the Goat); Ian McNeice (George Garrad); Ian Hart (Johnny Shellshocked); Kenneth Griffith (Reverend Jones); Tudor Vaughn (Thomas Twp); Hugh Vaughn (Thomas Twp Too); Robert Pugh (Williams the Petroleum); Robert Blythe (Ivor the Grocer); Garfield Morgan

(Davies the School); Lisa Palfrey (Blod); Dafydd Wyn Roberts (Tommy Twostrokes); Iuean Rhys (Sergeant); Anwen Williams (Mavis); David Lloyd Meredith (Jones the JP); Fraser Cains (Evans the End of the World); Jack Walters (Grandfather); Harry Kretchmer (Young Boy); Howell Evans (Thomas the Trains); Maisie McNeice (Girl in Classroom).

FILMS IN REVIEW, 7-8/95, p. 61, Pat Anderson

Anyone nostalgic for the great British Ealing comedies (*Kind Hearts And Coronets, The Lavender Hill Mob, Passport to Pimlico*, et al) of the 1950s, will not want to miss *The Englishman Who Went Up A Hill But Came Down A Mountain*. Ealing has been resurrected *pro tem* in Llanarhaedr, Wales. And here the English are played for suckers. The conflict pits this Welsh village against two Englishmen: Reginald Anson (Hugh Grant) and George Garrad (Ian McNeice).

In 1917 Anson and Garrad, both just returned from the war in France, are on an ordnance surveying tour of Wales and their object here is to measure the local mountain, Ffynnon Garw—1,000 feet being the minimum height for the legal designation of a mountain. And we know it's going to be short: by 20 feet.

Incensed, the villagers start muttering about the English changing the boundaries if this border Welsh mountain is discounted, God forbid. They plot a way to add the extra 20 feet. Led by innkeeper Morgan the Goat (Colm Meaney), the first thing they must do is keep the Englishmen from leaving next morning. So, in the middle of the night, Morgan and Ivor the Grocer (Garfield Morgan) collect some sugar to siphon into Anson and Garrard's gas tank, compounded in the morning by a little judicious sabotage by Williams the Petroleum (Robert Pugh). And then it is the turn of Thomas the Trains (Howell Evans), who is coached into insisting there are no trains leaving the station that day.

Now the village is galvanized: Garrad is plied with liquor; Anson is bewitched by the local beauty, Betty (Tara Fitgerald); while Reverend Jones (Kenneth Griffith), the Twp twins Thomas and Thomas Too (Tudor and Hugh Vaughn), Johnny Shellshocked (Ian Hart) and the rest of the village, men and women, proceed to dig up their fields and cart the soil to the top of Ffynnon Garw to make it 1,000 feet tall. But there are all sorts of snags, a death and many shenanigans before the film ends.

Writer/director Christopher Monger has created a very funny, gentle movie based on stories he heard as a child. The admirable cast is made up mostly of local people, while the principals are also all terrific. And certainly Hugh Grant and Colm Meaney will both add to their reputations with this delightful picture.

LOS ANGELES TIMES, 5/12/95, Calendar/p. 1, Kenneth Turan

"The Englishman Who Went Up a Hill but Came Down a Mountain" is an ungainly title for a light romantic trifle. It is, fortunately, the only cumbersome thing about this genteel crackup of a comedy, both deft and daft, that knows exactly how to do exactly what it is doing.

Cumbersome though it is, that title is fitting, because it reflects the quirky character of the Welsh village (here called Ffynnon Garw) where writer-director Christopher Monger grew up. It was a place where most everyone had appellations attached to their names, like Williams the Petroleum, who owned the garage, Davies the School, who taught therein, and Tommy Twostroke, who had possession of the town's only motorbike.

How then, young Monger once asked his grandfather, did a certain Mr. Anson come to be called the Englishman Who etc., etc.? The story he was told, a cherished local tale, is slight of plot, but so much wit and polish has gone into the telling that at its best "Englishman" recalls such cherished Ealing productions as "The Lavender Hill Mob" and "The Ladykillers" that made the 1950s the golden age of British comedy.

Set in 1917, when World War I was at its height, the film begins with the arrival of not one but two thoroughly English gentlemen in Ffynnon Garw. George Garrad (Ian McNeice) and Reginald Anson (Hugh Grant) are a team of cartographers, intent on measuring any and all mountains but not particularly eager to be where they are. "Pleasant enough place," says Anson, with Garrad replying with equal dryness, "I suppose so, given that it's Wales."

This constant English/Welsh sniping goes both ways, for the villagers are not particularly pleased to welcome these interlopers, especially when they realize they have come to measure the nearby summit, also named Ffynnon Garw, a source of intense local pride for being the first mountain inside the Welsh border.

When it turns out, as drama dictates it must, that Ffynnon Garw is just a tad short of the 1,000 feet necessary to be classified a mountain on official maps, a fury envelopes the town. "How could we face those who survived the war," one man passionately puts it, "if we lost the mountain?"

The threat of being dis-mountained even unites the unlikeliest allies, the fiery Rev. Jones (Kenneth Griffith), the guardian of local morality, and the biggest sinner around, innkeeper Morgan the Goat (Colm Meaney), who has taken unfair romantic advantage of the village's wartime lack of able-bodied men.

The idea is to do everything possible to delay the departure of the Englishmen until Ffynnon Garw can be somehow reconfigured and then remeasured. And everything includes getting the help of such village characters as the touched twins Thomas Twp and Thomas Twp, Too and the recruiting of local beauty Betty of Cardiff (Tara Fitzgerald, currently playing Ophelia to Ralph Fiennes' Hamlet in New York) to beguile the gentlemen's time.

Picking up where he left off in "Four Weddings and a Funeral," Hugh Grant proves that he has no current rivals in playing boyish, self-deprecatory, easily flustered and generally abashed young men who are awfully cute in the bargain. His performance is completely charming and nicely balances the work of Colm Meaney (familiar from "The Commitments" and "The Snapper") as the rough but canny Morgan.

Although writer-director Monger has worked in Hollywood without creating a stir, returning to his native Wales has proved a revivifying experience. "Englishmen" is notable for the pleasure it takes in language of all types, from the witty spoken word to the feast of knowing looks and smiles its characters indulge themselves in. Movies like this must be done just right to succeed, and, except for that title, "Englishman" has everything under the best kind of control.

NEW YORK POST, 5/12/95, p. 42, Michael Medved

"The Englishman Who Went Up a Hill But Came Down a Mountain" deserves to generate theater lines every bit as long as its unwieldy title.

This is an enchanting and original film that will leave its audiences feeling "mountain" high.

Based on a family legend passed on to writer-director Christopher Monger by his grandfather, the movie recreates a whimsical Welsh village in 1917.

At the height of World War I, the English authorities dispatch two surveyors (Hugh Grant and Ian McNeice) into Wales to prepare more accurate maps that will play a role in the national defense.

They stop first at the town of Ffynnon Garw (pronounced Finnen Garoo), perpetually proud of the fact that it's grown up in the shadow of "The First Mountain in Wales."

Unfortuntately, the cartographers explain that this natural wonder can only be designated as an official "mountain" if it's more than a thousand feet high, and definitive measurement shows the "hill" is only 984 feet.

Led by the elderly idealist Reverend Jones (indelibly played by the splendid Kenneth Griffith), the townspeople will do anything to preserve their local pride. "If this isn't a mountain then they might as well redraw the border and put us all in England, God forbid," they reason.

While the village unites in desperate measures to make their local peak rise to the occasion, the libidinous local inn keeper Morgan the Goat (the formidable Colm Meaney) conspires to keep the two map makers in town so they'll measure the hill again.

For that purpose, he deploys a maid played by the sensationally pretty Tara Fitzgerald (of "Hear My Song") to turn the head of the inevitable shy and bumbling Hugh Grant.

Filmmaker Monger (who previously crafted the uninspired Shirley MacLaine vehicle "Waiting for the Light") tells this strange little tale with such intoxicating affection for his native Wales and its people that the movie feels as nourishing to the spirit as a leisurely vacation at a cozy country inn during glorious spring weather.

Monger's cameras captures the hilly Welsh landscape with its patchwork fields and meadows in 200 different shades of green, shooting every detail in every scene the way an infatuated admirer might photograph the glowing body of his beloved.

Grant displays the same vulnerable boyish charm that made "Four Weddings and a Funeral" a smash hit, and Fitzgerald (who seemed unaccountably wan in their previous pairing in "Sirens") he provides him with admirable on-screen chemistry.

Meanwhile, the villagers of Ffynnon Garw—mostly played by real-life Welsh villagers who've never acted before—emerge with the fond, daffy and bittersweet flavor of the Dylan Thomas play "Under Milkwood."

You certainly learn the definition of the Welsh word "Twp" (pronounced "Tup," and meaning daft or batty) as you meet Johnny Shellshocked (home from the war with addled brains) and the dim local twins Thomas Twp and Thomas Twp Too.

In any event, moviegoers would have to be twp, too—or at least shellshocked—to allow themselves to miss the experience of the this splendidly satisfying and Hughgely entertaining motion picture.

NEWSDAY, 5/12/95, Part II/p. B2, John Anderson

Size matters. It determines confidence and self-esteem. It is especially important during times of stress, or loss, or national emergency.

It is, in other words, no laughing matter. Not for the people of Ffynnon Garw, the quaint Welsh folk who populate "The Englishman Who Went Up a Hill, But Came Down a Mountain." They take physical proportion and spatial displacement seriously. Movie audiences, however, may find Christopher Monger's Welsh-centric story amusing—and the increasingly popular Hugh Grant as boyishly charming as ever—even if the film is basically a situation comedy with a heavy bias toward situation.

The year is 1917, the young men of Wales are being slaughtered in France at the behest of their English governors, and as part of the war effort two English surveyors—the young and bemused Reginald Anson (Grant) and the goiterish George Garrad (Ian McNeice)—arrive to take measurements. It's a tense situation: Ffynnon Garw the town is named for Ffynnon Garw the mountain, a noted landmark that symbolizes local identity. So when Anson and Garrad report that their "mountain" is only 984 feet high—16 feet short of official mountainhood—the townsfolk decide to do something about it.

Much of the action concerns the nearly endless parade of earthmoving Welsh, who—by bucket, wheelbarrow and horsecart—make a mountain out of a hillock. And while it does take bravado to give a film such an lengthy title (hereafter referred to as "TEWWUAHBCDAM"), writer-director Christopher Monger never displays it on screen. His is an affectionate, if never particularly stimulating, portrait of a town and its people.

Keeping surveyors Anson and Garrad from leaving town before the mountain is finished occupies a plot of predictable screen time, but there's an array of eccentrics doing the work: the red-haired Morgan the Goat (Colm Meaney), who since the beginning of the war has begat a schoolroom's worth of ginger-headed babies about town; the Rev. Jones, Morgan's apoplectic bête noir, who's given a wonderfully twitchy performance by Kenneth Griffith; and Johnny Shellshocked (Ian Hart), a battle veteran who's a walking, and seldom talking, reminder of the horrors on the continent.

As the semi-bawdy Betty of Cardiff, Tara Fitzgerald, who starred with Grant in "Sirens," is his love interest here. Theirs is a curious chemistry in "TEWWUAHBCDAM": With her smoky, throaty voice and his natural delicacy, they gravitate toward an androgynous kind of Jazz-Age coupling. But Grant is a chameleon; his screen charm is like a series of tectonic plates that shift with each change in atmosphere, although nothing like a tremor ever results. Not in Ffynnon Garw, anyway.

SIGHT AND SOUND, 8/95, p. 47, Jo Comino

In 1917, two Englishmen, Reginald Anson and George Garrad, working for H.M. Ordnance Survey, arrive in the village of Ffynnon Garw, South Wales, in order to measure the local vantage-point, also called Ffynnon Garw. They put up at the pub run by the euphemistically-named Morgan the Goat. Only elevations above 1,000 feet qualify as mountains, and according to regional folklore Ffynnon Garw is the first mountain within the Welsh border. Betting on its height intensifies but accurate measurement reveals that Ffynnon Garw is, at 984 feet, only a hill after all. The villagers are devastated.

Reverend Jones calls a meeting at which it is decided to try and add the extra 20 feet to Ffynnon Garw so that it can qualify as a mountain. Various plots are hatched to detain the Englishmen while the work is carried out, including putting sugar in their car's petrol tank, slashing their tyres, and denying that passenger trains run from the railway station. Morgan's ultimate ploy is to summon an old flame, Betty from Cardiff, hoping her feminine wiles will persuade the Englishmen to dally awhile.

A torrential downpour results in further delay but also causes the earthworks to subside. Williams the Petroleum and Johnny Shellshocked—the brother of Blod, another of Morgan's girlfriends—are despatched up the hill with a tarpaulin. Lightning flashes precipitate one of Johnny's seizures. A rift between Morgan and Blod, who is upset by Betty's presence at the pub, ensues. As the rain persists Garrad sinks into a gin-sodden stupor while Anson, reticent at first, grows more intimate with Betty. On Sunday, after three days of rain, the sun comes out. Morgan attempts to persuade Reverend Jones to sanction work on the Sabbath so the project can be completed. The minister finds his own spiritual justification and exhorts his congregation to labour for Ffynnon Garw. Anson, assisted by Betty, agrees to undertake a new measurement. Applause breaks out as Johnny overcomes his phobias to wheel a barrowful of turf to the summit.

Just before sunset—with work nearing completion—Reverend Jones collapses and dies. His final wish is to be buried on the mountain top. Nevertheless, once the burial is over and the mound finished there is insufficient light for Anson to make an accurate calculation. He and Betty spend the night on the peak, descending next morning to a rapturous village to announce their engagement and a conclusive result—Ffynnon Garw is now officially a mountain.

Apart from a title of parabolic proportions, *The Englishman Who went Up a Hill, But Came Down a Mountain*—based on a semi-autobiographical story by Christopher Monger, a Welsh director living and working in Los Angeles—is remarkable in terms of its timing. Between Hugh Grant signing into the project and the production stage of the film came the runaway success of *Four Weddings and a Funeral*, and subsequently Grant's status has been thrown into doubt by his arrest for "lewd behaviour" in LA. Thus, a film which had become a star vehicle may now be adversely affected.

In a scenario where nationalities, Welsh and English, are pitted against one another in mock antagonism, Grant is cast as the sympathetic Englishman of the title and as a romantic lead who has to be coaxed into intimacy in a village dominated by a red-haired satyr. With his edges nicely blurred, Grant has free rein and an ideal screenplay for turning out a slightly understated reprise of his performance in *Four Weddings*. The whole range of mannerisms is up for grabs: the diffident grimace, the hand brushing aside the lock of hair that flops into the eye, the hint of a stutter. Costume details are strangely distracting in their appropriateness: crisp shirts, warm tweedy breeches with braces, Christopher Robin-like rainwear and galoshes. At one point there's even an elaborate plot device whereby Grant as Anson is compelled to lend Morgan the Goat his last clean shirt so that he can attend chapel with a semblance of respectability. The real reason seems to be to enable Grant to achieve an even softer look by means of a grandad vest at a key stage in his romance with Betty from Cardiff (Tara Fitzgerald, trying to match the stilted animal magnetism of Jennifer Jones in Powell and Pressburger's *Gone To Earth*). It all adds up to an impression of immense but fragile likeability. At one point Anson reveals to Betty that he, like Johnny Shellshocked, is a casualty of trench trauma, as if there's a need to justify his personality traits. "It's alright," he exclaims, "I'm alright, really I am." We know he is. He epitomises the ideal Englishman, his utter politeness reinforcing a set of certainties which his self-deprecatory manner immaculately undercuts. Like Christopher Monger, who 15 years ago was based firmly within the British independent sector at Chapter Arts Workshop in Cardiff, and whose more recent career has alternated between making films for S4C and Hollywood, *The Englishmen* is a hybrid. It deals with a discrete, indigenous community thrown into relief by the incursion of observing outsiders for the benefit of an audience of outsiders. The Welsh community portrayed here is depicted with a mixture of doughty characterisation (especially in the cases of Kenneth Griffith as Reverend Jones and Colm Meaney as Morgan the Goat) and caricature—take, for example, the obtuse sense of logic behind the naming of names which kicks off the narrative. For all the mythic qualities of Ffynnon Gawr, which are well-served by the cinematically stylish use of the mid-Wales landscape, we're placed firmly by the side of the Englishmen, benign onlookers at a whimsical, contained and fairly vapid spectacle.

VILLAGE VOICE, 5/16/95, p. 52, Georgia Brown

A mountain of promotion has been built around—and a spot in Cannes's *Un Certain Regard* competition secured for—a Miramax molehill quaintly titled *The Englishman Who Went Up a Hill but Came Down a Mountain*, hereafter to be known as *Hugh*. Apparently, Grant committed himself to Christopher Monger's coy farce before *Four Weddings and a Funeral* became the thing it became. For all I know, which is nothing, this new vehicle will prove another Hugh success.

I doubt it though. The average moviegoer's tolerance for pseudo-Welsh whimsy would have to be as high as Everest, and even Hugh as the Englishman hardly cuts a romantic swath. The tentative, stuttering, nice Mr. Anson is a roving cartographer for His Majesty's Ordinance Survey. He and a chubby, surly partner (Ian McNeice) arrive by motorcar in the Welsh village Ffynnon Garw for the purpose of measuring the local "mountain," also called Ffynnon Garw. They trek up F.G., but when they come down pronounce it, um, er, "a hill." It lacks 16 feet of the 1000 needed to qualify. Their pride at stake, the villagers contrive to keep the surveyors occupied while, toting buckets of dirt, they make up the necessary height.

The movie takes place in 1917, when all able-bodied men are off in places like Verdun getting shelled and gassed. This makes for jokes about the proliferation of babies resembling the randy innkeeper, Morgan the Goat (played by the gifted Colm Meaney, the dad in *The Snapper*). One of Morgan's women friends is Betty of Cardiff (Tara Fitzgerald, currently Ralph Fiennes's Ophelia), a serving maid at a nearby stately home. She's enlisted as bait to waylay shy Mr. Anson, and a most improbable romance blooms late in the picture.

I'm wondering who the audience for this kind of picturesque fluff might be. About six minutes into the picture, I felt trapped—as in a submarine. Gritting my teeth, I made it, barely.

Also reviewed in:
CHICAGO TRIBUNE, 5/12/95, Friday/p. F, Michael Wilmington
NEW YORK TIMES, 5/12/95, p. C16, Janet Maslin
NEW YORKER, 5/15/95, p. 96, Terrence Rafferty
VARIETY, 5/8-14/95, p. 65, Leonard Klady
WASHINGTON POST, 5/12/95, p. B1, Hal Hinson
WASHINGTON POST, 5/12/95, Weekend/p. 48, Desson Howe

ERMO

An Arrow Releasing presentation of an Ocean Film Co. Ltd. production in association with Shanghai Film Studio. *Executive Producer:* Li Ran. *Producer:* Jimmy Tan and Chen Kumming. *Director:* Zhou Xiaowen. *Screenplay (Mandarin with English subtitles):* Lang Yun. *Based on the short story:* Xu Baoqi. *Director of Photography:* Lu Gengxin. *Editor:* Zhong Furong. *Music:* Zhou Xiaowen. *Sound:* Hong Yi. *Art Director:* Zhang Daqian. *Set Designer:* Ma Ying and Tian Zhang. *Costumes:* Liu Qingli. *Make-up:* Lu Yingchun. *Running time:* 93 minutes. *MPAA Rating:* Not Rated.

CAST: Alia (Ermo); Liu Peiqi (Xiazi, "Blind"); Ge Zhijun (Ermo's Husband, Village Chief); Zhang Haiyan (Xiazi's Wife); Yan Zhenguo (Huzi, Ermo's Son); Yang Xiao (Xiu'er, Xiazi's Daughter).

LOS ANGELES TIMES, 6/5/95, Calendar/p. 4, Kelvin Thomas

Zhou Xiaowen's "Ermo," a bemused but compassionate riff on the eternal human comedy, takes its title from its peasant heroine (Alia) with a much-older, now impotent husband (Ge Zhijun) and their young son. Ermo supports her family working like a slave making noodles. Meanwhile, her fat and lazy next-door neighbor (Zhang Haiyan) not only has a lean, hard-working husband (Liu Peiqi) with a truck but also a color TV.

The entire film turns upon Ermo's determination to get a bigger set than her neighbor, and its unfolding allows for considering a wide range of questions of values and priorities. While Zhou is concerned with the impact of freer money—and also sexual attitudes—on China in general and Ermo in particular, he doesn't judge her.

NEW YORK POST, 5/12/95, p. 47, Thelma Adams

Meet "Ermo." She's tall, thin, shrewd, hardworking—she'd sell her last pint of blood to buy a 29-inch color TV.

In Zhou Xiaowen's contemporary Chinese comedy, Ermo (Alia) is an endearing but flawed figure of fun on the rural landscape.

She makes twisted noodles from scratch to sell at market. The first step is mixing the batter the old-fashioned way: with her feet.

The noodle-maker's home life isn't ideal. Her husband is impotent; her son's only joy is watching TV next door.

Ermo's neighbor, Blindman, so-called because of his small, close-set eyes, is as industrious as she is. His wife, Fat Woman, leads a life of relative luxury in the squat little mountain town on the edge of nowhere: she owns a color TV.

Ermo's nearly irrational desire to buy a TV bigger than that of her neighbors launches a chain of events that ultimately overwhelms her. The moral of this pleasing, small-scale, keeping-up-with-the-Joneses comedy is a familiar one: beware of what you wish for, you might just get it.

NEWSDAY, 5/12/95, Part II/p. B7, John Anderson

Is it money that's the root of all evil, or is it TV? In the China of "Ermo," its both. And according to veteran Chinese director Zhou Xiaowen, when the subsistence-level esthetic of the mysterious East meets the voracious, consumerist, couch-potato ethic of the decadent West, there's simply no contest. No contest at all.

In Zhou's dryly witty but ultimately saddening "Ermo," the title character (Alia) develops from a dissatisfied wife, mother and noodle vendor into the Madame Bovary of the idiot box: She'll risk everything—not over sex or boredom, but for the chance to watch "Oprah."

In what must be a salute to media surrender, Ermo and her relations are presented in classic sit-com-family style, devoid of history: Ermo's husband, Chief (Ge Zhijun), who in fact hasn't been the village chief in years, is considerably older than Ermo and impotent. Why they married or when is not explained; how their young son occurred isn't mentioned either. Theirs is an unhappy lot, with Ermo substituting work for sex; when she rises before dawn to knead noodle dough with her freshly washed and floured feet, the act possesses an erotic quality that transcends hemisphere.

Exacerbating Ermo's sexless, labor-intensive misery is her neighbor—referred to in the press notes as Fat Woman (Zhang Haiyan)—a well-fed harpy whose TV set has seduced Ermo's son. It's an unaffordable luxury for Ermo, who lives in a tightly shuttered world, undisturbed by the light of possibility—until Fat Woman's husband, Blindman (Liu Peiqi), introduces her to the joys of capitalism, tapping a relentless flow of entrepreneurial instinct.

Unlike other recent Chinese films, the enemy here isn't Mao or feudal ignorance. It's greed. But Zhou treats it like the apple in the Garden—this is Ermo's enlightenment, regardless of the ends. And along with the new view of evil comes a new look at modern peasantry: These folks are no simple country folk, mild in manner or pure of thought. The way Fat Woman and Ermo insult each other, they could become permanent guests of Sally Jessy Raphael. So who needs TV?

Ermo begins by poisoning Fat Woman's pig and ends up sleeping with her husband. She's ignorant, and cheap: when Blindman proposes to buy her lunch, she reacts almost violently to the "waste" of money. When Blindman gets her a job in a big city restaurant and a co-worker is injured, she's in anguish over donating blood—until she gets paid for it. Then she's willing to be drained.

Is Ermo a product of creeping Westernism? Somewhat. Her hair is set in a rather un-Chinese bob, and tradition means nothing to her. She has an insolent habit of spitting on her thumb—in order to count her money—that hints at a mercenary soul. She has the avarice gene; it's just been suppressed.

The sound of the film is full of delicate accessories: A crow laughs when Ermo buys her TV; the shrill cry of "twisted noodles!" that Ermo bellows in the marketplace echoes in various other sequences. Visually, Zhou relies on some standard Chinese cinematic anchors: the recurring portal, a formalized way of acknowledging change; the repeated shots of Ermo's noodle dough being pushed through a sieve, a metaphor for dreams and possibility, and the dusty wasteland that exists between the village and city, which presents the opportunity for reconsidering one's path.

When Zhou has an enormous sow walk through a scene, it's clearly a symbol, too—a bit unfair, perhaps, but befitting the general tenor of the piece. Ermo is tragic in the end, though, sitting beside her TV, an NFL game she can't possibly understand illuminating her dirt-floor hut. She's realized a dream, and found it means nothing. In this, Ermo is more than a symptom of cultural disintegration; she's part of an epidemic.

SIGHT AND SOUND, 7/95, p. 47, Tony Rayns

A village in North China. Ermo works hard making and selling twisted noodles to support her supposedly disabled husband (the former village chief) and their son Huzi, who is constantly going next door to watch television. She regularly trades insults with her overweight neighbour, mother of a girl named Xiu'er, but gets on well enough with Xiu'er's father, nicknamed Xiazi ('Blind'), who is the owner-driver of a truck. While her husband dreams of building a bigger house, Ermo determines to buy a television set of her own. Meanwhile, she attacks her hated neighbour by poisoning her pig.

Xiazi cajoles her into joining him in a trip to the nearest town, where she finds that she can sell her noodles at a much higher price—and sees a hugely expensive 29-inch television set in the department store. Ermo begins making frequent visits to town with Xiazi, and her husband begins to suspect them of having an affair. Xiazi finds her a job in the kitchens of a new restaurant; she stays in a cheap hostel and makes only occasional trips back to the village, compulsively saving her money. When she discovers that the hospital pays for blood donations she becomes a frequent blood donor, and her health begins to suffer.

During a drive back to the village one night, Xiazi stalls his truck and gropes her. They become lovers, but Xiazi is horrified to learn that she regularly sells blood and orders her to stop. Puzzled by receiving a fatter pay-packet than other workers at the restaurant, Ermo discovers that Xiazi has been secretly boosting her wages. Outraged at being treated like a whore, she quits the job and returns home, resuming her old job making and selling twisted noodles. Xiazi considerately deflects gossip from her by sleeping with a town prostitute and getting himself beaten up by her pimp.

By the time that New Year comes around, Ermo has saved enough to buy the 29-inch television set. Her noodle-strainer is pressed into service as an antenna. But she collapses from exhaustion and apparent anaemia soon after the set is switched on. Many villagers are soon visiting Ermo's house to watch television. But the only place to put the set is on the bed, and so Ermo and her husband and son sleep as best they can on wooden chairs.

In the story and character of Ermo, 'Fifth Generation' director Zhou Xiaowen has found a perfect cypher for the meaning and effect of change in rural China. Comparisons will obviously be drawn with Zhang Yimou's *The Story of Qiu Ju*—not only because it's about another feisty peasant woman with a mission, but also because Liu Peiqi (who played Qiu Ju's injured husband) reappears here as Xiazi, the richest man in the village—but *Ermo* rather cruelly exposes the political sleight-of-hand that underpins Qiu Ju. Zhou's film doesn't look or pretend to be like documentary, and has no pretension to make grand statements about the reliability of officials or the credibility of China's new legal system; it simply tells a story about a young woman who has the misfortune to get what she thinks she wants. The real comparison ought to be with Li Shaohong's brilliant *Bloody Morning (Xuese Qingchen*, 1990), the only recent film to offer a truthful and shocking account of all the obstacles to change in the Chinese countryside.

Ermo begins and ends with the sound of Ermo selling her twisted noodles by the roadside. The opening, a tightly-framed shot of Ermo squatting beside her food cart which becomes the film's visual leitmotiv, is scrupulously naturalistic. The ending, a slow track in on the 'snow' on the television screen after the close of broadcasting with the sound of Ermo's street-cry overlaid, is calculatedly ironic: it summarises the distance Ermo has travelled while underlining the emptiness of all she has achieved. In between, the film shows a tough but uneducated peasant woman struggling to come to terms with a barrage of new experiences: eating out in a restaurant, working in a semi-automated kitchen, selling her blood, buying a television set and being unfaithful to her wreck of a husband. She learns quickly but pragmatically, picking up only what she needs to know and never acquiring any larger perspective. The core of her experience remains the backbreaking work through which she supports her husband and son: the nights spent kneading dough with her feet, extruding noodles through the manual press and hanging them to dry on racks in the yard. Zhou's film is not a sentimental account of her 'education' but a cunningly formulated question. What, it asks, is the true nature of *satisfaction* in present-day China?

Zhou is smart enough to know that this question is as funny as it is tragic, and his film reflects that ambivalence precisely. But although Ermo's naivete generates much of the film's humour, Zhou never tries to get laughs at her expense. When Ermo first sees the television set in the town store, for example, it's playing a Chinese-dubbed tape of a western softcore sex film to a silent, rapt audience of peasants. Ermo registers her bafflement that the foreigners are speaking Chinese, but the real 'joke' is far more complex. What does it mean to show a shoddy foreign sex movie to people who have never met a foreigner or, indeed, travelled any further than the nearest county town? Like all peasants everywhere, these people have a matter-of-fact attitude to their own sexuality, but they also have a clear-cut sense of (Confucian) morality. Will seeing this sanitised foreign sex affect their thinking about sex itself. If so, how? Is watching this tape one of the factors that later convinces Ermo to betray her husband and succumb to Xiazi's advances? These are all funny/serious questions, and the film savours them—and many others like them—as such.

Zhou shoots the film almost entirely from static angles, trusting his compositions and choice of detail within the frame to produce all the questions and contradictions. (The only camera movements are tracking shots towards the television screen and occasional shots following foreground action.) This decision minimises the impact of visual rhetoric and throws the emphasis instead on to Zhou's very exact social observations, which are strong enough to take the weight. Everything is anchored in believable sociological detail: the weight problem of Xiazi's wife (reflecting his affluence and her consequent self-indulgence), the canniness of the peasant whose donkey is knocked over by Xiazi's terminally battered truck, the contrasted attitudes of state-employed shop assistants (rude) and privately employed restaurant staff (parroting courtesies), the squalor of the 'hotel' where Xiazi takes Ermo for sex and the grotesqueness of the anti-wrinkle cream he buys her as a gift. The fact that all of this rings so true depends to a large extent on Zhou's expert casting. Mongolian actress Alia (who made her screen debut in Zhou's long-banned *Black Mountain/Heishan Lu*, 1990) gives a truly fearless performance in the lead, and the actors around her match her absorption in the manners and gestures of peasant life.

The last thing seen on the television set which usurps Ermo's much-needed place on the family bed is the international weather forecast: the coming day's climate and temperatures in Tokyo, Bangkok, London ... This is both naturalistic (China's CCTV does indeed close its broadcasting each day with this forecast) and another of Zhou Xiaowen's seriously absurdist jokes. That information about tomorrow's weather in Europe is available to villagers in North China undoubtedly represents 'progress', but what does this progress mean? Ermo, of course, doesn't care what appears on the television screen; English lessons, American football and episodes of *Dynasty* are all the same to her. All she cared about was owning the biggest television set in the region, and she got it. As Zhou himself observes: "I love Ermo, because she's selfish and she's honest".

VILLAGE VOICE, 5/16/95, p. 61, Sally Eckoff

In a typical suburban comedy, you know something's up when you see a long shot of the neighborhood at night, all the identical houses dark and asleep but one. It apparently works the same in China: the person who can't sleep here is Ermo, a housewife who's incensed over a neighbor's TV.

Shot in an arid, mountainous region, *Ermo* is Zhou Xiaowen's ninth feature. Despite this landscape, the film is intimate, rich in detail, and bubbly with humor that doesn't go flat. Ermo attacks every day with mysterious zeal, making noodles to sell in the village, an apparently backbreaking job that her ailing husband and little son can do nothing to ease. The thorn in her side is Fat Woman, who lives next door and has a television that's not only the biggest one in what seems like creation but the only set in town. Tiger, Ermo's son, is getting addicted to it. Fat Woman's husband, Blindman, is an entrepreneurial wizard, while Ermo's mate, Chief, can't work, seems to be impotent, and doesn't want a big appliance in the house. One day, Fat Woman (hilariously played by Zhang Haiyan, chain smoking in a fuchsia jacket) tosses a pan of dirty water onto Ermo's twisty noodles and starts an all-out war. As Ermo, the fresh-faced actress Alia maintains the appearance of being more entertained than horrified. Her well-timed comic turns pop out strongly from the rough chaotic backdrops of village traffic and household drudgery. No matter how stressful the proceedings, the film is deftly funny.

The camera loves the constantly changing expressions of Ermo's scheming face, as well as the image of dough being laboriously pressed through a sieve, coming out the other side in snaky strands. That's our heroine: squeezed painfully through the mold of life, she's as common as a noodle. Zhou Xiaowen makes her story delicious.

Also reviewed in:
CHICAGO TRIBUNE, 8/4/95, Tempo/p. 3, Michael Wilmington
NEW REPUBLIC, 6/12/95, p. 33, Stanley Kauffmann
NEW YORK TIMES, 5/12/95, p. C10, Caryn James
VARIETY, 8/15-21/94, p. 44, Derek Elley
WASHINGTON POST, 6/9/95, p. B7, Hal Hinson
WASHINGTON POST, 6/9/95, Weekend/p. 42, Desson Howe

EROTIQUE

An Odyssey Group release of a Brandon Chase production in association with Group 1/Trigon/Tedypoly Films. *Running time:* 90 minutes. *MPAA Rating:* Not Rated

LET'S TALK ABOUT SEX—*Executive Producer:* Marianne Chase. *Producer:* Christopher Wood and Vicky Herman. *Director:* Lizzie Borden. *Screenplay:* Lizzie Borden and Susie Bright. *Based on a story by:* Lizzie Borden. *Director of Photography:* Larry Banks. *Editor:* Richard Fields. *Music:* Andrew Belling. *Sound:* James Thornton. *Casting:* Jerold Franks. *Production Designer:* Jane Ann Stewart. *Art Director:* Patrice Begovich. *Set Decorator:* Carla Weber. *Costumes:* Jolie Jiminez.

CAST: Kamala Lopez-Dawson (Rosie); Bryan Cranston (Dr. Robert Stern); Liane Curtis (Murphy).

TABOO PARLOR—*Producer:* Monika Treut and Michael Sombetzki. *Director:* Monika Treut. *Screenplay:* Monika Treut. *Director of Photography:* Elfi Mikesch. *Editor:* Steve Brown. *Sound:* Wolfgang Schukrafft. *Production Designer:* Petra Korink. *Costumes:* Susann Klindtwort.

CAST: Priscilla Barnes (Claire); Camilla Soeberg (Jukia); Michael Carr (Victor); Peter Kern (Franz); Marianne Sagebrecht (Hilde).

WONTON SOUP—*Producer:* Teddy Robin Kwan and Eddie Ling-Ching Fong. *Director:* Clara Law. *Screenplay:* Eddie Ling-Ching Fong. *Director of Photography:* Arthur Wong. *Music:* Tats Lau. *Editor:* Jill Bilcock. *Sound:* Gary Wilkins. *Casting:* Jerold Franks. *Production Designer:* Eddie Mok. *Running time:* 91 minutes. *MPAA Rating:* Not Rated.

CAST: Tim Lounibos (Adrian); Hayley Man (Ann); Choi Hark-kin (Uncle).

LOS ANGELES TIMES, 1/20/95, Calendar/p. 12, Kevin Thomas

The witty, steamy and audacious "Erotique" is composed of three deft, sexy tales from three of today's most venturesome female filmmakers—the U.S.' Lizzie Borden, Germany's Monika Treut and Hong Kong's Clara Law.

Although the film has been rated NC-17 for explicit sex, "Erotique" is not actually hard-core. The filmmakers' clear intent is not pornographic but rather to express a woman's bemused, often complex, view of sexuality. "Erotique," which has ample nudity and blunt language, is a stylish film with an attractive, capable cast that is definitely for sophisticated adults only.

Opening the film is Borden's "Let's Talk About Sex," which she wrote with well-known sex commentator Susie Bright. Vivacious Kamala Lopez-Dawson plays a struggling L.A. Latina actress who supports herself working at a phone sex agency, where she's becoming as fed up with fulfilling male fantasies as she is with discrimination in competing for acting roles. One day, however, she encounters a caller (Bryan Cranston) who is "man enough" to hear out her sexual fantasies. What happens next is delightfully unexpected, amusing and insightful.

Treut's "Taboo Parlor," set in Hamburg, finds lesbian lovers Claire (Priscilla Barnes) and Julia (Camilla Soeberg) deciding to pick up a man, Victor (Michael Carr), in a nightclub. He's arrogant and macho, but Treut is not content in giving him his comeuppance during fun and games with Claire and Julia, saving him for a fate that many—men, especially—will feel is rather too dire. Even so, "Taboo Parlor" is effectively outrageous. There are cameos by familiar faces: Peter Kern, as the nightclub's bartender, and Marianne Sagebrecht, as its emcee.

Arguably, Law's "Wonton Soup" saves the best for the last. It's the funniest, boldest and the most substantial of the episodes. An Australian Chinese, Adrian (Tim Lounibos), visiting Hong Kong for the first time, is having an amorous reunion after six months with Ann (Hayley Man), whom he met at college in Melbourne.

Eager for more passionate sex, Adrian turns to ancient Chinese sexual techniques, which leads to one of the most hilarious love scenes imaginable. The sequence, however, gives way to the underlying serious, potentially alienating, issue of cultural identity.

Both Adrian and Ann find skyscraper-ridden Hong Kong not very Chinese, and Ann craves to feel truly Chinese while Adrian admits that, try as he might, he cannot feel Chinese at all.

NEW YORK POST, 5/5/95, p. 37, Thelma Adams

What do women want? You won't find out watching "Erotique," an omnibus tease directed by Lizzie Borden, Monika Treut and Clara Law.

Borden made "Working Girls" (1985), one of the best films to demystify prostitution. The director sets her new fantasy, "Let's Talk About Sex," in a Los Angeles phone-sex factory. An attractive Latina actress wannabe, Kamala Lopez-Dawson, tires of dishing out male fantasies over the phone for money. When she varies from the formula and reveals her own dreams, her callers hang up—except for one. When their connection gets too heavy, her "regular" hangs up too. The obsessed actress calls on a butch woman cop to find the man for some al fresco fun and sex games.

Lopez-Dawson wants "a real man who'll get off on my fantasies for a change." But her dreams of dominance and submission, queenly postures and police uniforms, candlelit retreats and sponge baths, are the stuff of steamy daytime soaps.

What's the most fascinating, if not the most titillating, is the office routine at phone sex central: the slobby boss' constant badgering, the shabby surroundings, a frumpy woman knitting while talking dirty. Life's no party on the professional sex party line and, like "Working Girls," Borden's blunt style suits the near-documentary feel of these sequences.

Treut, the director of "Bondage" (1983) and "My Father Is Coming" (1991), doesn't seem to care if men get off on her fantasy. The German filmmaker follows a pair of upscale lesbians (Priscilla Barnes and Camilla Soeberg) as they cruise a Hamburg sex club looking for a man with whom to toy.

"Taboo Parlor" has the same pose-y, self-conscious feeling as Borden's short. Characters display flesh but aren't fleshed out. In a moment out of a trendy circus side show, actress Marianne Sagebrecht ("Bagdad Cafe") has a dance-on part as a dominatrix at a shipboard bar. The segment ends with a man-hating act so vicious it's not only unerotic, it's unforgivable.

By the time Clara Law's "Wonton Soup" arrives as the final course, the idea of mixing sex with love seems like a refreshing novelty. An Australian-Chinese boy (Tim Lounibos) visits Hong Kong to reunite with his Chinese-born college sweetheart (Hayley Man). Their first embrace after six months of separation is charged with passion and emotion.

The attractive pair are on the verge of a break-up. The cultural and emotional divide separating them is never as clear as it should be, but the boy's efforts to retrieve the romance provide the movie's most creative sex scene. He researches the ancient Chinese art of lovemaking and then dives in. During a strenuously athletic, buck-naked sequence, Lounibos and Man perform a dozen inventive positions (think wheelbarrow) with Man laughing most of the time.

The visually accomplished Law ("Temptation of a Monk") offers a love letter to Hong Kong, a city on the verge of breaking with the past and entering what could be considered an arranged marriage. This beautifully shot, bittersweet dimension underscores the only segment with emotional pull.

Who can say what women want, but I always find sex more erotic when it's coupled with real feeling, not just appetite.

NEWSDAY, 5/5/95, Part II/p. B2, Jack Mathews

The concept of "Erotique," an anthology of horny short stories made by, about and presumably for women of the '90s, gives the impression that it might double as an instructional film for men who don't know the difference between making love to a woman and hot-wiring a Lexus. But beware guys, there are more insults here than helpful hints, and a couple of fantasies that you won't want to try at home.

I can't be too specific about the depiction of men, since they deliver the punchlines to two of the three stories. But here's a clue: If you have a power tool lying around somewhere, identify with it.

The three independent filmmakers who contributed to this pastiche of gamy international erotica are America's Lizzie Borden ("Love Crimes"), Germany's Monika Treut ("Female Misbehavior") and Hong Kong's Clara Law ("Autumn Moon"). All three were paying attention when they were told to make the sex raw, raunchy and vigorous, but Law completely missed the point that they were to be anti-men.

Law's "Wonton Soup" is the only one of the three half-hour stories that deals with sex in a romantic context, and it is by far the most substantial. Amidst the sleek skyscrapers of westernized Hong Kong, a young Chinese woman's passionate reunion with her Australian-born Chinese boyfriend is tested by her growing fear of losing touch with her culture.

Realizing that his western arrogance is driving a wedge between them, Adrian (Tim Lounibos) takes a crash course in Chinese cooking and memorizes a book's worth of ancient Chinese sexual positions, all of which he tries out with Ann (Hayley Man) in one hilariously sweaty romp in a Hong Kong high rise.

In the end, there is not much hope for Adrian becoming truly Chinese, but it's the thought that counts.

The sensitivity theme underscores Borden's "Let's Talk About Sex" as well. In this soft-porn story, a Los Angeles telephone sex operator named Rosie (Kamala Lopez-Dawson) is about to lose her job because she keeps trying to talk to callers about *her* sexual fantasies. When one man does show interest, she draws him into an increasingly elaborate slave fantasy, which she eventually decides to enact for real.

Treut's "Taboo Parlor" is a black comedy about a pair of lesbian lovers (Camilla Soeberg and "Three's Company's" Priscilla Barnes) who pick up a narcissistic stud in a decadent Hamburg nightclub and bring him back to their apartment for a menage a trois that, for him, gives new meaning to the term unsafe sex.

All three episodes are well made and acted, and promote the theme that women have a right to their own fantasies and pleasures, regardless of how bizarre they may seem to men. If that comes as a shock to you, "Erotique" is too late to help.

VILLAGE VOICE, 5/9/95, p. 76, Laurie Stone

The heavy breathing films that make up *Erotique* are the work of three women: Lizzie Borden from the U.S., Monika Treut from Germany, and Clara Law from Hong Kong. In all, the female characters come out on top, rather than paying for pleasure with death or aloneness. What do women want? To live out the stroke movies playing in their heads.

Law's entry, "Wonton Soup" is the least lubricous, alternating between ponderous talk and sweaty sex, as an Australian-born Chinese man woos his drifting lover with ancient Chinese sexual stunts. The middle film, Treut's "Taboo Parlor" is juicier, a pastiche of killer-lesbian pulp and cabaret decadence. Julia (Camilla Soeberg) awakes upon satin sheets and suggests to her lover, Claire (Priscilla Barnes), that they hunt up a boy toy. They're off to an s/m club, where

Victor (Michael Carr) prowls. Imagining himself to be as studly in their eyes as in his own, he thinks he will have his way with both women, a folly they stoke by beginning their lovemaking on a bus. It's an outrageous escapade—a mirror held up to us, the softcore audience—as the leering, glassy-eyed passengers try to worm their way into the scene.

The opener, Borden's "Let's Talk About Sex," is the wittiest and hottest wedge. Latina actress Rosie (Kamala Lopez-Dawson) nimbly hopscotches a gauntlet of hustlers. On the street, she sasses back to a request for "mouth-to-dick resuscitation." At auditions, she declines the standard offer: "We'd like you to read for the hooker." At her job as a phone-sex worker, she rails against limited male fantasies and inadvertently hooks a fish named Robert (Bryan Cranston), who claims he's interested in her true desires.

With her hand on her crotch, she turns them both on for several weeks, conjuring a parade of men who go down on her and whose endeavors we're shown. She trades him a taste of her precariousness for a portion of his social power. "It excites me to see you with a man," she teases him, declaring, too, that he secretly wants her to top him. "You can fuck me with your cock," he allows, "but get that other guy out of here."

Lacking hardcore's uninhibited probes, *Erotique* sometimes frustrates, but all three directors handcuff rhetoric and serve up generous amounts of male tush.

Also reviewed in:
NEW YORK TIMES, 5/5/95, p. C8, Caryn James
VARIETY, 6/6-12/94, p. 38, Leonard Klady
WASHINGTON POST, 9/23/94, p. F7, Rita Kempley

ETERNITY

A Vivid Pictures release produced in association with the Australian Film Commission and the New South Wales Film and Television Office. *Producer:* Susan MacKinnon. *Director:* Lawrence Johnston. *Screenplay:* Lawrence Johnston. *Director of Photography:* Dion Beebe. *Editor:* Annette Davey. *Music:* Ross Edwards. *Sound:* Paul Finley. *Art Director:* Tony Campbell. *Running time:* 56 minutes. *MPAA Rating:* Not Rated.

NEW YORK POST, 5/10/95, p. 49, Larry Worth

[*Eternity* was reviewed jointly with *Is That All There Is?*; see Worth's review of that film.]

VILLAGE VOICE, 5/16/95, p. 60, Kathy Deacon

[*Eternity* was reviewed jointly with *Is That All There Is?*; see Deacon's review of that film.]

Also reviewed in:
NEW YORK TIMES, 5/10/95, p. C17, Stephen Holden
VARIETY, 10/3-9/95, p. 64, Emanuel Levy

FAIR GAME

A Warner Bros. release of a Silver Pictures production. *Executive Producer:* Thomas M. Hammel. *Producer:* Joel Silver. *Director:* Andrew Sipes. *Screenplay:* Charlie Fletcher. *Based on the novel by:* Paula Gosling. *Director of Photography:* Richard Bowen. *Editor:* David Finfer, Christian Wagner, and Steven Kemper. *Music:* Mark Mancina. *Music Editor:* Daryl B. Kell. *Sound:* Peter Devlin, Dick Church, and (music) Alan Mayerson. *Sound Editor:* Mark Stoeckinger. *Casting:* Jackie Burch. *Production Designer:* James Spencer. *Art Director:* William F. Matthews. *Set Designer:* Mark Garner. *Set Decorator:* Don K. Ivey. *Special Effects:* Bruno Van Zeebroeck. *Costumes:* Louise Frogley. *Make-up:* Sharon Ilsonn, Ronnie Spector, Marietta

Carter-Narcisse, and Jeni Kee Dinkel. *Stunt Coordinator:* Charles Picerni. *Running time:* 110 minutes. *MPAA Rating:* R.

CAST: William Baldwin (Detective Max Kirkpatrick); Cindy Crawford (Kate McQuean); Steven Berkoff (Kazak); Christopher McDonald (Lieutenant Mayerson); Miguel Sandoval (Juantorena); Johann Carlo (Jodi); Salma Hayek (Rita); John Bedford Lloyd (Louis); Olek Krupa (Zhukov); Jenette Goldstein (Rosa); Marc Macaulay (Navigator); Sonny Carl Davis (Baker); Frank Medrano (Guaybera); Don Yesso (Beanpole); Paul Dillon (Hacker); Gustav Vintas (Stefan); Christian Bodegaard (Farm Boy); Garry Francis Hope (Smile); Hank Stone (Ratso); Ski Zawaski (Bail Bondsman); Nancy Nahra (Forensic); Anthony Giaimo (Cafe Romano Manager); Carmen Lopez (Angry Mother); Erika Navarro (Little Girl); Pamela Berrard (Hotel Desk Clerk); Mark Wheatle (Stop & Shop Clerk); Bubba Baker (Hog Truck Driver); Scott Michael Campbell (Adam); Ruben Rabasa (Computer Store Manager); Jim Greene (Tow Truck Driver); Antoni Corone (Code Breaker).

LOS ANGELES TIMES, 11/3/95, Calendar/p. 6, Kenneth Turan

Imagine Cindy Crawford as a civil attorney who specializes in defending the downtrodden. Imagine William Baldwin as a Miami cop so tough he shrugs off beatings that would disable an ox. Imagine enough mayhem and explosions to keep 41 stunt players busy. But don't imagine there is any reason to see "Fair Game."

Even the recruited audience, without whose presence the filmmakers felt unsafe exposing their work to critics, seemed a little dumbstruck at how feeble a piece of business this is. By the time the much-anticipated Crawford-Baldwin love scene unspooled, it generated more giggles than gasps.

This is not a knock on the attractive leads, who gamely slog their way through a variety of grimy situations only to be over-matched by a desultory script by Charlie Fletcher and inept direction by Andrew Sipes, first-timers both and not particularly promising ones at that.

Baldwin, whose lines are of the "I need some answers" variety, goes through the heroic motions like a good soldier, while Crawford, in her feature debut, does the best she can without the benefit of, to put it gently, an overwhelming amount of talent. Both have personalities pleasant enough to make it regrettable that they're trapped in the lamest model-turned-actress movie since Lauren Hutton co-starred with Evel Knievel in the misbegotten "Viva Knievel!"

Crawford plays Kate McQuean, a Miami-based family attorney who defends women against abusive husbands and for some reason keeps the same "It's the Law" sign hanging in both her home and office. It requires a bit of doing to imagine that this ordinary citizen would attract the attention of the most feared group of killers in the Western World, but that is what "Fair Game" insists we believe.

Arriving in Miami intent on blasting McQuean to oblivion is a feared group of former KGB scum, led by the ruthless Col. Kazak (Steven Berkoff), whose tempers have not been improved by a protracted stay in Cuba. Irked at McQuean because a divorce action she initiated could compromise his attempt to steal much of the world's wealth (don't ask), the colonel is determined to turn her into chopped liver as soon as possible.

Equally intent on protecting her is Dade County homicide detective Max Kirkpatrick (Baldwin), who just happens to have the skills to go toe-to-toe with these ruthless Russkies. Yes, they have the capacity, a la "The Net," to track their prey anywhere using computers, but none of them are the least bit photogenic and in this movie the beautiful people inevitably come out on top.

Clocking in at 90 minutes, "Fair Game" has the feeling of a movie that's been trimmed, which, given what remains, may not be a bad thing. Both Fletcher's script, adapted from a novel by Paula Gosling, and Sipes' direction have a hurried feeling to them, as if they couldn't wait to get this movie over with and forgotten.

Which brings us back to Crawford, who spends a fair amount of the movie in demurely revealing outfits that expose carefully rationed areas of flesh. Though the credits indicate that three makeup people, two hairstylists, a vocal consultant and a dialogue coach all pitched in and helped her, the actress would have been better served by a single employee who knew how to read scripts and was savvy enough to advise her to stay away from this one.

NEW YORK POST, 11/3/95, p. 41, Thelma Adams

Its perhaps fitting to close Fashion Week with a few tips from supermodel Cindy Crawford, star of the much-delayed "Fair Game".

• If you're a lawyer on the lam from renegade KGB agents with hyper-computer capabilities, make sure you start out by wearing sexy undies. As mother always said, you never know when you will be, fire-blasted from your condo and have to survive in one skimpy outfit. Think lace; forget bras.

• In seeking protection, choose a lovesick cop (William Baldwin will do) who wears your jeans' size. Then, if you have to peel off your damp mini, his Levis will sculpt your butt as well as they do his.

• Life is a runway. Keep your hero near by pretending to spurn him but changing into one of his T-shirts al fresco. Flash a little nipple; who hasn't seen it by now??

• When all else fails and your makeup case is sleeping with the fishes, grime makes a fabulous cheek contour/eye shadow duo.

• Don't leave home without your concealer.

With these tricks of the trade, it's not surprising that the camera loves Crawford in "Fair Game." Audiences will be less enamored.

So the moled one isn't believable as a lawyer—in those micro-minis with the camera rolling up her legs like panty hose, that's beside the point. The problem is that Crawford's rapport with the camera doesn't extend to her fellow actors.

She can play to the lens, but not to flesh. The supermodel approaches long lines like tongue twisters. When it comes to slinging quips, she's banter-impaired.

Monster action producer Joel Silver ("Lethal Weapon") conceived "Fair Game" as a vehicle for Crawford's segue into movie stardom. He would have been wise to bolster her debut with a veteran team.

Andrew Sipes has a desk full of unproduced film scripts and a directorial debut, "The Champion," that only just hit his resume. He's not yet an actor's director, to say the least.

"Fair Game" is Charlie Fletcher's first produced screenplay. Besides relying on evil Russians, giving the movie a nostalgic air, the plot is full of holes. Why would this crack team of KGB castoffs risk their entire operation to kill Crawford and why are they leaving a trail of blood and bullet casings right to their doorstep?

It's not a mystery; it's just confusing. When one fiend calls the cop and the lawyer "idiots" we have to give the good guys the benefit of the doubt. They weren't born dumb, they were just written that way.

Baldwin gamely overcompensates. He leaps into space, He leaps glaring, before tumbling into Florida's Intercoastal Waterway to save the drowning damsel. He chases high-tech Russkies wearing only his manly smell, wet jeans and a Smith and Wesson.

By mid-movie, he can even bounce a joke off Crawford, a feat more daring than the high-speed chase for tow-truck and mini-van that leaves Baldwin dangling by his machismo like a hot-shot rodeo cowboy.

With all the squealing tires, shattered glass and high-caliber gun-play, "Fair Game" is noisy and exhausting. When the cop and the lawyer sail into the sunset after the fireballs-and-wet-T-shirt climax, Crawford isn't the only one who's comforted by Baldwins last line: "It's all right. It's over."

SIGHT AND SOUND, 3/96, p. 40, Chris Savage King

Miami family law attorney Kate McQuean is grazed in a shooting incident while out running. She reports the occurrence to Detective Max Kirkpatrick. Back at her office, she has an argument with a colleague about the division of property in one of her cases. She says she will invoke Maritime Law in order to get the title of a ship signed over to her client.

On board that ship, ex-KGB killer Kazak is overseeing a surveillance operation centred on Kate and her apartment, which then blows up, throwing Kate into the nearby canal. Max takes her to a hotel customarily used for witness protection. Kazak and his team trace them after Kate uses her credit card to order a pizza. Rosa, one of Kazak's assassins, replaces the pizza delivery boy, and a shoot-out follows. A .33 calibre bullet is discovered and Max contacts forensics to trace it.

An FBI agent—Baker—is called, but he turns out to be a fake. After another shoot-out, Kate and Max are on the run. They check into the Raleigh hotel and are threatened by Kazak over the phone. Meanwhile, forensics has traced the bullet to the KGB, and comments on ex-KGB agents' activity in Cuba: "if it's bad, they're doing it". Kate goes into a computer store and uses the assistant's computer to search her client database for Russian-Cuban connections. She locates Juantorena, a Cuban, and recalls the ship in which her client's interests are vested.

After another car chase, Kate has had enough and wants to quit. She jumps onto a train, but Max catches up with her. They fight, then have sex. Another assassin appears. Kate shoots him but she is then captured by Rosa and taken to the ship. Pursued by Rosa and a sidekick, Max sets a trap and eliminates them. While Kazak is busy finalising a computer heist, Max rescues Kate and they run off the ship as it explodes.

Fair Game is a collaboration between action producer Joel Silver (*Lethal Weapon I-III, Die Hard I* and *II*) and director Andrew Sipes (*The Champion*). It's a very basic product, with a few routine and casually nasty ingredients. The explosions are the film's real stars—hot, ballistic shocks, dissolving into dreamy slow motion. The plot logic is flimsy, but as this is Supermodel Cindy Crawford's first feature role, *Fair Game* is more interested in providing suitable settings for her physical charms. She has a more classic 'Hollywood' look than most current Hollywood actresses. With her Amazonian physique, big hair and unearthly white smile, she resembles a refugee from Hugh Hefner's *Playboy* mansion, or from a Jackie Collins novel, rather than anything more modern, or for that matter, real. Her face doesn't carry much impress of thought or feeling, but her body is something else. As Kate McQuean, the lawyer, she almost personifies the term 'doll', but occasionally performs like Action Man.

Whenever Crawford is required to run along in a skimpy vest and jeans, something magical kicks in. A tough athleticism is released, which doesn't detract from her stunning degree of natural grace. It's a real pity this film didn't make more of this unique selling point, because, as an actress, Crawford supplies but two expressions for her thin, woman-in-peril role: a rueful pout and a flustered, dry-eyed whimper—the latter making her hair more teased and distraught. The script doesn't serve her well. "How do you feel?" asks Max, after she has been catapulted out of her apartment by Semtex; "like my life just exploded," she replies. Although billed as an attorney, Crawford's part is lazily written as a standard-issue action ditz.

William Baldwin—very creditable in *Internal Affairs*—doesn't have a lot of scope either, but he and Crawford are physically well matched. Both of them are forcefully engaged in *Fair Game*'s employment of the just-out-of-the-trenches look—combat gear, splattered with dirt—first popularised in fashion magazines of the 70s and 80s. If she is required to be soaked as frequently as possible, then so is he, and his contours are shown to equally good effect. Their one sex scene is shot in virtual darkness, with occasional rays of electric blue light and chequered shadows. The camera focuses intently on Crawford's crisp white panties, and they're a fitting object of fascination for a film whose general outlook is both prurient and wholesome.

If *Fair Game* is held together by anything, it's by its blunt xenophobia. The ex-KGB assassins seem to have been hand-picked for their bad skin and generally rancid appearance. As Kazak, Steven Berkoff continues a now-familiar series of Hollywood roles (*Rambo, Octopussy*) as an all-purpose foreign villain. While apparently Russian, he speaks in the croaky posh English accent he used in his own film *Decadence*, except for a blurted Bogart imitation when he is briefly pretending to be American. It's a performance that's both impacted and airified, and seems to carry Berkoff the actor's private self-disgust as part of the package.

Kazak's mission and the progress of the heist aren't exactly clear—his team are mainly employed in tracking Kate and Max down. Kazak mumbles about various "politically incorrect" funds that he is hiving off, while Max confidently asserts that the villain has "no fucking conscience". History may have long put an end to the 'Commie Threat' motif but Russians and Cubans can still be cited as enemies. Kazak's crew are evidently evil enough for its female representative, Rosa (Jenette Goldstein) to be despatched by the hero with a knife thrust in the crotch. In an incidental scene, an Hispanic woman recriminates with her child, and Crawford attempts to display concern. Later, the mother and child show up again, acting similarly, and Kate belts the mother in the face. The action is gloatingly emphasised with an amplified sound effect.

Fair Game is hopelessly scattered in terms of general direction, but suddenly rears up to hammer random points home. "He said 'Dosvedanya asshole'," says Kazak, of Max, "he knows about the Russian connection." The film tries to provide Max with some kind of motive, on behalf of Kate and his police team, but there can be no emotional appeals when the threads of the narrative are so bare. This is an unimportant film, but even in unimportant films, beautiful bodies and explosions have to be set off within some functional context.

VILLAGE VOICE, 11/14/95, p. 94, Gary Dauphin

Cindy Crawford is not the worst thing about *Fair Game*. Her fully poseable action-figure performance is about what you'd expect: studied and empty at the same time. Far worse is *Fair Game*'s script. Playing a Julia Roberts-esque tough-cookie-in-miniskirt lawyer, Cindy runs afoul of the local remnants of the KGB and their nonsensical plot to tap an underwater cable handling bank transfers. Malevolently cunning bad guys come after Cindy and her Miami P.D. hero (William Baldwin) with more bogusly deployed high-tech window dressing than you can shake a modem at (laptop super computers, infrared night sights, Zodiac skiffs, et cetera). Explosions abound, director Sipes using them as punctuation to just about every encounter.

Cindy shows some dramatic range by wrapping her skinny legs around Baldwin's naked behind and tagging a baddie with a 9mm, all in the same fluid, humping motion. Having mastered the ability to flex various joints and talk at the same time for her workout videos, Cindy has the look of someone straining to cover up general mediocrity with a handful of assets. The net result could have been forgivable if anything else worthwhile had been thrown into the mix. However, since the non-Cindy aspects of *Fair Game* are actually a step *below* your average right-to-video thriller, forgiveness is impossible.

Also reviewed in:
CHICAGO TRIBUNE, 11/3/95, Friday/p. F, John Petrakis
NEW YORK TIMES, 11/3/95, p. C19, Stephen Holden
VARIETY, 11/6-12/95, p. 71, Brian Lowry
WASHINGTON POST, 11/3/95, p. F6, Hal Hinson

FAR FROM HOME: THE ADVENTURES OF YELLOW DOG

A Twentieth Century Fox release. *Producer:* Peter O'Brian. *Director:* Phillip Borsos. *Screenplay:* Phillip Borsos. *Director of Photography:* James Gardner. *Editor:* Sidney Wolinsky. *Music:* John Scott. *Music Editor:* Richard Bernstein. *Sound:* Michael McGee and (music) Dick Lewzey. *Sound Editor:* Bruce Nyznik. *Casting:* Linda Phillips Palo and Lynne Carrow. *Production Designer:* Mark S. Freeborn. *Art Director:* Yvonne J. Hurst. *Set Decorator:* Peter Louis Lando and Marianne Kaplan. *Set Dresser:* Jim Campbell and Scott Calderwood. *Special Effects:* John Thomas. *Costumes:* Antonia Bardon. *Make-up:* Stan Edmonds. *Stunt Coordinator:* Betty Thomas. *Running time:* 81 minutes. *MPAA Rating:* PG.

CAST: Mimi Rogers (Katherine McCormick); Bruce Davison (John McCormick); Jesse Bradford (Angus McCormick); Tom Bower (John Gale); Joel Palmer (Silas McCormick); Josh Wannamaker (David Finlay); Margot Finley (Sara); Matt Bennett (Ron Willick); St. Clair McColl (Himself); Jennifer Weissenborn (Labrador Helicopter Pilot); Gordon Neave (Flight Engineer); Karen Kruper (Nurse); Dean Lockwood, John LeClair, and Brent Stait (Sartechs).

LOS ANGELES TIMES, 1/13/95, Calendar/p. 2, Chris Willman

"Far From Home: The Adventures of Yellow Dog" is an old-fashioned boy-and-his-dog buddy movie, with an un-Lassie-like twist: It goes for gritty wilderness realism over fantastic feats of canine anthropomorphism.

Not just that, but—despite the pooch's singular billing in the subtitle—it's the boy actually pulling off more of the derring-do than his Labrador, when as shipwrecked strandees they journey together through the vast, inhospitable Northwestern wilderness. Think Timmy with a *load* of merit badges.

Fourteen-year-old Angus McCormick (Jesse Bradford, so good in "King of the Hill" and still remarkable here) is about to make a food run up the Canadian coast in an ocean vessel with his father (Bruce Davison), when a beatific four-legged visitor, Yellow Dog (Dakotah), mysteriously shows up at the ranch. The timing proves more than fortuitous when said dog is shortly washed ashore alongside his young master after a storm separates them from Dad, and these two finally head treacherously inland after days of waiting in vain to be sighted along a remote beach.

Angus' mother (Mimi Rogers) and her rescued husband are occasionally seen back in the civilized world, trying to keep the search parties going. But mostly it's Angus and Yellow Dog as increasingly miserable but determined backwoods survivalists: scraping with the occasional bobcat and such, but even more, just resorting to eating live insects or roasting mice on an open fire to stave off starvation. (You may notice that while the end credits carry the usual notice of no animals harmed during filmmaking, there's no disclaimer about, beetles. Sorry, vegans; sorry, anyone who just had dinner.)

The overcast wilderness of "Far From Home" looks as luscious as it is lonely under the terrific technical expertise of writer-director Phillip Borsos ("One Magic Christmas") and cinematographer James Gardner. There's a fascination in the middle stretch over how successfully—for a time—Borsos lets the harrowing woodsy hardships unfold in what seems like real time, with few concessions to the improbable twists children might expect out of a dog-driven adventure tale.

Maybe it could've used a couple of more of those concessions, though. You don't have to be a kid weaned on the talking critters of "The Incredible Journey" to balk at this movie's lack of an exciting third act—or any third act, really. After a strong, albeit leisurely paced, buildup, "Home" heads into the home stretch and ends unexpectedly just shy of the 80-minute point, right when your internal movie clock is telling you the high adventure is really about to kick into gear.

The relative grit is admirable, the locations awe-evoking; the kid is unusually good, and the dog has sex appeal. But even June Allyson might've tilted her head curiously at the sight of Lassie coming home—too soon.

NEW YORK POST, 1/13/95, p. 45, Michael Medved

In general, I'm not a notorious sucker for every sort of dog movie and for every sort of dog: In fact, the most recent addition to our family is a 13-week-old springer spaniel who's displayed a persistent tendency to tear up the house and to leave indiscreet reminders of his presence in every inconvenient corner he can find.

Even this problematic puppy, however, is easier to love than the new movie "Far From Home: The Adventures of Yellow Dog"—a cinematic mutt that is so far from adequate that it might convince Barbara Woodhouse that she was wrong when she famously declared "No Bad Dogs."

Actually, the canine star can't be blamed. He's a good-looking Labrador named Dakotah; the kind of dog you like to pat just for the solid, reassuring feel of his shoulders. Like many other action stars, in other words, he uses muscles and charisma to make up for lack of acting range.

The real problem here is the story—so painfully predictable that even my 5-year-old daughter, Shayna, normally the world's most forgiving movie critic, felt bored and annoyed.

Stray dog meets nice family ... Nice family adopts stray dog ... Dog and young master live through storm at sea and survive together in the wilderness ... In the end they're separated ... But will the heroic hound somehow find his way home?

It's just that deadly simple in "Far From Home," and neither the human acting nor the fecklessly photographed British Colombia scenery do anything to bring the tale to life. Every once in a while a scene turns up to remind you that the story's unfolding in one of the most rugged, spectacular environments in the world, but most of the time you literally can't see the forest for the trees.

The boy is played by 14-year-old Jesse Bradford, who did such a fine job of projecting edgy intelligence in Steven Soderbergh's "King of the Hill." Here he looks lost even when the script doesn't call for it.

His parents are played by Bruce Davison and Mimi Rogers, who make an undeniably handsome (and wholesome) screen couple, but spend far too many scenes with nothing to do but act desperately worried over their missing son.

Canadian writer-director Philip Borsos (who did the splendid western "The Grey Fox" and the sweet, underappreciated "One Magic Christmas") cuts back to these anguished moments on far too many occasions, as if trying to give some sense of perspective or purpose to the boy-and-dog's otherwise aimless (and endless) wandering in the forest.

Neither kid nor canine, have much of a clue what to do and the movie lacks dramatic tension because their ultimate deliverance depends on chance rather than their own determined efforts.

The movie does suggest some new direction for the Frugal Gourmet, however as it dramatizes the wanderers' attempts to stave off starvation.

The lost lad traps and roasts a mouse, swallows various worms and grubs, and makes a sticky paste from forest roots and the remains of stale, badly burnt cookies left in his pack.

Philip Borsos is a fine filmmaker who deserves credit for his consistent efforts to connect with family audiences, but even very young moviegoers deserve more appetizing—and nourishing—fare than this.

NEWSDAY, 1/13/95, Part II/p. B7, John Anderson

What's a boy-and-his-dog movie besides a buddy movie with half the dialogue? Ordinarily, it's a lesson in the ignobility of man and the superiority of nature. But not always.

In "Far From Home: The Adventures of Yellow Dog," the boy is as admirable as the pup—more so, perhaps, because he does at least as much as the dog to help them survive their grueling ordeal amid the virgin archipelago of British Columbia. This inter-species equality may be heretical, but it also lifts the film well above the usual nature adventure.

The talented Jesse Bradford seems to be specializing in adolescent boys surviving on hostile terrain. In Steven Soderbergh's underappreciated "King of the Hill," he was left to his own devices in a Depression-era St. Louis hotel, while his unstable family tried to right itself. At least his domestic situation has improved: As Angus, self-sufficient scion of the McCormick family, he lives a rather ideal life on the rough-hewn Canadian coast with a mother (Mimi Rogers) a father (Bruce Davison), a brother (Joel Palmer) and, after the dog adopts him, Yellow (Dakotah), a well-trained labrador who's turned up mysteriously one day and attached himself to Angus.

He's a remarkably self-sufficient lad—his father has taught him survival techniques, and in their rustic world these things are part of the nonacademic education. He's building himself a boat; when his parents say he can afford to either paint the boat or keep the dog, he takes the paint back to the store. And this precocious maturity will serve him well after he, Dad and Yellow are shipwrecked during a supply run that meets a Pacific storm. Dad will be rescued immediately, but Angus and Yellow are tossed up on an uninhabited shore and have to fend for themselves.

Kids will admire Angus' survival skills. So will adults. He fishes, he clams, he sews himself waterboots, he cooks outdoors, and makes a lean-to. The land is beautiful and Angus is Huck Finn. Then, the land turns harsh. The food disappears. The rain won't cease and Angus starts to pall. He has to demolish his boat so he can make a signal fire. He's always in the wrong spot when a plane flies overhead. He starts running out of matches. He finally cries, and it's about time.

"Yellow Dog" contains the obligatory battle-with-wolves scene—something that will compound that animal's already unfair image problem. There's also a lot of beautiful scenery, but it's never deceiving: The world out-of-doors is cruel and to survive one has to adapt—Angus, who we've already seen could not bring himself to kill a rabbit back home, has no compunction about killing one when his life is at stake. It's a harsh and perhaps useful lesson, especially for children whose exposure to the natural world consists solely of museum exhibits.

"Yellow Dog" is a solid little drama that offers moments of real fear for Angus' survival—for kids, at least. Those who've been down this kind of dog run before will know the outcome, but they'll find it entertaining just the same.

SIGHT AND SOUND, 4/95, p. 43, Louise Gray

14-year-old Angus McCormick lives with his parents, John and Katherine, and his younger brother, Silas, in a remote region of British Columbia. John, Angus and the boy's constant companion, a labrador called Yellow Dog, take out their boat, *Cormorant*. A sudden storm blows up, and the boat capsizes. John is rescued by a coast guard service headed by John Gale, but Angus and his dog are washed ashore on a remote coastline. They survive for a few days by eating fish, but on the ninth day, they decide to strike for home, walking through uncharted forest. Angus and Yellow Dog encounter wolves and other wild animals. With the dog leading the way, they survive by eating small animals, and eventually beetles and grubs.

On day 15, his father, Gale and the search party find Angus' campsite. Two days later, with no further clues, Gale suggests that the search be ended. Meanwhile, a weakened Angus spies a logging route on the opposite side of a high ravine, traversable only by a perilous log bridge. Midway across the ravine, a helicopter sees Angus. The boy is rescued, but Yellow Dog falls 200 feet into the water, and is presumed dead. Angus and his family are reunited, but the boy is stricken with anxiety about Yellow Dog's fate.

He makes forays into the forest to blow his dog whistle in the hope that Yellow Dog might hear it. Sara, Angus' schoolfriend, tells him he is a hero amongst his classmates and gives him a chaste kiss, but Angus retorts that Yellow Dog is the real hero. Three weeks pass and Angus sadly blows his whistle once more. A distant bark responds and Yellow Dog walks slowly into view. Angus and Yellow Dog's eyes meet. Followed by Silas, Angus races towards his dog as John and Katherine look on in tearful joy.

Taking the homeward bound theme from *The Incredible Journey* and combining it with a wilderness redolent of such environmentally-friendly films as *Once Upon a Forest*, *Far From Home* is an uncomplicated movie that celebrates family values and animal loyalty. Even the wilderness—so often used as a metaphor for wild and appetitive states that are contradictory to civilisation—is just what it is, nothing more. The terrain is certainly inhospitable, as the film's dazzling cinematography amply illustrates, bit it is not a place that threatens psychic dissolution as it does in, say, *Deliverance*. This film suggests that real shelter comes from the warmth (literal and metaphorical) of the family hearth. With family and dog on his side, Angus may be lost, cartographically speaking, but neither his nor Yellow Dog's homing instincts are damaged.

Also intact—and here is where suspension of disbelief is necessary—is Jesse Bradford as Angus. After nearly 20 days in the wild, fuelled by a diet of roast mice, Angus is the same chubby-faced boy as he was at the film's beginning. Presumably, child labour laws prohibit directors from starving adolescent actors in the interests of verisimilitude, so Jesse Bradford's pleasing plumpness will disappoint any vicarious dieters amongst *Far From Home*'s audience.

As an adventure story, *Far From Home* is paced entirely by its own events and shaped by the monumental environment in which it was filmed, with surging music for the emotive bits. The storm at sea, during which the *Cormorant* pitches and sways, makes for truly nauseating viewing, while the footage of remote British Columbia is breathtaking. With Mother Nature moving in on the film's starring role, the supporting performances look weak in comparison. The McCormick parents (Mimi Rogers and Bruce Davison) use two facial expressions only: grim determination, and grit-those-teeth and wipe-those-eyes happiness.

There are no attempts whatsoever at characterisation. No doubt Jesse Bradford constantly got his feet wet and his nails dirty slithering around in the forest, but the only acting beyond the call of duty required of him was to eat a live maggot. (Or did he? Admirably, *Far From Home* is a green movie, director Phillip Borsos' team was kind to critters, using prosthetic animals in the appropriate places.) The animal sequences, featuring wolves, a lynx, and canine performer Dakotah as the eponymous Yellow Dog are well organised, and carefully edited, showing them to maximum effect.

It is tempting to view Phillip Borsos' film as a subtle contribution to the general debate about how family values, sex and violence are portrayed by major feature films and perhaps it is: the kiss that Angus receives after his ordeal is assertively chaste. However, *Far From Home* is also an appealing adventure story in the time-honoured boy-and-his-dog tradition. The limitations of a pre-made mould are the limitations of this film.

Also reviewed in:
CHICAGO TRIBUNE, 1/13/95, Friday/p. H, John Petrakis
NEW YORK TIMES, 1/13/95, p. C10, Stephen Holden
VARIETY, 1/9-15/95, p. 71, Leonard Klady
WASHINGTON POST, 1/14/95, p. C3, William F. Powers

FARINELLI

A Sony Pictures Classics release of a Stephan Films/Alinea Films/Le Studio Canal +/UGC
Images/France 2 Cinema/Studio Images/K2 Productions/RTL/TV1/MG srl/Italian International
Film srl. With assistance from the Gouvernement de la Communaute Francaise de Belgique.
Producer: Vera Belmont, Linda Gutenberg, Aldo Lado, Dominique Janne, and Stephane Thenoz.
Director: Gérard Corbiau. *Screenplay (French with English subtitles):* Andrée Corbiau. *Based
upon the original screenplay by:* Andrée Corbian and Gerard Corbain. *Director of Photography:*
Walther Vanden Ende. *Editor:* Joelle Hache. *Music:* Christopher Rousset. *Sound:* Dominique
Hennequin and (music) Jean-Claude Gaberel. *Sound Editor:* Catherine O'Sullivan. *Casting:*
Gerard Moulevrier and Jose Villaverde. *Production Designer:* Gianni Quaranta. *Set Designer:*
Maria Cristina Reggio. *Special Effects:* Kuno Schlegelmilch. *Costumes:* Olga Berlutti and Anne
De Laugardiere. *Make-up:* Paul Le Marinel. *Running time:* 110 minutes. *MPAA Rating:* R.

CAST: Stéfano Dionisi (Farinelli/Carlo Broschi); Enrico Lo Verso (Riccardo Broschi); Elsa
Zylberstein (Alexandra); Caroline Cellier (Margaret Hunter); Marianne Basler (Countess
Mauer); Jacques Boudet (Philip V); Graham Valentine (The Prince of Wales); Pier Paolo
Capponi (The Father); Delphine Zentout (The Young Admirer); Omero Antonutti (Porpora);
Jeroen Krabbé (Handel).

LOS ANGELES TIMES, 3/17/95, Calendar/p. 19, Kevin Thomas

Belgian filmmaker Gérard Corbiau's "Farinelli" is in the grand European tradition of the
sweeping, epic historical romance, heady and histrionic, replete with sumptuous costumes and
decor. That its hero was one of the most famous castrati of the 18th Century has allowed Corbiau
and his wife, Andrée, his principal co-writer, to create a drama of extraordinary complexity, rich
in meaning.
    For all its emotional extravagance and sheer Baroque lushness, "Farinelli" is actually a triumph
of taut control and superb structuring. Especially dazzling is the film's simulation of the castrato's
3½-octave range achieved by combining the voices of counter-tenor Derek Lee Ragin and soprano
Ewa Mallas Godlewska. When Farinelli sings, he sounds like nothing you've heard before—eerie,
androgynous and electrifying.
    According to the Corbiaus, Farinelli—born in Andrea, Naples, in 1705 as Carlo Broschi—was
under the impression that at age 10 he was accidentally castrated during a fall from a horse that
left him unconscious and near death. In any event, Carlo (Stéfano Dionisi), who had had a
beautiful voice as a chorister, is a blessing to his older composer brother Riccardo (Enrico Lo
Verso), whose work shows off Carlo's amazing voice, which quickly captivates all of Europe.
Carlo is spectacularly handsome, and his voice and looks cause women to swoon. His condition
makes him a uniquely "safe" lover, but the Broschis' creative partnership extends to sharing their
women.
    An early meeting with composer George Frederick Handel (Jeroen Krabbé), however,
foreshadows Carlo's inevitable acknowledgment that Riccardo is second-rate, capable of virtuosity
rather than inspiration. Hired by a London theater to draw audiences away from Handel's operas
at Covent Garden, Carlo craves to perform Handel's work itself. Carlo, consequently, becomes
caught up in two conflicting, impassioned relationships. In his relationship with Riccardo we're
able to see, writ large, the contradictions in many a loving relationship, shot through with feelings
of guilt, betrayal, loyalty and obligation; in his relationship with Handel we discover the fierce
competitiveness between artists who simultaneously need and destroy each other.

Carlo has had to live with the perverse irony that castration has enabled him to become a star and idol of women. Now, through the, tension between these competing relationships, he begins discovering his destiny, which is to transform himself from a monster, a kind of freak music hall attraction—complete with feather headdresses à la Josephine Baker—into a great opera singer as a way of reclaiming and asserting his manhood. This is the heart of the film, yet the Corbiaus proceed, with a bold romanticism, to suggest that whereas the redemptive power of art can be treacherous that of love can be unequivocal.

Artistry abounds in every aspect of the film, which is as bravura in its acting as in its production design, and as glorious as its music. In addition to its three stars there are impeccable portrayals by Elsa Zylberstein as the young woman who loves both Broschis, Caroline Cellier as Carlo's worldly London impresario and Renaud du Pelotux de Saint Roman as her gallant crippled son, with whom Carlo identifies and loves as his own son. As in his earlier, also Oscar-nominated "The Music Teacher," Corbiau again finds profound meaning in the tempestuous world of music.

NEW YORK, 3/27/95, p. 84, David Denby

Farinelli (Stéfano Dionisi), star of the eighteenth-century opera stage, descends from the heavens in a floating cloud, plumes sticking straight up from his helmet. Before he opens his mouth, he might be any flamboyant singer in a campy opera. But the hero of *Farinelli* is a castrato, a virtuoso performer with the lung power of a man and the vocal range of a woman, and the sound of his voice is so penetrating, it causes people of both sexes to tremble and faint. After the performance, women go backstage and caress Farinelli's body. They don't need to be seduced; they're already aroused, and more than ready for sex, which poses no dangers—though castrati can get erections, they can't really ejaculate (a fact that would make them very popular in the anti-bodily-fluids nineties).

The castrati were the rock stars of the eighteenth century, and Farinelli (a real singer) was reputed to be particularly attractive. But who can play a role that combines glory and humiliation in so bizarre a fashion? Oddly, no actor or singer was willing to prepare for the role ... properly. (De Niro gained 60 pounds to play Jake La Motta, but even he might have hesitated before achieving authenticity for *Farinelli*.) Stéfano Dionisi, the handsome Italian who plays Farinelli, looks like Daniel Day-Lewis in his androgynous-lord-of-the-trees phase, but Dionisi's relation to Day-Lewis is rather like that of Richard Gere to Marlon Brando; he's self-involved and gloomily narcissistic. I'm not sure who *should* play a castrato. Camille Paglia, perhaps?

And what to do for the voice? The sounds that director Gérard Corbiau matched to Dionisi's lip movements were created electronically—"morphed"—by mixing together the voices of an American countertenor, Derek Lee Ragin, and the Polish soprano Ewa Mallas Godlewska. What results is extraordinarily agile and capable of holding notes for an eternity (a castrato specialty). But it doesn't sound real, and after a while, the hollow, slightly metallic tones gave me the creeps.

The castrato was an unnatural human invention that nevertheless had a certain musical logic to it. Modern technology can never quite simulate the sound, and the techno-wizardry only increases our sense of remoteness from an age both demanding and cruel in its pleasures. At the height of the castrato craze in the early eighteenth century, parents offered their 8- or 9-year-old boys to the knife on the slight chance that they might become famous singers; most of them, of course, got no further than the local church choir and led wretchedly unhappy lives (they were usually obese as well). Farinelli, born Carlo Broschi, was one of the rare great successes.

This movie, which Corbiau wrote with his wife, Andrée, is mostly devoted to Farinelli's tormented relationship with his older brother, Riccardo Broschi (Enrico Lo Verso), a minor composer who hangs on to his singing-genius brother as long as he can. The two travel around Europe, and Carlo performs music Riccardo writes for him—soulless virtuoso junk, with much ornamentation and floridly empty "runs." The collaboration goes further. After the performances, the women who go to bed with the great Farinelli discover that Riccardo, by prior arrangement, slips into his brother's place at a certain point and completes the act. The brothers have a pact: Carlo gets the women, and Riccardo gets the *"jouissance,"* as one countess, eyes gleaming, puts it. The rapt women accept this substitution, somewhat mysteriously, since it removes from their adventure its added frisson of contraceptive innocuousness.

Farinelli is more sensational than good. Sure, it's sexy in an uneasy, borderline-ludicrous way. Some of the red-velvet bedroom stuff, with beautiful ladies bursting out of impossibly revealing dresses, might be scenes from a *Playboy* costume party. The gently fantastic opera sets are enjoyable, and some of the music is lovely, especially Handel's *Rinaldo*, which, as everyone in the movie says, puts Broschi's empty compositions in their place.

But neither of the brothers is particularly appealing or commanding. Riccardo is a talentless, calculating poseur, and Enrico Lo Verso, who plays him, alternates between two expressions: a foolish grin and cringing remorse. As Carlo, Dionisi does a lot of beautiful suffering but never makes contact with us or—despite his alleged dependence on his older brother—with Lo Verso either. Held together by guilt and obligation, these two go through so many emotional crises that after a while, we collapse into boredom. The Corbiaus have created a lurid fantasia of mutual need that, dramatically speaking, has nowhere to go.

As if in desperation, the Corbiaus have turned the pragmatic genius Handel (Jeroen Krabbé) into a viciously sarcastic man, a competitive ogre who hates castrati because they have perverted natural writing for the voice. But it is unlikely that Handel ever advanced such an opinion, since the composer wrote some of his greatest roles for castrati (today, the music is usually transposed downward and sung by baritones). Emotionally violent, *Farinelli* is nevertheless irresolute and arbitrary; worse, it fails to dramatize the real irony in the material: that a man who arouses others to ecstasy can never find satisfaction himself. To be the prince of art and never know the simple joy of sex! The Corbiaus may take us to a world of complex pleasures, but they don't have the skill to make it anything more than a historical curiosity.

NEW YORK POST, 3/17/95, p. 49, Michael Medved

Carlo Broschi, known as Farinelli, reigned as the most celebrated singer of the 18th century and enjoyed many of the prerogatives of a contemporary rock star—adoring fans, a life of unimaginable indulgence, and beautiful women who swooned whenever he sang on stage.

In the most intimate arena of life, however, Farinelli could never quite compete with Mick Jagger: In a common practice of the era, he had been castrated at age 9 in order to preserve his piercing voice in all its purity.

The new film "Farinelli" presents that devil's bargain with surprising evenhandedness, entertaining the idea that the hero's supreme artistic achievements may have justified his boyhood mutilation.

Winner of the Golden Globe Award as best foreign-language film, and nominated for an Oscar in the same category. "Farinelli" explores an exotic subject in a slow, stately, but flamboyant style that's always impressive but never entirely satisfying.

The movie's main focus falls on the relationship between Farinelli and his older brother Riccardo, a mediocre but ambitious composer who used his younger sibling's famous voice to promote his own lackluster compositions.

The two brothers share everything, even their romantic conquests: The handsome Farinelli (played by Stefano Dioaisi, a Daniel Day Lewis lookalike) first seduces and arouses the women, then turns them over to Riccardo to finish the job.

The chief threat to the boys' close working relationship comes from the great composer Handel (Jeroen Krabbe), who offers Farinelli the chance to perform material more memorable than his brother's clumsy operas and battles the two Italians for popularity with music-loving audiences in London.

Meanwhile, our hero goes through a great deal of incoherent torment of the standard genius-is-pain variety, altogether unable to enjoy his phenomenal popularity.

Filmmaker Gerard Corbiau (director of 1987's Oscar-nominated "The Music Teacher") re-creates this bizarre baroque world as if he were handling science fiction rather than costume drama.

He certainly makes imaginative use of contemporary technology to simulate the voice of an 18th-century "castrato": electronically blending the singing of a male counter tenor with the soaring tones of a female soprano.

The effect is eerie—intensified by lavish, androgynous, plumed-and-masked costumes—but it's hardly magical, never approaching the "angelic" impact which contemporaries associated with the real Farinelli.

The plot is also unnecessarily convoluted, flashing back and forth between 1740 and 1722; following the brothers through handsome but indistinguishable locations in Naples, London, Dresden and Madrid.

The movie deserves credit for raising intriguing questions, but like its great subject's vaulting voice, they seem to hang endlessly in mid-air without ever really coming down to earth.

NEWSDAY, 3/17/95, Part II/p. B5, Jack Mathews

In 18th-century Europe, where a good opera life was more important than a good sex life, young boys who showed particular promise as singers were often castrated, saving their throats from the ravages of puberty, so they might go on to please kings and queens with their glass-shattering adult voices. A practice, you might say, of gelding the lily.

Carlo Broschi, born in Naples in 1705 and neutered seven or eight years later, was the greatest singer of them all, and he lived out a long life as a wealthy, revered music figure. But did he have any fun? Not according to "Farinelli," Belgian director Gerard Corbiau's putative true story of Broschi.

In this gorgeously staged but overwrought costume melodrama, one of the five Oscar nominees for Best Foreign Language Film, Broschi is more tortured than any of the songs he sings, and they are plenty tortured. Using the voices of two opera singers, counter-tenor Derek Lee Ragin and soprano Ewa Mallas Godlewska, and electronically blending them in a computer, Corbiau's crew attempted to re-create the pure, 3½-octave range of the so-called castrati and have their star, Stefano Dionisi, mime the performances. The quasi-synthesized music is impressively loud, but you'll have to key up your imagination to put the voice and Dionisi together. There are few moments when the lip synching illusion works, or when you're not aware that the high notes are being hit by a woman. "Farinelli" is certainly a great subject for a film biography. The castrati are fascinating tragic figures: children mutilated—often by their choirmasters or their own parents—for mass audience entertainment. Yet, with their children's voices and adult male lungs, they projected sounds out of the range of today's greatest opera stars, and were treated with the adoration reserved for our biggest rock stars. (No Michael Jackson jokes, please.)

How Farinelli, as Broschi was known, dealt with his mixed blessing is a promising dramatic concept. But Corbiau, who co-wrote the script with two others, has gone beyond creative license to science fiction in portraying the singer as a man with a huge sexual appetite (a rare trait in eunuchs), and concocting a Cain and Abel theme that reeks of psychoanalytic hooey. "Farinelli" is, in fact, the story of Carlo and his older brother, Riccardo (Enrico Lo Verso), who composes the mundane songs he sings, and satisfies the gorgeous women he seduces. "It's our pact," Riccardo reminds Carlo and his women, as he climbs into bed with them at the critical moment and takes over. What a sport!

The movie is at its best evoking the role of opera in the lives of the middle and upper classes of the period, in re-creating the passion of audiences and artists, and in exploring the political rivalries not unlike those of today—between opposing concert promoters. But "Farinelli" bogs down where it counts most, in developing the love-hate relationships between the brothers, and between Farinelli and the temperamental German composer George Frederick Handel (Jeroen Krabbe, in a persistent melancholic rage), whose work he loves. Every conflict and situation is blown up to operatic scale, and intentional as that may be, it undermines the integrity of the story, and its would-be mystery.

There is never much doubt about how and why young Carlo was castrated, yet Corbiau, using murky symbolism and confusing flashbacks, leads us to the revelation as if he were doing "Equus." Dionisi, while a bit too hunky for a man deprived of his hormones, gives a restrained and even moving performance, and Elsa Zylberstein, as Farinelli's strong and devoted companion, Alexandra, grounds her scenes with genuine character. But despite their performances, and the stunningly authentic sets and costumes, "Farinelli" is all theatrical artifice and trumped-up psychology. It's more soap than opera.

SIGHT AND SOUND, 11/95, p. 41, Peter Matthews

Madrid, 1740. Farinelli, the most celebrated singer in Europe, is staying at the court of King Philip V of Spain. It has been three years since he retired and parted from his brother and collaborator Riccardo. Now he lives in seclusion with his lover Alexandra.

Farinelli was castrated at the age of ten, allegedly after a fall from a horse. The angelic voice of his childhood has thus been preserved, and he makes even Riccardo's weak compositions sound good. His debut takes place in a public square in Naples in 1722, when he trounces a virtuoso trumpet player in an impromptu musical contest. The crowd ecstatically chants his name, and a legend is born.

Handel, the official composer of the English court, hears of Farinelli, and invites him to sing before the King. But he pointedly excludes Riccardo, and a bitter argument ensues in which Farinelli spits in Handel's face. The singer's fame increases. Farinelli's voice has a magical power over women; and he and Riccardo accomplish their seductions in tandem, with the castrato providing the foreplay and the elder brother finishing the job.

While Farinelli is on tour in 1734, Handel calls on him backstage and proposes again that he sing at Covent Garden. Confused by the offer, Farinelli is struck dumb on stage. Later in his dressing room, he waits for Handel, but is visited instead by a beautiful young woman, Alexandra Leyris. She begs him to follow her to London to save the Nobles Theatre from ruin at the hands of its more popular competitor—the royal opera house, run by Handel. As the Nobles is currently managed by Porpora, Farinelli's old teacher, he and Riccardo agree to go.

In London, Farinelli begins a passionate affair with Alexandra, supported in the usual way by Riccardo. At the Nobles, Farinelli defends Handel as a genius against his legion of detractors; but the composer spurns his friendly overtures. At the same time, Farinelli expresses doubts about the quality of his brother's music. Deeply hurt, Riccardo dissolves the partnership.

Alexandra has stolen the manuscript of Handel's new score, and Farinelli, determines to perform it. Seeking revenge, Handel finds the crestfallen Riccardo hiding in his attic, and whee-dles out of him the fact that it was Riccardo himself who castrated the young singer for their careers. Handel tells Farinelli what he knows; but Farinelli goes out and sings magnificently at the premiere. Crushed, Handel swears he will never compose another opera.

Farinelli's tranquil self-exile at the Spanish court is disturbed by the arrival of his brother, hoping to make amends. Riccardo slashes his wrists, but soon recovers. One last time, the two carry out their fraternal pact, and Riccardo leaves, having restored in some measure what he took away: Alexandra is pregnant.

Farinelli II Castrato has a garbled modernist structure involving shock cuts and bewildering shifts in time and it features a fair amount of casually kinky sex. But, really, this melodramatic embroidery on the life of the legendary eighteenth-century singer belongs to the pure old Holly-wood of such biopics as *A Song to Remember*, with sleek, sinister George Sand (Merle Oberon) flashing her eyes and instructing beefy Chopin (Cornel Wilde) to stop "that so-called Polonaise jumble you've been playing for days." In this case the historical heavy is Handel, who crushes a beetle remorselessly under his thick phallic cane and means to do the same to the high-strung castrato he sneers at as a "fairground attraction" and a "singing machine".

There's also the terrible secret Riccardo bears about the truth behind his brother Farinelli's bogus accident; and in general, one can understand the old-fashioned temptation to treat a singer's backstage life as grand opera (with select Freudian trimmings). At least on the level of romantic kitsch, the movie ought to be fun, and so it is, intermittently—as when Handel, skulking in the flies of the theatre, drops a threatening note down to Farinelli in mid-performance, then swoons when the castrato proceeds to trill more heroically than ever. This opulent production exhibits a lot of swooning, since it's the purple conceit of the writer-director Gérard Corbiau (who had a previous operatic turn with *The Music Teacher [Le Maitre de musique]* in 1988) that Farinelli's sustained high notes induce 'musical orgasms' among the flushed ladies in the stalls.

But *Farinelli* barely tweaks the cultural and psychological possibilities of its marvelous subject. There is a loose implication that the singer's androgynous, quasi-occult voice—here suitably 'morphed' from the separate efforts of a soprano and a counter-tenor—represents the eruption of Dionysus in the measured Apollonian world of the classical. The irony is that the god is also less than a man; and one may impute Oedipal rivalry to Farinelli's vocal triumphs without, however, being especially supported by the script.

Perhaps, then, the castration is a broad metaphor for the privations faced by any romantically driven, nonconforming artist? Apparently not, as Farinelli turns out to be a bit of a stud who, it is true, can't plant the seed, but nonetheless ploughs the field satisfactorily beforehand. Now it's quite plausible that a eunuch might need to prove his maleness; but the repeated scenes of energetic thrusting suggest rather an attempt to make Farinelli appear as 'normal' as his circumstances allow (he certainly keeps his mitts off Riccardo in their threesomes together). And there's something equally glib in the way our hero—who gets mobbed by groupies wherever he goes—is tipped as the first of the polymorphous superstars, a sort of Bowie or Prince *avant la lettre*. This, too, makes it easier on the audience and mitigates the strangeness and cruelty of the tale.

Stéfano Dionisi's pouty, brooding attitudes and his ornate get-ups—half Visigoth, half Las Vegas showgirl—have, however, been wittily worked out; and indeed, the delights on offer are mainly pictorial. The movie seems intended to horn in on the *Amadeus* and *Farewell, My Concubine* trade, but it misses the arch metaphysical duelling of the former and the historical density of the latter. You learn astonishingly little of the mixed social, economic and religious motives behind the *castrati* as an institution; but you obtain some first-class views of candelabra and periwigs. Even as fruity melodrama, *Farinelli* fails—ruined by the chaotic continuity, which churns up crises (such as a tremor the singer develops in his upper octaves), then forgets all about them. When at long last one reaches the big primal scene, it has no impact, since it's already obvious by then that the movie has no balls.

VILLAGE VOICE, 3/21/95, p. 56, Leslie Camhi

Brotherly love and castration—are they incompatible? Not in *Farinelli*, a strangely moving film based upon the life of Carlo Broschi (a/k/a Farinelli), reputedly the greatest castrato singer of the 18th century. His brother Riccardo began composing for little Carlo's voice and felt he had to save it from adolescent alchemy; he covered the dastardly deed with an alibi about the child's riding accident. The brothers kept collaborating; over the harpsichord and in bed with women, one supplied what the other was lacking.

Farinelli's voice and androgynous beauty captivated audiences in an age of artifice; he was courted by princes and adored by the people. Yet amidst the worldly glory, he suffered (understandably) from a sense of something missing; he wanted to sing the music of Handel, and to have a child.

Gérard Corbiau spares no lace and feathers in telling Farinelli's story; his public performances are charming spectacles of haute kitsch, though their historical accuracy is questionable. A particularly striking mise-en-scène has Farinelli tragically proposing marriage to his London patroness in the middle of an oyster-opening party. In spite of his fey accessories, Farinelli here is resolutely heterosexual; in several scenes, women seem to find him a perfect sexual partner. Stéfano Dionisi plays the wondrous singer with just the right mixture of noblesse, fragility, wounded dignity, and otherworldly strangeness; as the brother, Enrico lo Verso's vulgar masculinity seems overdone, but then, whose wouldn't?

But amidst the historical glitz, the real star of Corbiau's film (nominated for a foreign film Oscar) is the high technology that produced Farinelli's voice by digitally mixing a (female) soprano and a (male) countertenor. The result is impressive but somewhat incorporeal; aficionados may recall with nostalgia a 1902 recording of Alessandro Moreschi, *The Last Castrato*, whose haunting, childlike, unearthly voice seemed to sing of his own extinction.

Also reviewed in:
CHICAGO TRIBUNE, 4/14/95, Friday/p. C, Michael Wilmington
NEW REPUBLIC, 4/3/95, p. 28, Stanley Kauffmann
NEW YORK TIMES, 3/17/95, p. C3, Janet Maslin
VARIETY, 12/19/94-1/1/95, p. 74, Lisa Nesselson
WASHINGTON POST, 4/14/95, p. D1, Hal Hinson
WASHINGTON POST, 4/14/95, Weekend/p. 36, Desson Howe

FAST TRIP, LONG DROP

A Drift Releasing release. *Producer:* Gregg Bordowitz. *Director:* Gregg Bordowitz. *Screenplay:* Gregg Bordowitz. *Music:* Frank London, Lorin Sklamberg, and Alicia Svigals. *Running time:* 54 minutes. *MPAA Rating:* Not Rated.

WITH: Gregg Bordowitz; Bob Huff.

NEW YORK POST, 1/6/95, p. 43, Larry Worth

[*Fast Trip, Long Drop* was reviewed jointly with *The Darker Side of Black*; see Worth's review of that film.

NEWSDAY, 1/6/95, Part II/p. B7, John Anderson

[*Fast Trip, Long Drop* was reviewed jointly with *The Darker Side of Black*; see Anderson's review of that film.

Also reviewed in:
NEW YORK TIMES, 1/6/95, p. C6, Stephen Holden
VARIETY, 2/21-27/94, p. 52, Emanuel Levy

FASTER, PUSSYCAT! KILL! KILL!

A Strand Releasing release. *Producer:* Russ Meyer and Eve Meyer. *Director:* Russ Meyer. *Screenplay:* Jack Moran. *Director of Photography:* Walter Schenk. *Editor:* Russ Meyer. *Music:* Igo Kantor. *Running time:* 83 minutes. *MPAA Rating:* Not Rated.

CAST: Tura Satana (Varla); Haji (Rosie); Lori Williams (Billie); Ray Barlow (Tommy); Susan Bernard (Linda); Stuart Lancaster (Old Man); Paul Trinka and Dennis Busch (Sons).

NEW YORK POST, 1/13/95, p. 44, Thelma Adams

Russ Meyer's "Faster, Pussycat! Kill! Kill! is a four-star B-movie. "Serial Mom" director John Waters named this hilarious underground sex-and-karate classic his favorite movie, calling Meyer the "Eisenstein of sex films."

Made for $61,000 in 1965, the year of "Beach Blanket Bingo," Meyer's camera leers at three Amazonian professional go-go dancers on their day off.

While the director of "Beyond the Valley of the Dolls" for 20th Century Fox (scripted by movie critic Roger Ebert) got his start making skin flicks in the late '50s, there's no nudity here—this is Meyer doing "art."

Varla (Tura Satana)—in skintight jumpsuit, black boots made for kicking butt and Porsche to match—cracks the whip over her lover Rosie (Haji) and the free-spirited Billie (Lori Williams).

While playing chicken in their roadsters on the salt flats (Meyer maximizes his desert locations), the dancers meet two fresh-faced kids who look like they wandered off a beach party set. Tommy (Ray Barlow) and Linda (Susan Bernard, Playboy's Miss December 1966) have made a very wrong turn.

Varla plays butcher-than-thou with Tommy. After a few well-placed karate chops, she breaks the boy's back and kidnaps the bikini-clad Linda. They might both dance the watusi, but Satana is no Annette Funicello!

Afterwards, while gassing up their cars, the tarty trio tumbles on a money-making scheme to bilk a paraplegic geezer out of his insurance settlement. As Varla says, "and here's where our screenplay starts to unfold ..."

The old lecher and his two sons—a muscle-bound mental case named Vegetable and a weak goody-goody who falls for Varla have their own cache of dirty little secrets, including rape and murder. The patriarch, waits for stranded women in his ramshackle ranch like a spider in a web, but he doesn't realize that his prey is a black widow.

Meyer expertly milks both triangles for all possible melodrama; the dancers are as much a dysfunctional family as the cripple and his boys. When the two clans collide, and allegiances start to shift, a battle to the death is inevitable.

Part Japanese, part Apache, Satana's one of the best screen villainesses ever, a sexy sadist who'll stop at nothing for kicks—even aiming her Porsche at a wheelchair-bound senior. For Meyer, nothing is taboo.

"Faster, Pussycat! Kill! Kill!" captures the America of beach party movies as if seen through a warped looking glass held by Charles Manson. It's a hoot. No, make that four hoots.

NEWSDAY, 1/13/95, Part II/p. B7, Gene Seymour

Words like "incomparable" and "unique" raise yellow flags in the minds of newspaper editors who believe, with some justification, that such adjectives are often flashy adornments to someone's hype machine.

Nevertheless, I'll climb out on a limb and say there is nothing in cinema—*nothing*, do you hear—that compares with "Faster, Pussycat! Kill! Kill!" For starters, how many other movies can you think of whose central character is a leather-clad, bisexual, karate-chopping go-go dancer played by an actress (Tura Satana) who's half-Japanese, half-Apache? I thought not.

Satana's character, Varla, along with two other buxom dancers (Haji, Lori Williams), blow off steam by driving fast in the California desert, wrestling in the sand and snarling rococo insults at each other. One sunny afternoon, a clean-cut dork challenges the trio to a race. After he loses, he and Varla get into a fight. Bad move. Varla literally snaps him like a twig, much to the horror of his girlfriend (Susan Bernard).

With the girlfriend as hostage, the terrible three end up at a secluded ranch owned by a physically challenged pervert (Franklin Bolger) and his two sons, one of whom is a musclebound simpleton, the other a bookish twerp. None, clearly, is a match for these bimbos from hell.

Imagine how all this must have seemed to the drive-in crowd when it was first released back in 1965. They probably thought they were getting a routine highway thrill-kill machine instead of this kinky, scary juggernaut from director Russ Meyer, already well on his way to becoming sexploitation's main man.

Now it's a bona-fide underground classic, beloved by directors like Quentin Tarantino and John Waters. It's easy to see what those two especially see in "Pussycat," with its go-for-broke tackiness, rapid-fire pacing and self-perpetuating outrageousness.

And, daddy-o, what dialogue! It includes deathless declamations like,"You're real cute! Like a velvet glove cast in iron." One memorable exchange has Satana telling Williams how to keep their hostage drugged. Williams: "White pills for beddy-bye. Yellow pills for the wake-up call. What you got for love?" Satana: "That *depends*, Boom-boom, on what you got in mind!" What does that mean? Who talks like that? Does it matter? The last question's easy. It doesn't. Have a ball, cats and kittens.

VILLAGE VOICE, 1/17/95, p. 56, B. Ruby Rich

What becomes a legend most? In movieland, it's a rerelease. Enter *Faster, Pussycat! Kill! Kill!*, one of those rare legends that glides easily from its own time (1965) into our own, its charms intact and its powers as combustible as ever.

Faster, Pussycat's simple tale bears more than a passing resemblance to standard porn formula, devoid of hardcore but juiced on some kind of aesthetic steroids. Three chicks in search of kicks race their sports cats (one chick to a vehicle) across the desert. Varla is the leader, the lady in black, with nerves of steel and a sick sense of humor. Rosie is her besotted sidekick, forced by love to do Varla's bidding. Billie is the blond bombshell and the only card-carrying heterosexual, albeit a pill-popping boozing nympho.

It's out in the desert that the trio encounters such relics of Americana as a clean-cut hetero guy who underestimates the competition, his goody-goody girlfriend (played by Miss December of 1966), a salivating gas station geezer, and finally a depraved version of "Father Knows Best." Take one dirty old man and his mentally impaired sons, place them on a ranch with enough rumored cash to attract our revved-up females to lunch, then mix and pour.

Every expectation is fulfilled and no plot device left unturned in this cannily campy action flick. Someone gets kidnapped, someone gets drunk, and a lot of people get killed. Surprise: the all-male family is toxic. Surprise: the playmate is virginal. Surprise: the lesbian leader of the pack is heartless (well, can't have everything).

Plot alone, however, doesn't explain the sustained interest that *Faster Pussycat* generates. Camp aside, it is Russ Meyer's prescient avant-garde sense of cinematography, choreography, and editing that have been getting everyone so hot and bothered. Low-angle camera shots frame the vixens against the sky, quick cuts match the rhythm on the soundtrack, and montage rules the day as the disorientation of this world turned asunder is matched, frame for frame, by the cinematic deranging of our placid visual expectations.

"Welcome to violence, the word and the act." Spoken by a disembodied narrator as intent on exciting his already-captive audience as any sideshow barker bent on snagging customers, the smoothly mock-scientific opening voice-over goes on to warn us to be on the lookout for the pussycats, who "could be your secretary, your doctor's receptionist, or a dancer in a go-go bar." Armed and dangerous, va-voom, va-room, the pussycats interrupt the monologue and land, larger than life, in a frenzied watusi on the movie-theater screen. Welcome, indeed.

Who is this mystery storyteller, the unseen host whose words bind us to his vision? Russ Meyer was for decades America's favorite interpreter of stag-party sex in a size, Triple-D. He liked his women dominant and as hard-edged as his film, made with a tight circle of army cronies. "The sweetest kittens have the sharpest "claws!" read one *Faster Pussycat* ad. Meyer hasn't had an influential Hollywood fan pay tribute to him à la Tim Burton (unlike Ed Wood, of course, Meyer's still alive to defend himself). Nor has he had the luck à la Roger Corman of having his genre find favor and thereby retroactively redeem him (ironic softcore porn making for a trickier lineage than low-budget horror or action flicks).

But have no fear: the rediscovery of *Faster Pussycat* is an event that had to happen, and as chance would have it, the year of Newt could wish for no more fitting revival to usher in a first hundred days spirit of rebellion. With new prints from Strand Releasing and theatrical bookings across the country, *Faster Pussycat* is finally getting the attention it deserves. All it takes is one ticket for a first-hand graduate-seminar-quality lesson in how cultural artifacts, recycled, can serve entirely different purposes—and audiences.

Who, after all, was the "you" that the film's introductory monologue addressed? Me? Us? Them? The first time around, *Faster Pussycat* played to the folded-raincoat set with a taste for humor. Then it prospered on video in a delightful half-life as the favorite guilty pleasure of the hip intelligentsia, foremost among them John Waters. He declared it his favorite film of all time—and why not, since *Faster Pussycat*—shares his own theme of a kitschy universe of outcasts who are superior to the depraved normals set against them. In the '90s, post-*Basic Instinct* (whose screenwriter, Joe Eszterhas, should be given a lie-detector test if he doesn't cop to the influence), *Faster Pussycat* is back as an unexpected celebration of bad-girl empowerment. And, above all, it's a model that's being appropriated by dykes in search of some shit-kicking history and who find just the tonic in this band of frenzied femmes whose approach to men lies halfway between Sharon Stone and Hothead Paisan. Who'd have ever predicted that one decade's boy toys would become this decade's lesbian camp?

Time for a flashback, true-confession style. I first saw *Faster Pussycat* in the mid '70s, in the heyday of right-on feminism, when I was living in a loft in Chicago and programming art films at the Art Institute. A then-local critic by the name of Dave (*Daily News*) Kehr rang me up because, that fateful day being about 10 years BHV (Before Home-Video), he wanted to avail himself of the loft's prized 16mm projector and pull-down screen to watch an interesting film he'd come across.

I'd like to say the rest was history, but no. My pals and I were a combination of sensitive men, sophisticated dykes, and the above-mentioned ROF's, and we were kinda appalled by this low-life depiction of big-tit redeemers displaying their mammary talents for a presumably salivating male audience. After all, Russ Meyer had been known as the "King of the Nudies." We figured Kehr had procured this print from the notoriously nerdy University of Chicago Doc Film Society, which only clinched our hipper-than-thou, wet-dream suspicions. The fact that local newspaper scribe Roger Ebert had already written a script for Russ Meyer (*Beyond the Valley of the Dolls*) and lived to tell the tale of babes, babes, babes made our conclusion undeniable. This was retrograde male-objectification of women's bodies and desires further embellished by a portrait of lesbianism as twisted and depraved. Case closed.

That was then, this is now—and what a difference a day makes. Flash-forward 30 years and the empires of the senses seem decisively rearranged. From a contemporary perspective, the film inverts positive and negative images of "woman" to show just how interrelated the bad and the good have turned out to be, once sexuality is no longer deemed suspect. Further, *Faster Pussycat* deals a comparable body blow to the idea that women are victims: just sign up for a few aikido courses, buy a Mazda Miata, and you, too, can traverse the wide-open spaces of America, and woe to the man who crosses your path or the woman who tries to leave your orbit. In one fell swoop, then, the two most cherished ideologies of a certain kind of righteous feminism (positive role models, women as victims) have been inverted. No wonder the old man clasps his shotgun to his chest and warns: "They let 'em vote, smoke, and drive, even put 'em in pants, so what do you get? A Democrat for President." He understood the zeitgeist, even if he wasn't having any part of it.

Yes, *Faster Pussycat* seen through a 1995 filter is a veritable Rosetta stone of contemporary attitude; ironic, irreverent, sexually polymorphous, mixing high and low forms, reversing camera angles as handily as it does power and prurience, bending dialogue to suit its whims and wit, it's a film utterly revivified by its 1995 revival. Diamanda Galas has already claimed Tura Satana as her inspiration. There's been a lesbian bar named after the movie, and a rock 'n' roll band as well. There's even a CD out now of Russ Meyer soundtracks, including the notorious *Pussycat* monologue and a bonus photo album with shots of the girls. See, Mr. Meyer, we've caught up.

Also reviewed in:
CHICAGO TRIBUNE, 3/24/95, Friday/p. C, Michael Wilmington
NEW YORK TIMES, 1/13/95, p. C10, Stephen Holden

FATHER OF THE BRIDE PART II

A Touchstone Pictures release of a Sandy Gallin production. *Executive Producer:* Sandy Gallin and Carol Baum. *Producer:* Nancy Meyers. *Director:* Charles Shyer. *Screenplay:* Nancy Meyers and Charles Shyer. *Based on the screenplay "Father's Little Dividend" by:* Albert Hackett and Frances Goodrich. *Director of Photography:* William A. Fraker. *Editor:* Stephen A. Rotter. *Music:* Alan Silvestri. *Music Editor:* Andrew Silver. *Choreographer:* Peggy Holmes. *Sound:* Richard B. Goodman and (music) Dennis S. Sands. *Sound Editor:* Dennis Drummond and Greg King. *Casting:* Jeff Greenberg and Sheila Guthrie. *Production Designer:* Linda DeScenna. *Art Director:* Greg Papalia. *Set Designer:* Nancy Mickelberry, Masako Masuda, Yvonne Garnier-Hackl, and Dawn Snyder. *Set Decorator:* Ric McElvin. *Set Dresser:* Donn Piller, Sam Anderson, Mark Boucher, and Jennifer Pray. *Special Effects:* Dennis Dion. *Costumes:* Enid Harris. *Make-up:* Karen Blynder. *Make-up (Steve Martin):* Frank H. Griffin, Jr. *Make-up (Diane Keaton):* Marilyn Carbone. *Running time:* 106 minutes. *MPAA Rating:* PG.

CAST: Steve Martin (George Banks); Diane Keaton (Nina Banks); Martin Short (Franck Eggelhoffer); Kimberly Williams (Annie Banks-MacKenzie); George Newbern (Bryan MacKenzie); Kieran Culkin (Matty Banks); B.D. Wong (Howard Weinstein); Peter Michael Goetz (John MacKenzie); Kate McGregor Stewart (Joanna MacKenzie); Jane Adams (Dr. Megan Eisenberg); Eugene Levy (Mr. Habib); Rebecca Chambers (Young Woman at Gym); April Ortiz (Olivia); Dulcy Rogers (Ava, The Beautician); Kathy Anthony (Beautician #2); Adrian Canzoneri (Justin); Lori Alan (Mrs. Habib); Stephanie Miller (Annie, Age Four); Hallie Meyers-Shyer (Annie, Age Seven); Jay Wolpert (Dr. Brooks); Ann Walker (Dr. Brooks' Nurse); Sandra Silvestri (Jogging Mom); William Akey (Frantic Father #1); Seth Kaplan (Wild Four Year Old); Jonathan Emerson (Frantic Father #2); Joshua Preston (Tantrum Toddler); K.C. Colwell (Father Heading Off to Work); Chase Colwell (Adorable Toddler); Tony Simotes (Construction Foreman); Annie Myers-Shyer, Linda DeScenna, and Heidi Averill (Shower Guests); Chelsea Lynn (Matty's Friend); Sue Colwell (Nina's Customer); Rodriego Botero and Vince Lozano (Gang Kids); Caroline Lagerfelt and Ilene Waterstone (Check-in Nurses); Wendy Worthington (Prostate Nurse); Dorian Spencer (E.R. Nurse); Harris Laskawy (Prostate Doctor); Roxanne Beckford and Valerie Hemmerich (Nina's Nurses); Peter Spears (Dr. Wagner); Susan Beaubian (Annie's Nurse); Mychael Bates (Hospital Orderly); Jerri Rose White and Shannon

Kennedy (Baby Megan); Casey Boersma and Dylan Boersma (Baby George); Katie Pierce (Two Month Old Megan); Jonathan Selstad (Two Month Old George).

LOS ANGELES TIMES, 12/8/95, Calendar/p. 1, Kevin Thomas

"Father of the Bride Part II" is as bright and shiny as a Christmas tree ornament and will likely be cause for holiday season cheer in many a family feeling overdosed on brutality and depravity on the screen.

The seasoned husband-and-wife team of Nancy Meyers and Charles Shyer—she produces, he directs, they collaborate on the script—and their expert cast, virtually intact from the 1991 "Father of the Bride," knows exactly how to deliver the goods, just like Santa.

Having gone through the trauma of marrying off a cherished daughter, Steve Martin's George Banks finds himself on another dilemma: No sooner does his daughter Annie (Kimberly Williams) announce that she's expecting a baby than his wife, Nina (Diane Keaton), reveals that she too is pregnant. If George feels too young to be a grandfather, he also believes he's too old to be a father at his age, which his secretary has calculated as being exactly 31 days younger than President Clinton.

Unsurprisingly, Martin is adept at conveying the angst of middle-age male crisis, but the film doesn't develop his anxiety much beyond George high-tailing it to the gym—he's not really out of shape, for that matter—and the barbershop for a dye job. Very quickly the film settles into a kind of comfortable '50s sitcom in which a screenful of nice, affluent and intelligent people sort out their emotions and priorities in the face of inevitable changes created by the advent of babies in two households.

What Meyers and Shyer have accomplished is to create a pleasant, sentimental domestic comedy out of a family that really has no problems to overcome, not an easy feat. These people have everything: great looks—Martin and Keaton couldn't possibly make middle age look more attractive—good health, plenty of love and lots of money. Sure, they have to make choices and accept the passing of time like the rest of us. But they all live in homes worth hundreds of thousands of dollars; when George impetuously sells the Banks' gracious San Marino colonial only to buy it back, he has no problem paying $100,000 over his selling price.

Indeed, it is this transaction that blemishes "Father of the Bride II" as an otherwise innocuous fantasy of upper-middle-class American life. By making the purchaser of the Banks home an unshaven, tough-minding Arab (played with humor by Eugene Levy), Meyers and Shyer—in an amazing lapse of judgment for such pros—reinforce a nasty Southern California stereotype: that of the sharp-dealing Middle Easterner who tears down a gracious older home and replaces it with a monstrously over-scaled residence. The filmmakers clearly don't mean to be funny at the Arab's expense, but their film is too unreal for it not to play that way.

Ironically, they get away with a flamboyant gay stereotype in Martin Short's giddy party organizer supreme, the weirdly accented Franck Eggelhoffer, and in his equally campy cohort Howard (B.D. Wong). Franck has been written with genuine affection and imagination, and played with such panache by Short, that he could stand as an homage to Franklin Pangborn, that definitive screen sissy of Hollywood's Golden Era. Most important, Franck emerges as a three-dimensional individual who actually connects with the Banks family.

The film's best touch is when Franck talks George into constructing a new wing to his house especially for the baby—unnecessary since Annie's room is surely unused—and it turns out not to be the kiddie kitsch we're braced for but the most beautiful child's room imaginable with a refined, exquisitely appointed cream-colored interior reminiscent of early 20th century rooms featuring painted Louis XV and XVI-style furniture. But then production designer Linda DeScenna has good high-end WASP taste down pat, and her efforts have been given a burnished look by cinematographer William Fraker.

While Martin, Keaton, Williams and George Newbern as Nina's husband plus others form an ensemble, the film boasts another scene-stealer besides Short in Jane Adams, who plays a young, pretty, coolly competent obstetrician—exactly the kind of doctor you would want to have in any circumstances.

Well into the film you find yourself saying to yourself that Louis B. Mayer would have loved this film with its idealization of family life only to catch yourself realizing that, after all, it's a reworking of MGM's "Father's Little Dividend" (1951), the sequel to the original 1950 "Father of the Bride."

NEW YORK POST, 12/8/95, p. 51, Michael Medved

"Father of the Bride, Part II" provides few surprises—which is, of course, precisely the point of this sort of contrived, fluffy, sentimental sequel. Audiences aren't expecting broadened horizons or aesthetic envelope-pushing here; they crave another helping of those familiar elements that made the previous recipe so tasty.

In this case, the material feels even more reheated because the 1991 "Father of the Bride" was already a remake of a 1950 film (with Spencer Tracy), which spawned its own delightful sequel ("Father's Little Dividend") in 1951, which, in turn, loosely inspired this new film.

Despite the shadows of all these amiable ancestors, "FOTB2" still manages to provoke big laughs and some real tears with its supremely sunny vision of a refreshingly functional upper-middle-class family.

The story picks up a few months after businessman Steve Martin has married off his adored and beautiful architect daughter (Kimberly Williams)to a responsible and good-looking young man (George Newbern).

Approaching 50, Martin is contented with his mellow marriage (to Diane Keaton), his witty 12-year-old (Kieran Culkin), and their cozy Colonial on a leafy street in Pasadena, Calif. He is badly shaken however, when his daughter announces that she is expecting.

"I wasn't ready to be a grandfather," he admits in part of his consistently caustic voice-over narration. "What's so grand about it, anyway?"

Trying to reassure himself of his youth and vigor, George Banks (Martin) gets his hair dyed black, picks up a sexy something at Victoria's Secret, and comes home for an amorous afternoon with his bemused wife. A few weeks later, she's feeling so queasy she suspects menopause; instead, the doctor declares that she's expecting too, much to the consternation of her husband.

"The kid's gonna love spending his adolescence in a retirement home," Martin frets. "He certainly won't have to worry about us hearing him come in late ... because we won't be able to hear."

Director Charles Shyer and producer Nancy Myers (who also collaborated on the screenplay) have come to know and love all these characters; they portray their dilemmas with sweetness and sincerity, winning warm, effortlessly effective performances from everyone in the cast.

Even so, the movie at times feels as artificially padded as its two pregnant female leads—especially when it re-introduces "Franck" (Martin Short) the flamboyant wedding arranger with the impenetrable accent who tickled audiences in the first film.

Here, he stages a double baby shower, but since this chore doesn't give the popular character enough to do, the script strains to make him the family's architect, aerobics instructor, and all-purpose best friend—who is, wouldn't you know, conveniently on hand for the dramatic double delivery.

Another sour note involves a subplot in which the family home is threatened by a gratuitously insulting Middle Eastern stereotype named "Mr. Habib," amusingly played by Eugene Levy; Arab-American watchdog groups will promptly (and appropriately) protest.

Others might complain of fantasy elements in the whole setup; the Steve Martin character, for instance, impulsively writes a check for $100,000 to save his house, yet we got no glimpse of the toil that generates all this wealth.

Most moviegoers, however, will welcome characters who are so spectacularly fortunate and affectionate, and will feel fortunate themselves to spend two hours in their company.

NEWSDAY, 12/8/95, Part II/p. B7, John Anderson

Thanks to the inescapable parade of plugs and trailers advancing this film, disclosing the gimmick that's supposed to be giving CPR to "Father of the Bride PART II" is disclosing nothing: Both Nina Banks (Diane Keaton) and her daughter, Annie (Kimberly Williams) are pregnant at the same time, making bemused and bewildered father/husband/grandfather-to-be George Banks (Steve Martin) apoplectic.

I don't know about you, but I'm ready for an epidural.

When Spencer Tracy did this puzzled paternal stuff in the original "Father of the Bride" and its sequel, "Father's Little Dividend" (in which grandma Joan Bennett did NOT get pregnant), it was funny, because Tracy brought dignity to the role—and had something to lose by playing the buffoon. Martin has no such liability. Add to this the cavalier way money, pregnancy, Arabs and gays are tossed around, and what you have is probably the most insulting movie of the year. And in 1995, that's saying something.

Over the opening credits, we hear Steve Tyrell sing "Give Me the Simple Life" and watch a series of rooms glide by that suggest what Martha Stewart could do if she really had money. Then, we see Martin tapping his fingers impatiently, suggesting he wants to get out of this house. This, of course, is not the case: George Banks is in his armchair, awaiting his women ("they're my life ...") who are upstairs prepping for their two-pronged assault on the maternity ward. He then launches into a flashback that takes up most of the movie, complete with prolonged slo-mo sequences, much screaming, tinkly music, tinkly characters (Martin Short and B.D. Wong as Franck and Howard) and a diaperload of recycled jokes.

Never mind that no scene like this first one ever reappears, or that when the babies do arrive (with the portentousness of Charlton Heston parting the Red Sea, or the Valkyries coming home to roost) the situation is warmed-over "I Love Lucy"-style chaos. Questioning things like this in a film by Nancy Meyers (producer/co-writer) and Charles Shyer (co-writer/director) is like asking the Sphinx if he wants a drink.

You might. In the end, two women have had babies. That they happen to be mother and daughter is coincidental, and perplexing: Despite his protestations to the contrary, has the relationship between George and Nina disintegrated to such an extent that she's abandoned birth control entirely? Is there some Freudian inference we can draw to explain a middle-aged woman intentionally getting pregnant, perhaps to compete with her own child? The parent who has the more evident mid-life crisis is George, who dyes his hair, strains himself at the gym and lets his love light shine. But that Nina: She's a mystery. Or an idiot.

Meyers and Shyer, who turned out the first film (the first remake, that is) and also perpetrated "Private Benjamin," "Baby Boom" and "Irreconcilable Differences," are hacks supreme, which puts them at the top of the food chain in Hollywood. That, and this film, show just how disconnected Hollywood is from the lives of its customers.

As part of George's mid-life crisis, he decides to sell the house, which is purchased by the unpleasant Mr. Habib (Eugene Levy). When George discovers that Habib plans to tear it down and build two in its place, he throws himself in front of the wrecking ball and accedes to Habib's demand: $100,000 over and above the selling price. George, of course, lives in a fantasy world—for one thing, women don't generally look this composed and beautiful while having babies—so he simply writes Habib a check.

There was an awkward silence in the audience at the screening I attended, as George danced about his new/old front yard and celebrated having been gouged by Habib (Comical Arabs, like Conspicuous Affluence, are due for a comeback. See: "Sabrina"). Am I wrong, or is this still a lot of money? If George Banks can write a check of such manly proportions just to atone for his own stupidity, he shouldn't have had any problem paying for his daughter's wedding in the first film. And if someone had figured *that* out ahead of time, it would have saved us all a lot of aggravation.

SIGHT AND SOUND, 4/96, p. 45, Liese Spencer

Annie and her husband Bryan announce they are expecting a baby. Stunned, Annie's father George experiences a mid-life crisis. He visits the gym, buys a new outfit and has his hair dyed. On his return, he corners his wife Nina and they make love. Some days later, an Arab couple appear in his garden wanting to buy his house, offering to pay extra if he moves out in ten days. When George tells Nina about the sale she evicts him. He stays the night with Annie.

The next day, father and daughter play a last game of basketball before George and Nina move out. George and Nina stay at Bryan's parents' mansion. Feeling unwell, Nina suggests she may be experiencing the menopause. Tests show that she is pregnant. Deciding they must move back home, George buys back his house for double the price. Annie and Nina employ the flamboyant Franck Egglehoffer to design a nursery and baby shower.

When Annie is offered a new job in Boston and Bryan suggests they stay in California, she is upset. She visits George, who reluctantly tells her she must pursue the new career in Boston. When Bryan goes away on business, George is left in charge of preparations for the double birth. Exhausted, he takes a sedative and falls asleep. Annie begins labour and Frank has to drag George to the hospital where he is mistakenly admitted for a prostate examination. Nina also goes into labour and the women's babies are born on the same night. Some days later, Annie and Bryan leave for Boston. George waves goodbye, holding his baby daughter.

In *Father of the Bride*, narrator George Banks tells the audience that he "hates change". Director Charles Shyer apparently shares George's conservatism since this latest offering cheerfully recycles the set, cast and gags of that film. *Father of the Bride 2* is both a sequel to a remake and a remake of a sequel: the screenplay is based on the 1951 film *Father's Little Dividend*, Vincent Minelli's follow up to his original 1950 *Father of the Bride*. Such a straightjacketed formula allows little room for innovation, but proves ideal for Shyer's brand of reconstituted comedy, which here finds expression in a kind of studio soap opera.

Father of the Bride 2 plots a familiar trajectory of panic, preparation and celebration; swapping the trauma of marriage for the crisis of childbirth. As with most sequels, the film offers the repetition and continuity of a television series. Martin Short rehearses his role as a camp designer and a sheepish-looking Diane Keaton returns as Nina, the sensible foil to Steve Martin's mawkish hero. Returning to the idealised suburbia of the first film, *Father 2* shows George Banks' financial and emotional equilibrium threatened by a double pregnancy and a foreigner who colonises his ivy-clad home.

The fact that Shyer feels the need to import an Arab stereotype underlines just how poorly the film utilises Steve Martin's comic talent. As Banks, he is left to rail against soft targets, with the result that he comes across as self-pitying and unsympathetic. In comparison with the naturalistic acting of the rest of the cast, Martin's slapstick appears embarrassingly incongruous. Just as its predecessor did, *Father 2* explores the ambiguous feelings a father experiences when his daughter grows up and transfers her affection to another man, Martin's soulful appraisals of Annie are clearly meant to convey warm, paternal feelings, but instead appear as smouldering incestuous desire.

Luckily, any uneasy suggestions of sexual jealousy can be resolved by a spot of ball play. Basketball is here a metaphor for the exclusive relationship between father and daughter and acts as a symbolic space for George Banks' soppy reminiscences. As Annie shoots baskets, 'My Girl' replaces dialogue and soft-focus dissolves show her retreating through stages of childhood until she is a child once more. The motif is completed when Annie presents George with a miniature basketball for his new baby daughter.

But when Martin stops mugging, any residual traces of humour disappear. Throughout the film, air-brushed portraits of the family are larded with Martin's syrupy voice-over making observations about his enduring affection for his wife, or his protective pride in his daughter. When his brood tearfully vacates the family home, Banks quips, "Hey! What are we, the schmaltz family?", a question which assumes an unintentional rhetorical flavour. Anticipating the birth of his child, Banks' transcendental moment of fatherhood is wordlessly related in a scene where the camera greedily consumes the pastel perfection not of a nursery, but of a luxurious new "baby suite". Audiences who fail to discover any laughs in Shyer's toothless comedy can console themselves with the anodyne pleasures of such aspirational set appreciation.

VILLAGE VOICE, 12/19/95, p. 82, Amy Taubin

The woman sitting next to me coveted the Bennison pillows. I wanted the earthenware bowls. Neither she nor I had any desire to be pregnant at age 50, give or take a few years, as in Nina Banks (Diane Keaton) in *Father of the Bride* and remake of the sequel to the original *Father of the Bride, Father's Little Dividend*.

Since this is the '90s rather than the '50s and George Banks (Steve Martin) is a lot more affluent than the original Dad (Spencer Tracy), it's appropriate that Dad nouveau is expecting not one little dividend but two. George and Nina are about to become parents again just around the time that they become grandparents. And it will come as no surprise to anyone that, although Nina is due six weeks after daughter Annie (Kimberly Williams), the climax of the picture involves George running back and forth between Nina and Annie's delivery rooms, son-in-law Bryan (George Newbern) being conveniently away on business.

Plot, however, is merely the pretext for an orgy of Martha Stewart living, a two-hour inventory of the pleasures of being upper-middle-class—rich enough to build a $200,000 baby wing on a $2 million house in Pasadena though not so rich that a leaking roof or an infestation of termites passes without a show of concern. But George and Nina not only have a perfectly appointed, wonderfully comfortable home, they also run successful businesses that require them to put in zero hours on the job. Moreover, they are unfailingly good-humored and considerate and they've passed these virtues down to their kids, for whom sibling rivalry is nonexistent.

What gives *Father ... II* its special spin is the notion that age is not a factor for the Georges and Ninas of the world. The riddle of Oedipus no longer applies. Thus Nina, after an initial quip about her pregnancy being the stuff of *Enquirer* headlines, sails through it with narv a back spasm nor a mention of amniocentesis. And George, who panics at the sight of an obstetrician who looks young enough to be his daughter, warms to her when she points out that they're both wearing Hush Puppies.

Martin's performance is as impeccable as the set decoration, though one wishes he'd stop wasting his skill. Keaton flaunts her matronly hips, daring us to remember Annie Hall, but despite a jawline that's tighter than it was a decade ago in *Baby Boom*, she looks past the age of conception (no cosmetic surgery for wombs). *Father ... II* is a film for all the people who voted against their class interest in 1994. I'm sure it'll make a mint.

Also reviewed in:
CHICAGO TRIBUNE, 12/8/95, Friday/p. C, Michael Wilmington
NEW YORK TIMES, 12/8/95, p. C3, Janet Maslin
VARIETY, 12/11-17/95, p. 84, Brian Lowry
WASHINGTON POST, 12/8/95, p. F7, Hal Hinson
WASHINGTON POST, 12/8/95, Weekend/p. 43, Desson Howe

FEAST OF JULY

A Touchstone Pictures release of a Merchant Ivory production in association with Peregrine Productions. *Executive Producer:* Ismail Merchant and Paul Bradley. *Producer:* Henry Herbert and Christopher Neame. *Director:* Christopher Menaul. *Screenplay:* Christopher Neame. *Based on the novel by:* H.E. Bates. *Director of Photography:* Peter Sova. *Editor:* Chris Wimble. *Music:* Zbigniew Preisner. *Choreographer:* Sue Weston. *Sound:* Stuart Moser and Mike Shoring. *Sound Editor:* Colin Ritchie. *Casting:* Kathleen Mackie. *Production Designer:* Christopher Robilliard. *Art Director:* Roy Stannard, Caroline Smith, and Sonja Klaus. *Set Decorator:* Jill Quertier. *Special Effects:* Stuart Brisdon. *Costumes:* Phoebe De Gaye. *Make-up:* Tina Earnshaw and Susie Adams. *Running time:* 118 minutes. *MPAA Rating:* R.

CAST: Embeth Davidtz (Bella Ford); Tom Bell (Ben Wainwright); Gemma Jones (Mrs. Wainwright); James Purefoy (Jedd Wainwright); Ben Chaplin (Con Wainwright); Kenneth Anderson (Matty Wainwright); Greg Wise (Arch Wilson); David Neal (Mitchy Mitchell); Daphne Neville (Mrs. Mitchell); Mark Heal (Clerk at Shoe Factory); Julian Protheroe (Bowler-Hatted Man); Tim Preece (Preacher); Charles De'ath (Billy Swaine); Colin Prockter (Man in Pub); Richard Hope (Squire Wyman); Kate Hamblyn (Harvest Girl); Paddy Ward (Tom); Alan Perrin (Ticket Clerk); Dominic Gover (First Rowing Youth); Richards Hicks (Second Rowing Youth); Arthur Kelly (Game Keeper); Colin Mayes (Seaman); Mark Bazeley (Man in Restaurant); Stephen Frost (Tubby Man); David Belcher (Second Man); Frederick Warder (Captain Rogers); Tim Perrin (Hangman); Mark Whelehan (Assistant Hangman); Rupert Bates and Tom Marshall (Prison Wardens).

LOS ANGELES TIMES, 10/13/95, Calendar/p. 18, John Anderson

Since Eve, the sins of woman have been considered far more insidious than those of man. Why? Perhaps because by placing female error on a kind of cocked pedestal, men can get away with more. Let's face it: Helen of Troy hardly did a thing and launched a thousand angry ships. Odysseus didn't come home for 20 years, and when he did he was a hero.

What "Feast of July" is about is the wake of sin, a single sin, committed by a woman, in this case Isabella Ford (Embeth Davidtz). Seduced, abandoned and pregnant in the late 19th Century, she lumbers across the harsh winter landscape of the English Midlands, gives birth in a barn to a stillborn child and wanders stunned into a red bricked industrial town, where she is taken home by the kindly Ben Wainwright (Tom Bell).

There, she gets a skeptical eye from his wife (Gemma Jones) and an appreciative sizing-up by his three grown sons, who commence a barnyard-style mating dance over the comely young woman with the secret. Mom is not amused. And an air of dread hangs over the entire household.

Davidtz, who made such an impression in "Schindler's List," plays Bella, as she's called, with defiant restraint. Deeply wounded, scarred by the loss of love and child, she is determined to locate Arch Wilson (Greg Wise), the man who betrayed her. She finds him—and finds he's got a wife and child—and forsakes him. She flirts with brothers Matty (Kenneth Anderson) and Jedd (James Purefoy) and becomes engaged to the youngest, simplest Wainwright, Con (Ben Chaplin). But Bella's is a world without redemption: Her single moral lapse will haunt her, to a concluding tragedy so absolute it's farcical.

The film, by Christopher Menaul (who directed television's "Prime Suspect"), moves like Bella, with muted passion and determination. This is a Merchant Ivory production, but it eschews the lushness associated with most of its films for an aesthetic allegiance to the 19th Century. The cinematography by Peter Sova makes life seem positively claustrophobic, and the tone is so concentrated and constrained that when "Feast of July" does combust into violence—there is one scene of visceral brutality—you're stunned.

NEW YORK POST, 10/13/95, p. 47, Michael Medved

Do not scorn her words harsh and bitter
Do not laugh at her shame and downfall
For a moment just pause and consider'
That a man was the cause of it all ...

The words of this sentimental old song ("She Is More to Be Pitied Than Censured") evoke the spirit of a bygone age when society worried more about seductive cads than dead beat dads.

In the 19th century, a vulnerable young woman could be "ruined" in every sense of the word by false promises from a manipulating male, a tragedy played out struggling against the windy, wintry vastness of the moors of Western England. Finding her way to a stone ruin, she delivers—then buries—a baby in isolation and agony.

Determined to find the man who caused her suffering, she staggers into the red brick industrial town he had described as his home, a kindly lamp lighter (Tom Bell) and his deeply religious family. As she slowly gains strength, working to earn her keep, all three of the family's sons vie for her attention, regardless of her mysterious and troubled past. She eventually gives her heart to the youngest son (played by a prodigiously gifted newcomer, Ben Chaplin)—a shy, simple, down-trodden soul who spends his Sundays after church wandering nearby fields or communing with pigeons in an abandoned abbey.

When they announce their engagement, the boy's worried mother (played with incandescent intensity by Gemma Jones) puts aside her reservations to try to share their joy, but then the young woman accidentally crosses paths with the worthless, unrepentant smooth-talker who had dishonored her, producing tragic consequences for all concerned.

In this gorgeous retelling, this passionate, deceptively simple but deeply moving tale has the stark, ancient quality of Thomas Hardy's fiction. It's based on a novel by H.E. Bates, a superb British writer little known in the states, who died in 1974.

The movie features perhaps the most vivid evocation of the Late Victorian world ever captured on film—with sets and locations that look vital and lived-in, rather than painstakingly reconstructed.

Though released by the famed Merchant/Ivory production company, "Feast of July" avoids their normal focus on aristocrats and intellectuals, concentrating instead on poor, humble (but never idealized) country folk.

Director Christopher Menaul (a BBC veteran in his feature film debut) captures harvest time, workshop and seaport with poetic splendor and riveting detail. His cause is helped substantially by captivating, spectacularly sensitive musical accompaniment by Zbigniew Preisner ("The Secret Garden," "Europa Europa"), who ought to be considered a front-runner for the Oscar for best score.

South African Embeth Davidtz displays the same combination of vulnerability and unshakable strength she communicated so powerfully as Helen Hirsch in "Schindler's List"—here, playing an even more complex survivor.

Her richly textured characterization, accomplished with amazingly little dialogue, helps lend this old-fashioned tale of a woman wronged (and potentially redeemed) an unexpected edge of both immediacy and timelessness.

SIGHT AND SOUND, 9/96, p. 43, Geoffrey Macnab

Rural England, the late nineteenth century. Bella Ford, a young, pregnant woman staggers across a desolate moor. She stops alone in a little hut and miscarries. Then she continues on her way, eventually arriving distressed and confused, in a nearby town. She's looking for Arch Wilson, the lover who deserted her, but he is nowhere to be found. A local family, the Wainwrights, take pity on her and offer her a roof for the night. Learning that Bella's parents are dead and that her only living relative, her sister, is far away in Ireland, Mrs Wainwright decides to allow her to stay permanently. Gradually, Bella recovers her spirits and soon she becomes firm friends with the Wainwrights' three sons, Jedd, an army corporal, Matty, a shoemaker, and Con. All three sons seem enamoured of her, but at first she repels their advances.

As the brothers compete for her affections, a rivalry emerges between them. Jedd goes away with his regiment. Matty, frustrated by the lack of opportunity in his home town, decides to try his luck in London. Passionate but simple-minded Con is the only one left at home. He and Bella fall in love. She agrees to marry him after telling him about her earlier affair with Arch Wilson. She has since learned that Arch lied to her and already had a wife and child when she first met him. One afternoon, Bella and Con are rowing down river. By coincidence, they're spotted by Arch, who is fishing by the banks. He taunts them and humiliates Con by refusing to return Bella's hat, which fell off her head and floated down stream to him. Con reacts furiously, pummelling Arch to death with a stone. Con and Bella flee across country. They hope to escape to Ireland. When they arrive at a small port town, Con is racked with guilt. Despite Bella's entreaties, he turns himself in. He is sentenced to be hung. The Wainwright family are devastated and blame Bella for his misfortunes. She leaves for Ireland, pregnant with his child.

Although based on an H.E. Bates story and made under the auspices of Merchant-Ivory, *Feast Of July* is very different in tone from any of their E. M. Forster or Henry James adaptations. Despite the film's emphasis on costume and landscape, this is no celebration of country house living. Its characters are ordinary working folk in late nineteenth-century England, living in the shadow of the pub and the Providence Chapel.

The storyline clearly presented the film-makers with a dilemma. Bella Ford, the abandoned woman who stirs up fervent passions in the breasts of three brothers, sounds like a heroine straight out of a bodice-ripping Catherine Cookson melodrama. However, the opening scene in which Bella is seen stumbling across a desolate moor as solemn music from Zbigniew Preisner (Kieslowski's favourite composer) echoes on the soundtrack, makes it apparent that the material here is going to be treated in deadly serious fashion. Colours are muted. Except in the harvest sequences or in the early days of Bella and Con's courtship, skies seem overcast. Characters dress in dark costumes. The problem with this approach is that it risks dulling the emotions. What ought to be a full-blown tearjerker ends up curiously remote. With its cobbled streets and old terraced houses, Christopher Robilliard's meticulously detailed production design creates a world which seems as distant and rarefied as the one celebrated in Ridley Scott's old Hovis advertisements.

Director Christopher Menaul (*Prime Suspect, Fatherland*) plumps for grainy realism throughout. His only formal flourishes come early on, when Bella is exhausted and delirious, and sees the characters around her in almost blinding white light as she faints. She is presented as a victim of a patriarchal society in which women are held to blame for the way the men around them behave. (When her fiancé Con murders her former lover, Arch Wilson, he is sent to the gallows, but she is the one treated as if she is responsible for the killing.) There's a strangely ritualistic aspect to the way the narrative unfolds—from the very moment Bella first sets foot inside the Wainwrights' house, it is inevitable that her past will come back to haunt her. It comes as absolutely no surprise when events take their tragic turn.

Bates' original story is essentially pastiche Thomas Hardy. Its final stages, in which the lovers flee their crime and briefly find peace of sorts away from an oppressive community, could have been borrowed wholesale from *Tess of the D'Urbervilles*. In his film of that book, Polanski is able to invest his closing scenes with a ritualistic intensity. Here, disappointingly, Menaul fails to quicken the narrative pulse. The picture lumbers to its pre-ordained conclusion at the same even-handed pace it has struck throughout. As in Kieslowski's *A Short Film About Killing*, both the original murder and the execution of the murderer seem all the more brutal for the matter-of-fact way in which they're presented. But this is surely supposed to be a love story, not a polemical drama about the iniquities of capital punishment. The cross-cutting between Con as he is dragged away to the gallows and Bella as she boards ship to head for a new life in Ireland is bathetic in the extreme. Likewise, the concluding image, in which she stands by the prow patting her stomach as if to announce she's pregnant with Con's child and will keep his memory alive, seems insufferably smug.

Politely applauding the acting in British costume dramas is often a way of drawing a veil around other shortcomings. In this case, the performances are in keeping with the film as a whole—detailed, subtle and a little mannered. Neither cast nor director are able to animate Christopher Neame's screenplay with the passion necessary the movie into something other than a museum piece.

VILLAGE VOICE, 10/24/95, p. 84, Leslie Camhi

A wildly untoward event (which I won't reveal) marks the opening moments of *Feast of July*, the first feature from British director Menaul; then, for a long time, nothing much happens. Embeth Davidtz plays Bella Ford, a mysterious woman in tattered traveling gear who's taken in by the Wainwrights, a family living in a perfect 19th-century English village near the harsh and stunning moors.

The Wainwrights have three sons: Jedd (James Purefoy), a dashing cavalry officer; Matty (Kenneth Anderson), an entrepreneurial cobbler; and Con (Ben Chaplin), a dark Byronic brooder. As you might imagine, they battle for the love of our lassie, and one eventually wins. Unfortunately, Bella is a woman with a past that keeps reappearing.

Embeth Davidtz gives a sensitive and nuanced performance, and the rest of the cast is fine in support of her. Menaul has a sharp eye for character, landscape, and narrative detail, though the film's music drips with nostalgia. But if trains, cottages, and costumes all appeared carefully authentic, I couldn't help feeling that this story was deeply anachronistic. What about the keen suspicions that would have followed a working-class woman travelling alone in the 19th century? Chastity was not thrown to the wind so easily; love, our modern excuse and panacea, was not exactly the same for our ancestors. Sometimes, a close attention to a period's look leaves out the heart of history.

Also reviewed in:
CHICAGO TRIBUNE, 10/20/95, Friday/p. H, Michael Wilmington
NEW REPUBLIC, 11/13/95, p. 32, Stanley Kauffmann
NEW YORK TIMES, 10/13/95, p. C12, Stephen Holden
VARIETY, 8/28-9/3/95, p. 67, David Stratton
WASHINGTON POST, 10/21/95, p. H5, Hal Hinson

FIRST KNIGHT

A Columbia Pictures release. *Executive Producer:* Gil Netter, Eric Rattray, and Janet Zucker. *Producer:* Jerry Zucker and Hunt Lowry. *Director:* Jerry Zucker. *Screenplay:* William Nicholson. *Story:* Lorne Cameron, David Hoselton, and William Nicholson. *Director of Photography:* Adam Greenberg. *Editor:* Walter Murch. *Music:* Jerry Goldsmith. *Music Editor:* Kenneth J. Hall. *Sound:* Colin Charles and (music) Bruce Botnick. *Sound Editor:* John Morris. *Production Designer:* John Box. *Art Director:* Bob Laing and Michael White. *Set Decorator:* Malcolm Stone. *Special Effects:* John Evans. *Visual Effects:* Dennis Lowe. *Costumes:* Nana Cecchi. *Make-up:* Peter Robb-King. *Stunt Coordinator:* Greg Powell and Dinny Powell. *Running time:* 131 minutes. *MPAA Rating:* PG-13.

CAST: Sean Connery (King Arthur); Richard Gere (Lancelot); Julia Ormond (Lady Guinevere of Leonesse); Ben Cross (Malagant); Liam Cunningham (Sir Agravaine); Christopher Villiers (Sir Kay); Valentina Pelka (Sir Patrise); Colin McCormack (Sir Mador); Ralph Ineson (Ralf); John Gielgud (Oswald); Stuart Bunce (Peter); Jane Robbins (Elise); Jean Marie Coffey (Petronella); Paul Kynman (Mark); Tom Lucy (Sir Sagramore); John Blakey (Sir Tor); Robert Gwyn Davin (Sir Gawaine); Sean Blowers (Sir Carados); Alexis Denisof (Sir Gaheris); Daniel Naprous (Sir Amant); Jonathan Cake (Sir Gareth); Paul Bentall (Jacob); Jonty Miller (Gauntlet Man); Rose Keegan (Mark's Wife); Mark Ryan (Challenger); Jeffrey Dench and Neille Phillips (Elders); Oliver Lewis, Wolf Christian, and Angus Wright (Marauders); Jonathan Jaynes and Eric Stone (Guards); Ryan Todd (Young Lancelot); Albie Woodington (Scout); Richard Claxton (Child); Dido Miles (Grateful Woman); Michael Hodgson (Young Man in Crowd); Susannah Corbett (Young Woman in Crowd); Susan Breslau (Wedding Guest); Kate Zucker (Flower Girl); Bob Zucker (Little Boy with Birds); Charlotte Zucker and Burt Zucker (Bread Vendors).

CHRISTIAN SCIENCE MONITOR, 7/7/95, p. 12, David Sterritt

Judging from its punning title and the fact that Jerry Zucker directed it—he cut his teeth on comedies like "Airplane!" and the first "Naked Gun" picture—you might think "First Knight" was a spoof of good King Arthur and the many movies he's inspired over the years.

There were times during its 2¼-hour length when I longed for the Monty Python gang to barge into the action—telling shaggy Lancelot he needs a major haircut, perhaps, or turning the Round Table into the world's largest pizza tray. But no, the movie is serious if not actually sober, retelling the old legend with a straight face, a reasonably warm heart, and a whole lot of muscle in the action scenes that punctuate the story like clockwork.

Like many an Arthurian film of old, it cares more about the love triangle between its main characters than sweeping issues like the conflict between civic duty and self-indulgence, or the king's dedication to the rule of law. Zucker also directed the popular "Ghost," so it's not surprising that his camera dwells most convincingly on the moon-eyed gazes exchanged by Richard Gere's brash Lancelot and Julia Ormond's sensitive Guinevere, allotting just a few strong scenes to Sean Connery's regal Arthur and leaving the other knights mostly out of the picture.

Except the evil Malagant, of course, who struts through the story with a malevolent glare and a wicked yen to make life unpleasant for the Camelot crowd. He's played by Ben Cross with an antisocial gusto that nearly throws the film's romantic tone out of whack; but without him the battle scenes would seem even more perfunctory than they do.

More interesting than "First Knight" itself is the current spate of historical epics that it's part of—including the competently made "Rob Roy," with Liam Neeson in the title role, and the hyperactive "Braveheart," with Mel Gibson as director and star. Like those Scottish adventures, "First Knight" is proudly old-fashioned, combining nostalgia for premodern life with the dubious notion that love and death used to be simpler, nobler, and somehow more meaningful than they seem today.

FILMS IN REVIEW, 9-10/95, p. 56, Andy Pawelczak

In *First Knight*'s pre-credit sequence, we see a down-at-the-heels Lancelot challenging villagers to a playful sword fight—it's how this itinerant swordsman earns a living. And immediately we know something is wrong. This Lancelot is no hieratic figure come to life from a tapestry; as played by Richard Gere with a flirtatious smile and an endearing twinkle in his eye, he's a combination of an Errol Flynn-like Robin Hood and a Japanese samurai possessed of almost magical prowess with a sword. The confusion of signs is characteristic of a movie that never quite decides if it's a boy's adventure, a love story or a political allegory.

All of which is too bad. The Arthurian legends are part of the taproot of Western civilization, though it's hard to imagine how anyone working today could make a film based on them without being campy. In *Lancelot du Lac* (1974), Bresson—whose films admittedly belong to a different world of sensibility than *First Knight*—used the tales to mount a meditation on civilization and the paradoxes of religious faith. His knights encased in clanking armor were like precursors of our tanks, and when the men emerged from their metal carapaces they were as fragile and crepuscular as the glow of embattled, betrayed civilization itself. Jerry Zucker (*Ghost, Ruthless People, Naked Gun*) and his screenplay writer, William Nicholson (*Shadowlands*), do have an idea of sorts, but it's one that levels out the mythic power of the legend instead of giving it new life.

Lancelot first meets Guinevere (Julia Ormond) when he rescues her from the depredations of Prince Malagant (Ben Cross), a one-time Knight of the Round Table who has gone to the bad. It's a case of love at first sight—Gere, staring into Ormond's eyes, says he can always tell when a woman wants him—but Guinevere of course is betrothed to King Arthur (Sean Connery), and honor and all the imperatives of the medieval world demand that she marry him. In one of the film's big set pieces, she arrives at Camelot in the middle of the night to be greeted by Arthur who is flanked by a procession of torch-bearing men. The iconography is all wrong it's too grandiose, stentorian, almost fascist; it's as if the demonic monkeys who attend the Wicked Witch of the West have inexplicably become the guardians of Oz.

But never fear—Arthur is a good populist king and the black-clad Malagant is the fascist who, in a rapacious search for lebensraum, invades Guinevere's small state, Leonesse. As Malagant rails on about enlightened self-interest and the importance of leadership rather than brotherhood, Arthur blandly asserts that the only life worth living is one in the service of others. *First Knight* is that rarity these days—a tendentiously liberal movie—though the waters get a bit muddied when Malagant, a sophistical moral relativist, accuses Arthur of imposing his ideas of law and morality on the rest of the world. For Camelot, read America in the Kennedy era of muscular Cold War liberalism when this country still believed its mission was to defend weaker states.

The triangular love story gets lost in all these political maunderings—it never generates any heat or resonance. As Guinevere, Julia Ormond doesn't have much to do except look beautiful and occasionally troubled. Her role reminded me of anthropologist Levi-Strauss's famous remark that in primitive societies women are like pigs, a form of currency that circulates among the men. Sean Connery's Arthur looks regal enough but he's a paper cut-out king, and as Lancelot, Gere, with nary a gray hair, is once again acting out a coming-of-age scenario—his Lancelot has to renounce his rootless ways and accept responsibility, viz. join the Round Table and serve others. Ask not what Camelot can do for you, but what you can do for Camelot.

LOS ANGELES TIMES, 7/7/95, Calendar/p. 1, Kenneth Turan

Those who survived "Yes, Giorgio" won't be rushing to see Luciano Pavarotti as a romantic lead any time soon, just as veterans of "The Jazz Singer" were not disturbed that Laurence Olivier never managed another film with Neil Diamond. And anyone who made it through "King David" knows that taking Richard Gere out of the 20th Century is an extremely risky proposition.

It is a measure of the surprising resilience of "First Knight" that its casting of Gere as a cocky street tough who becomes Sir Lancelot does not decimate director Jerry Zucker's version of the King Arthur legend. But Gere is such a completely contemporary actor, so at sea in a suit of armor, that seeing him saunter through medieval halls as if he were a vice cop strolling Sunset Boulevard is shock enough to take us out of the story whenever he appears.

Aside from Gere, "First Knight" acquits itself honorably enough. Sean Connery scores points for typecasting as the noble Arthur: Julia Ormond, the ingenue of the moment, is appropriately fetching and feisty as Guinevere his bride, and 91-year-old Sir John Gielgud puts in a brief appearance to show everyone how it ought to be done.

And though certain over-choreographed segments play like halftime at the Camelot Bowl, "First Knight's" large-scale action set pieces are capably done and more than tolerably exciting. And Gere, coached by Bob Anderson, who worked with Errol Flynn 40-some years ago, not only did his own swordfighting but is actually quite good at it. The problem for him, and the film, comes when the non-physical acting begins.

This is not meant as a slur on Gere's ability. But the specifically here-and-now aspects of his persona that led to the considerable success of both "An Officer and a Gentleman" and "Pretty Woman" betray him here. To be a successful romantic fantasy, a film like "First Knight" must compel belief in its mythical setting, and perhaps the nicest thing to say about Gere's presence is that it doesn't make that any easier.

"First Knight's" William Nicholson script (from a story by Lorne Cameron & David Hoselton and Nicholson) takes several liberties with the Arthurian legend, which is mostly OK given that the particulars of the story have changed greatly over the 1,400 years it has been part of the Western literary tradition. Absent are the sword Excalibur, the magician Merlin and the mysterious Morgan le Fay, replaced by an elaborate back-story for Lancelot that takes pains to explain how a non-traditional figure like Gere ended up a knight.

This movie's Lancelot is a wandering swordsman from who knows where who makes a living hustling winner-take-all bouts with gullible locals. A devilish rogue who owes his success to his indifference about staying alive, Lancelot is so intent on going his own way you half-expect the Crystals' "He's a Rebel" to appear on the soundtrack when he's around.

Lancelot doesn't know it, but he is fated to cross paths with Guinevere of Leonesse, the good-hearted ruler of that tiny town who finds herself the target of predatory raids by the bad-to-the-bone Malagant ("Chariot of Fire's" Ben Cross in a splendid change of pace), a former member of the Round Table who believes, rather like some modern politicians, that "men don't want brotherhood, they want leadership,"

Those fierce raids cement Guinevere's decision to marry the powerful and protective King Arthur of Camelot, still dashing despite all those gray hairs. "How could I love anyone more?" she asks rhetorically, one of those fate-tempting statements that are reminiscent of the on-the-nose qualities of writer Nicholson's previous scripts for "Shadowlands," "Sarafina!" and "Nell."

Nearly captured by Malagant while on her way to Arthur, Guinevere is rescued by Lancelot, who just happens to be in the neighborhood. In the film's most embarrassing sequence, she fights off his romantic advances with a magisterial "How dare you treat me like this," and he insistently replies, "I can tell when a woman wants me, I can see it in her eyes." It's a good thing Tennyson and Thomas Mallory didn't live to hear this.

Chance also brings the young swordsman to Camelot and the attention of Arthur, who looks him over and says, "Lancelot, we won't be forgetting that name." Soon enough the three of them are involved in a "a woman who loved two heroes too well" love triangle that has been made so contemporary it seems to cry out for air time on Oprah.

Though it is hard to resist having some fun with "First Knight's" weaknesses—which include its decision not to emphasize Lancelot's traditional fierce loyalty to the king—director Zucker, in his first outing since "Ghost," has in truth made an acceptable attempt at a Camelot romance that, if not entirely convincing, stumbles less frequently than might be imagined.

Aside from Gere, presumably cast for his box-office appeal, "First Knight's" other failure of nerve comes in its ending, which, probably for the same reason, departs as far as it dares from the terrible sadness that has made the Arthur story last as long as it has. Long enough, presumably, to survive even this.

NEW YORK, 7/17/95, p. 49, David Denby

There's nothing startling in *First Knight*, another clanging-sword epic, but the picture, directed by Jerry Zucker (*Ghost*) and shot in Wales, is handsome, and satisfyingly romantic, with a strong traditional production designed by the great John Box. Richard Gere is perhaps too self-conscious to play a devil-may-care Lancelot modeled on Errol Flynn, but he's a lot less smarmy than he used to be, and his scenes with the Guinevere of Julia Ormond, a major actress in the making, actually generate some heat. *First Knight*, which also stars Sean Connery as an aging, noble King Arthur and Ben Cross as a black-eyed villain, has a pleasantly solid, old-Hollywood feeling to it.

NEW YORK POST, 7/7/95, p. 41, Michael Medved

At first blush, the idea of asking Richard Gere to portray Sir Lancelot seems like one of the most perverse pieces of Hollywood miscasting since John Wayne played Genghis Khan in 1954's immortally awful "The Conqueror"—or since Gere himself attempted to impersonate a biblical monarch in the titanic turkey "King David" (1985).

This time, however, Gere makes his performance work in its own odd terms, though in order to accept this audacious version of an American Gigolo in King Arthur's Court, you've first got to let it be forgot, that once there was a spot, for one brief shining moment that was known as Camelot.

The less you know about the ancient Arthurian legends, in fact, the better you'll like "First Knight." Producer-director Jerry Zucker (whose only previous solo directing effort was the mega-hit "Ghost") has completely restructured the Arthur-Guinevere-Lancelot triangle by creating a new, improved Lancelot who bears no resemblance at all to the aristocratic knight in shining armor who gallops through all the old stories.

This time, Lance is an unkempt, amoral, penniless wanderer who makes his living dueling peasants for money, and who by chance rescues the Lady Guinevere (Julia Ormond of "Legends of the Fall") from murderous thugs in the employ of the evil Malagant (played by the convincingly malevolent Ben Cross).

Though Guinevere is on her way to an arranged marriage with the much-older King Arthur (Sean Connery in a handsome silver hairpiece) she's instantly smitten by the sulky Lancelot.

It's a familiar movie situation: the spoiled rich girl is embarrassingly but irresistibly drawn to the moody, tender tough guy from the wrong side of the tracks. You almost expect this Lancelot to sport a black leather jacket and cigarette dangling from his lower lip.

In any event, Lancelot is similarly infatuated and follows Guinevere to Camelot, where he gets to rescue her from even more dire assaults, leading the grateful Arthur to reward this crazy, mixed-up kid by inviting him to join the most exclusive men's club in town: the Knights of the Round Table.

All of this plays much more effectively than it sounds because of Zucker's energetic and imaginative scenes of swordplay and derring-do, and consistently splendid production values.

John Box, legendary production designer on great films like "Lawrence of Arabia" and "Dr. Zhivago," here creates a hauntingly lovely, truly magical vision of Camelot, and Nana Cecchi provides stunning costumes that seem at once authentically ancient and startlingly original.

For most of the movie, director Zucker uses this visual splendor and the undeniable romantic electricity that crackles continuously among all three of his gorgeous stars, to sweep away all reservations concerning the film's shortcomings. By the conclusion of the picture, however, its mistakes and excesses seem to come home to roost as the whole movie collapses in a wretchedly contrived, insipidly "bittersweet" ending that will please no one.

Reaching that point you're left with the sort of sensation Apollo astronauts must have felt when they finally made it to the moon: Where you've arrived is absolutely nowhere, but getting there has been one hell of a ride.

NEWSDAY, 7/7/95, Part II/p. B2, Jack Mathews

Much of the good work, and all of the damage, was done on Jerry Zucker's fitfully entertaining "First Knight" when its three legendary characters—King Arthur, Queen Guinevere and Sir Lancelot—were cast. Sean Connery as the benevolent Arthur? A match made in casting heaven. The intelligent British beauty Julia Ormond as Guinevere? Perfect. Richard Gere as the dashing Lancelot? Get outta here!

What was Zucker thinking? Gere is the most contemporary of all contemporary actors, and about the most urban as well. And though he gamely tries to play Lancelot with the rakish charm of Errol Flynn's Robin Hood, he looks about as natural in this setting as graffiti on the Camelot gate.

As we might expect from the director of "Ghost," this interpretation of the Arthurian Legend focuses heavily on romantic sentiment and does away entirely with such literary accessories as the search for the Holy Grail, Merlin the Magician and the evil Mordred. "First Knight," with frequent forays to the battlefield, is about a strong, self-reliant woman torn by her love for two courageous but completely different men.

One is the beloved ruler of the magic kingdom of Camelot, a gleaming jewel of blue-roofed turrets and sanguine subjects, seemingly the only light left on during the Dark Ages. The other is a rootless vagabond, wandering the countryside living on wagers won from men taunted into testing his skill with the sword. One has everything to offer, including love and a wealth of philosophical purpose; the other can show her nothing except passion and a psychological scar left by a childhood tragedy.

Add the contrasting charms of Connery and Gere to the mix, and what's a girl to do?

Zucker and screenwriter William Nicholson ("Nell") attempt to make Gere a fair match for Connery by turning Lancelot into a literal super-hero. Not just good with a sword but invincible, and Gere handles his action scenes, many of them death-defying rescues of the grateful Guinevere, with an admirable (for a 45-year-old actor) athletic grace.

But "First Knight" succeeds or fails in the clinches, in the tender moments when this epic menage a trois is developing, and it's near agony watching the misplaced Gere, with his American accent and predatory "American Gigolo" moves, coming on to the defiantly sensible Guinevere.

When Lancelot and Guinevere are together for the first time and he says to her, "I know when a woman wants me," I thought she might laugh in his face. Instead, she does the first of many slow sexual burns, becoming so combustible at one point that she's on the verge of giving up happy-ever-aftering in Camelot for a little wow-now in the woods.

Zucker has created an appropriately fantastic setting. Camelot and the dark fortress of the black knight Malagant (Ben Cross), whose former seat at the roundtable is filled by Lancelot, suit the legend. And the pains taken to show the humanity of Arthur and Guinevere toward their people serve to add both depth to their characters and political context to the story.

But everything comes down to the relationships between Arthur, Guinevere and Lancelot, and the amount of emotion we're able to invest in them. No attempt is even made to develop other characters. Lancelot's fellow knights are as indistinguishable as a group of fraternity brothers, and though Cross strikes some sinister poses, as a megalomaniac intent on turning Camelot into a dictatorship, Malagant is a one-dimensional cartoon villain.

Connery is, as advertised, King Arthur—wise, generous, charismatic and romantic, an older version of the middle-aged Robin Hood he played to perfection in "Robin and Marion." And Ormond, who gave the only believable performance in "Legends of the Fall," gives us our most complex Guinevere yet.

But to be moved by the melodrama that ultimately unfolds, it is imperative that we accept her dilemma of being equally in love with Connery's Arthur and Gere's Lancelot. And that would require more than good acting; it would require recasting.

NEWSWEEK, 7/10/95, p. 56, Jeff Giles

According to legend, Lancelot was born to love only Guinevere: Lady Elaine had to spike his wine just to get him into ye olde sack. Now Richard Gere is playing the knight in the shiniest armor, so needless to say he's become a make-out artist who looks as if he'd lay the Lady of the Lake. Jerry Zucker's fun but perfunctory romance *First Knight* is ostensibly a King Arthur story. But Zucker and screenwriter William Nicholson have jettisoned so much of the epic—no Grail, no sword, no stone, no Merlin, no magic—it's a wonder they didn't just start from scratch. Zucker directed "Ghost," and is once more on the trail of endless love, focusing on the triangle between a fearless knight, a conflicted queen (Julia Ormond) and a beneficent, unsuspecting king (Sean Connery).

Guinevere is on her way to marry Arthur when her convoy is ambushed in the forest. She does battle—and looks terrific slamming one guy's head against a tree—until Lancelot charges up to save the day. Guinevere tells the wandering swordsman she's set to marry the king. He puts the moves on her right there in the woods anyway, saying, "I always know when a woman wants me." Guinevere fends Lancelot off after one kiss. But he follow's her to Camelot, where they exchange tortured glances as he becomes a knight and helps defend Arthur's kingdom against the evil Malagant (Ben Cross). Guinevere and Lancelot manage to kiss twice, but they never get down to serious cuckolding.

"First Knight" disappoints in a lot of ways: it's murky and sunless, its battle scenes are a letdown after "Braveheart." What's worse, the movie simplifies the famous love triangle almost beyond recognition. Lancelot no longer loves his king as much as his queen, so there's no dark thread running through his passion for Guinevere. Lady Elaine no longer exists, so the queen can't deliver the sort of bitchy asides she made in T.H. White's "The Once and Future King" ("Am I to watch you flirting with that turnip?"). Plus, there's an upbeat ending. Camelot was a hell of a lot more dysfunctional when White, Malory and Tennyson were calling the shots. All that said, Gere fights nimbly. Connery says "Camelot" in that nifty accent of his. And Ormond lives up to her considerable hype: Guinevere's love for Arthur is the only truly complicated emotion in the movie, and not many young actresses would have had enough range and regal cool to pull it off. "First Knight" is a half a glass of mead. Whether it's half empty or half full depends on how thirsty you are.

SIGHT AND SOUND, 8/95, p. 50, Kim Newman

In Camelot, King Arthur has established a rule of peace and freedom, prompting his former ally Prince Malagant to break away from the Round Table and establish an aggressive dictatorship. Between the lands of Arthur and Malagant lies Leonesse, a small territory ruled by Lady Guinevere and predated upon by Malagant's men. Guinevere contracts a semi-political engagement to Arthur, hoping to bring Leonesse under the protection of Camelot. As she travels to Camelot, her retinue is attacked by Malagant. She is rescued by Lancelot, a wandering swordsman who has reacted to the early loss of his family by swearing to love no land nor person. Later, Lancelot impulsively runs a gauntlet to win a kiss from Guinevere but refuses to collect, having promised not to kiss her until she asks him.

Malagant proposes to Arthur that Leonesse be divided between their kingdoms and, when Arthur refuses, kidnaps Guinevere. Lancelot rescues her and they confess their love for each other but realise their duty to the ideal of Camelot comes first. Arthur makes Lancelot a knight and then marries Guinevere. They help the people of Leonesse resist Malagant's invasion. Lancelot and Guinevere surrender to their feelings and kiss only to be discovered by a jealous Arthur. The King puts the lovers on public trial, an event which is interrupted by Malagant's attack on Camelot. Rather than yield, Arthur calls for his people to resist and is shot down by archers. Lancelot rallies and kills Malagant, driving off his armies. Arthur dies, passing their ideal of Camelot to Lancelot and Guinevere.

In its rigourous exclusion of the magical from the matter of mythical Britain, *First Knight*—a punning title that conceals a stodgy solemnity—is almost on a par with Robert Bresson's *Lancelot du lac*: no Excalibur, no Merlin, no Grail, no Morgana, no Green Knight, no Lady in the Lake, no Mordred, no sword in the stone, no Parsifal, no *quondam rexque futurus*. Set in some ahistorical Neverland with football, crossbows, Christianity, theme park rides and padded/studded armour that looks like the biker gear of George Romero's *Knightriders*, Jerry Zucker's post-*Ghost* epic trims away the romance and tragedy of the oft-told story. *First Knight* presents a Guinevere who is never an adulteress because she never actually sleeps with Lancelot, a Lancelot torn between his vow of emotional celibacy and the attractions of domesticity as he wields a fast sword like a wandering Western hero, and an Arthur whose declaration that the freedom of Camelot should be extended to all people everywhere sounds uncannily like the basis of America's post-war foreign policy.

It is pointless to lament the absence of much of the most poetical material in the legend and literature of Camelot from a Hollywood Summer blockbuster. After all, when John Boorman tried to cram *all* of Arthuriana into *Excalibur* he came up with an unwieldy mess shot through with brilliance and fudge—but it is notable that whenever Zucker and his collaborators try to 'improve' on the originals they come up with bathetic sequences that fall especially flat. Arthur dies of a few measly arrow wounds before the big battle and is shoved off into the lake on a burning bier in a Viking funeral. This is by a long sword a trite and unmagical alternative to Malory's *Le Morte d'Arthur*, not to mention Mark Twain's *A Connecticut Yankee at the Court of King Arthur*, T.H. White's *The Once and Future King*, the musical *Camelot* and even *Monty Python and the Holy Grail*. All great stories can be retold in an infinite number of ways, but this one bends only so far. Giving Lancelot and Guinevere a happy and morally pure ending, allowing them to hand the concept of godly monarchical democracy down to posterity, breaks so much that is vital, moving and important about the Arthur legend that we are left with extras scrapping, baddies leering and lovers simpering out of context.

Sean Connery, silver-grey wig given a fetching Tintin lick, would seem to be an ideal embodiment of King Arthur, and might even have the darkness to make the business about raping his sister and siring his eventual murderer play in Peoria. However, he simply gives another in his lengthening line of non-committal iconic performances, suggesting that he hasn't found a script he cares about in the last decade. Richard Gere's pretty-boy action man Lancelot handles his sword well, despite fight scenes that offer neither adventurous swashbuckling stunts nor grittily medieval violence, but he exhibits no screen chemistry at all, either with the King who is supposed to inspire him to greatness or the Queen (Guinevere graduates from Lady to Queen halfway through) who melts his heart. The lovely Julia Ormond is a spirited gel on horseback, capable of ripping her dress to leave a trail, but otherwise pitches fair to be the Rachel Ward of the 90s, offering smiles and *moues* as required.

Despite the fading male and rising female star power, this is a curiously characterless Round Table, with only a tiny and pointless John Gielgud cameo and Ben Cross' scowling villain providing recognisable faces and a curiously listless sense of the epic. Lancelot's rescues and gauntlet-running are Indiana Jones knock-off stunt sequences. The big battle scenes, however, depend on the supposed tactical genius of Arthur or Malagant having blind spots so that a fake camp can be constructed to lure an attack without any of Malagant's sheep-impersonating spies noticing. The villain's entire army creeps up on Camelot also unnoticed for the finale. In each clash of good and evil, one side displays remarkable stupidity in dashing into the field without thinking so that the foeman can inflict bloodless, inoffensive slaughter upon them.

TIME, 7/12/95, p. 58, Richard Schickel

Richard Gere's Lancelot is a cheeky existentialist. Julia Ormond's Guinevere is all up-to-date feminist spunk. Sean Connery's King Arthur is a leader for the Clinton era, well-meaning, essentially temporizing, as he impotently watches a great dream dwindle.

Camelot is, in spirit, more a modern gated community than a myth-enshrouded 6th century realm. And the great romance that was played out there—legend's Ur-Triangle—comes across in *First Knight* as not much more consequential than suburban adultery. Or, to be strictly accurate, adulterous yearnings. Guinevere and Lancelot never actually consummate their affair in this movie. A couple of kisses aside, they sin entirely in their heads, and then quite guiltily. One can easily imagine them as Gwen and Lance, furtively smooching on the 18th tee during a country-club dance, or stealing glances across a crowded PTA meeting—and perhaps living to regret their caution.

Yet every era has the right—maybe even the duty—to reinvent the Arthurian legend according to its lights, and so there is something instructive and entertaining about this version. Director Jerry Zucker has not spared the horses (or the broadswords) in mounting his handsome production. There are well-staged, smartly edited bursts of action at the approved modern intervals (every 10 minutes or so), the scenery is always pretty, and aside from Ben Cross's villain (imagine Pat Buchanan in not-so-shining armor), everyone is terribly nice, terribly agreeable. They are pleasant, altogether reasonable companions on this curiously jaunty ride into anachronism.

VILLAGE VOICE, 7/11/95, p. 45, Georgia Brown

There are those who blame *Star Wars* for all post-'77 action pictures. Andrew Sarris recently counted himself among them, though which summer F/X frolic he was reviewing at the time, I don't recall. Probably the campy *Batman Forever*. Me, I'd make a giant distinction between a sincere, personal film like *Star Wars*, which seems more like the end of something than the beginning—the next-to-last western, for example—and the pop-parodic flash of kinetic coaster-rides. For this I'd blame the careless uninventiveness of the studios as well as the millions who have $7.50 to burn. Lord knows, I bought enough Skywalker and C3-PO dolls in my young mothering days, but I'm still searching for a movie with *Star Wars*'s respect for myth and the old tales.

Maybe we should hold Malory's *Le Morte d'Arthur* accountable for Jerry Zucker's *First Knight*. There's a King Arthur in *First Knight*, also a Lancelot and Guinevere. Arthur dwells in a city called Camelot that glimmers in the vale like something out of the Broadway musical of that name (I didn't see it but can imagine the sparkling backdrop).

As far as the Arthur legend goes, the cinema that gave us Bresson's austere *Lancelot du Lac* also gave us *Monty Python and the Holy Grail*. You'd think that Zucker of *Airplane!* and *The Naked Gun* might lean toward the latter, but the tone of this is stupidly straight, like something he'd have spoofed in his better days. Narrative emphasis is on the Lancelot-Guinevere affair, although here "the most notable adulterers ever to be"— I'm quoting Thomas Berger's masterful *Arthur Rex*—never do it. They *kiss*. This, I suppose, is *First Knight*'s claim to novelty. The kiss, when it comes, is all slurpy dessert. I'll take the naked lovers in John Boorman's earnest *Excalibur*.

First Knight is a Richard Gere vehicle. I'm not amongst those who hold the silky Gere in contempt, though I do believe his milieu, his psychic period, to be the contemporary—his best films being hip urban dramas like *American Gigolo*, McBride's *Breathless*, the slimy *Internal Affairs*. *Sommersby*'s Civil War period was a time stretch. Gere's is the Armani era.

Set somewhat further back in time, *First Knight* opens up at a peasant fair where Gere's sword-wielding Lancelot takes on all comers. Writer William Nicholson (*Shadowlands*) takes off from the myth of Lancelot the invincible, Lancelot the unhappy itinerant swordsman, who wishes to die but is foiled by God. This scene is painful because Gere smirks and prances before a circle of spectators and behaves in a smug, unbecoming I'm-Richard-Gere-and-You're-Not way. Not even an I'm-Lancelot-and-You're-Not way.

When Lancelot meets Guinevere (Julia Ormond) he's full of himself: "I can tell when a woman wants me," says he in his Richard Gere way. She does want, but refuses. He swears he'll never kiss her until she asks him to, (Beg, bitch, and all that.) It would've been truer to have her mock him, humble him—*really* resist—since until this moment she's been presented as a strong-willed ruler of a small kingdom. Having been ambushed, kidnapped, and then saved by Lancelot while on her way to marry a certain King Arthur of Camelot, she's principled enough to honor her troth. One improvement here is that Guinevere isn't a temptress, and so a faithless woman isn't blamed for Camelot's fall.

Despite her nonexistent oeuvre, Ormond was recently the subject of a *Times Magazine* profile. (The publicity mill grindeth apace.) Ormond is likably vulnerable here, very present in the eyes, the way Genevieve Bujold used to be. Perhaps because she's more of a novice, she alone seems to be *acting* here; the male stars, old hands, may've instinctively cut their losses.

All armored up in Camelot, awaiting the bride's arrival, is Sean Connery's wizened Arthur. No matter that the actor is the actress's grandpa's age. Now things will pick up, think I. Not so. Never has Connery seemed so powerless to instill some gravity, coax some grace into a doomed project. Zucker may have employed O.J. to the fullest extent of his nonability, but he is powerless to capitalize on the filmdom's greatest resources. The script, too, all but writes Arthur out. His climactic scene—standing up to the villainous Malagant (Ben Cross of the giant head)—is so embarrassing it makes your teeth ache.

There's a venerable legend surrounding the death of Arthur. It involves the king's sword, Excalibur, and the death of all the knights. Apparently, this is a little drastic for the *First Knight* people. Isn't it a bit rash to have Camelot, as well as the civilized world, perish with Arthur? Why not leave Lancelot with the sword and Guinevere, as well as an intact and bustling Camelot?

Arthur's death here has teensy echoes—intentional, I'm sure—of the death of Robin Hood in Richard Lester's sublime *Robin and Marian*, where a younger Connery played the aging, wounded hero to Audrey Hepburn's piquant Marian. Oh, they shouldn't have reminded me.

Also reviewed in:
CHICAGO TRIBUNE, 7/7/95, Friday/p. C, Michael Wilmington
NEW YORK TIMES, 7/7/95, p. C10, Janet Maslin
NEW YORKER, 7/17/95, p. 84, Anthony Lane
VARIETY, 6/26-7/9/95, p. 78, Todd McCarthy

WASHINGTON POST, 7/7/95, p. F1, Rita Kempley
WASHINGTON POST, 7/7/95, Weekend/p. 36, Eve Zibart

FLUKE

A Metro-Goldwyn-Mayer release of a Rocket Pictures production. *Executive Producer:* Jon Turtle and Tom Coleman. *Producer:* Paul Maslansky and Lata Ryan. *Director:* Carlo Carlei. *Screenplay:* Carlo Carlei and James Carrington. *Based upon the novel by:* James Herbert. *Director of Photography:* Raffaele Mertes. *Editor:* Mark Conte. *Music:* Carlo Siliotto. *Music Editor:* Scott Grusin and Steve Livingston. *Sound:* Steve C. Aaron and (music) Lee De Carlo. *Sound Editor:* Mark Mangini. *Casting:* Lynn Stalmaster. *Production Designer:* Hilda Stark. *Art Director:* Richard Fojo. *Set Decorator:* Dayna Lee. *Set Dresser:* Robert Tate Nichols and Marshall Davis. *Special Effects:* Gene Grigg. *Costumes:* Elisabetta Beraldo. *Make-up:* Lynn Barber. *Stunt Coordinator:* M. James Arnett. *Running time:* 95 minutes. *MPAA Rating:* PG.

CAST: Matthew Modine (Fluke/Thomas Johnson); Nancy Travis (Carol Johnson); Samuel L. Jackson (Voice of Rumbo); Eric Stoltz (Jeff Newman); Max Pomeranc (Brian Johnson); Ron Perlman (Sylvester); Jon Polito (Boss); Bill Cobbs (Bert); Collin Wilcox Paxton (Bella); Federico Pacifici (Professor Santini); Clarinda Ross (Tom's Secretary); Adrian Roberts (Night Guard); Bart Hansard (Day Guard); Deborah Hobart (Dog Pound Vet); Libby Whittemore (Housekeeper); Dominique Milton (Schoolboy); Mary Ann Hagan (Woman #1); Yolanda King (Woman #2); Brian Katz (Paramedic #1); Mary Holloway (Paramedic #2); David Dwyer (News Stand Man); Michael H. Moss (Policeman #1); Duke Steinemann (Policeman #2); Georgia Allen (Rose); John Lawhorn (Farmer); Calvin Miller (Skeptical Man); Harry Pritchett (Priest); Duong Bl (Asian Dishwasher); Diego La Rosa (Security Guard); Angie Reno (Delivery Boy); Sam Gifaldi (Voice of Young Fluke).

LOS ANGELES TIMES, 6/2/95, Calendar/p. 6, Kevin Thomas

No wonder "Fluke" takes 50 of its 95 minutes to get to the heart of the matter, for in that time it has to sell us not only on the notion of reincarnation but also that humans can come back as dogs. That's an awful lot of suspending of disbelief to ask of an audience, but youngsters may be able to go along with it. Even so, parents should know at the outset that there are scenes of animal abuse too intense for the very young.

Fluke is a totally appealing mutt, an animal shelter escapee taken in tow by another likable canine, the streetwise Rumbo, who teaches the younger dog how to survive and even enjoy life in the big city (an unnamed Atlanta). But Fluke keeps dreaming of two young men (Matthew Modine, Eric Stoltz) racing their cars down a highway in the woods, with one of the men plunging off the road to his death.

Director/co-writer Carlo Carlei ever so gradually (at least for younger viewers) lets it sink in that Fluke is indeed the reincarnation of Modine. After those 50 minutes of urban adventures, Fluke does latch onto Modine's family, his lovely widow (Nancy Travis) and small son (Max Pomeranc), who live in a mansion in a nearby small town. It is Fluke's impression that Stoltz, Modine's partner in an "advanced mechanical design" corporation, is responsible for Modine's death; what's more, Stoltz is clearly intent on consoling the widow.

Carlei brings to "Fluke" the same urgency he brought to his terrific Italian debut film, the 1993 thriller "Flight of the Innocent," in which a 10-year-old boy—sole survivor of a Calabrian vendetta—runs for his life. On a technical level he succeeds in that he surely does allow us to see life from a dog's point of view. But if you have a tough time accepting that Fluke is Modine—and that Fluke and Rumbo can speak English "mentally" to each other—the first with the voice of Modine, the second with that of Samuel L. Jackson—then all of Carlei's earnestness seems increasingly silly and maudlin, an effect underlined heavily by Carlo Siliotto's relentlessly florid score. In fairness, Carlei—who's shamelessly manipulative—does score two good points: that as a dog Modine spends more time playing with his son than he did as his dad, and the way in which Fluke finally manages to reveal to Travis that he is indeed the reincarnation of her late husband.

Maybe if "Fluke," which might have been better as an animated feature, weren't such a lavish, big-deal production and closer to the modest level of the recent—and pleasant little-pig movie "Gordy," it wouldn't seem so overwhelmingly, at times even laughably, foolish. The film's human actors acquit themselves admirably under the circumstances, but there's no question that the stars are Comet (as Fluke) and Barney (as Rumbo), bolstered by excellent trainers and special-effects personnel.

NEW YORK POST, 6/2/95, p. 51, Michael Medved

Talk about movie star makeovers ...

For the new movie, "Fluke," the producers took a well-known, purebred golden retriever ("Comet," star of six years of TVs "Full House") and gave him a haircut and dye job so he could play the mongrel hero of this story.

Why bother with this mixed-breed impersonator, rather than casting a real-life mutt?

Comet's extraordinary performance more than answers that question. This is, to put it simply, the most intelligent and impressive acting job ever turned in by a canine, in part because of the unique demands of the role.

Fluke is a stray dog who gradually remembers he was a man in a previous life. Loosely based on a wistful novel by James Herbert, the story begins with Matthew Modine racing along a country road at night and then plunging to his death in a spectacularly staged crash.

Reincarnated as the world's most adorable puppy, he's taken to the pound with mother and siblings, then escapes to live on the streets with a homeless woman (Collin Wilcox Paxton) who gives him his name.

After her death, he befriends a junkyard dog named Rumbo (nicely brought to life with the street-wise voice of Samuel L. Jackson), though Fluke is haunted by vague recollections of a posh suburban life as a human being.

Eventually, Fluke connects with his own former family, including a grieving wife (expertly played by Nancy Travis of "Three Men and a Baby") and lonely son (Max Pomeranc of "Searching for Bobby Fischer") and longs to somehow tell them who he is.

He also yearns to protect them from danger, since he suspects that his former business partner (Eric Stoltz) conspired in his death.

All of this lays out far more moving than you might expect, thanks to the lovingly intense direction of Carlo Carlei, the young Italian master who previously made the justly acclaimed adventure "Flight of the Innocent."

The Atlanta-area locations, shot for the most part from a dog's point of view, emerge with poetic glow and sparkle, and the various animals project a truly astonishing range of emotions. No director has ever before captured such complex consciousness from the facial expressions of his hairy stars, so that he makes it easy to accept Fluke's haunting declaration, "Perhaps there are many out there like me. Hiding behind the eyes of simple creatures. Maybe even someone close to you."

The only major shortcoming in the picture is that it's too serious—and much too sad—for many of the very young moviegoers who seem to be its intended audience. "Fluke" is long on sentiment and pathos, but relatively short on the humor.

Above all, the picture seems obsessed with death, with three major characters perishing vividly before your eyes. Older children (and their parents) can certainly handle these disturbing moments, and thereby enjoy an original, thoughtful and caringly crafted entertainment, but be prepared to answer all sorts of pesky questions about reincarnation.

You might also have to deal with the sudden (and perhaps unwelcome) conviction that some beloved house pet is actually the recycled spirit of your late Aunt Sadie.

NEWSDAY, 6/2/95, Part II/p. B5, Jonathan Mandell

Fluke is a dog who speaks English to other animals, always wins in street-corner shell games, browses the newsstand and can even dial a telephone. If Fluke sounds almost human, that is because in a previous life he was indeed a man. But if "Fluke" sounds simply like a cute movie for kids, be warned: It isn't. It is something much more odd and grim.

We first see Fluke as Matthew Modine in a car driven off a narrow highway and crashing into a tree. As in a dream, the tree turns into a colorful tunnel, and we fall through it with him like

Alice entering Wonderland. On the other side, a huge dog fills up the screen, licking us. This is mother. The man has died and become reincarnated as a puppy.

The puppy goes through several adventures; it's adopted or befriended by a homeless woman, a junk-car dealer and a street dog named Rumbo, who begins speaking to him in the voice of Samuel L. Jackson. Fluke, who speaks with Modine's voice, is played as an adult by the golden retriever Comet, a star of ABC's "Full House," dyed to look like a mutt, with his soulful and intelligent gaze intact.

Fluke and Rumbo live a dog's life in Atlanta. But something keeps nagging at Fluke, something he can't quite grasp about his past. He has flashbacks, a ring catches his eye and he flashes back on the face of a beautiful woman (Nancy Travis). He sees a boy in a schoolyard and recalls the face of another boy (Max Pomeranc, who is as winning here as he was in "Searching for Bobby Fischer").

He slowly pieces together the fact that these we're his wife and son when he was a man. He becomes determined to find them, and eventually does. He tries to tell them who he is, which leads to some anthropomorphic humor, such as his wearing his old hat. But then the day comes when someone new enters their home: the person (Eric Stoltz) who, he remembers, ran him off the road. The plot moves toward a final, satisfying twist.

Mixing a sometimes cute, sometimes maudlin animal tale with a dark psychological mystery poses some big potential problems. Who is this movie for? "Fluke" is billed as "a magical adventure for the whole family," which is standard code for "kiddie movie." But while the animal action provides some adorable moments (perhaps' too adorable for some older kids), there is much here that seems either too subtle or, more often, too intense for the very young. There are several human and animal deaths, a couple of kidnapings and even some torture.

The worst of this is a series of scenes that are not in the James Herbert novel on which the film is based, and that bear a suspicious resemblance to scenes in the dog hit "Beethoven" (although in that film they were played for laughs): A growling, leather-jacketed human bully menaces, stalks and then kidnaps Fluke, taking him to a beauty-product company's animal-testing laboratory. There, Fluke is strapped into a contraption that forces his eyelids open and drops liquid into his eyes until he goes (temporarily) blind.

This drawn-out horror lingers even after Rumbo crashes through the window to effect a dramatic rescue, offering his tail to the blind Fluke and leading him out like a seeing-eye dog. He also opens the cages of all the other animals, so we get monkeys carrying little puppies to freedom—a victory for anti-vivisectionists everywhere, and a triumph of weirdness.

"Fluke" is as much an oddity as Fluke. It probably shouldn't work as a movie. But mostly, magically, it does.

VILLAGE VOICE, 6/13/95, p. 58, Tom Kertes

Fluke proves that, just because a film fits snugly under the dreaded heading of "entertainment for the whole family," it doesn't need to be syrupy glup that makes most discerning viewers over the age of eight OD from all that goodness and joy. At least not if the film is made with the dedication shown by Italian director Carlo Carlei (*Flight of the Innocent*), who had wanted to adapt James Herbert's novel for 12 years.

Proud puppy-puffers will tell you ad infinitum that their best friends are well-nigh human—well, this movie's title mutt was human at one time. After a fatal car crash on a lonely country road—shot amidst a shocking splash of color with amazing visual style—he returns as a pup with partial amnesia. (Who thought a movie could be a cross between *Hideaway* and *Lassie Come Home*) As Fluke's memories burst forth in mysterious bits and pieces, he begins to feel an irresistible yearning to see his young wife and son once again, to tie up all unfinished business, to "set things right." The mutt embarks on a lengthy journey to find them, and learns a lot about what he should have done with his life as a human during the cross-country ordeal. Naturally, there are some "messages" delivered, but at least they're not delivered with a hammer.

The pup is played by Matthew Modine in his human form, and by *Full House* (broken) star Comet as a mutt. Modine is just fine, but Comet ... well, Comet kicks butt. This is truly the Robert De Niro of dogs; if you think Bobby D, gaining 80 pounds to play Jake LaMotta was something, check out this pure golden retriever with his hair died a dark-hued brown to portray a mixed breed.

Much of the film is told, and shot, from the dog's point of view, and Carlei inventively shifts between human and puppyesque perspectives. The plot does have some holes the size of a doghouse and encounters some slow patches after all, even talking pups can do only so much—but this remains a quirky little film throughout, and one even most dour non-dog lovers should enjoy.

Also reviewed in:
CHICAGO TRIBUNE, 6/2/95, Friday/p. J, Michael Wilmington
NEW YORK TIMES, 6/2/95, p. C4, Caryn James
VARIETY, 6/5-11/95, p. 36, Emanuel Levy
WASHINGTON POST, 6/2/95, p. D6, Rita Kempley
WASHINGTON POST, 6/2/95, Weekend/p. 57, Desson Howe

FOR GOD AND COUNTRY

A Dor Film release. *Producer:* Danny Krausz and Milan Dor. *Director:* Wolfgang Murnberger. *Screenplay (German with English subtitles):* Wolfgang Murnberger. *Director of Photography:* Fabian Eder. *Editor:* Maria Homolkova. *Music:* Robert Steigler. *Art Director:* Renate Martin and Andreas Donhauser. *Running time:* 115 minutes. *MPAA Rating:* Not Rated.

CAST: Christoph Dostal (Private Berger); Andreas Lust (Rumpler); Andreas Simma (Moser); Marcus J. Carney (Kernstock); Leopold Altenburg (Tomschitz).

NEW YORK POST, 12/20/95, p. 38, Thelma Adams

Wolfgang Murnbergers's contemporary anti-war drama "For God and Country" begins so unexpectedly that I thought for a moment that I might be in the wrong theater.

A medieval knight rides through a stark winter forest. We view the trees from his perspective, sliced up by his visor, his breath magnified within the helmet. The knight enters a strange fortress and dismounts. Weighed down by his sword, stifled by his armor, he sees a robed woman performing a religious ritual. He kneels before her; she bares her breast and spritzes milk from her nipple.

Whoa! Wait a minute! Where are we?

Welcome to Private Berger's wet dream. We wake up with him (and damp sheets) in barracks on the eastern Austrian border. It is 1980 and the Austrians, fearing the Communists, are training conscripts for active duty. Eighteen-year-old Berger (Christoph Dostal) is there in body if not in soul.

With his handsome big eyes and full mouth that he has yet to grow into, Dostal has the promise of beauty without having shed his adolescent ungainliness. Dostal's Berger is a quiet presence, one of the guys who will always be accepted into a group, but who has no inclination to lead it.

Berger has one secret: He hides in the last stall of the latrine, "one square meter of freedom." In this room of his own, he draws and dreams and counts the days until he will regain civilian status.

Much of Austrian writer/director Murnberger's semi-autobiographical story proceeds in coming-of-age vignettes. The boys do their share of bootlicking. They learn to creep, crawl and inch over the Fatherland—while mostly consumed with what it would be like to pull these same maneuvers atop the motherland. Virginity and its loss are a frequent topic.

For those, like myself, who don't really want to share barracks games of concentration using X-rated cards and visits to shippers in dive bars with horny 18-year-olds, these episodes are a trial

Murnberger redeems his soldier's story with more pungent scenes. On a snowy overnight trek, the conscripts receive a treat: chicken dinner. The only problem is that the chickens are alive. For one Viennese youth, slaughtering the foul is a rite of passage, a soldier's first kill—and a messy botched job at that. The image of the slaughtered chicken head will find its way back to Berger's bathroom graffiti and into his dreams.

In "For God and Country" opening today at Film Forum after being discovered at the Rotterdam Film Festival in Holland, no sequence ever matches the haunting beauty of the first dream. Nevertheless, it's in the flights of fancy and fantasy that Murnberger transforms his mundane boot-camp diary into an offbeat, imaginative work.

Like the camera he places the viewer inside the head of a creative teen-aged conscript who has no desire for combat and no strong ethical reason to combat the status quo by any other means than escaping into his own imagination.

VILLAGE VOICE, 12/26/95, p. 70, Tom Kertes

"In case of a nuclear attack," the Austrian army captain shouts, "don't look straight into the explosion, boys. Cover your eyes well or you'll go blind."

Absurd? That's exactly the point.

For 19-year-old Private Berger, things are really confusing. The Austrian army is basically an oxymoron; the last time it had a chance to defend the homeland, it instead yielded to Hitler—an Austrian himself—with nary a shot fired. Now, in 1980, Berger is in a unit on the "easternmost border of the Western World," defending his country against the nearest "enemy," Hungary. But as soon as the army training is over, Berger's best bud leaves to vocation on Lake Bolaton, *in* Hungary, "working on improving international relations." Which, to these capitalistic teenagers, means "screwing East German chicks."

Based on youthful auteur Wolfgang Murnberger's own army experiences, this beautifully acted piece is so creatively put together—images, sounds, music, and rhythmic patterns rush at you from unexpected places throughout that, even when the too episodic story falters, interest rarely lags. The film is simply saturated with sex, both as a counterpoint to death and as a subject of fantasy for the bored-to-death conscripts. Again, the ambivalence: Berger longs for pure love with his high school girlfriend, who's only into light petting, but is engulfed at the same time by constant macho talk of sex with "prostitutes and sluts." "The ones I want don't want me," he ponders. "And the ones I don't want are no problem at all."

What does this sensible nonsense all add up to? At the end of the movie. Berger as narrator provides an answer: "When this film is over, you'll be 115 minutes closer to death."

Also reviewed in:
CHICAGO TRIBUNE, 3/1/96, Friday/p. K, Michael Wilmington
NEW YORK TIMES, 12/20/95, p. C16, Stephen Holden

FORGET PARIS

A Castle Rock Entertainment release of a Face production. *Executive Producer:* Peter Schindler. *Producer:* Billy Crystal. *Director:* Billy Crystal. *Screenplay:* Billy Crystal, Lowell Ganz, and Babaloo Mandel. *Director of Photography:* Don Burgess. *Editor:* Kent Beyda. *Music:* Marc Shaiman. *Choreographer:* Debbie Allen. *Sound:* Jeff Wexler, Don Coufal, Garry Holland, and (music) Dennis Sands. *Sound Editor:* Gregory King and Bobby Mackston. *Casting:* Pam Dixon Mickelson. *Production Designer:* Terence Marsh. *Art Director:* William Cruse and Jean-Michel Hugon. *Set Designer:* Roy Barnes. *Set Decorator:* Michael Seirton. *Set Dresser:* Scott "Berserker" Collins, James Gregory Evans, Chris "Chappy" Fielding, Thierry "T.T." Labbe, Carew "Big Ton" Papritz, and "Kurt V" Verbaarschott. *Costumes:* Judy Ruskin. *Make-up:* Peter Montagna. *Stunt Coordinator:* Mickey Gilbert. *Running time:* 95 minutes. *MPAA Rating:* PG-13.

CAST: Billy Crystal (Mickey Gordon); Debra Winger (Ellen Andrews); Joe Mantegna (Andy); Cynthia Stevenson (Liz); Richard Masur (Craig); Julie Kavner (Lucy); William Hickey (Arthur); Robert Costanzo (Waiter); John Spencer (Jack); Tom Wright (Tommy); Cathy Moriarty (Lois); Johnny Williams (Lou); Marv Alpert; Bill Walton; Charles Barkley; David

Robinson; Dan Majerle; Kevin Johnson; Paul Westphal; Sean Elliott; Patrick Ewing; Tim Hardaway; Kareem Abdul-Jabbar; Bill Laimbeer; Reggie Miller; Chris Mullin; Charles Oakley; Kurt Rambis; John Starks; Isiah Thomas; Spud Webb; Marcus Johnson; Rush Limbaugh; David Sanborn; Safe-T-Man (Themselves); Bert Copello (Airline Employee); Ron Ross (Insolent Official); Chris Shaver (Laker Girl); Mary Oedy (Knicks City Dancer); Joie Shettler (Spurs Silver Dancer); Andrea Toste (Sonics Dancer); Lisa Gannon (Attractive Woman); Richard Assad (Suitcase Man); Lisa Rieffel (Receptionist); Emmy Smith (Woman in Porsche); Margaret Nagle (Marilyn); Janette Caldwell (Andy's Date); Tim Halligan (Doctor); Tim Ahern (Fertility Doctor); Judyann Elder (Ivy); Deb Lacusta (Nurse); Tom Ohmer (Policeman); Robert Hunter, Jr. and Marty McSorley (Detroit Fans); Richard Haje (Dangerous Man); Clint Howard (Exterminator); Beverly Piper (Organist); Charlotte Etienne (3 Year Old Girl); Zachary Eginton (5 Year Old Boy); Jennifer Mickelson (7 Year Old Girl); Allan Kolman (French Waiter); Hedwige de Mouroux (Distinguished Business Woman); Roberto Bonanni (Distinguished Frenchman); Jean Shum (Waitress); Andre Rosey Brown (Huge Bodyguard); Rick Gunderson and Eric Christian (Motorcycle Cops); Liz Sheridan (Woman in Car); Irving Wasserman (Man in Car); Genelle Lee Baummgardner (Veronique).

CHRISTIAN SCIENCE MONITOR, 5/19/95, p. 12, Frank Scheck

What is the fascination that basketball players seem to hold for short men? Attend any New York Knicks game, and you'll see Woody Allen and Spike Lee on the sidelines. In the new romantic comedy, "Forget Paris," in which Billy Crystal plays a pro-basketball referee, one gets the feeling that the star, producer, director, and co-writer was just as eager to share screen space with such real-life sports luminaries as Charles Barkley as he was with Debra Winger.

The film, like Crystal's hit "When Harry Met Sally," is less interested in conventional romance than it is in exploring problematical aspects of relationships.

That picture asked the by-now familiar question of whether men and women can be friends without having a physical relationship, and the title characters didn't become lovers until nearly the final reel. In "Forget Paris," the man and woman meet, fall in love, and get married early on. But the film's true focus is about what happens after that, when the real work of a relationship begins.

In typical Hollywood fashion, the stars "meet cute." Crystal plays Mickey, who accompanies his father's body to Paris in order to bury him with his former war buddies. Winger plays Ellen, an airline representative who must deal with him when the casket, like any piece of luggage, is misplaced. Soon (after the crisis is resolved), the pair are frolicking amid highly photogenic Paris, enjoying a few days of romance before Mickey must return home.

Before long, Ellen, who is separated from her husband, leaves her job to marry Mickey and move in with him in Los Angeles.

The two are at first deliriously happy, but soon complications arise. Mickey's job keeps him on the road for weeks at a time, Ellen is miserable in her new job, and Mickey can't stand Ellen's senile father (William Hickey), who takes up residence with them.

What makes the film work is its sensitive examination of the way that couples must cope with the unromantic realities of trying to make a life together. Movies often present wildly disparate characters who meet and fall in love, but we rarely get to see what happens to them after the final clinch.

The title of "Forget Paris" refers to the advice that Mickey and Ellen get from friends whenever they long for the first few idyllic days that they spent together. It's rare that such sober, mature thinking permeates a Hollywood love story.

This being a Billy Crystal movie, there are also many moments of hilarity, with his crack comic timing and delivery making even the less witty lines seem wildly funny. Winger, who has been under-utilized in movies in the last few years, more than holds her own. In one wacky, episode involving a wounded pigeon, she displays quite a knack for physical comedy.

The film also has a clever structure, with the events being related as a story that Mickey's best friend (Joe Mantegna) is telling his nervous fiancee (the funny Cynthia Stevenson) while waiting for Mickey to join them for dinner. The original framing device enables us to see the story from various perspectives.

American filmgoers have embraced such recent romantic comedies as "French Kiss" and "While You Were Sleeping," but in both those films the couples got together at the end, with the last shot showing them walk off into the sunset hand in hand.

"Forget Paris" has the courage to begin where stories like this usually end.

FILMS IN REVIEW, 7-8/95, p. 55, Andy Pawelczak

Forget Paris begins on a melancholy note with Mickey Gordon (Billy Crystal), an N.B.A. basketball referee, flying to Paris to bury his unloved father in a French cemetery with the other members of his World War II unit. The coffin gets lost in the Paris airport and Mickey spends several days cooling his heels until Ellen Andrews (Debra Winger), an American employee of the airline, finally locates it. She shows up at the burial, commenting that nobody should bury their father alone—it turns out that she has father problems too, and lickety-split, they're having a whirlwind affair with all the postcard cliches of Paris as a backdrop. The Parisian photographs behind the credits by such photographers as Cartier-Bresson are much more invigorating.) Eventually, Mickey and Ellen get married and settle down in Los Angeles, and the movie turns into a lightweight *Scenes From A Marriage* sprinkled with not very funny one-liners.

Billy Crystal remains an appealing performer who made a great Academy Awards host, but as an auteur (he produced and directed the picture and collaborated on the screenplay) he's afflicted with the occupational disease of comics—the overreaching desire to be serious. Woody Allen pulled off the feat in a few pictures that were both funny and touching, but Crystal doesn't have Woody's finely tuned screen persona nor his stagecraft. The movie's conceit has Joe Mantegna, his fiance and two other couples waiting in a restaurant for Mickey and Ellen on the eve of Mantegna's wedding. As they wait, each tells a story about Mickey and Ellen's rocky marriage, and the resultant flashbacks have the quality of long winded barroom anecdotes without any real punch or point—you feet like interrupting with a one-liner of your own just to keep things moving.

The film has an Allenesque patina: vaguely ethnic N.Y./L.A. types, some Damon Runyon-like minor characters (including a cameo performance by Rush Limbaugh—maybe he'll pursue a career in movies and stay out of politics), and a conflicted, elusive heroine. Crystal does a disservice to Winger in this picture—she looks tired and washed out, and she has no sense of comic timing at all. Winger goes through her paces without heart—not even that Jean Arthur-like voice can save her—and a romantic comedy without heart is like tennis without a net, as Robert Frost once said about the practice of free verse.

Crystal gives the picture large infusions of hipness—the ravishing soundtrack of thirties and forties songs commenting on the action, saxophonist David Sanborn's bluesy rendition of the national anthem at a basketball game, a prolonged, pointless reference to *Prizzi's Honor* in the person of William Hickey, who played the shrewd, witch-like old don in that movie, as Ellen's senile father. But it all feels self-conscious and self-congratulatory. More than a whiff of narcissism clings to the picture; when Ellen says she fell in love with Mickey because he makes her laugh, it feels like special pleading on behalf of the comedian for the audience to love him. As Mickey, Crystal is the star of the show, the tender, melancholy lover who is a David among the Goliaths on the basketball court; when not looking sensitive and wounded, he beams and twinkles like the Tin Man in Oz. Perhaps Winger seems so disheartened because Crystal has a monopoly on heart in this film, and he wears it ostentatiously on his sleeve.

LOS ANGELES TIMES, 5/19/95, Calendar/p. 12, Peter Rainer

Billy Crystal plays a National Basketball Assn. referee in "Forget Paris," which means he makes a lot of jokes about a short guy yelling at tall guys. He milks his gift for yammering, he milks us for tears and he milks us for yocks too. Crystal's got quite a dairy farm going here. As the films's star/co-writer/director/producer, he keeps pumping away. Some of his antics are funny, but a lot of them run dry.

The film begins with a Woody Allen-ish framing device with a sportswriter, Andy (Joe Mantegna), and his fiancée, Liz (Cynthia Stevenson), waiting in a restaurant for the arrival of their guests to celebrate their nuptials. Andy fills in the time telling her about the on-and-off romantic odyssey of his friend Mickey (Crystal) and Mickey's friend Mickey's wife, Ellen (Debra Winger). As Andy's guests file in—car salesman Craig (Richard Masur) and his wife, Lucy (Julie Kavner, wonderful as always) and NBA coach Jack (John Spencer) and Lois (Cathy Moriarty), both on their second marriage—the Mickey Andy and Ellen saga is spun out in a series of flashbacks that stretch from Paris to Marina del Rey.

Crystal and his co-screenwriters Lowell Ganz and Babaloo Mandel are trying to anatomize the post-honeymoon blues that settle into most marriages. Meeting in Paris, Mickey and Ellen start out in a blissful trance. He's there to inter his father in a World War II burial ground with his comrades; she's the Paris-based airlines executive in charge of tracking down the coffin mislaid en route.

It's a contrived case of Meet Cute, and it's followed by a lot of Romance Cute, as Crystal takes us on a lickety-split swoon-a-thon that leads to marriage and not-so-happily ever after. Mickey's job, which he loves, keeps him on the road; Ellen chafes at her own indolence and overeats. Then it's his turn to stay home on job leave while she plays career woman. Her doddering father (William Hickey) moves in with them. It's like Ingmar Bergman's "Scenes From a Marriage" retooled by gag writers.

The core of any romantic movie-comedy or drama or any combination in between-is chemistry. And Crystal and Winger never seem to be in the same movie. Partly this is because Crystal doesn't seem to be acting with anybody else; his performance appears to be taking place in front of a vanity mirror. Winger can't get anything going with him except a wavering rat-a-tat-tat comic rapport. When she's in the movie's zoned-out post-bliss phase, she's blank.

And it's not the kind of expressive blankness that lets you into her unhappiness. It's more like a blah blankness. A movie about the disconnect between husband and wife turns into a movie about the disconnect between Crystal and Winger. As the film winds its weary way through all the permutations of fizzled ardor, we keep waiting for the explosive funny stuff to take us away from the "serious" stuff.

It could be that Crystal feels the same way. As filmmaker and performer, he doesn't seem to have his heart in the marriage woe material—or, to put it another way, all he offers is heart. Not since the heyday of Jerry Lewis has there been a comic actor so entranced with his heartfelt sappiness.

But you can't count "Forget Paris" out. Crystal is enough of a showman to work up some high-flown gags, and a few of them, particularly one involving Ellen and a pigeon glued to her head (trust me) are classics. Although they're finally overdone, the scenes with William Hickey puttering dazedly about the house are great, sick set-pieces, and so are some of the basketball moments, such as the sequence where Mickey self-destructs and throws Kareem Abdul-Jabbar out of his own farewell game. When he's not trying to strong-arm us into recognizing what a sensitive-souled laff-riot he is, Crystal creates a real comic buzz on-screen. It almost compensates for all the times you want him to buzz off.

NEW YORK, 5/29/95, p. 53, David Denby

Last week I complained about the unspeakable spoken narration in Gregory Nava's *My Family*, which added a glaze of sanctimony to oversimplified scenes. But I'm hardly against narration in general. Forties Hollywood, in its fatalistic, deep-shadowed *noir* period, depended on it heavily, and Woody Allen has used intermittent narration to charge up some of his best movies. In Billy Crystal's pleasant but bland romantic comedy, *Forget Paris*, the narration is perhaps the most intricate and creative element. *Forget Paris* is about a contemporary couple, Mickey (Crystal), an NBA referee, and Ellen (Debra Winger), an airline executive, who are both right and wrong for each other and who keep falling apart and then coming back together. In a New York restaurant, Mickey's best friend, a sportswriter, Andy (Joe Mantegna), tells his nervous bride-to-be, Liz (Cynthia Stevenson), how Mickey and Ellen met (we see the meeting) and then fell apart; and then, as Liz gets more and more alarmed (the story of the wayward couple seems to reveal to her the truth of her own impending marriage), other friends show up for dinner and relate further adventures and misadventures of Mickey and Ellen, each bit of narration leading into the scene itself. Will Mickey, who's working the Knicks game at the Garden, show up, too? Is he still together with Ellen? Liz is virtually in a state of nervous collapse before the last question is resolved. The lovely joke of the movie is that the narrated frame intrudes more and more on the picture, and finally becomes the picture itself.

Forget Paris is a huge improvement over Crystal's first film as director, the lugubrious *Mr. Saturday Night*. This time, Crystal, directing the screenplay he wrote with his longtime collaborators Lowell Ganz and Babaloo Mandel, works in fast-moving anecdotal style, with short scenes fitted to the narration. There are some wonderful moments. A great sports fan, Crystal captures the pressured excitement of basketball but from the unlikely point of view of the ref. A little white guy bursting out of a knot of jubilant black colossi, blowing his whistle and disallowing a crucial basket, Crystal's Mickey is a Napoleon on the court, holding his own with Charles Barkley or David Robinson, answering taunts and complaints with joking threats. He's as fast with his mouth as they are. Mickey is happy in his work and his hotel-centered bachelor life—until he falls in love, that is, and becomes miserable, and the fans screaming at him seem like morons with swollen red faces.

In the love scenes, Crystal's direction is far more tentative. Walking around Paris with Debra Winger, Crystal makes nervous jokes, as if he thought he didn't have the right to leave stand-up comedy behind and play a lover. We feel less of Mickey's anxiety (will this woman accept me?) than of the actor's anxiety (will the audience accept me?). Crystal has to learn to use himself boldly, even crassly, as Woody Allen does. Allen is unashamedly masochistic and unashamedly sexual, and it's the sexual aggressiveness that pushes the audience past the embarrassment of watching an unprepossessing man at the center of a movie. At the moment, Crystal is too cuddly, more a husband than a hungry male, and since the tough, smart Debra Winger seems to need a strong masculine presence to play against, they don't quite click together. He makes jokes, and she laughs and seems too intense and emotional for him. She's a good sport, and plays her role. But what is her role? Ellen seems like your generic intelligent, modern working woman.

Second-rateness is built into the filmmakers' conception of the marital drama. After some jokes about naive Americans discovering Paris, Crystal goes ahead and uses Paris in an entirely conventional way as a picture-postcard background for love. The Eiffel Tower! The Pont Neuf! Crystal and Debra Winger pose, spooning, in front of monuments. Back in the States, the newlyweds run into trouble. No fault on either side: Jobs pull them in different directions, and Ellen, having given up Paris, is trapped in Mickey's bachelor apartment, which she doesn't like (we're trapped in it, too, for many scenes). The screenplay tries for realism, and occasionally achieves it all too well and lands in banality. There are funny bits (gravel-voiced William Hickey turns up as Ellen's infuriating, muttering old dad), but Crystal hasn't figured out yet how to push the dialogue scenes beyond good television.

Do we want Ellen and Mickey to stay together? Yes, but not as much as we're supposed to—not as much as Liz, the woman in the restaurant who's hearing this story. I enjoyed the sociable, gossipy quality of *Forget Paris* (even strangers in the restaurant come over to talk to the people waiting for Mickey), but the marital-discord stuff is underpowered. *Forget Paris* is nice movie—maybe too nice. A more lyrical camera, a touch of bittersweet anguish, a woman whose charm possesses an intellectual edge. ... Crystal is close, but he's not quite there yet.

NEW YORK POST, 5/19/95, p. 39, Michael Medved

It's Crystal clear what Billy had in mind with "Forget Paris": He wanted to take a romantic comedy beyond the wedding bells that generally mark the conclusion of such pictures and to follow a couple in their sincere struggles to live neurotically ever after.

It's an admirable undertaking, and the movie definitely has its moments of both fun and feeling, but "Forget Paris" seems so contrived, superficial and self-consciously cute that it remains, well, forgettable.

The love story begins when Mickey (Crystal) meets Ellen (Debra Winger).

He's a hard-working referee in the National Basketball Association who takes time off to fly to France to bury his recently deceased father alongside fallen comrades in his Army unit.

She's an airline representative assigned to mollify the angry American when her company inadvertently loses his father's coffin.

After this awkward start, their relationship blossoms during several enchanted days together in the City of Light. They then fly back and forth across the Atlantic a few times to iron out complications in their circumstances before settling down to marriage in Mickey's beachside condo in Los Angeles.

The problems that plague this union are entirely believable, but so mundane and one-dimensional that there's no dramatic tension in their marital ups and downs.

Mickey loves his job with the NBA, but Ellen feels excluded when she tries to travel around with him in the macho world of big-time basketball.

Neither of them seems capable of sacrificing their own interests for the sake of the relationship, and that connection remains so shallow and insignificant that it's hard to blame them for dismissing it. The problem is that we know nothing about Debra Winger's character except the fact that she's from Wichita.

Winger is a consistently wonderful actress, but there's nothing even she can do with this shamefully underwritten part.

Crystal, by contrast, gets all the best laugh lines and a much richer portrayal in the script; it's no accident that he also happened to direct and co-write the movie.

As in his one previous film as a director (the earnest, overwrought "Mr. Saturday Night"), Crystal strains for seriousness, as if eager to prove to the world that he's more than just a likable funnyman.

In "Forget Paris" at least he remembers to throw in plenty of the witty comments his fans expect; in fact, several flimsily constructed scenes seem to exist solely to provide an excuse for that dialogue, rather than allowing smart talk to grow naturally out of the situations and characters.

There's also a problem with the overly elaborate framing device through which the story unfolds.

The central couple's best friends (Richard Masur, Julie Havner and Joe Mantegna) gather at a restaurant where they tell Mantegna's fiancee (Cynthia Stevenson) the Mickey and Ellen story.

We keep jumping back and forth between flash-backs of the two stars, and scenes of these increasingly restless raconteurs at the table, waiting for Crystal and Winger to show up so they can order their meal.

No wonder they're getting impatient and annoyed, munching on crackers and wine but—like the movie audience—denied any real nourishment or satisfaction.

NEWSDAY, 5/19/95, Part II/p. B3, Jack Mathews

Paris, the music of Cole Porter, Irving Berlin and the Gershwins, the voices of Billie Holiday and Ella Fitzgerald. One thing for sure, when Billy Crystal decides to host an evening of romantic entertainment, he knows how to set the table.

Crystal, who co-wrote, co-produced, directed and co-stars in "Forget Paris," also knows the importance of a sense of humor to courtship, and has learned—since the maudlin debacle of "Mr. Saturday Night"—how to keep the sentiment in check.

All of which makes for a very satisfying romantic comedy. If "Forget Paris" isn't quite the ode to marriage that Crystal calls it, it is terrifically entertaining and includes one scene—look for a pigeon and flypaper—that will have audiences rocking with laughter.

From the opening credits, with Billie Holiday singing "It's very clear, our love is here to stay ...", it's very clear what Crystal has to say. Married for 25 years himself, Crystal set out to make a movie about the work and compromise it takes for a marriage to endure beyond the honeymoon.

This is not exactly earthshaking news, but taking up where other romantic stories tend to end is a noble idea.

"Forget Paris," which Crystal wrote with his "City Slickers" and "Mr. Saturday Night" collaborators Babaloo Mandel and Lowell Ganz, doesn't go the distance with its couple, but in tracking their ups and downs through their first four years together, you get the idea.

The main issue testing the marriage of Mickey (Crystal) and Ellen (Debra Winger) is a persistent career crisis. He's an NRA referee, one of the best in the league, and is on the road six months out of the year. She's an airline executive who gives up a great job in Paris. After they meet, Ellen finds life as an NBA wife almost unbearable.

At least, that's where the story is headed. Structured in the style of Woody Allen's "Broadway Danny Rose," "Forget Paris" is a series of anecdotal flashbacks recalled by Mickey's friends in a restaurant where they're waiting for him to join them.

The beneficiary of these stories is an idealistic romantic (Cynthia Stevenson) who has just become engaged to Mickey's sportswriter friend (Joe Mantegna). The stories begin with Mickey and Ellen's whirlwind romance in Paris and get progressively more complicated. They are, as the group's newcomer begins to realize, not the best thing for a woman to hear on the eve of her own wedding.

Having the story broken up this way covers some serious flaws, chiefly that there is little chemistry between Crystal and Winger, that the case for why this marriage should survive is never really made. Other than their unforgettable time in Paris, Mickey and Ellen have next to nothing in common.

One of the things they do not have in common is the love for NBA basketball; indeed, Crystal shows more passion for that game than for the romance. Standing like a waist-high dwarf among some of the NBA's celebrated giants (Kareem, Ewing and—dare I mention him—Reggie Miller), Crystal virtually beams from the pleasure of their company.

The timing of the film's release, in the midst of the play-off season, may or not be inspired. The movie benefits from play-off frenzy, but people in New York don't want to think about "Forget Paris" when they're wondering if they'll be able to forget Indiana.

SIGHT AND SOUND, 10/95, p. 47, Peter Matthews

In a restaurant, Andy, a fortyish sportswriter, tells Liz, his fiancée, the story of his friends Mickey and Ellen, how they met in Paris and fell in love. As various guests arrive, each one picks up the story ...

When his father dies, Mickey Gordon, a top referee in the National Basketball Association, is obliged to fly with the body to France, so that the old man can be buried alongside his Second World War regiment. The airline loses the coffin, and a long trail of Gallic superciliousness leads to the office of Ellen Andrews, an expatriate American airline executive who locates the body. The funeral occurs in a small village, with Mickey the sole mourner ... until Ellen shows up. The two spend an idyllic week in Paris. Still, Mickey has his career to think of, and decides he must forget Paris. On the basketball court, however, he can't get Ellen out of his mind, and he flies back to France to propose. She confesses that she is already married—though separated—and confused. Mickey returns home but one night on the road, Ellen unexpectedly appears, having given up her husband and her job for him.

Mickey and Ellen get married but Ellen soon finds LA life nerve-wracking, abhors her inferior job at Burbank airport and resents all the time Mickey spends away. She convinces him to take up a new career selling cars, and they move to a nice suburban house in the Valley. Ellen gets a promotion, and the two achieve an uneasy peace until her senile father moves in with them. Feeling stifled and dissatisfied, Mickey returns to refereeing. In desperation, they go to a series of marriage counsellors. Finally, Ellen packs her father back to Wichita. Mickey and Ellen want a baby, but she has difficulty conceiving; it appears that nothing can be done. Ellen announces that she is leaving Mickey to accept a job back in Paris.

Now, some four months later, the assembled dinner guests are awaiting Mickey, who is late. Another patron interrupts the group to relate how, just moments ago, Mickey and Ellen were reunited on the basketball court to the jubilation of the crowd. The ecstatic couple arrives at the restaurant.

Some years ago, Billy Crystal made a perfectly acceptable romantic comedian in *When Harry Met Sally*. But there, he was obliged to knuckle down to a smart script (by Nora Ephron) and a director (Rob Reiner) who knew how to use his weaselly abrasiveness and harmonise it with Meg Ryan's soft dippiness. Most any good romantic comedy involves some such chemical reaction where two incompatibles foment violently before settling down to a poised and witty equilibrium. *Forget Paris* is a dreadful romantic comedy, and not because it doesn't play by the rules.

You can see that Mickey and Ellen are meant to be a pair of mixed nuts. Mickey is your standard all-American squirt, wily, hard-driving, untutored and beneath it all a quivering pile of goo; Ellen is the cool cosmopolitanite who knows about culture (although this amounts to a quick sighting of the Mona Lisa and a taste for Andrew Lloyd Webber) but longs for a belly-laugh. The ostensible trouble with these two is that neither will forget Paris—that is, climb down from their dream and face the compromises and mutual adjustments that an ordinary life together entails. The real trouble turns out to be the sustaining myth of all romantic comedy: men and women belong to alien species, and if that's terrible, aren't we lucky just the same?

But though the movie endorses the letter of the genre, it violates its democratic spirit. Maybe one can't really expect the beautifully attuned sparring of a Tracy and Hepburn; still, it's dismaying to watch Crystal, who directed and wrote the script (with Lowell Ganz and Babaloo Mandel), indulge in a display of shameless, unilateral mugging at the expense of his co-star. Debra Winger is tossed one gag where she must charge about with a live pigeon stuck to her head; and a few times, she gets to use that splendid horsey laugh. Otherwise, the whole show is Crystal's, and he sinks it with a persona so obnoxiously manic the subsidiary characters keep having to remind you what a charmer Mickey is reputed to be. The lack of teamwork has a not unexpected result: one doesn't much care whether the screwball duo irons things out, since there's not the slightest hint of chemistry between them.

Officially, the movie keeps its moral books on the up and up: it says that both parties are right, and both wrong. However, the emotional stress is made to fall squarely on Mickey during their numerous separations—so Ellen actually comes off as a bit of an inscrutable bitch who refuses this starved little sad sack the affection he continuously craves. Crystal hogs the pathos as greedily as he does the punchlines. One notices, for instance, how much gloppy sentiment gets squeezed out of Mickey's relationship with his dead father, whereas Ellen's senile one is used merely as the butt of his comic frustration (in this two-bit role, William Hickey still manages the most polished playing in the picture).

There's no denying that Mickey and Ellen's problems (conflicting schedules, independence versus security, and so forth) are recognisable. But they are also the hoariest of contemporary couple cliches, and require astute writing and acting to put them over. The tinny, perfunctory squabbles here carry little conviction, and the film-makers seem to know it for someone has elected to drown out everything with a wall-to-wall score (bastardised jazz, perky Parisian music and romantic standards made to sound incredibly tacky in context) that tries to cattle-prod the viewer into feeling something.

Winger is not the only wasted talent in the movie: there is also the likably hardboiled Cathy Moriarty and the terrific Julie Kavner (cracking the same dumb Weight Watchers jokes she did on *Rhoda* 20 years ago). They and the other minor players narrate the story in relays, but why bother with this device if you don't intend to throw contrasting lights on the protagonists (most obviously, along gender lines)? However, *Rashomon* this isn't, and Crystal seems afraid to go over his audience's head. From the evidence, that audience would appear to comprise those likely to be slain by the assorted cheese jokes (French and Swiss) or by such thigh-slappers as Mickey's strenuous efforts in the cubicle at the fertility clinic. True, romantic comedy can employ farcical or cartoonish elements successfully, as *Bringing Up Baby*—and later *Moonstruck*—so delightfully proved. But even low buffoonery takes tact, and that's what Crystal hasn't got a lot of.

VILLAGE VOICE, 5/30/95, p. 62, Ben Greenman

If you believe TV ads, there are two movies called *Forget Paris* in theaters now. One tells the story of Mickey Gordon (Billy Crystal), a tough NBA referee who goes face-to-stomach with hoop legends like Kareem Abdul-Jabbar and David Robinson. The other *Forget Paris* also stars Crystal as a ref, but it benches basketball in favor of a love story involving Mickey and an American expatriate named Ellen (Debra Winger).

The schizophrenic publicity, which comes in the heat of the NBA post-season, diagnoses the film's flaws as precisely as any critic can. Crystal's NBA fantasy intrudes elaborate simulated games and real-life stars, and the romance with Winger tries its darnedest to tell the truth about the compromises of adult love. But there's no harmony between the two main plots—watching one of them, it's hard to remember that the other ever existed. It doesn't help that the story is structured as a series of static anecdotes told by friends of the couple—although those friends, played by Cathy Moriarty, Richard Masur, Julie Kavner, Cynthia Stevenson, and Joe Mantegna (doing his best Bruno Kirby impression), are more compelling than Crystal and Winger.

Divided against itself, *Forget Paris* cannot stand. For a love story, it doesn't have enough heart. For a basketball story, it doesn't have enough bounce. For a story about Americans in Paris, it doesn't have enough Paris. Conspiracy theorists will be excused for feeling that the film colludes with Meg Ryan's *French Kiss* to create some sinister *When Harry Met Sally* confluence, and cynics will be pardoned for feeling that if Paris is cute enough for both Crystal and Ryan, it's too cute for the rest of us. There are enough jokes to stock two whole ads, but in the end, *Forget Paris* could learn a thing or two from the NBA—it's nice to take the open shot, but you need some muscle in the paint.

Also received in:
CHICAGO TRIBUNE, 5/19/95, Friday/p. J, Michael Wilmington
NEW REPUBLIC, 6/12/95, p. 32, Stanley Kauffmann
NEW YORK TIMES, 5/19/95, p. C16, Caryn James
NEW YORKER, 5/22/95, p. 98, Anthony Lane
VARIETY, 5/15-21/95, p. 95, Steven Gaydos
WASHINGTON POST, 5/19/95, p. D7, Hal Hinson
WASHINGTON POST, 5/19/95, Weekend/p. 57, Desson Howe

FOUR ROOMS

A Miramax Films release of a Band Apart production. *Executive Producer:* Alexandre Rockwell and Quentin Tarantino. *Producer:* Lawrence Bender. *Director (The Missing Ingredient):* Allison Anders. *Director (The Wrong Man):* Alexandre Rockwell. *Director (The Misbehavers):* Robert Rodriguez. *Director (The Man From Hollywood):* Quentin Tarantino. *Screenplay (The Missing Ingredient):* Allison Anders. *Screenplay (The Wrong Man):* Alexandre Rockwell. *Screenplay (The Misbehavers):* Robert Rodriquez. *Screenplay (The Man From Hollywood):* Quentin Tarantino. *Director of Photography (The Missing Ingredient):* Rodrigo Garcia. *Director of Photography (The Misbehavers):* Guillemo Navarro. *Director of Photography (The Wrong Man):* Phil Parmet. *Director of Photography (The Man From Hollywood):* Andrzej Sekula. *Editor (The Missing Ingredient):* Margie Goodspeed. *Editor (The Wrong Man):* Elena Maganini. *Editor (The Man From Hollywood):* Sally Menke. *Editor (The Misbehavers):* Robert Rodriguez. *Music:* Combusible Edison. *Music Editor:* Denise Okomoto. *Choreographer:* Sissy Boyd. *Sound:* Pawel Wdowczak and (music) Mutato Muzika. *Sound Editor:* Bruce Fortune and Victor Iorillo. *Casting:* Russell Gray. *Production Designer:* Gary Frutkoff. *Art Director:* Mayne Schuyler Berke. *Set Decorator:* Sara Andrews. *Animation Producer:* Kurtz and Friends. *Costumes:* Susan L. Bertram and Mary Claire Hannan. *Make-up: The Missing Ingredient/The Misbehavers:* Thomas G. Marquez. *Costumes: The Wrong Man/The Man From Hollywood:* Jacqueline Aronson. *Make-up: The Misbehavers/The Man From Hollywood:* Ermahn Ospina. *Costumes: The Missing Ingredient/The Wrong Man:* Lizbeth Williamson. *Running time:* 96 minutes. *MPAA Rating:* R.

CAST: Lawrence Bender (Long Hair Yuppie Scum); Kathy Griffin (Betty); Paul Hellerman (Taxi Driver); Quinn Thomas Hellerman (Baby Bellhop); Marc Lawrence (Sam the Bellhop); Unruly Julie McClean (Left Redhead); Laura Rush (Right Redhead); Paul Skemp (Right Redhead); Marisa Tomei (Margaret); Tim Roth (Ted the Bellhop).

THE MISSING INGREDIENT—Sammi Davis (Jezebel); Amanda de Cadenet (Diana); Valeria Golino (Athena); Madonna (Elspeth); Ione Skye (Eva); Lili Taylor (Raven); Alicia Witt (Kiva).

THE WRONG MAN—Jennifer Beals (Angela); David Proval (Sigfried).

THE MISBEHAVERS—Antonio Banderas (Man); Lana McKissack (Sarah); Patrick Vonne Rodriguez (Corpse); Tamlyn Tomita (Wife); Danny Verduzco (Juancho).

THE MAN FROM HOLLYWOOD—Jennifer Beals (Angela); Bruce Willis (Leo); Paul Calderon (Norman); Quentin Taratino (Chester);

LOS ANGELES TIMES, 12/25/95, Calendar/p. 12, Jack Mathews

[The following review by Jack Mathews appeared in a slightly different form in
NEWSDAY, 12/26/95, Part II/p. B2.]

Alexandre Rockwell, who came up with the idea for the anthology comedy "Four Rooms," says of the characters in his segment, "They are walking the line, and when you walk the line, sometimes you fall into hell and sometimes you trip into heaven."

Moviegoers run the same risk every time they plunk down the price of a ticket, and those who do so for this film will soon feel the heat of Satan's breath.

It's not enough to say that "Four Rooms" is a bad movie. It's four bad movies rolled into one, the sum being even worse than the parts. It's an embarrassment for its quartet of respected independent filmmakers, and an object lesson for investors suffering Sundance Syndrome, that bandwagon urge to throw money after talent unveiled at festivals.

It was on the film festival circuit where Rockwell ("In the Soup") and his collaborators Quentin Tarantino ("Reservoir Dogs"), Allison Anders ("Gas Food Lodging") and Robert Rodriguez ("El Mariachi") got to know one another, and it's no surprise they all went for his idea, which was for each to write and direct a segment about a nervous bellhop manning a rundown Los Angeles hotel by himself on New Year's Eve.

The surprise comes in the quality of the work they turned in.

After a credit sequence that is a "reasonably wacky knock-off" of "those done for the "Pink Panther" series, "Four Rooms" introduces the bellboy Ted (Tim Roth), who is left alone as the hotel—a chintzy version of the purgatory setting of "Barton Fink"—fills up with weirdos, and endures a nightmarish string of adventures in four of his guests' rooms.

In Anders' opening episode, "The Missing Ingredient," Ted delivers room service to a coven of witches—Madonna, Valeria Golino, Sammi Davis and Ione Skye among them and sticks around to donate sperm for an annual body fluids ritual. In Rockwell's "The Wrong Man," he walks in on a couple (David Proval, Jennifer Beals) enacting a dangerous game of bondage and is mistaken by the gun-toting husband for his bound and gagged wife's lover. In Rodriguez's "The Misbehavers," Ted is asked to look in on a pair of kids watching television while a corpse rots in the mattress beneath them. And in Tarantino's "The Man From Hollywood," the bellboy is offered $1,000 by three drunks (Tarantino, Bruce Willis and Paul Calderon) to wield the hatchet in a reenactment of an episode of "Alfred Hitchcock Presents."

Sounds better than it is.

Rodriguez's story is by far the best, something like a C-minus to the others' Fs. For one thing, it has Antonio Banderas, in the film's *only* restrained performance, playing a menacing Latino who offers Ted a $500 baby-sitting fee so he and his wife can go out on the town. For another, Ted isn't in it that much; it's mostly about the two kids playing "Home Alone," drinking champagne, smoking, playing darts with a syringe and blaming the corpse's odor on each other's feet.

We can only wonder what was on Tim Roth's mind when he got a fix on his character. It's as if he's doing an impression of Jim Carrey doing an impression of Jerry Lewis in "The Bellboy." Whatever you think of Carrey and Lewis, Roth's physical comedy skills are dwarfed by their genius. It is a gutsy performance, a blur of facial tics and weasely stammers, but we've slept in hotel rooms that are funnier.

It is either ironic or fitting that Rockwell's episode is the most pointless. "Four Rooms" has been cut by 26 minutes since its ridiculed premiere at the Toronto Film Festival. They might have been wiser to simply jettison this entire segment.

Anders' "The Missing Ingredient" is an aimless mess, with the witches wandering around moaning, a couple of them decorously topless, as they try to call up the spirit of their goddess, a '50s stripper named Diana, from the bridal suite's whirlpool bath.

But it is Tarantino's contribution that is the most disappointing. The least we'd expect from the creator of "Reservoir Dogs," "True Romance" and "Pulp Fiction" is some brittle dialogue and an engaging character or two. There's nothing of the sort here.

Tarantino, still fancying himself an actor, is "The Man From Hollywood," a drunken spendthrift determined to reenact the "Alfred Hitchcock" episode where Peter Lorre gets Steve McQueen to bet his little finger that he can get his cigarette lighter to work 10 straight times. It's a shaggy-dog story, again with no point, unless you want to bet how many times Tarantino can scream the F-word in 10 minutes.

You may feel like screaming it a few times yourself as you walk out of the theater, but at least you'll have a good reason.

NEW YORK POST, 12/23/95, p. 17, Thelma Adams

Making fun of "Four Rooms" is just too easy—it's like shooting goldfish in a coffee mug.

Usually, youngish filmmakers cut their teeth on student films and then make the leap to features. In this omnibus comedy set in an aging Hollywood hotel on New Year's Eve, Quentin Tarantino ("Pulp Fiction"), Robert Rodriguez ("Desperado"), Allison Anders ("Mi Vida Loca") and Alexandre Rockwell ("In the Soup") prove that they can still turn out a mediocre student film despite varying levels of success in the theatrical arena.

The animated opening credits of a doomed bellboy in various states of slapstick distress—a retro whiff of the "Pink Panther"—set a coy but comic-free tone. We begin to worry. We want them to be funny (c'mon, no one wants Tarantino and his gang of hipsters to fail—it could devalue all that "Pulp Fiction" adoration not to mention the coronation of "El Mariachi" director Rodriguez). They're just lame.

Ted the bellhop (Tim Roth) is the thread that links the four stories. With a pill-box hat, a blue bolero and a white shirt that refuses to stay tucked, we have Roth as Jerry Lewis. No twitch is left untried, no hip wiggle abandoned before its time, no shrill pitch of voice unexplored.

Roth stole "Rob Roy" out from under Liam Neeson. His brilliant portrayal of a Jewish hitman was the speeding bullet in James Gray's ballistic "Little Odessa" (among the year's best first films). But no actor, not even Roth, can serve four masters.

Over 96 minutes, twitchy Ted serves a coven of witches, a married couple who seek arousal with a revolver, a gangster with child-care problems and Tarantino doing schtick as an unstable stand-up comic with a wicked wager.

Up first: Madonna overexposes her cleavage in Anders' witch tale. The diva's bitchy bleached daughter of the dark arts has an annoying adolescent lesbian lover (Alicia Witt) in tow. The pop chameleon delivers her usual nuanced performance. (Like Tarantino in front of the camera, the advice remains: don't give up your day job. All that ego energy sucks up the light without reflecting brilliance.)

Despite the talent on ice—Ione Skye, Lili Taylor and Valeria Golino—this segment is plain goofy, the sexual high jinks too winky. What would Sabrina think of these amateurs? She'd twitch her nose and channel surf.

Rockwell's slice follows. It's barely a skit—and barely funny. Ted walks in on Siegfried (David Proval) and his wife, Angela (Jennifer Beals). The husband strung out on drugs and drink, has his wife roped to a chair and accuses Ted of sleeping with her. Proval and Roth go antic, along with a camera that won't stay still—perhaps to distract us from the fact that there's nothing really going on. For the climax, Rockwell's real-life spouse Beals recites slang words for penis.

The best of the bunch—everything is relative—is Rodriguez's slick outtake from the annals of the Addams' Family. Antonio Banderas tangos into the frame as a suave gangster who wants a night out with wife Tamlyn Tomita—and strong-arms Ted into babysitting his kids. Ever the entertainer, Rodriguez knows that when in doubt, cast cute kids, a devastating leading man, cue the gruesome corpses—and then torch the set when there's nowhere else to go (see "Desperado").

"Four Rooms" lands with a thud in the penthouse suite where, in one short year, Tarantino has squandered his "Pulp Fiction" cache. The former video clerk has searched his memory vaults to recycle an old episode from an Alfred Hitchcock TV show. Tarantino does himself a disservice as the obnoxious comic who wagers his sports car against his friend's pinkie finger over a party trick with a Zippo lighter.

As an actor, Tarantino displays the negative charisma he showed in "Destiny Turns on the Radio." The chinned one sports more lip sweat than Anthony Hopkins' Nixon. The writer/director also coaxes Bruce Willis' worst performance of the year. While next week's "Twelve Monkeys" presents the rehabilitated, smirk-free Willis, he appears here in that tiresome, manic, spoiled bar-boy frenzy we hoped he'd grown beyond.

Where's Johnny Depp when we need him to trash a hotel suite? Let's shut the door on "Four Rooms" (opening Christmas Day in hopes that few moviegoers will read the negative reviews) and raise a toast to better movies in the new year.

SIGHT AND SOUND, 2/96, p. 41, Mark Kermode

An old guy, Sam, hands over the mantle of bell-hop at the once-fashionable Monsignor hotel to young Ted, advising "stay away from night clerks, kids, hookers and marital disputes. Never have sex with the clientele. Always get a tip." On New Year's Eve, Ted is left alone by his boss Betty to tend to the clientele in four separate rooms.

The Missing Ingredient. In the Honeymoon Suite, a coven of modern day witches convenes to free the Goddess Diana from the stone into which she was turned by a jealous man on her wedding night, 40 years ago, in this very room. Ted is asked to supply rosemary, sea salt, spring water, ginger, and raw meat for their ceremony. Gathering around a large bathtub, the witches offer milk from a mother's tit, virgin's blood, the sweat of five men's thighs, and one year's worth of tears. Eva, however, has swallowed the semen which her lover Bill was to provide. Ted is offered $50 for some of his own. The witches complete their spell and conjure Diana from the bath.

The Wrong Man. Back in reception, Ted receives a demand for ice from Room 404. Arriving at the wrong room, Ted is held at gunpoint by the pill-popping Sigfried whose wife Angela is bound and gagged, Sigfried babbles incoherently that Ted is intimate with Angela, and forces Ted to nibble Angela's ear. Taunted by Sigfried about his name, Ted declares that no-one may call him Theodore. Sigfried is impressed, kisses Ted, and has a heart attack. Angela demands that Ted get nitro-glycerine from the bathroom to revive Sigfried. Ted fails to escape from the bathroom window, but is vomited upon by the tenant above, who actually ordered the ice. Sigfried wakes, declaring his attack a ruse to see if Angela loved him. Incensed, Angela declares Ted's penis to be enormous. In the confusion, Ted escapes, and passes another Theodore in the corridor, heading for room 404.

The Misbehavers. In room 309 a gangster-like man and woman pay Ted $500 to check up on their two children every half hour, telling them "Don't misbehave". Left alone, the children watch porno TV, puff cigarettes; drink champagne, deface the room and harass Ted with complaints. Ted arrives with milk and crackers and puts Mentholatum ointment on the children's eyelids to make them sleep. Resolutely awake, the children find a syringe in a bureau drawer, and trace an unpleasant smell to a corpse under the bed. Ted races upstairs where a stray cigarette sets the room ablaze. The man and woman return to a scene of carnage, and merely ask, "Did they misbehave?"

The Man from Hollywood. Distraught, Ted calls Betty's house, where a crack-smoking friend misunderstands his situation. Ted tells Betty he's quitting, but she begs him to attend to one last call from The Penthouse. Ted complies, and supplies Cristal Champagne, a block of wood, three nails, a roll of twine, and a sharp hatchet to movie mogul Chester, his associates Norman and Leo, and Angela, who has dropped in. After much small-talk, Leo reveals that the group want to re-play *The Man from Rio*, an Alfred Hitchcock Show episode in which Peter Lorre bets Steve McQueen his car against a little finger that McQueen cannot ignite his cigarette lighter ten times in a row. Chester has now bet his '64 Chevy Chevelle against Norman's 'pinkie' but doubts his own ability to cut off the finger should Norman lose. Ted refuses to help out until he is offered $1000. Norman puts his hand on the block and misfires his lighter on the first go. Ted cuts off his finger, takes the money and leaves. The bloodied party stagger to the lift with Norman's finger in an ice bucket. They drop it.

Portmanteau movies are by nature uneven beasts, but this showcase folly by four of Hollywood's 'hottest' stars plumbs new depths. Most damagingly, the first two segments are so ill-conceived that by half-time the audience still has no clue as to the intended tone of the collaboration. Quite apart from the difficulties of roping together four stylistically diverse works into a coherent whole, the first hour of *Four Rooms* is irredeemably inept. The only rational response to *Gas Food Lodging* and *Mi Vida Loca* director Allison Anders' saucy *The Missing Ingredient* is bemusement: is this meant to be funny, sexy, or perhaps satirical? We never know, and we never laugh.

From confusion, we lurch to tedium as the once-promising Alexandre Rockwell (*In the Soup, Somebody to Love*) delivers a slice of fever-pitched nonsense which revels in convoluted irrelevance. Rockwell seems to think it's clever to baffle an audience—it's engaging them that's difficult, and this he fails to do. Only in Robert Rodriguez's third section does an overall guiding vision become apparent, but while *The Misbehavers* is stylistically consistent (and builds upon his rigidly generic *El Mariachi* and *Desperado),* formally it amounts to nothing more than a crude one-line gag with a 20 minute set-up. (There are problems, too, with the level of nastiness which Rodriguez injects into the action, but by this juncture any uneasiness about his use of child actors must take a critical back-seat.)

The Man from Hollywood is clearly the best segment, using audacious single-takes and bubbling with Quentin Tarantino's well worn verbal pazazz. As a throwaway half-hour television special, it would doubtless achieve curiosity value for Tarantino fans, packed as it is with cine-literate in-jokes and fleeting genre nods. As the raison d'etre for a feature-length movie, however, this new twist on an old tiff solidly fails to justify the indulgent whole.

VILLAGE VOICE, 1/9/96, p. 58, Georgia Brown

You hear rumors that a movie's a dog but you go thinking, it can't be *that* bad. Reader, *Four Rooms* is worse. The conceit of this misguided show of hubris is that hotels harbor many stories, and why couldn't four talented (we'd assumed) filmmakers come up with four scintillating episodes? The new Hollywood brats—Anders, Rockwell, Rodriguez, and Tarantino—do their own *Paris vu par, New York Stories, RoCoPaC, Far from Vietnam.* And in the process help Tim Roth, playing the bellboy, destroy any career he might have as a comic.

Roth's Ted isn't just connective tissue, he's an integral part of each story. So we get to see Roth roll his eyes, wiggle his eyebrows and butt, ham and camp it up in *all four* tales. In Anders's stupid spoof, he's called on to deliver sperm to a witches' coven; in Rockwell's dreadful drama, he gets caught up with a feuding couple. These leadoff episodes are so leaden you'll need Krazy Glue to stay in your seat. Number three, Rodriguez's, has kinetic energy, two cute kids, and Antonio Banderas, although it, too, is no more than a one-note joke. Finally, Tarantino has the nerve to lift his plot from an old *Alfred Hitchcock Presents* and to star in it. No one else would let an actor this bad hog the screen.

Remember how buoyant *New York Stories* was (well, except for Coppola's portion)? Woody Allen and Scorsese, and even Coppola, worked at developing their material. The *Four Rooms* kids seem to think we'll be charmed to watch them clip their toenails.

Also reviewed in:
NEW YORK TIMES, 12/26/95, p. C13, Janet Maslin
VARIETY, 9/25-10/1/95, p. 93, Emanuel Levy
WASHINGTON POST, 12/25/95, p. D8, Hal Hinson
WASHINGTON POST, 12/29/95, Weekend/p. 32, Desson Howe

FRANKIE STARLIGHT

A Fine Line Features release of a Ferndale Films production in association with Channel Four Films/ Pandora Cinema/Rimb Productions/Eurinages, The Irish Film Board/Radio Teilifis Eireann/Canal Plus. *Producer:* Noel Pearson. *Director:* Michael Lindsay-Hogg. *Screenplay:* Chet Raymo and Ronan O'Leary. Based on the novel "The Dork of Cork" by: Chet Raymo. *Director of Photography:* Paul Laufer. *Editor:* Ruth Foster. *Music:* Elmer Bernstein. *Music Editor:* Kathy Durning. *Sound:* Kieran Horgan. *Sound Editor:* Nick Adams. *Production Designer:* Frank Conway. *Art Director:* David Walley and Linda Sutton. *Special Effects:* Gerry Johnson. *Costumes:* Joan Bergin. *Make-up:* Marie O'Sullivan. *Running time:* 101 minutes. *MPAA Rating:* R.

CAST: Anne Parillaud (Bernadette); Matt Dillon (Terry Klout); Gabriel Byrne (Jack Kelly); Rudi Davies (Emma); Georgina Cates (Young Emma); Corban Walker (Frank Bois); Alan

Pentony (Young Frank); Niall Toibin (Handy Paige); Dearbhla Molloy (Effa Kelly); Jean Claude Frissung (Albert Bois); Victoria Begeja (Anne Marie Bois); Barbara Alyn Woods (Marcia); John Davies (Tobin); Amber Hibler (Charleen); Jessie-Ann Friend (Lisa); Ulrich Funke (German Officer); Guy Verama (Interpretor); Julian Negulesco (Bernadette's Uncle); Corinne Blue (Bernadette's Aunt); Sage Allen (Bar Proprietress); Ann Weakley (Midwife); Elizabeth Keller (TV Interviewer); David Parnell (Photographer); Aidan Grennell (Bookshop Manager); Tristin Gribbin (Bookshop Assistant); Christopher Casson (Bookshop Gentleman); Owen Roe (Senior Customs Officer); Aisling Leyne (Girl in Gallery); Pauline Cadell (Prostitute); Alan Devine (Bernadette's Friend on Beach No. 1); Edward Naessens (Bernadette's Friend on Beach No. 2); Laurent Mellet (Bernadette's Friend on Beach No. 3); Christine Keane (Mother of Scabious Child); Darren Monks (Young Man in cinema); Kit Kincannon (Man in Bar); Martin Murphy (Guest at Wedding); Martin Dunne (Friend at Wedding No. 1); Derry Power (Friend at Wedding No. 2).

LOS ANGELES TIMES, 11/22/95, p. Calendar/p. 18, John Anderson

[The following review by John Anderson appeared in a slightly different form in **NEWSDAY, 11/22/95, Part II/p. B19.]**

There's a natural diminishment that occurs in the transference of autobiography to movie, just because so much about memoir has to do with personality. And personality on film, as we all know, is the exclusive domain of the actor.

So it was Michael Lindsay-Hogg's good fortune to have found and cast Corban Walker and Alan Pentony, two dwarfs who'd never acted before, as the older and younger versions of the title character in "Frankie Starlight." As Frank Bois—a writer whose adult life is intercut with recollections of his rather unorthodox upbringing in Ireland and Texas—both Walker and Pentony are the reasons to watch. Their emotional candor, their freshness and their endearing personalities make this quirky, quasi-magical little film the sweet thing it is.

But while Lindsay-Hogg—who has directed music videos, Beatles ("Let It Be") and the under-appreciated "The Object of Beauty" with John Malkovich and Andie MacDowell—gets wonderful performances out of Walker and Pentony, he fares less well with others, notably Anne Parillaud. As Frankie's mother, Bernadette—who flees postwar France for Ireland by becoming the sole source of recreation on a U.S. troop ship—Parillaud is paralyzed. She seems at times to need a nap.

She has a lot on her mind, though. Penniless, pregnant and deportable, she eludes immigration officer Jack Kelly (Gabriel Byrne), but then becomes his lover—an activity witnessed by Kelly's deeply traumatized daughter Emma (Georgina Cates). Crises ensue, but Kelly's very understanding wife, Effa (Dearbhla Molloy), insists that Bernadette and the infant Frankie come live in their home—where Jack instills in Frankie a knowledge and love of the stars. He also provides the unqualified affection a dwarf child—any child, for that matter—needs.

There is a sense, though, that detail from Chet Raymo's novel "The Dork From Cork"—which inspired this film—has been lost in the translation. Intercut with Frankie's childhood memories—which includes his brief relocation to Texas with Bernadette and her cowboy lover Terry Klout (Matt Dillon), an ex-GI who'd been aboard that troop ship—are the publication of the adult Frank's book, a combination of memoir, astronomy and his mother's life story. There are some truly funny moments between Frank and his agent Handy Paige (the celebrated Irish comedian Niall Toibin), which make one wish to linger in the present rather than revisit Frankie's past.

But it's a back-and-forth progression and a hot-and-cold experience for most of "Frankie Starlight," which ends with Frank's reunion with the adult Emma Kelly (Rudi Davies), and a miraculous, feel-good finale that perhaps only a non-actor/actor like Walker could pull off.

NEW YORK POST, 11/22/95, p. 48, Thelma Adams

You've no doubt been to the movies and come away wondering "Why on earth was this film made?"

Count "Frankie Starlight" among with this far-too-numerous group.

This painstaking and painful coming of-age movie orbits around a vertically-challenged Irishman. OK, I won't omit what the p.c. production notes couldn't cough up: Frankie is a dwarf. If I had said he was one of the little people, you might have thought he was a leprechaun.

But there's no particular magic in Michael Lindsay-Hogg's endlessly earnest literary adaptation of Chet Raymo's remaindered novel "The Dork of Cork." Raymo teamed with Ronan O'Leary to write a screenplay that snuffs out the book's whimsy magic and brings its astronomical allusions thudding to earth.

Who knows why jolly little Frankie (Alan Pentony)—beloved by his ESP-scarred French mother Bernadette (Anne Parillaud) and two foster fathers, Jack Kelly (Gabriel Byrne) and Terry Klout (Matt Dillon)—has grown into the bitter, bearded Lautrec-like character (Corban Walker) who narrates the story?

And while the filmmakers think that Frankie merits a soul (and some ache) and is rendered life-size in stature, the characters who surround him are dwarfed and ill-formed.

The beautiful Parillaud ("La Femme Nikita") plays Bernadette as if the actress has curled into a fetal position. She sulkily drifts through material that has her reading the future in one scene, then trotting off to Texas without a clue in another. Bernadette's sporadic visionary gift is reduced to a plot device (as in: hold the laundry, Frankie is in trouble across town, cut to Frankie cradling dead dog).

Playing Texan Terry, Dillon is saddled with an accent and a character without a legitimate motive. He rides into the story on a motorcycle and disappears into a beer bottle, tragically altering the course of Bernadette's life and leaving the audience befuddled as to why the American showed up at all.

Meanwhile, Byrne is on cruise control, hiding behind his craggy good looks until Kelly drops off the face of the script. One arbitrary scene follows another, as the script floats back in time and then whips forward to the present and the grouchy company of the grown Frankie.

All the labored flashbacks in the world—and Starlight's rehabilitation through the love of a good and tall redhead—can't overcome material that doesn't get any deeper than the writer's lament: "What is beautiful is always more desirable than what is not."

SIGHT AND SOUND, 5/96, p. 52, Geoffrey Macnab

Dublin, the present day. Frank Bois arrives at the office of literary agent Handy Paige, with a bulky manuscript entitled *Nightstalk*. The book tells of his childhood, his love of stargazing, and of how his French mother, Bernadette, came to live in Ireland.

The 1940s. As a young woman growing up in Normandy during the Nazi occupation, Bernadette narrowly avoids death in a bomb blast. Her father is executed by the Germans and her mother hangs herself. Bernadette flees France aboard an American troopship. During the voyage she is impregnated by one of the men on board, but is discovered by the ship's officers and put ashore in Dublin. Penniless, she is befriended by customs officer Jack Kelly. He briefly becomes her lover, and helps provide for her child, Frank, who is born a dwarf. Not long after Jack and his family are posted out of town, Bernadette meets an ex-GI from Texas, Terry Klout. He too becomes her lover and a father figure to Frank. Eventually, he takes them to Texas with him, but Bernadette isn't happy there. She works in a bar to save the money for her and Frank to return to Ireland. Not long after returning, she throws herself from a building to her death.

In the present day, the literary agent tells Frank his book has been accepted for publication. It proves a big success. One morning, as Frank is signing copies in a bookshop, he recognises Emma Kelly, Jack's daughter. The two mull over old times. Emma, an aspiring artist, invites Frank to her first exhibition. Their friendship blossoms and they marry.

Dotted throughout *Frankie Starlight* are sequences in which the diminutive hero, Frank Bois, sits on a rooftop, gazing at the heavens. For him, astronomy has almost alchemical powers: it is both a catalyst to his imagination and a means of escape from a world in which he is always going to be persecuted because of his size. He is a pint-sized visionary with a child's pellucid insight into human affairs; a clear descendant of *The Tin Drum*'s dwarf-savant protagonist. It can't be said, however, that his story offers much in the way of narrative momentum. Chet Raymo and Ronan O'Leary's screenplay (adapted from Raymo's novel, *The Dork of Cork*) is fragmentary and elliptical, lurching between past and present. We start with Frank in 80s Dublin. Then, through the unwieldy device of his autobiography, presented to a sceptical old soak of a literary agent, we are whisked back to his childhood and the story of why his French mother arrived in Ireland in the first place.

Frank fancies himself a poet. His frequent monologues are full of rich, allusive imagery about life, love and the stars. Unfortunately, director Michael Lindsay-Hogg (best known in this country for *Object of Beauty* and his television work) can't find a visual language to match them. He treats with leaden realism what ought to be a magical folk tale. By taking his material so literally, he exposes shortcomings in the characterisation and plot which a more imaginative style could have glossed over. His handling of his two 'star' actors also leaves plenty to be desired. As Frank's mother, Bernadette De Bois, Anne Parillaud comes across as a simple amalgam of Nikita (her own most famous role) and Beatrice Dalle's Betty Blue. She's the Gallic heroine as 'free spirit'—psychic, sexually voracious and ultimately suicidal. This is stereotyping at its crudest, without even a touch of irony to redeem it. Matt Dillon's ex-GI, Terry Klout, is an equally absurd creation. He drives a motorbike and speaks with a Texas drawl. He's supposed to be the quintessential 'Yank', as brash and fond of luxury as the country he comes from. In austere, post-war Dublin, he inevitably appears a wildly exotic figure, and Frank regards him with awe. But his reasons for beating a path to Bernadette's door are tenuous in the extreme. (His wife walks out on him so he comes to Ireland on a whim.)

Bernadette's decision to go back to Texas with him seems equally arbitrary. The little, self-contained American interlude, in which Bernadette, Frank and Terry briefly set up home together in the Lone Star state, is beautifully shot (all blue skies, wheat fields and smoke-filled bars) but doesn't have anything much to do with the rest of the film. The same might be said of the Normandy wartime sequences, in which the experiences of Bernadette's family during the Nazi occupation are sketched in cursory fashion. Arguably, the storytelling is supposed to be impressionistic—these are Frank's memories, strung together willy-nilly. He is enraptured by the past in the same way as he is by the stars he spends so much time gazing at. However, even if his imagination soars, the film-making seldom takes wing. As a consequence, the haphazard shifts in time and place seem jarring and arbitrary.

Producer Noel Pearson presumably saw Raymo's novel as source material for another screen adaptation in the tradition of his earlier successes, *My Left Foot* and *The Field*. The parallels with *My Left Foot*, in particular, are obvious: it too is about a writer who overcomes enormous obstacles to have his work published. But while that film, based on the true story of cerebral palsy victim, Christy Brown, was rude, boisterous fare, *Frankie Starlight* is a determinedly sentimental movie, a fact underlined by Elmer Bernstein's schmaltzy score. The film is most effective in its quietest moments. The scenes in which young Frank (played with great charm by freckled, doe-eyed 13- year-old, Alan Pentony) sits on the roof with Jack Kelly (Gabriel Byrne), just looking up at the heavens, or the moment when Frank spies on Kelly's red-haired daughter (Georgina Cates) washing her hair, are resonant in a way that much of the rest of the action is not. In an early scene, Frank is given a copy of Antoine De Saint-Exupery's classic fantasy, *The Little Prince*. *Frankie Starlight* is clearly supposed to be in a similar vein. What ultimately makes it so frustrating is the sense that there is something magical lurking within the story, but the film-makers have completely failed to uncover it.

VILLAGE VOICE, 12/5/95, p. 66, Georgia Brown

Frankie Starlight uses dwarfs to stoke sentiment, which isn't fair to dwarves. The movie's two dwarf actors, however, are so genuine and expressive that they're terribly good company. There is nothing false about them, though all around falseness glitters like stars in the movie's tricked-out skies. (Elmer Bernstein's treacly score is especially annoying.)

Directed by Michael Lindsay-Hogg and based on Chet Raymo's novel *The Dork of Cork*, *Starlight* starlight interweaves two stories, one from the past, about a Frenchwoman come to Dublin, and the other in the present, about the woman's reclusive grown son, Frankie, a dwarf. Bernadette (Anne Parillaud), however, never comes alive; she's merely a lovely figment in several men's imaginations. Frankie's story is more substantial, and as the child Frankie, Alan Pentony has such a handsome and piquant face, he's a pleasure to watch. Corban Walker, playing the elder Frankie, looks nothing like Pentony, but he is a wonderful conveyor of pain and humiliation as well as mischief and joy.

Bernadette's story begins in occupied France, where she survives a terrible accident and is thereafter credited with supernatural powers. The movie drops this subject once she leaves France by hiding out on a U.S. troop ship—this is where Frankie is conceived. When she's put off in Dublin, customs officer Jack Kelly (Gabriel Byrne) has an affair with her, but once his wife finds out and subsequently forgives him, he turns to simply caring for the mother and child. (It's Jack who teaches Frankie astronomy—hence, the movie's title.) Years later, an American from the troop ship (Matt Dillon) tracks down Bernadette and takes her and Frankie to Texas. About this time, Bernadette begins to seem mad rather than simply withheld. Intercut with these episodes from the past are passages showing the adult Frankie getting his book published and enduring people's casual rudeness.

The obvious comparison is to Jim Sheridan's *My Left Foot*, based on the autobiography of Christy Brown, the Irish writer with cerebral palsy. But that film was nothing if not hardheaded, whereas this one is mushy and ingratiating. The film's corny ending is particularly hard to take.

Also reviewed in:
CHICAGO TRIBUNE, 1/19/96, Friday/p. F, Michael Wilmington
NEW YORK TIMES, 11/22/95, p. C18, Janet Maslin
VARIETY, 9/18-24/95, p. 96, Leonard Klady

FRANZ KAFKA'S IT'S A WONDERFUL LIFE

A Manga Entertainment release. *Producer:* Ruth Kenley-Letts. *Director:* Peter Capaldi. *Screenplay:* Peter Capaldi. *Director of Photography:* Simon Maggs. *Editor:* Nikki Clemens. *Music:* Philip Appleby. *Production Designer:* John Beard. *Running time:* 24 minutes. *MPAA Rating:* Not Rated.

CAST: Richard E. Grant (Kafka); Crispin Letts (Gregor Samsa); Ken Stott (Woland); Elaine Collins (Miss Cicely); Phyliss Logan (Frau Bunofski).

NEW YORK POST, 11/29/95, p. 42, Larry Worth

[*Franz Kafka's It's a Wonderful Life* was reviewed jointly with *When Billy Broke His Head ... And Other Tales of Wonder;* see Worth's review of that film.]

VILLAGE VOICE, 12/5/95, p. 68, Leslie Camhi

[*Franz Kafka's It's a Wonderful Life* was reviewed jointly with *When Billy Broke His Head ... And Other Tales of Wonder;* see Camhi's review of that film.]

Also reviewed in:
NEW YORK TIMES, 11/29/95, p. C17, Janet Maslin

FREE WILLY 2: THE ADVENTURE HOME

A Warner Bros. release in association with Le Studio Canal+, Regency Enterprises and Alcor Films of a Shuler-Donner/Donner production. *Executive Producer:* Richard Donner, Arnon Milchan, and Jim Van Wyck. *Producer:* Lauren Shuler-Donner and Jennie Lew Tugend. *Director:* Dwight Little. *Screenplay:* Karen Janszen, Corey Blechman, and John Mattson. *Based on characters created by:* Keith A. Walker. *Director of Photography:* Laslo Kovacs. *Editor:* Robert Brown. *Music:* Basil Poledouris. *Sound:* Robert Janiger. *Sound Editor:* Louis L. Edemann, Charles L. Campbell, and Martin Maryska. *Casting:* Judy Taylor and Lynda Gordon. *Production Designer:* Paul Sylbert. *Art Director:* Gregory Bolton. *Set Designer:* Mindy R. Toback. *Set Decorator:* Casey Hallenbeck. *Special Effects:* Jon Belyeu. *Whale Effects:* Walt Conti. *Costumes:* Erica Edell Phillips. *Make-up:* Pamela Westmore and Whitney James. *Stunt*

Coordinator: Conrad E. Palmisano and Jeff Imada. *Running time:* 98 minutes. *MPAA Rating:* PG.

CAST: Jason James Richter (Jesse); Francis Capra (Elvis); Michael Madsen (Glen Greenwood); Jayne Atkinson (Annie Greenwood); August Schellenberg (Randolph Johnson); Mary Kate Schellhardt (Nadine); Elizabeth Peña (Dr. Kate Haley); Jon Tenney (John Milner); M. Emmet Walsh (Wilcox); John Considine (Commander Blake); Mykelti Williamson (Dwight Mercer); Paul Tuerpe (Milner's Assistant); Steve Kahan (Captain Nilson); Neal Matarazzo (Helmsman Kelly); Al Sapienza and Cliff Fetters (Engineers); June Christopher (Veterinarian); Marguerite Moreau (Julie); Christina Orchid (Donut Shop Lady); Edward J. Rosen (Environmental Man); Isaac T. Arnett, Jr. (Camper); Scott Stuber (Policeman); Chanel Capra (Teenage Girl at Ferry); Laura Gary (Whale Spotter); John Harms, Susan Brooks, and Jeff Brooks (Protesters); Joan Lunden (Herself).

LOS ANGELES TIMES, 7/19/95, Calendar/p. 4, Peter Rainer

The family that tends killer whales together stays together. That's the message of "Free Willy 2: The Adventure Home." When you're in need of some familial togetherness, sometimes only an orca will do.

The first "Free Willy," released in the summer of '93, was an ecology-era family film about a delinquent boy who bonds with an orca at the local sea park and, in so doing, bonds with his foster parents and a Native American teller of tales and a feminist seal handler. He ends up bonding with just about everything except the starfish.

In the sequel, young Jesse (Jason James Richter) is happily ensconced with his adoptive parents (Michael Madsen and Jayne Atkinson) when the arrival of his half-brother Elvis (Francis Capra) upsets the balance. Elvis and Jesse have never met. Their mother, a drug addict, has died, and now the tyke, who wears a Knicks cap backward and never tells the truth when a creative lie will do, is taken into the new family on a trial basis. In other words, we wait until a new round of bonding takes place.

And of course Willy, freed up from the first film, is there to help. Jesse re-encounters him when, camping with his family in Washington, he accidentally drops his harmonica in a cove and Willy pops up, jaws open, with the harmonica resting comfortably in his glottal area. Later, to impress the goddaughter (Mary Kate Schellhardt) of his Native American friend and protector (August Schellenberg), Jesse rides Willy in the surf.

Boy and girl bond—innocently, with a single kiss—by swimming around with Willy underwater. (Laszlo Kovacs' underwater photography has its allures.) Meantime, Elvis is trying to get his brother to like him, but he fibs so frequently that, when he passes along an overheard plot by oil-rig meanies and carny promoters: to filch Willy, nobody believes him. He's the Boy Who Cried Whale.

The OK-ness of the first "Willy" movie is repeated in the sequel, directed by Dwight Little and scripted by Karen Janszen and Corey Blechman and John Mattson. It's tolerable, and small children will probably have a rush of excitement whenever Willy bounces and flops and whistles through the foam.

Jesse and Elvis' search for family is mimicked by Willy and his sister Luna's attempt to reach their mother after a damaged oil tanker fouls the whale lanes. It's not exactly the most inspired example of plot cross-cutting—there's something absurd, maybe even for children, in all this whales-as-helpmates stuff—but it works on the kind of crude, basic level that children's fairy tales often inhabit.

And, as in the last film, there's even an 800 number to call during the end credits for Save the Whale info.

We also learn that "no whales were harassed or mistreated" during filming. That's good to know, too.

NEW YORK POST, 7/19/95, p. 33, Michael Medved

Its kind of tough to take a film seriously when its climactic scene depicts a killer whale rescuing a teen-age boy from ... a fire.

But this ludicrous sequence, like the rest of "Free Willy 2: The Adventure Home," is handled with such slick cinematic self-assurance, and such cheerful disregard for believability or common sense, that it's enjoyable in spite of itself.

As a sequel to the hugely successful family favorite of two summers ago, "Free Willy 2" may be stupidly conceived, but it's also handsomely well-executed, and it provides enough moments of excitement and sentiment to please audiences who loved the first film—especially the kids.

In fact, theaters ought to advertise this silly "Willy" with the following warning: "No moviegoer over the age of 13 will be admitted unless accompanied by a child."

Last time, you'll recall, a troubled 12-year-old named Jesse found redemption in his friendship with a lonely Orca whale, which he eventually freed from a seedy sea mammal theme park.

As the new film begins, both boy and whale seem to be thriving—with Willy splashing happily with family and friends in the waters of the Pacific Northwest, and Jesse (the soulful, appealing Jason James Richter) enjoying high school popularity and a warm relationship with his foster parents (Michael Madsen and Jayne Atkinson).

Before long, however, each buddy faces a dire menace. for Willy, it's a deadly oil slick and for Jesse it's an obnoxious, long-lost baby brother named Elvis (Francis Capra), who suddenly arrives from New York.

The various pieces of plot begin to come together when the foster parents take the two boys on a whale-watching camping trip, and the human family connects with the orca pod just in time to help them deal with environmental catastrophe and a greedy oil company.

One of the evil executives (M. Emmet Walsh) wants to capture Willy, who's trapped by the oil slick, and sell him back to captivity—a story line so tired that the producers might have appropriately titled this picture "Free Willy Already."

Impatience with all the churning subplots is considerably heightened when, out of nowhere, the spectral voice of Michael Jackson begins warbling on the soundtrack about his lost childhood, with lyrics like "No one understands me ... People say I'm not OK/Because I love such elementary things ..."

In addition to confronting such insipid drivel, Jesse gets his first girlfriend (played by bland, blank Mary Kate Schellhardt) as well as facing the challenge of working with a brand new co-star—in place of Keiko, the ailing, tank-bound Orca who played the title role in "Willy" One, "Willy" Two uses electronic, robotic whales to portray all the principal sea mammals.

These machines are spectacularly convincing—not only looking uncannily life-like, but actually giving more emotionally varied performances than the real whale in the first film.

Perhaps it's appropriate that these mechanical marvels steal the show in a movie that is, in every respect, triumphantly mechanical. Sure, it's inane, but feel free to enjoy it (with your kids)—even if people say "you're not OK" for loving "such elementary things."

NEWSDAY, 7/19/95, Part II/p. B3, John Anderson

Just another fish story? No, the same fish story. "Free Willy 2," knowing on which side its plankton is buttered, has reworked all the same formulas that made the original boy-and-his-whale tale such an enormous success—milking the sentiment, orca-strating the emotion, exalting the vistas and using Joan Lunden to provide journalistic gravity. But it's not until Michael Jackson's puerile-plaintive "Have You Seen My Childhood?"—during a sequence in which one of the young heroes has become a runaway—that the manipulation and marketing become a bit too much to swallow. This is a children's movie, after all, and the Jackson interruption just emphasizes the point that this underwater ballet of products, personalities and premeditation is being performed not by dolphins but by barracuda.

That said, "Free Willy 2" will entertain children largely because it empowers them. This is fiction, of course, but Jesse (Jason James Richter), whose abandonment by his mother and adoption by Glen and Annie Greenwood (Michael Madsen and Jayne Atkinson) was the original film's subplot, has become a person of character and responsibility. His knowledge of whales and his friendship with Willy—who was himself separated from his mother in the 1993 film—make him something of an expert. When a tanker runs aground and the resulting disaster separates Willy and his siblings from their mother, Jesse is consulted—by doctors, rangers and an oil company executive (Jon Tenney) whose plot to exploit the whales is squelched. And not by Jesse alone.

The maladjusted brat-turned-Jacques Cousteau role has been handed down to Elvis (Francis Capra), a lying, backward-Knicks-cap-wearing, sawed-off gangsta who also happens to be Jesse's brother. Half-brother. Their mother has died in New York, and Elvis—who claims at various times to be Al Pacino's son, an Alpine bungee-jumper and a black belt in karate—has been delivered to the Greenwoods, injecting social disarray into an almost normal Seattle (note the emerging theme of outdoorsy virtue versus urban corruption). Jesse could be happier. But Elvis comes around (young Capra makes him both irritating and sympathetic), though not before disrupting the romance between Jesse and Nadine (Mary Kate Schellhardt of "What's Eating Gilbert Grape?"), the pretty goddaughter of Jesse's mystical American Indian mentor, Randolph (August Schellenberg).

The whales? They perform admirably, bursting and plunging and swimming and laughing, often for no dramatic purpose at all. That's whales for ya. Amid the wide eyes and dropped jaws and the spectacular scenery—Laszlo Kovacs' cinematography is stunning—they're a wonderful thing to watch, even when you know that some of their antics are computer-generated and that an artificial orca is doing some of the stunts. All in all, "Free Willy 2" is best summed up by a 12-year-old at the screening I attended, who liked it a lot but said it was "really predictable." If you're any older—like, 13—this should tell you something.

SIGHT AND SOUND, 9/95, p. 51, Verina Glaessner

Teenager Jesse and his foster parents Annie and Glen spend their summers at a remote whale tracking station. Jesse hopes to make contact with Willy, the young whale he helped save from a marine wildlife park. He learns that his estranged mother has died and that his nine-year-old half brother Elvis is to spend the summer with him. The boys' initial mutual antagonism fades when they sight Willy's family of whales. Everyone is delighted when Willy remembers Jesse and performs his old tricks.

An oil tanker runs aground and spillage threatens the coastline. Willy's sister whale Luna becomes distressed and he fiercely protects her from human attentions. Jesse distracts Willy while the vet gives Luna an injection of antibiotics. Randolph, a Native American working at the tracking station, shows Jesse how to treat the animals naturally. Annie and Glen tend to the almost beached Luna, declining Elvis's offers of help. Elvis packs his bags to return to New York.

At the ferry terminal, Elvis overhears oil company executives planning to capture Willy and Luna and sell them as performing animals. Elvis tells the family and they unite against the oil company. Luna is released from a winch which has already removed her from the water and, through a series of slapstick manoeuvres, the plan to capture Willy is demolished. However, the oil spillage catches fire and when Jesse, Nadine (Randolph's god-daughter) and Elvis try to guide the beasts to safety, they become trapped. Nadine and Elvis are rescued by helicopter but Jesse looks lost until Willy rescues him. The family of whales escape the danger. Elvis hands Jesse a photograph of their mother which he had secretly kept for him.

For this sequel the Shuler/Donner production team have replaced Australian director Simon Wincer with the unknown Dwight Little and acquired Laszlo Kovaks as director of photography. It avails them nothing as realistic films which rely on gathered documentary content have a problem wedding the real antics of undoubtedly impressive and intelligent creatures with those of a palpably less winning cast of humans.

The small school of whales in this ecological disaster movie retains its dignity despite being represented mostly by animatronic models and despite the attempts of the narrative to entrap them in a dramatic farrago involving the death of foster child Jesse's 'real' mother, the arrival of his half-brother Elvis, a teen romance with Native American girl Nadine, and the ecological threat of a massive oil spillage. Just as Willy has bonded with his lost family since his return to the ocean, so Jesse and Elvis overcome their initial reluctance to find common ground.

Randolph, Nadine's father, is there to embody a pre-lapsarian, pre-industrial past, and to set his seal on the all-too-easy defeat of corporate villainy. The creatures themselves are there for their spectacular value, but they also mediate Jesse's transition to adolescence. Nadine and Jesse draw emotionally closer through their delight in the whales' antics and later, Jesse's stepfather Glen has a fatherly talk with Jesse, full of sexual misunderstandings.

Outside this family melodrama are the action-adventure sequences. These derive their strength not from the real-life drama of ecological damage, but from a quick fix of action involving fire and water, winchings to safety and miraculous survivals. The emphasis on action puts a brake on any but the most curt and obvious verbal exchanges between the characters. "Hey you guys, you alright?" serves most purposes.

This permits no one to make any kind of sense of what they see around them and simply wastes any potential interest the lives of those who man the tracking station might have for an audience. We still wait for that bold, timely and ecologically-informed film that will do more than simply pit city kids against the elements and decorate the edges with nature footage.

VILLAGE VOICE, 8/1/95, p. 51, Stan Dauphin

My editor gets somewhat nervous when I mention it, but I have to admit that I liked the first *Free Willy* movie. I caught it on cable one lazy Sunday afternoon while vaguely depressed, and it's saltwater-taffy sweetness cheered me up enough that *Willy*-1's by-the-numbers tale of a sullen foster kid (Jason James Richter) and his pet killer whale has a wet-eyed remembered sheen to it. I'm feeling better these days and am thus less able to fully wallow in *Free Willy 2*'s tearjerking. The sequel finds Jesse (Richter again) in fine spirits, whaleless, and settled into his new family. As Jesse has gone from sullen to girl-crazy between installments, the job of supplying the family angst that forms the runny core of both films falls to Jesse's long-lost little brother, Elvis (Francis Capra), who is most convincing when he's crying hysterically about their dead mother.

All of the first film's principals have been called back for the sequel, except for Lori Petty and the live killer whale who played Willy the first time around. Sold to a Mexican aquarium, the live whale has been replaced here by a mechanical one, the robot playing it aqua-muppet cute where the real thing showed flashes of intelligence that looked saddeningly sentient. Kids will like the footage of real killer-whale pods frolicking at sea, and Willy's climactic rescue of Jesse has the kick you'd expect of a good special effect, but all that saved *Free Willy 2* from becoming spoilt fish is the fact that it's so completely canned.

Also reviewed in:
CHICAGO TRIBUNE, 7/19/95, Tempo/p. 22, Michael Wilmington
NEW YORK TIMES, 7/19/95, p. C10, Caryn James
VARIETY, 7/17-23/95, p. 51, Leonard Klady
WASHINGTON POST, 7/19/95, p. D1, Rita Kempley
WASHINGTON POST, 7/21/95, Weekend/p. 38, Desson Howe

FRENCH KISS

A Twentieth Century Fox release of a Fox and Polygram Filmed Entertainment presentation of a Working Title production in association with Prufrock Pictures. *Executive Producer:* Charles Okun. *Producer:* Tim Bevan, Meg Ryan, and Eric Fellner. *Director:* Lawrence Kasdan. *Screenplay:* Adam Brooks. *Director of Photography:* Owen Roizman. *Editor:* Joe Hutshing. *Music:* James Newton Howard. *Music Editor:* Jim Weidman. *Sound:* John Pritchett and (music) Dennis Sands. *Sound Editor:* Robert Grieve and Stu Bernstein. *Casting:* Françoise Combadiere and Jennifer Schull. *Production Designer:* Jon Hutman. *Art Director:* Gerard Viard. *Set Decorator:* Kara Lindstrom. *Set Dresser:* Gerard James. *Special Effects:* Gilbert Pieri. *Costumes:* Joanna Johnston. *Make-up:* Paul Le Marinel. *Make-up (Meg Ryan):* Lutz Wesemann. *Stunt Coordinator:* Jean-Louis Airola. *Running time:* 108 minutes. *MPAA Rating:* PG-13.

CAST: Meg Ryan (Kate); Kevin Kline (Luc); Timothy Hutton (Charlie); Jean Reno (Jean-Paul); François Cluzet (Bob); Susan Anbeh (Juliette); Renee Humphrey (Lilly); Michael Riley (Campbell); Laurent Spielvogel (Concierge); Victor Garrivier (Octave); Elizabeth Commelin (Claire); Julie Leibowitch (Olivia); Miquel Brown (Sergeant Patton); Louise Deschamps (Jean-Paul's Girl); Olivier Curdy (Jean-Paul's Boy); Claudio Todeschini (Antoine); Jerry Harte (Herb); Thomasine Heiner (Mom); Joanna Pavlis (Monotonous Voiced Woman);

Florence Soyez (Flight Attendant); Barbara Schulz (Pouting Girl); Clement Sibony (Pouting Boy); Adam Brooks (Perfect Passenger); Marianne Anska (Cop 1); Philippe Garnier (Cop 2); Frédéric Therisod (Cop 3); Patrice Juiff (French Customs Official); Jean Corso (Desk Clerk); François Xavier Tilmant (Hotel Waiter); Williams Diols (Beach Waiter); Mike John's (Lucien); Marie Christine Adam (Juliette's Mother); Jean-Paul Jaupart (Juliette's Father); Fausto Costantino (Beefy Doorman); Jean-Claude Braquet (Stolen Moto Owner); Dominique Regnier (Attractive Passport Woman); Ghislaine Juillot (Jean-Paul's Wife); Inge Offerman, Nicholas Hawtrey, Wolfgang Pissors, and Nikola Obermann (German Family); Alain Frerot (Old Man); Dorothee Piccard (Mrs. Cowen); Jean Allain (Mr. Cowen).

CHRISTIAN SCIENCE MONITOR, 5/5/95, p. 13, David Sterritt

At first glance, "French Kiss" seems to be a nicely multinational comedy: It's about an American woman who chases her Canadian fiancé from Toronto to Paris, finding a new French boyfriend along the way.

Hollywood rarely puts much effort into portraying non-American people or places, however, and by the halfway mark it's clear that "French Kiss" has no more cultural diversity than the average studio romance. The heavily accented French hero is played by Kevin Kline, who hails from Missouri, and the parts of the story set in Paris and Cannes might as well have been shot on a California soundstage, so little authentic atmosphere do they carry.

Even the picture's genuine French actors, Jean Reno and François Cluzet, are most familiar to US audiences for English-language pictures like "The Professional" and "Ready To Wear," respectively. In all, "French Kiss" cares a lot more about the second word of its title than the first.

Also disappointing is the movie's oddly lackadaisical pace, which is enervating at best and slows almost to a crawl when Meg Ryan is expected to carry a scene.

She's an attractive actress, with a flair for comedy that has given a needed lift to pictures like "When Harry Met Sally ..." and "Sleepless in Seattle," two of her best credits. But she's not effervescent enough to rescue a really bad movie like "Prelude to a Kiss" or "The Presidio." In the hands of a laid-back stylist like director Lawrence Kasdan, her timing and delivery become perilously flat, draining energy from scenes that don't have much to begin with. Neither script nor director provide the support Ryan needs.

Kline fares better as the rogue she falls in love with, almost equaling the first-rate work he did in "Silverado" and "Grand Canyon," pictures that made good use of his flair for eloquent understatement. Reno and Cluzet make reasonably good showings, and Timothy Hutton is suitably shallow as the runaway boyfriend.

With an occasional burst of snappy dialogue in Adam Brooks's screenplay, the film is not entirely lacking in pleasures. But so many talented people should have come up with a confection more ingratiating, if not more inspired. Kasdan deserves most of the blame for its shortcomings. His previous pictures range from "The Big Chill" to "The Accidental Tourist." Many were hits, but none very deep. While he knows the skills of moviemaking, he rarely bestirs himself to do something exceptional with them.

The marvelous exception to this pattern is "Grand Canyon," which has a philosophical and spiritual resonance that carry it way beyond Kasdan's usual level. I've been waiting four years for him to reach that pinnacle again, and since it hasn't happened, I'm starting to suspect that his "Grand Canyon" writing partner, spouse Meg Kasdan, was the real creative force behind that picture.

I suggest *she* take the helm of the next Kasdan production and give it the same glow "Grand Canyon" had. That would be far more rewarding than the flimsy gratifications "French Kiss" has to offer.

LOS ANGELES TIMES, 5/5/95, Calendar/p. 1, Peter Rainer

The best reason to see "French Kiss" is for the early, funny scenes with Kevin Kline playing Luc, an avid leather-jacketed French thief with an industrial-strength mustache and perpetual 5 o'clock shadow. Before the movie turns him into a "sensitive" guy—i.e. an un-French Frenchman—Luc is a hilariously antiquated Gallic caricature. He's a wolf in wolf's clothing, and his accent pulls at vowels in a way the world hasn't heard since the heyday of Inspector Clouseau.

Luc is introduced to us sitting next to Kate (Meg Ryan) on a flight from Toronto to Paris. Overcoming a major case of fear-of-flying jitters and some passport problems, Kate is on a mission to track down her errant fiance (Timothy Hutton), who is in Paris for a weeklong physicians' conference where he has fallen for a leggy French bomb—shell (Susan Anbeh).

Kate believes that love should last forever. Her motive is simple: Get her man back. Luc chides Kate for her "girl's fairy tale" beliefs and provokes her with haughty homilies and sexual anecdotes culled from his vast backlog of lust. His motives are less simple: Is he provoking her because he's a rake or because he wants to distract her from her airborne fears? And, on the ground, is he just using her as an unwitting courier for a smuggled diamond necklace or is he also trying to get cozy?

"French Kiss" tries to be a glass of pink champagne, but some of the fizz has gone out of the bottle. There's no surprise in the warming romance between Luc and Kate, and most of the potshots at the snooty French are tired. But director Lawrence Kasdan and screenwriter Adam Brooks cram so many potshots into the piece that, after a while, it makes you laugh anyway. It's as if they assembled every possible joke-book gibe against the French into one movie.

The recession must really be over. Why else would Hollywood make a romantic comedy all about the vagaries of traveling abroad? This is the sort of thing that used to be big in the expendable-income eras of yore.

The axis of the movie's world is the lobby of Paris' George V hotel, with its almost surrealistically condescending concierge (Laurent Spielvogel) and lotharios ever on guard to light a lady's cigarette (and lift her purse). The standard attractions—the Louvre, the Eiffel tower, Arc de Triomphe—are photographed as great big tourist toys. This City of Light is anything but romantic. It's Wolf Central: the place to go if you want to give in to your worst impulses.

If the filmmakers had extended their view of snootsville Paris to the countryside, it might have grown into a great big nasty cartoon. It might have been a wonderful, shamelessly chauvinistic sick joke of a movie. But Kasdan and Brooks collapse into sentimentality. When they start in with the loamy salt-of-the-earth stuff in Provence, with the old papa leaning on his cane and the vineyards glowing green in the sunlight, we're in French Tourist Commission territory.

The confab between Luc and Kate gets awfully loamy, too. As they plot a reconciliation with Kate's fiance that neither believes in, we learn that, gosh, love can indeed last forever—as long as the right lovers are entwined. Luc loses his snap and Kate develops a whopping case of stars-in-eyes. The problem is not so much that we see all this coming but that, when it comes, it's just what we expected. The film dips its clichés in rose water, but the fragrance is faint.

Kline and Ryan have a trumped-up rapport that seems more energetic than magical. They go through a lot of romantic movie motions, including the obligatory train ride together and the one where they share a hotel room and he sleeps on the couch. They let us know they're Made for Each other.

But they make each other laugh a lot more than they make us laugh. Ryan overdoes her inno-cent-abroad adorability, and she has grown overfond of pratfalls and Lucille Ball-style mugging. Kline's underplaying opposite her comes across as a form of gallantry. He's a one-of-a-kind comic performer: a leading man with the fidgety, eccentric soul of a supporting player. He tricks his specialty into a full-scale performance. The bias in this movie is all on the side of the hearty, life-embracing Americans, but Kline's Luc gives the French the win. He could have gone a lot further into madcap passion if the movie had let him. This "French Kiss" is more like a little love peck.

NEW YORK, 5/15/95, p. 62, David Denby

There's a nice moment in *French Kiss*, a shaggy new romantic comedy directed by Lawrence Kasdan. Meg Ryan plays Kate, a will-driven American girl whose fiancé (Tim Hutton) goes to Paris on a business trip and falls in love with a pouty French beauty. Overcoming her fear of fly-ing, Kate gets on the plane to Paris to win back her man and is forced to endure the condescension of an overbearing, American-baiting Frenchman, Luc (Kevin Kline), who first sits down next to her and openly analyzes her sexual difficulties and then hides some stolen goods in her handbag. Kasdan and screenwriter Adam Brooks are using an old romantic-comedy trick: You force an unlikely pair to undergo adventures together until they begin to warm up to each other.

Luc is shabby, with greasy hair and a vain, pointed mustache, and he seems considerably less sensitive than a dog; Kate, by contrast, is strenuous, literal-minded, and hygienic—an all-American moral virgin.

In Paris, she loses her money to another con man, and when Luc retrieves some of it, she throws it down on the street. Then comes the nice moment: Kasdan holds the camera motionless across the way as Kate and Luc angrily part company at one of those odd, sharply angled Parisian corners in which one street goes up a hill, the other down. As we watch the two walk away, we wonder, Which one of them—the thief or the high-principled American girl—will come back and pick up the cash? The answer tells us reassuring things about both of them.

French Kiss is moderately enjoyable, a rough variant of the travelogue romances of the fifties and early sixties that starred Audrey Hepburn and Paris—the kind of skilled confectionary movie with whimsical waiters or policemen, boats on the Seine, and "bohemians" in berets. But like that Paris corner with the streets going high and low, most of *French Kiss* is a little off-kilter. The movie doesn't glisten, and except for a few scenes in Cannes, it's not elegant; some of the slapstick is rough, and a few scenes go on too long. I could be mistaken, but my guess is that the roughness was intentional, that Kasdan, after the fiasco of *Wyatt Earp*, wanted to run out and just make a movie.

Alas, his stars don't make magic together. With her puckered lips, superbright eyes, and easy emotions, Meg Ryan is like the liveliest girl in your high-school graduating class. She's a practical and resourceful performer, but there's something suburban and TV-ish in her facility. Kevin Kline is a different story, even though he suffers from anonymity on the screen. I'm speaking not of his gifts, which are abundant, but only of his lack of definition: He is a man perhaps too intelligent and modest to stylize his personality—to cut off possibilities for himself— the way lesser actors do. He's good at silliness and at characters who are pretending to be something, vain poseurs who themselves don't have any identity. In *French Kiss*, his Luc, the unsavory professional French charmer, turns out to be a man who has dispossessed himself, a man less evil than desperate. Kline plays him realistically; he's scruffy and rather touching, more acid than he's ever been before. He never does get a clean shave—not even Audrey Hepburn could have turned him into a prince.

NEW YORK POST, 5/5/95, p. 31, Michael Medved

Meg Ryan makes a specialty out of playing lovable neurotics, but in "French Kiss" she carries the bit too far.

Her characters in "When Harry Met Sally" and "Sleepless in Seattle" came across as endearing—and desirable despite their quirks, but the woman she plays in this film is such a mess that it's hard to imagine how either of the leading men could ever consider making a life with her.

Her character, Kate, is an unredeemable flake who sheds citizenships as easily as wardrobes—finding a new country twice within the same movie. She's utterly terrified of airplanes and dairy products and seems incapable of enjoying even a moment of her life.

It doesn't help that director Lawrence Kasdan is so intent on deglamorizing Ryan that she looks like a drowned mouse—with a bleached, brittle hairdo that suggests she may have borrowed one of the fright wigs Walter Matthau used to play Albert Einstein in her previous film, "I.Q."

As chief love interest to this grating kook, Kevin Kline, if anything, plays a character even less likable than she is. His leather-jacketed Luc is an unshaven, foul-smelling French thief whose interest in Kate after meeting her on the plane stems from his scheme to use her to smuggle some items through Paris customs.

Despite his despicable behavior and larcenous ways, we're supposed to go all squishy over Luc because he secretly nurses the ultimate yuppie dream—starting his own vineyard to make a truly refined bottle of wine.

In any event, he becomes Kate's only friend in Paris when she travels there to win back the yutzo fiance (Timothy Hutton) who has cruelly (but sensibly) jilted her for a sophisticated and gorgeous French woman (Susan Anbeh).

The only engaging presence in the cast is charming French actor Jean Reno ("The Professional"), playing a worldly-wise police inspector. But his participation raises the obvious question: Why cast a fake Frenchman (Kline) as your leading man when you could so easily have used the real thing?

Kevin Kline is, of course, a wonderful actor whose timing and warmth give the film what little charm it has—and he seems to be having fun with this exaggerated accent—but you can never forget for a moment that it's Kevin Kline working hard to impersonate a Parisian.

The movie also tries too hard to impersonate a fluffy comedy, with its big laugh-getting scenes featuring Meg Ryan falling into a pastry cart (a la Lucy) or losing her lunch when she eats too much exotic cheese on a train. There's also a lot of puerile humor about Kline's limp, er, performance; we're supposed to believe that this incurably macho Frenchman has somehow confessed to a total stranger that he is temporarily incapacitated in l'amour.

Lawrence Kasdan has directed some of the more intriguing films of recent years ("Grand Canyon," "Body Heat") but he's also made some outright stinkers, including "I Love You to Death," another surprisingly downbeat comedy with unappealing characters and his perennial star, Kline, doing a vaudeville accent.

"French Kiss" may indeed cause audiences to pucker up, but more in the style of sucking lemons than the thrill of touching tongues.

NEWSDAY, 5/5/95, Part II/p. B3, Jack Mathews

The current wave of romantic quest movies is certainly giving a boost to the European tourist industry. In Norman Jewison's "Only You" last fall, Marisa Tomei and Robert Downey Jr. tracked love all over Italy, pausing in romantic Venice and along the picturesque Amalfi coast. In Lawrence Kasdan's new romantic comedy, "French Kiss," we follow Kevin Kline and Meg Ryan from Paris to the Riviera, with a side trip to the vineyards of Provence.

Kline and Ryan, the most engaging romantic-comedy actors of their respective genders, are more fun to travel with.

"French Kiss" is no more profound or probable a story than "Only You," which had Tomei rushing off to Europe on the eve of her wedding to find a man bearing the name prophesied as that of her future husband by a fortune teller years before. Instead, she falls in love with the obnoxiously romantic fellow who tries to help her.

In "French Kiss," Ryan is jilted on the eve of her wedding and flies off to Paris to try to wrest her fiance (Timothy Hutton) from the arms of a voluptuous French hussy, and in the process becomes more and more attracted to the obnoxious Frenchman (Kline) she meets on the plane ride over.

If there are no big surprises in where the story is headed, getting there is half the fun. Kline and Ryan are perfectly matched, and though the pace of the story occasionally slows to a walk, there is an unself-consciousness about their performances, in the way their characters are gradually revealed to each other, that grounds the relationship in some reality and gives us a clear rooting interest in it.

That these two would find common ground seems unlikely when they meet. Kate is a history teacher who has driven her fiance away with her rigid game plan for their life together. Luc is a dreamer and a thief who talks a good game of romance but whose fear of commitment has rendered him—temporarily, he protests—impotent.

Somewhere on the flight to Paris, between Luc's clumsy attempts to get Kate over her fear of flying and getting her drunk with his supply of stolen airline vodka, Luc plants a diamond necklace in her handbag, and in doing so links his travel plans for the next few days to hers.

You get the impression from the views of the Eiffel Tower, the Louvre and other Paris landmarks that this may be Kasdan's first trip to France. Likewise, the train ride through the southern wine regions and the hilltop look at the jeweled setting of Cannes on the Riviera are shot like moving postcards. The idea may have been to capture the impression all this is making on Kate, but the scenery is so self-consciously gorgeous it occasionally threatens to upstage the actors.

With less engaging actors, it would have. But Kline, who has worked on four previous Kasdan movies, and Ryan, who has sort of taken over and upgraded the romantic innocent-roles once tailored to Goldie Hawn, manage to hold our interest. "French Kiss" isn't a powerhouse of passion—Luc and Kate don't get into a serious lip-lock until the coda tacked onto the end—but knowing it's coming is enough.

SIGHT AND SOUND, 11/95, p. 42, Max Schaefer

Toronto. Terrified of flying and averse to the French, Kate refuses to accompany her fiance Charlie to Paris. Once there, Charlie falls in love with a Frenchwoman, Juliette, and decides to stay. Kate determines to bring him home. On her flight to Paris, she meets Luc, a Frenchman who, while she is sleeping, slips a young vine plant and a diamond necklace into her handbag. His plans to retrieve them on the other side of Customs are unwittingly thwarted by Jean-Paul, a policeman whose life Luc once saved.

In Paris, Kate's bags are stolen. Luc helps her find the thief, get her handbag back and—most importantly to him—retrieve his plant. When Kate realises this was his motive they fight and part. Kate learns that Charlie and Juliette are in Cannes. She follows them; Luc, in search of the necklace, joins her. On the way, Luc teaches Kate to appreciate wine and describes his ambition to start a vineyard. On Luc's advice, Kate surprises Charlie and Juliette on the beach at Cannes and pretends to be sleeping with Luc. Jean-Paul finds Kate alone and begs her to speak to Luc—the necklace must be returned. That evening she has dinner with Charlie and wins him back. She sleeps with him, and Luc with Juliette, but both are unsatisfied.

Kate returns the necklace to Jean-Paul and, pretending to have sold it, gives Luc her life's savings and leaves. When Luc discovers what she has done—and that she has rejected Charlie—he pursues her and asks her to stay with him. Sometime later, they kiss in his new vineyard.

After Billy Crystal in *Forget Paris*, it is now Meg Ryan's turn with *French Kiss* to discover true love and unpasteurised cheese in the shadow of the Eiffel Tower. Both films can be seen as variants of *When Harry Met Sally*, the film that made these actors into household names. Here, as Kate and Luc, Ryan and Kevin Kline follow the Harry/Sally route from incompatibility and vague dislike to noble self-sacrifice and everlasting devotion—but without so much falling in love on the way.

In a scene which suggests a certain generic self-awareness but is more probably formulaic writing, the two leads diagnose each other as soon as they meet. "You are afraid to live," Luc tells her, "afraid of life, afraid of love, afraid of sex." Kate instantly dismisses him as a "nicotine-saturated and ... hygienically deficient Frenchman." Contrasts are laid on thick: Kate is afraid of flying, Luc loves it; Kate has broken the law only once (smoking pot), Luc is a professional thief; she lost her virginity at 18 with the class jock, he at 12 with the town prostitute; she aspires to placid domesticity, he is promiscuous, devious ("for me bullshit is like breathing"), a smoker and aggressive driver; in short, French.

Such stereotyping of the French, particularly of their sexual proclivities, applies throughout. (Adam Brooks claims to have based his screenplay on observations made over a year spent in France, but I suspect he was watching Renault ads.) Juliette professes true love for Charlie, but jumps happily into bed with his former fiancee's boyfriend. The thief who steals Kate's bags in Paris takes time out to offer her a *ménage à trois*. Even the concierge at the Hotel George V is proud that, unlike some countries, "France is not a country of puritanical hypocrites".

It turns out instead to be a country of photo opportunities. Paris does not seem to extend beyond the tourist haunts of Montmartre and the Champs Elysees. Outside the city, all France is cobbled squares and sun-flecked fields, prettily but predictably shot. The soundtrack meanders along on harmonica solos and bursts of Les Negresses Vertes, and climaxes with the absurdist masterstroke of Kline singing 'La Mer'.

Kline, his entrance signalled off-screen by consumptive gutturals, is nevertheless a slightly less ridiculous Frenchman than one might expect—he has clearly been practising, and even manages the occasional subtitled exchange with real French actors like Jean Reno—but he's unlikely to go down convincingly in Paris. Meg Ryan, the romantic comedy specialist, is disappointing here, forsaking the charm and vulnerability she displayed in *When Harry Met Sally* and *Sleepless in Seattle* in favour of furious mugging. She wants us to believe (as do most 'kooky' actresses) that quirkiness and hysteria are character-enhancing. She is therefore enchantingly hysterical on a crowded plane and charmingly quirky in her insular hatred of the French. Only her belching routine is cut short.

French Kiss (it might be subtitled *Canadians Don't*) gives the sometime-impressive director Lawrence Kasdan another chance to explain that we're all basically the same. This is a theme familiar from *Grand Canyon* and his script for *The Bodyguard*, which breezily swept racial divides aside. Here, abetted by Adam Brooks' enthusiastically wielded central metaphor—Luc's hopes of starting a vineyard echoing Kate's clucking domestic desire to "plant some roots and watch them grow"—he shows us how two white, middle-class Westerners overcome their cultural differences and find true happiness in the common language of kook.

VILLAGE VOICE, 5/16/95, p. 52, Georgia Brown

The first thing we see in *French Kiss*—a film developed by Meg Ryan's Prufrock Pictures—is Meg miming not an orgasm but a panic attack. You're meant to think this is the most adorable panic attack. Everything Meg does in *French Kiss* has adorable written on it. The pouchy little belly under a cutoff sweater, the dreamy blue eyes, the sheepdog hairdo,

The U Can Fly School, where Meg's character Kate has been trying to overcome her fear of flying by sitting on a mock plane, refunds Kate's money. Yet when Charlie (Timothy Hutton), her excitable fiance, goes off to a Paris medical conference and falls for a French goddess, Kate books the next flight. Which means we get to watch Meg perform those hysterics all over again.

This time around, a grouchy, unkempt Frenchman, Luc (Kevin Kline), sits beside her. A thief, as it turns out, Luc takes the opportunity to stash his contraband in Kate's knapsack—a device that keeps the two roped together long enough to "get acquainted." Pursuing Charlie and the statuesque Juliette (Susan Anbeh) from Paris's Georges V toward the Carleton in Cannes, Kate and Luc make an unexpected pit stop (she's adorably sick from the cheese) in a Provence village that just happens to abut Luc's family's vineyard. Wouldn't you know that Luc is the black sheep in a family of means in the loveliest spot on earth? The fatted calf is killed for a *repas* on the chateau terrace, and now we can breathe easy: We won't have to face Kate's return flight.

Kline has been known for excessive cuteness himself (*A Fish Called Wanda*), but here—no doubt in awe of Meg's prowess—Kline is blessedly restrained and even sexy. While it's hard to believe that Luc would be anything but bemused by Ryan's klutzy American moppet, the implication is that French women are all in the mold of Charlie's Juliette—tall, bitchy, and faithless. (The movie might be fun to watch with a French audience.) Director Lawrence Kasdan has had his ups and downs, but this travelogue comedy is a new low. A flop *royale*.

Also reviewed in:
CHICAGO TRIBUNE, 5/5/95, Friday/p. C, Michael Wilmington
NEW REPUBLIC, 5/22/95, p. 28, Stanley Kauffmann
NEW YORK TIMES, 5/5/95, p. C16, Janet Maslin
NEW YORKER, 5/22/95, p. 97, Anthony Lane
VARIETY, 5/1-7/95, p. 36, Brian Lowry
WASHINGTON POST, 5/5/95, p. B1, Rita Kempley
WASHINGTON POST, 5/5/95, Weekend/p. 49, Desson Howe

FRIDAY

A New Line Cinema release of a New Line Productions presentation of an Ice Cube/Pat Charbonnet production in association with Priority Films. *Executive Producer:* Ice Cube and Bryan Turner. *Producer:* Patricia Charbonnet. *Director:* F. Gary Gray. *Screenplay:* Ice Cube and DJ Pooh. *Director of Photography:* Gerry Lively. *Editor:* John Carter. *Music:* Frank Fitzpatrick. *Music Editor:* John Thomas and Thom Brennan. *Sound:* Robert Davenport and (music) David Tobocman and Tim Boyle. *Casting:* Jaki Brown-Karman and Kimberly Hardin. *Production Designer:* Bruce Bellamy. *Set Designer:* Maria Baker. *Set Decorator:* Michelle Harding Hollie. *Set Dresser:* Thomas J. Martinez and Larry Johnson. *Special Effects:* Robert Loftin. *Costumes:* Shawn Barton. *Make-up:* Rea Ann Silva and Cassi Mari. *Stunt Coordinator:* Julius LeFlore. *Running time:* 90 minutes. *MPAA Rating:* R.

CAST: Ice Cube (Craig); Chris Tucker (Smokey); Nia Long (Debbie); Tiny "Zeus" Lister, Jr. (Deebo); John Witherspoon (Mr. Jones); Anna Maria Horsford (Mrs. Jones); Regina King (Dana); Paula Jai Parker (Joi); Faizon Love (Big Worm); DJ Pooh (Red); Angela Means (Felisha); Vickilyn Reynolds (Joann); Ronn Riser (Stanley); Kathleen Bradley (Mrs. Parker); Tony Cox (Mr. Parker); Anthony Johnson (Ezal); Demetrius Navarro (Hector); Jason Bose Smith (Lil Chris); Bernie Mac (Pastor Clever); Justin Revoner (Kid #1); Meagon Good (Kid #2); Lawanda Page (Old Lady); Terri J. Vaughn (China); F. Gary Gray (Black Man at Store); Yvette Wilson (Rita); William L. Calhoun, Jr. (Shooter); Reynold Rey (Red's Father).

LOS ANGELES TIMES, 4/26/95, Calendar/p. 2, Peter Rainer

"Friday" is about two South-Central homeboys, Craig Jones (Ice Cube) and his best friend Smokey (Chris Tucker), and the long day they spend together hanging out in the 'hood. There's no plot really, just a series of lowdown comedy sketches that follow each other like skits in a variety show. If you don't like one sketch you may like the next.

It's the right format for this scattershot jokefest, which at times resembles a vaudeville act crossed with the kind of goofy bludgeoning antics that sometimes make it into gangsta MTV videos. The director, Gary Gray, has worked with Ice Cube on some of those videos, but they seem to be in a more loopy mood for "Friday." This is a kinder, gentler Cube—he even co-wrote the script, with DJ Pooh. The relief of "Friday" is that it's not another 'hood horror show. It makes fun of those shows.

The fun isn't always so funny. There's a flashback to a time when, without realizing it, Smokey smokes angel dust, and the scene is played for broad laughs. Did the filmmakers really think they could get away with this? And there are more toilet jokes per minute than in "Dumb and Dumber"—a dubious achievement. A lot of "Friday" plays like a mishmash of moments from shows like "Def Comedy Jam" and "The Wayans Bros." and "The Fresh Prince of Bel-Air." And, in fact, many in the cast, including Nia Long as Craig's would-be girlfriend, John Witherspoon as his father and Bernie Mac as a randy preacher who makes house calls, are regulars on some of these shows. They seem content to preen and mug as if they were still on the tube.

The commercial appeal of "Friday" may be helped by its TV familiarity. Movies used to compete with television by giving audiences bigger and broader experiences; now they try to give audiences a big-screen version of what keeps them cozy at home. Even the outrageousness of "Friday" isn't a heightening of what you see on television; it's just more of the same.

The movie is best when Craig and Smokey just sit back and watch the passing parade of humanity. These guys have a chummy clownish rapport: Ice Cube's disbelieving deadpan is the perfect foil for Tucker's rubber-faced, motor-mouthed antics. Tucker isn't the subtlest comedian you'll ever see but his hit-'em-with-everything style keeps the film percolating. He's not only the star of "Friday," he's its mascot.

NEW YORK POST, 4/26/95, p. 42, Bill Hoffmann

If you were a fan of Cheech and Chong's in-your-face marijuana comedies of the '70s, then you're likely to love Gary Gray's new gangsta farce "Friday."

If not, extreme boredom is likely set in for the 30 minutes or so the film dedicates to comedian Chris Tucker and his frantic efforts to get high and gab endlessly about how stoned he is.

I'll give this to Cheech and Chong: while I never found their sledgehammer drug humor funny, at least their early efforts were topical—mirroring the pastime of many young Americans at the moment.

In "Friday," the continuous clouds of dope smoke seem sadly passe. The catch phrase "just say no" has never seemed so appropriate.

Rapper Ice Cube co-wrote and stars in this mostly gentle, in-the-hood comedy that chronicles a day in the lives of two twenty-something dudes in South Central Los Angeles.

Cube plays Craig, whose life has just fallen apart. He's lost his job, his bitchy girlfriend is driving him crazy and his best friend, the stoned-out Smokey (Tucker), is being pursued by drug dealers he owes.

If that's not enough, his mother's on his case, trying to set him up with the neighborhood good girl ("She's in school and she's got all her teeth," Mom glows) and dear old Dad insists on lecturing him about life while he sits on the toilet spraying Lysol into the air.

What's a basically decent, down-on-his luck guy going to do? Move out of his folks' house? Get new friends? Leave the 'hood?

Yes, everything does resolve itself in the end. But maddeningly, we really never find out what's going on inside Cube's head. That's because screenwriter Cube infuriatingly allows actor Cube to be constantly upstaged by Tucker's mundane joint jokes.

Cube, one of the nation's top rap artists, has the makings of a sensitive young actor. Oddly though, his brooding, low-key style gets lost in a film that's full of over-the-top performances by an energetic cast of newcomers.

Even with its steady, raw stream of "energy, the comedy in "Friday" is strictly second rate and highly derivative.

Numerous comics have done the drug humor better; nobody beats Howard Stern when it comes to bathroom humor (and there's loads of that here); and rappers Kid 'n Play beat Cube and Tucker hands down as a gangsta comedy team.

Too bad, because director Gray's scrappy performers do manage to provide a laugh or two when they're able to rise above the bargain-basement material.

"Friday" is watchable in a pinch—thanks in part to a dynamite, foot-tapping, dance-inspiring soundtrack which features Curtis Mayfield, James Brown, War, and the Isley Brothers.

But this is one time I won't be saying, "Thank God it's Friday."

NEWSDAY, 4/26/95, Part II/p. B9, Gene Seymour

If comedian Robin Harris were still alive, he'd be doing routines like "Friday." Set in Harris' old stomping grounds of South Central L.A.,

"Friday" is packed with the kind of bluesy, grainy-toned and no-holds-barred ribaldry that made Harris' humor go down like home-cooking with his African-American fans.

Mainstream audiences may be surprised to find incendiary rap-*meister* Ice Cube playing the lead here, given that his screen credits include films ("Boyz N the Hood," "Trespass") that are far more intense and violent than this slacker comedy. But anyone who's paid close attention to Cube's work, especially in his N.W.A. days, knows he's capable of street humor as boisterous as anything in Harris' legacy.

Cube, who also co-produced and co-wrote the screenplay (with DJ Pooh), is Craig Jones, a 20-something guy living at home with his parents and sister because he can't hold onto a job. "How the _____ do you lose your job on your day off?" asks his father (the incomparable John Witherspoon), who suggests that his son might like to share the wonderful world of dog catching with him.

"But you hate dogs," Craig says. "That's right! That's right!," Pops replies. "All day long, I got my foot in a dog's ___ !" (Actually, it's the dogs who seem to get the better of Dad.)

With no job and no prospects, what's Craig going to do all day Friday? His friend Smokey (Chris Tucker), a pot-inhaling ne'er-do-well, suggests they just kick back on Craig's front porch and watch the world go by.

As morning turns to afternoon and then to evening, Craig and Smokey witness such diversions as the neighborhood pastor putting the make on a sultry neighbor across the street—only to be tossed out on his ear by her dwarf husband.

Not everything is that much fun. Smokey owes $200 to the neighborhood drug dealer (Faizon Love), who also happens to be the ice-cream man. The dealer vows revenge on both Smokey and Craig before midnight if he doesn't get paid. As they await their fate, the guys are bothered and beguiled by various women, including sweet, sane Debbie (Nia Long), who is one of the few who will stand up to the monstrous Deebo (Tiny [Zeus] Lister Jr.), a sullen sociopath who'll steal anything in the 'hood that isn't nailed down.

As noted, the plot ambles along with the improvisational haphazardness of a comedy routine. You laugh out loud a lot, but there are many places where the story seems to stop to catch its breath before deciding where to go next. If this were an actual routine, it would reach narrative perfection only after several run-throughs on a comedy-club tour. Right now, it's halfway there.

"Friday" compensates for such lapses with its laid-back pace and warm-hearted view of working-class foibles. Many caricatures, though broadly sketched, stop well short of wretched excess. (Although, the fingernails on Craig's jealous girlfriend must be seen to be believed.) It's nice to see Witherspoon given a movie role big enough to contain his outrageous talent and

Tucker is equally fun to watch. As for Cube, his smoldering persona proves as compatible with comedy as it is with drama. In the right hands, he could become one of the master slow-burn artists of our time.

SIGHT AND SOUND, 8/95, p. 50, Olly Blackburn

It's Friday morning in South Central LA and Craig has been fired from his job for stealing. His friend Smokey joins him on the front porch. He is in trouble with Big Worm, the local drug dealer, for smoking his weed rather than selling it. Deebo, the neighbourhood thug, drops by and forces Smokey to help him break into the house next door. They return with $200, which Deebo pockets. Smokey convinces Lil' Chris to share a joint with him. While the two are stoned, Debbie, a friend of Chris' sister, drops by. Smokey convinces her to give him the number of a girl who he arranges a date with. Meanwhile, Craig has been harried on the phone all day by his jealous girlfriend Joi. She arrives in time to see Debbie leaving the house.

Worm tells Smokey that unless he delivers $200 by 10pm he'll shoot both him and Craig. Smokey and Craig desperately try to come up with the money. Joi is about to lend it to Craig when Debbie's sister buttonholes him, asking him for a favour; in a fit of jealousy, Joi drives off. Craig's mother, father and sister all refuse to lend him the money. Meanwhile, Smokey's date arrives—she turns out to be grossly overweight and bald. Smokey tries to steal the $200 from Deebo while he's asleep with Debbie's sister, but fails to find the cash.

At 10pm, Craig and Smokey still haven't got the money. Worm tries to gun them down in a drive-by hit; they survive but the whole neighbourhood comes out to see who got shot. Deebo appears, followed by Debbie's sister who is badly bruised. Debbie yells at Deebo for hitting her sister and when Deebo slaps her, an incensed Craig attacks him. The two men fight and at one point Craig pulls a gun, but his family persuades him to settle the fight without it. Craig finally knocks Deebo out, Smokey takes the $200 from Deebo's shirt and arranges to pay back Worm. Craig and Debbie make a date for Saturday.

As Republican Party *gauleiters* Bob Dole and Bill Bennett have shown by their recent attacks on Hollywood films and Interscope records, rap and the cinema have a singular place in the middle-American imagination: as bearers of a cultural form of nerve gas. *Friday* is a movie made by rappers, starring one-time gangsta rapper *extraordinaire* Ice Cube. Nothing much happens in the film, it doesn't have anything particular to say and such characterisation as there is seems propped up on a zimmer frame of cultural stereotypes. Nonetheless, it is the sort of film that Republican commentators should be watching if they want to know what they're talking about.

Friday roughly appoximates what you get if you take the Corner Men from Spike Lee's *Do the Right Thing* and give them 90 minutes to themselves. A good half of the film is taken up with Ice Cube and Chris Tucker sitting on the porch. They observe cute girls jogging past, a cuckolded husband throwing his wife out onto the street, the next door neighbour's house being robbed. They never go anywhere except for a brief trip to the 'black-owned' grocery store (complete with a Korean counter boy—announced on the soundtrack by a gong). The film is content to describe the hermetic suburban universe that clusters around them.

The plot—such as it is—is pure stoop theatre. Cube and Tucker's dialogue is peppered with African-American suburban myths—the guy who mistook a PCP joint for weed and spent the night in a chicken coop, the philandering preacher who gets his just desserts and the paranoid girlfriend with five-inch blood-red talons for fingernails and braided hair like Medusa's locks. There's much fooling around and occasional contact with the neighbourhood thug, the local dealer and a stream of friends coming to visit Craig's sister. All the characters are standard models, with some idiosyncracies. On the women's side, for example, you have crusty, foul-tongued old bats going door-to-door for the Jehovah's Witnesses, slutty suburban housewives, tut-tutting wise-ass mammies, pathologically persistent girlfriends, troublesome tramps and tough cuties. One might accuse the film-makers of misogyny—but the male characters are no less cut and dried.

Friday is therefore a comic-strip of a movie, a rogues' gallery of African-American folk figures, each one getting his or her just desserts. Yet it isn't quite a sitcom; more a shaggy dog story told visually out of corner gossip. Perhaps the movie's closest equivalent in form is rap itself. *Friday* was written by two rappers—Ice Cube and DJ Pooh. A former helmsmen of the pioneer gangsta rap groups N.W.A., Ice Cube once argued that rap music doesn't exist to promote or reject, merely to report from the ghetto; to work as a broadcast for a black urban youth locked out of mainstream forms of communication. Equally, this would make a good justification of *Friday*.

Like freestyle rap, the stuff of the movie just pours out. Frequently it makes no sense but it is effortless to digest. Except for the brief climax of the film which advocates beating your opponent senseless rather than using a gun, *Friday* is mostly ephemeral stoop-side observation and front porch philosophy. It shows a potted African-American universe with its own urban myths instead of the crack-addled gun-toting woman-beaters of Republican nightmares.

VILLAGE VOICE, 5/9/95, p. 79, Gary Dauphin

Covering a South Central morning-to-night so cheerful even the local crackhead has a good sense of humor, *Friday* is basically a feature length riff on Ice Cube's "It Was a Good Day" video only with better jokes, its homey primal scene the smoked-up banter of two underemployed brothers sitting on a hot porch. Craig Jones (Ice Cube) lives in the house with said porch with Mom, Dad, and Sis, and he gets to spend this particular Friday home in his corduroy slippers after getting fired the day before ("How the hell'd you get fired on your day off?" goes the running joke). Craig's homeboy Smokey (stand-up comic Chris Tucker) has no job to speak of, except maybe slangin' 20 sacks of weed for ice-cream man-dealer Big Worm, but Smokey's too busy chain-rolling the stock to turn much of a profit. When Big Worm gives Smokey a 10 p.m. deadline to produce the money or the remaining weed, hilarity is sure to ensue, and does, albeit along slightly juvenile lines.

Friday is the product of a comic and rose-colored view of street life. The movie bears more than a passing resemblance to the *House Party* cycle, another entry in the can-we-do-X-before-Y-happens movie sweepstakes, a genre whose basic formula includes one-liners, romantic complications, comic stereotypes, and the ever handy moral lesson. Since its aims are modest to begin with, *Friday* has little trouble delivering on all those levels (bits of business like Smokey's flashbacks are a hoot), although the fact that most of its set-ups happen on that porch (with the sweet smell of chronic in the air) does give the movie a certain glassy-eyed inertia.

Friday is a do-it-yourself vanity project for sugar daddy Ice Cube. Despite having cowritten, starred, executive produced, and stocked it with friends (first-time director Gray did Cube's "Good Day" video, among others), Cube carries the weight of all that attention with his usual skill. An affable straight man, he exudes a certain gravity that neatly balances Smokey's hyperkinetic shtick, his mere presence giving *Friday* the street cred to do truly weird stuff like play a drive-by for yucks. Director Gray keeps things rolling with a smartly deployed soundtrack: Cube and Dre are heard of course, but so is Curtis Mayfield, the Isley Brothers, and the Rose Royce love theme from *Car Wash*. Gray and Cube probably figured that including "Good Day" might be overtipping their hand, but don't worry: It's a good *Friday* even without it.

Also reviewed in:
NEW YORK TIMES, 4/26/95, p. C16, Caryn James
VARIETY, 5/1-7/95, p. 37, Todd McCarthy
WASHINGTON POST, 4/26/95, p. C10, Richard Harrington
WASHINGTON POST, 4/28/95, Weekend/p. 44, Desson Howe

FUN

A Greycat Films/Neo Modern Entertainment release of a James R. Zatolokin presentation in association with Prerogative Productions and Lighthouse Entertainment of a Neo Modern Entertainment Corp. and Damian Lee production. *Executive Producer:* Rana Joy Glickman and Jeff Kirshbaum. *Producer:* Rafael Zelinsky. *Director:* Rafael Zelinsky. *Screenplay (based on his play):* James Bosley. *Director of Photography:* Jens Sturup. *Editor:* Monika Lightstone. *Music:* Marc Tschanz. *Music Editor:* David Trevis. *Sound:* Arnold Brown and Laurent Wassmer. *Casting:* Cathy Brown and Marki Costello. *Production Designer:* Vally Mestroni.

Special Effects: Denise Fischer. *Costumes:* Renee Johnston. *Make-up:* Denise Fischer. *Running time:* 105 minutes. *MPAA Rating:* Not Rated.

CAST: Renee Humphrey (Hillary); Alicia Witt (Bonnie); William R. Moses (John); Leslie Hope (Jane); Ania Suli (Mrs. Farmer); James J. Howard, Jr. and Frederick D. Adams (Male Prison Guards); Cindie Northrup (Prison Librarian); Rochelle Roderick, Steven Givens, and Gregory Steven Ferrett (Mrs. Farmer's Neighbors); Steve Adelson (Gas Station Attendant); Alan Shapiro (Record Store Manager); Victoria Radu (Nurse).

LOS ANGELES TIMES, 9/15/95, Calendar/p. 19, Kevin Thomas

"Fun" is how two pretty teenagers describe their fatal stabbing of a kindly elderly grandmother who extended her hospitality to them.

Bonnie (Alicia Witt), the 14-year-old strawberry blonde who did the actual stabbing, is capable of feeling pity for her victim (Ania Suli) and her family. But, no hypocrite she, Bonnie does not deny to her dark-haired pal—15-year-old Hillary (Renee Humphrey), who held down their frail victim—that she certainly did enjoy doing it. She admits she's even proud of herself.

A cautionary tale—and not an exploitation picture—adapted by James Bosley from his play, which in turn was, not surprisingly, based on a true incident, "Fun" is a thoroughly riveting experience that doesn't tell us anything new about disaffected youth but does get inside these kids' twisted psyches.

It's a kind of "Heavenly Creatures"—low-budget, no-frills, American-style. Bosley and his dynamic producer-director Rafael Zelinsky don't send any messages, they just tell it like it is. Yet the implications of their story are as dire as they are inescapable and wearyingly familiar: Turning loose young people from profoundly dysfunctional families into an open, impersonal, violence-saturated society like ours is an invitation to disaster: and far too many people are bringing into this world children they are either unwilling or incapable of raising in a responsible fashion.

In an exceptionally adroit adaptation of a play to the screen, Zelinsky and Bosley tear right into their story. Documentary-like black-and-white sequences open the film with the girls' arrival at L.A.'s Juvenile Hall, and Zelinsky establishes a rhythmic pace, cutting between a newsmagazine reporter, John (William R. Moses), trying to get Hillary to open up while a counselor, Jane (Leslie Hope), attempts to communicate with the hyperkinetic Bonnie.

Gradually, Zelinsky further intercuts flashbacks in color, revealing step-by-step the girls' meeting and leading up to the killing.

In similar ways, John and Jane are determined pros at interrogation. What emerges after much emotional fireworks is that from their point of view the seemingly senseless killing—the victim indeed picked at random—made perfect sense to the perpetrators.

Bonnie and Hillary meet while hitchhiking and are at once overwhelmed by their recognition of themselves in each other, followed by mutual onrush of the love they clearly had been deprived of their entire lives. In their ensuing celebratory mood of exhilaration and liberation, they almost unconsciously, in their pursuit of fun, move toward an act that will exorcise for them a lifetime's worth of rage at chronic abuse, neglect and deprivation. "Fun" therefore *does* make sense of that which is so easily described as senseless.

In doing so it gives an extraordinary opportunity to its actors. It is amazing that two actresses as young as Witt and Humphrey are able to sustain such a high emotional pitch throughout the film, and for their efforts they were rewarded with a special jury recognition for acting at the Sundance Film Festival. No less impressive, however, are Moses, who manages to make John a tenacious yet fundamentally decent journalist, and especially Hope, whose Jane is a woman who has survived her own terrible childhood and is dedicated to helping girls as troubled as she once was—at no small ongoing cost to herself. "Fun" looks great, thanks to Jens Sturup's bold, jarring camerawork, and boasts a rightly intense score by Marc Tschantz.

NEW YORK POST, 4/12/95, p. 35, Thelma Adams

Some people can't get enough movies about teen-age girls committing murder, but it looks like Rafael Zelinsky's "Fun" has been eclipsed by Peter Jackson's stunningly similarly themed chiller, "Heavenly Creatures."

What's so fun about murder? Werewolves of suburbia Bonnie (Alicia Witt) and Hillary (Renee Humphrey) worship at the altar of fun. "Hillary and I killed the old lady just for fun," says red-haired Bonnie. "Fun is the meaning of life."

The low-budget drama is most effective in the candy-colored scenes of the clean streets, barren strip malls and gas stations north of L.A. Cute outcasts Bonnie and Hillary meet and become blood buddies in a single day that unspools like "The Wonder Years" on acid.

Zelinsky goes arty in cinema verite flash-forwards to the girls' incarceration after the fact. These black-and-white sequences, loaded with forced confessions, introduce two caricatures: an attractive tabloid journalist (William R. Moses) and a chain-smoking prison counselor (Leslie Hope).

The hope is that through a series of interrogations, we will come to understand not only the girls motives but the idea that what is normal or functional—embodied in the callow reporter and troubled therapist—is less honest, less impassioned, less real, than the mall-struck murderesses.

Zelinsky's clumsiness in handling his themes aside, Witt and Humphrey capture the blunt hysteria and frenzy of two hormonally challenged teens who crash over the edge. Witt (of TVs "Cybill") has more energy than she can channel. She wheels and whirls and dances. She speaks like a speed freak. In a mass of fiery hair, she hides a face that promises Botticelli beauty beneath its last layer of baby fat.

If Witt is fire, Humphrey (the coming "Mall Rats") is earth. Resembling Ally Sheedy, she grounds the only centered character. A troubled poet, Hillary is the victim of the inevitable sex abuse that fuels these stories with canned psychology—and yet there's nothing canned about Humphrey's acting.

What's memorable, when all is said and overdone, is the energetic performances of two promising young actresses and a crude, child-wrought picture of "Grandma" tacked to the fridge and visible during the orgiastic knifing of a sweet old lady.

NEWSDAY, 4/12/95, Part II/p. B11, Jack Mathews

It is unfortunate that Rafael Zelinsky's "Fun," which had an acclaimed premiere at the 1994 Sundance Film Festival, took more than a year to make its way to commercial theaters. In the meantime, we've had a chance to examine the same subject—homicidal teenage girls in love—in Peter Jackson's brilliant "Heavenly Creatures," and "Fun" pales to the point of fade-out in comparison.

Both movies attempt to take us into the minds of young girls who, as a reaction to their environment, form a deep and ultimately unholy alliance that causes them to commit a horrible murder.

In "Heavenly Creatures," which was based on an actual 1950s case in New Zealand, the victim was one of the girls' mothers, and the killing was a desperate attempt to prevent their parents from separating them. In "Fun," the victim is an elderly woman, selected at random, and the motivation—for all the killers themselves know—is summarized in the title.

"This has been the best day of my life," says 14-year-old Bonnie (Alicia Witt) as she and her 15-year-old accomplice, Hillary (Renee Humphrey), celebrate their brutal crime with a pajama party for two.

"Awesome!" says Hillary.

"Nuclear!" says Bonnie.

"Fun," adapted by James Bosley from his one-act play, is a dramatized postmortem on a chance meeting between the two disturbed teenagers, who, after spending a day charging each other up with wild—and often prefabricated—tales of their sordid backgrounds, decide to christen their relationship with a thrill-kill.

The story is told on two parallel, intercut tracks. In color flashbacks, we relive with the girls their wild day together on the outside, and in black-and-white real time, we see them interacting separately with the hard-nosed social worker (Leslie Hope) and exploitative magazine writer (William R. Moses) interviewing them in the juvenile detention center where they are awaiting sentencing.

Zelinsky made some very effective choices in his narration, and in the contrasting styles of the two time periods. The flashbacks have the slick artifice of a Hollywood suburban horror fantasy, while the jail scenes are done in gritty, hand-held cinema vérité between the two perfectly re-creates the schizophrenic nature of the friendship, and forces the audience into the same agitated state of mind.

I'm not sure the movie is much more than an exercise in style, however. Where "Heavenly Creatures" took bold narrative leaps inside the girls' shared delusions and provided some understanding of their crime, "Fun" just sits outside and paws at them through a psychological prism. The actresses are very good, particularly Witt, who plays the psychotically manic Bonnie with such restless energy you'll feel like dropping a couple of thorazines yourself. But the more the counselor and the journalist attempt to plumb the killers' personalities, the more superficial it all becomes.

It may be that the title is intended to be taken literally, that the girls committed the murder because at that moment, with all their stars and hormones in conjunction, it seemed like an exciting thing to do. If so, the film barely qualifies as a cautionary tale. If the title is ironic, it is the most morbid sense of irony.

At times, the movie broaches the well-trod issue of cause and effect in the media—there are references to the music of Guns N' Roses and other pop-culture influences—but without anything new to add to that debate, there doesn't seem to be much point. There certainly isn't much fun.

SIGHT AND SOUND, 6/95, p. 42, Lizzie Francke

Having been convicted for the killing of an old woman, teenagers Bonnie and Hillary are kept at a detention centre. They are individually questioned by Jane, a counsellor, and John, a journalist, both of whom are attempting to find out why the girls committed the crime. Their story is told in intermittent flashbacks.

On the morning of the crime the girls strike up an instant friendship. They go on a shop-lifting spree, visit a photo-booth, but gradually become bored. They start to wander around the housing estates, playing various pranks on those who live there. They decide that they want to get into one of the houses. Pretending that Bonnie is not feeling very well, they inveigle their way into the house of an elderly woman who takes pity on them. When the woman gets suspicious they panic. For no apparent reason Bonnie stabs the woman to death and the two take flight, running back to Hillary's house.

As they try to piece the story together, Jane and John use different approaches to establish a rapport with Bonnie and Hillary. Jane reveals her own dysfunctional past to Hillary, while John promises to help reunite them. The two girls are kept apart despite protests. Hillary keeps a diary and writes poetry which John says he wants to publish. Later Hillary accuses Bonnie of lying. The two girls meet briefly during study time in the library and cause a commotion. A decision is made to send Bonnie to an another detention centre. She jumps from a high walkway, is hospitalized and later dies from her injuries. Hillary is seemingly unaffected by her death.

Fun could be described as a *The Girls Next Door* for the 1990s. It shares with the Penelope Spheeris film the same bleak and characterless suburban terrain that is now all too familiar: rows of neatly kept houses with clipped lawns and white picket fences and roads going nowhere other than from one shopping arcade to another. Similarly, Bonnie and Hillary are presented as ostensibly normal Gap-wearing kids, although their restlessness soon becomes apparent through the shrill and amateurish performances of Renee Humphrey and Alicia Witt. We glimpse them first in Hillary's bedroom where they are preparing for Bonnie's stayover, sharing make-up and pajamas. But swiftly the film makes manifest the nature of their crime as it segues between the detention centre and the events leading up to their committal. *Fun*'s concern, then, is not with what they did but why they did it.

With the prison interviews predominating, *Fun*'s theatre roots are only too evident. These scenes provide the substance of the film and one wishes that director Rafael Zelinsky had elaborated further on them rather than continually flipping into the past. When asked why they killed the old woman, the girls reply that it was for "Fun ... fun is the only thing that I believe in". They define fun as "doing something that I haven't done before." It's a suitably amoral slogan for the self-serve generation, but the film is less concerned with mulling over the disturbing implications of the murder as it is in investigating how such an act can be spun out retrospectively as drama. Tension is sought between the attempt to explain and the knowledge that—as with Hillary's diary of which she says: "some of it is true, some of it is made up"—there is always going to be some uncertainty about the girls' motives. This uncertainty defines the difference between Jane and John as investigators. As Jane tells John, it is he, as a journalist, who "has the license to connect the dots, fill in the blanks."

It is also clear that Jane and John have their own motives. John may feel that he has a story of social importance to tell, but he also wants journalistic glory. Jane assesses the girls for their own benefit but she also has personal reasons for helping them because she recognises something of herself in Hillary. It is therefore easy for the girls as media-literates brought up in the culture of *Oprah* to turn the tables. They talk about being abused as children—something which may or may not be true. John wants to know whether they have had a lesbian relationship: "That would be perfect for the TV movie—with Drew Barrymore," Hillary cannily replies. Their stance is a shrewd move on the part of the film-makers, since it contextualizes *Fun* in terms of the renewed interest in wayward girls (for example *Heavenly Creatures* and *Butterfly Kiss*) and it helps to distance the film from 'slammer chick' exploitation antecedents that might make *Fun* look more than a little anaemic.

VILLAGE VOICE, 4/18/95, p. 51, Amy Taubin

Two 15-year-old girls meet, bond, and kill an elderly lady—just for fun. Or so they claim. Rafael Zelinsky's uncommonly intelligent, haunting film, *Fun*, is the latest in the embryonic genre of the homicidal female buddy movie. When men kill, although it's not nice, it's within the realm of the expected, the far edge of boys just being boys. When women kill, it's a major transgression against the social order. Which is why everyone finds such stories fascinating, and why many women find them perversely empowering.

The scene is the archetypical, Southern California, low-end middle class 'burb with its rows of anonymous, two-story houses, each with its own tiny parched front lawn. The murderers, who look like your average 15-year-old valley girls, meet by chance at a bus stop, and instantly fall into the abyss they see in each other's eyes. It's love, or, technically speaking, symbiosis at first sight.

Hillary (Renée Humphrey) has the haggard, pent-up look of someone twice her age. Bonnie (Alicia Witt) seems like a giant three-year-old with her rounded face, tremulous mouth, and barely coordinated rag-doll body. Hillary is the control freak with a mind that's always working; Bonnie is all impulse, racing hyperkinetically in circles, motion revving her emotional engine. Different as they are, both seem horribly lonely, starved for attention, willing to do or say anything to be noticed, coming to life through the gaze of the other.

Within moments of their meeting, Hillary tells Bonnie that her father raped her, the details spilling from her defiantly maroon-lipsticked mouth. Bonnie matches her with her own tales of being deflowered by her brother and of orgiastic sex with her boyfriend in an amusement park house-of-horrors. One senses that Bonnie is making up what for Hillary is all too true. Bonnie's connection to reality is more tenuous than Hillary's; what she can't say but later has dragged out of her is that her mother walked out on her when she was a little girl. Bonnie needs Hillary to organize her rage; Hillary needs Bonnie to goad her into acting out her desire for revenge. They spend a day racing around, hysterically clutching each other, hurling rocks and screaming insults, the two of them fusing into a third entity capable of murder. Despite the dramatically condensed time frame, it all rings true.

Zelinsky isn't interested in suspense. In the first two scenes, we're given the facts of what happened and who did it. What the film does investigate are the how's and why's.

Fun is mostly set in the juvenile house of detention where the girls are held after their conviction. There, they are interviewed daily by the less-tough-than-she-looks prison counselor and a semi-sleazy reporter who's wangled his way in against the counselor's better judgment.

The interview device reeks of exploitation-movie cliché, but has the effect of heightening the sense of immediacy and authenticity. Zelinsky shoots the prison scenes vérité style in black-and-white, with a hand-held camera following the girls' every move. During the interviews, we're aware of the counselor's and the reporter's points of view. They are the eyes of society, mediating the girls' story. But Zelinsky also allows the girls fragments of subjectivity—flashbacks of their "awesome" day together shot in luminous color and arranged achronologically, the buildup to the murder alternating with the aftermath, until we get to the primal scene itself.

Zelinsky raises the dread specter of TV docudrama all the better to prove that *Fun* is something else again. The reporter, who tries to make Hillary confess that she's a lesbian until he gets it through his tabloided skull that something more complicated than sex binds the girls together, also threatens that unless she comes clean to him with the whole story, she'll see herself in a TV movie played by Drew Barrymore. "Drew Barrymore, she's a pussy," snorts Hillary, in one of the film's rare moments of humor.

Nor is *Fun* merely a cheap version of the overrated *Heavenly Creatures*, although, in fact, it cost way less than a million dollars. Unable to afford the sensuous surfaces—let alone the Claymation-style fantasy sequences (and just for the record, are there any women out there whose fantasies resemble, even remotely, the *Heavenly Creatures* special effects?)—Zelinsky goes for the inner truth and gives his exceptional actors the freedom they need to deliver it up. (And while I'm on the *Heavenly Creatures* comparison, there are no naked teenage knees in *Fun*, no attempts to charm the audience, no evasions of something so crucial as the mother-daughter relationship in the interests of shocking us at the end. The killing in *Fun* is all the more dreadful because it's so inevitable, the random choice of victim notwithstanding.)

Although fully scripted, *Fun* often seems improvised, in part because the rhythm of the scenes is determined by the actors rather than the editing. Witt and Humphrey, who each received a special acting award last year at Sundance, claim from the camera the attention their characters crave. Insecurity inspires them to act out. The camera records what they do with no particular emphasis. Although Witt has the showier (and more tragic) role, her performance would be impossible without Humphrey as a foil—and vice versa. Their interaction is heartbreaking because it's so familiar. What teenage girl hasn't ridden this kind of symbiosis almost to the edge. "It was like we fell in a big hole and the only way out was to kill her," says Bonnie. I know the feeling. *Fun* reminds me how lucky I am that something inside me (*superego* is too easy a term) kept me from acting on it.

Also reviewed in:
NEW YORK TIMES, 4/12/95, p. C16, Janet Maslin
VARIETY, 2/14-20/94, p. 39, Todd McCarthy
WASHINGTON POST, 8/4/95, p. D6, Rita Kempley
WASHINGTON POST, 8/4/95, Weekend/p. 40, Desson Howe

FUNNY BONES

A Hollywood Pictures release. *Executive Producer:* Nicholas Frye. *Producer:* Simon Fields and Peter Chelsom. *Director:* Peter Chelsom. *Screenplay:* Peter Chelsom and Peter Flannery. *Director of Photography:* Eduardo Serra. *Editor:* Martin Walsh. *Music:* John Altman. *Music Editor:* Dina Eaton. *Choreographer:* Christina Avery. *Sound:* Peter Lindsay. *Sound Editor:* Glenn Freemantle. *Casting:* Janey Fothergill, Maggie Lunn, Mary Gail Artz, Barbara Cohen, and Kate Dowd. *Production Designer:* Caroline Hanania. *Art Director:* Andrew Munro. *Set Decorator:* Tracey Gallacher. *Special Effects:* Tom Harris. *Costumes:* Lindy Hemming. *Make-up:* Pat Hay. *Stunt Coordinator:* Simon Crane. *Running time:* 128 minutes. *MPAA Rating:* R.

CAST: Ian McNeice (Sharkey); Richard Platt (Bellows); Peter McNamara (Canavan); Peter Martin (Skipper); Lee Evans (Jack); François Domange (Pirard); Ticky Holgado (Battiston); Olivier Py (Barre); Mouss (Poquelin); Harold Nicholas (Hal Dalzell); Oliver Platt (Tommy Fawkes); William Hootkins (Al); Jerry Lewis (George Fawkes); Ruta Lee (Laura Fawkes); Peter Pamela Rose (Jenny); Peter Morgan (Gofur); Richard Griffiths (Jim Minty); Peter Gunn (Nicky); Phil Atkinson and Nick Coppin (Policemen); Gavin Millar (Steve Campbell); Freddie Davies (Bruno Parker); George Carl (Thomas Parker); Christopher Greet (Lawrence Berger); George Khan (Francesco); Leslie Caron (Katie); Amir Fawzi (Little Tommy); Oliver Reed (Dolly Hopkins); Frank Harvey (Backward Talking Man); Sadie Corre (Poodle Lady); Rusty Goffe (Bag-Pipe Playing Dwarf); Freddie Cox and Frank Cox (Themselves); Eileen Bell

(Doggyduo); Brian Webb (Little Firewater); Andy Thompson and Peter Brande (Leo the Leprechaun); Terri Carol (Paper Tearer); Shane Robinson (Bastard Son of Louis XIV); The Ballet Hooligans and Lee Jellyheads (Themselves); Benji Ming (Plastic Cup Smasher); Maudie Blake (Musical Saw Player); Anthony Irvine (The Iceman); Fred Evans (Mr. Pearce); Terence Rigby (Billy Mann); Ruth Kettlewell (Camilla Powell); Zipporah Simon (Puppeteer); Phil Kelly (Himself); Tony Barton and Mike Newman (Comedians); George Raistrick (Club Owner); Jona Jones (Security Guard); Mickey Baker (Mayor); Mr. & Mrs. Mark Raffles (The Wychwoods); Ian Rowe (Ringmaster); Laci Endresz, Jr. (Juggler); Bobbie Roberts & His Elephants (Themselves); Andras Banlaki (Ring Boy).

LOS ANGELES TIMES, 3/31/95, Calendar/p. 4, Kevin Thomas

What are Jerry Lewis, Leslie Caron, Ruta Lee and Harold Nicholas doing in the same film?

They and a similar contingent of British stalwarts are lending stellar support to two young actors, Oliver Platt and Lee Evans, in "Funny Bones," the free-wheeling, risk-taking and altogether striking comedy from "Hear My Song's" Peter Chelsom.

With echoes of "Broadway Danny Rose," "The Sunshine Boys," "Hellzapoppin," plus touches of Fellini and Marcel Marceau, it heart-tugs while asking us to consider what's funny and why. A bold brew of show-biz schmaltz and serious inquiry, it's frequently hilarious, sometimes in an exceedingly dark and even surreal manner. Not everyone who loved the inviting, easy-going Irish blarney of "Hear My Song," however, is likely to connect with the wonderful weirdness of "Funny Bones."

Once past an opening credit sequence so bizarre you wonder if you're in the wrong theater, "Funny Bones" cuts to Las Vegas, where Platt's Tommy Fawkes is about to make his Strip debut before a crowd that includes his father, George Fawkes (Lewis), a fabled comic, and glamorous mother (Lee). Tap-dancing legend Nicholas is his opening act, and George can't resist coming onto the stage to warm up the audience. The overwhelmed Tommy—whose pompadour hairstyle makes him resemble the young Conway Twitty—finally comes out, tries a few jokes that he might have gotten by with at a comedy club, and flees, having bombed with atomic proportions.

Tommy surfaces in Blackpool, the irresistibly seedy and fanciful Atlantic City of England, where he spent the first six, very happy years of his life with his parents. Something tells him that tapping into what's left of music hall, the British equivalent of vaudeville, will give him a clue as to how to succeed as a comedian. As he auditions, with a certain arrogance, a series of vintage performers, many in their 70s and 80s (and maybe more), he has no idea what he's bargained for. He's set himself up to learn, not just about the sources of humor, more about himself and his father, and about life itself than he could ever have imagined.

Among the many people he encounters are Caron's Katie Parker, a family friend and former neighbor, her son Jack (Evans) and Katie's ex-husband Bruno (Freddie Davies) and brother-in-law Thomas (George Carl). Although they haven't worked in 12 years, Bruno and Thomas are a legendary show business team, a classic mime act. (Davies and Carl, not a team, are themselves beloved veterans in Britain.) Katie is a magician with endearingly campy Cleopatra trappings and Jack is a mime of astonishing brilliance and daring. Jack is also a wanted man, in a subplot that's a bit elusive, suggesting that there's been some cutting; press notes, for example, suggest that much of Oliver Reed's eccentric bad guy and his henchmen landed on the cutting-room floor.

Platt and Evans are formidable finds, young men with range and panache, and gratifyingly Chelsom has provided Lewis and Caron with major roles. Radiant and earthy, Caron sings "Englishmen Never Make Love by Day" with wisdom and élan, and she serves as the film's forthright artistic conscience. In recent years, Poland's Krzysztof Zanussi and France's Louis Malle have put Caron's dramatic abilities to good use, Chelsom does that and more: He gives her the chance to sing and dance as well.

Playing close to himself with a winning candor, Lewis shows us George's massive, endlessly competitive ego but also a genuine love for Tommy, and the movie's big moment of truth is delivered by Lewis in a terse, direct style. Among the film's many sterling British players are those hefty funnymen Richard Griffiths and Ian McNeice. At once giddy and substantial, "Funny Bones," which makes an inspired use of expertly staged flashbacks, is distinctive in the manner of Richard Rush's "The Stuntman," a film that it oddly recalls.

NEW STATESMAN & SOCIETY, 9/29/95, p. 49, Jonathan Romney

In one sequence of *Funny Bones*, the hero—a Las Vegas stand-up comic turned Blackpool talent-spotter—puts local entertainers through their paces, and faces a pandemonium of clowns, escapologists, musical saws, singing dogs and men who talk backwards. Peter Chelsom's strange patchwork of a comedy is one of the few ostensibly realistic films made since the glory days of the backstage musical to be structured like a succession of "turns". For the price of admission, you get stand-up routines: a Charles Trenet song that's supposed to be done Vegas-style but looks horribly end-of-the-pier; bendy British clown Lee Evans doing a frenzied mime to a tape of montaged racket; and an awfully coy ditty from Leslie Caron. Some of it you'll enjoy, some you'll loathe, but what's amazing is that there's so much of it. The only thing *Funny Bones* needs to make it more like a variety show, is to end with the entire cast waving adieu on a spangly carousel, in the bygone style of *Sunday Night at the London Palladium*.

Funny Bones is one of a handful of films that work on the premise that comedy is a hard, dreadful business. No, there are no teary-eyed Chaplin or Fellini clowns here—there are clowns, but they look terrifying and Chelsom has no time for the soft cliché about laughter warming the soul in dire days. Rather, humour is seen as a cruel necessity, a weapon of survival that gag-scarred comedians turn on the world and often on themselves. *Funny Bones* is not as tough or as chilly as Scorsese's *The King of Comedy*, which it salutes by casting Jerry Lewis in a role that once again resembles himself. Its theory of humour owes a lot to Trevor Griffiths' *Comedians*, but its real affinities lie within the quintessentially English shoddiness of Osborne's *The Entertainer*.

The two propositions that underpin *Funny Bones* are explained by comedian George Fawkes (Lewis) to his son Tommy (Oliver Platt). One is that you're either born funny or you have to work at it—you have funny bones or you speak funny lines. The other is: "I never saw anything funny that wasn't terrible, that didn't cause pain." Chelsom translates that frightening proposition into more manageable terms: much of the comedy here is painful in the sense of excruciating, ugly. It makes us wince the way a failed magic trick, or *Pets Win Prizes* might. The film relishes images of tawdry gruesomeness—from self-deludingly inept variety acts to a severed foot on Blackpool beach. In fact, the "funny bones/funny lines" distinction comes down to this: all comics have to grapple with the awfulness of the world, or their own awfulness. One way or another, it will be by foisting it onto others. Seen this way, comedy is something to be endured.

The film begins in Vegas as Tommy is upstaged by his own father, who pre-empts his best gag. Tommy dreams of "taking it to the edge": in fact, he goes for a trusty cheap-laughs routine, but when it starts folding up, he seems for a second to be on to something. If he had the confidence to take his hysteric sourness a jot further, he'd be on the verge of Lenny Bruce territory. But he doesn't, and besides he's in Vegas where that style won't go down well.

So he decides to leave for the place he imagines as the mecca of mirth—Blackpool, a town that haunts his childhood memories. But it's a wasteland of drizzle, novelty vicar acts and residual madness from the past. The place is haunted by a scary, reckless idiot boy (Lee Evans) and his strange uncles, a down-at-heel pair of Beckettian ancients. The poster for the films tells you everything you need to know: slumped blank-faced over their pints, the trio look like embalmers at leisure. The caption reads: "Beware: comic geniuses at work." Evans and the uncles (ante-diluvian troopers Freddie Davies and George Carl) have funny bones all right: the scene in which the uncles miraculously loom up in a ghost train is side-splitting, simply because it bows to none in its lugubriousness. They obviously don't have to try to be funny; but when they do, it's galvanising.

Chelsom works cleverly with the paradoxes of making a film from British imagery using Disney funds—he comes up with a lurid cartoon comment on the state of cultural misunderstanding between two nations. The America we see at the start of the film—all razzle dazzle, big cigars and yellow suits—looks like the imaginings of someone who's still not got round to seeing a Scorsese or a Spike Lee film. But then Tommy comes to Blackpool and the impression is equally arcane—fat ladies, timorous solicitors and all manner of Donald McGill horrors. This is as extreme, as imaginary an England (wolves howl here) as the hellish village-green society of Peter Greenaway's *Drowning by Numbers*, but it's grounded in a cultural reality: a half-buried collective memory of Ealing comedies, the Crazy Gang, all the English showbiz lore that's been relegated to the attic. Chelsom isn't so much reviving that humour as shaking down its dusty cadaver one last time. The laughter you hear in *Funny Bones* is very much laughter in the dark.

NEW YORK POST, 3/24/95, p. 44, Michael Medved

When unsuspecting moviegoers hear about a new film called "Funny Bones" that features Jerry Lewis in a rare screen role, they may go to theaters expecting an uproarious and outrageous comedy.

If so, they'll go home sorely disappointed—because "Funny Bones" isn't particularly funny.

It's one of those dark, brooding comedy-is-pain meditations in the tradition of the profoundly depressing Tom Hanks/Sally Field project "Punchline," or the previous Jerry Lewis vehicle "King of Comedy."

This time Lewis plays a world-famous comic who long ago retired from the spotlight but still easily overshadows his sweaty, insecure son, Tommy (Oliver Platt).

After the talentless Tommy bombs in Las Vegas, he runs off to Blackpool, a beach resort in the north of England that bears a bleak resemblance to Atlantic City and attracts world-class comedians to its clubs, pubs and circuses.

Tommy wants to make contact with the best of them and to buy their material to use in his act, and in his quest he stumbles upon two down-and-out brothers (Freddie Davies and George Carl), who are old friends of his father, now living in a shack beneath a roller coaster.

What happened to this comedy team, once considered the funniest in England?

Tommy soon learns that his infamous father stole their original act, as well as one of their women (the ageless Leslie Caron) and effectively ruined their lives.

Now their only hopes for a comeback rest with their moody but gifted son Jack (the talented British standup artist Lee Evans) who is trying to escape the consequences of his role in a drug deal gone sour—as well as an earlier scandal in which he brutally erased the supposedly thin line between comedy and violence.

This complicated tale, stitched together with a series of telling flashbacks, is co-written and directed by the unmistakably gifted Peter Chelsom, but it lacks the lyrical fairy tale atmosphere of his previous film, the splendidly satisfying "Hear My Song."

In "Funny Bones," by contrast, Chelsom (a native of Blackpool) emphasizes the gritty, shocking elements of his story—opening the picture with a sequence in which a French sailor loses both of his feet to the whirring blades of a ship's propeller. His many circus scenes invoke the spirit of Fellini rather than the Ringling Brothers.

Lewis is suitably grim and authoritative in his role, and Caron nearly steals the movie with her passionate portrayal of his former lover.

Platt, however, is a weak link in the cast—his character's one-dimensionally neurotic nervousness becomes tiresome to watch and prevents the audience identification which Chelsom seems to intend.

"Funny Bones" (the title refers to those rare natural comedians who have humor in their bones, not just on their lips) definitely has its moments, but it wears out its welcome by scoring its main points over and over again, making it clear that comedy, like sausage, is best appreciated if you don't know what went into it.

NEWSDAY, 3/24/95, Part II/p. B7, Jack Mathews

With his second feature, "Funny Bones," British director Peter Chelsom has stuck to some of the same familiar places and themes that brought him international attention with his first picture, the whimsically uplifting "Hear My Song," and the results are even better.

"Funny Bones" is a deliciously unpredictable comedy, with some serious notions holding it up, and it comes from—of all places—Disney, the home of both Mickey Mouse (that's good) and Pauly Shore (that's bad).

Chelsom, a native of Blackpool in northern England and a long-time member of the Royal Shakespeare Company, knows of what he writes and directs in "Funny Bones," which is set in Blackpool and energized, as was "Hear My Song," by his enchantment with the theater.

As you watch "Funny Bones," you can almost hear Chelsom asking himself, "What is it that makes some people take naturally to the stage, and audiences to them? Where does the talent come from, and where does it go?"

"Funny Bones," thankfully, doesn't try to answer those impossible questions, but it raises them in ways that seem to offer empirical evidence. When comics are performing on the stage within the movie, you know which ones are natural and which are not. Chelsom has made sure, casting brilliant British mimes and comedians in the key roles.

The performance of the movie belongs to the British stand-up comedian Lee Evans, making his film debut as Jack Parker, a young man raised by Blackpool vaudeville performers, but whose hilarious physical comedy routine conceals a darkly frightening secret.

Jack is a local star of the Blackpool comedy club that American comedian wannabe Tommy Fawkes (Oliver Platt) has come to visit, in hopes of buying an act that he can adopt and duplicate in Las Vegas. It was there, in a long and wonderfully staged sequence, that Tommy bombed in a casino debut arranged by his overbearing father, the world-reknowned kitsch comic George Fawkes (Jerry Lewis).

Now, Tommy has returned to Blackpool, where he lived with his parents the first six years of his life, intending to make himself funny by studying the same funny people who inspired his father. Blackpool is a beachside town with a ride park, a vibrant theater life and ample oddballs, and Chelsom captures all that with an honest affection that radiates off the screen.

There are wonderful plot twists and surprises throughout "Funny Bones," and I won't risk giving any of them away. The performances themselves are worth the price of admission. Evans is a tremendously talented mime, and you know the minute Jack begins performing onstage, acting out a crazy quilt of taped dialogue and sound effects, that they didn't hire an actor and train him to do this.

Platt, who is a fine comedy actor but no comedian, was a perfect choice for Tommy. He's a character who has been raised to believe stand-up comedy talent is handed down father to son, and before he walks out on that Las Vegas stage, you can sense both his insecurity and his incompetence.

But is his dad any funnier, or is he a man out of his time, getting reflexive laughs from people who knew him when? Jerry Lewis is really good at doing serious self-parody. He did it for Martin Scorsese in "The King of Comedy" more than 10 years ago, and he seems even more comfortable in "Funny Bones."

First, "Damn Yankees," now this. Is Lewis back in fashion?

NEWSWEEK, 4/17/95, p. 66, David Ansen

The language of comedy has always incorporated death: "I'm gonna kill 'em tonight," boasts the stand-up. "I died out there," moans the flopped gag man. The lethal underpinnings of the art of comedy are at the heart of *Funny Bones* a dark, breathtakingly quirky comedy from the director of the charming Irish tall tale "Hear My Song," Peter Chelsom. If most movie fare strikes you as generic and predictable, this may be the antidote: it's the most original, and the oddest, entertainment in some time.

Stand-up comic Tommy Fawkes (Oliver Platt) is struggling to emerge from the shadow of his father, a world-famous funnyman (Jerry Lewis). But his big Vegas debut is a disaster. Humiliated, he disappears to the seacoast town of Blackpool, England, the scene of his happy childhood and of his father's first triumph. Arrogant and armed with cash, he intends to buy for himself the best physical comedy routines in Blackpool, a town crawling with old vaudevillians and bizarre specialty acts (a biscuit-tin tap dancer, a backward-talking man). What he also finds is skeletons in the family closet.

It's also the home of the Parker brothers (Freddie Davies and George Carl), two old colleagues of his father, once great comics now appearing as ghouls in the amusement park's house of horrors. Bruno Parker's son Jack (Lee Evans) has inherited his comic genius—but his agility as a physical comedian is matched by his mental instability. His gift has come at a great and dark cost.

It wouldn't be fair to "Funny Bones" to disclose much more, and a synopsis couldn't begin to convey its unsettling and elating melange of tones. Chelsom and cowriter Peter Flannery delight in keeping the audience guessing where their flight of fancy is heading. One moment you're in an action movie on the high seas, where criminals are bargaining for mysterious smuggled eggs, the next you're in a Las Vegas showroom, the next on a Blackpool beach, where a severed foot washes ashore. It's the sort of movie where the funniest scene takes place in a morgue, the most horrifying in the middle of a comedy act, and Leslie Caron appears dressed as Cleopatra.

Chelsom and his motley, splendid cast transform these disparate, perilously whimsical elements into something rich and strange. (The dextrous Evans is astonishing; he does with his body what Robin Williams does with his brain.) One thing's for sure: you won't see anything like it.

SIGHT AND SOUND 10/95, p. 49, Louise Gray

When a shipboard drug deal goes awry off the Blackpool coast, Jack Parker, an edgy misfit, escapes with a portion of the drugs while a French sailor is killed by a boat's propellers. Meanwhile, in Las Vegas, Tommy Fawkes, the son of famous comedian George Fawkes, is preparing for his comedy debut in a club. When George upstages his son, Tommy heads for Blackpool, the town of his childhood, in search of new material.

In Blackpool, tourism director Jim Minty is trying to downplay the discovery of one of the dead sailor's feet on the beach, while Jack is threatening to jump off the Blackpool Tower. His father and uncle, Bruno and Thomas Parker—strange, sombre men, once feted as Blackpool's comic geniuses, but who now work the fairground ghost train—fail to coax him down, but Jack relents when his divorced French mother, Katie, arrives.

Tommy auditions acts to buy, realises that he has found his comic geniuses when he sees Jack, and wants to buy his act and that of the Parker Brothers, sight unseen. Gangster Dolly is impatient to find the lost drugs. The Frenchmen threaten Jack with retribution unless he helps them to retrieve their comrade's feet. Flashbacks detailing events in Jack and Tommy's early lives suggest links between them and reasons for the former's disturbance. When he sees the Parker Brothers' act, Tommy realises that George, who once had performed with them, stole their material, and that Jack is also his halfbrother. Tommy confronts George, who has arrived in England. Jack and Tommy steal the Frenchman's feet from the mortuary and return them to the French smugglers. Jack and Tommy rehearse their routine. Jack shows George a trick that involves an iron bar hidden in a rolled up newspaper. Flashbacks reveal further details of Jack's adolescence: he had killed a man in the course of an act involving the newspaper trick, and had spent time in a home for maladjusted children. George is shamed into arranging a show that will feature both the Parkers.

On the night of the show, Jack, disguised as a tramp, rushes into the ring. He climbs a 50-foot pole and sways wildly about the crowd. A policeman climbs up after him and Jack hits him. The policeman falls, but Jack catches him, saving him from death. Tommy is revealed as the policeman.

Following *Treacle* and *Hear My Song*, *Funny Bones* is the third in a trilogy of films based loosely upon director Peter Chelsom's Blackpool childhood. It is an affectionate portrayal of his hometown, replete with fleeting, rich caricatures of the type of people one might expect to find in a declining British holiday resort. Tommy and George remember Blackpool's comedy circuit as something golden and this is reflected in sumptuous cinematography. Beyond this, *Funny Bones* is also a highly successful film which explores convincingly the darker side of comic nature.

The vehicle for much of this is Lee Evans. A rubber-boned comedian whose repertoire of physical expression is truly remarkable, Evans brings to the central role of Jack a real, dangerous and indefinable tension. Having honed his talents on the stand-up circuit before making his recent transition to British television comedy, Evans fills the big screen with ease. The points at which he plays himself as a performer make for truly edgy viewing. The difficulties in making sense of the origins of Jack's behavioural problems have more to do with the slow, suspended way that Chelsom and his co-writer Peter Flannery have chosen to reveal the interconnecting histories of the Fawkeses and Parkers.

In retrospect, this approach generates few story problems. Chelsom's slow, revelatory narrative is coupled with a steady use of oddly-coloured flashback scenes as a device which—literally—illuminates the past. In this manner, Jack's sway-pole act might be read as the character's transition to a saner state, as if the emergence of Tommy, the truth about Katie's affair and the circus ring killing, all function to bring about a new clarity and a consequent abnormal reaction. A similar process operates around Tommy: by returning to Blackpool, and as it transpires, the truth of his own particular familial constellation, his separation from his father is complete. Chelsom's characters and actors are so strong that the discontinuities of the plot are effectively eclipsed. This is not to say that they are non-existent. The subplot surrounding the French sailors and Oliver Reed as Dolly—an improbably camp villain—seems tacked onto the film to provide respite from Evans' commanding role.

On a larger scale, *Funny Bones'* relationship to the film and televisual world is worth noting. Through Katie and the splendidly dour Parker brothers, Chelsom celebrates music hall, a tradition that has been lost in a televisual age. As George, the big shot American comedian whose lopsided charisma induces standing ovations across Middle America, Jerry Lewis recapitulates elements of his role in Martin Scorsese's *King of Comedy*. Lewis is not kidnapped by fanatics and held to ransom as he was in this earlier film, but his character here is nevertheless out of touch with the idea of comedy. "Some people just *are* funny," he tells Tommy, "others *learn* funny. You either have, or you don't have, funny bones." This is a neat line, but it glibly ignores the craft resources of the trained comic. Evans, with Oliver Platt's Tommy as his straight man, exploits perfectly the cusp that separates humour from tragedy. If laughter can be understood as the product, not only of surprise and dislocated scenarios, but as a release from tension, then Chelsom's film provides a deft exposition.

VILLAGE VOICE, 4/4/95, p. 57, Brian Parks

Poor Tommy Fawkes. He's a comic, and it's his big Vegas debut. Everyone's there, even Dad, the famous comedian George Fawkes. No wonder Tommy throws up long and hard in the bathroom before the show.

Taking the stage, Tommy stares deep into the maw of the cocktail-soaked audience. But when he launches into his sardonic routine his bitter jokes silence the tourists, who expect father George's lame one-liners (George played by a waxy Jerry Lewis). Devastated, Tommy flees the club, the country, and his dad's oppressive shadow. He retreats to Blackpool, England, where he was born and where his father got his start on the vaudeville circuit. There, Tommy (an appealing Oliver Platt) sets out to buy material from the local entertainers to take home for a new act.

But that isn't all Tommy finds. Amidst Blackpool's gaudiness he uncovers his family's secrets: a lost half brother (played by talented physical comedian Lee Evans) and dark news about his father's old vaudeville past.

Not too bad for a plot, except *Funny Bones* also tosses in a couple murders, a smuggling scheme involving "immortality powder," and a lot of weak philosophy on the nature of comedy. Oh, and a band of bumbling Frenchmen.

The film is a mess. At its best, *Funny Bones* is a wacky combo of *Bhaji on the Beach* and *Local Hero*, an oedipal seaside character comedy with a lot of overcast skies and brown clothes. It taps nicely into the pathos of jaded Blackpool, which writer-director Peter Chelsom presents as a washed-out Las Vegas, full of odd characters and little absurdities. Chelsom, who grew up there, has a good sense, of place and a fine surreal touch (a pair of severed feet figure prominently).

But as he tries to lash together his wildly disparate plots, as he forces father and son to duke it out over truth and creativity, the film loses its pleasant restraint, sinking into a tiring rant of madcap antics and personal revelations that are both unamusing and unearned. By the end, we're asked to believe that struggling Tommy has been born again in the font of vaudeville. No doubt Chelsom means to honor the performers he so admires, but this slide into pratfalls and trick emotions turns his movie both frantic and mawkish, trampling the modest, promising comedy he began with. All of which makes these *Funny Bones* pretty hard to swallow.

Also reviewed in:
NEW YORK TIMES, 3/24/95, p.C3, Janet Maslin
VARIETY, 1/30-2/5/95, p. 48, Leonard Klady
WASHINGTON POST, 4/28/95, p. D1, Hal Hinson
WASHINGTON POST, 4/28/95, Weekend/p. 44, Desson Howe

GEORGIA

A Miramax Films release of a CIBY 2000 production. *Executive Producer:* Ben Barenholtz. *Producer:* Ulu Grosbard, Barbara Turner, and Jennifer Jason Leigh. *Director:* Ulu Grosbard. *Screenplay:* Barbara Turner. *Director of Photography:* Jan Kiesser. *Editor:* Elizabeth Kling. *Music:* Steven Soles. *Sound:* Mark Weingarten *Casting:* Renee Rousselot, Jodi Rothfield, and Katie Ryan. *Production Designer:* Lester Cohen. *Special Effects:* Don Dumas. *Costumes:* Carol Oditz. *Make-up:* Micheline Trepanier. *Running time:* 117 minutes. *MPAA Rating:* R.

CAST: Jennifer Jason Leigh (Sadie); Mare Winningham (Georgia); Ted Levine (Jake); Max Perlich (Axel); John Doe (Bobby); John C. Reilly (Herman); Jimmy Witherspoon (Trucker); Jason Carter (Chasman); Tom Bower (Erwin Flood); Smokey Hormel (Leland); Jimmy Z. (Clay); Tony Marisco (Paul); Jamian Briar (Andrew); Rachel Rasco (Mish); Nicole Donahoo (Young Sadie); Aisleagh Jackson (Young Georgia); Coleen O'Hara (Ticket Agent); Bruce Wirth (Dan Ferguson); Thomas Kuhn (Bartender at Larry's); Bill Johns (Promoter); Mina Badie (Girl with Bobby); Chris Carlson (Reporter); Shawn Cox (17-year-old-boy); Jeff Steitzer (Drunk); Michael Shapiro (Brian); Barbara Deering (Nurse); Stephanie Shine (Nurse #2); Jay Keye (Gate Agent); Jo Miller (Herself); Gary Lanz (Backup Singer); C.W. Huston (Drunk in Crowd).

CINEASTE, Vol. XXII, No. 1, 1996, p. 37, Kent Jones

Georgia is about two sisters who haunt each other like ghosts. Sadie (Jennifer Jason Leigh) is a self-consciously unhinged bar-band singer who hangs on to the fringes of the Seattle music scene. She aggressively clings to her sister Georgia (Mare Winningham), a self-consciously 'together' woman of prickly serenity and a folkish, neotraditional singer with a large, adoring audience (her signature song is Stephen Foster's *Hard Times*). Dramatically, the film is simple: every time the sisters converge, one pulls the other a length further into the endless frustration of unresolved sibling conflict. Georgia is forever pushing her problematic junkie sister away with money and a bare minimum of acknowledgment, while Sadie is forever showering Georgia with praise that hits like cold needles. There is neither sweetening nor an imagined vision of sisterly utopia at *Georgia*'s core (as Miramax's ad campaign seems to suggest). Instead, we get the insidious anxiety of repetition compulsion as well as the vertigo of unresolved ambiguity, a specialty of director Ulu Grosbard. To what degree do family conflicts determine who we are and what we do! *Georgia*, like Grosbard's 1981 *True Confessions*, suggests that the biggest part of what we call life is an elaborate form of role-playing. This is not merely provocative Freudianism, but an instinctive response from one of our toughest-minded and most unheralded directors.

The common wisdom is that *Georgia* is a star vehicle for Leigh, that she's in so much of it that it's insane to name the film after Winningham's character, and that the movie has no ambitions beyond the recording of a virtuoso performance. As an actress, Leigh has always shoved her seemingly faceless anonymity and lack of star presence at the audience with her compulsive dedication and obvious talent. Far from the Woman of Many Faces you read about in the press, she's a single-track actress with a passive-aggressive stance: whenever she enters a scene, she looks like she's withdrawing from it and wants to be noticed doing so. Leigh's presence tends to overwhelm any scene she's in by sucking all the energy away from the other actors or the setting with her relentless solo act. Which might be a good way of describing the character of Sadie. In other words, even though Leigh, herself, initiated this project, and her mother Barbara Turner wrote the screenplay, *Georgia* is not a star turn. Rather, it is a film that draws its force from a finely tuned sense of human action in which Leigh's countenance, as well as those of Winningham, Max Perlich (as the haplessly sweet delivery boy Sadie marries) and Ted Levine (as Georgia's gently disenchanted husband), are allowed to interact and clash before a camera that registers the most intimate wavelength of communication.

This approach is a constant in Grosbard's best work (*Straight Time, True Confessions,* and the flawed but affecting *Falling in Love*). Grosbard has never been taken all that seriously as a filmmaker. 'He's good with actors' is a backhanded compliment. As we all know from film school or from its graduates, 'film is visual' and just filming actors acting isn't. 'Visual' basically means shock cuts, optical 'tremors,' and games with scale and perspective that were standardized and harnessed to the machine of popular culture in the early Eighties and that still pass as a sign of originality. In today's marketplace, such a quantitative idea of cinema often easily confuses esthetic and market value—the more visual the film is, the more value the audience gets for their money. I suspect that this is the truth behind the generally lukewarm, surface reception that *Georgia* has received. Where's the kineticism! Where's the visual excitement! Instead, we get a film that has the exploratory approach and humanly scaled action of a filmmaking style that went out of fashion in the mid-Seventies.

Let's look at the now (in)famous scene in which Leigh's Sadie sings a nine-minute version of Van Morrison's "Take Me Back" before a large audience at an AIDS benefit concert. Georgia has agreed to get a spot for her sister at the benefit as a way of lifting her spirits, at the urging of Axel (Perlich). "We're gonna kick the shit outa this thing!," shouts Sadie (she's referring to AIDS), before launching into an embarrassing tribute to her sister and then the song itself, a typically incantatory Morrison epic. Leigh (or Sadie) imitates Morrison nuance for nuance, and the song seems both wildly inappropriate for the occasion and completely beyond Sadie s limited vocal capabilities, while her performance is both embarrassingly emotional and ridiculously studied (it's crazy to think of anyone but Morrison singing it).

As he did for every song in the film, Grosbard shot "Take Me Back" live before a mostly real audience, and the scene develops a sort of ontological mystery: what are we looking at! First of all, it's clearly acting. But there's no actorly distance, because the performance and the film, as well, change gears for an unbroken, nine-minute performance. Is Sadie falling apart or is she wrenching this out of herself. What part of her does this performance come from! Is it proper just to call this bad singing, or to judge it as singing at all! Is it a joyous release for Sadie or a painfully manufactured catharsis! And what part of Leigh are we watching! The scene takes on even greater weight and complexity when Grosbard begins to cut to the still, judgmental Georgia waiting in the wings. How long will she wait before she comes out to save herself from further embarrassment! Or is it Sadie she will be saving! It's worth noting here that Winningham is an accomplished vocalist with a beautiful voice (she has a second career as a singer).

For such an allegedly uncinematic director it's a complex, subtle, and galvanic scene. Its force lies in the way it puts all the mysteries and questions it evokes into high relief with the utmost economy. Subtraction is central to Grosbard's work, not just as a clever way of telling a story but also as a crucial aspect of his hard-nosed vision: with everything but the chain of human actions stripped away, we are left to contemplate events that seem ordinary and hieratic at the same time. Unlike Monte Hellman or Maurice Pialat, two other directors for whom ellipsis is crucial, Grosbard operates from a strictly earthbound perspective, fixed on the sad tangles people create out of their own lives. What would be a 'touch' in someone else's film becomes the central event in a Grosbard film. When Sadie and Georgia meet for the first time in the movie, Georgia's icy nod to Sadie's spastic wave, which lasts a split second, tells us everything about their relationship. Similarly, their father, whom Grosbard has referred to as a crucial character, is in the film for a total of about fifty seconds, but the stoic decorum he evokes in his daughters tells you all you need to know.

Georgia is remarkably similar to *True Confessions*, in which Robert De Niro's careerist Monsignor has the same edgy relationship with Robert Duvall's short-fuse cop that Georgia has with Sadie: De Niro and Winningham quietly implode while Duvall and Leigh noisily explode. Just as *True Confessions* is more than just a good movie about brothers who don't see eye to eye, *Georgia* amounts to more than 'the love-hate relationship between sisters.' It's interesting that the music that Georgia sings falls in the neotraditionalist country-folk-new age vein of, say, k.d. lang or Mary-Chapin Carpenter, while many of the songs that Sadie sings are by people associated with the punk and new wave movements: the Velvet Underground, solo Lou Reed, Elvis Costello (John Doe, the former leader of the L.A. punk band X, plays the leader of Sadie's band). Those movements were notable for the way they challenged ideas of professionalism and quality with rushes of anger, emotional immediacy, and nonprofessional spontaneity. They were lively subcultures that were eventually coopted and dissolved by the music business during the Reagan era, with its triumph of a yuppie consumer culture that embraced the kind of immaculate, 'quality' music that Georgia sings.

In this sense, Georgia, with her exquisite taste and beautiful home and family, is a representative of the baby-boom middle class. The way she treats her fucked-up sister is a model of the way yuppies, as a class, aggressively avoided all difficulties by pretending that they weren't there. On the other hand, Sadie, with her tacky vintage clothing, rat's-nest hair, raccoon eye makeup and drunkenly sloppy emotionalism, represents the worst and most excessive aspects of the punk and drug cultures. Probably Leigh's idea, this iconographical set-up enables the well-scaled, unflinching *Georgia* to become what few American films have even attempted during the last ten years: a stinging reprimand to baby-boom complacency.

LOS ANGELES TIMES, 12/8/95, Calendar/p. 1, Kenneth Turan

It's not as if Jennifer Jason Leigh isn't a known quantity, not like the kind of intense, edgy, nervous work she specializes in has not been seen and appreciated up to now. But, even with all that as a backdrop, what she accomplishes in "Georgia" tears you apart.

Unlike performers desperate to try something out of their range, Leigh takes a more difficult, more rewarding route. Like a practiced athlete, she has gone deeper into herself and taken a familiar characterization to another level so forcefully that we've never seen anything like it before.

Of course Leigh had help. Without co-star Mare Winningham, an under-appreciated actress and an old friend, plus an insightful and intelligent script by Barbara Turner, the actress' mother, and the firm, naturalistic direction of Ulu Grosbard, such an excellent result wouldn't have been possible.

It's also fitting that there was a family aspect to "Georgia," because Leigh and Winningham play sisters, and what this downbeat, beautifully realistic film concerns itself with is how deep and troublesome are the ties of blood, how brutal an attachment a sibling relationship can be.

Though Leigh's character dominates the film, her name is not Georgia but Sadie. Yet the title is right because it is sister Georgia who looms largest in Sadie's mind, "the single person," Sadie is overly fond of saying, "I will miss when I leave this Earth."

With ratty hair, too short skirts and too much personality, Sadie looks and acts like the Little Match Girl on drugs. One of those irrepressible people everyone would give a lot to repress, Sadie is led by her relentless bravado posturing like a boxing champion even though she's never won a fight. "I'm great, this is great, things are gonna break for me" are her mantras, but in truth she has an almost unerring instinct for doing the wrong thing at all times.

Georgia is, of course, just the opposite. Introduced singing a knockout version of Stephen Foster's "Hard Times" to a huge arena audience, Georgia is a Linda Ronstadt/Bonnie Raitt type of star, a pulled-together individual who also keeps house, drives her two kids to school and has a husband so stable his name is Jake (Ted Levine).

The only thing Georgia cannot handle, in fact, is her sister. Being around Sadie unnerves her, makes her feel suffocated and ill at ease. And it's only partly because Sadie is a substance abuser addicted to "whatever's cheap or free" or even that the younger sister is uncomfortably determined to make a singing career out of her own questionable talent.

It's more that Georgia experiences Sadie as unbearably needy, someone who wants to try Georgia's life on for size as well as the clothes she frequently borrows. "Nothing is enough for you," Georgia tells her, and she complains to Jake with some truth that her sister "swallows people up."

"Georgia" is set in Seattle and its vibrant music scene, where the successful Georgia lives with her family in the sisters' childhood home and where Sadie returns after an indeterminate time away, a typical bit of which, spent with legendary singer Trucker (Jimmy Witherspoon), is shown in flashback.

Now that she's back in town, Sadie sets out to have the music career that, despite a voice on the far side of questionable, she is sure is coming. She hooks up with her ex-boyfriend Bobby (X's John Doe) and his band, singing backup at bowling alleys and weddings (her "Yossel, Yossel" is something special). She also gets romantically involved with the earnest Axel (Max Perlich), who thinks saying "very much so" is expressing an opinion, but her slide into decline and her looming conflicts with her sister are never far away.

"Georgia" took the unusual step of recording its 13 musical numbers live, a risk that has paid off spectacularly in terms of emotional intensity. Hearing Winningham sing in a rich voice that justifies the script line "God kissed her" underlines why Sadie is inextricably involved with her sibling. And to hear Leigh go through an extended, agonizing 8½-minute version of Van Morrison's "Take Me Back" is to understand better than any dialogue could convey the extent of Sadie's drive and desperation.

If there is one quality that defines "Georgia," its how nonjudgmental it finally is. With Leigh's exceptional performance to build on, Sadie is a person we come to care for despite herself. She is not a bad soul, just an impossible one who lacks so much as a clue about being an adult. And the film allows us to both despair for her as Georgia does and admire her for, in Jake's words, being "original and brave and without malice."

Turner, who has worked extensively in television since "Petulia," her best-known feature screenplay, has turned in a script that is a model of careful and thoughtful character development. And director Grosbard, whose previous films have included "The Subject Was Roses" and the memorable "Straight Time," brings an emphasis on the reality of the moment that allows even actors with smallish roles, like Perlich, John C. Reilly as stoned drummer Herman and Jason Carter as a would-be manager, to shine like stars. "Georgia" is not an easy film, but in the American independent arena, it outperforms everything in sight.

NEW YORK, 12/11/95, p. 68, David Denby

Sadie Flood (Jennifer Jason Leigh, the country-rock singer at the center of *Georgia*, is small and blonde, with hair so matted and scraggly it appears to have done earlier service as a mop. Sadie has got the punk-girl look down cold: She wears a Halloween mask of eyeliner, which runs down her face when she performs; her skin is generally smudged from inky tattoos. Rigid with tension, all nerves and no flesh, she claws her way through songs, scarring the music with rage. God knows that Sid Vicious and other punk-rockers have gotten by without musical talent; but Sadie, unfortunately, is singing country-and-western and rock ballads, which need a performer with a feeling for melody and the ability to release emotion within the formal boundaries of the songs. Sadie shatters the boundaries, interpreting with such a killer dose of pain and self-dramatization that every song turns into an existential crisis. Will she break down? Will her cracked voice simply quit? She's Courtney Love without talent. Sadie is also a heroin addict and an alcoholic, as well as a liar, a user, and a hanger-on, traits not uncommon in rock performers but intolerable in one so inept musically. She's a true pain in the neck, a woman who is madly jealous of her older sister, Georgia (Mare Winningham), who has become a big star singing exactly the same repertory and who has a large, womanly voice and an unforced and uplifting stage presence that audiences love. Sadie is obsessed with Georgia; she keeps on singing because of Georgia. But what is it that she wants from her sister? Love? Hatred? Recognition of her suffering, perhaps.

I can't say I was bored. In fact, much of the time I was fascinated. This is a remarkable and perversely brave movie—exactly the kind of thing that makes an independent cinema so necessary. But it's also an outrage—a scandal, really, for, as you may have guessed, the heroine of *Georgia* is not the successful sister but the talentless, bullying monster, Sadie Flood. We're supposed to think that Sadie has so much bottom-dog courage that she transcends failure. She's noble, driven, a martyr to her own incorruptible will—the pure essence of show business. There she is, sick, strung out, a dreadful reproach to the audience—Medusa at the orgy—but she keeps on singing in her cracked, toneless voice, dashing herself against the general indifference. The picture was written by Leigh's mother, Barbara Turner, a TV and movie veteran who expressly created a vehicle for her gifted daughter; the two women, script in hand, then approached director Ulu Grosbard, who has a well-deserved reputation for doing serious work with actors. It's highly unlikely that some ghastly miscalculation has been made, or that the star was betrayed by her collaborators. On the contrary, the filmmakers have probably made exactly the movie they wanted to make. But why did they want to make it? How instructive is the subject of misery and failure?

My guess is that Turner, Leigh, and Grosbard, like many people who have been successful in the arts, keep a soft spot in their hearts for madly ambitious losers like Sadie. Perhaps they consider themselves lucky, or sense that there's an element of mystery in their own talent. Looking at Sadie, they think, There but for the grace of God go I. In a generous mood, Robert Altman in *Nashville* paid homage to such people as Sadie. There was sexy Barbara Harris onstage, singing without success, and that coffee-shop waitress played by Gwen Welles, a woman who can't sing worth a damn and winds up stripping for the audience. Sadie, however, is not a minor character; she's the center. And she's not interested in giving pleasure, in entertaining; she wants to exhibit her pain, and she does it so gracelessly she punishes everyone who listens. Some greater demand than sympathy is being made on us. We are meant to believe in Sadie as the Life Force.

Georgia is set in the Seattle area, where it seems to rain more often than it did in Berlin in the old Cold War spy movies. Except for the successful Georgia and her family, who live in a beautiful house in the country, the characters molder in dreary furnished rooms, sitting around between gigs in a stuporous funk. Trying to make some money, Sadie performs with a band that does bar mitzvahs, but she's zonked all the time, and her Hebrew singing could scour pots. At some level, the filmmakers' anti-Hollywood bravado—the rueful portrayal of squalor and failure—is satisfying and funny, even liberating: Filmmakers need the freedom to sing the blues once in a while, and in standard commercial movies they don't often get it.

And Ulu Grosbard comes through. Grosbard, who coaxed a superb, little-seen performance out of Dustin Hoffman in *Straight Time* (1978), uses very simple camera setups, and he lets the scenes play at length, allowing the actors to create and sustain complex moods without the usual attention-deficit-disorder film editing that jerks us from one place to another. The acting is first-rate—intimate, detailed, psychologically penetrating. Yet Grosbard holds our attention with something unpleasant and strange. Almost every scene seethes with Sadie's unfulfilled ambition. She wants and wants, grabbing and devouring anyone nearby, and she puts a violent strain on the other characters, who squirm with embarrassment. After getting over our own embarrassment, we may become fascinated by Sadie's bad behavior, developing an almost prurient interest in it—the way we would become obsessed by some out-of-control person at the office. But this is not an interest sustained by drama; it's an interest sustained by voyeurism. It's like following Elizabeth Wurtzel's career as a self-immolating writer.

The movie is built around a paradox: Sadie has immense desire but no talent, whereas Georgia is a placid woman with an outsize talent who never wanted to be a singing star. A homebody, Georgia is perfectly happy in her kitchen, padding around with her big, sweet-tempered husband and her children. Mare Winningham looks radiant and sings well, and she pulls off the difficult role of an inherently kindly person who gets pushed too far and finally blows up. When she tells off Leigh, the anger is biting and clean—and more memorable for coming out of so much pained gentleness.

But *Georgia* is Jennifer Jason Leigh's movie. As always, her technique is astonishing. She fills in the ghastly details of Sadie's illusion that she's hip, she's cool, she's an insider, flinging up her arms onstage in mock acceptance of the nonexistent applause, tilting her head as she talks, letting it loll on her arm in would-be intimacy with people whose flesh is crawling with her every word. Sadie is not stupid, but she's blindly self-involved, and Leigh knows every desperate maneuver, every stratagem of the unloved. She goes all the way into the character, never commenting from outside it—never signaling us, for instance, that she's not this wretched person she's playing. In all, she gets about as far as an actress could get from Demi Moore and stay within the same profession. She's all honor. But is she an artist? I no longer think so.

My distaste for Jennifer Jason Leigh's recent performances has become almost visceral. For isn't Leigh doing to us almost the same thing that Sadie is doing to the people in the movie—daring us to reject her? Leigh keeps upping the ante. After her self-lacerating performances in *Last Exit to Brooklyn, Single White Female, Mrs. Parker and the Vicious Circle, Dolores Claiborne,* and now this thing, she seems to be slipping into a naive confusion of painfulness with truth, a confusion unworthy of her talent. Misery, after all, is no more true than any other emotion. And, at the risk of sounding like a college-outline Nietzschean: It is right and even moral to love health and beauty and to hate sickness and failure. But Leigh is turning sickness and failure into a mark of integrity. She might be a hysteric showing off her stigmata. Instead of building a career, she's building a cult.

In these performances, Leigh has got hold of one truth about human beings but not *the* truth. An actress of true greatness (say, Bette Davis) offers more variety and life, resources of pleasure as well as woe. The pitiful characters Leigh has been playing are simply not as interesting as she may think. Sadie Flood's fascinations, for instance, are severely limited by her flagrant narcissism; much of the time she's just a drag. In her own way, talented as she is, Jennifer Jason Leigh has become a bullying, even megalomaniacal performer. We've got to accept her conviction that anguish lies at the heart of life or reject her altogether: We're trapped by her talent, and by her ambitious masochism. She dares us to become philistines—a dare that many of us, unwilling to give up self-respect, may have to accept.

NEW YORK POST, 12/8/95, p. 43, Thelma Adams

Imagine they made a movie about your life and named it after your sister. Talk about taking another little piece of your heart out, baby.

"Georgia," Ulu Grosbard's searing tale of two sisters, is different from anything else you'll see this year: fearless, complex, ambling, ambitious and as painful as a corkscrew to the heart.

Georgia (Mare Winningham) is the perfect one. She's a graceful, scrubbed folk-rock star who has it all: adoring fans, a supportive husband, bright children and a wellspring of natural talent.

Georgia's little sister, Sadie (Jennifer Jason Leigh), has a hunger to devour the world in one bite and the ambition to make it as a modern-day Janis Joplin. There's just one problem: she has a voice of brass. As a singer, she'll never amount to much more than the blonde in the band at the bowling alley.

In a simple knife-twist of fate, it's Sadie's movie, but screenwriter Barbara Turner (Leigh's real-life mom) titled it "Georgia." The movie follows Sadie's downward spiral from bad to worse, from drunk to junkie. She burns through friends and family until, by the end, even Sadie's love for Georgia becomes too much of a weight for the successful sister to bear.

The movie opens with a brief, poignant flashback of two little golden-haired girls side-by-side in an upstairs window, holding pretend microphones and singing.

The glimpse of the past perfectly matches the drama's riskiest scene: an 8½-minute solo sung by self-professed mediocre singer Leigh. Georgia steps aside at a concert and lets her sister take the spotlight. Sadie sings a wrenching rendition of Van Morrison's "Take Me Back" with none of The Man's ticks and dramatic pauses left untried.

Leigh strips the emotional moment bare. Mute the sound and she can sell the song better than anyone. She comes alive performing. She just doesn't have the tubes to make it.

With this solo, director Grosbard unflinchingly captures the disparity between Sadie's desires and her reality. It's a crawl through glass that can't fail to touch anyone with even a shard of sibling rivalry. He caps the moment with a crushing blow; Georgia joins Sadie on the stage for an impromptu duet. In the interests of "saving" the song (and ending her embarrassment), she spoils Sadie's moment in the sun.

Grosbard uses the musical numbers (taped live in Seattle) to tap a strong emotional current. He has built the undercurrents of strife largely through indirection.

In a scene set in Georgia's ordered kitchen, she serenely stuffs oranges for a Thanksgiving feast, a musical Martha Stewart. The visual contrast with the spidery, alcoholic Sadie —her hand busy with jerky movements that lead nowhere—is loaded with tension. Sadie's hunger for Georgia's approval and the older sisters resistance is more devastating than later, confrontational dialogue.

Turner and Grosbard capture the endless small reminders of her and powerlessness that crowd a difficult relationship, the minor skirmishes that become walls in the maze of sisterhood. "Georgia" becomes less sure-footed as it follow's Turner's script in a downward spiral into Sadie's drug addiction that borders on bleak for bleak's sake.

Leigh has a shot at the Oscar as the alcoholic sister whose make-up stained eyes reflect a wall of unrealized ambition. She might have pushed these boundaries before in movies like "Mrs. Parker and the Vicious Circle," but Leigh's needy, charismatic Sadie is the best outing yet from an actress who takes risks in the parts she chooses and the way she chooses to play them. It's a performance so true it hurts.

NEWSDAY, 12/8/95, Part II/p. B2, Jack Mathews

In Ulu Grosbard's "Georgia," Jennifer Jason Leigh plays a Seattle punk rocker who has the look of a sick raccoon, the voice of a creaking door, the strength of a newborn fawn and enough pain to funk out the Dalai Lama. Mare Winningham plays a folk superstar who looks like Betty Crocker, has the voice of 10 angels, the strength of Mother Teresa and enough innate sunniness to chase the gray out of the Seattle sky.

They are sisters Sadie and Georgia, respectively, and if their contrasting talents and temperaments aren't enough, Georgia also got the father's love that younger sister Sadie desperately needed, and is now draining—like so much blood—from Georgia herself.

The story catches up with the sisters after Georgia has achieved a sort of legendary status among pop singers, and enough self-assurance to place her husband and her children ahead of her career, and after Sadie has nearly worn herself out on a treadmill of unacknowledged envy.

Sadie is equally addicted to drugs and self-pity, and her erratic behavior has ended what little career she's had as a bar singer and left her broke, friendless, jobless and compelled to accept the hospitality and saccharine kindnesses of the person she blames for her misery.

Calling "Georgia" a story of sibling rivalry doesn't quite get it. This is nuclear cold war, confined to a family operating under a perennially fragile truce, and though the unevenness of the story and its occasional pop cliches mark it as less than a great movie, it gets from Leigh and Winningham a pair of great performances.

The movie, written by Leigh's mother, Barbara Turner, was perfectly cast. Leigh cannot carry a tune, but neither can half the working rock singers in the country, and what she and Sadie lack in musicianship, they more than make up in passion. And Winningham, who (she'll be the last to tell, you) sang 20 years ago on "The Gong Show," does have the voice of 10 angels. Look for her next album; it's inevitable.

Their singing voices play perfectly for these characters. Sadie isn't being passed off as a good singer, just a bundle of raw emotional nerves making earnest noises on stage. She's Janis Joplin, with twice the grief and none of the talent, functioning in an alienated punk environment where the pain in a singer's voice can be more important than the timbre.

In the film's most remarkable sequence, filmed in two takes with more than 1,000 concert extras, Leigh does an 8½-minute version of Van Morrison's "Take Me Back," and for all the limitations of her voice, it leaves you drained from its emotional power. It may be the most courageous piece of acting on screen all year.

Sadie is clearly the dominant character in the film. We follow her whenever the sisters part, and watch her strain and destroy relationships with an assortment of friends and lovers. But "Georgia" is the right choice for the title. Good drama is about personal change, and though Sadie has a few ups to go with her many downs, her self-destructive course is pretty well laid out. It is Georgia who is compelled to reexamine her values and motivations, and face up to her own enormous anger, built up over years of emotionally babysitting a sister who loathes her for it.

Grosbard, a stage director with just a handful of movie credits ("Straight Time," "True Confessions"), has choreographed the musical numbers to perfection, but it is his handling of the actors—and particularly of the bountifully gifted Leigh—that makes "Georgia" one of the few keepers of the 1995 season.

NEWSWEEK, 12/18/95, p. 70, David Ansen

Georgia, a devastating study of sibling rivalry, is the tale of two competing Seattle sisters, Sadie (Jennifer Jason Leigh) and Georgia (Mare Winningham). Don't expect sisterly uplift or gender generalizations. Written with an acute ear by Barbara Turner—Leigh's mother—and directed with great emotional honesty by Ulu Grosbard, it's a resonant, grittily specific film. Anyone who's ever been locked in a love-hate relationship with a sibling will squirm with recognition.

Sadie, an emotional basket case, is all raw need and flaming exhibitionism—an aspiring rock singer whose lack of talent doesn't stop her from spilling her soul onstage, and whose reckless intake of booze and heroin keeps her bouncing from band to band and man to man. Georgia's life is as orderly as Sadie's is chaotic. A successful folk-rock singer with a voice like honey, she's constructed a life-caring husband (Ted Levine), loving children, the same placid country home she grew up in—designed to protect her deep need for repose and anonymity. So when the torn and frayed Sadie lands on her doorstep in need of shelter—not, you can be sure, for the first time—Georgia welcomes her with profound ambivalence. "She swallows people up," Georgia complains to her husband. Sadie is no less divided, revering her sister even as she drowns in her shadow.

Georgia has all the power, but is she really the stronger one? Is Sadie a self-indulgent monster or a brave, risk-taking soul? Which is the true artist, the gut raver or the seamless technician? Audiences take sides about the sisters; the movie doesn't. No easy judgments here, just raw psychological reportage. It's Grosbard's best movie since "Straight Time," and though its dogged realism denies it much cinematic rhythm it has a discomforting power.

And magnificent acting. Winningham has the subtler role, but she shades it with brilliant flickers of passive aggression. John C. Reilly, as a junkie drummer, Max Perlich as a gawky delivery boy Sadie impulsively marries, Jason Carter as Sadie's useless Brit "manager" are all pitch perfect. But it's Leigh's show, and she sets off a harrowing display of emotional fireworks. In the movie's key scene, she takes the stage for eight and a half magnificently appalling minutes and rips through a desperately heartfelt cover of Van Morrison's "Take Me Back." It's a mind-bending marvel: a great performance of a bad performance that's so great you have to wonder if it really is bad, or if some new category has to be applied.

It's invariably a shock to meet the shy, tiny, soft-spoken Jennifer Jason Leigh. In vain you look for signs of those raging, self-destructive heroines she seems compelled to portray. The psycho roommate in "Single White Female." The boozily brilliant Dorothy Parker. The tortured junkie in "Rush." The ravaged hooker in "Last Exit to Brooklyn." The housewife in "Short Cuts" who coos phone sex while diapering her baby. The sweetly vapid call girl in "Miami Blues."

None of these is remotely like Leigh. Indeed, if the actress resembles anyone in "Georgia," it's not the wild sister. "I'm much more like Georgia," she says, "in terms of needing quiet and treasuring my privacy." It happens that Leigh has a sister who is more like Sadie—Carrie, who "ran away from home and joined the carnival when she was 16," and for years, before she cleaned up, lived a life of heroin-laced abandon. "A lot of Sadie was inspired by Carrie. Carrie sometimes scared me and I was also awed. She would rage and was very gut, so I went into my head and became very cerebral.

"But in acting, that's where I could get my connection to that part of myself that I needed so desperately, what Carrie lived out and I didn't." Leigh does all her acting out in front of a camera—passionately. A fanatical researcher, she immerses herself in a role completely—even keeping a notebook in the voice of the character—until the metamorphosis is complete. But the method can take its toll. "I love that Sadie burns so intensely, but it's not my nature. After the movie was over I was 89 pounds, I was very sick, and just physically and emotionally exhausted. I really needed to come back to myself; I don't think I've ever felt that lost."

Now she's gearing up for another grueling role, a white-trash girl abused by her stepfather in Dorothy Allison's "Bastard Out of Carolina," which Anjelica Huston is directing. "I do roles because there's something in the character I haven't done before that I want to understand." It's character, not stardom, that drives her. "Those movie-star roles are deadening. There's just nothing human to connect to." But it's not only darkness that draws her, she insists. "I want to do more comedies, too. You know, it's nice to make audiences laugh."

TIME, 12/11/95, p. 82, Richard Corliss

The drumbeat began at the Cannes Film Festival in May, and it is now more insistent than a migraine pulse. Jennifer Jason Leigh's performance in *Georgia* has won the sort of critics' raves that fuel studio campaigns for an Oscar nomination. This racket must cease. To praise Leigh in this small, frail film is to mistake big acting for good acting, and shriek for soul.

The movie, written by Leigh's mother Barbara Turner and directed by Ulu Grosbard, is a two-hander about the edgy relationship of show-biz sibs. Georgia (Mare Winningham) sings pop; she's famous and sensible, a caring mom and sister. Sadie (Leigh) sings barroom rock and thinks the way to be Janis Joplin is to do drugs, embarrass herself onstage and lurch toward an early, ugly death. At the mike, in the van, at the airport, she goes self-destructively, picturesquely nuts.

A daring, often endearing actress, Leigh virtually patented the role of neurotic little-girl-lost in such cable-ready classics as *Sister, Sister* and *Miami Blues*. Lately, though, strenuous mannerism has clotted her work: bizarre accents in *The Hudsucker Proxy* and *Mrs. Parker and the Vicious Circle*, and, here, a surrender to the excesses of actressy masochism. As Sadie, she leaves no emotional scab unpicked. It's a role for which her voice, carriage and technique are ill suited; she's too small for these grandiloquent gestures. *Georgia*'s big set piece is an eight-minute (or possibly eight-hour) Joplinesque song in which Leigh screams, whines and pleads "Take me back" while falling to pieces onstage. It's a startling, exhausting spectacle—and, like the rest of Leigh's performance, very, very bad.

VILLAGE VOICE, 12/12/95, p. 72, Georgia Brown

Sadie and Georgia are sisters, Sadie and Georgia are singers. Georgia is famous, Sadie is not. Played to the hilt by Jennifer Jason Leigh, Sadie is the jittery, down-spiraling figure the movie *Georgia* tracks. But Sadie is forever drawn back—"Take me back, take me back," she insists à la Van Morrison—to her mostly enigmatic elder sister (a cool grave performance by Mare Winningham). The sweet paradox of Ulu Grosbard and Barbara Turner's fine film is that for all Sadie's self-destructive histrionics, the movie manages to tell Georgia's story, too.

Sister movies, or even serious family melodramas, are made in other countries. (*Georgia* is *Sweetie* minus the fish-eye lens.) Once upon a time someone in this country made a serious family melodrama and called it *Five Easy Pieces*. That was a quarter of a century ago. Financed with European money (CIBY 2000), *Georgia* is in a line with *Five Easy Pieces*—hold the mayo, hold the quirky plot.

I love the vignette that opens the movie: two little girls framed in the upper-story window of a country house lipsynching and gyrating to Otis Redding. Down below, on the lawn, parents and guests have arranged chairs to face the window. How timeless it is—the children's desire to put on a show, the grownups' bemused tolerance. Somewhere into the song, the littler of the two starts fidgeting.

If timelessness turns out to be Georgia's thing (she sings plaintive oldies, buys back the family manse, and prepares wholesome meals for husband and kids), grownup Sadie never stops fidgeting or messing up. In punkish makeup, she catches gigs where she can, though by the time we meet her she seems to have burned most of the bridges along the West Coast. Taken on by the legendary blues singer, Trucker (Jimmy Wltherspoon), she endures some dressings down and, spooked by Trucker's guns, runs away. What she's on at any given moment, you can't be sure. (Doing a wedding gig, she swigs Nyquil.) She speaks with a coy verbal twitch that betrays a vast inner awkwardness. She does lurid things with black eye makeup. As for Sadie's singing, she's a thief, stealing from Chet Baker, Van Morrison, Janis Joplin, the appropriated styles reflecting the rawness within.

Sadie's rancid sound seems designed to embarrass Georgia, whose voice is soothing and polite. At the same time, Georgia's control seems a reaction to Sadie's chaos. By cornering the market on doom, fury, and passion, Sadie doesn't give Georgia room to act out. Anything Georgia does is bound to look staid, boring, bourgeois, and drab. "I'm bolder than you," implies little Sadie, scoring again. (Mike Leigh's *Life Is Sweet* portrayed slightly younger versions of Sadie and Georgia.)

You can see the grimness on Georgia's face when she discovers her little sister is in the same city (a drenched Seattle). From across the room, Sadie waves goofily while delaying her approach. Picking up on Mom's mood, Georgia's eldest child can barely greet her aunt. But Georgia's warm and accepting husband, Jake (Ted Levine), welcomes Sadie, invites her into their circle—partially because he identifies with Sadie's burning desire to *get to* Georgia. "Best man in the world," says Sadie of Jake. Georgia is the loneliest person in the movie. Like many sad cases, Sadie's a demon.

At one point Sadie is adopted by a fresh-faced 23-year-old grocery delivery boy, Axel (Max Perlich). Like Jake, Axel is content with being an adjunct, with hero worship and rendering services. From a brief glimpse at the sisters' zombielike father, he was an adjunct, too.

On the one hand, *Georgia* is extremely painful; on the other, there's joy in the enterprise. Screenwriter Turner (who wrote *Petulia*) is Leigh's mother. Leigh has two sisters, one of them, a gifted musician, ran away from home at 16. I can't believe any woman with a sister, wayward or no, won't cherish this movie.

Also reviewed in:
CHICAGO TRIBUNE, 1/10/96, Tempo/p. 5, Michael Wilmington
NATION, 12/18/95, p. 803, Stuart Klawans

NEW YORK TIMES, 12/8/95, p. C18, Janet Maslin
NEW YORKER, 12/11/95, p. 110, Anthony Lane
VARIETY, 5/22-28/95, p. 93, Todd McCarthy
WASHINGTON POST, 1/12/96, p. D1, Rita Kempley
WASHINGTON POST, 1/12/96, Weekend/p. 32, Desson Howe

GERMANY YEAR 90 NINE ZERO

A Brainstorm Productions release of a Brainstorm-Antenne 2 production in association with Gaumont, Peripheria. *Producer:* Nicole Ruellé. *Director:* Jean-Luc Godard. *Screenplay (French and German with English subtitles):* Jean-Luc Godard. *Based on "Nos Solitudes,"* by: Michel Hanouon. *Director of Photography:* Christophe Pollock, Andreas Erben, and Stephan Brenda. *Editor:* Jean-Luc Godard. *Sound:* François Musy and Pierre Alain Besse. *Production Designer:* Romain Goupil. *Running time:* 62 minutes. *MPAA Rating:* Not Rated.

CAST: Eddie Constantine (Lemmy Caution); Hanns Zischler (Count Zelten); Claudia Michelsen (Charlotte/Dora); André Labarthe (La Narrateur); Nathalie Kadem (Delphine de Stael); Robert Wittmers (Don Quixote).

CHRISTIAN SCIENCE MONITOR, 1/25/95, p. 13, David Sterritt

[*Germany Year 90 Nine Zero* was reviewed jointly with *JLG by JLG*; see Sterritt's review of that film.]

LOS ANGELES TIMES, 1/29/96, Calendar/p. 10, Kevin Thomas

The fall of the Berlin Wall inspired Jean-Luc Godard in this one-hour "Germany Year 90 Nine Zero" to bring back his "Alphaville" private eye Lemmy Caution and imagine him as the Last Spy, a mole planted in East Germany for more than 50 years.

As Caution (the late Eddie Constantine, fittingly in his final role) makes his way to the West, he confronts the ghosts of Germany's dark past. "Germany Year 90 Nine Zero" unfolds in fragments structured like musical variations in which Godard draws upon archival footage in ways that make the technique seem fresh. He incorporates the footage with his usual barrage of philosophical declarations, this time contemplating the nature of history.

Constantine, his deep voice as strong as ever, is ever the trench-coated icon, and serves as the film's commentator as well as traveler. Godard's heart lies clearly with the East, despite its failings, rather than with the glittery, ultra-materialist West, and there are flashes of his characteristic bleak humor. As is generally the case with Godard, he floods us with more ideas, propositions and insights than we can possibly absorb, at least in only one viewing. But his command of his medium is so effortlessly complete that "Germany Year 90 Nine Zero" is tremendously moving even when you know that there's probably lots that's whizzing right past you.

NEW YORK POST, 1/20/95, p. 42, Larry Worth

The concept of avant-garde director Jean-Luc Godard making a film about himself is akin to imagining Robert Motherwell painting a self-portrait: All the elements would be there, but you couldn't necessarily tell the nose from the mouth.

And since Godard hasn't even flirted with cohesive narrative for nearly three decades, "JLG by JLG" is what his fans might expect: a puzzling, ever-intriguing homage to abstract thought, stunning imagery and fascinating footage of the great man himself.

Visually, the film is beautiful, with its postcard-perfect shots of wintry landscapes and violent rainstorms. But when complemented by classical music and Godard's stream of consciousness philosophizing ("The past is never dead. It hasn't even passed yet."), the result takes shape as celluloid poetry.

And that's not even mentioning the engaging clips of Godard alternately captured in the editing room (surrounded by posters of films like "Helas Pour Moi"), on the tennis court, wandering the seashore or just chatting with his scantily clad housekeeper.

So does it add up to a cohesive whole? Not really, but that's part of Godard's unique allure, further evidenced by "Germany Year 90 Nine Zero," Godard's follow-up to his futuristic 1965 saga, "Alphaville."

Godard has taken "Alphaville's" hero, Lemmy Caution—again played by the wonderful Eddie Constantine, in what turned out to be his last role—and placed him in Germany after the Berlin Wall's fall. There, the former spy travels across a bleak landscape that's as otherworldly as anything in "Alphaville," confronting a brotherhood of fellow outsiders led by a still-deluded Don Quixote.

Separated into segments bearing title cards like "roads which lead to nowhere," and filled with great lines such as "periods of bliss are history's blank pages," Godard's vision artfully reflects on alienation while addressing how Germany's ghosts jibe with its future.

But make no mistake. Both "Germany" and "JLG" (which each require $6 admission, or $10 for both) are targeted for a select audience, namely, Godard's loyal followers. Those filling that bill will find them required viewing, and unqualified treats.

NEWSDAY, 1/20/95, Part II/p. B7, John Anderson

In "Alphaville," his 1965 "sci-fi" film, Jean-Luc Godard introduced Lemmy Caution (Eddie Constantine), a granite-faced special agent who crossed intergalactic space to confront a world run by computer, while Godard embarked on the more abstract approach that would mark his later films. It was a tale of alienation and conformity, but more about the modern world than any futuristic fantasy.

In "Germany Year 90 Nine Zero," Lemmy Caution is back. Older, brittler, he's the "last spy" returning from the cold of East Germany and facing a world that's heading full-bore into an orgy of consumerism. It's a contemporary tale—if, in its collage style, it can be called a tale—as well as a prophesy.

Godard, whose film employs so many obscure literary and cinematic references it should be released in an annotated edition, sees Germany as the conscience of the world, in a way. Using stock footage, some of it from concentration camps, he portrays that country as a laboratory of forgetfulness. How can the world recall, or never forget, the last crisis when there's a new one brewing? His use of anachronistic elements camp victims, fin-de-siècle socialites, Lemmy, a vendor of Holocaust souvenirs—makes the case for convenient memory.

For his part, Lemmy is a walking recrimination, both of the West ("Which way is the West?" he bellows, and gets no answers) and of art. Particularly Godard's art: Whatever cinema has attempted has failed, he says, otherwise the world wouldn't be in the shape it's in. The failures of his medium have become a regular theme in Godard's more recent work (including "JLG by JLG," which is being shown with "Germany" and was reviewed here when it was at the Museum of Modern Art last year). "Germany" itself occasionally feels like a lovely exercise in futility.

At the same time, Godard creates beautiful pictures, even if they are, at the same time, another kind of recrimination. His pacing varies wildly but assumes a musicality that's invigorating. It's Godard's painterly ability to merge the disparate elements he uses—including allusions to his own work—into an emotionally fulfilling whole that sets him apart.

Back in 1966, the year after "Alphaville," Godard made "Masculin/Feminin," which was a pointed portrait of a particular place and time and the "children of Marx and Coca-Cola." "Germany Year 90 Nine Zero," too, is about a specific time and place in the metamorphosis of the world. But his characters, this time, are merely the misbegotten offspring of Coca-Cola.

VILLAGE VOICE, 1/24/95, p. 49, J. Hoberman

If the Public Theater's current double bill of two recent movies by Jean-Luc Godard seems particularly fin de siècle, it may be because the new year marks two anniversaries. As the movies enter their second century, Godard—the epitome of "young cinema" and the single most influential personality of the post-1960, pre-Steven Spielberg film world—turns 65.

Germany Year 90 Nine Zero (1991) concerns the end of the Cold War, *JLG by JLG* (1994) just the end of time. Each packs a universe into an hour; both are suffused in solipsistic rue. *Germany Year 90* had its origins in a French television request to make a movie about "solitude," while the similarly commissioned self-portrait *JLG by JLG* emphasizes the aging artist's isolation. Godard, after all, is an exotic creature. Although *Breathless*, arguably, the most significant debut film since *Citizen Kane*, is virtually Godard's lone commercial success, he may be cinema's last universal master—a figure who has impacted on every mode of production (Hollywood, avant-garde, Third World, video, television) and each critical discourse, from auteurism through structuralism, cine-semiotics, Lacano-feminism, the new historicity, and beyond.

Emerging from the depths of the Cinémathèque Française, Godard was among the first to read the history of film as a text or—said another way—the first to understand that the period of classic cinema was over. His current ongoing project, the multipart *Histoire(s) du cinéma*, begun in 1989 for French television and produced entirely at his studio in Rolle, Switzerland, may prove to be his magnum opus, addressing the "splendor and misery" of the 20th century as documented by the movies: the "Newsreel of History" as the "History of Newsreels."

It was Godard who taught the movies to quote and who proposed to criticize one film by making another. A practicing movie journalist throughout the '50s, Godard defines the notion of cine-critical consciousness. Indeed, the New York Film Critics Circle marks *its* 60th anniversary this week by presenting him with only the seventh "special award" in the organization's history. According to NYFCC chairman Armond White, the six previous honorees have been *Snow White*, *Fantasia* the *Why We Fight* series, *The Sorrow and the Pity*, *Voice* movie critic Tom Allen, and Film Forum. The combination sounds like nothing so much as a Godard scenario. It was he, after all, who cubed the radical juxtaposition of Soviet montage, splicing together B movies and Picasso, documentary and pulp fiction, film and video, Marx and Coca-Cola, and every conceivable permutation of sound and image.

In *JLG by JLG*, Godard references old movies as readily as he pulls books out of his shelves—the VCR gives him access to all. *Germany Year 90 Nine Zero* is no less layered with allusions. (Continually combining German and Russian music and movies, *Germany Year 90* first evokes the Third Reich with a stutter-stop sequence of Nazi officers dancing the tango, apparently excerpted from *The Damned*, newly set to Rachmaninoff.) As the title *Germany Year 90* evokes *Germany Year Zero*, Roberto Rossellini's 1947 neorealism drama of post-World War II Berlin, so the casting evokes Godard's own *Alphaville*, the (now 30-year-old) movie that portrayed then contemporary Paris as the galactic capital of a comic-book future—a film that half the cineastes in Alphabet City have longed to remake.

Contemporary critics cited *Alphaville*'s "East Berlin" ambience. In *Germany Year 90*, Godard takes advantage of the new freedom to film in East Germany to track *Alphaville*'s tough-guy hero Lemmy Caution (Eddie Constantine) through the decomposing DDR of December 1990. To the degree that the movie has a plot, it follows Lemmy—a/k/a "The Last Spy," having evidently been installed as a mole in some East German backwater—as he makes his confused and gloomy way back West, after the collapse of the Berlin Wall.

Is this the New World Order? "With no more Cold War, where's the benefit to being American?" a spy-master wails, then backs his car over the fallen sign for Karl-Marx Strasse. Asking directions from, among others, a distracted Don Quixote, Lemmy (naturally) searches for the West on the immense Babelsburg movie lot in the former East Berlin: A title identifies this sequence as "The Last DEFA [East German] Documentary Film." No longer ground zero, Berlin remains Europe's haunted house. A wealth of 20th-century history is compressed into a single reference to the one-sentence intertitle from F.W. Murnau's 1922 *Nosferatu* that Surrealist honcho André Breton said contained the movie's entire poetic charge. "Once I crossed the frontier, the phantoms came out to meet me," Lemmy muses, approaching the site of the former Wall.

At last, Lemmy arrives on the Ku'damm, glamorous new center of the old West Berlin where the cigarette ads invite newly arrived Ossies to "Test the West." Gazing on shop windows ("Christmas with all its ancient horrors"), visiting the *sex kino* zone, settling into a soulless hotel suite, Lemmy has returned. It's Alphaville once more—although this time forever.

When *Germany Year 90* was shown by MOMA as part of Godard's 1992 retro, Amy Taubin called it "the first film of Godard's old age." *JLG by JLG* confirms her observation, personalizing the melancholy implicit in the end of the post-World War II political order.

Germany Year 90 celebrates the austere beauty of chilly fields, barren parks, the mist rising off icy streets, the nocturnal frozen glow of Berlin's neon-limned Aeroflot office. No less wintry (or taken with cold afternoon light on "empty" country landscapes), *JLG by JLG* is subtitled "December self-portrait." The movie opens with Godard wheezing into the mike, a photograph of his childhood incarnation Jeannot prominently displayed upon his mantlepiece—already, the artist says, "in mourning for myself." Outside, whitecaps roll the surface of Lake Geneva, beside which Jeannot grew up and to which he has since returned.

In *Germany Year 90*, the late Eddie Constantine played his signature role as a sort of excavated fossil—in one scene, sitting alone in a suitably desolate churchyard and, by way of a memento mori, removing his battered fedora to reveal a bald pate. Another manifestation of "The Last Spy," the Godard of *JLG by JLG* ponders a tiny flickering tele-image or lavishes long close-ups on his weathered hands. As Constantine perches on a mound of old tires, listening to, or imagining, the soundtrack of an old French movie (perhaps one of his own), so JLG underscores a shot of cold Lake Geneva with the dialogue from a movie that he has never ceased to champion, Nicholas Ray's *Johnny Guitar*. Significantly, the scene chosen has Sterling Hayden demanding that Joan Crawford lie to him, rather than admit to the ravages of time.

Godard's celluloid self-portrait celebrates the cacophony of his bookshelves, muses upon images of women, makes humorous reference to his past mistakes, (Where the militant Godard had called for "two, three, many Vietnams," there are now, he observes, "two, three, many United States.") He is self-absorbed and alone—except for the sexy young maid whose goodbyes he ignores (and whose name he gets wrong) and a mysteriously blind film editor. Her scissors poised over the unspooling reels of celluloid, she suggests a modern equivalent to the Greek goddess of fate.

There is a sense in which Godard will be forever young—at least as long as there are projectors and film. But, as a moment of spring gives way to a black screen, *JLG by JLG*, like *Germany Year 90*, ends on a diminuendo of unbearable sadness. Art is that which lasts. Film, which Godard once called truth 24 times per second, is as transitory as life.

Also reviewed in:
NEW YORK TIMES, 1/20/95, p. C8, Stephen Holden
NEW YORKER, 2/6/95, Terrence Rafferty
VARIETY, 9/16/91, p. 90, David Stratton

GET SHORTY

A Metro-Goldwyn-Mayer Pictures release of a Jersey Films production. *Executive Producer:* Barry Sonnenfeld. *Producer:* Danny DeVito, Micahel Shamberg, and Stacey Sher. *Director:* Barry Sonnenfeld. *Screenplay:* Scott Frank. *Based on the novel by:* Elmore Leonard. *Director of Photography:* Don Peterman. *Editor:* Jim Miller. *Music:* John Lurie. *Music Editor:* Bobby Mackston. *Sound:* Jeff Wexler, Don Coufal, Gary Holland, and (music) Patrick Dillett. *Sound Editor:* Philip Stockton and Skip Lievsay. *Casting:* David Rubin and Debra Zane. *Production Designer:* Peter Larkin. *Art Director:* Steve Arnold. *Set Designer:* Erin Kemp. *Set Decorator:* Leslie E. Rollins. *Set Dresser:* Douglas McKay. *Special Effects:* Danny Gill and Gary Bierend. *Costumes:* Betsy Heimann. *Make-up:* Ellen Wong. *Make-up (John Travolta):* Michelle Buhler. *Stunt Coordinator:* Brian Smrz. *Running time:* 105 minutes. *MPAA Rating:* R.

CAST: John Travolta (Chili Palmer); Gene Hackman (Harry Zimm); Rene Russo (Karen Flores); Danny DeVito (Martin Weir); Dennis Farina (Ray "Bones" Barboni); Delroy Lindo (Bo Catlett); James Gandolfini (Bear); Jon Gries (Ronnie Wingate); Renee Props (Nicki); David Paymer (Leo Devoe); Martin Ferrero (Tommy Carlo); Miguel Sandoval (Mr. Escobar); Jacob Vargas (Yayo Portillo); Linda Hart (Fay Devoe); Bobby Slayton (Dick Allen); Ron Karabatsos (Momo); Alison Waddell and Amber Waddell (Bear's Daughter); John Cothran, Jr. (Agent Curtis); Jack Conley (Agent Dunbar); Bernard Hocke (Agent Morgan); Big Daddy Wayne (Ray Barboni's Bodyguard); Xavier Montalvo (Big Guy with Escobar); Carlease Burke (Rental Car Attendant); Vito Scotti (Manager at Vesuvio's); Rino Piccolo (Waiter at Vesuvio's);

Alfred Dennis (Ed the Barber);   Ralph Manza (Fred the Barber);   Zed Frizzelle (Kid at Lockers);   Harry Victor (Limo Driver with Sign);   Patrick Breen (Resident Doctor);   Barry Sonnenfeld (Doorman);   Donna W. Scott (Screaming Woman);   Zack Phifer (Ivy Restaurant Maitre d');   Gregory B. Goossen (Duke, Man at the Ivy); Stephanie Kemp (Ivy Restaurant Waitress); Rebeca Arthur (Las Vegas Waitress); Jeffrey J. Stephan (Bones' Buddy); Ernest "Chili" Palmer (Bones' Buddy #2).

CHRISTIAN SCIENCE MONITOR, 10/27/95, p. 12, David Sterritt

The real comeback kid of the mid-90s is neither a politician nor an athlete. He's an actor named John Travolta, who clearly hopes "Get Shorty" will consolidate the resurgence of star-power that galvanized his appearance in "Pulp Fiction" last year. This would reverse the neglect he suffered in the low-glamour period after "Welcome Back Kotter" and his early movies lost their glow.

Not that "Get Shorty" offers the charged-up intensity of "Pulp Fiction," a movie so hyperkinetic that Travolta's comparatively laid-back hit man came off as one of the more relaxing characters. The new picture is cooler in tone, more modest in ambition, less flamboyant in achievement. While it provides another neat spotlight for Travolta's newly mature talents, it surrounds these with story ingredients that aren't quite as clever, surprising, or amusing as they'd like to be.

Based on Elmore Leonard's bouncy novel, "Get Shorty" offers the unusual spectacle of a Hollywood satire aimed at Hollywood itself. Travolta plays Chili Palmer, a mob money collector who flies into Los Angeles on the trail of a client who's absconded with a bagful of cash. Among the people he meets are a small-time producer who wants to graduate from Grade Z productions to bigtime cinema; the producer's girlfriend, a former leading lady in those Grade Z productions; and a Major Motion-Picture Star who's eager to learn gangster-speak by hanging around with an expert like our hero.

Leonard's novel gets most of its humor from three sources: the raffish rhythms of subtly exaggerated speech patterns, the goofy interplay among folks who embody variegated forms of sleaziness, and the inspired idiocy of the unproduced film script that sparks heated rivalry among the main characters. Written by Scott Frank, the movie version tones down the dialogue, smooths out some character conflicts, and eliminates most details about the fought-over script. This adds to the economy and punchiness of the movie, but it reduces the story's overall impact. It becomes more a smart-alecky trifle than the wicked show-biz parody it might have been with more fidelity to Leonard's vision.

This said, the picture has enough assets to please moviegoers willing to put up with its many four-letter words and the bursts of violence that spring from nowhere at unexpected moments.

Travolta is wry and winning as the discreetly dangerous hero, Gene Hackman is his usual jovial self as the glitz-minded producer, and Rene Russo makes the most of her thankless role as the former horror-flick actress. Danny DeVito is predictably perfect as the character referred to in the title—an improbable star who's more pretentious than profound—and there's good supporting work by Bette Midler and Delroy Lindo, who seems to be in half the pictures now playing. A handful of real-life Hollywood stars juice up the movie with cameo appearances that I won't give away here.

Don Peterman did the colorful cinematography and John Lurie, whose sounds also enliven the current "Blue in the Face," composed the perky music. The picture was directed by Barry Sonnenfeld, who concocted more memorable laughs in the "Addams Family" pictures but still shows a considerable flair for comedy. If his next project combines a stronger screenplay with an equally distinguished cast, it will be an entertainment to be reckoned with.

LOS ANGELES TIMES, 10/20/95, Calendar/p. 1, Kenneth Turan

The town, of course, is Hollywood, and the genial premise of Leonard's novel and the diverting film that's been made from it is that being a success in the movie business is a piece of cake for those schooled in more traditional criminal pursuits.

The crook in question is Chili Palmer, a smooth Miami loan shark and movie fan who finds himself in L.A. on mob business. Once he discovers that "I don't think the producer has to know too much," he sees no reason why he shouldn't be getting some of that action as well.

Wittily directed by "Addams Family" veteran Barry Sonnenfeld and adapted from Leonard's effortlessly wised-up work by Scott Frank, "Get Shorty" is light comedy in an amoral setting. The jokes are quick, with clever jibes alternating with double-crosses and the occasional murder, and the streamlined plot unrolls like a colorful ball of twine.

At the center of it all, an island of calm with every hair carefully razor cut, is Chili, a hard guy with a soft heart. John Travolta plays him as a Mafioso Cary Grant in a black leather coat, and the fit is perfect. Sexy, funny and completely charming, Travolta gives a splendid, old-fashioned star performance that pushes the picture to a level that would not have been possible without him.

Chili gets to L.A. via Las Vegas, where he went looking for a nervous Miami dry cleaner in hock to the mob who supposedly died in a plane crash. The dry cleaner, however, turns out to be alive enough to be spending his way through the $300,000 he scammed from the insurance company.

As a favor to a Vegas pal, Chili also pays a visit to a producer named Harry Zimm (Gene Hackman) who owes money to a casino. Though Harry's credits are of the "Slime Creature" variety, Chili has heard of them and, almost as a lark, pitches the dry cleaner story as a major motion picture. Harry is interested, but the B-picture scream queen (Rene Russo) in whose house Harry is crashing is not amused—though we can tell she finds Chili kind of cute.

The longer Chili stays in L.A., the more complicated things become. Harry has his hands full with nasty Bo Catlett (Delroy Lindo), who runs both drugs and a limo service and, yes, is also eager to move into producing. For his part, Chili has to deal with a surly Miami associate, Ray (Bones) Barboni (Dennis Farina). And everyone has to cope with Martin Weir (Danny DeVito), the hottest actor in Hollywood off his starring role in "Napoleon," the man with the power to turn everyone's movie dreams into gold.

This is the briefest outline of a pleasantly complex criminal confection that Sonnenfeld and Frank keep moving at an amusing pace. Though the entire cast (including unbilled cameos by Bette Midler and Harvey Keitel) contributes, Travolta is the man who keeps this souffle from collapsing. Watching him charm his way through continual difficulties, it's hard to believe that the movie business all but ignored him for years and that he himself turned down this dream assignment twice before "Pulp Fiction's" Quentin Tarantino, the godfather of the actor's current rebirth, convinced him to do it.

Elmore Leonard's novels and short stories have been made into numerous films, but "Get Shorty" comes the closest to re-creating his casual yet dazzling verbal style, characterized by sentences that surprise you and dialogue that knows its way around. And the film also does a good job with the book's gentle digs at the inane way the movie business tends to function.

Less successful are the film's new twists, including a visiting drug lord subplot that doesn't contribute anything and the addition of a more conventional ending, the book being so lacking in one it even jokes about its lapse. Unlike Chili, "Get Shorty" is not going to knock anybody out, but in the category of amiable diversions it's awfully tough to improve on.

NEW YORK, 10/23/95, p. 54, David Denby

In *Get Shorty*, a movie of inspired chat, there are many voices talking, but we hear only one voice—that of Elmore Leonard, the language-obsessed crime novelist whose 1990 book serves as the basis for the movie. Leonard's grip on the vernacular is so profound that you come out of *Get Shorty* cursing a blue streak, just like the characters (I advise you not to take your 12-year-old son to it, which is what I did). Leonard recognizes that the world is corrupt and everyone is out for himself; his dialogue, for all its threat and menace, is essentially satirical. *Get Shorty*, which was adapted by screenwriter Scott Frank and directed by Barry Sonnenfeld (*The Addams Family*), preserves a splendid Leonardian joke—that the ways of gangsters and of Hollywood players are essentially the same. The movie is set in the kind of high-sleaze sub-world that in real life financed Coppola's *The Cotton Club*, a world that produced a corpse as well as a bad movie. Chili Palmer (John Travolta), a Miami loan shark, coolly confident, with dominating eyes, goes to Los Angeles to collect a debt; falls in with producers and actors, including the great, diminutive movie star Martin Weir (Danny DeVito); and becomes obsessed with the movie business. Chili can certainly talk and swagger, and he has access to money. That makes him a producer. What *else* is required? In the movie business, ideas are meaningless until they become pitches. The movie that then gets made is almost a footnote to the pitch meeting.

Chili winds up producing a true story, a series of events still unfolding as he makes his way about town. This "story" is a peculiar affair involving a poor schmuck of a dry-cleaning-store owner (David Paymer) who runs away from Miami with some insurance money; a seriously sunburned Miami gangster (Dennis Farina) who thinks the money belongs to him; and some more gangsters, from Colombia and Los Angeles, pursuing money from a botched drug sale that is parked in a Los Angeles airport locker. This story keeps happening in the background of *Get Shorty*. The hoods show up and rip each other off; Chili even intervenes a few times and moves "the plot" along. At a certain point, the movie we're watching merges into the movie Chili wants to make.

Not unlike *Smoke, Get Shorty* is a playful work about stories and the way that storytelling affects life—a reflexive postmodern game, but lightly done, without the clunky ambitions that destroyed *The Last Action Hero*. Sonnenfeld works in a racy, fluent, light-fingered style, all gleaming surface and decor, but he's not slick, exactly. He takes his time; he's less interested in momentum and tension than in personality and language. At the risk of doldrums (and there are a few), he lets people talk, sometimes cutting back and forth between conversations going on simultaneously. *Get Shorty* isn't a gangster film; it's a movie about gangsterish people who make movies. The violence, when it comes, is staged in semi-slapstick style. The real violence is conversational, the pleasures of talking in all its more aggressive varieties—conning, intimidating, pitching, turning the tables.

Sixty years ago, the actor George Raft imitated the mannerisms and moves of actual gangsters, and it was said that gangsters in turn imitated Raft. Warren Beatty later added another mirror: In *Bugsy*, he was a movie star playing a gangster, Bugsy Siegel, who was himself, in his own mind, a movie star. In John Travolta's performance in *Get Shorty*, the distinction between gangster and actor has vanished altogether. Recovering his ripe-handsomeness at the age of 41, Travolta wears dark clothes, and he has swept-back dark hair and a broad smile. He's a low-key, suavely amusing thug, intimidating but usually not violent (he doesn't have to be). In all, this is Travolta's wittiest and most glamorous performance. The extra weight, which he carries well (the dark clothes help conceal it), becomes an added element in his new, substantial presence, and he's so charming that we simply accept that this sleek-looking shylock carries off everything he tries. "Look at me," he says to everyone, and they do, unable to look away. He's got the eyes. Eyes, of course, are what make a movie star, and when Chili, trying to collect a debt for someone else, breaks into the house of the junk-movie producer Harry Zimm (Gene Hackman), Harry, who has been awakened from a drunken sleep, thinks Chili is an actor looking for a role.

The two men form a partnership to produce movies, and with the help of an aging B-movie starlet (Rene Russo), who knows which side her bread is buttered on, they pursue the great Martin Weir. In the best scene of the movie, Chili challenges Weir to use his eyes the way *he* does, to look at someone as if he were saying, "You're mine, asshole." DeVito, playing this self-serious kingpin star (Dustin Hoffman?), goes a through a series of scowls and squints, and before long, he's hooked. Chili is just teasing him, mastering him, but Martin thinks it's a pitch, the greatest pitch of all time: He's already playing a loan shark, and he hasn't even heard the story yet! A movie deal is concluded right there. I don't know if movies happen that way, but it's a very satisfying little myth of macho vanity, and DeVito, quiet and meditative, earnest as a priest, shows sides of thoughtfulness and vulnerability he's never shown before.

Get Shorty is vivacious and volubly funny, and both the Miami and Los Angeles sections look great. That crack-voiced ruffian Farina gives a wonderful performance as a Miami gangster whose brains have been bleached by too much sun, and the invaluable Delroy Lindo is on hand as a Los Angeles limo driver-gangster who thinks he's qualified to get into the movie business (and who's to say he isn't?). Yet *Get Shorty* is not quite a great movie: Sonnenfeld needed to bring his comedy a little closer to reality; he needed to scare us, to be a little more sober and not always such a nifty jokester. *Get Shorty* doesn't have much dramatic tension, and we feel a letdown when we realize the movie is just an entertaining conceit. But it has many pleasures. Once agin, Hollywood has offered itself as a juicy subject for satire. Its willingness to do so is one of the few redeeming things about the place.

NEW YORK POST, 10/20/95, p. 37, Michael Medved

"Rough business, this movie business. I may have to go back to loan-sharking, just to take a rest."

So says Chili Palmer (John Travolta) a low-level mob operative in Miami who's sent to California to collect on a gambling debt from struggling B-movie producer Harry Zimm (Gene Hackman).

Zimm, a shameless schlocky exploiter whose graying goatee signifies his imperishable aspirations as an "artist," is trying to put together the classiest project of his career. ("This time, no mutants or maniacs. This is gonna be my 'Driving Miss Daisy.'")

Chili decides to help him, in part because of his attraction to Karen Flores (Rene Russo), the glamorous, seen-it-all star of many of Harry's scream-fests, and in part because of his pure, boyish love of movies.

Unfortunately, other underworld types also attempt to get in on the act, including a drug-running entrepreneur in the limousine business (Delroy Lindo), and his hulking henchman, a former stuntman named Bear (James Gandolfini).

The success of the project that inspires all of them depends upon signing up the most acclaimed actor in Hollywood, the "Shorty" of the title (Danny DeVito), a temperamental genius who happens to be Karen's ex-husband and is just coming off the triumphant title role in the film "Napoleon."

DeVito is hilariously effective in his (ahem) small part, a character reportedly inspired by another notoriously mercurial and short actor, Dustin Hoffman.

In fact, "Shorty" is long on brilliant performances—suggesting that this incomparably accomplished cast makes California's real "Dream Team." (The movie is so deep in talent that no less than Bette Midler turns up in a very funny but altogether uncredited bit part).

Travolta stakes a strong claim to another Oscar nomination, creating a far richer, more intriguing character than he did in his somewhat overrated work in "Pulp Fiction."

His Chili is a mellow, soft-spoken, easy-going tough guy who projects a formidable edge of menace behind his bemused and sparkling gray eyes. Travolta swaggers through his role with a feline grace and jazzy self-assurance he hasn't equaled since "Saturday Night Fever."

In fact, the whole movie projects the same sort of easy, loose-limbed rhythm—and marks a triumph for director Barry Sonnenfeld, whose previous work (both "Addams Family" movies and the forgettable "For Love or Money") showed no hint of such subversive humor and insinuating charm.

The shaggy-dog plot, taken from Elmore Leonard's brilliant novel, may be hard to follow or remember, but the juicy characters and zingy dialogue are impossible to forget. "You think I go to see your movies, Harry " taunts Delroy Lindo's character. "I seen better film on my teeth."

You can see a much better film—and easily one of the year's most original and unexpected comedies—with the savory and sensational "Get Shorty."

NEWSDAY, 10/20/95, Part II/p. B2, Jack Mathews

Mystery writer Elmore Leonard has spent more time than he would care to remember in Hollywood, negotiating with agents and studio executives. And with his best-seller "Get Shorty," he let us know what he thinks of the place.

Leonard's view is not the usual vengeful satire, a much visited genre capped by Robert Altman's "The Player." Leonard sees Hollywood not as the habitat of sharks and soul-sucker's, but as a place where incompetence and desperation lead to a sort of creative gridlock, where a good, take-charge mob guy could come in and get the traffic moving.

Such a guy is Chili Palmer, one of Leonard's most memorable creations, and, thanks to a fabulous star turn by John Travolta, a soon-to-be classic film character.

In Barry Sonnenfeld's adaptation of "Get Shorty," Travolta lights up the screen in the classic sense of the phrase. It's a movie filled with wonderful characters and great performances—in fact, the most enjoyable film I've seen this year. But Travolta, his own confidence renewed by last year's "Pulp Fiction" and subsequent Oscar nomination, dominates the stage as few star's can.

Travolta's innate enthusiasm and affability have always been the great strengths of his characters, as far back as "Welcome Back, Kotter" and "Saturday Night Fever." They are even more appealing now, in middle age, when he's playing characters you'd expect to find filled with cynicism.

There is no cynical edge to Travolta, which may limit him elsewhere but makes him perfect for Chili, a cool Miami loan shark so adept at the art of leverage he can turn any situation into a career opportunity. Which is what he does when a collections job brings him to L.A. and he's bitten by the movie bug.

The story, with a crafty screenplay adaptation by Scott Frank ("Dead Again"), places Chili in the company of a hustling schlock-horror movie producer (Gene Hackman), a jaded actress (Rene Russo), her movie star ex-husband (Danny DeVito) and a local mob figure (Delroy Lindo), all connected by their interests in film careers. They are joined by Chili's Miami boss, Bones Barboni (Dennis Farina), who can't resist reaching for the stars himself.

The action is driven by illicit loot in a locker being watched by feds at L.A. International. The temptation to try to grab it, with a key that keeps changing hands, is heightened by its usefulness in getting a movie into production.

It's that sense of desperation again, and only Chili, cool incarnate, can handle the pressure. He's got a script that everyone loves—it happens to be the case he is currently working—and he knows how to move it along.

"Get Shorty" has enough plot to hold our interest, and it is one of those rare films with the perfect ending. However, its joys come through the characters and the actors, every one wonderful.

Hackman, whose comedy performances in "Young Frankenstein" and the "Superman" movies are often overlooked in his respected resumé of dramatic work, is hilarious as Harry Zimm, the prototypical Hollywood hustler, and he has a high time chewing the scenery and mocking every fool he's met.

DeVito has never been better cast than as Martin Weir, a superstar whose short stature is no obstacle as long as his performances in movies like "Napoleon" keep packing in audiences. In the film's best sequence, Weir gets an acting lesson in gangster demeanor from Chili; Travolta and DeVito interact with a sly knowingness that absolutely defines the tone of the picture. Russo may not have enough to do in this male world, but women can take solace in knowing her character is the smartest, and Farina is a riot as the comically evil Barboni.

NEWSWEEK, 10/23/95, p. 75, David Ansen

Hollywood has been in love with mobsters since the beginning of movies, but the other side of the equation—that mobsters are smitten with Hollywood—has seldom been considered. That is, until *Get Shorty*. It was novelist Elmore Leonard's inspired jest to set his 1990 crime novel in the balmy fishbowl that is the movie industry. Into this tank he drops two species of sharks—the predatory hustlers of show business and the carnivores of crime—and watches the results (part mating dance, part struggle for survival) with an amused grin. It's no contest. The Hollywood boys may flash pearlier teeth, but the hoods beat them at their own game. Reality bites deeper.

In director Barry Sonnenfeld and screenwriter Scott Frank's bouncy, immensely likable adaptation (which wisely retains Leonard's gift for lowlife gab) we follow Miami debt collector Chili Palmer (John Travolta) to L.A. A wiseguy with a passion for the movies, Chili muscles in on horror-film producer Harry Zimm (Gene Hackman), who owes the mob $150,000. First he threatens Zimm, then pitches him an idea for a movie—a story about a shylock tracking down a dry cleaner who's faked his own death and absconded with a bundle of mob money. The shylock, of course, is Chili, and the story is one we've been watching. But, as Zimm complains, it lacks a third act.

"Get Shorty" will supply that ending, and lots more, as Chili pursues his dual career as a debt collector and aspiring Hollywood producer. Without revealing too much of Leonard's clever plot, we should mention that it involves a star-struck drug dealer (Delroy Lindo) who wants to invest his profits into a Zimm production; Chili's mobster nemesis Ray (Bones) Barboni (a hilarious Dennis Farina), who thinks Chili is cheating him, and the towering (but short) Hollywood actor Martin Weir (Danny DeVito), whom Chili pursues to star in his project.

Chili's romance with Hollywood is surpassed only by Hollywood's infatuation with Chili. He has the one thing these self-obsessed artistes know they lack: authenticity. And they want a piece of it. Soon Weir is wearing a Chili-style jacket and driving the same van. Travolta makes it easy to see why this loan shark conquers Hollywood: with the piercing stare he uses to intimidate his prey and the charming smile that seduces everyone including Harry's girlfriend Karen (Rene Russo), Travolta turns his own star wattage on full blast. His innate sweetness sets the tone of this good-natured jape, which tweaks Hollywood foolishness without making a federal case of it. Sonnenfeld ("The Addams Family" movies) paints in bright, bold brush strokes, putting a cartoon outline around his characters. It's possible to imagine a different, grittier rendition of Leonard's tale, but why ask for the moon when you've got these stars?

SIGHT AND SOUND, 3/96, p. 42, John Wrathall

En route to Los Angeles on the trail of Leo Devoe, a dry cleaner who has faked his death and absconded owing money to the mob, Miami loanshark Chili Palmer picks up another assignment from a Las Vegas casino to collect the gambling debts of 'B' movie film producer Harry Zimm. After following Harry to the house of his sometime girlfriend and star Karen Flores, Chili breaks in, and ends up pitching Harry an idea for a movie about a loanshark who comes to LA on the trail of a man who faked his death. The only trouble with the story, Harry tells him, is that it doesn't have an ending.

At the airport the next day, gangster Bo Catlett picks up a suitcase of drugs from a Colombian courier, leaving $500,000 in a luggage locker as payment. When the courier, scared away by a DEA stakeout at the airport, comes to Catlett's home to get the money, Catlett kills him.

Meanwhile Chili decides to try his hand at film producing after Harry tells him about *Mr Lovejoy*, the hot script he is trying to develop, which he sees as a vehicle for Karen's ex-husband, movie star Martin Weir. But Harry also owes money to Catlett, who wants a share in the project, and Catlett is trying to pressure Harry and Chili into picking up the drug money from the staked-out luggage locker and turning it over to him.

Having collected from Leo, Chili visits Martin with Karen to sound him out on *Mr. Lovejoy*. Wondering what has happened to Chili, his Miami boss Ray 'Bones' arrives in LA and tracks down Harry, whom he beats up and frames for the shooting of one of Catlett's men. Out of hospital, Harry discovers that Chili has set up his own movie instead of *Mr Lovejoy* with Martin.

When the Colombians arrive to find out what happened to their courier, Catlett kidnaps Karen to try and pressure Chili into giving him the money he needs to pay them off. Chili takes the money to Catlett's house, where Catlett tries to kill him—but ends up falling to his own death from the terrace. Back at the hotel, Chili is surprised by Ray, who finds the key to the locker and assumes that this is where Leo's money is stashed. Ray goes to the airport and, as he opens the locker, we jump forward to the studio where a film is being made of Chili's story.

Though they might seem ideally suited for adaptation to the big screen, the crime novels of Elmore Leonard have, until now, spawned a sorry selection of films—*Stick, Glitz, 52 Pick-Up, Cat Chaser*—which have enjoyed neither critical nor commercial success. Leonard's more lasting contribution to cinema has come indirectly, via his influence on Quentin Tarantino. Tarantino's hallmarks—intricate yet accident-strewn plots, unheroic protagonists whose criminal ambitions never free them from more mundane concerns, split-second jumps from comedy to violence—can all be found in Leonard. It was a fitting tribute that Tarantino blew some of his *Pulp Fiction* earnings on the rights to a handful of his idol's works. It's equally fitting that the first mainstream studio attempt to emulate the Tarantino style (Danny DeVito, star and producer of *Get Shorty*, also executive produced *Pulp Fiction*) should return to Leonard as its source.

Get Shorty's other inheritance from *Pulp Fiction* is, of course, John Travolta, perfectly cast here as the movie-obsessed loanshark whose direct, almost innocent manner captivates Hollywood folk accustomed to more Byzantine dealmaking. ("I think you're a decent type of man even if you are a crook," Leo's 'widow' tells Chili early on, in case we don't get the message.) Overflowing with movie in-jokes, *Get Shorty* is certainly entertaining. Yet despite the richness of the subject matter (small-time mobster becomes Hollywood player) and the impressive cast (Gene Hackman, Rene Russo, Dennis Farina, Delroy Lindo, an unbilled Bette Midler) the end result is disappointingly trite. Leonard's characteristically roundabout plot, in which every action has an unforeseen consequence, seems contrived and inconsequential when compressed into Scott Frank's screen-play, while Chili's continual reference to old movies comes over as 'Tarantino Lite'—he knows the dialogue of *Touch of Evil* off by heart (especially Dietrich's lines "Isn't somebody going to come and take him away", and "He was some kind of a man ... what else can you say about people?"), and even with a gun to his head takes the trouble to lecture Catlett about the difference between *Rio Bravo* and *El Dorado*.

Barry Sonnenfeld first persuaded DeVito to buy the rights to the novel in 1992, so it's not his fault that in the meantime two other films have ploughed the same furrow with more trenchancy—*The Player* (with which *Get Shorty* also shares its film-within-a-film punchline) and, more tellingly, *Bullets Over Broadway*. As does Cheech in that latter film, Chili turns out to be a more genuine and less pretentious storyteller than the 'artists' he falls in with, while his creativity and his criminal life are inextricably intertwined. (Chili doesn't have an ending for the story he pitches until real life provides him with one when Ray 'Bones' tries to collect the money from the locker—the scene we see being shot for the film within the film.)

Where Sonnenfeld does fall short, however, is in matching Leonard's famously deadpan tone ("If it sounds like writing," the novelist once said, "I rewrite it"). Fresh from *The Addams Family* films, the director opts for a broad, farcical style which robs the story of any sense of danger, and reduces the deaths to throwaway jokes. Worse, with the commendable exception of Russo as Karen and Lindo as Catlett (who's almost as good here as he was in *Clockers*) Sonnenfeld allows the cast to camp it up. DeVito has always been a ham, but Hackman here gives his most trivial performance since Lex Luthor.

VILLAGE VOICE, 10/24/95, p. 71, J. Hoberman

John Travolta became a superstar, first on TV and then in the movies, playing a version of the late '50s-early '60s urban youth type variously known as a Greaser, a Hitter, and (in my neighborhood) a Rock. Rocks cultivated their pompadours and extorted your lunch money; they carried switchblades, copied homework, repeated grades, and flouted the Board of Ed dress code; they were reputed to shoot dope, steal cars, and fuck their girlfriends (known, in my junior high, as Skanks or Hoo-ahs).

The Rock was already a nostalgic figure when Travolta embodied Vinnie Barbarino on the mid-'70s sitcom *Welcome Back, Kotter*. Travolta's particular genius was to turn the strutting, inarticulate Greaser into a suave gentle man, if not a real pussycat. Travolta played the Hitter as closet Fred Astaire—menacing slit eyes transformed by a baby-faced smile. The actor abandoned this magic formula after *Grease* and only regained it, some 15 years in celebrity wilderness later, as *Pulp Fiction*'s affable hit man. *Get Shorty* is the inevitable follow-up.

A genial, intermittently sprightly hoodlum comedy, directed by Barry Sonnenfeld from the novel by Elmore "Dutch" Leonard, *Get Shorty* is calculatedly warmed by Travolta's beaming presence as Miami mob enforcer Chili Palmer. Collecting debts for his loan-shark bosses, Chili is the tough guy as psych-out artist and, indeed, Travolta's comeback enjoyment is contagious—implicitly bound up with the audience's own pleasurable identification. Far more than in Leonard's novel, the movie Chili is a movie fan. He even borders on movie geek; introduced as a hood who loves Jimmy Cagney flicks—and knows the dialogue from Orson Welles's *Touch of Evil*, he's not above referencing his interpreter's own career.

Its drama predicated on absurd, violent situations (a film-long vendetta is triggered by one gangster borrowing another's leather jacket) and enlivened by a variety of insane coincidences, cartoonish flashbacks, and free-floating riffs, *Get Shorty* is likable, if fashionably thin, From the ad campaign and the retro *Miami Vice* pink-and-turquoise credits through the reiterated James Brown riff that provides the basis of John Lurie's score through the fade-out gag, *Get Shorty*—presents itself as Tarantino lite. A few faces may be bludgeoned, punks shot point-blank, airplanes shown to crash—it's all cool! (As ostentatiously knowing as the movie is, the most inadvertently au courant reference is the attention given *Touch of Evil*. Hollywood might well ponder a movie about a rogue cop who makes his career framing suspects who are already guilty.)

Get Shorty's action shifts from Miami Beach to Brooklyn to Vegas, before settling comfortably down in Beverly Hills to satirize the rabid self-absorption of the indigenous species. The basic scenario is not unlike that of *Bullets Over Broadway*. ("What the fuck do you know about movies?" Chili's pal will wonder, "I don't think the producer has to know much," is his answer.) Sent to collect a debt from schlock producer Harry Zimm (Gene Hackman in turtleneck, gold chain, and ostentatiously capped teeth), the naturally gifted Chili winds up pitching him a boffo movie story. Welcome to L.A. *Get Shorty* is never more itself than when Zimm pads downstairs in the middle of the night to find an unknown hoodlum sitting on the living-room sofa watching Letterman and bursts out: "I thought you were an actor, for chris-sakes."

Well cast and entertainingly written, *Get Shorty* suffers mainly from Sonnenfeld's slow-footed direction. The editing is slack. The framing could be tighter. The premise, however, never falters. Among the movie's numerous ensuing complications is Zimm's prior involvement with tough-guy Bo (Delroy Lindo), another thug whose greatest desire is to break into pictures. The parallel to Chili's successful improvisation—making up, living out and casting his own movie—is the hilarious concentration with which *Get Shorty*'s elusive, elfin, eponymous object of desire, egomaniacal Hollywood star Martin Weir (Danny DeVito), assimilates Chili's performance into his own tough-guy persona.

In a more perfectly Dutch universe, DeVito and Travolta would have had each others parts. Sonnenfeld who directed both Addams Family chronicles, is more at home with broadly comic monsters: Bette Midler provides a welcome shot of manic energy, and as Chili's nemesis Bones, Dennis Farina stalks through the movie like a decomposing corpse. DeVito plays another sort of mummy, surrounded heroic busts and portraits of himself. Best is Hackman's Zimm—a '70s fossil dwelling in a musty Hollywood Boulevard office. Not only might the title of his *Slime Creatures* be taken as autobiographical when he rises from his hospital bed to take a meeting, he's a vision from Morticia's crypt.

Also reviewed in:
CHICAGO TRIBUNE, 10/20/95, Friday/p. C, Michael Wilmington
NATION, 12/4/95, p. 724, Stuart Klawans
NEW REPUBLIC, 11/13/95, p. 32, Stanley Kauffmann
NEW YORK TIMES, 10/20/95, p. C1, Janet Maslin
NEW YORKER, 10/23/95, p. 96, Terrence Rafferty
VARIETY, 10/9-15/95, p. 61, Todd McCarthy
WASHINGTON POST, 10/20/95, p. D1, Hal Hinson
WASHINGTON POST, 10/20/95, Weekend/p. 44, Desson Howe

GLASS SHIELD, THE

A Miramax Films release of CBY 2000 presentation of a Byrnes/Schroeder/Walker production. *Executive Producer:* Chet Walker. *Producer:* Tom Byrnes and Carolyn Schroeder. *Director:* Charles Burnett. *Screenplay:* Charles Burnett. *Based on the screennplay "One of Us" by:* Ned Welsh. *Director of Photography:* Elliot Davis. *Editor:* Curtis Clayton. *Music:* Stephen Taylor. *Sound:* Veda Campbell. *Production Designer:* Penny Barrett. *Art Director:* Joel Carter. *Costumes:* Gaye Burnett. *Running time:* 109 minutes. *MPAA Rating:* PG-13.

CAST: Michael Boatman (J.J.); Lori Petty (Deborah); Ice Cube (Teddy Woods); Michael Ironside (Baker); Richard Anderson (Massey); Bernie Casey (Locket); Elliott Gould (Greenspan); M. Emmet Walsh (Hal); Don Harvey (Bono); Sy Richardson (Mr. Taylor); Natalija Nogulich (Judge Helen Lewis).

LOS ANGELES TIMES, 6/2/95, Calendar/p. 2, Peter Rainer

Charles Burnett, the writer-director of "The Glass Shield," doesn't make movies like anybody else. And since his new film is a police drama, his uniqueness, at least initially, is doubly welcome.

He doesn't try to give us a big-screen TV cop movie; he doesn't jiggle his cameras and pour on the profanities and the blood. We're watching a small-scale, closed-in tale of moral outrage, and Burnett's core of intelligence keeps it from edging into a rant.

The problem is that Burnett, who had difficulties with his production company over the film's final cut, works in such large, broad strokes that the film becomes melodramatic and lifeless the more it tries to ram home its points of social injustice. Based loosely on real incidents involving John Eddie Johnson, the first minority officer in an all-white L.A. sheriff's office, the film follows J.J. (Michael Boatman) as he endures the racism, at first casual, then overt, of his fellow officers.

J.J. is potentially a great character. He has always wanted to be a cop and, for a while, he goes along with the lying in the department because he wants to be "one of them." He genuinely believes in cleaning up the streets, and when he falsely implicates a black kid (Ice Cube) in the murder of the wife of a white businessman (Elliott Gould), he believes he's working for a greater good.

J.J. is torn apart by his allegiance to a sheriff's office that is characterized as clearly racist and as willing to sacrifice him when the going gets rough. He feels like a traitor to the community that is clamoring for justice on another police brutality case involving an African American street kid who suspiciously expired in jail. When J.J. and fellow harassed officer Deborah (Lori Petty)—the department's only female trooper—try to turn the tables, they walk into a jungle of conspiracies.

Burnett, in films such as "To Sleep With Anger" and "Killer of Sheep," has constructed such densely packed emotional landscapes that "The Glass Shield," with its ringing declarations and cardboard villains, seems flat by comparison. The actors don't provide much shading; even J.J., conflicted as he is, doesn't resonate. He's in the movie in order to make the move from naive to wised-up, but his story seems more a demonstration than a drama. His sacrifice is too ringingly symbolic.

J.J.'s story is all too real but Burnett, by making virtually every white officer in the sheriff's department a cringing cur, makes it seem overscaled. (The curs are played by, among others, Michael Gregory, Richard Anderson and M. Emmet Walsh.) The corrupt cops in this film spend a lot of time talking out their plots; what's probably closer to the truth is that the kind of corruption that goes on here isn't discussed with hand-rubbing glee. The truly corrupt don't *need* to be told how to be corrupt—that's why they're favored in the first place.

Burnett keeps a tight control over the production, and it takes on the quality of an enveloping nightmare. It's a rigorous, angry piece of work, but it misses out on the psychological depths that have made Burnett's previous films among the glories of recent American independent moviemaking. He's fashioned a manifesto, and the suit doesn't quite fit him.

NEW YORK POST, 6/2/95, p. 50, Thelma Adams

Road to hell paved; see good intentions.

Charles Burnett had the best of intentions with his new cop drama, "The Glass Shield." More mainstream than the domestic dramas and comedies that made the writer/director's reputation—"To Sleep With Anger" and "Killer of Sheep"—his latest outing sticks close to his home turf, South Central Los Angeles.

Like the rest of Burnett's small but important body of work, "The Glass Shield" is a moral tale that peels away at racial, class and sexual differences in contemporary America. He humanizes ghetto life, focusing on working and middle-class heroes. Burnett resists sensationalizing violence; robberies and shootouts remain at the screen's margin.

In "The Glass Shield," Burnett departs from chamber studies of individuals and families rooted in the community. Instead, he focuses on an institution that plays a significant part in the life of the area without ever being integrated into it—the sheriff's department.

J.J. Johnson (the boyishly charming Michael Boatman, who made a splash as the mortician on "China Beach") has always wanted to be a policeman. When he finally gets his chance, the black rookie finds himself in a rogue sheriff station in South Central.

The agreeable, athletic, gently sexist young man genuinely wants to be a good cop. He rolls with the subtle and not-so-subtle racist comments aimed at him and struggles to fit in. Early in his career, he makes a moral misstep that has large repercussions: To back up a white fellow officer and convict a black murder suspect (Ice Cube), J.J. perjures himself on the witness stand.

J.J. soon becomes the man torn in the middle. Despite his efforts, he can't fit in with the rough-riding band of sheriffs led by villains Richard Anderson and Michael Ironside. The extent of their illegal activity—the cops provide the community with no more protection than a glass shield—gradually becomes clear as does their framing of the angry but innocent Ice Cube.

J.J. bands with another uniformed outsider, Deborah Fields ("Tank Girl" Lori Petty), to purge the department. His identification with the cops is so complete, what it takes him a while to get over his own prejudice against the woman who walks softly and carries a big stick.

In a subplot, Burnett opens a window on J.J.'s family life. His younger brother has wed recently and his stable, middle-class parents are pressuring the rookie to marry his devoted but not uncritical girlfriend. The family drama might have been more developed in earlier versions, but it's sketchy here. It should either yield emotional intensity, or be deleted.

Burnett seems to be clear overall on what he wants to say in this movie—he places responsibility solidly at the door of the individual and not the system—but incapable of dramatizing the issues. "The Glass Shield" lacks the smooth veneer and assured storytelling of "To Sleep With Anger" and the rough, raw energy of "My Brother's Wedding."

Burnett remains an important director to watch, but this time around he has tried to shoehorn his vision into a police thriller devoid of thrills, satisfying neither mainstream audiences nor die-hard fans.

NEWSDAY, 6/2/95, Part II/p. B2, Gene Seymour

The comic book panels of police chases and shoot-'em-ups flashing within the opening credits of "The Glass Shield" hint at the junk-culture notions fueling the soon-to-be thwarted dreams of the film's rookie-cop protagonist, J.J. Johnson (Michael Boatman). They also show the kind of hackneyed, two-dimensional crime melodrama whose garish surface elements are duplicated by writer-director Charles Burnett.

But it soon becomes clear that while Burnett wants the, film to *look* like a routine tale of crooked cops; and rapid-fire injustice, he wants complexity to insinuate its way into the pulp archetypes the way menace sneaked into the working-class family depicted in his seminal 1990 film, "To Sleep With Anger."

For the most part, he succeeds—though the suspicion you're watching a made-for-TV movie isn't eased by the presence of such tube stalwarts as Boatman, Richard Anderson and Linden Chiles. Still, they, along with the rest of a strong cast, show big-league chops in this riveting saga.

Boatman's Johnson starts out as the eagerest of beavers as he joins an all-white sheriff's division in L.A. Yet his bucolic, Eddie Attaboy patina does little to endear him to his fellow officers, most of whom look like mean clones of Tom Selleck. The only collegue who bothers to treat him as an equal is Deputy Deborah Fields (Lori Petty), who, as the unit's only woman, receives the same gruff condescension as Johnson from their alleged superior (Anderson), who's been presiding over a cesspool of corruption and cover-up. Fields knows this, but can't do anything about it.

Johnson so wants to prove himself to these slugs-with-badges he's even willing to lie on another cop's behalf in the trial of Teddy Woods (Ice Cube), who was stopped at a gas station by the white cop on "suspicion" (i.e., being black) and then falsely charged with the murder of a white woman whose husband (Elliott Gould) claims, Charles Stuart-like, that a black man was the culprit.

Soon, Johnson, with nudging from Fields and Woods' powerhouse lawyer (Bernie Casey), begins to figure out that Woods isn't the first African-American to get railroaded—or worse—by his fellow officers, around whom both he and Fields start to feel less safe. Burnett leaves out much of the gratuitous violence and excoriating language one expects from gritty crime movies and replaces it with tension that, while beautifully modulated, loses nothing in sheer momentum or pure grip.

What's even more impressive is Burnett's free-flowing humanism, whose impact isn't apparent until after the movie is over. Only then do you realize you've just seen a cop movie whose wronged victim (Woods) isn't always sympathetic, whose bad guys don't entirely lack humanity and whose hero deserves much of the bad stuff that happens to him at the end. I've got problems with the *very* ending—which, one hears, was changed by the film's distributors from a less hopeful, but more logical conclusion. But it doesn't soften the overall impact of what may well be the only summer movie around that doesn't put your mind on cruise control.

VILLAGE VOICE, 6/6/95, p. 47, Georgia Brown

Charles Burnett is so original he can make an LAPD noir without using either the F-word or the N-word. Well, almost. Although the N-word is never uttered in *The Glass Shield*, at one point we see it scrawled across a station house mirror into which the precinct's only African American must search for his face. Burnett—MacArthur recipient, iconoclast, one of the most poetic filmmakers of our time—believes such words shouldn't be said and he won't. Meditate on this, Quentin T. and F. Lee Bailey.

Language aside, *The Glass Shield* in its eerie, cartoony, deep-hued beauty is unlike any contemporary cop movie you've seen. Its stylized underwater look sometimes resembles those color-saturated crime recreations in Errol Morris's *The Thin Blue Line*, and there are more venetian blinds here than in Sternberg, Sirk, and Fassbinder combined. Light slides in like slices of stained glass.

I first saw *The Glass Shield* in the Cannes marketplace a year ago, at the *Pulp Fiction* hour, and, like Alex Cox's *Highway Patrolman* three years before, it stayed with me long after *beeg* competition movies had melted into Mediterranean mist. In *The Glass Shield*, nobody shoots anybody point-blank, no wounds open up like bougainvillea, there're no slurpy kisses—no sex scenes at all. A murder takes place, but we come upon the victim's body, as in the old movies, slumped in her car seat. She's not a blond in a negligee but a middleaged woman in a *shmatte*. It's to the old movies Burnett has turned, albeit adding a pop, comic-book glaze.

J.J. Johnson (the impressive Michael Boatman) is a rookie cop as wide-eyed and fresh-faced as a child. No chips on these shoulders. J.J. seems to have emerged from some conflict-free bubble. When a cop caustically shoos him from the precinct's officers-only parking, J.J. grins eagerly and shows his badge as if the fellow's acid tonalities have nothing to do with the color of J.J.'s, and, by contrast, the other cop's skin. When one veteran refuses to shake his hand in welcome, J.J. looks puzzled, not bitter. The only one to greet him warmly is fellow outsider, Deputy Debbie (Lori Petty), not openly female but Jewish.

J.J. is mocked for his grammar and spelling ("What did I spell wrong?" "Sepulveda!", barks the supervisor, referring to the boulevard), harassed just for being there. His clear-eyed honesty interferes with business as usual. Two old-timers (played by M. Emmet Walsh and Richard Anderson, who bears more than a passing resemblance to LAPD detective Phillip Vanatter), aided by the junior officers, are involved in various shady matters.

Burnett doesn't seem interested in clarifying the nature of these deals. Even the main event, with a dazed Elliott Gould playing the nefarious Mr. Greenspan, left me confused. What's clear is that J.J. is willing to lie on the stand to back up a fellow officer. Initially, this cop stops Teddy Woods (a low-key Ice Cube) because, guess what, he's black; finding a gun in the car, he brings Teddy into the precinct where he's framed for murdering Mrs. Greenspan. Being a credulous fellow, J.J. assumes he's doing the world a favor by getting scum like Teddy off the streets.

The precinct is not merely corrupt but, to the last white man, hateful. Outside in the community, good people like J.J.'s father, his fiancée and an activist pastor try to get J.J. to see the light. A bluff, Johnnie Cochran-type defender (Bernie Casey) takes Teddy Woods's case and, in the process, exposes J.J.'s perjury. Although *The Glass Shield* wrapped way before the O.J. thing, it lays out a frame-up much like the one conjured by Simpson's defense team.

Burnett's original ending, the one I saw at Cannes, was shocking, bleak, and terribly lonely. It showed a black man crying. The new, softer version—reshot for Miramax distribution—has the tears taken out but is still powerful. This one has comfort but no joy.

Also reviewed in:
CHICAGO TRIBUNE, 6/2/95, Friday/p. H, Michael Wilmington
NATION, 7/10/95, p. 68, Stuart Klawans
NEW YORK TIMES, 6/2/95, p. C4, Caryn James
NEW YORKER, 6/12/95, p. 109, Terrence Rafferty
VARIETY, 5/30-6/5/94, p. 44, Todd McCarthy
WASHINGTON POST, 6/2/95, p. D1, Hal Hinson

GOLD DIGGERS: THE SECRET OF BEAR MOUNTAIN

A Universal Pictures release of a Bregman/Deyhle production. *Executive Producer:* Louis A. Stroller. *Producer:* Martin Bregman, Rolf Deyhle, and Michael S. Bregman. *Director:* Kevin James Dobson. *Screenplay:* Barry Glasser. *Director of Photography:* Ross Berryman. *Editor:* Stephen W. Butler. *Music:* Joel McNeely. *Music Editor:* Michael T. Ryan. *Sound:* Ralph Parker. *Sound Editor:* William Hopper, William Jacobs, and Charles Maynes. *Casting:* Mary Gail Artz and Barbara Cohen. *Production Designer:* Michael Bolton. *Art Director:* Eric A. Fraser. *Set Decorator:* Elizabeth Wilcox. *Set Dresser:* Patrick Kearns. *Special Effects:* Mike Vezina. *Costumes:* Mary McLeod. *Make-up:* Connie Parker. *Stunt Coordinator:* Betty Thomas. *Running time:* 92 minutes. *MPAA Rating:* PG.

CAST: Christina Ricci (Beth Easton); Anna Chlumsky (Jody Salerno); Polly Draper (Kate Easton); Brian Kerwin (Matt Hollinger); Diana Scarwid (Lynette Salerno); David Keith (Ray Karnisak); Gillian Barber (Grace Briggs); Ashleigh Aston Moore (Tracy Briggs); Jewel Staite (Samantha); Amy Kirk (Molly Morgan); Dwight McFee (Sgt. Weller); Andrew Wheeler (Hank); Roger R. Cross (Paramedic); Kimberley Warnat (Girl); Jesse Moss (Adam); Scott Augustine (Doug); Steve Makaj (Deputy Ted); Betty Phillips (Mysterioius Woman); Jay Brazeau (Everett Graham); Dustin Brooks and Philip Josef (Fight Boys); Carren Learning (Voice of Adult Beth).

LOS ANGELES TIMES, 11/3/95, Calendar/p. 4, Kevin Thomas

At the beginning of "Gold Diggers: The Secret of Bear Mountain" a charming yet substantial adventure movie aimed at adolescent girls—13-year-old Beth (Christina Ricci), arriving in a picture-book Oregon village nestled in the most spectacularly beautiful mountain setting imaginable, asks petulantly, "Where's the mall?"

Fearing the prospect of a boring summer, Beth, a deep-dyed L.A. girl is completely oblivious to the magnificence of her surroundings. Never fear, for very swiftly she discovers such excitement that her very life is in danger. What happens is that she strikes up a friendship with the town's rebellious outcast, Jody (Anna Chlumsky), who tells her of a legend concerning an Irish immigrant lass, disguised as a boy, who discovers gold in nearby Bear Mountain—and who may have survived a tunnel cave-in that killed the rest of the miners long, long ago. Jody is convinced that there's still gold in them thar hills.

Writer Barry Glasser hits just the right note, creating a lively Nancy Drew-style entertainment for girls on the threshold of womanhood yet giving them adult respect. There's a serious subplot in which the source of the self-reliant Jody's seeming acts of defiance are a response to the apparent fact that she and her alcoholic mother (Diana Scarwid) are at the mercy of her mother's unemployed boyfriend (David Keith), an attractive good ol' boy on the surface but physically abusive in private. Glasser shrewdly keeps us guessing at the truth of the situation while making the larger point that young people can have a very hard time getting adults to investigate such a matter let alone believe them.

Kevin James Dobson's direction matches the judiciousness of Glasser's script, resulting in an intelligent entertainment enlivened with first-rate performances all around, including a nicely drawn portrait by Polly Draper of Beth's mother, a recent widow caught in the dilemma of how far to trust her daughter in her new friendship with the unpredictable and widely shunned Jody. Cinematographer Ross Berryman captures the grandeur of the film's setting, but at times Joel McNeely's grandiose score threatens to overwhelm this unpretentious picture. It's a testament to the film's sturdiness that it survives McNeely's unintended efforts to drown it.

NEW YORK POST, 11/3/95, p. 41, Michael Medved

Two whining, self-conscious young actresses; cheesy special effects; an incomparably insipid plot; and an out-of-left-field ending as annoying as anything you'll see this year—what possible excuse could there be for a major studio to release such bilge?

The producers of the god-awful "Gold Diggers" would no doubt defend it as an example of "family entertainment," an old-fashioned adventure story designed to appeal to children. But if this is the excuse for this film's existence, then how can they justify inserting a frightening subplot involving alcoholism and brutal abuse? Despite its odd intentions, the film fails on every level: It's much too inane and inept for adults, while it's far too dark and disturbing for kids.

This misguided mess begins harmlessly enough, with lots of attractive Pacific Northwest scenery (with British Columbia standing in for the state of Washington), as the 13-year-old main character, a sophisticated L.A. girl played by Christina Ricci of "The Addams Family" and "Casper," moved to a picturesque small town with her recently widowed mother (Polly Draper).

She quickly makes friends with a rebellious tomboy (Anna Chlumsky of "My Girl"), a social outcast who divides her time between stealing from her school and wandering in the woods. It turns out that Chlumsky is obsessed with a local legend about a fortune of gold buried deep within Bear Mountain. By carefully reading an out-of-print biography of a 19th century miner girl, she's convinced she can find her way to the treasure.

Unfortunately, her single mother (Diana Scarwid) tolerates a violent, drunken boyfriend (played a much-too-menacing, David Keith) who's determined to bully Chlumsky into revealing her secrets. The result is a series of endless chase scenes through tacky, papier-mache mountain caves that look considerably less convincing than the caverns at Tom Sawyer's island at Disneyland.

There's also a scene where Ricci finds her leg crushed under a pathetically staged avalanche; though she's trapped under a ton of rocks for four hours, with the water level steadily rising to her nose, she eventually gets up and walks away with no ill effects.

Both Ricci and Chlumsky display glimmers of star quality, but their acting here is absolutely appalling; they seem to be trying to upstage each other in nearly all the scenes they share and their overdone efforts to "emote" are often painful to watch. Ricci comes across as especially uncomfortable and unconvincing. In fact, she seems far less natural than she did behind her heavy makeup for the Addams Family movies.

It's easy to sympathize with the apparent motivation behind this project—to create a rare adventure story in which two resourceful female protagonists search for hidden treasure in the spirit of an affirmative action answer to "The Hardy Boy's."

It's only a shame that the lame production values and the graphic depictions of abuse in a pathetic attempt at "social relevance" altogether undermine the sense of fun. The teen-age heroines may be digging for precious minerals, but the frustrated moviegoers will get only fool's gold.

Also reviewed in:
CHICAGO TRIBUNE, 11/3/95, Friday/p. G, John Petrakis
NEW YORK TIMES, 11/3/95, p. C12, Stephen Holden
VARIETY, 10/30-11/5/95, p. 72, Leonard Klady
WASHINGTON POST, 11/4/95, p. C3, Hal Hinson

GOLDENEYE

A United Artists release of an Albert R. Broccoli presentation. *Executive Producer:* Tom Pevsner. *Producer:* Michael G. Wilson and Barbara Broccoli. *Director:* Martin Campbell. *Screenplay:* Jeffrey Caine and Bruce Feirstein. *Story:* Michael France. *Director of Photography:* Phil Meheux. *Editor:* Terry Rawlings. *Music:* Eric Serra. *Music Editor:* Bob Hathaway. *Sound:* David John. *Sound Editor:* Jim Shields. *Casting:* Debbie McWilliams. *Production Designer:* Peter Lamont. *Art Director:* Neil Lamont. *Set Decorator:* Michael Ford. *Special Effects:* Chris Corbould. *Miniature Effects:* Derek Meddings. *Costumes:* Lindy Hemming. *Make-up:* Linda Devetta. *Stunt Coordinator:* Simon Crane. *Running time:* 130 minutes. *MPAA Rating:* PG-13.

CAST: Pierce Brosnan (James Bond); Sean Bean (Alec Trevelyan); Izabella Scorupco (Natalya Simonova); Famke Janssen (Xenia Onatopp); Joe Don Baker (Jack Wade); Judi Dench (M);

Robbie Coltrane (Valentin Zukovsky); Tcheky Karyo (Dimitri Mishkin); Gottfried John (General Ourumov); Alan Cumming (Boris Grishenko); Desmond Llewelyn (Q); Samantha Bond (Moneypenny); Michael Kitchen (Bill Tanner); Serena Gordon (Caroline); Simon Kunz (Severnaya Duty Officer); Pavel Douglas (French Warship Captain); Olivier Lajous (French Warship Officer); Billy J. Mitchell (Admiral Chuck Farrel); Constantine Gregory (Computer Store Manager); Minnie Driver (Irina); Michelle Arthur (Anna); Ravil Isyanov (MIG Pilot); Vladimir Milanovich (Croupier); Trevor Byfield (Train Driver); Peter Majer (Valentin's Bodyguard).

FILMS IN REVIEW, 1-2/96, p. 63, Victoria Alexander

Disregard *GoldenEye*'s widely quoted remark by James Bond's new female boss "M" that he's "nothing but a sexist, misogynist dinosaur." He's really a "Destroyer of Cities"—that city being St. Petersburg, Russia. Immediately before the collapse of the Soviet Union, I spent ten days in St. Petersburg. It is a truly gorgeous city cluttered with imperial palaces, thanks to the ruthless conduct of its post-modern monarchies. Bond (Pierce Brosnan) spends a scant few hours in St. Petersburg before commandeering a Russian tank and causing major property damage. A tank can be quite a nasty piece of machinery, and it's a credit to *GoldenEye*'s production that the wholesale destruction looked startlingly realistic.

With *GoldenEye*, Brosnan takes his rightful place in the pantheon of movie stardom. Through the grace of some unknown god, he was destined to play James Bond. Like a mythological Greek warrior, Brosnan's quest has been long, treacherous and the path scattered with rumored usurpers to the prize. Brosnan confidently steps forward and takes what always belonged to him after Roger Moore abdicated (or was pushed). Brosnan doesn't have Sean Connery's majestic bearing—yet. But he does resurrect James Bond, liberating him from Moore's interpretation as a fleshy buffoon and Timothy Dalton's overworked, tired, put-upon secret agent. Now, thankfully, we return to a stylized and demonized 007. This Bond is fearless, cruel, and an unrepentive lover of women. It also gives us the mandatory Bond special effects, outrageous stunts, pyrotechnics, plane/train/car wrecks, and wide scale killings.

The Bond women also return with ferocious delight. Famke Janssen plays Bond's female nemesis and requisite orgiastic mass murderer. Izabella Scorupco is Bond's beautiful good-girl Russian love interest. But both these women are tough cookies. The film moves at a hyper-acccelerated pace. It's the fastest, tightest, coolest Bond since Connery stopped playing baccarat. No one eats, sleeps, or gets sensitive.

Brosnan's lithe appearance on screen suggests an approachability, until the camera gets close. He's beautiful in a pensive, disturbing way. You don't expect someone so beautiful to have been tarnished by life in ugly little ways, but Brosnan looks like he's seen it all early on and it's damaged him. When conveyed subliminally and skillfully, this "unjustly punished beauty" is mesmerizing. It's as if we now realize James Bond came from a poverty-stricken, abusive, alcoholic home. He didn't overcome his background, he suppressed it. Brosnan telegraphs this backstory with his sensual face. You can actually watch him use his facial muscles to convey thoughts! This certain "thing" makes icons out of stars. Furthermore, while this Bond's confidence is the only sexual prowess we see (Connery's women always moaned "Oh, James" afterwards), Brosnan delivers on one of the toughest leading man minefields—he knows how to kiss.

LOS ANGELES TIMES, 11/17/95, Calendar/p. 1, Kenneth Turan

Like men of a certain age who persist in wearing tiny ponytails, "GoldenEye," the latest James bond film, is a middle-aged entity anxious to appear trendy at all costs. A mildly successful attempt at updating a relic, its appeal depends greatly on an audience's willingness to go along for a familiar ride.

"GoldenEye" is the 17th Agent 007 film in a series that dates back to "Dr. No" in 1962, and while Bond is no rival to either Charlie Chan or Sherlock Holmes in the numbers department, that span is long enough for certain traditions to have developed. And, like conscientious pilgrims, the makers of "GoldenEye" have ensured that the film stops at all the stations of the cross of this particular religion.

So Bond fans will be relieved to know that Britain's preeminent secret agent still drives an Aston Martin DB5 (as well as a new BMW Z3) and fiddles with gadgets like a ballpoint pen that becomes a grenade, all courtesy of the venerable Q, played by Desmond Llewelyn, who's had the part for more than 30 years. And 007 is still a font of glib remarks and pithy comebacks who delights in trading ribald ripostes like "one rises to the occasion" with an assortment of eye-catching women.

Pierce Brosnan, the fifth actor to play Bond (don't forget George Lazenby), won't replace Sean Connery in anyone's mind, but that is really asking too much. Brosnan does have the right kind of self-confident swagger and he bears up as well as possible under the film's determination to bring Bond into a world where his unrepentant sexism is not quite as charming as it may once have seemed.

So while Bond is allowed to leer at villainess Xenia Onatopp (Famke Janssen) and captivate heroine Natalya Simonova (Izabella Scorupco), he is taunted with accusations of sexual harassment and has to put up with a tongue-lashing by M (tartly played by Judi Dench) for being "a sexist, misogynist dinosaur." It's all more creaky than convincing, like a homework assignment no one was particularly eager to carry out.

One traditional Bond element that retains its appeal is the impressive pre-title sequence. This one involves what may be the world's longest bungee jump (nimbly executed by stuntman Wayne Michaels), a stunning 750-foot leap off the top of a dam that gets Bond into position to take on a chemical weapons plant in the old USSR.

Mostly, however, "GoldenEye" takes place in the new Russia, where criminal mafias have more power than the enfeebled state. In fact Onatopp, a feisty operative who finds violence sexually exciting, works for Janus, a potent crime syndicate that is a major player among the world's arms dealers.

When Janus manages to get its hands on a top-secret helicopter and activate GoldenEye, a terrifying weapon based in outer space, Bond is called into action once again by a reluctant M. Aided by Simonova, much too attractive to have died with everyone else in a GoldenEye attack, Bond takes on turncoat Russian generals, renegade Cossacks and all manner of threats to the world's peace and security.

Working from a shaky script by Jeffrey Caine and Bruce Feirstein that is, if anything, overloaded with plot turns, director Martin Campbell has concentrated his attention on keeping the explosions coming at a regular clip. Not much time is allowed to pass without people fleeing from either a plane, train or car crash—the showier the better.

Though "GoldenEye" is an acceptable Bond picture, it's a reasonable facsimile more than any kind of original, and it's hard not to feel a certain weariness while watching it unfold. Despite Brosnan's smile and amusing touches like Joe Don Baker's CIA operative calling Bond "Jimmy" and "Jimbo," the gap between then and now makes this one Bond picture that isn't as light on its feet as its protagonist.

NEW YORK, 11/27/95, p. 78, David Denby

I went to see *GoldenEye*, the new Bond, when I was dead tired, and it suited me just fine. This is a perfectly silly and perfectly pleasant entertainment. Pierce Brosnan, handsome in a slightly fatuous way, has finally found something to do with himself—put on a tuxedo and run across catwalks. Brosnan, a slender man, is a lightweight Bond in every sense, without menace, but his dimpling smile can pass for irony. It's amusing to see Bond physically overmatched by a woman—nearly crushed between the muscular thighs of Famke Janssen, the Dutch amazon who plays Xenia Onatopp, a Russian criminal with tigerish bedroom appetites. The director Martin Campbell, born in New Zealand, has the right feeling for the comedy of exaggeration. Campbell had the audience roaring with appreciation right at the beginning, when Brosnan falls off a mountaintop and skydives right into a little propeller plane that has lost its pilot and appears headed for the bottom of a canyon. Campbell is so good with large spaces, he even gets a good joke out of the tired subject of bungee-jumping. The Bond franchise shows every sign of continuing indefinitely.

NEW YORK POST, 11/17/95, p. 43, Thelma Adams

Does TV's former Bond-lite, Remington Steele, spit in the "GoldenEye" or make it sparkle?

A little group therapy first: Some things can't be changed and we have to let them go. No one will ever play James Bond better than Sean Connery. But can Pierce Brosnan rescue the franchise from the Roger Moore-Timothy Dalton-George Lazenby years?

Brosnan's Bond walks the walk and talks the talk. He plays the role straight, without self-irony. He looks smart in his Brioni tux. He shoots a gun and a sarcastic comment at the same time. He can handle a BMW and a woman at high speeds. And he swills his shaken-not-stirred martinis without slurring a word, shirking a double-entendre or missing a shot.

Brosnan also sails through the difficult swimsuit competition. He can display a forest of chest hair, keep his posture straight in skimpy briefs and still pull his Walther pistol out of a rolled towel and not look silly. Now that's acting.

The new Bond slips a little in the self-confidence arena. Brosnan rates high as a lady killer, but he's less believable as a cold-blooded assassin. More comfortable with a quip than a poisoned quill, Brosnan could take lessons from turncoat agent 006, played with dead menace—and sexy good looks—by Sean Bean ("Patriot Games").

In this post-Cold War clash between Her Majesty's Secret Service and a coterie of bad Russians (who have seized control of the GoldenEye, a gadget capable of zapping all electrical circuits and reducing London to its knees) Brosnan's greatest skill is in being the perfect host.

Brosnan bonds all the traditional elements of the good, basic Bond flick. "GoldenEye" showcases one of the best Bond babes ever, Russian minx Xenia Onatopp (Famke Janssen), who crushes her victims during sex with vise-like thighs.

As love interest Natalya Simonova, Swedish model Izabella Scorupco is smarter than your average Bondette, but she doesn't let that stop her. She braves the Russian winter in a short skating skirt and heels, and she has mastered the pitiful piquant scream of the distressed damsel: "Jaaaames."

There is an unforgettable stunt with an airplane, a motorcycle and a cliff. The locations are far-flung, from Monaco to St. Petersberg to Puerto Rico. The cheesy credits with dancing girls mixing it up in an orange soup with various phallic symbols are suitably retro, while Tina Turner belts out the instant Top 40 title song written by Bono and the Edge.

As directed by Martin Campbell ("No Escape") and written by Jeffrey Caine and Bruce Feirstein, Bond is an unreconstructed male. But this old-schooler now has to take orders from Dame Judi Dench as M.

But Bond is a fantasy hero, not a New Age role model. We don't want him tied to apron strings or last year's girl any more than we want him to drive last year's Chevy.

When we go to a boys-with-toys movie, we want boys with toys. When we go to a Bond movie, we want a hero who takes himself seriously, even if he raises his tailored eyebrows at the world around him. In "GoldenEye," Bond is back.

NEWSDAY, 11/17/95, Part II/p. B3, Jack Mathews

The makers of "Goldeneye," the latest James Bond movie in Hollywood's longest-running and most exhausted series, were very calculating in giving Bond a new boss—a woman—and having her confront him in their first meeting as "a sexist, misogynist dinosaur."

In the 33 years since "Dr. No" got things under way, the world has become a different place, and though Bond has been physically reborn from time to time, the character that Ian Fleming created as a Cold War techno-hero has grown increasingly out of date.

With a brand new Bond (Irish-born Pierce Brosnan becomes 007 No. 005), and a six-year hiatus in the series, the producers took the opportunity to raise his consciousness. He's still the personification of cool—still dressing impeccably, driving great sports cars, ordering his vodka martinis shaken-not-stirred, and possessing a quip for every occasion. But when it comes to dealing with the '90s woman, Bond is almost deferential. In fact, the two Russian women of "GoldenEye"— the villainess Xenia Onatopp (Famke Janssen) and Natalya Simonova (Izabella Scorupco), the ally who becomes his lover—are both as smart and tough as he is.

As one who has had very little interest in Bond since Sean Connery abandoned the role to Roger Moore 20-plus years ago, the makeover doesn't make it particularly worthwhile. Brosnan is unquestionably the best Bond since Connery, but it isn't just the character who's become a dinosaur. The series is a dinosaur. The Cold War is over, the Big Bad Commies are baby capitalists, and today's best-paid spies can be seen digging through Roseanne's garbage looking for items for the National Enquirer.

Nevertheless, the franchise beckons, and writers have come up with another outrageous comic book story, a plot to rob the banks of London and cover the crime by blowing the city up with a commandeered Russian weapons system. Bond's nemesis is fellow intelligence officer 006 (Sean Bean), who has aligned himself with some ex-KGB agents, and the race against the clock takes them and Bond from the frozen tundra of Russia to Monte Carlo to the Caribbean.

There are a couple of stunning action sequences for Bond fans to behold. The traditional curtain-raiser features a gut-turning, 175-foot bungee jump stunt from the rim of a giant dam, followed by Bond's plunge into a canyon—minus parachute or bungee cord—to catch up with a runaway plane, climb aboard and pull it out of a dive before it crashes.

The other main action sequence, a spectacle unto itself, has Bond chasing a KGB caravan through the streets of architecturally wondrous St. Petersburg in a huge tank, destroying scores of cars, trucks and buildings along the way. The sequence was shot partially on location in St. Petersburg, but most of the destruction was enacted on an elaborate two-acre English set that duplicated St. Petersburg facades.

Those two set pieces, plus the extended finale on a giant satellite dish (actually, the world's largest spherical telescope, located in Puerto Rico), rank "GoldenEye" with the best of the Bond films on the level of pure action. But the producers have some work left in their makeover of Bond as a contemporary hero looking ahead to the 21st century.

Somehow, they have to make up for what Bond loses in becoming a "nice guy." There are some laughs from his fights with Onatopp, a Russian gangster who makes hand-to-hand combat look like wild sex, but she never becomes anything more than comic relief. And as interesting as the stunning European model Scorupco is as Natalya, there is a curious lack of sexual tension between her and Brosnan.

It seems that once they decided to make Bond more respectful of women, they couldn't figure out how to retain his sex appeal. What is he doing, penance? Even Miss Moneypenney (Samantha Bond), gets into the act, playfully threatening Bond with a sexual harassment suit for making innuendos.

The days of disposable "Bond girls" are over, but give the guy a break. Fleming conceived James Bond as a superhero who, for saving the world time and again, could expect something more for his trouble than a government check.

NEWSWEEK, 11/27/95, p. 86, Jack Kroll

GoldenEye opens with one of the best of the James Bond "teasers"—the precredit stunt sequences that kick-start 007 on his escapades. In this one Bond does a bungee jump off the top of a gigantic dam, falls 750 feet and is yanked to a whiplashing stop as he fires a grappling hook into the ground. Thank you, stuntman Wayne Michaels, and you, Pierce Brosnan, take over for the close-up. After nine years, since NBC wouldn't free him from his contract so he could replace Roger Moore, Brosnan gets to make his inaugural address: "The name is Bond—James Bond."

Your heart goes out to Brosnan, finally getting the role of his dreams. He's handsome, there's a touch of his native Ireland in his acccent, he can throw a punch ... oh, lets face it, James Bond is mythic or he's a zilch. Brosnan is OK, but OK isn't mythic. Sean Connery, the most magnetic male animal since Cary Grant, established the myth. Moore's touch of ironic self-parody added a nuance that kept the going. Timothy Dalton didn't seem to have his heart in it. Brosnan has his heart and everything else in it. But he seems ... small, as if he bears the scarlet letters TV on his tux. Years of playing Remington Steele will do that. When Connery walked into a Monte Carlo casino, the necklaces of the rich bimbos seemed to jump out of their cleavage. When Brosnan walks in, well, have a good evening, James.

Entropy, the inexorable running down of an energy system, may have overtaken the Bond saga. Technology has squeezed character to a few measly pixels on the digital screens. Explosions have replaced dramatic climaxes. Movies now die hard with lethal weapons wielded by terminators. Bond's creator, Ian Fleming, can't help anymore: "GoldenEye" is an original story by Michael France, with script credit to first-timers Jeffrey Caine and Bruce Feirstein. It's a tangled story involving Mafia-infested Russia, with Bond battling an attempt to blow out the world's high-tech communications. A swarm of villains keeps bumping into one another, all played by terrific actors, including Germany's Gottfried John, Britain's Robbie Coltrane and Alan Cumming, and especially Ireland's Sean Bean as Bond's former colleague 006, who switches sides, because he's really from a Cossack family, so that ... Please! Bring on an explosion!

And they do come on, a soporific succession of similar smithereenings. The fun in this 17th Bond comes mainly from the Bond girls. (That's girls, not women; we're dealing with cultural history here.) Good girl is Izabella Scorupco (Polish) as Natalya Simonova, a Russian cyberexpert. Bad girl is Famke Janssen (Dutch) as Xenia Onatopp, a scorcher in S&M leather whose specialty is squeezing the life out of guys with her mighty thighs. New Bond director Martin Campbell lays down on the job here, showing us her victims' gasping faces when we want to see a precise picture of this lasciviously lethal operation. Actually, there is one woman, the first female M, Bond's boss, played by the great actress Judi Dench. "You're a sexist misogynist dinosaur," she berates Bond. Brosnan looks a bit chagrined. Connery would have withered M with a laser look. And turned her on.

SIGHT AND SOUND, 1/96, p. 40, José Arroyo

James Bond (Secret Agent 007) is on a mission with Alec Trevelyan (006) to blow up a Soviet chemical weapons facility. 006 is caught by General Ourumov and 007 is forced to choose between completing the mission or saving his friend. Before he is shot, 006 encourages Bond to blow up the base. Bond does so and escapes.

We next see Bond nine years later on the road to Monaco. Inside his Aston Martin, a young British woman is trying to evaluate him psychologically for his job; on the road, a beautiful woman races him with her red sports car. That evening Bond meets the other driver, Xenia Onatopp, at the casino. He flirts with her and beats her at baccarat. She leaves with an admiral whom she later kills during sex. The next day, she and General Ourumov steal a stealth helicopter, return to Russia and there blow up a base in Siberia to gain sole access to GoldenEye, a secret satellite electronic-pulse weapon. Only two people, both computer experts, survive the destruction of the base: Natalya Simonova and Boris Grishenko.

Bond's boss "M" sends him to Russia. He meets a former KGB agent who directs him to the plot's organisers. Bond avoids getting killed by Onatopp, but is then captured by the mastermind, Trevelyan, who is still alive. Natalya, betrayed by Boris, is strapped with Bond into the helicopter which is primed to self-destruct. They escape only to be arrested. In captivity, they meet the Russian Defence Minister and tell him that Ourumov is a traitor but Ourumov shoots the Minister and kidnaps Natalya. Bond chases after them through the streets of St Petersburg in a tank. The villains board a train but Bond derails it and shoots Ourumov, but the others escape. Natalya pinpoints the location of Trevelyan's headquarters in Cuba. Trevelyan intends to disable every electrical device in London. Bond and Natalya infiltrate the base and destroy it, eliminating Trevelyan and Onatopp.

The Bond films are such an institution that their producers know if they don't screw up they've got a guaranteed audience. We want to like most movies we pay to see but we already know the Bond formula—it has already earned our good will—so our pleasure revolves around seeing how the film-makers execute their turn. *GoldenEye* doesn't blow it.

In *GoldenEye*, the usually spectacular pre-credits sequence must also present a new star as Bond. We first see Pierce Brosnan running, bungee-jumping from an incredible height and sneaking into a military facility to blow it up. The scene has all the integral elements of the series: great scale, witty repartee, a sense of duty, and spectacular stunts. When Bond free-falls after his aeroplane, the very notion is so ridiculously Bond the audience I saw it with burst into applause.

The Bond films are a fantasy bred from the Cold War (and from the need to produce films that could compete with television). Part of the fantasy was that the appearance of the Iron Curtain created new sites of conflict as well as new types of heroism. Since the battle was international and covert, the hero's manhood could be tested in luxury hotels and resorts all over the world rather than in grimy battlefields. The skills required were no longer merely physical and moral but also social, intellectual and sexual. Another part of the fantasy was that Great Britain still had a role to play as a major power in this conflict.

One would think that the fall of the Soviet Union and the decline of Britain as an international power would have affected the potency of these fantasies, but seemingly they haven't. Perhaps we've seen the Bond films so often and for so long that we understand *GoldenEye* more in relation to the history of Bond films rather than feel the need to relate it to a broader history through some notion of realism. If anything, the fall of the former Soviet Union has allowed Western film-makers to represent Russia in ways they would not have dared before *glasnost*. *GoldenEye*'s credit sequence, like all the Bond films, has semi-naked girls dancing. Except this time they are doing it on a giant hammer and sickle while Communist icons collapse. The audacity of the sequence springs from seeing such powerful symbols reduced to mere camp props. What bothered me most is that *GoldenEye* pulls this off so well that it didn't bother me at all.

GoldenEye follows the Bond formula well—all the familiar characters are back and the gadgets are demonstrated. The film offers luxury, beautiful women, a strong villain and an elegant hero in exotic locales. Set pieces bookend the film; there is a good car chase and the rest offers a fine mixture of wit and action. However, *GoldenEye*'s greatest success, especially in the light of how *The Living Daylights* and *Licence to Kill* failed, is in modernising Bond.

It seems that though the Bond series need pay little attention to history, a greater degree of verisimilitude in its portrayal of contemporary sexual mores is deemed essential. If not in the avant-garde of the 60s Playboy ethos, the Connery Bonds were certainly in tune with it; the Dalton Bonds attempted to catch-up with the times. *GoldenEye* does not attempt to change Bond by making him a New(ish) Man as the Dalton Bonds did. Instead the film nods slightly towards the present by changing the attitudes of those around him. Miss Moneypenny jokes with him about construing his advances as sexual harassment. "M" is now a working mother who tells Bond he is a sexist, misogynist dinosaur. The film positions Bond as beleaguered by powerful women ("M", his psychological evaluator, Onatopp) even though the Bond himself seems not to have a problem with female authority.

There is likely to be some debate about the effectiveness of Brosnan as Bond, but a large measure of *GoldenEye*'s success is due to him. He's arguably as handsome as any of the previous Bonds and he's a much better actor than George Lazenby. He doesn't read all of his lines as if they were in quotation marks as Roger Moore did, or seem embarrassed to be playing the role like Timothy Dalton. Brosnan is the fittest Bond we've had since early Sean Connery. He is elegant and moves well. The moment when he's running over everything in sight with his tank and takes time to rearrange his tie is quintessential Bond. Inevitably, all new Bonds are compared to Connery. Both he and Brosnan give the impression that there is a mystery behind the martinis and the guns. Dalton had that as well but there was stiffness in his characterisation that reduced mystery to distance or blankness. With Dalton one didn't want to resolve that mystery. With Brosnan, as with Connery, one does.

Director Martin Campbell (whose credits include *Edge of Darkness* and *No Escape*) can be credited for his staging of the film's action and humour. At a time when so many villains in American action films signify their villainy through their Britishness it is also a pleasure to have a British hero in a big budget movie. I do have one serious gripe: that despite all the spectacle the only thing one would miss by watching the film on video is the scale. Now scale in itself is reason enough to see a film in the cinema. But I resented the amount of close-ups; the feeling that the action seemed to take place on only one plane, that all the possibilities of staging on a big screen were reduced to maximise the limitations of a small one. Limited use of screen space is one element which prevents *GoldenEye* from being what some other Bond films were—a particular kind of great cinema.

TIME, 11/27/95, p. 92, Richard Schickel

James Bond movies are as stylized as a Noh play—or should one say a Dr. No play?—and the 17th film in the series raises only one question. How well do Bond's established conventions survive after a third of a century's hard use, the post cold war deglamourization of espionage and the arrival of yet another actor in the central role? The short answer is, on wobbly knees. But herewith some further reflections—007 of them on a *GoldenEye*:

001 The Character Issue: Pierce Brosnan is not as gravely witty as Sean Connery, not as insouciant as Roger Moore and not a pompous twit like Timothy Dalton. He's a mid-range James Bond, on whom a certain self-consciousness has been imposed. He continues to register emotions mainly by arching or furrowing an eyebrow. But in the age of sexual correctness they have cut back his double entendres, and people keep telling him he lacks the capacity for mature relationships with women. Worse, he seems to believe them. What next? Sensitivity training? A condom in his wallet? Teetotaling, with perhaps a demand that his Perrier be served in a bottle, not a can?

002 The Supervillain: He may, as usual, have a superweapon trained on a Western capital, but Alec Trevelyan (Sean Bean), a freelance mastermind operating in today's chaotic Russia, has a dreary back story explaining how he went wrong instead of truly evil élan. Big mistake: we don't want motivation in a Bond nemesis; we want psychosis on a joyous, cosmic scale. Gert Frobe, you are missed.

003 The Supervixen: She's got the right sort of name—Xenia Onatopp (get it?)—the right sort of attitude—sado-masochistic—and the right sort of wardrobe—parodically sexy—but Famke Janssen is more aggressive than seductive. You know too soon where she's coming from—out of an abnormal psychology text.

004 The Henchman (or -woman): Oddjob, Jaws, Rosa Klebb—this is a job for grotesques. Gottfried John as a rogue Russian general looks weird all right, but he has no unique killing skills—just a sneer and a routinely itchy trigger finger. Richard Kiel, you are missed.

005 Vehicular Manslaughter: The usual planes, trains, automobiles crash and burn with noisy, deadening regularity, sending many a nameless extra to his unmourned, uninvolving and unimaginative doom.

006 M: Big switch—a sex change, no less—here. Judi Dench, the distinguished English stage actress, is now running Bond. She has a butch hairdo, a brusque Thatcherite manner and a license to kill with unkindness. She calls Bond a "sexist, misogynistic dinosaur" right to his face. There's a chic in her cheek the rest of the movie direly misses.

007 Q: He's still being played by Desmond Llewelyn as a cranky English eccentric, still making fountain pens that explode and wristwatches that do more than tell time. He's the last link to the boyish silliness that once animated this series. One wishes him good health and long life, for if, as the closing credits threaten, "James Bond Will Return," they—and we—are going to need him.

VILLAGE VOICE, 11/28/95, p. 64, Georgia Brown

Smoother than an unbruised vodka martini, *GoldenEye* opens with a handsome aerial view of a massive mountain dam (it's in Switzerland) and of our hero poised for a spectacular dive. The fairly lengthy pre-credit sequence is capped by a bravura escape; another dreamy free fall, this time aimed to end up inside the cockpit of a diving pilotless plane. The movie's first line, spoken somewhere inside the bowels of that mighty dam, has 007 (Pierce Brosnan) assuring fellow operative 006 (Sean Bean), "I'm alone." Whereupon his colleague replies playfully, "Aren't we all!" Oooooh. Veering on the poignant. If only they could keep it up.

In the past week, a *Voice* arts editor, who, I gather, doesn't see all that many movies, mentioned that he wouldn't miss the new Bond. At the time, I, who see too many, wondered why. Everything now is Bondishly self-parodying. But for a few minutes into the cool, opulent *GoldenEye*—18th Bond in 33 years—I thought maybe revisiting Bond is a way back to a golden, gentler past. (Remember when the Bonds were jumped on for sadism!)

During Tina Turner's title number, shadowy Amazon's climb erect stone Lenins as hammers and sickles float by like clouds. (Where would MTV be without Magritte!) When the icons fall, the women seize the hammers to compound the breakage. Communism's end as capitalism's music video. A sign, in case you were wondering, that the new Bond is sticking with old antagonisms: as always, to and from Russia with love.

What follows is too busy to begin to summarize. Someone got carried away. Marvel, marvel, yawn, yawn. Massive explosions, maximum damage. The cinematography by Phil Meheux (you'd never know he shot Alan Clarke's *Scum*) is sumptuous. So is the geography. Bond flits around the globe like George Soros: Mediterranean spas, Siberia, St. Petersburg, London, Russia again, the Caribbean. Where the movie scrimps is on actors, but here it gets especially good value. There's Fassbinder regular Gottfried John as a vicious Russian general, Joe Don Baker as a clunky CIA operative, Robbie Coltrane as an arms merchant, Tcheky Karyo as Defense Minister Mishkin, and Alan Cumming as a meglomaniacal computer nerd.

Low rent, thankfully, extends to the leads. Tailored by Brioni, our newest Bond looks impeccable if a trifle slight. In his forties now, Brosnan's prettiness is only slightly cut by wrinkles, but as Flemings dandy he has the requisite grace and class. Not that he has Connery's ease and swagger or the mischievous irony around the eyes (Brosnan's eyes are small and hard to read). With women, the character is warier now—more acted upon than acting—and there's no conviction to his lechery. Of course, a contemporary Bond has more reason to beware women, what with their recently discovered competence.

In one progressive touch, the new chief of M16, M, is played with butch grace by the great Judi Dench. The traditional treacherous beauty—and the movie's only outsized comic villain—goes under the apt surname Onatopp (she's Dutch-born Famke Janssen). This former fighter pilot's modus operandi is to bite men's lips while squeezing them breathless between viselike thighs (a strenuous effort to make *Diamonds Are Forever*'s Bambi and Thumper look quaint). She also appears to orgasm after accomplishing anything cruel. *GoldenEye*'s nice girl and love interest is Russian computer expert Natalya Simonova (Polish-born, Swedish-bred Izabella Scorupco). The movie is too chicken to kill her off, although it toys with the idea. It's she who inquires of James, "How can you be so cold?" James's uninspired answer: "It's what keeps me alive." (*GoldenEye*'s writers don't contribute much new wit. That "Boys with their toys" refrain hardly qualifies as deconstruction.)

Smartly directed by New Zealander Martin Campbell (best work: BBC's *Edge of Darkness*), *GoldenEye* wears out its welcome by piling on climaxes when line would do perfectly. Still and all, my colleague was right; you could do worse than see the new Bond.

Also reviewed in:
CHICAGO TRIBUNE, 11/17/95, Friday/p. C, Michael Wilmington
NEW YORK TIMES, 11/17/95, p. C17, Janet Maslin
NEW YORKER, 11/27/95, p. 105, Anthony Lane
VARIETY, 11/20-26/95, p. 47, Todd McCarthy
WASHINGTON POST, 11/17/95, p. F1, Hal Hinson
WASHINGTON POST, 11/17/95, Weekend/p. 44, Desson Howe

GOOFY MOVIE, A

A Walt Disney Pictures release. *Producer:* Dan Rounds. *Director:* Kevin Lima. *Screenplay:* Jymn Magon, Chris Matheson, and Brian Pimental. *Story:* Jymm Magon. *Editor:* Gregory Perler. *Music:* Carter Burwell. *Music Editor:* Tom Carlson and Adam Smalley. *Sound:* Mike Boudry and (music) Michael Farrow and Armin Steiner. *Sound Editor:* David E. Stone. *Casting:* Jamie Thomason. *Production Designer:* Fred Warter. *Art Director:* Wendell Luebbe and Lawrence Leker. *Running time:* 76 minutes. *MPAA Rating:* G.

VOICES: Bill Farmer (Goofy); Jason Marsden (Max); Jim Cummings (Pete); Kellie Martin (Roxanne); Rob Paulsen (PJ); Wallace Shawn (Principal Mazur); Jenna Von Oy (Stacey); Frank Welker (Bigfoot); Kevin Lima (Lester); Florence Stanley (Waitress); Jo Anne Worley (Miss Maples); Brittany Alyse Smith (Photo Studio Girl); Robyn Richards (Lester's Grinning Girl); Julie Brown (Lisa); Klée Bragger (Tourist Kid); Joey Lawrence (Chad); Pat Butrum (Possum Park Emcee); Wayne Allwine (Mickey Mouse); Herschel Sparber (Security Guard).

LOS ANGELES TIMES, 4/7/95, Calendar/p. 12, Peter Rainer

Goofy finally gets his own movie in—"A Goofy Movie." He had his own TV show, "Goof Troop," which started up in 1992, but that wasn't enough for him. After all, what's a TV series compared to big-screen stardom?

These days even animated animals are acting like David Caruso.

In a sense, "A Goofy Movie" is still a TV show. Several of its characters are drawn from "Goof Troop" and the Disney Television Animation team was hired to oversee the work of artists in Disney's animation studio near Paris, where many of Disney's afternoon TV episodes are concocted. Compared to the lavish detailing that Disney expends on its Grade A features like "Aladdin" and "The Lion King," "A Goofy Movie" is cut-rate. It wouldn't look out of place on the small screen.

But it's not slipshod. A few of the voice-over actors, like Wallace Shawn as a school principal or Bill Farmer as Goofy, provide some joys. Small children will probably find the film sporty and painless, and it has six musical numbers and a hilarious subplot involving Bigfoot. Directed by Kevin Lima and produced by Dan Rounds, it moves briskly, and, if it doesn't make a star out of Goofy, it doesn't trash him either. It lets Goofy be Goofy.

Most of the movie, however, is taken up with Goofy's teen-age son Max. Goofy wants to bond with the boy; at the start of summer vacation they go on a fishing expedition that turns into a series of mini-disasters. That's where Bigfoot comes in; he traps the duo in their camper and does a little dance from "Saturday Night Fever." (Don't ask.) Max starts out distancing himself from his goof of a dad and ends up becoming best buddies with him. And, in the process, he wows his high school heartthrob Roxanne. This Cyrano gets the girl.

Animated movies are generally at their best when they're not trying to be civic-minded. "A Goofy Movie" is fairly funny but, with its father-son confabs and bond-a-thons, it's a bit too drippy with life lessons for tots. The lessons seem to be in the movie to impress parents and make them feel as if they're doing a Good Thing in bringing their children.

If you're going to make something called "A Goofy Movie," why dampen the goofiness?

NEW YORK POST, 4/7/95, p. 44, Bill Hoffmann

The Disney magic is nowhere to be seen in "A Goofy Movie," the studio's cheesy attempt to give cartoondom's favorite floppy-eared, ah-shucks pooch a movie of his own.

After amazing achievements like "The Lion King" and "Aladdin," what went wrong?

It's easy to answer that question after only five minutes of viewing. "A Goofy Movie" looks slapped together with about as much care as a kid takes making mud pies at the beach.

The script is abysmal and the animation just barely adequate. Those traits may be perfectly acceptable for Saturday morning TV fare—but not for a feature-length film with the Disney stamp on it.

The soggy plot concerns the efforts of Goofy's son Max to try to gain the affections of a cute classmate named Roxanne by pretending he's pals with Powerline, a dreary Prince-like rock band.

He further boasts he'll be on stage with the group at their upcoming Los Angeles concert. But the chances of that happening vanish when Goofy decides he and Max should go off on a weeklong camping trip for a little bonding.

Max hates the idea: His father doesn't understand him, is totally behind the times and is an embarrassment to his friends. Still he goes and by the end of trip is—gee, what a surprise—totally in tune with dear-old dad.

The movie explores an age-old dilemma most parents have had with their kids at one time or another. But instead of relying on the personalities of the Disney characters to drive their point home, screenwriters Jymn Magon, Chris Matheson and Brian Pimental load up on ill-placed '90s references to try to be hip.

Some of them are quite disturbing for a G-rated movie.

There's a weird reference to getting high when one of Max's pals, in euphoric ecstasy, sucks down a bottle of cheese spread as if he's inhaling a joint. Then there's the takeoff on a well-known profanity when Max cries out, "I'm in deep sludge!"

It's obvious there wasn't a lot of care taken in making "A Goofy Movie." Perhaps Disney figures it can dash off a series of animated cheapies in between its classics. If that's the case, what a shame.

NEWSDAY, 4/7/95, Part II/p. B7, Gene Seymour

With Tim Allen and Forrest Gump, those twin towers of addlepated awkwardness, ruling pop culture these days, it's inevitable—and only right—that Goofy be given a full-length movie all his own. Conceived back in 1932 as a comic foil for Mickey Mouse, Disney's klutz-of-klutzes has also been its most versatile clown. Happiness is watching him ambushed by every inanimate object in the known universe, from garden hoses to golf clubs, barbells to spatulas, water skis to lawn mowers.

In "A Goofy Movie," it's the mechanics of fatherhood that have got the Goofster flummoxed. Max, his 14-year-old son, looks like a smaller version of his dad. (Wouldn't you just love to know who the mother was?) The strong family resemblance (including a furtive "hyuk" that sneaks into Max's otherwise normal voice) is just one of the things that doesn't thrill the kid about his life. He's also smitten with a pretty little classmate named Roxanne and goes to outrageous means to get her attention. After pulling a stunt that brings him within a razor's edge of expulsion, Max gets a date with her.

Dear old dad has other plans. Concerned about his son's mercurial behavior (and not knowing that it's only love that's driving Max crazy), Goof decides that what the boy needs is some serious bonding on the open road. So he overstuffs the old jalopy with fishing gear and forces Max to head west with him for a fishing trip.

That's just his first mistake. Many others (as you'd expect with Goof) follow. One of them results in an impromptu visit by the funniest incarnation of Bigfoot in recent memory. But it's the tension between restless teen and clueless parent that looms over their quality time like a storm cloud. Don't sweat it, folks. Things never get as solemn as I'm making it sound. You know they'll work it out.

Still, I'm not entirely sure a character as cheerfully uncomplicated as Goofy needs as many emotional levels as this film gives him, though Bill Farmer does a good job bringing varied moods and tones to the Goof's familiar voice. I'm also not sure the film needs even one of its six songs to keep it going, though we have Disney's success to blame for making gratuitous musical interludes mandatory in feature-length cartoons.

But let's talk about Disney's success, shall we? While not even the studio would place "A Goofy Movie" in the same epochal realm of achievement as "Beauty and the Beast" or "Pinocchio," the film shows within its modest aspirations why nobody does this sort of thing better. Even the little things—a reflection in a window or a shrug—are carried out with careful attention to detail and a keen sense of personality. Maybe "A Goofy Movie" is nothing more than an extended animated sitcom episode, ready-made for home video. If so, it's the best of its kind you'll see anywhere from anyone.

SIGHT AND SOUND, 11/96, p. 50, Leslie Felperin

Somewhere in the USA, the present. Goofy is a single, canine father who lives with Max, his adolescent son. Max has a crush on a schoolmate named Roxanne. On the last day of school, Max interrupts the principal's speech with his impersonation of the pop star Powerline. This so impresses Roxanne she asks him on a date. However, the principal has phoned Goofy to warn him that Max is on the road to ruin. Encouraged by his workmate Pete's paeans to father-son togetherness, Goofy decides to take Max on a summer-long cross-country drive to a favourite Goofy-family fishing spot. Max tries to explain to Roxanne why he can't go out with her, but he lies and says that he and his father have been invited by Powerline to join the star on stage during his Los Angeles concert.

Goofy and Max take to the open road, closely following a map-route used by generations of the Goofy family. They have a huge row at a dilapidated attraction, Lester's Possum Park. Later, they accidentally meet up at a campsite with Pete and his son P.J. who are travelling in their huge, well-equipped RV. Goofy accidentally snags Big Foot while casting his fishing line and he and Max are forced to hide in their car for the night. When Goofy offers Max the role of navigator as appeasement, Max secretly changes the route to take them to Los Angeles. Pete tells Goofy of the ruse, and though he goes along with it, at a crucial junction the truth comes out. While arguing, Goofy loses control of the car and it ends up in a river, but Max saves his father's life.

Reconciled, Goofy agrees to go to LA with Max and help him invade the stage at the concert. They are successful and all of Max's friends see him on television dancing and singing with Powerline and Goofy. Back home, Max tells Roxanne the truth about what really happened but she tells him she still likes him, especially his 'goofy' laugh, of which he had been so ashamed.

Although *A Goofy Movie* resurrects a major character of the Disney short cartoons of the 30s-50s—the gormless canine star, Goofy—viewers expecting a nostalgic recreation of the old-fashioned, small-town world he once lived in are in for a shock. Like the family in *The Brady Bunch* movies, Goofy may have stayed the same but the world around him has changed. Now Goofy is the patriarch of a slightly dysfunctional cartoon family. The dysfunction and the film's present-day setting are both unusual for a straight-out Walt Disney picture (not a subsidiary-- produced film such as *James and the Giant Peach*). The premise is that Goofy is now the father of a son who is ashamed to have inherited his dad's 'goofy' laugh and comic clumsiness.

The film is thus almost an allegory of the studio's changing values (hotly contested by the religious right in the US) and coded plea that the new regime can reconcile the values treasured by its older audience with those favoured by a younger audience. The Oedipal rivalry and embarrassment is played out as an antipathy to each other's tastes and interests which are clearly flagged as Old-Disney v. New Disney: on the car stereo, Goofy wants to sing along to 'High Hopes' while Max prefers thrash-metal.

Up until the gooey ending, the tension is reasonably interesting. What spoils it is that the film's icon of coolness, the naff pop star Powerline, looks like a deviant Devo member and sounds like late-period Michael Jackson. Since everyone in the film is a dog, I was expecting some parodic variant on Snoop Doggy Dog at the very least, but I suppose the filmmakers dare not frighten the parents too much with the kind of stuff kids *really* like. Even the animation is cautious, bar a few interesting 'effects' such as an imitation of a black-and-white camcorder's view.

In the film's favour though, there is one priceless sequence when they visit a seedy Disneyland- wannabe theme park called Lester's Possum Park. Goofy drags Max to a display of inept water mammals, clucks over a possum-suited staff member, and buys Max a possum-hat that resembles a badly stuffed roadkill victim. One would almost suspect that some shadowy faction within the Disney-empire is having a veiled go at Disneyland itself, or at the whole utopian and faintly fascistic theme-park ethic. All the same, if there is dissent brewing within the Magic Kingdom, the conclusion of *A Goofy Movie* is poised to cancel any self-criticism.

Also reviewed in:
CHICAGO TRIBUNE, 4/7/95, Friday/p. H3, John Petrakis
NEW YORK TIMES, 4/7/95, p. C16, Stephen Holden
VARIETY, 4/10-16/95, p. 45, Todd McCarthy
WASHINGTON POST, 4/7/95, p. D7, Hal Hinson

GORDY

A Miramax Family Films release in association with RAS Entertainment, Ltd. of a Robson Entertainment production. *Producer:* Sybil Robson. *Director:* Mark Lewis. *Screenplay:* Leslie Stevens. *Story:* Jay Sommers and Dick Chevillat. *Director of Photography:* Richard Michalak. *Editor:* Lindsay Frazer. *Music:* Charles Fox. *Sound:* Mary H. Ellis. *Casting:* Shari Rhodes. *Production Designer:* Philip Messina. *Costumes:* Barcie Waite. *Running time:* 89 minutes. *MPAA Rating:* G.

CAST: Doug Stone (Luke MacAllister); Kristy Young (Jinnie Sue MacAllister); Michael Roescher (Hanky Royce); Deborah Hobart (Jessica Royce); Ted Manson (Henry Royce); James Donadio (Gilbert Sipes); Tom Lester (Cousin Jake); Tom Key (Brinks).

LOS ANGELES TIMES, 5/12/95, Calendar/p. 12, Kevin Thomas

"Gordy" is a sweet little movie, ideal for youngsters and easy to take for parents, about the adventures of a pig so adorable that he could turn us all into vegetarians. Gordy is one of six piglets who live happily with their parents at the idyllic Meadowbrook Farm. Hard times, however, have hit its owner, and only narrowly escapes being shipped "up North" for auction with the rest of his family. What's Gordy to do but to take off to try to find his relatives?

Director Mark Lewis, who has a crucial light touch, and writer Leslie Stevens, working from a story by Jay Sommers and Dick Chevillat, skillfully anthropomorphize Gordy and his animal friends, who are capable of speech but are understood mainly by children, who have the patience and credulity, also the "pureness of heart," to listen to and understand them.

Gordy lucks out by crossing paths with a pretty girl (Kristy Young) and her widowed father (Doug Stone), who are country-Western singers on tour. When they perform at a garden party at the Arkansas governor's mansion, Gordy saves a little rich boy (Michael Roescher) from drowning, becoming an instant media hero.

There's a silly, poorly motivated development in which an evil PR man (James Donadio) for Roescher's tycoon grandfather means to do away with Gordy. But this contrivance does propel the plot, and most youngsters aren't likely to be bothered by its flimsiness.

Newcomers Young and Roescher are appealing, the adult actors competent enough for the circumstances, and the entire film is well-crafted. Animal lovers of all ages should be delighted with "Gordy," which also boasts a number of pleasant musical numbers and performers.

NEW YORK POST, 5/12/95, p. 46, Thelma Adams

"Mothers, don't let your sons grow up to be bacon."

That could be the country-western song for "Gordy," a dated family comedy about an Arkansas piglet who saves his family from the slaughterhouse.

Directed by Mark Lewis, the movie opens with a pig's-eye-view of Meadow Brook farms. Gordy watches two rednecks in a pickup truck with an "America: Love It or Leave It" sticker round up his papa to take him "up north," the place from which pigs never return.

The traumatized talking pig has a tearful split with his father. "Don't leave us, father," Gordy cries as he follows the truck, pounding the pavement on little pink legs. Back at the sty, Gordy discovers that his mother and five siblings have also disappeared.

The little-pig-that-could sets out to find his family. Along the way he meets a lot of people who's names end in "Y." Jinnie Sue MacAllister (Kristy Young) is a pre-teen country-western singer; Hanky Royce (Michael Roescher) is the scion of a food empire.

When Gordy saves Hanky from drowning ("The pig saved the boy!"), he becomes a "Hero Pig" and the trademark for Royce industries. All this distracts the young porker from his quest.

The movie is based on the idea, voiced by Hanky's grandfather, that "people just can't resist a baby animal." In fact, Gord is very resistible. Dressed up in printed pajamas or scuba gear, given the wisest comments and the best one-liners the meager script has to offer, backlit and only occasionally slobbering, the piglet star (actually 25 piglets over the course of shooting) lacks charisma.

Gordy's talking is also a problem. While apparently pure-of-heart humans can understand the beast, sometimes he talks English and sometimes he snorts pig Latin. In a technique that makes "Mr. Ed" look sophisticated, Gordy's piggy mouth moves in a way that doesn't match the speech. As for the rest of the animal kingdom, roosters and chickens seem chatty, but horses and cow's speak in monosyllabic moos or whinnies.

Of course, Gordy saves the day. He retires to Meadow Brook farm with Hanky, Jinnie Sue and their respective families. In the final, family reunion scene, kooky cousin Jake ("Green Acres" vet Tom Lester) sets the barbecue ablaze and everybody laughs.

Wait a minute! What are they barbecuing? Where's Gordy?

Snort.

NEWSDAY, 5/12/95, Part II/p. B5, Jonathan Mandell

To get a quick fix on "Gordy," the latest in a long tradition of pig movies, do not think Wilbur in "Charlotte's Web," and definitely forget Miss Piggy in "The Muppets Take Manhattan." Think Arnold in "Green Acres."

Not just because Gordy is real, rather than a cartoon or puppet pig, nor because the film takes place in "the heartland of America" and is full of country songs. More to the point, the two creators of "Green Acres," that hick-chic TV series featuring a cute little pig treated like a child, also thought up the story behind "Gordy"... 19 years ago. That is when Tom Lester, who played Eb on "Green Acres" (and has a small role here), first optioned the story. It has taken him all this time to get a producer to turn it into a movie. Would it be swinish to say they probably should have spent a few more years on it?

"Gordy" begins promisingly on the Meadow Brook Farm in Arkansas, where the piglet is rushing past the other animals looking for his kin.

"Have you seen my family?" he squeaks to a cow, who replies with an utterly believable moo that really does sound like "no." The filmmakers seem to have worked most diligently on the animal conversations, which are a mix of genuine animal noises and dubbed English; the movement of the actors' mouths (or beaks or snouts) is more convincing than in most dubbed movies.

Gordy's family, we soon discover, has been kidnaped by evil men who, we learn much later, are intent on turning them into sausage. The harsh and shadowy scenes in the slaughterhouses could have been filmed by a vegetarian crusader.

Gordy sets out on a journey to find (and finally save) his family, and on the way 1) is discovered by a girl (14-year-old Kristy Young) who lost her mother, and is the singing daughter of the character played by country-music star Doug Stone, who also sings a lot; 2) saves from drowning the grandson of a rich industrialist (10-year-old Michael Roescher); 3) becomes a national hero, a company spokesman and then the chief executive officer of a conglomerate, interviewed by Louis Rukeyser on "Wall Street Week"; 4) is kidnaped by the henchmen of an evil p.r. man and ... what began as charming and childlike becomes much too complicated and broad.

Since the piglet seems to change size in every scene, it is not surprising to learn that Gordy was played by 25 different pigs. Only one still lives with the real teenage girl. Did the film wrap with a big barbecue?

Also reviewed in:
CHICAGO TRIBUNE, 5/12/95, Friday/p. J, John Petrakis
NEW YORK TIMES, 5/12/95, p. C18, Caryn James
VARIETY, 5/8-14/95, p. 66, Joe Leydon
WASHINGTON POST, 5/12/95, p. B6, Rita Kempley

GORILLA BATHES AT NOON

An Alert Film/Extaza/Von Vietinghoff Filmproduktion coproduction. *Producer:* Alfred Hürmer, Bojana Marijan, and Joachim von Vietinghoff. *Director:* Dusan Makavejev. *Screenplay (German and Russian with English subtitles):* Dusan Makavejev. *Director of Photography:* Aleksander Petkovic and Miodrag Milosevic. *Editor:* Vuksan Lukovac. *Music:* Brynmor Llewllyn-Jones. *Sound:* Uros Kovacevic. *Production Designer:* Veljko Despotovic. *Special Effects:* Srba Kabadajic. *Running time:* 83 minutes. *MPAA Rating:* Not Rated.

CAST: Svetozar Cvetkovic (Victor Borisovich); Anita Mancie (Miki Miki/Lenin); Alexandra Rohmig (German Girl); Petar Bozovic (Trandafil); Andreas Lucius (Policeman); Eva Ras (Mother); Suleyman Boyraz (Turk); Natasa Babic-Zoric (Frau Schmidt); Aleksander Davic (Dealer).

NEW YORK POST, 3/29/95, p. 32, Larry Worth

Since "Gorilla Bathes at Noon" won the international critics' prize at the '93 Berlin Film Festival, it's safe to assume the pickings were slim.

Or maybe the crowd just liked the film's Berlin setting, which, without doubt, serves as the production's chief asset.

At any rate, the movie marks the end of a five-year disappearing act for Yugoslavian director Dusan Makavejev. But since "Gorilla" has neither the cutting edge of Makavejev's classic "W.R.: Mysteries of the Organism" nor the mainstream appeal of "The Coca-Cola Kid" and "Montenegro," the return calls for a muted celebration.

The hard-to-follow plot concerns a Russian officer in present-day Berlin who remained after his fellow soldiers' desertion. He spends his time sleeping on rooftops, dealing with black marketeers, fantasizing about a female Lenin impersonator and dreaming of better times.

In addition to documenting those dreams, Makavejev intersperses clips from 1949's celluloid schlocker "The Fall of Berlin," full of dying comrades bemoaning their failure to reach the Reichstag or lovers united under Stalin's glowing gaze. Sadly, the propaganda seems more interesting than the story at hand.

To be fair, the director's quirky sense of humor and deliciously surreal eye surface on various occasions. Yet, the unique appeal that has mesmerized Makavejev's following for almost three decades is merely dangled before viewers like a tease, then quickly enveloped in the project's mire.

In addition, Svetozar Cvetkovic, looking like Liam Neeson's Slavic cousin, does his best to make the hero charismatic. But while nicely conveying diehard patriotism and childlike innocence, Cvetkovic can't make the character into a cohesive whole. Then again, neither could Makavejev's script.

The good news for Makavejev fans is that they don't have to settle for his least interesting effort. Starting Saturday and continuing through April 9, the Museum of the Moving Image in Astoria, Queens, will show a collection of the director's gems, with the great man himself introducing each program this weekend.

But should the subject of "Gorilla" arise, he'll have a lot of explaining to do.

NEWSDAY, 3/29/95, Part II/p. B9, John Anderson

Like a battered wife, the people of the formerly Communist Eastern Bloc have a tough time leaving their abusive spouse (i.e., Lenin) behind. The situation may have been ugly, but it was familiar. It was home. In many ways, it was easier to be dependent than entrepreneurial.

Especially in a world that wanted you to change and now doesn't want you at all. This is the thrust of Dusan Makavejev's darkly funny and resignedly sad "Gorilla Bathes at Noon," a 1993 film that is on one level about a Russian soldier left behind in Berlin but—given Makavejev's Yugoslav background—is also about much, much more.

Makavejev—the subject of a retrospective at the American Museum of the Moving Image in Astoria beginning Saturday—is one of the acknowledged geniuses of the current cinema. Like Jean-Luc Godard, his films since the '60s (which have ranged from "The Coca-Cola Kid" to the subversively erotic collage film "WR: Mysteries of the Organism") have challenged perception and film vocabulary. Unlike Godard's, his films have had local political repercussions. Attacked by Stalinists and patriotic Americans alike, he is a citizen of the world who, to paraphrase a line from the film, has no real home.

And neither does Viktor Borisovich (Svetozar Cvetkovic), a Soviet officer whose army left Berlin while he was recuperating in a mental hospital. Just who or what is insane is a constant question in Makavejev's film. But Viktor is rather stoically adrift in a changing, roiling world.

He says he is the son of a Soviet war hero, and some of the more effective moments in "Gorilla" juxtapose Viktor with his alleged father: a character in Mikhail Chiaureli's 1949 "The Fall of Berlin," complete with heroic music and the Red Army storming the Reichstag. It is ludicrously overblown imagery, but when intercut with Viktor's current homeless state, makes a good case for artifice and selective memory.

Makavejev employs his trademark collage technique, and his melding of old film with new reinforces what he establishes through his more conventional narrative—a forsaking not only of people but of values and mores that once transcended political systems. Viktor tries to reclaim Lenin, and is mocked, both by the people and the director. But his attempts to find a home—be it political or otherwise—should say much to everyone about the state of the world.

VILLAGE VOICE, 4/4/95, p. 45, J. Hoberman

Once upon a time, Dusan Makavejev was the leading cine-satirist and social psychologist of communist Europe, a Marxist artist who specialized in biting the Marxist hand that fed him.

WR: Mysteries of the Organism (1971), Makavejev's scandalous burlesque of totalitarian repression, effectively exiled him from his native Yugoslavia; Sweet Movie (1974), his deliberately revolting evocation of consumer frenzy, severely compromised his subsequent Western career.

Since then, Makavejev's homeland has disappeared and his greatest foil fallen apart. The radical counterculture that supported him is long gone; even the cinephilia that nourished his movies verges on the obsolete. The 62-year-old filmmaker might be a creature out of Alice's Wonderland—a Cheshire Cat for whom everything has vanished but his grin.

A practitioner of intellectual slapstick and a montage specialist working in the gaps separating East from West and documentary from fiction, Makavejev cultivates contradictions. In an unselfconsciously obtuse book-length memoir of Makavejev's ill-fated *Manifesto* (1988), British actor Simon Callow complained that although Makavejev "wants the professionals to somehow be more amateur ... he reproaches the amateurs for not being professional enough," dubbing the director, "king of contrariness." Given the current climate of right-minded stupidity, what better time than for the Mak retro that opens this weekend at AMMI in conjunction with the Public's theatrical premiere of his 1993 *Gorilla Bathes at Noon*?

An affably episodic travelogue following the adventures of the last Soviet soldier in post-Wall Berlin, *Gorilla Bathes at Noon* finds Makavejev up to his old tricks: diapering a baby with an East German flag; parodying the most famous of Soviet statues, Vera Mukhina's heroic *Worker and Collective Farm Girl*, by relocating its forward-striding, hammer-and-sickle-brandishing couple to a mound of junk in an automobile graveyard. The most elaborate textual reference interpolates florid Sovcolor chunks from *The Fall of Berlin*, the 1949 World War II extravaganza aptly described by one historian as the ultimate in "Stalinist piety" (at one point, overdubbing its soundtrack with excerpts from *Triumph of the Will*).

Among other things, *Gorilla Bathes at Noon* proposes itself as *Fall of Berlin*'s absurdist sequel: The Fall of East Berlin. *Gorilla*'s protagonist, Major Victor Borisovich (Svetozar Cvetkovic, who played the studly Yugoslav innocent in *Montenegro*, the most enjoyable of Makavejev's late films) is introduced in juxtaposition with the bombastic battle sequence where *Fall of Berlin*'s triumphant Red Army storms the Reichstag—except he's squatting on an apartment rooftop. Subsequently, he's revealed to be the child of the lovers, Alexei and Natasha, who are reunited in the presence of a suitably divine Stalin at *Fall of Berlin*'s ecstatic climax.

Makavejev, who has a well-developed appreciation for Communist kitsch, has called *Fall of Berlin*'s finale "naive and pathetic, grandiose and moving. Its author believed he was producing an important epochal historic fresco, but it was just a beautiful comic strip." Of course, Makavejev himself is an author who sets out to make beautiful comic strips and, almost accidentally, produces world-historic frescoes. Having been stripped of his raison d'être, if not his uniform, Victor Borisovich is like an infant in the cold post-Cold War world—a situation with which Makavejev can perhaps identify. "I am a soldier whose army deserted him," the Russian explains to a sympathetic fräulein.

As his film's title suggests, Makavejev wonders if this new Soviet "new man" constitutes an evolutionary advance. Is the defeated Victor an innocent bumpkin or a noble savage? An updated version of Turgenev's "superfluous man" or first cousin to Dostoyevsky's "idiot"? Trading on his goofy charm and impassioned, alcohol-fueled rants, Victor wanders through the curiously tranquil city, taking up with a rogues' gallery of black marketeers, stealing food from the animals in the zoo, getting himself locked up in prison, dreaming that he is wed to a female Lenin who sits at home and darns his socks: "What' a great honor, Vladimir Ilych, to be married to you!"

In his memoir, Callow explains that, while making *Manifesto*, he began "to believe that Makavejev's temperament creates spontaneous Makavejevian happenings." (His example is a scene of ridiculous bureaucratic subterfuge interrupted, midshot, by the unexpected appearance of actual, similarly uniformed functionaries.) *Gorilla Bathes at Noon* is similarly predicated on such resonant, semidocumentary sequences—the most remarkable of which concerns the disposition by decapitation of Nikolai Tomsky's 60-foot Lenin statue, supposedly the world's largest, in the former East Berlin.

"*Ich bin ein Berliner,*" Victor Borisovich cries to the TV crew that attempts to interview him as he makes a perfunctory attempt at cleaning the paint-spattered statue. In addition to Makavejev and his crew, the abandoned monument has attracted spontaneous offerings—flowers, ribbons, an invitation to public spitting, some Communist folk singers, and—a gaggle of drunks and crackpots. There's also a sign reading "Hands Off History," a injunction that has more than once been hurled at Makavejev.

Also reviewed in:
CHICAGO TRIBUNE, 6/16/95, Friday/p. J, Michael Wilmington
NEW YORK TIMES, 3/29/95, p. C14, Stephen Holden
VARIETY, 3/1/93, p. 58, David Stratton

GREAT DAY IN HARLEM, A

A Castle Hill Productions release of a Jean Bach production with financial assistance from The Jane and Lloyd Pettit Foundation/Flo-Bert/New York Foundation of the Arts. *Producer:* Jean Bach. *Director:* Jean Bach. *Screenplay:* Jean Bach, Susan Peehl, and Matthew Seig. *Director of Photography:* Steve Petropoulos. *Editor:* Susan Peehl and Phil Fallo. *Music:* Mark Cantor. *Sound:* Steven Hertzog, Judy Benjamin, and Neil Gettinger. *Running time:* 60 minutes. MPAA *Rating:* Not Rated.

WITH: Quincy Jones (Narrator); Dizzy Gillespie; Art Blakey; Art Farmer; Chubby Jackson; Paula Morris; Marian McPartland; Eddie Locke; Ernie Wilkins; Mona Hinton; Robert Benton; Sonny Rollins; Hank Jones; Johnny Griffin; Scoville Browne; Taft Jordan, Jr.; Bud Freeman; Gerry Mulligan; Elaine Lorillard; Robert Altschuler; Steve Frankfurt; Buck Clayton; Horace Silver; Milt Hinton; Felix Maxwell; Everard Powell; Max Kaminsky; Benny Golson; Nat Hentoff; Mike Lipskin.

LOS ANGELES TIMES, 2/20/95, Calendar/p. 9, Kevin Thomas

Back in 1958, Esquire magazine's young graphics editor Robert Benton, now the esteemed filmmaker, gathered some 60 jazz musicians for a group photograph in front of a Harlem brownstone for a cover story on the golden age of jazz. Documentarian Jean Bach, in the irresistible, Oscar-nominated, 59-minute "A Great Day in Harlem" persuaded the surviving musicians to speak of those who have since died—legends such as Thelonious Monk, Lester Young, Charles Mingus and Pee Wee Russell.

As luck would have it, bass player Milt Hinton and his wife Mona brought along their 8mm camera to film the occasion, and their footage complements the now-famous photograph, taken by Art Kane, as do snapshots taken by others of the historic gathering.

Bach has been able to make that day come alive through image as well as sound—all the departed greats are seen and heard performing in film clips—and through the insightful reminiscences of their peers.

NEW YORK POST, 2/17/95, p. 48, Chip Deffaa

In "A Great Day in Harlem," you'll find an informed quality, a rightness in the details that you'll find in the very greatest of jazz documentaries (such as "The Story of Jazz," "Billie Holiday: The Many Faces of Lady Day," and "Satchmo") and which is conspicuously absent in so many others (such as last year's Benny Goodman documentary).

It's a matter of setting up the interview subjects right, choosing the best quotes and the best musical examples.

Producer/director Jean Bach's understanding of—and obvious affection for   the jazz musicians she has interviewed has enabled her to capture them with rare naturalness.

Such greats as Art Blakey and Dizzy Gillespie, who could be curt with interviewers who weren't hip, talk to her (and thus to the film's viewers) as an old friend—which she was.

Her first husband, the late Shorty Sherock, was a jazz musician. And anyone who spends much time in jazz clubs soon meets "La Bach," whom Whitney Balliett profiled in a book as the world's "number one jazz fan."

So Bach (aided by writer Matthew Seig and editor Susan Peehl, who've worked on most of the top jazz documentaries of the past decade) brings us musicians as they are. Hank Jones explains why Lester Young was unique; Benny Golson tells a wonderful story on himself, dreaming up his ultimate composition.

And reminiscences about departed greats lead to superbly chosen clips, in which strongly self-confident, highly individualistic stylists like Roy Eldridge, Red Allen, Maxine Sullivan, and Jimmy Rushing show what they did best. And make many of their young successors of today seem bland by comparison.

Ostensibly, the film is about a day in 1958 in which musicians gathered in Harlem to be photographed for Esquire magazine, but Bach conjures up a whole era in a manner sweet and sad.

Minor flaws? The Lester Young clip isn't the best example of his art. The generally sharp editing cuts from Bud Freeman to Max Kaminsky with confusing abruptness. And talk from non-musicians sometimes sags.

New York still is, no less than in 1958, the world's jazz capital. But Bach's valentine to so many departed greats certainly leaves you feeling things ain't what they used to be.

NEWSDAY, 2/17/95, Part II/p. B5, Gene Seymour

Rarely has the process of capturing a moment in time been given as thorough and satisfying a treatment as Jean Bach serves up in "A Great Day in Harlem." Though not quite an hour in length, this Academy Award-nominated documentary's slender dimensions are tightly packed with enough evocative recollection, shrewd observation and enlightening information to inspire several movies, nonfictional or otherwise.

The moment commemorated by "Great Day in Harlem." came at about 10 a.m. on a morning in August, 1958, when, at the behest of Esquire magazine, 58 jazz musicians assembled at 126th Street between Fifth and Madison Avenues for a group photograph taken by Art Kane, who had virtually no experience as a photographer before the gig—and became famous as a photographer afterwards.

The picture, to be included in a special jazz issue of the magazine in January, was arranged by Robert Benton, the magazine's art director, who later became a celebrated film writer-director.

Kane and Benton contribute memories and observations to Bach's narrative. But here, as with the photos, it's the musicians who take center stage. It makes one feel all warm and gooey inside just to see and hear such recently departed masters as Art Blakey, Dizzy Gillespie, Bud Freeman and Buck Clayton recall the moment, the era and the musicians.

The first thing Freeman mentions is how *unusual* it was to find so many of his colleagues up and about so early, since jazz musicians are, by professional inclination, creatures of the night.

Yet there they were. And together they made a staggeringly diverse panoply of jazz in the late 1950s—a time which marked, arguably, its last great convergence of mass popularity and creative ferment.

Bach can string together anecdotes as if she were making a pearl necklace. It's a hoot to hear about how the enigmatic, truculent Thelonious Monk made sure he wore a light-colored coat so he could stand out in the crowd. And if those familiar with Kane's legendary photo ever wondered how Gillespie made his hero, Roy Eldridge, turn away from the camera or why Count Basie was the only musician sitting on the curb with neighborhood kids, their questions are here—with answers. And there are sweet sketches of Charles Mingus, Pee Wee Russell, Luckey Roberts and many others now long gone. Except for their music—and this lovely little film.

SIGHT AND SOUND, 6/95, p. 43, Mark Sinker

A black and white still of a crowd in a street opens the film. It's a unique and immensely famous photograph in the jazz world, of 57 musicians and one club owner. It was taken one August morning in 1958, and first published in 1959 in a special jazz issue of Esquire; it's unique because well-known figures from every jazz generation then active were present, among them Coleman Hawkins and Henry 'Red' Allen from the 20s, Lester Young from the swing era, Dizzy

Gillespie and Thelonious Monk from bop, and Horace Silver and Sonny Rollins, young men who would come to jazz stardom in the decade that followed. Mostly in their Sunday best, they're arrayed along the curb, or standing behind on the walk-up to a Harlem brownstone. A gaggle of small boys sits in front of them. We move in close and see that, on the extreme right, Dizzy Gillespie has just tapped Roy Eldridge on the shoulder, and, as he turned, put his tongue out. "This probably is the greatest picture of that era of musicians ever taken," says an as-yet unidentified voice. "And I'm so proud of it."

A documentary about the circumstances surrounding the photo, *A Great Day In Harlem* cuts together a multiplicity of rival takes, other photos and home movies from the same day with talking-head and voice-over reminiscences from surviving musicians and others involved in the shoot's organisation, and with archive stills, promo shorts and extracts from the 50s *Sound of Jazz* television series, and others.

First the scene is set: we learn how Robert Benton, art director at Esquire, and jazz fan, asked photographer and freelance art director Art Kane, a novice without a studio, to come up with something for the special edition. Then the focus is turned to the music and personalities of some of those present: Luckey Roberts the stride pianist, the oldest present; the enigmatic Monk; Mary Lou Williams, the first woman in jazz actually to impress her male colleagues. We hear from those who took their own pictures: bassist Milt Hinton and his wife Mona, who'd brought a little colour cine-camera, and one Mike Lipskin, a devotee of pianist Willie 'The Lion' Smith. We hear the story of the morning, from musicians rising far earlier than normal, to the panic of the inexperienced Kane and his assistants; we learn why Basie is seated on the curb, and of how all the kids came to be in the photo also; we learn how Dizzy made it his business to bug his idol Eldridge, and how—in the opinion of his peers—this photo catches the essence of both men, and many others.

In the film's closing moments, trumpeter Art Farmer discusses how strange it is to look at this picture and consider those no longer with us: because for "us", he says (meaning jazz musicians), "We don't think about people not being here ... Lester Young is here. Coleman Hawkins is here. Roy Eldridge is here. They are in us, and they will always be alive." Think of the film—conceived when Jean Bach realised that only a handful of those in the picture still survived—as a classic Big Band performance. In jazz, the improvisation fills in, deflects, re-scripts, and animates the original tune. Here, the picture itself is the tune; the solos are the promo shorts and old television clips of particular musicians playing, and—crucially, affirming Farmer's point—the tales and memories and plain fandom of musicians still alive towards these players. So that the matter of the documentary riffs off the matter of the photo, with all its visible and hidden little narratives, honing some 60 hours of interview down to clusters of different takes on similar ideas. Some of the best of Susan Peehl's editing, of blow-ups of Kane's unused takes, turns the stills into a kind of flickerbook movie, so that people jostle, joke and chatter. This, together with the gentle shock of the Hintons' grainy, colour home-movie footage, desolidifies the iconic, turning a frozen public media-moment back to semi-private street party. The records of this era still have a striking lived immediacy; so do the films. The documentary strives, with their help, to counter the intimations of mortality that any old photo is thick with.

It isn't always successful in this. The opening credits are frenzied, as if to "jazz up" the still in a rather trivial sense. The use of music sometimes tumbles into mere generic backing track, tasteful but anonymous, especially when removed from context, or used for links. We've learnt too well, after decades of jazz soundtracks, to hear without listening: paradoxically, more silence might have done the musicians less of a disservice, by heightening the pleasures of the times when we did get to listen. As it is, some of the most potent, intriguing, unstable moments are provided by the shorts and black and white TV fragments: plump, impeccably turned-out Henry 'Red' Allen, a clown-showman in the Armstrong mould when singing, becomes a trumpeter with a brooding, quietly cracked tone when playing; mournful and sallow-faced Pee Wee Russell plays old-school clarinet with a fabulous, slithering oddness; there's a bafflingly unlikely clip of bassist Charles Mingus in *All Night Long*, the 1961 British jazz thriller, alongside Patrick MacGoohan and a youthful Richard Attenborough (who calls Mingus "man"). In a 40s short, Maxine Sullivan is heart-stoppingly cute, the Toni Braxton of her day; in a photo seen only for a moment, Sonny Rollins has a mohawk.

Hinton looks at one of the photos he took, and sees Sullivan: "very young, beautiful". Beautiful, yes, but very young? She was born a year after Hinton, who was 49 in 1959. When old men reminisce, they also sentimentalise a little. Almost no one attempts in the interviews and anecdotes to challenge or jolt this mood; pianist Hank Jones comes closest, his deadpan contribution being to analyse every participant in relation to their gain in or loss of weight since that day. Kane demystifies himself likeably: "This idiot kid," he calls himself. "I never felt so alone in my life." But it's hard to avoid the irony that with this project he was contributing to exactly the iconography which was to stifle the music's meaning and to alienate newcomers to it" The film's title-typography is a homage to the design world of the late 50s, with its arty magazines and album covers; Benton and Kane belonged to this world, of course, but it spoke to a haughty up-scale hipness curiously divorced from the lives of the musicians it framed, for whom the thrill of this day is meeting one another rather than getting into *Esquire*. (There's another sadness here: Kane, this well-meaning, talented, courageous jazz fan, committed suicide this February.)

There are omissions. We never learn why, if Willie 'The Lion' Smith took the trouble to get up early and come to the shoot, he isn't actually in the picture: several other (admittedly minor) figures are neither interviewed nor mentioned. In a wider sense, the historical context is left unspoken: 1958 was actually a threshold year, as no one here could have known. Free Jazz—in the shape of Ornette Coleman—was soon to cause a lasting, angry, politicised rift in jazz: the formality of these suits and the courteous reserve of some of those wearing them would be suc-ceeded by dashikis and rage. The kids in the foreground would not, on the whole, grow up to be even mildly interested, let alone fans. There's a mortality that all the clips and talk and casual, intimate movement cannot quite cast a spell against; that of the music itself, in its full, living unity and community. The old guard might have been around for some years yet, but this was surely the last possible moment when such a project could have been undertaken. The very magazine media that so lovingly set out to record this scene were with their "special jazz issues" unwittingly helping occlude it as a living, changing thing, embalming it in within the celebration of itself.

Which does matter; though the failure to touch on it only very slightly mars a likeable, intelligently original and moving documentary.

VILLAGE VOICE, 2/21/95, p. 56, Henry Cabot Beck

This documentary describes the events surrounding a 1958 *Esquire* photo session, which is downplayed as a sort of fluke, a whim on the part of art directors Robert Benton (pre-*Bonnie and Clyde*) and Art Kane to gather as much jazz talent as was available for a once-in-a-lifetime group shot. Among those on that Harlem street at the obscenely early hour of 10 a.m.: the acidly eccentric Thelonious Monk, tenor colossus Sonny Rollins, Count Basie parked on the curb with some local kids, lined up like the keys on a toy piano, Lester Young in porkpie regalia, the still vital Coleman Hawkins, Dizzy Gillespie sharing yuks with his hero Roy Eldridge, Charles Min-gus, Willie "the Lion" Smith, the beautiful and brilliant Mary Lou Williams, Gene Krupa, the old-timers and young turks, idols and idolizers, from four decades of jazz. The photograph only begins to hint at the guard-changing drama of the moment, when the hot postbop breath of Miles and Coltrane (both absent) was on the necks of those who had made their emergence possible.

Archival musical footage and personal recollections are added to a reel of remarkable 8mm ama-teur footage shot by shutterbug jazz star Milt Hinton and his wife Mona. The result is a 60-minute film that tells the story of an era already fading from view, of a world that exists beyond the CD box set. Several of the commentators interviewed for the film have died, including Gillespie and Art Blakey, but the documentary, like the photo itself, is so full of warmth that a preview audience laughed like children at their wry reminiscences. *A Great day in Harlem* is first-rate in every respect, honoring a handful of men and women who lived singular lives by dint of their will, talent, and wealth of character—as one voice recalls, "the most original people you ever met."

Also reviewed in:
CHICAGO TRIBUNE, 5/19/95, Friday/p. N, Howard Reich
NEW YORK TIMES, 2/17/95, p. C12, Stephen Holden
VARIETY, 2/20-26/95, p. 74, Godfrey Cheshire
WASHINGTON POST, 6/16/95, p. F7, Richard Harrington
WASHINGTON POST, 6/16/95, Weekend/p. 46, Desson Howe

GROSSE FATIGUE

A Miramax Zoe release of a Gaumont/TF1 Films production. *Producer:* Patrice Ledoux. *Director:* Michel Blanc. *Screenplay (French with English subtitles):* Michel Blanc. *Based on an original idea by:* Bertrand Blier. *Director of Photography:* Eduardo Serra. *Editor:* Maryline Monthieux. *Music:* Rene-Marc Bini. *Sound:* Pierre Befve. *Set Decorator:* Carlos Conti. *Special Effects:* George Demetrau. *Costumes:* Elizabeth Tavernier. *Running time:* 87 minutes. *MPAA Rating:* Not Rated.

CAST: Michel Blanc (Michel/Patrick Olivier); Carole Bouquet (Carole); Philippe Noiret (Philippe); Jacques Buron (The Inspector); Francois Morel (The Deputy); Dominique Besnehard (Michel Blanc's Agent); Jean-Louis Richard (The Psychiatrist); Raoul Billerey (Michel Blanc's Father); Josiane Balasko; Marie Anne Chazel; Christian Clavier; Guillaume Durand; Charlotte Gainsbourg; David Halliday; Estelle Halliday; Gerard Jugnot; Dominique Lavanant; Thierry Lhermite; Mathilda May; Roman Polanski; Regine.

LOS ANGELES TIMES, 7/12/95, Calendar/p. 4, Kevin Thomas

In "Grosse Fatigue," a pitch-black comedy on the perils of fame, the popular French star Michel Blanc is writer, director and casts himself in dual roles, playing himself and a vicious, reckless impersonator bent upon destroying Blanc's life and career.

Based on an idea by writer-director Bertrand Blier, for whom Blier starred in "Ménage," this quirky and original film is by turns funny, scary and finally, a meditation on the question of identity for an actor—and by extension, for ourselves—and even a lament for the decline of the French cinema.

It's important to the enjoyment and appreciation of "Grosse Fatigue," which translates idiomatically as "Dead Tired," to try to see it as a French audience would see it. Usually when actors play themselves in a film they are treated as being more famous than they actually are, and this effect is magnified greatly by the fact that in the United States the bald, diminutive Blanc is memorable to us mainly from Patrice Lecomte's "Monsieur Hire."

Yet Blanc has made some 40 films and in France is also a TV star. Similarly, while the tall, beautiful Carole Bouquet, who also plays herself, is familiar to fans of French films since making her debut in Buñuel's 1977 "That Obscure Object of Desire," she is best known in the United States as a star of the James Bond film, "For Your Eyes Only," and as the face for Chanel No. 5.

In short, if Blanc is not to strike us as awesomely self-important, we have to take it on faith that he—and Bouquet too—are on home ground instantly recognized and pursued by fans everywhere they go.

Once past these considerations "Grosse Fatigue" proceeds with dispatch and a fine mastery of tone that allows Blanc's predicament to seem often excruciating and excruciatingly funny at the same time.

Blanc's double goes beyond freeloading at Cannes and boorish behavior at Regine's to a rape of actress Josiane Balasko (also playing herself). In a momentary stroke of luck Balasko drops charges, allowing Blanc's old friend Bouquet, for whom he's been struggling to write a script for years, to whisk him off to the solitude of her elegant country estate in Provence.

Instead of rest, however, Blanc by chance at last encounters his impersonator, whose real name is Patrick Olivier, who at 40 has simply flipped out, claiming his life has been ruined by being mistaken for the star his entire adult life. Yet just as things are looking up for Blanc, the film takes a dark swerve no Hollywood film would dare.

Blanc is adept at playing himself and his tormented and tormenting look-alike—it's as if Blanc were revealing the bad as well as the good sides of his own psyche. He is also able to draw sparkling portrayals from others, especially the charming, unself-conscious Bouquet. In his imaginary self-portrait, Blanc moves from feeling sorry for himself to an acceptance of self in the most extreme of circumstances.

NEW YORK POST, 7/12/95, p. 34, Thelma Adams

"After the orgy, it's the cold shoulder," a man driving a red car calls out to actor Michel Blanc, played by actor Blanc, in the frothy French comedy "Grosse Fatigue." If Blanc seems confused, it's because Patrick, an identical impostor also played by Blanc, has been living it up and leaving the tab for his more famous, less fun-loving, twin.

The tiny, bald comic has found ample fame in France to inspire him to write and direct this souffle about the wages of celebrity.

Blanc is a Gallic Woody Allen, amusing to everybody but himself. Like Allen, the die-hard New Yorker, Blanc, the die-hard Parisian, is allergic to the country. Lured to the Provence estate of actress Carole Bouquet (played by the radiant Chanel model and former Bond babe), Blanc barricades himself in his room, moaning about the din of peace and quiet.

Unlike Allen, Blanc has the wisdom to pair his neurotic alter-ego with an actress who couldn't be more firmly grounded. Bouquet, who debuted in Luis Bunuel's "That Obscure Object of Desire" (1977) towers over Blanc wearing her comic sense as casually as her fabulous wardrobe.

For the first hour, the movie pops along, with Bouquet playfully dominating Blanc in a lively game of poking fun at the bald guy. A number of French celebrities drop by to take part in the fun, including Charlotte Gainsbourg, Cannes Film Festival honcho Gilles Jacob and the restaurateur Regine. Depardieu's name gets dropped and his ego dunked repeatedly.

But the souffle falls in the final third. Having set up an improbable situation and squeezed it for its comedic possibilities, Blanc doesn't know where to take his doppelganger comedy. Patrick takes over Michel's life and Michel finds himself in the shadows, auditioning to be a Blanc lookalike.

While the air has gone out of the plot by this time, there's still an opportunity for some shaggy humor. Actor Philippe Noiret ("The Postman") turns up playing himself, claiming to be a victim of the same "evil double" phenomena. The two wander Paris, bashing easy targets like Yankee cultural imperialism ("We'll all end up mice in their f--king amusement parks," Noiret laments) and mourning the death of French cinema.

"Grosse Fatigue," which translates as "dead tired," proves that all this ranting about the death of French cinema should be taken about as seriously as Woody Allen's whining.

NEWSDAY, 7/12/95, Part II/p. B9, Jack Mathews

The rhetorical question "What price fame?" gets answered with an outrageous French twist in actor-writer-director Michel Blanc's "Grosse Fatigue," a darkly comic satire about a well-known French star—Blanc himself—whose life is turned upside-down by the appearance of an opportunistic double.

Casting a host of other good-natured French actors as themselves—Carole Bouquet, Philippe Noiret and Josiane Balasko among them—Blanc invites us into his life at its most vulnerable moment. He's in the midst of a seven-year case of writer's block, he's become depressed and grumpy, and to make matters gravely worse, he's being confronted with a mountain of evidence that he has been living a duplicitous life.

Bouquet reports a rumor that he has offered a role written for her to Emmanuelle Beart. A stranger approaches him on the street and reminds him about the other night's orgy. Balasko is pressing charges against him for tying her to a radiator and raping her. And he has just been thrown in jail with three guys who call him Mimi.

I don't know how many dozens of times between "The Prince and the Pauper" and "Dave" the idea of an unknown person assuming the role of an eminent look-alike has shown up on the screen, but it's never been done quite like this. Most satire is aimed at the arrogance of power and class. Blanc has trained his gun on himself, on the state of French cinema and on the mixed blessing of celebrity.

It is a gutsy piece of self-flagellation. Telling a story that begins with an assumption of your own fame and popularity may be the ultimate conceit. But Blanc, perhaps best known in the United States for his title role in "Monsieur Hire," has made himself as much of a fiction as the impostor, and, in fact, a far less interesting character.

"Grosse Fatigue," from an idea suggested by the French director Bertrand Blier, offers a Kafkaesque view of what can happen to a public figure unfortunate enough to have a look-alike with no scruples. That's not quite fair to the imposter, a petty thief named Patrick, who makes the reasonable case that if he is to spend his life being mistaken for the short, bald and pudgy star, he ought to have some of the perks, if not the life itself.

Underneath the spiraling lunacy of the story is some very savvy commentary on being a celebrity in the late 20th Century—the compromised privacy, the constant self-delusion, the fragility of fame. Through Noiret, who shows up as an actor whose life and career have long been taken over by his imposter, Blanc makes a severe attack on the current state of French cinema, which is dominated by American action films.

Blanc's frustration is understandable. It is a true scandal that the French have allowed mundane Hollywood product to erode the unique visions of their own filmmakers. But the point is made much too bluntly for the style of this otherwise marvelous satire.

VILLAGE VOICE, 7/18/95, p. 45, Georgia Brown

Something similar [the reference is to *Living in Oblivion*; see Brown's review] is the premise of Michel Blanc's droll *Grosse Fatigue*, a more complex but also very broad farce about stardom, its perks and perils. Blanc plays himself, meaning he plays his usual screen persona, a sour, deadpan, nerdy little guy. The difference here is that he's rich and famous, star of movies like *Menage, Les Bronzes*, and *M. Hire*, and occasional (as here) writer-director. When we meet Blanc, he's being accused by cops of grosse behavior: not paying a taxi driver for the whore he supplied. "I haven't done whores since '77," sputters the indignant Blanc.

Next we see the little fellow checking into Cannes's Carleton at festival tim, and, since he hasn't a reservation, commandeering the suite of Gerard Depardieu, who's run off to a wine tasting (this may be a French in-joke). Anyway, Blanc behaves boorishly at Cannes, trying to fuck actresses Mathilda May and the child-like Charlotte Gainsbourg. When Gainsbourg goes to fetch him a Valium, he steals from her purse.

Well, just as that dear, shy Hugh Grant was recently embarrassed by *his* horny double, Blanc turns out to be the victim of an unscrupulous impersonator, a look-alike named Patrick (also, of course, played by Blanc). Not only does Patrick cash in—doing signings at malls, judging topless contests, et cetera—he rapes Blanc's friends, like Josiane Balasko. (Somehow these rapes stay on the level of nasty jokes.) After a while, no one believes Blanc except the serenely poised Carole Bouquet (herself), who whisks him off to her country estate to work on his script, even though his double has already promised the role to Emmanuelle Beart. It's here that they happen upon the nefarious Patrick, whose mother actually believes her son is Blanc acting under a stage name. She's thrilled that he's finally brought home a trophy such as Bouquet. Finally confronting his double, however, Blanc ends up making a pact with the devil that I'll leave you to discover for yourself.

I first saw *Grosse Fatigue* over a year ago at Cannes—at which time it was slated to wind up as an American remake—and on French soil it seemed more exciting than it does here and now. The idea (attributed by Blanc to Bertrand Blier, who *would* have made dark work of it) is richer than the execution, which gets tedious and is bland to look at. The film does have a truly inspired ending, however, the message of which is that fakes have taken over everywhere, are now running the works, while originals are obscure and unemployable: They can't even get hired to play their own standins.

In this brief, charmed moment, Blanc extends his critique to cinema itself, implying—through the gentle, intelligent authority of Philippe Noiret—that films aren't what they were, that the Americans are the rapacious usurpers, the uncouth pretenders. (The small hitch here is that there's been no French cinema to usurp for over 20 years.) Of course, the underlying joke—on the audience—is that even here we're taking Noiret for his persona, just as we've taken Depardieu for a flake, Bouquet for a cool cucumber, Gainsbourg for an innocent, and Blanc for a schlemiel. Outside this inner circle with fixed identities are dolts and boors and dupes with no identities. Us. The film invites you to chummy up with the stars and then yanks them back to the firmament.

Also reviewed in:
CHICAGO TRIBUNE, 7/21/95, Friday/p.C, Michael Wilmington

NATION, 8/14-21/95, p. 181, Stuart Klawans
NEW YORK TIMES, 7/14/95, p. C6, Janet Maslin
VARIETY, 5/23-29/94, p. 55, Leonard Klady
WASHINGTON POST, 7/21/95, p. C7, Rita Kempley
WASHINGTON POST, 7/21/95, Weekend/p. 38, Joyce Jones

GRUMPIER OLD MEN

A Warner Bros. release of a John Davis/Lancaster Gate production. *Producer:* John Davis and Richard C. Berman. *Director:* Howard Deutch. *Screenplay:* Mark Steven Johnson. *Director of Photography:* Tak Fujimoto. *Editor:* Billy Weber, Seth Flaum, and Maryann Brandon. *Music:* Alan Silvestri. *Sound:* Edward Tisse. *Casting:* Sharon Howard-Field. *Production Designer:* Gary Frutkoff. *Art Director:* Bill Rea. *Costumes:* Lisa Jensen. *Running time:* 105 minutes. *MPAA Rating:* PG-13.

CAST: Jack Lemmon (John Gustafson); Walter Matthau (Max Goldman); Ann-Margret (Ariel Gustafson); Sophia Loren (Maria Ragetti); Burgess Meredith (Grandpa Gustafson); Kevin Pollack (Jacob Goldman); Daryl Hannah (Melanie Gustafson); Ann Guilbert (Francesca Ragetti); Katie Sagona (Allie Gustafson); Wayne A. Evenson (Handsome Hans).

LOS ANGELES TIMES, 12/22/95, Calendar/p. 18, Kevin Thomas

[*The following review by Kevin Thomas appeared in a slightly different form in* NEWSDAY, 12/22/95, Part II/p. B13.]

"Grumpier Old Men" brings back Jack Lemmon and Walter Matthau as feisty seniors John and Max, next-door neighbors in a small Minnesota town, and Ann-Margret as John's lovely wife of six months. Joining them is Sophia Loren, a big plus in an overly contrived comedy, strewn with less-than-hilarious geriatric sex jokes, that gets by on its formidable star power.

The glowing, eternally gorgeous and witty Loren arrives on the scene with her cagey old-country mother (Ann Guilbert) to turn John and Maxs' beloved bait shop into an Italian restaurant. The guys start sabotaging her efforts in actually quite nasty ways, but it's clear from the start that Loren's unlucky-in-love Maria and lonely widower Max are going to end up with each other.

Meanwhile, John's lecherous 95-year-old father (Burgess Meredith, a shameless scene-stealer) pursues Guilbert while John's daughter (Darryl Hannah) and Max's son (Kevin Pollak) are trying to overcome parental interference in planning their wedding.

Unfortunately, plot developments do not emerge often enough from writer Mark Steven Johnson's characters but more frequently from Johnson's arbitrary dictates. However, he does give his veteran stars, Matthau and Loren especially, enough to work with so that under Howard Deutch's easy-going direction they can fill out their roles with their strong, familiar presences and well-honed comedy skills.

The picture works best when the romantic skirmishing begins in earnest between Max and Maria. When Loren turns provocative and Matthau draws upon his crusty basset-hound charm, their sparring recalls Mae West and W.C. Fields in "My Little Chickadee." "Grumpier Old Men" needs more of this and less of Matthau and Lemmon indulging in pranks that make them look childish. Lemmon and Matthau, however, do have a funny scene in which they stop off on the way to their children's wedding to land a huge fish.

It's great to see cherished, long-time stars in big roles to which they can bring so much spontaneity and finesse, you wish only that this movie were sturdier and had aimed higher. Judging from the bloopers that unreel during "Grumpier Old Men's" end credits, the cast had lots of fun making this movie—more fun, it would seem, than it is to watch.

NEW YORK POST, 12/22/95, p. 51, Thelma Adams

"Grumpier Old Men"—and the gorgeous women who love them.

Am I the only one taken aback by the image of the still-luscious Sophia Loren smooching with that old sock puppet, Walter Matthau? Hers are the lips that kissed Cary Grant!

I think I've only just recovered from last year's "Grumpy Old Men" and its pairing of Jack Lemmon and Ann-Margret. In this sequel senior sex fantasy, even Burgess Meredith, who plays Lemmon's dad with a lusty combo of smut and senility, gets lucky. Lemmon has a nude scene!

For all the kissin' and cleavage (mostly Loren's and a bit of Lemmon's), the real love couple is Lemmon and Matthau—grumpy and grumpier. The women are just an excuse for America's oldest living boys to hurl insults at each other. "The Odd Couple" vets know how to do hostility.

"Grumpy Old Men" screenwriter Mark Steven Johnson has returned to pack insults and slapstick gags onto the flimsiest candy shell of a plot. Perpetual rivals and best buds Gustafson (Lemmon) and Goldman (Matthau) are planning the marriage of Gustafson's daughter (Daryl Hannah) to Goldman's son (Kevin Pollak). Gustafson, himself a newlywed, married Ariel (Ann-Margret) at the end of the last movie. Feeling left out, Goldman watches "Geraldo" ("oh, lesbians, yummy") and grumbles—until a new girl arrives in town (Loren).

Director Howard Deutch ("Pretty in Pink") whips through the formula like a math whiz doing fractions. He lets his two well-baked hams carry the show. Like "Grumpy Old Men," the humor here is geezers talking dirty—and fumbling their chances to do the nasty.

Lensed by cinematographer Tak Fujimoto ("Philadelphia"), the movie looks too good for a routine comedy. Loren and Ann-Margret look too good for their co-stars. The surprise is that Matthau and his straight man Lemmon can make even the most routine jokes and rude insults sound funnier than they are. This time around, the boys are grumpier but they're as funny as ever.

Also reviewed in:
CHICAGO TRIBUNE, 12/22/95, Friday/p. A, Michael Wilmington
NEW YORK TIMES, 12/22/95, p. C3, Stephen Holden
VARIETY, 12/18-31/95, p. 66, Leonard Klady
WASHINGTON POST, 12/22/95, p. C1, Rita Kempley

GUMBY: THE MOVIE

A Arrow Entertainment release of a Premavision production. *Producer:* Art Clokey and Gloria Clokey. *Director:* Art Clokey. *Screenplay:* Art Clokey. *Director of Photography:* Art Clokey. *Editor:* Lynn Stevenson. *Music:* Ozzie Ahlers. *Sound:* James Allen. *Art Director:* Gloria Clokey. *Running time:* 90 minutes. *MPAA Rating:* G.

WITH: Charles Farrington; Art Clokey; Gloria Clokey; Manny La Carruba; Alice Young; Janet McDuff; Bonnie Rudolph.

LOS ANGELES TIMES, 12/4/95, Calendar/p. 5, David Kronke

[The following review by David Kronke appeared in a slightly different form in
NEWSDAY, 12/11/95, Part II/p. B7.]

Sometimes big stars are better served taking on a supporting character role in a popular film than in trying to carry their own lame vehicle. Case in point: Had Gumby appeared in a supporting capacity in "Toy Story," his popularity and figure sales would now be soaring; alas, his ego drove him to headline "Gumby the Movie," which may be out on video before you finish reading this review.

Written, produced, directed and just about everything else by Gumby creator Art Clokey and his family, "Gumby the Movie" (in the film itself, it's somewhat more hopefully titled "Gumby 1") is like that new Beatles song: It won't exactly taint your fond childhood memories of the little green slab of clay, but it certainly doesn't do anyone involved any favors.

In this age in which computers can create lovable, sympathetic characters, "Gumby's" jittery claymation has something of a quaint appeal (a dog rides a skateboard in the movie, less because skateboards are cool nowadays than because it's easier to animate that way).

But there's nothing quaint or charming about the tired and listless screenplay, which sort of dawdles from situation to situation (the main plot involves the malevolent Blockheads' efforts to prevent Gumby and his pals from organizing a Farm Aid benefit).

Characters occasionally mouth groaners so lame it takes a few seconds to realize that the lines were intended as jokes. It's admirable, in a way, that Clokey and Co. haven't felt the need to update their hero for a '90s audience, but they should realize that movies should have dialogue much sharper than that slapped together on a tight TV production schedule.

Even Pokey seems a little embarrassed by the proceedings.

NEW YORK POST, 12/9/95, p. 17, Larry Worth

Long before Woody and Buzz Lightyear captured children's imagination in "Toy Story," a clay boy named Gumby and his orange horse Pokey romped through a delightfully surreal universe in a series of six-minutes shorts.

The gang got updated in the '80s when creator Art Clokey lensed some brand-new adventures for Gumby and company, then decided they were ready for the big screen. The result: "Gumby: The Movie."

Thankfully, the end product is more imaginative than the title. Producers, however, might have had their own doubts; the film virtually snuck into town and opened without a critics' screening.

Not to worry. Gumby and Pokey have stood the test of time. Sooner than he can scratch his asymmetrical head, Gumby is up to his old tricks: letting his feet of clay step into a series of oversized books like Alice passed through the looking glass. And the refreshingly cynical Pokey is never far behind.

Hopi Indians, whirling dervishes, animals from Old McDonald's farm and knights of the Round Table come into play, along with a whole new set of Gumby regulars: a yellow dinosaur named Prickle, a blue Goo sporting yellow yarn braids, the skateboard-riding dachshund Lowbelly and three rockers to round out Gumby's band, the Clayboys.

There's no shortage of hilarious moments, from parodies of John Mellencamp's Farm Aid concerts to spoofing Luke Skywalker and Darth Vader's "Empire Strikes Back" light-swords duel. But what becomes increasingly obvious is Clokey's inability to string those energetic bits into a cohesive storyline.

Too much time is spent on a yawnable framing device concerning a deadly Gumby clone and the inevitable kidnap plot. And while the new characters are lots of fun, they can't compensate for a lack of Gumby in the film's first half.

Granted, it's great to see the clay heroes back in the spotlight, along with the innocence and charming simplicity that became their trademark. But if Clokey's going to keep up with the likes of "Toy Story," his feature-length scripts can't bend, stretch, and ultimately squish viewers' attention spans. Better to leave the bending, stretching and squishing to Gumby and Pokey.

Also reviewed in:
VARIETY, 12/11-17/95, p. 84, Dennis Harvey

HACKERS

A United Artists Pictures release. *Executive Producer:* Iain Softley. *Producer:* Michael Peyser and Ralph Winter. *Director:* Iain Softley. *Screenplay:* Rafael Moreu. *Director of Photography:* Andrzej Sekula. *Editor:* Christopher Blunden and Martin Walsh. *Music:* Simon Boswell. *Music Editor:* Paul Rabjohns. *Sound:* Peter Lindsay. *Sound Editor:* Glenn Freemantle. *Casting:* Dianne Crittendon. *Production Designer:* John Beard. *Art Director:* John Frankish. *Set Decorator:* Joanne Woollard. *Hacker Consultant:* Jack Hitt and Paul Tough. *Visual Effects:* Tim Field. *Costumes:* Roger Burton. *Make-up:* Christine Blundell and Liz Daxauer. *Stunt Coordinator:* Jery Hewitt. *Running time:* 105 minutes. *MPAA Rating:* PG-13.

CAST: Jonny Lee Miller (Dade); Angelina Jolie (Kate); Jesse Bradford (Joey); Matthew Lillard (Cereal); Laurence Mason (Nikon); Renoly Santiago (Phreak); Fisher Stevens (The Plague);

Alberta Watson (Lauren Murphy);   Darren Lee (Razor);   Peter Y. Kim (Blade);   Ethan Browne (Curtis);   Lorraine Bracco (Margo);   Wendell Pierce (Agent Dick Gill);   Michael Gaston (Agent Bob);   Marc Anthony (Agent Ray);   Penn Jillette (Hal);   Liza Walker (Laura);   Bob Sessions (Mr. Ellingson);   Blake Willett (S.S. Agent, Seattle);   Max Ligosh (Young Dade);   Felicity Huffman (Attorney);   Paul Klementowicz (Michael Murphy);   Richard Ziman (Judge);   Bill Maul (Norm);   William DeMeo (Jock);   Denise George (Denise);   Jeb Handwerger and Mitchell Nguyen-McCormick (Freshmen on Roof);   Gary Klar (Mr. Simpson);   Terry Porter (Joey's Mom);   Johnny Myers (1st Sysops Technician);   Kevin Brewerton (2nd Sysops Technician);   Sam Douglas (English Teacher);   Kal Weber (1st V.P.);   Jeff Harding (2nd V.P.);   Tom Hill (2nd S.S. Agent);   Jennifer Rice (Reporter);   Douglas W. Iles (Addict Hank);   Annemarie Zola (Addict Vickie);   Michael Potts (Tow Truck Driver);   Nancy Ticotin (Phreak's Mom);   Mmike Ciccetti (Ellingson Guard);   Mick O'Rourke (Phone Repairman);   Dave Stewart (London Hacker);   Naoko Mori (Tokyo Hacker);   Roberta Gotti (Italian Hacker);   Ravil Isyanov and Olegario Fedoro (Russian Hackers);   Eric Loren (News Technician);   Kristin Moreu (Flight Attendant);   Ricco Ross (Second Reporter);   Tony Sibbald (Jail Guard);   Richard Purro (Talkshow Host);   Enzo Junior (Da Vinci Virus);   Yoshinori Yamamoto (3rd V.P.);   Ralph Winter (4th V.P.);   Kimbra Standish (Receptionist);   Steven Angiolini (Rollerblader).

LOS ANGELES TIMES, 9/15/95, Calendar/p. 8, David Kronke

"Hackers" is one of those movies that explore a cool misunderstood teen sub-culture with a breathtaking lack of verisimilitude. As a result, it gives you more insight into the minds of Hollywood hacks than of computer hackers.

It's about five kids at a New York high school who all just happen to be elite hackers, meaning they've each caused a major pile-up somewhere along the information superhighway. (Multiply these five kids by the number of high schools in this country and you wonder how any computers manage to get anything done if so many smart-alecky punks are routinely fooling with them.)

Despite goofy nicknames like Cereal Killer, they're the hippest computer nerds on the planet. The fact that they spend every spare moment fiddling with their laptops hasn't prevented them from ferreting out trendy underground clothing (costume designer Roger Burton's look could be called Road Warrior of Beverly Hills). Rather than discussing the nuances of "Star Trek: Voyager" over the Internet in their lonely rooms, they jam in a club that's equal parts acid house and virtual reality arcade.

Exquisite sexual tension is provided by Dade (Jonny Lee Miller), the new kid in town with a secret past, and Kate (Angelina Jolie), who initially dates a guy whose occupation is "just [looking] slick all day"—only in Hollywood can that pay the bills. As young lovers will, Dade and Kate flirt by showing off their hacking skills, competing to see who can ruin the lives of others more ingeniously.

For the rest of the cast, sexual tension is provided solely by their hardware: If real life made fetishes of computers as much as this movie does, Bill Gates would be People Magazine's Sexiest Man Alive. One guy plays with his nipple while describing an act of corporate sabotage, while another plants a big, wet kiss on his computer screen. Kate even abandons a bout of heavy petting at one point to show off her hard drive.

If the kids stand in one spot long enough to have a conversation, inevitably a sign will sprout up behind them reading, "Trust your technolust." If these guys got carpal-tunnel syndrome, you can bet they'd accessorize with studded black leather wrist braces.

Eventually, a semblance of plot surfaces, which can be summed up fairly thoroughly by a mere two lines of dialogue:

First: Corporate villainess Margo (a dazed Lorraine Bracco) asks skateboarding cyber-weasel The Plague (Fisher Stevens, one of the least menacing bad guys in cinema history), "You've created a virus that's gonna cause a worldwide ecological disaster just to arrest some hacker kids?"

Later: Discussing a beleaguered comrade, a pal of Dade's says, "The Secret Service is really out to get him—hey, there's a big party tonight, you wanna go?" At least their priorities are straight.

And the hardware! These kids' equipment come with options CompUSA declines to tell you about when you're browsing through PowerBooks: Keyboards have sound systems that, when tapped upon, create cool, futuristic echoes and ear-splitting guitar riffs (Simon Boswell's music seems intent only on blowing out THX Dolby theater speakers from coast to coast). Screens splash their images across the faces of their users and extemporaneously depict animated bytes flowing through circuitry as the hackers explore corporate files, which are apparently accessed as easily as pointing a mouse at an icon. (Can Windows 95 do all this?)

All this is courtesy of the short-circuited imagination of Rafael Moreu, making his feature screen-writing debut, and director Iain Softley, who hopes that if he piles on the attitude and stylized visuals, no one will notice just how empty and uninvolving the story really is. All the sound and fury in the world can't disguise the fact that yowling music, typing montages and computer animation do not a gripping finale make. This movie megabytes.

NEW YORK POST, 9/15/95, p. 43, Thelma Adams

Grab your Jolt, the ultra-caffeinated cola favored by "Hackers," and plug into the revenge of the computer nerds.

You'll probably need the extra charge to keep up with all the tangled story lines in Iain "Backbeat" Softley's boy-meets-girl, computer virus-meets-worm, cyber thriller.

Newcomer Rafael Moreu's energetic but muddled script networks a group of gifted hackers at Manhattan's Stuyvesant High School.

Dade (Jonny Lee Miller), the new boy on campus, has a past. He dabbled in white-collar computer crime before he was out of T-shirts and he's still on probation.

Everywhere Dade turns, he bumps into brilliant, acne-free hackettes: the young (Jesse Bradford), the black (Laurence Mason), the freaky (Renoly Santiago) and the hard-to-get but kissable Kate (Angelina Jolie).

As if getting a date wasn't hard enough for the gifted and socially challenged, Dade and the gang stumble across an elaborate industrial espionage scam that threatens the ecological balance of the world.

The mastermind behind the scheme is The Plague, a computer security specialist—in other words, a hacker with a single, steady source of income for his noodling skills.

As played with his usual smarm-charm by Fisher Stevens, Plague has the same feeling of retro futurism that burdens most of the recent spate of cyber schlock Imagine Ming the Merciless as a touch typist.

The moll to Stevens' Ming is the bubble-headed exec Margo (Lorraine Bracco in a steady acting decline) whose only words in her defense are that she can't even program a VCR. Do we hear Hollywood calling?

After "Hackers," "Johnny Mnemonic," "The Net," and "Virtuosity," I've discovered the first lesson of cyber movies. It's nearly impossible to dramatize computer usage.

You can chase computer nerds across electric landscapes, erase their identities, or revive high-wattage psycho killers, but that's all a distraction from the central conundrum: There's no drama in a guy flailing away at a keyboard.

How many typing thrillers were there in cinema's first 100 years?

"Hackers" tries to crash through this barrier by putting its characters in kinetic motion. The kids sprout rollerblades; Plague slings a mean skateboard.

What works in "Hackers" has nothing to do with things cyber. Miller's computer hot-shot with a bad haircut is increasingly charming as the movie progresses. His hunt-and-peck relationship with Jolie's brain in a bustier has some real spark.

Once the script pushes through its muddled middle of plots and sub-plots, the nerds come into complete focus and bond. The final hour achieves an appealing energy. It's as if director Softley finally breaks finally breaks the code of the funky side of the hacker subculture in the same way he improvised a riff on the early, underground German rock'n'roll days of The Beatles in "Backbeat."

NEWSDAY, 9/15/95, Part II/p. B4, John Anderson

You can't give it much, but give "Johnny Mnemonic" one thing: In it futuristic world-gone-wired, computers had made life considerably worse for the man/woman on the street. The monopolization of information wasn't a good thing, as Martha Stewart might say. It didn't improve schools, it didn't make people look better. It simply didn't provide.

And although "Hackers" is supposed to be set in present time, it is a technological and economic leap from here to there—there being the imaginary city of 1995 New York, a place where schools are clean, everyone looks like a model, everyone is on the Internet and there are enough opiates to keep the masses happy and productive—not trying to infiltrate corporate computer systems and wreak havoc.

"Hackers," like "Johnny Mnemonic," is a movie trying to get online while the getting's good, and a total fantasy, a joke of sorts, and as such it can be forgiven many sins. It may also be a western, since it has all the standard characters: Corporate, computerized America is the railroad; the government is, well, the government, and the hackers, high-school-age techno-wonks who can worm their way into any data base, are the last bastions of individuality in these here United States. (Keep repeating: It's only a movie.)

Dade (Jonny Lee Miller) is a hacker with a record: When he was 9 he infected Wall Street with a virus that crashed 1,507 computers. He lives to hack, and when a job for his mother (Alberta Watson of "Spanking the Monkey") brings them to New York, he falls in with a bunch of similarly addicted youth, all of whom are well equipped to undo the feeble security precautions of small-timers like AT&T and the major banks. The Plague (Fisher Stevens), however, is planning a rip-off of his own corporation, and when the hackers get in his way, he frames them with a virus that's set to sink a flotilla of oil tankers, thus causing pollution and bad karma.

Iain Softley, who directed the Beatles movie "Backbeat," flounders a bit. He resorts to the usual quick cuts, pumped-up music and flash graphics to impart a sense of cruising speed on the Internet—cheesy schtick at this point. His characters and their dynamics—especially Dade and Kate (Angelina Jolie), the computer queen who takes exception to Dade's existence—are pretty standard (they hate, they develop mutual respect, they find love, etc.). None of which is as current as the ostensible subject matter of the movie. One routine, having Dade's inner thoughts expressed in fleeting snippets of pop-cultural refuse, seems straight out of cable's "Dream On." Softley then drops it, as inexplicably as he introduced it.

The film does make the teenagers the heroes—they're smarter, they're faster, they don't have more insurance, but they do have the numbers—who undo Plague's evil scheme, but then they are left curiously adrift. Are we to think, even remotely, that one foiled plot will liberate data and benefit humankind? Or that the pranks of hackers aren't simply teaching the huge horders of information how to deflect infiltration? Or that the lone rangers of the information highway aren't going to go the way of the cowboy?

SIGHT AND SOUND, 5/96, p. 53, Jim McClellan

Seattle, 1988. Dade Murphy, an 11-year-old hacker whose computer virus has crashed Wall St, is arrested. Seven years later, Dade moves to New York and is soon hacking into a cable television station, where he locks horns with another hacker, Acid Burn. Next morning Dade meets (and is rebuffed by) Kate at his new school. He goes to techno-club Cyberdelia, where he again annoys Kate by beating her at a video game. That night he hacks into the school's computers, reprogramming the sprinkler system so everyone gets soaked the next day.

Dade is quickly accepted into the school's hacker gang by Phantom Phreak and Cereal Killer—unlike Joey who, desperate to prove himself, hacks into the Ellingson Mineral Corporation, unwittingly stumbling into a scam set up by the Plague, a hacker-turned-security-man. Plague alerts secret service agent Gill, suggesting Joey is part of a terrorist hacker cadre threatening to sink the company's computer-controlled supertankers. Joey is arrested but crucial files remain hidden. Plague then suggests to Dade that they join forces. Dade refuses.

Dade discovers that Kate is Acid Burn. Plague threatens Dade's mother. Enlisting extra help via the Internet, Dade, Kate and the others attempt to stop Plague from sinking the tankers, all the while being pursued by Gill. A chase across New York shifts into cyberspace, as hackers bombard the Ellingson computers with viruses. Though Plague is foiled, the teen hackers are arrested. Plague seems likely to escape but Cereal Killer, still free, hacks a television station and reveals the truth.

The Hollywood studios have yet to come up with an effective way of putting all things 'cyber' on-screen. Recent efforts to move computer technology front and centre (*The Net, Johnny*

Mnemonic, Virtuosity) demonstrate the limitations of the current formula—update an established genre (woman in peril, serial thriller) and play to the mass market's technophobia. Unfortunately, this is the approach adopted by *Hackers*, Iain Softley's follow-up to *Backbeat*. The result is a standard-issue post-MTV John Hughes-ish teen pic with techno-trimmings, a 90s juvenile delinquent picture in which the misunderstood hero doesn't ride a motorbike down the interstate but guns his hard drive up the infobahn.

The hacker may be an authentic modern folk devil—perhaps even the true heir of the beats—but unfortunately, computers don't look as good as motorbikes. Users may be taken to all sorts of info-mystical realms, but on screen, the machines just don't move. Consequently, the script's insistence that these black boxes are sex machines capable of delivering a fearsome erotic charge (there's a scene in which everyone drools over the 'killer refresh rate' of Kate's high-powered computer), can't help but look vaguely silly.

This is symptomatic of the general problem which bedevils most cyberfilms—the fact that all the real action happens in an immaterial realm—cyberspace and Softley often resorts to techno-cliché. As in so many other films, logging on to the net is figured as hallucinatory information-overload, a 2000-style trip. But Softley also attempts to map the urban landscape onto cyber-space—New York's skyline is depicted as computer circuitry; a corporate mainframe looks like massed ranks of neon skyscrapers. This pays off nicely in scenes suggesting the multi-mediated consciousness of Dade and the other hackers, for whom the real world is always bleeding away into an imaginary map of data flows and digital networks. Less effective is the idea that hackers are representatives of some kind of cyber youth culture, about to take the world by storm. The resulting assemblage of video games, rave videos and fractal club flyers looks like it was thrown together after a cursory flick through the West Coast cyber magazine *Mondo 2000*.

However, *Hackers'* real problem—aside from the fact that it accepts too readily hackers' rather sentimental vision of themselves as 'information freedom fighters'—is that anxiety over the 'immateriality' of its subject has provoked an anxious over-reaction in which potentially decent ideas are touched on only briefly. For example, the paranoia about the vulnerability of computer databases to manipulation, which *The Net* turned into a lumbering two-hour slog, is here the basis for a five minute comic routine in which Dade and Kate compete to change Agent Gill's records in ever more outrageous ways. In the end, though the idea of hackers serving as scapegoats for more powerful interests ostensibly provides the basic plot, the real narrative dynamics are those of the Hughes-style teen flic. So, for all the talk of "hacking the planet", what Dade really wants to do is get a date and be accepted for what he is. By the end of the film he's writing his and Kate's names in lights on the city skyline—by somehow hacking a nearby sky scraper's lighting system. Cute sentimental pay-offs go with the teen territory, but you end up feeling that if digital technology does have to appear on-screen via the filter of standard genres, why not at least pick something appropriate. Surely there's enough in hacker culture to produce a useful variant on the conspiracy movie.

VILLAGE VOICE, 9/26/95, p. 80, Amy Taubin

As techno savvy as *Mute Witness* is rough hewn [see Taubin's review], *Hackers* delivers a similar ratio of style to substance, although next to *The Net*, it seems absolutely brilliant (no way should this be used as ad copy). I see it as *The Net* crossed with *Kids* with a little bit of *Batman*. My friend Larry who understands the industry from the inside says the model is *WarGames* with the threat of nuclear extinction diminished to an all-engulfing oil spill. Larry was pissed off that *Hackers* didn't deliver on its thriller component. With a villain who's an easy mark, how could it? I was happy that it was an above-average teen comedy with the same premise as the all but forgotten *Real Genius*, that smart kids have more fun.

Directed by Iain Softley, who takes the same genius-lite approach to a multiculti bunch of New York teenage hackers as he did in *Backbeat* to the Beatles in their Hamburg days, *Hackers* has lots of attitude, great clothes, amusing dialogue, winning performances, and, if you like this sort of thing, an abundance of computer animation providing an imaginative landscape for what happens when one jacks into the secret world of corporate mainframe with a laptop. What it lacks in socio-economic logic—how do the public school kids come by their state-of-the-art hardware—it more than makes up for in its casually ultrademocratic politics: Hackers of the world unite against the corporate state.

Dade Murphy (Jonny Lee Miller) is the new boy in school, a hacker with a past. Dade was once Zero Cool, the 11-year-old who crashed 1500 Wall Street computers. Now as Crash Override he quickly wins the admiration of an elite crew of hackers, among them Cereal Killer (Matthew Lillard), who emulates Sean Penn in *Fast Times at Ridgemont High* but with pigtails, and Phantom Phreak, the terror of NYNEX (Renoly Santiago), who has the wittiest lines and a Latino throwaway delivery to match. Dade falls for Kate, a/k/a Acid Burn (Angelina Jolie), whose hacking prowess has hitherto gone unchallenged. Kate is a rich girl with huge eyes, bee-stung lips, and a tomboy stance. "I hope you don't screw like you type," she says as she contemplates Dade's fingers flying over the keys.

In comic-book fashion, the heroic hackers find their nemesis, The Plague (Fisher Stevens), a former freelance hacker who's become a hired hand for a big oil corporation. When The Plague realizes the hackers are on to his scheme to steal millions by planting a worm in the oil companies accounting files, he tries to frame them for industrial sabotage telling the FBI that they're responsible for the Da Vinci virus, which, if activated, will cause a dozen super tankers to spill their oil. "A worm *and* a virus!" exclaims the bemused Cereal Killer. "The plot thickens."

While real keyboard cowboys/girls may resent *Hackers* for ripping off and polishing up their subculture, the film is clearly on their side. Being a hacker is presented as the most glamorous and subversive identity a kid can aspire to, easily eclipsing being a film director or a rock star. What could be better than "to hack the planet" from atop the Empire State Building?

The young actors give enthusiastic performances (although Miller, a ringer for Chris O'Donnell in *Batman Forever*, sometimes seems a bit too posed). As Dade's mom, Alberta Watson is as much an object for adolescent fantasy as she was in *Spanking the Monkey*. In fact, the film is populated with bad dads and good moms. Darren Lee and Peter Y. Kim score as pair of punked-out Asian VJs, media icons, and elite hackers who come online for the final showdown with the message "Are we fashionably late!" As the villains, Fisher Stevens and Lorraine Bracco fare less well. The bewigged Bracco would be unrecognizable if not for her breathy Brooklyn baby-doll voice.

Special praise to Roger Burton's medieval-mixed-with-athletic-wear costumes. I coveted every one.

Also reviewed in:
CHICAGO TRIBUNE, 9/15/95, Friday/p. C, Michael Wilmington
NEW YORK TIMES, 9/15/95, p. C25, Janet Maslin
VARIETY, 9/18-24/95, p. 94, Joe Leydon
WASHINGTON POST, 9/15/95, p. D7, Hal Hinson
WASHINGTON POST, 9/15/95, Weekend/p. 44, Joe Brown

HALLOWEEN: THE CURSE OF MICHAEL MYERS

A Dimension Films release of a Nightfall production. *Executive Producer:* Moustapha Akkad. *Producer:* Paul Freeman. *Director:* Joe Chappelle. *Screenplay:* Daniel Farrands. *Director of Photography:* Billy Dickson. *Editor:* Randy Bricker. *Music:* Alan Howarth. *Sound:* Mark Hopkins McNabb. *Casting:* Ross Brown and Mary West. *Production Designer:* Bryan Ryman. *Art Director:* T.K. Kirkpatrick. *Costumes:* Ann Gray. *Special Make-up Effects:* John Carl Buechler. *Running time:* 88 minutes. *MPAA Rating:* R.

CAST: Donald Pleasance (Dr. Loomis); Mitch Ryan (Dr. Wynn); Marianne Hagan (Kara Strode); Paul Rudd (Tommy Doyle); Leo Geter (Barry Simms); George P. Wilbur (Michael Myers); Devin Gardner (Danny Strode); Mariah O'Brien (Beth)

LOS ANGELES TIMES, 10/2/95, Calendar/p. 8, Jack Matthews

It is considerate of the shlock-meisters still toiling in the realm of slasher movies launched in the late '70s to put the name of their immortal bogey men in the titles. You wouldn't want to be sitting next to a horror buff expecting Jason and getting Freddy.

So, hats off, in that respect, to the producers of "Halloween: The Curse of Michael Myers," the latest in a numbing series begun in 1978 by John Carpenter, and repeated five times since, with only a few plot and casting changes to detract from the brilliant slice-and-dice work of its masked hero, Mike may be getting older, but he can still sling a knife around like a chef at Benihana.

In Part 6, Michael Myers, who died in an explosion at the end of Part 5, returns unsinged to trick-or-treat the folks in his hometown of Haddonfield, where he began killing as a child on Halloween, and where the holiday has been outlawed in his memory.

His agenda, we are told by old Doc Loomis (the late Donald Pleasence, almost unrecognizably frail) and Tommy Doyle (Paul Rudd), a young man who survived an earlier slaughter, is to murder the family now living in his old house, and—as a special bonus—a newborn baby who bears the sign of evil.

The body count mounts quickly as Michael picks off members of the targeted family, along with the doctors, nurses, real estate brokers, deejays and other rubes who amble into his view. A slit throat here, a crunched skull there, here a hatchet, there a pitchfork, eee-iii-eee-iii-ohhhh!

"Enough of this Michael Meyers. B.S.!," says a disgruntled Haddon-fielder, as news spreads of the returning native son.

Dream on.

NEW YORK POST, 9/30/95, p. 17, Thelma Adams

Just when you thought it was safe to carve that pumpkin again, along comes "Halloween: The Curse of Michael Myers."

The curse of Mikey—the masked serial killer who began by snuffing his sister one Pumpkin Day and then did Freud one better by slaughtering every member of his family—is his addiction to sequels.

"The Curse" is the latest entry in the slaughterfest begun by horrormeister John Carpenter in 1978. Carpenter has had the good sense to take his cut but skip his spot at the helm ever since, letting unknowns like Joe Chappelle turn the franchise into drive-in fodder.

The sixth in the line of slasher slush films is a hack job. First, Myers, a bit of "pure evil," impales a postpartum mom. Then he whacks an unhappy homemaker (Tide aside: How do you remove those nasty bloodstains?) and drills her drunken hubby. Then he ...

"The Curse" follows the time-worn don't-open-that-closet, don't-go-into-that-house, don't-turn-on-that-washer-dryer format.

Enter the Druid subplot. Tommy (Paul Rudd), traumatized by witnessing his babysitter's murder years before (she was Myers' niece), sees an ancient rune left by Myers at a murder site. The young man leaps to the conclusion that the psycho is practicing human sacrifice.

As quickly as this idea is raised it's dropped like last-year's Druid. Back to Myers as pure evil. But what's the purest evil of them all? The ending is sequel-ready.

The movie is dedicated to the late Donald Pleasence, who wearily stares down the grave in his sixth and final performance as Myers' nemesis. In his case, Rest in Peace means never having to appear in "Halloween 7: The Relentless Search for Profit."

Also reviewed in:
NEW YORK TIMES, 9/30/95, p. 15, Stephen Holden
VARIETY, 10/2-8/95, p. 40, Daniel M. Kimmel
WASHINGTON POST, 10/2/95, p. D6, Richard Harrington

HARLEM DIARY: NINE VOICES OF RESILIENCE

A Discovery Channel release in association with Gabriel Films. *Executive Producer:* Steve Burns. *Producer:* Jonathan Stack. *Director:* Jonathan Stack. *Screenplay:* Terry Williams. *Director of Photography:* Maryse Alberti and Samuel Henriques. *Editor:* Suzanne Szabo Rostock. *Music:* John Hicks. *Sound:* Stuart Deutsch. *Running time:* 96 minutes. *MPAA Rating:* Not Rated.

WITH: Jermaine Ashwood; Amir Williams-Foster;   Michael Counsins;   Barr Elliot; Nikki Matos; Kahil Hicks; Christina Head; Kass Kalanzo; Salaim Shabazz; Amir Williams-Foster; Damon Williams; Rasheem Swindell; Akida Bailey; Diarra Cummings; Errol Kenya James; Kahli Hicks; Nikki Matos; Rasheem Swindell; Damon Williams.

LOS ANGELES TIMES, 10/20/95, Calendar/p. 12, Kevin Thomas

The arrival of Jonathan Stack's "Harlem Diary: Nine Voices of Resilience," in the immediate aftermath of the Million Man March, couldn't be timelier, for it sends the same basic message of taking responsibility for one's own life even in the face of overwhelming adversity.

In their stirring, illuminating documentary, producer-director Stack, co-director Spencer Style and writer/co-producer Terry Williams introduce us to nine distinctive, thoroughly engaging African Americans, ranging from 12 to 26, who tell us their stories for both Stack's camera and through their own. The result is a well-structured, well-paced film that flows with grace and spontaneity and has been masterfully edited by Susanne Szabo Rostock. Aiding greatly to the film's varying moods is John Hicks' evocative score.

All nine speak of a determination to make something of their lives. You fear not only that all of them may not succeed but, because of the neighborhood violence that endangers everyone who lives there, you also fear for those well on their way to their goals. What "Harlem Diary" makes so very clear is that the lives of each of these individuals is valuable, that each has a potential for accomplishment for themselves and their communities. Significantly, fathers are virtually absent from their lives: One gets out of prison shortly after his son, another is a white man who lives in Virginia.

The film's scene-stealer is unquestionably its youngest participant, Amir Williams-Foster, a 12-year-old near-lifelong actor starring in the soap opera "All My Children." Amir is as brilliant as he is handsome, breathtakingly articulate and, as a filmmaker and a photographer, he speaks of "narrative" and "structure" and the need to see beyond the surface of his photos. We for sure will hear more from him.

Christina Head, a 17-year-old beauty raised by her staunch grandmother, takes us with her as she visits her Greek father for her half-sister's wedding in Virginia Beach, Va. Half-black, half-white, Christina was taught to think of herself first as a person rather than as a member of either race, but she arrives at her father's home with an understandable apprehension as to how she will be accepted. Her fears prove unfounded, yet afterward, she's glad to be back home.

Akida Bailey, 21, finds success in a mid-town Manhattan brokerage firm but has trouble getting a cab, despite his business suit and briefcase. Gradually, his unhappiness grows, and he risks quitting his good job to pursue some kind of position in Harlem that would allow him to work with children.

Many but not all of the rest of the film's young people are as centered as these three, and it's hard to be optimistic about some of them, no matter how strong and true their insights into themselves and society, given the crushing circumstances of their lives.

These nine people are so adroit at speaking for themselves that the occasional on-screen narration by Williams, a sociologist, often seems academic and redundant. In most instances, we'd like to know more about the young people's families—where did all those fathers go, how does it happen that one mother has nine children, ranging from 17 to a baby, without a man in sight? What are the families' sources of income?

"Harlem Diary" is nonetheless a fine, moving accomplishment filled with truths about all people, young and old, and not just African Americans.

NEW YORK POST, 10/27/95, p. 46, Bill Hoffmann

Give video cameras to nine young residents of Harlem, ask them to put their lives on tape and you'll get powerful images.

That's what director Jonathan Stack did—ending up with a jarring, often powerful documentary called "Harlem Diary."

These amateur filmmakers dive head first into a world many New Yorkers can only dream or read about in the papers and shake their heads: a world in which street violence, broken homes, rampant drug use, substandard housing and shattered dreams are the daily norm.

Stack's subjects hit you with the horrors of urban poverty for 90 harrowing minutes; but amazingly, "Harlem Diary" isn't a downer.

The young people who chronicle their lives here are resilient, headstrong individuals determined to beat the odds and make it in the world.

One is Damon Williams, 20, a Riker's inmate whose mom has died of AIDS and whose dad and brother are also behind bars. Now, with the birth of his daughter, Damon wants to learn a trade and go straight.

Another is Nikki Matos, an 18-year-old single mother, who organizes a street play and mural as a memorial after her best buddy, Mark, is shot dead in random gunfire.

"I have been to so many funerals that the faces of the dead have disappeared," she explains.

Sad and depressing stories, yes. But these kids refuse to give up—and that ultimately makes the film a tribute to the incredible strength of the human spirit.

My one beef with "Harlem Diary" is its annoying use of an optical process in which scenes are given a herky-jerky, stop-motion look.

This technique has been done to death on music videos and cop shows and its use here adds a hokey look to sequences that need to be played straight. Stack's material is rock-solid, but the cheap effects dilute its power.

VILLAGE VOICE, 10/31/95, p. 76, Gary Dauphin

Using the footage produced by Harlem young people enrolled in a video-diary program, documentarian Jonathan Stack has assembled an understated mix of set pieces, monologues, neighborhood tours, and reenactments as different and diverting as their under-25 directors.

Narrated by writer Terry Williams, *Harlem Diary* features nine segments, the best of them from Christina Head, a thoughtful princess of Greek and African American descent trapped in the high-rise tower from some nightmare urban fairy tale, and Kahlil Hicks, a onetime "bouncer" at a crack house. Christina brings her camera along to a white half sister's wedding down south, an evil eye to protect her from rejection from the other side of the family. What she comes back with instead are quiet home movies of dancing and laughter so wholesomely average that the racial divide and her fears evaporate on screen. In contrast, Kahlil pulls a talk-TV sting, taking his camera into his old place of business and pointing out the habits of the users with clinical detachment. His film includes *Harlem Diary*'s only movie-movie image: one of the crackheads singing a blues song while accompanied by a fellow lost soul on a broken-down bass, Kahlil's handheld swirling around as he fights to get the right angle.

The most technically polished is by a self-described child actor and photographer, his black Bohemian pretensions already fully in place at the age of 12. In the end, though, you have to like the kid the way you do any cute, talkative youngster who's smarter than you are. He might be the weak link in this film but that's just because he's young, and in a climate marked by the demonization of young people of color, Stack and *Harlem Diary* have the wisdom to know that that's no crime.

Also reviewed in:
NEW YORK TIMES, 10/27/95, p. C14, Walter Goodman
VARIETY, 10/23-29/95, p. 46, Leonard Klady

HEAT

A Warner Bros. release in association with Regency Enterprises of a Forward Pass production. *Executive Producer:* Arnon Milchan and Pieter Jan Brugge. *Producer:* Art Linson. *Director:* Michael Mann. *Screenplay:* Michael Mann. *Director of Photography:* Dante Spinotti. *Editor:* Dov Hoenig, Pasquale Buba, William Goldenberg, and Tom Rolf. *Music:* Elliot Goldenthal.

Music Editor: Lee Scott, Stephan Lotwis, Michael Connell, Jay Richardson, and Denise Okimoto. *Sound:* Lee Orloff and (music) Stephen McLaughlin and Joel Iwataki. *Sound Editor:* Per Hallberg and Larry Kemp. *Casting:* Bonnie Timmermann. *Production Designer:* Neil Spisak. *Art Director:* Marjorie Stone McShirley. *Set Designer:* Robert Fectman, Steven Schwartz, and Paul Sonski. *Set Decorator:* Anne H. Ahrens. *Special Effects:* Terry D. Frazee. *Costumes:* Deborah L. Scott. *Make-up:* John Caglione, Jr. *Stunt Coordinator:* Joel Kramer. *Running time:* 161 minutes. *MPAA Rating:* R.

CAST: Al Pacino (Vincent Hanna); Robert De Niro (Neil McCauley); Val Kilmer (Chris Shiherlis); Jon Voight (Nate); Tom Sizemore (Michael Cheritto); Diane Venora (Justine); Amy Brenneman (Eady); Ashley Judd (Charlene); Mykelti Williamson (Drucker); Wes Studi (Casals); Ted Levine (Bosko); Dennis Haysbert (Breedan); William Fichtner (Van Zant); Natalie Portman (Lauren); Tom Noonan (Kelso); Kevin Gage (Waingro); Hank Azaria (Marciano); Susan Traylor (Elaine Cheritto); Kim Staunton (Lillian); Danny Trejo (Trejo); Henry Rollins (Hugh Benny); Jerry Trimble (Schwartz); Marty Ferrero (Construction Clerk); Ricky Harris (Albert Torena); Tone Loc (Richard Torena); Begonya Plaza (Anna Trejo); Hazelle Goodman (Hooker's Mother); Ray Buktenica (Timmon); Jeremy Piven (Dr. Bob); Xander Berkley (Ralph); Rick Avery and Bill McIntosh (Armored Guards); Brad Baldridge (Children's Hospital Doctor); Andrew Camuccio and Brian Comuccio (Dominick); Max Daniels (Shooter at Drive-in); Vince Deadrick, Jr. (Driver at Drive-in); Charles Duke (Cop); Thomas Elfmont (Desk Clerk Cop); Kenny Endoso (Bartender); Kimberly Flynn (Casals' Date); Steven Ford (Officer Bruce); Farrah Forke (Caludia); Hannes Fritsch (Miracle Mile Bartender); Amanda Graves (Linda Cheritto); Emily Graves (Anita Cheritto); Niki Harris (Marcia Drucker); Ted Harvey and Daniel O'Haco (Detectives); Patricia Healy (Bosko's Date); Paul Herman (Sergeant Heinz); Cindy Katz (Rachel); Brian Libby (Captain Jackson); Dan Martin (Harry Dieter); Rick Marzan (Basketball Player); Terry Miller (Children's Hospital Nurse); Paul Moyer (News Anchorman); Mario Roberts (Bank Guard); Phillip Robinson (Alphonse); Thomas Rosales, Jr. (Armored Truck Driver); Rainell Saunders (Dead Hooker); Kai Soremekun (Prostitute); Rey Verdugo (Vegas Cop); Wensy L. Walsh (News Anchorwoman); Yvonne Zima (Hostage Girl).

FILMS IN REVIEW, 3-4/96, p. 60, Victoria Alexander

Heat has got to be Michael Mann's dream cast, with Al Pacino as cop Vincent Hanna and Robert De Niro playing arch criminal Neil McCauley. The supporting cast is equally impressive, with McCauley's crew including the always interesting Tom Sizemore, Val Kilmer, and Jon Voight. After a long film hiatus, it's nice to see Voight again, although I couldn't understand a word he said in the film (and this in a role essential to the plot since he plays the moneyman behind the scenes).

Writer-director Mann knows how to create feverish tension. Movie icons Pacino and De Niro are given adversarial roles loaded with characterization, depth, and sexiness. With *Raging Bull* the exception, De Niro doesn't play sexy often. Here, De Niro is sexy, but his sexual dynamic is displayed in a scene with Pacino, instead of with his lonely girlfriend Eady (played by TVs Amy Brenneman of *NYPD Blue*). The subplots follow the relationships both cop and criminal have with the respective women in their lives. Pacino has the more colorful scenes with his wife, played by Diane Venora; De Niro's character is ice cold and distant.

The gist of *Heat,* that these two men are equally matched professionals, with ace teams backing them up, makes for exciting entertainment. It's a fast, mesmerizing three hours of stylized moviemaking. Unfortunately, Pacino slips into an alternate screen personality who, every once in a while, is given to yelling like a methamphetamine maniac. Perhaps someone thought *both* men were too cool, and Pacino drew the short straw.

As in his *Miami Vice* TV series and the film *Manhunter,* Mann seems fascinated by cops with a dark side. Wasn't Detective Sonny Crocket a hair's breadth away from committing a felony, week after week? *Heat*'s cop Hanna so admires the skill of McCauley, he uses a police helicopter to find him and off they go for coffee. However, without this lapse in protocol, we'd never get one of the film's most electric and enjoyable scenes: Pacino and De Niro face to face.

My husband weighed in with his evaluation of *Heat*, since many years ago he had worked as a vice cop in Miami. He just couldn't abide the glaring inaccuracies that plague *Heat* and many other police dramas. He's right about several major points in *Heat* and, frankly, Mann has the skill and expertise to know better. It shows lazy writing and sloppy research. When Pacino and his men observe the crew breaking into a warehouse, they let them go instead of arresting them for a burglary-in-progress. Just being in each other's company would constitute a parole violation, sending them back to the "joint" pronto, and as with most movies, uniformed cops are portrayed as simply dumb. Why, I know housewives who wouldn't leave a mall unless they checked to see if they were being followed.

The cops in *Heat* fall for the dopiest of ploys: McCauley pulls a fire alarm in a hotel to settle a score with a former crew member hiding out there. The police are expecting McCauley and he knows it. They are not only with the guy, they are outside guarding his room. When the fire alarm goes off, they run to see what the trouble is, leaving the guy alone. McCauley easily enters the room and kills him. And in the final shoot-out, Hanna disregards standard police procedure by not calling for backup, pursuing McCauley alone through an active aircraft runway.

I can't stand stupid victims and thank goodness they keep them out of *Heat*. Everybody here (except the men in blue) are at the top of their game. I certainly don't want to see movies about cops typing out reports all day or arguing the fine, legal points of an arrest. But intelligent, well thought-out crime dramas, such as 1995's *Seven* and *The Usual Suspects* rank much higher in authenticity than the high-gloss, high-concept *Heat*.

LOS ANGELES TIMES, 12/15/95, Calendar/p. 1, Kenneth Turan

What's old has been made fine and new in "Heat." Writer-director Michael Mann and a superlative cast have taken a classic heist movie rife with familiar genre elements and turned it into a sleek, accomplished piece of work, meticulously controlled and completely involving. The dark end of the street doesn't get much more inviting than this.

Though Mann is best known for directing "The Last of the Mohicans" and executive producing TV's "Miami Vice," moviegoers with a fondness for crime stories will remember "Thief," his polished 1981 feature debut starring James Caan as a master safecracker and Tuesday Weld as the woman in his life.

With its poetically heightened dialogue and fascination with character and the mechanics of crime, "Heat" is a satisfyingly new venture into that same territory. No one sees as much epic existential heroism in the romantic fatalism of hard men and the women who try to love them as Mann does. Sometimes he even sees too much, and "Heat" (which at 2 hours and 45 minutes wouldn't be harmed by a trim) does overreach at times. Yet its narrative pull, as unrelenting as a riptide, creates more than enough tension to compensate.

The story of the battle of wills between master criminal Neil McCauley (Robert De Niro) and LAPD detective Lt. Vincent Hanna (Al Pacino), "Heat" is an intensely masculine film, bent on mythologizing the lonely, driven men on both sides of the law it shows to be as disciplined and directed as warrior monks.

"Heat" also makes explicit one of the themes implicit in films like these, that criminal and cop, hunted and hunter, have more in common than not. Obsessed and obsessive, dedicated to doing what they do best to the exclusion of anything else in their lives, the cool McCauley and the passionate Hanna are closer to each other than to their nominal partners in and out of crime.

"Heat" opens with one of the film's beautifully re-created criminal actions, McCauley and his regular crew of Chris (Val Kilmer) and Michael (Torn Sizemore) are joined by a new guy named Waingro (Kevin Gage) in a carefully planned attack on an armored car. Everything doesn't quite work out as intended, however, and detective Hanna gets to try on a new case for size.

Though Hanna is introduced making love to his wife, Justine (Diane Venora), don't be fooled. Justine is wife No. 3, and the marriage is not going well. Smart, ferocious and tireless, the detective barely has a life outside of pursuing those who break the law. Afraid that unburdening himself will make him lose his edge, Hanna is unwilling to share any of himself with anyone. "All I am," he admits, "is what I'm going after."

That's a sentiment Neil McCauley wouldn't have difficulty echoing. An ascetic criminal mastermind who lives in a furnitureless house by the Pacific, McCauley accurately describes his emotional state as "a needle starting at zero going the other way."

At ease with all forms of violence but unwilling to raise his voice or say an unnecessary word, McCauley lives by the strictest code: "Allow nothing in your life you can't walk out on in 30 seconds flat." Still, for all his caution and savvy, McCauley, with Hanna on his tail, ends up trying for that one last job no movie criminal can resist.

At the core of "Heat's" success is the strength of its ensemble acting. By paring away nonessentials and clamping down on mannerisms and tricks, Mann has helped his actors both uncover and rediscover the core of their appeal, the innate qualities that made them stars in the first place. There is no one in the film, including Pacino, De Niro, Kilmer, Sizemore and a ravaged-looking Jon Voight, who does not give the kind of restrained yet powerful performance that ranks with the very best work of their careers.

And surprising for a film that deals with outsized macho emotions, this concern for acting and characterization carries over into the opposite sex. Mann pays close attention to human moments, to what the script laconically calls "husband and wife stuff," and the gifted trio of Diane Verona, Ashley Judd and Amy Brenneman have more impact on this film than would ordinarily be the case.

"Heat" does other things equally well. Its use of L.A. locations is excellent (as was the case with Mann's earlier "Manhunter") and its violence is for the most part carefully parceled out, potent without causing revulsion. Mann's dialogue can sound overwrought and self-consciously operatic, but it is more often muscular and to the point.

The notion of criminals as lonely, existential warriors is of course not new (Jean-Pierre Melville's "Le Samourai," starring Alain Delon, did it especially well), but it's rarely done with as much dexterity and panache as Mann and company have provided.

NEW YORK, 12/18/95, p. 50, David Denby

In *Heat*, Michael Mann is back on the streets again, which is very good news. Mann's previous movie, *The Last of the Mohicans*, offered such pictorial enchantments as waterfalls, forts, and Daniel Day-Lewis au naturel, swinging through the woods like Tarzan just out of the shower. It was all very pretty, and sometimes violent and spectacular, but the director of *Manhunter* and the creator of the television series *Miami Vice* and *Crime Story* belongs in those dark alleys among cops and criminals every bit as much as John Ford belonged among cowboys and cavalry officers. *Heat* is about crime in Los Angeles, a familiar movie subject, God knows, but Mann has mounted the production with high intelligence and on a grand scale—an epic scale really. There are not one but two obsessional figures—Neil McCauley (Robert De Niro), the head of a frighteningly determined and brutal group of thieves, and Vincent Hanna (Al Pacino), a haggard but still potent and resourceful LAPD detective. We see the planning and then the execution of the heists and the way the police, a step or two behind, struggle to catch up; and we get the aftermath, the bloody mopping up, with its furious displays of loyalty and betrayal. Mann's staging of the crime scenes is extraordinary—concentrated, businesslike, physically inventive, and extremely violent. But Mann wanted to do more than action. The criminal and the cop are seen as parts of a social group, surrounded by partners and friends, and also by the women who carry the burden of their lives and who, for once, emerge as complex individuals rather than the usual languorous molls. By the end, we feel we've gotten to know both sides of the law extremely well.

The mental duel between hunter and quarry—redoubled by the implicit rivalry between Pacino and De Niro—holds the picture together. Mann demythologizes his two figures without making them any less frightening or heroic. De Niro's McCauley certainly becomes one of the most impressive of all movie criminals, a man who never stops thinking and is therefore gentle as well as brutal—he looks after his men so they will be there when he needs them. (Gentleness, we learn, can be one of the criminal's principal tools.) This implacable man doesn't come back from the dead like the vicious movie villains of recent years, but he does keep on coming, and coming; he's a genius of thoroughness, and De Niro plays him without a wasted moment or emotion. A perfect criminal, McCauley has no weaknesses. When his loneliness temporarily leads him to an innocent young woman (Amy Brenneman), he protects her against himself.

Pacino doesn't try to be cooler than De Niro. He goes for the contrast. He's hoarse-voiced, wrought up, with a shambling walk, his arms flying. Intimidating some poor rat-fink informer, he's antic and noisy. The lieutenant is an explosive man who prizes his anxieties, which keep him alert. With the other cops, however, Hanna is all command—there's a wonderful episode in which he takes control of a crime scene, analyzing evidence and rapping out orders. You see him thinking all the time, too. On the job, Hanna gives and gives, but at home, he's numb, recessive, and his wife (Diane Venora) feels shut out. That situation is not unusual for movie cops, but I've never seen a police detective's wife like Diane Venora, who has a long neck, bangs, and a tense and unusual presence. You can see why these two belong together—also why they will never be happy together, as if she had just stopped in from a Village coffeehouse.

Under the skin, McCauley and Hanna are really very similar—both of them driven, violent men, great at what they do and unable to imagine doing anything else. At one point, they pause in their furious activities and meet over coffee, exchanging views with ironic politeness, like two rival bankers or novelists. Mann has created a mythic moment: Pacino and De Niro have never appeared in the same scene together. But he purposely underdramatizes the meeting, not wanting to do anything obvious, and the double meanings catch up to us slowly. These are two killer actors who despite all their differences in technique have come together. *Heat* is yet another exploration of that perennial movie subject, the male mystique of professionalism and violence, yet it's one of the best—an action film with an intellectual grip that never once, in almost three hours, lets go.

NEW YORK POST, 12/15/95, p. 52, Thelma Adams

Michael Mann wrote the book on testosterone. Think Don Johnson in "Miami Vice." Think Daniel Day-Lewis running, running, running in "The Last of the Mohicans." Think Robert De Niro and Al Pacino in the sprawling L.A. crime saga "Heat."

Think again.

The always entertaining producer/writer/director Mann demonstrates a Mount Rushmore respect for these two acting icons. He would have been better off treating them like just two more members of the unbeatable supporting cast, a gang that includes hormone heavy Val Kilmer (my kingdom for those lips), Tom Sizemore, Ted Levine, Diane Venora, Wes Studi and the fantastically tart Ashley Judd.

The aging Italian stallions play mirror images of each other. De Niro's Neil McCauley is a pro who pulls off crack, high-level robberies with a tight crew; Pacino's Vincent Hanna is a robbery/homicide lieutenant who always gets his man.

Both are loners, a fact externalized through decor (we've seen enough "Miami Vice" and "Crime Story" to know how essential interior design is to Mann's pulp fiction). McCauley owns a beach house ripped from the pages of "Architectural Digest," with hardly enough glasses to fill one cabinet in his custom kitchen. Hanna bunks with his third wife in the overwrought, post-modern nightmare, she got in the divorce settlement from her previous husband; the only thing in the house that's his is the TV.

"I'm alone, I'm not lonely," McCauley protests too much.

For most of the cat-and-mouse movie, Mann separates De Niro and Pacino. They share one hoot of a kitschy, crackpot scene at the movie's hinge. Hanna pulls McCauley over and takes him to a diner. Leaving the characters behind, the two actors go into coffee-klatch mode, sharing their dreams and fears, their tics and trade secrets, and dropping those hard-boiled lines they've been chewing ever since they began playing big-screen cops and robbers on the cusp of the '70s. As Pacino says, "You do what you do, and I do what I gotta do."

Before the climactic (or, at nearly three hours, anti-climactic) scene at LAX, where the dueling method actors confront death under the jets, the doppelgangers frame a familiar Mann universe. The action set pieces are slick and riveting; the complicated personal lives of the individuals are given their series of intense scenes of passion or discord (no couch potato evenings here!); the internal conflicts of men on both sides of the law are threshed up and Mann marks his urban territory with neon lights and unusual locations.

There are enough plot twists, romantic complications and divine bad guys to fill a year of series television. In fact, in the '80s, Mann dealt with all these issues and more in his awesome—and little seen—Chicago to Vegas gangster panorama "Crime Story." Propelled by an unbeatable Todd Rundgren score, Mann generated more heat with pock-marked Dennis ("Get Shorty") Farina in the lead as the driven cop than he does with Pacino.

With "Crime Story," Mann achieved art through pulp fiction. Occasionally, "Heat" rises to the level of good slush TV, but when Mann succumbs to De Niro and Pacino worship and takes himself too seriously, the results are lukewarm.

NEWSDAY, 12/15/95, Part II/p. B7, Jack Mathews

For a movie that seems to have been cooked up in a Crock-Pot, Michael Mann's "Heat" gives off plenty of heat.

It's too slick, with an MTV veneer and an overloaded electronic score, it has a Los Angeles cops'n robbers plot more implausible than the O.J. Simpson defense theory, and at nearly three hours, it has approximately three times more glib yammer and phony macho posturing than an episode of Mann's "Miami Vice." But with Robert De Niro and Al Pacino working together for the first time in their storied careers, it goes where no Mann has ever gone before.

Writer-director Mann pulled off a major coup in getting the two New York acting dynamos for his movie, and though they play direct adversaries who meet only twice—once in a wordless shootout—their awareness of each other charges every scene. It is huge commercial grandstanding by all involved, and will satisfy no one hoping for a mano-a-mano acting clinic. But hey, it could have been Nick Nolte and Eddie Murphy.

Set in contemporary Los Angeles, a sprawling carpet of lights we see most often from balconies and windows in the Hollywood Hills, "Heat" is the story of an obsessive robbery/homicide detective named Vincent Hanna (Pacino) who allows his marriage to crumble while pursuing Neil McCauley (De Niro), the stealthy head of a gang plotting a $12-million bank job.

Mann attempts a couple of fine balancing acts, telling his story from the points of view of both the hunter and the hunted, and mixing, in equal parts, his kind of explosive action melodrama with honest character study. He succeeds marvelously with the first act, cutting back and forth from Hanna and McCauley, each of whom is trying to resolve personal problems of loneliness and connection, while moving closer and closer to a showdown that only one is likely to survive.

Pacino is given more opportunity for those explosive outbursts that have become hallmarks of both actors' screen personas. Hanna is a sort of feral detective, full of nervous energy and passion, qualities that make him a star on the force but a lousy companion at home. With a wife (Diane Venora) on the verge of a nervous breakdown, and a teenage stepdaughter (Natalie Portman) becoming alienated and morose, Hanna's two lives are about to tear each other apart.

McCauley, on the other hand, is the personification of the cool arch criminal, a thief with great ambition and keen instincts, who knows when to hit and when to walk away. He's a crook who spends as much time casing the police as the bank. But after meeting and falling in love with a young bookstore clerk (Amy Brenneman), McCauley's getting used to the idea of not being alone, and that sentiment—in his line of work—is a serious liability.

That these two men would meet over coffee to discuss their relative agendas is the film's most ridiculous and successful conceit. There is something in their conversation, in their interaction, that has more to do with the actors' careers than with those of their characters, and it's about worth the price of admission.

There are a lot of other things—too many other things—going on. Mann's attempting, in ways that become glaringly superficial, to depict the other thieves as full, psychological beings, family men being tugged in opposite directions by their antisocial habits and their desires for normal lives. But because these guys have to deliver the firepower required of the action genre, they think nothing of slaughtering innocent, presumably normal people, and after the first couple of excessive shoot-outs, you want to flush the whole bunch out of your mind.

In any event, the secondary characters among them, Val Kilmer as McCauley's gambling-addicted sidekick, Ashley Judd as Kilmer's fed-up wife, and a sickly Jon Voight as the gang's financier—serve more to confuse than clarify the story. The time spent with them dilutes the film's real strength and stretches its thin story 30 to 40 minutes too far.

"Heat" would have been a lot hotter if Mann had trusted more in the power of De Niro and Pacino and less in his own imagination.

NEWSWEEK, 12/18/95, p. 68, David Ansen

Neil McCauley (Robert De Niro) and Vincent Hanna (Al Pacino) are good at their work. McCauley executes high-stakes heists. Hanna stalks crooks for the LAPD. The cop is a high-strung guy with two bad marriages behind him and a third on the rocks. The robber, a veteran of Folsom, wants no distracting attachments. Cautious, methodical, he's an emotional ascetic. Both McCauley and Hanna are obsessives who find their deepest sense of themselves in the single-minded pursuit of their passion. It's not justice or money that provides the rush, but the action itself. They are the formidable antagonists, the existential cat and mouse, in Michael Mann's *Heat*, a stunning crime drama that shares its protagonists' rabid attention to detail—and love of adrenalin.

A genre movie with epic ambitions, Mann's sprawling saga starts with a bravura heist: McCauley and his crew topple an armored car, leaving three dead guards behind. Hanna starts his investigation, and Mann starts his, delving into the hearts and minds of the thieves in McCauley's crew, the women who choose to live with them, and the cops, informers and petty crooks whose lives become entangled in the wake of the crime. Mann's not interested in good and evil, but in behavior: the choices people make, the internal pressures that can cause the best-laid plans to go awry. When the heat comes down, Mann watches these human atoms implode, setting off a violent chain reaction that few will survive.

You know you will get high style and hard-bitten romanticism from the man who made "Thief" and "The Last of the Mohicans," and TV's "Miami Vice" and "Crime Story." There are set pieces here—a gunfight in an abandoned drive-in movie, a chaotic shoot-out on the downtown L.A. streets—that leave you open-mouthed. He films L.A. in bold, unhackneyed style, finding in its vast industrial spaces a mirror of the void his characters are trying to fill.

It's that void—and those characters—that make "Heat" an unusually soulful action movie. This may be the most impressive collection of actors in one movie this year. Pacino and De Niro are in great form, but there's also Val Kilmer as the crew member with a gambling problem, and Ashley Judd as the unfaithful wife he can't let go of. There's Amy Brenneman as the lonely bookstore clerk who penetrates McCauley's solitary armor, and Diane Venora as Hanna's brainy, unhappy wife. There's also Tom Sizemore, Jon Voight, Ted Levine and choice bites for Kim Staunton and Ricky Harris. Just when it seemed that the only hope for crime movies lay in the postmodernist artifice of films like "Pulp Fiction," Mann reinvests the genre with brooding, modernist conviction. This one sticks to your gut.

SIGHT AND SOUND, 2/96, p. 42, John Wrathall

Neil McCauley and his crew, Chris Shiherlis, Michael Cheritto and Trejo, plan the armed robbery of a security van carrying bearer bonds; the job goes perfectly, except that a new recruit to the crew, Waingro, shoots a guard. Afterwards, McCauley tries to kill Waingro, but he escapes. Vincent Hanna, a homicide cop whose third marriage is falling apart because of his devotion to his job, examines the scene of the crime and admires the professionalism of the job; the only clue is that one of the robbers was overheard calling a security guard "Slick". McCauley's associate Nate arranges to sell the bearer bonds back to their original owner, Van Zant, but the meeting in a deserted drive-in turns out to be an ambush; McCauley and his crew kill Van Zant's men and escape.

A chance lead from the brother of one of Hanna's informers identifies Cheritto as the man who calls people Slick. Hanna puts Cheritto under surveillance and starts tracking the crew around Los Angeles as they prepare their next heist. Meanwhile McCauley, who prides himself on his lack of attachments, has met and fallen in love with Eady, a graphic designer who knows nothing about his criminal career, and with whom he plans to leave for New Zealand after one last job. While burgling a metal depository, however, McCauley realises that they are being watched and calls the job off; because they have not stolen anything yet, Hanna doesn't arrest them. Even though they know the police are onto them, the crew decides to carry out one final bank robbery.

Following him one night, Hanna stops McCauley, takes him for a cup of coffee and tries to warn him off. The same night, the crew all shake off their tails, except for Trejo. The crew goes ahead without him, and the bank robbery they have planned goes smoothly; but after a tip-off, the police arrive as the robbers are leaving. A gun battle ensues, in which Cheritto is killed and Shiherlis wounded. Aiming to settle scores before he leaves town on a plane arranged by Nate, McCauley traces the tipoff to Trejo, who has been tortured into betraying the plan by Waingro, who has been recruited by Van Zant to get revenge on McCauley. After tracking down and killing Van Zant, McCauley persuades Eady to leave with him that night. But, learning that Waingro is holed up in a hotel near the airport, he can't resist having a go. Although the hotel is staked out by the police, McCauley manages to kill Waingro, but Hanna spots him on his way out of the hotel, chases him across the airport runways and shoots him down. Hanna holds McCauley's hand as he dies.

After a journey into the eighteenth-century wilderness for *The Last of the Mohicans*, Michael Mann returns to the urban terrain of his television series *Miami Vice* and *Crime Story* and his features *Manhunter* and *Thief* with a film which can be read as a compendium of his work to date. Like James Caan's safe-cracker, Frank, in 1981's *Thief* (released in this country as *Violent Streets*), Neil McCauley is single-mindedly devoted to his profession .("What are you?" Hanna asks him, "A monk?"), and only loses control of his own destiny when he tries to buy himself what Hanna, when he confronts him in the coffee shop, dismisses as "a regular-type life". Vincent Hanna, meanwhile, is a variation on William Petersen's Will Graham from *Manhunter* in his talent for putting himself in the shoes of his prey and seeing what they see, and in the way this leaves him closer to those he is pursuing than those he is protecting.

In one breathtaking sequence in *Heat* which evokes the voyeuristic, hall-of-mirrors feel of *Manhunter*, Hanna and his men watch McCauley's crew scouting out a refinery. When they have gone, Hanna stands exactly where they stood, trying to guess what they were looking at—before realising that they were looking at *him*, and that McCauley has now lured him into the open. The camera then pulls back to show McCauley taking his picture. Hanna can ultimately catch McCauley because they are just alike (Mann suggests this early on with near identical shots of Hanna picking up his gun from the table before he goes to work, and McCauley putting his down when he gets home). Both have their matching crews, and the presence of Wes Studi, the formidable Magua from *The Last of the Mohicans*, as Hanna's right-hand man Casals, alerts us to *Heat*'s echo of that film, as the bands of modern-day Mohicans and Hurons track each other across the jungle that is Los Angeles.

Mann reinvents LA here with the same visionary gaze he turned on Miami in *Miami Vice*, Las Vegas in *Crime Story* and Atlanta in *Manhunter*. From the "dead-tech, post-modernist" home where Hanna's marriage falls apart, to McCauley's beach-side glass box, bathed in blue light (just like Graham's home in *Manhunter*), to the red-and-white-checked concrete cubes by the runway where McCauley dies, there's not a boring building in the film. Mann is the best director of architecture since Antonioni. In fact, few film-makers at work today can rival Mann's control of every detail of the film-making process—perhaps this is why his films are so infrequent—from the fluent but unostentatious camera movements (worthy, as David Thomson has pointed out, of Max Ophüls), to the precise, almost expertly chosen soundtrack, which manages to make artists as diverse as Moby and György Ligeti sound like they belong on the same record.

David Thomson has singled out another Mann trademark, his peerless use of vivid supporting players, and *Heat* certainly doesn't disappoint in this respect. Mann discovers compelling new sides of Jon Voight (Nate, who could be Jack Palance's younger brother), Val Kilmer (blond, ponytailed, puffy-faced and petulant as the safe-cracker Shiherlis) and Tom Sizemore, typecast as a cartoon psychopath in the likes of *Natural Born Killers* and *Devil in a Blue Dress*, but here reinvented as the solid, grey-haired foot soldier, Cheritto. Tom Noonan, the serial killer from *Manhunter*, has a great cameo, bearded like an orthodox priest, as the source who tips McCauley off about the bank job, while Ted Levine—the killer in *Manhunter*'s de facto sequel, *The Silence of the Lambs*, and a veteran of *Crime Story*—turns up balding and moustachioed as one of Hanna's men. Mann also takes the trouble to populate his man's world with interesting women: Diane Venora, barely glimpsed since *Bird*, as Justine Hanna; Natalie Portman of *Léon* as her suicidal daughter; Ashley Judd, finally fulfilling the promise of *Ruby in Paradise*, as Charlene Shiherlis. Only *NYPD Blue*'s Amy Brenneman, in the pivotal role of Eady, fails to make much of an impression.

The real casting coup, of course, lies in the first pairing of De Niro and Pacino (they were father and son in *The Godfather Part II*, but never shared a scene). The first half of *Heat* plays absorbingly off the mounting tension about when the two will meet. Hanna first sees McCauley's Satanic image through a heat-vision viewfinder while staking out the metal depository; McCauley gets his look at Hanna through a telephoto lens. When it finally arrives, two hours in, their single scene together (bar the final shootout) is all the more highly charged for the banality of the setting, in a coffee shop. Rewardingly, the confrontation seems to have the same significance for the actors as it does for the characters: two driven professionals, frequently compared to each other and both at the peak of their powers, finally get the chance to size each other up at close range. In the same way that McCauley and Hanna's duel inspires each to greater feats of ingenuity, so the actors bring out the best in each other. Pacino is on edge here, with an alarming habit of suddenly shouting his words, but such is his authority that he makes it seem like the character's mannerism rather than the actor's; Hanna is not the loose cannon of cop-movie cliché, but a man who pretends to be when he needs to intimidate people, whether an informer or his wife's lover. De Niro, meanwhile, rises to the challenge with his most compelling work since *The King of Comedy*. Thankfully free of tics, his McCauley is so ruthlessly controlled that he barely moves his head; his eyes do all the work. If *Heat* were a play, you could imagine De Niro and Pacino swopping the roles every night, like Olivier and Richardson in *Othello*.

"All I am is what I'm going after," says Hanna near the end of his quest, a motto that could serve as well for McCauley, or for any of Mann's protagonists. In Mann's universe, as in that of Howard Hawks, professionalism is all that counts; but, unlike Hawks, Mann shows the cost of such a code in widows and wrecked marriages. In fact, for a cop movie, *Heat* seems unusually suffused with an awareness of death. Hanna's wife Justine, who, like her husband, always wears black, keeps telling him that he is walking dead through life. When McCauley and Hanna meet, they compare their dreams—and both have been dreaming of death, of time running out. (For Mann and his leads, all into their fifties, this seems to carry a real weight.) And, in the film's only superfluous scene, Waingro announces himself as the Grim Reaper before murdering a prostitute—leaving Hanna, who, in his wife's haunting words "lives among the remains of dead people", to pick up the pieces.

Of all the directors in America today who are set on keeping *film noir* alive, Mann seems the most willing to invest the genre with real characters and morality, and the most reluctant to fall, back on cliché. (Which doesn't mean he fails to deliver on the set pieces: the bank robbery here, which spirals into a pitched battle on the streets of downtown LA that's as ferocious as anything in *The Last of the Mohicans*, will surely stand as one of the great failed-heist sequences.) For those who cherish *Thief, Manhunter* and *Mohicans*, and for those who believe that Martin Scorsese's post *King of Comedy* output has slipped into a sort of flashy self-parody identified by Gilbert Adair as "Scorsese", as in journalese or legalese, *Heat*, placed by the accident of its British release schedule within a month of *Casino*, another, more vigorously hyped three-hour De Niro crime story, only serves to bolster the case for Michael Mann as the key American auteur of the last ten years.

TIME, 12/11/95, p. 81, Richard Schickel

Neil McCauley (Robert De Niro) is an orderly and calculating man. Like many entrepreneurs managing small, risky businesses, he has put the rest of his life on hold lest emotional distractions disrupt more profitable pursuits. Though that business consists of planning and executing complex, high-stakes robberies, the man is actually as risk averse as an actuary, and about as romantic.

Vincent Hanna (Al Pacino) is, in contrast, a disorderly and incautious man. A Los Angeles detective who is all hot-wired impulses, he has never learned to control his emotions or wall off his professional from his personal life; he's heading helplessly toward a divorce from his neglected wife (Diane Venora) even as he sniffs his way toward Neil and his mob.

Dispassion vs. passion, intellect vs. instinct, the implosive vs. the explosive style—as writer-director Michael Mann develops the duel between this cop and this robber in *Heat*, his film becomes a compassionate contemplation of the two most basic ways of being male and workaholic in modern America. It also becomes a critique of pure reason. For Neil is placing impossible demands on himself, on his associates, on a chance universe in which they inhabit one of the chancier corners. He can't prevent himself from falling in love (with Amy Brenneman's innocent bookstore clerk). He can't prevent his most valuable henchman and his wife (Val Kilmer and Ashley Judd) from marital misbehavior that threatens his enterprise. He can't, in general, prevent blighted human nature, from scribbling all over his neat blueprints. This leaves him vulnerable to a policeman—nice irony here—who is more accepting of the world's anarchy than he is.

All this adds good weight and tension to the movie and provides a lot of very good actors with the opportunity to do honest, probing work in a context where, typically, less will do. But Mann's aspirations don't stop there. Having revived the historical saga in *The Last of the Mohicans*, he obviously wants to do the same thing for what has become a much more familiar (and tiresome) genre, the urban action picture.

This Mann achieves with truly epic sweep, maniacal conviction and awesome technical proficiency. He announces his intentions in an opening sequence that may be the best armored-car robbery ever placed on film. He proceeds to a crazily orchestrated bank heist that goes awry and finishes in a wild fire-fight on a crowded downtown street that is a masterpiece of sustained invention. He ends with a chase that takes Pacino and De Niro into wholly original realms of hellishness, the back end of an airport, where their passions are nearly drowned out by the thunderous comings and goings of heedless flight.

There, in case you've missed it, is Mann's point. Throughout the movie, he has given us a vision of Los Angeles that goes beyond the usual sheen-and-scuzz contrasts it amuses most directors to observe. His L.A. is a void, a blankness, something like an empty movie screen—or an empty modern soul—waiting to be filled up with that most hypnotic of abstractions, violent action. This, he's saying, is what some of us are good at. And, all pieties aside, look how much we like it.

VILLAGE VOICE, 12/26/95, p. 66, Amy Taubin

In Michael Mann's wide-screen, west Coast gloss on his own *Miami Vice*, the locations almost upstage the stars, Al Pacino and Robert De Niro. Mann is a locations visionary. He sees a city not so much for what it is for what it might become. Just as Miami remade itself to better resemble its image in *Miami Vice*, L.A. may rise eventually to *Heat*'s desolate, sand-blasted impersonality.

Mann's City of Lights, where Vincent Hanna (Pacino) and Neil McCauley (De Niro) go through their paces as the last of the existential cops and criminals, couldn't be more removed from the gothic, phosphorescent L.A. of David Fincher's *Seven*. *Heat*'s color scheme is ultracool. In one inconsequential scene set at a construction site, Mann finds a 20-foot-high pile of baby-bunting yellow sand that perfectly balances the film's basic bleached blues and grays. The image stays in the mind's eye long after the formulaic plot has faded. So does the ultimate showdown between Vincent and Neil on the far reaches of an airport runway, where the immediate question of who lives and who dies is dwarfed by the planes roaring overhead. Mann's use of scale is as meaningful as any great modernist painter's.

The splendid visuals aside, *Heat* is a cosmically silly movie—which doesn't make it any less entertaining. Mann manages to have his romance of obsessed masculinity and send it up too. The joke is in the casting. Pacino and De Niro are as much dinosaurs as the parts they play; Mann doesn't demand a suspension of disbelief. If anything, the competition for acting honors between these two ethnic superstars (relics of the wilder side of '70s cinema) eclipses the fictional face-off of cop and criminal.

Though there are no big surprises in either performances, my preference is for Pacino, whose head-fakes and erratic speech rhythms have the improvisatory flair of the new Knicks. Pacino manages to be playful even when he's excessive and never less than true even when he's over the top. Moment to moment, he's a pleasure to watch.

Pleasure has never been part of De Niro's game. He's a lot better here than in *Casino* (which isn't saying much), and just about as proficient as he was in *GoodFellas*. At his best, these days, De Niro seems admirable rather than awesome. Once upon a time, his rigidity was a desperate defense against a rage that might erupt at any moment. He could make one both fear long for the return of the repressed. But over time, that rage imploded into a black hole, sucking the life from him—and from anyone who watches. Here, that inner heaviness, though it doesn't make for a thrilling performance, is right for the character—a career criminal who's ultimately undone not by the desire for love he so carefully guards against as by a need for revenge that is the one thing he can't control.

Mann has never gotten the credit he deserves as an actor's director. In *Heat*, he does well not only by his two stars but also his supporting cast, particularly Val Kilmer as the most volatile of the partners in crime, Ashley Judd as his intermittently loyal wife, and Diana Venora as a woman who knows she's too smart to stay married to a cop. She's so smart, in fact, she almost gets away with using the word "detritus" in the middle of a love scene.

Also reviewed in:
CHICAGO TRIBUNE, 12/15/95, Friday/p. C, Michael Wilmington
NEW YORK TIMES, 12/15/95, p. C18, Janet Maslin
NEW YORKER, 12/25/95 & 1/1/96, p. 145, Anthony Lane
VARIETY, 12/11-17/95, p. 82, Todd McCarthy
WASHINGTON POST, 12/15/95, p. F1, Hal Hinson
WASHINGTON POST, 12/15/95, Weekend/p. 49, Desson Howe

HEAVEN'S A DRAG

A First Run Features release of a TDF production in association with The London Lighthouse with the participation of British Screen. *Executive Producer:* Stephen Garbutta. *Producer:* Gary Fitzpatrick. *Director:* Peter Mackenzie Litten. *Screenplay:* Johnny Byrne. *Story:* Paul McEvoy and Peter Litten. *Director of Photography:* John Ward. *Editor:* Jeffrey Assenault. *Music:* Roger Bolton. *Choreographer:* Roy Rowlands. *Sound:* Julian Dawton. *Art Director:* Geoff Sharpe. *Special Animatronix Effects:* Richard Pirkis. *Costumes:* Else Curtis. *Make-up:* Victoria Wright, Darren Phillips, and Helen Lennox. *Running time:* 96 minutes. *MPAA Rating:* Not Rated.

CAST: Thomas Arklie (Simon); Ian Williams (Mark); Tony Slattery (Terry); Dilly Keane (Siobhan); Jean Boht (Mrs. Downs); John Altman (Dogger); Caroline Munro (Mrs. Pignon); Gordon Milne (Drop Dead Gorgeous); Nicholas Harrison (Siobhan's First Lover); Ian McKellen and Sinitta (Quilt Documentary Narrators); Paul Cottingham (1st Poxy Shirt Lifter); Lloyd Williams (Bodybuilder); Robert Sturtz (Chris); Benjamin Sterz (Man in Gym); Brian Carter (Leather Man); Mark Hutchinson (Hospital Visitor); Janet Allen (Ward Sister); Nigel Fairs (Mark Lookalike); Robert Whitson (Man in Cruise Bar); Philip Curr (Skinhead); James Greaves (Man in Lavatory); Brian Ross (Nick); Tony London, Richard Cope and Dick Bradnum (Yobs); Ken Kennedy (Mr. Willoughby); Andrew Kennedy (Steve); Alan Lowe (Young Man in Club); Will Pollet (Young Mark); Wayne Amiel and Henrique da Silva (Go-Go Dancers); John Cannon (Jessie Biscuit); Brian Carter and Mike Shear (Jessie's Men); David Ingram (Archangel).

LOS ANGELES TIMES, 10/27/95, Calendar/p. 10, Kevin Thomas

"Heaven's a Drag" is not nearly as good a picture as it could have been, and like the similarly uneven "Jeffrey," it at once grapples with the challenge of gay relationships in the age of AIDS while nakedly tugging at the heart.

Originally titled "To Die For," it was renamed so as to avoid confusion with the current Nicole Kidman film. This modest British production, however, does cover considerable territory in gay life, throws in some campy humor, and it is well-sustained by Thomas Arklie, who excels in the film's starring role.

Arklie plays Simon, a muscular, sexy London TV repairman whose lover Mark (Ian Williams) is a boyish-looking drag performer with AIDS. The two have an open relationship, which means that while on stage Mark not infrequently witnesses Simon picking up a guy and taking off, not returning till morning. Twenty minutes into the film Mark dies suddenly, only to return as a ghost, fully materialized to Simon but invisible to everyone else. Describing himself accurately as "the clinging queen," Mark's spirit becomes suffocatingly possessive of Simon.

Where director Peter Mackenzie Litten and writer Johnny Byrne go wrong is not in taking pains to establish Mark and Simon's relationship credibly in the first place. What attracted Simon to Mark, who dead or alive is not particularly good-looking and is often a petulant martyr, remains a mystery. Yet they've clearly been together a substantial length of time.

That we never get to know why the two became a couple undermines what eventually concerns the filmmakers most, which is the problem many men, straight or gay, have in experiencing and expressing love for another human being. Not only is Mark hectoring Simon insufferably from beyond the grave for the love he never got from him while he was alive, but also is forcing Mark to face up to his inability to love and why, this is.

Mark's coming to terms with himself and his emotions is the heart of the matter, and the film's strongest aspect. The getting there is not as satisfying, however. Williams' Mark, although often admirably brave, is a truly trying individual, and the filmmakers don't help matters with some tedious comic relief from Simon's tiresome busybody Irish neighbor (Dilly Keane) and her relentlessly politically correct boyfriend (Tony Slattery). Despite flaws, "Heaven's a Drag" is likely—and perhaps deservedly—to draw audiences, just as "Jeffrey" has, because it dares to wear its heart on its sleeve.

NEW YORK POST, 6/23/95, p. 38, Larry Worth

A movie's name can be its biggest drawback, as evidenced by the low-budget "To Die For." After showing in a few film fests, that title—perfect for a supernatural thriller or "Love Story III"—was wisely dropped.

Then, somebody dreamed up an even worse one: "Heaven's a Drag," which invokes images of Jim Bailey impersonating Judy Garland for cloudfuls of cherubs.

Ironically, the essence of this gay fantasy-drama lies somewhere in between its monikers.

Johnny Byrne's script concerns Simon, a handsome, seemingly superficial hustler in London, who refuses to grieve when Mark, his drag queen lover, dies of AIDS. Simon's no sooner back in circulation than Mark's lonely spirit materializes, determined to make Simon confront his demons.

While the plot rips off certain aspects of "Ghost" (particularly the bittersweet finale), it's closer in spirit to the less flashy "Truly, Madly, Deeply," wherein the joys of having a loved one back from beyond prove more trial than treat.

Using that premise as a launching pad, director Peter Mackenzie Litten gains strength from the script's dramatic moments, which consistently steer clear of maudlin. For that matter, even Mark's deathbed scene occurs off camera.

To cover numerous intricate subjects (homophobia, gay bashing, a "respectable" mourning period, sex vs. love, the art of cruising, denial of feelings), Litten zeros in on details which advance the story while moving viewers, like finding an answering machine message from a dead friend, or dealing with a concerned parent's disapproval.

Unfortunately, Litten's Jekyll-Hyde nature is also revealed—and when his penchant for slapstick surfaces, it's not pretty. A subplot about the guys' upstairs neighbors—a sex-starved matron and her do-gooder boyfriend—is on the level of "Three's Company." Meanwhile, some less-than-special effects and the old talking-to-air joke hearken back to "Topper."

As if to compensate, the mostly-unknown actors give their all, including a delicately-nuanced turn from Thomas Arklie, as the complex Simon and Ian Williams ensuring that the flamboyant Mark rarely goes over the top. In addition, Jean Boht's too-fleeting scenes as Simon's mother are beautifully realized and unexpectedly wrenching.

The bottom line: "Heaven" is like a battle between good and evil, where virtue ultimately triumphs. Maybe the title's apt after all.

NEWSDAY, 6/23/95, Part II/p. B4, John Anderson

Is a holocaust film automatically mawkish, and trivial, and exploitive of tragedy? Probably, given the weight of the subject matter and its natural diminishment on screen. In the case of "Heaven's a Drag," the holocaust is AIDS, and the aim is sincere. But the execution not only makes you squirm, it makes you scratch your head at the same time. Which isn't easy.

Simon (Thomas Arklie) is a hunky, HIV-negative habitué of leather bars; his live-in lover Mark (Ian Williams) is a drag performer with AIDS who spends his off hours watching a tape of the AIDS memorial quilt and sewing his own. The two have an open relationship, with Simon keeping up a brisk pace in various beds while Mark waits, basically, to die.

After Mark's death, Simon begins to see things: Margaret Thatcher's face on TV turns into Mark's; an inviting smile at a gay bar turns into Mark's; during a date, his stereo spontaneously combusts into Mark's signature song. Simon's being haunted, by a ghost intent on screwing up his love life.

Simon's an insensitive ass, to be sure, but Mark's modus operandi isn't exactly generous, or logical, unless you accept the subtext of keeping Simon negative. As played by the elfin-faced Williams, Mark is overbearingly campy, a non-living, non-breathing stereotype of queenly histrionics with dialogue to match. Although the film—25 percent of whose profits are going to London Lighthouse, the English AIDS hospice—attempts some strong statements about love in the age of AIDS, it too often gets in its own way.

Much more effective are the scenes of Simon with his mother (Jean Boht), with whom he sorts out his ambiguous feelings about his late father. And although they are stereotypes themselves, the straight characters in Simon's universe offer some relief from the earnestness. Siobhan, the upstairs neighbor and Greek chorus, is a cross between Joan Blondell and Barry Fitzgerald. Her boyfriend Terry (Tony Slattery), a local P.C. do-gooder, is comical, and Dogger (John Altman), Simon's co-worker who's unaware his friend is gay, is an on-target, if ludicrous, example of virulent homophobia and repressed inclinations. All in all, though, "Heaven's a Drag" (formerly titled "To Die For") is an example of the road to movie hell being paved with good intentions.

SIGHT AND SOUND, 12/94, p. 54, Robert Yates

Present-day London. When Mark dies of Aids, he leaves his lover, Simon, a TV repairman, the panel he was working on for the Aids Memorial Quilt. Spending little time mourning, Simon is soon out cruising in clubs, for which close friend Siobhan reproaches him. Yet, whenever Simon attempts to hook up with other men, he sees Mark's face—on another's shoulders or on a TV screen. Running home, he clears the flat of all traces of Mark, but reminders of him linger, including an old message on the answering machine, which only he can hear.

Simon brings a man home, but as they kiss, Simon's car alarm begins to wail, and lights and electrical equipment take on lives of their own. Later, in bed alone, Simon wakes up at some-body's touch, and discovers Mark there with him. He has returned, as a ghost—invisible to others—dismayed that Simon appears to have forgotten him so quickly. Mark proceeds to rearrange the flat in his image. Outside the flat, he interferes with Simon's attempts to flirt. The two vex each other.

When Simon's work mate Dogger arrives to pick him up, Mark rebukes Simon for keeping his sexuality hidden from Dogger. Later, after Dogger has amused himself at the expense of a middle-aged homosexual, Simon invites him for a drink, taking him to a gay bar where he kisses a few friends and frightens Dogger away. Walking home, Simon is confronted by a homophobic gang and only escapes a beating when Mark creates a diversion. But still Simon insists that Mark has to let him go, and tells him he never loved him.

Restless, Simon visits his mother. They talk about his late father, and how he hurt Simon by rejecting him for being gay. His mother shows Simon a letter her husband wrote just before his death, regretting painfully the break with his son. Simon rushes back to his flat, and begins to cry out for Mark. He returns and they kiss before Mark is collected by a group of angels. Simon begins to work on Mark's unfinished quilt.

To Die For is as much about bereavement as it is about HIV and the gay community. In relation to other 'Aids films', it shares with Richard Glatzer's *Grief* a concern with the effects of early death on the lover left behind. The narrative centres on Simon's response, and traces his difficulties in expressing grief. Or rather, the narrative seems driven towards persuading Simon to cry.

The film's premise appears straightforward. Simon keeps his feelings in check because he has been hurt before, by his father. Equally simple is its resolution. When Simon realises his father's love, he can open up and grieve. Yet, between premise and resolution, the script—by Johnny Byrne who, among other TV credits, created *All Creatures Great and Small*—seems to develop by ignoring its own evidence, pulling us in one direction while what we see takes us in another. Ghost Mark is mostly tiresome (as is Alan Rickman's ghost in *Truly, Madly, Deeply*, a film whose tonal range, coupling humour with sentimentality, *To Die For* aims for). His behaviour seems designed to send Simon running all the more quickly to a pickup joint.

Of course, the convention of the ghost only being visible to the bereaved always invites us to read ghostly appearances as inner dialogue made flesh. In this case, Simon's summoning up anger directed at Mark's ghost could be interpreted as his attempt to fend off the pain he feels. But it's difficult to invest in this line, since although Mark is not seen or heard by others, the results of his interventions are. His supernatural forays only contribute to the film's uncomfortable mix of tones.

First-time director Litten, inspired to make the film by the death of a friend, moves between the would-be comic and the mawkish. The 'comic' takes in a quite stunning series of hackneyed characters. There's Siobhan, an Irish woman who loves the 'crack' and, fighting her body clock, is desperate for a man. Terry, the man, is a fool of a trendy leftie who gets entangled in PC terms he barely understands. Then there's Dogger, Simon's crudely drawn homophobic work mate who crashes into another caricature, a middle-aged effete homosexual. Indeed the main couple itself—butch TV repair man and delicate professional—is straight out of pink central casting.

Litten is no more successful at tugging our heart strings. When, before the final twist, Simon tells Mark that he simply did not love him, the admission might not be heart-lifting but it is at least credible, given what has gone before. At the climax, however, with the music swelling (it does little else) and angels descending, the film lacks any persuasive force. Neither inevitable nor apt, the ending comes across as woozy wishful thinking.

VILLAGE VOICE, 6/27/95, p. 62, Gary Dauphin

A modest British import, *Heaven's a Drag* is a matter-of-fact blend of light supernatural comedy and old-fashioned tear-jerking. Mark (Ian Williams) and Simon (Thomas Arklie) are lovers who share a nice flat and an open relationship. Whether this arrangement grew out of Simon's cooly distant demeanor or Mark's HIV status (and steadily worsening health) is left unclear, but it's obvious that Mark is definitely the aggrieved and emotionally neglected partner. When Mark enters the hospital and quietly passes away off screen, Simon quickly announces that he wants to get on with his life. But before you know it Mark's ghost is back in the picture, taunting the neighbors and foiling Simon's attempts to get laid.

Director Litten tries to soften the abruptness of Mark's demise with (straight) comic relief and steadily smart side patter. The film's deadpan visuals match Simon's general attitude, and the haunting is played more for laughs than special-effected chills. Unfortunately, the story never quite stretches enough to encompass Litten's intended metaphor about mixed-HIV-status couples. Soon the earlier exchanges of wry dialogue fall by the wayside as Mark and Simon engage in increasingly shmaltzy arguments about who didn't love who and why, Mark waxing existential about death being a state of nothingness lit only by his love for Simon. Although things work out for the pair in all too predictable fashion, *Heaven's a Drag* does manage to collect itself for a fairly satisfying finale. Too bad it's one borrowed from Isaac Julien's much more effective tableaux of gay glory.

Also reviewed in:
CHICAGO TRIBUNE, 9/29/95, Friday/p. L, Stephen Holden
NEW YORK TIMES, 6/23/95, p. C16, Stephen Holden
VARIETY, 6/27-7/3/94, p. 87, Emanuel Levy
WASHINGTON POST, 10/20/95, p. D6, Megan Rosenfeld

HEAVYWEIGHTS

A Walt Disney Pictures release in association with Caravan Pictures. *Executive Producer:* Judd Apatow and Sarah Bowman. *Producer:* Joe Roth and Roger Birnbaum. *Director:* Steven Brill. *Screenplay:* Judd Apatow and Steven Brill. *Director of Photography:* Victor Hammer. *Editor:* C. Timothy O'Meara. *Music:* J.A.C. Redford. *Music Editor:* Michael T. Ryan. *Sound:* Mary H. Ellis and (music) John Vigran. *Casting:* Judy Taylor and Lynda Gordon. *Production Designer:* Stephen Storer. *Art Director:* Harry Darrow and Jack Ballance. *Set Decorator:* Chris Spellman. *Set Dresser:* Andrew J. Krish. *Set Dresser:* Leonard M. Smith and Joseph R. McGuire, Jr. *Special Effects:* Bill Purcell. *Costumes:* Kimberly A. Tillman. *Make-up:* John Bayless. *Prosthetic Make-up (Ben Stiller):* Michael Burnett. *Stunt Coordinator:* Steve Boyum. *Running time:* 98 minutes. *MPAA Rating:* PG.

CAST: Tom McGowan (Pat); Aaron Schwartz (Gerry); Shaun Weiss (Josh); Tom Hodges (Lars); Leah Lail (Julie); Paul Feig (Tim); Kenan Thompson (Roy); David Bowe (Chris

Donelly); Max Goldblatt (Phillip); Robert Zalkind (Simms); Patrick La Brecque (Dawson); Jjeffrey Tambor (Maury Garner); Jerry Stiller (Harvey Bushkin); Anne Meara (Alice Bushkin); Ben Stiller (Tony Perkis/Tony Perkis Sr.); David Goldman (Nicholas); Joseph Wayne Miller (Sam); Cody Burger (Cody); Allen Covert (Kenny); Tim Blake Nelson (Camp Hope Salesman); Nancy Ringham (Mrs. Garner); Seth St. Laurent (Camp MVP Racer); Bobby Fain (Camp MVP Pitcher); Robert E. Spencer III (Soccer Goalie); Dustin Greer (Blob Master); Matthew R. Zboyovski (Hope Wall Climber); J.T. Alessi (Baloon Shaver); Chris Snyder (Baseball Scorekeeper); Jonathan Clark (Gerry's Double); Aubrey Dollar, Mary Holt Fickes and Jamie Olson (Camp Magnolia Girls); Lauren Hill (Angelic Girl); Landry M. Constantino (Kissing Girl); Lois Yaroshefsky (Camp Magnolia Counselor); Matthew Bradley King (Gerry's School Buddy); Deena Dill (Stewardess); Tom Kelley (Man on Plane); Lars Clark (Jack Garner); Judd Apatow (Homer).

LOS ANGELES TIMES, 2/17/95, Calendar/p. 4, Peter Rainer

Is it politically correct these days to be fat and proud or thin and proud.

Disney's new kidpic "Heavyweights" plays it both ways: It says it's fine to be chubby and then goes ahead and makes all the usual chubby jokes. It's a case of having your hi-cal cake and eating it too.

Gerry Garner (Aaron Schwartz) is sent by his parents to a summer camp for overweight kids called Camp Hope. (Is this a sly dig at Bill Clinton?) Quickly bonding with his fellow heavies, including Josh (the amusing Shaun Weiss) and Roy (Kenan Thompson), Gerry finds himself for the first time among kids who don't make fun of him. In fact, none of the kids make fun of each other—which seems a bit too idyllic. Wouldn't the least fat kids make fun of the fattest?

Instead, they make fun of the camp's new director, a fitness guru horror named Tony Perkis (Ben Stiller), who plans to use the summer activities as the basis for a bogus infomercial. (Perkis appears to be based partially on motivation guru Anthony Robbins.) Perkis puts the kids through boot camp paces, and he gets more and more wacko, in ways that are more disconcerting than funny, as the film dribbles on.

Co-written by director Steven Brill and Judd Apatow, "Heavyweights" is an inoffensive dawdler for kids under 10. It might have been funnier if the filmmakers had taken a good look at the summer camp scenes from "Addams Family Values," where a pageant involving Native Americans and settlers turns into a race war. Is it too much to ask for a little subversiveness in these toddler fests?

The funniest moment in "Heavyweights" is when the camp's original owners, played by Jerry Stiller and Anne Meara, break down and sob in front of their campers as they declare bankruptcy. It's Stiller and Meara's only scene in the movie, which is a waste far more upsetting than the mounds of uneaten ribs and cheeseburgers that litter the campgrounds.

NEW YORK POST, 2/17/95, p. 49, Bill Hoffmann

Gerry Garner has a weight problem. He's the type of kid who goes to the neighborhood lemonade stand and instead of paying 10 cents for a cup, plunks down two bucks and downs the whole pitcher.

It's no wonder Gerry's parents decide to send him to a "fat camp" for the summer.

Gerry (Aaron Schwartz) fits in right away with his fellow campers, most of whom come back year after year and don't lose an ounce of weight.

But then, thin isn't in at "Camp Hope." Rather, it's what's underneath, in one's heart, that really counts.

That's the heartwarming, if rather sappy message of Disney's new comedy, "Heavyweights," a middling shaggy-dog tale of triumph in the face of overwhelming odds.

As Gerry gets to Camp Hope, it turns out the old place is in no great health either.

Run for years by a kindly old couple (Jerry Stiller and Anne Meara), the camp has now been taken over by Tony Perkis (Ben Stiller), a fly-by-night fitness freak who wants to force the kids into shape and film an infomercial around it to get rich quick.

Instead of showing movies and having weenie roasts, Perkis presents lectures like "Liposuction: Option or Obsession?"

The camp's sweet-natured, compassionate counselors are replaced by obnoxious health nuts like the Nazi-like German, Lars (Tom Hodges).

You know its only going to be a matter of time before the kids rebel and throw their weight around to overthrow the bad guy's.

The kid actors are engaging, particularly Kenan Thompson, who plays Roy, a wise-cracking black kid who does some great mugging for the camera.

The trouble is that most of the humor here is terribly forced and never laugh-out-loud funny. Too often, director Steven Brill resorts to crude jokes for cheap laughs. Passing wind and mooning are two that come to mind, (schticks that probably will have old Walt Disney rolling in his grave!)

The result is a flabby concoction of rather bland, TV sitcomish comedy.

A totally over-the-top Ben Stiller is sadly wasted as the fitness guru/psycho.

It's not giving away the picture to say that fat wins over physique. The fat guy even gets the girl.

It's just too bad that "Heavyweights" is such a lightweight.

NEWSDAY, 2/17/95, Part II/p. B5, John Anderson

Firm, round and fully packed, the bus to Camp Hope—the combination paradise/purgatory of "Heavyweights"—feigns a right to McDonald's, barely resists the allure of roadside roast beef and skirts dangerously close to a few doughnuts shops before getting back on the straight and narrow. Fat may be funny, but enabling is no joke.

What is? In "Heavyweights," the first feature from director Steven Brill, (who wrote the two "Mighty Ducks" movies), it's the idea that a bunch of good-natured, overweight pre-adolescent males might get together for a summer of fun and commiseration—and then be subjected to an obsessive health guru who wants to make their vacation his infomercial. With a helping of "Meatballs," and a dash of "Revenge of the Nerds," it's a full-frontal assault on fitness Nazis and the national spandex obsession—which is good, and makes fat kids people, too. All too often, though, the movie is like that bus: flirting with empty calories while knowing, in its cholesterol-clotted heart, that it can do much better.

The kids have a weight problem, not a neurological disorder, but Brill can't resist garnishing his film with pratfalls that have a circus-freak quality: Gerry (Aaron Schwartz), for instance, has such trouble throwing a foul ball back onto a field in the film's opening moments that he appears to have both aplastic anemia and Epstein-Barr syndrome. His pals at camp—Roy (Kenan Thompson), Josh (Shaun Weiss), Cody (Cody Burger) and their chief counselor, Pat (Tom McGowan) have similar problems with physical space. This becomes a kind of Victim Art—the oppressors being sluggish genes or and eating it: We're supposed to feel a mix of sympathy and admiration for these kids, but anyone not in stretch pants gets to feel superior, too.

The hefty cast is a novelty, but the plot is institutional: Gerry arrives at camp only to find that its owners, Harvey and Alice Bushkin (Jerry Stiller and Anne Meara) have sold the place to Tony Perkis—an increasingly psychotic fitness entrepreneur who, as played by Ben Stiller, looks and acts like a cross between the Joker and Christina Baranski's demented camp counselor in "Addams Family Values." Bad food, no fun overactive appetites—as well as a case of having your cake and a disco nightmare mixer with the girls camp (music by Hot Chocolate and the Bay City Rollers) drive the boys to insurrection. They and their displaced counselor Pat bond in their loathing of Tony and all he stands for. The revolution is afoot.

Despite the utter predictability of it all, there are plenty of fortifying moments—a slo-mo, post-liberation food orgy accompanied by Strauss, for instance—but the laughs arrive mostly via the dialogue, delivered by the portly but promising young actors (themselves proving what's important and what's not). Schwartz is solid, Thompson has a nice dry delivery and Shaun Weiss as the wiseguy Josh is a natural comic; having disappeared from his bunk under mysterious circumstances, he returns doing a takeoff of the lobotomized Jack Nicholson in "Cuckoo's Nest" that's a hoot.

Most memorable, however, may be little Nicholas (David Goldman), the English camper, who wins the academic portion of the inter-camp competition by rattling off the names of five American vice presidents. There hasn't been a more satisfying transatlantic cultural coup since Charles Laughton recited the Gettysburg Address in "Ruggles of Red Gap."

Also reviewed in:
CHICAGO TRIBUNE, 2/17/95, Friday/p. M, John Petrakis
NEW YORK TIMES, 2/17/95, p. C16, Stephen Holden
VARIETY, 2/20-26/95, p. 74, Leonard Klady
WASHINGTON POST, 2/17/95, p. F7, Hal Hinson

HIDEAWAY

A TriStar Pictures release of an S/Q production. *Producer:* Jerry Baerwitz, Agatha Hanczakowski, and Gimel Everett. *Director:* Brett Leonard. *Screenplay:* Andrew Kevin Walker and Neal Jimenez. *Based on the novel by:* Dean R. Koontz. *Director of Photography:* Gale Tattersall. *Editor:* B.J. Sears. *Music:* Trevor Jones. *Music Editor:* Bill Abbott. *Sound:* Rob Young and (music) John Richards. *Sound Editor:* Stephen Hunter Flick and Dean Beville. *Casting:* Amanda Mackey and Cathy Sandrich. *Production Designer:* Michael Bolton. *Art Director:* Sandy Cochrane. *Set Decorator:* Elizabeth Wilcox. *Set Dresser:* Matt Reddy, James Clare, Peter Stoffels, and Patrick Kearns. *Special Effects:* Mike Vezina. *Visual Effects:* Tim McGovern. *Costumes:* Monique Prudhomme. *Make-up:* Todd McIntosh, Jayne Dancose, and Victoria Down. *Stunt Coordinator:* Jacob Rupp. *Running time:* 112 minutes. *MPAA Rating:* R.

CAST: Jeff Goldblum (Hatch); Christine Lahti (Lindsey); Alicia Silverstone (Regina); Jeremy Sisto (Vassago); Alfred Molina (Jonas); Rae Dawn Chong (Rose Orwetto); Kenneth Welsh (Detective Breech); Suzy Joachim (Dr. Kari Dovell); Shirley Broderick (Miss Dockridge); Tom McBeath (Morton Redlow); Joely Collins (Linda); Roger R. Cross (Harry); Michael McDonald (Young Cop); Don S. Davis (Dr. Martin); Rebecca Toolan (Female Doctor); Hiro Kanagawa (Nurse Nakamura); Jayme Knox (Mother of Baby); Norma Wick (TV Announcer); Michelle Skalnik and Gaetana Korbin (Victims); Tiffany Foster (Samantha); Mara Duronslet (Zoe); Iris Quinn Bernard (Jonas' Wife); Natasha Morley (Jonas' Daughter); Sarah Strange (Second Girlfriend).

LOS ANGELES TIMES, 3/3/95, Calendar/p. 14, Peter Rainer

"Hideaway" is not for the faint of heart. It *is* for the faint of mind.

Jeff Goldbloom plays Hatch Harrison, who apparently dies in a car accident only to be brought back from "the other side" by a crack team of resuscitators. His wife, Lindsey (Christine Lahti), who also survived the accident with their daughter, Regina (Alicia Silverstone), doesn't quite know what to make of the new Hatch. As soon as he leaves the hospital he gets touchier and touchier. But he's got a right. His doctor (Alfred Molina): counsels Lindsey to stay calm. "He's really on edge. You know, dying and all."

It's too bad that the resuscitators worked on Hatch couldn't have worked their wonders on "Hideaway." The film may be full of wormy whiz-bang vortex effects but it's near-dead. The plot has something to do with a spiritual connection between another once-dead guy, Vassago (Jeremy Sisto), a serial-killing Satanist who specializes in virgin sacrifice—with Regina at the top of his wish list.

Hatch sees murders through Vassago's eyes, Vassago sees more mundane stuff through Hatch's eyes—he is, after all, an antique dealer. The family's deceased daughter—a hit-and-run victim—reappears to Hatch in his voyagings. If you ran the scripts for the "Poltergeist" movies and "Resurrection" and "Eyes of Laura Mars" and "The Omen" through a shredder, you might end up with "Hideaway."

Maybe that's just what director Brett ("Lawnmower Man") Leonard and screenwriters Andrew Kevin Walker and Neil Jimenez did. Or is Dean Koontz, whose novel sparked this mess, the culprit?

The supernatural effects are meant to be state-of-the-art interactive, but a little of this movie's woozy candy-colored spiraling between life and death goes a long way. The film's conception of the afterlife resembles sea-sickness.

Are we supposed to recognize Hatch's ordeal as a parental guilt trip? Does he represent the backwash of the '60s? (He describes his post-death heebie-jeebies as "acid flashbacks." Bummer.) Goldblum doesn't do anything ordinary in this movie, and neither does Lahti. And yet these two wonderful actors seem pinioned by all the rampaging dumbness.

You get the feeling they would have killed to play this one as a comedy.

NEW YORK POST, 3/3/95, p. 48, Michael Medved

Within its first five minutes, before the titles even roll across the screen, "Hideaway" offers a grotesquely gory teen suicide for Satan, then follows that tormented soul on a spectacular special effects thrill-ride from this world to the very gates of hell.

As you might expect, this sort of all-stops-out opening does succeed in grabbing your attention, but what's more surprising is the way this slick shocker keeps the audience absorbed all the way through its convoluted plot, right down to the climactic confrontation in a (groan!) abandoned amusement park. In fact, "Hideaway" is so expertly executed that it almost—but not quite—transcends its own dubious genre.

That class of movie might best be described as "King Krud"—noisy gorefests in which ordinary people are tortured by vast diabolical forces for no logical reason other than straining the imagination of the filmmakers.

These supernatural thrillers are often, but not always, based on the work of horrormeister Stephen King. In the case of "Hideaway," the source material is a novel by Dean R. Koontz, one of King's colleagues who's become a hugely successful fright novelists in his own right.

This time, the victim of the deviltry is a successful antiques dealer solidly played by Jeff Goldblum. While returning from a weekend in the mountains, Goldblum, his wife (Christine Lahti) and their pouty 16-year-old daughter (played by Alicia Silverstone of "The Crush") suffer one of the more terrifyingly well-staged (and brilliantly edited) highway accidents ever captured on film. Before his heroic spouse can pull Goldblum's lifeless body from the waters of a freezing river, his heart has stopped and all vital signs are gone. But a dedicated doctor at a local hospital (played by Alfred Molina) succeeds in bringing him back from the beyond.

In the days that follow, he's happy to be alive, but inexplicably plagued by horrific visions in which he's viewing the world through the eyes of a psychotic serial killer who preys on teen-aged girls.

When the victims' faces from these visions turn up in news broadcasts as either missing or dead, he gets increasingly hysterical—especially since his sadistic alter ego (a surly teen-ager with shades and an attitude, played with eerie effectiveness by newcomer Jeremy Sisto) communicates to Goldblum that his own daughter will be a future victim. Could this murderous rampage relate in some way to the gruesome suicide at the film's beginning?

You don't learn the answer till the film's conclusion, but when you do, the connection seems more satisfying than you might expect—despite the fact that the final struggle is surrounded by an altogether unnecessary explosion of showy, heaven-vs.-hell dazzlement.

This technological wizardry is the real selling point of the film, and the trademark of director Brett Leonard who previously crafted the surprisingly successful low-budget fantasy "Lawnmower Man." Here, he places the special effects in the service of creating characters and telling a story which, despite its predictable and inconsistent elements, still has the power to send you out of the theater feeling shaken and disturbed.

NEWSDAY, 3/3/95, Part II/p. B5, Jack Mathews

In the opening moments of Brett Leonard's psychological thriller "Hideaway," we follow a dying man's soul through a kaleidoscopic tunnel to hell, and though it is returned to mortal life, only slight singed, we are pretty much stuck there until the movie's over.

There are bad movies, which don't aspire to much to begin with, and there are gargantuan miscues, which squander large budgets, embarrass respected actors, and insult the intelligence of the audience. "Hideaway," adapted from the Dean Koontz model, collapses into the second category.

Leonard is being billed as some sort of New Age visual effects guru, thanks to the exhilarating imagery in "The Lawnmower Man," where he took his characters and the audience into the dizzying world of virtual reality. But in "Hideaway," he goes beyond virtual reality into virtual nonsense, imagining the near-death experience as a video exhibit at the Museum of Satanic Art.

We take that first trip through the soul tunnel with a satan worshiper (Jeremy Sisto) who has just impaled himself on a pair of scissors (accompanied by a heavy metal version of "Nearer My Devil to Thee"), and a second one with Hatch Harrison (Jeff Goldblum), a responsible family man who drowns in an auto accident. Both victims are brought back to life after two hours of death by the ethically challenged head of a local hospital's "advanced resuscitation unit," and linked by a metaphysical snafu that allows each to see through the other's eyes.

For Hatch, it's not a pretty sight. He sees young women being murdered by Vassago (Sisto), and is horrified to learn his own daughter, Regina, (Alicia Silverstone) is Vassago's ultimate target. Since he can convince neither the police nor his wife (Christine Lahti) of his clairvoyance, Hatch sets out alone to get to Vassago before Vassago gets to Regina, and take him on mano-a-mano in the Fifth Dimension.

Even as an excuse for a lot of computer-generated effects, "Hideaway" fails. The after-life tunnel is filled out with obvious good vs. evil symbolism; Vassago sees demons in hot red, Hatch gets a cool blue reception from angelic figures, even spends a moment with the soul of a younger daughter whose death he is still grieving. And as spectacle, the effects pale—at least emotionally—compared to Stanley Kubrick's psychedelic blast into God's country in "2001: A Space Odyssey" 27 years ago!

Goldblum and Lahti, who is among the best criers of her generation, go all out to give the story emotional depth, and newcomer Sisto, playing his entire role in sunglasses and chapped lips, is an effectively creepy villain. But there is no saving this stiff; its soul departs in the opening scene and never returns.

VILLAGE VOICE, 3/7/95, p. 61, Tom Kertes

The film opens as a young man, having just propped up his recently murdered mother and sister in a praying position in front of a nifty homemade altar, commits suicide by falling on a knife while humming some catchy tunes in praise of Satan. Considering that this is one of the kinder and gentler parts of *Hideaway*, you may want to, well, hide away when it explodes into a theater near you. However, should you decide to see it, this is not a film you'll easily forget.

A psychological horror movie with techno-thriller pretensions (think *Jacob's Ladder* crossed with *Silence of the Lambs*), Brett Leonard's follow-up to his equally "different" *Lawnmower Man* features characters far larger than life: Mom and Dad are so Good they could make you retch. The teen daughter is Innocence of the widest-eyed kind. And the aforementioned No More Mr. Nice Guy is so uniformly Evil that he makes Newt Gingrich look like Father Theresa.

These stylized stick figures are almost given depth by their outward appearance (Jeff Goldblum's Good Dad looks Satan-esque at times, Evil Guy is a doppelganger for angelic-looking Jim Morrison). Strangely enough, this makes sense in a movie that's obviously intended as an unrelenting assault on the senses. The spectacular computer-generated effects, mostly dealing with the soul's journey to the "other side," are there to experience rather than think about; they should thrill believers to near-death. And the intermittent pounding of heavy metal music evokes an aura of ever-looming danger and impending doom.

It can't be easy to act in a film where the characters come in second to the sensory joys; the charismatic Goldblum, fine in patches but rankly amateurish in others, certainly proves that. As Mom, Christine Lahti once again does a lot with little. But *the* find of the film has to be Very Bad Person Jeremy Sisto. He'll occupy your nightmares for a while.

Also reviewed in:
CHICAGO TRIBUNE, 3/3/95, Friday/p. M, Michael Wilmington
NEW YORK TIMES, 3/3/95, p. C14, Janet Maslin
VARIETY, 2/27-3/5/95, p. 70, Leonard Klady
WASHINGTON POST, 3/4/95, p. C1, Rita Kempley

HIGHER LEARNING

A Columbia Pictures release of a New Deal production. *Producer:* John Singleton and Paul Hall. *Director:* John Singleton. *Screenplay:* John Singleton. *Director of Photography:* Peter Lyons Collister. *Editor:* Bruce Cannon. *Music:* Stanley Clarke. *Music Editor:* Carlton Kaller. *Sound:* Veda Campbell. *Sound Editor:* Greg Hedgepath. *Casting:* Jaki Brown-Karman and Kimberly Hardin. *Production Designer:* Keith Brian Burns. *Art Director:* Richard Holland. *Set Designer:* Charles Daboub, Jr. *Set Decorator:* Michael C. Claypool. *Costumes:* Carol Oditz. *Make-up:* Alvechia Ewing and Beverly Jo Pryor. *Stunt Coordinator:* Bob Minor. *Running time:* 127 minutes. *MPAA Rating:* R.

CAST: Omar Epps (Malik Williams); Kristy Swanson (Kristen Connor); Michael Rapaport (Remy); Jennifer Connelly (Taryn); Ice Cube (Fudge); Jason Wiles (Wayne); Tyra Banks (Deja); Cole Hauser (Scott Moss); Laurence Fishburne (Professor Maurice Phipps); Bradford English (Officer Bradley); Regina King (Monet); Busta Rhymez (Dreads); Jay Ferguson (Billy); Andrew Bryniarski (Knocko); Trevor St. John (James); Talbert Morton (Erik); Adam Goldberg (David Isaacs); J. Trevor Edmond (Eddie); Bridgette Wilson (Nicole); Kari Salin (Claudia); John Walton Smith, Jr. (Coach Davis); Randall Batinkoff (Chad Shadowhill); Malcolm Norrington (Cory); Antonio Todd (Adam); Tim Griffin (Orientation Advisor); Patricia Forte and Sheila Ward (Counselors); George LePorte (Starting Judge); Warren Olney (TV Reporter); D-Knowledge (Himself); Skip O'Brien, Joe Bugs, and Bill Evans (Security Guards); Ernie Singleton, Dedrick Gobert, and Bruce Williams (Fudge's Homies); Richard D. Alexander (Big Shorty); Michael Buchman Silver, Graham Galloway, and Paul Anthony Kropfl (Frat Members); James W. Smith, Walton Greene, and Mary Bakjian (Race Officials); Mista Grimm (Drunk Student); Alicia Stevenson (Monet's Friend); Colleen Ann Fitzpatrick (Festival Singer); Robby Parker (Dogman); Pola Maloles (Flyer Girl); Ingrid Walters (Party Girl); Kiante Elam (Black Pepper); Jamie Jo Medearis (White Salt); Rick Avery (Guard Beats Malik); Tony Donno and Cole McLarty (Gay Victims).

LOS ANGELES TIMES, 1/11/95, Calendar/p. 1, Kenneth Turan

Because he accomplished so much so early, it is easy to forget how young John Singleton is. "Higher Learning" reminds us.

Signed by a major agency while still a student at USC, Singleton saw his first film as a writer-director, "Boyz N the Hood," debut to exceptional notices and make him at age 23 the youngest person and the first African American to be nominated for the best director Oscar.

Singleton followed "Boyz" with the disappointing "Poetic Justice," and now, still in his 20s, comes his third feature, and its youthfulness shows in more than its college setting. In both how much Singleton wants to say and the difficulty he has in being dramatically effective with all that to express, his age is showing.

Focusing on a trio of incoming students at the fictional multicultural Columbus University (shot largely at UCLA), "Higher Learning" has more on its mind than an entire year's worth of standard studio films. It explores, among other things, racism both casual and blatant, ethnic polarization, date rape neo-Nazis, bisexual experimentation, and the pressures society puts on black men in general and black athletes in particular.

In a "Dumb and Dumber" world, it is undeniably heartening to see someone trying to address what is going on in society, a filmmaker who wants to use the medium to do the right thing. But presenting problems is not the same as dramatizing them successfully, and as strong as his message is, Singleton has not found the best way to deliver it.

Two of "Higher Learning's" three protagonists bump into each other in a dormitory elevator early on, but since they're on separate life paths, they don't reconnect until the film is nearly over and they've both experienced quite a lot.

Kristen Connor (Kristy Swanson) is a sheltered young white woman from Orange County whose family has lately fallen on hard financial times. Clearly unused to people of color, she nervously clutches her handbag when Malik Williams (Omar Epps) enters the elevator, an act that Malik, a high school track star on an athletic scholarship, observes with a kind of resigned disgust.

Having even more difficulty connecting with anybody is Remy (Michael Rapaport), a lonely outcast from Idaho whose identity as a heavy-metal fan is not enough to make him feel at home or figure out where he belongs on a campus that is much more diverse than anything he's anticipated.

Around these three revolve a small galaxy of subsidiary characters. There is Monet (Regina King), Kristen's acerbic African American roommate; Deja (Tyra Banks), an attractive fellow runner Malik has his eye on; Taryn (Jennifer Connelly), a campus feminist who befriends Kristen; Wayne (Jason Wiles), Malik's easygoing white roommate; and Fudge (Ice Cube), a sixth-year senior who is a master of glacial cool.

With its cast fairly evenly divided, "Higher Learning" mostly avoids the trap of patronizing either race. In fact, "Zebrahead's" Michael Rapaport gives the film's most interesting performance as the troubled Remy, and Singleton has taken care to make the film's neo-Nazi skinheads, especially their leader, Scott (Cole Hauser), recognizable.

What "Higher Learning" does have difficulty doing is making a coherent whole out of its mass of shifting focuses. Without the aid of the recognizable faces that Robert Altman uses to keep the identities of his characters from becoming confusing, it is often hard to remember if we've met someone before and, as, for instance, with nice guy Wayne, what exactly it was he did the last time we saw him.

Adding to the difficulty is that Singleton can't always manage to bring enough nuance to his characterizations. Too many of the people in "Higher Learning," like Taryn the feminist, tend to come off as billboards more than people, staking out positions when they should be becoming human, a difficulty that extends to two of the film's most revered characters, Fudge and Professor Maurice Phipps (the always magnetic Laurence Fishburne).

Of all the characters in the film, Singleton, not surprisingly, seems to have invested the most in Malik Williams, smart and talented but unsure about how to handle the pressures placed on a successful young African American. Fudge and Phipps, because they see his promise, try in their own ways to educate Malik, to awaken him to his potential and his responsibilities.

But while the professor can't be argued with when he says "information is power," and Malik is similarly correct when he says, "as a black man in America, stresses come from everywhere," the accuracy of their words is not the issue. Though Singleton has a youthful desire to preach to his audience and show them the light, those kinds of statements are best absorbed when they flow out of meaningful situations, not just the character's mouths.

Despite a weakness for trying to tie things up with melodramatic violence, Singleton remains a fluid filmmaker who works well with actors. And when he is not trying so hard to make points—for instance, in a playful scene of Malik flirting with Deja—his skill is evident. Still finding his way after that expectation-raising early success, Singleton probably already knows the truth of the Frederick Douglass statement he has Professor Phipps quote: "Without struggle, there is no progress." He may not be there yet, but he is on the road.

NEW YORK POST, 1/11/95, p. 36, Michael Medved

Make no mistake: "Higher Learning" is a dreadful movie, but at least it's not a total, irredeemable disaster like John Singleton's last outing, "Poetic Justice."

This time, the young writer-director coaxes a few solid performances out of his large cast, and even delivers a handful of gripping action scenes that recall the cinematic flair he brought to his now legendary debut film. "Boyz N the Hood."

For the most part, however, "Higher Learning" remains a mess—tendentious, phony, inept, indulgent and one of the longest, dreariest two-hour-and-seven-minute sits you're likely to endure at the movies any time in 1995.

Omar Epps plays an inner-city track star who gets an athletic scholarship to fictional Columbus University. During freshman year, he crosses paths with a mousy young thing (Kristy Swanson) from Orange County, who's promptly date-raped by a smirking frat boy, before she falls in love with another woman (Jennifer Connelly)—angelic leader of campus feminists.

Meanwhile, the third freshman in Singleton's survey of contemporary campus life is a geeky kid from Idaho (Michael Rapaport) who makes few friends—until he's recruited by the local cell of drooling Nazi skinheads, who equip him with firearms and eventually precipitate the movie's biggest (and bloodiest) scenes.

None of these young actors is bad, exactly; Swanson, for instance, is vastly more adequate than she was in her prior starring role in "Buffy, the Vampire Slayer."

The problem is that the characters are all so appallingly underwritten that not even the world's greatest thespians could make us care about them.

For instance, Epps' character enjoys a passionate love affair with a fellow track star (played by supermodel Tyra Banks), but other than lots of closeups of body parts, we know nothing about these people or their relationship.

To try to give weight to this manipulative melodrama, Singleton trots out Laurence Fishburne as the voice of wisdom and authority—the same basic role he played in "Boyz N the Hood."

This time, however, the redoubtable Fishburne comes equipped with beard, bow tie and silly, unexplained accent (is it Jamaican?) in his role as a political science prof given to delphic pronouncements meant to be vaguely inspiring.

Throughout the picture, Singleton's hammer-handed approach trivializes everything it touches: On the serious issue of date rape, he shows Kristy Swanson objecting not so much to the fact that she's forced to have sex, but that her attacker refuses her request that he put on a condom.

Worst of all, the movie reduces significant problems of campus racism to a tiny band of cartoon Nazis. Wouldn't it be nice if all examples of real-life university intolerance came so conveniently identified with swastika tattoos and iron-cross medallions?

Meanwhile, the soundtrack blares out an eclectic selection of 28 songs and snatches that are generally more diverting than the action on screen.

These musical selections include such worthy offerings as "Super Monkey" (by Stanford Prison Experiment), "A Pimp" (by Otis O'Solomon), and the appropriately titled "Situation: Grimm" (by Mista Grimm).

Those who enjoy this music would be well advised to buy the soundtrack album (sure to be a big seller) and skip the experience of suffering through this miserably, misfired motion picture.

NEWSDAY, 1/11/95, Part II/p. B9, John Anderson

At the center of Columbus University—the fictional setting of John Singleton's campus drama, "Higher Learning"—stands a statue of the school's namesake, wearing a look than can only be described as dazed. It's as if he'd heard someone call him an imperialist, racist, conquering swine, despoiler of nature, befouler of Eden, slaver, sadist and unrepentant white male European.

Or, made him sit through this movie.

"Higher Learning" should be advertised as the first drive-by feature—random, vicious, ultimately pointless. Singleton, who at age 23 received an Oscar nomination for the successful and affecting "Boyz N the Hood," has since produced the lackluster Janet Jackson vehicle "Poetic Justice." Now, he has turned his talents to making a film that, while technically adequate, is a jumble of angry stereotypes, scattershot philosophy, opaque thought and cartoon characters, all of which reinforce rather than question any biases its audience might have. This is, clearly, not a filmmaker with a generous, or even developing, vision.

Whether "Higher Learning" is an accurate portrayal of contemporary campus life I can't say—what constitutes the contemporary campus anyway? But if it is, the college budget crises can be cured by selling the books and putting the teachers on workfare. Their effectiveness as educators is nil, including the imperious Prof. Phipps (the ever-charismatic Laurence Fishburne) whose pronouncements—"Strip yourself of the attitude that the world owes you something"—are largely contradicted by the movie.

Rather than an institute of learning, Columbus University is, instead, a social laboratory, in which the three main characters prove the director's half-baked sociological hypotheses, most of which seem to be based on hearsay.

Malik, portrayed by the talented Omar Epps ("Juice"), was a high school star whose tepid track time and hot head almost lose him his partial college scholarship. And he is just one of Singleton's galloping contradictions: An athlete who resents "feeling like a thoroughbred," who realizes that, "They wouldn't give a ___ about me if I wasn't running for this school" (which is probably true, and he should listen to Phipps), but who really, really wants a full scholarship. Apparently, the ghettoization of the scholar-athlete is only as acceptable as the size of the grant.

Malik's political enlightenment is being administered by Fudge, the most puzzling, or revealing, of Singleton's characters. Played with appropriate disdain by rap star Ice Cube, Fudge is a natural leader, a student of life and Frederick Douglas, who's been at college six years and exhibits nothing but contempt for anyone who (1) studies, (2) goes to class ("Y'all trained Negroes"), or (3) attempts to get anything out of his or her college education. As an agitator he's gifted, provoking the racist campus security force and the Bud-befuddled frat boys. But his existence at Columbus prompts questions. Why is he there at all? As the director's mouthpiece, of course.

Singleton's most troubling and racist characterization, though, is that of Remy (Michael Rapaport of "Zebrahead"), a social misfit whose failure to fit in turns him from wallflower to murderous Nazi skinhead. He's the kind of quiet loner whom no one noticed until he began firing from a tower. His racism, born of Fudge's refusal to turn down his stereo, is virulent.

And then there's Kristen (Kristy Swanson), who after downing tequila shooters for several hours accompanies another drunk student back to his frat house room, where they wiggle out of their clothes and create the beast with two backs. At this point, Kristen makes a request that he put on a condom, he ignores it, and she runs screaming and weeping from the room. A victim of date rape? We're supposed to sympathize, but only because of her naivete. Granted, the situation comprises all the reasons there's a date-rape debate, but Singleton rubs our noses in what he sees as her insignificance: When she's taken back to the party by Fudge and Co. to identify her "date," it's so they can avenge not Kristen but her roommate, Monet (Regina King), whom the suspect has called a "black bitch."

This is a cruel dismissal of both the issue and Kristen, who will turn for comfort to the feminist organizer, Taryn (Jennifer Connelly), a woman whose lesbianism, in Singleton's mind, must be the last resort of the rape victim. We're never sure what they actually do together—Singleton cuts confusingly between Kristen and Taryn and Kristen and the sensitive Wayne (Jason Wiles).

But the Kristen storyline is a lesson in logic compared to Remy's. His evolution is a broad burlesque of so-called white rage that would be laughable if it weren't so inflammatory, and so symptomatic of what's tragic and predictable about "Higher Learning."

NEWSWEEK, 1/16/95, p. 66, David Ansen

The first screen-filling image in John Singleton's *Higher Learning* is the American flag, removing any doubt that the young director of "Boyz N the Hood" is after big game. His fictitious Columbus University is going to be a microcosm for America in all its fractious multi-cultural diversity. As big metaphors go, the college campus offers ripe possibilities, throwing together unformed souls of every possible class, race and ethnic background. Mix these cultural collisions with the volatility and confusion of kids whose identities are still up for grabs—like the three freshman protagonists here—and Singleton comes armed with enough explosive social issues for a half dozen dramas.

Malik (Omar Epps), a runner on a partial athletic scholarship, is a struggling student who feels his worth is measured only by his track performance; Kristen (Kristy Swanson), an Orange County blonde who's date-raped by a frat boy, is awash in sexual ambiguities and Remy (Michael Rapaport), an isolated Idaho rube, is desperate to fit in anywhere. Each of them is lost and looking for role models. Malik, a chronic complainer, gets little overt sympathy from his West Indian political-science professor (Laurence Fishburne), a stern sage who rejects Malik's ethos of victimization. But another student, Fudge (Ice Cube)—the unofficial guru of the black students—senses his intellectual potential. Kristen, reeling from her brutal encounter with the frat boy, drifts into sexual confusion: she's romantically torn between a wise lesbian political activist (Jennifer Connelly) and a sensitive hunk, having sex with both. Remy, the outcast, can only find a place at the extremes: he falls in with the campus skinheads, a loutish gaggle of swastika-waving brutes.

When Singleton unfurls those swastikas (accompanied by some doom-laden Stanley Clarke music) you know there's trouble ahead—both for the characters and for the movie. For, its first hour, "Higher Learning" keeps you absorbed, even when the waiting feels didactic: it's accurate about the tribal instincts of students, the way kids band together around music and style and half-formed ideologies. But Singleton doesn't get inside these students the way he did with the homies in "Boyz N the Hood"—they're representative figures in an earnest allegory about fractured America. And as soon as Singleton lets his plot go the skinhead route—fist-fights, assassinations, gay-bashings, an innocent black victim and vengeance—"Higher Learning" sells its soul (and its brain) for overwrought melodrama.

As a filmmaker, Singleton's caught in the old form/content bind. The message he thinks he's sending—that kids need to question all premises, to find their own answers, to "unlearn" the prejudices built into the system—is at odds with the Hollywood visual vocabulary he practices with slick but unconscious finesse. He wants to criticize the overemphasis on athletic performance, but films the track scenes with glamorous, Nike-ad brio. (When Malik calls his relay teammates "slaves" after one of these lyric running scenes, it's impossible to know whether we're meant to take him seriously.) He wants to question authority, but his camera angles worship his heroes and demonize his villains in expressionistic shadows. The audience isn't allowed to discover anything on its own: Singleton underlines every big moment, and adds exclamation points. And yet you leave more confused than illuminated—what do mad skinhead assassins really have to tell us about anything? Do Nazi skinheads go to college?

Watching "Higher Learning" work itself up into a frenzy, you can feel the burden that Singleton's success has placed on him: he feels he has to address so many burning social issues—and pump up a crowd pleaser—that he's left himself no room as an artist. There's no spontaneity in his college kids—he doesn't give his actors much breathing space—and no buoyancy in the filmmaking. Singleton is too young, and too talented, to trap himself in the robes of a spokesman. Maybe if he unlearns the overcooked language of Hollywood melodrama he'll find his true voice.

SIGHT AND SOUND, 10/95, p. 50, Mark Sinker

It's a new academic year at Columbus University, and the lives of Kristen and Remy (both white) and Malik (black) intertwine. Remy clashes with Fudge (black) over the latter's loud rap music, and is repeatedly rebuffed and mocked. Kristen meets Taryn (white) who invites her to a feminist meeting.

Professor Phipps (black) teaches Kristen and Malik politics. Malik realises he will have to train harder if he wants a full sports scholarship. Kristen gets drunk and has unpleasant sex with a student named Billy. He insults Kristen's black room-mate Monet, and is nearly beaten up by Fudge's posse. Kristen, isolated and humiliated, goes to Taryn's meeting. Malik borrows the autobiography of Frederick Douglass from Fudge. Phipps lectures on democracy, property and liberty: the assignment for the semester is to formulate your own personal ideology.

Malik meets Deja, a smart black female athlete, and they start dating. Kristen is in love with Taryn, but meets Wayne, Malik's untidy white roommate, and likes him. Unable to choose, she has sex with both. Led by Scott, armed Nazi skinheads have recruited the friendless and resentful Remy: he clashes violently with Malik, who is thrown into doubt about continuing at Columbus. Later, the skinheads and Fudge's posse skirmish.

Kristen organises a Peace-Fest but the skinheads attack it. Remy, on the roof with his rifle, kills Deja: Professor Phipps fails to save her. Malik chases Remy, and fights him. Security drag Malik off and beat him up, then chase Remy, who shoots himself.

At the memorial site for Deja, Malik meets Kristen, who feels responsible and desolate. Malik tells her she can't blame herself. They exchange names for the first time, and shake hands.

An accurate technician, John Singleton is no screen dialectician, no Spike Lee. You won't leave the theatre arguing loudly with your partner. There's nothing that surprising in this choices-tragedy, but by refusing to decide quite what he believes, Singleton throws doubt on some of the Hollywood liberal clichés—of character, of solution—that threaten to shape it. He sets these doubts up architecturally rather than dramatically, through the cross-play of affinities and contrasts between characters in not-quite-connected storylines: Kristen/Malik, Fudge/Scott, obviously, but also Fudge/Taryn, Remy/Malik, Remy/Kristen. It's a very *symmetrical* movie.

This works against the urgency it needs: the action (the fight scenes, Deja's bloody death) is episodic, and somewhat defanged. But the symmetry pushes to the front Phipps, the film's key character (and without formal counterweight; he's in fact the only teacher we meet). Pipe-smoking, courteous, Caribbean, he's untypical territory for Laurence Fishburne. It's almost a John Houseman role: a curmudgeon because he wants his pupils to make the most of themselves, and therefore loveable (ultimately). He pushes Malik to do better; not to fall back on excuses or victimhood but to work the system to his advantage. Yet Singleton injects doubt here too. A refusal to guide those who don't guide themselves may be what turns them toward unthinking tribalism; crusty commitment to higher learning as a good in itself seems irrelevant in the wake of violent death. Is knowledge for the getting of power, or to challenge it? Hasn't education been undermined by the politicisation of information? Although Phipps is exasperated by Kristen's refusal to take a stand in her essays, her sexual confusion is as close to a symbol of civic decency as the film gets; as if not being able to choose is the way out. The heart of the film's central Douglass quote, "without struggle there is no progress", may be the word "struggle"—but the skinheads are reading Hitler's *Mein Kampf* (trans: *My Struggle*).

It was brave to take on multicultural intolerance; braver still to refuse the sentimental cop-outs (such as sporting achievement, or the objectivity of the learned). Singleton is mordant about officialdom's institutionalised unfairness, financial, cultural and practical: Security guards always intervene against blacks first, and other things don't come out right, either. He's almost too careful with the complex ecologies and etiquettes of American campus life. Even his skinheads are not mere boneheads; indeed, Cole Hauser gives the performance of the film as their sinister-because-foresightful leader. Remy is so whinily unlikeable why would even Nazis put up with him? Malik has good lines, including a 13-word *précis* (which *Hoop Dreams* took three hours to say), hurled at a teammate he's just let down: "All you ever gonna be is a runner. Like a horse. A slave." But the other main characters seem unformed; the secondary characters are little more than ciphers, numbered points in a position paper, which is intelligently presented, but (like Fishburne's Phipps) disappointingly cool and (like Swanson's Kristen) just too vague to be memorable.

TIME, 1/23/95, p. 57, Richard Schickel

It is difficult to be a young black filmmaker like John Singleton. His race tends to impose racism on him as subject. His youth and his status as a generational spokesman oblige him to assume a particular attitude, an outraged political correctness that extends to other, nonracial matters (notably sexism). His audience, which is also young, meanwhile makes, or seems to make, contradictory demands on him—for violently dramatic confrontations on one hand; for hopeful, or at least not entirely bleak, conclusions on the other.

Higher Learning is the desperately confused response to all these pressures. It finds on a single college campus every imaginable youthful type: a track star on an athletic scholarship (Omar Epps), who is convinced he is being exploited; his very smart, very pretty girlfriend (Tyra Banks), who is coolly intent on using the system to her advantage; a young white woman (Kristy Swanson), victimized by date rape, tempted by lesbianism, ultimately redeemed and betrayed by her idealistic political activism; a socially maladroit loner (Michael Rapaport), who finds a dank spiritual home with the local neo-Nazis. The rapper Ice Cube is on hand as a perpetual graduate student and guru to the black activists. Laurence Fishburne represents adult authority as an arrogant, challenging and ultimately wise and sympathetic political-science professor.

These aren't really characters; they are points on a rigidly conceived political spectrum. From the moment you meet him, you know, for example, that Rapaport's miserable character has only one fate and one function: to bring the movie to a predictably bloody, conventionally instructive but emotionally abstract conclusion. Singleton has made all the right political moves given his complicated circumstances, but he hasn't really made a movie of them.

VILLAGE VOICE, 1/17/95, p. 52, Gary Dauphin

The main beneficiary of Hollywood's recent (and belated) fascination with young black male writer-directors long before he'd even released his first film, John Singleton has always been a relentlessly prepackaged product. The two major studio releases to his credit, (not to mention the *New York Times*-endorsed media persona) fit so neatly between Spike Lee's edgy auteurisms and the black demimonde of rap-comedy franchises that you'd think Singleton was born to fill the gap between commercial poles, which of course he was.

Already anointed as the next Spike by Columbia Pictures before he was 22, Singleton's career was laid out before him well into the next century solely on the basis of the script he wrote for *Boyz N the Hood*. Besides being a pretty good read, *Boyz* gave Hollywood the sellable black male commodity it privately hoped for, namely an easier-to-deal-with Spike Lee, The (valid) presumption of talent in the Spike-not-Spike tag might have spared Singleton the indignity of having to ply a trade in lowbrow *House Party* clones and quickie gang flicks, but it also hasn't prevented him from making a movie like his latest, *Higher Learning*, a middling first-year-of-college picture that goes from reasonably arresting to maddeningly corny with such frequency that "hodgepodge" is the only word to properly describe it.

Perhaps because Singleton-the-commodity's adoptive mother was the notoriously fickle Industry that nurtured him, the choice of surrogate fathers is the key to how his stories have factored out. That was certainly the case in *Boyz*, where the Ice Cube and Laurence Fishburne characters vied for the nascent buppy soul of Cuba Gooding Jr., and it's certainly true in *Learning*. Set at Columbus University, a fictitious West Coast college, *Learning* follows the intertwined stories of a trio of every-undergraduates, black track star Malik (Omar Epps), bland white girl Kristen (Kristy Swanson), and a slightly dim-witted Idaho hick named Remy (Michael Rapaport). Having found their rooms, the three put up posters and play their music, a campus ritual outlining their characters for the audience in clean and concise strokes. Malik pins up an antique-seeming Vanessa Williams calendar as Remy unfolds his Danzig poster; Kristen tapes up baby pictures while Tori Amos croons in the background. Despite their racial differences and divergent tastes, they're all pretty much your run-of-the-mill dumb freshmen, empty heads whose education will comprise the bulk of *Learning*'s story.

Since Malik will be Singleton's stand-in, his enlightenment takes center stage throughout. Presumably fresh off the slide from an inner-city adolescence only slightly less stressful than that of the surviving male protagonist in *Boyz*, Malik arrives on Columbus's verdant lawn full of ego and undirected talent but not much else. After Malik pimp-strolls onto the practice field wearing sunglasses, his first potential mentor, a black track coach, chews him out for a bit too much showboat, while his poli-sci teacher, Professor Phipps (Fishburne again), kicks him out of class over an unpaid tuition bill. Although Phipps and Malik will come to a later understanding, Fishburne is oddly underutilized here. His Phipps is a cardboard cutout, a peppermint candy-popping West Indian suit who is basically all manners and platitudes about how the problem with black people today is their expectation of handouts, their laziness, and so on.

As *Learning* is Singleton's test foray into the world of white leading actors, Kristen and Remy's adjustment issues share semi-equal billing with Malik's. Remy's basic problem is that he's a few chromosomes short of a full 46. Gangly and insufferably stupid, he lopes around campus asking people to play video games with him or "Hey man, where's the party?" so dull-witted and lonely that when he's adopted by the local cell of neo-Nazi skinheads, you almost feel happy for him. Kristen, like most white women in Singleton's vaguely afrocentric universe, is equally empty. When Professor Phipps asks her, "What are you?" she shrugs at him, her identity opaque to herself until Singleton has her date-raped after a night of tequila shots.

In the aftermath, Kristen drifts into the local undergraduate feminist collective, headed up by a junior named Taryn (Jennifer Connelly). Written by Singleton as the really supportive type whose open smile and smooth maturity might very well hide the heart of a touchy-feely cliché, Taryn and her subsequent affair with Kristen are treated with a matter-of-factness that's surprising—although whether the evenhandedness is a sign that Singleton is over his male paranoia or just didn't know what to do with the topic except put it on screen is unclear throughout.

Besides Phipps and Taryn and the skins, though, *Learning*'s main example of positive mentoring comes from Fudge (Ice Cube). A sixth-year senior, Fudge is the unofficial mayor of the Black Hole (Columbus's African American ghetto), and whether he's rolling a joint, loaning Malik black studies books or listening to Kristen and her black roommate complain about the date-rapist like some Afroed Solomon, he's the living and breathing heart of *Higher Learning*. Cube's screen presence is, as always, undeniable, and in Fudge he's found a character that actually allows him to take a slight side step out of the gang-banger archetypes he's been inhabiting on screen. Getting his e-mail or tormenting some white folks just for the fun of it, Cube is all good, which unfortunately can't be said of the other mentors in *Learning*.

Since Singleton imagines his political credibility with black audiences is dependent on tackling the race issue in the most bluntly head-on way imaginable, it isn't long before Malik and Kristen's various paths to mental uplift are forced on a particularly violent detour by Remy and his neo-Nazi pals: Although the third act of *Learning* is supposed to be its most "explosive," the climax is strictly TV-movie, basically a recapitulation of shooter-in-the-tower scenes from *The Deadly Tower*, the 1975 docudrama on the University of Texas at Austin massacre of August 1966.

By the time the dust has settled, not much has changed except that Malik and Kristen get to exchange their first supportive words of the film while standing over candles and flowers memorializing Columbus University's fallen. Intended as a bittersweet moment (it counters Kristen and Malik's only other encounter, wherein Kristen clutches her purse at the sight of him), it's by far the most annoying and telling scene in the movie. Looking for all the world as if the entire previous two hours were solely intended to bring them together, Kristen and Malik stiffly mourn the death of their innocence before walking into the hazy future. But I'm thinking it's really John Singleton crying. Once upon a time he was the new kid on the yard with the umblemished academic record and the boundless future, but like the four years of college, wunderkindhood only lasts but so long.

Also reviewed in:
NEW YORK TIMES, 1/11/95, p. C13, Janet Maslin
VARIETY, 1/9-15/95, p. 71, Todd McCarthy
WASHINGTON POST, 1/11/95, p. C1, Rita Kempley
WASHINGTON POST, 1/13/95, Weekend/p. 39, Desson Howe

HIGHLANDER: THE FINAL DIMENSION

A Dimension Films release of a Transfilm/Initial Group/Fallingcloud production. *Executive Producer:* Guy Collins and Charles L. Smiley. *Producer:* Claude Léger. *Director:* Andy Morahan. *Screenplay:* Paul Ohl. *Based on the story by:* William Panzer and Brad Mirman. *Based on characters created by:* Gregory Widen. *Director of Photography:* Steven Chivers. *Editor:* Yves Langlois. *Music:* J. Peter Robinson and Paul Di Franco. *Sound:* Daniel Masse, Claude Hazanavicius, Jean Philippe le Roux, and Louis Kramer and (music) Robert Fernandez. *Sound Editor:* Michel B. Bordeleau. *Casting:* Nadja Rona, Vera Miller, and Françoise Combardière. *Production Designer:* Giles Aird and Ben Morahan. *Art Director:* Alain Paroutaud. *Set Decorator:* Paul Hotte, Jean Kazemirchuck, and Gillie Delaf. *Set Dresser:* Ginette Robitaille, Daniel Breton, Annie Régol, and Rafael Vicent. *Special Effects:* Louis Craig. *Visual Effects:* Stuart Galloway. *Costumes:* Jackie Budin, Mario Davignon, and Micheline Rouillard. *Make-up:* Nicole Lapierre, Penny Lee, Johanne Gravel, Agnès Tassel, Amanda Knight and Tazi Asmaa. *Special Make-up Effects:* Stephen Dupuis and Charles Carter. *Stunt Coordinator:* Dave McKeown and Yves Langlois. *Running time:* 94 minutes. *MPAA Rating:* PG-13.

CAST: Christopher Lambert (Connor MacLeod/Russel Nash); Mario Van Peebles (Kane); Deborah Unger (Alex Johnson/Sarah); Mako (Nakono); Raoul Trujillo and Jean-Pierre Pérusse (Warriors); Martin Neufeld (Stern); Frederick Y. Okimura (Old Japanese Man); Daniel Do (Takamura); Gabriel Kakon (John); Louis Bertignac (Pierre Bouchet); Michael Jayston (Jack Donovan); Zhenhu Han (Innkeeper); Akira Inoue (Inkeeper's Son); Darcy Laurie and George Vitetzakis (Bangers); David Francis (Doctor Malloy); Lisa Vitello (Nurse); Matt Holland (Intern); Richard Jutras (Uniform); Liz Macrae (Interviewer); Emidio Michetti (Detective); André Oumansky (Marquis de Condorcet); Charles S. Doucet and Garth Gilker (Cowboys); Paul Hopkins (Tommy); Michael McGill (Medical Examiner); Chip Chuipka (Charlie); Patrick Fierry (Captain); Clifford Spencer (Guillotine Man); John Dunn-Hill (Loony Napoleon); Morven Cameron (Receptionist); Vlasta Vrana (Vorisek).

LOS ANGELES TIMES, 1/30/95, Calendar/p. 8, Kevin Thomas

Like its two predecessors, "Highlander: The Final Dimension" is elementary and vague, is purportedly last installment works well enough on a comic book level. Music video veteran Andy Morahan, in his feature directorial debut, has the right idea: Go for as much energy, pace and visual panache as possible.

Christopher Lambert returns in the title role as the 16th-century Scotsman Connor MacLeod, who cannot die except by decapitation. It seems that there is a handful of these immortals on

Earth who will duel until only one is left. The survivor then becomes the winner of the Prize of Ultimate Knowledge and Power. Since Sean Connery did not return as the Highlander's mentor, he has been replaced by the Japanese sorcerer, Nokono (Mako), whose cave, as it turns out, has been just discovered under a present-day power plant in Japan.

Having been buried alive in that cave for 400 years by Nokono, who sacrificed his life in doing so, Kane (Mario Van Peebles), the Master of Illusion, is not in the best of tempers when he emerges, naturally determined to do in MacLeod, the sorcerer's pal and accomplice in keeping him out of circulation for so long.

The entire film also has but a single goal, which is to keep moving until the Highlander and Kane have their inevitable, entirely predictable big showdown, which takes place in New Jersey in what looks to be an oil refinery complex.

In between the considerable action, Lambert does get a chance to convey the Highlander's essential isolation, and Van Peebles goes for gleeful, stylish villainy, which is just what is needed. Deborah Unger, who also plays MacLeod's love in the 18th Century, is an elegant archeologist who falls in love with the near-500-year-old Highlander—but, of course, he doesn't look a day over Lambert's 37.

NEW YORK POST, 1/28/95, Part II/p.15, Larry Worth

A wise old sage tells the superhero: "A most feared and evil enemy is among us. You are the only one who can stop him. If he wins, the world will suffer eternal damnation."

Viewers will relate, since suffering is the name of the game for witnesses to "Highlander: The Final Dimension."

But a putrid screenplay didn't stop Christopher Lambert from participating in the third big-screen installment about a Scottish immortal with otherworldly powers.

This time, he's up against nose-ringed master magician Mario Van Peebles, attired in Sherpa get-up as a latter-day Attila the Hun. Seems the Highlander walled him up in a Japanese cave 400 years ago. Having finally escaped his bonds, he's mad as hell and ready for his next trick: making his adversary disappear.

Don't like that ol' chestnut? Witless screenwriter Paul Ohl has lots more cliches up his sleeve, like the one about Highlander Jr., who's just waiting to be kidnapped and used as a pawn for the titans' final clash. Then there's the reincarnation of Highlander's French Revolutionary love (creating a subplot to the subplot that actually rips off "A Tale of Two Cities").

Director Andy Morahan, whose only experience behind the camera is lensing MTV videos, gives away his origins by jumping continents and centuries without rhyme or reason as blaring rock selections assault the eardrums.

Add to that a collection of bargain-basement special effects, featuring the most hilarious styrofoam and cardboard sets since "Plan 9 from Outer Space" and an avalanche that looks like a cloud of talcum powder.

It's probably for the best that both Lambert and Van Peebles let their swords do most of the talking, just as generic love interest Deborah Unger relies on her bodice-busting attributes. Thankfully, veteran actor Mako takes an early dive as a live-action Yoda.

Then again, who could bring conviction to lines like "nothing is what it seems, Highlander"? Particularly when "Highlander" is exactly what is seems: a silly waste of time, effort and nose rings.

NEWSDAY, 1/28/95, Part II/p. B5, Jonathan Mandell

If you are not already a fan, it may be a mystery to you why the Highlander cannot die—not just the character of the Scottish swordsman (who can only be killed if his head is chopped off, played by the Neanderthal-browed, semi-comatose Christopher Lambert, but the movie itself. The original 1986 film was a complete flop in moviehouses throughout the nation, not just critically but commercially. Yet it spawned a sequel ("Highlander: The Quickening") even more hokey and less intelligible, and then a Saturday afternoon TV series. Now, nine years later, comes a third installment, "Highlander: The Final Dimension."

The answer to this mystery of immortality lies in a new dimension, a final frontier—actually two final frontiers: the international market and the local video store, where the first Highlander alone earned more than $100 million.

So the producers have brought back the formula, mumbo jumbo intact, spending a bit more on the special effects and shamelessly lifting plot lines and even whole scenes from the first Highlander. The results are more entertaining than they should be, for those who don't try too hard to follow what's going on, and don't mind that the filmmaker shifts times and locales like a channel-surfer on speed—medieval Scotland, where Conner MacLeod was born, 18th-Century France, techno-modern Japan, sandy Morocco, and a comically brutal and cynical present-day New York straight out of the "Death Wish" series. This is a city where the villain—this time Mario Van Peebles with bad teeth, a Darth Vader-deep digital bass, the shaggy outfit of a Mongol warrior, a wild wig and a ring through his nose—seems to fit right in.

SIGHT AND SOUND, 3/95, p. 37, Tom Tunney

The sixteenth century. Following the deaths of his wife Heather and friend Ramirez, 'Immortal' Highlander Connor MacLeod goes to Japan and seeks enlightenment from the sorcerer Nakano in his mountain lair. Rival Immortal Kane surprises the two men, stabbing MacLeod and beheading Nakano. However, the energy released as Nakono's magic transfers itself to Kane causes the chamber to collapse. Kane and his accomplices are trapped inside. MacLeod escapes.

1994. An archaeological dig on the mountain allows Kane and his accomplices to break out, murdering a security guard. Kane sends one associate to seek out MacLeod and murders the other. The Japanese police and US archaeologist Alex are baffled by the two corpses but Alex finds a fragment of tartan cloth which she identifies as belonging to the sixteenth century Scottish clan MacLeod. Sensing that a rival Immortal is hunting him, MacLeod leaves his adopted son John in Morocco and goes to New York. Mugged and shot several times, he is taken to hospital. Believing him insane, the authorities put him in an asylum. MacLeod escapes and beheads an emissary of Kane. He thinks back to eighteenth-century France and his relationship with the English woman Sarah.

Arriving in New York, Kane sees a television report about the dig. This leads him to Alex's lab, then to MacLeod's New York apartment; the two men have an initial skirmish. Detective John Stern is convinced that the hospital slaying is linked to a rash of beheadings in the mid-80s in which MacLeod was also involved. Alex refuses to tell him anything. In Scotland, MacLeod and Alex meet, and he fashions a new sword. They adjourn to the pub before making love.

Meanwhile, as Kane searches MacLeod's New York apartment, MacLeod's son phones. Using his shape-shifting powers, Kane meets the boy at Newark airport in the guise of MacLeod and kidnaps him. MacLeod arrives too late to save the boy, but Kane has left a message telling MacLeod where they should meet for their final battle. In the struggle which follows, MacLeod beheads Kane, despite his briefly adopting the guise of Alex. Reunited with his son and Alex, MacLeod returns to a new life in Scotland.

The original *Highlander* film was set mainly in mid-80s New York, with flashbacks to 1536 Scotland. The first sequel begins in 1999, with most of the action set in 2024. The odd decision to make *Highlander III: The Sorcerer* a sequel to one and a prequel to the other is clumsy in the extreme, and infuriating to audiences who have sat through the earlier films.

Highlander II may not have made much sense, but it did have a gloriously tongue-in-cheek turn from Sean Connery, and its action scenes were presented with commendable kinetic verve. *Highlander III* suffers immeasurably from Connery's absence, while its action scenes are comparatively tired. But its biggest problem is an utter failure of imagination on the part of its writers. The reluctance to push what is essentially a sword-and-sorcery saga even further into sci-fi territory is understandable, but instead the script offers no more than a rehash. Given all of history since 1536 to choose from, they merely give the plot of the first film some Japanese trimmings. Mario Van Peebles, his voice electronically deepened, steps lamely into the cardboard villain's shoes, and Deborah Unger has the supportive female role, previously parcelled out to Roxanne Hart and Virginia Madsen.

The most telling moment is when we learn in passing that Hart's character Brenda, from the original *Highlander*, was murdered in 1987. Only in this cursory fashion is that movie's happy ending explained away. By implication, *Highlander III*'s equally trite ending will have to be superseded by 1999 to explain the opening of *Highlander II*. Attempting to link the three films in any logical sense is futile; the series' priority is simply to engineer MacLeod into a climactic situation where he can chop the head off the next opponent to come along. Its cyclical logic is less that of a conventional narrative than of a computer game. Switch it on and Kane, Kurgan, Katana or another villain will be along for another bout of cut-and-thrust. "There can be only one!" is MacLeod's catchphrase, but it now seems to refer as much to the plot as to the cosmic order he supposedly upholds.

Such a repetitive structure plays havoc with conventional notions of character. In *Highlander III*, MacLeod still grieves for his first wife Heather, and there are flashbacks to his relationship with Sarah during the French Revolution. Brenda, in narrative terms only seven years dead, is barely mentioned. The audience loses track of who MacLeod is grieving for at any one time. Christopher Lambert, who has a limited acting range, here faces an impossible task—putting emotional flesh on a character with all the weight of a computer image.

Highlander III lacks the second film's manic energy in its action scenes and fills the gaps in between with such a clumsy exposition that it becomes an object lesson in how not to construct a screenplay. Every action is telegraphed in advance and the sole function of the eighteenth century flashbacks ("They need you in Paris, the Revolution has started!") seems to be to pad out the running time. The well-worn device of the hero having a son purely so that he can be kidnapped is disappointing enough; but the way in which this is accomplished is only one of several mind-numbingly obvious links between the set pieces. Kane just happens to be in MacLeod's apartment when the boy phones, and just happens to be in a New York bar when there is news about the archaeological dig.

So much coincidence and contrivance is intrusive, as is the film's hand-me-down visual style. The scenes in Scotland look like ads either for the Scottish Tourist Board or for woolly menswear; and the action scenes are all set in that sanitised netherworld where MTV, bad science fiction and ads for drinks, cars and the privatised electricity industry become one.

Also reviewed in:
CHICAGO TRIBUNE, 1/29/95, Tempo/p. 7, Johanna Steinmetz
NEW YORK TIMES, 1/28/95, p. 16, Stephen Holden
WASHINGTON POST, 1/28/95, p. D3, Richard Harrington

HOME FOR THE HOLIDAYS

A Paramount Pictures and Polygram Filmed Entertainment release of an Egg Pictures production. *Executive producer:* Stuart Kleinman. *Producer:* Peggy Rajski and Jodie Foster. *Director:* Jodie Foster. *Screenplay:* W.D. Richter. *Based on a short story by:* Chris Radant. *Director of Photography:* Lajos Koltai. *Editor:* Lynzee Klingman. *Music:* Mark Isham. *Music Editor:* Craig Pettigrew. *Sound:* Chris Newman and (music) Steven Krause. *Sound Editor:* Gloria S. Borders. *Casting:* Avi Kaufman. *Production Designer:* Andrew McAlpine. *Art Director:* Jim Tocci. *Set Designer:* Carl Stensel. *Set Decorator:* Barbara Drake. *Costumes:* Susan Lyall. *Make-up:* Kathrine James. *Stunt Coordinator:* George Aguillar. *Running time:* 103 minutes. *MPAA Rating:* PG-13.

CAST: Holly Hunter (Claudia Larson); Robert Downey, Jr. (Tommy Larson); Anne Bancroft (Adele Larson); Charles Durning (Henry Larson); Dylan McDermott (Leo Fish); Geraldine Chaplin (Aunt Glady); Cynthia Stevenson (Joanne Wedman); Steve Guttenberg (Walter Wedman); Claire Danes (Kitt Larson); Austin Pendleton (Peter Arnold); David Strathairn (Russell Terziak); Zachary Duhame (Walter Jr); Emily Ann Lloyd (Brittany Lace); Sam Slovick (Jack Gordon); Angela Paton (Mary); Shawn Wayne Hatosy (Counterboy); Randy Stone (Young Puppy); Nat Benchley (Airport Cop); James Lecesne (Ron Brewer).

LOS ANGELES TIMES, 11/3/95, Calendar/p. 1, Kenneth Turan

Comedy loves misery, and few things manufacture discontent as efficiently as ritualized family gatherings. "Home for the Holidays" hopes to find the laughs in the mad chaos of one miserable Thanksgiving, but like many holiday wishes it doesn't quite get fulfilled.

Directed by Jodie Foster and written by W.D. Richter, "Holidays" isn't able to differentiate between reproducing the insanity of a Thanksgiving run amok and making that nightmare amusing. What results is a film with some bright spots but whose effect is finally as muddled and wearying as the event itself sometimes is.

For Claudia Larson (Holly Hunter), the annual family reunion could not come at a less promising time. Suffering from a wicked head cold and just fired from her job as an art restorer, Claudia is also worried about leaving her 16-year-old daughter Kitt (Claire Danes) home alone, a concern that is intensified when Kitt tells her, at the Chicago airport no less, that she is going to use the weekend to have her first sexual experience.

Waiting for Claudia back home in Baltimore are her stress-generating parents. Mother Adele (Anne Bancroft) is a nonstop talker and chain-smoker who thinks Claudia is wasting her life "filling in holes in dead people's pictures." Her heedless babbling has inevitably turned husband Henry (a still light-on-his-feet Charles Durning) into the silent partner in their marriage.

Worn down by the deluge, Claudia hopes that her gay younger brother Tommy (Robert Downey Jr.) will join the group, but when he does she half wonders why she cared. A terrible practical joker, with emphasis on the terrible, Tommy shows up with a handsome hulk with the unlikely name of Leo Fish (Dylan McDermott), leading Claudia to wonder what happened to Tommy's partner Jack.

Through the arrival of Tommy is supposed to get "Home for the Holidays" into high comic gear, it has the opposite effect. While the film believes him to be a lovable scamp whose idea of fun is taking embarrassing nude Polaroids of his sister, he comes off more like an immature jerk who is part of the family problem, not a potential solution.

This inability to correctly judge the emotional impact its characters are having on viewers causes problems for "Holidays" from beginning to end. Claudia manages to remain sympathetic, but few of her relatives duplicate that feat.

Adele's sister Glady (Geraldine Chaplin), for instance, who lives with 210 plants and her memories, is supposed to be a pure spirit but comes off as a shopworn eccentric. And Claudia and Tommy's sister Joanne and her husband, Walter (Cynthia Stevenson and Steve Guttenberg), are such feeble foils as the token squares that the fun we are supposed to have at their expense seems hardly worth the effort.

As the big day wears on and on, various family members drink too much and reveal a variety of troublesome secrets. It's all supposed to be great fun, but Foster is not the first beginning director (this is her second time behind the camera, after "Little Man Tate,") to prove that this type of material is a lot tougher to get right than it seems. Farce is by nature arbitrary, but we should be so dazzled by events we don't notice, which is not at all what happens here.

Foster and Richter, of course, want to do more than make audiences laugh: they want us to be touched by their characters' humanity and take an interest in a budding romance, but that rarely is the case. Instead we end up marking time and wishing we were elsewhere. When father Henry turns a garden hose on some particularly obstreperous family members, it's hard not to wish he would soak the whole movie and be done with it.

NEW YORK POST, 11/3/95, p. 35, Michael Medved

If you view the approach of Thanksgiving and its sometimes testy family reunions with an unshakable sense of dread, then you're part of the core audience, for "Home for the Holidays."

I should confess at the outset that I'm not a member of this group, since I'm enough of a cornball (or butterball) to have always loved the yearly turkey feast and eagerly anticipated its celebration.

Nevertheless, the acting in this sad, fun film is so superb, and Jodie Foster's direction is so unexpectedly skillful, that the picture can draw anyone—at least temporarily—into its seductively nasty vision of the holiday.

Holly Hunter plays a struggling single mother who, just hours before she leaves work for her Thanksgiving break, gets fired from her job at a Chicago art museum. She also learns that her 15-year-old daughter (Claire Danes) won't be accompanying her to the family get-together in Baltimore and will, instead, spend the holiday at her boyfriend's home where she's tentatively planning to lose her virginity.

As if this weren't enough bad news for one November, Hunter also loses her coat on the flight east and after her arrival must contend with the disapproval of her warmhearted but obtuse parents (Anne Bancroft and Charles Durning). In addition, there's an eccentric, emaciated spinster aunt (Geraldine Chaplin), and an uptight sister (Cynthia Stevenson) who's trying hard to be a conventional yuppie mom and supportive wife to a stuffy, self-important banker (Steve Guttenberg).

Most obnoxious (and endearing) of all is the family's baby brother (Robert Downey Jr.), who arrives unexpectedly from Boston with a handsome business associate (Dylan McDermott), and proceeds to torture everyone with his wit, insight, cruelty and whirling dervish energy.

There's not much of a plot, but screenwriter W.D. Richter (who wrote and directed "Buckaroo Bonzai" and "Late for Dinner") provides plenty of well-scripted sniping over sweet potatoes and stuffing as each character reveals key elements of his past and personality.

Of course, everything goes entertainingly wrong at the table, but not so cruelly or disastrously wrong as to strain credibility; all the mishaps and misunderstandings feel both real and familiar. Thanks to ensemble acting of the very highest order, the family members all emerge as vivid, sympathetic characters, with (usually conflicting) points of view you can understand.

Director Foster displays such heartfelt affection for these people that the film builds an altogether unexpected emotional richness and lyrical intensity even while it's accumulating bitter laughs. The weakest item on her Thanksgiving menu involves a contrived, overly convenient romance between Holly Hunter and Dylan McDermott, but even here the chemistry between the two fine actors is undeniable.

Foster's first film as a director, "Little Man Tate," won widespread praise but struck this critic as stilted and clumsy. This time, however, no one can mistake her formidable filmmaking gifts, as she lets her holiday pageant unfold with humor, heart, savvy, and a solid sense of place. The entire film is captured in burnished images that offer an altogether appropriate autumnal glow.

Even as gravy spatters all over a starched new dress, parents argue, or kids scream in the background, every frame of this contentious family get-together is unmistakably infused with love.

SIGHT AND SOUND, 12/96, p. 47, Claire Monk

A picture restorer at a Chicago museum, single mother Claudia Larson is dreading her Thanksgiving visit to her parents in Baltimore. Just before the holiday, she is made redundant by the elderly boss she has recently slept with. Then Kitt, her assured 15-year-old daughter, drops the bombshell that she plans to lose her virginity while staying with her boyfriend's family. Dazed by events, Claudia leaves an ansaphone message for her crazy brother Tommy telling, him all her recent woes and pressing him to come to Baltimore to support her. Back in the stifling family bosom, she grits her teeth at her inactive father Henry's eccentricities and her overworked mother Adele's refusal to treat her as an adult.

Tommy arrives without warning from Boston in a 'surprise' night-time raid, along with a handsome friend, Leo Fish. Assuming that Leo is Tommy's boyfriend, Claudia is disappointed that Tommy seems to have split up with his steady partner Jack Gordon. The family gather, including Adele's semi-senile unmarried sister Aunt Glady and Claudia's estranged, ultra-conservative housewife sister Joanne, her banker husband Walter and children. Thanksgiving dinner instantly erupts into chaos and conflict. Glady's memories of a kiss from Henry when she was 21—the emotionally peak of her life—prompt so much embarrassment that her revelation is simply ignored. Tommy tells everyone the full contents of Claudia's phone message, and Joanne launches an hysterical attack on Tommy's 'exotic' lifestyle. Tommy has been through a gay marriage ceremony with Jack; Joanne, who heard the news through friends, sees this as a personal humiliation.

It turns out that Jack is spending Thanksgiving with his 'real' family, the Boston gay community, and that Leo is a straight friend who has come along because he was curious to meet Claudia. In the aftermath of the dinner, Kitt rings to tell Claudia that, annoyed by her boyfriend's immaturity, she's decided not to take things further with him. An attraction develops between Claudia and Leo but, convinced they live too far apart, Claudia bids him goodbye. Brought closer to her parents by their handling of the crises, she is sad to leave. She finds Leo has booked himself onto her flight home, and agrees to give their relationship a try.

The second film to emerge from the three-year deal between Jodie Foster's Egg Pictures and Polygram (the first was *Nell*), and also Foster's second film as director (following the 1991 child-prodigy drama *Little Man Tate*), *Home for the Holidays* doesn't, at first sight, have precedent in its favour. There's nothing in the earnestness of the two earlier films to suggest a comic touch, nor does the conservatism of *Nell* augur well for a comedy about two sacrosanct American institutions: Thanksgiving and the family.

Moreover, *Home for the Holidays* starts unpromisingly. Holly Hunter's daffy Claudia, with her limp hair, embroidered skull-cap and borrowed coat, at first seems like a kook too far. It's too easy to envisage the role being played by Barbra Streisand two decades back. The comedy takes a while to gather pace. Comic set pieces start to accumulate early on—as Claudia passes through an airport terminal it seems that every payphone is being used by someone caught up in a Thanksgiving trauma—but a lot of the jokes are of a kind that you don't actually laugh at.

This slowness to catch fire is partly due to the script by W.D. Richter (screenwriter of *Nickelodeon* and the 1978 *Invasion of the Body Snatchers*). Its humour relies heavily on character—the central joke being that Claudia's bohemian chaos pales into insignificance compared to the craziness of most of her family—but some of the characterisation is enigmatic. Claudia's parents are ambiguous figures who make it hard for the viewer to know how to respond (Why does Henry play the electric organ while watching *Wheel of Fortune?*) despite wonderful performances from Charles Durning and a bewigged Anne Bancroft. Such uncertainty is hardly the stuff of belly-laughs and it's significant that the film only starts functioning as a comedy with the introduction of characters who work as instantaneous archetypes, particularly Claudia's prankster brother, Tommy, a show-stopping outrageous creation from Robert Downey Jr.

Tommy—an adult gay man who approaches life with the cheeriness and unstoppability of a four-year-old, but whose energy feeds on considerable anger—is emblematic of what *Home for the Holidays* gets right. Refreshingly, this is a film which stretches the definition of family comedy beyond the maternal preoccupations of recent Hollywood examples, from *Nine Months* to *Parenthood*. Its main focus is not adult-as-parents but adults-as-children, a distinction which also neatly encapsulates its audience appeal. This is a comedy for baby-boomers who, if not necessarily empty-nesters (Hunter's Claudia is a single mother, after all), feel detached from the child-rearing ideal, and perhaps feel that they are still children themselves. A running joke in Claudia's two scenes with her daughter Kitt is that the 15-year-old appears not just more chilled than her mother but more mature, more in control.

By virtue of his gayness, Tommy can be seen as the character most distanced from the conventional family ideal. Yet it's through him that the film makes clear that it's not against the family per se, just conservative family values. Tommy and his partner Jack's choice of a 'marriage' ceremony to please themselves rather than their biological families, Kitt's 'mothering' of Claudia and Claudia's 'mothering' of her own mother all suggest that family is wherever we find it and whatever we make of it. In Foster's comedy it's the nuclear family—the miserable, bigoted Joanne and her dull husband—who are left out in the cold.

VILLAGE VOICE, 11/4/95, p. 90, Georgia Brown

Enduring Jodie Foster's *Home for the Holidays* is to yearn for *The Piano*, i.e., Holly Hunter silenced. Trapped with Hunter and a lunatic Robert Downey Jr. is far more punishing than a visit to any nutty family I know. At least at home you can ask to be excused.

Holiday divides into chapters with heads such as "Mom & Dad," "Company," "Relatives," and "More Relatives." At the end, there's one called "The Point." I'll get to that.

Hunter's character is the plucky, churning Claudia, single mom and restorer of old masters, at least until she's fired the day before Thanksgiving vacation. Reeling and sneezing (she has a nasty cold), she takes off for Baltimore leaving behind in Chicago an improbably staid 15-year-old daughter (Claire Danes). "Mom & Dad" turn out to be Anne Bancroft and Charles Durning in a flakiness contest. Mom is a bewigged, chain-smoking hysteric; Dad, full of vinegar, is tuned to the music of the spheres. (I wondered if Dad was in the early stages of Alzheimer's, but no, he turns out to be the film's most stable character.) Claudia's maiden aunt, Glady (Geraldine Chaplin), shows up to emit an alarming fart and confess a long-standing crush on Dad.

The central bond is between Claudia and her gay brother Tommy (Downey), who gets outed to his parents over the course of the weekend. Tommy brings along a mystery guest, Leo Fish (Dylan McDermott): Will he turn out to be a Lytton or a Leonard? Both Tommy and Claudia show nothing but contempt for their, ugh, *married* sister Joanne (Cynthia Stevenson). This pathetic thing arrives with her humorless hubby (Steve Guttenberg) and their obnoxious brood.

Indulged might be a better word than *directed* for Foster's role here. She has obviously encouraged Downey to let it all hang out and mostly he's in a contorted frenzy. It's not long before I'm siding with tightass Joanne. (When she accuses Claudia of feeling "superior to everyone," I seconded it.) For his Tommy, assuming, with good reason, that it turns Claudia on.

Written by W.D. Richter (*Slither, All Night Long, Buckeroo Bonzai*) based on a short story by Chris Radant *Home for the Holidays* is—it begs for this—a turkey.

Also reviewed in:
CHICAGO TRIBUNE, 11/3/95, Friday/p. C, Michael Wilmington
NEW YORK TIMES, 11/3/95, p. C8, Janet Maslin
NEW YORKER, 11/13/95, p. 128, Anthony Lane
VARIETY, 10/30-11/5/95, p. 70, Emanuel Levy
WASHINGTON POST, 11/3/95, p. F1, Rita Kempley

HOTEL SORRENTO

A Castle Hill Productions release of a Bayside Pictures production in association with Horizon Films/Australian Film Finance Corporation. Developed and produced with the assistance of Film Victoria. *Producer:* Richard Franklin. *Director:* Richard Franklin. *Screenplay:* Richard Franklin and Peter Fitzpatrick. *Based on the play by:* Hannie Rayson. *Director of Photography:* Geoff Burton. *Editor:* David Pulbrook. *Music:* Nerida Tyson Chew. *Sound:* Lloyd Carrick and (music) Robin Gray. *Casting:* Greg Apps. *Production Designer:* Tracey Watt. *Set Decorator:* Jill Eden. *Costumes:* Lisa Meagher. *Running time:* 112 minutes. *MPAA Rating:* Not Rated.

CAST: Caroline Goodall (Meg Moynihan); Caroline Gillmer (Hillary Moynihan); Tara Morice (Pippa Moynihan); Joan Plowright (Marge Morrisey); Ray Barrett (Wal Moynihan); Nicholas Bell (Edwin); Ben Thomas (Troy Moynihan); John Hargreaves (Dick Bennett).

LOS ANGELES TIMES, 7/14/95, Calendar/p. 8, Kevin Thomas

"Hotel Sorrento" has lots on its mind but expresses it with exceptional grace. Nothing less than the nature of the Australian character in all its contradictions is what concerns its makers, but it emerges through a classic intimate drama of reunion, as three sisters gather at their sunny, spacious family home in the seaside resort of Sorrento in the state of Victoria. So hospitable has the Moynihan place become over the years that it's a virtual hotel.

Today, however, the atmosphere is anything but friendly. Long a London resident, Meg (Caroline Goodall) and her English publisher-husband (Nicholas Bell) have arrived for a visit in the wake of her well-received novel, which she regards as purely fictional but which her sisters believe is so autobiographical that she has merely changed the names.

Also down for a visit is the Manhattan-based Pippa (Tara Morice), who's back in Australia to explore the possibilities of setting up a chain of American sandwich stand franchises. Meanwhile, Hillary (Caroline Gillmer), a widower with a 16-year-old son (Ben Thomas), has stayed at home, looking after her widowed father (Ray Barrett) and running a coffee shop. Nearby is a divorcée (Joan Plowright), who has a weekend place in Sorrento and has a frequent guest (John Hargreaves), who is editor of a bimonthly paper concerned with Australian cultural issues.

Director Richard Franklin, himself an Australian expatriate with a long stint in Hollywood, and his co-writer Peter Fitzpatrick have pulled off an effective adaptation of Hannie Rayson's play. Wisely, they have opened it up only when it seems natural to have done so.

"Hotel Sorrento" plays like a contemporary Chekhov drama in which personal matters interact with larger issues. Franklin doesn't worry about being too talky, nor should he when he's working with such crisp, witty and intelligent dialogue and actors.

On one level, then, the sisters thrash out their feelings for each other while trying to sidestep an old secret that links them painfully. Meanwhile, there emerges a raft of questions about

Australian cultural identity—questions dealing with a lingering sense of colonial inferiority and *machismo*, with the   resentment toward critical expatriates, with the waning yet pervasive influence of Britain and the growing impact of American cultural/economic imperialism.

It is no small achievement that "Hotel Sorrento" manages to deal with all of these matters and more with style and grace—and to involve our hearts as well as minds.

NEW YORK POST, 5/26/95, p. 43, Thelma Adams

"Sisters, blisters": That's the memorable first line in a poem my older sister penned in high school. Fortunately, she went into TV news and that festering autobiographical novel about our relationship never got written.

In "Hotel Sorrento," a sharp, small-scaled Australian film with the aching tug of hard-won truth, the conflict among three far-flung sisters surfaces after Meg (Caroline Goodall, the wife in "Schindler's List," "Disclosure," and "Hook") publishes a thinly veiled autobiography.

The conflict comes to a head during a reunion at the family home, nicknamed Hotel Sorrento. Meg returning from England to get in touch with her roots, Pippa ("Strictly Ballroom" star Tara Morice), a sales agent for an American franchising firm, comes home to push Yankee sandwiches on the natives and prove how much she has changed since she moved to Manhattan.

In the absence of her sisters, Hillary (Caroline Gillmer), the "ordinary and sensible" one, has become the family matriarch. A widow herself, she cares for her widowed father Wal (Ray Barrett), her son Troy (Ben Thomas) and Hotel Sorrento.

Hillary and Pippa have recently read "Melancholy," Meg's novel about growing up dysfunctional down-under in the male-dominated backwater of a seaside resort. The book has received critical acclaim abroad but Hillary and Pippa are tougher critics.

The high-strung Pippa tells Hillary, "Our childhood's been sort of raided ... It's as if [our memories] aren't ours anymore."

Hillary tells Meg that the line between fact and fiction is wearing thin: "The only difference is you haven't used our real names."

As siblings, Hillary and Pippa aren't so quick to buy into Meg's theory that the only way to gain success in macho Aussie society is to betray your sisters. Nosy neighbor Marge, the wonderful Joan Plowright ("Enchanted April"), enters the fray like a fairy godmother whose arm you can't resist taking. Marge tries to plot a middle course, appreciating Meg's art and respecting Hillary's backbone, trying to reconcile art and family.

As produced, directed and cowritten by Richard Franklin, and based on Hannie Rayson's play, the sisters represent the larger cultural conflicts between Australia, England and America. Australians look for high-culture and approval among the Shakespeare-and-Chaucer set in the mother country, but are seduced by American pop culcha.

Franklin, an Australian who has built a career on second-tier Hollywood productions like "Psycho II," relies largely on witty dialogue to propel "Hotel Sorrento." The movie climaxes in a stinging set piece around the dinner table when the sisters face off about Meg's novel.

The movie's virtues are those the script ascribes to Australians: Down under, they call a spade a spade. At the very end, when Franklin wanders away from direct and bracing confrontations and reaches for subtler effects, he digs deep into Ingmar Bergman's pockets. A derivative shot of the three silent sisters framed by the windows of Hotel Sorrento, cuts the legs out of the drama and the movie goes limp.

As the three sisters attempt to define themselves separately and together and fail to purchase a reconciliation at bargain rates, it's worth noting that this movie about women struggling in a male dominated society was produced, directed, and written by men.

NEWSDAY, 5/26/95, Part II/p. B5, John Anderson

Much is asked of the Moynihan sisters of "Hotel Sorrento." Each has to occupy a specific position in the pecking order of contemporary female aspiration. Each has to symbolize a different degree of alienation from the suffocating hominess/cultural stagnation of Australia. Each has to deal with the idiosyncratic crankiness of the other two, which is no small feat in itself.

And they all have to cope with the perpetually percolating Joan Plowright, who, as Marge Morrisey, supplies the Greek chorus to the minor tragedy of their lives.

Meg (Caroline Goodall) is a writer living for the past 10 years in England, where her novel "Melancholy" has been nominated for the Booker Prize. Pippa (Tara Morice), who's been in New York, has come back home to open a chain of American fast-food franchises. The widowed Hillary (Caroline Gillmer) has never left the family home—which the locals refer to as Hotel Sorrento—"choosing" instead to care for their father, Wal (Ray Barrett), and her son Troy (Ben Thomas) while her sisters have made their way in the world. Choice, naturally, is a big question here. "I thought when they had their babies it would slow them down," Hillary says, "and I could catch up." But her sisters have betrayed her with childlessness.

Goodall, the wife of Schindler in "Schindler's List" and Michael Douglas' spouse in "Disclosure," gets to cut loose here, and she and her costars are effectively morose and bitter. The somewhat mysterious Marge—you simply don't know who or what she is for some while—turns out to be a fan of Meg's, and her readings from "Melancholy" supply a narrative framework for this Richard Franklin-directed version of Hannie Rayson's play. The story is in no hurry to get anywhere. Once it does, it delivers pointed dissertations on national pride, family loyalty, the occasionally self-destructive turn of female relationships and the burdens men assume women will tote.

But while women power the action here, they're considerably less than inspired, or inspiring. Meg's book is a thinly veiled autobiographical memoir of their town, which paints her sisters in not-always-flattering shades of condescension or outright bile. Their lifetime of regrets and resentments come bubbling up, and they face off in the expected clash of egos. But as we're given little reason to be sympathetic, their plaints sound like whining. Overall, "Hotel Sorrento" is like a memory, no one is really all that fond of recalling.

SIGHT AND SOUND, 8/96, p. 51, Nick James

Sorrento, Australia. Wal Moynihan, an elderly widower, lives with his eldest daughter Hilary—herself a widow whose husband died in a crash—and her son Troy in their ramshackle family home, nicknamed 'Hotel Sorrento'. Wal's youngest daughter, Pippa, has just returned from New York to help set up a sandwich franchise. Tension among them increases when a novel, *Melancholy*, written by a third sister, Meg—who lives in London—is shortlisted for the Booker prize.

Some of the characters in the novel closely resemble family members. Meg and Pippa have read and are upset by the book. Wal asks Troy to read it to him. Meanwhile, Meg decides to come home for the first time in ten years, bringing her husband Edwin with her. Before she arrives, Wal drowns while taking his morning swim.

Dick, a political journalist, has become friendly with Hilary. His companion, Marge, is a big fan of Meg's novel. Hilary invites them to a family meal, in which an argument about Australian culture breaks out, with Meg mocking the progress vaunted by Dick. This leads to a confrontation between the sisters: Meg accuses Hilary and Pippa of selfishness for not even mentioning her book; they in turn accuse her of hypocrisy for arguing that *Melancholy* is fiction when it's clearly taken directly from their lives.

Later, the three sisters debate what to do with the house—Pippa's for selling it, so that Hilary can move to Melbourne; Meg is horrified by the idea. Marge advises Hilary not to take the self-sacrificial route in life. Troy asks Meg to tell him what really happened to his father, Hilary's late husband. Meg admits that she was in love with him, and felt that he knew it. He asked her to meet him, but to her surprise it was to confess that he was having an affair with Pippa. Afterwards, he drove his car into a tree. Meg is sure that Hilary doesn't know about this. Shortly afterwards, with Meg's acquiescence, the house is sold.

With its three sisters reunited in their childhood Australian home after their father's drowning to ruminate on their lives in a sub-Chekhovian manner, *Hotel Sorrento* is so openly a filmed play it makes all complaints about its staginess redundant. As directed by Richard Franklin (*Psycho II*), visual ideas about how to deal with the film's long speeches are so lacking that actors walk for no apparent reason other than to give the camera some movement to record. Whenever one of three bereaved sisters begins to muse on the past, she starts walking, often away from whoever she's talking to. This gives *Hotel Sorrento* the feeling of a walk-and-talk documentary, with character auditioning for the part of the presenter. The unintentional comedy this style provides is the best film has to offer in terms of entertainment.

Considering that a sense of place is what both the film and the original by Hannie Rayson (apparently a big success in Australia) are all about, it's ironic that Richard Franklin fails to make anything more of Sorrento than an archetypal, flyblown seaside resort. There's no sense of the unique and beautiful place described in the novel *Melancholy* which the middle sister, Meg, has written as a distillation of her love/hate relationship with her family and Sorrento itself. Against the dead weight of such a non-specific backdrop, the passionate argument between Meg and the patriotic newspaperman, Dick, at the heart of the film seems forced. When the expatriate novelist mocks Dick's belief in a new, sophisticated Australia, we are meant to despise her, but the debate, like the film, is so ill-at-ease with what constitutes 'culture' that it is undermined front the start. After all, if stodgy morality plays full of long political speeches such as this are its measure, that would suggest that Australian cultural life, unbelievably, has not progressed since the 1890s. In that sense, *Hotel Sorrento* to seems to have come from a different planet than the vivid likes of *Strictly Ballroom* or *The Adventures of Priscilla, Queen of the Desert*.

This is merely one wound in a film which seems determined to shoot itself in the foot at every turn. All the characters are given to constant musing about who they are, where they come from, and what it means to be Australian, but they all seem to be committing the ultimate Australian social crime of whinging. If there's a genuine note in the whole thing it is Ray Bennett's portrait of the Ocker father, Wal, a symbol of the tight-lipped patriarchal past that his daughters are striving to redefine themselves against. It's a measure of this film's clumsiness that his death by drowning seems inconsequential—the idea that he may have killed himself because of what Troy had read him of the novel just doesn't fit.

Given its faithfulness to its stage origins, *Hotel Sorrento* ought at least to have provided meaty central roles for the three film actresses, but each of the Moynihan sisters is more a conduit of Politically Correct anxieties than a complex character. Pippa, the one-time callous vixen trying to assuage her guilt by 'saving' her sister Hillary from domestic servitude, is also a representative of a American fast-food outlet. Hillary herself, a maternal rock that her sisters look to for anchorage, stands for Australia's hardy settler women. Meg is the focus of the debate about cultural responsibility. Regrettably, none of them comes across as anything more than a badly written soap opera character given a script with long and windy pretensions to profundity.

VILLAGE VOICE, 5/30/95, p. 52, Georgia Brown

The welcoming *Hotel Sorrento*, directed by Richard Franklin, is from a play, and it shows but not offensively. (The playwright is Hannie Rayson, whom I'd assumed was female because of the name and the narrative's focus on the three sisters, but like Chekhov, he's not.) What's rare and refreshing about *Sorrento* is its honest, straightforward treatment of family quarrels, compared with Hollywood's usual cutesy clichés. Named for the Moynihan family homestead, the film covers a lot of psychic ground, from sister rivalry to the touchy relations between Brits and Aussies—another family feud.

Sorrento's three sisters are the stolid Hillary (Caroline Gillmer), widow, mother of the 14-year-old Troy (Ben Thomas), still living in the family home in Australia; Meg (Caroline Goodall), a spunky London-based novelist whose *Melancholy* is short-listed for the Booker Prize; and the sullen Pippa (Tara Morice), a New Yorker returned home to scout the region for an American sandwich franchise. That the sisters have scattered themselves onto three separate continents reflects the breadth of their mutual distrust.

Currently, tension flares over Meg's semiautobiographical novel. Neither of her sisters has discussed the book with Meg—even to admit that she's read it—and both disapprove of her using family material and feel exposed and betrayed. "It makes you feel your childhood has been raided," whines Pippa. Hillary, as is her habit, keeps mum. Meanwhile, in her chic London loft, the volatile, dashing Meg is furious at their silence, their "cowardice" as she calls it. Her husband, Edwin (Nicholas Bell), the typical little Brit, happily dissects the situation in her favor.

Back in Sorrento, Hillary-the-nurturer take care of her father and son, as well as the visiting Pippa who's touting Yank can-do: "In America they *believe* in change." She claims that in

America she *has* changed, and is annoyed that it doesn't show back home. As the youngest, Pippa is the least secure, and seemingly the most peripheral, until we find about her central part in a family tragedy. She's the one sister, however, that the script doesn't see from within. Or perhaps Morice—she was the Cinderella girl in *Strictly Ballroom*—doesn't bring her into focus.

As the film's chorus, Joan Plowright's Marge Morrisey, divorcée and painter, muses on the Moynihans, taking issue with an old friend, Dick (John Hargreaves), who has a grudge against "bloody expatriates" like Meg. Dick is what you might call a serious journalist. He and Marge are probably the only Sorrentonians up on the Booker competition and intrigued by the novelist and, by extension, her family. When Meg returns to Sorrento for her father's funeral (his death comes less as a blow than a device), they contrive to meet her—Marge to express a fan's gratitude, Dick to argue aggressively with the novelist's opinions on the "new" Australia.

As plays do, the movie contrives to drop in a "revelation"—a family secret—toward the end. I wish it hadn't. Nothing significant is really illuminated. Fortunately, the movie withstands this distraction because the material is intelligent and the acting so fine—especiaily the two Carolines, Goodall and Gillmer, who convey the long familiarity of sisters who are nevertheless at odds because of their innate personalities. One expects they'll reach a deep rapprochement in late middle age. I could have stayed cooped up with these women a lot longer.

Also reviewed in:
NEW YORK TIMES, 5/26/95, p. C10, Stephen Holden
VARIETY, 4/24-30/95, p. 54, David Stratton

HOUSEGUEST

A Hollywood Pictures release in association with Caravan Pictures. *Executive Producer:* Dennis Bishop. *Producer:* Joe Roth and Roger Birnbaum. *Director:* Randall Miller. *Screenplay:* Michael J. Di Gaetano and Lawrence Gay. *Director of Photography:* Jerzy Zielinski. *Editor:* Eric Sears. *Music:* John Debney. *Music Editor:* Allan K. Rosen. *Sound:* David MacMillan and (music) John Richards. *Sound Editor:* John A. Larsen and Lewis Goldstein. *Casting:* Rick Montgomery and Dan Parada. *Production Designer:* Paul Peters. *Art Director:* Gary Kosko. *Set Decorator:* Amy Wells. *Set Dresser:* Sarah Jackson Burt and James Schneider. *Special Effects:* Richard L. Thompson. *Costumes:* Jyl Moder. *Make-up:* Alvechia Ewing. *Stunt Coordinator:* Jeffrey J. Dashnaw. *Running time:* 108 minutes. *MPAA Rating:* PG.

CAST: Sinbad (Kevin Franklin); Phil Hartman (Gary Young); Kim Greist (Emily Young); Chauncey Leopardi (Jason Young); Talia Seider (Sarah Young); Kim Murphy (Brooke Young); Paul Ben-Victor (Pauly Gasperini); Tony Longo (Joey Gasperini); Jeffrey Jones (Ron Timmerman); Stan Shaw (Larry); Ron Glass (Derek Bond); Kevin Jordan (Steve 'ST-3'); Mason Adams (Mr. Pike); Patricia Fraser (Nancy Pike); Don Brockett (Happy Marcelli); Kevin West (Vincent Montgomery); Wynonna Smith (Lynn); Kirk Baily (Stuart the Manager); Valerie Long (Sister Mary Winters); Jesse Rivera (Little Kevin); Melvin Brentley II (Bobby); Brandon Alexander (Kid #1); B'nard Lewis (Local Guy #1); Jonathan Floyd (Local Guy #2); Vondria Bergen (Ticket Saleswoman); Susan Richards (Happy's Wife); Palma Greenwood (Myrna); Chuck Aber (Big Spin Host); Larry John Meyers (Mr. Ichabod); Jody Savin (Rosie the Caterer); Alex Coleman (Tom Miller); Lee Cass (Stern Man); Marilyn Eastman (Society Woman); John Hall (Preppy Man); Bob Tracey (Priest); Vicki Ross-Norris (Woman in Red Dress); Tina Benko (Waitress); William Cameron (Jerry Jordon); Patti Lesniak (Jane Jordon); Kate Young (Michelle Castel); Randall Miller (Drunk at Party); Donald Joseph Freeman (Happy's Thug); Mindy Reynolds (Burger Counter Girl); Catherine Cuppari (Kelly); Bingo O'Malley (Ticket Vendor); Susan Chapek (Nurse); Ron Newell (Dr. Kraft); Alvin McCray (Dental Student); Nicole Armstrong (Little Girl #1); Alana Hixson (Little Girl #2); Damien Luvura (Tough Kid #1); Ben Hanlan (Tough Kid #2); Jason Walczuk (Tough Kid #3); Jan Eddy (Biker); Lisa Davis (Secretary); David Early (Security Guard); Greg Collins (Cop); Bernie Canepari (Mayor); Patricia Cray (Serious Woman); Harold Surratt (Guy in Crowd); Donna Leichenko (Counter Girl); Robert Le (Don Woo); Dante Washington (Yogurt Store Kid).

LOS ANGELES TIMES, 1/6/95, Calendar/p. 8, Kevin Thomas

"Houseguest," a rowdy fish-out-of-water comedy, is as good-natured as its big, beefy star, comedian Sinbad. His Kevin Franklin is a Pittsburgh dreamer steeped in get-rich-quick schemes but now dangerously in debt to a local Mafioso. Deciding to make a run for it, he finds salvation when, at the airport, he's mistaken for a childhood friend by Phil Hartman's Gary Young, an Ivy League lawyer who lives in the lush suburb of Sewickley and has come to pick up his old acquaintance.

Gary hasn't seen his summer camp pal Derek Bond for 25 years, and Kevin is as in the dark about the reason for the reunion as we are. Writers Michael J. Di Gaetano and Lawrence Gay amusingly string Kevin and us along as to what Derek's profession is; indeed, Kevin, posing as Derek, manages to get through a career-day speech at a local school—the reason for the visit—before finally learning that the man he is pretending to be is an eminent dentist.

All of a sudden, then, an on-the-lam inner-city black man finds himself a house guest in an upper-middle-class suburban white household. Gary, his wife Emily (Kim Greist) and their children Jason (Chauncey Leopardi), Sarah (Talia Seider) and Brooke (Kim Murphy) live in a turn-of-the-century Colonial Revival mansion.

Directed in lively fashion by Randall Miller, "Houseguest" manages some deft social satire of WASP mores, but the emphasis is on broad comedy. The film has such vitality that it could easily have set its sights higher; a couple of credibility-defying car chases and other examples of reckless driving could have been jettisoned to spend more time on Kevin's developing relationships with his hosts. (The film also carries product placement to new heights—or depths, depending on your point of view.)

Kevin is so warm, expensive and natural that the uptight Young family takes to him quickly. He gives the kids the time they so desperately need from their self-absorbed workaholic parents. in turn, he discovers for the first time that he has something to offer to others that is of value. However, such self-discovery tends to take a back seat to the bumbling pursuit of Kevin by the Mafioso's thugs (Paul Ben-Victor, Tony Longo).

Even so, Miller gets fresh portrayals from a fine cast that includes Stan Shaw as Kevin's baffled best pal and Jeffrey Jones as Gary's neighbors a *real* dentist understandably a tad suspicious of Derek. Although "Houseguest" is tailored to show off the engaging Sinbad, a man of much wit and presence, Hartman makes Gary an actually quite likable square. Greist's quizzical Emily, coolly unapologetic about steeping herself in her expanding yogurt parlor empire, is especially distinctive. As for the real Derek Bond, he turns out to be an insufferable stuffed shirt, played delightfully by Ron Glass.

NEW YORK POST, 1/6/95, p. 43, Michael Medved

"The rich are different from you and me," Scott Fitzgerald sighed, in one of the most famous exchanges in American literary history.

"That's right," Ernest Hemingway reportedly responded. "They have more money."

They have more problems, too—or at least that's the suggestion of the likable new comedy "Houseguest." Phil Hartman, durable veteran of "Saturday Night Live," plays a prosperous lawyer in a picturesque suburb of Pittsburgh, but he hates his job under a nasty, callous boss (Mason Adams), and his wife (Kim Greist) resents Phil's refusal to respect her new career (as a frozen-yogurt entrepreneur).

Meanwhile, the kids are a mess—especially a teenaged daughter (Kim Murphy), who's a suicidal existentialist with a smug delinquent of a boyfriend.

Compared to the dilemmas of this mildly dysfunctional family, the problems of the movie's main character are simplicity itself: All he's got to worry about is staying alive, by avoiding the murderous gangster goons (Tony Longo and Paul Ben-Victor) who've been dispatched by an angry loan shark to permanently erase the chronic deadbeat from their books.

TV comic Sinbad plays this fast-talking inner-city kid with a bundle of get-rich-quick schemes, who at least succeeds in gabbing himself to safety: When the hit man chase him to the airport, he bumps into Phil Hartman, who's waiting to meet a long-lost buddy from summer camp he hasn't seen in 25 years.

Sinbad passes himself off as the visitor goes home with the family for the weekend and then struggles to keep up the charade.

It's the old reliable "wrong man" plot, even if it isn't exacly Hitchcock. Sinbad eventually discovers that the fellow he's impersonating is a world-renowned dentist, and the scene in which he makes novel use of Novocain while performing a painful procedure isn't for the faint of heart.

There are also too many slapstick car chase scenes, with our masquerading hero terrifying various characters with his wild driving.

Moreover, the movie asks us to believe in the life-affirming power of the tacky old Commodores song "Brick House"; it's played so insistently on the sound track that it sticks in your mind for days after the movie.

Despite these shortcomings, "Houseguest" is an enjoyable romp, thanks only to the powerful appeal of its star. Sinbad combines the high-energy, smart-mouthed edge of an Eddie Murphy with an underlying decency and even sweetness.

Fortunately, Phil Hartman makes the perfect straight man for his costar's antics, and the easy-going chemistry between them gives this tired material more life than it deserves.

Director Randall Miller (who previously devised the dreadful high school comedy "Class Act") wisely avoids heavy-handed messages about the cross-cultural lessons that the uptight suburbanites can learn from their earthy African-American visitor. Sinbad charms them (and us) with sheer likability and honest emotion, not superior street smarts.

The emphasis on making time for friendship and family might be a fuzzy/feel-good cliche, but when packaged by these expert performers even the silliest sentiment is easy to swallow.

NEWSDAY, 1/6/95, Part II/p. B7, John Anderson

Boldly rushing into Whoopi Goldberg territory, television star Sinbad breaks into the big time as a savvy, street-smart black man who, while avoiding mobsters and probable death, hides out with a family of white misfits, teaching them the true meaning of love, trust and what's important in life. If this isn't stereotyping, Stepin Fetchit was Chinese.

But Sinbad is a charmer, which may make "Houseguest"—not "House Party," not "Housesitter" but "Houseguest"—a little easier to swallow, although one shouldn't count on it. The jokes are stale, the plugs for a certain burger chain are shameless, and the slapstick was old when Lucille Ball was a pup.

The plot, which you've heard before, involves Kevin Franklin (Sinbad), an enthusiastic if unlucky fortune hunter whose faith in get-rich-quick schemes has landed him in big trouble with loan sharks, who send two sibling hitmen—named, of course, Gasperini (Tony Longo and Paul Ben-Victor)—to get him.

In flight and trying to get on one, Kevin runs into Gary Young (Phil Hartman), who's waiting at the airport for a friend he hasn't seen in 25 years. Convinced that Kevin is the friend, he takes him home to his wife; Emily (Kim Greist), who looks as if she just lost the Vampira role at the "Ed Wood" auditions, and his warped children. Kevin's warmth, humanity, common sense and innate charisma win them over and make real people of them: But first, he has to avoid being killed.

Much of the humor, as it were, is generated by Kevin's confusion over what he's supposed to be. A linguist? A pro golfer? No, he's impersonating a world-renowned dentist, and the result is slightly less painful to watch than "Marathon Man." Sinbad is game, though, and makes the most of a less than sparkling script. Phil Hartman as his foil and best-friend-to-be is less irritating than usual, even if his persona as self-aware shlemiel gets old quick. And so does "Houseguest," which in the end—dare we say it?—sorely abuses its welcome.

Also reviewed in:
CHICAGO TRIBUNE, 1/6/95, Friday/p. J, Michael Wilmington
NEW YORK TIMES, 1/6/95, p. C2, Caryn James
VARIETY, 1/2-8/95, p. 73, Joe Leydon
WASHINGTON POST, 1/6/95, p. C7, Richard Harrington
WASHINGTON POST, 1/6/95, Weekend/p. 37, Desson Howe

HOW TO MAKE AN AMERICAN QUILT

A Universal Pictures release of an Amblin Entertainment production. *Executive Producer:* Walter Parkes, Laurie MacDonald, and Deborah Jelin Newmyer. *Producer:* Sarah Pillsbury and Midge Sanford. *Director:* Jocelyn Moorhouse. *Screenplay:* Jane Anderson. *Based on the novel by:* Whitney Otto. *Director of Photography:* Janusz Kaminski. *Editor:* Jill Bilock. *Music:* Thomas Newman. *Music Editor:* Bill Bernstein. *Choreographer:* Peri Rogovin. *Sound:* Russell Williams II and (music) Dennis Sands. *Sound Editor:* Terry Rodman. *Casting:* Risa Bramon Garcia and Mary Vernieu. *Production Designer:* Leslie Dilley. *Art Director:* Ed Verreaux. *Set Designer:* Evelyne Barbier, William J. Law III, and Josh Lusby. *Set Decorator:* Marvin March. *Special Effects:* Martin Becker. *Costumes:* Ruth Myers. *Make-up:* Valli O'Reilly. *Stunt Coordinator:* Dan Bradley. *Running time:* 109 minutes. *MPAA Rating:* PG-13.

CAST: Kaelyn Craddick and Sara Craddick (Young Finn); Kate Capshaw (Sally); Adam Baldwin (Finn's Father); Winona Ryder (Finn); Dermot Mulroney (Sam); Ellen Burstyn (Hy); Anne Bancroft (Glady Joe); Maya Angelou (Anna); Alfre Woodard (Marianna); Lois Smith (Sophia); Jean Simmons (Em); Kate Nelligan (Constance); Denis Arnot (James); Rip Torn (Arthur); Derrick O'Connor (Dean); Johnathon Schaech (Leon); Samantha Mathis (Young Sophia); Loren Dean (Preston); Melinda Dillon (Mrs. Darling); Krysten Lee Wilson and Kellie Lynn Wilson (Baby Duff); Brrian McElroy and Michael McElroy (Baby Pres); Paige Kettner and Ryanne Kettner (Little Evie); Annie Mae Hunter (Little Duff); Matt Zusser (Pres); Ari Meyers (Duff); Kaela Green (Evie); Joanna Going (Young Em); Tim Guinee (Young Dean); Jane Alden (Em's Mother); David Williams (Em's Father); Richard Jenkins (Howell); Tamala Jones (Anna's Great Grandmother); Harvey E. Lee, Jr. (Anna's Great Grandfather); Esther Rolle (Aunt Pauline); Rae'ven Larrymore Kelly (Little Anna); Gail Strickland (The Mrs.); Debra Sticklin (Lady Guest); Jared Leto (Beck); Maria Celedonio (Young Anna); Charles Parks (Male Guest); Claire Danes (Young Glady Joe); Alicia Goranson (Young Hy); Holland Taylor (Mrs. Rubens); Will Estes and Jonah Rooney (Boys at Party); Mykelti Williamson (Winston).

CHRISTIAN SCIENCE MONITOR, 10/6/95, p. 12, David Sterritt

Movies focusing primarily on women are so unusual in Hollywood that "How to Make an American Quilt" takes on news value simply by making it to the screen.

Based on Whitney Otto's popular novel, it features a largely female cast in a series of brief stories dealing with love and loss as seen through distinctly feminine eyes. While it doesn't bring many new insights to the familiar situations it explores, it has enough dignity and charm to win over audiences looking for an evening of quietly sentimental entertainment.

True to its title, "How to Make an American Quilt" is stitched together from a number of separate story-patches united by a common theme. The picture's main setting is a fine old house in California where a graduate student named Finn comes to spend a relaxing summer with her grandmother and great aunt. She wants to finish her thesis on female rituals and handiwork, and decide whether she really wants to marry her current boyfriend.

Since her grandma's home serves as headquarters for a long-established quilting bee, she spends many hours observing local women as they complete their latest project, a quilt with "Where Love Resides" as its motif. While they work, they regale Finn with tales of romantic attachment from their own lives, guiding her to a better understanding of human relationships.

The stories in "How to Make an American Quilt" are fairly varied, covering an extended time period—one anecdote—begins way back in the 19th century—and dealing with everything from marriage and commitment to passion, jealousy, and resentment. The characters are also racially and ethnically diverse and represent a wide range of age groups.

This being the case, it's disappointing that the filmmakers tell the different tales in pretty much the same style, giving the movie a sameness that contradicts its heterogeneous subject matter. The picture remains cool, collected, and attractive even when the narrative goings-on cry out for a more unpredictable approach.

This lack of flexibility is surprising from Australia-based director Jocelyn Moorhouse, who made the tough-minded "Proof," a boldly eccentric drama about a blind photographer, and produced the inventive "Muriel's Wedding," a wild and woolly comedy about a perpetual outsider. Aiming for enough conventionality to ensure good box-office results, she has chosen the warmth of familiarity over the excitement of discovery—an understandable choice, given the rules of the Hollywood game, but not a very stimulating one.

Jane Anderson wrote the screenplay, which does a neat job of connecting the various plot-lines while putting an emphasis on death, infidelity, and extramarital sex that may be off-putting for some moviegoers. Winona Ryder continues her rise to full maturity as Finn, with firm support from Alfre Woodard, Kate Capshaw, Anne Bancroft, Kate Nelligan, Ellen Burstyn, Jean Simmons, and poet Maya Angelou, among others.

The film was produced by Sarah Pillsbury and Midge Sanford, sustaining their ongoing commitment to movies by and about women. The gifted Janusz Kaminski, best known for his superb work on "Schindler's List," did the picture-perfect cinematography.

LOS ANGELES TIMES, 10/6/95, Calendar/p. 6, Kenneth Turan

With its impressive cast and its women's perspective on the nature of romantic relationships, "How to Make an American Quilt" sounds appealing before the fact. And once it's over, its aftertaste is warm and pleasant. But while the film is on the screen, things are not all they should be.

For though made with care by Australian director Jocelyn Moorhouse, whose edgy "Proof" was a memorable debut, "American Quilt" is a rather ordinary experience. It has its effective moments but it tends to indicate emotions more than deliver them, and is finally more conventional and unadventurous than its elements would lead you to believe.

The critical element was Whitney Otto's extravagantly reviewed novel about the varieties of emotional experience. How did a novel that excited such justified acclaim end up just adequate on film? The answer is really a case study in the often unexamined difficulties that must be faced in transferring a book to the screen.

Otto's novel briefly introduces us to a woman named Finn, engaged to a young man named Sam. With her life situation about to change, she decides to spend the summer with her grandmother Hy and Hy's sister Glady Joe in the small Northern California community of Grasse, to take a little time to think before the married part of her life begins.

Hy and Glady Joe are members of a quilting circle in Grasse, and as the summer progresses, its members not only sew a wedding present quilt for Finn (who basically disappears from the book), but they also reveal the stories of their lives, passing on wisdom along with their different experiences with love and emotion.

With its unusual structure (the stories alternate with "instructions," the author's meditations on quilting and life) and its fine writing, it's not surprising that "Quilt" captured Hollywood's heart. But like some of the characters in the book, the filmmakers loved too well but not necessarily wisely.

For one thing, "Quilt" comes in pieces; it's as much a short story collection as a novel. The kind of potent narrative line audiences are believed to hold dear is absent, and no character has a strong beginning-to-end presence. Keeping things together on paper is Otto's writing style, something not available on screen, even if the choice is made, as it is here, to extensively use, voice-over.

What the filmmakers are forced into is a devil's bargain. They have to graft a narrative structure onto a novel that doesn't have one and hope like hell that it won't look like a third wheel, that enough of the book's magic will survive the surgery. In "The Joy Luck Club," an episodic novel-to-film project with a number of similarities, the changes were minimal and the operation a success. In "Quilt," a great deal has been changed, and the additions stand out as awkward.

Screenwriter Jane Anderson has some solid credits, including "The Positively True Adventures of the Texas Cheerleader Murdering Mom," but what has been concocted for "Quilt" is consistently prosaic and not nearly on the same level as the original material.

The role of Finn, for example, has been artificially bulked up so that star Winona Ryder is given as much screen time as possible. Not only is her relationship with Sam (Dermot Mulroney) made predictably rocky, a totally new and rather inane rival boyfriend named Leon (Johnathon

Schaech) is fabricated out of very familiar whole cloth, just so audiences can wonder who she is going to end up with. All of this distracts from the quilters' stories, which, given how some of them have been blanded out, is at times just as well.

"Quilt" does have that remarkable cast, including Ellen Burstyn, Lois Smith, Jean Simmons and Kate Nelligan, most of whom—especially Maya Angelou as Anna, the magisterial matriarch of the quilting society—do excellent if brief work. But Alfre Woodard is underused in the undeveloped role of Anna's daughter Marianna, Anne Bancroft is considerably over the top as Hy's sister Glady Joe and the actresses never manage to cohere into a believable community.

There are moments, mostly in the strange unhappy story of Sophia (excellently played as a young woman by Samantha Mathis) where the skill that director Moorhouse showed in "Proof" is evident. But given the nature of the original material and the people involved, it's disappointing not to feel more consistently positive about "How to Make an American Quilt." It doesn't have to be a mistake to make a tricky novel more accessible to a mass audience, but sacrificing as much as this project did should not be necessary.

NEW YORK, 10/30/95, p. 136, David Denby

The many parts of *How to Make an American Quilt* are fused so smoothly, and with such shrewd and loving craftsmanship, that I would describe the movie not as a quilt but as something more solid and complicated. *Quilt* is a Biedermeier film, perfectly fitted and joined. The Australian director Jocelyn Moorhouse (*Proof*), in her first American outing, and the producing team of Midge Sanford and Sarah Pillsbury have gathered together a collection of legendary actresses and regal personalities (Jean Simmons, Anne Bancroft, Ellen Burstyn, Kate Nelligan, Maya Angelou, and Lois Smith) and by some miracle have kept them off one another's toes while molding them into a selfless ensemble. In a golden California town, a Berkeley graduate student, Finn (Winona Ryder), is spending the summer with her grandmother (Burstyn) and her great-aunt (Bancroft), ostensibly to finish her M.A. dissertation but actually to escape her alarmingly serious boyfriend (Dermot Mulroney), who has proposed marriage. At the house, the two senior ladies are joined by friends in their annual summer quilting bee. Making a quilt, we understand, is not an affair to be taken lightly (Ms. Angelou adds a note of ceremoniousness), but the long periods of sewing and patching also allow a free range of gossip and rivalry. As Finn fusses over her decision to marry or not, the older women share with her their memories of husbands and lovers.

The house is set among orange groves; the summer lingers on, and the movie has the feeling of a fairy tale. But it's a bittersweet tale, a group of love stories held together by the theme of impermanence. The women's loves haven't turned out the way they had hoped—though they haven't turned out badly either. The men have left or died or strayed into adultery, but something strong was there in each of those marriages. *How to Make an American Quilt* is a testament to the pleasures and disappointments of half-good marriages (which is to say, most marriages). In this movie conceived and made by women, the memories of early love are re-created (in flashback) with a rich infusion of feeling that is both romantic and biting—the men are seen for their sexual possibilities, ardently, but with a dash of rueful satire. Sophia (Lois Smith), now in her sixties has become an embittered woman; we see her as a beautiful young girl (Samantha Mathis) romanced by a handsome and self-confident geologist (Loren Dean), and we see as well why her later unhappiness is almost inevitable. The movie shifts easily between present and past, regret and desire, and just when things are getting a little too soft and resigned, Kate Capshaw shows up as Winona Ryder's overgrown-flower-child mom and charges the movie with the energy of the undefeated. By the end of the summer, Finn knows what she has to do.

NEW YORK POST, 10/6/95, p. 45, Michael Medved

"How to Make an American Quilt" is, at best, patchy—with a few strong performances and striking images haphazardly assembled in an ill-planned pattern that amounts to almost nothing.

Based on the best-selling debut novel by Whitney Otto, the movie centers on eight women who form a "Quilting Bee" in the fictional farming community of Grasse, Calif.—sort of a white, Afro-American version of the "Joy Luck Club," in which the long-suffering old ladies work together on quilts rather than playing mah-jongg.

The group meets at the home of Ellen Burstyn, who welcomes a visit from her granddaughter (Winona Ryder), a Berkeley grad student who is, appropriately enough, writing her master's thesis on "women's handiwork in tribal cultures."

She's also trying to decide whether to accept a marriage proposal from boyfriend Dermot Mulroney, and so listens to romantic recollections from all the stitching stalwarts.

In place of the novel's richness and detail, however, the movie gives only a chintzy glimpse of each of these ladies—offering one brief melodramatic flashback before moving on to the next member of sewing circle.

You learn, for instance, that Ellen Burstyn enjoyed a brief affair with the husband (Rip Torn) of her sister (Anne Bancroft), and that the recently widowed Kate Nelligan indulged a similar dalliance with the chronically philandering artist husband (Derrick O'Conner) of fellow quilter Jean Simmons.

The regal quilting queen (poet Maya Angelou) was once seduced by a smooth-talking white boy, and the product of that passion (Alfre Woodward) fell heartbreakingly in love with a married poet (Mykelti Williamson) during a sojourn in Paris.

The problem is that you learn nothing else about these women other than one tragic, quickly sketched love affair that each of them endured. For a movie that purports to celebrate the joys of female bonding with an "enlightened" feminist consciousness, it's ironic that each of the characters is exclusively defined in terms of unhappy relationships with men—and it doesn't help that every one of these men is demonstrably worthless.

No wonder that the young central character (a whining, insecure Generation X stereotype, performed with uncharacteristic confusion and clumsiness by the usually capable Ryder) is so uncertain about her marriage plans.

Getting into the spirit of the movie, she conducts a mindless affair with a muscular farm worker (handsome newcomer Johnathon Schaech)—a dumb, indulgent distraction that never appeared in the book.

Director Jocelyn Moorhouse (who previously created the quirky, absurdly over-praised Australian film "Proof," about a blind photographer) treats this shallow material with the solemnity and self-importance of some new cinematic version of "Gotterdammerung" or "The Trojan Women," and the brilliant cinematographer Janusz Kaminski ("Schindler's List") presents lyrical, glowing, larger-than-life images of orange groves and Victorian homes that seem especially ill-matched to the movie's thin, soap-opera substance.

A few of the actresses (especially the radiant Joanna Going as they young Jean Simmons, or Samantha Mathis as the young Lois Smith) make vivid impressions in minor roles, but for the most part "American Quilt" is sloppily stitched together, blanketing the viewer with banality and boredom.

NEWSDAY, 10/6/95, Part II/p. B3, Jack Mathews

The work that went into Jocelyn Moorhouse's adaptation of Whitney Otto's best-seller "How to Make an American Quilt" is as sincere and meticulous as the work that goes into the art form itself. The movie, like the book, is a patchwork of stories, each individual but working together toward harmony, and nearly every moment of it is steeped in affection.

So why does it remain so cool and uninvolving?

The answer, I believe, is that "Quilt" is simply not movie material. The symbolic storytelling of the American quilt provided a perfect blueprint for Otto's finely detailed novel, but in being condensed and reconfigured for a two-hour film it fell into a never-land where it has neither the richness of a novel nor the poetic impact of a quilt. It is instead an anthology of fractured short stories, about the youths, passions and heartaches of the women summarizing their lives in a sewing circle.

The beneficiary of these stories is Finn (Winona Ryder), a young graduate student who has come to spend the summer with her two great-aunts, Hy (Ellen Burstyn) and Glady Joe (Anne Bancroft), with the dual purpose of making notes on their quilting group for a thesis and mulling over her relationship with her lover Sam (Dermot Mulroney).

Once you know that the current project of the Grasse Quilting Bee is Finn's wedding gift, the scene is set for a round-robin of reminiscence, and it is only a matter of time before someone lays it on the line, Gump-like, that romance is like a quilt: Young lovers expect perfection; old lovers accept the frayed edges and faded colors that come with enduring passion. "The Quilts of Madison County."

Okay, it's a woman's movie. The novel's author, the screenwriter, the producers, the director and all of the main characters are women, and so is its target audience. But like "Moonlight and Valentino" and most of the other films in the current wave of women's movies, the specter of men hangs over every scene, scoundrels and lovers without whom a woman's life, we might conclude, cannot be told.

So we drift back into the lives of the seven quilters to learn of the romantic tragedy that left Sophia (Lois Smith as the older woman, Samantha Mathis in her youth) embittered and cynical, and of the betrayal that scarred the relationship between Hy and Glady Joe. We are reminded of the womanizing husband who continues to hurt and embarrass Em (Jean Simmons, Joanna Going as the young Em), of the white man who impregnated Anna (Maya Angelou, Maria Celedonio as the young Anna) when she was a teenager and of the poet who got away from Anna's grown daughter (Alfre Woodard).

The performances of the actresses are uniformly good, but you can tell by the preceding paragraph that there are probably too many of them. By necessity the stories are skimpy, and in their abbreviated form most come off as tragic. The sentiments sewn into Finn's finished quilt seem to be recommending pain and suffering.

Fear of failure is the cause of Finn's ambivalence about marriage, and screenwriter Jane Anderson has added to her confusion a temptation not in the book. It's a chance meeting with a local hunk with whom she shares an immediate sexual attraction; then she seeks advice from her wizened elders as to whether she should stick with solid Sam or take her chances with the hot bod in the adjacent orchard.

The add-on romance is a strained contrivance, and though Ryder plays it with conviction, it undermines both her character and the symbolic harmony of the quilt. In the end, "How to Make an American Quilt" fulfills only the promise in the title; you'll know what it takes to make a great one, but the movie is no museum piece itself.

SIGHT AND SOUND, 6/96, p. 45, Liese Spencer

Graduate student Finn Dodd is dropped by her boyfriend Sam at her Grandmother Hy's mansion in California. Inside are members of the Grasse quilting bee, Finn's great aunt Glady Joe, family friend Anna, her daughter Marianna and their friends Sophia, Em and Constance. On the porch that evening, Hy and Glady Joe tell Finn the story of their antagonistic relationship. As Hy's husband lay dying, Hy drove into the countryside with Glady Joe's husband Arthur and they slept together. When Glady Joe found out, she smashed all her ornaments. Glady Joe shows Finn the storeroom where the broken china is plastered into the wall.

At the swimming baths the next day, Finn is approached by Leon, a handsome stranger, and hears the story of Sophia's unsuccessful marriage. As a girl, Sophia loved to dive, and met her future husband, Preston, at the baths. Once married, she gave up swimming and kept house while he travelled. They were unhappy and one day Preston abandoned her with the children.

That evening, Sam appears. Finn is annoyed that he has interrupted her study, they argue and he leaves. Phoning him later that night, Finn is upset to hear a woman's voice on the phone. The next day Em describes to Finn the nature of her relationship with philandering artist Dean. She confides that she is going to leave him. Anna criticises Constance's patch and the other women ask her to go. Constance tells Finn about her happy marriage to Hal and subsequent affair with Dean.

Finn postpones a date with Leon to view Anna's old quilts. Anna tells Finn the story of her grandmother's marriage. Released from slavery in 1860, she wandered until intuition told her to follow a crow. The crow led her to her future husband. In the 30s, Anna became pregnant with an illegitimate child, and went to work for Hy and Glady Joe's family as a maid. That night Finn sleeps with Leon in the orchard.

Looking through a photo album with Marianna, Finn hears the story of her various lovers, including her brief meeting with the love of her life, a Parisian poet. Some days later, Finn's mother appears at the house to tell her that she is remarrying her father. That evening a storm blows Finn's typewritten thesis from her desk, out into the gardens and orchards. Em retreats to

Dean's studio where she finds hundreds of loving portraits of herself. The following morning Glady Joe chips the ornaments from her wall and Finn collects her manuscript. Some days later the quilt is completed. The next morning Finn wraps herself in it and follows a crow to Sam's van, parked in the orchard, waiting to take her home.

From its female production team to its ensemble narrative, *How To Make an American Quilt* is an exemplary 'woman's picture' for the 90s, skilfully embroidering the once-despised form with modern mores. Like its generic forebears of the 40s and 50s, the film takes its screenplay from women's writing. But whereas such weepies traditionally plundered the flushed prose of magazine fiction and bedside-table novellas, *How To Make an American Quilt* owes its storyline to a thesis-turned-novel that made it onto *The New York Times* bestseller list.

The film's genesis in 'quality' rather than pulp fiction provides a clue to its gently revisionist nature. In contrast to the lush sentimentality of *Steel Magnolias* or the girlie bonding of *Waiting To Exhale*, this is a quality movie that leisurely maps a muted, liberal feminism. Visiting her grandmother's house for the summer, student Finn tries to finish her thesis on the rituals of women's handiwork in tribal cultures, and to decide whether to marry her boyfriend Sam. On arrival she discovers a "quilting bee", an extended family of older women, hard at work on her bridal quilt. The metaphors at play here are not hard to unpick and could easily have made for a movie weighed down by homespun wisdom. Instead, the film works surprisingly well, weaving a narrative patchwork that gradually reveals the tribal culture of small town America through a series of flashback reminiscences.

Switching between Finn and the other women, director Jocelyn Moorhouse maintains a good equilibrium between past and present. As a photograph album, swimming trip, or smoke on the porch segues seamlessly into recollection, there is a comforting rhythm and inevitability to the stories. In tales ranging from Marianna's illegitimate birth to Hy's mournful fling with her sister's husband, the film privileges the established generic themes of romance and female desire, but gives them a contemporary spin. Thus it is Finn, rather than her boyfriend, who fears the constraints of marriage and domesticity, and desire is not figured solely through her youthful and beautiful protagonist, but refracted through all seven characters.

Ellen Burstyn and Anne Bancroft are particularly good as the rival sisters, conveying a sense of testy interdependence, while Lois Smith brings real pathos to her child-scaring Sophia, scarred by a half-lived existence as a reluctant homemaker. However unhappy, these women are not victims, but firmly in control of their own destinies. Maya Angelou is a particularly inspired choice for the role of Anna; presiding over the film as a strict and stately matriarch.

The film's effectiveness also owes much to Moorhouse's flexible direction, which uses voice-over, home movie footage, or stylised fable to distinguish each slice of history. There is more invention here than in her quirky arthouse hit *Proof*. Striking cinematography from Janusz Kaminski, meanwhile, helps to infuse a distinct visual style. The dreamlike courtship of Sophia and Preston, for example, is photographed with a chilly, glittering clarity in cool blues.

One criticism that could be levelled is that the film substitutes cosy liberalism for the more disruptive desires that erupted in such classic meldodramas as Douglas Sirk's *All That Heaven Allows* and *Written on the Wind*. One might argue that this politically correct seven ages of woman represents a safe, attenuated version of the genre; a bourgeois rewriting of the old populism. To do so, would be unfair. *How To Make an American Quilt* remains a movie about "how women love men", and its narrative offers familiar stories of domestic frustration (Sophia) along with its modern models of strong, single women (Anna, Finn). The film avoids straight-laced preaching and, in Finn's dalliance with Leon the strawberry-picking dreamboat, it offers the traditional pleasure of swooning escapism. Unlike weepies of old, the affair is simply a sweet distraction for the heroine rather than the prelude to soul-searching misery and punishment. It is, however, a fantasy world that is closed off by marriage to the sensible, unexotic Sam.

Where the film differs most significantly from its predecessors, is that it is written, directed, produced and acted by women. This might explain its ability to offer a romantic tale that is intelligent about its women characters.

TIME, 10/9/95, p. 84, Richard Schickel

Men stray from domesticity and tend to die prematurely. Women are victimized by both of these predilections and devote their leftover lives to regrets, resentments and needlework.

That's pretty much the message of *How to Make an American Quilt*, as received by Finn (Winona Ryder), a graduate student who spends a small-town summer with her grandmother and aunt (Ellen Burstyn and Anne Bancroft), working on her thesis and getting her head together. As things work out, she seems to devote most of her time to gathering instructive reminiscences from them and the rest of the ladies in their quilting bee. They are neither so genteel nor stridently feminist as you might fear.

The mood of this adaptation of Whitney Otto's novel by writer Jane Anderson and director Jocelyn Moorhouse is sweetly subversive. It usefully insists that beneath the placid surface of middle-class life strong currents rush and eddy, carrying everyone in directions utterly unpredictable when they are young and sure of themselves. And if it doesn't provide fully developed roles for them, it does evenhandedly offer a lot of underutilized actresses (among them Jean Simmons, Lois Smith and Kate Nelligan and the poet Maya Angelou) a moment or two to remind us how good they are.

There's something abrupt about the way these ladies are brought forward one by one to tell their often archetypal tales of dreams betrayed. But there's also a nice tartness, a lack of self-pity, in their telling. *Quilt* is a patchwork, but when it's finally stitched together, one sees a certain artless intricacy in its design, a certain glow in its blend of colors.

VILLAGE VOICE, 10/24/95, p. 76, Georgia Brown

My grandmother died in her eighties (forgive me for waxing personal this week), her closet stuffed with thousands of quilt pieces. Ever on the lookout for material—our clothing discards, remnants to be got free from fabric departments—Nanny would cut out and piece together tiny triangles, squares, hexagonals, then stack and box the shapes according to their intended patterns. Whole quilts, however, materialized only in her dreams. Soon after her mother's death, my mother sat down and finished maybe five of Nanny's quilts, and then went on to other things.

My lonely grandmother would have benefited from a supportive sewing circle such as we find in the Jocelyn Moorhouse-directed ensemble piece, *How To Make an American Quilt*. Working collectively, the women not only spur each other on creatively but pass the time confiding, reminiscing, and cementing, or in some cases testing, bonds. Adapted by Jane Anderson from Whitney Otto's bestseller, the movie raises issues close to a woman's heart although most of its sentiments seem rhetorical rather than movingly dramatized.

At the center of the circle and the beneficiary of their labors—since this particular work will be her wedding quilt—sits Winona Ryder's Finn Dodd, a 26-year-old masters candidate working on her third thesis: something along the line of Woman's Handiwork as Social Force in Tribal Cultures. Their labor is the subject of her labor. Pressured by the devotion of her longtime boyfriend, Sam (Dermot Mulroney), Finn wonders if any mate can suit her for a lifetime (and if any thesis topic is worth sticking to until the end). When a local hunk picks her up at the town swimming pool, she takes the dip. Like *Persuasion*'s Anne Elliot but differently, Finn is unable to choose. (Usually a Ryder fan, I find her dopey and vacant here, relying too heavily on a deliberately awkward smile.)

As their bittersweet lives flashback by, the women generate serial object lessons. Placid Grandma Hy (Ellen Burstyn) is still paying for an impulsive fling with the husband (Rip Torn) of her drama-prone sister Glady Joe (a mischievous Anne Bancroft). The long-suffering Em (ever-graceful Jean Simmons) watches as her compulsively unfaithful husband takes up with the recently widowed Constance (Kate Nelligan). Presiding sternly, Anna (Maya Angelou) represents the circle's staid artistic director, only subtly challenged by her semiotics-trained daughter (Alfre Woodard).

Sound complicated! You bet.

Quilt's cluttered construction—with separate actresses (including little women Samantha Mathis and Claire Danes) playing the quilters in bygone days—makes for *mucho* viewer confusion. No doubt fans of the novel will find this less taxing, but for the rest of us, Universal should pass out little family trees.

Also reviewed in:
CHICAGO TRIBUNE, 10/6/95, Friday/p. F, Johanna Steinmetz

NEW REPUBLIC, 10/30/95, p. 34, Stanley Kauffmann
NEW YORK TIMES, 10/6/95, p. C12, Caryn James
VARIETY, 10/2-8/95, p. 61, Leonard Klady
WASHINGTON POST, 10/6/95, p. B1, Linton Weeks
WASHINGTON POST, 10/6/95, Weekend/p. 44, Eve Zibart

HUNTED, THE

A Universal Pictures and Bregman/Baer Productions release of a Davis Entertainment Company production. *Executive Producer:* William Fay. *Producer:* John Davis and Gary W. Goldstein. *Director:* J.F. Lawton. *Screenplay:* J.F. Lawton. *Director of Photography:* Jack Conroy. *Editor:* Robert A. Ferretti and Eric Strand. *Music:* Motofumi Yamaguchi. *Music Editor:* Robin Katz. *Sound:* Larry Sutton. *Sound Editor:* Robert Shoup and Gloria S. Borders. *Casting:* Karen Rea and Doreen Lane. *Production Designer:* Phil Dagort. *Art Director:* Sheila Haley. *Set Dresser:* Glenn MacDonald, Jeff Davies, Annastacia McDonald, Tony Sorgnese, Susan Kosola, and Perry Battista. *Special Effects:* Bob Comer. *Costumes:* Rita Riggs. *Make-up:* Margaret Solomon. *Stunt Coordinator:* Buddy Joe Hooker and John Wardlow. *Stunt Fight Coordinator:* Tom Muzila. *Running time:* 110 minutes. *MPAA Rating:* R.

CAST: Christopher Lambert (Paul Racine); John Lone (Kinjo); Joan Chen (Kirina); Yoshio Harada (Takeda); Yoko Shimada (Mieko); Mari Natsuki (Junko); Tak Kubota (Oshima); Masumi Okada (Lt. Wadakura); Tatsuya Irie (Hiryu); Hideyo Amamoto (Mr. Motogi); Michael Warren (Chase); Bart Anderson (John); James Saito (Nemura); Seth Sakai (Dr. Otozo Yamura); Toshishiro Obata (Ryuma); Ken Kensei (Sujin); Hiroyasu Takagi (Misato); Michio Itano (Sumato); Jason Furukawa (Bartender); Naoko Sasaki (Officer Naoko); Warren Takeuchi (Officer at Hospital); Dean Choe (Ninja #1); Victor Kimura (Medical Technician); Iris Salmon (Surgeon #1); Jack Mar (Surgeon #2); Hisami Kaneta (Nurse); Anthony Towe (Fumio); Kuniharu Tamura (Noraki); Tong Lung (Detective); Reina Reyes (Small Girl); Hiroshi Nakatsuka (Taxi Driver); Jay Ono (Train Controlman); Hiro Kanagawa (Lieutenant); Mercedes Tang (Mistress); Ryoto Sakata (Officer on Train); Ken Shimizu (Rookie); Sumi Mutoh (Sumi); Chieko Sugano (Dancer).

LOS ANGELES TIMES, 2/25/95, Calendar/p. 4, Kevin Thomas

In J.F. Lawton's handsome, ambitious "The Hunted," New York businessman Christopher Lambert checks into a luxury hotel in Nagoya, Japan, encounters at the hotel bar beautiful, enigmatic Joan Chen. He spends the night with her, only to then witness her assassination by ninja John Lone.

Nearly murdered himself, Lambert gains the protection of martial artist Yoshio Harada and his wife/partner Yoko Shimada, only to learn that he's become a pawn in Harada's obsession with avenging his family's decimation centuries earlier by Lone's ninja clan.

In his directorial debut, Lawton, screenwriter of "Pretty Woman" and "Under Siege," sets up his story smartly, struggles a bit as he shifts gears to concentrate more on Harada's implacability than on finding out why Chen was killed, but regains his footing for a strong, compelling finish in which the whole improbable notion of a samurai saga set down in modern-day Japan becomes credible.

The film gets a big charge from Motofumi Yamaguchi's driving drum score, performed by Kodo. Lawton clearly knows Japanese samurai movies, and "The Hunted," in which Lambert, Chen and Lone make solid impressions, explores thoroughly the ironies, paradoxes and absurdities within the samurai code of honor.

NEW YORK POST, 2/24/95, p. 45, Larry Worth

Whoever said that the pen is mightier than the sword never saw "The Hunted."

In this tale of samurai in modern-day Japan, flashing steel rules the day. And the bloodier the weapon, the more writer-director J.F. Lawton seems to thrive.

The tale kicks into gear when New York businessman Christopher Lambert sees his one-night-stand, Joan Chen, murdered by black-clad assassin John Lone. And the chase is on, with Lone and his henchman ripping apart—literally—everyone who gets in the way of offing Lambert.

Though the plot's dramatics hold scant surprises, Lawton tosses in a few wild cards with some amusing one-liners, perhaps to balance the increasingly stomach-churning violence.

And, like it or not, the carnage—particularly a lengthy sequence when screaming train passengers become targets for Lone's satanic henchmen packs a visceral punch that both exhilarates and horrifies.

It's almost enough to gloss over the production's failings, like a ghost story sub-plot that goes nowhere and less-than-breathtaking travelogue footage.

In addition, a better actor than Lambert was needed for the title role. Lambert's sole strength is his skills with a broadsword, some thing he probably picked up from his efforts in the "Highlander" trilogy.

Sadly, the always-reliable Chen barely heats up the hot tub with Lambert before meeting her maker. But Lone compensates as a magnetically frightening villain aided nicely by Yoshio Harada's turn as Lambert's athletic mentor.

Still, Lawton emerges as the man to keep an eye on. He'll never be mistaken for Akira Kurosawa, but he makes "The Hunted" into grudgingly entertaining trash. And a graphically bloody good time.

NEWSDAY, 2/27/95, Part II/p. B9, John Anderson

A large order of ninja, hold the turtle. Side order of French pastry stuffed with 1,000-year-old eggs. Cold sake cocktail with an umbrella. Stir with samurai swords. Brrrrrrrrrpppp.

"The Hunted" is a classic recipe for international casting, even if the end results argue for an immediate closing of all borders. A martial-arts morality fable that will probably do very well in overseas rentals, it stars French actor Christopher Lambert as American businessman Paul Racine, whose late-night tryst with a Japanese *nouvelle* geisha named Kirina—played by Chinese film star Joan Chen—ends very badly: Having mixed up their keys, he returns to her room to find her being executed by the invincible *terminator san* Kinjo (Hong Kong's John Lone). Racine survives his wounds, but then becomes the target of Kinjo's relentless ninja family, the *Makato*.

The beautiful Chen must be a star, because even though she's decapitated in the first 10 minutes she still gets third billing. She'll be back to haunt Racine's dreams, though, providing an opportunity for the set-design and special-effects guys to strut their stuff, when they're not painting Japan in broad strokes of superstitious mysticism and electric urban squalor (perhaps that's why so many Chinese are playing Japanese). As the ads say, Paul is "trapped in a world where killing is an art and revenge is an obsession." Asia, in other words, is no place for a nice, unintelligible, unarmed capitalist.

Paul—who to the movie's credit is less instant ninja than everyone's choice for most Likely to be Dead Meat—comes under the protection of Takeda (Yoshio Harada), a traditionalist descendant of a long line of samurai, who has a vendetta (I know? it's Italian) against the Makato for offenses committed two centuries earlier. The rivalry between Kinjo and Takeda leads to a bloodbath on a bullet train, the slicing and dicing of many innocent Japanese (I think they're Japanese) and, of course, provides the setup for a climactic battle. Paul, meanwhile, provides the bait for Takeda to lure Kinjo to his island encampment.

Does any of this sound familiar? Good. Because if "The Hunted" invented all this stuff, someone would have to be arrested. Lambert, he of the serious eyebrows, is believable as a sitting duck, less believable when he challenges Takeda, the human Vegamatic. The bloodshed is cruel and abundant, which for some will sound like an endorsement. It's not. "The Hunted" is a sukiyaki of clichés, a pot-au-feu of gratuitous violence, a hot-and-sour soup of sloppy dialogue. It may, however, be quite useful as an appetite suppressant.

Also reviewed in:
CHICAGO TRIBUNE, 2/26/95, Tempo/p. 4, Michael Wilmington
NEW YORK TIMES, 2/25/95, p. 13, William Grimes

VARIETY, 2/27-3/5/95, p. 69, Brian Lowry
WASHINGTON POST, 2/25/95, p. D3, Rita Kempley

I AM CUBA

A Milestone Films release of an ICAIC and Mosfilm coproduction. *Director:* Mikhail Kalatozov. *Screenplay (Spanish, Russian and English with English subtitles):* Yevgeny Yevtushenko and Enrique Pineda Barnet. *Director of Photography:* Sergei Urusevsky. *Editor:* Lida Turina. *Music:* Carlos Fariñas. *Sound:* Vladimir Sharum. *Set Designer:* Evgueni Svidietelev. *Running time:* 141 minutes. *MPAA Rating:* Not Rated.

WITH: Luz Maria Collazo (Maria/Betty); Jean Bouise (Jim); Sergio Corrieri (Alberto); Mario González Broche (Pablo); José Gallardo (Pedro); Raúl Garcia (Enrique); Salvador Wood; Alberto Morgan; Fausto Mirabal; Roberto García York; Maria M. Diaz; Celia Rodriguez (Gloria); Barbara Dominique; Iris del Monte; Rosendo Lamardriz; Raquel Revuelta.

CHRISTIAN SCIENCE MONITOR, 3/10/95, p. 13, David Sterritt

Confounding the conventional view that the newest movies are the most exciting movies, rediscoveries from bygone years are providing some of this season's most interesting fare.

At the head of the list comes "I Am Cuba," a remarkable 1964 picture that literally defies description.

Belatedly brought to theaters by Martin Scorsese and Francis Ford Coppola, who have admirable records of digging out overlooked cinematic gems, the movie has an episodic plot about freedom fighters, urban rebels, sugar-cane harvesters, and other figures from Cuban society just before Fidel Castro's revolution ousted the old capitalist regime.

The film meanders from one storyline to another, sometimes pausing long enough to build effective suspense, sometimes moving on before anything of consequence has happened. If its forced nostalgia for Cuban socialism were all it had to offer, it would be little more than a historical curiosity even if it does boast a loquacious screenplay by Yevgeny Yevtushenko, the legendary Russian poet and Enrique Pineda Barnet, his respected Cuban counterpart.

What ranks "I Am Cuba" among the most thrilling films in recent memory is neither its subject nor its soundtrack, but the astounding cinematic style of Russian director Mikhail Kalatozov, whose pyrotechnics are more imaginative than 95 percent of the stuff Hollywood cranks out with special-effects resources never dreamed of by this comparatively low-tech artist. His camera flies, dives, swoops, and soars, enveloping the viewer in a dazzling cascade of almost hallucinatory visions.

While the content of the shots is often little more than public relations flack for Cuban-Soviet solidarity, the imagery is so visually transcendent that it lifts the picture far above its literal level, just as a superb musical setting may render the words of a song largely irrelevant.

Open your eyes to "I Am Cuba," and it may be a long time before you see movies in the same way again. A big vote of thanks is due to Milestone Films for teaming with Scorsese and Coppola to bring this hidden masterpiece to light.

LOS ANGELES TIMES, 7/21/95, Calendar/p. 8, Kevin Thomas

Mikhail Kalatozov's 1964 "I Am Cuba" is a great poetic epic that blends the stirring visual daring of Russia's cinema of revolution with an intoxicating Latin sensuality.

It is a triumph of collaborative strategy, with Kalatozov and his dazzling cinematographer Sergei Urusevsky in perfect rapport with each other and with their writers, renowned poet Yevgeny Yevtushenko and eminent Cuban novelist Enrique Pineda Barnet. It is said that Kalatozov, best known for "The Cranes Are Flying" (1958), a World War II romance of uncommon passion and candor (and a big art-house success in the United States) wanted to make a "Potemkin" for Castro's revolution and for the people of Cuba, and he certainly succeeded.

"I Am Cuba," composed of four episodes set in late 1956, when Castro was raising an army in the Sierra Maestra, had apparently not been shown outside the Soviet Union or Cuba until is was presented at the Telluride Film Festival in 1992.

It is a major discovery, and the long delay in its U.S. release has resulted in its impact compounding irony with irony. That's because the revolution that was to wipe away the corruption of the Batista regime is now, three decades later, mired in economic catastrophe and marked by a bleak history regarding human rights.

The film inescapably confronts American audiences with our own sorry role in Cuba's misery, past and present, in that it reminds us that if the United States was to such a large extent responsible for Batista, it is also responsible for Castro.

"I Am Cuba," which has a glorious, emotion-charged score by Carlos Fariñas, is a superb example of imaginative planning yielding an effect of constant spontaneity.

Punctuated by stanzas of the poem that gives the film its title, it most resembles in style, not surprisingly, Sergei Eisenstein's incomplete "Que Viva Mexico" in its folkloric passages. In its immediacy and passion, it brings to mind the volatile cinema of revolutionary Cuba itself and of Allende's Chile as well as the films of the Russian masters. It is at its most Soviet in spirit in its stirring but doctrinaire finish.

In the opening stanza of that poem, Columbus' fateful remark, "This is the most beautiful land ever seen by human eyes," accompanies a Fellini-like helicopter shot over the Cuban coast, capturing images of poverty before settling on a Havana hotel rooftop, where a beauty contest is in progress.

Soon we're swept up in a swirl of driving Afro-Cuban music and dance as the least boorish of several American businessmen (noted French actor Jean Bouise) spends the night with a beautiful, reluctant prostitute (Luz Maria Collazo) only to awaken in a vast makeshift village of far greater poverty than he had ever imagined.

Kalatozov next acquaints us with a worn peasant (José Gallardó), who, as he looks out into a rainstorm, recalls how he lost everything when he was duped into leasing his sugar cane land only to have it sold out from under him to the United Fruit Co.

The camera then picks out a young man (Raúl García), part of a group of students who throw Molotov cocktails at a drive-in screen showing a newsreel celebrating U.S.-Cuba relations, this sequence, depicting the ever-widening student-led anti-government demonstrations, culminates with one of the most bravura tracking shots ever attempted.

Appropriately, "I Am Cuba" concludes in the ruggedly beautiful Sierra Maestra with tremendous cumulative power as a peasant casts his lot with Castro's guerrillas. In this post-Soviet era, however, the idealistic zeal that fuels all of this fiery film takes on a cast that's truly tragic.

NEW YORK, 3/20/95, p. 60, David Denby

I Am Cuba, playing at Film Forum, is an outlandish hybrid of propaganda and aestheticism. It's as if a boar had mated with a macaw, or a potato with a row of sugarcane. The result: The newborn spud sprouts feathers. The Soviet director Mikhail Kalatozov and cinematographer Sergei Urusevsky, who had worked together on the celebrated 1958 Soviet movie *The Cranes Are Flying* went to Havana in 1962, right around the time of the Cuban Missile Crisis, to make a propaganda film. Poet Yevgeny Yevtushenko tagged along; the three hooked up with Cuban novelist Enrique Piñeda Barnet. In 1964, after much travel, considerable immersion in prerevolutionary (i.e., colonial) culture and many meetings with officials, they concocted this fabulous monster, which has never been commercially distributed in this country. (The movie is being brought out by Francis Coppola, Martin Scorsese, and a small distribution company; it will soon be released nationwide.) Set in the final days of the corrupt Batista regime, the movie is nominally a work of propaganda. But the filmmakers, escaping the austerities of the Soviet film bureau, Mosfilm, fell under the spell of the brilliant sky, the heat, the sullen-sexy, full-bodied women and handsome men. Whatever their intentions, they wound up making a sensuously beautiful movie. *I Am Cuba* is certainly propaganda, but the stiff, Marxist-Leninist platitudes are embodied in a languorous, art-for-art's-sake visual scheme that contradicts the message at every turn.

There are no central characters, only long vignettes of prerevolutionary oppression. American businessmen in white suits sit around in bars, laughing and making crude jokes. Saintly Latin girls are menaced by carousing Marines. A resolute sharecropper sets fire to his land rather than let it fall into the hands of the United Fruit Company. Fidel and Communism are irresistibly on the march. Heroic student radicals, bursting with idealism, go proudly to their deaths for *la revolución*. "I am Cuba ...," intones a nameless female, over and over, in the kitschy drone of Yevtushenko prose poetry. *Viva la revolución!* Yet from the opening sequence, in which the camera, borne aloft in a helicopter, approaches the gleaming island from the sea and then passes over it, the black-and-white images are astoundingly fluid and expressive. Using filters, the filmmakers made the palm trees look like huge white feathers scraping a darkened sky. At the Havana nightspots, the camera, intoxicated, spins through a phantasmagoria of faces; it glides down an outdoor hotel elevator and then wanders, insinuating as a gigolo, through crowds of vamping, luscious girls in bathing suits; finally, it ducks into a swimming pool and heads underwater, as if to cool itself off. Capitalist decadence has never looked more enticing, more fantastic. *I Am Cuba* could be a hymn to the liberation of appetite.

The movie doesn't work, of course, either as art or as propaganda. The filmmakers become so excited about the visual possibilities of each episode that they keep forgetting what revolutionary points they're supposed to be making. Even when an oppressed peasant grandiloquently dies, they spin off into sheer fantasia, whirling the camera around like maniacs. After a while, the meanings slide into reverse: Sinful Havana looks so beautiful that one longs for the continuation of Batista's rule.

I Am Cuba is the first, and perhaps the only, work of Communist decadence, and it suggests that what the Soviets saw in Cuba was not all that different from what the Mafia saw there—sex, sunshine, freedom from restraint. Compared with such splendor, the movie's revolutionary promises of "land" and a more equitable future come off as pallid clichés. Communism was never right for Cuba, and this movie suggests why. That none of Castro's dreams came true only enhances *I Am Cuba*'s irresistible, bittersweet aura as a sport of history, an ironic found object.

NEW YORK POST, 3/8/95, p. 32, Larry Worth

In "I Am Cuba," the exhilarating photography says it all: The characters are all black-and-white as the footage, and the tales are as distorted as the wide-angle lens.

But there's a method to Martin Scorsese and Francis Ford Coppola's madness in bringing this 1964 Soviet-Cuban production to the United States. "I Am Cuba" is more than an historical time capsule of a controversial time and place. It's a dizzyingly wild ride to cinematic glory.

Georgian director Mikhail Kalatozov evokes the genius of Fellini's "La Dolce Vita" as he opens with a pool party of filthy-rich Americans in one astonishing tracking shot, concluding as the camera follows a curvaceous bombshell into the deep end for some underwater high jinks.

And that's just for starters. Kalatozov's camera defies gravity as it climbs buildings, swoops over land and water or descends into the earth's bowels, always without an edit. Cinematographer Sergei Urusevsky ups the ante with his brilliant use of filters, as when turning dense jungle foliage into a kaleidoscope of shimmering fronds.

The plot is divided into four unrelated, increasingly politicized segments, each of which reflects the film's blatantly anti-Batista, pro-Castro sentiments. Naturally, the downtrodden or intelligentsia is always the hero and those in control—aided by American capitalists—are despots.

The bottom line: All the scenarios are incredibly over-the-top. But audiences will be sucked in by the words of writer/poets Yevgeny Yevtushenko and Enrique Pineda Barnet composer Carlos Farinas' lovely score, and—of course—imagery which must be seen to be believed.

Is it propaganda? Of course. But as Leni Riefenstahl demonstrated so perfectly in "Triumph of the Will," well-photographed propaganda can both mesmerize and entertain. You just can't take it seriously.

NEWSDAY, 3/8/95, Part II/p. B9, John Anderson

A cold war relic and a cinematic oddity, "I Am Cuba" is a collision of visual sophistication and revolutionary naiveté, Latin passion and Russian sobriety, moral righteousness and the sweet smell of decadence. It may induce cultural whiplash, but it's a feast for the eyes.

Begun in 1963, with the Cuban Missile Crisis casting its long shadow, this Cuban-Soviet coproduction—which is being presented under the imprimatur of Francis Ford Coppola and

Martin Scorsese—presents in episodic form the struggle of the Cuban people to throw off the yoke of their oppressors, namely Fulgencio Batista and the United States.

In one chapter, a young woman spends her days being wooed by a simple fruit vendor, and her nights being pawed by the boorish American patrons of a seedy nightclub. Her prostitution is the handiwork of drooling capitalists, one of whom steals her crucifix and presumably her soul. In another segment, a hard-working farmer's sugar cane is sold out from under him to United Fruit. He burns the place down and dies. When a young Cuban woman is pursued through the dark Havana streets by a cretinous group of American sailors, it takes just one student revolutionary to back them down. He will die, however, and at the hands of the same fat policeman whose life he spared—a lesson that the revolution cannot afford compassion.

This is not-so-pure propaganda, thanks to the freewheeling and wildly romantic direction of Mikhail Kalatozov ("The Cranes Are Flying") and the delirious black-and-white cinematography of Sergei Urusevsky, whose voluptuous textures and dizzying camera angles—and homages to Sergei Eisenstein, whose "Potemkin" this film was intended to answer—make "I Am Cuba" so visually exciting. For all the sophomoric storytelling, the film has a sensuousness that never lets up, from the party scene that opens the film—in which bikini-clad women parade for American hedonists—to the student's funeral cortege, in which mourners jam the streets in a show of proletarian strength. Urusevsky's imagery and esthetic are the real stars of "I Am Cuba" and it is perhaps not so odd that the purely artistic qualities of the film are what have survived best after 30 years.

VILLAGE VOICE, 3/14/95, p. 49, J. Hoberman

There are film fossils for which cine-paleontologists search and film fossils that just miraculously appear. *I Am Cuba* is among the latter—as unexpected a find as a Siberian woolly mammoth preserved beneath the sands of a coconut grove.

Thirty-odd years after its evidently disastrous premiere, Soviet director Mikhail Kalatozov's deliriously stodgy two-hour-and-20-minute paean to the Cuban revolution emerges from the vaults and onto Film Forum's screen. If the film seems a bit stiff and blinking, that's nothing compared to the disorientation it inspires. *I Am Cuba* has the quality of a Communist hallucination.

History barely records that *I Am Cuba* was one of three fraternal projects that the then-fledgling Cuban film institute coproduced with its new Warsaw Pact allies as a means of educating homegrown moviemakers. Two were banal genre pieces: *Prelude 11*, by the intermittently distinguished East German director Kurt Maetzig, was a thriller about CIA-sponsored counterrevolutionaries; *For Whom Havana Dances*, by Czech hack Vladimir Cech, set a story of contemporary Cuba against the picturesque backdrop of Havana's carnival.

I Am Cuba, cowritten by youthful bard Yevgeni Yevtushenko, was less easy to categorize. A throwback to the revolutionary formalism of the 1920s or belated tribute to Sergei Eisenstein's incomplete *Que Viva Mexico*, Kalatozov's sun-struck evocation of life before and during the Cuban revolution was a critical and commercial failure—never shown outside the USSR or Cuba until it surfaced as part of a Kalatozov tribute at the 1992 Telluride Film Festival.

A veteran director and former camera operator, the Georgian-born Kalatozov (1903-73) enjoyed a varied career before venturing out into Havana's searing tropical light. His first feature was the experimental, staged-ethnographic doc, *Salt for Svanetia* (1930). He subsequently served as Soviet consul in L.A. during World War II, shored up his credentials with the notorious Cold War melodrama *Conspiracy of the Doomed* (1950), and signaled the post-Stalin "thaw" with a visually expressive World War II romance, *The Cranes Are Flying* (1957). The last marked the beginning of a three-film partnership with virtuoso cameraman Sergei Urusevsky (1908-74), disciple of the Cubo-Futurist painter-photographer-graphic designer and all-around red modernist, Alexander Rodchenko.

Relentlessly visual, *I Am Cuba* employs relatively sparse dialogue in the service of four narrative vignettes, more or less delineating the progress from pre-revolutionary despair to armed struggle. The movie opens with a bird's-eye view of pristine beaches and primordial palm trees, the wide-angle lens warping space and elongating natives as the narrator sonorously intones how "Ships took my sugar and left me in tears." Almost immediately, suffering is upstaged by aestheticism. Apparently using a specially constructed external elevator, Urusevsky's camera swoops among Havana's skyscrapers, lands on the deck of a luxury penthouse, pans over a gaggle of bikini-clad jet-setters, and then, still in a single continuous shot, plunges beneath the chlorinated water of the roof-top swimming pool.

Downstairs in the cabaret-designated site of Cuban degradation and American imperialism, here visualized as something out of *La Dolce Vita*—two slick rockers croon a ballad in praise of *"loco amor"* as American tourists ogle writhing dancer-prostitutes, when not amusing themselves by rendering them in suitably degenerate Picasso-like sketches. Urusevsky films an orgiastic floorshow, treating the nightclub interior like the material of a taffy pull, bobbing and weaving through a foliage of foreground clutter and masklike faces. For all the contorted performers, the camera is the star.

Throughout, Urusevsky's wildly tilted, mainly handheld, deep-focus, chiaroscuro compositions keep the viewer in a permanent state of vertigo. Some shots feel as if filmed from a hammock, others from a dolly whose tracks are laid across the sky. (The cranes are really flying here.) The second, shorter episode leaves decadent Havana (where even the taxis are Cadillacs) for the countryside—although even a farmer's humble hut offers an arena for Urusevsky's loop-the-loop camerawork.

A dispossessed peasant sends his teenaged children to town (where they spend his last peso swilling Coca-Cola and playing the jukebox), then torches his crop—the camera spinning like a corkscrew through the flaming cane field.

Maintaining the fiery metaphor, while picking up the revolutionary pace, the movie's third and longest section returns to Havana. A newsreel of Cuba's pre-Castro dictator Fulgencio Batista is revealed, as the camera tracks back, to be projected on a drive-in screen. A group of student Fidelistas hurl firebombs at the image, setting it aflame. When police shoot a student distributing antigovernment leaflets from a campus balcony, the swirling camera accentuates the trajectory of his fall—shadows of fluttering leaflets caress him as he lies on the pavement. (Topping even this overheated symbolism, a dead dove falls from the sky as other students march toward the waiting firehoses of the police.)

The murder of another student leader provides material for one more visual tour de force—the victim advancing into swirling smoke and spattered by water even as he is gunned down—but the most extraordinary shot is reserved for a funeral procession. As the young martyrs are borne through the narrow streets of downtown Havana, the camera ascends over the crowd to a fifth-story loft, observes a group of cigar workers leaving their tables to unfurl a commemorative banner from their window, and then—still in one unbroken take—floats out into space to follow, overhead, the parade of mourners.

Finally, having established the traditional worker-peasant-intellectual triumvirate, *I Am Cuba* visits the rebel stronghold of Oriente Province for a minidrama of revolutionary conversion. A peon family shelters a fugitive Fidelista—although his attempt to raise their consciousness fails until they are subject to gratuitous bombing by Batista's air force.

Saturation bombast is the operative strategy. *I Am Cuba* is a movie in which drunken American sailors saunter past Havana's illuminated storefronts, declaring themselves "the heroes of old Uncle Sam," while stalwart guerrillas march singing into battle, smiling through the explosions. (When captured and interrogated as to the whereabouts of their leader, the revolutionaries paraphrase *Spartacus* by individually proclaiming, "I am Fidel.") As the narrator informs us in a burst of official bluster, "These are the people about whom legends will be told."

Everything is as true as its pose. History is made with the inevitable monument in mind. Thus, for all its splendid expressionist frenzy, *I Am Cuba* is a formidably static work—memorializing, as if in granite, the hopes, illusions, and hysteria of 1963. At once stirring and stultifying, the movie is as hubristic as its title. *I Am Cuba* petrifies the moment when already moribund Socialist Realism dared to cha-cha-cha.

Also reviewed In:
CHICAGO TRIBUNE, 12/8/95, Friday/p. C, Michael Wilmington
NATION, 3/20/95, p. 394, Stuart Klawans
NEW YORK TIMES, 3/8/95, p. C15, Stephen Holden
NEW YORKER, 3/20/95, p. 107, Terrence Rafferty
VARIETY, 5/17/93, p. 97, Dennis Harvey
WASHINGTON POST, 5/19/95, p. D6, Hal Hinson

I CAN'T SLEEP

A New Yorker Films release of an Arena Films/Orsans Productions/Pyramide/Les Films de Mindif/France 3 Cinema/MG Films/Agora Film/Vega Film coproduction. *Producer:* Fabienne Vonier and Ruth Waldburger. *Director:* Claire Denis. *Screenplay (French with English subtitles):* Claire Denis and Jean-Pol Fargeau. *Director of Photography:* Agnes Godard. *Editor:* Nelly Quettier. *Music:* John Pattison. *Art Director:* Thierry Flamand and Arnaud de Moleron. *Running time:* 110 minutes. *MPAA Rating:* Not Rated.

CAST: Katerina Golubeva (Daiga); Richard Courcet (Camille); Alex Descas (Théo); Beatrice Dalle (Mona); Line Renaud (Ninon); Sophie Simon (Alice); Irina Grjebina (Mina); Tolsty (Ossip); Vincent Dupont (Raphael); Patrick Grandperret (Abel); Laurent Grevill (Doctor).

NEW YORK POST, 8/11/95, p. 43, Thelma Adams

Death stalks Paris, the city of great cheekbones and dangling ashes. "France is afraid," screams a Le Figaro headline.

Someone is snuffing grannies. No one feels secure. The true case of "The Monster of Montmarte" inspired Claire ("Chocolat") Denis to direct a movie that trades on grisly violence to pose tired existential questions: What is safety? Do we really know our neighbors? Who can we trust?

In "I Can't Sleep," Denis worries these questions with an insomniac's doggedness—and a bleary-eyed incoherence.

While Denis shows callous, granny-murdering scenes, they fail to shock because the director is interested in deflating, rather than heightening, tension. Denis and co-screenwriter Jean-Pol Fargeau are not interested in the police dragnet, but in the net of social relations that radiates around the killer.

Denis cuts off a potentially interesting slice of Parisian life. Aspiring actress Daiga (Katerina Golubeva) emigrates from Lithuania to chain smoke in limbo on the margins.

Black transvestite singer Camille (Richard Courcet) revels in the margin, carving out small-scale stardom in the gay netherworld. Camille's brother Theo (Alex Descas) dreams of escaping Paris for his native Antilles, but Theo's white wife Mona (Beatrice ["Betty Blue"] Dalle) resists and they pull their son between them.

Theo beats his wife, Camille roughs up his lover, Daiga rear-ends the car of the stage director who lured her to Paris with unkept promises. Theo's superficially normal next-door neighbors have an unhealthy obsession with German shepherds that bleeds into their sex life.

Theo reveals a central theme, an insecurity more fundamental than the threat of random violence when he confesses to the Paris police: "My brother is a stranger to me." In fact, Theo, desperate to flee Paris for the simpler life of Martinique, has also become a stranger to himself.

The problem here is that Denis uses the serial murder mysters as a lurid thread to pull us into the world that she wants to dissect, and that microcosm never comes into focus. At the end, the characters are as enigmatic as they were as in the beginning. Like Theo, we feel that they are strangers to us.

NEWSDAY, 8/11/95, Part II/p. B5, John Anderson

Where did perestroika get anyone? "Nowhere," says Daiga (Katerina Golubeva), who's just driven from Lithuania to Paris, and found out it's nowhere too.

In Claire Denis' "I Can't Sleep," there are various circles nowhere. And various degrees of death. At the bottom of the heap are the victims of the so-called "granny killers," left rotting in their fly-infested walk-ups. But the real corpses are just punctuation for the self-obsessing miseries of Denis' wounded characters, for whom security is an illusion and who cross paths and purposes with an obliviousness that's startling and true.

Denis has spun her story off the real-life account of Thierry Paulin, a Parisian night crawler who with his lover, Jean-Thierry Mathurin, murdered more than 20 elderly women before their arrest in 1987. Paulin died in prison of AIDS in 1989, and remains a cipher. What made him fascinating to Denis, clearly, was the way he symbolized not just the unpredictability—and utter banality—of violent crime, but how its practitioners become anonymous monsters. And how the eruption of evil, which we live with every day, is impossible to contain. Or understand.

"I Can't Sleep" opens with an incongruous sequence featuring two helicopter pilots laughing hysterically over the Parisian skyline. What does this mean? Perhaps that the air is thin. Or that they're happy to be free of the striated terrain of the earthbound. There's the sexual no-man's-land of the transvestite homosexual Camille (Richard Courcet) and his lover Raphael (Vincent Dupont), who are committing the murders. There's the terror-laced joie de vivre of Ninon (Line Renaud), who instructs self-defense classes for elderly women (and rents rooms in her hotel to Camille and Raphael). There's the economic desert confronted by Camille's Theo (Alex Descas), an Antillian carpenter with a young son and wife (Beatrice Dalle), who wants to flee to the islands. And there's the promised land of refugee Slavs, for whom even a dangerous Paris is better than home.

On the road below the copter, to the sounds of Rat Pack jazz—Dean Martin singing "Relax-Ay-voo"—Daiga, an aspiring actress, is motoring along French freeways en route to a promised part that doesn't exist. She is introduced rudely to real life—part of her introduction involves an answering machine, which together with Denis' reliance on coincidence and fate recalls Kieslowksi's "Red" without the charity. But she'll adapt—quickly, cynically, angrily—and by the time the film ends and she's made off with the loot, she's become the model for Europe's new world order. "When you don't know how to do anything, beauty can be a big help," she is told. She already knows.

VILLAGE VOICE, 8/15/95, p. 41, Georgia Brown

One of the best films to open this year, Clair Denis's I Can't Sleep (J'ai pas sommeil) is a rich and startling noir that manages to evoke Wenders and Jarmusch at the same time as Chabrol and Hitchcock, (Denis was assistant director on Down By the Law, Paris, Texas and Wings of Desire, before going on to shoot her best known film, the 1988 Chocolat. Less a thriller than a densely atmospheric portrait of a quartier, Sleep proceeds quietly and mysteriously and with the tact of an ethnographic doc. Since this sensational film has been kicking around without a distributor for nearly two years, we should all be grateful to New Yorker Films for making it available.

I Can't Sleep has a wonderfully odd opening. Inside a police helicopter hovering over highways outside Paris, a couple of cops—the sort to have a nude pinup on the instrument panel—start laughing. The laughter picks up and eventually the guys grow hysterical. You begin laughing along, then wonder what you're laughing at. You're laughing at laughing. Call it the power of suggestion, or the beginning of mass hysteria.

Without (ever) explaining what the above is all about, point of view shifts to the highway below where Daiga Bartus (Katerina Golubeva), an attractive young woman from Lithuania, steers her decrepit East bloc auto into the city. Over the car radio come news reports of a sinister "Granny Killer," but as Daiga doesn't understand much French, she can't be alarmed. Throughout the film she moves like a sleepwalker, a spy in the quartier, but unlike the natives she figures out two or three things she needs to know. The old Dean Martin song "Relax-Ay-voo" comes up—it could be her theme song—as she heads into the neighborhood behind the Sacre Coeur; it's the arrondissement favored by the Granny Killer.

Sleep was inspired by a true news story, the 1987 murders of at least 20 elderly women. A black homosexual, Thierry Paulin, and his lover were arrested for the killings, although Paulin died of AIDS before coming to trial. His white partner, Jean-Thierry Mathurin, is serving a 20-year sentence (one year per granny). Given that the killers were gay lovers and one was black, this is a charged subject. Yet Denis nonchalantly relegates the murders to the very periphery of the picture and fills in the space around them. This is far from a sensationalist treatment; the film is not scary or suspenseful. It has the kind of cool, distanced attitude toward crime—especially to the social territory surrounding crimes—usually associated with Chabrol, Simenon, and Highsmith.

At the movie's center sit three silent outsiders: Daiga and two brothers, Camille and Théo, from Martinique. Daiga's movements are intertwined, though in a glancing, impersonal way, with those of the beautiful Camille (Richard Courcet), a tall, uneffeminate, sometimes transvestite singer. Théo (Alex Descas) she never meets. When she comes to town she camps on the stairwell outside her aunty's apartment—rather as the killers, as we find out later, would. Later, she watches neighbors watch the removal of an old woman's body from her ransacked apartment. Daiga takes a job in the same hotel where Camille lives. Its proprietor, Ninon (Line Renaud), also teaches karate to frightened grannies. Sometimes Camille stays with his strangely silent, brooding brother, Théo. Théo and his wife Mona (Beatrice Dalle) struggle over their adorable young son. The kid has trouble sleeping.

Théo is the principal "I" who can't sleep. A carpenter doing handyman's work, he wants to return to Martinique, to find a safer, saner place. A next-door neighbor keeps Théo awake practicing some bizarre but unspecified sex rite (his apartment is decorated with representations of German shepherds). Late in the film, Théo finds his neighbors' door ajar and wanders through their rooms searching for clues, the way Grace Kelly in *Rear Window* goes to Raymond Burr's. Like her, he gets caught, although the woman who finds him—the supposed victim?—doesn't turn him in. Théo worries about his brother. His curiosity resembles Daiga's—although Théo attempts to intervene whereas she, exercising the perfect cool of the young, doesn't. As a chambermaid, Daiga exercises her right to rummage through the rooms of the residents. She also peers into rear windows, inspecting the secrets of this Paris, this strange world.

I'm impressed by Denis's control, and her hubris. She doles out information so sparingly. Like Daiga, the mute witness, who comes to Paris and just as quietly leaves, the movie lingers here and there, refusing to judge its characters. Except perhaps for an oily theater director named Abel.

This is not a portrait of a serial killer. The murders are so distanced, you don't experience them as real and Camille never really becomes a murderer in the viewer's eyes. (He seems more comprehensible as an embodiment of the filmmaker's longtime fascination with large, beautiful black men, victims and silent revengers.) Like many noirs, *I Can't Sleep* is more about community (or lack thereof) than the criminal. The killer, this sort of movie says can be any one of us. Its Paris is a shadowy pool of transients, where those alone are easy prey. Who will care for the helpless? the film asks, with Théo, the one most aware of the danger, hugging his child to him and plotting to get away.

Also reviewed in:
CHICAGO TRIBUNE, 1/12/96, Friday/p. L, John Petrakis
NATION, 8/28 & 9/4/95, p. 216, Stuart Klawans
NEW REPUBLIC, 8/21-28/95, p. 30, Stanley Kauffmann
NEW YORK TIMES, 8/11/95, p. C3, Caryn James
VARIETY, 5/23-29/94, p. 57, Deborah Young

I, THE WORST OF ALL

A GEO Cinematografica release. *Executive Producer:* Gilbert Marouani. *Producer:* Lita Stantic. *Director:* Maria Luisa Bemberg. *Screenplay (Spanish with English subtitles):* Maria Luisa Bemberg and Antonio Larreta. *Based on the novel "The Traps of Faith" by:* Octavio Paz. *Director of Photography:* Felix Monti. *Editor:* Juan Carlos Macias. *Music:* Luis Maria Serra. *Sound Editor:* Jorge Stavropulos. *Production Designer:* Voytek. *Art Director:* Daniel Mora. *Special Effects:* Enrique Gandaras, Rodolfo Denevi, and Hugo Sica. *Costumes:* Graciela Galan. *Make-up:* Mirta Blanco. *Running time:* 105 minutes. *MPAA Rating:* Not Rated.

CAST: Assumpta Serna (Sister Juana Inés de la Cruz); Dominique Sanda (Maria Luisa, Viceroy's Wife); Héctor Alterio (Viceroy); Lautaro Murua (Archbishop of Mexico); Alberto Segado (Father Miranda); Franklin Caicedo (Santa Cruz, Bishop of Puebla); Graciela Araujo (Sister Ursula); Gerardo Romano (Siguenza).

LOS ANGELES TIMES, 11/24/95, Calendar/p. 6, Kevin Thomas

When, at the beginning of Maria Luisa Bemberg's superb "I, the Worst of All," the archbishop of Mexico (Lautaro Murua) and the viceroy of Spain (Hector Alterio), both newly appointed, toast harmonious relations between church and state, you just know it's not going to last. After all, this is the 17th Century, when the Inquisition was in full force, and the archbishop proves to be as religiously fanatic as the viceroy is worldly.

The really serious, inevitable clash, however, is not in fact going to be between these two men but between the archbishop and a singular young woman, Sister Juana Ines de la Cruz (Assumpta Serna), who entered her convent at age 20, persuaded by her priest that a life as a nun would not be incompatible with a life as an intellectual.

With a kindly, open-minded abbess supporting her, Sister Juana has had it her way: holding a singing class for children, tending to the convent's accounts but spending most of her time in her garret library—considered the finest in the Americas at the time—studying and writing the poetry that would rank her among the greatest poets of Spain's Golden Age. Her abbess sees her as the pride of the convent, but the woman-hating archbishop sees her activities as evidence of "scandalous dissipation."

Not helping matters in the long run is that Sister Juana, apparently latently lesbian, has captivated the beautiful new vicereine (Dominique Sanda), who sees both of them imprisoned by the rigid proscriptions placed upon women at the time. The very existence of their friendship flouts convention, but as long as the viceroy's tour of duty lasts Sister Juana is safe.

Initially, the beautifully designed "I, the Worst of All," adapted from a novel by Nobel Prize-winning Octavio Paz, bristles with a spirit of feminism and has us pondering its inescapable implications for the Roman Catholic Church of today: What of the status of its women, of freedom of expression and intellectual pursuit or, for that matter, the plight of Mexico's poor?

But just as we're sure that Sister Juana is headed for a burning at the stake, Bemberg takes us into the heart of the Catholicism's enduring paradox: What the Church does to Sister Juana is abominable in its closed-mindedness and virulent misogyny but in doing so it provides her with the kind of testing that results in an astounding spiritual redemption. "I, the Worst of All" is charged with an ambiguity and an irony that is electrifying. Well-supported by Sanda, Alterio and others, Serna is, as always, a fine actress; here she give us a portrayal of the kind of range, passion and intelligence that is demanded in portraying Joan of Arc.

Bemberg's "I, the Worst of All" has proved to be the fitting valedictory for one of the most unusual careers in film; actually, "I Don't Want to Talk About It," an extraordinary fable of unexpected love starring Marcello Mastroianni, was the last of her six films. In her 40s the elegant Maria Luisa Bemberg turned her back on her life as a rich Argentine aristocrat to turn to filmmaking, making her directorial debut at 58. Each of her films, all of them feminist, but not militant in spirit, reflected her rapid maturity as an artist. The late U.S. arrival of "I, the Worst of All" (1990) allowed Bemberg, who died in May of cancer at 73, to leave us with a masterpiece.

NEW YORK POST, 9/22/95, p. 44, Larry Worth

Long before a chorus of nuns asked how to solve a problem like Maria, a 17th century bride of Christ gave the Catholic church an even bigger headache.

In Mexico of 1660, a feminist viewpoint was a dangerous thing—as proven by the real-life travails of Sister Juana Ines de la Cruz. Now recognized as one of Spain's greatest poets, her tragic attempts to pursue an intellectual life inside the convent have been captured in the magnificent, "I, the Worst of All."

Maria Luisa Bemberg—whose artistic penchants were showcased in "I Don't Want to Talk About It" and "Camila"—proves the perfect director to expose the soul of a poet, as well as documenting its destruction in the name of Catholicism.

As Sister Juana's story opens, she's seen as a somewhat unconventional nun, with her roomful of books, telescopes and gadgetry symbolizing a thirst for knowledge and literature. Clearly ahead of her time, she boldly states that "intelligence has no sex. Neither is the freedom to explore the secrets of the universe a privilege of men."

The stern archbishop begs to differ, elevating politicking and power plays within the church to an art form. Enraged by Sister Juana's growing celebrity status, the jealous cleric takes extreme measures to silence her voice in verse.

On the side of the angels is the Spanish viceroy to colonial Mexico and his beautiful wife—Sister Juana's liberal-minded mentors. And the fight is on.

Bemberg (who made the film in 1990) handles the challenging tale with her trademark grace and subtlety. That's particularly manifest in the depiction of a growing attraction between Sister Juana and the viceroy's wife. Seen through Bemberg's lens, it meshes harmless flirtation with a passionate meeting of minds.

Further, Bemberg gets great use from the austere sets. Beyond allowing the convent to seem a virtual prison, their stagy quality foments an appropriate "Twilight Zone" feel as an innocent takes on the Inquisition in a godless ambience.

Then there's the superb cast. Whether reciting Sister Juana's heartbreakingly lovely passages or confronting the plague, Assumpta Serna is a radiant if beleaguered heroine. Equally compelling is Dominique Sanda's eloquent vicereine, glowing with the same beauty—and hints of Sapphism—she brought to "The Conformist" 25 years ago.

The riveting result works on many levels: as a treatise on repression, as an ode to a supremely gifted woman and—most clearly—as one of 1995's loveliest cinematic gems.

SIGHT AND SOUND, 11/91, p. 56, Verina Glaessner

Mexico, the late seventeenth century. Sister Juana is famed throughout Mexico—and indeed Spain—for her learning. She writes and produces a play in the convent to celebrate the visit of the new viceroy and his wife, the vice-reine, Maria Luisa, who is immediately much taken with Juana. Many of her fellow nuns are envious of her, however, and the strict, embittered Sister Ursula determines to forestall any move to make Juana the Mother Abbess. She is aided in her campaign by the equally fanatical Archbishop.

Maria Luisa becomes a regular visitor at the convent and Sister Juana, having found a kindred spirit despite the superficial differences in their lives, composes increasingly passionate poems to her new patroness and protector. When Sister Ursula mounts a campaign to strip the nuns of their personal possessions, Maria Luisa intervenes on Sister Juana's behalf, saving her precious library, her telescope, and other curiosities in which she delights.

When Sister Ursula becomes abbess, Juana's library is closed, and her books dispersed or burnt. The viceroy is dismissed and returns to Spain with his wife, and even Father Miranda, Sister Juana's confessor, turns increasingly against her. Called to her mother's deathbed, she remembers her decision as a young girl to enter the convent, and attempts unsuccessfully to learn the identity of her father.

Back at the convent, she finds that only the ex-Jesuit Siguenza supports her. Tricked into writing a religious pamphlet she believes will be for private circulation only, she is horrified to find it published behind her back. As Mexico succumbs to floods and plagues, Juana devotes herself to the sick and dying; seeing her complete selflessness, Father Miranda offers once more to become her confessor. As the worst of the plague abates, Juana agrees to renounce her former ways, her quest for knowledge and the life of the intellect, and signs a statement to this effect in her own blood, with the words, "I, the worst of all".

Maria Luisa Bemberg has put herself in triple jeopardy with a subject that encapsulates three areas the cinema has notoriously found difficult to handle: the world of the intellect, artistic creativity, and the vagaries of convent life. In her bio-pic of one of Mexico's greatest poets, Juana Ines de la Cruz, Bemberg does not always avoid the pitfalls. Her heroine gazes rapturously heavenwards and having rejected sexuality ("To me, the body is abstract"), suffers the physical world's revenge on her through the plague. What saves the film is Bemberg's single-mindedness. Both director and script—based on an Octavio Paz essay—have fastened on Juana as closely as a penitent gazing on a devotional painting, which mirrors the heroine's 'obsessive' desire for knowledge.

Bemberg's anti-naturalistic style usefully sets the film at a distance from the novelettish world of costume drama. *I, the Worst of All* is also unusual among stories of convent life in that it is not about the discovery or loss of vocation but about a woman joining the church for quite other reasons, to find, as Bemberg has put it, "a room of her own", a world of intellectual challenge from which women are otherwise excluded, a world symbolised by the masculine garments she dons as a young girl. Juana's vow to dress as a nun because she is not permitted to dress as a man has a ring of childish defiance. But it is, the film suggests, determined by the wider history of Mexico itself, a society engaged in combating strains of primitivism and provincialism with notions of a greater purity. Spain, as the dialogue between the various scheming clerics makes plain, is a touchstone of corruption (rather than a source of learning), against which Mexico's purity may be measured.

Juana is caught between her love for her protectress, the vice-reine Maria Luisa (played by Dominique Sanda as someone quite physically at odds with her domestic and social role) and her initially dutiful respect for Father Miranda, her confessor. Juana and Maria Luisa are linked romantically—it is not the first time that Bemberg has shown the homosexual relationship in a therapeutic light—but also by the bonds of possibility. Maria Luisa embodies the life from which Juana has so decisively turned away; Juana acts out Maria Luisa's desires.

If their relationship is an exchange of equals, Juana's with Father Miranda is built on the premise of her ultimate and complete submission. Just as Miss Mary, in Bemberg's earlier film, closed the door on her brief moment of fulfilment, so Juana here completes her subjection to Father Miranda's will in a gesture of total self-abnegation, a paradigmatic example of female submissiveness. It's the fact that Bemberg has alerted us throughout to quite other possibilities that makes this ending so shocking, and lends it an icy defiance that reverberates back through the film, erasing its hesitancies and occasional awkwardness.

Also reviewed in:
NEW YORK TIMES, 9/22/95, p. C10, Stephen Holden
VARIETY, 10/8/90, p. 62

IN THE MOUTH OF MADNESS

A New Line Cinema release. *Executive Producer:* Michael De Luca. *Producer:* Sandy King. *Director:* John Carpenter. *Screenplay:* Michael De Luca. *Director of Photography:* Gary B. Kibbe. *Editor:* Edward A. Warschilka. *Music:* John Carpenter and Jim Lang. *Sound:* Owen A. Langevin. *Sound Editor:* John Dunn. *Casting:* Back Seat Casting Associates. *Production Designer:* Jeff Steven Ginn. *Art Director:* Peter Grundy. *Set Decorator:* Elinor Rose Galbraith. *Set Dresser:* Peter P. Nicolakakos, Clive Thomasson, and Carlos Caneca. *Special Effects:* Martin Malivoire Pictures and Ted Ross. *Visual Effects:* Bruce Nicholson. *Costumes:* Robert Bush and Robin Michel Bush. *Make-up:* Donald J. Mowat. *Make-up (Special Effects):* Robert Kurtzman, Gregory Nicotero, and Howard Berger. *Stunt Coordinator:* Jeff Imada. *Running time:* 95 minutes. *MPAA Rating:* R.

CAST: Sam Neill (John Trent); Jurgen Prochnow (Sutter Cane); Julie Carmen (Linda Styles); Charlton Heston (Jackson Harglow); David Warner (Dr. Wrenn); John Glover (Sapirstein); Bernie Casey (Robinson); Peter Jason (Paul); Frances Bay (Mrs. Pickman); Wilhem von Homburg (Simon); Kevin Rushton (Guard #1); Gene Mack (Guard #2); Conrad Bergschneider (Axe Maniac); Marvin Scott (Reporter); Katherine Ashby (Receptionist); Ben Gilbert (Young Teen); Dennis O'Connor (Cop); Paul Brogen (Scrawny Teen); Sharon Dyer (Homeless Lady); Sean Ryan (Bicycle Boy); Lance Paton (Little Boy); Jacelyn Holmes (Little Girl); Hayden Christensen (Paper Boy); Garry Robbins (Truck Driver); Sean Roberge (Desk Clerk); Robert Lewis Bush (Hotel Man); Louise Beaven (Old Lady); Cliff Woolner (Bus Driver); Deborah Theaker (Municipal Woman); Chuck Campbell (Customer); Carolyn Tweedle (Nurse); Thom Bell (Farmer); Mark Adriaans (Window Teen); Jack Moore-Wickham (Simon's Son, Johnny).

LOS ANGELES TIMES, 2/3/95, Calendar/p. 6, Kevin Thomas

"In the Mouth of Madness" is a thinking person's horror picture that dares to be as cerebral as it is visceral. An homage to the master of the macabre, novelist H.P. Lovecraft, on the part of its writer Michael De Luca, this handsome, intelligent New Line Cinema production also finds its director, John Carpenter, in top form and provides Sam Neill with one of the most challenging roles of his career—which is saying a lot.

Charlton Heston, Julie Carmen and Jurgen Prochnow round out the key roles impressively; this is hardly your usual roster of horror stars.

Opening with a captivating prologue, "In the Mouth of Madness" gets off to a decidedly film noirish start with Neill cast as a crack insurance investigator, a cynical guy De Luca has compared to Fred MacMurray's character in "Double Indemnity."

Heston's commanding Jackson Harglow—now that's a name it takes a Heston to get away with—is a top Manhattan publisher who has hired Neill's John Trent to track down horrormeister novelist Sutter Cane, who outsells even Stephen King—and whose new manuscript is due to be delivered in a few days. Heston sends Trent and Cane's tart, take-charge editor Linda Styles (Julie Carmen) off to New Hampshire in search of Cane, who lives there in a small town, Hobbs' End.

That the town is not on the map is not the first weird phenomenon in the darkly humorous film—and there's a torrent of strange happenings to follow, of course. When Trent and Styles manage to locate the picture-postcard village, it is all but deserted.

When they register at the community's charming inn, they cannot see that its elderly, Mildred Dunnock-like proprietor (Frances Bay) likes to keep her naked husband handcuffed to her ankle! Carpenter begins in a low key, building tension slowly but steadily, in a first-rate display of style and craftsmanship.

Understandably, Trent thinks that he's become a patsy in some kind of publicity stunt perpetrated to generate publicity for the latest Cane book. But soon he's caught up in what seems to be a nightmarish Cane novel, loaded with effective eerie occurrences, courtesy of Industrial Light & Magic, that brings him into a confrontation with the sinister, malevolent Cane (Prochnow), who has become the instrument of an ancient evil force—that is, if Trent somehow hasn't lost his mind and is imagining all that is happening to him. (You even begin to think that Trent just may be Cane himself.)

"In the Mouth of Madness" is concerned with the power of imagination, the very human tendency to have more confidence in the strength of evil than good, and it may—or may not—be invoking Lovecraft's notion that we're engaged in a struggle for control of the universe with an ancient species that is its true ruler. In any event, you'll most likely be inclined to agree with this engrossing film's most memorable line, "Reality isn't what it used to be."

NEW YORK POST, 2/3/95, p. 46, Michael Medved

John Carpenter's "In the Mouth of Madness" tells the story of a novel so terrifying that it drives readers mad. This movie version is also guaranteed to make you mad—but in the sense of angry, not insane.

Sam Neill plays an insurance investigator who, at the beginning of the film, arrives in straitjacket at a prison for the criminally insane. His tale unfolds in flashback, as he describes his efforts to locate a bestselling horror novelist whose resume bears a striking resemblance to Stephen King's. Sutter Cane (played with smirking hamminess by the distinguished German actor Jurgen Prochnow) has disappeared on the eve of the release of his latest and greatest fright fest.

Despite suspecting a publicity stunt by a profit-hungry publisher (led by an executive played by none other than Charlton Heston), Neill agrees to track down the absent author, accompanied by Cane's no-nonsense editor (Julie Carmen).

These two intrepid souls drive together to rural New England (where else?), and after crossing a covered bridge they arrive at the fictional town of Hobbs End—which appears on no maps, but serves as the center of Cane's scary universe. They are then randomly menaced by mobs of ax-wielding zombies, packs of bloodthirsty dogs, slobbering lizard monsters, haunted churches, sudden fires and other horrors that turn up for no apparent reason beyond their echoes in the works of Stephen King.

Meanwhile, the movie never decides whether Sutter Cane's victims have been seduced into a nightmare world by the writer's powerful imagination, or whether the novelist actually enjoys demonic powers to alter reality. In any event, we can only assume that the terrifying elements in his book that supposedly scare people crazy have nothing in common with the silly and mediocre special effects (by the ubiquitous Industrial Light and Magic people) that we see deployed on screen.

There's no tension at all in this circuitous story, since we already know from the beginning of the film that Sam Neill will lose his mind and surrender to Cane's nefarious power. There's also no real acting, because there's no characterization: You know as much about these people as you learn about the characters in 30-second TV ads.

As simply displayed by films like "Halloween," "The Fog" and "Escape From New York," John Carpenter knows how to direct a straight-ahead action picture with force and style, but he's utterly powerless to give shape to these maze-like meanderings.

In fact, you might wonder how this lame script ever got produced, until you take note that the screenwriter (Michael De Luca) also happens to be president and chief operating officer of the film studio New Line Cinema. He's salted his labor of love with all sorts of cutesy allusions to his favorite writer, H.P. Lovecraft, but in place of Lovecraft's customary complexity, this film offers only confusion. There's no chance at all the picture will scare you to death, but boring you to death is a serious risk.

NEWSDAY, 2/3/95, Part II/p. B7, Jack Mathews

A curious thing happens when reality and fiction are merged in horror movies, as they were last year in "Wes Craven's "New Nightmare" and are now in John Carpenter's "In the Mouth of Madness." You become so intrigued by the cleverness of the writing, in the ways real people find themselves being pursued by fictional monsters, that you forget to be scared.

"In the Mouth of Madness" is full of marvelously clever twists and turns and I enjoyed every minute of it. But not for a second did I lose touch with reality and feel the rush of fear that has addicted moviegoers throughout the history of the medium.

But that's OK. I also liked "Wes Craven's New Nightmare," in which Freddy Krueger's creator loses control of his monster and has to race him to save the world. Craven and Carpenter ("Halloween," "The Thing") are such solid directors of horror that the pleasure is often in the inventiveness of their work.

The world, as it happens, is also at stake in "In the Mouth of Madness," the story of an insurance-fraud investigator named John Trent (Sam Neill) whose search for the fabulously popular, suddenly missing, horror writer Sutter Cane (Jurgen Prochnow) leads him into the author's latest novel. That work-in-progress takes Trent to the fictional New Hampshire town of Hobb's End, where he not only finds Cane, but is led to believe he may be a figment of the writer's imagination, a character designed as a conduit between the fictional and real worlds.

Cane's new book is titled "In the Mouth of Madness," an apt description of Trent's journey, which ends—at the beginning of the movie—with his being thrown into a padded cell. There, he recalls for a dubious psychiatrist (and us) the events that brought him there and warns of the imminent takeover of mankind by the demons drawn up by Sutter Cane. It is no coincidence, he assures the shrink, that American cities suddenly are plagued with random violence committed by spellbound readers of Cane's latest best-seller.

"Madness" is a pack rat's horror movie, with echoes of "Nightmare on Elm Street," "Angel Heart," "Invasion of the Body Snatchers," "Total Recall" and a dozen other movies, all seamlessly combined in what plays like an elongated, tongue-in-cheek episode of "Twilight Zone."

Neill, an underused actor until "Jurassic Park" and "The Piano" spiced up his resume, is a strong protagonist as Trent, whose demeanor changes from cool film noir detective to confused traveler to raving maniac, with a hint of lothario thrown in. He is, you see, at the mercy of the writer creating his life script, and it is full of surprises.

Helping pull off those surprises, as either real or imagined characters, are Jackson Harglow (Charlton Heston), the publisher who hires Trent to find Cane, and Linda Styles (Julie Carmen), the sexy but uninterested editor assigned by Harglow to accompany him to Hobb's End. The creatures they find there would lower the property values in Hell, but it's all in good fun.

"Reality is not what it used to be," Cane tells Trent. Neither is horror fiction.

SIGHT AND SOUND, 8/95, p. 52, Philip Kemp

A man, John Trent, is carried kicking and screaming into a hospital and locked in a padded cell, where he draws crosses all over the walls. Interviewed by a senior medic, he tells his story...

An experienced insurance fraud investigator, Trent is being briefed on a new assignment over lunch when he narrowly escapes attack by an axe-wielding maniac. His assignment involves a publishing company who claim their top author, horror writer Sutter Cane, has vanished, leaving his latest novel, *In the Mouth of Madness*, incomplete. Impatient Cane fans are rioting outside bookshops. The head of the company, Jackson Harglow, introduces Trent to Cane's editor, Linda Styles, adding that the axeman, now dead, was Cane's agent.

Suspecting a publicity scam, Trent starts reading Cane's books. They give him weird nightmares, but he deduces that the cover designs make up a coded map of New Hampshire and show the location of Hobbs End, the fictional setting of Cane's last novel. He drives there with Linda, along a route that becomes steadily more outlandish. Hobbs End proves to be exactly as Cane described it, including the Pickman Inn, where Trent and Linda check in, and a huge, forbidding church with Byzantine domes. Villagers with guns attack the church, but Cane appears at the entrance, and the villagers are savaged by a pack of mastiffs.

Linda insists they are now living Sutter Cane's new book, but Trent is still sceptical. Visiting the church, Linda finds the author. He shows her his completed novel, which he claims was dictated to him by an alien race who plan, via his writings, to destroy humanity and take over the earth. When Linda returns to the hotel she seems oddly changed. Trent tries to escape with her from the town, where a mob is rioting in the streets, but Linda begins to mutate and each time Trent drives out of the town he finds himself back in it. Finally he crashes, waking up in the church where Cane gives him the finished typescript and points him down a tunnel which returns him to the normal world.

Narrowly escaping the irrupting aliens Trent finds himself near the highway and makes his way to a motel where he burns the typescript. Back in the city Harglow, denying all knowledge of Linda, tells him *In the Mouth of Madness* was published months ago and has now been made into a film. All over the world riots are breaking out, with people mutating or killing each other. Outside a bookshop Trent kills a Cane-reader with an axe, and is committed to an asylum ...

Dr Wren leaves Trent in his cell. That night Trent hears screams and sounds of slaughter. The next morning the hospital is wrecked, bloody and deserted. Making his way into the abandoned city, Trent finds a cinema showing the film *In the Mouth of Madness*. As the film we have just seen unrolls on the screen in front of him, he sits shrieking with deranged laughter.

Even if John Carpenter has yet to recapture the gleeful, buzzsaw energy of his earliest work, several of his subsequent films have come sufficiently within striking distance to keep his admirers hoping for a return to form. *In the Mouth of Madness* isn't that; but it's an accomplished and well put-together piece of work—one that moreover achieves a rare balancing act in parodying the horror genre without sending it up. True, the plot is derivative; but then that's the whole point.

The chief source of the film, as screenwriter Michael De Luca readily admits, is H. P. Lovecraft's Cthulhu mythos, in which an ancient and loathsome race who preceded us, and whose image survives in our earliest myths and nightmares, waits to repossess the world. The ingenious twist in Carpenter's film is that the channel by which they achieve this is the writings of someone like Lovecraft himself, whose imagination has created the requisite alternative reality, centring on the archetypal spooky New England village of Hobbs End. The process is never made too clear—are the humans being taken over, Body Snatchers-style, by the aliens, or simply being driven to destroy each other? It hardly matters; the film is far more concerned with playing off the different levels of reality, with Sam Neill's cynical investigator first finding himself trapped within the pages of a book he despised, and finally watching himself—as we are—in the film of that same book as apocalypse cracks open around him.

In playing games with genre conventions and competing realities, *In the Mouth of Madness* strays into much the same territory as the recent, unlooked-for turnaround in the Freddy series, *Wes Craven's New Nightmare*. But comparison with Craven's film, which managed to combine post-modern jokiness with genuinely scary moments, shows up the chief weakness of *Madness*: for all its skill and ingenuity, it just isn't very frightening. Rather than screams or shudders, it's more likely to provoke knowing grins from horror aficionados as they check off the references: now a nod to Lovecraft, now a glance at King, now an echo of Carpenter's own work. (Linda's metamorphosis into a scuttling spider-creature with her face on upside-down was done, and better, in *The Thing*.) Other horror-movies are drawn on, too: Hobbs End recalls the Hobbs Lane tube station of *Quatermass and the Pit*, and the intern at Trent's nuthouse is a Dr Sapirstein, like Ralph Bellamy's urbane gynaecologist in *Rosemary's Baby*.

The film is something of a virtuoso performance. But virtuoso technique notoriously precludes much digging into the depths, and Carpenter here rarely touches the emotions his earlier, cruder efforts so readily got to. Lovecraft's writings, at their best, are genuinely disturbing, lingering somberly in the mind; given such a source, it's disappointing that *In the Mouth of Madness* should provide not much more than a diverting hour-and-a-half.

VILLAGE VOICE, 2/7/95, p. 51, Georgia Brown

Horror movies are fairy tales, too. When they're frighteningly coherent, I should say. *In the Mouth of Madness*, directed but not written by John Carpenter (the writer is Michael De Luca), strives for Lovecraftian terror but the end result is so confused, you're mostly struggling to figure out what's supposed to be frightening you. (*Mouth* makes you appreciate the clarity of Stephen King.)

The basic conceit—I got this—is that the bestselling horror novels of Sutter Cane (Jurgen Prochnow) are so persuasive they're literally usurping reality. Sucked into the Cane vortex, readers around the country find their faces breaking out in ugly splotches; they utter cryptic warnings like, "We *see* you." Some wreak havoc on public property.

With the latest apocalyptic tome due in the stores, Cane himself suddenly disappears. The publisher (Charlton Heston) hires a hotshot insurance investigator, John Trent (Sam Neill), to track him down. A Cane virgin, Trent nevertheless figures out that the writer is holed up in a remote, off-the-map area of New Hampshire. Accompanied by Cane's sexy, smart-mouthed editor (Julie Carmen), Trent drives north, into the world of the novels—snow-covered, small-town New England as a cryptic sort of hell. The couple finds Cane typing away in a neo-Orthodox church, while slimy, tentacled things ooze from doorways.

The squids—always, as I recall, seen pushing through cracks—may've been added at the last minute for a bit of conventional yuck. What they have to do with Cane's Weltanschauung, God knows. The great writer himself is an enigmatic, vaguely messianic figure with a whiff of Teutonic decadence, but mostly his machinations are limited to trapping Trent and his companion in a time/space warp. This is a tease, since they're suddenly, inexplicably released. (Maybe this reviewer missed the whole point here, but she even had the use of production notes.)

For the most part, Neill's Trent functions as a "perfectly sane" everyman—our stand-in—insisting that Real Is Real (knock wood). We know, however, that he's succumbed at some point, since, at the movie's beginning, he's dragged struggling into a stately loony bin. The body of the film is in flashback, Trent-the-patient's account of his investigation as told to another investigator played by David Warner. For a few fleeting moments, Warner's presence lends a measure of subtle gravity and high comedy. I'm only mentioning it because there's not much here to hold onto.

Also reviewed in:
CHICAGO TRIBUNE, 2/3/95, Friday/p. J, John Petrakis
NEW YORK TIMES, 2/3/95, p. C17, Janet Maslin
NEW YORKER, 2/13/95, p. 92, Anthony Lane
VARIETY, 2/6-12/95, p. 73, Leonard Klady
WASHINGTON POST, 2/3/95, p. D6, Richard Harrington

INCREDIBLY TRUE ADVENTURE OF TWO GIRLS IN LOVE, THE

A Fine Line Features release. *Producer:* Dolly Hall. *Director:* Maria Maggenti. *Screenplay:* Maria Maggenti. *Director of Photography:* Tami Reiker. *Editor:* Susan Graef. *Music:* Terry Dame. *Sound:* Steven Borne. *Casting:* Heidi Griffiths. *Production Designer:* Ginger Tougas. *Art Director:* Betsy Alton. *Costumes:* Cheryl Hurwitz. *Make-up:* Frances Sorensen. *Running time:* 95 minutes. *MPAA Rating:* R.

CAST: Laurel Holloman (Randy Dean); Maggie Moore (Wendy); Kate Stafford (Rebecca Dean); Sabrina Artel (Vicky); Toby Poser (Lena); Nelson Rodriguez (Frank); Dale Dickey (Regina); Nicole Parker (Evie Roy); Andrew Wright (Hayjay); Katlin Tyler (Girl #1); Anna

Padgett (Girl #2);   Chelsea Cattouse (Girl #3);   Stephanie Berry (Evelyn Roy);   Babs Davy (Waitress);   John Elson (Ali);   Lillian Kiesler (Old Lady #1);   Maryette Charlton (Old Lady #2).

CINEASTE, Vol. XXI, No. 4, 1995, p. 46, Frann Michel

Maria Maggenti's light romantic comedy, *The Incredibly True Adventure of Two Girls in Love* offers a cheerfully normalizing view of queer relationships. The film is weakened by some amateurish acting, and the plot climaxes with a bit of heavy-handed wackiness, but writer-director Maggenti has a sure visual style: the film's tone is winningly sunny and bright, both visually and emotionally, and Maggenti seems to try to make all the politically correct choices. A story of teen love, the film includes a mature lesbian couple as well as a glimpse of two old women lovers in a motel; a story of love between girls, it also notes the solidarity between lesbian and gay male teens. The film maintains its light tone by glossing over the difficulties of the many issues it raises.

The two girls of the title are high-school seniors Randy and Evie, and they and their households are presented as cultural opposites. Randy is working class, her home a place of genial chaos. Evie is upper class, and lives with her doting mother in a large and elegantly furnished house. Randy likes rock and roll and draws cartoons; Evie likes opera and reads poetry. Randy is flunking math and won't be able to graduate; Evie finds school easy and is headed for college. Randy roller-skates to her job at a gas station; Evie is flutteringly ignorant about her expensive car. Randy is white, and Evie is black, a configuration that disrupts the stereotypical conflation of race and class hierarchies. Love bridges all these apparent gaps as the two girls meet and fall in love, and the potential conflicts of race and class are touched on only gently. Evie worries that Randy's aunt Rebecca has a problem with her being black; Randy suggests instead it might be a problem with people who can afford to go to Paris.

Similarly, the problems of being a queer teen are acknowledged but downplayed. Randy's mother, an Operation Rescue fanatic, has kicked her out, but the happy upshot is that Randy now lives in "just your normal, regular, typical lesbo household" with Rebecca and Rebecca's lover Vicky. Evie's friends abandon her when she tells them about her relationship with Randy, but by the end of the film they are reading *Rubyfruit Jungle* and eager to see Evie again. Evie herself seems to experience no conflict about her feelings for Randy, and though Randy warns her that they could be beaten up for holding hands in public, no such violence occurs. Homophobic verbal harassment is marginalized by long shots, and physical threat is answered by a straight ally with a fly swatter.

By placing teen romantic love in context of the love of family, friends, and former lovers, the narrative foregrounds the theme of love rather than the politics of identity. Certainly, the film takes queer pride for granted. When Randy mentions that she "came out to a girl at school today," her aunt responds "That's great, hon, I'm proud of you"; triangles, rainbow flags, and ACT-UP logos are prominently displayed in their house and on buttons and T-shirts worn by Randy and her friend Frank. But this is not a coming-out film. Randy is already out, and Evie tells her shocked friends, "I didn't say I was gay, I said I was in love." Indeed, many in the film move comfortably between same-sex and other-sex relationships. When the movie opens, Randy is involved with Wendy, a married woman. The normal lesbo household is soon joined by Rebecca's ex-lover Lena, who needs a place to stay after breaking up with a boyfriend. The two old women seen briefly near the end of the film refer to their husbands. That the word 'bisexual' is never mentioned is in keeping with the emphasis on celebrating (lesbian) romance rather than on defining lesbian identity.

Unlike many romantic comedies, however, *Two Girls in Love* offers plenty of reminders that love doesn't last. Evie herself says as much early in the film, when she breaks up with her boyfriend. When Randy tells her coworker Regina she's in love with Evie, Regina reminds her that that's what she said about Wendy. Evie's parents are divorced; Rebecca has an ex; and the ex has an ex. Indeed the film's closing dedication suggests that perhaps love shouldn't last forever: it reads, "For my first girlfriend, may our relationship finally rest in peace." But the film also affirms the endurance of ties, both in that dedication and in Rebecca's insistence that her home is always open to people she loves. If some of the humor of the film comes from the girls' naive belief that they can promise to love each other forever, the fallacy of this lies not in anything specific to lesbian love, but in the patterns of love in general.

LOS ANGELES TIMES, 6/16/95, Calendar/p. 10, Peter Rainer

The experience of first love is a movie perennial but rarely is it believably rendered. The best thing going for "The Incredibly True Adventure of Two Girls in Love"—an amateurish, sweet, little piddle of a movie—is that it captures a bit of the freshness, and the awkwardness, of the moment. Partly this is because writer-director Maria Maggenti seems to be carrying on her own first love with movies. This is her first feature, and even though, to put it gently, it's no great shakes as a piece of filmmaking, it allows the performers lots of freedom.

With the exception of the two leads, Laurel Hollomon and Nicole Parker, this freedom results in overacting so broad as to be burlesque. (The fact that the overacting may be deliberate doesn't help much.)

But the Two Girls in Love—Randy (Hollomon) and Evie (Parker)—are frisky and personable. They seem like real people, and so their budding romance strikes a few remembered chords. Randy is on the outs in her high school because she's openly lesbian; she lives with her lesbian aunt and her aunt's lover in a working-class sprawl. Evie, terrifically popular and upper class, is in Randy's senior class. They Meet Cute when she has to get her Range Rover fixed at the repair shop where Randy works after school.

Randy looks more imposing than she really is; she's a frail tomboy. Evie, who has up to this point been heterosexual, warms to her in stages, while her friends and, finally, her family, observe in horror.

Maggenti presents the romance in such a dewy, matter-of-fact way that the film is like a babes-in-the-woods fantasy of lesbian interracial harmony. (Randy is white; Evie African American.) In place of the tortuous suffering that often accompanies these stories, Maggenti substitutes benign bliss. Each approach is a species of make-believe, but at least Maggenti's is more entertaining.

NEW YORK POST, 6/16/95, p. 41, Michael Medved

The problem with most movies about high school romance is that they condescend to their protagonists, treating them the way that inept anthropologists might present South Sea islanders.

This tendency to portray infatuated adolescents as members of some primitive, incomprehensible race turns up in the current Drew Barrymore vehicle "Mad Love", as it does in countless other films.

In "The Incredibly True Adventure of Two Girls in Love," on the other hand, debuting writer-director Maria Maggenti resists any temptation of emphasizing the exotic status of her characters—despite the movie's focus on lesbian love.

Like all effective films about teen-age romance (remember Cameron Crowe's superb "Say Anything"?), this project seems universal and timeless rather than trendy. At its best, it can remind anybody—gay or straight, boomer or Gen X'er—what it feels like to experience love's first punishing pangs at age 17.

Randy (Laurel Hollomon) is a sulky tomboy who lives with her aunt, her aunt's current lover, and her aunt's former lover in a shabby little house on the wrong side of the tracks. "It's just your normal, typical lesbo household," she says of this assemblage of four bickering blue-collar women.

Randy, works after school in her aunt's service station, where she one day checks tires for Evie (Nicole Parker) a flighty, self-absorbed member of their high school's untouchable social elite. Evie is a drop-dead gorgeous, African-American princess, adored daughter of a wealthy (and divorced) economist (Stephanie Berry), inevitably bound for Ivy League glory at the conclusion of senior year.

Despite huge differences in social status, academic ability, race, resources and sexual orientation, the two young women develop a surprising friendship, which gradually (and very plausibly) drifts into something more.

The stunned reaction of the various people in their lives is humorously but sympathetically explored; filmmaker Maggenti seems more interested in colorful characters and amusing situations than scoring political points.

In several ways, in fact, she seems to challenge prevailing notions of political correctness. Evie doesn't discover some innate attraction to other women; the movie strongly suggests that she's drawn to Randy's vulnerability and integrity in spite of the fact that she happens to be female, not because of it.

Both these unknown actresses come across so forcefully, so naturally in their roles that you can't help wondering how closely they resemble their characters in real life—a huge tribute to the director and her performers.

Nicole Parker as Evie is such an especially electrifying, athletic and graceful screen presence that future stardom seems assured; "Two Girls in Love" could be best remembered in future years as the audacious little film that introduced the world to a major leading lady.

In its own right, the picture will win no points for promoting family values or responsible behavior among teens: At one point, the two heroines make indulgent use of Evie's home while her mother's away on business, even availing themselves of illegal substances which they most definitely inhale.

Nevertheless, the gentle, affectionate tone (aided considerably by a nostalgic, woodwind-heavy musical score by Terry Dame) provides so much insinuating charm, and so many surprises, that this "Adventure" does seem both incredible and true.

NEWSDAY, 6/16/95, Part II/p. B5, Jack Mathews

The title of novice writer-director Maria Maggenti's "The Incredibly True Adventure of Two Girls in Love" and her bittersweet dedication at the end capture the earnestness that, for many, will overcome the film's wholesale clumsiness.

The movie seems almost a film version of a vanity book—amateurishly written, directed and acted, and absent any sense of visual style. Yet its depiction of the first love between two high-school seniors is so sincere and knowing, it's impossible not to be moved by it.

Yes, first love is an incredible adventure, even more so for lovers of the same sex who have to deal with their own conflicting feelings of trepidation and desire, and the disapproval of society around them. Maggenti dedicates the movie to her first girlfriend, with a whimsical nod to the pain they both endured, and the truth of that experience is the truth of the film as well.

The two girls are Randy (Laurel Holloman), a socially ostracized tomboy who lives with her working-class aunt and her aunt's lesbian lover, and Evie (Nicole Parker), a classmate with wealthy, divorced parents. In a mostly white upstate New York community, Evie also happens to be black, an intentional non-issue in the relationship. Maggenti made the romance interracial as a way of showing that when it comes to prejudice among teenagers, racism is no match for homophobia.

It's an endless process of coy glances and awkward conversation that leads to romance for Randy, the school "dyke," and Evie, the popular campus beauty who's perplexed by her attraction to another girl. The awkwardness of the girls' growing relationship rings true enough, but Maggenti has no sense for staging or pacing the events, and when the romance finally does kick in, the tone makes a radical shift to comic farce.

It's as if Maggenti was telling her story on the fly, and decided, after the girls' first night of lovemaking, that she'd better throw some humor in quickly, and lots of it.

As over-the-top as the final scenes are, with the girls on the run from their cartoonishly confounded friends and family members, they are able to keep us on their side. If the movie achieves nothing else, it makes us believe that Randy and Evie are in love.

SIGHT AND SOUND, 10/96, p. 41, Amanda Lipman

Randy Dean, a high school student, jeered at by most of her peers for being a lesbian, lives with her aunt Rebecca, Rebecca's lover, Vicky, and Lena, a former girlfriend of Rebecca's. Randy is having an on-off affair with Wendy, who is married to the jealous Oliver. Randy also works after school at a gas station. When fellow-student Evie Roy comes to adjust her tyre pressure, Randy immediately falls in love with her.

Evie feels uncommitted to her. boyfriend, Hayley, and when she meets Randy in the school lavatories, tells her about it. The pair are caught smoking and given detention together. Randy writes Evie a letter and Evie responds by giving Randy Walt Whitman's *Leaves of Grass*. Evie's friends are amazed by her behaviour. Randy is threatened by Oliver, but finishes with Wendy anyway on account of Evie. Evie invites Randy to stay at her house for her birthday while her mother is away. Randy discovers that she has not earned enough credits to graduate from school and does not dare tell her aunt.

Evie, meanwhile, is rejected by her friends because of her feelings for Randy. Randy, pretending to her aunt that she is staying with friends, arrives at Evie's house and the pair cook a huge meal and drink Evie's mother's best wine. They make love and it is the first time for both of them. The next morning, Evie's mother comes back unexpectedly. She is horrified by the mess and throws Randy out of the house. Evie follows her, and the pair drive to a motel. Stuck without any money, Randy phones Wendy, who arrives to help them. Rebecca, Vicky, Lena, and Evie's mother discover where they are and converge on their motel room. The young women swear their eternal love for each other and decide to face the mob together.

Teen dykes are a new and welcome variation on the high school movie theme, but it goes without saying that, while they might provide some positive identification for a teenage lesbian, they do not automatically make for a good film. The *Incredibly True Adventure of Two Girls in Love* pays a little bit of lip service to the teen movie with a jokey aside about the fantasy of going to the prom (the goal of so many films such as this) with a woman—the well-heeled Evie, who looks as if she could have walked straight out of *Clueless*. But it also distances itself from the genre. For while the best teen movies, such as *Heathers* and *Clueless,* combine humour, satire and sympathy through a series of pert observations, allowing us easily to warm to them, *Two Girls* opts instead for melodrama—that good old-fashioned vehicle for gay romance. The problem is that when, as here, melodrama does not achieve its heightened emotional expectations, it seems rather pedestrian.

So the bucketful of dramatics in the sub-plot around Wendy, the tacky married woman with whom Randy is having a fling, is irksome rather than enthralling—just a lot of empty screaming and shouting (and heinous overacting) on the part of Wendy and her jealous husband Oliver. More potent is a raucous scene in which Rebecca, Vicky and Lena move back and forth in front of a fixed camera in their kitchen. Randy and Evie stand dazed behind them, conveying a feeling of ambiguity towards the communal but clamorous house that speaks volumes.

Randy's tough exterior—tough walk, tough talk, tough guitar playing—is meant to hide a touching vulnerability which is never properly explored. When we see the sensitive side of her emerge, through reading the sensual poetry of Walt Whitman, what is shown is a predictable teenage cliché, not her experiencing herself change. Evie, the rich black girl in her mansion, with her Range Rover, her absent father and over-protective mother, is even more tantalisingly unknown. She talks the language of the mind, using phrases such as "adolescent impulses" and "emptiness syndrome" in dealing with her mother. She mixes with the bland, rich, bigoted kids at school. Yet we never see how these aspects affect her relationship with Randy. Instead, we are given a polarised account of different lifestyles—beer, dope and rock music for Randy; wine, good food and opera for Evie—and the complicated issue of their unlikely friendship is reduced to them trying each others' Walkmans and grimacing. In effect, the two girls are rarely brought close to us. And this is emphasised, perhaps unconsciously, in the film's rise of a number of shots from the ceiling downwards. For example, in one scene we see Randy and Evie from above, heads together, like co-conspirators. The film seems to be asking us to be right in there with the voting women, yet the effect is to distance us from them.

By setting out to be a 'serious' film, *Two Girls,* the first feature to be directed by Maria Maggenti, could have explored what it is like to be isolated from a peer group, or to define yourself as a lesbian teenager. This does not happen enough here, but there are two moments at which the film does come to life in this way: first, in a diner, when the girls, having pulled apart once, steadfastly hold hands under the gaze (disapproving, we assume) of a waitress with her back to us; and secondly, when Evie and Randy are about to make love and we discover that it is the first time for both of them. The ensuing scene, though, is a sudden change of direction. It is beautifully and sensitively shot, but it is also, surely, a foray into the fantasy movieland of gleaming bodies and breathless, perfect sex.

VILLAGE VOICE, 6/20/95, p. 48, Amy Taubin

Randy and Evie are high school seniors. Randy works part-time in a gas station. One day Evie drives up in her Range Rover; she needs air in her tires. The two of them do this skittish little dance around each other. Soon they're trading quips, then confidences, then kisses. Think you've seen it all before? Think again. Randy and Evie are both female.

Tender, witty, and unabashedly romantic, Maria Maggenti's *The Incredibly True Adventure of Two Girls in Love* puts a sexual-preference twist on the teen coming-of-age film. It makes a play for the audience that embraced *Go Fish* but it also exhibits more of a crossover potential. Coming out of a preview screening I heard a twentyish gay man remark, "It really made me want to go to bed with a woman."

If there weren't so few English-language, lesbian, entertainment movies (you can count them on one hand), the comparison between *Two Girls in Love* and *Go Fish* wouldn't be quite so inevitable. For starters, *Two Girls* embraces genre conventions more tightly than does *Go Fish* (although I suspect it was only a lack of filmmaking experience that held *Go Fish*'s genre aspirations in check). And then there's the major difference between the settings of the two films. *Go Fish* stays within the confines of a tight, well-defined, lesbian subculture. *Two Girls* places its vulnerable protagonists within the casually hostile environment of a suburban high school—given the rigors of comedy, the worst they suffer is a few snubs and a bunch of name-calling.

What connects *Two Girls* and *Go Fish* to each other also makes them of a piece with almost every other romantic comedy ever made a boundless optimism about the power of true love and a pair of potential sweethearts who seem so right for each other that we never stop rooting for them to get together.

Two Girls has great chemistry—the result of boldly written characters and off-beat casting choices. If the script sometimes edges close to cliché, the understated, slightly awkward performances of Laurel Hollomon as Randy and Nicole Parker as Evie ground the film in something closer to life. Opposites attract, even when they're the same sex.

Randy, the skateboarding tomboy, lives on the wrong side of the tracks with her aunt and her aunt's lover in what she calls "just a regular lesbo household." In the eyes of her classmates, "she's like a total pothead, number one, and she's a total diesel dyke, number two." (Maggenti's ear for teenspeak is infallible.) As close as Randy's come to love—before meeting Evie—is the occasional grope session behind the garage with the older, married Wendy (Maggie Moore), who fancies herself an omnisexual Anita Ekberg. Plus, she's failing math which makes graduation unlikely.

Evie on the other hand, is smart, popular, rich, and pretty with softly rounded features, shiny hair extensions (yup, she's black), and breasts that demand notice. Unlike Randy, she hasn't come out—even to herself—although her well-worn copy of *Leaves of Grass* suggests she's felt the pull of unorthodox desire.

Spirited and very smart, *Two Girls* is a no-budget film that makes a virtue of its limited resources. The cinematography is crisp; the framing thoughtful, even when it's a matter of one master shot after another. Maggenti makes the inexperience of the leading actors work for the film. Real-life camera-shyness reads on screen as the shyness of young love. What Hollomon and Parker lack in emotional range, they more than make up for with physical energy and spontaneity. If directorial talent is an ability to balance all the elements so they fuse in a coherent vision, then Maggenti's the real thing.

But don't go to *Two Girls* expecting an art film. Maggenti's no Chantal Akerman (I doubt that she wants to be). She's made a teen comedy with a difference. Gender, race, and class explicitly figure in the picture, *Two Girls* goes where *Desperately Seeking Susan* never dared; and though it transgresses, it's never threatening. (The absence of threat has a lot to do with casting: Hollomon and Parker don't spark fantasy in the viewer like Rosanna Arquette and Madonna.) If Maggenti were interested in making heterosexual romances, Hollywood would be hailing her as, finally, a female John Hughes, or at least, a Richard Linklater. Committed as she is to the representation of lesbian pleasure, her future is, at best, uncertain. Something about *Two Girls* suggests, however, that she won't settle for the margins.

Also reviewed in:
CHICAGO TRIBUNE, 6/30/95, Friday/p. M, John Petrakis
NEW REPUBLIC, 7/31/95, p. 26, Stanley Kauffmann
NEW YORK TIMES, 6/16/95, p. C3, Caryn James

VARIETY, 2/6-12/95, p. 75, Emanuel Levy
WASHINGTON POST, 6/30/95, Weekend/p. 44, Joe Brown
WASHINGTON POST, 7/1/95, p. C2, Rita Kempley

INDIAN IN THE CUPBOARD, THE

A Paramount Pictures and Columbia Pictures release of a Kennedy/Marshall production in association with Scholastic Productions. *Executive Producer:* Bernie Williams, Robert Harris, and Marty Keltz. *Producer:* Kathleen Kennedy, Frank Marshall, and Jane Startz. *Director:* Frank Oz. *Screenplay:* Melissa Mathison. *Based on the novel by:* Lynne Reid Banks. *Director of Photography:* Russell Carpenter. *Editor:* Ian Crafford. *Music:* Randy Edelman. *Music Editor:* John Finklea. *Sound:* Arthur Rochester and (music) Dennis Sands. *Sound Editor:* Ron Bochar and Skip Lievsay. *Casting:* Lara E. Spotts. *Art Director:* Tony Fanning and Jim Feng. *Set Designer:* Erin Kemp, Barbara Ann Jaeckel, Jr., Cosmas Demetriou, John Dexter, and Richard Fernandez. *Set Decorator:* Chris L. Spellman and Gretchen Rau. *Special Effects:* Michael Lantieri. *Costumes:* Deborah I. Scott. *Make-up:* Felicity Bowring. *Stunt Coordinator:* Dennis R. Scott and Lynn Salvatori. *Running time:* 96 minutes. *MPAA Rating:* PG.

CAST: Hal Scardino (Omri); Litefoot (Little Bear); Lindsay Crouse (Jane); Richard Jenkins (Victor); Rishi Bhat (Patrick); Steve Coogan (Tommy); David Keith (Boone); Sakina Jaffrey (Lucy); Vincent Kartheiser (Gillon); Nestor Serrano (Teacher); Ryan Olson (Adiel); Leon Tejwani and Lucas Tejwani (Baby Martin); Christopher Conte (Purple Mohawk); Cassandra Brown (Emily); Christopher Moritz (Sam); Beni Malkin (Ramon); Juliet Berman (Tina); Stephen Morales (Kiron); George Randall (Indian Chief); Gia Galeano (Yard Teacher); Kevin Malaro (School Kid); Tom Bewley (Darth Vadar); Keji Johnston (G.I. Joe); J.R. Horsting (Robocop); Michael Papajohn (Cardassian); Eric Stabenau (Firengi).

LOS ANGELES TIMES, 7/14/95, Calendar/p. 1, Kenneth Turan

"The Black Stallion," "E.T." and now "The Indian in the Cupboard." When it comes to writing films that both involve and captivate children, Melissa Mathison is the one you want to call.

Mathison's forte is not necessarily coming up with original ideas: "Indian," like "Stallion" (which she co-scripted), is based on a modern classic of children's literature, first published in 1980. Written by Lynne Reid Banks (who also wrote "The L-Shaped Room" for adults), this story of a magic cupboard that brings toy plastic figures to life has more than 5 million copies in print and many more of its three sequels.

Mathison's gift is rather her understanding of the sense of wonder and her ability to infuse it as well as an honesty of spirit, into the material she works on. And not many screenwriters can match her in putting emotion on screen in a way that is effective without being excessive.

Although audience members, from presidential candidates on down, don't seem to care or even notice, this has been a superb year for children's films. Starting with John Sayles' "The Secret of Roan Inish" and extending through "A Little Princess" and this, several different approaches to material for young people have been tried with equal success.

Although its story makes it the most dependent on special effects, "The Indian in the Cupboard" is also the most self-effacing of films, a gentle and low-key effort directed in a determinedly non-flashy manner by Frank Oz, best known for his longtime association with the Muppets.

That unobtrusiveness extends to Mathison's script, which has an effortless quality yet is able to seamlessly effect a major change from the original novel, set in Britain and featuring boys who have tea after school and say such things as "Now look here" and "How dare you."

Although his name has remained the same, 9-year-old Omri has been transferred to Manhattan and his part taken by a young American actor, Hal Scardino, who debuted as a defeated opponent in "Searching for Bobby Fischer."

With tousled hair and large eyes, Scardino is one of the few child actors who actually seems like a real kid, not a wily show-biz veteran, and his skill as a reactor, his ability to sharply register everything from delight to pain on his face, is essential to this story of a boy who has an awful lot to react to.

Omri gets the wooden cupboard (it's metal in the novel, more like a bathroom medicine cabinet) as a birthday present from one of his brothers. From his best friend Patrick (Rishi Bhat) he gets an ordinary-looking plastic Indian, one of those mass-produced figures to which even children rarely give a second thought.

Omri absently puts the figure in the cupboard, locks it up with a key his mother got from her grandmother and then forgets all about it. Until the next morning, when he hears something rattling the small door. He rushes to open it and is understandably astonished to discover that the plastic Indian has become a flesh-and-blood little man, all of 3 inches tall and furious at finding himself in the land of the giants. "You are so real," Omri marvels. "I am, are you?" the warrior answers back.

The man's name, Omri learns, is little Bear (played by Litefoot, a Cherokee Nation recording artist in his acting debut). An Iroquois who has been somehow removed from his real life in 1761 (the film, like the book, gracefully chooses not to explain how), Little Bear can speak English because his tribe is allied with the colonizing British.

Beside himself with pleasure and amazement, Omri tries to help Little Bear adjust to his new world, supplying him with material to build a lodge house and protecting him from the perils of modern life.

All this would be difficult enough, but Omri lets Patrick in on the secret, and, against his better judgment, a plastic cowboy goes into the cupboard and out comes Boohoo Boone (engagingly played by David Keith), a lachrymose 19th Century cowboy who sounds like Gabby Hayes and is less than pleased to discover a miniature Native American in his neck of the woods.

Dangers of varying degrees confront Omri in his role of sorcerer's apprentice, but it is consistent with "The Indian in the Cupboard's" simplicity and fidelity to the original that they are modest ones and suitable to the scale of a child's imagination.

Although it is not flashy, "Indian" is indebted to the effects work of Industrial Light & Magic. Using a combination of blue-screen technology and enormous, specially constructed props, including a sneaker 14 feet high and 35 feet wide, ILM and cinematographer Russell Carpenter make this bit of magic completely convincing.

From Omri's realization that having Little Bear dependent on him is "an enormous, huge responsibility" to the film's thoughts on trust and the importance of getting along with those who are different, "Indian" is intent on teaching lessons, but it does so easily, with a welcome lack of pretension. Like many of the classic works for children, it is finally about the rough passage to adulthood, and Hal Scardino's ability to convey that change is another reason why even in a year of wonders children this quiet film still manages to impress.

NEW YORK POST, 7/14/95, p. 43, Michael Medved

Every child fantasizes at one time or another about some particularly beloved toy that springs magically to life to become a secret and cherished companion.

"The Indian in the Cupboard" makes those dreams startlingly real for moviegoers of all ages in an utterly engaging piece of entertainment that deserves the embarrassingly overused designation of "classic."

Like "The Wizard of Oz," or "E.T." (which shares a producer and a screenwriter with this new film) or "A Little Princess" from earlier this year, "The Indian in the Cupboard" will still produce joy and wonder when watched by children (and their parents) 50 years from now.

Based on the book by Lynne Reid Banks the story begins when a sensitive New Yorker named Omri (played by a marvelous appealing and unaffected newcomer named Hal Scardino) receives a mundane assortment of gifts for his ninth birthday.

These include an old wooden cupboard his big brother has retrieved from the street and cleaned up, and a miniature plastic Indian from his best friend (Rishi Bhat).

That night, Omri locks the Indian in the cupboard with an heirloom key passed from his grandmother, but the next morning when he looks in on his toy, it's been miraculously transformed into a 3-inch-tall living Indian named Little Bear—an Iroquois brave transported from his forest life in 1761 who view's the shocked boy before him as some sort of giant or Great Spirit.

Immediately, Omri takes responsibility for hiding the Indian in his room, while providing him with food, tiny weapons and tools, plus the materials he needs to build an authentic Iroquois long house.

Before long, Little Bear (played by a charismatic Cherokee rap musician named Litefoot) also gets companionship in the person of a grubby, drunken Texas cowpoke (David Keith) who comes to life when Omri's best friend (the only one who shares his secret) uses the cupboard to transform another toy. At first these two tiny figures do what cowboys-and-Indians do naturally—shooting at each other from behind the sneakers and baseballs on the floor of Omri's room.

Eventually, however, they become friends, learning from one another (just as Omri from both of them) and together facing the unspeakable danger posed by a pet rat owned by the boy's brother. That pesky rodent, by the way, delivers the single most heart-stopping shock I've experienced in movies all year.

The special effects work flawlessly—which means they never seem special at all, making the movie's premise believable and almost ordinary.

Director Frank Oz (who's specialized in smart character comedies like "Dirty Rotten Scoundrels" and "Little Shop of Horrors") handles the material with humor and tenderness, but with no trace of cloying sentimentality.

Even politically correct invocations of Native American nobility—including the historically questionable notion that the Iroquois Confederation inspired the U.S. Constitution—can't spoil the prevailing mood of warmth and decency, or undermine the movie's messages about compassion and responsibility.

Even if you don't believe in magic cupboards and living toys, this altogether amazing film is enough to prove that movie magic, in the right hands, remains potent and powerful.

NEWSDAY, 7/14/95, Part II/p. B2, Jack Mathews

Frank Oz, one of the original creative forces behind Jim Henson's Muppet and "Sesame Street" franchises, has shown distinct dark and light sides during his career as a filmmaker. On the light side, three "Muppet" movies. On the dark, "Little Shop of Horrors" and "The Dark Crystal." It's an age thing—I'm over 10—but I prefer the Oz with the edge.

Oz' new film, "The Indian in the Cupboard," adapted from Lynne Reid Banks' award-winning children's book is so light it nearly drifts off the screen. Youngsters may be enchanted by the story of a young boy whose toys come magically to life, but parents tagging along will have to take their thrills vicariously.

"Indian" is the story of Omri (Scardino), an imaginative 9-year-old who discovers that an old cabinet, given him by his brother, when locked and unlocked with an antique key, transforms his plastic toys—an American Indian, a cowboy and his horse, a World War I British medic—into breathing miniatures. It's the ultimate toy set until Omri discovers that his new friends have left real lives behind in other periods to join him, and that he must take responsibility for getting them back.

Not a lot happens in the meantime. The Indian (Cherokee rap artist Litefoot), who is transported from the late 18th Century, and the cowboy (David Keith), from the 1870s, fight like cats and dogs until they discover the humanity in each other and become brothers under the skin. The medic (Steve Coogan) is called in occasionally to administer to their injuries and make a few wisecracks, and then returned to the battlefield in Europe. An assortment of other objects, among them a T-rex, are no sooner animated than sent back.

An enormous amount of effort went into these illustrations. Omri and his best friend, Patrick (Rishi Bhat), who claims ownership of the cowboy, interact with the tiny characters throughout the movie, and with sets duplicated for the perspectives of both sets of characters, it does begin to take on a sense of reality. Hollywood, of course, has been pulling off similar stunts, with varying degrees of success, throughout its history. But to every new generation, it's an amazement.

Unfortunately, too much of the imagination expended by Oz and his crew went into the production and not enough into the story. The real pleasure, for kids of all ages, is in the actual magic, seeing Omri stick another plastic character in the cabinet and have it come alive. Instead, we spend most of our time playing a PC version of cowboys and Indians, and though it delivers the right message—all lives and cultures have values, and deserve respect—it becomes tedious.

There is also a huge gap in the seriousness with which the actors take their assignments. Litefoot plays Little Bear with such dignity and gentleness of spirit, I kept thinking what a great date he would have been for Pocahontas, while Keith's besotted half-wit Boone is sort of a cross between Gabby Hayes and "Cat Ballou's" Kid Sheleen.

Oz has whipped up one genuinely exciting sequence, involving Omri's brother's pet rat and Little Bear, that may have parents out-screaming their kids. "Indian in the Cupboard" could have used a lot more like it.

NEWSWEEK, 7/17/95, p. 60, David Ansen

Melissa Mathison has worked on the screenplays for two of the most wondrous family films to emerge from Hollywood—"E.T. the Extra-Terrestrial" and "The Black Stallion." She's now done the adaptation of Lynne Reid Banks's award-winning children's book, *The Indian in the Cupboard*, and though director Frank Oz's movie doesn't reach the pop poetic heights of those two (few films do), it's an engaging and touching flight of fancy.

The 9-year-old hero, Omri (Hal Scardino), gets three presents for his birthday—an old cupboard, a special antique key and a miniature plastic Indian. It proves to be a magical combination, for when he puts the three-inch figure in the cupboard, it comes to life as a real, albeit tiny, Iroquois named Little Bear (Litefoot), transported from 1761 and terrified by the giant New York City kid peering down at him.

Omri soon discovers that the cupboard can transform all his inanimate objects—dinosaurs, knights, Darth Vader—into flesh and blood. A bright, sensitive kid, he grasps that with this awesome power comes responsibility. Little Bear is dependent on him for survival, and the child suddenly has to act like a parent. When his pal Patrick (Rishi Bhat) insists on adding a toy cowboy on horseback to the mix—the weepy, trigger-happy Boone (a very funny David Keith)—Omri finds he needs the skills of a U.N. peacekeeper. In one startling sequence, Little Bear and Boone get their first exposure to TV—a racy blast of MTV sex, followed by a violent Indian massacre from an old Western. This movie shoot-'em-up incites near-lethal passions in Boone and Little Bear. Coming from Hollywood, it's a startlingly explicit metaphor (and *mea culpa*) for the connection between on- and off-screen violence.

The didacticism is, for the most part, gracefully meshed with the storytelling, and the special effects never take over the show. "Honey, I Shrunk the Kids" and others have played with scale before, but Oz's film differentiates itself by its intimacy—it's a kind of presexual love story between a boy and his man/toy, who is both his mentor and his charge. Growing up is seen as the discovery of compassion—recognizing that others have needs too. For a change, this is a fable in which a child discovers his "inner adult."

Ultimately, "Indian in the Cupboard's" claim on the heartstrings is the result of the off-beat casting. Scardino—found by casting director Margery Simkin after 500 auditions—has a lovely, goony charm, and Litefoot, a Cherokee rap artist with no acting experience, is a delightful discovery. That these two generate such a convincing bond is no mean feat: the trick perspective required them to play all their scenes together solo. Their friendship is the film's most indelible special effect.

SIGHT AND SOUND, 1/96, p. 42, Nick James

Omri is a young boy living in the big city. On his ninth birthday he is given a 3-inch toy Indian by his friend Patrick and a wooden cupboard by his brother Gillon. Omri finds an old key that fits it. That night he puts the Indian inside and locks the door. The following morning, he hears a noise coming from the cupboard and finds that the miniature warrior has come alive and that he speaks some English. Omri learns he is an Iroquois named Little Bear. Hearing his mother coming, Omri locks the cupboard.

Opening it again that evening, he finds Little Bear has turned back into a toy, so he relocks the door. Later he hears the noise again—Little Bear has returned. Realising how the cupboard works, Omri transforms several figures at once but they start to fight so he changes them all back except for Little Bear. The Indian resents his being plucked from his eighteenth-century life. He demands food and tools to build a house, Omri asks his father, Victor, for money to buy hacksaw blades. He goes to the shop and buys some, but is robbed of the change by a bigger boy.

Omri injures Little Bear's leg by accident. He brings Tommy, a First World War British medic to life to care for him. When he is recovered, Omri shows Little Bear to Patrick and swears him to secrecy, but Patrick insists on having a miniature friend of his own. Omri's plastic cowboy becomes Boone, a drunken drifter from the 1890s. At first Boone and Little Bear fight but they soon get along. Then one night, Omri, Patrick, Little Bear and Boon watch television, and during a Western fight scene, Little Bear becomes confused and fells Boone with an arrow. Omri brings back Tommy to save Boone. He realises he must send Little Bear and Boone back. In a magic ceremony, Little Bear asks Omri to close his eyes, and he finds himself in a forest. Little Bear, now full-sized Indian, embraces Omri and calls him a young warrior. Returning to himself, Omri bids Little Bear farewell before turning the key.

Despite its title, *The Indian in the Cupboard* seems as if it were devised as a perfect politically correct fairy tale, and it succeeds as such to a much greater extent than Disney's elegant but worthy *Pocahontas*. The narrative never loses its sense of wonder or its steady drive, despite the weight of historical guilt that representation of Native Americans now carries. Where the animated tale *Pocahontas* was an over-sensitive if even-handed version of a more hopeful interlude in the arrival of colonialism in America, *Indian* is happy to be in keeping with more traditional children's fictions. It is respectful of fact, yet keen to take imaginative flight and the special effects are both convincing and enchanting.

Thus *Indian* makes fun of its diminutive Iroquois' struggle to survive the terrors of a Brobdingnagian bedroom as much as it takes his iconography and religious beliefs seriously. It has a touching and convincing faith in the idea that an imaginative small boy would be bound to discover nobility and beauty in an Iroquoian brave whatever propaganda about 'savages' he may have unwittingly consumed. The film is equally unafraid to boost Boone the cowboy as a fun-loving drunk and to kill off a regenerated old Indian with fright at seeing the giant Omri. But then this story is not, after all, of the politically correct era, being adapted from the *Indian in the Cupboard* novels of British author Lynne Reid Banks which were themselves based on stories she told her son some 14 years ago.

As is proper to the bedtime story, the film's focus (generally much sharper here than in Oz's adult comedies such as *The Little Shop of Horrors*, *Dirty Rotten Scoundrels* and *Housesitter*) is on the child's world in which parents and teachers are mere peripheral ghosts dispensing approval or blame. Although it is not overtly signalled in any way, what Omri experiences—an omniscient view of a warrior's life-or-death struggle—is not that far from a computer game, but the difference is that there are consequences to his participation that must be dealt with—even bodies to be buried (the old Indian's). While the point of view remains with Omri—a sickly, timid, wide-eyed dreamer—much of his vulnerability is projected into his tiny but stern companion, and an obvious but pertinent analogy is drawn between Little Bear's natural forest habitat and the cruel city through which Omri must soon travel. Such a projection makes Little Bear cousin to other diminutive representatives of the child's inner voice—not least Disney's Jiminy Cricket from *Pinocchio*, and perhaps even Timothy the mouse from *Dumbo*, (although we are spared the kitsch touch of a magic feather).

However, Little Bear does more than these non-combatant ringside whisperers. He gets involved, living his giant friend's anxieties out in a landscape of mountainous beds and prairie-like carpeting inhabited by huge rats and clumsy human colossi. That Little Bear also takes on the role of an Iroquois uncle by preparing Omri for impending manhood might in a less subtle film be a substitution for an absent father or worse. Certainly in his distinctly non-urban plaid shirt, Omri's dad is an uncomfortable reminder of the sinister protagonist of *The Stepfather* and the cavernous, multi-storey house that they live in is of the familiar 'how can they afford that?' variety seen in such films as *The Hand That Rocks the Cradle*, *Hider in the House* and even *Mrs. Doubtfire*, each of which also deals with a hidden domestic presence. Against this background creepiness however, *The Indian in the Cupboard* is capable of creeping up on you and aiming straight for the heart.

VILLAGE VOICE, 7/25/95, p. 58, Gary Dauphin

Frank Oz's genuinely heart-warming children's movie *The Indian in the Cupboard* actually manages to accomplish something rare for a contemporary fairy tale. It takes the small frame of childhood fantasy and expands it through solid storytelling and winning effects to the level of a grandly resonant morality play. This is no mean feat considering that some of *Indian*'s stars are a bit over three inches tall, and that its main relationship is between a pint-sized 18th-century Iroqois Indian and a nine-year-old pale-faced New York City boy who holds him captive with his magic cupboard. Oz and screenwriter Melissa Mathison (who penned *E.T.*) navigate these potentially perilous waters with special effects that never falter and, most importantly, Hal Scardino's expressive and wonder-filled performance as the cupboard's owner.

Also reviewed in:
CHICAGO TRIBUNE, 7/14/95, Friday/p. D, Gary Dretzka
NEW YORK TIMES, 7/14/95, p. C3, Janet Maslin
VARIETY, 7/17-23/95, p. 51, Brian Lowry
WASHINGTON POST, 7/14/95, p. D1, Frank Ahrens
WASHINGTON POST, 7/14/95, Weekend/p. 36, Joe Brown

INNOCENT, THE

A Miramax Films release of a Lakeheart/Sievernich Film coproduction in association with The Berlin Film Board, The Brandenburg Film Board, and the North Rhine Westfalia Film Board. *Executive Producer:* Ann Dubinet. *Producer:* Norma Heyman, Chris Sievernich, and Wieland Schultz-Keil. *Director:* John Schlesinger. *Screenplay (based on his novel):* Ian McEwan. *Director of Photography:* Dietrich Lohmann. *Editor:* Richard Marden. *Music:* Gerald Gouriet. *Choreographer:* Eleanor Fazon. *Sound:* Axel Arft. *Sound Editor:* Nick Stevenson. *Production Designer:* Luciana Arrighi. *Art Director:* Dieter Döhl. *Set Decorator:* Olaf Schiefner. *Special Effects:* Adolf Wojtinek. *Costumes:* Ingrid Zore. *Make-up:* Joan Hills. *Running time:* 118 minutes. *MPAA Rating:* R.

CAST: Anthony Hopkins (Glass); Isabella Rossellini (Maria); Campbell Scott (Leonard); Ronald Nitschke (Otto); Hart Bochner (Russell); James Grant (MacNamee); Jeremy Sinden (Lofting); Richard Durden (Black); Corey Johnson (Lou); Richard Good (Piper); Lena Lessing (Jenny); Dana Golembek (Charlotte); Susanne Jansen (Mermaid Singer); Christine Gerlach (Woman with Dog); Ludger Pistor (German Informer); Meret Becker (Ulrike); Christianne Flegel (Frau Eckdorf); Klaus-Jürgen Steinmann (Herr Eckdorf); Jessica Cardinahl, Franziska Brix, and Forest Ashley Knight (Maria's Children); Matthew Burton (Flight Officer); Rupert Chetwynd (Air Commodore); Martin Becker and Natascha Bub (Offenders at Police Station); Hans Martin Stier, Helmut Bernhoffen, and Gerch Hofmann (Police Inspectors); Friedrich Solms-Baruth (Hotel Receptionist); Martin Honer (Left Luggage Officer); Stefan Taufelder (East German Checkpoint); Hubertus Brand and Peter Meseck (East German Border Guards).

LOS ANGELES TIMES, 9/4/95, Calendar/p. 5, Kevin Thomas

"The Innocent," a ponderous, old-fashioned love story set in postwar Berlin, would surely have been far more effective had it actually been told in the '50s, the era in which it is set. In any event, it's altogether the wrong movie at the wrong time, despite the earnest efforts of its stars—Campbell Scott, Isabella Rossellini and Anthony Hopkins—and their distinguished director, John Schlesinger.

Scott lives up to the title role with a vengeance. He's cast as a British telephone engineer enlisted in a top-secret project run by British and American intelligence, an actual operation, lasting from 1954 to 1956, involving digging and equipping a massive underground tunnel in order to eavesdrop on communist communications in the Russian sector. No sooner does he arrive than he enters the tunnel, despite his new boss, a tough, crude American (Hopkins) telling him he must not do so until he obtains a clearance.

Much more seriously, he disregards Hopkins' admonition to be wary of romantic entanglements and promptly falls in love with Rossellini's beautiful woman of mystery the moment he casts eyes on her at a nightclub. In no time at all Scott has plunged headlong into disaster, endangering the project and his life as well.

No one gets much help from Ian McEwan's script, adapted from his own novel. Scott's humorless engineer generates little or no sympathy, and Hopkins is mainly on hand to give a mannered interpretation of a classic Ugly American. The master German cinematographer Dietrich Lohmann gives the film a wonderfully dark, shadowy look, making splendid use of seedy locales in the former East Berlin, but McEwan gives us very little in the way of genuine suspense or intrigue to go along with some terrific atmosphere; there's not that much sense of Cold War tensions.

A framing story, set as the Berlin Wall crumbles, both trivializes that momentous event and reveals that Scott's engineer is essentially the same dense prig he was when we met him some 35 years earlier. And the considerable presence of Rossellini, for all her unique radiance and talent, perversely has the effect of making us feel as if we're looking at one of Ingrid Bergman's lesser old movies.

NEW YORK POST, 9/2/95, p. 17, Larry Worth

The opening and closing scenes of "The Innocent" show the toppling of the Berlin Wall. But in between, nearly everything else crumbles.

That includes the talents of director John "Midnight Cowboy" Schlesinger and a cast led by Anthony Hopkins, Isabella Rossellini and Campbell Scott. Granted, the results occasionally amuse as "fun trash," but it's easy to see why the film remained on Miramax's shelf for the last two years.

The story is based on Ian McEwan's best-selling novel about espionage, murder and lost love in Cold War Berlin. Yet, Schlesinger fails to generate suspense, romance or much interest along the way.

The chief entertainment is watching the hackneyed spy plot rip off everything from the Kit-Kat Klub in "Cabaret"—this time with pneumatic tubes subbing for telephones to communicate between tables—to the legendary finale of "Casablanca," with Rossellini on the airfield instead of her mom. (Though screenwriter McEwan could also be accused of stealing the dismembered corpse scene from "Shallow Grave," that early '95 drama was filmed and released while this one collected dust in a vault.)

Surely intended as a classic thriller, the real mystery is why Academy Award winner Hopkins went on cruise control as an Ugly American intelligence officer. Meanwhile, Rossellini makes her woman of intrigue as transparent as Saran Wrap. As for Scott's titular secret agent, his only convincing moment involves play-acting as Frankenstein's monster.

The bottom line: Only the most naive will fall for "The Innocent."

SIGHT AND SOUND, 8/94, p. 42, Philip Strick

As the Berlin wall is torn down in 1989, ageing business Leonard Marnham returns to the city at the invitation of Maria, the woman he loved and lost there during the Cold War. He recalls that when he first came to Berlin in 1955, he was a telephone engineer recruited to assist a British-American operation. Assigned to work under American officer Bob Glass, he gradually learns about Operation Gold: the CIA and MI6 secretly run a tunnel under the Russian sector in order to tap into Soviet telephone lines, recording coded calls for analysis in London and Washington. Obsessed with security, Glass strictly supervises Leonard's activities, watching with concern as the young man becomes involved with Maria, a girl he meets at the Resi Dance Hall. In turn, Leonard is instructed by MacNamee, his British superior, to spy on Glass to ensure that all information about Operation Gold is shared.

Infatuated with Maria, Leonard clumsily spoils their passionate relationship by becoming violent one night. Maria runs away, and Glass promptly takes her in for questioning; cleared by his security team, she later returns to Leonard on the run from her former husband Otto, who has beaten her up. Although horrified at this revelation, Leonard is ecstatic at their reunion; Maria introduces him to her parents and relatives, and soon they announce their engagement party. The celebrations are gate-crashed by Leonard's downstairs neighbour, Geoffrey Black, who appears mysteriously well-informed about all the guests. Afterwards, Leonard and Maria find Otto waiting for them: he will only sign Maria's divorce papers in return for cash and full details of Operation Gold. There is a fierce struggle, and Otto is killed.

Leonard collects two equipment cases from his office, and he and Maria fill these with Otto's dismembered corpse. Struggling to dump the cases, Leonard runs into Black and explains that they contain decoding equipment; back in his own apartment, Black makes a hasty phone call in Russian. As a result, no sooner has Leonard, with immense difficulty, deposited the cases in the tunnel than Operation Gold is uncovered by Soviet troops and the cases are handed over to the West German police. Throwing herself into Glass' embrace, Maria persuades him to arrange for Leonard to be flown immediately out of Berlin to escape trial for murder. At the airport, at the last minute, she tells Leonard he must leave without her, and only now, when at last they meet again, does Leonard realise that this was an act not of betrayal but of self-sacrifice. Among the crowds cheering the destruction of the wall, Leonard and Maria look forward to life together.

In adapting his novel, set in 1987, for the screen Ian McEwan has created the film's opening and closing sequences from what was the book's postscript, timeslipped a scant but significant two years forward. As a result, the fall of the Berlin Wall becomes the vantage point for a story told in flashback, and the relationship between Leonard and Maria is paralleled by two significant episodes in Cold War history. What began as an affair of tunnelings, misapprehensions and concealments survives to celebrate the removal of a final symbolic obstacle to peace. In the novel, the sundered couple remain apart at the end, their potential reconciliation unconfirmed.

In both versions, McEwan cheats on his characters. The 30-year separation in which Maria sensibly gets on with her life, possessing all the facts and coming to terms with them, while Leonard remains gloomily frozen in a condition of ignorance and emotional impairment, is singularly unconvincing. The truth of the matter, despite McEwan's careful scene-setting, is that neither tunnel nor wall actually has much bearing on the lovers' basic problem: it is the intrusive Otto and his demise, rudely and somewhat puzzlingly spiked on a cobbler's last, that causes all the damage. Fascinated by technical detail, McEwan writes of environment, espionage and dismemberment with the same intricacy; on the page, there is no question that the segmentation of Otto will haunt the lovers for many years. But on screen, dissection has evidently been judged less easy to enact than a few glimpses of blood-splashed faces gasping for air, and the film's emphasis has been unhelpfully shifted.

Firstly, the killing itself, an ugly and rather ludicrous outburst of fast cutting and orchestral hysteria, abruptly destroys the urbanity of mood (Schlesinger's earlier scenes of the rivalries surrounding Operation Gold evoke the seediness of *An Englishman Abroad*, only to leave a bizarre irrationality in its place. More extendedly, the challenge of hiding Otto's remains, a series of encounters in which the corpse seems perpetually on the point of discovery by kids, dogs, railwaymen and armed sentries, has a Hitchcockian humour which confirms the implicit silliness of Leonard's previous brushes with authority and the comical awkwardness of the youth himself. Most crucially, the shared revulsion with which, in the book, the lovers try to conceal their crime, is lost: instead, the burden is largely shouldered by Leonard, while Maria slips too easily into the guise of self-serving betrayer.

The result of the failure of their onscreen relationship to gel is that the big farewell scene at the airport, its echoes of *Casablanca* enhanced by Isabella Rossellini's striking resemblance to her mother Ingrid Bergman, enjoys little prospect of being taken seriously, while the jump forward into a profusion of grey hair and wrinkles carries no weight at all. Schlesinger, though unable to resist the usual clichés whenever he encounters a spiral staircase, directs with restraint and keeps to a minimum flourishes like the serpentine opening shot that encompasses a babble of reporters in the hotel lobby. For what it's worth, the monumental dullness of post-war Berlin comes over loud and clear—an ominous grey labyrinth of tension and exhaustion in which only the Resi Dance Hall retains vestiges of tinsel vivacity.

Anthony Hopkins as Bob Glass creates a solid performance from an underwritten sketch; extraordinarily, he manages with a single tear to provide the revelation, slightly fumbled by McEwan, that the story's true romance lies elsewhere, in Glass' unrequited love for Maria. In the thankless role of the ingenuous Leonard, Campbell Scott is unable to substantiate the behaviour that McEwan, too, has been unable to render plausible—the sudden stupidity of his attempt to rape Maria. With this one dislocation, for all the absurd authenticity of the Operation Gold fiasco itself, the fiction that McEwan has constructed becomes unreliable and nonsensical.

Also reviewed in:
CHICAGO TRIBUNE, 9/22/95, Friday/p. O, Michael Wilmington
NEW YORK TIMES, 9/2/95, p. 11, Caryn James
VARIETY, 9/27/93, p. 40, Rebecca Lieb
WASHINGTON POST, 9/2/95, p. D3, Rita Kempley

IS THAT ALL THERE IS?

A Yaffle films release for BBC Scotland. *Executive Producer:* John Archer. *Producer:* Trevor Ingman. *Director:* Lindsay Anderson *Screenplay:* Lindsay Anderson. *Director of Photography:* Jonathan Collinson. *Editor:* Nicolas Gaster. *Music:* Alan Price. *Sound:* John Anderton. *Running time:* 54 minutes. *MPAA Rating:* Not Rated.

WITH: Lindsay Anderson; Alexander Anderson; Bernard Kops; David Sterne; Mark Sigsworth; Brian Pettifer; Andrew Eaton; Tom Sutcliffe; David Sherwin; Jocelyn Herbert; David Storey; Alan Price; Murray Anderson.

NEW YORK POST, 5/10/95, p. 49, Larry Worth

Everyone from Bergman to Bronson has used film over the decades to plumb the inscrutable give-and-take of life and death.

But those who think there's nothing left to say haven't seen "Is That All There Is?" and "Eternity," two documentaries that stunningly complement the theme at hand, and each other.

"Eternity" has a bit more universal appeal, courtesy of a mysterious phantom named Arthur Stace who traversed Sydney, Australia, writing the word "Eternity" 500,000 times over a 40-year period. His palette: a yellow piece of chalk; his canvas: whatever wall or sidewalk struck his fancy.

Writer/director Lawrence Johnston puts a deliciously eerie twist on the tale, making the late Stace look like a benevolent Jack the Ripper in gorgeously-shot re-creations. Initially, he's photographed as a silhouette in trench coat and fedora, prowling the pre-dawn alleys to deliver his one-word sermon.

So what did the message mean, and who *was* Arthur Stace? Well, a series of "witnesses" relate their brushes with the shadowy figure—and how the passion, commitment and focus of Stace's mission haunted their lives.

But while Johnston thoroughly addresses Stace's emergence as a cultural phenomenon Down Under, he leaves too many questions about Stace's personal life.

Thankful, an ethereal score and crisp black-and-white cinematography distract from the oversights, with a surreal, near-ghostly ambience treading a fine line between dreams and nightmare.

The existence of late director Lindsay Anderson was also consumed by dreams and nightmares, as superbly recorded in Anderson's final film, "Is That All There Is?"

The man who lensed classics like "If ...," "O Lucky Man" and "This Sporting Life" spent his senior years in a London apartment filled with posters and photos from his salad days.

The production follows a typical 24 hours of the elderly Anderson's life, which mesmerizes—and amuses—in its ordinariness. The great man is consumed by baths, pills, newscasts, friends and the most mundane of errands.

What separates Anderson from the hoi polloi is his deliciously serrated wit (exemplified in comments about Michael Caine's hair) and a tough-as-nails nature (rebounding effortlessly after a bookstore clerk informs Anderson that his treatise on John Ford sells better if not autographed).

The film falters only when dipping into the obvious. Seeing Anderson cross-cut his food-shopping forays with news clips of starving Africans is neither original nor thought-provoking. Far more moving is Anderson's unconventional tribute to the memory of actresses Rachel Roberts and Jill Bennett.

That eclectic mix of sense and sentience—in both "Is That All There Is?" and "Eternity"—is what ultimately imbues new life in this deceptively moribund genre.

VILLAGE VOICE, 5/16/95, p. 60, Kathy Deacon

In the 1930's long before the birth of Calvin Klein's perfume, the word *Eternity* began appearing in the streets of Sydney, Australia. Written in chalk with great precision using copperplate script, it came to grace virtually every sidewalk in the city, and was for many years a mystery. The agent of this mad redundancy was eventually revealed to be a Mr. Arthur Stace, a former alcoholic and petty criminal who experienced a profound transformation upon hearing a sermon at age 45. The Lord said, Go out and write *Eternity*, which Stace did a half a million times over the next 40 years. Celebrating Stace as an art icon and folk hero, Lawrence Johnstone's documentary *Eternity* downplays the monotonous obsessiveness of his single theme. Fellow Australians ponder whether he's an artist or eccentric. Offering archival photographs of early 20th-century Sydney by turns quaint, gritty, and graphic, the solemn tone of the project is offset by its surreal re-creations of the lone figure of Stace writing his tag against the backdrop of the city.

Eternity is oddly paired with *Is That All There Is?*, a 54-minute rendering of a day or so in his own life that Lindsay Anderson made for the Scottish BBC just prior to his death in 1994. A founder of the Free Cinema movement in Britain in the '50s, Anderson went on to make films such as *This Sporting Life* and *If* that dealt with the straitjacket of the British class system. He later worked more in theater than in cinema. The succession of short scenes in this documentary, consisting largely of insider shoptalk with thespian cronies, has a near anthropological feel; yet in recording his diurnal motions, a sense of emotional connection seems nearly absent. A momentary break in the tedium is supplied by a nephew's startlingly violent outburst—he looks like a '60s rebel, until we see him in the last scene at a cocktail party, fitting in nicely. Anderson's detached self-examination, which may be of interest mainly to buffs, shows the septuagenarian, weary with his marginal niche in British cultural life, regarding himself as something of a relic.

Also reviewed in:
NEW REPUBLIC, 5/29/95, p. 26, Stanley Kauffmann
NEW YORK TIMES, 5/18/95, p. C17, Stephen Holden
VARIETY, 12/29/93, p. 35, Derek Elley

IT TAKES TWO

A Warner Bros. release of a Rysher Entertainment presentation of an Orr & Cruickshank production in association with Dualstar Productions. *Executive Producer:* Keith Samples and Mel Efros. *Producer:* James Orr and Jim Cruickshank. *Director:* Andy Tennant. *Screenplay:* Deborah Dean Davis. *Director of Photography:* Kenneth Zunder. *Editor:* Roger Bondelli. *Music:* Sherman Foote and Ray Foote. *Sound:* David Lee. *Casting:* Amy Lippens. *Production Designer:* Edward Pisoni. *Art Director:* Vlasta Svoboda. *Costumes:* Molly McGuiness. *Running time:* 100 minutes. *MPAA Rating:* PG.

CAST: Kirstie Alley (Diane Barrows); Steve Guttenberg (Roger Callaway); Mary-Kate Olsen (Amanda Lemmon); Ashley Olsen (Alyssa Callaway); Philip Bosco (Vincenzo); Jane Sibbett (Clarice Kensington); Michelle Grisom (Carmen); Desmond Roberts (Frankie); Ernie Grunwald (Harry Butkis); Ellen Ray Hennessey (Fanny Butkis); Lawrence Dane (Mr. Kensington); Gerard Parkes (Priest).

LOS ANGELES TIMES, 11/17/95, Calendar/p. 2, Kevin Thomas

There's a show-biz axiom about actors not going up against kids on the screen, but in the giddy, lively "It Takes Two," Kirstie Alley more than lives up to her star billing—even if she and her equally adept co-star Steve Guttenberg are teamed with those practiced scene-stealers, the Olsen twins of TV's "Full House."

Alley is Diane Barrows, a hearty Manhattan orphanage caseworker looking for Mr. Right and wishing he and she could then adopt feisty 9-year-old Amanda Lemmon (Mary-Kate Olsen). Barrows knows she should keep her detachment, but she finds streetwise Amanda irresistible. Meanwhile, 9- year-old Alyssa Callaway (Ashley Olsen) is in an opposite predicament: how to keep her long-widowed father Roger (Guttenberg) from marrying the dreadful socialite Clarice (Jane Sibbett)—a grasping, child-hating airhead. As it happens the vast Callaway country estate—Roger is a pioneer cellular-phone tycoon worth $20 billion—is across the lake from a summer camp he has established and where Diane has taken her young charges.

Anyone the age of Amanda and Alyssa and above will be able to figure out instantly that after the two girls cross paths, have fun and adventure exchanging lives, that they're going to play Cupid.

Writer Deborah Dean Davis and director Andy Tennant are fully aware of the absolute predictability of their material and therefore make the getting to an inevitable ending as much fun as possible. They turn a plot that is entirely a contrivance into a sturdy structure for farce.

Davis is a skilled writer, but it's Tennant—here moving from TV to films—who makes exhilarating what in lesser hands could so easily have seemed a stale and old-fashioned "Princess and the Pauper" turn. It would seem he persuaded everyone involved that an affectionate tongue-in-cheek approach was the only way to go.

In both knockabout physical comedy and quizzical repartee, Alley exudes a roll-with-the-punches good nature.

Guttenberg brings a self-deprecating charm to the unpretentious Roger, and Philip Bosco is the perfect butler, discreet but loyal, unobtrusive in attempting to steer his boss away from a disastrous course. At first you have the feeling that Sibbett, in playing the hilarious woman-you-love-to-hate Clarice, won't have any place to go with her, but she becomes the constant foil, against which everyone else evolves.

As for the Olsen twins, they're perky, precocious types, throwbacks to an earlier Hollywood in which children tended to perform rather than act and are therefore ideal for "It Takes Two."

NEW YORK POST, 11/17/95, p. 48, Michael Medved

"It Takes Two" isn't going to win any awards for blazing originality: It shamelessly recycles two of the sturdiest, most familiar plot devices around, throwing together elements of "The Prince and the Pauper" and "The Parent Trap."

Nevertheless, it is so splendidly well-acted, so crisply and lovingly directed, that it will charm and entertain even the most skeptical curmudgeons.

Mary-Kate and Ashley Olsen, the talented 9-year-old twins already known to millions of kids from their videos, CDs, and shared role on TVs "Full House," here play two-unrelated little girls from different strata of society. Amanda (Mary-Kate) is an orphan who lives at a children's shelter on the Lower East Side: Alyssa (Ashley) is an heiress who attends a snooty boarding school.

Both girls long for a normal family life: Amanda wishes she could be adopted by her orphanage case worker (Kirstie Alley), a feisty single woman who's just about given up on ever meeting Mr. Right. Alyssa, meanwhile, wants to spend more time with her widower father (Steve Guttenberg), a fabulously wealthy cellular-phone tycoon.

Both girls face a crisis when they arrive for the summer at different shores of the same mountain lake: Amanda at a camp for orphans and Alyssa at her father's palatial vacation home. Amanda wants to avoid adoption by a cloying, creepy family on Staten Island, while Alyssa learns that her dad is about to marry a social-climbing fashion plate (Jane Sibbet) with instinctive hostility toward children.

When the two little girls bump into each other accidentally and see that they look exactly alike, they decide to switch identities and hatch a plot to get Guttenberg and Alley romantically interested in one another.

Director Andy Tennant (a TV veteran who here makes his auspicious big-screen debut) handles this material with wit and energy, creating a dazzling series of colorful, sunny storybook images.

The adorable Olsen twins are natural charmers, while Alley and Guttenberg—who come across as two of the nicest people on the face of earth—generate real and refreshing romantic sparks.

Guttenberg also displays a suave knack for perfectly-timed physical comedy that will win some big laughs.

The dependable Philip Bosco is on hand as a kindly, all-knowing butler, while Jane Sibbet (in her first major film) nearly steals the movie with her hilarious but believable role as the prospective stepmother from hell, projecting some of the same nasty sex appeal as the evil queen in "Snow White."

Many mothers in the audience will feel especially grateful for the fact that the likable romantic heroine (Alley) is, to put it gently, generously proportioned, while the villainess (Sibbet) wraps her bitchiness in an outrageously svelte and leggy package.

This year's other finest family films—"A Little Princess," "Indian in the Cupboard" and "Babe"—offered a bit of edification and inspiration along with their entertainment value, but "It Takes Two" is pure, unpretentious diversion. It offers, however, such a fleet-footed, frisky, frolicsome sense of fun that both kids and parents will find plenty of reason to celebrate.

NEWSDAY, 11/17/95, Part II/p. B6, John Anderson

With all the journalistic thumb-sucking going on lately about whether the movies have become less relevant—and less entertaining—than television, along comes "It Takes Two" to settle the argument: The movies aren't inferior to television. They are television.

With a plot that's been heisted from "The Parent Trap"—but has all the predictable sloth of any "TGI Friday" sitcom—the film stars Ashley and Mary-Kate Olsen, late of ABC's "Full House," as the filthy rich Alyssa Callaway and the streetwise orphan Amanda Lemmon. The former plays Chopin and rides Lear jets; the latter lives a lowly life in a New York children's shelter that seems to be situated on Sesame Street.

Amanda's surrogate mother is social worker Diane Barrow, played by Kirstie Alley ("Cheers"), who in her singularly sad-sack manner keeps whining that she really needs a man. Dream boy comes along in the person of cellular-phone magnate Roger Callaway, played by Steve Guttenberg (pick a credit), who's inconveniently engaged to the scheming, witchy Clarice Kensington (Jane Sibbett, of "Friends" and the formerly "Famous Teddy Z"). The entire package is the work of those creative geniuses James Orr and Jim Cruickshank, who are responsible, among other things, for "Father of the Bride" (a remake), "Sister Act 2" (a sequel) and "Three Men and a Baby" (a remake).

Oh yes, and the writer, Deborah Dean Davis, according to her bio, "has written more than forty episodes of prime-time television ... and sold several projects that were developed by all three major television networks." Now you know who's responsible.

With all this talent, is it any surprise that "It Takes Two" is the unwatchable thing it is? Not really, although it does owe a huge debt to prime-time TV. The jokes are clichéd bits of preciousness that you can't believe have been reworked: The poor kid eating escargot and retching, for instance, or the rich kid running to the wrong goal during her first football game.

The plot itself is simply recycled: Amanda and Alyssa change places, maneuver Diane and Roger into close proximity, foil Clarice's plans to marry Roger, and thwart Amanda's adoption by a family of ghouls from Staten Island. The casting is absurd: Guttenberg and Alley are no more believable as a love match than Bill Clinton and Ruth Bader Ginsburg. And Philip Bosco as the wise and avuncular butler Vincenzo is the most shameful waste of talent since Laurence Olivier did Polaroid commercials.

"It Takes Two," essentially, is the kind of film that gives "family entertainment" a bad name. Perhaps it's a plot. Certainly, if Bob Dole had to watch this, he'd never open his mouth about Hollywood again.

Also reviewed in:
CHICAGO TRIBUNE, 11/17/95, Friday/p. G, John Petrakis
NEW YORK TIMES, 11/17/95, p. C19, Stephen Holden
VARIETY, 11/20-26/95, p. 48, Leonard Klady
WASHINGTON POST, 11/17/95, p. F7, Hal Hinson

J.L.G. BY J.L.G.

A Gaumont/Peripheris production. *Producer:* Jean-Luc Godard. *Director:* Jean-Luc Goddard. *Screenplay (French with English subtitles):* Jean-Luc Godard. *Running time:* 65 minutes. *MPAA Rating:* Not Rated.

WITH: Jean-Luc Godard.

CHRISTIAN SCIENCE MONITOR, 1/25/95, p. 13, David Sterritt

Jean-Luc Godard probably the greatest filmmaker active in Europe today, has been challenging the lazy patterns of commercial cinema ever since his first full-length movie, "Breathless," launched the influential New Wave movement 3½ decades ago. As bold and experimental as ever, he keeps churning out films and videos at an impressive clip.

The new works having American theatrical premières at the Public Theater are "JLG by JLG," a moody self-portrait, and "Germany Year 90 Nine Zero," an avant-garde thriller with a sociopolitical theme.

An unabashed intellectual with a prodigious appetite for art, painting, and philosophy, Godard enjoys stuffing his movies with so many references and quotations that even his fervent admirers are hard-pressed to sort them out in a hurry.

This is especially true of an essay-film like "JLG by JLG," which assembles elements of his own life—from his ideas and theories to his home and his favorite movies—into a densely edited montage that's as difficult to decode as it is gorgeous to see and hear.

The results are oddly wrongheaded at times, as when Godard expounds a symbolic "theory of stereo" that dissects Middle East tensions in muddled terms. Yet even the film's weakest passages are never less than stimulating, and it's clear that Godard has retained a taste for self-deflating humor, as when he costumes himself in a winter hat that slyly recalls a jester's cap of old. Full of exquisite music, passionately filmed images, and snippets from all sorts of literature, this "December self-portrait" is a unique achievement.

"Germany Year 90 Nine Zero" borrows its main character from "Alphaville," a 1965 science-fiction movie in which Godard skewered totalitarian tendencies he detected in modern French society. Older and wiser now, hero Lemmy Caution starts his new adventure as a spy in East Berlin just after the Berlin Wall has tumbled. Heading back to West Germany, he passes through a series of situations involving figures from the past few centuries of European history. He ends his journey in a post-cold-war world that Godard finds both alluring and appalling.

In a recent interview, Godard told me that a movie should be half "spectacle" and half "investigation," using motion-picture technology to uncover truths that would otherwise be undiscernible in our complex world.

"Germany Year 90 Nine Zero" fits this formula, combining the last performance of B-movie star Eddie Constantine with Godard's somber ruminations on culture, creativity, and commercialism. It would be more convincing as an investigation if its spectacle aspects weren't quite so quirky and meandering. Still, it's as fascinating as anything Godard has given us in years, making up in adventurousness what it lacks in easy access.

NEW YORK POST, 1/20/95, p. 42, Larry Worth

[*J.L.G. by J.L.G.* was reviewed jointly with *Germany Year 90 Nine Zero*; see Worth's review of that film.]

NEWSDAY, 1/20/95, Part II/p. B7, John Anderson

[*J.L. G by J.L. G.* was reviewed jointly with *Germany Year 90 Nine Zero*; see Anderson's review of that film.]

VILLAGE VOICE, 1/24/95, p. 49, J. Hoberman

[*J.L. G by J.L. G.* was reviewed jointly with *Germany Year 90 Nine Zero*; see Hoberman's reviewed of that film.]

Also reviewed in:
NEW YORK TIMES, 1/20/95, p. C8, Stephen Holden
NEW YORKER, 2/6/95, Terrence Rafferty, p. 92
VARIETY, 7/11-17/94, p. 44, David Rooney
WASHINGTON POST, 3/31/95, p. D1, Hal Hinson

JADE

A Paramount Pictures release of an Evans/Adelson/Baumgarten production. *Executive Producer:* William J. Macdonald. *Producers:* Robert Evans, Craig Baumgarten, and Garry Adelson. *Director:* William Friedkin. *Screenplay:* Joe Eszterhas. *Director of Photography:* Andrzej Bartkowiak. *Editor:* Augie Hess. *Music:* James Horner. *Music Editor:* Jim Henrikson. *Sound:* Kirk Francis and (music) Shawn Murphy. *Sound Editor:* Sandy Berman. *Casting:* Ronnie Yeskel. *Production Designer:* Alex Tavoularis. *Art Director:* Charles Breen. *Set Designer:* Robert Goldstein and John Chichester. *Set Decorator:* Gary Fettis. *Set Dresser:* Christopher Carlson, Fred Paulsen, John Lister, Scott Newell, and Scott Whitten. *Special Effects:* R. Bruce Steinheimer. *Costumes:* Marilyn Vance. *Make-up:* Robert Ryan and Michael Laudati. *Make-up (Special Effects):* Chris Walas Inc.. *Stunt Coordinator:* Buddy Joe Hooker. *Running time:* 90 minutes. *MPAA Rating:* R.

CAST: David Caruso (David Corelli); Linda Fiorentino (Trina Gavin); Chazz Palminteri (Matt Gavin); Richard Crenna (Governor Lew Edwards); Michael Biehn (Lt. Bob Hargrove); Donna Murphy (Karen Heller); Ken King (Petey Vesko); Holt McCallany (Bill Barrett); David Hunt (Pat Callendar); Angie Everhart (Patrice Jacinto); Kevin Tighe (D.A. Arnold Clifford); Jay Jacobus (Justin Henderson); Victoria Smith (Sandy); Drew Snyder (Executive); Bud Bostwick (Justin Henderson's Brother); Darryl Chan (Tommy Joy); Graham Cowley (Deputy Coroner); Nellie Cravens (Governor's Secretary); Ron Ulstad (Kyle Medford); Allen Gebhardt (Forensic Man); Garrett Griffin (Police Officer); Julian Hill (Forensic); Mini Mehra (Resident); Nicholas Tarvid (Pilot); Harold Morrison (Co-pilot); William Piletic (Priest); Olimpia Saravia (Maid); Tina J. Spangler (Secretary); Issac Spivey (Homeless Man); Victor Talmadge (Lawyer); Kenneth Tigar (Corporate Man); Bill Tolliver (Medical Examiner); James Edward Veurink (Executive); Victor Wong (Mr. Wong); Ron Winston Yuan (Technician).

LOS ANGELES TIMES, 10/13/95, Calendar/p. 10, Kenneth Turan

Watching "Jade" is such a hollow experience it's hard to work up the energy to dismiss it. A movie where the car chases have more personality than the people, its monotone acting and recycled plot make one wonder, not for the first time, how something this tired ever got made.

Prime mover here is screenwriter Joe Eszterhas, last heard from on "Showgirls," whose career is not exactly going from strength. His script baldly rips off his earlier "Basic Instinct" and leaves a collection of loose ends as tangled as Medusa's head and just as likely to petrify viewers.

Based, like "Basic Instinct," in San Francisco, "Jade" familiarly opens with the murder of a wealthy man in his handsomely furnished mansion. Inside the dead man's safe the police discover a roll of film depicting the governor of California (Richard Crenna) having sex with a prostitute (model Angie Everhart).

Instead of a detective, the investigator this time around is Assistant Dist. Atty. David Corelli (David Caruso), who, in typical Eszterhas fashion, soon finds himself up to his neck in the sleazy side of life and searching for a prostitute named Jade who may be the key to the case.

Also drawn into the affair are clinical psychologist and best-selling author Trina Gavin (Linda Fiorentino), Corelli's ex-lover, and her current husband, top defense attorney Matt Gavin (Chazz Palminteri), who also happens to be Corelli's best friend. All three leads are coming off successful work elsewhere and presumably took these stick-figure roles because their agents were able to negotiate hefty salary increases all around.

With its pseudo-raunchy dialogue and slimy situations, "Jade" retreads familiar territory for both director William Friedkin and Eszterhas. And despite the writer's recent public protestations that his women are strong masters of their own fate, he once again hasn't been able to come up with female protagonists who aren't victims or hookers or, more likely, both.

Even if you can stomach that kind of nonsense, "Jade" has a fatal problem in its lackluster ending, so unfocused it seems like part of the movie has been lopped off with scissors. After placing several characters in considerable jeopardy, "Jade" neglects to explain who did what to whom and why. For all the information we're given, the filmmakers might as well have stuck a "tough luck, suckers" logo on the screen.

Director Friedkin, who made his reputation with the chase-heavy "The French Connection," has provided a couple of well-crafted jaunts through Chinatown here, and veteran cinematographer Andrzej Bartkowiak brings a fine degree of professionalism to the visual side. But apparently the director spent so much time worrying about the subliminal visual clues he says he put into "Jade" that he forgot to include any real ones.

NEW YORK POST, 10/13/95, p. 44, Michael Medved

Unsuspecting moviegoers might be enticed into seeing "Jade" based upon the impressive credits of its creators. This, after all, is a steamy new thriller from the director of "The French Connection" (William Friedkin), the producer of "Chinatown" (Robert Evans), and the writer of "Basic Instinct" (Joe Eszterhas).

In this case, however, it would be more appropriate to remember that it's a product of the director of "Cruising," the producer of "Oliver," and the writer of "Showgirls."

In other words, "Jade" has more in common with the worst work of these uneven filmmakers than it does with their best.

The movie begins with an embarrassingly obvious nod to "Basic Instinct," showing a ritualized sexually-tinged murder in an elegant San Francisco mansion. Though we never see either killer or victim, we hear horrible screams and watch a spreading pool of blood, as Stravinsky's "Rite of Spring" fills the soundtrack at deafening volume.

The scene then shifts abruptly to a charity ball, where we meet three school chums from Stanford: wealthy lawyer Chazz Palminteri, crusading assistant District Attorney Caruso, and psychologist/socialite Linda Fiorentino.

Fiorentino is married to Palminteri, but she used to be in love with Caruso, who still carries a torch for her. As if this wasn't enough to keep her busy, she's soon the prime suspect in the murder that opened the film, with Caruso assigned to prosecute the case.

He eventually learns that his old flame's been leading a tawdry double life as an insatiable call girl named "Jade," whose rich, powerful customers include the governor of California (an understated and effective Richard Crenna).

With these high-level connections to the case, it's no wonder that Caruso's star witnesses begin to disappear, leading to an elaborate chase scene in which director Friedkin displays some of his old "French Connection" flash (also in evidence in his under-appreciated "To Live and Die in L.A.").

The problem is that the Eszterhas plot never begins to make sense, and the supposedly revealing conclusion is so muddled, confusing and poorly edited that a half-dozen intelligent, observant friends who talk about the movie afterward won't be able to tie up its many loose ends.

Fiorentino is also a big disappointment—especially after her sizzling, commanding performance in last year's "The Last Seduction." Here, she's preposterous as a brilliant psychologist (where she delivers a supposedly insightful lecture as if reading the phone book) and as an all-powerful sexual predator (here the fascination men are supposed to feel for her is never comprehensible).

Lit and groomed in a surprisingly unflattering manner, she fatally lacks the glamour this role demands—coming across as a bored, slightly frumpy, middle-aged housewife.

None of the characters emerge as anything more than smudged ciphers, so "Jade" fails in its attempts to convey raunchy and exotic eroticism. Actually, it could play in future double-features with "Showgirls" as a staple of high school abstinence classes; it makes sex look dumb and ugly enough to cool the ardor of even the most hormone-addled adolescent.

This murder mystery, in other words, is no "Basic Instinct"; it's better summarized as "Basically, It Stinks."

NEWSDAY, 10/13/95, Part II/p. B6, Jack Mathews

It is a little frightening to think that Joe Eszterhas, the hightest-paid screenwriter in history, and one of the sickest, may be sitting in front of his computer at this very moment coughing up something I will one day be obliged to look at in a theater.

God knows what it might be. The story of a serial necrophiliac who infiltrates the New York City Morgue? A prison psychologist who acts out her patients' violent fantasies? A wealthy socialite who, when her husband's out of town, doubles as a call girl in the rough sex trade?

Whoops, scratch that last one. Done. It's the premise of "Jade," the most recent Eszterhas-written fever dream, arriving less than a month after his Las Vegas lap dance fiasco "Showgirls."

"Jade," directed by William Friedkin, is much more in the vein of "Basic Instinct," the blockbuster erotic thriller that has had studios paying the writer $3 million for every bonehead topless, bottomless or pantyless idea he gets. But this one is so facilely written, so absent of either thrills or eroticism, it might beat "Showgirls" to the video bin.

All the elements of Eszterhas' high-trash formula are present in this story about a passionate San Francisco district attorney (David Caruso), his old friend and courtroom rival (Chazz Palminteri) and the sexual adventuress, (Linda Fiorentino) both men love but neither really knows. The murky plot has Caruso investigating the murder of a wealthy and kinky San Francisco art collector, which leads him to suspect first the governor of California (a rancid Richard Crenna), then Fiorentino.

"Jade," whose title refers to Fiorentino's nom de tarte, merely rehashes the theme (sex is dangerous, if you do it right), characters and setting of "Basic Instinct" without coming close to matching the earlier film's mesmerizing tawdriness.

In the two clear character parallels, Caruso's David Corelli is a soft and wasted version of the cop played by Michael Douglas, and Fiorentino, though her manner is unquestionably sultry, will convince no one she has as earnest a sexual appetite as Sharon Stone. Only Palminteri, as the ethically challenged lawyer, appears to be having any fun.

Besides the dubious plots, bad dialogue, corrupt characters and sexual peccadilloes that distinguish Eszterhas' thrillers, he also gets the big money for writing unsatisfying endings. "Jade" doesn't end, not in the sense of resolving anything. It just stops on a revelation. I would give the writer the benefit of the doubt and say that the original ending appears to have been trimmed in the editing room, except that experience tells me that whatever Eszterhas had in mind, I don't want to know.

NEWSWEEK, 10/23/95, p. 75, David Ansen

Joe Eszterhas is misunderstood. The guy who wrote "Showgirls" and "Basic Instinct" is always getting knocked for creating degraded women characters. Jade puts the lie to this: he can't create credible human beings of either sex. This tired "psychological thriller," directed by William Friedkin, has no psychology and few thrills. Linda Fiorentino (badly lit) plays a cool clinical psychologist who, unknown to her powerful San Francisco attorney husband (Chazz Palminteri), leads a double life as a call girl. Did she also murder a millionaire with an antique ax? That's what her lover, the ambitious D.A. (David Caruso), wants to know. What we want to know is why we should care about any of these stick figures. Eszterhas seems as bored with them as we are. He's just moving his dopey plot. along, leaving Friedkin to fill in the gaps with car chases and irrelevant chinoiserie.

SIGHT AND SOUND, 12/95, p. 47, Mark Kermode

Ambitious San Francisco DA David Corelli enjoys a close friendship with prominent lawyer Matt Gavin and his alluring wife Trina, with whom Corelli once had an affair. When millionaire socialite Kyle is found brutally murdered with one of his prized antiquities (an ancient axe) Corelli is assigned to investigate. In Kyle's safe, Corelli finds photographs of California Governor Lew Edwards making love to an unidentified woman. Against the wishes of Lt. Bob Hargrove and his superiors, Corelli confronts Edwards and suggests that Kyle was blackmailing him. Investigations lead to a lavish beach-house brothel, the scene of the Edwards photographs where video cameras have been secretly installed.

As police scientists struggle to reconstruct a half-burned video tape found there, Correlli and his team trace Patrice Jacinto, Edwards' sexual partner. Jacinto had been asked by her client to act like 'Jade', a hooker of legendary prowess who "took it every way". When fingerprints taken from the axe match those of Trina Gavin and an old beach-house neighbour identifies her as a regular visitor, she is unofficially questioned. Trina claims she visited Kyle on the night of the murder to discuss antiquities and he showed her the axe. Corelli arranges to meet Patrice at a local restaurant, but she is mown down by a black car. The videotape evidence reveals Trina having aggressive sex with a man not her husband. Trina and Matt are summoned to the police station where they react angrily to the taped evidence. Hargrove attempts unsuccessfully to remove Corelli from the case. Trina tries to seduce Corelli and convince him of her innocence. Shunned, Trina has sex with an unidentified man. The beach house neighbour is found murdered. Realising that Trina was with him at the time of the murder, Corelli dashes to the Gavin household where he and Matt kill Hargrove who is attacking Trina. Corelli accuses Governor Edwards of masterminding the murders, and instructs him to leave Trina alone or he will release the photographs. Matt confesses that he killed Kyle, and tells Trina to be 'Jade' for him the next time they make love.

The prospect of director William Friedkin tackling a script by hackneyed erotic-thrills merchant Joe Eszterhas is not one which devotees of either's work should relish. A master of crime-suspense thrillers with a flair for muscular action, Friedkin remains perhaps the single most sexless director currently working in Hollywood. To date, the only one of his movies to forefront erotic visuals is *Cruising*, a savage gay serial killer movie with a sado-masochistic charge which the director would doubtless disavow.

Friedkin's sexlessness is catastrophic for Eszterhas, as the writer has increasingly chosen to rely on voyeuristic titillation and *not* upon a rational engagement with the plot. In the hands of a Verhoeven, whose forte is violent screen sex, Eszterhas's scripts provide an amusing join-the-dots, enabling the action to move from one eye-popping set piece to the next. Strip *Jagged Edge, Basic Instinct* or *Sliver* of their enticing soft-porn trappings, and you're left with a trio of dopey whodunnits with laughably predictable plot twists.

Enter Friedkin, the prince of police-procedurals, who tackles *Jade* like a serious crime thriller, concentrating upon the half-witted plot. Clearly floundering with the narrative, Friedkin throws in a couple of miserably botched salacious fancies before resorting swiftly to the one party-trick he knows he can pull off with aplomb—a rip-roaring car chase through San Francisco and right into the middle of a Chinese New Year Parade. If *Jade* is a failure on almost every other level, this sequence at least joins the elevated train chase from *The French Connection* and the Long-Beach Freeway run from *To Live and Die in LA* in confirming Friedkin as the best car-chase director since Peter Yates. Sadly, this crown Friedkin will have to wear with enough pride to satisfy all his ambitions, for as a serious modern A-list director, he is way out of his depths. As for Ezsterhas, there are video directors such as Alexander Gregory Hippolyte who are tackling erotic thrillers with far more panache. Perhaps he should give Hippolyte a ring; the results could hardly be worse than this.

VILLAGE VOICE, 10/24/95, p. 80, Georgia Brown

Jade is the latest piece of garbage from Joe Eszterhas. The limited appeal of the writer's *Basic Instinct* had a lot to do with Sharon Stone's sly naughtiness, the wry way she, and, to some extent, Jeanne Tripplehorn led Michael Douglas's lust-crazed detective around the Bay Area by his dick. Directed woodenly by William Friedkin, *Jade* is *Basic Instinct* redux, but *B.I.* minus the drollery. Plot and milieu are basically similar, with Linda *The Last Seduction* Fiorentino called on to exhibit the female of the species's kinky predatoriness. The movie features a backless black dress with ropy straps—you see it on the ad, the wearer scaling the wall like a black widow.

The opening shot—a shopper's tour of a male crime victim's lair—shows just what standards of taste have been breached by the filthy (in a double sense) rich owner. In the bedroom are a Balthus (looking so fake the buyer must've been blind) and hundreds of pricey chotchkes, including a collection of silver boxes containing women's hair. Instinctively, an assistant D.A. on the case, David Corelli (David Caruso), goes right for the one bearing the Chinese character for jade (picking it up without donning plastic gloves). He tracks down a jealous red-maned hooker who is eager to reveal that a rival called "Jade" takes it "from behind," takes it from anywhere, for that matter. The redhead, however, has scruples. Of course, *she* is one of the first to get splattered on the roadway.

Small surprise when Jade turns out to be Trina Gavin (Fiorentino), a clinical psychologist specializing in violence in the workplace (in *Basic Instinct*, Tripplehorn was a cop shrink) and the trophy wife of powerful defense attorney Matt Gavin (Chazz Palminteri). Since both are college friends of Corelli, they get special treatment when Trina is accused of offing one of her clients with a ceremonial axe (fancier than an ice pick). Here, too, there's an all-boys interrogation of the suspect, though this time the lady keeps her knees together.

Fiorentino's one-note bitch in *The Last Seduction* was lavishly overpraised, and here the actress looks jittery, plain, and out of her element. But so, I'd say, does everyone. Caruso is particularly washed out and unglamorous and shows none of his NYPD steam. Although looser than his two costars, Palminteri has trouble posing as a high-toned swell, a man of wealth and taste. *In Bullets Over Broadway*, he glowed with good old New York gruffness, whereas in this vulgar production, he's being called on to hide anything coarse and genuine. Maybe you could call me jaded.

Also reviewed in:
CHICAGO TRIBUNE, 10/13/95, Friday/p. J, Michael Wilmington
NEW REPUBLIC 11/13/95, p. 33, Stanley Kauffmann
NEW YORK TIMES, 10/13/95, p. C10, Janet Maslin
VARIETY, 10/16-22/95, p. 93, Brian Lowry
WASHINGTON POST, 10/13/95, p.F6, Rita Kempley
WASHINGTON POST, 10/13/95, Weekend/p. 44, Desson Howe

JAR, THE

An Artistic License Films release. *Producer:* Alireza Zarrin. *Director:* Ebrahim Foruzesh. *Screenplay (Persian with English subtitles):* Ebrahim Foruzesh. *Director of Photography:* Iraj Safavi. *Music:* Mohammed Reza Aligholi. *Running time:* 85 minutes. *MPAA Rating:* Not Rated.

CAST: Behzad Khodaveisi (Teacher); Fatemeh Azrah (Khavar).

NEW YORK POST, 9/27/95, p. 40, Larry Worth

The opening camera shot slowly pans over mountains of desert sand, suggesting an epic to rival "Lawrence of Arabia." But don't hold your breath looking for Peter O'Toole on the horizon.

"The Jar" is about as far from big-budget extravaganzas as movies get. And therein lies both its charm and chief drawback.

The action—or what passes for such—takes place in a remote Iranian village as youngsters drink from the schoolyard's terracotta water jug. Tragedy comes in the form of one student's startling discovery—a crack in the side of the jar.

In a Third World locale where water and survival go hand-in-hand, that's a pretty dramatic turn. And since driving to the nearest Pottery Barn isn't an option, the sentient schoolmaster (handsome newcomer Behzad Khodaveisi) must ponder all options.

The nearest city to stock such luxury items is a long donkey ride away. And that's assuming funding is available, which it isn't. As for the hamlet's only repairman, he refuses to lose a day's pay on a freebie.

The teacher's solution sets off a Rube Goldberg-like chain of traumas that ultimately pits villager vs. villager. And in documenting that process, director Ebrahim Foruzesh initially offers a thought-provoking look at a unique culture.

His penchant for detail—subtly focusing on a child's decayed teeth or letting the light catch in a communal tin cup's dents—makes the production ring true, along with effective portrayals of responsibility, shame and divided loyalties.

Ditto for shots of the spartan countryside and its palette of browns and tans, with bloodletting offering the sole splashes of red.

But a little goes a long way when the plot ranges from thin to non-existent. After the first hour, the cast and crew's lack of sophistication becomes somewhat trying, And the longer the story continues, the more it seems much ado about nothing.

As tedium ultimately takes over, the final segment proves arduous. The whole thing's only 85 minutes, but "The Jar" is one case where less would definitely be more.

NEWSDAY, 9/20/95, Part II/p. B7, John Anderson

Among the world's emerging cinemas, the films of Iran contain a naivete that is refreshing and instructive. They allow us to see what has become cliched with new eyes, to revisit shopworn allusion, with a revitalized appreciation for what really speaks to us as cinema (or literature). Allegorical exercises that would seem precious from a U.S. director are presented without inhibitions. Angst and archetype are married for a vital kind of neo-classicism.

We can see it in the work of even the most sophisticated Iranian filmmaker, Abbas Kiarostami, whose "Under the Olive Trees" was a movie-within-a-movie-within-a-movie but remained grounded in rustic storytelling. Or Darius Mehrjui, whose "Sara"—based on "A Doll's House"—gave blunt immediacy to a play whose message the West generally takes for granted. Or Ebrahim Foruzesh, whose 1992 film "The Jar"—his second feature as a director is a poetically simple tale that is both a portrait of a town and a transcending parable of communality and ego.

At a remote school in a parched Iranian village, the lone teacher (Behzad Khodaveisi) is in a situation known to educators everywhere: He gets little money and his school is overcrowded. He does get the villagers' respect—which is where he parts company with most of his American counterparts—but also their resentment: His education gives him a social standing above his students and their parents, which prompts rumor-mongering and ill will when a crisis occurs.

The crisis is a leak in the school's ceramic water jar. If not for the jar, the children would have to drink from a brook that is both a good distance; away and dangerous for the children (they are predominantly boys, by the way). The teacher knows he can request a new jar from the government, but he also knows that if he gets one it will take weeks. So when a child suggests that another boy's father could fix the leaking jar, the teacher goes to the man for help.

So begins a parade of petty bickering and selfishness. The father demands three ingredients for his cement: ash, lime and eggs. Everyone is happy to contribute ash and lime; few kids come with eggs. When a child repeats what he's heard at home—that the teacher will be using the whites for the cement and eating the yolks himself—the teacher gets angry.

He's actually a generous man and the handsome Behzad Khodaveisi makes him an inspiring presence, one who turns his flaws into assets: When he strikes a child whose fighting has injured a classmate, he atones for his impatience by offering rice his mother has sent him. He feeds the kids his own jam (his mom sent that too) and contributes money for the jar fund (no, the egg whites don't work).

"The Jar" is straightforward and unstylized, but Foruzesh is affectionate and discreet in what he shows about his cranky town. He probably has more respect for his villagers than they have for the teacher—but generosity, of course, is what "The Jar" is all about.

VILLAGE VOICE, 10/3/95, p. 80, Elliott Stein

The emergence of Abbas Kiarostami as a major figure of the world film scene has prompted curiosity about other Iranian cineastes. Ebrahim Foruzesh seems a significant player—he has produced more than 80 films, although *The Jar* is only his second directed work. His first, *The Key* (1987), was written by Kiarostami.

The Jar is set in 1967, years before the Islamic revolution, in a remote but highly photogenic village in the central desert of Iran. Its linear narrative has the limpid simplicity of a fable. There are no fountains in the village—the only sources of water are the large communal jar in the schoolyard and a dangerous stream outside of town. When the jar springs a leak, a major crisis develops. Lining up at the jar had been a socializing activity for the children; its disrepair creates anarchy. No one seems able to fix it; the authorities are in no hurry to replace it. The affair throws the entire power structure of the village into question; this modest society, finding itself inexplicably endangered, seeks a scapegoat—the teacher, an outsider, becomes the target of malicious gossip. Disgusted, the man resolves to leave town.

Foruzsesh's mise-en-scène, sans directorial flourishes, emphasizes the engaging performances of the nonprofessional locals, especially the children. His film's only problem is its length. Bresson might be able to keep us on the edge of our seats with little more than a leaky jar for 90 minutes—at this point in his career, Foruzesh can't.

Also reviewed in:
NEW YORK TIMES, 9/27/95, p. C16, Caryn James
WASHINGTON POST, 11/24/95, p. D9, Hal Hinson

JEFFERSON IN PARIS

A Touchstone Pictures and Merchant Ivory Productions release. *Executive Producer:* Donald Rosenfeld and Paul Bradley. *Producer:* Ismail Merchant. *Director:* James Ivory. *Screenplay:* Ruth Prawer Jhabvala. *Director of Photography:* Pierre Lhomme. *Editor:* Andrew Marcus and Isabel Lorente. *Music:* Richard Robbins. *Music Editor:* Gerard McCann. *Choreographer:* Beatrice Massin and Elizabeth Aldrich. *Sound:* Mike Shoring. *Casting:* Sylvie Brocheré, Joanna Merlin, and Celestia Fox. *Production Designer:* Guy-Claude François. *Art Director:* Thierry François. *Set Decorator:* Bernadette Saint Loubert. *Costumes:* Jenny Beavan and John Bright. *Make-up:* Carol Hemming and Tina Earnshaw. *Make-up (Special Effects):* Pauline Heys. *Running time:* 144 minutes. *MPAA Rating:* PG-13.

CAST: AT JEFFERSON'S HOUSE, THE HOTEL DE LANGEAC; Nick Nolte (Thomas Jefferson); Gwyneth Paltrow (Patty Jefferson); Estelle Eonnet (Polly Jefferson); Thandie Newton (Sally Hemings); Seth Gilliam (James Hemings); Todd Boyce (William Short); Nigel Whitney (John Trumbull); Nicolas Silberg (Monsieur Petit); Catherine Samie (Cook); Lionel Robert (Cook's Helper); Stanislas Carré de Malberg and Jean Rupert (Surgeons); Yvette Petit (Dressmaker); Paolo Mantini (Hairdresser); F. Van Den Driessche, Humbert Balsan, and Michel Rois (Mutilated Officers); Bob Sessions (James Byrd); Jeffrey Justin Ribier (Mulatto Boy); Marc Tissot (Construction Foreman); AT LAFAYETTE'S; Greta Scacchi (Maria Cosway); Simon Callow (Richard Cosway); Lambert Wilson (Marquis de Lafayette); Elsa Zylberstein (Adrienne de Lafayette); Jean-Pierre Aumont (D'Hancarville); Christopher Thompson (Interpreter); Olivier Galfione (Chevalier de Saint-Colombe); Anthony Valentine (British Ambassador); Steve Kalfa (Dr. Guillotin); André Julien and Jacques Herlin (Savants); Elizabeth Kaza and Agathe de la Boulaye (Card Players); Abdel Bouthegmes (Lafayette's Indian); AT VERSAILLES; Michael Lonsdale (Louis XVI); Charlotte de Turckheim (Marie Antoinette); Damien Groelle (The Dauphin); Valerie Toledano (Madame Elizabeth); Vernon Dobtchev (King's Translator); Mathilde Vitry, Catherine Chevalier, and Laure Killing (Ladies of the Court); Felix Malinbaum (Captain of the Guard); Hervé Hiolle (King's Messenger); Christian Vurpillot (Archbishop); Philippe Girard and Eric Berg (Post Office Spies); AT THE PANTHEMONT ABBEY; Nancy Marchand (The Abbesse); Jessica Lloyd (Julia); Olivia Bonamy, Sarah Mesguich, and Virginie Desarnault (Schoolgirls); Sylvie Laguna (Nun); Ndrine Piau and Sophie Daneman (Singers); Denis Fouqueret (Bishop); Annie Didion (Crazed Nurse); AT DOCTOR MESMER'S; Daniel Mesquich (Mesmer); Yan Duffas and Thibault de Montalembert (Assistants); Magali Leiris and Valentine Varella (Patients); Gabrielle Islwyn (Singer with Megaphone); AT THE OPERA; William

Christie (Conductor); Jean-Paul Fouchécourt (Dardanus); Ismail Merchant (Tipoo Sultan's Ambassador); Martine Chevalier (Mademoiselle Contat); Valerie Lang (Demented Woman); AT THE PALAIS ROYAL; Vincent Cassel (Camille Desmoulins); Jean Dautremay (Shopkeeper); Alban Thierry, Alain Picard, and Jean-Marc Hervé (Puppeteers); PIKE COUNTY, OHIO; James Earl Jones (Madison Hemings); Beatrice Winde (Mary Hemings); Tim Choate (Reporter).

CHRISTIAN SCIENCE MONITOR, 4/4/95, p. 13, David Sterritt

"Jefferson in Paris," the new movie from Merchant Ivory Productions, couldn't arrive at a more auspicious moment.

In recent times, pundits and politicians have revived the fashion of invoking early American history as a utopian epoch, shaped by uniquely gifted men blessed with a political wisdom that has since been mysteriously lost.

Bringing into play the artistic wisdom that has brought them to the front ranks of world cinema, director James Ivory and writer Ruth Prawer Jhabvala use their new film to probe not the super-human abilities but the all-too-human complexities of those who faced the, moral and intellectual challenges of 18th-century democracy.

Full of surprises as usual, Ivory and Jhabvala set their story not in the newborn United States but in faraway Europe, using Thomas Jefferson's five-year stint as an ambassador to address such imposing issues as freedom, equality, and revolution.

While the story swings between sweeping historical study and intimate biographical conjecture, its steady focus on Jefferson's complicated nature keeps the film consistently warm and engaging, avoiding the twin pitfalls of neatly mythologizing or crudely debunking the protagonist and his era.

Add the brilliant sensitivity to period detail that has become one of Ivory's most striking trade-marks—every object has the ring of truth, from buildings and furniture to clothing and table set-tings—and you have a work of art that's satisfying on every level, showing that the makers of such literate entertainments as "A Room With a View" and "Howard's End" are still at the peak of their powers.

The film begins in 1784, eight years after Jefferson drafted the Declaration of Independence and—at least as important to the course of his life—two years after the death of his wife, from which he has still not recovered. Arriving in Paris to assume his post as ambassador to the French court, he finds himself in an uneasy land presided over by a weak-willed king and a self-indulgent queen. The two fail to grasp the import of the revolutionary tremors generated by their angry populace with increasing frequency.

Himself a committed revolutionary with a healthy respect for political turmoil, Jefferson ob-serves the growing upheaval with a sort of fatherly approval—reinforced by the respect he receives from progressive French thinkers—while taking an attitude of bemused fatalism toward the obliviousness of his royal hosts. Where a more conventional drama might show him becoming preoccupied with these developments, however, "Jefferson in Paris" depicts him as a fully rounded individual who needs to devote much of his energy to his own concerns.

He keeps up his activities in architecture, agriculture, and other practical fields. He installs his elder daughter in a Roman Catholic school, hoping she'll get a good education while keeping her Protestantism intact, and becomes somewhat distressed when events require him to put his theories of religious freedom into personal practice. He grieves the death of a child in Virginia, and sends for his remaining daughter to join him in Europe.

Busy as all this makes him, he also finds time to strike up a romantic relationship with the British-Italian wife of a foppish French painter—and to begin a second affair, perhaps more de-voted and certainly more sensual, with a slave named Sally Hemings, sister of his personal ser-vant and nursemaid to his youngest child.

Jefferson's involvement with Hemings has inspired every kind of discourse, from prurient gossip to earnest scholarship, in the years since it became widely known. Ivory is no prude—films like "Quartet" and "Maurice" show him to be quite the opposite—but in keeping with the civilized sensibility that always distinguishes his work, he and his collaborators refuse to capitalize on obvious possibilities for sensationalism.

Their treatment shows a Jefferson motivated more by loneliness, insecurity, and the simple need for affection than by the lusts and aggressions so eagerly traded in by conventional movies.

The filmmakers also dodge the temptation to moralize about the relationship in racial terms; instead they portray both white master and black subordinate (not technically a slave while on French territory) as people of their time, reaching to one another for reasons too intricate to explain.

First-rate acting provides firm support for Ivory's approach. Nick Nolte sets his career on a new path with his depiction of Jefferson, combining maturity with vulnerability in a manner that perfectly suits Jhabvala's artfully constructed narrative.

Thandie Newton plays Hemings with a smartly balanced mixture of dignity and playfulness. Greta Scacchi brings a different inflection to the same qualities as the European artist who also captures Jefferson's heart.

The supporting cast includes James Earl Jones as a mixed-race descendant of the Jefferson-Hemings affair; Michael Lonsdale as the sadly bewildered French monarch; and Simon Callow, a normally dependable actor who brings more caricature than conviction to the effeminate painter.

Pierre Lhomme did the finely toned cinematography, charged with the visual luster that Ivory films invariably contain. Richard Robbins composed the nicely functional music, and Guy-Claude François created the impeccable production design. As always, Ismail Merchant is the inspired producer who coordinated these contributions.

FILMS IN REVIEW, 7-8/95, p. 55, Andy Pawelczak

This must be the season for eighteenth century decadence. Along with the villains in *Rob Roy*, we now have Simon Callow in rouge, eye-makeup and lipstick as the effete British painter Richard Cosway in the Merchant/Ivory production *Jefferson in Paris*. Besides Callow's furiously campy performance, nothing much else stands out in this oddly misconceived project in which the drama disappears almost without a trace into the upholstery.

Part of the problem comes from Ruth Prawer Jhabvala's script which never decides what it's all about. She seems to have conceived of Jefferson as a kind of Jamesian hero set loose in revolutionary France. A pragmatic idealist full of longing for Monticello's pastoralism, he's emphatically a man of the New World—on a visit to Notre Dame, he complains about its gloomy, aesthetic monstrosities. Jhabvala, who wrote the screenplay for James' *The Bostonians*, even gives him a classic Jamesian moment when he says the earth belongs to the living—it's like Lambert Strether's famous peroration on "living" in *The Ambassadors*. What the script completely misses is any real sense of Jefferson's intellectual and political passions. We see him writing letters on a contraption that produces duplicates—Jefferson was a profligate and elegant correspondent—and at one point he delivers a speech about private property as a means to happiness, not an end in itself. But it feels patched in to remind us that this is, after all, Thomas Jefferson, an icon of American history. Otherwise, the film spends most of its time charting Jefferson's affairs of the heart with Maria Cosway (Greta Scacchi) and his 15-year-old slave girl, Sally Hemings (Thandie Nevdon), as the Ancien Regime collapses around his feet.

As Jefferson, Nick Nolte ambles through the role. I suppose the filmmakers chose Nolte partly for his quintessentially American looks—with that big, lumbering body capped with long blond hair and the weathered face that still has some traces of boyishness, he looks like a cross between an aging surfer and a classic private eye cum frontiersman. As Jefferson wanders around Paris observing the decadent antics of its upper class citizens and the revolutionary ardor of the rabble—which Ivory signifies, ridiculously, with a shot of a mob rushing through the streets with a head on a pike—Nolte keeps his innate dignity but seems bewildered, not in the manner of an innocent abroad but in that of an actor who can't find the living pulse of his character.

The movie finds its real subject—race—about halfway through, but things don't get any better. Shortly after Jefferson hurts his hand while showing off to Maria Cosway, Sally Hemings arrives in Paris and miraculously cures the wounded member with a home remedy. We're meant to understand that Sally's earthiness and emotional directness—in contradistinction to the artificiality of the Europeans—is just what the doctor ordered, both for Jefferson's hand and his aching heart. This is reinforced when Sally performs a grotesque little dance—it's supposed to be a slave folk dance—and Jefferson is visibly charmed. It's all a cliche and would even be open to the charge of racial stereotyping, if the whole film weren't so swathed in tasteful decor and lifeless acting. The seduction scene itself is carefully ambiguous; as Sally lingers over the sleeping Jefferson, she brushes an imaginary fly from his face and his now powerful hand shoots up to grab her wrist. Seduction? Rape? End scene.

Jefferson in Paris, amidst all its confusions and cop-outs, does have a few minor pleasures: in addition to the aforementioned performance by Simon Callow, there's a quietly intelligent one by Gwyneth Paltrow as Jefferson's daughter with whom he has an unwholesomely close relationship. There's also the shock of recognition when we realize that the old roue who periodically appears is played by Jean-Pierre Aumont. But never has decadence been so little fun, and as a serious film about race in America, the movie has less than nothing to say.

LOS ANGELES TIMES, 3/3/95, Calendar/p. 1, Kenneth Turan

Thomas Jefferson's idea of having fun in Paris was knocking down the walls of his house and putting up new ones. He enjoyed spending his evenings reading thick books and making multiple copies of his diary with the aid of a cumbersome machine. And when he really got worked up emotionally he'd say things like "For an American, freedom of religious conscience is one of our great privileges." Is it any wonder that "Jefferson in Paris" is not exactly crackling with romance and excitement?

Architect, philosopher, writer of the Declaration of Independence and America's third President, Jefferson fits any definition of an extraordinary man, but the more this listless, 2-hour-and-22-minute epic unfolds, the more unclear it becomes why anyone thought the five years he spent in France's capital on the eve of that country's revolution would make an engrossing film. Could it be that the filmmakers got Jefferson confused with the man he succeeded as America's representative at the court of Louis XVI, party animal Benjamin Franklin, and only discovered their mistake once it was too late?

Given that the people involved in the project were the impeccably tasteful trio of producer Ismail Merchant, director James Ivory and screenwriter Ruth Prawer Jhabvala, that is not likely. Responsible for some of the most satisfying films of recent years, including "A Room With a View," "The Remains of the Day" and the masterful "Howards End," the team has also created its share of stiff misfires like "The Bostonians" and "Maurice," a group "Jefferson in Paris" is closely akin to.

Because this is a Merchant Ivory film, the look of the past has been beautifully re-created with great care and the (relatively) little cost of $15 million. "Jefferson" not only outfitted more than 1,500 extras (with fabric manufactured in low-cost India) but pulled off some quite elaborate set pieces, including a festive night at the opera and a memorable day when a robin's-egg-blue hot-air balloon rose above Versailles.

But the successful Merchant Ivory ventures have done more than look attractive, they've forged emotional connections with the audience, something "Jefferson in Paris" is unable to do. A wax-museum movie that is both bland and reverential despite its focus on the great man's love life, "Jefferson" is hampered by its disconnected protagonist, accurately described as a gentleman who "wears his heart under a suit of armor."

Given the prodigious amount of research involved, the film's portrait of Jefferson as grave, formal and unbending, both serious and seriously repressed, is presumably accurate. But accuracy does not ensure interest, and watching this exacting gentleman diffidently cope with not one but two romantic attachments is not the stuff that dreams are made of.

Though he does a better job than scoffers will expect, selecting Nick Nolte to play Jefferson was not inspirational casting. Nolte took the part seriously enough to acquire a Jefferson library of some 200 volumes as well as an on-again, off-again Virginia accent, but he is not one of those actors who plays period easily and the strain affects his performance.

One of these relationships is a liaison historians have bickered about ever since Fawn Brodie's 1974 biography publicized the assertion that Jefferson had several children with a slave named Sally Hemings, his late wife's half-sister. "Jefferson" opens in Pike County, Ohio, in 1873, with a kind of teaser trailer for the Hemings liaison, as Madison Hemings (James Earl Jones), one of those children, claims to a startled reporter that President Jefferson was his father.

The film then flashes back to widower Jefferson's arrival in Paris, where the only woman in evidence is his daughter Patsy (Gwyneth Paltrow). She turns out to be an emotional obstructionist, possessive of her father to the point of hostility toward any potential rivals.

The first woman she faces off against is Maria Cosway (Greta Scacchi), the wife of the celebrated but sexually ambiguous painter Richard (Simon Callow). She and Jefferson archly flirt from almost the moment they meet (if you can call dialogue like her "Tell me about America" and his "The subject is as large as the land itself" flirting), but Jefferson's romantic obtuseness is not so easily disposed of.

Next to catch the Virginia's eye is a young slave named Sally Hemings, who arrives in Paris as a companion for Jefferson's youngest daughter. Though British actress Thandie Newton looking suitably attractive, she does not come off as young (14 going on 15) as the film claims, and she is further handicapped by the script's use of dialect.

The issue of slavery is one of "Jefferson's" main concerns, brought up both by Sally's freedom-seeking brother James (Seth Gilliam) and the high-minded French aristocrats such as the Marquis de Lafayette (Lambert Wilson) who tediously chide Jefferson in two languages for his tolerance of that peculiar institution.

This same inability to fascinate holds true for the film's look at the French Revolution, whose early stirrings Jefferson was witness to. With the exception of a salacious, anatomically correct puppet show, its scenes of a nation in turmoil are on the ponderous side, a situation not even a dinner party with clever Dr. Guillotin demonstrating his new invention on unsuspecting vegetables can alter. "Jefferson in Paris" is what Merchant Ivory films have been unjustly accused of being in the past: pictures at an exhibition, no more, no less.

NEW STATESMAN & SOCIETY, 6/16/95, p. 33, Jonathan Romney

The lunatic diversity you find in even a modest week of cinema releases mocks the notion coherence in a film reviewer's job. Most literary critics wouldn't have to deal with a Mallarmé sonnet in the morning and a Barbara Taylor Bradford after lunch. But this week it struck me that I'd had two intensely unpleasurable experiences from two entirely different films. Both filled me with a sense not just of boredom, but of gaping emptiness; both epitomised my idea of cinema as hell. It occurred to me that they were so far apart, somehow, according to the law of circularity, they had to be essentially of the same kind. You may detect a hidden agenda here—that under cover of seeking out hidden affinities between two unconnected films, I am actually attempting a quite bogus rhetorical exercise. That may be the case. But for a critic, boredom is the most grievous burden of all (after all, we're talking about two hours out of someone's life here), and sometimes rhetoric is the only retaliation we've got.

The films in question are *Jefferson in Paris* and *Bad Boys*—one an historical drama of the grand school, by the reputable firm of Merchant Ivory and Jhabvala; the other, a "flying glass" action movie by the equally renowned team of Don Simpson and Jerry Bruckheimer, the producers of *Beverly Hills Cop* and *Top Gun*. I say *Bad Boys* is "by" them, because their names are highlighted on the publicity material and in the film itself, at the expense of its efficient and hitherto unknown director Michael Bays (which gives a new twist to the idea of anonymous direction).

So, one lofty offering from the most eminent team of Sunday-supplement *auteurs*; and one chunk of fodder so transparently factor-farmed as to have no *auteur* at all. In fact, both films were made by establishments rather than directors and both carry brand names rattler than signatures. I'm inclined to think of "Merchant-Ivory" and "Bruckheimer-Simpson" as resembling not the old Hollywood studio insignias like Paramount or MGM, but culinary labels, so attuned is their work to easy recognition and digestion. It may be Fortnum and Mason in one case and Burger King in the other, but it's all fodder. It's hard to see either film as anything but the latest flavour in a successful line.

Both films fall within instantly recognisable genres—with all the accoutrements. Fine brocades and fine acting in one, guns, girls and jovial effing-and-blinding in the other. In fact, the costume drama and the action movie are arguably the only stable genres that now exist in mainstream cinema, the only ones impervious to the ebb and flow of re-invention and cross-fertilisation. Otherwise, "pure" genre largely exists only in the straight-to-video market where you find strains like the real-life problem movie (*Oprah* operas) or that mix of psychodrama and lingerie ad, the erotic thriller.

Jefferson and *Bad Boys* are as purely generic as they come. *Bad Boys* simply ups the ante on *Beverly Hills Cop*. There's not one feisty, *witz*-spouting black cop, but two—a harassed suburban husband (stand-up comic Martin Lawrence) and a muscular super-lothario (sometime "Fresh

Prince" rapper Will Smith), at comic logerheads. They bust jaws, smash cars, question the size of each other's dick, and get next to a variety of faceless vamps. Business as usual.

It may seem cynical to suggest that the painstakingly crafted *Jefferson in Paris* is every bit as routine a product as *Bad Boys*, but I believe it is. Ismail Merchant and James Ivory simply offer a refinement of the familiar, a new bloom of gravitas they haven't handled before. This time it's the 18th century rather than the late 19th, Paris rather than the Home Counties, fact (supposedly) rather than fiction, Nick Nolte rather than Anthony Hopkins. But we're still being sold the same values. We get diligently researched authenticity, sumptuous tableaux, the work of several "distinguished" players—in short, we know that we're in the hands of experts. Watching both films, we're trusting in the capabilities of technicians: in *Jefferson*, a reputed trio of what the blurbs usually call "expert storytellers", in *Bad Boys*, armies of specialists in ballistics, stunt driving and the deployment of blue neon lighting.

The trouble is, when you know you're in good hands, you tend to lean back and settle into the ride. Fundamentally, these are both in-flight movies that lull you into a trance while you're in transit. One film may hypnotise you with exquisite landscapes after Boucher, the other with bangs and crashes and small-willy jokes; one may be overtly dumb, while the other proclaims itself as "thought provoking" (stimutainment?). But both encourage you to leave your critical faculties at the door.

In his recent book *Flickers*, Gilbert Adair, covering the school of "high culture" drama that Merchant-Ivory films exemplify, says: "It's a type of cinema which excludes us from what might be termed the materiality of film as effectively as a sweet-shop window excludes a craning child from the goodies within—our noses are flattened against the screen."

You could extend that metaphor to the *Bad Boys* school, which excludes us by repeatedly making us start back from the window in alarm—by forever showering broken glass in our faces. Whether it remains augustly intact or splinters in shock after shock, in both cases it's ultimately the window itself that we're aware of; it's the window that displays the name of the film running the show.

So it wouldn't be too much of a surprise if one day Bruckheimer-Simpson were to sink millions into an historical epic, or if Merchant-Ivory did make an action movie—the world's first flying porcelain blockbuster?

NEW YORK, 4/17/95, p. 106, David Denby

Can't we leave the founding fathers to historians and biographers? No good American movie has ever been made about an intellectual in a powdered wig. The clothes are impossible—the ruffles and breeches comically impede physical ease—but an even greater hurdle is the eighteenth-century manner. We enjoy bluster and mere panache in this country, but genuine superiority makes us nervous; and the Founding Fathers, with their unaffected gravity, their rhetorical brilliance and eloquence (in prose, at least), are now as far beyond our comprehension as the sacred statues on Easter Island. In its new production, *Jefferson in Paris*, the Merchant Ivory team approaches this Founding Father with piety and criticism, and the results are forced both ways.

The title *Jefferson in Paris* is dismayingly accurate. The movie offers a generalized view of the great man's years in Paris (from 1784 to 1789) as ambassador, lover, and observer of revolution. The filmmakers show off Jefferson's protean interests so proudly, they seem eager to dispel some vagrant suspicion that Jefferson wasted his time in Paris—as if we thought he were a dissipated undergraduate sprawling among whores. We learn that he set up a beautiful house and then enjoyed the social life of the salons; he dined, collected, visited churches, traded epigrams with aristocrats; he studied new inventions and architecture and flirted with great ladies. He also wrote and wrote, using a primitive but effective device that made a simultaneous copy. All of which is elegantly staged and photographed, and highly pleasing, but so what? The problem is not Nick Nolte, who, at 54, is a mite elderly (Jefferson was 41 when he arrived in Paris), though otherwise fine—straightforwardly and effortlessly masculine, with a strong high forehead. The trouble is that Merchant Ivory cannot make a film about Thomas Jefferson. Anxiety about historical detail seems to stymie their imagination.

They try for a dark side. A widower, Jefferson suffered from melancholy and loneliness, and he became passionate friends with the talented painter—a miniaturist—Maria Cosway (Greta Scacchi), who was young, beautiful, and unhappily married to the twisted fop Richard Cosway

(Simon Callow), another miniaturist. The Jefferson-Cosway friendship, which probably never developed into sexual intimacy, is documented in scads of letters. But screenwriter Ruth Prawer Jhabvala also offers up as uncontested fact Jefferson's love affair with the teenage mulatto slave Sally Hemings (Thandie Newton), the authenticity of which has been much debated by historians. According to this movie, Jefferson lost interest in Maria Cosway because he was entertained nightly by his slave girl.

Merchant Ivory mean to expose the uneasy hypocrisy of an American icon of liberty who arrives in Paris with human property. But Ivory and Jhabvala fail to bring the love affair to anything remotely approaching life. Thandie Newton plays Sally as seductive and cuddlesome, a cloying, tarty flirt who lightens the burdens of the great man's soul. Jefferson is brought low, but the filmmakers, eager to maintain their hero's dignity, give Nolte nothing to do; he's merely amused and affectionate, and when it comes to sex, the film recedes hastily into discretion. But if Jefferson slept for years with a mulatto girl who belonged to him, the affair must have had a perversely erotic charge, a touch of dirty white lust in the slave cabins. Merchant Ivory step into their own trap: They want to make Jefferson into a fabulous monument and a low sex scoundrel at the same time. Their insistence on his hypocrisy has the nagging obviousness, and the timidity, of an academic exercise. Instead of being outraged, we may think something like, "If only we had hypocrites of this quality today!"

Merchant Ivory can't do passion. They never could. They can only do repressed passion—the repressed passion of a woman for another woman (*The Bostonians*), a woman for a man (*A Room With a View*), a man for a man (*Maurice*), a father for his daughter (*Mr. & Mrs. Bridge*), a butler for a great house (*The Remains of the Day*). The intimate foreground of *Jefferson* is wan and rather polite (Nick Nolte and Greta Scacchi stand upright in their elaborate costumes and talk perfect prose at each other). But Merchant Ivory are ideal producers of background; their control has become masterly, in an impersonal way. They don't go in for Stanley Kubrick's weird painterly effects (*Barry Lyndon*) or Peter Greenaway's mocking perversities (*The Draughtsman's Contract*). Instead, the production is limpidly beautiful and unmannered—lavish but never tawdry, active but never frenzied. The trouble is, James Ivory, Ismail Merchant, and production designer Guy-Claude François have rather better taste than the French royalty of the 1780s. So elegant and witty seem the entertainments of Louis XVI, so harmless the pathetic amusements of Marie Antoinette, that the French people come off as rather beastly to have spoiled the royal fun with that nasty revolution. The perfect poise of Merchant Ivory's nostalgia plays them false. It almost always has.

NEW YORK POST, 3/31/95, p. 44, Michael Medved

"Jefferson in Paris" is a lavish 2½-hour costume drama that tries to do so many different things that it loses all focus and falls apart before our eyes.

The celebrated team of producers Ismail Merchant, director James Ivory and screenwriter Ruth Prawer Jhabvala can't decide whether to concentrate on the love life of Thomas Jefferson, the unfolding tragedy of the French Revolution, or the corrupting influence of African slavery on everyone associated with the "Peculiar Institution."

The movie stars the capable Nick Nolte and dramatizes five crucial years in Jefferson's life beginning in 1784 when, at age 41, he arrived in Paris to represent his new nation as ambassador to France.

The lonely widower from Virginia is both repulsed and fascinated by the decadent court of Louis XVI and is especially captivated by the charming Maria Cosway (a perfectly cast Greta Scacchi), flirtatious wife of a prominent painter.

Meanwhile, Jefferson's younger daughter crosses the Atlantic to join him in France, accompanied by her nurse Sally Hemings (Thandie Newton), a 14-year-old slave girl.

Historians still argue about Jefferson's alleged relationship with Hemings, and question the widely circulated story—initiated by political opponents during his presidential campaigns—that he fathered four children with his own slave.

The movie version, however, leaves no doubt about the passionate attachment between them in part because Thandie Newton (the Zimbabwean-born actress who starred in the film "Flirting") is the film's single most formidable asset.

She balances innocence with long-suffering worldliness, and deftly highlights both the horror and the attraction in her "master's" involvement with a mere child who is legally his property.

Seth Gilliam is primarily impressive as Sally's brother James, who covers his resentment toward his owner with a mask of admiring servility.

The movie's frequent depictions of revolutionary France are far less persuasive than its recreations of Jefferson's domestic arrangements, and will probably confuse anyone who is not already familiar with the historical record.

These scenes have the feeling of stilted waxworks tableaux, and function like a long, complicated story with no punch line—since the climactic storming of the Bastille, which took place just weeks before Jefferson's departure from Paris, isn't dramatized at all.

Jefferson's personal stature is also diminished by the emphasis on his dithering, indecisive attraction to Maria Cosway, largely ignoring all his other achievements and interests.

Nolte tried his best to add dignity to the role, struggling with strangely stilted speech meant to echo the language of the great man's letters, but he seems utterly unable to convey the dazzling, kinetic, quick-silver intelligence, and insatiable curiosity, that made Jefferson one of the most remarkable minds of his or any century.

In the end, the movie's shapeless structure reminds us that nearly all of the past triumphs of the acclaimed Merchant-Ivory team ("A Room With a View," "Howards End," "The Remains of the Day") have been reasonably faithful adaptations of distinguished novels; by contrast, the filmmakers seem to be floundering with the freedom afforded them in this original screenplay.

"Jefferson In Paris" (enriched by a splendid musical score by Richard Robbins) represents a rare disappointment for this supremely gifted team, but even their ambitious failures are more intriguing than the solid successes of others.

NEWSDAY, 3/31/95, Part II/p. B5, Jack Mathews

At a presidential reception for Nobel Prize winners in 1962, John Kennedy told his guests that they represented the most extraordinary talent and knowledge ever gathered at the White House, "with the possible exception of when Thomas Jefferson dined alone."

Kennedy was speaking for a lot of historians who regard Jefferson, author of the Declaration of Independence and our third president, as the best and brightest of America's early political leaders. But if the man we meet in James Ivory's "Jefferson in Paris" gives an accurate picture of what he was like to be around, it's no wonder he dined alone.

This is one egocentric, morally ambivalent, sexually confused, wig-headed bore, a man who by all but the most redneck standards of today would be considered both a racist and a misogynist. He was a prig about the casual sexual morality of the French aristocracy, but greedily bedded down with the 15-year-old slave he brought over from Monticello. And in bringing his slaves to a country where owning people was illegal, then encouraging the leaders of the mounting people's revolt, he may also qualify as the first Ugly American.

That is not exactly the impression Ivory and his spectacularly miscast star Nick Nolte were trying to leave. "Jefferson in Paris," a dramatized condensation of Jefferson's private life while serving as U.S. ambassador to France, intends to present a brilliant statesman who, more as a paradox than a hypocrite, found his libertarian idealism at odds with his aristocratic Virginia background. It's easy to understand why the Kennedys identified with him.

All this makes "Jefferson in Paris" sound more interesting than it is. The Merchant-Ivory team, known for such impeccably fine literary adaptations as "Howards End" and "The Remains of the Day," hit the history books for this one and came up with a monumental yawn.

The period backdrops of Paris and its countryside make it as elegantly detailed as any of their previous films, and the story moves with the same deliberate speed. But in trying to fill the gaps in the historical record of Jefferson's private life in Paris, screenwriter Ruth Prawer Jhabvala raised more questions than she answered.

What was the nature of Jefferson's relationships with the Anglo-Italian artist Maria Cosway (Greta Scacchi), with whom he fell madly in love in Paris, and Sally Hemings (Thandie Newton), the slave who became pregnant there with the first of several children she would ultimately bear him?

Biographers poring over the passionate love letters exchanged between the widower Jefferson and the married Cosway disagree on whether they consummated their affair, and the filmmakers, for reasons of drama rather than discretion, sided with the naysayers. Instead, they use Jefferson's sexual frustration to rationalize his affair with Sally Hemings, (debated by biographers, treated here as fact) and to intensify his nearly incestuous passion for his teenage daughter Patsy (Gwyneth Paltrow).

"Jefferson in Paris" is a soap opera trying to pass itself off as psychological biography, and doesn't work as either. Turning Sally Hemings into a precocious vamp who senses her master's sexual unrest and lures him into their first liaison is taking cruel creative license. This learned genius, moralist and control freak can't resist the charms of an illiterate child?

Through the narrative perspective of one of the Jefferson-Hemings offspring (James Earl Jones) speaking to a reporter half-a-century later, the film acknowledges Jefferson's deep ambivalence about slavery, and explains for us the quid pro quo relationships (favored treatment for sexual favors) common between landowners and their slaves. But even if you accept that Sally, the product herself of a slave-master coupling, was merely following the example of her mother, making her the sexual aggressor is a cheap way of softening Jefferson's exploitation of her.

Whether any of this might have been compelling drama was lost with the casting of Nolte, who looks ridiculous in a white wig, and even more ridiculous trying to hide his macho persona behind the arch mannerisms of an 18th-Century aristocrat. This sort of casting against type works better in comedies.

After an excruciating two hours and 24 minutes, the Thomas Jefferson we know is more dilettante than statesman, and rather than humanize their larger-than-life subject, the filmmakers have shrunk him to an emotional weakling who felt sexual power only over his daughter and his concubine. It gives whole new meaning to the phrase "founding father."

NEWSWEEK, 4/3/95, p. 69, David Ansen

One of the intriguing 18th-century artifacts featured in the lavish new Merchant Ivory production *Jefferson in Paris* is a loomlike contraption Thomas Jefferson employs when writing letters, enabling him to produce a simultaneous copy of his text. Director James Ivory has always been fascinated by period details, so you can't be sure if the prominence given this machine is decorative or metaphorical. Is it a comment, perhaps, on the double nature of Jefferson himself, the complex, brilliant statesman/architect and champion of liberty who drafted the Declaration of Independence, yet lived in Paris as the American ambassador to France attended by his black slave James Hemings (Seth Gilliam)?

The Virginian, played by Nick Nolte, was a 41-year-old widower when he landed in Louis XVI's France, a country on the verge of a revolution inspired in part by Jefferson's own words. It's fascinating to learn, as Ruth Prawer Jhabvala's heavily researched script reveals, that at the time Jefferson was minister to the Versailles court, Congress was insolvent, and that one of his accomplishments was procuring a loan from Dutch bankers to remunerate the French volunteers who had fought alongside us in our revolutionary struggle with England.

American movies so seldom delve into our 18th-century roots that one gratefully absorbs the historical details sprinkled throughout this always handsome spectacle. "Jefferson in Paris" is, alas, a better history lesson than a drama. Smart but inert, stately but rhythmless, it circles its contradictory, polymathic hero for nearly two and a half hours without ever quite bringing him to life. Nolte makes a gallant effort but can't entirely disguise that he's not to the manor born.

Ivory and Jhabvala approach Jefferson through his relationship with three women. The first is his beloved daughter Patsy (Gwyneth Paltrow), a highly strung, possessive girl on whom he dotes with a passion bordering on the illicit. The second is Maria Cosway (Greta Scacchi), the married English-Italian aristocrat he gives his heart to, then pulls away from when she offers to leave her husband and Europe for him. The third is Sally Hemings (Thandie Newton), his young mulatto slave and lover, with whom he may have fathered several illegitimate children. Here, the filmmakers are taking their lead from Fawn M. Brodie's controversial best seller "Thomas Jefferson: An Intimate History." The historians can debate the facts of this relationship, but there's no doubt Sally's arrival midway through comes not a moment too soon. Between Nolte and Scacchi there are a couple of sweet moments, but no romantic or erotic *frisson*. With Newton and Nolte the movie finally registers a pulse.

Jhabvala and Ivory aren't out to rake Jefferson over the coals for his racial hypocrisies; they cast a cool, objective eye on both his moral lapses and his intellectual virtues. But judiciousness can take you only so far. What this movie needs is great scenes, and it doesn't have any. When the Merchant Ivory team is at its best—in "Howards End" and "A Room With a View"—you can feel the passion behind the tasteful reserve. But there's no moment in "Jefferson in Paris" when you can feel why the filmmakers *had* to tell this story. All dressed up, this elegant movie has nowhere to go.

SIGHT AND SOUND, 6/95, p. 46, Mike Atkinson

On the eve of the French Revolution. Thomas Jefferson—41, widowed and accompanied by his teenage daughter Patsy and his slave manservant James—comes to Paris as the American ambassador to France. Immersed in the richness of art, architecture and invention, Jefferson begins to court Maria Cosway, a free-spirited painter and society flirt whose marriage to the effete Richard Cosway in no way impairs her love life.

Their affair is restricted to exchanging love letters and beatitudes however, due to Jefferson's lingering feelings for his dead wife and for Patsy, who shares a rather intense intimacy with her father, and because of his various social and professional engagements. Meanwhile, Jefferson gets word that one of his younger daughters has suddenly died in Monticello, the Virginian family home, and he summons his third daughter, Polly, to him. She arrives with her nurse, Sally, James' sister. Soon, just as James begins considering running away to be a free man in France, Sally and Jefferson begin a sexual liaison that results eventually in a pregnancy. Maria finds out through Patsy about Sally's late night visits to the ambassador's bedroom, and breaks off their attachment. As the French Revolution commences and Jefferson is summoned back to the States to be Washington's Secretary of State, he agrees to set free James, Sally and her children back in Monticello, upon his death. He does, and their mixed race progeny live on to tell the tale years later.

Even its committed detractors must admit that the *maestoso* style machine of Merchant/Ivory has made their particular variety of literary costume drama seem effortless. And indeed, with *Jefferson in Paris*, they seem to apply very little effort. Coasting since long before *A Room with a View* on the cozy allure of bustles, mahogany interiors, garden idylls, Edwardian nostalgia and easily adaptable classic novels, Merchant/Ivory (and that includes busy scriptsmith Ruth Prawer Jhabvala) depend so blindly on their heritage details and decor in *Jefferson in Paris* that even the customary degree of grace and assurance has vanished from the formula.

At least the previous Ivory towers were superbly fashioned, however repetitive and quaint. In *Jefferson* there's not much that's convincing on any level—you never forget about the strangers sitting next to you in the theatre. The story, a potentially fascinating gallimaufry of history and speculation (it remains unproven that Jefferson sired children through his slaves), is diffuse and clubfooted. Fitfully, Jefferson courts a married woman, sleeps with a slave, makes and breaks devotional promises to his daughter, but we are given no idea why Jefferson does what he does, or how he feels about it. With Jhabvala's first original screenplay since the Ivory team hit it big adapting Henry James and E.M. Forster, *Jefferson* has the narrative energy of a wax museum and the insight of a primary school history text.

Decor and costuming are meticulous, as well they should be. Yet, although set and shot in France (including Versailles) and despite Jefferson's enthusiasm for architecture, the film's closely framed interiors and *jardin* strolls give us little sense of place—it could've been shot in Toronto. Nick Nolte, looking the part rather smartly, sleepwalks through a drastically underwritten role as if unaware that the entire film pivots on Jefferson's inner turmoil and romantic yearnings. Greta Scacchi as Maria tries in vain to show she's worthy of attention, and even the fiercely talented Gwyneth Paltrow (playing Patsy) is wasted.

No amount of radical historical perspective would have improved *Jefferson In Paris* as a movie, but it might have at least raised a few scholarly and political hackles. As it is, the film's approach to history, politics and especially race relations is disappointingly blinkered. We only see the Parisian rabble as they run by, burning effigies. Perhaps intended to reflect aristocratic tunnelvision, the film's hermetic view of royal life unfortunately comes off as simply decadent. The blazingly apparent conundrum about Jefferson's character—that he was both a fervent, Declaration of Independence-drafting democrat and a slave owner—is, come 1995, the central issue, and the filmmakers know it. Sally and James are therefore at the narrative core. Once there, however, they're given stock conflicts, while Jefferson, whose will and whim is the film's primary topos, remains virtually silent. James hankers for freedom, but he's portrayed as an ungrateful, headstrong drunk. Sally, obviously the more sensible of the two, wants to go back home to Monticello. It's as if the film thinks that it's doing the black characters a favour simply by giving them screen time. Only once is Jefferson pressed by a French statesman as to why negroes aren't included in the Jeffersonian "all men are created equal" definition of democracy, and Jhabvala gives Jefferson no comprehensible answer. The subject is never broached again, although audiences are forced to consider both it and why the film has gone silent on the matter, in every scene.

When Jefferson agrees to free Sally and her kin only after he has died, the film ponders the scene as if it's a moment of great historical import. He in fact died 37 years later; if it were Ivory's intention to reveal Jefferson as a hypocritical lout, there's plenty of ammunition, but the film still attends to the man as if he were a pillar of principle and wisdom. Jhabvala, Merchant and Ivory have devised the scenario to raise questions about Jefferson's legitimacy as a broker of ideals, they answer them by focusing on inane and bloodless romances.

TIME, 4/10/95, p. 82, Richard Schickel

One day long ago, Harry Cohn, the legendary film mogul, found himself contemplating the miniscule grosses of some historical epic set in the 18th century and decreed that henceforth no picture emanating from his studio would feature men in wigs and knee breeches writing with quill pens.

Jefferson in Paris brings this bit of vulgar wisdom back to mind. Regrettably so, for it is the work of that redoubtable trio consisting of producer Ismail Merchant, director James Ivory and screenwriter Ruth Prawer Jhabvala. With films like *Howards End* and *Remains of the Day*, they have, almost alone, kept alive what in Cohn's day was one of Hollywood's more agreeable genres: the handsomely made, well-acted literary-historical drama. These movies reflected the cultural aspirations of producers like Irving Thalberg and David O. Selznick while serving the needs of that portion of the audience not enamored of car chases and tommy-gun fire.

The problem with this kind of filmmaking has always been caution. And that's what is wrong with *Jefferson in Paris*. It's as if everyone was just a little too much in tasteful awe of its subject, who is played rather stolidly by Nick Nolte. They are afraid to grant him his full vitality or give full dramatic life to the issues, public and personal, that stirred him during the five years (1784-89) when, recently widowed, he served as the new American republic's ambassador to France.

At the time, Jefferson had much of interest on his mind. The nation to which he was accredited was in a pre-revolutionary condition, and members of the liberal aristocracy (his particular friends) were trying to ameliorate the situation. At the same time the great deist's daughter Patsy (Gwyneth Paltrow) is flirting with Catholicism, even thinking about taking vows. Their relationship is not improved when Jefferson starts courting a married woman, the painter Maria Cosway (Greta Scacchi), and deteriorates farther when Sally Hemings (Thandie Newton), one of Jefferson's slaves, arrives from Virginia and they begin their notorious (though historically unconfirmed) love affair.

There is plenty of material here for a gripping story about a man whose habits of life and belief are being challenged in all sorts of ways. But essentially the movie settles for pretty pictures. The love stories are presented with gingerly discretion. Jefferson's affair with Maria is all arch, twittering banter in an antique style; nothing in it elevates their pulses (or the audience's). Hemings is presented as a wise, if untutored, child, more of a nursemaid to Jefferson than a believably sexual being. It's hard to see what he saw in either of them, and the script does not provide any fully developed scenes of dramatic conflict between them. Even Jefferson's endless intellectual curiosity is seen more as an eccentricity than a vital force—like his sexuality, muted and eventually strangled in fastidious gentility.

VILLAGE VOICE, 4/4/95, p. 50, Gary Dauphin

Essentially a tony update of Dino De Laurentiis's slave-ploitation production *Mandingo*, *Jefferson in Paris*, has the gall to treat American chattel slavery as a complication of merely Clintonesque proportions (Jefferson owned slaves, but didn't inhale), having the drafter of the Declaration of Independence and third president call slavery an "evil" in its first half even as the same institution allows him to bed down and impregnate Sally Hemings, his daughter's 15-year-old nurse for a second act.

While these are the facts of Jefferson's life, the Merchant Ivory brain trust is so smug in the conviction of their Midas filmmaking touch that they must have figured all this story needed to be told was James Ivory's obsessive-compulsive attention to the details of costume and furnishing, and Ruth Prawer Jhabvala's ear for Byronic exchanges. They were wrong. Lurid as it might have been, at least De Laurentiis's softcore flick had the perverse intelligence to know that certain forms of racial ugliness are a cesspool best understood through wallowing, whereas *Jefferson* is a mannered and unacceptable invitation to traverse the same rank site with petticoats hiked and no more than an aristocrat's cloak (albeit prettily woven) for a footbridge.

Screenwriter Jhabvala opens the film with a reporter's visit to the post-Civil War home of Madison Hemings (James Earl Jones, playing the alleged son of Thomas Jefferson), aligning *Jefferson in Paris* with a revisionist view of history even as its subsequent episodes are strictly racial business as usual. Satisfied to have that historical wrinkle out of the way, the next hour of the film covers the five years TJ ambassadored his way around pre-Revolutionary France. Surprisingly, Nick Nolte manages to convey the title character's contradictions ably enough. Recently widowed and taking a dim view of his continental hosts' foibles, Nolte's Jefferson is a mix of distraction and Kevin Costner-ish moral earnestness, a credible early American in Paris. This TJ is a strong silent type who happened to pen one of the great documents of the democratic tradition.

Over time (lotsa time: *Jefferson* proceeds at a gilded snail's pace), TJ's main occupations settle into apologizing for slavery and the juggling of various women. In one scene, after his formulation that "all men are created equal" is tossed back at him during a discussion of slavery, Jefferson blames the institution's continued existence on the democratic process, explaining that he'd wanted slavery abolished but was outvoted. As for the ladies, first and foremost there is TJ's own daughter Patsy (Gwyneth Paltrow), whose loving relationship with her father threatens to tip over into the incestuous every time she's alone with him. Having replaced her dead mother as the Lady of Monticello, Patsy is constantly promising TJ that she will never leave his side, the pair nearly giving each other open-mouthed busses at least twice. (Patsy's later outburst about slavery seems honest despite the fact that it's bound up with her sexual confusions.)

Then there is Mrs. Cosway (Greta Scacchi). Since this is, after all, a Merchant Ivory production, a more traditional impossible romance is called for than Patsy, and Maria Cosway fits the bill perfectly. A thoroughly continental (i.e., "liberated") woman, Maria wittily flirts her way into TJ's estimation, their affair aided and abetted by her preening fop of a husband, English portraitist Richard Cosway. At first TJ throws himself into the affair with equal enthusiasm, but when he breaks his wrist while jumping over a pile of logs (this in order to prove his mad, mad love for her), he reevaluates things, distancing himself from Cosway and the foolish European ways she's come to represent.

Jefferson is typically wonderful to look at (the scenes of the French court are textural marvels) and its white-white romantic goings on would be material enough for most historical melodramas. But by focusing on these particular five years of Jefferson's life, Ivory and Prawer Jhabvala set themselves the task of telling a third "love" story, and one whose dominant metaphor has historically been understood by most thinking people as rape. *Jefferson* prefers to view it as a combination of homesickness and seduction: Sally Hemings (a shucking and living Thandie Newton, who last appeared as mulatto finger food in *Interview With the Vampire*) arrives in France, and before you can say "I ain't scared ah you, Massa" (which, incidentally, Sally, does say), she's happily carrying her master's child. TJ is oblivious to her charms until Sally, buxom and homespun creature that she is, takes it upon herself to mix up a poultice of mustard and ash "foh dat dere wrist, Massa," a concoction that causes Jefferson to exclaim: "Sometimes our good old American remedies really are the best!"

Best remedy indeed, TJ, for the fact of the matter is that his comfortable slide into an offscreen liaison with a young slave (not to mention the negotiated return of Sally and her brother, James, to slavery) is as slave-holding American as apple pie. The facts of Thomas Jefferson's life though they may be, there's a fundamental ugliness to them that no amount of pretty pictures can hide. History is history, but it's the desire to give that ugliness the "Merchant Ivory" treatment which makes *Jefferson in Paris* a failure and an insult.

Also reviewed in:
CHICAGO TRIBUNE, 4/7/95, Friday/p. C, Michael Wilmington
NEW REPUBLIC, 4/24/95, p. 30, Stanley Kauffmann
NEW YORK TIMES, 3/31/95, p. C1, Janet Maslin
VARIETY, 3/27-4/2/95, p. 74, Todd McCarthy
WASHINGTON POST, 4/7/95, p. D7, Hal Hinson
WASHINGTON POST, 4/7/95, Weekend/p. 45, Eve Zibart

JEFFREY

An Orion Classics release of a Workin' Man Films presentation in association with the Booking
Office. *Executive Producer:* Kevin McCollum. *Producer:* Mark Balsam, Mitchell Maxwell, and
Victoria Maxwell. *Director:* Christopher Ashley. *Screenplay (based on his play):* Paul Rudnick.
Director of Photography: Jeffrey Tufano. *Editor:* Cara Silverman. *Music:* Stephen Endelman.
Music Editor: Shari Schwartz. *Choreographer:* Jerry Mitchell. *Sound:* Matthew Price and
(music) Jon Goldberger. *Sound Editor:* Anthony "Chic" Ciccolini III. *Production Designer:*
Michael Johnston. *Set Decorator:* Andrew Baseman. *Set Dresser:* Donna Drinkwater.
Costumes: Daniele Hollywood and Alan Markinson. *Make-up:* Debbie Zoller. *Make-up
(Sigourney Weaver):* Vincent Longo. *Stunt Coordinator:* George Aguilar. *Running time:* 92
minutes. *MPAA Rating:* R.

CAST: Steven Weber (Jeffrey); Peter Jacobson (Man #1); Tom Cayler (Man #2); David
Thornton (Man #3); Lee Mark Nelson (Crying Guy); John Ganun (Tourist); Michael T. Weiss
(Steve); Joseph Dain (Movie Theater Guy #1); Jeffrey Ross (Movie Theater Guy #2); Irma St.
Paule (Mother Teresa); Patrick Stewart (Sterling); Nicky Paraiso (Salesman); K. Todd Freeman
(Barney's Waiter); Robert Klein (Skip Winkley); Patti Ann O'Connell (Cheryl the Showgirl);
Patrick Kerr (Waiter/Actor/Policeman); Peter Bartlett (Casting Director); Christine Baranski
(Ann Marwood Bartle); John Seidman (Boss); Victor Garber (Tim); Bryan Batt (Darius);
Barton Heyman (Elderly Man); Darryl Theirse (Homeboy); Camryn Manheim (Single Woman);
Sigourney Weaver (Debra Moorhouse); Kathy Najimy (Acolyte); J. Smith Cameron (Sharon);
Ethan Phillips (Dave); Lou Sumrall (Thug #1); Robert Capelli, Jr. (Thug #2); Vinny Capone
(Thug #3); Nancy Ticotin (Woman in the Window); Peter Maloney (Dad); Debra Monk
(Mom); Marcus Lovett (Memorial Guest); Michele Pawk (Young Mother); Demetri Corbin
(House Manager); Alexander Cohen Smith (Child); Nathan Lane (Father Dan); Mary Bond
Davis (Church Lady #1); Lenka Peterson (Church Lady #2); Olympia Dukakis (Mrs.
Marcangelo); Gregory Jbara (Angelique); Peter B. (Master); Albert Macklin (Slave); Michael
Duvert (Sean); Alison Sheehy (Network V.O.); Sarah Peterson (Nurse); Marylouise Burke
(Aunt Phyllis); Joe Ponazecki (Uncle Barney); Alice Drummond (Grandma Rose); Henry Stram
(Cousin Gary).

FILMS IN REVIEW, 9-10/95, p. 57, Kenneth L. Geist

The biggest laugh in *Jeffrey* comes from a cut from the gay protagonist kissing his boyfriend
to a pair of straight couples watching them in a movie theater. The repulsed young men in the
audience jeer and turn away while their women dates huddle closer.

By anticipating heterosexual antipathy to gay osculation this isolated commentary in the film
seeks, unsuccessfully, to disarm it.

Jeffrey is a cartoon-like comedy which jeers at the possibility of its horny title character (Steven
Weber) remaining celibate in the AIDS era.

Catholic clergy will find the film's scoffing at Jeffrey's choice as irritating as the portrayal of
a lecherous priest (Nathan Lane) who awkwardly puts the make on Jeffrey when he comes to
church for guidance in his struggle to deny his sexual instincts.

Jeffrey is a too faithful screen adaptation by Paul Rudnick of his successful, 1993 Off-Broadway
play. The movie version reminds us that highly stylized scenes, which can work well in the more

artificial medium of the theater, are hard to bring off when you are actually shooting in Sheridan Square, especially for a first time filmmaker like Christopher Ashley, who directed the stage play. (A number of the play's theatrical highlights—such as the opening bedful of Jeffrey's sexual partners—are sadly missing.)

To compensate for the specialized nature of the film and the obscurity of its curiously unphotogenic leads (Weber and Michael T. Weiss as a the HIV bartender who is Jeffrey's intended), the production has enlisted a number of name players to lure an audience: Patrick Stewart plays a haughty decorator, Sigourney Weaver does a cameo as an egotistical TV evangelist, while Olympia Dukakis drops in for two scenes as the enthusiastic mother of a pre-op transsexual. These actors don't serve to redeem the displaying enterprise. Even the cinematography of Jeffrey J. Tufano often looks dim, and he does little to make the unappealing male leads look attractive.

The film's theology of divine fate as a balloon, capricious in its suspension and fall, is as philosophically lightweight as the rest of the fluffy script.

When the snide decorator sobs over the death from AIDS of his lover (a dancer in *Cats*), you realize the picture wants us to cry as well as laugh. I already knew Rudnick's swell jokes from the play and left the film dry eyed.

Hollywood may well point to the failure of this low budget film to confirm its belief that gay films don't sell and that gay AIDS subjects are best left to television.

LOS ANGELES TIMES, 8/4/95, Calendar/p. 4, Kevin Thomas

"Jeffrey," the popular Paul Rudnick gay romantic comedy, makes the transition from stage to screen so awkwardly that its heavy-handed flamboyance threatens to subvert its brave and important message: Hate AIDS, love life!"

Some genuinely funny lines do sparkle, and there are some staunch portrayals (especially by Patrick Stewart) as well as truly poignant moments, but they're all but overwhelmed by an overdose of raucous, bitchy, sledge-hammered camp humor.

Although the film is abundantly affectionate in its depiction of gays—stereotypical and otherwise—it is no more successful a screen adaptation than the clunky film version of Harvey Fierstein's "Torch Song Trilogy."

Rudnick, who adapted his own play, and Christopher Ashley, the play's director in his film debut, don't seem to grasp the need to scale down performances and to rethink the entire play in visual terms or how to control tone. It's axiomatic that the more theatrical its material, the more visually stylish a film must be to sustain it.

"Jeffrey" is wildly uneven, and it aims at the lowest common denominator in its exceedingly broad comedy. It's like the difference between experiencing a fine production of "Steel Magnolias" on stage and its overblown film version.

The film opens with its most effective device, a montage showing how gay waiter/aspiring Manhattan actor Jeffrey (Steven Weber) discovers his love life withering away out of an escalating, all-consuming fear of AIDS.

Just when he's sworn off sex, he meets at his gym a hairy-chested, sweet-natured hunk named Steve (Michael T. Weiss), who experiences love at the first sight of Jeffrey. Right away, there's a credibility problem: Jeffrey is an ordinary-looking guy with a rather colorless personality aside from his fear of sex, whereas Steve is a spectacular-looking, macho but tender man. You have to wonder why Steve, who is in fine health but has been HIV-positive for five years, bothers with the diffident, retreating Jeffrey.

As Jeffrey and Steve skirmish, Rudnick and Ashley take us on a tour of Manhattan gay life—a gay parade, an AIDS fund-raising ball with an outrageous dancing waiter sequence and hosted by a shrill Christine Baranski, a strident cameo by Olympia Dukakis as the loud-and-proud mother of a "pre-operative transsexual lesbian son," and a frenetic encounter with a lecherous Broadway musical-lover, gay priest-philosopher (Nathan Lane).

There's also a fantasy game show "It's Just Sex," hosted with apt unctuousness by Robert Klein, plus a funny turn by Sigourney Weaver as a bullying, double-talking New Age evangelist who tries to buffalo a troubled acolyte (Kathy Najimy) as well as Jeffrey. (At one point Jeffrey is cared for by Mother Teresa after a gay bashing.)

The film spends much of its best time, however, with Stewart as a hilariously acerbic but strong and gallant interior designer whose young lover Darius (Bryan Batt), a "Cats" chorus boy, is bravely slipping from HIV-positive to full-blown AIDS. Peter Bartlett has a nifty, comical cameo as a waspish casting director.

Weber was probably cast as Jeffrey because he has an Everyman look with which many people can identify, straight or gay, but Jeffrey is so nerdy, it's hard to go along with the film's great concern for him as to whether or not he flees home to Wisconsin.

As Steve, Weiss has terrific presence and real potential, but like most of the cast, has been directed as if he were playing under a proscenium instead of for the camera. "Jeffrey" certainly has enough going for it to connect with easily pleased audiences, but is sure to disappoint more demanding moviegoers, straight or gay.

NEW YORK POST, 8/4/95, p. 44, Thelma Adams

As Sterling, a preening interior design queen, Patrick Stewart commands the sales floor at Barneys with all the shoulders-back bravura of Capt. Picard—but with a better color sense. Stewart's performance cuts high camp with just the right amount of understated tragedy, delivering one of the keenest pleasures of "Jeffrey." Engage!

The delirious Nathan Lane (Nathan Detroit in the Broadway revival of "Guys and Dolls") flies in the face of convention and will no doubt ruffle feathers as a horny, gay Catholic priest. Father Dan sees shades of the divine in sex and musical comedy. His notion of God is lighter than air: He's the guy at a picnic who taps the balloon aloft just before it hits the ground.

Who can compete with the dead-on social satire of the "Hoe-Down for AIDS" set at the Essex House ballroom? Dr. Sidney Greenblatt and his Mount Sinai Ramblers provide the musical accompaniment for a Busby Berkeley-style dance number in which the cater waiters ("the gay National Guard") circle the red-ribboned hostess (Christine Baranski of TVs "Cybill") before leaping into each other's arms and simulating sex.

At one time, an AIDS comedy would have been considered an oxymoron. Writer Paul Rudnick ("Addams Family Values") can sling a mean one-liner and torch a taboo with the best of them. He joins forces with his off-Broadway partner, director Christopher Ashley, to transplant their award-winning play from the stage to the screen.

The story line is as thin as Stewart's hair: It's a tale of two couples, one at the end and the other at the beginning of a relationship.

Fed up with the demands and tensions of safe sex, gay guy about town Jeffrey (the appealing Steven Weber of TVs "Wings") is ready for celibacy. Just when he's ready to "just say no," he meets dreamboat bartender Steve (newcomer Michael T. Weiss). There's a glitch: Steve is HIV positive; Jeffrey isn't, and he just can't handle entering into an intimate relationship with death so close at hand.

Meanwhile, Sterling downplays the health of his much-younger, HIV-positive lover. Darius (Bryan Batt), a chorus boy in the musical "Cats," has begun to have dizzy spells. Sterling believes he can will the symptoms away, drape them in denial, wrap them in wit, but he ultimately learns "the limits of style."

Stewart and Weiss carry the emotional weight in a universally strong cast. When Jeffrey stands Steve up, the bartender does an angry disco dance alone in his apartment, a tarantella to exorcise his own fear of death and frustration, that hit me in the gut.

With "Jeffrey," the greatest pleasures play scene by scene rather than revealing themselves dramatically. One-liners, though they alternately tickle or sting, cannot carry the weight of a story that must shift effortlessly between keeps the movie from gaining power as the set pieces accumulate. The final message, delivered by Darius, reduces to an epigram suitable for embroidering on a pillow: "Hate AIDS, love life."

NEWSDAY, 8/4/95, Part II/p. B9, Jack Mathews

In attempting to sell Christopher Ashley's comedy/drama "Jeffrey" as a gay love story for a crossover audience, the filmmakers have taken to comparing the movie to the Rock Hudson/Doris Day doodles of the late '50s and early '60s. While the comparison holds on one level—the films share a severe case of the courtship cutes—this "Pillow Talk" is definitely not for everyone.

"Jeffrey," with a script adapted by Paul Rudnick from his 1993 Off-Broadway play, is the story of a young gay man (Steven Weber, from TV's "Wings") who has moved from rural Wisconsin to Manhattan, presumably for the more liberal lifestyle, and has since become convinced that the only way to live with the threat of AIDS is to live without sex.

The triggering incident for Jeffrey's decision, played out under the sheets in the opening scene, is his discovery that his condom has ruptured during sex. It's a shock and an embarrassment to him, and a true mood killer for his lover, who leaves in a huff. Talking directly to the camera, as he does throughout the movie, Jeffrey swears off sex, even though he regards its pleasures as God's most divine gift to the human race.

But no sooner has Jeffrey made his decision than he meets the hunk of his dreams at the local gym, and just as his will is about to yield to temptation, the other man (Michael T. Weiss) responsibly announces that he is HIV-positive. The conflict of fear and desire that follows, leavened with some hilarious comic bits, is the source and substance of the movie.

If anybody can find humor in a plague, it's Rudnick. The playwright and screenwriter ("The Addams Family Values") is sort of a Henny Youngman of pop culture; his punch lines never seem to follow the setups, which makes the jokes all the better. He is also a great sketch writer, and while the episodic nature of "Jeffrey" exposes the underlying weaknesses of the story, some of those cameo-studded episodes are priceless.

Sigourney Weaver has a grand time chewing the scenery as a pop-psychology guru who administers tough love to an auditorium filled with the walking wounded. Nathan Lane is a riot as an aggressive gay priest who comes on to Jeffrey in the confessional. And "Star Trek's" Patrick Stewart, in the most sustained supporting role, is perfect as an aging queen with the biggest heart in the Big Apple.

But the sentimentality and coyness of the on-again, off-again romance between Jeffrey, who is a perpetual whiner, and Weiss' ardent Steven is excruciatingly shallow. It begins as a relationship fueled entirely by lust—for Jeffrey, it's love at the first sight of muscle and crotch—and then, in the absence of quick sexual gratification, evolves into something like adolescent infatuation.

Ashley, who directed the play, is on his first outing as a film director, and his inexperience shows. Though the film has opened up the play in airy fashion, with scenes shot in outdoor settings from Central Park to Washington Square, the intimate moments between Weber and Weiss are strained and unconvincing, particularly when the core issue—how can a moral person reject a lover with a terminal illness?—turns the last act into a pointed lecture.

Despite its jarring leaps from exuberance to maudlin sentimentality, "Jeffrey" is hard not to appreciate. It offers what seems an honest glimpse into a lifestyle permanently altered by the presence of a killer virus, and into a culture that has not lost its sense of humor.

SIGHT AND SOUND, 4/96, p. 47, Peter Matthews

It's New York City in the mid-1990s, and Jeffrey has a problem. He's a single gay man who loves sex; the trouble is that erotic encounters in the Aids era get bogged down in complex rules and paranoias. After a series of pick-ups in which safe sex is taken to ever more bizarre extremes, Jeffrey makes a decision: he will give up sex entirely.

To sublimate his libidinal energy, Jeffrey starts going to the gym. However, during a bench-press exercise, he meets the dishy Steve, who immediately comes on to him. Jeffrey is sorely tempted, but escapes without making a date. On the street, he is knocked down by a car—and apparently comforted by Mother Teresa. He runs into his best friend Sterling, an interior designer, and the two discuss his new resolve in the course of a shopping expedition. Sterling, Jeffrey and a sales assistant are then transported to a fantasy game show called "It's Just Sex", where the most stylish answer wins. Jeffrey loses when he admits he is an actor.

Trying to channel his energy into his career, Jeffrey auditions for the role of a tough cop on a television series—but gets cast as the effeminate neighbour instead. Discouraged, Jeffrey returns to his job as a 'cater-waiter' at a "Hoe Down for Aids", he again meets Steve, who is working as a bartender. All the waiters join in a sexy Busby Berkeley style dance routine, but Jeffrey still eludes Steve. Sterling and his boyfriend Darius, a dancer in *Cats*, have Jeffrey over to dinner, and he sees how contented they are, despite Darius' HIV positive status. But the couple has also secretly invited Steve, who at last persuades Jeffrey to date him. Soon after, however, Steve confesses that he too is HIV positive.

Reeling from the news, Jeffrey seeks counsel from Sexual Compulsives Anonymous, from a self-styled post-modern evangelist and even from his parents (who suggest phone sex as the solution). In the end, he can't go through with the date. After an awkward chance meeting with Steve, Jeffrey gets queer-bashed, and again Mother Teresa appears. Still looking for answers, Jeffrey visits a church, where he meets the lecherous Father Dan. The latter, an aficionado of Broadway musicals, tells him to grab at happiness where he can.

Instead, Jeffrey plans to run back home to his parents in Wisconsin. At the Gay Pride festival, he encounters Steve and his new boyfriend, Sean. Some time later, Darius collapses at the ballet and dies in hospital. A devastated Sterling berates Jeffrey for his cowardice; but then Darius appears in a celestial vision and dares Jeffrey to take on life. Steve and Jeffrey finally have their date—an intimate dinner for two, with Mother Teresa tinkling away at the piano.

It seems mean to knock *Jeffrey*, a modest and well-intended romantic comedy about sex in the Aids era. The movie isn't designed to bear close scrutiny, nor do the film-makers appear to care about this particularly—nor did the preview audience, who howled delightedly at even the most faded instances of fag bitchery. It's all fairly pleasant if one relaxes one's critical faculties, and there are perhaps good reasons why gay audiences (at whom *Jeffrey* is mainly targeted) choose to do just that. Still, hold the movie up to any decent standard—say, Richard Glatzer's incredibly fresh and sweet-natured *Grief* (which needs no sort of indulgence to enjoy)—and its awkwardness comes depressingly into view.

The mildly *risqué* premise is that anxiety about HIV can operate as a romantic impediment in pretty much the same way Cary Grant's fidgety trepidation once kept Katharine Hepburn temporarily at bay. Jeffrey must learn to stop being such a droopy-drawers and seize the day—because his suitor Steve may not, after all, have so many days left. Paul Rudnick's script (based on his 1993 off-Broadway play) eschews the morbid tone of earlier Aids dramas, and tries very hard for brio and effervescence. The point is that whatever has traditionally been called shallow in gay culture—the campness, the style-consciousness, the compulsive cruising (here persevered with even at a memorial service)—actually comprises its best spiritual defence against mortality.

Rudnick wheels on a number of flighty, frivolous queens to make the message explicit and he doesn't forget that surefire laugh-getter, a randy priest, who explains how the presence of God can be felt in Lerner and Loewe musicals. There is shallowness and shallowness, however, and the movie would be more plausible if it remotely lived up to its own philosophy. One registers the odd bright line (such as the swishy interior designer Sterling's outraged "Leave this house!" on discovering that his partner Darius has never heard of Ann Miller); but the dawdling episodes and their squat, ugly staging seem calculated, on the whole, to disprove the idea that gay men have better taste than other people.

The film is really just a series of throwaway skits which Rudnick and the director Christopher Ashley (who was also responsible for the stage version) have attempted to lard with parody and freaky fantasy. Characters are apt to be whisked off to a sexy quiz show or find themselves in the middle of a production number, and Mother Teresa materialises for one running gag (which, however, works only if you think her proximity to homosexuals is intrinsically hilarious). The effect is—to put it charitably—hit-or-miss; and one feels faintly sorry for such guest stars as Sigourney Weaver and Olympia Dukakis, who get trotted out like goodwill ambassadors and then look clueless at the shapeless weirdness of their few scenes.

On the bonus side, there is Patrick Stewart (the authoritative Captain Picard in *Star Trek: The Next Generation*), whose Sterling takes the concept of casting-against-type into a new dimension. Somewhat provocatively, the movie claims this old-style flaming creature as the genuine article compared with 'normal', respectable queers. Too bad, then, that Jeffrey himself is so drippy a point of audience identification. Steven Weber tries gamely, but his strenuous mugging fails, by a long shot, to convince us that our hero is a funny guy. In fact, the character is quite exasperating in his wimpish refusal to get on with things; and though this seems in part deliberate, it's also because his fears have no real bite. How could they in the pedagogic sitcom format the film-makers have chosen? The miracle is that Stewart and Michael T. Weiss (who plays the spurned Steve) occasionally break through the plastic proceedings with something more viscerally felt. As for Jeffrey, the movie gangs up on him with so many glib exhortations to happiness that one eventually develops a sneaking sympathy for his doubt. At least it's halfway human.

TIME, 8/28/95, p. 69, Richard Corliss

[*Jeffrey* was reviewed jointly with *The Usual Suspects* see Corliss' review of that film.]

VILLAGE VOICE, 8/8/95, p. 54, Gary Dauphin

As the movie adaptation of Paul Rudnick's well-regarded Off-Broadway play about one gay man rediscovering sex and his sense of humor as friends slowly die around him, there are a number of things riding on *Jeffrey*. First and foremost, there's the question of Hollywood's phobia about putting gay subject matter front and center. Although *Jeffrey* deals with that through a prominent onscreen kiss in its early going, there's a sign of other complications when just after planting his two male leads in a close-up clinch, director Christopher Ashley (who also directed the play) cuts away to a shot of two white-bread breeder couples looking stupidly aghast in a hypothetical—and empty—multiplex. The fact that comic disgust gets almost as much screen time as the kiss indicates that even in a film as gay positive as *Jeffrey*, there are compromises involved in moving from stage to screen.

After its title character (played by Steven Weber of NBC's *Wings*) swears off sex out of fear of contracting AIDS, *Jeffrey* spends most of its time working out his neurotic kinks using Rudnick's well-turned vignettes and comic exchanges. Jeffrey falls for an HIV-positive hunk at the gym (Michael T. Weiss), and the film finds the wit and heart to play that setup for laughs as well as poignancy. Most of the jokes aren't Weber's (his best punchlines are nonverbal, sitcom-honed double takes and eye-pops); they belong to Rudnick's cast of side characters, from Sigourney Weaver's psychotic self-help guru, to Nathan Lane's Broadway-worshiping Catholic priest, to Captain Patrick Stewart's crisply dignified interior designer. Stewart steals the movie numerous times: Just when you get the feeling you're watching some secret holodeck program Jean-Luc Picard keeps hidden in the bowels of the Enterprise, he reaches deep and displays Shakespearean chops. Ashley's stage roots show in theatrical hiccups that seem lifted from Broadway (right down to a production number), with Jeffrey often turning to the camera as if he's playing to the front-row seats.

The other thing that's riding on *Jeffrey*, of course, is Steven Weber's movie career. Straight star of the small screen on *Wings*, Weber's portrayal of Jeffrey is amicably low key, giving nary a whiff of heroic do-gooderism or overreaching. Ever the straight man (pun intended), Weber brings a particularly small-screen kind of comfort to a setup that could otherwise hold a great deal of discomfort and dislocation, keeping *Jeffrey* steadfastly funny and hopeful while portraying the open-ended tragedy of the plague years.

Also reviewed in:
CHICAGO TRIBUNE, 8/18/95, p. J, Michael Wilmington
NEW REPUBLIC, 7/31/95, p. 27, Stanley Kauffmann
NEW YORK TIMES, 8/4/95, p. C10, Caryn James
VARIETY, 7/24-30/95, p. 70, Greg Evans
WASHINGTON POST, 8/18/95, p. G6, Hal Hinson

JERKY BOYS, THE

A Touchstone Pictures/Caravan Pictures release. *Executive Producer:* Tony Danza and Emilio Estevez. *Producer:* Joe Roth and Roger Birnbaum. *Director:* James Melkonian. *Screenplay:* James Melkonian, Rich Wilkes, John G. Brennan, and Kamal Ahmed. *Director of Photography:* Ueli Steiger. *Editor:* Dennis M. Hill. *Music:* Ira Newborn. *Sound:* Michael Barosky and (music) Frank Wolf. *Sound Editor:* John A. Larson and Harry B. Miller III. *Casting:* Douglas Aibel. *Production Designer:* Dan Leigh. *Art Director:* C.J. Simpson. *Set Decorator:* Ronnie Von Blomberg. *Set Dresser:* Chris Nelson and Dennis Causey. *Special Effects:* Steve Kirshoff. *Costumes:* John Dunn. *Make-up:* Michael Bigger. *Stunt Coordinator:* Peter Bucossi. *Running time:* 82 minutes. *MPAA Rating:* R.

CAST: John G. Brennan and Kamal Ahmed (The Jerky Boys); Alan Arkin (Lazarro); William Hickey (Uncle Freddy); Alan North (Mickey); Brad Sullivan (Worzic); James Lorinz (Brett Weir); Suzanne Shepherd (Mrs. B); Vincent Pastore (Tony Scarboni); Brian Tarantina (Geno); Peter Appel (Sonny); Daryl Theirse (Connley); David Pittu (Doorman); Frank Senger (Bouncer); Michael Louis Wells (Roadie); Ozzy Osbourne (Band Manager); John Norman Thomas (Cabbie); Hope Shapiro (Tolly); Paul Bartel (Host); Danny Dennis (Comedian); Brenda Forbes (Rich Woman); David Stepkin (Old Man); Robert Weil (Quigley); Joe Lisi (Foreman); Ron Ostrow (Fast Food Family Man); Garfield! (Guard); Susan Blommaert (Sister Mary); Angela Pupello (Brett's Date); Jorjan Fox (Lazarro's Young Lady); Ronald Rand (Angry Commuter); David Klein (Young Johnny Brennan); Coach Cox (Young Kamal); Christopher Conte (Young Brett Weir); Charlotte Moore (Mrs. Weir); Dennis Hutchinson (Newsman); Maria A. Corbo (Newswoman); Jerry Dunphy (Anchorman); Tom Jones (Himself); Christopher Harrison (Sparky the Clown); John DiLeo and Marc Webster (Reporters); Michael E. Giammella (Waiter); Al Cerullo (Helicopter Pilot).

NEW YORK POST, 2/3/95, p. 47, Thelma Adams

You've seen "Dumb and Dumber." Now along comes the dumbest!

Get in touch with your own inner jerk with Disney's "The Jerky Boys." Let's just say it's not "The Lion King."

The Jerky Boys are a homegrown phenomenon two working-class beer drinkers from Queens named Johnny Brennan and Kamal. The pair got their jollies making crank phone calls while other people were getting a life.

Then a miracle happened. The boys taped their pranks and pals loved them. A cult formed. The Jerky Boys made two records and both went gold.

Producer Roger Birnbaum got turned on to the boys while making "The Three Musketeers" in the Alps. Maybe it was the altitude, but he evidently became convinced that the dialing duo and their pranks would make a good movie—or at least earn a return on his investment.

Hello! Didn't anyone ever tell Birnbaum that film is a visual medium?

The jerry-rigged plot involves dumb cops, dumb mobsters and dumb boys converging when Brennan and Kamal let their fingers do the walking in godfather territory. It might not be nice to fool mother nature, but it's dangerous to play phone pranks on the mafia.

Alan Arkin has a low-impact role as mob kingpin Lazarro. Singer Tom Jones, director Paul Bartel, and rocker Ozzy Osbourne have cameos.

VILLAGE VOICE, 2/21/95, p. 58, Jeff Salamon

In "The Gay Model," a skit off the Jerky Boys' first official collection of prank phone calls, Johnny Brennan is trying to get a job. Crystal, who has unfortunate enough to answer the phone, has been listening to him describe his résumé for about two minutes when he goes for the gold as the climax to his runway act, he brags, he likes to "pull large pieces of furniture from my ass." Crystal shrieks with laughter. "He pulls large pieces of furniture from his *ass!*" she squeals to her coworkers, not even bothering to cover the mouthpiece. By this point, the question of whether this gag is noxious or transgressive—i.e., whether Johnny is spoofing gay sexuality or straight people's delusions about gay sexuality—is moot; he's pushed his shtick as far as it will go, and now it's up to Crystal to decide where this routine is headed. And Crystal, of course, has figured out that her leg is being pulled—hasn't she? Maybe, or maybe not, or maybe she's not sure. She doesn't hang up on him or ask him to come clean, and she continues to answer all his questions. The gap between her sense of reality has opened up enough to pull a large piece of furniture from.

The Jerky Boys movie never gets anywhere near that level of subversion. The problem lies in the mismatch between the two media. The telephone is low-fidelity, high-interactive, and profoundly utilitarian. The Hollywood movie, on the other hand, is high-fidelity, non-interactive, and primarily a vehicle for fantasy. So where's the kick in watching some guy with a mullet haircut pick up a phone and complain about his hemorrhoids to an actress who's been paid to pick up the other end of the line and act offended? The thrill of the Jerky Boys recordings isn't just in listening to Johnny and Kamal's Mamet-esque monologues but in hearing how far real people can be pushed by increasingly outlandish provocations. A sort of Milgrom Experiment played for laughs.

The Jerky Boys might have clicked had Johnny or Kamal or director-coscreenwriter James Melkonian worked inside of their middle-class Queens milieu rather than fabulizing it with a dopey gangster plot—think of how Kevin Smith's *Clerks* wedded a similar gift for proletarian male chatter to a genuine sense of place. Instead, Johnny and Kamal get ground beneath genre dictates. Back in 1964, Marshall McLuhan noted that the advent of the talking picture put an end to telephone-inspired dialogue comedy records. And so again: Cinema killed the telephone star.

Also reviewed in:
CHICAGO TRIBUNE, 2/5/95, Tempo/p. 7, John Petrakis
NEW YORK TIMES, 2/4/95, p. 13, Stephen Holden
VARIETY, 2/6-12/95, p. 77, Joe Leydon
WASHINGTON POST, 2/4/95, p. D3, Rita Kempley

JOHNNY MNEMONIC

A TriStar Pictures and Peter Hoffman release of an Alliance production. *Executive Producer:* Steffan Ahrenberg, B.J. Rack, Victoria Hamburg, and Robert Lantos. *Producer:* Don Carmody. *Director:* Robert Longo. *Screenplay (based on his short story):* William Gibson. *Director of Photography:* François Protat. *Editor:* Ronald Sanders. *Music:* Brad Fiedel. *Music Editor:* Allan K. Rosen and Patty von Arx. *Sound:* Doug Ganton. *Sound Editor:* Patrick Dodd. *Casting:* John Buchan. *Production Designer:* Nilo Rodis Jamero. *Art Director:* Dennis Davenport. *Set Decorator:* Enrico Campana. *Set Dresser:* Mike Franklin. *Special Effects:* Rory Cutler. *Costumes:* Olga Dimitrov. *Make-up:* Linda Gill. *Stunt Coordinator:* Dwayne McLean. *Running time:* 98 minutes. *MPAA Rating:* R.

CAST: Keanu Reeves (Johnny); Dina Meyer (Jane); Ice-T (J-Bone); Takeshi (Takahashi); Denis Akiyama (Shinji); Dolph Lundgren (Street Preacher); Henry Rollins (Spider); Barbara Sukowa (Anna K); Udo Kier (Ralfi); Tracy Tweed (Pretty); Falconer Abraham (Yomamma); Don Francks (Hooky); Diego Chambers (Henson); Sherry Miller (Takahashi's Secretary); Arthur Eng and Von Flores (Viets); Victoria Tengelis (Pharmakom Receptionist); Warren Sulatycky (Yakuza Operator); Celina Wu (Mikiyo); Gene Mack (Laslo); Jamie Elman (Toad); Simon Sinn (Man in Hotel Lobby); Caitlin Carmody and Erin Carmody (Twins in Hotel Lobby); Doug O'Keefe (Pharmakom Security); Marlow Vella (LoTek Kid); Howard Szafer (Strike); Paul Brogren (Stump); Arthi Sambasivan (Nurse); Silvio Oliviero (Stick); Coyote Shivers (Buddy); Lynne Adams (Rocket Launcher Yakuza); Mike Shearer (Yakuza Partner); Susan Tsagkaris (Opera Singer); Christopher Comrie (Beijing Riot Newscaster); Robin Crosby (Girl in Hotel Room).

LOS ANGELES TIMES, 5/26/95, Calendar/p. 1, Peter Rainer

In "Johnny Mnemonic," set in 2021, Keanu Reeves plays a courier who transports nefarious top-secret corporate information in his chip-enhanced, mega-storage capacity noggin. He has made room for the info by dumping most of his own memory, which may or may not explain why Johnny is such a blank. But do the filmmakers realize how blank this hero is?

Visual artist Robert Longo, directing from a script by cyberpunk author William Gibson, isn't big on funniness. A movie that partially takes place inside the cranial cyberspace of an empty-headed character ought to be more kicky and satiric than this glum, punchy blowout. And the race by the bad guys to capture Johnny's head—intact should be kickier, too. It should be, as more than one critic' has already pointed out, "Bring Me the Head of Johnny Mnemonic."

There's a messianic streak in the movie—it's present in most apocalyptic sci-fi—but the punk religiosity is all swagger and attitude. If the film is about holding onto your humanity during the apocalypse, it would help to have a little more humanity on view.

It would also help if an occasional glint of brightness would penetrate the film's glowering grunginess. It's as if production designer Nilo Rodis Jamero were trying to turn us all into bats; the recreations of central Beijing and the Free City of Newark are darker than dark. This Information Superhighway could use a few street lamps. We're supposed to be wowed by all the dankness: the crunched, blasted cables and catwalks and spare mechanical parts that crowd this world. But it all has an undifferentiated dullness—kind of like the inside of Johnny's mind.

Now that we're primed for an onslaught of cyberpunk movies it would be helpful to point out that all this cyber stuff still requires a few old-fashioned dramatic virtues, like gripping, well-told stories and characters you can connect with. If you burn away all the newfangledness from this film you're left with a lot of blotchy noir-ish bits from James Bond and Raymond Chandler, with none of the bits coming together.

The Gibson short story that "inspired" the film was a brief, amusingly punky piece of futurism—hard-boiled gumshoe pulp for the cyberpunk generation. The movie goes way beyond Gibson's slim enjoyments into a gross fatigue of sodden plots and counterplots. In the 21st Century, the world is divided into warring corporate fiefdoms with technologically enhanced samurai bodyguards and Yakuza overlords and anarchic urban guerrillas—they're the good guys—called LoTeks. There's even a dolphin named Jones, an ex-Navy code-breaker, who helps Johnny download.

The cast is full of striking faces, belonging to such performers as Ice-T, Japanese superstar Takeshi, Udo Kier, Dina Meyer (as Johnny's samurai sweetie), Barbara Sukowa and Henry Rollins. But most of them can't break through the gloom. The one exception is Dolph Lundgren, playing a crazed evangelist with messianic hair and a hair-trigger temper. Lundgren is explosively fanatical and funny. Wonder of wonders—he actually gives the best performance in the movie.

Considering the void at the center of his character, Reeves isn't bad. He's worked up some tricky robotic movements but his dialogue can't match their invention.

NEW YORK POST, 5/26/95, p. 43, Michael Medved

A mnemonic is, of course, a memory aid, but "Johnny Mnemonic" is a movie you'll want to forget as soon as you've seen it.

This is an ugly, empty, infuriating piece of cinematic refuse—CyberJunk masquerading as futuristic CyberPunk—and easily one of the worst movies of the year.

Keanu Reeves plays the title character, a corporate courier in the year 2021 who holds precious information in a computer chip implanted in his brain.

Unfortunately, he's dumped his own memories to make room for the data he carries for his shadowy clients, which perhaps explains the dazed, pallid, amazingly uninflected performance that Reeves delivers in impersonating Johnny.

His screen presence is so blank and his acting so invisible that it makes one long for his relatively well-rounded and nuanced characterization in "Bill and Ted's Excellent Adventure"—let alone his genuinely impressive and versatile work in "Speed" and "Little Buddha."

In any event, Johnny wants to download the information before his poor abused brain explodes of overload, or one of the movie's grotesque bad guys manages to cut off his head to retrieve the data himself.

Prominent among these villains is "Street Preacher" (played by noted thespian Dolph Lungren) a hateful stereotype who wears Christ-like beard and flowing hair and declares "Come to Jesus" as he murders people with his crucifix tipped with a dagger.

Johnny's allies are also bizarre, such as Jane, his technologically enhanced "street samurai" bodyguard, played by knockout newcomer Dina Meyer in the movie's single most adequate performance.

These rebels, the sole remaining resistance to the evil, greedy, all-powerful corporations that now rule the world, are secretly guided by an all-knowing dolphin named Jones, whose superior mind is electronically connected to various contraptions from his murky tank under the bridge.

This papier-mache sea mammal represents the movie's single most embarrassing prop, since the dark, demented, gleaming visual surfaces of the picture are for the most part intriguing and impressive.

Directed by the provocative and prominent painter and installation artist Robert Longo in his feature-film debut, the production design seems to request an uneasy meld of "Blade Runner,"

"Mad Max" and "Tron," and should be enough to help with the sales of the forthcoming (in two weeks) CD-ROM version of the movie.

As it is, however, his grimy, grim literalism (including extraordinarily graphic scenes of sadistic dismemberment) and plodding pace make the movie all but unwatchable, full of wretched deer-in-the-headlights performances that we associate with Godzilla movies.

Next time, they might want to try letting a dolphin direct it.

NEWSDAY, 5/26/95, Pat II/p. B2, John Anderson

"Snatch back your brain, zombie! Snatch it back and hold it ..." Is this a public-service announcement? Affirmative, dude. In the 21st Century of "Johnny Mnemonic," computer pirates regularly interrupt the scheduled broadcasts of the multinational oppressors, fomenting revolution in a world gone corporate. We of the second millennium should consider it words to the wise.

In literary "cyberspace" (his term), novelist William Gibson reigns as chief architect and contradiction. A writer in a realm where words are irrelevant, he chronicles a future held hostage by information and a society crippled by hubris and technique. Put him together with yet another director slumming his way from the '80s art world to film (Robert Longo) and an actor who's spent much of his career subordinating emotion in favor of attitude (Keanu Reeves) and what you have is a movie crippled by hubris and technique.

For a "futuristic" film, it certainly has a lot of the cookie cutter about it; strip away the high-tech graphics and you have a standard Hong Kong thriller without the muscle. Johnny, whom we meet in a hotel room (cliché No. 1), is a free-lance information courier for the omnipotent, malevolent corporate structure. Civilization has disintegrated; NAS (nerve attenuation syndrome) threatens everyone; information equals currency and is under constant siege by anarchic hackers. Johnny, who's had to dump his own memories to make room for the megabytes he stores and delivers, is an enemy of the people—until he's overloaded with invaluable, corporate data and has to outrace both the clock and the Japanese mob (clichés 2, 3 and 4) in order to save himself and the world (5, 6).

"Johnny Mnemonic," taken from Gibson's short story and starring Reeves as the human chip, is full of itself—from the video kaleidoscope that we see in Johnny's bursting head, to the post-apocalyptic terrain where familiar landmarks have been computer-tortured into caricatures, to the "Blade Runner"-esque ruthlessness that embraces most of the characters—but doesn't quite have the nerve or generosity to let us in on the joke. So we're subjected to a dubious roller coaster of a film that wants to make serious statements about the world economy's inhumanity to man without being a bummer. Man.

The movie is traditional in one sense: Filmmaking has always had to ease its way into technological innovations; the most satisfying films are seldom innovative, and the innovative film is seldom a total success. (What's "The Jazz Singer" remembered for? The acting?) "Johnny Mnemonic's" hallucinatory graphics are a curiosity, but not much more than exercises. The sequence in which Johnny puts on gloves and enters virtual reality is fascinating, though, especially if, like me, you have little driving time on the information highway. But that may be the difference between loving "Johnny" and finding him insufferable.

All is not bleak: Ice-T, who plays the leader of the rebel LoTeks, proves himself once again to be a charismatic screen presence; Dolph Lundgren, as the lethal, implant-powered Street Preacher, shows a certain self-deprecating sense of humor while wreaking havoc. Rock star Henry Rollins (as Spider, the renegade doctor) shouldn't quit his day job, though. And, as his bodyguard and love interest (cliché No. 7), Dina Meyer has little chemistry with Reeves. But then, as a man supposedly tortured by his appliance-like qualities, the star does a pretty good impersonation of an ice-maker.

NEWSWEEK, 6/12/95, p. 65, Jack Kroll

Two hot pop icons, Keanu Reeves and Drew Barrymore, regale us with cold new movies. Reeves is *Johnny Mnemonic*, a 21st-century courier who carries secret data via a brain-implanted memory chip. Will his overloaded noggin explode before he can download it, will the evil data swipers lop off his head? Cyberpunkmeister William Gibson's script is a hollow inflation of his hip, *haute*-pulp short story. And debut director Robert Longo, a hot painter of the art-boom '80s, has produced a derivative flick; call it "Bladeless Runner." Still, it has its engaging moments (Henry Rollins as a wacked-out doctor, stunner Dina Meyer as a cyborg samurai).

This can't be said for *Mad Love*, in which bad girl Casey (Barrymore) inflames nice guy Matt (Chris O'Donnell) at their Seattle high school. She freaks out, he springs her from a psychiatric ward and off they vroom. This must be the lowest-octane road movie ever, in the hands of British director Antonia Bird. O'Donnell is amazing: his face never registers one significant expression. Barrymore's does; but Paula Milne's script allows her little beyond an all-purpose teen angst. "Mad Love" contains not much madness or love, not one fresh insight into kids or parents. At a moment of stress, Matt starts chomping on Cap'n Crunch. That's scarier than the visions of dystopia by William Gibson.

SIGHT AND SOUND, 2/96, p. 45, Lizzie Francke

In the dystopian future, the world's population is being decimated by Nerve Attenuation Syndrome (NAS). Johnny Mnemonic works as a courier, carrying information in a micro-chip implanted in his brain, for which he has had to dump part of his own memory. Even then his capacity is still less than he is being asked to carry. He is sent to Central Beijing for his latest mission where, shortly after loading Johnny with the information, the clients are wiped out by Shinji and other cohorts of a ruthless Yakuza, Takahashi.

Returning to the free city of Newark, Johnny is pursued by the Yakuza. After one particularly nasty scrape, he is rescued by a young woman, Jane who takes him to J-Bone, leader of a rebel tribe of LoTeks who live on the fringes of the city. Because of the memory overload, it becomes crucial that Johnny downloads as soon as possible. Part of his access code (three random television images) has been stolen from him.

Johnny discovers that he is carrying the cure for NAS. J-Bone leads Johnny to a whizz-kid flesh mechanic Spider whose solution to the problem could endanger Johnny's life. A ruthless lulling machine, known as the Street Preacher, is sent after Johnny and kills Spider before the information can be extracted. Johnny's only hope is now the code-breaker, Jones, a highly trained dolphin. Just as the two are hooked up, Takahashi attacks. Shinji, however, mounts a coup, killing Takahashi. As Takahashi dies, he hands to Johnny the missing code image. Johnny lulls Shinji. The Street Preacher turns up, but Jane and Johnny destroy him. J-Bone and Jones are able to facilitate the downloading of Johnny's memory banks and retrieve the information. Johnny is finally given back his own memories.

As a cult concept, the cyberpunk chiller *Johnny Mnemonic* has everything going for it: novelist William Gibson writing the screenplay from one of his early short stories, the internationally renowned artist Robert Longo making his feature film directing debut after a string of pop-promos, an eclectic cast that includes not only Keanu Reeves on a post-*Speed* high ("meet the ultimate hard-drive" runs the legend), but also 'Beat' Takeshi, Dolph Lundgren, Ice-T and Udo Kier. As such it seems the ultimate in cyber-chic. The messy result, however, proves just how little one can rely on packaged ingredients, no matter how fascinating a combination they ought to add up to. For while there are blinding flashes of brilliance here, such as when Johnny navigates an animated cyberspace, they are brief and quickly forgotten.

One of the most disappointing aspects of *Johnny Mnemonic* is a rather drab sense of *deja-vu*. Japanese corporation global domination, the tribal style DIY LoTeks, the neon-studded stygian gloom of the cyberjunk future, unpleasant forms of execution—in this case a lethal cheesewire laser—all seem rather passé after the post-*Blade Runner* and post-*Brazil* advert blitz. Even the novel reference to the "Free City of Newark" seems as though it has been done before. Meanwhile the central premise of a man who has traded in his own memories seems like something that Philip K. Dick dreamt up long ago. While on paper Gibson's furious, compressed style gave the story new linguistic currency, Longo has not been able to translate that into cinema.

With his robotic acting style, Reeves on screen for almost the entirety of *Johnny Mnemonic*—might seem to be the biggest problem. He certainly looks the part: Longo styles him as a sleek-suited urbanite (echoing Longo's series of drawings 'Men in the Cities') and his blur of Caucasian and Asian genes fits in with the global future presented here. Yet as an actor he is a perfect example of the binary method: on and off seem to be his only modes and the whole point about Johnny is that he is not wholly computerised. There is still supposed to be something human to him and so this stilted playing cannot be excused as being part of the film's project.

Consequently *Johnny Mnemonic* starts to work as a joke against Reeves—the very idea that his head could carry anything much, let alone the solution to the world's problems, becomes miraculous. This is particularly evident when Reeves is required to deliver a big third-act speech, prompted by his ally Jane who tells him to think about more than himself as he attempts to save his own skin. His speech ("I want room service...") starts out like a set piece on the contradictions of multi-corporation late capitalism, as Johnny, perched on top of a slag heap, extols the virtues of a swanky hotel lifestyle. The momentous mood, though, is skewered by Reeves' two-dimensional delivery.

Reeves' stumbling performance suggests that Longo might have been happier if *Johnny Mnemonic* had been conceived entirely as a piece of animation. The iconography of the other *dramatis personae* reinforces this feeling, for it is iconography at the expense of characterisation. With tumbling golden locks and swirling robes Dolph Lundgren is conceived as a Teutonic Charlton Heston figure from a Technicolor biblical epic, and Takeshi Kitano's Yakuza has dragons tattooed all over his body. One can only presume that Longo's ideas raced far ahead and the actors just got in the way.

VILLAGE VOICE, 6/6/95, p. 52, Amy Taubin

The cybernetically enhanced memory courier Johnny Mnemonic arrives on the big screen in a brain-dead $30 million movie directed by painter Robert Longo. William Gibson is credited with the script adapted from his own *Johnny Mnemonic*, the most haunting short story in his 1986 cyberpunk collection *Burning Chrome*. It's the first bit of Gibson fiction to reach the screen; let's hope it's not the last, although a disaster of this proportion can't help but have a chilling effect.

An antihero who is nothing less than a metaphor for the struggle between the individual psyche and corporate ideology, Johnny has been recycled, courtesy of Sony, as a multimedia event. If you find the prospect of going out to the movies less than appealing—and that wouldn't be surprising, given some of my recent experiences in some of New York's finest theaters—you might have a glance at *Johnny Mnemonic*, the screenplay, published by Ace in a slim volume along with the original story and some tacky black-and-white production stills. This version, which lacks the charming facility of the bestselling *Pulp Fiction*, also mysteriously omits the most flat-footedly amusing speech in the actual movie (Johnny's frantic attempt at self-definition: "I want room service, I want a club sandwich, I want a cold Mexican beer"). In any event, it's not going to replace *Chinatown* as the model for aspiring screenwriters.

Or, you might try *Johnny Mnemonic*, the CD-ROM, which as several online addicts informed me, presents an interactive software advance in that you can actually edit the picture on the fly. In other words, you can direct Johnny to go left or right, kick or hit, and he'll respond immediately without any of those annoying menus or time lags breaking the narrative flow. Before you start imagining, however, how fun it would be to order Keanu Reeves around with a flick of your finger on the keyboard, you should know that the CD-ROM employs a cast of unknowns as well as a different director, set designer, et al.

As for *Johnny Mnemonic*, the movie, well, it's a mess, although not nearly as pretentious and pernicious a mess as *Search and Destroy*, the other debut film by that other '80s painter, David Salle. A talent for making compelling single-frame, static images (that's what painting is) does not necessarily translate into a talent for conceiving the dynamics of movement in space and *time* (which is what filmmaking is about).

Novice directors embarking on Hollywood-style epics need lots of support from their crew ($30 million won't get you *Blade Runner* these days, but it could go a long way, especially in Canada, which is where *Johnny Mnemonic* was made). Here, the cinematography is murky, the sound design is as flat and muffled as in a 16mm student film, and the production design, which tries for a merger of the 1930s *Flash Gordon* with *Blade Runner*, foils all attempts at action. Standing in for "the free city of Newark" in the 21st century, Toronto looks like Toronto with a little extra neon and smog. And the terrifying "killing floor"—the climactic battleground of the original story, which suggested CBGB during an earthquake—is nowhere to be found.

Likewise absent is the noirish romanticism of the original. Johnny's situation has been hyped-up in action-movie style. He's still a mnemonic courier, hired by industrial smugglers to transport information hidden in a data-storage chip implanted in his brain. In the story, however, the secret info is nothing more than a great whatzit (pointless except as a pretext for the exercise of power);

in the film, it's nothing less than the formula for the cure for NES (the AIDS of the future), which defectors from the ruthless Pharmakom corporation are attempting to deliver to the NES underground—the ACT up division of the LoTeks (the good guys).

Johnny's difficulties are not entirely external. Having recklessly agreed to transport more info than his chip will hold, he is suffering from data seepage (which comes to him, and us, as rushes of computer animation so tired that it could have been lifted from *Tron*). If Johnny doesn't download in 24 hours, his brain will explode.

Inept though it is, the film has certain likable aspects, first among them its politics, which support a creative humanist subculture against the totalitarian corporate state. (Among Pharmakom's hired guns is a self-styled "preacher" who crucifies his victims.) The LoTeks shack up in "Heaven," which looks a lot like a Nam June Paik installation filled with ancient TV's and technological detritus made to function in innovative ways. Longo originally planned *Johnny Mnemonic* as a low-budget black-and-white movie, shot *Alphaville* style. Instead he's made a medium-budget (by industry standards) techno-dinosaur that gives lip service to the values of DIY culture.

In supporting roles, Ice-T and Henry Rollins triumph. Molly, the LoTek punkette of the original story who made Tank Girl seem like a wuss, is glammed-up to no end in the movie and her name inexplicably has been changed to Jane (Dina Meyer). Which leaves us with Keanu Reeves—terrific, except when he opens his mouth, and what a great haircut.

Also reviewed in:
CHICAGO TRIBUNE, 5/26/95, Friday/p. J, Michael Wilmington
NEW YORK TIMES, 5/26/95, p. C23, Caryn James
NEW YORKER, 6/12/95, p. 111, Terrence Rafferty
VARIETY, 5/22-28/95, p. 92, Todd McCarthy
WASHINGTON POST, 5/27/95, p. C3, Rita Kempley

JOURNEY OF AUGUST KING, THE

A Miramax Films release of an Addis/Wechsler production. *Executive Producer:* Bob Weinstein, Harvey Weinstein, and Richard N. Gladstein. *Producer:* Nick Wechsler and Sam Waterston. *Director:* John Duigan. *Screenplay (based on his novel):* John Ehle. *Director of Photography:* Slawomir Idziak. *Editor:* Humphrey Dixon. *Music:* Stephen Endelman. *Sound:* Paul Ledford. *Casting:* Billy Hopkins, Suzanne Smith, and Kerry Barden. *Production Designer:* Patricia Norris. *Art Director:* Bill Davis. *Set Decorator:* Deborah Winship. *Special Effects:* Ray Bivins. *Costumes:* Patricia Norris. *Make-up:* Lori Hicks. *Running time:* 97 minutes. *MPAA Rating:* PG-13.

CAST: Jason Patric (August King); Thandie Newton (Annalees); Larry Drake (Olaf Singletary); Sam Waterson (Mooney Wright); Sara-Jane Wylde (Ida Wright); Eric Mabius (Hal Wright); Bill Whitlock (Samuel); Muse Watson (Zimmer); John Doman (Bolton); Andrew Stahl (Harrison); Danny Nelson (Felix); Collin Wilcox Paxton (Mina); Dean Rader Duvall (Gabriel); Billy Ray Reynolds (Ben); Marlus C. Harding (Sims); Lisa Roberts (Meg); John Burnett Hall (Travis); Roy Bush Laughter (Tom); Clint Menacof (Ralph); A. Duncan Shirley III (Porter); Chase Conley (Harry, Son); E. George Betz (Bridge Attendant); Nesbitt Blaisdell (Mr. Cole); Graham Paul (Wade); Joan Cope (Elsie); Terry Nienhuis (Fisher).

CHRISTIAN SCIENCE MONITOR, 11/16/95, p. 11, David Sterritt

Anyone who thinks Americans have reached "the end of racism," as a widely discussed new book puts it, should see the movies at their local multiplex.

"Strange Days" builds its story around a murdered rap singer and an incipient race riot, then defuses the social issues by pinning all the trouble on a couple of rogue cops. "Dangerous Minds" presents glamorous Michelle Pfeiffer taming a schoolroom full of inner-city troublemakers. "Mighty Aphrodite" again finds Woody Allen portraying New York as the world's whitest city.

And now we have "The Journey of August King," a well-meaning movie that sets out to fight racial insensitivity, but ends up reinforcing it by adhering to old movie formulas that should have been discarded long ago.

The title character is a 19th-century mountain man who meets a runaway slave by chance, and reluctantly decides to help her escape the cruel master who's been tormenting her. Stowing her in the bottom of his wagon, he transports her through a North Carolina landscape that's as deadly as it is picturesque. The countryside is full of hiding places, but it's populated by slavery-supporting citizens who wouldn't hesitate to pounce if they knew the purpose of his journey. Along the way he develops a complex relationship with his secret passenger.

Although some of today's intellectuals claim the legacy of slavery has faded from American life, only a few generations have passed since slaveholding was ended, and some elderly people now alive actually knew former slaves when they were children. Since the social and psychological effects of slavery still linger, I'm predisposed to applaud any film that reminds us how destructively evil the practice was.

The trouble with "The Journey of August King" is that it's less about the persecuted female slave than the sturdy male adventurer who rescues her. This might make sense in box-office terms, since most moviegoers are middle-class white people. But it works against the film's apparent desire to attack racism by depicting the plight of a beleaguered and sympathetic victim.

I call this the "Glory" syndrome, after the slickly produced hit that purported to celebrate a black Civil War brigade, yet managed to fill the screen with Matthew Broderick's handsome face at every opportunity.

Memo to Hollywood: Deciding to produce a film about historical racism is only the first step in making a constructive contribution. The second step—and evidently the hardest—is letting African-Americans actually have the leading roles, even if this means reversing decades of habit.

The same admonition goes for movies about sexism. Why isn't this called "The Journey of Annalees," in honor of its brave heroine? After all, the whole narrative is set in motion by her courageous decision to flee the tyrant—her father as well as owner, it turns out—who's been ruthlessly oppressing her.

As a conventional film story, "The Journey of August King" is affecting if not exciting, punctuating its leisurely plot with bursts of action and occasionally savage violence. Jason Patric makes the hero believably stolid, and Thandie Newton—playing her first major role since "Jefferson in Paris" introduced her to moviegoers—makes the heroine as three-dimensional as the limits of the screenplay allow.

The supporting cast includes Sam Waterston as August's friend and Larry Drake as the slave-owning farmer who's determined to hunt down his runaway property.

Filmed with much atmospheric beauty, the picture is of a piece with earlier work by John Duigan, the Australian-born director who counts great-looking productions such as "Sirens," "Flirting," and "Wide, Sargasso Sea" among his credits. John Ehle wrote the screenplay, based on his novel.

LOS ANGELES TIMES, 11/10/95, Calendar/p. 14, Jack Mathews

[The following review by Mathews appeared in a slightly different form in **NEWSDAY, 11/10/95, Part II/p. B7.]**

On Hollywood's shamefully slim list of movies dealing with American slavery, there are next to none about the attitudes of non-plantation whites toward the runaways they encountered. Or about the relationships that were often forged between them.

We've got Huck Finn and Jim and that's about it.

And now, with John Duigan's smart and finely detailed adaptation of John Ehle's 1971 novel "The Journey of August King," and a pair of terrific performances from Jason Patric and Thandie Newton, the short list expands to include North Carolina settler August King and slavegirl Annalees.

August's three-day journey, from a trading post back to his mountain home with the runaway hiding in his cart, doesn't have the dramatic highs of Huck Finn's adventures, and there aren't many moments you would consider remotely fun. Ehle, who also wrote the screenplay, was looking back with a century's more perspective and guilt than Mark Twain, and has zeroed in on the emotional issue of what it was to have been both human and property at the same time.

Beautifully shot in the pine forests of western North Carolina by Polish cinematographer Slawomir Idziak, "August King" takes us back to the pre-abolitionist, pre-Underground Railroad years of the early 19th Century, when runaway slaves were tracked like game in the woods north and west of the plantation South.

The punishment for aiding a runaway was the destruction of the abettor's own property, and in the harsh environment where the settlers survived on subsistence farming and barter, that was nearly the same as a death sentence.

That's the situation facing August King—a recently widowed farmer whose worldly possessions include the log cabin, a cart, a horse, a milk cow, a pig and pair of geese—after he is approached on the trail by the 17-year-old Annalees and offered her owner's silver watch in exchange for his help. August rejects the watch, but having met her abusive owner (Larry Drake) can't reject her plea.

Ehle and Duigan, the Melbourne director perhaps best known for his erotic films "Sirens" and "Wide Sargasso Sea," have packed a lot of human dynamic into this simple, straightforward story. The movie stumbles at the beginning, introducing August as a passive Christ-like figure pausing to feed a biscuit to a dying dog (surely, this man will love all God's children), and at the very end, when he nicely summarizes the lessons of his experience. But the story itself is handled with such delicacy, finesse and fundamental humanity that its casual pace becomes a pleasure.

Patric underplays August in a way that limits the emotional payoffs but which seems absolutely in keeping with the character's lifestyle, education and predicament.

The filmmakers set some traps for themselves that they carefully avoid stepping into. There is sexual tension between August and Annalees that grows out of their vulnerabilities and—as the pack closes in on them—their interdependence. But it is unspoken, and very deliberately held in check, which charges their scenes instead of undermining them.

NEW YORK POST, 11/10/95, p. 49, Thelma Adams

"The Journey of August King" is the fall's most earnest movie.

It is 1815. The mountains of North Carolina. Farmer August King (a run silent, run deep Jason Patric with a hairpiece nearly as serious as his expression) is returning from market with a cow, a boar and some geese.

King accidentally bumps into scrumptious runaway slave Annalees (Thandie Newton, the bed-warming serf of "Jefferson in Paris"). The encounter forces a moral dilemma: Should the broken-hearted widower harbor the girl and break the law and his own intense isolation, or should he return her to her repulsive owner, Olaf Singletary (Larry Drake).

Drake (Benny from TVs "L.A. Law") does a surprisingly good job playing Olaf as the tortured ogre, a physically powerful man torn by his love for the slavegirl. It's the classic she's my daughter, she's my lover, she's my property situation.

In a season of peculiar love triangles, King, Singletary and Annalees make for a remarkably chaste grouping. Director John Duigan (of steamy "Sirens" fame), working from John Ehle's script, underplays the increasing heat between King and Annalees, although he does indulge in one silly stroke-the-balm-on-the wounds scene between the pair.

Cinematographer Slawomir Idziak ("The Double Life of Veronique") overindulges in that sepia-toned historical perspective that makes me want to rub my eyes to get rid of the dust. The poetic images tend to collect in pairs (if we are lucky and they are not hammered in more often) as in a shot of Annalees' blood on a thorn, followed shortly with a reminder shot of blood and thorn.

Still, "The Journey of August King," is a decent film, decently told. It's quiet, plodding pace allows those actions that do occur to resonate. When events force King to slaughter his recently bought cow to protect Annalees, we know the emotional cost without a line of dialogue. When the travelers pass the single scene of grim violence that gives the movie its PG-13 rating—an atrocity committed against a second, male runaway—the image has a power lacking in most Hollywood movies because the constant repetition of violent images numbs us to the horror.

"The Journey of August King" reminds me of the slice-of-Americana independent movies of the late '70s and early '80s—the small-lives, small-stories regional dramas with their painstaking attention to period detail.

Those Off-Hollywood movies ("Heartland" was among the best) were often easier to respect than they were to love, but they did offer an alternative to the genre movies that now even the indies imitate.

"King" is a kinder, gentler family film that might appeal to self-appointed Hollywood critics like Sen. Bob Dole, but the underlying realty is that the public will vote with their ticket money and see "Ace Ventura: When Nature Calls" or "Seven." And why shouldn't they? You can try to legislate Hollywood, but you can't mandate taste.

VILLAGE VOICE, 11/14/95, p. 94, Beth Coleman

North Carolina, 1815: settler August King (Jason Patric) goes to market to make final payment on his land. In the years he's been living in the mountains he's lost his wife, but he's got his property and some new livestock to show for his perseverance. By the end of his return journey, all King has left is cinders, a beautiful view, and the proud memory of aiding a runaway slave in her escape. Annalees (Thandie Newton, who just played another love-slave, Sally Hemings) is so charming and pretty its easy to see why her owner-father is reduced to Old Testament-style justice in his search for the girl gone running.

Journey offers a simple, fairy tale-like parable of selflessness and virtue over the meanness of ownership. It's a surprisingly serene trek, meditating on the ethics of responsibility and sexual desire in ways that interestingly overstep the trail the movies has trotted out.

Also reviewed in:
CHICAGO TRIBUNE, 3/24/96, Tempo/p. 11, Mark Caro
NEW YORK TIMES, 11/10/95, p. C14, Janet Maslin
VARIETY, 9/11-17/95, p. 109, Todd McCarthy
WASHINGTON POST, 3/22/96, p. B7, Rita Kempley

JUDGE DREDD

A Hollywood Pictures release of an Andrew G. Vajna presentation of an Edward R. Pressman/Cinergi production in association with Charles M. Lippincott. *Executive Producer:* Andrew G. Vajna and Edward R. Pressman. *Producer:* Charles M. Lippincott and Beau E. L. Marks. *Director:* Danny Cannon. *Screenplay:* William Wisher and Steven E. de Souza. *Story:* Michael De Luca and William Wisher. *Director of Photography:* Adrian Biddle. *Editor:* Alex Mackie and Harry Keramidas. *Music:* Alan Silvestri. *Music Editor:* Kenneth Karman. *Sound:* Chris Munro and (music) Dennis Sands. *Casting:* Jackie Burch. *Production Designer:* Nigel Phelps. *Art Director:* Les Tomkins. *Set Decorator:* Peter Young. *Special Effects:* Joss Williams. *Costumes:* Emma Porteous. *Costume (Judge Dredd):* Gianni Versace. *Make-up:* Nick Dudman. *Make-up (Special Effects):* Chris Halls. *Stunt Coordinator:* Marc Boyle. *Running time:* 91 minutes. *MPAA Rating:* R.

CAST: Sylvester Stallone (Judge Dredd); Armand Assante (Rico); Rob Schneider (Fergie); Jurgen Prochnow (Judge Griffin); Max von Sydow (Judge Fargo); Diane Lane (Judge Hershey); Joanna Miles (McGruder); Joan Chen (Ilsa); Balthazar Getty (Olmeyer); Maurice Roeves (Miller); Ian Dury (Geiger); Chris Adamson (Mean Machine); Ewen Bremner (Junior Angel); Peter Marinker (Judge Esposito); Angus MacInnes (Judge Silver); Louise Delamere (Locker Judge); Phil Smeeton (Fink Angel); Steve Toussaint (Hunter Squad Leader); Bradley Savelle (Chief Judge Hunter); Mark Morghan (Judge Killed by Robot); Ed Stobart (Barge Crew Member); Huggy Lever (Brutal Prisoner); Alexis Daniel (Brisco); John Blakey (Border Guard); Howard Grace (Pilot); Dig Wayne (Reggie); Martin McDougall (Twist); Ashley Artus (Squatter 1); Christopher Glover (Squatter 2); Brendan Fleming (Squatter 3); Stephen Lord (Zed Squatter 1); Phil Kingston (Zed Squatter 2); Ewan Bailey (Aspen Guard); Stuart Mullen (Co-Pilot); Pat Starr (Lily Hammond); Adam Henderson (Fuppie); Mitchell Ryan (Hammond).

LOS ANGELES TIMES, 6/30/95, Calendar/p. 1, Peter Rainer

The opening credits of the new futuristic Sylvester Stallone clobber-movie "Judge Dredd" are crowded with the comic-book covers of the cartoon super-hero. That's a tip-off that we're about to see a comic-book movie.

Then a windy, wordy preamble describing the apocalyptic Third Millennium world we are about to enter rolls down the screen. Just in case your comic-book appreciation skills are still in the preliterate stage, the words are intoned by James Earl Jones. That's a tip-off that it's OK to shut off your verbal skills for this film.

You won't need them.

"Judge Dredd" tries to create a cartoon universe that is simultaneously grungy and bespangled, with a story by turns campy and straight-arrow. At the center of it all is Stallone's Joe Dredd, based on the character originally created for the British comics magazine 2000 AD, a visored guardian of the law in the apocalyptic world of Mega-Cities where populations exist beehive-like in high-rises and regularly rout each other. Dredd clanks through these mean streets in designer armor-wear that makes him look like a flavorsome crustacean; and he keeps his pronouncements clipped and to the point. Sample dialogue: "I *am* the law!"

Dredd is a stickler for the law—actually, he's kind of a pain about the law. In the comics, Dredd is a blasted commando who never removes his visor, never cracks a smile, never questions his role as combination judge, jury and executioner. Stallone's Dredd removes his visor, cracks an occasional semi-smile, and, when he finds himself framed for murder and sent to the penal colonies, questions authority (sort of).

Well, it's a start.

The appeal of Dredd, both in the (relatively) straight-faced comic books and in his jauntier, clunkier movie incarnation, is his direct-action approach to justice. He's the Dirty Harry of the digital effects generation. Within the first half hour of the film he's splattering bad guys and, even better, blowing up a snooty futuro-yuppie's sports car.

Dredd is like an embodiment of the audience's wildest revenge fantasies, but 26-year-old director Danny Cannon and his screenwriters William Wisher and Steven E. deSouza, don't really get into the full reactionary nastiness of it. They don't target too many sacred cows. It's as if they were afraid a social-satiric edge would alienate all the hormone-pumped teen boys who represent the core audience for this film. (Their fears are probably grounded.)

They also shy away from anything richer in the scenario. (Comic-book extravaganzas *can* be psychologically rich—just look at "The Empire Strikes Back."), Dredd has his counterpart in Rico (Armand Assante), like Dredd a product of the finest DNA science can devise but as malevont as Dredd is staunch. Rico, with his sparked eyes and Gila monster profile, plots with Judge Griffin (Jurgen Prochnow) to rule Mega-City One. Dredd and Rico are mirror images—literally good cop and bad cop—but we never sense in Dredd a pull to the dark side.

We never sense much of anything in him. Where he's supposed to show a bit of warming in his scenes with his beauteous legal protector Judge Hershey (Diane Lane) he seems about as programmatic as Mr. Spock. He's like Spock on steriod overload. Stallone plays Dredd with a hulky half-humor; his great jaw and froggy-scary voice are already the stuff of comics.

Stallone seems to have resigned himself—rather lucratively—to playing overdeveloped, sub-verbal cartoons. This sort of thing may go over big with the overseas market that can't abide subtitles on their movies or complexity in their heroes, but it's straitjacketed Stallone into the role of kiddie kingpin superstar. Dredd's humor functions only on the rebound—he's the butt of jokes from his petty-thief side-kick "Fergie" (Rob Schneider). But really, we don't need all of Fergie's jibes. We in the audience do a good job supplying our own.

The filmmakers go for an over-the-top approach to mayhem and sometimes they pull off a rip-roaring moment or two. There's a flying motorbike chase through Mega-City One's inky skies that's a digitalized wingding; and the production design by Nigel Phelps and the visual effects by Joel Hynek take us *inside* the city's mega-grunge in a way most of these futuro-fantasies don't. The action, which seems truncated yet overlong, piles on so many things that a frame-by-frame comic-book effect is fitfully achieved. The director doesn't provide much kinetic movie making pleasure but he knows enough to jam the screen with clamor. It's not excitement, exactly. It's simulated excitement.

NEW YORK POST, 6/30/95, p. 37, Thelma Adams

"Judge Dredd" is as overblown as its star, Sylvester Stallone.

Based on the popular futuristic British comic book, the splashy special effects shoot 'em up plays like a big-budget B-movie western. The year is 2139. Sly rides into the anarchy-torn streets of Gotham, a lawman on the frontier of a new millennium. He's just an old-fashioned loner who sees the world in black and white while everyone else is living a Technicolor dream.

Dredd—a public servant who is simultaneously judge, jury and executioner—is a role tailor-made for Stallone. Pounding the pavement in big boots and a Gianni Versace storm trooper get-up, his cleft chin slicing the wind, his oversized lips twisted in a sneer, he is the ultimate straight man, the big shoulders carrying the weight of all that techno-crud.

Stallone's lawman is mono-syllabic. His first line is "I am the law" and he lays it down on the soundtrack like a welder. Occasionally, he'll toss off a deadpan quip, but he's so busy sneering he doesn't even slow down for much pucker time with the sweet Judge Hershey (blandly played by Diane Lane).

Let's say the part is no strain on Stallone's emotional range. Dredd's a chip off "RoboCop," without the personality.

The supporting characters provide the fun. "Saturday Night Live"'s Rob Schneider does the Joe Pesci, annoying-sidekick thing as a computer hacker who links up with Dredd on the wrong side of the law. The "what me worry?" boy rivals Macaulay Culkin in mugs-per-second, but he lightens Sly up considerably. The star amiably accepts being the butt of the joke: he must be used to it by now.

Virtually unknown British director Danny Cannon lines up a slew of highstrung villains. Armand ("The Mambo Kings") Assante's Rico is Dredd's evil twin, a megalomaniacal Italian stallion—hold the sense of justice. Jurgen Prochnow ("Das Boot") does the slow boil as a Machiavellian chief justice with a taste for totalitarianism. Joan Chen ("Twin Peaks") has a scowl-and-cleavage role as a bio geneticist who gets in a hair-pulling match with Lane.

If there's a feeling of deja vu, it's only because you've seen it all before in other movies. From "The Texas Chainsaw Massacre" comes a futuristic family of cannibals complete with an updated version of Leatherface. Cue the ominous thunder and lightning from "Frankenstein." Hold the climactic Statue of Liberty scene from Hitchcock's "Saboteur." Chalk up nods to "Blade Runner" and "The Silence of the Lambs."

"Judge Dredd" is a stone-solid Stallone vehicle. It might be set on the frontier of the future, but it doesn't need to break any new ground to keep fans satisfied. It's meat-and-potatoes, Saturday afternoon action fare, a painless way to chill the summertime blues in an air-conditioned theater for 91 minutes.

NEWSDAY, 6/30/95, Part II/p. B3, Jack Mathews

On the face of it, "Judge Dredd" seems a perfect comic-book adaptation. Its futuristic setting is imaginatively re-created on screen; its arsenal of voice-activated assault weapons is an NRA lifer's dream; the action is fast, furious and frequent, and its superhero is played by a man who was to comic-book acting born.

Sylvester Stallone is Judge Dredd!

So, why is it—to quote someone leaving the theater ahead of me—so "dreddful"?

Two insurmountable problems faced young British director Danny Cannon and screenwriters William Wisher and Steven de Souza. The first is that Judge Dredd, a dispassionate 21st-Century lawman who arrests, convicts and punishes criminals all in one motion, has about as much inherent personality as RoboCop, whom he resembles. And the other is that Stallone doesn't have enough personality of his own to give the character even a smidgeon of charm.

Wisher, who wrote "Terminator 2," and de Souza, whose credits include "Running Man" and the first two "Die Hard" movies, tried to liven Dredd up with glib lines tailored to action heroes normally played by Arnold Schwarzenegger or Bruce Willis. "Court's adjourned," after tossing a villain off a skyscraper roof. That sort of thing.

But Stallone, who wore a Superman outfit under his clothes in grade school, takes himself and his heroic alter egos too seriously to toss those lines off with any sense of comic irony. Dredd is as real to him as Rambo, which was self-delusion enough, and he seems to be on a mission that transcends the modest ambitions of comic-book fantasy.

An audience that isn't provided humor in a film like this will find some on its own, and I predict some hefty guffaws where none are intended. Specifically in scenes between Dredd and his slinky partner, Judge Hershey (Diane Lane), who has some weird romantic interest in him, and between Dredd and his evil brother Rico (Armand Assante), who is putting brotherly love to a stern test by using Dredd to take over the city.

In fact, there is a pretty good laugh the moment Dredd appears, in a gold and black, crypto-Nazi uniform topped by a snappy two-tone helmet and half-visor. All we can see of Stallone is that famous twisted mouth, the fixed snarl and square jaw. Then he says, "I am the law!," and we're howling.

As silly as Stallone looks in that costume, the backdrop is truly marvelous. Production designer Nigel Phelps, who worked with the late Anton Furst on "Batman," has blended live-action sets with matte paintings and miniatures to create a dizzying three-dimensional comic-book environment. And, with just a couple of glaring exceptions, the special-effects team has filled out the scenery with some terrific optical stunts.

"Judge Dredd," an 18-year-old comics series inspired by contemporary fears of over-population and rising crime, is set in 2039, after environmental and social disasters have divided America into three mega-cities separated by barren deserts. To combat lawlessness in these cities, cops have been given authority to dispense justice on-the-spot to everyone from scofflaws to armed killers. And in Mega-City One, a New York 10 times higher and more populated than it is today, no one is swifter or more just than Dredd, who is as purebred to his task as a Doberman pinscher guarding a junkyard.

The plot pivots on the attempt by Rico and a corrupt political ally (Jurgen Prochnow) to drive out the ruling chief justice (Max von Sydow), create an overwhelming force of identical test-tube cops and turn Mega-City One into a managed police state they can run with lucrative self-interest. No easy task with Dredd out to stop them.

The movie is not totally without humor. Assante is one of the great scene-chewers of his time, and can get off lines like "Send in the clones!" with some panache. And "Saturday Night Live" alum Rob Schneider livens things up as the hapless thief who becomes Dredd's wisecracking and unwanted companion.

But there are a lot more opportunities to laugh *at* "Judge Dredd" than *with* it—and after a while, there is not much fun in that.

SIGHT AND SOUND, 9/95, p. 55, Nick James

In Mega City One, 2139 AD, law and order is dispensed by a force of judges who can arrest, judge, convict and carry out sentence with autonomous authority. An armed riot is in full swing in the Ground Zero ghetto. Fergie, a petty felon returning from the Aspen penal colony, ducks for cover as two Judges come under heavy fire. They call for backup and get the veteran Judge Dredd. The Judges attack the rioters, and one is killed, but Dredd and the other survivor, Judge Hershey, finish off the gang. Dredd finds Fergie hiding and convicts him to another penal term.

At the penal colony, a psychotic former Judge, Rico, murders the governor and escapes from his force field cell. Soon a television journalist campaigning against the high-handed methods of the Judges is murdered, apparently by Judge Dredd. The weapon used, a "Lawgiver", is encoded with Dredd's DNA. Dredd is arrested and put on trial by the Council of Judges led by Dredd's mentor Judge Fargo. Hershey defends him well, but the DNA evidence proves decisive. The only way that Dredd's sentence can be reduced from death to penal servitude is by Fargo retiring and asking for the reduced sentence as a final request. Retirement for Judges means exile to the wasteland known as the Cursed Earth.

Dredd is chained into the same transport as Fergie, which is then shot down over the Cursed Earth by a renegade gang. Dredd and Fergie survive the crash but are taken prisoner. Fargo rescues them but is fatally wounded in the attempt. Before dying, Fargo tells Dredd that he is not a natural born human but the result of the Janus project, a genetic experiment to produce the perfect Judge, and that the renegade Rico is his cloned brother. Back at Mega City One, the new Chief of Council, Judge Griffin, is in league with Rico. A campaign of sabotage leads to the slaughter of dozens of Judges giving Griffin enough leverage to force the Council to agree to revive the Janus project to re-man the Judiciary.

Dredd and Fergie break back into Mega City One and attack the Council headquarters. They chase Rico to the Janus experiment laboratories where, with his henchwoman Ilsa, Rico begins cloning new warriors from his own DNA rather than the original prototype. In the ensuing battle, the laboratory is destroyed and Rico falls to his death. Afterwards, Dredd is offered the leadership of the Council but he declines, stating that he will always be a "street Judge".

The context for discussion of *Judge Dredd* in the British media has been almost exclusively a matter of tribal enthusiasms, as if the majority audience for this film will be made up of diehard fans of the comic 2000 AD on which the film is based. This is, of course, unlikely; no cult audience could generate the returns the producers of a big budget (reported as $80 million) film of this kind need for success. Yet this same yardstick of authenticity has also been used to measure *Tank Girl* and *Batman Forever*, both of which have been deemed to fall short of their origins. It is one of the peculiarities of the current critical passion for pop culture that snobbery is inverted: few critics argue these days that a Joseph Conrad or an E. M. Forster adaptation should be strictly true to the book, but if a comic strip is substantially reworked, it denounced as a violation.

Judge Dredd the movie is in any case an effective visual realisation of the comic strip which spawned it. The strip's urban terrain, Mega City One, is here seen as an entirely apt ad-hoc assemblage of cinematic influences, including *Metropolis, Ben Hur, El Cid* and *Blade Runner*, an anarchic upward sprawl of gleaming towers. The objects within it—the Judges' epaulette-heavy uniforms, their weapons and vehicles—are also suitably iconic. If, in imitating comic strips, cinema's dystopias are beginning to look more alike, no-one who has read a lot of comics will be surprised; it's a medium so voracious that few science fiction ideas are fresh to its readers. In that sense, imagined futures are now self-generating feedback systems: movies scavenge from the comic books which in turn scavenge from movies. The film's youthful British director, Danny Cannon, proves himself to be a natural builder of such hybrids and he is reasonably well served by the script for the first 40 minutes or so.

The reins of *auteur* power on this particular movie, however, were undoubtedly shared with Cannon's star Sylvester Stallone. No-one can doubt that a movie version of Dredd needs a star of Stallone's magnitude and he embodies a suitably implacable, thoroughly new Judge Dredd with some panache. What eventually sinks the narrative, however, is the insistence on providing him with a romantic foil, Diane Lane's Judge Hershey. Stallone does his best to begrudge Hershey's insinuations into his life but, coupled with his unlooked for anxiety about his test tube origins, her presence seems to imply that Dredd is an agonised candidate for therapy.

Here's where the comic book fan's complaints are more telling. Stallone's triumphal removing of his helmet, shifting the focus from those much-vaunted crooked lips, may be an act of self-confident freedom from the comic book. But the consequence of the new-found Dredd's emotional depth is that he can easily be dismissed as just another cop with a unspoken beef about the dehumanising effects of the job (as if he were in *NYPD Blue*) when the whole point about Mega City One is that *everyone* is dehumanised.

Once the strategy to make Dredd a person becomes clear, then the nihilism and quirkiness so cleverly established at the beginning recedes, and the struggle for control of a lawless city is superceded by Dredd's quest to redefine himself. This leaves Stallone in need of a core cathartic and satisfying antagonist than Armande Assante as his ranting brother clone Rico. Assante seems happy to join the very British line of villainy that might be called the Blofeld school of blowhard. He's like a *muy macho* Malcolm MacDowell or Keith Allen and he leads Dredd towards a finale that is worthy of James Bond: an exploding lab which fails to complete the making of a single Rico clone. By destroying his brother, Dredd can truly stand alone without any blood ties to the society which he must police. However, the movie Judge Dredd has only himself to blame if he is haunted by his comic book shadow.

TIME, 7/10/95, p. 59, Richard Corliss

Sly Stallone stares out at the tortured futuristic landscape of *Judge Dredd* with a macho hauteur that seems to say, "Who's tougher than me?" And the answer is, the bosses of the major film studios. Compared with them, Stallone and his fellow summer-movie heroes—those mean-eyed, pumped-up, epigram-expectoratin' cinema studs—are prissy little honor-roll students. The real tough guys are fellows named Semel and Pollock and Roth; their battlefield is the summer calendar; they show their guts by slotting their big pictures to open in just the right week in hopes of killing the competition. This is the art of war, New Hollywood-style.

Sometimes it pays off: *Batman Forever* grabbed $106 million in its first 10 days in North American theaters. But the strategy has a sort of kamikaze logic. Since there are more big movies than early-summer weekends, most films—even the hits—will be seven-day wonders. So it has been, with few exceptions, this season. *Crimson Tide* gives way to *Die Hard with a Vengeance* is vaporized by *Casper* gets eaten by *Congo* is beaten by *Batman Forever* gets a poke in the eye from *Pocohontas*. Hey, it's a jungle out there. One weekend you're the lion king; the next, you're vulture chow.

So the burly, bombastic *Judge Dredd*, based on a popular series of British graphic novels, is best seen as a metaphor for the movie wars. As policeman, jury and executioner in the 22nd century, Joseph Dredd (Stallone) is supposed to be one potent dude, but he is manipulated and programmed by a ruling council. This Mega-City is fascism as fashion statement; Dredd's uniform has enough leather and metal to stock an S&M boutique. But he's just a soldier for hire, or a star looking for his next project. Dredd's warped mirror image is a renegade named Rico (Armand Assante), as dangerous to Dredd as the next action film on the release schedule. "Guilt and innocence—it's a matter of timing," Rico says. He could be describing the difference between summer hit and flop.

For all its superficial pleasures—like some clever production design and the splendor of a fight between two gorgeous women, Diane Lane and Joan Chen—*Judge Dredd* couldn't have worse timing. For one thing, it surfaces at the end of a 15-year line of dark sci-fi films; imagine *Blade Runner* inside a *Tron* video game. For another, the movie tries for the same combination of facetiousness and majesty that *Batman Forever* mined only two weeks before. *Dredd*, written by Michael De Luca, William Wisher and Steven de Souza, plays like an instant clone of the Gotham Gothic.

Alas, director Danny Cannon hasn't the skill to make majestic melodrama plausible. As for the facetiousness, Rob Schneider sweats arsenals of ammunition as Dredd's sarcastic sidekick. But the effect is redundant since Sly is his own comic relief. By now Stallone has become a symbol for all that is goofy and grandiloquent in Hollywood's live-action summer cartoons. The hormone that courses through his movie veins could be called preposterone.

VILLAGE VOICE, 7/11/95, p. 45, Georgia Brown

Set in the American dark age of 2139 A.D., the dreddful *Judge Dredd* (there, I said it!) draws heavily on *Star Wars* but even more shamelessly on the postapocalyptic apparatus of *Blade Runner* and the *Mad Maxes*. Due to the convergence of sources, it isn't surprising that certain contrivances in *Dredd* and *First Knight* overlap. For instance, in each a main character immediately declares himself with a rousing, "I am the law!" (It must be a screenwriter rule: Begin with a blunt statement of purpose.) In *First Knight*, the clause is shouted by the villainous Malagant after his gang polishes off a meek, undefended village (he may've said, "I am the Lord!" but, hey, what's the difference?). In *Dredd*, the declaration of hubris is flung by the movie's eponymous superhero (Sylvester Stallone) at unruly citizens he's about to arrest, try, sentence, and punish in one efficient action. The movie's topical premise: chaotic times—population overload, triumph of the scum—call for meaner justice. A third millennium Dirty Harry.

Thanks to the cut of his helmet, Dredd (the character is out of a British comic book), like RoboCop, is all mouth. Stallone's mouth acts the same way the rest of him acts—broadly. Grimace, sneer, smirk. As in *First Knight*, the movie's only bit of eros boils down to a kiss. And on those pouty lips.

Dredd suffers from a complicated personal history which I will only say resembles that of certain key figures in *Blade Runner*. (I forgot to mention that *Knight*'s Lancelot uncovers his childhood trauma with Guinevere's help; she's the Barbra Streisand figure from *Prince of Tides*.) It's no wonder with Dredd's passion for rough justice that he's framed for murder—so many killings occur here, I can't recall any particular victim. His prisoner transport plane, however, is shot down over the vast wasteland that makes up the U.S. outside its three population centers—Mega-Cities they're cleverly named. Surviving the crash, Dredd finds himself prisoner of a warped family of cannibals, desert-rats out of *Texas Chainsaw Massacre*. They string Dredd up the way the enemy did Rambo.

By now Dredd has been joined by Fergie (Rob Schneider), a little-guy heckler and sidekick reminiscent of the Joe Pesci character in the *Lethal Weapons*. Whereas *First Knight* features John Gielgud as Guievere's (useless) sage advisor, *Dredd* has hired Max von Sydow to play the tormented Chief Justice. During Dredd's stay in the desert cave, von Sydow shows up in a brown hooded monk's cloak, a dead ringer for Alec Guinness in *Star Wars*.

Once the helmet is off, Stallone is lighted the way Warren Beatty is in *Love Affair*. The body—once the shirt is off—is Schwarzenegger's in *Conan*. (It's the Michael Jackson theory: surgery, body sculpting, cosmetology as art.) Did Stallone have blue eyes the last time we saw him? Were they always so big? Here the eyes, once revealed, often glisten with tears despite Dredd's supposed curse—a paucity of emotion. "Emotions? There ought to be a law against them," the character snorts to a female colleague (Diane Lane), who would like to appeal to such. Dredd seems not to count as emotions the contempt he evinces, the fury he feels.

As for *Dredd*'s "ideas" on the current immigration debate, the forces of good here consist of a lofty, if flawed, Swede, our hot-blooded Italian stallion, a devoted Anglo dame, and a smart little Jew (he's a hacker). These, I take it, are meant to be a cut classier than the evildoers: crafty Chinese scientist (Joan Chen), treacherous German bureaucrat (Jurgen Prochnow), and psycho/macho Latin (Armand Assante).

The last, the movie's chief villain, is Dredd's evil twin, Rico, who, unlike his *Scarface* namesake, has no holy mother to mourn his end. This end is an event out of *Blade Runner*, or, if you prefer, *King Kong*. The end's locale is the Statue of Liberty, a monument used more inventively in *Ghostbusters II*, *Batman Forever*, and Hitchcock's *Saboteur*. But enough. This reviewer's faulty memory runneth down.

Also reviewed in:
CHICAGO TRIBUNE, 6/30/95, Friday/p. F, Michael Wilmington
NEW YORK TIMES, 6/30/95, p. C3, Caryn James
VARIETY, 7/10-16/95, p. 35, Todd McCarthy
WASHINGTON POST, 6/30/95, p. D1, Rita Kempley

JUMANJI

A TriStar Pictures release of an Interscope Communications/Teitler Film production. *Executive Producer:* Ted Field, Robert W. Cort, and Larry J. Franco. *Producer:* Scott Kroopf and William Teitler. *Director:* Joe Johnston. *Screenplay:* Jonathan Hensleigh, Greg Taylor, and Jim Strain. *Story:* Greg Taylor, Jim Strain, and Chris Van Allsburg. *Based on the book by:* Chris Van Allsburg. *Director of Photography:* Thomas Ackerman. *Editor:* Robert Dalva. *Music:* James Horner. *Music Editor:* Jim Henrikson. *Sound:* Randy Thom, Gary Rydstrom, and (music) Shawn Murphy. *Sound Editor:* Richard Hymns. *Casting:* Nancy Foy. *Production Designer:* James Bissell. *Art Director:* David Willson and Glen Pearson. *Set Designer:* Pamela Klamer and Elizabeth Lapp. *Set Decorator:* Tedd Kuchera and Cynthia T. Lewis. *Special Effects:* Stan Parks and Rory Cutler. *Costumes:* Martha Wynne Snetsinger. *Make-up:* Sandy Cooper. *Make-up (Special Effects):* Charles Porlier. *Visual Effects:* Stephen L. Price and Ken Ralston. *Running time:* 100 minutes. *MPAA Rating:* PG.

CAST: Robin Williams (Alan Parrish); Jonathan Hyde (Van Pelt/Sam Parrish); Kirsten Dunst (Judy); Bradley Pierce (Peter); Bonnie Hunt (Sarah); Bebe Neuwirth (Nora); David Alan Grier (Bentley); Patricia Clarkson (Carol Parrish); Adam Hann-Byrd (Young Alan); Laura Bell Bundy (Young Sarah); James Handy (Exterminator); Gillian Barber (Mrs. Thomas); Brandon Obray (Benjamin); Cyrus Thiedeke (Caleb); Gary Joseph Thorup (Billy Jessup); Leonard Zola (Cop);

Lloyd Berry (Bum); Malcolm Stewart (Jim Shepherd); Annabel Kershaw (Martha Shepherd); Darryl Henriques (Gun Salesman); Robin Driscoll and Peter Bryant (Paramedics); Sarah Gilson and Florica Vlad (Girls); June Lion (Baker); Brenda Lockmuller (Pianist); Frederick Richardson (Barber).

LOS ANGELES TIMES, 12/15/95, Calendar/p. 1, Jack Mathews

[The following review by Jack Mathews appeared in a slightly different form in **NEWSDAY, 12/15/95, Part II/p. B3.]**

If you've seen "Toy Story," you know how computer animation can be used to charm the socks off of young children. If you see "Jumanji," you'll learn how it can be used to scare the hell out of them.

"Jumanji," adapted from Chris Van Allsburg's children's book by director Joe Johnston ("The Rocketeer") and starring a very subdued Robin Williams, is filled with magnificent, computer-animated fantasy images. But virtually every one of them exists as a lethal threat to the people, primarily children, populating the story. It's like a spectacular Halloween prank being played on the audience, with gull-size mosquitoes, roaring lions, snapping monkeys, stampeding elephants, flesh-eating plants and monsoon storms thundering off the screen.

Something bad happened on the way from the book to the movie. Van Allsburg's award-winning story is a fanciful adventure about an ancient board game whose consequences are real. The players roll the dice, and if they land on, say, that African stampede, so many elephants, giraffes and rhinos come crashing through their wall.

But there is a huge difference between suggesting those events, even with Van Allsburg's detailed illustrations, than having it played out in a series of harrowing, noisy adventures with real children in seeming peril. Obviously, the filmmakers were encouraged by the success of "Jurassic Park," but even Steven Spielberg said he wouldn't take his kids to see it. How "Jumanji" got away with a PG rating is something ratings architect Jack Valenti may have to explain to some perturbed parents.

"Jumanji" opens in the small New England town of Bantford in 1969, with the discovery by 12-year-old Alan Parrish (Adam Hann-Byrd) of a board game in a rusty old trunk dug up next to his father's shoe factory. When Alan and his friend Sarah (Laura Bell Bundy) start to play the game, he immediately disappears and she is chased down the street by a colony of giant African bats.

Cut to Bantford, 1995, long after Alan's parents have spent their fortune looking for him, and died broken-hearted, and Sarah has become the town's eccentric outcast. A new family has just moved into Alan's abandoned and dilapidated home, and when some ominous drumbeats lead the two kids to his Jumanji game in the attic, it's show time again.

The sick joke of Jumanji is that once you start the game, you cannot stop until someone wins, meaning that the game Alan and Sarah started in 1969 is still open. When the new players Judy (Kirsten Dunst) and Peter (Bradley Pierce) roll the dice, inadvertently bringing an adult version of Alan (Williams) back from exile in the board's other-world jungle, they have to find Sarah and take turns rolling for horrors.

Johnston and his writers attempt a sort of "It's a Wonderful Life"-fulfillment ending, where lessons are learned and tragedies undone, and cap it with an all's well ending in storybook (alliterates with Bedford Falls) Bantford.

It's hardly the same. George Bailey was a confused man forced by an angel to look back and find the good in an eventful life. Alan Parrish is a kid in a man's middle-age body, wrestling crocodiles and running from a bog-game hunter (Jonathan Hyde) who bears a striking resemblance to the father whose love he never had.

Resolving the father-son conflict is a bit too Freudian for kids, and the sanguine ending, in any event, won't erase whatever emotional trauma they endure getting there. Using both computer animation from Industrial Light & Magic and animatronics by Amalgamated Dynamics, "Jumanji" creates a hostile world of heightened realism. As much as you may admire the computer's creations, the adventures themselves make you squirm more out of impatience than anything you'd describe as a thrill.

NEW YORK POST, 12/15/95, p. 45, Michael Medved

In an era of Nintendo, Sega Genesis and dazzling CD-ROMs, how could you possibly get young people excited about a decidedly old-fashioned board game?

One way to accomplish the purpose is to scare the dickens out of them, a function which "Jumanji" performs with admirable intensity, originality and imagination.

Loosely inspired by the award-winning (and much less scary) 1981 children's book by Chris Van Allsburg, this wildly whiplashing thrill ride is totally inappropriate for young children—as I discovered much to the dismay of my 6-year-old daughter.

This poor kid spent more than half the screening with her sweater drawn over her head, and she has already complained of several "Jumanji"-inspired nightmares. Any parents who terrify similarly sensitive kids with this particularly potent "PG" entertainment should feel even more guilty than I do, since they have herewith been warned.

Older children, on the other hand, will be exhilarated rather than traumatized—as will most of their parents. The story centers on an ornately carved board game of jungle adventure discovered by 12-year-old Alan Parrish (Adam Hann-Byrd) in a small town in New Hampshire in 1969. Players are supposed to roll dice to follow a tortured path toward "home" but Alan lands on a particularly unlucky square and finds himself sucked into the nightmarish game and disappearing from his ordinary world.

Because his pal Sarah (Laura Bell Bundy) is too frightened to continue playing, the unfortunate boy remains trapped in the jungles of Jumanji for 26 years until two new children (Kirsten Dunst and Bradley Pierce) discover the old game in the attic of Alan's boyhood home.

Their roll of the dice brings Alan back (now as a hirsute 38-year-old survivalist nicely played by Robin Williams) but the various squares on which they land also release plagues of nearly biblical proportions on the quaint New Hampshire town, including giant mosquitoes, stampeding elephants and rhinos, man-eating plants, roaring lions, monsoons, earthquakes, crocodiles, huge spiders and an implacable big-game hunter (Jonathan Hyde) determined to bag human quarry.

Alan explains that the only way to put an end to the horrors is to play the game to its conclusion, and for that purpose he must reconnect with his childhood friend, Sarah, now a nervous psychic played by Bonnie Hunt. Along the way, Williams and his companions discover how his long-ago rolls of the dice had a terrible impact on his family and the fate of the whole town.

Williams is usually the world's most manic and riveting performer, but not even his energetic antics could upstage the special effects—a dazzling blend of animatronic robot animals with computer-generated imagery (in the style of "Jurassic Park"). Among all these cunning critters, only the mischievous monkeys seem oddly mechanical and unconvincing.

Director Joe Johnston (who previously crafted "Honey, I Shrunk the Kids" and the splendid but underappreciated adventure "The Rocketeer") doesn't let up for a moment, giving no chance to catch your breath between one "wow!" and the next, yet somehow managing to inject fleeting touches of wit and sentiment.

It's a virtuoso performance all the way, though by the ingenious conclusion even the most thrill-happy moviegoers will feel drained and exhausted, as if they've been mercilessly trampled by a rampaging sensory stampede.

NEWSWEEK, 12/18/95, p. 71, John Leland

Jumanji, the award-winning children's book by Chris Van Allsburg, is a delicately creepy fable about the adventures that await children who wander away from their parents' apron strings. Some are enchanting, some scary; all shimmer with the playful spirit of the game that brings them to life. That shimmer, unfortunately, never makes it to the screen. For $65 million, director Joe Johnston ("Honey, I Shrunk the Kids") and the wizards at Industrial Light & Magic turned this gentle fantasy into a mean-spirited exercise in terror.

Jumanji is an ancient board game "for those who seek to find/A way to leave their world behind." With each roll of the dice, the game conjures up an element of the jungle. The point is that the yoke of parental civilization keeps us from beauties, but also from beasts. But for Johnston's four players—Robin Williams, Kirsten Dunst, Bonnie Hunt and Bradley Pierce—the game stirs up pure malice: man-eating plants, gun-toting monkeys, a stampede, a great white hunter hellbent on bagging Williams just for sport. The players have to keep going until somebody wins or the special-effects budget runs out.

It's a sleek premise: what better field for fantasy than a world in which the membrane between civilization and the wilds opens at a roll of the dice? But the filmmakers seem interested in the jungle creatures only for their capacity to kill. The movie has no sense of wonder or play. Williams, reportedly, paid $15 million for his role, is wasted. Tied to the rhythms of its computer-generated scenes of mayhem, the film has no time for fooling around. The jungle beasts are gratuitously nasty, the New England townsfolk no better. When elephants and rhinos are stampeding down the main drag, all the citizenry can think to do is loot the local department store.

The film may be inappropriate for the book's young audience. At a screening, my 7-year-old crawled into my lap, terrified, and never left; I spent most of the film worrying for him, denied the cheap pleasures even a bad movie can deliver. In the end, he felt it was fun and not too scary, though he suggested a PG-8 rating. But as family Christmas movies go, "Jumanji" has all the cheer of a lump of coal.

SIGHT AND SOUND, 3/96, p. 44, Philip Strick

Brantford, New Jersey, 1969. Bullied by his classmates, 12-year-old Alan Parrish takes refuge at his father's shoe factory. On an adjacent building site, Alan unearths a box that was buried a century ago, containing a board game called Jumanji. After a row with his father, Alan shows Jumanji to his friend Sarah Whittle. At the first roll of the dice the game startlingly reveals its powers: Alan is sucked into the Jumanji board and Sarah is pursued from the house by a cloud of bats.

26 years later, young Judy Shepherd and her brother Peter move into the former Parrish residence with their Aunt Nora. Nervously investigating noises from the attic, the children soon find Jumanji. A tentative roll of the dice produces giant mosquitoes and a riot of monkeys; reading the rules, Judy finds that each Jumanji contest, once started, has to be played to the end and they have no option but to continue the game originally begun by Alan and Sarah. The next roll produces a rampaging lion but at the same time releases Alan from his 26-year confinement; he suppresses the lion and begins to celebrate his return. But celebrations are premature: his parents are dead, the shoe factory is derelict, Carl Bentley is now the local cop, and a plague of strange creatures is infesting Brantford.

Persuaded by Judy and Peter to resume the game, Alan realises they need Sarah's participation as well; reclusive since the night of Alan's disappearance, Sarah is reluctant to get involved again but at last joins a pact to see the game through. Fresh apparitions are soon unleashed, including a murderous big game hunter, Van Pelt, whose prime target is Alan himself. When Peter tries to improve matters by cheating he pays the penalty by beginning to change into a monkey. With Bentley's assistance they trap Van Pelt in the wreckage of a supermarket and hurriedly return to the game. The next roll produces a monsoon which floods the house; escorted by Bentley, Aunt Nora comes home just in time to be carried away by the torrent.

Finally, they are trapped in the attic, where giant spiders advance. Judy is felled by the poison from a tropical plant and Alan struggles to free himself from quicksand. Van Pelt has Alan squarely in his sights when a last desperate throw of the dice produces the winning move and the game is over. Van Pelt and the wildlife hordes disintegrate back into the Jumanji board and Alan and Sarah are restored to their childhood, promptly hurling the game into a nearby river. Alan embraces his father and their differences are forgotten. Years later, at one of Alan and Sarah's Christmas parties, Judy and Peter turn up with their parents, who are quickly talked out of a proposed holiday trip. Meanwhile, washed up on a distant beach, Jumanji awaits new game-players.

Given Joe Johnston's central role as special effects designer for the *Star Wars* trilogy and two of the Indiana Jones films, it is tempting to interpret the Jumanji board game as a symbol, to the director at least, for the whole filmmaking process. Sprouting crises and challenges at every move, demanding extremes of ingenuity and stamina, and refusing to relax its grip until completion, the game creates its own ground rules and can only be outwitted by the combined effort of all its players together with a reasonable dose of good luck. At the same time, like the unruly mechanisms of Johnston's previous features, *Honey, I Shrunk the Kids!* and *Rocketeer*, the magical device offers access to an array of enthralling and spectacular hazards, extraordinary adventures in which participation is reward enough.

More deliberately, the main *Jumanji* subtext is of the "Luvya, Daddy" kind, repeating what has become the obsessive refrain in Stateside films and soaps ever since mass hugging was rediscovered by family therapists. Cast adrift by their separate ways of life, children and adults in *Jumanji* struggle on the brink of open warfare, unable to access harmony until interdependence has been exposed, recognised and embraced. Belabouring the point, the 'lost' boy's father and the big game hunter who has pursued him for 26 years through the *Jumanji* jungle are played by the same actor (Jonathan Hyde, with a nice line in moustache-twirling villainy). In fact, although in the warmth of the moment we may be disinclined to argue, this renders the final reconciliation less plausible: why should Alan so easily welcome the menace he has evaded for so long?

Initially bullied by his classmates and dismissed by his father, what Alan learns from *Jumanji* is survival, a lesson which he passes on not only to his resurrected parents but also, eventually, to the parents of his co-survivalists by smartly dissuading them from what would be—and has already been, once—a fatal enterprise. Conveniently producing the gift of a clean slate when the game ends, the *Jumanji* board enables its participants to avoid the heartaches of an alternate world. Perhaps as a reflection of the inherent alternatives, or simply as part of the adaptation from Chris Van Allsburg's children's book, there are curious gaps in the lives of all the *Jumanji* characters. A major absence is any clear description of Alan's jungle boy existence, an upbringing which, with a brisk shave and a change out of his Robinson Crusoe/Peter Pan outfit, he is remarkably quick to discard.

His friends are also vaguely sketched, from the neurotic Sarah to the dependable Carl Bentley who, mysteriously progressing from shoe shaper to beleaguered cop, suffers the brunt of the *Jumanji* plagues without any obvious compensation. The long-suffering Aunt Nora, similarly, has no apparent purpose other than to react amusingly to passing absurdities: despite Bebe Neuwirth's poised performance and a careful montage of her single-handed restoration of the Parrish mansion, she finally vanishes, underemployed and unrewarded. With a nudge from its *Wizard of Oz* reference, *Jumanji* comes across as a tale of blusters and deceits, not only in these elusive biographies but also in the failed evasions of its four central game-players, one of whom even becomes part-animal for having attempted to cheat.

Not that ethical considerations should distract the film's audiences for long. The pleasure of *Jumanji* lies in its echoes of *Jurassic Park*, the incontrovertible evidence that magic exists and can, almost harmlessly, stampede a herd of elephants and rhinos down a front hall which, too palatial for its own good, more or less deserves invasion anyway. Although a touch grey at the edges as if recently formed from smoke, these trundling giants step up the next rung of the special effects ladder from Spielberg's dinosaurs by having hair and personality, like the rhino at the rear of the parade who glares irritably at an astonished motorist, or the lion which has taken hints from Disney in roaring and stretching only to be shut in a broom cupboard. Some rather spindly overgrown spiders are outclassed by a demonic troop of monkeys which, Gremlin-like, spread chaos through the town, resulting in a jaundiced touch of realism as the townsfolk ransack their own supermarket, by a wonderful pelican that carries the Jumanji game briefly out of reach, and by an offshoot of the ravenous plant from *The Little Shop of Horrors* that zestfully spits poison darts. Through the mayhem, Robin Williams cuts an unusually restrained figure, apart from the frenzy of his first release from Jumanji; even astride a crocodile or up to his neck in floorboards, he must have recognised that the stampede would steal his thunder.

TIME, 12/18/95, p. 75, Richard Corliss

This is the way Hollywood wants it: before long, all movies will be made by guys sitting at computers or playing with giant mechanical toys. The lions and raptors and aliens will go *Boo!* as they are programmed to do, and audiences will go *Eek!* as they are programmed to do. Occasionally, the films will require actors, listed in the credits as "Special Human Effects," but they won't need viewers with minds of their own. These movies will be ideal for the cybergeneration: machines playing to machines.

If *Jumanji* finds an audience, our point will be proved. Director Joe Johnston's elaborately dressed kids' movie—about a board game that sucks its players into a perilous jungle overrun by lions, rhinos, monkeys, crocodiles and spiders—spends so much time on the *how* of special effects that it neglects the *why* of characterization. *Jumanji* wastes the gifts of two terrific comic actors, Robin Williams and David Alan Grier, and some other good people (Kirsten Dunst, Bonnie Hunt). Like the viewer, everyone on-screen pretty much sits back, gets strapped in and takes a bumpy techno-thrill ride through a haunted house.

Jumanji's plot (from Chris Van Allsburg's book and a script by Jonathan Hensleigh, Greg Taylor and Jim Strain) is the 486th rewrite of a Spielbergian fantasy: lost child meets the Dead Parents Society. The story doesn't advance; it just piles up, like a multiple-car wreck. And its whimsy is spiked with way too much spite. In this nightmare replay of *Toy Story*, everything is demolished: a pretty old home, a local mall, an innocent town. It's destruct-o-rama, kids! Fun for the whole dysfunctional family! Because it exploits children's weakness for noise, clutter and anarchy, *Jumanji* is a perfect Christmas gift—for Bob Dole. Let's see if the Movie Morals Monitor goes after a PG film that really deserves a righteous swat.

VILLAGE VOICE, 12/19/95, p. 82, Gary Dauphin

A Byzantine suburban fantasy in F/X-driven kid-pic drag, *Jumanji* is two movies in one, part nicely turned action comedy aimed at kids and part holiday race card mailed not so subtly to accompanying parents. Based on Chris Van Allsburg's award-winning children's hook, the film follows the adventures young Alan Parrish, who in 1969 finds a magical chutes-and-ladders-like game called Jumanji. When he and his friend Sarah start to play, pieces move by themselves and African bats fly out of the fireplace, Jumanji's jungle versions of "Go directly to jail" somehow manifesting themselves in the real world.

An unlucky roll of the dice transports Alan to said jungle, where the game dictates he must wait until another player rolls a six or an eight. Pudgy little Alan has a long wait ahead of him, as Jumanji flashes forward from there to the present day. the dusty board is discovered by the Parrish home's new young occupants, Judy and Peter (Kirsten Dunst and Bradley Pierce). Unaware of what they're getting themselves into, they roll Jumanji's dice, unleashing a lion, poisonous mosquitoes, and a plague of Gremlin-like digital monkeys in short order. One of their rolls is an eight, so a wooly-haired Alan (Robin Williams) pops out of the game as well, all grown up after 26 years trapped in the jungle.

Alan finds a transformed town: Main Street is hidden under layers of for-sale signs and graffiti, his parents are dead, and his family's shoe factory has been closed for years, some of these changes the result—à la *It's a Wonderful Life*—of his own disappearance, Jumanji's rules stipulate that, once started, a game has to be played through to completion, this in order to get rid of the various critters and minor disasters it produces, so alan agrees to finish the game with Judy and Peter. Sarah's adult self (a loopy Bonnie Hunt) is enlisted to make it an even four, and from there the movie's more spectacular jungle-related hell breaks loose as every roll of the dice brings them closer to game's end.

Jumanji's visual effects are first-rate (especially the stampede and monsoon sequences), and the cast handled itself well enough. Williams, as always, plays himself. Despite decades of isolation in the jungle, he still manages to drop one-liners about trailer parks. *Jumanji*'s most interesting adult-sized action is in the side bits, though. As the game progresses, the African wilds spill out of the Parrish home into the surrounding town, its lily-white residents either fleeing wildebeest or slyly looting stores at the edge of the frame.

These are weird elements to find in a childrens' film, and although they might make *Jumanji* more "adult friendly," they're also what made me so wary of the film's inevitable Christmas-cheery ending, as a decades long race to get the jungle out of the suburbs comes down to a roll of some racially loaded dice.

Also reviewed in:
CHICAGO TRIBUNE, 12/15/95, Friday/p. H, John Petrakis
NEW YORK TIMES, 12/15/95, p. C24, Janet Maslin
NEW YORKER, 12/25/95-1/1/96, p. 148, Anthony Lane
VARIETY, 12/11-17/95, p. 83, Leonard Klady

WASHINGTON POST, 12/15/95, p. F7. Rita Kempley
WASHINGTON POST, 12/15/95, Weekend/p. 51, Desson Howe

JUPITER'S WIFE

An Artistic License release. *Producer:* Michael Negroponte. *Director:* Michael Negroponte. *Screenplay:* Michael Negroponte and Gabriel Morgan. *Director of Photography:* Michael Negroponte. *Editor:* Michael Negroponte. *Running time:* 78 minutes. *MPAA Rating:* Not Rated.

LOS ANGELES TIMES, 9/8/95, Calendar/p. 10, Kevin Thomas

Michael Negroponte's beguiling "Jupiter's Wife" takes us into the unique universe of Maggie Cogan, a longtime resident of Central Park, with the utmost sensitivity and discretion. Negroponte approaches Cogan with a passion for discovery and understanding. The result is an illuminating, beautifully wrought film of charm, humor and unexpected emotional impact. Dismiss all those feelings of dread at the prospect of watching a documentary on a homeless person and you're in for a treat that may lift your spirits while expanding your horizons.

Cogan is a sturdy, weathered, middle-aged woman with a hefty backpack and four dogs on leashes. She is witty, articulate, clearly of superior intelligence. She also declares that she is the wife of the Greek god Jupiter—and the daughter of the late actor Robert Ryan.

She also claims she has ESP—and she very well may be right on that score.

Never does Negroponte make Cogan feel that she's a crazy woman but instead befriends her, gradually gaining her trust. Clearly Cogan, who says she became homeless in 1986, is formidably self-reliant and, as it turns out, has something of a support network, even a guardian angel, in the vibrant Katina Pendleton, wife of actor Austin Pendleton.

What emerges with a grace that is as spiritual as it is aesthetic is a celebration of living close to nature—never did Central Park ever seem so lyrical. Yet the film also becomes an exemplar of how caring individuals can help a homeless person—provided that he or she is capable of accepting and receiving help.

At heart, however, "Jupiter's Wife" is a detective story requiring the utmost delicacy and soundness of judgment. Understandably intrigued, Negroponte attempts to discover what traumas or series of traumas so completely devastated Cogan at some point in her past. Remarkably, he manages to get answers without betraying or exploiting Cogan—or anyone else. "Jupiter's Wife," a kind of cosmic mystery story, is too full of surprises and revelations to give anything away here. The key point is that Cogan was able to draw upon her knowledge of Greek mythology to help her make sense of her life after it was shattered.

As this wonderfully affecting film progresses, so, seemingly, does Cogan's self-awareness. But the great thing about "Jupiter's Wife" is that it doesn't go too far in any aspect. It doesn't exploit Cogan, it takes leave of her grateful that she's better off at the film's end than when we meet her, and it is wise enough to know that her future can only be viewed tentatively.

NEW YORK POST, 8/18/95, p. 46, Thelma Adams

She claims to be "Jupiter's Wife," but the schizophrenic homeless woman at the center of Michael Negroponte's documentary is more akin to Jerry Garcia's sad-sack sister. Acid casualty Maggie Cogan inhabits Central Park with a pack of stray dogs and a buoyant smile that has no relation to her life's harsh realities.

Working solo with a hand-held, Super-VHS camcorder, Negroponte cast his beautifully shot, intimate documentary as carefully as any Hollywood director. Maggie has a weathered, wooden doll face: pink cheeks, full lips and a Howdy Doody gap-toothed smile that reaches right through the camera. Her eyes dance under headlight-shaped wire-rimmed glasses; her sinewy, athletic body has a mountain man's vitality.

What interests Negroponte are the myths Maggie weaves about her life: she is married to the god Jupiter; she is the daughter of the actor Robert Ryan; she is a changeling, separated at birth from her real parents and raised by a wicked couple in suburban Long Island. She believes in

ESP, hears voices (largely Jupiter speaking in romantic tones), and maintains a constant conversation with her extended canine family.

Negroponte sets about to decode these myths, to get to the bottom of Maggie's personal history, to find the "why" behind the vital, wandering figure.

At its worst, "Jupiter's Wife" falls victim to the pet homeless person syndrome: an individual adopts a street person to reconnect with his own humanity by finding the humanity in her. Negroponte occasionally swoons under the spell of Maggie's cosmic schizophrenic spoutings ("Maggie sees things that I don't," he says somberly on the soundtrack). These ramblings can seem less profound than monotonous for the viewer.

Negroponte takes a vacation in the Catskills with his family, but intones: "I'm 100 miles from Central Park and Maggie's enigma will not release me." He's got the pet homeless person syndrome bad!

But "Jupiter's Wife" gradually gains in power, taking on the urgency of a mystery story. Using fragments of memory, interpreting hallucinations and doing a little detective work, the director begins to form a profile of Maggie Cogan.

Maggie grew up with the standard alienation of a suburban '50s teen, graduated with the class of '61, got tumbled about by the social changes of the '60s and peaked in her early 20s as one of the first female horse-drawn carriage drivers in Central Park.

By the early '70s, Maggie's life had begun to unravel. At some point, between having two kids by two different fathers who didn't stick around for long, Maggie dropped acid and began to lose the reins on reality. She lost her heart, lost the kids, lost her way and ended up, years later, walking her dogs, her babies, on the Central Park Rambles.

In one of the movie's most unexpected moments, Negroponte inserts a clip of a 1968 "What's My Line?" TV show hosted by Wally Bruner. There's Maggie, fresh-faced with her open, gap-toothed smile, challenging the panel to guess her occupation. After a panelist picks carriage driver, Bruner cheerfully sends Maggie off with the question: "And your future is in Central Park?"

"Could be," Maggie answers. Little did Wally know.

VILLAGE VOICE, 8/22/95, p. 52, Amy Taubin

For years, I used to see Maggie and her family of dogs hanging out in front of the Cooper Union library. Whenever I'd run into her, I'd slip her a five or a ten, or sometimes I'd give her a spare carton of cat food, which she said the dogs liked a lot. It's hard enough being homeless, but being homeless with animals is next to impossible. No one will let you sleep in their hallway, much less crash in their apartment, with five dogs. I worried about Maggie, but I resisted getting involved.

Documentarian Michel Negroponte did get involved sufficiently to produce a film about Maggie titled *Jupiter's Wife*. Shot for $400 on super-VHS and then transferred to 35mm, it proves that compelling films can be made for no money. The subject is what counts, and Maggie is a great subject.

Negroponte followed her with his camera for two years—from her residence in Central Park to the Long Island City apartment she rented with the help of a network of friends who also got her on Supplementary Security Income. Maggie is a schizophrenic, which in her case means that she has created an elaborate parallel universe for herself, a cosmology that collapses categories of human and animal, past and present, actuality and myth, everything tied together with a string of metaphors that Negroponte is ardent to unravel.

Maggie is more than willing to open herself to the camera and Negroponte cleverly picks out clues to her past life from her wildly associative stories. He discovers '60s newsreel footage of the young Maggie during her carriage-driving days in Central Park and her six minutes of fame on *What's My Line*. The problem is that Negroponte is so anxious for us to understand Maggie that he imposes a formulaic linearity on her fragmented psyche. He never lets her chaotic sense of time take over the film. Worse, his voiceover narration has a fake overawed quality that would irritate even a three-year-old. Still, Maggie survives the straitjacket the film puts her in. I wish I felt as confident about her off-screen future.

Also reviewed in:
NEW YORK TIMES, 8/18/95, p. C8, Walter Goodman
WASHINGTON POST, 10/27/95, p. D7, Rita Kempley

JURY DUTY

A TriStar Pictures release of a TriStar and Triumph Films presentation of a Yoram Ben-Ami/Peter M. Lenkov production in association with Weasel Proudctions, Inc. *Producer:* Yoram Ben-Ami and Peter M. Lenkov. *Director:* John Fortenberry. *Screenplay:* Neil Tolkin, Barbara Williams, and Samantha Adams. *Story:* Barbara Williams and Samantha Adams. *Director of Photography:* Avi Karpick. *Editor:* Stephen Semel. *Music:* David Kitay. *Music Editor:* Chris MacGeary. *Choreographer:* Peggy Holmes. *Sound:* Itzahk Magall. *Sound Editor:* Edmund J. Lachmann, Glenn Auchinachie, Brent Winter, Tom Scurry, Greg Conway, and Reid A. Woodbury, Jr. *Casting:* Ferne Cassell. *Production Designer:* Deborah Raymond and Dorian Vernaccio. *Set Designer:* Daniel Bradford. *Set Decorator:* Nancy S. Fallace. *Set Dresser:* Barbara Cole. *Special Effects:* Frank Ceglia. *Costumes:* Terry Dresbach. *Make-Up:* Suzanne Sanders. *Stunt Coordinator:* Dan Bradley. *Running time:* 86 minutes. *MPAA Rating:* PG-13.

CAST: Pauly Shore (Tommy); Tia Carrere (Monica); Stanley Tucci (Frank); Brian Doyle-Murray (Harry); Abe Vigoda (Judge Powell); Charles Napier (Jed); Richard Edson (Skeets); Richard Riehle (Principal Beasely); Alex Datcher (Sarah); Richard T. Jones (Nathan); Sharon Barr (Libby Starling); Jack McGee (Murphy); Nick Bakay (Richard Hertz); Ernie Lee Banks (Ray); Shelley Winters (Mom); Dick Vitale (Hal Gibson); Billie Bird (Rose); Jorge Luis Abreu (Jorge); Siobhan Fallon (Heather); Gregory Cooke (Reece Fishburn); Mark L. Taylor (Russell Cadbury); Sean Whalen (Carl Wayne Bishop); Laurelyn Scharkey (Harry's Bombshell); Steven Hy Landau (Tuna Salad Guy); Melissa Samuels (Club Announcer); Paul Stork (Transvestite); William Newman (Judge D'Angelo); Susan Lentini (Judge Swartz); Tom Booker (Press Runner); Jay Kogen (Russell's Assistant); Paul Thorpe (Goliath); Michael Reid Mackay (Steer Shack Employee); David McMillan (Friendly Falafel Employee); Saemi Nakamura (Wiener Boy Employee); Efren Ramirez (Pirate Pete's Employee); J.D. Hall and Bruce Economou (Guards); Lynn Ziegler (Mrs. Woodall); Yolanda Miro (Spanish Reporter); Y. Hero Abe (Japanese Reporter); Michael Feresten (Folk Singer); Fritz Mashimo (Japanese Suicide Man); George Christy (Dr. Brookings); Gizmo (Peanut).

LOS ANGELES TIMES, 4/12/95, Calendar/p. 2, Kevin Thomas

"Jury Duty" would be a terrible be a terrible comedy at any time, but its lame references to the O.J. Simpson trial and puny jabs at the media circus surrounding such events only make it seem worse.

Pauly Shore plays Tommy, an inept, none-too-ambitious guy, who having failed as a male stripper, winds up as the jury foreman on a serial murder case. It seems an open-and-shut matter, but Tommy, having promoted himself to the presidential suite in the hotel where the jury is sequestered and being otherwise unemployed, starts stretching out deliberations, understandably driving his fellow jurors, including the beautiful Tia Carrere, nuts. Shamelessly, the film's director John Fortenberry, in a less-than-encouraging feature debut, and its various writers then have Tommy and Tia's Monica start having real doubts about the accused killer's guilt.

Shelley Winters, as Shore's doting trailer park mother, and Charles Napier, as her salvage collector fiancé, liven up this increasingly grim business.

NEW YORK POST, 4/12/95, p. 35, Thelma Adams

Pauly Shore's shtick is to be so freakily pathetic that the audience wants to punch him. Then, when Mr. Grating Personality gets smacked, we laugh, sometimes despite ourselves. His ecstatic repulsiveness is the key to Shore's anti-charm.

"Jury Duty," Shore's latest fish-out-of-water comedy—he saved the free world as a dysfunctional private "In the Army Now"—finds him fighting for truth, justice and a free lunch as a juror on a murder trial.

Call it "12 Angry Weasels." An unemployed man allegedly killed seven fast-food restaurant managers. Shore's out-of-work schlump stretches deliberations on the case to keep himself sequestered, fed and with a roof over his head. So, the jury be hanged—and, valley boy, are they angry!

John Fortenberry makes his directorial debut with a formulaic comedy that's not quite as endless as the O.J. trial. The courtroom setting allows Pauly to take cheap pot shots at the Simpson circus. "Judge Ito bite on my burrito," Shore whines over the closing credits.

The comic highlight, such as it is, comes early on. Shore auditions for a job as a male stripper doing a naughty milkman routine. The female onlookers leave the club, but a lone transvestite remains to purr, "Let's go back to my place and curdle."

And that's the highlight!

Shore's greatest gift is giving other actors work. Shelley Winters, who plays his mom, would be embarrassing herself on "The Tonight Show" if it weren't for Pauly. Here, "The Poseidon Adventure" star overacts just grabbing a newspaper off her porch before disappearing minutes after the opening credits roll.

Abe Vigoda, Brian Doyle-Murray, Stanley Tucci and Richard Edson pick up paychecks while Tia Carrere plays the juror of Pauly's dreams. The "Wayne's World" dreamgirl has to kiss Shore and look turned on—now that's acting!

NEWSDAY, 4/12/95, Part II/p. B9, John Anderson

Remember when one had to actually *buy* something to get the girl? Aftershave. Automobiles. Beer. You at least had to make a contribution to the economy. Now all you need is an IQ lower than your age. Adam Sandler. Chris Farley. Or The King, Pauly Shore, who in "Jury Duty" acts like a total waste of space and walks away with Tia Carrere.

And how about Tia? First she rocks Wayne's world and now she's washed up on Shore. What is she? A serial loser?

And isn't this all contrary to a healthy marketplace? Shouldn't people like Pauly be put on workfare? Am I taking this all too seriously? It's probably just overexposure. I actually thought about writing that "Jury Duty" was funnier than "Tommy Boy." And what would that have meant, other than that my brain had turned to building material?

No, Kato Kaelin is not in "Jury Duty," but his ethos presides. After the shiftless, unmotivated, uneducated and unemployable Tommy Collins (Shore) fails at erotic dancing—in a particularly unsavory scene that features another of this movie's patron saints, Andrew Dice Clay—he heads back to the mobile home to leech off Mom (Shelley Winters) and her fiancé, Jed (Charles Napier) When the folks decide to go on a Las Vegas honeymoon, the house goes with them. Tommy, homeless as well as witless, has no alternative but to actually answer his summons to jury duty, and hope to be sequestered.

He maneuvers himself onto the high-profile case of Carl Wayne Bishop (Sean Whalen), the so-called "Drive Thru Killer," who's accused of slaying seven fast-food employees. Why? Or why only seven? It doesn't matter. What's really important is that Tommy, by making a blatant plug for the jury's hotel during the nightly news, gets himself a deluxe room and will delay the trial indefinitely to keep it that way.

And except for Tommy's solving the case and walking off with Monica (Carrere) the law student (uh huh), that's the story. The dog Gizmo, who plays Peanut, is good, and he upstages Shore. There are a few funny moments, but thinking back, I realize most of them involved Pauly being in pain. Oh yes, and Abe Vigoda as the judge. It's nice to know Fish got a promotion.

Also reviewed in:
CHICAGO TRIBUNE, 4/12/95, Tempo/p. 2, John Petrakis
NEW YORK TIMES, 4/13/95, p. B4, Janet Maslin
VARIETY, 4/10-16/95, p. 45, Brian Lowry
WASHINGTON POST, 4/14/95, Weekend/p. 36, Desson Howe

JUST CAUSE

A Warner Bros. release of a Lee Rich production in association with Fountainbridge Films. *Executive Producer:* Sean Connery. *Producer:* Lee Rich, Arne Glimcher, and Steve Perry. *Director:* Arne Glimcher. *Screenplay:* Jeb Stuart and Peter Stone. *Based on the novel by:* John Katzenbach. *Director of Photography:* Lajos Koltai. *Editor:* William Anderson. *Music:* James Newton Howard. *Music Editor:* Thomas Drescher. *Sound:* James Sabat and (muisc) Shawn Murphy. *Sound Editor:* Michael Kirchberger. *Casting:* Billy Hopkins, Suzanne Smith, and Kerry Barden. *Production Designer:* Patrizia von Brandenstein. *Art Director:* Dennis Bradford. *Set Designer:* Mark Garner. *Set Decorator:* Cloudia and Maria Nay. *Set Dresser:* Peter Muller. *Special Effects:* Mike Meinardus. *Costumes:* Ann Roth and Gary Jones. *Make-up:* Scott Eddo, Shelly Woodhouse, and Melanie Hughes. *Stunt Coordinator:* Charles Picerni. *Running time:* 105 minutes. *MPAA Rating:* R.

CAST: Sean Connery (Paul Armstrong); Laurence Fishburne (Tanny Brown); Kate Capshaw (Laurie Armstrong); Blair Underwood (Bobby Earl Ferguson); Ed Harris (Blair Sullivan); Christopher Murray (Wilcox); Ruby Dee (Evangeline); Scarlett Johansson (Kate); Daniel J. Travanti (Warden); Ned Beatty (McNair); Liz Torres, Ida Conklin, and Lynne Thigpen (Delores); Taral Hicks (Lena); Victor Slezak (Sergeant Rogers); Kevin McCarthy (Phil Prentiss); Hope Lange (Libby Prentiss); Chris Sarandon (Lyle Morgan); George Plimpton (Elder Phillips); Brooke Alderson (Dr. Doliveau); Colleen Fitzpatrick (Prosecutor); Richard Liberty (Chaplin); Joel S. Ehrenkranz (Judge); Barbara Jean Kane (Joanie Shriver); Maurice Jamaal Brown (Tanny's Son); Patrick Maycock (Jordan F. Vaughn); Francisco Paz (Concierge); Marie Hyman (Clerk); S. Bruce Wilson (Party Guest); Erik Stephan (Student); Melanie Hughes (Receptionist); Connie Lee Brown and Clarence Lark III (Prison Guards).

FILMS IN REVIEW, 7-8/95, p. 56, Russ G. Gregg

It is very tempting to completely write *Just Cause* off as another typical sloppy Hollywood thriller, but it deserves at least some critical attention. It is basically the same old story: executive-producer Sean Connery portrays the good lawyer, Paul "strong-arm-of-the-law" Armstrong, who searches for the buried truth about a gross injustice suffered by an "innocent" young man, played by Blair Underwood. But there is a real twist to this thriller because you can't trust anything the plot tells you. The viewer's expectations, shaped with implicit trust in the veracity of the plot's information, are completely overturned by the plot itself by the time the credits roll. Such trickery is fine, especially for the thriller genre; but *Just Cause* fails to achieve a "pure shock" because it does not tease the viewer with the truth and insight throughout the story; instead, it misleads with conspicuous calculation. Character deceives character in the story, so director Arne Glimcher, likewise, deceives his audience. With every aspect of the film's form geared to completely mislead the audience, *Just Cause* is almost a blatant cinematic lie, a bit too pretentious. Not that lies are always completely bad. All people need lies; for, arguably, truth cannot exist without deception.

But *Just Cause* does not simply tell the viewer a few innocent white lies. This film weaves infinite webs of celluloid deception through its cinematography and elusive editing, both of which, like an impromptu alibi, occasionally lack grace. These elements earn their merit, however, by effectively misleading the viewer, an appropriate gesture for a thriller about a deception. Gearing the story to Armstrong's perspective, Glimcher attempts to force the viewer to experience the same deception he experiences, not that anyone would really care about this stereotypical Atticus Finch-like character by the end.

For example, the recurring low angle shots of Chief Tanny Brown, deftly performed by Laurence Fishburne, force the viewer to see him as a powerful and abusive man; naturally, any viewer would believe Bobby's story after seeing such a signpost. He towers above the camera and Bobby Earl during the interrogation scene, kicking Bobby out of the frame into the next shot. Remember also the ending of the scene at the Brown household, in which Brown ejects Armstrong before he goes to the swamp. The low angle shot of the ominous Chief Brown in front of his house, in a flourish of Eisenstenian deception, cuts to the swamp with a level shot of a submerging crocodile. An intellectual montage? Hardly, for as such, the cut suggests no narrative truth which makes the metaphor work. This particular "visual metaphor" does not accurately describe Brown as he appears in the story, but it lies to the viewer. It describes only what the director wants you to think of Brown at that point, before the plot gives away its own self-conscious lie about his true character.

But who needs subtle editing and cinematography with such a deliberate director who tailors every other element of this film to trick his audience? Recall when Chief Brown (remember, he's a good guy), dressed in a black hat, walks into the low angle shot of the interrogation chamber as the soundtrack plays menacing music of impending doom. With this blatantly deceptive and excessive stylization, there is no room to doubt that Brown is the bad guy by the end of the shot, although he is really a good guy. The only cue to Brown's true, gentle nature, ironically, is this film's conspicuous overstylization, so excessive that it verges on complete affectation. With every single stylistic element of the medium pointing to Brown's malevolence, a very practiced viewer could feasibly smell the deception, and expect just the opposite.

Chances are, however, that most people allow themselves to be, for lack of better words, lied to, which is fine for some. Consider the deceptiveness of the various acting styles in the film and how the director must have affected these performances. There lies an inconsistent and irreconcilable difference in Larry Fishburne's (and, for that matter, Blair Underwood's) performance at the beginning of the film and at the end. A threatening and conniving smokey (and most likely suspect for the murder at hand) at the film's beginning, the true Tanny Brown is revealed to be a kind, fatherly man-of-the-law bereft by Joanie Shriver's death. But nothing happens in the plot to justify these changes in his manner, unless he is schizophrenic. Imagine how unbelievable a performance like this would seem in a play, with no low-angle shots and suggestive cutting to force the idea of Brown's corruption on the viewer. Without a life-changing incident involving a character in the plot, there is no way to explain such antithetical acting styles other than the director's blatant trickery.

All stories, in general, are lies, and it is an obvious fact that thrillers, by their nature, usually entail some kind of deception; Glimcher, however, seems to be a very bad liar. Constructing his entire film around those various surprise character turns detracts from the film's suspense, a must in every thriller. The viewer never wonders, for example, who the murderer is because the film basically reveals that it is Tanny Brown. Of course, the story entertains as it surprises the viewer with the truth; anyone can surprise by telling a lie and contradicting themselves with the truth.

There seems to be room for a lot more than deception in this story, especially racial themes, since the script successfully uses both the "C" and "N" words within the first 15 minutes of the film. Instead, Glimcher, trickster that he is, sloppily discards everything for the empty and sudden surprise of overdirected character twists. After seeing this film, it is hard not to share William Burroughs' disdain with most modern art, that it is not art at all, but trickery. Not to say the film is terrible in its entirety; on the contrary, it has extremely competent and enjoyable sections. American cinema has seen few interrogations as horrifying as Chief Brown's harassment of Bobby Earl. The camera movement during Bobby's confession creates such a desperate helplessness and sense of injustice (false as it may be) that it can be compared to the highest caliber of "moving camera" films, like *Blow Out*. Though far from cathartic, it is both entertaining and familiar to see Bobby become crocodile food at the poachers' stand. After all, most of us were told as children that we would share the same fate for telling a lie.

LOS ANGELES TIMES, 2/17/95, Calendar/p. 4, Peter Rainer

The murder thriller "Just Cause," starring Sean Connery and Laurence Fishburne, is set in the Florida Everglades. And a good thing, too. This is a thriller that needs all the fronds and storks and gators it can get.

It doesn't bog down in the bogs, but it's slow-moving just about everyplace else. It's the kind of legal-eagle mystery where someone is always stopping someone else every 10 minutes to recap the action—just in case we weren't paying attention. This two-steps-forward-one-step-back approach makes for one jerky ride.

Scripted from the Jonathan Katzenbach novel by Jeb Stuart and Peter Stone, and directed by Arne Glimcher, "Just Cause" comes across like a mishmash of moments from "Cape Fear" and "In the Heat of the Night" by way of "Strangers on a Train." Connery plays Paul Armstrong, a

Harvard Law professor who decides to take on the case of Bobby Earl (Blair Underwood), a young man on death row he believes unjustly accused eight years earlier of murdering a 10-year-old girl. Armstrong hasn't practiced law in 25 years but, as his prosecutor wife (Kate Capshaw) tells him, "Every once in a while you gotta get a little bloody—it's good for the soul."

Since academia is considered something less than the real world in this movie, Armstrong's descent into the Everglades is depicted as if it were a jaunt into Hades. (The notion that life in Harvard's upper echelons might be as back-stabby as life in the backwater small-town precincts of Florida never seems to have crossed the filmmakers' minds.) The condemned man and the Harvard prof turn out to have something in common—they were both the first in their families to go to college.

But Earl, who passed through the portals of Cornell, is black, and he sees his conviction as an example of old-style racism in the New South, where high-level blacks carry out white supremacist policy. (The arresting officer was black; the murdered girl was white.) He believes his refusal to shuck and jive has condemned him, his confession, obtained after 22 hours of torture at the hands of the local arresting officer, Tanny Brown (Laurence Fishburne), is openly disbelieved by his sympathizers.

The attempt to turn "Just Cause" into some kind of racial statement wears thin fast. And maybe that's just as well, since, if you bother to examine what the film is ultimately saying, it's a sweet slice of reactionary-ism.

But you don't have to get heavy-duty political to poke holes here. Start with the casting. Connery is such a staunch and worldly presence that casting him as a bookish prof tiptoeing through the marshes is a hoot. When a particularly nasty cop tries to scare Armstrong by shaking his hand—hard—you expect Connery to cleave the guy in two instead of wince. And when Brown tries to scare Armstrong by choking him with his seat belt, you expect more of a retaliation than a mere gasping for air.

Connery's heroic presence is scaled down to near-invisibility here (just as Nick Nolte's was in "Cape Fear") and it throws the entire film out of whack. Connery shouldn't be cast as the common man risen to mythic heights. He's *already* mythic. Everyone in this film is supposed to have a double identity but the doubleness is rote. Armstrong is a strong opponent of the death penalty so, of course, we expect his principles to be put to the test. Earl is enraged all right—but is he also guilty? Brown begins the movie as murderous thug-cop who holds a gun inside Earl's mouth to provoke a confession; in his later scenes he appears to have undergone a sadism-ectomy. His family romps and joshing badinage with Armstrong are played straight, without irony. Sadism in this movie is a spur of the moment thing—it gets written out of the script when it's no longer required to get a rise out of the audience.

The one exception to all this is Ed Harris' performance as Blair Sullivan, the Hannibal Lecter-like death row inmate who also claims to have killed the 10-year-old girl. Harris gives his role a fearful grace: He looks like a skinned rabbit, and when he goes into one of his crazy-man trances, his eyes seem to slide upward into his skull. Harris has always been good at playing lethal, but he's never before been this scary.

If the movie had been about Sullivan it would have kept its viewers awake nights. But audiences for "Just Cause" will be able to sleep soundly, perhaps even catch a few winks in the theater.

NEW YORK POST, 2/17/95, p. 49, Michael Medved

The new thriller "Just Cause" contains so many preposterous and arbitrary twists and turns that a more appropriate title might be "Just Because."

Characters go off and on tangents and the story tilts idiotically on its axis for no other reason than the illogical decrees of the shamelessly manipulative plot.

Based on a novel by former Miami Herald crime reporter John Katzenbach, the movie centers on a brilliant professor at Harvard Law School, played by Sean Connery.

We know he's supposed to be brilliant because we first see him while he's denouncing capital punishment in a public (and puerile) debate against a hapless George Plimpton.

After this meeting, Connery's approached by a member of the audience (played by Ruby Dee in an effective cameo), who's traveled up to Cambridge to ask the great professor to intervene to save the life of her grandson, a death row inmate in Florida.

After discussing the matter with his wife, a former prosecutor played by Kate Capshaw, Connery heads down to the Everglades to investigate the case.

The condemned man (a suitably suave Blair Underwood) says that he confessed to the rape and murder of an 11-year-old girl only after brutal beatings and torture by local cops.

The principal police official, and the chief obstacle to Connery's investigation, is a surly, suspicious hothead played by Laurence Fishburne—who calls to mind all the old stereotypes of the racist Southern small-town cop except for the fact that he happens to be black.

There's an obvious resentment between this Fishburne character, a hard-working, blue-collar African-American, and the Underwood character, a more upwardly mobile type who once enjoyed a scholarship to Cornell. But like all the other potentially intriguing elements in the story, it goes absolutely nowhere.

The movie's other significant character is a psychotic serial killer who, from his jail cell on death row, might just help Connery solve the murder mystery.

Played by the scenery-chewing Ed Harris as a sort of cornpone Hannibal Lecter, this figure recycles one of Hollywood's most obnoxious recent stereotypes (see Scorsese's "Cape Fear") of a Crazy Convict Killer Christian; he is constantly invoking the name of Jesus or quoting the Bible while gleefully discussing murder and mayhem.

The movie's overall "things are seldom what they seem" theme never pays off because the characters are equally phony and one-dimensional both before and after the key revelations that turn the plot on its head; the indestructible star power of Fishburne and Connery (who also served as executive producer) counts for nothing.

A climactic and hopelessly hackneyed chase scene, in which every single participant behaves in an absurd and implausible fashion, only intensifies the annoyance factor.

Director Arne Glimcher battled some similarly clumsy plot elements in his one previous outing, "The Mambo Kings." But at least that film offered some intoxicating atmosphere.

Here, even the purportedly creepy Everglades locations seem fraudulent—as primal and dangerous as the Jungle Cruise at Disney World—and the picture quickly sinks beneath the murky waters.

NEWSDAY, 2/17/95, Part II/p. B2, Jack Mathews

Arne Glimcher, the Pace Gallery founder who has segued from fine art to mass audience movies, has proven to be a quick study in his Hollywood career. "Mambo Kings," which marked his directing debut, showed that he could make a melodrama as ripe as anything Arthur Hiller has ever done. And with his new film, "Just Cause," he demonstrates a spectacular flair for the clichés of the suspense thriller genre.

Suspense fans will tolerate clichés—cling to them like lifejackets!—if we're being led through a taut, scary and unpredictable story. And for two-thirds of the way through "Just Cause," we follow willingly along. But that last third is so completely mundane, the script ought not to have even made it to television.

"Just Cause," adapted from the John Katzenbach novel by Jeb Stuart ("The Fugitive") and the veteran Peter Stone ("Charade," "Sweet Charity"), stars Sean Connery as a Harvard law professor and death penalty opponent who gets drawn out of the halls of academe to take up the cause of a black prisoner awaiting execution in Florida.

It's been 25 years since Connery's Paul Armstrong has practiced law, and while his lawyer wife (Kate Capshaw) makes much of his need to stoke the old advocate's fire, it isn't law that he's going to practice in Florida. He's going to become a detective, and reinvestigate the cheesy case that put the handsome articulate Bobby Earl Ferguson ("L.A. Law's" Blair Underwood) on Death Row.

Ferguson claims he was beaten and tortured into confessing to the rape and mutilation murder of an 11-year-old white girl, then rushed through a trial designed to calm the fury of the community. Further, the lunatic who actually committed the crime, says Ferguson, is in an adjacent Death Row cell, cackling over Ferguson's predicament.

Who does Armstrong believe, Ferguson or the black cop (Laurence Fishburne) he insists railroaded him? And in any event, will Armstrong sustain his moral objection to the death penalty?

That's all the plot I can comfortably reveal, but be warned. The rest is pure malarkey, ruined not so much by predictability as improbability. Virtually everything that occurs in the last half-hour is either banal or beyond the pale.

Clearly, it is his choice of material, more than any artistic shortcomings, that seems to define Glimcher as a budding studio hack. "Mambo Kings" was a flashy Cuban-American soap opera that allowed him to show off his senses of color, music and composition. With "Just Cause," which allows him to test his palette on the black-green swamps of the Everglades, he seems more determined to buff up his resume as a mainstream director.

Glimcher can have that career. His films are inventively shot and gracefully paced, and he works well with actors. He got a performance from Armand Assante in "Mambo Kings" that I would have thought was out of that actor's range, and there is uniformly good work on display in "Just Cause."

Connery is as engaging as ever, playing a wise old owl of a lawyer who actually gets in over his head in a southern redneck town. Fishburne commands the screen every bit as much as Connery, but in a completely different way. The camera need only turn in his direction and he fills the frame with what I can only describe as a charismatic dread.

The showpiece performance, however, is given by Ed Harris, playing the Death Row maniac Blair Sullivan as a Hannibal Lecter on speed. Harris is a sight, shackled to a conference room table, the veins popping out of his bald head and the spit flying, as he tries to both intimidate and manipulate Armstrong.

But all the goodwill built by the performances is squandered by the ludicrous twists and clichéd action sequences in the final moments. No saving graces are possible in a thriller with a bad ending.

SIGHT AND SOUND, 5/95, p. 47, Claire Monk

Florida 1986. A white police Lieutenant, Wilcox, and his black assistant, Detective Tanny Brown, arrest Bobby Earl Ferguson, a young black man. In custody, Wilcox beats him and asks leading questions about a sex attack. Eight years on at a Harvard University symposium, law academic Paul Armstrong lectures on the disproportionate number of blacks who are executed for murder. A woman tells him her grandson, Bobby Earl, is on Death Row for a crime he didn't commit, Paul is reluctant to help but his wife Laury—like him a former DA—persuades him.

In Florida Paul reads up on the rape and murder of Joanie Shriver which Bobby Earl says Tanny Brown framed him for. Bobby Earl claims Tanny extracted the confession by forcing him to play Russian Roulette. Bobby Earl's dental records were never matched to the bite marks on the body and no semen traces were mentioned in the white female pathologist's report. Tanny drives Paul along the killer's route to the murder spot in the Everglades and almost strangles him with the seatbelt—supposedly to show that Joanie's screams would have been inaudible five minutes from town.

Tanny reveals that Bobby Earl had been charged with kidnap (and acquitted) in another state. Bobby Earl says his 'victim', a white girl, wanted to come out in his car. He claims her *real* killer is a serial killer, Blair Sullivan, held on the same Death Row. Tanny mentions that Laury was the prosecutor at Bobby Earl's kidnap trial—which Paul didn't know. Laury had plea-bargained the case but it was thrown out. During an adjournment, Bobby was badly beaten in the cells; Laury's guilt made her persuade Paul to help him. Paul visits Sullivan, who claims not to remember if Joanie was one of his victims, but who tells Paul, in Biblical riddles, the location of the murder weapon. Tanny joins Paul in a hunt in the Everglades. Paul finds a knife—a scimitar consistent with Joanie's unusual wounds—hidden in a culvert.

Letters from Sullivan about "carving up" Joanie secure Bobby Earl's release on probation. Sullivan phones Paul: his death warrant has been signed, and he asks Paul to say goodbye to his family on his behalf. Paul arrives at the Sullivans' house to find dead, decaying bodies. Sullivan confesses that he never met Shriver. Tanny tells Paul the confession is useless if Sullivan isn't alive to testify, but Sullivan is electrocuted.

Having slashed Wilcox's throat, Bobby Earl abducts Laury and Katie. Paul and Tanny lose their trail and head for the Everglades where, in a hut, they find Laury and Katie bound and gagged. Bobby Earl attacks Tanny and, entering the hut, announces that during his kidnap trial beating he was also castrated. Paul calls his bluff by claiming that Blair Sullivan has had a stay of execution. Tanny reappears alive; Bobby Earl is stabbed by Paul with his own knife, then devoured by a crocodile. In relief and shock, the reunited family stagger to Tanny's car.

"This is a case that hangs together by the thinnest of threads, explains Laurence Fishburne's black Florida cop to Sean Connery's liberal white Harvard law academic. "Now, if you start pickin' at them threads, they collapse." The same could be said of this big, expensive legal thriller.

As an adrenalin-generator, *Just Cause* can't be argued with, and there are enough acerbic pleasures of script, acting and detail for it to convince—at first—that it's the classy, intelligent vehicle it thinks it is. The movie is mature enough, for instance, to include a marital relationship in which cynical mutual knowledge between partners is the sign of a bond rather than breakdown. When Laury tells Paul, after the revelation of her role in Bobby Earl's kidnap trial, that she wants him to "make it right" for Bobby Earl, he ripostes: "No honey—you want me to make it right for you." Blair Underwood makes a persuasively clever, bitter Bobby Earl until the script starts making his job impossible. Then there's Connery: his arrival at Miami airport hemmed in by slack-wearing seniors—probably no older than he is—is a hoot. But take away the adrenalin rush and *Just Cause* starts looking incoherent, derivative and fundamentally hokey. What begins promisingly as a clever, Scott Turow-ish legal twister with a campaigning streak changes halfway through into a pale echo of *The Silence of the Lambs* before plundering *Cape Fear* to conjure a last-minute women-in-peril climax. In the process, a complex black protagonist is sidelined in favour of a near-parodic white serial-killer narrative, with all the attendant clichés.

Possibly this shift in tone has been conceived to keep audiences amused; what it actually does is destroy the film's psychological credibility. When Paul enters Sullivan's cell, recent generic convention requires the brilliant lawyer to fall under the born-again nutter's hypnotic spell—a development not only at odds with Paul's shrewdness but also with Ed Harris's amusingly camp personification of Sullivan. The *übermensch* status of the formulaic movie serial-killer ensures that Sullivan enjoys not only charismatic power but unexplained prison privileges: no third-party witness is ever present at the pair's encounters. In a similar vein, Capshaw's detention worker Laury—self-assured enough to cover up for a young offender who has hit her in the face by telling a judge the bruises were caused by Paul—is hardly the likeliest woman to end up under the thumb of a sexual psychopath.

But then *Just Cause*'s one coherent message is that nothing is as it seems: a 'true' flashback showing that Tanny Brown really did extort Bobby Earl's confession at gunpoint is followed by a misleading one showing Joanie getting into Tanny's car outside the school. But where a smart thriller wrong-foots us by showing us truths before we can make sense of them, *Just Cause* plays with verisimilitude so promiscuously that it ought to be charged with wasting audience time. Such psychological basics as the question of Laury's murky motivation are avoided. The corollary of this message is that good and evil, truth and lies are all one and the same. The 'lesson' Paul learns—that integrity may cause harm and lies may bring about good—is essentially illiberal and anti-ethical. It is not until he breaks with the morality which the film initially seemed to advocate—by lying that Sullivan is alive and murdering Bobby Earl with his own knife—that 'justice' is finally done.

The unwitting result is a film which is narratively and morally perverse, since everything we are shown or told is in danger of not ringing true. Plot credibility rests on a revelation so ludicrous—Bobby Earl's hilariously casual announcement, five minutes before the end, that the police castrated him—you'll need nerves of steel not to laugh. The ultimate targets of this nihilism are the very same liberal and intellectual principles which the film initially held up for our admiration. While Paul's scholarly rationality and commitment to justice nearly precipitate the rape and murder of his wife and daughter, small-town and racially-motivated prejudices against a black high-achiever are shown to be rooted in sound instinct. *Just Cause* is just another instance of the currently flourishing Hollywood ideology of reactionary liberalism, in which stupidity and prejudice are held to be somehow superior to thought.

VILLAGE VOICE, 2/28/95, p. 76, Abby McGanney Nolan

Pace gallery founder-turned-film director Arne Glimcher, who took the mambo out of *The Mambo Kings*, doesn't give us any reason for *Just Cause*, a star-studded John Grisham-Thomas Harris pastiche. There are twists and turns aplenty but not one genuine thrill as Harvard Law professor Paul Armstrong (Sean Connery) maneuvers to save convicted Cornell scholarship student Bobby Earl Ferguson (Blair Underwood) from the executioner's ax.

The setting is the Florida Everglades; it isn't long before we are knee-deep in a swamplike script. Underwood sits on death row for the rape and murder of a 10-year-old white girl. Connery has a 10-year-old white girl of his own but takes the case because of his anti-capital punishment sentiments and because his lovely wife (Kate Capshaw) wants him to visit the "real world" for a change. Thanks, honey. He flies south *en famille* and plays Sherlock Dershowitz. Awaiting him is Tanny Brown (Laurence Fishburne), an inexplicably tough cop with a penchant for gratuitously violent scenes.

Glimcher refines the plodding formula of *The Firm* and *The Pelican Brief* by perfecting the way in which all major plot reversals are preceded by a moment of obviously false calm. Reviewers have been asked not to reveal the nature of these twists (or the lame *Cape Fear* finale), but, yes, the tables are turned and toppled and turned, all over again. This doesn't necessarily make the tale any more compelling—or even surprising. Ed Harris does manage some bone-chilling moments as a serial killer with a scary haircut. But far more creepy is the ridiculous "good black man versus bad black man" setup.

Connery usually manages to avoid prosecution for his mercenary moves—who blames him for *Rising Sun*? *Just Cause*, which he executive-produced, may not be so easily erased from his rap sheet.

Also reviewed in:
CHICAGO TRIBUNE, 2/17/95, Friday/p. C2, Michael Wilmington
NEW REPUBLIC, 3/20/95, p. 29, Stanley Kauffmann
NEW YORK TIMES, 2/17/95, p. C18, Janet Maslin
VARIETY, 2/13-19/95, p. 47, Todd McCarthy
WASHINGTON POST, 2/17/95, p. F7, Hal Hinson
WASHINGTON POST, 2/17/95, Weekend/p. 42, Desson Howe

K.K.K. BOUTIQUE AIN'T JUST REDNECKS, THE

Producer: Camille Billops and James V. Hatch. *Director:* Camille Billops and James V. Hatch. *Screenplay:* Camille Billops and James V. Hatch. *Director of Photography:* Dion Hatch. *Editor:* S.A. Burns. *Music:* George Brooker and Christa Victoria. *Running time:* 76 minutes. *MPAA Rating:* Not Rated.

NEW YORK POST, 3/3/95, p. 49, Bill Hoffmann

Imagine an ongoing stream-of-consciousness workshop where people can go to discuss their ideas about racism.

That's the premise behind "The KKK Boutique Ain't Just Rednecks," a 76-minute exploration of who's racist and why.

The boutique is actually a dark warehouse staffed by politically hip performance artists who lead racially mixed groups through a series of mind exercises to get to the root of their racist tendencies.

And there is a real boutique here, a place that sells neo-Nazi blouses and goose-stepper boots.

"The KKK Boutique" assumes that everybody is instilled with some form of racism and the only way it can be exorcised is by talking it through.

There's the elderly black woman who tells of the time in 1928 when her family bought a house in an all-white neighborhood and got a visit from the Ku Klux Klan.

Then there's the prejudice some young black women harbor against dark-skinned blacks and how they would never go out with one. Black is OK, they say, but the lighter the better.

The problem with "The KKK Boutique" is that it's too sophomoric in approach sort of like an elementary school class putting on a play about racism.

Costumed members of the boutique's staff use skits and songs to coax the audience into baring their souls.

Only there's little new, and the prejudices that are expressed won't shock anybody.

After decades of fine documentaries on racism on outlets like PBS, "The KKK Boutique" seems like little more than an adult cartoon, albeit a cartoon with some interesting social issues.

NEWSDAY, 3/3/95, Part II/p. B7, John Anderson

Racism is our Delilah: It saps our strength, makes us less productive, divides us and distracts us. It also makes us look ridiculous. And we embrace it like a lover.

So Camille Billops and James V. Hatch, the married makers of "The KKK Boutique Ain't Just Rednecks," are certainly on the right track with their so-called "docu-fantasy," which alternates broadly comedic sketches with deadly serious testimony about race, sex and hatred in these here budget-balancing United States. Their aim is to make bias look ludicrous—while at the same time establishing that everyone, no matter how enlightened they think they are, harbors prejudices of some kind, toward someone, with varying degrees of acknowledgement and vitriol.

But the balance is a bit off, because of the very seesaw sensibility the couple exercises. Taking us through the Boutique itself—set up in Dante-esque levels of hell—we're given the most baggy-pants kind of comedy and then confronted with actual witnesses telling real stories about fear and hate. The trouble is, you're not always sure about what's what, and not always ready for it.

Some scenes are painfully acute. The Public Theater's George C. Wolfe, for instance, as an Alistair Cooke-style TV host, sings a turn-of-the-century song titled "Coon, Coon, Coon," and his self-conscious loathing makes it an uncomfortable burlesque. Conversely, a mock quiz show called "May I Touch Her Here?" is supposed to be a satirical dart at male sexual hang-ups about women of other races but is less than pointed. And there's no corresponding send-up of female attitudes—suggesting the film has a blind spot of its own.

The jarring lack of delicacy in tying segments together is supposed to force the viewer to confront his or her presumptions, but occasionally the segue is counterproductive. At one point, a black man appears, recalling a friend, a World War II vet, who was dragged off a bus, beaten and his eyes gouged out for failing to abide by southern racial etiquette. While you're digesting this bit of horror, the film cuts to a harlequin-faced fiend wrapped in American flags who asks "Why are niggers so black?" The result is resentment toward the filmmakers for puncturing the moment.

Billops and Hatch—who made the acclaimed 1991 documentary "Finding Christa," about Billops' reunion with the daughter she'd given up for adoption—are themselves the most affecting aspect of "The KKK Boutique."

Opening the film in a field of sunflowers, cutting and combing each other's hair, they reminisce about what it's been like as an interracial couple—Hatch is white, Billops is black—and their candor and ease with each other confirms that what they're trying to do is worth the effort, even if they don't always hit the target squarely.

VILLAGE VOICE, 3/7/95, p. 61, Leslie Camhi

Cutting and combing each other's hair in a field of sunflowers, filmmakers Camille Billops and James Hatch chat about the racism they've encountered during some 30 years as a happy interracial couple. In their new documentary, *The KKK Boutique*, conversations between the couple and their friends alternate with fantasy sequences in which they blend Brechtian and flower-child aesthetics to create a vision of racial hell, a darkly Disney-esque version of Dante's *Inferno*.

"Our workshop on racism is going to be a very personal journey for each of you," Billops promises visitors to their "KKK Boutique." Like a cross between Dante's Virgil and the Mad Hatter, she leads her "boutiquers" through several way stations of prejudice: from a shop of racial fashions to a sinister sexual parody of a TV game show, *May I Touch You Here?* ending at the "pit," the final circle, where elaborately costumed creatures are frozen in their hatred.

A dramatic recital of "Coon! Coon! Coon!" a 1901 song about passing ("I wish my color would fade/I'd like to be a different shade"), proves to be a malignant revelation; unfortunately, the conversations that punctuate the more visionary antics tend too often toward banality. Billops bitingly defines racism as her "general dislike of everyone on the street," but Hatch later categorizes it as exclusively "a male testosterone reaction." Nevertheless, the couple's black humor and childlike seriousness are endearing and undoubtedly hard-earned, and the sheer strangeness of the demons that populate their racial hell makes the film worth viewing. How often, after all, does one get to see a nice white man all dressed up as Mammy?

Also reviewed in:
NEW YORK TIMES, 3/3/95, p. C14, Stephen Holden

KICKING AND SCREAMING

A Trimark Pictures release of a Joel Castleberg/Sandollar/Trimark production. *Executive Producer:* Sandy Gallin, Carol Baum, and Mark Amin. *Producer:* Joel Castleberg. *Director:* Noah Baumbach. *Screenplay:* Noah Baumbach. *Story:* Noah Baumbach and Oliver Berkman. *Director of Photography:* Steven Bernstein. *Editor:* J. Kathleen Gibson. *Music:* Phil Marshall. *Casting:* Ellie Kanner. *Production Designer:* Dan Whifler. *Costumes:* Mary Jane Fort. *Running time:* 96 minutes. *MPAA Rating:* R.

CAST: Josh Hamilton (Grover); Sam Gould (Pete); Catherine Kellner (Gail); Jonathan Baumbach (Professor); John Lehr (Louis); Olivia d'Abo (Jane); Peter Czernin (Lester); Carlos Jacott (Otis); Chris Eigeman (Max); Eric Stoltz (Chet); Eliza Roberts (Josselyn); Jason Wiles (Skippy); Parker Posey (Miami); Chris Reed (Friederich); Noah Baumbach (Danny); Jason S. Kassin (Freddy); Cara Buono (Kate); David Deluise (Bouncer); Thea Goodman (Friederich's Date); Lauren Katz (Stephanie); Alexia Landau (Nose Ring Girl); Perrey Reeves (Amy); Anthony Giglio, Jr. (Singing Freshman #1); Richard Tacchino (Singing Freshman #2); Nico Baumbach (Random Freshman); Jose Ignacio Alvarez (Stunt Knight #1); Solier Fagundez (Stunt Knight #2); David Kirsch (Ike); Matthew Kaplan (Omar); Dean Cameron (Zach); Elliott Gould (Grover's Dad); Marissa Ribisi (Charlotte); Kaela Dobkin (Audra); Sal Viscuso (Bar Teacher); Jessica Hecht (Ticket Woman); Nora Perricone (Door Person); Melanie Koch (Girl at Bar).

LOS ANGELES TIMES, 10/25/95, Calendar/p. 1, Kevin Thomas

Noah Baumbach's "Kicking and Screaming" takes many of us back to one of life's more painful periods: the immediate aftermath of college graduation. For a lot of us, especially those whose years on campus preceded the rancor of the Vietnam War era, college was four years in a cocoon, filled with hard work and fun and more friends than perhaps we ever had before or ever would again.

Some of us graduates were plunged into uncertainty because of a change in goals. But this film's four young men, whom we meet at their graduation party, don't seem to have thought about life after college, and they are clinging to the past with all their might.

For a first film, "Kicking and Screaming" is at once ambitious and uncompromising; it is in fact quite serious even though it is essentially a comedy. It's the kind of film that is worth more for what promises in Baumbach's future than for what he actually delivers.

Two remarks, both made by women, cut to the heart of the matter: that these four guys talk alike and what they talk about is trivia. They even resemble each other in that all four are slim young men with dark hair and regular rather than handsome features. As a result it takes some time to be able to distinguish Grover (Josh Hamilton), Max (Chris Eigeman), Skippy (Jason Wiles) and Otis (Carlos Jacott) from one another. They are well-spoken, even at times erudite. Eigeman was also in Whit Stillman's "Metropolitan" and "Barcelona," the films that "Kicking and Screaming" most resembles in tone and attitude.

It's a difficult film to get into, for it is punctuated with flashbacks of Grover's longing memories of the radiant young woman (Olivia d'Abo) he let get away from him and with periodic bottom-of-the-screen announcements like "Spring Break"; at times we wonder if the whole picture may be a flashback. It isn't, it's just that the guys, who share a nice old Craftsman cottage, behave as if they were still in school, with Skippy even continuing to take classes.

The film is also hard to connect with because Baumbach is tough-minded enough not to try to work up undue sympathy for these four, who spend a large hunk of their time at a local bar, presided over by Chet (Eric Stoltz), who has settled for life as a permanent student.

Baumbach might well have dared to be a bit more conventional and shown them at least trying to get jobs. Only Otis does, finding work at a video store. Meanwhile, we're left wondering just how they're supporting themselves in this protracted limbo of feeling sorry for themselves; whatever misery they experience is self-inflicted and not from trying to make their way in the world.

Baumbach, however, pushes his rigorous stance to the extent that you begin to wonder why you're bothering to watch the aimless lives of these four unfold. Baumbach surely does make these characters, all of whom are impeccably acted, absolutely real, but at 25 he may be too close to the material to achieve the detachment from which irony and meaning flow. Besides d'Abo's Jane, the other young women are Parker Posey's Miami, who has outgrown Skippy, and Cara Buono as a vivacious 16-year-old townie.

All three are lots more grown up than the men, which is certainly true to life. Elliott Gould is refreshing as Grover's father, as open as Grover is self-absorbed. Finally settling on Grover as his key character, Baumbach builds unobtrusively to a knock-your-socks-off finish that allows "Kicking and Screaming" to conclude on its strongest note.

NEW YORK POST, 10/6/95, p. 50, Thelma Adams

As "Kicking and Screaming" opens, a graduation reveler asks, "Would you rather be stranded on a desert island with McNeill or Lehrer?" From that moment on, the dry one-liners whiz by like bullets in a western.

Noah Baumbach ponders the question, "Is there life after college?" While the 25-year-old writer/director has been busy hatching his first movie (which had the distinction of screening at the New York Film Festival), the four recent grads at the story's center are victims of inertia, terrified by their own witty worst-case scenarios.

The slacker quartet includes Grover the heartsick writer (Josh Hamilton), Max the curmudgeon ("Barcelona's" Chris Eigeman), Otis the neurotic (Carlos Jacott) and lost boy Skippy (Jason Wiles). The buddies hover at the edge of campus, drinking beer, chasing freshman girls and living in fear that they will turn into the local Yoda—Chet (Eric Stoltz), the 28-year-old perennial student.

The movie skips lightly forward on a sea of quips, pausing only to look back at Grover's lost love, Jane (Olivia d'Abo). A fellow fiction writer, she has grabbed a grant to study in the Czech Republic and moved on. Prague," says Grover, "you'll come back a bug."

"Kicking and Screaming" follows the romance between Grover and Jane in flashback. The two met in writing class. Jane's first words were a critique of her future lover's fiction: the characters in Grover's stories spend all their time discuss inconsequential things."

Grover is from the Ann Beattie, Raymond Carver, college workshop school of contemporary American fiction. Baumbach also tries to build toward an epiphany, a moment of deep feeling, through indirection, conflicts that avoid the great divide between characters, snappy remarks delivered as a defense against heartfelt feeling. He hopes, through the careful accumulation of small, familiar moments that ring true for how we live in the present, to push through to a deeper resonance.

As a filmmaker, Baumbach evokes Whit Stillman, the chronicler of Upper East Side culture. Both create an ironic social commentary by setting up sharp, well-cast navel-gazers and sending them spinning with a barrage of pointed dialogue.

In contrast, Stillman's milieus—Manhattan's rising upper crust in "Metropolitan" or the Yank expatriates and Spanish flames of "Barcelona"—are rarely under the camera's lens. His themes—patriotism or a critique of liberalism—go against the Hollywood grain. Stillman strays far from the Generation X crowd, whereas Baumbach's slackers, though compelling, are familiar, kin to the cast of "Reality Bites."

Baumbach, however, is more generous to his characters than Stillman. He indulges his boys like paper-trained puppies, but he adores the women who cast critical gazes from the periphery. Jane strikes out to test herself as a writer. Skippy's girlfriend Miami (the playfully pungent Parker Posey) has an internal guidance system that will never let her get as lost as her boy. Even Max, who does nothing but grouse and do the crossword puzzle, finds a teen-aged blue-collar babe (Cara Buono) who doesn't balk at adult responsibility.

It's Baumbach's grounded women who lead their men, "Kicking and Screaming," into adulthood—or leave them in the dust.

NEWSDAY, 10/4/95, Part II/p. B7, Jack Mathews

Who said talk is cheap? It's precious in Noah Baumbach's "Kicking and Screaming," and I mean that in the most flattering way.

The dialogue, the droll humor, the way his characters relate through a coded language is remarkably sharp and mature work for a first-time filmmaker, let alone one who was in the predicament of his own characters—college grads going not so easily into the real world—when he began writing it.

You do not have to have gone to college to be cued to the truths of "Kicking and Screaming." It's about that point in most men's lives when they face separation from their friends, from the comfort of those tight little fraternal orders of buddies that boys tend to form in adolescence and cling to—through thick and thin, through the good times and the bad, for better or worse—until death do them part, if possible.

You guys all talk the same, it is noted a couple of times by girls mixing with "Kicking's" four friends. And they do. They've developed a subtle dialect; not just in the use of words, but in the ideas, outlooks and humor expressed, and in the rhythm of their delivery. What starts out as self-conscious bonding ritual grows into something familial, and, of course, a constant annoyance for wives and girlfriends who feel excluded by it.

Baumbach catches that dynamic at the flash point, as Grover (Josh Hamilton), Max (Chris Eigeman), Skippy (Jason Wiles) and Otis (Carlos Jacott) graduate from college and face uncertain futures with massive insecurities, among them the prospects of love lives more complicated than having sex with incoming freshwomen.

Their instincts are not to do anything rash. Grover declines to follow his girlfriend Jane (Olivia d'Abo) to Prague, and sticks around to eat his heart out with the guys. Otis decides to defer his graduate scholarship in Milwaukee. The aptly named Skippy, who looks like he'd rather be skateboarding, is missing the hints that his girlfriend Miami (Parker Posey) has outgrown him. And Max is so dedicated to reminiscing, he reminisces the very moments he's in.

Baumbach is working very much in the style of Whit Stillman, who made a remarkable debut of his own with 1990's "Metropolitan," then slipped a bit with "Barcelona," a postgraduate "Metropolitan" in which the dialogue became precious in the worst sense; the lines were so self-consciously crafted, they could have been framed and mounted.

We'll see where Baumbach goes from here, but "Kicking and Screaming" is a smart beginning. He clearly has the most important powers of a storyteller—the ability to observe people and events and place them in perspective—and an apparent ease with the medium. (He got tremendous help from "Like Water for Chocolate" cinematographer Steven Bernstein.)

"Kicking and Screaming" has its rough spots, some sophomoric jokes and sight gags scattered among the many laugh-out-loud scenes, but it's an honest, engaging first film, with characters we can only hope Baumbach will revisit now and then.

NEWSWEEK, 10/23/95, p. 75, David Ansen

Remember the name Noah Baumbach. He's the 25-year-old writer/director of Kicking and Screaming, a smart and delicately rueful comedy about the terrifying leap from college into what is commonly known as real life. At first, the young, brainy and paralyzingly self-conscious graduates may strike you as cousins of Whit Stillman ("Metropolitan") and Richard Linklater ("Slacker"). But the arch wit of these kids is only their defense against entropy and angst. Baumbach himself is not afraid to strike deeper and sweeter emotional chords, as he takes us through a year in the lives of four inseparable male buddies, who nervously cling to their collegiate routines, while the women they know forge ahead with much less fuss and trembling. The expert ensemble includes Josh Hamilton and the delightful Olivia d'Abo as lovers whose affair doesn't survive graduation; the wonderfully petulant Chris Eigeman; the deft Parker Posey, and a very droll Eric Stoltz as a perpetual student and bar-stool philosopher content to have no ambitions at all. This modest, witty movie, with its fine ear for the undertone of aimless chatter, never raises its voice to make hollow Gen-X proclamations. Baumbach puts his trust in the details, and he gets them right.

TIME, 12/4/95, p. 87, Richard Corliss

Once it was the un-genre; now it is in danger of overpopulation. We speak of the post-modern comedy of manners, in which hyperarticulate twentysomethings talk—and talk and talk—about the imminent threat of becoming thirtynothings. They are the Sons of *Seinfeld*, and among the brightest of their number is Noah Baumbach's *Kicking and Screaming*, the little fable of half a dozen or so college grads. It's an upmarket *Clerks*, a less fraught *Jeffrey*, *Barcelona*, with a faster pulse—or maybe *Friends* on PBS. Grover (Josh Hamilton) doesn't want his girlfriend Jane (Olivia d'Abo) to go study in Prague—she'll "come back a bug." Max (Chris Eigeman), a guy so jaded that every new experience is déjà vu, falls in with cheeky Kate (Cara Buono). Chet (Eric Stoltz) is a professional student, and Otis (the delightfully morose Carlos Jacott) apparently plans to make a career of losing. They all share an avocation: chatting. The young men, especially, are "media slaves," infomaniacs. Who would win, Freddy or Jason? Does BANKRUPT come up more often on *Wheel of Fortune* now?

Cool is something these folks wear like a dinner jacket; their offhand wit is so studied that their bull sessions seem like a final they crammed for. But the writer-director is canny enough to salt the stew with poignancy, so that by the end these attitude machines have become human beings—more than the sum of their chiseled jokes. Baumbach is a find, of sorts: he has both comic sense and camera sense. Imagine Quentin Tarantino without the guns.

VILLAGE VOICE, 10/10/95, p. 69, J. Hoberman

Among other things, *The Addiction* [see Hoberman's review] slyly evokes the timeless self-importance of the student milieu—it may be the first vampire movie to include a thesis defense. What, one wonders, would willful Kathleen make of the reluctant graduates in Noah Baumbach's *Kicking and Screaming*—and what for that matter, would these sensitive wiseacres make of the outrageously ambitious movie which spawned her!

Kicking and Screaming, which conveniently opens next door to *The Addiction* at the Angelika (itself a student milieu), is a most auspicious debut by 25-year-old writer-director Noah Baumbach. Addressing the stimulating aimlessness of college life and the existential terror of graduation, it's a kind of slacker *No Exit* in which Grover (Josh Hamilton) and his three buddies stay on at school (at least through the fall semester), while Grover's senior-year girlfriend, Jane, leaves to study abroad.

Any movie romance between two aspiring undergraduate writers is bound to be self-conscious, and *Kicking and Screaming* is self-reflexively so—founded on overlapping dialogue and hyperverbal pyrotechnics, employing a worked-out back-and-forth structure that's punctuated by Jane's recurring calls from Prague. Although basically a guy thing—Eric Stoltz, the grand old man of ambitious youth comedies, even appears as a suitably bemused perpetual student—the female characters are more individuated than their male counterparts.

Jane may not be quite the wonder she's intended to be, but Olivia d'Abo is a fount of oddball mannerisms while Parker Posey, who has a cartoon character's hard-edged profile, confirms her status as a wired scene stealer. The precise shoddiness of the student mise-en-scène compensates for the vagueness of the generic locale—Cara Buono's Brooklynoid townie is a fully realized conception, but what planet does she come from!

If the ensemble performance and reliance on generational one-liners sometimes suggests a higher grade of *Friends*, the dialogue is as smart and funny as the camera placement is impeccable. That *Kicking and Screaming* is a notably literate (and film-literate) production should not be too surprising—the writer-director is the son of two writers, Jonathan Baumbach and our colleague Georgia Brown. If any child of mine produced a movie half so accomplished, I'd be bursting—even if it did include as mischievous a parental portrait as the one provided here by '60s fossil Elliott Gould.

Also reviewed in:
CHICAGO TRIBUNE, 11/10/95, Friday/p. J, Michael Wilmington
NEW YORK TIMES, 10/4/95, p. C16, Janet Maslin
VARIETY, 10/9-15/95, p. 61, Greg Evans
WASHINGTON POST, 11/17/95, p. F7, Hal Hinson

KID IN KING ARTHUR'S COURT, A

A Walt Disney Pictures release in association with Trimark Pictures and Tapestry Films. *Executive Producer:* Mark Amin. *Producer:* Robert L. Levy, Peter Abrams, and J.P. Guerin. *Director:* Michael Gottlieb. *Screenplay:* Michael Part and Robert L. Levy. *Director of Photography:* Elemer Ragalyi. *Editor:* Michael Ripps and Anita Brandt-Burgoyne. *Music:* J.A.C. Redford. *Music Editor:* Mark Green and David Cates. *Sound:* Otto Olah. *Sound Editor:* Gavin Myers, Gareth Vanderhope, Martin Bayley, and James Harvey. *Casting:* Allison Gordon-Kohler, John Hubbard, and Ros Hubbard. *Production Designer:* Laszlo Gardonyi. *Art Director:* Beata Vaurinecz. *Set Dresser:* Istvan Toth. *Special Effects:* Ferenc Ormos. *Costumes:* Maria Hruby. *Make-up:* Julia Vitray. *Stunt Coordinator:* Bela Unger. *Running time:* 91 minutes. *MPAA Rating:* PG.

CAST: Thomas Ian Nicholas (Calvin Fuller); Joss Ackland (King Arthur); Art Malik (Lord Belasco); Paloma Baeza (Princess Katey); Kate Winslet (Princess Sarah); Daniel Craig (Master Kane); David Tysall (Ratan); Ron Moody (Merlin); Barry Stanton (Blacksmith); Michael Mehlnan (Shop Owner); Melani Eoettinger (Peasant Woman); Rebecca Denton (Washer Woman); Michael Kelly (Apprentice); Louise Rosner (Lady in Waiting); Paul Rosner (Peasant Boy); Bela Unger (Head Guard); Shane Rimmer (Coach); Tim Wickham (Ricky Baker); Daniel Bennett (Howell); Debora Weston (Mom); Vincent Marzello (Dad); Catherine Blake (Maya); J.P. Guerin (Umpire).

LOS ANGELES TIMES, 8/11/95, Calendar/p. 4, Kevin Thomas

On a sunny day in the San Fernando Valley a nervous 14-year-old, Calvin Fuller (Thomas Ian Nicholas), steps up to bat and strikes out. Suddenly, an earthquake hits and a fissure opens up in the ground, with Calvin falling into the void only to plop down in a 12th Century English countryside.

No, it's not the San Andreas Fault acting up, but rather Merlin the Magician (Ron Moody), sending out a call for a hero to rescue an aging King Arthur (Joss Ackland) from the evil clutches of the ambitious Lord Belasco (Art Malik). It seems both the Valley kid and the monarch are suffering from a lack confidence, but you can be certain that they will have recovered triumphantly by the time Disney's fine family comedy-adventure "A Kid in King Arthur's Court" is over.

This lively time-travel fantasy is the clear result of imagination and reflection on the part of writers Michael Part and Robert L. Levy and director Michael Gottlieb and their colleagues, who possess a crucial light touch. Shot extensively—and most handsomely—in Czechoslovakia using a number of real castles, "A Kid in King Arthur's Court" strikes just the right balance in its conception and design. In conversation the citizens of Camelot use "thee" and "thou" but speak in a natural manner, and the look of the film is neither grotty nor overly glamorous. The film, in short, evokes the Middle Ages effectively, creating an aura of authenticity without going over-board about it.

Understandably, Calvin is not just a little confused by what's happened to him, but he's more resilient than he could have ever imagined. True, it doesn't hurt that he quickly becomes a friend of Arthur's younger daughter, Princess Katey (Paloma Baeza), recreating for her a Big Mac and keeping the village smithy busy—and confounded—by showing how to forge such items as roller-blades and a bicycle. Still, things really are rotten in Camelot. Grieving the loss of his queen, Guinevere, Arthur has lost touch with his people, who have begun to turn against him, thanks to the chicanery of Belasco, who intends to gain the throne via marriage to Arthur's elder daughter (Kate Winslet) upon her impending 18th birthday.

"A Kid in King Arthur's Court," which has a zesty, lilting score by J.A.C. Redford, is enlivened by solid portrayals all around, headed by the likable Nicholas and the veteran Ackland, whose imposing presence and majestic voice make both a credible yet wistful and vulnerable Arthur.

NEW YORK POST, 8/11/95, p. 42, Michael Medved

Already this summer, the Arthurian legend has survived the bone-headed casting of Richard Gere as Sir Lancelot (in "First Knight"), so it's reasonable to expect that the ancient Camelot myths will also outlive the amiable silliness of "A Kid in King Arthur's Court."

This new Disney release provides the sort of adequate (if uninspired) entertainment that will satisfy themselves wishing that this sturdy premise—and the movie's talented young star—had been employed to more memorable effect.

The movie begins on a Little League baseball diamond—familiar territory for 15-year-old Thomas Ian Nicholas, who previously starred in "Rookie of the Year"—where the embarrassment of striking out is soon forgotten when a massive California earthquake opens a huge crack in the ground that leads our hero all the way to medieval Camelot.

As he adjusts to his new environment he discovers that King Arthur (Joss Ackland) has also been striking out a lot: the aging monarch is detached, feeble and possibly senile since the death of his beloved Guinevere, and easily dominated the evil Lord Belasco (Art Malik, the terrorist villain in "True Lies").

Fortunately, the king's been blessed by two brave beautiful daughters (Paloma Baeza and Kate Winslet from "Heavenly Creatures") who hope that the adolescent visitor from another world can help return their father to rigorous rule.

This hope is encouraged by Merlin (Ron Moody) who, though long dead, appears magic-mirror style in a well in a secret passageway of the castle. Meanwhile, the peace of the realm is occasionally affrighted by a mysterious black knight, who hides his identity inside a plumed helmet.

There is, in short, enough going on to keep moviegoers engaged. Director Michael Gottlieb (who previously perpetrated the tawdry turkey "Mannequin") this time employs an appropriately breezy, light-hearted style and manages for the most part to conceal the film's obviously limited budget.

The problem is a nagging sense of missed opportunities. In Mark Twain's original "A Connecticut Yankee in King Arthur's Court" the great fun of the story comes from the inventive way the hero uses his everyday 19th-century knowledge to become an instant big shot in the Dark Ages, but this script never exploits the similar possibilities in showing a hip, computer-savvy teen-ager dazzling the benighted knights of the Round Table.

Instead, the film goes much too far in making its hero "Everykid": his only ability to impress Arthur and Co. arises from equipment (a portable CD player, rollerblades, a Swiss Army Knife) he's carried with him in his book bag.

Needless flat-footed dialogue ("What are the girls like in Reseda?" "Well, Princess, they're nothing like you!") further detracts from the merriment.

Thomas Ian Nicholas nevertheless makes the most of his role, protecting the perplexed, indestructible likability of a teen-aged Tom Hanks and generating real romantic sparks with the elegant Paloma Baeza as one of the princesses.

The surprises and celebration that comprise the uplifting ending make no sense at all, but should leave most summertime customers grateful for even this contrived rush of good feelings.

NEWSDAY, 8/11/95, Part II/p. B5, Jonathan Mandell

Mickey Mouse has become a monster. They have been writing about this in the business pages and the opinion pages for several weeks, and now somebody subversive at Disney has made it literally true in "Runaway Brain," the 119th cartoon short starring the world's most famous mouse—and the first Mickey short, so the Disney flacks proclaim, in 42 years.

Mickey's benign image may have allowed the Disney corporation to take over Times Square, and ABC, and much of the rest of the world, but this particular cartoon has some refreshingly seditious touches. Mickey is less blandly cute, closer in look to the original rodent who made his debut in "Steamboat Willie" in 1928. And "Runaway Brain" has the kind of wise-guy throwaway gags that you'd expect more in Warner Bros. cartoons like Bugs Bunny; it begins with Mickey at home playing a video game in which the witch kills off each of Snow White's seven dwarves one by one. As soon as she scores, a tombstone pops up with the words "R.I.P. Dopey" or "R.I.P. Doc."

So wrapped up are Mickey and his dog Pluto in the game that he forgets his anniversary with Minnie Mouse. He promises to make it up to her, and she misunderstands this to mean a vacation in Hawaii that he can't afford. To get the money for the trip, he answers an ad "for a mindless day's work" at 1113 Lobotomy Lane, where after ringing the front bell, he falls down a trap door and finds himself the prisoner of mad ape scientist Dr. Frankenollie (the voice of "Frasier" star Kelsey Grammer).

"It's not just a job," the doctor says. "It's an adventure."

"I hate adventures," Mickey says.

"Perfect, you're hired."

Dr. Frankenollie switches Mickey's brain with that of a libidinous monster. Adventures ensue: a raucous pas-de-trois with the monster as Mickey trying to manhandle Minnie, and Mickey as the monster trying to save her—until they switch bodies again. The whole cartoon is seven minutes long. But it is seven minutes that may restore your faith in the Disney franchise.

At least, that is, until you begin watching the main feature, "A Kid in King Arthur's Court," which stars Thomas Ian Nicholas, the endlessly mugging star of "Rookie of the Year," as a clumsy, timid adolescent Little Leaguer transported back in time to Camelot, where he befriends one princess, saves another, jousts with the villain, teaches and learns from the king.

"Kid" fits the kind of blandly jokey fare that Disney used to offer in its long-running TV show of the 1960s, "Walt Disney's Wonderful World of Color," the most colorful part of which, if I remember correctly, was almost always the opening credits.

Rather than the inspired time-clash anachronisms of "Back to the Future," we get mostly a sampling as boring as the contents of the kid's schoolbag: CD player, Swiss army knife, flashlight.

"Cool," the boy says at one point, voicing his teenage vernacular approval.

"Cool?" the king asks and smothers him, first with a big animal pelt. It's like that.

Not all the touches fall so flat. The boy commissions a blacksmith to make him, first, a second set of roller blades and then a medieval bicycle.

"How does the boy know so much?" the blacksmith asks, astonished.

"Metal shop, eighth grade," he says with assurance.

But don't expect much of such quirkiness or any wit. Art Malik, who played the villain in Arnold Schwarzenegger's "True Lies," plays another villain here. We know this in the very beginning because he scowls, and because he wears a ponytail—a sign of individual expression strictly forbidden in Disney World.

Also reviewed in:
CHICAGO TRIBUNE, 8/11/95, Tempo/p. 28, John Petrakis
NEW YORK TIMES, 8/11/95, p. C16, Caryn James
VARIETY, 8/14-20/94, p. 55, Leonard Klady
WASHINGTON POST, 8/11/95, p. F6, Hal Hinson

KIDS

An Excalibur Films release of an Independent Pictures and The Guys Upstairs presentation. *Executive Producer:* Gus Van Sant, Michael Chambers, and Patrick Panzarella. *Producer:* Cary Woods. *Director:* Larry Clark. *Screenplay:* Harmony Korine. *Story:* Larry Clark and Jim Lewis. *Director of Photography:* Eric Edwards. *Editor:* Christopher Tellefson. *Music:* Lou Barlow and John Davis. *Sound:* Charles R. Hunt and Jan McLaughlin. *Sound Editor:* Wendy Hedin. *Casting:* Alyssa Wishingrad. *Production Designer:* Kevin Thompson. *Set Decorator:* Ford Wheeler. *Set Dresser:* Mike Preston and Jennifer H. Alex. *Costumes:* Kim Druce. *Make-up:* Tracy Warbin. *Make-up (Special Effects):* Tim Considine. *Stunt Coordinator:* Manny Siverio. *Running time:* 95 minutes. *MPAA Rating:* Not Rated.

CAST: Leo Fitzpatrick (Telly); Sarah Henderson (Girl); Justin Pierce (Casper); Joseph Chan (Deli Owner); Jonathan S. Kim (Korean Guy); Adriane Brown (Little Girl); Sajan Bhagat (Paul); Billy Yaldes (Stanly); Billy Waldeman (Zack); Javier Numez (Javier); Luis Nunez (Luis); Christian Bruna (Christian); Alex Glen (Alex); Chloe Sevigny (Jennie); Rosario Dawson (Ruby); Julia Mendoza (Susan); Gillian Goldstein (Linda); Priscilla Forsyth (Diane); Francine Fuertes (Jennie's Nurse); Deborah Draper (Ruby's Nurse); Alan Wise (Accordian Player); Billy Solomon (Dancing Boy); Johanna Ignatov (Singing Woman); Raymond Batista (Legless Man); Julie Stebe-Glorius (Telly's Mom); Christiana Stebe-Glorius (Telly's Little Brother); Dr Henry (Rasta Drug Dealer); Harold Hunter (Harold); Jon Abrahams (Steven); Hamilton Harris (Hamilton); Jeff Pang (Jeff); Atabey Rodriguez (Misha); Tony Morales and Walter Youngblood ("Jungle Fever" Couple); Elsworth "Cisco" Davis (Hoodlum); Joseph Knopfelmacher (Taxi Driver); Michele Lockwood (Kim); Carisa Glucksman (Joy); Scot Schwartz (Bennie); Yakira Peguero (Darcy); Sidney Prawatyotin (Sid); CarlLy-Min (Security Guard); Avi Korine (Fidget); Zulaika Velazque (Gertie); Nick Lockman (Nick); Joey Alvarez (Joey); Gerry Smith (Gerry); Lavar McBride (Lavar); Julie Ho (Tamara).

FILM QUARTERLY, Winter 1995-96, p. 41, Jesse Engdahl & Jim Hosney

Larry Clark's *Kids* opens with a bang. Splayed out on a flowered bedspread are two adolescents—he looking like Huckleberry Finn, she like a pre-Raphaelite angel—locked in one of those endless, sucking French kisses that only teenagers can perform, awkwardly expressing their desires within the bounds of pre-coital sex. An uncomfortable duplicity is established: the camera captures a vision of innocence slipping toward a blissful fall, but the familiar elements of soft lighting and romantic music are eerily absent, making everything *too* raw, too "real." More cold and harsh than warm and wet, the kiss is finally broken and they speak, betraying themselves as distinctly nonprofessional actors. "You know what I want to do?" the boy asks bluntly. "Yeah ... you want to fuck me," the girl answers matter-of-factly. She can't be more than 13, a fact reinforced by the battery of teddy bears looking on. The scene offers a painfully transgressive voyeurism; shock, embarrassment, and the absolute need to see more are mixed in equal measure.

These two are definitely not Molly Ringwald and Anthony Michael Hall, but, at the same time, they don't have the decadent glamour of Warhol's "kids"; the distances provided by both "entertainment" and "art" films seem to be lost. The camera does cut away from the young bodies before they actually fuck; rather, the audience sees the effect of the action on these two: a close-up of the boy's face shows an utter lack of sensitivity as he savagely pounds into the young girl; her face is a mixture of agony and resignation as she receives him. It's not gentle or pretty; in a voice-over the boy, Telly, waxes: "Virgins. I love 'em. No diseases, no loose-as-a-goose pussy, no skank. No nothin. Just pure pleasure." Cut to black, hit the music, hard, roll credits. It's clear what *Kids* is all about.

Nothing like this has ever been put on screen before. With this opening sequence, Larry Clark assaults our cinematic sensibilities, just as Luis Buñuel did in 1928 by slitting a woman's eyeball: both directors open our eyes to new realities. What are we looking at? Why are we watching? What can't be shown? What shouldn't be shown? These questions are given new urgency by the film's opening. As *Kids* progresses, its raw, pseudo-documentary style allows the events to unfold "naturally," which makes them all the more believable and disturbing.

"I don't want no baby," says the girl from the opening scene, clearly aware of one risk of sex; but it's a risk she will overlook with Telly's (Leo Fitzpatrick) empty promises that it won't happen and that he cares for her. Of course, the audience wonders why she still doesn't make him wear a condom; her vulnerability to him is as frightening as her seeming ignorance of AIDS. The callowness of Telly's seduction underscores its reality—how many girls give it up to a player like this every day? An equally disturbing prospect for the audience is that this very vulnerability is what makes her, and him, so appealing. Despite the many unattractive elements in Telly's character, he is a *kid*, and his quest for virginity is a child's game that resonates much deeper, broader needs. And the very fact that these two kids are so unglamorous serves to enhance their authenticity and, paradoxically, renders them more attractive to an audience jaded by hollow movie fantasies.

Telly comes out of the bedroom triumphant and cocky, so cocky that he spits on the expensive oriental rug in the dining room. He meets Casper, his best friend (Justin Pierce), and immediately begins to brag about his conquest, revealing his obsession with virgins as a goal, a profession, the only thing meaningful in his life: "Was'up, bitch? ... You fucked it? ... that girl was like twelve and you hit it up! ... Who am I? The motha fuckin' virgin surgeon!" Full of attitude, these boys dress, walk, and talk with the hiphop style that signifies street authenticity, but a visit to Telly's house reveals he's a lower-middle-class kid with two parents at home. The film cuts across class and race lines, pointing to issues that affect many different "types" of kids.

At the core of *Kids'* power is its shockingly accomplished cinéma-vérité look that in some ways recalls the roughness of another teen film almost equal in power, Jonathan Kaplan's *Over the Edge*. "The reason why I like that movie," said Larry Clark, "was that they used kids the right age, they actually used kids, Real kids. I knew my film had to be from the inside .... I think when you see *Kids* that most of us—not all of us, but most of us—will say 'Yeah, that's the way we were, that's the way kids are.'" (*Artforum*, May 1995.)

The camera rests on the faces of Kids' "real" teens, probing, revealing, betraying all that is beautiful, ugly, attractive, repulsive, alluring, and repugnant. That the gaze is adult, that it is male, that it is often unmistakably erotic/homoerotic makes it all the more disturbing. Despite the fact that many of the girls are more conventionally attractive, the camera remains fascinated by the boys and their homosocial bonding. In a crucial sequence, we watch the closeness and physicality among the skaters in Washington Square Park as Telly and Casper greet their friends, hugging, slapping five, enjoying deep affection. Tales are told and marijuana is shared in a ritual "spleef twistin'." In her book *Between Men: English Literature and Male Homosocial Desire*, Eve Kosofsky Sedgwick points out that" ... 'male bonding' ... may, as in our society, be characterized by intense homophobia, fear and hatred of: homosexuality" (1-2). Proving Sedgwick's concept of the homosocial, the skaters are repelled by an interracial gay couple who walk past. But the skaters are also an interracial group—it's the open display of the couple's homosexuality that disturbs these young boys. It's as if they're trying to deny what's at the heart of their subculture. At the end of the film, when Casper rapes the passed-out Jennie (Chloe Sevigny), his desire is fueled by the fact that his best friend has just had sex with another virgin; having sex with Jennie is as close as he can come to having sex with Telly. Homosociality can never consciously become homosexuality.

As much as the film disturbs us with images of young girls acquiescing to Telly, we also see these girls talking with a rare and brutal honesty and sense of humor about sex and even pushing boys away—not because they don't like sex or don't trust boys (in fact, it's fascinating how these girls seem to accept these boys for what they are), but because it's not what they want or when they want it. It's unusual for a film to show not only females, but young females openly explaining how much they prefer foreplay to sex, or at the same time how they love "hard-core fuck pounding!" The film that demystifies teenage sexuality allows female desire a voice that's rarely heard in American cinema. The girls unabashedly express their love of pleasure, appreciating and extolling the talents of boys who have "magic fingers" and complaining when the sex it leads up to is anticlimactic: "It either takes them too long or too short to come." The scene of the girls discussing sex is intercut with Telly and Casper arguing with six other boys about what girls want. The boys claim that girls do indeed "love to give head ... they just act like they don't in front of their friends." Cut to the girls exclaiming, "I hate sucking dick ... it takes so long and you're fucking gagging ... and you're not getting anything out of it." The girls come out of this sequence seeming much more sophisticated, sensitive, interesting, and complex than the boys, whose sexuality is animal and competitive, graceless, even primitive.

This open discussion of sexuality removes the film from the conventions of the teen melodrama genre where sex is usually the central conflict and any broad social ramifications of a repressive society are glossed over by the "family romance," which asks us to believe that if the romantic problems are solved then true resolution is achieved. Clark also subverts Hollywood melodrama by playing with one of its classic devices, the cross-cutting of two narrative strands destined to meet in climax and resolution. Two narratives are indeed cross-cut in *Kids*: Jennie attempts to find Telly after she learns that he has infected her with the AIDS virus and Telly heads towards the seduction of another virgin, Darcy (Yakira Peguero). We expect these two strands to intersect at a moment of "truth," providing us with a dramatic payoff; we wonder if Jennie will "save" Darcy. But that not what she's trying to do. The fact is, she doesn't know what to do. In a direct attack on the simplistic morality melodrama, Clark uses his pseudo-documentary style to hollow out the audience's expectations.

This tension plays off another traditional narrative trajectory, the romantic unification of the couple. The strands again intersect, but once more the dramatic payoff is denied. When Jennie finds Telly, he's already deflowering Darcy, and she can only stand there and stare, completely lost. There is no resolution, no closure; nor is the couple united, except possibly in having AIDS. With devastating irony, Jennie passes out and is then raped by Casper, with the AIDS virus possibly being passed on to yet another person. Yet we'll never know what Jennie feels or thinks as she sees Telly with Darcy—jealousy, disgust, despair? Similarly, we'll never know whether Darcy or Casper got infected. Does it make a difference? Is that what the film is about? Although *Kids* may not be about *all* kids, it's not just about *these* kids. Dismay and disgust is exactly the reaction of most adults to this fact, which is one of the reasons these kids are the way they are.

Adults are out of touch and also out of sight in *Kids*. When they do appear, they are worn out, beaten down, hardened by life—and by these teens who refuse to be disciplined or follow warnings. Most adults in the film are ignored, mocked, or lied to; Telly's mom asks him if he'll be home before 4 A.M. for once, while explaining how she can't give him money because she's broke (she's lying because she does have money that Telly then steals); the free-clinic nurses must deal with 16-year-old girls who've had unprotected sex and are dying on them; the Korean clerk from the corner market is ripped off. The exceptions are adults from the street: a drug dealer, a street musician, and a legless beggar. In a sequence that obliquely refers to another unrelenting look at kids—Luis Buñuel's *Los Olvidados*—where the kids throw a legless beggar off his cart, Casper gives the beggar money. It's one moment of compassion for a character who will brutally crack a kneeling man across the face with a skateboard, then later rape the unconscious Jenny.

This sequence adds complexity to the characterizations of Casper and Telly and shows us the world in which they live, a world that also includes a mother who breast-feeds while smoking a cigarette, and a cab driver who offers Jenny his view on how a young girl should look at life: "Whatever it is, just forget about it. Life's too short. Make yourself happy."

The film ends with Casper waking up out of a alcohol/drug stupor and saying "Jesus Christ, what happened?" Earlier in the evening, one of the younger boys admires a gold crucifix, insisting that he believes in Jesus. But when Casper invokes the name it's only a exclamation of surprise and loss; there's no salvation offered by the film. His question is addressed to the audience, who must grapple with the issues the film raises. Whatever salvation the kids achieve can only come through their own efforts—they have replaced religion with skateboarding, deflowering virgins, smoking dope, and drinking malt liquor. God belongs to the adult world, not theirs. Telly gets the last word as he tells us of his need for virgins, because that's all he's got in this world: "When you're young, not much matters. When you find something that you care about, then that's all you got. When you go to sleep at night, you dream of pussy. When you wake up, it's the same thing. It's there in your face, in your dreams, you can't escape it. Sometimes when you're young the only place to go is inside. That's just it. Fucking is what I love. Take that away from me, and I really got nothin."

With nowhere to run, nowhere to hide, these kids take what they can get because, as Casper bluntly says, they may be sick but "that's how I'm livin ..." Whatever these kids use, they it use to fill a void in their lives; the world of adults is another planet, one the kids visit only when they have to. "I don't know no *kid* who's got no AIDS," says one boy to Telly (again in patently unmelodramatic fashion), indicating that the disease is seen only as another adult scare tactic, like those against rap music and wearing your baseball cap backwards.

Kids attempts to deromanticize its subjects through its nonconventional elements: the jarring visual style, the nonprofessional actors, the raw perspectives on sex and violence, and the nonsensationalized pleasure taken in the presentation of spectacle. Yet the more it strips away melodramatic conventions, the more we see how compelling and even attractive its subjects are. That's the uncanny quality of teens: not innocent children, not corrupted adults, but somehow in a magic nether world, fighting to stay free from an inevitable fall. "When you grow up, your heart dies," says Ally Sheedy in *The Breakfast Club*; the line may not seem true to adults now, but did it back when they were young? The brilliance of *Kids* lies in the fact that it is presented to us without the overt moralizing of a John Hughes film.

One of the film's most fascinating aspects is the range of reactions it provokes—anger, disgust, and denial seem to come in slightly ahead of resignation, respect, and even pleasure and acclaim. For adults to recognize that they can see where these kids are coming from, or even that these types of kids exist, would somehow validate the kids' actions; worse, they may have found the kids, and their behavior, just as attractive as repulsive. What may be most troubling is that the film's message *isn't* nihilistic: *Kids* is one of the most exuberant cautionary tales ever. The beauty, the life, the hope of the film is in its aesthetic reverence for its subjects. The real-life drama of sex, drugs, and violence, presented in all its pathetic beauty, leaves many wondering why these kids just don't get it. Yet maybe we're the ones who don't get it.

LOS ANGELES TIMES, 7/28/95, Calendar/p. 1, Kenneth Turan

It may be too late to save you from "Kids."

Not save in the moral sense, because, as New York City Mayor Jimmy Walker famously commented, "No one was ever ruined by a book." Or a movie. But bored, bored is a different matter.

A fictionalized look at a day in the life of streetwise, sexually active teen-agers in New York, "Kids" does know how to get talked about. Though it fizzled at Cannes after a ballyhooed Sundance debut, its NC-17 status caused the Weinsteins of Disney-owned Miramax to form an independent company called Excalibur just to distribute it without a rating.

But despite considerable publicity from media outlets fearful that the hipness bandwagon will pass them by, "Kids" is more tedious than titillating, one of those cinematic irritations more interesting to read about than to see.

Directed in neo-documentary style by photographer Larry Clark in his feature debut, "Kids" follows the exploits, such as they are, of teen-age Telly (Leo Fitzpatrick), known to intimates as "the virgin surgeon." The film opens with him operating on his next victim, and then, in the most explicit language screenwriter Harmony Korine could dream up, sharing all the details with his drooling pal Casper (Justin Pierce).

Most of the rest of "Kids" is a *cinéma-vérité*-influenced look at how these benighted young people and their friends pass the time. Those who have the stamina will be treated to weed smoking, gay bashing, throwing up, thieving and brawling, food fights and a general weakness for getting stoned and creating a mess. As to sex, it occurs sporadically but—happily, given the age of those involved—it is much more talked about than visible.

Perhaps sensing that the film needed one, Korine and Clark do throw in a single strand of plot, so antiquated it would have looked familiar to D.W. Griffith. Jennie (Chloe Sevigny), one of the surgeon's victims, finds out she is HIV-positive and, with time out for getting stoned and being sick, desperately tries to contact Telly before he can deflower another innocent. If Telly were old enough to have a mustache to twirl, the scene would be complete.

When it comes to the film's authenticity, nominally a selling point given that Korine was but 19 when he wrote the script, that is also dicey. The filmmakers take great public pleasure in proclaiming "Kids'" fidelity to current teen reality, but when challenged on particulars tend to insist with equal intensity that it's all just a script.

But even if "Kids" were a paragon of documentary verisimilitude, it wouldn't matter much. Because once the initial jolt of seeing case-hardened babies who look barely out of diapers having sex and talking dirty wears off, "Kids" is incapable of doing anything to transform these layabouts into people worth caring about. Few adults would want to spend time with such obnoxious truants in real life, and "Kids" does not make them compelling or involving on film.

One adult, however, cares a great deal. Director Larry Clark has been interested in young people and sex since his celebrated photography collections, "Tulsa" in 1971 and "Teenage Lust" in 1983. Clark is apparently one of those individuals (protege and executive producer Gus Van Sant is another) who are intoxicated by teens, who considers the years between 12 and 20 as the apogee of human existence, with only a long slide into senility left after they're gone.

Given that a familiarity with Clark's work makes it clear that "Kids" owes its existence to the working out of his lifelong personal obsessions, certainly a legitimate source, it is disingenuous at best to blandly insist that the project is some kind of public spirited anti-AIDS manifesto, as one of its executive producers did when claiming "we did the film because we felt America is asleep. We hope to wake everyone up." Truly, what people have said about this film is more disturbing than anything put on the screen.

For, so like the teen-agers it portrays, what "Kids" wants to do more than anything is not alert society but rather gross out the grown-ups. Its spirit is nakedly visible in a few loving close-ups of a legless beggar on a city subway car. The man has no purpose in the film except to further the filmmaker's dreary hopes of getting a rise out of the squares. The fast talk and sexual abandon of the under-age kids is presented in exactly the same spirit, as a kind of compassionless carnival sideshow aimed at the bad traffic accident segment of the audience, viewers determined to believe that the worst things put on screen are by definition the most true to life.

That reference to carnival sideshows is especially apt, for the films "Kids" most resembles are the traveling exploitation films with titles like "Mom and Dad" and "The Story of Bob and Sally" that were toured around America in earlier decades by mobile entrepreneurs who referred to themselves as "the forty thieves."

The main lure of these films, hard as it is to believe today, was documentary footage of a baby being born, considered racy material at the time. But they were sold as, yes, wake-up calls to America. Here's how the advertising material for "Bob and Sally" reads: "It's boldly frank! It's humanly true! It's more than just a story ... it's life itself! The passionate problems of today's youth who forget about consequences and defy convention."

It would all fit quite nicely on a poster for "Kids."

NEW YORK, 7/31/95, p. 44, David Denby

Telly (Leo Fitzpatrick), the skanky 17-year-old "hero" of Kids, sleeps with a frightened but willing young girl and then runs down the steps of the girl's brownstone and shares the details with his best friend, Casper (Justin Pierce), who is waiting for him on the front stoop. Telly is coarse and mean, and he lives only to get laid. Yet he's at the center of Kids, the first movie to be directed by photographer Larry Clark, the self-mythicizing "outlaw" whose life is said to have inspired Gus Van Sant's Drugstore Cowboy ["What's the Matter With Kids Today?," New York, June 5]. A sort of low-life Modigliani, Larry Clark is possessed by an erotic ideal. In both Kids and his book of photographs, Teenage Lust, Clark, 52, feasts on teenagers thickheaded and dreamy with sex, the girls very young, with ripening breasts, the boys slender, unmuscled, naked. Clark turns the youth of his subjects into aesthetic shock. His teens have arrived at decadence without passing through maturity. They seem to have no dimensions—intellectual, spiritual, even physical—apart from carnality. They're all tongues.

Is Larry Clark an artist or a creep? Both, I think. Kids is the work of an artist who is also a voyeuristic hanger-on. Clark made Kids from a script by a screenwriter who was then 19 years old, Harmony Korine, and cast the movie with nonactors, most of them skateboarding friends of Korine's who were scouted in Washington Square Park. Clark gives himself utterly to losers and predators, leaving out moralizing or tears. His absorption is so complete that it dissolves perspective and finally sense. Despite the atmosphere of casual viciousness, the picture is anything but casual; it's rigorously structured, and the structure has the finality of death. As Telly discourses nonstop on the pleasures of deflowering 14-year-olds, he and Casper skateboard around the East Side, steal from Korean grocers, and smoke dope in Washington Square with friends; later, they invade a school swimming pool and finish the day at an all-night party that turns into a teen near-orgy (many hands reaching into many crotches), at the end of which Telly bags another virgin and Casper gives up his humanity altogether. All this takes place in a single hot summer day in Manhattan. But there's a countermovement to the boys' pleasure. As Telly and Casper rampage through town, one of Telly's past victims, Jennie (Chloe Sevigny), now HIV-positive, forlornly tries to find her lover. What seems like a celebration of unruly life turns into a celebration of inexorable death. Telly is a loose cannon.

Is this a tragic vision? It is not. Kids is fascinating but stunted. Telly comes on with a sweet line of rubbish ("I care for you, I just want to make you happy," etc.), and he's very successful with 14-year-olds, but he's more limited in consciousness than a drunk who won't leave his barstool. Cunning yet low-minded, with a grinding sameness to his talk, he's not even handsome, just avid, with pimples and a long neck that makes him look rather like a penis. And his friend Casper is a buffoon, albeit sneakily likable. By taking us low, Larry Clark gives the appearance of presenting New York adolescence without hypocrisy or cant. He doesn't bother with the kind of square sociological "understanding" that made fifties juvenile-delinquent movies so lugubrious; nor does he offer the glamorous romance of doomed youth. The scenes of older, crippled people in the city getting by—surviving—seem to represent the only possible future for these kids. For some people in the audience, the lack of moral feeling will come as a jolt. They will find the movie disturbing and hip—or at least "real." But in its own way, *Kids* is as constructed, as unreal, as a Hollywood youth picture with clean-scrubbed actors and a dog.

Kids is Clark's first film, but his technique is remarkably fluent. Eric Alan Edwards, Van Sant's cinematographer for *My Own Private Idaho*, uses a handheld camera much of the time, and Clark and Edwards sweep along with the kids on the streets and move in close as they sit in the park cursing and smoking. When the camera catches things on the fly, the trash talk seems newly sprung, almost "overheard," much like the exchanges in a cinéma-vérité documentary. In a memorable sequence, Clark cuts back and forth between separate groups of boys and girls, the boys boasting about sex, the girls laughing and complaining about the taste of sperm, and the editing (by Chris Tellefson) sustains the lewdly exuberant mood. The entire sequence seems like a single dirty outburst with both sexes getting in their licks. Clark, I think, is offering not a faithful portrait of teenagers but an exposure of his own erotomania, a fantasy of perpetual arousal. But he's good at it: Whatever resistance or revulsion we may feel, we're caught up in Larry Clark's teen-sex dreamworld. *Kids* isn't pornographic, but it has an itchy erotic surface, and it's saturated in physical intimacy. When two girls start kissing each other at a swimming pool, and the boys stand around and jeer, one knows that Clark has done things never seen before in teen movies.

At times, the boorishness feels right. Most kids don't need or want beauty; they trust it less than squalor. Clark and Korine capture the way white kids have picked up African-American street talk, echoing the sound of the dispossessed because it feels cool to them. *Bitch. Nigger. Fuck.* For Telly and his friends, everything besides those words sounds prissy. But there isn't much they can do with the words—they don't have the subtlety of emphasis and nuance that some black kids have, and the talk becomes boring. In other ways, the movie is unconvincing and devious. Who are these kids? They appear to live on the East Side, but what part of the East Side? They certainly aren't rich, but they have endless access to apartments that are always empty, as if waiting to be wrecked in a party. This, of course, is fake—those apartments have been emptied so a movie can be shot in them. Apart from Telly's mom, who appears in a single ambiguous scene, parents don't exist. Nor do teachers, cops, or older friends. The kids are caught in a vacuum. They have no hopes, no interests, no models. In brief, Clark has drained them of qualities so we can be shocked by how empty they are. They're even vile to one another, without the group loyalty that adolescents usually turn against adults.

I'm not asking for paragons who act honorably and speak in grammatical sentences, like the white-gloved teenagers in a Whit Stillman movie. I'm asking for a richer range of motivation and feeling in Clark's chosen turf of mangy teens. But Clark's fantasies, and the methods he has used to realize them, may make that impossible. My guess is that the characters seem unreal because neither the teenage screenwriter nor the teenage nonactors have the experience or the technique to create a rounded human being. (Only an actor can act a real person; a real person doesn't know how.) With the camera rolling, the "actors" probably fall back on what Clark wants from them—the raunchy "truth," which may actually be a form of showing off. Trying for authenticity, they wind up misrepresenting themselves.

Kids is ultimately more depressing and naive than illuminating. Apart from the skateboarding, the kids do not show any grace in their antics. But you don't have to be a sentimentalist to expect that even street trash will occasionally shine with human glory. The girls in particular come off as zombies. Teenage girls may not always want gentleness, but do they really want contempt? None of them has a thought; not one gets up and walks away from this pack of losers. The equality of that scene of boys and girls talking separately of sex is only an illusion. *Kids* is a boy-centered vision. Though Larry Clark's boys may be dogs, at least they can bark.

But there's a real oddity: If the kids are so free, why is the picture such a downer? The answer is that fantasy is instrumental; it has a particular use, and then it ends. If the characters drift meaninglessly and unconsciously toward death, that may be because they don't, outside their creator's erotic dreams, have much hold on life. Horribly—and unforgivably—death completes the fantasy and makes it perfect.

NEW YORK POST, 7/21/95, p. 41, Thelma Adams

It's 10 p.m. Do you know where your "Kids" are?

Larry Clark's powerful docudrama is every parent's worst nightmare. Following a jargon-laden script by teen-ager Harmony Korine, famed photographer-turned-director Clark throws himself into the testosterone-driven world of two shameless Manhattan teens, Telly (Leo Fitzpatrick) and Casper (Justin Pierce).

Telly worships at the altar of sex—and practices virgin sacrifice. The movie starts with a black screen and the sound of kissing, stripped of all eroticism. Telly beds a blonde who still carries baby fat in her chin, even if her tan body has the taut attraction of a swimming champ. Behind them are her swimming trophies, her stuffed animals, a Beastie Boys poster.

Telly cons the blonde out of her virginity and leaves immediately afterward, pausing only to spit into her parents' tasteful living room. He links up with Casper to gloat and proclaim his addiction to virgins, the ultimate in safe sex. "That's why I love virgins—purity ... If you deflower a girl, you're the man".

And some man Telly is. His body has the stretched-out look of a boy who has grown five inches in the past year but has yet to fill out. His hairless face is uneven, like a flat soccer ball that has been kicked in at the side. But zits, a pixie haircut and pouty jowls don't keep him from sweet-talking one girl after another into going all the way with him.

Clark follows a day-in-the-life, you-are-there format. We trail Telly and Casper around Manhattan as Telly selects his next victim, the 13-year-old Darcy (Yakira Peguero). The tension builds as Jennie (Chloe Sevigny), one of a legion of Telly's castoffs, seeks out the roughshod Romeo with an explosive piece of news.

One thing that makes "Kids" (which has been released as unrated after first earning an NC-17 rating) so explosive is the candid way in which this demented dead-end gang gab about sex and drugs. Clark gains power with an unflinching style that pulls viewers into the action: We can almost taste the stale beer, smell the vomit after a late-night parent-free party, feel the blood in our mouths as the boys brutally beat a black man in Washington Square Park. After seeing this movie, I wanted to gargle with Lysol, leap into a hot shower.

Clark's Manhattan is a city where everyone is kissing but love is banished. It would be a flash of paranoia to see "Kids" as telling a universal story, a portrait of the American nightmare. Telly and Casper, Jenny and Darcy, are city kids. They run wild as city kids have always run wild—but certainly, with sexual mores as lax as they have ever been and with the AIDS crisis, the ante has been upped.

Watching "Kids," I couldn't help but mourn the idealism of the sexual revolution of the '60s. Free love is one thing when practiced by college students with access to student health centers and parents' money to get them out of scrapes. But when "if it feels good, do it" trickles down to the teen-age population in the age of AIDS, it becomes a dangerous and disruptive force, a deadly legacy of selfishness.

Rarely have the words "trust me" become so sinister as when Telly mouths them to the unsuspecting Darcy. Like most kids, he lives in the present without regard for the future. What sets Telly apart—and makes "Kids" so bleak—is that he has no regard for anyone but himself; no personal expression except the pursuit of carnal pleasure. His final words are: "F---ing is what I love. Take that away from me and I've got nothing."

NEWSDAY, 7/21/95, Part II/p. B5, John Anderson

Thanks to the indigestible sugar glaze applied to so much of what the media feed us, there's a countervailing esthetic that says ugly is real. And if that's true, then Larry Clark's "Kids" is as real as a plane crash—not as enjoyable, perhaps, but it does provide all the same physical sensations associated with downward spiral, crash and burn.

The prerelease hype on Clark's film—a much-written-about foray into teenage sex, drugs and lack of hope—was predictable; that the Weinstein brothers of Miramax bought it for $3.5 million and then put it in the foster home of Excalibur Films (thus keeping it separate from parent Disney) was guaranteed to set off alarms. They fought their NC-17, but they never had a chance for an R rating.

There's one encouraging thing about "Kids," though: Here is a film that strips adolescents down to their barest instincts and language, that charts in frank and brutal terms the heedless, naked collision of hormone-raging bodies, freed from minds that might actually care about Rainbow

Curriculum-supplied condoms and caution. It's provocative and nasty enough to inspire conversation about the ordinarily unspeakable. And that's the good news.

The bad news is that despite the film's gritty documentary feel, its sticky-fingered take on teenage lust and its appallingly naked dialogue, what Clark seems to be doing much of the time is putting dirty old fantasies in dirty young mouths. Written by then-19-year-old Harmony Korine (that he's the grandson of Bowery Boy Huntz Hall is somehow hilarious), the script sounds like something intended by a post-adolescent to arouse a middle-aged director. It's also an exercise in outrage, the kind perpetrated by a particularly obnoxious child sticking french fries up his nose. The characters are memorable—thanks to the talents of the young actors—and the situations are no doubt factual enough: Adolescent AIDS cases are rising, and polls consistently report a lack of interest among the young in the safe aspects of safe sex. But as a film, "Kids" is progressively startling, relentless and boring—like a naked mime, perhaps, or a wired cokehead explaining his detailed plan to take over IBM.

Clark, whose photo essay "Tulsa" of two decades ago was a graphic peek at Oklahoma speed freaks and their libidos (the subsequent "Teenage Lust" plowed much of the same ground), is a voyeur, naturally. But just as naturally, and cynically, "Kids" is presented as some kind of cautionary tale for the post-plague generation, when the only real purpose served is titillation and a certain degree of disgust. Telly (Leo Fitzpatrick), the antihero of what passes for a story, is first seen sucking serious face with a 14-year-old virgin (Sarah Henderson) whom he will, shortly, sweet-talk into sex. It's a wet, sloppy, prolonged close-up of tongues and volatile complexions (Eric Alan Edwards' cinematography is uncompromisingly frank and fluid), but you get that uneasy feeling that you're being buffaloed. And the film, and kiss, are only a minute old.

Telly, the self-proclaimed "virgin surgeon," makes a specialty of first-time seductions—virgins are young, sweet, and they have no diseases, he says, although a disregard of diseases is what this film is all about (the fact that Telly would use the word "deflower" is another clunker). He doesn't limit his theater of operations, however: One of his conquests, Jennie (Chloe Sevigny), has learned that she's HIV-positive. Since Telly's the only one she's slept with, she goes off to find him. Why? I was hoping for violence, but when she eventually does find him, in the middle of his latest deflowering, there's no confrontation.

And no point. Jennie's search for Telly, the one flimsy dramatic thread that runs through the movie, amounts to nothing. There's no Jennie-Telly scene—it's hard to imagine how Clark would have directed it—and no specific moral, given that the film falls off as it does. Casper, Telly's demented friend (it's the equivalent of the DeNiro role in "Mean Streets"), awakens as the film ends, asking, "What the hell happened?" Good question: He's raped Jennie while she's unconscious, in the film 's most repellent moment, and the room is a carpet of half-naked bodies. But what's really happened is a con job. Even Jennie, the most sympathetic character, is impossible to accept: Sure, she's been given a death sentence, but would she care? Clark has created a milieu of youth with no future and no concerns. None of the other children ever acknowledge the dangers of sex, or that there are any. So a test result from a clinic? Without any accompanying symptoms! It would all be dismissed, like a bad lover, or fear of death.

NEWSWEEK, 7/24/95, p. 52, John Leland

[*Kids* was reviewed jointly with *Clueless*; see Leland's review of that film.]

SIGHT AND SOUND, 5/96, p. 54, Leslie Felperin

Manhattan teenager Telly talks a young girl into surrendering virginity. He then meets up with his friend Casper, a skateboarding ace and they discuss Telly's preference for virgins and shoplift some beer en route to their friend Paul's flat. There, the boys watch home videos of their skateboarding feats with other friends, sniff nitrous oxide, and further discuss sex. In another apartment, a group of girls is discussing the same topic. Jennie, reveals that she lost her virginity to Telly some time ago and hasn't yet had sex with anyone else. A flashback shows her going for an HIV test with her more promiscuous friend Ruby. In the present, the two collect their results and though Ruby is in the clear, Jennie is HIV positive. She sets off to find Telly.

Telly and Casper steal some money from Telly's mother. Telly plans to look up a 13-year-old he knows named Darcy and deflower her. At Washington Square park, Casper scores some marijuana and lights up, sharing his joint with his friends, including a boy named Harold. The boys practice their skateboarding moves. A collision with an older skateboarder leads to a fight. The entire gang set on him with vicious blows and then run off. Jennie keeps just missing Telly.

Casper, Harold, two girls named Kim and Misha, and Telly go round to Darcy's house so that Telly can persuade her to come out with them. They climb over the fence of a public swimming pool and go for a swim together before setting off for a party at a boy named Steven's house. Jennie goes to a club where she is given a tab of some unnamed drug and told that Telly is at Steven's. By the time she arrives, everyone is inebriated. Jennie stumbles in on Telly deflowering Darcy, but gives up on trying to interfere and collapses on the sofa. In the morning, Casper pulls down Jennie's jeans and has sex with her while she is still comatose.

There is an almost mathematical relationship between how controversial a given film's topic is—glamorised serial killing, say, or Aids—and how much hype it will generate. In turn, the degree of hype begets in prospective viewers an inclination to prejudge the film in relation to the topic. Given any exposure to pre-publicity for such films as *Natural Born Killers* or *Philadelphia*, it becomes almost impossible to have an unmediated reaction. Many reactions are possible, but invariably the aesthetic judgement of the film is predicated on the viewer's ideological position vis-à-vis the topic. Even the bemused assumption of neutrality becomes a 'position'. So it is with *Kids*, which finally arrives in Britain stirring up controversy about under-age sex and teenage mores ahead of its release. *kids* is, on the surface, a relatively simple film. It's the story of a group of pubescent and pre-pubescent middle-class people goofing off, hanging out, taking drugs, and having sex. The controversy concerning *kids* rests on several points: the realism of the representation itself, the appropriateness of representing it at all, and the intentions of its filmmakers.

As far as realism is concerned, *kids* works very hard to establish its credentials. Shot on grainy stock with an often jittery hand-held camera, the film's cinematography and muffled voice-recording connote the style of low-budget documentary, as if this were an ethnographic study of native New York wildlife. Director Larry Clark even presents himself in the film's publicity material as a participant-observer who stumbled upon the film's subculture by accident, while teaching his teenage son to skateboard. *Kids* may have been written by a 'real' 18-year-old skate-punk, Harmony Korine, but signs of writerly craftsmanship are scrupulously effaced so that the dialogue sounds improvisatory and naturalistic, thick with swear words, slang and adolescent speech rhythms. The editing hangs on a shot a beat longer than one expects in scene after scene, as if the decision where to cut was an entirely arbitrary one, as if this was real life. Clark has hitherto been best known for his still photography of street life and teenage subcultures, and the *mise en scène* of *kids*, using mostly New York locations and unknown actors, springs from much the same milieu as this earlier work.

Yet realism is also the most artificial of genres, relying on a meticulous grooming of imperfection to achieve its effect. Those shots go on *just* too long enough and no more. Those actors look *just* ordinary enough while still managing to look fairly attractive. While many of the activities depicted certainly do go on amongst teenagers, dramatic necessity dictates that the film should cram a lot of hedonism into one day. Most teenagers lives are filled with a lot more television-watching, game-boy playing, and acne picking. *kids* has been compared by some to the films of Andy Warhol and Paul Morrissey, but if more typical teenage life were the subject, the result would be less like the rather glamorous *Chelsea Girls* and more like *Empire*, Warhol's 8-hour one-shot epic depiction of the Empire State Building.

However, Clark is more interested in anomie than ennui, and this is why defenders of the film have championed its unflinching focus on teenage sex. Equally, it has also become the focus for strident moral outrage. The film's aesthetics support both arguments. Clark plays the documentary detachment wild card very cannily. The opening scene, in which Telly persuades a girl to have sex with him is typical of this both-ways strategy. The sound of their first kiss is amplified to catch every slurp of saliva, drawing us into the sensuality of the moment. It's both seductive and highly uncomfortable. Once the sex starts, the pained expression of the girl's face subverts any pleasure that might have been aroused, and the film nudges slightly towards censure. Yet the story doesn't stay with the girl, and the next scene is wholly concerned with Telly bragging to Casper. We're invited to share his exuberance in his conquest, rather than her pain, as he offers Casper his finger to sniff ("Smells like Butterscotch," Casper remarks).

Throughout, the disposition of points of view keeps sympathies spinning like a gyroscope. Telly's day is tightly counterbalanced by that of Jennie, the girl he infected with HIV who is pursuing him. One reading would suggest that we are meant to read Telly as wholly vile and Jennie as wholly a victim, but a single scene with Telly's preoccupied mother (the only parent we see) suggests he is emotionally neglected, and how much blame can be apportioned to someone who is still a minor themselves? Jennie is hardly a saintly martyr anyway. We see her as very much a part of the same social set, gaining access to a fashionable nightclub with enviable ease and then casually dropping a tablet which results in her losing her ability to complete her mission to find Telly with the same carelessness with which one might mislay a handbag. The last scene of Casper effectively raping her while she's unconscious is just as craftily ambiguous. Are we to read it as punishment for her indulgence, or less loadedly as yet another instance of how easily HIV might be transmitted through the casual-causal chain of teen sex?

Given the way the film strains so hard to avoid judgement, the advocacy of safe sex is the only clear moral message the film seems to transmit. Mind you, with an expected '18' certificate in this country and an 'R' in the US, that message has a much-reduced chance of reaching the age group which the film depicts. Which brings us to the murky final question of what were the intentions of the film-makers themselves. Clark has said that he wanted to make a film about adolescence, to show that, "kids have sex, kids take drugs, kids party, kids have fun". This blunt ambition to 'tell it like it is' has much to recommend it, especially since filmic depictions of adolescent sexuality and recreation are so frequently timid and sanitised. kids is a very brave film for daring to chip away at the taboos surrounding its subject.

But is honesty the only policy here? This is not a documentary, but a highly constructed, one might even say contrived, work of fiction. Take off the adulatory ring to the phrase, and one could call it, merely descriptively, a work of art (it is certainly an 'art-film'). This begs the question of whose pleasure this art is fashioned for. Is it for the teenagers who can't legally see the film? Or is it for the adults who can, but only if they suspend any scruples they might have about watching teenagers fuck, even if it is faked? The film makes these questions all the more uncomfortable because its style in the sex scenes recalls, if not hard porn, certainly the softer, arty porn of Warhol et al. This is especially notable in the swimming pool scene where Misha and Kim 'put on a show' for the boys with their kissing in which both the characters themselves as well as the film-makers seem aware off the scene's proximity to that hackneyed of porn clichés, the lesbian scene. Perhaps the most fundamental question of all is whether it is possible to explore the sexuality of the young without simultaneously exploiting it.

In the end, each viewer of the film will have to run these questions through their own private morality computer. It's unlikely that any two people's final sums will add up the same way. Personally, this film has left flash-frames and memory triggers in my mind that won't quite shift, and there has to be something said for any work of art that's that powerful.

VILLAGE VOICE, 7/25/95, p. 53, Georgia Brown

It'd be easy to write off Kids—I wouldn't mind writing it off as aggressive and exploitative and irritatingly pretentious, except that it's so very good, too, and probably useful as a cautionary tale. Photographer Larry Clark certainly knows how to direct a vérité camera, get vérité performances from adolescent nonactors, and take full advantage of the throbbing city backdrop. The movie's implicit claim to being the thing itself (it looks so raw, it must be real) dares you to call it exaggerated, distorted, or a partial view, although it is all of these. Like its creator, Kids carries a built-in Fuck You factor, as well as more than a whiff of radical chic. It's hard to see how Tina mixed the boat.

The movie's setting is a hot summer day, with much of Manhattan in heat. It opens with a close-up of a boy and girl deep kissing; their mouths work away, making smacking noises that sound magnified on the sound track. The camera pulls back to show the couple wearing realistic underwear and sitting entwined on her bed with stuffed animals looking on. The boy, Telly (Leo Fitzpatrick), has freckles on his bony shoulders and a gawky, rather geeky boy body. (Clark's taste has always run to caved-chest skinniness; contrast Bruce Weber's for hunky development.) She, being at a more graceful stage, a girl at the crack of puberty, is lovelier, though her baby-cheek face is beaded with sweat and she doesn't look nearly as comfortable (in front of the camera?) as he. The air conditioning in her parents' brownstone must not be on.

"If we fucked you'd love it," says he. She asks whether he cares about her; the reply is affirmative. The next thing we know he's pumping away on top of her and his cocky voiceover comes up: "Virgins, I love 'em. ... Pure pleasure," The look on the poor, dumb thing's face: pure pain. (In the credits, this one is known as Girl #1.)

He's a killer, Telly, even if he weren't, as we soon learn, HIV positive. He's a cold little fucker whose mission is to wipe out innocence in what has usually been considered one of its classic forms. Goodbye childhood, hello cruel world. Trust me, Telly tells his girls, on the verge of murdering trust. He's just a kid. That's what these kids are like, implies Clark, whose obsession with teenage lust (the title of one of his photo collections), painful puberties and their dire consequences (suicide, patricide), has been out front for years.

Bouncing out of the girl's house, Telly joins his buddy, Casper (Justin Pierce), who's been waiting on the stoop. Telly lets Casper sniff his hand, crows over his conquest, and together they dissect, in clinical and philosophical terms, the finer points of virgin fucking. It confers a kind of immortality. "Nobody has the power to do that again!" brags Telly. Fifty years from now, marvels Casper, you'll still be the one.

The basic plotline—follow the kids through 24 hours while Telly tracks down the next virgin and one of his former virgins, Jennie, tracks *him*—is 52-year-old Clark's, although he picked a skateboarding acquaintance, Harmony Korine, to write the script. *Kids* is more interesting as another solid block in Clark's highly respected oeuvre, although Korine's wiseass media savvy may wind up grabbing the mainstream press. Korine is a tiny 22-year-old film buff, who looks 13 and gets off on fibbing to reporters. At Cannes, he told the press he grew up around circuses where his father sold goldfish.

Clark, on the other hand, is scary. His *Tulsa, Teenage Lust, Larry Clark 1992* are collectors' items. (A signed *Tulsa* was selling for $1200 in last Sunday's Chelsea flea market. A $50 "deductible" fee was being charged for examining it. Wait until *Kids* comes out.) His thing is boys 'n' their dicks, though these are often posed with props like guns and needles. If the *Kids* milieu seems like one where knives or guns might pop up, Clark deliberately limits the film's weapons to dicks, skateboards, and, if you will, the camera. Clark has said he suffered a late puberty, missed out on his own teens, and wants to be one of the "normal" kids he photographs, though "normal" here is a judgment call. In linking his adolescence with theirs, you could say that Clark sucks up normality the way Telly does virginity.

Kids is a radical film somewhat in the way of Mike Leigh's *Naked*, which you might say picks up the same kids further down the road. They both rub your nose in things you may prefer to miss, although Leigh's film offers a space for melancholy contemplation whereas *Kids* doesn't. Also, *Naked* uses very expert actors, whereas *Kids* uses kids. Clark's singular ability to elicit natural-looking performances clearly comes from proximity and personal familiarity.

The paradox of *Kids* is that its documentary-style realism masks a grand imaginary construct. Let's start with its fantasy about girls. Those who lie down for Telly without a proper courtship are uniformly ripe and beautiful. The blond, blue-eyed Jennie in her blue and white (nun-colors) T-shirt, is played by Chloe Sevigny, profiled in *The New Yorker* as the new "It" model. Darcy (Yakira Peguero), the 13-year-old Telly sets out to conquer, is radiant, unsullied innocence itself. Wearing her backpack over both shoulders, she walks out exuding a wholesome, childlike (untouchable) glow. That such prizes would fall to one so callous makes girls appear brain-dead, even unable to bargain. (Yes, I know that the mightiest of female minds routinely fail, but this takes it a bit far.)

Another white boy fantasy realized is beating a tough-talking, good-looking black guy (he's objected to being bumped by Casper's skateboard) to a twitching pulp in the middle of Washington Square Park. And then spitting down on his bloodied face. The skaters—Telly, Casper, et al.—are distinctly homeboys, calling each other bitch and wearing their pants around the groin; and like many white homeboys they're rednecks.

Some *Kids* commentators have marveled at the gang's rainbow composition. I don't think so. The sole black boy in the core group, Harold (Harold Hunter), is more mascot than friend and he's singularly ugly. Girls are repelled by him. When they break into the Carmine St. pool at night, Harold amuses the white kids by twirling his black dick. (Asked at Cannes why they didn't show the dick, Korine quipped, "It was too big for the screen.")

Clark's world is conspicuous for its lack of adults. One creepy cab driver dispenses corny advice to the distraught Jennie while obliquely coming on to her. Telly's slovenly Mom smokes and is fixated on the TV while breast-feeding her baby. (Another stupid female, she's oblivious as Telly steals her blind.) This glimpse of maternal breast so unhinges Casper that he takes one of her Tampax, soaks it in cherry Kool-Aid, and sucks—a merry conflation of blood, milk, and probably fears.

Meanwhile, a younger generation rises, embodied by four little fellows—perhaps 11 or 12 years old—who hang out with big kids in mysteriously available apartments. The little ones laugh at the jokes, drink, do whippets and whatever drugs come their way. Clark carefully chose the four for their adorable, piquant faces and lines them up on the sofa for the viewer's horrified delectation. Audiences also can take them as comic relief. One of these tykes is posed at the end, passed out beside a rape in progress, to look like a sleeping, or dead, angel.

When Casper inquires of another *puti*, the one with the turned-up nose, what kind of bitch he likes to fuck, you see the kid's face crumple while simultaneously trying to keep up his front. This is a kid reacting, not acting. The expression signals not unmediated documentary but Clark's spontaneous creation of an environment to record. The same kid shown a little later lies on his back while a bigger girl licks his bare chest; he giggles nervously as if he's being tickled. Something is happening and he's doesn't want to show what it is. (I'm curious how the parents are rationalizing their consent.) Clark may be less offensive than Jock Sturges, more upfront than Sally Mann, but he and they and Woody Allen with his polaroids of Soon-Yi are manipulators of children. Clark may complain on about the ersatz teen flicks of his youth—how corny that they used overage actors—but what we're really talking about is the need to use real children to stoke fantasy.

As I wrote from Cannes, it's an old fiction, the debauching of innocence, and specifically the deflowering of virgins. *Clarissa* comes to mind, so does *Les Liaisons Dangereuses*, which has practically been appropriated as a text of our times. But Richardson and De LaClos purport to speak about evil, whereas Clark, in contemporary style, doesn't, taking his story to a sordid ending. AIDS, of course, can be viewed at the sinners' punishment, although this cautionary tale aspect can in turn be seen as a cover. An effective cover. Most girls after seeing *Kids* will insist on condoms.

A colleague's theory is that those who have kids won't like the movie and those who don't will. I'm sure I would've had the same ambivalences if I weren't a mother. Putting it bluntly, my most serious problem with *Kids* is that I hated these monsters from beginning to end.

Also reviewed in:
CHICAGO TRIBUNE, 7/28/95, Friday/p. L, Michael Wilmington
NATION, 8/28-9/4/95, p. 216, Stuart Klawans
NEW REPUBLIC, 8/14/95, p. 25, Stanley Kauffmann
NEW YORK TIMES, 7/21/95, p. C1, Janet Maslin
NEW YORKER, 7/31/95, p. 80, Terrence Rafferty
VARIETY, 5/29-6/4/95, p. 52, Todd McCarthy
WASHINGTON POST, 8/25/95, p. D6, Rita Kempley
WASHINGTON POST, 8/25/95, Weekend/p. 44, Desson Howe

KINGDOM, THE

An October Films release of a Zentropa Entertainment/Danmarks Radio production in association with Swedish Television/WDR/Arte. *Executive Producer:* Svend Abrahamsen and Peter Aalbaek Jensen. *Producer:* Ole Reim. *Director:* Lars von Trier. *Screenplay (Danish and Swedish with English subtitles):* Lars von Trier, Tomas Gislason, and Niels Vorsel. *Story:* Lars von Trier and Niels Vorsel. *Director of Photography:* Eric Kress. *Editor:* Jacob Thuesen and Molly Marlene Stensgaard. *Music:* Joachim Holbek. *Sound:* Per Streit. *Art Director:* Jette Lehmann and Thomas Ravn. *Special Effects:* Niels Skovgaard and Niels Fly. *Make-up:* Lis Olsson and Birthe Lyngs Sorensen. *Make-up (Special Effects):* Kim Olsson and Lis Olsson. *Running time:* 279 minutes. *MPAA Rating:* Not Rated.

CAST: Ernst Hugo Järegard (Stig Helmer); Kirsten Rolffes (Mrs. Drusse); Ghita Norby (Rigmor); Soren Pilmark (Krogen); Holger Juul Hansen (Dr. Moesgaard); Annevig Schelde Ebbe (Mary); Jens Okking (Bulder); Otto Brandenberg (Porter Hansen); Baard Owe (Bondo); Solbjorg Hojfeldt (Camilla); Birgitte Raabjerg (Judith); Louise Fribo (Sanne); Peter Mygind (Mogge); Ole Bolsen (Christian); Vita Jensen and Morten Rotne Leffers (Dishwashers); Michael Simpson (Man from Haiti); Bente Eskosen (Night Nurse); Nis Bank-Mikkalsan (Priest); Dick Kays (Security Manager); Soren Lanander (Young Man); Finn Nielsen (Madsen); Motte Munk Plum (Mona's Mother); Solveig Sundborg (Miss Kruger); Helle Virkner (Mrs. Mogensen); Else Petersen (Old Lady); Claus Strandberg (Hypnotised Patient); Tove Maes (Mrs. Zakariasen); Kurt Ravn (Zakariasen's Son); Svend Ali Haman (Haman); Morten Eisner (Mechanic); Claus Nissan (Jensen); Gunnvor Noisse (Charlady); Henning Jensen (Hospital Manager); Lars Lunse (Minister of Health); Lea Bragger (Mary's Mother); Laura Christensen (Mona); Udo Kier (Aag Kruger); Soren Elung Jensen (Man in Top Hat); Paul Huttel (Dr. Stenbaek); Holger Perfort (Professor Ulrich); Benny Poulsen (Senior Registar); Henrik Koefoed (CT-Scanner Operator); Lene Vasegaard (Gynecologist); Klaus Wegener (Doctor in Casualty); Michael Moritzen (Ear Specialist); Julie Wieth (Pediatric Nurse); Annette Katcher (Casuality Nurse); Birte Tove and Lise Schroder (Nurses); Mette Marckman (Young Nurse); Thomas Stender (Student); Soren Hauch-Fausboll (Auxiliary Nurse); Soren Staen (Porter OK); Gordon Kennedy (Assistant Animal Collection); Ole Emil Riisager (Narrator).

LOS ANGELES TIMES, 11/10/95, Calendar/p. 19, Kevin Thomas

Lars von Trier's monumental, 271-minute "The Kingdom" goes beyond its hilarious, brazen satire of incompetence and corruption at a vast Copenhagen hospital to warn of the lack of spirituality in modern life and to suggest that we must never forget that evil is an eternal adversary.

Presented in two parts with an intermission, it was made by Trier last year for Danish TV and is composed of four segments; next year Trier will resume shooting the series, eventually to number 13 segments.

A kind of Danish answer to "Twin Peaks" and then some, it is remarkably entertaining and consistently imaginative throughout its daunting length yet becomes sufficiently wearying to make us remember that we are not seeing "The Kingdom" in the form for which it was designed.

Although it shares the visual bravura and dark vision of Trier's "Zentropa," a film noir fable of corrupt postwar Germany, it thankfully has none of the insufferably pretentious obscurantism of the earlier film. Essentially, "The Kingdom" is the Arthur Hiller-Paddy Chayefsky "The Hospital—plus a swath of "General Hospital" for good measure—and given cosmic, supernatural dimension.

It unfolds like one of Joe Frank's bizarre odysseys for radio and has been shot from the hip by endlessly flexible cameraman Eric Kress. To ensure a grainy, sepia cinema-verite look to "The Kingdom," Trier filmed it in 16mm, transferred it to video, then back to film and finally blew it up to 35mm.

A weird, dream-like prologue showing peasants bleaching fabric in a murky pond announces at the start that, according to Trier, the National State Hospital in Copenhagen, nicknamed the Kingdom for its immense size (and perhaps also for its self-contained world), has been constructed, highly symbolically, on a marsh.

A recently arrived, self-important Swedish consulting neurosurgeon, Stig Helmer (Ernst-Hugo Järegard), a jowly, wavy-haired middle-aged man forever condescending to the Danes, sets an increasingly convoluted plot in motion when he embarks on a barrage of petty complaints when a young junior physician, Jorgen Hook (Soren Pilmark), goes ahead and orders a CAT scan for an elderly patient, Sigrid Drusse (Kirsten Rolffes), because Helmer is late for the morning staff meeting.

Mrs. Drusse is no ordinary patient. She may in fact be a malingerer, but far more important she is a dedicated spiritualist who senses the tormented spirit of a little girl lurking at the bottom of an elevator shaft. A formidable actress of humor and intellect, Rolffes' Mrs. Drusse becomes, along with Helmer, the story's other major character. Although an amusing figure in her indomitable nosiness, she and her cause are key in creating an underlying and ever-increasing seriousness and poignance to the film's glorious outrageousness.

The hilarity blooms from humanity's infinite capacity for absurd, often tragicomic behavior. The pompous Helmer is driven to comical ends in trying to cover up his incompetent surgery that has left a little girl brain-damaged. The neurosurgeons form their own Masonic-style lodge, complete with rituals, to create a protective system of highly elastic ethics.

The head of neurosurgery, Dr. Moesgaard (Holger Juul Hansen, very Leslie Nielsen), is a fool who's embarked on a program of "Operation Morning Air," which amounts to launching daily staff meetings with a silly song exuding false good cheer. Pity the poor patient who ends up at "The Kingdom."

With so much screen time at its disposal and an exceedingly large cast with a substantial core of principals, "The Kingdom" crackles with good acting. In addition to those actors already mentioned, others who excel include Ghita Norby as a middle-aged physician intent on landing Helmer; Jens Okking as Mrs. Drusse's long-suffering son, a hospital porter; and Birgitte Raabjerg as Pilmark's attractive colleague and eventual lover.

Ubiquitous German actor Udo Kier serves as the film's creepy symbol of evil, a role he's played effectively many times before. While its sheer length makes "The Kingdom" demanding, it is not only as rewarding as many other ambitious screen odysseys but a lot more fun.

NEW YORK POST, 1/6/95, p. 42, Larry Worth

If Stanley Kubrick, David Lynch, Paddy Chayefsky and Robert Altman were rolled into one, the result might be Lars von Trier.

The Danish director's latest—"The Kingdom"—is the best ghost story since "The Shining," with the weirdest characters since "Twin Peaks," set in the most bizarre madhouse since "The Hospital," and containing the bloodiest good humor since "M*A*S*H."

If that sounds like an impossibly odd combo, so be it. But von Trier, who earlier lensed the imaginative "Zentropa," has crafted a five-hour epic unlike anything cineastes have witnessed, or are likely to again.

The action takes place in the eerily lit corridors and operating rooms of a Danish hospital, nick-named the Kingdom, as a cross-section of eccentric doctors, nurses and orderlies deal with a head-severing intern, a power-mad neurosurgeon, a zombie-plagued dream center, an ambulance from Hell, two all-knowing but retarded dishwashers, an alien pregnancy and Haitian voodoo. That's in addition to basics like malpractice, murder and revenge.

But the most intriguing thread concerns the apparition of a crying child who haunts the main elevator shaft, seen and heard only by an elderly woman who conducts seances with fellow patients. Her obsession to reach the girl and solve the mystery is irresistibly captivating, and creepy.

But it's thanks to the healthy doses of sly humor, graphic operations and surreal photography (shot in otherworldly shades of sepia) that von Trier's script gains intensity, coalescing into nearly unbearable suspense. Ironically, that leads to the production's one drawback: a finale that will leave many feeling let down.

But don't be deterred by the ending—or running time. Aided by a superb ensemble cast, von Trier's undeniable brilliance reigns supreme in "The Kingdom."

NEWSDAY, 1/6/95, Part II/p. B7, Jan Stuart

As the national health-care debate is quietly pre-empted by the great hospital show bakeoff ("ER" vs. "Chicago Hope"), America is witnessing the biggest obsession with doctors' dirty little secrets since the heyday of Ben Casey and James Kildare. While Hollywood's latest scalpel soap operas deliver heart-tug and open-heart surgery with equal aplomb, neither can hold a candle to Denmark's "The Kingdom" for giddy, pull-out-the-stops cheap thrills.

In all honesty, this 279-minute loop-the-loop ride from director Lars von Trier ("Zentropa") is no more your garden-variety medical drama than "Twin Peaks" (to which it has been likened) was a detective series. Set in a Danish hospital built on haunted wetlands, "The Kingdom" is at soul an old-fashioned ghost story with techno-age cheek.

Yeah, there's a David Lynch tease to it, but von Trier has also clearly spent some time with Paddy Chayevsky's blackly comic "The Hospital" and Stanley Kubrick's grimacing "The Shining."

What you get is Stephen King sporting a hipper-than-thou face-lift.

Divided into four hour-plus episodes, "The Kingdom" scans a monolithic state hospital as it (literally) comes apart at the seams. The troubled ghost of a young girl who died there decades back hovers in the elevator shafts; the evil secret surrounding her death, coupled with the cancerous corruption at the hospital, is causing the building's foundation to crack. The ghost's comings and goings are monitored by a pair of dishwashers with Down's syndrome and a spiritualist named Mrs. Drusse (Kirsten Rolffes), one of those lovable-loathsome busybody characters that kept Helen Hayes off unemployment lines in the last 20 years of her life.

Trying to keep the place spiritually intact, at least, is Moesgaard (Holger Juul Hansen), a good-natured medical director who hopes to rescue this mammoth bureaucracy from impersonality with new-age reach-out programs. Doing their best to corrode the system is Moesgaard's son Mogge (Peter Mygind), a philandering intern who gives decapitated heads to women doctors who reject his advances, and Krogen (Soren Pilmark), a young doctor who runs a medical black market that thrives on favors and blackmail.

The real spark plug of "The Kingdom" is Dr. Helmer, a spectacularly arrogant neurosurgeon from Sweden with an ethnocentric disdain for anything Danish or nonscientific. As played with hammy relish by Ernst Hugo Jaregard, he's a wonderfully malevolent lightning rod for the hospital's outlandish constellation of misadventures. When he finds himself shanghaied by a Masonic fraternity that runs the hospital, you almost feel for the jerk: He's like, some dreadful reactionary power broker you guiltily agree with every now and again.

"The Kingdom" moves like a house afire. Cowritten by the director with Niels Vorsel, it's refreshingly free of the high-mindedness that often made von Trier's formal experiments in "Zentropa" so exasperating. The labyrinthine plot is peppered with parent-child axes and references to family that implies a link between the hospital's degeneration and an aberration of family values. But it's a thematic red herring, finally. Von Trier is happy to merely pile on the absurdities for the fun of it; we were particularly fond of a squeamish female intern who wallows in slasher flicks but can't sit still to watch an injection.

The silliness goes flaccid now and again. That Greek chorus of Down's syndrome dishwashers wears out its welcome by the second of several sanctimonious appearances, while dear old Mrs. Drusse indulges in a bit of death trafficking that resurrects medium Zelda Rubenstein's "move-into-the-light" hooey from "Poltergeist." But "The Kingdom" is high-style trash that needs no apologies. You'll want a Hefty-sized bag of popcorn for this one.

SIGHT AND SOUND, 1/96, p. 43, Geoffrey Macnab

The Kingdom is a large hospital in Copenhagen. Dr Stig Helmer, a cantankerous Swedish neurosurgeon who can't stand the Danes, is late for the morning meeting. In his absence, Junior Registrar Hook has booked in an elderly patient, Mrs Drusse, to have a brain scan. Helmer is furious to have his authority usurped. He orders Mrs Drusse's immediate discharge. Medical student Mogge, is spurned by beautiful nurse Camilla. He reacts by chopping off the head of a corpse in the mortuary and leaving it in her room in a plastic bag. The joke backfires when somebody else opens the bag. His professor, Bondo, hears about his antics, and threatens him with expulsion.

The hospital administrator, Dr Mosegaard, warns Helmer that the mother of a young girl he recently operated on is going to sue him for negligence. In a bid to protect himself, Helmer joins "the lodge", a secret, masonic-style society. Mrs Drusse has no sooner been discharged from the hospital than she re-admits herself. She is a psychic, and has heard a young girl crying in the lift shaft. Her son, Bulder, a hospital orderly, wheels her round the hospital as she tries to work out whom the voice belongs to. She discovers that a little girl, Mary, was murdered in the Kingdom hospital by her father, a prominent doctor by the name of Kruger, back in 1919.

Helmer is now being investigated by the Medical Council. To clear his name, he tries to break into the hospital archive and to destroy the carbon copy of the operation notes which incriminate him. Mogge also wants these notes. Hook has stolen the severed head, but has promised to give it back in return for help in discrediting Helmer. Mrs Drusse also turns up at the archive, looking for the notes detailing Mary's death. Hook starts an affair with Judith, another young doctor who's pregnant by a former boyfriend. Mrs Drusse holds a funeral service for Mary after finding her body pickled in embalming fluid in Professor Bondo's office. Hook uses the carbon copy of the operation notes to blackmail Helmer. Mogge enrols on the 'sleep treatment' course that Camilla runs. Bondo has the diseased liver of a dead patient transplanted into his own body so he can carry on his research into hepatomas a liver disease.

Hook has a hunch there's something wrong with Judith's pregnancy. He compares a photo of her ex-boyfriend with a picture of the old murderer, Dr Kruger. Realising they both look identical, he urges her to have an abortion. He also helps Mrs Drusse as she again tries to lay Mary to rest by ushering her back to the place where Mary died—now the site of the lift shaft. Helmer absconds to Haiti with a kitchen porter who introduces him to the local voodoo witchdoctors. He pays for needles to be stuck in effigies of his enemies. The Minister of Health arrives on a sudden visit to check up on the hospital's 'Operation Morning Air' scheme. He's appalled to discover Professor Bondo having 'his' transplanted liver removed against his will, Mogge making love to Camilla on an operating table, and Judith having an abortion. Judith's operation is going very badly. Suddenly Kruger's oversized, bloody head appears from between her legs. An intertitle announces "To Be Continued..."

There really is a hospital in Copenhagen called The Kingdom, a solid, modern edifice built, like the rest of the city, on ancient marshes. Von Trier's film about it begins in brooding fashion with a slow motion pan across what seems like a medieval landscape. Hands are shown, bleaching and squeezing cloth. Fog and steam are all around. A voice-over murmurs apocalyptic warnings that scientists' "arrogance and their persistent denial of the spiritual" will one day see the Kingdom slip back into the bog. The prelude ends with blood seeping through a wall. It's arresting imagery, for sure, but not exactly what you expect from a movie that is billed as a hospital soap opera.

Then again, hospital soap operas aren't exactly what you expect from Lars von Trier, "the ageing *enfant terrible*" of Danish movies and director of *Europa*. His dark opening flourish is about his only concession to his own cinematic past. Immediately it's over, there's a brash credits sequence with ambulances screeching down the highway to remind us that *The Kingdom* was shot for television, and we're plunged into the chaotic, pell-mell world of neurotic doctors, angry patients and bureaucracy gone haywire, a world familiar from countless other small-screen hospital dramas. There's a clear sense that von Trier relishes the freedom television gives him after the painstaking business of making features. Everything about *The Kingdom* suggests speed. The director and his co-screenwriters knocked together the story in a month and a half, apparently without revision. The shooting style, all hand-held camera, jump cuts and random reframing, has the same kind of vertiginous fluidity as *Homicide* or *e.r.*

There are multiple storylines and as colourful a collection of oddballs as you could wish to see on the wards. The chief comic creation is the peevish Swedish neurosurgeon, Stig Helmer (played with magnificent pomposity by Ernst Hugo Järogärd), a character so disdainful of all things Danish that he rushes out of the hospital at every opportunity to gaze longingly toward his homeland. He drives a Volvo, speaks admiringly of Bjorn Borg, and has a favourite refrain for his colleagues: "Danish scum." While the satire about Swedish/Danish relations is liable to be lost on foreign audiences, Helmer remains a memorable grotesque. Most equally ridiculous is Dr Moesgaard, the vacillating hospital administrator who initiates 'Operation Morning Air' in a bid to make his staff more polite to one another. Von Trier exercises a magnetic effect on Danish actors, most of whom clamour to work for him, and it comes as no surprise that he's assembled so strong a cast here. He encouraged his performers to "play with their emotions" and would shoot the same sequences with them acting first happy, then angry or sad. He chose which version of any given scene he preferred at the editing stage. This lends the performances an improvisatory air utterly in keeping with the film-making itself.

The Kingdom is itself a microcosm of society. Dysfunction and incompetence are rife. Fat cat doctors who care more for their own dignity than their patients, woefully incompetent bureaucrats and fraudsters are all on display. Von Trier mocks them mercilessly. But the film is as much a ghost story as a satire, an eerie, often quite horrific one which starts with an old lady, Mrs Drusse, hearing a girl cry out in a lift shaft. Gradually, as secrets about old evil-doings emerge, the grim opening sequence, with its emphasis on impermanence and decay, begins to make sense. Von Trier uses the supernatural elements to show how sterile what he refers to as "the concrete sciences" seem when confronted with the spiritual world. The mystery of who the ghost is and where she comes from also gives the narrative a focus. As Mrs Drusse bumbles her way closer to the truth, the tempo accelerates and all the disparate elements of the story begin to come together.

Throughout the film, a pair of Down's Syndrome children, working in the kitchens, make Delphic utterances about how events will turn out. "The wicked will laugh, the good will cry," is their last prediction. By then, everything is building to a feverish climax. Even in these concluding sequences, von Trier manages to leaven the horror with humour, (the Minister of Health makes a surprise visit at the hospital's darkest hour), but he abandons us at the crucial moment. Just when we're on tenterhooks, desperate for some kind of resolution, the film grinds to an untimely halt. If this is an ironic joke on the director's part, it's a hugely frustrating one. Rumour has it that von Trier is shortly to start work on new episodes. He'll be hard pressed to pick up from where he left off or to trump this astounding effort.

VILLAGE VOICE, 1/10/95, p. 45, J. Hoberman

Some of the best television in New York is projected these days on movie screens—the timidity of American TV creating opportunities for the city's alternative venues. The CBC's *Boys of St. Vincent* played Film Forum for months; the BBC's *Buddha of Suburbia* is currently held over at the Public Theater; MOMA is poised to revive its Alan Clarke retro; and *The Kingdom*, a four-episode miniseries, coproduced by Danish and Swedish television, opens Friday for a weeklong run at the Walter Reade.

The Kingdom is set almost entirely in a vast Copenhagen hospital, but unlike *The Boys*, *The Buddha*, and most Clarke, it has nothing to do with television's unofficial mandate for social realism. Directed and cowritten by Denmark's aging enfant terrible Lars von Trier (known here mainly for his dank and voluptuous *Zentropa*, a porno "movie-movie" that brazenly began with a bid to hypnotize its audience), *The Kingdom* suggests a mad exaggeration of ordinary commercial TV. Inspired perhaps by *Twin Peaks*, von Trier concocts an unholy mix of hospital soap opera, Saturday-morning supernaturalism, and genteel detective story—spiking the punch with cheap gross-out effects and an abundance of sneering attitude.

The mood in *The Kingdom* is doomsday sensationalism. The infectious, blaring credit sequence feels like a parody of the overture to *The Fox 5 News*—a frantic montage connoting urban disaster, an ambulance caterwaul mixed with a lugubrious rumbling vocal and set to a disco beat. A portentous introduction informs us that "the Kingdom Hospital rests on an ancient marshland [and] cracks are starting to appear in the edifice." Eye fixed on the millennium, von Trier orchestrates a visceral return of the repressed—unseen forces are pushing up through the hospital parking lot, a sign that the Kingdom is about to yield up its trove of Gothic secrets.

For all the intimations of apocalypse, however, there are fewer showboat effects here than in previous von Trier films. *The Kingdom*, which the Walter Reade is showing as an uninterrupted 279-minute extravaganza, was shot partially on video and printed on monochromatic amber-tinted stock. The look is programmatically cheap and lurid, the style aggressively pseudo-vérité. A nervous, handheld camera constantly peers over people's shoulders, jockeying for position in this almost entirely self-enclosed world.

Increasingly baroque, *The Kingdom* establishes an absorbing atmosphere of smoldering idiocy. Like any self-respecting miniseries, it deploys a large cast of characters, a fair amount of erotic intrigue, and a convoluted tangle of corrupt schemes. The doctors belong to a lunatic secret fraternity. One runs a black-market operation out of the hospital basement, another tries to further his career by browbeating the family of a dying man into allowing him to dissect the man's diseased liver. Seeking to implements a reform program called Operation Morning Air, the hospital's inane director leads staff meetings in song even as his medical-student son attempts to impress a sultry nurse by leaving a decapitated head at her station. (The mordant hospital humor includes some horrifically graphic operations—one involving power tools.)

The star patient is Mrs. Drusse (Kirsten Rolffes), the elderly mother of one of the hospital's porters, who has been admitted to the Kingdom some 26 times; an amateur spiritualist, she fakes symptoms so as to be able to conduct seances for the patients. Having established contact with the ghost of a child who haunts the elevator shaft, Mrs. Drusse pads dogged through the corridors in her terry-cloth robe, trying to solve the Kingdom's ultimate mystery. (Also in tune with the vibes are the two Down's syndrome dishwashers who, while never interacting with any other characters, function as a Greek chorus.)

Meanwhile, in a parallel narrative, the irascible Swedish neurosurgeon, Dr. Stig Helmer, seeks to cover himself for botching the brain surgery of another little girl. A superb comic creation (embodied by rumpled Ernst Hugo Järegard), Helmer is both overbearingly self-important and extravagantly paranoid. He systematically removes the hubcaps from his Volvo before leaving the hospital parking lot, publicly browbeats colleagues as well as patients, complains constantly, and is consumed with an insane hatred for Denmark—periodically retiring to the hospital roof to gaze longingly toward Sweden and rail against the "Danish scum" surrounding him.

As adroit as he is funny, von Trier keeps all the plots bubbling. By the third episode, everything comes to a boil and converges on the hospital archives—the various characters making repeated attempts to uncover and destroy assorted documents. By the final hour, the entire Kingdom is unhinged—most spectacularly when a group of government ministers tour the hospital, blundering onto a series of illegal organ transplants, exorcisms, and late-term abortions, intercut with the application of voodoo rituals.

A dedicated punk, von Trier trashes New Age spiritualism as well as medical science—not to mention the Scandinavian sense of a rational, orderly society. When it comes to administering the Kingdom, enlightened liberals are no less foolish than Neanderthal conservatives. Nor is the audience spared. Be forewarned that, while it does make a kind of retrospective sense, the end of von Trier's monumental, tawdry, and hypnotic jape is cruelly abrupt—or maybe it's a ploy to have you tune in next year.

VILLAGE VOICE, 11/7/95, p. 72, Georgia Brown

Like police precincts, hospitals prove natural sites for soaps, sitcoms, and even serious drama. Small worlds. Issues of life and death (death in particular) are always close at hand. (We'll wait in vain for that other qualifying principality, the prison, to come to prime time.) When Erving Goffman studied mental hospitals as closed systems, he chose as a title the double-edged *Asylums*—places of horror, places of safety and rest. For his brilliant black comedy, situated in a vast medical institution, Danish filmmaker Lars von Trier (known for *Zentropa*) comes up with *The Kingdom*, with its quasi-feudal, quasi-religious ring. Think of it as *The Exorcist* goes to *The Castle*.

Made for Danish TV, von Trier's first four installment (out of a projected 13) are far zanier, spookier, and cannier than anything likely to materialize on our tube. Episodes are prefaced by an eerie yellow-tinted title sequence showing that the gigantic present-day hospital (aerial views look like Co-op City) has been built on a landfill—a marshland and centuries-old site of "the bleachers," primitive launderers utilizing swamp gases. The inexorable pull back to primordial waters, including the womb, is a reassuring image throughout. (Perhaps there's a connection here, too, to the leeching of color from the film stock. The effect of muted sepia tones—you can just make out color—is to suggest that the viewer suffers from drastic color blindness. We see through a glass darkly since face-to-face is far too dangerous.)

Drama begins with the admission of moon-faced, moon-driven Mrs. Drusse (the marvelous Kirsten Rolffes), complaining of "pins and needles" in her right hand. When a CAT scan reveals nothing out of the ordinary, Mrs. D. is scornfully dismissed by chief neurosurgeon Stig Helmer (renowned Swedish actor Ernst-Hugo Järegard) as a malingerer. But it takes more than orders to get Mrs. D. to vacate the premises. Having made contact with one of the hospital's unhappier ghosts—a crying child in the elevator shaft—the old lady checks herself right back in.

Meanwhile, the darting, circling camera has introduced us to several other principals, such as hospital head Dr. Moesgaard (Holger Juul Hansen)—handsome head very little brain—and his handsome, brainless son, med student Mogge (Peter Mygind). Then there's tall, blond Dr. Hook (Soren Pilmark), who lives, unbeknownst to authorities, in the buildings bare basement corridors (he takes the term *resident* literally). Hook is a sort of alternative chief, ruling over a mini-kingdom of his own. Abhorring waste, he collects and recycles the institution's throwaways—extracting, for example, pure cocaine from eye drops and selling it back to the staff. Hook isn't exactly the series's hero (that would be Mrs. Drusse), but he leads the opposition against the vain and incompetent Helmer. (One of the film's hilarious running jokes is the pompous Swede's contempt for everything Danish.)

As for romance, *The Kingdom* has its share, though none of it predictable or reassuring. Aside from Mogge's clumsy wooing of the sleep-lab nurse, there's the otherwise competent Dr. Rigmor (Ghita Norby, the mother in *The Best Intentions*), who is mad about Helmer and really believes he might move in with her. The lovely Judith (Birgitte Raabjerg), a neurologist pregnant by her runaway boyfriend falls for her colleague Hook who is happy to receive her in any state—until, that is, he's spooked by a ghost.

Tenderer than any lover's caress are choric conversations between two beatific mongoloids (Vita Jensen and Morten Rotne Leffers) who work in dishwashing—making them descendants, perhaps, of "the bleachers." Filmed in slow motion and lit it seems, from within, these two stigmatized seraphim comment cryptically on the action: "When things are sad, children cry./When things are sorrowful, adults cry./What is it called when buildings cry?" As the hospital's foundation is undermined by drips, leaks, and floods, these underground waters mingle with the patients' own blood, mucus, and tears.

"Some blood cannot be washed off," comments one of the holy fools polishing plates that won't come clean.

In hospital-land, sins are hushed up and expected to wash. Pathetic victim of Helmer's incompetence, the nine-year-old Mona locks, drools, and finger paints with what looks like blood. This once beautiful girl links up with the ghost of Mary, a child long ago murdered by her doctor-father (a cameo by Fassbinder's Udo Kier) and left a pickled specimen in the labs.

Episode four caps a crescendo of incident with a grotesque birth: Inside the living, the undead wait for an opening. That such uncompromising irreverence premiered during a recent Christmas season and was wildly popular is tribute to the Danes' sense of humor. Strangely, it's not bitter but joyful.

Also reviewed in:
CHICAGO TRIBUNE, 11/24/95, Friday/p. L, John Petrakis
NEW YORK TIMES, 1/6/95, p. C6, Stephen Holden
VARIETY, 9/25-10/2/94, p. 63, Derek Elley
WASHINGTON POST, 2/2/96, Weekend/p. 39, Desson Howe

KISS OF DEATH

A Twentieth Century Fox release. *Executive Producer:* Jack Baran. *Producer:* Barbet Schroeder and Susan Hoffman. *Director:* Barbet Schroeder. *Screenplay:* Richard Price. *Story:* Eleazar Lipsky. *Based on the 1947 motion picture screenplay by:* Ben Hecht and Charles Lederer. *Director of Photography:* Luciano Tovoli. *Editor:* Lee Percy. *Music:* Trevor Jones. *Music Editor:* Bill Abbott. *Sound:* Les Lazarowitz and (music) John Whynot and Simon Rhodes *Casting:* Paula Herold. *Production Designer:* Mel Bourne. *Set Decorator:* Roberta J. Holinko. *Set Dresser:* Daniel K. Grosso, Chris Vogt, Richard Nelson, Jr., and William Durnin, Jr. *Special Effects:* Steve Kirshoff. *Costumes:* Theadora Van Runkle. *Make-up:* Allen Weisinger. *Stunt Coordinator:* Mike Russo. *Running time:* 101 minutes. *MPAA Rating:* R.

CAST: David Caruso (Jimmy Kilmartin); Samuel L. Jackson (Calvin); Nicolas Cage (Little Junior); Helen Hunt (Bev); Kathryn Erbe (Rosie); Stanley Tucci (Frank Zioli); Michael Rapaport (Ronnie); Ving Rhames (Omar); Philip Baker Hall (Big Junior); Anthony Heald (Jack Gold, Lawyer); Angel David (J.J.); John Costelloe (Cleary, Calvin's Partner); Lindsay J. Wrinn and Megan L. Wrinn (Corinna, Toddler); Katie Sagona (Corinna, 4 Years Old); Anne Meara (Bev's Mother); Kevin Corrigan (Kid Selling Infinity); Hugh Palmer (Naked Man Dancing); Hope Davis (Junior's Girlfriend); Richard Price (City Clerk); Edward McDonald (U.S. Attorney); Alex Stevens (Convoy Drunk); Mark Hammer (Judge); Joe Lisi (Agent at Bungalow); Frank Dileo (Big Junior's Friend); Jason Andrews (Johnny A.); Sean G. Wallace (Bobby B.); Ed Trucco (Calvin's Partner); Bernadette Penotti (Molested Dancer); Debra J. Pereira (Sioux Dancer); Shiek Mahmud-Bey (Federal Agent); John C. Vennema (Angry Federal Agent); Tony Cucci (Junior's Crew #1); Allen K. Bernstein (Junior's Crew #2); Dame (J.J.'s Crew #1); Jose De Soto (J.J.'s Crew #2); Lloyd Hollar (Prison Chaplain); Nicholas Falcone

(Priest at Funeral); James McCauley (Cop Outside Bar); Michael Artura (Emergendy Room Cop); Tom Riis Farrell (EMS Supervisor); Juliet Adair Pritner (Female Agent); Henry Yuk (Chinese Restaurant Owner); Chuck Margiotta (Escort at Cemetery #1); Jay Boryea (Escort at Cemetery #2); Joseph Pentangelo and Alan Jeffrey Gordon (Riker's Security Officers); Dean Rader-Duval and Willie M. Watford (Sing Sing Guards).

FILMS IN REVIEW, 7-8/95, p. 57, Andy Pawelczak

Forties and fifties films noirs—such movies as *Out of the Past* (Tourneur, 1947), *Criss Cross* (Siodmak, 1948), and *The Big Heat* (Lang, 1953) had a black-and-white deadpan quality that made them look like X-rays of the American Dream, and what they revealed just below the surface was simultaneously disquieting, subversive, and, of course, viscerally exciting and hugely entertaining. *Kiss of Death*, Barbet Schroeder's new film, loosely based on the forties movie of the same title in which Richard Widmark debuted as a psycho-killer, doesn't have quite that kind of resonance—perhaps no contemporary noir can in our hyped-up, wised-up age—but it's a smart movie with all its pieces in the right places and some terrific performances, the kind of movie Hollywood used to make as a matter of course.

The plot is generic, the tale of a small time crook, Jimmy Kilmartin (David Caruso), who is trying to go straight and is coerced by the police into acting as a confidential informant. A lot of critical ink has been spilled about Caruso's transition from *NYPD Blue* to the big screen. As Jimmy, Caruso is operating in familiar territory—cops and bad guys in Queens—but he has screen presence to spare and a face that seems stamped with guilt and pain. In the original forties movie, Victor Mature brought a wounded spirituality to the role—in both that film and Siodmak's *Cry of the City*, he had a sheen of saintliness that played well against the dark background of the noir world. Caruso's Jimmy is more visibly a product of his environment—he's a working class stiff with an anachronistic sense of honor and a longing to do the right thing in a corrupt world. Caruso holds his own against Nicolas Cage in the much flashier role of Little Junior Brown, an out-of-control hood who worries about a spot of blood on his new cassette player after he beats someone to death. Cage seems to have modeled his performance on Dennis Hopper's in *Blue Velvet*—with bulging eyes and puffed up chest, he has a comic book ferocity as he sniffs an asthma inhaler and intimidates everyone in his domain.

Richard Price's dialogue gives the movie the authentic sound of Queens. At one point, Jimmy helps a man who has been badly beaten by Little Junior, and another character accuses him of being a "liberal," a peculiarly Queens usage of the word. The characters all add a scatological tag to the ends of their sentences, as in "Let's have a serious conversation about life, and shit," and there's a nice moment when Jimmy tells Little Junior that whatever doesn't kill you makes you stronger—it's a quote from Nietzsche but in the mouths of these characters it sounds like hard won jailhouse wisdom, and Little Junior is suitably impressed.

Barbet Schroeder has an interest in the underside of American life, as he demonstrated in *Single White Female* and *Reversal of Fortune*. Here he captures the noir landscape in unnerving, hyper-real color—car junkyards, vacant lots, sad small houses on the outskirts of Queens. Little Junior runs a topless joint called Baby Cakes that Schroeder renders as a Bosch-like antechamber of hell—painted a garish pink, it's all fake palms, glaring neon, and casually naked girls gyrating in a wilderness of mirrors. He also gets some stunning performances from his supporting players, particularly Mark Rapaport as Jimmy's oily, treacherous cousin and Stanley Tucci as a creepy D.A. who would sell his mother for a federal judgeship. Samuel Jackson, who seems to be in everything these days, plays a cop whose eye perpetually tears as a result of a bullet would—he's the crying policeman of this dank, dark world.

LOS ANGELES TIMES, 4/21/95, Calendar/p. 1, Kenneth Turan

The dark, twisty kingdom of film noir, a shadow world that leaks fatalism, pessimism and romantic despair, is the drug of choice for today's directors. Hardly a month passes without one filmmaker or another attempting a modern-day noir knockoff, so strong is the lure of this brooding bad-guy genre. But it takes the arrival of a film as compelling as "Kiss of Death," one of the most effective neo-noirs, to underline why so many of the others haven't been able to go the distance.

While most of the modern copies are content to mimic the surface moodiness of the classics, "Kiss of Death" duplicates their emotional impact as well. Written by Richard Price, directed by Barbet Schroeder and starring "NYPD Blue's" David Caruso in his first post-stardom movie role, "Kiss" is not after dispassionate admiration. Its depiction of fallible characters whipsawed by pitiless antagonists on both sides of the law is wrenching to experience, and that is as it should be but hardly ever is.

As noir fans will know at once, "Kiss of Death" takes its title from a 1947 film remembered for showcasing Richard Widmark as the unbalanced Tommy Udo, whose idea of fun was pushing frail old ladies down flights of stairs. But rather than a conventional remake, screenwriter Price has come up with a new story suggested by the original's theme of a loner pressured to break the criminal code and turn against his own kind.

A successful novelist ("Clockers") as well as an accomplished screenwriter ("Sea of Love," "Mad Dog and Glory" and the Oscar-nominated "The Color of Money"), Price gives "Kiss of Death" all the noir essentials: an intricate plot that flows and eddies in unexpected places, dialogue that is juicy as well as wised-up and characters, whose anguish is easy to connect with.

With brisk economy, "Kiss of Death" introduces its protagonists, Jimmy Kilmartin (Caruso) and his wife Bev (Helen Hunt). Just the looks they exchange in their Queens apartment indicate how difficult it has been for them to remain in love, how grateful but skittish they are about having survived the rigors of alcoholism (for her) and a prison stretch for stealing cars (for him).

Later that night, with Bev out and Jimmy baby-sitting their daughter, there is hysterical knocking at the door. It is Jimmy's cousin and former cohort Ronnie (Michael Rapaport), and he is desperation itself. If he can't get one small final criminal favor from Jimmy, he's going to end up a dead man. Jimmy, out on parole, knows he should say no, we all know he should say no, but this isn't that kind of picture.

Inevitably, nothing is as easy as Ronnie says it will be, and much against his will Jimmy gets sucked into the dark heart of amorality where it's difficult to tell the criminals from the crusaders. Everyone wants something from him, from ambitious Dist. Atty. Frank Zioli (Stanley Tucci) to a relentless cop (Samuel L. Jackson) to Little Junior (Nicolas Cage), a mesmerizing crown prince of crime.

Jimmy's instinct is to refuse everyone, but no one is willing to leave it at that. Decisions about cooperation are forced on him, as Jimmy desperately tries to balance what he believes in against the effects his actions will have on the family he values so much because it has been so hard to create and maintain.

Stories like this don't work unless the actors hit all the right notes, and in "Kiss of Death" they do. The very warm Hunt, star of TV's "Mad About You" and also a vibrant presence in "The Waterdance," deftly establishes Bev's character, and Jackson brings his usual extra dimensions to the role of a wary, embittered cop.

On the other side of the law, Rapaport, last seen as the confused neo-Nazi in "Higher Learning," adds another to his list of idiosyncratic Iagos. And Cage, one of the few American actors who gets more interesting from film to film, comes close to kidnaping the picture as Little Junior, a pumped-up but asthmatic thug who, like King Kong, is a gorilla with a wistful air about him. Adroitly written and beautifully realized, Little Junior is a character whose words and actions defy prediction. Except that no one is likely to forget what happens when he's around.

Fine as Cage is, without an equal presence in the leading role, "Kiss of Death" would not satisfy. And Caruso turns out to have a classic film noir look about him. Although his face never loses its pose of cool, there is a sadness around his eyes, a vulnerability modifying his surface toughness. As "NYPD Blue" proved, Caruso knows how to make you care, and that ability has survived intact on the big screen.

A fair share of the credit for all this must go to Barbet Schroeder, a director since 1969 who has worked largely in France but sporadically (most recently with "Single White Female") in this country. Collaborating with veteran cimematographer Luciano Tovoli, Schroeder's experience and expertise are visible from the opening shot, a smooth crane movement revealing an enormous auto junkyard, immediately establishing a sense of place, of a New York only native New Yorkers ever see.

What Schroeder also brings to the mix is a welcome unobtrusiveness and sense of balance. This is the kind of film where the violence is parceled out in small, intense doses, and a key sexual event is signaled by nothing more than an open top button on a pair of jeans. Although his interest in the dark side has been evident at least as far back as the kinky "Maitresse," except for Nicholas Kazan's Oscar-nominated effort on "Reversal of Fortune," his American films have until now suffered from below-par scripts. With a fine piece of work in his hands, Schroeder has brought all his skill to bear on "Kiss of Death," and it has made all the difference.

NEW YORK, 4/24/95, p. 68, David Denby

At the beginning of the new crime picture *Kiss of Death*, I sighed in relief and pleasure: The camera, high on a crane, slowly glides through an automobile junkyard located just beyond the outfield of Shea Stadium, and though we can't immediately tell what's going on, we know that it's got to be something dirty. After such piffling, ineptly directed works of fantasy as *Muriel's Wedding* and *Don Juan DeMarco*, we're back in the essentially serious world of New York. The auto boneyard is, of course, a chop shop, one of those advanced deconstructive enterprises in which stolen automobiles are broken down, or disguised and shipped overseas; and soon the hero, an ex-con named Jimmy Kilmartin (David Caruso), is driving a truckload of stolen cars through the night. The trip is dangerous for Jimmy, who, in language that now seems quaint to us, is trying to "go straight." Shot, then arrested, Jimmy goes back to prison; and when he comes out, a man with almost nothing in life but a beloved baby daughter, he falls into the hands of a Manhattan D.A. and the Feds, who use him to trap higher-ups in Jimmy's old criminal organization. Though Jimmy is as smart as anyone, he still gets exploited—his streak of decency makes him vulnerable.

Kiss of Death is the best crime movie since Scorsese's *GoodFellas*, and part of the pleasure of it lies in its ritualized elements. There is, for instance, Jimmy's scuzzbag cousin Ronnie (Michael Rapaport), who persuades Jimmy against his better judgment to make that nighttime drive. Ronnie is the type of groveling, hysterical movie punk whose entreaties always lead to disaster. And there's his counterpart, Zioli, the unscrupulous D.A., who, in the person of Stanley Tucci (you'll recognize the arrogant nostrils), is so cynical he will only respond to people who try to practice fraud on *him*. The picture is based on a 1947 gangster *noir* of the same title directed by Henry Hathaway, written by Ben Hecht and Charles Lederer, and starring Victor Mature and the grinning giggler Richard Widmark. This new version shares the original's fatalism, but even with its crime-movie feel, it's a less stylized work, more realistic and matter-of-fact.

The writer, Richard Price, justly famous for his heightened naturalistic dialogue, creates an entirely malevolent world of thugs and law-enforcement officials. Everyone lies and betrays, and the most vicious cynicism is offered in ordinary tones. And director Barbet Schroeder (*Reversal of Fortune*) supports Price's gratifyingly nasty screenplay. Schroeder doesn't give the movie the dynamic or luscious visual scheme—a unified visual look of a Scorsese or a De Palma. But Schroeder is impressively businesslike. He skips the obvious steps, presses ahead, and holds us very tightly. There's a great deal of violence in this movie, but it's done soberly—Jimmy, for one, can see the blows coming and accepts them as the price of living in the criminal world. The matter-of-factness has its own kind of wit: The cops, arresting a suspect, always manage to sneak in a punch or bang the guy's head on a car door.

Caruso's Jimmy Kilmartin is a fairly simple man. He's in his thirties, and has been a screwup his whole life; now he wants nothing more than to be close to his daughter. Caruso's voice is low and flat, and his creased, lived-in face, pale as Crisco, manages to suggest both a Catholic schoolboy and an elderly alcoholic lying in the gutter. The performance is infused with a powerful neo-Hemingwayesque mystique: Jimmy is a man with an internal sense of honor that allows him to endure pain and defeat and still go on. This may not be an original idea, but Caruso, who became a star on television in *NYPD Blue*, uses a quiet voice and slight movements of his facial muscles to suggest a man who's always thinking.

Somber as he is, Barbet Schroeder has learned one thing from Scorsese—when you do punks and meatballs, you can go far over the top without compromising the seriousness of your movie. Schroeder gets what should become a legendary performance from that powerful loose cannon Nicolas Cage. With his short black beard, furious stare, and militant chest hair, Cage, as Little Junior, an enforcer and minor mafioso, is as erect as a steel brush. Everything affronts him—he would rage at a bumblebee for disturbing a buttercup. Cage is extremely funny, and at times he just dispenses with naturalism and leaps into space. When Little Junior's father dies, Cage, working off the grief at Baby Cakes—the strip club Little Junior's family runs in Queens—hops up and down on the dance floor, screaming and gasping for breath. Little Junior is an asthmatic, and many of his rages end in a strangled wheeze.

In the face of such hysteria, Jimmy Kilmartin has to draw on all the guile of the criminal world. *Kiss of Death* has a mythlike structure, reminiscent of a medieval quest, except that the search here is for nothing more than his daughter. The man must go on and on, with only his faith to sustain him, until he reaches the end.

NEW YORK POST, 4/21/95, p. 39, Thelma Adams

David Caruso won't be phoning Don Johnson for career advice any time soon. The Queens-born, redheaded heartthrob took the heat for leaving the cast of the popular TV show "NYPD Blue." The move won't be the "Kiss of Death" to his career that many predicted: Caruso clicks in Barbet Schroeder's remake of the 1947 film noir classic.

Following in Victor Mature's footsteps, Caruso plays Jimmy Kilmartin, a standup, blue-collar family man and former car thief. This fallen choirboy has gone straight, clean and sober, but it hurts. Kilmartin's vulnerable and that's why women love him. The part is tailormade for Caruso.

Kilmartin's nemesis is Little Junior Brown (Nicolas Cage). Unlike the unadulterated psycho Tommy Udo played by Richard Widmark in his unforgettable film debut in the 1947 "Kiss," Little Junior is vile but not pure evil.

He's an asthmatic enforcer, killing guys who threaten the family car-theft business. Bulked-up and hard-boiled, one minute Junior is lifting a blonde bimbo like a barbell above his head while vainly seeking his father's approval, the next he's pogoing in a fever of grief after his dad, Big Junior, dies.

Little Junior is vulnerable and people still fear him. What role can't Cage play?

Kilmartin and Little Junior are the pistons of this character-driven "Kiss of Death." As Kilmartin's wife, Helen Hunt, the Emmy-winning star of "Mad About You," leaps from small to big screen even more sensationally than Caruso.

In a heartbreaking visit to her jailbird husband, she admits: "I can't make it out there without you." She proves the truth of her words with downcast eyes and wobbly steps when she falls off the wagon shortly thereafter.

Samuel L. Jackson and Ving Rhames (both of "Pulp Fiction") give strong support, while Michael Rapaport ("Higher Learning") adds to his weasel portfolio as Kilmartin's twitchy, doomed cousin.

Director Barbet Schroeder ("Barfly") and novelist/ screenwriter Richard Price ("The Color of Money") have kept the original thriller's central tension: a low-level thief gets squeezed between the law and the mob. He squeals to protect his family, but that action only makes them vulnerable to a violent, hardened criminal for whom the legal system is no match.

A 1958 attempt to transplant this story to the West, Cordon Douglas' "The Fiend Who Walked the West" with Robert Evans in the psycho role, failed.

The original, shot on New York locations, had a monochrome morality to match its black-and-white photography. There were standup guys and bad guys. Mature was a thief, but he wasn't a bad guy. Cops might be inept, but they held the moral high ground over cold-blooded killers like Widmark.

Schroeder and Price trade black-and-white for a dirty, dusty color. They start their story deep in tank-top territory under the shadow of Shea Stadium and discover a mongrel beauty among the wrecked cars stranded in a chop shop lot.

Like the shift to color, the filmmakers have updated the movie's morality, introducing a post-modern ambiguity. Little Junior commits murder, but he is consistent with his code of honor; he's true to his word. The good guys, however, are not uniformly good. District Attorney Frank Zioli (Stanley Tucci) compromises Kilmartin's safety for his personal ambitions. He scraps with federal agents and the forces for justice drop the ball.

Richard Price's tightly written, dryly amusing script is less a remake of Henry Hathaway's "Kiss of Death" than a variation on a theme. Gone are Widmark's grotesque giggles, gone is the scene of Udo pushing a wheelchair-bound woman down a flight of stairs. Also banished is the gloriously grim, self-sacrificial ending, in which Mature crumbles in a hail of bullets in order to bring Widmark down.

Kiss that kind of guts good-bye. Having established a hard-boiled world of ambiguity and double-dealing, Schroeder's "Kiss of Death" makes a deal with the devil. The dark, gritty thriller takes a final Technicolor twist, serving up a soft-boiled happy ending that might suit Hollywood but would be laughed off the set of "NYPD Blue."

NEWSDAY, 4/21/95, Pat II/p. B2, Jack Mathews

All the enmity directed at "NYPD Blue" dropout David Caruso seems a little weird to those of us who noticed him in such pre-"NYPD" films as "Thief of Hearts," "The King of New York" and "Mad Dog and Glory," and have always thought of him as a budding movie star.

Yes, the hit TV show made him a household name, and rich, but it didn't indenture him, and no actor with the choice would prefer playing the same character every week on TV when he could play him in an occasional movie. More money, less work, a bigger mystique, and he gets invited to better parties.

Caruso certainly had the choice, and would have had a good film career regardless. Whether playing good or bad guys, he's always displayed the same edgy presence—a combination of explosive temperament and intelligence—that has mesmerized us in the likes of Nicholson, Pacino and De Niro. Fury is a prized commodity in Hollywood stars.

I don't know whether Caruso will ever join that exclusive club, but Barbet Schroeder's "Kiss of Death," a loose remake of the 1947 Henry Hathaway gangster classic, is a perfect vehicle for him to make a run at it. Richard Price's updated and seriously altered screenplay has a role tailored to Caruso's sensitive tough guy image, and whatever he lacks in imposing stature—frankly, he looks a little soft and pink here—he makes up for in spring-wound emotion.

There's no point in belaboring comparisons to the original "Kiss of Death," which is badly dated now and of lingering interest only to sadistic fans of Richard Widmark's performance as a giggling psycho who pushes an old lady in a wheelchair down a flight of stairs. That scene is mercifully missing from the remake, and though the characters played by Caruso and costar Nicolas Cage have the same general conflict as that between Victor Mature and Widmark, their energy levels are totally different.

Caruso plays Jimmy Kilmartin, a reformed auto thief who, in negotiating for his freedom from prison, agrees to help an ambitious assistant district attorney (Stanley Tucci) collect evidence on a mob boss known as Little Junior (Cage). Mature played the stoolie as a kind of a pathetic burnout case; Caruso plays him as a guy high on life.

The always-inventive Cage manages to make Little Junior as crazy as Widmark's Tommy Udo, but in a way that defies pathological labeling. Wearing a menacing goatee and pumped up to the size of an NFL linebacker, Cage is either in a full galloping rage or on the verge of one at all times. Junior is like a plane crash at the moment of impact.

The gamesmanship and eventual bloodletting between Cage and Caruso is all "Kiss of Death" is about. This is an old-fashioned Warner Bros.-style gangster movie, slicked up with color and production values, state of the art violence, and a gallery of museum quality bare breasts (the major setting is Junior's flaming pink, topless Baby Cakes bar).

Caruso, in the most literal sense, is the central figure of "Kiss of Death." Every other character evolves out of his or her relationship with him. Junior, the DA, the good cop Calvin (Samuel L. Jackson) with whom Jimmy forms an unlikely bond, his double-crossing cousin Ronnie (Michael Rapaport), and his two wives—ill-fated Bev (Helen Hunt), and the babysitter (Kathryn Erbe) who grows up and, in a courtship scene so brief you might miss it, takes her place.

In a recent television interview, Caruso attributed the "difficult" label slapped on him by coworkers to his single-minded quest for an absolute truth on the job. That's the kind of baloney that gives method actors a bad name, particularly when discussing something as slight as "Kiss of Death." The movie is a lot of fun, and Caruso deserves much of the credit. But there is more substance in an episode of "NYPD Blue," and that's the absolute truth.

NEWSWEEK, 5/1/95, p. 69, Karen Schoemer

The age of Tarantino is turning out to be a cruel time for the American thriller. A year or two ago, the average villain simply had to fire a gun to kill his victim dead; nowadays the bullet has to go through one wretch's hand, ricochet off the face of another and leave everybody a mangled mess. Before Tarantino, killers merely had to skulk and scowl; now they all need some wacky identifying quirk, like sucking on an inhaler marked with the initials B.A.D. or being afraid of the color red. *Kiss of Death* is director Barbet Schroeder's ("Single White Female") attempt at neo-noir. Loosely based on the 1947 crime classic starring Victor Mature, it showcases David Caruso in his first film since leaving "NYPD Blue." He plays a reformed crook who gets suckered into one final heist, winds up in the can and upon his release goes back to the underworld to help the police. You'd think Caruso would look pretty good, because everyone around him looks awful. Nicolas Cage, playing bad guy Little Junior, weight-lifts strippers instead of barbells, pummels people to death and reminds us that if there ever was a time when his acting wasn't completely over the top, that day is long gone. Helen Hunt, as Caruso's beleaguered first wife, barely has a scene where her eyes aren't puffy and her mascara isn't smeared. The usually wonderful Samuel L. Jackson is reduced to dabbing a runny eye with a handkerchief; in this film, tics pass for characterizations. Caruso snarls and flexes his muscles a lot, but for a man supposedly racked by moral dilemmas he gives a remarkably one-note performance. Today Victor Mature is widely considered a Hollywood joke, the archetypal beefcake stud with no talent to back up his looks. But his quiet, tight-lipped performance gave the original much of its allure. Caruso may be a heartthrob, but he's no Victor Mature.

SIGHT AND SOUND, 6/95, p. 48, Nick James

Jimmy Kilmartin is a reformed car thief from Queens NY who is devoted to his wife, Bev, and baby daughter, Corrina. Jimmy's cousin Ronny begs him to come on a truck-stealing job in place of a drunk. Otherwise, he says, gangster Little Junior will kill him. Against his better instincts, Jimmy agrees. He finds the semi-conscious drunk in the truck cab and pushes him aside. When the police stop the truck convoy, Jimmy gives himself up, but the suddenly roused drunk shoots one of the arresting officers, Calvin. Jimmy takes the punishment for the cop's wounding, but he says nothing and begins his time in prison.

Ronny promises Jimmy he will look after Bev, who has a drink problem. One night Ronny deliberately gets Bev drunk. When she wakes up at Ronny's apartment, she bolts into the street. Trying to drive Ronny's car away, she is killed in a collision. Jimmy offers the cops a deal in which they indict everyone, including Jimmy, for the robbery except Ronny. Incensed at being arrested, Little Junior assumes that Ronny is the snitch. Out on bail, he finds Ronny and he punches him to death.

Jimmy gets out of prison and marries neighbour Rosie, but the District Attorney forces him to work for the cops, assigning Calvin as Jimmy's cop minder. Jimmy tries to buddy up with Little Junior at his club Baby Cakes while wearing a 'wire', getting rid of the device just in time before being searched. Little Junior then takes Jimmy to a meeting with black gang leader Omar. Jimmy performs well, and, at a second meeting, Little Junior uses Jimmy unwittingly as a decoy to divert Omar's attention while he shoots him. Jimmy has recorded the killing but his expected reprieve is ruined when Omar turns out to have been an undercover FBI agent.

The FBI want Little Junior left alone as he is the key to a drugs network, but the police arrest him. Knowing that Jimmy is an informer, Little Junior has Corrina temporarily kidnapped, but she is later found unharmed. Meanwhile, the District Attorney has agreed to the FBI's offer to drop Little Junior's prosecution in return for a judge's post. Jimmy confronts Little Junior at Baby Cakes, causing a fight which leads to Calvin arresting Little Junior for assaulting a police officer. When the DA tries to have this arrest quashed, Jimmy plays him a recording he made when the DA admitted being bought off by the FBI. He threatens to send copies to the newspapers if Little Junior doesn't serve his time, or if Kilmartin or his family are ever bothered again.

Much of the history of the American crime film is in the fabric of *Kiss of Death*. As a remake of Henry Hathaway's 1947 *film noir* of the same name, it harks back to the gritty, cops-on-the-street strain of *noirs* that includes *The Asphalt Jungle*. Hathaway's film was also notorious for Richard Widmark's chilling portrayal of a sadistic killer, Tommy Udo, and, while little remains here of the original film's plot beyond its premise, there is an almost comic attempt from Nicolas Cage to match Widmark in inspired criminal lunacy. This involves Cage taking the more ludicrous aspects of his character Little Junior—his outrageously kitsch nightclub, his vivid sportswear, his pet acronym B.A.D (Balls, Attitude, Direction)—very seriously indeed. As well as a *noir* pedigree there are also at least three sets of recognisable *auteur* fingerprints on the film, each, in their own way representing a different tradition.

Firstly, the plot's painstaking evocation of police and criminal procedures bears the page-thumbing researcher's digits of screenwriter Richard Price. Secondly, in the film's fetishistic juxtapositions of muscle and steel in motor shops, prisons and girlie bars, and in the high-camp flourishes of Little Junior's gangster lifestyle we have the unmistakably steely touch of director Barbet Schroeder. Thirdly, *Kiss of Death* bears Quentin Tarantino's influence. *Pulp Fiction* has clearly had an impact on the way the film has been put together. The use of firearms to pack narrative shocks—for example when Omar is suddenly shot without warning—is post-*Pulp*, as is the knowing black humour and the casting of sexy actors as gangsters, particularly *Pulp*'s own Samuel L Jackson and Ving Rhames.

The traditions that each of these influences represent are not usually found together in the same film. Richard Price's screenplays and novels such as me *Colour of Money*, *Sea of Love*, *Night and the City* and *Clockers* have a degree of realism which never allows imagination as substitute for an establishable fact or pattern of demotic speech. In *Kiss of Death*, Jimmy Kilmartin's miserable fate is weighed, quantified and dealt out with an attention to plausibility that Schroeder's overblown *mise-en-scène* often undermines. If Price's work is the logical extension of Hathaway's gumshoe perspective, then Schroeder's approach owes more to the designer flash of *Miami Vice*. This uneasy stylistic alliance is further complicated by the Tarantino influence. His fan worship of pulpy crime novels couldn't be further from Richard Price's addiction to the unfolding of real lives.

Kiss of Death might have benefited from the tension between these different moods if it had a more compelling central performance. On this evidence, David Caruso will not find the transition from the televisual fame he enjoyed as the morally-upright but quick-fisted cop in *NYPD Blue* to the role of a feature film leading man easy. As Jimmy Kilmartin, he is required to tone down his former intensity to a loser's baleful glow, kindling the slow-burning anger of a family man's protective instincts. Caruso's performance tries to imply deep emotional torment but he hasn't yet got the knack of being a blank screen onto which the audience can project their emotions. The stony cockiness he offers here is no substitute. Besides Kilmartin's character is often implausible. For example, given his supposed pride in and loyalty to his family, what are we to make of the ease with which he switches his affections to his babysitting neighbour after his first wife has been killed?

Kiss of Death has several scenes of agonising suspense—for example Kilmartin rocking his daughter on an exposed see-saw while surrounded by police protection officers peering at distant trees—but they are outnumbered by others of seemingly false significance that drag on interminably. Schroeder lacks the ability to marry the ponderously authentic exposition with such bitter comedic exchanges as Kilmartin's response to Little Junior's suggestion that he get an acronym of his own. "How about F.A.B.—Fucked At Birth". Like *Pulp Fiction*, *Kiss of Death* is self-aware of its historical place in the crime film genre, but it fails to carry its tradition lightly or, crucially, to imaginatively reinterpret what the crime film is capable of.

TIME, 5/1/95, p. 84, Richard Schickel

According to director Barbet Schroeder, by the time he started shooting his remake of *Kiss of Death*, "only the title and one plot point remained from the 1947 original. Sure.

According to some impressionable reviewers, David Caruso, late of *NYPD Blue*, made the right decision when he quit the hit ABC show to play leads in the movies. He is, they say, an authentic star. Yeah, right.

Don't you get tired of being treated as if you were born yesterday? The fashionable novelist Richard Price has done a reasonably good job of slipcovering the source of this remake's screenplay, and Schroeder has energetically tarted up his version of a film Henry Hathaway originally shot in a rather austere semi-documentary style. But the fact is that the basic situation, most of the main narrative beats and all the major characters are essentially as they were 48 years ago (as a trip to any well stocked video store will prove)

As for Caruso, he's a fairly crude update too—of Victor Mature, whose role he has taken on. Mature also came off as a self-absorbed egocentric, but that was more an accident of looks than a matter of intent, and he fought against it, sometimes with self-parody. We will not live to see the day Caruso sends himself up. For he seems to believe inwardness is a guarantee of integrity, a signal that a whole lot of serious acting—too fine for him to share fully with us—is going on inside his head. Me? I'll have the ham sandwich, thanks.

Once past the truth-in-advertising issues, though, you have to admit that there's something sturdy, maybe even indestructible, about *Kiss of Death*. It's the story of a not-too-bright crook and family man named Jimmy Kilmartin (Caruso) caught in a well-carpentered claustrophobic invention. Busted for his reluctant role in a big-time car theft, he gets the book thrown at him when he refuses to inform on his confederates. Then his wife dies, and his fatherly obligations to his little girl start calling. So does the D.A. (Stanley Tucci), who makes a proposal: help him catch the rest of the mob, and Jimmy can go back to daddying. The trouble is that while Jimmy is away, that old gang of his is taken over by Little Junior, played by the peerlessly creepy Nicolas Cage. Even though he doesn't get to push a wheelchair-bound woman down a flight of stairs, as giggly Richard Widmark did memorably in the original, hypnotic psychopathy is never in short supply when Cage is aslither.

A half-century ago, this figure was a revelation; people hadn't seen criminal lunacy of this kind on the screen, before. What's most effective about the new *Kiss of Death* is Tucci's marvelously slimy prosecutor. This character was once a symbol of society's rectitude. Now he's as hard and amoral as the gangsters, someone we snicker at knowingly. He, and our reaction to him, may be the scariest thing about this movie—scarier than Cage's performance. Or the good reviews for Caruso's nonperformance.

VILLAGE VOICE, 5/2/95, p. 45, J. Hoberman

An editor of mine once proposed a piece attacking the "dead hand of film noir" that had clutched the fresh young throat of American indies. A leftist, he was surely paraphrasing the passage in *The 18th Brumaire of Louis Bonaparte* wherein Marx evokes the "tradition" of "dead generations [weighing] like a nightmare on the brain of the living." Marx's crack sounds like a noir scenario to me—if the original noirs of the 1940s pondered the burden of an unhappy fate, present-day noir labors under the weight of movie history.

Barbet Schroeder's *Kiss of Death*, based on the 1947 Henry Hathaway film of the same title, and Steven Soderbergh's *The Underneath*, a remake of Robert Siodmak's 1949 *Criss Cross*, update movies that now are familiar only to cinema studies majors or habitués of AMC. But these current features seem less examples of revivalist neo-noir than exercises in a kind of meta-noir. Each director, in his way, rises to the challenge to take the original material, acknowledge its particular relevance, and then somehow make it new.

In their day, neither *Kiss of Death* nor *Criss Cross* were throwaway productions. Both were considered innovative "location" movies distinguished by enigmatic titles and eye-catching set pieces. And both featured hard-luck protagonists trapped and pummeled by their unfortunate pasts. *Criss Cross* is more classically noir for employing a fatal woman to embody historical inevitability; albeit a generally blowsier film, *Kiss of Death* may be considered more progressive for making that personal heritage a criminal environment.

Updated by Richard Price from the original Ben Hecht-Charles Lederer script, the new *Kiss of Death* likewise means to be a crime film with heart. It's a drama of the little guy—presented to the 1947 audience in the unlikely form of Victor Mature and to us as David Caruso. Playing his *NYPD Blue* persona's unlucky twin, Caruso is here a domesticated ex-con living frugally with wife (Helen Hunt) and infant daughter somewhere beneath the approach to LaGuardia. An erstwhile car thief, Caruso has gone straight and likes it, but when a lowlife pal calls in a debt, he agrees to pilot a truckload of hijacked cargo through nocturnal Queens right into a police set-up. A cop gets shot; trying to prevent it, Caruso takes a bullet in his hand but also takes the rap.

Sincerely ravaged, the pasty but intense Caruso makes a sensitive punk. He's meant to be a good liar and a bit of a daredevil as he battles Nicholas Cage's pumped-up crime boss for possession of the movie. As the original *Kiss of Death* featured neophyte Richard Widmark playing a giggling, twitchy psychokiller who famously shoves a wheelchair-bound old lady down a flight of tenement stairs, so the remake presents Cage as a neurotic sadist who runs his crime ring out of the most sumptuous strip-joint on Queens Boulevard. (In a curt nod to history, his father is confined to a wheelchair.)

The musclebound pasha of the pink-stucco Baby Cakes lounge, hyperstylized Cage bench-presses his bored dancers for exercise, then punishes a drunk who harasses one by making the guy prance naked under the lights. Cage turns the movie into his own personal snarlfest while angst-ridden Caruso, released from Sing Sing and trying to protect his family, is compelled to turn stoolie and deliver this monster to the cops. To help make the informer more simpatico, *Kiss of Death* ups the cynicism level. Caruso gets caught in a procedural crossfire between FBI robots and NYPD funkballs—everybody running for cover and making deals over his head.

The first major gangster film to follow World War II, the 1947 *Kiss of Death* expanded the level of acceptable screen violence and was praised for the naturalism of scenes shot in the Tombs, Sing Sing, the Chrysler Building, and elsewhere. (Writing in *Time* magazine, James Agee found it "something new and welcome in U.S. crime movies. None of its criminals is glamorous, nor does anyone piously point out that crime does not pay.") As briskly understated and moodily anachronistic as one of Jean-Pierre Melville's mock-American *policiers, Kiss of Death* makes particularly skillful use of indirect violence. A sometime documentarian, Schroeder goes the original one better in evoking an atmospheric white-ethnic world of chop shops, topless joints, and total brutality on the Brooklyn waterfront.

In the best noir tradition, the movie bristles with sharp-elbowed secondarios competing to perform their pet turns. Samuel L. Jackson's irate cop, Stanley Tucci's smarmy D.A., Michael Rapaport's neighborhood jerk, Ving Rhames's paranoid thug, and Anthony Heald's sleazeball lawyer are all old and welcome friends. Indeed, *Kiss of Death* is so excellently typecast, one might almost forget its commercial raison d'être as Hollywood's first David Caruso vehicle.

Also reviewed in:
CHICAGO TRIBUNE, 4/21/95, Friday/p. C, Michael Wilmington
NATION, 5/22/95, p. 736, Stuart Klawans
NEW REPUBLIC, 5/22/95, p. 29, Stanley Kauffmann
NEW YORK TIMES, 4/21/95, p. C1, Janet Maslin
NEW YORKER, 5/1/95, p. 93, Terrence Rafferty
VARIETY, 3/27-4/2/95, p. 74, Todd McCarthy
WASHINGTON POST, 4/21/95, p. D1, Hal Hinson
WASHINGTON POST, 4/21/95, Weekend/p. 44, Joe Brown

LAMB

A Capitol Entertainment release of a Flickers Productions/Limehouse Pictures production in association with Chanel 4. *Executive Producer:* Al Burgess. *Producer:* Neil Zeiger. *Director:* Colin Gregg. *Screenplay (based on his novel):* Bernard MacLaverty. *Director of Photography:* Mike Garfath. *Editor:* Peter Delfgou. *Music:* Van Morrison. *Sound:* Bill Burgess. *Sound Editor:* John Delfgou. *Production Designer:* Austen Spriggs. *Art Director:* Val Wolstenholme. *Special Effects:* Gordon Coxon. *Costumes:* Monica Howe. *Make-up:* Vivien Placks. *Stunt Coordinator:* Bill Weston. *Running time:* 110 minutes. *MPAA Rating:* Not Rated.

CAST: Liam Neeson (Brother Sebastian, Michael Lamb); Harry Towb (Priest); Hugh O'Conor (Owen Kane); Frances Tomelty (Mrs. Kane); Ian Bannen (Brother Benedict); Ronan Wilmot (Brother Fintan); Denis Carey (Mr. Lamb); Eileen Kennally (Neighbor Woman); David Gorry (O'Donnell); Andrew Pickering (Murphy); Stuart O'Connor (O'Halloran); Ian McElhinney (Maguire); Bernadette McKenna (Jeweler's Assistant); Jessica Saunders (Bank Teller on Boat); Robert Hamilton (Stranger at Holyhead); Roger Booth (Farmer on Train); Marjie Lawrence (Department Store Assistant); Nicola Wright (Hotel Receptionist); Freddie Stuart (1st Crook); Roy Glascock (2nd Crook); Al Ashton (Aquarium Attendant); Doreen Keogh (Landlady, Cheap Hotel); Nick Dunning (Football Spectator); Nigel Humphries (Policeman); Tony Wredden (Pharmacist); Dudley Sutton (Haddock); Larrington Walker (Newtan); Walter McMonagle (Carpenter); Colum Convey (Plumber); Emer Gillespie (Avis Girl).

MONTHLY FILM BULLETIN, 6/86, p. 174, John Pym

Owen Kane, aged ten, is delivered by his mother into the untender care of Brother Benedict, the disaffected principal of a boys' remand home on the West Coast of Ireland. Brother Sebastian (Michael Lamb), whose ailing father, a widower, is not far from death, takes an interest in Owen, an epileptic, whose mother (if the boy is to be believed) once nearly smothered him. An uneasy, unspoken friendship begins when Brother Sebastian gives back cigarettes which an older boy has extorted from Owen. Later, Sebastian ineffectually remonstrates with Brother Benedict for unjustly thrashing Owen for the graffiti "Benny Dies OK". Returning from his father's funeral, Sebastian catches Owen fleeing from the home: he does not report him. Brother Sebastian's disillusionment with the priesthood finally boils over when the principal intimates that he should donate his forthcoming inheritance to the order. Having obtained a £2,000 advance from the family solicitor in Dublin, Lamb goes on the run with Owen, whom he passes off as his own son. They take the ferry to Holyhead and then the train to London. Their idyll, with Lamb the indulgent father giving Owen what he has never had, is inevitably shortlived. Lamb's money (depleted by three-card tricksters) runs low and, having begun in modest hotel luxury, they soon find themselves living in a squat with Lamb working as a casual labourer. The police slowly close in. At an Arsenal football match, Owen has a fit and Lamb only narrowly gets him out of the grounds before the authorities intervene. The problem of the boy's diminishing supply of prescribed pills soon becomes acute, however, and they fly back to Dublin. In the country, Lamb prepares a cocktail of drugs. On a beautiful strand, after a tranquil last meal, Owen suffers another fit and is carried into the ocean by Lamb. Having drowned the boy—having delivered him, that is, from suffering and hopelessness—Lamb discovers that, despite his best efforts, he is unable to end his own life.

At the beginning of *Cal*, the first of Bernard MacLaverty's concise, direct novels to have been adapted for the cinema (and they adapt, it should be noted, very well), the protagonist, a Roman Catholic youth, finds himself the unwilling participant in the murder of a Protestant policeman: he must then live with the rending consequences of his action. In *Lamb*, matters are reversed. The murder is, however, ordained and foretold, and there is precious little that the misguided priest, his options decreasing by the hour, can do to prevent himself from committing it. What makes the film of *Lamb* more directly affecting (and less subtle) than that of *Cal* is that the victim is a child and, despite an opening shot warning of the end, there is always a hope that the worst may not in fact occur.

Michael Lamb is as innocent—perhaps more properly, naive—as his name suggests. On a visit to his father, shortly before the latter's death, he rolls up his sleeves and puts on the kettle with a genuine enthusiasm for being of help. He cannot, however, do anything to alleviate the old man's paralysis. In this, his faith does not help him. He is thirty years old, but not yet really a man; the debilitating obedience required by the priesthood has saved him from that. Brother Benedict, his assured superior, treats him as if he were a child, and sometimes not even a very bright one. Like a delinquent, it seems, Sebastian must be threatened. "If you decide to vamoose, I can make it difficult for you", Brother Benedict warns. "The church in Ireland has as many fingers as there are pies".

Sebastian is a child, too, in the sense that he is incapable of capitalising on his impulses. In London, he has not the faintest idea what to do with Owen , once the boy has been kitted out in new clothes and once his few, not very extravagant wishes have been indulged. No wonder he falls for the three-card trick. If one could believe that Lamb had thought about his actions, instead of simply reacting against circumstance, his fate—shivering on the beach beside the body of the boy he loved—might have struck one as tragic. As it is, he cuts on almost every level a most pathetic figure. The tragedy, such as it is, is the boy's: he bears the mark implied by his name—scars on his body, a pimple on his face, epilepsy, a tendency to wet the sheets: "Kane the Stain". But he embodies a youthful gumption—very different from Lamb's Boy Scout leanings—which one feels would have seen him through had he not had the ill luck to be taken up by Brother Sebastian.

MacLaverty has a clear, observant eye—and in this he may be compared to two other Ulster writers, Seamus Heaney and Louis MacNeice. In one of the novel's flashbacks, for example, Lamb remembers his father's respect for "every living thing". "Although he was plagued by rabbits, when the myxomatosis came he would take the trouble to kill them with a blow of his hand as they sat trembling, saying he did not want to waste a cartridge on them". Colin Gregg and his cameraman Mike Garfath have adopted a comparably clear and unsentimental style. The inexorability of the plot is matched by the swift, sharply lit style of its execution. The detailing is correct, from the carpentry shop at the boys' home to the plastic apron which Brother Benedict wears to dust and catalogue his books. London has the feel of a foreign city. The brutality of the end is counterbalanced by the bright matter-of-fact sequence of events which precedes it. This is not, significantly, another rainswept Irish saga, but one which, at the key moments, is suffused with light—and it is the more disturbing for that.

The dire influence of the priesthood on the education of Irish children has been a theme frequently, and profitably, turned over by Irish writers. And MacLaverty, who was himself once a teacher, clearly takes pleasure in giving the devil— Brother Benedict—the best lines. This is a tight moral tale (152 pages), and on the whole the players must fulfil their parts in it and little more. But Brother Benedict, as portrayed to relishable effect by Ian Bannen, inhabits a world of his own. Of course, he knows that the boy who wrote "Benny Dies OK" was not signing his own initials (Owen Kane). An example has been made; the boys now know that Benny has risen. It was his little irony: KO. All of which is beyond Brother Sebastian, whose inability to understand God's love in these paradoxical terms is in part the cause of his ruin.

NEW YORK POST, 2/24/95, p. 44, Thelma Adams

"Discipline is love disguised."

Thus speaks the bromide-spewing headmaster Brother Benedict (Ian Bannen) to the idealistic Brother Michael Lamb (Liam Neeson), justifying his authoritarian rule over a home for delinquent boys on the crusty coast of Ireland.

In "Lamb," Irish director Colin Gregg's dreary docudrama about the spiritual slaughtering of the innocent, you don't need a score card to identify the saints and sinners. The characters are so heavily drawn by screenwriter Bernard MacLaverty (based on his novel of the same name), all that's been left, out are the halos and the pitchforks.

"Lamb" had a theatrical release in Britain in 1986 and has belatedly washed onto our shores on the crest of Neeson's popularity. As the naive Lamb, the Irish actor makes an awkward monk. He does a lot of fussing with his long, black robe when he's not clasping his hands behind his back like a figure skater.

Neeson's broad face and limpid bovine eyes express the kind of generalized concern that could have been inspired by the thought: "Did I leave my oven on?"

In this case, the cause of Neeson's wrinkled brow is a crisis of faith brought on by the death of his father and the arrival of Owen Kane (Hugh O'Conor), a new student ripe for bullying by students and teachers alike.

Kane (read Cain, never a lucky name for a child) comes across as a composite of documentary ticks. The 10-year-old is a jug-eared, pink-cheeked, elfin epileptic who smokes, swears and steals when he's not wetting the bed.

Since this is victim art, even Kane's vices are forgivable as he was abused by his parents and beaten by Benedict.

Lamb decides to rescue his own tortured soul and the klepto kid by fleeing to England. Predictably, the police, spurred on by the wily Benedict, view this flight to freedom in a more limited way—they call it kidnapping.

Lamb didn't think this half-baked scheme through and, clearly, neither did the screenwriter. The overlong movie follows the surrogate father and son through a series of misadventures that fail to resonate.

When all else fails, writer MacLaverty telegraphs the point. Lamb reads Kane the story of Daedalus and Icarus. In Greek mythology, the inventor built wings of feather and wax to escape Crete. His son Icarus flew too close to the sun and fell to his death when the wax melted.

A father's desire to fly kills the son. Innocence is slaughtered. The conclusion of "Lamb" is less shocking than it is abrupt.

Van Morrison provided the brooding score.

NEWSDAY, 2/24/95, Part II/p. B4, Terry Kelleher

From World War II Poland in "Schlinder's List" to backwoods America in "Nell" to auld Scotland in the forthcoming "Rob Roy," Liam Neeson is clearly an actor on the move. "Lamb" takes us back to his Irish roots.

The 10-year-old drama finds Neeson playing a Catholic brother assigned to a harsh reform school in County Galway. Sitting on a windswept pile of rock at the edge of the cold Atlantic, the institution is run with pious malevolence by Brother Benedict (a masterly Ian Bannen), who speaks of classism and capital punishment as if they were divine precepts.

Neeson's Brother Sebastian is starting to doubt God, and he's certainly finished believing in Brother Benedict. But he hasn't entirely lost his faith; he just isn't sure where to place it anymore. The death of his father, who had urged him into the religious life, leaves Brother Sebastian shaken and even more restless.

The plight of 10-year-old Owen Kane (Hugh O'Conor, who played Christy Brown as a child in "My Left Foot") moves him to an act of faith in human redemption. An epileptic raised by abusive parents, Owen obviously faces more pain under Brother Benedict's regime. Impulsively—and, it must be said, not so plausibly—Brother Sebastian decides to quit the order, liberate the boy and flee with him to England.

Neeson and O'Conor are touching, believable and sometimes quite funny as, essentially, two children of strikingly different sizes and attitudes. Brother Sebastian is a bit flummoxed by the great, secular world. Owen, already accomplished at smoking and swearing, is quick to pick the forbidden fruit. But Brother Sebastian, born Michael Lamb, learned the meaning of love at his father's knee, and this he is determined to teach.

When Michael helps Owen build a model airplane, and reads to him of the mythical Daedalus and Icarus, we sense that the two fugitives ultimately will be lambs sacrificed on the altar of symbolism. But even those who find fault with the wrenching conclusion will admire the way Neeson conveys his character's tenderness and anguish.

VILLAGE VOICE, 2/28/95, p. 74, Natasha Stovall

Starring Liam Neeson, his Irish brogue, and his furrowed brow, *Lamb*—released in Europe in 1987 is a *Boys Town* for those who know the Newt has orphanages pegged all wrong. Below the unforgiving sky of Ireland's Antrim coast, the Remand Home is as cruel and barren as its surroundings. The young foundlings occupy themselves pounding nails through Jesus's palms in woodshop, skinny-dipping in the frozen sea, and beating each other silly—while brothers of an unspecified order sweep about in black robes barking admonishments and beating the boys silly.

Delivered unto this depressing scene is young Owen Kane (Hugh O'Conor), a spindly, epileptic 10-year-old saddled with scars from his absentee da and an abandonment complex courtesy of his neglectful ma. He's a magnet for an idealistic young brother, Michael Lamb (Neeson), who's drawn to Owen's defiant neediness ("Fok you!" is Owen's fondest retort), and the two slowly amble toward an awkward closeness. But Michael's superiors take issue with any sort of tenderness, it seems"Oh, a favorite?" leers sadist-in-charge Brother Benedict (Ian Bannen), eyebrow cocked. "You know what that can lead to."

With faith fading fast, Michael spirits Owen to London, ostensibly to save him from the home's brutality, but clearly also to nurture a relationship that has grown beyond simply ward and keeper.

Director Colin Gregg records London's blaring neon and seedy interiors with the same chilly detachment with which he caresses Antrim's rocky shore—neither place offers safety for the fugitives, and they're left with only each other to cling to. So *Lamb*'s story unfolds within the subtleties of two faces, two minds, two bodies, as Michael struggles to assume the responsibilities of fatherhood, and Owen the unfamiliar, absolute trust of childhood.

As the pair's world quickly collapses inward, there's a palpable unwillingness on Gregg's part to follow the story to its tragic end. *Lambs*'s resolution doesn't make sense because its cruelty isn't built up to in the body of the story. *Lamb* would have us believe in the transcendent power of human bonds over society's narrow traps, but when Gregg finally brings himself to drop his bomb, it's not unexpected, just unbelievable.

Also reviewed in:
NEW REPUBLIC, 3/27/95, p. 29, Stanley Kauffmann
NEW YORK TIMES, 2/24/95, p.C17, Stephen Holden
VARIETY, 11/20/85, p. 15

LAMERICA

A New Yorker Films release of a C.G.G. Tiger Cin.Ca and Arena Films coproduction in collaboration with Raiuno and Vega Film and supported by Eurimages. *Executive Producer:* Enzo Porcelli. *Producer:* Mario Cecchi Gorri and Vittorio Cecchi Gori. *Director:* Gianni Amelio. *Screenplay (Italian with English subtitles):* Gianni Amelio, Andrea Porporati, and Alessandro Sermoneta. *Director of Photography:* Luca Bigazzi. *Editor:* Simona Paggi. *Music:* Franco Piersanti. *Sound:* Alessandro Zanon. *Set Designer:* Giuseppe M. Gaudino. *Costumes:* Liliana Sotira and Claudia Tenaglia. *Running time:* 120 minutes. *MPAA Rating:* Not Rated.

CAST: Enrico Lo Verso (Gino); Michele Placido (Fiore); Carmelo Di Mazzarelli (Spiro); Piro Milkani (Selimi); Elida Janushi (Selimi's Cousin); Sefer Pema (Prison Warden); Nikolin Elezi (Boy Who Dies); Artan Marina (Ismail); Besim K. Kurti (Policeman); Esmerald Ara (Little Girl).

LOS ANGELES TIMES, 6/13/96, Calendar, p. 1, Kenneth Turan

"Lamerica" is a miracle, a reason to believe. Dramatic, intelligent insightful and ambitious, this exceptionally moving film is strong enough to rank with the masterworks of Italy's cinema. In a town that believes that box office is the sole test of greatness, it is both chastening and heartening to encounter the real thing.

The path of films of piercing quality is not, however, an easy one. Though it won numerous awards in Italy, as well as the prestigious Felix for best European film of 1994, "Lamerica" was ignored by the Academy Awards' predictably fallible foreign language committee. And it arrives in Los Angeles nearly a year after its New York Film Festival debut, at only one theater for only one week. It's enough to make you weep.

A profound emotional experience, "Lamerica's" always-human story touches delicately but tellingly on questions of personal and national identity, on the immigrant's desire to better himself elsewhere and the stranger's parallel passion to return home. Its title, an unlettered reference to the United States, is as much metaphor as anything else, an allusion to the fabled place of dreams that is finally as elusive as El Dorado.

"Lamerica" is only the third theatrical feature (the first, "Open Doors," was Oscar nominated, and the second, "Stolen Children," won the Grand Jury Prize at Cannes) for director Gianni Amelio, a quiet but forceful filmmaker whose natural empathy with his characters and adept use of non-professional actors places him directly in the Italian neo-realistic tradition.

Like "Stolen Children," which followed a carabiniere as he escorted a child prostitute and her brother across Italy to a new home, "Lamerica" uses the device of a geographical journey to move characters on unexpected voyages of interior discovery.

And with "Lamerica," the director himself took a journey, for this film is entirely shot in Albania, just 70 miles across the Adriatic from Italy's boot. Perennially impoverished, Albania, as old newsreel footage that runs alongside "Lamerica's" opening credits shows, was invaded by Italy in 1939 and forced into an unequal political union "in the name of fascism."

In 1991, the year "Lamerica" is set in, a new pair of opposing invasions is taking place. On the one hand, thousands of Albanians, desperate to improve their lot, are pouring into port cities, intent on fleeing over the water to the earthly paradise they've glimpsed on glossy Italian TV.

Coming into Albania from Italy, on the other hand, are exploiters looking to make a profit out of the country's desperation and naivete. Fiore and his young partner Gino (Michele Placido and Enrico Lo Verso, the film's only professional actors) are practiced and prosperous deceivers who are looking to set up a dummy corporation that will take advantage of the Albanians while bilking money from the Italian government.

Arrogant about their wealth and contemptuous of the desperate locals, Fiore and Gino need a docile Albanian figurehead to head their board of directors. In the disease-ridden ruins of a former prison camp, they come across their ideal man: Spiro Tozai (Carmelo Di Mazzarelli).

Encrusted with the misery of half a century in detention, Spiro has so lost touch with reality he thinks he's 20 years old. Incontinent, unwilling to speak, possibly feeble-minded, Spiro is capable only of signing his name, which is all the Italians care about.

Fiore heads back to Italy, which means that Gino is left alone when a crisis occurs. Spiro is needed to sign more papers, but the old man has precipitously fled from the orphanage where he's been incongruously warehoused and Gino, much against his will, has to head out into Albania proper to find him.

It's a journey into a world of unimaginable chaos that, like a bog, sucks Gino in deeper and deeper, involving him in complex and unforeseen emotional situations. With his illusions and his bravado gradually peeled off the way the wheels are stripped from his expensive car, Gino is forced to confront the implications of his own and his country's history and culture when he discovers that Spiro Tozai has a voice after all.

Enrico Lo Verso, who starred in "La Scorta" and "Farinelli" as well as playing the wistful carabiniere in "Stolen Children," is an ideal actor for director Amelio's aims. With soft, pouting lips and sad eyes, he has a face to which emotional confusion comes easily, a face that can make the transition from arrogance to uncertainty believable.

The wonder of this film, however, is 80-year-old Carmelo Di Mazzarelli, a retired fisherman Amelio met by chance on a pier. With no previous acting experience, Di Mazzarelli has, in the tradition of neo-realism, been able to give a performance, that seems to go beyond acting to convey something essential about the human spirit.

As much as any of the actors, Albania and its people are critical to "Lamerica's" success. Amelio has a particular gift for faces and types, picking images—like a tiny girl doing slick hip-hop dance moves in a ruined hotel—that are indelible. It's only one of the many things to marvel at in this remarkable, unforgettable film.

NEW YORK POST, 12/20/95, p. 38, Larry Worth

It's a buddy movie, a road movie and a love story—even though Wesley and Woody are MIA, Bob and Bing have traveled elsewhere and there's not so much as a lip-lock.

In "Lamerica," director Gianni Amelio reinterprets each genre while lensing a neo-realist drama to rival Rossellini, De Sica or Antonelli's finest.

The incisive screenplay—co-written by Amelio, Andrea Porporati and Alessandro Sermoneta—concerns two Italian hucksters determined to exploit 1991 Albania's weak economy. Their plan is simple: establish a dummy shoe factory in the once-communist territory. And since an Albanian resident must head the business, they find a 70-year-old political prisoner who thinks he's 20 and manages a spidery scrawl.

So far, so good. Until Gino—the younger, cockier, more condescending carpetbagger—dumps the old man in an orphanage, from which the senior promptly wanders. Chasing him onto a passing bus, Gino unwittingly embarks on a journey of self-discovery. But as he finds his values, he becomes as much a victim as everyone around him.

Appropriately, the Albanian landscape proves even bleaker than the story. It's mile after mile, vista after vista of sand and dirt, disturbed only by a dried-up riverbed. But even in the country's most remote corners (the history of which is summarized in an opening newsreel), it's survival of the fittest.

As in his last effort, the brilliant "Stolen Children," Amelio stresses that man's cruelty to man knows no bounds. Yet, right in the middle of unending horrors (the worst of which takes place in a sewer-like prison, with zombie-like inmates advancing on outsiders a la "Night of the Living Dead"), Amelio sneaks in the unexpected.

For instance, as Gino and his charge find lodging in a rat-infested, once-fashionable hotel, they catch sight of a dirty rag-clad girl in the hallway, joyfully dancing with precision-like moves to rock tunes on the radio. It's the equivalent of the peacock-in-the-snow scene from Fellini's "Amarcord" or the white stallion galloping through war-torn city streets in Costa-Gavras' "Missing."

Such tableaus, which continue through the heartbreaking finale, have more power and conviction than anything Hollywood has mustered this year.

Amelio's other strength is inspired casting. He chose a non-actor, Sicilian fisherman Carmelo Di Mazzarelli, to play the delusional old man, with amazing results. Every crease on Di Mazzarelli's face tells a story, with only his eyes betraying the vital life force trapped within.

Enrico Lo Verso's Gino is the film's other phenomenon. The actor, best known from "Farinelli" and "Stolen Children," mesmerizes with his mop of curly hair, thick lips and high cheekbones. But his multi-layered conveyance of a soul beneath the tough-guy facade makes his performance a revelation.

Further enhanced by a subtle score and nightmarishly stark lighting, "Lamerica"—the title of which refers to a dream for happiness that's always out of reach—emerges as one of 1995's most extraordinary productions.

NEWSDAY, 12/20/95, Part II/p. B7, Jack Mathews

In Italian director Gianni Amelio's fine 1992 "Stolen Children," the young actor Enrico Lo Verso plays a Milan cop who is ordered to escort a pair of kids who have been taken from their abusive mother to an orphanage hundreds of miles away and through the adventure undergoes some serious introspection.

Amelio, who's single-handedly reviving Italian neo-realism, and Lo Verso, one of the most interesting European actors to come along in a while, are reunited with "Lamerica," and though the new setting is Albania, the core humanity of the story and the lessons learned are very similar.

Again, Lo Verso is playing a man escorting a lost child across country and getting a good dose of self-revelation along the way. But this time, the child is an 80-year-old Sicilian named Spiro who came to Albania with the Italian army at the beginning of World War II, was left behind to be warehoused in a Communist prison and, when suddenly reawakened to reality, has forgotten it all.

What brings Lo Verso's Gino and the non-professional Carmelo Di Mazzarelli's Spiro together is a shameless plot by Gino and his business mentor Fiore (Michele Placido) to exploit Albania's political and economic weaknesses in the aftermath of the fall of communism. The two Italian con men come to Albania intending to set up a bogus corporation with a titular Albanian president and rob a few investors blind before they're found out.

How quick a hit they intend to make is evident in their choice of a company president, a disheveled old man so confused he doesn't even think to deny he is Albanian. He speaks both Italian and Albanian, but his thoughts are gibberish, and it is not until a series of darkly comic events has put him and Gino on the road together—alongside scores of Albanians hoping to rendezvous with a boat that will take them to America—that Gino begins to learn the truth of the old man's life.

"Lamerica" is as spare as the land it's set on, essentially a simple tale of people on the run from certain despair to an imagined paradise. But Amelio sees the current Albanian experience as a direct parallel to life in postwar Italy, and he is probing human issues that go far beyond contemporary politics.

Gino and Spiro, in some ways, represent the extremes of human nature in good and bad times. Gino gives in relative prosperity, is driven by greed and yet is cynical. Spiro, for 60 years, has done nothing more than survive, using madness as a defense, and remains an optimist.

The relationship that develops between the men is fascinating. It begins with Gino as exasperated guardian, tracking the old man for no reason other than to preserve the con. But the dusty trail of parched Albania quickly takes him beyond that point, making him as vulnerable as Spiro and the others they meet on the road, and Gino begins to see in the old man's searching eyes a sense of truth he's not known before. Amelio's deeply human story ends with some memorably poetic images and on revelations that leave the theater with you

There are endless stories to be culled from fragments of the shattered Iron Curtain, and just glimpsing the lifestyles in Albania, where some people were so cut off from Western culture that they hadn't seen a working television set before 1991, is an eye-opener.

Like Spiro, Albania has been asleep for 60 years, and it has a lot of catching up to do. And so do we.

NEWSWEEK, 1/29/96, p. 58, David Ansen

Lamerica, the best new Italian film to reach our shores in years, is shot in CinemaScope, the format of epics, wide-screen adventures and sweeping American vistas. But the harshly impressive landscapes in Gianni Amelio's powerful movie belong to a country we haven't been allowed until now to see on screen. Welcome to Albania, a country that from 1944 to 1991 was sealed off to the West under the draconian communist dictatorship of Enver Hoxha. Though it's only 70 miles from the coast of Italy, the chaotic, poverty-stricken land Amelio captures in his indelible images seems to belong to another century, if not another planet.

Now open to the capitalist West, the country is rife for plunder. Enter two Yuppie Italian scam artists, Fiore (Michele Placido) and his younger partner, Gino (Enrico Lo Verso), who need to find an Albanian straw man to sit as "chairman" of their phony shoe factory, for which they hope to get Italian government grants. In the hellish remains of one of Hoxha's prison camps they find their perfect sap—a feeble-minded 70-year-old named Spiro (Carmelo Di Mazzarelli). They clean him up, coach him to sign documents and install him in a Catholic orphanage.

"Lamerica" has more on its mind than exposing the dark side of the new world order. Spiro slips away from the orphanage, and the frantic Gino sets out in pursuit. So begins an odyssey across the bunker-strewn, beggar-infested landscape of Albania—where feral children steal the shoes from your feet. During his journey Gino discovers that the man he' searching for isn't who he seems. He's not even Albanian. Nor will Gino's identity survive intact. His precious Jeep stripped, his documents confiscated, he's caught up in a nightmare that forces him to acknowledge his kinship with the desperately poor Albanians dreaming of escape to the promised land of Italy. And, in a moving, transcendent climax, we see as well Gino's kinship with his Sicilian forefathers, who once dreamed of making the voyage to a magical America.

Amelio, who made the stunning "Stolen Children," is a master. His haunting images have a stately elegance that put one in mind of both John Ford and Bernardo Bertolucci. But he also has roots in neorealism: except for Lo Verso and Placido, his cast is composed entirely of nonprofessionals. From the 80-year-old Di Mazzarelli, a former fisherman, he coaxes a performance of remarkable poignance. His traumatized Spiro, who's spent 50 years as a prisoner and still thinks he's a 20-year-old in World War II, and the callow, opportunistic Gino develop a strange bond. It's built on deceit but evolves into something more complex—a shared yearning that links the Italian past to the Italian present. Amelio's eloquent but unsentimental humanism asks us to reconsider our relationship to the wretched of the earth. Though his film, which won the Felix Award as the best European Film of 1994, will obviously have a special resonance for Italians, it's no less relevant to America in 1996, in the grips of anti-immigrant fever. Don't miss this beauty of a film.

VILLAGE VOICE, 12/26/95, p. 60, Georgia Brown

Knowing that Gianni Amelio's *Lamerica* has already reaped praise (the *Times* called it the triumph of the New York Film Festival") and won several prestigious prizes (a Felix for Best European Film Venice's Best Director), I feel slightly less churlish for finding it solemn and sentimental. A better *professóre* than he is an artist, Amelio has terrific ideas for films.

Like Amelio's 1992 *Stolen Children* (another Felix winner), *Lamerica* traces a journey into the interior. This time the country to be traversed is the wretched Albania long considered Europe's wildest, most backward part. Again, the film focuses on the vacant young actor, Enrico Lo Verso, playing the film's guide, its tainted but basically decent point of view. Here, Lo Verso plays Gino, first seen as the callow apprentice to veteran entrepreneur Fiore (Michele Placido). Crossing Albanian customs, the enterprising Italians pick up their eager, chatty interpreter, Selimi (Piro Milkani), who clamors into the open back end of their fancy Jeep.

Fiore and Gino conduct business Italian-style. They've come to establish a dummy corporation, but since law requires an Albanian GEO, they're searching for a human dummy to install as company head. Selimi takes them to a former labor camp where they pick the dazed, seemingly docile Spiro (Carmelo Di Mazzarelli). Fiore says Spiro reminds him of his dead father; it's Gino, however, who's left behind in Albania to watch over the child-like old man, and, when Spiro escapes, to track him down.

In 1991, the year the movie takes place, thousands of Albanians managed to slip through to Italy (only to be shipped back later by Italian authorities), and Amelio's Albania is a surreal sea of desperate young men running, walking, hitching in one direction—toward the ports, toward Italy (One volunteers that he and his buddies plan to become soccer stars since that's the best job.) As America, North and South, represented hope to impoverished Italians 50 or so years ago, so a conspicuously prosperous Italy is today's l'America (Amelio drops the apostrophe).

In their smart, well-made Italian clothes, and hardly bothering to conceal their visceral revulsion for Albanian poverty, the two visitors are the real amnesiacs. Like con artists everywhere, they've forgotten what it was like to do honest work.

Although nearly the whole film takes place inside Albania, *Lamerica* is meant as a scathing critique of contemporary Italy. The sulky Gino first shows signs of life upon spotting a TV tuned to an Italian channel—to one of those stupid game shows. And once he takes up his journey into the interior, stupid game shows mockingly turn up. TV gives Albanians their notions of Italy. The film's loveliest moment shows a beautiful blonde child dancing to the MTV of her dreams. "You like her?" laughs an old woman. "Take her to Italian television."

Following a classic narrative, "civilization" falls away in stages. Gino loses his Jeep, then his luggage, his classy Italian sunglasses, his job, and finally—jailed for corruption—his passport and clothes. To a weary functionary, he pleads the case for corruption: "You aren't used to capitalism. ... That's how things work in Italy. ... We're *businessmen.*"

If Gino from Sicily essentially becomes an Albanian—miserable, tattered, desperate for Italy—the gentle Spiro turns out to be a fellow Sicilian: one of many soldiers who went into Albania with Mussolini and were left behind when Fascism fell. Under Hoxha's brutal Communism, Spiro was locked away in a labor camp for 50 years. Spiro only lost his mind, however; back in Italy, they were losing their souls.

Lamerica is more interesting to think about than to sit through. Amelio's filmmaking feels agonizingly dull. I'm not talking about the respectably slow episodic plot (more or less the same one he used in *Stolen Children*), but the quality of images. For one, Amelio relies heavily on faces, yet he doesn't know how to find a face's life. The 80-year-old retired fisherman he picked to play Spiro is practically winking at the camera.

Okay, I know I should be grateful for any serious content at all.

Also reviewed in:
CHICAGO TRIBUNE, 12/24/95, Tempo/p. 12, Michael Wilmington
NATION, 1/1/96, p. 35, Stuart Klawans
NEW REPUBLIC, 1/29/96, p.26, Stanley Kauffmann
NEW YORK TIMES, 12/20/95, p. C16, Janet Maslin
VARIETY, 9/12-18/94, p. 45, Deborah Young
WASHINGTON POST, 2/16/96, p. F6, Richard Harrington
WASHINGTON POST, 2/16/96, Weekend/p. 47, Desson Howe

LAST OF THE DOGMEN

A Savoy Pictures release of a Mario Kassar presentation of a Joel B. Michaels production in association with Carolco Pictures Inc. *Executive Producer:* Mario Kassar. *Producer:* Joel B. Michaels. *Director:* Tab Murphy. *Screenplay:* Tab Murphy. *Director of Photography:* Karl Walter Lindenlaub. *Editor:* Richard Halsey. *Music:* David Arnold. *Music Editor:* Laurie Higgins Tobias. *Sound:* David Ronne and David M. Kelson. *Sound Editor:* Michael O'Farrell. *Casting:* Amanda Mackey and Cathy Sandrich. *Production Designer:* Trevor Williams. *Art Director:* Ricardo Spinace. *Special Effects:* David Kelsey. *Costumes:* Elsa Zamparelli. *Make-up:* Allan A. Apone. *Stunt Coordinator:* Chuck Waters. *Running time:* 120 minutes. *MPAA Rating:* PG.

CAST: Tom Berenger (Lewis Gates); Barbara Hershey (Lillian Sloan); Kurtwood Smith (Sheriff Deegan); Steve Reevis (Yellow Wolf); Andrew Miller (Briggs); Gregory Scott Cummins (Scars); Graham Jarvis (Pharmacist); Mark Boone Jr. (Tattoo); Helen Calahasen (Yellow

Wolf's Wife); Eugene Blackbear (Spotted Elk); Dawn Lavand (Indian Girl); Sidel Standing Elk (Lean Bear); Hunter Bodine (Kid); Parley Baer (Mr. Hollis); Georgie Collins (Senior Editor); Sherwood Price (Tracker); Molly Parker (Nurse); Antony Holland (Doc Carvey); Robert Donley (Old Timer); Brian Stollery (Grad Student); Mitchell LaPlante (Wild Boy).

LOS ANGELES TIMES, 9/8/95, Calendar/p. 2, Kenneth Turan

"Last of the Dogmen" doesn't have an original bone anywhere near its body, but that's what makes it an unexpectedly sweet-natured experience.

Durable, familiar, unpretentious, "Dogmen" is a family adventure tale notable for its modest aims and the respect with which it treats its old-fashioned material. Seeing the film's sweeping vistas peopled by stalwart men and heroic women is like going back in time to an era when movies did not try too hard to be what they were not.

Narrated with predictable Western gumption by an uncredited Wilford Brimley, "Dogmen," though filmed in Canada and Mexico, is set in the Oxbow, an area of northwest Montana genially referred to as "4,000 square miles of the roughest country God ever put on a map."

Three escaped convicts have fled into this territory, so remote "places haven't seen a footprint." Though we can tell he doesn't want to, a troubled sheriff Deegan (Kurtwood Smith) tells his deputy, Lewis Gates, to find them.

The gruff, cantankerous Gates (Tom Berenger), aided by his wonder dog Zip, is the best tracker in the state, drunk or sober. Mostly he's in the former state, mourning the death of his wife in an accident his father-in-law, that same Sheriff Deegan, irrationally believes Gates could have prevented.

About to close in on the evildoers, the tracker is stunned to find the men have disappeared, leaving just enough bloody traces to indicate they've come to a deservedly bad end. And he discovers one thing more: part of an arrow.

Fortunately for the mystified Gates, an anthropology professor named Lillian Sloan (Barbara Hershey) is doing field work conveniently nearby. She identifies the arrow as belonging to the Cheyenne, more specifically to a fierce military society within the tribe called the Dog Soldiers. But Dog Soldiers, she says, have not been seen in these parts for 130 years or more.

Gates—who thinks he may have spied something, he's not sure what, moving around in the distance in the Oxbow—is eager to return and investigate further, and he wants Sloan, who he doesn't particularly like but who does speak fluent Cheyenne, to make the trek into the wilderness with him. What they discover shocks them, but anyone familiar with the conventions of this particular genre will not be quite as surprised.

Tab Murphy, who wrote and makes his directing debut with "Dogmen," got a co-story credit on the Oscar-nominated script for "Gorillas in the Mist" in 1988 and has had other projects in varying stages of development since. "Dogmen" is apparently the first script he wrote after he left film school, and he directs it with a likable straight-ahead quality that does not over-hype the unpretentious story.

In this he is helped considerably by his two leads, neither of whom are seen on screen as often as their abilities warrant. The convincingly rugged Berenger is at home as tobacco-chewing Gates, and Hershey is, as always, a luminous graceful presence. "Last of the Dogmen" is neither challenging nor ambitious, but as a Boys and Girls Own Adventure it does fine.

NEW YORK POST, 9/8/95, p. 49, Michael Medved

Whenever Hollywood presents some version of vast, virginal, unexplored wilderness, there's almost always something mysterious lurking "out there." Could it be a lost world of dinosaurs? A giant ape, the elusive big foot, or a legendary temple of gold?

In "Last of the Dogman," the surprise behind the trees is a pristine Native American society, totally uncontaminated by Western civilization, descended from a handful of "Dog Soldier" or "Dogmen" Cheyenne warriors who survived the historic Sand Creek massacre in 1864.

According to the movie's intriguing script (by Tab Murphy of "Gorillas in the Mist," who also makes an auspicious debut as director) they fled deep into the rugged Montana back-country where, for 130 years, they've scrupulously avoided all contact with the murderous white man.

Their isolation ends, however, when an alcoholic mountain man and bounty hunter, played by Tom Berenger, goes into the wilderness to pursue three vicious escaped convicts. Before he can bring them back alive, they're mysteriously killed by antique Cheyenne arrows. Determined to solve this enigma, Berenger recruits a noted anthropologist (Barbara Hershey) to accompany him on a trek back to the mountains.

From this point forward, the thrust of the story is entirely predictable. Of course, the bickering between Berenger and Hershey ("Just because I let you come along doesn't mean I have to like it!") only masks their underlying attraction; and, of course they'll both be utterly captivated by the innocence of the primitive, natural life they discover among the Cheyenne.

Their big challenge will be to protect their new friends from other, less sympathetic, white intruders—especially Kurtwood Smith as a hard-bitten, angry local sheriff, who happens to be Berenger's former father-in-law.

Thanks to superb cinematography (by Karl Walter Lindenlaub of "Stargate") and breathtaking, exceptionally well-chosen locations (the movie was shot in both the Canadian Rockies and a national park outside Mexico City), this strange tale, reminiscent of an odd combination of "Dances with Wolves" and "Brigadoon," plays out far more strongly than you'd expect.

Tom Berenger settles comfortably into his role, giving far richer dimension to this character than his sleepy half-hearted recent work elsewhere. Barbara Hershey also makes the most of her convenient love interest role, generating surprisingly potent chemistry with her co-star. A real scene stealer throughout the movie is Zip, an 18-month-old Queensland Heeler rescued from a dog pound to play Berenger's heroic canine companion.

Despite sincere attempts at accurately rendering Cheyenne culture and customs, the movie fails at its key efforts to convince us that we're watching a 19th-century tribe that's somehow survived into the edge of the 21st century.

The warriors and their families are too unfailingly warm-hearted and nice, and their existence too idyllic and picturesque, to give an authentic sense of the hardships and grandeur of their little survivors' society. The music is also a major problem—with the intrusive, soppy symphonic score by David Arnold undermining even some of the film's most spectacular visual elements.

Nevertheless, the ineptly titled "Last of the Dogmen" remains a big, bold, energetic outdoor adventure that's unexpectedly well-suited for family viewing. If the feathered Cheyenne arrow doesn't exactly hit the bull's-eye, at least it comes reasonably close to the target.

NEWSDAY, 9/8/95, Part II/p. B4, John Anderson

That a tribe of unassimilated Cheyenne warriors might exist in the isolated Shangri-la of the Montana Rockies is not just an intriguing notion, it's a consoling one. It suggests that the cultural (if not quite literal) genocide perpetrated in this country fell short of success, that certain ways of life can outlast time and progress. That there's such a thing as a second chance.

It's a notion that's highly implausible but certainly appealing. And so, in many ways, is "Last of the Dogmen," a lumpy, bumpy adventure that matches a crusty Tom Berenger with a classy Barbara Hershey and tells much of their story via the quasi-curmudgeonly Wilfred Brimley—who, speaking of lumpy and bumpy, is as convincing here as he, is selling oatmeal.

But Berenger and Hershey are pros, and despite a less than polished script by first-time director Tab Murphy (he wrote "Gorillas in the Mist"), the story has a certain charm. And a certain predictability.

Berenger is Lewis Gates, who, if we are to believe Brimley's voice-over, is one of those mountain-type men they don't make anymore: the best tracker, the best bounty hunter, a rugged individualist so rugged and individual he only talks to his dog (Zip, played by Zip). His wife drowned some years earlier; Lewis was unable to save her, and he's never forgiven himself. Her father, Sheriff Deegan (Kurtwood Smith), hasn't forgiven him either. But occasionally, the sheriff needs his son-in-law's services, such as when three convicts lull a guard aboard a prison bus and hightail it into the mountains.

Lewis finds them easily enough, but the trigger-happy cons are killed—by arrow—before he can capture them. And so begins Lewis' Cheyenne autumn.

It's a curious twist on an old theme that Murphy employs here: Lewis, hard-drinking, cynical, skeptical and en route to an early grave, is completely taken with the idea that a tribe is loose in the so-called Oxbow: He's found a bloodstained arrow and the tracks of unshod horses. He tells Deegan that the men he wanted are dead and goes looking for more proof.

What he gets is more skepticism. Lillian Sloan (Hershey), an anthropologist and expert in Indian culture, is completely dismissive of Lewis' theory—which is understandable, although it's usually her type of character who harbors enthusiasm for the unprovable in these kinds of movies. After Lewis does some additional research—she is an academic, after all—she decides to head for the hills with him, where they get captured.

Led by Yellow Wolf (Steve Reevis), the son of Chief Spotted Elk (Eugene Blackbear), the Cheyenne warriors treat them roughly, but spare their lives because Lillian speaks Cheyenne (I think that's why). What they find is a kind of aboriginal Oz where nothing has changed for 128 years. The happy captives (they're a bit too blase about being prisoners) help save a life, become accepted by the tribe and manage to preserve the Cheyenne's isolation at the same time. Which raises the nagging question about "Last of the Dogmen" that goes unanswered: When the savvy Lillian and Lewis first decided to find the Cheyenne, didn't they realize that the tribe's extinction was the only possible result? Ah, but asking *that* question, to paraphrase Brimley, wouldn't be the right thing to do.

SIGHT AND SOUND, 6/96, p. 45, Tom Tunney

After three convicts escape into the Montana wilderness, Sheriff Deegan hires bounty hunter Lewis Gates to hunt them down. Gates successfully trails the fugitives but, before he can capture them, they are killed by a band of Cheyenne warriors. Once known as the "dog men", these Cheyenne are descendants of the 20-odd survivors of the 1864 Sand Creek Massacre who fled into the mountains.

Gates tracks down a railway man who once briefly captured a wild Cheyenne boy. Then he seeks the advice of anthropology professor Lillian Sloan. A fluent Cheyenne speaker, Sloan finally agrees to accompany him into the wilderness. After a week of friction on the trail, the duo are finally confronted and captured by the Cheyenne war party and taken to their isolated settlement.

Sloan convinces the tribe of their good intentions and Gates agrees to go back to get medicine for Chief Yellow Wolf's son, who was badly injured during the fight with the convicts. Gates holds up the town drugstore, but he's surprised outside by the police and pursued through the town. Sheriff Deegan raises a posse which Gates attempts to hold off while the Cheyenne and Sloan move to higher ground. Deegan confronts Gates in the waterfall entrance to the tunnel and gets the drop on him, but Yellow Wolf, at the other end of the tunnel, detonates Gate's dynamite charge with an arrow. This seals the tunnel and sends Gates and Deegan flying into the water below. Gates rescues the sheriff and then, after briefly returning to town and making his peace with him, he heads back up into the mountains where he is reunited with Sloan and the tribe.

The Last of the Dog Men is the work of first-time director Tab Murphy. Apparently, this was his first screenplay, written some 14 years ago, but the finished film shows all the signs of having been refashioned and fatally compromised in order to reproduce the box-office success of both *Gorillas in the Mist* (which Murphy co-wrote) and *Dances With Wolves*. Repeatedly, David Arnold's dire John Barryesque score oozes and surges like a musical syrup, while the camera tilts upwards to celebrate the scenic vistas of the unspoilt Montana uplands.

Typically, these interludes include a look of rapt wonder on Barbara Hershey's face invoking memories of Sigourney Weaver as Dian Fossey in *Gorillas in the Mist*. Hershey is presented as the conscience of the film, the person whose knowledge of the Native American heritage goes hand in hand with a desire to protect and celebrate it. The tribe thus explicitly becomes something like Fossey's mountain gorillas: a fundamentally innocent, passive community which has to be nurtured and protected from the depredations of modern life.

However, all of this cosy politically correct condescension squares very awkwardly with the action premise of the film. The idea of a small band of warriors cut off from civilisation for several generations recalls such prime cuts of exploitation as *The Island* (about descendents of a gang of Caribbean pirates) and *Death Line* (the flesh eating progeny of nineteenth-century navvies who lurk in the London Underground). In those two films, the highly improbable plotting was all part of the fun.

At first, *The Last of the Dog Men* seems to be going down that promising action and exploitation route. The brutal slayings of the three escaped convicts could have been the cue for a bizarre modern-day battle of cowboys and Indians. But Murphy clumsily switches gear and focuses on the film's tired love story. With its mismatched couple stuck on the trail together, the film laboriously opts for a battle-of-the-sexes romantic comedy. Then in a third section, the film switches gear yet again and it becomes a pastoral idyll with the duo as awestruck observers of a Native American *Lost World*.

For Murphy, the whites still have to be the villains, but rather than warriors, the Cheyenne of the latter part of the film resemble nothing so much as the pacifist inhabitants of a late 60s commune. The convention of the Western hero having to engage in a gruelling test of courage to gain the trust of the tribe (*Run of the Arrow*, for instance) is also avoided because Murphy wants to keep his Indians in their place as peace-loving victims. Any ritualised violence on their part would hardly fit with his scheme of things.

So, we're asked to believe that a community, which has remained undisturbed in its mountain hideaway for over 120 years, would suddenly uproot itself because of the approach of a few townies, when previously their warrior skills had enabled them to dispose of all trespassers. The Cheyenne are further insulated by Gates acting as their protector. A kind of "Magnificent One", he fights off the posse in a holding action while they make their escape.

These scenes, particularly Gates' gallop along the town's front street and across a busy road, are excitingly staged, but from the moment the movie decides to present its Cheyenne warriors as innocent children of nature it has nowhere to go but steadily upwards into an increasingly foolish fantasy. Needless to say, there is a huge credibility problem with the script. Why has this society not expanded greatly in size over the intervening century? Why have they never been spotted before? And would Lillian really walk out on her college career to spend the rest of her life camping out on a mountain?

If this was an exploitation movie, such questions would be swept aside by the brutal thrust of the narrative. However, since Murphy won't travel that route, they're allowed to congeal around the story's increasingly soggy idealism and the result is a film which succeeds neither as an action movie nor as a love story. It's a pity, because the rugged mountain landscapes on display here are some of the most majestic to grace a Western since the great days of Anthony Mann and James Stewart. Of course, the key to Mann's cinema was the way in which his magnificently rugged landscapes perfectly matched his morally ravaged heroes. Tab Murphy, by contrast, insists on a simplistic moral dichotomy which is more stupefying than sublime.

Also reviewed in:
CHICAGO TRIBUNE, 9/8/95, Friday/p. H, Michael Wilmington
NEW YORK TIMES, 9/8/95, p. C4, Caryn James
VARIETY, 9/4-10/95, p. 72, Leonard Klady
WASHINGTON POST, 9/12/95, p. B8, Rita Kempley

LAST GOOD TIME, THE

A Samuel Goldwyn Company release. *Executive Producer:* Klaus Volkenborn. *Producer:* Dean Silvers and Bob Balaban. *Director:* Bob Balaban. *Screenplay:* Bob Balaban and John McLaughlin. *Based on the novel by:* Richard Bausch. *Director of Photography:* Claudia Raschke. *Editor:* Hughes Winborne. *Music:* Jonathan Tunick. *Choreographer:* Pattie Meyer. *Sound:* Antonio L. Arroyo. *Sound Editor:* Steve Visscher. *Casting:* Billy Hopkins, Suzanne Smith, and Kerry Barden. *Production Designer:* Wing Lee. *Art Director:* Michael Shaw. *Set Decorator:* Betsy Alton. *Set Dresser:* Kara Cressman and Christine Welker. *Costumes:* Kimberly A. Tillman. *Make up:* Angela Johnson. *Stunt Coordinator:* Jim Lovelett. *Running time:* 95 minutes. *MPAA Rating:* Not Rated.

CAST: Armin Mueller-Stahl (Joseph Kopple); Maureen Stapleton (Ida); Lionel Stander (Howard); Olivia d'Abo (Charlotte); Andrian Pasdar (Eddie); Zohra Lampert (Barbara); Kevin Corrigan (Frank); Molly Powell (Dorothy); Jody Wilson (Mrs. Wilder); Beatrice Winde (Nurse

Westman); Burtt Harris (Supermarket Manager); Ken Simmons (Bartender); Gino Lucci (Bus Driver).

LOS ANGELES TIMES, 4/14/95, Calendar/p. 6, Peter Rainer

"The Last Good Time" opens with an old widower's reverie of his wife dancing for him in the firelight. It's a bittersweet memory he returns to again and again, and it's a bit too gauzy and precious to be believed. The old man—Joseph Kopple (Armin Mueller-Stahl)—keeps a photo of his wife on the wall of his dank, tidy one-bedroom apartment in Brooklyn, and her image stands out as a kind of offering. He's enshrined her memory and closed himself off from any further feeling. He's only nominally in this world.

"The Last Good Time" is also a bit too gauzy and precious to be believed. It's a tender fable about tough-tender people, and it makes a show of how unsentimentally sentimental it is. Adapted from the Richard Bausch novel by John McLaughlin and Bob Balaban, who also directed, it's self-consciously coy. We're always aware that we're watching a fable. When Joseph takes in Charlotte (Olivia d'Abo), a battered twentysomething neighbor on the run from her boyfriend (Adrian Pasdar), their communion is framed as a life-affirming growth experience: She drops her tough-cookie edginess, and he drops his Old World severity.

It's a touching relationship, and the performances are sensitive, but the filmmakers are so concerned about not exploiting these two that they end up sanctifying them. Their wary, tentative friendship that leads to a little romance is missing the befuddling fear and exhilaration that we would expect. It's a prim, bedewed good time.

Balaban is trying to show old age in ways that most movies don't. He's trying to dignify old people and not turn them into coots. Another of Joseph's neighbors, Ida (Maureen Stapleton), and his expiring friend Howard (the great, gruff Lionel Stander in his last feature film role), who is laid up in a nursing home, have a do-not-go-gentle-into-that-good-night feistiness. And Joseph, who fills out his days reading Plato and Wittgenstein and making diary notes about errands, is oddly admirable in his refusal to whimper.

These people are a welcome change from the cartoon cutups that often pass for oldsters in the movies, and yet the film may move too far in the other direction. It's a tribute to feistiness that turns the story of their lives into a how-to guide in perseverance.

Like Charlotte, Balaban may admire Joseph's Old World gravity too much. Joseph is dignified all right, but ultimately he's not that much more expressive than the strong, silent types who turn up in action films. (His deepest emotions come out when he plays the violin.) And yet you wish him well. When he's with Ida, you can see what he doesn't—that he needs someone to care about.

Balaban's directing debut, the 1988 "Parents," was a disturbing, highly original black comedy that should have put him on the map big time. But that film was too off-putting for general audiences, and "The Last Good Time," his third feature, seems like a retreat into comfiness. It's a well-crafted, very well-acted mood piece that lulls instead of startles.

NEW YORK POST, 4/7/95, p. 46, Thelma Adams

There is a poignant scene in the middle of "The Last Good time." Kopple (Armin Mueller-Stahl), a retired violinist, tells the reclining twentysomething Charlotte (Olivia d'Abo) about the grief he shared with his late wife when their son died.

He sits in shadow on his bed with his back to the camera, lit only by the bathroom light in the background. In a quiet, measured voice, Kopple revealed how difficult it was to support his spouse while overcome by his own loss.

It's a small, beautiful moment of restraint, delicacy and human dignity. Bob Balaban, who directed "Parents" but is best known as a New York actor who made his debut in "Midnight Cowboy," makes a gift of such moments to his actors and the audience.

The scenes in which Kopple visits his former neighbor and accountant Howard (the late Lionel Stander of the original "A Star Is Born" in his final role) at a Brooklyn nursing home are alive with available light and generous feeling. The two seniors have a refreshing ease and naturalness as they convey the feeling that they've known each other for years.

Howard cracks a Chinese cookie and cracks wise: "I'm so old my fortune is blank."

Given the grace with which Balaban treats his elderly characters, including the lonely but self-sufficient Ida (Maureen Stapleton), it's a shame that the central conceit is about a 70-year-old man having a last fling with a young girl.

I don't know about you, but I'm tired of this fantasy. Clearly Richard Bausch, whose novel was adapted by Balaban and John McLaughlin, was not.

Thrown out by her thuggish boyfriend Eddie (Adrian Pasdar), Charlotte (d'Abo, formerly of TVs "The Wonder Years" doing the Rosanna Arquette waif) lands at Kopple's door.

They briefly set up housekeeping. The relationship's unlikely, consummation (where are all these nubile nymphs dropping their clothes for grandpas for free?) is actually well-done and erotic.

Charlotte's concern for Kopple's health is touching. The next day Kopple tells Howard in jocular amazement, "Now they tell you what they want you to do at times."

Mueller-Stahl ("Avalon") gently unfolds as the orderly, compassionate musician living in the past who, through his encounter with a younger woman, come to embrace the present and realize that his future is anything but blank. It's a generous, thoughtful performance in a small movie with a big heart.

Still, I'm ready for a small, sensitive movie about a granny (why not Maureen Stapleton?) and her leather boy (calling Keanu Reeves). It's been over 20 years since "Harold and Maude."

NEWSDAY, 4/7/95, Part II/p. B5, Jack Mathews

In the pre-credit opening of Bob Balaban's exquisite "The Last Good Time," a supple young woman lying in the pulsing glow of a fire is aroused by a violin solo, and begins to dance—swaying, turning, reaching, as if she were trying to make love to the music itself.

Moments later, as the camera seems to follow the music into an urban neighborhood, through an open apartment window, and past an elderly man asleep in a chair, we see the same woman's face in a framed photograph on the wall. Suddenly, there is a commotion in another apartment, waking the old man, ending the music and, for the moment, his dream.

Rarely is a movie set up more deftly, or developed with more care. Balaban, a character actor who has directed one other feature (the forgettable "Parents") and several TV shows, has a genuine passion for this old man and an understanding of what that image of the dancing lady means to him.

Adapted by Balaban and John McLaughlin from the Richard Bausch novel, "The Last Good Time" is the story of Joseph Kopple (Armin Mueller-Stahl), a retired German violinist living out his remaining years in a five-story walkup in Brooklyn. Fastidious, proud and aloof, Kopple spends his time reading old philosophers, playing his violin, cleaning his room and visiting an old friend (the late Lionel Stander) who is nearing death in a nursing home.

For Kopple, the last good time was a night 50 years earlier when his wife danced for him in front of a fireplace, and that memory is the only true emotion he allows himself. He even rejects the overtures of companionship from the widow living upstairs (Maureen Stapleton) because he wants nothing to intrude on his time with his wife.

But someone breaks in anyway. Charlotte (Olivia d'Abo), the girlfriend of an abusive drug dealer (Adrian Pasdar) living in the same building, asks Kopple for sanctuary in his apartment for a couple of days and the relationship grows in subtle, unexpected ways. Kopple becomes the gentle figure missing from Charlotte's life, she draws him out of his reverie and rekindles some of his passion for life.

The subtext to the relationship is a drug deal gone bad, which puts Kopple in the middle of a dangerous situation. But what little plot there is just gets in the way of the compelling action, which is the effect that two people born a half-century and cultural light years apart have on each other.

The movie's mundane sub-plot is not resolved well, and there are a few too many senility jokes surrounding Stander's character. But Balaban, with the superb internal performance of Mueller-Stahl, has created a tremendously complex and sympathetic character in Joseph Kopple and treats his subject matter with the respect and patience it deserves.

"The Last Good Time" is ultimately a love story, with moments of sublime tenderness. But more important, it is about how our connections with people can change our lives at any age. If you don't live in the past, the last good time is always in the future.

VILLAGE VOICE, 4/18/95, p. 60, Leslie Camhi

Aging has its moments, and *The Last Good Time*, a sad and funny film, explores them with warmth and without sentimentality. Armin Mueller-Stahl is quietly sexy as the geriatric Joseph Kopple, a retired German violinist who lives in Brooklyn. Beyond making lists and doing his shopping and laundry, Joseph's days are occupied with visits to Howard (Lionel Stander), his ailing accountant, now in a nursing home. In the evenings he practices the violin a little and spends a lot of time remembering his deceased wife and vanished happiness.

This orderly routine is slightly disrupted when the IRS informs him that, due to the senile Howard's error, he owes them all his money. It is utterly unsettled a few days later, when he offers refuge to Charlotte (Olivia d'Abo), a young woman whom he finds sleeping in his hallway after a fight with her abusive boyfriend. Vast gaps of age and class loom between this unlikely couple, yet their scars slowly bring them together.

Carrying this tender film are fine performances by all the actors, including Maureen Stapleton, who plays Joseph's lonely, concerned, and elderly neighbor. Bob Balaban's discreet direction errs only in re-creating a kitschy moment of sensuality from Joseph's past that might better have remained a private memory. But the many ways in which time weighs upon young and old alike are touchingly rendered. Bette Davis's immortal words might here be amended; if, as she noted, "Old age is not for sissies," neither is youth.

Also reviewed in:
CHICAGO TRIBUNE, 5/5/95, Friday/p. F, John Petrakis
NEW YORK TIMES, 4/7/95, p. C5, Caryn James
VARIETY, 10/31-11/6/94, Emanuel Levy
WASHINGTON POST, 5/5/95, p. B7, Hal Hinson
WASHINGTON POST, 5/5/95, Weekend/p. 50, Kevin McManus

LEAVING LAS VEGAS

A United Artists release of a Lila Cazès production. *Executive Producer:* Paige Simpson and Stuart Regen. *Producer:* Lila Cazès and Annie Stewart. *Director:* Mike Figgis. *Screenplay:* Mike Figgis. *Based on the novel by:* John O'Brien. *Director of Photography:* Declan Quinn. *Editor:* John Smith. *Music:* Mike Figgis. *Sound:* Pawel Wdowczak. *Sound Editor:* Nigel Heath. *Casting:* Carrie Frazier. *Production Designer:* Waldemar Kalinowski. *Art Director:* Barry M. Kingston. *Set Decorator:* Florence Fellman. *Set Dresser:* Amy H. Abrams. *Special Effects:* William Harrison. *Costumes:* Laura Goldsmith. *Costumes (Elisabeth Shue):* Vivienne Westwood. *Make-up:* Katy Bihr. *Stunt Coordinator:* Russell Towery. *Running time:* 112 minutes. *MPAA Rating:* R.

CAST: Nicolas Cage (Ben Sanderson); Elisabeth Shue (Sera); Julian Sands (Yuri); Richard Lewis (Peter); Steven Weber (Marc Nussbaum); Kim Adams (Sheila); Emily Procter (Debbie); Stuart Regen (Man at Bar); Valeria Golino (Terri); Graham Beckel (L.A. Bartender); Al Henderson (Man at Strip Bar); Shashi Bhatia (Hispanic Prostitute); Carey Lowell (Bank Teller); Anne Lange (Business Colleague); Thomas Kopache (Mr. Simpson); Vincent Ward (Business Man #1); Lucinda Jenney (Weird Woman); French Stewart (Business Man #2); Ed Lauter (Mobster #3); Waldemar Kalinowski (Mobster #2); Mike Figgis (Mobster #1); David Kriegel (Hotel Manager); Bill Thompson (Midwest Man at Poolside); Marek Stabrowski (Pawn Shop Owner); R. Lee Ermey (Conventioneer); Mariska Hargitay (Hooker at Bar); Danny Huston (Barman #2); Laurie Metcalf (Landlady); David Brisbin (Landlord); Shawnee Smith (Biker Girl); Paul Quinn (Biker Guy); Julian Lennon (Bartender #3 in Biker Bar); Tracy Thorne (Waitress at Mall); Bob Rafelson (Man at Mall); Susan Barnes (Desk Clerk); Marc Coppola (Dealer); Michael Goorjian (College Boy #1); Jeremy Jordan (College Boy #2); David Lee Willson (College Boy #3); Xander Berkeley (Cynical Cabbie); Sergio Premoli (Stetson Man at Casino); Gordon Michaels (Security Guard); Lou Rawls (Concerned Cabbie).

FILM QUARTERLY, Summer 1996, p. 38, Albert Johnson

It was only a matter of time before the American cinema offered more lower-depth perceptions of Las Vegas people; not the average, everyday denizens of that town, who have to work and thrive through its sunlit days, but the ephemeral night people who exist within the gaudy cocoon of gambling casinos, cocktail lounges, and the pavements of the neon-splendoured strip. Over the past decades, some efforts have touched upon the more venal aspects of Las Vegas, either romantically *(The Only Game in Town, One from the Heart,)* or semi-dramatically, as if surveying the amoralities with sardonic humor *(Oceans Eleven, The Las Vegas Story, Five Against the House).* The 90s have explored an uncensored view of Las Vegas: Martin Scorsese's *Casino* (exposing the gangster milieu on a more psychological level than the too fictional *Bugsy)* reworked the interplay of ethnic loyalties and emotional betrayal (born in Hawks' *Scarface),* with DeNiro and Pesci as icons of this genre. Paul Verhoeven's *Showgirls* promised an insightful, authentic look at the women who performed in gaudy imitations of Paris's Lido, but settled for a sophomorically vulgar exercise in softcore pornography. Not surprisingly, it is Mike Figgis's *Leaving Las Vegas* that has caught the essence of tragedy in that city, as a background for doomed refugees from failed American dreams.

Two of Figgis's previous films, *Stormy Monday* and *Liebestraum,* should have prepared one for the indigo-hued evocation of despair and violence associated with the underworld, and he seems to have a pessimistic fascination with the human propensity for self-destruction. As writer-director, Figgis displays a wry detachment from his characters, half-sympathetic, half-disdainful. His omniscience is cruel, and *Leaving Las Vegas* is stripped of all sentiment, except pity perhaps, but even if this threatens to touch the spectator, the vile bodies before one are abruptly beheld as emblems of irrevocable disgust.

The story follows the decline and fall of a once successful Hollywood script-agent, Ben Sanderson (Nicolas Cage), who, after losing a wife and son through divorce, wholeheartedly decides to leave his shattered life and position and set off alone for Las Vegas. His goal is to kill himself consuming inordinate amounts of alcohol, and to submit to whatever fleshly blandishments come his way. Before the title credits of the film, there is a prelude to this exasperated acceptance of death: Ben's embarrassing encounters with former associates in a nightclub; Ben's supermarket forays with a liquor cabinet of a grocery cart; his shame-faced acceptance of his final paycheck: each of these glimpses prepare one for Figgis's meticulous attention to Ben's determined self-obliteration.

His suicidal quest coincides with the emotional and physical struggles of a beautiful young prostitute, Sera (Elisabeth Shue). Sera's emotional enslavement to Yuri, her belligerent Latvian pimp (Julian Sands), is made more horrifying when it is later revealed that in moments of pique, he had punitively inscribed knife carvings on her buttocks (her revelations of abuse are confided to an offscreen person, which occasionally confuses the time sequence of the plot).

Ben and Sera meet as client and doxy, but their happenstance encounter is marked by the same undercurrent of despair that social outcasts can intuitively recognize in one another. The mechanics of loveless sex, familiar to her, become important as she decides to yield to a sympathetic attraction to Ben. At this point, Figgis and his cinematographer (Declan Quinn) move constantly closer to the protagonists: skin textures, garments, and the imagined odor of empty liquor bottles touch one's reactions, and the various tormented and tragic episodes in Ben and Sera's downward spiral continuously lower their self-esteem and disturb the spectator. These are truthful observations of people beyond rescue.

The crosscurrents of fate affect both characters as Figgis shows Sera's sudden loss of protection. Yuri has been on a doomed flight from vengeance, and his pursuers happen to be at the same gas station where Ben stops en route to Las Vegas. Ben crosses paths again with Yuri in a pawnshop, and later, Sera walks past the assassins as they close in on their prey. Sera's professional appeal is wavering as well, her gruff dismissal by a prospective middle-aged client at a casino-bar is made particularly wrenching because a more glamorous hooker (Mariska Hargitay) watches the scene bemusedly. Affected by Ben's honesty and need for solace, Sera decides to try and save his life, as a human antidote that will keep him on balance. When Ben warns, "Never, never ask me to stop drinking," it only brings out more of her ardor. The realism is palpable: Figgis's ear for the dialogue of his personal Las Vegas, for these miserable miscreants, makes every sentence ring true. Tentative gestures of compassion (Sera's gift of a hip flask), the images of these two in the red-blue-green neon nights, or their daylight moments of normalcy in a mall (when Sera tries on her gift of new earrings)—these things bring one closer to the brief happiness along their tragic journey. When separated from one another, Ben succumbs to bouts of delirium tremens, and Sera is victimized in a violent assault by a trio of collegians (Quinn provides a chilling close-up of one of their faces, the boyish face caught in a mask of evil).

There are certain great performances of the alcoholic hero in American films (Van Heflin in *Johnny Eager*, Gig Young in *Come Fill the Cup*, and Ray Milland in *The Lost Weekend* come to mind), and Nicholas Cage's portrayal of Ben Sanderson now joins them. His physical appearance and body language attest to the skill of his delineation of one who has lost the zest for caring. At one point, lying askew on Sera's couch in a boozy haze, he resembles a giant marmoset whose eyes move swiftly from joy to total despair, but their luster of indifference never fades. Elisabeth Shue complements Cage's portrayal. Her wholesome, athletic beauty camouflages deep psychic scars, and in the indefinable pain of her performance lies the effective understatement of tragedy as she is pushed farther and farther away from society. One knows that Sera survives Las Vegas, but that is not the same as knowing that she will survive her future.

Since Cage and Shue dominate the film, the minor roles are very fleeting; only Julian Sands remains vivid as Sera's temporary nemesis, and his role exemplifies an amazing range of portrayals during his international film career. There are a few surprise cameo roles: Lou Rawls is a cabdriver who sympathizes with Sera; and in wordless glimpses, Mike Figgis is seen as one of Yuri's assassins, and director Vincent Ward is a partygoer when Yuri introduces Sera as the chief orgiaste.

Mike Figgis has arranged an excellent, soft-jazz musical score which also uses famous standards ("Come Rain or Come Shine" and, almost as a love motif, "My One and Only Love"), and Sting is heard on the sound track, giving voice to several threnodies which aptly evoke the blue-lit motels and brighter lights of Las Vegas that illuminate the pleasure-seekers and eliminate the shadowy struggles of those lost inhabitants who either fight for life or fight to flee from it.

FILMS IN REVIEW, 11-12/95, p. 102, Barbara Cramer

Here's the good news: Nicolas Cages phenomenal *pas de deux* with Elisabeth Shue should finally earn him an overdue Oscar nomination. Now the bad news: Who's going to see it? *Leaving Las Vegas* is *Midnight Cowboy* for the mid-Nineties, and it'll be a tough sell before it finds its audience. It is *slice-of-life* cinema with a crust almost too hard to swallow. It's a *downer*, but so well-acted and executed, so utterly believable, that this intermezzo between a drunk with a death wish and a hooker with no place to go is one of the most beautiful love stories of our time.

Cage's Ben is a gentle charmer—somewhat on the order of a Don Quixote with a grave drinking problem, though we're not sure why. (As he says along the way, he doesn't know if he drinks because his wife left him, or his wife left him because he drinks.) His booze of choice is anything that fits in a bottle, and he polishes off more than a squadron of sots. Gin, Vodka, Beer. By the case. He's not particular; whatever he can keep down.

He's a pricey Hollywood screenwriter, but his working days are numbered. His love affair with the bottle is so obvious, so intrusive and debilitating, you'd think his superiors would get him into rehab. They don't, and he's canned, with enough of a golden parachute to keep him in booze for the rest of his short, unhappy life. So off he goes to Las Vegas to drink himself to death. As he says, "Three or four weeks at $350 a day should do it." (Before he leaves his home, he burns all his possessions, including his passport and photo of his wife and child. You're forewarned this could be a dead-end trip.)

It's on the streets of Vegas that he teams up with Sera (Shue), a beautiful, young L.A. hooker on the outs with her Russian pimp (Julian Sands) because she feels she can make more money in the gambling mecca. She thinks of herself as "a service." No excuses. She's also young, beautiful, and on the skids. Ben might not be ideal, but she's in love with this guy with "101 proof breath" and "tired of living alone." Sera says, "You're like some kind of antidote mixed with the liquor that keeps me in balance." Ben's retort to Sera is, "You can never ever ask me to stop drinking. Do you understand?" She does and they bond. They both realize they don't have that much time, or that he'd change.

What makes their coupling so memorable, so credible, is a rarity—onscreen as in real life. Their love is entirely non-judgmental and completely accepting of each other's frailties. It's not about sex.

What matters is not so much the plot, but the pair's performances: elegant by any standards, moving, and uncommonly difficult to pull off. But they do, imparting a sensitivity that keeps you half hoping for a happily ever after ending you don't really expect to happen. Its poignant climax, fraught with tenderness and compassion, is filled with a most humane expression of love and devotion seldom seen onscreen.

One caveat is in order here. This film is a strange hybrid; it's neither a standard terminal illness weepy nor alcohol dependency drama, though there might be a knee-jerk tendency to compare it to such classics as *The Lost Weekend, Days of Wine and Roses*, or those of the *Dark Victory* variety.

Cage, perhaps better known as being quirky and offbeat in lighthearted romances (*Moonstruck, Peggy Sue Got Married)* emerges as the gifted dramatic actor he truly is. He's the drunk as noble savage. His humanity remains intact. (One might compare the power of his role to that of Tyrone Power's descent as the geek in 1947's *Nightmare Alley*.) Ditto for Shue. It's her best, most accomplished work to-date, after years of playing the all-American girl (*Cocktail, Soapdish*).

British director Mike Figgis (*Internal Affairs, The Browning Version*), who also scripted and composed the film's fine score, masterfully moves his leads—and, for that matter, all the supporting players (including Julian Lennon, Lou Rawls, Richard Lewis and Steven Weber, among others)—with the sure hand of a maestro conducting a classic requiem. Instead of sadness, you're left energized, with a renewed sense of awareness in the common decency and nobility of man.

Sadly enough, John O'Brien, writer of the semi-autobiographical novel on which the film was based, and himself an alcoholic, killed himself two weeks after signing the movie deal. His father said the book was his suicide note.

In a poetic aside, I was reminded of William Ernest Henley's "Invictus" which begins: Out of the night that covers me/Black as the Pit from pole to pole,/I thank whatever gods may be/For my unconquerable soul ... and concludes with: I am the master of my fate:/I am the captain of my soul.

Powerfully, exquisitely, this film illuminates those lines.

FILMS IN REVIEW, 3-4/96, p. 61, Harry Pearson, Jr.

To richly enjoy *Leaving Las Vegas*, one must see it as a metaphor, sort of an American *Tristan and Isolde* that takes place in our own heart of darkness, the city of Las Vegas. Something like this has been done before in a section of that wildly diverse movie, *Aria*. Franc Roddam, using Wagner's Liebstodt (from Tristan, of course), sets his picture perfect lovers down in Las Vegas, bound for suicide. This they accomplish, nude, in a backroom bathtub, by slashing their wrists, but not before a sensuous roll in the sack. Why? Well, you have no idea.

In *Leaving Las Vegas*, we have a hero determined to drink himself to death. Why? Well, we have no idea. He staggers across the path of a hooker, who, it later appears, will eventually wind up dead herself (at least I think that's the purpose of an otherwise gratuitous and artistically miscalculated rape sequence). Why is she a hooker who takes such risks? Well, we have no idea. Both, in other words, are emblematic of inescapable aspects of the human condition and both are, without question, seriously flawed souls.

If you stay away from this film (as I almost did) because the subject matter—a guy drinking himself to death—is just too depressing, you'll be making a mistake. No, it doesn't have a happy ending. He succeeds (and the love-death motif is made explicit as he does). But this is not literally, a film about self-immolation through the potion of booze. If it were, it would be unwatchable. Nicolas Cage, as the drunk, goes out quite as cleanly as Bette Davis in *Dark Victory* (that is, with a bare minimum of the gross physicalities that would actually occur), and he goes out, evidently orgasmically (at last) with the hooker (Elizabeth Shue) riding atop him. What this really is is a kind of myth, a sort of serious American fairy tale for grownups.

The film is, as such, well nigh perfect, hugely entertaining and at times awfully, awfully funny thanks to a performance by Cage that is a pure marvel. I've liked Cage's acting in the past, even as I found something about his bassett hound looks offsetting. Here he uses those looks with a creative vengeance and turns them to the purposes of High Comedy and, just as sharply, uses them to suggest a kind of winsome hangdoggedness that lets us believe that a seasoned hooker (who would have ever thought that Shue had this kind of depth as an actress?) would fall for him. Cage and Shue are so good together that you take the myth seriously and believe in their dilemma and its deeper truths.

The director, Mike Figgis, has taken chances before and occasionally (as in *Liebstraum*) dropped the Big One. Ah, but check out one of his earlier works, the moody and noir-ish *Stormy Monday* which works almost perfectly. *Vegas* is a risky film. Not the least of which is because it's unbelievable. I mean, get this. A successful screenwriter has determined to drink himself to death (this is an intellectual decision). He is, conveniently, fired and given severance so he can go out in style in Vegas. (A beautifully played scene this one, with Cage overjoyed at the prospect but trying to hide it and his boss suffering because he has to fire Cage.) He comes across a hooker with an Albanian pimp (would you believe Julian Sands?). She likes him. The pimp is assassinated (really), so she is free to do what she wants and what she wants is to move Cage into her place (remember he is a falling down, often destructive drunk).

But *Vegas* succeeds on any number of levels. Its pacing is, except for a brief section toward the end when Cage is off camera for nearly ten minutes, flawless. It moves with a surety of purpose rare in these days of the playing-it-safe cinema. The background music includes not a few torch songs alluringly sung by Sting (of all people), who, by the way, distinguished himself as an actor in *Stormy Monday* which fit the mood lock to key. But it mostly succeeds because of the acting of Cage and Shue, who not only imbue their characters with the kind of three-dimensionality rare in American film, but who also have an interactive chemistry that clicks.

More than this, though, is what the movie turns out to be all about, and this we discover as she is prodding a reluctant Cage to move in with her—he says he will only if she doesn't try to stop his drinking. In other words, you'll have to accept me just as I am. She agrees. And, a little later on, she similarly requires of him that he say not one word about her hooking. (Ironically, she knows that he is always so drunk that he cannot achieve orgasm, though that doesn't remove the erotic component from the relationship. It seems to have quite the opposite effect.) And so we come to see that *Leaving Las Vegas* is really about unconditional love, which makes it, insofar as I know, just about unique.

LOS ANGELES TIMES, 10/27/95, Calendar/p. 1, Kenneth Turan

"Leaving Las Vegas" is a film laden with virtues but difficult to embrace. Beautifully put together, sensitively acted by Nicolas Cage and Elisabeth Shue, directed by Mike Figgis with assurance and style and making exceptional use of its musical score, this doomed romance is finally not as satisfying as all of that would have you believe.

One reason is an obvious one, intentionally crafted by the filmmakers themselves. The uncompromisingly downbeat story of a love affair between a hard-luck prostitute and a man hellbent on drinking himself to death, "Leaving Las Vegas" is one of the bleakest romances in memory, a totally despairing film, complete with a wrenchingly explicit scene of anal rape, that is shrouded in a miasma of hopelessness. If this is what great romance means, audiences may feel like settling for whatever's in second place.

In addition, the more "Las Vegas" makes a fetish out of authenticity, implicitly telling you that if you're uncomfortable it's because what you're watching is unbearably real, the more it stylizes, glorifies and romanticizes its despair. Though everything seems realistic at first, it doesn't take much scrutiny to reveal the gloss of artificiality. And if this film turns out to be just another Hollywood fantasy, its rationale for inflicting pain on viewers becomes increasingly shaky.

Writer-director Figgis, who also wrote the film's moody score, has had a career as ambivalent as this picture, similarly balanced between grittiness and artificiality. Besides doing his share of standard fare including "Mr. Jones" and the recent "The Browning Version," he also directed a pair of small but artful paeans to despair, "Stormy Monday" and "Liebestraum."

Connecting to the semi-autobiographical novel by John O'Brien that "Las Vegas" is based on, Figgis determined to make it without compromising his vision, even though there was apparently not much of a budget to work with. Collaborating with cinematographer Declan Quinn, Figgis shot the whole movie on inexpensive Super 16 film, working documentary style on Las Vegas' streets and infusing Cage and Shue with a passion for their characters.

Cage plays Ben Sanderson, a Hollywood fellow-traveler whose life in L.A. is displayed in an extensive pre-credits prologue. For reasons that are left vague if they exist at all, Ben is a palsied wreck of an alcoholic, determinedly drinking himself out of job, friends and any kind of human sympathy. Though some of Cage's natural charm leaks into the role, Ben on a bender is a terrifying sight, alienating everyone in his path.

The movie proper begins when arrives in Las Vegas, checks into a misbegotten motel and runs into a prostitute named Sera (Shue, best known for "Karate Kid"-type ingenue roles) cruising the Strip. Sex doesn't really interest him, he wants to talk and what he mostly wants to say is that he is set on drinking himself to death in as short a time as possible.

Having just escaped from a relationship with a sadistic pimp named Yuri (Julian Sands), Sera is at loose ends herself. Warily, she and Ben dance around a loving, mostly non-sexual relationship that is based on avoidance of mental attitudes all around: He isn't to complain about her line of work and she is under no circumstances to try to get him to stop drinking.

Though the artifice in this setup is obvious in print, on the screen impassioned actors and Figgis do a convincing job of making it resemble reality, partially by piling painful misery on top of painful misery for its protagonists, until it seems like the entire movie is in the shadow of an enormous black cloud.

Yet to concentrate only on the misery is to gainsay the great skill Figgis brings to his work here. Determined to do nothing the ordinary way, he has put a distinctive visual flourish into almost every scene. And the way he has complexly layered music into the film to establish mood, using not only his own score but soulful versions of standards (Sting singing "It's a Lonesome Old Town," Don Henley doing "Come Rain or Come Shine") will be admired for years to come.

But more than the miserable existences Ben and Sera live end up becoming troublesome. The film cheats on its honesty, first, through a series of flash-forwards, by taking pains to assure us that at least one of these lovers will have a happy future. Figgis' script makes both characters more poetically articulate than they ought to be, and certainly experienced streetwalkers are rarely as attractive as Shue. As for Cage's character, though Ben suffers mightily, anyone who has walked around L.A.'s Skid Row knows that he looks almost glowing compared to those who are truly drinking themselves to death.

What we're left with is a superbly constructed sham that makes you suffer by pretending it's real. "Leaving Las Vegas" is so marvelously put together it's sure to have an effect, but despite how hard it pushes, in the final analysis it's too much of a pose to break your heart.

NEW STATESMAN & SOCIETY, 1/19/96, p. 33, Lizzie Francke

The very title of Mike Figgis' new film is resonant of so much—*Leaving Las Vegas*. It's in the "leaving"—suggesting business that is not quite completed for the transient who cannot quite quit. In a way, the film, which is adapted from the semi-autobiographical novel by John O'Brien, is about the final last tug as the hero Ben (Nicholas Cage) prepares to move on. Only, the next stop is oblivion, for Ben has chosen to drink himself to death.

Fleeing Los Angeles, where his alcoholism estranged him from his family and career as a screenwriter, he chooses to lose himself in the garishly lit Las Vegas. For him the gambling town becomes some grotesque departure lounge where he just waits it out, filling himself with the contents of bottle after bottle. It is also where he meets Sera (Elisabeth Shue), a smart young prostitute, equally adrift in life. Her addiction is the need to be needed. Their tragic emotional entanglement is the plain substance of what is an extraordinary riff of a movie.

Particularly extraordinary is the way the film just stays just there with those two restless characters, who are underpinned by two shattering performances from Cage and Shue. Figgis, who came to cinema out of an experimental theatre background—famously he was involved with the *People Show*—has had a choppy time in Hollywood, particularly with his penultimate movie *Mr Jones*. But here, working on a $3-million budget and shooting in Super 16mm, he frees himself creatively.

One could imagine the false move into a sentimental journey of redemption, with Sera providing Ben with a new reason to live as he checks into a rehab clinic while she quits the game, but it studiously avoids that. Their relationship is founded on each unquestioningly accepting the other. "You can never, never ask me to stop drinking", says Ben at the outset of their affair, while Sera presents him with a gift of a hip flask as a sign of her solid commitment. Likewise, we, the audience, are also asked to accept Ben's alcoholism. It is a painful fact of his character, a choice that we are asked to respect. Meanwhile, there are no explanations of why he is driven to drink in the first place, no flashbacks to a brutalised childhood with a bourbon-swigging dad, no insights into the stresses and strains of the months and years leading up to his Vegas trip. His past is left a blur: "I don't know if I started drinking because my wife left me, or my wife left me because I started drinking." Life with the bottle is the beginning and the end. But, crucially, while *Leaving Las Vegas* doesn't moralise about drinking, it doesn't glamorise or romanticise it either; rather it is presented in the raw.

Indeed it is the raw characterisation that is at the heart of the film. One might flinch at Sera's relationship with her paranoid pimp Yuri (Julian Sands with an impeccable Lithuanian accent, proving that he can act after all)—but even when she submits to him there is a defiance, as though she is still ultimately in control whatever the humiliation. His death, a third of the way through the film, cuts her loose, but it also sends her drifting. She plays Sera as resilient to a point; someone desperate to secure her own boundaries, who finds emotional safety in a profession that just requires her to act something rather than be.

Cage's acutely observed performance gets under the tight skin of an alcoholic. Playing a barfly can bring out the worst in an actor—as though being a character out of control were in itself an excuse to give an out of control performance. And one could expect the worst from Cage, given his shaky track-record especially his rather too freewheeling turn in such films as *Wild at Heart*. But here, with his puffy, almost gray face and shadowed, caved-in eyes, he seems to document the heavy drinker who is a danger to himself, who strains to keep a raging energy within. Ben's excesses are mostly embarrassing rather than abusive to others. At the beginning of the film he interrupts an old colleague's dinner date at a swanky LA restaurant (all uplighting, linen and lilies). The party comprises superficial Hollywood shoptalk, with one young starlet blessed with the hilarious line, "The nicest thing about this film is that we get to handle guns." In this instance, his expansive, provocative behaviour is welcome, to the audience at least, in being so wonderfully at odds with the bland atmosphere. But in the very next scene the bravado turns sour as he attempts to pick up a young woman at a bar and finally has to be cautioned by the barman.

At this point, it becomes clear that *Leaving Las Vegas* works to pull us into Cage's wayward state of mind. Figgis plays with the bluesy score (which he also composed), daring to drain the film into silence to imply the isolation and the chaotic sense of environment as Cage goes on a bender. In this respect, Vegas is the perfect final resting place—a neon numbing pain of a town that won't switch off. Yet with all the harsh pinks and greens and blues that flash through *Leaving Las Vegas*, it is the darkness that seems more visible. It is a film saturated with despair that is a long time lifting after it has wound to its end.

NEW YORK, 11/13/95, p. 88, David Denby

Ben Sanderson (Nicolas Cage), a faltering Hollywood screenwriter, chugs a half-bottle of gin and shudders under the assault of the booze. For a moment, he appears to sink into himself. But then, like a diver coming up fast and breaking the surface with a toss of his head. Ben shakes off the alcohol and crows in delight. Ben is drinking himself to death—purposefully, and without fear or regret. In *Leaving Las Vegas*, an extraordinary American film written and directed by the British writer-director-musician Mike Figgis, the reason for Ben's alcoholism is never seriously addressed. Ben himself doesn't know, for instance, whether his wife left him because he started drinking or whether he started drinking because his wife left him. In any case, it doesn't matter. Ben's spectacular boozing is just a given fact of his existence—beyond reason or cause—and his death, from the beginning of the movie, is a certainty. And thus, having dispensed with the usual maudlin suspense of such movies (when will the hero hit bottom and pull himself out of it?), Figgis is free to open his film to mystery and to art. *Leaving Las Vegas* turns into an awed celebration of obsession and of romantic love. Despite a few awkward scenes, *Leaving Las Vegas* is the most accomplished American movie of the year—the most active visually, the strongest and purest in emotion.

What's new about *Leaving Las Vegas*—and possibly, for parts of the audience, what's outrageous about it—is the absence of lamentation, the refusal to grieve over a wasted life. The movie changes tempo now and then, but it never becomes punishing or cautionary or merely realistic. In the early sections, Ben makes a fool of himself, spouting Hollywood-insider gibberish about "Dickie" Gere and so on, all the while sponging off his agent buddies; and for a moment, I thought we were heading for a long, painful slide into humiliation. But then Ben gets fired from a production company (a delicately comic moment, since his boss is trying hard to be gentle and Ben can barely conceal his delight), and he is liberated. So is the movie. Ben goes on a spree without end, and Figgis swings the camera joyously into grungy Los Angeles bars and strip joints. The movie turns sleek and black, with flashes of brilliant light against the dark, and we experience an overwhelming mix of excitement and dread: This man is happy, and he's going to die.

Figgis's first film, *Stormy Monday*, a thriller set in an English provincial city, was soaked in melancholy and general *noir*ishness; it was a good movie, but Figgis sat on his moods too long, and they became ambiguous and emptily portentous. In *Leaving Las Vegas*, he moves along swiftly, and some of the cutting is boldly discontinuous, the sections held together by a common emotion or by verbal association. The picture never sags or falls into bathos. Falling-down drunk, sozzled beyond sozzlement, Ben embraces the ecstasy of letting go completely. Since he's also an amazingly selfless man, with no interest in justifying or excusing himself, no desire to make trouble for other people, we can like him without disgust. He's a casualty, but not a loser.

Nicolas Cage makes it work. Cage doesn't windmill his arms and shout, as he has in the past. Most of the time, he's soulful, with earnest eyes and a quiet voice. There are a few wild flights of self-dramatization, but they pass quickly. Ben is consciously constructing a personality on top of a self that has been burned away by drink. Polite, even courtly, he propitiates the world, overarticulating his words in that solemn imitation of sobriety that so many drunks resort to. He beams at people as if he were a successful salesman; he tries to sound debonair. But nothing quite comes out right, and his mishaps are often funny. The movie doesn't stint on his physical disintegration—the paleness and weakness, the shakes and DTs—but that sort of sorrowful spectacle has been done before. What's fascinating and original in Cage's performance is the mental processes of a man tearing away at an old self and building a new one over nothing. The precariousness of Ben's effort seems gallant, even admirable, and Cage's achievement is heroic.

After making a bonfire of his belongings, Ben heads for Las Vegas. (The title, I assume, is a morbid joke: There is really only one way you "leave" Las Vegas.) On the street, he meets the one girl for him, a good-looking hooker, Sera (Elisabeth Shue), who has some sort of longtime relationship with a Latvian pimp (played in crazy-Latvian-pimp style by the very English Julian Sands). Sera's scenes with the pimp feel unanchored and not really necessary. And we could do without Sera's post hoc confessions to a psychiatrist, in which she explains why she fell in love with Ben. We don't need explanations; we can see that she's touched by him, and that she needs to feel she's a decent person as well as a good whore. That he can't perform sexually, and doesn't even want to, is a kind of relief (at first). He obviously needs tending, and her taking care of him is a way of leaving prostitution without leaving it. She becomes his "wife" and still goes out at night and earns a living, defiant and masochistic at the same time.

Apart from her general likability and intelligence, I have never registered anything special about Elisabeth Shue. In my mind, she blurred into Lea Thompson (both nice girls without much temperament), which is probably unfair to both actresses. But Shue, it turns out, has been guarding immense reserves of ambition. In *Leaving Las Vegas*, she goes out on a limb again and again and pulls off moments that some of the most famous movie actresses of the past might not have attempted. Sera agrees to accept Ben as he is and never to ask him to stop drinking, and the movie turns into a romantic epic, as weighted and expansive, as lyrical and crazily emotional, as any movie romance I can think of (this is also as close as the movies have ever come to the somber exaltation of Wagner's *Tristan und Isolde*). Elisabeth Shue plays a woman in love, physically in love, with a man who loves her but doesn't want her sexually, and her performance is overwhelmingly erotic. Again and again, she turns her body to Nicolas Cage. In a scene at the side of a pool, in a desert motel, she is naked at last and almost breathing fire.

Ben and Sera have gone deep into self-hurting pleasures, and they're not coming back. Figgis accepts them with something like awe: The doomed nature of their love transfigures it. *Leaving Las Vegas* will infuriate therapists and twelve-steppers, because it suggests that hope is a shallow illusion, and that a few weeks of glorious intimacy are worth more than a hundred chat sessions. In some ways, it's a very hip movie, though its character is different from that of most hip movies. A picture like *Pulp Fiction* stays cool, even nihilistic. Quentin Tarantino is an ironist; he doesn't open himself to emotion for fear of losing his edge. But *Leaving Las Vegas* is both hip and supersaturated with feeling, and it takes us to far-out places where movies don't often go.

Perhaps such a work can be made only the way this one was, cheaply (for a reported $3.5 million) and with stars not of the first rank. The dedication of everyone involved appears to have been absolute. *Leaving Las Vegas* is based on a novel by a writer named John O'Brien, who killed himself two weeks after Figgis had formally committed himself to the project. Hearing that, one has to suppress a laugh: O'Brien's suicide is an astonishing fact entirely consistent with the mood of the movie. As for Figgis, he not only adapted the book and directed but plays the trumpet in the bluesy-sexy music he wrote for the picture. *Leaving Las Vegas* is as close as we get to art in the American cinema of the nineties. Now the question is whether there's an audience out there to support it.

NEW YORK POST, 10/27/95, p. 42, Michael Medved

Sitting through "Leaving Las Vegas" is such a powerfully unpleasant experience that some observers will automatically hail the picture as a triumph of courageous, cutting-edge cinema.

Nicolas Cage plays a prodigious consumer of every sort of booze who gets fired from his executive job at a Hollywood production company. He has already chased away his wife and child (who appear only in a snap shot that Cage burns), so he takes his severance pay and heads for Las Vegas where he proudly plans to drink himself to death in one final, four-week bender.

While staggering down the Strip he picks up a cynical streetwalker (Elisabeth Shue) who begins to feel pity for him when it's clear that he's too far gone, physically, to get anything like his money's worth. As their friendship develops, he moves into her apartment and they demonstrate a purportedly admirable acceptance of one another's weaknesses.

"I know I'm a drunk. I know you're a hooker," Cage declares "I just want you to know that I'm a person who's totally at ease with this." To show just how much at ease he is, Cage cheerfully sends her out each night to ply her trade, while she devotedly facilitates his non-stop drinking to the point of excruciatingly realistic D.T.s and blackouts.

Cage is always an audacious, unconventional actor, and he does manage to infuse his bleak role with surprising wit and warmth. Shue is also passionately committed to her part, but she is disastrously unsuited for this role: She is simply too beautiful, too radiantly healthy and athletic to play a battered street-corner whore who's regularly tossed out of casino gambling floors.

(Actually, the appearance of Harvard graduate Shue as this golden-hearted, street-wise hooker may represent part of a disturbing mini-trend coming, as it does, in the same week that fellow Harvard graduate Mira Sorvino appears in a similarly stereotyped role in "Mighty Aphrodite." Alert the alumni association!)

Based on an autobiographical novel by John O'Brien (who killed himself just as work commenced on the film version of his book), "Leaving Las Vegas" is painfully tedious and repetitive, reveling in its clinically detailed and bloody scenes of brutality and rape, barroom brawling, and drunken rolls through broken glass, not to mention the expected abundance of vomit and urine.

Writer-director Mike Figgis ("Stormy Monday," "Internal Affairs," "Mr. Jones") also wrote the ironically romantic musical score, and his careful craftsmanship shows he is clearly in love with this dreary, monochromatic material.

He's even enlisted a number of well-known friends (Valeria Golina, Richard Lewis, Julian Lennon, Lou Rawls) to make cameo appearances for an occasionally diverting game of spot-the-star, but it's still a good idea to leave "Las Vegas" to movie-going masochists.

NEWSDAY, 10/27/95, Part II/p. B6, Jack Mathews

People travel to Las Vegas from all corners of the earth for all sorts of reasons, and many never return. Some lose their shirts and take up careers as cab drivers and dealers. Some like Paul Anka, become permanent floor shows. And some just relish the self-destructive possibilities in a town without a clock.

Nicolas Cage's Ben in "Leaving Las Vegas" definitely falls into the latter category, and falls and falls and falls. He is a terminally depressed alcoholic, in the last stages of a disease he embraces, having arrived with just enough money left from his high-paying Hollywood job to drink himself to death. He figures it will take him four, maybe five weeks to reach the last blackout, and he does not want to be disturbed. Not even by the hooker (Elisabeth Shue) who becomes his companion, lover and soul mate.

"Leaving Las Vegas" is the toughest, most uncompromising and disturbingly bleak major studio film of the year, and one of the best. There has never been a movie about alcoholism quite like it. There are no overarching themes about the dangers of social drinking, as in "Days of Wine and Roses." Or the hell of addiction, which scared up a batch of Oscars for director Billy Wilder and star Ray Milland a half-century ago in "The Lost Weekend." Or drinking as self-prescribed medication for mental illness, Jack Nicholson's excuse in "Ironweed."

Ben is simply suicidal, and although his alcoholism is beyond his control, he continues to drink for the reason others hold a gun to their head, swallow pills or hurdle the railing at the Golden Gate Bridge. He wants out, and plans to do it—in the style of the most famous Las Vegas performer—his way.

The question is, why would you want to watch? For starters, because you'll see one of the most versatile actors of his generation at his absolute best. Cage can do more things well than anybody. He can be as tough and menacing as Robert DeNiro, as funny and sensitive as Tom Hanks, and anything in between, or outside of them.

It is hard to place Ben on the continuum because the character is virtually devoid of ego. He is neither bitter nor self-pitying, and though we learn of the losses of his family, friends, dignity and job, they were all the result of his drinking, never the cause.

Figgis, who adapted the screenplay from the novel by John O'Brien, has abandoned the cliches of melodrama to focus on the connection Ben makes with Sera (Shue), a hooker for whom dependence is her own drug of choice. Through the gallons of booze, the drunken outbursts and Ben's rapid deterioration, a love grows between these disparate Vegas losers that is both sweet and moving.

Shue makes Sera almost too good to be true. She seems too smart and self-confident to have gotten herself into a fix with her sadistic Albanian pimp (Julian Sands), and it's a bit of a stretch to believe she would take on a project as self-destructive as babysitting a terminal drunk, no matter how charming and loving he may be between bouts.

But "Leaving Las Vegas" tests all of your preconceived notions of movie romance and tragedy. Figgis, the gifted director of "Internal Affairs" and "Stormy Monday," is going for the kind of poetic truth that comes from real life experience and not from a screenwriter's imagination.

The truth underpinning "Leaving Las Vegas" received something of a morbid reminder from O'Brien, who drew the novel from his own unending battle with alcoholism, and who committed suicide two weeks after learning that it was to be made into a movie.

NEWSWEEK, 10/30/95, p. 81, David Ansen

A love story like no other, Mike Figgis's *Leaving Las Vegas* is a bleak, mesmerizing rhapsody of self-destruction, defiantly uninterested in peddling Hollywood-style uplift. Figgis doesn't pretend, and I won't either, that this movie is for everybody. Its milieu is sordid, its language explicit and its lovers—an alcoholic screenwriter named Ben (Nicolas Cage) and a Vegas prostitute named Sera (Elisabeth Shue)—aren't in the market for reformation. But anyone who cares about ravishing filmmaking, superb acting and movies willing to dive into the mystery of unconditional love will leave this dark romance both shaken and invigorated.

The movie takes its tone of manic, frazzled lyricism from its sozzled hero. All we know about Ben is that he's lost his wife and child because of his drinking, and now he's lost his writing job. Burning his possessions, he heads for Las Vegas with the simple goal of drinking himself to death. Beyond hope, fortified with massive quantities of booze, he attains at moments (when he's not racked with the shakes) the benign, loquacious cheerfulness of a man for whom there's no difference between free fall and freedom. He picks up Sera on the Strip and takes her back to his motel. Sex, in his state, is out of the question. They drink together, pass out together and, several encounters later, move in together. He has one condition—that Sera will never ask him to stop drinking. She agrees. Nor will he ask her to stop hooking.

They have no future, but writer-director-composer Figgis, a bona fide existentialist, gives them a now that is harrowing and heartbreaking in its precisely observed details. "Leaving Las Vegas," based on a John O'Brien novel, doesn't have much plot, and doesn't need it. It lives on its noirish, sexualized atmosphere, its vivid minor characters, its haunting, ballad-laden score and the startling editing, which suggests the lurching, almost hallucinatory rhythms of a drunken mind. And most of all it lives in the risky, honest performances of Cage and Shue, whose tough-tender poignance and raw physicality will astonish everyone who remembers her from her bland roles in "Cocktail" and "Adventures in Babysitting." You can feel that everyone involved was digging deep; they've struck tarnished gold.

SIGHT AND SOUND, 1/96, p. 44, Philip Kemp

Ben, a Los Angeles screenwriter and dedicated drunk, visits a smart Beverley Hills restaurant to borrow money from Peter, an agent he knows. Embarrassed in front of his friends, Peter gives Ben some money and tells him never to contact him again. The next day Ben's boss reluctantly fires him, giving him a generous payoff. Having ceremonially burnt all his possessions, Ben heads for Las Vegas where the bars are open 24 hours a day.

In Las Vegas Yuri, a Latvian pimp, catches up with Sera, a hooker who evaded him in Los Angeles, and coerces her into working for him. Driving drunkenly into Las Vegas, Ben nearly knocks Sera down at an intersection. The next day they meet again, and he pays her to come to his motel room. Ben is impotent, but they affectionately spend the night together. In the morning Yuri beats Sera for not earning enough. However, three Russian mafiosi on Yuri's trail catch up with him, leaving Sera free to do as she likes. She has dinner with Ben, then invites him to move in with her.

Accepting that Ben is set on drinking himself to death, Sera even buys him a hip flask as a present. They visit a casino, but get thrown out when Ben in a drunken fit smashes a blackjack table. At a bar a biker girl makes advances to Ben, and her boyfriend headbutts him. Since Ben is unhappy that Sera continues to work as a hooker, she suggests a stay at a motel out in the desert. At the motel's poolside they almost get to make love but Ben smashes a glass table and the motel owner tells them to leave immediately.

Back in Vegas, Sera suggests Ben should see a doctor. He angrily rejects the idea. After she leaves for work he goes out gambling and hits a lucky streak. His winnings attract a hooker, and they go back to Sera's place, where she finds them in bed together. Furious, she throws Ben out; later she searches for him, but in vain. Off her guard, she lets herself be picked up by three college boys who rape her and beat her up. Her landlords, shocked by her appearance, give her notice to quit. Ben phones and Sera rushes to him, finding him near death in a skid-row motel. At last they make love. The next morning he dies.

Since the undeserved failure of *Liebestraum*, his darkest and most labyrinthine film, Mike Figgis' career has stalled. *Mr Jones*, intended as a study of a manic-depressive, was mutilated by the studio who cut out all the depressive bits. *The Browning Version*, an odd choice of material, was a workmanlike but unneeded remake. But *Leaving Las Vegas*, at least for its first half hour or so, looks like a major return to form. Right from his first cinema feature, *Stormy Monday* (set in Newcastle during "America Week", thus allowing for a strong dose of Stateside imagery), Figgis has been fascinated by that peculiarly American mix of glitz, sleaze and violence that finds its apotheosis in the nightmare neon carnival of Las Vegas, Nevada. Figgis and Vegas (the two names even coalesce) were surely made for each other.

And Nicolas Cage was surely made to portray a terminal alcoholic on self-destruct. Deploying a fearsome battery of gulps, twitches and off-the-wall gestures, Cage turns in a performance of such flailing physicality as to make his Sailor in *Wild at Heart* look like a model of sober good citizenship. At moments of stress—which are frequent—his whole body goes into a spasm, and he even seems able to make his eyeballs pulsate. It says a lot for Elisabeth Shue, grabbing with both hands the chance to escape from a string of bland nice-girl roles, that with far less pyrotechnics at her command she can still hold her own against Cage, matching him in pain and desolation if not in intensity.

Like all the best alcoholic movies—*The Lost Weekend, Days of Wine and Roses*—*Leaving Las Vegas* doesn't waste time on trite motivations. No tortured childhood, no tragic love affairs: Ben is drinking himself to death because that's what he wants to do. The only problem with this—since we can tell early on that a last-reel commitment to a rehab clinic is scarcely on the cards—is that it makes for a relentlessly linear storyline. With the poisonous Yuri disposed of, there's not another countervailing force to prevent Ben achieving his purpose; which he eventually does.

This being so, it falls to the actors and the script to keep us caring what happens. Cage and Shue, as discussed, work wonders; but Figgis' script does them few favours, with much of the dialogue clumsily spelling out the obvious. "I am not here to force my twisted soul into your life," Ben tells Sera. "We both know that I'm a drunk and you're a hooker." Figgis also uses the soundtrack, usually one of the strongest elements of his work, to ram things home. "Are you some sort of angel visiting me in one of my drunk fantasies?" asks Ben, cueing Sting to launch into 'Angel Eyes'; and when the pair at last get it together in the final reel, they're accompanied by 'You Turn Me On'. As if this wasn't enough, the action's punctuated with scenes of Sera relating the affair to an unseen listener. "We realised we didn't have much time," she explains in the very last shot, "and I accepted him for what he was." By this stage, that's hardly a revelation.

Not all the writing's on the debit side, however. Now and then the film regains a touch of the sardonic sharpness it needed all along: checking into a motel, The Whole Year Inn, Ben sees the sign above the desk metamorphose into The Hole You're In. Moreover, *Leaving Las Vegas* looks great, without question. Declan Quinn's dark, moody photography and John Smith's raw-nerve editing build a cumulative sense of temporal and spatial disjunction, drawing us insidiously into Ben's unravelling perception. But their work is undermined by the flatness of the dialogue and an underlying sentimentality. A kindly, philosophical black cabbie (played by singer Lou Rawls) is introduced to restore Sera's self-esteem, and the long-delayed deathbed fuck gets the apotheosis treatment—a high, distant trumpet and a wordless choir. Ben's dying, but he's been redeemed by the love of a good hooker. In all fairness, *Pretty Woman* it's not—but in the end we're a lot closer to that tart-with-a-heart story than one would ever have expected from this director.

TIME, 11/6/95, p. 75, Richard Schickel

In its opening moments *Leaving Las Vegas* establishes the fact that Ben (Nicolas Cage) quite self-consciously intends to drink himself to death on a maniacally accelerated program. What better place to do so than the title city, world capital of self-loathing?

Soon after arriving there he meets Sera (Elisabeth Shue), a masochist who is perhaps not quite as smart and tough as she thinks she is, and thus obviously in line for a painful comeuppance. What could be more appealing to her than a relationship with the visibly doomed Ben?

So she invites him to move in with her—no sex, please, we're preoccupied—and the audience is invited to watch their downward spiral. We're not talking high, morally instructive tragedy here, just a hard lesson in postmodernist outlawry and its sad little anarchies. Writer-director Mike Figgis (*Stormy Monday, Internal Affairs*) places a few opportunities to arrest their course along this pair's path, but Ben and Sera don't notice them, and he refuses to exploit them for dramatic purposes or even for ironic effect.

Figgis is a refusenik in every way. Even the neon glitz of his milieu; visual catnip to most directors, is muted. This Las Vegas is mostly low-wattage motel rooms and morning-after grayness. Cage, that most daring of actors, practically cha-chas through the gloom, high on the freedom that the loss of all amour propre bestows. Shue's character hasn't yet reached that heady state. She's engaged in a complex struggle between self-awareness and self-destruction. One has only the smallest hope for her. And none at all for the commercial fate of a movie that may be just a bit too pleased with its own artful bleakness.

VILLAGE VOICE, 10/31/95, p. 76, Georgia Brown

Bring back the sad songs. Laceration time again. Bruise season. Moviewise, October looks to be the cruelest month (except that *Georgia* opens officially in November. Mike Figgis's soulful *Leaving Las Vegas* harks back to the lyric masochism and achy melancholia of certain noirs—a mood that will always hang on in novels and plays but is seldom found in movies anymore, In Figgis's bluesy exercise in *nostalgie de la boue*—sans too much *boue*—a man determined to drink himself to death meets a young woman, pretty low herself, determined to cuddle him to the bitter end.

If Figgis hadn't cast Nicolas Cage as alcoholic screenwriter Ben Sanderson, maybe he would've asked Jeff Bridges. But Bridges would make a moody, grown-up Ben whereas Cage is a puppyish lush, mixing a kind of sexy goofiness with endearing tics, cagey irony, and a ruined physical appearance. Cage's hair is disappearing, his chin is multiplying, and those hooded eyes look ghoulish enough for *The Addiction*. We first meet Ben in a characteristically playful mood, bopping down the aisle of a supermarket booze section, snatching at bottles on the fly. Ben is stocking up. (He can easily go enough a fifth for brealfast.) At the moment Ben is still technically employed but once he shows up at his Hollywood office, this too is over. Leaving the bulk of his belongings in green garbage bags (ever so neatly lining the curb), Ben sets off for nearby Las Vegas to carry out his self-destructive project.

The first person he meets—since he chugs while driving, he nearly runs her down—is Sera (Elisabeth Shue), an all-American-looking call girl in thrall to a nasty Russian pimp (a sinister Julian Sands). Fortunately, Yuri's days are numbered. His demise leaves Sera free to concentrate on Ben who will proceed to torture her in his own way. Sera has a talent for self-humiliation (several times she presents her backside), although she appears to be working on some of this business with a shrink.

Vegas is virtually a two-character psychodrama and both performances are stunning. Cage's role may be flashier, but Shue's is more naked. She's so natural, and the confused pain on her face makes it look as if she's not acting at all. Sera looks like the Wellesley girl Shue at one time was—a Wellesley girl gone down fast, though never to the bottom. (Sera's apartment is stylish and well-stocked with books, and the character is dressed by Vivienne Westwood.) Some of Shue's most touching scenes show Sera falling back on her ingrained good manners ("I'm so sorry to put you to this trouble, I'll never let it happen again") but Ben gives these manners a workout. At other times Sera puts up a tough cookie pose. "You can fuck my ass, you can come in my face," she tells Ben casually on their first, um, date. "Just keep it outta my hair, I just washed it."

(Parenthetically I would like to note a trend: movies written by middle-aged men that get kicks from having young women talk dirty—besides *Vegas*, there're *Showgirls, Strange Days*, and *Mighty Aphrodite*. Moreover, three out of the four contain very nasty rapes.)

Figgis's ballad of codependency is no *Barfly*. No one looks poor. This is down-the-tubes with style, self-destruction minus grunge. Except for an occasional tantrum, Ben is an upbeat drunk. Falling backward into a glass table, he walks away grinning despite the splinters in his back. In that instance, he's accomplished what he meant to: putting out Sera's flame. Ben's principal form of violence lies in distancing himself. Come too close and watch him betray you. Though no case histories are written into the movie, the implication of a burning family photo is that betrayal is Ben's thing. Sera, meanwhile, seems to have spent her short life on the receiving end.

I hesitate to add—considering all my colleagues already in love with it—that this beautiful-losers lullabye just doesn't thrill me. (While I don't understand alcoholics, I do understand Wellesley girls tripping on the wild side.) Still, it's the sort of film I will always welcome back: a well-spent low budget, a nice handheld camera (Declan Quinn shooting Super 16), a lovely romantic score (especially that piano theme bubbling up when love is in the air), and a suitable, uncompromised ending.

Also reviewed in:
CHICAGO TRIBUNE, 11/10/95, Friday/p. C, Michael Wilmington
NATION, 11/27/95, p. 684, Stuart Klawans
NEW YORK TIMES, 10/27/95, p. C3, Janet Maslin
NEW YORKER, 11/6/95, p. 176, Terrence Rafferty
VARIETY, 9/18-24/95, p. 93, Leonard Klady
WASHINGTON POST, 11/10/95, p. F7, Rita Kempley
WASHINGTON POST, 11/10/95, Weekend/p. 45, Desson Howe

LEONA'S SISTER GERRI

Produced in association with Newton Television Foundation. *Producer:* Jane Gillooly. *Director:* Jane Gillooly. *Director of Photography:* Andrew Neumann. *Editor:* C.L. Monrose. *Music:* Caleb Sampson. *Running time:* 57 minutes. *MPAA Rating:* Not Rated.

WITH: Leona Gordon; Roberta Brandes Gratz; John Twerdy; Joyce Carboni; Joanne Griffin; Judy Blare.

NEW YORK POST, 12/13/95, p. 42, Larry Worth

It's been said that a picture's worth a thousand words . But in "Leona's Sister Gerri," a picture's definitely worth a documentary.

That picture is a gruesome 31-year-old police photo of a woman's naked corpse, hunched over bloody towels in a motel. The victim, Gerri Santoro, died from a botched abortion.

While pro-choice advocates used that shot as a rallying point for their cause, director Jane Gillooly steers clear of a polemic. Instead, she explores what brought Gerri to her demise at age 28, with illuminating, heartbreaking footage.

Viewers learn that Gerri was the mother of two little girls, the wife of an abusive husband and the bearer of unflagging courage and integrity. That comes through loud and clear via detail-laden interviews with her devoted sister (the titular Leona). Gerri's grown daughters and the best friend who still blames herself for not reacting differently to trouble signs.

The rest of the tale is told through pictures, as in the shot of Gerri and Leona as youngsters growing up on the family's Connecticut farm, the definition of sweetness and innocence to their parents and 13 siblings.

Gillooly proceeds in a straightforward, chronological approach to Gerri's complex life and times. And by objectively reporting on a tragedy in the making, thus skirting the situation's political overtones, audiences are left—refreshingly—to draw their own conclusions.

Before closing, the production also reveals how the police photo found its way into Ms. magazine in 1973, with Gillooly contrasting family members' surprisingly divergent reactions to its publication.

One daughter tearfully says: "You look at some woman lying there, dead, and those who are against abortion think of her as some scum. But she wasn't. She was a beautiful, beautiful woman."

In "Leona's Sister Gerri," Gillooly ensures that the beautiful woman is duly immortalized.

Also reviewed in:
NEW YORK TIMES, 12/13/95, p. C19, Janet Maslin
VARIETY, 3/27-4/2/95, p. 77, Godfrey Cheshire

LES MISÉRABLES

A Warner Bros. release in association with Les Films 13/TFI Films Production with the participation of Canal+. *Executive Producer:* Tania Zazulinsky. *Producer:* Claude Lelouch. *Director:* Claude Lelouch. *Screenplay (French with English subtitles):* Claude Lelouché. *Inspired by the novel "Les Misérables" by:* Victor Hugo. *Director of Photography:* Claude Lelouch. *Editor:* Hélenè de Luze. *Music:* Francis Lai, Philippe Servain, Erik Berchot, Michel Legrand, and Didier Barbelivien. *Sound:* Harald Maury. *Sound Editor:* Jean Gargone. *Casting:* Arlette Gordon. *Art Director:* Jacques Bufnoir. *Set Designer:* Laurent Tesseyre. *Set Decorator:* Laurent Tesseyre. *Special Effects:* Dominique Colladant and Georges Demétrau. *Costumes:* Dominique Borg. *Make-up:* Charly Koubesserian and Magali Ceyrat. *Stunt Coordinator:* Daniel Verite. *Running time:* 174 minutes. *MPAA Rating:* R.

CAST: Jean-Paul Belmondo (Henri Fortin/Jean Valjean); Michel Boujenah (André Ziman); Alessandra Martines (Elise Ziman); Salome Lelouch (Salome Ziman); Annie Girardot (Farmer's Wife); Philippe Leotard (Thenardier Farmer); Clémentine Célarié (Catherine/Fantine); Philippe Khorsand (Policeman/Javert); Ticky Holgado (Kind Hoodlum); Rufus (Thenardier Father/Son); Nicole Cruisille (Thenardiere 1830/1900); William Leymergie (Toureiffel); Jean Marais (Bishop Myriel); Micheline Presle (Mother Superior); Darry Cowl (Bookseller).

LOS ANGELES TIMES, 10/20/95, Calendar/p. 10, Kevin Thomas

[The following review by Kevin Thomas appeared in a slightly different form in **NEWSDAY, 10/20/95, Part II/p. B6.**]

Claude Lelouch's extravagant melodrama "Les Miserables" is neither a film of the musical nor the umpteenth remake of the Victor Hugo novel, but rather an epic saga of an Everyman whose life parallels that of the hapless Jean Valjean as it embodies the history of France in the turbulent first half of the 20th Century. No new Lelouch film has made it to American screens for nearly a decade, but he proves to be just as swooningly romantic a filmmaker as ever.

That's not the case with his star, Jean-Paul Belmondo, who hasn't been seen in a new film in the United States for about 20 years. Belmondo still has the magnetism, the easy masculine authority that brought him international renown 35 years ago with "Breathless." Belmondo remains rugged and reasonably trim, but his face is deeply creased. Just past 60 when he made this film, he looks his age, even though for most of the film he plays a man between 45 and 50. What the heck, Belmondo's Henri Fortin has had the tough kind of life that will age you fast enough; besides, seeing Belmondo in action after such a long time is the best and ultimately only reason for sitting through this tempestuous near-three-hour chronicle.

Like most Lelouch films, "Les Miserables" is energetic, emotion-charged, flashy and drenched in thundering Liberace-like piano crescendos while expressing his by now rather touching belief in an intensely schematic working of coincidence and fate. Life for Lelouch may be filled with drastic ups and downs but by golly, it proceeds like clockwork, striking a perfect balance between the eternal cycle of joy and sorrow.

Somewhere around the film's halfway point, Belmondo's Fortin, an illiterate ex-boxer turned furniture mover who becomes obsessed with the legend of Jean Valjean, watches the 1934 version of "Les Miserables" starring the great Harry Baur as Valjean. "The second half of the film is a bit much—it's over the top," he says later, an appraisal that applies perfectly to *this* "Les Miserables."

For quite awhile Lelouch's impassioned observation of the working of fate is fun but eventually it becomes needlessly drawn-out, lapsing into the mechanical in the process. As the century turns, 5-year-old Henri's father (also Belmondo) is wrongly convicted of murder, reducing his mother to prostitution. As his parents meet their grim fates, little Henri grows up to be a champion boxer, quite literally at the stroke of the World War armistice.

Jumping ahead to the increasingly perilous '30s, Henri an apparently happy-go-lucky furniture mover, is transformed by the simultaneous discovery of "Les Miserables," which he has to have read to him, and by meeting the Zimans, a Jewish couple who are fleeing Paris and who have hired Fortin to move their furniture to a large old house in Normandy.

Betrayed in their attempt to flee to Switzerland, Mons. Ziman (Michel Boujenah) ends up being hidden by a farm couple (Annie Girardot, Philippe Leotard); Madame Ziman (Alessandra Martines), a famous ballerina, falls into the clutches of the Nazis; but Henri has managed to place their little daughter Salomé (Salomé Lelouch, the director's daughter) in the safety of a beatific Micheline Presle's Catholic convent.

Lelouch milks interminably the question as to whether the Zimans will survive the war and be reunited, and it involves a contrived and protracted change of heart by Girardot and Leotard toward Ziman. An exhausting cross-cutter, Lelouch throws in more subplots and developments than can be described here and inserts several vignettes—famous scenes from the actual "Les Miserables," one of which provides a delightful cameo by Jean Marais as the priest whose spirit of generosity and kindness changes Jean Valjean's life.

At all times, "Les Miserables" is a spectacular-looking film with those great settings and costumes that are a hallmark of French period films. In well-drawn parts the cast is staunch—as it has to be to bear up under this weighty endeavor—but Belmondo, even though off the screen for considerable stretches, easily walks away with the picture.

NEW YORK POST, 10/20/95, p. 43, Michael Medved

The worst thing about the ambitious new French film "Les Miserables" is the misleading and miserable title.

No, this is not another version of Victor Hugo's 1842 classic; it is, rather, an original and often gripping melodrama from director Claude ("A Man and a Woman") Lelouch that follows a dozen people through the first 50 years of this century.

These characters are all obsessed with Hugo's novel, and comment with tiresome frequency on the strained resemblance between episodes in their lives and the plot of the famous book.

This device is obviously intended to give the movie a timeless resonance ("There are only two or three stories in the world and we must all live them over and over"), but Lelouch doesn't really need the annoying references: his new story is absorbing and well-acted enough so that it easily could stand on its own.

The sprawling tale begins with an aristocratic New Year's celebration of the year 1900, ironically recapturing the high hopes with which Europe welcomed this tragic century.

After leaving the party, a troubled businessman commits suicide on a lonely road and his loyal chauffeur (Jean-Paul Belmondo) is wrongly accused of murder.

While the driver suffers in jail, his wife is forced into prostitution and his young son escapes to become an army boxing champ during World War I.

Some 23 years later, this young man has retired from the ring and entered middle age (played again by Belmondo), operating a moving service and helping a Jewish family flee the Nazis.

That family consists of a tempermental lawyer (Michel Boujenah), his ballerina wife (played by the resplendently lovely retired ballerina Alessandra Martines) and their precocious daughter (portrayed by Salome, daughter of director Lelouch), and during their flight they read their illiterate moving man (and protector) long passages from—you guessed it—"Les Miserables."

After a horrifying betrayal, the family is separated and the father is hidden by a farmer (Philippe Leotard) and his wife (Annie Girardot), whose initial kindness is corrupted when they devise a scheme to squeeze money from the Jewish lawyer's secret account.

As it careens through the years, the plot is full of far-fetched coincidence—but no more far-fetched than some actual stories of Holocaust survival, including boyhood recollections of director Lelouch.

The film also features some truly spectacular action sequences, including an unforgettable prison break and a re-creation of the D-Day landing in Normandy.

Belmondo, once heralded as the Marlon Brando of France, has aged far better than his American counterpart; he settles comfortably into his salt-of-the-earth, working class hero role (as a latter-day Jean Valjean) and remains an irresistibly appealing screen personality.

It's easy to forgive this film's uneven pacing and manipulative story-line because of consistently fine performances, a lush, old-fashioned film score (by veteran composers Michel Legrand and Frances Lai) and a few moments of profound emotional impact.

SIGHT AND SOUND, 2/96, p. 49, Mark Sinker

At a grand ball in 1899, an imposter aristocrat is uncovered, and flees. His car breaks down, and while his chauffeur Henri Fortin tinkers with the engine, he shoots himself. Fortin is arrested, convicted of his murder, and imprisoned. His wife Catherine and son (also called Henri) find work in a rough bar in a tiny Normandy sea-village, but the wife has to prostitute herself to pay for Fortin's lawyer. Fortin attempts to escape, is betrayed, and chooses to fall to his death. His wife kills herself. Henri grows up to be a boxer, retaining the championship for 13 years after World War One, when he becomes a furniture remover.

The Zimans are a mixed-race couple living in 40s Paris under the Nazis: André is a Jewish lawyer, Elise a Catholic ballet dancer. They have a daughter, Salome. Jews are under threat, so the Zimans move to Vichy. Fortin drives the truck, helping them evade a checkpoint. As they drive, he asks them about Victor Hugo's *Les Misérables*; he recently saved two men's lives by lifting a piano off them, and people have called him "Valjean" ever since (Jean Valjean, the central character in Hugo's classic novel *Les Misérables*, is famously strong and save lives by lifting things). Fortin is illiterate: so the Zimans begin reading him the novel. They arrive at their new house, but are threatened with exposure, and decide to flee again, this time to the Swiss border. Fortin, pretending to be Salome's father, helps place her in a Catholic school. At the border, the Zimans join other fleeing Jews, but are betrayed. Most are shot: André is wounded, but escapes. A farmer and wife help him recover. Elise is captured, recognised as the famous ballet dancer, made to dress up and escort Nazi officers at parties, before being sent to a Polish death camp. In Salome's school, the Mother Superior guesses her background and protects her.

Fortin is arrested for transporting Jews, and tortured. He says nothing, escapes, and joins a band of burglars in Paris. André writes regular letters to Salomé from hiding, paying the farmer couple from a secret Swiss Bank Account. The wife falls in love with him. Her drunken husband, although jealous, tolerates this unrequited passion, but concocts a plan to rob him. Nazi war fortunes are waning, but Ziman is told that his family are dead and he can never come out of hiding. The burglars realise the war is ending, and belatedly join the Resistance. In the Normandy village where Fortin grew up, they blow up a pillbox during the Allied landings. Fortin becomes a hero, and then Mayor. Salome joins him there; then Elise, liberated from the deathcamps. His old burglar pals turn up, police in pursuit, among them the ex-Vichy policeman who once tortured Fortin. Fortin helps the burglars, but there's a siege, and they take the policeman hostage. Torn, Fortin rescues him; after a shoot-out, the police arrest Fortin. He confronts the policeman with his Vichy past: the policeman exits the car and shoots himself. Fortin is charged with his murder. Ziman, still hiding, doesn't know the war is over. The farmer couple, planning to poison him, have withdrawn all his money, but they argue and kill one another. After a time, Ziman ventures out, finds the bodies, his money and newspapers proclaiming the Nazi surrender. He arrives in the Normandy village in time to defend Fortin, successfully. Fortin becomes Mayor again, and Salome marries the grandson of the bar-owners who gave Fortin and Catherine work long ago.

In part a film version of Victor Hugo's vast, baggy, nineteenth-century social-conscience melodrama, a French-Lit institution reshaped to explore life under occupation during The Second World War, Les Misérables is also a film about the pleasures and power of reading. Both projects risk disaster, and yet Claude Lelouch—though a notoriously manipulative sentimentalist, as the soft-focus vapidity of his not-so-new-wave Un homme et une femme (1966) shows—rather unexpectedly wins us over with the second, and thus evades the more egregious pitfalls of the first. After a somewhat creaky start (40 years of plot exposition), and in the teeth of unavoidable narrative unlikeliness, the director has managed something rather impressive.

Much of the Ziman/Fortin plot echoes Hugo's, despite obvious differences of historical context and possibility. But Lelouch also constantly revisits famous scenes in the book itself, with its decades-long plot and miasma of coincidence, using the same actors to dramatise the readings: thus Belmondo plays Fortin and Valjean, while Philippe Khorsand plays Fortin's torturer and Valjean's pitiless-but-honourable nemesis Javert. What this achieves, against all odds, is a credible rendering of the way all kinds of people are brought together (or indeed kept apart) by a book they know. Artfully, Lelouch plays as much with readerly impatience as well as readerly devotion—when Fortin and a burglar pal duck into a cinema to hide out, and find themselves watching Les Misérables on-screen, Fortin summarises what they've missed, laughing at the over-the-topness of some of the plot. When Ziman summarises the plot, Salome has always to correct him. At other times, the lush physicality of reading is slyly invoked, a celebration of books as sensuous objects. The implication is that when the world turns sour this great story is all our stories; which Lelouch 'proves' by juggling differences as well as similarities. Unlike Hollywood, he refuses to fawn on literature, which is fun to watch.

Sometimes the deep argument seems awry: unlike scheming French collaborators obeying Vichy laws, Fortin was just a housebreaker, but if he does good because he's illiterate and knows no better, why are we cheering his induction into the Hugo readers' club? Lelouch's argument is probably that Les Misérables, as universally loved popular culture, should be distinguished from all Literary and Art Elitisms and Legalisms that challenge and distort the good in all of us, however lowly born. Which is a hard row to hoe in discussion of France under Occupation, and we may not be convinced (intellectually) that the forms, devices and assumptions of the classic Hugo novel tell us that much about doing the right thing in the hardest of times: the evil of circumstance was hardly the only peril French Jews faced in the 40s, and did Victor Hugo readers really make better moral choices than non-readers in this regard?

But Lelouch after all knows two or three things about applied heart-tugging, and deploys his own childhood memories of this period and evacuation, combining them with a genuine gift for striking moments: a huddle of nervous Jews, in their best bourgeois travelling clothes, waiting in eerie blue dawn-light to dash across the snow to freedom or doom; a vast school-hall full of small French girls banging pianos to cheer their black American liberators; the relentlessly sinister return to a Nazi commandant who is also a brilliant pianist, and whose demonically expressionist playing merges into several of the soundtrack's emotional climaxes. Though Michel Boujenah is something of a cartoon as regards his 'Jewish' look (his make-up not that far from plastic glasses-nose-moustache), the Zimans' husband-wife arguments are well-observed, especially their spats of superficial recrimination (as if each considers the war the others' fault). The drunken banter between farmer and wife is even better, Philippe Leotard, his usual excellent self, weak and villainous yet strangely sympathetic. Belmondo is also well used: his unsurprisable fleshy blankness gradually softening and sunnying up as the written word enters his soul, and as the hardest of times ends around him. When we find ourselves tearfully pleasured at Claude Lelouch's wholly implausible happy ending, at once a giddy *hommage* to Renoir (painter/*père*, not film-maker/*fils*) and the virtues of uncorked uprush and silly delighted release from the terrors that went before, we realise that the irrational grip of human scale decency clutches at film reviewers too, sometimes. And what's wrong with that?

TIME, 11/6/95, p. 76, Richard Schickel

Spectacular sweep, romantic grandeur, narrative richness, an improbably happy, morally instructive ending—*Les Misérables*, which is less an adaptation of Victor Hugo's novel than a melodramatic, meditation on its themes, has all the old-fashioned, totally unfashionable virtues.

Claude Lelouch's film, which relocates the French national epic in the 20th century, mostly during World War II, also has all the defects those virtues imply. It is full of absurd coincidences, broadly archetypal characters and situations (yes, a Nazi thumps out a piano concerto while a prisoner is being tortured nearby), and a sentimentality that verges at times on the woozy. It's as if the writer-director, who in certain high-toned circles will never be forgiven for making *A Man and a Woman*, had never heard of modernism, let alone postmodernism.

Yet his *Les Misérables* is more sophisticated than the feelings it evokes, and infinitely more compelling than you can imagine a film derived from such a familiar source might be (there have been at least seven movie adaptations of it, not to mention an unstoppable, stage musical). Lelouch understands that Jean Valjean and his friends, foes and milieu have long since permeated our consciousness, that you can't just uproot them, plunk them down unchanged in modern times and expect anyone to see the result as more than a gimmick.

What Lelouch does instead is divide Valjean in two, a father and son (both played by a wonderfully battered Jean-Paul Belmondo, whose son Paul plays the character in a transitional passage). Then he provides him with adventures that analogize, rather than slavishly imitate, those of his literary model. This figure, called Henri Fortin, is throughout aware of his resemblance to Hugo's original. He sees movie versions of the story, and people keep telling him that his physical strength, moral fortitude and frequent bad luck remind them of Valjean. He wouldn't know. He's illiterate, a retired boxing champion who drives a moving van.

It is this work that brings him into contact with the Ziman family, middle-class Parisian Jews who hire him to help them escape the Nazi occupation—promising, in return, to read *Les Misérables* to him on the way to the Swiss border. Much of the film focuses on the fracturing of this family and their terrible struggle to survive. In the meantime, of course, Fortin is obsessively pursued by his version of Inspector Javert, here a nameless policeman collaborating with the Nazis and a man seemingly as outraged by Fortin's lack of complexity as he is by his untutored goodness.

The question of whether that goodness can survive, whether it can extend its grace to the tormented Zimans and at the same time triumph over the fateful malignity of the relentless cop, remains the central question, for Lelouch as for Hugo. But this is not, finally, a movie that encourages such abstract considerations. It is all shameless pace and jostle, a compendium of evil (war, suicide, poverty, injustice, exploitation) that yet asks us to believe that common decency (and a strong back) can eventually triumph over it. Maybe so, maybe not. But how pretty it is to believe it may. And how pleasurable it is to be absorbed into the bloodstream of this movie and be borne along on its racing pulse.

VILLAGE VOICE, 10/31/95, p. 76, Georgia Brown

Nick Cage isn't the only actor to entrust his face to time and the weather. [The reference is to *Leaving Las Vegas*.] One can sit through Claude Lelouch's *Les Misérables* quietly marveling at what has become of '60s heartthrob Jean-Paul Belmondo. Well it doesn't really take all three hours to come to terms; one to two would have been quite sufficient. (Given a choice, by all means pick the last half.)

A gloss on the Hugo novel, Lelouch's convoluted *Les Mis* takes considerable time working up steam. Opening at the crack of the century—New Year's Eve 1900—a clumsy first section centers on Henri Fortin *père* (Belmondo), loyal chauffeur wrongly blamed for killing his employer. Fortin goes to prison, an institution he never succeeds in getting out of, and his wife and young son must fend for themselves. (This early section resembles 1994's *Germinal*, everyone with their black-streaked faces looking like bystanders too close to a bomb blast.) An opportunistic innkeeper turns Fortin's wife to prostitution; the son (played in his early twenties by Belmondo's son Paul) turns to boxing and becomes lightweight champion. Suddenly, we zip to the late '30s and the Occupation, with Belmondo *père* now playing the fortyish Fortin *fils* (and looking every day of the actors 62 years).

Although the story of Fortin *père* was rife with *Les Mis* parallels, analogies get cooking once Fortin *fils* lifts a grand piano off a man pinned underneath. Since Hugo's hero performed a similar feat with a carriage, townspeople call the illiterate Fortin Jean Valjean. Burning to read Hugo's novel, Fortin gets his wish while transporting a Jewish family to the Swiss border. The fleeing Zimans—father (Michel Boujenah), mother (former ballerina Alessandra Martines), and child (Lelouch daughter Salomé)—know the novel so well they can almost recite it. As Fortin marvels over parallels to his own family history ("Valjean is me! Cosette is me!"), the intellectual M. Ziman observes sagely, "It's the history of the world. There are only two or three stories and we must all live them over and over."

The point is made also that each of us plays several characters, villains as well as heroes.

As Hugo's tales are brought up, Lelouch dramatizes them, with Belmondo as a white-wigged Valjean and the film's other actors playing their 18th-century counterparts. As the Occupation with its various treacheries sets in, scenes continue to be interwoven with those from the novel. (The three Zimans get split up, with Salomé in a friendly convent, Mme. Ziman sent to a concentration camp, and Monsieur hidden in the cellar by two farmers played by two other familiar faces, Annie Girardot and Philippe Léotard.)

At its best the film begins to take on manic slapstick elements of silent comedy. A few scenes are powered for the associations one brings to them. Lelouch also has incorporated his own families wartime experience into details of the Zimans' terrible odyssey.

But back to the man with the craggiest face since Auden's—or Michel Simon's. The question as to whether Belmondo is still capable of a great performance is certainly not settled here. Given the banality of Lelouch's direction, Belmondo is blatantly coasting through this epic-sized curiosity piece. Stare dutifully, for three hours and you wonder, Pierrot le Fou, is it you?

Also reviewed in:
CHICAGO TRIBUNE, 11/3/95, Friday/p. J, Michael Wilmington
NEW REPUBLIC, 11/20/95, p. 33, Stanley Kauffmann
NEW YORK TIMES, 10/20/95, p. C18, Janet Maslin
VARIETY, 4/10-16/95, p. 46, Derek Elley
WASHINGTON POST, 11/3/95, p. F1, Rita Kempley
WASHINGTON POST, 11/3/95, Weekend/p. 43, Desson Howe

LESSONS OF DARKNESS

A Film Forum presentation. *Producer:* Paul Berriff. *Director:* Werner Herzog. *Director of Photography:* Paul Berriff. *Editor:* Rainer Standke. *Running time:* 50 minutes. *MPAA Rating:* Not Rated.

WITH: Werner Herzog (Narrator).

FILMS IN REVIEW, 1-2/96, p. 63, Andy Pawelczak

The between-the-wars Italian Futurist art theoretician Marinetti wrote that war is one of the great aesthetic spectacles of the modern age. Walter Benjamin, a German literary critic, remarked that Marinetti, and the fascist artists who succeeded him, would make the destruction of humanity into an aesthetic object for our contemplation. Werner Herzog (*Aguirre, the Wrath of God*) is far from being a fascist, but his documentary about the aftermath of the Gulf War, *Lessons of Darkness*, comes close to realizing Marinetti's vision. The movie is a mythological tone poem about the end of the world.

With minimal commentary, Herzog shows us the ecological devastation of Kuwait, his somnambulistic camera gliding over scenes of eerie, sinister beauty: oil wells that erupt into pillars of fire, wrecked bunkers and vehicles that glow like the shards of being, a forest covered by oil whose surface treacherously reflects the sky. Many of the images are indecipherably abstract, and it's characteristic of this paradoxical movie about the horror of war that it evokes art historical references. The textures of oil, ash, and burned metal recall German artist Josef Beuys' fetishized honey and felt, and the rough, pebbly surfaces of Dubuffet's primitivist canvasses. A brief, quiet shot of a long table covered by burned hand tools gives a clue to Herzog's aesthetic strategy here: taken out of their context of equipment, ordinary hammers, pliers, toasters, et al., become strange, faintly sinister artifacts in a post-modern art work. Cinematic references abound also. The smoky, infernal mise-en-scene and aerial camera recall *Blade Runner*, and a brief lyrical interlude of a bubbling lake of oil ironically evokes Disney's pastoral fantasies.

The absence of a human presence in most of the movie makes the two interviews that Herzog includes even more powerful. In one, a traditional Kuwaiti woman in robe and black headdress tries to communicate through hand gestures how her children were killed by rampaging soldiers; she was rendered mute by the trauma. In the other, a woman tells how her child hasn't spoken since soldiers brutalized him and killed his father. He weeps black tears, we're told, as a result of the omnipresent oil well fires. People appear again in the form of Texas oil well firefighters, but as filmed here they're barely human. Dressed in heavy fire-retardant uniforms and helmets and masks, they're like sadomasochistic underworldlings gleefully stoking the fires.

Lessons of Darkness is a Wagnerian Gesamtkunstwerk, a total work of art, its darkly beautiful images accompanied by a ravishing soundtrack of Wagner, Schubert, Verdi, and others. The picture's strongest trope is the contrast between its highly civilized artistic means and the primitive violence it depicts. It's Herzog's Gotterdammerung.

Lessons of Darkness, which is only 50 minutes long, was accompanied at New York City's Film Forum by the 30-minute long *Satya: A Prayer for the Enemy*. Produced and directed by Ellen Bruno, the film is a documentary about the persecution of Tibetan Buddhist nuns by the Chinese. Bruno tells the story through interviews and fragmentary, hypnotic imagery: a bare stone dungeon, a naked light bulb, a grainy black-and-white shot of a prisoner and a guard with a cattle prod. Opening and closing with a close-up of a burning butter-lamp, the film is a testament to the great, sacrificial effort to keep the light of civilization burning in a time of darkness. The teenage nuns—who suffered imprisonment, torture, and, in one case, rape for protesting the Chinese oppression, of their country—are far from primitive fanatics, and their prayer at the end that all living beings be set free from suffering is a powerful reminder of what it means to be human. The film made a good counterpoint to *Lessons of Darkness*, and the Film Forum, one of New York's great cultural resources, is to be congratulated once again for screening these two pictures which otherwise might not have been seen at all.

NEW YORK POST, 10/25/95, p. 41, Thelma Adams

Black lagoons of oil. Dense charcoal swirls of smoke suffocating the sun. Plumes of fire.

What better spot than post-Gulf War Kuwait to point out man's penchant for remaking his home into an inferno on earth? With stunning aerial photography, somber narration and the music of Wagner, Mahler and Verdi, German director Werner Herzog composes a gorgeous, disturbing visual poem in his 50-minute documentary "Lessons of Darkness."

Herzog has made a brilliant and extreme career clutching his head and exclaiming "madness, madness." In "Aguirre, the Wrath of God," "Nosferatu the Vampyre" and a string of docu mentaries he has dissected the human condition with a dark vision forced by his birth in the final years of the Nazi regime.

With "Lessons of Darkness," Herzog reprises a favorite theme: beauty and devastation confronting each other on a desert plain.

A Kuwaiti who has lost her speech tries to explain the torture of her sons by soldiers; another mother holds her toddler, who has said nothing since he saw his father murdered during the war. But their testimony—and the images of masked men fighting the blazing Kuwaiti oil fields—are purposefully inarticulate. Man as an individual is minimized; as a group, his legacy is ruin and suffering.

Herzog presents a god's-eye-view on road kill of an epic proposition. Unless you are hypnotized by boiling pools of oil and smoke forming the devil's face as it races up to pollute the, atmosphere, a little bit of darkness goes a long way.

Opening the program at the Film Forum, Ellen Bruno's short documentary "Satya: A Prayer for the Enemy" is a gentle, urgent call for nonviolence.

The jewel-toned film focuses on the plight of nuns in contemporary Tibet. The Buddhists testify to their torture by the Chinese who have occupied their nation since 1950.

NEWSDAY, 10/25/95, Part II/p. B9, John Anderson

German director Werner Herzog has created hellish visions in his almost three-decade film career, but few can match the infernal imagery captured in "Lessons of Darkness," his astonishing meditation-documentary on the devastation of the Gulf War.

Shot largely from a helicopter—by Herzog's coproducer and cinematographer Paul Berriff—the film surveys a Kuwaiti landscape of endless damage and environmental sin. Thirty-foot oil tanks have melted and collapsed like plastic toys; geysers of petroleum burn across a smoke-blackened plain of oil-puddled earth and greasy ash. The expansiveness of it all is awe-inspiring, the waste and the ecological violence is terrific—as is the realization that none of this has been revealed, not by the U.S. government, not by CNN.

Throughout it all, Herzog's ice-cold narration and ethereal score—by Mahler, Prokoviev and others—lends an otherworldy slant to the film. Herzog intended the world in his movie to be viewed the way aliens might see it. What they see could only be considered ungodly, along with the creatures who perpetrated it. In addition to the massive, lurid environmental destruction, there are smaller human tragedies. A woman who watched her sons tortured to death—and was rendered mute—tries to speak to Herzog; her strangled sounds are less than words, and more than pain. There is a silent survey of weaponry—clubs, hammers, whips, a blood-stained cleaver, other implements of torture. A child who has never spoken since being abused by soldiers (presumably Iraqi, although Herzog never says) casts an accusatory stare at the camera.

It's an amazing film, one that must be seen to be believed. Of course, even after seeing it, there are those who won't believe it, but that of course is how these things happen and continue to.

VILLAGE VOICE, 10/31/95, p. 71, J. Hoberman

Horrific and awe inspiring, Werner Herzog's 50-minute documentary *Lessons of Darkness* can most simply be described as a travelogue of hell: white-hot skies, black seas of bubbling pitch, flaming lakes, fiery geysers, billowing toxic fumes, an arid wasteland littered with the dinosaur bones of twisted metal debris.

This powerfully visionary film, which begins by quoting Blaise Pascal on the grandeur with which solar systems die and is interspersed with tersely poetic intertitles, could have been made to illustrate the Book of Revelation. Children are reported to weep black tears. Temperatures on the ground are said to reach 1000 degrees. A sequence called "Satan's National Park" shows a scorched, gnarled, partially submerged forest. The douds are reflected on its liquid surface, but "everything that looks like water is, in actuality, oil," remarks Herzog in his measured Vincent Price voice-over.

This catastrophic landscape is the Kuwaiti desert in the aftermath of the Gulf War. "The war lasted only a few hours ...," Herzog says by way of introducing a few minutes of televised flares and aerial explosions. No further explanation is offered. There's an emphasis throughout on the failure of language. "The first creature we encountered tried to communicate something to us,"

Herzog explains, adopting the persona of a bemused space traveler. A traumatized woman wants to tell us her tale—two sons tortured to death before her eyes—but finds that she can no longer speak. A young child whose head was trampled by Iraqi soldiers has also lost his power of speech.

Eventually, Herzog and his intrepid DP, coproducer Paul Berriff, get down with the firefighters—men wearing Darth Vader helmets and speaking Texan who, spraying oil-rig volcanoes with massive jets of water, precipitate an infernal black rain. Herzog defamiliarizes their attempt to shut off and secure the oil wells through the use of slow motion, so that the sequence titled "The Closing of the Wells" becomes pure science fiction. In the film's final segment, the men torch a gusher and rekindle the blaze. "Others, seized by madness, follow suit," Herzog reports. "Now they are content, now there is something to extinguish again."

One of the most original documentary filmmakers of the past quarter century, Herzog has described himself as a director of landscapes. Here the use of solemn, surging rhapsodies (Grieg's *Peer Gynt*, Mahler's *Second Symphony*, Wagner's *Parsifal*) to underscore his unprecedented images suggests a desire to conduct cosmic upheaval. Meditating on the perverse grandeur of a man-made apocalypse, flying over a smoldering death star whose sole sign of life is the shadow cast by his helicopter, the filmmaker is totally in his element. *Lessons of Darkness* is a masterpiece—the culmination of Herzog's romantic Doomsday worldview.

The litter of burnt cars and transports, the collapsed radar station, and shattered bunkers are ruins of a vanished city: "All we could find were traces." It is as if Herzog were tapping into some primordial memory. If the tortured vistas of *Lessons of Darkness* bring to mind surrealist painter Max Ernst's celebrated canvas *Europe After the Rain*, it may be that those vistas are Herzog's heritage. Born in 1942, he grew up amid the craters and wreckage of defeated Nazi Germany. His earliest recollection, according to the film notes, is "the red sky over the burning town of Rosenheim."

Herzog's passion for destruction has a quasi-religious fervor. Indeed, this "requiem for an uninhabited planet" might have the galvanizing effect on eco-activists that a Gruenwald altarpiece had for believers during the bubonic plague. In this spirit perhaps, Film Forum is showing *Lessons of Darkness* with Ellen Bruno's *Satya: A Prayer for the Enemy*, a 28-minute documentary about Buddhist resistance to the Chinese occupation of Tibet. Bruno too exhibits a shocking aestheticism—step-printing her footage throughout to slow down and blur the motion and give her tract movie an unexpectedly smoky, sensuous quality.

Also reviewed in:
NATION, 11/27/95, p. 684, Stuart Klawans
NEW YORK TIMES, 10/25/95, p. C16, Janet Maslin

LIABILITY CRISIS

A FilmHaus release of a Wilkesfilms production. *Executive Producer:* Andrew Wilkes. *Director:* Richard Brody. *Screenplay:* Richard Brody. *Director of Photography:* James Maxton-Graham. *Editor:* Richard Brody. *Music:* Ludvic Beethoven and Francine Trester. *Sound:* Rob Taz. *Running time:* 80 minutes. *MPAA Rating:* Not Rated.

CAST: Mirjana Jokovic (Dunia); Jim Helsinger (Paul); Shari Meg Seidman (Wendy); R. Ward Duffy (Larry); Caren Alpert (Susie); Sylvia Weber (Mother); Sidney Annis (Father).

NEW YORK POST, 6/9/95, p. 58, Larry Worth

Plenty of good ideas are buried in Richard Brody's "Liability Crisis." And you'd need a pile-driver to unearth them.

Ostensibly, it's about a Manhattan-based Jew who's obsessed with the Holocaust. He's the kind of guy who, when shushed in a moviehouse, yells back, "Nazi."

Then, it's about a Yugoslavian woman consumed by isolation from everyone and everything, conveniently paralleling her country's dissolution and the ensuing political turmoil.

Don't like either storyline? Hold on. Another one comes along about every 15 minutes. The problem: Almost none are played out with enough conviction or compassion to make any impact. And by the time Brody finally hits pay dirt—over an hour into the alleged plot, he turns to Jews feeling discriminated against, while continuing to discriminate against others—it's too little, too late.

Brody, who doubled as screenwriter, clearly suffers from a lack of experience. That explains his plethora of wannabe-arty closeups, as of the protagonist writing ad infinitum in his journal, and meaningless black-and-white fantasy sequences. Ditto for a wildly inappropriate score.

The production's failures are unfortunate since two of the performers show potential. Making his big-screen debut, Jim Helsinger exhibits enough drive and ambiguities to fuel the central character. Meanwhile, Mirjana Jokovic has undeniable presence as his understandably confused lover.

But neither can compensate for Brody's overpowering amateurishness and penchant for the numbingly dull. Accordingly, he's the biggest liability in "Crisis."

NEWSDAY, 6/9/95, Part II/p. B7, John Anderson

Paul (Jim Helsinger), the protagonist of "Liability Crisis," is a would-be Manhattan filmmaker who works as a temp, takes a job in advertising and attributes each of life's pitfalls to anti-Semites, or otherwise good people being good Nazis. It is the work of Richard Brody, who also is a would-be filmmaker, worked as a temp, took a job in advertising and will probably find in this review something of the Third Reich.

Set up as a triptych of Paul's emotional, ethical and spiritual worth—or lack thereof—the film is largely about unlovable people in love, which is just one of its insurmountable obstacles. The other? The fact that you're not exactly sure how the director intends Paul: as a smug, lying manipulator of emotions and history, or (as the director seems to think) a paragon of modern intellectual yearning, or at least of sympathetic moral bemusement.

Chastized at his latest job for not working, Paul compares his boss' attitude with that of Germans who stood by as Jews were murdered. He draws a swastika on the door of a German neighbor with a war record, who subsequently kills himself. He hears an "achtung beat" in most popular music. He tells a would-be employer that '90s poverty is the moral equivalent of Hitler's final solution—glibly, condescendingly, exasperatingly.

He has a lover, Dunia, played by Mirjana Jokovic (of the recent Cannes honoree "Underground"), who's only slightly less irritating than Paul. A Yugoslavian—thus giving her ties to the latest thing in genocide—she resents the rejection of Paul's family because she's not Jewish, but she resents Paul, too, for reasons not entirely clear. But that's OK: He's had a fling with his neighbor, Wendy (Shari Meg Seidman), he lies about it, and he puts himself in compromising positions with women so he can then reject them on the grounds that he's being faithful to Dunia. He's a twisted dude, and unwatchable.

What's more troubling about "Liability Crisis" is the way it belittles Paul's obsession with the Holocaust, without distancing him from the rest of the so-called Jewish "obsession" with the Holocaust, which is a way for real anti-Semites to reject the horrors of the war altogether. Amid all the pretentious celebrations about ethnicity and ethics, director Brody doesn't really have a grip on his material and ends up juggling lighted matches and gasoline.

VILLAGE VOICE, 6/13/95, p. 58, Leslie Camhi

New York Jewish culture, at its worst, can seem insular and narcissistic, and in *Liability Crisis*, it does. This first feature written and directed by Richard Brody convincingly captures the fishbowl effect of one young man's fixations, but leaves viewers gasping for air.

Paul (Jim Helsinger), an aspiring filmmaker, has problems with women and is obsessed by Hitler. His only documentary consists of interviews with old men talking about their wartime experience. By day he temps, by night he philanders with Wendy, his Jewish neighbor, while waiting for his Yugoslavian girlfriend Dunia (Mirjana Jokovic) to return from study in China. She gets back and their romance turns existential; she meets his overbearing family, and the film becomes a Yugoslav nouvelle vague version of *Guess Who's Coming to Dinner*.

Jokovic makes for a soulful, displaced shiksa, but we never learn that much about her character; in fact, everyone but Paul comes perilously close to being simply his projection. At one point, he passes a black woman reading *Mein Kampf* in the hallway. Is he hallucinating? A strain of daring, dark hilarity, and a few good Jewish jokes, make the film worth seeing.

But I couldn't help wondering, can't we ever talk about anything different?

Also reviewed in:
NEW YORK TIMES, 6/9/95, p. C10, Stephen Holden
VARIETY, 6/12-18/95, p. 60, Godfrey Cheshire

LIE DOWN WITH DOGS

A Miramax Films release of a Walrus Productions film. *Executive Producer:* John Pierson. *Producer:* Anthony Bennett and Wally White. *Director:* Wally White. *Screenplay:* Wally White. *Director of Photography:* George Mitas. *Editor:* Hart F. Faber. *Art Director:* Reno Dakota. *Running time:* 86 minutes. *MPAA Rating:* R.

CAST: Wally White (Tommie); Reno Dakota (Square Joe); Jonathan Pauldick (Political Guy #1); Anthony Bennett (Political Guy #2); Devin Quigley (Political Woman); Raymond Capuana (Dick Guy #1); Dennis Davis (Dick Guy #2); Eli Kabillio (Dick Guy #3); Eddie Encarnacion (Dick Guy #4); Matthew Gambino (Tommie's Body Double); Kevin Mayes (Toby); David Matwljkow (Charlie); Darren Anthony (Jose); James Sexton (Eddie); Chester Hinsfield (Flyerman); Al Marz (Scalper); Nevada Belle (Church Lady); Christine Hull (Tourist Lady); J.D. Cerna (Peter & Sal); Darren Dryden (Ben); Hans Hoppenbrouwers (Dan); Nonny Kulecza (Bob); Hart F. Faber (Bob's Voice); Vann Jones (Glen & Herbert); Ty-Ranne Grimsted (Carmelota Pessums); Jack Hazan (Simon); Wendy Adams (Sally); Michel Richoz (Michi); Bash Halow (Guy); Randy Becker (Tom); Richard B. Olson (Jeffrey); Brian Quirk (Ru); Julie Wheeler (Prep-Girl); Kevin Shenk (Waitress); Scott James Jordan (Driver & Groper); Ken Bonnin (Chris); Denis Gawley and Paul Rex Pierson (Sex Boys); Jesus Cortez (Stripper); Tim McCarthy (Dorothy Stratton Killer); Carol McDonald (Margaret); Martha J. Cooney (Doctor); Rob Cardazone ("Trip"); Steve Lent (Benjamin); Charlie Fieran (Anthony); Deborah Auer (Dubbing).

LOS ANGELES TIMES, 7/28/95, Calendar/p. 16, Kevin Thomas

In his wry, jaunty "Lie Down With Dogs," Wally White immediately dispenses with the twin expectations of gay filmmakers: to be politically correct and/or pornographic. White, in his feature debut, then proceeds with his bittersweet romantic comedy/coming-of-age tale, set in quaint Provincetown, Mass., long a favored gay resort. The boys may be here, but a gay "Where the Boys Are." White himself spent the summer of '91 in P-town.

White casts himself as Tommy, a whimsical, boyish-looking young man fed up with the Manhattan rat race and ready to take his chances on a summer in Provincetown, where he might just find some romance.

Arriving with $50 and not quite maxed-out credit cards, he's immediately propelled into the hectic task of trying to find work and a place to stay when virtually all of the jobs and affordable lodgings are already taken. Resilient and plucky, Tommy makes friends easily and learns to cope with transitory work and places to stay. Almost immediately he commences an affair with a free-spirited, handsome man (Randy Becker).

White is highly ingenious in the ways in which he makes a shoestring budget work to his advantage. He makes asides to the audience, moves back and forth in time and creates amusing montages, all of which serve both his narrative and also to create the sense that Tommy, his friends and lovers aren't going anywhere—even when they're moving at a frenetic disco beat.

For all its period charm, Provincetown emerges frankly as a pretty dreary place to spend a vacation—even if you are young and attractive. White suggests that young men without funds find themselves considering jobs where the line between houseboy and hustler blurs to nonexistence.

Tommy discovers that hot but safe sex is out there but that romance tends to be shallow. There's also a surfeit of hard drinking and aimless partying.

By the end of the summer, Tommy may have learned something about himself and about life, yet he remains an optimist—he is, after all, young. Consequently, Tommy's summer may leave you with more of a sour aftertaste than it does Tommy himself.

"Lie Down With Dogs"—a cautionary title if ever there was one—is nevertheless pretty funny with lots of campy, bitchy humor, and White never lets up even when his energy occasionally exceeds his inspiration. He's an engaging actor himself, and Becker plus Bash Halow and James Sexton as Tommy's pals are sharp. Without an ounce of pretension or self-consciousness White has come up with a pithy sketch of certain aspects of gay society.

NEW YORK POST, 7/28/95, p. 40, Thelma Adams

Let's pause for a minute of silence to recognize what a monumental achievement it is for an independent filmmaker simply to complete a project and get it into the theaters.

That said, not every young genius who maxes out his credit cards to make a feature film is the next Spike Lee.

Consider Wally White.

The New York University film grad has turned the grammar school theme "what I did on my summer vacation" into the full-length feature "Lie Down With Dogs." While I'm sure that the young writer, director and star had one great summer in the so-called "gay ghetto" of Provincetown on the Cape, his whiny tale of looking for a job, bedding boys, taking drugs and searching for the meaning of life would hardly make a gold short story, much less a movie.

White approaches his subject with brio and a sense of humor—the credits unfold on Calvins sported by buff young men. But, as the tortured post-grad Tommie, the chipmunk-cheeked dynamo natters directly at the camera in a way that (my apologies to Wally's mother) is simply not as adorable as he thinks it is. His deepest fears run to taking the risk of going on a summer vacation without any money and running up his credit cards. It's not exactly Hamlet.

Rarely has hedonism been so painful!

With the success of recent low-budget, gay- and lesbian-themed movies like "Go Fish" and "The Incredibly True Adventures of Two Girls in Love," it's not, enough for a film to fly out of the closet. It also has to be engaging. As the ever-critical Tommie would say, "This is lame."

NEWSDAY, 7/28/95, Part II/p. B11, Jack Mathews

Writer-director-star Wally White attempts to become the Woody Allen of gay film with this jaunty tale of a neurotic young New Yorker who decides to shuck his guilt for a summer of fun and sun in the gay haven of Provincetown, Mass. It's a "Where the Boys Are" for the boys. White talks to the camera incessantly, as if the audience were the blank paper upon which he was chronicling his great adventure, and in one scene he even walks out of the movie to declare to his crew that it is the filmmaker's responsibility not to be boring. Despite his evident enthusiasm for his character and the material, however, boring he is.

VILLAGE VOICE, 8/1/95, p. 50, Stan Dauphin

[*Lie Down with Dogs* was reviewed jointly with *She Lives to Ride;* see Dauphin's review of that film.]

Also reviewed in:
CHICAGO TRIBUNE, 7/28/95, Friday/p. K, John Petrakis
NEW YORK TIMES, 7/28/95, p. C5, Caryn James
VARIETY, 2/20-26/95, p. 80, David Stratton
WASHINGTON POST, 7/14/95, p. D6, Rita Kempley

LITTLE ODESSA

A Fine Line Features release of a Live Entertainment presentation of a Paul Webster/Addis-Wechsler production. *Executive Producer:* Nick Wechsler, Claudia Lewis, and Rolf Mittweg. *Producer:* Paul Webster. *Director:* James Gray. *Screenplay:* James Gray. *Director of Photography:* Tom Richmond. *Editor:* Dorian Harris. *Music:* Dana Sano. *Music Editor:* Richard Bernstein and Philip Tallman. *Sound:* Tom Paul. *Sound Editor:* John A. Larsen and Lewis Goldstein. *Casting:* Douglas Aibel. *Production Designer:* Kevin Thompson. *Art Director:* Judy Rhee. *Set Decorator:* Charles Ford. *Set Dresser:* Mike Preston, Annie Ballard, Mike Murphy, and Stuart Montgomery. *Special Effects:* Drew Jiritano. *Costumes:* Michael Clancy. *Make-up:* Karen Nichols. *Stunt Coordinator:* Roy Farfel. *Running time:* 99 minutes. *MPAA Rating:* R.

CAST: Tim Roth (Joshua Shapira); Edward Furlong (Reuben Shapira); Moira Kelly (Alla Shustervich); Vanessa Redgrave (Irina Shapira); Maximillian Schell (Arkady Shapira); Paul Guilfoyle (Boris Volkoff); Natasha Andreichenko (Natasha); David Vadim (Sasha); Mina Bern (Grandma Tsilya); Boris McGiver (Ivan); Mohammed Ghaffari (Pahlevi); Michael Khumrov (Yuri); Dmitry Preyers (Victor); David Ross (Anatoly); Ron Brice (Man with One Leg); Jace Kent (Mechanic); Marianna Lead (Clara); Gene Ruffini (Janitor).

LOS ANGELES TIMES, 6/2/95, Calendar/p. 8, Peter Rainer

"Little Odessa" is about Russian Jewish émigrés in Brooklyn's Brighton Beach, and the 26-year-old writer-director James Gray, making his feature film debut, turns the wintry neighborhood into something resembling the steppes. The community is so ingrown that its denizens appear to have transferred all their Old World enmities and passions intact to the New World.

But there's nothing convivial or warming about the transference. Clearly the Russians who came to America were hoping for something more than this blasted, scrounging existence. They have the world-weary look of souls in torment.

If atmosphere alone made a movie, "Little Odessa" would be first-rate. But Gray doesn't really trust his own best gifts, he's so young that he's trying to work up as many different crosscurrents and plot contrivances as possible, hoping, perhaps, that something will stick and a reputation will be made. The film is a grab bag of melodramatic incident—a high-class résumé movie.

Tim Roth plays Joshua, a hit man for the *organizatsya,* the Russian mob. Banished by his father Arkady (Maximilian Schell) from visiting his family, Joshua nevertheless finds a way to reconnect with his younger brother, Reuben (Edward Furlong), who idolizes him, and his mother Irina (Vanessa Redgrave), who is wracked with a brain tumor.

Joshua is back in the old neighborhood for another reason too. He has one more hit to carry out before he can return to his homeland. It's a film noir-like development, and, like the hit-man stuff in general, it seems airlifted from a pulpier, more movie-ish scenario. Joshua is a romanticized killer. His love for his brother and his mother and his erotic tenderness toward one of the neighborhood girls (Moira Kelly) are supposed to make him a tragic figure in our eyes. When he and his father come to blows, we're meant to recognize how the old man's burly incomprehension of his sons' lives is to blame.

If only Gray had chucked the low-end gangster material and worked a bit closer to the feel of the streets. If only he risked everyday passions instead of cooked-up ones. The scenes between Joshua and his brother are complexly moving, and, throughout, there is a fine eye at work. Roth is tense and cryptic, and a few of the other performers, including Furlong and Redgrave—although she overdoes the wailing—are strong. (Schell carries on a bit too hammily.) Gray hasn't filled out the emotional terrain he's surveyed here. He hasn't quite grown into the emotions he wants to put on screen. When he does, he'll come up with something lasting.

NEW YORK POST, 5/19/95, p. 39, Thelma Adams

"Brooklyn is no good for me," says Joshua Shapira (Tim Roth, wielding his slight body like a stiletto, narrowing old eyes in a young face). When you're a hit man, you can't go home again.

For Jewish mobster Shapira, home is "Little Odessa." Gun in hand, Shapira follow's a contract back to the faded seaside community turned Russian emigre Mecca of Brighton Beach, Brooklyn. Once there, he unloads a legacy of violence on his family's doorstep.

Physical violence, largely underplayed by writer/director James Gray in his first feature film, takes a back seat to the emotional swells within the Shapira clan.

Joshua's father Arkady (the harnessed thunder cloud of Maximilian Schell) is a portrait of dreams disappointed, an intellectual confined to a sidewalk newsstand. Joshua's mother Irina (a red-eyed, pain-twisted Vanessa Redgrave in a brief, devastating dance of death) clings to her deathbed, the tumor eroding her brain a symbol of the family's failure to root in the new world.

Joshua's bittersweet reunion with his younger brother, Reuben (Edward Furlong), reminds him of lost innocence—even though the teen-ager is no innocent himself. There is an instant physical bond between Roth and Furlong, both instinctual actors whose personalities melt into the characters. Sharing Nathan's hot dogs under the boardwalk becomes an act of communion, a race across the winter snow promises a future spring that will never come.

Shot on location in and around Brighton Beach in the winter of 1993, "Little Odessa" benefited from the freak snow storms that lend a dirty, "Dr. Zhivago" sweep to the landscape. The heartbreaking images of Coney Island adrift—the frozen Wonder Wheel, the ruined roller coaster, the shadow of the sea—form a magical backdrop for Gray's elegiac tragedy.

The movie drifts in the wrong direction when it leaves the highly charged family drama and concentrates on the less coherent mobster tale that forces "Little Odessa" to its operatic conclusion. This is the rare, memorable movie debut where the dramatic shot to the heart is more deadly than any bullet in the head.

NEWSDAY, 5/19/95, Part II/p. B5, John Anderson

Joshua Shapira, the not-so-tortured Russian-Jewish hitman played by Tim Roth in "Little Odessa," moves with shoulders hunched, arms slightly spread and a forward motion that's part business, part bravado and totally unnecessary. It's the walk of someone who wants to prove he's a bad-ass. Joshua has nothing to prove.

By the time he makes it back to the snow-scattered streets of Brighton Beach, Brooklyn—painted by writer/director James Gray with a post-autumn palette of wintry gray and aged yellow—we've seen him cold-bloodedly execute a man on a Moscow park bench, and then make a phone call. It's a matter-of-fact exchange of commercial information: The voice, told the job is done, say's there's another in Brooklyn, where Joshua isn't wanted and shouldn't go. But he goes, because there's no escape from his fate or himself.

He know's it, and we do, too: "Little Odessa"—the 25-year-old Gray's more-than-auspicious debut and an award-winner at last year's Venice Film Festival—is as dire and doomed a tale of irredeemable sin as we're likely to see in the current age of romance. Gray makes it abundantly clear—through his resigned rhythms, his nighthawk's perspective and his penchant for anguished faces—that Joshua is lurching toward disaster. What we don't know is how many members of his family he'll take with him.

It's a mordant clan. Joshua's younger brother, Reuben (Edward Furlong), is a chain-smoking truant who reveres his lethal sibling; their father, the alternately brutal and brooding Arkady (Maximilian Schell), runs a newsstand, tries to stay clear of the local Russian mob chief, Volkoff (Paul Guilfoyle), and is cheating on his terminally ill wife, Irina—who, although we see her only briefly, becomes a tragically dominating presence via the peerless Vanessa Redgrave. Theirs is a New World Disordered, a Moscow-on-the-precipice.

Reuben is a headphone-wearing, movie-watching American, but Joshua represents the link between Russia and New York, and an unstable link it is. Told that his mother's dying, he asks, "Pop still with the stand?" His sense of ethnicity is erratic. "We're Jews. We wander," he tells Reuben, when asked where he's going to go. After his brother's bar mitzvah—which he misses—Joshua asks, "You got a lotta money? You can make a lot of money from those things."

His mind is a place where money and murder crowd out almost everything else, making this a movie in which displays of affection or tenderness are not only infrequent but startling—including those with Alla (Moira Kelly), the neighborhood beauty Joshua courts in his scarish manner ("We'll go out this week") and who confirms his damned view of himself. "Did you think of me?" he asks. "Not really. I guess I wondered where you went," she says, confirming his suspicion that when he's gone he won't be remembered at all.

Gray takes an even, studied tone that seldom wavers, seldom lifts "Little Odessa" beyond gloom and desperation. None of the characters is particularly endearing, not even Reuben, who's given a pasty, punkish portrayal by Furlong. And even the violence is understated, maintaining the pace of slow doom. This may not conform to everyone's taste, but it isn't a wrong decision. It shows, in fact, a good deal of integrity on the part of the director, who seems to hit precisely the target for which he's aiming.

SIGHT AND SOUND, 5/95, p. 49, Philip Kemp

Joshua Shapira, an American of Russian Jewish descent, has become a hitman for the Russian mafia. Assigned to hit an Iranian jeweller in the Brighton Beach area of Brooklyn, he protests that this is his home territory which he can't enter, but his boss insists. Having reluctantly checked into a local hotel, he is drawn towards the family home where his dying mother Irina lives with his father Arkady, his grandmother Tsilya and his younger brother Reuben. Lingering outside the house, Joshua is recognised by a young layabout, Sasha, who tells Reuben of his brother's return. Joshua, contacted by Reuben, agrees to visit their mother, but seeks out Sasha and intimidates him and his friends into helping with the hit.

Accompanying Reuben home, Joshua is thrown out by Arkady, who attacks Reuben for bringing his disgraced brother into the house. In the street Joshua is recognised by a henchman of Volkoff, the local godfather, whose son he killed; Joshua shoots the man before he can contact his boss. He encounters Alla, a young woman he used to know, and they become lovers. Joshua confronts Arkady coming home after a night with his mistress, Natasha. They negotiate a truce, and Joshua visits his mother, who entrusts Reuben to him.

At Tsilya's 80th birthday party Arkady is warned by Volkoff not to shield Joshua. Meanwhile Joshua, aided by Sasha and his friends, kidnaps the jeweller, shoots him at the city dump and incinerates his body. Reuben, who has followed them, witnesses the execution and retrieves the murder gun. When Joshua comes to say goodbye to his family, he sees bruises on Reuben inflicted by Arkady. He holds Arkady at gunpoint and humiliates him. Arkady contacts Volkoff and tells him where to find Joshua.

Irina, alone with Reuben, collapses and dies. On his way to transmit the news to Joshua via Sasha, Reuben encounters Volkoff's hitmen. Both he and Sasha rush to Alla's house, where she and Joshua have been making love. One of the hitmen kills Alla; Reuben shoots the hitman but is accidentally killed by Sasha. Joshua takes his brother's body to the furnace and incinerates it.

"I suppose it was crazy of me," muses Maximilian Schell's saturnine patriarch, lamenting his attempts to instil culture in his son Joshua, "to think of reading *Crime and Punishment* to a two-year-old." Crazy probably, but at least he can't complain it didn't take. Joshua, and indeed virtually the entire cast of *Little Odessa*, is sunk in enough coagulated Slavic gloom to make the Brothers Karamazov seem like the Brothers Marx. Anyone to whom Brighton Beach (New York version) hitherto meant Neil Simon is in for a surprise. In James Gray's depiction of the Brooklyn Jewish colony—his debut as a feature director—snappy one-liners are as rare as bacon sandwiches.

The same funeral pall infects the visuals. Most scenes take place at night or in fusty, underlit apartments with wallpaper the colour of tobacco juice. Over the rare daytime exteriors there hangs a brownish haze, less a New York smog than the doomy exhalations of the film's characters. Almost everybody wears dark grey or black, and the soundtrack drips grief, with choirs intoning lugubrious Yiddish or Russian chants. "We'll wait ten seconds," Joshua tells his victim, as the wretched Iranian kneels whimpering on a garbage heap, "and see if God saves you." Ten seconds wasted, since by this stage it's clear that neither salvation nor any other form of comfort is on offer in *Little Odessa*. The sole available option is death.

It's largely this ingrained fatalism that gives the film its ethnic specificity. Otherwise, despite the copious display of local colour, there's oddly little in terms of plot or character that couldn't work equally well for several other US immigrant communities: add a touch of surface bonhomie, and the film could replay practically unchanged on the Italian-American Lower East Side. The plot doesn't work all that well though, even on its own terms. Twice we see Joshua, the icy efficient contract killer, in action: he walks up to his target in broad daylight, pumps a bullet through his skull and departs. The third killing of the Iranian, however, involves an elaborately-planned kidnapping and the recruitment of three young amateur helpers. Hard to see why, except that this gives time for Joshua to hang around and re-engage with his disintegrating family. Yet, for all its contrived plotline and self-conscious solemnity, the film still exerts a grip. Even within a narrow tonal palette Tom Richmond's cinematography achieves subtle gradations of mood, from the sombre near-monochrome of the family apartment to the high contrast, *film-noir*-ish backlighting of the garbage dump execution. The actors likewise turn the limitations of their roles to strengths, digging down to the emotional bedrock. This is especially true of Schell's Arkady, bedraggled and pot-bellied, smouldering with the resentment of an intellectual reduced to shameful domesticity. *Little Odessa* verges on the risible, but its faults no less than its virtues are those of an intense personal vision. Gray's talent as a film-maker is unmistakable; maybe next time he could just lighten up a bit.

VILLAGE VOICE, 5/23/95, Film Special/p. 28, J. Hoberman

An unusually somber, even tormented, gangster film, *Little Odessa* is chilly enough to coagulate blood. This first feature by 25-year-old James Gray, set in the Russian-Jewish enclave of Brooklyn's Brighton Beach, hides from the light—there are scenes where the screen can't wait to fade to black.

Little Odessa's morose energy is mirrored by its antihero: A hit man for the Russian mafia, Joshua Shapira (Tim Roth) is summoned back from an unspecified exile to the old neighborhood. His ostensible job is to eliminate a wealthy Iranian Jew; his unconscious mission, as the prodigal son, seems to be his family's obliteration. Shapira's grandmother (veteran Yiddish performer Mina Bern) is tottering into her ninth decade as his mother (Vanessa Redgrave) lies dying of a brain tumor. Meanwhile, his father, Arkady (Maximilian Schell), plays the tragic patriarch, deceiving his wife and bullying his young son Reuben (Edward Furlong), the plague-ridden family's sole sign of life.

Gray recasts the immigrant saga in utterly downbeat terms. If Russian-speaking Arkady is a ravaged, fallen aristocrat—operating a newsstand under the El—the half-Americanized Joshua is an oily little thug whose greatest talent is the capacity to walk up to some guy on the snow-covered boardwalk and casually blow him away. (*Little Odessa* gains considerably for having been shot in New York amid the blizzards of '94.) Attuned to the movie's emotional climate, Joshua is so cold-blooded his idea of a good time is to take his adoring kid brother to visit the fellow reptiles in the Coney Island aquarium.

Little Odessa makes much of its exotic fauna but the movie's ethnic particularity is spotty at best. (Unlike those of Quentin Tarantino, Gray's gangsters are down—but then neither does anyone else, except the impressively tormented Vanessa Redgrave (who, according to the press notes, shot all her scenes in three days). Schell does a lugubrious Tevye. Joshua and his buddies talk as if they learned English by studying *Mean Streets*. But when, outside a suitably dark and gloomy synagogue, the lonely hit man reencounters a kindred spirit in the form of a depressed dumpling named Alla (Moira Kelly), vocal inflections turn bizarrely British. (More naturalistic, perhaps, is their subsequent notably spacy and unsentimental sex scene—a bit of tender mauling, after which Alla just wants to sleep.)

While *Mean Streets* remains the template, *Little Odessa* might also be derived from Allen Baron's awful but compelling 1960 indie, *Blast of Silence*, in which a taciturn, out-of-town contract killer stalks his prey through a wintry Manhattan. The locations here are likewise strong—the Shapira's live in a convincingly musty and disheveled apartment where the stale reek of cigarettes complements the pervasive atmosphere of fear, illness, and death—but the context is similarly weak. At one point the Americanized Reuben brags to Joshua that he hangs with *shvartzers*, although we only see one black character and an elderly one at that. The milieu is visceral but synthetic.

"Big" Odessa, of course, was the home of the colorful Jewish underworld celebrated by Isaac Babel in his sardonic tales of the pre-Revolutionary "gangster king" Benya Krik. The transplanted Little Odessa is diminished and deracinated. Gray's literary model is more Dostoyevsky in Brooklyn. (At one point, Arkady brags of reading *Crime and Punishment* to two-year-old Joshua.) The air of grim suffering is intermittently spiritualized with a heavy overlay of Russian liturgical music.

Joshua is an unexplained evil for whom history is an inexplicable burden. "We're Jews, we wander," he tells his brother at one point. This terse formulation is only one of the inert relics the movie ambiguously puts on display. The various references to Jewish rituals have the sense of ancient pottery shards. Did Gray excavate or drop them? Even a Jewish funeral is scored with a mock Russian Orthodox mass.

Most heartfelt are the movie's subliminal references to Nazi terror—the summary execution of whimpering victims, the inevitable annihilation of unlucky innocents, the bodies bundled in bloody sheets and burnt in a garbage-dump crematorium. In this scenario, Joshua is the survivor—a golem whose rabbi is an invisible crime lord, a killer who suffers like Job.

Also reviewed in:
CHICAGO TRIBUNE, 6/2/95, Friday/p. K, Michael Wilmington
NEW REPUBLIC, 6/5/95, p. 33, Stanley Kauffmann
NEW YORK TIMES, 5/19/95, p. C12, Caryn James
VARIETY, 9/12-18/94, p. 44, David Rooney
WASHINGTON POST, 7/14/95, Weekend/p. 36, Desson Howe
WASHINGTON POST, 7/15/95, p. D8, Rita Kempley

LITTLE PRINCESS, A

A Warner Bros. release of a Mark Johnson/Baltimore Pictures production. *Executive Producer:* Alan C. Blomquist and Amy Ephron. *Producer:* Mark Johnson. *Director:* Alfonso Cuarón. *Screenplay:* Richard LaGravenese and Elizabeth Chandler. *Based on the novel by:* Frances Hodgson Burnett. *Director of Photography:* Emmanuel Lubezki. *Editor:* Steven Weisberg. *Music:* Patrick Doyle. *Music Editor:* Roy Prendergast. *Sound:* José Antonio Garcia and (music) Paul Hulme. *Sound Editor:* Bob Newlan. *Casting:* Jill Greenberg Sands. *Production Designer:* Bo Welch. *Art Director:* Tom Duffield. *Set Designer:* John Dexter and Larry Hubbs. *Set Decorator:* Cheryl Carasik. *Special Effects:* Alan E. Lorimer. *Costumes:* Judianna Makovsky. *Make-up:* Julie Hewett and Robert N. Norin. *Stunt Coordinator:* Charles Croughwell. *Running time:* 100 minutes. *MPAA Rating:* G.

CAST: Eleanor Bron (Miss Minchin); Liam Cunninham (Captain Crewe/Prince Rama); Liesel Matthews (Sara Crewe); Rusty Schwimmer (Amelia Minchin); Arthur Malet (Charles Randolph); Vanessa Lee Chester (Becky); Errol Sitahal (Ram Dass); Heather DeLoach (Ermengarde); Taylor Fry (Lavinia); Darcie Bradford (Jesse); Rachael Bella (Betsy); Alexandra Rea-Baum (Gertrude); Camilla Belle (Jane); Lauren Blumenfeld (Rosemary); Kelsey Mulrooney (Lottie); Kaitlin Cullum (Ruth); Alison Moir (Princess Sita); Time Winters (Frances the Milkman); Lomax Study (Monsieur Dufarge); Vincent Schiavelli (Mr. Barrow); Pushpa Rawal (Maya); Rahi Azizi (Laki); Ken Palmer (John Randolph); Helen Greenberg (Flower Lady); Norman Merrill (Doctor in Hospital); Peggy Miley (Mabel the Cook); Robert P. Cohen (Ermengarde's father); William Blomquist (Rich Boy in Street); David Fresco (Beggar Man in Fantasy Forest); Judith D. Drake (Bakery Woman); Chris Ellis (Policeman).

LOS ANGELES TIMES, 5/10/95, Calendar/p. 1, Kenneth Turan

"Magic has to be believed to be real," an understanding father tells his daughter in "A Little Princess," a philosophy this enchanting fantasy has taken as its own. Unlike the creators of far too many children's films, those responsible here have taken their story's events exactly as seriously as they expect their small audience to, with appealing results.

Adapted from a novel by the venerable Frances Hodgson Burnett, who also wrote "Little Lord Fauntleroy" and "The Secret Garden," "Princess" is dependent on its fairy-tale elements, but the filmmakers have smartly seen to it that these are not overdone. In fact, the straightforward way the picture treats its magical and sentimental sequences enhances its tangible sense of wonder.

While this well-mannered "Little Princess" is always nice, it's not immediately apparent if that's all it's going to be. For as initially presented, little Sara Crewe is reminiscent of the creatures in Agnieszka Holland's precious version of "The Secret Garden," a film so well-scrubbed and respectful it crossed over the border into cloying.

Sara (10-year-old newcomer Liesel Matthews) is discovered in Simla, India, in 1914, frolicking on a riverbank and recounting tales of monsters and heroes from the Sanskrit epic the Ramayana. Here she first hears, from her Indian nanny, the film's not exactly gender-blind philosophy that all women and girls are princesses, each in their own way.

Reality, however, soon asserts itself: Sara's father, the wealthy but first-name-deprived Captain Crewe (Liam Cunningham), has to leave India to fight the good fight in the Great War, and Sara must be taken to Miss Minchin's School for Girls in New York, the alma mater of her dear departed mother.

Though the haughty, overbearing Miss Minchin (Eleanor Bron) and her flighty, rotund sister Amelia (Rusty Schwimmer) are in awe of Sara's wealth, they are less enamored of the girl's disregard for rules, her tendency to be a freer spirit than this rigid place allows.

There is a potential pitfall in this setup, because paragons of childhood tend to be great bores with too much of the wrong kind of princess about them. Saving Sara from this trap is the innate feistiness of actress Matthews and the genuineness of her character's desire to be a friend to the friendless, especially the downtrodden servant girl Becky (well done by Vanessa Lee Chester). Soon almost the whole school is sneaking into Sara's room every night to hear her spirited versions of the tales she heard in India.

Then, once again, a reversal of fortune occurs, and this time it is a shocking one. A lawyer arrives at the school and the news he brings of her father's disappearance in battle and the confiscation of his wealth unhinges Sara's life. Overnight she is turned from a cosseted, indulged pet into an overworked drudge, forced to scrub floors, move to the attic with Becky and exist on bitter gruel.

It is this devasting plot twist that keeps "A Little Princess" honest and lifts it above ordinary. For one thing, Sara as a chastened orphan, her spirit crushed, plays much more effectively on our sympathies than Sara as the oblivious heiress, and Matthews' acting seems to improve as her character's situation worsens.

This change of life is especially touching because what the Richard LaGravenese and Elizabeth Chandler script does best is delineate what is essentially a father-daughter love story. Though the screenwriters have taken a number of understandable liberties with the original novel, including successfully softening and Hollywoodizing the book's ending, they have also, in tender scenes like the Captain's goodby to Sara at Miss Minchin's, enhanced and amplified that key emotional connection.

As always when a film more than fulfills expectations, many factors contributed to the success of "A Little Princess," notably the acting of Eleanor Bron, expert at giving Miss Minchin just a twinge of humanity, and Errol Sitahal, who brings appropriate majesty to Ram Dass, the Asp-like Indian who happens to live next door. The soaring music by Patrick Doyle (who scored both of Kenneth Branagh's Shakespearean films) sets the emotional tone, and production designer Bo Welch has beautifully constructed Sara's fantasy India and the ominous oversized plushness of Miss Minchin's.

Finally, a great deal of credit has to go to Mexican director Alfonso Cuarón, whose only previous feature was "Love in the Time of Hysteria." Though Cuarón has had other domestic projects fall through (he was at one time slated to direct "The Perez Family"), this became his Hollywood debut and it is an impressive one.

Working with "Like Water for Chocolate" cinematographer Emmanuel Lubezki, Cuarón perfectly understands how a combination of simplicity and restraint help to create a sense of wonder on screen, how a gust of snow blowing open a window can take your breath away more than the most elaborate of machine-made special effects. Under his sure, quiet direction, "A Little Princess" casts the type of spell most family films can only dream about.

NEW YORK POST, 5/10/95, p. 47, Michael Medved

What makes a children's classic? It's not just a matter of sunshine or butterflies or talking bunnies or catchy tunes. The common element in the most memorable cinematic entertainment for young viewers, from "The Wizard of Oz" to "E.T." to "The Lion King," is emotional intensity—pitched at a level that kids can understand. Sure, the best family movies produce their share of smiles, but they also generate tears along the way.

That's certainly the case with "A Little Princess," the gorgeous new version of a nearly hundred-year-old book and play by Frances Hodgson Burnett, the beloved author who also wrote "Little Lord Fauntleroy" and "The Secret Garden."

Though the writers of this film (led by Richard LaGravanese, who previously created "The Fisher King") have taken liberties with the original story, they've preserved most of its harsh elements; the young heroine, Sara, is exposed to death, sudden poverty, and wanton cruelty. Nevertheless, as in all cherished fairy tales, the frights and horrors only serve to intensify the ultimate feelings of joy and celebration.

At the beginning of the story, Sara (played by 10-year-old newcomer Liesel Matthews) lives an idyllic and exotic life in colonial India with her widower father, Captain Crewe (Liam Cunningham). It is, however, 1914 and the Captain is soon called away to fight in the Great War, moving his daughter to an exclusive boarding school in New York for safe keeping.

When he's reported missing in action, her financial support disappears and the school's unnaturally nasty headmistress (Eleanor Bron) moves Sara to the attic and forces her to labor as a Cinderella-like servant girl.

Sara nevertheless maintains her optimism and imagination, regaling the other girls at school with tales from Hindu mythology. Meanwhile, the mysterious and mystical Indian manservant in the building next door (Errol Sitahal), assisted by his versatile trained monkey; keeps a watchful eye on the situation.

This storyline may seem like weak tea for a generation accustomed to spectacular sci-fi monsters and shoot-'em-up' video games, but the gifted director, Mexico's Alfonso Cuaron, invests the material with so much passion and visual virtuosity that even the most jaded viewer will be properly spellbound.

With its stunning sets and costumes, "A Little Princess" feels like a splendid old story book full of dazzlingly detailed illustrations, all bound up in richly scented leather with burnished gold trim. The lavish fantasy sequences, depicting Sara's stories of Prince Rama and Princess Sita, are a feast of dreamlike color and imagination. A lush evocative score by composer Patrick Doyle (who also worked on Kenneth Branagh's "Henry V' and "Much Ado About Nothing") adds significantly to the magic.

Liesel Matthews is a down-to-earth and capable young actress who is perfectly cast as Sara. Unlike Shirley Temple in the fondly-remembered 1939 version of the story, she never overwhelms the material with her cuteness.

"All girls are princesses," her character stubbornly insists. "It's our right." In any event, this triumphant film should be more than, enough to make your own little princesses feel like royalty.

NEWSDAY, 8/4/95, Part II/p. B7, Jack Mathews

Next to "Apollo 13," Alfonso Cuaron's "A Little Princess" is probably the best reviewed movie of the summer of '95. Yet, when I've mentioned it to friends looking for a good children's picture, they've looked at me with blank stares, as if they'd never heard of it.

Most people haven't, even though the film was playing in more than 1,300 theaters in May. Warner Bros. had simply miscalculated in its marketing strategy, and opened the movie before the traditional Memorial Day summer kickoff, before families had entered the "how do we entertain the kids?" zone, and by the time their radar screens were turned on, the movie was gone.

Now, in a rare example of consumer thoughtfulness, Warner Bros. is bringing this wonderful movie back—so we're reviewing it again—and if you've got young children, you've got a second chance to show them a good time.

"A Little Princess," adapted from either the Frances Hodgson Burnett classic short story or the 1939 Shirley Temple movie, whichever you best remember, is the story of Sara Crewe (Liesel Matthews), a rich English girl with an even richer imagination, who is taken from exotic India, where she was being raised by her widowed father, and placed in a private boarding school while he serves in the British Army.

The boarding school has been relocated from London to New York for this version, and the period has been moved forward from the Boer War to World War I, but the magic of her experience is the same. With her equally strong beliefs in magic (the romantic Indian myth of Ramayan that she loves is enacted in sublimely colorful fantasy sequences) and in her father (Liam Cunningham, who also plays the prince in the Ramayan), Sara keeps herself and her schoolmates buttressed against the whims of the school's greedy and mean-spirited headmistress (Eleanor Bron).

Parents looking for characters that their young daughters can identify with (Pocahontas became college age in Disney's hands) need look no further.

SIGHT AND SOUND, 2/96, p. 47, Jo Comino

Simla, India, 1914. Sara Crewe listens avidly to her ayah's tale of Prince Rama and Princess Sita. At the outbreak of The First World War her widowed father, bound for the trenches, leaves her at Miss Minchin's boarding school for girls in New York. Although Captain Crewe's wealth earns Sara prize pupil status, Miss Minchin detests her candour and intelligence. Sara's flair for storytelling alleviates the stifling regime and wins over the majority of her classmates. She even manages to establish a rapport with the black servant girl Becky.

Sara's lavish birthday party is disrupted by the news that her father has been lost in action and his assets seized. Penniless and alone, Sara is stripped of her possessions by a wrathful Miss Minchin and banished to Becky's attic. She rises above the drudgery and deprivation of her new life thanks to Becky's companionship, her ex-classmates' loyalty and the power of her imagination. Her compassion to those as needy as herself is observed by Ram Dass, an Indian manservant who lives next door. Overnight he transforms the attic into the palace of the girls' dreams.

When Miss Minchin discovers the remains of a magnificent banquet in the garret she accuses Sara and Becky of thieving and summons the police. Perilously Sara escapes next door over the roof. Ram Dass' master has taken in a casualty of war, an amnesiac who tried to save his son's life—none other than Captain Crewe. Sara comes face to face with her father. Only when she is dragged away screaming does his memory return. While Sara leaves with her father and Becky, the school is liberalised under new patronage and Miss Minchin reduced to penury, a chimney sweep's assistant.

Film versions and television serialisations of *A Little Princess* by Frances Hodgson Burnett (author of *The Secret Garden* and *Little Lord Fauntleroy*) abound, notably the 1939 Shirley Temple vehicle in Technicolor with dance routines and a dream sequence. The latest offering gives the nineteenth-century Christian/capitalist morality of the novel ("Give as ye shall receive" and redemption through suffering) a multicultural spin with a dose of Indian folk-legend and a codicil on inter-racial harmony. It is significant that Sara and Becky become 'sisters' in a happy ending vague enough to imply a levelling of status rather than a perpetuation of the servant/mistress relationship. Homelessness too is a topical issue, here cast with a reassuring Dickensian glow which celebrates altruism.

A Little Princess is aimed first and foremost at pre-teen girls for whom it provides an admirable juvenile female lead—sassy, priggish, emotional but no goody-two-shoes. The soundtrack teeters on the brink of mawkishness with lyrics of the "Take my heart" variety delivered in a piping tone. But then this is the way of many successful Disney hits. The responsibility for Sara's imaginary life, is left to the film's art department rather than the script's characterisation. *A Little Princess* has a striking picture book quality to it which is sometimes distracting. Miss Minchin's school is a mock-Gothic castle in a bilious shade of green which recalls the Wicked Witch of the North in *The Wizard of Oz*. Its gloomy interiors, with their exaggerated opulence and scale, are intercut, with tableaux of trench warfare, uniformly sludge brown, and episodes from Sara's Indian background, in dazzling whites, yellows and saffron. Sara's fall and rise is mirrored by instalments of the *Ramayana* as she recounts them to the other girls. They feature her father as Prince Rama and her dead mother as a Princess Sita threatened by a many-headed monster Ravanna (who stands for Miss Minchin) in full-blown Indian film epic style replete with special effects. Although vivid, the colour symbolism is heavy-handed on occasion: Sara's fateful party, for example, when a black balloon detaches itself, drifts towards the camera lens and pops.

Putting aside the sheer cinematic suspense of the denouement where Sara gets to negotiate a rickety plank at a dizzying height in a full electric storm, the film is at its most potent when it deals with pretend play—the delight children get from the conviction that their wishes are as good as tangible. This happens to Sara and Becky when they wake up to discover their god-forsaken garret has been transformed into a sumptuous parlour, laid out with a banquet of sausages and muffins; it's the detail which counts. It's encouraging too that Eleanor Bron's splendidly spiky Miss Minchin, with her febrile harp-playing, is neither rehabilitated nor psychoanalysed as you dread she will be. In a world where "all girls are princesses" you need an unredeemed witch or two.

VILLAGE VOICE, 5/23/95, Film Special/p. 30, Georgia Brown

It's telling that Warner's opened Alfonso Cuarón's enchanting *A Little Princess* at just one New York City theater, at 64th Street and Second Avenue. Somebody thinks all the real princesses reside on the Upper East Side. The studio should trust its movie's message. "All women are princesses," says the heroine's Indian nurse. "It is our right."

When the dashing captain Crewe (Liam Cunningham) tells his daughter Sara (Liesel Matthews), "You are and will always be my little princess," the friend next to me, who may one day have a daughter of his own and change his mind, found the speech a bit weird. Creepy. In the following scene, on a ship carrying the couple from India to America, Captain Crewe presents Sara with her dead mother's old locket, then takes her in his arms and waltzes around the first-class deck in the moonlight. Could it be he's one of those "unnatural" fathers who want to "marry" their own daughters? In which case it's lucky it's 1914 and as a British officer he's about to be sent to the front. But first, he must take Sara to New York and enroll her in the same exclusive boarding school her mother attended.

As a daughter, I found the shipboard scene stirring. The little girl just wants to marry Daddy, sit at the foot of his table, and bear his many babies. Richard LaGravenese, who wrote *The Fisher King*, and Elizabeth Chandler have liberally adapted Frances Hodgson Burnett's novel, originally called *Sara Crewe*, and rather than shy away from the oedipal content, the writers play it up. They've also deepened the story by making Sara's father a soldier rather than an investor in diamond mines. (In the novel, he dies back in India of jungle fever having believed he'd lost his fortune.) Besides giving him a cause, the war setting opens the ending to a thrilling recognition scene, one that involves the father's battle-induced amnesia, which functions as a defense against desire, a sign of time passing, a necessary distance between parent and child. It also invokes the child's worst nightmare, that the parent will forget.

But I'm getting ahead of my story. The Crewes find the famed Miss Minchin's School for Girls at the end of a lively Manhattan cul-de-sac. (In the novel, the school is in London.) Bo Welch's production design is as witty as it is attractive. A cross between a mansion and a fortress, the brick building is a sickly chartreuse and everything inside, from the girls' uniforms to the brocade drapes to the apples on the table, is in shades of green—all of this a bitter joke on a "green world" where growth is free and unfettered. The sinister headmistress, Miss Minchin (Eleanor Bron), makes her entrance gliding down the staircase as if on tiny rollers, and, as the evil stepmother equivalent, intervenes between the lovers like bad breath. The movie has lots of laughs.

Like the Kuwaitis, Sara has too much. Her father has no sense of boundaries; he needs to grow up, too. She's ensconced in a suite so lavish it's a parody of opulence. But since she's clever and kind, the other girls aren't that jealous, except for the inevitable snide rival—here named Lavinia. Sara befriends the school's chubby girl, tames a tantrumy younger child, and is the first to speak to the scullery maid, Becky (Vanessa Lee Chester).(Making Becky black seems to me the film's one false move, since she inevitably seems the object of Sara's noblesse oblige.) Sara copes with the loss of her father by telling stories, and the film is unusually shrewd in keeping India forefronted as a source of myth—and of colors more vivid than green. Here India is a stronger, richer presence than it is even in Burnett's *The Secret Garden*. As in *Little Women*, the heroine's story-telling shows how writers develop out of grief.

Although princesses are born, to grow worthy of the title they must evolve. For a time, they wear tatters, sleep in the ashes, and keep company with mice—or, as in Burnett's novel, rats. (Lucky girls get to complete the process in a decent number of teenage years, some take forever.)

When word comes midway through the movie that Captain Crewe has been killed, Miss Minchin appropriates Sara's fine things and makes her into a scullery maid. Living in the dreary attic near Becky, she goes from despair to perseverance. Although Sara saves herself, the connection to India gives sustenance, and she's aided by the fairy tale's traditional genie as well as an animal helpmeet.

These days, as Hollywood stumbles along, its record on children's films is amazingly solid: *The Secret Garden, The Lion King, Little Women,* and now *A Little Princess.* All of them grave, comforting, and in the best instructive tradition. As Todd McCarthy points out in his elegant *Variety* review Warner's would do well to treat this new Cinderella like royalty. It's on my 1995 Top 10.

Also reviewed in:
CHICAGO TRIBUNE, 5/19/95, Friday/p. L, Michael Wilmington
NEW YORK TIMES, 5/10/95, p. C13, Janet Maslin
NEW YORKER, 5/29/95, p. 96, Terrence Rafferty
VARIETY, 5/1-7/95, p. 35, Todd McCarthy
WASHINGTON POST, 5/19/95, p. D1, Rita Kempley

LIVING IN OBLIVION

A Sony Pictures Classics release of a JDI Productions/Lemon Sky Productions film. *Executive Producer:* Hilary Gilford. *Producer:* Michael Griffiths and Marcus Viscidi. *Director:* Tom DiCillo. *Screenplay:* Tom DiCillo. *Director of Photography:* Frank Prinzi. *Editor:* Camilla Toniolo. *Music:* Jim Farmer. *Sound:* Mathew Price. *Sound Editor:* Hal Levinsohn and Eliza Paley. *Casting:* Marcia Shulman. *Production Designer:* Therese Deprez. *Art Director:* Scott Pask and Janine Michelle. *Set Dresser:* Betsy Alton. *Costumes:* Ellen Lutter. *Make-up:* Chris Laurence and Laura Tesone. *Running time:* 91 minutes. *MPAA Rating:* Not Rated.

CAST: Steve Buscemi (Nick Reve); Catherine Keener (Nicole); Dermot Mulroney (Wolf); Danielle von Zerneck (Wanda); James Le Gros (Chad Palomino); Rica Martens (Cora); Peter Dinklage (Tito); Hilary Gilford (Script); Michael Griffiths (Sound); Matthew Grace (Boom); Robert Wightman (Gaffer); Kevin Corrigan (Assistant Camera); Tom Jarmusch (Driver); Ryan Bowker (Clapper); Francesca DiMauro (Food Service Supervisor); Norman Field (Hair/Make-up Artist); Lori Tan Chinn (Costume Designer); Vincenzo Amelia (Cook); Laurel Thornby (Nicole's Mother).

LOS ANGELES TIMES, 7/21/95, Calendar/p. 4, Kenneth Turan

"Living in Oblivion" is a crooked valentine to the independent film world, a bemused and caustic billet-doux to the boys and girls who don't quite have the clout to figure in "The Player" but end up addicted to the business anyhow.

As the cinematographer of Jim Jarmusch's "Stranger Than Paradise" and the director of the Brad Pitt-starring "Johnny Suede," writer-director Tom DiCillo has certainly been there. And he has turned his experience into a clever and consistently funny inside-movies comedy, a witty revenge against the dream factory, low-budget division, that won the Waldo Salt Screenwriting Award at the Sundance Film Festival.

Starring some of the best actors in the independent world, including Steve Buscemi, James Le Gros and Dermot Mulroney, "Oblivion" is an intricately constructed film-within-a-film, gathering in one small place every problem, both conceivable and otherwise, a struggling film might encounter.

Originally concocted as a half-hour short to showcase actress Catherine Keener (the co-star of "Suede" and Mulroney's wife), "Oblivion" has a quirky three-part structure in which film, reality and fantasy double back on one another. Each section involves a single scene that put-upon director Nick Reve (Buscemi), the kind of intense young *cineaste* who has a poster for Fritz Lang's "M" on his bedroom wall, is trying desperately to commit to film.

The first section, which approximates the half-hour short, is the most ingeniously structured, with color (for the film-within-a-film, also called "Living in Oblivion") alternating with black-and-white. As take succeeds take, with problems piling up like cordwood, we meet the movie gang, in many ways more compelling than the material they're struggling with.

Nicole (Keener), whose big "Ellen Talks to Mom" scene is being shot, wants to be taken seriously as an actress but is universally known as the girl who had a celebrated shower scene with Richard Gere. And her confidence isn't helped by overhearing crew members cattily ripping her to bits.

Not initially prone to doubt is Wolf (Mulroney), the self-absorbed director of photography who lives with forceful assistant director Wanda (Danielle von Zerneck), and, as his leather vest, beret and eventual eyepatch indicate, fancies himself the artist on the set.

The funniest member of this team, though he doesn't know it, is Nicole's co-star, Chad Palomino (Le Gros), who appears in the second section. A Hollywood player set to star next as "the sexy serial killer Winona Ryder shacks up with," Palomino is a fatuous oaf slumming in the indie world who drives everyone crazy with his womanizing, his improvisations ("Just stop me if I'm out of line") and his scattershot flattery. "I want to learn from you," he tells Nick earnestly. "You're the genius." This is easily the most pointed portrait in the film, as well as the most humorous, fueling speculation at Sundance that DiCillo had drawn just a bit on his previous experience with Brad Pitt.

"Oblivion's" third section has poor Nick trying to shoot a dream sequence while coping with a troublesome dwarf and a rambunctious smoke machine. It's not quite up to the standard set by the first two, but it does provide an opportunity to nicely wrap things up.

Though "Living in Oblivion" may sound like a one-joke movie, the pleasure of the endeavor is that it has no trouble holding your interest without feeling repetitive. Mark it down to the excellence of the acting, including the smallest roles, and the amusing and accurate way the ambience of bargain-basement filmmaking is captured.

This realism extends from the physical look of the production to movie terminology to, most important, the psychology of the business. Everyone in the production, from the gaffer to the director, is to varying degrees ambitious, egocentric, rife with insecurities, in constant need of reassurance and eager to push his or her own agenda. But, hey, it's only a movie. Isn't it?

NEW STATESMAN, 11/10/95, p. 35, Jonathan Romney

8½, that bottomless abyss of film on film, would probably not have seemed as magisterial if Fellini had decided to top up the extra half by adding another explanatory layer—by publishing his own notes on making the film. The new American comedy *Living in Oblivion*, on the other hand, rather benefits from the pithy, self-deprecating diary, *Eating Crow*, that Tom DiCillo has collated to accompany his script. For one thing, it lets you know just why DiCillo is so sardonically downbeat about the role of the director—a job that *8½* doesn't exactly demystify. Fellini's alter-ego in his film is a rather grand demiurge of an anti-hero riddled with confusion and embarrassment, but at bottom secure in the knowledge that from his very embarrassment wonderful jewelled monsters would burgeon.

For DiCillo's battered creator Nick—played by the eloquently frazzled Steven Buscemi—creative agony isn't in it; that might come later, *after* you've persuaded the boom operator to stop dropping his mike into shot, *after* you've dealt with the tender ego of the narcissistic male lead, or in DiCillo's own case, *after* you've realised that you only have $50 left in your pocket to see you through the Sundance Festival. It's a far cry from the new Antonioni film *Beyond the Clouds*, in which the film director hero wanders through Europe searching for a story to tell. But there's the traditional distinction; we look to European cinema for art, to the American independents for more pragmatic angst among the baseball caps and gaffer tape.

Living in Oblivion is that thoroughly unfashionable thing, a film about film-making. Both in his film and his notes, DiCillo milks the insider gags for all they're worth, but why shouldn't he? It looks as though they're the only compensation for the hellish job he's in. This is a one-joke film, but then so was *8½*, and that joke, in a nutshell, is: so you think this is easy? It's the account of director Nick's hideous experience attempting to shoot what looks like a hideous film, entitled, of course, *Living in Oblivion*. Nick's film has everything you'd expect to find in a lousy US indie film: a heartfelt confession about parental abuse, an incongruously upmarket love scene in evening dress, and a dream sequence involving a top-hatted dwarf bearing an apple. The scene is only there, in fact, so that the actor Nick hires for the part can give him a furious harangue about the stereotypical idiocy of using a dwarf as a dream image.

The humour flows remarkably smoothly, bearing in mind the film's overall tone-tense, constantly balanced on the verge of hysteria. In fact, the whole thing looks deceptively like an improvised diversion—a sketch grown to feature proportions, coasting thanks to a witty cast who have the well-seasoned feel of familiar sitcom players. In fact, as the diary reveals, the film started life as a short that DiCillo decided to knock together with some friends, while waiting in desperation to get his next feature financed. It expanded almost by accident, but DiCillo's account makes you realise how traumatic and laborious even such happy accidents can be.

Casual as it looks, there's a remarkably sophisticated game of structuring going on in the film, part of which goes to disguise the join between the original short—which provides the first part of the film—and the final version. Without spoiling its best surprises, suffice to say that it's done by juggling levels of narrative and different types of film stock, and springing some surprising new changes on the old truism that in cinema, it is *not what is seems*. DiCillo also takes some brilliant risks with his cast—for example, in the way he shows us his lead actress Catherine Keener making wonderful sensitive work out of Nick's appalling script, only to wreck her performance deliberately with a stray microphone or a duff bit of lighting. In his notes, DiCillo makes it clear how much he owed to the good will of his cast: all you can say is, they must *really* have been good friends.

DiCillo portrays himself on paper as a desperate case, a bitter ironist with a negligible income after his first feature—the over-mannered *Johnny Suede*—became a *succès d'estime* and not much else. *Eating Crow* is brilliant on several counts—on the rivalry between independent film-makers who loathe their peers for getting the funding that eludes them, on the vapid business mores that mean that anyone with half a name will be surrounded by no-hope sycophants and ambulance chasers, and by petty moguls only too happy to better their fragile egos even further. DiCillo portrays film-making as a job that no one in their right mind would want—the only thing worse than hanging around between takes is hanging around between films, but he turns the chagrin to brilliant advantage. As a way to get even with an abnormally demanding day job, *Living in Oblivion* is a serious undertaking; but it avoids giving the impression of taking itself at all seriously. As an exercise in celluloid navel-gazing, it's a lot more fun than comparable exercises by Wim Wenders, Abel Ferrara and, if it comes to that, Fellini too, who never had qualms about using dwarves in dreams.

NEW YORK, 7/31/95, p. 45, David Denby

In the funniest sequence of *Living in Oblivion*—a neat independent film about the making of an independent film—a nervous young actress (Catherine Keener), playing a big scene with her "mother," goes through take after take of the same emotions, each take destroyed by some tiny error of the crew's. Gradually, the actress's concentration shreds. Watching this, we may become so impressed by this dis-illusioning of the film medium that we forget that Keener and director Tom DiCillo are creating a new illusion right before our eyes. *Living in Oblivion* might be called an on-the-cheap *Day for Night*. We're in downtown Manhattan, not the south of France, and the grunge and desperation levels are rather high. Among the movie's satirical pleasures, one must count the appearance of James Le Gros doing a sensational sendup of Brad Pitt, and the performance of Peter Dinklage as a huffy dwarf actor who doesn't like being essentialized ("Do you dream of dwarves? Even *I* don't dream of dwarves").

NEW YORK POST, 7/14/95, p. 42, Thelma Adams

In Tom DiCillo's jaundiced view, filmmaking is one big pain in the butt—and crammed with comic potential. Writer/director DiCillo's "Living in Oblivion" darts behind the scenes on a low-budget shoot to check out the dreamers and schemers spooling around in cinema's low-rent district.

A temperamental dwarf, a preening star, a neurotic starlet, a desperate director, a beret-wearing cinematographer and a wandering mother cross paths in the airless sound stage that's the setting for a mediocre movie-within-a-movie and a hilarious sendup of "the collaborate art."

DiCillo structures his hip soap opera among the shooting set in three parts: two anxiety dreams and a day of shooting a dream sequence from hell. In this omnibus nightmare that switch-hits between black-and-white and color, the bits are better than the whole, but the laughter's a constant.

Steve Buscemi plays Nick Reve. The harried helmer looks like an R. Crumb messiah with his hobo chin growth, lank long hair and I-have-suffered saucer eyes. Low-budget staple Buscemi ("Reservoir Dogs") tears into a lead role tailor-made for him. For Reve (French for dream), filmmaking is one big anxiety dream that he can only control by piercing through his fear with caustic humor.

DiCillo began this film as a short to showcase Catherine Keener, the star of his first, overlooked feature "Johnny Suede." Keener plays Nicole, an actress whose claim to fame is a shower scene in a Richard Gere flick. Trying to break through to stardom with a lead in a small movie, Nicole is plagued by the nightmare that she will end up slinging hash at a diner.

Keener's best moment comes early on. Shooting—and reshooting—a scene entitled "Ellen talks to Mom," the actress-within-the-actress must get progressively worse as take follows take. Nicole finally digs deep and transforms the flat dialogue into raw emotion. She hits her mark—but the cameras aren't rolling. It's riotously funny and a keen reminder of how much goes into every frame and what a small fraction the viewer actually sees.

Keener's real-life husband, Dermot Mulroney ("Bad Girls"), camps it up playing Wolf, the black-leather-wearing, self-involved cinematographer whose macho image belies a soft-hearted chump who trails puppy-like after ambitious assistant director Wanda (Danielle von Zerneck).

Wanda has her eyes on the most powerful guy on the set: Chad Palomino (James Le Gros). Le Gros does a broad riff on Brad Pitt (the star of "Johnny Suede"), creating a ladykiller airhead under a shock of honey-colored hair. Chad is taking a break from Hollywood because, he tells Nick, "I'm not into that Hostess Twinkee s--t."

"Living in Oblivion" played to receptive insider audiences at the Sundance Film Festival, where DiCillo won the Waldo Scott Screenwriting Award, and New Directors/New Films at the Museum of Modern Art. The challenge facing this offbeat comedy is attracting the wider audience it deserves among those who appreciate Hostess Twinkees but occasionally have a yen for a lemon tart.

NEWSDAY, 7/14/95, Part II/p. B5, Gene Seymour

It's possible to imagine half the Quentin Tarantino wannabes who see "Living in Oblivion" being frightened into the insurance business by the film's broad, agonizingly funny depiction of independent moviemaking. Just as possibly, the other half will think: "Whoa! This is *way* cooler than I thought it would be!"

That writer-director Tom DiCillo's second feature is capable of drawing both reactions says a lot about his ability to temper the bitter and the sweet of his experience into an entertaining whole. "Living in Oblivion" (an odd title for such a knockabout farce) has some of the same poky charm of DiCillo's first feature, "Johnny Suede," without that film's coy, hand-me-down surrealism. The dreams and nightmares swirling through *this* movie seem, by contrast, far more real, especially when things go over the top, which they often do.

Anxiety is "Oblivion's" drive wheel and DiCillo couldn't have found a more appropriate actor than Steve Buscemi for the wheel's hub. Best known as one of "Reservoir Dogs'" hot-wired thugs, Buscemi is a seething pile of jitters as Nick Reve, who's trying to direct a masterpiece on a shoestring while holding onto his sanity.

The film is told as a series of anxiety dreams, the first of which is done in black-and-white as Nick struggles to capture an intimate mother-daughter scene over New York street noise. Every take is spoiled by some snafu. The catering's a health hazard, the crew's a platoon of space cadets and the equipment's as second-rate as Nick's script.

Nicole (Catherine Keener) is Nick's leading lady, a talented, magnetic but hopelessly insecure actress known only for an oft-cited "shower scene with Richard Gere." She has a quickie with her leading man, an overbearingly narcissistic movie star named Chad Palomino (James Le Gros, who's a howl). Nick can't finish shooting a love scene between the two without serious ego spillage from Chad.

The third segment isn't a dream. (I don't think.) But, in a way, it's the most nightmarish of all. Nick tries to film a surreal scene involving Nicole in a wedding dress and a grim dwarf in formal dress (Peter Dinklage).

Murphy's Law is enacted once again: Wolf (Dermot Mulroney), Nick's leather-garbed cinematographer, can't concentrate on the shoot because his girlfriend (Danielle von Zerneck), who's also the assistant director, has just dumped him. The dwarf is ticked off at being used as a prop. (He's got a point.) And Nick's mother has wandered from her institution onto the set. Even the fog machine's in an uncooperative mood.

As with "Johnny Suede," "Oblivion" often assumes a zoned-out state that mirrors the fictitious crew's mental capacity. But DiCillo's laugh-out-loud moments compensate for the movie's lapses. Whaddya say, kids? Wanna make a movie?

SIGHT AND SOUND, 11/95, p. 46, Ben Thompson

In New York, director Nick Reve struggles to make a low-budget film. His lead actress Nicole Springer, is nervous about a very difficult scene in which she confronts her mother with her feelings about traumatic events in her childhood. This is because this scene echoes one in real life that her real mother died too soon for her to play out. A complex mix of characters are at work on the shoot—among them bossy assistant director Wanda and temperamental cinematographer Wolf—and a series of mishaps frustrate them; a sound boom keeps dropping into the frame, focus is lost, a light explodes. The actresses run through their lines again to collect themselves, and achieve the perfect take with no film in the camera. A persistent beeping noise sends Nick into a tantrum. It's the noise of his alarm clock. He wakes from his nightmare.

Nicole wakes up after an ill-advised one-night-stand with her moronic leading man Chad Palomino. The next day's filming goes very badly. Palomino's macho antics distract the crew and his increasingly absurd suggestions for the big love scene plunge the whole set into chaos. When Nicole overhears him complaining about her to Nick, and boasting about their sexual liason, she humiliates him in front of the camera and a fist-fight develops which Nick joins in with. As a battered Palomino limps off the set, Nick tells Nicole the whole film is really about her and they kiss. She wakes from her dream.

On the real set, the filming of a dream sequence becomes the stuff of nightmares. Nick's mother (who bears an uncanny resemblance to the mother actress in his dream) turns up, having escaped from her old people's home by walking through walls. The smoke machine explodes and the dwarf hired to lend a sinister quality to the dream sequence takes umbrage at his stereotypical role and marches off the set. Nick is about to throw in the towel when his mother steps into the dwarf-shaped breach and—to universal sighs of relief—a suitable dream sequence is completed.

Tom DiCillo's second feature (after 1992's widely-praised but disappointingly soulless *Johnny Suede*), *Living in Oblivion* has been a long time coming but it turns out to be richer and more entertaining than anyone had a right to expect. At first glance the subject matter looks alarmingly self-indulgent—the opening shot is a slowly looming close-up on a well-used movie camera—and how much mileage can possible be left in that old "It was only a dream" device? Quite a lot, as things turn out.

There's a whiff of self-referential flannel about the writer/director's insistence that the stuff going on behind the camera is often a lot more interesting than the stuff going on in front of it, but it only takes a few moments of *Living in Oblivion* to realise that something authentic and intriguing is going on. The grainy black and white opening segment sucks the viewer into the film-making process with consummate skill. The sequence in which Catherine Keener's performance progressively deteriorates through seven retakes is not only superbly-acted, it also invites the audience to make the kind of judgements about what constitutes a convincing characterisation that they routinely entrust to the director. The fine gradations that divide success and failure are compellingly hard to discern under this kind of intense analysis.

The opening third of *Living in Oblivion*—the director's dream sequence—was originally shot as a complete short with a view to possible expansion to full feature length. It would have been easy for the completed film to lose its way from there on in, but the characters and their inter-connecting tensions expand happily to fill the available space. The atmosphere broadens and gets progressively more comic with accrued complexity. The scenes in which Chad Palomino lets his creative juices flow with ever more ridiculous suggestions are hilarious, even without remembering that DiCillo is the man whose debut film gave the mighty talent of Brad Pitt its first significant cinematic exposure.

All the actors appear to be enjoying themselves. If Catherine Keener resents the fact that a film which was originally conceived as a showcase for her eventually becomes one for the rat-like loveability of Steve Buscemi, she does not show it. This is the second film in the last couple of years (the first was the excellent *In the Soup*) in which Buscemi has shone in the potentially irritating role of struggling film-maker. Someone somewhere has got the message, because he is currently shooting his own debut feature.

Tom DiCillo's greatest achievement here is to demystify the film-making process without robbing it of its thrill, its beauty or even, in the end, of its mystery. The man still best known as Jim Jarmusch's one-time cinematographer has given a beguilingly human face to the dreams and nightmares of American independent cinema.

TIME, 8/28/95, p. 69, Richard Corliss

[*Living in Oblivion* was reviewed jointly with *The Usual Suspects*, see Corliss' review of that film.]

VILLAGE VOICE, 7/18/95, p. 45, Georgia Brown

The wonder is that there aren't more movies about moviemaking given that this fraught group activity readily provides plot essentials such as interpersonal tension and intrapersonal delusion (not to mention mass hysteria). If *The Player* kicked off the recent trend of satires about the business, on-the-set pictures so far have been rare, with Truffaut's *Day for Night* still being the one to beat. With half of all high school grads (I'm taking an informal survey) thinking about going into movies, clearly there's a public primed to see beyond the frame. Or thinking that they can. Demystification can create more mist. A minor but effective character in Tom DiCillo's charming *Living in Oblivion* is a quirky fog machine.

DiCillo—cinematographer on Jarmusch's *Stranger Than Paradise* and director of the whimsical yet melancholy *Johnny Suede*—divides his cryptically titled second feature into three parts: The first turns out to be the director's anxiety dream; the second, an actor's anxiety dream; the third, the real-life shooting of an anxiety dream sequence. If I'm blithely giving away a couple of punch lines, let me just say that dreams, here as in *Johnny Suede*, are no stranger than reality and that reality—represented tentatively by the final segment—serves up the oddest images. *Oblivion*'s three skits are of equal weight, yet DiCillo poises the film more to turn on itself than to progress.

Our fictional indie filmmaker, played by Steve Buscemi, is named Nick Reve, and you should know that *rêve* is French for dream. Nick may be dreaming, but he's also revving up for another brutish day on the set. Today, he's shooting a difficult, supposedly critical sequence, "Ellen talks to Mom." Ellen is played by Nicole, a winning though insecure actress, who, in turn, is played by Catherine Keener. Nervous Nicole gets picked up by an inscrutable driver (Tom Jarmusch, brother of Jim), who next picks up Cora (Rica Martens), the actress playing Mom in the day's psychodrama. On the set, Nick is patient but tense, as shot after shot is spoiled by screwups—a boom entering the frame (twice), the focus-puller's distraction, a passing boombox. Nicole eventually loses it but the spacey Cora, a true Mom, comes to her rescue and the two improvise a poignant sequence that has onlookers weeping. Too bad the lovesick leatherboy cameraman, Wolf (Dermot Mulroney), is in the john vomiting his guts out.

Oblivion's first third was shot as a half-hour short, a valentine to Keener, who'd been in *Johnny Suede*. Then DiCillo was encouraged to turn the piece into a feature—a pleasure, he say's in the press notes, since the small ensemble shoot was so easy compared to *Suede*'s aggravations.

Much in this farce will appeal to those who've spent time on a set—meaning just about every New Yorker. For example, Wanda-the-assistant director (Danielle von Zerneck), all honey-toned with Nick and foul-mouthed with the crew. Like every other woman on the set, Wanda is panting to get into bed with the leading man, a callow cad named Chad Palomino (James Le Gros). After spending one night with his costar, he's ready for the next victim. Le Gros, who's only in the second segment (Nicole's nightmare), is as puffed in his tux as an Emperor Penguin. You can't say DiCillo favors his director over actors and crew, however. Buscemi's stressed-out Nick is a chump and appears to have no talent whatsoever; his precious movie looks incredibly dopey. Which gives you an idea of the movie's quite severe limitations. This may be a comedy about moviemaking but it's not a movie about movies.

If you believe rumors, *Living in Oblivion*'s in-joke is that the jerky Palomino is based on *Suede* star Brad Pitt. If this seems hard to believe, given Pitt's sweet, low-key, perfectly modulated Johnny, it just goes to show how smoothly the camera lies, how impossible it is for fools like you and me to tell actors from roles, stars from the luster they cast, or angels from assholes.

Also reviewed in:
CHICAGO TRIBUNE, 8/25/95, Friday/p. J, John Petrakis
NATION, 8/14-21/95, p. 181, Stuart Klawans
NEW REPUBLIC, 8/14/95, p. 24, Stanley Kauffmann
NEW YORK TIMES, 7/14/95, p. C8, Janet Maslin
VARIETY, 1/30-2/5/95, p. 47, Todd McCarthy
WASHINGTON POST, 8/11/95, p. F6, Hal Hinson
WASHINGTON POST, 8/11/95, Weekend/p. 39, Desson Howe

LORD OF ILLUSIONS

A United Arrtists Pictures release of a Seraphim production. *Executive Producer:* Steve Golin and Sigurjon Sighvatsson. *Producer:* JoAnne Sellar and Clive Barker. *Director:* Clive Barker. *Screenplay:* Clive Barker. *Director of Photography:* Ronn Schmidt. *Editor:* Alan Baumgarten. *Music:* Simon Boswell. *Music Editor:* Paul Rabjohns. *Choreographer:* Alexandre Magno. *Sound:* Stephen Halbert and (music) Rick Winquest. *Sound Editor:* John A. Larson and Lewis Goldstein. *Casting:* Sharon Howard-Field. *Production Designer:* Stephen Hardie. *Art Director:* Marc Fisichella and Bruce Robert Hill. *Set Decorator:* David A. Koneff. *Special Effects:* Lou Carlucci. *Visual Effects:* Thomas C. Rainone. *Costumes:* Luke Reichle. *Make-up:* Gigi Williams. *Make-up (Scott Bakula):* Laura Gorman. *Stunt Coordinator:* Cliff Cudney. *Running time:* 109 minutes. *MPAA Rating:* R.

CAST: Trevor Edmond (Young Butterfield); Daniel Von Bargen (Nix); Kevin J. O'Connor (Philip Swann); Joseph Latimore (Caspar Quaid); Sheila Tousey (Jennifer Desiderio); Susan Traylor (Maureen Pimm); Ashley Lyn Cafagna (Young Dorothea); Michael Angelo Stuno (Lead Male Cultist); Keith Brunsmann (Snakeman); Barbara Patrick (Lead Female Cultist); Scott Bakula (Harry D'Amour); Wayne Grace (Loomis); Mikey LeBeau (Exorcised Boy); Robb Humphreys (D'Amour's Demon); James Brandon Shaw (Motel Bellboy); Johnny Venokur (Tapert); Jordan Marder (Ray Miller); Barry Del Sherman (Butterfield); McNally Sagal (Detective Eddison); Famke Janssen (Dorothea Swann); Joanna Sanchez (Clemenzia); Joel Swetow (Valentin); Stephen Weingartner (Stage Manager); Daniel Edward Mora, Jr. (Stage Technician); Billy McComb (Walter Wilder); Vincent Schiavelli (Vinovich); Lorin Stewart (Billy Who); Barry "Shabaka" Henley (Dr. Toffler); Bergen Lynn Williams (Nurse); Mike Deak (Apparition in Repository).

FILMS IN REVIEW, 11-12/95, p. 103, Victoria Alexander

[*Lord of Illusions* was reviewed jointly with *The Prophecy*; see Alexander's review of that film.]

LOS ANGELES TIMES, 8/25/95, Calendar/p. 10, Kevin Thomas

Imagine Charles Manson, possessed of supernatural powers, locked in combat with Philip Marlowe and you'll have some idea of stylish horrormeister Clive Barker's latest blood-and-guts thriller, "Lord of Illusions."

It's Barker's most ambitious venture to date, and he projects a vision of evil with such implacable cinematic impact that it sustains its substantial gore quotient better than its predecessors—and even survives a number of moments of unintended humor. "Lord of Illusions" looks sensational, and it gives Scott Bakula a long overdue chance to show he can carry a big picture on the big screen.

Rugged, intelligent and sensitive, Bakula is ideally cast as Barker's New York private eye Harry D'Amour, who's hired to go to Los Angeles to track down a man wanted for insurance fraud. It looks to be a piece of cake until Harry follows his quarry into a Venice fortuneteller's parlor, which proves to be a veritable Gates of Hell.

A couple of plot convolutions later he's caught up with a hugely popular magician, Philip Swann (Kevin J. O'Connor), who promptly dies—or does he?—on stage in a misfired Sword(s) of Damocles act, leaving a beautiful, elegant but clearly haunted widow Dorothea (Famke Janssen). The attraction between Dorothea, ensconced in a vast mansion, and Harry is mutual and immediate but stays unspoken.

What Harry doesn't yet know—but we do, thanks to a prologue set in 1982 in a derelict compound in the Mojave Desert—is that she and Swann were both once in the thrall of the Manson-like Nix (Daniel Von Bargen, very scary), whose powers seem to go beyond the ability to levitate and to get into other people's heads, both of which he certainly does impressively.

It may well be that Nix has imparted to Swann genuine magical powers—that Swann is, in turn, something more than a Lord of Illusions.

The film is loaded with glimpses and portents of unspeakable degradation, and while Barker is fortunately not one to linger morbidly, he confronts Harry with a series of nasty, sadistic types who are far more evil than anyone Marlowe ever had to tackle.

Within its classic noble-knight-strifes-to-save-fair-lady plot, Barker raises the question of whether, within the realm of magic, the line between trickery and the supernatural can actually blur. Barker, who uses Hollywood's Magic Castle as a key setting and source for magic lore, aptly refers to Harry Houdini in this regard.

Houdini believed that he could contact his wife after his death, but after he failed to do so, some years later Mrs. Houdini appeared in a movie exposing phony spiritualists who preyed on those desperate to contact their dead loved ones.

Like "Mortal Kombat," "Lord of Illusions" has superb production design, special effects and cinematography—plus a driving score that capture the jolting contrasts of Southern California life in which a tasteful, seemingly secure existence of wealth and luxury and the sordid and bizarre not infrequently collide. "Lord of Illusions" belongs to Bakula, but he gets staunch support on both sides of the camera. Be sure to stay for the end crawl, during which Diamanda Galás is heard singing "Dancing in the Dark" as you've never before heard it.

NEW YORK POST, 8/25/95, p. 40, Michael Medved

For the most part, Clive Barker's "Lord of Illusions" is a gruesome mess, but somewhere, rattling around beneath all the gore and goo, the prolific horror specialist has fastened onto some intriguing ideas.

The movie's main concern seems to be the hazy dividing line between illusionists and true magicians. From Harry Houdini through David Copperfield, there's always been something inescapably creepy about the most talented practitioners of "magic."

Even though rational people recognize that what the performer does is just sophisticated trickery, these impressive stunts can lead the audience—and even, at times, the illusionist himself—to suspect some supernatural power.

That's certainly the case for Philip Swann (Kevin J. O'Connor) the millionaire Las Vegas-style magician at the center of "Lord of Illusions." He boasts a spacious mansion in the Hollywood hills and a stylish wife (former model Famke Janssen), but also bears the burden of a dark past.

At one time, he studied with a whacked-out wizard named Nix (Daniel von Bargen), a master performer who ultimately inspired a religious cult whose members combined the least attractive features of the Branch Davidians and the Manson gang. In any event, the movie begins with a bloody scene from 1982 when young Swann helps murder his one-time mentor, then buries the body—with an iron mask clapped over the face and screws drilled deep into the temples—somewhere in the desert.

Thirteen years later, something goes horribly wrong in Swann's glitzy stage show, and this mishap bears some obvious connection to plans by surviving followers of the diabolical Nix to bring their boy back from the dead. Meanwhile, Swann's wife finds comfort from this confusion in the arms of a hard-boiled film noir private detective (Scott Bakula) she has summoned not only from another city (New York), but seemingly from another movie altogether.

As author of some 30 popular books, Clive Barker knows how to keep a story moving along; there's so much going on, in fact, you hardly have a chance to slap your forehead over the film's many idiotic moments. Barker's previous directorial effort, "Hellraiser," demonstrated that subtlety isn't exactly his strong point, but he knows how to deploy memorably disgusting special effects without altogether stopping the momentum of the narrative.

The main problem here is the acting, which seldom rises to a professional level. TVs Scott Bakula takes a Quantum Leap in the wrong direction, embarrassing himself with the same confused, furrowed-brow expression as reaction to everything from romantic ecstasy to excruciating pain.

And speaking of pain, the film's over-produced conclusion, with Nix's partially decomposed body rising from the slab, makes obnoxious attempts at deeper resonance by invoking well-known Christian imagery. "Jesus!" one observer exclaims, while another declares, "Christ in heaven!"

Meanwhile, the sadism and mutilation in scene after scene begin to take a toll on our patience. This isn't just the goriest film of the year, but the abundance of its blood-spurting horrors easily exceeds the combined total of any 10 other 1995 releases. If this seems to you any sort of recommendation, then you should be consulting a psychiatrist rather than a film critic.

NEWSDAY, 8/25/95, Part II/p. B4, John Anderson

Who is the title character in Clive Barker's new and eagerly awaited "Lord of Illusions"? Barker, of course. In a tale that coyly poses the artifice of showbiz sleight-of-hand against the evils of "real" magic, the filmmaker sits back (smiling, we like to think) and spins the whole thing like a bewitched basketball.

Not that he doesn't score. On the basis of the "Hellraiser" series and his prolific writing, Barker is the uncrowned king of the horror hill, and his stories and films always take an overworked genre a few steps beyond—beyond what, of course, usually being the operative question (and the deciding factor in whether you want to indulge yourself. For fright fans, though, "Lord of Illusions" has plenty of qualities, even if consistency isn't among them.

We arrive in the Mojave, 1982, where Barker drops us in the middle of what looks like a Manson family argument. As two vehicles race toward a house on a dusty desert road, we pass dead chickens and fire, two sure signs of bad hoodoo; inside, a group of spaced-out disciples is watching Nix (Daniel von Bargen) balance fire in his hand. Swann (Kevin J. O'Connor) arrives with his posse in tow, armed to the teeth and out to get Nix, who's kidnapped a 12-year-old girl and is menacing her with a leashed mandrill. Nix asserts his considerable authority, which he has appropriated from the very bowels of hell. Swann is momentarily disoriented by the Nix mind-warp. He comes to his senses. Shots are fired. Nix is ventilated. Swann and the others make sure his grave is very deep.

Up to this point, "Lord of Illusions" is a riveting, state-of-the-art creep show. We're left hanging to a great degree, because we have no idea what's going on, but it doesn't matter: While films of horror and fantasy work best when they supply a dramatic infrastructure—some kind of mythology, even an invented one, that explains why people are doing what they do—Barker gets away without it, because he compensates with an air of such dread.

But can he keep it up? Of course not. He peaks too early, but it's fun while it lasts—even if it makes the rest of the film last twice as long as it might have.

We skip ahead 13 years and 3,000 miles to New York, where private investigator Harry D'Amour (Scott Bakula) has just saved a young boy during an exorcism. Again, we're not supplied with many details, just the implication that Harry and the supernatural may be old friends. Getting down with the devil is hard work, though: When he's offered a trip to Los Angeles to track a low-rent swindler on an insurance scam, Harry says OK. He could use the tan.

Once there, naturally, he runs smack into the Swann-Nix psychodrama, which is claiming victims and real estate as Butterfield (Barry Del Sherman), one of Nix' lost boys, tries to find his master's grave and raise him up again; one pictures Nix aging like a fine wine, just waiting for that special occasion. Well, the occasion has arrived.

Bakula, formerly of TV's "Quantum Leap," is a kind of undergraduate Harrison Ford. He's pleasant enough onscreen but, lacking any dark edge, isn't really what we want. He's obviously what Barker wanted, though, since the story—in which Swann has become a David Copperfield-style illusionist with the skills Nix taught him—grows continually more preposterous and less dreadful as time goes on. The plot takes detours to romance with Harry and Swann's wife Dorothea (Famke Janssen) destined for each other—one passionate kiss elicited gales of laughter at the screening I attended, it was so inappropriate/predictable. What's most disappointing in "Lord of Illusions" is the way Barker has to keep accelerating the mayhem to maintain his momentum. This leads to some impressive special effects and makeup, but just as many ludicrous turns in the story, which wasn't so bad to begin with.

VILLAGE VOICE, 9/5/95, p. 74, Gary Dauphin

Fright meister Clive Barker has gone from the typewriter to the directors chair three times, but his best film to date is still *Hellraiser*. Barker's fascination with baroque visual texture (ornate masks, torture chambers, s/m costumes, and rigorously symmetrical production design) dovetailed with the horrific turn of his literary imagination in *Hellraiser*; inspiring the "visionary" moniker that might soon seem like empty hype if Barker keeps making unfocused films like *Lord of Illusions*.

Lifted from his series of short stories about psychic PI Harry D'Amour (a serviceable Scott Bakula), *Illusions* is less interesting as a traditional horror movie than as a kind of Los Angeles nightmare: New York-based D'Amour goes to LA on a simple insurance fraud case and becomes enmeshed in a war of the illusionists, a heebie-jeebie battle royale that pits a showman with real powers and his lady friend (newcomer Famke Janssen) against a desert madman replete with his own cult. D'Amour's investigation doesn't seem to have much to do with the mysteries of power and evil that consumed a film like *Hellraiser*. Instead, Barker takes you on a tour of the atmospheric but slightly flat locales he imagines must compose L.A.'s magical underworld: Venice tarot parlors, Hollywood Boulevard theaters, the opulent hillside dwellings of rich adepts, and the rotting, rural compounds of dupes in starch of transcendence. As far as chills, this film has a few but they're tame compared to the visual shocks of *Hellraiser* and some of Barker's written work which makes you wonder if the Lord of Illusions might not turn out to be Barker himself.

Also reviewed in:
CHICAGO TRIBUNE, 8/25/95, Friday/p. H, Michael Wilmington
NEW YORK TIMES, 8/25/95, p. C6, Stephen Holden
VARIETY, 8/21-27/95, p. 67, Joe Leydon
WASHINGTON POST, 8/25/95, p. D6, Richard Harrington

LOSING ISAIAH

A Paramount Pictures release. *Producer:* Howard W. Koch, Jr. and Naomi Foner. *Director:* Stephen Gyllenhaal. *Screenplay:* Naomi Foner. *Based on the novel by:* Seth Margolis. *Director of Photography:* Andrzej Bartkowiak. *Editor:* Harvey Rosenstock. *Music:* Mark Isham. *Sound:* Thomas Nelson. *Casting:* Aleta Chappelle. *Production Designer:* Jeannine C. Oppewall. *Art Director:* William Arnold. *Set Designer:* Suzan Wexler and Cydney M. Harris. *Set Decorator:* Jay Hart. *Costumes:* Mary Malin. *Running time:* 108 minutes. *MPAA Rating:* R.

CAST: Jessica Lange (Margaret Lewin); Halle Berry (Khaila Richards); Davidd Strathairn (Charles Lewin); Cuba Gooding, Jr. (Eddie Hughes); Daisy Eagan (Hannah Lewin); Marc John Jefferies (Isaiah); Samuel L. Jackson (Kadar Lewis); Joie Susannah Lee (Marie); Regina Taylor (Gussie); La Tanya Richardson (Caroline Jones); Jacqueline Brookes (Judge Silbowitz).

FILMS IN REVIEW, 7-8/95, p. 58, Andy Pawelczak

Losing Isaiah wants to have it every which way. It raises serious questions about racial animosity and alienation and then blurs all the issues in the manner of a sentimental TV movie, Jessica Lange is beautiful and charismatic—a shot of her smoking a cigarette in the rain evokes an almost forgotten Hollywood romanticism—but her character is so undeveloped—as are all the others—that at the end you'd be waiting for the film to begin if you weren't so relieved that it's finally over.

Margaret Lewin (Lange) is a hospital social worker who insists on saving an abandoned crack child that a white doctor has callously given up on. She decides to adopt the child, for reasons not altogether clear—one brief scene suggests that she's an idealistic workaholic with compelling unmet needs. Lange's performance hints at forces working in Margaret that the script doesn't begin to touch on—it's a classic case of an actress making something out of almost nothing. What comes through most clearly is a radiant maternal archetype—Margaret is full of passionate solicitude for the difficult, hyperactive child, a solicitude which at times verges on the obsessive, though the film doesn't go anywhere with that idea either.

Margaret's opposite number is Khaila (Halle Berry), the child's crack-addicted biological mother. In the early scenes of the movie, we see her wallowing in melodramatic degradation, but once she undergoes rehabilitation—which seems to take place painlessly—she turns into a stable young woman who wants her child back. She gets the help of a lawyer—perhaps a toned-down version of C. Vernon Mason, played by the versatile Sam Jackson—for whom the case has political reverberations. The rest of the film focuses on the courtroom drama in which the ideological issue is laid out should poor black children be adopted by affluent white parents who can't provide them with a black identity? It's a real question, one filled with history and anguish, but don't expect an answer, at least not one that will satisfy any of the contending parties on the dangerous ground of race in America.

As Khaila, Halle Berry is in over her head, or she would be if the script gave her anything real to do. Mostly she just looks good in the manner of a high-fashion model displaying the latest street styles. David Strathairn as Margaret's frustrated, philandering husband (his infidelity is exposed in the witness box in a moment reminiscent of the O.J. trial) does his usual competent job, and Cuba Gooding, Jr. appears in an utterly inconsequential role as a fast-talking young man interested in Khaila. The movie's most striking performance is given by the child who plays Isaiah as an explosive bundle of high strung nerves and overreactions. The direction, by Stephen Gyllenhaal, is no more than it should be. *Losing Isaiah* won't add anything to the national discourse on race, and if remembered at all it will be for a few shots of Jessica Lange that might have come out of a different movie.

LOS ANGELES TIMES, 3/17/95, Calendar/p. 1, Peter Rainer

"Losing Isaiah" is highly affecting balancing act. It has all the elements of a TV movie-of-the-week tear-jerker: A white social worker, Margaret Lewin (Jessica Lange), adopts an African American crack baby, Isaiah (played as a 3-year-old by Marc John Jeffries), and the baby's biological mother Khaila (Halle Berry) tries to get him back. The scenario—by Naomi Foner, based upon the Seth Margolis novel—plays, at least superficially, like a compendium of socially conscious playlets. We're enlisted in a guided tour of controversy about transracial adoption, single motherhood, black-white racism, day care and marital infidelity.

And yet, "Losing Isaiah" doesn't come across as a screed or, despite a few swerves into mawkishness at the end, a weepy. Director Stephen Gyllenhaal brings out the passion in the material without slobbering all over us. He understands the importance of what is ultimately at stake here—Isaiah's future.

We first see Margaret in the Chicago hospital where Isaiah has been rushed after nearly being crushed to death inside a garbage truck compactor. Khaila, out of her mind on crack, had deposited him the night before in a cardboard box in an alley and then forgotten to retrieve him. When she comes to, she thinks she's killed him and gets herself arrested for shoplifting and then incarcerated for three years in an inmate-run drug rehab program.

Margaret has the worn, somewhat blowzy look of a woman who has been wrung out by caring. She has developed a professional stance: gregarious and a bit peremptory. She has disdain for the doctors who consider babies like Isaiah, born with multiple defects, low priority.

But we also sense something distinctly missing in her life. Her husband, Charles (David Straithairn), doesn't appear to satisfy her need to connect emotionally: He's an intelligent, somewhat closed-off man who wants more care from his care-giver wife. Isaiah brings out in Margaret her own wounded, valiant fortitude, her need to turn love into a crusade. She's enamored of Isaiah's fighting spirit—and she wants to be a part of his triumph.

The bulk of the film's conflict comes when Khaila, out of prison and living in an overcrowded apartment in the projects, discovers her baby is still alive and sues to get him back. She has been rehabilitated, although her life is a constant, grueling temptation to return to crack, and the news that Isaiah is alive sends her into a messianic state equal to Margaret's. In a way, the boy has become both Margaret's and Khaila's reason for living; and one of the most vivid crosscurrents in the movie is the way both women inspire their claims for motherhood.

They are divided by their opposing interests, and yet their love for Isaiah can't help but unite them too. (When Margaret first sees Khaila in the courtroom, she's thunderstruck by her beauty.) Fighting for Isaiah, these dueling mothers are like twin spirits. It seems unspeakably cruel that their very love should have brought them to this place.

The film crosscuts between the lives of Margaret and Khaila, and the back-and-forth movement reinforces the slugged, abrupt quality of their days once the battle begins. It also cuts back on the amplitude of the performances. Lange and Berry work in potent, compact episodes and sometimes, especially with Lange, one wants to be with them for a longer stretch. It's a testament to the film's emotional power that you always want more than it gives you—but it's also an indication of how overextended it sometimes is.

The filmmakers bring front and center the issues of transracial adoption; they position Isaiah as a kind of test case. In this they mimic the lawyers for both sides, especially Khaila's (played by Samuel L. Jackson), who appear to be using the child as a political football. The courtroom scenes are gripping but also more conventional than the film at its best, where political considerations take second-billing to the deep, conflicting passions of the two women. The court proceedings frame those passions, but they also subtract from them—emotionally, we've already gone beyond them.

Even though the conflict in "Losing Isaiah" is, literally, black and white, Gyllenhaal and Foner don't stack the deck for either Margaret or Khaila, and that's as it should be. They've taken a situation that is, almost by design, unsolvable (even though a solution is finally provided). They give themselves over to the women's competing claims without preconception; they allow each woman her due. The actresses respond with an all-out fervor.

Few current directors can match Gyllenhaal's work with actresses: Barbara Hershey has never been better than in his TV movies "A Killing in a Small Town" and "Paris Trout," and Sinead Cusack in "Waterland" and Debra Winger in "A Dangerous Woman" were also startlingly good. Halle Berry, whose previous movie work has mostly been decorative, comes through with a powerful piece of work.

Jessica Lange does too—nothing new in that. Her Margaret seems to be harboring some deep sorrow, even before Isaiah enters her life. When she fears Isaiah may be taken away from her, she has a brief scene where she whispers fairy tales to him in bed, and there's a mysterious, compelling suspense in her whisperings, as if she yearned to be whisked away from this world with Isaiah to a real fairy-tale realm. Lange gives the film its core of knockabout sadness.

In the best sense, "Losing Isaiah" is the kind of film that makes audiences want to talk about it afterward.

NEW YORK, 4/3/95, p. 59, David Denby

In *Losing Isaiah*, Jessica Lange gives all of herself, every breath and stray hair. There's something peasantlike about her; she has the physical power of a farm woman cutting wheat. Lange is a great actress stuck in an inferior period of Hollywood moviemaking, and in such films as *Blue Sky*, playing a nymphomaniac Army wife, she seemed cast adrift. But Lange is surprisingly effective in *Losing Isaiah*, a much more conventional movie. Her Margaret Lewin, a Chicago social worker, adopts an abandoned black baby—a boy dumped into the garbage—and then refuses to give him up when his natural mother, repentent and shipshape, wants him back. The screenwriter, Naomi Foner (adapting a novel by Seth Margolis), doesn't simplify things. She makes it clear that Margaret, somewhat estranged from her daughter and husband, latches on to the baby as her salvation (as well as the baby's salvation); and Lange makes the woman stiff and will-driven and not always intelligent, with a streak of righteousness approaching fanaticism. Halle Berry, as the crack-addicted mom who goes straight, doesn't have as interesting a role to play, but she's skillful and moving too.

The material, generically and stylistically, is TV-movie-of-the-week, with each scene making one point and one point only. But Foner and director Stephen Gyllenhaal don't soften anything; they examine the conflicting claims (a stable home against a natural mother of the same race), and they discover that both women are right, both wrong. *Losing Isaiah* is a decent, upright piece of work. The two women fight for the child with logic and emotion, and the movie holds both forces in balance. I wasn't entertained, exactly, but at least I was not insulted. Yet *Losing Isaiah* is not enough. If we're going to have women in pairs, let's have them freed from exhausted old fictions.

NEW YORK POST, 3/17/95, p. 49, Michael Medved

In a Chicago alley in the dead of winter, a crack-addicted young mother (Halle Berry) places her 3-day-old baby in a cardboard box beside a dumpster.

Rushed to the hospital at the point of death, the infant manages to hang on, and attracts the attention of a dedicated white social worker (Jessica Lange).

Eventually, she and her husband (David Strathairn) adopt the baby, who grows into an enchanting, affectionate toddler. By the time he's 3, however, his birth mother emerges from prison and a tough drug rehabilitation program to track Isaiah down and claim him as her own.

She wins the aid of an idealistic lawyer (the always formidable Samuel L. Jackson) who accepts the case for political reasons. "Black babies belong with black mothers," he flatly declares. Predictably, the adoptive family refuses to give up without a fight and the conflict moves to a courtroom confrontation.

That legal battle represents the core of "Losing Isaiah," a new movie that hopes to capitalize on the public's fascination with several well-publicized recent cases involving birth parents who try to take their babies back from couples who have adopted them.

What makes the struggle in the film even more dramatically compelling than its real-life counterparts is the script's careful balance between the claims of the child's two mothers; screenwriter Naomi Foner ("Running on Empty") takes "great pains to show there are no villains here and arms both sides with potent arguments.

The problem is that unequal performances by the principals throw all calculations out-of-whack and destroy the movie's intended "you-be-the-judge" objectivity.

Halle Berry, a splendid actress who's hovered for years at the verge of the super-stardom she deserves, delivers a characterization that is a triumph of both subtlety and substance; Jessica Lange, on the other hand, comes across as washed-out, whiny and one-dimensional, playing all her big scenes in such an unhinged, hysterical tone that she sacrifices much of the audience sympathy her character would otherwise attract.

It hardly helps matters that Berry is one of the most radiant and dynamic young stars in today's Hollywood, while the supremely gifted Lange never before has been presented as so dowdy, tired and middle-aged.

The movie's contrived conclusion makes matters even worse, offering a surprise plot twist that seems designed to satisfy every sensibility in the audience, and incongruously fastens a huggy-hopeful resolution onto an inherently tragic situation.

Nevertheless, Stephen Gyllenhaal (director of last year's over-praised "A Dangerous Woman," with Debra Winger) wins solid performances from most of his cast) including an amazingly intense and varied acting job from a beautiful 4-year-old named Marc John Jeffries as Isaiah. The moody, jazz flavored musical score by Mark Isham offers another significant plus, as does Cuba Gooding Jr. in a brief part as a fast-talking charmer from the projects who is pursuing Berry.

With such substantial assets, "Losing Isaiah" isn't entirely a lost cause, but it remains so unbalanced that even its most wrenching emotional moments leave as intrigued, but unmoved.

NEWSDAY, 3/17/95, Part II/p. B5, Jack Mathews

Do black babies, under all circumstances, belong with black parents? Is a crack baby found in a trash bin at birth better off with the ex-crack addict mother who discarded him than he would be with the affluent white couple who adopted him? Did director Stephen Gyllenhaal or anybody else involved in the making of "Losing Isaiah" really want to answer these questions?

I have not read the Seth Margolis novel from which "Losing Isaiah" is adapted, but I'll take it on faith that the book had something pertinent to say about the grotesque rise in the number of cocaine-addicted Dumpster babies, and how these children may be best served by society. The filmmakers did nothing more than raise the issue, lay out some of the arguments, then walk away from it themselves.

Jessica Lange, whose interest in the project is the only explanation for its having eluded the more suitable made-for-TV format, acts up a storm as the social worker who adopts a newborn rescued from a Chicago alley, and two years later has to battle the birth mother in court for the right to keep him. But for all the love, pain and anguish her Margaret Lewin goes through, and which seems to drain the life right out of Lange's face, we don't learn the most basic thing about her. Why was she obsessed with having the baby in the first place?

The answer, I'm afraid, is that it was in the script. Gyllenhall and screenwriter Naomi Foner, his wife and collaborator (they worked together on "A Dangerous Woman"), were so anxious to get to the conflict of the film—the racial arguments over Isaiah's welfare—that they glossed over the character motivation leading to it.

There are hints in the beginning, and nothing more, that Margaret may be trying to fill an emotional void. Her teenage daughter is in the separation-from-parents stage, and the look we see her husband (David Strathairn) give one of the women at work suggests that all may not be well in the marriage.

But nothing really explains Margaret's impulsiveness at the hospital, where she is smitten by the struggling abandoned baby and, like a kid with a stray puppy, insists on bringing him home.

The movie rushes along on parallel tracks for 40 minutes or so, showing the adjustments in the Lewin household to Isaiah in their all-white community, and the gradual recovery of his guilt-ridden mother Khaila (Halle Berry) in the inner city. When Khaila learns that her son is still alive and that a black advocacy group is willing to fund and represent her in a custody fight, the scene is set.

If you know your TV movies, this is where the sociology and data are laid out in dramatic speeches. One expert witness testifies to the neurological damage inflicted on crack babies. Another talks about the problems of identity for a black child raised outside the black culture. And the judge has to decide the nature-nurture merits of motherhood; which is best for Isaiah, the person he knows and loves as his mother, or the stranger who *is* his mother?

"Losing Isaiah" makes some very dubious arguments before it cops out and makes no argument at all. You can admire the earnestness of the performances of Lange and Berry, though the latter's short-term transition from addled, illiterate junkie to concerned, clear-headed mother is a bit too much to swallow. But if the filmmakers had no point of view to espouse, no answers to any of their own questions, we have to ask one more thing.

Why did they bother?

VILLAGE VOICE, 3/21/95, p. 57, Gary Dauphin

Isaiah has two mommies: There's Khaila Richards (Halle Berry), the black crackhead and prostitute who forgets her baby Isaiah on a dumpster while "buggin' and druggin'"; and then there's Margaret Lewin (Jessica Lange), the friendly social worker who falls in love with the shrieking foundling and adopts him into her sunny, white suburban home. As Isaiah (played by a remarkably expressive four-year-old named Marc John Jefferies) grows and grows, he bonds with Margaret and the Lewins, hyperactive and prone to outbursts in the way generally ascribed to crack babies but otherwise snug in the understanding folds of Margaret's mother love. On the dark side of Chicago, Khaila goes through jail, rehab, literacy training, and a hellish rented room in the projects, alternately hostile to her counselors and gentle to the children similarly consigned to the graffiti-ridden Henry Horner houses.

As fundamentally conservative as it is earnest, *Losing Isaiah* has the difficult task of having to push two conflicting sets of sympathy buttons, which instead of producing a complex look at its various social problems (addiction, rehabilitation, poverty, transracial adoption) settles into a gauzy haze of good intention that never lifts. When Khaila discovers that Isaiah is still alive (after having resigned herself to the idea that he'd died in the trash), it takes about five minutes for her to start spying longingly on him in the playground, 10 for her to take up legal counsel (an upright and smirky Samuel L. Jackson), setting the Lewins' attitude that possession is nine-tenths of the law against Khaila's need to finally mother her child.

The conflict between Khaila and Margaret is a pretty odd one as race-based battles royale go. Margaret's first reaction to Khaila (besides noting that junkies who abandon their babies should be in jail) is to swoon with terror that "she's so beautiful," whereas Khaila mounts a self-improvement campaign, which among other things includes getting religion and blowing off a suitor (a pleasantly goofy Cuba Gooding Jr.). Berry gives the performance of her career, her character conveying a moral certitude as dependent on Berry's slim-necked good looks as it is the script's belief in Khaila's sincerity. Lange is, as ever, an avatar of fortysomething white female skittishness, as credible cooing for Isaiah as she is breaking down and calling Khaila an animal or blacks "you people." It doesn't take a Solomon to know how things will end for Isaiah, but call it a sign of the times when the law finds that black children should be with black mothers, but black mothers have to concede that sharing is the highest form of caring.

Also reviewed in:
CHICAGO TRIBUNE, 3/17/95, Friday/p. C, Michael Wilmington
NEW YORK TIMES, 3/17/95, p. C8, Janet Maslin
VARIETY, 3/20-26/95, p. 47, Todd McCarthy
WASHINGTON POST, 3/17/95, p. B1, Rita Kempley
WASHINGTON POST, 3/17/95, Weekend/p. 38, Desson Howe

LOVE AND HUMAN REMAINS

A Sony Pictures Classics release of a Max Films/Atlantis Films coproduction. *Executive Producer:* Roger Frappier and Pierre Latour. *Producer:* Roger Frappier. *Director:* Denys Arcand. *Screenplay (based his play "Unidentified Human Remains and the True Nature of Love":* Brad Fraser. *Director of Photography:* Paul Sarossy. *Editor:* Alain Baril. *Music:* John McCarthy. *Music Editor:* Bruce Lange. *Sound:* Dominique Chartrand and Marcel Pothier and (music) Earl Torne. *Sound Editor:* Marcel Pothier. *Casting:* Deirdre Bowen, Lynn Kressel, Lucie Robitaille, and Stuart Aikins. *Production Designer:* François Seguin. *Set Decorator:* Jean Kazemirchuk, Michèle Nolet, and Ginette Robitaille. *Special Effects:* Louis Craig. *Costumes:* Denis Sperdouklis. *Make-up:* Micheline Trépanier. *Stunt Coordinator:* Yves Langlois. *Running time:* 99 minutes. *MPAA Rating:* R.

CAST: Thomas Gibson (David); Ruth Marshall (Candy); Cameron Bancroft (Bernie); Mia Kirshner (Benita); Rick Roberts (Robert); Joanne Vannicola (Jerri); Matthew Ferguson (Kane); Aidan Devine (Sal); Robert Higden (Editor); Sylvain Morin (Drag Queen); Ben Watt (Native Boy); Karen Young (Singer); Serge Houde (Cowboy); Alex Wylding, Polly Shannon, and Annie Juneau (Victims); Maurice Podbrey (Theatre Director).

LOS ANGELES TIMES, 6/23/95, Calendar/p. 4, Kenneth Turan

English has not been good to Denys Arcand.

Working in his native French, Arcand became one of Canada's most accomplished directors. His previous works include the intelligent and witty "The Decline of the American Empire" and "Jesus of Montreal," both international successes. And now comes the runt of the litter, "Love and Human remains."

Arcand first film in English, "Remains" is based on a play by Brad Fraser, who also wrote the screenplay. Though the original was reputedly a success in several countries, it is hard to see why based on what's provided on screen.

"Remains" is yet another "love in the age of AIDS and anxiety" saga, with the camera following seven loosely connected characters as they search for relationships in the most tedious places. It's not so much that we've seen all this before, though we have, it's that the protagonists this time around are maddeningly dreary.

The story pivots around two roommates, David (Thomas Gibson) and Candy (Ruth Marshall), who were lovers before David realized he was gay and took to saying clever things like "Honey, I'm homo" when he enters their apartment.

As if this weren't troublesome enough for Candy, she is dissatisfied with her job as an underpaid book reviewer and is having trouble sorting out her social life. Should she get involved with that nice bartender (Rick Roberts) who keeps mooning over her or try something completely different with the persistent lesbian (Joanne Vannicola) she's met at the gym?

David is by far the more prominent and off-putting of these characters, a former actor who says he became a waiter because "it's more artistically satisfying." A bored, sarcastic club-hopper, David may be unpleasantly smug and self-centered, but that doesn't stop everyone else from finding him simply fascinating.

That group of admirers include a 17-year-old busboy (Matthew Ferguson) who has a crush on him, a bemused dominatrix with a psychie streak ("Exotica's" Mia Kirshner) and a childhood friend (Cameron Bancroft) whose most noticeable characteristic is that he just might be the only person in town who's even more unpleasant than David.

Adding a certain undefined quality to the mix is the fact that a serial killer is stalking the un-named city where these people live, and the film offers periodic chances to watch the evil-doer at work. That's about as edifying as it sounds.

Few things are as enervating as a movie that thinks it's hip but isn't. Filled with deluded emotional deadbeats, "Love and Human Remains" offers no reason why anyone should want to chart the progress of its characters' insect lives. As for Denys Arcand, he has done better than this before and surely will again.

NEW YORK POST, 6/2/95, p. 51, Thelma Adams

Corny, kinky Canadian killer movie—now that's a genre!

Angularly attractive David (Thomas Gibson) loves boys, the younger the better.

Leather-clad baby doll Benita (Mia "Exotica" Kirshner) whips men while telling them Campfire Girl ghost stories.

Navel-gazing Candy (Ruth Marshall) dabbles in girls.

Square-jawed civil servant Bernie (Cameron Bancroft) is simply yuppie scum.

Love eludes them; death doesn't.

The aptly titled "Love and Human Remains" crosses sex among the sublet set with a movie-of-the-week serial killer plot. It's an uneasy mix that never quite comes together in Brad Fraser's pithy but spineless script.

The characters are more fashionable than fresh—and their psychologies are pure "Oprah." David is a recovering child star; Benita hints at sexual abuse at her father's hands; Candy binge eats; and, well, Bernie wears a trench coat and a tie.

Denys Arcand ("Jesus of Montreal") seems to be sucked into the same vacuum as his characters in the talented French-Canadian director's first English-language movie. Arcand's social commentary cum sex thriller hungers for a strong identity but remains split and uncertain.

A drawing room farce, scene provides the movie's high point. Boys and girls cross paths in a gender-bending crescendo of snappy wit and snapping tempers. Real pain begins to surface in a group so lost, alone and self-possessed that they need the Mounties to help them find the way back to their own hearts

NEWSDAY, 6/2/95, Part II/p. B5, John Anderson

When considering crime fiction, the idea seems natural enough: Present a cast of characters with ordinary, or even not so ordinary, problems—but in situations that are well within the limits of belief.

Then, introduce murder into the mix—not as something the audience has expected all along but the way it usually happens, as a stark, raving disruption of the existing universe. The result? The grimmest kind of realism and a dramatic catharsis worthy of the subject matter.

So why isn't it done, and done often? Because it doesn't work, and it really doesn't work in "Love and Human Remains," Denys ("Jesus of Montreal") Arcand's screen version of Brad Fraser's play. The convergence of the heinous and the humdrum simply renders everything inconsequential: Personal problems lose their gravity when contrasted with the violent loss of life; murder, when treated as an afterthought to dating anxiety, loses weight. The audience feels trivialized, too—especially when the film's thrust isn't the murder at all but a septet of young Canadian urbanites wrestling with their uncertain sexuality and interlocking relationships.

David (Thomas Gibson), for instance, is a scathingly cynical waiter and former teenage sitcom star for whom homosexuality is both a wound and a shield. He lives, unthreateningly, with Candy (Ruth Marshall), a book editor and loser at love who thinks a lesbian relationship might be the answer—one the elfin Jerri (Joanne Vannicola) will be happy to provide, if she can nip Candy's budding interest in bartender Robert (Rick Roberts). Meeeeeanwhile, David's attentions are split between his Pan-like busboy Kane (Matthew Ferguson), his friend Benita (Mia Kirshner), a psychic/dominatrix, and his hetero-sexual buddy Bernie (Cameron Bancroft), whose attitude toward women needs some major structural overhauling.

It's one big extended unhappy family. Within this "Big Chill"-meets-"Go Fish"-meets-"Melrose Place" scenario, someone is killing young women (there is also safe and unsafe sex, which is far less shocking than the movie seems to think). Is there a parallel between the sexual violence on the street and the psychosexual injuries being sustained by our erotic tag team? Perhaps. There may also be a parallel between the "Geraldo" show and 100 chimps with typewriters. Whether it's worth the examination is a whole other question.

Here's another: Do the problems of "Love and Human Remains" belong to Arcand or Fraser? Both—one for writing banality, the other for filming it. Arcand, however, has done a lot more for Fraser than Fraser's done for him.

SIGHT AND SOUND, 8/94, p. 44, Trevor Johnston

Montreal. David, a former actor waiting tables, bemoans changing times with old friend Bernie, a city office worker. Dominatrix Benita whips a customer. A young girl is brutally murdered by an unknown assailant. After unprotected oral sex with occasional male lover Sal, David returns home to his flatmate Candy, a struggling book reviewer, with whom he previously had an unsuccessful heterosexual relationship. Bernie arrives, blood-stained from a scuffle and looking for a place to crash.

The next day, Candy is approached at the gym by female teacher Jerri, but later agrees to a date with bartender Robert. Teenage waiter Kane recalls with some affection David's role in a popular TV series. Having subsequently agreed to Jerri's offer of a date, Candy leaves Robert's apartment when his physical designs on her become too apparent. As the killer claims another female victim, David takes Kane to see Benita, whose psychic gifts reveal that the latter is in love with him. Jerri reveals her feelings for Candy, while Bernie confesses his despair to David. Dismayed by a tape of his old TV show, David later eschews sex with Kane, returning home to discover Candy has forsaken awkward love-making with Jerri for the sanctuary of his bed. The following evening, however, her sex with Robert is interrupted by a female caller on the answerphone.

Candy is at home waiting for Robert when Kane arrives to talk to David. Even more inconveniently, the increasingly obsessive Jerri arrives with a gift for Candy, who treats her harshly—much to the dismay of Robert, who arrives late. After everyone leaves, Candy accuses David of heartlessness, but he maintains his emotional independence. David plays back a phone message from Sal, who reveals he has been diagnosed HIV positive. Candy unsuccessfully tries to patch things up with Robert, while David ferries an aggressive Bernie to see Benita. Her psychic insights identify Bernie as the local serial killer and he swiftly leaves. Back at the flat, Candy is confronted by Jerri, then assaulted by Bernie. Kane saves the day before David returns to confront Bernie, who reveals his love for David before jumping to his death. Later, Kane and Candy accompany David to his first audition in years. Sal meets them at the door to confirm his good health before David tells his two friends, "I love you".

Denys Arcand broke through to international critical and box-office success in his film *The Decline of the American Empire*. In it, he juggled the manifold sexual manoeuvrings among a group of determinedly bourgeois college academics as the pretext for testing the primacy of individual over collective fulfilment within a de-politicised society in terminal moral decay. 1989's *Jesus of Montreal* played out a nudgingly put on Passion amid the triviascape of contemporary media culture, to probe our bases for belief in an era where faithlessness has become the norm.

In both films, the veteran Canadian radical managed to balance the sense of lofty pronouncement with a deft and only half-serious satiric touch, accurately zeroing in on whatever it was the chattering classes were chattering about that week. With this latest offering, however—significantly, not written by Arcand but adapted by Brad Fraser from his play *Unidentified Human Remains and the True Nature of Love*—that appearance of poise seems to have gone awry. There is enough in the film to suggest that Arcand has his finger somewhere near the pulse of anxiety-haunted sex in the 90s, but here his typically non-judgmental stance of uncommitted observer on a world gone mad seems increasingly like a glossily urbane cover for a worrying paucity of positive insight.

With its Generation X-ish cast of metropolitan fringe dwellers and looming reminders of the spectre of AIDS in the two signposted sequences of unprotected sex, the film seems to tick off as many of today's cultural worry-beads as it can gamely get through. From serial killers, to the legacy of child abuse (dominatrix Benita), to the babble of meaningless media proliferation, it flits hither and thither like the zap of David's remote control, as he grazes idly through multiple TV channels. This is an image Arcand pointedly repeats, underlining its metaphoric associations with the divergences in moral certainty that throw up a climate of choice upon choice but little conviction or guidance.

What is fresh and true about the film, however, is the authentic seam of physical and emotional need that Arcand and Fraser mine through such diverse individuals as Thomas Gibson's sardonically aloof homosexual David and Ruth Marshall's desperate literary reviewer. The latter wavers between unsatisfactory experiences with both men and women—all of whom, in turn, are looking for their own Ms Right. Like some lonely hearts column made celluloid, the film certainly appreciates the scale of the issue, yet having to shuttle between so many significant characters does necessarily reduce the audience's potential emotive identification with each of them on an individual level, attractive performances notwithstanding.

As a screenwriter, Fraser has not quite managed to disguise the piece's theatrical origins. The farcical set-piece that brings David, Candy, Kane, Jerri and Robert agonisingly together in the same flat at the same time remains one of the film's funniest moments. But the climactic assault that wheels Jerri into the apartment to confront Candy over their failed liaison, brings the now-deranged Bernie in through the window to attack her and then manages to have teenager Kane on hand as her salvation, is notably unconvincing. Although the opening-out for the screen has allowed the resident serial killer more scope to roam the Montreal underpasses, Arcand seems as uninterested in the mystery slayer angle as a plot motor as he is by the psychic interludes with barely integrated plot device Benita, throwing red herrings at the rather dim Robert ("Nice tofu!" he proclaims, sitting down on Candy's prize futon) and supplying a weak, vaguely suspect motivation for the all too obviously unhinged Bernie. Here is a character who turns mass murderer in rage at his repressed, unrequited love for the best male friend who abandoned him: let the protestors who railed at *The Silence of the Lambs* make of that what they will.

Finally, the suicidal Bernie's last words are echoed by David's (genuinely) cheery fade-out line, "I love you", suggesting that the world would really be a much better place if we all cared about each other that little bit more. For someone who sets himself up as a knowingly chic commentator on our vanities and mores, this is a bathetic point of arrival. There again, with Arcand, a man whose eyebrow seems permanently raised, one can never be sure whether it is 'seriously' intended or not. He may tacitly tut-tut at our deficiencies in moral gravitas, but his own wry ambivalence looks more and more like a smokescreen around a hollow centre.

VILLAGE VOICE, 6/6/95, p. 47, Georgia Brown

Even when Canadian director Denys Arcand (*The Decline of the American Empire*) tries to be passionate and indignant (*Jesus of Montreal*), his work comes out stone cold and calculated. Such is the curse on Canadian art (think of Atwood, Egoyan, Cronenberg). Arcand's latest, *Love and*

Human Remains—adapted by Brad Fraser from his, *Unidentified Human Remains and the True Nature of Love*—is a zeitgeist film that sends Arctic gusts down the spine. Its chic thrills remind me of the recent *Shallow Grave*; perhaps it will enjoy the same brief vogue.

One difference between the extended circle in *Human Remains* (played by a young ensemble, many of them making screen debuts) and the frolicsome trio in *Grave* (note title convergence) is that the Scots are more yuppily employed. In *Remains*, the main character, David (Thomas Gibson), takes pride in being a waiter after having once starred in a sitcom. "I find being a waiter more artistically satisfying," he boasts. For sex, David visits gay clubs; for guy talk, he gabs on a rooftop with his childhood friend Bernie (Cameron Bancroft); for puppy love, he encourages the affections of a 17-year-old busboy (Matthew Ferguson). Another friend (Mia Kirshner from *Exotica*) happens to be a psychic dominatrix with a fairly pathetic set of clients. For swift banter as well as old-fashioned cuddles, there's his roomie and former lover, Candy (Ruth Marshall), a book reviewer who's considering, in the abstract, turning lesbian. When the intense Jerri (Joanne Vannicola) comes on to her in the gym, Candy follows through but is more attracted to a freckled, risky bartender, Robert (Rick Roberts).

Plus, one of these confused souls is a serial killer. Young women who wander at night keep turning up dead, earlobes bloody where their earrings were ripped off. Leads, or misleads, point to several members of the above circle. With psychos and AIDS—definitely a factor here—whom can you trust? There's every contamination except the Ebola virus. The creepy stuff signals how frightening contemporary life is and how dangerous love is.

Production notes report that all vegetation was carefully eliminated from the film to enforce the urban nightmare aspect. Arcand trains his lens on empty stretches of interstate and sections of cloverleaf (the concrete kind) as metaphors for sterility and anomie. But where a film like *Shallow Grave* was at least consistent, ending in a rousing defeat for human kindness and solidarity, *Human Remains* suddenly turns, yikes, mushy. At least it tries to. Such a chill hangs over the theater, however, that a few "I love you"s are hardly bracing enough. Maybe they should've planted bushes and trees.

Also reviewed in:
CHICAGO TRIBUNE, 6/23/95, Friday/p. J, Michael Wilmington
NEW YORK TIMES, 6/2/95, p. C4, Caryn James
VARIETY, 9/20/93, p. 28, Todd McCarthy
WASHINGTON POST, 7/7/95, p. F6, Frank Ahrens

MAD LOVE

A Buena Vista Pictures release of a Touchstone Pictures presentation. *Producer:* David Manson. *Director:* Antonia Bird. *Screenplay:* Paula Milne. *Director of Photography:* Fred Tammes. *Editor:* Jeff Freeman. *Music:* Andy Roberts. *Music Editor:* Steve McCroskey. *Sound:* Nelson Stoll and Fred Runner. *Sound Editor:* Fred Judkins. *Casting:* Dianne Crittenden. *Production Designer:* David Brisbin. *Art Director:* Mark Worthington. *Set Designer:* Mary Finn. *Set Decorator:* Gene Serdena. *Set Dresser:* David M. Bowen and Chris Karges. *Costumes:* Michael Joseph Long. *Make-up:* Fern Buchner. *Stunt Coordinator:* Webster Whinery. *Running time:* 99 minutes. *MPAA Rating:* PG-13.

CAST: Chris O'Donnell (Matt); Drew Barrymorre (Casey); Matthew Lillard (Eric); Richard Chaim (Duncan); Robert Nadir (Coach); Joan Allen (Margaret); Jude Ciccolella (Richard); Amy Sakasitz (Joanna); T.J. Lowther (Adam); Kevin Dunn (Clifford); Elaine Miles (Housekeeper); Sharon Collar (Librarian); Selene H. Vigil (Singer); Valerie M. Agnew (Drummer); Roisin Dunne (Guitar); Elizabeth F. Davis (Bass); Todd Sible (Bartender); Leslie Do Qui (S.A.T. Monitor); Patrick Ryals (Vice Principal); Angela Hall (Dr. Laura Genel); Hunt Holman (Nurse Barry); Sandra Singler (Orderly); Allen Galli (Medication Nurse); Greg M. Gilmore and David J. Guppy (Patients); Liev Schreiber (Salesman); Angelina Calderon Torres (Landlady); Stefan Enriquez (Waiter); Yvonne C. Orona and Pedro Garcia (Mechanics).

LOS ANGELES TIMES, 5/26/95, Calendar/p. 14, Kevin Thomas

Chris O'Donnell and Drew Barrymore soar in "Mad Love," but the film itself is grounded in a TV-movie feel. It lacks the style and personality to make its young-lovers-on-the-run tale seem fresh rather than way too familiar.

Within the luminously beautiful Barrymore, there's both a shimmering, mercurial expressiveness and a wounded vulnerability that makes her perfect casting for Casey. She's the new girl across the Seattle-area lake from the home of O'Donnell's Matt.

Casey is so much more sophisticated than the boyish-looking Matt, who is drawn to her surely in part because of her streak of recklessness. Casey zeros in on Matt's vulnerability, which is that his mother deserted him, his father, his younger brother and sister. It's amazing yet credible—given Casey's charisma and passion and his own suppressed, troubled history—that the steady, self-disciplined Matt so swiftly throws over the traces and runs off with Casey only to discover how dangerous her anarchic spirit can be.

Antonia Bird, director of the controversial "Priest," has inspired her two young stars to take the kind of risks that yield portrayals of terrific range, depth and appeal. Unfortunately, this seems the limit of her and writer Paula Milne's inspiration. We never learn the root cause of Casey's instability, and just what role her authoritarian father (Jude Ciccolella) may or may not have in her condition.

More effective are her mother (Joan Allen), who gradually asserts herself against her dominating husband, and Matt's father (Kevin Dunn), who's a conscientious single parent.

If it accomplishes not a whole lot else, "Mad Love" does show to great advantage O'Donnell, who underplays in impressively sustained fashion, and especially Barrymore, who radiates a timeless, indelible star quality.

NEW YORK POST, 5/26/95, p. 42, Michael Medved

Lady Caroline Lamb famously described her lover, Lord Byron, as "mad, bad and dangerous to know"—a description that is equally apt for Casey Roberts, the character Drew Barrymore plays in "Mad Love."

Casey represents the worst nightmare for any parent of adolescent boys: a glamorous nutcase so passionately alive and appealingly unpredictable that it's easy to see how an otherwise well-adjusted kid could forget about family and future to follow her down the path of self-destruction.

Chris O'Donnell lays her admirer, Matt, a cleancut high school senior who selflessly helps his single father raise two much-younger siblings.

He's the last person you'd expect to fall for irresponsible Casey—which is one of the reasons he falls so hard.

After one of her semi-annual suicide attempts, she winds up in a psychiatric hospital, from which Matt helps her to escape.

They hit the road, hoping to build a new life together in New Mexico.

It's a challenging premise for a motion picture, and in Drew Barrymore, British director Antonia Bird (the Controversial "Priest") has found a formidable leading lady.

Barrymore's own well-publicized hospitalizations and suicide attempts closely resemble the experiences of the character she plays, a connection which perhaps contributes to the air of total vulnerability she brings to the role.

Co-star O'Donnell as previously demonstrated in "Scent of a Woman" and "Circle of Friends," can project a powerful combination of sweetness and strength, though he does seem a bit too solid (and somewhat too old) for the part he's playing here.

Director Bird overstates nearly everything. When Matt spots Casey for the very first time, he's looking at the stars with his telescope, but then trains his sights on the giggling, buck-naked neighbor girl who's enjoying a moonlit jet-ski frolic on the lake that fronts their houses.

And there's a problem of consequences: In their merry flight, the mad lovers smash up one car, steal another, play with firearms, and illustrate other forms of dysfunctional and anti-social behavior with no lasting repercussions.

The movie goes soft and easy on these kids: Casey's supposed to be "ill," not rotten and manipulative, and the ending included the maddening suggestion that all she needs is a bit of medication and a spot of "therapy" and she'll be good as new.

Barrymore's so bewitchingly watchable in the role that she makes us care about this character even though, like the other people in this movie, we ought to know better.

NEWSDAY, 5/26/95, Part II/p. B5, Jonathan Mandell

"Mad Love" begins like a "Sleepless in Seattle" for teenagers, a date movie with love songs not by Jimmy Durante and Nat King Cole but by Nirvana and 7 Year Bitch.

He first sees her manically kicking the trunk of her yellow Volkswagen in the parking lot of their Seattle high school. His eyes light up and so do hers, but they do not meet.

He next spots her accidentally with his telescope (he's an astronomy buff) through the window of her bedroom across the lake. She is jumping up and down manically to the latest grunge rock.

Shy, he has his kid brother drop an envelope containing a concert ticket anonymously in her mailbox. She goes to the rock club. He joins her on line. Finally, they meet.

"If you want to go out on a date," she says, "you're going to have to ask me."

He asks her.

Will this be love? Of course, Chris O'Donnell—Al Pacino's pal in "Scent of a Woman," and the new Batman's pal Robin in this summer's "Batman Forever" (as well as an Irish heartthrob in "Circle of Friends")—has striking blue eyes and a (frequently unclad) torso suitable, for Teen Beat, but he is also decent and goofily earnest, a cross between a pubescent Paul Newman and an adolescent Ron Howard. (Maybe there's a little Tom Hanks in there too.) Drew Barrymore—E.T.'s pal grown into Whoopi's boy-crazy pal in "Boys on the Side" (and a character named Sugar in "Batman Forever")—is vampy and wild, but also needy, a platinum blond with pouty red lips and expressively inked eyebrows who can both smolder and stew; she's part early Madonna, part baby Bette Davis. (Maybe there's a little Meg Ryan in there too.) This is a pairing made in Hollywood.

But the title "Mad Love" turns out to be something of a pun. So, soon after they have gazed up at the nighttime stars, strolled before a sun-dappled waterfall and had their first few smooching sessions (the camera zooming in sensuously on PG-rated parts of their anatomy), Barrymore's character begins to act a bit strange. She pulls a fire alarm during an SAT test to get his attention. She jumps in the lake late at night. She tries to commit suicide.

She's institutionalized; she suffers, it turns out, from manic depression. Though he's supposed to be a responsible straight arrow, he helps her escape. Suddenly the Seattle high-school romance has turned into a desert road movie, and a tale of adolescent angst.

"Mad Love" is well-intentioned, aimed at teens (with a sound track annoying at times to anyone over 20) but with a responsible resolution that parents can support. Rarely as mindless as such fare often can be, it is, also never as sensitive as it pretends to be. It is surprising that "Mad Love" was directed by Antonia Bird, the same British woman who made the complex and controversial "Priest," because the characters in "Mad Love" seem guided in their actions and interactions less by some complicated mix of passion and compassion, desire and despair than by simple Hollywood convention.

This is a teen movie, so the parents exist only to yell a lot at their kids, and sit around looking concerned. This is a romance, so rather than act like a regular teenager he's a romantic lead, instantly devoted and bafflingly tolerant of her frighteningly erratic behavior. This is a road movie, so it is less important that her symptoms be clinically accurate than that they help create a sense of adventure and suspense.

But don't let's ask for the moon. We have two soon-to-be stars.

NEWSWEEK, 6/12/95, p. 65, Jack Kroll

[*Mad Love*, was reviewed jointly with *Johnny Mnemonic*; see Kroll's review of that film.]

SIGHT AND SOUND, 1/96, p. 45, Nick James

In lakeside Seattle, Matt Leland is a young high-school student helping his father raise his younger brother and sister—Matt's mother left when he was nine. Matt uses his telescope to stargaze, but one night he observes a young woman living on the opposite bank. She, Casey Roberts, turns out to be a new girl at school. Her impulsive behaviour fascinates him. After taking Casey to a concert, they fall passionately in love with one another.

On the day when Matt is sitting an SAT exam, Casey wants to see him so badly she sets off the fire alarm. That night, Matt observes Casey's parents remonstrating with her. She dives into the lake and swims across to him. The following day, Matt learns that Casey has been suspended. Her father tells Matt he can't see Casey any more. Discovering that Casey has been admitted to psychiatric hospital, he pretends to be her brother and finds her tied to her bed because she tried to kill herself. He promises to get her out.

They break out during his next visit and head for Mexico. Casey insists that Matt drive blind for a while under her guidance. He succeeds in overtaking a truck, but then another truck pulls out in front and they career off the road, breaking Matt's Jeep's axle. They catch a ride from a travelling salesman who puts his hand on Casey's knee. She stabs a cigarette in his face and, after a struggle, Casey and Matt steal his car. Casey finds a gun, but doesn't tell Matt.

They take a room in a New Mexican town. Having sold his telescope, Matt goes to buy Casey a dress. While she waits outside, the world crowds in on her. That night Matt finds Casey pasting cut-out eyes on the walls. Later, in a restaurant, Casey breaks down completely. While she is sleeping, Matt calls Casey's mother. Casey wakes, sees him on the phone and drives off in the car. Matt follows, arriving in time to prevent her shooting herself. He persuades her to go back to her parents. Later, back in Seattle, he receives a postcard from her telling him the treatment for manic depression is going well.

The move from experienced British television director to Hollywood auteur is a notoriously difficult one, with many possible pitfalls. There's the sometimes distracting joys of the best and most technologically advanced equipment that Hollywood money can buy, and the more unexpected matter of working with actors who want to embody their roles intuitively before they learn their lines. Stephen Frears and Beeban Kidron are perhaps typical of directors who have made that transition yet neither has taken as bold a plunge as Antonia Bird, who directs here that most quintessentially American of genres, the teen-angst road movie (albeit with a script by a British author).

Not that *Mad Love* is of the glib 'live fast, die young' school of road movie. Paula Milne's script is properly thought out, compassionate for its troubled heroine and keen to make the consequences of the young couple's breakaway from their Seattle families at least logical. Matt and Casey's mad love is not the driven doom-oppressed *amour fou* of French poetic realism or 40s *film noir*, but a more fragile bloom, like a constant game of 'Truth or Dare' played by two shy adolescents—except that one of them, Casey, is a severe manic-depressive. Antonia Bird was suggested for the project because of her frantically-paced but sensitive portrayal of disturbed homeless London youth in the BBC drama *Safe*, which gained a small theatrical distribution outside the UK, and her involvement in *Mad Love* came before the *success de scandale* of her feature film debut *Priest*. The care with which she explores the couple's respective family pressures and sets up their fascination with each other in the first half hour has many of the hallmarks of her British work on such television series as *EastEnders, Casualty, The Men's Room* and *Inspector Morse*—an easy naturalism magnified by a powerful sense of intimacy that is only weakened by the fact that Drew Barrymore and Chris O'Donnell often seem uncomfortable with one another.

And it's appropriate that the physical apparatus of institutional neglect that characterised *Safe*—the reinforced doors, entryphones and ragged mattresses—should here in suburbia be replaced by a psychologically oppressive landscape. The relative ease with which Matt and Casey gain access to one another and flout their parents' wishes doesn't alleviate the sense of distance between Matt's worshipful gaze and Casey's self-obsession. They are misfits drawn together but neither completes the other, even when they make their getaway to New Mexico.

The surface character of Casey—the free-spirited family rebel that Matt assumes her to be at first—is one that Drew Barrymore has played often before (in *Poison Ivy* and *Gun Crazy* for example). While always a magnetic presence, Barrymore's Casey is pretty indistinguishable from her other *femmes fatales*. With Barrymore, you know you are going to get the sultry looks and the sultry dance routine, and it's a pity that she rarely convinces us of Casey's inner torment, especially when O'Donnell has Matt's awkward complexity simmering from the start.

Barrymore is given both the best and the most clichéd moments of the film. Stunt posing on the back of the jeep, cutting eyes out of magazines and pasting them on the wall, staring like a doomed angel from above while Matt 'betrays' her on the phone—these are hoary clichés from the cinema's lexicon of wacky-to-unwell behaviour. Yet against these Bird can craft a beautifully realised scene in which Casey waits outside while Matt is buying her a dress from a thrift store. The camera picks out incidents from the street—a bunch of good ol' boys appraising Casey sexually, a group of mothers and children, the dress being lifted off a tailors dummy in the window. On the one hand these seem like signposts to the many possible futures for Casey but on the other they are part of the ceaseless threatening hubbub of a world that's closing in on her. Barrymore's fierce angel's face is truly poignant here.

But what *Mad Love* really lacks is the pungency of *Safe* and *Priest*. For a road movie, it's so responsible: there is little overt sex and virtually no profanity. While on the run, Matt phones home at every opportunity as if he was *Happy Days'* Richie Cunnigham taking his father's car for a Sunday drive. He and Casey choose to do the most ordinary things together because, for Casey, it's the struggle to do ordinary things that is so difficult. As such they are not the teen rebels that the genre demands, but rather a Tin Man and a Scarecrow Girl without even a wizard to disappoint them. Perhaps the lack of an edge can be put down to the film's bid for a US NC-13 certificate. Even the LA thrash music that drones on behind every action and the postcard coda, in which Casey is "doing fine", feels tacked on and bland. Nevertheless, *Mad Love* is more a near miss than a failure.

VILLAGE VOICE, 6/6/95, p. 52; Amy Taubin

At the *Johnny Mnemonic* "all-media" preview, the audience hooted and talked back to the screen. There were few walkouts, however, which is more than I can say for the "all-media" preview of *Mad Love*. There, the audience began exiting after 20 minutes, although whether the hasty departures should be attributed to the quality of the film or to the large rat dashing up and down the center aisle of what was once Woody Allen's favorite theater is an open question. (When I asked an usher if he knew that there were rats in the hallowed Beekman Theater, he replied, "I wouldn't doubt it.")

Mad Love is as much about *l'amour fou* as one could expect a PG-13 movie could be. Meaning it isn't. The only mad aspect of the relationship between Matt (Chris O'Donnell) and Casey (Drew Barrymore) is that they don't use a condom when they make love for the first time, or anytime thereafter. This has nothing to do with the personal recklessness of the characters and everything to do with the exigencies of the PG-13 rating. In order to insure a PG-13, the film must allow the more naive members of the audience to believe that when the screen fades to black, Matt and Casey stop their kissing and groping and go straight to sleep. To bring a condom into the picture would make things too explicit. Better to encourage unsafe sex than risk an R. The hypocrisy is that *Mad Love* can be released as a PG-13 film while Larry Clarke's *Kids*, a cautionary tale about the perils of unsafe teen sex if ever there was one, will be lucky to get an NC-17.

Mad Love's premise is thinner than the average after-school special. Matt, a responsible high school senior (except in the condom department) falls in love at first sight with the madcap Casey, the new girl in Seattle who drives a yellow VW and grooves to L7. Although Casey seems no more impulsive than Katharine Hepburn in *Bringing Up Baby*, her art professor father—a regular Hilton Kramer he is—has her committed after she's expelled for pulling the fire alarm during the SATs. The film suggests for a while that the cause of Casey's instability may in fact be her father. But as it turns out, her problem is neither bad parenting nor the contradictions of growing up female, but a *chemical imbalance*—which needs to be regulated by prescription drugs administered under psychiatric supervision. The message of the film: straight-up guys should beware a girl who wears her estrogen on her sleeve.

O'Donnell plods through his part like a young Jeff Daniels but without Daniels's hint of self-mockery. Barrymore delivers her lines like Madonna and seems bored out of her mind. Antonia Bird's idea of direction is to insert as many picturesque landscapes as possible. Bird once directed an unflinching piece about London street kids for the BBC. She's better known for *Priest*, a hyperbolic exercise in crosscutting that combines manipulative sentimentally with the polemics of *Hard Copy*. (Friends who were moved to tears by the film tell me that I don't appreciate it because I wasn't raised a Catholic.) *Mad Love* merges the teen milieu of *Safe* with the sexual obsession of *Priest*. If it's meant as a career move, it's in the wrong direction.

Also reviewed in:
CHICAGO TRIBUNE, 5/26/95, Friday/p. L, Connie Lauerman
NEW REPUBLIC, 6/19/95, p. 30, Stanley Kauffmann
NEW YORK TIMES, 5/26/95, p. C16, Stephen Holden
VARIETY, 5/29-6/4/95, p. 54, Emanuel Levy
WASHINGTON POST, 5/26/95, p. F7, Hal Hinson

MAGIC IN THE WATER

A TriStar Pictures and Triumph Films release of an Oxford Film Company/Pacific Motion Pictures production. *Executive Producer:* Karen Murphy and Tony Allard. *Producer:* Matthew O'Connor and Rick Stevenson. *Director:* Rick Stevenson. *Screenplay:* Rick Stevenson and Icel Dobell Massey. *Director of Photographer:* Thomas Burstyn. *Editor:* Allan Lee. *Music:* David Schwartz. *Music Editor:* Sharon Smith. *Sound:* Michael McGee. *Sound Editor:* Jacqueline Cristianini. *Casting:* Debra Zane and Stuart Aikins. *Production Designer:* Errrol Clyde Klotz. *Art Director:* Eric Norlin. *Set Decorator:* T. Michael O'Connor. *Set Dresser:* Richard Patterson and Michael Rouse. *Special Effects:* Randy Shymkiw and Rory Cutler. *Visual Effects:* Gene Warren, Jr. *Costumes:* Monique Prudhomme. *Make-up:* Sandy Cooper. *Stunt Coordinator:* Jim Dunn. *Running time:* 98 minutes. *MPAA Rating:* PG.

CAST: Mark Harmon (Jack Black); Joshua Jackson (Joshua Black); Harley Jane Kozak (Dr. Wanda Bell); Sarah Wayne (Ashley Black); Willie Nark-Orn (Hiro); Frank Sotonoma Salsedo (Uncle Kipper); Morris Panych (Mack Miller); Ben Cardinal (Joe Pickled Trout); Adrien Dorval (Wright Hardy); Marc Acheson (Lefty Hardy); Anthony Towe (Taka); John Proccacino (Frank); Thomas Cavanaugh (Simon, 1st patient); Garrett Bennett (Christian, 2nd patient); Brian Finney (Bug-Eyes, 3rd patient); David Rasche (Phillip, 4th patient); Tamsin Kelsey (Sheriff Stevenson); Benjamin Ratner (FX Man); Lesley Ewen (Private Nurse); William Sasso (Shy Young Orderly); Teryl Rothery (Beth); Norma Wick (Reporter); Nathan Begg (Kid in Cowboy Hat); Philip Baer and Peter Baer (Boys in Boat); Elisa Wayne (Girl in Tutu); Cole Halleran (Boy on Leash).

LOS ANGELES TIMES, 8/30/95, Calendar/p. 4, Kevin Thomas

There may be "Magic in the Water," for it surely isn't up there on the screen—or at least not in sufficient quantity to make this film anything special among the summer's many family films.

On the plus side are some very good performances by Mark Harmon and by Joshua Jackson and Sarah Wayne as his children: on the minus side are a heavy-handed dose of political correctness and a needless flight into dubious whimsy in an already fanciful situation.

Harmon plays a sour, tough-talking Seattle talk-show psychiatrist, divorced and indifferent to his kids. His former wife has shamed him into taking them on a vacation to a Canadian resort community, whose lake is supposed to contain its own elusive Loch Ness-style monster.

Nobody, however, is having a very good time until Harmon gets knocked on his head. This hoariest of devices not only transforms his personality—suddenly, he's a loving, caring father—but he also becomes part of a group of men who feel that the gentle spirit of the mythical lake monster, Orky, has inhabited them. It's an apparently transcending spiritual experience, but one that brings them into group therapy administered by local medico Harley Jane Kozak (whose idea of a performance seems to be a series of increasingly tiresome quizzical expressions).

This development comes across as mainly silly and extraneous and tends to sidetrack us from the children's growing conviction that there really is a wonderful creature lurking at the bottom of the lake. This notion has real dramatic possibilities, but it's coupled with great dollops of mystical Canadian Native wisdom and ecological protest in such a bald, trite manner that it's an instance of enough already.

Director Rick Stevenson and his writers are most adept at making real Harmon's errant but transformed father and Jackson's teenage son and Wayne's 10-year-old charmer and their evolving relationships with each other.

Stevenson directs them into winning, involving portrayals, but fantasy clearly is not his strong suit. As a result, it's hard to imagine all but the very young getting caught up in this sweet, well-meaning movie.

NEW YORK POST, 8/30/95, p. 42, Michael Medved

"Magic in the Water" is an ambitious piece of family entertainment that tries hard to convey wholesome, uplifting messages—in fact, it tries much too hard.

By the end of the movie, all its obvious good intentions begin working against one another, as the plot goes through increasingly absurd contortions to re-enforce non-controversial virtues like defending the environment, making time to cherish your children, respecting Native American traditions, and preserving the innocence and enthusiasm of the younger generation.

That's a lot of water for any movie to carry, even if it is magic—and this confused, fumbling exercise emphatically is not.

The story centers on a divorced, workaholic media shrink (Mark Harmon) with a popular Seattle radio show who takes his two children for a few weeks of summer vacation in a rented cabin on the shores of a Canadian lake.

Those kids (a teen-ager played by Josh Jackson and a 10-year-old portrayed by winning newcomer Sarah Wayne) have been waiting all year for these precious days with their father, but when they get to the lake he spends all his time trying to finish a book and leaves them to fend for themselves.

The little girl is soon fascinated with local tales of a Loch Ness-style monster known as Orky, and she discovers some mysterious creature that rises from the depths to devour the Oreo cookies she places as an offfering on the dock.

Meanwhile, her father suffers an accident in the lake, after which he joins a group of disturbed locals who meet regularly with the attractive, unattached town psychiatrist (Harley Jane Kozak).

Each of her patients is convinced that he has been dragged into the water by a creature who then inhabits their bodies and miraculously restores a childlike sense of wonder and joy. The only problem is that this therapeutic sea serpent is slowly dying due to a nefarious conspiracy secretly dumping toxic waste into the lake. The greedy bad guys have even seen to it that the elderly medicine man (Sotonoma Salsedo), who is the only one who understands the creature, is so heavily drugged that he can't do anything to rescue Orky.

The only way this convoluted mishmash might have worked at all would have been treat Orky like Kriss Kringle in "Miracle on 34th Street"—never definitely answering the question of whether or not the mystical creature is real. Unfortunately, director/co-writer Rick Stevenson erases all doubts, displaying an embarrassingly bad electronic sea serpent that looks about as lifelike as a concrete roadside dinosaur at a gas station in South Dakota.

Stevenson has in the past produced some fine independent films ("Restless Natives," "Promised Land" "Some Girls"), but he's never directed before, and that lack of experience shows in an unsteady tone that wavers between seriousness, silliness and shameless sentimentality.

The British Columbia scenery is spectacular, and Mark Harmon makes an appealing leading man—especially in one scene where, rejuvenated by Orky, he teaches his kids how to lie on their backs and "move" clouds across the sky. But he's wasted in a film that's a heavy, klutzy monster that can't possibly survive in such shallow water.

NEWSDAY, 8/31/95, Part II/p. B7, Gene Seymour

Several times during "Magic in the Water" Ashley (Sarah Wayne), the lonely, wistful little girl who believes the ripples on a lake in the Pacific Northwest mark the path of a mythic sea monster, mentions a foul odor coming from the water. She's certain it's the creature's bad breath. "My mom says if you have bad breath, it means you're sick," she tells the ripples.

Actually, Ashley, what you're probably sniffing is the movie's script, which reeks from stale family melodrama, turgid plot contrivances and half-baked New Age concepts. Too bad, because the basic idea behind "Magic in the Water" offered many possibilities for sweet, inventive whimsy.

Ashley's vision of the monster comes while she's vacationing by the lake with her teenaged brother, Josh (Joshua Jackson), and their divorced dad, Jack Black (Mark Harmon), an egocentric radio psychiatrist whose advice comes in bite-sized homilies like "Stop whining!" Hard to believe, but Josh and Ashley idolize this blowhard, who spends more time growling over his three cellular phones than having heart-to-hearts with the children.

They spend their quality time in Glenorky, a Canadian town that gets the second part of its name from Orky, a legendary lake monster. The whole town is practically a theme park for Orky lore, with restaurants, souvenir stands and underwater surveys. There are a lot of Orky-related things, however, that aren't on the tour. Like a therapy group of grown men whose inner children have been awakened by what they believe is a visit from Orky's spirit.

Ashley, beguiled by the Orky legend from the time she arrives, decides to leave Oreo cookies for the monster overnight. When she sees that the cream filling on each cookie has been eaten, Ashley is moved to tell her skeptical brother and distracted dad that Orky's real. Then again, the filling could have been eaten by the mysterious old American Indian next door. Or even a local booster who's trying to persuade tourists that the creature exists.

But as far as Ashley's concerned, Orky's real. And soon Jack himself bumps his head and becomes one of the Orky-possessed grown-ups. He also becomes a warm, fuzzy guy and a sharing, playful dad—digging a hole to China, building a sand castle and orchestrating cloud patterns for Josh and Ashley's amazement.

The town shrink (Harley Jane Kozak) is more than amazed. She's convinced that Jack needs meditation and observation. Ashley, meanwhile, senses that both her dad's wooziness and Orky's "bad breath" are somehow connected with some kind of mortal danger.

All this sounds a lot better than it plays. What should be a buoyant, lilting tale trudges and plods along with unpleasant dialogue and unconvincing story elements. I'm not going to say whether or not there's an Orky. But I will say that children under the age of 7 (and possibly way older) will probably do a lot of squirming in their seats before they find out.

Also reviewed in:
CHICAGO TRIBUNE, 8/30/95, Tempo/p. 18, John Petrakis
NEW YORK TIMES, 8/30/95, p. C10, Caryn James
VARIETY, 5/1-7/95, p. 38, Joe Leydon
WASHINGTON POST, 8/30/95, p. D1, Hal Hinson
WASHINGTON POST, 9/1/95, Weekend/p. 31, John F. Kelly

MAJOR PAYNE

A Universal Pictures release of a Wife 'N Kids production. *Executive Producer:* Damon Wayans and Harry Tatelman. *Producer:* Eric L. Gold and Michael Rachmil. *Director:* Nick Castle. *Screenplay:* Dean Lorey, Damon Wayans, and Gary Rosen. *Based on a story by:* Joe Connelly. *Director of Photography:* Richard Bowen. *Editor:* Patrick Kennedy. *Music:* Craig Safan. *Music Editor:* Darrell Hall. *Choreographer:* Russell Clark. *Sound:* Rosa Howell-Thornhill. *Sound Editor:* Michael Wilhoit and Kelly Oxford. *Casting:* Aleta Chappelle. *Production Designer:* Peter Larkin. *Art Director:* David Crank. *Set Decorator:* James V. Kent. *Set Dresser:* Cliff Eubank, Jamie Bishop, Steve Shifflette, Catherine Lynn McKenney, Gordon McVay, Eric R. Link, and Mark Kersey. *Special Effects:* Joey DiGaetano, III. *Costumes:* Jennifer L. Bryan. *Make-up:* Selena Evans-Miller. *Stunt Coordinator:* Greg Elam. *Running time:* 97 minutes. *MPAA Rating:* PG-13.

CAST: Rodney P. Barnes (Weight Lifter); Ross Bickell (Colonel Braggart); Scott "Bam Bam" Bigelow (Huge Biker); Joda Blaire-Hershman (Cadet Bryan); Orlando Brown (Cadet Tiger); Peyton Chesson Fohl (Cadet Johnson); Stephen Coleman (Cadet Leland); Mark Conway (Police Sergeant); David DeHart (Wellington Cadet Captain); Joshua Todd Diveley (New Cadet); Robert Faraoni, Jr. (Smart-Ass Soldier); Michael Gabel (Lt. Wiseman); Albert Hall (General Decker); William Hickey (Dr. Phillips); Michael Ironside (Lt. Colonel Stone); R.J. Knoll (Blind Kid); Andrew Harrison Leeds (Cadet Dotson); Dean Lorey (Mr. Shipman); Mark W. Madison (Cadet Fox); Brad Martin (MP); Steven Martini (Cadet Alex Stone); Chris Owen (Cadet Wuliger); Karyn Parsons (Emily); Seymour Swan (Soldier); Leonard Thomas (Bleeding

Soldier); Hechter Ubarry (Guerilla Leader); Carolyn L.A. Walker (Woman); Damien Wayans (Cadet Williams); Damon Wayans (Major Payne); R. Stephen Wiles (Cadet Heathcoat); Tommy Wiles (Cadet); Christopher James Williams (Marksman); Al Cerullo and John Louis Fischer (Chopper Pilots).

LOS ANGELES TIMES, 3/24/95, Calendar/p. 12, Kevin Thomas

While "Major Payne" is too predictable for most adults, it's an ideal entertainment for youthful audiences that allows Damon Wayans to be at his best in a dream part. In the title role, Wayans is a Marine so dedicated that "gung-ho" doesn't remotely begin to describe his zeal in the line of duty, a quality that Wayans and his co-writers happily push to comical extremes. Having distinguished himself in Iraq, Panama and Kuwait, the major has come to the end of the line.

In short order, the man hoping to find some line of work that make use of "my exemplary skills as a trained killer" winds up at Madison Academy commanding its junior ROTC misfits, who have been last-place finishers in the Virginia Junior Military Games eight years in a row. You scarcely need a crystal ball to figure out how things will turn out for Payne and his boys.

Although overly familiar, "Major Payne"—a reworking of the amusing 1955 "The Private War of Major Benson" starring Charlton Heston—does give Wayans a chance to stretch in a role that finds him adopting, to hilarious effect, the craziest folksy twang and quaint expressiveness imaginable.

Emotionally, Payne verges on the robotic, but he's canny and has an ultra-dry sense of humor. Trying her best to break through to the major both as a man and a teacher is the school's sensible counselor, played appealingly by lovely Karyn Parsons. The young actors cast as the students are similarly capable, and Steven Martini, in his film debut, is especially effective as one of the older students, troubled by a sneering alcoholic father (Michael Ironside). Orlando Brown is irresistible as the resilient Cadet Tiger: Parsons has to remind the major that Tiger is, after all, only 6 years old.

Directed with verve by Nick Castle, "Major Payne" is a handsome production, filmed almost entirely at the Miller School in Charlottesville, Va., which boasts a large and beautiful campus and a wonderful collection of fine old buildings.

NEW YORK POST, 3/24/95, p. 46, Michael Medved

"Major Payne" is aptly named; it is, in fact, so sloppily thrown together that it insults the intelligence of even the drooling, dumb-and-dumber pre-adolescent male audience for which it seems to be intended.

Damon Wayans plays Major Benson Winifred Payne, a ruthlessly efficient Marine Corps "killing machine" who's served his country in bloody conflicts around the world but is suddenly discharged because his warrior ways don't fit the kinder, gentler image of the new Corps.

"It's been two whole weeks since I killed a man and already I'm starting to get the itch," he declares.

He eventually stifles those primal hungers to take a job as head of the junior ROTC program at a picturesque private school in Virginia.

The cadets in his charge are the same group of oddly assorted losers you've seen a hundred times before in formula movies about tough-tender military men (or coaches, or teachers) who magically whip a group of rebellious kids into a winning team.

Meanwhile, a sensitive, enlightened teacher at the school (played by former model Karyn Parsons) wants Payne to go easy on the boys, while hoping to humanize him by injecting a note of romance in his desolate life.

This creaky plot is based on "The Private War of Major Benson," a pleasant 1955 comedy with Charlton Heston as a hard-bitten officer who mellows out as commander of a military school—which, in the original, is incongruously run by an order of nuns.

At least that 40-year-old chestnut has the courage to play its sentimentality straight, but in "Major Payne," Wayans tries to have it both ways—recycling all the ancient cliches at the same time that he mocks them.

In the end, "Major Payne" seems like a mildly amusing one-joke sketch that's been stretched out to intolerable length.

NEWSDAY, 3/24/95, Part II/p. B7, John Anderson

While Adam Sandler, Jim Carrey, Chris Farley and the rest of the dumber-than-dirt mob of movie comedians do backflips to amuse us, Damon Wayans can just stand there and be funny. He's a natural, and one who's style is in direct defiance of the currently popular crypto-Jerry Lewis brand of film humor: He knows that we know that he knows what's going on. You just wish he knew how to pick a movie.

One of these days, Wayans is going to find himself a project that doesn't rely on insults, flatulence and scatology to make its comedic points, and the whole genre will be elevated. But that day is not "Major Payne," which relies on insults, flatulence and scatology to score its comedic point. That the film is bearable at all is because of Wayans' goofiness, and it's barely watchable.

It's does accomplish one amazing feat: I never thought I'd see "To Sir, With Love" cross-pollinated with "The Dirty Dozen," but here it is, complete with war games, career crises, tests of loyalty, and the cloyingly climactic emotional bonding between students and teacher. Or, rather, students and psycho. Because that's what Major Payne (Wayans) seems to be most of the time, when he's not being pathetic or inspirational.

Benson Winifred Payne, as he is apt to call himself, is a veteran of Panama, Kuwait and Iraq, but his place in the New World Order is leading the Junior ROTC of Madison Academy, where men are boys and Payne doesn't know the difference. His relentlessly, sociopathically gung-ho attitude puts him in direct confrontation with the school's beautiful director, Dr. Emily Walburn (Karyn Parsons), whose effect on Payne has its amusing aspects but which doesn't make much sense, given how single-minded and brutal Payne can be.

And he can. He treats each boy, regardless of age, size or infirmity (he calls a deaf student "Mr. Handicapped Man" and refers to another as "ass eyes") as raw military recruits. He'll say and do anything. And, of course, once you've established this you have to keep making his behavior more and more outrageous until it really isn't all that funny anymore.

You could argue that Payne is on the right track. His spoiled charges—especially the too-old-for-prep school Alex Stone, played by Steven Martini in a reprise of the John Cassavetes role in "Dirty Dozen"—put laxative in his food, and try to photograph him in bed with a cadet wearing a dress. They will, of course, grow to love and respect Major Payne—who at one point buries them all up to their necks and waters them like flowers—with the emotional process being handled so perfunctorily that no one even thinks of believing it.

But this isn't about believing anything, or making a story that isn't a hackneyed collage of old movie and TV bits—one of the funnier sequences has Payne fantasizing about life with Emily, to the theme song from "The Donna Reed Show" (and yes, Alex Stone was the name of Carl Betz' character). No, Major Payne is about giving Wayans something to do. And he can do much better than this.

Also reviewed in:
CHICAGO TRIBUNE, 3/24/95, Friday/p. H, Michael Wilmington
NEW YORK TIMES, 3/24/95, p. C16, Caryn James
VARIETY, 3/20-26/95, p. 48, Leonard Klady
WASHINGTON POST, 3/24/95, p. C1, Rita Kempley

MALLRATS

A Gramercy Pictures release of an Alphaville production in association with View Askew Productions. *Producer:* James Jacks, Sean Daniel, and Scott Mosier. *Director:* Kevin Smith. *Screenplay:* Kevin Smith. *Director of Photography:* David Klein. *Editor:* Paul Dixon. *Music:* Ira Newborn. *Sound:* Jose Araujo. *Casting:* Don Phillips. *Production Designer:* Dina Lipton. *Art Director:* Sue Savage. *Set Decorator:* Diana Stoughton. *Costumes:* Dana Allyson. *Running time:* 97 minutes. *MPAA Rating:* R.

CAST: Shannen Doherty (Rene); Jeremey London (T.S. Quint); Jason Lee (Brodie); Claire Forlani (Brandi Svenning); Michael Rooker (Svenning); Priscilla Barnes (Ivannah); Renee Humphrey (Tricia); Ben Affleck (Shannon); Joey Lauren Adams (Gwen); Stan Lee (Himself); Jason Mewes (Jay); Ethan Suplee (William); Brian O'Halloran (Gill); Art James (Gameshow Host); Kevin Smith (Silent Bob); David Brinkley (TV Executive No. 1); Jonathan Brodie (The Priest); Sven Thorsen (Security Guard).

LOS ANGELES TIMES, 10/20/95, Calendar/p. 2, Kenneth Turan

[The following review by Kenneth Turan appeared in a slightly different form in:
NEWSDAY, 10/20/95, Part II/p. B6.]

If the Sundance Institute or the AFI ever offers a course advising directors of successful first films what to avoid the second time around, "Mallrats" could be at the heart of the curriculum.

Written and directed by the talented Kevin Smith, whose ultra-low-budget "Clerks" was an exuberant and anarchic delight, "Mallrats" is a numbing and dispiriting experience aimed at the least discriminating parts of the teenage audience. The only reason anyone old enough to vote might want to attend is to learn from someone else's experience what mistakes not to make.

Lesson One: Don't repeat yourself. Magic is not going to strike twice. Though having random folks hanging out at a convenience store was hilarious in "Clerks," having random folks hanging out in a suburban mall feels false, contrived and nowhere near as clever.

Lesson Two: Don't go out with a slapdash script. An afternoon spent at that mall by two pals who are dumped by their girlfriends may arguably be enough to base a movie on, but this picture's forced and unfocused dialogue sinks "Mallrats" like a stone.

For the record, Rene (Shannen Doherty) has broken up with Brodie (Jason Lee) because he spends too much time with his comic book collection and his Sega games. And Brandi (Claire Forlani) has split with T.S. (Jeremy London) because he can't understand why she has to be a contestant on her dad's "Truth or Date" TV game show. Or something.

Lesson Three: Don't think the addition of the name star you can now afford is going to help you out, Shannen Doherty of "Beverly Hills, 90210" does as adequate a job as anyone else in this unchallenged cast, but her presence can in no way rescue a film that has forgotten Lessons One and Two.

Lesson Four: Don't assume bathroom humor is cool. Yes, Jim Carrey made millions for all concerned with that particular brand of juvenalia, but Carrey is not in this movie and running jokes about bodily functions are not automatically winning if you're old enough to cross the street by yourself.

Lesson Five: Don't count on the good feelings generated by your first film to carry over to you your second. At one advance screening of "Mallrats," the most frequently overheard conversation was those who'd seen "Clerks" desperately trying to convince those who hadn't, that it really was a movie worth watching.

About the only thing to survive from "Clerks" are the characters of Silent Bob (played by Smith himself) and his sidekick Jay (Jason Mewes) and even they have lost a good deal of their comic effectiveness. When this film ends with the on-screen notice that "Jay and Silent Bob will return in 'Chasing Amy,'" it feels more like a warning than a prediction.

NEW YORK POST, 10/20/95, p. 42, Michael Medved

If you found last year's "Dumb and Dumber" a bit too genteel or your tastes, then "Mallrats" is the movie for you.

It's so cheerfully mindless, so proudly puerile, that it defeats all attempts at reasonable criticism. One could properly point out that the film is gross, stupid, childish, oafish and offensive—but then the producers might turn around and happily quote such adjectives in newspaper ads touting this messterpiece.

Like "Clerks," the previous over-praised, low-budget effort from writer-director Kevin Smith (which set a world's record for the number of fellatio jokes in a single movie), this film forces a few laughs from its own unpretentious amateurism, and the rude, crude energy of its characters.

Chief among the title vermin in "Mallrats" are Jeremy London and Jason Lee as two talkative layabouts supposedly enrolled in New Jersey colleges but devoting most of their lives to comic books, Sega games and, of course, shopping malls.

As this cinematic epic unfolds, they're both dumped by their girlfriends (Claire Forlani and Shannen Doherty) and they dedicate a full day to winning back the affection of these lovelies.

That effort takes place within the precincts of the local mall (actually filmed in Minnesota), leading up to the broadcast from that shopping center of a new game show called "Truth or Date," produced by the disapproving father (Michael Rooker) of one of the girls under pursuit.

Aiding the two heroes in their romantic quest are a pair of local pot-heads (Jason Mewes and director Kevin Smith) making return appearances from "Clerks."

Opposing the course of true love are a muscular security guard (Sven Thorsen) and the smug proprietor of a mall men's store (Ben Affleck), who inflicts a far-too-realistic beating in a scene of gratiutious violence.

We also encounter a topless fortune teller with three nipples (Priscilla Barnes) and the legendary real-life comic book creator Stan Lee.

The women don't have much to do here except look gorgeous, a function performed especially well by the luminous Shannen Doherty, and by Joey Lauren Adams as a pert, promiscuous temptress.

Jason Lee, a real-life skate-boarding champ making his starring debut, exudes an impish charm as he spouts dialogue that is simultaneously coarse and high-falutin.

In addition to innumerable references to farting, vomit, anal sex, masturbation and other bodily functions, there's a running gag about rubbing fingers inside sweaty, stinky underwear, then shaking hands with an enemy so the smell attaches to him for hours afterward.

In a similar spirit, "Mallrats" may seem intermittently amusing as it unspools on screen, but the unpleasant odor seems to stick around long after the feeble fun is forgotten.

VILLAGE VOICE, 10/31/95, p. 76, Gary Dauphin

In case you're wondering where *Mallrats*'s head is at, let me tell you now that it's lodged firmly up some guys hairy butt. In other movies, this could be considered a bad thing but here it's a good and funny one, writer-director Kevin Smith starting his follow-up to *Clerks* off with an old dumb joke about putting a cat where the sun don't shine and going from there to identify his two main bad guys via jokes about derrieres.

In comedies about slacker autodidacts, the story is just an excuse for the side bits, which is exactly as things should be. Suffice it to say that comic collector Brodie (pro skateboarder Jason Lee in his first movie role) is the joke teller, and *Mallrats* opens the fine morning when he and his buddy T. S. (Jeremy London) get dumped by their respective girlfriends (Shannen Doherty and Claire Forlani). A trip to the mall ensues for some of those good food-court cookies, and from there subplots cheerfully lifted from Road Runner cartoons, *The Dating Game*, and *The Empire Strikes Back* pile on until a fortune-teller with three nipples and Marvel Comics god Stan Lee (playing himself) tell our heroes how to win back their girls.

Since Smith is still a better writer than he is a director, the idiot-savant dialogue is *Mallrats'* main pleasure. This is a boy's fantasy, so the girls are mostly prettily empty props here, Doherty a screaming bore. Jason Lee's Brodie on the other hand is the perfect slacker hero: the actor and Smith obviously know that in Slackerland the ability to comically recirculate very particular kinds of useless information is the only superpower worth having. Jason Mewes (a holdover from *Clerks*) is hysterical as alt.rock stoner Jay, and Smith himself does a nice turn as Jay's partner-in-anarchy Silent Bob, a weird cross between Yoda and Batman. These performances and Smith's ear for the groaner joke and generational references are what make *Mallrats* so funny, which is why Smith will probably be better remembered than the previous mass-cult's nerd avenger, Jeff Kanew.

Also reviewed in:
CHICAGO TRIBUNE, 10/20/95, Friday/p. L, Michael Wilmington
NEW YORK TIMES, 10/20/95, p. C8, Janet Maslin
VARIETY, 10/16-22/95, p. 94, Leonard Klady

WASHINGTON POST, 10/20/95, p. D6, Hal Hinson
WASHINGTON POST, 10/20/95, Weekend/p. 44, Desson Howe

MAMMA ROMA

A Milestone release of an Arco Film production. *Producer:* Alfredo Bini. *Director:* Pier Paolo Pasolini. *Screenplay (Italian with English subtitles):* Pier Paolo Pasolini and Sergio Citti. *Director of Photography:* Tonino Delli Colli. *Editor:* Nino Baragli. *Music:* Carlo Rustichelli. *Set Designer:* Massimo Tavazzi. *Art Director:* Flavio Mogherini. *Running time:* 110 minutes. *MPAA Rating:* Not Rated.

CAST: Anna Magnani (Mamma Roma); Ettore Garofolo (Ettore); Franco Citti (Carmine); Silvana Corsini (Bruna); Luisa Orioli (Biancofiore); Lamberto Maggiorani (Patient).

CHRISTIAN SCIENCE MONITOR, 1/25/95, p. 13, David Sterritt

"Mamma Roma," directed by the late Italian filmmaker Pier Paolo Pasolini, was made in 1962 but has never played in American theaters until now. This lapse of time is inexplicable, given the remarkable power of the movie and the fact that it stars Anna Magnani, one of Italy's most internationally popular actresses.

Whatever the reason for its long sojourn on the shelves of some obscure vault, its arrival at Film Forum is cause for celebration. It's a stirring drama that reaffirms Magnani's gifts while shedding new light on the early stages of Pasolini's career.

The title character is a prostitute who gives up her profession and moves to a run-down neighborhood of Rome where she hopes to make a decent life for herself and her son. She opens a food stand, makes new acquaintances, and settles down to watch over young Ettore, a feisty adolescent who's as likely to get into mischief as she was at his age. Much of the film is marked by humor; heartiness, and respect for the earthy details of working-class life. Things turn darker when Mamma Roma's former pimp arrives on the scene, and tragic when Ettore finds himself in dangerous trouble.

The plot and characters of "Mamma Roma" are too familiar to be very surprising, as Pasolini seemed to recognize a few years later when he admitted the "unforgivable" presence of repetition in this movie, which was only the second feature film he had ever directed.

Nonetheless, two assets bring the picture to vivid life. One is Magnani's bravura performance, marked by a superbly nuanced sense of emotional energy. The other is Pasolini's sensitive directing, which inflects the kitchen-sink naturalism of Neo-realist cinema with a complex mixture of poetic elements. These elements reflect his longtime (and paradoxical) commitments to Marxist protest, Christian compassion, and the sensuous pleasure of aesthetics for their own sake. This early drama stands with his finest work.

CINEASTE, Volume XXI, No. 3, 1995, p. 42, Peter Bondanella

Mamma Roma was first screened at the 1962 Venice Film Festival, where it was immediately sequestered on absurd charges of immorality and not released for theatrical distribution in Italy until a month later. It was shown in the United States only in 1990 at a Museum of Modern Art retrospective. The present version, released by Milestone Film (with the assistance of Martin Scorsese), has been struck from the original Italian negative with new English subtitles and represents the first American theatrical release of a film that is of great importance in Pasolini's collected cinematic works. Its release now is a welcome event, as Pasolini's reputation as a filmmaker and intellectual has grown since the almost two generations that separate us from his violent death in 1976.

Mamma Roma shares many of the characteristics that made Pasolini's first feature-length film, *Accatone* (1961), such an important and original work. Pasolini's first films grew out of a complex intellectual transition that bridged the gap between the great canonical works of Italian neorealism, such as Rossellini's *Open City* or *Paisan* and De Sica's *The Bicycle Thief*, on the one hand, and a new generation of filmmakers, such as Bellocchio, the Taviani brothers, Bertolucci, and Pasolini himself, who saw the French New Wave and its more self-conscious attitude toward cinematic style and political ideology as an alternative to pure social realism. The pastiche style Pasolini made famous in his first work long before the concept gained popularity in postmodernist theory is repeated on numerous occasions in *Mamma Roma*. Ugly, ghetto-like locations in the neighborhoods inhabited by the film's protagonists are photographed with classical music (Vivaldi) on the soundtrack. When Pasolini frames the down-and-out characters from Rome's suburbs in his shots, he often does so by direct citations from classical Old Master art. Thus, the death of Mamma Roma's son Ettore surely refers to the familiar iconography of Mantegna's famous portrait of a superbly foreshortened dead Christ. Functional illiterates in a prison hospital cite Canto IV of Dante's *Inferno* as a matter of course in another scene.

Pasolini employed the pastiche juxtaposition of high and low cultural signifiers in an attempt to ennoble the sordid world to which he was philosophically, politically, and sexually attracted—an attraction that ultimately proved fatal and led to his brutal murder by one of the *ragazzi di vita* that figure so prominently in *Mamma Roma* and *Accatone*. For Pasolini, such individuals possessed an epical-religious quality because they were not yet part of the consumer society he hated and which he identified with the petit bourgeois (a class to which he admittedly belonged himself). What is most interesting about *Mamma Roma* is precisely how Pasolini visualizes the distinction between this shadow world he loved and the petit-bourgeois world of Mamma Roma, played by a superb Anna Magnani in one of her greatest roles.

Pasolini selected Magnani for the part of the ex-prostitute who wants middle-class respectability for her ne'er-do-well son because, for him, she personified everything that he despised in the *piccolo borghese* class. Because of her classic role in Rossellini's *Rome, Open City* (1945), she was also identified iconographically with the artistic expression of Italian neorealism, a cinematic moment Pasolini admired but wished to transcend with his own unique form of mythical realism. During work on the set, Pasolini and Magnani constantly quarreled over the style of the film, with Pasolini preferring short takes and a complete reconstruction of the material he was shooting through radical editing, while Magnani naturally preferred a star-centered cinematography privileging close-ups of the actress in dramatically engaging states of emotional stress.

Certainly, the most pronounced aspect of Pasolini's style in this second excursion into the poet-novelist into the cinema must be considered his short takes (some so jerky and 'unprofessional' that mainstream cinematographers will no doubt find them irritating) and his rapid, often radical editing. It was precisely this rough texture in the imagery of Pasolini s first film that moved Bernardo Bertolucci to remark that while he apprenticed with Pasolini on his debut in the cinema, it was as if Bertolucci were witnessing the invention of the cinema on the set. But in fairness to Pasolini's intelligence, it is important to note that the 'rough' texture of his early works was completely a product of his esthetic principles and not simply the result of a lack of professional training. In fact, Pasolini was not only capable of 'professional' touches, but he was also quite competent in planning entirely different kinds of shots. An excellent example of such a diametrically opposed style takes place on two different occasions in the film where Pasolini follows Mamma Roma with an extremely long take down a long road. Its sudden appearance in the film shocks the viewer who has, by this time, come to expect the abrupt editing and frontal close-ups that characterize much of the film. One critic of the film (Maurizio Viano) has aptly remarked that the scene not only responds indirectly to André Bazin's arguments in favor of the inherent realism of long takes but also interjects a note of professional artifice into a film supposedly created by a rank amateur.

Mamma Roma will not add luster to Pasolini's posthumous reputation, since he is at present almost universally lionized, at least by academic critics. Much of the credit for publicizing Pasolini's legacy must go to the Fondazione Pier Paolo Pasolini headed by the director's friend Laura Betti. Largely because of her efforts, Pasolini not only is available in easily purchased videotapes but is the artist represented by more laserdisc titles than any other Italian director—even more than Antonioni, Bertolucci, or Fellini. Academic film critics and politically involved intellectuals in Europe and America seem fascinated by Pasolini's works; his violent death, and the sordid details of that unfortunately abrupt end to his career, have prompted some critics to transform his image into that a homosexual martyr (a role Pasolini himself would most certainly have rejected).

While film historians can certainly applaud the distribution of this important work, the reappearance of *Mamma Roma* should also be the occasion for a reconsideration of Pasolini's role in postwar Italian cinema. Such a reconsideration will not prove completely positive, for there are elements in Pasolini's idiosyncratic ideology which, examined in the calm light of a dispassionate analysis of such early and precocious films as *Mamma Roma*, may strike the obiective viewer as not only remarkably naive but even, on occasion, irresponsible. Take, for example, the admittedly humorous treatment of work and the working class in both *Accatone* and *Mamma Roma*. We all know Pasolini's Marxism is of a peculiar variety, but what kind of Marxist (or humanist, for that matter) denigrates the nobility of labor in favor of exploiting others, economically and sexually? Yet, this is precisely what Pasolini does in both films. In the midst of Italy's economic miracle which transformed an agricultural nation into one of the world's most dynamic societies, Pasolini quite rightly sees this wrenching change in Italian society, personified in the character of Mamma Roma and her son Ettore, as a step toward the destruction of traditional popular culture.

But Pasolini's hatred of the *piccolo borghese* mentality blinds him to the courage displayed by Mamma Roma, who attempts to leave a life of prostitution to make a better life for her son. Pasolini's overt admiration and implicit sexual desire are directed, instead, toward Ettore, who proves to be not only a petty thief but to have absolutely no concern for bettering himself in life. In an era when every Western society is reconsidering the foundations of the welfare state, on the one hand, and redefining the place of labor in a free market economy, on the other, would anyone but Pasolini praise unemployment as a condition preferable to gainful employment among the underprivileged classes? The notion that Pasolini's *ragazzi di vita* should somehow remain uncontaminated by the contemporary world was always a utopian notion in Pasolini's ideology, especially if such lack of contamination required that they refrain from any kind of participation in the Italian economy.

Pasolini's view of the people who populated the *borgate*—the shanty towns, urban slums, and newly developed housing projects around the periphery of Rome—has always struck me as strikingly similar to the attitude of American tourists and expatriates who fell in love with Italy immediately after the war when a full meal could be bought for less than a dollar and any small amount of U.S. currency guaranteed the owner a carefree life in a sun-drenched country full of beautiful monuments and charming people. Today, many of these individuals constantly lament the fact that times have changed in Italy and that the cost of living is far higher there than in America (not concerning themselves with the fact that in the process of raising the costs, the standard of living for the average Italian has risen by leaps and bounds). Ultimately, this embodies a colonialist mentality, and Pasolini, in some respects, was guilty of the same kind of thinking about the people who populate Mamma Roma's world.

Viewing *Mamma Roma* three decades after its first appearance should raise some hard questions about Pasolini's legacy, questions that admiring critics all too often fail to raise. But the distribution of the film also underlines what an original and stimulating talent Pasolini brought to the cinema and how much Italy has lost from the contributions he might have made to Italian culture during the two decades since his death. *Mamma Roma*'s stylistic originality and its reinterpretation of the heritage of Italian neorealism certainly justify its re-release, and it can only be hoped that videotape and laserdisc versions will soon follow.

LOS ANGELES TIMES, 3/20/95, Calendar/p. 4, Kevin Thomas

Pier Paolo Pasolini's second feature, 1962's "Mamma Roma," which begins its first local run Wednesday at the Nuart, is one of the director's finest. We meet its heroine (Anna Magnani, at her incomparable, volcanic best in the title role) just as she has given up streetwalking, having scrimped and saved for years, to open a produce stand in an open-air Roman market and to reclaim her teen-age son (Ettore Garofolo), who has been raised in a small town and whom she overwhelms with an almost seductive mother love.

The film is marked by some extraordinary tracking sequences as Mamma Roma strides through the night, proudly announcing her dreams and feelings to a chorus of passersby—and also by a cinemactic image of crucifixion. The late film historian Ephraim Katz aptly remarked that Pasolini's entire career was characterized by "a brave attempt to reconcile his allegiances " to Marx, Freud and Jesus Christ."

NEW YORK, 2/13/95, p. 101, David Denby

At the beginning of *Mamma Roma*, Anna Magnani, a retired prostitute, shows up at the country wedding of her ex-pimp, driving three pigs before her and roaring with laughter. This great Pier Paolo Pasolini film from 1962 has an outsize sense of life's pleasures and dangers—the glory and terror of life lived at the utmost—that shrivels our pathetic contemporary cinema to nothing. The whole tragedy of Mamma Roma is there in the opening scene (which is staged as a blasphemous Last Supper)—the prostitute's exuberant release from bondage, her love of children, the pimp's resentments. Mamma Roma is a feisty, street-smart woman who means well but goes too far in her reactions, and Magnani plays her with the full power of her thick and vibrant Michelangeloesque torso, her strut and intimidating temper, her roof-raising laughter. Pasolini's view is essentially tragic: Our doom grows out of our healthiest and most vital instincts. After a long, sordid history as a streetwalker (and we get to see how she handles clients in a few stunning sequences), Mamma Roma wants to join the middle class and raise her 16-year-old son as a respectable man. In the person of ugly-beautiful non-actor Ettore Garofolo, the son has moments of shambling grace, but this country boy, transported to the Rome suburbs, is overwhelmed by city freedoms and pleasures, and he sinks rapidly. Some of this movie is carelessly done (the ending is rushed), but there are great sequences throughout and a poetically expressive use of the camera (as well as some Christian symbolism that seems arty and over-formalized—the abiding Pasolini vices). In this movie Pasolini said his farewell to Neo-Realism. What followed, in the years before his death in 1975, was a mix of avant-garde formalism and Catholic/Marxist mysticism. He never again achieved the power and emotional directness of *Mamma Roma*, a memorial of the great director he could have become.

NEW YORK POST, 1/18/95, p. 39, Thelma Adams

"Mamma Roma" opens with a laugh and ends with a howl.

Pier Paolo Pasolini's passionate tragedy stars Anna Magnani, the diva of the Italian neo-realist movement ("Rome, Open City").

With her shock of black hair, open-mouthed laugh, and full-to-overflowing figure, the Academy Award-winning actress is a force of nature, equal parts joy and rage.

(Meryl Streep studied Magnani's "Mamma Rosa" while researching the part of Francesca, the fortysomething Italian-American whose passion is released in the coming movie "The Bridges of Madison County.")

Pasolini—filmmaker, poet, novelist, homosexual and murder victim—attracted Magnani's attention with his directorial debut, "Accattone," and cast her in this, his second film.

Released to controversy in Italy in 1962, "Mamma Roma" makes its U.S. theatrical debut today at the Film Forum, 20 years after the director's death at age 53.

Set in the drab Roman suburbs, ex-hooker Mamma Roma (Magnani) tries to go straight and push her teen-age son, Ettore (Ettore Garofolo), into the middle class.

Pasolini's masterful drama—Mildred Pierce, Italian-style—proves that there's nothing easy about being an easy woman.

The beautiful but feckless Ettore, a cross between a Caravaggio angel and Elvis on velvet, has the awkward but riveting sensuality of an adolescent on the verge of manhood.

In a vibrant scene, Mamma Roma teaches Ettore the tango. They trip and crash to the floor, entangled, laughing heartily.

But every joy bears the seeds of tragedy. Later, Ettore steals his mother's tango records and sells them in order to buy a gold chain for the scrawny, slutty Bruna (Silvana Corsini).

"At your age, the only woman you need is your mother." Mamma Ro' tells Ettore. She would climb on the cross for her son—and he would gladly let her.

Mamma Ro,' is an optimist born for tragedy, a creature so filled with life's fire that the world, in its eternal jealousy, must extinguish it.

From the opening image of a country wedding constructed like the Last Supper to the crucifixion at the movie's close, "Mamma Roma" is a psychological drama fraught with religious overtones.

Pasolini the poet sharpens every image, hones every phrase, layers meaning upon meaning, pushing the frontiers of the neo-realism he inherited from Roberto Rossellini and Vittorio de Sica to get at a raw emotion that is realer than real, a howl born in laughter.

NEWSDAY, 1/18/95, Part II/p. B9, John Anderson

Pier Paolo Pasolini was a snaggle of incongruities: A devout Marxist who was obsessed with religious imagery; a devotee of Italian neo-realism who remade that very genre; a moralizer against urban violence and decay who was under constant scrunity by the law and who, in November, 1975, was bludgeoned to death during a sexual tryst with a much younger man.

Considering the contradictions, "Mamma Roma," a 1962 work that is having its U.S. debut at Film Forum in Manhattan for the next three weeks, is as representative of Pasolini and his art as any other film he made. Simultaneously an economic manifesto, a Lutheran screed and a moral fable, it is also a star vehicle for Pasolini's leading actress star, Anna Magnani—who happened to be his antagonist during the making of this movie.

As the title character, Magnani is a billowing force of maternal instinct, street smarts and potential sexual energy. We meet her at the marriage of her pimp, Carmine (Franco Citti), where the wedding table resembles the Last Supper and the room resembles a vault. She laughs too loud, makes too-crude jokes, embarrasses the bride and should be embarrassed herself. But while her joy may seem forced—Magnani greets each small setback in Mamma's life with a gale of hilarity—the wedding has freed her from the streets.

She's bringing her son, Ettore (Ettore Garofolo), back from the country to live in Rome. And she truly believes that she has control of her life.

Mamma Roma is exhibit A in Pasolini's indictment of Italy's church, state and class system. When she recites her family history, we see that her fate is prescribed, that one's opportunities and worldview are dictated by the weight of one's wallet. "Why am I nobody and you're the King of Kings?" she asks, eyes upward, during a moment of despair. There is no answer, either from heaven or from us.

Pasolini's use of symbolism is blunt—the landscapes on the outskirts of Rome, where Mamma runs a vegetable stand and Ettore becomes involved with a group of thugs, mixes youth and ruins, and the constant backdrop is of a disinterested city under reconstruction. The Virgin-and-Child motif, the relative morality on which Roman life operates, Ettore's love for the slutty Bruna (Silvana Corsini), and the parallels between Mamma and Ettore, and Bruna and her baby, are presented like overdue bills.

At the same time, Pasolini attained a vitality in his picture that owed much to Fellini, Antonioni and his own idiosyncratic preference for the quick take—which apparently annoyed his star, an actress accustomed to a lingering camera. Ironically, the most memorable scenes are two extraordinarily long shots that bookend the movie. Each features Mamma, strutting her usual Roman thoroughfare, reciting her history and philosophy as a succession of customers join her and then fall away like scales. But the first, taken as she prepares to leave the streets, is triumphant. The second, after Carmine sends her back there, is desperate.

Ettore's fate clinches Pasolini's Christ metaphor. Strapped to a hospital bed after he's been arrested and gone hysterical, he's as good as crucified; our point of view is from the base of his cross. And Mamma's point of view is from a window, looking out at St. Peter's Basilica across a dusty, and all but impassable, field.

VILLAGE VOICE, 1/24/95, p. 54, Georgia Brown

There's a fly on the opening credits to *Mamma Roma*. Pasolini's signature, maybe? I see it as a ghost. If Pasolini's spirit visited, it would surely come back, not as a shooting star or some sweet-throated bird, but as this durable, despised insect of the slums. On the scrap heap where Pasolini died—where he was bludgeoned to death by a kid he'd picked up—flies must have sipped his blood.

Mamma Roma, which takes place in the same sort of end-of-the-world landscape as the one where its director was murdered, is a great, great movie, one of Pasolini's best. How strange that until now it has never formally opened here (it's played in a few museum shows over the years). Back in 1962, *Mamma Roma* provoked the Italian authorities—they probably didn't like that the movie was based on a true story where a boy died in prison strapped to a medieval-style rack—but why U.S. distributors avoided the film is beyond me.

The opening scene will take your breath away. The setting is a stark, vaulted, whitewashed chapel. The low, centered camera takes in the whole of a long crowded banquet table, making this resemble so many Last Supper frescoes. In the middle sits a bride and groom: Carmine (Franco Citti of *Accattone!*), a former pimp, has just taken a more or less respectable wife. The celebration, however, is turning ugly; like the 13th fairy, one of the guests, Mamma Roma (Anna Magnani), begins heckling the couple. Carmine was her pimp and lover, the father of her son. Fueled with spite, she lets it rip, mocking the couple by bringing in three pigs—fratelli d'Italia, Italy's three brothers, she calls them, and the bride's "new in-laws." At one point, the principals sling insulting lyrics of a popular song at each other. Taking in the whole spectacle is two-year-old Ettore.

Sixteen years later. Mamma Roma returns to the town to fetch her grown son. In the interim, she's moved to Rome, worked the streets, and put aside enough lire to buy the license for a vegetable stall and a decent apartment. Now she's ready to turn a new leaf and give Ettore (Ettore Garofolo) a proper home. She finds him riding the town's dinky carousel—a sad young prince huddled sullenly in the corner of an empty chariot and going nowhere. "What will I do in Rome?" he asks her. "You'll keep an eye on the ruins" she snaps. Pure Magnani.

Pasolini never liked using professional actors. The skinny Garofolo was discovered waiting tables. Carrying a basket of fruit, he reminded Pasolini of—what else?—a Caravaggio. (Actually, with his punched-in baby face, he looks like Citti and even more like Pasolini.) The volatile Magnani, on the other hand, *was* an actress, and she kicked up a ruckus when Pasolini the purist, a hater of naturalism, tried to get her "to say each line one at a time as if they each were a tiny bit of gold." It was a style of underplaying she was entirely unsuited for. The shoot was troubled in other ways. In the middle, Citti—who wasn't far from the slums himself—was arrested and jailed, and Pasolini refused to replace him.

Like all of Pasolini's films, *Mamma Roma* resonates with the director's personal story. After the young Pasolini was arrested in his hometown of Casara on a morals charge and lost his teaching job, he and his devoted mother sneaked out of town and headed for the more tolerant and anonymous Rome. (In real life, he, not the mother, is the whore.) His Fascist, militaristic father, whom he hated, followed—as Carmine the pimp does here. The point is that in *Mamma Roma*, Pasolinia true mamma's boy—identifies closely with the martyred son.

The film's main setting is Rome but not "Rome." The famous white city—represented here by the squat gold dome of a cathedral—gleams off in the distance, whereas the immediate landscape is a series of boxy housing projects set out on the edge of weed fields. On these stark, beautiful plains, among crumbling ruins of the Holy Empire, the local kids play their not-so-innocent games.

Magnani's marvelous, monumental Mamma—everyone in the new neighborhood knows her immediately—is bursting with bourgeois visions, yet her tactics are hardly bourgeois. When Ettore takes up with Bruna, a dazed 24-year-old used by the *ragazzi* as their private sex toy, Mamma arranges for one of her former coworkers to seduce him away. The distraction is temporary. To get the idle Ettore a job, Mamma sets up and then blackmails a prosperous restaurant owner. Though the scheme works, the boy quits when Bruna tells him his mother is a whore. Drifting into petty crime, the boy falls ill with a mysterious fever—it's like the TB that takes the hero of Pasolini's novel *A Violent Life*. The last we see of Ettore, he's in his undershorts, strapped flat on a prison hospital table, and photographed from the soles of his feet to resemble Mantegna's blunt, brutally foreshortened Christ.

Having recently seen Bresson's *The Devil, Probably*, and now *Mamma Roma*, I'm marveling once more how terribly moving these distanced, stylized films can be. You can know the ending beforehand, be semidetatched throughout (or so you think), and then get hit by a ton of grief. Here as elsewhere, Pasolini counterbalances narrative with set pieces, like shots of boys running, Ettore's playful romp among the ruins, or the heroine's garrulous monologues while she strolls under a bank of streetlights. Then, for all Mamma Magnani's magnificently noisy theatrics, Pasolini gets his way: It's the child's quiet, lonely convulsions that pierce the heart.

Also reviewed in:
CHICAGO TRIBUNE, 5/19/95, Friday/p. P, Michael Wilmington
NEW YORK TIMES, 1/18/95, p. C16, Janet Maslin
VARIETY, 8/29/62, p. 19
WASHINGTON POST, 5/12/95, p. B6, Rita Kempley

MAN OF THE HOUSE

A Walt Disney pictures release of an All Girl production in association with Orr & Cruickshank Productions. *Executive Producer:* Margaret South. *Producer:* Bonnie Bruckheimer and Marty Katz. *Director:* James Orr. *Screenplay:* James Orr and Jim Cruickshank. *Story:* David Peckinpah and Richard Jefferies. *Director of Photography:* Jamie Anderson. *Editor:* Harry Keramidas. *Music:* Mark Mancina. *Music Editor:* Curtis Roush. *Sound:* Rob Young and (music) Jay Rifkin and Alan Meyerson. *Sound Editor:* Craig Berkey. *Casting:* Amy Lippens. *Production Designer:* Lawrence G. Paull. *Art Director:* David Willson. *Set Designer:* Alex Kameniczky. *Set Decorator:* Rose Marie McSherry. *Set Dresser:* Brent Bennett. *Special Effects:* Mike Vezina. *Visual Effects:* Michael Lessa. *Costumes:* Tom Bronson. *Make-up:* Victoria Down. *Make-up (Chevy Chase):* Lee C. Harman. *Stunt Coordinator:* Betty Thomas. *Running time:* 98 minutes. *MPAA Rating:* PG.

CAST: Chevy Chase (Jack Sturges); Farrah Fawcett (Sandra Archer); Jonathan Taylor Thomas (Ben Archer); George Wendt (Chet Bronski); David Shiner (Lloyd Small); Art LaFleur (Red Sweeney); Richard Portnow (Joey Renda); Richard Foronjy (Murray); Peter Appel (Tony); Leonard George (Leonard Red Crow); George Greif (Frank Renda); Ron Canada (Bob Younger); Chris Miranda (Hank Sweeney); Zachary Browne (Norman Bronski); Spencer Vrooman (Darryl Small); Nicholas Garrett (Monroe Hill); Jimmy Baker (Young Ben); John DiSanti (Romeo Costanza); Walter Marsh (Judge #1); Judith Maxie (Judge #2); Jim Smith (Minister); Sean Orr (Baliff); Tony Sampson (Big Kid at School #1); Shane Meier (Big Kid at School #2).

LOS ANGELES TIMES, 3/3/95, Calendar/p. 8, Kevin Thomas

"Man of the House" is a serious comedy that works serious. It cuts to the heart of a contemporary phenomenon all too familiar to countless youngsters, that of having to adjust to a stepparent or to a parent's lover. An understated Chevy Chase couldn't be better as a fearless Seattle-based federal prosecutor who faces his greatest challenge trying to win over the 11-year-old son (Jonathan Taylor Thomas) of his girlfriend (Farrah Fawcett).

Thomas' Ben has had his adoring mother all to himself for five years, and at his adolescent stage the boy's jealousy of Chase's Jack Sturges is completely understandable. It's further complicated by Ben's unconscious fear that if he does become attached to Jack that Sturges may walk out on him and his mother, just as his own father did.

Director James Orr and his co-writers develop the difficult but evolving relationship between the man and the boy credibly, and this helps sustain the film throughout. Despite its considerable wide appeal, "Man of the House" could be a better film on several counts. The key problem is that Ben has been conceived as your typical tough-talking, quick-on-the-uptake Hollywood brat; Thomas is clearly a capable actor, but the way in which director Orr and his co-writers have conceived his role, Thomas' Ben seems too often synthetic instead of sympathetic.

Not helping matters is that Fawcett's Sandy, as level-headed and fair-minded as she is presented to be, seems to have failed to prepare Ben for Jack moving in with them, with the idea of eventual marriage if everything works out. You'd have thought that she would have taken pains to see that Ben and Jack got to know each other *before* planning for Jack to move in—and, when he does, to make it clear up front that she and Jack would be sharing the same bed.

There's a false rather than funny ring to the adults dutifully going along, at least initially, with the boy's insistence that his mother and her lover sleep in separate rooms. The filmmakers are on much firmer comic ground in working in a couple of klutzy routines for Chase and making him a target for an underworld reprisal for having sent up a big-time gangster.

Looking gorgeous and still possessing the toothiest smile in the world, Fawcett is likable as a woman trying hard to be fair to both son and lover, and George Wendt is a real asset, bringing the film warmth and humor as a down-to-earth guy who sees Jack through the perils of Indian Guides with Ben. "Man of the House" has its moments—but it could have used more of them.

NEW YORK POST, 3/3/95, p. 49, Michael Medved

Thanks to the spectacular success of "Mrs. Doubtfire" and "The Santa Clause," Yearning Fathers have become one of Hollywood's flavors-of-the-month. Both movies showed sensitive divorced dads (played by leading comics) who would do anything to restore their damaged relationships with their kids.

With "Man of the House," the Disney company offers a new variation on the theme: a *prospective* stepdad who will do anything to win acceptance from the resentful and suspicious son of the woman he loves.

This time, Chevy Chase is the comedian in the lead role, playing a fearless prosecutor in Seattle who's devoted his life to putting vicious mobsters behind bars.

"I can stand up to some of the toughest hoods in the country, and that doesn't faze me a bit," he declares. "But facing an 11-year-old kid—that's really tough!"

The tough kid in question is played by Jonathan Taylor Thomas (Tim Allen's son in TVs "Home Improvement") who doesn't want any interloper moving in on his divorced mom (the perpetually perky Farrah Fawcett).

In order to overcome this resistance, Chase and the boy enroll together in the YMCA Indian Guides program, under the theory that rain dances and tomahawk throws will help to build their relationship. Actually, Chase bonds more successfully with George Wendt (another stepdad struggling to win over a reluctant boy) than he does with the kid.

It's only when three stereotyped gangsters bent on revenge come after Chase during a weekend camping trip that all the Indian Guides must learn to work together in order to fight off the vicious hit men in the worst slapstick "Home Alone" style.

This embarrassingly awful resolution highlights a major flaw in the film's structure: By making Chase a crusading prosecutor they stack the deck too much in his favor.

If the character had been given a more ordinary, less glamorous job, his insecurity in approaching the boy would have felt more sympathetic and believable.

Chase nevertheless exudes his usual charm and makes us identify with his eagerness to play a father's role, while Jonathan Taylor Thomas makes an effective foil, taking his scheming kid character right up to the edge of obnoxiousness without altogether sacrificing the affection of the audience.

He does display one irritating mannerism, however, that detracts from his performance. In the same way that the young Christian Slater used to sound uncannily like Jack Nicholson, Taylor Thomas sounds uncannily like Christian Slater, trying to sound like Jack Nicholson.

Another distraction involves the widespread pubic awareness of the recent losing streak for Chevy Chase, including his disastrous TV talk show, a big screen box-office bomb (last year's forgettable "Cops and Robbersons"), and some highly publicized personal problems.

In this cruel context, a few observers may jump on "Man of the House" as further evidence of his decline, but that's not fair to the film.

It's true it's no masterpiece, but it does provide a pleasant and sometimes touching diversion, until the climactic campout when an otherwise likable picture gets hopelessly lost in the woods.

NEWSDAY, 3/3/95, Part II/p. B5, Jack Mathews

Chevy Chase's transformation from sardonically hip "Saturday Night Live" news anchor to cornball suburban movie mensch was completed many years ago. Still, I never expected to find him playing the Dean Jones role in a Disney movie.

But there he is in "Man of the House," looking a little bewildered himself, as Jack Sturges, a U.S. attorney who can stare down the toughest mobsters in Seattle but wilts under the withering glare of an 11-year-old boy whose mother he hopes to marry.

This is an old-fashioned Disney family movie, cute as a "Love Bug" if you have a small, non-discriminating child with you—preferably a boy—and a fate worse than death if you don't. I was alone.

Chase is bad enough when he's playing a character tailored to his particular brand of physical comedy; here, he is reduced to playing a simpering weenie constantly being upstaged by kids and a bunch of middle-aged men dressed up as Indians. They are the fathers and sons of a spectacularly square club called the Indian Guides, whose members wear feathered headbands, call each other things like Little Wing and Running Bear, and play such neat games as potato bowling.

Jack Sturges is talked into joining the Guides by young Ben (Jonathan Taylor Thomas of "Home Improvement"), who hopes the geekiness of this particular bonding exercise will convince his mother's lover to hit the road. Ben doesn't want a father to replace the one who took off with a secretary five years earlier, because he can't bear another disappointment.

Sturges' challenge: To show Ben and his mother (Farrah Fawcett, of the still cascading curls) that he will withstand any humiliation, even being renamed Squatting Dog, to prove his sincerity, his dependability and his accuracy at hatchet throwing. The question—and don't give it a thought—is whether Ben will come around to Jack's side, and perhaps even help him thwart the mobsters lurking in the background.

Taylor Thomas has a very appealing presence onscreen, and a great voice (you heard him as the young Simba in "The Lion King"). The story is told from his character's precociously cynical point of view, beginning with the departure of his father to his adoption of a suitable replacement, and kids will eagerly identify with him.

The older actors are, to use the idiom of the Indian Guides, in heap big trouble. Chase does a couple of obligatory pratfalls, but most of the time he walks around looking as if he's brooding over the assignment.

And George Wendt, the mountainous beer-guzzling regular from "Cheers," actually looks embarrassed in the scene where the Guides all hop around in a rap music rain dance. Even the gifted mime David Shiner, playing a mute dad who has to act out his thoughts, is made to look like a klutz.

Disney scheduled only one advance screening of "Man of the House," on a Saturday morning, and stacked the theater with kids who sounded as if they were still on a sugar high from their Froot Loops. God, I envied them.

SIGHT AND SOUND, 7/95, p. 51, Philip Kemp

Eleven-year-old Ben Archer lives with his mother, artist Sandra Archer, in Seattle. Deeply hurt when his father deserted them both five years ago, he has since contrived to see off all Sandra's boyfriends, so he is dismayed when she announces that she plans to marry Jack Sturges, a successful prosecuting attorney in the District Attorney's office. Still worse, Jack moves in with them. Egged on by his school friend Monroe, Ben sets out to sabotage the relationship, working on Sandra's guilt feelings and preventing the couple from sleeping together. Meanwhile, Jack is being shadowed by the vengeful Joey Renda, the son of a drug trafficker he sent to jail, and Joey's sidekicks Murray and Tony.

Despite Ben's efforts, Jack persists in trying to win him over. From a younger boy at school, Norman Bronski, Ben learns about the Indian Guide Club, where fathers and sons bond together through practising supposedly Native American rituals. Calculating that the sophisticated Jack will find this utterly humiliating, Ben professes enthusiasm and drags him to a session where they meet the other members: Norman's easy-going stepfather Chet, stickler-for-detail Red Sweeney and his son Hank, and mute circus artiste Lloyd and his son Darryl.

Initially Jack is as embarrassed as Ben had hoped. But after Jack enlists the help of Leonard Red Crow, Chief of the Salish Indians, to teach genuine Native American skills with bow and arrow and tomahawk, both he and—despite himself—Ben find themselves becoming enthusiastic, and a bond grows between them. When the group arrange a canoeing trip, Jack fails to show up: his car brakes have been sabotaged by Joey Renda, and he fetches up in the harbour. He survives unscathed, but conceals the full story from Sandra and Ben. Bitterly disappointed, Ben reverts to hostility.

The group plan a camping trip in the woods. Bob Younger, Jack's boss, orders him to leave town for a while; Jack refuses, determined not to let Ben down again. Joey and his sidekicks follow the group to the woods, and Ben overhears them plotting to kill Jack. Jack tells Ben and the others to fetch help while he decoys the heavies, but falls and injures his leg. Ben returns to help him; using their new-found skills they booby-trap Murray and Tony, but are caught by Joey, who is about to kill them when the rest of the group show up and capture the hoods. All the group attend Jack and Sandy's wedding, while Ben muses how well things have turned out.

In the credits, *Man of the House* is billed as an "All Girl Production". The name's anything but apt, since this is a All Boy Production if ever there was one. Barring one brief bit-part, the sole woman in the cast is Farrah Fawcett, and all she gets to do is flash her teeth, look gauntly sexy and spot-weld the odd lump of metal in the cause of portraying an artist. Male/female relationships, in any case, are largely irrelevant here: father/son bonding is what the movie's about, and once Jack and Ben have got their problems sorted out, it stands to reason that everything will be just fine between Jack and Sandra. So boys must learn to be men, men must get the chance to act like boys, and the compact is sealed (how else?) by heading off into the wilderness and wielding lethal weapons.

In the intervals of all this Junior League Iron-Johnnery, and despite being stuck with a grindingly predictable plot, the film does rack up a few diverting moments. It's best in its earlier reaches, when the abrasion between stepfather and son is at its height: Ben, surveying the newly-installed array of aftershaves and deodorants in the bathroom cabinet, mutters, "What's wrong with the guy—is he decomposing?" There's some neat role reversal too, with the two adults trying to sneak off for some nocturnal nookie, but stopped dead by the appearance of a censorious 11-year-old glaring down from the landing.

Apart from a couple of crudely stuck-on slapstick episodes, most of the humour preserves this drily sardonic tone, to which the cast respond with relish. As Ben, Jonathan Taylor Thomas is likeably uncute, and there's particularly good support from George Wendt (Norman from *Cheers*) and Leonard George, son of Chief Dan George, who's clearly inherited his father's laconic charm. What none of them can overcome, though, is the film's relentlessly didactic intent, culminating in a finale that rams home its trite message ("Sometimes you have to trust people") with all the subtlety of a piledriver on steroids. A couple of years ago the BBC broadcast *Goggle Eyes*, adapted by Deborah Moggach from Anne Fine's novel, which treated an almost identical subject with far more wit and imagination, and infinitely less moralising, not that there's any question of plagiarism. More's the pity; if the makers of *Man of the House* had seen *Goggle Eyes*, it might have improved their film no end.

Also reviewed in:
CHICAGO TRIBUNE, 3/3/95, Friday/p. L, Michael Wilmington
NEW YORK TIMES, 3/3/95, p. C6, Stephen Holden
VARIETY, 3/6-12/95, p. 63, Brian Lowry
WASHINGTON POST, 3/3/95, p. B7, Hal Hinson

MANGLER, THE

A New Line Cinema release of a Distant Horizon, Filmex (Pty) Ltd. production in association with Allied Film Productions. *Executive Producer:* Harry Allen Towers. *Producer:* Anant Singh. *Director:* Tobe Hooper. *Screenplay:* Tobe Hooper, Stephen Brooks, and Peter Welbeck. *Based on a short story by:* Stephen King. *Director of Photography:* Amnon Salomon. *Editor:* David Heitner. *Music:* Barrington Pheloung. *Sound:* Richard Sprawson and (music) David Hunt. *Casting:* Christa Schamberger. *Production Designer:* David Barkham. *Set Dresser:* Jeanne Henn and Hamid Croukamp. *Special Effects:* Max Poolman. *Costumes:* Moira Anne Meyer. *Make-up:* Tracy Crystal, David Miller, and Barry Koper. *Stunt Coordinator:* Gavin Mey. *Running time:* 105 minutes. *MPAA Rating:* R.

CAST: Robert Englund (Bill Gartley); Ted Levine (John Hunton); Daniel Matmor (Mark Jackson); Jeremy Crutchley (Pictureman/Mortician); Vanessa Pike (Sherry Oulette); Demetre Phillips (Stanner); Lisa Morris (Lin Sue); Vera Blacker (Mrs. Frawley); Ashley Hayden (Annette Gillian); Danny Keogh (Herb Diment); Ted Leplat (Doctor Ramos); Todd Jensen (Roger Martin); Sean Taylor (Derrick Gates); Gerrit Schoonhoven (Aaron Rodriguez); Nan Hamilton (Mrs. Ellenshaw); Adrian Waldron (Mr. Ellenshaw); Norman Coombes (Judge Bishop); Larry Taylor (Sheriff Hughes); Irene Frangs (Mrs. Smith); Megaan Wilson (Ginny Jason); Odile Rault (Alberta); Ron Smerczak (Officer Steele).

LOS ANGELES TIMES, 3/6/95, Calendar/p. 7, David Kronke

Consider, for a second, what you might honestly expect from a movie called "The Mangler." Well, it doesn't even aim that high.

This cheapo horror flick lacks a whit of sense—narrative coherence is mangled more than anything else. Otherwise, it's a glum, lackluster affair. Its ostensible selling points—it's based on a story from The Stephen King factory, directed by Tobe Hooper, the best friend a Texas chain saw ever had, and stars Robert Englund, whose performance here makes his work as Freddy Krueger seem positively subtle—don't add up to much.

It concerns the grisly fates that befall all those at an industrial laundry in rural Maine, apparently just outside OSHA's jurisdiction. Seems there's an elephantine steam iron and speed folder that routinely gobbles up the help and clankily cranks them into pulpy squares.

This doesn't stop most characters in the movie, however, from turning their backs to this eviscerating eyesore and resting their hands before its menacingly gaping maw. Nor does the laundry's crazed owner (Englund) seem too put off by the inefficient nature of his prized monstrosity: All that blood would be hard to get out of the sheets it stains.

In town is a dyspeptic cop (Ted Levine) who sputters profanity apoplectically if a truck slows down traffic—you can imagine how he reacts to a string of deaths. He and a New-Age nitwit (Daniel Matmor) swap lines of dialogue most actors wouldn't dare touch ("I don't suppose you know anything about industrial laundries"; "You know, I used to work in an industrial laundry"), then decide the machine is possessed.

Levine finally reveals why he is so grouchy throughout this movie: He knew he would have to shoot a monumentally stupid scene in which he tries to perform an exorcism on a bucket of bolts that looks like a reject from Fritz Lang's "Metropolis."

This might have been mildly interesting if someone had put an ounce of effort into the script and if Hooper had set the story far in the past. As is, he and the design team are seeking an eerily Gothic look.

Hooper could have also made at least a token attempt to create one interesting or sympathetic character and shot more than one take per scene—even by horror standards, the acting here is lame. Call it "The Bungler."

NEW YORK POST, 3/4/95, p. 15, Bill Hoffmann

There's no question that doing laundry is a real drag.

But for the employees of Gartley's Blue Ribbon Laundry, it's especially hellish.

That's because of a huge piece of pressing equipment, known as "The Mangler," which looks like a demonic cross between a newspaper printing press and "Alien."

And in the first 10 minutes of Tobe Hooper's dopey new movie, "The Mangler" mercilessly gobbles up a kindly old lady who works there and spits out her bloody body parts.

Yes, folks, it's the world's first movie about a killer laundry machine!

"The Mangler" is owned by a mean, disabled old slave driver named William Gartley (Robert Englund, better known as Freddy Krueger), who doesn't care how many people get chewed up in the monstrosity. And over the years, too many have.

"There's a little of that machine in me and a little of me in it," he explains with a deep cackle.

Enter Officer Johnny Hunton (Ted Levine), a cop with some demons of his own, who is bound and determined to shut the ghastly device down.

With the aid of a bearded occultist Mark Jackson (Daniel Matmor), Hunton discovers that the machine is possessed and may have a thirst for the blood of young virgins.

Hunton and Jackson hunt to find the magical mumbo-jumbo that will kill the metal monster before it mangles again.

Based on a short story by Stephen King, "The Mangler" is a mess, trying to mix too many horror genies and succeeding at none.

Bits from "The Exorcist," "Maximum Overdrive," "Alien" and countless gore movies are all represented here.

The situation isn't helped by the amazingly wooden performance of Ted Levine, who was so effective as the skin-'em-alive killer in "The Silence of the Lambs."

There are some effective set designs here—particularly Gartley's creepy office—but the script kills any potential they have to scare.

Director Hooper is the same man who scared our pants off with "The Texas Chainsaw Massacre" and "Poltergeist."

The only thing he succeeds at here is making you want to send your laundry out from now on.

NEWSDAY, 3/4/95, Part II/p. B5, John Anderson

Few attend the cinematic works of Tobe Hooper—which have included "Poltergeist," "Invaders from Mars" and two "Texas Chainsaw Massacres"—looking for Noël Coward. No, they want fear, they want chills, they want possession by demons, imperiled women and temporarily impotent but ultimately victorious men. Actually, that *is* Noël Coward.

But you know what we mean, and all of the above can be found in "The Mangler," Hooper's latest, if far from his greatest. Lifted from a Stephen King story, it has as its centerpiece a mangle—a huge, industrial iron—that in the purgatorial laundry of a sleepy-but-haunted Maine town gives new meaning to the words "pressing the flesh."

The machine is Moby Dick to laundry owner Bill Gartley (Robert "Freddy," Englund), who hobbles about on two prosthetic legs and keeps his business staffed with nubile young women—occasionally, the mangle needs to chew on a 16-year-old virgin, and Gartley is obliged to provide one. Coming to the rescue, sort of, is police officer John Hunton (Ted Levine), who joins forces with parapsychologist Mark Jackson (Daniel Matmor) to take the starch out of Gartley.

The sheets hit the fan once John and Mark discover the secret of the mangle, which wants to fold, spindle and mutilate Sherry (Vanessa Pike), Gartley's niece and the most annoying whiner and screamer since Fay Wray. Levine and Matmor are a good team, though, even if Levine's cop is too cynical to be indignant over the town's dirty laundry. Jeremy Crutchley does nice double duty as a creepy police photographer and a mortician who talks to his corpses. While this is hardly a seamless story, Hooper has given his audience what he thinks it wants: blood, mayhem, but no new wrinkles.

SIGHT AND SOUND, 7/95, p. 50, Philip Strick

On the outskirts of Rikers Valley lies a vast laundry processing plant, where exhausted women slave for the cruel and deformed owner. Bill Gartley, and his industrial steam-iron, "the mangler". A series of strange accidents is triggered when an icebox falls on the machine, wounding a young worker named Sherry Ouelette who is Gartley's niece. Blood drips on the mechanism, which soon gobbles an old lady, Mrs Frawley. Officer John Hunton is called in to investigate.

Already on the scene is a photographer, Pictureman. Mark Jackson, Hunton's brother-in-law, tries to convince Hunton that the mangler is possessed, but the Sheriff records a verdict of accidental death. Subsequently, a small child is found suffocated inside the plant's icebox from the plant. When Hunton batters the object with a mallet a huge whirlwind of energy is released. Pictureman suddenly dies of cancer, bequeathing to Hunton a scrapbook of cuttings. These reveal that many virginal daughters of the town's powerful elite have gone missing on their sixteenth birthdays. Hunton confronts Gartley. There is a struggle and Gartley's foreman, Stanner, gets caught in the mangler.

Hunton is warned off the case. Most of the town turn out to be in league with Gartley and the machine. Gartley initiates his lover Lin Sue into the demonic club and when the machine demands a new sacrifice, they present it with Sherry, who is turning sixteen. Hunton and Jackson arrive just in time. Lin Sue is rollered and crushed, whilst Gartley is folded to death. But an attempted exorcism only succeeds in bringing the mangler fully to life. Jackson is killed and Hunton and Sherry escape—but not before Sherry has lost some blood to the machine. Later, when Hunton visits Sherry at the plant he discovers she has developed similar handicaps to her dead uncle, is in charge of the factory and everything is running as normal.

The Mangler assembles something of a modern horror-genre hall of fame: director Tobe Hooper (*The Texas Chain Saw Massacre, Poltergeist*) is teamed with Robert Englund (of Freddy Krueger fame) and Ted Levine (*The Silence of the Lambs*) in yet another adaptation for the screen of a Stephen King short story. The film scores high on production finesse: new digital editing techniques give many of the cast amputated fingers, the gore is viscerally convincing and the sequence where the 40-foot machine becomes a kind of giant mechanical bullfrog is well done. Yet all this fails to add up to a frightening movie; the giant laundry machine does not translate from the page to the screen as a motor of menace.

Stephen King worked in a laundry while making his name as a writer, and the force of *The Mangler*, seems to derive in part from his desire to revenge himself on his old job. In his story, fear is generated not simply by the figure of the possessed machine, but by the gradual uncovering of the human consensus which nurtures and supports it. The tale takes as its premise Nietzsche's vision of a perfect society whose social cohesiveness is provided by mystical forces released by the sacrifice of children.

Thus in Rikers Valley, the town elite have agreed to feed to the mangler demon their middle fingers and a proportion of their virginal offspring in return for a life of saccharine suburban bliss. But, in the film, the device is used cheaply, dispelling its power: libidinousness is purchased easily by having the machine demand only daughters, and not sons, and since Gartley is the only member of the elite that we actually meet, the necessary mood of paranoia is never achieved. The human evil of Rikers Valley never gains enough weight to compensate for the steam-iron's failure to terrify.

Englund, having honed his horror acting to a fine degree in all of those *Elm Street* movies, does a good job as the deranged and deformed capitalist who has to tweak his throat knob to stop himself gargling with excitement when he watches his young lover undress. But despite his efforts the film's major theme— the melding of human with machine—fares badly. Englund's character has been maimed by the mangler in his youth and is practically a cyborg. Encased in leg braces and sporting a mis-matched artificial eye he drools to Hunton: "There's a little bit of me in that machine, and a little bit of it in me."

Again we are short-changed by the simplicity of the film's conceptual framework, in which human plus machine equals evil, and existential hero plus righteous outrage equals good. Ted Levine's cop with a past (not a patch on his Buffalo Bill in *The Silence of the Lambs* fails to carry the protagonist's burden: he can't seem to decide whether to go for a detached parody or try to generate audience identification, and in the end manages neither. The audience is left, like Hunton in the final scene, bemused that things have turned out like they have, but not really that bothered either way.

Also reviewed in:
CHICAGO TRIBUNE, 4/7/95, Tempo/p. 16, Rene Rodriguez
NEW YORK TIMES, 3/4/95, p. 16, Stephen Holden
VARIETY, 3/6-12/95, p. 66, Godfrey Cheshire
WASHINGTON POST, 3/6/95, p. D6, Richard Harrington

MARTHA AND ETHEL

A Sony Pictures Classics release of a Canobie Films production. *Producer:* Jyll Johnstone and Barbara Ettinger. *Director:* Jyll Johnstone. *Screenplay:* Jyll Johnstone and Barbara Ettinger. *Director of Photography:* Joseph Friedman. *Editor:* Toby Shimin. *Sound:* John D. McCormick. *Sound Editor:* Mary Ellen Porto. *Running time:* 80 minutes. *MPAA Rating:* G.

WITH: Jyll Johnstone and Barbara Ettinger (Narrators); Martha Kneifel; Ethel Edwards.

CHRISTIAN SCIENCE MONITOR, 2/6/95, p. 15, David Sterritt

What makes some documentaries valuable is the light they shed on subjects far outside our normal rounds of experience. But sometimes the most involving nonfiction films are those dealing with material quite close to home.

Proving his point, a quiet and compelling movie called "Martha & Ethel" has become one of the rare documentaries to go into regular theatrical release—courtesy of Sony Pictures Classics, which is distributing the film after its well-received premiere at last year's Sundance Film Festival.

"Martha & Ethel" focuses on a time-honored profession: that of the "nanny" who raises children when parents are reluctant or unable to do the job alone.

The movie's director, Jyll Johnstone, first conceived the project as a 20-minute study of the German-born nanny who raised her and four siblings over a 30-year period starting in the early 1940s. The film took on feature-length proportions when Barbara Ettinger became coproducer, bringing in the African-American nanny who played a central role in her household during the same period.

Although both are nannies in the classic sense of the term, Martha and Ethel prove to be very different as people and as professionals. Martha became a baby nurse in her native Germany, taking a comfortable job with a wealthy Jewish family. This position disqualified her for further employment when the Nazis came to power, so she moved to the United States and eventually settled into the Johnstone's home. As interviews with Martha and the now-grown family show, she was a disciplinarian who never questioned Old World notions that coolness, strictness, and sparsely granted affection are just what children need.

Ethel, also left home in the '30s trading her Southern sharecropper roots for a more exciting life in cities to the north. Her job with the Ettingers assumed new importance when the couple divorced, greatly increasing her responsibility for their six teenagers. Again, a series of on-camera interviews and shared recollections give fascinating glimpses into her personality, which appears to be exceptionally warm, caring, and outgoing.

If this double nanny-biography were all "Martha & Ethel" had to offer, it would be a likeable but unmemorable movie. Lending extra resonance is the portrait it paints of the Johnstone and Ettinger families, and of the filmmakers who grew up within them. Both families hired a nanny by choice rather than necessity, and present-day interviews with the children indicate a lingering uneasiness with the distant parent-child relations that resulted.

Although the movie draws no definite conclusions, it raises important questions about how to balance order and convenience with love and affection while raising children in a materialistic society. It also brings needed attention to the nanny profession itself; which is often taken too much for granted—as are individual nannies, to the point where Sony's production notes for "Martha & Ethel" don't bother supplying last names for either of the women in its title.

The film might have been more revealing if it had been made by outsiders who could look at all these nannies, parents, and children with fresh and unprejudiced eyes; yet some of its appeal stems from the honesty and generosity shown by the filmmakers in sharing their experiences. Moviegoers who decry the sorry state of mainstream films should make a point of seeking out "Martha & Ethel."

LOS ANGELES TIMES, 3/8/95, Calendar/p. 8, Kevin Thomas

As a dual portrait of two very different women who became nannies for two equally different families, "Martha and Ethel" offers a unique view of servants' lives and also gives us a rare glimpse of upper-crust American life over the past half-century.

The downtrodden and the disenfranchised tend to attract filmmakers lots more than nannies and the rich, but then producer-director Jyll Johnstone and co-producer Barbara Ettinger, friends since childhood in Manhattan, are telling us about their own nannies and their own families.

They are, thankfully, in no way apologetic about their privileged backgrounds, and they get their nannies, Martha and Ethel, respectively, to open up as they do their parents and siblings.

When so many wives are working as well as husbands, nannies are no longer the province of the wealthy. It was different when the Johnstones hired Martha Kneifel in 1941, just before the birth of their first of five children, and when the Ettingers in 1954 hired Ethel Edwards, who helped raise their six children.

The most significant thing about both Martha, who died at 91 last fall, and Ethel, now in her 90s, is that they were following their calling and that they seem truly to have no regrets in devoting their lives to other people's children.

Ethel is a tall, elegant black woman from a South Carolina sharecropping family with a radiant personality. When we meet German-born Martha, who is plain and short, she's vivacious and affectionate, but the Johnstone children remember her as a stern disciplinarian, as strong and detached as their glamorous, fashion-plate socialite mother.

The Johnstones don't seem to have been harmed by the influence of Martha and their equally formidable mother, and they admit that their nanny did instill in them a sense of discipline. Much of Martha's portion of the film involves an attempt on the part of several of the children to connect emotionally with her.

Ethel's relationship with the Ettingers has been entirely different. While not losing a sense of who she is, Ethel, a woman of warmth and wisdom, really became a part of the Ettinger family, loving its six children as if they were her own. When the Ettingers' marriage broke up, Ethel gradually became Mrs. Ettinger's friend and companion as the children grew up. To this day the two women, in a "Driving Miss Daisy" relationship, live under the same roof, deeply appreciative of each other—but, yes, Ethel continues to wear her uniform.

There's a great deal of self-satisfaction in Mrs. Johnstone, who feels she and Martha both did their jobs well. Mr. Johnstone and Mr. Ettinger don't figure much in the film, both seem politely grateful about the women who did most of the raising of their children.

All of this information about Martha and Ethel and the families they worked for unfolds like a good novel, and we're left with both a sense of particular lives lived. You have the feeling that there's lots more to be explored about the Johnstones and their relationships with one another, but that's a whole other movie.

NEW YORK POST, 2/3/95, p. 47, Thelma Adams

"Martha and Ethel" are two 90-year-old former nannies.

Wiry German disciplinarian Martha Kneifel fled Hitler and raised producer/director Jyll Johnstone and her brothers and sisters.

Ethel Edwards migrated from South Carolina seeking better opportunities. She found her lifelong niche nuturing co-producer Barbara Ettinger and her siblings.

Childhood friends Johnstone and Ettinger have created a portrait of two seniors which reveals as much about the filmmakers as their subjects.

The fascinating documentary contemplates upper-class family life, parenting, and the bonds and fissures between daughters, mothers and nannies.

As a new generation of women not homebound mothers but working professionals—hands its children off to intimate strangers, "Martha and Ethel" becomes more than an artifact about the past. It is a window on the future.

Johnstone grew up hating Martha. She initially asks: "Why my parents hired someone else to bring us up?" Jyll begins trying to unearth the roots of her emotional numbness; she concludes understanding Martha as an individual with a history separate from her own.

For Ettinger, who still crawls into Ethel's lap fully grown, The movie begins as a celebration of the woman whom she loved with a devotion that rivals what she felt for her mother.

"Martha and Ethel" is a document of psychological separation, of adults coming to see their "mothers" as beings distinct from themselves with their own secrets, longings, disappointments and joys.

NEWSDAY, 2/3/95, Part II/p. B7, John Anderson

"Following World War II," reads the "Martha & Ethel" press material, "a generation of women willingly relinquished their mothering responsibilities to hired women ..." When I read this to my mother, she was surprised, because she distinctly remembers caring for some children back in the '50s, and is pretty certain they were her own.

She could be wrong, of course. And "Martha & Ethel"—Jyll Johnstone and Barbara Ettinger's affectionate, if deeply myopic, documentary about their nannies/surrogate mothers—could be right in positing that the filmmakers had a kind of privileged upbringing that was more normal than anomalous, that America in the post-war years really was the land of June Cleaver Unchained. If this sounds highly personal on my part, it is. But so is "Martha & Ethel," a film that takes the documentary form, which is always subjective anyway, and turns it into group therapy.

The women at the center of this film couldn't be more different, or less likely subjects of a movie. Ethel Edwards, who came from a black sharecropper family in South Carolina, is portrayed as a common-sensical woman who raised the Ettinger children with kindness and a bit of a jaundiced eye toward her employers. Martha Kneifel, who fled Germany in 1936 (having been blackballed for her work with Jewish families) and was hired in 1941 by the Johnstones, was a martinet who subscribed to a regimen of rigid control and parsimonious affection.

How these women's characters affected their respective charges isn't something that's pursued with particular diligence by the filmmakers. It just sort of leaks out through the voiceover narration, the interviews with siblings, parents and the women themselves, and the archival television and movie footage from the period. And it becomes clear before too long that both Ettinger and Johnstone are using their nannies to launch a flank attack on their parents—and likely are not even aware of it.

The parents—the fathers are virtual absentees, the mothers fonts of warped values—are case studies in self-absorption and fear of adulthood. Johnstone's mother was born in Monaco, played piano and, although not orphaned, was adopted by a wealthy American couple who encouraged her concert career. She later became a fixture on the New York charity circuit (the footage concerning her various social appearances is archeological); for her, parenthood seems to have been, at best, an inconvenience. Ettinger's mother, who still lives with Ethel, admits that she was unequipped for child-rearing; just who is the child is another inadvertent question raised by the film. Less villainous than vacuous, these women are oblivious either to the intentions of this film or to their children's various maladjustments.

This is fascinating stuff, but so is a car crash. It isn't very good filmmaking, though, because the filmmakers ultimately abdicate their responsibility as blithely as their parents. When one of the fathers, addressing what it meant to hand over your children to virtual strangers, says, "That's just the way it was done," you ask yourself why Ettinger or Johnstone didn't simply say, "No, it wasn't," and give voice to their deep-seated resentments.

SIGHT AND SOUND, 9/95, p. 56, Louise Gray

Martha, now aged 87, left Baden-Baden in 1936 for the United States. A trained children's nurse, her previous work with a Jewish family made her ineligible for work in Hitler's Germany. In 1941, she was hired by the Johnstones, an upper middle-class family, to raise their five children. Martha remained with the family until her retirement in 1971.

Ethel, an 88-year-old, is black, the daughter of sharecroppers from South Carolina. Ethel came to know the Harlem night life of the 20s before entering service in 1954, becoming nanny to the six Ettinger children. A sequence of interviews, intercut with archive footage detailing the aspirations of 40s, 50s and 60s life, explores each nanny's impact on various members of the families they served, as well as supplying details of Martha and Ethel's own lives.

Martha, who imported a strict German discipline to the Johnstone household, is described in loving terms, although the children were often frightened of her. Ethel, on the other hand, is spontaneously affectionate, a 'natural' mother. She continues to live, as an employee, with Mrs Ettinger in Connecticut, although both she and the family acknowledge that the relationship they share is difficult to define. At the end of the film, each family make an effort to embrace the backgrounds of their respective surrogate mothers. Martha visits her home town and is feted like a returning heroine. On her return, the Johnstones are concerned that Martha is becoming infirm and that, consequently, life alone in her New York apartment will become arduous. One of the daughters arranges for her to move to California, close to her. The Ettingers take Ethel to visit her younger, 86-year-old sister and relatives. We see photographs that Barbara Ettinger has taken of Ethel. A further sequence of photographs, which includes one of Martha and Ethel together, concludes the film.

Over the course off this intensely personal and affectionate documentary, certain questions become increasingly insistent. What about Martha and Ethel's own lives, one wants to ask. And, for that matter, what about the children these feisty, vivacious, octogenarian spinsters never had? These are difficult questions. One of the most revealing moments of the film shows Martha in her New York apartment, introducing her teddy bears and rag dolls as her children. But Martha and Ethel, after all, have been surrogate mothers to a cumulative 11 children. "You don't have to bear children to love them," says Ethel at one point, and Martha and Ethel are, in turn, well-loved and cared for. Each child and each parent has a relationship to each nanny respectively. Ethel, who receives Mother's Day cards from 'her' children is now a working companion to Mrs Ettinger, a salaried friend.

Salaried friend? No wonder an infant Ettinger is surprised to discover that Ethel has a different surname. Another describes her momentary sense of betrayal and confusion upon learning that her nanny is a paid hand. Both sets of parents, caught up in the social whirl of their milieux, had passed day-to-day responsibilities to the nannies. What price, one might ask, does love command?

But such questions are unanswerable and it is to the credit of director Jyll Johnstone and her co-producer, Barbara Ettinger, that this film offers no simplistic analyses of the nannies. *Martha & Ethel* is a slowly revealing film, punctuated with a humour born of careful editing. It is concerned to trace the marks that these two women have made on their 'families' lives, and to contextualise them within points of Martha and Ethel's own experience. This is done with a deft touch. An adult Johnstone child talks about being beaten with a wooden spoon by Martha; archival footage, from *Mädchen in Uniform*, illustrates Martha's training environment, and she speaks about her own childhood spankings, administered by, yes, a wooden spoon. Mrs Johnstone, a Monaco-born former concert pianist who was adopted by American parents, speaks of the child's need for discipline, and one is aware that her own security—with its concomitant requirements for an identifiable framework within which to manoeuvre—may be on the agenda. Further film clips portraying 50s advertisements about how the ideal wife should behave expand upon the social context of the mother's life. Despite Martha's Germanic approach to child-rearing, it is interesting, indeed moving, that some decades after leaving her homeland, she is still only able to whisper Hitler's name.

One is left with a film that produces its own weave of relationships and ties. Johnstone's historical context is never reductionist and the personalities of her interviewees are strongly represented. Above all, Martha and Ethel come across as courageous women, whose attachment to children knows no racial or national divide. But the issue of employee, or even chattel, status never really vanishes. Mrs Ettinger relates packing kids, luggage and Ethel into the station wagon during her and Mr Ettinger's divorce. There is a nagging feeling that, given the confusion between master, servant, mother and friend roles, that this is possibly *Driving Miss Daisy* writ large. Johnstone is unflinching on these subjects. Certainly, the family environments of the Ettingers and Johnstones represent a particular social class in a particular economic climate. In her portrayal of these two women, the differences of race and nationality are barely mentioned. Some may consider this a grave oversight. But then *Martha & Ethel* is not a hectoring film, merely an honest and touching attempt to represent a series of relationships and commemorate the extraordinary love that characterised them. Given Britain's own propensity towards a nanny culture, this film will undoubtedly speak to several generations here.

VILLAGE VOICE, 2/14/95, p. 52, Georgia Brown

Jyll Johnstone's *Martha & Ethel* poses as a portrait of two nannies. Since the elderly women—an African American from South Carolina and a German emigrant—are touching, complex, and vigorous, this part is easy. Look closer and the nannies are a screen for Johnstone's real subjects: her parents, class, and—a practice more stunting than foot-binding—the relinquishing of parenting. What struck me most in this sly, brave documentary is the pathos of two pinched society women—call them breeders—who gave up, along with their children, a chance to do productive work. Too much money, the film indicates, is lethal.

First the nannies. One—Johnstone's own—is Martha Kneifel, a tiny, steel-willed *mädchen* who imposed Germanic ideals of cleanliness, order, and discipline on five resentful charges. The other is Ethel Edwards, a skinny, wonderfully warm sharecropper's daughter who raised coproducer Barbara Ettinger and her five sibs. (It might be pointed out that neither nanny's last name is provided in the movie's production notes. In the film, Ethel's surname becomes an issue when an Ettinger daughter recalls her shock as a child discovering it was not the same as hers.)

Publicity bills this picture as reflecting the "new prosperity" of the '50s when "a generation of women willingly relinquished their mothering responsibilities." I beg to differ. I grew up in the '50s (though not in the East) and didn't know anyone with a nanny. As I recall, women stayed home and took care of their own kids more than ever before. (After all, they'd been "liberated" by those new labor-saving devices.) If you really want to talk of relinquishing mothering responsibilities, nothing this century beats the '80s. On this level, decisions faced by the Johnstones and Ettingers are those faced today.

In one case, money bought love; in the other it didn't. None of the Johnstone kids felt loved by Martha, and Martha, graduate of a Third Reich school of child rearing, never considered love one of her duties. Given her goals, it would have been counterproductive. Just one of the principles she was taught in nanny school: "The child's will must be broken." (One parodox of aging: She may not have known how to love, but in her eighties, Martha seems perfectly lovable.) Even today, the Johnstone parents don't regret choosing Martha—an attitude that underlines their continuing alienation from the resentful children.

Blithely, Mrs. Johnstone recalls how the babies were brought home from the hospital and "they were *hers* from that time on." She laughs about once trying to look in on her crying son and Martha's turning her back: "I learned to keep away." Here is a cowardly couple who have contrived to spare themselves the honest emotions of real parents everywhere—torment, anguish, and guilt.

But I'm reading in. Johnstone herself is reticent about family business. Clearly she's made a pact not to go into details. We don't know any of the siblings' or the two fathers' professions. There's talk about Martha's weapon of choice, the wooden spoon, but we don't learn what consequences her paddlings and other harshness had on the children: All we can say is that the younger generation looks prosperous. (Someone collects handsome nouveau lamps.) If I'm correct, one Johnstone son doesn't appear. But if no secrets are explicitly shared, there's plenty of funny business lying open for inspection, even in the luckier Ettinger household.

Having been raised under the gentle, permissive Ethel, the Ettinger kids do look looser, less abashed. Instead of criticism and raps with the spoon, they got hugs and indiscriminate approval. Ethel, says Mrs. Ettinger, even adjusted to the horrid excesses of the '60s, whereas she was appalled having to sit down to dinner with hippies. Ethel herself discloses that success depended on never losing sight of her *place* as a black person. When she got to sit with the family in restaurants, for instance, "I never let it go to my head." Always, lurking in the shadows, there was the dirty fact that this love was hired. At one point, an Ettinger daughter describes how confused and betrayed she felt on discovering Ethel was being *paid*.

In both families, the dads made (or inherited?) the money to hire Ethel and Martha, yet each is barely articulate—their very mouths don't seem formed for intimate disclosure. Briefly on screen here, they merely ratify the wisdom of long-ago decisions. "Martha was a great disciplinarian," marvels Mr. Johnstone in his Florida retirement outfit. "How did we know she loved the children? She was so *busy*."

But it's the biological mothers who get you most. Apparently in her sixties, the elegantly brittle Mrs. Ettinger, though perfectly capable, is still being waited on by the 88-year-old Ethel. When she has a cold she calls Ethel to the kitchen to find the decaf tea. Ethel dutifully opens the cupboard where the tea is in plain sight. "At first it was employer/employee," Mrs. Ettinger explains, "now it's more of a friendship." Ethel calls her friend "Mrs. Ettinger."

Fear of babies. That's how both wives explain their initial decisions. They plead no prior training. Little do they know that in rejecting their infants, then their growing children, they missed a real chance to grow up.

Also reviewed in:
CHICAGO TRIBUNE, 2/24/95, Friday/p. J, Johanna Steinmetz
NEW YORK TIMES, 2/3/95, p. C8, Janet Maslin
VARIETY, 2/7-13/94, p. 40, Emanuel Levy
WASHINGTON POST, 3/10/95, p. C7, Rita Kempley
WASHINGTON POST, 3/10/95, Weekend/p. 36, Desson Howe

MARTHA AND I

A Cinema Four release of an Iduna Film (Kirch Gruppe), Progefi, TF1 Films coproduction in collaboration with ZDF, ORF, Canal Plus, and Raidue. *Producer:* Sabine Tettenborn and Marius Schwartz. *Director:* Jiri Weiss. *Screenplay (German with English subtitles):* Jiri Weiss. *Director of Photography:* Viktor Ruzicka. *Editor:* Gisela Haller. *Music:* Jiri Stivin. *Production Designer:* Karel Vacek. *Costumes:* Maria Frankova. *Running time:* 107 minutes. *MPAA Rating:* Not Rated.

CAST: Marianne Saegebrecht (Martha); Michel Piccoli (Ernst); Vaclav Chalupa (Emil as a Youth); Ondrej Vetchy (Emil as an Adult); Bozidara Turzonvovas (Rosa Kluge); Jana Brezinova (Ida Fuchs); Sona Valentova (Elsa Fuchs); Jana Altmanova (Kamila Fuchs); Zuzana Kocurikova (Ilona); Klaus Grunberg (Bertl); Michael Kausch (Werner); Jiri Menzel (Dr. Benda).

LOS ANGELES TIMES, 4/21/95, Calendar/p. 2, Kevin Thomas

Jiri Weiss' beautiful, heart-rending "Martha and I," a love story told with uncommon poignancy and meaning, stars Marianne Saegebrecht and Michel Piccoli as an unlikely couple whose mutual devotion develops limitless depths.

For Saegebrecht, the plump, radiant star of Percy Adlon's comedies "Sugarbaby," "Bagdad Cafe" and "Rosalie Goes Shopping," the film is a personal triumph, signaling her emergence as a serious actress of remarkable range and understatement. For Piccoli, it marks yet another splendid performance of wit and passion.

At first, Saegebrecht's Martha is strictly peripheral, the devoted, unobtrusive housekeeper to Piccoli's Ernst, a successful, urbane obstetrician. But about a year after he's kicked out his glamorous, adulterous, much-younger wife, he sizes up Martha and abruptly announces, much to her understandable astonishment, that they're getting married.

What ensues is amusing and affectionate as Ernst transforms a servant into a prosperous doctor's well-turned-out wife. The humble Martha resists mightily, unable to believe she can be—or even deserves to be—attractive.

Great love blossoms between them, but Martha and Ernst are the right couple in the wrong place, a charming town on the German-Czech border in the late '30s. For Ernst is a Jew, never mind that he's a free-thinking agnostic who regards himself as a Czech through and through: Martha is from sturdy German peasant stock.

Ernst's many sisters are silly snobs who condescend to Martha, but she has a brother who's far worse: a rabid, nakedly anti-Semitic Nazi. As "Martha and I" grows darker, the actions of Martha and Ernst reveal the magnitude of true love.

Exquisitely nuanced and possessed not of a single false note, "Martha and I"—set largely in settings of deceptively solid, well-upholstered upper-middle-class comfort—proceeds with warmth, humor and a profound sense of loss.

Weiss, the veteran Czech-born writer-director, unflinchingly confronts with powerful calm and detachment the evil of the Holocaust on the most personal, intimate level. Every frame of his film is suffused with love and respect for Martha and Ernst, bespeaking Weiss' assured, unfussy mastery of screen storytelling and the fact that he's telling a true story; indeed, the film unfolds from the point of view of Weiss' alter ego, Ernst's teen-age nephew, played by Vaclav Chalupa and, as an adult, by Ondrzej Vetchy.

It took Weiss, long a Los Angeles-area resident, decades to get to make this film—and five years to get it distributed in the United States. "Martha and I" warrants every ounce of Weiss' persistence and patience.

NEW YORK POST, 3/24/95, p. 44, Thelma Adams

See "Martha and I" for Marianne Saegebrecht's performance. With her Bruegel face, peasant figure and delicate movements that defy the roughhewn charms of both, the "Bagdad Cafe" actress creates a memorable, understated character.

Her gentile German housekeeper blossoms under the love of Ernst (Michel Piccoli), her Jewish employer, and discovers despair when historical events separate them.

Piccoli ("Atlantic City") brings shadows and light to the part of a cultured, assimilated gynecologist who perceives himself as a Czech first and foremost—until the advent of the Nazis.

Ernst, however, is not the "I" of the title. His nephew Emil (played as a child by Vaclav Chalupa and as an adult by Ondrej Vetchy) narrates this autobiographical tale written and directed by 83-year-old Czech filmmaker Jiri Weiss.

Made in 1990, "Martha and I" kicked around the festival circuit, winning numerous prizes. It finally makes its New York debut today at the Quad in the West Village.

The movie is a labor of love, but Weiss' alter ego Emil's coming-of-age in Czechoslovakia under the rise of Hitler is almost a distraction from that part of the story that generates the most heat.

Neither Chalupa nor Vetch is as engaging as the major stars, and we feel restricted looking over Emil's shoulder at the action. Weiss falls prey to coming-of-age cliches that are not in evidence in the Martha/Ernst romance. Emil loses his virginity and, presto, the girl is pregnant.

The movie is at its most original when it veers from a Holocaust memoir and gives way to a complicated love story set against dangerous times.

Together, Saegebrecht and Piccoli forge a believable and moving bond.

NEWSDAY, 3/24/95, Part II/p. B8, John Anderson

Practicing 20-20 hindsight on the Holocaust is a rather comfortable occupation for a filmmaker. Even the most mawkish subject matter becomes imbued with tragedy; poignancy is not just easy, it's unavoidable.

In "Martha and I," writer-director Jiri Weiss ("The Wolf Trap," "Ninety in the Shade"), working from his own boyhood memories of Nazi-shadowed Prague, is dealing with some pretty mundane material: adolescent lust, middle-age adultery, abortion, mixed marriages and bourgeois class conflicts. But even if the world Weiss creates was not on the verge of obliteration, "Martha and I" would work, because the director's story is so rich in detail and his own personality.

It also succeeds because of the subtle and tragic performance by Marianne Saegebrecht ("Bagdad Cafe," "Sugarbaby") who makes Martha a mix of insecurity and love, and the receptacle of everyone's selfish indulgence. Long in the employ of Ernst (Michel Piccoli), an esteemed Jewish physician in a Czech border town, the homely house servant clearly adores him, but is discreet enough to keep secret his wife's philanderings. When he finds out anyway, and gets a divorce, he marries Martha—defying conformity, and setting the stage for a mini-disaster mirroring the larger one en route from Berlin.

All of this is witnessed by Ernst's teenage nephew Emil (Vaclav Chalupa) who, having been caught in all but flagrante delicto with his mother's maid, is shipped to live with his uncle. There, Ernst introduces him to erotica, wine and the vagaries of adulthood. And by observing Ernst's life, Emil receives an education.

Weiss abandons Emil after a while, though—despite the title's suggestion, this is not an Emil's-eye view of the world. And neither is Weiss particularly subtle about much of what goes on in "Martha and I." The objections to the marriage by Martha's virulently German and anti-Semitic brothers, and by Ernst's own class-conscious sisters, make the political parallels more than abundantly clear. What Weiss does do well, however, is make us care: Piccoli is a charismatic Ernst, whom the villagers call the "doctor with the golden hands." His wisdom may be flawed—he virtually remakes Martha, to her shame and discomfort—but their relationship, which begins as a platonic affection, grows into unblinking devotion. Martha, the everywoman who has nothing but love, represents all things human, and non-Nazi.

The film, shot in a number of languages and dubbed—Saegebrecht spoke German, Piccoli French and the other actors their native tongues—was deemed anti-German, pulled from distribution by its producers and finally shown on television in an abbreviated form. What the Quad is showing is the uncut version, which is worth seeing not just for Saegebrecht and Piccoli, but because it's a moving piece of propaganda, emotional and otherwise.

VILLAGE VOICE, 3/28/95, p. 55, J. Hoberman

Jiri Weiss's bittersweet *Martha and I*, which had its German premiere on TV to mark the 53rd anniversary of Kristallnacht (and was shown here, soon after, at the Jewish Museum's 1992

Payson Media Festival), is very much an old man's movie—" a look back to the time of dreams," per its writer-director.

Born in Prague on the eve of World War I, the scion of a wealthy Jewish family, Weiss was a militant socialist and a precocious documentary filmmaker. He escaped to England when the Nazis occupied Czechoslovakia, served in a British army film unit, then returned to his liberated homeland to help construct the newly nationalized movie industry. Weiss was a major Czech director during the 1950s, even as his highly crafted neorealist films gave way to more psychological dramas—several of which explored Czech-Jewish subject matter. Leaving his birthplace for good after the 1968 Soviet invasion, Weiss taught film at various American universities. He was nearly 80 when he came out of retirement and returned home to make his last, explicitly autobiographical film.

Familiarity with Weiss's CV gives *Martha and I* added poignancy. A sexually curious teenager in the bustling Prague of 1935, Emil is dispatched by his uptight mother to the countryside to stay with his uncle, Dr. Ernst Fuchs (Michel Piccoli). The eccentric, autocratic obstetrician educates the lad with Balzac and *Decameron*, as well as with the spectacle of his own household intrigues. When the doctor is betrayed by his young wife, he divorces her and, largely because a man in his position must have a wife, marries his faithful cook, the ample, placid Martha (played with unusual restraint by Marianne Sägebrecht).

Martha and I is a love story so unromantic it verges on fairy tale. When Ernst brings his bride to meet his four properly bourgeois sisters in Prague, they are appalled—as much for reasons of ethnicity as class. Martha is not only an uneducated middle-aged woman with bad teeth but a Sudeten German. The wedding feast, which only her family attends, is replete with German-Czech tension; only afterward does the movie acknowledge that the Fuchs are not only Czechs but Jews.

Like the greatest of Czech Holocaust films, Alfred Radok's 1948 *Distant Journey, Martha and I* marks the destruction of Czech Jewry by the accretion of bureaucratic detail. When, first, the Czechs are forced from the Sudetenland, Martha moves with Ernst to live with his panicky sisters in Prague. When Jews are forbidden to work, she refuses to abandon him—braving hostile crowds, who curse her as a German, to apply for immigration forms, stealing the New York phone book from the Prague post office so that she can write to every Fuchs in New York. (Presented as an instance of Martha's devotion, the scene left me wondering whether this was a true Weiss family anecdote and, if so, how many of my own Prague cousins missed, for lack of a phone book, the opportunity to contact their American relatives.)

Ernst thoughtfully divorces Martha against her will. It's a measure of Weiss's tact, however, that, before the doctor can be deported, Martha's brothers come to kidnap her. She's the one dragged away screaming. As boisterous as *Martha and I* opens, as sentimental as it can be, its ending is devastatingly underplayed. A postwar postscript makes it clear that Martha, no less than Ernst, vanished in the smoke of Central Europe.

Also reviewed in:
NEW REPUBLIC, 3/13/95, p. 30, Stanley Kauffmann
NEW YORK TIMES, 3/24/95, p. C14, Stephen Holden
NEW YORKER, 4/1/95, p. 95, Terrence Rafferty
VARIETY, 9/17/90, p. 99
WASHINGTON POST, 4/21/95, p. D7, Hal Hinson
WASHINGTON POST, 4/21/95, Weekend/p. 45, Eve Zibart

MATTER OF LIFE AND DEATH, A (RESTORED VERSION)

Producer: Michael Powell and Emeric Pressburger. *Director:* Michael Powell and Emeric Pressburger. *Screenplay:* Michael Powell and Emeric Pressburger. *Director of Photography:*

Jack Cardiff. *Editor:* Reginald Mills. *Production Designer:* Alfred Junge. *Special Effects:* Douglas Woolsey and Henry Harris. *Running time:* 104 minutes. *MPAA Rating:* Not Rated.

CAST: David Niven (Peter Carter); Kim Hunter (June); Roger Livesey (Dr. Frank Reeves); Robert Coote (Bob Trubshaw); Marius Goring (Conductor 71); Raymond Massey (Abraham Farlan); Kathleen Byron (An Angel); Richard Attenborough (English Pilot); Bonar Colleano (American Pilot); Joan Maude (Chief Recorder); Abraham Sofaer (The Judge); Robert Atkins (The Vicar); Bob Roberts (Dr. Gaertler); Edwin Max (Mr. McEwan); Betty Potter (Mrs. Rucker).

LOS ANGELES TIMES, 4/14/95, Calendar/p. 1, Kenneth Turan

There was a time when romantic, sentimental movies were not the exclusive property of dolts and simpletons, when filmmakers of wit and sophistication made clever fantasies about the triumphant power of love. "Stairway to Heaven" is such a movie, and Michael Powell is the only director who could have made it.

First released nearly half a century ago and beginning a two-week revival run at the Nuart in West Los Angeles today, "Stairway" was Powell's personal favorite, which is saying a lot, because the output of the Archers—the production company he formed with writing and directing partner Emeric Pressburger—included such lush and inventive visual extravagances as "Black Narcissus," "Tales of Hoffman" and the beloved "The Red Shoes."

Powell, who died in 1990 at age 85, lived long enough to see his bravura filmmaking style go in and out of fashion and then in again. After a time of neglect, Powell was championed by Martin Scorsese and editor Thelma Schoonmaker, who became Powell's wife. Scorsese is one of the forces behind "Stairway's" re-release, which coincides with the American publication of "Million Dollar Movie," the second volume of Powell's autobiography, and a multi-city tour of Powell-Pressburger features that belatedly will reach Los Angeles early next year.

In the meantime, we have "Stairway" to wonder over. The film has never been on video and has not been seen theatrically in 15 years, and the current British Film Institute restoration includes a bucolic scene of a nude boy playing on a reed pipe that was inexplicably considered too racy for American taste and deleted from all previous U.S. versions.

And that was not the only example of domestic obtuseness. The original British title for the film is the more fitting "A Matter of Life and Death," but as Powell mischievously relates in the first volume of his memoirs, "A Life in Movies," tyro distributors Arthur Krim and Bob Benjamin were aghast. "'You can't have "death" in the title,' they screamed. ... It was only the United States that had to be protected from the realities of life and death."

All that was quite ironic because, the initial impetus for the film came when someone in authority asked Powell and Pressburger: "Can't you two fellows think up a good idea to improve Anglo-American relations?" What they came up with was, to quote a voice-over near the start of "Stairway," "a story of two worlds, one we know and another which exists only in the mind of a young airman."

David Niven, more dashing than any human could possibly be, plays Peter Carter, an RAF squadron leader near the end of World War II. The picture of blithe heroism, Peter is thrust at the audience as the only man left alive in the fiery cockpit of his bomber.

His parachute gone, Peter is about to jump anyway, but still has time to recite some beautiful poetry to June, the plucky British-based American servicewoman he chances to be in radio contact with. She's played by Kim Hunter, later to win an Oscar as Stella in "A Streetcar Named Desire," who was brought to Powell's attention by old Hollywood hand Alfred Hitchcock.

Peter is next glimpsed in the English Channel, having miraculously survived his jump. He not surprisingly thinks he's in heaven but is soon set right and almost immediately catches sight of a woman bicycling near the beach. It is, of course, June and, as Powell put it, "in the magic way of lovers, they recognize each other and fall in love."

In the Other World (except for a brief shot of a very young Richard Attenborough saying, "It's heaven, isn't it?," Powell and Pressburger went to pains to avoid the word), things are not going so smoothly. Conductor 71 (Marius Goring), an aristocratic French victim of the guillotine whose job it was to escort Peter to the hereafter, has somehow missed him and now must visit Earth to try to rectify his mistake.

But Peter, when told that his still being alive is all a mistake, refuses to go quietly. During his new time on the planet, he explains, he has fallen in love, and that has changed everything. He tells his dilemma to June, who confides it to Frank Reeves (Roger Livesey), the local doctor who just happens to be a frequent contributor to Brain magazine. He theorizes that Peter is suffering from a series of highly organized hallucinations that tricky surgery might cure.

While the operation is being set up, in the Other World Peter is granted the right to appeal. The prosecutor will be the Brit-hating Abraham Farlan (Raymond Massey), the first Englishman to die in the Revolutionary War. And who will Peter choose to be his counsel? He can't seem to decide.

This back and forth between two worlds, the familiar one on Earth and the Other out there, is made more striking by the film's inventive use of three-strip technicolor.

With Jack Cardiff (a future Oscar winner for "Black Narcissus") as cinematographer and Geoffrey Unsworth (ditto for "Cabaret") as camera operator, "Stairway" saves its gorgeous colors for conventional reality. The Other World is shot in a kind of pearly monotone, which was actually the three-strip film painted without the dyes. The difference leads to the film's most memorable line, recited to the audience by Conductor 71 after we've watched the hues flow back into his clothes when he arrives on Earth: "One is starved for Technicolor up there."

Though it gets a bit talky once the trial starts, "Stairway to Heaven" remains remarkable for being a film that believes that heroism is reciting poetry as your plane goes down in flames and exults at the sight of a lover's single tear on a red, red rose. Another world indeed.

NEW YORK POST, 4/14/95, p. 40, Thelma Adams

When I was a kid, my image of the afterlife didn't come from a synagogue or church. I got it from "Stairway to Heaven." I saw the marvelous British fantasy on the "Million Dollar Movie" when the old black-and-white TV set got three channels if the rabbit ears were properly arranged.

It wasn't so much a stairway as an escalator that ferried souls to a bureaucratic heaven where individuals were invoiced and delivered in a stripped-down Oz. With its beams of light, standard-issue wing sets and salesgirl angels, it was a sedate, approachable place—like Sears first thing on a Sunday.

While you could rub shoulders with famous historical icons from Abe Lincoln to Paul Bunyan, this heaven was a child-free zone. That was when I still believed that because my sister was 4 years older than me, her death would precede mine by four years.

In the Michael Powell-Emeric Pressberger movie, which was released in 1946 as "A Matter of Life and Death," there was also a loophole, a way to cheat the inevitable. David Niven's R.A.F. pilot leaps from his injured plane over the English Channel without a parachute. He survives because the angel assigned to guide him got lost in the fog. The fabulous Marius Goring plays Conductor 71, the effete Frenchman who "lost his head" in the French revolution and is still a little addled by the experience.

The movie becomes an appeal to heavenly court for Niven to remain on earth. The pilot's chief argument is that he has fallen for Kim Hunter, the American soldier he bonded with over the radio as his plane plunged. Conductor 71's mistake has resulted not only in a delayed death, but in the birth of a true love.

"A Matter of Life and Death" is a matter of love and propaganda. What I couldn't have known when I was watching the movie on a Sunday afternoon before bath and Disney's wonderful world was that the Archers, as the Powell-Pressburger team are known, were men with a mission. They began shooting on V-J Day with an assignment: encourage British and American amity in the post-war era.

While the movie celebrates abandoning reason and embracing love, there are a number of pointed scenes that I saw in a new light with a little historical perspective. Niven says of his Yankee girl-next-door, "Her accent is foreign, but it sounds sweet to me."

The climactic heavenly trial is not a pitched debate about mortality, but a grudge match between the British and the Americans who air all sorts of mutual cliches before finding common ground, a code of law in which the rights of the individual are protected against the system.

Watching the new, restored 35mm print, I discovered a major difference from the upbeat-titled TV version I remembered: heaven is black and white but earth is in glorious color.

British spring is heaven on earth, with azaleas in bountiful bloom and lush greenery. The Conductor's tossaway phrase suddenly has bite; when he comes down to England to retrieve Niven, he says, "One is starved for Technicolor up there."

NEWSDAY, 4/14/95, Part II/p. B5, Joseph Gelmis

Of the handful of memorable romantic fantasies about shuttle diplomacy between heaven and Earth, only "A Matter of Life and Death" has ever rated a national rerelease.

Hollywood's contributions to the subgenre were remade rather than revived: "Here Comes Mr. Jordan" was remade by Warren Beatty as "Heaven Can Wait" and "A Guy Named Joe" was remade by Steven Spielberg as "Forever."

See "A Matter of Life and Death" and you'll know why they were able to simply spruce up the 49-year-old film and rerelease it. Now that some legal rights issues that prevented it from being seen have been cleared up and the Technicolor print has been restored to its original opulence, "A Matter of Life and Death" is as effective and seductive an entertainment for supreme romanticists as it was in 1946.

Originally issued in the United States as "Stairway to Heaven" the film transcends with grace and wit and elegant style what sounds corny and precious on paper. This is the story of an RAF pilot who miraculously survives bailing out of his blazing bomber over the English Channel without a parachute ("I'd rather jump than fry"), falls in love with the last person he talked to before jumping, an American WAC, and then resists his extradition to heaven when the delinquent "soul-collector" arrives a day late.

The film is a litmus test for romantics. If your tear ducts aren't pumping and you don't have goose bumps within the first five minutes, as fearless and blithe David Niven and smart and decent Kim Hunter reveal the essence of their beings by radio and fall in love, then consider yourself a retired romantic.

As filmmaking, "A Matter of Life and Death" is deliriously sumptuous fun, full of quirky and mysterious moments. Of the 17 films by The Archers (Michael Powell and Emeric Pressburger) that preceded this series-concluding two-week run, the biggest crowds at Film Forum were attracted to "I Know Where I'm Going," another sublime romance (in which the lovers are united by the forces of nature rather than the negligence of divine bureaucrats). In these two films, Powell and Pressburger, worldly men with romantic streaks, used their filmmaking talent and finesse to create enduring visceral experiences out of what they themselves wanted to believe—that love is the strongest force on Earth.

VILLAGE VOICE, 4/18/95, p. 60, Elliott Stein

The most whimsical propaganda picture ever made, *A Matter of Life and Death* (1946) was the result of a British Ministry of Information request for a film that would help improve strained Anglo-American relations. Screenwriter Emeric Pressburger and director Michael Powell obliged with an oneiric flight of fancy, a spectacular paean to *amour fou*

Returning from a bombing operation over Germany, RAF pilot Peter (David Niven) should have been killed when he bailed out of his doomed plane without a parachute, but the ethereal Messenger sent to collect him got lost in the fog. Will a heavenly tribunal allow him to remain on earth to enjoy life with his lover, American WAC June (Kim Hunter)? One guess.

This virtuosic film's main visual conceit is that Heaven is all black and white (in point of fact it's in a Technicolor bleached of color, reduced to pearly monochromatic tones), a dreary bureaucratic monumental Utopia, populated by unsmiling regimented hordes, whereas Earth is awash in color. England—its seashore, countryside and human-scale townscapes—is the picture's true Heaven. Indeed, *A Matter*'s best remembered line, delivered by the Messenger (Marius Goring), is: "One is starved for Technicolor up there."

Although shot through with striking imagery, *A Matter* is patchy and uneven, a notch below P and P's finest work: *Blimp, Black Narcissus, I Know Where I'm Going, The Red Shoes*. Its propagandistic agenda becomes downright clunky during the High Court proceedings held in the vast amphitheater of a sort of celestial Hollywood Bowl where ghostly representatives of all nations and ages attend the debate on Peter's fate. The restored and burnished print on view at Film Forum does live up to the claims made for it—I felt I could lift up my hands and warm them with the glow from the hues on screen.

Also reviewed in:
CHICAGO TRIBUNE, 4/20/95, Tempo/p. 9A, Michael Wilmington
NEW YORK TIMES, 12/26/46, p. 28, Bosley Crowther
WASHINGTON POST, 7/28/95, p. B1, Hal Hinson

MAYA LIN: A STRONG CLEAR VISION

An Ocean Releasing release. *Producer:* Freida Lee Mock and Terry Sanders. *Director:* Freida Lee Mock. *Screenplay:* Freida Lee Mock. *Director of Photography:* Eddie Marritz and Don Lenzer. *Editor:* William T. Cartwright, Sr. *Music:* Charles Bernstein. *Sound:* Robyn Hutman and Judy Carp and (music) Rick Ash. *Running time:* 96 minutes. *MPAA Rating:* Not Rated.

LOS ANGELES TIMES, 11/10/95, Calendar/p. 16, Jack Mathews

The ease against the parochialism of the documentary committee of the Academy of Motion Picture Arts and Sciences has not been made better by its critics than it was by the committee itself in presenting the Oscar this year to abstaining chairwoman Freida Lee Mock's totally unremarkable "Maya Lin: A Strong Clear Vision."

With the committee's snub of "Hoop Dreams" still the ranking embarrassment of the year in Hollywood, we finally get a look at the winner and what we see is a film that should have gone directly to the Discovery Channel or been pared down for the one-hour format of "A&E's Biography."

No disrespect to Maya Link the gifted Chinese American architect and sculptor who, as a 20-year-old Yale undergraduate, submitted the winning design for the Vietnam Memorial in 1980. Hers was chosen from 1,400 entries, by a panel of professionals evaluating them without knowing the designers' identities, and it resulted in one of the nation's most inspirational and frequently visited monuments.

How Lin came up with the design for a class project, submitted it to the national competition as an afterthought and then weathered the storm of protest and racist taunts from some angry Vietnam veterans is a terrific story, and recapping it with the reflections of Lin 15 years later gives the documentary noble purpose.

We also learn a good deal about how art connects to the national psyche, and how smart the judges on that panel were. While many of the professional architects and designers sent in sculpted models, three-dimensional drawings and detailed blueprints, Lin submitted simple pastel impressions, with her monument standing out as an angled black stripe against a blue-green field. With that, and the essay she spent two months writing, the judges divined a work of genius, and were proven right.

But "Maya Lin" is only compelling while focused on the Vietnam Memorial, which takes up perhaps a third of its one-hour, 45-minute running time. The rest details the work Lin has done since and takes a cursory look at her background.

The only thing Lin has done that approaches the psychological power of the Vietnam Memorial is her fountain design for the Civil Rights Memorial in Montgomery, Ala. The other pieces we see her working on—a crushed-glass sculpture garden, a wavy-roofed house, the Peace Chapel at Juniata College in Pennsylvania—seem, in comparison, to be self-indulgent and slight,

The film's problems, however, are journalistic. Mock includes news footage of Vietnam veterans spokesman Tom Carhart's 1980 press conference outburst, during which—with Lin looking on sadly and a little cowed—he called her design a "black scar" and an insult to veterans. The protest was taken up by others, and the plan nearly abandoned.

Has time and the memorial's impact tempered the views of its original critics? The movie calls out for an answer that Mock never provides.

Finally, "Maya Lin" is not even particularly compelling to look at. Scenes of Vietnam veterans weeping at the memorial are always moving, whether in this film or in annual Memorial Day news coverage. But Mock was unable to capture the visual power of the monument itself. Or of the fountain in Montgomery. Hers is simply the most fundamental kind of documentary filmmaking, absent any poetic sense or social point-of-view of its own.

In the end, "Maya Lin" is less a portrait of the artist than an admiring tribute, fit for a dinner when her magnificent wall celebrates its 20th anniversary. The only explanation for its Oscar victory is that the documentary committee members confused the quality of the film with the quality of its subject.

NEW YORK POST, 11/3/95, p. 44, Larry Worth

Long before the public knew anything about it, "Maya Lin: A Strong, Clear Vision" had garnered a flood of ill will and resentment. As 1994's Academy Award-winning best feature documentary, it earned the honor that everyone assumed would go to "Hoop Dreams."

But the truth of the matter is that director Freida Lee Mock's look at the Yale University student who designed the Vietnam Veterans' Memorial is just as compelling, unique and thought-provoking as the highly acclaimed "Dreams."

Instead of charting two young black men's physical and emotional journeys on the basketball court, it tells of a 20-year-old woman plucked from obscurity when her idea for a Washington, D.C., landmark-to-be won approval over 1,400 other submissions.

Using a combination of newsreels and current footage of the now 35-year-old Lin (and various mentors), Mock shows how the soft-spoken architect employed wisdom beyond her years to combat veterans angered by her vision, along with hate-mongers asking, "How can you let a gook design the memorial?"

History shows that Lin handled the firestorm with the grace, dignity and composure which became her trademarks. They also served as necessities on the projects ahead, all of which are chronicled by Mock in a refreshingly straightforward manner.

Indeed, the film's latter half surfaces as an amazing mosaic of the designer's accomplishments, including the Civil Rights Memorial in Montgomery, Ala., the Women's Table sculpture at Yale and the Park Presidio environmental project in San Francisco.

But what sets the film apart is how Mock captures the passion and focus of Lin's work, whether she's sitting idly at a drafting table or deciding *exactly* how much water should flow over the letters chiseled into a piece of stone.

Ironically, Mock's examination of artistic vision seems deceptively simple, much like Lin's granite masterpieces. But on closer examination, "Maya Lin" takes shape as a soaring testament to undeterred courage—never mind exhilarating moviemaking.

VILLAGE VOICE, 11/7/95, p. 72, Gary Susman

As documented in *Maya Lin: A Strong Clear Vision*, the architect who created the Vietnam Veterans Memorial is a woman of talent, courage, and perseverance, Maya Lin was only 20 and an undergraduate at Yale when, for a class project, she entered the competition to design the memorial, little imagining that her submission would beat 1440 other entries. She faced down slurs against her youth, sex and Asian heritage to build the monument as she designed it, and its austerely eloquent testament to the human toll of the war has made it one of the most beloved attractions in Washington.

Lin seems an unassailable human being, so I feel churlish picking on Freida Lee Mock's tribute to her. Nevertheless, the movie is sloppily organized and remains vague on what motivates Lin as an artist, as a person, and as a creator of social justice-oriented public spaces. The film opens with its most powerful segment, the story of the Vietnam Memorial, followed by a numbing travelogue through Lin's résumé, with a midpoint detour revisiting her happy middle-class childhood.

Maya Lin won the documentary Oscar for 1994 leading to charges of cronyism, since Mock had been the selection committee chair (she recused herself last year). Certainly its first 20 minutes are as worthy as any documentary; as a whole, though, it's hardly a better choice than *Hoop Dreams* and *Crumb*, which weren't even nominated. The film deserved less maladroit handling, but then, so did Lin.

Also reviewed in:
NEW YORK TIMES, 11/3/95, p. C12, Janet Maslin
VARIETY, 3/13-19/95, p. 53, Dennis Harvey
WASHINGTON POST, 10/20/95, p. D6, Linton Weeks

MEET THE FEEBLES

A Greycat Films release of a Wingnut Films production. *Producer:* Jim Booth and Peter Jackson. *Director:* Peter Jackson. *Screenplay:* Danny Mulheron, Frances Walsh, Stephen Sinclair, and Peter Jackson. *Director of Photography:* Murray Milne. *Editor:* Jamie Selkirk. *Music:* Peter Dasant. *Puppet Designer:* Cameron Chittock. *Production Designer:* Mike Kane. *Running time:* 94 minutes. *MPAA Rating:* Not Rated.

VOICES: Donna Akersten; Stuart Devenie; Mark Hadlow; Ross Jolly; Brian Sergent; Peter Vere Jones; Mark Wright.

NEWSDAY, 2/22/95, Part II/p. B13, John Anderson

The knife-throwing frog is a Vietnam vet and a junkie. The elephant is facing a paternity suit brought by a chicken. The rabbit has a sexually transmitted disease and the tabloid reporter is a toilet-habituating housefly. And they're only bit players.

"Meet the Feebles," a 1989 film by Peter Jackson—whose vaunted "Heavenly Creatures" is the likely reason this is opening here at all—rides one basic joke from slap-happy theme song to climactic massacre: Making otherwise innocent, Muppet-like creatures vulgar, avaricious, sexually malevolent and maladjusted. In other words, human.

But "The Muppet Show" did all that long ago, imbuing its own fluffy cast with a raft of idiosyncracies and, more important, a refusal to acknowledge their own semi-animate status. Jackson's contribution to this quasi-genre is to take the joke to its gamey extreme.

The characters are stock, although their voices and species show some imagination: Bletch, the Feebles' cigar-chomping producer, is a walrus involved in a drug war with a cockney-accented boar named Cedric, and is using cast members to make backstage S&M films (the compliant cow wears udder rings). His loathsome aide-decamp, Trevor the rat, sounds like Peter Lorre and eats whatever or whomever is lying about. Recent acting-school graduate Robert (or Wobert, since he has a speech impediment) is a hedgehog in love with Lucille the poodle, whom Trevor is trying to turn into a porn star. Dr. Duck sounds like Paul Lynde; Wynyard the dope-fiend frog sounds like Jim Ignatowski on "Taxi."

Heidi the hippo, Belch's former love, is betrayed at every junction, and turns understandably homicidal. She gets her revenge in a Sam Peckinpah-inspired orgy of bullets and bile that is, not surprisingly, over the top: Jackson, like a driver trying to outrace red lights, accelerates the violence and bad taste but can't get out of the way of his own collapsing shtick.

VILLAGE VOICE, 2/28/95, p. 74, James Hannaham

Perhaps it's worthwhile to restate the obvious—Peter Jackson is a sick fuck. Harboring unnatural fetishes for vile puppets, blood, gore, and matricide, the New Zealander's four films to date have included three, "splatter comedies," and one film of incredible sophistication, beauty, and intelligence, *Heavenly Creatures*.

Creatures probably inspired Film Forum to give the metro area another bad taste of the old Peter Jackson, as located in the twisted foam bodies of a third-rate Muppet knockoff ensemble with a TV variety hour, *Meet the Feebles*. Despite their innocent appearances, these stuffed animals have vices all too human. The Miss Piggy analogue, Heidi the Hippo cracks when producer Bletch the Walrus betrays her. Toting a semiautomatic weapon, the artiodactyl mammal shoots the stuffing out of the Feebles in a nihilistic final sequence Jackson would later perfect in *Dead Alive*. Bletch operates a drug ring from his office, with Barry the Bulldog acting as his enforcer. His assistant, Trevor the Rat, makes porno films where cows with pierced udders wince under the whips of cockroaches in the sewer beneath the soundstage. He ain't making no nature films.

Originally planned as a seven-minute short, *Meet the Feebles* feels very much like the one joke that it is, hastily slapped together by matching stereotypes up with animals. Heidi's rival for Bletch's affections, for example, is a Siamese cat. The only genuinely cute character is a nebbishy hedgehog with a lisp, in love with a showgirl poodle, with whom he carries out the expected narrative: Hedgehog meets Poodle, Hedgehog loses Poodle, Hedgehog gets Poodle back in the end. Combining such sickening sweetness with flying organs gives you a feeling you might get from downing alternating glasses of Manischevitz and Zima.

Few of these grotesqueries make you laugh in spite of yourself, except for Wynyard the smack freak frog's tour-of-duty-in-Vietnam sequence. Puppet frogs playing GIs in 'Nam while puppet cats spout communist dogma is so tasteless that it scrapes genius. But if *Heavenly Creatures* made you a Peter Jackson fan, stay away from these hellish creatures.

Also reviewed in:
CHICAGO TRIBUNE, 5/5/95, Friday/p. P. H, Michael Wilmington
NEW YORK TIMES, 2/22/95, p. C18, Janet Maslin
VARIETY, 5/30/90, p. 32
WASHINGTON POST, 6/3/95, p. H3, Richard Harrington

METAL AND MELANCHOLY

An Ariel Films release. *Producer:* Susanne Van Voorst. *Director:* Heddy Honigmann. *Screenplay (Spanish with English subtitles):* Heddy Honigmann and Peter Delpeut. *Director of Photography:* Stef Tijdink. *Editor:* Han Hendricks and Danniel Danniel. *Sound:* Piotr van Dijl. *Running time:* 80 minutes. *MPAA Rating:* Not Rated.

NEW YORK POST, 4/5/95, p. 35, Thelma Adams

"Life is hard but beautiful." So says a Lima cab driver. Did we have to travel all the way to Peru to discover this? Perhaps not.

Heddy Honigmann's documentary "Metal and Melancholy" focuses on Peruvian cabs and their drivers. It's a backseat view of a society that's fallen and can't get up. The middle class has been squeezed dry. In order to keep up, managers, actors, teachers, cops and housewives slap "taxi" stickers on their old cars and moonlight on the streets of Lima.

One cabby refers to his fellows as the "seafarers of the 20th century." They spread news, tell stories, bellyache about the way things used to be.

Each driver has a soulful tale: a father reveals his daughter's struggle with cancer; a woman describes an out-of-body experience; a thespian re-enacts an emotional scene from "The City and the Dogs" (which played the Film Forum in 1987); a single mother breaks down about her mate's infidelities and her father's violent rages; and a cop admits he ratted out radical professors during his secret service days.

There are a million stories in the naked city—and cabbies know their share. Seduced by the storytellers, Honigmann falls into the road-movie trap: the documentary is episodic and shapeless. Lima emerges less as a city than as a series of cramped back seats. Except for signs advertising Inca Kola, we could be anywhere in Latin America.

"Metal and Melancholy" would have made a great short. At 80 minutes, it's a long taxi ride.

VILLAGE VOICE, 4/11/95, p 64, Michael Atkinson

A documentary-cum-road movie that travels in endless U-turns around the depressed streets of Lima, *Metal and Melancholy* is quite like the Peruvians themselves—relaxed, persevering, nakedly emotional, and tougher than seat leather. Dutch (but Lima-born) filmmaker Heddy Honigmann's portrait of Lima's enormous cabbie subculture often approaches a mild sort of dystopian vision—a demolished society surviving out of their cars by way of surreal gypsy cunning. You could mistake it for Australian sci-fi, except that Honigmann's people drive to live, not live to drive.

Indeed, the economic crater of present-day Peru is the cabbie's primary text. Poverty has apparently forced most of the population to buy a $1 taxi sign, slap it on their family jalopy's windshield, and prowl the streets. Bureaucrats, scientists, teachers, cops, even movie actors (including a player from *The City and the Dogs*) all augment their dismal earnings by hacking. (One wonders, who are the fares?) The film's pretext is the craft of survival, but by simply plopping the camera down in the front seat next to the drivers and paying for innumerable $2 trans-Lima jaunts, Honigmann also reawakens the road movie's old and mysterious meditation on our complex relationship with the interior of the automobile. One cabbie sings to his car to keep it running; another devoutly maintains a decimated bomb that no one can steal because it would essentially fall apart without the right rituals. Cars become characters; there are swarms of old VW Beetles. Like all good hack movies, *M&M* is also a cruel gerbil-wheel tour of the Transitional City's badlands, which, in Lima, might make even Travis Bickle blanch: Honigmann visits a communal grave stacked high with bloody children, and if the smell lingers in her nose too long, her seasoned hack cohort tells her to use her own sweaty clothes to clean it out. ("A doctor advised me.")

Honigmann's film, however, is no more despairing than the Limans—"the resilience of the human spirit" is a platitude, but it applies: nearly every cabbie is bursting with dead-real insight, compassion, wit, and poetry. One impoverished gentleman observes that his green wreck is "the color of hope"; a woman cabbie totters disarmingly from sobs to laughter describing her harrowing life; even the urchins hawking stolen cigarettes on the night streets are impish and buoyant. Simply shot, and serenely edited, Honigmann's movie is a rueful B-side ballad to David Letterman's rollicking Oscar night taxi dance: truer, sweeter, and worldlier.

Also reviewed in:
CHICAGO TRIBUNE, 8/2/96, Friday/p. H, Michael Wilmington
NEW YORK TIMES, 4/5/95, p. C23, Stephen Holden
VARIETY, 5/23-29/94, p. 59, Dennis Harvey

MIAMI RHAPSODY

A Hollywood Pictures release. *Executive Producer:* Jon Avnet and Jordan Kerner. *Producer:* Barry Jossen and David Frankel. *Director:* David Frankel. *Screenplay:* David Frankel. *Director of Photography:* Jack Wallner. *Editor:* Steven Weisberg. *Music:* Mark Isham. *Music Editor:* Tom Carlson. *Choreographer:* Adam Shankman. *Sound:* Michael Tromer and (music) Stephen Krause. *Casting:* Renée Rousselot. *Production Designer:* J. Mark Harrington. *Set Decorator:* Barbara Peterson. *Set Dresser:* Philip Schweighardt. *Special Effects:* Kevin Harris. *Costumes:* Patricia Field. *Make-up:* Isabel Harkins. *Running time:* 95 minutes. *MPAA Rating:* PG-13.

CAST: Sarah Jessica Parker (Gwyn Marcus); Gil Bellows (Matt); Antonio Banderas (Antonio); Mia Farrow (Nina Marcus); Paul Mazursky (Vic Marcus); Kevin Pollak (Jordan Marcus); Barbara Garrick (Terri); Carla Gugino (Leslie Marcus); Bo Eason (Jeff); Naomi Campbell (Kaia); Jeremy Piven (Mitchell); Kelly Bishop (Zelda); Mark Blum (Peter); Norman Steinberg (Charlie); Ben Stein (Rabbi); Donal Logue (Derek); Mary Chernoff (Grandma Lil); Elodia Riovega (Antonio's Mother); Chaz Mena (Ted); George Tapia (Carlos); Avery Sommers (Nurse); Ed Arenas (Photographer); Frank Fong (Chinese Host); Lisa Banes (Gynecologist).

LOS ANGELES TIMES, 1/27/95, Calendar/p. 8, Peter Rainer

"Miami Rhapsody," a comedy about marital jitters starring Sarah Jessica Parker, is full of funny performers and beautiful Miami scenery and classic pop tunes but it still seems awfully familiar. It's not just that it keeps reminding you of Woody Allen—reportedly it's working title was "Miami." It also reminds you of Neil Simon and a barrage of sort-of-bright TV sitcoms.

Writer-director David Frankel, making his feature-film debut, has created a number of TV series, including "Doctor, Doctor" and "Teeth," and his approach to the audience is very punchy and direct. He times the scenes for quick, flip giggles; the film practically comes with its own laugh track. And the "serious" moments are just as glib—they come with their own sob track.

Parker plays Gwyn Marcus, a frizzy-haired neurotic who opens the film by telling us—she's actually addressing her psychiatrist—about the time her boyfriend Matt (Gil Bellows) proposed to her a year before. As we see in flashback, Gwyn has a Commitment problem. To make matters worse, she instinctively looks to her immediate family for encouragement to take the plunge and discovers their marriages are awash in infidelity.

Her younger sister Leslie (Carla Gugino) marries a football hero (Bo Eason) who turns out to be less tight end than tightwad; Gwyn ends up walking in on her dalliance with an old high school flame. Her brother Jordan (Kevin Pollak), one of those guys who always seems to have a cellular phone retrofitted inside his ear, ditches his pregnant wife (Barbara Garrick) for his business partner's mate (Naomi Campbell, looking every inch the supermodel). Her mother, Nina (Mia Farrow), turns out to be carrying on with her grandmother's male nurse, Antonio, a Cuban smoothie played by—who else?—Antonio Banderas. Her father, Vic (Paul Mazursky, in a fine, wry turn), who suspects his wife's affair, is doing some dallying of his own with his travel agent (Kelly Bishop).

Gwyn is looking for any excuse not to marry and gets more than she bargained for. The most enjoyable moments in "Miami Rhapsody" are the ones in which the characters are dazed by their own libidos—Gwyn most of all. She even develops a hankering for her mother's paramour, which brings the film into freaky-Freudian territory, but lightly so. Nina, in her scenes with Antonio, seems entranced by her own good fortune; it's pretty clear she has no intention of leaving her husband for him but she can't resist a momentary fantasia. It brings out her girlishness. Vic has the edgy, humbled uncomfortableness of a man who can't reconcile his wife's affair with his own. He feels bad about both.

Parker has never had this large a starring role, and she confirms her bright, addled, quicksilver gifts for comedy. She's such a spirited performer that she elevates the sitcom Woodman material into something fluffier and funnier than it has any right to be.

Frankel doesn't really take this material very far into the kind of eccentric looniness that might have made it memorable. He sandbags the comedy by inserting strategic life lessons—the movie is intended as a learning experience for us as well as for the characters. Even though the movie's collision of New York Jewish comic rhythms and sultry Miami Pop is promising, it never ignites. Frankel does well by his actors, though. He indulges their love of performing and they repay him threefold.

NEW YORK, 2/13/95, p. 100, David Denby

Miami Rhapsody, David Frankel's first film, is a flagrant copy of mid-period Woody Allen, but that's the least of what's wrong with it. Imitativeness, I think, is a pardonable fault in a new director. A more pressing difficulty is that the picture isn't very good. *Miami Rhapsody* begins with Louis Armstrong singing Cole Porter under plain titles; and then Sarah Jessica Parker, as the heroine, Gwyn, looks right into the camera—addressing her gynecologist, who is offscreen—and tells us, in rueful-glib style, what is wrong with her family. She then makes self-deprecating remarks and such jokes as "It's a good rule of thumb never to be older than your gynecologist." We are in Woodyland, all right, but a plumply mediocre and depressed Miami version of it, where second- and third-best are good enough. Parker delivers her lines clearly and with a comic's emphasis, but the jokes just pop out as if they had nothing to do with her. They sound like ... lines.

Gwyn, it turns out, has a cute boyfriend (Gil Bellows), a zoologist who handles chimps but isn't one himself; he wants to marry her, but everyone in Gwyn's family—her mother, father, sister, brother—is cheating, and Gwyn is too dismayed by all these infidelities to get hitched. But wait a second. Everyone is cheating? Isn't that a rather mechanical situation? It's an idea, perhaps, for a standup comedy routine ("and then I went to see my brother, and he introduced me to his mistress ..."), but it's too skeletal an idea for a movie. It would work dramatically only if we got involved with the different people and saw what was at stake in the relationships, and if the various elements in the milieu added up and explained the emotional allure of adultery (as they did in *Shampoo*). But Frankel, 35, who has worked extensively in television, just skips along from one person to the next, and he makes so little contact with some of the actors that their behavior seems entirely arbitrary.

Carla Gugino, who plays Gwyn's fleshy, dark-haired sister, simpers and giggles as she abandons her new husband for an unappealing old boyfriend; and the ferrety Kevin Pollak, as Gwyn's brother, rattles off cheaply cynical remarks and seems like a lesser Ray Sharkey, who used to play tense no-goods with an alert intelligence. If Frankel wanted to expose Gwyn's family as shallow and greedy, the shallowness of his treatment of them makes the whole thing seem like a setup. Paul Mazursky, as the hypocritical dad who mourns the loss of his wife's love while cheating himself, adds some heavyset melancholy. Mia Farrow, however—who may be present to take the sting out of the charge of Woody imitation by this sheepish acknowledgment of it—is dreamy, vague, and disconnected, and her alleged mad fling with Antonio Banderas, a Cuban-émigré male nurse, is a bust. These infantile pleasure-seekers not only lack conscience, they lack consciousness. They seem to have emerged from a diminished gene pool—that is, from a bad sitcom. Banderas, speaking his English more clearly than in *Interview With the Vampire*, is the only grown-up among them, but Frankel and cameraman Jack Wallner don't photograph him well, and we can't see his eyes, his most arresting feature. A man without eyes can't be a great seducer.

The movie is set in a pastel-pink-and-blue Miami, a city the movie conceives (explicitly) as an alternative to Los Angeles. But the tone of generalized anxiety and self-deprecation doesn't seem to fit the prosperous, sunshiny milieu. Where does Gwyn's guilt come from? From New York, maybe? There's nothing supporting her attitudes, and so the imitation Woodyisms stick out: The tone is Woody's without Woody's roots. Sarah Jessica Parker gets off some decent one-liners, but in *Miami Rhapsody*, one thing happens and then another, and none of it matters emotionally, so the petty narcissism grows rancid and trivial. In between the jokes, you may look away from the screen in embarrassment. The next time out, David Frankel needs to move toward realism—or all the way into farce. At the moment, he's still in television.

NEW YORK POST, 1/27/95, p. 53, Michael Medved

From its opening credits (with plain lettering against a black background, accompanied by a jazz standard) to its ironic concluding monologue (delivered by the main character straight to the camera), "Miami Rhapsody" is a painfully obvious homage to Woody Allen—and therein lies both its main strengths and its chief weakness.

Like Woody's vintage work in "Hannah and Her Sisters," this movie offers a complex plot and an abundance of vivid characters, along with crisp, witty dialogue to keep things moving along. At the same time, both style and content feel so shamelessly derivative that you can't escape the feeling that you're watching a clever recycling of various old movies (including "Blume in Love," "Lovers and Other Strangers" and more), rather than seeing any heartfelt version of real life.

The Woody Allen stand-in at the center of this new story has moved to Miami, lost 30 years in age and apparently undergone a sex change operation—since she's a young woman of 20-something, fetchingly played by Sarah Jessica Parker.

As the movie begins, this wise-cracking advertising copywriter (and aspiring comedy writer) has just gotten engaged to a mellow veterinarian (Gil Bellow), when she begins to discover that every single member of her family is having an affair. Mama Mia Farrow is stepping out with the handsome male nurse (Antonio Banderas) who cares for the family's invalid grandmother; Papa Paul Mazursky's been fooling around with his travel agent for years.

Big brother Kevin Pollak leaves his pregnant wife to move in with stunning Naomi Campbell, the wife of his business partner; while little sister Carla Gugino risks her new marriage to a pro football player for a fling with an old flame from high school. No wonder the main character begins to question her own wedding plans.

Writer-director David Frankel, who cut his creative teeth on the TV series "Grapevine" and "Teeth," makes an auspicious big-screen debut and delivers a few genuinely hilarious scenes. There's a lavish wedding, for instance, at which the rabbi (played by Ben Stein) announces that he will read a poem with which bride and groom wish to consecrate their love; he then solemnly intones doggerel that recalls the work of Dr. Suess in "Green Eggs and Ham."

In the end, however, the movie's attitude is too breezy for its own good, straining credibility when each and every one of the extramarital relationships ends happily—leading either to renewed, strengthened marriage, or an exciting new relationship.

Like her Woody prototype, Sarah Jessica is supposed to function as the movie's moral center, but in view of the film's shallow, glamorized view of infidelity, there is no moral center.

Still and all, the talented cast is fun to watch and the dialogue is a consistent pleasure to hear. "Marriage is a lot like Miami," the main character concludes. "It's hot and stormy and sometimes it's dangerous. But if it was really so awful, then why is there so much traffic?"

This film itself is never awful, and will probably generate a good deal of traffic.

NEWSDAY, 1/27/95, Part II/p. B7, Jack Mathews

The publicists who put together the production notes for writer-director David Frankel's "Miami Rhapsody" rate a pat on the back for noting that the film is "reminiscent" of Woody Allen's "Hannah and Her Sisters." Reminiscent isn't exactly the word I'd use—imitation is more like it—but it is a surprising bit of honesty.

They could afford it because what they have here is a very good imitation, one that manages to rework in clever ways all of Allen's neurotic romantic impulses, without the annoying whininess that too often dominates his characters.

"Miami Rhapsody" is the story of Gwyn Marcus (Sarah Jessica Parker), an advertising writer in Miami whose doubts about her impending marriage are compounded by the revelations of troubled marriages in her own family. Her mother (Mia Farrow) is having an affair with a young Cuban nurse (Antonio Banderas), her father (Paul Mazursky) has been sleeping with his travel agent (Kelly Bishop), her brother (Kevin Pollak) has left his pregnant wife (Barbara Garrick) for the wife (Naomi Campbell) of a business associate, and her sister (Carla Gugino) is a newlywed already cheating on her husband.

In many ways, "Miami Rhapsody" plays out as a situation comedy, with Gwyn being surprised by these infidelities through a series of comic sketches. But it's much more than that. Frankel's messages are that women are often just as unsure of marriage as men, and that for relationships to endure, they have to withstand some devastating assaults.

Frankel, a television writer making his directing debut, writes with a wonderful sense of irony, and Parker gives a delightful comic performance as the angst-ridden central character and narrator of the story. The movie opens and closes in Gwyn's psychiatrist's office, and in between we learn all of the circumstances that brought her there.

There is no mistaking the inspiration for her character. She's doing Woody Allen, punctuating nearly every sentence with some cryptically sardonic observation. But Gwyn is less egocentric and more lovable than Allen; the weight of the world may be on her shoulders, but she's also laden with worries for the well-being of her spectacularly screwed-up family.

Frankel handles this material with a sure-handedness unusual in a first-time director, but it is the writing and the ensemble performances that make "Miami Rhapsody" sing. Farrow is terrific as the middle-aged mom, drunk with the excitement of having a young lover, and Banderas plays Antonio with a conviction that removes all doubt of his motivation.

The movie is not without its weaknesses. Frankel may be a good mimic of Allen, but he can't maintain his level of humor. Some of Gwyn's lines are just too pat to be taken as spontaneity, and though we spend a lot of time with her and her sincere and unsentimental fiancé (Gil Bellows), we're never quite sure why she accepted his proposal in the first place.

Still, this is an unexpected pleasure. I wrote in a column the other day that this is trash time for Hollywood, the period when the studios dump last year's leftovers on the market. With the arrival of "Miami Rhapsody" and "Before Sunrise," which also opens today, I hereby eat those words.

SIGHT AND SOUND, 7/95, p. 51, Jonathan Romney

Gwyn Marcus, an advertising copywriter living in Miami, tells her analyst about her family and her love life ...

Gwyn has accepted a marriage proposal from her zoologist boyfriend Matt. She attends the wedding of her sister Leslie to Jeff, a pro footballer with the Miami Dolphins. At the reception, Gwyn's father Vic tells her that he is convinced her mother Nina is having an affair. Later, Nina admits to Gwyn that she is involved with Antonio, the Cuban nurse who is looking after Gwyn's stroke-afflicted grandmother. Nina tells her how the affair began, with a night out at a Cuban restaurant and a visit to his apartment.

Visiting her brother Jordan, Gwyn finds him in rowing with his pregnant wife Terri, who has learned that he is having an affair with Kaia, the model wife of his business partner. He tells Gwyn how the affair started. Gwyn runs into Antonio, and they discuss his affair with Nina. She tells Nina that she and Matt have set the wedding date, but that she is reluctant to sacrifice her own identity. Nina confesses that she finds Antonio too passionate, and that things are now going better with Vic. At her office, Gwyn learns that she has lost one of her clients, who thinks that, as a woman, she will want to leave work and have children.

In a Chinese restaurant, Gwyn encounters a distraught Zelda, a travel agent that Nina has always suspected Vic of having an affair with. Vic admits that he is, but says that he now feels trapped in the relationship and is in love with Nina again.

Gwyn visits Jordan and Kaia, now living together, but in a state of conflict. She returns to her apartment to find Leslie using her bed to make love to an old school friend, Mitchell; Leslie tells her how they met. Panicked by all these revelations, Gwyn calls off her engagement. Antonio is expecting a visit from his mother, who wants to see him with a girlfriend; he asks Gwyn to pose in the role, and he takes her for a wild night on the town.

Gwyn's coveted project, a sitcom script, has been accepted by a producer friend of Vic's. Matt tells her he has been accepted for a new job in Zaire, and that their romance is over. Meanwhile, Leslie and Jeff split up, Jordan and Terri begin a tentative reconciliation, and Vic and Nina are getting on well. Antonio accompanies Gwyn to Orlando for her script meeting; they are about to make love, but her anxiety stands in the way. Nina phones to tell Gwyn her grandmother has died. At the funeral, Jordan learns that Terri has given birth to a baby girl; in hospital, they are finally reconciled. In her analyst's office, Gwyn philosophises about love, life and Miami.

David Frankel's high-gloss comedy of manners pull off a neat balancing trick, providing brittle urban humour on one hand, and on the other a mood every bit as opulent and romantic as the title suggests. Much of the film's appeal comes from the way that the setting, with its rather factitious tropical sultriness, offsets the characters' angst-driven verbals. Cynically down-to-earth on one hand, lushly overwrought on the other, the film makes for an odd hybrid: *Miami Witz*.

Learning that both her parents are having affairs, Gwyn laments, "It's not the norm. It's not L.A." But it's not quite Miami either: David Frankel's setting is a non-specific fantasy land that allows the writer-director to create a particular comic style, blending the traditional pessimism of Jewish humour with the escapism of what could best be called Jewison humour. Not a few moments of *Miami Rhapsody* suggest that director's *Moonstruck*, with palms replacing pizzas. Most of all, though, this Miami resembles a particularly well-heeled district of Woody Allen's Manhattan, and at times, the parallels are so glaring as to seem careless. Most obvious is the casting of Mia Farrow, too obtrusively WASPy to make a convincing mother to Sarah Jessica Parker's engagingly wiseacre heroine. There's a narrative comprising overlapping tales of romantic disaster, recounted—ostensibly by Gwyn, then by her family and friends—in a series of voice-overs and flashbacks between flashbacks. There's also the use of a sumptuous mainstream jazz soundtrack to counterpoint the narrative's cynical undertow—for every small-time betrayal or moment of disillusion, a swathe of Gershwin or Ellington sugars the pill. Charming though the film is, it's charming in the way that lighter Allen films are, and we're likely to be distracted counting the echoes. The family saga structure resembles a looser, more whole-heartedly comic variant of *Hannah and Her Sisters*, while the story about Gwyn's father and his mistress seems to be decanted straight from the Martin Landau-Angelica Huston relationship in *Crimes and Misdemeanors*.

Consequently the film comes off as a rather disjointed set of anecdotal sequences and one-liners that result in something of a sitcom feel. (Frankel is, in fact, best known for his television work, directing and writing the CBS series *Grapevine*.). Frankel lays on the life-lessons with a commendably light touch and manages to avoid the sentiment that US sitcoms and romantic comedies invariably fall prey to. There are even some good visual gags. Best of all is the moment when Jordan visits Kaia on a photo shoot. The camera describes besotted circles around Naomi Campbell; just as Kevin Pollak comes into view in the crowd of onlookers, she takes off her top, and he collapses in a dead faint.

As for Miami, city resident Frankel is scrupulous in giving us an exhaustive tour of real locations, from the Zoo to the Beach to Coconut Grove, and cinematographer Jack Wallner contrives a high-gloss look that makes the city as intensely tropical as it's ever been on film: searing neons, hot oranges and greens, interiors decked in jungle vegetation wallpaper. The atmosphere, though, is more tangible than the city itself, which remains an idea, a luxury playpen for the characters to enjoy their troubles in.

It's when Frankel attempts to deal with the Hispanic Miami that he comes unstuck. Despite an attempt in the script to defuse these middle-class Jewish ladies' romantic misconceptions about 'dangerous' Antonio, the evenings that Gwyn and Nina spend with him are straight out of the absurd salsa-and-seduction fantasy of *The Mambo Kings*—another film featuring Antonio

Banderas, who seems to have become Hollywood's rent-a-fake-Cuban. Nina and he don't simply go out for a meal, they go to a wild nightspot where he, naturally, gets up and jams with the band on congas. The most stereotypical note is Antonio's over-protective, bustling mother, who simply wants to see him with a nice girl—something of a Hispanisation of the Jewish mother joke.

The rather smug depiction of an enclosed, incestuous circle is redeemed by some memorably absurd moments: notably Leslie and Jeff's awful dippy wedding ritual, with their personalised touches of doggerel—"Will you love him in a boat, and will you love him on a float?"—and ample jokes about nose jobs and dentistry. And the cast—with the exception of Naomi Campbell and her transatlantic Mick Jagger diction—is uniformly excellent. Sarah Jessica Parker makes a galvanisingly prickly centre to it all, in her best turn since *L.A. Story*. If this isn't the film that makes her a star on celluloid, at the very least she'll get her own sitcom series—a *Rhoda* with de luxe cocktails.

VILLAGE VOICE, 1/31/95, p. 50, Georgia Brown

In comparison with a garish comedy like David Frankel's *Miami Rhapsody*, the eccentricities of *Before Sunrise* become truly lovable. Although he's reputedly the son of the *Times*'s Max, Frankel seems to be announcing in his debut that his real sire is Woody Allen. Here he mixes one cup *Hannah and Her Sisters* with a quarter cup *Husbands and Wives*, adds two tablespoons *Alice*, plus a pinch of *Crimes and Misdemeanors*. Bakes and serves.

Once the discreet pink deco credits roll to Louis Armstrong's "It Was Just One of Those Things," the movie opens onto a tight close-up of Gwyn Marcus (Sarah Jessica Parker) speaking to the camera. It turns out she's being interviewed not by a shrink but a new, inquisitive gynecologist. Flashback to an explanation of how, just a year ago, Gwyn got engaged, yet today is not "sexually active." Mia Farrow has been called on to play Gwyn's slightly spacey, sexually active, and apparently *Jewish* mother. It's no doubt meant as an in-joke when Mia delivers the line, "You can't have kids forever."

Coincidentally, a favorite granny is a touchstone here, too. Settled in a nursing home, Gwyn's grandmother is mute from a stroke and pleasantly attached to Antonio (Antonio Banderas), her hunky Cuban nurse. In the movie's first few minutes, Gwyn finds out her mother is having a fling with Antonio while her father (Paul Mazursky) is dallying with Zelda, his travel agent. (Here's Gwyn objecting to Dad's confidences: "I can't imagine Mom having sex with another man! I still have trouble imagining her having sex with you.")

Next, Gwyn watches as brother Jordan (Kevin Pollack) gets thrown out by his pregnant wife Terri (Barbara Garrick) because he's slept with her best friend. "I need sex!" protests the sleazy Jordan who is already on to his business partner's wife (she's a model played by Naomi Campbell). Meanwhile, Gwyn's younger sister Leslie (Carla Gugino) marries a Miami Dolphin (Bo Eason) in a ceremony straight out of *Green Eggs and Ham*. It seems like just days later that Leslie is using Gwyn's apartment for trysts with a long-lost high school classmate, now a dentist. So much family infidelity inevitably takes its toll on Gwyn's engagement to Matt (Gil Bellows), a perfectly prosaic, but faithful, zoologist.

You can take the couples out of Manhattan, but you can't take *Manhattan* out of the couples. Still, Woody's personal comedies look both hilarious and profound next to *Miami Rhapsody*, where the one-liners are stunningly derivative and psychology is strictly from sitcoms. Frankel's comedy centers not on personal angst and neurosis but on random acts by fictitious personalities. Moreover, there are some disturbing undercurrents here that he seems blithely unaware of. One scene between Kevin Pollack and Naomi Campbell is truly ugly, and the movie's only black man, a professional, when pressed, fires the movie's only gun.

Also reviewed in:
CHICAGO TRIBUNE, 2/3/95, Friday/p. C, John Petrakis
NEW REPUBLIC, 2/27/95, p. 26, Stanley Kauffmann
NEW YORK TIMES, 1/27/95, p. C6, Stephen Holden
VARIETY, 1/23-29/95, p. 71, Todd McCarthy
WASHINGTON POST, 2/3/95, p. D1, Hal Hinson
WASHINGTON POST, 2/3/95, Weekend/p. 36, Desson Howe

MIDNIGHT DANCERS

A First Run Features release of a Tangent Films production. *Executive Producer:* Richard Wong Tang. *Director:* Mel Chionglo. *Screenplay:* Ricardo Lee. *Director of Photography:* George Tutantes. *Editor:* Jess Navarro. *Music:* Nonong Buenoamino. *Sound:* Ramon Reyes. *Production Designer:* Edgar Martin Littaua. *Running time:* 115 minutes. *MPAA Rating:* Not Rated.

WITH: Alex Del Rosario (Joel/Jimmy); Gandong Cervantes (Dennis/Raffy); Lawrence David (Sonny); Luis Cortez; Richard Cassity; Danny Ramos; Perla Bautista (Mother); Soxy Topacio (Dominic); R.S. Francisco (Michelle); Nonie Buencamino (Dave).

LOS ANGELES TIMES, 9/28/95, Calendar/p. 8, Kevin Thomas

Mel Chionglo's "Midnight Dancers" inevitably brings to mind the late Lino Brocka's masterful "Macho Dancer" in that they both delve into the precarious lives of the young men who work as entertainers and prostitutes in Manila's garish gay night-life district.

Both point up the economic hardships that drive such youths to sell themselves and reveal the widespread corruption and crime to which they become vulnerable. And along with considerable skin, they reveal the staunch, sustaining friendships that develop between the dancers.

For all such similarities between the two pictures, "Midnight Dancers" actually ends up more closely resembling the Luchino Visconti masterpiece "Rocco and His Brothers" in that it is first and foremost a family saga. It begins in classic fashion with the youngest son, Sonny (Lawrence David), arriving in Manila from his native Cebu, where the family has lost its land. A bright student and trophy-winning basketball player, Sonny has dropped out of school to go to work to help out his hard-pressed family. His older brothers Joel (Alex Del Rosario) and Dennis (Gandong Cervantes) are already dancer-hustlers who work at the   Club Exotica, and inevitably the handsome, naive Sonny joins them.

What is significant and distinctive here is that Chionglo and his perceptive writer, Ricardo Lee, (who co-wrote "Macho Dancer") show the brothers as part of society and of a sturdy family structure. The family is held together by their loving mother (Perla Bautista), who accepts that her sons are macho dancers because that's the way they can make the most money, but you feel that, not surprisingly, she's into denial about their hustling.

Chionglo celebrates an unexpected acceptance of diversity. Joel, whose working name is Jimmy, is a devoted husband and father yet has a tender, longstanding relationship with a young, adoring client, Dave (Nonie Buencamino), who helps out the family financially from time to time.

Nobody is taken aback when Sonny's first romance is with a drag performer (R.S. Francisco), who says he wouldn't mind if Sonny had a "real" girlfriend because that would prove he's a "real" man. Meanwhile, at the Club Exotica we also become acquainted with a number of the other dancers, including one who has developed AIDS. (Oddly, both Brocka and Chionglo downplay the specter of AIDS). Like Spike Lee, Chionglo can create deceptively idyllic moments amid a dangerous world. The irony is that a gesture of hospitality to a street urchin on the part of the mother brings about tragedy.

Warm, sensitive, vital, humorous and emotion-charged, "Midnight Dancer," is a powerful urban epic on an increasingly grinding struggle for survival, beautifully photographed and scored in a surprisingly low-key fashion. Like "Macho Dancer," it shows the dancers in action, on stage and in bed, forth-rightly but discreetly. (There is, however, one quick glimpse of a stage routine that would surely get the film an NC-17 rather than an R, were the film to be submitted for rating). Chionglo, who inspires his cast to live rather than act their parts, looks to be a worthy successor to the courageous and talented Brocka, who was killed in a car accident in 1991.

NEW YORK POST, 7/28/95, p. 40, Larry Worth

Nineteen ninety-five could go down as the year of the gay art film. Countless variations on men having a having a sexual identity crisis, an AIDS crisis or simply a bad hair crisis are filling local "alternative" screens.

Separating "Midnight Dancers" from the pack is its Philippines-based locale. Director Mel Chionglo's examination of Manila's seamy environs, poverty-stricken barrios and residents' reaction to homosexuality make for an intriguing cultural study.

According to Ricardo Lee's script, gay couplings are a way of life in the Philippines. The cavernous expanse of a gay bar—where much of the plot takes place—is packed with family guys who want to ogle boys undulating in their skivvies, despite the occasional police raid.

Further, the ruggedly handsome main character has a wife, child and male lover, all of whom get along quite well. He dances in the local hotspot next to his younger, equally macho brother, who runs with one of Manila's roughest street gangs.

When the baby of the family returns to Manila, it's only natural that he join his siblings on stage. Their iron-willed mother, meanwhile, is content to take their money and save any judgments.

Viewers with double-digit IQs quickly realize that this isn't "My Three Sons." Yet, Chionglo sledge-hammers that point home via gratuitous shots of the perfectly-toned, well-oiled dancers doing their thing. The question remains: How many times must the camera dote on pretty boys lathering their pectorals? And that's just for starters.

The attempts at titillation not only distract from the story line, but contribute to a sense of befuddlement. Had more time been spent on the innumerable subplots, peripheral characters would seem less like afterthoughts.

Actually, there's also confusion when it comes to the principals; the siblings look almost too similar, making viewers constantly concentrate on who's who, particularly in bedroom scenes where faces take a back seat to writhing limbs.

Chionglo somewhat compensates with a final half hour of melodramatic twists, social conundrums and a tragic denouement. Better still, the hard-working cast—led by Alex Del Rosario, Grandong Cervantes and Lawrence David—seems adept at going with the ever-changing flow.

The bottom line: "Midnight Dancers" takes two giant steps past its gay brethren for a refreshingly unique atmosphere—and one step back for playing like a cheap Chippendales audition.

VILLAGE VOICE, 8/1/95, p. 50, Stan Hannaham

Midnight Dancers starts out with a ratio of beefcake to plot that makes you wonder why they don't start flashing a 900 number on the screen. The oiled-up title characters are a group of amazingly attractive straight young men who have dropped out of school to enter the lucrative world of gay prostitution in the Philippines. The film follows three brothers who introduce a fourth to their polymorphous lifestyle. These guys may take it up the rear every night, but if you put them down for it, they'll beat the crap out of you. All "macho dancers" have girlfriends, and in one case, wives and children in addition to their male lovers.

Screenwriter Ricardo Lee presents everything in the brothers' world as business-as-usual until about halfway through *Midnight Dancers*. Moral judgements are left to the viewer. The macho dancers' parents have resigned themselves to their sons' professional choice—"It's just a job ... what was I going to do, cry?" Mom says, though you get the feeling she hasn't read the whole job description. The tiffs between coworkers who steal each others' briefs, the slick sex scenes, the brothers' squalid yet quaint home life, even the overdose of a fellow hustler, have remarkably little weight, because these peripheral mishaps keep saying the same thing in slightly different ways: these are troubled, poor and desperate boys, downtrodden but hard-working and virtuous.

The first real tragedy, at the separation of the boys' parents after a Mother versus Mistress fistfight in the street, gives way to many more. An orphan who stays with the family turns out to be a thief, the police raid Club Exotica, and so on. If the first half of the film seems dangerously close to softcore pornography, the second half plunges into Save the Children infomercial dramatization territory. One brother, tagging along on a car theft, gets hacked to death with a machete by drug dealers, and the mother's wailing body-identification scene takes *Dancers* up and over the top. The characters are too flat to take seriously; there's little difference between the brothers, and the only insight into their mother is that she's overly generous. The filmmakers might want to take a hint from Sally Struthers, who though she begs you to feed the children, sure doesn't starve herself.

Also reviewed in:
CHICAGO TRIBUNE, 2/23/96, Friday/p. N, John Petrakis
NEW YORK TIMES, 7/28/95, p. C10, Stephen Holden
VARIETY, 10/24-30/94, p.71, Emanuel Levy

MIGHTY APHRODITE

A Miramax Films release of a Sweetland Films presentation of a Jean Doumanian production. *Executive Producer:* Jean Doumanian and J.E. Beaucaire. *Producer:* Robert Greenhut. *Director:* Woody Allen. *Screenplay:* Woody Allen. *Director of Photography:* Carlos DiPalma. *Editor:* Susan E. Morse. *Music:* Dick Hyman. *Choreographer:* Graciela Daniele. *Sound:* Gary Alper. *Sound Editor:* Bob Hein. *Casting:* Juliet Taylor. *Production Designer:* Santo Loquasto. *Art Director:* Tom Warren. *Set Decorator:* Susan Bode. *Set Dresser:* Dave Weinman. *Costumes:* Jeffrey Kurland. *Make-up:* Fern Buchner and Rosemarie Zurlo. *Running time:* 93 minutes. *MPAA Rating:* R.

CAST: F. Murray Abraham (Leader of Greek Chorus); Woody Allen (Lenny); Helena Bonham Carter (Amanda); J. Smith Cameron (Bud's Wife); Steven Randazzo (Bud); David Ogden Stiers (Laius); Olmpia Dukakis (Jocasta); Jeffrey Kurland (Oedipus); Tucker Robin (Infant Max); Donald Symington (Amanda's Father); Claire Bloom (Amanda's Mother); Nolan Tuffey (Two-Year Old Max); Jimmy McQuaid (Max); Yvette Hawkins (School Principal); Karin Haidorfer and Garry Alper (Park Avenue Couple); Rosemary Murphy (Adoption Coordinator); Peter McRobbie (Linda's Ex-Landlord); Kathleen Doyle (Ex-Landlord's Wife); Jennifer Greenhut (Lenny's Secretary); Sondra James (Operator); Paul Giamatti (Extras Guild Researcher); William Addy (Superintendent); Peter Weller (Jerry Bender); Kenneth Edelson (Ken); Danielle Ferland (Cassandra); Mira Sorvino (Linda Ash); Dan Mullane (Messenger); Thomas Durkin (Race Announcer); Dan Moran (Ricky, The Pimp); Paul Herman (Ricky's Friend); Tony Sirico, Tony Darrow, and Ray Garvey (Boxing Trainers); Michael Rapaport (Kevin); Jack Warden (Tiresias); Kent Blocher (Voice of Zeus); Joseph P. Coleman and Georgette Pasare (Porno Film Stars).

CHRISTIAN SCIENCE MONITOR, 11/3/95, p. 12, David Sterritt

There he goes again. Woody Allen has long complained that moviegoers draw too many connections between him and the characters he plays.

If he's so peeved about this problem, though, one might ask why he keeps writing this character over and over—the reasonably brainy, moderately nerdy Jewish guy who's such an obsessive New Yorker that not even rocky love affairs (which he endures in film after film) can shake him out of Manhattan.

Allen might answer, as he did when I interviewed him years ago, that his narrow acting range requires an equally narrow assortment of roles. Still, he can't expect audiences to draw clear lines between his on-screen and off-screen personas as long as he patterns important aspects of his characters on traits, mannerisms, and idiosyncrasies that are part of his own personality.

And this is bound to lead to trouble. It did in 1980, when he starred in "Stardust Memories" as a filmmaker who despised his audience. And it's happening this year with his new comedy, "Mighty Aphrodite," which leaves uncomfortably large openings for moviegoers to draw parallels—however strained or unfair these might between his cinematic work and the personal troubles that have made him a tabloid staple in recent years.

Allen plays a sportswriter whose wife talks him into adopting a baby. After a bit of initial terror, he falls goofily in love with the kid, but his affection takes a peculiar turn when he becomes fixated on locating the mother who gave the child up for adoption. She turns out to be a good-natured prostitute whose coarse exterior masks a diamond-in-the-rough inner self.

The plot takes many turns as our hero tries to help the prostitute improve her life, manage his own romantic feelings toward her, and hold his marriage together as he and his wife are both tempted by outside relationships.

Some observers have seized on a minor story point—the prostitute is younger than Allen's character—to accuse Allen of exploiting May-December romance in the wake of his own widely publicized involvement with a much younger woman. I think this is a cheap shot at Allen, given the vast differences between the fanciful screenplay and the facts of his real-life troubles.

Still, it seems clear that parts of "Mighty Aphrodite" are meant as self-justifications. Much of the opening portion shows Allen's character as an excellent adoptive dad, countering public charges that he badly failed in this department. The overall thrust of the narrative is to show him as a bumbling yet good-hearted man who may stumble into temptation but would never allow things to get too far out of hand.

The very title of the movie suggests that romantic attachment—here symbolized by Aphrodite, the Greek goddess of love—is a matter of destiny more than decision, and what's a poor guy to do when his emotions take over?

There's more than a trace of hypocrisy in this, of course. Allen has presented himself for decades as a hip intellectual with a healthy skepticism about bromides and platitudes. So it's hard not to cringe when he relies on an old saw like "love conquers all" to justify self-indulgences on or off the screen.

This aggressively shallow approach to life and love coupled with a badly condescending attitude toward the story's working-class characters, makes "Mighty Aphrodite" one of Allen's least satisfactory films. This is too bad for the excellent cast, including Mira Sorvino as the prostitute, Helena Bonham Carter as the wife, and F. Murray Abraham as the leader of a Greek chorus that punctuates the action with hilarious commentary.

FILMS IN REVIEW, 1-2/96, p. 64, Andy Pawelczak

The joke begins with the clangy doggerel rhyme in *Mighty Aphrodite*'s title and continues with the Zorba bouzouki music which accompanies the opening credits. Woody Allen's new film is part throwback to the inspired sophomorism of *Bananas* and *Everything You Always Wanted to Know About Sex* and part continuation of the East Side saga of tangled relationships and upscale angst that we're accustomed to from Woody's later films. The good news is that the combination works: the two sides of Woody throw each other into high relief. Aristophanic it's not, but *Mighty Aphrodite* is full of funny literate conceits and uninhibited vulgarity, and Woody himself seems rejuvenated by this resurrection of an earlier self.

Lenny Winerib (Allen) is a sportswriter married to Amanda (Helena Bonham Carter), an ambitious fledgling art dealer too busy to have a child. Against Lenny's better judgment, they adopt (attention voyeurs: this is the only reference to the real-life Woody's problems) and six years later, when the marriage is foundering, Lenny becomes obsessed with finding his son's biological mother. She turns out to be a hooker and porn film actress and the rest of the movie is about Lenny's Pygmalion-like attempt to remake her into a lady and find her a husband.

The film's central scene is Lenny's first meeting with Linda (Mira Sorvino), a towering, dirty-mouthed but sweet-tempered Aphrodite whose apartment is filled with phallic tschotkes. When she tells Lenny that her best film was "The Enchanted Pussy," he does a stuttering, embarrassed double take, as did some members of the audience in the Lincoln Plaza Cinema where I saw the picture. The joke here is on Woody's genteel, faintly snobbish persona, and if the lower class sex-goddess Linda is not quite Shaw's life force, by the end she does awaken something dormant in the repressed Lenny.

The picture's other major joke is the use of a campy Greek chorus that comments on the actions at vital moments. In some horrible space/time warp, Woody would be not altogether incapable of putting a chorus on stage for real—remember the Bergmanesque pretensions of *Interiors*—so the chorus here functions partly as a ironic commentary on Woody's own cultural propensities. Dressed in robes and masks and filmed in the ruins of a Greek amphitheater in Sicily, the chorus swings and sways, cries out oracular warnings, and at one point even croons a Cole Porter song. When Lenny decides to search for his son's mother, there's a crack of thunder and the chorus tells him not to be a schmuck. In addition to the chorus, there are also a Jocasta (played by Olympia Dukakis) and Oedipus about whom the chorus remarks that they started a whole new profession. As in Mel Brooks' *History of the World Part One*, the joke consists of the contrast between the archaic, portentous figures and the Borscht Belt wisecracks they utter.

As Lenny, Allen is the familiar neurotic but ineluctably charming denizen of New York's tonier neighborhoods. Lenny's profession of sportswriter makes him into a less rarefied Everyman than the usual Woody character, and it enables Allen to populate the film, as in *Broadway Danny Rose*, with a variety of Damon Runyon types. Helena Bonham Carter as Lenny's wife is a suitable foil to Sorvino's hooker: she's beautiful, cool, and inexorably upwardly mobile. Class is the great repressed in Allen's films, and in this picture it almost breaks through the screen fantasies in the contrast between the working class Sorvino and the WASPish Carter. Sorvino, the daughter of actor Paul Sorvino, dominates every scene she's in. Her alarming habit of talking dirty is rendered even funnier by her high piping voice and appealing innocence.

In the supporting cast, F. Murray Abraham makes periodic appearances as the chorus leader, Jack Warden is a very contemporary Tiresias, and Peter Weller, of *RoboCop* and *Naked Lunch*, is a lecherous art dealer with designs on Lenny's wife. Michael Rapaport, who played an oily thug in the recent *Kiss of Death*, deserves special mention as Kevin, a prizefighter who falls for Linda and is so dumb that when Lenny says he feels superfluous Kevin asks if he's sick or something.

Mighty Aphrodite reminded me, more strongly than some other recent Allen movies, of where Allen comes from. His is a world where the Freudian demi-urge still reigns, where mothers and whores still bedevil the psyches of tottering, embattled males, and where a well aimed wisecrack can right the balance for at least a moment. In some ways, Allen's closest literary counterpart is Philip Roth. Both men come out of a tradition of Jewish humor, moral probity, and social striving, and both have outlasted their social contexts by reinventing themselves several times over. *Mighty Aphrodite* is a palimpsest of old and new Allen. It made me anxious to see where he will go in his next film, which he was already shooting the week *Aphrodite* opened in New York. Mighty Woody.

LOS ANGELES TIMES, 10/27/95, Calendar/p. 2, Kenneth Turan

Like the tortoise in Aesop's celebrated fable, Woody Allen has used not flash but persistence to become one of the most prolific of active American filmmakers. "Mighty Aphrodite" is his 25th feature as a writer-director in an impressive string that would have been difficult to predict when "Take the Money and Run" started things off in 1969.

A sketchy trifle that is sporadically amusing but also off-putting around the edges, "Aphrodite" is an example of how Allen has been able to make just about a film a year for more than a quarter of a century. Because he is funny when he wants to be, because comic lines and situations come easily to him, Allen rarely turns out a film that doesn't give you something to laugh at. But his movies also have a tendency, as this one does, to feel insubstantial, like a first draft he didn't have the patience to pound into shape.

Most of the laughs in "Aphrodite" come from a clever framing device. The film opens in a stone amphitheater that hosts a genuine Greek chorus declaiming lines from English translations of several classic plays. But suddenly the chorus is saying, "Take, for instance, the tale of Lenny Weinrib, as timeless as anything Greek," and into a tale of modern Manhattan we go.

This chorus reappears periodically, offering New York sportswriter Lenny (played by Allen himself) counsel and even once breaking into a spirited rendition of Cole Porter's "You Do Something to Me." Also showing up in costume in Manhattan are the chorus leader (F. Murray Abraham), the blind seer Tiresias (Jack Warden) and other robed characters, all of whom have lots of advice to offer Lenny, who needs it.

Lenny's problems begin with a conflict with wife Amanda (Helena Bonham Carter). An art dealer who wants a gallery of her own, she is also eager for children but feels that "too many exciting things are happening in my business" to produce one the old-fashioned way. So, despite Lenny's serious protests, they adopt an infant boy named Max.

As the boy grows up, Lenny comes to cherish Max. But his relationship with Amanda drifts as she begins to pay increasing attention to her patron, Jerry Bender (Peter Weller). Partly to compensate, Lenny starts to obsess about finding Max's birth mother, who he increasingly imagines to be the repository of all possible virtues.

Well, not exactly. Once Lenny locates Linda Ash (another pleasant surprise from the versatile Mira Sorvino), she turns out to be a bubble-headed prostitute who has a squeak for a voice and is quite serious about her work in pornographic films.

Not telling her why he's interested, and against the advice of the Greeks and everyone else, Lenny pursues his interest in Linda, telling himself he wants to straighten out her life for Max's sake. It turns out to be more of a job than he anticipated.

Though there is a fair amount of amusement to be found in Lenny's story, it is difficult to watch it and merely laugh. Another way Allen can make so many films, aside from not always honing the scripts, is by working in variations off his own situations and possibly even his own fantasies. One can't help, for instance, thinking of ex-love Mia Farrow in Allen's dismissive skewering of a woman who considers herself too busy to have children of her own.

And though Allen's fascination with older men/younger women relationships has yielded successes like "Manhattan" and "Husbands and Wives," the older he gets the more uncomfortable these liaisons are to watch. And throwing in the venerable male fantasy of getting involved with an attractive prostitute adds to the off-putting taste that not even a finely tuned sense of humor can totally erase.

NEW STATESMAN & SOCIETY, 4/12/96, p. 33, Lizzie Francke

Woody Allen might be in his autumnal years—and there is something very, autumnal about his bark-brown demeanour in *Mighty Aphrodite*—but his latest film seems like something he might have produced when he was greener. It opens in a sun-dried amphitheatre where a Greek chorus—heavily robed and with pale, mugging faces—bemoan the fates of Oedipus, Jocasta and Co, only to turn their attention away from Thebes to Manhattan's Upper East Side, where the actions of one Lenny Weinrib are beginning to worry them a bit. And throughout the film, they are on hand to lend comment either in chunks of cod Sophocles or jaunty bursts of Cole Porter. Now, seeing a Greek chorus (courtesy of Dick Hyman and his orchestra) prance their way through "When You're Smiling" might not appeal to all. It tickled me, but the night I saw the film I was in a ticklish sort of mood where anything vaguely silly would prompt hysterics. Back at the word processor, I now recognise it as a jape that might pall for some. It is the kind of gag one might find in Allen's juvenilia files but then Allen turns his films around with such mighty gusto that one can hardly blame him for dusting down an old idea. Remember over 20 years back to *Play It Again, Sam*—how the "Humphrey Bogart" was on hand to offer the nervy Allen advice on his love life. In the same way, the leader of the chorus (F Murray Abraham), flowing garb and all, strides incongruously through Manhattan offering occasional counsel—a weird flip in a film that is otherwise visually stylistically modest.

This light conceit with its highbrow leanings (which allows for jokes about what a party-pooper that old moaning Cassandra can be), however, rather rattles *Mighty Aphrodite*. For when it comes down to it, the film pits Upper East Side erudition against downtown dumbness. The story follows Lenny (Allen, the familiar angsty persona), a whizz of a sports writer, and his art buyer wife Amanda (Helena Bonham Carter—breaking her fragile mould with a very neat performance as waspish chainsmoker that seems to owe a tad of homage to Mia Farrow), who are considering having a child. Not their own, mind you, for Amanda, who has designs on opening her own gallery, maintains that she couldn't possibly fit it into her schedule right now. So this well-heeled couple acquire a child in the same way that Amanda might get her hands on a rare object—she has a good contact at the right agency. The little bairn as well have arrived gift-wrapped (and one wonders if this is Allen's little dig at the child collector Farrow). Certainly, his parents seem more interested in the boy as a delightful accessory, particularly as young Max seems to be so clever, though he swiftly recedes from the view of the film as it shifts focus on to Lenny and Amanda's growing disaffection for each other.

Soon Lenny is musing as to who might be the real mother of his smart kid. He goes in search, hoping to find some latter-day oracle, only to discover to his horror that the prodigy springs from the loins of Linda Ash, a brassy hooker turned soft-porn star who delights in the screen moniker of Judy Cum and whose apartment is chock full with the kind of phallic objects that, had they been in Amanda's gallery, would prompt enthusiasm from the chattering classes, but here just look like cheap kitsch.

In Allen's last film, *Bullets Over Broadway*, the playwright hero ended up being artistically aided—and ultimately outwitted—by a seemingly monosyllabic hood. In *Mighty Aphrodite*, there is the same edgy meeting between seemingly high and low lives. For the film pivots on Lenny's need, Professor Higgins-style, to overhaul Linda and turn her into the kind of mother he thinks his son should have and that might include paying off her pugnacious pimp while advising her to take up a respectable profession like hairdressing.

Linda might not prove to outwit him, but with Mira Sorvino in the role, she eclipses all expectations. The actress won her Oscar for best supporting actress on the strength of it. Best supporting actress is apt, for from the moment she appears she promptly carries the entire film, towering over the spindly Allen. In her flower-print capri pants and tight-knit sweaters that keep afloat a capacious bosom, Sorvino plays Linda—"the state of the art fellatrix"—with a touch of Marilyn Monroe or Judy Holliday. Indeed, at one point she is reading from the script of *The Philadelphia Story* to practise for an audition (Linda yearns to be taken seriously as an actress), while we know it is another George Cukor film that she should be considering: *Born Yesterday*, where Holliday plays the broad who gives the wise guys a run for their money. Her voice is helium high, but there's nothing cartoonish about her characterisation. Indeed, like Monroe or Holliday, she brings a pathos to the role that indemnifies it from a patronising stance while at the same time she has wonderful comic delivery. Allen is deft at writing roles for women—if you think back over his *oeuvre*—but more importantly he is shrewd about casting. Sorvino grabs the script and runs off with it, making something substantial out of its lightness. It may be green, but it puts a spring in the step.

NEW YORK, 10/30/95, p. 108, David Denby

There's a Greek chorus in Woody Allen's new movie *Mighty Aphrodite*, an actual Greek chorus, men and women standing in a magnificent ancient amphitheater and raising their arms in supplication, and although the movie itself is not a success, the chorus is one of the funniest of Woody's many formal inventions. Allen has often left someone standing around for his characters to talk to—ghosts, a shrink, innocent people on the street, and sometimes just the camera itself, applied to in bewilderment, for solace. But this is a Greek chorus wearing masks and cloaks and led by F. Murray Abraham, who often sounds like a chorus all by himself, and it talks as well as listens. "Woe unto man!" it announces at the beginning, enunciating its laments in crisp unison. After much sculpturing of body and hands, and many references to Achilles and Zeus and other celebrities of the Greek imagination, the chorus gets down to business: Lenny Weinrib is about to do something foolish. The mortal in question, a New York sportswriter (Allen), is rather improbably married to an ambitious art-gallery employee, an intense young woman who, in the person of Helena Bonham Carter, walks about with her head bent in sorrow (she appears to be keening, like the chorus). The couple adopts a baby, who grows up to be a handsome and brilliant little boy, and then Lenny becomes obsessed with a pointless question: Who are the biological parents? Where could this little paragon have come from? He has to know. And he sets off on a quest to find out. The chorus, which has begun to metamorphose into a group of kibitzers (more Carnegie Deli than Delphi), now chants things like "Let sleeping dogs lie! ... Please, Lenny, don't be a schmuck!"

The mother, Linda (Mira Sorvino), turns out to be a vulgar, dumb hooker who wears floral pants and fluffy pink bunny sweaters, with her breasts squeezed up high, like some poor thing escaping from the set of *Showgirls*. In an excruciating (and excruciatingly misguided) scene, Lenny goes to see her in her Manhattan apartment. She's a nice girl and wants only to please him sexually and get on to the next client, but he refuses sex, and, without ever telling her why he's there, he tries to talk to her about her life—even argue her out of her life, which annoys Linda a great deal. There might, I suppose, be some comedy in the spectacle of a high-minded little man frightened by a strapping, guileless whore who keeps coming on to him, but the scene is more embarrassing than funny. Woody Allen, who will be 60 in a few weeks, looks shriveled, even wizened, next to the huge, fleshy 25-year-old Sorvino. When she tries to get Lenny undressed, he nearly faints.

All this is tough to sit through, even though we realize that Woody Allen created the scene as a joke on poor, obsessed Lenny, and perhaps as a joke on himself. Lenny has to learn that genes are not stitched together but rolled like dice, and the child that follows conception is rarely the intellectual and temperamental copy of the parents. Is Woody Allen warning himself against excess curiosity? Adopting those two kids with Mia Farrow, and then having a love affair with another of Farrow's adopted children (from Mia's marriage with André Previn), he might well wonder where some of these many vulnerable children came from. Is Allen working out a personal obsession? I wouldn't ask such a philistine question if Lenny's behavior made much sense. But *Mighty Aphrodite* is not a very convincing fiction. Lenny says he doesn't want his son to meet his own mother someday and find a whore, and he doesn't seem to recognize the peculiar snobbery in the idea. Woody Allen may not recognize it, either. Despite the Greek chorus, which is supposed to be Lenny's superego (it never lets up on him, and he never listens to it), this is an unconscious film. When Lenny keeps returning to Linda, we have no idea whether Woody Allen means him to be secretly excited by her; whether Lenny is perhaps looking for his own mother, or a new wife, or a way of being a good Samaritan; or whether he's just a dirty old man playing at fantasies of redemption, like Prime Minister William Gladstone, who liked to invite the London streetwalkers in for tea and a stern little chat.

Like Mia Farrow's chippy in *Broadway Danny Rose* or the pile-driving Elaine Stritch character in *September*, Linda the hooker, with her endless appetite for sex, is one of Allen's indomitable-force-of-life women, but he patronizes her terribly, showing her up again and again as hapless. There's a huge class difference between Lenny and Linda, and we feel Allen's discomfort; he can't reach across that divide except to embrace a cliché: the whore with the heart of gold. He seems caught between disdain and pity. He may think he's humanizing Linda when he shows that all she wants is to be appreciated and loved, but she just seems a simple thing with appalling taste. A more generous-minded creator might have shown that the little boy *has* taken something wonderful from his mother, but no connection with the child is established. Linda's part is lazily, insensitively written, and the untried Mira Sorvino gives a disconnected, defenseless performance, speaking in a high, forced voice that is uncomfortable to listen to—she sounds like a man using his upper register in a puppet show.

The choral laments and injunctions put a joshing frame around the action, but Lenny never listens to the chorus, and the movie shows that he's right to ignore them. None of the chorus's more dire predictions come true, and the picture turns into a pleasant fable. Life is not riddled with catastrophes; life is a comedy. As if defeated, the chorus gradually lightens up and changes into something else—it's a wonderful joke, and I won't spoil it. Woody Allen may want to believe that he can safely ignore his conscience, that some of his wilder flights into foolishness with adopted children are perfectly okay. In *Mighty Aphrodite*, he's not dramatizing an obsession; he's in the grip of one—but the roots of it are obscure and unproductive, and the movie, despite its clever frame, remains an uneasy experience.

NEW YORK POST, 10/27/95, p. 37, Michael Medved

"Mighty Aphrodite" is a somewhat undernourished comic trifle with only two things going for it—but at least Woody Allen fully exploits both of them.

The film's most original touch is the use of a Greek chorus, wearing grey robes and tragic masks, filmed in dramatic natural light at an ancient amphitheater. As the story opens, these archaic figures declaim and gesture in unison in the ultra-serious style associated with "authentic" productions of Sophocles.

Before long, however, the chorus (led by F. Murray Abraham) begins loosening up as they comment on the tribulations of a nervous New Yorker (Woody Allen, of course) and offer advice like "Please, Lenny—don't be a schmuck!"

The other big asset of "Mighty Aphrodite" is a bawdy, hilarious, genuinely touching performance by rising star Mira Sorvino, who is likely to get a supporting-actress Oscar nomination for her efforts. She is so good, in fact, that she single-handedly saves the movie, at the same time throwing the story out of balance by showing up the other characters for the thin, bloodless creations that they are.

Woody, for instance, plays the same insecure nebbish we've met as many time before, this time called Lenny Weinrib and making his living as a sportswriter. He's married to a glamorous but unsmiling gallery owner (played by British actress Helena Bonham Carter with an impeccable American accent) who's increasingly preoccupied by her work and by her wealthy, adoring business partner (Peter Weller).

Lenny, meanwhile, begins a secret quest to find the birth-mother of their 5-year-old son, reasoning that any woman who produced this bright funny, beautiful kid must be worth meeting.

This fantasy eventually brings him to Sorvino, a chirpy hooker with a room temperature IQ and the stereotyped heart-of-gold, who also plays bit parts in porno movies under the name "Judy

Cum." Without ever telling her the basis for his interest, Lenny begins a friendship while resisting her frequent attempts to demonstrate her professional competence.

He even faces down her menacing pimp (using the ultimate bribe for sports-mad New Yorkers) and tries to arrange a serious relationship for her with a hay-seed prize fighter ("I had 16 fights and I won 'em all but 12") played by Michael Rapaport.

The "Aphrodite" in the title is, of course, the Greek goddess of love, but there's precious little romance in the film—certainly nothing like the grand passions in previous Allen efforts such as "Manhattan" or "Hannah and Her Sisters." The relationship between Lenny and his wife is particularly disappointing; the chorus insists that we should care deeply about saving this marriage, but her character is such a shallow sourpuss that you much prefer watching Woody with the far more endearing Sorvino.

The chorus itself also gets to be a bore, as Allen beats his one gag to death and beyond. By the time these robed-and-sandaled figures break into a jazzy, light-footed dance, you can't help realizing that Allen's "Aphrodite" is diverting and flighty," but never quite mighty.

NEWSDAY, 10/27/95, Part II/p. B6, John Anderson

The difference between vulgarity and wit, it suddenly occurs to me, is effort. Even the most tasteless gag can be a bon mot, if the joker isn't trying too hard to be funny.

Woody Allen is trying too hard. "Mighty Aphrodite," his latest and most self-referential send-up of modern mores and neuroses, is occasionally funny. More often, though, it's uncomfortable to watch, because the man is tying himself in knots.

His jokes are cruder, his characterizations ruder. Allen has always had a mean streak—his nebbishy personas frequently are tortured by inferior beings who can't be avoided—but he's meaner here. If he were funnier it might all work, but the slightness of the jokes only amplifies the harshness of his glare.

This clearly has to do with the subject matter—the anxieties of an adoptive father, something we all know he knows something about—and the possibility that, in trying to exorcise himself of demons, he's also strangled his sense of humor. The one consistently funny bit is a literal Greek chorus led by F. Murray Abraham (half mensch, half deity) that begins by making Homeric observations about Allen's character and ends up singing show tunes. But as the only reliable recurring routine, it also grows desperate.

Lenny Weinrib (Allen) is a sportswriter married to an art gallery employee (Helena Bonham Carter) who is inspired by a pregnant friend to adopt a child. Her motives are immediately suspect—and as the presumed stand-in for Mia Farrow, her characterization is a bit vicious. But Lenny, like Woody's own self-image, is a soul adrift, devoid of power or control: He resists the adoption idea, but they adopt anyway, and he becomes obsessed with love for the boy. This may be understandable, but when he then becomes obsessed with finding out who his son's mother is, it's not. It is, in fact, thoroughly inexplicable. Is this some adoptive-parent thing the rest of us don't know anything about? If it is, Allen is so constrained by his own self-involvement that we're never told, and we never care.

What he finds when he does locate the mother is an Amazonian hooker with a heart of gold, and a mind of mush. As Linda Ash—one of several *noms de brothel* she's going by—Mira Sorvino is captivating, her Victoria Jackson impersonation quite ridiculous but endearing. She dwarfs Lenny, and breathes life into the movie, which is a paradox, given how broad and unsavory her character actually is.

Lenny becomes Pygmalion, his wife becomes distracted, the kid disappears and Linda is transformed. Woody? He's caught between incipient tragedy and uncontrolled hubris. Cue up Bobby Short.

SIGHT AND SOUND, 4/96, p. 48, Nick James

Lenny is a New York sportswriter. His wife Amanda, a successful art dealer, persuades him that they should adopt a baby boy. By the time the child, Max, is three years old he is a prodigy and Lenny begins to wonder where the talent came from. With Amanda increasingly absorbed by her art career, Lenny decides to track down Max's mother. Told by the adoption agency that the mother's name is privileged information, he sneaks a look at the file for her address. He soon learns that she is a woman of many names, who acts in porn movies as Judy Cum, although her real name is Linda Ash. A boxing contact finds out that she turns tricks and gives Lenny her phone number. He arranges to see her at her apartment. After a friendly beginning, his interest in Linda's private life makes her think he's a threat. She throws him out.

Lenny accosts Linda on the street and offers to take her for lunch. They have a delightful day at the racetrack but he finds out that Linda's family is anything but prodigious. In the meantime, Amanda has decided to open her own gallery, but her backer, Jerry Bender, makes a pass at her and she is emotionally confused. Linda turns up at Lenny's office to tell him that her pimp, Richy, will not allow her to give up the game, and that he's threatening to kill Lenny. Lenny goes to see Richy, is threatened himself, but eventually wins Linda's freedom in return for some good seats to see the Knicks play basketball.

Lenny decides to matchmake Linda with a young boxer, Kevin, about to return to life upstate in Wampsville as an onion farmer. Meanwhile, Amanda has told Lenny that she's moving out because she needs to find out whether she's in love with Jerry. Lenny goes to see Linda but finds Kevin outside in a fury because he's found out about Linda's past. Lenny and Linda find solace in each other's arms for one night. Afterwards, Lenny and Amanda both realise they still love one another and are reunited. Linda drives to Kevin's farm to beg him to take her back but he refuses. On her way back to New York she stops her car for a helicopter pilot in distress. They are soon married and they raise a baby girl, conceived on that single night with Lenny. Some years later, Lenny and Linda bump into one another at a toy store with their kids and say a brief hello.

With such an edifice of a career as he's built up over the years and with his recent, albeit reluctant, admission that comedy is his true forte, Woody Allen has every right to feel comfortable with himself—as comfortable as anyone who has made anxiety the fragile substance of his art can be. His last movie, *Bullets Over Broadway*, in particular, with its clever, multi-layered narrative and pithy, affectionate wit, seemed a return to the form of his peak years—those of *Annie Hall* and *Manhattan*, obviously, but also of *The Purple Rose of Cairo, Zelig, Broadway Danny Rose* and *Radio Days. Bullets* gained tremendously from Allen not acting in it himself; we could appreciate his directing and writing talent without the interference of mitigating feelings about his screen persona. *Bullets* came after a couple of respectable ground-regaining experiments that helped dispel the unsavoury publicity around Allen's breakup with Mia Farrow—*Husbands and Wives* with its shaky, verite camera and his quirky *Manhattan Murder Mystery*. His is now such an impressive body of work that even long term doubters (such as myself) are obliged to admire him.

Mighty Aphrodite, however, has no visual innovations, concentrates on people in rooms and brings back Allen's favourite long-faced nebbish screen persona. A sportswriter this time, Lenny is essentially the same character that Allen always plays. With his aspirant art-dealing wife, Amanda (Helena Bonham Carter as an utterly plausible neurotic, chain-smoking Manhattanite), he is as much a part of the well-heeled Upper East Side cultural elite as is the director himself. Equally, *Mighty Aphrodite* is absolutely a product of that elite. The film is circumscribed by familiar Allenist devices—great mainstream jazz on the soundtrack, and theatrical conventions brought to the cinema. Like a parlour game of allusion for the cognescenti, *Mighty Aphrodite* opens with a masked Greek chorus in an amphitheatre, led by F. Murray Abraham, declaiming the fates of Achilles, Hector and Oedipus only to turn to Lenny's more mundane fate. They soon become the comic replacement for the analyst sounding-board figure of Allen's earlier films.

With some partial realisation that he is, perhaps, getting too old for this sort of thing, Allen does not, for once, make his plot revolve around his character's love life. Instead, Lenny is seen as a man of wisdom trying to sort out another person's life for them, against the hectoring advice of the Greek chorus (a device pushed well beyond its comic limit), while his own love life is drifting away from him. Needless to say the recipient of Lenny's wisdom is not from the Upper East Side, but a happy, bubbly prostitute, Linda Ash, who Lenny, a connoisseur of unintelligent flesh (he's a boxing fanatic), admits is "pretty and quick". As the statuesque, squeaky-voiced Linda, happily showing off her sex toys, Mira Sorvino really lifts the film into the light, bantering comedy it aspires to be. However, Linda is also treated as an exotic species of the lower classes.

Amazed that his talented adopted son could have come from such low-life genes, Lenny is confident that he can get Linda out of prostitution and into hairdressing, which his aunt did for all her life. And really, it proves very simple. He buys off her pimp with some Knicks tickets and then tries to set her up in marriage with a boxer, Kevin, who is truly stupid. Kevin is clearly all Linda can manage in Lenny's book. That the relationship doesn't work out and she ends up with a literate helicopter pilot of her own volition is neither here nor there, because in this cosy tale, it's the interaction between opposite poles that matters. The vivacious giantess with the heart of gold helps the ageing writer to realise that he loves the neurotic wife who earlier forces him to adopt a child because, as she says, "I can't take a year out right now". In turn Lenny's anxiety about his adopted son forces him to act as the enabling eminence who gets Linda out of her dangerous criminal rut. There's at least one awkward thread that the apparently neat ending—with its matching of one unknowing parent with another—fails to tie up. If it is nurture (by the home help, it would seem), not genetics, that has made Max a prodigy, can we therefore assume that Linda's new daughter will fail to blossom as well?

For despite Allen's attempts to build in a knowing perspective on the class boundaries being breached by Lenny, *Mighty Aphrodite* remains deeply patronising about Linda and Kevin. Most of the humour (not a rich Allen vein by anyone's standards), is at the expense of their ignorance. We are invited to gently mock and chide their limited aspirations as they make slow progress towards some kind of Upper East Side vision of whatever it is nice, ordinary, uncultured folks do. And Allen, as Lenny, lectures Linda in exactly the same way as his character chided the teenage Mariel Hemingway in *Manhattan*. It would be a pity if such a talent as Woody Allen were to see out the rest of his career playing passive-aggressive moral bullies of this order.

TIME, 10/30/95, p. 91, Richard Corliss

Stardom can offer airtight insulation from the fact that he is famous, a celebrity too often creates the fiction that he is revered. O.J. Simpson, for instance, translated an acquittal verdict by 12 jurors into the claim that most Americans really believe he's innocent. And Woody Allen, who three years ago was show biz's most notorious middle-age male, keeps making movies whose plots reflect, excuse and promote his lustlorn escapades. Both guys are fallen idols who have trouble understanding what all the fuss was about. They want America to take an amnesia pill so they can get back to their work: being loved in public.

We don't for a moment equate capital crimes with romantic misdemeanors. Still, there's something icky in Allen's compulsion to write scripts about fiftysomething guys ready to dump their wives for nubile waifs the approximate age of Soon-Yi Farrow Previn. This is the plot of Allen's 1992 *Husbands and Wives*, of his brutally funny playlet in the off-Broadway *Death Defying Acts*, and of his exasperating, finally engaging new film, *Mighty Aphrodite*.

Here he's Lenny Weinrib, a sportswriter with a pretty, peckish wife (Helena Bonham Carter) and, to his joy, a five-year-old adopted son Max. Curious about the boy's lineage, Lenny finds Max's natural mom, Linda (Mira Sorvino), a prostitute who also does porn work. How can this lost soul, with her Vargas body and "state-of-the-art fellatrics," be the wellspring of a brilliant child? Lenny must save this creature, for Max and from herself. His anguished pursuit of Linda, in which he tries mating her with a dim boxer (Michael Rapaport), is tracked by a Greek chorus that's all singing, all dancing and so Yiddish you could plotz. "I see catastrophe," one chorus member darkly intones. "Worse—I see lawyers."

More perilous still, we see Allen rewriting his tabloid sins at an age (he'll be 60 this year) when he looks like a pensive Rumpelstiltskin; boyish roguery ill suits him. In TV revivals of Broadway farces, he plays crabby geezers: the tourist with tsuris in *Don't Drink the Water*, a decrepit comic in a new version of *The Sunshine Boys*. Yet in his films Allen is the Woody of old—or, rather, of young. To Lenny, the raw, vibrant Linda makes Amanda seem stale and shrewish. Bonham Carter (who's a radiant 29 and certainly doesn't look shrewish) must play that standard Woody marplot the older woman. Sure, Linda's got the screwball charm of the early Judy Holliday, but does every Allen superbabe have to be born yesterday?

And can't Amanda be more than a grab bag of weaknesses? Poor trite thing: she's bored by Lenny's name games and love play. She insists on adopting a child, then all but ignores him. ("I'm the boss," Lenny insists to Max. "Mommy's only the decision maker.") And she cheats on Lenny before he can on her. Her dalliance is a betrayal; his is a quest. Once again Allen's take on marriage is biased and bleak; he sees it as a prison for two, where the condemned may finally rise to a level of reciprocal pity. They achieve awareness by admitting defeat.

Fortunately, Allen eventually dumps the wife stuff to concentrate on one of his classic characters: Linda, whom Sorvino wonderfully incarnates with a weenie voice and a brassy poignancy. The distracting visual trope of Allen's last few movies—that virtually every scene, no matter how long, must be filmed in one shot with a very fidgety camera—pays off in the first meeting of Lenny and Linda; the comic tension is deliciously built and sustained. And when the chorus breaks into some dreamy Cole Porter harmonies as background to an unlikely amour, the goofiness is almost magical.

The suspicion lingers that Woody Allen deserves a good spanking, and not from a prostitute with a heart of gold. But, listen: humor and sentiment can triumph over stern morality any day. Once the picture gets going, it reminds us that Allen is also an artist with an acute feel for movie romance. So scruples be damned. This time, *Mighty* makes all righty.

VILLAGE VOICE, 10/31/95, p. 71, J. Hoberman

Like *Lessons of Darkness*, [see Hoberman's review] which opens with the poured-concrete equivalent of Doric columns limned against a luridly orange sky, Woody Allen's *Mighty Aphrodite* plays off the notion of classical tragedy; the first image has a masked Greek chorus in a ruined amphitheater promising us a "tale as timeless as life itself."

This prologue notwithstanding, *Mighty Aphrodite* is a relatively modest Allen opus—straightforward farce without even the art-and-artist bushwa of *Bullets Over Broadway*. Rather than life itself, the subject is Woody Woodso Woodman—here impersonating a middle-aged sportswriter, Lenny Weinrib, whose young, workaholic wife (Merchant-Ivory axiom Helena Bonham Carter) insists on adopting a baby. O dread, long-postponed paternity! Ignoring the warnings of the Chorus—"Please Lenny, don't be a schmuck!"—not to mention those of the actual Cassandra, Lenny goes in search of his son's birth mother.

Since the quest is couched as a sublimated extramarital affair, it should be no surprise that his child's mother is a happy hooker and occasional porn star (blond-bewigged Mira Sorvino) whose apparent low IQ reproaches Lenny's insistence on his son's brilliance—despite the child's proplike performance. The exaggeratedly statuesque, ridiculously attentive Sorvino towers benignly over her dithering director, scooping up most of the movie's laughs by talking dirty in an uninflected Minnie Mouse falsetto. Considering how many gags Woody wrings from her character's stupidity, it's remarkable how much dignity the actress brings to the role—albeit insisting overmuch in interviews on her Harvard pedigree.

Just as Allen's comic vision is predicated on the unlikely coupling of high art and shtick (Jack Warden as Tiresias; Greek Chorus singing "When You're Smiling"), so his comic persona has always been founded on whining and self-justification. The good news is that Woody's post-Mia fall from grace has given him license to make jokes about dildos and blow jobs; the bad news is that the scandal has left him with a permanent ax to grind. Here, he virtually steps out of the movie to sound out against the practice of adopting children while simultaneously projecting the image of a doting father. Similarly, the consummation of Lenny's paternal interest in a comely call girl is rationalized by his wife's self-absorption and her almost-affair with a reptilian smoothy (Peter Weller).

In a preemptive strike that must have sent Allen's publicists around the bend, an outraged Maureen Dowd attacked this scenario weeks ago on the *Times* Op-Ed page as "a sentimental exercise in self-promotion." Dowd read *Mighty Aphrodite* as a kind of salvo launched in the court of public opinion ("I recognize spin when I see it"), and *Mighty Aphrodite* may indeed be Allen's advertisement for himself. Still, it's a promo tempered by a comic lack of perspective. (Woody, after all, is a man who saw Terry Zwigoff's wartfest *Crumb* and was inspired to ask Zwigoff to make a celluloid portrait of him.) The ritual evocation of Oedipus notwithstanding, Narcissus is the movie's presiding hero.

Mighty Aphrodite is thoroughly solipsistic. (The most excruciating instance is Allen's idea of a kindergarten interview—Mr. and Mrs. Lennie grill their son's prospective head mistress as though she were their household domestic.) Yet *Mighty Aphrodite* is a weirdly satisfying movie. In the same way that the repetition of every joke contributes to its formal rigor, so the exaggerated decrepitude produced by Allen's proximity to the firm young flesh of his female costars contributes to its pathos. Offering a flash-forward to the artist as a querulous old man, *Mighty Aphrodite* manages to be amusing without really being funny.

Also reviewed in:
CHICAGO TRIBUNE, 11/3/95, Friday/p. C, Michael Wilmington
NEW REPUBLIC, 11/27/95, p. 28, Stanley Kauffmann
NEW YORK TIMES, 10/27/95, p. C1, Janet Maslin
NEW YORKER, 10/30/95, p. 112, Anthony Lane
VARIETY, 9/4-10/95, p. 73, Todd McCarthy
WASHINGTON POST, 10/27/95, p. D7, Hal Hinson
WASHINGTON POST, 10/27/95, Weekend/p. 50, Desson Howe

MIGHTY MORPHIN POWER RANGERS: THE MOVIE

A Twentieth Century Fox release of a Saban Entertainment/Toei Company production. *Producer:* Haim Saban, Shuki Levy, and Suzanne Todd. *Director:* Bryan Spicer. *Screenplay:* Arne Olsen. *Story:* John Kamps and Arne Olsen. *Director of Photography:* Paul Murphy. *Editor:* Wayne Wahrman. *Music:* Graeme Revell. *Music Editor:* Joshua Winget. *Sound:* Bob Clayton and (music) Dan Wallin. *Sound Editor:* John A. Larsen. *Casting:* Liz Mullinar and Christine King. *Production Designer:* Craig Stearns. *Art Director:* Colin Gibson. *Set Designer:* William Passmore. *Set Decorator:* Tim Ferrier. *Set Dresser:* Tara Kamath and Lon Lucini. *Special Effects:* Tad Pride. *Visual Effects:* Erik Henry. *Costumes:* Joseph Porro. *Make-up:* Lynn Wheeler. *Stunt Coordiantor:* Rocky McDonald. *Running time:* 95 minutes. *MPAA Rating:* PG.

CAST: Karan Ashley (Aisha/Yellow Ranger); Johnny Yong Bosch (Adam/Black Ranger); Steve Cardenas (Rocky/Red Ranger); Jason David Frank (Tommy/White Ranger); Amy Jo Johnson (Kimberly/Pink Ranger); David Yost (Billy/Blue Ranger); Paul Schrier (Bulk); Jason Narvy (Skull); Paul Freeman (Ivan Ooze); Gabrielle Fitzpatrick (Dulcea); Nicholas Bell (Zordon); Petea-Maree Rixon (Alpha 5); Jean Paul Bell (Mordant); Kerry Casey (Goldar); Mark Ginther (Lord Zedd); Julia Cortez (Rita Repulsa); Jamie Croft (Fred Kelman); Paul Pantano (Kids); Mitchell McMahon and Tim Valka (Kids); Peter Mochrie (Mr. Kelman); Scott McGregor (Security Guard); Paula Morrell (Reporter); Paul Goddard and Robert Simper (Construction Workers); Robyn Gol (Zombie Parent Dancer).

LOS ANGELES TIMES, 6/30/95, Calendar/p. 1, Kevin Thomas

"Mighty Morphin Power Rangers: The Movie" brings the popular TV series to the screen with a barrage of spectacular special effects, a slew of fantastic monsters, a ferociously funny villain—and, most important, a refreshing lack of pretentiousness.

Director Bryan Spicer and his writers have held onto a crucial sense of proportion; they've jazzed up the production values for the big screen but have kept an appealing make-believe comic-book look and sense of wonder. And no matter how far they soar into outer space, the Power Rangers remain likable, well-scrubbed, wholesome high school kids—all parents of teenagers should be so lucky.

You'd think that when construction workers in the large city of Angel Grove—Sydney, Australia, actually—come upon what looks to be a decidedly outsize manhole cover bearing a satanic monster face upon it, they'd call in the archaeologists. But *nooooo*—and once the cover is removed, a gigantic metallic claw clutching an immense egg emerges. Popping out of the egg after 6,000 years of incarceration is none other than the terrible Ivan Ooze (Paul Freeman), a figure "of evil beyond imagination," who is eager to make up for lost time in destroying the planet, and then the universe itself.

After all, he points out, he's missed the Spanish Inquisition, the Black Plague—and "the Brady Bunch reunion." The Power Rangers have their work cut out for them. With a head like a horned toad, Ivan is a sharp, witty figure of malevolent fun who overshadows more familiar evildoers like Lord Zedd and Rita Repulsa.

So potent is Ivan's evil that the Power Rangers' leader Zordon (Nicholas Bell), encased like a holograph in his elaborate command center, begins losing his life force. The Power Rangers must travel to a distant planet to obtain the Great Power if Zordon is to survive.

Be warned that the film is intended for youngsters, for whom the triumph of good over evil won't seem quite so predictable as it is to adults. Similarly, the six Rangers—Karen Ashley, Johnny Yong Bosch, Steve Cardenas, Jason David Frank, Amy Jo Johnson and David Yost—probably won't strike kids as being so bland since they've come to know them on TV.

Beyond its extravagantly gleeful villain, nonstop action and visual razzle-dazzle, it has a simple but important message, delivered by a lovely warrior queen (Gabrielle Fitzpatrick) on that distant planet. She tells the Power Rangers that "the strength is inside you. Trust it."

NEW YORK POST, 6/30/95, p. 37, Michael Medved

For anyone over the age of 8, "Mighty Morphin Power Rangers: The Movie" will be a mighty morphin bore. But for the little kids who comprise its core audience, the film is considerably worse than that—a piece of toxic trash that ought to inspire serious concerns among responsible parents.

While it's easy to shrug off the harmless stupidity, the movie version is so vastly improved in terms of production values that its potential impact is far more worrisome. With splashy special effects and elaborately edited fight scenes, it will produce nightmares for some children, and encourage many others to imitate all sorts of dangerous and obnoxious behavior.

The movie's intensity may be unfamiliar to fans of the TV series, but the plot line reads like a rehash of several weeks of small screen adventures. We first meet our six teen-aged super hero's when they're sky-diving for charity, then roller-skating through their home town of Angel Grove (actually Sydney, Australia).

Their fun ends when a construction crew unearths a long-buried egg that contains "an evil beyond all imagination"—Ivan Ooze (Paul Freeman), a purple monster who looks like a medieval gargoyle of Satan and is intent on destroying the universe.

He not only hypnotizes all local parents, getting them to abandon their kids and walk toward lemming-like destruction at the edge of a cliff, but invades the inner sanctum of Zordon, the omniscient controller who play's the same role with Power Rangers that Charlie used to play with his TV's "Angels."

With Zordon lying near death and their mystical morphin abilities destroyed, the Rangers journey to the distant planet of Faydos to find a new source of power. There, they encounter "the perfect warrior," Dulcea (Australian starlet Gabrielle Fitzpatrick), who seems to have purchased her wardrobe at Frederick's of Faydos—resembling Raquel Welch in her fur bikini in "One Million Years B.C."

The stunning Fitzpatrick also boasts a remarkable ability to deliver silly lines with a straight face. "Buried deep within each of us is an animal spirit waiting to be released."

The movie is full of such New Age, non-pagan nonsense. In between, the Rangers battle an assortment of hideous armored dinosaur skeletons and huge insect-like machines while their stunt doubles jump off cliffs, deliver karate kicks and turn endless somersaults in the air.

The six stars (familiar to fans of the TV series) are clean cut young people who smile and say "yeah!!" a lot but display no discernable acting ability, shouting out their lines as if they were providing voice-overs for wretched Japanese cartoons.

The climatic battle, with each Ranger commanding a huge "zord" (a fighting machine in the shape of his respective "sacred animal") displays some truly impressive computer-generated effects, which go on much too long, and help to make this noisy, noxious annoyance even more unsuitable for kids.

NEWSDAY, 6/30/95, Part II/p. B2, Gene Seymour

To those parents who are no doubt cringing over the prospect of "Mighty Morphin Power Rangers: The Movie" we say: Take heart. Yes, the movie is cheesy like the TV show. But it's not the bland, processed stuff doled out in daily half-hour segments. It's bigger, tangier, tastier. Children will swallow the movie whole, but adults digesting its contents will find enough sharpness to make the experience bearable. At the very least.

Most of the edge is provided by Paul Freeman (Belloq from "Raiders of the Lost Ark"). In "MMPR: The Movie," Freeman is a hoot as the "galactically revered, universally despised" Ivan Ooze, a purple, primordially slimy villain stirred from several millennia of slumber by the Power Rangers' regular antagonists, Lord Zedd and Rita Repulsa. Ooze has big plans.

First, he's going to beat up on Zordon, the positive life-force and mentor to the Power Rangers, who forced Ooze to spend eternity in a pink egg. Then he's going to turn all the parents of Angel Grove, the Rangers' hometown, into zombie slaves by selling jars of purple slime to their kids. Then if he's got a spare minute, he'll wipe out the Power Rangers and take over the world—in that order.

Guess who stands in his way? You got it! The Power Rangers (Jason David Frank, David Yost, Amy Jo Johnson, Karan Ashley, Steve Cardenas and Johnny Yong Bosch). Don't expect much from these guys in the way of a stretch—except, of course, in the physical sense.

The scenery stretches, too. The Rangers have to go to a faraway planet to renew their lease on galactic energy. There they encounter a scantily clad good witch who gives them new animal personas. Which of course means ... new toys to buy!

Director Bryan Spicer, whose previous credits have all been in television (mostly on clever, now-canceled Fox network stuff like "The Adventures of Brisco County, Jr."), moves things along at a brisk clip with plenty of breezy, antic humor to offset the inevitable corniness.

During one of the movie's many noisy battles, Ooze remarks to one of his henchmen, "Oh, here comes that cute Pink Ranger!" The henchman replies, "Oh, you think she's cute, too, huh?" One imagines this exchange repeated in thousands of households between older and younger siblings. Here and elsewhere, "Mighty Morphin Power Rangers: The Movie" shows it knows how to wink at itself while remembering what it's there for in the first place: to sell a new line of action-toy accessories.

SIGHT AND SOUND, 9/95, p. 57, Louise Felperin

Angel Grove, California. The present. Six teenagers—Aisha, Adam, Rocky, Tommy, Kimberly, and Billy—have been chosen by an extraterrestrial being, named Zordon, to be Power Rangers, though their identities remain a secret. In order to help fight the forces of evil, the Rangers have various accoutrements, including power coins, giant mechanical vehicles in the shapes of totemic animals called Zords, and tight, figure-hugging body suits. The rangers wage a constant battle with Lord Zedd and Rita Repulsa and their hordes of evil minions.

The precarious status quo is upset when an accident at a building site releases the nefarious Ivan Ooze, Zordon's chief rival, from an imprisonment that has lasted millennia. Ooze takes over Zedd and Rita's headquarters, and sends a plague of hench-creatures to bedevil the Rangers while he sacks Zordon's headquarters. When they finally arrive at Zordon's, the Rangers find the Power dissipated, their Zords destroyed and their power coins gone, making it impossible to "morph" into their Power Ranger guises. With what little energy is left, Alpha 5, Zordon's robot assistant, transports the six teenagers to the distant planet of Phados to get help.

On Phados, with the help of the voluptuous witch Dulcea, the Rangers gain fresh power with new totemic spirits. Meanwhile, back in Angel Grove, Ooze has started marketing a sticky ooze which when touched turns parents into zombies. Fred Kelman, a pre-pubescent friend of the Rangers, has organised the children of Angel Grove in an effort to stop their parents plummeting over a precipice at the building site. The Rangers return, summon their new Zords and ride into battle with Ivan's ectomorphicons, huge mechanical insect-like weapons. Eventually, they triumph, the parents awake from their spell, and Zordon, who was lying on his death bed, is restored to his former self by the Rangers channelling the Power.

In a heroic struggle to fill newspaper and magazine space, the noble forces of journalism world-wide have battled to generate column inches on the topic of cartoon and comic book characters being translated into feature film formats. *Mighty Morphin Power Rangers*—in both the movie version and the television series—has been sucked into this maelstrom of genre building and containment. Have the Rangers colluded with the powers of darkness? Or are they really victimised refugees, unfairly huddled together with the likes of *Tank Girl, Judge Dregg, Batman*, and *Casper* who truly deserve blame for this morass of merchandising and opinion forming? The answer, with caveats, is yes to both questions: the transition to feature film has blotted out some of the charms of the original format, but the *Power Rangers* phenomenon remains intrinsically different from the comic-book-to-film ventures mentioned above.

Mighty Morphin Power Rangers: The Movie had a fundamentally different genesis. It isn't based on a comic book or an animated cartoon, but on a popular children's television show. This is a crucial fact in understanding the attraction and popularity of the *Power Ranger* concept. Being ghettoised on Saturday morning children's television endows the series with exclusivity—it is a kids' thing which grown-ups largely cannot, nor wish to, follow. The strength of the series lies in its profound innocence: like early cinema, it seems to be groping for a new visual grammar that will suit its content. The influences—Hong Kong martial arts films, *Godzilla* movies, anodyne teen-angst television series—are always obvious, but they function as shameless steals rather than as clever borrowings. Unlike the *Batman* franchise and the recent *Casper* movie, nostalgia plays no part in *Power Rangers'* appeal, neither can pre-built subcultural hipness (pace *Tank Girl* and *Judge Dredd*) tarnish it. Quite simply and literally, the original series can't afford to be clever. Ruthlessly formulaic, it ends up looking like a touchingly cheap *bricolage* of *Monkey* (the Far East Asian paganistic television series) and *Beverly Hills 90210* (the American pap-and-pimples series).

Unfortunately, the makers of *Mighty Morphin Power Rangers: The Movie* have been infected by the Hollywood urge to lure the widest possible audience. Armed with loads of money to spend in comparison to the series' budget, they drafted in special effects teams, wrote a distressingly coherent script, and threw in some lame Freddie Krueger-style humour. Gone are the gloriously weird battles between puppets and men in Zord-suits that looked like they were taking place in another dimension (or at the very least, in a Toho Studio backlot). Instead we get shiny new ectomorphicons and Zords which look like characters from an expensive but dull CD-rom game. Gone are the curiously old-fashioned cameo-insets that framed the Rangers as they shouted the names of dinosaurs at "morphin time". Instead we're given discreet, zooming graphics which unimaginatively respect the conventions of the 'frame'. Gone is Trini (my favourite Ranger) substituted by Aisha, the new Yellow Ranger who lacks Trini's intelligence and wit, but is played by pop singer Karan Ashley of KRUSH. The plangency of the original series is almost wholly drained, except for the rather touching sequence where the children try to save their parents from the lure of Ooze's consumerist cant.

Stylistically homogenised throughout, *Power Rangers*, although far more enjoyable, is now formally barely different from any of the other schlocky tie-ins and rip-offs that are clogging our multiplexes at present. Blown up to fill a big screen and stretched to two hours, the *mise en scène* is sparse and the pace stumbles, whereas the television series seems bursting with bodies and swift as a kick to the chest. (Indeed critics have decried the film and series' violence.) Others may be seduced by its slick computer-generated hyper-realism and its predictable shape-shifting villain, but I'm waiting on my couch for the re-runs.

Also reviewed in:
CHICAGO TRIBUNE, 6/30/95, Friday/p. H, John Petrakis
NEW YORK TIMES, 6/30/95, p. C3, Caryn James
VARIETY, 7/10-16/95, p. 35, Joe Leydon
WASHINGTON POST, 6/30/95, p. D1, Frank Ahrens
WASHINGTON POST, 6/30/95, Weekend/p. 42, Kevin McManus

MINA TANNENBAUM

A New Yorker Films release of an IMA Films production in association with UGC Images/Christian Bourgois Productions/La Sept Cinéma/FCC/SFPC (France)/Les Films de L'Etang (Belgium)/Belbo Film Productions (Netherlands) with the participation of Canal+/Soficas Sofinergie 2/Sofinergie 3/Centre National de la Cinématographie/RTBF Télévision Belges/Eurimages. *Producer:* Georges Benayoun. *Director:* Martine Dugowson. *Screenplay (French with English subtitles):* Martine Dugowson. *Director of Photography:* Dominique Chapuis. *Editor:* Martine Barraqué and Dominique Gallieni. *Music:* Peter Chase.

Choreographer: Lucia Coppola.   *Sound:* Alain Villeval.   *Sound Editor:* Laurent Quaglio. *Casting:* Gigi Akoka.   *Art Director:* Philippe Chiffre.   *Set Decorator:* Pierre Decraen.   *Costumes:* Yan Tax.   *Make-up:* Nancy Baudoux.   *Running time:* 128 minutes.   *MPAA Rating:* Not Rated.

CAST: Romane Bohringer (Mina Tannenbaum); Elsa Zylberstein (Ethel Bénégui); Florence Thomassin (The Cousin); Nils Tavernier (François); Stéphane Slima (Didier); Chantal Krief (Daisy); Jany Gastaldi (Gisèle); Dimitri Furdui (Henri); Eric Defosse (Serge); Jean-Philippe Ecoffey (Jacques Dana); Harry Cleven (Gérard); Alexandre Von Sivers (Devas); Atrus De Penguern (Naschich); Elise Benroubi (Mina, Age 10); Hugues Quester (Choumachère); Shirley Kleinman (Ethel, Age 10); Tony Cecchinato (Gypsy); Sabrina Germeau (Mina, Age 5); Gwenola de Luze (Muriel); Elodie Grosbois (Ethel, Age 5); Julien Kafaro (Man in the Street).

LOS ANGELES TIMES, 5/26/95, Calendar/p. 16, Kevin Thomas

For much of "Mina Tannenbaum," French filmmaker Martine Dugowson makes you wonder why she didn't call her film "Mina and Ethel," since it's the story of two women, both born in 1958, who meet at age 7. But by the time the film is over you understand only too well why it bears the title it does, although on screen Mina and Ethel are of equal importance.

You come away understanding much more, for this is a major film on the meaning of friendship. Dugowson, a cinematographer in her smashing feature-directing debut, leaves us with a heightened awareness that the most important of friendships can be fragile and possess limits and that friendship, like life itself, is invariably provisional. This is a real depth-charge of a movie, one that you can't—and shouldn't—easily shake off.

Movies don't get much more deceptive than "Mina Tannenbaum." Dugowson invites us to assume that we're going to see a cozy, intimate little movie that the French are so good at—one that will be a vehicle for two of France's brightest young stars, Romane Bohringer and Elsa Zylberstein, both of whom are consistently dazzling. Dugowson makes us forget how skilled the French also are at pulling the rug out from under us—even when providing some hints of what's to come right at the start.

Dugowson, who won a best screenplay award at Cannes in 1992, hopscotches over the decades, but most of her story, set entirely in Paris, takes place in 1974 and 1989. At 16, Bohringer's Mina is already set on a career as a painter but is convinced that she's homely, although we can see the beauty behind the thick glasses. Zylberstein's Ethel, who's not sure yet what she's going to do with her life, is also clearly a beauty—but, in her friend's accurate estimation, is about 25 pounds overweight.

When Dugowson cuts to 1989 she shows us a chic Mina, who's discovered contact lenses, has had a lover for four years—and predecessors to him—and is experiencing acclaim as an artist, while Ethel has slimmed down but is struggling to break through as a free-lance journalist. This first glimpse of Mina is misleading: She hasn't got it made as an artist, and she's actually mired in her teen-age self-image.

Dugowson has let us know from the start that Mina and Ethel are both Jewish but hasn't made anything of it, letting us accept the information as matter-of-factly as we take note of the color of the women's hair. Dugowson in time reveals a crucial distinction: that while *we* shouldn't make a federal case over anyone's religion or anything that makes him or her a member of a minority, we must deal with whatever makes *us* in any significant way different from the majority.

Dugowson rightly brings a bittersweet humor to Ethel's all-too-familiar predicament of the over-bearing mother adamant about her daughter marrying a Jew. In a stunning moment we discover that the crucial chasm between Mina and her mother, a child of the Holocaust, is that she cannot understand how her daughter could possibly be unhappy—that she doesn't even have the right to be so.

"Mina Tannenbaum" belongs to its radiant stars, but Nils Tavernier and Jean-Philippe Ecoffey excel as key men in the women's lives. Finally, Dugowson makes every minute count of her handsome film's substantial 128-minute running time.

NEW YORK POST, 3/3/95, p. 48, Thelma Adams

One paints; the other doesn't. Martine Dugowson's Gallic Thelma et Louise pairs uncompromising artist "Mina Tannenbaum" (Romane Bohringer) and eager-to-please journalist Ethel Benegui (Elsa Zylberstein) in a lengthy but mortal friendship.

Females can be fickle, even to each other. Writer/director Dugowson won the Grand Prize for Best Screenplay at the 1992 Cannes Fest.

Her breezy, heartfelt feature debut reinvents stock material—a quarter-century friendship between two outcasts of the fatty and four-eyes mold—with fresh and vibrant characters culled from the French Jewry.

"Mina Tannenbaum" guides us through deliciously familiar territory—the bad hair, bad shoes, '60s and '70s yielding to the polished '80s and '90s.

Through the years, the women's relationship rings true: affection tempered by jealousy; mutual rebellion against mothers anchored in a previous era; relief at finding a soul-mate gradually giving way to the drive toward separateness, toward defining oneself as an individual in the world.

Dugowson adds to this a level of whimsy bordering on magic realism. Cigar-smoking guardian angels bicker in the sky above the girls' first meeting.

Later, during an argument between Mina and her mother, the parent suddenly shrinks to her inner-child, a forlorn dark-eyed girl with a yellow star sewn to her sleeve. Bohringer and Zylberstein lose themselves in their roles.

The daughter of French star Richard Bohringer has the charisma to carry the movie. As in "The Accompanist," a steely strength underlies her doe-like frame. Bohringer is unafraid to show the welds in her armor, although her climactic expressions of anguish push the edge of melodrama.

NEWSDAY, 3/3/95, Part II/p. B2, John Anderson

Like "Thelma and Louise" on the love highway, or "Jules and Jim" without Jules and Jim, "Mina Tannenbaum is about friendship, but perhaps only tangentially. In her marvelous debut feature, writer-director Martine Dugowson mixes generous helpings of mawkish emotion and magical realism with a tragicomic take on the melodrama that is us.

No one wants to imagine his or her death as the pedestrian event it usually is, and Dugowson introduces her title character (played as an adult by Romane Bohringer) the way we'd all like to be remembered: As the subject of posthumous tribute—and a documentary. Having introduced the late artist to us through this introductory filter of sentimental recollection, she spends the rest of the movie proving that first-hand facts are no less subjective and illusory.

As fictional film biography, this is right out of "Citizen Kane," and "Mina" even has its Rosebud—of sorts: a painting of two women, a paraphrase of a Gainsborough that Mina executes at age 10 (Elise Benroubi). It becomes the totem of friendship between her and Ethel (played at 10 by Shirley Kleinman and later by the memorable Elsa Zylberstein). Born on the same day, in the same hospital, and nursed in adjoining cubicles—Dugowson plays fast and loose with coincidence—their lives will be intertwined forever.

Why? friendship has seldom been more unlikely, or more devoid of natural sympathy. But that's Dugowson's persistent point. Although both her heroines are children of unforgiven mothers—Ethel's has a malignant obsession about her marrying a Jew; Mina's is a Holocaust child choking on a caul of anger—each views the other as an extension of herself. As they grow up together through the '70s and '80s, taking failed stabs at love and torturing themselves with self-doubt, neither senses when the other is embroidering a story—flashbacks and revised flashbacks punctuate the narrative. Neither shares the other's impulses, except regarding men. And yet their common bond is what they live for—or rather, what keeps them going when all else lets them down.

Dugowson applies many fantastic elements to the fabric of "Mina Tannenbaum," with mixed results. When Ethel and Mina meet as young girls, their grandfathers appear in the sky, observing from heaven. When Mina moons over her would-be lover, we see them dance in costumes lifted out of a Degas. Rita Hayworth or Bette Davis might appear, echoing whatever passion is gripping Mina or Ethel; Dugowson's film quoting is accurate, if coy. But she has a liberated sense of imagery: At the hospital where both girls are born, she first shows us the earth outside it, which is alive with worms. It's an elusive but somehow perfect foreshadowing of the squirming abstractions Mina will one day create on canvas, and of the slippery nature of her and Ethel's relationship.

Romane Bohringer ("Savage Nights" "The Accompanist") is among the best young actresses alive; she buries her own beauty in Mina, who is always the flightless sparrow. Elsa Zylberstein is nearly her equal as Ethel, whose career path into journalism (couldn't she have become a doctor?) marks her and Mina's basic spiritual differences, differences they overlooked all their lives, but which haunted them all the same.

SIGHT AND SOUND, 10/94, p. 49, Ginette Vincendeau

The story of Mina Tannenbaum is told in flashback after her death. Mina was born in Paris in 1958 in a Jewish milieu on the same day as Ethel Bénégui. The two girls meet at a ballet class in 1968 and despite their differences (Mina is thin and difficult, Ethel plump and placid) become close friends. In 1974, Mina has become a gifted though shy art student. She falls in love with François, a fellow student.

Partly because of her shyness, her love remains unrequited. Her relationship with her mother, a traumatised concentration camp survivor, is strained. Ethel falls in love with Didier, a pianist. On the point of having sex, she is overcome with embarrassment at her 'fat' body.

By 1989 Mina, transformed from ugly duckling to trendy beauty, is a successful artist living with the handsome Serge. Ethel tries to establish a career in journalism while hiding from her mother the fact that she is living with a 'goy', Gérard. Mina sells three paintings to a well known art dealer, Jacques Dana, who flirts with her. Ethel gets a job on an arts magazine by impersonating Mina, who is shocked by Ethel's unscrupulousness; soon Ethel's journalistic career blossoms. An accident leaves Mina's face scarred and her paintings don't sell any more; she takes copying work. Ethel's mother is terminally ill and accuses her daughter of killing her with her lifestyle. Wracked by guilt, Ethel advertises for a Jewish husband in a newspaper, and Jacques Dana, amused, replies.

Although Ethel's mother dies and the marriage does not take place, Mina feels betrayed and stops seeing Ethel. Serge leaves her. Mina's father is mentally ill and her mother sells the family flat; she feels increasingly lonely and desperate. Later, she hears that Ethel is back with Gérard and that they have a baby. She engineers a chance meeting, and they decide to spend the following Saturday together. Ethel postpones the meeting because of a holiday. This triggers Mina's deepest depression and she lulls herself. We learn that Ethel's baby girl is called Mina.

Martine Dugowson's first feature is an unusual, sometimes uneven mixture of comedy and melodrama. Yet it is a film of immense charm and humour which works surprisingly well. If *Mina Tannenbaum*'s central theme of friendship has a universal ring to it, the film also occupies that relatively rare territory in French cinema, the mainstream woman's film.

The centrality of the two women, their tribulations (relationships with mothers and men and with each other, the traumas of emergent sexuality) and the disposability of the men, all foreground women's experiences and desires. The oscillation between sameness and difference at the core of female friendship also serves as a comment on female identity, especially in relation to the mother. In this respect, a fascinating aspect of *Mina Tannenbaum* is the way the girls rebel against their mothers, yet end up in similar positions to them. Mina loathes her mother's morbidity, but commits suicide; Ethel is stifled and repelled by her Jewish mother, who is forever pushing her to conform, yet she ends up with a man and a baby.

The bitter-sweet observation of adolescent growing pains in the streets of Montmartre inevitably evokes Truffaut, while the female friendship and period reconstruction prompt comparisons with Diane Kurys. But although Dugowson's recreation of the aesthetic horrors of 1970s platform shoes, floppy hats, unflattering crushed velvet dresses, ghastly haircuts and so forth is very funny, she keeps period details to a minimum and manages to suggest the decade economically through a knowing use of French popular singers such as Enrico Macias, Dalida and Serge Gainsbourg. Mina's descent into failure and loneliness is far from the universe of these two directors, and a departure from the classic woman's coming of age picture. Whereas the genre leads us to expect both women to grow (as in Kurys' *Diabolo Menthe* and *Coup de foudre*) through their various traumas, Mina's tragic ending is not redeemed and her suicide is truly shocking. And where some will see the divergent trajectories of the heroines as realistic—Ethel the pragmatist is a survivor, Mina the tortured artist a loser—feminist spectators will also see Ethel, the conformist with a good job, man and baby, survive Mina the transgressor, whose art, hitherto a raison d'être, suddenly becomes meaningless. But, as with classic Hollywood melodrama, however much Mina, and occasionally Ethel, are victims, *Mina Tannenbaum* is pleasurable because of the strength of Bohringer and Zylberstein's performances.

Romane Bohringer, on whose name this film was probably picked up for UK distribution, builds on her performance in Cyril Collard's *Les Nuits fauves* and Claude Miller's *L/Accompagnatrice*. She elaborates on her well-established persona of highly strung and hypersensitive young woman, whose success in France is associated with its appeal to a young generation (Charlotte Gainsbourg, considered for the part, occupies a similar terrain). She manages however to flesh out what already verges on type casting by displaying a fine sense of comedy, especially in the early scenes. The relative newcomer Zylberstein (previously seen in Maurice Pialat's *Van Gogh*) is also impressive and manages well the physical and mood changes demanded by her role. Above all, the two actresses form a great duo.

Mina Tannenbaum's depiction of the Jewish petite bourgeoisie of the Montmartre area provoked strong reactions in France. It is not difficult to see why, since the mothers, the traditional central figures of Jewish culture, are turned into monsters. While such stereotypes serve to highlight the generation gap they also occasionally jar with the naturalistic project of the film. Ethel's mother eating chocolates and watching TV in bed is very funny, while her emotional blackmail on her death bed is unsettling. Similarly, Jacques Dana, the gallery owner, is rather crudely drawn, as is the arrogant art teacher (though Hughes Quester turns this part into a wonderful cameo).

Ultimately what awkwardness and lack of subtlety there may be are compensated for by the sense of enthusiasm and experiment that permeates the film—surprisingly, in view of its downbeat ending. Dugowson uses a number of devices which provide an ironic distance, while not being in any way avant-garde. The film is framed by scenes featuring a cousin who does not appear in the main story, nurses break into a dance when the girls are born, and at various points characters—the mothers, the art dealer, the art school lecturer, dead grandfathers 'in the sky'—address the camera directly with details of Mina's life or comments on the action. Occasionally, the grown-up Mina confronts herself as a child or the two young women are juxtaposed with their idealised visions of themselves in the same shot. *Mina Tannenbaum* may not be autobiographical, but Dugowson (distantly related to the director Maurice Dugowson) is the same age as her protagonists, and is clearly talking from the heart about an era and a milieu she knows.

VILLAGE VOICE, 3/7/95, p. 58, Amy Taubin

I don't want to damn Martine Dugowson's *Mina Tannenbaum* to box-office oblivion by calling it a women's picture, but yes, that's precisely what it is—a film directed by a woman and suffused with female subjectivity about a symbiotic attachment between two women. For viewers who've waited 25 years for an antidote to the Jungian misogyny of Bergman's *Persona*, this almost does the trick.

In France, where *Mina Tannenbaum* was nominated for a César (the French Oscar) for best first feature, women directors have given new life to a nearly moribund national cinema. In fact, three of the five César-nominated first features were directed by women. Besides *Mina Tannenbaum*, they are Pascale Ferran's *Coming to Terms With Death* and Marion Vernoux's *Nobody Loves Me*, both screening in MOMA's New Directors series later this month.

In the U.S., however, where merely to have a uterus, let alone a uterus unpledged to the patriarchy, is a sign of subversion, *Mina Tannenbaum*'s future is by no means assured. Let me hasten therefore to inform you about some of the film's other virtues: It has the kind of insight into claustrophobic Jewish family life in Paris that Woody Allen might envy; it's a thoroughly unromanticized depiction of a talented young painter knocking around the French art world; and it's powered by a mercurial performance from Romane Bohringer.

Mina Tannenbaum opens with the untimely death of the eponymous hero, the cause, at this point, unspecified. Almost immediately it flashes back to Mina's birth in 1958, then leaps to the initial meeting 10 years later of Mina and her future best friend Ethel (Elsa Zylberstein). There's an uprising taking place on the steps of the Sorbonne, but the young girls know only that they are social outcasts in their ballet class. Ethel is overweight and none too bright. Mina wears thick glasses, acts the clown to disguise her anger, and is making paintings that reveal her confusion about the boundaries between herself and others.

They already have suffered the narcissistic wounds that will make their emotional lives disasters. Mina's mother, herself the child of Holocaust survivors, has no love for her own daughter. "As the Talmud says, one who doesn't marry isn't a human being." Ethel's mother warns her daughter that she'll shoot her if she gets involved with a goy. (If the film has a flaw, it's that the mothers are portrayed as villains rather than as the unconscious victims of a misogyny that's endemic to a ghettoized patriarchal culture.)

Jump to 1974, the year of Dalida and Serge Gainsbourg, chunk-heeled shoes, bell-bottoms, long leather vests, and skinny deco scarves. Mina and Ethel have their first romances, which fall apart—Ethel, ever self-conscious about her weight, flees her boyfriend's bed when the time comes to take off her clothes, and Mina breaks a date with the boy who adores her because she doesn't want him to see her bad haircut.

Jump again, now to 1989. Mina's career is off to a fast start. She's been through several love affairs and is living with a young painter who worships her. Ethel, now willfully svelte, is involved with a non-Jew whose existence she keeps a secret from her family. Ambitious, but less directed than Mina, she talks her way into a job as a journalist. The first rift between the friends occurs when Ethel uses Mina's name to get an interview with a famously reclusive artist. It's all downhill from there. Mina has an accident that leaves her face slightly scarred. The wound, which a more stable personality might have shrugged off, pierces her fragile sense of self. In no time, she's alienated her lover, her dealer, and her best friend.

Wildly erratic in tone, *Mina Tannenbaum* is like three films packed into one, and it's a sign of Dugowson's intelligence as a director-writer that she nearly gets away with merging the fantastical comedy of the opening scenes (replete with dancing baby-nurses and red-winged angels) with the psychological melodrama of the end. But it's not until the last 20 minutes that the relationship between Mina and Ethel comes into focus, and it's not until the final shot that the mystery of that relationship, fraught with as much desire and taboo as any Oedipus complex, is revealed.

Also reviewed in:
CHICAGO TRIBUNE, 8/25/95, Tempo/p. 2, John Petrakis
NEW REPUBLIC, 3/6/95, p. 30, Stanley Kauffmann
NEW YORK TIMES, 3/3/95, p. C17, Janet Maslin
VARIETY, 3/28-4/3/94, p. 70, Lisa Nesselson
WASHINGTON POST, 6/23/95, p. F6, Rita Kempley

MONEY TRAIN

A Columbia Pictures release of a Peters Entertainment production. *Executive Producer:* Frederick Pierce, Tracy Barone, and Adam Fields. *Producer:* Jon Peters and Neil Canton. *Director:* Joseph Ruben. *Screenplay:* Doug Richardson and David Loughery. *Story:* Doug Richardson. *Director of Photography:* John W. Lindley. *Editor:* George Bowers and Bill Pankow. *Music:* Mark Mancina. *Music Editor:* Thomas Drescher. *Sound:* James J. Sabat. *Casting:* Francine Maisler. *Production Designer:* Bill Groom. *Art Director:* Dennis Bradford and Sarah Knowles. *Set Decorator:* Beth Rubino. *Set Dresser:* Joseph Badalucco and Gary Aharoni. *Special Effects:* Phil Cory. *Costumes:* Ruth E. Carter. *Make-up:* Laini Thompson and Margot Boccia. *Stunt Coordinator:* Jack Gill. *Running time:* 103 minutes. *MPAA Rating:* R.

CAST: Wesley Snipes (John); Woody Harrelson (Charlie); Jennifer Lopez (Grace Santiago); Robert Blake (Patterson); Chris Cooper (Torch); Joe Grifasi (Riley); Scott Sowers (Mr. Brown); Skipp Sudduth (Kowalski); Vincent Laresca and Nelson Vasquez (Subway Robbers); Vincent Patrick (Bartender Frank); Aida Turturro and Alvaleta Guess (Women on Platform); Vincent Pastore, David Tawil, and Ron Ryan (Gamblers); Greg McKinney, Mitch Kolpan, and Jeremy Roberts (Guards); John Norman Thomas (Detective); Oni Faida Lampley and Jack O'Connell (Dispatchers); Saul Stein, Manny Siverio, and Johnny Centatiempo (Brown's

Enforcers); Enrico Colantoni (Dooley); Christopher Anthony Young (Guard with Dooley); Richard Grove (Motorman); Steven Randazzo (Guy at Bar); William Charlton (Businessman); Josefina Diaz (Young Woman); Moss Porter (Mickey); Keith Leon Williams (Darryl); Jose Zuniga (Victor); Thomas G. Waites (Barricade Captain); Leikili Mark (Punk Girl); Kevin Guy Brown (Punk Guy); Bill Nunn (Crash Train Motorman); Sharon Schaffer (Token Clerk); Angel Caban and Joe Bacino (Decoy Cops); Jose Soto, Larry Gilliard, Jr., and Flex (Hoods); Michael Artura (Second Captain); Mark Weil (Stockbroker); Joseph Wilson Ayesu (Little Joe); Katie Gill and Cody Gill (Crosswalk Children).

LOS ANGELES TIMES, 11/22/95, Calendar/p. 10, Kenneth Turan

"Money Train" is a by-the-numbers action-buddy picture, and few directors run through those numbers as smoothly as Joseph Ruben. With buddies du jour Wesley Snipes and Woody Harrelson as the leads, this turns out to be an acceptable if undemanding venture that has to overcome several bumps along the way.

Ruben, with credits including "The Stepfather," "True Believer" and "Sleeping With the Enemy," has a fairly deft touch with the kind of pulp popular entertainment that might have been B-picture material in Hollywood's golden days.

Snipes and Harrelson are reteamed after making quite a splash in "White Men Can't Jump." A hipper version of the Mel Gibson-Danny Glover "Lethal Weapon" pairing, they have a genuine rapport that is often stronger than the actual lines they have to read.

Here, in a goofy twist, they play foster brothers John (Snipes) and Charlie (Harrelson), two tough transit cops who roam the New York City subway system observing the motto of "Serve, protect, break a mugger's neck." Loaded with attitude, they take no guff off anyone but can't do enough for each other.

Actually it's mostly John who does things for kid brother Charlie, an inept high-stakes gambler and perpetual screw-up who is always needing to be bailed out according to Donald Patterson (Robert Blake), Charlie is "a wreck looking for a place to happen."

As chief of the Metropolitan Transit Authority, Donald Patterson is the boss of bosses which means he spends most of his time obsessing about the money train, so-called because it collects the $3 million to $4 million in cash receipts the subway system takes in daily. (Those tokens do add up.) Naturally, the brothers fantasize about knocking it off, but they are cops after all, so all they do is dream.

The other thing they fantasize about is Grace Santiago (Jennifer Lopez), the newest and most attractive member of their subway detail. This wouldn't be an movie if both men didn't fall out of love with Grace and how they work out that relationship as well as they lust for those millions is the main order of business.

The most successful parts of "Money Train" are its action sequences which include the hectic pursuit of a twisted psychopath called the Torch (Chris Cooper) and scenes involving subway trains (shot by second unit director and action veteran Terry Leonard) that were so involved that a replica of a chunk of the New York system called the longest set in film history, had to be constructed in downtown Los Angeles.

But especially compared to something like "Speed," "Money Train" doesn't have quite enough thrills in it. Rather extra attention is paid to the buddy comedy aspects of Doug Richardson and David Loughery's script, even though it's not as strong as the relationship that Ron Shelton wrote in "White Men."

In fact, there are signs that "Money Train" was possibly written for a different kind of pairing. Much is made of conflicts between the two brothers, but Harrelson and Snipes have so much innate rapport that the bickering and hostility the plot forces them to engage in is never momentarily convincing.

Snipes and Harrelson perform like the veterans they are, and Jennifer Lopez mostly holds her own with them. Her best scenes, including a memorable conversation held in a boxing ring, tend to be with Snipes, who is such a one-man charm school it's a shame he doesn't appear in sophisticated romantic comedies as often as action films.

"Money Train's" biggest surprise, though it shouldn't be, is Robert Blake, who hasn't made a feature appearance in years. Looking lean and acting lethal, Blake is ruthless and effective as the transit twins' fierce boss, and seeing more of him in the future would be a pleasure.

NEWSDAY, 11/22/95, Part II/p. B5, John Anderson

Certain movies are going to be guilty pleasures no matter how you try to intellectualize your way out of it. Take, for instance, an action/adventure/train chase/romance/buddy flick starring Wesley Snipes and Woody Harrelson set at Christmastime in Manhattan and featuring a massive ripoff of the Metropolitan Transportation Authority. How can you resist?

The MTA stuff alone is enough to make me dismiss all the illogic, bad taste and questionable criminal activity in "Money Train," a fast-moving if slightly daffy hybrid of "The Taking of Pelham One Two Three" the "Die Hard" films and Snipes and Harrelson's own "White Men Can't Jump." In this one, the two actors arc brothers—adoptive brothers—who are also maverick Transit Police officers and rivals for the affection of one Officer Grace Santiago (movie newcomer and former "Fly Girl" Jennifer Lopez). Their lives are made more complicated by MTA chief Donald Patterson (Robert Blake), a sociopathic martinet who doesn't like their act and whose chief obsession is the subway car that picks up the Transit Authority receipts—the money train.

Director Joseph Ruben ("The Good Son," "Sleeping With the Enemy") and his screenwriters, Doug Richardson and David Loughery, know it's better to give than to receive. So amid all of Ruben's frenetic, action sequences—he filmed largely in New York, but also built, and wrecked, a subway set in Los Angeles—the filmmakers also provide four, count 'em, intersecting plot-lines.

The one you presume is going to be the main one concerns a scarred psycho known as the Torch (Chris Cooper) who is setting token booths on fire, with the vendors inside. John (Snipes), Charlie (Harrelson) and Grace are in hot pursuit, but the odd thing is they catch him: The Torch turns out to be a red herring, not the main story point he seems to be.

Running on a parallel track is the tale of Charlie, inveterate gambler, and his poker debts to one Mr. Brown (Scott Sowers), a lethal mobster with a crew of equally bad-tempered henchmen. Charlie has always been the screwup, ever since he ran away from the orphanage (sniff) and John's family adopted him. And, once again, John has to bail him out. Which he does, in the typical Wesley Snipes butt-kicking manner.

John won't go so far as to give up Grace, who has enchanted Charlie but finds herself attracted to John. Charlie's loss at love, his dismissal from the force by Patterson and his financial difficulties with Brown drive him to take a crack at the money train on New Year's Eve—the fourth plotline, and the nail-biting finale to a curiously constructed film.

Cops as thieves, instruction on how to torch token vendors, one overheated sex scene and a sprinkling of gratuitous violence—"Money Train" has everything a holiday movie needs (remember: they're showing the traditional "King Kong" tomorrow on Ch. 21). Even the subway system isn't portrayed quite rightly—which is probably wise, given how many knuckleheads might want to hijack a real money train. But this is a popcorn movie that basically does what it's supposed to, even if you have to overlook a lot—like the climactic train chase itself: If Patterson wanted to stop the train, wouldn't he just cut the power? Oh, well. Details, details. The subway system should run as well as this movie.

SIGHT AND SOUND, 6/96, p. 46, José Arroye

Foster brothers John and Charlie are undercover transit cops for the New York subway system. Their job is to act as bait for criminals and, when necessary, to protect the money train which collects millions of dollars each night from the subway stations. They successfully bait some petty crooks but fail to catch a pyromaniac who has set fire to a woman ticket collector in her booth. John and Charlie have a reputation for being trigger-happy and there is no love lost between them and Patterson, the chief of the Metropolitan Transit Authority.

Grace Santiago, a rookie cop, gets assigned to their beat. Charlie promptly falls for her and tries to woo her but she falls for John instead. When Charlie drops by John's place, he finds him in bed with Grace and this results in a fight. Charlie feels inferior to his brother and has a gambling problem. He decides to pay off his losses by gambling some more and ends up deeper in debt. He shows up drunk for work the next day. When the pyromaniac turns up again, Charlie's inebriate state endangers the lives of Grace and some civilians and he is promptly fired. John lends him the money but he gets his pocket picked by an old lady. Creditors are about to throw him off a tall building when John arrives, resolves the problem, but tells Charlie he never wants to see him again. When Charlie next sees his creditors, they give him a brutal beating, warning him that John's life will also be in danger unless he pays up.

In despair, Charlie puts his plan of robbing the money train into action on New Year's Eve. He sends John a model of the money train they had stolen from Patterson's office to let him know the plan is on. He and Charlie successfully take over the train but the planned escape route is blocked by Patterson. By mixing in with the crowds, Charlie and John avoid being identified as the thieves. Meanwhile, the pyromaniac burns in his own petrol. Grace arrests Patterson for putting passengers lives in danger. As the New Year is announced in Times Square, John finds that Charlie has some of the stolen money still hidden in his anorak.

Money Train is designed to cash in on the success of Wesley Snipes and Woody Harrelson as the star partnership in *White Men Can't Jump*. The film's advertising is built around the tag line "Wesley and Woody are back" but they're not really "back" in the full sense of the word. What was likeable about the two actors in *White Men*—they looked good, sparked wit off one another, and played characters who were lovably picaresque—is absent. Perhaps actors 'having chemistry' is another way of saying they are well-directed and have a servicable script that can support an interactive display. If so, to say Wesley and Woody lack chemistry here is another way of saying the film isn't very good.

It's hard to understand why a film that is indisputably a star vehicle should be so careless with the presentation of its major assets. Charlie is an unattractive, irresponsible character: he drinks, gambles and steals. There is nothing to explain why people within the film put up with him, let alone why the viewer should like him. Woody Harrelson needs an opportunity to be charming (that's what helped make *White Men* a hit), but it is not forthcoming. He is given shaggy hair and baggy clothes that are at best unflattering. To make him seem more lovable, he sings James Brown's 'Say It Loud! I'm Black and I'm Proud'. Maybe with Ron Shelton directing, that scene could have been funny. Here it's just awkward.

If Woody Harrelson is not shown to advantage, Wesley Snipes is sabotaged. He gets top billing and wins the girl but these are the only concessions the film makes to his stardom. The scene in which John and Grace get it on together is typical. We see them moving closer in medium shot. As they begin to dance, Snipes looks as if he can really move, but the camera denies us the chance to find out. It's bad enough that we don't see Snipes in action, but on the print I saw he's sometimes hard to see at all. Bit players in *Money Train* get better lighting than Snipes; whenever there's a white person in the frame, discerning Snipes' features becomes a matter of eyestrain. A look at him in *Jungle Fever* or even *Waiting to Exhale* gives some measure of how little the cinematographer John W. Lindley seems to understand about filming black actors.

If *Money Train* fails to provide the pleasures associated with its stars, it also denies us those of genre. There are some conceptually exciting action scenes (with bullets and fists flying, and gunfire in speeding vehicles) but they are poorly executed. Quick cuts of fast-moving vehicles do not neccessarily make an exciting action sequence. In *Money Train*, the frenetically roving camera actively prevents us from seeing the action. We never see either of the stars completing a movement from beginning to end. Part of the pleasure of watching Antonio Banderas in *Desperado* is to see how he moves and Robert Rodriguez makes sure that we do. In *Money Train*, the action scenes present us with a stilted breakdown of the various moves, rather than the illusion of movement.

Among the more disagreeable aspects to the film, Charlie's desire to be black which means dancing to James Brown and saying "bro"' a lot is, at best, tasteless. It is dishonest not only because of what we know about racism in the United States, but also because of the way Wesley Snipes is disadvantaged by the lighting. Also unsavoury is Charlie's keeping of the money. Legalities don't matter much in action movies but Charlie is given no reasonable motivation for hanging on to what is public money. The film's cynicism also infects its attitude to the viewer—a few jokes, lights and explosions are meant to be enough of a return for the ticket price.

VILLAGE VOICE, 12/5/95, p. 68, Gary Dauphin

No one involved with *Money Train* would invoke political courage as one of the film's strong suits, but perversely enough it's the better movie. [The reference is to *White Man's Burden*.] A rail-thin but effective action cash-in on the chemistry Wesley Snipes and Woody Harrelson established in *White Men Can't Jump, Money Train* follows in the long tradition of black cop-white cop buddy movies, its New York City subway locale making it a kinder, gentler version of *Die Hard III.*

The money train in question is the MTA collection car, a rolling safe that makes only periodic appearances until the film's final, stunt-fest reel. This slow buildup makes *Money Train* an odd action outing: Wesley and Woody play foster brothers as well as partners here, so a good half of the film is spent working through various relational sub-plots, little things like Woody's gambling problem or Wesley's tendency to always get the girl. (Jennifer Lopez handles the Rosie Perez role well—and actually manhandles Wesley.) These issues don't ever approach real drama, but Snipes and Harrelson exude so much comfortable fellow feeling that it's impossible not to root for the happy ending when Woody starts to see the train as his way out off debt and Wesley fears it's what will bring his foster brother finally and irrevocably down. This is all resolved in a predictably crowd-pleasing fashion, of course, but as a daily subway rider I found nothing clichéd about a film where the MTA is ripped off for a change.

Also reviewed in:
CHICAGO TRIBUNE, 11/24/95, Friday/p. C, John Petrakis
NEW YORK TIMES, 11/22/95, p. C12, Stephen Holden
VARIETY, 11/20-26/95, p. 48, Brian Lowry
WASHINGTON POST, 11/22/95, p. B4, Hal Hinson

MONTH BY THE LAKE, A

A Miramax Films release of an Anuline production developed in association with Tamara Asseyev Productions. *Producer:* Robert Fox. *Director:* John Irvin. *Screenplay:* Trevor Bentham. *Based on a novella by:* H.E. Bates. *Director of Photography:* Pasqualino De Santis. *Editor:* Peter Tanner. *Music:* Nicola Piovani. *Music Editor:* Robin Clarke. *Sound:* David Crozier. *Sound Editor:* Les Wiggins. *Production Designer:* Giovanni Giovagnoni. *Set Decorator:* Mauro Passi. *Costumes:* Lia Morandini. *Make-up:* Nilo Jacoponi. *Stunt Coordinator:* Franco Salamon. *Running time:* 96 minutes. *MPAA Rating:* PG.

CAST: Vanessa Redgrave (Miss Bentley); Edward Fox (Major Wilshaw); Uma Thurman (Miss Beaumont); Alida Valli (Mrs. Fascioli); Alessandro Gassman (Vittorio); Carlo Cartier (Mr. Bonizzoni); Natalia Bizzi (Mrs. Bonizzoni); Paola Lombardi (Enrico); Sonia Martinelli (Maria); Frances Nacman and Veronica Wells (American Ladies); Riccardo Rossi (Guido); Ajanta Barilli (Italian Girl); Bianca Tognocchi (Angel 1); Carlotta Bresciani (Angel 2).

LOS ANGELES TIMES, 9/22/95, Calendar/p. 16, Jack Mathews

[The following review by Jack Mathews appeared in a slightly different form in NEWSDAY, 9/22/95, Part II/p. B4.]

Somewhere after the midpoint of John Irvin's "A Month by the Lake," Uma Thurman, playing an American nanny for rich Italians in 1937 Italy, blurts out an alcohol-amplified insult to Edward Fox, her middle-aged companion at an evening party.

"You're so boring," Thurman says, accent on the last word. "I want to have fun."

Well, so do we. We've come to watch a movie billed as light romantic comedy, set on the glorious shores of Lake Como, which has been the playground for generations of wealthy Europeans, and all we've done so far is watch a bunch of mostly middle-aged blue bloods behave as if they were in the full flush of adolescence.

Thurman and Alessandro Gassman, the young beach boy who fancies himself a Lothario for vacationing matrons, aren't that far removed from their comings-of-age. But Fox and co-star Vanessa Redgrave, both of whom were born in the year of the film's setting, are, and "A Month by the Lake" is their story.

Adapted from a novella by H.E. Bates, "A Month" is a memory piece, a reflection by a woman looking back on her first solo vacation on Lake Como and her meeting with the man who would become her husband.

It happened "during the last fantastic summer before the war," Redgrave's voice informs us over opening credits, as we watch her come ashore at the hillside villa where she and her late father had vacationed the preceding 16 years. She'd had a long romance with a married man, we'll learn, but as she arrives here, on the eve of the second World War, she has the wiles of a helpless schoolgirl and becomes infatuated with the first man she sees with well-shaped ears.

"You can tell a lot about a person by his ears," Redgrave's Miss Bentley tells Fox's Maj. Wilshaw, a wealthy Brit on holiday, and she assures him and us that his are worth a thousand words.

There are no close-ups of those expressive ears, so we have to take Miss Bentley's passion for the major on faith. As the diminutive Fox, who's towered over by both Redgrave and Thurman, plays him, Major Wilshaw is a major loser, a self-absorbed, supercilious twit whose stiff upper lip quivers at the first sign of rejection.

She, on the other hand, is a live wire, a woman of boundless energy, curiosity, patience and determination, stepping aside while the major makes a fool of himself chasing the flirtatious nanny, inventing a fictitious affair with young Gassman to stir the major's jealousy, devoting days and nights to massaging his overstuffed ego.

"A Month by the Lake" would have been a much better story if Miss Bentley had simply slept with the beach boy and learned to play the mandolin.

Irvin, who has produced some noted BBC shows ("Tinker, Tailor, Soldier, Spy") and directed some terrible Hollywood movies ("Raw Deal," "Next of Kin"), sort of waits out his story rather than pushing it forward. The actors are left to ham it up innocuously while their characters wait for the story to overtake them.

There are allusions to the dark storm building over Europe, and one unnerving scene of ardent Fascists parading through the cobbled streets of a medieval lakeside village. Obviously, we're looking upon a moment sandwiched between tranquillity and the apocalypse.

But nothing of substance ever really seems to be at stake. The war is far removed from these idlers' minds, and the romance between the gushing Redgrave and the comically pathetic Fox fades as quickly as a ripple on that immense and beautiful lake.

NEW YORK POST, 9/22/95, p. 44, Thelma Adams

John Irvin's "A Month by the Lake" magically transforms 96 minutes of film into 30 days on a leaky lifeboat.

It is one of those precious, nostalgic romances set on a beautiful location—the shores of Italy's Lake Como—that leaves behind nothing much except a memory of oversized hats, the rustle of dinner dresses, and the flouncy entrances and exits of its stars.

Itinerant middle-age photographer Miss Bentley (Vanessa Redgrave) has returned to her favorite watering spot after her father's recent death. She casts her eye on a fellow Englishman, stuffy but attractive Major Wilshaw (Edward Fox). Almost before they can say tea, a young American nanny, Miss Beaumont (Uma Thurman), arrives and steals the major's gaze.

As a backdrop to this skirmish between young and old, a larger battle looms. Shadows accumulate over the lake in the form of fascists. The black shirts goose-step on the fringe of otherwise silly scenes, reminding the viewer of what the characters cannot know: This is the last frivolous summer before the onslaught of WWII. Life is exquisitely more precious, cry the specters of war, than you tea-taking twits realize.

Thurman plays the disruptive American beauty with all the naughty skips, coy head turns and fluttery hands of a girl portraying Zelda Fitzgerald in a high school play. Under Irvin's lax direction, Thurman is closer to "Even Cowgirls Sing the Blues" here than "Pulp Fiction."

In the pivotal role of the major, Fox struggles to wring some charm out of a role that, as written by Trevor Bentham, is largely off-putting. Picture Hugh Grant continuing a life of vice until late middle age so that his boyish allure has hardened like a cynical mask and that gives you the look of the man at the fulcrum of this romantic seesaw.

"A Month by the Lake" is, after all, Redgrave's movie. Her Bentley is a gift-wrapped feminist role model, a vision of self-sufficiency and independence in the prewar era. She is middle-age but slim-middled, athletic and attractive, engaged in an avocation that gives her great pleasure and a world that she savors. She is looking for love but she's not defined by it. Redgrave fairly glows in this role and, aside from occasionally rocking onto the toes of her sensible shoes as if she were about to take flight, she resists the overacting of her fellows.

If you love Redgrave, spend "A Month by the Lake." For those who can take or leave her, the romance is a choppy pleasure at best, rocked by editing so haphazard that it invites us to wonder if there was another month at Lake Como that has been left out—not that I'd want to extend my stay.

SIGHT AND SOUND, 8/96, p. 58, Geoffrey Macnab

Lake Como, Italy, 1937. Miss Bentley, a single, middle-aged Englishwoman, arrives for her annual holiday at the luxurious villa run by Signora Fascioli. Her fellow guests range from the Bonizzonis, an Italian family she has known for years, to a pair of American spinsters and a handsome, if severe, Englishman, Major Wilshaw. She takes a shine to Wilshaw, but every time she organises a date with him, something goes wrong: he's furious when he beats her at tennis, exasperated when she causes them to miss their boat and very angry when she's late for cocktails. She tries to patch up their quarrels, but he always finds some fresh cause for grievance. Only his attraction for the Bonizzonis' beautiful, high-spirited nanny Miss Beaumont prevents him from returning immediately to London. Miss Beaumont is happy to string him along, but privately she regards him as a ridiculous figure.

In a bid to attract the Major's attention and make him jealous, Miss Bentley begins to spend all her time with a handsome young Italian, Vittorio. This has the desired effect. Humiliated by Miss Beaumont during a conjuring performance he gives at the villa, Wilshaw now devotes his attentions to Bentley instead. Towards the end of the holiday, there is a picnic in the mountains. The event is tinged with gloom—the war is not far off, and everybody realises there will be no more summers at the lake until it is over. Bentley and Wilshaw walk off into the woods together, finally acknowledge their mutual attraction, and kiss. Meanwhile, Miss Beaumont, sacked by the Bonizzonis, begins to flirt with Vittorio.

In a voice-over, Bentley explains how she and Wilshaw subsequently became lovers and companions.

Directed by John Irvin, who is best known for all-action movies such as *Raw Deal, Hamburger Hill* and *Robin Hood, A Month By the Lake* unfolds at such a languorous pace that it quickly becomes apparent that it doesn't have a story to tell. Its real purpose is to foreground landscape (it's set around Lake Como), period (the 30s as experienced by the leisured classes) and performance. A mood of self-indulgent nostalgia is evident from the outset, as Miss Bentley (Vanessa Redgrave) sets the scene with a plaintive voice-over, rekindling the past. She has an eye for the foibles of her fellow holidaymakers; she notices the amount of gin and vermouth the wealthy but bad-tempered American guests at the villa drink; she details the eccentricities of the Italian servants, and tries to surmise the personalities of the people she meets by the shape of their ears. Her character's determination to fix moments in time is underlined by her passion for photography. Throughout the film, Bentley carries a camera, ready to capture any person or event she deems worthy of preservation. Her continued snapping inevitably gives the narrative an episodic, disjointed feel. It's as if we're seeing her holiday pictures. They may have an emotional resonance for her, but they seem esoteric, even pointless, to us.

Miss Bentley is surely intended as a detached observer, the spinster as spy, eccentric yet acute. This isn't how she comes across. Redgrave approaches the role in fiery, passionate fashion, as if she's playing Isadora Duncan or one of Chekhov's tragic heroines. Her sheer vitality makes her obsession with staid, pompous Major Wilshaw (Edward Fox), the archetypal Englishman abroad, all the more perplexing. He's as "stiff as a candlestick," Miss Beaumont (Uma Thurman) observes after trying to dance a waltz with him. Fox's mannerisms in the role, his gap-toothed smile and clipped delivery, are bizarrely reminiscent of Terry Thomas. His lines ("you're not a bad sort, Miss Bentley") often sound as if they've been cobbled together from a P.G. Wodehouse novel.

There's something contrived, too, about the setting. The original H.E. Bates novella on which the screenplay is based was written in the 60s. Transplanting the action to the 30s, the filmmakers deck out their characters in period finery: evening dresses, dinner jackets and old-fashioned swimming costumes are all self-consciously paraded. There are also a few token references to the politics of the time. In between the tennis matches, boat trips and dinner parties, we're given fitful hints that this was the Mussolini era. Every so often, a fighter plane darts overhead. Miss Bentley gets a little bruised when she tries to photograph a fascists' match. One or two characters talk about military service. Bentley's voice-over occasionally strikes an elegiac note, is if to warn us that the storm clouds are gathering over Europe and that this idyllic summer was the last of its kind before the war changed everything. But such gloom is belied by a postscript in which she tells us that her idyllic holidays at Lake Como were soon resumed. The war, it seems, was nothing more than an inconvenience.

At least *A Month By the Lake* looks as ravishing as any tourist brochure. The cinematographer Pasqualino De Santis, (who shot *Death in Venice* and *The Damned* for Visconti, *Lucky Luciano* and *Illustrous Corpses* for Rosi and *Lanceot du lac* and *The Devil, Probably*, for Bresson), captures spectacular views. It's not difficult to understand why the characters are all so enraptured by the landscapes which surround them. Against such a backdrop, though, most of the cast look as animated as waxwork dummies. Uma Thurman as the Siren-like nanny flits in and out of frame in flirtatious, quicksilver fashion, lending a much-needed dynamism to affairs. Redgrave, too, shows plenty of vitality. But with a director who specialises in unnecessary close-ups and a storyline which meanders, this isn't exactly a vacation to remember.

Also reviewed in:
CHICAGO TRIBUNE, 9/29/95, Friday/p. H, Michael Wilmington
NEW REPUBLIC, 10/23/95, p. 28, Stanley Kauffmann
NEW YORK TIMES, 9/22/95, p. C3, Stephen Holden
VARIETY, 9/18-24/95, p. 97, Leonard Klady
WASHINGTON POST, 9/29/95, p. F7, Hal Hinson
WASHINGTON POST, 9/29/95, Weekend/p. 44, Desson Howe

MOONLIGHT AND VALENTINO

A Gramercy Pictures release of a PolyGram Filmed Entertainment presentation of a Working Title production. *Producer:* Alison Owen, Eric Fellner, and Tim Bevan. *Director:* David Anspaugh. *Screenplay (based on her play):* Ellen Simon. *Director of Photography:* Julio Macat. *Editor:* David Rosenbloom. *Music:* Howard Shore. *Music Editor:* Tom Kramer. *Sound:* Bruce Carwardine and (music) John Kurlander. *Sound Editor:* Scott Hecker. *Casting:* Amanda Mackey and Cathy Sandrich. *Production Designer:* Robb Wilson King. *Art Director:* David Ferguson. *Set Decorator:* Carol Lavoie. *Special Effects:* Michael Kavanagh. *Costumes:* Densie Cronenberg. *Make-up:* Patricia Green. *Running time:* 107 minutes. *MPAA Rating:* R.

CAST: Elizabeth Perkins (Rebecca Trager Lott); Whoopi Goldberg (Sylvie Morrow); Jon Bon Jovi (House Painter); Shadia Simmons (Jenny Morrow); Erica Luttrell (Drew Morrow); Matthew Koller (Alex Morrow); Gwyneth Paltrow (Lucy Trager); Kathleen Turner (Alberta Russell); Scott Wickware (Policeman); Kelli Fox (Nurse); Harrison Liu (Mr. Wong); Wayne Lam (Mr. Wong's Son); Ken Wong (Mr. Wong's Father); Carlton Watson (Henrik); Jack Jessop (Sid); Josef Sommer (Thomas Trager); Jeremy Sisto (Steven); Alan Clifton (Street Vendor); Judah Katz (Marc); Julian Richings (Hairstylist).

LOS ANGELES TIMES, 9/29/95, Calendar/p. 4, Jack Mathews

[The following review by Jack Mathews appeared in a slightly different form in
NEWSDAY, 9/29/95, Part II/p. 4.]

A bad tactical decision was made by writer Ellen Simon and director David Anspaugh at the very beginning of "Moonlight and Valentino," and the movie neither backs away from it nor recovers from it. In setting up their story of a young widow's stand-off with grief, the filmmaker's chose not to introduce us to the subject of her loss: rather, they have him die off-screen, hit by an unseen car while jogging in an unseen park, and leave us to wonder what kind of person he was and what sort of relationship they had.

True, the movie is about healing, not loss. It's about how Rebecca (Elizabeth Perkins) becomes dependent on the emotional support of the three women closest to her, and how that dependency affects *their* lives. But it's pretty hard to understand her feelings after the tragedy without knowing what they were before, and from her reaction, you might think she'd lost the keys to her car.

Simon, daughter of playwright Neil Simon, adapted "Moonlight" from an autobiographical play she wrote in 1989, the year after her husband was killed while jogging in New York City. The three members of Rebecca's support group—her sister Lucy (Gwyneth Paltrow), best friend Sylvie (Whoopi Goldberg), and stepmother Alberta (Kathleen Turner)—represent the circle that gathered around Simon in her time of need.

That's a promising subject for dramatizing, and timely, given Hollywood's emerging interest in women. But it remains nothing more than a subject, a premise for a lazy dramatic comedy where everything is implied and nothing revealed. Its payoffs, such as they are, come through Rebecca's trio of rescuers, each of whom has her own problems.

Lucy is an awkwardly virginal college student still emotionally unhinged by the death years earlier of her mother. Sylvie is clinging to a marriage she knows is over. And Alberta seems to be dividing her time equally between her flourishing investment career and her compulsive campaign to win the acceptance of her stepdaughters.

None of these crises, or their resolutions, is very compelling. They're just there, subplots providing some nice moments of comic relief and some gaggers of sentimentality.

Cutting grief with humor is a daunting task, particularly when the pain is personal. Neil Simon himself failed while mourning his wife's death in "Chapter Two," and Ellen, who shows a measure of dad's gift for sardonic one-liners, has followed suit.

The actresses do their best with the thin material, and are actually very engaging when simply interacting. Goldberg gets the biggest laughs, naturally, and Paltrow gives Lucy a combination of flakiness and innocence that makes her the most interesting of the quartet.

The title is a reference to Rebecca's hunky house painter (Jon Bon Jovi) who takes his shirt off and buckles the knees off the four onlookers. Bon Jovi is making his film debut in the Brad Pitt role, the sexy drop-in who knows how to put bounce back in a lonely girl's step.

But this is no career-maker. Bon Jovi seems hunky enough, with his Kato Kaelin locks and toned abs, but he has no screen presence whatsoever, and his lines—which must have looked so cool and seductive on paper—are delivered as if he were slightly embarrassed by them.

NEW YORK POST, 9/29/95, p. 49, Michael Medved

"Moonlight and Valentino" does better with a dead husband than with a live lover—and that's not because that lover is played by Jon Bon Jovi.

Actually, the rock star is unexpectedly effective in his acting debut, though he can hardly make up for an underwritten role and a meandering story line that has lost its way long before he appears on the scene.

Director David Anspaugh (who previously shaped the splendid, sensitive sports sagas "Hoosiers" and "Rudy") deserves full credit for coaxing magnificent performances from everyone in his varied cast, but no amount of acting brilliance can compensate for the absence of shape and structure in the source material.

Perhaps those weaknesses stem from the story's autobiographical origins. In 1988, Ellen Simon (daughter of playwrite Neil) lost her husband when he was struck by a car during his morning jog, and she later based a sensitive play on her experience.

The movie adapts that drama, beginning with poetry professor Elizabeth Perkins' reaction to the sudden death of a beloved spouse we never see.

In her grief, she's comforted by her earthy best friend, an eccentric potter played by Whoopi Goldberg; her ill-adjusted but endearing baby sister, who is a chronically disorganized college student played by the gifted Gwyneth Paltrow; and her one-time stepmother (Kathleen Turner), a business woman and control freak who had been married for a decade to Perkins' widowed father (Josef Sommer).

The movie describes the experience of loss and mourning with eloquent intensity. "There are all these friendly people walking around my house," says Perkins, "Telling all these stories about Ben and making him sound like this fabulous stranger I'm never going to meet."

As Perkins (who is ferociously fine in her showy, emotionally charged part) reassembles her shattered life, the movie delicately traces the intricate tie of dependents and affection connecting her to three women who mean most to her life, but the plot then has no place to go.

Goldberg frets over the kids and her kiln, fearing an inevitable divorce, while Paltrow enters her first full-scale romance under the urging of big sister.

Kathleen Turner simultaneously conspires to throw the still-grieving Perkins together with a hunky house painter (Bon Jovi) all four women lustfully admire.

Actually, he's a character of female fantasy about as realistic as the old male favorite of the gorgeous hooker with the heart of gold: Bon Jovi's supposed to play a macho, blue-collar guy who's also sweet, sensitive, (his dog's name, Valentino, helps provide the title) innocent, adoring and (implausibly) unattached.

With lustrous images of an idyllic, unnamed New York suburb (actually shot near Toronto), director Anspaugh employs the same poetic touch he used in his lyrical movies about sports, but with little drama or story line to sustain it, this game is over and begins to drag long before its final quarter.

SIGHT AND SOUND, 7/96, p. 48, Claire Monk

When her husband, Ben, is killed by a car, Rebecca Lott, a young poet lecturer, fends off her initial shock with wisecracking humour. Her best friend, Sylvie, younger sister, Lucy, and divorced stepmother, Alberta, rally round to give their support, but their personal conflicts leave her little space for grieving. Sylvie feels that her own marriage is dead; Lucy has never had a relationship because of low self-esteem and still resents Alberta's intrusion into the family after her mother died; Alberta, a high-powered company directors alienates everyone by taking over the funeral arrangements. Only in private can Rebecca really start to express her grief.

Alone one night, Rebecca is startled by a visit from a collie dog. The four women are soon thrilled by the sight of the dog's good-looking owner, a decorator working nearby. They hear him call the name "Valentino" and imagine it must be his own name but it is actually the dog's. "The Painter" soon becomes the women's main diversion, a source of sexual speculation and fantasy, especially for Sylvie. But her panic when she thinks, wrongly, that her husband has left her, makes Sylvie realise she still needs him. As a gift for Rebecca's first birthday without Ben, Alberta hires The Painter to paint Rebecca's house. Rebecca is disconcerted to find him painting in the moonlight; he takes her out for pizza as an apology. They have a great evening but, wanting to keep her bereavement private, Rebecca does not correct his guess that she has just dumped a boyfriend. Later, he drops by just as Rebecca is throwing some of Ben's things away. He learns the truth and the two end up in bed.

Rebecca shares all the details of their lovemaking with Sylvie, but guilt, fury and grief follow and she retreats from all outside contact, allowing The Painter to fade out of her life. Finding her raging about a row with Ben in which she refused his wish for a child, Sylvie suggests that the four women should 'let go' of Ben. In the cemetery one night, they pay tribute to one another and confront their unfinished emotional business. As Rebecca formally bids Ben farewell, a thunderclap announces a rainstorm and the dawn.

In a recent interview, the actress Holly Hunter was quoted as saying: "The way (women's issues) are depicted in scripts is often very flat, very two-dimensional, with women talking about their periods and babies ... kinda politically correct, and the women are always coming to these emotional catharses at the end, dancing together and stuff." Hunter was voicing an ambivalence shared by many of us as she tried to justify her involvement in *Copycat*, the derivative serial killer movie. *Moonlight and Valentino* does indeed end with its four female protagonists variously reconciled with themselves and each other, cavorting in witchy robes and face paint in a rain-lashed cemetery. But this cringe-making conclusion is a one-off let-down in a movie of sparkling wit and psychological acumen which is, until that point, a joy. Even the graveyard visit prompts an Iron John gag: "Isn't this fun?," says Alberta (Kathleen Turner), "I've read about men's groups doing this sort of thing and I've always felt really excluded."

With a screenplay adapted by *thirtysomething* writer Ellen Simon (daughter of Neil, the comedy dramatist) from her own partly autobiographical stage play, *Moonlight and Valentino* shows its theatre origins. Yet Simon's exceptional script and the emotional tact of the direction by David Anspaugh (*Hoosiers* aka *Best Shot*) make this theatricality more often a strength than a weakness. There are intrusive moments of wordiness, and some of Rebecca's self-conscious speeches about her feelings as a new widow ("I have just realised that I am the W word, and I am going to wake up first thing tomorrow and look like Georgia O'Keeffe, aged 85.") should have been spared the trip from stage to screen. Bur character-driven writing and A-list performances are the film's main pleasures.

Complex and contradictory, the four main characters are roles to die for, and Elizabeth Perkins as Rebecca, Kathleen Turner, Gwyneth Paltrow as Lucy and Whoopie Goldberg as Sylvie all rise to the occasion—although Goldberg, as often, is short-changed in a role where her very presence is supposed to signify eccentric, colour-blind bohemianism. As the dreadlocked tarot reader, Sylvie, she seems an odd match for her yuppie WASP husband and her fantasy about having The Painter paint a question mark on her thigh in aquamarine because it would look great with her skin tone is the sole indication that the film-makers have noticed she is black. Paltrow's Lucy, a beatnik slacker who longs for a Marcello Mastroianni tattoo, fares better in an amusing addition to her growing gallery of neurotics.

Simon's script succeeds against the odds in extracting comedy from a narrative grounded in her own experience of loss and grief (her husband Jeff Bishop was killed in 1988, in an identical manner to the film's fictional character, Ben). *Moonlight and Valentino* is good at conveying the fluctuating, paradoxical emotions of the bereaved: the jarring, self-protective humour which can provoke shock or censure in those around them. "Hey guys! It's been a great week—I'm just gonna wear black, read a little Sylvia Plath," says Rebecca to Sylvie, Lucy and Alberta after Ben's funeral. But the flipside of this cracked wit is despair. The hospital sequence showing in slow-motion Rebecca's unprepared reaction to the news of Ben's death and the later scenes of her private grief (shot from a scrupulously unvoyeuristic mid-distance) are wordless.

Simon understands that the difference between good and bad taste is here a matter for the bereaved: those who have been through grieving will understand the social comedy of the funeral, with Rebecca listening politely to bizarre tributes to Ben from colleagues of his she has never met before. Her script does not shrink from the sniping such occasions provoke: "I think it's interesting how you deny yourself food and always wear black," Alberta snaps at Lucy, before forgetting Lucy's dead mother's name for the umpteenth time and phoning *The New York Times* to hustle a high-profile obituary of Ben.

In such a thoroughly woman-centred picture, the fantasy figure of The Painter is an obvious, but still amusing, device. His performance has a tongue-in-cheek quality heightened by Alberta's comically mistaken claim that he neither speaks nor understands English (making him literally a dumb blond)—an error which frees the women to comment on his 'great ass' and to hand him a dish of butter as a wordless way of picking a paint colour. This promising conceit is over all too soon, but speaking or dumb, MTV rocket Jon Bon Jovi is entirely likeable and convincing in the role.

VILLAGE VOICE, 10/3/95, p. 82, Beth Coleman

In the first five minutes of *Moonlight*, Rebecca (Elizabeth) loses her husband to a most banal tragedy—car intersects with jogger. Ben is dead, which is the excuse for Rebecca and her circle of women to gather. Despite the corny, romantic title, it's mourning, gossip, and healing that's being sold here as women's work. And the girls go at it with a gusto that makes you think death and divorce are what keep suburban communities lively. Moving between Columbia University, where Rebecca teaches poetry and Ben taught astrophysics (yep), and what looks like Larchmont, *Moonlight* tries to figure out why the men—husband, fathers—keep disappearing while the women get more and more hysterical.

Best friend Sylvie (a schizy Whoopi Goldberg jumping from earthy mama to spiritual guide) wants to know when her own marriage hit half-life. Stepmother Alberta (Kathleen Turner flexing her comedy muscles) makes a business out of mothering. All in black, younger sister Lucy (played by a delicious Gwyneth Paltrow) seems happy for an excuse to cry. Different ages and dress sizes, they all want to know what *is* a woman without a man?

Jon Bon Jovi comes in to save the libidinal day but ends up making more friction than hay. It's not just Rebecca, played with a deftness by Perkins that defies a cliché-heavy script, who falls apart, but the whole coven. *Moonlight* moves into areas of depression and confession that its lip-gloss sheen cannot handle. The final appeal is to Mother—how to be one or how to find one—who always knows how to make bad things better.

Also reviewed in:
CHICAGO TRIBUNE, 9/29/95, Friday/p. D, Michael Wilmington
NEW YORK TIMES, 9/29/95, p. C6, Stephen Holden
VARIETY, 10/28/95, p. 40, Emanuel Levy
WASHINGTON POST, 9/29/95, Weekend/p. 46, Desson Howe

MORTAL KOMBAT

A New Line cinema release of a Lawrence Kasanoff/Threshold Entertainment production. *Executive Producer:* Bob Engelman and Danny Simon. *Producer:* Lawrence Kasanoff. *Director:* Paul Anderson. *Screenplay:* Kevin Droney. *Director of Photography:* John R. Leonetti. *Editor:* Martin Hunter. *Music:* George S. Clinton. *Music Editor:* Joanie Diener. *Sound:* Steve Nelson and (music) John Whynot. *Sound Editor:* Marc Fishman. *Casting:* Fern Champion and Mark Paladini. *Production Designer:* Jonathan Carlson. *Art Director:* Jeremy A. Cassells. *Set Designer:* Brian Jewell and Galia Nitzan. *Set Decorator:* Susan L. Degus. *Set Dresser:* Merry-Beth Noble. *Special Effects:* Daniel Lester. *Costumes:* Ha Nguyen. *Make-up:* Mony Mansano. *Stunt Coordinator:* Pat E. Johnson. *Running time:* 95 minutes. *MPAA Rating:* PG-13.

CAST: Christopher Lambert (Lord Rayden); Robin Shou (Liu Kang); Linden Ashby (Johnny Cage); Cary-Hiroyuki Tagawa (Shang Tsung); Bridgette Wilson (Sonya Blade); Talisa Soto (Kitana); Trevor Goddard (Kano); Chris Casamassa (Scorpion); François Petit (Sub-Zero); Keith H. Cooke (Reptile); Hakim Alston (Fighting Monk); Kenneth Edwards (Art Lean); John Fujioka (Chief Priest); Daniel Haggard (Assistant Director); Sandy Helberg (Director); Steven Ho (Chan); Peter Jason (Master Boyd); Lloyd Kino (Grandfather); Gregory McKinney (Jaxx); Mikal Moore and Brice Stephens (Singers at Techno Club); Kevin Richardson (Voice of Goro); Ed Boon (Voice of Scorpion).

LOS ANGELES TIMES, 8/21/95, Calendar/p. 3, Kevin Thomas

"Mortal Kombat," which thrives as an arcade game, an animated video and even a touring stage show, arrives on the big screen with terrific, high-energy panache. A martial arts action-adventure with wondrous special effects and witty production design, it effectively combines supernatural terror, a mythical slay-the-dragon, save-the-princess odyssey and even a spiritual quest for self knowledge.

Through its frequent scenes of combat it manages to remind youthful audiences to confront their fears and to take responsibility for their own destiny. Director Paul Anderson and writer Kevin Droney and their many colleagues clearly thought through all they have managed to accomplish. These various layers of meaning reveal themselves through the unfolding of a plot that is simplicity itself. A sleek, leather-jacketed evil sorcerer. Shang Tsung (Cary-Hiroyuki Tagawa), who rules from his sinister, supernatural Outerworld, has led a powerful prince to victory against mortal contenders for nine generations. Should he win a 10th round, he will be able to control the world forever.

To accomplish this, Shang Tsung has announced a Mortal Kombat to be held in a Southeast Asian island kingdom, which is in actuality the Outerworld. Drawn to this remote place are Liu Kang (Robin Shou), a young martial arts whiz who comes to realize that he cannot escape his destiny as a descendant of a Kombatant of 500 years ago, Johnny Cage (Linden Ashby), a martial arts movie star who sees the tournament as a once-and-for-all chance to prove to the world that he really does perform all his own stunts; and Sonya Blade (Bridgette Wilson), a humorless Special Forces Team agent in pursuit of a hated enemy who bravely confronts more than she bargained for. In Shang Tsung's thrall is the beautiful Princess Kitana (Talisa Soto), eager to aid his defeat. Meanwhile, the Kombatants have a crucial mentor in Lord Rayden, the Thunder God (Christopher Lambert), a priestly figure possessed of much wisdom as well as his own supernatural powers.

The film is a constant test of these Kombatants' skills in defending themselves against all manner of monsters, supernatural terrors and temptations that Shang Tsung unleashes as the tournament draws near. As impressive as the special effects are at every turn, even more crucial is Jonathan Carlson's superb, imaginative production design, which combines Thailand exteriors with vast sets that recall the barbaric grandeur of exotic old movie palaces and campy Maria Montez epics. John R. Leonetti's glorious, shadowy camera work and George S. Clinton's driving, hard-edged score complete the task of bringing alive the perilous Outerworld.

Robin Shou emerges as a reflective, courageous hero, and Linden Ashby nicely spoofs his movie star role, but the key acting honors go to Lambert and Tagawa, who bring a light, humorous touch to their embodiments of Good and Evil.

NEW YORK POST, 8/19/95, p. 18, Larry Worth

The ads proclaim: "Nothing in the world has prepared you for this."

That's true—if you've avoided kung fu movies like the plague, missed every rerun of the "Seventh Voyage of Sinbad" (and its ilk) and never walked past a video arcade.

For everyone else, "Mortal Kombat" has a very familiar ring. In fact, the ghosts of Ray Harryhausen and Bruce Lee appear to be squaring off on a regular basis. And that's one of the chief problems: The film can't decide whether fighting or effects should take precedence.

Neither imagination nor originality is found in either category, but the target audience—kids addicted to the video game on which the story's based—probably won't even notice. They'll be too busy screaming for kool kombat killers Scorpion (who unleashes a deadly snakelike creature every time he opens the palm of his hand) or Sub-Zero, (who can freeze anyone and anything in his path).

That's not even mentioning the all-powerful sorcerer who's organized the titular battle between the forces of good and evil, a four-armed, cloven-hoofed cretin and a statue that turns into a cousin of those "Jurassic Park" raptors.

Actually, the attractive heroes, on whose well-muscled shoulders the future of mankind balances, are a less-interesting lot: a handsome but obnoxious action movie star, a pectoral-perfect martial-arts expert and a gorgeous Special Forces Team leader. They're each disciples of the luminous Lord Rayden, protector of the earth and god of lightning (which explains his electric-zap stares).

Director Paul Anderson takes those characters and throws them in the blender with genre staples like candle-illuminated caves, sunset-silhouetted island landscapes, and ancient Buddhist temples. And plenty of the aforementioned warring and wizardry.

The results range from passable to hokey, with the latter worsened by screenwriter Kevin Droney's lame sense of humor. In fact, the only real laughs come from Christopher Lambert's tongue-in-cheek turn as Rayden, who makes quite a fashion statement in his flowing robes, coolie hat and gray Veronica Lake wig.

It all culminates in a cliffhanger finale which clearly begs for a sequel. That may leave some filmgoers unsatisfied. But like it or not, at least "Mortal Kombat" goes down fighting.

NEWSDAY, 8/19/95, Part II/p. B7, Jonathan Mandell

In the century since humankind first marshaled light for a new form of entertainment known as the motion picture, filmmakers have plumbed all of western civilization for stories to tell; they have based their movies on works of classic literature or great drama, poignant short stories or moving memoirs, beloved popular tales of TV shows, deeply felt personal experience and shrewd observations of the social scene. Now, in the case of "Mortal Kombat," we have a movie based on "a series of interactive game cartridges."

Because "Mortal Kombat" is more a business deal than a movie, it is worth quoting this full sentence from the production notes: "A multimedia licensing bonanza, the popular characters from 'Mortal Kombat' appear in such diverse platforms as a nationally touring, live-action stage show; an animated video; three arcade games; a series of interactive game-cartridges, and action figures."

All this in just two years. First introduced as a video game in 1993, "Mortal Kombat" was bought by about 6 million children in that first year alone; that's $300 million worth of gore and mayhem. "Mortal Kombat II," introduced a year later, sold about $50 million in its first week, which was way more that week than the ticket sales for "The Lion King" and "Forrest Gump" combined.

With such a track record, a film was inevitable, and the result nearly review-proof, at least for its committed fans.

Still, a job's a job. So here, roughly, is the plot: Three earthlings agree to engage in mortal combat with the assorted monster's, sorcerers and bare-chested Ninjas of the Outerworld, for very different reasons. Liu Kang (Robin Shou, a muscular martial arts actor from Hong Kong) is out to avenge the murder of his brother, or to fulfill the destiny of his heritage, or perhaps he likes to kick people in the face.

Johnny Cage (Linden Ashby) plays a movie star out to prove he's not the fake martial artist the magazines accuse him of being. (Any objective person would judge his effort unsuccessful.) The blond Sonya Blade (Bridgette Wilson) is a member of a Special Forces Team that gets caught up in the combat while pursuing somebody else. They fight different creatures one by one, or together, especially Shang Tsung (Cary-Hiroyuki Tagawa), under the guidance of the god Rayden, played by Christopher Lambert of "Highlander" fame, which should tell you something.

If it doesn't, then it's time to be more explicit: "Mortal Kombat" is incoherent, poorly edited and laughably acted. The neo-gothic sets are not bad, and the special effects are the best part of the movie, although they seem mostly to involve Ninja fighters turning into monsters or skeletons, and then oozing worms, snakes and beetles. But even on its own terms, "Mortal Kombat" is kablooey. There are no more than 15 minutes worth of exciting fight scenes.

At the end, having successfully conquered the enemies, the three heroes stand before a gothic castle that explodes, revealing a huge monster who tells them, "I've come for your souls."

The four get into fighting stance.

Oh no, already sequel.

SIGHT AND SOUND, 11/95, p. 47, Leslie Felperin

In China, martial arts combatants are summoned to take part in a tournament called Mortal Kombat to decide whether Outworld—a ravished: alternative universe—and its inhabitants shall be allowed to cross into our world and blight it. Amongst others defending the earth are Liu, who was raised by martial arts fighting monks, Sonya, a law enforcer and Johnny Cage, an action movie star. They are assisted and advised by a demigod named Rayden. The main contestants representing Outworld are led by Shang, an evil wizard. Under his command are Kano, an English underworld crime boss, Goro, a multi-armed monster, plus Sub Zero and Scorpion, who have unique supernatural powers. The loyalties of the 10,000-year-old Princess Kitana, the rightful heir to Outworld, are more ambiguous.

The forces representing Outworld soon prove their lethal might, but Sonya snaps Kano's neck in combat. Cage battles and defeats Scorpion. Liu draws with Princess Kitana, who surreptitiously gives him advice on his next fight which helps him later defeat Sub Zero. Eventually, Cage beats the seemingly undefeatable Goro. Rayden reveals that he knows each earth's warrior's deepest fears. Shang drags Sonya into Outworld and Cage and Liu follow. There the latter two battle monsters, but are helped by Princess Kitana. Liu challenges Shang to a final bout, and having faced his worst fears (himself, and his destiny) in the process, emerges victorious. Princess Kitana regains the rule of Outworld. Back in our world, the winners' happy reunion with Rayden is cut short when the godlike Emperor emerges on the horizon.

Many recent action films induce a sense of déjà vu. See one 'concept' and you are more than likely to see it again a few months later. Thrillers set on submarines (*Under Siege, The Hunt For*

Red October, Crimson Tide), men-in-kilts films (*Rob Roy, Braveheart*), and a slew of comic-book based movies drop off the production line. It seems we've only just recovered from the mind-batteringly silly *Street Fighter* when *Mortal Kombat* comes forth to wrest control of the joystick. In their previous incarnations as video games, *Street Fighter* and *Mortal Kombat* were sworn foes, fighting for the forces of Nintendo and Sega respectively. Most consumers tended to agree that *Mortal Kombat*, with more blood and better animation, was the superior game. With elegant cosmic symmetry, *Street Fighter* (actually based on the game *Street Fighter*) has proved to be the better film, if only for its delightful camp outréness and refusal to take itself too seriously.

The problem with *Mortal Kombat* is its pace. After a striking opening dream sequence in which Liu's brother has his back broken, the first 40 minutes flits peripatetically from location to location. The script presents a lot of overly-elaborate back-stories to digest, but they go down awkwardly. When the climax comes with the Mortal Kombat tournament, the fights are so bland and stodgy, a feeling of cinematic dyspepsia never really dissipates. "Finish him!," exhorts Shang near the end of many of the contests, a catchphrase of the original game. "Finish it!," you feel like shouting back at the screen.

Director Paul Anderson, whose previous film was the dismal British ram-raiding teen-pic *Shopping*, overindulges in slow-motion photography, neglecting to generate a sense of speed to offset the film's many dull stretches. He lacks flair for action, so the overall impression is of watching someone playing the game badly rather than feeling as if you are in the game itself. A nightclub scene, thronged with trendy ravers, provides a nasty flashback to Anderson's previous *Shopping* trip, but there are no new goods on display. Too much energy seems to have been spent designing elaborate sets of leering gargoyles and orientalist clutter that recall Korda's *The Thief of Bagdad*. Yet, nothing spectacular ever happens. There are scenes involving boats, forests, underground taverns and sports arenas, yet everything is so darkly lit and densely decorated it looks like one location.

Several lurid monsters literally rear their ugly heads, often putting in finer performances than the 'living' players. As Rayden, Christopher Lambert reprises his weary immortal act from the *Highlander* films—the lightning bolts from his eyes seem to be the only thing keeping him awake. What most of the cast and stunt people are good at is shouting, kicking, and throwing punches, which they perform admirably. The real stars of this film are the foley artists, who produce the wonderfully realistic sounds of bones breaking and flesh being pummelled. With so many action films coming out these days, all so heavily reliant on these sound effects, one hopes these noble technicians are reaping the financial benefits. They ought to get a share of the grosses.

VILLAGE VOICE, 9/5/95, p. 72, Gary Dauphin

Officially the last summer movie on my calendar, *Mortal Kombat* is also the only film I've really looked forward to this season. Part of a rabid fan of gamers that drove Kombat to a $23 million opening weekend, I had anticipatory jitters for months due to a cunningly designed trailer that produced hard-ons in anyone who'd ever gotten off on the words "FINISH HIM!" or "FLAWLESS VICTORY."

For those of you who don't know Mortal Kombat is a video game, hugely popular and occasionally controversial, whose only purpose and reward is the administering and appreciation of martial arts-style violence. As the game's allure was in offering realistic mayhem boiled down to its most repetitive aesthetic elements, *Mortal Kombat* the movie would have failed dismally if it messed too much with the basic vid-game formula, the problem with last year's *Street Fighter*. A flop on every possible level, that Van Damme vehicle didn't realize that its only reason for being was to provide a big-screen reproduction of the pain-pleasure loop the game, a mistake that *Kombat* evades by smartly dispensing with trifles like character and plot in order to fully concentrate on the real action: volume, lengthy fight scenes, and lewd special effects.

This film does have a scenario and it could appropriately fit on the back of a cartridge box. Lapsed monk Liu Kang (Robin Shou), lady cop Sonya Blade (Bridgette Wilson), and movie star Johnny Cage (Linden Ashby) are all tricked or lured into a martial-arts tournament against other-worldly forces, with the fate of the planet hanging in the balance. It's that simple and stupid but for fans of the game, *Mortal Kombat* transcends its obvious limitations by pushing a series of visceral buttons that have been hard-wired into our brains by too many hours in front of a game console. Each character (whether villain or hero) fights in a style consistent with their small-screen moves, and the film strategically deploys the secret techniques and powers that are hidden throughout the game (like Liu's flying kick or Sonya's reverse-handstand wrestling hold), throwing them at the audience at the precise moment when they'll elicit maximum cheers and the most acute shock of extra-narrative recognition. There is some very B-movie dialogue here and the good guys win just the way you would if you were them (and you have been, of course), but director Paul Anderson smoothes this over with a steady attack of game samples, techno beats, and layered digital effects that boost the game's already intricate visuals. All of which makes for an experience that some might find chillingly Pavlovian, but which will suit the initiates better than fine.

Also reviewed in:
CHICAGO TRIBUNE, 8/20/95, Tempo/p. 1, Chauncey Hollingsworth
NEW YORK TIMES, 8/19/95, p. 11, Stephen Holden
VARIETY, 8/21-27/95, p. 67, Leonard Klady
WASHINGTON POST, 8/19/95, p. C3, Richard Harrington

MOVING THE MOUNTAIN

An October Films release of a Xingu Films production. *Producer:* Trudie Styler. *Director:* Michael Apted. *Screenplay (Mandarin and English with English subtitles):* Michael Apted. *Director of Photography:* Maryse Alberti. *Editor:* Susanne Rostock. *Music:* Liu Sola. *Sound:* Scott Breindel. *Running time:* 83 minutes. *MPAA Rating:* Not Rated.

WITH: Wang Dan; Wang Chaohua; Wu'er Kaixi; Chai Ling; Li Lu; Wei Jingsheng (Themselves); Zhang Jin-Ming (Li Lu, Age 10); Huang Yi-Ming (Li Lu, Age 4).

LOS ANGELES TIMES, 5/19/95, Calendar/p. 10, Kevin Thomas

Michael Apted's "Moving the Mountain" is a major achievement, illuminating China's student-led democracy movement that culminated so tragically in the Tian An Men Square massacre in June, 1989.

Drawing upon his formidable skills as both a director and documentarian, Apted confidently clarifies the complex chain of circumstances that led to that brief but profound outcry for democracy. Inevitably, "Moving the Mountain" is devastating but ends with a Chinese parable expressing the belief that the mountain can be moved—that democracy will eventually flower.

When the film's British producer, Trudie Styler, met with a number of the democracy movement's student leaders within days of their escape to the West, she found in Li Lu, now completing a law degree and a master's in business administration at Columbia, a way to encompass China's tumultuous history of the past three decades within the young man's own story. Thus, setting the stage for all that is to come, Apted acquaints us with Li, who's handsome, personable, fluent in English and a passionate campaigner for change in China while living in exile. As he recounts his life, Apted commences flashbacks in a deft mix of archival footage and scenes from his early youth re-created in Taiwan.

Born in April, 1966, a month before the beginning of the Cultural Revolution, separated from his out-of-favor parents during infancy, a survivor of the 1976 Tangshan earthquake—one of the deadliest in history—Li learned self-reliance early on. On April 26, 1989, Li, then an economics major at Nanjing University in China's central coast, sneaked aboard a train bound for Beijing, where thousands of people, mainly students, were beginning to gather in the wake of the death of ousted Communist Party General Secretary Hu Yaobang, a progressive economic and political reformer.

As we move toward Tian An Men Square, Apted brings Li together in New York with other escaped leaders: Chai Ling, commander-in-chief of the student headquarters during the demonstration, to whom Li had been a deputy; Wang Chaohua, the eldest of the students, who had crucial ties to the nation's intellectual communities; and Wu'er Kaixi, a feisty, early leader in the movement. In China, Apted also managed secretly to film Wang Dan, a fearless, key leader, only recently released from prison, and Wei Jingsheng, a veteran dissident, the students' hero and inspiration and also fresh from prison, where he had been serving a near-15-year sentence in horrendous conditions.

This beautifully structured film acquires epic dimension as the confrontation with armored tanks of demonstrators, hunger strikers and just plain citizens draws ever-closer.

Apted's mastery of structure, his classic sense of the tragically inevitable, his seamless blend of amazing archival footage, re-creations of the students' perilous escapes and their present-day observations come together like a thundering cataract, with much of the impact of D.W. Griffith's four stories colliding at the climax of "Intolerance." "Moving the Mountain" not only communicates (and commemorates) the meaning of Tian An Men Square in majestic fashion but also expands the possibilities of film itself.

NEW YORK POST, 4/26/95, p. 42, Larry Worth

Michael Apted has made his fortune with the likes of "Coal Miner's Daughter," "Nell" and "Gorillas in the Mist." But he deserves his fame for documentaries.

Indeed, Apted's skills honed the "7 Up" series, and "Incident at Oglala" into breathtaking productions to rival any piece of fiction.

Now, with "Moving the Mountain," he taps both genres as he traces the lives of six student heroes from China's Tiananmen Square tragedy.

In the process, he not only showcases an important chapter in world history but presents the fight for democracy in a universal light.

Deputy commander of the student headquarters under martial law Li Lu eloquently notes at the film's outset that the world only remembers the image of one young man standing in front of a column of tanks; but an entire generation was standing behind him. And this is their story.

Initially, Apted focuses on grainy, black-and-white re-creations of Li Lu's childhood. Horror stories about parents imprisoned at Chairman Mao's whims, being shuffled between adoptive families, watching the public humiliation of dissidents, and—most memorably—forced to bond with lizards result in Li Lu's outrage at the Cultural Revolution.

Unrest is fanned by the deadly Tangshan earthquake of 1976 and continued atrocities under Deng Xiaoping, ultimately setting the scene for Tiananmen Square.

At that point, Li Lu is seen hooking up with the film's five other principals—two women and three men—who later reflect on the chain of events. Specifically, each tells—sometimes through a veil of tears—about the blood shed in Tiananmen Square and the nightmarish aftermath of being on the government's "most-wanted" list.

The words take on heightened poignance since Apted dispenses with arty flourishes for a straightforward storytelling approach. He seamlessly pieces the facts and faces into a passionate, truly spellbinding production.

Aided by producer Trudie Styler (whom Apted previously worked with when lensing "Bring on the Night," a fine rock-umentary on her husband, Sting), "Moving the Mountain" takes shape as a soaring—and sobering—tribute to the human spirit.

NEWSDAY, 4/26/95, Part II/p. B9, Gene Seymour

"Moving the Mountain" vividly reminds its audiences that there was much more to the quixotic movement for Chinese democracy six springs ago than the Tiananmen Square massacre. The film treats the student-led movement for democratic reform as culmination of more than 20 tumultuous, agonizing years of Chinese history.

Michael Apted, director of "Coal Miner's Daughter" and the generation-tracking documentary series that began with "7 Up," has a well-developed instinct for biography-as-metaphor. So it's not surprising that he finds a framework for recounting this history in the life of Li Lu, one of the movement's leaders, who was born just one month before Mao Tse-Tung launched the Cultural Revolution in 1966, which punished those believed to be enemies of Mao's revolution.

Li Lu's own parents were among the purged, and he spends much of his childhood as an outcast. Through re-enactments, Apted shows Li Lu developing his own sense of self amidst his country's physical (the 1976 earthquake) and political (Mao's death the same year) upheavals.

For much of the succeeding decade, new boss Deng Xiaoping eases restrictions on free trade and permits criticism of the regime. Mao's regime, that is. Not his. *Never* his. Eventually, spoils of economic reform like inflation, corruption and greater access to Western ideas inspire in students like Li Lu an urge to compel drastic, lasting change.

The April, 1989, death of progressive hero Hu Yaobang, coming in the midst of a government crackdown on reforms, sets off the series of events demonstrations, riots, confrontations with government leaders—that made up the democracy movement. Catching the world by surprise and then capturing its imagination, the students put all their hopes in a hunger strike at Tiananmen Square. At one point, Li Lu's girlfriend travels to the square to join the protest. They marry in one of the film's bittersweet sequences. Now in exile, he says he hasn't seen her since.

When the movement's terrible climax comes to pass on the Beijing streets, we get even less of a visual sense of the killing than we got six years ago through journalists' eyewitness accounts. Perhaps it's best that a student's face-down of an army tank remains the movement's defining image. An excess of blood can numb one's impulse to hope.

And hope is just about all Li Lu and the four other movement leaders interviewed here were able to carry with them when they escaped their homeland. "Moving the Mountain" achieves its most compelling moments not in reconstructing or recounting events, but depicting the stoicism and grief haunting the faces of these thwarted, but undaunted, idealists as they make their way bravely through an uneasy exile.

VILLAGE VOICE, 5/2/95, p. 50, Georgia Brown

I forget why the old man wants to move the mountain. To get to the other side? At any rate, he directs his children to begin shifting rocks and dirt. A neighbor scoffs: "Old man, you think you can move a mountain!" The old man replies, "If my children's children and their children (etc.) work steadily, one day the mountain will be moved."

This is the parable Michael Apted and Trudie Styler adopt for the title of their documentary on China's democracy movement and the 1989 events in Tiananmen Square. My mind, such a stubborn instrument, stalls on analogies. The mountain, in the case of Tiananmen and thousands of protesters, didn't move. Turning the parable on its head—with the old man as any Chinese leader of this century—the children's children might have better things to do than carry rocks for the capricious old bugger.

Title aside, *Moving the Mountain* provides a moving reminder of Tiananmen and an overdue update on the fates of several participants. At 83 minutes, the documentary is more tantalizing overview than complete or definitive picture. It should be seen, although it is already being argued over by many close to the subject.

At some point, Apted or, more likely, Styler—the London-based moving force behind the project—chose to gather their narrative around Li Lu, a lieutenant in the uprising. In near-perfect English Li tells his own story as his childhood is restaged in black-and-white. Born in 1966 along with the Cultural Revolution, Li is wrenched from his parents and farmed out to a series of peasant families all of whom, he reports smiling, "didn't like me." He winds up in a state orphanage with a Dickensian culture of bullying. In 1976, Tangshan, the region where he lives, is hit by what is called the worst earthquake since the 16th century; 240,000 perish, so does Li's known world, though once again he miraculously escapes. In April 1989, a college student, he heads for Beijing, where he quickly rises to "deputy commander" of the fateful hunger strike. When the tanks roll in, Li escapes once more, this time to the West. He's currently getting an MBA and law degree from Columbia.

It's a terrifying story told heartwarmingly. Unfortunately, on film, Li Lu comes across as smooth, almost jocular, with some of the American politician about him—qualities that make him the least compelling of the four former student leaders filmed sitting around a table in New York in 1993. The others are Wu'er Kaixi, number two on the authorities' most-wanted list and the young man widely photographed meeting with Party leaders in his pj's; Chai Ling, four on the list and the prime mover of the hunger strike; and Wang Chaohua, number 14, the oldest of the leaders, forced to leave behind her husband and four-year-old son. Wang Chaohua, in particular, seems terribly anguished, tormented over her role in the uprising.

Interviewed secretly in China are two activists who seem heroic by any standards: Wang Dan, the number one most wanted, who was caught and served five years in prison, and the older Wei

Jingsheng, the students' hero, who spoke out for human rights as far back as the late '70s and served nearly 15 years. (Amnesty International currently reports Wei ominously "missing.") Both Wang and Wei are lean, and, perhaps because they are not filmed strolling under the magnolias of American campuses, possess unmistakable gravity. Here Wei is critical of the Tiananmen leadership, though he isn't given space to elaborate. Both men speak of the necessity of staying in China.

The burden of exile itself is a poignant subject here—much of it presented implicitly. How to reconcile the material success these students enjoy in the U.S. with the failure of the movement, the renewed repression in China? Joining Russians and East Europeans before them, the former students meditate on losing roots, maybe souls. What none of the Chinese shown here seem to have developed is anything approaching Kundera's bitter irony or Brodsky's Odyssean stoicism. They're still young.

Objections to Apted's film are already being aired and I shall repeat some here. The movie, it's said, minimizes ideological differences among the leaders—particularly on the issue of the hunger strike. Also—a minor matter perhaps, but one showing carelessness with fact—it looks here as if the massacre of protesters takes place in the square rather than in the sidestreets. Although the subject of money funneled to the protesters is raised, tougher questions as to where the money went are not. Another messy issue left unexplored is the participation of Hong Kong triads—perhaps even the CIA-in facilitating the escapes from China.

But *Moving the Mountain* doesn't pretend to be a muckraker. Just as Shu Kei's emotional *Sunless Days* presented Tiananmen from Hong Kong's so-near-yet-so-far perspective, this film's vantage is from across a vaster gulf. It brings back vividly, often very painfully, a time when for us China was nearer.

Also reviewed in:
NEW YORK TIMES, 4/26/95, p. C11, Janet Maslin
VARIETY, 10/3-9/94, p. 63, Joe Leydon
WASHINGTON POST, 6/2/95, p. D1, Hal Hinson

MURDER IN THE FIRST

A Warner Bros. release of a Le Studio Canal+ production in association with the Wolper Organization. *Executive Producer:* David L. Wolper and Marc Rocco. *Producer:* Marc Frydman and Mark Wolper. *Director:* Marc Rocco. *Screenplay:* Dan Gordon. *Director of Photography:* Fred Murphy. *Editor:* Russell Livingstone. *Music:* Christopher Young. *Music Editor:* David Cates. *Sound:* Ed White and (music) Robert Fernandez. *Casting:* Mary Jo Slater. *Sound Editor:* Barney Cabral. *Production Designer:* Kirk M. Petruccelli. *Art Director:* Michael Rizzo. *Set Decorator:* Greg Grande. *Set Dresser:* Gregg Bruza, Jon Bush, Ed Nua, and Jonathan Mikita. *Special Effects:* Kevin McCarthy. *Costumes:* Sylvia Vega Vasques. *Make-up:* Lisa Rocco. *Stunt Coordinator:* Doug Coleman. *Running time:* 122 minutes. *MPAA Rating:* R.

CAST: Christian Slater (James Stamphill); Kevin Bacon (Henri Young); Gary Oldman (Associate Warden Glenn); Embeth Davidtz (Mary McCasslin); Bill Macy (William McNeil); Stephen Tobolowsky (Mr. Henkin); Brad Dourif (Byron Stamphill); R. Lee Ermey (Judge Clawson); Mia Kirshner (Adult Rosetta Young); Ben Slack (Jerry Hoolihan); Stefan Gierasch (Warden James Humson); Kyra Sedgwick (Blanche); Alexander Bookston (Alcatraz Doc); Richie Allan (Jury Foreman); Herb Ritts (Mike Kelly); Charles Boswell (Simpson); David Sterling (Inmate Rufus "Roy" McCain); Michael Melvin (Inmate Arthur "Doc" Barker); George Maguire (Inmate #1); Nick Scoggin (Inmate #2); Douglas Bennett (Inmate #3); Joseph Richards (Inmate #4); Julius Varnado (Inmate #5); Tony Barr (Winthrop); Stuart Nisbet (Harve); Gary Ballard (Alcatraz Guard Swenson); Randy Pelish (Alcatraz Guard McKeon); Neil Summers (Alcatraz Guard Whitney); Sonny H. King (Alcatraz Guard Wimer); Ray Quartermus, Lee E. Mathis, and Wayne Parks (City Jail Guards); Warren Spottswood (Cable Car Conductor); Thomas Fenske and Robert Lee (Newsreel Reporters); Sheldon Feldner (Men on the Street #1); Fred Franklin

(Man on the Street #2); Danny Kovacs (Man on the Street #3); Joseph Lucas (Man on the Street #4); William Hall (Man on the Street #5); Bill Barretta (Man on the Street #6); Randall Dudley (Man on the Street #7); Wally Rose (Shopkeeper); Amanda Borden (Rosetta Young, Age 9); Eve Brenner (Winthrop's Secretary); Joseph Cole (Marshall Gates); Richard Kwong (Chinese Monk); Gary Lee Davis (Giant of a Man).

FILMS IN REVIEW, 3-4/95, p. 59, Andy Pawelczak

When Orson Welles, at the age of 25, first saw the R.K.O. studio, he remarked that it was the world's biggest electric train set for a boy to play with. Marc Rocco, the director of *Murder in the First*, must have felt something similar. The film is full of unmotivated shots and fancy camera pirouettes—Rocco never shoots a scene straight on if he can use an overhead shot or turn the camera on its side. He worries the camera to death and as a result the movie has the dead-in-the-water, pictures-at an-exhibition look of an exercise in film technique.

The script doesn't help. It's the standard story of an innocent man brutalized by prison authorities. Henri Young (Kevin Bacon) has spent 11 years in Alcatraz for pilfering five dollars from a post office in order to feed himself and his younger sister. The film opens with a grainy, black-and-white newsreel report of his attempted prison break. We see the warden announcing that the rehabilitation process is about to begin, and then, in the kind of dime store irony that the movie abounds in, Rocco cuts to a shot of Henry being savagely beaten and thrown in the hole. After spending three years in solitary confinement, he's returned to the general population where, in a dazed, incoherent state, he kills the man who betrayed him in the prison break. The rest of the movie is a courtroom drama in which Henri's young legal aid lawyer James Stamphill (Christian Slater), defends his client by attempting to indict the prison authorities for crimes against humanity.

The inexperienced Stamphill is assigned the case because it's a lost cause—no one wants him to win or challenge the politically connected prison administrators—but the trial brings out his underlying idealism and passion for justice. Rocco pays a lot of attention to forties ambience—fedoras, long topcoats, longshoreman's caps, old cars—but the big, obtrusive shot of a theatre marquee announcing Capra's *Meet John Doe* is more than period detail—it's telling us that Stamphill is a populist hero fighting for the little guy against the corrupt powers-that-be. The problem is that the role, as written by Dan Gordon and played by Christian Slater, is so pallid that we almost need that caption to clue us in. Slater doesn't have the powerful romantic presence of the young Gary Cooper and James Stewart—he just ends up reminding you how much less adult both the actors and the movies are today than they were in the forties.

Kevin Bacon has the meatier role. As Henri, he's semi-autistic and feral, and the film's central scenes chart Stamphill's attempts to reach him and the emerging friendship between the two very different men. With blackened teeth, scarred face, hobbled gait, and a jerky, nervous delivery of his lines, Bacon is very convincing and even manages to overcome the role's heavy overlay of Christ symbolism. Rocco italicizes the Christ-of-Alcatraz theme by shooting the early scenes in the hole as if they were Renaissance crucifixions with Bacon's naked, bloody body lit up by a refulgent white light. These shots are so studied—they must have taken hours to set up—that they become tableaux; all that's lacking is a title: Ecce Homo.

Murder in the First boasts a good, restrained performance by Gary Oldman as a sadistic warden, but it's not enough to save the picture from portentousness and self-importance. At one point Rocco tries to lighten the tone with a shot of Slater walking down a San Francisco street as the Andrews Sisters sing "Tuxedo Junction" on the soundtrack, but the shot, like so many others in the film, stands out like a sore thumb—it's irrelevant and immaterial.

LOS ANGELES TIMES, 1/20/95, Calendar/p. 8, Kenneth Turan

There are films that confuse excess with honesty—noisy, unpleasant screeds that believe that the best way to serve the truth is by being as overwrought and in-your-face as possible. Only by rubbing the audience's nose in something unpleasant, the theory goes, can anything worthwhile be done.

This theory is put into irritating practice in "Murder in the First," directed by Marc Rocco from a script by Dan Gordon. If, as these gentlemen insist, inhuman conditions can drive a man to murder, many of this film's viewers will be streaming out of theaters with mayhem on their minds.

Those conditions are located on the rock they call Alcatraz, the island in San Francisco Bay that was a functioning federal prison in 1938 when "Murder" begins with an attempted escape that goes awry. In obviously faked newsreel footage (the first of a stream of unconvincing sequences), we see the convicts being led back inside and prison officials vowing that "rehabilitation" is about to begin.

For escapee Henri Young (Kevin Bacon), rehabilitation takes on a particularly horrific form. Though prison rules forbid solitary confinement for more than 19 days, Young is thrown into a dungeon-like hole for three years. By the time he comes out, he's a twittering basket case who resembles the wild man of Borneo. That escape attempt, it seems, was taken personally by associate warden Milton Glenn (Gary Oldman), a quiet sadist who is not averse to perpetual revenge.

As conveyed through the aesthetics-of-excess lens of director Rocco (whose debut feature was "Where the Day Takes You"), Young's years in solitary are dwelt on in loving, almost masochistic, detail. We see him naked and bloody, scrawling and muttering, his haggard face twitching from perpetual torture. And just in case the point is somehow missed, there is the inevitable shot of his body hung Christ-like against prison bars. Anything worth doing, this film believes, is well worth overdoing.

Not surprisingly, no sooner is Young out of solitary than he goes a little psycho and commits the act that bring him to the attention of attorney James Stamphill (Christian Slater), who has been narrating this little tale in portentous voice-over.

Though a graduate of Harvard Law, Stamphill is languishing in the nether regions of the San Francisco public defender's office when Young's case is handed to him because, in his boss's comforting phrase, "the guy is guilty, a monkey could try it." Fighting words to young Mr. S., a combination of Jimmy Olsen and Jimmy Stewart whose heroes just happen to be Emile Zola and Clarence Darrow.

Though he has trouble getting syllable one out of Young, so spooked by what he's been through that he's turned catatonic, Stamphill throws himself into the case. Helped by co-worker and girl-friend Mary McCasslin (Embeth Davidtz), he comes up with an unusual defense, and one that fits perfectly with today's don't-blame-me ideology: It was Alcatraz that turned Henri Young into a bad person. Why, left to his own devices, he might have had a shot at winning a Nobel Prize.

Slater is acceptable as Stamphill, and it is a measure of the emotional heights that "Murder" is pitched at that Gary Oldman as the vile associate warden is the most low-key actor in the ensemble. As to Kevin Bacon's performance as the much-abused Young, it is adept technically and certainly a challenge physically, but its virtues end up being beside the point because the film is so woefully over-manipulative and over-the-top.

Apparently based on a true story "Murder in the First" turned everyone into a bear for authenticity: Director Rocco spent a weekend in Alcatraz locked up in solitary and Kevin Bacon, according to the press notes, "slept in the dungeon prior to filming to gain a greater understanding of Henri's ordeal."

But the more this film makes a fetish of reality, the phonier it ends up seeming. Touches like having Stamphill dressed by Armani have a way of not ringing true, and dialogue references to "a media circus" are plainly anachronistic. And the film's twirling camera work, intended to bring you closer to Young's state of mind, induces only dizziness. The most trying thing about "Murder in the First," however, is that it is convinced it's saying something of significance. Now that really is a crime.

NEW YORK POST, 1/20/95, p. 33, Michael Medved

In 1938 a petty thief named Henri Young attempted to escape from the federal penitentiary on Alcatraz Island. When authorities dragged him back to the Rock, they punished him by locking him for three uninterrupted years in solitary confinement—chained and naked in a 5-foot-high dungeon cell underneath the prison.

The day he finally emerged from this ordeal, dazed and shattered, blinking at the light and noise in the crowded prison mess hall, Young spotted the prisoner who had betrayed his escape attempt.

Without hesitation, and in front of 200 witnesses, he rushed over and savagely killed the man by opening his throat with a spoon.

In the court case that followed, Young faced the gas chamber, but his lawyers attempted to put the whole prison on trial. They argued that the wanton cruelty of wardens and guards had deprived their client of any meaningful control over his own actions—he had become a frightened animal, an unthinking weapon no more responsible for the killing than the spoon he held in his hand.

This historic trial provides the basis for "Murder in the First." which tells its story with riveting intensity and blazingly brilliant performances. An all-but-unrecognizable Kevin Bacon (who lost 25 pounds to play the part) portrays Henri Young with such heartbreaking force that he should be remembered next year at Oscar time; he makes the character's suffering unforgettably vivid without smoothing over his rough edges, or ever sentimentalizing his victim status.

Christian Slater is convincing in a far less demanding part, though the script occasionally undermines his good work by building the role around cliches. His character, a fictionalized composite of Young's several defenders, is a recent graduate of Harvard Law who takes on Henri's cause as his first big case, risking his whole career to challenge the corrupt system.

While Slater's role is too one-dimensionally heroic, Gary Oldman's part is a study in unrelieved villainy: he plays a fictionalized assistant warden who brutalizes Henri Young with sadistic beatings and straight-razor mutilations.

From Sid Vicious to Lee Harvey Oswald to the ill-conceived characterization of Beethoven in "Immortal Beloved," no one plays dangerous psychos more brilliantly than Oldman—and he's never more chilling than he is when he's as soft-spoken and understated as he is here.

Director Mark Rocco shapes each scene with a restless, swooping, constantly moving camera that heightens tension without ever calling undue attention to itself or slowing the forward momentum of the story.

The 30-year-old filmmaker (who previously directed "Where the Day Takes You," an honest but lyrical look at homeless teens) also gets his period details remarkably right—despite a few minor slips, like references to a "media circus" in a simulated newsreel from 1941.

As political statement, "Murder in the First" follows a cunning strategy: at a time when many Americans believe we've gone too far to accommodate prisoners' rights, the movie focuses on the bad-old-days when no one could deny that convicts were shamefully mistreated.

Despite its shortcomings, the picture marks the arrival of a major film-making talent who displays something even more valuable and rare than skill with actors or visual flair: young Marc Rocco has, of all things, a social conscience.

NEWSDAY, 1/20/95, Part II/p. B2, John Anderson

Despite what the trailers seem to be saying, "Murder in the First" is not a murder mystery. In fact, there's very little mystery at all: Within hours of being released after three years in solitary confinement, Henri Young (Kevin Bacon) takes one look at the man who was responsible for his little trip to hell and opens up his throat with the blunt end of a spoon.

Since there were 200 witnesses, and nobody sees a need for a trial anyway, the case is assigned to fresh-faced public defender James Stamphill (Christian Slater), who's never tried a case before. Young is being written off, but before you know it, Stamphill is putting Alcatraz on trial, and focusing national attention on its barbaric methods of "rehabilitation."

Based on a true story, which is a phrase that never fails to set off alarms, "Murder in the First" is a little bit "Each Dawn I Die," a little bit "Miracle Worker"—Stamphill's coaxing Henri out of his catatonic state has the air of crusade about it—and a little bit Goya. Director Marc Rocco loves to dwell among the shadows, and the film's opening scenes of the horrors inflicted on Young in the dungeons of Alcatraz are gruesome.

But his stylistic flamboyance gets out of hand. The arty camera angles, the multitude of overhead shots, and Henri's occasional sensory overload—depicted by a kaleidoscopic/impressionistic image stampede—seem to contradict the gritty prison atmosphere Rocco ostensibly is after. His use of "newsreels" is a particularly good example of style gone wild: Ordinarily, such newsreels emphasize just how shallow the pool of public information is in a case like this. Here, the newsreels are as arty as the rest of the film—hand-held news footage from the '30s is certainly a rarity—and also serve as blatant propaganda for Alcatraz' side of the story, which is a cheap way of getting us on Henri's side.

We're already there, of course. Henri was sent to prison for stealing $5 to feed his baby sister, became involved in an escape attempt at Alcatraz and as a result became the literal whipping boy of Warden Glenn (Gary Oldman), who explains very calmly to Henri that an escape might cause him to lose his job. And then how would he feed his family, he asks, before slicing Henri's Achilles tendon and laming him for life. The callous violence comes easily in "Murder in the First," but one senses it's the director's way of impressing us with how serious a story this is.

Oldman is the best thing in the movie; his Glenn is a portrait in rationalized sadism, and his moments on the witness stand—vaguely reminiscent of the Cruise-Nicholson scene in "A Few Good Men"—is startling, because we've seen such little acting throughout the rest of the movie. Slater is impossible to buy as a first-time trial attorney. He manages to bring down the prison, humiliate J. Edgar Hoover's hand-picked penal administrator and save the life of an admitted murderer, all the while maneuvering around the courtroom like F. Lee Bailey on roller skates. And Bacon? Well, in a movie season rife with mental deficients and misfits, he seems right at home.

SIGHT AND SOUND, 12/95, p. 48, Nick James

In Alcatraz penitentiary in 1938, Henri Young, imprisoned for stealing five dollars from a mail office, is caught trying to escape with two other inmates. As punishment, he is stripped naked and placed in one of the 'dungeons' of Alcatraz, an enclosed five feet high chamber that leaks seawater and has no light source. The normal time limit for this form of solitary is 19 days but Henri remains there for more than three years, interrupted only by regular beatings from sadistic Associate Warden Glenn and one half-hour exercise session outside. Each and every time, Henri is led to believe it is his release into normal captivity.

When finally released into the prison population in 1941, he has become wild and disturbed. In front of 200 witnesses, he attacks and murders with a blunt spoon the prisoner who leaked the escape plans. The Public Defender's Office allocates a rookie lawyer, James Stamphill, to defend what is regarded as a lost cause. Stamphill fails at first to get Young to talk to him, but he begins to piece together the true horror of Young's story.

On the first day of the trial, Stamphill accuses the Warden and the Associate Warden of the murder, claiming that Young was only the weapon. After putting both Wardens on the stand, providing photographs of the 'dungeon' and proving that the beatings took place, Stamphill is confident that Young will only be convicted of manslaughter. However, Young is so scared of being returned to Alcatraz that he insists on changing his plea to guilty. Stamphill avoids this by getting him to testify to his reasons for changing. Young is convicted only of manslaughter and returned to Alcatraz, where his dead body is found in his cell sometime later.

Murder in the First is Marc Rocco's second feature (his first *Where the Day Takes You*, which also starred Christian Slater, was never released theatrically in the UK.) At heart it's a straightforward courtroom drama with a few newsreel nods to the Warner Bros gangster movies of the 30s and a long prologue depicting petty thief Henri Young's brutal treatment in Alcatraz. Yet the static camera conventions of courtroom drama, upheld in such films as *Presumed Innocent* and *A Few Good Men,* barely restrain Rocco's delight in askew angles and sweeping movements. If his work was not enhanced by two impeccably controlled central performances from Kevin Bacon as the brutalised prisoner Henri Young and Christian Slater as Young's lawyer, James Stamphill, Rocco's omniscient crane shots and constantly shifting focus might well have proved unbearably irritating and superficial.

But Rocco strives to make a virtue out of restlessness. Young's three-year ordeal in the Alactraz 'dungeon' is portrayed with a relish for self abasement and confined spaces reminiscent of much performance art. As blue-lit shots frame Bacon's filthy and bloodied form contorted on the wet stone floor, several other art gallery images come to mind: Robert Mapplethorpe's nudes when Young is fresh, crop-headed and relatively unscathed; William Blake's Nebuchadnezzar when he is half-crazed, bearded and crawling on all fours. Yet this conscious visual stylisation does not distract from the horror of Young's experiences. Only when the trial begins does Rocco's prowling surveillance of Young in his holding cell start to grate. As Bacon hunches into himself and Slater pounds away with unanswered questions you feel that some of the more subtle gestures of performance are being lost to the constantly passing prison bars and the low-key lighting. Given the opportunity for exploiting nervous tics offered to Bacon, he is laudably restrained, building his performance on fearful blinking and fidgeting hands. Slater, on the other hand, is smooth and upstanding enough to have been cast in a studio film of the period.

If there is a serious flaw in *Murder in the First*, however it is not the hyperactive camera style but rather the fact that the audience need never struggle with their affections. With right clearly on Young's side from before the start of the trial, Slater has the unenviable job of keeping the fires of indignation burning in us long after their cause has been removed from our eyes. Clarence Darrow-style grandstanding is now so familiar a trope of the courtroom drama and the rules of it are so flexible (prosecution objections are rarely raised to a defending attorney's final cross-examination, no matter how conjectural or opinionated) that Slater can get away with cross-examining at breakneck speed, leaving a more regular movie grandstander, such as Gary Oldman as Warden Glenn, with little to do but fume. Nevertheless, by the time the debate about Young wishing to change his plea comes around, Slater's hectoring tone has begun to nag and it takes the curious dignity that Kevin Bacon gives to the hobbled Young to keep you watching to the final credits.

VILLAGE VOICE, 1/31/95, p. 52, Gary Dauphin

The true-to-life story of one Henri Young (played with scoliotic fragility by Kevin Bacon), *Murder in the First* is what I imagine insiders call a "real movie-movie": A-list Hollywood fare gifted with a strong story, crystal clear production values, and a trio of talented and youngish leading men (Bacon, Christian Slater, and Gary Oldman). A courtroom drama that mixes broad shouldered (and slightly clichéd) themes like "justice" and "friendship" with brutal cell-block beat-down sequences, *Murder*'s ostensible subject is the wave of reform that shook America's penal system during the '40s, but don't you believe it. *Murder* is about acting first and foremost.

Bacon's Henri Young is less a character than a collection of abused body parts; Marc Rocco's direction makes the most of his constantly shaking, in-turned ankles, the broken, purplish finger nails, and a neck so used to cringing from blows that it seems permanently bent. Until his 1939 murder trial set off a newsreel feeding frenzy, the actual Young was an anonymous loser whose only crime was a $5 theft that landed him in the federal pen at Leavenworth. (He happened to rob a grocery store that doubled as a post office.) For reasons elided by the film, Young is transferred to Alcatraz and promptly attempts to escape. Alcatraz is well worth fleeing: the island home of hard-cases from Capone to Machine Gun Kelly, it's also a police city-state, prisoners squeezing out existences between the flowered quarters of guard's families above and the medieval dungeon hidden below. Young was tortured for close to three years for the attempted breakout; he spent over 1000 days straight in Alcatraz's lightless solitary confinement level, (the usual stint was 19), allowed out for one half hour of exercise a year, and regularly beaten by guards on the orders of Alcatraz's associate warden. Oldman makes the most of his role as Warden Glenn. Tight around the mouth even when he's beating bound prisoners, Oldman manages to coil himself around a character with little to do beyond loosening his cuff links before picking up a blunt or sharp object.

Driven certifiably looney by his isolation, the first thing Young does upon being released back into the population is kill the prisoner who ratted him out. The task of handling Young's subsequent trial is given to James Stamphill (Slater), a 24-year-old court-appointed attorney fresh out of Harvard. Slater's rather theatrical line of defense? Young "was just a weapon, but Alcatraz was the killer."

All this is, of course, the type of material that has launched a thousand bad movies, but *Murder*'s principals do their jobs so well that you will forgive a familiar misstep or two. In the end memorable details are never really Young's or Stamphill's or Glenn's: They're Kevin Bacon's as he inhabits the rotting pieces of Young's lice-ridden body or Slater's as he imagines himself Clarence Darrow, his growing affection for Young kept from bubbling soap suds because Slater is such a smug bastard in the courtroom. Bacon's never lived up to the promise he showed in Barry Levinson's *Diner* (*He Said, She Said*, anybody?), but down to his last shell-shocked tick, he muscles *Murder* into a first-rate Hollywood feature, which is precisely what youngish and talented leading men are supposed to do.

Also reviewed in:
CHICAGO TRIBUNE, 1/20/95, Friday/p. D, John Petrakis
NEW YORK TIMES, 1/20/95, p. C3, Janet Maslin
VARIETY, 1/16-22/95, p. 95, Todd McCarthy
WASHINGTON POST, 1/20/95, p. D6, Rita Kempley
WASHINGTON POST, 1/20/95, Weekend/p. 36, Desson Howe

MURIEL'S WEDDING

A Miramax Films release of a CiBy 2000 presentation in association with the Australian Film Finance Corporation of a House and Moorhouse Films production. *Producer:* Lynda House and Jocelyn Moorhouse. *Director:* P.J. Hogan. *Screenplay:* P.J. Hogan. *Story:* Jocelyn Moorhouse and P.J. Hogan. *Director of Photography:* Martin McGrath. *Editor:* Jill Bilcock. *Music:* Peter Best. *Choreographer:* John O'Connell. *Sound:* David Lee, Glenn Newnham, Livia Ruzic, and Roger Savage. *Casting:* Alison Barrett. *Production Designer:* Patrick Reardon. *Art Director:* Hugh Bateup. *Set Decorator:* Jane Murphy and Glen W. Johnson. *Special Effects:* Ray Fowler. *Costumes:* Terry Ryan. *Make-up:* Noriko Watanabe. *Stunt Coordinator:* Rocky McDonald. *Running time:* 105 minutes. *MPAA Rating:* R.

CAST: Toni Collette (Muriel Heslop); Bill Hunter (Bill Heslop); Rachel Griffiths (Rhonda); Jeanie Drynan (Betty Heslop); Gennie Nevinson (Deirdre); Matt Day (Brice); Daniel Lapaine (David Van Arkle); Sophie Lee (Tania); Belinda Jarrett (Janine); Rosalind Hammond (Cheryl); Pippa Grandison (Nicole); Chris Haywood (Ken Blundell); Daniel Wyllie (Perry); Gabby Millgate (Joanie); Katie Saunders (Penelope); Dene Kermond (Malcolm); Susan Prior (Girl at Wedding); Nathan Kaye (Chook); Cecily Polson (Tania's Mother); Rob Steele (Higgins); Genevieve Picot (Store Detective); Richard Sutherland (Constable Saunders); Steve Smith (Constable Gillespie); Jeamin Lee (Chinese Waitress); Jon-Claire Lee (Chinese Maitre'd); Kuni Hashimoto (Akira); Ken Senga (Victor Keinosuke); Des Rodgers (Island MC); Rodney Arnold (Ejected Diner); Steve Cox (Cruise Taxi Driver); Kevin Copeland and James Schramko (Sailors); Barry Crocker and Richard Morecroft (Themselves); Richard Carter (Federal Policeman); John Gaden (Doctor); Heather Mitchell and Penne Hackforth-Jones (Bridal Managers); Heidi Lapaine and Kirsty Hinchcliffe (Bridal Assistants); Diane Smith (Physiotherapist); Darrin Klimek (Rhonda's Taxi Driver); Robert Alexander (Barrister); Troy Hardy (Young Boy); Robyn Pitt Owen (Singer at Muriel's Wedding); Annie Byron (Rhonda's Mother); Vincent Ball (Priest); John Hoare (Well-wisher at Muriel's Wedding); Frankie Davidson (Sergeant); Louise Cullen (Deidre's Friend); Basil Clarke (Funeral Priest); John Walton (Taxi Driver).

LOS ANGELES TIMES, 3/10/95, Calendar/p. 1, Kenneth Turan

"Muriel's Wedding" is the event Muriel wants so much to happen but fears never will. How is she to feel otherwise when her frightful best friends insist she surrender a bridal bouquet she's just caught. "Give it back, give it back," they yap at her like well-dressed terriers. "Nobody's ever going to marry you."

That scene, which opens P.J. Hogan's marvelous debut film, sets the tone for what is to come. Wickedly mocking but empathetic, able to laugh at its characters while paying attention to their sorrows, this subversive comedy about self-esteem resists the notion that films have to timidly remain within tidy genre rules.

Winner of four Australian Academy Awards, including best picture, "Muriel's Wedding" is the latest in a series of brash and rowdy comedies from that country that includes "Strictly Ballroom" and "The Adventures of Priscilla, Queen of the Desert." Made with energy, raucous good humor and noticeable wit, its ability to recognize the poignancy in its situations makes it special even in that uninhibited group.

Played with take-no-prisoners comic enthusiasm by Toni Collette, 22-year-old Muriel Heslop is the kind of hapless young woman who wears a shoplifted leopard-skin dress to a wedding—and gets caught by the store detective. Overweight, with bad skin, a braying laugh and a frighteningly wide grin, aggressively unattractive Muriel is known locally in Porpoise Spit for saying and doing the wrong things. Even her taste in music, her devotion to Abba's bubbly but outmoded melodies, makes her nominal friends wince.

And when it comes to matrimony, Muriel is so in love with the idea of being married that she is on intimate terms with every frame of Princess Di's wedding tape. Glassy-eyed and obsessive on the subject, Muriel looks on a marriage license as a membership card in the human race that will prove to everyone, herself most of all, that she has finally become a worthwhile person.

Muriel comes by her insecurities the way most people do, through her dysfunctional blood relatives. Father Bill Heslop (veteran Australian actor Bill Hunter), known as "Bill the Battler" to his intimates, is a politician and influence-peddler whose hobby is running down everyone in his family, from his catatonic wife, Betty (Jeanie Drynan), to his horde of professional couch-potato children.

But though Muriel takes her fair share of abuse, she has something rare, and that is spirit. Though it tends to come out in unhelpful ways, like her weakness for telling strings of lies, that quality makes Muriel believe that some day things will go her way. "I know I'm not normal," she says earnestly, "but I can change."

That passion also makes Muriel defy logic and seriously bend some rules to accompany her horrified trio of harpy girlfriends when they take a Club Med-type vacation on Hibiscus Island. There Muriel meets Rhonda (Rachel Griffiths), a full-bore party animal who truthfully says, "My whole life is one last fling after another."

Unexpectedly, Rhonda responds to the free spirit in Muriel and the validation of that friendship proves liberating. It starts Muriel on a wild and chaotic journey of self-discovery, filled with wacky and eccentric plot turns, that will gradually cause her to rethink almost all her most cherished ideas.

Clearly, "Muriel's Wedding" would be much less than it is without the right stars, and Collette, who has the courage not to shortchange Muriel's more off-putting qualities, and Griffiths, who looks like a mature Juliette Lewis and makes Rhonda's character believable, were both remarkable enough to win Australian Academy Awards. And the rest of the cast, even an old warhorse like Bill Hunter, completely catches the spirit of the piece and join forces as a gifted ensemble.

The credit for this has to go to writer-director Hogan and a production team led by co-producers Lynda House and Jocelyn Moorhouse (who directed the memorable "Proof" and is Hogan's wife). They've come up with a slashing guerrilla attack on accepted notions of marriage, family and self-improvement that never allows us to forget the doubt that makes its characters human. Though it is consistently funny, "Muriel's Wedding" is savvy enough not to play things just for laughs.

NEW STATESMAN & SOCIETY, 4/14/95, p. 35, Jonathan Romney

What's the most representative image of new Australian cinema? Possibly the scene in *The Adventures of Priscilla, Queen of the Desert*, in which a gang of drag queens in the Outback lip-sync flamboyantly to "I Will Survive", while an impromptu Aboriginal audience cheers them. A resplendent picture of understanding and community under one big desert sky, regardless of the barrier of race and sexuality—all in all, such an archly obvious image that having seen the clip, I really couldn't be bothered to go and see the film.

I'm not normally that easily put off any film, but having been to *Strictly Ballroom*, the previous year's big sequinned Australian hit, I felt I'd seen enough Antipodean glitterkitsch for a lifetime. In a culture that's traditionally the domain of rough, rugged geezers, you can see why camp and artifice should be of some political importance; but Australia is seriously in danger of losing its cultural credibility if it's becoming known as the world's prime exporter of ABBA coverbands.

I didn't fancy the look of *Muriel's Wedding*, after seeing the trailer, which features a gang of giggly lasses in glaring prawn-and-pineapple hula costumes, and the heroine and her best mate going through the motions of "Waterloo", done up in clingy white satin like French and Saunders playing to the gallery. What did hook me, though, was that the film is co-produced by Jocelyn Moorhouse, who made the remorselessly grim *Proof* a few years back; her husband, P J Hogan, is the writer and director.

Sure enough, *Muriel's Wedding*, is not what it seems. It *is* a larky, rude, lurid feel-good farce—up to a point. Then it turns decidedly chilly—which, indeed, it has been right from the beginning. It's a film about learning to deal with a hopeless life and the largely futile fancies which bolster it. Muriel Heslop lives in the dreary, aimlessly civic-prided town of Porpoise Spit, where her dad (Bill Hunter) is a corrupt local councillor. He's known as "Battling Bill", but his battles are largely fought with his down-trodden family, and comprise a war of attrition to keep them cowering. Muriel, lumpy and insecure, escapes from family hell and the rejection of her snooty, Barbie-like peers by worshipping ABBA and fantasising about being a dream bride. The other girls, in between bitching and doling out blow-jobs to each others' men, put her down mercilessly; when she catches the bouquet at a wedding, the others demand a rematch.

Muriel's day comes at a hideous Fantasy Island resort, where she finds a kindred spirit in the unruly Rhonda (Rachel Griffiths); together they do that ABBA routine to a reception of dropped jaws from the girls and leery grins from the beach boys. Because of the skill with which Hogan negotiates a contrast between Muriel's loveless reality and this new over-lit world of Pina Colada fantasy, the apotheosis works marvelously. This really *is* a feel-good moment.

Any other film might have left it there, on this crowd-pleasing girls' bonding triumph. But *Muriel's Wedding* doesn't swallow momentary happiness so easily. It's at this point, just as Muriel is finding a new self, that Hogan begins to build on the petty moral bleakness he's been hinting at so far—and, for my money, he gives rather better value than Mike Leigh's version of the same. The Heslop family horrors really start to bubble up—the no-hope slobbishness of her siblings, Dad's viciously abusive tyranny and the blasted emotional void inhabited by Muriel's mother. Played brilliantly by Jeanie Drynan, this role, on the surface all dishmop stooge, becomes a dangerously still pool concealing unfathomable depths of hurt.

Muriel leaves for Sydney and changes her name to Mariel, but can't leave herself behind—she's soon indulging her wedding dress dreams, obsessively trying on confections of silk chantelle, bursting like a monster meringue. The reality principle intrudes on her new life in another, uncomfortably melodramatic way, as Rhonda is suddenly stricken by cancer and ends up in a wheelchair. She's suddenly forced to drop her hard-forged wild-child identity, just as Muriel's beginning to construct her own. Her fate represents a challenge to Muriel's self-absorbed, escapist drives. It's a narrative flaw, though, that Rhonda loses the use of her legs just as she's been enthusiastically shagging a couple of sailors, and just as Muriel's about to lose her virginity too; the implication of this exceptionally contrived turning point is that Rhonda is punished for her sexuality, as well as being used as a temporary obstacle to Muriel's sexual maturing. Hogan tries to allay the doubt by having an anxious Rhonda reassured that her cancer's not the result of too much sex, but it's harder for us to be reassured that this plotline isn't a rather cavalier narrative expedient.

But otherwise the film is beautifully knitted together, and very acute in its reading of how fantasy operates in a context of everyday drabness; it's one of the best films about adolescence and fanhood (not that I can think of many others). And, despite its theme, it's neither about getting the man, nor too obviously about *not* getting the man. The superhunk who falls into Muriel's lap isn't really of much consequence to her. Her bridal obsession is entirely about herself—it's purely a dream of her own personal graduation, of shining brighter than the rest. *Muriel's Wedding* is actually a cynical examination of the idea of what all feel-good movies aim for—a brief image of earthy ecstasy. The film is happy to celebrate such dreams, to string them along, but it doesn't buy them for a second, even though it recognises their necessity. By the time "Dancing Queen" rolls round for the end credits, *Muriel's Wedding* leaves you feeling pretty exhilarated—but strangely sobered too.

NEW YORK, 4/3/95, P. 58, David Denby

Of late, movies have failed at something that once virtually defined their existence—putting men and women together in couples for our delight, excitement, and edification. With rare exceptions like Mike Newell's *Four Weddings and a Funeral* or Richard Linklater's *Before Sunrise*, recent romantic pictures have been depressingly functional and crude, still stuck in old Tracy-Hepburn or Rosalind Russell-working-girl formulas. In the void, filmmakers have begun doubling up women the way the early-seventies rash of buddy movies doubled up men.

I didn't review the Australian comedy *Muriel's Wedding* because I found it too embarrassing to write about. But I keep hearing that people enjoyed it, so it may be time to deposit a little poison into the appropriate ears. *Muriel's Wedding* is about a heavyset girl from the Australian resort town of Porpoise Spit, an excruciatingly shy, inarticulate slug, bullied by her father, dismayed by her beaten-down mother. Muriel (Toni Collette) haunts the bridal stores, thinking of nothing but old Abba tapes and marriage; the film's first-time director, P.J. Hogan, seems to wallow in her troubles—her physical awkwardness, her rejection by her bitchy Barbie-doll friends. Hogan must think he is creating sympathy, but he doesn't realize how offensive it is to ask the audience to sympathize with a blob. Hogan makes everyone look bad—all the characters are caricatures, vile and loud, or so utterly depressed they might be zombies from a horror movie.

Muriel is meant to be a prisoner of false values, but the picture itself has been conceived at the infantile level of tabloid fantasies. Another lonely young woman (Rachel Griffiths), a spike-haired toughie with no fears, takes up with Muriel, becoming her one true friend. Then this dream buddy contracts, in her twenties, cancer of the spine and winds up in a wheelchair. Muriel, meanwhile, marries a beautiful South African athlete with an interesting curl to his upper lip. He doesn't really want her at first—he marries to attain citizenship—but he warms up to her after he, too, discovers her superior qualities. Will she blossom? No—just as this male dish goes to bed with her at last, she leaves him in order to take care of her friend. She has escaped one prison, her father's miserable house, in order to enter another, as a nurse-companion, and this is presented as a victory for her and for the human spirit. I had the same queasy feeling I had during *Boys on the Side*, when Whoopi Goldberg, as a good-hearted lesbian who never has any sex, nurses her friend who has AIDs. Women can do without men, apparently, but they have to be punished in some way. They die or wind up taking care of invalids. This sickly new canonization of female friendship may be a setback for women.

NEW YORK POST, 3/10/95, p. 47, Thelma Adams

There must be a German word—bridalust or something—for that mania a woman of a certain age gets for choosing a wedding dress, casting herself at the center of a marriage ceremony, and feeling her adult life click into place. This desire has little or nothing to do with the groom.

If there's not a German word, at least there's an Australian comedy that captures the delight and desperation of the wedding gown complex.

P.J. Hogan's warm-hearted "Muriel's Wedding" doesn't pre-frost the cake with a bride-to-be that's everybody's dream girl. Muriel Heslop (Toni Collette) is a gangly, freckled, slack-jawed ostrich who hopes that putting on the veil will make her a swan.

Muriel has her share of problems not the least of which is coming from Porpoise Spit, Australia. Her troika of pretty, petty pals dumps her. Her father (Bill Hunter) says she's "useless" and, though he's tactless and coarse, he has a point—she has no visible skills to launch a career. As for boyfriends, the gap in her love-life was big as the one between her teeth.

Muriel's dreams and aspirations are framed by the '70s pop sensation ABBA (a bigger phenomenon down under than in the States). With their peppy, pop tunes and bittersweet lyrics, ABBA holds out the promise that Muriel could be having the time of her life—but it just isn't happening in Porpoise Spit.

Muriel's antic adventures proving herself provide frisky, crowd-pleasing laughs, but the movie distinguishes itself with its poignancy.

The cruelty of Muriel's friends is unyielding and true and Muriel buys into it at an enormous cost to herself. "I know I'm not normal," she tells them as they brush her off, "but I'm trying to change."

Muriel's father loves her and crushes her simultaneously—and he has ground her birdy, sweet mother (Jeanie Drynan) into a non-entity. At every family dinner out, Mr. Heslop's mistress Dierdre (Gennie Nevinson) arrives with a cheery wave and mock shock at the "coincidence" that they should meet. Muriel need look no further to know that a wedding dress is not necessarily a prelude to bliss.

In the end, Hogan takes a few melodramatic turns but that didn't keep the movie from winning the Australian Academy Award for best film in 1994. Collette won best actress for her robust portrayal of an ordinary gal who becomes extraordinary in her desire not to settle or be settled in a dreary backwater.

NEWSDAY, 3/10/95, Part II/p. B2, Jack Mathews

Muriel Heslop is the ugly duckling of Porpoise Spit, Australia, the overweight, under-loved, socially inept daughter of a corrupt local politician and a timid, chronically depressed mother. And, in P.J. Hogan's warmly hilarious and uplifting "Muriel's Wedding," things are going to get worse before they get better.

There is a quality to Australian comedy, that works on audiences like a laughing gas, a buoyancy that seems to lift the film right off the screen and dangle it overhead like a giant balloon. We saw Baz Luhrmann work that trick on us a couple of years ago with his exhilaratingly good-natured "Strictly Ballroom," we saw it last year with Stephan Elliott's drag comedy "The Adventures of Priscilla: Queen of the Desert," and Hogan, on his very first feature, has reproduced the magic here.

It takes no small amount of gas to give Muriel lift-off. Brilliantly played by Toni Collette, who gained 40 pounds for the role, Muriel is a big girl, and dead weight at that. She grew up in sloth, one of three inert children whose lives are embarrassing footnotes to that of Bill Heslop (Bill Hunter), their egomaniacal father.

However, unlike her vegetating mother, brother and sister, Muriel at least dreams of a better life, of meeting her Prince Charming (or Prince Bozo; just about any man will do) and being swept down the aisle in a blur of white taffeta and lace. We learn just how great a fantasy that is in the opening moments when Muriel catches the bridal bouquet at a friend's wedding, and is asked to give it back.

A great deal of cruelty is heaped upon Muriel—her father belittles her as a typing school dropout, her friends declare her too uncool and dumpy to hang out with them—but her dream of marriage and her addiction to the music of ABBA keep her going against all odds. The turning point in her self-discovery comes when she drains her father's bank account, treats herself to a tropical vacation, then slips off to Sydney to try on wedding gowns and respond to mail-order bride ads.

The fictional name of Porpoise Spit captures the tone of the entire movie, and yet, there is just enough heft beneath the whimsy to make the film touch down once in a while. Muriel is a stand-in for all people, male or female, who feel they were last in line when God handed out looks, and though its beauty-is-only-skin-deep theme is an ageless cliché, it is done with great imagination and flare.

For "Strictly Ballroom," Baz Luhrmann used a fisheye lens at one point to underscore the distorted reality he was after, and that is the feeling we get—without the fisheye view—watching "Muriel's Wedding." The characters and situations are both authentic and wildly exaggerated, the film manages to deal seriously with Muriel's delusion, her mother's depression, and a friend's struggle with cancer without undermining its essential lightheartedness.

"Muriel's Wedding" dominated the Australian equivalent of the Oscars, winning acting awards for both Collette and Rachel Griffiths, a revelation as Rhonda, the worldly, free-spirited woman who becomes Muriel's best friend and mentor in the art of living. The other stand-out performances are given by Hunter, the cartoonishly evil father, and Jeanie Drynan, as the mother who loathes her circumstances but lacks the will to do anything about them.

But it is Collette who, pardon the pun, has to carry most of the weight, and she is sensational. She invests Muriel with an ebullience of nature that makes her shine from within. No matter how pathetic or dark Muriel's situation, Collette keeps us assured of the specialness of her character, and we gladly dream along with her.

When Muriel finally makes her trip down the aisle, she is physically the same ugly duckling we meet in the opening scene. And she's beautiful.

SIGHT AND SOUND, 4/95, p. 49, Robert Yates

Porpoise Spit, a small town in Australia. When Muriel catches the bride's bouquet at a wedding, her old school friends, led by the vicious Tania, cruelly insist that she gives it up since no-one will ever marry her. She is then reported to the police for wearing a stolen dress. Only the intervention of her father, a local political bigwig, prevents them from questioning her. Muriel has neither job, nor friends. Her contemporaries tell her she's an embarrassment. When her father secures her some work in his lover Deirdre's beauty salon, Muriel cashes a blank cheque intended for Deirdre and takes off to the Pacific island where Tania and her gang are on holiday. There she finds the gang and Rhonda, a schoolfriend none of them has seen for years. Disliking the others, Rhonda adopts Muriel, who spins her a story about the holiday being her last fling before she gets married. On returning to Porpoise Spit, having had a great time, Muriel decides not to face her father and follows Rhonda on to Sydney. They share a flat, enjoying themselves until the day that Rhonda collapses and a cancerous tumour is diagnosed. She loses the use of her legs, and Muriel, renamed Mariel, takes care of her. In bridal shops, assistants take photos of her in dresses to show to her "ailing mother". When Rhonda discovers these, Mariel breaks down, complaining that everything would be okay if only she could marry.

Rhonda discovers she'll never walk again. Meanwhile Mariel's father is facing corruption charges. Mariel answers a newspaper ad, agreeing to marry Brice—a rich, handsome South African swimmer who needs Australian nationality. The wedding is a grand affair with all of Porpoise Spit invited, but Mariel's mother arrives late and her daughter fails to see her. Some time later, Mariel's mother commits suicide. After the funeral Mariel decides to leave Brice. As Muriel once again, she tells Rhonda she would like to take care of her. The two set off for Sydney.

Muriel would make a good guest for Oprah Winfrey. After a wretched childhood, she begins to make a new life for herself. Then her only friend contracts cancer, her father is exposed as a corrupt politician, and her mother commits suicide. Yet it's more than the run of misery that lends her *Oprah* potential. Despite everything, she also pulls through—the perfect prime-time confessional pay-off. Indeed, P.J. Hogan, the Australian debutante director, explains Muriel's journey in terms we'd recognise from television pop psychology. "Her victory," he says, "was to find out who she was." Hogan plays this melodramatic stuff for laughs, using humour as a bulwark against mawkishness. But slipped into this comedy is a morality tale, suggesting the downside of psychobabble through its depiction of Muriel's self-obsession. Although we are invited to approve of Muriel's growth, and cheer along at the film's close when she and Rhonda take joyous leave of Porpoise Spit, her behaviour along the way suggests an underdog's potential for a blind cruelty equal to that she receives from Tania. Muriel is so lost in her fantasies of triumph that she forgets all about her disconsolate mother and abandons Rhonda for her Prince Charming.

Porpoise Spit is an Australian version of the small town so often depicted in the American cinema of the 80s, where homely qualities barely veil routine dysfunction. While there's little that's really sinister in Hogan's town beyond a general unhappiness and frustration, this is tarted up in the gaudiest of clothes (production and costume design are well over-the-top). The holiday scenes especially are rendered in dazzling colours. Muriel's family home is exaggerated in a different way. Her father and siblings form a collection of grotesques that wouldn't be out of place in a Harry Enfield sketch, the father lamenting continually the likelihood that his children will turn out to be dim-witted failures (and so establishing a self-fulfilling prophesy which—the film's pop psychology tells us—Muriel battles against).

The heightened colours, the melodramatic sweep of the story, the dashes from wretched reality to drunken fantasy—all these are features the film shares with the pop music Hogan employs. He spent months wooing Abba, eventually persuading the band to let him use six of their songs. Abba is Muriel's favourite group, and she acts out her daydreams to their songs. When life is good, she says, it feels just like 'Dancing Queen.' But in her behaviour lies an age-old cautionary tale about the dangers of an unbridled fantasy life. Hogan's poignant take on the theme can be traced in the way that Muriel assembles her wedding album: as a *Madame Bovary* for the *Photo Love* generation. The tragic touches—Rhonda collapsing in the middle of a particularly enjoyable night of sex with a couple of sailors (later, finding herself paralysed)—are only plausible in such an outsize context. In essence *Muriel's Wedding* is an intentionally humorous dayglo soap opera, cogent and occasionally affecting.

TIME, 4/10/95, p. 82, Richard Schickel

The most astonishing thing about *Muriel's Wedding* is that critics and civilians alike keep referring to it—favorably and unfavorably—as a romantic comedy. This says a great deal about our hunger for the innocent pleasures of the sort of film that (*Four Weddings and a Funeral* excepted) no one knows how to make anymore, but not much useful about writer-director P.J. Hogan's film.

There's nothing romantic about *Muriel's Wedding* and, a few sardonic laughs aside, very little comedy in it either. It is instead a relentless assault on what Marxists used to call petit-bourgeois values and what we have since learned to identify as middle-class dysfunction. Hogan's horrid examples are the Heslop family of Porpoise Spit, Australia. Dad is a crooked low-level politician, Mom has been rendered virtually speechless by chronic depression, and the kids all lie around watching telly and putting on weight. Daughter Muriel (played with brave, ponderous dimness by Toni Collette) is no better than the rest of this awful lot, and maybe worse, since she thinks things would be magically perfect if she could just have a church wedding with all the lacy trimmings.

How she achieves that goal (but nothing like true love) and in the process confounds false friends and temporarily betrays her only true one (a hot-wired Rachel Griffiths), finally gaining such wisdom as she can handle, forms the substance of the movie. Muriel is really a sort of Weight Watchers' Forrest Gump, only a little more dreamy and larcenous and a lot more damaged by cultural junk food; what little she knows of life she has absorbed from Abba songs. But she is a cautionary, not an exemplary, figure, and there is something bleakly bracing in the way Hogan tells her story.

VILLAGE VOICE, 3/21/95, p. 56, Georgia Brown

What is it with Australia and vulgarity? Make that New Zealand, too. *Strictly Ballroom, Heavenly Creatures, Priscilla Queen of the Desert*, all are films reveling in, rolling in, crassitude. Jane Campion's wonderful early films were vulgar in this direction, too—cartoony melodramas peopled with earthy, unglamorous, bordering-on-grotesque characters. But look where this dangerous trend has led: To P.J. Hogan's *Muriel's Wedding*, an ostentatiously shallow comedy riddled with disfiguring close-ups and so stupendously garish that theaters should provide throw-up bags. It was a huge hit in the homeland.

Muriel (Toni Collette), a large, lonely girl with splotches on her face, is obsessed with weddings. (Not with marriage, mind you, just the ceremony and trappings.) Conveniently, the movie opens at a wedding, apparently so we can gauge just how out of her element this cringing mound of flesh is. When Muriel catches the bouquet, the catty bride and her maids demand that she toss it back. At home with her lumpish family, however, Muriel comes off half normal. Her sibs too are fat and traumatized, Mum (Jeanie Drynan) moves through the kitchen like a dazed sheep, and Dad (Bill Hunter), a corrupt local official, gets off on humiliating his offspring in public.

Running away for a holiday, Muriel is taken up by the rebellious Rhonda (Rachel Griffiths), a free spirit who persuades her to move from provincial Porpoise Spit to Sydney's fast lanes. Here, Muriel gets a job in a video store, a becoming haircut, and even a shy boyfriend. But wedding gowns still exercise their peculiar power and our girl begins stopping into bridal outfitters, pretending to be a bona fide customer.

My second favorite line in the movie: When Muriel tells the saleslady the big day is in September, this woman sighs, "Spring!"

The first comes after the plucky Rhonda, now in a wheelchair, has tried to hide from the glamorous, made-over Muriel. When she spots her old pal, Muriel coos softly, "I saw your wheels."

In the end Muriel gets to have her wedding cake, eat it, and throw it in all the familiar faces. Nothing beats wish fulfillment. I'm glad I sat all the way through because I hated it a teensy bit less.

Also reviewed in:
CHICAGO TRIBUNE, 3/17/95, Friday/p. G, Johanna Steinmetz
NEW YORK TIMES, 3/10/95, p. C15, Janet Maslin
VARIETY, 5/23-29/94, p. 55, Todd McCarthy
WASHINGTON POST, 3/17/95, p. B7, Hal Hinson

MUTE WITNESS

A Sony Pictures Classics release of a Cobblestone Pictures production. *Executive Producer:* Richard Claus. *Producer:* Alexander Buchman, Norbert Soentgen, and Anthony Waller. *Director:* Anthony Waller. *Screenplay:* Anthony Waller. *Director of Photography:* Egon Werdin. *Editor:* Peter Adam. *Music:* Wilbert Hirsch. *Sound:* Albert Avramenko and (music) Frank Reinke. *Production Designer:* Matthias Kammermeier. *Art Director:* Barbara Becker. *Special Effects:* Victor Orlov and Pavel Terchov. *Costumes:* Svetlana Luzanova. *Make-up:* Irina Morozova. *Stunt Coordinator:* Sergei Vorobiov. *Running time:* 98 minutes. *MPAA Rating:* R.

CAST: Marina Sudina (Billy); Fay Ripley (Karen); Evan Richards (Andy); Oleg Jankowskij (Larsen); Igor Volkow (Arkadi); Sergei Karlenkov (Lyosha); Alexander Buriew (Strohbecker); Alec Guinness (The Reaper); Alexander Piatov (Wartschuk); Nikolai Pastuhov (Janitor); Stephen Bouser (Lovett); Valeri Barahtin (Mitja); Nikolai Chindjaikin (Inspector Pekar); Vasheslav Naumenko (Officer Mlekov); Larisa Husnolina (Victim); Olga Tolstetskaya (Actress); Denis Karasiov and Igor Iljin (Fake Policemen); Oleg Abramov (Double); Uri Sherstiniov (Angry Neighbor); Ludmilla Makeeva (Neighbor's Wife); Vladimir Salnikov (Lab Assistant); Sascha Buchman (Alex); Natalie Poliushkina (Natasha); Konstantin Sitnikov (Angry Props Manager); Regina Peter (Telephone Operator's Voice); Norbert Soentgen (Peeping Tom).

LOS ANGELES TIMES, 9/15/95, Calendar/p. 14, Kevin Thomas

"Mute Witness" is an ingenious but exceedingly savage and protracted lady-in-distress thriller that benefits considerably from its key setting, Moscow's vast, seedy old Mosfilm Studios complex. For all its nervy style, it aims steadfastly at the lowest common denominator among exploitation picture audiences.

Billy (Marina Sudina), a mute special-effects makeup artist working on a low-budget American production for an understandably self-absorbed young director (Evan Richards), inadvertently becomes locked in the immense, maze-like sound stage and its surrounding structure. To her horror she witnesses a couple of Russian members of the crew shoot a snuff film—a particularly gory sequence involving sex. Once her presence is detected by these villains, the cat-and-mouse pursuit is on full force.

Writer-director Anthony Waller unfailingly comes up with one gimmick after another to keep Billy and eventually the director and the director's spunky girlfriend (Fay Ripley), who is also Billy's sister, in constant danger, but after awhile the suspense becomes increasingly credibility—defying and mechanical. Meanwhile, the brutality increases, and the overall effect is one of growing morbidity, despite Waller's broad strokes of comic relief.

In fairness, Waller does pack a few jolts for thrill-seekers, mainly early on before the film becomes such a wearying blood bath, and he shrewdly keys into the gangsterism currently plaguing the former Soviet Union. The film's strongest asset by far is Egon Werdin's fluid and strikingly lit cinematography.

NEW YORK POST, 9/15/95, p. 43, Michael Medved

At the very least, you have to give "Mute Witness" high marks for resourcefulness and audacity.

It's a slick low-budget gore fest about the making of a clumsy low-budget gore fest. The fictional filmmakers are inept Americans who shoot their picture in Moscow in order to save money on production costs, just as the real-life movie people behind this production cleverly make the most of their wintry, atmospheric Russian locations.

The main character in the story, an American make-up artist named Billy, is skillfully played by a rising Russian star (Marina Sudina) with presumably limited English skills; the script effortlessly overcomes this obstacle by making her the "Mute Witness" of the title, a brave but lonely soul who can't say a word in any language.

The horrors begin one night after cast and crew finish their day's work and accidentally lock the voiceless makeup artist inside the deserted film studio. She's just about resigned to spending the night in this creepy place when she hears noises on one of the sets and sees two of the Russian technicians from the project busily shooting their own scene. One of them operates the camera, while "the other enthusiastically plays his part in a porno encounter with a naked blonde floozy, who is understandably shocked when her on-screen partner suddenly begins hacking her to bloody bits.

Billy is the only witness to this snuff film rampage and as she runs off in terror, the killers are tipped off to her presence. What follows is an elaborate, stunningly well-staged chase scene through the empty building, including an especially chilling bit of business in a gloomy cellar that served in real-life as the site for thousands of executions during the Stalin era.

Later that same night, the police fail to believe Billy's account of what of what she's seen and her only allies are the klutzy "boy wonder" director (Evan Richards) of the shoddy movie that employs her, and her protective big sister (Fay Ripley), who also happens to be the director's girlfriend.

A suave, initially sympathetic Moscow police official (played by Russia's top box office star, Oleg Jankowskij) may or may not be part of the snuff film conspiracy, headed by an omnipotent crime boss known as "the Reaper." The actor who plays this role is identified in the credits only as "The Mystery Guest Star," but he's instantly recognizable as one of the most distinguished actors of this century, who met the director by chance in Moscow and agreed to shoot his one scene in the morning just before his plane returned to England.

The entire production is characterized by this sort of improvisatory energy and irreverent wit, and it's easy to overlook technical shortcomings (like Oleg Jankowskij's sloppily looped English dialogue) because the dark, paranoid atmosphere of a chaotic, gang-infested, post-Communist Moscow is so well conveyed. Anthony Waller, the 36-year-old director/writer/producer (a leading creator of commercials in Germany and England) makes no attempt at an artistic statement, but this is the sort of smart, stylish project that will open doors for him everywhere.

"Mute Witness," in other words, offers eloquent testimony to a promising new talent.

NEWSDAY, 9/15/95, Part II/p. B4, Jack Mathews

In a dark movie studio in Moscow, an American special-effects makeup artist for a slasher film being made there happens onto a scene more horrifying than anything she'd ever wasted a barrel of stage blood on. Locked in and looking for a security guard, the young woman instead finds two Russian crew members apparently in the midst of shooting a snuff film.

The witness screams, as she watches the terrified blond victim being slashed to death with a knife, but makes no sound. She is completely mute.

The next hour or so of Anthony Waller's "Mute Witness" is flawless Hitchcockian suspense, as Billy (Marina Sudina) tries to stay a step ahead of the Russians chasing her through the labyrinthine studio. She can phone her sister (Fay Ripley) and her director (Evan Richards), who are waiting dinner on her, but can't speak to them. Like blind Audrey Hepburn in "Wait Until Dark," Billy has only her remaining senses to help her escape.

Writer-director Waller, making the leap here from TV commercials to features, knows how to ratchet up the tension and keep the audience guessing. Were the Russians really shooting a snuff film, or testing the special-effects equipment, as they insist? Are those body parts lying next to Billy in the bottom of the elevator shaft, or props? What's the importance of the key she's desperate to find, and the computer disc everyone seems to want? And can Waller sustain this crafty mind-puzzle to the end?

The answer to the last question is, not quite. Waller, who planned this project for 10 years and actually shot Russian underworld boss Alec Guinness' small role back then, got caught up in his own cleverness, contriving a confusingly cute ending that seems to come from a different, and lesser movie. The gags that he tries to work in, primarily through Richards' obnoxiously insensitive Andy, are more grief than relief.

Still, "Mute Witness" is a better thriller than Hollywood seems able to crank out these days. Moving the story's setting from Chicago to Moscow, and the underworld from American to Russian, was probably not the smartest commercial move, but the strangeness of the new locale and culture adds immeasurably to the sense of alienation and suspense.

The murkiness of the studio and nighttime Moscow, where the story eventually spills out, fills the air like London fog, and when it comes to understanding what the Russians are saying to each other, Billy is effectively deaf, as well as mute.

Waller used mostly Russian actors, including the marvelous Sudina, a veteran of two dozen features and TV movies, and that also adds to the Americans-in-peril theme. If Billy can't tell the good guys from the bad, the police from the Russian mafia, neither can we. And not knowing is delightfully unnerving.

SIGHT AND SOUND, 1/96, p. 46, George Macnab

On a film set inside a dilapidated Moscow studio, the crew finish for the day. American director, Andy, his girlfriend, Karen, and Karen's sister, Billie, a mute special-effects make-up artist, get ready to leave. Just as they're about to drive off, Billie informs the others in sign language that she's going to collect a mask to work on for the next day's shoot. The studio gates are closed and Billie is left locked inside. She hears noises from the set, investigates, and witnesses what looks like the brutal stabbing of a woman. A technician has filmed the entire murder. He hears her drop her handbag and comes after her. They go on a nerve-wracking chase which culminates with Billie falling from a height onto a pile of discarded film cans as she tries to escape.

The police are called. The technician and his accomplice deny the crime, claiming they were testing out special effects. The only officer who believes the allegations is Larsen formerly of the KGB. He mentions a brutal criminal gang run by a shadowy figure, the Reaper, which specialises in snuff movies. If this gang is involved, he warns, Billie could be in serious danger herself. Billie goes back to her flat. While she's having a bath, the technician and the actor break down her door and demand to know where she's hidden a diskette. Larsen rescues her. They flee. He tells her the diskette contains vital information about the Reaper's operations. She eventually remembers seeing it in the studio. They head back there, as do Andy and Karen.

Larsen takes the diskette from Billie and shoots her in front of the Reaper, who is waiting outside the studio in his limousine. The Reaper drives off. Only when Billie rises to her feet do Andy and Karen realise the scene was a stunt performed with blood bags. Larsen also is about to drive away when Billie desperately beckons him to get out of the car. He does so just in time, rolling to safety as a huge bomb explodes.

Mute Witness is a virtuoso exercise in cinematic sleight of hand. Each time its Byzantine narrative seems to reveal some fresh nugget of information that will elucidate the mystery, a piece of trickery pulls the carpet from beneath viewers' feet and leaves them flailing for new clues. The games it plays with storytelling and film form may suggest a self-conscious, avantgarde approach, but Anthony Waller's debut also works as an ingenious, multi-layered thriller: a Macguffin—a diskette which looks as if it holds the key to the entire shebang but is really just another distracting plot device—is thrown in for good measure, and the often quite horrific happenings are leavened with the kind of gallows humour that Hitchcock used to love.

At first, it appears this is a straightforward slasher movie. The very first sequence shows a woman in her apartment who thinks she's alone. Little does she realise that her husband's corpse is in a bloody heap behind the door and a masked killer is coming towards her with a knife. As we fret for her to notice the murderer, she fiddles around with her lipstick and insists on looking in the wrong direction. It's only after she's been stabbed and gone through an elaborate dying swan routine in which she all but destroys the apartment that we learn it's not for real. The murderer sits down to light himself a well-earned cigarette and, gradually, make-up artists, prop people, lighting technicians, and an entire motley film crew appear from the shadows behind him. It's a brilliantly funny little opening. This film-within-a-film is a sort of shadow play of what is to follow. But Waller cheats right from the outset. The sequence, with its myriad close-ups and reaction shots, could never have been filmed by his fictional camera crew in one continuous take.

Writing about this sequence highlights a problem most reviewers are likely to face, namely that it's impossible to address the film in any detail without giving at least some part of the plot away. Every scene seems to boast its own pet revelation. Even describing the cast is problematic. The key cameo role of 'The Reaper' is played by a "Mystery Guest Star." As he's an instantly recognisable figure, keeping his identity secret is bound to be a forlorn task. Perhaps he only agreed to appear in the film uncredited, but you suspect Waller is using him as just one more piece of bait to entice audiences.

At its best, *Mute Witness* has a feverish, dream-like quality. This is exemplified in the protracted sequence in which the mute heroine, Billie Hughes, is chased down the long corridors of the film studio by a technician she presumes wants to kill her. There's one of those giddy, disorientating shots in which the camera zooms toward her while simultaneously tracking backward. Stairwells, basements, fire escapes and lift shafts are used as Billie's hiding places. As the technician draws ever closer, Waller manages to generate the same kind of awful tension that characterised the chase sequence in *Night of the Hunter*. As in that film, the audience, too, is likely to feel it is being pursued. The fact that the picture unfolds almost in real time adds to the momentum. The few scenes of relative tranquillity are themselves laced with menace. As Billie relaxes in her flat, you're always aware that something nasty this way comes.

Unsurprisingly, given that the movie was shot in Moscow with a mix of Russian, American and British actors, the dialogue is the weakest point. Sometimes interpreters are needed. Sometimes Waller provides clumsy excuses for the Russians to speak in English. But even the communication problems are in keeping with the nightmarish mood the film-maker is trying to engender. Not just Billie but every other character struggles to understand and be understood. The film's tone, like its narrative, is constantly shifting. Knockabout comedy-action (hoodlums being electrocuted in baths or shot by accident) is combined with moments of bloody, Grand Guignol-style horror. ("You never forget the look in the victims' eye when they realise they're about to die," observes one character in the aftermath of the very nasty snuff movie sequence.) As the policeman hero, Oleg Jankowskij (a Russian actor best known to western audiences for his role in Tarkovsky's *Nostalgia*) comes on like a character out of a James Bond film. Billie Hughes (Marina Sudina) at first seems a vulnerable heroine along the lines of Audrey Hepburn in *Wait Until Dark*, but then develops into a feisty, self-reliant figure.

There's no gainsaying the writer-director's cleverness or conjuring ability, but his consummate cleverness risks backfiring, if only because it is sometimes hard to work up much sympathy for characters that you know are only supposed to be ciphers. It's a tribute to the freshness of the performances that you root for them anyway. Even if *Mute Witness* is short on emotional depth, the sheer promiscuity of its references and the delight Waller takes in the medium make it an exhilarating experience all the same.

VILLAGE VOICE, 9/26/95, p. 80, Amy Taubin

A shabby-chic, English-language, made-in-Moscow horror film about an American film crew making a horror film in Moscow on the cheap, *Mute Witness* seems bound for a lucrative life on the midnight movie circuit. When I first saw it at a late-night screening at the Sundance Film Festival, I screamed in all the appropriate places and then walked alone through the dark corridors of my hotel without once looking over my shoulder. Though expertly timed and wittily reflexive, *Mute Witness* lacks the psychological resonance that could leave you feeling creepy about show-ers—or, in this case, Russian film studios—for the rest of your life.

Our hero Billy (Marina Sudina), a mute makeup and special-effects artist, witnesses the making of a snuff film when she's inadvertently locked in a labyrinthine Moscow film studio after her American colleague have departed for the evening. Although Billy's enough of an expert in fake blood to know when she's seen the real thing, no one believes that she actually saw a woman being hacked to death on camera. Nevertheless, the murderers decide they would feel more comfortable if Billy were out of the picture.

Mute Witness's high point is a bravura, nearly silent 20-minute chase scene in which a terrified but agile Billy is pursued through the hallways, elevator shafts, and garbage pits of the dilapidated film studio by the snuff film director (a Russian Liam Neeson lookalike) and his henchman. Shot and edited for maximum surprise and with an attention to spatial logic that's rare these days in Hollywood films with 15 times the budget, it's an excellent calling card for British director Anthony Waller. *Mute Witness* is Waller's first feature; he spent the previous decade making TV commercials.

Drawing on early De Palma and Michael Powell's definite *Peeping Tom*, Waller uses his limited means of production to send up the ludicrous aspects of exploitation filmmaking, especially the

Euro-pudding variety (mix 'n' match locations, wooden acting, awkward dubbing). But despite his considerable ingenuity, *Mute Witness* gets predictable down the stretch, leaving one time to meditate on the sleazier aspects of the script. (Why, I wondered, to no avail, is the hero mute?) Best not to probe for deeper meaning when the tongue-in-cheek message is staring you in the face: Sometimes filmmaking is more trouble than it's worth.

Also reviewed in:
CHICAGO TRIBUNE, 9/15/95, Friday/p. J, Johanne Steinmetz
NEW YORK TIMES, 9/15/95, p. C4, Janet Maslin
VARIETY, 2/13-19/95, p. 50, Emanuel Levy
WASHINGTON POST, 11/3/95, p. F6, Rita Kempley
WASHINGTON POST, 11/3/95, Weekend/p. 43, Desson Howe

MY FAMILY: MI FAMILIA

A New Line Cinema release of a Francis Ford Coppola presentation in association with Majestic Films and American Playhouse Theatrical Films of an American Zoetrope-Anna Thomas-Newcomm production. *Executive Producer:* Francis Ford Coppola, Guy East, Tom Luddy, Lindsay Law, and Sergio Molina. *Producer:* Anna Thomas. *Director:* Gregory Nava. *Screenplay:* Gregory Nava and Anna Thomas. *Story:* Gregory Nava. *Director of Photography:* Edward Lachman. *Editor:* Nancy Richardson. *Music:* Mark McKenzie and Pepe Avila. *Choreographer:* Miguel Delgado. *Sound:* José Araujo. *Sound Editor:* Marian Wilde. *Casting:* Janet Hirschenson, Jane Jenkins, and Roger Mussenden. *Production Designer:* Barry Robinson. *Art Director:* Troy Myers. *Set Decorator:* Suzette Sheets. *Set Dresser:* Jeff Snyder, Rochelle Seldin, Mark W. Gantt, Adam R. Pinkstaff, and Teusa Koiwai. *Costumes:* Tracy Tynan. *Make-up:* Ken Diaz and Mark Sanchez. *Stunt Coordinator:* Rick Baker. *Running time:* 120 minutes. *MPAA Rating:* R.

CAST: Jimmy Smits (Jimmy Sanchez); Edward James Olmos (Pacos); Esai Morales (Chucho); Eduardo Lopez Rojas (Jose Sanchez); Elpidia Carrillo (Isabel Magana); Jenny Gago (Maria Sanchez); Enrique Castillo (Memo "Bill" Sanchez); Rafael Cortes (Roberto); Ivette Reina (Trini); Amelia Zapata (Roberto's Girlfriend); Jacob Vargas (Young Jose); Emilio del Haro and Abel Woolrich (Ox Cart Drivers); Leon Singer (El Californio); Rosalee Mayeux (Maria's Employer); Jennifer Lopez (Young Maria); Alicia del Lago (Maria's Aunt); Thomas Rosales (Boatman); Anthony Gonzalez (Baby Paco); Cassandra Campos (Baby Irene); Michael Gonzalez (Little Paco); Susanna Camposs (Little Irene); Constance Marie (Toni); Benito Martinez (Young Paco); Greg Albert (Young Memo); Maria Canals (Young Irene); Jonathan Hernandez (Young Jimmy); Cris Franco (Young Gerardo); Michael DeLorenzo (Butch Mejia); Eddie Ayala and Valente Rodriguez (Chucho's Friends); Romeo Rene Fabian (Eddie); Bel Hernandez (Eddie's Mom); Jeannette Jurado (Rosie); Seidy Lopez (Lena, Chucho's Girlfriend); George Lopez, Jr. and Moses Saldana (Ballplayers); Brian Lally (Officer); Ernie Lively (Sergeant); Bart Johnson (Young Officer); Peter Mark Vasquez (Prison Guard); Scott Bakula (David Ronconi); Lupe Ontiveros (Irene Sanchez); Ruben Sierra (Gerardo); Mary Steenburgen (Gloria); Willie C. Carpenter (I.N.S. Guard); Delana Michaels (Judge); Pete Leal (Old Man on Balcony); Valerie Wildman (Sunny, Gloria's Friend); Michael Tomlinson (Dr. McNally); Saachiko (Nurse); Emilio Rivera (Tamalito); Paul Robert Langdon (Carlitos); Angelina Estrada (Woman with Groceries); Dedee Pfeiffer (Karen Gillespie); Bibi Besch (Mrs. Gillespie); Bruce Gray (Mr. Gillespie).

LOS ANGELES TIMES, 5/3/95, Calendar/p. 1, Kenneth Turan

Your head may insist you resist the unashamed sentimentality of "My Family," but your heart will encourage you to give in, and for once your heart will be right. Old-fashioned and proud of it, this mixture of soap opera and folk opera envelopes you in a warm hug of such heroic proportions that reasoned opposition is futile. Go ahead, indulge yourself. You earned it.

Co-titled "Mi Familia," this "Roots"-type examination of 60 years in the life of a Mexican American family in Los Angeles has been preceded by numerous attempts to deal with the culture of the barrio, but none of them has been this rich or this effective. Persuasively acted by what amounts to an all-star team of Latino actors and actresses, "My Family" is not perfect, but it does add an unexpected amount of spirit to the sentimental nostalgia that is its core attraction.

Given that "My Family" is made by Gregory Nava and Anna Thomas (he directed and she produced their co-written script), the same husband and wife team that created "El Norte" more than a decade ago, this film's pervasive rosy glow and reliance on melodrama and big emotions is not hard to predict.

What is something of a surprise is the film's effective use of self-kidding humor, and its refusal to be sanctimonious. Unafraid to flaunt its weepy elements, "My Family" also doesn't flinch from the tough times. It has an unexpected willingness to be close to astringent when it needs to, to allow its characters to experience painful passion and anger. And in Esai Morales and especially Jimmy Smits, who gives a career remaking performance, it has actors who know how to take advantage of that opportunity.

"My Family" covers so much family territory that all its main characters are played by at least two and sometimes as many as three actors. Holding it all together is the extensive voice-over of Paco, the oldest son and an aspiring writer. Edward James Olmos, who plays Paco, does not have a great deal of screen time, but it is hard to imagine this film without his soothing narration and the Godfather-like quality of his voice.

"I have to begin where millions of stories have begun before, in a small village in Mexico," says Paco. The village is in Michoacán, where, for reasons that are amusingly unclear, teen-aged José Sanchez (Jacob Vargas) departs in the mid-1920s to seek out his only living relative in "Nuestra Reina de Los Angeles," a place so impossibly far away it took him a year to get there.

Once in Los Angeles, José soon falls in love with and marries Maria (Jennifer Lopez). Their life together was not uneventful then and became even more tumultuous in the film's other two time periods, the 1950s and the 1980s (when the couple is equally well played by Eduardo Lopez Rojas, one of Mexico's most respected actors, and Jenny Gago).

The Sanchezes had six children, with each one having at least one story. There is Paco, as noted, the writer; Irene, the daughter with the serious appetite; Toni, the sister with a will of iron; and three more sons: Chucho, the rebellious pachuco; Memo, the homework-loving good son; and Jimmy, the cherished youngest child.

Since part of the pleasure of "My Family" is to be astonished by the soap opera plot twists the script never fails to come up with, it need only be said that everything from macho turf rivalries to heroic river-crossings to the always malevolent shadow of La Migra, the immigration police, gets touched on here in Nava's casually mythologizing style.

One of the reasons "My Family" is successful is that the simple concept of focusing on the real family, not the substitute gang family that many previous Latino films have latched onto, is a surprisingly effective one. And both the script and direction have taken care to give the film's characters what they themselves would consider essential: simple dignity.

Though many elements, including a sonorous music and an eye-opening pastel-themed visual scheme, help "My Family," its biggest asset is its bilingual cast, which brings so much belief to their parts that it rubs off and helps convince us these people really are a family.

This conviction also adds more dimension to the characters than is necessarily on the page. Morales is appropriately passionate as the unbending Chucho, and Smits as the smoldering, exasperated loner Jimmy finally gives the kind of movie star performance that has been expected of him for years, personally invigorating the entire second half of the film.

And among the actresses, mention should be made of newcomer Constance Marie as the surprising Toni, and especially Elpidia Carrillo; whose quiet performance as the Salvadoran immigrant Isabel is in some ways the emotional heart of the picture.

As with any film that walks this close to the edge of bathos, there are moments when "My Family" stumbles and even falls. But most viewers will prefer to focus on the parts that feel effortlessly successful, like a memorable sequence when two people are observed falling in love while dancing to the music of a car radio. For times like that, almost anything can be forgiven.

NEW YORK, 5/22/95, p. 78, David Denby

The immigrant's journey to America—the drama of arrival and immersion in the swirling native stew—is obviously one of the central American stories. For the artist, however, it's a story full of traps. The immigration theme can fall all too easily into a series of archetypal events and moods—the dangers of the journey; prejudice and poverty in the new country; economic failure followed by success. Only an artist of real delicacy can avoid triteness and didactic redundancy. Of the two new versions of the immigration story, Latino division—*My Family* and *The Perez Family*—Gregory Nava's *My Family* is pretty much a calamity. Young children might learn from it, but for anyone above the moral age of 10, it's a stupefying experience. Some years after the Mexican Revolution, a peasant heads north, arrives in Los Angeles, marries a Mexican woman of deep religious faith, and raises a large family in the East Los Angeles barrio. The movie is built almost entirely around sunlit clichés and exemplary moments, both happy and sad. Whenever the story develops a little power, Edward James Olmos, narrating in his mossy drone, tells us things that we can see for ourselves.

Nava goes right down the center; he's incapable of surprising us. He simplifies the characters—to make them more universal, no doubt—and each member of the family represents a different possibility of Mexican-American experience. The father, sweating and shrugging, is an icon of Noble Toil; the mother illustrates Simple Religious Faith; and so on. The actors hit the same square emotions over and over again. Esai Morales plays the Bad Son in such a familiar, soft-edged style that we lose interest in him before the gringos gun him down. Showing up in the middle of the movie, Jimmy Smits relieves the tedium simply by conveying grown-up intelligence. Smits, with his bulky, forbidding forehead and dark eyes, seems a force of great good or great evil—we can't tell which. He holds himself in readiness; when Elpidia Carrillo, playing his young wife, brings him to life, the movie begins to breathe. Carrillo, however, immediately dies in childbirth, another victim of white indifference. It's not that such things don't happen to poor immigrants—they do. It's that Nava hasn't found a way of making tragedy anything more than an illustration of general principles.

In the end, *My Family* has all the moral interest and spiritual excitement of a foundation-grant application. It's a paint-by-numbers epic, a movie that enrages in a way that routine commercial hackwork does not. Why? Because vanity and complacency presided at its birth, as well as indifference to the hard work of entertaining an audience. The same movie has been made before; in one form or another, it will be made again. The institutions that sponsor it, such as *American Playhouse* and Francis Ford Coppola, will not suffer any damage to their self-esteem. They can always justify the boringness as an obligation to "tell the story of the people," a claim that, in the arts, is the first and last refuge of a faker.

NEW YORK POST, 5/3/95, p. 31, Michael Medved

In the 1920's, young Jose Sanchez (Jacob Vargas) leaves his home in the mountains of Mexico to search for his only surviving relative. Traveling on foot, he looks for the village known as "Los Angeles," at first not realizing it's in another country and, for all practical purposes, another world.

Hundreds of miles and seven decades later he's made California his home, settling into a comfortable house in East L.A. supported by his hard work as a gardener, and raising six American children.

"My Family (Mi Familia)" tells the story of those children (and their children) with so much love and passion that the characters emerge as distinctly as members of your own family.

Edward James Olmos plays the oldest son, an aspiring writer who narrates the tale while Esai Morales is memorably charismatic as his tough-tender rebellious young brother. Jimmy Smits is searingly brilliant as the baby of the family—a withdrawn and suffering soul who tries to build loving relationships between prison terms.

Lesser-known performers also make indelible impressions—especially Constance Marie as an impetuous sister who leaves her life as a nun to marry an activist priest (Scott Bakula) and the magnetic Jennifer Lopez, who plays Maria, the matriarch of the family, as a young woman.

One of the movie's most spectacular sequences shows her swept up by "La Migra" (the immigration authorities) in the 1930s and deported to Mexico, but fighting overwhelming forces of nature to return to her husband and children in Los Angeles.

Director Gregory Nava (who previously created "El Norte," a stunning low-budget account of impoverished immigrants from Guatemala) paints such scenes in the heightened colors of melodrama.

The movie's evocations of the past have been captured with a burnished, golden, sunset glow, which seems appropriate for tales that have been told many times to become part of the family's (perhaps exaggerated) lore, complete with the sudden appearances of angels in clouds or white owls as supernatural messengers.

His film is also well-anchored in everyday details, especially concerning the family's sprawling house in east L.A. that changes and grows over the decades like another character in the story.

If the plot seems, at times, suggestive of soap opera in the honored tradition of "All My Children," it nonetheless delivers so many powerfully moving moments that you can forgive the manipulation.

Especially magical is a scene in which sulky Jimmy Smits, who has married a Salvadorian immigrant (the radiant Elpidia Carrillo) in order to prevent her deportation, is slowly but subtly seduced by his wife.

When she overcomes his resistance and finally persuades him to dance with her to some infectious salsa music, the pair generates enough heat to melt theater seats—not to mention the people sitting in them.

At film's end, when the aged Jose and Maria (Eduardo Lopas Rojas and Jenny Gago) sit around their table staring at the empty chairs left by the children who've moved out and are on their own, they assure one another that, despite heartbreak, their life in America has been good—in fact, very good. By the same token, despite its shortcomings and excesses, "My Family" has been very good indeed.

NEWSDAY, 5/3/95, Part II/p. B7, Gene Seymour

There's so much about "My Family (Mi Familia)" that's movie-of-the-week-sappy you wonder, as you're watching it, why you're enjoying it so much. No mystery, really. Even if it were only halfway decent, the film would swallow up our wandering attention spans because nearly all of us are suckers for heavily layered family melodrama, whether we're close to our own families or not.

"My Family" is more than just halfway decent. It is evocative, well-crafted and performed with verve and passion by a first-rate cast of Latino actors. They, along with director Gregory Nava, bring the kind of depth to the Mexican-American experience that commercial movies rarely if ever, convey.

It all starts with the very long walk young José Sanchez takes from his central Mexican village to East Los Angeles. This was in the 1920s when, as Paco (Edward James Olmos), the family griot, says, "The only border [between Mexico and the United States] was a line in the sand." José finds steady work manicuring Beverly Hills lawns. On one such lawn, he finds Maria, a pretty young housekeeper, whom he marries.

As the Great Depression takes hold, José and Maria struggle to keep food on the table for their two young children. While pregnant with her third, Maria, though a U. S. citizen, is caught up in an immigration sweep, loaded into a railroad car and sent back to the Mexican highlands. Cut off from the rest of her family, Maria takes her newborn son, Chucho, with her back to the States, despite their near-fatal encounter with a torrential river along the way.

The film moves to the late 1950s where Chucho (Esai Morales from "La Bamba") has grown into a charismatic and volatile young man who's become part of a street culture as full of peril as the river that almost drowned him. A rift develops between José (Eduardo Lopez Rojas) and Chucho that serves as a grim prelude to the tragedy that follows.

The legacy of that tragedy is borne most acutely by younger son Jimmy (Jimmy Smits), who, by the early 1980s, is even more of an accident waiting to happen than Chucho was. Older sister Toni (Constance Marie), an ex-nun-turned-activist, extracts Jimmy's reluctant willingness to marry a Salvadoran woman (Elpidia Carrillo) in danger of deportation. Eventually, they fall in love and she gets pregnant. But as is often the case in this tale, "happily ever after" is out of reach.

Nava, who wrote the screenplay with his wife, producer Anna Thomas, seasons this generational epic with quasi-mystical imagery, voluptuous colors and a delicate feel for period detail. Even when the story goes over the top, its rich design and fine performances keep you engrossed.

Many of the lesser-known actors, like Rojas and Carrillo, are revelations. You wish there were more of the redoubtable Olmos, but what little there is is surprisingly frisky. You also wish Morales could find roles that don't require as much smoldering. He's very good at it, but when you watch his Chucho leading little kids in an impromptu mambo lesson, you sense a graceful comedian inside Morales yearning to bust through the Angry Young Man.

Of Smits' performance, it's enough to say that the producers of "NYPD Blue," having weathered the loss of David Caruso, may need to worry again about sacrificing their leading man to the movies. OK, so his face becomes a teary sponge once too often. The rest of the time, he's as enigmatic and compelling as Bobby Simone—and just a little scarier.

SIGHT AND SOUND, 10/95, p. 53, Lucy O'Brien

In the early 1920s teenager Jose Sanchez leaves his remote village in Mexico in search of his last living relative, an old man in far-away Los Angeles. After a long journey on foot Sanchez reaches the city, finds the cantankarous El Californio, one of the original California settlers, and stays. While working as a gardener in Beverly Hills he meets his future wife, a housekeeper named Maria. By the 30s they are happily married with two children, but when pregnant with her third, Maria is picked up during an anti-immigration sweep and deported to Mexico. It is two years before she makes the dangerous journey back with her baby son, and the family are reunited.

In the 50s, Chucho has grown up to become a rebellious young man, caught between American cultural values and his Mexican heritage. After his sister's wedding, Chucho becomes involved in a dance hall fight and accidentally kills a man. Hunted down by the police, he is shot dead in front of his younger brother Jimmy. By the 80s Jimmy emerges as a withdrawn and troubled soul, fresh out of jail for armed robbery. Through the intervention of his social activist sister Toni, he becomes the reluctant partner in an arranged marriage to keep a young immigrant woman, Isabel, from deportation. They eventually fall in love, but when Isabel dies during childbirth an enraged Jimmy estranges himself from his son, Carlitos. After time in prison, he returns for a reconciliation with his five-year-old boy. Carlitos continually rejects him until Jimmy decides despairingly that he has to leave. It is at this point that his son accepts him, and the two are able to cement their relationship.

Gregory Nava, the director of *El Norte*, originally envisaged this epic Latino family saga as full of "colour and life like a novel by Márquez". While the photography is stunning—conveying warm, honey-coloured light in the opening village scenes, the vibrancy of the 50s wedding, the gritty heat of 80s streets—there is little of the seductive surrealism that marks out say, Alphonso Arau's *Like Water for Chocolate*. Nava's only nods towards Magic Realism are when the young Sanchez gazes up at a shiny cloud with his new bride and finds an angel, and a large owl that appears every so often as an inconvenient omen of death.

Spanning three generations, the story is a simple study of the squishy heart of 'La Familia', narrated in a Mexican John Boy Walton style by the eldest living son Paco, an aspiring writer played by Edward James Olmos. Although three decades are covered—the 20s, 50s and 80s—there is little sense of the complexities of American immigrant experience. The first period, for instance, which begins with subtitles, charts with a mawkish sincerity Sanchez's slow struggle for his family's survival in the new Los Angeles.

There is a bewildering change of pace when the film leaps into the 50s and a full-blown Mexican-American wedding. Again, it is beautifully shot, with memorable images such as a long line of sparkling Chevys. But the characters lapse into parody: there is Esai Morales' hot youngblood Chucho, facing up to the leader of a local gang with his knives and "macho bullshit"; Eduardo Lopez Rojas' sentimental patriarch, gathering the *familia* together for a group photograph and suppressing a sob of pride, and Constance Marie's Toni, the typically fiery Chicano daughter who bursts into tears when she catches the bride's bouquet. "Whatever's the matter?" asks her long-suffering mother. "I will never marry," she says amid the mayhem. She is going to be a nun. "She will be marrying Jesus!", cries mother Maria victoriously.

Soon after the family celebrate Toni's entry into the sisterhood, her brother Chucho battles it out on the dance floor, *West Side Story*-style. His violent death at the hands of trigger-happy Los

Angeles police could have been used to underscore the tensions that destabilised the Latino community, but instead it is explained away as the revenge of the barn owl, the evil spirit who nearly claimed him as a baby.

When the film moves into the 80s, the mood changes again with the overlay of slightly more sophisticated political grit. By now Toni has left the holy order to marry an ex-priest and become a somewhat implausible social activist, urging her younger brother Jimmy (played by Jimmy Smits of *NYPD Blue* and *LA Law* fame) to "use the system to fuck the system." With his deftly-cut sideburns and burning biceps Smits is easy on the eye but wooden in performance. The pace flags as first Toni and then his determined young wife (gushingly over-played by Elpidia Carrillo) try to break his impenetrable lone wolf pose.

It's not until the final scenes that the drama begins to bite, first with a comic edge when successful lawyer brother Memo brings his WASP fiancee and her parents home—a wonderfully observed cultural clash between the two families. There is also soulful pathos in the way Jimmy finally wins over his estranged son, the conflict between them slipping beyond stereotype into a heart-wrenching exploration of love, loss and trust. These moments, however, are not enough to give this film the substance it badly needs. While Jimmy is glibly written off by the narrator as "the family fuck-up who carried the shit for the rest of us," Ma and Pa sit at the kitchen table reflecting on their lives in a manner reminiscent of a coffee commercial. *The Godfather* this ain't.

VILLAGE VOICE, 5/16/95, p. 6, Ed Morales

[*My Family* was reviewed jointly with *The Perez Family*; see Morales' review of that film.]

Also reviewed in:
CHICAGO TRIBUNE, 5/3/95, Tempo/p. 24, Michael Wilmington
NEW YORK TIMES, 5/3/95, p. C18, Caryn James
VARIETY, 2/6-12/95, p. 74, Todd McCarthy
WASHINGTON POST, 5/5/95, p. B15, Rita Kempley

MY LIFE AND TIMES WITH ANTONIN ARTAUD

A Leisure Time Features release of an Archipel 33/Laura Productions/La Sept/France 2 production with the participation of Centre National de la Cinématographie/Centre National des Lettres/La Maison des Écrivains/Ministère de la Culture et de la Francophonie/La Sacem—Société des auteurs compositeurs et editeurs de musique/Conseil Régional de Haute-Normandie/Conseil Général du Val de Marne/13 Production/Conseil Général des Bouches du Rhône. *Executive Producer:* Denis Freyd. *Director:* Gérard Mordillat. *Screenplay (French with English subtitles):* Gérard Mordillat and Jérôme Prieur. *Based on the diaries by:* Jacques Prevel. *Director of Photography:* François Catonné. *Editor:* Sophie Rouffio. *Music:* Jean-Claude Petit. *Sound:* Pierre Lorrain and Dominique Dalmasso. *Art Director:* Jean-Pierre Clech. *Set Decorator:* Martine Faure. *Special Effects:* Geroges Demetrau, Olivier Zemenski, and Grégoire Delage. *Costumes:* Caroline de Vivaise. *Make-up:* Maud Baron and Kathia Fontaine. *Running time:* 93 minutes. *MPAA Rating:* Not Rated.

CAST: Antonin Artuad (Sami Frey); Marc Barbé (Jacques Prevel); Julie Jézéquel (Jany); Valérie Jeannet (Rolande Prevel); Clotilde de Bayser (Marthe); Charlotte Valandrey (Colette).

LOS ANGELES TIMES, 1/26/96, Calendar/p. 14, Kevin Thomas

Antonin Artaud is most widely known today for his intense portrayal in Carl Dreyer's "Passion of Joan of Arc" as the handsome young priest, the only cleric sympathetic to the Maid of Orleans and her martyrdom.

He was also a poet and theoretician, lamenting the loss of spirituality in modern life. He founded his influential Theater of Cruelty with the belief that what was presented on the stage ought to have real-life consequences. By the late '30s, however, Artaud (1896-1948) was committed to a mental institution.

Gerard Mordillat's bleak but compelling "My Life and Times With Antonin Artaud" concentrates on the final two years of his life after he gained his freedom in 1946 from a large asylum not far from Paris. Mordillat and co-writer Jerome Prieur have based the film on the diaries of Jacques Prevel, a struggling poet who had sent Artaud some of his work, received an encouraging return letter and sought him out, once Artaud could venture into Paris again.

Specifically, Prevel (Marc Barbe) wanted Artaud's permission to use the letter, as an introduction to a collection of his poetry and hoped that Artaud (Sami Frey), who swiftly denied his request, would become his mentor; what he did instead was to turn Prevel into his supplier of large quantities of opium and laudanum.

Yet Mordillat, in the developing connection between the two men, discovered a rich opportunity to consider the nature of friendship in such depth and complexity that we can recognize ourselves in these two men, both of whom would seem so different from most of us.

In a great portrayal, Frey—who bears a certain resemblance to Artaud—creates a ravaged-looking yet still dynamic Artaud steeped in paranoia and flights of megalomania and delusion. "I've survived my own death," he remarks wryly. His Artaud can be crazed, savage and yet, in quieter moments, kind, gentle and concerned for others. He's a resilient artist who has learned to fuel his art with his myriad demons; for him self-destruction has become an art form.

By contrast Prevel, on the verge of tuberculosis, apparently has received virtually no recognition, does a lot of Left Bank hanging out and spends most of his time with his waif-like mistress Jany (Julie Jezequel, who recalls Edie Sedgwick with her shock of blond hair and sad eyes), leaving his pregnant wife, Rolande (Valerie Jeannet), to cope for herself—and to do his laundry. Whatever the sources of Prevel's income may be, they are slender. Barbe manages to engage us in the fate of a not particularly sympathetic man.

Those who have had the experience of being close to an artistic genius will recognize that familiar sense of isolation Artaud experiences, even in the midst of acolytes, and the challenge such a remarkable individual has in dealing with us lesser mortals.

How honest can the great man of vision be with the work and accomplishments of his inferiors? Artaud is notably cagey in rendering opinions of Prevel's poetry when the younger man seeks them out. Yet even living legends need companionship, and Prevel's reward for living in reflected glory was the opportunity to make a record of Artaud's final years (which were far more productive than the film suggests).

Shooting in a harsh black and white, Mordillat evokes the humorless Existentialist atmosphere of the Left Bank in postwar Paris.

NEW STATESMAN & SOCIETY, 5/24/96, p. 35, Jonathan Romney

Cinema seems by nature more inclined to hagiography than iconoclasm; it is the way it leaves you sitting in the dark gazing up silently at other people's luminous presence. In the theatre you always have the option of walking out, as indecorously as you fancy.

The theatrical career of Antonin Artaud, both as theorist and producer, was one long provocation to enraged mass walkouts; the inventor of the Theatre of Cruelty would rather have seen an audience succumb to bubonic seizures of pain and passion than have them queue for autographs after the show. All the stranger then to see a film that pays such polite homage as *My Life and Times With Antonin Artaud,* based on a memoir by the poet Jacques Prevel. Its French title is *En Compagnie d'Antonin Artaud;* a better translation might have been *Hanging Out With Antonin Artaud.* That is all Prevel does: hang on the great man's coat-tails in the hope that some glory will rub off.

This belongs to the school of apprenticeship films in which we gaze on a luminary through the eyes of a devoted, long-suffering tyro who at last emerges spiritually enlarged. It most resembles Bertrand Tavernier's *Round Midnight,* in which a Paris jazz buff adopts an ailing sax-player as mentor and co-dependent. There is the same marvelling at the sheer authoritative anarchy that such figures supposedly exude, and uncritical belief that to frequent one for long enough will revolutionise your own life.

The only film I know that at once celebrates and successfully ironises such a relationship is *Ed Wood,* where the flamboyantly inept subject sat at the feet of Bela Lugosi, a legend no less absurd than himself. Affectionate but hardly reverent, Tim Burton's film let us revel in the fallibilities of icon and acolyte alike.

Antonin Artaud is directed by Gerard Mordillat, who seems as obsessed with his subject as Prevel was; he has already made two documentaries about Artaud and Prevel, this fictionalised account being a spin-off from his research. It is set in 1946, when Artaud was on his uppers and soon to die. Released from the Rodez asylum, he came to Paris and was paid assiduous court by Prevel who, according to the film, supplied his laudanum.

If you didn't know why Artaud was important, this film would leave you none the wiser. It doesn't claim to be a biography but, for all the specific references, Artaud comes across as simply that shadowy figure, the pain-stricken genius. He is too glamorous: the saturnine Sami Frey still has the looks of the *nouvelle vague* heart-throb, whereas in two decades, Artaud had gone from the very figure of angelic intensity to looking like Max Wall on a rough day.

The period looks wrong, too, despite the elegantly stark black-and-white photography. This 1946 looks more like the late 1950s, largely because of the doomed-hipster appearance of Marc Barbe's Prevel, all cheekbones and cowlick. There is also the odd giveaway glimpse of distinctly 1990s graffiti.

Mordillat might have done better to ditch the period effect altogether and instead cultivate a flagrantly artificial world that would have been more in keeping with Artaud's dramatic theory (he once prescribed the use of "puppets 30 foot high, representing King Lear's beard in the storm"). At only three moments does Mordillat seem consciously to be making cinema: a slow motion funeral; a silent theatre recitation in which the actress and audience are lit by intense flashes; and Artaud's first appearance, wandering half-glimpsed through crowds at a station.

Frey's Artaud is effective because he has a clipped sense of measure, even when ranting; his shrieks and bellows sound as though they might be the rigorous language of breath and muscle that Artaud imagined, and he expounds his paranoid theories with the monotone distraction of a doctor filling out a prescription. But the film really belongs to Prevel and his ego. Behaving wretchedly towards his girlfriend and wife, he is as abject as film heroes come, even by *poète maudit* standards; but all seems justifiable in terms of his destiny as Artaud's attendant.

The film hints at some anatomy of obsessional fan worship, but overall it settles for a mystificatory celebration of stormy charisma. It is not a film that would remotely have interested Artaud, a passionate Marx Brothers fan; *Ed Wood* might have been more up his street.

NEW YORK POST, 7/19/95, p. 35, Larry Worth

When it comes to madness, King George had nothing on Antonin Artaud. And when it comes to acting, the brilliant Nigel Hawthorne has nothing on lesser-known Sami Frey, as demonstrated in "My Life and Times With Antonin Artaud."

Frey's portrait of the frenzied Artaud—a real-life French poet/actor/theater impresario—is such a fascinating, scaring exploration of genius on the verge of insanity that he's almost frightening to watch.

As given life by Frey—complete with ravaged face, fingertip-raked hair and smoke curling up from an omnipresent cigarette—Artaud is alternately laid-back and volatile, like a live wire whose sputters erupt into luminous sparks.

Taking place in Paris of 1946, the screenplay covers the final years of Artaud's life, shortly after winning his freedom from a mental asylum. Ensconcing himself in the City of Light's cafe society, Artaud befriends Jacques Prevel, a young poet doomed to pen mediocre sonnets.

Basking in Artaud's shadow makes Prevel block out the relationship's real *raison d'etre*: Artaud convinces Prevel to get him the desperately needed drugs to which he's now addicted.

The tale, which is told from Prevel's perspective, also covers the young man's juggling of his pathetic mistress with his justifiably sullen bride and their newborn child.

Though there's clearly no shortage of story, director Gerard Mordillat concentrates on the wild array of characters and the legendary ambience of St. Germain-des-Pres in the '40s, photographed in appropriately grainy black-and-white.

Unfortunately, Mordillat's penchant for details (like the wall-to-wall clutter of Artaud's garret) or emphasis on squalor and desperation (honed by the soundtrack's wailing harmonica) overpowers the narrative. Further, those unfamiliar with Artaud's eclectic career will be at a disadvantage since much is erroneously taken for granted.

That's where Frey's mesmerizing performance comes in, easily compensating for lapses with one gimlet-eyed glance. In addition, Marc Barbe nicely holds his own as the eager-to-please protege while Valerie Jeannet's frustrated spouse and Julie Jezequel's turn as Jacques' hopeless lover are fine supports.

Granted, "My Life and Times With Antonin Artaud" will never be mistaken for breezy summer entertainment. Instead, it challenges audiences right through the final riveting image. And, with the likes of "Nine Months" at the box office, that's a refreshing change indeed.

SIGHT AND SOUND, 6/96, p. 48, Geoffrey Macnab

Paris, 1946. Struggling young poet, Jacques Prevel, learns that the celebrated writer and actor, Antonin Artaud, is shortly to be released from the mental asylum where he has spent the last nine years. The two are introduced in a cafe. Although Artaud acknowledges he received Prevel's letter and poetry in the prison, he is brusque and offhand with the younger man. Prevel comes away from the encounter bitterly disappointed.

Not long afterward, Prevel is summoned. Artaud needs laudanum and sends Prevel to buy it for him. An unlikely friendship springs up between the two men. They spend time sitting in cafes and walking the streets of Paris. Artaud is introduced to Prevel's wife, Rolande, and his mistress, Jany. Despite Artaud's encouragement, Prevel still can't get his poetry published. A publisher tells him that his work is impressive in some respects, but also seems lazy and incomplete.

Artaud's health is failing, and Prevel himself is growing increasingly sickly. One night, while in bed with Jany, Prevel suffers a violent fit during which he coughs up blood. Jany fetches Rolande and together the two women rush him to hospital. While he convalesces, Artaud comes to visit him. This is one of their last meetings. Ravaged by cancer and drugs, Artaud soon dies. Prevel is left to reflect on his brief friendship with the great man.

The laid-back jazz soundtrack, sleek black and white photography and post-war setting in *My Life and Times with Antonin Artaud* come as a surprise. Artaud, after all, was no dapper Left Bank man-about-town. Whether expounding outlandish theories on the links between theatre and the plague, shrieking out his poetry on the radio, writing manifestos and surrealist screenplays, or glowering at the camera in febrile, hollow-eyed fashion for Abel Gance and Carl Dreyer, his persona was always that of the anguished, visionary madman.

Gérard Mordillat's film, based on a memoir by writer Jacques Prevel, unfolds in the last two years of Artaud's life, between his release from a mental asylum in 1946 and his death in 1948. Initially, there's a sense that he is already a spent force; a relic from a bygone era. "He looks like my father just before he died," Prevel (Marc Barbe) observes to his mistress after meeting Artaud for the first time, a neat irony considering that Prevel himself is a consumptive wreck. In real life, Artaud's teeth had fallen out as a result of all the electric shock treatment he received in the asylum; he was riddled with cancer and hopelessly addicted to drugs. Actor Sami Frey can only hint at this level of physical dilapidation. He is charismatic and imposing, but at times his Artaud seems more *boulevardier* than tortured artist. Even when he speaks about "sickness as strength," and inveighs against healthy, bourgeois society, his robust appearance belies his words.

Not that his suffering is entirely downplayed. In the centre of his nursing-home room, there is a large block of wood which he attacks with a hammer in moments of frustration. He talks frequently in a frenzied way of how he is being assaulted by malevolent spirits. "Every time a man and a woman have sex," he tells Prevel, "it deprives me." A fly, he informs the young poet, is "an evil thought from someone far away." Perhaps perversely, these final years of Artaud's life were among his most productive. Whatever his mental or physical state, he never lost his formidable work ethic. Throughout the film, Mordillat shows him drawing, writing, reciting, and thereby exposes the paradox inherent in the myth of the mad artist—Artaud is at once chaotic and disciplined.

One of Artaud's last published essays, "Suicide Of Society", was on Van Gogh, a painter with whom he clearly felt a close affinity. Given their resemblance, one might have expected Mordillat to follow the path of Minnelli's *Lust For Life* (1956) and make this an overwrought, expressionistic biopic in which the film-making is as stylised as the subject matter. There are occasional flourishes, notably the delirious sequence at the railway station, when Artaud is due to arrive back in Paris, and the surreal funeral procession which rounds off the film. Generally, though, Mordillat's approach is cool and restrained. François Cantonne's camera work depicts Parisian street and cafe life in a crisp, observatorial style reminiscent of Magnum Agency photographers.

Artaud is always seen obliquely, through Prevel's eyes. The movie is as much about the younger writer as it is about Artaud himself. Prevel is a dedicated disciple. He rushes hither and thither from chemist to chemist to procure laudanum for his new mentor. The two take bracing walks on the city streets. They sit in smoke-filled cafes, discussing poetry and philosophy, but never anything trivial.

With two such self-indulgent central characters and a largely incident-free storyline, matters might have been expected to drift along nowhere in particular. Instead, as the unlikely friendship between the artist and his acolyte blossoms, this develops into a macabre, gently comic, buddy movie, albeit one with a high-art gloss. For a tortured madman, Artaud is a surprisingly humorous figure. His words, Prevel says at one point, are "like bombs". He certainly comes up with some choice one-liners. Whether serving disgusting meals for Prevel and his wife, having his daily shave or being helped over the wall and back into his asylum late at night by police officers when he loses his keys, he has a large measure of the clown about him. (Not for nothing did he call himself "Le Momo"—the fool.) Prevel, too, is an endearingly quixotic figure, struggling with his never-to-be-published poems, emulating Artaud, even at the cost of his own health.

Mordillat seems somewhat obsessed by his subjects. As well as this dramatisation of their relationship, he has also made two documentaries about them, *La Véritable Histoire d'Artaud le Mômo* and *Jacques Prevel, de colère et de haine*. Here, though, their identities don't necessarily matter. Even without their name tags attached, *My Life and Times with Antonin Artaud* would still work as a dark comedy about friendship and literary obsession.

VILLAGE VOICE, 7/25/95, p. 58, Leslie Camhi

Some people's destiny is to stand by the side of genius, its burning incandescence reflected in their own lesser light. *My Life and Times With Antonin Artaud* is based on the diaries of Jacques Prevel, a French poet who lingered in obscurity. In moody black and white, the film evokes the Paris of 1946, full of smoky jazz clubs and petty bohemians Antonin Artaud—poet, essayist, artist, addict, theatrical presence, mad surrealist—returns from nine years internment in an insane asylum. At 50, he's a furious virtuoso and a haggard ruin. Jacques Prevel is a young poet anxious for attention, Artaud becomes his mentor; in return, Prevel supplies him with laudanum and opium, the bread and butter of his existential anguish.

Prevel shuffles back and forth between his beautiful, pregnant wife and his tawdry mistress, a peroxide blond living in a squalid hotel. Artaud is attached to both an arty brunette and a blond actress whom he tortures during extended rehearsals. While the men create, the women whine, rage, and sniffle. From such unpromising circumstances, a strangely delicate and moving film about art and friendship is born.

As the elder poet, French actor Sami Frey is brilliant, alternating pitiful, childish helplessness with wild aesthetic majesty. Overwhelmingly empathetic and narcissistic, his Artaud suffers from true grandeur as well as its delusions. His face, a mobile wreck as fascinating as Artaud's late self-portraits, acquires a grotesque splendor. Marc Barbé's Prevel is tubercular and soulful. Above all, this film is haunted by Artaud's unearthly language—dispatches from the brink of madness—that Prevel had the good sense to scribble down for posterity.

Also reviewed in:
CHICAGO TRIBUNE, 2/16/96, Friday/p. M, John Petrakis
NEW REPUBLIC, 8/7/95, p. 28, Stanley Kauffmann
NEW YORK TIMES, 7/19/95, p. C10, Stephen Holden
VARIETY, 10/10-16/94, p. 85, Emanuel Levy
WASHINGTON POST, 10/13/95, p. F6, Hal Hinson

MYSTERY OF RAMPO, THE

A Samuel Goldwyn Company and Team Okuyama release of a Shochiku/Rampo Project production. *Executive Producer:* Kazuyoshi Okuyama. *Producer:* Yoshihisa Nakagawa. *Director:* Kazuyoshi Okuyama. *Screenplay (Japanese with English subtitles):* Kazuyoshi Okuyama and Yuhei Enoki. *Story:* Rampo Edogawa. *Director of Photography:* Yasushi Sasakibara. *Editor:* Akimasa Kawashima. *Music:* Akira Senju. *Music Editor:* Narushito Imaizumi. *Sound:* Kenichi Benitani and (music) Tomoyoshi Ezaki. *Production Designer:* Kyoko Heya. *Art Director:* Kyoko Heya. *Set Decorator:* Masahiro Furuya. *Special Effects:* Michihisa Miyashige and Atsuki Sato. *Costumes:* Sachico Ito. *Running time:* 103 minutes. *MPAA Rating:* Not Rated.

CAST: Naoto Takenaka (Edogawa Rampo); Michiko Hada (Shizuko/The Mystery Woman); Masahiro Motoki (Kogoro Akechi, Private Eye); Mikijiro Hira (Marquis Ogawara); Teruyuki Kagawa (Masashi Yokomizo).

LOS ANGELES TIMES, 5/19/95, Calendar/p. 16, Kevin Thomas

Kazuyoshi Okuyama's "The Mystery of Rampo" is a supremely elegant and sensuous romantic fantasy that imagines prolific mystery writer Edogawa Rampo (1894-1965) becoming involved in one of his own stories.

A box-office champ in Japan, it fittingly marks the centennial of Shochiku Co. Ltd., proprietor of the renowned Grand Kabuki and one of the oldest, most distinguished film studios in the world. "Rampo" has much of the swirling style, lush decor and costumes and extravagant emotions of "Farinelli."

Everything about the film is bravura, including Akira Senju's heady, mood-setting score with its mournful waltz theme. After an opening montage of prewar newsreels, we meet briefly Edogawa Rampo (Naoto Takenaka)—his name is a phonetic homage to his hero Edgar Allan Poe—just before his latest novel unfolds for us in a quaint animated sequence.

A seemingly demure housewife finds her semi-invalid husband inside her hope chest while she's playing a game of hide-and-seek with their children—and instead of helping him out, locks him in to suffocate death.

Japan is at the brink of World War II, and the government censor not surprisingly bans this novel, which is hardly in the militaristic spirit of the times. Rampo then reluctantly attends the reception for a movie based on one of his novels at the magnificent Art Deco-style Hotel New Grand. Fleeing the crowds, he experiences the apparition of a beautiful woman in black in a deserted reception area of the hotel.

Life then begins to imitate art as he learns of a woman believed to have deliberately suffocated her husband in the same way his heroine did. Rampo soon seeks out this woman (Michiko Hada, the gorgeous "face" for Shiseido Cosmetics)—and she looks exactly like the woman in black.

Rather than deal with the real-life woman, who may or may not be guilty of murder, Rampo imagines her becoming the woman in black, the mistress of an extravagantly decadent marquis (Mikijiro Hira) who lives in an immense Beaux Arts palace perched on a cliff overlooking a suitably stormy sea. The beauty longs for escape; Rampo has his handsome perennial hero, private detective Kogoro Akechi (Masahiro Motoki), attempt her rescue.

At times darkly humorous and boldly Freudian in its symbolism, "Rampo" is implicitly a comment on a society careening toward chaos, but on a more personal level is unsettlingly expressive of a man's fear of a woman whose purported drastic behavior could be an extreme response to her frustrated craving for love and support.

Everything about the film is impeccable, from its perfectly modulated performances to its glorious cinematography (by Yasushi Sasakibara) to the smallest prop.

Amazingly, veteran producer/co-writer Okuyama took over the directorial reins from Rintaro Mayuzumi and proceeded, in his directorial debut, to guide some 60% of the film—amazing because "The Mystery of Rampo" is such a risky, ambitious undertaking and yet seems all of a piece.

NEW YORK POST, 6/2/95, p. 50, Thelma Adams

In Kazuyoshi Okuyama's "the Mystery of Rampo." Rampo is Edogawa Rampo, the famed Japanese mystery writer whose pen name is the Japanese pronunciation of Edgar Allen Poe. Not since "Naked Lunch" has a movie nailed the hallucinatory relationship between a fiction writer and his subject, between the world of imagination he creates and the reality he distorts.

Rampo (Naoto Takenaka) pens a story about a woman who kills her invalid husband. He has crawled into her hope chest in a failed game of hide and seek with local urchins. She discovers him later that day, half-dead. Instead of freeing him, she shuts the lid. The story unfolds in exquisite animation—the wife's delicate figure flaming into a demon as she smothers her spouse, the distant call and response of kids playing hide and seek.

What passes for reality intrudes; live actors return. Rampo's publisher, Masahi Yokomizo (Teruyuki Kagawa) produces a newspaper clipping. A woman named Shizuko (Michiko Hada) has allegedly committed an identical crime. But, since the government has censored the story, how could Shizuko have read it?

Rampo investigates. He discovers that Shizuko resembles his imaginary murderess. Shizuko appeals to Rampo for aid. He shuns the physical comfort she seeks, but returns to his desk to write his heroine out of her current predicament.

In this new manuscript Rampo conjures up his alter-ego, Akechi (Masahiro Motoki), to head the inquiry. The dashing Akechi finds the widow co-habiting with a perverse marquis. The movie takes a tense erotic turn. Rampo realizes his love for this woman as he watches through Akechi's eyes as the marquis physically humiliates Shizuko.

Akechi, the marquis and their object of desire refract off the author. "I like to control people," says the marquis. Isn't that also true for the mystery writer who creates a mirror world where he is all-powerful?

Shizuko tells Rampo "you mean everything to me." She describes a character's dependence on her author as well as romantic feeling. There's a reciprocal truth here: An author falls for his creations and they can bleed into his real life.

"The Mystery of Rampo" reveals itself in unforgettable images. As the handsome Akechi enters a room, his reflection in a mirror is that of Rampo, the bald man in the gray flannel kimono.

NEWSDAY, 6/2/95, Part II/p. B7, Gene Seymour

"The Mystery of Rampo" is so rich and luscious that you don't want to watch it so much as bite into it. Slowly. Few films anywhere provide the mental gymnastics and sensual intoxication of this Japanese-made speculative fantasy drawn from the life and work of Edogawa Rampo (1894-1965), who wrote detective stories in the classic tradition of Arthur Conan Doyle, G.K. Chesterton and Edgar Allan Poe, from whose name Rampo phonetically derived his own *nom de plume*.

Set in the 1930s, when Japanese militarism was at its ominous, pre-World War II peak, the movie begins with an enchanting animated sequence depicting the plot of a Rampo novel. It's about a provincial housewife who finds her semi-invalid husband accidentally locked inside her hope chest, where he was playing hide-and-seek with their children. Instead of letting him out, she locks the trunk again, sealing his death. Despite Rampo's popularity, this tale is censored by the government because of the heroine's immoral character.

Rampo (Naoto Takenaka) takes his melancholy mood to a party celebrating a movie version of one of his previous books. As he leaves, he follows what he believes to be a beautiful woman dressed in black widow's weeds. She vanishes so quickly that he believes her to be an apparition. Imagine the writer's astonishment when he finds a newspaper article suggesting that this same woman (Michiko Hada) may have killed her husband in the same way that the heroine of his censored story killed hers.

Thus begins the kind of elegant, bewildering tango of illusion and reality that author Jorge Luis Borges, another fan of the classic tale of detection, loved to compose. Rampo seeks out the woman, with whom he feels a vague but powerful kinship. But it seems he can only engage his feelings by imagining the fate of his censored heroine.

So a new tale begins, in which the widowed housewife becomes the beautiful, doom-haunted mistress of a decadent marquis (Mikijiro Hira) living in a huge mansion on a cliff above a rocky shore. Into this scene of gothic depravity parachutes detective Kogoro Akechi (Masahiro Motoki), Rampo's perennial hero and "alter-ego," who tries to save her from the marquis' creepy clutches.

Rampo is supposedly writing this story. But the visual red herrings scattered throughout make both him and us wonder whether the story's writing him. Much like David Cronenberg's "Naked Lunch," this isn't a film about a writer so much as about the agonizing, difficult, oddly triumphant process of writing itself and how the imagination copes with limitations—whether they're imposed by the government or the self.

Director Kazuyoshi Okuyama's film literally bursts at the seams with harrowing jolts worthy of David Lynch. (An overworked comparison, I know. Trust me. Here it applies.) Much like Lynch, Okuyama gets carried away by his own audacity often enough toward the end that the movie almost ceases to be interesting or fun. But such excesses are easily overcome by the bold cinematography of Yasushi Sasakibara, the sumptuous production design of Kyoko Heya and the haunting score of Akira Senju.

VILLAGE VOICE, 6/6/95, p. 58, Christian Finnegan

Japanese mystery writer Edogawa Rampo once said, "Life is but an illusion, the dreams of a night are real." It is fitting, then, that the movie that bears his name should so closely resemble a nightmare—confusing, disorienting, yet disarmingly resonant.

Using actual persons and events as a springboard, Japan's *The Mystery of Rampo* soon catapults into the supernatural, culminating in an actual confrontation between Rampo and his fictional characters. The plot revolves around a woman who is accused of killing her husband in the exact manner that Rampo has described in a short story. He soon becomes obsessed with this living, breathing version of his imagined heroine until the wall separating fantasy and reality collapses in on him.

Despite being based on the life of a writer, *Rampo* is an overwhelmingly visual affair. Director Kazuyoshi Okuyama's kitchen-sink approach utilizes everything from animation to Artaudian montage sequences. And while its unabashed artiness sometimes feels self-conscious and arbitrary, the film is redeemed by the extreme vividness of the images Okuyama conjures up; he gives himself an impressive backdrop to play against, setting *Rampo* against the splendor of pre-WW II rural Japan. But perhaps most affecting is Akira Senju's score, so rich and textured that it makes even mundane moments seem riveting.

The Mystery of Rampo is not without its faults—though all of the performances are fine, the actors sometimes seem like window dressing. Also, the plot asks you to take enormous leaps of faith, and even then you feel like you've missed a couple of scenes by the time the credits roll. But as difficult as it is to buy into the world of *Rampo*, the payoff is worth it.

Also reviewed in:
CHICAGO TRIBUNE, 9/15/95, Friday/p. K, Michael Wilmington
NEW YORK TIMES, 6/2/95, p. C12, Stephen Holden
VARIETY, 5/23-29/94, p. 58, David Stratton
WASHINGTON POST, 6/2/95, p. D6, Hal Hinson

NADJA

An October Films release of a Kino Link production. *Executive Producer:* David Lynch. *Producer:* Mary Sweeney. *Director:* Michael Almereyda. *Screenplay:* Michael Almereyda. *Director of Photography:* Jim DeNault. *Editor:* David Leonard. *Music:* Simon Fisher Turner. *Sound:* William Kozy. *Casting:* Billy Hopkins, Suzanne Smith, and Kerry Barden. *Production Designer:* Kurt Ossenfort. *Set Dresser:* Joan Lucke, Jr. *Special Effects:* Arthur Jolly. *Costumes:* Prudence Moriarty. *Make-up:* Dina Doll. *Stunt Coordinator:* Arthur Jolly. *Running time:* 92 minutes. *MPAA Rating:* R.

CAST: Suzy Amis (Cassandra); Galaxy Craze (Lucy); Martin Donovan (Jim); Peter Fonda (Dr. Van Helsing/Dracula); Karl Geary(Renfield); Jared Harris (Edgar); Elina Löwensohn (Nadja); David Lynch (Morgue Attendant); Nic Ratner (Bar Victim); Jack Lotz (Boxing Coach); Isabel Gillies (Waitress); Jose Zunga (Bartender); Bernadette Jurkowski (Dracula's Bride); Jeff Winner (Young Dracula); Sean (Bela); Bob Gosse and Rome Neal (Garage Mechanics); Giancarlo Roma (Romanian Kid); Anna Roma (Romanian Mother); Thomas Roma and Aleksander Rasic (Romanian Policemen); Miranda Russell (Lucy's Baby).

LOS ANGELES TIMES, 9/1/95, Calendar/p. 1, Kevin Thomas

In the title role of Michael Almereyda's "Nadja," an elegant, witty but also sometimes tedious spin on the legend of Dracula, Elina Lowensohn is a black-caped beauty with a bold Frida Kahlo face. A rich, restless denizen of Manhattan's night life, she admits that it's "hard not to think of everything as superficial."

She soon believes she has reason to hope that things will change, for this film's Dr. Van Helsing (Peter Fonda, dressed Ivy League-style but sporting long, wispy hair) announces that he has driven a stake through the heart of her father, Count Dracula himself. Longing for love and some meaning in her life, she unsurprisingly has a tough time escaping the family heritage.

This black-and-white film has a steel-engraving look as stunning as Nadja herself, but Almereyda has formidable cinematographer Jim DeNault alternate between 35mm and Pixelvision cameras. Production notes helpfully tell us that the blurred shot-through-a-honeycomb grid look created by Pixelvision is meant to transport us "into the hazy universe of the vampiric unconscious." The effect, however, is primarily distracting, which is also the case in trying to sort out the entangled relationships between the film's people.

Van Helsing wants his nephew (Martin Donovan) to help him destroy Nadja and her twin brother Edgar (Jared Harris), but Nadja has already seduced Donovan's wife (Galaxy Craze) and his half-sister (Suzy Amis) has fallen in love with Edgar. And this is just the beginning of the complications.

Although it's difficult not to try to sort out all this and much more, Almereyda probably means to make the larger point that everybody is connected to everybody else anyway and that we all have within ourselves the capacity to devour each other emotionally, like vampires. Almereyda attempts a large, philosophical appraisal of modern life and its ills and to set it off with frequent jabs of spiky, subtle dark humor and a lush sensuality. He by and large succeeds at this, but his film suffers from a malaise typical of fledgling filmmakers: a prolonged middle section that bogs down, inviting audience attention to wander before it regains momentum. In simply choosing to rework "Dracula," Almereyda has given himself the daunting task of trying to discover fresh meaning in the over-mined vampire genre; vampirism as a metaphor for AIDS, for example, is not new.

Almereyda, on the other hand, has a real knack in giving his cast the confidence to play close to the edge of spoofery, requiring them to reel off line after line of deliberately portentous dialogue while keeping straight faces, which allows for quite a few droll, dryly funny moments. Another strength is a vibrant contemporary score by Simon Fisher Turner, long an associate of the late Derek Jarman. Although "Nadja" proclaims Almereyda's distinctive witty sensibility and talent, it also suggests that he needs to aim higher and that Dracula needs to be laid to rest, at least for awhile.

NEW YORK POST, 8/25/95, p. 41, Thelma Adams

Michael Almereyda's dotty downtown Dracula movie, "Nadja," flaunts such irresistible lines as vampire hunter Van Helsing's description of the Count's death: "He was like Elvis in the end. Drugs. Confused. Surrounded by zombies. The magic was gone."

It's a campy touch that '60s fossil Peter Fonda—nearly bloodless, with every late night he ever spent having taken its toll on his pale face—plays both the famed bloodsucker and his nemesis.

When daddy dies, the family cape falls to Nadja (Elina Lowensohn) and her sickly twin, Edgar (Jared Harris). Since Nadja lives in Greenwich Village, wearing a funky wrap, dressing in black and keeping nightcrawler hours never arouses suspicion.

With her chocolate-pudding eyes, high forehead, cruelly curved lips and homegrown Romanian accent, Lowensohn makes a sexy yet somber vamp.

It wouldn't be a downtown Dracula in the '90s if Ms. D. didn't suffer from existential angst. Like Lowensohn's character in Hal Hartley's "Amateur," Nadja proclaims: "I want to change my life." She's undead, but she longs for rebirth.

Nadja might suck blood, but she suffers like any other transplanted bohemian twentysomething: she tries to define herself against her dysfunctional family, she searches for love, she takes solace in one-night stands and looking cool.

Nadja meets Lucy (Galaxy Craze) in a bar. They connect because Lucy and her husband, Jim, Van Helsing's nephew, are so individually down they can't communicate with each other. Lose the fangs, and we're dangerously close to the deadpan comedies of modern mannerlessness that mark Hartley territory.

After an hour, "Nadja" loses its bite. Executive-produced by David Lynch, it succumbs to "Twin Peaks" disease. It falls in love with its own campiness and forgets the audience is still watching.

Whatever else Almereyda wants "Nadja" to be—a hip meditation on love and death and the whole, damn dysfunctional thing—he still needs it to work as a horror movie. But when "Nadja" becomes an exercise in cooler than thou, it plants a stake in the heart of audience interest.

As Lucy states in a rare moment of clarity: "I want to be over this. I want to move on."

NEWSDAY, 8/25/95, Part II/p. B7, Jack Mathews

David Lynch is the executive producer of Michael Almereyda's contemporary vampire yarn "Nadja" and appears briefly as a New York morgue attendant in a scene where Dracula's daughter comes to claim her father's decapitated, heart-staked body. You've been warned.

Lynch's predilection for dark, weird and campy material is well-documented, and though "Nadja" is unworthy of his name, it's easy to understand his interest in Almereyda. The younger filmmaker shares Lynch's tastes and comes at his material with admirable, and sometimes annoying, disregard for convention.

As convoluted as it is, Almereyda's script, seemingly inspired by "Love at First Bite" and "Vampira: Queen of the Dark," is the most normal thing about it. It's New York at night, and Dracula has finally met his end at the hand of a manically klutzy, bike-riding Van Helsing (Peter Fonda), who wants to ram a stake through his daughter's heart before she can reanimate the corpse.

Fonda gives camp a bad name with his performance. He delivers some of Almereyda's best lines ("Blood is like chewing gum to these people"), but he still may be the first Van Helsing you'd like to see lose the eternal struggle.

Fortunately, the central character is Nadja, and Elina Lowensohn gives her an almost mesmerizing, seductive quality. With a thick Hungarian accent and all but her face enveloped in black, Nadja casts her spell first on some unlucky bozo she picks up in a bar (a scene that can be taken as either an AIDS metaphor or a call for prohibition) and then on Van Helsing's niece-in-law Lucy (Galaxy Craze).

Nadja is the only even marginally interesting character in the story, a vampire with a thirst for blood and a clear conscience. But good as she is, Lowensohn cannot lift "Nadja" out of the low-rent district of independent film. And despite Jim DeNault's excellent 35-mm black-and-white cinematography, all that people are likely to remember are the ridiculous impressionist sequences shot on a $45 Fisher-Price toy camera that make it appear as if you're looking through a shower door.

In moviemaking, as opposed to moviegoing, you get what you pay for.

SIGHT AND SOUND, 4/96, p. 49, Kim Newman

New York, Nadja, a beautiful vampire, senses Dracula, her father, has been killed. Jim, nephew of Van Helsing, learns his uncle has been arrested for murder and bails him out. Nadja and Renfield, her slave, steal Dracula's body from the morgue. Nadja meets Jim's wife Lucy in a bar: Nadja reveals she is estranged from Edgar, her twin brother, and that her mother died in childbirth. Nadja and Lucy begin an affair; though Nadja is genuinely enamoured of her lover,

Lucy falls ill. Van Helsing deduces that Dracula's children have stolen the Count's body and enlists the reluctant Jim's aid in his anti-vampire crusade, revealing to the young man that he is his father. Nadja visits Edgar in Brooklyn, and finds him comatose, tended by Cassandra, a nurse who happens to be Jim's sister. Edgar stirs, and Nadja tells him their father has been killed. Lucy realises she is being enslaved by Nadja, and tries to resist.

Lucy and Jim intervene as Nadja tries to attack Cassandra in a Brooklyn garage, and Nadja is injured in an explosion. The Van Helsing faction joins forces with Edgar, who thinks his sister is dangerously out of control. Lucy is still under Nadja's influence. Nadja flees with the captive Cassandra to Castle Dracula in Romania, pursued by Jim, Lucy, Van Helsing and Edgar. Van Helsing drives a stake through Nadja and cuts off her head, but she lives on in Cassandra, who later marries Van Helsing.

Given that the genre has produced such exercises in frozen beauty as Carl Dreyer's *Vampyr* and Werner Herzog's *Nosferatu*, Michael Almereyda's second feature doesn't make it as the artiest vampire movie of all time, although not for the want of trying. Shot in ravishingly sharp black and white, with inserts in Almereyda's trademark Pixelvision to suggest the inhuman visions of its undead, *Nadja* makes imaginative use of New York locations, finding effective stand-ins for the Black Sea and Castle Dracula on Staten Island and in a derelict hospital. With exploitation elements blurred or eliminated (no nudity, little blood) and a group of blankly miserablist characters spouting doom-haunted self-analysis ("I have walked behind the sky, we are all animals, but there is a better way to live"), *Nadja* tries hard not to be a horror movie.

Concerned with characters whose states of being don't really count as life (the family-traumatised Jim and Lucy just as much as the undead Edgar and Nadja) *Nadja* runs the risk of being entirely unapproachable. Indeed, the film is almost completely devoid of urgency or warmth. A calculated attempt to evoke the zero degree existential dreadfulness of its immortal predators' lifestyles, the film is a pretty slow one to watch. Elina Löwensohn, glimpsed in *Schindler's List* and featured in *Amateur*, is a model—gorgeous Nadja, her blankly impassive beauty more creepily suggestive than all her downbeat dialogue, while Jared Harris matches her briefly as Edgar and Karl Geary has a few odd moments as a winsome, Irish Renfield. Executive producer David Lynch pops in for a cameo as a morgue attendant, though his customary weirdness means that when he is hypnotised into serving the vampire, it's hard to tell the difference.

Suzy Amis, Martin Donovan and Galaxy Craze are stuck with the human roles: lifeless stooges, they are dragged along by a plot which establishes absurdly complex relationships between all the characters and blithely winds up with Nadja-as-Cassandra marrying someone who is legally her uncle and also—if Van Helsing's irrelevant mid-point revelation is to be credited—perhaps biologically her father. The only loose cannon in the cast is Peter Fonda, cast as a cycling fearless vampire killer with long hair and granny glasses who gets to rant that the dying Dracula "was like Elvis ... drugs, confused, surrounded by zombies" and seems to have picked up from his prey the habit of sleeping in a piano. Fonda is also glimpsed as a PixelVision Count writhing on a stake, sharing the role with clips of Bela Lugosi's hypnotic eyes taken not from Universal's 1930 *Dracula* but from the public domain *White Zombie*. Fonda's turn is amusing and brings more pep to the film than its one burst of apparent action: the garage fight in which Nadja crushes a few heads with black and white gore effects and seems to be destroyed in a low-budget explosion that has no effect on the plot.

As if under the impression that a vampire movie should literally be a parasite on other movies, Almereyda has taken his plot almost intact from Lambert Hillyer's *Dracula's Daughter*, a swift and underrated 1934 sequel to *Dracula*. In 'updating' it, *Nadja* brings out the lesbian theme by having Dracula's daughter—Gloria Holden in the old film—fall for the heroine rather than the hero, and in bulking out the tight plot, the film throws in the character of Nadja's turncoat vampire brother. Otherwise, this is character-for-character and beat-for-beat a remake of the earlier movie. While Hillyer and Holden were content to let their despairing, self-loathing Countess be subtly sympathetic, *Nadja* fumbles its attitude to the heroine. First, she is a tragic survivor of a bathetically dysfunctional family ("My father was a cruel and distant man who didn't care we existed"); then, an out-of-control madwoman unaware of the damage she does. The over-familiar possession finale, old when *The Hunger* borrowed it from *Daughters of Darkness*, doubles back again to suggest, incoherently, that maybe the vampire-killers are the destroyers of beauty and tenderness. The contrast with *Dracula's Daughter* only shows that unconscious art can often be more profound than ironic icon-invocation and gallons of mood.

TIME, 8/28/95, p. 69, Richard Corliss

[*Nadja* was reviewed jointly with *The Usual Suspects*; see Corliss' review of that film.]

VILLAGE VOICE, 8/29/95, p. 51, Georgia Brown

The lushest film of the year thus far is Michael Almereyda's *Nadja*, a comic vampire tale, or portrait of the young as a lost tribe of bloodsuckers. Shot in shimmering, undulating black and white-part Fisher-Price Pixelvision, part silvery 35mm—*Nadja* follows, the path of Dracula's, moody daughter, who, discontented with the routine, intends somehow to start over, be born again.

Nadja (Elina Löwensohn) is a Romanian in New York, a predator looking for a human arm, or lap, to rest her faithless head on. Her heart isn't in the nightly rite, this exchange of fluids that leaves the other lifeless. (Yes, this too is an AIDS movie.) When her father, Count Dracula Ceauçescu, dies, Nadja believes herself free to change her life. "I'll find someone; I'll be happy." In a bar she finds the melancholy Lucy (Galaxy Craze), and entertains her with stories of the Black Sea ("It's blue"), the Carpathians, and her lost twin, Edgar. Lucy: "Does he live in the shadow of the Carpathians?" Nadja: "Brooklyn. I've never been there." But she does mean to go.

Nadja doesn't make Lucy or herself very happy. "The pain I feel is the pain of fleeting joy," she broods. Their lovemaking (in a stunning pixilated sequence) leaves Lucy drained, bleeding at both ends, and something of a zombie, although not yet "one of them." Lucy's worried husband, Jim (Martin Donovan), and Jim's goofy uncle, Van Helsing (Peter Fonda in the Crispin Glover role), set out to save her, which means ridding the world of Nadja. Nadja, meanwhile, has set off for Brooklyn where she plans to revive the comatose Edgar (Jared Harris).

It takes some time for viewers, and then the movie's characters, to assimilate above information, but sooner or later everything that rises here does converge. And not only is Jim's uncle really his father, but Cassandra (Suzy Amis), devoted nurse to Edgar, turns out to be Van Helsing's other child, and, ipso facto, Jim's sister (At this point I suspected the story might turn out to be about the Fondas. Come to think of it. Peter Fonda with stringy silver locks quite resembles Jared Harris's father, Richard, in *Unforgiven*.)

The Pixelvision passages are the beating heart, the shadow text, of *Nadja*, usually, but not always, I think, representing vampire-vision—a fresh, fracturing eye on a tired old scene. Blown up to 35, the tiny squares are magnified into a floating, mutating grid that Almereyda slyly rhymes with various items in the exterior world like a quilt, a coffee cup with checkerboard frieze, a wall cupboard of cubes.

Watching *Nadja*, I'll admit, can be like wading upstream in a swiftly moving current—one step forward, two back. You aren't swept along. (A sensational score by Simon Fisher Turner aids progress.) The movie falls somewhere in between Guy Madden's beautiful intellectual whimsy and one of Hal Hartley's solemn picaresques. (The presence of Hartley regulars Donovan and Löwensohn doesn't help. Or maybe it does if you're a Hartley devotee.)

And then there are wonderful, privileged moments straight out of Almereyda's wacky 1988 *Twister* (Amis was here, too), as when Renfield (Karl Geary), Nadja's slave, insists on sitting in the patterned wing chair where Cassandra sits. At times like this you realize that *Nadja*'s theme is blood ties, bloody ties, sibling rivalry, sibling lust, the secret language of families family curses, and, always, the undying longing for home. The film's final few minutes, musing on merging, are exquisite.

Also reviewed in:
CHICAGO TRIBUNE, 9/1/95, Friday/p. G, Michael Wilmington
NEW YORK TIMES, 8/25/95, p. C5, Caryn James
VARIETY, 9/26-10/2/94, p. 61, Todd McCarthy
WASHINGTON POST, 9/22/95, p. D7, Hal Hinson
WASHINGTON POST, 9/22/95, Weekend/p. 44, Desson Howe

NAKED KILLER

A Rim Film Distributors release of a Wong Jing's Workshop production. *Executive Producer:* Wong Jing. *Producer:* Wong Jing. *Director:* Clarence Fok Yiu-leung. *Screenplay (Cantonese with English subtitles):* Wong Jing. *Director of Photography:* William Yim and Peter Pau. *Editor:* Wong Chi-hung. *Music:* Lowell Lo. *Choreographer:* Stephen Lee. *Art Director:* Ngai Fongnay. *Costumes:* Shirley Chan. *Martial Arts Director:* Lau Shung-fung. *Running time:* 95 minutes. *MPAA Rating:* Not Rated.

CAST: Chingmy Yau (Kitty); Simon Yam (Tinam); Carrie Ng (Princess); Svenwara Madoka (Sister Cindy); Kelly Yao (Baby).

NEW YORK POST, 3/17/95, p. 48, Thelma Adams

"Naked Killer" is a live-action cartoon for adults only. Direct from Hong Kong, it flaunts a quartet of female assassins: mentor Sister Cindy (Svenwara Madoka); her pupils Kitty (Chingmy Yau) and Princess (Carrie Ng); and Princess' lover, Baby (Kelly Yao).

On the side of good is goofy-but-handsome cop Tinmam (Simon Yam). Ever since he accidentally shot his brother, the addled detective vomits at the sight of guns—and shoots blanks below the waist. Kitty changes that and he's, uh, grateful.

Kitty tells the lovesick Tinmam she's not the girl for him: "I'm a professional killer now. We have conflicts in our jobs."

Director Clarence Fok teams with writer/producer Wong Jing for a stylish, giddy comedy of emasculation. Charles Bronson's "The Mechanic" enters hormone hell.

In one contract hit, Princess and Baby tag team a trendy triad in a luxurious swimming pool. Afterwards, they pause for post-slaughter sex in the shallow end while the man's blood billows into the shot. There swimming in Bond waters, but with a twist. The look is slick, the colors saturated, the fashion high, the cuts switchblade quick.

Fok and Jing have made a hard-boiled hoot that revels in and breaks the rules of the game in a way that's empowering and rude and thoroughly entertaining. The women are strong, the men are weak, but the mayhem remains the same.

NEWSDAY, 3/17/95, Part II/p. B7, John Anderson

Do "The Quick and the Dead," and the recently rereleased "Faster Pussycat, Kill! Kill!" indicate that cheesy, action-movie feminism has reached its golden age? No, as the utterly insane "Naked Killer" clearly shows, cheesy, action-movie feminism has reached its gelded age.

Like a Chanel commercial shot by John Woo, "Naked Killer"—about a gang of lethal hitwomen who sexually mutilate their male victims and are being pursued by an impotent cop—is pure style and pure action. There's not enough, but what's there is choice. The film is almost entirely devoid of logic, plot structure or intelligible subtitles. A few examples:

"Brother, how will you get hurt?"

"Are you nuts? Sure!"

"Do you dare play some exciting sex game?"

"Sorry, I mistake you as one of my best friends."

"Let's eat beef set."

"Something you can't do it by force."

"For men, it's no reason for them to reject vodka."

"He is not worth dying."

"Men, go and eat _____."

"Don't you afraid I am coming to kill you?"

And, of course, the memorable "_____" which sounds exactly like _____ in English.

As the one cop who suspects that a recent string of mutilation murders is being committed by women, Tinam (Simon Yam) is the "Vertigo"-like hero: Having accidentally shot his brother to death, he becomes nauseated at the sight of a gun and confesses to problems below the waist. But he's on the right track. The murders are the work of Sister Cindy (Svenwara Madoka), the queen of assassins, who takes Tinam's friend Kitty (Chingmy Yau) under her wing after she shoots up an office building to gain revenge for her father's death. Cindy helps her escape, in the movie's best sequence, an absolutely fantastic parking-garage shootout. Cindy and Kitty, in turn, are being pursued by the malevolent Princess (Carrie Ng) and her lover Baby (Kelly Yao). Death and dismemberment will ensue.

Unlike the horrific but honest gunplay of a Woo, "Naked Killer" is cartoonish, and weird and fun and in the baddest of taste. I didn't love it, oddly enough. But it's worth a shot.

VILLAGE VOICE, 3/21/95, p. 58, Richard Gehr

Ushering in a wave of slick Hong Kong product combining softcore porn with old-fashioned ultraviolence, Clarence Fok's 1992 feature opens with a parodied cliché—woman in jeopardy on an empty, rain-slicked street—then shifts gears abruptly into one of the more baroque and ferociously inverted strangle-stab-and-shoot'em-ups ever.

The ensuing story is nearly comprehensible: Detective Tinam (Simon Yam), impotent and pukingly allergic to guns since accidentally shooting his brother, figures out that a string of man-murders was committed by women—a quartet of faster, hornier pussycats than Russ Meyer ever imagined. Impressed by her ability to dispatch an abusive boyfriend, Tinam falls for Kitty (Chingmy Yau), who's seen reinvented as "Vivian" by Sister Cindy (Svenwara Madoka), an older avenging vixen. Psychobisexual fireworks ignite when gorgeous dyke icon Princess (softcore queen Carrie Ng) is contracted to kill Cindy and her luscious new protégé. In set pieces frenzied even by HK standards, the women whip through the air like cinematic furies compensating for decades of action negligence. (To celebrate their success, Princess and her cute sidekick share girlish caresses in a swimming pool ribboned with their latest victim's blood.) A high-tech kitchen appliance whirring toward a fiery apocalyptic conclusion, *Naked Killer* processes *Vertigo* with *Ms. 45* and *Faster Pussycat! Kill! Kill!* with *Heroic Trio*, kicking evil male butt all the way.

Also reviewed in:
CHICAGO TRIBUNE, 7/21/95, Friday/p. H, John Petrakis
NEW YORK TIMES, 3/17/95, p. C8, Stephen Holden
VARIETY, 6/20-26/94, p. 42, Derek Elley

NATIONAL LAMPOON'S SENIOR TRIP

A New Line Cinema release of an Alliance Communications production. *Executive Director:* Peter Morgan, Michel Roy, and Neil Stearns. *Producer:* Wendy Grean. *Director:* Kelly Makin. *Screenplay:* Roger Kumble and I. Marlene King. *Director of Photography:* François Protat. *Editor:* Stephen Lawrence. *Music:* Steve Bartek. *Sound:* Tom Hidderley. *Casting:* Ross Clydesdale. *Production Designer:* Gregory Keen. *Art Director:* John Dondertman. *Set Decorator:* Jeff Fruitman. *Set Dresser:* Bruce Mailing. *Special Effects:* Michael Kavanagh. *Costumes:* Sharon Purdy. *Make-up:* Lesley Haynes. *Stunt Cordinator:* Ted Hanlan. *Running time:* 94 minutes. *MPAA Rating:* R.

CAST: Matt Frewer (Principal Todd Moss); Valerie Mahaffey (Miss Tracy Milford); Lawrence Dane (Senator John Lerman); Tommy Chong (Red); Jeremy Renner (Dags); Rob Moore (Reggie); Eric "Sparky" Edwards (Miosky); Kevin McDonald (Travis Lindsey); Michael Blake (Herbert Jones); Tara Charendoff (Carla Morgan); Nicole deBoer (Meg Smith); Sergio Di Zio (Steve Nisser); Fiona Loewi (Lisa Perkins); Kathryn Rose (Wanda Baker); Danny Smith (Virus); Lori Anne Alter (Shirley); Jack Jessop (Mr. Bloom); Kay Tremblay (Mrs. Winston); Jack Newman (Larry Diplo); Simon Sinn (Mr. Woo); Grace Armas (Mrs. Woo); Daniel Lee (Wong Woo); Paris Chong (Pablo); Carol Ng (Du Mi Wong); Wayne Robson (Frank Hardin); George R. Robertson (President Davis); Rachel Wilson (Teen Girl, Susie); Philip DeWilde

(Teen Boy, Fast Eddie); Richard Partington (Doctor); David Sparrow (Lerman's Limo Driver); Marvin Ishmael (Ish); Jim Warren (Detective); Lindsay Leese (Hotel Registration Clerk, Peggy); Monique Kavelaars (Mandy); Ingrid Kavelaars (Candy); James Millington (Senator Johnson); Warren Davis (Senator Duffield); Gerry Quigley (Congressional Aide); Michael Kohut (Honor Guard); Addison Bell (Congressional Chairman); Matt Piche (Teen Boy, Rick); Kim Schraner (Teen Girl, Caroline); Joanne Reece (Press Member); Robert Bidman (Gus Freely, TV Reporter); Megan Kitchen (Scared Little Girl); C.J. Fidler (Nurse).

LOS ANGELES TIMES, 9/11/95, Calendar/p. 6, David Kronke

"National Lampoon's Senior Trip" opens with an apparent bid to recall the glory days when the National Lampoon moniker meant something besides lame movies that last in theaters a week or two: Shots of a high school yearbook, with an earnestly empty quotation from its principal, play off of memories of the magazine's classic yearbook parody of the '70s.

And that's about all that recalls those happy times when the name National Lampoon was associated with humor. Immediately thereafter, the first three gags in the movie involve a pratfall, a fat guy belching and stoners smashing up things. Most of the rest of the film's jokes center around those concerns as well.

"Senior Trip" focuses on a group of high school losers who, under dubious pretenses, are invited to Washington by the President to appear before a Senate hearing on education. The filmmakers don't sweat the issue of characterizations beyond stoner, slut, geek, brown-noser, lesbian, grunger, sullen black dude, smart girl and fat guy, all led by Dags (Jeremy Renner), a ne'er-do-well with a good heart. Principal Moss (Matt Frewer), a fidgety disciplinarian, and new instructor Miss Milford (Valerie Mahaffey) chaperon the expedition, as poorly as one might imagine.

One might expect all sorts of comic invention as these misfits shame our hallowed nation's capital, but this scarcely occurs to screenwriters Roger Kumble and I. Marlene King, who turn most of the movie into an interminable road trip aboard a bus (piloted by Tommy Chong, so you can imagine where the gags there lie).

There's a tiresome subplot involving a crazed crossing guard (Kevin McDonald of "Kids in the Hall") pursuing the bus decked out in a "Star Trek" outfit, and a pointless subplot involving a corrupt senator. Neither would have likely survived the editing room had the movie had any energy or wit, but all the filmmakers are interested in is having the kids get drunk and piling up sex-capades. (The teen-agers in this movie make those in "Kids" seem like bright and shining hopes for our country's future.)

Frewer, perhaps sensing the chance to rise above the general paucity of wit around him, tries hard, infusing Moss with prissily rigid body language and manic desperation as he tries to remain in control but, ultimately, he's simply trying to build laughs out of nothing. Mahaffey manages not to look too embarrassed despite her insultingly stereotypical character, Renner lacks the charisma to serve as a decent anti-hero and the actors portraying the students go through obvious motions or get lost in the shuffle.

By the time the field trip arrives in D.C., an hour of the film has been frittered away, leaving the kids with only a half-hour to see the sights (actually, only one—J. Edgar Hoover's grave site, where of course the only joke anyone could think up involves the fat guy passing gas), have sex all around and suddenly and inexplicably get serious about the issue of education reform.

Which means we're even denied the chance to see them make a mockery of the political process. That's another way in which "Senior Trip" differs from the National Lampoon sensibility of old—once upon a time, humor writers could make telling points with cutting satire, not with witless, insincere bromides.

NEW YORK POST, 9/9/95, p. 17, Larry Worth

Washington, D.C. is the destination of "National Lampoon's Senior Trip," but they should have gone to Wally World. After all, the site of "Vacation's" biggest laughs also symbolizes the last time a National Lampoon flick earned more than a snicker.

Twelve years later, Lampoon writers are way past the bottom of the barrel. They're simply recycling their own swill.

Ripoffs of the "Animal House" gang are all here: a pair of anti-establishment heroes, preppy class president, sex-crazed nerd, black radical, food-crazy fat guy, and virginal heroine. Mercifully, one knows the end is in sight when Miss Goody-Two-Shoes surrenders to the call of the wild.

And naturally, the troops are led by a fascist principal and a gawky math teacher who'll be easy targets for the students' pranks. Yep, nothing new here.

That also extends to a subplot about an evil senator who's trying to scuttle the president's national education bill. (Coincidentally, the chief executive bares an eerie resemblance to scandal-plagued soon-to-be-former Sen. Bob Packwood.)

But the D.C. business takes a back seat to unending beer-blast scenes—and, consequent bathroom and vomit jokes. Writers Roger Kumble and I. Marlene King show their desperation to get giggles when a small girl is run over in a school crosswalk. They'd probably find humor in the Susan Smith saga, too.

Along the way, no talent director Kelly Makin coaxes woefully over-the-top performances from Matt "Max Headroom" Frewer, Valerie "Northern Exposure" Mahaffrey and Kevin "Kids in the Hall" McDonald. But the nadir comes as Tommy Chong drags his bong-toting '60s idiot out of the cliche closet one more time.

With virtually no redeeming features, even diehard Lampooners will see "Senior Trip" as a 90-minute excursion to no-man's-land.

Also reviewed in:
CHICAGO TRIBUNE, 9/11/95, Tempo/p. 5, Michael Wilmington
NEW YORK TIMES, 9/9/95, p. 12, Janet Maslin
VARIETY, 9/11-17/95, p. 105, Daniel M. Kimmel
WASHINGTON POST, 9/9/95, p. D2, Frank Ahrens

NEKROMANTIK

A Film Threat Video production. *Director:* Jorg Buttgereit. *Running time:* 74 minutes. *MPAA Rating:* Not Rated.

CAST: Daktari Lorenz (Rob); Beatrice M. (Betty).

NEW YORK POST, 7/7/95, p. 40, Larry Worth

A boy, a girl and the decomposing corpse they both love ... in every sense of the word.

That's the gist of "NekRomantik," a controversial German horror film that expands the definition of menage a trois, and tries shattering the final taboo in the process.

Specifically, the tale centers on Rob (Daktari Lorenz), a pasty morgue attendant who can't leave his work at the office: jars of eyeballs, intestines and assorted organs decorate his apartment, along with bone-enhanced furniture and a Charles Manson poster overseeing all.

Further, Bob's beautiful live-in ghoul friend, Betty (Beatrice M), shares his morbid passions. What more could a guy want? Well, a head-to-foot, bonafide carcass, for starters. But what's that old saying about being careful what you wish for?

No sooner does Rob sneak a cadaver home than he's competing with its maggot-ridden body for Betty's affections. And that's just the beginning.

Indeed, director and co-writer Jorg Buttgereit isn't content until he's pressed every button in an ill attempt to make audiences nauseous. And while the lovingly detailed carnage can be largely dismissed, Buttgereit sinks to new lows as a bunny gets its throat slit before being gutted and skinned.

Attempts at tongue-in-cheek humor would have seemed a natural. As is, the only sign of creativity is having the subtitles in an appropriately gothic script. But that contributes little to any sense of entertainment, satire or suspense.

Clearly, "NekRomantik" (which Germany has tried to ban since its 1987 release there) is just a series of gory tableaus—capped by an ungodly finale—intended solely to repulse.

Just as plain and simple is the one element separating Buttgereit from horror meisters like George Romero, John Carpenter, Tobe Hooper. Talent.

NEWSDAY, 7/7/95, Part II/p. B4, Jack Mathews

If you find nothing erotic or humorous about a couple of a shacked-up necrophiles who use jarred body parts as aphrodisiacs, bathe in bloodied water and make passionate love to a decomposing corpse, read no farther. I am obligated to push on.

Jorg Buttgereit's 1988 "Nekromantik" includes all of the above, plus the actual killing and cleaning of a bunny, and it has become something of a cult classic in Germany, where it has prompted both a sequel and an attempt by the government to have its negative destroyed.

That's making too much of a bad thing. "Nekromantik" is a date movie for gross-out freaks, college students mostly, who find this stuff more challenging than a spitting contest. These movies, particularly the German imports, are disgusting, revolting, vile, and they go way, way too far, which is why so many people claim to love them.

If it weren't for the killing of the rabbit, which is shown in scenes intercut with the mock autopsy of a human body, "Nekromantik" would be merely sensational. Rob and Betty, who seem barely alive themselves, put on a foul show with that corpse, and there is a combination suicide-masturbation scene that is genuinely depraved. The movie does produce a few choking laughs, and one really funny idea; after losing his dream job with a company that picks up human road-kill, Rob wakes up to discover that Betty has run off with the corpse.

The use of the rabbit footage suggests one of two things: that Buttgereit didn't think his dramatized gore was shocking enough on its own or that he was actually trying to comment on the grotesqueness he was creating. That second option has been used by some critics as proof that "Nekromantik" is a piece of art. Now, *that's* scary.

VILLAGE VOICE, 7/11/95, p. 54, Richard Gehr

Nearer the New German Cinema of Fassbinder's *The Merchant of Four Seasons* than the old American horror of *Night of the Living Dead*, Berlin filmmaker Jorg Buttgereit's second "leichenfick" (corpse-fuck) flick plumbs serious emotional depths with mordant wit and low-budget gore. A seemingly contented young couple residing in an apartment decorated with Charles Manson photos and a bed of bones, Rob (Daktari Lorenz) and Betty (Beatrice M.) Share a passion for dead viscera. (*Nekromantik* draws obvious but often forgotten parallels between the meat most of us eat and the meat we are.) Betty bathes in blood while Rob works on his collections of assorted organs and fetuses.

Employed by Joe's Streetcleaning Agency, Rob gathers the human remnants of the sort of grisly auto wreck that opens the film. After a lackadaisical gun owner accidentally plugs his apple-picking neighbor one fine day, the victim's decomposed corpse eventually provides Rob and Betty with the makings of a memorably romantik three-way. When rob loses his job, however, Betty and the body take a powder. Her note—"I'm not wasting the best years of my life"—could have been left by any number of Fassbinder swine. Deep in despair, Rob seeks solace at a perfectly parodied slasher film, whose distanced, formulaic thrills just bore him, then with a dead prostitute, whose body he violates on a tombstone. Still despondent, he eviscerates himself as his engorged member spews forth sperm and blood, a sloppy waterworks of life and death. But since necrophilia means never to say goodbye, the film's final image sets the stage for Buttgereit's cult-fave sequel, *Nekromantik 2*.

A powerful piece of transgressive cinema, *Nekromantik* combines a haunting score, economical montage, and a gutsy take on horror's potential for illuminating both our bodies and our selves. For all its shock value, this Film Threat Video bestseller, originally released in 1987, actually boasts substantially less gore than the typical contemporary American horror film. It affects us at the place where love is even colder than death.

NET, THE

A Columbia Pictures release. *Producer:* Irwin Winkler and Rob Winkler. *Director:* Irwin Winkler. *Screenplay:* John Brancato and Michael Ferris. *Director of Photography:* Jack N. Green. *Editor:* Richard Halsey. *Music:* Mark Isham. *Music Editor:* Will Kaplan and Tom Carlson. *Sound:* Richard Lightstone. *Sound Editor:* Michael O'Farrell. *Casting:* Mindy Marin. *Production Designer:* Dennis Washington. *Art Director:* Tom Targownik. *Set Designer:* Anne Harris. *Set Decorator:* Anne D. McCulley. *Computer Consultant:* Todd Aron Marks. *Special Effects:* Dale L. Martin and Leo Leoncio Solis. *Costumes:* Linda Bass. *Make-up:* Pamela Westmore. *Stunt Coordinator:* Buddy Van Horn. *Running time:* 118 minutes. *MPAA Rating:* PG-13.

CAST: Sandra Bullock (Angela Bennett); Jeremy Northam (Jack Devlin); Dennis Miller (Dr. Alan Champion); Diane Baker (Mrs. Bennett); Wendy Gazelle (Imposter); Ken Howard (Bergstrom); Ray McKinnon (Dale); Daniel Schorr (WNN Anchor); L. Scott Caldwell (Public Defender); Robert Gossett (Ben Phillips); Kristina Krofft (1st Nurse); Juan Garcia (Resort Desk Clerk); Tony Perez (Mexican Doctor); Margo Winkler (Mrs. Raines); Gene Kirkwood (Stan Whiteman); Christopher Darga and Charles Winkler (Cops); Julia Pearlstein (2nd Nurse); Rick Snyder (Russ Melbourne); Gerald Berns (Jeff Gregg); Tannis Benedict (Elevator Woman); Vaughn Armstrong and Wren T. Brown (Troopers); Lynn Blades (Remote Reporter); Israel Juarbe (Thief); Julia Vera (Mexican Nun); Lewis Dix (FedEx Man); Lili Flanders (Embassy Worker); Adam Winkler (Computer Nerd); Brian Frankish (Shuttle Driver); Wanda Lee Evans (Desk Sargeant); David Winkler (Computer Technician); Kerry Kilbride (WNN Reporter); Roland Gomez (Limo Driver); Melvin Thompson (Fire Official); Rich Bracco (Fireman); Lucy Butler (Female Officer); John Livingston and Cam Brainard (Computer Technicians); Dennis Richmond and Elaine Corral Kendall (Newscasters); Alfredo Lopez (Guitar Player); Thomas Crawford (Waiter); John Cappon (ICU Doctor); Barbara Abedi (CCU Nurse); Kevin Brown (The Bunny); Hope Parrish and William B. Hill (Security Officers); Danny Breen (Supervisor); Andrew Amador (Dermot Conley); Melissa Bomes (Reservation Clerk).

FILMS IN REVIEW, 9-10/95, p. 57, Andy Pawelczak

At the beginning of *The Net,* a man says into a telephone, "This really is reality." We don't find out what he means until the end of the movie, but the remark could stand as an ironic emblem for the whole film. Reality in this cyberthriller directed by Irwin Winkler (*Guilty By Suspicion, Night And The City*) all but disappears in a chase down the information highway. There's nothing very new in the movie—it's a formula picture with echoes of *The Fugitive* and half a dozen other films—but it has an appealing performance by Sandra Bullock and despite some murky cyberspeak it more-or-less holds your interest almost to the end.

Angela Bennett (Bullock) is the ultimate computer nerd. A free-lance computer trouble-shooter, she communicates with the world through the Internet and even orders dinner through her computer, eating it in the glow of a computer-simulated blazing health. The screenplay, by John Brancato and Michael Ferris, doesn't make more than a minimal gesture towards explaining her alienation—something about an absent father in childhood—and at one point has her remark that computers are a good hiding place. But we get the point—she's a neurotic loner, a character in search of a plot.

Angela's self-contained, artificial world is disrupted when a colleague sends her a strange program and is then killed in an airplane crash. On vacation in Cancun (an opportunity for Bullock to wear a bikini), she meets a smooth, charming Englishman (Jeremy Northam) who first romances her and then tries to kill her. Before long, her identity is wiped out on computer records and replaced by a false one that labels her a fugitive from justice. Reduced to an anonymous Everywoman, she's out there alone in LA on the lam from both the police and a shadowy organization that is infiltrating the nation's computer systems.

The plot has several twists and surprises, but it basically comes down to Hitchcock's formula for mesmerizing audiences—threaten the female characters. As Angela, Bullock manages to make something entertaining out of the old vulnerable-but-surprisingly-tough-and-resourceful-woman role. And it's refreshing to see a female lead without a love interest. The closest Angela comes to a romantic involvement is with her ex-psychiatrist with whom she once had a brief affair and on whom she calls for help in her dilemma. As played by Dennis Miller, he's a bumbling knight in shining armor; when Angela tells him her story of conspiracy and assassination, he initially suggests that it's all a fantasized "reaching out" to the world—it's a case of psychobabble meets cyberspeak.

Irwin Winkler's direction isn't very energetic or imaginative but it gets the job done; we have to scan a lot of computer screens but that's par for the course in a movie like this. *The Net* is another cautionary tale for the computer age, and it reminded me of the underlying premises of the cyberthriller: a) for the average moviegoer, the Internet is still an almost metaphysical concept with a potential for Kafkaesque menace; and b) paranoia is the appropriate code of response to our comings and goings in cyberspace.

LOS ANGELES TIMES, 7/28/95, Calendar/p. 12, David Kronke

Since computer culture is seeming as impenetrable and imposing as ever to the layman, it's as good a time as any for a good wallow in technophobia. Still, it's hard to get caught up in "The Net."

Sandra Bullock stars as Angela, a hotshot computer dweeb so ensconced in cyberculture that there's only one person in the whole of L.A. County who can reliably identify her. (For someone who has become famous because she exudes such a natural likability, Bullock has been cast in her last two films as someone who is virtually friendless.)

About to embark on her first vacation in six years, she receives a bizarro computer program that apparently grants access to the most powerful and secret files in the country (and does so accompanied by menacing sound effects, which one would think should require a special program unto itself). She shrugs off the ramifications of such a thing, though, as blithely as she handles the suspicious death of a colleague who was coming to visit her to talk about it.

In Mexico, she breaks the second rule of cheap literary symbolic devices: Never fall for someone whose name is an inept anagram for "devil," particularly if your name is Angela. "Nice piece of hardware," she flirts coquettishly with a suave fellow named Jack Devlin (Jeremy Northam)—referring of course, to his portable computer.

Big mistake—before long, Devlin and his operatives and their seemingly inexhaustible control over government computer networks threaten to take Angela permanently off-line. And the script, credited to John Brancato and Michael Ferris, soon veers off into blithering idiot territory, stocking up on the contrivances, plot holes and flat-out mistakes with jaw-dropping regularity. This is one of those movies where everything could be cleared up with an early trip to the authorities.

Just a few examples: Angela arranges to meet with a fellow computer nerd within 30 minutes, is consequently waylaid by hours, but still bothers to show up. Even when Devlin often has no idea where she is, he conveniently seems to be within a couple of minutes of her—even after she spirits away to San Francisco. Angela enters a building in daylight; minutes later, it's pitch-black outside. And, of course, there's that rather implausible key plot hinge that there is *no one* in town that hasn't somehow taken note of the fact that this perfectly attractive young woman exists and can vouch for her identity to the authorities.

That anyone manages to care remotely about what's going on despite all this is a tribute to Bullock's appeal. She remains a disarmingly winning performer, though here she's saddled with some clunky, clichéd bits of behavior: Angela recites the words she types (sort of the cyber-equivalent of moving your lips while reading).

Irwin Winkler has produced more than his fair share of terrific movies (including a number of Martin Scorsese films), but has yet to prove his mettle as director. Winkler's previous efforts, "Guilty by Suspicion" and "Night and the City," suffered from a dramatic inertia that returns here—he just seems incapable of bringing a sense of urgency to the material. Mark Isham's music works overtime to try to juice the proceedings, as does Richard Halsey's frenetic editing, which occasionally render sequences incoherent—you just take it on faith, for example, that Angela is able to escape from Devlin by riding on a carousel.

In the end, some of the problem with "The Net" may lie in the inherent nature of its subject matter. Sure, there's a lot of running and shooting and car-crashing and other sundry thriller staples, but ultimately, a lot of the ostensibly most suspenseful scenes depend on Angela's typing abilities—and those of you who have ever manned a keyboard are aware just how riveting a pastime typing can be.

NEW STATESMAN & SOCIETY, 10/6/95, p. 34, Jonathan Romney

The Net—a thriller about one woman and her laptop—looks at first glance as if it's going to be one of those new computer-hip movies by which Hollywood is currently (and a touch desperately) attempting to hack into the rival excitements offered by the Internet and Virtual Reality (forthcoming are *Johnny Mnemonic, Virtuosity,* et al). In fact, *The Net* only sells itself as a cyberthriller; really it's a conservative tract that is distrustful not only of computers, but also of the new film languages that computer-literate *zeitgeist* might entail. It has no interest in the online experience as a springboard for new narrative and visual techniques: in fact, it would much rather not mess with fancy software at all. If you want to gawp at smart graphics, you'd be better off with *Donkey Kong County.*

The Net is about solitary, obsessive, but likeable computer expert Angela (Sandra Bullock). She accidentally stumbles on some obscure but dangerous information on a disk, spends most of the film fending off the heavies who are out to silence her, then finally cracks their dark secret and saves the day. What we have here is exactly what the dreary *Disclosure* was, under all the flash trimmings an old-fashioned office-bound paranoia thriller, a tarted-up version of the sort of film where a character stumbles on the wrong document and ends up having to find another document in someone else's office before the security guards arrive. The makers of these films can change the fact that searching for a file on a computer desktop is not *per se* any more exciting than rifling through dusty filing cabinets by torchlight. It's simply John Grisham with added megabites.

No one seems to have considered the possibility that a rather riveting thriller might be made simply about someone sitting at their table with a Powerbook. Immobility isn't inimical to excitement—imagine a sort of virtual *Rear Window.* But director Irwin Winkler has his heart set on Hitchcock pastiche of a more boisterous kind (the smooth English baddie, preposterously scowled by Jeremy Northam, is called Devlin, presumably after the Cary Grant character in *Notorious*). He wants his action to take place in the real world, or some absurd genre version of it. So Angela jets off to Mexico for a bit of Bond romance in an open boat, then returns to LA for a laborious bout of skullduggery, involving an extended stalk-out at a fairground—one thriller staple that no one should attempt unless able to face uncomfortable comparisons with *Strangers on a Train.*

The premise too is out of *North by Northwest*—an innocent, comfortable in her enclosed world, stumbles into something she doesn't understand and is thrown into a scary reality, her own identity being challenged in the process (it's an unfortunate by-product of Bullock's self-deprecating good humour that we just can't take Angela's paranoid dilemma that seriously). And instead of looking for something interesting in the iconography of the display screen itself, the film ends up being about a concrete McGuffin; the thing that everyone's chasing is a boring old floppy disk.

The plot seems expressly designed to get us away from the keyboard and into the fresh air; *The Net* is remarkably moralistic about the ill-effects of staying in too much. It goes to painful lengths to stress Angela's sad isolation. She has never actually met the people she's closest to—other hackers remain voices on the phone, or on-screen icons, like her virtual date *Cyberbob* (this is deep nerd territory). She has one ex-lover, a soft-headed but fundamentally abusive shrink who has no idea what she's talking about. She's so dysfunctional that she stays in every night alone, ordering pizza on-line, and mooning about to Annie Lennox on the soundtrack. She also speaks aloud all the instructions she types into her machine—an inexcusably sloppy way of ensuring we don't have to tax our minds over what she's doing.

The message is simply that computers are screwing up the world, beginning with our social skills. If Angela had gone out on a few more dates instead of staying in and swapping E-mail with smiley icons, none of her woes would have happened. This is a bit rich. Considering how the film is being sold. It would be like an 18th century epistolary novel complaining about the way that people sit at home waiting for the post to arrive. A particularly shoddy metaphor of the social collapse that the film bemoans is the fact that Angela's mother has Alzheimer's and can't recognise her; the implication is that if we insist on messing around with machinery, our mental files will get wiped too.

The usual modern-world terrors are here: surveillance, technocratic omniscience. Angela's life is erased on line, which is possible because no one knows her. Computers crash at LA airport and Wall Street; hospital records are tampered with. Angela signals her revolt against technology by smashing a hospital computer—a gesture of defiance that's crushingly banal just because it's, once again, so *concrete* (and a touch anti-social, surely). She sees the folly of hacking and gets real, as suggested by a silly visual metaphor near the end—a screen full of pixels melting and blurring into a nice pinkflower bed.

There may also be another, more down-to-earth agenda to the film's techno-fear. *The Net* features a lot of very obvious product placement for Apple Macintosh, which is thanked at the end credits; oddly enough, the villain of the piece turns out to be a company headed by a figure not unlike Bill Gates, and responsible for a product called Gatekeeper. I'm not saying that *The Net* is a concerted piece of industrial defamation aimed by one company at a successful rival that happens to be heavily invested in the Internet; but a little paranoia never did any harm.

NEW YORK POST, 7/28/95, p. 39, Michael Medved

Hollywood has compiled a decidedly mixed record with its attempts to make the power and excitement of computers come to life on the big screen.

"WarGames" and "Sneakers" enjoyed moderate success, while more bizarre cyber-fantasies like "Demon Seed," "Tron" and—heaven help us—"Johnny Mnemonic," quickly crashed at the box office. The key question with all of these movie is whether they will appeal to that substantial portion of the potential audience that may not care all that much about computers.

By this standard, "The Net" is one of the best of its breed. The technological menace comes across as comprehensible and even vaguely believable, while the more important human dimension provides an array of intriguing characters.

Sandra Bullock plays a brilliant but lonely computer analyst in Venice, Calif., who spends her time on free-lance assignments finding bugs and battling viruses. Just before departing on a desperately needed vacation to Mexico, she agrees to one more favor for a colleague by looking at a "beta" prototype of a new Internet program that inexplicably provides access to top-secret data bases like the IRS, the Federal Reserve, and others.

Before Bullock can figure out what's happening, the associate who discovered the program dies in a mysterious plane crash and a massive computer breakdown at LA airport further delays her own departure.

Finally arriving at the beach in Yucatan, she meets a suave British businessman (superbly played by stage actor Jeremy Northam) who not only shares her passion for computers but also knows every scene in her favorite movie, "Breakfast at Tiffany's."

The romance that follows is as seductive for the viewer as it is for Bullock's character, but it's rudely interrupted when she's nearly killed for the computer diskette carrying the mysterious program. All her identification papers are lost, and someone begins using the Internet to alter every aspect of her identity. They've given her a new name and a falsified police record, so even after she manages to return home she can't resume her life.

Bullock's reclusive habits leave no neighbors able to vouch for her, so she's forced to turn to her former lover, a married psychiatrist smirkingly played by comedian Dennis Miller, but the two of them are hardly a match for the omnipotent forces deployed against them.

Like all such preposterously paranoid thrillers, "The Net" depends heavily on its ominous mood and cinematographer Jack Green ("Unforgiven," "Bridges of Madison County") does a superb job of creating a grim yet realistic atmosphere. Sandra Bullock, as always, displays an everywoman quality that emphasizes her vulnerability; at the same time, she makes it easy to believe her character possesses untapped strengths.

The climatic chase scene needlessly intersects with a big AIDS demonstration in San Francisco (making some point about the connection between computer and human viruses?) but as staged by director Irwin Winkler ("Guilty By Suspicion") it's still an arresting piece of cinema.

In one telling line, Bullock's character admits that computers are her "whole life" because "they're a perfect hiding place." This irresistibly involving film also makes a good place to hide for a few hours, forgetting your own problems while you're entangled with this chilling "Net."

NEWSDAY, 7/28/95, Part II/p. B2, Jack Mathews

You do not have to own and operate a personal computer to follow the plot complications of Irwin Winkler's cyberspace thriller "The Net." The story, about a professional computer nerd who has her life electronically erased by an Internet terrorist, is such derivative Hollywood suspense it could have been titled "Hitchcock for Dummies." "The Net," written by enough people to start a basketball team, stars Sandra Bullock as Angela Bennett, a free-lance software doctor who tracks down and kills viruses in corporate computer programs and gets them back online. Computer viruses, which may be the only technical concept you need to know, are programs inserted into other programs that multiply, spread and screw everything up.

Angela's work is her life. She is the ultimate computer shut-in, glued to a pair of computers that connect her to her clients, her bank and her nearest pizza delivery. She ventures out of her suburban Los Angeles home only to visit her Alzheimer's afflicted mother (Diane Baker), and with the exception of a brief affair with her married psychiatrist (Dennis Miller), she has kept her human contacts at an electronic arm's length. Her only confidantes are disembodied Internet chat buddies with names like Cyberbob and Ice Man.

Then one day, while enjoying her first vacation in six years, Angela meets a computer-literate Mr. Right (Jeremy Northam) on a Mexican beach, and has an impulsive one-night stand that turns into a never-ending nightmare. Seems the man is less interested in her than in the computer disk she's carrying around, and she soon finds herself being chased from Mexico to Los Angeles and across cyberspace.

Much of the computer hooey is fun. Winkler makes what could be deadly passive scenes—Angela typing—both playful and tense, and the idea of a person having her computer records rewritten to obliterate her true identity is a nice projection of both high-tech paranoia and Hitchcockian drama. Angela is a classic suspense character, a woman who knows too much, and she spends half the movie on the run before she realizes the fix she's in and what she should do about it.

Unfortunately, Winkler devotes most of his energy to a series of shamefully banal chase sequences. If you're going to do Hitchcock, you ought to at least have some fresh ideas for staging action.

The saving grace of "The Net" is Bullock, whose sunny disposition and warm accessibility make her an irrepressible protagonist, even while putting the lie to her character. Angela is written as a woman so socially isolated she hasn't a person in the world to call on when Devlin (Northam) changes her computer history to that of a wanted criminal (mom's brain is pertinently suffering from its own form of computer virus), and try as you might, you can't see Bullock as someone without friends.

SIGHT AND SOUND, 10/95, p. 55, John Harkness

Computer wizard Angela Bennett lives a reclusive life in Southern California, where she hunts for viruses in computer programmes. She doesn't really seem to know anyone except her mother, who suffers from Alzheimer's disease and doesn't recognise Angela as her own daughter.

Angela receives a strange piece of software from Cathedral, the company she works for. Even though she is about to go on vacation to Mexico, she agrees to meet her boss Dale to go over the disc. On his way to meet her, Dale's plane crashes because of a mysterious computer instrument malfunction. Nevertheless, Angela goes to Mexico where she meets handsome Jack Devlin, who seems to have a lot in common with her. When a local steals Angela's bag, we discover that Devlin is an assassin, his knowledge of her garnered from computer databases. Discovering his gun, Angela knocks him unconcious, then she too is knocked out in a boating accident.

After three days in a Mexican hospital, Angela gets back to her hotel to find that she has already been checked out. When she applies for temporary papers so she can get back to the US, they come back with another name, Ruth Marks, on them. On returning to LA, she finds that her car is missing, her house has been emptied and put up for sale, and that the police believe she's a criminal. She can't find anyone who can identify her, gets busted, and is helped out of jail by a seemingly friendly but actually fraudulent FBI agent. She turns to her ex-therapist/boyfriend Dr Alan Champion for help. He gets her to a hotel room and a laptop, and she discovers that there is a massive conspiracy involving a software mogul and a gang of renegade hackers, The

Praetorians, who are selling a data protection programme with a hidden flaw that enables them to manipulate every system that installs it.

Champion succumbs to an altered medical prescription and dies. Angela eludes Devlin for the second time and infiltrates Cathedral Software where her identity has been taken by a Praetorian imposter (the real Ruth Marks). There she gets to the heart of the conspiracy and later, at a computer trade fair, she gets back on-line and destroys the Praetorian database with a favourite virus. Devlin shoots Marks by mistake and in a final struggle he falls to his death.

Irwin Winkler is an honoured producer, with a Best Picture Oscar for *Rocky* and enormous prestige for producing several of Martin Scorsese's best films. Unfortunately, what he really wants is to direct, and he has the clout to do it. So he has foisted a trio of exceedingly mediocre films upon an unsuspecting public: *Guilty By Suspicion, Night and the City* and now *The Net*. *Guilty By Suspicion* was dull and *Night and the City* had the unexpected effect of making Jules Dassin's original film (on which Winkler's film was only loosely based) look like a masterpiece, but at least they were coherent. *The Net* simply doesn't make sense.

Supposedly, the renegade hackers can get into any database in the world and change the data. This is fine if you believe that one can access police data banks through the Internet. (You can't.) What this film neglects to consider is that anyone who has owned a computer for any length of time has had at least one major system crash and the bigger the system the more likely it is to crash, so that anyone who owns a large database has backups for their backups. Supposedly, Jeremy Northam's Jack Devlin is a cold-blooded professional killer. Why then is he defeated at every turn by Angela Bennett, a computer geek whose idea of a big evening is ordering a pizza and chatting on the Internet?

The Net also violates basic thriller rules, particularly the one that demands that the hero must confront and defeat the villain. Angela never even meets the big villain, choosing instead to dispose of his henchman. This is like making a James Bond movie in which Bond never gets to meet Goldfinger. Winkler has no real eye. He has a decent cinematographer and the film looks competent—and at the price of Hollywood movies today it ought to—but it seems that no thought has been given to how the film should function as a coherent visual entity.

Winkler and company have devoted millions of dollars worth of technology and a few thousand man-hours to create a neo-Luddite thriller that resembles a cross between *Sneakers* and *Three Days of the Condor*. It spends its 100 minutes or so showing us all the cool things one can supposedly do with technology and then denounces that technology as dehumanising. With all the talk about the new computer-oriented and virtual reality films—*The Net, Virtuosity Hackers*—we seem to have been here before. In Hollywood terms this is old news. *WarGames* warned us about the dangers of rampant computer technology more than a decade ago, as did Donald Cammell's *Demon Seed*, and the great virtual reality movie, Douglas Trumbull's *Brainstorm*, is almost 15 years old.

The Net is an old-fashioned woman-in-distress thriller with cyberpunk trappings and a nod to contemporary feminism—Sandra Bullock's Angela gets to brain the villain with a fire extinguisher instead of waiting for a man to come along and shoot him, but its trappings dress up a mentality that comes from the horse and carriage era. In its favour, *The Net* offers another charming Sandra Bullock performance. (Is it just me or does she bear an uncanny resemblance to the Gelfings, the little humanoid pixies in Jim Henson's *The Dark Crystal*?) It also gets some comic juice from Dennis Miller as her exboyfriend. Miller is turning into the male Rosie O'Donnell, showing up for a few scenes, goosing the picture into life, and then leaving.

The Net is the work of a print-era intelligence rejecting the evolutionary future, fearing that if everyone has a computer people who can write software will control the known universe. People expressed similar fears about the introduction of the automobile, but people who can fix the transmission on a Buick have yet to achieve lasting political power.

TIME, 7/31/95, p. 66, Richard Schickel

She's shy, lonesome and doesn't do much with her natural prettiness. It's only after you get to know her that you realize she's bright and eager to break out of her shell and that crisis is her preferred cosmetic. It is the source of the transfiguring glow that makes Sandra Bullock's screen character into a doofus dream girl, a sex symbol the nerdy '90s can relate to.

In *The Net*, as opposed to *Speed* and *While You Were Sleeping*, she at least has a decent job, as a computer-systems analyst. But her Angela Bennett still doesn't have a life. She works at home, orders in pizza via the Internet and has only one hands-on relationship—with her mother, who has Alzheimer's disease. Through no fault of her own, Angela comes into possession of a program that is being marketed as a vaccine for computer viruses but is itself an electronic Ebola. It can gather data from the most secret sources and spread false information anywhere it wants. Needless to say, Angela must be deleted before she can delete it.

To this end, an old-fashioned hit man (Jeremy Northam) is employed and constantly, pluckily frustrated by her. What's much more difficult for Angela to handle is the near terminal case of technoparanoia her enemies induce in her by erasing her true self from everyone's data bank and substituting a false identity (as a prostitute-drug addict) in the world's records. There are some logical jump cuts in *The Net*'s narrative. But director (and co-writer) Irwin Winkler has a confident sense of pace and scale, a healthy skepticism about the morals and motives of cyberspace cadets and, in Bullock, an actress whose gumption and vulnerability can penetrate any plastic pocket protector and jump-start the most shriveled hacker's heart beneath it.

VILLAGE VOICE, 8/1/95, p. 46, Jeff Taubin

"I am I because my little dog knows me," wrote Gertrude Stein. Stein was deeply attached to her dog, Basket, but she here also was pondering the problem of modernist identity. In *The Net*, Angela Bennett (Sandra Bullock) finds herself in an even more precarious situation than Stein suggests, with absolutely no one, except those who want her dead, to confirm that she is she. Angela doesn't have any pets but she does have a mother. Unfortunately, her mother has Alzheimer's disease. Who is Angela when her mother doesn't know her? This anxiety-provoking question is proposed at the opening of *The Net* but is soon suppressed in the interest of summer entertainment.

A cyberspace riff on *The Fugitive*, *The Net* gives us a female systems analyst whose specialty is tracking down computer viruses. Except for occasional visits with her forgetful mom, Angela lives entirely on the Net. Freelancing out of her home, she communicates exclusively via electronics. It's been a long time since she's had face-to-face contact with anyone but the odd delivery person. Thus, she's an easy mark for anyone who wants to make her disappear.

Suspecting that she knows their secret, a group of terrorist hackers, bent on world domination, try to murder Angela in the flesh. When she eludes them (for a woman who never ventures out of the house, she's in fabulous physical condition), they take the precaution of deleting her identity from the various information systems in which she's encoded. Who am I if someone's stolen my pocketbook, and the records of my social security, credit cards, and driver's license no longer exist? Such is the riddle of identity in the postmodern information age.

Blandly directed by Irwin Winkler (who before he turned "creative" was a first-class producer) but neatly photographed by Jack Green (a favorite of Clint Eastwood), *The Net* is likely a vehicle for Bullock, who exhibits a more calculated version of the self-sufficiency that seemed so fresh just a year ago in *Speed*. In addition to *The Fugitive*, Hitchcock's *North by Northwest* also makes it into the mix. A little Hitchcock is a distracting thing. I got through *The Net* by trying to imagine what the master would have done in cyberspace.

Also reviewed in:
CHICAGO TRIBUNE, 7/28/95, Friday/p. F, Michael Wilmington
NEW REPUBLIC, 8/21 & 28/95, p. 30, Stanley Kauffmann
NEW YORK TIMES, 7/28/95, p. C3, Caryn James
NEW YORKER, 8/7/95, Terrence Rafferty
VARIETY, 7/24-30/95, p. 69, Todd McCarthy
WASHINGTON POST, 7/28/95, p. B7, Hal Hinson
WASHINGTON POST, 7/28/95, Weekend/p. 38, Desson Howe

NEVER TALK TO STRANGERS

A TriStar Pictures and Peter Hoffman release of an Alliance production. *Executive Producer:* Rebecca DeMornay. *Producer:* Andras Hamori, Jeffrey R. Neuman, and Martin J. Wiley. *Director:* Peter Hall. *Screenplay:* Lewis Green and Jordan Rush. *Director of Photography:* Elemer Ragalyi. *Editor:* Roberto Silvi. *Music:* Pino Donaggio. *Music Editor:* Yuri Gorbachow. *Sound:* Chaim Gilad. *Sound Editor:* Jane Tattersall. *Casting:* Jon Comerford. *Production Designer:* Linda Del Rosario and Richard Paris. *Set Decorator:* Richard Paris. *Set Dresser:* Elizabeth Calderhead and Doug McCullough. *Special Effects:* Frank Carere. *Costumes:* Terry Dresbach. *Make-up:* Desne Holland. *Stunt Coordinator:* Rick Forsythe. *Running time:* 102 minutes. *MPAA Rating:* R.

CAST: Rebecca De Mornay (Dr. Sarah Taylor); Antonio Banderas (Tony Ramirez); Dennis Miller (Cliff Raddison); Len Cariou (Henry Taylor); Harry Dean Stanton (Max Cheski); Eugene Lipinski (Dudakoff); Martha Burns (Maura); Beau Starr (Grogan); Phillip Jarrett (Spatz); Tim Kelleher (Wabash); Emma Corosky (Young Sarah); Susan Coyne (Alison); Joseph R. Gannascoli (Carnival Attendant); Reg Dreger (Flight Attendant); Frances Hyland (Mrs. Slotnick); John Bourgeois (Uniformed Cop); Kevin Rushton (Corridor Guard); Kelley Grando (Young Girl); Bruce Beaton (Taxi Driver); Tony Meyler (Cop #1); Rodger Barton (Plain Clothes Cop); Nolan Jennings (Waiter); Bret Pearson (Accomplice); Teresa Hergert (Anchorwoman).

NEW YORK POST, 10/21/95, p. 17, V.A. Musetto

When a movie starring superhot Latin heartthrob Antonio ("Assassins") Banderas opens without advance screenings for critics, you know it must be a bomb.

And so it is with "Never Talk to Strangers."

Banderas plays a tatooed, ponytailed hunk on a motorcycle who picks up a shrink (Rebecca De Mornay) in a liquor store. Before you know it, she finds herself the victim of a mysterious stalker.

Could the culprit be Banderas? Or perhaps her horny upstairs neighbor (Dennis Miller)? Or her estranged dying father (Len Cariou)? Or even, somehow, the serial killer-rapist (Harry Dean Stanton) she's studying to see if he's fit to stand trial?

You've seen it all before. The predictibility is compounded by a script that never fleshes out its characters, lifeless acting, static direction (by Peter Hall), dumb dialogue ("F--k you." "No, f--k you."), and dull, washed-out cinematography.

Even the sex scenes (Banderas and De Mornay both get to show off their bodies) are yawners.

The surprise (at least to me) denouement provides the movie's sole redeeming quality. Trouble is, you have to sit through an hour and a half of mediocrity to get to it.

NEWSDAY, 10/23/95, Part II/p. B10, David Kronke

There's a scene deep into "Never Talk to Strangers" (you may have already dozed off) in which Antonio Banderas' character, Tony, has abused Rebecca De Mornay's Sarah, sending her packing. Inexplicably, she returns to his grungy loft, slaps him, takes down his jeans and bites his backside. Sure enough, they're off in the over-the-top realm of carnal corn, and the mystery becomes, who let Joe Eszterhas take over this movie?

No one, it turns out, and believe it or not, more's the pity. Screen writer Eszterhas demonstrated with "Showgirls" and "Jade" that, at least he tackles his erotic thrill shows with a trashy exuberance. The folks behind "Never Talk to Strangers" have some misguided notion that they're doing something with loftier goals, and in this genre, nothing is more deadly than pretension.

Sarah, a criminal psychologist brilliant everywhere but in her personal life, gets involved with Tony despite her better judgment. He's a charmer with a fuzzy past and a talent for making every gesture seem just a wee bit ominous. Her jealous pal, Cliff (Dennis Miller), does a slow burn while Tony makes nice with her, and her estranged father (Len Cariou), who also keeps a skeleton or two in his closet, struggles to re-insinuate himself into her life. Sarah's current assignment—she works for an outfit pointedly named the Veer Institute—is evaluating a serial killer trying to cop Hannibal Lecter's best moves from "Silence of the Lambs" (alas, Harry Dean Stanton is not up to the job).

So it's to the surprise of no one but Sarah that her life veers into unpleasantness. She receives—gasp!—a bouquet of dead flowers; even more perturbing incidents prod her to discover who's behind all these shenanigans.

Trouble is, it's pretty obvious if you pay attention—at least two visual cues and an expository bit of dialogue hand you the solution, a variation of which is a staple plot line on any TV mystery series that lasts a season or two—and frankly, aside from obvious red herrings, there's nothing going on in this movie to hold your interest.

The film's biggest surprise is that it marks the Hollywood directorial debut of Peter Hall, the founder and director of England's prestigious Royal Shakespeare Company. Hall doesn't appear to possess the heart or stomach for this kind of lurid melodrama; his contribution seems to consist solely of protractedly purposeful pacing and advising his performers, "Look like you're really guilty of something."

De Mornay also served as executive producer on this project, which supposedly indicates she wielded enough clout to keep from embarrassing herself—let's just say her performance here will not be interpreted as a feminist tract on self-reliance. Banderas is becoming the Dennis Quaid of the '90s—each time out, those in the know predict that this, finally, will be the project that makes him a huge star; each time out, they're proven frustratingly wrong. Here, he smolders on cue, but never succeeds in creating a plausible character.

SIGHT AND SOUND, 5/97, p. 51, Liese Spencer

New York, the present day. Criminal psychologist Dr Sarah Taylor is analysing Max Cheski, a serial killer, to determine whether he has Multiple Personality Disorder. That evening, she resists her neighbour Cliff's friendly attempts at seduction and goes shopping. At the supermarket, a guy named Tony Ramirez tries to pick her up. She gives him her number and returns home where she finds her estranged father on the doorstep. The following evening Sarah goes to Tony's flat. He tells her he is a surveillance consultant. She talks about her mother's death and how a past fiancé disappeared without a trace.

The next day, Max's lawyer tries to intimidate Sarah into dropping his case. She returns home to find a box of dead flowers. On a date with Tony that evening, Sarah reluctantly tries a fairground shooting gallery which triggers flashbacks of her mother's death. She faints and when she comes round at Tony's flat she sees him going through her handbag. Sarah accuses him of sending her the dead flowers and storms off. Changing her mind, she returns and they have passionate sex.

The following day, Sarah meets with Max's lawyer and confronts him about the threats, but he denies them. When Sarah receives her dead cat in a parcel, she goes to the police who tell her to hire a private detective. After following Tony, the detective tells Sarah that Tony is researching her past. At Sarah's apartment Cliff sees an intruder leaving Sarah's flat. He chases the intruder but is knocked out by an iron bar and taken to hospital. Meanwhile, Sarah has gone to Tony's apartment and discovered his file on her. At her flat, Sarah narrowly escapes electrocution when a wall heater falls in her bath. Detectives decide to treat her case as attempted murder. After the police leave Sarah's father at the flat, Tony also arrives and admits that he has been investigating her over the disappearance of her ex-fiancé—his brother. Tony shows Sarah video footage from a hidden camera which shows that she broke into her own flat. Sarah's repressed memories of her mother's death resurface and she tells Tony how her father sexually abused her and killed her mother to make it look like an accident. Sarah shoots her father, then kills Tony dead after admitting she murdered his brother. She tells the police that Tony shot her father and she killed him in self-defence. The police say she won't have to stand trial.

Early in *Never Talk to Strangers*, the heroine is surprised on the steps of her house and drops her shopping. A close-up of a jar of thick tomato sauce oozing over her doorstep gives advance warning of the subtlety of director and former theatre director Peter Hall's visual metaphor, but it still comes as a surprise to be bombarded with quite such a tired combination of steamy sex and broad horror. From the electric heater wobbling over the vulnerable heroine as she takes a bath to the compulsory pet slaughter (this time a dead cat in the post), the film packs generic clichés into almost every scene. Like many of the best thrillers, this suspenser is premised on a fashionable new psychological disorder. Unfortunately, Repressed Memory Syndrome, which could have made ideal meat for a complex flashback potboiler, is squandered here on a film whose implausible plot and tasteless direction are so risibly hackneyed it borders on pastiche.

Set-bound voyeurism and a familiar, spiralling rhythm of shock editing creates an overall flavour of a 70s stalk-and-slash flicks, but *Never Talk to Strangers* also bears the mark of a number of more recent films. The dangerously anonymous and passionate relationship between Sarah and Tony, for example, echoes the compulsive affair of *Fatal Attraction,* with Hall offering audiences interminable sex scenes choreographed with enthusiastic vulgarity around an industrial wire grill. Elsewhere, in Sarah's sparring interviews with her insane case study Max, there's echoes of the Lecter/Clarice relationship in *The Silence of the Lambs*, as Stanton's wily sex killer manipulates the interview to make Sarah the object of his interrogation.

In spite of a brutally pragmatic, script, dealing out basic exposition rather than character development ("I'm Sisyphus with a hard on" says Sarah's neighbour in one of the few lines which might pass for wit), *Never Talk to Strangers* does feature decent performances. Five years ago, Rebecca De Mornay raised her career profile as a pretty psychotic nanny in *The Hand that Rocks the Cradle*. As executive producer and star of this equally low-brow concoction, she uses her cool blonde looks to similarly unnerving effect, reprising the role of a damaged woman whose professionalism masks a tightly controlled insanity.

Of the creepy male suspects who surround her, Antonio Banderas and Harry Dean Stanton are well cast in stock rôles. Banderas plays the oily, Latin lover stereotype with gusto. His ponytailed, leather jacketed he-man charges around on a phallic motorbike and speaks in a cod Puerto Rican accent. Harry Dean Stanton, meanwhile, adds a much needed hint of macabre humour as the wisecracking serial killer. (It's a pity then that the relationship between Stanton's Max and Sarah is quietly shelved half way through the movie.)

Given the overall crudeness of *Never Talk to Stangers*, there's something inevitable about its violent and illogical climax which, with a laughable opportunism, decides to combine Multiple Personality Disorder and Repressed Memory Syndrome for maximum melodramatic impact. Sarah, it transpires, has not only repressed memories of sexual abuse and her mother's death but developed a peculiarly lethal strain of man-hating Multiple Personality Disorder to deal with those traumas. "You're shit, like all men," she explains to Tony before blowing him away. If the psychology is a bit of a tangle then the message is depressingly familiar: inside every 'controlling' career woman there's a hysterical, sexually aggressive little girl waiting to get out. Rebecca De Mornay plays her well, but do we really need to see any more of her in this part—or of this kind of trashy, exploitative thriller, for that matter?

Also reviewed in:
CHICAGO TRIBUNE, 10/23/95, Tempo/p. 1, John Petrakis
NEW YORK TIMES, 10/21/95, p. 14, Caryn James
VARIETY, 10/23-29/95, p. 46, Brendan Kelly
WASHINGTON POST, 10/21/95, p. H5, Hal Hinson

NEW JERSEY DRIVE

A Gramercy Pictures release. *Executive Producer:* Spike Lee. *Producer:* Larry Meistrich and Bob Gosse. *Director:* Nick Gomez. *Screenplay:* Nick Gomez. *Story:* Nick Gomez and Michael Marriott. *Director of Photography:* Adam Kimmel. *Editor:* Tracy S. Granger. *Music:* Dawn Soler. *Sound:* Jeff Pullman and (music) Eric Liljestrand and Patrick Derivaz. *Sound Editor:* Stuart Levy. *Casting:* Tracey Moore and Todd Thaler. *Production Designer:* Lester Cohen. *Set Decorator:* Lynn-Marie Nigro. *Set Dresser:* Guido DeCurtis. *Special Effects:* Steve Kirshoff. *Costumes:* Barbara Presar. *Make-up:* Ellie Winslow. *Stunt Coordinator:* Phil Neilson. *Running time:* 100 minutes. *MPAA Rating:* Not Rated.

CAST: Sharron Corley (Jason Petty); Gabriel Casseus (Midget); Saul Stein (Roscoe); Gwen McGee (Renee Petty); Andre Moore (Ritchie); Donald Adeosun Faison (Tiny Dime); Conrad Meertins, Jr. (P-Nut); Devin Eggleston (Jamal); Koran C. Thomas (Ronnie); Michelle Morgan (Coreen); Samantha Brown (Jackie Petty); Christine Baranski (Prosecutor); Robert Jason Jackson (Lionel Gentry); Roscoe Orman (Judge); Dwight Errington Myers (Bo-Kane); Gary DeWitt Marshall (Jessy); Ron Brice (Tiko); Shawn McClean (Reebo); Paulie Schulze (Booking Sergeant); Leslie Nipkow (Female Officer); Arthur Nascarella (Mr. Chop Shop); Michael Tancredi (Officer Clueless); Ian Kelly (Incarcerated Knucklehead); Emilio Mayes and Ian Kelly (Young Guns); Arabella Field (Female Jury Member); David Butler (TV Reporter); Oran Jones (Ron Q.'s Dad); T.K. Kirkland (House Rules); Leslie Segar (Angry Resident); Kellie Turner (Agitated Neighbor); Maurice Carlton (Irate Friend); Monique Maxwell and Monet-Cherise Dunham (Jackie's Homegirls); James McCauley (Whiteboy in Jeep); Teisha Panely (PJ Spokesperson); Damon Chandler (Detective); Andy Radcliffe (Buff); Ellsworth "Cisco" Davis (Cisco).

LOS ANGELES TIMES, 4/19/95, Calendar/p. 8, Peter Rainer

The best thing about "New Jersey Drive" are the nighttime scenes of joy-riding Newark street toughs cruising and spinning up and down the boulevards in merry chaos. The cars, mostly stolen, are like creatures out of an urban night-world, and they're both frightening and beautiful to watch.

Writer-director Nick Gomez, whose first film was the micro- budgeted "Laws of Gravity," is entranced by the way these cars move, and he's also drawn to the joy-riders. Jason (Sharron Corley) and his shaven-headed buddy Midget (Gabriel Casseus), like the other rootless black teenagers whom we see, cruise through the movie. (They can break into a car in the time it takes to read this paragraph.) They're always in motion, going in circles, and their dialogue has a street jive lilt.

Gomez finds all this hypnotic—and that's the movie's limitation as well as its strength. He tries to keep the finger-pointing to a minimum but the film is not nearly as evenhanded as its free-floating technique would indicate. Ultimately it's a kind of apologia for these kids. It's a tribute to their *style*.

The point may be that, when you have nothing else going on in your life, style is your salvation. We don't get much beneath the style, though. There's a sameness to the incidents in this movie—it's like a tape loop of trouble.

Jason, who lives with his sister and mother and her boyfriend, narrates the movie, which flashes back from his entrance into a detention hall. He is portrayed as a good kid caught up in a bad scene; he's emblematic of what urban despair can do to you. But Jason doesn't really develop as a character, perhaps because the actor playing Jason—who was a member of a gang in the Brownsville section of Brooklyn—strikes too many attitudes. He poses tough, and so does Gabe Casseus as Midget, though he smiles more. As their lives spin more and more out of control, you can spot the warning flags a mile away.

When one of the boys says, "We were just trying to make our own mark in the world," a note of special pleading comes into play. Since it is the (mostly) white racist cops in this movie who are the brutalizers—chief among them Saul Stein's burly bad Roscoe—"New Jersey Drive" comes across as a soft-pedaling of urban crime. (Spike Lee was the executive producer.)

Despite the semi-documentary look and the up-from-the-streets banter, the film is just about as romanticized as "Rebel Without a Cause" or "The Wild One." It's a youth-in-trouble fantasia with a hip-hop beat, and it's primed for audiences who want to enter into dangerous terrain without getting their shoes scuffed. The danger in this movie is a turn-on for audiences in the same way that it appears to be for Jason and Midget and the others, and there's something a little disreputable about that.

NEW YORK POST, 4/19/95, p. 34, Thelma Adams

"New Jersey Drive" is an "American Graffiti" for the 90s.

"We couldn't wait until it was our turn to get behind the wheel," says Newark teen Jason Petty (Sharron Corley). Is that so different from what drove Richard Dreyfuss, Ron Howard and Paul LeMat onto the drag strip in 1962?

In most of America outside Manhattan, a driver's license is a one-way ticket out. It paves the way for an escape from the family home. The driver tests his wings, carves out a place where he can be himself with his friends away from his parents. Driving is a teen form of power, a portal to the adult world, a rite of passage,

The difference in "New Jersey Drive" is that teenagers like Petty aren't just driving cars, they're stealing them. They're taking a shortcut to one of the fruits of the American dream—a cherry car.

Set in Newark, considered the car-theft capital of the world, and based on a series of articles published in the New York Times, "New Jersey Drive" is exhilarating. Writer/director Nick Gomez takes us on a fast and fluid joy ride with the radio blaring and our stomachs in our throats.

Gomez exploded onto the independent cinema scene with "Laws of Gravity," a tight downward spiral about Brooklyn small-timers made for $35,000 and change. On his second feature, the director has a bigger budget, Spike Lee as an executive producer, and less control.

The car culcha scenes that showcase Petty and his pal Midget (Gabrielle Casseus) are tight and assured. But the ride falters with the entrance of Officer Roscoe (Saul Stein), a big-headed, rogue cop so stereotypically malevolent with his joyless, horsey grin and bruised knuckles that he could be rolling out of a Road Runner cartoon.

That said, the movie's strength is its understanding of these teen car thieves without rationalizing their crimes. Standing curbside on the brink of a theft, Petty has the option to avoid the car. He has a supportive mother and an attractive girlfriend who discourage his rolling ways.

And yet, given the choice, Petty does the wrong thing, the stupid thing, the shortsighted thing: He hops in a car that isn't his and drives away.

NEWSDAY, 4/19/95, Part II/p. B9, Jack Mathews

Remember when a cops 'n' robbers movie was one about good guys chasing bad guys? Not anymore, not since journalism and the arts have begun probing behind the badges to reveal that police are often as corrupt and criminally violent as the people they're after.

Writer-director Nick Gomez' gritty "New Jersey Drive," inspired by a series of New York Times articles about criminal behavior among Newark police assigned to the inner city, is the latest in the new thugs 'n' thieves genre. Did I say police? These men in blue are vigilantes, uniformed Dirty Harrys who are as apt to crack the skull of a black suspect as clap the cuffs on him.

For them, a cop's job is to defeat the enemy, not to serve and protect, and their enemies are the street gangs who've adopted wholesale auto theft as both a livelihood and a pastime. Kids from broken or never-were families with nothing else to do and no regard for their futures define themselves by their skill at stealing cars, which they either joyride into oblivion or sell to chop shops.

Gomez, whose first film, "Laws of Gravity," spent three days with a pair of ill-fated young Brooklyn thieves, is not as successful at building sympathy for the youths in "New Jersey Drive." These aren't kids forced into lives of crime, though their environment certainly encourages it (as a disorganized community youth activity). Stealing cars—which they can do faster than you can say "Is that my $500 alarm?"—is great fun, and even greater fun when it ends in a police chase—the ultimate joyride.

The thing "New Jersey Drive" does best is demonstrate why the confrontations between police and street gangs are so personal. The kids are having a ball flaunting their nihilistic lifestyles in the faces of the hated police—they even steal a cop car now and then—and the police are frustrated by their powerlessness to stop them.

But Gomez has loaded the deck against the cops in such a way that you either root for the thieves—who, by the way, don't spend their money on anything stronger than beer and pot—or sit back dispassionately and watch the two sides slug it out. From the opening moments, when we see the police ambush a pair of kids in a stolen car, shoot one of them and then report it as a defensive action, siding with the law is not an option.

The central figure of the story is Jason (Sharron Corley), a high-school dropout torn between his loyalties to his gang—particularly to his wild friend, Midget (Gabriel Casseus)—and to his concerned mother (Gwen McGee). Jason narrates the story from a juvenile detention center, recalling both the events that led him there and his relationship with the vicious rogue cop Roscoe (chillingly portrayed by Saul Stein).

Gomez and the talented young actors in his cast have vividly recreated the street culture of inner-city Newark, using street language so idiomatic that it is at times nearly impossible to understand, and you watch the sometimes violent interaction of the kids with a dread that borders on hopelessness. Despite the evolving maturity of Jason, and the condemnation of police brutality, "New Jersey Drive" doesn't do anything more than admonish both the police and the gangs to behave better.

I would be remiss not to raise the specter of violence that has often followed these films into the theaters. However good their intentions, recent movies focusing on gang culture—"Boyz N the Hood," "Menace II Society," "Juice"—have attracted the attention of gang members too, and their behavior doesn't necessarily change when they go out to see themselves portrayed on the screen.

VILLAGE VOICE, 4/25/95, p. 62, Gary Dauphin

There's a chronic and shared loneliness that runs through Nick Gomez's compelling tale of Newark black boys and the cars they steal, only the characters in *New Jersey Drive* suffer most of their losses before the first credit rolls. In Gomez's first feature, *Laws of Gravity*, characters seemed caught mid-slouch and devices like the no-frills, cut-to-black transitions said as much about the director's inventiveness in getting the film made as they did the random pointlessness that filled his wannabe wiseguys's day to day. By giving that emptiness wholly back to its characters and subtracting some of the guerrilla filmmaking window dressing, *New Jersey Drive* marks a more mature effort in many ways, but how it strikes you will depend on how far you're willing to ride with Gomez into this cramped and understatedly downbeat world.

For a film whose operative metaphor is the teenage joyride, *New Jersey Drive* proceeds with a laconic disregard for the souped-up thrills some viewers might sit down expecting. Taken loosely from a series of articles by *New York Times* reporter Michel Marriott, *Drive* opens with Jason Petty (gifted "non-professional" Sharron Corley) taking a long walk into juvenile hall, and flashes back from there to a night when he and a homeboy are shot at while joyriding by Officer Roscoe (Saul Stein). A violent blip in the droning monotony of street-corner life, Roscoe pursues Jason and his friends like a white ethnic fury.

For their part, Jason and his main man Midget (Gabe Casseus, blessed with a menacingly disingenuous smile) kill their obvious surplus of time by stealing cars, their lives otherwise a series of cool tempo'd exchanges and moments. An almost old-fashioned form of career crime (when the local drug dealers tell them "this isn't a fuckin' drag strip," Midget quips: "Get a job"). Jason and Midget's joyrides are mostly for show, high-speed balm for wounds whose exact nature (race, age, masculinity, the missing fathers?) Gomez only hints at from the margins of *New Jersey Drive*'s scenes.

Whether spinning doughnuts and 360s or just cruising by their friends real slow, *New Jersey Drive*'s nominal heroes are the feature floats in an almost stately parade of lifted rides, as nondescript urban scenery scrolls past their rolled-down windows. Corley bears the weight of being a moral anti-center with the kind of nonchalance that allows him to step into a stolen ride (while on probation, even) without the shadow of a second thought. Except for his mother (Gwen McGee), no one makes much of an impression on him. Jason's "yeah, whatever" equanimity about his situation—whether it be juvenile hall, Roscoe's abuse, or the larger problem of being black, young, and poor—is only broken when his friends transgress streetlife golden rules along the lines of "Yo. Don't mess with my sister." Jason has a core lack of irony (not to mention a certain thoughtlessness) that befits someone his age, and *New Jersey Drive* reflects that inside and narrow p.o.v. to a tee. If Jason or any of his friends are to survive this part of their adolescence, it won't be because *New Jersey Drive* forces that ending on them. Lifting cars might be child's play, but knowing when to stop is the hard part.

Also reviewed in:
CHICAGO TRIBUNE, 4/19/95, Tempo/p. 5, Gary Dretzka
NEW YORK TIMES, 3/24/95, p. C8, Caryn James

VARIETY, 1/23-29/95, p. 71, Todd McCarthy
WASHINGTON POST, 4/19/95, p. C10, Hal Hinson

NICK OF TIME

A Paramount Pictures release. *Executive Producer:* D.J. Caruso. *Producer:* John Badham. *Director:* John Badham. *Screenplay:* Patrick Sheane Duncan. *Director of Photography:* Roy H. Wagner. *Editor:* Frank Morriss and Kevin Stitt. *Music:* Arthur B. Rubinstein. *Music Editor:* Abby Treloggen. *Sound:* Willie Burton and (music) John Richards. *Sound Editor:* John Benson. *Casting:* Carol Lewis. *Production Designer:* Philip Harrison. *Art Director:* Eric Orbom. *Set Designer:* Nancy Mickelberry, Louis Montejano, and Linda King. *Set Decorator:* Julia Badham. *Special Effects:* Jeff Jarvis. *Costumes:* Mary E. Vogt. *Make-up:* John Elliott, Jim Scribner, Sheila Evers, and Patty York. *Stunt Coordinator:* Shane Dixon. *Running time:* 90 minutes. *MPAA Rating:* R.

CAST: Johnny Depp (Gene Watson); Courtney Chase (Lynn Watson); Charles S. Dutton (Huey); Christopher Walken (Mr. Smith); Roma Maffia (Ms. Jones); Marsha Mason (Governor Eleanor Grant); Peter Strauss (Brendan Grant); Gloria Reuben (Krista Brooks); Bill Smitrovich (Officer Trust); G.D. Spradlin (Mystery Man); Yul Vazquez (Gustino, Guest Services); Edith Diaz (Irene, Domestic Maintenance); Armando Ortega (Hector, Guest Services); C.J. Bau (Mixologist); Cynthena Sanders (Beverage Server); Dana Mackey (Transport Reception Manager); Christopher Jacobs (Comestible Server); Charles Carroll (Sanitation Engineer); Miguel Najera (Franco, Governor's Bodyguard); Jerry Tondo (Chief Aide); Lance Hunter Voorhees (Weapons Security); John Azevedo, Jr. (Security Associate); Lance August (Personal Security); Peter Mackenzie (JBN Reporter); Rick Zieff (JBN Videographer); Tom Bradley (Himself); Michael Chong (Asian Man); Cynthia Noritake (Asian Woman); Holly Kuesport (Physically Attractive Woman); Pamela Dunlap (Centerpiece Poacher); Jan Speck (Rally Orienter); Tom Lawrence (Personal Waste Facility User); Robert Buckingham (Illegal Security Access Carrier); J. Clark Johnson (Hackney Transportist); Antony Sandoval (French Man); Isabel Lorca (French Woman); Nicole Mancera (Young Hispanic Girl); Yolanda Gonzalez (Her Mother); Antonette Saftier (Mrs Wentzel); Teddy Beeler (Union Station Security); Alison Stuart (Verbally Abusive Spouse).

LOS ANGELES TIMES, 11/22/95, Calendar/p. 12, Kevin Thomas

The taut suspense thriller "Nick of Time" plunges Johnny Depp into a nightmare minutes after arriving at Union Station. On a catwalk overlooking the main waiting room, a man (Christopher Walken) and a woman (Roma Maffia) are scanning the crowds intently, finally zeroing in on Depp's Gene Watson and his little daughter, Lynn (Courtney Chase).

Flashing a badge, Walken tells Watson he's under arrest. In a blink of an eye Lynn has been taken hostage by Maffia, and Watson has roughly 80 minutes to get over to the Bonaventure and assassinate the governor of California (Marsha Mason), participating in a political rally, if he is to get his daughter back alive.

"Nick of Time" is like "Speed" in that you might not be able to go along with it if you had time to think about it. But director John Badham is not about to let that happen, and from the get-go writer Patrick Sheane Duncan is hard at work building credibility for Watson's dilemma. Even at the risk of his daughter's life, Watson, a decent man—and made totally convincing by Depp—is determined to try to avoid having to try to kill the governor.

This handsome Paramount production is a clever piece of work. Shrewdly, the filmmakers have one of Walken's employers remark that he is less than impressed by his tactic of blackmailing an innocent man into becoming an assassin; surely, there could be an easier, surer way of rubbing out the governor.

Yet Walken, who can embody pure, scary evil better than just about anybody, makes his icy professional killer the sort of guy you'd be tempted to hire in the first place; at the same time, he's also the kind who'd have a screw loose enough to want to get off on terrorizing an individual picked out of a crowd to do his dirty work. OK, it's a premise right out of a paperback you'd buy at the airport as a diversion during a long flight, but one that is really made to work on the screen. Besides, at this crazy point in history, how can any political assassination gambit be dismissed as preposterous?

As part of the impressive economy that is the film's hallmark, "Nick of Time," which is spectacularly photographed by Roy H. Wagner, pares down exposition to a bare minimum. In time we learn that Depp and his daughter are returning from the San Diego funeral of his estranged wife; we never know for sure the governor's party—just that a conspiracy of his conservative backers feel sufficiently betrayed by her liberal policies to want to kill her.

What the filmmakers have done instead is to cast the picture right down the line with actors of such skill and presence that you don't need to be told much about them. Marsha Mason's warmth, attractiveness and intelligence suggests in a flash that the governor is just the sort of person who would grow in office.

Peter Strauss (as the governor's campaign manager husband) and Charles S. Dutton (as a shoeshine man who hears more than he says he does) have similar sharp impact, and there's a wonderful all-in-a-day's-work matter-of-factness about Maffia's kidnaper that makes her all the more chilling. Indeed, the bantering between Maffia and the spunky Chase, parked in a van across from the Bonaventure, becomes a source of dark humor.

That the credits read "A John Badham Movie" instead of the *de rigueur* "Film" is indicative of "Nick of Time's" lack of pretentiousness; except for the Union Station prologue, it takes place entirely at the Bonaventure. For Depp, the most venturesome young actor in Hollywood, "Nick of Time" represents a smart move into a genre that could expand his audience without diminishing his stature.

NEW YORK POST, 11/22/95, p. 47, Michael Medved

"Nick of Time" uses its 90-minute length to depict 90 minutes in the life of its main character, allowing dramatic events to unfold on screen in "real time," but nothing else about this unfortunate film feels in any way real.

In one sense, the project is a victim of its own central gimmick. In real life, even our most dramatic hours are interrupted by stretches of tedium, as we, ride in an elevator, go to the bathroom, or take a cab from one place to another.

In most movies, the camera shows a character getting into the cab or the elevator, then getting out once he reaches his destination. In a real-time epic like this one, however, every elevator ride, every trip to the john, must deliver some jolt of significance to the plot. The "authentic timing" thereby gives rise to a bang-bang series of staccato surprises, creating a hyperactive surface that undermines the very sense of reality the device was intended to convey.

In "Nick of Time" the plot is so preposterous anyway that no adjustments in mere timing could save the film. Johnny Depp plays a bespectacled accountant who arrives in Union Station in downtown L.A. for a series of business appointments. He's bringing along his 6-year-old daughter (Courtney Chase), who he clearly adores, though the script remains foolishly ambiguous on whether he's a grieving widower or recently divorced.

In any event, father and child are intercepted at the station by two businesslike figures (Christopher Walken and Roma Maffia) who flash police badges, then proceed to kidnap the little girl and threaten her dad. Depp is given a loaded gun and ordered to a nearby hotel to assassinate the idealistic governor of California, a "flaming liberal" played by Marsha Mason. If he goes to the authorities, or fails to complete the assignment by precisely 1:30 p.m., the bad guys will murder his daughter.

It turns out that the assassination plot involves a conspiracy so pervasive and powerful that it puts even the feverish fantasies of Oliver Stone to shame, and raises big questions about why the plotters need an unreliable, randomly chosen stranger like Depp in the first place.

In a bow to political correctness, the film also follows a tiresome scheme in which the menaced governor's only reliable protectors are all people of color (including a one-legged shoeshine man, well-played by Charles Dutton), a pattern which becomes so predictable that it destroys surprises in the plot.

Christopher Walken is appropriately ferocious and frightening in his scene-stealing performance, but Johnny Depp is disastrously bland in the Everyman role. He's done well in the past playing eccentric, otherworldly creatures "Edward Scissorhands," "Benny & Joon," "Ed Wood," "Don Juan DeMarco") but as an "ordinary guy" facing extraordinary challenges, he shows little emotion and comes across like a cipher.

Director John Badham has enjoyed success with past thrillers ("WarGames," "Stakeout") that blend wit and action, but he seems ill-suited for a humorless, self-important, paranoid project like this one. Though the film is intriguing in its opening moments, it loses all energy long before its silly series of multiple climaxes and, like a second-rate team with no game plan, the players simply run out the clock.

NEWSDAY, 11/22/95, Part II/p. B19, John Anderson

The big gimmick in "Nick of Time"—in which widowed father Johnny Depp is given the choice of assassinating the governor of California or losing his little daughter—is also its big handicap. Done in real time, so that the movie is precisely as long as the drama within it, the film not only establishes at the outset how much time Depp's character has, it apprises us regularly how much time is left. Since thrillers don't generally resolve, until they're over, the tension goes slack almost every time you see where the big hand is.

Despite this self-created obstacle to suspense, director John Badham ("Stakeout," "Saturday Night Fever," "Point of No Return") does manage to create some nervousness, even if the story is more than vaguely implausible: Mild-mannered accountant Gene Watson (Depp), en route by train from his estranged wife's funeral with their 6-year-old daughter (Courtney Chase), is waylaid in L.A.'s Union Station by two counterfeit police officers (Christopher Walken and Roma Maffia). They make him an offer: Kill the incumbent governor, Eleanor Grant (Marsha Mason), or they'll murder his daughter.

He has an hour. And, as she various clocks tick the time away, Watson will try to avoid doing what they want, all the while knowing he'll do it if it means saving his daughter.

What's unlikely about all this? That the assassination conspiracy reaches all the way to the top of the governor's campaign, and is, presumably, highly professional. And yet, Walken and Maffia's unnamed characters search out their killer at random, looking for someone with something to lose. They latch onto Watson, who's so ironically law-abiding that once he sees a badge he follows them to a van, gets in and is trapped. His unwillingness to kill Grant, of course, throws their precisely laid plan into complete disarray.

Add to this the fact that Walken's character is like Watson's shadow: Whenever the latter seeks help from a stranger—Huey the shoeshine man (Charles S. Dutton) for instance—Walken is there at his elbow. This ability to appear at will becomes something of a joke throughout "Nick of Time," and it adds to the credibility crisis: If Walken and Co. can get to anyone and anywhere in the governor's hotel, why do they need Watson?

So, outside of these fine points of contradictory plot construction, there's no problem. Except for the clock. And the fact that this assassination movie is opening on Nov. 22, the 32nd anniversary of the assassination of John F. Kennedy—bad taste? No, judging from the rest of the film, they probably just didn't notice.

SIGHT AND SOUND, 5/96, p. 57, Kim Newman

Union Station, Los Angeles. Getting off a train at midday, accountant Gene Watson and his six-year-old daughter Lynn are accosted by a Mr Smith and Ms Jones, who pose as police officers. Smith gives Gene a gun and tells him that unless he goes to the nearby Westin Bonaventure Hotel and murders a certain woman by 1.30pm. Lynn will be killed. The potential murder victim turns out to be California Governor Eleanor Grant, who has annoyed conservative interests by reneging on campaign promises to big business. Gene tries to alert the governor's security staff but they are in on the conspiracy. At gunpoint, he makes her aide, Krista Brooks, take him to Brendan Grant, the governor's husband and advisor. Brendan, in the thrall of a mysterious tycoon, is also involved, and Smith, who is on the security staff, murders Krista.

Just after 1 pm, Gene convinces Huey, the shoeshine man, of the problem, and is helped to evade Smith's surveillance long enough to tell the governor of the situation. She doesn't believe

Gene but when she tries to call off the speech she is due to give at 1.30pm, Brendan insists that she goes ahead, which convinces her that Gene has been telling the truth. During the speech, Gene fires wildly, causing a panic. Huey prevents Ms Jones from killing Lynn. Smith is about to murder the girl when Gene guns him down. The true story of the conspiracy begins to filter through to the television news.

Given the super-inflation that has afflicted the thriller/action genre in the 90s, which increasingly values the meaningless kinesis of action over any narrative involvement that might actually be thrilling, it is a shame that *Nick of Time*, which at least has modesty going for it (as well as a very experienced action director in John Badham) does not work better. Real-time plot-unfolding is not, of course, new and here (as in *Rope* and *High Noon*) it prompts fudgings of physical space and narrative progression to keep the machine working. Insistent cutaways to clocks and the confinement of most of the action to a hotel (which has already been seen as the site of a foiled assassination in *In the Line of Fire*) work hard to establish an artificial urgency. But even with the proper suspense mechanisms in place, any real-time telling of this story, involving all the waiting for lifts and hailing of taxis to get Johnny Depp from one scene to the next, would more likely resemble something by Chantal Ackerman than the kind of high-octane nail-biter we expect from the director of *Bird on a Wire*, *The Hard Way* and *Drop Zone*.

Nick of Time also stumbles over simple matters of credibility: since the governor's entire staff (with the exception of the disposable ethnic Krista) is in on the plot to kill her, it is probable that someone as ingenious and ruthless as Smith could come up with a far less unwieldy plan. Christopher Walken coasts through another bad guy role, working hard to spark some life into this stock character, but the crucial relationship between his human fiend and Johnny Depp's ordinary Joe—as he dies, Smith gloats that he has indeed managed to turn Gene into a murderer never clicks, because Depp as an average bespectacled accountant is about as well cast as Charles Bronson was as a pacifist architect in *Death Wish*.

For Depp, this must have seemed an opportunity to go straight like Keanu Reeves in *Speed*, sublimating his fondness for eccentricity and integrity to the demands of a product picture. However, his pretty-pretty looks and reliance on neurotic tics work against a role that could have been a career-maker for a less talented actor. In a suit and tie, establishing hero credentials by seeing off some roller-bladers hassling his daughter at the station, Depp does his best to be a regular leading man. But he delivers an early speech so intently that it's difficult on a plot level to work out whether his claim to a cab driver to have come from his wife's funeral is the literal truth or a made-up excuse to explain his distress. Given his screen history and the visible wires of angst that animate his model-perfect face, one feels Depp's natural reaction to this situation would be to retreat into catatonia for an hour and a half, pondering Hamlet-like on the tug between action and inaction, stirring himself to murder just after Walken has killed the little girl.

VILLAGE VOICE, 12/5/95, p. 61, J. Hoberman

Another sort of masculine imperative may be found in John Badham's *Nick of Time*—a trimly efficient assassination thriller that successfully overrides most logical objections to its premise. [The reference is to *Wild Bill*.]

Paramount decided to open this Johnny Depp vehicle on the 32nd celebration of JFK death day and there are instant intimations of social breakdown as the train carrying Depp's bespectacled widower and his generically adorable six-year-old daughter pulls into L.A.'s Union Station. The homeless are fighting in the storm drains; predatory rollerbladers can skate through the station at will. Then, a sinister pair of operatives (Christopher Walken and Roma Maffia) snatch Depp's daughter, hand him a gun, and tell him he has 90 minutes to shoot California's governor (Marsha Mason) if he ever wants to see the child again.

It's assassin as victim. Written by Patrick Sheane Duncan, whose subjective-camera *84 Charlie Mopic* was perhaps the most conceptually interesting of late-'80's Vietnam films, *Nick of Time* has a similar gimmick. The movie more or less approximates real time and is set almost entirely in the hermetic, privatized urban environment of the massively cylindrical Westin Bonaventure Hotel-cum-deluxe mall. The premise produces an inescapable tension—there's only one patently unfair lapse into action hallucination—even as the disorienting location (known to the grad students of the past decade for being a paradigm of the new "total space," according to Fredric

Jameson's 1984 essay "Postmodernism, or, the Cultural Logic of Late Capitalism") becomes a sort of vulgar equivalent of Kafka's Castle.

Not only is the Bonaventure a seamless, inescapable environment, the governor's crime is basically existential. She's not a candidate for higher office. She has been sentenced to death for being a politician—or perhaps, in this California-centric universe, for being soft on the unnamed Proposition 187. The necessity for her elimination suggests some combination of immigration laxness and multicultural excess; she is accused by one conspirator of having "turned the governor's office into the United Nations."

Pondering the experience of the Bonaventure's imposing glass elevators, Jameson wrote that the traditional stroll had been superceded by "a transportation machine which becomes the allegorical signifier of that older promenade we are no longer allowed to conduct on our own." Similarly, participation in the democratic process is represented by this parable of theme-park America, in which a diminished patriarch bounces off the chrome and glass walls, fruitlessly seeking empathy from his fellow hyper-citizens.

Those who might save Depp from his killer instincts are inevitably those who, in the movie's color-coordinated schemata, have the most to lose from the governor's death. Politics is predicated on self-interest after all.

Also reviewed in:
CHICAGO TRIBUNE, 11/22/95, Tempo/p. 1, Rick Kogan
NEW YORK TIMES, 11/22/95, p. C14, Janet Maslin
VARIETY, 11/27-12/3/95, p. 80, Brian Lowry
WASHINGTON POST, 11/22/95, p. B4, Rita Kempley
WASHINGTON POST, 11/24/95, Weekend/p. 54, Desson Howe

NINA TAKES A LOVER

A Triumph/TriStar release. *Executive Producer:* Graeme Bretall and Shelby Notkin. *Producer:* Jane Hernandez and Alan Jacobs. *Director:* Alan Jacobs. *Screenplay:* Alan Jacobs. *Director of Photography:* Phil Parmet. *Editor:* John Nutt. *Music:* Todd Boekelheide. *Sound:* Dan Gleich. *Casting:* Richard Pagano and Sharon Bialy. *Production Designer:* Don De Fina. *Set Decorator:* Victoria Lewis. *Costumes:* Marianna Astrom-De Fina. *Running time:* 100 minutes. *MPAA Rating:* R.

CAST: Laura San Giacomo (Nina); Paul Rhys (Photographer); Michael O'Keefe (Journalist); Cristi Conaway (Friend); Fisher Stevens (Paulie).

LOS ANGELES TIMES, 5/5/95, Calendar/p. 10, Kevin Thomas

"Nina Takes a Lover"—but even though she's played by Laura San Giacomo it's hard to care one way or another. Writer-director Alan Jacobs, in his feature debut, takes us into a self-enclosed world only to inhabit it with uninteresting people; it's even hard to connect with Nina through her occupation, owner of a small San Francisco shoe store, not exactly the most captivating of endeavors.

Jacobs means to grapple with the challenge facing couples several years into marriage, a time when romance has begun to fade, making the relationship vulnerable. Nina is being interviewed by a newspaper journalist (Michael O'Keefe) who is writing a piece on this very subject, and the film commences to unfold in flashbacks. Nina tells the reporter that, inspired by a fling one of her married friends (Cristi Conaway) is having with an espresso bartender (Fisher Stevens), she entered an affair with a Welsh photographer (Paul Rhys) while her husband was out of town for three weeks.

None of these people has much personality or individuality or much on their minds except their emotions, and it's hard for San Giacomo and Rhys, for all their magnetism and skill, to keep us intrigued. What's more, Jacobs resorts to a gimmick for his payoff when he hasn't created enough substance to make it work as well as it should. "Nina Takes a Lover" is the sort of picture the French make so very intense and involving, charged with insights and ironies.

It's a shame that "Nina Takes a Lover"—the kind of small, intimate film one wants to like—hasn't more going on to hold our attention more firmly, because it is nicely crafted, nicely acted and unfolds with a certain grace and charm.

NEW YORK POST, 5/12/95, p. 42, Thelma Adams

To be faithful, or to be unfaithful, that is the question. In "Nina Takes a Lover," reporter Michael O'Keefe is researching a lifestyle piece about marital infidelity. His interviews stir up a chamber piece about sex and marriage that never quite rises above the level of a Cosmo article, although the comedy is an offbeat departure from typical Hollywood scenes from a marriage.

Set within San Francisco's upscale coffeehouse culture, "Nina Takes a Lover" showcases the underused talents of espresso-voiced beauty Laura San Giacomo, ("sex, lies and videotape"). As Nina, the chic owner of a shoe store, the archly named Arches, San Giacomo plays a modern married woman who seems to have everything. But something is missing when she tosses that salad or sells those espadrilles: The thrill of a new romance is gone and she can't find anything to take its place.

Nina meets a photographer (Paul Rhys) while her husband is away on business. The tall, broad-shouldered, dreamy-eyed British actor is as ripe as the apple Nina crunches to get his attention.

When they're not forced to talk like characters from an Obsession ad, Rhys and San Giacomo have excellent chemistry. The seduction by apple and an interlude in the back of the shoe store where the photographer seduces Nina on a ladder are fresh and appealing.

The scenes that pair Nina and her best friend play like Betty and Veronica making it with Jughead and Reggie while Archie is away. As written and directed by newcomer Alan Jacobs, the structure is the movie's central flaw. Whenever the narrative returns to the coffeehouse for interview segments with O'Keefe, the flames of passion frizzle out and the characters' narcissism surfaces.

By the conclusion of "Nina Takes a Lover," we're glad to end the affair.

NEWSDAY, 5/12/95, Part II/p. B5, Jack Mathews

First-time writer-director Alan Jacobs has boasted that he spent only four days writing "Nina Takes a Lover," the story of a San Francisco woman who has a mad affair while her husband is out of town. After watching it, you may wonder what took him so long.

This is not a movie, it's a shaggy-dog story, an hour-and-a-half of exposition to reach a conclusion that makes you feel like a fool for having paid attention. Everybody loves a surprise ending, but only if all that precedes it becomes instantly logical, as if the truth had been hovering just beyond your perception all along.

"Nina," which focuses on the ennui that often settles over a marriage after the first years of passion, is much too coy—and its characters much too narcissistic—to keep us hanging on the outcome. The story is told through a series of fragmented interviews between a magazine writer (Michael O'Keefe) and two sets of lovers—Nina (Laura San Giacomo) and the British photographer (Paul Rhys) she meets in a park, and Nina's best friend (Cristi Conaway) and her lover (Fisher Stevens).

What the writer learns, when he's not chewing his cud over his own marriage revelations, is that the two women have entered affairs for totally different reasons and with different levels of commitment. Nina's friend is stuck in a bad marriage, and figures she deserves all the extra-marital action she can get, while Nina, reluctant at first, cannot resist the opportunity to rediscover the romantic passion that has faded between her and her husband.

The brassy Conaway and Stevens, playing an espresso shop Lothario with an Italian flair, have some fun with their roles, but the others are so serious, so devoid of personality, that you really don't want to know what's eating them. It's like being stuck in the waiting room at a marriage counselor's office with strangers who insist on *sharing*!

What Jacobs might have remembered had he taken ... say, five days to write the script, is that one of the essential elements of romantic passion, and of a successful marriage, is a shared sense of humor. That's why they call it whoopie.

Also reviewed in:
CHICAGO TRIBUNE, 5/5/95, Friday/p. I, John Petrakis
NEW YORK TIMES, 5/12/95, p. C12, Stephen Holden
VARIETY, 1/31-2/6/94, p. 67, Todd McCarthy

NINE MONTHS

A Twentieth Century Fox release of a 1492 production. *Executive Producer:* Joan Bradshaw and Christopher Lambert. *Producer:* Anne Françios, Chris Columbus, Mark Radcliffe, and Michael Barnathan. *Director:* Chris Columbus. *Screenplay:* Chris Columbus. *Based on the film "Neuf mois" by:* Patrick Braoudé. *Director of Photography:* Donald McAlpine. *Editor:* Raja Gosnell. *Music:* Hans Zimmer. *Music Editor:* Adam Smalley. *Sound:* Nelson Stoll and (music) Jay Rifkin. *Sound Editor:* Robert Shoup. *Casting:* Janet Hirshenson and Jane Jenkins. *Production Designer:* Angelo P. Graham. *Art Director:* W. Steven Graham. *Set Designer:* Richard Berger and Steve Saklad. *Set Decorator:* Garrett Lewis. *Special Effects:* John McLeod. *Costumes:* Jay Hurley. *Stunt Coordinator:* Glenn R. Wilder. *Running time:* 100 minutes. *MPAA Rating:* PG-13.

CAST: Hugh Grant (Samuel Faulkner); Julianne Moore (Rebecca Taylor); Tom Arnold (Marty Dwyer); Joan Cusack (Gail Dwyer); Jeff Goldblum (Sean Fletcher); Robin Williams (Dr. Kosevich); Mia Cottet (Lili); Joey Simmrin (Truman); Ashley Johnson (Shannon Dwyer); Alexa Vega (Molly Dwyer); Aislin Roche (Patsy Dwyer); Priscilla Alden (Older Woman); Edward Ivory (Older Man); James M. Brady (Bicyclist); Charles A. Martinet (Arnie); Brendan Columbus (Little Boy on Beach); Eleanor Columbus (Little Girl in Ballet Class #1); Anna Barnathan (Little Girl in Ballet Class #2); Zelda Williams (Little Girl in Ballet Class #3); Peter Bankins (Tow Truck Driver); Betsy Monroe (Bobbie); Ngaio S. Bealum (Sean's Friend #1); Cynthia Urquhart (Sean's Friend #2); Tim Moffet (Sean's Friend #3); Mia Liban (Sean's Friend #4); Kumar Singh (Sean's Friend #5); Amanda Girard (Praying Mantis); Val Diamond (Dr. Kosevich's Receptionist); Jerry Masan (Clown Outside Toy Store); Irene Columbus (Woman in Toy Store); Violet Columbus (Baby in Toy Store); Brittany Radcliffe (Child #1 at Toy Store); Porscha Radcliffe (Child #2 at Toy Store); Cody Lee Dorkin (Child #3 at Toy Store); Emily Gosnell (Child #4 at Toy Store); Bradley Gosnell (Child #5 at Toy Store); Kristin Davis (Tennis Attendant); Angela Hopkins (Ultrasound Receptionist); Emily Yancy (Dr. Thatcher); Hayley Rose Hansen (Baby in Ultrasound); Shawn Cady (Roller Blade Girl); George F. Mauricio (Moving Man); Paul Simon (Car Salesman); Frank P. Verducci (Car Lot Customer #1); Barabara Olson (Car Lot Customer #2); Morgan Miller (Kid Being Choked in Park); Carol De Pasquale (Maternity Floor Receptionist); Bruce Devan (Doctor in Hallway); Cheryl Lee Thorup (Christine); Clarke Devereux (Emergency Attendant #1); Tommy Banks (Emergency Attendant #2); Susan Ilene Johnson (Delivery Room Head Nurse); Maureen McVerry (Pregnant Woman #1); Velina Brown (Pregnant Woman #2); Joy M. Cook (Pregnant woman #3); Sue Murphy (Pregnant Woman #4); Lee Ann Manley (Pregnant Woman #5); Diane Amos (Rebecca's Nurse); Betsy Aidem (Gail's Nurse); Terence McGovern (Anesthesiologist); Geoff Bolt (Male Delivery Room Nurse); Gwen Holloway (Female Delivery Room Nurse).

LOS ANGELES TIMES, 7/12/95, Calendar/p. 1, Kenneth Turan

Recent events notwithstanding, the biggest threat to Hugh Grant's career is not his vice arrest but the indifferent performance of forgettable material. Films like "Nine Months" can kill a career faster than the tabloids.

The story of one man's resistance to becoming a father, the nominally comic "Nine Months" is the latest effort from writer-director-producer Chris Columbus, the boy conglomerate best known as the director of "Home Alone," a film that looks cutting-edge compared to this predigested pap.

Only 35, Columbus is turning into the youngest business-as-usual filmmaker in the business, with an unerring instinct for the predictable and the hackneyed. Though his films (including "Mrs.

Doubtfire") are such consistent moneymakers that the press kit trumpets Columbus as "the fifth most successful motion picture director of all time," they are not going to win any awards for originality. Nor, apparently, do they particularly want to.

Set in San Francisco, "Nine Months" (based on the French film "Neuf Mois") posits a familiar situation. Rebecca Taylor (Julianne Moore) and Samuel Faulkner (Grant) have spent five wonderful years together, but the over-30 Rebecca feels something is missing from her life, and it's not the heartbreak of psoriasis.

No, Rebecca wants a family, but Samuel, who just happens to be a child psychotherapist, is horrified at the thought. "Why change what's perfect?" he asks, an attitude that is intensified by a random encounter with a family of breeders, Marty and Gail Dwyer (Tom Arnold and Joan Cusack) and their trio of out-of-control monster children.

But guess what? Rebecca accidentally gets pregnant and, guess again, Samuel is not overjoyed. What, sell his red Porsche convertible for a family car? In fact, Samuel so strenuously resists fatherhood that Rebecca starts to question whether this indeed is the man she wants to spend the rest of her life with. And so on.

Though Columbus says he likes to mix comedy with emotion, there is little enough of either here, and no real story to speak of, witness the film's culmination in a particularly leaden farce in a hospital delivery room. Though he is a sincere director who has the commercially enviable knack of embracing tired contrivance as if it were fresh invention, making things believable and moving is not, at least at this point in his career, one of Columbus' strengths.

Not benefiting from his direction is Grant, who gives a performance that doesn't edge into self-parody, it embraces it wholeheartedly. Rather than act, Grant has chosen the easier path of immersion in a sea of movie star mannerisms: He winks, raises his eyebrows, flutters his lids, fools with his hair, rubs his nose, forces a grin and then starts over again.

If Grant is victimized by doing too much, Moore is handicapped by having too little to do. After her impressive work in "Vanya on 42nd Street" and the current "Safe," watching her trying to cope with this film's lightweight dialogue and situations is like watching Michael Jordan trying to fit himself into a schoolyard pickup game. While it is gratifying to see such a gifted actress getting a commercial payday, it's too bad it had to be this one.

As for Arnold and Cusack, perhaps it's enough to say that both have done better work elsewhere. And their jobs are not made any easier by the peculiar burden of their characters, which are written to be half comic grotesques and half sensitive role models who, teach silly Samuel that having children can be more satisfying than that red Porsche convertible. In case you had any doubts.

Coming off best are a pair of sidemen who are allowed to mostly concentrate on being funny. Robin Williams adds a welcome note of pure anarchy as Dr. Kosevich, newly arrived from the former Soviet Union and not used to human patients. And Jeff Goldblum, looking surprisingly muscular with a cute earring, makes a strong impression as Samuel's best friend and confidant.

Though it strives to be clever, the only time "Nine Months" manages to be genuinely witty is in its closing credits, when it displays baby pictures of its stars. It's a small touch but it's not overdone, which is probably why it provides such a contrast with its surroundings.

NEW YORK POST, 7/12/95, p. 33, Michael Medved

At one point in "Nine Months" Hugh Grant tells his best friend, an eccentric artist played by Jeff Goldblum, that his latest painting looks like "hotel room art."

And that's just how "Nine Months" should be categorized—it's the kind of by-the-numbers work that's as garish and vacuous as the images of farms or bridges you'd find on the wall of any Holiday Inn.

Grant portrays a child psychiatrist in San Francisco who's been happily involved for five years with a ballet instructor played by Julianne Moore. He describes their life as "dangerously close to perfect," until the sunny afternoon when she announces she's unexpectedly pregnant—and he immediately proceeds to crash his shiny red Porsche.

That crash gives an indication of the elbow-in-the-ribs nature of the film's attempts at humor; you almost expect these clumsy comedic moments to come accompanied with a laugh track.

It's a pity. In the enjoyable "Four Weddings and a Funeral," Hugh Grant became an international star by playing a charming bumbler who kept finding himself in ridiculous but believable situations. Here, nothing feels real: Grant beats up a guy in a dinosaur suit at a toy store, runs down a bicyclist on the way to the hospital, and gets into a free-swinging brawl with the doctor (and others) in the delivery room. He's particularly ill-suited for this sort of slapstick: mugging toward the camera with bug-eyes and open mouth, or executing awkward and exaggerated pratfalls.

Tom Arnold is only slightly less stilted as a loud-mouth car salesman who insists on befriending Grant when he learns that their woman are expecting at the same time. Robin Williams also makes a brief but amusing appearance as an inept, warm-hearted Soviet emigre obstetrician who's (implausibly) assigned to Julianne Moore even though his only experience involves delivering animals back in Russia. He's also given to embarrassing malapropisms—like suggesting to a patient who's howling in pain that she needs a "pedicure" when he means to say "epidural."

Writer-director Chris Columbus has made a fortune by deftly mixing slapstick and sentiment in films like "Home Alone" and "Mrs. Doubtfire," but this time the feeling comes across far more effectively than the funny stuff. That's due in large part to the touching performance by Julianne Moore as a sexy, down-to-earth woman who's heartbroken that the man in her lift, can't seem to share her joy in the new life she's carrying.

Obviously, much of the speculation concerning "Nine Months" centers on the box office impact of off-screen scandals involving Hugh Grant. It's unfortunate that people drawn to the movie will be inundated with lewd content to add to the minor titillation of the star's recent arrest for lewd conduct.

The movie is full of smarmy double-entendres like Robin Williams telling Moore she has a "small pussy" after examining her and finding cat hairs on her clothes—and considerably more graphic references and four-letter words than you'd expect in a PG-13 release.

These gratuitous elements represent a sad attempt to lend an edge to an otherwise bland comedy that is, for the most part, painfully unfunny.

NEWSDAY, 7/12/95, Part II/p. B2, Jack Mathews

Hugh Grant's bad times are behind him. With writer-director Chris Columbus' "Nine Months," the British star can get on with a career that was barely nudged by an event that was scripted in tabloid heaven.

In this romantic farce, written and directed by Chris Columbus ("Home Alone," "Mrs. Doubtfire"), Grant plays Samuel Faulkner, a child psychologist who does not like kids, but does love the toys and lifestyle their business provides him. His bright red Porsche, his fashionable San Francisco apartment, the tennis club membership, a five-year relationship with Rebecca (Julianne Moore) that comes "dangerously close," he tells her, "to perfection."

Then she gets pregnant, and during the panic, accusations, confusion, conflict and soul-searching that follow, the pathologically self-absorbed Samuel is born again.

To say the story, adapted from the French film "Neuf Mois," is predictable is to state the obvious, Columbus' movies are all predictable; the pleasures, if you find them, are in the lines, the situations and the performances. Columbus has a penchant for wretched sentimentality, and it's a frequent intruder here. But he also has a wonderful ear for sly comic dialogue, and a developing gift for the kind of physical farce we used to get in gut-clutching waves from Blake Edwards.

Those farcical set pieces don't always work. There's a badly overreaching scene in the maternity ward, where two women are giving birth simultaneously while their husbands are fighting, that undermines much of the good work that precedes it. But with all screwball comedy, you either accept the excesses and enjoy, or resist and anguish.

"Mrs. Doubtfire" was anguish for me, because Robin Williams' frantic freeform comic style was ultimately suffocated by sentiment. Hugh Grant is a comedy actor, as opposed to a comedian, which gives us a different set of expectations and allows him to shift moods less jarringly. And though Samuel is the central focus of the story, Grant is given plenty of comic support, not least by Williams himself, who appears in an unrestrained cameo as Rebecca's Russian doctor, a former veterinarian looking forward to his first human delivery.

Also around are Tom Arnold and Joan Cusack, as a couple of eager breeders with a pack of obnoxious children, and Jeff Goldblum, who uses the script's subtlest lines to steal every scene he's in, as Samuel's equally self-absorbed best friend.

Moore does the best she can with the straight and underwritten role of the suffering Significant Other, a woman whose nesting instinct puts her at odds with the man she loves. But it's a losing cause. It's hard enough to create a real character amidst chaos, and impossible when all she is asked to do is wait around for Samuel to change.

Grant's mannerisms—the nervous tics, the bashful shrug, the James Stewart stammer—are going to grow old soon, but it's all pretty effective now. Both in "Four Weddings and a Funeral" and this, he turns egotism into rakish charm. He manages to seem both self-assured and vulnerable at the same time, whimsical and pained, and based on his performance on Jay Leno's show, I would say it's a style to which he comes naturally.

During Monday's show, Leno led a camera crew outside to the throng of media and fans who'd gathered for Grant's first post-bust appearance. Among the crowd was a young woman holding up a sign saying "I would have paid you Hugh."

I don't know how much use Grant has for that sort of devotion, but after "Nine Months," all he'll have to do is ask.

SIGHT AND SOUND, 10/95, p. 56, Claire Monk

English child psychologist Samuel Faulkner has lived happily in San Francisco with his girlfriend Rebecca for five years but recoils from commitment. When Rebecca announces that she is pregnant, he is so shocked he crashes his Porsche. He visits his friend Sean, who shows no regrets that his partner Christine has just left him because he refused to start a family. Sean's sister Gail and her husband Marty arrive with their three intrusive daughters, intensifying Samuel's horror.

Samuel plans to tell Rebecca she must end the pregnancy, but loses his nerve. After a hospital check-up with Dr Kosevich, a newly arrived Russian émigré obstetrician, Samuel persuades Rebecca to keep her pregnancy quiet, but their secret is revealed when they are spotted by Gail and Marty who are attending a checkup for an expected fourth child. Rebecca tells Gail she is unhappy about Samuel's negative attitude to their baby. Sean, admits to Samuel that losing Christine and the chance of fatherhood have left his life empty, and tells Samuel not to make his mistake.

Too late to share Rebecca's first ultrasound appointment, Samuel is moved to hear that the child is a boy and healthy. Warned by the doctor that Rebecca is upset and needs his support, he arrives home contrite to find her packing. Alone with the ultrasound video of his son, he cries. Eventually, Samuel apologises to Rebecca for his selfishness and she accepts his offer of marriage.

Rebecca goes into labour. The couple are horrified to find Dr Kosevich in charge and have to share a delivery room with Gail and Marty. In the ensuing chaos, Marty is disappointed to acquire a fourth daughter, and Samuel is overwhelmed to see his new son.

Just before *Nine Months'* US release back in July a rumour drifted across the Atlantic that the 'disgraced' Englishman's $35 million big studio debut was, according to one source, "the worst movie to come out of Hollywood since *9½ Weeks*". Sadly, Nine *Months* isn't even that interesting. If it weren't for the Lewd Hugh factor, this would just be another routine Chris Columbus comedy—except that this time the cynicism about conventional family set-ups which gave Columbus' *Mrs Doubtfire* and *Home Alone* their edge has been unconvincingly papered over in the name of saccharine pro-family propaganda.

That motherhood and marriage are the only 'natural' outcomes for Rebecca is never really in doubt. In case we miss the message, Rebecca tells Gail "I know it's fashionable to be a strong single mother, but I want this baby to have a mother and a father." What Senator Robert Dole—the Republican leader—will make of *Nine Months* is a mystery. Coherently coupling as it does coy sex with self-consciously explicit language, and girlie sentiment with 'comic' male violence; it comes across as a self-defeating shotgun wedding of high concepts, tacked together by committee in the desperate hope that slinging in something for everyone will please someone somewhere.

The success of *Four Weddings and a Funeral* had much to do with its makers' freedom to by-pass this kind of corporate bad faith. By contrast, the executives who control *Nine Months* and its star's image really need not have bothered. They removed a sequence in which Grant gets arrested for breaking a window to rescue his cat reputedly on the bizarre grounds that it would reduce his appeal for female audiences. No less likely to have the same negative effect are a scene in which he is accused of French kissing Tom Arnold while the latter is giving him mouth-to-mouth resuscitation and one where he repeatedly kicks a toy-store employee wearing a dinosaur suit in the head.

The oddest thing about watching *Nine Months* is noticing how uneasily Grant fits this formulaic comedy-romance. In *Four Weddings* his tongue tied confusion, elaborate self-denigration and disastrous lack of tact were over-played but came off because they seemed real. In *Nine Months* the same traits, extravagant verbal nuances and facial tics are duplicated so closely that his performance comes across as self-conscious, insincere self-pastiche—an extension, in fact, of the same performance he has spent the past year perfecting in public. However, in the process his hypertrophied 'Englishness' has mutated into something nastier: his wit now comes across as arrogance, his self-belittlement as a front for self-regard and his tactlessness as rudeness and even cruelty.

This performance might have provided an acerbic foil for the movie's sentimentality—but in a film which requires us to believe in his transformation into a dream husband and father it's a disaster. It's fitting that the film assigns more importance to an exchange of commodities than it does to a change of heart: Samuel's refusal to part with his two-seater Porsche is presented as definitive proof of his hostility to the future child, so his purchase of a family car and an engagement ring are deemed sufficient to silence any misgivings about the pairing.

In fact, the main thing Rebecca and Samuel seem to have in common is their shared xenophobic terror of Robin Williams' highly-strung Russian obstetrician, offensively portrayed as having earned his professional honours by practising on monkeys. If Williams is still the funniest person in the film, it's no thanks to a script which makes him mouth ancient malapropisms like "Now I'll take a look at your Volvo."

In a sad come-down from her famous pube-flashing in Robert Altman's *Short Cuts*, the talented Julianne Moore is here given the ignoble task of tempting Grant with the most sanitised cinematic strip-tease in living memory. But then *Nine Months'* idea of what women want is so impoverished that when Samuel carries his heavily pregnant bride over the threshold, her wedding-day treat proves to be a lavishly equipped, pastel-hued nursery.

Also reviewed in:
CHICAGO TRIBUNE, 7/12/95, Tempo/p. 16, Michael Wilmington
NEW REPUBLIC, 8/14/95, p. 24, Stanley Kauffmann
NEW YORK TIMES, 7/12/95, p. C11, Janet Maslin
VARIETY, 7/10-16/95, p. 34, Todd McCarthy
WASHINGTON POST, 7/12/95, p. D1, Rita Kempley
WASHINGTON POST, 7/14/95, Weekend/p. 36, Desson Howe

NIXON

A Hollywood Pictures release of an Andrew G. Vajna presentation of an Illusion Entertainment Group/Cinergi production. *Producer:* Clayton Townsend, Oliver Stone, and Andrew G. Vajna. *Director:* Oliver Stone. *Screenplay:* Stephen J. Rivele, Christopher Wilkinson, and Oliver Stone. *Director of Photography:* Robert Richardson. *Editor:* Brian Berdan and Hank Corwin. *Music:* John Williams. *Music Editor:* Ken Wannberg. *Sound:* David Macmillan and (music) Shawn Murphy. *Sound Editor:* Wylie Stateman and Gregg Baxter. *Casting:* Billy Hopkins, Heidi Levitt, and Mary Vernieu. *Production Designer:* Victor Kempster. *Art Director:* Donald Woodruff, Richard F. Mays, and Margery Zweizig. *Set Designer:* Henry Alberti, Peter J. Kelly, and Charlie Vassar. *Set Decorator:* Merideth Boswell. *Set Dresser:* Roger Knight. *Special Effects:* F. Lee Stone. *Costumes:* Richard Hornung. *Make-up:* John Blake. *Running time:* 190 minutes. *MPAA Rating:* R.

CAST: Anthony Hopkins (Richard M. Nixon); Joan Allen (Pat Nixon); Powers Boothe (Alexander Haig); Ed Harris (E. Howard Hunt); Bob Hoskins (J. Edgar Hoover); E.G. Marshall (John Mitchell); David Paymer (Ron Ziegler); David Hyde Pierce (John Dean); Paul Sorvino (Henry Kissinger); Mary Steenburgen (Hannah Nixon); J.T. Walsh (John Ehrlichman); James Woods (H.R. Haldeman); Brian Bedford (Clyde Tolson); Kevin Dunn (Charles Colson); Fyvush Finkel (Murray Chotiner); Annabeth Gish (Julie Nixon); Tony Goldwyn (Harold Nixon); Larry Hagman ('Jack Jones'); Ed Herrmann (Nelson Rockefeller); Madeleine Kahn (Martha Mitchell); Saul Rubinek (Herb Klein); Tony Lo Bianco (Johnny Roselli); Corey Carrier (Richard Nixon at 12); Tom Bower (Frank Nixon); David Barry Gray (Richard Nixon at 19); Tony Plana (Manolo Sanchez); Dan Hedaya (Trini Cardoza); John Cunningham (Bob); John C. McGinley (Earl); John Diehl (Gordon Liddy); Robert Beltran (Frank Sturgis); Lenny Vullo (Bernard Barker); Ronald von Klaussen (James McCord); Kamar de los Reyes (Eugenio Martinez); Enrique Castillo (Virgilio Gonzales); Victor Rivers (Cuban Plumber); Drew Snyder (Moderator); Sean Stone (Donald Nixon); Joshua Preston (Arthur Nixon); Ian Calip (Football Player); Jack Wallace (Football Coach); Julie Condra Douglas (Young Pat Nixon); Annette Helde (Happy Rockefeller); Howard Platt (Lawyer at Party); Mike Kennedy (Convention Announcer); Harry Murphy (Fan #1); Suzanne Schnulle Murphy (Fan #2); Michael Kaufman (Fan #3); Bridgette Wilson (Sandy); Pamela Dickerson (Girlfriend); O'Neal Compton (Texas Man); John Bedford Lloyd (Cuban Man); Christian Renna (Family Doctor); Michael Chiklis (TV Director); Wilson Cruz (Joaquin); James Pickens (Black Orator); Mikey Stone (Edward Nixon); Robert Marshall (Spiro Agnew); Marley Shelton (Tricia Nixon); James Karen (Bill Rogers); Richard Fancy (Mel Laird); Peter Carlin (Student #1); Joanna Going (Young Student); Michelle Krusiec (Student #2); Wass Stevens (Protester); Tom Nicoletti (Secret Service Agent #1); Chuck Pfeiffer (Secret Service Agent #2); Alex Butterfield (White House Staffer); Mark Steins (White House Security); Ric Young (Mao-Tse-Tung); Bai Ling (Chinese Interpreter); Peter P. Starson, Jr. (Air Force One Steward); Jon Tenney (Reporter #1); Julie Araskog (Reporter #2); Ray Wills (Reporter #3); John Bellucci (Reporter #4); Zoey Zimmerman (Reporter #5); Mary Rudolph (Rosemary Woods); Clayton Townsend (Floor Manager #1); Donna Dixon (Maureen Dean); John Stockwell (Staffer #1); Charlie Haugk (Staffer #2); Boris Sichkin (Leonid Brezhnev); Fima Noveck (Andre Gromyko); Raissa Danilova (Russian Interpreter); Marilyn Rockafellow (Helen Smith); Bill Bolender (Bethesda Doctor); Melinda Renna (Bethesda Nurse); George Plimpton (President's Lawyer).

CHRISTIAN SCIENCE MONITOR, 12/20/95, p. 14, David Sterritt

The life and times of Richard Nixon have come to the Hollywood screen—expletives undeleted. They come by courtesy of Oliver Stone, who evidently considered the controversy over his explosive "JFK" a mere warm-up for future excursions into American history as seen through his proudly irreverent eyes.

Not that "Nixon" raises as much ruckus as "JFK" did with its wild speculations, volatile mixtures of fact and fiction, and quicker-than-the-eye editing. The new picture is calmer, more contemplative, even a bit melancholy in its portrait of an aspiring world-changer whose bravest plans are forever undercut by deep-lying personality flaws.

In the true Stone tradition, though, it's bound to earn widespread attention while outraging just about everyone at some point in its three-hour running time.

Nixon admirers won't like its portrait of the president as a foul-mouthed bigot, spewing venom about minorities into his hidden White House microphones, and a heedless geopolitical killer, sending bombers to Southeast Asia with hardly a shrug. Nixon detractors won't like its compassion for the president as a three-dimensional human being who might have been a 20th-century giant if, as the Henry Kissinger character suggests, someone had just loved him enough when it counted.

My own view of the movie lies between these extremes. Stone does a masterly job of balancing two Nixons, the ruthless powermonger and the sadly vulnerable man, allowing each to flourish as a fully rounded screen figure. Yet here, as in many of his other movies, Stone pushes the envelope a little too far, allowing his own similarities to Nixon—a driven personality, a thirst for power in his profession, an attraction/repulsion relationship with the press—to skew his movie in the direction of synthetic drama rather than audacious "countermyth."

Stone's ability to both praise and excoriate Nixon may be related to the wobbly political views I've detected in his movies over the years. In pictures like "Platoon" and "Talk Radio" and "Born on the Fourth of July," he seems to be a Hollywood liberal, criticizing the political and military establishments for their conservative leanings. But the recent "Natural Born Killers" strikes me as antiliberal in the extreme, brimming with contempt for the media and scorn for the powerless members of society. The ideological oscillations in "Nixon" may reflect Stone's own uncertainties about the public sphere, suggesting that he's more interested than illuminated when it comes to political matters.

His weakness in this area shows most clearly in the film's worst sequence: a last-minute coda accompanying the final credits, when we hear Nixon bid farewell to the White House after his resignation over the Watergate scandal. Like countless others, I saw that event live on television and vividly remember the president being barely in control of his emotions as he vented his sorrow at the most wrenching moment of his career.

Putting an ornery twist on this scene, Stone makes it seem almost triumphant, with the departing chief executive giving inspirational advice in a rock-solid voice instead of groping for words through poorly concealed tears. It's an inexplicable choice, ending a richly complex film on an oddly simplistic note.

Out-of-kilter as it is, Stone's approach to this finale injects the only false ingredient into Anthony Hopkins's superb portrayal of the title character, which seamlessly blends Nixon's physical traits with the actor's own interpretive brilliance.

The supporting cast is similarly strong: James Woods and J.T. Walsh as H.R. Haldeman and John Ehrlichman, the president's top henchmen; Ed Harris as E. Howard Hunt, pictured as a weirded-out conspirator; Bob Hoskins as J. Edgar Hoover, given flagrantly gay mannerisms; E.G. Marshall as John Mitchell, steely and guilty in equal measure; Joan Allen and Mary Steenburgen as Nixon's long-suffering wife and discipline-conscious mother; and above all Paul Sorvino, who plays Kissinger as a smooth-talking concoction of Ivy League intelligence and Dr. Strangelove inscrutability.

In cinematic terms, "Nixon" is far more conservative than the daring "JFK," harking back to relatively straightforward Stone pictures like "Wall Street" and "Heaven and Earth." Still, it contains some breathtaking moments of filmic ingenuity, as when John F. Kennedy's assassination is conveyed in a sequence of exquisitely evocative shots.

Robert Richardson's cinematography is crisp and imaginative, if less dazzling than his work in the current "Casino," and John Williams's music lends a classical touch to the proceedings. Stone wrote the screenplay with Stephen J. Rivele and Christopher Wilkinson.

FILMS IN REVIEW, 3-4/96, p. 62, Andy Pawelczak

Oliver Stone's three-hour-long Nixon begins with a quote from the Bible—"What does it profit a man if he gains the whole world and loses his own soul"—and right away we know we're in for some serious sledding on slippery ice. Stone, in an act of hubris that almost puts him on a par with Nixon himself, wants to tap into the political unconscious of America in two of its most traumatic decades. It's all here, either referred to or directly presented in reenactments and documentary footage—Vietnam, the Cambodian sideshow, Kent State, the Kennedy assassinations, Watergate. The cast of characters is immense—Mao Tse Tung, Leonid Brezhnev, Henry Kissinger, the White House Plumbers, J. Edgar Hoover, John and Martha Mitchell, et al. At the center of it all is Nixon (Anthony Hopkins), Tricky Dick himself, who keeps dissolving into the spectacle as if he were America's uneasy dream of itself, or America were his dream, a nightmare from which he is trying to awaken. Asking if the film works is like asking if a Rube Goldberg device works. Gears engage, wheels spin, sparks fly, and the net result is—phfft. But this is not to say that the film is without interest.

In JFK, Stone mythologized the Kennedy assassination into the primal crime, patricide. In Nixon, with copy-book Freud in one hand and his revised version of the Kennedy assassination in the other, he moves on to fratricide. Stone's Nixon is haunted by the childhood deaths of two brothers as a result of which he was able to go to law school. Eventually, he transfers his brother fixation onto Kennedy in their rivalry for the presidency. Kennedy is everything Nixon isn't and wants to be; he's rich, handsome, Ivy League-educated, charismatic, beloved, and Hopkins makes Nixon's class resentment and envy palpable. In Stone's version of history, the Kennedy assassination is the key to the Nixon mystery: the team that engineered the assassination was formed during the Eisenhower/Nixon administration to assassinate Castro, so Nixon feels indirectly responsible for Kennedy's death—he's Cain to Kennedy's Abel. The film suggests that the Watergate coverup was partially motivated by Nixon's desire to keep E. Howard Hunt, one of the burglars, quiet because he was privy to the truth about the assassination.

Anthony Hopkins' performance as Nixon is more impersonation than from-the-inside-out acting, but he gets many of the details right: the frozen grin, the hunched posture, the mechanical flailing of the arms in a victory gesture. The picture begins with Watergate and then kaleidoscopically flashes back to Nixon's childhood and early campaigns—at times we're not sure what time zone we're in—so Hopkins' performance doesn't gain any momentum for the first two-thirds of the movie. In the last third, though, with Nixon barricaded in the White House, Hopkins gets a sense of tragic pathos as Nixon drinks and sweats and rants about his enemies. Inside this huge, frequently confused movie there's a small, painful drama about a little man who longs for greatness and makes some truly horrible decisions out of pride and neurotic compulsion.

Nixon's secondary characters never really emerge into sharp individuality, as no doubt the real-life dramatis personae in the White House never emerged from the maw of Nixon's insatiable neediness. As portrayed here, they're mostly opportunistic sycophants who feed Nixon's self-destructive fantasies. James Woods as H.R. Haldeman gives an uncharacteristically restrained performance, as does J.T Walsh as John Erlichman, and Paul Sorvino accurately captures Kissinger's vocal intonations and wooden imperturbability. Joan Allen as Pat Nixon looks surprisingly glamorous at times, particularly with a cigarette in her hand. Mary Steenburgen is miscast as Nixon's castrating, repressive mother, and Bob Hoskins contributes an egregious caricature of J. Edgar Hoover as a sinister homosexual with wandering libido. Ed Harris deserves special mention for a brief appearance as E. Howard Hunt. He delivers the film's most memorable line when he describes Nixon as "the darkness reaching out for the darkness," an image that Stone dramatizes in the closing scenes as the White House shadows enclose Nixon.

Stone's direction is what we've come to expect of him: sometimes incisive, excessive at other times, often leaden and flat. In yet another act of hubris, he models the picture after *Citizen Kane,* the movie is constructed like a jigsaw puzzle whose solution will answer the question, who is Nixon? Stone includes several direct references to the Welles picture: a newsreel that ends with a blank screen and a dying soundtrack, Nixon and Pat arguing over a huge dinner table, a broken Nixon wandering through White House corridors. There's even a Rosebud—the missing 18 minutes of White House tapes. But where Welles' narrative was still linear, Stone breaks his up into stroboscopic sound and image bytes, and you have to pick up information on the run. The editing room technology here almost overwhelms the human drama.

Is the film a whitewash? Stone doesn't focus much on the blood Nixon spilled in Vietnam and Cambodia, and the night I saw the movie some people booed while others hushed them. In an important scene late in the picture, Nixon goes out in the middle of the night to talk to Vietnam War protestors at the Lincoln Memorial. (Throughout the movie, Nixon has imaginary conversations with Lincoln's portrait in the White House; Lincoln's struggle to save the Union is another variation on the fratricide theme.) Hopkins is quite moving in this scene. As Nixon pumps hands campaign-style and talks awkwardly about football, a pained, mutilated sincerity comes through the familiar rictus-like smile. Finally, a young girl says the government is a wild animal and Nixon himself is powerless to stop the war. The comment strikes deep, complex chords in Nixon: his childhood feelings of impotence, guilt about Kennedy, an emerging messianic belief that only he can save a fratricidally divided America. And for a moment the suffering man betrayed by his own demons comes powerfully into focus.

Stone could have used a line from another Welles movie as his epitaph for Nixon. At the end of *Touch of Evil,* Marlene Dietrich says about the dead Welles character: "He was some kind of man. What does it matter what you say about people?" *Nixon*'s reach exceeds its grasp—this has always been Stone's failing—but the movie is an honorable attempt to portray some kind of man.

The folowing commentary by Stephen F. Rogers appeared in FILMS IN REVIEW, 3-4/96.

Oliver Stone, America's most provocative and controversial political filmmaker, has returned to the murky waters of "official" United States history—first explored in his landmark *JFK*—with *Nixon,* a lengthy portrait of the only president ever forced to resign the office. As with *JFK,*

Stone's latest film boasts an all-star cast, three hour—plus running time, an intriguing blend of fact and speculation, and a real-life drama of Shakespearean proportions. And, as with *JFK*, Stone has once again incurred the wrath of political pundits, newspaper columnists, and various other media denizens. Most have joined forces to accuse him, once again, of tampering with the facts to create his own version of history.

But wait a minute. Whose history is it anyway? Long before *JFK*, the vast majority of Americans believed John F. Kennedy had been assassinated as the result of a conspiracy and many were convinced that elements of their own governmental agencies may have been involved. Only the mainstream media and our political leaders continued to foster the lone assassin theory on a public that wasn't buying. But Oliver Stone and *JFK* caught the thought police off guard. *JFK* vividly portrayed the duplicity and deceit inherent in the machinations of American government and hinted at the powerful and unseen forces in control of that government. The film spurred renewed public interest in the Kennedy assassination. As a direct result, Congress passed the JFK Records Act of 1992, resulting in the release of thousands of formerly classified documents relating to the Kennedy assassination.

Ironically, many of these documents, presided over by the Assassination Records Review Board, have done more to elucidate and vindicate the investigation of Jim Garrison (upon which Stone centered *JFK*) than many would have thought possible. Indeed, one recently unearthed memorandum written by a staff counsel with the House Select Committee on Assassinations in 1977 stated that committee members had reason to believe Clay Shaw (who has since been documented as a CIA asset during the 1960's) was possibly involved in the "high level" planning of the assassination. The same Clay Shaw that the media had accused Jim Garrison of victimizing during the trial and Oliver Stone of demonizing in his film. But you didn't hear about this development in any of the major dailies or newsweeklies that have so ardently criticized Stone's cinematic versions of history. Whose history is it anyway?

And now, *Nixon*. In a way, the film serves, as Oliver Stone recently noted, as a bookend to *JFK*. Watergate and the Kennedy assassination share many of the same key figures and events, and the director crams as many of them as he can into this epic drama. While the film ostensibly purports to be a biography of sorts about Richard Nixon (and it is that, to a degree), in reality the main focus here is on Watergate and the various motives of the players involved in that labyrinthine scandal. There are also references in *Nixon* to Track 1 and Track 2, respectively the failed Bay of Pigs invasion of Cuba, and the CIA-Mafia attempts to assassinate Castro. Stone pulls his punches here, barely hinting at Nixon's involvement with these covert operations, although it is the specter of this sordid past that returns to haunt him as the Watergate affair unfolds. Nixon obviously had good reason to fear E. Howard Hunt, Frank Sturgis, and the rest of their CIA-connected Cuban cronies.

Much has been made in the press, *Newsweek* in particular, of the reference by Nixon to Bob Haldeman concerning "the Bay of Pigs thing." In his book, *The Ends of Power* Haldeman stated that Nixon was referring to the Kennedy assassination when he used that euphemism. *Newsweek* debunked the Haldeman quote, stating that the president's former chief of staff claimed his ghostwriter, Joe DiMona, had fabricated the theory on his own, while Haldeman was in prison. In a recent interview though, DiMona claimed that Haldeman proofread the entire manuscript five times and never touched the passage in question.

Interestingly enough, it was Haldeman who Nixon sent to CIA director Richard Helms in an attempt to pressure Helms and the CIA to back off the oval office during Watergate. Helms, who was eventually fired by Nixon, threatened to sue Oliver Stone for depicting him as having tried to blackmail Nixon by exposing the latter's role in Track 2. Stone eventually cut the scene with Sam Waterston as Helms, but claimed it was strictly for length purposes. In *JFK*, Stone was forced to trim a scene featuring Lee Harvey Oswald and his CIA-connected, White Russian mentor George DeMohrenschildt, presumably for length purposes also. This scene later appeared on the director's cut of *JFK* issued for home video. Maybe Waterston will end up there, too.

Ultimately, *Nixon* succeeds brilliantly in portraying a powerful but repressed personality, caught up in—and victimized by—events beyond his control. A control freak unable to control anything by the end of his political career. As Nixon, Anthony Hopkins is mesmerizing in his capacity to evoke the essence of the Nixon personality. He doesn't really look like him, but he sure feels like him. Other standouts in the immense cast include Joan Allen, who transforms the essentially inanimate Pat Nixon into a most human persona; James Woods as the stony-faced Haldeman; Paul Sorvino, with a dead-on impersonation of Henry Kissinger; and Bob Hoskins, who adds the requisite dose of sinister sleaze to his J. Edgar Hoover as he huddles with mob figures and practices his vitriolic brand of political gamesmanship. Larry Hagman has a choice role as "Jack Jones," a pseudonym for one of the Texas oilmen who dominated the arena of behind-the-scenes politics in the age of Nixon. It could be Clint Murchison, or possibly H.L. Hunt, but it doesn't really matter. Nixon owed them all and they knew it. A clever piece of casting when one considers Hagman's most popular role as J.R. Ewing, the fiendish, wealthy oilman on TVs Dallas.

Oliver Stone's greatest achievement with Nixon, though, is motivating his audience to think and to question the "official" versions of history. What was Watergate really about? What propelled Nixon from his obscure beginnings to the pinnacle of power? Is the presidency really the pinnacle of power in America? And who was really calling the shots during these momentous events in American history? Oliver Stone wants moviegoers to seek out the answers themselves, instead of relying on media spin doctors for the truth. The resultant search is the process of democracy and it's something Stone can be proud of.

LOS ANGELES TIMES, 12/20/95, Calendar/p. 1, Kenneth Turan

Richard Nixon reincarnated and reinvented himself so often there seemed to be a new Nixon for every phase of the moon. So it is fitting that "Nixon," the latest interpretation of our most resilient president, is presented by, of all things, a new Oliver Stone.

Mostly (though not completely) gone is the disturbing, lunatic Oliver Stone, the bad-boy writer-director who infuriated the political establishment with "JFK" and outraged sensibilities nationwide with "Natural Born Killers." He's been replaced by a filmmaker very much on his best behavior, a thorough researcher who consulted 80 books and published a heavily footnoted screenplay. If Quentin Tarantino made a film in the style of Sir Richard Attenborough, the surprise could not be greater.

And "Nixon" is in many ways an impressive; well-crafted piece of work. With name actors in more than 20 parts, it is as intelligently cast (by Billy Hopkins, Heidi Levitt and Mary Vernieu) as any movie this year, and includes at least one exceptional performance, though not the one you're expecting.

Collaborating once again with cinematographer Robert Richardson and editors Hank Corwin and Brian Berdan, Stone has not completely abandoned the visual fireworks, the odd angles and the multiple looks that have characterized his work.

But even though Stone could, and often did, drive everyone crazy with his exhaustive excesses, that doesn't mean that restraint necessarily suits him. This "Nixon," serious and filled with good intentions though it is, lacks the one element Stone movies have rarely done without before, and that is pulsating excitement. It is possible to nod off during "Nixon" and, for an Oliver Stone picture, that is a first.

Partly this is because considerable chunks of the film are taken up with Nixon in meetings and strategy sessions, an inside-baseball approach that will appeal largely to political junkies. So much time is spent watching Nixon being Nixon (as opposed to showing how he became Nixon) that the drama is hard to find.

Stone and co-scripters Stephen J. Rivele and Christopher Wilkinson see Nixon as the kind of tragic figure that would justify the celebrated quote from Matthew that begins the film, "What shall it profit a man, if he shall gain the whole world, and lose his own soul?"

"Nixon's" Nixon is a seriously troubled individual, given to self-pity and tortured by insecurities. The son of a father who professed that "struggle, not victory, gives life meaning," he believed in America and accomplished much, but was not strong enough to overcome his personal demons and ended up cast into a slough of alcoholic despond by the Watergate fiasco.

Whether the president actually was a problem drinker is one of the key areas where historians have already begun to quibble with Stone, the other being Nixon's involvement with Track 2, an abortive CIA anti-Castro plot the picture connects with (surprise) the Kennedy assassination. But unlike "JFK," what's on screen is so non-incendiary by nature, no one besides specialists and Nixon's immediate family are likely to be much troubled by its lapses.

It is Nixon himself who presents a more serious difficulty. Despite some time spent showing his formative years in Whittier, it is possible to watch this entire three-hour-and-10-minute movie and not feel you understand this president any better than when you came in. His masks, whatever they might have been, were simply on too tight; he remains opaque and unknowable despite the best efforts of the filmmakers to analyze him.

And, heroic and impressive though it is in some ways, Anthony Hopkins' performance in the title role does not satisfy. Part of the problem is physical, the scrunched-over Hunchback of Notre Dame way this Nixon walks. And the man's voice is so familiar that Hopkins' choice of accent, defensible though it may be, inevitably feels wrong. All told, these touches help turn Nixon into a kind of grotesque, lacking in traits that would make his leadership of anything more important than a Kiwanis Club believable.

"Nixon" starts, like a horror movie, on a dark and stormy night, with the president prowling around a room of the White House like Dracula in his lair, listening to the secret tape recordings he made in the oval Office. That triggers the film's intricate flashbacks-within-flashbacks structure, which by the time it's over manages to at least touch on all the major milestones of Nixon's career, including conflicts with Alger Hiss and Helen Gahagan Douglas, the Checkers speech and the Kennedy debates, the bombing of Cambodia and the opening of China.

Back, too, like an unsettling dream, are the dozens of disturbing characters from the Nixon years, from Henry Kissinger (Paul Sorvino) and John Mitchell (E.G. Marshall) to twin terrors H.R. Haldeman (James Woods) and John Ehrlichman (J.T. Walsh). All these roles are well done, with the actors who find humor in their parts—notably Bob Hoskins as a J. Edgar Hoover who cruises the kitchen help and Madeline Kahn as Martha Mitchell coming off best.

Easily the most memorable performance in this film, however, is Joan Allen's exceptional work as Pat Nixon, the loyal wife Nixon liked to call "buddy." Able to get deeper into her character than anyone else, Allen, a highly regarded stage actress who played the mother in "Searching for Bobby Fischer," turns every scene she's in into eye-opener drama. She shows us a more complex, more human Pat Nixon than we imagined, and, in doing so, underlines that the film hasn't managed to do the same for our 37th president.

NEW YORK, 1/8/96, p. 44, David Denby

Anguish is not an emotion that Oliver Stone has ever shied away from—or that he has allowed his audience to escape. Stone put us through hell in his three Vietnam films, hectoring us again and again for not sufficiently sharing the troubles of the GIs and the Vietnamese. But tenderness is a new emotion for Stone, and the most surprising thing about *Nixon*, his obsessional, painful, fascinating new movie, is how much warmth the director extends to the unlikely figure of Richard Milhous Nixon (Anthony Hopkins). For here is a portrait of the most wretched man who ever lived. Clumsy and trapped, a bear carrying his own zoo bars around with him—even into his bedroom—the president is a harsh and fraudulent personality, deaf to others but far too intelligent not to notice how many people loathe him. For Nixon-haters, the movie is the moment of truth: Will they give up enough of their distaste to accept a complex view of their lifelong nemesis? Intellectuals in particular have always favored a satirical treatment—Nixon as malevolent clown and self-pitying opportunist. Two dimensions are enough for such a man! But now we get more. Two and a half, perhaps. We are asked to see Nixon as monstrous but afflicted, tough but infinitely troubled—a typical Stone character caught in perpetual anguish.

Stone has attempted Shakespearean tragedy within the form of a whirling, cyclical montage structure; the movie is an open homage to *Citizen Kane*, and that doesn't always work. As always, Stone overloads the medium, surrounding us with *film*. There are newsreels of the real Nixon, mock newsreels with Hopkins morphed into scenes with Kennedy or Khrushchev, childhood miseries from long-ago California. Color, black-and-white, and sepia footage clamor for attention, sometimes all three in the same sequence. The movie is exhaustingly expressive, as if Stone were afraid we wouldn't get it somehow. Just before Nixon's resignation in 1974, as the president falls into drunkenness and despair, an entire lifetime plays through his head with increasing violence. Stone also cuts back to earlier moments in Nixon's career—the 1960 presidential and 1962 gubernatorial elections, the assassination of Kennedy—and those events set off memories as well. Poor Nixon! He can't ever escape the tragic Oliver Stone movie pounding inside his head. He gets dissolved into a hundred fragments and then reassembled as a man intolerably burdened by his past. *Nixon* is bullying and redundant—aesthetic terrorism, a friend calls the style. Yet there's a generous soulfulness here, an intimacy with defeat and rage, and a strain of shocked pity, particularly in the scenes between Dick and Pat. I was often moved.

It appears necessary to say that *Nixon* is an interpretation—necessary because some very distinguished journalists cannot understand this commonplace idea. Drawing on archival and biographical materials, Stone and his screenwriters, Stephen J. Rivele and Christopher Wilkinson, combine, condense, recast, and rewrite. So does every maker of narrative nonfiction, from Mailer to movie-of-the-week. For instance, the filmmakers reworked the dead, cold, all but impenetrable language of the Watergate tapes into scenes that crackle with conflict and dark hints. The mad, circumlocutory evasiveness of the originals is gone, replaced by something more simply and plainly evil. Is this falsification? Can there be drama without something like it?

In all, *Nixon* sticks much closer to ascertainable fact than did *JFK* (which was, I admit, entirely reckless on the subject of Lyndon Johnson and the assassination of John F. Kennedy). Stone offers only one major speculative line—Nixon's alleged involvement as vice-president in CIA plots to assassinate Castro. The plots failed, and the plotters, including Mafia gangsters and Cuban émigrés who became furious at Kennedy after the Bay of Pigs, connived in JFK's assassination. (Or so Stone's Nixon thinks.) Years later, even though he had nothing personally to do with Kennedy's death, Nixon muses incoherently over the old conspiracies and secrets. Veiled references fall into his conversation, baffling his closest adviser, Bob Haldeman (James Woods). The obsession becomes a figure in the thick carpet of Nixonian guilt, where it mixes with memories of the two brothers who died young of TB years earlier in rural California. In Nixon's mind, both pairs of dead brothers—Arthur and Harold Nixon, Jack and Bobby Kennedy—sacrificed themselves so that Nixon could be president. He carries his unhappiness with him and, according to Stone, guiltily undoes himself by first making the tapes and then choosing not to destroy them. At some level, he wants to be found out.

Now, it's fine for journalists to point out actual errors and inventions, but the implication that Oliver Stone is merely lying is ludicrous and philistine. Stone, after all, does not write newspaper articles. Such things as dramatic shaping, acting, pace, mood, counter-mood, and so on are not just dressing but the substance of whatever it is a director wants to say. Stone's journalistic critics won't, or can't, take notice of such complex moments as that eerie scene on the presidential yacht, when, after the Kent State killings, Nixon thinks of his brother Harold, who died at roughly the same age as the students. Depressed as he is by Kent State, Nixon cannot offer condolences to the students' families—"Nixon can't do that," he says, unconsciously switching to the third person so the public figure, rather than himself, refuses sympathy and grief. Regret, rage, and contempt pass through the moment like shifts in the wind. Now, if *Nixon* isn't a good movie, it's because scenes like these don't work, not because they diverge from the historical record. The journalists who hate Stone clearly want him off their turf, but they aren't always convincing about what his films "say," which is never something simple like "LBJ had JFK killed." The journalists belittle whatever they can't simply paraphrase.

I have mixed feelings about Anthony Hopkins's work. Despite sedulous imitation of the Nixon manner—sudden smile, flung-up arms, a tendency to top-heaviness—he doesn't much look or sound like Nixon. But that's not really the point. Hopkins gets some things dead right—the impersonality, the bluff, unconscious rudeness. The trouble is that Hopkins is too busy. He acts like crazy—cringing, cowering—and it's too much. Presidents are generally cold bastards, and none colder than Richard Nixon, but Hopkins responds emotionally to everything and hides nothing. A man this vulnerable could not have come close to the White House. Hopkins, who has often played remote ordinary men, bizarrely forgets the remoteness of power.

The fault is Stone's, perhaps, more than Hopkins's. If we had seen more of Nixon the executive, Nixon the masterful strategist, the president's fall into bathos and incoherence would have been more striking. But *Nixon* begins with the president at the end of his tether, in 1974, and the flashbacks don't offer much contrast. Nixon is always a seething, resentful mess. Hopkins gives us a theater actor's overwrought projection of inner states of feeling. It works best in the scenes with Pat (Joan Allen), in which Nixon, gruff and clumsy, finds himself overmatched by a woman whose candor and whose sexuality intimidate him. Yes, this is Pat Nixon we are talking about. Joan Allen is a revelation, and Oliver Stone should be proud—he has gotten a whole woman on the screen at last.

Setting up Richard Nixon as the heir to soulless, power-mad Charles Foster Kane makes a kind of sense: the same public success and personal emptiness, the same tendency to fraud and cynicism. But does imitating the structural shape and expressive devices (the Gothic atmosphere, the multiple voices) of *Citizen Kane* also make sense? *Kane* is an extraordinarily entertaining masterpiece. The doomy, heavily shadowed, movieish quality of the atmosphere consorts well with its overall spirit, which is satirical and mischievous. But in *Nixon*, which shares the same atmosphere (the White House as a Gothic castle), the almost campy doominess is made to consort with grief and paranoia, and the two don't fit together. If Nixon is a tragic figure, Stone should have portrayed him with a simpler, more dignified technique. In all, I wish to God Oliver Stone would lighten up a bit. But this punishing, lugubrious yet oddly tender movie is at least a step in a new direction. Stone, 49, hasn't finished making himself yet. There may be a whole new range of expression within his grasp.

NEW YORK POST, 12/20/95, p. 37, Michael Medved

The problem with Oliver Stone's portrait of Richard Nixon isn't that he makes the man look evil, but that he makes the man look small.

In his view, the 37th president of the United States is neither wicked nor great, formidable liar nor formidable leader. He is, rather, a wretched, psychotic, consistently inept little man who can inspire only pity and scorn.

This dismissive portrayal is not only bad history (even Nixon's most outspoken critics recognized his toughness and competence), it is also dramatically disastrous. Director and cowriter Stone asks us to take a convoluted 3-hour-and-10-minute trek through the twisted mind of a doomed politician who is never anything more than pathetic—giving us no reason whatever to care about this Incredible Shrinking Nixon.

Consider, for example, the way Stone distorts the first televised debate of the 1960 presidential campaign. The movie offers actual of John Kennedy looking spectacularly handsome, energetic and intelligent, and these images are then skillfully cut together with Anthony Hopkins performing his feckless non-impersonation of Nixon—looking frightened, mumbling, incoherent, embarrassed and obviously out of his league.

Film of the real-life Nixon, however, tells a very different story. Yes, he looked tired on TV (and a bad makeup job accentuated his 5 o'clock shadow), but in terms of rhetorical command he easily held his own with Kennedy. In fact, surveys showed that Americans who heard the debate on radio, undistracted by visual imagery, felt by an overwhelming margin that Nixon had won the confrontation.

Stone's determination to cut his anti-hero down to Lilliputian size makes even his familiar nickname of "Tricky Dick" seem incomprehensible, since the clumsy, bumbling geek we meet in the film never looks the least bit tricky or slick.

Even as president, he is regularly humiliated by people around him, as in the ludicrous scene where the fawning chief executive (implausibly unaccompanied by either staff or Secret Service) visits a gathering of conspiratorial Texas oilmen (led by Larry Hagman), who looks as if they were part of "JFK" outtakes.

"Dick, aren't you forgetting who put you where you are?" Hagman darkly warns. "That can be changed in a heartbeat."

Another embarrassing encounter shows a grinning Nixon meeting with FBI director J. Edgar Hoover (Bob Hoskins) in 1968 and listening to America's top cop drop unmistakable hints that he will clear the way for Tricky Dick's election by arranging the assassination of Bobby Kennedy—and of Martin Luther King, too, while he's at it.

Of course, wild conspiracy theories are no surprise in an Oliver Stone film, so that the only shock here is how poorly Stone makes his case. Whatever one may think of the paranoid postulations of "JFK," it's impossible to deny the film's cinematic power—or the effectiveness with which Stone advanced his ideas. "Nixon," on the other hand, is as incoherent, muddled and forlorn as its fictionalized protagonist.

The non-linear time sequence (lurching from 1972 to 1974 to 1960 to 1920 to 1952, with flashbacks within flashbacks) is dizzying and almost impossible to follow. Those who know little about the historical events will be lost; while those who do remember the history will be appalled at the fabrications. For instance, Nixon is shown deciding to run for president only after Lyndon

Johnson had taken himself out of the race when, in fact, Nixon had been campaigning hard for a year (and had already won the New Hampshire primary, for heaven's sake!) when LBJ withdrew in March of '68.

The fundamental problem with the film isn't so much that it makes dubious points as the fact that it makes no coherent point at all. From "Natural Born Killers," Stone borrows the technique of wacky, illogical, surrealistic montages—treating the White House dirty tricksters as if they were "Natural Born Plumbers." He absurdly inserts irrelevant images of a horse's eye, a crucifix, aerial shots of desert, JFK licking an ice cream cone and—again and again—close-ups of bombs dropping over the jungles of Vietnam.

These jumbled visions, perhaps meant to represent the main character's madness, and in Stone's view even Pat Nixon herself (unforgettably well-played by Joan Allen in the film's single most moving performance) holds the president in utter contempt.

"Dick, sometimes I understand why they hate you," she says during one drunken rant. "I remember Alger Hiss. I know how ugly you can be. You're capable of anything."

Beyond Allen's heartfelt, professional work, the other most impressive turn comes from Paul Sorvino, improbably transformed into an altogether convincing version of Henry Kissinger, investing his lines with a wealth of sly hints.

At the other extreme, James Woods offers a ridiculous portrayal of Bob Haldeman, rendering the president's solemn, soft-spoken chief of staff as an edgy, hyperkinetic slickster.

The major acting challenge of course falls to Sir Anthony Hopkins, who neither sounds nor looks like the all-too-familiar Nixon. Hugging his own elbows, with his head pulled unnaturally into his shoulders, he more closely resembles a bad Ed Sullivan imitator.

Nevertheless, Hopkins is too fine an actor to leave an audience entirely unmoved, and as the president comes unglued in the last stages of the Watergate coverup the star is finally effective and affecting.

His single finest moments come at the very end when the credits roll, as Stone recreates Nixon's farewell speech just before leaving the White House following his resignation. Suddenly, for the first and only time, Stone and Hopkins manage to convey the character's stature and eloquence, and make you feel the grandeur of his tragedy. They do so by using his actual words, virtually unedited.

It makes you all the more frustrated at Stone's insistence on toying with the other public utterances he attempts to reproduce, as part of the director's personal need to upstage and overshadow the historical figure he's trying to portray. In the end, his petty, pitiable, unfocused "Nixon" is very difficult to pardon.

NEWSDAY, 12/20/95, Part II/p. B3, Jack Mathews

For those expecting to feel the heavy hand of Oliver Stone in the biographical docudrama "Nixon," you won't be disappointed. But it will not be as heavy as you're used to, and the full weight of it won't descend until the movie is essentially over. In fact, you can avoid most of it by following these simple instructions:

When you hear Stone's own voice kick in at the end of the movie, cover your ears and run for it.

The director's updating postscript about Richard Nixon's place in the political cosmos violates a basic tenet of storytelling—if you can't dramatize it, forget it—and dampens the emotional punch of a moment Stone spent more than a year and the audience more than three, hours getting to.

Having grown up in Southern California, assured by my working-class parents that homeboy Nixon was the incarnation of evil, and learning nothing in my adult life to disprove that, I thought it impossible that I could feel the slightest tug of sympathy for the man. But by the end of Stone's meticulous and surprisingly fair-handed film, as Anthony Hopkins re-enacts the disgraced president's final departure from the White House, an uncomfortable knot of ambivalence had formed in my throat.

For the first time, 21 years after celebrating Nixon's historical comeuppance, I saw it from his point of view, and it is profoundly sad. Then, Stones voice cuts in, drawing unnecessary perspective from the future, and the fragile emotional connection is lost.

There are other moments where Stone lays things a little too much on the line, and some characterizations—Bob Hoskins' bitch-queen J. Edgar Hoover, Paul Sorvino's somber Henry Kissinger—that cross over into caricature. But recent history, with its facts and personalities still fresh in the minds of many viewers, is the most difficult for film biographers to recreate, and Stone has succeeded beyond anything "The Doors," "Born of the Fourth of July" and "JFK" would have predicted.

In fact, "Nixon" is the most straight-forward of Stone's "Sixties movies" since "Platoon." There are no delirious conspiracy theories, total conjectural history, or fantastic leaps of psychological interpretation. It is essentially an unsentimental portrait of a tragic American figure, an attempt to fathom a man who rose from origins as humble as Abe Lincoln's to become the most powerful person on earth, only to be consumed and destroyed by his own petty instincts.

Hopkins takes some getting used to as Nixon. He's too short, he looks nothing like him, and his voice—though the words and inflections are familiar—misses by a mile being a good impression. But once we're past the superficial comparisons, Hopkins takes us into regions of the character we never saw in the public Nixon.

In turns generous and mean-spirited, confident and insecure, gentle and vicious, good dad and Tricky Dick, Hopkins' Nixon is a study in contradiction, and though Stone doesn't for a moment accept Nixon's view of himself as a victim, Hopkins makes us understand why he felt that way.

Of the large ensemble surrounding Nixon, Joan Allen's Pat Nixon is the surprising stand-out. Far from her stiff, stand-by-her-man First Lady image, Allen's Pat is a woman whose superior personal strength, moral courage and devotion are finally sapped by the growing cruelty and self-destructiveness of her husband. It's a painfully moving performance that, more than anything else, shows just how lost Nixon became.

Stone, with a script culled and sculpted from scores of biographies, oral histories, government papers and the famed "Nixon tapes," opens his story in the office of the so-called White House plumbers, the Gordon Liddy-led gang whose bungled crimes would unravel Nixon's presidency, and tracks forward and back, in nonlinear fashion, through his childhood and his early political career, settling down in the last hour to dramatize the final days.

Near the end, Kissinger shakes his head at the pathetic spectacle Nixon has become, and says to Al Haig (Powers Boothe), "Imagine what this man would have been if he'd been loved."

It's a line that makes you cringe, but when you take it in context, and complete the sentence—" ... if he'd been loved BY THE PEOPLE"—you are at the core of Nixon's flawed existence, and of the film's overarching theme. Stone covers a lot of other material on the road from Whittier to Watergate, but continually returns to the essential conflict between Nixon's driven ambition and his crippled ego.

"Why do they hate me so?" he asks, in a forlorn cry of exasperation, and it is true in the film, as it was to the end of his life, that he never knew the answer.

Stone verges on some "Citizen Kane" mythologizing at times, but he pursues the enigma of Nixon's character with unusual restraint. It would have been a disaster if, as with "JFK," he pretended to know more than anyone else and provided his own smoking gun. Certainly, it must have been tempting, after establishing Nixon's respect for his grocer father's honesty and his Quaker mother's convictions, to dramatize some breech in those relationships to explain the loose grip he'd have on morality throughout his life.

We do see the president being haunted by the memory of his mother (Mary Steenburgen), who shows up as a disapproving ghost in the White House, and by that of his older brother (Tony Goldwyn), whose early death from tuberculosis made it possible for Nixon to go to college. However, the strength of "Nixon" is its refusal to draw clear conclusions.

There is no question that Nixon was burdened by a life-long inferiority complex, exacerbated by the popularity of the privileged Kennedy clan and the whole "Eastern intellectual establishment" that rejected him and became the target of his enormous bitterness. But how a man who saw and seized the opportunity to become one of the century's leading architects of global politics also came to symbolize cheap political tricks, character assassination and betrayal of public trust remains the elusive legacy of America's most confounding leader.

Stone's film, and Hopkins' extraordinary performance, shed light on the subject, and though we can't quite make out everything we see scampering around there, it's quite a sight.

SIGHT AND SOUND, 3/96, p. 48, José Arroyo

In 1972, Richard Nixon, the President of the United States, begins the process of covering up the break-in at the Watergate Complex in Washington by a slush-funded dirty tricks team of 'plumbers' originally hired to fix leaks to the press, one of whom is on the White House payroll. At the time, Nixon says "I haven't got time for this shit," but from that date until 1974 we see the Watergate investigation creep closer to the President until he is forced by impeachment to resign. As this drama unfolds, a number of flashbacks illustrate the life of Richard Nixon.

Nixon was born into a strict Quaker family. His mother's faith and discipline are major influences. The death of two brothers from tuberculosis gives him the opportunity to go to study law at university. He wins him a seat at Congress at the age of 33. His role in the House Un-American Activities Committee, especially his indictment of Alger Hiss, brings him to national attention and he becomes Vice-President under Dwight D. Eisenhower.

When his tax record comes under investigation, he gives the famous 'Checkers' speech on national television in which he itemises exactly what he owes. He wins back public sympathy by demonstrating love for his dog. In 1960 he loses the closest Presidential race in US history because Kennedy uses privileged information and thus makes a fool of him on national television. After he loses the gubernatorial race for California in 1962, his wife Pat, who loves him and has supported him all along, decides to leave him unless he drops out of politics, which he does for a while. He is in Dallas the day Kennedy is shot, talking to rich Texans and Cuban refugees, who suggest he could win the presidency but he turns them down. J. Edgar Hoover offers to support him if he should race again. Robert Kennedy's assassination makes Nixon a sure thing and he wins. His interventions in Vietnam are seen as cynical; his rapprochements with China and the Soviet Union as major achievements.

As the White House's involvement with the Watergate burglary begins to gain currency. Nixon sacrifices all his cronies to protect himself, cutting himself off from his wife and lying to his children right up until the final resignation. At his funeral, he is acclaimed a great President.

Nixon justly begins with Watergate. After showing us, in black and white, the now-infamous burglars about to break into the Democratic National Committee headquarters, the film cuts to 1973. It is raining. The camera moves through an iron fence and approaches a White House adorned with the Stars and Stripes. Then thunder roars, lightning strikes, and the American flag waves wildly in a storm of light and darkness. It is a typical Stone touch (or rather wallop). With this shot Stone isn't simply telling us that Watergate shook up the American government. To Stone it's such an earth-shaking event, even the elements must tremble. I trembled to think that this film had three more hours to go. Before I knew it, the end credits were rolling. *Nixon* is riveting.

Nixon is an ideal subject for Stone. In most of his other films the leading characters are just vehicles through which to examine an issue. In *Nixon* they *are* the issue. The film can focus on the man and still discourse on the rise of the military-industrial complex, the Vietnam war, how the combination of greed and power can lead to evil, the assassination of John F. Kennedy and how the media has corrupted American political and social life. In other words, Nixon's life gives Stone the opportunity to re-examine subjects he has already explored in *Salvador, Platoon, Wall Street, JFK* and *Natural Born Killers*. One of the many interesting things about *Nixon* is that these issues are looked at from the centre of power.

The life of Richard Nixon easily lends itself to epic treatment. The quote from Matthew 16:26 which prefaces the film, "what shall it profit a man if he shall gain the whole world but lose his soul," telegraphs the story. However, as the film anchors the narrative in 1973, when Watergate was closing in on the President, its focus is on the latter part of the question. As we see him break several constitutional amendments, lie, cheat, shut out his family and sacrifice his colleagues in order to hold on to power, every flashback is a measure of his fall from grace.

The descent seems all the more steep because the film shows the high moral and ethical standards with which Nixon was brought up. When the film flashes back to Whittier, California, in 1925, black and white footage depicts an angelic Richard growing up in a poor but loving Quaker family, a strict one that lives by the good book and believes in duty, discipline, hard work and community. If we were to judge him by how his mother expected him to behave, the verdict would be harsh. But the film, while it does not shy away from tracing his ambition or his ruth lessness, is kinder: we are shown that Nixon likes to win but we are also shown that he wants to do good and that, in his own mind, he mostly uses his power to do so.

The film's explanation of the rise and fall of our hero hinges on three elements: the lie, the deaths of brothers and the influence of the military-industrial complex. Lying is established as a character flaw when Richard is a child and his mother catches him in one. While forgiving him, she lets him know that lying is a great sin, carrying a terrible punishment. Catching Alger Hiss in a lie is what helps make Nixon's name, paving his way to the vice-presidency. Being caught in a lie over Watergate is what makes his fall complete and irreversible. Lying is the foundation of the moral decline that transforms Richard Milhouse Nixon into Tricky Dicky.

What gives *Nixon* emotional resonance is the idea that its hero's success is built on the deaths of two sets of brothers: Nixon's own and the Kennedys. His brothers' deaths enable Nixon to go to University; the Kennedys' smooth his path to the White House. The film makes a point of comparing Harold, Richard's elder brother, to JFK. Tony Goldwyn, as Harold, is given a similar haircut and flashes the same brilliant smile as John Kennedy. Both are depicted as having what Nixon lacks: good looks, social ease, a carefree, fun-loving manner. Nixon and Kennedy had parallel careers and the film depicts their relationship as complex. Class resentment on Nixon's part against the Ivy League is evident, as are pride and paranoia but these do not temper his need to be liked by the ruler of Camelot. That Nixon is forever burdened by the suspicion that fate (or God) may have sought the sacrifice of his brothers as the price of his success gives him a tragic depth.

Nixon uses the military-industrial complex as the political explanation for the President's rise and fall. A combination of very rich Texans, anti-Castro Cubans and J. Edgar Hoover stands in for these vested interests. The film briefly hints at what *JFK* made explicit: that these interests may have been responsible for Kennedy's assassination because he was going to withdraw troops from Vietnam. We know Nixon is in bad company when we meet J. Edgar Hoover just after the latter has eaten fruit from his houseboy's lips. (Bob Hoskins doing homosexual lasciviousness is hilariously distanciating.) The President's realisation that real power lies not with his office but with anonymous para-military, para-governmental and corporate interests is the climax of the film. This is represented by his discussing power with young activists underneath the stern shadow of the Lincoln Memorial. (The image of Abraham Lincoln, like Kennedy's, recurs throughout the film as a reminder of Nixon's failed aspirations). A young woman makes him realise that the power to change things is now held by invisible forces. "It's taken me a lifetime to learn what that young girl already knows," says Nixon. Anthony Hopkins says the line convincingly, but the scene remains an embarrassment.

Stone's films have always featured superlative acting and *Nixon* is no exception. Joan Allen as Pat Nixon and Paul Sorvino as Henry Kissinger stand out for their excellent depictions of still-famous people. Mary Steenburgen, as Nixon's mother, evokes a gentle intransigence so powerful that one knows the how and why of her influence on young Richard. But the glue to the narrative is Anthony Hopkins' tour de force performance which makes clear the banality of evil. Ambition, insecurity, greed, hope, paranoia and love register on Hopkins' face, which transforms into a sweaty setting for Nixon's shifty eyes and overly eager smile. It's an embodiment so extraordinary that a shot of his back is not only recognisable as Nixon, but communicates something of his complexity.

Visually, the film falls somewhere between *JFK* and *Natural Born Killers*. Stone's experiments with mixing different types of film stock, in black and white, colour and even sepia, finally pay off. In *JFK*, the mix was more an affectation. In *NBK*, it served a shallow expression. Here, judicious matching of images evokes the period and creates a texture that layers time and character, creating a visual impression of a social history while at the same time helping to tell a personal one.

Nixon's perspective is post-modern. During his resignation, an aide tells him "history will remember you kindly." "Depends on who writes the history books," replies the President. The film evokes that attitude through its layering of quotations from famous newsreels, television shows and photographs (many of them doctored), and stirs them in with the rest of the images, manipulated by various processes. This collage effect simulates a collective memory of the American culture of the period that, in the realm of fiction, easily passes as history.

I'm not sure that *Nixon* treats Nixon kindly. But in representing his life as the tragic drama of a powerful man involved in mythic struggles against himself and invisible but extraordinary forces, the film compliments Nixon with grandeur. It may not be history but it makes for a fascinating film.

TIME, 12/18/95, p. 74, Richard Corliss

Poor Richard Nixon: the most human President of the television age. A better statesman than politician, a tireless but graceless campaigner, a successful salesman who was liked but not *well* liked, the man seemed uncomfortable in his own skin. The canniest moments in the three-plus hours of *Nixon*, Oliver Stone's dense, ultimately disappointing biopic, capture Nixon at his most pathetically endearing—the Commander in Chief as klutz. In a telling vignette lifted from Woodward and Bernstein's *The Final Days*, Nixon (Anthony Hopkins) gets so frustrated at his inability to remove a medicine safety cap that he finally bites it off.

Stone typically bites and claws at his subjects, then spits out phantasmagoric movie melodrama—terrific stuff like *Platoon* and *JFK*. This time he's almost mellow. The script, which he wrote with Stephen J. Rivele and Christopher Wilkinson, argues that Nixon had a dark role in anti-Castro mischief; the Cuba connection keeps echoing. The movie also nails him for the Cambodian bombing that set in motion the destruction of a beautiful country. Oddly, Stone doesn't find Nixon guilty of starting the Vietnam War or killing John Kennedy. He does pock the film with right-wing poobahs who anticipate, with frothing pleasure, the deaths of J.F.K. and his brother Robert.

The film ricochets through 50 years of Nixon's life; it suggests that he never outgrew a severe rural childhood or an attachment to his stern mother; it includes both a *March of Time* summation of his career and a scene in which the great man argues with his wife across the expanse of a long dinner table. *Citizen Nixon*, anyone? You might expect that Stone, our most vigorous and cinematically ambitious director, would be drawn to create a prismatic, *Kane*-like portrait of a potentate who was an enigma, not least to himself. But no. Stone is content to dramatize major episodes from the life. Some have voltage, but others are dry re-enactments inserted for the record. This gives much of the film an oddly pageant-like, perfunctory tone. It's a $43 million term paper.

In a huge cast of good actors, James Woods stands out as steely Bob Haldeman, and Joan Allen suggests in deft brush strokes a Pat Nixon condemned to stand by her ungiving man. Hopkins, though, is a failure. He finds neither the timber of Nixon's plummy baritone, with its wonderfully false attempts at intimacy, nor the stature of a career climber who, with raw hands, scaled the mountain and was still not high or big enough.

The real Nixon was a tragicomic figure; he doesn't need Stone's demonizing or mythologizing touch. His saga, moreover, is familiar from a quillion docudramas and *Saturday Night Live* skits. It is also imprinted in the TV memories of Americans over 35. The President's bizarre farewell speech, nicely re-created by Hopkins, captures that spooky poignancy. Then as he boards Air Force One, Hollywood gives way to archive videotape, and we see the real Nixon with his implausible grin and victory wave of the arms—apotheosis and self-parody in one indelibly weird moment. For once, the gonzo director has met his match. Real life, if it's real Nixon, is more dramatic than an Oliver Stone movie.

VILLAGE VOICE, 12/26/95, p. 53, J. Hoberman

He may be just a homely little face on a postage stamp but as candidate Bob Dole last year eulogized our 37th president: "The second half of the 20th century will be known as the Age of Nixon. Now, thanks to Oliver Stone's *Nixon*, we may climax that epoch in the second half of December 1995.

Attempting to make sense of Nixon's rise and fall and rise and fall and current rise, the long and winding road from Whittier to Watergate to Eternity, Stone has clearly bitten off more than he can swallow. The director may quote the New Testament, cite Shakespeare, and genuflect toward *Citizen Kane*, but his cautiously self-described "dramatic interpretation," with Sir Anthony Hopkins miscast in the title role, arrives so thoroughly chewed over in the media it already seems regurgitated.

Something less than a total rehab job, *Nixon* finds Stone chastened but still in *JFK* mode. The movie is markedly more "responsible" than his last presidential election year extravaganza, albeit a kindred chronology-jumbled, all-format mix and match. Hopkins is repeatedly gumped into historical events—facing off against the actual Kennedy in the 1960 TV debate, for instance—but the nudging visual interpolations are here more restrained. There will never be a *Nation* symposium on this three-hour morass. Unlike *JFK*, *Nixon* is more often turgid than flashy, explicitly devoted to the reality principle. "When they look at you they see what they want to be," Stone's Nixon tells a JFK portrait late in the movie. "When they look at me, they see what they are."

Satisfying as it is to at last have Nixon as a Disney character, Hopkins's overheated, self-consciously self-conscious performance doesn't get the overall nuttiness of Nixon's unctuous rage, his failed regular guy-ness, his sonorous gloom, his vicious opportunism, his iron-butt single-mindedness. Nixon's blatant cheesy neuroses have provided juicy fodder for a variety of actors—Jason Robards Jr. in the 1977 miniseries *Washington: Behind Closed Doors*, Rip Torn in the 1979 miniseries *Blind Ambition*, Philip Baker Hall in Robert Altman's 1984 *Secret Honor*, Lane Smith in the 1989 *The Final Days*. Not here. Hopkins swills Scotch and curses, maladroitly pulls the doorknob off a door and repeatedly twitches into a mirthless public smile—his performance is an inorganic checklist of "Nixonian" traits. Hopkins is having less fun than even the real Nixon. When he perfectly reproduces the demented free association of Nixon's farewell address, he's upstaged by Stone's decision to show a bit of the actual thing on tape.

Given this penchant for inadvertent exposure, Nixon was made for psycho history. It's a pity that Warren Beatty turned down the role, particularly since Stone pegs Nixon as terminally unloved. The movie's most painful sequences are the black-and-white flashbacks to the grim Nixon childhood—working with his brothers in the family gas-pump grocery, in thrall to his severely "saintly" Quaker mother (Mary Steenburgen). She's reincarnated in the movie in the person of Nixon's wife Pat (Joan Allen), a near perfect simulacrum who shows up every once in a while to reintroduce the notion of the pychosexual and provoke her husband's displeasure: "Brezhnev is coming in three days—I don't want to deal with him and them and *you!*"

Oliver Stone, it's well known, can't make a movie without finding himself in it. No less than Nixon the filmmaker must feel himself underappreciated, if not persecuted. Stone is no stranger to truculent self-pity; Nixon, moreover, may be the only American politician whose paranoia matches his own. In the Stone schemata, E. Howard Hunt the former CIA op turned spy novelist and Watergate burglar, signifies conspiracy. "I know what he is and what he tracks back to," Nixon mumbles in the course of the famous missing 18 minutes on the June 20, 1972, White House tape.

The erased conversation is, as Stone suggested in *Newsweek*'s cover story, *Nixon*'s "rosebud"—Nixon's fear that the murder of JFK was blowback from the CIA-Mafia plot to kill Castro that according to Stone, Nixon helped organize. This of course somewhat contradicts the premise of *JFK* but, seizing upon the coincidence (coincidence?) that brought Nixon to Dallas on the eve of the Kennedy assassination, Stone introduces Larry Hagman as a kind of politically minded J.R. Ewing and takes the opportunity to reprise Dealy Plaza—this time superimposing some sort of God brooding over the sky.

Nixon is basically conceived as its subject's slow-motion assassination. Thus, Nixon's legendary post-Kent State, 4 a.m. visit to the young protestors camped out at the Lincoln Memorial is less an instance of stunted, perhaps alcohol-sodden sentimentality (surrounded by bewildered students, the president droned on about football—and Neville Chamberlain, unable to make eye contact with anyone) than the mystical moment when he receives the revelation of what Stone calls "the Beast." One coed realizes that, much as Nixon may want peace, the System won't let him stop the Vietnam War.

Nixon, per Stone, regards his greatest triumph as having extricated the U.S. from Vietnam without precipitating a right-wing revolt. What the movie more usefully hints is that Nixon's opening to China, his Soviet détente, and "peace with honor" Vietnam settlement, were all founded on a demonstrable capacity for mass murder. Stone makes much of the *Macbeth* or *Richard III* notion of Nixon advancing to power "over the bodies" of the fallen Kennedys but rather less of Nixon's role in the slaughter of hundreds of thousands of Vietnamese and Cambodians. While the movie's most effective bit of business has Nixon talking mad bomber as his too-rare steak starts bleeding all over his plate, Stone is hardly immune to the *realpolitik* scenarios invariably used to justify Nixon's foreign policy.

Sub-Carlyle hero-worshiping romantic that he is, Stone ultimately buys Nixon's Great Man self-explanation, although, of course, in that he's not alone. Played for maximum, sepulchrally croaking buffoonery by Paul Sorvino, Henry Kissinger is the movie's biggest kiss-ass until the real Bill Clinton enlivens the interminable final credits to deliver a mealymouthed eulogy at the real Nixon's funeral.

This may be Stone's final trip to the '60s and he can scarcely bear to let the movie end. In a final *Citizen Kane* flourish, Stone reintroduces his cast. The pomposity factor is raised by his choice of the Mormon Tabernacle Choir's "Shenandoah" for the walkout music. If *JFK* was scurrilous hero worship, *Nixon* is uplifting whitewash. To achieve the full Shakespearean grandeur, he really should be showing a pile of corpses.

Also reviewed in:
CHICAGO TRIBUNE, 12/20/95, Tempo/p. 1, Michael Wilmington
NEW YORK TIMES, 12/20/95, p. C11, Janet Maslin
VARIETY, 12/18-31/95, p. 65, Todd McCarthy
WASHINGTON POST, 12/20/95, p. C1, Hal Hinson
WASHINGTON POST, 12/22/95, Weekend/p. 42, Desson Howe

NO MERCY

An Inca Films release of an Inca Films/Amaranta Foundation of New Latin American Cinema production. *Executive Producer:* Gustavo Sanchez. *Producer:* Francisco J. Lombardi. *Director:* Francisco J. Lombardi. *Screenplay (Spanish with English subtitles):* Augusto Cabada. *Based on the novel "Crime and Punishment" by:* Feodor Dostoyevsky. *Director of Photography:* Phil Flores Guerra. *Editor:* Luis Barrios. *Music:* Leopoldo La Ross. *Sound:* Daniel Padilla. *Casting:* Monica Dominguez. *Production Designer:* Cecilia Montiel. *Running time:* 117 minutes. *MPAA Rating:* Not Rated.

CAST: Diego Bertie (Ramón); Adriana Dávila (Sonia); Jorge Chiarella (Portillo); Hermán Romero (Alejandro); Marcello Rivera (Julián); Mariella Trejos (Mrs. Aliaga).

NEW YORK POST, 9/13/95, p. 38, Larry Worth

The priest tells the penitent. "Your story doesn't impress me. It's the way you tell it."

And in those two lines, the characters of "No Mercy" have pretty much summed up the production.

As the umpteenth cinematic reworking of Fyodor Dostoyevskys "Crime and Punishment," a young man commits murder, then wrestles with his conscience when another is accused. But director Francisco J. Lombardi offers a refreshing new spin—and sense of relevance—by placing the classic tale in present-day Lima's slums.

The Peruvian capital's high crime rate and gloomy ambience lend themselves perfectly to the air of desperation that propels the youth from wide-eyed college student to wild-eyed killer.

Screenwriter Augusto Cabada has also updated the supporting players: the wily inspector investigating the case, a filthy rich Humbert Humbert and the object of his lust: a teen-aged hooker.

That quartet deftly wrestles definitions of justice, good vs. evil, and multiple looks at existentialism. But never to the action's detriment. In fact, Lombardi's pacing has the effect of a vortex drawing audiences in from the outset.

The director's penchant for subtlety also proves a driving force, most effectively at the all-important murder scene. He makes the violence's impact quick and disturbing, then wisely cuts away when the act is to be repeated. He's well aware that viewers already have the message.

Understatement applies to a religious theme as well. It gradually surfaces through the 15-year-old prostitute, a modern-day Mary Magdalene who survives her nights via beliefs in God and the

Bible. The protagonist, meanwhile, has a vaguely Christ-like appearance, though his angst-stricken transgressor seems closer to Judas.

Throughout, there are no easy answers, intensified by a cast that delivery portraits drawn in shades of gray. Diego Bertie's tortured anti-hero is a particular standout, with Adriana Davila's fallen woman-child delivering haunting support.

While Argentinian cinema has been getting a boost from the likes of Maria Luisa ("I Don't Want to Talk About It") Bemberg and Adolfo ("A Place in the World") Aristarain, Lombardi's inspired work in "No Mercy," opening today at Film Forum, promises to do the same for Peru—and then some.

VILLAGE VOICE, 9/19/95, p. 71, Georgia Brown

[*No Mercy* was shown jointly with *Clockers*; see Brown's review of that film.]

Also reviewed in:
NEW YORK TIMES, 9/13/95, p. C16, Stephen Holden
VARIETY, 5/30-6/5/94, p. 44, David Stratton

NOBODY LOVES ME

A CFP Distribution release of a Cobra Film Productions film in association with ZDF. *Producer:* Gerd Huber and Renate Seefeldt. *Director:* Doris Doerrie. *Screenplay (German with English subtitles based on her short story):* Doris Doerrie. *Director of Photography:* Helge Weindler. *Editor:* Inez Regnier. *Music:* Niki Reiser. *Sound:* Wolfgang Wirtz. *Production Designer:* Claus Kottmann. *Costumes:* Siegbert Kammerer. *Make-up:* Evelyn Dohring. *Running time:* 104 minutes. *MPAA Rating:* Not Rated.

CAST: Maria Schrader (Fanny Fink); Pierre Sanoussi-Bliss (Orfeo de Altamar); Michael von Au (Lothar Sticker); Elisabeth Trissenaar (Madeleine); *ALSO WITH:* Ingo Naujoks; Joachim Krol; Peggy Parnass; Lorose Keller; Anja Hoffmann.

NEW YORK POST, 11/3/95, p. 40, Thelma Adams

Sex and death and the single frau; the Fanny Fink story.

Twenty-nine-year old Fanny wears black. Skeletons dangle from her ears. She works days at Cologne airport frisking female passengers; at night, she's "making friends with death" at a New Age class on "Conscious Dying." Fanny hasn't been in love for four years.

Self-sufficient and dissatisfied, Fanny's whining mantra provides the movie's title: "Nobody Loves Me."

German writer/director Doris Dorrie ("Men") takes this slender situation and comically turns it on its head, sounding surprising depths and creating a world that is simultaneously familiar and fresh. Fanny lives in a dreary housing project, but she could be any black-clad, East Village waif searching for Mr. Right in all the wrong places while trying to find herself at an age when her mother was already settled with children.

Dorrie both understands and chides this state of protracted adolescence. She doesn't put urban angst on a pedestal; she deflates it for the self-indulgent waste it so often is among the middle classes. "I wouldn't fall in love with me if I were you," Fanny tells the camera at a video-dating service with a winsome pout.

Dorrie casts Fanny's lot in with a character who lives down the hall at the housing project: an outrageous psychic and transvestite torch singer named Orfeo (Pierre Sanoussi-Bliss). He is everything Fanny is not: poor, marginal, facing death as a reality rather than as a hobby and spiritually centered. He doesn't have to wear black; he is black.

Fanny seeks Orfeo out to tell her fortune. It's not the information Orfeo gives her by throwing bones in exchange for deutsche marks but the friendship he offers that seals Fanny's fate. From a liberating and ecstatic dance they perform to African drums in his apartment, through tender scenes of intimacy in which this gay man and straight woman bond, to Orfeo's impatience with Fanny's ingrown angst, their partnership is vivid and alive.

Against a backdrop of the Cologne Carnival, antic comic scenes and an offbeat mysticism, Dorrie constructs a relationship between two rounded and unusual characters usually relegated to supporting roles. True friends call each other on their B.S. Orfeo, for all his funky modernity, teaches Fanny an old-fashioned lesson: you have to give love to get it.

If nobody loves Fanny, it's because, locked away in her black-clad funk, she lacked the capacity or compassion to care for someone else. She learns that the power to change her life does not lie with some future Mr. Right but within herself. For Dorrie, Fanny serves as a metaphor for modern Germany; her story supplies a critique of a country where the supply of compassion is inversely proportional to material wealth.

VILLAGE VOICE, 11/7/95, p. 76, Leslie Camhi

Near her 30th birthday, shy Fanny Fink (Maria Schrader) begins to wonder whether she'll be alone forever. She lives by herself in bleak high-rise building in an utterly unlovely corner of Germany. By day, she frisks passengers at the local airport; at night, she's drawn to classes that teach her to "make friends with death," through suicide lessons and mock burials. In church, she lights a candle: "Not a smoker or a drinker, with good health insurance and an apartment of his own," she prays. "Is your biological clock digital?" her single mother, a hot-tempered, second-rate novelist, chides her. "Don't you hear it ticking?"

One day, in the elevator, a tall black man wearing a fur coat and copious body paint offers her his card; "Orfeo de Altamar, Psychic and Palm Reader." Desperate Fanny pays the fey Orfeo (Pierre Sanoussi-Bliss) a visit, and he makes a prediction involving Lothar, their building's comely if obtuse new super. As Orfeo's health slowly fails, Lothar pursues his own plans for the general eviction of all such marginals and eccentrics.

Nobody Loves Me is a charming romp through the angst-ridden world of celibate singledom—a wry reminder of all the tricks you use to get out of bed on an unloved morning, and all the lonely evenings you spend lying in your homemade coffin. I found the AIDS subtext largely unconvincing; Orfeo's pseudo-African pastimes and mystical prophecies were eventually wearying. But Dorrie has managed to approach the seemingly exhausted subject of women living alone with fresh humor, tenderness and hope.

Also reviewed in:
CHICAGO TRIBUNE, 1/19/96, Friday/p. M, Michael Wilmington
NEW YORK TIMES, 11/3/95, p. C3, Stephen Holden
VARIETY, 1/16-22/95, p. 97, Eric Hansen

NOVEMBER MEN, THE

A Northern Arts Entertainment release of a Rohd House Investments and Sun Lion Films production. *Producer:* Paul Williams and Rodney Byron Ellis. *Director:* Paul Williams. *Screenplay:* James Andronica. *Director of Photography:* Susan Emerson. *Editor:* Chip Brooks. *Music:* Scott Thomas Smith. *Sound:* James Dehr and Vince Garcia. *Running time:* 90 minutes. *MPAA Rating:* Not Rated.

CAST: James Andronica (Duggo); Leslie Bevis (Elizabeth); Beau Starr (Agent Granger); Paul Williams (Arthur Gwenlyn); Coralissa Gines (Lorina); Rod Ellis (Agent Clancy); Robert Davi (Himself); Lexie Shine (Morganna).

NEW YORK POST, 11/3/95, p. 40, Larry Worth

Oliver Stone is going out of his way to help promote "The November Men." And it's no wonder; the film boils down to "JFK" meets "Day for Night."

Homages aside, the production holds an even more enticing carrot for inveterate rabble-rouser Stone: "The November Men" is virtually guaranteed to make waves.

Set in the summer of 1992, the paranoia-fueled plot centers on fictional left-wing director Arthur Gwenlyn's latest movie project—a thriller about a conspiracy to knock off President George Bush. But Arthur's lovely girlfriend cum cinematographer can't help wondering—with good reason—if the movie is a convenient cover for a *real* assassination of Barbara's better half.

Most of the tightly-written dialogue has audiences gamely ping-ponging between fact and fantasy as the director makes his vision come to life. One minute, the horrifying violence is part of the movie-within-a-movie; in the next, the blood spilled is for keeps.

That's where Paul "The Revolutionary" Williams—the film's *real* director—comes in. As an appropriately jaunty score sets the mood, he taunts viewers with myriad twists and unexpected turns, even managing to fool the most savvy with the old "dream" standby. Sure, it's been done before, but rarely with tongue planted as firmly in cheek.

But Williams dangles one other trick from his bag, and it's a doozy: He lensed his principal actors as a real-life Bush event (without having obtained the proper authority's permission, according to opening credits). Going a step further, he then put the former chief executive in a rifle's cross hairs. Enter controversy—which will only be fanned by the disturbing conclusion.

A competent cast, with Williams playing Arthur and screenwriter James Andronica standing out as a tightly-wound Vietnam vet, blend nicely into the cleverness. Only Coralissa Gines strikes a wrong note as Andronica's Asian wife.

Granted, the production has other flaws, ranging from an occasional amateurishness to loose ends. Even so the countless assets of "November Men" should have audiences applauding well into December.

VILLAGE VOICE, 11/7/95, p. 67, J. Hoberman

Does producer director Paul Williams imagine himself a low-rent Oliver Stone? Or, trickier than that, does he just play one on the screen?

Paranoia folds drolly in upon itself in Williams's *The November Men*. The filmmaker casts himself as a sort of late-60s Encino Man ("the last Communist," as somebody says), encouraging speculation as to what sinister forces delayed his movie's release for two years, after a well-received premiere at the 1993 Chicago Film Festival.

The November Men belongs to a genre that had its moment in the early '70s with Watergate-era conspiracy flicks like *Executive Action* and *The Parallax View* and has now, thanks in part to *JFK*, come around again as comedy—kinda. (I'm thinking of *Dave* and *Bob Roberts* and inadvertently, *The Bodyguard*.) *The November Men*'s historical import is signified by the tense drumroll and mournful trumpet flourish that underscore its title credits.

Maverick director Arthur Gwenlyn, played by maverick director Williams, gravely watches the televised image of his state senator, Tom Hayden, holding forth on the JFK-MLK-RFK assassinations. "Our lives were wrecked" is Hayden's concluding formulation.

Defrosted in his cryogenic crypt by the smoldering fire of midlife crisis, Arthur is thus inspired by Hayden to consider the idea of a world-historic left-wing presidential assassin—at least as the basis for a movie. The filmmaker enlists the support of his highly skeptical live-in DP Elizabeth (Leslie Bevis) and hustles a few actors—mainly an irate, unemployable Vietvet named Duggo (James Andronica, author of the actual screenplay)—to appear in his "guerrilla" production, *Crosspoint*. Almost immediately, the authentic George Bush (who?) is deplaning Air Force One directly in their sights. Pan to Arthur explaining to Elizabeth: "They killed our guys. Now we kill theirs."

"President Bush" may be an anachronism, but then so is Arthur, not the least in his *cinema = truth 24 times per second* aesthic. Arthur wants everything else in his movie to be "real"—like advertising for an HIV-positive actor to play the role of an HIV-positive potential assassin. After a while, things get too real. The *Crosspoint* cast includes all manner of nonprofessional malcontents, including an angry white lesbian-feminist, an unemployed black man, and a pair of sullen Iraqis wishing to wreak vengeance on Bush with a remote-control minihelicopter. And Arthur, who tracks a planned presidential motorcade, setting up coordinates for a "killing zone" with a multi-level Los Angeles parking lot serving as the Texas Book Depository, has begun calling Duggo's wife Lorina "Marina"—as in Oswald.

Once the befuddled Duggo starts to crack, Arthurs movie (and Williams's) begins to suggest Rambo as the Manchurian Candidate. Small wonder that Elizabeth—played by Bevis in a constant state of lip-gloss anxiety—concludes that Arthur is "using the movie to make his own assassin" and reports her lover to the secret service. Of course, the secret service is also in the business of amassing documents and constructing scenarios. A double agent tells his secret service colleague that he thinks he's being set up by Arthur to be the patsy: It's "pure Oswaldism". Or, from Arthur/Williams's perspective, ready-made Zapruder.

A lost member of the De Palma-Schrader-Scorsese generation, Williams wrote and directed his first independent feature—a quasi-autobiographical evocation of suburban high school angst—at the age of 23, back in 1967. Then praised, now forgotten, *Out of It* was followed by two soberly fashionable youth pix, Jon Voight as *The Revolutionary* (1970) and *Dealing: Or the Berkeley-to-Boston Forty-Brick Lost-Bag Blues* (1972), based on a book cowritten by the young Michael Crichton and featuring a juvenile John Lithgow in the role of a suave campus pot connection. The rest is mainly silence. Does *The November Men* then follow "The September Song"? Given that Arthur is played by his own lanky, balding director, the character's inscrutably fanatical glint complicates *The November Men* as self-portrait.

Carefully composed, well-shot, and decently acted (even if Bevis prevailed on Williams, or was it vice versa, to write her a sequence requiring a leather Catwoman suit), *The November Men* is a modest '60s movie made today—complete with an abundance of self-parodic '60s-style blood bags. Despite, or perhaps because of, the rock-head bust of Ronald Reagan that presides over the final confusion the final twist seems like pure eau de Trip. Trying to make *JFK* in real life, *The November Men* wants to give movie-industry megalomania a political meaning, although Williams seems too genuinely movie-struck to satirize cinephilia let alone take more than a few potshots at Hollywood. (He's an amateur in both senses of the world.)

Where *Get Shorty* pokes fun at the industry, *The November Men* waxes philosophical. This chintzy Pirandello is at once a documentary pseudo-event and a two-dimensional psychodrama, most impressive for its unfaltering borderline attitude. Williams's comeback blurs the distinction between his contriving a movie and his character's provoking a "revolution." The solipsistic underlying premise is that making a movie makes everything permissible—mainly itself.

Also reviewed in:
NEW YORK TIMES, 11/3/95, p. C16, Stephen Holden
VARIETY, 11/15/93, p. 31, Leonard Klady

NOW AND THEN

A New Line Cinema release of a Moving Pictures production. *Executive Producer:* Jennifer Todd. *Producer:* Suzanne Todd and Demi Moore. *Director:* Lesli Linka Glatter. *Screenplay:* I. Marlene King. *Director of Photography:* Ueli Steiger. *Editor:* Jacqueline Cambas. *Music:* Dawn Soler and Cliff Eidelman. *Music Editor:* Bill Abbott. *Sound:* James Thornton and (music) Armin Steiner. *Sound Editor:* Craig Berkey. *Casting:* Valerie McCaffrey. *Production Designer:* Gershon Ginsburg and Anne Kuljian. *Art Director:* Gershon Ginsburg. *Set Decorator:* Anne Kuljian. *Set Dresser:* Scott A. Lawson, Suzann Sims, and Thommie Hicks. *Special Effects:* Morgan Guynes and Andre Ellingson. *Costumes:* Deena Appel. *Make-up:* Deborah Larsen. *Make-up (Demi Moore & Melanie Griffith):* Ronnie Spector. *Stunt Coordinator:* Dean Mumford. *Running time:* 96 minutes. *MPAA Rating:* PG-13.

CAST: Christina Ricci (Young Roberta); Thora Birch (Young Teeny); Gaby Hoffmann (Young Samantha); Ashleigh Aston Moore (Young Chrissy); Demi Moore (Samantha Albertson); Rosie O'Donnell (Roberta Martin); Rita Wilson (Christina Dewitt); Melanie Griffith (Tina Tercell); Willa Glen (Angela Albertson); Bonnie Hunt (Mrs. Dewitt); Devon Sawa (Scott Wormer); Travis Robertson (Roger Wormer); Justin Humphrey (Eric Wormer); Bradley Coryell (Clay Wormer); Janeane Garofalo (Wiladene); Lolita Davidovich (Mrs. Albertson); Ric Reitz (Mr. Albertson); Walter Sparrow (Crazy Pete); Cloris Leachman (Grandma Albertson); Kellen Crosby (Kenny); Joey Stinson (Outfielder); James Paul Cleckler (Catcher); Tucker Stone

(Young Morton); Jamison B. Dowd (Jimmy); Hank Azaria (Bud Kent); Beverly Shelton (Eda); Geoff McKnight (Tractor Driver); T.S. Morgan (Limo Driver); Carl Espy (Morton Williams); Alice Tew (Baby).

LOS ANGELES TIMES, 10/20/95, p. F14, John Anderson

[The following review by John Anderson appeared in a slightly different form in **NEWSDAY, 10/20/95, Part II/p. B6.**]

Childhood is embraced in life and fiction because it's presumed to represent our better selves—more innocent, more pure. Not, however, more intelligent. And therein lies the major rub in "Now and Then," a memory film that derails into a smoldering heap before leaving the station.

The idea that Christina Ricci, Thora Birch, Gaby Hoffman and Ashleigh Ashton Moore—four of the best young actresses in film—could grow up to become, respectively, Rosie O'Donnell, Melanie Griffith, Demi Moore and Rita Wilson isn't just unlikely (the Ricci-O'Donnell metamorphosis is particularly jarring), it's depressing.

Roberta (Ricci and O'Donnell), Teeny (Birch and Griffith), Samantha (Hoffman and Demi Moore) and Chrissy (Ashleigh Aston Moore and Wilson) are best pals—their undying friendship is affirmed at regular intervals—and grew up in the sleepy town of Shelby, Ind., to be quite different people.

Roberta has become a doctor, who also excels at sports (her dubious sexual proclivity is delivered with something like a wink). Samantha is a best-selling novelist. Chrissy, fussy and uptight as a child, is more so as an adult; she's also *really* pregnant and still living in her mother's house (which she's never redecorated). The sexually precocious Teeny has become a bombshell, of the cinematic variety.

They've reunited at Chrissy's to await the birth of her child (anyone want to bet it's a girl?) and relive some memories. We're cautioned, by the dulcet tones of Demi Moore: "Thomas Wolfe once said, 'You can never go home again ...'" Well, after "The Scarlet Letter" I wouldn't take her word for it, but in this case both she and Tom are right.

Propelled by enough '70s pop hits to stock several soundtrack albums, the girls are introduced through character-defining vignettes that never develop into anything like a real story. There's a thread of a plot about a long-ago murder and how the girls try to solve its mystery, but director Lesli Linka Glatter is more concerned with putting her foursome into situations that prompt them to realize how much they mean to each other. And we get the point a long time before they seem to.

As the narrator, Demi Moore delivers greeting-card profundities and Griffith gets to strut her stuff; O'Donnell has a nice wry delivery when the infrequently funny line comes her way. But it's the younger women's movie, and they acquit themselves admirably, even if most of the creative energy in the film seems to have gone into the costumes and set design. It's too bad, but in a year when female bonding is all over the screen, and uniformly dreadful to watch, "Now and Then" merely continues the trend.

NEW YORK POST, 10/20/95, p. 43, Larry Worth

If director Lesli Linka Glatter were to don a chef's hat, her specialty might be a palatable tuna sandwiched in stale bread. In the meantime, she's made the cinematic equivalent: "Now and Then."

Though advertised as a vehicle featuring Demi Moore, Melanie Griffith, Rosie O'Donnell and Rita Wilson, the quartet show up at the beginning and end of the *real* story: an extended flashback with Gaby Hoffmann, Thora Birch, Christina Ricci and Ashleigh Aston Moore (respectively) as their younger selves.

Coming of age in the summer of 1970, the quartet of 12-year-olds play truth-or-dare games, deal with a bunch of bullies, try to a solve a decades-old murder mystery, experience romance, face death and deal with divorce. A busy summer, indeed.

And through it all, friendship sustains the sometimes tenuous bonds between tomboy Ricci, glamour girl Birch, naive Aston Moore and wise-beyond-her-years Hoffmann. Heck, they even learn to look beneath others' facades.

It's no wonder the adult foursome finds itself rooted in the past, particularly since their reunion revolves around a horrifyingly slapstick wait for Wilson to give birth. Without doubt, the delivery's more painful for viewers.

First-time director Glatter would have done herself—and audiences—a big favor by focusing solely on the youngsters. That would have canned Wilson and Griffith's histrionics while nixing questions over how the adorable Ricci grew into less-than-adorable O'Donnell.

Moore, who also co-produced, is the only adult who doesn't embarrass herself, not counting humorous cameos by Cloris Leachman, Bonnie Hunt, Janeane Garofalo and Brenda Fraser. But they're all outacted by the teen-age co-stars, each of whom delivers a distinct personality "type" while avoiding cliches.

Though nearer to the recent "Baby-sitters Club" than a distaff "Stand by Me," "Now and Then" stands out as one case where children—unlike their grownup counterpoints—should be seen and heard.

Also reviewed in:
CHICAGO TRIBUNE, 10/20/95, Friday/p. J, Michael Wilmington
NEW YORK TIMES, 10/20/95, P. C12, Caryn James
VARIETY, 10/23-29/95, p. 46, Joe Leydon
WASHINGTON POST, 10/20/95, p. D6, Laura Blumfield

OLD LADY WHO WALKED IN THE SEA, THE

A CFP Distribution release of a Blue Dahlia Productions, Sociète Financiere de Coproduction, Films A2, Little Bear, J.M. Productions coproduction. *Director:* Laurent Heynemann. *Screenplay (French with English subtitles):* Dominique Roulet. *Based on the novel by:* San Antonio. *Director of Photography:* Robert Alazrald. *Editor:* Jacques Comets. *Music:* Phillipe Sarde. *Set Decorator:* Valerie Grail. *Costumes:* Catherine Leterrier. *Running time:* 95 minutes. *MPAA Rating:* Not Rated.

CAST: Jeanne Moreau (Lady M); Michel Serrault (Pompilius); Luc Thuillier (Lambert); Geraldine Danon (Noëmie).

LOS ANGELES TIMES, 11/15/95, Calendar/p. 6, Kevin Thomas

In Laurent Heynemann's delightful yet acerbic and exceedingly wise "The Old Lady Who Walked in the Sea," Jeanne Moreau looms into view like a galleon at full mast, strolling slowly in the surf, not in a bathing suit but in dramatic attire and a big hat.

Moreau's Lady M, who walks with a cane, is trying to soothe her arthritic hip, but the brazen glamour of her exaggerated wardrobe, jewels and wigs proclaims loudly her defiance of age. Moreau has the appearance and demeanor of a woman who has unapologetically lived a life of pleasure, and her fading beauty is perfect for playing Lady M.

The setting is Guadeloupe, and Lady M and her dapper, silver-haired companion, Pompilius (Michel Serrault), seem a rich retired couple on vacation. Rich they are, but we're genuinely surprised when we soon discover that Lady M, in partnership with Pompilius, is a world-class con artist whose entire life has been given over to grand affairs and great capers. She's not about to give up either, and when she discovers Lambert (Luc Thuillier), a handsome beach boy—and petty thief—she devises to engage him in both.

After these three have returned to Lady M's fabulous mansion on the Riviera, it becomes clear that we're watching "Sunset Boulevard on the Grand Corniche"—but with a crucial difference: Lady M is a tough-minded realist, not a crazed Norma Desmond. Pompilius may have been a long-ago lover, but he's no Max Mayerling, encouraging any self-delusion in Lady M. To the contrary, these two trade insults with aplomb. However, Lady M is falling in love with Lambert against her better judgment.

The film's jewel-heist plot is but a device to develop the relationship between Lady M and Lambert. This in turn allows Moreau to work her magic. The way in which Lady M has been written and played so mesmerizingly by Moreau is to reveal her as a woman who has not merely lived by her very sharp wits but also according to her own code.

Lady M is a great star part for Moreau, who receives deftly underplayed support from Serrault and Thuillier. More comedy of manners than romantic comedy, "The Old Lady Who Walked in the Sea" skirts neither the remorselessness of aging nor the cruelty it can sow, but it leaves us admiring Lady M.

NEW YORK POST, 9/15/95, p. 42, Thelma Adams

"I'm an old bitch," crows Jeanne Moreau in "The Old Lady Who Walked in the Sea." As the high-class grifter Lady M., on the prowl for young blood and old money, Moreau is not a woman who invites disagreement.

Laurent Heynemann's brightly colored comedy follows two aging con artists, Lady M and her dried-up lover, Pompilius (Michel Serrault). The constant companions have reached a golden age of swindles, coasting along Guadeloupe and the French Riviera, exchanging stinging insults and constructing high-return stings.

Lady M, with her arthritic hip that she tries to appease by seawater strolls, and the impotent Pompilius are closer to the grave than the cradle. While Pompilius resigns himself to the inevitable decline with a whimper, the lady finds the fountain of youth in a piece of larcenous blond beefcake named Lambert (Luc Thuillier).

Lady M adopts the petty thief, intending to transform him into a gentrified grifter. Pompilius is skeptical—and jealous. Moreau, whose name became synonymous with the menage a trois after Truffaut's French New Wave classic "Jules and Jim," has returned to familiar territory. The sexy senior becomes the apex of a comically charged love triangle—call it Harold and Maude and Pompilius.

The comedy is at its giddy best when Pompilius and Lady M trade insults. "You're an old sow in heat," hurls the dapper old man. She tosses back a curdled term of endearment, addressing her ex-amour as "my old love wreck."

As a caper film, Dominique Roulet's otherwise tart script could have used restructuring. The heists pulled by the trio have little tension; they are just speed bumps as Lady M changes partners on love's superhighway. The big events seem forced or fall flat, but the interlocking scenes are lit up by Moreau's vibrant character.

"The Old Lady Who Walked in the Sea" showcases the talents of the aging but not aged Moreau. The 67-year-old actress was always able to project a beauty more radiant than the sum of her features, to bare her soul even if the picture wasn't pretty. Here, Moreau fearlessly projects desire even if she is less desirable than she once was. I would follow her into the sea and so, if you believe farcical French fairy tales, would the hunky Lambert.

NEWSDAY, 9/15/95, Part II/p. B7, John Anderson

Sex and the elderly are not subjects that usually gravitate to each other. Together—or separately, for that matter—they make Americans uncomfortable, although not Mike Wallace, who during a recently aired "60 Minutes" interview was more than happy to grill the French actress/-monument Jeanne Moreau about her alleged litany of lovers.

Moreau, showing more class than CBS will ever have, was unperturbed, handling the subject matter with frankness and a healthy respect for lust—which is exactly what she brings to "The Old Lady Who Walked in the Sea," a darkly cynical comedy about the undampened fires of the heart, the loins and cupidity.

(This 1991 film was to have been a presentation of the now-defunct Film at the Public but instead will be shown at two other Manhattan theaters.)

Moreau—whose expansive career has included such films as Louis Malle's "Les Amants," Antonioni's "La Notte" and Truffaut's "Jules et Jim"—plays Lady M, a foul-mouthed diva with a passion for diamonds and sex. With her longtime companion Pompilius—they were lovers once but now exhaust their ardor in a congress of mutual insults—she runs blackmail schemes and extortion scams; they stroll the beaches of Guadeloupe like boulevardiers, their thoughts never straying too far from money or hormones.

But when Lady M. meets Lambert (Luc Thuillier), a callow beach stud who becomes her obsession, Pompilius' days are numbered. The three set out to pull off a risky heist—the theft of a jeweled tiara from a maharaja's daughter—which sets the stage for Pompilius' eventual betrayal. One wonders if Lady M is just a stand-in for death, a voracious feeder on souls.

Whatever she is, Moreau makes her a memorable old reprobate, one who prays to God that her plans—which include Lambert—will be fulfilled, while never ceasing to plot and plan, and hunger for her misspent youth.

And whatever else "The Old Lady Who Walked in the Sea" pretends to be about, it's simply very funny—partly because of Moreau and Serrault, partly because we don't expect mature people to act this way and partly because we're all maturing quickly and might well picture ourselves in their orthopedic shoes and fits of passion.

VILLAGE VOICE, 9/19/95, p. 76, Leslie Camhi

French culture once shocked the world with its decadence and perversion, but in *The Old Lady Who Walked In the Sea*, the cherished national vices now seem quaintly anachronistic. This star vehicle features Jeanne Moreau as the aging whose golden years are paved with lust and diamonds. On a working holiday in the Antilles, while blackmailing fellow vacationers with her partner, Pompilius (Michel Serrault), an erudite con artist, Lady M. meets Lambert (Luc Thuillier), a blond beach boy who she quickly decides is ripe for "adoption." This sexless ménage à trois soon retires to a fabulous villa on the Côte d'Azur, where they plan their next caper and Lady M. tries refining her protégé's vulgar gift for graft into something sharper.

Thuillier's a crude hulk, and her project is doomed to failure. The film's charm lies in watching Moreau and Serrault, two great French stars, trade increasingly ornate invectives aimed at each other's wrecked and elderly condition. He calls her young lover a "fossil fondler," while she tells him to go and rest his calcified bones. The florid script skillfully mingles gallantry with decrepitude and a creepy, Old World racism, but sometimes the champagne goes flat; the happy ending is unconvincing. Moreau is, yes, a beautiful woman, but I'd like once to see a role for an older actress that didn't feed endlessly off the spectacle of her aging.

Also reviewed in:
NEW YORK TIMES, 9/15/95, p. C12, Stephen Holden
VARIETY, 11/18/91, p. 31, Suzan Ayscough

ONCE WERE WARRIORS

A Fine Line Features release of a Communicado film in association with the New Zealand Film Commission/Avalon Studios/New Zealand On Air. *Producer:* Robin Scholes. *Director:* Lee Tamahori. *Screenplay:* Riwia Brown. *Based on the novel by:* Alan Duff. *Director of Photography:* Stuart Dryburgh. *Editor:* Michael Horton. *Music:* Murray Grindlay and Murray McNabb. *Maori Music Consultant:* Hirini Melbourne. *Choreographer:* Kepe Stirling. *Sound:* Michael Hedges. *Sound Editor:* Don Paulin, Ray Beentjes, and Emma Haughton. *Casting:* Don Selwyn Wellington and Riwia Brown. *Production Designer:* Michael Kane. *Art Director:* Shayne Radford. *Costumes:* Michael Kane. *Make-up:* Debra East. *Fight Coordinator:* Robert Bruce. *Running time:* 108 minutes. *MPAA Rating:* R.

CAST: Rena Owen (Beth Heke); Temuera Morrison (Jake Heke); Mamaengaroa Kerr-Bell (Grace Heke); Julian Arahanga (Nig Heke); Taungaroa Emile (Boogie Heke); Rachael Morris, Jr. (Polly Heke); Joseph Kairau (Huata Heke); Clifford Curtis (Bully); Pete Smith (Dooley); George Henare (Bennett); Mere Boynton (Mavis); Shannon Williams (Toot); Calvin Tuteao

(Taka); Ray Bishop (King Hitter); Ian Mune (Judge); Te Whatanui Skipworth (Te Tupaea); Rangi Motu (Matawai); Robert Pollock (Policeman); Jessica Wilcox (Policewoman); Stephen Hall (Prosecuting Officer); Wiki Oman (Youth Advocate); Israel Williams and Johnathon Wiremu (Youths); Richard Meihana (Taunter in Court); Edna Stirling and Ngawai Simpson (Women); Spike Kem (Old Drunk); Arona Rissetto (Nig's Friend); Fran Viveare (Nig's Girlfriend); Brian Kairau (Joking Man Outside Pub); Charlie Tumahai (Karaoke Singer); Tama Renata (Party Guitarist); Guy Moana (Evicted Partygoer/Pub Customer); Maree Moschonas (Gang Rape Victim); Riwia Brown (Bully's Girlfriend).

CHRISTIAN SCIENCE MONITOR, 3/1/95, p. 12, David Sterritt

Once Were Warriors hails from New Zealand, but the problems it tackles—domestic violence, racial tension, youth gangs—have relevance around the world. The story focuses on Jake and Beth, whose 18-year marriage has spawned a host of problems. Many are caused by Jake's outbursts of drunken abuse. Others stem from Beth's lingering doubts about whether she was right to marry him over the objections of her parents, ethnic Maoris who wished their daughter would stay away from decadent white culture.

The movie gains much of its strength from the hard-hitting style of director Lee Tamahori, whose ability to construct scenes of sustained emotional force is greater than one might expect from a newcomer who developed his skills making TV commercials.

Even more impressive are the performances by Temuera Morrison, a New Zealand soap-opera star of surprising depth, and Rena Owen, whose explosive portrayal of Beth won the best-actress award at last year's Montreal World Film Festival.

The movie itself won the best-film award at Montreal and has been praised at other European and American festivals. It isn't a success only on the movie-buff circuit, moreover: At box offices in New Zealand, it has become the top-grossing picture of all time, outdoing even "Jurassic Park" and other high-profile releases.

This doesn't mean it's a masterpiece; as I observed in a report from Montreal, it's less artful than powerful, in the sense that a locomotive or a sledgehammer is powerful. But its cry of anguish over domestic abuse has clearly struck a resonant chord.

LOS ANGELES TIMES, 3/3/95, Calendar/p. 1, Kenneth Turan

Blue skies, lush green hillsides, a limpid lake. The first picture "Once Were Warriors" presents of New Zealand is the classic, expected one. But then the camera pulls back and that image is unmasked as a deceptive billboard sitting in a quite different environment, the trash-strewn, dead-end slums of gritty urban Auckland.

The highest-grossing film in New Zealand history, "Once Were Warriors" is unblinkingly intent on exploring the reality behind its country's benign facade, on exposing the dirty underside of the glowing picture postcard.

A relentless sledgehammer of a film, "Warriors" is raw by design, intentionally sacrificing subtlety and nuance to enhance the impact of its passionate muckraking. And while the picture's nightmarish scenario is undeniably powerful, getting beaten up by a movie is not a sensation everyone cherishes.

"Warriors" focuses on the predicament of the Maoris, the Polynesian group that ruled the island before the Europeans came and trashed and burned their way of life. Now, like so many indigenous groups, the film's ghettoized Maori are a culture that has lost its way, its members living on alcohol and the dole without any noticeable hope for better lives.

The film concentrates in particular on the family of Beth and Jake Heke. Married for 18 years, parents of five children, Beth and Jake still have moments (like the sentimental love duet they sing at one of their frequent all-night beer parties) when the initial attraction they had for each other is still strong and visible.

But mostly life for Beth and Jake, especially for Beth, is a catalogue of horrors. Though Jake says modestly, "I got a temper on me, who doesn't?," in fact he has a terrifyingly short fuse. A legendary bar brawler nicknamed Jake the Mus (for muscle) who thrashes strangers just to stay in practice, loses it one night and inflicts a horrific, stomach-turning beating on Beth that leaves her looking as grotesque as the Hunchback of Notre Dame.

Living in a household like this, it is no surprise that many of the couple's children are troubled. Their oldest son, Nig (Julian Arahanga), is totally estranged and thinking of joining a motorcycle gang characterized by intimidating face and body tattoos in the Maori tradition. And his younger brother Boogie (Taungaroa Emile) is hanging out with petty thieves and in danger of being removed from the family and placed in a state institution.

Only Grace (Mamaengaroa Kerr-Bell), the sweet-smiling oldest daughter, seems to have escaped the influence of this pestilent environment. A would-be writer who keeps her two youngest siblings entertained with stories, she confides her hopes to Toot (Shannon Williams), a glue-sniffing homeless teen-ager who lives in an abandoned car under a freeway underpass.

Aside from simply presenting these people and their environment, impressing this grim side of New Zealand life on the world's cinematic consciousness, director Lee Tamahori (a maker of commercials in his feature debut) follows several related themes. Can anyone escape from this sink of despair, what path will they need to follow, and how much suffering needs to go down before any of that can happen?

With a screenplay by Riwia Brown based on a best-selling novel by Alan Duff, "Once Were Warriors" is helped greatly by its unmistakable tang of actuality, the sense that the problems it describes are valid and inescapable. For the largely Maori cast, particularly Rena Owen as the strong-willed Beth and Temuera Morrison as the appalling Jake, that connection to reality enhances performances potent enough to make audiences feel they're experiencing the horrors as they're happening.

But, as often happens when films are intent on getting a message across, "Once Were Warriors" can't stop itself from overdoing things. This is one of those films where indignities schematically pile up and up and up, where if something bad can come out of a given situation, it will. Even its nominally uplifting subplot about the restorative power of Maori tradition barely makes a dent in the gloom.

By choosing to bludgeon the audience with ever-worsening tales of woe, "Once Were Warriors" paradoxically blunts its power, though the truth is that people may be too shell-shocked. to notice.

NEW YORK, 3/6/95, p. 54, David Denby

A little over twenty years ago, I traveled to New Zealand and met a great many sheep, some of them with four legs. I was visiting on behalf of the USIA, which sends Americans all over the map on cultural duties. I felt a bit sheepish myself. Film cans under my arm, I gave innocuous talks about Chaplin, Ford, and, yes, Preminger, and drank innumerable cups of tea, fed to me by white New Zealanders who lived in small Hempstead-style houses. They informed me solemnly that New Zealand could do without pornography, though why they considered this an issue I never discovered, since as far as I could see there wasn't any pornography in New Zealand. In each city, the local cultural officials took me to museums to see Maori art—masks and totems and huge canoes—but I never met any Maori, the indigenous people who constitute about 12 percent of the population. New Zealand seemed a quiet place indeed, genteel and evasive. When fistfights erupted at closing time in the Auckland bars, the newspapers carried on as if the nation were enmeshed in a major social crisis. I marveled at a country that seemed dull and provincial in many ways but was nonetheless sufficiently blessed to settle arguments with fists rather than knives or guns.

On the evidence of *Once Were Warriors* a powerful new movie from New Zealand, fists remain the preferred method of combat. But everything else comes as a shock; the picture reveals sides of Maori life and New Zealand temperament kept well out of sight two decades ago. *Once Were Warriors* is based on a novel by Alan Duff; it's a portrait of a brawling working-class Maori family, and particularly of a violent husband and father, that caused a stir in New Zealand, dismaying many who wanted a more positive image of the country's Maori population. Adapting the book into a movie, director Lee Tamahori, who is part Maori, brought in a woman screenwriter, Riwia Brown, and shifted the focus from the husband, Jake, to his wife, Beth. Since Beth is played by a magnificent New Zealand actress named Rena Owen, who's half Maori herself, the shift seems a stroke of genius. The movie—crude in places but startling too—is now the story of a woman's awakening, set against the backdrop of the destructive pop-cult life of the Maori underclass.

Jake (Temuera Morrison), a powerful man with short hair and piercing eyes, gets laid off, goes on the dole, and starts an endless party with his mates that moves from a huge bar to home and back again. His wife adores him, but he beats her and ignores the children, who are drifting toward chaos. If *Once Were Warriors* is to be trusted, gangsta rap and biker regalia have fused with the emblems of Maori culture. The urban young toughs in their black leather vests and pants undergo vicious rites of initiation, then get themselves tattooed in the fantastic circular patterns of the old tribesmen.

Director Lee Tamahori seems split in his feelings about all this, but split in an interesting way. The Maori live on the wrong side of the freeway, on streets littered with junked cars, rubble, and graffiti. The cluttered and blackened urban squalor gives Tamahori a terrific visual subject, and working with cinematographer Stuart Dryburgh (who shot *The Piano*), he revels in the lurid, angry rawness. Yet he also uses red and brown earth colors whenever he can, as if the old communal land of New Zealand were calling the Maori away from their disastrous city life. The movie is a work of pop culture driven by a strong anti-pop animus.

The men can escape; the women cannot. Rena Owen has high, strong cheekbones, a mane of thick unruly hair, and a smile that transforms her face into pure, distilled merriment. Her masklike beauty reminds me of Jeanne Moreau's, but the way Owen uses her body—all of it, in every shot—is entirely her own. Walking through the neighborhood, her Beth, perhaps 35, is still a beautiful young woman with a lioness's hauteur. Like the other women in the neighborhood, Beth has been brought up to "keep your mouth shut and your legs open." Her rough life doesn't bother her; she revels in it, enjoying the rude, hard-drinking parties as much as anyone. But when Jake boils over—slams her against the wall and pummels her face—she's in danger of losing her life. Coming in the middle of the raucous but jovial party, the violence is horrifying. I don't think I've ever seen a woman hit in a movie with this much ferocity. So fists can do damage, too.

People always ask, How can a woman who's not a masochist put up with abuse? Beth suggests one answer: As she describes her first attraction to Jake—and how she rebelled against everyone by going off with him—we can see that, eighteen years later, she's hanging in out of pride, not masochism. But for Beth, what's lawless and exciting about her husband is also what's likely to destroy her. She's caught in the bind of many women attracted to tough guys, and Rena Owen, taking everything to extremes, shows us love fighting back rage, and then shame and despair tearing away at love. Owen's performance is classic, but Temuera Morrison, as Jake, doesn't have material of the same richness to work with. Jake has been conceived as a brute, a man who thinks that sex is all he owes his wife (and who secretly believes that sex is all he can give her). He's little more than an unreachable brawler, and he's unnecessarily diminished when his self-hatred as a Maori is used against him to explain why he beats up the woman he loves.

The director, Tamahori, has worked in commercials in the past, but his movie isn't slick in the Western style. *Once Were Warriors* is hard and true. City life has a strong emotional pull—the lure of pleasure and irresponsibility—which may be something Americans understand all too well. But I would guess that American audiences will be less convinced when Jake and Beth's middle son, shipped off to some sort of national reform school, winds up in the hands of a Maori sage, who teaches him and other young men to beat their chests and chant and receive the spirits of their ancestors. This is where the movie turns pious, and I was reminded of my dutiful trips twenty years ago to see canoes and masks. How are tribal rites supposed to heal the ruptures of modern industrial society, with its structural unemployment, its imported mass culture, its programmed hedonism? For us, the movie is more about the man and the woman—about what might happen when Beth tells off Jake and risks another beating.

So let's hear it for New Zealand, the land of 3 million people and 50 million sheep. This obscure, underpopulated, once-pacific country has made a film that couldn't possibly intersect more crucially with our bitterest preoccupations.

NEW YORK POST, 2/24/95, p. 45, Thelma Adams

There's a point in Lee Tamahori's "Once Were Warriors" when Beth Heke (Rena Owen) and her unemployed husband Jake (Temuera Morrison) sing together in their living room surrounded by a rowdy after-hours party.

The handsome Maori pair share a moment of raucous harmony, projecting pure, sexual, married love. Beth and Jake are the golden couple of their low-rent circle.

The camera cuts upstairs. The five Heke kids are huddled in a shabby room. Hearing their parents' song, the children are relieved.

The moment passes quickly.

The joyous drunk dissolves into a bitter feud between the Hekes. The volatile Jake turns on Beth. Physical love becomes physical abuse. Husband tosses wife around the room like a rag doll and slams her against the wall.

The next morning, the children awake to a trashed house. Blood smears the dirty walls. The eldest daughter, Grace (Mamaengaroa Kerr-Bell), starts to tidy up.

Tamahori sets his powerhouse debut feature among the Maoris in the urban projects of contemporary New Zealand, but his themes are timeless and universal. It's the children who suffer at the hands of their parents' problems.

Few viewers will fail to make a connection with O.J. and Nicole Simpson, another golden pair caught in a downward spiral of passion, drug abuse and brutality.

"Once Were Warriors" shows domestic violence as grand and destructive passion. Sexual abuse is a betrayal of intimacy when a kindly uncle adopts a disturbing nocturnal face during a midnight raid on a child's bedroom.

Riwia Brown's script, based on Alan Duffs novel, spans the razor's edge between physical love and physical violence. It captures the rage beneath the substance abuse that rises uncontrollably to the surface in volatile individuals, aided, but not caused by, alcohol. Jake is not evil incarnate; he's a charming guy with a dark side beyond his control.

The chemistry between Owen and Morrison clinches "Once Were Warriors." Owen has the looks of Jeanne Moreau, the raw emotional power of Anna Magnani, and a slim athleticism all her own. She received the best-actress award at the Montreal Film Festival last summer for her strong, gutsy portrayal of Beth. (In addition, "Warriors" was named the festival's best film.)

As subtle as a sledgehammer, "Once Were Warriors" would have benefited from a little restraint in the final plot twists. That said, the movie gains its power by pounding the audience until our senses are raw and wired, our sympathies profoundly aroused.

"Once Were Warriors" is unforgettable.

NEWSDAY, 2/24/95, Part II/p. B2, Jack Mathews

What a difference a culture makes. In America, and many other countries around the world, "Jurassic Park" is the highest-grossing picture ever released. In New Zealand, the movie that has packed them in in record numbers is first-time director Lee Tamahori's "Once Were Warriors," a searing portrait of a dysfunctional family of urban New Zealand Maoris.

The best explanation for "Warrior's" popularity at home is the desire of New Zealanders—of the dominant, European-descended stock; of the native Maori; and of the huge population of mixed blood—to better understand what has become the nation's chief social problem, the assimilation of Maoris into an industrialized, city-centered culture.

"Warriors," adapted from a novel by Alan Duff, burrows to the core of this problem by focusing on the Heke family—father, mother and five kids caught in a welfare system that does more to encourage poverty, alcoholism, domestic violence, and gang activity than it does to help people out of the economic ghetto.

Jake Heke (Tamuera Morrison), a muscle-bound, quick-tempered, wife-beating alcoholic, was hard enough to live with when he had a job. As we meet him, he's been laid off, which gives him more time to spend drinking and brawling with his buddies (unemployment makes up for all but $17 of his weekly pay), while it further cuts into the dream of his wife, Beth (Rena Owen), of moving out of the tough neighborhood and buying a home of their own.

Meanwhile, one son (Julian Arahanga) is venturing into a gang, another (Taungaroa Emile) has been taken away to a school for delinquents, and their innocent 13-year-old daughter Grace (Mamaengaroa Kerr-Bell), is coming of age in a place where innocence is doomed.

In many ways, "Warriors" seems to mirror America's urban minority communities. Every square inch of the landscape is covered with graffiti, teenagers collect on street corners drinking and doing dope, tattooed gang members face off like territorial animals, police sirens wail through the night. But the Maoris aren't so much an oppressed minority as they are a people struggling with their own identity. Some of them wear the ornately geometric full-body tattoos of the ancient tribes; others are covered with scorpions, spider webs, hearts and daggers, and seem to be striving for some idolized biker image from B movies.

The conflict of "Warriors" is between the Maoris who cling to their tribal past and those who want to shuck it altogether. Jake, who sees himself merely as a descendant of slaves, loathes the native culture that still exists in rural New Zealand, and from which he had lured Beth 18 years earlier. She merely wants a better life for her children, and accepts her abuse as the inevitable consequence of moving to the city.

"Just keep your mouth shut and your legs open," a friend advises Beth, after one of Jake's drunken rampages. But the same booze that makes him dangerous makes her defiant, and the pattern is repeated.

Tamahori has a passion for the kind of choreographed, smash-face violence you expect to find on the straight-to-video shelf, and the frequent barroom fights seem to have been designed for people who resemble those in the bar. At the same time, the beating administered to Beth and Jake, in the film's most startling sequence, is terrifyingly realistic. If you think violence is entertaining, Tamahori is saying, take a look at the real thing.

"Warriors" is a marvelously directed film, and the cinematography of Oscar-nominated Stuart Dryburgh ("The Piano") draws us so deeply into its gray-brown setting, you can almost smell the despair. But it is the performances of its Maori cast that make it so profoundly compelling.

Owen, who has worked mostly on stage in London, plays Beth with a deft mix of vulnerability and strength, and New Zealand soap opera star Morrison, beefed up to the proportions of a character out of Popeye, is both a monster and a charmer as Jake.

And finally, there is Kerr-Bell, a novice discovered when she accompanied a friend to the auditions for "Warriors." Kerr-Bell is a beautiful teenage girl with a luminous smile, and her lack of acting experience adds to the innocence of Grace, the aptly named character upon whom the story, and the future of the still unassimilated Maoris she represents, ultimately hang.

NEWSWEEK, 3/6/95, p. 68, David Ansen

In New Zealand, the homemade *Once Were Warriors* has recently surpassed "Jurassic Park" to become the most successful film in the country's history. The brutal domestic realism of Lee Tamahori's film couldn't be further from Spielberg's theme-park fantasy, but there is one metaphoric connection: both films are about endangered species turned dangerous. Those facing extinction here, however, are the descendants of Maori warriors now living deracinated lives of squalor and crime in the urban ghettos of Auckland. Their culture long since decimated by the English, who banished their language, their rage has turned inward. There are few white faces on view in Tamahori's movie, which is concerned less with the injustices done to the Maori in the past than with the way a stigmatized culture sometimes turns violently upon itself. Any resemblance to ghettos closer at hand hardly needs belaboring.

Adapted from an Alan Duff novel by playwright Riwia Brown, "Once Were Warriors" puts us in the shoes of Beth Heke (Rena Owen), a battered woman struggling to keep her family together and her children out of trouble. Her jobless giant of a husband, Jake (Temuera Morrison), spends his days guzzling beer with the boys and getting into fights, and throwing parties at home at night. Beth likes a drink and a song herself, and she obviously thinks her hunk of a husband is sexy, but the price is high: in his alcoholic rages, Jake bashes her to a bloody pulp. Domestic violence has never been more savagely portrayed on screen.

The whole family suffers the repercussions. One son joins a gang (the tattooed members resemble something from "The Road Warrior"). Another lands in a reform school, where he learns his first lessons in Maori pride,. Thirteen-year-old Grace is raped by a family friend in her own home. The raw power of "Once Were Warriors" is undeniable. And Rena Owen, wired with nervous energy, makes a formidable heroine. She exudes an angry earthy sensuality that brings Jeanne Moreau to mind. But the movie's visceral bluntness is both its strength and its weakness: almost every point is hit square upon the nose. It's not surprising that Tamahori has been signed to direct a Hollywood studio film: he knows how to work up an audience's outrage. But for all its gritty urban details, the writing never ventures far from melodramatic formula. Beth's big speeches are just that—speeches. The urban Maori milieu, however, is something we haven't seen before, and the images stay with you. You can smell the beer on the barroom floor, taste the food in the Heke household and feel the fear in the air every time Jake lurches home, spoiling for a fight.

SIGHT AND SOUND, 4/95, p. 50, Lizzie Francke

Jake and Beth live with their five children in a poor suburb of Auckland, New Zealand. Jake has just lost his job and Boogie, his teenage son, has been cautioned yet again by the police. The couple host a party while their 13-year-old daughter Grace looks after the smaller kids. She promises Boogie she will accompany him to his court appearance the following day. During the party, Nig, the eldest son, alienated from his father, turns up to ask his mother for money. But Beth finds the house-keeping money has disappeared and when she starts quarrelling with Jake, who has been drinking and gambling it away, he beats her up.

Next day Grace cleans up the mess and takes Boogie to court where they learn he is to be sent to reform school. Beth is devastated. Meanwhile, Nig is initiated into the local gang. Weeks later, Jake and Beth are still distant, with Jake spending all his time drinking with friends. *Rapprochement* occurs when Beth persuades Jake to take the family to visit Boogie. They hire a car and take a picnic. The visit goes fairly well but on the return journey Jake stops off at his favourite bar. Beth takes the children home in a taxi. Grace is angry at her mother for allowing her father to treat them so badly.

That night Jake holds another impromptu party. Beth refuses to join him. Jake's friend Bully slips into Grace's room and rapes her, threatening to do worse if she tells her parents. The following day, Beth, sensing something is wrong, tries to talk to Grace but she runs away to visit her friend Toot, who lives in a car. When he tries to kiss her affectionately she again runs away?. While Beth and a friend are out searching for her, Grace returns home. Her father shouts at her for refusing to kiss her "Uncle Bully" goodnight. She goes into the back yard and hangs herself from a tree.

Beth finds her. On the following day she arranges a traditional Maori funeral. During the ceremony, Jake stays at home drinking with friends. Beth returns, having asked Toot to join the family. Later, she reads Grace's diary and discovers the truth. She goes to confront Bully in the local bar. At first Jake refuses to believe her, but after seeing the diary, he attacks Bully. Beth walks out, telling Jake she is leaving him for good and taking the children with her.

Celebrated as the top-grossing film of all time in New Zealand, *Once Were Warriors* is also the first Maori work to reach an international art-house audience. In terms of genre, however, it fits neatly with recent Afro-American urban films in dealing with a community disenfranchised through economics and race. Rap music and a punchy credits sequence indicate that, for director Lee Tamahori, the genre connection is important. Quick-fire editing and burnished visuals give the film a rich appearance, far from the sober, social-realist tradition that the subject matter might ordinarily suggest. In style then, this story of an imploding dysfunctional family borrows more from Hollywood melodrama than from Ken Loach. Although the film is adapted from Alan Duff's novel, the producer/scriptwriter team of Robin Scholes and Riwia Brown agreed to "shape it more to Beth's story". With Beth as the emergent protagonist, *Warriors* is thus clearly a woman's comment on the status quo, gaining much of its dynamism from Rena Owen's sparky performance as the matriarch.

Nevertheless, *Warriors* also shares with such films as *Boyz N the Hood* a concern with male codes of behaviour and social emasculation. Physical strength is all that these adult men have left for themselves. The camera lingers on their musculature, emphasising an erotic quality which Beth seems at first to admire. Jake, having lost his job, finds other ways to prove himself, whether by drinking his mates under the table or punching out Beth. It is perhaps this view of the working class Maori male that has made Duffs novel so controversial. His characterisation of Jake treads a delicate line between the negative stereotype of a wife-beater and a more complex psychological portrayal. In the film, however, Jake's behaviour is more obviously the result of his alienation from his Maori roots. His gambling, drinking and mistreatment of his wife mark him out as a victim of the corrupt and decayed values of the Europeans. Beth, reminding Jake that his forebears were slaves, tells him: "You're still a slave to your fist, the drink, yourself..."

In contrast, Jake's sons Nig and Boogie learn to channel their aggression and disaffection into more ritualistic expressions of anger. The local gang that Nig joins is a very urban tribe. Augmenting shades and leather jackets with myriad tattoos, the members seem to be nodding towards some sort of tradition—the initiation ceremony even includes a punch-up with the leader. Yet the cosmetic, gestural nature of these warrior clichés becomes clear in scenes shot in cool shades of blue—the gang look more like style guerillas than anything more effective. It is Boogie who gets inducted into more serious Maori rites, learning tribal dances and the philosophy that inspires them from a social worker at the reform school. When Boogie smashes the windows in the school hall, the worker tells him: "You think your fist is your weapon. When I finish with you, your mind will be your weapon, which you will carry inside."

Spiritual loss is the film's ultimate diagnosis, particularly of a kind associated with the land. The opening shot of green hills proves to be a billboard inscribed with the words "En/power". The camera pulls away revealing a tangle of motorways bathed in a nicotine yellow haze. These polluted surroundings are far from Aoteara, the promised haven of Maori myth (Aoteara means thin white cloud). Ironically, the one strong tree in their yard is where Grace chooses to hang herself. Beth mourns her own dislocation from a rich tradition during a visit to the part of the country where her family comes from. Yet there's a sense that, despite her putting up with Jake's abusive behaviour, she alone never lost touch with the spiritual armoury of her ancestors' warrior past.

VILLAGE VOICE, 2/28/95, p. 68, Gary Dauphin

An odd spin on the family-abuse melodrama, *Once Were Warriors* is hard to watch but even more difficult to look away from. This is partly because its down-under locale (a Maori enclave in urban New Zealand) revitalizes what would otherwise be all-too-familiar source material (drunken dad beats mom on a regular basis), but it's also because *Warriors's* principals remain so working-class stylish throughout that you don't quite know how to process the brutality that fills their day to day. As violent as *Warriors* is, it's also filled with very pretty people, its complicated codes of hair, clothes, and tattoos as important to the development of the characters as their dialogue and action.

Besides the burly new jacks at the local bar, Jake Heke's favorite punching bag is his wife Beth (Rena Owen). A barrel-chested bull-terrier of a man ("a hard man," Beth calls him), Jake loses his job early in the picture, drinking the day away with his similarly underemployed cronies. With his buzz cut and tight black T's, Jake (New Zealand soap star Temuera Morrison) is an engagingly terrifying monster, and when he's not hurting people he's strangely chivalrous and impulsive, hovering somewhere between the English louts of the Loach-Leigh axis and the walking elegies of Allison Anders's *Mi Vida Loca*. Jake's violence is complicated like any good monster's should be, and Morrison even manages the perverse trick of getting the audience to root for him at times, no small feat with the memory of Beth's abused face fresh in one's mind.

A vivid screen presence in her own right, Beth has somehow managed to keep her edgy beauty and spirit despite five kids and 18 years with Jake. Beth loves her husband but worries about how his failings are affecting her children. After she's beaten to a swollen pulp by Jake, he keeps telling her how irresistible she is until she falls for his lame explanations again ("Just stay out of my way when I get like that," Jake offers). But when Jake reneges on a make-nice promise to visit a son locked up in juvey hall, that particular sin is more significant to her than the danger he poses to her. Ever the loving mother, Beth is more proud than angry when elder son Nig (Julian Arahanga) returns from a gang initiation with a face full of Maori tribal tattoos; 13-year-old Grace (Mamaengaroa Kerr-Bell) isn't just the love of Beth's life but the film's quiet-eyed center. Set up immediately as an avatar of hope and possibility, Grace gets through Jake's drunken fits by copying her emotional scars into a spiral notebook, transmogrifying them into fairy tales she reads for a homeless gluehead chum.

Written, directed, and acted by savvy Maori flies in New Zealand's buttermilk film and TV scene, *Warriors's* up-front theme is the lost dignity of indigenous peoples. What's replaced that lost dignity is male posturing and attitude, the film's indie look (director of photography Stuart Dryburgh also shot *The Piano* and saturates the screen with earth tones and shadows) underscoring Tamahori's brand of smoothly hip identity politics. The Hekes and the Maori once were warriors, but life in New Zealand's flatland concrete ghettos has made Jake and his boys masculine clichés, their saving grace their constant flashes of street charisma.

But then there's the problem of how the Hekes' living-room walls are so artfully splattered with Beth's blood in the aftermath of a fight. *Warriors* is too unflinching in its look at the Hekes' tribulations to be so precious in its attention to detail, even if those details are slick production design or the endlessly fascinating elements of Maori subculture. A surfeit of movie smarts and slickness makes it easier for Tamahori to raise his stakes, but by the time the film's central tragedy has come to pass you might be too numbed (or distracted) to care.

Also reviewed in:
CHICAGO TRIBUNE, 3/3/95, Friday/p. K, Michael Wilmington
NEW REPUBLIC, 3/27/95, p. 28, Stanley Kauffmann
NEW YORK TIMES, 2/24/95, p. C12, Janet Maslin
VARIETY, 5/30-6/5/94, p. 48, David Stratton
WASHINGTON POST, 3/3/95, p. B1, Rita Kempley
WASHINGTON POST, 3/3/95, Weekend/p. 38, Desson Howe

1-900

A Zeitgeist Films release of a Dino Film produkties production. *Producer:* Theo van Gogh. *Director:* Theo van Gogh. *Screenplay (Dutch with English subtitles):* Johan Doesburg, Marcel Otten, Ad van Kempen, and Ariane Schluter. *Based on the stage play by:* Johan Doesburg. *Director of Photography:* Tom Erisman. *Editor:* Ot Louw. *Music:* Ruud Bos. *Sound:* Ben Zijlstra. *Art Director:* Ruud van Dijk. *Running time:* 80 minutes. *MPAA Rating:* Not Rated.

CAST: Ariane Schluter (Sara); Ad van Kempen (Thomas).

LOS ANGELES TIMES, 10/20/95, Calendar/p. 8, Kevin Thomas

The perils—and pleasures—of phone sex are illuminated in "1-900," Theo van Gogh's audacious, persuasive film of a controversial Dutch play, which he adapted to the screen with its playwright Johan Doesburg, his actors and two other writers.

Although suffused with blunt sex talk, the film is actually discreet, firmly focused on its two characters' inner longings more than on their bodies. Ariane Schluter and Ad van Kempen do an outstanding job of involving us in their characters.

Schluter's Sara, who is a stunning twentysomething professional living in a tastefully decorated apartment, initiates the contact with Van Kempen's Thomas, a divorced architect whose apartment is also his workplace. After some mutual self-consciousness, the two of them are soon turning each other on with sex fantasies, but ever so gradually their once-a- week contact develops into a power play and beyond that, in violation of the rules of the game, a desire for an actual meeting.

The point is that they've in effect painted each other in the corner. How can they live up to the fantasy image each has of the other? Thomas has described himself as a terrific 33-year-old stud when instead he's a short, somewhat paunchy guy with thinning hair at least a decade older.

He's nonetheless a warm, attractive guy, but Sara would surely be disappointed by him in person, considering the image he has projected to her. If that is sad, perhaps it's even sadder that a knockout like Sara would feel the need to resort to phone sex.

Van Gogh—yes, he's Vincent's nephew several generations removed—and Doesburg manage the tricky business of not condemning phone sex while suggesting how it reveals the terrible isolation and loneliness so many people, even nice-looking men and women, can feel in urban contemporary society.

Van Gogh and his ace cinematographer, Tom Erisman, have also created an elegant, highly visual film that takes place in only two sets with only two people. "1-900" is one film for adults that actually is grown-up.

NEW YORK POST, 9/8/95, p. 49, Thelma Adams

Loneliness and the long-distance operator: That's the claustrophobic world Theo van Gogh calls up in his phone-sex drama from Holland, "1-900."

Living proof that artistic talent isn't hereditary, the great-great-nephew of Vincent, has produced and directed one of the year's least sexy movies—despite the fact that its two protagonists, Sara (Ariane Schluter) and Wilbert (Ad van Kempen), are constantly rubbing their privates.

Told in a series of short scenes followed by blackouts, we see the development of Sara and Wilbert's telephone trysts. Their first exchange is halting, awkward and comic. They pass through stages of intimacy, tenderness, frustration, anger and, finally, sadism.

The movie is at its most touching in the opening scenes as the two professionals, an architect and an art history professor, indulge in verbal flights of self-puffery. When asked what he looks like, Wilbert describes a much younger, thinner man named Thomas. Sara's petite blonde becomes a voluptuous, brown-eyed brunette.

Sara can reinvent herself for "Thomas," but she can't squelch her hysterical giggles or make her protest, "I'm not lonely," sound like anything but its opposite. In a face-to-face meeting, Wilbert, the divorced architect, would never get to first base with her.

The couple soon fall into a routine. Every Thursday night, Sara and Wilbert volley masturbatory fantasies: a visit to the hairdresser, a drunken homosexual exchange at a disco, a bit of incest. In the cracks between their sex talk, they begin to develop a dependency. But their connection is limited by Sara's power over Wilbert: She has his number, but he lacks hers.

Phone sex might be safe but, if it's anything like these dry dialogues, it's nothing to get out of bed for. In "1900," the fantasies are feeble, the drama trumped up and, if anyone had bothered ask the audience "was it good for you?" The answer would have been a resounding snore.

Van Gogh, whose previous films include "Luger" and "No Potatoes," has adapted his movie from Johan Doesburg's play, "06," the numbers for the Dutch phone-sex exchange. Rather than opening up the drama to take advantage of the screen, the director reduces "1-900" to a radio play.

NEWSDAY, 9/8/95, Part II/p. B7, Jack Mathews

I have to admit I've never understood the attraction to phone sex. Talking your way through a sexual encounter strikes me as being a little like talking your way through a good meal, as if imagining a bite of tender squab will end your craving for it.

Nevertheless, Dutch director Theo Van Gogh, of the ear-cutting Van Goghs, has fashioned a compelling 80-minute feature on the subject by going past the "he sighs, she sighs" eroticism to the psychological danger of becoming intimate with a phone mate from another area code.

"1-900," the American equivalent of Holland's 06 pay-talk prefix, stars Ariane Schluter and Adrian Kempen as two lonely professionals who assume false identities and meet for phone sex every Thursday. The conversations evolve from playful awkwardness to explicit fantasies to tenderness, cruelty and—most dangerous of all—curiosity about each other's true identities.

They fall in love, without ever seeing each other, and gradually realize that what started out as the most impersonal and nonthreatening of relationships has become a tangle of emotions and lies. How does a man tell a woman who thinks he is 33, well-built and rangy that he is really 49, potbellied and stumpy!

It's no small trick for Van Gogh, the grand-nephew of Vincent, to hold our attention throughout a film that has only two sets—his pad and hers—and in which every line of dialogue is spoken into an inanimate object. He achieves it through some gracefully choreographed camerawork and editing, which turns us into the ultimate eavesdropper, and through the terrific performances of his actors, particularly Schluter.

The U.S. distributor has self-applied an X rating to "1-900," and while there is no nudity, there is plenty of self-abuse, and the sex talk is as graphic as it gets, or—depending on who's calling—as it needs to be.

VILLAGE VOICE, 9/12/95, p. 70, Michael Atkinson

If nothing else, our culture's acceptance of verbal-virtual intimacy in the face of viral terror is a hardy display of sociological adaptation, as the Dutch couple in *1-900* prove. Phone sex is the mode of intercourse, and like a kind of masturbatory *My Dinner with Andre*, *1-900* hits the runway at full yak. Directed by Theo van Gogh (his greatnephew), this elliptical, two-voice play-into-film harbors nothing but sympathy for its dueling fantasizers as they reach across a North Sea of telecommunicative loneliness, and jerk themselves off as if that's what phones were made for.

Sara (Ariane Schluter) and Wilbert (Ad van Kempen) are both first-timers and surprisingly relaxed. She is a thirtyish Helen Mirren type, he's a fiftyish Brian Dennehy, and they both lie about their looks. The awkwardness gives way quickly to cooperative sex natter, and the frigging is constant if not always blissfull. Of course, as time passes, libidinal action becomes standard and real, relationship issues surface, along with a few closeted skeletons. Its simple, lean-to structure would surely collapse if not for the acting—Schluter is especially believable and haunted.

Nicholson Baker's novel *Vox* is a far more complex essay on the topic, and it might take you less than *1-900*'s 80 minutes to read it. Though limited in concept and helplessly stagebound, *1-900* is fairly unpredictable and cliché-free—what the circumstances are of each call is often a complete mystery, and often unresolved. Equally mysterious is why audiences guffaw at images of a man masturbating, and fall silently awestruck at images of a woman doing the same. I was put out; perhaps Shere Hite could look into it for me.

Also reviewed in:
NEW YORK TIMES, 9/8/95, p. C10, Caryn James
VARIETY, 10/10-16/94, p. 86, Derek Elley

ONLY THE BRAVE

A First Run Features release of a Pickpocket Productions film in association with the Australian Film Commission and the Independent Filmmakers Fund of Film Victoria. *Producer:* Fiona Eagger. *Director:* Ana Kokkinos. *Screenplay:* Ana Kokkinos and Mira Robertson. *Director of Photography:* Jaems Grant. *Editor:* Mark Atkin. *Sound:* Craig Carter. *Art Director:* Georgina Campbell. *Costumes:* Margot McCartney. *Running time:* 62 minutes. *MPAA Rating:* Not Rated.

CAST: Elena Mandalis (Alex); Dora Kaskanis (Vicki); Maude Davey (Kate Groves); Helen Athanasiadis (Maria); Tina Zerella (Sylvie); Bob Bright (Reg); Mary Sitarenos (Athena); Peta Brady (Tammy).

NEW YORK POST, 5/5/95, p. 37, Larry Worth

In their '60s heyday, double features were a mixed bag: an alluring main attraction usually teamed with a B-movie that couldn't stand on its own.

Apparently, some things never change, as evidenced by the pairing of "Only the Brave" and "Playing the Part." The former is an intelligent, disturbing look at troubled teens; the latter a self-indulgent documentary on a college student trying to tell her parents she's a lesbian.

Sadly, "Part" director Mitch McCabe offers no insight to her dilemma. Her relationship with conservative, upper middle-class parents in Grosse Pointe, Mich., is portrayed in a cloying, irritating and ultimately cruel manner.

A lack of spontaneity—capped by a scene where she baits Mom into an argument, having first whispered her game plan to the camera—brings new meaning to vanity productions.

Thankfully, all that becomes a bad memory when "Only the Brave" takes over. First-time director Ana Kokkinos establishes herself as a woman with tremendous insight, and instincts. Her subjects aren't necessarily entertaining, but they're well worth addressing.

Kokkinos' screenplay, co-written with Mira Robertson, tells of two adolescent girls (nicely played by Elena Mandalis and Dora Kaskinis) in suburban Melbourne, struggling with dreams that don't seem meant to be.

An early scene of one reciting from William Golding's "Lord of the Flies" as the other gouges her desk with a pen-knife is only a shadow of what's to come.

They're typical students in a girls-will-be-girls kind of way, caught up in parties, social cliques, drugs, rebelling against parents, searching for love, and mining sexual confusion. But too often, their angst leads to violence, and paves the path to tragedy.

Kokkinos never errs by making the heroines overly sympathetic. Instead, there's a nice mix of vulnerability, thoughtlessness and self-destruction. Harsh lighting and evocative photography contribute to the appropriately bleak mood.

The chief flaw here is the running time. At slightly under an hour, too many developments are compressed into the last 15 minutes. Another half hour could have rounded out all the rough edges.

Regardless, "Only the Brave" comes off as a finely nuanced portrait of characters in pain. Just as "Playing the Part" finely exemplifies what to avoid.

NEWSDAY, 5/5/95, Part II/p. B5, John Anderson

The common conceit of Ana Kikkinos' dire, dreamy "Only the Brave" and its recent sister acts—"Fun" and "Heavenly Creatures"—is that violence looms as an inevitable and ultimately liberating product of frustrated homoeroticism, sexual abuse and social awkwardness. And that the rolling, surging passions of the lesbian heart—latent or otherwise—cannot be subdued.

Just how inevitable the mayhem, or how latent the passion, is where Kokkinos parts company with her male colleagues (Peter Jackson of "Heavenly Creatures" and Rafael Zelinsky of "Fun"). Rather than reflect her heroines against a malevolent, film-house mirror, á la Jackson, or contrast crime with delirious, desperate adolescent love, as Zelinsky does, she sets her self-destructive women down in a world primed to immolate them—so much so that when Alex (Elena Mandalis) and Vicki (Dora Kaskanis) set a hedgerow ablaze in the film's startling opening moments it feels like self-defense.

Both are teenaged Australians of Greek extraction, which makes for a double social handicap; both find entertainment in vandalism, drugs, fighting and aimless drifting. Vicki engages in cheap, bitter sex with men; Alex can't find her sexual bearings, but finds some recognition and encouragement in her teacher, Kate Groves (Maude Davey). Vicki wants to emulate Alex' runaway mother and become a singer; Alex just wants to find her mother.

Disheveled, angry and determinedly unattractive, Alex and Vicki traverse a high-school world of punchups and betrayals, petty jealousies and sexual hostility, all of which might have been banal without Kokkinos' super-realistic storytelling—the denouement is a shocker—and her dark portrayal of a nasty, brutish and none-too-short adolescence.

Paired with "Only the Brave" is Mitch McCabe's perkier-than-a-prom-dress "Playing the Part," in which this privileged Grosse Pointer and Harvard student—the school helped fund the film—goes about trying to find the nerve to tell her parents she's a lesbian; the film itself, of course, is the resolution and the joke. Being on the same bill with Kokkinos' film only makes McCabe's look more trite, but the level of self-absorption lends credence to two otherwise, questionable hypotheses: that homosexuality is the natural result of rabid self-love and that an Ivy League education provides practical knowledge without an emotional or ethical mooring. Neither is true, I'm sure, but McCabe mounts a good argument.

"Playing the Part" moves along smartly, and is well edited and occasionally funny. But unless McCabe is trying to create a fictional persona for herself, her obtuseness renders the technical accomplishment moot. Filming her plastic-surgeon father in his office with an unclothed mastectomy patient—who shows nerve and good humor in allowing herself to be filmed—McCabe says only that, "It's weird to think that this is what paid for my college education." Preparing for a society dance she co-chairs with her ice-queen mother, McCabe observes, "I'm about to be the only lesbian among 600 Grosse Pointers." Oh, really? And when she intentionally enrages her mother with her sloppiness so she can film Mom clandestinely—and to not great effect—it pushes the old art-ethics envelope.

In the credits, McCabe thanks her adviser, Ross McElwee, which explains a lot. McElwee, director of the monumentally smarmy "Sherman's March," is the king of self-celebratory documentary. (That his more recent "Time Expired" acquired resonance was only because everything went wrong.) In Mitch McCabe's ungenerous and indulgent "Playing the Part" he has a gifted student, and a dubious legacy.

VILLAGE VOICE, 5/9/95, p. 72, Georgia Brown

Books are burned in Ana Kokkinos's edgy, doom-laden *Only the Brave* (fresh from New Directors), and when this happens it's a sign of a character's propensity to go too far. Two teenage girls are on fire; one makes it through the flames.

Kokkinos's grim drama is a scant 62 minutes, so it works fast and elliptically, rather like a fever dream. Since viewers work more slowly, it takes us a while to catch up and on. That the film's look is murky—it wears its grunge on its sleeve—gives us the feeling of just barely making out life in the shadows.

Alex (Elena Mandalis) and Vicki (Dora Kaskanis) are Greek Australian best friends, part of a pack hanging out on the verge of some bleak industrial park, the migrant's outpost. They attend a shabby high school but only to give the teachers fits, fight turf wars, and escape joyless homes. Alex grudgingly participates in English, a concession to the semicool Miss Groves (Maude Davey) who is pressed into lending Anaïs Nin's *Little Birds*. The relation inspires Vicki's contempt, i.e., jealousy. From flashbacks and dreams we learn that Alex pines for her mother, a singer, who ran off to big-city bars. Vicki has worse problems. (Neither actress is a professional, but Mandalis, especially, delivers a tough, concentrated performance.)

Here is new Australian work displaying none of the whimsical hyperbole or ironic grotesquerie of the usual Campion-inspired fare. Like her characters, Kokkinos makes her own way.

Miles apart but paired theatrically is Mitch McCabe's 38-minute pouting, coming-of-age, coming-out piece, *Playing the Part*. With its gentrified milieu, McCabe's Harvard thesis film would make a better double bill with *Martha & Ethel*, the recent retrieving-our-nannies doc. This, too, is a poison-pen letter to a perfectly coiffed mom.

Mom is Mrs. McCabe of Grosse Pointe, Michigan, a middle-aged Linda Montag, an interior decorator—she's made their home her showcase. Mitch—or as she's called by the family, Michelle—is obsessed with Mom, dressed up in her clothes and posing for a series of photos. Phototherapy she calls it (and I got the impression one can take the class for credit). Dad—her buddy, Mitch calls him—is a plastic surgeon specializing in breasts; his favorite patient shows off his fine work. The plastic boob seems a perfect emblem for this family.

Drama centers on McCabe's failed efforts to tell her parents she's gay. Her camera rolls, but the words don't come. "Wait till they see my movie!" seems to be *Playing the Part*'s subtext. Docutherapy 101 we'll call it.

Also reviewed in:
NEW YORK TIMES, 3/24/95, p. C8, Stephen Holden
VARIETY, 8/1-7/94, p. 45, Emanuel Levy

OPERATION DUMBO DROP

A Walt Disney Pictures release of an Interscope Communications production in association with PolyGram Filmed Entertainment. *Executive Producer:* Ted Field and Robert W. Cort. *Producer:* Diane Nabatoff and David Madden. *Director:* Simon Wincer. *Screenplay:* Gene Quintano and Jim Kouf. *Based on the story by:* Jim Morris. *Director of Photography:* Russell Boyd. *Editor:* O. Nicholas Brown. *Music:* David Newman. *Music Editor:* Tom Villano. *Sound:* Ben Osmo and (music) Robert Fernandez. *Sound Editor:* Tim Chau and Donald J. Malouf. *Casting:* Mike Fenton and Julie Ashton. *Production Designer:* Paul Peters. *Art Director:* Lisette Thomas and Steve Spence. *Set Decorator:* Jim Erickson. *Special Effects:* Brian Pearce. *Visual Effects:* Michael Lessa. *Costumes:* Rosanna Norton. *Make-up:* Judy Lovell. *Make-up (Danny Glover):* Diane Hammond. *Stunt Coordinator:* Guy Norris. *Running time:* 108 minutes. *MPAA Rating:* PG.

CAST: Danny Glover (Captain Sam Cahill); Ray Liotta (Captain Doyle); Denis Leary (David Poole); Doug E. Doug (Harvey Ashford); Corin Nemec (Lawrence Farley); Dinh Thien Le (Linh); Tcheky Karyo (Goddard); Hoang Ly (Nguyen); Vo Trung Anh (Quang); Marshall Bell (Pederson); James Hong (Y'B'ham); Long Nguyen (Jhon); Tim Kelleher (C-123 Pilot); Scott N. Stevens (C-123 Co-Pilot); Kevin La Rosa (Huey Pilot #1); Christopher Ward (Huey

Co-Pilot); Robert Kevin Miller (Huey Gunner #1); Michael Lee (Village Elder); Le Minh Tien (NVA Captain); Mac Van Nam (NVA Lieutenant); Ton Nguyen That (Feed Salesman); Somsak Hormsabat (Bike Driver); Lionel Douglas (Lieutenant); Tien Nguyen Van (NVA Anti Aircraft); Doi Chettawat Kanboon (Lihn, 6 years); Chern Dao Van (Lihn's Father); Steve Countouriotis (Huey Co-Pilot #2); Mark S. Bryant (C-130 Pilot); Jared Chandler (C-130 Co-Pilot); Nick Satriano (Red); Hing Hang Quang (Old Villager); Thanh Nguyen (NVA Soldier); Wichien Nguyen Thi (Peasant Woman).

LOS ANGELES TIMES, 7/20/95, Calendar/p. 14, Kevin Thomas

As a pleasing family adventure-comedy. "Operation Dumbo Drop" is as familiar as its setting is unlikely: Vietnam, 1968. Even more unlikely, however, is that it was inspired by an actual incident in which some Green Berets delivered an elephant to a small village in the midst of war.

"Operation Dumbo Drop" is not about to displace such films as "The Deer Hunter," "Platoon" and "Full Metal Jacket" as landmark depictions of the Vietnam War, but that is hardly its intention. Actually, its arrival couldn't be more timely, with the normalizing of relations with Vietnam just 20 years after the war ended. Most everyone past adolescence will find the picture easily predictable, yet certainly a Vietnam War movie in which the Americans are persuasively admirable is a refreshing change of pace.

Ray Liotta's cynical Capt. T.C. Doyle, a West Point graduate looking for action, arrives in a Montagnard village hard by the Ho Chi Minh Trail to take over a command from Danny Glover's Capt. Sam Cahill, who respects the villagers and their culture. That includes a ceremonial ritual involving an elephant, who is regarded as sacred.

No sooner does Doyle espouse his by-the-book views than a contingent from the North Vietnamese Army kills the elephant as punishment to the villagers for their cooperation with the Americans, who are there to protect them from the NVA and the Viet Cong. A sensitive, humane man, Cahill pledges to the village elder that he and his men will replace the elephant.

Any grown-up—and many children, too—could tell you that the profoundly reluctant Doyle will join forces with Cahill, as will three other Green Berets—Doug E. Doug's superstitious H.A., Corin Nemec's farm boy Farley and Denis Leary's con man Lt. Poole, who's just the guy who can produce a new elephant with little more than a snap of his fingers. The village elder forces the men to take along an elephant boy, the hostile, anti-American Linh (12-year-old Dinh Thien Le) on their quest for a replacement elephant.

Of course, this group's 200-mile journey back to the village with the new animal will be fraught with incidents both perilous and amusing; of course, everyone will shape up and honor Cahill's commitment to the village.

Although this is the least violent and bloody Vietnam War movie you are ever likely to see, "Operation Dumbo Drop," handsomely photographed by Russell Boyd, does not downplay the danger of Cahill's mission. More important, writers Gene Quintano and Jim Kouf, in adapting a story by Jim Morris, don't skirt the seeming folly of Cahill's odyssey and do illuminate its significance.

There's a linchpin scene, crucial to making the entire film work, when Cahill accuses Doyle of a lack of moral consciousness in regard to the Vietnamese, and Doyle stunningly retorts that Cahill is in fact risking the lives of his men in transporting the elephant so that if and when he makes it back to the United States, he can arrive home with a clear conscience.

Under Simon Wincer's brisk, efficient direction, Glover, Liotta, Leary, et al., give the kind of full-bodied portrayals essential to making basically formulaic material come alive. It's no small feat to pull off a traditional comedy in the context of the Vietnam War, which lends itself so much more easily to the freewheeling, absurdist humor of "Good Morning, Vietnam."

NEW YORK POST, 7/28/95, p. 38, Michael Medved

"Operation Dumbo Drop" coughs up so many stale gags about elephant vomit and pachyderm poop that you begin wonder why they didn't call it "Operation Dumbo Droppings."

These scatological sequences may produce titters among the 10-year-old boys who appear to be this film's target audience, but for the rest of us they only add to the wealth of witless time-wasting before the story finally staggers to its surprisingly spectacular and rousing conclusion.

In that finale, for the second time in the history of the company, the Disney people make an elephant fly. In this case, the beast doesn't flap its ears and float gracefully above the ground; instead, it plunges to earth from a height of 10,000 feet, trumpeting in terror because it's locked on a platform attached to a parachute that won't open.

It's an oddly thrilling movie moment (thanks to brilliant photography and a convincing animatronic elephant), made all the more so when Ray Liotta's character jumps out of a plane to go after the plummeting beast, hoping to connect in mid-air and to fix the parachute before pachyderm and paratrooper both go splat.

Unfortunately, the movie itself has gone splat long before we arrive at this stirring climax. Inspired by one of the more bizarre true stories to come out of the Vietnam war, the tale unfolds in 1968 as Liotta, a guts-and-glory Green Beret captain, arrives in a Montagnard village to replace Danny Glover, a more warm-hearted and unconventional officer.

Glover is concerned because the friendly villagers, who have always supported the American cause, need a replacement for the prize elephant recently slaughtered by North Vietnamese forces.

The two captains are ordered to cooperate in securing them a suitable beast, and their expedition covers 200 miles of difficult terrain while producing the inevitable bickering-buddy bits between them.

Even gifted pros like Glover and Liotta can't make this material come to life, and adding to the strained sitcom atmosphere is another member of their team, a cheerfully amoral operator (and Sgt. Bilko stand-in) nicely played by Denis Leary.

Also along for the ride is an orphaned "elephant boy" played 13-year-old newcomer Dinh Thien Le. Unfortunately, Dinh delivers nearly all his lines in the same urgent, nasal and heavily accented whine, making it all the harder to accept the notion that his mere presence melts the heart of even hard-bitten GIs, producing innumerable scenes of insipid group hugs.

Australian director Simon Wincer is becoming something of a specialist in big mammal movies, having previously helmed the original "Free Willy," but here key scenes showing his elephant star (a 26-year-old, 8000 pounder named Tai) on board a truck, a boat, and planes (twice) seem splotchily edited.

The director also displays a ham-handed touch for comedy (as he previously demonstrated on Paul Hogan's "Lightning Jack," one of the most painfully unfunny movies of the century) and here again, in some of the movie's purportedly uproarious antics (all in the uncomfortable setting of the Vietnam war), Wincer's humor can make you well ... wince.

NEWSDAY, 7/28/95, Part II/p. B5, Jonathan Mandell

Almost nobody dies in the Vietnam of "Operation Dumbo Drop," the latest Disney fable, which, according to the closing credits, was "inspired" by a true story. The biggest fatality is a village elephant.

He is shot by the stern, red-collared soldiers of the North Vietnamese army as a warning, when they find the wrapper of a Nestle's Crunch bar in the mountain village of Kak Nhe, evidence that the villagers have been in contact with Americans.

Capt. Sam Cahill (Danny Glover), a Green Beret who has come to love the villagers, knows how important the elephant is to them, and he is determined to get them another one. He enlists his imminent replacement, Capt. Doyle (Ray Liotta), as well as an Oz-like trio of fellow soldiers—a cynical Mr. Fix-it, a country bumpkin afraid of animals and a funny coward (played by Doug E. Doug of "Cool Runnings"). They are accompanied by a young boy, played by newcomer Dinh Thien Le, who is a recent immigrant to the United States from Vietnam.

"He has no family," explains the Vietnamese man who sells the Green Berets the new elephant.

"Killed in the war?"

"No, killed by foreign star," the man says sarcastically, and then adds (since this is a children's movie): "Yes, killed by the war."

Together the men, the boy and the elephant undertake an arduous and dangerous journey through jungle land, sea and air. Since this is a movie, the journey is full of self-discovery, as well as schmaltz and slapstick—loading the elephant onto a truck or a plane; administering a tranquilizer anally; trying to stop him from wreaking havoc on a well-traversed village street; dropping him from a plane with a parachute—and some stabs at wit. The soldiers of the North Vietnamese army, who monitor their moves with binoculars, are baffled that the Americans are bothering with an elephant. Finally, a lieutenant figures it out: The elephant is a symbol of the American Republican party," he says in Vietnamese, with English subtitles. "Nixon is a Republican."

Though these soldiers frequently shoot their weapons at the Green Berets, and the Green Berets frequently shoot back, the Disney corporation has gone out of its way to make sure nobody gets killed. When the Green Berets triumph, it's because they knock the weapons out of the enemies' hands. The Americans do blow up a boat, but the North Vietnamese all jump off the boat first.

This might be Disney's effort to protect its 8-year-old viewers from violence (or at least protect Disney shareholders from an anti-violence protest). But it is, of course, a lie, a sanitized version of Vietnam that falls as flat as the title. (The real mission, in a perhaps telling contrast, was called Operation Barroom.) The Americans are all basically good, the other side bad; the Vietnamese villagers, who like to laugh a lot, are all pro-American, and the wholesome South Vietnamese soldiers wear well-pressed suits. On the 20th anniversary of the end of the Vietnam War, as the United States restores diplomatic relations with this complicated Asian country, we get a Bob Hope vision of Vietnam—Vietnam as World War II—only worse, because this movie is aimed at children, who are not likely to know about the complexity and the real pain, and the stupidity, and the many, many, many deaths.

VILLAGE VOICE, 8/8/95, p. 55, Gary Dauphin

Complaining about the many ways in which *Operation Dumbo Drop* is corny, trite and stupid is a bit like whining that water's wet. Disney's *Dumbo Drop* is a studio pro's comedy with low intentions about a group of GI's trying to do the right thing in the mountains of Vietnam. There's an element of the surreal about this trek through verdant countryside to replace elephants lost to war, but there's a true story behind it, concerning the U.S. Army project of parachuting these two-ton pack animals into rural villages as part of the hearts-and-minds campaign.

Dumbo Drop fits nicely in the company of comic soft-pedalings of the Vietnam War from *Air America* to *Good Morning, Vietnam*. There are predictably solid performances. Danny Glover is in fine form as Sam, a savvy Green Beret, and Ray Liotta play's his by-the-book replacement like the controlled psycho I've always believed him to be. Comic Doug E. Doug has a nice (albeit slighty spooked) turn as a superstitious short-timer, and there are slides galore in piles of elephant manure. Director Simon Wincer (of, you guessed it, *Free Willy*) shoots the climactic elephant-drop scene for honest thrills, but if there is a real surprise up *Dumbo Drop*'s trunk it's how, despite three or four encounters with North Vietnamese soldiers, our boy's settle every fight with fists instead of bullets. As has been said on numerous occasions: Disney is truly the magic kingdom.

Also reviewed in:
CHICAGO TRIBUNE, 7/28/95, Friday/p. H, Gary Dretzka
NEW YORK TIMES, 7/28/95, p. C12, Janet Maslin
VARIETY, 7/31-8/6/95, p. 36, Joe Leydon
WASHINGTON POST, 7/28/95, p. B7, Hal Hinson

OTHELLO

A Castle Rock Entertainment release of a Dakota Films/Imminent Films production. *Executive Producer:* Jonathan Olsberg. *Producer:* Luc Roeg and David Barron. *Director:* Oliver Parker. *Screenplay (adapted for the screen from William Shakespeare's play):* Oliver Parker. *Adapted from the play by:* William Shakespeare. *Director of Photography:* David Johnson. *Editor:* Tony Lawson. *Music:* Charlie Mole. *Music Editor:* Andrew Glen. *Choreographer:* Stuart Hopps. *Sound:* Peter Glossop. *Sound Editor:* Rodney Glenn. *Casting:* Debbie McWilliams. *Production Designer:* Tim Harvey. *Art Director:* Desmond Crowe. *Costumes:* Caroline Harris. *Make-up:* Tina Earnshaw. *Running time:* 125 minutes. *MPAA Rating:* R.

CAST: Laurence Fishburne (Othello); Irene Jacob (Desdemona); Kenneth Branagh (Iago); Nathaniel Parker (Cassio); Michael Maloney (Roderigo); Anna Patrick (Emilia); Nicholas Farrell (Montano); Indra Ove (Bianca); Michael Sheen (Lodovico); Andre Oumansky (Gratiano); Philip Locke (1st Senator); John Savident (2nd Senator); Gabriele Ferzetti (The Duke of Venice); Pierre Vaneck (Brabantio).

CHRISTIAN SCINECE MONITOR, 1/17/96, p. 13, David Sterritt

[*Othello* was reviewed jointly with *Richard III*; see Sterritt's review of that film.]

LOS ANGELES TIMES, 12/14/95, Calendar/p. 1, Kevin Thomas

Laurence Fishburne is superb as the noble Moor of Oliver Parker's sleek, refreshingly unpretentious "Othello." Fishburne has everything it takes to make Shakespeare's tragic hero work: talent, intellect, depth, imposing physical presence, innate dignity, handsomeness, sex appeal and a resonant voice. His Othello adds further luster to a notable, wide-ranging career highlighted by such indelible portrayals as his corrosive Ike Turner in "What's Love Got to Do With It" and the strong, loving father of "Boyz N the Hood."

Although Parker has pared down the play, created a real movie out of it and made it as accessible as "Fatal Attraction," he has in fact celebrated rather than diminished the grandeur of Shakespeare's dialogue. He has allowed no theatrical flourishes, none of those tours de force of vocal inflections so beloved by the British that can strike American ears as distractingly artificial and mannered, and has instead gone for a simple eloquence in the way his actors speak that allows us to appreciate the full majesty of Shakespeare's dialogue.

He has said that he approached the play as an erotic thriller, and there is no question that the grand passion of Othello and Desdemona (Irene Jacob) ignites as well as illuminates Shakespeare's profound grasp of how fate and human psychology can conspire in intricate, inevitable fashion to bring about tragedy.

Racism, that persistent evil, triggers the downfall of Othello as much as his own jealousy in Parker's telling. Othello may be one of Venice's most celebrated warrior mercenaries, but he is a black man. Desdemona's father Brabantio (Pierre Vaneck), a Venetian nobleman, is not only quick to express his outrage over her elopement but also to say cruelly to Othello: "She has deceived her father—and may thee."

At the outset, therefore, the seed of jealousy has been planted in Othello's mind. It won't blossom until Iago (Kenneth Branagh), furious at being passed over as Othello's right-hand man after a decade in his service, starts fanning it in earnest. You have got to believe that Iago would not have embarked on such a relentless, despicable course of revenge had his master not been black.

Ironically, were not Desdemona as truly pure in character she might well have detected Iago's infernal machinations long before her bridegroom was blinded by jealousy. Yet surely Othello would not be so quickly consumed by such destructive emotions were he not so subjected to bigotry.

Parker has surrounded Fishburne, who shaved his head and wore a beard and tattoos for the part, with a first-rate ensemble of players. Fishburne adopts a cultivated, understated English accent that blends well with a predominantly British cast, and Jacob's own slight French accent is unimportant when measured against the radiance and poise she brings to Desdemona. The key to Fishburne's admirable portrayal is that he has managed to bring meaning to his every word of dialogue, thus setting a standard for clarity essential for comprehending Shakespearean usage, so much of which has vanished from English discourse.

With his disarming, open-faced good looks and warm manner, Branagh is able to underline Iago's infamy, even allowing him a few stricken glances to suggest that he might well have flashes of regret over what he has set in motion. Anna Patrick brings out the full measure of ambivalence in her Emilia, Desdemona's lady-in-waiting, who has the misfortune to be Iago's exploited wife. Nathaniel Parker's Cassio and Michael Maloney's Rodrigo, two more innocent victims of Iago's plotting, round out the key figures capably.

Oliver Parker (Nathaniel Parker's brother) hasn't the image-making genius that Orson Welles was able to bring to his "Othello," but then who has? Yet his "Othello," photographed with an elegant simplicity by David Johnson amid authentic period settings and costumes in Italy, has a rich, cinematic fluidity. Most important, Parker has shown how involving and moving Shakespeare can still be on the screen.

NEW YORK, 1/15/96, p. 49, David Denby

The new *Othello* is a more conventional affair—realistic, unimaginative, even depressingly literal-minded. [The reference is to *Richard III*.] When Othello (Laurence Fishburne) and Desdemona (Irene Jacob) retire to the bedroom, the director, Oliver Parker, serves up soft-core sex in a lyrical-schlock style I associate with the Playboy channel. Limbs, limbs, limbs. Much of the body play, on the other hand, has been cut away, (a far greater loss than in *Richard III*), and what is left is generally spoken with great clarity but (with one exception) no special illumination. Parker, trained as an actor, has simplified the play in ways that reduce it. In this *Othello*, everyone is very young and inexperienced. Othello and Desdemona are freshly in love—each in love, perhaps, for the first time—and so little known to each other that their sexual passion seems unconnected to anything else in their natures. Iago's subtlety and cruelty, we feel, are not even needed to destroy their love; almost anything, even ordinary life, would have brought it down from this daring, vulnerable, and thoughtless height. In a word, neither of them seems very bright.

Iago has been made almost superfluous, yet Kenneth Branagh's performance is still the best thing in the movie. This Iago is also very young, an ordinary man, plainspoken, not super-subtle, just more daring and clearheaded than anyone else. Indeed, he's so young and energetic that we're a bit puzzled. Surely this chipped fellow has more to live for than destruction? Coleridge spoke of "motiveless malignity," but a great Iago, with a few more years under his belt, can suggest the rage of disappointed ambition. Branagh's Iago has little reason for rage—his whole life seems before him. But Branagh, as always, speaks the verse with a vigorous directness of manner, as if he and Shakespeare had just spent some time together at a local tavern, and he creates a rough-and-ready Iago, very physical, jocular, companionable, and dangerous. Of all the actors I've seen, he most obviously justifies Othello's spectacular misperception of his character as "honest Iago."

Laurence Fishburne pronounces his part rather than acting it. He glowers and holds his dignity through everything, even in moments of utmost horror, and sometimes one gets the impression that dignity is more important to him than expression. Fishburne is awfully tight. We can believe that this man is a commander, because self-control is paramount to him. The point, however, is that Othello loses his command of himself, and Fishburne won't let himself out. The next time around, he needs to take a flying leap. The whole movie is intimate and very quiet, almost subdued. Oliver Parker has eliminated every trace of theatricalism—and, alas, almost every trace of excitement.

NEW YORK POST, 12/14/95, p. 66, Michael Medved

The new version of "Othello," from director Oliver Parker, is one of the most erotically charged Shakespearian productions ever committed to film.

It's not just the addition of torrid, wordless bedroom scenes between a muscular, formidable Othello (Laurence Fishburne) and a passionate Desdemona (Irene Jacob); even the vicious Iago (Branagh) gets into the act rewarding his devoted wife, Emilia (Anna Patrick) for unwittingly cooperating with his dark plots by pinning her to the bed and sliding sinuously between her legs.

There's also steamy interaction between the handsome Lieutenant Cassio (Nathaniel Parker, the director's brother) and the saucy Bianca (Indra Ove), as well as inventive (and effective) directorial additions in which we repeatedly enter Othello's tormented imagination to see fevered images of his nude wife in joyous frolic between the sheets with Cassio.

The entire film seems to be permeated by a sweaty, Mediterranean heat—which is entirely appropriate, given that most of the action of the play takes place on the island of Cyprus, where Othello and company have been dispatched from Venice to fight the Turks.

Director Parker (in an enormously impressive feature film debut after previously creating three acclaimed short films) is assisted in his carnal emphasis by the ingenious casting of Fishburne.

In contrast to the noble, grandiose flourishes of most Othellos (including Orson Welles and Laurence Olivier in previous film version), Fishburne brings an unmistakable edge of danger, moody menace and barely tamed barbarism to the part.

With his battle scars and tattoos, this mercenary Moor is menacing and potent from the first moment we meet him; we understand why the 16th century Venetian nobles might fear the black stranger at the same time they rely on his warlike ferocity as their general.

Branagh also makes a superb Iago, aided immeasurably by his indestructible on-screen charm.

In this remarkable performance, he offers an unusually persuasive answer to the nagging problem of the play; why is Iago, for many years a loyal officer, suddenly determined to ruin the life of his commander by stirring up groundless jealousy toward his new wife?

Branagh seems to suggest that Iago is so amazed and thrilled when he begins to see the effect of his own manipulative powers, that he gradually gets carried away. The actor's electrifying joy in his own villainy is intoxicating, and makest the audience accomplices in his scemes.

The only disappointing bit of casting involves Irene Jacob (Swiss-born star of Krzyzstof Kieslowski's "Red" and "The Double Life of Veronique"), whose thick French accent makes her Shakespearian lines pointlessly difficult to understand. There's also a problem with her age: at 30, she's only three years younger than Fishburne, undermining all the many textual references to the vast age difference between Othello and the young wife he steals from her protective father.

Parker's determination to provide a youthful, more virile, more fearsome Othello, should have been accompanied with a corresponding insistence on an even younger (and more headstrong) Desdemona.

Nevertheless, the director deserves credit for a film that crackles with energy and rushes at breathless pace from scene to scene; his condensation of the original play, reducing its line count by nearly half, is seamless and supremely skillful.

If Shakespeare's soaring poetry seems, at times, slighted by this approach (particularly when clumsily pronounced by Jacob) that's the price we pay for Parker's more naturalistic, intensely cinematic style.

We never once watch orotund actors declaiming famous lines at full voice, Parker is in love with images and passions, rather than beautiful words, and that infatuation has produced a handsome, praiseworthy production that consistently sizzles.

SIGHT AND SOUND, 2/96, p. 51, Geoffrey Macnab

Venice, 1570. A moonlit night. Desdemona, daughter of respected Venetian aristocrat, Brabantio, pledges her love to Othello, the Moor and celebrated soldier. They're spied on by Iago, who is jealous that Othello has promoted Cassio instead of him. He and Roderigo, Desdemona's spurned suitor, waste no time in alerting Brabantio to what has happened. Othello is called to the Doge of Venice's council chambers. He is told to prepare for war in Cyprus. Brabantio, an old friend of his, reluctantly agrees to the marriage with Desdemona, but warns the Moor that if she's capable of deceiving a father, there's no reason why she shouldn't deceive a husband.

The army, under Othello's command, establishes headquarters at a garrison in Cyprus. Othello and Desdemona spend their first married night together, but Iago is already busy plotting their downfall. He gets Cassio drunk and lures him into a violent brawl. Othello learns of Cassio's misdemeanour and dismisses him from his service. Iago steps into the breach. Now with easy access to Othello, Iago begins to hint that Desdemona is unfaithful. He tells the Moor that she is having an affair with Cassio. At first, Othello doesn't believe him, but Iago has arranged matters so craftily that it looks as if there is something between the couple. The first gift Othello ever gave Desdemona was a handkerchief. When he sees Cassio with that handkerchief, he is sure that his wife is unfaithful. He vows to kill her.

Iago orchestrates a fight between Roderigo and Cassio. The former is killed, the latter badly wounded. Othello, meanwhile, wakes Desdemona from her sleep, warns her to say her prayers, and then suffocates her. Desdemona's maid, Emilia, learns of the murder. She tells Othello that she herself had stolen the handkerchief on the orders of Iago, who is her husband. Othello realises he has been duped by the man he most trusted into committing a hideous crime. Distraught at what he has done, he commits suicide. Iago is left to his punishment. The film ends with Desdemona and Othello being buried at sea.

Think of the funeral procession that opens Orson Welles' *Othello*. As the cortege passes, seen in silhouette, Iago (Michael MacLiammoir) is thrown in an iron cage and hoisted aloft. Throughout the sequence, his eyes are fixed intently on the dead Moor. It's a spectacular overture which both works as grand cinematic set-piece and hints at Iago's lustful obsession with the man whose downfall he has just engineered.

Oliver Parker's new *Othello*, his debut feature, starts in much tamer fashion with a shot of a gondola gliding across the waters. Parker's beginning makes perfect sense. Desdemona is on a clandestine journey to meet her lover, Othello. In Venice, why not travel by gondola? Nevertheless, the comparison with Welles, unfair though it may be, underlines Parker's basic problem. He has assembled an impressive cast. His film is sumptuously lit and designed. He has cleverly tailored Shakespeare's text, foregrounding the love affair between Othello and Desdemona. He could hardly have hoped for two more magnetic stars to play the couple than Laurence Fishburne and Irene Jacob. But this Othello lacks one vital ingredient—visual flair.

All too often, framing is static. This is Shakespeare done talking heads-style. Characters are filmed in medium close-up as they deliver their monologues. The film-makers' pet trick is to pull focus so that one face in front of the camera will blur and another behind it come into definition. Action and dialogue are rarely matched. When Desdemona dances to lyre music or Othello and Iago engage in mock combat with cudgels, it's as if these scenes have no bearing on the narrative. The costumes and elaborate tableau effects lend proceedings a stiff, formal air. Take the sequence in which everybody assembles in the Doge's council chambers. As individuals state their case, the rest of the cast mill around like extras behind them. An inept, slow motion flashback sequence in which Othello remembers his old, now sullied, friendship with Brabantio emphasises the leaden quality of the film-making.

Parker claims he saw the play as "an erotic thriller." If so, it is not an especially steamy one. The words get in the way of the passions. Parker's frank treatment of the sexual relationship between Desdemona and Othello is refreshing. But even this doesn't extend much beyond one or two corny, slow-motion lovemaking sequences.

Parker's most successful formal conceit is to allow Iago to address the camera directly. There's little of the sleek malevolence that MacLiammoir brought to the part in Branagh's playing of the villain. This Iago is more of a winking, chubby-cheeked prankster in the *Just William* mould, eager to see how far his scheming will go. As he weaves his mischievous web, there's a moment in which he pulls his hand over the camera lens while he talks of "the net that shall enmesh them all." It's never quite clear what motivates him. But in its own inscrutable way, this is an immensely enjoyable piece of acting.

Fishburne, too, is impressive. His Othello is a saturnine, imposing figure, with a more or less permanent scowl fixed to his face. He looks ungainly when he's forced to ride into frame on a huge stallion. But he is suitably authoritative when it comes to barking out orders to his underlings and speaks the verse, especially the more lyrical passages, quite beautifully. And there's nothing wrong with Irene Jacob's Desdemona, even if her French accent is at first a little disconcerting.

It's telling that it is easiest to write about the film in terms of the performances. An established stage and television actor (he played Mark Calder in *Casualty*), Parker seems more interested in these than in the quality of the film-making. The overblown music and occasional visual flourishes (for instance the *Piano*-like sequence in which Othello and Desdemona's coffins are dropped into the sea) come across as trimmings rather than an integral part of the movie. It probably wouldn't make much difference if they were stripped away. Events do warm up in the final reel with the sword fight between Roderigo (who gurgles blood as he dies) and Cassio, as well as Othello's murder of Desdemona, but there's no escaping the prevailing sense of theatricality. Parker clearly has a strong sense of the play as a violent, *noirish* melodrama, but, although he elicits fine performances, he hasn't rendered it in cinematic terms.

TIME, 1/15/96, p. 67, Richard Corliss

[*Othello* was reviewed jointly with *Richard III*; see Corliss' review of that film.]

VILLAGE VOICE, 12/19/95, p. 82, Amy Taubin

And speaking of remakes, [The reference is to *Father of the Bride Part II*; see Taubin's review of that movie.] there's *Othello*, so incoherently directed by Oliver Parker that it wasn't until hours after I left the theater that I thought of O.J. The wonderfully talented Laurence Fishburne makes a game try at one of the most difficult parts ever written, but like any actor he would have needed years of preparation to get his tongue around the text (and if the press notes are to be believed, he plunged in with only a few weeks rehearsal). Irene Jacob is similarly at a loss as Desdemona. Kenneth Branagh plays Iago as an opportunistic political hack, thus bringing the enigmatic villain down to his own level of mediocrity. Still, there's logic, if no charisma, in his performance. I daresay this *Othello* means to be about something besides the opportunity to design a poster of a white woman blowing in a black man's ear, but whatever interpretation was in Parker's mind, it's nowhere to be found on the screen.

Also reviewed in:
CHICAGO TRIBUNE, 12/29/95, Friday/p. C, Michael Wilmington
NEW REBUBLIC, 2/12/96, p. 30, Stanley Kauffmann
NEW YORK TIMES, 12/14/95, p. C11, Janet Maslin
NEW YORKER, 12/18/95, p. 126, Terrence Rafferty
VARIETY, 12/11-17/95, p. 83, Todd McCarthy
WASHINGTON POST, 12/29/95, p. F1, Rita Kempley
WASHINGTON POST, 12/29/95, Weekend/ p. 32, Desson Howe

OUTBREAK

A Warner Bros. release of an Arnold Kopelson production in association with Punch Productions. *Executive Producer:* Duncan Henderson and Anne Kopelson. *Producer:* Arnold Kopelson, Wolfgang Petersen, and Gail Katz. *Director:* Wolfgang Petersen. *Screenplay:* Laurence Dworet and Robert Roy Pool. *Director of Photography:* Michael Ballhaus. *Editor:* Neil Travis, Lynzee Klingman, and William Hoy. *Music:* James Newton Howard. *Music Editor:* Jim Weidman. *Sound:* Richard Lightstone and (music) Shawn Murphy. *Sound Editor:* Wylie Stateman and Gregg Baxter. *Casting:* Jane Jenkins and Janet Hirshenson. *Production Designer:* William Sandell. *Art Director:* Nancy Patton and Francis J. Pezza. *Set Designer:* Carl J. Stensel, Stella Furner, Thomas Reta, and Eric Orbom. *Set Decorator:* Rosemary Brandenburg. *Set Dresser:* Glenn Roberts. *Special Effects:* John Frazier. *Visual Effects:* Mark Vargo. *Costumes:* Erica Edell Phillips. *Costumes (Biohazard Suits):* Christopher Gilman and Maralyn Madsen. *Make-up:* Susan A. Cabral, Ellis Burman, and Monty Westmore. *Make-up (Special Motaba Make-up Effects):* Matthew W. Mungle and John E. Jackson. *Stunt Coordinator:* Budy van Horn and Keith Tellez. *Running time:* 125 minutes. *MPAA Rating:* R.

CAST: Dustin Hoffman (Colonel Sam Daniels); Rene Russo (Dr. Robby Keough); Morgan Freeman (General Billy Ford); Kevin Spacey (Casey Schuler); Cuba Gooding, Jr. (Major Salt); Donald Sutherland (General Donald McClintock); Patrick Dempsey (Jimbo Scott); Zakes Mokae (Dr. Benjamin Iwabi); Malick Bowens (Dr. Raswani); Susan Lee Hoffman (Dr. Lisa Aronson); Benito Martinez (Dr. Julio Ruiz); Bruce Jarchow (Dr. Mascelli); Leland Hayward III (Henry Seward); Daniel Chodos (Rudy Alvarez); Dale Dye (Colonel Briggs); Cara Keough (Sarah Jeffries); Gina Jeffries (Mrs. Jeffries); Per Didrik Fasmer (Mr. Jeffries); Michelle Joyner (Sherry Mauldin); Donald Forrest (Mack Mauldin); Julie Pierce (Erica Mauldin); Tim Ransom (Tommy Hull); Michelle M. Miller (Darla Hull); Maury Sterling (Sandman One); Michael Emanuel (Sandman One Co-pilot); Lucas Dudley (Viper One Pilot); Robert Alan Joseph (Viper Two Pilot); Joseph Latimore (Viper Two Co-Pilot); Michael Sottile (Gunner Pilot); Ed Beechner (Gunner); Matthew Saks (Sergeant Wolf); Diana Bellamy (Mrs. Pananides); Lance Kerwin (American Mercenary); Brett Oliver (Belgian Mercenary); Eric Mungai Nguku (African Nurse); Larry Hine (Young McClintock); Nicolas H. Marshall (Young Ford); Douglas Hebron (Ju-Ju Man); Jae Woo Lee (Korean Captain); Derek Kim (Seaman Chulso Lee); Bill Stevenson

(Biotest Guard); Kellie Overbey (Alice); Dana Andersen (Corrine); Patricia Place (Mrs. Foote); Nicholas Pappone (Little Boy on Plane); Traci Odom (Little Boy's Mother); Herbert Jefferson, Jr., Thomas Crawford, and Buzz Barbee (Boston Doctors); Jenna Byrne (Tracy); Brian Reddy (Tracy's Father); Ina Romeo (Mrs. Logan); Teresa Velarde (Nurse Emma); J.J. Chaback (Nurse Jane); Carmela Rappazzo (Hospital Receptionist); Kurt Boesen (Mayor Gaddis); Jack Rader (Police Chief Fowler); Robert Rigamonte (County Health Official); Mimi Doyka (Frightened Mother); C. Jack Robinson (Biotest Manager); Robert Alan Beuth (George Armistead); Gordon Michaels (Man in Line); Peter Looney (White House Counsel); Conrad Bachmann (California Governor); Cary J. Pitts (Anchorman); Cynthia Harrison (Co-anchor); Marcus Hennessy (Station Mangager); Albert Owens (Broadcast Director); David Silverbrand (TV Reporter); Julie Arqskog (Janet Adams); Frank Rositani (Senator Rosales); George Christy (Senator); Bruce Isacson (Jaffe); Marilyn Brandt (Ford's Secretary); Philip Handy (Sergeant Meyer); Ralph Miller and Mark Drown (Officers); Jim Antonio (Dr. Drew Reynolds).

FILMS IN REVIEW, 7-8/95, p. 58, James M. Welsh

Outbreak is the flip side of *Jurassic Park*, a techno-thriller that threatens to put the Future of Humanity in jeopardy, but it is mainly a thriller, competently directed by Wolfgang Petersen and well acted by Dustin Hoffman, Rene Russo, Cuba Gooding, Jr., and Morgan Freeman.

A deadly virus breaks out of Africa and ends up in picture-perfect middle America. The town is called Cedar Creek, California, and its future doesn't look very good. An epidemic is killing people off with alarming speed, and a rogue general (Donald Sutherland in another dismal villainous role) wants to firebomb the town off the map, partly to get rid of the virus, but mainly to cover up his own "national security" deviousness.

There is just too much going on in this overloaded plot. The virus plot would be enough ("more deadly than the Black Plague, more contagious than the common cold") and the race against time to find the host monkey. But the first complication is a personal one between Colonel Sam Daniels (Hoffman) and his wife Roberta (Russo), who are headed for a divorce. They are both doctors. She works for the Center for Disease Control and he is with the U.S. Army Medical Research Institute for Infectious Diseases. He gets sent to a "hot" zone in Zaire, where he first encounters the virus.

The virus gets carried by an infected monkey smuggled by merchant seaman Jimbo Scott (Patrick Dempsey) into California. When he cannot sell the monkey to a pet shop, he releases it in a redwood forest before flying to Boston, where he falls ill and dies. Somehow the virus mutates and becomes airborne in California, making it a possible catastrophic killer.

It turns out the Army knew about the original virus and had developed it for biological warfare purposes. The villain in this plot is General McClintock (Donald Sutherland), in league with General Billy Ford (Morgan Freeman), Sam Daniels' (Hoffman's) commanding officer. Daniels eventually figures out this conspiracy after General McClintock orders him reassigned to another project. But Daniels disregards orders, determined to save the day and his wife, who has become infected. Daniels and his sidekick Major Salt (Gooding) steal a helicopter and go after the host monkey, which they miraculously manage to locate. In record time they somehow manage also to isolate an antibody to stop the virus. To pump up the action, the miraculous plot includes a helicopter chase with McClintock trying to blow Daniels out of the sky. Daniels is lucky to have a scientific sidekick who is also a crack helicopter pilot.

The viral epidemic represented here is based on a close call that actually occurred in suburban Virginia during the 1980s when it was feared the Ebola Zaire virus had mutated into a human-threatening strain. Richard Preston first told this story for *The New Yorker* in 1992, a long essay that later became his book *The Hot Zone*. Producer Arnold Kopelson read *The New Yorker* piece and went after the movie rights. According to Bernard Weinraub, Dustin Hoffman consulted with scientist Peter Jahrling, (who originally identified the Ebola-Reston virus) because the script did not make sense to him. Five additional writers were brought in to "doctor" the script but only managed to make it more absurd. In the film it only takes the Hoffman character 24 hours to create and synthesize antibodies from the captured host monkey, but Jahrling estimated that in fact such a process could take up to a year. The film both sensationalizes and trivializes a serious issue, exploiting contemporary fears concerning AIDS and its spread worldwide. The first strain of the fictional "Motaba" virus in the film is communicated through body fluids.

The first half of the movie is a fairly convincing scare machine and is especially effective when it shows the airborne virus being spread by a coughing victim in a crowded movie theater; but ultimately the threat is too conveniently defused in the latter half. *Entertainment Tonight* described the plot as being "ripped from today's headlines," Ripped off might be closer to the mark. An earlier treatment of the virus from hell motif can be traced back 25 years to *The Andromeda Strain*, which Robert Wise directed from Michael Crichton's novel.

Dustin Hoffman is a very likeable actor who deserves a better script than this film provides, but, then he must have agreed to take the role, knowing the film could be no more than a second-rate thriller, dressed up nicely with production values and the visual skills of cinematographer Michael Ballhaus. So maybe Hoffman got exactly what he deserved here. The film has been well promoted, however, and is likely to make money, even though it cost something like $60 million to produce, and that's always the bottom line in Hollywood. This movie should play well in the city and country. It's a fright.

LOS ANGELES TIMES, 3/10/95, Calendar/p. 1, Peter Rainer

"Outbreak," starring Dustin Hoffman encased in a germ-free suit and helmet, is the kind of movie that's usually described as "visceral." It sure ain't "cerebral." Despite a lot of high-tech gizmology and oodles of data about hemorrhagic fevers and viral strains, it's basically a so-spreadable-it's-incredible creeping glop movie. It's a B-movie with A-accouterments.

Even though "Outbreak" is grounded in some very real global fears about viral crises-in-waiting, it quickly mutates into an action-adventure winging that's about as plausible as "True Lies." Which is probably just as well. If the film were truly effective it might set off a nationwide panic—a "War of the Worlds" for the '90s, with microbes instead of Martians.

The mystery virus—nicknamed "Motaba"—that is the real star of the film first turns up in 1967 in a mercenary camp in Africa. Next thing you know the village and all its expiring inhabitants are mysteriously nuked. Cut to the present: Motaba is back and Zaire's got it. Col. Sam Daniels, M.D. (Dustin Hoffman), is sent into the African rain forest to check out the damage by Gen. Billy Ford (Morgan Freeman), his longtime friend and commanding officer at the U.S. Army Medical Research Institute for Infectious Diseases. Sealed off in his germ-free jumpsuit, Sam surveys a village littered with corpses, liquefied organs, gaping mouths. His associate, Maj. Salt (Cuba Gooding Jr.), is a little green. He throws up in his helmet, pulls it off his head and survives—which proves the virus isn't airborne. Yet.

One of the perverse enjoyments of "Outbreak" is watching Hoffman, who is notorious for inhabiting characters bollixed by the blips of indecision, playing a no-nonsense action hero. Hoffman is such a cerebral actor that his new damn-the-torpedoes style has an almost parodistic edge. Hoffman appears to be winking at us, as if to say, "And you thought maybe I couldn't make a blow-'em-up movie?" (Perhaps he and Meryl Streep will share a river raft on their next outing.) Sam gets to shout down the top brass, drop onto a moving freighter from a helicopter blinded by fog, stand up to AWACS and fighter choppers. Then his ex-wife, Robby (Rene Russo)—she works for the Center for Disease Control and Prevention—comes down with the virus after it spreads to sleepy Cedar Creek, Calif. Sam and Robby, recently splitsville, still cast lingering looks of smoldering affection at each other. So it's inevitable Sam should brave airborne environments to save her. He removes his headgear at her bedside. Love means never having to keep your helmet on.

Director Wolfgang ("In the Line of Fire) Petersen, working from a script by Lawrence Dworet and Robert Roy Pool, likes to juice his movies with a barrage of bad guys. In "Outbreak," he's somewhat at a disadvantage because his chief meanie, Donald Sutherland's Gen. Donald McClintock, is no match for Motaba. McClintock has a simple solution to everything: When in doubt, nuke. His new baby is Operation Clean Sweep, where he plans to do to Cedar Creek what he did to the rain forest. But the killer virus is something else again. As Sam says, "It's a billionth of our size ... and it's *beating* us."

"Outbreak" has its eco-advocacy side: Messing with the rain forest unleashes plagues. The actual transmission of the virus from Africa to Cedar Creek is well-handled. (The film could use more scenes of scientific detective work.) We see how a single infected monkey, hijacked and sold to a pet store, then released into the wilds of Northern California after nibbling and regurgitating on a host of humans, can quickly turn the planet into a hot zone. But the preposterousness of the plot—the hair-raising rescues and daredevil standoffs—tends to turn everything, even the very real dangers of rogue viruses, into sci-fi. And this may be intentional.

It's possible to view "Outbreak" as a kind of *faux* thriller about AIDS. Infected blood is exchanged, people are accidentally stuck with infected needles. And, in true melodramatic fashion, "Outbreak" posits a comprehensible, targetable enemy—the military. A rogue officer is the only thing standing between us and health. Of course, an antiviral serum in this movie can be concocted and mass-produced in about the time it takes to cook a Pop-Tart.

"Outbreak" plugs into mass audience fears about AIDS and then exoticizes those fears and disposes of them. It's preposterousness with a mission: the '90s equivalent of the 1956 "Invasion of the Body Snatchers," where the virus was a creeping conformity that turned everybody into pod people. You can always count on Hollywood to capitalize on the infectious.

NEW STATESMAN & SOCIETY, 4/28/95, p. 41, Jonathan Romney

The biggers scare a film ever gave me came directly after Philip Kaufman's remake of *Invasion of the Body Snatchers*. It wasn't so much the film itself that got to me, with its story of parasitic alien spores reducing earth's population to hordes of shuffling, blank-eyed zombies. It was emerging from the auditorium only to realise that I was one of hordes of shuffling, blank-faced zombies.

It's often been said that video culture is destroying what is most specific about cinema-going: the collective nature of the experience—with the cinema as either a glorified funhouse or church. That's fine for *Singin 'in the Rain* or Tarkovsky, however. But a more alarming aspect of film-going, which has contributed to cinema's social disrepute, is the idea of the mob—a mass squeezed promiscuously and, potentially uncontrollably, into a small space. It's a notion that makes for both excitement (who doesn't dream of some impossible, truly orgiastic cinema?) and terror. Hence the regimental nature of multiplex architecture—keep them ranked and filed at all costs.

One extension of this is the idea of cinema as plague ward, the place of epidemic and its containment. Kaufman's *Invasion*—and Don Siegel's 1956 original—play brilliantly on the menace of the crowd as a constituent part of movie-going. It's generally taken as gospel that cinema is best enjoyed en masse, with reactions spreading from one part of the auditorium to another. But going to the cinema is in this sense a perilous undertaking—you have to open yourself up to contact with other people's emotions.

Artaud said much the same about theatre, in his *Theatre and the Plague*, a wonderful piece that describes the body bubonic as surging and pulsating with black, noxious fluids, then tells us that theatre has much the same effect on an audience. Artaud didn't really extend the argument to cinema—although he did write a delicious encomium to the Marx Brothers—but cinema is the epidemic form *par excellence*. On stage, actors communicate their passion directly to us, but the surpassing wonder of the cinema epidemic is that it comes to us out of nowhere, out of light, thin air. What are the dust motes suspended in the projector beam but Siegel's alien spores, noxious microbes?

It's hardly surprising, then, that cinema has taken the theme of contagion very much to heart, and there's a rich vein of plague paranoia movies—from Elia Kazan's *Panic in the Streets*, to David Cronenberg's cycle of sex-parasite chillers, to Todd Haynes' *Poison*, in which a body-mutating virus becomes the vehicle for a complex argument about otherness, queerness and Aids. By the time of *Poison*'s release in 1991, it had become a critical commonplace to assume that all contagion movies could be made to yield an Aids-specific reading (the same goes, with dreary reductiveness, for vampire films).

Clearly, cinema's affinity with contagion makes it the perfect vehicle for Aids debates and metaphors. But to rely too much on the Aids reading is to limit the resonance of this particular quality of cinema. Plague cinema's particular strength is its ability to make us aware (almost physically, as horror and suspense films can) of the connection between physical proximity and mental contagion. It can trace the subliminal notions of mass hysteria. Plague films always produce some sort of diagnosis of the social body, even if it's only through what they avoid saying.

One such case of avoidance is Wolfgang's Petersen's new epidemic thriller *Outbreak*, in which the US army moves in on a small town infected by a deadly virus. The scenario seems to owe a lot to George Romero's *The Crazies*, in which martial law is similarly imposed on a town whose poisoned inhabitants are taking leave of their senses. Rather than saving the world, the central husband and wife characters end up tearing each other apart. There's something infinitely more cathartic in Romero's absolute, circularnihilism—another town, another apocalypse—than there is to Petersen's blockbuster. For a start, we can be sure of *Outbreak*'s ending—you don't pay millions for a star like Dustin Hoffman and then deny him the chance to be humanity's saviour.

Outbreak is the plague movie in its extreme degeneracy—stripped of any real paranoia, reduced to the anaemic shades of the straight-up action movie. As an action movie it gives good value: it knows how to handle pathos, humour and helicopters. But as a film about what it purports to be about, it's a void—it's about the epidemic as much as *Disclosure* is about sexual politics. It's genuinely parasitic cinema, with the plague acting as living host to the mortifying blockbuster bug. It comes with a clipboard-full of genre commonplaces, each neatly slotted into place. The plague comes from elsewhere (Africa), which chimes with a popular tradition of Aids paranoia; but its spread is occasioned by US military skullduggery, and apart from one transmitting kiss, it is shorn of sexual overtones. From Aids culture, the film simply draws the fear of epidemic; it painstakingly avoids making any comment of it.

As in *The Crazies*, the military presence that aims to save the world has first to destroy the town. But where Romero forced us to be paranoid all round, making us at once identify with the townspeople and fear them, the innocents here—the great American public—are simply faceless pawns who supply a chance for plucky scientist Hoffman to redeem himself, win back his estranged wife (Rene Russo) and do a lot of fee-enhancing copter-jumping. *Outbreak* is a strange thing—a body horror movie without horror, a feel-good movie about feeling bad, Apocalypse lite. They do get one thing right, though. The plague first breaks out in a cinema.

NEW YORK, 3/20/95, p. 60, David Denby

The early scenes of *Outbreak* ratchet up our anxiety fast. In a Zairean mercenary army encampment, back in the late sixties, a deadly virus from the rain forest attacks the soldiers' immune system with ferocious speed. Contained, then seemingly obliterated, by the American military, the virus nevertheless emerges from the jungle 25 years later and kills again. Once more, it seems contained. But not quite: A tiny monkey that may be a host animal—a screecher, with sharp little teeth—gets taken to the United States and innocently let loose in the Northern California redwoods. What follows is an initially convincing horror story. Routines that seem utterly normal—inadvertent gestures, shuttling between coasts, the usual displays of greed and carelessness—spread the deadly virus as rapidly as the flu. A kiss, a cough in a crowded theater become unwitting murder.

Outbreak, which was directed by Wolfgang Petersen (*In the Line of Fire*), gets to the theaters before the movie version of Richard Preston's book *The Hot Zone*. (That movie may be canceled anyway.) This movie exploits the audience's fear of AIDS as an element of cinematic technique, but the opening scenes are so well done I was too fascinated to get angry. Petersen, jumping from one location to another, has a reassuring big-movie competence: He moves men and material around fast; he's good with groups of people and scenes of disorder. As the disease settled into a small Northern California town, my feelings of anxiety receded and something like pleasure took over: The genre hokiness, the echoes of a fifties sci-fi classic like *Invasion of the Body Snatchers* made the movie less scary than fun. Tanks and men pour in to herd the terrified population here and there, and Dustin Hoffman, as the supersleuth Army doctor, gives such a lip-biting, anguished performance he absolves the movie of slickness. Hoffman isn't good, exactly; he's tense, edgy, and righteous, like a B-movie actor from the fifties, but at least he's not Kevin Costner.

Somewhere in the middle, though, *Outbreak* falls off a cliff. The movie becomes a lamely conventional melodrama in which the tough little humanist Dustin Hoffman fights the tall, cynical military nihilist Donald Sutherland, and all its terror fades. The government has been storing the virus and also the antidote as part of its secret campaign to ... You can figure out the rest. There are fake-looking helicopter chases with actors emoting like crazy in copter mock-ups a few yards above the ground, snarling confrontations between top military officers, and a dreadful scene in which Hoffman tearfully begs two young pilots not to bomb a small town. The commonplace movieishness becomes ludicrous and insulting. *Outbreak* doesn't exploit AIDs so much as trivialize it. All it takes to lick a deadly new virus, it turns out, is a couple of gutsy guys in a whirlybird—if only all those AIDS researchers at the Centers for Disease Control had thought to rent a chopper!

NEW YORK POST, 3/10/95, p. 37, Thelma Adams

The viral thriller "Outbreak" has a healthy first hour before catching the flu.

Director Wolfgang Petersen ("In the Line of Fire") jump-starts the movie with a breathless 1967-set prologue showing a loathsome epidemic in "Zaire" and the American military's scorched-earth response. (Gaffe squad alert: the equatorial country, formerly the Democratic Republic of the Congo, didn't become Zaire until 1971.)

When the lethal bug breaks out in the present and threatens to end the millennium with a black plague revival, who you gonna call? Bug busters.

Enter military doctor Sam Daniels ("Rain Man" Dustin Hoffman) and his ex-wife, Robby (Rene Russo).

Hoffman's little brick neurotic pauses before hurtling off to Zaire to have a final spat with career woman Russo ("In the Line of Fire"). Russo, who still shares her husband's profession but not his bed, has just left the army to battle bugs for the Center for Disease Control and Prevention. Yes, it's the B-plot, the romantic fuse that's as inevitable as a third-act discovery of an antidote.

Fellow bug-buster Kevin Spacey ("Glengarry Glen Ross") plays referee in the post-marital spats. The actor can punch even the straightest lines. He adds a tartness to the proceedings before he virtually disappears in the second half.

Petersen makes the engine of his thriller machine purr. Like "In the Line of Fire," the director achieves a breathless, beautiful forward motion, the complicated tracking shots and dynamic editing creating an exquisite tension.

Cinematographer Michael Ballhaus ("Quiz Show") gives strong support and the pair take the camera to rare extremes for a mainstream thriller. In a movie theater scene, suddenly a virus-cam follows the microscopic bacteria, like the evil twins of Lawrence Welk's bubbles, flying from a disgusting infected, open-mouthed cough into the gaping, laughing mouth of another cinema patron.

The fear of contagion becomes so absolute that when a person coughs in the audience, you want to exile them.

Then the tension vanishes. Laurence Dworet, M.D., and Robert Roy Pool, in their first produced screenplay, having created an interesting dilemma, become feverish in the second half. It takes 90 minutes for Hoffman to discover the missing link between the African outbreak and the ones on our shores, and then only five to find the offending monkey who is living in the wilds of California and has only been seen by one wee girl.

Dworet and Pool indulge in the most simple-minded military paranoia. Donald Sutherland plays a wire-lipped albino general with a messiah complex who is willing to raze a California town to cover his own butt in a biological weapons scam.

Good neighbors make good fences and good villains make good thrillers. Sutherland, in a one-dimensional role bordering on parody, doesn't hold the fascination of a Mensa psycho like John Malkovich in "In the Line of Fire." The virus, though deadly, is short on personality.

Academy Award nominee Morgan Freeman ("The Shawshank Redemption") is wasted as Hoffman's boss, a doctor torn between his Hippocratic oath and the just-following-orders mentality of Hollywood's army.

Early on, Freeman dispatches Hoffman on a trip to Zaire with a cautionary: "Get in, get out." The screenwriters should have heeded their own advice.

NEWSDAY, 3/10/95, Part II/p. B2, Jack Mathews

During the first hour of Wolfgang Petersen's "Outbreak," I kept wondering why Warner Bros. hadn't opened the film before the end of the year and given it a shot at the Oscars. It was playing as a powerful, beautifully shot medical drama about the threat of a runaway virus brought into the United States by an African monkey, and there in the middle of it all, the perpetually intense Dustin Hoffman.

Then the second hour arrived, bringing with it some of the most banal conventions of the popcorn thriller, and it seemed that the studio was making a big mistake not holding the film until summer.

The problem with "Outbreak," at least for those apt to prefer the first hour over the second, is typical of Hollywood pictures exploiting scientific issues that threaten society at large. Screenwriters, whether they're working from the atom bomb, an invasion of killer ants or a mysterious disease, imagine the worst-case scenario, invent outsized heroes and villains, throw in a love story and turn it all into a race-against-time disaster movie.

In this case, the inspiration came from the hushed-up Ebola Zaire virus scare that occurred in Virginia a few years ago and was reported in terrifying detail in a New Yorker article written by Richard Preston (whose subsequent book, "The Hot Zone," has been on the New York Times best-seller list for five months). "Outbreak" writers Lawrence Dworet and Robert Roy Pool deny that they contracted the idea from Preston's article, but clearly that was what motivated the studio to finance it.

In any event, Dworet, a medical doctor on an extended screenwriting sabbatical and his partner, Pool, have done a good job of dramatizing the effects of Ebola Zaire, a highly communicable virus that is carried in monkeys in the African rainforest and kills humans by attacking their cells and essentially liquefying their internal organs.

The Virginia incident occurred when scientists brought African monkeys in for laboratory study and, after a tense period during which they feared the Ebola virus might escape into the civilian population, they halted it by destroying the host monkeys. The true story is dramatic enough, almost beyond belief, but it's no match for the apocalyptic arc of "Outbreak."

Here, Ebola Zaire is used as a pawn in a mad general's design for biological warfare, and though the immediate crisis is the fate of a small town visited by the virus, the dramatic conflict is between the medical experts trying to isolate and beat the disease and the Army troops ordered to get in their way.

Petersen, the German director of "Das Boot" and the hit 1993 thriller "In the Line of Fire," knows how to build and hold suspense, and before "Outbreak" turns into a chase film, he has us by the throat. With two trips to Zaire, where the virus has broken out in separate incidents, we meet the killer bug and are convinced he's as awesome an opponent for man as the creature in "Alien."

The next thing we know, he's on his way to America, carried by a monkey destined for a pet shop in a town on the California coast. When the outbreak occurs there, the choices facing the government are (a) quarantine the town and destroy everyone in it, or (b) find that damn monkey and use his antitoxins to mass-produce a cure.

Hoffman's intelligence and intensity seem perfectly suited to Col. Sam Daniels, the driven medical investigator for the Army's infectious disease unit, and as Daniels mobilizes his team for the search and destroy mission against Ebola, Hoffman operates on a level of borderline hysteria that gives the film its desperate sense of urgency.

But the role is undermined by a painfully contrived romantic subplot between Daniels and Dr. Roberta Keough (Rene Russo), a colleague and ex-wife with whom he's engaged in a cute custody battle over their two dogs, and when the story escalates into pure action, he seems lost in scenes where we'd expect to find Harrison Ford.

Elsewhere, the characters aren't developed beyond the conventions of the genre. Kevin Spacey has some fun as Daniels' wisecracking co-worker, but Donald Sutherland's villainous general is a parody of nutty military hawks and Morgan Freeman, as the officer ordered to do the wrong thing, isn't asked to do much more than sulk.

Still, there is enough scientific reality beneath the Hollywood cliches—a germ of truth, if you will—to make "Outbreak" the first must see movie of the new year.

NEWSWEEK, 3/20/95, p. 65, Jack Kroll

You could do a history of movies based on threats to mankind: gangsters, war, the bomb, aliens. The next major cycle may be about the smallest and scariest menaces: viruses. *Outbreak* is the first thriller to deal with the increasingly lethal and proliferating microbe mafia. Another project, "Crisis in the Hot Zone," starring Robert Redford and Jodie Foster, succumbed to the deadly E virus: ego. Both its stars wanted to be the hero. No such problem with "Outbreak," since Dustin Hoffman is a much bigger star than Rene Russo. They play a divorced couple, both experts in infectious diseases, fighting the mysterious Motaba virus that comes out of Africa via a smuggled monkey and infects the entire town of Cedar Creek, Calif.

Army medic Col. Sam Daniels (Hoffman) heads a team of "disease cowboys," as they're called in Laurie Garrett's book "The Coming Plague," which along with Richard Preston's "'The Hot Zone" sparked the current interest in the viral menace. Through its first half, "Outbreak" is a gripping genre movie about these intrepid doctors. Director Wolfgang Petersen ("In the Line of Fire") knows how to make a pleasurable wreck of your nervous system with his kinetic camera and triphammer editing. He whirls you through a formulaic but irresistible narrative that has Daniels and his sidekicks battling not only the mutating virus but the mutating duplicity of the army brass, in the persons of General Ford (Morgan Freeman) and General McClintock (Donald Sutherland). To contain the plague before it spreads across the country, these Hippocratic hypocrites have prescribed the ultimate unthinkable dosage (take one Kaboom and get lots of sleep). To head off this therapeutic apocalypse, the desperate Daniels takes off in a chopper to search for the escaped "host" monkey, which would supply the antibodies for a serum.

At this point "Outbreak" becomes "Breakdown." The screenplay, credited to Laurence Dworet and Robert Roy Pool (but mutated by several other writers), collapses into a series of world-record implausibilities. The president agrees to subtract one town from the U.S. atlas. Daniels's pilot, a young *doctor*, outmaneuvers a guy who's been introduced as "the best damn pilot in this man's army." To lure the lethally infected monkey, an *unprotected little girl* is sent out, making kitchy-koo noises. The army chain of command melts down into a ludicrous succession of insubordinations. Petersen even spoils his aerial-stunt scenes by inserting shots of Daniels in his chopper, obviously shot on a sound stage with projected backgrounds, breaking the momentum with palpable fakery.

Good thrillers may ask you to suspend your disbelief, but not your intelligence. "In the Line of Fire" was a model of its kind. With "Outbreak" you could say Petersen trivializes a major world health problem just for thrills, but if "Outbreak" tingled your spine without betraying your brain, well, that's entertainment. Genre movies are fun because they take us into some recognizable world and excite us by threatening that world. Are Daniels and his ex-wife Robby gonna get back together? Will one of them catch the plague? It's fun to see our corny hopes answered with style. But not even the intelligent intensity of Hoffman and the warm appeal of Russo (or the architectural splendors of her face in giant closeup) can override the plague of inanity that overtakes "Outbreak." Scientists now think that these microorganisms are man's ultimate adversaries. If they take over the planet, one consolation will be that viruses don't make silly movies.

SIGHT AND SOUND, 5/95, p. 31, Philip Kemp

Zaire, 1967. A mysterious fever devastates a mercenary camp. American medics fly in and promise help will be sent. Soon after they leave, a covert US military air strike obliterates the camp.

Present-day Maryland. Colonel Sam Daniels, a doctor at a US army viral research centre, is splitting up with his wife, Dr Robbie Keough. His superior, General Billy Ford, sends him to investigate an outbreak of deadly fever in Zaire, along with his assistant Major Casey Schuler and a new team member, Major Salt. They arrive to find all the villagers in the affected area dead or dying from a new, lethally fast-acting virus. Meanwhile a monkey, captured in the nearby jungle by animal traders, is on a Korean ship bound for California.

Back at the lab, Sam identifies the disease as motuba, a haemorrhagic virus which caused the 1967 outbreak, but Ford, warned by senior General Donald McClintock, refuses to declare an alert. The ship docks and an animal supplier, Jimbo Scott, smuggles the monkey in, taking it to Rudy's Pet Shop in the small town of Cedar Creek. Rudy rejects the animal, which scratches him, and Jimbo releases it in the woods before flying to Boston to meet his girlfriend, Alice. He collapses on arrival, and he and Alice are examined by Robbie, who has been notified, before they die. In Cedar Creek Rudy falls ill and dies; his blood infects a lab assistant, Henry, who is taken ill in a crowded cinema. As the infection spreads, Sam (defying Ford's orders) arrives with massive army backup, and quarantines the whole town. Robbie flies in with her team.

The monkey, loose in the woods, is adopted by a little girl, Sarah Jeffries. Casey deduces that the virus has mutated, and that the original host carries both strains—as well as the antidote. The source of infection is traced back to the pet shop. In Washington a Presidential Committee briefed by McClintock decides to bomb Cedar Creek to eliminate the virus. When quantities of antidote to the original virus (though not to the mutated strain) are sent by Ford, Sam realises that motuba was deliberately developed for germ warfare purposes. Casey and Robbie succumb to the fever, while Sam, threatened with arrest by McClintock, flees with Salt in a hijacked helicopter.

Sam and Salt trace the Korean ship and board it, finding a picture of the monkey which they broadcast on television. Sarah's mother contacts Sam; the monkey is captured and taken back to Cedar Creek, despite McClintock's pursuing helicopters. The antidote is synthesised and patients start recovering, but despite Ford's opposition and Sam's desperate pleas, McClintock orders the bombing to proceed. Sam and Salt take off and block the bomber's path with their helicopter. The bomb falls in the sea, and Ford places McClintock under arrest. Robbie, saved by the antidote, is reconciled with Sam.

Outbreak takes its inspiration from a true incident and a persistent rumour. In 1989, an incurable haemorrhagic viral infection broke out among imported Phillipino monkeys in Reston, Virginia; and for years the myth has circulated, insidious and alarmingly plausible, that Aids originated in a germ warfare experiment that went badly wrong. There's clearly enough makings here for a powerful and disturbing film that could, within the potent metaphor of disease as warfare, align the criminal irresponsibility of government agencies with the protean opportunism of viruses (some of which can mutate so fast now antidotes are obsolete before they reach the patent stage). Every so often, *Outbreak* gets within shouting distance of being such a film, which makes it all the more frustrating that what we finally end up with is a cross between *Mission Impossible* and an episode of *The X-Files*.

One of the film's more unnerving moments occurs in a small-town cinema. A man in the audience slumps, coughing convulsively, and the camera pulls focus to show us, floating in the projector's beam, tiny airborne spores of infected spittle shot from his mouth, drifting into other mouths that laugh or gulp popcorn. It's a chilling image of unwitting vulnerability—especially if you're sitting in a cinema at the time. And later, as the casualties mount and the medico-military occupation of Cedar Creek tightens its grip, patients are shunted into a makeshift huddle of huts ringed with barbed wire that inescapably recalls a Nazi death camp.

However, intimations like these, and Michael Ballhaus's shadowy, haunted photography, go for little in the face of a script set on running headlong into every available banality, with points rammed crassly home. "These people are casualties of war, Billy," says Donald Sutherland's perfidious general, referring to the doomed citizens of Cedar Creek, "I'd give them all a medal if I could", to which Dustin Hoffman pleads desperately, "It's not the town you're killing—it's a big piece of the American soul!"

Along with this verbal overkill goes a squeamishness in the physical depiction of the disease. We're constantly being told how horrendous it is, but all we get are a few aghast reaction shots and actors with fake blood round their eyes. And when Rene Russo is stricken, she shows all the symptoms of a moderately bad cold. (This whole estranged wife plot strand merely serves to give the hero a little extra motivation in case saving the American soul wasn't quite enough.)

"Idiocy is our only option!" announces Dustin Hoffman, hijacking a helicopter. The film-makers evidently agree, since from here on we descend into a welter of Action Man cliché laced with inane coincidence. (The monkey is identified thanks to a Korean sailor being so taken with it, he kept its photo above his bunk as a pin-up.) In the hands of, say, David Cronenberg, *Outbreak* could have emerged as a disquieting fable of how a healthy body/society can be invaded, subverted and destroyed from within. As it is, it's a classic example of how a potentially good film can be trashed by lazy studio formula thinking.

TIME, 3/20/95, p. 71, Richard Corliss

Young, gung-ho Major Salt (Cuba Gooding Jr.) is eager to impress his bosses by describing the fatal cunning of the Motaba virus—how it rapidly turns a healthy body into a bloody, pustulous corpse. "That's very good, Major," says Colonel Sam Daniels (Dustin Hoffman) wryly. "We've read that in a book too."

Not quite. They—or rather, producer Arnold Kopelson—read it in a *New Yorker* article in 1992. "Crisis in the Hot Zone," Richard Preston's true story about the near escape of the Ebola virus from a Virginia lab, threw Hollywood into a bidding frenzy, and Kopelson was one of the pursuers. When Preston sold his rights to 20th Century Fox, Kopelson decided to make a fictional plague film, *Outbreak*. It scurried into production while the *Hot Zone* project dithered in development and then aborted. So if you want to see a virus epic, *Outbreak* is it.

What you get is a big, bustling, intermittently dippy melodrama that takes the Preston premise a few steps further. The virus becomes airborne and infects a California town. Now sneezing in a crowded theater can spread an instant epidemic. And a cute monkey may be the innocent agent of genocide.

Sam, an Army doctor, is the only person with the expertise, the guts and, dammit, the nobility to solve this apocalyptic poser. Screenwriters Laurence Dworet and Robert Roy Pool have given him a requisition brainy-dishy ex-wife (Rene Russo), an agitated boss (Morgan Freeman), a helpful colleague (Kevin Spacey, who is very good) and plucky Major Salt to steer Sam through an unlikely airplane battle at the climax. But in movies like this, a man must stand alone. It's a mild hoot to watch Certified Great Actor Hoffman play an action hero. Note the Clint-like glint in his eyes, the terse authority he gives such endearingly daft phrases as "Idiocy is our only option."

Sam could stanch the epidemic in a trice were it not for that old bogeyman the nut case Army general (Donald Sutherland, eyes rolling goofily). Apparently a killer virus, the threat of plague, a White House crisis—oh, and a pretty blond child set up for a big bad monkey bite—aren't enough for one doomsday movie; the military has to go bats as well. We can only surmise that back in 1986, when he produced *Platoon*, Kopelson contracted a deadly strain of the conspiracy virus from Oliver Stone.

Director Wolfgang Petersen (*Das Boot, In the Line of Fire*) handles it all proficiently and at times artfully, as in two elaborate tracking shots that reveal various levels of biological contamination and the spread of the disease through hospital vents. Still, the whole operation looks musclebound. *Outbreak* is really about the lumbering, quasimilitary maneuvers that go into big-budget filmmaking. If Preston's virus story were a virus, the *Outbreak* team would aim an H-bomb at it. And the *Hot Zone* people would be sitting around apprehensively, waiting for it to develop.

VILLAGE VOICE, 3/21/95, p. 47, J. Hoberman

Outbreak, the high-powered epidemiological thriller that opened last weekend, doesn't make a whole lot of sense or leave very much behind. Still, given the health of the competition, its single-minded sense of importance is (designated pull quote) mildly contagious.

Indeed, having proved hardier than a rival monkey-driven killer-virus movie—the never made Redford-Foster vehicle *Crisis in the Hot Zone*—*Outbreak* already owns Hollywood's petri dish. Its topicality has been insured, if not by a new incident of some mysterious flesh-rotting microorganism, then at least by the recent appearance of Laurie Garrett's well-publicized *The Coming Plague*.

A mysterious, virulent contagion originating in Zaire, *Outbreak*-itis begins like the flu, rapidly escalates to pink lesions, and, within 24 hours, liquifies the sufferer's insides. The epidemic may suggest a sped-up time-lapse vision of HIV, but the movie hews to a more old-fashioned End of the World scenario. As briskly directed by Wolfgang Petersen, *Outbreak* is strongest when mapping the geography by which the virus spreads. A monkey, brought to San Francisco from Africa on a South Korean freighter, infects a pet shop; a California carrier gets off a plane in Boston, kisses his waiting girlfriend, and dies.

At its best, *Outbreak* is a hideous comedy of errors. Back in idyllic Cedar Creek, California, a clumsy hospital technician spatters contaminated blood all over his lab, and then, once infected, coughs up a noxious cloud of diseased sputum in the midst of a crowded movie theater inexplicably showing *What's Up Doc?* Petersen's most inspired bit of business—an act of humorous aggression (or self-hatred) reminiscent of similar tropes in *Targets* or the original version of *The Blob*—the scene gives new meaning to the term "word of mouth" with mega-close-ups of guffawing, popcorn-chomping audience members breathing in the toxic vapors.

Thanks to the movies, all Cedar Creek comes down with the plague, overwhelming the facilities at the local hospital. First the Centers for Disease Control (Rene Russo) and then the U.S. Army Medical Research Institute for Infectious Diseases (Colonel Dustin Hoffman and General Morgan Freeman) invade the town to establish makeshift concentration camps of sickness and death. As riots errupt on Main Street, the medics realize that the virus has already mutated and that the original carrier must be found to provide an antibody.

With its emphasis on professionalism, collective heroics, and male groups, *Outbreak* is basically a Howard Hawks situation, albeit denuded of erotic rivalries and snappy retorts. The untalented dialogue by Dr. Laurence Dworet and his writing partner, Robert Roy Pool, reinforces the routine failure of language: "It is, in a word, frightening" is how one TV reporter articulates the situation. But that is not to call the movie "understated." Where Elia Kazan's 1950 *Panic in the Streets* used a laconic, quasidocumentary style to represent an instance of pneumonic plague in New Orleans, *Outbreak* prefers whenever possible to swing its technological dick, juicing the story with exciting helicopter chases and cool explosions.

Events even set off a White House alarm. Although the president is unseen, the film is basically Clinton-esque. The plague is explicitly visualized as the return of a Vietnam era repressed—including the evil premise that in order to save the town it became necessary to destroy it. Replete with a Defense Department cover-up, illuminated by the pale fire of rogue general Donald Sutherland's refined malevolence, *Outbreak* refers in a glancing, iconographic way to such liberal classics as *Dr. Strangelove* and *The China Syndrome*. (Some free-floating images are more evocative: The stack of zip-up body bags in a northern California hamlet suggests reverse versions of the pods from *Invasion of the Body Snatchers*.)

Cast against type in the Harrison Ford (or is it Keanu Reeves?) role, Hoffman is typically driven—pursed, craggy, and something of a bore with his compulsive hunches as well as the torch he carries for ex-wife Russo. Despite their lab smocks, there's a marked absence of chemistry between these two doctors. When the Hoffman character brings his two pet Saint Bernards over to the Russo character's home for baby-sitting, it's the scene that has fleas.

Once *Outbreak* shifts gears into chopper-adventure mode, Hoffman bonds with a young, emphatically gung ho medic cum helicopter pilot (Cuba Gooding Jr.). Meanwhile, Freeman, as Hoffman's weary, compromised superior officer, is the most complicated, if underwritten, character. Or maybe Freeman just has the knack for conveying inner life. It's a pity he and Hoffman couldn't exchange roles.

Also reviewed in:
CHICAGO TRIBUNE, 3/10/95, Friday/p. C, Michael Wilmington
NEW REPUBLIC, 4/10/95, p. 30, Stanley Kauffmann
NEW YORK TIMES, 3/10/95, p. C8, Janet Maslin
NEW YORKER, 3/20/95, p. 105, Terrence Rafferty
VARIETY, 3/13-19/95, p. 49, Todd McCarthy
WASHINGTON POST, 3/10/95, p. C1, Rita Kempley
WASHINGTON POST, 3/10/95, Weekend/p. 36, Desson Howe

PANTHER

A Gramercy Pictures release of a PolyGram Filmed Entertainment presentation of a Working Title production in association with Tribeca Productions/MVP Filmz. *Executive Producer:* Eric Fellner and Tim Bevan. *Producer:* Preston Holmes, Mario Van Peebles, and Melvin Van Peebles. *Director:* Mario Van Peebles. *Screenplay (based on his novel):* Melvin Van Peebles. *Director of Photography:* Eddie Pei. *Editor:* Earl Watson. *Music:* Larry Robinson. *Music Editor:* Christine Cholvin. *Sound:* Susumu Tokunow and (music) Dan Wallin. *Sound Editor:* Dane A. Davis. *Casting:* Robi Reed. *Production Designer:* Richard Hoover. *Art Director:* Bruce Hill. *Set Decorator:* Robert Kensinger. *Set Dresser:* Bill Butler. *Special Effects:* Beverly Hardigan. *Costumes:* Paul A. Simmons. *Make-up:* Kim Davis. *Stunt Coordinator:* Bob Minor. *Running time:* 125 minutes. *MPAA Rating:* R.

CAST: Kadeem Hardison (Judge);   Bokeem Woodbine (Tyrone);   Joe Don Baker (Brimmer); Courtney B. Vance (Bobby Seale);   Tyrin Turner (Cy);   Marcus Chong (Huey Newton);   Anthony Griffith (Eldridge Cleaver);   Bobby Brown (Rose);   Nefertiti (Alma);   James Russo (Rodgers); Jenifer Lewis (Rita);   Chris Rock (Drinker #1);   Roger Guenveur Smith (Pruitt);   Michael Wincott (Tynan);   Richard Dysart (Hoover);   M. Emmet Walsh (Dorsett);   Wesley Jonathan (Little Bobby);   Kahlil Nelson (Boy on Bike);   Thayis Walsh (Bernadette);   Anthony Jones (Sabu); Dick Gregory (Reverend Slocum);   Kool Moe Dee (Jamal);   Lahmard Tate (Gene McKinney); William Fuller (Sgt. Schreck);   David Greenlee (Patrolman);   Melvin Van Peebles (Cynical Jail Bird);   Adam Powers (White Hippie);   Sharrif Simmons (Poet);   Emory Douglas (Bret Schaefer); Emory Douglas (Bret Schaefer);   Aklam (Bakar);   Mark Curry (Lombard);   Dario Scardapane (Student);   Reginald Ballard (Brother at Meeting);   Ralph Ahn (Mr. Yang);   James Bigwood and Martin Bright (Grove Street Cops);   John "Doo Doo Brown" Gordon, Marvin Young, and D-Knowledge (Recruits);   Mark Buntzman (Pushy Reporter);   Robert Peters (Cop at Ramparts); Shanice Wilson (Singer at Punk Panthers);   Jeffrey Carr (Denzil Dowell);   Ann Weldon (Mrs. Dowell);   Steven Carl White (George);   Brian Turk (Deputy);   Charles Cooper (Sheriff);   Jay Koch (Governor Reagan);   Tim Loughrin (Reporter at Capitol);   Tony Beard (Guard at Capitol); Jerry Rubin (Defense Attorney);   Beau Windham (Hoover's Aide);   Jamie Zozzaro (Girl Buying Drugs);   Yolanda Whitaker (Pregnant Junkie);   Roberto L. Santana (Matty);   Arthur Reed (Blind Man);   Gunnar Peterson (Cop at Gas Station);   Christopher Michaels (Reporter at Police Station); John Harwood (Cop at Line Up);   James Legros (Avakian);   John Knight (Cop at Panther Office); Joseph Culp (Baby Faced Cop);   Erik Kohner (Nervous Cop);   Preston L. Holmes (Prison Guard);   Robert Culp (Charles Garry);   Chris Tucker (Bodyguard);   John Snyder (Cop);   Tracey Costello (Kathleen Cleaver);   Mario Van Peebles (Stokely Carmichael);   Jeris Poindexte (Black Cop);   Steve Gagnon (Prosecutor);   Brent Sincock (Judge);   Manny Perry (Shorty);   James A. Earley (Angry Cop);   William Brennan (Partner).

LOS ANGELES TIMES, 5/3/95, Calendar/p. 1, Kenneth Turan

Jean-Luc Godard called the well-brought-up radicals of the 1960's "the children of Marx and Coca-Cola" and a twist on that celebrated phrase is applicable to "Panther," an examination of the Black Panther Party, and its director Mario Van Peebles, both of which are the children of an equally unlikely pairing: Black Power and Hollywood.

As the son of Melvin Van Peebles, the renegade filmmaker whose 1971 "Sweet Sweetback's Baadasssss Song" was a groundbreaking success in the black community, Mario Van Peebles was raised with a firm sense of the political aspects of culture. "Sweet Sweetback" was a favorite of Huey Newton, the B.P.P. minister of defense, and the senior Van Peebles wrote the "Panther" script based on his own time spent with the party leadership.

But the reason Mario Van Peebles was able to make "Panther" was that his Hollywood credentials are also in excellent order. Though they had a politics of color overlay, both his previous films as a director, "New Jack City" and "Posse,'" are definitely in the commercial mainstream when it comes to plotting, characterization and the manipulation of on-screen violence.

What Van Peebles wanted to do with this look at the early days of the ever-controversial Panthers is to unite those two aspects of his style, to make what he himself called an "edutainment" that would use show-biz tools in such a way that "today's kids will see that great, positive things can be accomplished when you come together as a community."

The hoped-for fusion does not totally happen, however, and though the film's partial fictionalization of Panther history was done in search of a larger reality, what results instead is a frustrating amalgam of truth, violence, supposition and inspiration.

The most compelling part of "Panther" is a sincere attempt at celebratory, spirit-raising filmmaking in the "Malcolm X" mold, a romanticized but effective attempt at creating heroes and showcasing the positive aspects of the Panther Party and its message of black empowerment and self-respect.

However, the potential danger with inspirational films, whatever their stripe, is that they tend to be peopled exclusively by one-dimensional folks, heroes or villains with no shades of gray, and from a dramatic point of view "Panther" suffers from this.

When you add in a tired gangster plot involving shoot-outs, double-crosses and explosions, the upshot is a piece of work that presents different public faces depending on the point of view it is approached from, a film sure to be both over-criticized and over-praised.

Throwing yet another element into the mix is "Panther's" "JFK" aspects, its detailing of nefarious conspiracies against the Panther Party in particular and the African American community in general. Some of its more incendiary accusations turn out to be well-documented, but others are not, and the difficulty of telling them apart adds to the confusion.

Melvin Van Peebles' impressionistic script has chosen to focus on the Panthers in their early, most idealistic years, stopping before government-encouraged internal dissension and internecine violence began to tear the organization apart. Rather it details, through the composite character of Judge (Kadeem Hardison), a Vietnam veteran who is a reluctant convert, how the party came to be born in Oakland in 1966 with the two words "Defend yourself."

Those words were uttered by the party's founders, Bobby Seale (Courtney B. Vance) and Huey Newton (Marcus Chong). After watching a peaceful protest led by the Reverend Slocum (Dick Gregory) for a much-needed neighborhood stoplight turn into a police riot, they began to feel that "black folk been praying to God for 400 years. Maybe its time we tried something else."

That something else turned out to be the Panther Party, which emphasized discipline, self-improvement, feeding the hungry and an end to "police shooting black people like it was going out of style." Initially funded by the heavily marked-up sale of Mao's Little Red Book to Berkeley students, the Panthers, garbed in black leather jackets with rifles at the ready, soon became known for standing up to what they considered to be oppressive authority, and the scenes of their confrontations with "the pigs" are easily the film's most celebratory.

This attitude did not meet with the approval either of Bay Area law enforcement officials or FBI poobah J. Edgar Hoover (Richard Dysart), who declared the Panthers public enemy No. 1 and proceeded, with the help of a local cop played by Joe Don Baker, to sow discord within the party.

The FBI's campaign against the Panthers, funneled through a program called COINTELPRO, is in fact confirmed by documents released through the Freedom of Information Act. What is not well-documented, however, is the film's final "JFK"-type contention that a single meeting led to a massive government-Mafia conspiracy to neutralize the black community. Even if this event happened, Van Peebles, directing only his third theatrical feature, lacks the Oliver Stone-type manipulative skills necessary to make it at all plausible.

If it is strongest in its agitprop attempt to reclaim and potently repackage an important part of recent black history (though the little-seen documentary "The Murder of Fred Hampton" makes similar points to greater effect), "Panther" is weakest in its simplistic treatment of human nature.

Perhaps fearful that the power and larger truth of their message would be diluted, the filmmakers have allowed hardly any characters, no matter what their skin color, to be multidimensional, and while that may help in terms of propaganda, it hurts in terms of involving drama. But films with political agendas rarely have any use for subtlety, have never cared how they made their points, and there is no reason "Panther" should be any different.

NEW YORK POST, 5/5/95, p. 31, Thelma Adams

"I'm black and I'm proud." It's been ages since I heard that slogan aloud and it still resonates.

In Mario Van Peebles flawed, ambitious "Panther," it's hard not to wax nostalgic for a '60s that never was, a time when Afros were big, crack was a line you jumped over on the sidewalk, and the Black Panther party rose from the ranks of ghetto choir boys.

Based on a script by Melvin Van Peebles, the director's father, "Panther" joins the ranks of recent movies like Merchant Ivory's "Jefferson in Paris," Oliver Stone's "JFK," and Spike Lee's "Malcolm X" that pick and choose among the history books, finding facts that suit their theories about the past rather than drawing theories from the facts.

When it comes to history, mainstream movies, with their prime directive to entertain, are no substitutes for objective research. That said, Van Peebles, father and son, leap into a fertile period of the American past: the rise and fall of the Black Panther party in Oakland in the late '60s.

Van Peebles pulls historical figures Huey Newton (Marcus Chong), Bobby Seale (Courtney B. Vance) and Eldridge Cleaver (Anthony Griffith) into the spotlight. The drama actually centers on a fabricated figure, Judge (Kadeem Hardison), a Vietnam vet and Berkeley student. Judge gets pulled into the Panthers and then pulled apart when Newton encourages him to become a double agent, passing information to the FBI.

Hardison, tamped down from the motor-mouthed Dwayne Wayne character he played on TV's "A Different World," makes for a strong, thoughtful presence at the center of a cultural storm. If he doesn't quite seem to have, the scars of a veteran, or the study habits of a Berkeley student, Judge's motives for joining the Panthers are sympathetic, neither naive nor radical. He wants to protect his neighborhood from police brutality on the one hand and indifference on the other. As he says in the restrained voiceover, his radicalization "started in my mom's front yard."

As in Van Peebles' "New Jack City," the ensemble of young, black actors is particularly fine. The depiction of the inner struggles of the radical cell contains "Panther's" most dramatically sure material.

Chong's Huey is a natural leader who finally finds a place to put his abundant energy (and a justification for his egotism). Vance's Seale jockeys for dominance in a battle of the head over the heart, Griffith's Cleaver, the Panther's Minister of Information and a powerful orator, is as entranced by the power of his rhetoric as his listeners. It's Cleaver who leads an organization that has gotten too big for its founders into violence in response to the assassination of Martin Luther King.

As the Panthers grow in size and the movement steamrolls, the movie escapes from Van Peebles. The energy is in the interaction of Newton, Seale, Judge and Cleaver. When the plot turns on an FBI conspiracy, complete with a twisted, one-note J. Edgar Hoover played by father-figure Richard Dysart, the power and insight drain away.

The movie does well to remind viewers of the extra-legal (and documented) activities of the FBI in snuffing out the Black Panthers. However, much that has been revealed in articles and books on the subject by scholars and ex-Panthers has been shunted aside, including the uneasy and often exploitative relationship with women among many male Panthers, drug abuse and Panther-on-Panther violence.

Despite its flaws, watching "Panther" is like a shot in the head. It entertains, it provokes, it energizes. Van Peebles captures the excitement and hope of a time when the phrase "come the revolution" was not yet soaked in irony, when social change—and change for the better—seemed not only possible but inevitable.

NEWSDAY, 5/5/95, Part II/p. B2, Jack Mathews

Where is Spike Lee when we need him?

If ever a filmmaker and a subject were right for each other, Lee and the '60s Black Panther Party of Huey Newton, Bobby Seale and Eldridge Cleaver are they. And now, on the eve of the 30th anniversary of the Watts Riots that helped move them to action, is the time.

After "Do the Right Thing," which examined the conditions and circumstances that occasionally lead to spontaneous revolt, and "Malcolm X," about the charismatic leader of the Black Muslim Movement, Lee's voice—angry, uncompromising and informed—is the one most likely to help us understand the confrontational politics of the Panthers.

Instead, Mario Van Peebles and his father, Melvin, director and writer respectively of "Panther," are the first to have weighed in on the subject, and instead of peeling away the layers of myth surrounding the organization, they've exploited them in a shockingly conventional action-melodrama. In the same way that inner-city drug trafficking served as a gateway to the rough stuff in Mario Van Peebles' "New Jack City," the politics of Newton, Seale and Cleaver open the guns of opportunity in "Panther."

The issues that inspired the Panther party—the persistent police brutality, joblessness and futility that define life in the inner city—are all here, but shaped in ways that oversimplify history, romanticize violence and patronize the young African-Americans who form its target audience. There will be cheering in the theaters when Newton (Marcus Chong) and Seale (Courtney Vance), armed with rifles and a working knowledge of the California Penal Code, back down some redneck cops, but the movie turns so many historical moments like that into theatrical set pieces that they quickly lose their impact.

"Panther," told from the point of view of a returning Vietnam veteran (Kadeem Hardison) who joins the fledgling Panthers in 1966 Oakland, covers about the first 18 months of the party's existence, from its formation after one-too-many police assaults on peaceful black protesters to the full-court press put on it by J. Edgar Hoover's FBI.

It is hard to overstate the antagonistic role of law enforcement in the violent events of the '60s, but the Van Peebles have done it. The Oakland police are rogue gangs of thugs and killers, and the FBI agents seem to have been body snatched by Nazi seedpods from another planet. The only bad blacks are drug dealers used as FBI informers.

To portray all of the police as racist villains and all of the African-Americans as either victims or martyrs is to turn that complex chapter of social history into something literally black and white. And the suggestion that the FBI's ultimate counter-Panther strategy—of lowering the anger level in the ghetto by flooding it with heroin—is responsible for today's inner-city drug epidemic is a stunning leap. Hoover was more powerful than a gas leak in a sleeping bag, but we can't blame him for everything foul in the land.

What "Panther" does best, in the early going before it becomes a revenge fantasy, is demonstrate how everyday police brutality in minority communities heightens tension and makes violent confrontations inevitable. It was excessive police force that ignited the fires of Watts in 1965 (and indirectly 27 years later in L. A., after a white jury found Rodney King guilty of his own beating) and a similar incident in Oakland the next year that opened the community to the revolutionary politics of the Panthers.

Just how far we haven't come was evident last week with videotaped news footage of a black man being thrown to the ground and kicked and beaten by out-of-control cops in Cincinnati.

"Panther" makes us feel the community's outrage over these indignities, and makes Newton's and Seale's gun-toting militancy seem the most reasonable reaction in the world. But as the movie wears on, they evolve from local heroes into action heroes, traditional Hollywood protagonists standing up to the overwhelming forces of evil.

With the exception of Hardison, who makes his fictional character the film's most realistic one, the cast seems more determined to play legends than to play people. Certainly, the filmmakers were more interested in re-enacting the battles than in providing insights into the war. "Panther" is more the legacy of Superfly than of Malcolm X.

SIGHT AND SOUND, 12/95, p. 49, Amanda Lipman

Judge, a black Vietnam veteran putting himself through college, explains in voice-over how the Black Panther Party was formed in 1966 by two students in Oakland, California—Huey Newton and Bobby Seale. Judge is drawn into the group after he witnesses the Panthers standing up to policemen who have been beating up a black man. When the FBI leans on Dorsett, the California police chief, to do something about the Panthers, he sends Brimmer, one of his cops, to keep watch on them.

At Newton's suggestion, Judge starts to infiltrate the police via Brimmer. An innocent black man is killed by the police and the Panthers arrange a demonstration calling for justice. Meanwhile, Brimmer is pressurising Judge to come up with some information about the Panthers. When Seale takes a group of Panthers to the State Capitol they are all arrested and thrown into jail after which J. Edgar Hoover has the Panthers disarmed.

Eldridge Cleaver becomes the Panthers' Minister of Information. When Judge's best friend, Cy, is murdered (by the police, as he wrongly thinks), he makes a deal with Brimmer. Judge fakes a robbery at a gas station and a carful of Panthers are arrested. But at the identity parade the victim turns out to be blind. Brimmer comes after Judge and beats him up. The FBI brings in a black agent and starts a war of attrition, looting Panther offices and beating up members. Newton is set up on a charge of murdering a cop and thrown into prison.

When Martin Luther King is murdered, Cleaver calls for violent action. Seale does not agree and the party is split. But after a young Panther is killed by the police, Cleaver is made to leave. Amidst a huge campaign, Newton goes on trial and wins his case. Meanwhile, the FBI begins to flood the black community with cheap heroin. Brimmer, disillusioned with the police force, leaks this to Judge. Seale is arrested by the police and the FBI pretends that Judge betrayed him. Judge manages to clear his name and, with two others, heads for the warehouse where the dope is stored. After a violent shoot out, one of the Panthers dies a hero's death acting as decoy. Now, in 1995, Judge recalls how the Black Panthers were finally broken up by the FBI.

Chronologically speaking, *Panther* could be a sequel to *Malcolm X*. Apart from Angela Bassett reprising her role as Betty Shabazz, what it also has in common with Spike Lee's film is an insistently black perspective. It may be a truisim, but like a black director (here, Mario Van Peebles, son of writer and one-time director Melvin, on whose novel the film is based) to give a voice to black characters taking their destiny into their own hands. Consequently, it may seem unnecessary to add that parts of this film owe a little to Lee—not least the use of humorous to-camera discourses as various talking heads explain why they want to join the party. But *Panther* also bears some of the slick, high-speed hallmarks of Mario Van Peebles' first movie, *New Jack City*.

Panther bulges with material. Part of this is 'real life' history, part ideology and part fiction. The interaction of historical characters—notably Panther founding fathers Huey Newton and Bobby Seale—with the fictional, phlegmatic narrator Judge, brings up questions of cinematic truth. Is this a history or a fiction? Given that all histories are also fictions, does it matter? Not necessarily, but so much of this film is made with the simplicity of an educational introduction to the Black Panther Party that it implies an accuracy that it does not have. Then again, the brutal treatment of black people has such resonances for a modern audience for whom the Rodney King beating and subsequent riots in LA are still a recent memory that there is enough essential if not literal truth here.

The Black Panther Party was formed as a response to economic and social racism, and fired up by both Martin Luther King and Malcolm X. It seems perfectly reasonable for the film to crystallise this in specific incidents: a chirpy little boy being run over because no one bothered to put up a stop light in a black area of Oakland; a man killed by the police just for being the wrong colour in the wrong place at the wrong time. But *Panther* more or less maintains this level of simplicity throughout. Huey Newton and Bobby Seale are both great guys—heroes and visionaries. This allows for some rousing moments, when, for example, Newton quotes the law so rigorously at a cop trying to intimidate him that the police just have to let him go about his business. The way in which the Panthers utilise the law to enable them to carry guns, to use their right of free speech or of silence to stay free of the largely racist police force makes stirring entertainment, while the emphasis on the fact that they were formed to serve the community, rather than to act as a separatist paramilitary, may be a useful piece of didacticism. There is no effort, however, to explore the contradictions between the wearing of black leather uniforms and rifles and the group's sickle cell anaemia testing drives. The Panthers were an unashamedly Marxist organisation but here they come over merely as sartorially conscious humanists, ridding the community of drug dealers and providing free, funky outdoor concerts.

The in-fighting that tore the party apart is only seen through the intervention of Eldridge Cleaver, depicted as a wicked witch who favours violence, and is ousted with such rapidity you wonder what ended up on the cutting room floor. There are hints of differences of opinion between other African American groups and the Panthers, and there is an uneasy sense of division when Newton makes Judge promise to tell no one about his double agent work. There is also a strong feeling that something is missing from the story when Newton, the anti-drugs campaigner, is killed in a drugs raid.

If the film simplifies, at least it turns away from a fatuous black-is-always-good argument. For not only is there the Eldridge Cleaver factor, but the FBI agent in charge of "neutralising" the Panthers is also black—though he looks white. Confronted by a black cop, he claims that it is not a racist issue but a political one. Yet as the film makes implicitly clear, it is precisely the fact that the two issues are closely intertwined that makes the Panthers seem so dangerous to J. Edgar Hoover.

Panther also contains some stylisation not unlike that of Oliver Stone's *Natural Born Killers*. On the night he hears of Martin Luther King's death, Judge stands against a backdrop of a city in flames; a landscape that both depicts the exterior world and his own feverish mind. At another point, he lies in bed, his brain full of violent images: Vietnam, the looting of the party offices. Suddenly we are catapulted into an interior world—a rare moment in a film that is mostly concerned with action. While *Panther* deals with sexual politics in allowing the women to act as equals, most of this action is physical, masculine conflict. This is where Mario Van Peebles hits *New Jack City* territory: good versus bad in a male world that is irredeemably violent. *Panther* also opts for a loose ending: the struggle continues, says Judge—the good guys do not win and a happy ending is nowhere in sight.

TIME, 5/15/95, p. 73, Richard Corliss

How did Oliver Stone let this one get away? A gang of '60s rebels, an aura of righteous violence, the charge that J. Edgar Hoover and the Mafia flooded our nation's cities with cheap drugs—why, it's all so lurid, it must be true. And if it's not, it can still be a movie.

Panther, the new film directed by Mario Van Peebles *(New Jack City)* from a screenplay by his father Melvin *(Sweet Sweetback's Baadasssss Song)*, is indeed a movie: an earnest, naive, fitfully engrossing film with urgent performances and a final plot twist that stretches credulity to the snapping point. But because the subject is the Black Panther Party for Self Defense—the notorious cadre of black radicals that incited and attracted much of the '60s edgiest violence—*Panther* is more than a movie. It's the cause of raucous dispute, a chance for opening and licking old wounds about the party, an excuse for debating both the sorry condition of today's urban blacks and the responsibility, if any, of filmmakers to get the facts straight.

A committee of black entertainers and athletes, including Danny Glover, Spike Lee and Magic Johnson, took out ads in *Daily Variety* to support Van Peebles *père et fils:* "We laud their efforts and their courage for making a movie that sends a message of strength, dignity and empowerment to the African American community—especially to our youth." This was in response to an earlier ad, declaring *Panther* "a two-hour lie," that was placed in *Daily Variety* by David Horowitz's Center for the Study of Popular Culture, a neoconservative outfit in Los Angeles. Horowitz, a reformed leftie who worked for the Panthers in the '70s, now believes that "the overwhelming impact of the Panthers was negative." And he fears *Panther* will have a toxic effect: "I fully expect that there will be people who will die because of this film."

Mario Van Peebles demurs: "The kids don't see this movie as a call to arms but as a call to consciousness." In this Molotov cocktail of fact and fancy, the party's founders, Huey Newton (Marcus Chong) and Bobby Seale (Courtney B. Vance), are two street-wise dreamers from Oakland, California, who live their slogan: "Power to the People." They arm themselves and talk instructive trash to the pig cops—but within the letter of the law. They also serve food to kids and educate them in Afro awareness.

In real life, the free lunches came at a hefty price. The early Panthers—who took their rhetorical cues from that noted protector of civil liberties, Chairman Mao—were a confused blend of boys' club and militia. Their gun battles with police were macho street theater run amuck. And their thug posture, as later adopted by drug gangs and rap artists, further isolated the black male from the American mainstream. In the film, though, iconography tells the story. The Panthers are young and handsome; virtually all whites are old and fat, decadent crypt keepers of a corrupt culture.

The film's main new charge is that with the Mafia's connivance, Hoover sent the Black Revolution a toxic sedative: cheap dope. And it worked too well, enslaving whites as well as blacks. As *Panther* notes, America has 10 times as many drug addicts now as it did in the '60s. The notion of the FBI's fomenting a domestic opium war is piquant—but preposterous. And what if it's true? Are we to blame aboriginal Americans for introducing tobacco to the Europeans?

The filmmakers stress that *Panther* is fiction; some of those who were there see it as flawed fact. "In part, Mario and his father have done a very good job of showing our history," says David Hilliard, former Panther chief of staff. "But the characterization of Bobby Seale being dominant over Huey Newton is certainly a reversal of history. Unfortunately, most of the people in the party leadership who could have helped are on my project." Hilliard, you see, is working with Seale on their own film for Warner Bros. These days Panther adversaries don't have shootouts, they have rival development deals with movie studios.

It's one more proof that sooner or later, everything is show biz—fodder for the great infotainment maw of gossip, nostalgia and exploitation. An ad for the movie's sound track announces: "The Panthers had a calling. Now, so do you. Call 1-800-8-PANTHER to win $1,000 instantly in the Panther 'Power to the People' Sweepstakes." As for Horowitz, his potent grievances have been so well publicized that Mario Van Peebles grouses, "He must have a bigger promotion budget than our film does."

As Melvin Van Peebles advises, "The movie is a Rorschach test. Your perception of the past completely colors the way the movie strikes you." No doubt. But in offering the Panthers as idealists and objects of veneration to today's youth, the movie surely stands guilty of criminal naiveté. What's the politically correct term for whitewash?

VILLAGE VOICE, 5/9/95, p. 67, J. Hoberman

Mario Van Peebles's *Panther* follows Spike Lee's *Malcolm X* in celluloid '60s replay as the real Black Panthers followed the actual Malcolm. Still, the current post-Oklahoma City, militia-obsessed, FBI-friendly climate gives Van Peebles's down-home celebration of earlier political outlaws an unexpected relevance. The movie's print ad, in which a clenched black fist towers over a toppling state capitol building, is half of Timothy McVeigh's alleged wet dream.

Panther opens as close to May Day as commercial release patterns will permit and, directed by Van Peebles from a script by his father Melvin, it's cautiously incendiary and mildly revisionist. Invoking the muse of docudrama with the requisite images of Martin, Malcolm, and JFK, as well as a newsreel montage of beatings and riots set to James Brown gutbucket funk, the movie is proudly, loudly chaotic—an act of media mythmaking enlivened by all manner of factoids, cameos, and extra-textual cross-references. For all the variously compressed points of view that *Panther* represents, Van Peebles remains constant to the aesthetic of the hectic jumble.

Van Peebles doesn't romanticize the Panthers; he treats them, fondly, as legendary ancestors—a lost breed of two-fisted social workers, revolutionary martyrs, and anti-authoritarian daredevils. The Panthers' unprecedented capacity for confronting the virtually all-white, famously brutal Oakland police was the bedrock of their popular appeal. The cops in *Panther* are so monstrous they attack even a peaceful, church-led prayer vigil for the child victim of an automobile accident. The street is abuzz when, armed mainly with his knowledge of the law, Huey P. Newton faces them down.

Featuring non-stars Marcus Chong and Courtney B. Vance in the roles of BPP founders Newton and Bobby Seale, with stand-up comic Anthony Griffith as their distinguished recruit Eldridge Cleaver, *Panther* dramatizes a number of key incidents from the party's early history—addressing *Malcolm X* as much as the actual period. Acting as bodyguards for Betty Shabazz (played by Angela Bassett, who now owns the part) on a visit to San Francisco, the Panthers successfully out-posture a rival Afrocentric group and attract Cleaver to their ranks, Buying Mao's little red book in bulk from a Chinatown store, they establish their Third World-ist credentials as well as their entrepreneurial smarts by hawking marked-up copies to white students on the Berkeley campus, then use the proceeds to buy guns from a sympathetic Japanese revolutionary.

Masters of the semiotic guerrilla warfare that characterized the '60s, the Panthers not only furnished the so-called Revolution with a designated vanguard but a number of catchphrases, slogans, and pin-ups. The Panther uniform invented by Newton conflated the French resistance-fighter's military beret, the Communist organizer's leather jacket, the hipster's shades and goatee, and the Westerner's carbine. That the BPP's chosen nemesis was California governor Ronald Reagan only enhanced their showbiz aura—although the BPP's was a theatrical performance that courted and included real death.

Although harder to merchandise than Malcolm, in part because they managed to project themselves beyond the ghetto of cultural nationalism, the Panthers seem ripe for revival. Hugh Pearson's critical but not unsympathetic 1994 history, *The Shadow of the Panther*, has been followed by reissues of Philip Foner's *The Black Panthers Speak* and Huey Newton's *To Die for the People*. (Later this month, a new play by Arthur Laurents reconfigures the famous New York fundraising party for the Panther 21 that provided Tom Wolfe with the essence of "radical chic.")

In a better world, Pearson's book would serve as the basis for a long Lanzmann-style documentary-meditation on the BPP's rise and fall. In this one, the Van Peebles *père* and *fils* have concocted a fictional narrative that reinscribes certain blaxploitation conventions back into the tale of those bad muthafuckas and their female cohorts who would be superceded by the imaginary exploits of Shaft, Superfly, Slaughter, Hammer, and Cleopatra Jones. Back from the Nam, disillusioned vet Judge (TV star Kadeem Hardison) is recruited first by the Panthers and then, as an informant by a local cop (Joe Don Baker) who is himself reporting back to the FBI—immediately interested, as well they might be, in a street-smart black revolutionary socialist party with ties to the international left.

Panther takes pains both to explicate the FBI's illegal COINTELPRO operation directed against the BPP and, if rather less, explicate the role of women and sexism as well as the sometimes fatal power struggles within the party itself. Van Peebles stages Newton's October 1967 shoot-out with the Oakland cops for maximum ambiguity and action pow (this is, after all, the moment of the Barrow Gang), but the murder of Bobby Hutton stands in for a series of often defenseless Panthers gunned down by police across America. You be the Judge. The worst of the white devils, J. Edgar Hoover, orders the "ultimate contingency" and floods the ghetto with cheap smack. Indeed, the most significant mythmaking may be the attribution of Newton and the Panthers' own drug involvement to an FBI-Mafia conspiracy.

Twenty-four years ago, Newton devoted an entire issue of the party journal, *The Black Panther*, to his detailed exegesis of *Sweet Sweetback's Baadasssss Song*. Now Melvin Van Peebles returns the favor. Still, however admiring, *Panther* is by no means hagiographic. Marcus Chong, himself a son of the counterculture, could hardly be said to dominate the screen. Slight as he is, Chong often seems physically overshadowed by events. The movie presents Newton as brilliant and fearless, but also unstable, manipulative, and increasingly paranoid. In its way, *Panther* critiques the Great Man theory of history (and filmmaking) implicit in *Malcolm X*. The BPP is shown to emerge organically, even collectively, out of a particular moment and milieu.

Climaxing with an instance of absurd B-movie triumph, the Van Peebles team only alludes to the Panthers' subsequent devolution into a street gang. (It's as if the page has turned in the comic book of history.) *Panther* opens, like an urban riot, with a car running down a child at a dangerous Oakland intersection. It ends on a self-deprecating diminuendo. "Well, we finally got the stoplight." Yes indeed, and the movie too.

Also reviewed in:
CHICAGO TRIBUNE, 5/3/95, Tempo/p. 24, Michael Wilmington
NEW YORK TIMES, 5/3/95, p. C18, Janet Maslin
VARIETY, 5/1-7/95, p. 35, Todd McCarthy
WASHINGTON POST, 5/3/95, p. C1, Rita Kempley
WASHINGTON POST, 5/5/95, Weekend/p. 49, Desson Howe

PARTY GIRL

A First Look Pictures release of a Party Pictures production. *Producer:* Harry Birckmayer and Stephanie Koules. *Director:* Daisy von Scherler Mayer. *Screenplay:* Daisy von Scherler Mayer and Harry Birckmayer. *Story:* Daisy von Scherler Mayer, Harry Birckmayer, and Sheila Gaffney. *Director of Photography:* Michael Slovis. *Editor:* Cara Silverman. *Music:* Anton Sanko. *Sound:* Antonio Arroyo. *Casting:* Candice Sinclair. *Production Designer:* Kevin Thompson. *Set Decorator:* Jennifer Baime. *Costumes:* Michael Clancy. *Running time:* 98 minutes. *MPAA Rating:* R.

CAST: Parker Posy (Mary); Omar Townsend (Mustafa); Sasha von Scherler (Judy Lindendorf); Guillermo Diaz (Leo); Anthony DeSando (Derrick); Donna Mitchell (Rene); Liev Schreiber (Nigel); Nicole Bobbitt (Venus).

LOS ANGELES TIMES, 6/9/95, Calendar/p. 8, Peter Rainer

Mary (Parker Posey), the party girl of "Party Girl," is the Gen X Holly Golightly of the Manhattan club scene. She's a camp diva who carries her club cool with her like a portable ornament. Her deadpan and the sonorous flatness of her voice are put-ons—and put-downs too.

Unlike most of the Hollywood Gen X movies, "Party Girl" actually looks as if it were made from the inside. It's addled and inconsequential, but at least it's not condescending. Director Daisy von Scherler Mayer and her co-screenwriter Harry Birckmayer don't get all anthropological about the club scene; they don't film it as if they were dropping in on Mars.

They also don't overvalue what they're showing us. "Party Girl" has the courage of its own no-braininess.

Posey takes some getting used to. Her bubbliness isn't particularly infectious; it's more like a piece of pop art. And her funkiness is blanker than blank. A little of her voguing goes a long way, but Posey varies the rhythms of her act. Mary is a party girl who works days as a library clerk, and she has her epiphany when, flying high, she files books at night and boogies about the stacks. The Dewey Decimal system for her is like some ancient code; it's a code she finally breaks, and it opens up her life. In a flash of inspiration, she arranges the record-album collection of her deejay roommate (Guillermo Diaz). (He thinks she's gone bonkers.) She becomes the library's No. 1 helpmate.

The melting pot world of this movie, with its wraparound soundtrack of hip-hop and funk, is pleasantly checkerboard. Mary is hooked on a Lebanese falafel vendor (Omar Townsend), her roommate is Latino, her best friend (Anthony DeSando) is gay. The club scene is heavily black. What's original about Mary's coming-of-age saga is that she ends up the quintessential good girl but with a twist. She's "good" in the same way that she's "bad." It's all a performance, a pose.

Will librarians forever have their image changed by this film? Will the literacy rate rise? Don't count on it.

NEW YORK POST, 6/9/95, p. 33, Thelma Adams

Have Wonderbra, will travel. That's Parker Posey, who pulls on the title role of "Party Girl"—a downtown club kitten named Mary—like a pair of blue satin elbow gloves. On the slim, sly brunette both part and gloves—and the Wonderbra—are a perfect fit.

Posey stole scenes as the bitchy Darla in Richard Linklater's "Dazed and Confused" and a blase squatter in Hal Hartley's "Amateur."

With her skinny frame, angular face and pasty skin, she's not a chip off the 90210, exchangeable beauty block. She takes what she has—an inefffable smile, an extravagant neo-Salvation Army style, an ability to make a fashion statement by the mere part of her hair—and she works it.

And now Posey emerges from "Party Girl" a star, a "Funny Face" for the '90s. There's nothing plastic about her. The actress is frothy, sexy, smart and has wicked comic timing.

Co-written by Harry Birckmayer and Daisy von Scherler Mayer, who also made her directorial debut, the "Party Girl" story couldn't be simpler. At 24 Mary has fab friends, a great wardrobe, a nightlife to die for—and no future.

"I don't have a job. I'm a loser. So shoot me," Mary tells her godmother Judy (Sasha von Scherler, the director's mother). Librarian Judy does the unthinkable: She offers Mary a gig shelving books.

The rest of the movie plots Mary's belated coming-of-age, her transformation from gaga downtown diva to responsible citizen. If the script, though witty, is short on surprises and the plot squeaks at every turn, it's a small price to pay for a film this effervescent and good-natured.

NEWSDAY, 6/9/95, Part II/p. B5, John Anderson

Parker Posey, best known thus far as the despotic high-school senior of "Dazed and Confused" and for drop-in roles as soap sirens and slacker sluts, is going to be big.

Ask anyone. Why? Because her screen personality is deliciously split: Exuding vulnerability and disdain in equally generous doses, she is simultaneously adorable and irritating, the human equivalent of a particularly captivating TV commercial.

So what does Parker Posey mean? Perhaps nothing, which would make her the "It" Girl of the '90s—"It" being attitude in search of ideas (or even values, to use an oft-abused word). But Posey does seem to embody something youthful and ungainly and caught on the fence between ennui and hope. Which also makes her perfect as "Party Girl."

Daisy von Scherler Mayer's lighter-than-nitrous-oxide confection starts out as a celebration of downtown hedonism, segues into an old-fashioned redemption fable, and finally laughs up its sleeve, lest anyone take its sincerity seriously. As the archetypically named Mary, Posey is a kind of post-backlash feminist backslider, as well as a born hustler—when her illegal loft party is busted, she tells the Asian-American cop it's a benefit for the "United Coalition for the Children of Chinatown." She's also a fashion slave with a progressively retro sensibility—her closets are full of vintage and designer clothing and HATS—and she's looking for love, in all the wrong places. The right place is, in keeping with the movie's forthright sense of prescribed unpredictability, a falafel stand.

Between shifts at the local library where she clerks for her ragingly menopausal godmother, Judy (Sasha von Scherler), Mary meets Mustafa (charismatic newcomer Omar Townsend), who in Lebanon was a teacher but on Houston Street sells babaganoush. His erudition sparks something in her, including a revelation: For all her late-night know-how and wide network of acquaintances, she basically knows nothing. So the queen of the clubs becomes a convert to knowledge, with the convert's single-mindedness and drive.

For all its ultra-hip accoutrements—which include the buoyant supporting cast of Scherler, Guillermo Diaz, Anthony DeSando and Donna Mitchell—"Party Girl" unfolds like the most standard of standard melodramas: Misguided heroine sees error of her ways and turns over new leaf, but then has to contend with the biases and past impressions of the as-yet-unconvinced.

These include Judy, who fails to recognize the depth of Mary's bibliographical passion, and Mustafa, who compares her interest in him with "traveling to a foreign country without having to buy an airplane ticket:" But Mary is sincere—as sincere as anything here is supposed to be. Calling "Party Girl" insubstantial, of course, would be like buying a big vat of extra creamy, super-smooth, blended, whipped vanilla pudding and complaining that there aren't any lumps.

VILLAGE VOICE, 6/13/95, p. 60, Gary Dauphin

As familiar and cutely inconsequential as a visit to your favorite (and DJ'd) downtown bar, *Party Girl* isn't so much a portrait of New York nightlife as it is the listings version. Her Houston-to-Canal playground notwithstanding, Mary (*Dazed and Confused*'s Parker Posey) is your basic twentysomething slacker chick, only decked out here in ample *Paper/Interview* magazine attitude and Betsy Johnson-esque gear, a house mix spinning in the background. Strategically stocked with pre-chewed New York types the way Mary's clothing rack is *très* stocked with styles, *Party Girl*'s main action involves putting Mary through a variety of rent-and romance-related paces. Jobless and with no marketable skills, Mary begs employ as a library clerk from her aunt ("Librarians have master's degrees," Auntie tries to explain), partying by night with her Latin DJ roommate Leo (Guillermo Diaz, doing a nice turn channeling early John Leguizamo). Along the way Mary takes a liking for Mustafa (Omar Townsend)—a falafel-stand jockey—and before you can say "like white on couscous," Mary is doing a cappella renditions of Rai songs, visions of a shirtless Mustafa dancing in her head.

Too cheerful to pursue the *Looking for Mr. Goodbar* anxieties that the librarian-by-day/diva-by-night scenario might provide, *Party Girl* instead sends Mary on a soul search for her responsible side, setting the Dewey decimal system up as her climactic and comic antagonist. First-time director von Scherler Mayer has a good feel for comic pacing and Posey is a cool spark plug of post-everything white-girl energy, but *Party Girl* is less fun than I'd hoped it would be. The film has lots of insider touches—The Lady Bunny makes an opening cameo—but it's still much more of a *9 to 5* workplace comedy than it is a club-life *After Hours*.

Also reviewed in:
CHICAGO TRIBUNE, 7/7/95, Friday/p. H, Michael Wilmington
NEW YORK TIMES, 6/9/95, p. C17, Stephen Holden
VARIETY, 1/23-29/95, p. 72, Todd McCarthy
WASHINGTON POST, 9/8/95, p. F7, Hal Hinson
WASHINGTON POST, 9/8/95, Weekend/p. 44, Desson Howe

PATHER PANCHALI

A Sony Pictures Classics release. *Producer:* Satyajet Ray. *Director:* Satyajet Ray. *Screenplay:* Satyajet Ray. *Based on the novel by:* Bibhuti Bhushan Bandapaddhay. *Director of Photography:* Sabrata Mitra. *Editor:* Dulal Dutta. *Music:* Ravi Shankar. *Art Director:* Banshi Gupda. *Running time:* 112 minutes. *MPAA Rating:* Not Rated.

CAST: Kanu Banerjee (Harihar, the Father); Karuna Banerjee (Sarbojaya, the Mother); Uma Das Gupta (Durga, as a Young Girl); Runki Banerjee (Durga, as a Child); Subir Banerjee (Apu); Chunibala Devi (Old Aunt); Reva Devi (Mrs. Mukerjee); Rama Gangopadhaya (Ranu Mukerjee, her Daughter); Tulshi Chakraborty (Schoolmaster); Harimoran Nag (Doctor).

FILMS IN REVIEW, 7-8/95, p. 59, Andy Pawelczak

Pather Panchali (Song of The Little Road) inaugurated Satyajit Ray's distinguished career. Released in 1955, the film had an immediate worldwide success, winning a special jury prize at the 1956 Cannes Festival, and was followed up by the equally renowned *Aparajito* (1956) and *The World Of Apu* (1959), the three films comprising the "Apu Trilogy." A restored print financed in part by the Merchant/Ivory Foundation allows us to see Pather as it was meant to be seen and to reassess Ray's cinematic art.

To begin with, the print, though not flawless, is luminously beautiful and points up Ray's fascination with light. The shots of people wandering through a shimmering, dappled forest integrate man and nature in a pastoralism reminiscent of Jean Renoir with whom Ray worked in 1950 on *The River*. The repeated shots of water also recall Renoir; in one extended sequence, the camera fixes on dragonflies dancing across a lotus pond to the accompaniment of Ravi Shankar's sitar improvisations on the soundtrack. Ray's lyrical abstractions aren't mere mood setting decor; the lotus pond sequence, for example, represents in a concrete image a woman's sense of relief after receiving a letter from her long absent husband. In another sequence, two children follow a rotund candy vendor down a forest path, and a shot of their reflections in a pond somehow captures all the poignancy of childhood and lost time.

The film has a loose, episodic structure, partly derived from Italian neorealism, particularly De Sica's *The Bicycle Thief*, which deeply impressed the young Ray. It tells the story of an impoverished Bengal family over a period of several years. By contemporary movie standards, nothing much happens, and if you come to this film for the first time you may be put off by its leisurely, meandering pace. There are a birth, two deaths, a woman's humiliating struggle with poverty, a child's slow coming-to-awareness of the world. The film has been described with such adjectives as universal, timeless, humanistic, but much of its power comes from the specificity and accuracy of its details. The acting isn't so much acting as it is a kind of being-before-the-camera, if you'll forgive the Germanic neologism. A few glances and a stray caress from the mother tell us that the boy-child is the hope of the family, and the father's addiction to tobacco conveys worlds about his ineffectual dreaminess. Some of the best scenes involve a toothless crone who is irredeemably alive right up to her last breath. The children's discovery of her body in the forest is one of the great moments in world cinema.

But the film is full of indelible images: the crumbling family compound, half gone back to nature, which looks like a cottage in a fairy tale; the old crone smearing guava paste on her mouth, watched by the wide-eyed young girl, Durga; the tragic expression on the mother's face as she cradles her dead daughter on her lap; the child Apu's first look at a train in which you can feel the tug of distance and mystery (it's significant that Durga trips and doesn't see it—she will die, and Apu will go to Benares and become a man of the city). In her review of another Ray film, *Devi*, Pauline Kael wrote: "Like Renoir and De Sica, Ray sees that life itself is good no matter how bad it is. It is difficult to discuss art which is an affirmation of life, without fear of becoming maudlin. But is there any other kind of art, on screen or elsewhere?" To use an unfashionable word, *Pather Panchali* is a beautiful film, and I'm grateful to the Merchant/Ivory Foundation for producing this print.

VILLAGE VOICE, 4/11/95, p. 51, J. Hoberman

Pather Panchali, the 1955 masterpiece that launched Satyajit Ray's career and, newly restored and resubtitled, inaugurates the rerelease of nine features by the Bengali master, is a serene heart-wrencher.

Propelled by Ray's death (and deathbed Oscar) in 1992, *Pather Panchali* was for the first time listed in *Sight and Sound's* once-a-decade critics' poll of the 10 greatest films. It was not always so regarded. The story of a poor, Brahmin family in rural Bengal was described, in its initial *New*

York Times review by Bosley Crowther, as "a rambling and random tour of an Indian village ... a baffling mosaic of candid and crude domestic scenes."

Indeed, *Pather Panchali* is less a linear-narrative than a series of rhyming incidents—arrivals and departures, both cosmic and mundane—which continually dissolve into the underlying spectacle of the natural world. A dreamy poet, and sometime Hindu priest, periodically goes to the city in search of work, leaving his anxious, practical wife in charge of two big-eyed children-10-year-old Durga and her younger brother, Apu—as well as the toothless, bent crone they call Auntie. The family's ramshackle courtyard and the forest that surrounds their dusty village are the perimeters of a cruel Eden in which nothing much happens. The wind moves in the trees, the weather changes, itinerant entertainers come to town, meals are prepared, and people die—disappearing as if into the depths of the lily-choked pool in the forest beyond the house.

The inevitability of death in *Pather Panchali* is all the more affecting for the archetypal vividness of the movie's characters. A maddeningly selfish and useless creature, Auntie is the personification of pure, heedless Being. Her decrepit vitality is matched by the intensity of Durga's hunger for fruit pilfered from a neighbor's garden, for candy and gewgaws and pure sensation. When a monsoon arrives, the girl runs outside in the rain, her upturned face drinking in the experience.

Although Apu is the protagonist of *Pather Panchali*'s two sequels, *Aparajito* and *The World of Apu*, he is here largely an observer—watching kittens play in the courtyard, running to see the train to Calcutta roar through a field, absorbing his mother's shame at their poverty, taking in the accusations leveled against the sister he has displaced from the family center. Still, Durga is the film's soul—she, it's been said, has to steal life itself.

Born in 1921 into a distinguished literary family, Ray was first an enthusiast. He confounded a Calcutta film society and was inspired to become a filmmaker after seeing *The Bicycle Thief*, Vittorio De Sica's neorealist account of a poor Rome family. In 1949, Ray met neorealism's most important precursor, Jean Renoir, who was in Calcutta shooting *The River*; Ray helped Renoir scout locations. Renoir, who had extensive experience working outside the French film industry, encouraged the young graphic designer to make his own film.

Ray spent nearly two years trying to raise money for *Pather Panchali*, which, although adapted from a popular 1928 novel, was deemed so uncommercial a project as to be beyond comprehension. (Ray was not the only would-be independent in Bengal; Ritwik Ghatak, the tormented filmmaker unfairly eclipsed by Ray's subsequent prominence, was already in the midst of his never released first feature.) Finally cashing in his life insurance, Ray plunged in. He assembled his cast, few of whom had any prior screen experience, and went on location—shooting on weekends for the better part of a year until he ran out of money. His 4000-foot rough cut generated no interest. Time was against him: Durga and Apu were growing up, Auntie (a former stage actress living in Calcutta's red-light district) was an octogenarian who needed a daily dose of opium to get through her scenes.

Shooting had again been suspended when, almost by chance, a curator from the Museum of Modern Art heard about *Pather Panchali*, saw the footage, and enthusiastically offered a venue for the finished film. Around the same time, a sympathetic government minister got wind of the project and provided state funds to complete the movie. After struggling for nearly four years, Ray suddenly had six months to deliver the completed project. To make the MOMA deadline, he and his editor virtually moved into the film lab. In a burst of virtuosity, Ravi Shankar composed and recorded the trilling, rolling score—at once plaintive and exhilarating—in an all-night session.

Ray had yet to see the finished film, which was shipped without subtitles and screened in New York in the spring of 1955 as *The Story of Apu and Durga* for a small but enthusiastic audience. *Pather Panchali* opened in Calcutta that summer to word-of-mouth success. Overcoming opposition from both state and national governments (in part because Prime Minister Nehru was enlisted to its cause), *Pather Panchali* was shown at Cannes in 1956 where, despite some hostility on the jury, the movie won a special award.

In its vicissitudes and ultimate triumph, *Pather Panchali* is also the quintessential indie production. John Cassavetes's similarly hand-to-mouth *Shadows* was already shooting when Ray's film opened commercially in September 1958 at the Fifth Avenue Cinema. For some it seemed all but underground. The director "provides ample indication that this is his first professional motion picture job," *The New York Times* complained. "Any picture as loose in structure or as listless in tempo as this one is would barely pass for a rough cut in Hollywood."

From start to finish, *Pather Panchali* was unlike anything produced in the commercial Indian cinema. Not only were there no stars, there was no romance, no singing, no dancing—Ray used the original score only as background. Even the *Times* noted the absence of sentimentality.

All exteriors were shot on location, but *Pather Panchali* was no more cinema vérité than Ray himself was an aesthetic primitive. Calcutta, the capital of the British raj, gave the Bengali intelligentsia a unique vantage point; Ray continued the fusion of Eastern and Western art forms associated with his family friend, Rabindranath Tagore. *Pather Panchali's* performers were mainly professionals; only the smaller roles are played by actual villagers. What the movie did was to immerse neorealism in the flow of life, documenting the sophisticated city dweller Ray's discovery of rural Bengal. Unlike his subsequent movies, *Pather Panchali* never had a proper script. Ray worked from a treatment and the sketches he had shown producers.

As long as *Pather Panchali* took to complete, it retains a powerful spontaneity. This quality is unique to Ray's first film; his subsequent features are far more conventionally skilled, nuanced, and detached. Still, although a recent tribute to Ray published by Michael Sragow in *The Atlantic Monthly* posits Steven Spielberg as heir to the Renoir—Ray tradition of "luminous observation," none of these later films are exactly a *Temple of Doom*.

Pather Panchali is fascinating for its pragmatic use of linking dissolves and offscreen space. Ray's somewhat studied compositions—his characteristic two-shot has one performer face the camera while listening to another who looks away—are given texture by the splotched emulsion and mismatched film stocks. To some Indian observers, *Pather Panchali* seemed a regression to silent cinema. Ray used close-ups to show reactions while dubbing his post-synchronized dialogue over long shots and cutaways.

Thus, *Pather Panchali* is not only the paradigmatic independent and last masterpiece of neorealism, it's also a model for that "imperfect cinema" extolled in the late '60s by Cuban cultural theorist Julio Garcia Espinosa—the new Third World film practice that "can be created equally well with a Mitchell or with an 8mm camera ... no longer interested in predetermined taste, and much less 'good' taste." With his skillfully unmatched compositions and suggestively elliptical editing, tricky sound bridges and understated dramatics, intuitive structure and humble subject matter, Ray made a formal virtue out of necessity.

While commercial movies were by definition opulent, *Pather Panchali* was, almost shockingly, concerned with hunger. (One recent critic, born in Guyana and experiencing firsthand the shock of recognition, counted 47 incidents that revolved around food.)

As lyrical as *Pather Panchali* was, as uninsistent as its flow of imagery can be, as steeped as it is in random existence, no movie has ever been more concerned with physical survival.

Also reviewed in:
NEW YORK TIMES, 9/23/58, p. 37, Bosley Crowther

PEBBLE AND THE PENGUIN, THE

A Metro-Goldwyn-Mayer Pictures release of a Don Bluth Ireland Limited production. *Executive Producer:* James Butterworth. *Producer:* Russell Boland. *Screenplay:* Rachel Koretsky and Steve Whitestone. *Editor:* Thomas V. Moss. *Music:* Barry Manilow. *Music Editor:* Dominick Certo. *Choreographer:* Kevin Carlisle. *Production Designer:* David Goetz. *Special Effects:* David Tidgwell. *Running time:* 74 minutes. *MPAA Rating:* G.

VOICES: Shani Wallis (Narrator); Scott Bullock (Chubby/Gentoo); Martin Short (Hubie); Annie Golden (Marina); Louise Vallance (Priscilla/Chinstrap 2); Pat Musick (Pola/Chinstrap 1); Angeline Ball (Gwynne/Chinstrap 3); Kendall Cunningham (Timmy); Alissa King (Petra); Michael Nunes (Beany); Tim Curry (Drake); Neil Ross (Scrawny); Philip Clarke (King); B.J. Ward (Magellenic 1); Hamilton Camp (Magellenic 2); Will Ryan (Royal); Scott Bullock (Gentoo); Stanley Jones (McCallister); James Belushi (Rocko); Will Ryan (Tika).

LOS ANGELES TIMES, 4/12/95, Calendar/p. 1, Kevin Thomas

"The Pebble and the Penguin" is pure enchantment, a beguiling animated fantasy of assured style, boasting some rousing new songs by Barry Manilow and Bruce Sussman and the aptly cast, highly expressive voice talents of Martin Short, James Belushi, Tim Curry and Annie Golden.

Narrated by Shani Wallis, this charmer for all ages from veteran animator Don Bluth's company is all of a piece.

Rachel Koretsky and Steve Whitestone's screenplay turns up a penguin mating ritual in which a male penguin presents a pebble to a female penguin: If she accepts, they're mated for life. The shy, timid Hubie (Short) comes up with a gorgeous, emerald-like gem to place before the beautiful, demure Marina (Golden), but before we can discover whether she'll accept, the looming, villainous penguin Drake (Curry) has propelled Hubie into a journey that takes him all the way from the Antarctica to Bounty Island in the South Seas.

How will Hubie ever get back in time to give Marina the jewel by the time of the Full Moon Ceremony? And if Marina should refuse Drake she will be banished!

For Bluth's formidable team of artists and technicians, the writers have come up with a series of terrific confidence-building adventures for Hubie and his hearty, stalwart new pal, Rocko (Belushi), a Rockhopper penguin with a topknot and fierce eyebrows.

The penguins and other animals are drawn in the straightforward Disney style, but what's such a plus are the film's simple yet elegant stylized backgrounds that make an imaginative use of pure, clean colors and give the film a crucial contemporary feel.

Manilow and Sussman have written a love song, an anthem in the full-bodied Manilow manner, "Sometimes I Wonder," which could become a cabaret standard as well as part of Manilow's concert repertoire. For Drake they've come up with the suitably menacing "Don't Make Me Laugh," which makes full use of Curry's penchant for comic evil, and there's a jaunty song-and-dance tune for Hubie and Rocko, "Looks Like I Got a Friend." Rounding out this animation winner is Mark Watters' lively, romantic score.

NEW YORK POST, 4/12/95, p. 35, Michael Medved

"The Pebble and the Penguin" is one of those pleasant, well-intentioned G-rated animated movies full of pretty colors and hummable tunes (by Barry Manilow), but with a story line so flimsy, and characters so grotesque and unappealing, that it leaves its audience out in the Antarctic cold.

The plot, such as it is, was inspired by the curious real-life mating ritual of the Adelie Penguins. Upon reaching adulthood, the male of the species searches for a pebble and presents it to the penguinette of his choice. If she picks up the rock, they than mate for life.

In the movie, a shy, overweight bird named Hubie (the voice of Martin Short) wants to stone a pretty little number named Marina (the voice of Annie Golden), but she's also pursued by the puffed-up, villainous penguin, Drake (the voice of Tim Curry).

You know he's not a suitable match for the heroine because he looks nothing at all like a penguin (or any other sort of animal on the planet) and, in fact, vaguely resembles Disney's "Big Bad Wolf," complete with sharp teeth inside his beak.

In any event, Drake hurls his soft-spoken rival Hubie into the sea, where he's picked up by "The Good Ship Misery," taking assorted caged penguin species to imprisonment in zoos. Naturally, he escapes (with the aid of a raffish Rockhopper Penguin played by the voice of Jim Belushi) and the rest of the movie depicts his attempts to get back home in time to prevent Marina's marriage to the dastardly Drake.

The animation (by Don Bluth's preternaturally productive Irish film factory) is smooth and accomplished, and at times—especially when portraying hungry killer whales who want to munch on a penguin lunch—it's downright impressive.

These ornery Orcas are so frightening and formidable, in fact, that they may instantly erase years of benign "Save the Whales" propaganda aimed at our kids.

Unfortunately, the penguins themselves are much less life-like than their enemies in the natural struggle for survival; the artists are so desperate to make Hubie the hero engaging and adorable, in fact, that they have to rely on equipping him with a funny hat with ear flaps. Attempts at witty dialogue ("Goodness glaciers!" or "Wake up and smell the seaweed!") seem similarly forced.

It doesn't help that nearly all the movie plays itself out against icy, surreal Antarctic backdrops that quickly become monotonous, despite the animators efforts to tint them with shifting colors.

Since leaving the Disney stable in 1979 and setting up his own operation, Don Bluth has achieved a decidedly mixed record of success, pleasing audiences with "An American Tail" and "The Land Before Time" (both coproduced with Steven Spielberg, and striking out with "All Dogs Go to Heaven," "Rock-a-Doodle," last year's abysmal "A Troll in Central Park" and many others.

His experience reminds us that Walt Disney's true genius never involved his drawing ability; it centered on his status as the best story editor in the business. In this arena, Bluth definitely needs help, since it's the writing above all that leaves "Pebble" on the rocks.

NEWSDAY, 4/12/95, Part II/p. B2, Jack Mathews

Nature dealt a series of cruel blows to the penguins of Antarctica's Adelie Coast. Not only were the little birds given no means of flight and then sequestered in the coldest place on Earth, but the males and females were made to look so alike in size and appearance that the "Me Tarzan, You Jane" courtship ritual of most animal species was rendered impossible.

To make up for that procreational design flaw, nature gave the Adelie penguins another way to find each other. Males pick up pebbles and offer them to females. If the females accept, the honeymoon is on. This is also done with small stones in Beverly Hills.

That real-life ritual provided the inspiration for Don Bluth's "The Pebble and the Penguin," an animated musical fairy tale about one lovesick penguin's attempt to present his precious pebble to the bird of his dreams before the Full Moon Ceremony that kicks off the annual mating season.

Would that the movie were as imaginative as the actual ritual. Bluth's Dublin-based animators have done a superb job of visualizing and drawing the story, but writers Rachel Koretsky and Steve Whitestone didn't come up with enough compelling events, characters, romance or humor to hold it together for children or their parents for 75 minutes. And the songs written by Barry Manilow and Bruce Sussman offer little musical relief.

Hubie (voice of Martin Short) is a lovable enough hero, a shy, stammering romantic who's fallen for a beauty already picked out by the rookery's reigning bully, Drake (Tim Curry). When Drake realizes that Marina (Annie Golden) prefers the gentle Hubie to him, he sets Hubie adrift in an angry sea populated by leopard seals, killer whales and human penguin-nappers.

Most of the film is taken up by Hubie's adventures on the high seas and his relationship with Rocko (James Belushi), the crabby penguin with whom he shares a seemingly endless series of repetitious escapes and a few corny duets. Hubie drops his magic green pebble in harm's way so many times I was wishing the animators had drawn the poor guy a belly purse.

Will Hubie and Rocko become friends? Will they find their way back to Antarctica? Will Hubie learn to defend himself and stand up to Drake, and will Rocko fulfill his dream of flying? The answers are not as satisfying as they should be, and young children may be too frightened by the scary underwater chases to care.

"The Pebble and the Penguin" is a Disney wannabe that has the look of Disney and the wit of Hanna-Barbera. Every cell is a framable piece of art, and the action sequences move with the grace of "The Lion King." But "Pebble" doesn't come close to meeting the expectations set by Disney's latest run of animated musicals, and given that studio's franchise on the medium, you have to wonder if it would make any difference if it did.

SIGHT AND SOUND, 3/96, p. 49, Nick James

Hubie, a shy and awkward penguin, is in love with Marina and so he must find a shapely stone to present to her as part of the full-moon mating ritual. After a day squabbling over pebbles he wishes for the perfect stone. Out of the sky crashes a meteorite, leaving a small gemlike rock in its crater. But Hubie is assaulted by the evil Drake, who wants Marina for himself. He falls into the ocean and narrowly escapes a killer whale by clambering onto an iceberg which is swept away.

The crew of a ship called Misery catch Hubie and throw him in the hold with other penguins. They are soon joined by the fierce Rocko who is determined to escape. Hubie and Rocko get away and are washed ashore on a south seas island where Rocko mocks Hubie's determination to get back home. He confesses to Hubie his dream of learning to fly. Hubie says he has a friend back home who has managed to fly and so Rocko agrees to accompany Hubie.

After a run-in with a seal, in which Hubie shows his bravery, Rocko teaches him how to fight and Hubie confesses that the flying-friend story was a ruse. They are attacked by killer whales. Hubie escapes but there's no sign of Rocko or the pebble. Drake has kidnapped Marina. Hubie challenges him to fight but is immediately knocked unconscious. He revives, fights ferociously and Drake falls into a chasm. Rocko turns up alive with the pebble. Drake reappears but causes his lair to crumble on top of himself. Hubie, Marina and Rocko are falling to their doom when Rocko begins to fly and saves them all. Hubie presents Marina with the pebble, which she accepts.

The Pebble and the Penguin takes its keynote from the Barry Manilow songs that pepper its narrative: like them the film smoothly follows a routine structure, is full of naggingly familiar borrowings and sticks rigidly to the conventions of its genre. Forced away from home to suffer several trials of fortitude, Hubie the shy penguin returns to get his girl and win the day. This may look like a simple folktale, but in practice it is something more desperate. Hubie never has to convince Marina to admire him, and Drake, his adversary, stays out of the storyline for the bulk of it. With so little narrative drive to the love story, the film has no emotional core and it struggles for effective diversionary moments to match the genius of so many recent Disney animated classics. (Compared to this film, *Beauty and the Beast, Aladdin* and even *Pocahontas* are works of genius). Drake is a lacklustre version of *Beauty and the Beast*'s Gaston, Rocko, an aerially-inclined Dumbo in disguise and Marina, an analogue of any number of simpering cartoon damsels.

Yet for a film that so relentlessly solicits our sentimental attachment, *The Pebble and the Penguin* looks as if it were designed to depress. The lovers Hubie and Marina are unintentional grotesques, looking, with their splayed beaks and oversized eyes, like savage Otto Dix caricatures of a dope and a dreamboat. Maybe animator Don Bluth was overly concerned to avoid the cutely waddlesome appeal of the penguins in *Mary Poppins*. Certainly there is a manic quality to much of the action that recalls the heyday of *Loony Toons* but it is strangely at odds with Manilow's scoring. The feeling of accidental unease that Bluth's penguins engender is only enhanced by the generally drab colouring of the backgrounds, in particular the ocean sequences—this a film whose transfer to video will be a technological miracle if it manages to avoid creating a murky soup of greys and browns.

Details one probably wouldn't care about if the film was working irritate and nag at the viewer. Why is Drake the only penguin with teeth? Why is he wearing a superman cape? Why would penguins who value smooth round pebbles be suddenly entranced by a chunky gem? Perhaps the biggest disappointment is that the film never lives up to the cheesiness of Manilow's first song 'Now and Forever' which promises a black-tie *Grease* on ice. Instead, *The Pebble and the Penguin* skids all-too-smoothly into anonymity.

Also reviewed in:
CHICAGO TRIBUNE, 4/13/95, Tempo/p. 6, John Petrakis
NEW YORK TIMES, 4/12/95, p. C21, Caryn James
VARIETY, 4/10-16/95, p. 45, Leonard Klady
WASHINGTON POST, 4/13/95, p. C3, Hal Hinson

PEREZ FAMILY, THE

A Samuel Goldwyn Company release of a Samuel Goldwyn Company production. *Executive Producer:* Julia Chasman and Robin Swicord. *Producer:* Michael Nozik and Lydia Dean Pilcher. *Director:* Mira Nair. *Screenplay:* Robin Swicord. *Based on the novel by:* Christine Bell. *Director of Photography:* Stuart Dryburgh. *Editor:* Robert Estrin. *Music:* Alan Silvestri,

Jellybean Benitez, and (traditional music) Arturo Sandoval. *Sound:* Henri Lopez. *Casting:* Billy Hopkins, Suzanne Smith, Kerry Barden, Laura Ekstrand, and Ellen Jacoby. *Production Designer:* Mark Friedberg. *Art Director:* Ken Hardy. *Set Designer:* Michael Delgado. *Set Decorator:* Stephanie Carroll. *Set Dresser:* Skip Shields. *Costumes:* Eduardo Castro. *Make-up:* Hallie D'Amore, Jay Cannistraci, and John Sobeck. *Make-up (Marisa Tomei):* Joanne Gair. *Stunt Coordinator:* John Zimmerman. *Running time:* 112 minutes. *MPAA Rating:* R.

CAST: Alfred Molina (Juan Raul Perez); Marisa Tomei (Dottie); Anjelica Huston (Carmela); Lazaro Perez (Armando Perez); Jose Felipe Padron (Felipe); Diego Wallraff (Angel Diaz); Trini Alvarado (Teresa); Celia Cruz (Luz Paz); Ranjit Chowdhry (Ranjit); Chazz Palminteri (Officer Pirelli); Bill Sage (Steve); Angela Lanza (Flavia); Ellen Cleghorne (Officer Rhoades); Billy Hopkins (Father Aiden); Ruben Rabasa (Father Martinez); Melissa Anne Acosta (Isabel); Jose Manuel Cabrera (Hermaphrodite); Roberto Escobar (Rivera); Norman "Max" Maxwell (Gate Guard); Sarita Choudhury (Josette); Oscar Gonzalez (Old Guajiro #1); Florencio Santana (Old Guajiro #2); Magaly Aguero (Angel's Secretary); Maite Arnedo (T.V. Reporter); Gustavo Laborie (Official); Glenda Diaz-Rigau (Giovanna); Vivian Ruiz (1st Official); Jody Wilson (2nd Official); Clarence Charles (Black Owner); Elodia Riovega (Middle-Aged Mama); Marc MacCauley (Male Volunteer); Eduardo Corbe (News Photographer); Antoni Corone (Security); Jorge Luis Ramone (Young Guard); Bernard Fouquet (Customer, Saks Fith Avenue); Salvador Levy (Middle-Aged Man/Customer); Vincent Gallo (Orlando); Melissa Ramone (Young Carmela); Sandor Juan (Vendor); Mel Gorham (Vilma/Raquel); Luis E. Torres (Guajiro Drummer #1); Angel Gonzalez (Guajiro Drummer #2); Jose Maldonado (Airplane Pilot).

CHRISTIAN SCIENCE MONITOR, 5/12/95, p. 13, David Sterritt

"The Perez Family" is the latest film by Mira Nair, who made her first big film impression on audiences when "Salaam Bombay!" won an Oscar nomination seven years ago.

Less acclaim has greeted her more recent work, but she remains an important screen artist because of the fundamental project underlying her career: to represent the faces, voices, and lives of marginalized people who are overlooked by filmmakers too mindful of commercial pressures.

It's this ambition that led Nair to focus on an Indian street urchin in "Salaam Bombay!" and to center "Mississippi Masala" on the complex relationships between Indian immigrants and their African-American neighbors in a quiet Southern town. Nair was raised in India before moving to the United States, and knows firsthand the difficulties that confront displaced people.

"The Perez Family" looks at another situation spiced with ethnic and cultural complications. It begins during the Mariel boat lift of 1980, which brought a huge influx of unexpected Cuban refugees to Miami's already crowded Little Havana neighborhood.

Among the travelers is Juan, just released from a Cuban prison and eager to reunite with his wife, who came to Florida with their infant daughter two decades earlier. On the same boat is Dottie, a barely reformed prostitute who's convinced her new country will offer sensual pleasures undreamed of by Castro's cronies.

Reaching the shore of Miami is easier than gaining permanent entry, though, and both voyagers find themselves stalled in the stadium where unprocessed arrivals are held. Learning that families have higher priority than individuals, Dottie seizes on a convenient coincidence—she and Juan both have the last name Perez, as do many others in the holding camp—and puts together a phony clan consisting of herself, the reluctant Juan, a scrappy boy designated as their son, and a bewildered grandpa who spends much of his time on trees and rooftops, hoping for a glimpse of the homeland he left behind.

Other characters add more layers to the tale. One is Juan's wife Carmela, long established as a Floridian but still pining for her long-missing husband. Another is her disreputable brother, whose concern for her well-being is rooted in machismo rather than respect. Also present is an Italian-American police officer who finds Carmela as attractive as she is melancholy. Add the colorful background of Little Havana itself, swirling around these follow with nonstop energy, and you have the recipe for Nair's celebration of liveliness, inventiveness, and hopefulness among people facing more than their share of challenges.

What keeps the celebration from being persuasive is Nair's wish to explore more subplots and personality twists than she's prepared to handle. She shows an impressive ability to spin from one interest to another—now studying Juan's loneliness for Carmela, then spying on Dottie's seduction of a friendly cop, suddenly zooming to Carmela's house for her daughter's view of things, and so on. But none of these episodes is developed as fully as it might have been if the film were focused and concentrated, instead of edgy and easily distracted. While its spirits are enjoyably high, its dramatic scenes seem arbitrary, and many comic interludes fall flat.

With these difficulties noted, I'll add that everyone involved deserves the proverbial "A" for effort, starting with Nair, who remains heroically single-minded in her concern for characters rarely given a place on movie screens.

FILMS IN REVIEW, 9-10/95, p. 58, Maria Garcia

Mira Nair's *The Perez Family* resonates with the spirit and energy of the feminine. Not since Ridley Scott's *Thelma and Louise* and Martha Coolidge's *Rambling Rose* have we seen such fully realized women characters in an American film. Although *The Perez Family* features an ensemble cast, Nair manages to create a level of intimacy that endears us to each character, but especially to the women, whose strength and sensuality shape the events of this film.

At the heart of the Perez family—an unrelated group of Cuban immigrants with the same surname—is Dottie (Marisa Tomei), a sensuous Latino earth mother. Dotie organizes the Perez family by adopting Juan Raul (Alfred Molina), a political prisoner, as her husband, and a boy (Jose Felipe Padron) and an older man (Lazaro Perez) as her son and father-in-law, all in order to get assigned as a sponsor-families get placed first. Unlike Juan Raul, whose genteel heritage anchors him in Cuba's past, Dottie's humble background always places her squarely in the present. As soon as she boards the boat for America, she kicks the dust of the sugar cane fields from her high heels, freshens her lipstick, and tells Juan about the first thing she's planning to buy in Florida, a pocket mirror with shells on it.

Juan Raul's real wife, Carmela (Anjelica Huston), is an aristocrat. She lives in Coral Gables where she raised a daughter and a brother while Juan Raul languished in a Cuban jail for 20 years. But Carmela is not the long suffering madonna she would be in almost any other film, just as Dottie is not the stereotypical whore-with-a-good-heart; these women are the spiritual daughters of their American counterparts, the women who settled the frontier, our foremothers. If William Wellman were making *Westward the Women* in 1995, Dottie and Carmela would be aboard the wagon train.

Dottie is the Ava Gardner of the nineties, a barefoot contessa, a woman whose sexuality is integrated and fully realized. We see such a woman in Melanie Griffith whose passion and depth remind us of Marilyn Monroe, the quintessential feminine spirit of yet another era. In Italian cinema, Dottie is Anna Magnani and in France, Simone Signoret. Carmela is Greta Garbo in *Queen Christina* and *Ninotchka*, Grace Kelly in *High Society*, and Audrey Hepburn in *Robin and Marian*. These women and the characters they portray represent the eternal feminine spirit which inspires and matures masculine energy.

In a minor role, Angela Lanza plays Flavia, a cabaret singer, and Angel's girlfriend. (Angel is Carmela's deceptive and neurotic brother, a Castro supporter.) Flavia is another example of Nair's remarkable characterization of women—instead of the stereotypical Hollywood showgirl, an empty-headed, self-involved creature who can barely mask her ambition, Flavia is a self-assured performer, always aware of the effect her presence is having on others. If Carmela and Dottie represent a departure from the traditional portrayal of womanhood—the mature, devoted mother, and the budding young woman—Flavia is a more three-dimensional version of the playful feminine muse. Although she continually inspires Angel to reach beyond his rather limited potential, Flavia doesn't exist purely as an instrument of his psychic growth. She's in a symbiotic relationship with Angel.

No doubt women have played the role of muse throughout history, but in reality, they also compel men to confront the quotidian realities, the necessity of living in the present. Juan Raul and John (Chazz Palminteri), Carmela's *innamorato*, relinquish the past in order to begin their new lives with the women they love. Significantly, both men are middle-aged, that time of life when one begins to feel one's mortality, perhaps for the first time.

Dottie senses that the woman Juan Raul married no longer exists, just as the Cuba he knew can never be again. His loss is healed by Dottie whose strength and presence of mind releases him from the illusions that previously sustained him. The man who once owned sugar cane fields in

Cuba now happily sells flowers on a busy boulevard in Florida, secure in his ability to build a new life.

John is a man adrift, a divorced cop, a guy for whom a good woman would mean everything. His brand of masculinity—palpable, like John Wayne's and William Holden's—finds life in Carmela's mature instincts. When John is looking for an excuse to hang around, Carmela puts him to work in her home. In his rolled-up shirtsleeves, he epitomizes the protective masculine spirit which has come alive under Carmela's loving gaze.

Although a relative newcomer, Mira Nair is an excellent director in every respect. In *The Perez Family*, as in *Mississippi Masala* and *Salaam Bombay*, she manages to create a visual style that merges perfectly with the subject matter of the film. Nair also keeps us squarely focused on the emotional lives of her characters. She seems to have that unerring instinct which all good directors share—that characterization is everything.

LOS ANGELES TIMES, 5/12/95, Calendar/p. 2, Peter Rainer

"I am like Cuba. Used by many, conquered by none!" This is the anthem of Dottie Pererez (Marisa Tomei), the Mariel boatlift refugee and hip-swinging free spirit of "The Perez Family." And if you can believe anybody actually saying a line like that and meaning it, backed by the full, gleeful endorsement of the filmmakers, you may be able to buy into this movie, which is chock-full of such ringingly phony moments.

Everything in "The Perez Family" is overheated and undercooked. Set mostly in Miami in 1980, it's a pastel-colored jamboree of clichés about the family and romantic love in which just about everyone is hotblooded or hot-under-the-collar or hot-to-trot or just plain hot. That heat represents the Life Force. It's as if all of Miami were a griddle for its populations.

The 1988 Christine Bell novel upon which the film is based was larky and bustling and crammed with folksy-phony epigrams. Director Mira Nair and screenwriter Robin Swicord have taken Bell's salsa rhythms and jacked up the volume a full notch. They're trying for something voluptuously ecstatic to match the mood of the Cuban immigrants awash in their newfound capitalist wonderland. The results are certainly giddy, but are they good?

Dottie Perez, who is in love with John Wayne and rock 'n' roll and all things "American," has come ashore with Alfred Molina's Juan Raul Perez (no relation) on the last Mariel boat lift to Miami. Released from a Cuban jail after 20 years, Juan hopes to be reunited with his wife, Carmela (Anjelica Huston), and his now-grown daughter, Teresa (Trini Alvarado).

Dottie and Juan connect with two other Perezes, the young street urchin Felipe (Jose Felipe Padron) and a batty codger, Armando (Lazaro Perez)—also no relation. Because it is easier to remain in America as a family, they become one: They fob themselves off to the immigration authorities as married couple, son, grandfather.

The inevitable happens—the fake family becomes a real one. The movie becomes a paean not so much to family as to love. Family is where you find it.

At least that's the game plan. The problem is that this "family" never really comes across as anything more than a conceit. The actors are so frenetically "ethnic" that they never convince as real people. Tomei, normally one of the most likable of actresses, traipses about in a heavy Coppertone tan and flouncy garb and a Charo accent. Molina is so intensely sodden that he's like a great big scowling dark cloud.

And then there's Juan's real family, equally cartoony. As Juan's pining, forever hopeful wife, Huston at least fills the screen. She looks like an empress, and her imperious sensuality has a real kick to it. But her brother Angel (Diego Wallraff) is another yammering hotblooded hell-raiser— we're introduced to him when he buys his sister a pistol for safekeeping. Later, in a fit of pique, he rams his fist through a wall.

There's also a baffling subplot involving the local police lieutenant (Chazz Palminteri) who casually romances Carmela. We're supposed to regard these tentative love birds as a fairy-tale couple—they parallel the twinkling rapport that develops between Dottie and Juan.

Nair ("Salaam Bombay," "Mississippi Masala") is a gifted filmmaker, but her best range doesn't get full play here. She has a strong eye for documentary detail, and she fills the screen with color, but she can't reconcile her performers to her feeling for realism. She captures the florid carnival atmosphere of Miami in glints and spurts. Whenever the performers take center stage, which is most of the time, the film turns into a play-act charade.

NEW YORK, 5/22/95, p. 78, David Denby

The Perez Family, which is about Cubans coming to Miami, is an altogether different affair. Mira Nair, the Indian-born, American-educated director of *Salaam Bombay!* and *Mississippi Masala*, does the immigration story the right way—eccentrically, as a sort of unstable comedy of confusion. In the past, I've complained about a kind of United Nations, family-of-man-ism in Nair's work. In *Mississippi Masala*, she assembled the elements of ethnic comedy without making them flow together. This movie flows—like lava, from the opening shot to the last. Stuart Dryburgh, who shot *The Piano* for Jane Campion, does the cinematography in a rich yet precise style, the color palette a doubling of sensual Miami and *Cubano* tones, reds and oranges and greens crowding together. *The Perez Family* is a scruffy, not always first-rate, but full-bodied and immensely likable movie. Nair and screenwriter Robin Swicord (adapting a novel by Christine Bell) suggest that entering this country is an experience less of misery than of bedlam, in which misunderstanding and incongruity play the largest part. You survive—if you survive—by using your wits, staying loose, and improvising.

Juan Raul Perez (Alfred Molina), a former sugar-plantation owner who has been moldering in a Cuban prison, doesn't have that kind of ease. Haggard and sallow, with jagged teeth and matted hair, Molina—an English actor of Spanish-Italian descent—convincingly makes Juan Raul a wreck of a once-handsome man. We see Juan Raul's dreamy memories of his old life in flawless white suits; in the present-day scenes, he is seedy, even a sad sack. When Castro lets him go, he becomes one of the *Marielitos*, the criminal and dazed people foisted on the U.S. by the supreme leader in 1980. On the boat to Key West, Juan Raul is out of it, and he's taken in hand by Dottie (Marisa Tomei), an ex-prostitute who's all hot for Yankee freedom.

No doubt there will be complaints about Tomei's performance. She's not Cuban (though she worked on her tan), and she has added a good twenty pounds of flesh, which she swings around with abandon, her hips and breasts floating up and down like a raft on a boiling sea. At first it seems that Nair and Tomei have wildly exaggerated the clichés of Latin sensuality. It takes us a while to see who Dottie is: Ruby-lipped and dreamy, she's less a whore than a woman in love with the idea of herself as a freedom-loving hot tomato. Tomei turns a caricature into a person. Tough Dottie is a mover; when Juan Raul falls into a daze, she keeps thinking. Arriving in Mi-Yammi, they're forced to find some sort of life under the stands at Miami's Orange Bowl, where Immigration piles them in with the drag queens. Amazingly, rather than emphasize the squalor, Nair turns the Orange Bowl into a comic theater of disorientation.

Nair was also shrewd, I think, to view all the characters as slightly addled fantasists rather than as noble sufferers (they suffer, but they fool themselves, too). This way, we warm up to them; we see their stories not as aspects of tragic destiny or universal exile but as part of the crazy-quilt pattern of American life. Juan Raul dreams of the wife he hasn't seen in twenty years, Carmela (Anjelica Huston), who's now a sedately sexy bourgeois lady living in suburban Coral Gables and working at the perfume counter at Saks. She dreams of her husband, too, but does she really want him back? Wouldn't it be better to hook up with the FBI agent (Chazz Palminteri) who gravely courts her while fussing over the dangers she may face from the *Marielitos*? Huston has never been as delicately self-mocking as she is here. *The Perez Family* turns into a loopy romantic comedy and a loopy family drama. The title is ironic: In order to get free of Immigration, Dottie puts together a "Perez family" out of *Marielito* named Perez, including a young hoodlum as "son" and a crazy old man as "granddad." The slapped-together Perez family becomes the American Family incarnate.

Some people may be put off by the movie's volatile shifts in mood, from comedy to pathos and then back again. *The Perez Family* is melodramatically plotted, and the ending is a shambles (a couple of transitional scenes appear to be missing). Nair needs to smooth a few things out, but she's become a comic-romantic director of great originality, a sort of spicier, more sensual Paul Mazursky. *The Perez Family* is held together by immense affection for its characters and its chaotic milieu. With any luck, this luscious and happily absurd movie will serve as the taking off point for a great career.

NEW YORK POST, 5/12/95, p. 43, Michael Medved

Is there anything Marisa Tomei can't do?

After winning her supporting-actress Oscar for hilarious work in "My Cousin Vinny" she single-handedly carried two slightly soggy, shamelessly sentimental romances ("Untamed Heart" and "Only You") through the sheer force of her charisma, charm and on-screen vulnerability.

Now in "The Perez Family," she displays a completely different side to her cinematic personality—and at first she is scarcely recognizable. For one thing, the normally taut, trim Tomei has gained some 20 pounds for this role. To use an old-fashioned word, she is shockingly (and seductively) zaftig.

She plays Dottie, a saucy sugar cane worker who is a formidable force of nature. "I am like Cuba," she declares. "Used by many, conquered by no one."

Inspired by the impossible idea that she will go to Hollywood and seduce John Wayne, she joins the 100,000 refugees in the celebrated Mariel boat lift of 1980. During the brief cruise to Florida she meets Juan Raul Perez (played with perfect irony by Alfred Molina), a one-time aristocrat who's just been released after 20 years as a political prisoner.

He's eager to reunite with his adored wife (the always-elegant Anjelica Huston and daughter (Trini Alvarado) in Miami. But in the mass confusion of the boat lift, they're led to believe that the beloved Juan Raul has been left behind as Castro slams shut the doors to further immigration.

Meanwhile, Dottie discovers that if she and Juan Paul pretend to be husband and wife they stand a better chance of getting the favored immigration status that will allow them to escape the overcrowded detention camp that's been established for Marielistas in the Orange Bowl.

Since they both bear the same last name ("Perez" being the Cuban equivalent of "Smith") the masquerade is possible, and she soon recruits another Perez, a dotty old man, to pose as their grandfather, and yet another namesake, a thieving juvenile, to serve as their son. While this makeshift "Perez family" is assembling, Juan Raul's lonely real-life wife is succumbing to the attentions of a kindly, philosophical police lieutenant (Chazz Palminteri).

As in her previous films, "Salaam Bombay!" and "Mississippi Masala," director Mira Nair displays prodigious flair for dazzling colors and unexpected cultural collision. "Few filmmakers can so memorably convey the vibrant pulse of daily life with its spicy tastes and pungent smells.

This time, she has the additional advantage of a purposeful dramatic arc to her story, courtesy of a fine screenplay by Robin ("Little Women") Swicord, based on a novel by Christine Bell. At times, the plot seems to toy too cruelly with its characters, but the sense of all-powerful and benign destiny is re-established with the help of a luxuriant, lyrical, profoundly moving musical score by Alan Silvestri (who missed out on the Oscar he deserved for "Forrest Gump").

Activists may protest that, with the overall shortage of parts for Latino performers, plum roles shouldn't go to "Anglos" like Tomei and Huston. But they are so superb that complaint seems churlish. "The Perez Family," like its characters, is an unpredictable life force that is ultimately irresistible.

NEWSDAY, 5/12/95, Part II/p. B5, John Anderson

"I have a solooochun," announces Dorita Perez (Marisa Tomei), the overheated Cuban ex-prostitute who arrives, along with ex-political prisoner Juan Raul Perez (Alfred Molina), in Miami via the Mariel boatlift. The problem? They've got no sponsors, single people are Immigration's last priority, and life in the Orange Bowl has lost its appeal. Dorita's answer? Find a few more unrelated Perezes and form an instant family.

It's hard to imagine a movie crying out for Rosie Perez, but "The Perez Family" takes such a la cucaracha attitude toward Hispanics, and such a blithely casual stance on the crisis of the 1980 boatlift, that a little more stereotypical hot-cha-cha probably wouldn't hurt.

Tomei, her head in a cascade of ringlets and her body in perpetual motion, plays a woman in heat and looking for John Wayne (when she learns he's dead, she weeps bitter tears). Molina as Juan, wearing a post-crucifiction posture with broken resolve, is looking for his wife, Carmela (Anjelica Huston), whom he hasn't seen in 20 years. Carmela has been waiting so long she lives to wait. Their daughter (Trini Alvarado) comes off like a social worker. And Carmela's hot-blooded (naturally) brother, Angel (Diego Wallraff), is less than interested in reuniting Juan and Carmela.

Mira Nair, the director of "Mississippi Masala" and "Salaam Bombay," has an eye for color and a sense of daring about story structure. She balances the disparate, parallel stories of Juan and Carmela and their hesitant romances—Juan with Dorita, Carmela with a friendly fed (Chazz

Palminteri)—smoothly. But regardless of technique and Robin ("Little Women") Swicord's snappy script, little about the characterizations are believable. They are, on occasion, a little bit unsettling.

One would think that with no actual Cubans in any leading roles, Nair would have reined in her cast, especially Tomei, who is sexy and entertaining and way over the top. But amid the occasional bits of magic realism and the energy she imparts, Nair has a problem with scope: Visually, it's too tight, dramatically it's too wide and slack. You can see it in the cramped, claustrophobic way she shoots Juan's flashbacks, in which he revisits former life, white-suited on a Cuban beach. You can see it in the ungenerous way she shoots the climactic fiesta. And you can see it in the broad—no pun intended—performances.

The allegorical aspects of the story are two-pronged: What is family? And what is prison? Both are valid, especially concerning people of an oppressed nation coming here and being oppressed. But Nair's take on U.S. policy, her avoidance of the nasty facts about the criminals Castro sent here, and her offhand way of turning what was basically an internment camp into Club Babalu, gives optimism a bad name.

SIGHT AND SOUND, 9/96, p. 50, Peter Matthews

Juan Raul Perez is a former plantation owner who has languished 20 years in a Cuban prison for setting fire to his cane fields when Castro tried to expropriate them. He has lived on memories of his wife Carmela and daughter Teresa, who emigrated to Miami before his arrest. Now in 1990, Castro has initiated a policy of releasing political prisoners and unloading them on the unsuspecting Yankees. Juan is duly let go, and on shipboard meets the irrepressible Dottie, an agricultural worker and ex-prostitute.

In Miami, a mistake by an immigration official results in Dottie being listed as Juan's wife. Carmela's brother, Angel, sent to meet Juan at the boat, fails to recognise his much-changed brother-in-law. At their suburban home, Carmela and the now-grown Teresa are desolate at Juan's nonappearance. Meanwhile, all the new immigrants have been herded into a compound at the Orange Bowl Stadium, where they await sponsors who will arrange jobs for them. Learning that stable family units are favoured, Dottie persuades Juan to pose as her husband. She then sets about assembling a family, out of the various Perezes in the compound: Armando, a senile old man, will do as Papa; Felipe, a street kid involved with gangsters, can serve as her long-lost son.

Carmela has a noisy row with Angel, who is paranoid about the rising crime rate in Miami and wants his sister to pack a gun. The police are called, and Carmela meets Officer Pirelli, a federal agent. Juan discovers Carmela's address, but their reunion is aborted when he sets off the burglar alarm Angel has installed. Carmela is frightened by the intruder; Officer Pirelli is again summoned, and the two soon begin dating. At a disco, they run into Dottie, who has escaped curfew with the help of Steve, a security guard. Returning to camp, Dottie learns that the 'Perezes' have obtained sponsorship from the Church of the Resurrection. On the outside, she and Juan sell flowers to the passing traffic.

Juan spots an ad for Angel's bed shop, and visits him but Angel tells him to stay away from Carmela. Juan spies Carmela kissing Pirelli and hastily retreats from meeting her. Soon after, Felipe overhears Juan and Dottie discussing their hidden savings. He steals the money and is killed in a fight with a former crony. Drawn together by the tragedy, Dottie and Juan realise they are in love. Angel admits to his girlfriend Flavia that he recognises Juan. Flavia informs Teresa, and the two organise a surprise reunion for husband and wife at a Cuban festival. It all goes wrong when Carmela, still mistaking Juan for a derelict, tries to shoot him. In the ensuing fracas, Steve wounds Angel in the hand. When the dust settles, Juan and Carmela agree that they have both moved on in their lives and they part.

The Perez Family, begins well with a magical title sequence depicting a golden-hued memory of Cuba. The setting is perhaps the 50s, but the impression is of some timeless idyll of gracious living remote from the din of cities and revolution. An affluent bourgeois clan, each member arrayed in dazzling white, is having a picnic on the beach and the camera tracks lovingly over the faces, food and children's games as if greedy to preserve the evanescent details. Yet the imagery is too honeyed and hallucinatory to be quite credible and the scene ends with a surreal shot off half a dozen of the revellers bathing fully-clothed in the sea. There is an abrupt cut to a darkened cell which confirms what we may already suspect: the whole has sprung from the starved imagination of the 'political' prisoner, Juan Perez, now obsessively reciting the names of the family he has lost.

The director Mira Nair, with considerable help from the cinematographer Stuart Dryburgh, imbues this opening section with a stylised lyrical intensity comparable to the Cuban passages in Oscar Hijuelos' novel *The Mambo Kings Play Songs of Love,* (an intensity absent from Arnold Glimcher's bland 1992 film adaptation *The Mambo Kings*). Memory exerts its tidal pull on a character who sets about seeking the lost object he has idealised. The difference is that in Hijuelos, the irretrievable object is the mother's smile, which traps the dreamer in a circle of fatalistic longing. Juan's memories of his young wife belong to a more conscious order and he learns to shake them off. The movie is about the painful, necessary process of breaking with the past, with family and tradition. It's about accepting loss and freeing oneself to forge new, unanticipated ties and, as in the oldest immigrant drama, America still serves as the melting pot for this social and emotional reconfiguration.

But if Juan wakes up to disillusionment, so does the viewer. The movie never again attains the resonance or beauty of its Cuban prelude—and this is due less to the failure of America to live up to the characters' dreams than to Nair's (and her screenwriter Robin Swicord's) failure to keep track of what the story is saying. As Nair showed in *Salaam Bombay!*, and even in the doubtful *Mississippi Masala,* she has great empathy for cultural outsiders and a talent for putting the most delicate, intangible emotions on the screen. There are many such stray moments here, most of them involving Anjelica Huston as Juan's wife Carmela, a quiet, unassuming woman who has spent half a lifetime in the shadow of her husband's absence and now suddenly rediscovers her own desires. But Nair's sense of pace and of structure have always been seriously defective; and the plot-heavy script, combining as it does elements of romantic comedy and haywire melodrama, seems designed to expose all her weaknesses.

The effect is a bit dithering: the movie can never decide whether it means to be a slender, bittersweet fable about growing apart or a stylised farce (like a Latino *A Midsummer Night's Dream*) with sombre undertones. Nair and Swicord get us to care a good deal about who ends up with whom. There are sufficient streaks of maturity in the acting, writing and direction to make one resent such stupid contrivances as having Carmela tote a gun so that the crossed wires can precipitate a gaudy near-tragedy (as if her inner conflict of loyalties weren't interesting enough). It ought to be piercing and sinister that Carmela sees in the prison-ravaged Juan only a dangerous piece of Cuban flotsam; but the tone is too diffuse and uncertain to drive home the class irony (which may have been clearer in Christine Bell's original novel). In perhaps an excess of niceness, the movie underplays Carmela's snobbery and it barely indicates how Juan, the ex-sugar-cane boss, must feel to find himself vending flowers on the street.

Still, there is a lovely scene near the end where husband and wife talk across the abyss of their differences, express their discomfort with each other and agree to part like sane, civilised people. This outcome is a vast relief, and not so much because Juan's deracinated status makes him a fit helpmeet for the ornery survivor Dottie. Actually, these two belong together only by default—Marisa Tomei's shrill, amusing imitation of a Rita Moreno-ish spitfire strikes no particular sparks against Alfred Molina's drab depressiveness. But one desperately wants Carmela to get her shy, courtly policeman Officer Pirelli, and that's largely a tribute to the unstressed teamwork of Anjelica Huston and the increasingly attractive Chazz Palminteri.

The movie is a rocky ride, but Huston calms and centres it whenever she is on screen. Here is a performer who is the reverse of a technician: instead of building a part brick by brick from outside, she seems to draw on the dormant possibilities in herself. These possibilities are limitless: one feels that Huston could play anything from Medea to a Magnani-esque peasant, since she pays every character the compliment of a reserved inner life, a soul. The role of Carmela is perfunctorily written, and yet Huston turns it into an indelible portrait by the precise understatement of her acting. One obtains a sure grasp of the contrary qualities making up this placid, rather conventional woman: her pragmatism, her diffidence, her propriety, her occasional sense of mischief. But something remains, some mystery of composure and of passionate attentiveness, which Huston has the fine instinct to leave intact. It's a sublime performance, and the best reason to see *The Perez Family.*

TIME, 5/29/95, p. 69, Richard Schickel

A man languishes for 20 years in a cruel dictator's prison. A wife passes that time in exile, faithfully awaiting his return. We know what's supposed to happen when he's released: a period of adjustment (serio or comic, according to taste) and then a triumphant assertion of true love's unconquerable power.

That's life according to the movies and the rest of a pop culture devoted to offering us emotionally reassuring clichés on a weekly basis. (A good current example is *My Family*, another immigrant saga, in which any seasoned moviegoer can foretell the fate of every character the minute he or she appears, as well as the shamelessly sentimental ending.) But life according to life is usually not so predictable. So, when you run into something like *The Perez Family*, a movie that is full of lifelike bestartlements but still comes out kind of nice in the end, you have to treasure it.

It's Fidel Castro who sundered the marriage of Juan and Carmela Perez (Alfred Molina and Anjelica Huston). It's the political amnesty and boatlift of 1980 that promises to reunite them. It's another Perez, no relation, who gives them a new life utterly unlike the one they yearned for all those years. Her name is Dottie. She is a hooker-turned-sugarcane-cutter, and Marisa Tomei plays her, most wonderfully, as a force of nature, a small hurricane gusting along on her own headlong agenda, ripping the roofs off everyone's expectations.

She meets Juan on the boat to Miami, gets mistaken for his wife by an overtaxed immigration officer and decides to exploit the error. Families, it seems, have a better chance of attracting sponsorship—and thus escaping from the refugee camps—than singles do. For good measure, she adds a son (a street kid) and a grandpa (a silent, nutty old guy with a habit of shedding his clothes and climbing trees, hoping to glimpse his lost homeland) to her surrogate brood.

This has a good effect on Juan, whose long incarceration has, understandably, made him depressed and withdrawn. In his condition, as he slowly realizes, he doesn't need or want a simulacrum of his old life back; what he requires is an energizing new deal from a fresh pack. Oddly (and luckily) enough, Carmela is coming to the same conclusion at the same time, propelled by the appearance of a cop (Chazz Palminteri) who starts responding to her wistful, if discreetly displayed, charms as well.

But you can't contain or adequately characterize *The Perez Family* in a plot summary. For, writer Robin Swicord (*Little Women*) and director Mira Nair (*Mississippi Masala*) have crammed their film to bursting with wayward characters and strangely arresting incongruities. Nair has called the movie "an overripe mango," and that's as good a metaphor as any for a juicy, messy, exotic and utterly delicious treat.

VILLAGE VOICE, 5/16/95, p. 56, Ed Morales

When Hollywood makes films about Latinos, it can make me boiling mad, sort of like water for chocolate. Ever since *West Side Story*—a film most Puerto Ricans regard as just this side of *Birth of a Nation*, with some cute dance numbers—there has been an unrelenting trickle of deeply cheesy, phony-accented stereotyping and flagrant misrepresentation that can only make me wonder, what have I done to deserve this? After the brief tease of Darnell Martin's excellent indie Latin hiphop *I Like It Like That*, Hollywood returns to spixploitation mode with two different takes on the ultimate Latino cultural obsession, the clan.

Gregory Nava's *My Family* and Mira Nair's *The Perez Family* correspond to two of the three major formulas for recent films about U. S. Latinos—the former, like *American Me*, a socialist-realist Chicano soap opera with a mostly Latino cast and the latter, like *Mambo Kings*, a Cuban American migration drama with non-Latino "stars" and Latinos in minor roles. (The third formula, Nuyorican gangsta flick, was most recently revived by *Carlito's Way*, in which Brian De Palma and honorary Latino Al Pacino tried to fuse *Q&A* with *Sea of Love*.) Neither of these strategies has been very satisfying—the Chicano movies are generally cornball affairs that lack a sense of humor while the Cuban ones play up the dancing shtick while making a cartoon farce of the typical Spanish-accented American.

You'd think Mira Nair, who made *Mississippi Masala*, a very sweet and affecting movie about the Indian diaspora in Africa and the South, would be somewhat sensitive to portraying Latinos accurately—after all, "We people of color have to stick together" was *Masala*'s unspoken mantra.

But just as that film's black-Indian romance seemed to fulfill that slogan, Nair here flouts it by creating a dismal, embarrassing minstrel show starring Hollywood-approved pseudo-Mediterraneans like Angelica Huston, Alfred Molina, and Marisa Tomei (in tanning-machine brownface) passing for Miami Cubans. As much as I have admired Tomei's spunky Brooklyn presence in *Untamed Heart* and elsewhere, here, as Dottie, a Mariel boatlift chick in uncontrollable heat, she makes me cringe. "I yam like Cuba," she blurts, fending off a lecherous field worker, "used by many and conquered by no one." No one except for John Wayne, whom she inexplicably wants to fuck.

Tomei's hip-swiveling coochie-coochie girl act (see Charo) supplies most of the dramatic tension in a lifeless plot that purports to reunite the "real" Perez family: fellow Marielito Juan Raul (Molina) and his wife Carmela (Huston), who left him behind 20 years before at the onset of the Revolution. Pining away for her husband in a Valium-like stupor, Carmela's energy is drained by her frantic brother Angel, who spends the entire film raging like Joe Pesci, waving a blood-streaked bandaged fist. Chazz Palminteri plays a suave federal agent trying to track down stray Marielitos, and it isn't long before they're thrown together and Carmela falls for his shit-eating grin. Meanwhile Dottie, when she's not busy humping a detention-camp guard and shaking her prominent butt all over South Beach, creates a dysfunctional family unit, adopting fellow detainees Molina, an insane old general, and a young street thief, as a gambit to gain a church sponsor for their release from the Marielito camp.

This second, faux Perez family is supposed to capture our hearts with their colorful, inarticulate struggle to live the American Dream, but it's just a new setting for another round of bad acting. When Dottie finally seduces Molina—a forlorn Pacino—she moans with ecstasy ("Joo smell like flowers"), and the rose petals that shower down on yet another round of multiple Tomei orgasms provide us with a moment of magical realist comic relief. After an absurd climax—a shooting at a big dance concert—the romantic pairings shuffle out and the message for Latinos seems to be not "Love the one you're with" but "Marry an Italian."

Gregory Nava's *My Family*, is an entirely different story. Cowritten by Nava and employing an ensemble of Chicano, Nuyorican, and Latin American actors, the film is an ambitious multigenerational portrait of the Mexican American experience told through the fictional, arche-typal Sanchez family. Although it gets off to a creaky, overly melodramatic start, the film gains momentum and clarity through strong performances from Nuyoricans Esai Morales and Jimmy Smits, as two of the four Sanchez brothers. There's also a distinct Coppola aura (he's an executive producer) that lurks behind the lush cinematography, which peaks with a *West Side Story*-like fight sequence between Morales and rival gang leader Michael DeLorenzo at a dance that shows how Mexican America put its own spin on rock and roll.

The problem with *My Family* is that despite, or perhaps owing to, its well-meaning, identity-affirming ideology (its treatment of Mexican and Central American immigration amounts to a searing rejection of Prop. 187; the viewer is often reminded that California was once part of Mexico), it lacks a sense of irony and often comes off as naive, awkward agitprop. Given Edward James Olmos's tremendous accompilshments, from early Chicano theater to his performances as a wily math teacher in *Stand and Deliver*, his voiceover narration as the "writer" of the family still borders on self-parody. The use of a plaintive, hooting moan from a cosmic owl, combined with Olmos's somber intonations about evil spirits that live in rivers, plays like unintended camp.

Still, the best moment of this film may do more for Latinos than any offered up by the studio system so far. On an East L.A. street, a Salvadoran refugee, whom Smits marries as a favor to his activist sister, coaxes Jimmy into a lesson on how to dance Latin. There are many different interpretations of this scenario: It's a union between the salsafied East Coast and banda-dominated Cali; it's a reminder to sold-out Hispanics that you can always learn how to dance; it's a choreographed representation of the subversive matriarchal streak in the barrio. But what lingers in the memory is the sight of Jimmy Smits growing into a hardcore homeboy role he's never before been cast in, looking almost as if he were finally getting comfortable being *himself*.

Also reviewed in:
CHICAGO TRIBUNE, 5/12/95, Friday/p. H, Michael Wilmington
NEW REPUBLIC, 6/5/95, p. 33, Stanley Kauffmann
NEW YORK TIMES, 5/12/95, p. C17, Caryn James

VARIETY, 5/15-21/95, p. 95, Emanuel Levy
WASHINGTON POST, 5/12/95, p. B8, Hal Hinson
WASHINGTON POST, 5/12/95, Weekend/p. 48, Desson Howe

PERSUASION

A Sony Pictures Classics release of a BBC Films/Mobil Masterpiece Theatre/Millesime Productions presentation. *Executive Producer:* George Faber and Rebecca Eaton. *Producer:* Fiona Finlay. *Director:* Roger Michell. *Screenplay:* Nick Dear. *Director of Photography:* John Daly. *Editor:* Kate Evans. *Music:* Jeremy Sams. *Choreographer:* Geraldine Stephenson. *Sound:* Terry Elms. *Casting:* Siobhan Bracke. *Production Designer:* William Dudley and Brian Sykes. *Art Director:* Linda Ward. *Visual Effects:* Colin Gorry. *Costumes:* Alexander Byrne. *Make-up:* Jean Speak. *Stunt Coordinator:* Helen Caldwell. *Running time:* 103 minutes. *MPAA Rating:* PG.

CAST: Amanda Root (Anne Elliot); Ciaran Hinds (Captain Frederick Wentworth); Susan Fleetwood (Lady Russell); Corin Redgrave (Sir Walter Elliot); Fiona Shaw (Mrs. Croft); John Woodvine (Admiral Croft); Phoebe Nicholls (Elizabeth Elliot); Samuel West (Mr. Elliot); Sophie Thompson (Mary Musgrove); Judy Cornwell (Mrs. Musgrove); Simon Russell Beale (Charles Musgrove); Felicity Dean (Mrs. Clay); Roger Hammond (Mr. Musgrove); Emma Roberts (Louisa Musgrove); Victoria Hamilton (Henrietta Musgrove); Robert Glenister (Captain Harville); Richard McCabe (Captain Benwick); Helen Schlesinger (Mrs. Smith); Jane Wood (Nurse Rooke); David Collings (Mr. Shepherd); Darlene Johnson (Lady Dalrymple); Cinnamon Faye (Miss Carteret); Isaac Maxwell-Hunt (Henry Havter); Roger Llewellyn (Sir Henry Willoughby); Sally George (Mrs. Harville); David Acton and Justin Avoth (Naval Officers); Lonnie James (Jemima); Roger Watkins (Landlord); David Plummer (Apothecary); Richard Brenner (Coachman); Bill McGuirk and Niall Refoy (Tradesmen); Ken Shorter (Lady Dalrymple's Butler); Dermot Kerrigan (Footman); Tom Rigby (Little Charles); Alex Wilman (Little Walter); Rosa Mannion (Concert Opera Singer).

FILMS IN REVIEW, 9-10/95, p. 59, Pat Anderson

Like all Jane Austen novels, *Persuasion* deals subtly with the manners and mores of her characters, but the delicacy of her writing is not well served here. Since this picture was financed by France 2 and the BBC, one would at least expect it to be up to the standard of the best of Masterpiece Theater or a Merchant/Ivory book adaptation. Instead, we have a cast of seasoned, classically trained British actors performing like rank wooden amateurs.

Thus, in the spirit of the one-eyed man being king in the country of the blind, Corin Redgrave as Sir Walter Elliot, at least shows some life and finesse in the role of the vain, impecunious paterfamilias—for instance, when he picks up a highly polished silver knife at the dinner table, using it as a looking glass and proceeding to adjust his hair. And there's a credible performance by Sophie Thompson as the self-absorbed Mary Musgrove. In one sequence, while lying on a sofa declaring herself deathly ill, after much urging, she consents to try to eat a little something to keep up her strength, and then proceeds to tuck into the food and drink with gusto.

Sir Walter Elliot of Kellynch Hall in Somersetshire, is obliged, for financial reasons, to rent his property, while removing himself to Bath with his eldest daughter Elizabeth (Phoebe Nicholls) and her widowed friend, Mrs. Clay (Felicity Dean), who has designs on Sir Walter. Dean unaccountably plays Mrs. Clay as a sort of languid 1920's lounge lizardess.

While Sir Walter's party leaves for Bath, his middle daughter Anne (Amanda Root) goes to help her younger sister, Mary Musgrove, cope with her children, husband and in-laws. Amanda Root, though, seems to think she is in a silent movie. She stares intently at everyone and exaggerates all her movements. Anne Elliot is not one of Jane Austen's most endearing heroines, but she deserves better than this.

For Austen heroines, love never runs smoothly. And so it is for Anne, At the age of 19 she had become engaged to Captain Wentworth (Ciaran Hinds, with a perpetual Don Johnsonish two-day beard), but had broken the engagement at the behest of her father and godmother Lady Russell (Susan Fleetwood, playing Austen's aloof, haughty character as a grungy middle class woman). Now, seven years later, they meet again; Anne has at last repaired to Bath, where she is being courted by her cousin and father's heir William Elliot (Samuel West). The plot and various subplots involving Mary's sisters-in-law, Wentworth's best friend, William Elliot and Mrs. Clay all come to their logical ends.

Director Roger Michell comes to *Persuasion* with an impressive record as Resident Director of the Royal Shakespeare Company, but here he appears out of his depth. The outdoor Bath sets look palpably false-like '30s and early '40s Hollywood back lot sets. And there is no way that Anne and Wentworth, at the turn of the 19th century, would, in full public view, kiss passionately in the center of Bath.

LOS ANGELES TIMES, 10/6/95, Calendar/p. 1, Kenneth Turan

Jane Austen never married, possibly never received so much as a passionate kiss, and formed her closest emotional bonds with her spinster older sister. Yet, in one of the enduring mysteries of genius, few writers have had a more acute sense of romantic psychology, or had more piercing insights into the relationship of people in love. No place in the human heart was unknown to her, which is why her popularity not only endures, but increases. Especially in Hollywood.

"Persuasion" is the first (except for the "Emma"-based "Clueless") of a projected series of Austen adaptations, and it is going to be difficult to improve on. Literate, sophisticated, bitingly funny, it's a Cinderella romance so delicious you want it never to end.

The film's source is Austen's last completed novel, published posthumously in 1818. Though not as well known as "Pride and Prejudice" or "Sense and Sensibility" (which Emma Thompson is currently filming), "Persuasion" is a favorite among readers for several reasons.

Its heroine, Anne Elliot, is 27, no longer young by the standards of Regency England. Its lovers are more emotionally experienced than is usual with Austen, probably because by this time she was more knowing herself, and its story has a poignance that director Roger Michell and screenwriter Nick Dear (both veterans of the Royal Shakespeare Company) effectively blend into the usual Austen mix of courtship and clever satire.

"Persuasion" starts with a brisk dose of Austen fun, a scathing look at Sir Walter Elliot of Kellynch Hall (superbly played by Corin Redgrave, Lynn's and Vanessa's brother), an obtuse monument to snobbishness and pretension, who is at the moment having to face the unpleasant reality of a lack of funds.

Though he despises the Navy (calling it, in one of Austen's typically bracing lines, "the means of bringing persons of obscure birth into undue distinction"), Sir Walter is convinced by his neighbor Lady Russell (Susan Fleetwood,) to move to Bath and rent the hall to one Adm. Croft and his wife (John Woodvine and Fiona Shaw). Sir Walter and his entourage depart at once, but daughter Anne (Amanda Root) is left behind to tend to all the tedious details of moving.

The good, sensible, sympathetic daughter, Anne is used to this kind of treatment, but as she goes about her duties, including visiting her married sister Mary (Sophie Thompson), a thoroughly imaginary invalid, one thing troubles her. Now that Mrs. Croft is established in the neighborhood, her brother, Frederick Wentworth, is sure to make an appearance, and there is more than a little history between these two.

Eight years earlier, Anne was engaged to Wentworth, at the time a spirited young man with no prospects. Under the persuasive influence of Lady Russell, she was convinced to break off the match, and now her former beau is returning as a wealthy, supremely eligible naval captain and Anne, who can barely say his name, is terrified they will meet.

Naturally, they not only meet, but circumstances also throw them together a good deal. Though the Captain (played with enviable posture and self-possession by Ciaran Hinds) tells friends that he finds Anne "so altered, he would not have known her," it's impossible not to wonder how much of a spark remains between them. The business of "Persuasion" is to answer that question, and to show how both Anne and Wentworth deal with the obstacles society (and the appearance of possible new matches for each of them) throws in their way.

Making this story difficult for filmmakers is that Austen's world was not known for frank speech or dramatic action. Fortunately, director Michell and screenwriter Dear, working with cinematographer John Daly and a splendid troupe of actors, are up to doing what's needed. Which is capturing a nuanced society of looks and smiles, where more is implied than spoken and the subtle pressure of a hand helping a woman into a carriage can be as dramatic as a slap across the face.

And though fine period recreations are not scarce, a telling effort has been made to make the physical atmosphere as real as possible. The actors wear little makeup, the costumes and furnishings all seen lived in, not merely worn, and no face, no matter how minor, has been anything but carefully chosen. And Dear has succeeded in his stated aim of trying to marry the wit of Austen to some of the psychological reality of Ingmar Bergman.

Because the nature of Regency society was such that Anne can't act very much on her own, can't be the mistress of her fate, an actress with the skill to win over an audience via quiet persuasiveness was necessary, and Amanda Root, another RSC veteran with great, deep, soulful eyes and a delicately expressive face, does that beautifully.

Director Michell, whose debut theatrical feature this is, does a superior job of marshaling all these resources and enforcing a uniformly engaging tone. Both for veteran Janeites and those new to the religion, "Persuasion" is a most persuasive place to be.

NEW YORK, 10/23/95, p. 57, David Denby

Persuasion, on the other hand, [the reference is to *The Scarlet Letter*] is the real thing, a generally intelligent and moving BBC adaptation of Jane Austen's last completed novel (Roger Michell directed). I admit that at first it's something of a shock seeing Jane Austen mounted on the screen at all—everything appears bigger, more theatrical and obvious than one had imagined, the manners more brutal, the contrasts of rich and poor more overt. On a few occasions, the filmmakers get carried away: Surely it is a mistake to show the Cinderella heroine, Miss Anne Elliot, leaving the family estate in an animal cart;   and surely Anne and her suitor, Captain Wentworth (Ciaran Hinds), would not kiss in the daylight, and on the streets of Bath. But apart from these errors, most of the movie goes extremely well. I would have preferred as Anne an actress without Amanda Root's prim, tight-lipped demeanor (*Persuasion* is about delayed passion, not repression), but Corin Redgrave is excruciatingly funny as the snobbish Mr. Elliott, and many of the other British stalwarts are wonderful—pale, mope-mouthed Sophie Thompson, for instance, as the complaining sister Mary. Wonderful, too, was the sight of the fields and towns and great houses of England. *Persuasion* was written during the Napoleonic Wars and is warmed by love of the British Navy and that sacred place, home. The movie preserves the glow.

NEW YORK POST, 9/27/95, p. 40, Thelma Adams

Some of the year's ugliest characters surface in the most genteel of settings in "Persuasion." Some of the sexiest scenes occur with characters swathed in gloves and empire-style gowns, tongues tied with formal discourse.

Roger Michell's pristine adaptation of Jane Austen's 1818 novel is a shrewd interplay of surface and depth that mirrors one of the key conflicts in Austen's fictional world: the struggle between the superficial and the profound.

Because the British novelist was such a keen observer of human nature, her novels are less historical relics than modern tales of women struggling to find their place in the world while they battle the constraints of society and their own hearts.

Set in 1814, "Persuasion" is a Cinderella story about a level-headed heroine who, faces spinsterhood at 27. Anne Elliot (Amanda Root) tends her spendthrift father (Corin Redgrave) and her ungrateful sisters.

Regrets, Anne has a few. Eight years earlier she had been poised to marry Frederick Wentworth (Ciaran Hinds). A family friend persuaded Anne to nix the match because the naval officer was poor. By the time Wentworth returns from the seas, he has made a mint and risen in rank while the Elliot family fortune has eroded.

Wentworth's return revives Anne's repressed feelings. For anyone who has ever regretted not following their heart in life's big decisions, who has been counselled to make a dreadfully wrong turn in the past, this ache resonates. The desire to put things right again, to go back to that fateful juncture and undo past decisions, gives the story its emotional tension.

We want to reunite the lovers, to knit the raveled edges of their lives neatly together. This desire to set other people's affairs in order, often without tending to our own, is a common theme in Austen's books—a topic central to the summer sleeper "Clueless" which was loosely based on Austen's "Emma."

Unlike the familiar high-gloss BBC adaptations that "Persuasion" initially resembles, Michell never gilds the lily. The production never overwhelms the drama.

Amanda Root's Anne blossoms in front of the camera. She begins as a dowdy woman with dead brown eyes who fulfills a vital but unappreciated role in her family. As the great listener, the reliable shoulder to lean on in all disputes great and small, she is by definition a supporting character in life's drama. By movie's end, Anne finds her voice and follows it to center stage to become a memorable romantic lead who cannot be persuaded twice to abandon the man closest to her heart.

NEWSDAY, 9/27/95, Part II/p. B7, John Anderson

The same impulse that drives yuppies to buy BMWs and high-end tequila has made Jane Austen the Martha Stewart of social constraint. This is something of a joke, considering that, Austen's characters live in a world that consistently fails to live up to its own suffocating standards—and where happiness is usually attained only by resisting the tug of conformity. But the search for perfection by the shallow through the immaterial has a model universe, in Austen's oeuvre, especially if the searcher misses the point.

Director Roger Michell doesn't miss the point—which is the strongest argument on behalf of "Persuasion," his cool, static adaptation of Austen's posthumously published 1818 novel, and a film that continues the Austen mini-renaissance ("Clueless" was based loosely on "Emma"; Ang Lee is bringing out "Sense and Sensibility" in December). It relates the torturously romantic pas de deux of Anne Elliot (Amanda Root) and Capt. Frederick Wentworth (Ciaran Hinds), whose betrothal was squashed eight years earlier—Anne unwisely having accepted the advice that Wentworth was unwealthy and therefore unsuitable. She has regretted her decision ever since, as has the captain, but when circumstances thrust them together again they have to contend not just with their own modulated emotions, but with the convoluted reasoning of everyone around them.

The story has been given a sort of "Masterpiece Theater" treatment by BBC veteran Michell ("The Buddha of Suburbia") and was first aired on British television. But despite its sense of underpopulation and lack of cinematic energy, Michell maintains the integrity of Austen's commentary on the wages of being proper, while rooting the story in its time and place and not trying to make it relevant or current.

Amanda Root, whose previous appearances have been on the English stage or the BBC, is a delightful Anne Elliot, a woman who knows that her most promising years (for matrimony) are behind her, but who isn't sure she should care. (On the other hand, when someone states that "No one is more capable than Anne," she isn't sure she hasn't been insulted.) Root plays her as a crushed flower who knows her unhappiness is her own fault and whose reactions are beyond her: When Mrs. Croft (Fiona Shaw), Wentworth's sister, announces that her brother has married, Anne has a perfectly physical reaction (it's the wrong brother, of course); later, when she glimpses Wentworth on a street, there's the same kind of gasping for breath, clutching of breast. Anne's love is not purely cerebral.

Her father—the profligate, indebted Sir Walter Elliot (Corin Redgrave)—is a serious stuffed shirt who must vacate the ancestral home of Kellynch Hall and head for Bath to retrench. This raises the curtain on a troop of characters and an equal number of situations. Anne's older sister, Elizabeth (Phoebe Nicholls), is a disappointed schemer; her younger sister, Mary (Sophie Thompson), is purely insufferable. Mary is married to Charles Musgrove (Simon Russell Beale), whose sisters, Louisa and Henrietta (Emma Roberts and Victoria Hamilton), engage in a torrid (well, not exactly) flirtation with Wentworth, who is still nursing his Anne-inflicted wounds. Mrs. Croft becomes a confidante to Anne—who is everyone else's confidante—as does Capt. Benwick (Richard McCabe), whose true love died while he was away at sea. "You have no conception of what I have lost," he tells Anne. "Yes. I have," she answers. Happily, Wentworth overhears.

In contrast to our indelicate times, personal passion isn't a justification for violating the social order. It becomes clear to Anne and Wentworth that their heat has never died, but their reserve keeps getting in the way: Wentworth thinks Anne is involved with William Elliot (Samuel West), a distant cousin with base designs on Anne's fortune; Louisa, who is injured in a fall (the slo-mo is absurd), becomes, in Anne's eyes, an impediment to her happiness.

In the great tradition of the 19th-Century novel, there are a multitude of problems caused by misunderstandings and unspoken words. But Root and Hinds bring a special kind of understated heat to their roles, and to Austen's world, where the fires always burn beneath a delicate veneer of frost.

NEWSWEEK, 10/9/95, p. 78, David Ansen

The unlikeliest movie mini-trend of the year, right up there with movies about Las Vegas low life, is the sudden spate of films inspired by Jane Austen, a writer who, having died in 1817, never got to weigh in on the subject of lap dancing. The trend began almost subliminally, with "Clueless," a liberal teen update of "Emma." In December we will get "Sense and Sensibility," starring and adapted by Emma Thompson and directed by the Taiwan-born Ang Lee ("Eat Drink Man Woman"). The BBC will soon air its new production of "Pride and Prejudice," and writer/director Douglas McGrath is preparing the original "Emma," without the 90210 Zip code. It wouldn't seem that we're living in an age that's particularly welcoming to Austen's bracing ironies, her intimately calibrated dissection of manners or her finely chiseled moral distinctions. But perhaps that's the point of her newfound popularity: she's a splash of clear, cool water on our morally groggy foreheads.

Whatever the reason, we can only be grateful for the first arrival, *Persuasion*, faithfully adapted from Austen's last, posthumously published novel. It sets a standard the rest will be hard pressed to equal. Two men of the English theater, director Roger Michell and playwright Nick Dear, and an exquisite ensemble of actors (many are veterans of the Royal Shakespeare Company) have subtly but brilliantly refurbished the conventions of the costume drama. "Persuasion" is free of the plummy scent of greasepaint and theatrical oratory—it's very much a movie—and it doesn't look like a glossy brochure for Old Country Estates. The upper-middle-class Regency world it evokes feels scuffed and lived in, and the urgency of its emotions, however quietly spoken, can pierce the heart.

Austen's heroine, Anne Elliot (Amanda Root), faces spinsterhood at the age of 27, having been persuaded, eight years earlier, to reject the proposal of the man she loved—and still loves. Her trusted friend Lady Russell (Susan Fleetwood) deemed him unsuitable, owing to his lack of fortune. The Elliot family's fortunes, in the meantime, have fallen into decline: Sir Walter Elliot (Corin Redgrave, wonderfully loathsome), Anne's peerlessly snobbish widowed father, has been forced to rent their ancestral home to Admiral Croft (John Woodvine) and his wife (the dazzling Fiona Shaw). Sir Walter and his oldest and favorite daughter, the haughty Elizabeth (Phoebe Nicholls), remove themselves to Bath. The unwanted Anne is sent off to attend to her hypochondriacal sister Mary (the hilarious Sophie Thompson). who lives with her husband Charles Musgrove (Simon Russell Beale) on a neighboring country estate.

It is there that Anne first re-encounters the lost love of her life. Frederick Wentworth (Cioran Hinds) is now a wealthy captain of the navy, having returned from the Napoleonic war with riches and honor. But he finds Anne "so altered he would not have known her." His bitterness toward her is self-evident, and he turns his attentions toward the silly Musgrove sisters, Louisa (Emma Roberts) and Henrietta (Victoria Hamilton), who find him a most eligible catch. Is there any hope that Anne and Frederick can rekindle their aborted love?

Written in the final year of her life, "Persuasion" is considered the most autobiographical of Austen's novels. It's a comedy tinged with melancholy and the ache of missed opportunities. From an author who satirized the follies of romanticism, and tweaked moonstruck romantic excess, it's the closest she came to revealing her own yearning soul. Michell is wonderfully sensitive to the shifting tones of the tale, which can pivot from acid social satire to Cinderella fable at the turn of a gossip's neck. The movie is hushed, sotto voce: we become eavesdroppers on a society caught in those intimate moments when its public mask is down. My one complaint is technical: the sound is second rate. With dialogue this sterling, it's a shame to miss a single line.

Amanda Root's Anne is hardly a conventional screen heroine. plain and sad eyed, she doesn't make much of an initial impression, which is part of Michell's strategy. Anne has been shunted off to the side of her family. She's an observer, a listener, but we gradually come to see the inner beauty that distinguishes her from her sisters: an unsanctimonious virtue that sets her apart from her family's naked social ambitions. The source of the painful comedy that separates her and Frederick is that neither lover ever gets the chance to speak his or her heart. Hinds, who resembles Peter Finch, and has some of Alan Rickman's snaky sexuality, is as physically commanding as Root is unprepossessing, and therein lies their surprising chemistry. "Persuasion" is proof that the most repressed love stories can have the sweetest payoff. Like Anne herself, the movie reveals its wonders slowly. By the time it's reached full bloom, you may find yourself in an unreasonably happy state.

VILLAGE VOICE, 10/3/95, p. 80, Georgia Brown

Set in 1814, Jane Austen's *Persuasion* is also about property, station, rank, and the minuscule loopholes that allow a man to get a leg up. Especially it is about value: how worth is measured and whether virtue matters. But most of all, the novel is an exquisite tale of gratification delayed, love that alters not, even over eight years of separation and despair.

Austen isn't subtle in her rendering of the Elliot family and neither is director Roger Michell in this clever adaptation (the adroit screenplay is by Nick Dear). Anne Elliot (Amanda Root), middle daughter of the vain and stupid Sir Walter Elliot (Corin Redgrave), is the novel's heroine, its point of view, yet in the beginning she's nearly inarticulate—drowned in the chatter and clutter surrounding her. (Perhaps this is the significance of an opening shot from underwater.) Her elder sister, Elizabeth (Phoebe Nicholls), pops chocolates, has a frivolous nose and perpetual sneer; the younger sis, Mary Musgrove (Sophie Thompson, sister of Emma) is less sinister but sillier, forever pleading ill and evading responsibility. In the beginning, the satire of these sisters, this widowed father with his obviously dyed hair and bigoted opinions, seems overdone. But this just makes us more solicitous of Anne.

The notion behind the title is that Anne can't exercise her own will. She's not a voice but an ear; others enlist her to hear their troubles. She's at their disposal. She plays the piano while the others dance. The salient persuasion took place eight years ago when the Elliots' mother-surrogate, Lady Russell (Susan Fleetwood), persuaded Anne to turn down a proposal from Frederick Wentworth because he had only himself to recommend him. Now a naval officer, Captain Wentworth returns to the neighborhood because his sister and her husband, Admiral and Mrs. Croft, are renting Sir Walter's ancestral house. Having squandered his fortune, Sir Walter is persuaded by Lady Russell to retreat to Bath where he can live cheaply. Having gained a fortune in the meantime, Wentworth is looking for a wife, and while Anne looks on, he proceeds to court the ditzy Musgrove sisters.

Since a woman's role was to be receptive rather than active, so much depends here on Amanda Root's brown eyes. In the Royal Shakespeare Company, Root played Juliet to Daniel Day-Lewis's Romeo, Cressida to Ralph Fiennes's Troilus, and in her first leading film role she shows herself capable of acting via facial expression, upholding the more subtle values of reticence, modesty, and patience. At the beginning, Anne seems plain and mousy; by the end—thanks also to Michell's delicious pacing—she blossoms into the fairest at the ball. As Wentworth, Cialan Hinds, a tall man with an especially large face, carries off the trick (one sees it rarely) of making a withheld, virile man gradually turn into a smoldering, lovesick wretch. (His antecedents are Cary Grant in *An Affair To Remember*, Rock Hudson in *Magnificent Obsession*, Depardieu in *The Woman Next Door*.)

The enthusiasm for *Persuasion* already evinced by the boys at *The Observer* shows that this is not a woman's picture but a fairy tale for adults. It's what we all like to see: Suffering validated (it's necessary for growth), virtue rewarded, things turning out as they ought to turn out.

Also reviewed in:
CHICAGO TRIBUNE, 10/27/95, Friday/p. H, Michael Wilmington
NEW REPUBLIC, 10/9/95, p. 26, Stanley Kauffmann
NEW YORK TIMES, 9/27/95, p. C18, Caryn James

NEW YORKER, 9/25/95, p. 107, Anthony Lane
VARIETY, 5/29-6/4/95, p. 60, Derek Elley
WASHINGTON POST, 10/20/95, p. D1, Hal Hinson
WASHINGTON POST, 10/20/95, Weekend/p. 44, Desson Howe

PICTURE BRIDE

A Miramax Films release of a Thousand Cranes Filmworks produced in association with Cécile Co. Ltd. *Producer:* Lisa Onodera and Diana Mei Lin Mark. *Director:* Kayo Hatta. *Screenplay (Japanese and English with English subtitles):* Kayo Hatta and Mari Hatta. *Director of Photography:* Claudio Rocha. *Editor:* Lynzee Klingman and Mallory Gottlieb. *Music:* Mark Adler. *Music Editor:* Joanie Diener. *Sound:* Susan Moore-Chong and (music) Dennis Sands. *Casting:* Anna Fishburn and Yumi Takada. *Production Designer:* Pual Guncheon. *Special Effects:* Archie Ahuna and Mike Van Arkel. *Costumes:* Ada Akaji. *Make-up:* Bryan Furer. *Stunt Coordinator:* Colin Fong. *Running time:* 90 minutes. *MPAA Rating:* PG-13.

CAST: Youki Kudoh (Riyo); Akira Takayama (Matsuji); Tamlyn Tomita (Kana); Cary-Hiroyuki Tagawa (Kanzaki); Toshiro Mifune (The Benshi); Yoko Sugi (Aunt Sode); Shoin Hoashi (Buddhist Minister); Keiji Morita (Photographer); Michael Hasegawa (Immigration Officer); Peter Clark (Christian Minister); Lito Capiña (Augusto); Warren Fabro (Felipe); Michael Ashby (McCullum); Glenn Cannon (Mr. Pieper); James Grant Benton (Antone); Kati Kuroda (Yayoi); Hatsuko Otsuka (Fumi); Kyle Kakuno (Yamamoto); Dawn Saito (Geisha); Christianne Mays (Miss Pieper); Moe Keale (Hawaiian Fisherman); Traci Toguchi (Uto); Melvin Miranda (Miguel); Natasha Mamiya and Jessica Louie (Kei-chan); Riki Sugimoto (Gambler); Shuji Kumagata (Benshi Cart Drummer); Chizuko Nishimura Endo (Shamisen Player); Nobu McCarthy (Narrator).

LOS ANGELES TIMES, 5/5/95, Calendar/p. 8, Kevin Thomas

Between 1907 and 1924 more than 19,000 Japanese woman immigrated to Hawaii to marry Japanese sugar-cane workers. These couples knew little of each other beyond an exchange of photos upon the actual experiences of many such women, some of them still living in their 90s, director Kayo Hatta and her sister and co-writer Mari have created the exquisite "Picture Bride," a gentle and eloquent tale of perseverance that blossoms finally into the most tender of love stories.

Diminutive Youki Kudoh, who was one-half of the funny punk couple in Jim Jarmusch's "Mystery Train," plays a traditional Japanese girl, the 16-year-old Riyo. Arriving in Hawaii in 1918 full of apprehension, she quickly decides she's made a terrible mistake. Her soon-to-be-husband Matsuji (Akira Takayama) proves to be 43, a good 20 years older than the photo of himself he sent her.

A virile man of the soil, he attempts to take her roughly on their wedding night in his modest cottage. He repels Riyo, who rejects his clumsy advances, to the extent that she becomes determined to save up her earnings to pay for her way back to Japan. We know very well that with a pay rate of 65 cents a day, *minus* expenses, that she is as unlikely to attain this goal as she is to give it up, so badly does she need it sustain her in her first rugged months in the cane fields.

Once Riyo has taken considerable ribbing for being a "city girl"—she's from Yokohama—she begins to gather strength from the earthy camaraderie of the other women, forging a friendship with the beautiful but disillusioned Kana (Tamlyn Tomita), whose handsome husband Kanzaki (Cary-Hiroyuki Tagawa) has degenerated into a drunken wifebeater.

Kanzaki has given in to the bitterness and frustration of a particularly vicious and racist cycle: The fieldworkers are supervised by a lethally brutal Portuguese, who in turn can never rise above his own station because of Anglo discrimination. Meantime, he refuses to pay Filipino workers as much as the Japanese. In short, Hatta reminds us that the racial harmony so vaunted in today's Hawaii was not so long ago far from the norm. (Shortened considerably from its showing at Cannes last year, "Picture Bride" curiously tells of a brewing strike only to pull away from it completely.)

Hatta and her collaborators, however, bring to Riyo's odyssey an epic vision in which the natural and the supernatural blend effortlessly, as they so often do in Japanese films. "Picture Bride" unfolds as a series of ravishingly beautiful, highly sensual images, captured by "Like Water for Chocolate" cinematographer Claudio Rocha and accompanied by Mark Adler's shimmering score, which incorporates motifs from both Japanese and Hawaiian music.

It's the scope and depth of Hatta's vision, combined with its intense particularly of time and place, that gives Riyo's story such universality; "Picture Bride" couldn't be more Japanese—or more American. Hatta's perspective, furthermore, allows her to be fair-minded to the disappointed, well-meaning Matsuji, even to the hateful Portuguese. The film glows with a feminine sensibility—a sensibility that reveals that strength and delicacy can go hand in hand.

Hatta is not only a visionary but also a fine director of actors. Who could have guessed at the depths Kudoh is capable of from her off-the-wall character in "Mystery Train"? Like Kudoh, Takayama shows us an individual in the process of growing, changing, adapting. Tomita makes the kind of impression you hope will be indelible with the award-givers. And Tagawa, although on screen only briefly, conveys Kanzaki's torment fully.

Like the cherry on an ice cream sundae, "Picture Bride" is topped with a genial cameo by Toshiro Mifune as a *benshi*, or narrator, of the silent films he presents to the workers right smack in the fields.

NEW YORK POST, 4/28/95, p. 43, Michael Medved

"Picture Bride" is as gentle and refreshing as a tropical breeze.

It tells the story of Riyo (Youki Kudoh), a Yokohama teen-ager in 1918 who feels disgraced by the death of her parents—though we don't learn the nature of the scandal until the film is nearly over.

Fleeing from her troubled past, she sails to faraway Hawaii as a "picture bride," committed to marry a Japanese sugar cane worker she has never met.

Upon her arrival in Honolulu, she is shocked to discover that her new husband (Akira Takayama) is an old man of 43, and that the handsome photograph he had sent to her is more than 20 years old.

Moreover, the island paradise he described in his letter (complete with a plagiarized Haiku) is actually a crude shack set amidst the sugar cane fields.

No wonder that she rejects all her husband's fumbling physical advances, and finds her only real friendship with another woman from her work crew, beautifully played by Tamlyn Tomita of "The Joy Luck Club."

This earthy survivor soon teaches Riyo to earn a few extra pennies doing laundry, facilitating the young bride's dream of saving enough money to buy passage back to Japan.

The story is based on the family history of "Hawaiian-born director Kayo Hatta, and it's so lyrically told and superbly well-acted that it's easy to understand why the film drew admiring attention at both the Cannes and Sundance festivals.

Hatta avoids the temptation of making her characters into larger-than-life, picture book pioneer heroes; these are ordinary people with plenty of ordinary (and maddening) shortcomings.

The film may try a bit too self-consciously to introduce glimpses of other ethnic groups in Hawaii (Filipinos, Chinese, Portuguese, Native Hawaiians and the dominant European Haoles), but its re-creation of the daily life of impoverished immigrants is full of poetic intensity. Riyo, for instance, pauses to listen to the night wind sighing through the sugar cane and hears the voices of family ghosts, just as this memorable film brings haunting life to the forgotten songs of the filmmaker's own departed ancestors.

NEWSDAY, 4/26/95, Part II/p. B5, Jonathan Mandell

Near the beginning of "Picture Bride," the sensitive first feature film that took two Japanese-American sisters 10 years to make, the man and the woman who have just met are sitting in two wooden bathtubs side by side, a wall between them. She asks how old he is.

Never mind, he says.

She insists.

"I'm 43," he says finally.

She gasps. "Older than my father was."

The man and the woman are newlyweds. They are Japanese but they are not in Japan. Outside the thin walls of the Japanese-style bath, a reminder of home, is the strange new sky-high land where they now must live, full of towering sugarcane fields and the wind-swayed stirrings of ghosts.

They are in the frontier Hawaii of 1918, and the man, Matsuji (Akira Takayama), has worked in the fields for years in order to afford to send away for a Japanese bride, a common practice at a time and place where men outnumbered women 30 to 1.

A matchmaker chose Riyo (Youki Kudoh), an orphan from the city of Yokahama escaping some unspoken past. She decides to marry Matsuji based only on the beautiful haiku poem he has written her, and the photograph he has sent. But the photograph is of a handsome young man. "I didn't have a recent photo of myself," he says lamely, when the ship docks and they meet. "I'm sorry," he says, and lowers his head.

For those of us for whom 40 seems a perfectly reasonable age, the woman's revulsion toward the man simply because of his age—her determination to earn enough money working the fields and doing extra laundry to buy her passage back—might seem extreme, superficial, unfair. But part of the film's beauty is its willingness to create less-than-always-noble characters whose imperfections, including some outdated and disturbing beliefs, are neither mocked nor condemned.

"Picture Bride," winner of the Audience Award at this year's Sundance Film Festival, is as spare, as deceptively simple and as affecting as haiku. Like haiku, it might strike some viewers as incomplete, with too many questions unasked or unanswered, but what is there is powerfully observed, and well acted. The good acting is symbolized, rather than embodied, by the presence of Toshiro Mifune, the world's most famous Japanese actor, who only appears in this movie for about five minutes, and for little purpose.

"Picture Bride" is lushly filmed by Claudio Rocha, the cinematographer who also shot "Like Water for Chocolate," and like that movie, most viewers will probably focus on the slowly evolving love story. But "Picture Bride" is based on historical fact, and alludes to, if inadequately explains, the conditions of the times—the exploitation, ethnic tension, labor strife, and general hardship of the women and farm workers and immigrants from Japan, who struggled with sorrow and pain and also unexpected joy on their way to become Japanese-Americans. That is why Al D'Amato should see this picture.

SIGHT AND SOUND, 2/97, p. 52, Philip Kemp

Yokohama, 1918. 18-year-old Riyo Nakamura, orphaned by the death of her father, is persuaded to become a 'picture bride' whose photograph will be circulated to men seeking wives. She hears from a Japanese in Hawaii, Matsuji Kimura; he includes a haiku in his letter and describes Hawaii as "a paradise where it's easy to become rich." His photo shows him as young and handsome. Arriving in Honolulu, Riyo discovers he's 43 (older than her late father) and that someone wrote the haiku for him. After a brief mass-marriage ceremony, she learns that she's expected to toil long hours in the sugar-cane fields. Wretched and lonely, Riyo spurns Matsuji's amorous advances, dreaming only of amassing enough money to return to Yokohama.

Touched by Riyo's misery, other women cane-cutters take pity on her and protect her from Augusto, the brutal Portuguese foreman. Yayoi, an older woman soon to return to Japan, takes a motherly interest, and Riyo forms a close friendship with Kana, a woman nearer her own age with a feckless drunken husband and a small child, Kei-chan. Besides cane-cutting, Kana earns money running a laundry service. Riyo starts to help her. Her relationship with Matsuji remains distant, and he talks despondently of saving up for another wife.

A travelling cinema, run by the sophisticated Benshi, arrives to show samurai films, deepening Riyo's homesickness. On Kana's advice, Matsuji tries to woo Riyo and takes her for a day in the country. They get on better, but she still rejects his advances. One day when the wind is right Augusto insists on setting light to the canes (a necessary process prior to harvesting), refusing to let Kana first check if Kei-chan is safe. With the field alight she finds the child missing, and plunges desperately into the flames after him. As the other workers gaze in horror, mother and child are burnt to death.

That evening Matsuji starts to organise a strike. He asks Riyo to contribute to strike funds from her savings, but she won't give more than $2. Later that night, she confesses her "shame": both her parents died of TB. Matsuji, shocked, turns away when she touches him in bed. Mortified, she runs away across the island, falls asleep on a beach and dreams of Kana, who tells her to forget about returning to Japan. Riyo comes home to find Matsuji drunk and miserable at her absence, and they make love for the first time. The next day in the canefield, she happily joins in the other women's bawdy songs. Matsuji builds a shrine to her parents; they pray before it, then float lanterns down the river for her parents' souls and those of Kana and Kei. The Japanese community joyfully celebrates the Feast of Lanterns. In voice-over, Riyo talks of her daughter and granddaughter, and of her home—in Hawaii.

Films about mail-order brides—Jan Troell's *Zandy's Bride* furnishes another example—mostly follow a standard three-act pattern. (Truffaut's *La Sirène du Mississippi* offers a rare quirky exception.) Firstly, disillusionment—the husband is far older, the existence harsher, than expected; secondly estrangement: she resentfully spurns his remorseful advances; and lastly, reconciliation: realising the old man isn't such a bad sort really, she finds happiness of a kind.

In terms of plot, then, *Picture Bride* springs no surprises. The interest lies in the telling, and it's to the credit of all concerned—especially Kayo and Mari Hatta's script, Kayo Hatta's sensitive direction, and Youki Kudoh's touching performance as Riyo—that our interest is sustained, and steadily heightened. Partly, this derives from the fascination of crossed realities, the Mizoguchi-meets-*Blue-Hawaii* anomalies gleaned from watching familiar Japanese gestures and mores played out against a lush, tropic-paradise setting. (Thor Fridriksson's 1995 Japanese-Icelandic comedy, *Cold Fever,* offered the snow-zone equivalent.) But mainly it's because, however predictable the storyline, the film-makers succeed in making us care about the characters right from the start.

Though a fiction, this is intended as a distillation of countless similar narratives. Between 1907 and 1924, an onscreen prologue tells us, over 20,000 young women from Japan, Korea and Okinawa travelled to Hawaii to marry men they knew only through photographs. Riyo's experience may or may not be typical, but it's never sensationalised and feels wholly convincing. Matsuji is occasionally drunken and crude, but never brutal, and despite his frustration, keeps his distance from her in bed. Indeed he's often kindly and considerate after his fashion: there's a touchingly comic tenderness in his attempt to win Riyo over, following Kana's advice to "make romantic, like in movie—like Rudoff Barentino". Even the film's nastiest character, the Portuguese foreman Augusto, is no melodramatic villain. His bullying, one senses, stems from his inability to get close to them in any other way.

The racial tensions on the island are sketched in: Augusto resents having a young Anglo foreman placed over him, the Japanese canecutters bad-mouth the Chinese, a fight nearly erupts between the Japanese and the lower-paid Filipinos. But all this, though adding to the atmosphere of the film, plays a relatively minor part in the action. There's rather more significance (though it's a brief episode and in no way rammed home) in Riyo's encounter with a Hawaiian fisherman. Though evidently attracted, he doesn't hassle her but merely observes on hearing she works in the cane-fields that no Hawaiian would touch such a job. As a fisherman, he explains, he can enjoy five years pleasant labour and a long, relaxed retirement—and hints that anyone who does otherwise is a fool. Riyo, who has been slaving all hours in the desperate attempt to amass her fare home, takes note.

The scene is typical of the strengths of the film—unforced, uncontrived, it makes its point quietly and with no undue emphasis. The same goes for the lead performance (and for all the acting, come to that): Riyo's transformation from scared, doll-like waif to confident, fulfilled young woman occurs gradually and convincingly, without histrionics. (The only slightly hammy performance comes from Toshiro Mifune in his cameo as the travelling showman. But then it's that kind of role.) Like Mark Adler's delicate pastiche-Japanese score, subtly evocative with its soft guitars and bamboo flutes, *Picture Bride* gently insinuates itself into the memory but never overplays its hand.

VILLAGE VOICE, 5/2/95, p. 56, Luis H. Francia

Upon her arrival in 1918 Honolulu, Riyo, a beautiful but fragile 16-year-old picture bride from Tokyo, is infuriated when her betrothed, Matsuji, turns out to be middle-aged. One of thousands of Japanese laborers working on Hawaii's sugarcane plantations, he barely resembles the 20-year-old photograph he'd sent her. With no money for return passage, Riyo is forced to marry him, in a mass ceremony with other picture brides, common at a time of anti-miscegenation laws.

When the unrelieved hardships of plantation life become abundantly clear, Riyo's heart turns implacably cold; Matsuji attempts to thaw it. His patient, often clumsy but ardent wooing, and Riyo's gradual softening, form the emotional, delicate core of Kayo Hatta's lyrical debut, *Picture Bride*. Youki Kudoh as Riyo and Akira Takayama as Matsuji etch convincing portrayals, with an appealing mix of genteel stubbornness and gentle roughness.

Their uneasy, evolving relationship contrasts with that of another seemingly more compatible couple (played lustily by Tamlyn Tomita and Cary-Hiroyuki Tagawa) whose marriage ends tragically. In exploring these parallels, Hatta gives us a vivid sense of Hawaiian plantation life during the early years of this century. Forced to live in ghettos, the plantation workers had to deal with a racist hierarchy, bossed by often cruel Portuguese overseers, who themselves answered to haole, or white American, owners and managers.

Part of the film's resonance lies in our recognition, no longer shocking in a Republican America, that even as we approach the end of the millennium, the plantation spirit still lives on.

Hatta, herself born in Hawaii, handles the skein of events to suggest the complexities—including intra-ethnic feuding—of plantation society. And through her quiet, effective attention to daily-life details, we get a vivid sense of how, despite merciless exploitation, the field hands attempt to recreate home in a setting so very different from Japan.

Hatta's empathetic feel for these now-vanished lives makes us overlook her failure to explore larger political issues, alluded to when talk of a pan-Asian strike surfaces. We have come by then to care for this peculiar marriage, knowing it will endure and seeing how, without the personal, the political remains a cold stew of abstractions.

Also reviewed in:
CHICAGO TRIBUNE, 5/19/95, Friday/p. P, John Petrakis
NEW YORK TIMES, 4/28/95, p. C16, Janet Maslin
VARIETY, 5/23-29/94, p. 56, Todd McCarthy
WASHINGTON POST, 5/20/95, p. H3, Rita Kempley

PIGALLE

A Seven Arts Releasing presentation of a Premiere Heure LM, UGC, FCC, Delfilm production with the participation of Canal Plus, Sofinergie 3, Federal Office of Culture of the Federal Department of the Interior (Switzerland). *Producer:* Romaine Bremond and Patrice Haddad. *Director:* Karim Dridi. *Screenplay (French with English subtitles):* Karim Dridi. *Director of Photography:* John Mathieson. *Editor:* Lise Beaulieu. *Sound:* Jean-Pierre Laforce. *Art Director:* Gilles Bontemps. *Costumes:* Jean-Louis Mazabraud. *Running time:* 93 minutes. *MPAA Rating:* Not Rated.

CAST: Vera Briole (Vera); François Renaud (Fifi); Raymond Gil (Fernande); Philippe Ambrosini (Malfait); Blanca Li (Divine); Jean-Claude Grenier (The Emperor); Bobby Pacha (Pacha); Younesse Boudache (Mustaf); Patrick Chauvel (Jesus le Gitan); Jacky Bapps (Forceps); Roger Desprez (Elegant Roger).

NEW YORK POST, 12/8/95, p. 51, Larry Worth

Paris is synonymous with picture-perfect vistas like the Eiffel Tower, Arc de Triomphe and Notre Dame Cathedral. But part of the City of Light's glow comes from the flashing neon of Pigalle.

The naughty part of Gay Paree—where strip-tease shows and drug dens are de rigueur and streetwalkers, pimps, hustlers and tourists crowd the sidewalks—could enliven the most lackluster narrative.

So what went wrong with "Pigalle," director/writer Karim Dridi's dramatic look at Paris' seamiest side? First and foremost, he ignored the Moulin Rouge area's unique allure, failing to differentiate between the former stomping ground of Toulouse-Lautrec and any other sex-for-sale hotspot.

Instead, the focus falls on a dopey love triangle between a handsome pickpocket, a stripper trying to avoid prostitution and a scheming female impersonator. The trio is also caught up in the machinations of three sets of drug dealers, with predictably tragic results.

But since all the characters—right down to an evil, cackling dwarf—are mere stereotypes, why should audiences care if they start dropping like flies? Worse, the obtuse narrative makes the reason for the killings—never mind who's actually responsible—an ongoing source of confusion.

Finally, Dridi's tableaus of bumping, grinding and groping get redundant fast. Rather than advancing the storyline, they cater to leering viewers. Meanwhile, the cinema verite approach—complete with bleached-out hues and grainy camerawork—gets lost in the shuffle.

The film's only real asset is Vera Briole as the flesh-peddling dancer. Briole effectively conveys the pain and confusion beneath her shellacked facade. Unfortunately, Blanca Li is a less-than-arresting drag queen while Francois Renaud—the object of everyone's lust—comes off as a cipher.

So, despite Briole's brave efforts, "Pigalle" doesn't merit a peep.

NEWSDAY, 12/8/95, Part II/p. B8, John Anderson

Part melodrama, part autopsy, Karim Dridi's "Pigalle" is named after the red-light district of Paris, where the film takes place, a human soup of transvestites, junkies, killers and pathetic misfits. We've seen it all before.

Which is not to say that Dridi, making his feature debut, doesn't produce a gritty, kinetic excavation of Paris' sex industry and underbelly and make some cogent statements about humanity's unhealthy and *amour*-starved fringe. It's just that his film often seems to be about the place rather than the people. Martin Scorsese has used scuzzy locales, too, but few people would say "Taxi Driver" was about Times Square.

"Pigalle" is, to a large degree, an album of sleazy snapshots decorating a sordid tale of human desperation. Vera (Vera Briole) is an exotic dancer and peep-show stripper who's trying to keep a safe distance from the gangsters who run Pigalle. Fifi (Francois Renaud) is a James Dean-ish drifter who's attracted to Vera while also being in love with Divine (Blanca Li), a drag queen who's become a pawn in a drug war between competing—and quite vicious elements of Pigalle's criminal hierarchy. When Divine is sadistically killed (there are generous portions of brutality in "Pigalle"), the film sets off on a new plot line of revenge, manipulation and murder.

The garish, gamy atmosphere of Pigalle is captured in helter-skelter fashion by British cinematographer John Mathieson, who manages to make the picture fluid and staccato at the same time. Dridi, meanwhile, isn't afraid to mine the humor in his milieu—the class commercialism of a sex-shop exchange, for instance, or the pointed absurdity of a drunken subway driver's stripping for a bar full of cheering idiots—while keeping his characters poised on the edge of hysteria.

Dridi also makes clear the toll that the flesh market takes on its product. The characters, like Vera and Fifi or the maternalistic drag performer Fernande (Raymond Gil), aren't given much history, but they don't really need it. They are in many ways your standard castoffs, looking for love in all the wrong places—because for one reason or another they are incapable of giving or receiving it, on what most of us consider normal terms. For all the flashing lights and the pathetic "glamor" within his film, Dridi knows the score and keeps it in our face.

VILLAGE VOICE, 12/12/95, p. 67, Leslie Camhi

Pigalle is a neighborhood story, set on the hill that once made Paris the international capital of pleasure and is now a place of shopworn sex and tacky glory. For his first feature, director Karim Dridi hung out and picked his cast from among the *quartier*'s copious riffraff.

Vera, a talented stripper, works for her lover, the Gypsy. She betrays him for Fifi, a baby-faced bisexual and small-time thief, who is cheating on Divine, his long-suffering, transvestite companion. Are these slight characters underdeveloped or are they simply pawns in the grip of raw desire and insidious underworld forces? This Pigalle gangster network includes the handsome, reptilian drug-and-porn merchant Malfait, the sleazy, seemingly Sephardic Pacha, and the "Emperor," a commanding dwarf.

Compared to old-time Times Square, this European marginal milieu seems to profit from a touching sense of community. No one appears entirely desperate, the single child goes unmolested, and even the sex workers enjoy sex, at least part of the time. In one scene, a semi-beloved neighborhood drunk (naturally, a subway conductor) does a cute striptease on a bar.

Pigalle's casual camerawork and astute casting lend the film true local grit, though Dridi's directing errs occasionally on the side of the obvious; the acting veers into melodrama as the gangland murders soon start piling up. But both sex and the sex trade, with its business men buying whips and hot peep-show numbers, appear real enough, as does the dual moral of this fairly trifling story: the sex trade will continue no matter what; trust in the love of transvestites.

Also reviewed in:
NEW YORK TIMES, 12/8/95, p. C10, Stephen Holden
VARIETY, 9/19-25/94, p. 81, David Rooney

PLAYING THE PART

A First Run Features release. *Producer:* Mitch McCabe. *Director:* Mitch McCabe. *Screenplay:* Mitch McCabe. *Director of Photography:* Mitch McCabe. *Editor:* Mitch McCabe. *Running time:* 38 minutes. *MPAA Rating:* Not Rated.

NEW YORK POST, 5/5/95, p. 37, Larry Worth

[*Playing the Part* was reviewed jointly with *Only the Brave*; see Worth's review of that film.]

NEWSDAY, 5/5/95, Part II/p. B5, John Anderson

[*Playing the Part* was reviewed jointly with *Only the Brave*; see Anderson's review of that film.]

VILLAGE VOICE, 5/9/95, p. 72, Georgia Brown

[*Playing the Part* was reviewed jointly with *Only the Brave*; see Brown's review of that film.]

POCAHONTAS

A Walt Disney Pictures release. *Producer:* James Pentecost. *Director:* Mike Gabriel and Eric Goldberg. *Screenplay:* Carl Binder, Susannah Grant, and Philip LaZebnik. *Story:* Tom Sito. *Supervising Animator:* (*Pocahontas*) Glen Keane, (*John Smith*) John Pomeroy, (*Governor Ratcliffe*) Duncan Marjoribanks, (*Meeko*) Nik Ranieri, (*Powhatan*) Ruben A. Aquino, (*Thomas*) Ken Duncan, (*Percy, Grandmother Willow & Wiggins*) Chris Buck, (*Ben & Lon*) T. Daniel Hofstedt, (*Flit & Forest Animals*) Dave Pruiksma, (*Nakoma*) Anthony Derosa, and (*Kocoum*) Michael Cedeno. *Editor:* H. Lee Peterson. *Songs (music):* Alan Menken. *Songs (lyrics):* Stephen Schwartz. *Music:* Alan Menken. *Music Editor:* Kathleen Fogarty-Bennett. *Choreographer:* D.J. Giagni. *Sound:* Doc Kane and (music): John Richards. *Sound Editor:*

Larry Kemp and Lon E. Bender. *Casting:* Brian Chavanne and Ruth Lambert. *Art Director:* Michael Giaimo. *Visual Effects:* Don Paul. *Native American Consultant:* Shirley "Little Dove" Custalow McGowan. *Running time:* 80 minutes. *MPAA Rating:* G.

VOICES: Irene Bedard (Pocahontas); Judy Kuhn (Pocahontas, Singing Voice); Mel Gibson (John Smith); David Ogden Stiers (Governor Ratcliffe/Wiggins); John Kassir (Meeko); Russell Means (Powhatan); Christian Bale (Thomas); Linda Hunt (Grandmother Willow); Danny Mann (Percy); Billy Connolly (Ben); Joe Baker (Lon); Frank Welker (Flit); Michelle St. John (Nakoma); James Apaumut Fall (Kocoum); Gordon Tootoosis and Geefwee Boedoe (Kekata).

CHRISTIAN SCIENCE MONITOR, 6/23/95, p. 12, David Sterritt

Near the beginning of "Pocahontas," the new Walt Disney animation, the heroine and her father come up with different interpretations of the river that runs through their land. Stodgy parent that he is, Powhatan sees it as a reliable presence that's always stable and dependable. But his daughter finds it a changing, dynamic force full of excitement and surprise.

Disney likes to think of its 33 feature-length cartoons as belonging to the latter category—a moving, shifting stream always ready to embrace new material. The variety of that material is certainly broad, ranging from age-old legends and fairy tales to contemporary stories like "101 Dalmatians," literary yarns like "The Little Mermaid," and original projects like "The Lion King."

After a little thought, though, one realizes that Disney's animated oeuvre is more like the river as Powhatan sees it: large, pleasant to look at, and comforting in its consistency. But it doesn't encompass the world with the flexibility Pocahontas values. Quite the contrary, it bends the world to suit its needs, dictated by a narrow vision of the marketplace Disney serves.

This explains how "Pocahontas" can mark an innovation for the studio—it's their first animation based on a real-life person—without giving the slightest sense of entering fresh territory.

The heroine is beautiful and frisky, the hero is square-jawed and sturdy, the animals are adorable and anthropomorphic. The drawings are equally irresistible, combining time-tested imagery with fashionable touches. All of which fits the pattern of Disney cartooning. The movie gives a delightfully smooth ride, and you always know where you're going. But don't raise your expectations too high if you share Pocahontas's taste for free-spirited adventure.

Most moviegoers will find nothing to complain about as "Pocahontas" spins its well-known story about an Indian princess who falls in love with an English colonialist, schools him in native American ways, and saves him from her father's deadly wrath when warfare breaks out. Indeed, the steadiness of Disney films is considered pure gold by parents looking for child-friendly entertainment.

What bothers me isn't the relative worth of any Disney picture, but the way these movies have evolved—or failed to evolve, clinging to formulas that refuse to grow in any but superficial ways.

True enough, "Pocahontas" tips its hat to such trendy (and worthy) causes as conservation and environmentalism, and even delivers a hearty endorsement of interracial dating. Yet the studio can hardly be congratulated for "taking a stand" on socially relevant issues, since it's careful to wrap its ideas in an aura of nostalgic fantasy that neutralizes their ability to challenge or stimulate us. This suggests that the issues in question aren't deep or important anyway, since a sprightly song and a colorful image are always enough to drive away uncertainty and restore the feel-good glow that made the Disney folks famous.

I like to feel good as much as anyone, but I can't help questioning Disney's insistence on molding all material to fit the requirements of its committee-approved blueprints—even when the material is supposedly based on historical fact—rather than steering the kind of come-what-may course that Pocahontas seeks.

Some critics are lauding the new movie for breaking out of the mold, with its strong female characters and its willingness to allow a bittersweet ending instead of a triumphant finale. This strikes me as being overly grateful for small favors, though, given the picture's overall adherence to Disney's game plan.

Looking at "Pocahontas" for plain old entertainment value, it passes the test, although there's a slightly mechanical feeling to the drawing, dialogue, and directing that makes one suspect the crew was doing it by the numbers. The film's best asset is its voice-only performers, including

Irene Bedard as the title character; Mel Gibson as her British boyfriend; native American activist Russell Means as the heroine's father; Linda Hunt as a talking tree ; Michelle St. John as Pocahontas's sister Nakoma; and David Ogden Stiers as Ratcliffe, the new colony's nasty governor.

For an example of Disney's self-imitation, note how Ratcliffe's dog serves as a sort of familiar spirit, like the animal accomplices of Disney's fairy-tale villains. For an example of Disney's expertise at winning its audience's heart, note how vividly the interplay between Pocahontas and Nakoma is sketched, making us feel their sisterly relationship.

No studio turns out animations with more dependable production values. And no studio more consistently implies that its version of reality is more compelling than any of the real-life complexity it so conveniently avoids.

LOS ANGELES TIMES, 6/16/95, Calendar/p. 1, Kenneth Turan

Disney animation is one of the wonders of the modern movie age. Whether it is the magic of making drawings move or the emotional link the films have to childhoods past, there is something perennially enchanting about the elaborate feature-length cartoons that come from the house that Walt built.

Yet even magic isn't forever and pixie dust doesn't perennially bubble out of the ground like water from a spring. And with "Pocahontas," Disney's 33rd animated feature and the latest in the increasingly popular modern series that has gone from "The Little Mermaid" to "The Lion King," the spell, though hardly broken, is showing increasing signs of wear.

Not that "Pocahontas" won't justifiably delight children or is lacking in its share of animation's good things. Among its strengths is a gorgeous look, replete with sweeping vistas and colorful panoramas, and a fearless, strong-minded and athletic heroine (albeit one whose form-fitting buckskins make her resemble a close personal friend of Fabio's).

But adult viewers, spoiled by what has come before, may feel that this film, which relates the legendary romance between a chief's daughter and English adventurer John Smith in the New World, is more by-the-numbers than inspired. Directed by Mike Gabriel and Eric Goldberg, "Pocahontas" is on the formulaic side, a copy that duplicates what its predecessors have done, only a little less adroitly and with a little less style.

So if the previous films featured cute animal sidekicks for its heroes, Pocahontas hangs out with Meeko the raccoon and Flit the hummingbird, undeniably amusing but no match for the lusty companions of "The Lion King." And the film overall lacks the bursts of irresistible humor that have powered its predecessors.

This blandness is especially noticeable in "Pocahontas'" seven songs, with music by Alan Menken and lyrics by Stephen Schwartz. They mean well (more about that later), but they lack the wit and zest that came naturally to Menken's earlier partner, Howard Ashman, whose loss to AIDS has left a gap that looms larger with each successive film.

Disney has tried to break new ground in one area, with uneven results. Criticized in the past, and with reason, for promulgating racist stereotypes, the studio has walked the extra mile, making Pocahontas' tribe as noble as the day is long, living in mellow harmony with nature until the dread "pale visitors" arrive. Though this scenario (written by Carl Binder, Susannah Grant and Philip LaZebnik) is preferable to the one that came before, it would be nice if the pendulum stopped in the middle sometime instead of swinging from one side to the other.

Titular leader of the British expedition that founds what is to become the Jamestown colony in Virginia in 1607 is the bloated and evil Governor Ratcliffe (voiced by David Ogden Stiers), who is accompanied by the officious valet Wiggins and an insect dog named Percy and who is continually searching for gold that isn't there. Having the British as villains, apparently, is still socially acceptable.

The man the new colonists respect, however, is John Smith (Mel Gibson), a hunky blond with the looks of a beach volleyball champion who somehow acquired a reputation as a Native American fighter despite never having encountered any until this trip.

On the Native American side of things, Powhatan (Russell Means) is having troubles of his own. His daughter Pocahontas (Irene Bedard, with singing by Judy Kuhn) is not exactly wild over his plan to marry her to a humorless warrior with the strength of 10, and good advice of the "even the wild mountain stream must someday join the great river" variety is not helping much.

For Pocahontas is wondering if life might have something more exciting in store for her. She's encouraged in this by Grandmother Willow (Linda Hunt), an anthropomorphized tree that looks like Robin Williams in bark drag and is the film's most amusing presence.

Naturally Smith and Pocahontas are fated to meet, but in addition to falling in love under a steamy waterfall, they engage in a political debate over ecology and correct land use that sounds like a contretemps on the "MacNeil/Lehrer Newshour." But while these two are spooning (and singing the score's best song, "Colors of the Wind"), the opposing sides are preparing for war, and soon enough Pocahontas will dramatically plead for Smith's life in the situation that has linked their names for hundreds of years.

Much has been made of the fact that the real Pocahontas was probably 12 or 13 when she met Smith and unlikely to look as much like a "Dating Game" contestant as she does here, but that is beside the point. Anybody who goes to a film like this for a history lesson is at best misguided.

Among the things people do go for, however, is romance, which makes the film's half-hearted "we'll always have Paris" ending something of a misstep. It is closer to the historical truth, but then this film hasn't exactly been bitingly realistic in other respects. If you're going to make a pro-ecology, anti-colonialism animated feature, you might want to throw in a conventional happy ending to lighten things up. It couldn't hurt.

NEW YORK POST, 6/12/95, p. 31, Michael Medved

First, the good news: "Pocahontas" is a gorgeously animated extravaganza with some catchy songs and colorful characters.

The bad news involves the burden of the magical "Disney" name and the sky-high expectations it generates: As successor to mass appeal masterpieces like "Beauty and the Beast" and "The Lion King," this new production must be deemed a mild disappointment.

Part of the problem is that "Pocahontas"—which was screened Saturday night in Central Park and opens in theaters June 23—is, well, pokey.

Though its running time is barely 85 minutes, the picture feels much longer because of an acute shortage of story.

Everybody knows about the climax where the title character intervenes with her father, Chief Powhatan, (the voice of Indian activist Russell Means) to save the life of English settler John Smith, but while we wait for that dramatic denouement the movie merely kills time with cute raccoons, talking trees, and earnestly forgettable songs about learning to respect alien cultures.

As the first Disney animated feature ever to dramatize real-life figures from the past, "Pocahontas" tries to combine entertainment with a history lesson, but falls short on both counts.

The movie rightly depicts the Jamestown settlers of 1607 as motivated by greedy delusions of discovering gold, but the colony's pompous governor (who appears here under the wrong name and even with the wrong flag) is nothing more than a silly cartoon villain.

The portrayal of Capt. John Smith is even worse: The movie gives us a 17th-century surfer boy, blond and bland—despite the robust vocal talents (and surprisingly strong singing voice) of Mel Gibson.

Pocahontas herself is, on the other hand, an altogether captivating creation, so lovingly drawn and athletically animated that viewers of all ages (and genders) will fall for her.

Never mind the fact that the real Pocahontas was only 11 at the time of this story and could hardly qualify as a politically correct poster girl for the Native American pride and multiculturalism so passionately stressed by the movie.

The Pocahontas of history abandoned her people, married an Englishman (not John Smith), embraced Christianity, changed her name to Rebecca and traveled to London, where she died at age 22.

While the movie can't be faulted for avoiding such complex story elements, it still maintains an unexpectedly gloomy atmosphere, in part due to the dark palette of blues and grays the animators used to recreate the primeval Virginia wilderness.

There's also an abrupt, unsatisfying, downbeat (and historically absurd) ending that will send no one out of the theater with a song in his heart—though we may have a few tunes on our lips, thanks to the seductive score by Alan Menken.

POCAHONTAS 1101

In place of the late lyricist Howard Ashman (his collaborator on "Little Mermaid" and "Beauty and the Beast") he's now working with Stephen Schwartz ("Godspell") who sorely lacks Ashman's grace or wit. This is particularly obvious in several heavy-handedly New Age, "Can't-we-all-get-along" ballads, though early in the movie the music briefly soars with "Just Around the River Bend"—a memorable expression of yearning and expectation reminiscent of "Something's Coming" in "West Side Story."

This splendid song, enhanced by the movie's undeniable visual dazzlements, makes one yearn for the next Disney musical just around the river bend, even while savoring the mixed pleasures of "Pocahontas."

NEWSDAY, 6/23/95, Part II/p. B2, Jack Mathews

Walt Disney Studios' 33rd animated feature, "Pocahontas," is its first to be based on a historical character. Let's hope they don't try that again.

With one eye on history and one on the box office, Disney attempts to wrap a conventional fairy tale romance in a cloak of political correctness, and suffocates the life and humor right out of the movie. "Pocahontas" is fabulously drawn, of course, but nearly every other element of the modern Disney animated musical—the songs, the villains, the animals—pales in comparison to its predecessors, "The Little Mermaid," "Beauty and the Beast," "Aladdin" and "The Lion King."

Forget the chest-beating Disney has done over its use of American Indian actors as the voices for the Indian characters, for its efforts to authenticate native culture references, and for depicting the early white settlers as the intruders, despoilers and thieves many of them were. *Kids won't care!*

And if you want to use "Pocahontas" as a conversation starter about the ill treatment and distorted image of Indians, how are you going to explain the hot flashes Pocahontas gets over the first white guy she sees? You tell me, when an Indian rejects her own customs and a suitor from her own tribe for a blond hunk with a gun, what's the message for children?

The Indians in the old Hollywood westerns who said "white man speak with forked tongue" had that right. What hubris of Disney to age Pocahontas from 11 to jailbait, give her a body that would test the pacemakers at the Beverly Hills Racquet Club, then go out and say, "Look at all the Indians we hired for this movie!"

The greater problem is that they took themselves seriously. They did away with the voices of Flit and Meeko, Pocahontas' hummingbird and raccoon buddies, turning them into frustrated mimes, and bypassed the colorful production numbers that have become the signature of the New Era of Disney Animation.

Instead, we have a relatively sedate tale of a spirited native girl (speaking voice of Irene Bedard, singing voice of Judy Kuhn), who, at the advice of a talking tree she calls Grandmother Willow (Linda Hunt), follows her heart right into the arms of John Smith (Mel Gibson). Their love sends them back to their respective camps ready to lay down their lives to prevent war between the settlers, led by the gaseous Governor Ratcliffe (David Ogden Steirs), and the natives, led by the wise—and yes, noble—Chief Powhatan (Russell Means).

The songs, written by Alan Menken and Broadway lyricist Stephen Schwartz, include this year's probable Oscar winner, a hummable ballad about the sanctity of nature called "Colors of the Wind." But most of the songs are memorable mostly for the heavy-handed sermonettes contained in them.

No one should expect a history lesson from a movie, unless it's billed as one, but Disney squandered a great opportunity in deciding to recast the Pocahontas tale as a sort of "Romeo & Juliet" knockoff. It's hard to imagine kids wouldn't have more fun and get more out of the real legend, that of a curious and carefree child who saved John Smith in, order to save peace.

In real life, Pocahontas did end up marrying an Englishman and became a celebrity in London society. They could have used that in the sequel.

NEWSWEEK, 6/19/95, p. 77, Laura Shapiro

Hollywood wisdom has long decreed that boys won't go to girls' movies, but somebody at Disney must be feeling rebellious: *Pocahontas* is unabashedly girl-driven. Apart from the occasional burst of gunfire, just about everything in this lavish, animated feature is for the pigtail set, especially a big romance between Pocahontas (Irene Bedard, with Judy Kulm's singing voice) and the strapping John Smith (Mel Gibson). Pocahontas even has a best girlfriend (Michelle St. John). And there's something strangely familiar about the Indian maid herself, tall and shapely in a buckskin minidress, with miles of floating hair: she's Native American Barbie.

Disney takes liberties with the 17th-century legend, but "Pocahontas" is certainly true to current pedagogy. The British are ill shaven and greedy for gold, while the Indians led by Chief Powhatan (Russel Means), are gentle and wise, know all about nature, have family values and have even invented lacrosse. Look, up until now, Disney's most memorable American Indian was Princess Tiger Lily; the company owes them one.

Alan Menken's music is inflated, and Stephen Schwartz's lyrics are stilted; but this is a gorgeous-looking movie with a star worth cheering for. Assertive, fearless and the first great athlete among Disney heroines, Pocahontas doesn't hesitate a moment to risk her life for Smith and world peace. And as a 6-year-old New Yorker put it, heading out of a "Pocahontas" screening with a blissful look on her face, "Finally, I got to see a movie where the girl has black hair."

SIGHT AND SOUND, 10/95, p. 57, Leslie Felperin

London. 1607. Captain John Smith helms the ship taking Governor Ratcliffe of the Virginia Company to the New World where the latter hopes to found a colony and, more importantly, find gold.

The Native Americans living in the area the adventurers are bound for are lead by Chief Powhatan, who wants his free-spirited daughter Pocahontas to marry Kocoum, the tribe's fiercest warrior. Pocahontas confides her troubles and her dreams to her friend, an ancient spirit which resides in a willow tree named Grandmother Willow. Pocahontas sees the ship arrive and the men claim the land for Britain. After briefly meeting Smith in the woods, she runs back to the tribe to report the arrival of the strangers. The tribal shaman sees visions of the white men as rapacious wolves who will eventually devour their people.

While the British establish their fort and dig fruitlessly for gold, Pocahontas and Smith meet by a waterfall and are soon conversing fluently with each other. When a member of the tribe is shot in a scuffle with the settlers, Powhatan decrees that no one should have contact with the white men, but Pocahontas and Smith, falling in love, continue to meet in secret.

Tensions escalate between the two groups, despite Pocahontas and Smith's pleas for peace. When Pocahontas' friend Nakoma tells Kocoum that Pocahontas is with Smith, he and Smith fight and Kocoum is shot by Ratcliffe's equerry Thomas. Smith is captured by the tribe and condemned to death, but Pocahontas insists they must kill her first. Powhatan is moved by this, and considers making peace with the settlers. When Ratcliffe tries to shoot Powhatan, Smith takes the bullet instead while attempting to save the chief. He recovers and the British put Ratcliffe under arrest and set off for home. Smith beseeches Pocahontas to come with him back to England, but she insists on staying behind with her people and the two sadly part company presumably forever.

There is something about the sheer scale of the success of Disney's animated films, breaking box-office records with the nonchalant regularity of a butcher snapping the necks of chickens, that raises the hackles of critics. Ever since the publication of the Dorfman and Mattelart's 1971 Marxist critique, *How to Read Donald Duck,* the Disney company has been constructed as an exemplar of capitalist cultural imperialism, permeating every nation on the earth with its seductive, easily translatable pop propaganda.

Dorfman and Mattelart were mainly concerned with the more disposable Donald Duck comic books, rather than the films. Yet, as the latter have grown in popularity and success and as "The Mouse"—as *Variety* likes to refer to the voracious rodent which is the Walt Disney Company proper—has grown to its global status, it has seemed ever more urgent to be vigilant of what subtextual messages might be contained within the cartoon texts. The Disney Version of stories is put under as much scrutiny as the testimony of policemen in Los Angeles courts. Thus, there were accusations of racism concerning *Aladdin* and *The Lion King*, and critics and academics have questioned the images of women portrayed in *Beauty and the Beast* and *The Little Mermaid*. It is as if we are holding the films responsible for much more than just entertaining children on a wet afternoon.

Pocahontas is fascinating because it bears witness to the company's attempt to grapple with these criticisms as well as to produce another record-breaking blockbuster that will soak up receipts as well in the midwest of America as that of Africa. Inevitably, it is fraught with contradictions and ironies. It is large and contains multitudes, as Walt Whitman said of himself; and like Whitman's poetry, it is baggy, drawing on a distinctly American vernacular (both verbal and visual), and full of moments of real poetry, sharp pathos and patronising kitsch.

Pocahontas is as politically correct as oatmeal cookies. Its heroine is tall, muscular and graceful, can steer rapids as well as Meryl Streep in *The River Wild*, and has a face so scrupulously uncaricatured she lacks cheekbones and any more nose than a pair of nostrils lest she be confused with her hook-nosed ancestors in cartoon history. All her expression resides in her eyes, as dewy and doe-eyed as Bambi's mother before she gets shot. The rest of the tribe are equally circumspectly drawn, while the white settlers range from exaggerated grotesques (baddies like Ratcliffe) to more realistic figures depending on how likeable they are. The film's world view constructs a great chain of being in which the Native Americans are poised at the pinnacle, neatly inverting Renaissance concepts of hierarchy.

The film-makers here seem acutely aware that they are dealing for the first time in a major way with 'true story', albeit one clouded in myth and predictably revised here. No matter how ersatz, the viewer is constantly aware of how historical details are being mobilised for verisimilitude. When Smith describes Pocahontas' people as "savages" in his accurately seventeenth-century way, her offence is assuaged by his explaining that it is "just a word". Indeed, a curious concern with language permeates the film, with the natives speaking an authentic North American dialect which quickly morphs into American-accented English. Much magical play is made of Smith and Pocahontas' immediate grasp of one another's languages, literalised in a kiss. One would almost imagine that the story—people had been brushing up on the linguist-philosopher Tzvetan Todorov's *The Conquest of America*, which posited that the Native Americans apparent inability to understand Western language became the cornerstone of a whole discourse which explained their 'savagery'.

The anxiety of accuracy muddles much throughout the film. It showcases how much animation's motion-control and background-generating technology has advanced movements, especially Pocahontas' hair (tricky stuff to animate), are perfectly done, and some of the shots 'underwater' are nothing less than exquisite. However, the palette feels all wrong. The British scenes and characters are rendered in drab sepia colours so that the Native American setting, all bright and brutally blue skies, will seem all the nicer and friendlier. It would seem to me that a more muted natural palette would have been more appropriate to the latter culture, but I suppose the merchandisers, who favour a more garish, child-luring range of hues, had to be appeased.

The art direction alone belies the forces that threaten to tug *Pocahontas* apart: on the one hand, the natural world must be stylised, with faint native symbols accenting the wind sweeping the leaves to suggest the harmony of their culture with the environment; but on the other hand the film's commitment to corrective historicising and verisimilitude reigns in the exaggeration which is animation's stock-and-trade. As a solution the film resorts to the gestures of the epic—huge landscapes, swelling choruses, even split-screen effects at the climax which recall Abel Gance's *Napoléon*.

In the end, the film does get to you. It's Disney's darkest and most tragic animated film, even though it pulls back from telling the true historical ending—the real Pocahontas came back to England with Smith, died shortly after arriving and was buried in Gravesend. And though most children probably won't yet know it, they'll soon learn that this story with its 'happy' ending depicting a final concord between natives and settlers only begins a more chilling history concerning a genocide that would span centuries of horror. It's this 'front-story' which truly brings tears to the eyes when the credits roll, and by suggesting it, perhaps in a cloudy but well-meaning way, this film tries to expiate a little of the guilt that might be felt by one of the West's most successful capitalist organisations.

TIME, 6/19/95, p. 59, Richard Corliss

Ah, innocence! These days, can a movie be made on that subject, or any other, without stepping into a puddle of trouble? With the Christian Right and its political cronies on one side and a gaggle of cultural protectionists on the other, it's now possible for even a G-rated film to annoy somebody, anybody, with a special interest and access to a fax machine.

This week's example: *Pocahontas,* the handsome, deeply felt, even more deeply reverent animated musical from the Walt Disney Co. In retelling and retooling the 17th century encounter between the Powhatan princess and English Captain John Smith, the film takes the American Indians' self-image at face value. These are men of probity, women of dignity, curators of the land, weavers of white magic. Their standoff with the white man is one of eco-heroes vs. strip miners, defenders of an idyllic homeland against greedy invaders.

Yet many historians and aboriginal Americans are at odds over the film's version of the tale. The historical Pocahontas was a child of 11, not a buxom woman of 20, when she met John Smith—with whom she did not have a romance (though she did marry an Englishman and move to London). "I wish they would take the name Pocahontas off that movie," Shirley "Little Dove" Custalow McGowan, a storyteller of the Powhatan nation and for a time a Disney consultant on the picture, told the *Washington Post.* On the other side, Russell Means, the Wounded Knee insurgent who provided the voice of Chief Powhatan, said, "It is the finest film ever done in Hollywood on the Native American experience."

Both could be correct, at least politically, and still miss the main point. Yes, the Indians are very nice people here, which is a nice thing. And yes, the real Pocahontas probably didn't have Tina Turner's posture and Iman's neck. She probably didn't sing Broadway-style songs either or talk to a clever raccoon and a persnickety hummingbird. Maybe John Smith didn't look like Fabio and sound like Mel Gibson (who speaks the role). But this is a movie—a cartoon, for goodness' sake! It is a boy-meets-girl, boy-gets-girl, boy-loses-girl story whose plot is familiar in every weepie affair, from Romeo and Juliet to *The Bridges of Madison County.* And it follows the rule of historical romance: Print the legend.

In fact, *Pocahontas,* smartly directed by Mike Gabriel and Eric Goldberg, has a political agenda, but of a more general sort. In designating as its hero the spunky but idealistic princess and as its villain the English Governor Ratcliffe, head of the Jamestown expedition, the film takes the side of every available underdog: the working-class English sailors fighting the avaricious aristocrat, the Indian conservators over the white predators, the female spirit of conciliation over the male itch to resolve every dispute by going to war. Boldly eco-liberal, Pocahontas even pokes fun at the Disney Co.'s recent attempt to buy Virginia land and build a historical theme park, Disney's America, not far from Jamestown. "With all ya got in ya, boys,/ Dig up Virginia, boys!" sings Ratcliffe, as his toadying manservant sculpts exotic animal topiary of the sort found at every Disney park.

All this is to say that every work of popular art is political, and the good ones are more than that. Like this one. *Pocahontas* takes a while to get going, but when it does it becomes a wistful meditation on lost love in what it depicts as the last age of innocence. The lovers Pocahontas (voiced by Irene Bedard) and John Smith are from a gentler, more serious movie era; and so, to its credit, is this film. The picture has its light moments and patentedly adorable characters, notably Meeko the raccoon, a most fastidious glutton with a lot of personality. But *Pocahontas* lacks the menagerie of cuties that filled *The Little* Mermaid and *The Lion King,* and the absence must be intentional. For this is an animated film for adults who have a touch of the moony adolescent in them. The movie passionately argues that, of all causes, love is the one most worth fighting for.

And singing about. Of all the fine scores Alan Menken has composed for Disney animated features (*The Little Mermaid, Beauty and the Beast, Aladdin*), this is the most complex and rhapsodic, full of swelling passages that are artfully complemented by the Disney artists' imagery of pristine streams and forests. Menken's lyricist, Stephen Schwartz of Broadway's *Godspell* and *Pippin,* has a poetic righteousness that deftly avoids propaganda. *Colors of the Wind*—among the loveliest ballads composed for a Disney cartoon, and sung to fierce perfection by Judy Kuhn—ends with the admonition, "You can own the earth, and still/ All you'll own is earth until/You can paint with all the colors of the wind."

Political arguments aside, this had to be called *Pocahontas.* It is not the story of John Smith and his Indian girlfriend; it is the portrait of a princess of the spirit. Instead of reducing the historical character to a cardboard placard of goodness, the film gives her an impish curiosity and willfulness. Because she also has a classical heroine's sense of quest, the picture's Pocahontas rises above stodgy old legend into the sky of myth; and there she soars, eagle-like, watching over the land and its contentious people. That's apt for a role model for any child, red or white. And it's perfect for a film romance that earns a place of honor among Disney's latter-day animated film stunners.

VILLAGE VOICE, 6/27/95, p. 62, Gary Dauphin

A faint shadow of *The Lion King* (not to mention of something like *Snow White*, or even *101 Dalmatians*), *Pocahontas* sleepwalks through the popular myth of the title character's encounter with John Smith (voiced by Mel Gibson and looking here like some blond superhero), hitting all the main points of contention without offering any of the potential excitements. Played by Irene Bedard and sung by Judy Kuhn, Pocahontas meets Smith, falls in love with him, and rescues him from her sage and wise father (Russell Means, who should have known better but probably just couldn't resist), all in that order and with little else to hold your interest.

This is an oddly live action love story, with Pocahontas sexy in the way of recent Disney starlets of color (c.f. the princess in *Aladdin*) but no Jessica Rabbit, and Smith's essentially bland virility riding on the associations provided by the recognizable sound of Gibson's he-man voice. Where's the Disney magic you ask? In the hype, unfortunately. Visually attractive in a glazed over sort of way, the film's most arresting feature is Disney's stated desire to do the multicultural mythmaking thing, presenting a picture of history that is simultaneously bogus and generally friendly to the natives. There will be valid critiques of this film from the left, but from a six-year-old's p.o.v., there's some pretty heady stuff: the rape of the land, the obvious sophistication and moral superiority of Native American peoples, the avarice of gold-greedy explorers and colonials. Too bad the other elements of interest to a six-year-old are absent, like funny animals (the ones here goof but don't talk), scary villains, villains, impressive magic, songs with lyrics they'll be able to remember, et cetera. If you want to expose a child to *Pocahontas*'s more edifying aspects, make sure they're small enough that you can just force them to go. Otherwise you'll have to sweeten the deal with the promise of a *Batman/Power Ranger* double feature and a large order of fries, and even then they might still get mad at you.

Also reviewed in:
CHICAGO TRIBUNE, 6/23/95, Friday/p. C, Michael Wilmington
NATION, 7/31-8/7/95, p. 145, Stuart Klawans
NEW YORK TIMES, 6/23/95, p. C6, Janet Maslin
VARIETY, 6/12-18/95, p. 59, Jeremy Gerard
WASHINGTON POST, 6/23/95, p. F1, Rita Kempley
WASHINGTON POST, 6/23/95, Weekend/p. 38, Desson Howe

POSTMAN, THE (IL POSTINO)

A Miramax Films release of a Cecchi Gori Group/Tiger Cinematographica/Pentafilm Esterno/Mediterraneo Film coproduction in association with Blue Dahlia Productions/Studio Canal+. *Executive Producer:* Albert Passone. *Producer:* Marrio Cecchi Gori, Vittorio Cecchi Gori, and Gaetano Daniele. *Director:* Michael Radford. *Screenplay (Italian with English subtitles):* Anna Pavignano, Michael Radford, Furio Scarpelli, Giacomo Scarpelli, and Massimo Troisi. *Story:* Furio Scarpelli and Giacomo Scarpelli. *Based on the novel "il postino di Neruda"* by: Antonio Skarmeta. *Director of Photography:* Franco di Giacomo. *Editor:* Roberto Perpignani. *Music:* Luis Enrique Bacalov. *Sound:* Angelo Raguseo and (music) Franco Finetti and Fabio Venturi. *Sound Editor:* Ezioi Marcorin. *Production Designer:* Lorenzo Baraldi. *Costumes:* Gianna Gissi. *Make-up:* Alfredo Marazzi, Simone Marazzi, and Leone Noël. *Running time:* 113 minutes. *MPAA Rating:* Not Rated.

CAST: Massimo Troisi (Mario); Philippe Noiret (Pablo Neruda); Maria Grazia Cucinotta (Beatrice); Linda Moretti (Rosa); Renato Scarpa (Telegraph Operator); Anna Bonaiuto (Matilde); Mariano Rigillo (Di Cosimo); Bruno Alessandro (Pablo Neruda's Voice).

LOS ANGELES TIMES, 6/14/95, Calendar/p. 6, Kenneth Turan

"The Postman" ("Il Postino" in the original Italian) is a tender and wistful comedy about the friendship between a celebrated poet living in exile and the simple local man who delivers his mail. Made under unique and wrenching circumstances, it gained poignancy and a kind of purity from its troubles, and an already affecting film ended up suffused with emotion.

"Postman" stars Massimo Troisi, an adored Neapolitan comic actor and director whose previous work never managed American distribution. And this film, directed by Michael Radford ("White Mischief"), an English friend fluent in Italian, was made under the worst kind of duress.

Troisi, born with congenital heart troubles, got increasingly weaker as production continued. But though he could work no more than an hour or two a day, the actor refused to postpone filming and instead put off an essential heart transplant. "Postman's" restrained, poetic style, its director says, "was born out of this adversity, as if it had been predestined."

The idea, based on a combination of fact and fancy, also came from Troisi, who is one of five credited screenwriters. It germinated from a novel set in Chile about the imagined relationship between Pablo Neruda, that country's great Nobel Prize-winning poet, and a postman. The film smoothly transfers the setting to the island of Capri, off the southern coast of Italy, where Neruda was in fact exiled in 1952.

Troisi plays Mario Ruoppolo, a fisherman's son vaguely discontented at the thought of a life at sea, a quasi-innocent whose life gets turned around by a few twists of fate.

At the movies one night, Mario sees a newsreel celebrating the arrival in Rome of Neruda, exiled for his passionate Communist beliefs. The man's political stance, however, does not impress Mario as much as Neruda's reputation as "a poet beloved by women."

On the way home from the theater, Mario notices a help wanted sign. It turns out that the great Neruda will be moving to his island, and, the postmaster explains, a special mailman will be needed to handle the volume of correspondence this "great and kind person" will be receiving.

Fascinated enough by the eminence he is serving to look Chile up in an atlas, Mario slowly but doggedly begins to chat with the poet when he drops off the day's mail, and "Postman" is especially convincing in showing how a tentative relationship could develop between these thoroughly unlikely soul mates.

For Mario the attraction at first is the stubborn hope that knowing Neruda, perhaps even getting him to autograph a book, will help in the pursuit of women. But, almost without his knowing it, Mario begins to think about poetry as well, to ask the kind of naive, original questions about verse that can't help but intrigue the writer. And when Mario, after not knowing what a metaphor is, comes up with one unawares and then, in a masterful acting moment, hides his head in pleased chagrin, their friendship is sealed.

Neruda is played by French actor Philippe Noiret, one of the venerable pillars of European acting, and he handles the part with grace and aplomb. But, obviously, this picture is the uncontested property of Troisi.

With superb timing, an impressive variety of facial expressions and the hangdog demeanor of an Italian Buster Keaton, Troisi brings a truth and simplicity to his character that means everything. The actor's clear empathy with his audience keynotes his great popularity, and the plaintive weariness that illness adds to his character seems not special pleading but rather an intensification of Mario's essential nature.

"Postman's" mainplot mechanism has Mario seeking Neruda's poetic assistance when he falls helplessly in love with Beatrice (Maria Grazia Cucinotta), the beautiful local barmaid.

But the film, surprisingly, goes considerably beyond questions of love and romance to deal with the nature of friendship, the power of the written word to change and enlarge lives in unanticipated ways, and the price that invariably will be asked for any such changes.

"The Postman" has given Troisi the kind of international acclaim he hoped for, but it is a success he did not live to witness. Within hours of completing work on this project, the actor died in his sleep, and 10,000 shocked admirers attended his funeral. Troisi told friends that he wanted the last piece of his old heart to get into this movie, and though the cost was overwhelming, there can be no doubt that he succeeded.

NEW YORK, 8/14/95, p. 43, David Denby

The late Massimo Troisi, star of the charming Italian film *The Postman*, had a stalled, foggy voice in which the words got lost somewhere between the conception and the delivery. In *The Postman*, set on a tiny, primitive island off the coast of Italy, Troisi's Mario Ruoppolo has no one to speak to, which is a pretty good reason for not speaking much. And then, in the early fifties, the island is visited by a kind of god—the exiled Chilean poet Pablo Neruda, who, in the person of the courtly, genially overweight Philippe Noiret, takes up residence in an empty villa. Mario, who becomes his postman, suddenly cannot stop speaking, and the poet, at first brusque, then wary, gradually gets drawn into the miracle of Mario's awakening, reciting poetry to the word-hungry mail-carrier. They have a memorable moment on the beach in which Neruda makes up a sea poem, with a pounding, wave-tossed rhythm, and Mario suddenly understands what poetry is.

The movie is a fable of creation: Mario is literally created by the words he learns to speak. The English director Michael Radford, working in Italian, keeps the tone light and charming and on the whole rather chaste (whimsy is a danger successfully avoided). In a noisy season, it's easy to be lulled by such enchanting episodes as Mario's poetry-rich courtship of a sultry island beauty who becomes aroused by his words. The girl's overprotective aunt, in a series of hilarious pot-banging tirades, denounces that mysterious force, "metaphors," as the traducer of her niece's virginity. She's right, of course. Once you've lost your innocence with words, you never want to regain it.

NEWSDAY, 6/14/95, Part II/p. B9, John Anders

The postman ring a lot more than twice Michael Radford's "The Postman"; sentiment seems to have its sticky fat finger stuck in the bell. You'll let them in, though, because both are delivering kind of simple truth—even poetry—that justifies opening the door and being walked all over.

Adapted from Antonio Skarmeta's quasi-factual novel, "Burning Patience," "The Postman" is a sweetly poignant film for real as well as dramatic reasons: Massimo Troisi, the celebrated Italian comic actor, die shortly after the movie wrapped. He looks like a dying man, and was.

But the film draws its pathos from many sources and is about many things, including personalized mail service. In a small Italian village in 1952 (a change from the book), the unemployed Mario (Troisi) spies a want ad and thus becomes a postman with one customer: Pablo Neruda (Philippe Noiret, of "Cinema Paradiso"), the Nobel laureate-to-be who has moved to a house just outside town and is enjoying the sunny comfort and attention befitting a world-renowned poet and Chilean political exile.

How Mario and "Don Pablo" become intimates; how Neruda plays Cyrano for the unassuming Mario, helping him win the lovely Beatrice (Maria Grazia Cucinotta); how Neruda's Communist politics are absorbed by Mario—half through indignation, half through hero-worship—are all part of this tale of unlikely friendship.

But "The Postman" is also about celebrity and selfdefinition: Why does the proximity of a famous man make Mario blossom, even before they've gotten to know each other? Mario, himself a kind of exile—he's lived in a fishing village all his life and hates to fish—comes out of his shell in response to Neruda's poetry and its implied power. But he's also drawn out by the idea of the man, who represents something Mario's never seen, or expected to see.

One of the lovely things about "The Postman" is how Radford convinces us of the highly unlikely possibility that two such disparate men would meet, and just as the arcs of their lives had intersected: Neruda, a sculptor of polished words who responds to simplicity with unspoiled instinct; Mario, the simplest of men, who responds instinctively to art. Despite his characters' growing affection for each other, though, Radford regularly isolates his two poets, emphasizing the point that both are totally alone: Neruda in his poetical-political diaspora, Mario in his melancholy.

This becomes even more sadly evident after Neruda, the warrant for whose arrest has been revoked, returns to Chile. There are no letters—save one asking Mario to forward some belongings—and the now-unemployed postman has to live on the memory of his famous friendship. Neruda does return, but by then Mario is gone, his search for truth having taken a fatal turn. Neruda, last seen as a speck on a beach, knows that neither poetry nor politics respects any truth but its own. Neither does film for that matter, but at least in the "The Postman" fact accommodates fiction in the service of something larger.

NEW YORK POST, 6/14/95, p. 36, Thelma Adams

It's tough when fishing is the family business and you're allergic to boats.

The sniffling, sad sack Mario (Massimo Troisi seems bound for a life of quiet desperation. He lives on a tiny island off the Italian coast that, with its terra cotta days and jewel-toned nights, looks like paradise. To Mario, it's more like Alcatraz.

Mario's father, as crusty as a heel of bread, has no patience for his son's sensitivities. "Go to America or Japan if you want to, but get, yourself a job," says the fisherman.

The son's luck turns when he becomes "The Postman" to the islands single celebrity: the Chilean poet Pablo Neruda (the acclaimed French actor Philippe Noiret).

Director Michael Radford ("White Mischief") and famed Italian comic actor Troisi adapted Antonio Skarmeta's Chilean novel "Burning Patience" to the screen.

The filmmakers transposed Skarmeta's fiction about Neruda's friendship with a postman from Chile to an island off Naples. They drew on the historical fact that the Communist poet spent a period of political exile in Italy.

The plump, teddy-bearlike Noiret ("Cinema Paradiso") serves as a foil for the bony, angular Troisi. Together they create a comedy of contrasts. Like the sad clown, Troisi builds humor from tragedy. In this case, the tragedy was just beyond the screen. The Italian actor suffered from a congenital heart disease and needed a heart transplant during the shooting of this labor of love. The 41-year-old star postponed the operation and died the day after filming ended.

"The Postman" builds on small moments to tell an ineffably sweet story about poetry's transformative power. Through his contact with Neruda, Mario is not only able to see the beauty in the world around him but to woo a beauty, Beatrice (Maria Grazia Cucinotta), with new-found words.

"Poetry doesn't belong to those who write it, but to those who need it," says Mario.

"The Postman (Il Postino)" is a delightful call to reclaim poetry, to bring it back down to earth and put it to work in everyday life where it is as necessary as a job, a loaf of bread, a beloved companion and a true friend for life.

SIGHT AND SOUND, 11/95, p. 49, Julian Graffy

1952. Mario, the unemployed son of an Italian fisherman, learns from a cinema newsreel that the exiled Chilean poet, Pablo Neruda, is to take up residence on their island. Impressed by the number of women mobbing the poet's train, he secures the job of Neruda's personal postman, though his boss is more interested in Neruda's reputation as Communist 'poet of the people'. Daily, Mario brings piles of letters and parcels to the villa where Neruda lives with his wife, Matilde. He reads the poet's verse, and gradually incites Neruda to talk to him about poetry, in particular about the workings of metaphor. Neruda, too, warms to Mario's natural perceptiveness. Mario begins to wonder if he too is a poet.

In the local bar, Mario is smitten by the beautiful Beatrice, the owner's niece, and tries to enlist Neruda as scribe of his passion. Neruda refuses, but gives him a book "for his metaphors," which he signs in front of the girl. Metaphor works its spell on her, too, and she falls for Mario. Neruda is witness at their wedding, but at the reception he announces that he can now return to Chile. The men part affectionately, and Neruda promises to write, but time passes. The Christian Democrats win a landslide election victory, and then rescind their local promise to supply running water. Mario, radicalised by his experience, votes Communist, and insists that his future son will be named Pablito.

Eventually, a formal letter from Neruda's secretary requests the forwarding of items from the villa. Mario's family take this as evidence that he was exploited by the poet, but Mario insists that it was he alone who gained from their encounter. Fulfilling an earlier promise, he makes a tape of the sounds of the island for Neruda. Ten years later, Neruda and Matilde return to the island and meet the child, Pablito. His widowed mother explains that Mario never saw his son. He was killed at a Communist demonstration at which he was to read his workman's poetry. She plays the tape, 'Canto per Pablo Neruda', and Neruda is last seen pensively walking the island's beach.

Michael Radford apparently wanted to cast Massimo Troisi in the lead role in his first feature, *Another Time Another Place*, but it was not until ten years later that the two worked together on *The Postman*, a sort of reversed reworking of the concerns of the earlier film. In *Another Time Another Place*, Italian prisoners of war brought passion and experience to the repressed, marginal community of northeast Scotland; here it is the Italian who is the marginal figure, waiting to be ignited by poetry and Pablo Neruda. Troisi, who initiated the project, is central to the film's effect—he is scarcely off-screen, and at the beginning his combination of nuanced gesture and vocal hesitancy is compulsive; he does not so much play as inhabit the role of Mario. Philippe Noiret gives a more conventional performance as Neruda, and the contrast in acting styles serves as an effective register of contrasting experience and sensibility.

Most of the film is devoted to the repeated encounters between the two men, however, and all the actors' skill cannot prevent a certain narrative lethargy. The central early plot motif, the islanders' fear of the contagion of 'metaphor' spreading through them, produces amusing moments, as they each use metaphor to express their unease, but Mario's sudden insight that maybe the whole world is a metaphor is left undeveloped. Instead, the film abandons poetry for a lazily predictable tale of Mediterranean backwardness, stocked with cliché characters—local fishermen, smouldering dark beauty (called Beatrice to invoke the poetry of Dante), black-clad widow, seedy politician, anti-Communist local priest implying that Neruda may have eaten his own children—and helped along with sentimental detail. Despite Troisi and three other Italians being credited, with Radford, for the screenplay, this is fake Italy, Italy for export. It is particularly ludicrous that Neruda should be required to school the Italian peasant, a man in his thirties, not just in poetry, but in love. In the original novel, set on an island off the Chilean coast, the hero was a 17-year-old boy. The exiling of the novel to Italy, and the need to cast Troisi, has exacted a heavy cost in credibility, a cost that extends to Neruda, who remains slightly perfunctory, with his tangos, his smug refusal to discuss his poetry, and his fretting about the Nobel Prize (which he was not to win until 19 years later). Neruda turns into another lovably curmudgeonly oldster, melting and transmitting his knowledge and artistic passion to a neophyte, a variant of Noiret's role in a similarly glutinous vision of Mediterranean life, Tornatore's *Nuovo Cinema Paradiso*.

Eventually, the film seems to realise the absurdity of its vision, as Mario admits to himself that his curiosity and his naive questions can have been little more than a diversion for Neruda, and that his ideas about his own poetic gift are a delusion. This belated attack of intellectual rigour is welcome, and produces the most original and persuasive scenes in the film, but it is sadly short-lived, as the film-makers succumb once more to 'heart-warming' cliché, making their hero a martyred worker poet, whose doe-eyed son can avenge his abandonment by leading Neruda to his rueful final stroll.

The Postman is well served by its actors, and does contain amusing details—watching the newsreel at the start, the villagers are far less impressed by the grand foreign poet than by the shots of themselves and their island. But its fundamental falsity and miscalculations are ever more evident, miscalculations encapsulated in a banal and intrusive musical score by Luis Enrique Bacalov.

VILLAGE VOICE, 6/20/95, p. 43, Georgia Brown

In 1952, while Pablo Neruda was on a reading tour of Italy, a nervous Italian government decided to heed Chile's request and kick him out of the country. By the time the police could escort Neruda to Rome, protestors were swarming the streets chanting, "Let the poet stay!" The government relented and Neruda and his new amorata, Matilde Urrutia, were offered a splendid villa on the island of Capri. (Whereas Neruda professed himself delighted to discover "the hidden Capri of the poor," the villa belonged to the man who owned half the island.) Here they stayed for several months, until Chile revoked the warrant for Neruda's arrest and he could return home. In his *Memoirs*, Neruda describes the Capri interlude as a period of work and solitude spent "among the simplest people in the world."

In the rich, delightful conceit that fuels Michael Radford's *The Postman (Il Postino),* one of these simple people is Mario Ruoppolo (Massimo Troisi), a 31-year-old fisherman, albeit one not cut out for the family line of work. At the local cinema, Mario sees the pro-Neruda marches on newsreels and hears that the poet (played with bemused reserve by Philippe Noiret) will be coming to live on his island. Impulsively, he applies for a job as a temporary postman whose sole job is to deliver, by bike, Neruda's voluminous fan mail. Since Italian postman made (make?) their living by tips, the job promises little remuneration, but Mario-the-dreamer has his sights on higher rewards.

In his letter-carrier capacity, Mario discovers that women, in particular, are Neruda's correspondents. To be a poet, he surmises, is to win fame, wealth—or wealthy sponsors—and the love of women. But to become a poet, Mario must first learn what poetry is. After buying a collection of Neruda's poems, he asks the great man to sign it: Something intimate, to impress the girls in Naples. When the author signs merely "Regards," Mario is crushed: As a Communist, a "man of the people," Neruda should know better.

Besides chronicling the meeting of a Marxist intellectual and a real, live oppressed worker, *The Postman* describes what is now closer to our hearts, a close encounter between a star and a fan. The former is aloof, absorbed in work, hardly aware of the existence of this functionary; the latter, focused entirely on the prominent figure as a source of dreams and fantasy life. And the fan expects everything; he thinks it his due. (Perhaps it is.) Such a relation, as we know, has many possible outcomes. Unlike *Taxi Driver, The Postman* is a sweet tale of innocent eras, or less aggressive parts of the world.

Based on Antonio Skármeta's novel, *Burning Patience (Ardiente Paciencia), The Postman* also describes the more specific encounter of writer and reader. In most cases this is a meeting that takes place in the circumscribed space of the page, in the rarefied medium of print. Readers are not meant to color in the white space between words. (All, the perils that may befall those who insist on violating this barrier, encountering their idols face-to-face.)

Once he begins reading, Mario has questions. What do you mean that "the smell of barbershops" should make you sob? The point of poetry, Neruda patiently advises, is it works only in the form it's in; explaining poetry makes it banal. Mario latches onto Neruda's line, "I'm tired of being a man." I, too, have felt that way, he says.

Empowered by poetry, Mario falls for a sexy waitress and steals a Neruda poem to woo her with. Rebuked by the author, he replies with a swell line, "Poetry belongs not to those who write it but to those who need it." The woman's name, fittingly, is Beatrice, although Mario has not yet heard of Dante. When Neruda sets eyes on Beatrice (the luscious Maria Grazia Cucinotta) he looks like he wouldn't mind adding her to his fan club. (When Beatrice's protective momma rushes to the rescue, the movie makes clear that locals spouted metaphors long before poets vacationed there.) But if this sort of betrayal isn't the direction our fiction takes, the friendship, such as it is, between somebody and nobody is shown to have real dangers.

Italians like their movies the way Americans like breakfast cereals, with plenty of sugar. Director Radford may not be Italian, but the production is, and *The Postman* teeters at times toward sentimentality and the merely picturesque. Then there's the fact that the moving force behind the project, Troisi, Naples's beloved Pulcinella, was visibly dying on the set. Having been told he needed a heart transplant, the 41-year-old insisted on finishing the film and died the day after production ended.

Once you're in possession of this morbid information, Troisi's performance seems horribly, pointlessly, valiant. As it is, his Mario looks inexplicably decrepit. Thin, stooped, sweating, Troisi could barely stand and worked no more than two hours a day. *The Postman* should be called *The Sacrifice.*

Also reviewed in:
CHICAGO TRIBUNE, 6/23/95, Friday/p. G, John Patrakis
NEW REPUBLIC, 7/3/95, p. 27, Stanley Kauffmann
NEW YORK TIMES, 6/14/95, p. C15, Janet Maslin
WASHINGTON POST, 6/23/95, p. F7, Rita Kempley
WASHINGTON POST, 6/23/95, Weekend/p. 38, Desson Howe

POWDER

A Hollywood Pictures release in association with Caravan Pictures of a Roger Birnbaum/Daniel Grodnik production. *Executive Producer:* Riley Kathryn Ellis and Robert Snukal. *Producer:* Roger Birnbaum and Daniel Grodnik. *Director:* Victor Salva. *Screenplay:* Victor Salva. *Director of Photography:* Jerzy Zielinski. *Editor:* Dennis M. Hill. *Music:* Jerry Goldsmith. *Music Editor:* Ken Hall. *Sound:* Steve C. Aaron and (music) Bruce Botnick. *Sound Editor:* Anthony Mazzei and Peter Austin. *Casting:* Junie Lowry-Johnson. *Production Designer:* Waldemar Kalinowski. *Art Director:* Barry Kingston. *Set Decorator:* Florence Fellman. *Set Dresser:* Grant Sawyer. *Special Effects:* Ron Trost. *Visual Effects:* Stephanie Powell. *Costumes:* Betsy Cox. *Make-up:* Kris Evans. *Special "Powder" Make-up:* Thomas R. Burman and Bari Dreiband-Burman. *Stunt Coordinator:* David Sanders. *Running time:* 111 minutes. *MPAA Rating:* PG-13.

CAST: Mary Steenburgen (Jessie Caldwell); Sean Patrick Flanery (Powder); Lance Henriksen (Sheriff Barnum); Jeff Goldblum (Donald Ripley); Brandon Smith (Duncan); Bradford Tatum (John Box); Susan Tyrell (Maxine); Missy Crider (Lindsey); Ray Wise (Stipler); Esteban Louis Powell (Mitch); Reed Frerichs (Syke); Chad Cox (Zane); Joe Marchman (Brennan); Philip Maurice Hayes (Greg); Dannete McMann (Emma); Tom Tarantini (Steven Barnum); Woody Watson (Mr. Kelloway); Alex Allen Morris (Dr. Roth); Brady Coleman (Dr. Deggan); Barry Berfield (Paramedic #1); Paula Engel (Anna); Meason Wiley (Arturo); Dee Macaluso (Nurse #1); James Houston (Doctor Associate #1); Bill Grant-Minchen (Doctor Associate #2); Bonnie Gallup (Nurse).

LOS ANGELES TIMES, 10/27/95, Calendar/p. 8, John Anderson

[The following review by John Anderson appeared in a slightly different form in NEWSDAY, 10/27/95, Part II/p. B9.]

One part "Nell," one part "Frankenstein" and one part Michael Jackson, "Powder" supposes that the thing we fear is our more-perfect reflection. The title character (Sean Patrick Flanery) has reached the limit of human potential—his mind is greater, his body is stronger, he has powers beyond human comprehension. And of course, he has a heart to match. What he doesn't have is a film that casts more than pale tribute at such perfection.

Found after the death of his grandparents, in the house where closed-minded old crones had kept him hidden, Powder turns out to be a lightning rod, literally and figuratively. His mother was struck by a thunderbolt while he was still in the womb (he remembers it all) and his affinity for electricity is supernatural. As a human oddity, he also attracts all the small-minded fears and hatreds of the rural Americans around him (wouldn't we like to think it's only them) and we know early on he can't survive. He's too pure, too perfect, too white. And too silly.

The actors seem to share our mirth. Mary Steenburgen, as the noble Jessie Caldwell, social worker/psychologist, strikes some spectacularly overwrought poses. She's no match, however, for Jeff Goldblum, who as math teacher and Powder confidant Donald Ripley (believe it or not) enters each room at the state orphanage as if were Randolph Scott poised at swinging saloon doors.

Lance Henriksen, as Sheriff Barnum (more, references to hokum!), is stern and kind and completely confusing (why is he so intent on keeping Powder at the home?) while Brandon Smith does a nice portrayal of a stupid, prejudiced police officer, who can only instill deep confidence and security in the townsfolk, knowing he is armed and ignorant.

As Powder, Flanery gives a convincing enough portrayal of a young man totally unfamiliar with the world, who's learned everything he knows from books (which he can recite by heart) and who exhibits more courage than is called for. He does, however, look a lot like Michael Jackson, with his complexion, his rolled-up trousers and his fedora. Given the Barnum and Ripley allusions, I wonder how accidental all this was.

Powder may have a good soul, but he's very white. Startlingly white. Whiter than any albino person has ever been. And he changes. Sometimes he looks like a person without pigment. Other times, he seems to have been buttered and floured. The "special makeup" credited to Thomas R.

Burman and Bari Dreiband-Burman is one of the distracting flaws in the film. (This week's revelation that writer-director Victor Salva is a convicted child molester also might skew audience response to the film.)

But something's got to keep your attention, and if it's Powder's complexion ... well, you could be waiting for Goldblum to collapse in laughter, which never quite happens.

NEW YORK POST, 10/27/95, p. 46, Thelma Adams

Oh, "Nell"! What is it about all these freakish geniuses, raised away from human kind in root cellars and rotted cabins who are exposed to the cruel world at the death of a relative and turn out to be so much smarter, purer and better than society at large that they just can't help bringing out the worst in those around them before they transform the local folks into the best they could possibly be?

About the only thing that "Powder" doesn't have is Jodie Foster dancing naked in the moonlight. Here is the adolescent nicknamed Powder because of his Casper ghostly complexion, placed like a cross between Nosferatu, Michael Jackson and the Beaver by Sean Patrick Flanery (TVs "The Young Indiana Jones Chronicles"). He might have a shocking personality (his pregnant mom was struck by lightning), but he's a certifiable genius who can recite "Moby Dick" by memory—just call out a page number.

When his godfather dies, the pathos-dripping Powder leaves the family farm and changes the lives of three people who have no right to be hanging out in Texas backwater. Mary Steenburgen (get a new agent!), Jeff Goldblum and Lance Henriksen are three actors in search of a moment of grace as they try to inject Southern sensitivity, East Coast humor and Swedish drama into a script by director Victor Salva, that had no reason to be produced in the first place.

If he was such a genius, what was Powder doing in this movie anyway?

SIGHT AND SOUND, 5/96, p. 57, Nick James

Texas, 1978. A comatose pregnant woman is rushed into hospital. A doctor tells her husband that he's managed to save the baby, but the woman has died. The child is albino and hairless with an astonishing level of brain activity. On seeing him, the father recoils yelling, "That's not my son!"

Wheaton County, Texas, the present. Sheriff Barnum and his deputy, Duncan, are called to a remote farmhouse where an old man has been found dead of natural causes. Living in the basement is his grandson, a hairless, pale-skinned boy who's never been to school. Barnum brings in Jessie Caldwell, head of a local home for young adults, who discovers that Powder has high intelligence and strange electrical powers. Installed at the home, Powder sees off bullies with his kinetic control of the canteen cutlery but he is soon unhappy. He tries to leave, only to be brought back by Barnum.

We learn that Powder's mother was struck by lightning causing his premature birth and that his father abandoned him to be raised by his grandparents. In a science class at high school, teacher Donald Ripley is demonstrating an electrical arc device which suddenly sends an arc across the classroom, lifting Powder off the ground until the power is switched off. The home's inmates go on a camping trip, and some of the boys sneak off to go deer hunting with Deputy Duncan. Powder tracks them down, too late to prevent the deputy from shooting a stag. But, by gripping Duncan's arm with superhuman strength and laying his own hand on the deer's neck, he makes Duncan experience the deer's death agony.

Sheriff Barnum becomes so convinced of Powder's powers that he brings the boy to visit his wife Maxine who is stricken dumb by terminal cancer, yet will not die. Powder enables Maxine to speak, telling Barnum that she can't die until the Sheriff reconciles with his yuppie son Steven. Barnum takes the hint and his wife passes peacefully away. Meanwhile, Powder has formed a close attachment with a local girl, Lindsey. When he ventures to kiss her at the county fair, her father threatens and vilifies him. Powder runs away again and this time makes it to his grandparents' house, only to find that all his things have been sold. Barnum and Duncan come to take him back, but Caldwell and Ripley persuade Barnum to let him go. He runs off as an electrical storm begins and before the others can catch him, he is absorbed into the ether by a flash of lightning, becoming one with the universe.

It is easy to list the unsophisticated ways in which *Powder* feeds off the genre-history of neurotic teen outsiders. For a start, the character of Powder is almost a textbook case of how to project adolescent alienation into a paranormal sci-fi scenario, recalling the constant use of adolescence as a gateway to the unknown in such films as *Carrie, Poltergeist* and the *Nightmare on Elm Street* series. Powder's powers—granted in the womb when his mother was struck by lightning—make him super-sensitive to the horrors of the adult world (people are sometimes less than kind), and super-bright enough to represent hope for mankind's future (someday we'll all be all-knowing and all-loving, stop being less than kind and become one with the universe).

As such he combines the otherworldly vulnerability of David Bowie's alien in *The Man Who Fell to Earth* with the chilling preternatural wisdom of the infants in *The Children of the Damned*, as well as having kinetic powers over objects to rival those of his adolescent counterpart in *Carrie*. But there's a much more blatant model for Powder's acute superiority complex even than these. With his pancake-white skin, eerie helium voice and adoption of a trilby hat and shades, Powder so resembles the public persona of singer Michael Jackson that the part might have been devised for him. With Jackson in mind one might expect a script of unbearable kitsch sentimentality containing panaceas of love for the whole world and *Powder* does provide several moments of ingratiating cuteness, including a sexless fairground love scene and Powder's television evangelist-style intercession for Mrs Barnum's dying wishes.

Yet, despite severely testing the straight faces of its high-quality cast, *Powder* sometimes shakes off sentiment and achieves a rare, compelling strangeness. The film is paced and shot in a hyperreal style in which textures of clothing and skin, land and skyscapes are highly detailed and dwelt upon at unnerving length. It's a patient aesthetic that works best in the confrontations between Powder and the other institutional boys, in which the boys' physical differences attain a level of metaphor. A similar sense of the uncanny is achieved in parts of Phil Alden Robinson's *Field of Dreams* and less successfully in Michael Tolkin's *The Rapture*. The constant, hypnotic low-key tension means that the few special effects showpieces are made all the more exhilarating. So frugal is the writer/director Victor Salva with the supernatural, he never stretches the limits of movie plausibility.

For much of the time, Powder is an ordinary teen outsider, a sort of neutered rebel. Our belief in his extraordinary powers becomes in these moments an act of communal faith. Sean Patrick Flanery plays him well as a sensitive recluse, but his character's supposed superabundant wisdom is never much in evidence. It requires the conviction with which Mary Steenburgen as Jessie Caldwell, Lance Hendrikson as Sheriff Barnum, and Jeff Goldblum as Donald Ripley play at being awestruck for the movie to be as effective and original as it sometimes is.

As concerned professional carer, softened cop and curious teacher, they represent the receptive aspects of an otherwise closed community. Taking into account the boy's electrically enhanced intelligence, *Powder* can be easily read as a parable of the coming of the electronic revolution. In this context, the fear and wonder of these adults can be read as symptomatic of the greying of the baby boom generation. As the first among them reach 50, they are faced with a rampant new technology that, as one television advert has it, will seem the norm to the children of today. It would be no surprise then if *Powder* proved to be the first of a glut of films in which fear of the young is the primary theme.

Also reviewed in:
CHICAGO TRIBUNE, 10/27/95, Friday/p. J, John Petrakis
NEW YORK TIMES, 10/27/95, p. C14, Caryn James
VARIETY, 10/30-11/5/95, p. 72, Joe Leydon
WASHINGTON POST, 10/27/95, p. D7, Rita Kempley
WASHINGTON POST, 10/27/95, Weekend/p. 48, Desson Howe

PRIEST

A Miramax Films release of a BBC/Electric Pictures/PolyGram Filmed Entertainment production. *Executive Producer:* Mark Shivas. *Producer:* George Faber and Josephine Ward. *Director:* Antonia Bird. *Screenplay:* Jimmy McGovern. *Director of Photography:* Fred Tammes. *Editor:*

Susan Spivey. *Music:* Andy Roberts. *Sound:* Dennis Cartwright. *Casting:* Janet Goddard. *Production Designer:* Raymond Langhorn. *Art Director:* Sue Pow. *Costumes:* Jill Taylor. *Make-up:* Ann Humphreys. *Running time:* 97 minutes. *MPAA Rating:* R.

CAST: Linus Roache (Father Greg Pilkington); Tom Wilkinson (Father Matthew Thomas); Cathy Tyson (Maria Kerrigan); Robert Carlyle (Graham); James Ellis (Father Ellerton); Lesley Sharp (Mrs. Unsworth); Robert Pugh (Mr. Unsworth); Christine Tremarco (Lisa Unsworth); Paul Barber (Charlie); Rio Fanning (Bishop); Jimmy Coleman (Funeral Director); Bill Dean (Altar Boy); Gilly Coman (Ellie Molloy); Fred Pearson (Patrick); Jimmy Gallagher (Mick Molloy); Tony Booth (Tommy); Charley Wilde and Euan Blair (Tommy's Children); Giuseppe Murphy (Man in Lift); Kim Johnson (Mrs. Gobshite); Keith Cole (Mr. Gobshite); Adrian Luty (Jehovah's Witness); Bobby Martino (Bobby); Rupert Pearson (Man on Skateboard); Victoria Arnold (Girl in Confessional); Gareth Potsig (Boy Car Thief); Ray Williams (Boy with Stutter); Valerie Lilley (Sister Kevin); Kevin Jones (Boy at Beach); Michael Ananins (Charge Sergeant); Mickey Poppins (Reporter); Marsha Thomason (Nurse); Matyelok Gibbs (Housekeeper); John Bennett (Father Redstone); Gareth Milne (Fight Arranger); Mauricio Venegas (Chilean Band Leader).

FILMS IN REVIEW, 7-8/95, p. 60, Maria Garcia

Antonia Bird's *Priest* is so improbable and so badly envisaged that it can hardly be called a film at all. Driven by the most mind-numbing and sophomoric polemics, it resembles a theater class improvisation rather than a cohesive cinematic narrative. The characters are stereotypes shaped by Ms. Bird's considerable distress with the institutional Catholic Church. Unfortunately, that distress is based upon a schoolgirl's understanding of the Roman Catholic faith, and upon a basic lack of understanding about institutions in general. Even if *Priest* were less didactic, its implausibility destroys any shred of credibility it may have possessed: one would be hard pressed to find a small English parish inhabited by a liberation theologist and a closet homosexual, in a diocese run by a corrupt, acquisitive bishop.

In places, the screenplay (by Jimmy McGovern) is so silly that I kept expecting Torquemada the Grand Inquisitor (Mel Brooks in *History of the World, Part I*) to appear. Unfortunately, this never happened. The opening sequence is a good example of how ridiculous the film gets: a priest who has been forced to retire drags a crucifix through the streets to the bishop's office to use it as a battering ram. Clearly, Ms. Bird meant to be profound but it's a scene out of a satire, not a drama. Then, in the first love scene between Father Greg (Linus Roache)—the homosexual priest—and Graham (Robert Carlyle, who gives the film its only really effective performance), Graham asks Greg whether he's Catholic; he says it takes one to know one. I could not help but wonder what betrayed Father Greg—it couldn't be his preference for the missionary position, could it? Maybe he just yelled "Oh God" once too often? But the best chuckle of all was the Marquis de Sade-inspired proclamation from Father Greg that he's aroused by the naked body of Christ hanging on the cross. To my surprise, no one else in the audience laughed.

Which brings me to the dilemma of *Priest*'s popularity. It seems angry films will always find audiences, just as this one has. Blaming institutions, the government, the Catholic Church, our parents and even other outside influence for our shortcomings is far easier than engaging in a discernment process which would reform these influences. Movies like *Priest*, which require no emotional or intellectual involvement, allow people to project their pain and emptiness onto the screen, rather than involving them in the revelatory and cathartic process which great films inspire. These films are like the aging priest's crucifix/battering ram, which released his frustration but provided neither the bishop nor his church (nor the audience, I might add) with any deeper understanding of his dilemma. Films like *Priest* are the soap operas, the dime store novellas, the peep shows of the cinema.

Even more disturbing is the fact that *Priest* does not even aspire to artfulness—it is totally uncinematic. There is never a moment in this film, with the possible exception of the final shot, in which the audience grasps the director's intentions visually. Since Father Greg is so badly conceived, narrative structure is also completely undermined. That's why the film requires the director's overbearing presence, and why it relies so heavily on dialogue to explain everything—the emotions the audience should be experiencing through the main character are unformed and incomplete. Without the presence of a well-conceived protagonist, no film can hope to achieve the emotional are so necessary for narrative integrity.

On a purely personal level, every Roman Catholic questions the practices of the institutional church but many of them persist, just as Father Greg does, and Father Matthew (Tom Wilkinson), because they are somehow perfected through the underlying principles which govern their faith. The Church is the best expression of their spirituality. She is Mother Church, and she still symbolizes the power of love and acceptance, even for the homosexual and the liberation theologist, the edge-dwellers of the institutional Church.

Robert Bresson's *The Diary Of A Country Priest* (1951), based on the novel by Georges Bernanos, remains the only cinematic expression of Catholic spirituality. It depicts one priest's quest for faith and spiritual perfection in a world that makes that quest almost impossible to accomplish. And for those who can remember even further back, Carl Dreyer's *The Passion Of Joan Of Arc* (1928) illustrates the power of one woman's faith in her struggle against the institutional Church. Perhaps it's unfair to place *Priest* against these two masterpieces but I feel compelled somehow, if only to illustrate that Bresson and Dreyer, both highly critical of the institutional Church, were able to elevate the stories of their protagonists to an archetypal dimension which enriches the spiritual dilemmas of people in institutionalized religions—something Antonia Bird can only aspire to.

LOS ANGELES TIMES, 3/24/95, Calendar/p. 10, Kenneth Turan

What are we to make of "Priest"? Created for British television, it arrives on American theatrical screens laden with all the plaudits an extensive tour of the world's festivals can bestow on it, from audience awards to standing ovations. And, to a limited extent, it deserves them.

But the harder truth about "Priest" is that it is also an unintentional sham that offers the trappings of reality without its essence, a well-meaning film most adept not, as it likes to think, at grappling with difficult subject matter but at making viewers feel good about themselves.

Certainly "Priest" gets points for staking out so many of Catholicism's incendiary areas that the filmmakers hope even the Pope will be impelled to watch. The torments of a homosexual priest, the regrets of a non-celibate heterosexual colleague, the nightmare of incest, the agony of wanting to break the inviolate seal of the confessional to right a terrible wrong, all get an airing. Bing Crosby in "Going My Way" this is defefinitely not.

But although there is a danger of making "Priest" seem less involving than it is, the film's take on most of these issues is depressingly simplistic and predigested. Having determined to wade into this great dismal swamp of material, screenwriter Jimmy McGovern and director Antonia Bird haven't been able to resist compulsively tidying it up. All the film's emotions and motivations are neatly boxed and labeled; everything possible, in fact, is done to make it easy for audiences to feel they're on the side of the angels.

"Priest" begins with the forced retirement of an elderly cleric, who, in a typically theatrical gesture guaranteed to get our attention, responds by ramming a lifesize crucifix through the window of his bishop's study.

Coming in as a replacement in the poor Liverpool parish of St. Mary's is Father Greg Pilkington (Linus Roache), a young man eager, in the bishop's cynical words, "to do his bit for the inner city." Quite handsome in a boyish way, Father Greg causes a bit of a stir when he arrives and immediately gets into a philosophical spat with fellow priest Matthew Thomas (Tom Wilkinson).

Father Matthew is a recognizable type, a progressive, socially conscious cleric who keeps a large photo of Sitting Bull around and sees himself as a focus for change. Father Greg, by contrast, is traditional, conservative and more than a little self-righteous, believing that moral guidance is the sole reason for a priest's existence.

Who can doubt but that this officious prig is going to have to be taken down a peg or two and learn some lessons in humanity and humility. And, soon enough, Father Greg gets his first taste when Maria (Cathy Tyson), the parish housekeeper, makes the kind of carefully reasoned yet off-the-cuff speech about her questionable private affairs that no one could manage in real life.

This kind of platform speaking turns out to be typical of the way "Priest" allows its characters to behave. Even the parishioner who practices incest speaks out on his own behalf with such an articulate position paper on the subject that you half expect him to hand Father Greg a sheaf of footnotes when he's finished.

"Priest's" subplot about incest, which is as arbitrary as it sounds, is the film's weakest, most schematic area. Is it really necessary to have the symbolic fires of hell (in the form of a trash can blaze) flaming over the malefactor's shoulder when he talks, or have his daughter's carefully constructed game of building blocks collapse when he enters the room? The restraint practiced by the powerful and austere "The Boys of St. Vincent," a TV movie from Canada that also deals with scandals within the church, would not have been out of place here.

What humanizes Father Greg most, however, is having to deal with the difficulties inherent in being a gay priest, and this is where the film is at its strongest and most convincing. Star Linus Roache, a veteran of British TV and theater, creates a quiet and believable portrait of a man torn between his spiritual vocation and his sexual behavior.

But balanced against this is "Priest's" determination to confirm its viewers' core prejudice, that all the world's troubles come from the way other people, never us, act out of narrow-mindedness and prejudice. If we in the audience were faced with the problems shown on screen, tolerance and understanding surely would be the orders of the day.

Aside from its obvious flaws, that kind of thinking makes "Priest" increasingly unrealistic. The difficulty with reality, which "Priest" is unable to come to grips with, is not so much that obviously bad things happen to obviously good people but that the lines are often more blurred than clear-cut, the consequences of behavior not nicely tied up with a ribbon.

Subtlety, nuance and the willingness to let audiences experience uncertainty would be necessary for this film to be as courageous as it sincerely believes it is. But, given the state of movie audiences, if it had those qualities, all those standing ovations would be a lot less likely.

NEW STATESMAN & SOCIETY, 3/17/95, p. 33, Jonathan Romney

The history of British cinema, for better or worse, is a history of realism. It's all very well invoking the spirits of Powell and Pressburger, of left field artificers like Jarman, Greenaway or Sally Potter. The British directors who really win international acclaim tend to be the die hards whose work could carry that proud Hollywood tag-line: "Torn from today's headlines!" In a recently filmed TV discussion on British cinema, directors Stephen Frears and Michael Apted—who have gone on to become dependable mainstreamers—paid homage to *Play for Today* and the definitive tradition of British cinema. In fact, Apted claimed, his country-and-western biopic *Coal Miner's Daughter* was his conscious attempt to import that style into America.

It's the phantom of TV kitchen-sink drama that makes it so hard to get a purchase on why British realism remains unsatisfying as a language. For a film critic, there's always a danger in complaining that a film looks "like a TV film"—quite apart from opening yourself to charges of snobbery, it's a hard accusation to make meaningful. You know what British TV films feel like, because you've seen them; but there's no specific code that defines them, other than the fact that eight out of ten feature Julie Walters. Otherwise, you have to resort to a circular argument—this is a TV film because it's about the sort of thing we see on TV.

The other argument, though, that defines British TV drama is a sense of being auxiliary to wider debate, rather than self-contained. British TV has always had the benefit of a closely tied support industry geared to debate—the *Listener*, when it existed, near-instantaneous discussion on *Points of View* or *Right to Reply*. It's partly because these mechanisms exist and need to be fuelled that the BBC tends to make dramas that keep the Reithian mill churning. And people are more likely to phone in to discuss questions of housing or inner-city crime than a film's formal qualities. That's the problem with a film like Ken Loach's *Ladybird Ladybird*, whose agenda has everything to do with the real. All discussion of the film tends to be around journalistic questions—does or doesn't it get its facts right about the social services? Consequently, discussion of the film as a film seems frivolous, the sort of thing only an aesthete would fret about.

That's the problem too with the BBC-produced *Priest*. Again, it's tempting to say that it feels like a TV film, but that's largely because we're used to seeing Liverpool only on the small screen. Its makers are known TV names—director Antonia Bird, who worked on *Inspector Morse* and the hugely acclaimed drama *Safe*, and Jimmy McGovern, TV's drama man of the moment. No surprise, then, that watching *Priest* you can't quite get the taste of soap out of your mouth. What's most televisual about it is the thoroughness with which it tries to sort through its issues, as if obliged to give maximum value for your licence fee. Idealistic young hardliner Father Greg (Linus Roache) arrives in Liverpool to find this dogmatic faith confronted by feisty right-on colleague Father Matthew (Tom Wilkinson), who is cohabitating with his housekeeper Maria (Cathy Tyson). Greg fulminates, but is soon sneaking out to the gay clubs and getting embroiled in his own surreptitious affair. He also learns that a young girl in his congregation is being abused by her father, an unrepentant figure whom a more metaphysically inclined Catholic drama might have made into Satan incarnate; of course, Greg feels bound by the sanctity of the confessional. Celibacy, homosexuality, the reality of evil, the pragmatics of liberation theology—this one has it all. It shouldn't happen to a Jesuit.

It's this exhaustiveness that makes *Priest* so much like a TV film, with the convincingly sensual Roache facing a key issue every 20 minutes. It might have been more upfront, in fact, to make it into a series and simply have him deal with one crisis a week—you can see the mileage in an austere cross between *The Moral Maze* and *Doctor Finlay's Casebook*. As it is, the film is obliged to tie up all its ethical knots before the end, and it does it too cathartically for comfort—there should be some sort of tax on using "You'll Never Walk Alone", however ironically. For all the insistence on making this a materialist drama, you can't help feeling *Priest* might have breathed more had it taken on some of the headier abstractions of religious drama risen to the Bresson challenge. Otherwise, Father Greg just looks like a social worker saddled with an unreasonably tough code of practice.

NEW YORK, 4/17/95, p. 104, David Denby

Linus Roache, the star of *Priest*, is a serious, sweet-faced young man with mild blue eyes that tend to flare with a sci-fi-like intensity. Roache's effects may be calculated, but his inflammability is a beautiful thing to watch. He's the latest in a line of handsome young Brits (including Daniel Day-Lewis and Ralph Fiennes) whose attitude toward acting is, by American standards, extraordinarily unspoiled. Whatever may be wrong with England, the habit of training actors in theatrical rep companies still produces a selfless dedication to craft. Linus Roache will undoubtedly do many good things in the future, but for the moment, he has found his identity as Father Greg Pilkington, a solemn young priest—and guilt-ridden gay man—who arrives in bedraggled contemporary Liverpool, joins a pasty-faced-poor parish, and promptly gets himself into one mess after another.

Roache's Father Greg is both a sensual young man and a highly orthodox Catholic, and he experiences the satisfactions of the flesh as an inexpressible relief and an excruciating trial. I have to admit that when I first heard about *Priest*, I groaned. The sins of the flesh are a concern that most of us, Catholic and non, straight and gay, have long since dismissed, and I was in no mood for overwrought spiritual anguish. But I was wrong in my assumptions about the film, which turns out to be much broader in its reach. It is not only Greg's sexual desires but his moral instincts that are at war with church doctrine and his vocation. A forlorn teenage girl with a crumpled face tells him at confession that she's being abused by her father, which puts Greg in a dreadful position: His vows forbid him to violate the confessional, and so he hesitates to take action to save the girl—a reluctance he experiences as both a fulfillment of his priestly role and a betrayal of his Christian duty. Almost everything in Greg's life pulls him apart. His troubles mount up with near-comic dolorousness and bring him to the point of kneeling with ridiculously blasphemous thoughts before his God, a beautifully shaped naked man hanging on a cross.

Priest, which was produced by the BBC, is a terrifically vital and surprisingly funny movie. The Liverpool writer Jimmy McGovern works with pungent, colloquial force and in broadly emotional, popular terms. But McGovern, who was educated by priests, also raises some of Catholicism's deeper questions: Is it morally right for Greg to abase himself before 2,000 years of institutional history? Or does the church afford him a dignity that makes his personal sufferings trivial? Director Antonia Bird works broadly, too, at times too broadly. She likes to whip up storms of emotion, and she goes for melodramatic contrasts and shock cutting. There is a show-offy opening scene, in which a disgruntled old priest ramrods the bishop's headquarters with a huge crucifix. But then the movie settles down and takes hold; you feel tied to Greg's anxiety, his nausea, his moral impotence.

Greg boards with another priest, Father Matthew Thomas, who is played by the wonderfully bearish actor Tom Wilkinson. A defiant liberal who separates the institutional church from the teachings of Christ, Father Matthew has a happy sexual relationship with his beautiful housekeeper (Cathy Tyson), and he's appalled by the almost sanctimonious Greg, who believes that sexuality is a sin and that the church has the right to punish him. With an onslaught of argument and jokes, Matthew attempts to rescue the young priest from despair. The growing friendship between these two is one of the most satisfactory emotional relationships in recent movies. Bird creates the ebb and flow of the friendship with elemental force, and she has a gently lyrical way with the gay-sex scenes—Father Greg's nights on the town as he glides around on his bicycle offer sweet freedom. *Priest*, which seems cramped and ugly in the beginning, grows physically more beautiful as it goes on, an opening to sensuous pleasure that suggests where the movie's heart lies. Not that *Priest* mocks the clergy or Catholicism. This is one of the rare truly Christian movies, and it says in the end that priests who offer not only the Sacraments but the embrace of forgiveness are as necessary to the faithful as Jesus. *Priest* turns out to be ... a revelation.

NEW YORK POST, 3/24/95, p. 45, Thelma Adams

From the startling opening image of a raging, aging priest ramming an altar-sized crucifix into a bishop's window to the final cathartic communion between a young priest and his parishioner, Antonia Bird's "Priest" is, in the director's words, "A celebration of Catholicism, but a questioning of certain rules within the church."

It is the most intelligent, insightful and entertaining movie thus far this year.

Linus Roache, from the Aidan Quinn school of drop-dead handsome, plays Father Greg, the conservative young priest newly assigned to a parish in Britain's toughest city, Liverpool. Greg is certain of his vocation, but events in Liverpool sorely test his faith.

Greg's first shock is that his fellow father, Matthew Thomas (Tom Wilkinson), a "hugging" priest with progressive politics, is living in sin with their housekeeper, Maria (Cathy Tyson).

"There's just sin," Greg scolds Matthew. "You can't change the rules just because it pleases you."

Before long, Greg's certainty begins to erode. Watching Matthew and Maria, Greg gains a heightened awareness of his own loneliness and lack of companionship. One night, he removes his clerical collar and picks up Graham (Robert Carlyle) at a gay bar.

Breaking the vow of celibacy—with a man—begins Greg's crisis of faith. But when young Lisa Unsworth (Christine Tremarco) confesses that her father is molesting her, the priest must decide whether to break the seal of the confessional to protect her from future attacks.

Catholic, Liverpuddlian screenwriter Jimmy McGovern (TV's "Cracker") sets up these conflicts with humor and compassion, developing a dialogue between good and evil, left and right, young and old.

In an effective scene, the incestuous father (Robert Pugh) enters Greg's confessional. His pale face framed by a square mesh, The blue-eyed fiend justifies his actions in a cunning whisper: "Incest is human. It's the one thing we'd all like to do, deep down, in here. I've dedicated my life to the study of incest. I don't need help. I don't need therapy."

Facing this "grinning, sickening evil," Greg's faith crumples. Bird follows the confession with an emotionally wrenching sequence. She intercuts Mrs. Unsworth's discovery of her husband en flagrante delicto with Lisa and Greg's impassioned plea to an image of Christ to protect the girl, while he tearfully acknowledges the depths of his despair.

Roache deftly handles the transformation from an earnest, by-the-book neophyte to a man who has weathered the storm and seen his faith reborn. The naturalistic performance begins with a buttoned-down control and then opens up as the actor begins to unbutton his character and, then, as the buttons fairly fly, his emotions quaver with intensity.

Bird delicately directs the sex scene between Greg and Graham; it's erotic in a gentle, almost solemn, way—a thanksgiving to human ecstasy. The guilt that immediately follows for Greg is overpowering, but the script is less convincing in translating a young relationship based on sex into one of love. When Graham tells Greg, "I love you," it's the movie's single false note.

Bird's stunning directorial debut ushers provocative issues of hypocrisy, faith, forgiveness and homosexuality in the priesthood into the mainstream. Her achievement is making them accessible by solidly grounding the drama in traditional techniques. Bird and McGovern treat their characters and the audience with intelligence—and the love and compassion that is the theme of "Priest."

NEWSDAY, 3/24/95, Part II/p. B8, Gene Seymour

Though top-loaded with fiery rhetoric, "Priest" starts off with a mostly wordless scene that is also one of its best: A sad old Catholic priest, about to be put out to pasture, decides to get a head start on his retirement by ramming a large crucifix through his bishop's window.

The feisty old geezer is immediately replaced by Father Greg Pilkington (Linus Roache), young, handsome and seemingly circumspect, who comes to this working-class Liverpool parish armed with conservative politics and a strictly by-the-book approach to Catholicism.

This puts him at odds with Father Matthew Thomas (Tom Wilkinson), the parish's senior priest, who is liberal and mildly libertine, since he's having intimate relations with the rectory's housekeeper ("Mona Lisa's" Cathy Tyson). After trading dueling sermons (Greg's for "individual responsibility," Matthew's for "compassion"), they achieve an uneasy peace under the same roof.

It doesn't take long, however, for cracks to appear in Father Greg's assurance about the Church and about himself.

He is confronted with the kind of torment Montgomery Clift's priest faced 40-odd years ago in Hitchcock's "I Confess." During confession, a teenaged girl tells Greg that her father has been raping her regularly. He doesn't know how to get help without breaking the sanctity of the confessional, and the father (a frightening Robert Pugh) tells him to keep out of his business. Evil appears, an anguished Greg confides to a friend, "and faith runs away in terror."

This friend's name, by the way, is Graham (Robert Carlyle), whose companionship Greg sought in a gay bar. Graham, who's also Catholic, comes to a church service to receive communion from Greg, who refuses to give it to him. Both these crises peak at the same time, tossing Greg into public, as well as private, agony.

"Priest" was first conceived as a four-part BBC-TV series by writer Jimmy McGovern, who is best known on these shores as the creator of the idiosyncratic "Cracker" detective-movie series that occasionally surfaces on the A&E cable network. More often than not, the strain of compressing all these complications into an hour-and-a-half movie shows in its thick gouts of declamatory dialogue and heavy-handed dramaturgy. And while there's enough of "Cracker's" zesty, pungent wit around to make "Priest's" shriller passages bearable, there's too little of interesting characters like Tyson's, who gets only one big speech of her own.

McGovern's hard-driving approach is perfectly matched by director Antonia Bird, another BBC veteran. For every lyrical sequence Bird designs in "Priest," she makes half-a-dozen others that come at you like hard blows to the senses. Yet, both despite and because of its blunt-edged, big-hearted bluster, "Priest" deserves its shattering, heart-tugging—and mostly wordless—conclusion.

NEWSWEEK, 3/27/95, p. 72, David Ansen

"We're priests, not bloody social workers!" screams the young doctrinaire Father Greg (Linus Roache) to the middle-aged, activist Father Matthew (Tom Wilkinson), whose working-class Liverpool parish he's just joined. Their theological disputes begin almost as soon as the handsome, gym-fit Greg arrives. To his ear, Matthew is just fobbing off glib liberal pieties to his flock, when he should be discussing the spiritual. He's doubly shocked to discover that Matthew has taken the presbytery's pretty housekeeper (Cathy Tyson) as his mistress. "Get rid of her," he advises sternly, brooking no argument. "There's just sin."

Before Antonia Bird's *Priest* comes to its highly charged conclusion, all Greg's notions of sin, of his vocation, of the Roman Catholic Church's role in the community and of his own identity will be subject to painful re-examination. During confession a 14-year-old girl (Christine Tremarco) reveals that her father is molesting her. Horrified, Greg wants to intervene but can't—it's forbidden to break the seal of the confessional. Burdened with her secret, he then must grapple with his own. How can he be so contemptuous of Matthew's breach of celibacy when his own desires lead him to Liverpool's gay bars—and a night of unpriestly ecstasy in the arms of a man?

"Priest" is loaded with enough live-wire issues to fuel a mini-series. Director Bird and writer Jimmy McGovern take on incest, homosexuality, the church's civil war between conservative and liberation theologies, and the age-old conflict between one's obligation to God and to one's conscience. It's solid, intelligent moviemaking and, at its best—in the scenes involving the abused Lisa, her self-justifying father (Robert Pugh) and her outraged mother (Lesley Sharp)—emotionally wrenching.

But in packing in so many thematic controversies, "Priest" can't quite escape that TV-movie feeling that the issues are dictating the drama, and the characters are just along for the dialectical ride. To these secular eyes, the bearish, feistily compassionate Father Matthew is hugely sympathetic, but I kept wondering why he bothered being a priest in the first place, since he refuses to play by any of the rules. Bird finds nice pockets of humor to counteract the melodrama, but at the climactic moment she uses a music cue so corny it undermines the genuine feelings she's worked hard and honestly to evoke. Nonetheless, "Priest" shouldn't be missed—much of it is strong and moving. My reservation is not that it bites off more than it can chew (these days, big teeth are welcome) but that there's something mechanical about its mastication. Its controversies feel predigested.

SIGHT AND SOUND, 3/95, p. 48, Philip Kemp

A young Catholic priest, Fr Greg Pilkington, newly appointed to a working-class Liverpool parish, arrives at the presbytery where he meets Fr Matthew Thomas and the housekeeper, Maria Kerrigan. In his first sermon Greg offends Matthew by preaching that individuals, not society are responsible for their sins. For his part Greg objects to Matthew singing karaoke in a pub and is scandalised to find he shares a bed with Maria.

Against Matthew's advice, Greg tries to visit his parishioners on a housing estate, meeting with rejection and abuse. After officiating at a boozy wake he puts on civilian clothes and visits a gay club, where he picks up a young man, Graham. They make love at Graham's flat. The next day Greg takes confession from a group of schoolchildren; one of them, Lisa Unsworth, tells him her father is sexually abusing her. Greg confronts Unsworth, who is defiantly unrepentant.

Lisa has a fit in the classroom while Greg is teaching. He drops hints to Lisa's mother and her teacher but, trapped by the seal of the confessional, is unable to speak out. Graham, whom Greg has continued to see, comes to Mass, but Greg withholds the sacrament from him. Desperate about Lisa, he urgently prays to Christ to intervene. Mrs Unsworth, coming home unexpectedly, catches her husband and Lisa in bed together. Realising Greg knew, she publicly denounces him.

Greg and Graham, embracing in Greg's car, are caught by the police. Greg pleads guilty and his case is splashed across the headlines. He attempts suicide and is told by the Bishop to quit the diocese. Having vainly tried to see Lisa, he retreats to a remote country parish presided over by the censorious Fr Redstone. Matthew arrives and persuades Greg to come back and say Mass with him. Despite Matthew's impassioned plea for tolerance, half the congregation walk out, and those that remain queue up to take communion from Matthew. Only Lisa comes for communion from Greg. He breaks down and weeps in her arms.

Snorting like a bull limbering up for the matador, an elderly priest levels the wooden beam he's carrying and charges full-tilt at the elegantly diamond-paned windows of the Bishop's palace. His improvised battering-ram is a five foot crucifix. Outrageous, powerful and brutally funny, the pre-credit sequence of *Priest* gives fair warning of what's in store: a none-too-subtle but trenchant assault on the smug hypocrisies of our time, using organised religion, and specifically the Catholic church, as the chosen blunt instrument.

Jimmy McGovern, here making his debut as a feature film writer, has never scrupled to show his hand, and the sermon he puts in the mouth of the radical Fr Matthew makes it clear enough where he thinks the Church should be standing: "If you exploit your workforce, shut down schools and hospitals ... aren't you interfering in Creation and spitting in the face of God?" "That wasn't a sermon, it was a party political broadcast for the Labour Party," comments Greg sourly. But the film pitilessly exposes the futility of his own attempts at priestly duties, gabbling Last Unction over an insensible body on a speeding hospital trolley, or embarking on an ill-fated round of pastoral visits. (Gratified at last, after countless slammed doors and obscenities, to be invited in, he finds himself faced with two Jehovahs Witnesses eager to make converts.)

Not that *Priest* attacks religion as such; if anything, it affirms the validity of faith by setting it against a backdrop of those who abuse it, the time-servers and bigots—recalling G.K. Chesterton's comment that Christianity wasn't tried and found wanting, but found difficult and not tried. The film never descends to facile anti-religious jibes, and even—by tight cross-cutting between Greg's desperate prayer and Mrs Unsworth catching her incestuous husband in the act—hints at the possibility of direct divine intervention. In the final reel Greg, forgiven by the abused child Lisa, achieves something close to a Bressonian grace.

Bressonian austerity, though, is in fairly short supply. This final scene already packs a massive emotional punch; garnishing it with a solo piano rendition of 'You'll Never Walk Alone' might be thought to verge on overkill. Still, lapses like this scarcely matter, given the fury and savage humour of McGovern's writing and the energy of Antonia Bird's direction. Bird draws from her cast—especially Tom Wilkinson as Matthew and Christine Tremarco as Lisa—performances of raw intensity, but the film's most chilling moment goes to Robert Pugh as Lisa's father, justifying himself ("It's the one thing we'd all like to do") with wet-lipped relish. The Catholic hierarchy probably won't be any too pleased about *Priest*. They should be, though—if only for a film that pays religion the compliment of taking it so seriously.

TIME, 4/10/95, p. 80, Richard Corliss

Father Greg (Linus Roache), the young priest at a Catholic parish in Liverpool, is handsome, theologically conservative—and gay. His boss, Father Matthew (Tom Wilkinson), spouts socialistic dogma and has sex with his live-in housekeeper. The husband of the parish's hardest-working volunteer forces sex on their daughter. The local bishop is a ward heeler in a cassock.

Priest, then, is no *Going My Way*. And Good Friday was perhaps not the ideal day for Miramax Films to schedule *Priest* for wide release. Small wonder that a few of the faithful were miffed. The Catholic League threatened a boycott of Miramax's owner, the Walt Disney Co., before Miramax moved the date back. Disney hardly needs the aggravation; last week it told Miramax that the studio could not distribute *Kids*, a scalding and graphic film about an HIV-positive teen. If *Kids* receives a proscriptive NC-17 rating, Miramax may be obliged to sell the film (with its hefty $3.5 million price tag) to another distributor.

Priest, directed by Antonia Bird, is sensational only in its content. At heart it is a TV drama with a one-track mind; Jimmy McGovern's script has no fewer than four scenes in which someone intrudes on a couple's sexual intimacy. Bird cues every emotion with spell-it-out reaction shots and a soupy sound track. What movie dares use *You'll Never Walk Alone* with no irony? *Priest* does, which is one reason why it leaves fat, hot tears on many spectators' faces. The film delivers on its promise to edify at any cost.

For many modern Catholics, the question of a gay clergy inspires a big shrug. Why shouldn't homosexuals (and women) be priests? These days, they are among the few who want to be. The real issue, blithely dodged in this movie, is the Catholic sin of giving scandal. A priest is, after all, Christ's salesman and stand-in. He need not be infallible—since he is human and conceived in sin—but he'd damn well better be discreet. So it is one thing for old Matthew to keep a woman quietly in the rectory; it is another for young Greg to go cruising in a gay bar near his parish. Or surrender to rapture on a public beach. Or have oral sex in a car on the street. Poor Greg: he may not be damned, but he surely is dense.

If Greg were to come to this confessor, his penance would be 10 Hail Marys and an I.Q. test. As for *Priest*, it would be made to sit in sackcloth and ashes at the church door as a cautionary example to all filmmakers who truckle to noble sentiment.

VILLAGE VOICE, 3/28/95, p. 55, J. Hoberman

If most imported movies have a liberal bias, it may be because their only possible audience is one sufficiently live-and-let-live to tolerate the very idea of a foreign film. In that context, the British *Priest* and Czech/German/French *Martha and I*, both opening Friday, are a rowdy pair of crowd pleasers.

Priest is the more commercial of the two releases. Where *Martha and I* concerns Nazis and Jews in pre-World War II Czechoslovakia, *Priest*'s pounding melodrama conflates various strains of Catholicism with incidents of homosexuality and incest. Directed from TV writer Jimmy McGovern's script by Antonia Bird (an admirer of Ken Loach, with ample experience of her own in BBC soaps), *Priest* is a prize liberal weepie—heavy-handed, good-hearted, unself-consciously self-righteous, and shamelessly manipulative.

Set in a working-class Liverpool parish, the movie opens with a grizzled ex-priest venting his frustration against the Church by using a crucifix as a battering ram. Father Greg (Linus Roache), the handsome young priest who has been chosen to replace this old malcontent, turns out to be a social conservative. His first sermon—a high-minded argument for individual responsibility—offends the senior priest, Father Matthew (Tom Wilkinson), who is not only a political liberal but a doctrinal one as well, having shacked up with his comely housekeeper (*Mona Lisa's* Cathy Tyson).

Salt of the earth that he is, Father Matthew functions as the filmmakers' megaphone: "If you exploit your work force, shut down schools and hospitals ... aren't you interfering in Creation and spitting in the face of God?" he cries from the pulpit. ("That wasn't a sermon," Father Greg sourly observes. "It was a political broadcast for the Labour Party.") As a raving Thatcherite, Father Greg must be punished. His inability to comprehend his parishioners is amusingly underscored by a series of failed home visits, a hospital disaster, and a bizarre wake in which—as mourners dance around the coffin—the widow confides in the horrified young priest that she had been praying for her husband's death.

It soon develops that Father Greg has his own guilty secret. He goes incognito to a gay disco and picks up a guy for some fairly explicit sex. This "sin" is bracketed with an instance of father-daughter incest within the parish, which, bound as he is by the rules of the confessional, Father Greg cannot expose. (The movie's creepiest scene has the abusive father taunting his confessor with the thought that he is merely acting out what all men desire.) Father Greg can't deal with the incest. Nor, in one of the movie's more dramatic scenes, can he bring himself to give his new boyfriend communion. The two scandals simultaneously come to light.

Inclusive as it is, *Priest* is not exactly anti-Catholic, or even anti-religious. Faith has its rewards: "When I turn to Him for help," Greg agonizes, "I see a naked man, totally desirable." Nor is Bird a particularly subtle filmmaker. She has her camera spin 360 degrees around a homosexual kiss, intercuts the revelation of incest with shots of Father Greg praying so as to suggest a form of divine intervention, and, most egregiously, twice slaps "You'll Never Walk Alone" on the soundtrack. (I'm told that the song is Liverpool's soccer anthem, but call me closed-minded, I cannot separate its bombastic bathos from an American context.)

Of course, there's no denying the feel-good communion of the movie's made-for-Miramax ending. *Priest* won the People's Choice Award at the 1994 Toronto Film Festival; with my own eyes, I saw it accorded a rapturous standing ovation last January at Sundance. Bird, meanwhile, has alighted in Hollywood, where she is currently directing Drew Barrymore in *Mad Love*.

Also reviewed in:
CHICAGO TRIBUNE, 4/7/95, Friday/p. O, Michael Wilmington
NEW REPUBLIC, 5/15/95, p. 26, Stanley Kauffmann
NEW YORK TIMES, 3/24/95, p. C23, Janet Maslin
NEW YORKER, 3/27/95, p. 107, Anthony Lane
VARIETY, 9/19-25/94, p. 77, Brendan Kelly
WASHINGTON POST, 4/7/95, p. D1, Rita Kempley

PRINCE BRAT AND THE WHIPPING BOY

A Jones Entertainment Group Ltd. release. *Producer:* Ellen Freyer. *Director:* Syd MacCartney. *Screenplay:* Sid Fleischman. *Director of Photography:* Clive Tickner. *Editor:* Sean Barton. *Music:* Lee Holdridge. *Production Designer:* John Blezard and Norbert Scherer. *Running time:* 96 minutes. *MPAA Rating:* G.

CAST: Truan Munro (Jemmy); Nic Night (Prince Horace); George C. Scott (Blind George); Kevin Conway (Hold-Your-Nose-Billy); Vincent Schiavelli (Cutwater); Karan Salt (Annyrose); Andrew Bicknell (The King).

NEW YORK POST, 9/28/95, p. 52, Larry Worth

The title sounds like a gross hybrid of kiddie film and S&M weirdness. Sure enough, "Prince Brat and the Whipping Boy" is not only juvenile but painful to watch.

Based on Sid Fleishman's children's novella with a distinct "Prince and the Pauper" theme, the tale centers on a spoiled king's son who dragoons a salty street lad into service as his "whipping boy." In other words, every time the prince is naughty, his stand-in gets paddled.

It wouldn't take B.F. Skinner to realize that A) the disciplinary system here is doomed to fail, and B) a little attention from the royal dad would solve the whole problem.

But as circumstances—and the cumbersome. script—dictate, the bickering boys are later thrown into the forest, where the tables are turned and the crowned scion suffers. Naturally, a lasting friendship is only a fairy-tale ending away.

But predictability is the least of the problems here. From beginning to end, director Syd MacCartney virtually redefines incompetence.

For starters, he can't even establish where this nonsense is set. The kingdom of Brattenburg sure seems Germanic, but its French chateau castle and characters with atrocious English accents make for a schizophrenic locale.

Worse, the child actors—Truan Munro's stalwart urchin, Karen Salt as his precious little sister and princely Nic Knight, who waddles around like a young but talentless Charles Laughton—put the Culkin clan on a level with the Barrymores.

Screen veterans Kevin Conway, Vincent Schiavelli and Mathilda May are no better, understandably trying to hide themselves under a ton of makeup and vaguely Edwardian costumes. Most hilarious is George C. Scott, camping it up beyond belief in eyepatch, grizzled beard and tri-corner hat as a landlocked Long John Silver.

Clearly perceived as a dud by its producers, "Prince Brat and the Whipping Boy" showed up more than a year ago on the Disney Channel. Too bad they didn't keep it an exclusive.

Also reviewed in:
NEW YORK TIMES, 9/28/95, p. C13, Janet Maslin

PROFESSION: NEO-NAZI

A Drift Releasing release of an OST-Film and Hoffman & Loeser Produktion film. *Producer:* Andrea Hoffmann. *Director:* Winfried Bonengel. *Screenplay (German with English subtitles):* Winfried Bonengel. *Director of Photography:* Johann Feindt. *Editor:* Wolfram Kohler. *Sound:* Paul Oberle and Ronald Gohlke. *Running time:* 87 minutes. *MPAA Rating:* Not Rated.

NEW YORK POST, 5/19/95, p. 38, Larry Worth

It's almost impossible to shock moviegoers in the '90s. But even the most jaded will be jarred by the opening of "Profession: Neo-Nazi."

The camera pans the room of a Toronto meeting of hate-mongers. OK, no big deal. Until the composition of those gathered sinks in: silver-haired grannies, cherubic children and average-looking joes who could pass as—and may be your next-door neighbors. As they rise en masse to shouts of "white power," the movement's hideous horror sets in.

And that's just for starters. The real subject of Winfried Bonengel's startling documentary is Ewald Althans, a handsome, smart, charming 28-year-old who's not-so-quietly doing his part to "create a new order for Germany."

The film's most talked-about scene will surely be Althans' visit to Auschwitz, where he interrupts a tour guide's speech to tell tourists that no atrocities took place at the camp. One young American challenges him, and the riveting exchange pits a voice of compassion against Althans' smug smile and unflinching arrogance.

An equally fascinating dialogue takes place as Althans sits at a table with his parents, both of whom try to come to terms with having raised an angel-faced monster.

To his credit, director Bonengel lets his subjects do all the talking. Although that decision led to controversy in Germany (where speeches denying the existence of the Holocaust are illegal), viewers can decide if the film is a soapbox for neo-Nazi rhetoric or a chance to let present-day goose-steppers dig their own graves.

Either way, Bonengel earns kudos for destroying cliches about neo-Nazis. Yes, the stereotypical leather-clad skinheads are on hand, but so's a sweet-faced octogenarian who cradles her picture of Rudolf Hess and defends Adolf Hitler's actions. Even more alarming is a scene of grinning children being taught to load guns and shoot at communists.

With donations from ultra-rightwingers pouring in (as depicted in still another eye-opening tableau), the group is clearly growing stronger. That alone guarantees to chill the spine of all but the comatose. And those who state—"Profession: Neo-Nazi."

NEWSDAY, 5/19/95, Part II/p. B5, Jonathan Mandell

Young, blond, good-looking and articulate, Ewald Althans travels the world happily full of hate. "This is my fate: Cameras in my face and Jews at my heel," he says with a smile in "Profession: Neo-Nazi," a German-made documentary that caused an outcry when it was shown in Germany two years ago.

The closest Althans comes to the United States is Canada, where he visits a Nazi publisher who likes to wear fake concentration-camp garb and ships millions of brochures and tens of thousands of videocassettes promoting fascist views. "He can create a new order for Germany," the publisher says of Althans. "What Hitler wanted is still valid."

Such relentlessly offensive material turns tedious quickly, as does meeting after meeting of the like-minded throughout Europe. A viewer soon hungers for some context, some independently verified facts; it is not clear how large these groups are, and how interconnected—there is mention of "our fighting in Iraq and Croatia," with little elaboration. We do not learn what, if anything, the police know about these groups, and if any legal action has been taken against them.

But "Profession: Neo-Nazi" is partially redeemed "by a few scenes that stand out in their fascination and horror. An old lady compares Hitler to Jesus, favorably, and recalls in detail the heavenly moment when her mother met the führer. Althans' parents, a pleasant-looking middle-aged couple who "reject" their son's glorification of the Third Reich, talk of his childhood, right in front of him. "As a small child, you always had extreme behavior," his mother says, as he sits next to her. "To be noticed at all costs. I think you were unhappy."

Most memorably, Althans visits Auschwitz—taunting visitors who are walking through the killing ovens, shouting about how the Holocaust was a hoax. A young American takes him on: "What was this, a vacation camp?"

Filmmaker Winfried Bonengel has genuine leftist credentials; his previous portrait of a different would-be führer resulted in the man's leaving the movement, which led to a second film, "A Neo-Nazi Drops Out." Yet, when "Profession: Neo-Nazi" was shown in Germany, protests led to its withdrawal from movie houses, with critic's and prosecutors complaining that without commentary the filmmaker's intentions are unclear and "the neo-Nazi is left with the last word."

The film now opens with a long statement saying explicitly that the views of the subjects are different from those of the filmmaker, whose aim was to point out how dangerous the movement is. But, mirroring in a way the original error, these particular words are in German, without any translation, and are inaccessible to the average viewer.

VILLAGE VOICE, 5/23/95, Film Special/p. 28, J. Hoberman

Where *Little Odessa* [see Hoberman's review] unfolds in a dead Jewish world, the controversial German documentary *Profession: Neo-Nazi* showcases an all-too-vivacious Hitler wannabe. Handsome, smiling Ewald Althans, 27 when Winfried Bonengel shot this portrait, may dress like James Dean in *Rebel Without a Cause* but, expounding his "orthodox National Socialism" with a fanatical glitter, there's no doubt that he has one.

Profession: Neo-Nazi opens in Toronto where Althans has gone to visit his exiled führer, Ernst Zündel. The middle-aged Zündel, a major publisher of neo-Nazi, white supremacist, and anti-Semitic propaganda ("My mouth waters when I plan world rule," he chuckles), is himself a prize piece of work—he delights in baiting Jewish survivors by dressing up and demonstrating in the uniform of a concentration-camp inmate. "Zündel is such a warm-hearted person," Althans gushes, informing us that he is prepared to be the requisite "cold-blooded Prussian."

As Althans confidently predicts his future ("cameras in my face, Jews at my back"), Bonengel dredges up a bit of the young Nazi's past, returning to Germany to interview Althans with his parents. Seemingly liberal bourgeois intellectuals, they are confounded by their son's politics. Recalling his childhood antics, mother Althans accuses him of always seeking negative attention: "Your motive was to be noticed at all costs." As if to prove her point, Althans is next seen visiting Auschwitz where he disrupts a tour group visiting the gas chambers by loudly proclaiming that the Holocaust is a hoax.

The Auschwitz sequence is the movie's most disturbing—nobody except for one upset and inarticulate American kid seems capable of addressing Althans's provocation. Althans, of course, is enormously pleased with his own performance; back in Germany, he entertains his cohorts with slides taken of the Auschwitz "swimming pools." Althans aside, *Profession: Neo-Nazi* features copious incidental ranting—an old lady explaining that "Hitler just wanted to bring peace to the whole world," a German volunteer bragging of the Serbs he's killed in defense of Croatia. The movie ends with Althans delivering a tirade as expert as it is well received. The sequence, bizarrely reminiscent of Christopher Jones's smirking teenage Hitler riff from *Wild in the Streets*, can be construed as a sympathetic glorification or a damning revelation depending on what knowledge the viewer brings to the movie.

Counting on an informed audience, Bonengel's strategy was clearly to allow Althans sufficient rope and hope he would hang himself, while presumably Althans's plan was to use Bonengel (whose previous documentary, *A Neo-Nazi Drops Out*, portrayed recovering fascist Ingo Hasselbach) as a means for self-promotion on the logic that even one convert is worth a thousand armchair anti-fascists. Neither got precisely the anticipated response. *Profession: Neo-Nazi* was banned in several German states while Althans and his followers circulated the movie abroad. Ironically, it was a screening at the 1994 Rotterdam Film Festival that discredited the young *Übermensch* in neo-Nazi circles—he was recognized and outed by Dutch journalists who linked him to the Amsterdam gay scene.

Incidentally, Althans is evidently no stranger to our shores. As James Ridgeway noted in the *Voice* several weeks ago, the newsletter *Germany Alert* has reported his ties to Norman Olson, commandant of the now notorious Northern Michigan Regional Militia.

Also reviewed in:
NEW YORK TIMES, 5/19/95, p. C12, Stephen Holden
VARIETY, 2/21-27/94, p. 49, David Rooney

PROMISE, THE

A Fine Line Features release of a Bioskop-Film/Odessa Films/J.M.H. Productions Lausanne/WDR-Fernsehen production in collaboration with Studio Babelsberg/Canal PLUS/CNC. *Producer:* Eberhard Junkersdorf. *Director:* Margarethe von Trotta. *Screenplay (German with English subtitles):* Peter Schneider and Margarethe von Trotta. *Script Collaborator:* Felice Laudadio. *Director of Photography:* Franz Rath. *Editor:* Suzanne Baron. *Music:* Jürgen Knieper. *Sound:* Christian Moldt. *Sound Editor:* Max Hoskins and Harry Schnitzler. *Casting:* Doris Borkmann and Helenka Hummel. *Production Designer:* Martin Dostal. *Art Director:* Benedikt Herforth. *Set Decorator:* Franz Bauer. *Costumes:* Petra Kray and Yoshio Yabara. *Make-up:* Irmela Holzapfel. *Running time:* 119 minutes. *MPAA Rating:* R.

CAST: Corinna Harfouch (Sophie); Meret Becker (Sophie as a Young Woman); August Zirner (Konrad); Anian Zollner (Konrad as a Young Man); Jean-Yves Gaultier (Gerard); Eva Mattes

(Barbara); Susanne Uge (Barbara as a Young Woman); Hans Kremer (Harald); Pierre Besson (Harald as a Young Man); Tina Engel (Sophie's Aunt); Otto Sander (Professor Lorenz); Hark Bohm (Mueller); Dieter Mann (Konrad's Father); Simone von Zglinicki (Konrad's Mother); Ulrike Krumbiegel (Elisabeth); Monika Hansen (Sophie's Mother); Klaus Piontek (Sophie's Stepfather); Christian Herschmann (Alexander, 12 Years-old); Joerg Meister (Alexander, 20 Years-old); Heiko Senst (Wolfgang); Anka Baier (Monika); Sven Lehmann (Max); Udo Kroschwald (Secret Police Agent); Wolfgang Winkler (Stasi Man at School); Andreas Mann (Party Secretary at School); Hagen Oechel (Army Instructor); Christian Tschirner (Uwe, Border Guard); Robert Hummel (Escape Aide); Gilles Gaudis (Man in Court); Franz Viehmann (Stasi Man in Court); Waltraut Kramm (Guide); Horst Hiemer (Prison Director); Bernd-U Reppenhagen (Border Officer); Karl Kranzkowski (1st Border Official); Noella Dussart (Helenka).

LOS ANGELES TIMES, 11/3/95, Calendar/p. 12, Kevin Thomas

Margarethe von Trotta's beautiful, stirring love story "The Promise" reveals, through the lives of one young couple, the profound impact the Berlin Wall had on all Germans, East and West alike. It is a splendid example of classic screen storytelling by a renowned international filmmaker, a work of strength and simplicity that illuminates with flawless craftsmanship many complex issues and contradictions. Epic in scale, spanning the entire 28-year existence of the Wall, it is at once political yet ultimately personal.

In the fall of 1961, by prearranged signal, five young East Berliners, three men and two women, leave a dance floor as Bill Haley's "Rock Around the Clock" is blasting away and head swiftly for a dark street where they disappear beneath a manhole cover. A loose shoelace causes one young man, Konrad, to stop for a second, just long enough for troops to swoop down him. The other four make their way through the sewer to the safety of West Berlin, where Konrad's lover Sophie leads her friends to the home of her aunt, a successful fashion designer.

Now on different sides of the Wall, Konrad and Sophie will soon learn the huge toll that it will exact of their lives as it does for so many other Germans. While Sophie can start working for her aunt as a model and designer, Konrad finds himself instantly at the mercy of the East German government, which his father tries to appease by claiming his son tried to talk his friends out of their flight.

To clear himself Konrad must enter military service—as a border guard—prior to commencing his higher education, where he will emerge as a brilliant, ground-breaking astrophysicist.

"The Promise" is primarily more Konrad's and East Germany's story. It is that of a man marked permanently by his association with that escape. He sees his only way out a zealous pursuit of career, which in fact does yield him a more comfortable material existence than most East Berliners enjoy. Yet it is no more than a gilded cage as he is under constant surveillance and cannot leave the country until he's allowed to attend a scientific congress in Prague, but wouldn't you know that it would be 1968 and that Konrad and Sophie reunite just as the Soviet talks roll in?

It is the mark of von Trotta and her co-writers' skill and perspective that the timing of this reunion doesn't seem like piling it on their star-crossed lovers but rather as one of the more major incidents in a relentless, systematic repression on the part of the Eastern bloc geared to snuffing out all personal freedom.

Beyond this, von Trotta does not paint the West as an earthly paradise and from the outset she makes clear, that as soundly as she condemns the Soviets, she never loses sight that the Wall is a cruel legacy of a war started by the Germans themselves.

Furthermore, she allows Sophie to insist that when all is said and done that Konrad must ultimately take responsibility for choosing to remain in the East—his growing international professional stature could conceivably create viable opportunities for flight—yet wisely does not judge him herself.

In thinking of everything—much, much more in regard to the Wall and its devastating, ironic and profound emotional and psychological effects—von Trotta is able to move on to show us, post-Prague Spring, Sophie and Konrad going about creating separate lives for themselves yet always in the shadow of the Wall and a love that endures despite them both yielding to other priorities. (Sophie, after all, could return to East Germany, though at great price.)

A handsomely designed film with a suitably romantic score, "The Promise" abounds in full-bodied portrayals, starting with Anian Zollner and August Zirner, who play the younger and older Konrad, and Meret Becker and Corinna Harfouch, who play the younger and older Sophie.

In support are such major German actors as Otto Sander as Konrad's professor, a representative of the Socialist ideal betrayed by East German corruption and totalitarianism; Tina Engel, for once getting to took glamorous as Sophie's staunch aunt; and Hark Bohm, as an especially repellent Stasi agent. Eva Mattes plays Konrad's activist aunt, and Hans Kremer her idealistic husband.

For all its specificity, "The Promise" tells a universal story of separation and oppression, of love and loss.

NEW YORK POST, 9/8/95, p. 48, Thelma Adams

Imagine "Doctor Zhivago" without Omar Sharif and Julie Christie, without sweeping snow-scapes and that haunting theme, and you've got Margarethe von Trotta's dreary historical romance "The Promise."

East Berliners Sophie and Konrad are teenage lovers. In 1961, they attempt to escape through the sewers to the West. Konrad trips at the last minute, but is there to secure the manhole cover over his beloved. Sophie swims through excrement to freedom—an apt metaphor for "The Promise."

The pair are reunited during the Prague Spring of 1968. Sophie gets pregnant, but Konrad will not let her return to the repressive East with him. However, Konrad's plans to flee West are scuttled. A dozen years pass before they meet again.

By now it's 1980. The two are passing into middle age with new partners. Their son, Alexander, is nearing the terrible teens. He's the only one who believes a reunion between his parents is possible and, when the Berlin Wall tumbles in 1989, Alex makes sure that his mom and dad connect.

Respected German director von Trotta navigates the story line—based on a script she co-wrote with Peter Schneider and Felice Laudadio—with all the passion of a foreign tourist following a subway map. Konrad and Sophie remain ciphers whose love never reaches epic portions.

Did Konrad really trip on that fateful night above the Berlin sewers? Or was he too much the son of his papa, a card-carrying member of the Communist Party? Did he fumble his later opportunities to rip through the Iron Curtain in order to preserve a healthy scientific career, romance be damned?

It's never very clear. Von Trotta doubles the confusion when she switches her leads mid-Wall. The young Konrad, a pretty, pale, artistic-looking boy with Rushmore cheekbones and flaxen hair played by Anian Zollner, becomes the elder Konrad, a haunted, tentative, shorter man with a ruddy complexion and a thatch of coarse, dark hair played by August Zirner.

Admittedly, the course of true love never ran smooth, but the lovers themselves ring false. It's potentially interesting to see the ways in which history and the Wall divide the pair and the way the East German government manipulates their families and colleagues to keep Sophie and Konrad separate. But there remains the nagging feeling that this couple wouldn't have lasted out a year if she was living on Long Island and he had a Manhattan studio.

Von Trotta has a heavy pedigree. The "Rosa Luxemburg" director ranks as a contemporary of Rainer Werner Fassbinder and the collaborator/wife of Volker ("The Tin Drum") Schlondorff. But, with her back against the Wall and a title ripped straight off a romance novel, von Trotta is adrift in mini-series territory here. The problem is that she is no more willing to commit to her oh-too-ordinary lovers Konrad and Sophie than they are to each other. Either pump up the "Sophie" theme and cue the snow machines, or get out of the way.

NEWSDAY, 9/8/95, Part II/p. B4, John Anderson

The Berlin Wall, like a Capulet balcony or a plane leaving for Lisbon, is such an obvious symbol of love gone bad that you almost wonder why Margarethe von Trotta ("Rosa Luxembourg") bothers to rework it again. But her aim in "The Promise"—whose East-West lovers see each other only four times in 30 years—is to be definitive. Instead, she's got one leg over the wall.

That she doesn't quite scramble over from melodrama to archetype has less to do with the breadth of her and Peter Schneider's story than with the less-than-crystalline nature of her characters. Konrad (played as a youth by Anian Zollner, as an adult by August Zirner) is feckless and flawed, and persistently fails to do right by Sophie (as a girl, Meret Becker; as a woman, Corinna Harfouch). And yet, we're never sure exactly what's motivating him—or not—as he continues to let her down and she continues to love him.

Even at the start, Konrad is a question mark. Cutting from newsreel-style footage of the Berlin Wall to a party scene out of "American Bandstand," von Trotta makes it clear something's up: Several teenagers, including Konrad and Sophie, are going to flee to the West through the sewers. But just as Konrad is about to go down the manhole and elude a military patrol, he trips—and thus begins his and Sophie's long night.

Did he fall or did he fake it is the question that persists throughout "The Promise," which is more about promises not kept. Sophie is strong-willed and loyal; she goes to meet Konrad, who has become a prominent scientist, in Prague, where they hope to live together, but it's '68 and the Soviets have other plans. Konrad is compromised by a colleague and can't keep his vow to meet Sophie in the West. Their son, conceived during a brief (but not too brief) reunion, becomes an obstacle to their happiness, as do their respective marriages.

Von Trotta is honest and unsentimental about the desperation felt by many Germans and the complexities faced by those who would actually flee East Berlin; it was never as simple as the West would have had one think. At the same time, Konrad's pathetic wavering—which is supposed, I assume, to symbolize an aspect of the German national character—grows wearying. Throughout the film, which became the first German work in years to open the Berlin Film Festival, one wishes he were more like Sophie: A scene of her as a tour guide, talking to a group of Japanese tourists about national complicity in war crimes, is rather startling. And welcome, given the sentiment and indecision that mars much of "The Promise."

SIGHT AND SOUND, 9/96, p. 52, Nick James

Berlin, August 1961. The Berlin Wall goes up. In East Berlin, students Konrad and Sophie are in love. Autumn, 1963. They and their friends Max, Wolfgang and Monika have obtained a map of the sewer system and intend to escape to the West where Sophie's wealthy aunt can set them up. At the last minute, Konrad falls over, and urges the others on. They make it to the other side but Konrad turns back. The East German authorities interrogate him. Konrad's father, a workers' official, takes a dim view of his involvement.

Sophie is desperate for Konrad to get away. Friends let Konrad know about an escape service, but he arrives at the rendezvous just as his contacts are being bundled into Stasi cars. Called up for the army, Konrad is posted as a border guard. He again tries to escape, but his patrol partner prevents him. Discharged from the army, Konrad is soon working as a brilliant research scientist investigating sunspots. His work eventually allows him the chance to go to Prague, and he invites Sophie to meet him there. After brief recriminations, their life together is fleetingly happy until the 'Prague Spring' is ended by the invasion of Soviet tanks. Sophie is obliged to return to the West. Konrad is offered promotion due to his boss's indiscretion in having dared to criticise the system.

Sophie tries to visit East Berlin to tell Konrad she is now pregnant, but is turned away. She sends Konrad an ultimatum to break free or forget her. He remains in the East, marries and has a daughter. Sophie also finds a partner, but her son wants to see his real father. In 1980, Konrad is allowed into West Berlin on a visit and he plucks up the courage to visit Sophie and his son. Konrad's 'loyalty' to the East and rising eminence makes it possible for his son to start visiting him, but the favour of further visits is used as insurance against Konrad's defection. Konrad and Sophie are not finally reunited until, in 1989, the wall is taken down by a popular uprising, and Konrad's son comes to fetch him across.

Margarethe von Trotta's *The Promise*, her first film to be distributed in Britain since *Three Sisters* (*Paura e amore*) in 1990, is as purposeful and heartfelt a work as might be looked for from a director who was once one of the mainstays of the New German Cinema of the 70s and 80s. It is the kind of European film that invites grand comparisons—as epic in its scope as, say, Sergio Leone's *Once Upon a Time in America*; as sweeping in its melodrama as Sydney Pollack's *The Way We Were;* as well acted and staged as Luchino Visconti's more operatic works. And yet, while tackling 28 years of German history through the eyes one man and woman in love, it is at same time, only a modest achievement.

The Promise keeps its scale down to small units of people pulled about by the train of history: friends, family, lovers, workmates. The Berlin wall going up in '61 is done newsreel style; the tanks arrive in Prague in '68 on one street corner. The central story of Konrad and Sophie, whose love burns slowly down from the time they are separated as youngsters in 1963 to their reunion when the wall is broken up in 1989, might indicate a grand passion out of *Doctor Zhivago* as the film's main concern. (It is beautifully acted by two sets of actors, Anian Zollner and Meret Becker as the young couple, August Zirner and Corinna Harfouch as the adult pair). However, politics is the film's true focus. The chess game of cold war calamities is mirrored in the couple's variously anguished expressions. On the level of melodrama, Konrad's need for Sophie is not quite powerful enough to convince him that everything about Communist East Berlin is wrong, so he trips over his shoelaces while Sophie is escaping through the sewers. Metaphorically, he is, no doubt, East Germany, the reluctant lover held back from embracing the West by bonds of filial loyalty as well as coercion. Sophie, in turn, is the careless, freewheeling West, growing insensitive and intolerant during the long wait for the wall to crumble.

Despite all that irony-smothering iconic weight—the need to explain what happened to Germany through the couple's various attempts at reunion—Konrad and Sophie resemble Celia Johnson and Trevor Howard in *Brief Encounter* more than they do two halves of a broken pfennig. Despite the clear desire on the part of von Trotta for a melodrama that analyses (*á la* Fassbinder) the social and political components of their relationship, her affection and sympathy for these characters and the near-miniseries level of coincidence she inflicts on them is as likely to mist up the cold microscope of realism as it is to put hearts under glass. For this is a very emotional film; and yet the dominant mood is romantic yearning of a different kind to sexual love. *The Promise* is suffused instead with nostalgia, a fug of mourning for a time of political certainties when, as can be gleaned from von Trotta's seminal 70s films *The Second Awakening of Christa Klages, Sisters* and *The German Sisters*, it was possible to find the finance to refute the workings of Capital on film. There is something a little specious about this sense of loss, no matter how well it chimes in with the current mood of disillusionment in Germany. It seems to have as much to do with von Trotta's loss of youth and bohemian comradeship as it does with the political void. After all, sentimental remembrance is hardly the most politically useful of feelings to invoke in an audience. But then a return to 'old-fashioned' socialist values may be all that von Trotta wants to recommend.

Even with 28 years of history and passion to deal with, *The Promise* still labours its political and emotional points with long takes, soporific editing, and a sometimes clumsy use of melodrama. If, as it seems, European *auteur* cinema is slowly losing the wider audience, one reason might be because of a reluctance on the part of established film-makers to recognise the speed with which viewers now read films (and how transparent the clichés of literary/European cinema have become). To say that is not to deny von Trotta's seriousness or the subtlety with which she treats Konrad and Sophie's relationship. At its best, *The Promise* makes us identify with the adult passions of people tossed about by events. Whether its partisan nostalagia leads to understand those events any better is another matter.

VILLAGE VOICE, 9/19/95, p. 80, Devon Jackson

Apparently, critics both German and non-German have been quite upset at von Trotta for making this film. For looking at East Berlin and the former CDR through rose-colored glasses. As if she'd simply taken *West Side Story* and *The Way We Were* and put the two doomed lovers on opposite sides of the Berlin wall for three decades and in the process trivialized not just history and politics but filmmaking and love to boot. Hardly.

The Promise opens in 1961 at a sock hop in East Berlin as Konrad and Sophie spend their last slowdance together before escaping with friends via the sewer into the freedom of West Berlin. Sophie goes first but Konrad hesitates—and we all know what that leads to: a 28-year future wherein the two see each other only four more times.

In that virtual lifetime, von Trotta and screenwriter Peter Schneider explore not just the vows of two split-up lovers trying to stay committed to each other, but of other couples and individuals and whole societies and political systems trying, often contradictorily and hypocritically, to stay true to who and what they say they are and want to be. (Spanning so many years, *The Promise* employs two Sophies and two Konrads, a casting decision that works fine with the women but is rather jarring in the case of the Konrads, who look nothing like each other.

If it were a bigger picture, more epic á la *Dr. Zhivago,* more arrogant á la *Wings of Desire,* it might have been granted a certain automatic respect. Even so, von Trotta here successfully spins her obsessiveness with sisterly dopplegängers into a tale of halved dualities aiming for an emotional and physical recoupling. (To her credit, too, von Trotta never ironizes the Wall or its meaning.) Sure, the heavy-stringed score can be a bit overwrought, the sweeping camera movements might wear, and there is a scene of Konrad and Sophie doing the clichéd run into each others arms, but there are plenty of moments of romantic and political poignancy. The final shot, of Sophie's oh-so-loaded reaction to Konrad calling to her across a crowd of reunited Berliners, is stunning; and the boy, whom I will not identify since it would give away the plot, is incredibly moving particularly when he and Konrad go out for a walk along the Berlin Wall (c. 1980), and the boy tosses a ball over the Wall, waits two beats, and the ball sails back over to him. "How do you do that?" asks Konrad. "I don't know," says the boy, "but it happens everytime."

Also reviewed in:
NEW REPUBLIC, 10/9/95, p. 26, Stanley Kauffmann
NEW YORK TIMES, 9/8/95, p. C8, Stephen Holden
VARIETY, 2/13-19/95, p. 49, Leonard Klady

PROPHECY, THE

A Dimension Films (a division of Miramax Films) release of a First Look Pictures presentation of a Neo Motion Pictures production. *Producer:* Joel Soisson, W.K. Border, and Michael Leary. *Director:* Gregory Widen. *Screenplay:* Gregory Widen. *Director of Photography:* Bruce Douglas Johnson. *Editor:* Sonny Baskin. *Sound:* Al Rizzo. *Casting:* Don Phillips. *Production Designer:* Clark Hunter. *Set Decorator:* Michele Spadaro. *Set Dresser:* Phil Fracasi. *Special Effects:* Gary King. *Mechanical Effects:* Jor Van Kline. *Costumes:* Dana Allyson. *Make-up:* Martha Cecilia. *Special Make-up Effects:* Scott Patton. *Stunt Coordinator:* Dan Bradley. *Running time:* 91 minutes. *MPAA Rating:* R.

CAST: Christopher Walken (Gabriel); Elias Koteas (Thomas Dagget); Virginia Madsen (Katherine); Eric Stoltz (Simon); Amanda Plummer (Rachel); Adam Goldberg (Jerry); Viggo Mortensen (Lucifer); Moriah Snyder (Mary); Emma Sheneh (Grandmother); Nik Winterhawk (John); J.C. Quinn (Burrows); Albert Nelson (Grey Horse); Steve Hytner (Joseph); Jeremy Williams-Hurner (Brian); Emily Conforto (Sandra); Nick Gomez (Jason); Christina Holmes (Allison); Sandra Lafferty (Madge); Jeff Cadiente (Usiel); John Sankovich (Deputy #2); Bobby Lee Hayes (Deputy #1); William Buck Hart (Grave Keeper); Rrandy Adakai-Nez (High School Kid); Sioux-Z Jessup (Nurse).

FILMS IN REVIEW, 11/12/95, p. 103, Victoria Alexander

The Prophecy, written and directed by Gregory Widen, outclasses its companion film, Clive Barker's *Lord of Illusions,* which played last summer. I generally ignore our local newspaper's rating system, but *Lord of Illusions* got three stars. Maybe this time I would have to go see a "slash-em-up" movie. The review, however, neglects to caution that the movie is an absolute bloodfest. Sitting in the dark theater, watching between my fingers, my mind started to wander. I'd read Clive Barker's collection of short stories, *Books of Blood,* many years ago. Even by my indulgent standards—I have a large number of non-fiction books on human sacrifice and torture—Barker was depraved, but he had a distinct flair for it. Obviously, his fascination with bloodletting hasn't been sated by seeing it all visually displayed in his very successful *Hellraiser* movies. This thing about blood must go deeper. All the actors, and most of the sets, end up covered with blood. Just about the time my friend whispered, "Oh, just don't bother to look up,"

I concluded (without the benefit of a Ph.D. in psychology) that Barker is mining the primal fear of menstruation. Perhaps this is why he's so popular with his adolescent target audience.

To the primitive mind, birth and death contained magical properties. With the onset of menstruation, pregnancy can occur. With birth, man begins his journey to death. In primitive initiation rites, young boys must shed their blood—the female blood they fed on in the womb. This is all subliminally intertwined in *Lord of Illusions* where we meet Swann (Kevin J. O'Connor), a famous magician whose extravagant illusions are really exhibitions of psychic power. Swann fakes his own bloody narcissistic end, echoing the fear of death inherent in menstruation. He survives the bloodletting, as women do each month. Nix (Daniel Von Bargen), a powerful supernatural being, really livens things up. He's a fairly primitive example of a dark force himself. Swann had been his way-too-favorite disciple. Nix's obsession with Swann also caught my jaded attention. It was an intended sacrifice, an adolescent virgin—now Swann's wife—who had come between them. A browless, spandex-wearing disciple of Nix's goes through a great deal of trouble to assemble a group of followers, find Nix's body, and bring him back to life. Is Nix grateful for being resurrected after spending 13 years underground surrounded by dirt, and eaten by worms? Summarily revived, Nix kills all his hapless followers. Repulsive even before Swann wired an iron mask to his face and buried him, Nix rises from the grave a man-beast. I kept thinking, "There, now you've done it. No followers—so who's going to get you a new set of clothes?"

The Prophecy is an entertaining and thought-provoking film. Screenwriter/director Widen not only knows his Bible, but a lot of Hebrew Cabala as well. After the angelic revolt in Heaven, Satan got his own kingdom and a big playground of souls to harvest and torment. God became so interested in his creation, "man," that He elevated him above all else. He began interfering in a major way: making laws and rules, watching over everything. God got so involved with this "stiff-necked people" that when they fouled things up, He sent His "only begotten Son" to redeem them. (And if that wasn't enough help, immediately after His Son's death, He sent The Holy Spirit to look after things.) A fraction of the remaining loyal angels became jealous of man and began a second war in heaven. As our story unfolds, a renegade seraph, Gabriel (Christopher Walken), comes to earth to capture the soul of the most vile man on earth, a recently deceased Korean War army colonel guilty of horrific war crimes. Gabriel needs this soul to form his expansion team. And as with any expansion team Gabriel must recruit a cadre of exceptional talent.

The Old Testament contains many stories about angels coming to earth and interacting with man. Often, as the angel Gabriel proclaims, the job was to do God's dirty work by destroying cities, killing first-born sons, and generally meting out God's punishments. (Other angels are assigned less stressful work such as birth announcements, desert marches, and guardian duty.)

A failed-priest-to-be turned New York City homicide cop, Thomas Dagget (Elias Koteas), is drawn into this second revolt of angels when a copy of his seminary thesis is found at a brutal crime scene. Simon (Eric Stoltz), a good angel, finds the Colonel's soul before Gabriel does and places it in a little Navaho Indian girl's mouth for safekeeping. The girl is brought to a shaman to exorcise the Colonel's soul from her body. Meanwhile, this Second War has closed heaven and final judgments are in abeyance, so Satan (Viggo Mortensen) turns up as the rightful owner to the Colonel's soul, demanding it himself.

Christopher Walken is terrific as the arrogantly witty, stern, and charming jealous angel. Gratefully, he understood the subtlety and dimensions of this complex role. Most of Walken's dialogue as Gabriel shows the screenwriter knew his material thoroughly. All the supporting characters are well-written and bizarrely funny, especially Gabriel's pulled-from-the-brink-of-death companions (Adam Goldberg and Amanda Plummer).

Immediately after leaving the theater, my husband and I began a very heated debate about angels, By the time we'd gotten home, it had escalated to the "show me" stage. It was "dueling Bibles" as we both read aloud from different translations. Mine is heavily annotated and I just happened to be reading it the night before; my husband hasn't picked up a Bible in years.

This is the best recent film of the genre and should have been better promoted by its releasing studio. However neglected, it's an impressive showcase for writer/director Widen, who also did a wonderful job of creating images of fallen angels and special effects (especially the last image of Satan bursting into a flock of crows).

LOS ANGELES TIMES, 9/4/95, Calendar/p. 6, David Kronke

Here's the ultimate statement for our era of diminished expectations: "Heaven isn't heaven anymore," laments the angel Simon (Eric Stolz) early on in the frankly bizarre religious thriller "The Prophecy."

Seems even God his trouble finding good help these days. The angel Gabriel (Christopher Walken), upset that God doesn't hold him in such high favor anymore (apparently, heaven isn't above office politics), is planning a palace coup. Enraged that God is more interested in the activities of "talking monkeys" (i.e., humans), Gabriel has descended upon Earth to claim the soul of a demented Army colonel that will help him muck up heaven's heavenliness (it's explained that although angels do know quite a bit when it comes to atrocities, they have nothing over us humans).

Even Lucifer (Viggo Mortensen) is chagrined—"Two hells is one hell too many," he grumbles reasonably; hence, he advises the only people who can stop this sinister plan, Thomas (Elias Koteas), a cop who abandoned the priesthood, and Katherine (Virginia Madsen), a small-town schoolteacher concerned that one of her students is possessed by said colonel's soul.

No, it's not a comedy. Essentially, a sequel to the biblical tale of Lucifer's fall from grace, only with car crashes and gunplay (one would presume that Gabriel might have learned a lesson or two from his colleague's missteps). This foray into spiritual torment is the directorial debut of screenwriter Gregory Widen ("Highlander," "Backdraft"), who as a former firefighter has insight into earthly infernos. Though Widen proves himself capable enough behind the camera, his script here is simply too loopy for him to render it in any credible fashion.

Walken, who would probably not rank high on any casting director's list of names seeking more run-of-the-mill angels, won't receive an endorsement from heaven's Chamber of Commerce for his frequently over-the-top performance as Gabriel, who, although vaguely omnipresent and multipowerful, for some reason can't drive a car. Resplendently creepy with his ghostly pallor, blue fingernails and jet-black hair, Walken parades through this thing like Jack Nicholson in "The Shining" or Dennis Hopper in just about anything he's done recently. Stoltz, with ratty hair, black fingernails and the long coat favored by Euro-trash villians in bad cop movies, is the good angel. The rest of the cast puts an admiral amount of commitment into their performances given the material.

Still, "The Prophecy" has an odd appeal that keeps you engaged, if only to find out just how strange it dares to get. Thomas, the cop who quickly unlocks the mystery, accepts everything that unfolds around him with little or no problem, but audiences will likely be filled with doubting Thomases.

NEW YORK POST, 9/2/95, p. 17, Bill Hoffmann

The plot of "The Prophecy" sounds ridiculous enough to keep you miles away from your local movie house. Two rival archangels fly to Earth to steal the soul of a dead military man, whose evil genius on the battlefield they believe can help them wrest away Heaven from God's servants.

But give writer/director Gregory Widen credit—he almost pulls it off. With a top-notch cast, excellent photography and the spooky setting of the Arizona desert, "The Prophecy," until its final 20 minutes, is a breezily entertaining horror picture with an edgy, butt-kicking sense of humor.

Much of the credit goes to Christopher Walken, who with his pasty-white face, jet-black hair and bug-eyes, resembles a haunted Billy Crystal, rattling off macabre one-liners like a psychotic Borscht Belt comic.

As arch-angel Gabriel, Walken, with a tongue-in-cheek verve, yanks out eyeballs, tears out hearts and sets bodies afire in his bid to achieve his mission.

That's a tough assignment because Gabriel's competitor, Simon, (Eric Stoltz) has already sucked the soul from Hawthorne's corpse (by planting a soul kiss on him!) and implanted it in Mary, a young, cherub-faced Navajo girl.

Soon Mary starts spouting Linda Blair-like nonsense such as "We've got to cut their hearts out!"

Luckily, the unearthly plot is uncovered by cleric-turned-cop Tom Dagget (Elias Koteas) and Mary's school-teacher Katherine (Virginia Madsen), who protect Mary and battle Gabriel all through a bloody climax.

It's here that the piece falls apart, though, when the devil—in the form of a pretentious, bearded yuppie with an attitude—joins in the gory festivities.

Walken's tour-de-force performance, however, is worth the price of admission. Amanda Plummer also scores big as a dying young woman whose journey to eternal sleep is interrupted so she can be Walken's unholy partner-in-crime.

"The Prophecy" is like junk food you may kick yourself later, but it tastes pretty good going down.

Also reviewed in:
CHICAGO TRIBUNE, 9/3/95, Tempo/p. 7, John Petrakis
NEW YORK TIMES, 9/2/95, p. 15, Stephen Holden
VARIETY, 8/14-20/95, p. 58, Eric Hansen
WASHINGTON POST, 9/2/95, p. D3, Hal Hinson

PURE FORMALITY, A

A Sony Pictures Classics release of a C.G. Group Tiger Cinematografica/Film Par Film coproduction. *Executive Producer:* Bruno Altissimi and Claudio Saranceni. *Producer:* Mario Cecchi Gori and Vittorio Cecchi Gori. *Director:* Giuseppe Tornatore. *Screenplay (French with English subtitles:* Giuseppe Tornatore and Pascale Quignard. *Story:* Giuseppe Tornatore. *Director of Photography:* Blasco Giurato. *Editor:* Giuseppe Tornatore. *Music:* Ennio Morricone. *Sound:* Pierre Gamet. *Production Designer:* Andrea Crisanti. *Costumes:* Beatrice Bordone. *Running time:* 107 minutes. *MPAA Rating:* PG-13.

CAST: Gérard Depardieu (Onoff); Roman Polanski (The Inspector); Sergio Rubini (Andre, the Young Policeman); Nicola Di Pinto (The Captain); Paolo Lombardi (The Warrant Officer); Tano Cimarosa (The Old Attendant); Maria Rosa Spagnolo (Paula).

LOS ANGELES TIMES, 5/26/95, Calendar/p. 14, Kevin Thomas

Giuseppe Tornatore's "A Pure Formality," from the maker of "Cinema Paradiso," quite literally opens with a bang—and with the sound of a gunshot ringing in our ears the camera assumes the point of view of a person running through a dark, rainy forest. Eventually we discover the person is a large, heavy man (Gerard Depardieu), wet, disheveled and distraught. On a road he's stopped by police and taken into custody for questioning when he can't produce identification.

Once at the police station—an ancient, crumbling stone structure with the leakiest roof in the world and seemingly in the middle of nowhere (but apparently in France)—Depardieu behaves with hostility and outrage, complaining that he'll be late for a meeting with the minister of culture. His situation initially doesn't improve with the arrival of the station's inspector (Roman Polanski). He has a hard time convincing him that he is in fact Onoff, a renowned writer and a particular hero of the Inspector, who can quote from Onoff's novels at length.

Things now are looking up: dried off and cleaned up, Onoff is all set to leave, ready to be driven home to his nearby mountain retreat. That's when the Inspector, with deceptive casualness, says that he has a few more questions to ask Onoff, who can't account for the two hours leading up to his arrest or why he was out wandering in the mud and the rain in the first place. It's "a pure formality," the Inspector insists.

We know, better, for from the outset Tornatore, who co-wrote his film with Pascale Quignard, has created an unsettling atmosphere, the kind that makes you feel something in not quite right, but you're not sure what. In any event, the Inspector—diminutive, humble yet fundamentally sharp and steely—commences a remorseless interrogation that has the effect of confronting Onoff with his life and his failings, all that memory tends to erase.

Punctuated with fragments from Onoff's memories, "A Pure Formality" becomes a crackling duel of wits—brilliantly written and directed—between two formidable presences: Polanski, in his first substantial acting role since his own macabre "The Tenant" nearly 20 years ago, and Depardieu, who is towering as a man baring his soul. The result, in part, is a remarkable revelation of what it can mean to be a writer and what writing is all about, in particular the notion that to write is "to lose consciousness."

With its mood-setting Ennio Morricone score, "A Pure Formality" is quite compelling, but you have to be alert throughout to feel fully the strong, reeling impact of its out-of-left-field finish. Right after Onoff is arrested he mutters that his predicament seems out of a "Hollywood B-movie." Precisely. For what Tornatore has done is to bring a rich intellectual and philosophical dimension to a familiar '40s Hollywood plot. The beautifully crafted "A Pure Formality" plays the way an Agatha Christie novel unfolds: When it is over you realize in retrospect that Tornatore has planted clues all along the way.

NEW YORK POST, 5/26/95, p. 42, Thelma Adams

Columbo meets Kafka in the latest movie from the director of "Cinema Paradiso," Giuseppe Tornatore.

I could envision the back of Peter Falk's raincoat and then the swivel of his hips, his finger raised to his nose as one more not-so-insignificant question formed on his chapped lips, as the inspector (Roman Polanski) drops the phrase he uses to describe his interrogation of an alleged murderer, the phrase that gives the film its title: "A Pure Formality."

During a downpour (a tribute to Columbo and his trademark raincoat?), a man runs headlong down a country road. The police detain him. He lacks identity papers and there has been a murder in the woods nearby. The drenched man is Onoff (Gerard Depardieu), a famed novelist in the throes of a mid-life crisis.

If Onoff has committed the murder, he doesn't seem to remember it—or is that just a clever dodge by a practiced storyteller?

The police station is the main set, the site of a two-man tug-of-war about guilt and innocence, memory and art. So drab is the institution of justice that the rooms are almost colorless. The lights fail, the phones don't work, there is no corner of comfort in this purgatory. The extravagant rain drips through the roof into vessels of all sizes. The water rises until it must be bailed out in buckets.

Depardieu dominates this operatic set. He is the movie's heart, soul and stomach. The star of "Danton" and, "Colonel Chabert" has always been an actor whose brute physique contrasted with his emotional vulnerability. Now, at 47, his body has also become vulnerable.

Like Marlon Brando in "Don Juan De Marco," Depardieu's size is breathtaking. But unlike the American "Don Juan," in this European co-production (in French with English subtitles) we see the actor stark naked with a belly that would have suited Falstaff.

Polanski, best known as a director ("Repulsion," "Chinatown") and fan of underage girls, plays the inspector, an educated bumpkin who is the novelist's biggest fan. With his beady eyes, wizened elf face and five-o'clock shadow, Polanski is a guarded actor, shutting the audience out. His rages are teapot tempests, his raised voice a shrill whistle. With his schizophrenic, one-man good-cop, bad-cop routine, Polanski is no match for Depardieu.

This good-looking, poorly dubbed, hip-pocket psychological thriller builds drop-by-drop, book chat by chat, the favored language of North American Euro-wannabes. In the end, rather than feeling the floodgates of revelation releasing within me, I just wanted to bail out.

NEWSDAY, 5/26/95, Part II/p. B5, John Anderson

Movies with trick endings and overly shrewd resolutions can leave you feeling that there's no exit. That you can infer no good from any of it. That, hereafter, you'll think twice before putting your faith and hope in some film director's hands.

One might say the same about cloyingly clever openings of film reviews. But here, at least, you're in on the gag at the outset. When a film ends with a twist that all but negates what you've been feeling for the previous hour-and-a-half, there's a sense that a fraud has been perpetrated—even when the ending isn't all that tough to figure out in advance.

In "A Pure Formality," the latest by Italian director Giuseppe Tornatore ("Cinema Paradiso"), we hear panting, look down a gun barrel, see a shot and embark on a confusing dash through the woods, in a downpour, toward the flashlights of three policemen. "Pneumonia for sure," one says, looking at the rain-soaked runner (Gerard Depardieu), who has no ID and is taken in for questioning.

Who is he? The gunman? The victim? Tornatore toys with us here, and will throughout. Eventually—after an untidy beating and some other unpleasantness with his captors—Depardieu's character claims to be Onoff, a reclusive French novelist who has not published for six years. To the police inspector who arrives to question him (Roman Polanski), he is one of the greatest authors of all time. To Onoff, the police investigator is a torturer and his detainment an outrage.

Their exchanges are intriguing and Tornatore's eye for detail and acrobatic camerawork can be arresting. But the director uses the visuals not to enhance the action but to distract from it. It's as if, in a desperate fear that he'll lose us with the words, he has to keep shifting the focus to another charged image. Which becomes redundant, as do the images.

Depardieu is among a handful of the more riveting actors to watch work—even when he takes his clothes off and flaunts all that generously proportioned Gallic expanse. Polanski plays badger to Depardieu's bear, and they make not-so-beautiful but dramatic music together. Which is partly why, when the music stops, you're left standing around like a goof.

VILLAGE VOICE, 5/30/95, p. 52, Georgia Brown

I have a friend who worked for Polanski on *Repulsion*. For years after he kept the director's picture pasted inside one of his shoes, "So every time I took a step I'd crush the wretched dwarf." Roman Polanski has no problem playing the prick. He can also play a smarmy civil servant or a sentimental fool aching to be victimized. Terrorized children—Polanski eluded the Nazis—pick up useful tricks. If he hadn't needed to control things, he could've been an actor of Ben Kingsley's stature.

In *A Pure Formality*, Giuseppe Tornatore's mousetrap drama, Polanski the actor steals the show, snatches it from the beefy paws of a massive, hard-working Gerard Depardieu. This isn't to say that Depardieu isn't wonderful in his usual colossus mode, but the wily Polanski, hunched into the padded shoulders of his cheap, functionary's suit, is brilliant. And his good cop/bad cop rolled into one is the one in charge; he's the director of the piece.

Like *Death and the Maiden*, *A Pure Formality* depicts an inquisition; it's an inquiry into character, an anatomy of evasion. Depardieu plays the accused and Polanski his interrogator. The crime—judging by a cryptic image of a gun firing, the sound of a body failing—is murder. After the shot, Depardieu crashes through trees and sloshes forward in the rain until he's picked up and, confused and evasive, hauled into a backwater police station. Where, this is, exactly, isn't clear. France supposedly, but, once he arrives at the station, it looks more like some leftover Czech or Polish border crossing. At first, the influence is *The Trial*, later it's *The Twilight Zone*. Morricone has supplied one of his jittery scores.

When I saw the film a year ago in Cannes, I felt sure Tornatore was filming a play. But no, this is an original film script by the director and Pascal Quignard *(Tous les matins du monde)*. In any case, it's a drastic departure from the director's semi-autobiographical, Sicily-drenched *Cinema Paradiso*. The acting is far more subdued, or shall we say, French. *Paradiso,* a tale about growing up inside movies, was a swell idea crudely realized, farcical and overstated. A *Pure Formality*—a lite idea, seamlessly wrought—could easily be the work of a different director. The only elements it has in common with *Paradiso* are those two men in a booth and the artist as a subject.

Onoff (Depardieu) is a novelist of stature, literally and figuratively. (Tornatore encouraged Depardieu to gain weight for the part. One time here he falls to the ground, rolls on his back, and his great, quivering white belly looms up like moonrise.) When Onoff reluctantly gives the Inspector his name, the Inspector, a great fan, doesn't believe him. "And I am Leonardo da Vinci," he scoffs. Off the top of his head, M. Da Vinci quotes a passage that Onoff himself has forgotten. Aha, an imposter! But when Onoff recites a passage of his own choosing, tears spring to the little functionary's eyes. *Now* he recognizes his idol—who has shaved his beard and, for a moment, it seems the two will spend the evening speaking of cabbages and kings. But the duel has just begun.

Outside, the storm rages; inside, the ceiling leaks and eventually the power falls (as it did in *Death and the Maiden* and countless psychodramas before that one). A shy, sweet-natured assistant (Sergio Rubini) empties buckets, mops up overflow, and takes down the suspect's words on an ancient typewriter. The magnified sounds of the drips and the typewriter mechanism aid in the breakdown process. The cunning, ferret-faced Inspector alternates delicacy and brutality and eventually Onoff lets go of his secret and so does Tornatore.

Death and the Maiden had a good political reason for being. *A Pure Formality*, pure hokum, wishes to play a metaphysical trick. Who cares? As an actor's demo, it's a giddy adventure. Afterward I felt like pasting Polanski's picture on my refrigerator. Apologies to my good friend.

Also reviewed in:
CHICAGO TRIBUNE, 7/14/95, Friday/p. H, Michael Wilmington
NEW REPUBLIC, 6/19/95, p. 30, Stanley Kauffmann
NEW YORK TIMES, 5/26/95, p. C10, Caryn James
VARIETY, 5/23-29/94, p. 53, Deborah Young
WASHINGTON POST, 6/30/95, p. D6, Rita Kempley

PUSHING HANDS

A Cinepix Film Properties release of a Central Motion Picture Corporation presentation in association with Ang Lee Productions and Good Machine. *Executive Producer:* Jiang Feng-chyi. *Producer:* Ted Hope, James Schamus, Emily Liu, and Ang Lee. *Director:* Ang Lee. *Screenplay (Mandarin and English with English subtitles):* Ang Lee and James Schamus. *Director of Photography:* Jong Lin. *Editor:* Tim Squyres. *Music:* Xiao-Song Qu. *Sound:* Paul Thomas Christian. *Casting:* Wendy Ettinger and Jeff Berman. *Production Designer:* Scott Bradley. *Art Director:* Michael Shaw. *Costumes:* Elizabeth Jenyon. *Running time:* 100 minutes. *MPAA Rating:* Not Rated.

CAST: Sihung Lung (Mr. Chu); Lai Wang (Mrs. Chen); Bo Z. Wang (Alex Chu); Deb Snyder (Martha Chu); Haan Lee (Jeremy Chu); Emily Liu (Yi Cui).

LOS ANGELES TIMES, 6/16/95, Calendar/p. 2, Kevin Thomas

Although "Pushing Hands" is the last to arrive, it is the first of what has been called writer - director Ang Lee's "Father Knows Best" trilogy, in which a parent confronts a changing world. It includes "The Wedding Banquet" and "Eat Drink Man Woman."

It's also Lee's debut feature, filmed in New York and suburban Westchester in 1991. As such, it hasn't quite the scope of his subsequent films, but it does have much of their warmth and wisdom. It begins on a somber note, sketching a near-silent day in an expensive, tasteful modern home in a woodsy suburb. Seventy-year-old Mr. Chu (Sihung Lung, who also plays the father in the two later films) goes about his solitary rituals, exercising, preparing his food, watching Chinese videos while his writer daughter-in-law Martha (Deb Snyder) sits at her computer in the next room in increasing desperation. She lashes out at the father-in-law who knows no English— "No metal in the microwave!"—and thrusts earphones at him.

In time we learn that the widowed Mr. Chu, a tai chi master, has arrived from Beijing to live With his son's family only about a month earlier and that his presence is making it impossible for Martha to work. Lee doesn't set up this situation as deftly as he does conflicts in his subsequent films. He makes us feel that Martha is unnecessarily unsympathetic—that he's loaded the dice in making her such a shrew, especially since her father-in-law is clearly a nice, well-meaning man freshly arrived in a new and vastly different world. (Simply installing a door, for example, between the living room and Martha's workroom surely would be a help.)

Nonetheless, Lee has set Mr. Chu's story in motion, which involves the cruel discovery that American society by and large really makes no time (or space) for its older generation, a shocking realization for a Chinese and a painful predicament for Mr. Chu's loving son Alex (Bo Z. Wang). A picture that gets better as it goes along, "Pushing Hands" simultaneously grows deeper and funnier as Chu commences working out his own destiny.

"Pushing Hands'" title refers to a tai chi exercise designed to help you keep your balance while destroying that of your opponent, and therefore suggests Chu's struggle against his fate. It is a lovingly observed, nicely acted, human comedy with Lung emerging as the shrewd, witty delight he is in all three Lee films.

NEW YORK POST, 6/2/95, p. 51, Thelma Adams

"Punishing hands is a way of keeping your balance while unbalancing your opponent," Alex Chu tells his wife Martha, explaining his father's Tai Chi technique.

"Like marriage," Martha retorts. Ang Lee's 1992 "Pushing Hands" is about balance. Mr. Chu (Sihung Lung), a retired martial-arts master, emigrates from Beijing to America. When Chu moves into his son's Westchester house, he upsets the equilibrium between Chinese-born Yankee Alex (Bo Z. Wang) and his American princess wife (Deb Snyder).

Lung plays the first of three traditional fathers who form the spine of Lee's trilogy—"Pushing Hands," "The Wedding Banquet" and "Eat Drink Man Woman." Mr. Chu is the movie's immovable center, its Rock of Gibraltar. When things become intolerable at home, Chu moves to Chinatown and becomes a dishwasher. When the boss tries to fire him for being too slow, Chu refuses to leave the sink. The entire kitchen staff, a Chinese gang, and the NYPD fail to move the Tai Chi master from his spot.

Unbalanced because he no longer needs to push against the political and social turmoil that defined his life in China, superfluous in his son's home, unwanted outside of it, Chu befriends a fellow immigrant, Mrs. Chen (Lai Wang). The couple survive their children's matchmaking schemes and are on the verge of providing each other with comfort and dignity at the movie's close. Their connection presages the delicacy and insight of Lee's later movies. Lee understands that we can only be ourselves when we have someone with whom to share our selves.

Even at his most hard-headed, Chu is tremendously sympathetic. He has the body of an athlete, the skills of an artist, the powers of a faith healer, the soul of a poet: he's an Asian uber Dad.

For all of Chu's strength, "Pushing Hands" is severely out of balance. Chu pushes his unworthy opponents and the movie topples over.

Martha is straight out of the shrew-of-the-month club. Portrayed by the flouncy, raccoon-eyed Snyder, Alex's wife is a self-involved novelist who twists herself into a bleeding ulcer while the Zen master sits in the next room, the object of her discord. It takes a while for the audience to develop any sympathy for her; Lee seems to have even less.

Alex is also hard to grasp. We don't quite get him in his quiet, yuppie, honey-I'm-home moments so that when Wang launches into angry tirades they seem more like actor's tricks than expressions of true emotion.

Alex and Martha's marriage feels like a plot device—Asian immigrant and curly blonde wife. We never really believe that the pair share a history. We must take their intimacy on faith. We haven't seen them living in harmony, so that there's no contrast with the life out of balance initiated by Mr. Chu's arrival.

"Pushing Hands" shows Lee's promise, but the reason that the first film in his "father knows best" trilogy is the last to open in Manhattan is readily apparent.

NEWSDAY, 6/2/95, Part II/p. B5, John Anderson

There's something déjà vu-ish about Ang Lee's new movie, probably because it's Ang Lee's old movie. "Pushing Hands" was the first in/last out of Lee's "father knows best" trilogy—includes "The Wedding Banquet" and "Eat Drink Man Woman"—and deals with many of the same themes as those two films. What it doesn't have is their polish. What it does have is their eye and their heart.

One of Lee's pet themes is assimilation—and not just of the recent arrival. In "The Wedding Banquet," the gay Chinese son has never reconciled his life in New York with his traditional upbringing and is living two lives. In "Eat Drink Man Woman," the three modern daughters are caught between their father's traditional expectations and their own independence. No one is, excuse the expression, grounded: There's a free-floating quality to their lives that needs a steely, slap in the face with the velvet glove of tradition. Enter Dad.

In "Pushing Hands," Mr. Chu (veteran Taiwanese actor Sihung Lung, the father in "Wedding Banquet"), a master of the martial art of tai-chi and a recent emigre from Beijing, is a walking disruption for his American daughter-in-law, Martha (Deb Snyder). And a worry for his son, Alex (Bo Z. Wang), and an object of devotion for his grandson, Jeremy, (Haan Lee). Director Lee creates tension immediately and masterfully, with a near-silent sequence of Martha and Chu moving about their Westchester house like two hostile armies—Martha trying to write her second novel, Chu executing his tai-chi exercises. It's a tension that will remain unrelieved until two things happen: Martha, who has her own assimilation problems, becomes ill (Martha's character is the film's major flaw; were she at all sympathetic it would be richer); and Chu begins to move beyond the tiny China he carries in his mind, and where he's been living since coming to America.

Much of "Pushing Hands"—the name of a tai-chi technique Chu teaches at a local school—is about willful blindness, and making one's life whole. Chu will find a bit of romance with Mrs. Chen (Lai Wang), leave his son's home in humiliation after being set up on a date with her and become a minor celebrity after a Chinatown restaurant melee. He'll also learn that, though he may know best, he doesn't know everything. And that just because one's life is whole doesn't mean it can't be reshaped.

VILLAGE VOICE, 6/6/95, p. 58, Sally Eckhoff

In Ang Lee's first two major releases, 1993s *The Wedding Banquet* and last year's *Eat Drink Man Woman*, he outlined the widening rifts between Old World parents and their American children. Now, with the release of *Pushing Hands*—actually the first of Lee's "father knows best" trilogy—he also confirms what many of his viewers may already suspect: cluttered shots and slightly irritating personalities are favorite devices for creating emotional tension. Lee has poignant stories to tell, but arouses his audience's appetite for harmony by nearly driving them to distraction first.

"Pushing hands" is a tai chi exercise in which the fighter maintains his stability while unbalancing his opponent. The film's title refers to the inner struggle of Mr. Chu, a retired, lovably serene tai chi master who leaves Beijing for Yonkers to live with his married son. Young, handsome Alex (Bo Z. Wang) is the picture of filial concern. But Alex's sour-faced, galumphing American wife (Deb Snyder) can't wait to get Granddad out of the house. In desperation, the elder Chu takes off for Chinatown. His martial arts skills are put to the test when he's fired from a dishwashing job.

Sihung Lung's Mr. Chu would be a delight in almost any cinematic milieu. However, when the director crams his domestic scenes with bric-a-brac and other visual distractions, we see the old man's contrasting virtue painted with too broad a brush. And by adding the jarring textures of amplified household noise (sizzling oil, slamming doors), Ang Lee ups the ante in situations already fraught with chaos. The sensory overload doesn't completely deflate the story's original charm. Yet one can't help but feel that given a less hysterical atmosphere, the actors would have more than a fighting chance.

Also reviewed in:
CHICAGO TRIBUNE, 7/21/95, Friday/p. I, Michael Wilmington
NEW YORK TIMES, 6/2/95, p. C12, Janet Maslin
VARIETY, 3/16/92, p. 60, Derek Elley
WASHINGTON POST, 6/9/95, p. B7, Rita Kempley
WASHINGTON POST, 6/9/95, Weekend/p. 42, Desson Howe

PYROMANIAC'S LOVE STORY, A

A Hollywood Pictures release. *Producer:* Mark Gordon. *Director:* Joshua Brand. *Screenplay:* Morgan Ward. *Director of Photography:* John Schwartzman. *Editor:* David Rosenbloom. *Music:* Rachel Portman. *Sound:* D. Bruce Carwardine. *Casting:* Amanda Mackey and Cathy

Sandrich. *Production Designer:* Dan Davis. *Art Director:* Peter Grundy. *Costumes:* Bridget Kelly. *Running time:* 96 minutes. *MPAA Rating:* PG.

CAST: William Baldwin (Garet); John Leguizamo (Sergio); Sadie Frost (Hattie); Erika Eleniak (Stephanie); Michael Lerner (Perry); Joan Plowright (Mrs. Linzer); Armin Mueller-Stahl (Mr. Linzer); Mike Starr (Sgt. Zikowski); Julio Oscar Mechoso (Jerry); Floyd Vivino (Ass Pincher); Babz Chula (Ass Pincher's Wife); Richard Crenna (Mr. Lumpke).

LOS ANGELES TIMES, 4/28/95, Calendar/p. 12, Peter Rainer

"A Pyromaniac's Love Story" practically pants for your approval. It's a strenuous, sweet-natured romantic comedy that never really works its way into your heart—or your head. Maybe it's the fault of the premise—a bakery burns down and, as a sign of their passion, four love-struck souls each try to take credit for it. It's an unwieldy conceit for a comedy.

Successful adult fairy tales have made do with far less, but director Joshua Brand (creator of such TV shows as "Northern Exposure" and "I'll Fly Away") and screenwriter Morgan Ward don't provide much genuine romanticism. It's a film about ardor made with a careful tastefulness. A comedy about would-be pyromaniacs needs more inspired lunacy.

John Leguizamo plays Sergio, a Puerto Rican pastry boy at a failing German bakery run by the Linzers (Joan Plowright and Armin Mueller-Stahl, recapping their husband-and-wife act from "Avalon"). When the bakery burns, the police are besieged by a raft of confessors: Sergio, Mr. Linzer, Mrs. Linzer and Garet Lumpke (William Baldwin), whose wealthy father (Richard Crenna) wants Sergio to take the rap in exchange for a bundle of cash that will allow him to properly romance Hattie (Sadie Frost), who works as a waitress but wants to see the world.

Sergio is an innocent who believes in the power of passion. Hattie, who clonks guys on the make for her, doesn't seem like the type to inspire such ardor. But, it turns out, she's an innocent too. Garet, more gushy about, his feelings, spouts windy odes to love and in general carries on like a reject from a roadshow production of "Cyrano." (He has a bum leg like Lord Byron.) He carries a torch—literally—for the well-to-do Stephanie (Erika Elenjak) before switching over to Hattie.

The filmmakers are trying to bring the torch metaphor to life. These people are supposed to be inflamed by love, but there's nothing combustible about the way they connect. In this Anytown, U.S.A. locale, the characters—German, Puerto Rican, rich, poor—seem like wholesome puppets. Leguizamo, who, from some angles, resembles a young John Garfield, is peppy, and Plowright and Mueller-Stahl may turn out to be the next Hume Cronyn and Jessica Tandy. But "A Pyromaniac's Love Story" is no hunka hunka burnin' love.

NEW YORK POST, 4/28/95, p. 42, Larry Worth

Long before cameras started rolling, someone should have taken a match to the "Pyromaniac's Love Story" script.

It's the kind of movie in which a convoluted plot—and this one's a doozy—takes second place to wondering how it ever got made. Or signed on a cast that includes John Leguizamo, Sadie Frost, Erika Eleniak, Armin Mueller-Stahl, Joan Plowright and William Baldwin.

Actually, Baldwin was smarter than some: He doesn't show up until 35 minutes into the story. But with a 96-minute running time, he'd have been smarter to delay for another hour.

First-time director Joshua Brand attempts to mold the production into an adult fairy tale about the vagaries of amour, with three couples serving as perpetually star-crossed lovers. The result is a modern-day variation on "Midsummer Night's Dream," sans any trace of wit, talent or Shakespeare.

Further, any film that centers on the spirit of romance better have actors with charm to spare, like Johnny Depp add Marlon Brando in "Don Juan DeMarco." Here, Leguizamo and Baldwin have never been less appealing.

They're among those who—for reasons too complicated to explain—are claiming to have committed arson at a neighborhood pastry shop. And lest any trace of malice creep into this game of musical jail cells, all the suspects claim to have done it for love.

That's hard to believe in the best of circumstances, but especially when there's zero sparks between the pals. As the object of Leguizamo's obsession, Frost shows none of the potential exposed as the vampiric minx of "Francis Ford Coppola's Dracula." Ditto for Eleniak's dull turn as Baldwin's bitchy main squeeze.

Only pastry shop owners Mueller-Stahl and Plowright—reunited from Barry Levinson's "Avalon"—survive with dignity intact. And that's an accomplishment after being forced to recite Morgan Ward's pathetic dialogue.

The bottom line is that cast and crew have produced a farce without, laughs. Accordingly, "A Pyromaniac's Love Story" is a five-alarm fiasco.

NEWSDAY, 4/26/95, Part II/p. B5, Jack Mathews

Whoever wrote the production notes for Disney's "A Pyromaniac's Love Story" made a gallant effort to fob off fire as a metaphor for love. Both are ignited, both are affected "by sudden shifts in wind or mood," both can blaze out of control. And both, I would add, can lead to disaster.

"A Pyromaniac's Love Story," the first feature by TV director-producer Joshua Brand ("A Year in the Life," Northern Exposure"), is another misfired comedy from the company that thinks Pauly Shore is funny. Somebody in that studio's live-action division has a low threshold for humor and is determined to persuade the rest of us that minor talents are major.

Comedian John Leguizamo, who gets the Disney star treatment here, is not exactly a minor talent. He has done brilliant one-man shows on Latino stereotypes and now has his own TV series ("The House of Buggin'"). But he registers almost zero as a romantic lead, and not even Robin Williams could get a laugh out of this ill-conceived, dreadfully written mess.

The script, by recent film school grad Morgan Ward, revolves around the torching of a small pastry shop in an unidentified American city (it was actually shot in Toronto) and the series of misunderstandings and false confessions inspired by it. Those taking blame include the shop's pastry boy, Sergio (Leguizamo), its owner, Mr. Linzer (Armin Mueller-Stahl), and the owner's wife (Joan Plowright).

Yes, the pastry shop blaze is a metaphor for love, lame as it may be. The shop is actually torched by a lovestruck delusional (William Baldwin) trying to make a point with a girlfriend he erroneously believes is in love with Sergio. As one of the characters suggests, women appreciate small romantic gestures—the opening of a door, a bouquet of flowers, a Class A felony. (Taking her to this movie, however, will not have the desired effect.)

At the same time, Sergio and the Linzers are ready to take the fall out of their own misguided senses of passion. Sergio is actually taking a bribe from the arsonist's father, thinking he can do the time and then use the money to set off on a romantic world tour with the restless waitress (Sadie Frost) down the block.

Only the romance between the Linzers has an electron of spark, and that owing entirely to the yeoman-like work of old pros Mueller-Stahl and Plowright. Some real feeling passes between the immigrant couple they portray, and in this film, that smidgen of sincerity is like finding an unsinged keepsake in the ashes of a burned-down building.

There is nothing else to commend "A Pyromaniac's Love Story." Baldwin, its best known star, is its greatest liability, so operatically over-the-top as the lame, lovestruck arsonist that you're hoping he won't find true romance until he gets to prison.

It's hard to know how many more of these comic hairballs are clogging the drain in Disney's live-action factory, but I suggest they send them all to Pauly Shore's house and make him watch them.

Also reviewed in:
CHICAGO TRIBUNE, 4/28/95, Friday/p. D, Michael Wilmington
NEW YORK TIMES, 4/28/95, p. C18, Stephen Holden
VARIETY, 5/1-7/95, p. 36, Joe Leydon

QUICK AND THE DEAD, THE

A TriStar Pictures release in association with Japan Satellite Broadcasting, Inc. of an IndieProd production. *Executive Producer:* Toby Jaffe and Robert Tapert. *Producer:* Joshua Donen, Allen Shapiro, and Patrick Markey. *Director:* Sam Raimi. *Screenplay:* Simon Moore. *Director of Photography:* Dante Spinotti. *Editor:* Pietro Scalia. *Music:* Alan Silvestri. *Music Editor:* Kenneth Karman and Thomas Drescher. *Sound:* Dennis L. Maitland and (music) Dennis Sands. *Sound Editor:* Lawrence H. Mann and Uncle J. Kamen. *Casting:* Francine Maisler. *Production Designer:* Patrizia Von Brandenstein. *Art Director:* Steve Saklad. *Set Decorator:* Hilton Rosemarin. *Set Dresser:* Daniel Boxer, Jeff Debell, Armando Quiroz, and Saul Leiberman. *Special Effects:* Al Di Sarro. *Costumes:* Judianna Makovsky. *Make-up:* Gary Liddiard. *Make-up (Sharon Stone):* Tricia Sawyer. *Stunt Coordinator:* Terry Leonard. *Running time:* 103 minutes. *MPAA Rating:* R.

CAST: Sharon Stone (Ellen); Gene Hackman (John Herod); Russell Crowe (Cort); Leonardo DiCaprio (Kid); Tobin Bell (Dog Kelly); Roberts Blossom (Doc Wallace); Kevin Conway (Eugene Dred); Keith David (Sgt. Cantrell); Lance Henriksen (Ace Hanlon); Pat Hingle (Horace the Bartender); Gary Sinise (Marshall); Mark Boone, Jr. (Scars); Olivia Burnette (Katie); Fay Masterson (Mattie Silk); Raynor Scheine (Ratsy); Woody Strode (Charles Moonlight); Jerry Swindall (Blind Boy); Scott Spiegel (Gold Teeth Man); Jonothon Gill (Spotted Horse); Sven-Ole Thorsen (Gutzon); Lennie Loftin (Flat Nose Foy); Matthew Gold (Foy's Boy); Arturo Gastelum (Carlos Montoya); David Cornell (Simp Dixon); Josef Rainer (Virgil Sparks); Stacey Ramsower (Young Ellen); Tony Boggs (Zeb); Scott Ryder (Gunfighter); Timothy Patrick Quill (Man in Bar); Solomon Abrams (Man on Veranda); John Cameron (Bordello Swell); Bruce Campbell (Wedding Shemp); Michael Stone (Counselor); Butch Molina (Saloon Patron); Gregory Goossen, Mick Garris, and Oliver Dear (Young Herod's Men).

CHRISTIAN SCIENCE MONITOR, 2/13/95, p. 13, David Sterritt

The "Quick and the Dead," about a sheriff who keeps order by holding nonstop shootouts in the town square, is the liveliest western I've seen in ages. But many moviegoers will be slow to see it, since the western genre has been more dead than quick at the box office in recent years.

True, an occasional horse opera becomes a hit with audiences. The acclaimed "Unforgiven," the ambitious "Dances With Wolves," and the dreadful "Legends of the Fall" come to mind.

"Wyatt Earp" was a more typical case, though, falling off its horse despite a big-name director and an all-star cast. Once a Hollywood staple, the western genre was killed off in the 1970s and '80s by science fiction, which adapted its conventions to a more trendy, effects-oriented framework. The granddaddy of this change was "Star Wars," which set its story not in the future but "a long, long time ago ..."

Playing their cards cleverly, the makers of "The Quick and the Dead" have plugged into all sorts of current fashions. Key roles in the story are played by a no-nonsense woman, a fresh-faced youngster, and a weather-beaten old man—no sexism or ageism here—supported by a cast of ethnically diverse characters (liberals can smile) treated irreverently enough (conservatives can also smile) for the mixture to seem reasonably uncalculated.

Equally to the point, director Sam Raimi has juiced up the action with the energetic style he developed in the sardonic horror movies that launched his career. To my eye, Raimi shockers like "Darkman" and "The Evil Dead" are more tricky than scary, using an onslaught of gimmicks to mask an absence of thought and feeling. His new western also has plenty of self-conscious devices, from superswift editing to the year's weirdest camera angles. But what makes them more than ostentatious inside jokes is the respect he shows for the conventions he affectionately parodies.

At once an old-fashioned adventure and a post-modern pastiche, "The Quick and the Dead" walks a slim tightrope with impressive skill and humor. Its main reference point is the work of Sergio Leone, the Italian maestro whose "spaghetti westerns" reinvigorated the genre during its last major phase about 30 years ago. Raimi draws on pictures like "The Good, the Bad, and the Ugly" and "Once Upon a Time in the West" as freely as George Lucas drew on John Ford's classic "The Searchers" in his "Star Wars" scenario, rediscovering the dark poetry Leone found in the anarchic stretches of an untamed frontier.

None of this means "The Quick and the Dead" has the operatic sweep of a Leone masterpiece. Simon Moore's screenplay is repetitious, and while Raimi tries to make this a virtue, the story fades before its 103 minutes are over.

Touches of pretentiousness also creep into the otherwise breezy atmosphere, starting with the fact that Redemption is the name of the Arizona town where the picture takes place. References to redemption are now in vogue, from the title of "The Shawshank Redemption" to the license plate reading "grace" in a "Pulp Fiction" episode. A philosophical filmmaker like Paul Schrader can get away with this, but I'm not the first critic to wonder if schlockmeisters like Stephen King and Quentin Tarantino really spend their time pondering the theme of salvation. Raimi's movie would seem more sincere if Shoot-'Em-Up or Mow'Em-Down were the setting for its explosive action.

Gene Hackman brings his usual professionalism to the sadistic sheriff who forces his citizens into showdowns they'd rather do without. Sharon Stone is strong as a vengeful woman who rides into town, and Leonardo DiCaprio makes a solid impression as a fledgling gunfighter, although he doesn't find the amazing originality he brought to "What's Eating Gilbert Grape" a couple of years back. Roberts Blossom, Pat Hingle, Gary Sinise, and the late, great Woody Strode are standouts in the supporting cast.

Dante Spinotti did the eye-dazzling cinematography, and Pietro Scalia gets credit for the hyperactive editing. Alan Silvestri composed the score, which has a moody charm reminiscent of Ennio Morricone's memorable music for various Leone epics. It couldn't be more appropriate.

LOS ANGELES TIMES, 2/10/95, Calendar/p. 1, Kenneth Turan

Wearing a long tan duster, black hat, leather pants and a shirt cut to the navel (gunfighting is such hot work), a young woman named Ellen rides into the dusty Western town of Redemption with repartee on her mind. An oafish local croaks "You're pretty" and gets "You're not" as a reply. He tries "I need a woman" only to be trumped by "You need a bath." No wonder they're calling this "The Quick and the Dead."

In truth (no surprise here), the new Western starring Sharon Stone as the laconic woman-with-one-name is not really about an epic battle of wits. It's a tale of test, a kind of Super Bowl of gunslingers, complete with NFL-type playoff brackets, that pits killer against killer in what is, inevitably, a single-elimination tournament.

And who could ask for a more impressive bunch of competitors? There is Ace Hanlon (Lance Henriksen), resplendent in a leather outfit that is pure Hollywood Boulevard; Kid (Leonardo DiCaprio, of all people), a glib youthful prodigy; and Gutzon (Sven-Ole Thornsen), the fastest draw in all of Sweden. Yes, Sweden.

Clearly this is the delirious as opposed to the historical West, a place that is excessive and self-parodying by design. And though the studio is calling "The Quick and the Dead" "a Western, unlike any seen before," those familiar with Sergio Leone and the long line of spaghetti Westerns that "A Fistful of Dollars" spawned will know exactly where this film is coming from.

A careful knockoff of Leone, complete down to the blighted, surreal landscape and the grotesque characters with awful teeth (the leather designers apparently arrived in this part of the West well before the dentists did), "Quick" relies on its star just as much as Leone relied on his.

As the female Clint Eastwood, a woman with a mission, Stone proves she can smoke a cheroot and stare down a dunce with the best of them. An actress whose strength has always been her considerable on-screen presence, Stone understands the kind of posing and posturing this film requires much better than either DiCaprio, who seems a bit lost in his part, or co-star Gene Hackman.

Hackman plays Herod (so much for subtlety), the fearless malefactor who has turned Redemption into his own private money machine. Greed aside, Herod has a philosophical reason for sponsoring the quick-draw competition. Cort (Russell Crowe), his former partner in crime, has become a priest given to saying tedious things like "I have renounced violence" and "Killing people is wrong." But can a killer truly change? Herod is determined to find out.

The real stars of this extravaganza, however, are not people but hardware, the highly polished handguns that no one walks around Redemption without. The film's crew includes an armorer/gun coach, an assistant armorer, even a holster fabricator, and the camera caresses the revolvers with an almost fetishistic glee.

Written by Simon Moore and directed by the energetically cartoonish Sam ("The Evil Dead") Raimi, "The Quick and the Dead" is showy visually, full of pans and zooming close-ups. Rarely dull, it is not noticeably compelling either, and as the derivative offshoot of a derivative genre, it inevitably runs out of energy well before any of its hotshots runs out of bullets.

NEW YORK, 2/27/95, p. 108, David Denby

As a boss lady of the old West, Barbara Stanwyck was insinuating and tough—a smart cookie who could be dangerous. Sharon Stone doesn't have anything like Stanwyck's force. She has something else. In *The Quick and the Dead*, riding into town in leather pants, vest, black hat, and one of those fab, calf-length Western coats—a very big coat, a major coat—she seems to have cleaned out half the shops in Milan. You have to laugh at first. Yet she's an extraordinarily glamorous woman. Sharon Stone has the tall, lean body of the Western hero, and she's developed an amusingly minimal, narrowed-eyed style that may remind you of mid-period Clint. She's still a good model, and just enough of an actress to triumph in this crazy movie. Stone plays Ellen, a lone gun who cleans up the town of Redemption, a sinkhole of corruption and vice ruled by a wicked gangster named Herod (Gene Hackman). Given Stone's clothes, I thought, for a while, that I might have heard Hackman's name as "Harrods," the department store in London. But no, the filmmakers want us to think of the nasty king of Palestine who ruled at the time of Jesus' birth and ordered the slaughter of the Innocents. In *The Quick and the Dead,* the light breaks through the skies, and periodic rainstorms wash away the blood of the sinners. Ellen has come as the redeemer. We're in pop-apocalyptic Hollywood, where Christ is always ready to do service at the box office.

The Quick and the Dead is preposterous but far from boring. Herod rules over the decrepit, burnt-out town as a kind of Old West mafia boss, exacting 50 cents of every dollar that changes hands. Each year he stages a quick-draw tournament in which anyone can duel anyone else. At the end of the contest, having knocked off all the local hotshots who might threaten him, Herod alone is left standing. The plot is no more than a chart, like the basketball playoffs: The winners along the way have to keep fighting, so friends and family members, as well as criminals, wind up plugging one another. Oddly, no one leaves the town or complains about the rules. People itch to prove that they're the best. Even Ellen. She has a blood score to settle with Herod, but rather than just shoot the bastard in the back like any rational person, she enters the contest. Apparently Americans in the Old West enjoyed nothing so much as getting shot and falling down in the street. When people are shot, daylight literally shines through the bullet holes.

Herod's contest is such a brazenly commercial idea—the Western reduced to its climactic moment, the duel—that paradoxically it may strike many people as hip or even pure, like a horror film with nothing in it but stalking and slashing. I found the movie less hip than calculated, but I was entertained. You're not supposed to take *The Quick and the Dead* as real life or even as a real Western. The director, Sam Raimi, known for his chic-horror movies (*The Evil Dead, Darkman,* etc.) abandons all memory of the classical Westerns of Ford, Hawks, Anthony Mann, and late Clint Eastwood (*Unforgiven*); instead, he further stylizes the preoccupations of the mannerist masters Sam Peckinpah, Sergio Leone, and early Clint Eastwood, focusing on flourishes and gestures and the grotesque rituals of death.

The Quick and the Dead could have been a cultish bore like *The Crow*, yet what's remarkable about the many duels is how much of the personalities of the various shootists comes through. Raimi has an effectively ruthless shorthand style—anecdote reduced to iconography. This director and the screenwriter, Simon Moore (an Englishman), have little interest in psychology, depth, motivation. The movie is all short, vivid strokes: A man is what he looks like and talks like. I doubt whether so many raunch-faced, walleyed, scrofulous plug-uglies, and also so many high-style studly gunslingers, have ever been assembled to shoot at one another in a single movie. Yet as each one dies, we know who he is, what his fantasy of himself was, and why he thought he was better than anyone else. Raimi's camera brings the audience close, and the movie's "dark" tonalities—the sadism and ghoulishness, the bizarre death obsessions—seem more like an outré B-movie style than a moral vacancy to get upset about. How can you hate a director this flamboyant?

And then there's Gene Hackman, who's reason enough to see anything. The unglamorous, stocky man sitting in the backseat of Warren Beatty's jalopy in *Bonnie and Clyde* has built one of the great careers in modern movie acting. One would think Hackman had squeezed all the juice out of the role of an evil Westerner in *Unforgiven,* but here he is, squeezing some more. Again, he takes a complex kind of amusement in evil, but he's drier this time, and colder, more purely focused on power. And then he surprises us: His Herod is an evil man who knows what goodness is. Therefore, when he chooses evil, he is chilling and perverse. Even in this malevolent playpen of a movie, Hackman seems like a grown-up.

NEW YORK POST, 2/10/95, p. 37, Michael Medved

The new equal-opportunity western "The Quick and the Dead" is just quick enough—and slick enough—to overcome its gimmicky plot about a tough, leather-clad female gunslinger.

Sharon Stone plays this mysterious angel-faced avenger who rides into the corrupt, grimy town of Redemption to compete for the big cash prize in its annual quick-draw tournament—a sort of U.S. Open for gunfighters.

The long-reigning champion of this event is John Herod (Gene Hackman), the brutal boss of the town, who this year faces not only the unconventional challenge from Sharon Stone, but must also confront an African-American professional shootist (Keith David) who's been hired by the town's oppressed Mexican peasants to rid them of the tyrant.

Even worse, Herod must confront an Oedipal subplot, shooting it out with the cocksure "Kid" (Leonardo DiCaprio)—a favorite at the local bordello who claims to be his only son.

Even a pacifist preacher (Russell Crowe) is forced into the fighting.

This heavy-handed material would have been unwatchable had the director taken it too seriously.

Fortunately, Sam Raimi, eccentric genius of "Darkman" and "The Evil Dead," has the good sense to treat this story as a gun-in-cheek comedy. When quick-draw competitors absorb bullets, they don't just bleed, their bodies develop gaping holes the size of the Holland Tunnel.

Each shootout is rendered with such cunning, stunning originality that Raimi keeps you guessing—not about what will happen in the silly story, but which cinematic trick the director will spring next.

The movie's most telling special effect remains, however, an actor named Hackman—who invests his ruthless villain with so much chuckling charisma that it's an unmitigated pleasure to watch him work.

As for Sharon Stone, she's been blessed with a role that seems specifically designed to fit her unique thespian skills; since her character is supposed to be the strong silent type, she has few lines to deliver.

This means that she gets little chance for embarrassingly flat delivery that generally mars her performances.

She thereby achieves a high point in her motion picture career: In her previous starring roles, she has seldom been so ... adequate.

Whatever the movie's shortcomings in terms of characterization or story line, its visual brilliance carries the day. Cinematographer Dante Spinotti captured natural splendors in "The Last of the Mohicans" and "Nell," and here he draws similarly glowing world of a deliberately artificial western town.

Production designer Patrizia Von Brandenstein (who won the Oscar for creating the somewhat different setting for "Amadeus") re-creates that town with loving, evocative detail, calling to mind the existentialist never-never lands of Sergio Leone, rather than any authentic view of the frontier.

In fact, the whole picture conveys the energy (and insanity) of classic spaghetti westerns—and like the best of them, it's, a saucy, spicy dish.

NEWSDAY, 2/10/95, Part II/p. B2, Jack Mathews

There are two ways to watch Sam Raimi's "The Quick and the Dead," and only one way to enjoy it.

If you look at it as a conventional revenge Western, with a soft, blond-haired babe (Sharon Stone) in the role usually reserved for such leathery heroes as John Wayne or Clint Eastwood, you'll be puking in your popcorn box. If you watch it as a hip parody of Sergio Leone's spaghetti westerns, if you think of its setting as a metaphor for purgatory, you'll have a wonderful time.

Raimi has developed a cult audience for his wryly funny horror movies ("The Evil Dead," "Darkman") and he brings the same irreverent touch to the western genre in "Quick and the Dead." The movie includes virtually every cliche of the western, but Raimi turns them into a series of comic notes; once you catch the rhythm of what he's doing, you look forward to the cliches, knowing they'll be turned upside-down.

Written by British playwright and TV writer Simon Moore, "Quick and the Dead" creates a classic western setting—a lawless border town whose cowering town folk, posturing gunslingers and rouged whores are all lorded over by a ruthless land baron (Gene Hackman)—and frames the entire story in a quick-draw contest that vaguely follows the rules of modern tennis.

The participants' names go on a board, and each day, at prescribed hours, they pair off and face each other in individual matches in the middle of town. The survivors move into the next bracket, and fight again the next day.

The annual contest is sponsored and always won by the baron, a career sociopath so cruel his name is John Herod. He lives in baroque splendor in the midst of dusty Redemption, and uses the violent game to both thin the herd of outlaw immigrants and to satisfy his own taste for blood.

Into this scene comes Stone's Lady With No Name, a cheroot-smoking chick in chaps, who has been preparing for the shootout since she was a little girl, and saw—as we do in intermittent black-and-white flashbacks—her lawman dad (Gary Sinese) ordered murdered by Herod. She seems to have also spent a lot of time watching old westerns.

The gender twist is really the film's weakest element. Stone plays it straight, as if she were one of the boys, and she has the macho gestures down pat. The squint, the way she slugs down whiskey from water glasses, the explosive temper. But, hey, it's Sharon Stone, her blond tresses hanging like strands of gold, her saddle bags filled with an endless supply of designer western-wear, and the gag just doesn't hold up all the way.

There are other minor problems. There are lapses where the movie seems to take itself too seriously, and Leonardo DiCaprio, as Herod's gun-happy son, looks more like a woman in drag than does Stone. But even that casting turns out to be something of a stroke for Raimi; DiCaprio plays the Kid with such flat-out enthusiasm for the competition that he comes off exactly like some crazed skateboarder who doesn't know how close he is to death.

Hackman has a field day with Herod, playing him as a combination of Little Bill Daggett in "Unforgiven" and Lex Luthor in "Superman." He is evil incarnate, a sadist who enjoys making people kill each other as much as he enjoys killing them himself, and he'll draw on his own son before he'll give him the fatherly respect he wants.

Redemption is clearly a fantasy western town, a way station on the road to hell, filled with a loathsome assortment of scarfaced, rot-toothed ex-cons, phonies, fortune-hunters and vultures. Besides Stone, the only "good guys" are a see-no-evil blind boy, a teenage prostitute and Cort (Russell Crowe), a former killer who has turned preacher and sworn off violence (temporarily).

Raimi has instilled this with the gothic flavoring of horror movies. Tilted camera angles, quick zooms, foreboding artifice (there are heavy downpours from a sunny sky, after which the streets are as bone dry as before) and always the irreverent touches of humor.

"I've always wanted to fight you, Cort, ever since I first saw you," says Herod, in a tone that seems vaguely sexual. "It's just this itch I had to scratch."

You never heard John Wayne say that.

NEWSWEEK, 2/20/95, p. 72, Jeff Giles

Moviemakers love to give women guns nowadays. That may sound like empowerment, but you've got to ask yourself one question: is Hollywood interested in the women or the guns? In "The Quick and the Dead," Sharon Stone looks fabulous in a dust coat and spurs. But the role reversal at the heart of Sam Raimi's uneven movie is just a gimmick; a script doctor could have turned this into a Kevin Costner vehicle in 15 minutes. Stone's character, a sullen gunslinger named Ellen, rides into a town called Redemption and enters a quick-draw competition. Among her ornery foes are the town's kingpin, Herod (Gene Hackman, in his familiar evil-bastard mode), and his blustery illegitimate son, Kid (Leonardo DiCaprio, working his usual minor miracles). "The Quick" is just a simple story of revenge. Still, it takes Raimi forever to explain the facts of the case: namely, that Herod terrorized Ellen's family once upon a time in the West. Early on, "The Quick" is damnably slow. But Stone gives a nice, brooding performance—a tip of the cowboy hat to "Unforgiven." And Raimi, who also directed "Darkman," keeps the dark humor and the arty shots coming. (The cameramen must have been on Dramamine.) In the end, this Western is serviceable enough. Herod says if you're born bad, you're bad forever. "The Quick" was born bad, but it got better.

SIGHT AND SOUND, 9/95, p. 58, Ben Thompson

John Herod, the psychotic *de facto* ruler of a Western town called Redemption, is holding a gunfighting contest. Drawn by a huge pot of money, gunslingers have come from afar, but the only one Herod cares about is Cort, a reformed outlaw turned preacher. In the saloon, Herod has Cort strung up and is shooting away the legs of the chair which supports him to force him to take part in the contest. Ellen shoots the rope and saves Cort's life. She enters the contest, but Cort still refuses, even in the face of savage beatings and humiliation. When he is given a gun and someone draws on him, however, his reflexes take over and he shoots the man dead. He gives the nervous Ellen advice which helps her through her first round contest.

During a drunken liaison with Herod's son Kid, Ellen happens upon a store of dynamite. She is tormented by memories of a childhood trauma involving Herod. He invites her to his rooms, and she plainly wants to kill him but can't go through with it. The competition progresses and Herod decrees fights should now be to the death. Having killed a hitman hired by the townsfolk, he demands more taxes from the cowering residents. Ellen tries to leave Redemption, but the vengeful force which drives her is too strong.

Ellen and Cort become lovers, but are impelled to fight in the semi-final. With his connivance, she plays dead. Herod kills his son in the other semifinal, but as he and the preacher—who turns out to be a former compadre—face each other, the town is consumed in a massive dynamite conflagration, from which Ellen emerges to confront Herod. When she was a little girl in Redemption and her father was town sheriff, Herod strung him up and gave her the chance to save him by shooting the rope. She missed and shot him in the head. Ellen now kills Herod, gives Cort her father's marshall's badge, and rides out of town.

The Quick and the Dead is a rather unappetising prospect at first sight: Sharon Stone clambering onto the virago Western bandwagon long after most people thought it had left town, with the gnarled and entirely untrustworthy Sam Raimi clutching the reins. This film's feminist credentials could hardly be less convincing. Stone's Ellen has a mysterious tendency, apparently common in the old west, to forget to do up her shirt buttons when she leaves the house—but in its own warped way, *The Quick and the Dead* is something of a classic.

There is more to this film than Sharon Stone striking another heroic blow for womankind by shooting male chauvinists with her big gun, although obviously that does play a big part. Simon Moore's dialogue—"I'm gonna kill you if I have to ride all the way to hell to do it"—is mostly on auto-sass, but there is the odd piquant exchange. "I need a woman" grunts one of Redemption's many unappetising specimens of masculinity. Our heroine ripostes, "You need a bath".

Stone's performance is not entirely as anticipated though. She might have been expected to do the ice-cold avenger thing—resolute and iron-willed with perhaps the odd flickering eyebrow to betray a moment's anxiety. Instead she opts for perpetual quaking irresolution. Far from stone-faced, her mouth trembles with fear every time the splendidly villainous Gene Hackman hoves into view. This might be stretching her acting abilities to places they were never meant to go but it actually contributes substantially to an amusingly overwrought atmosphere.

There are some fine supporting acts, with Leonardo DiCaprio particularly cheeky as the ill-fated son of the estimable Hackman, but the real star of the film is its director. Sam Raimi's project—to chop up spaghetti Western languor with an extra hit of slasher movie malevolence—seems a simple one, but he sets about it with such sadistic vigour that what might have been dreary pastiche becomes gleeful mischief. Spaghetti Western quotes—blind boy, coffin maker measuring up the hero etc.—start out a little too obvious, but the longer the film continues, the more Raimi's malicious sense of fun takes hold. There are some splendidly nasty touches. His camera lurches into viciously phased close-ups with the psychotic inevitability of a drunk walking into a door frame. And if the heroine's return from the dead does not exactly come as a surprise, the true horror of her childhood trauma—not you killed my paw but I killed my paw—is cunningly held back till the very last.

The rococo cinematography is a joy from start to finish too. There's one moment when the camera shoots up Hackman's leg to get to a clock face ... how often have you seen an entire auditorium moved to spontaneous applause by a camera angle?

VILLAGE VOICE, 2/21/95, p. 47, J. Hoberman

Sam Raimi's latest live-action cartoon, *The Quick and the Dead,* is by far the most entertaining and bloodthirsty of recent postwestern western pastiches. The mode is revenge, with a tensely inexpressive Sharon Stone playing the Charles Bronson role from Sergio Leone's *Once Upon a Time in the West* (albeit outfitted more like Clint Eastwood in *High Plains Drifter),* the even prettier Leonardo DiCaprio helping out as a hilariously brash ingenue, and Gene Hackman exaggerating his villainous turn in *Unforgiven.*

The Quick and the Dead is actually pastiche pastiche—an artfully reheated spaghetti western. The half-gutted, horseflop-filled set that represents the town called Redemption; the near constant corrida music scored to increasingly ceremonial gunfights; the cast of gross pug-uglies baring their rotted teeth, striking matches off each other's stubble, or (in one case) cutting a commemorative notch in a forearm rather than a gun, suggest Leone sent up by *Mad* magazine. Raimi garnishes his pasta with a few trademark Gothic touches—Stone frequents the town graveyard, bad guy Hackman dresses like an undertaker and lives in a frontier version of the Addams Family mansion—and serves it up with hyperbolic gusto. You get to see daylight through the body of more than one plugged gun fighter.

Predicated on a fast-draw elimination tournament, *The Quick and the Dead* is basically one ritual contest after another—and hence a sort of meta-western. As schematic, and fundamentally vacuous as it is, Raimi is compelled to come up with increasingly baroque variations on the basic theme. (The novelty eventually wears thin although the movie rallies for the climactic blowout.) What's most conventional is Stone's star turn. Not much pussy power here. Her characterization is as asexual as her daytime wardrobe and, although the script flirts with images of gentle Jesus, Oedipus, and Billy Budd, it turns out that Stone is avenging the Law of the Father after all.

Also reviewed in:
CHICAGO TRIBUNE, 2/10/95, Friday/p. C, Michael Wilmington
NEW YORK TIMES, 2/10/95, p. C8, Janet Maslin
NEW YORKER, 3/13/95, p. 111, Anthony Lane
VARIETY, 2/13-19/95, p. 47, Todd McCarthy
WASHINGTON POST, 2/10/95, p. B7, Hal Hinson
WASHINGTON POST, 2/10/95, Weekend/p. 37, Desson Howe

REASON TO BELIEVE, A

A Castle Hill Productions release of a Pioneer Pictures presentation. *Producer:* Ged Dickersin and Douglas Tirola. *Director:* Douglas Tirola. *Screenplay:* Douglas Tirola. *Director of Photography:* Sarah Cawley. *Editor:* Sabine Hoffman. *Sound:* Alex Wolfe. *Sound Editor:* Louis Bertini. *Casting:* Laura Adler. *Production Designer:* Carol O'Neil. *Art Director:* Constance Lemasson. *Set Decorator:* Tracy Keegan. *Set Dresser:* Christine Frey. *Costumes:* Yvens De Thelismond. *Make-up:* Karen Caldwell. *Running time:* 109 minutes. *MPAA Rating:* R.

CAST: Allison Smith (Charlotte Byrne); Jay Underwood (Jim Current); Danny Quinn (Wesley Grant); Georgia Emelin (Linda Berryman); Kim Walker (Judith); Keith Coogan (Potto); Lisa Lawrence (Alison); Christopher Birt (Gary); Obba Babatunde (Professor Thurman); Mark Metcalf (Dean Kirby); Robin Riker (Constance); Holly Marie Combs (Sharon); Afton Smith (Becky); Joe Flanigan (Eric Sayles); David Overlund (Frehley); Tim Keiffer (Dave Brown); Michelle Stratton (Amy); Mary Thomas (Tracy); Rachel Parker (Donna); Sally Kenyon (Daisy); Andy Holcomb (Harvey); Cary Spadafori (Nancy); Terek Puckett (Lazy Student); Matt Johnson

(Hippie Student); Heather Weber (CJ's Happy Girl); Christopher Trela (Kinko's Brother); Don Handfield (Nuj); Claire Cundiff (Captain Pepper); Christian Meinhardt (Editor); Tulane Chartock (Dean's Secretary); Carol O'Neil (Feminist); Alex Wolfe (Asshole in Quad); Noah Lanich (Puking Brother); Amy Smith (Bartender); Frank Martana (Scared Brother); Jeff Niles (Treefort Brother); Doug Devine (Tequila Shot Brother); Dave Trachtenberg (Biggest Brother); Jon Huffman (Dean); Fathers of the Id (Bar Band); Material Issue (Band at Viking Party).

LOS ANGELES TIMES, 10/27/95, Calendar/p. 6, Kevin Thomas

With "A Reason to Believe" writer-director Douglas Tirola makes a courageous, thoughtful attempt to tackle the very serious problem of rape on the campus, but unfortunately he's come up with an illustrated sermon rather than an involving drama. It's a picture in which everything that happens is all too credible but seldom comes alive, despite conscientious acting. As it so often happens with such films, those most in need of receiving its message the least likely to hear it. Its greatest value will be as an educational tool for women's groups encouraging women to speak out on sexual abuse, rape in particular.

Filmed at Tirola's alma mater, Miami University, the story's setting is a typical large institution of higher learning with a strong fraternity and sorority system. It stars Allison Smith as Charlotte, a pretty, popular, sometimes bitchy and brittle young woman who's miffed when her boyfriend Wesley (Danny Quinn), unable to attend his fraternity's big Viking costume bash because of his uncle's funeral, tells her he doesn't want her to go without him. Clearly used to having her way, Charlotte goes, gets drunk, lies down on Wesley's bed, where his best friend Jim (Jay Underwood) starts making unwanted advances. Too wasted by booze to fight him off but not too far gone to protest verbally, Charlotte ends up being raped by him.

To Tirola's credit this all-crucial scene is not only discreetly filmed but also allows us to understand how Jim could believe in his own mind that this sexual encounter did not constitute rape because Charlotte did not put up that much of a struggle. He's sorry about what happened, but is not about to admit to himself, let alone anyone else, that Charlotte was in no condition to stage much of a resistance.

By, the next day a numbed Charlotte is further devastated to discover that not only can she not keep her fate (witnessed by a voyeuristic frat bro) secret, but that no one, starting with Wesley, is prepared to believe her. Gradually, she allows herself to be recruited by Linda (Georgia Emelin), the fiery leader of the campus women's group, to speak out and demand a hearing from weak-willed, publicity-sensitive university administrators.

At this point the preachiness, present from the start, takes over the film in earnest. If the film devolves into a lecture, it is one that does try to cover all the key issues: the very difficult business facing a woman attempting to prove that she has been raped, and then getting the powers that be to do anything about it.

Tirola's view includes that sticking point between some men and women: that a woman has absolutely no responsibility whatsoever in regard to her attire and behavior, no matter how provocative, in the matter of rape. Tirola also seems to be aware that a man can after all be falsely accused.

Not surprisingly, the fraternity system, which has never been presented on the screen in a balanced fashion, is shown in the worst possible light, with Wesley's fraternity dominated by a bunch of crude male chauvinist party animals. But then none of the film's key people, with the exception of Linda, is Phi Beta Kappa material in the first place.

NEW YORK POST, 9/22/95, p. 51, Thelma Adams

"A Reason to Believe" is an excuse to pursue a hot campus topic—date rape—with a single-mindedness suitable for Oprah but tiresome in a high-gloss drama.

As the opening credits roll in "A Reason to Believe," a gang of fraternity men and sorority women play a drinking game that involves confessing to such things as urinating in the shower and performing oral sex in public.

They might talk dirty, but Charlotte (Allison Smith) and Jim (Jay Underwood) and Wesley (Anthony Quinn's son Danny) are perky and well-groomed. At this unnamed college, fraternities and sororities square off against the only visible student activists—radical feminists, their ranks swollen with lipstick lesbians. With all the mousse and mascara worn by the actors, it's hard to tell the difference between the Greeks and the "don't call us girls" gals.

After a violent clash between feminists and frat boys, the afternoon before Beta Sigma's annual bacchanal—the Viking party—27-year-old writer-director Douglas Tirola sets up the crucial event. Wesley leaves town. His steady, Charlotte, attends the party without him, gets sloshed and crashes on his bed. Jim follows Charlotte upstairs, sucks her toes, loosens her toga and proceeds to have sexual intercourse. A nearly unconscious Charlotte feebly defends herself.

With nary a diverting subplot, Tirola lays out the perspectives of the alleged victim and attacker, the fraternity boys, the sorority sisters, the activists and campus officials, charting the radicalization of Charlotte along the way.

Don't even bother to mull the finer points of the controversy over in your mind. The script will answer all questions and tie them up with a bow before the final scene.

Novice lenser Tirola puts a professional sheen on this varsity drag, and coaxes respectable performances from his appealing and experienced cast, but he can't overcome the limitations of a by-the-numbers script which unfolds like an R-rated After-School Special.

NEWSDAY, 9/22/95, Part II/p. B6, Jonathan Mandell

Charlotte hangs out with her boyfriend Wesley, his fun-loving frat brothers and their girlfriends, talking giddily about sex, getting drunk and going to toga parties.

She ignores the humorless feminists on campus whose conversations are long harangues about sexual harassment or the "epidemic" of rape. But then, at a party at her boyfriend's frat house, while Wesley is out of town, Charlotte is raped.

The rapist is a frat brother, a friend of Wesley's, who attacks her when she is drunk and all but passed out. She is too embarrassed to tell anybody. But he boasts about his conquest, as if it were consensual, to the entire fraternity. They roar approval; one member proclaims the encounter the "play of the week."

"A Reason to Believe" is a serious, nearly clinical look at the aftermath of this "acquaintance rape"—the reaction of her boyfriend, who breaks up with her, and her friends, who largely don't believe her, and of the rest of the campus once the story gets out. It is also about Charlotte's own reaction.

Made for a mere $175,000, "A Reason to Believe" is admirable in many respects: its important subject matter, its professional cinematography and soundtrack, the high quality—and even high pedigree—of its actors. Charlotte is played by Allison Smith, the youngest Annie on Broadway, who went on to play Jane Curtin's daughter on "Kate & Allie"; the cast includes Danny Quinn, son of Anthony Quinn, and Keith Coogan, grandson of Jackie Coogan.

Only the script is amateurish, so earnest and obvious that it sometimes seems just a few cuts above one of those instructional/cautionary films in your high school hygiene class. While there are several poignant or revealing scenes, most are choppy and confusing, or pedantic.

First-time filmmaker Douglas Tirola seems so eager to tell us everything he has learned about rape that, in place of what could have been a complex drama, he gives us every reaction, every emotion, neatly summed up in long predictable speeches ("Research shows ...") that are divvied up judiciously among the attractive cast.

If its flaws suggest that it will not last long in movie theaters, "A Reason to Believe" deserves an honorable run—at freshman orientation, where the ensuing conversation can focus on the subject rather than the film.

VILLAGE VOICE, 9/26/95, p. 88, Gary Dauphin

Writer-director Tirola isn't too for from his own bright college days, but from the film he's made about campus politics, date rape, and the Frat House, you get the impression that he spent an awful lot of time at the kegorator when he should have been picking up fundamentals like how to shoot a two-person conversation. Tirola might have had the best intensions, but what transpires onscreen after popular-chick Charlotte (Allison Smith) is raped by her boyfriend's frat brother is not so much campus angst as first-time director meltdown. From its static shots to its uninspired performances, *Reason* is difficult viewing, a film about rape that left an otherwise feminist woman I know muttering that the assaulted protagonist annoyed her. There are some nicely grotesque set pieces involving the fraternity boys, but even I found this crew a bit too caricatured, an odd thing considering that I've never met an over-generalized portrait of abusive white men I didn't like. To paraphrase one of the characters: There are no victims here, only survivors in the audience.

Also reviewed in:
NEW YORK TIMES, 9/22/95, p. C18, Stephen Holden

RECKLESS

A Playhouse International Pictures release in association with The Samuel Goldwyn Company. *Executive Producer:* Lindsay Law. *Producer:* Amy J. Kaufman. *Director:* Norman René. *Screenplay (based on his play):* Craig Lucas. *Director of Photography:* Frederick Elmes. *Editor:* Michael Berenbaum. *Music:* Stephen Endelman. *Production Designer:* Andrew Jackness. *Costumes:* Walter Hicklin. *Running time:* 92 minutes. *MPAA Rating:* PG-13.

CAST: Mia Farrow (Rachel); Scott Glenn (Lloyd); Mary-Louise Parker (Pooty); Tony Goldwyn (Tom); Eileen Brennan (Sister Margaret); Stephen Dorff (Tom, Jr.); Giancarlo Esposito (Game Show Host).

LOS ANGELES TIMES, 11/17/95, Calendar/p. 6, John Anderson

[The following review by John Anderson appeared in a slightly different form in **NEWSDAY, 11/17/95, Part II/p. B5.]**

Bing Crosby is singing, snow is falling down, the world is falling down: Rachel (Mia Farrow), pajamaed and "cocoa'd," is telling husband Tom (Tony Goldwyn) her Christmas dreams on Christmas Eve. And a tearful Tom is telling Rachel that he's hired someone to kill her.

Funny? It is, in fact, the one laugh-out-loud moment in Norman René's "Reckless," a "dark comedy" and a fantastical meditation on holidays and forgetfulness and fact-facing and denial, and a disorienting and disturbing film. It doesn't do, exactly, what "Home for the Holidays" does for Thanksgiving; what writer Craig Lucas and director René are after is far darker and morose.

Rachel is the kind of person who dismisses all knowledge that contradicts her world view. When Tom is crying, for instance, and Rachel doesn't know why, she assumes that the cause is the TV news. "I'll turn it off," she says. "It's not real."

This gets to the point of Lucas' play, which he's now adapted to the screen: Rachel is an archetypal American in the sense that she refuses to disbelieve this is the best of all worlds and that dissenting information can't simply be dismissed. Lucas sees it as a form of cowardice and it is. It's also what has driven Tom to bring the hit man into their Springfield home on Christmas Eve. And it's what makes Rachel's subsequent journey—kind of "It's a Miserable Life"—such a troubling trip.

It's not a pleasant film, but in its challenging way it makes us look at ourselves a bit differently and it certainly puts a spin on Christmas. Some audiences will be more than disturbed by what goes on, although divulging too much of the storyline would dilute its effect.

When Rachel flees her house to avoid being killed—the worst rebuke she can spit at Tom is "This is so meeeeaaan!"—she meets Lloyd (Scott Glenn), a kind but slightly mysterious man who brings Rachel home to his wife, Pooty (Mary-Louise Parker), a paraplegic who also communicates through sign language. Together, the three form a family based on assumptions that eventually splinter and crack. Lloyd and Rachel take to the road, visiting every Springfield in the nation ("There's one in every state," Lloyd says) searching for ... what? Rachel's self-realization is a good bet, as is the essence of America, the root of its happy myopia and the resulting aversion to perceiving the truth.

Farrow, who seems to pick and choose her roles with care, is quite affecting as Rachel because she mixes vulnerability and self-absorption as few others can. And she's backed by a cast that's not only capable, but whose members seem somehow content to find themselves in a film that asks so much of them, and of us.

NEW YORK POST, 11/17/95, p. 49, Michael Medved

"Reckless" is intended as an antidote to the great gobs of holiday cheer that begin descending, like the first snowfall, on the American public this time of year; it's a cynical cinematic response to Jimmy Stewart and Frank Capra that might as well have been titled "It's a Disgusting Life."

The problem is that the alternate Christmas universe the movie sets up is neither realistic nor funny—just bizarre and painful and sadistic. Director Norman Rene and writer Craig Lucas (who previously collaborated on "Longtime Companion" and "Prelude to a Kiss") claim to be offering a more honest vision of this society's tacky seasonal obsessions, but through most of the movie it feels like their characters are wandering the surface of another planet.

It's a planet that no sane space traveler would ever want to visit. The nightmare begins with a chirpy, bespectacled homebody named Rachel (Mia Farrow) dressed in a flannel nighty, tucking her two boys in bed and then snuggling up to her handsome husband (Tony Goldwyn) on Christmas Eve.

In a fit of guilt, he confesses that he's hired a hit man to kill her, so she runs away in the nick of time. Freezing in a phone booth at a filling station, she's picked up by a kindly social worker (Scott Glenn) who takes her home to the paraplegic, deaf mute wife (Mary-Louise Parker) he nurses and adores.

Later, Farrow discovers that the deafness is just an act to win the husband's sympathy, and that this perfect, nurturing man is a former drunk who cruelly abandoned his previous family. It is also turns out that the big-hearted humanitarian agency where Mia gets a job is really a front for embezzlement and, ultimately, murder.

As she and Glenn hit the road together, traveling between towns named Springfield in all 50 states, he begins drinking again, passing out repeatedly and vomiting over his Santa Claus beard. She nevertheless maintains her "Candide" optimism about his best of all possible worlds until she finally arrives, filthy and forlorn, in a homeless shelter where she lives for years without speaking a word.

Farrow's performance is full of ticks and grimaces, and her character is so insufferably flaky that it's hard to work up much sympathy for her plight; in fact, it's far too easy to see why her husband would want to rub her out. The other people in this picture aren't vivid characters, they're just grotesque cartoons and much of the acting has a slapdash, one-take quality.

The only notable signs of artistry come in the fanciful production design (by Andy Jackness) which offers a snowy, surreal variant on Currier & Ives or Capra's Bedford Falls.

Beyond these deliberately artificial surfaces, which underline the film's basic theme about the essential phoniness of Christmas cheer and "family values" there's nothing worth watching in "Reckless."

In sharp contrast to Jodie Foster's "Home for the Holidays," which offered its own (far more provocative) revisionist version of holiday fare, there's no one here to like or care about for a moment. "Reckless," in short, is a wreck.

VILLAGE VOICE, 11/21/95, Film Special/p. 22, Georgia Brown

Luckily, Mia Farrow hasn't lost face. In Craig Lucas and Norman René's wonderful *Reckless,* she's as piquant and moving as in *Alice* or *Purple Rose of Cairo.* If, like me, you've been wondering if Farrow would ever again find a worthy comic role, I'm happy to announce that she's found one here. *Reckless* (terrible generic title, the movie's only blatant flaw) is a bizarre, highly original farce, and Farrow, who's in every scene, is brilliant.

She also looks like she's 15. Well, 25. In the opening scene she wears braids, flutters about in bed chattering on blithely, childishly, about Christmas Eve and snow and mistletoe and presents under the tree. Suddenly, the man beside her (Tony Goldwyn), father of her two children, confesses he's put out a contract on her life. For the insurance. The killer will show up any minute. "This is so *mean!*" Rachel (Farrow) whines as she's forced out the upper-story window into deep snow. *(Into the Snow* would've been a good title.) What follows is Alice's adventures in a cruel winter wonderland, a therapeutic journey into adult responsibility.

Freezing in her nightie (plus a scarf plucked from the childrens snowman), Rachel is picked up by a faintly sinister social worker, Lloyd (Scott Glenn), who invites her home for the holidays. Lloyd lives in a cozy log cabin with his paraplegic wife, Pooty (Mary-Louise Parker). Pooty, who motors around in a wheelchair, is a deaf-mute as well.

It'd be a shame to give away more of the movie's picaresque plot since the fun is in the wild ride, the daft, unpredictable leaps. (I'll just say that Giancarlo Esposito turns up as the host of a game show—"Your Mother or Your Wife"—and Eileen Brennan is a nun who practices primal-scream therapy.) For a long time I was thinking, they can't keep up this pace; so much stream of consciousness will surely wear thin. Amazingly, they did. *Reckless's* hyper-normal landscape resembles that of *Blue Velvet* (Frederick Elmes photographed both), and if René isn't the director Lynch is, a delirious energy rises in waves from Lucas's lyrical, nutty script. Next to this, *Mighty Aphrodite* looks even worse.

Also reviewed in:
CHICAGO TRIBUNE, 11/17/95, Friday/p. I, Michael Wilmington
NEW YORK TIMES, 11/17/95, p. C12, Stephen Holden
VARIETY, 9/25-10/1/95, Leonard Klady
WASHINGTON POST, 11/17/95, p. F7, Hal Hinson

RED FIRECRACKER, GREEN FIRECRACKER

An October Films release of a Yung & Associate Company production in association with Xi'an Film Studio and Beijing Salon Films. *Executive Producer:* Yong Naiming. *Producer:* Chan Chun-Keung and Yong Naiming. *Director:* He Ping. *Screenplay (Mandarin with English subtitles):* Da Ying. *Based on the story:* Feng Jicai. *Director of Photography:* Yang Lun. *Editor:* Yuan Hong. *Music:* Zhao Jiping. *Choreographer:* Qiao Ruiming. *Sound:* Gu Changning and Zhang Wen. *Choreography:* Qiao Ruiming. *Art Director:* Qian Yunxiu. *Set Decorator:* Zhang Deqin. *Costumes:* Chen Changmin. *Make-up:* Ma Shuangyin. *Running time:* 111 minutes. *MPAA Rating:* Not Rated.

CAST: Ning Jing (Cai Chun Zhi); Wu Gang (Nie Bao); Zhao Xiaorui (Man Dihong); Qiao Yang (Chief Servant); Xu Zhengyun (Old Master Xu); Zhao Liang (Hei Liu); Ju Xingmao (Bao Ge); Li Yushen (Manservant); Lu Hui (Old Boss Wang); Wang Liyuan (Wang Ma); Zhang Bolin (Businessman).

LOS ANGELES TIMES, 6/2/95, Calendar/p. 6, Kevin Thomas

He Ping's exquisite "Red Firecracker, Green Firecracker" takes us to northern China at the turn of the century, where the Cai family rules over territory so vast that a peasant remarks that one could walk through it three days and three nights and still not cross it from border to border.

The source of the family fortune may seem surprising: the humble firecracker, which we learn is used not only for celebrations but also for breaking up iced-over rivers and, most important of all, as medicine formulated from its ingredients. Alas, it has come to pass that there is no longer a Cai male heir, which means that at 19 the beautiful Chun Zhi (Ning Jing) has assumed severe male attire, sworn never to marry and is always addressed as master.

Chun Zhi's lot is much like that of the elderly empress, presiding over the waning Qing Dynasty in Beijing's Forbidden City. Her whims may be of iron, but she is imprisoned in her ancient palace along the Yellow River by her gender.

Chun Zhi rules firmly but wisely, displaying the imperiousness expected of her, but tradition places her under the firm guidance of an elderly family retainer, Mr. Zhao (Gai Yang). She may make the final decisions—and her word is law—but the actual administration of her business and her estate is carried out by her major domo Mr. Mann (Zhao Xiaorui), obsequious to her but brutal to those below him.

Chun Zhi has already resigned herself to her lonely fate, when she hires, sight unseen, an itinerant painter to decorate all 72 of her palace's doors. Mutual attraction sparks instantly between this stunning young woman and the strapping, clean-cut young artist, Nie Bao (Wu Gang) that inevitably will not be denied. What's more, he's a firebrand—proud, outspoken, headstrong.

"Red Firecracker, Green Firecracker," adapted by Da Ying from a novel by Feng Jicai, brings to mind Zhang Yimuo's "Raise the Red Lantern" in its depiction of the closed world of the palace with its intrigues and power plays, and also Huang Jianxin's "The Wooden Man's Bride," which by coincidence is screening at the Nuart Saturday and which depicts a young woman forced to marry a carved effigy of her dead bethrothed.

The celibacy required, of Chun Zhi is actually even more absurd, for how is she to carry on the dynasty that supports so many people if she is not allowed to marry and have children? Chun Zhi's people are such hidebound traditionalists that none of them seem to be able to perceive this absurdity, thus undermining the very economic security they crave dearly.

This film is long and leisurely yet seems never draggy nor tedious because He Ping has done such a splendid job of transporting us to an exotic time and place, and of eliciting flawless portrayals from his cast. The most complex and intriguing figure is actually Mr. Mann; he's not sympathetic, yet Zhao Xiaorui shows us an obedient man struggling to do what is expected of him in unprecedented circumstances.

Gorgeous looking—as are most Chinese films—"Red Firecracker, Green Firecracker" benefits crucially from a plaintive, mood-setting score by Zhao Jiping, who creates the music for many of China's major contemporary films.

NEW YORK POST, 4/14/95, p. 41, Thelma Adams

He Ping's "Red Firecracker, Green Firecracker" is a sensual fairy tale. A princess in an ivory tower falls for a peasant. Will they live happily ever after?

The setting is turn-of-the-century China. The sole heir to a prosperous firecracker empire is female. To keep the business intact, the elders instruct Chun Zhi (Ning Jing) to don menswear and assume the master's role, denying her femininity.

Handsome artist Nie Bao (Wu Gang) arrives to paint murals at the family estate. "We have lots of rules here. Break them and you'll be punished", Chun tells him.

Despite the master's stern warning, we can see the romance coming like a speeding train from Shanghai. Before long, Chun yens to strip off her dour blacks and wear feminine red. This threatens the elders and the status quo.

The conflicts between rich and poor, master and servant, male and female, art and commerce frame the lavish story of sexual awakening and societal constraints that opened the New Directors/New Films series at MOMA last month.

The imagery—the raging Yellow River at sunset, a single tear captured in golden light during lovemaking, the painter's gilded icons—is painstaking and seductive.

"Red Firecracker, Green Firecracker" has many of the elements we've come to associate with Chinese cinema: gender-bending complications, beautified cinematography, exquisite costumes and set design, superb acting, and a historical setting. It even has an explosive climax.

But this gilded lily lacks depth of feeling—the emotional transcendence or political punch shared by the best Chinese movies, such as "Farewell, My Concubine," "To Live" and "The Blue Kite."

NEWSDAY, 4/14/95, Part II/p. B3, Jack Mathews

Fireworks, as Marco Polo first informed the West, were invented in ancient China and have been an integral and elaborate part of Chinese culture ever since. So it is not surprising to learn, as we do in He Ping's "Red Firecracker, Green Firecracker," that there were dynasties of fireworks families within the broader political dynasties ruling the country.

What is surprising about the movie is how well He Ping and screenwriter Da Ying have used that manufacturing backdrop to turn a simple love story into an explosive—both literally and figuratively—allegory about China's transformation from a feudal to a capitalist society in the early years of this century.

The romance driving the story is between a vagabond artist named Nie Bao (Wu Gang) and Chun Zhi (Ning Jing), the 19-year-old heir of the Cai family fireworks dynasty. Nie Bao has been hired by a Cai emissary to redecorate the family's mansion. His presence there, as a free-spirited outsider with little regard for tradition, arouses the suppressed passions in Chun Zhi, a woman who, as the sole heir to the Cai business, has been raised, costumed and addressed as a man.

The layers of contrast and conflict are laid out with the simplicity of a pie chart. The Cais' feudal compound is on one side of a river, across from a village of money lenders and merchants. Chun Zhi is living a life prescribed by ancestral law; Nie Bao is following his impulses. The Cai palace art is out of the past; Nie Bao's is being drawn from the heart. But the emotional, political and social currents beneath those layers run as deep and with as much force as the raging Yellow River, which He Ping uses as his central metaphor.

Despite some acute overacting by Wu Gang, Nie Bao is an engaging Bohemian rake, and given the severe restrictions placed on her as "master" of the Cai house, it is easy to understand Chun Zhi's attraction to him. His dangerously personal art—a simple sketch of her is a minor scandal among the underlords running the family enterprise—stirs feelings in her she has never felt, and though her first reaction is to recoil from them, and to have Wu Gang punished, her lust has been ignited.

As Nie Bao and Chun Zhi consummate their romance, "Red Firecracker" indulges in some pretty mundane soap opera, with jealous suitors, shocked elders, even a scandalous pregnancy. And Zhao Jiping's obtrusive score sounds as if it were canned with a 100-piece orchestra in Hollywood. But, to use He Ping's own mixed metaphor, all of the events between the lovers, their enemies and the villagers across the way flow into one stream that sweeps us toward the political allegory's explosive climax.

Yes, there is a fireworks show, but not one you'd want to see on July Fourth. Having given up on dissuading Chun Zhi from living her life as a woman, the family elders revive an ancient courtship ritual that would allow her to marry Nie Bao if he can defeat all other declared suitors in an open competition. The man who survives the most dangerous stunt with explosives wins her hand.

The competition, with men detonating bombs on their heads, in their teeth and between their legs, is awkwardly staged and edited, and hasn't nearly the dramatic impact implied. Still, it serves the purpose of bringing the combustible forces of the past and future together at this one moment in Chinese history, and the movie introduces to Western audiences a strong new voice (He Ping is 37) at a time when Chinese tradition is undergoing another tug-of-war with the temptations of free enterprise.

SIGHT AND SOUND, 9/95, p. 59, Tony Rayns

Travelling artist Nie Bao arrives in a town on the Yellow River and is hired to paint traditional New Year pictures for the Cai family, whose wealth is founded on a fireworks factory. The family owns the entire region, and is the biggest local employer. Nie Bao finds that the head of the family, Chun Zhi, is a 19-year-old woman, who dresses and behaves like a man. Nie Bao is warned that the household has many rules; he will be punished if he breaks them. He is quartered in the house's South Chamber, and begins work on the 'door god' paintings.

He initially commands respect from the household's head of staff Man Dihong, but Man soon comes to resent Nie Bao's independence of spirit. And when Man realises that Chun Zhi is interested in the newcomer, he turns against him and tries to humiliate him. Chun Zhi is shocked to discover that Nie Bao has painted her as a woman and slaps him; but the picture awakens her latent desire to be a woman. Nie Bao, however, mocks her conservatism, and she turns him over to senior retainer Qiao and Man Dihong for punishment. In the event, Chun Zhi cannot bear to see him beaten and threatened with castration. She releases him, and he leaves the district.

Nie Bao returns to the house in the late spring, announcing his presence by throwing a defiant firework in to the courtyard. Chun Zhi visits his lodging at night and they make love. Chun Zhi begins dressing as a woman and wearing make-up, throwing the Cai household into disarray. When Nie Bao admits to Man Dihong that he has slept with Chun Zhi, Man organises a gang to beat him up. Qiao and old retainer Xu categorically forbid Chun Zhi to marry Nie Bao, and organise a three-day ritual to propitiate the Cai ancestors. Nie Bao again leaves the district.

But his love for Chun Zhi draws him back. The household elders meet to discuss how to deal with him, and recall that an outsider was allowed to marry into the Cai family in the Ming Dynasty by winning a fireworks contest. Man Dihong is chosen to represent the Cai family in a new contest, with the promise that he can marry Chun Zhi if he wins. The contest takes place in a stone quarry. Both men allow fireworks to explode on or near their bodies, but Nie Bao is finally defeated by his attempt to launch a series of fireballs from a tube gripped between his thighs. He is stretchered off, and disappears without seeing Chun Zhi again.

Some time later, Chun Zhi is married to Man Dihong and expecting her first child. She consoles herself with the private thought that Nie Bao is the child's real father.

Red Firecracker, Green Firecracker one of the few 'serious' Chinese movies of recent years to have absolutely no subtext: all of its phallic play, gender subversion and castration fantasies are right up there on the screen. The film fits squarely into the Chinese genre inaugurated by Zhang Yimou's *Red Sorghum* in 1987, being set in the backwoods of Republican China and using a fairly torrid narrative to raise the issues of desire, sexuality and repression. The genre has latterly included such movies as Huang Jianxin's *The Wooden Man's Bride (Yan Shen*, 1993) and Zhou Youchao's *Sweet Grass (Huang Sha, Qing Cao, Hong Taiyang*, 1995), but *Red Firecracker, Green Firecracker* is arguably the best of them. It's expertly judged visual style—austere framing and classical editing patterns contradicted by sumptuous dark colours and textures—gives it the edge.

He Ping came to this project as a hired hand, and says he doesn't consider it as 'personal' a film as *The Swordsman in Double-Flag Town (Shauang-Qi Zhen Daoke*, 1990), certainly the most innovative and fully realised genre movie made in China in recent years, a Leoneesque transposition of codes and conventions from the western into Chinese frontier terms. *Swordsman* was the last project green-lighted by Wu Tianming during his time as head of the Xi'an Film Studio, and it saved He Ping from a career directing such turgid historical dramas. The international success of *Swordsman*—which has been distributed and/or seen on television virtually everywhere except Britain—was a surprise for both the studio and He Ping himself. *Red Firecracker, Green Firecracker*, by contrast, reflects the effective collapse of the Xi'an studio as a production entity and the new order in Chinese film production; the project was put together and packaged by private companies in Hong Kong and Beijing.

To acknowledge this is not to devalue the film, which has solid conceptual roots in the social changes in present-day China. Chinese women restricted to having single children increasingly refuse to see themselves as procreators, a change which has led to widespread rethinking of traditional sex roles and attitudes to sexual pleasure. The film's account of Cai Chun Zhi's flowering as a woman and Nie Bao's literal emasculation as a sensitive-but-macho male goes some way further than Zhang Yimou did in *Red Sorghum* to explore these new ideas and attitudes, and the director's playfully explosive imagery brings the issues to life in a way that's not in the least parochial.

The film's weaknesses are mostly in the script. The adaptation of a story by Feng Jicai, a specialist in folkloric exotica, is plodding and repetitive. Nie Bao leaves and returns at least once too many times, and the machinations of the clan elders against him are thinly sketched. Similarly, details like Nie Bao's bonding with a street urchin are dropped in opportunistically, with no real attempt to integrate them into the narrative flow. On the other hand, the aural cross-cutting between voice-overs spoken by Chun Zhi and Nie Bao works well to anchor the narrative sprawl in the central characters' shifting sense of their relationship and, in the case of Chun Zhi, her own identity. The effect is curiously touching, and mitigated only slightly by the coarseness of Ning Jing's performance once she has discovered her femininity.

Visually, though, He Ping and his cinematographer Yang Lun acquit themselves with great aplomb. Predictably, they use formal compositions to render the stultifying atmosphere of the Cai household and fluid tracking and hand-held shots to render the onset of unbridled passions, but the control of colour and the flair of the design are strong enough to counter the sense of *déjà vu*. The film is full of individual arresting images: Nie Bao removing his shoes on entering the Cai household, because the soles contain metal nails which are potentially dangerous in the proximity of so much gunpowder; the debris from a firecracker falling like snow in the household courtyard; the climactic fireworks contest enacted in a safe stone quarry hung with Cai family banners in five colours. In its way, in fact, *Firecracker* points a way forward for "Fifth Generation" film-making in China as clearly as *Farewell My Concubine* did. It rises to the challenge of telling a story rooted in Chinese history and culture in terms that will be accessible to any viewer, Chinese or not.

VILLAGE VOICE, 4/18/95, p. 60, Lisa Katzman

In Red Firecracker, Green Firecracker, Chinese director He Ping puts a kinky spin on the tragic immutability of traditional Chinese gender roles. Living as a female eunuch in her ancient family compound, surrounded by a passel of grizzled elders, Chun Zhi inherits her parents' firecracker factory with the proviso that she never marry. Though she struts around in male garb and metes out equal measures of charity and punishment to her workers, her life in drag is less self-expression than obeisance; it doesn't take much for Nie Bao, a temperamental itinerant artist she hires, to awaken her conflicted desires. Under the jealous eye of an arrogant manservant, Chun Zhi engages Nie Bao in a minuet of approach/ avoidance that takes a nasty tum for the artist when he breaks one of his master's rules.

He Ping chips away at the concept of Confucian fate, showing how it's well-paved by calcified and often cruel traditions. But even this doesn't fully explain why the film's theme of sexual punishment feels less character-driven and more like an inconsistent structural device. When Chun Zhi loses her virginity to Nie Bao she gives up her sadistic edge, dons a dress and announces to the gray-faced elders that she wants to be treated like a woman. Played without a trace of irony, her transformation from dominatrix to femme is almost campy. You'd think she would have doped out the difference between her life and those of other women and realized what she's asking for. Yet when Nie Bao announces his intention to marry "the Master," and the elders arrange a firecracker competition between suitors, we hear nary a peep from Chun Zhi. Unlike the wonderfully, madly resilient women played by Gong Li in Zhang Yimou's films, Chun Zhi sadly isn't much of a heroine. And so if we come to care more about Nie Bao during the film's spectacularly brutal climax, it's more because he's a fighter, and because He Ping really has more to say about how Chinese custom maims men.

Also reviewed in:
CHICAGO TRIBUNE, 4/21/95, Tempo/p. K, John Petrakis
NEW YORK TIMES, 3/17/95, p. C19, Stephen Holden
VARIETY, 2/28-3/6/94, p. 71, Derek Elley
WASHINGTON POST, 5/5/95, p. B7, Hal Hinson
WASHINGTON POST, 5/5/95, Weekend/p. 49, Desson Howe

RESTORATION

A Miramax Films release of a Segue Productions/Avenue Pictures production in association with Oxford Film Company. *Executive Producer:* Kip Hagopian. *Producer:* Cary Brokaw, Andy Paterson, and Sarah Ryan Black. *Director:* Michael Hoffman. *Screenplay:* Rupert Walters. *Based on the novel by:* Rose Tremain. *Director of Photography:* Oliver Stapleton. *Editor:* Garth Craven. *Music:* James Newton Howard. *Music Editor:* Jim Weidman, Robin Clarke, and Bob Hathaway. *Choreographer:* Quincy Sacks and Kate Flatt. *Sound:* Simon Kaye. *Sound Editor:* Martin Evans. *Casting:* Mary Selway and Patsy Pollock. *Production Designer:* Eugenio Zanetti. *Art Director:* Alan Cassie. *Set Decorator:* Eugenio Zanetti. *Set Dresser:* Marina Morris. *Special Effects:* Peter Hutchinson. *Costumes:* James Acheson. *Make-up:* Paul Engelen. *Running time:* 113 minutes. *MPAA Rating:* R.

CAST: Robert Downey, Jr. (Merivel); Sam Neill (The King); David Thewlis (Pearce); Polly Walker (Celia); Meg Ryan (Katherine); Ian McKellen (Will Gates); Hugh Grant (Finn); Ian McDiarmid (Ambrose); Mary Macleod (Midwife); Mark Letheren (Daniel); Sandy McDade (Hannah); Rosalind Bennett (Eleanor); Willie Ross (Man with Visible Heart); David Gant (Chiffinch); Benjamin Whitrow (Merivel's Father); Neville Watchurst (Latin Doctor); Bryan Pringle (Watchman); Roy Evans (Fleeing Man); John Quarmby (The Chancellor); John Dallimore (The Secretary); Roger Ashton-Griffiths (Mr. Bung); Janan Kubba (Pretty Wench); Henrietta Voigts (Female Patient); Simon Taylor (Second Doctor); Selina Giles (Fair Lady);

Susanne McKenrick (Dark Lady);   Nick Hutchison (Pinworth);   Andrew Havill and Tony Gardner (Gallants);   David Ryall (Lord Bathurst).

LOS ANGELES TIMES, 12/29/95, Calendar/p. 8, Kevin Thomas

"Restoration" vividly recreates one of the most colorful chapters in English history: the return of the reign of Charles II in 1660 after a decade of dour Puritan rule under Oliver Cromwell. A libertine but also a modernist, Charles returned the court to a life of pleasure-seeking while encouraging a flourishing of arts and sciences.

It's a rich background for a period adventure, and in the '40s novelist Kathleen Winsor drew upon it for her "Forever Amber," a bestseller about a resilient fictional favorite of the merry monarch that became a memorable, though necessarily bowdlerized, 1947 Otto Preminger film.

Director Michael Hoffman and writer Rupert Walter, in adapting Rose Tremain's 1989 novel, have been able to capture the bawdiness of the era with a great deal more candor than Preminger was permitted, but that's not enough to keep "Restoration" from seeming an increasingly ponderous and old-fashioned costume melodrama. Not helping matters is that the filmmakers are saddled with a hero remarkably passive for the genre.

So depressed is young physician Robert Merivel (Robert Downey Jr.) over the primitive state of medicine in 1663 London that he spends his evenings in debauchery. By chance he comes to the attention of Charles II (Sam Neill), who orders him to court—to treat one of the king's cherished spaniels. The poor animal, tortured by the barbaric medical practices of the day, is beyond treatment but miraculously recovers, thus cementing Merivel's fortunes, or so it would seem. In time, Charles decrees that Merivel shall be knighted and given one of England's stateliest mansions—in returning for marrying one of the king's favorite but most troublesome mistresses. The hitch is that the doctor must not fall in love with his beautiful bride (Polly Walker).

If you remember your English history—or "Forever Amber"—you know that there will be big challenges ahead for Merivel, even if he had been able to live up to the king's condition in regard to his bride. Bubonic plague will break out in 1665, followed by the Great Fire of London the following year.

As Merivel becomes increasingly buffeted about by fate the film becomes increasingly mechanical; despite Downey's ability to register Merivel's bemused, perplexed reactions to his abrupt and startling changes of fortune, the man resists mightily taking responsibility for his own destiny.

By the time he's predictably thrust onto the road to redemption he's spent so much time in debauchery it's hard to accept his bursts of brilliant medical intuition. And why would a physician, no matter how eager to serve others, head for a plague-ridden London with a pregnant wife?

As in "Chaplin," Downey is really better than the film, embracing the strengths and weaknesses of Merivel in credible fashion. Although Neill lacks the amusing hauteur of George Sanders in "Forever Amber," he is a magnetic, cynical and capricious Charles, of whom it was famously remarked that "he never said a foolish thing or did a wise one."

Hugh Grant has some delicious moments as a supremely foppish, painter in the king's favor, and Ian McKellen is suitably wise and deferential as Merivel's manservant. Meg Ryan brings vitality and conviction to her tricky role as a deeply disturbed young Irishwoman cured mainly by love. Rounding out the key players is David Thewlis as Merivel's saintly physician friend.

In the encouraging opening sequences you hope that the feel for satire and sense of the absurd that Hoffman brought so successfully to "Soapdish" will flourish and dominate throughout "Restoration," but the film is overcome by the rumbling workings of a creaky plot as the story grows more serious. Gorgeously mounted and elegantly scored, "Restoration" is not without charm or pathos or even wit and intelligence, but it's ultimately a disappointment.

NEW STATESMAN & SOCIETY, 3/8/96, p. 38, Lizzie Francke

Restoration is a heritage movie in every way. Not least in that the film, which is loosely based on Rose Tremain's novel of the same name, has been chosen by Cinema 100, the Department of National Heritage backed organisation responsible for the centenary celebrations, to be the royal gala screening in the presence of HRH, the Prince of Wales. One just can't imagine why—as it reflects on the period after Cromwell's revolution, and portrays the mark II version of Charlie's namesake ancestor as the enlightened king whose reign brought light into the darkness through his patronage of science and the arts. This, after all, is a time that saw the founding of the Royal Society, the building of the Greenwich Observatory and the publication of Newton's first theoretical writings. And after at least a decade of serge and stiff collars, flouncy fun was back in fashion by royal appointment. "The theatres are open, milliners are working and a rich man may go to heaven again," quips one dissenting artisan. Kings here are a rather good thing—though they may be a little daft. Charles appoints a young physician, Merivel, to care for his favourite, the poorly Lou-Lou, a floppy eared spaniel, but His Majesty has bright plans for the future and a particular interest in architecture. Sound familiar? (I would love to be at that screening, when mention of Charles II's amorous exploits is made.) With a retinue of favoured mistresses as well as some willing gals from the theatre, the King's "royal tool" was want to "waggle about". (No doubt there will be much schoolboy chortling at this line.)

Otherwise *Restoration* is just the kind of cinematic dish to set before a future king. It is the *1066 and All That* kind of history and includes such choice moments from Charles' reign as the Plague and the Great Fire of London. The intellectual revolutions only find their way into the film in obvious ways. But then it is hard to dramatise ideological flashpoints in history. (Witness the incredibly dreary *Jefferson in Paris*.) *Restoration* re-upholsters the period with the picaresque, fictional tale of Merivel, a dilettante hero who must learn to put his expanding knowledge of medical matters to more useful effect. But while much mention is made of the marvels of the new age, it is bereft of the requisite wonder, despite the opening scene in which Merivel examines a man whose beating heart can be seen through a hole in his chest. This visceral peep show provides the film with a jolt start that it proceeds never quite to match.

Restoration is not meant to be a challenge, but rather a cushioned tour. The poster campaign purloins from that of *The Madness of King George,* which was a far wryer romance with history; perhaps the distributors hoped to market it as a prequel. It is, as the press book puts it in bold, a *British film*, produced by the Oxford Film Company no less. One might add that the director Michael Hoffman's debut back in 1982 was a film called *Privileged*—a title that was used without so much as a whiff of irony—in which a group of young students put on a production of *The Duchess of Malfi* in the quad and punt about a bit on the Cherwell. Hoffman is an American and certainly seems rather enamoured with the more swanky side of British life and history. (Meanwhile, *Restoration*'s screenwriter, Rupert Walters, has just penned *True Blue* about the Oxford and Cambridge boat race insurrection of the late 1980s.) Unsurprising, then, that much of *Restoration* seems to be catering to an American audience. Indeed, the Oxford Film company might have made it, but the pugnacious US independent company Miramax financed the project along with another Stateside enterprise, Avenue Pictures. The casting of New Zealander Sam Neill as King Charles and Americans Robert Downey Jr as Merivel and Meg Ryan doing an Oirish accent as an inmate of an asylum bears this out. The Brits have the bit parts here, whether Ian McKellen as an old retainer, or Hugh Grant doing a Rupert Everett as a pursed mouth, foppish artist. David Thewlis is the only one to have more than just a fleeting appearance—here playing Merivel's scholarly pal, John Pearce, who is a little more earnest about the medical profession. Though fine in itself, it's a safe choice of actors.

The cinematography also puts one firmly in one's place and does not let us doubt that this is an opulent "Golden Age". Apparently the intention was for a "painterly look", though the result, particularly for the court scenes, is more something akin to the gaudy Ferro-Roche ad school. Did someone smear syrup all over the camera lens? It may be meant to be that sickly. After all, Merivel's fascination with all things royal is meant to be rather circumspect, while at one point someone demurs: "I find much of the decoration disturbing." The film itself seems rather a little too hooked up on such sumptuousness. At least in one way *Restoration* is about the fabric of the past.

NEW YORK POST, 12/29/95, p. 39, Michael Medved

On rare occasions, a movie can sweep away reservations and resistance through the sheer force of its ambition.

That's the case with "Restoration," a movie that tries to do so much—and does so much of it so well that it's easy to overlook some serious shortcomings.

Based on a superb, sweeping historical novel by Rose Tremain, the movie attempts nothing less than the re-creation of a dazzling moment in human history—the explosion of light and learning, color, culture and corruption associated with the restoration of the monarchy to Britain in 1660, after 11 years of sober and serious Puritan rule.

The "Merry Monarch" Charles II (played here with commanding presence by Sam Neill) established a court of resplendent decadence, at the same time he encouraged advances in science, architecture, and the arts. A mere six years after he assumed the throne, however, a series of disasters devastated London, including an outbreak of bubonoic plague that killed at least 20 percent of the population, followed by the Great Fire which destroyed more than 80 percent of the city's buildings.

"Restoration" tries to capture all this on film, from the seductive glitter of King Charles' court to the heaped and rotting bodies of plague-ridden urban streets, at the same time, it tells the story of an intriguing fictional character.

Robert Downey Jr. plays Robert Merivel, a dedicated student of the rapidly advancing science of medicine who becomes a royal favorite at the palace. Charles entrusts him, in fact, with a most delicate mission: a sham marriage to the monarch's favorite mistress (the luminous Polly Walker) in order to keep her convenient to the king.

Merivel, however, ultimately breaks the one royal rule laid down for his union: He falls in love with his own wife. His infatuation is duly reported by a wonderfully foppish portraitist (Hugh Grant) and our hero is suddenly out of favor.

Finding his way to a humble Quaker hospital, he is powerfully drawn to one of the patients—a half-mad, impoverished Irish girl, hauntingly played by Meg Ryan in the film's single strongest performance.

Unfortunately, Downey's acting never approaches her level and represents the movie's central weakness. Though he's adequate as a shallow hedonist and social climber, when his character is supposed to discover new depths and gravity (along with an almost sacred calling for medicine), Downey seems woefully miscast. Regarding romance, Downey conveys greater love for his own flamboyant costumes than he does for the woman in his life.

The movie also suffers from a lack of bite and sparkle in the script. The Restoration represented the golden age of English wit, but the one salient example of sophisticated humor in this picture involves the ability of Downey's character to break wind on cue.

Nevertheless, director Michael Hoffman (previously associated with far less challenging fare like "Soapdish" and "Promised Land") provides enough sumptuous visual stimulation to overwhelm these weaknesses. Sets, locations and especially costumes are all magnificent—and amazingly lavish for the modest budget of $18 million.

Gorgeously composed interiors specifically recall the rich, crowded sunlit world of the painter Vermeer—who was working across the channel in Holland in precisely the same era.

Like the Restoration itself, the movie is thrilling, sensuous, and consistently fascinating, despite its follies and flaws.

NEWSDAY, 12/29/95, Part II/p. B7, John Anderson

Just in case you needed more evidence that the film industry is a universe run amok, consider this: For $18.5 million a filmmaker can't hire Tom Cruise, but he can produce something that looks like "Restoration."

Set at that historic moment when Cromwell was out and monarchy was in, Michael Hoffman's energetic and enthusiastic period melodrama has a quite winning and persuasive Robert Downey Jr., but it does need a bit of a push getting where it wants to go. Long getting released and long the object of unkind rumors, "Restoration" is nowhere near as unwieldy as some feared it would be. But it is, basically, a 17th-Century soap opera long on episodic highs and lows, short on narrative crescendo. It has a great look, some moving moments, but occasionally feels like it needs a transfusion of dramatic purpose.

Downey gives a galloping performance as the bewigged and brocaded Robert Merivel, who progresses from pest-house quack to King Charles II's court physician on the strength of some dumb luck and one bit of brio: When the debauched doctor and his colleague (and conscience) John Pearce (David Thewlis) are confronted by a man with an exposed beating heart—the result of a wound that never healed—Pearce can't bring himself to touch it. Merivel can, and does, and is witnessed by the king, who's impressed enough to bring him to court.

Once there, Merivel virtually abandons medicine in favor of the fleshy pleasures available—and there are plenty. Director Hoffman and production designer Eugenio Zanetti replicate a monarchy drunk on its own excesses and gleeful at being restored; Sam Neill's slightly dangerous Charles is a man who knows just how good it is to be the king. The world is gilded and plush, and Merivel gets intoxicated, literally and spiritually. He's overripe for a fall, of course, which arrives when he becomes the king's beard—by marrying the royal mistress Celia Clemence (Polly Walker)—and then has the bad taste to fall in love with her.

Stripped of his land and title, Merivel begins a literal and spiritual journey that brings him to Pearce's Quaker-run asylum, where he meets and beds an Irish madwoman named Katherine (Meg Ryan) and fathers her child (there is a rather absurd scene in which Merivel delivers their baby by Caesarean, without anesthesia; Katherine barely whimpers). From there, he travels to London, becomes a hero of the bubonic plague, survives the Great London Fire of 1666 and as a result is restored to his lands and title. We are left to presume that Merivel will become the gifted healer he was meant to be.

Hoffman is clearly fascinated by the medical practices of the period, which were a mix of modem technique and pure superstition, and he's equally enraptured by England's split personality—the mud and gore of life outside court vs. the gilded glory of the palace. He doesn't quite get past his own infatuation with surfaces—which, it must be said, are quite beautiful—and probe the underside of "Restoration." He does, however, give us the big, broad picture.

SIGHT AND SOUND, 4/96, p. 51, Nick James

London, 1663. Robert Merivel, a student physician with a "gift for healing", works in the Royal College Hospital with his best friend John Pearce. They examine a man with a gaping but healed wound that exposes his beating heart. Pierce declines to touch the heart, but Merivel grasps it; the man feels nothing. He is observed by the newly restored King Charles II, who later summons Merivel to attend a sick Spaniel. After reviving the dog, he is invited to court and soon becomes a libertine buffoon.

Needing a stooge for a "paper marriage" to one of his mistresses, Celia Clemence, the King chooses Merivel, offering him in return a knighthood and a Suffolk estate, Bidnold. Ordered never to touch Celia, Merivel falls instantly in love with her but is confined to Bidnold without her, where he languishes drunkenly until she is herself banished there for expressing jealousy of other royal mistresses. Merivel intrigues with his chief servant, Will Gates, to keep Celia ignorant of the King's renewed desire for her; he makes a pass at her which she rejects by spitting in his face. He is stripped of his house and title.

Merivel seeks out Pearce, and is welcomed into the Whittlesea Quaker group caring for the mentally ill. He realises that one inmate, Katherine, is not a lunatic but simply grieving for her drowned child. While Merivel and Katherine become lovers, Pearce contracts the plague. After Pearce dies, Merivel and a pregnant Katherine are obliged to leave. They arrive in plague ridden London. Faced with a breach birth, Katherine insists on undergoing lethal surgery to save the baby (named Margaret) and dies. Merivel flings himself into caring for plague victims, invoking Pearce's name. Mistaken for Pearce by them, his legend grows.

Believing Celia infected by the plague, the King summons 'Pearce', who attends concealed by a mask. 'Pearce' tells the King that Celia has a less lethal malady, one easily treated if the King will confess his true affection for her. News of the Great Fire sends Merivel hurrying to save his daughter. Stairs collapse beneath him and he falls unconscious into a small boat which drifts downstream to the Suffolk bank. He wakes in bed at Bidnold, attended by Will Gates. The King arrives bringing Margaret safely with him. Celia had recognised 'Pearce' as Merivel and so Bidnold is returned to him by a grateful King.

The title of the Rose Tremain novel adapted here proves to be a fecund pun. Apart from meaning the return of the British monarchy after the death of Cromwell with the coronation of Charles II in 1660, *Restoration* also stands for the rebuilding of London after the ravages of the plague and the conflagration of 1666. In narrative terms it refers to the story of hero Robert Merivel, who is flattered away from doctoring by the King, falls back to obscurity and then 'finds himself' as a single parent and a 'new man' when he returns to medicine (thus finding the King's favour again). Merivel's powers are themselves restorative. Finally there's the irony that the film, as a sumptuous heritage costume drama, is entirely dependent on a convincing 'restoration' of the period depicted.

A lot of effort, research and money has gone into this. The viewer is bombarded with enjoyable visual information about the seventeenth century and made to feel quite giddy with the unaccustomed grandiosity of it all. *Restoration* proves that it is possible to do over-the-top Baroque, carrying out projects that were too expensive even for the Merry Monarch—such as the wedding on water in which the King's mistress Celia Clemence, while plucking a lyre, floats towards her "paper bridegroom" Merivel, flanked by rows of carved and gilded swans. There are some very effective images of the old London Bridge and the Thames teeming with life. The film is just as arresting with its grim material: the Great Fire, the man with the exposed heart and the strange, beak-like plague mask that Merivel wears are images that linger. These last two have a grotesque quality that might, under Peter Greenaway's analytical gaze, have been central to the project of *Restoration*. In Michael Hoffman's film, however, they are part of the fusillade of period bric-a-brac that seems designed as much to draw attention away from weaknesses of narrative.

These fault lines spring mainly from the reshaping of Tremain's picaresque story of seventeenth century vicissitude into the kind of heroic mythic structure so influential with Hollywood executives, one very big on contrasts. Merivel and Pearce, respectively lecherous rake and pious Quaker, are unlikely pals but their relationship wouldn't be quite so implausible if Robert Downey Jnr and David Thewlis didn't seem to be in different movies. The deadpan Thewlis is in something dour and realist—Ken Loach doing a puritan *Marate/Sade*, perhaps whereas Downey Jnr is wide-eyed in a Richard Lester musketeer romp one minute and a dewey-eyed Lawrence Nightingale the next. One extremity of mood follows another, busting genre boundaries in their wake: there are sections like *The Draughtsman's Contract*, others like *The Madness of King George*. The movie suffers badly from this lack of a consistent tone, something that also afflicted Hoffman's *Restless Natives* (but not his brat pack movie *Promised Land*).

The Madness of King George, managed a fine balancing act between psychological tragedy and dry wit. *Restoration* prefers farce to irony and its tragedy is entirely melodramatic. The plague and the Great Fire look very impressive, but they are treated narratively as brief impediments to Merivel's personal fulfilment. Sam Neill's Royal prerogative as Charles is as arbitrary and unpredictable a force as that of Nigel Hawthorne's George III, but Hawthorne didn't affect the Douglas Fairbanks' twinkle in his eye that Neil does. Neil's is one of many performances here that could have slipped in from Lester's Musketeer films—Meg Ryan's embarrassing asylum colleen, Katherine, and Ian McKellen's formula factotum, Will Gates, are two others. The effect is to push design to the fore, with all the sweetness of a flummery, and that is sometimes pleasure enough.

VILLAGE VOICE, 12/26/95, p. 60, Georgia Brown

Given Albania's miserable history as a strategic pawn, it's hard to know what the country lost that is currently worth restoring. [The reference is to *Lamerica;* see Brown's review.] In Britain, on the other hand, they once took the monarchy away for 11 years and then had much fun bringing it back. This was called the Restoration, and what a time was had by a privileged few.

Restoration the movie is based on the novel by Rose Tremain, and what virtues the book has I can't guess (as it was short-listed for the Booker Prize, it may have some). The movie, directed by Michael Hoffman of *Soapdish,* is a dopey, picaresque comedy with an exotic backdrop: Charles II's indecent court, the Great Plague of 1665, and the great fire of London of 1666. It's what I call a Big Wig movie.

Our hero is a gifted (or so everyone says) playboy doctor, Robert Merivel (Robert Downey Jr.), who is taken up by a quixotic King Charles II (Sam Neill) and made the royal vet (the King keeps 18 pampered spaniels). Later, the King marries him off to Celia (Polly Walker), one of the royal mistresses, and he becomes the royal beard. When Merivel makes a (rejected) pass at Celia, the king kicks him out into the cold.

Despite what the movie would have us to believe, Charles doesn't seem to have been the jealous sort. If you believe Graham Greene's *Lord Rochester's Monkey,* "Charles expected constancy in women as little as he practiced it himself." The likelier cause of someone like Merivel's disfavor is that he fails to amuse. Downey acts very silly—running naked with plumes attached to his dick, for example—but he's neither funny nor witty. The movie's few giggles go to Hugh Grant's foppish turn as a Court Painter with Big Moles.

Plume between his legs, Merivel joins up with a solemn old med school chum (David Thewlis) now running a Quaker insane asylum. One of the inmates, Katherine (Meg Ryan doing a very silly walk), takes a shine to Merivel and subsequently gets pregnant. At this point the lovers set off for London where Katherine dies in childbirth and Merivel works off his grief by fighting the black death.

Judging from primary sources like the diaries of Pepys and Boswell, the era was sex-obsessed even by contemporary standards. (See, too, Lawrence Stone's rollicking *The Family, Sex, and Marriage in England, 1500-1800.*) If at first, Pepys is shocked to learn that the sovereign feels up his mistress in the middle of chapel or a theatrical performance, lo, when humble subject Pepys goes and does likewise, he meets with success! Royal tastelessness sets the pace again. Pepys's infatuation (from afar) with the king's mistresses makes these ladies seem the Restoration equivalent of movie stars. On hearing some gossip about his favorite, Lady Castlemaine, he observes, "Strange how it is for her beauty I am willing to construe all this to the best and to pity her ... though I know well enough she is a whore."

Restoration is too hopelessly prudish to get any of this right. (Though I wouldn't care to see the result, Peter Greenaway might be the right talent for the subject.) It seems to think that garishness and some random details are enough. The prominent inclusion of pineapples, for example, will remind those in the know that it was Charles's royal gardener who produced the first domestically grown specimen.

The screening I attended happened to benefit the Whitney, providing Whitney director David Ross with the awkward task off convincing $95-a-ticket guests that *Restoration* would be a match for their superior tastes. Here were his reasons: our eras have a plague in common; in the picture they would be able to detect echoes of Caravaggio and Rembrandt; and, best of all, "Beauty is timeless." So is bullshit.

Introducing Ross, Harvey Weinstein had confided that *Restoration* was his favorite Miramax film of the past year and a half. Tough year and a half, Harvey?

Also reviewed in:
NEW YORK TIMES, 12/29/95, p. C3, Janet Maslin
VARIETY, 12/18-31/95, p. 65, Godfrey Cheshire
WASHINGTON POST, 2/2/96, p. B1, Rita Kempley
WASHINGTON POST, 2/2/96, Weekend/p. 39, Desson Howe

RHYTHM THIEF

A Strand Releasing release of a Film Crash production. *Producer:* Jonathan Starch. *Director:* Matthew Harrison. *Screenplay:* Christopher Grimm and Matthew Harrison. *Director of Photography:* Howard Krupa. *Editor:* Matthew Harrison. *Music:* Danny Brenner, Hugh O'Donovan, John L. Horn, and Kevin Okerlund. *Sound:* Charles Hunt. *Casting:* Meredith Jacobson. *Art Director:* Daniel Fisher. *Costumes:* Nina Carter. *Running time:* 88 minutes. *MPAA Rating:* Not Rated.

CAST: Jason Andrews (Simon); Eddie Daniels (Marty); Kevin Corrigan (Fuller); Kimberly Flynn (Cyd); Sean Hagerty (Shayme); Mark Alfred (Mr. Bunch); Christopher Cooke (Jules); Bob McGrath (Rat Boy).

LOS ANGELES TIMES, 12/15/95, Calendar/p. 16, Kevin Thomas

Wedged among a thicket of year-end prestige pictures, Matthew Harrison's "Rhythm Thief," is a triumph of economy in all senses that pops up to deliver a knockout punch. Harrison yanks us right down to the mean streets of Manhattan's Lower East Side, where Simon (Jason Andrews) and most everyone he comes in contact with is living the most marginal of existences.

Simon survives by selling bootleg cassettes on the streets. He's a compact, virile young man, self-possessed and self-reliant. He's also a man of his word, tough and resilient, and he exudes an inner strength, a cool self-discipline that makes him a magnet for the desperate and the outright demented.

He's always fending off a hyper kid (Kevin Corrigan) who wants to be his pal and his partner. A woman (Kimberly Flynn) drops by his stark, dingy tenement apartment regularly for "sex and nothing else," but gets hysterical when he flatly insists she live up to these terms which, he reminds her, are her own.

Simon clearly has decided that survival depends upon abiding by his own code and by maintaining a detachment from others. He is really only open, if you can call it that with a philosophical older neighborhood man (Mark Alfred), who appreciates his intelligence and integrity and wishes Simon do more with his life.

Out of the blue a waiflike young woman, Marty (Eddie Daniels), from his past turns up to tell him that his mother, who had been a mental patient, has died. Simon reflexively rebuffs Marty, a dreamy type who loves to write on walls (and on her arms too), but she persists. A series of events propel Simon and Marty to Far Rockaway Beach, where he at last feels able to reveal his vulnerability and capacity for tenderness.

In telling Simon's story, Harrison has been aided by an exceedingly vital and fluid cameraman, Howard Krupa, who shot in black and white. In expressing Simon's concern that his life means nothing, Harrison reveals a style that is at once as rigorously minimalist as Simon himself yet exudes the raw drive and energy of the film's extraordinarily intense and captivating score by Danny Brenner, Hugh O'Donovan, John L. Horn and Kevin Okerlund.

Andrews is an actor of admirable reserves and concentration, and he's supported by actors as capable as he is. Often funny in its sense of absurdity and finally wrenching, "Rhythm Thief" - which reportedly cost only $11,000 to make—exudes a sense of life being lived on the edge.

NEW YORK POST, 11/15/95, p. 44, Larry Worth

Nine months ago, the judges at Sundance were split over which film should walk off with the grand jury prize. Ultimately, they went with Edward Burns"'The Brothers McMullen."

After seeing the other contender, Matthew Harrison's "Rhythm Thief," it's easy to understand the quandary.

In his directorial debut, Harrison has lensed a gritty, wonderfully original drama that's downright exhilarating, filled with the wildest set of off-the-wall eccentrics since "The Road Warrior."

As in George Miller's post-apocalyptic opus, the protagonist and all the peripherals are scary, funny and ultimately endearing, taking precedence over plot with their fascinating manners and mores.

Regardless, the plot comes with an intriguing premise: Anti-hero Simon is a somber but driven individual who spends his time going to clubs and tape-recording the music, which he then sells on bootleg cassettes. All that's well and fine until the ultra-feminist lead singer of an underground band takes umbrage, and revenge—setting the wheels in motion for adventure, romance and tragedy.

But Harrison adds his own spin on the mix via some grainy, in-your-face camerawork that lends a jarring intensity. It serves as the perfect touch for the East Village setting, imbuing the proceedings with an authentic look and feel.

Harrison also earns kudos for co-writing (with Christopher Grimm) a wealth of deliciously loopy dialogue for the sundry druggies, lunatics and psychos populating the fringes, of Simon's world. What evolves is a form of sly, gimmick-free humor that offsets the jangly ambience.

Even the hot, urgent sex scenes carry a striking ferocity, despite their intended lack of passion. Then, just when one least expects it, there's a gentle moment to catch viewers off guard—right before a burst of unexpected violence. And so it goes.

The relatively unknown actors effortlessly keep pace with the mood swings, led in high style by Jason Andrews as anything-but-simple Simon. Eddie Daniels, Kevin Corrigan and Kimberly Flynn furnish inspired support.

Collectively, cast and crew ensure that "Rhythm Thief" rarely misses a beat.

VILLAGE VOICE, 11/21/95, Film Special/p. 24, Michael Atkinson

Chump-change indie filmmakers are prone to engage themselves with tiny, circular stories that pace leopard-like over a filthy square foot of urban turf and lead, fatalistically, to nowhere—they're cheap to make, easy to write, properly imbued with hipness. After stalking the margins for decades making hilariously saber-toothed shorts, and having his first feature, the '93 midget-bowling noir farce *Spare Me*, fail to find a New York screen, Matthew Harrison has toughened up and taken the safe way out.

A winner at Sundance, *Rhythm Thief* is a dry, sober, whimsical but never satiric runt-movie take on downtown lowlife, in which a self-loathing bootlegger (Jason Andrews) tries to keep his dismal life hermetically sealed despite the invasive efforts of crazy neighbors, a weird old girlfriend, and an angry local band whose music he's stolen. It's *Aquarian Weekly* noir. Harrison has abandoned his instinctive absurdism for a bargain-basement Scorsese-ism, bopping along the emptier lower 'hoods with his Andy-Garcia-after-six-rounds hero, hanging out for wads of tough, all-white, fuck-you banter and jagged MTV cutaways. Made on the requisite shoestring (do we really care how much anymore?) and shot in grit-on-the-tongue black-and-white, Harrison's character study is as whittled down as its hero's social calendar. Everyone talks so much about him surviving, you know he's doomed. If it's sometimes less than convincing (a local club band out to murder street-vending copycats?), *Rhythm Thief* still finds time for ersatz lyricism—a madwoman's poetry written up and down a young girl's arms, a romantic idyll between subway cars passing over the East River. "I'm going to sleep," the loopy girlfriend slurs with her eyes closed, "Will you come with me?" If only there were half the story of *Laws of Gravity*, or even *Space Me*.

Also reviewed in:
CHICAGO TRIBUNE,2/2/96, Friday/p. H, Michael Wilmington
NEW YORK TIMES, 11/15/95, p. C15, Stephen Holden
VARIETY, 9/19-25/94, p. 82, Ken Eisner

RICHARD III

A United Artists Pictures release with the participation of British Screen of a Bayly/Paré production developed in association with First Look Pictures. *Executive Producer:* Ellen Dinerman Little, Ian McKellen, Joe Simon, and Maria Apodiacos. *Producer:* Lisa Katselas Paré and Stephen Bayly. *Director:* Richard Loncraine. *Screenplay:* Ian McKellen and Richard Loncraine. *Based on the stage production by:* Richard Eyre. *From the play by:* William Shakespeare. *Director of Photography:* Peter Biziou. *Editor:* Paul Green. *Music:* Trevor Jones. *Sound:* David Stephenson and (music) Kirsty Whalley and Paul Golding. *Sound Editor:* Phillip Bothamley. *Casting:* Irene Lamb. *Production Designer:* Tony Burrough. *Art Director:* Choi Ho Man and Richard Bridgland. *Special Effects:* John Evans. *Costumes:* Shuna Harwood. *Make-up:* Pat Hay. *Make-up (Special):* Daniel Parker. *Stunt Coordinator:* Jim Dowdall. *Running time:* 105 minutes. *MPAA Rating:* R.

CAST: Christopher Bowen (Prince Edward); Edward Jewesbury (King Henry); Ian McKellen (Richard III); Bill Paterson (Ratcliffe); Annette Bening (Queen Elizabeth); Matthew Groom (Young Prince); John Wood (King Edward); Nigel Hawthorne (Clarence); Maggie Smith (Duchess of York); Kate Steavenson-Payne (Princess Elizabeth); Robert Downey, Jr. (Earl Rivers); Tres Hanley (Air Hostess); Tim McInnerny (Catesby); Stacey Kent (Ballroom Singer); Jim Carter (Hastings); Roger Hammond (Archbishop); Dennis Lill (Lord Mayor); Jim Broadbent (Buckingham); Edward Hardwicke (Stanley); Ryan Gilmore (George Stanley); Dominic West (Richmond); Donald Sumpter (Brackenburry); Kristin Scott Thomas (Lady Anne); Adrian Dunbar (Tyrell); Andy Rashleigh (Jailer); Marco Williamson (Prince of Wales); Bruce Purchase (City Gentleman); James Dreyfus (1st Subaltern); David Antrobus (2nd Subaltern).

CINEASTE, Vol. XXII, No. 1, 1996, p. 34, Gary Crowdus

The theatrical vogue for updated versions of Shakespeare's plays inspired by Jan Kott's 1964 book, *Shakespeare, Our Contemporary*, never really caught on in the cinema. Kott's book argued persuasively for the continuing relevance, even timeliness, of the playwright's work, and theatrical productions worldwide in the years since have been replete with Hamlets in blue jeans, Shylocks in business suits, and Montagues and Capulets feuding with guns, chains, and flick knives. The Shakespeare films produced during the same period, however—including those by Franco Zeffirelli, Roman Polanski, Peter Brook, and Kenneth Branagh, among others—invariably presented the plays in their traditional historical settings.

Ironically, Kott never advocated the historical transposition of Shakespeare, since he believes the relevance lies not in modern-dress productions but in the social, political, and human issues dramatized in the plays. For Kott, whose wartime experience of the German occupation of Poland and anti-Nazi underground resistance was succeeded by the establishment of communism and years of repressive Stalinist rule, the world portrayed by Shakespeare—one fraught with civil war, ideological turmoil, political persecution, and brutal repression—was very much like his own. Kott saw Shakespeare's image of history as one of a "Grand Mechanism" in which each successive chapter repeats the previous one, representing a never-ending struggle for power, with every step marked "by murder, perfidy, and treachery."

This metaphor of history as a cruel, self-repeating cycle is most evident in the English history plays, especially *The Tragedy of King Richard III,* one of Shakespeare's earliest and most popular plays. While the playwright's later, more mature plays presented complex psychological characterizations, *Richard III* borrowed from earlier, cruder dramatic forms, notably the moralizing and bloody revenge tragedies of the first century Roman playwright Seneca. Combining this dramaturgical style with the politically biased historical accounts of later Tudor chroniclers of Richard's reign, Shakespeare fashioned a memorable portrait of a bright, witty, but ruthless political despot—physically deformed, to boot—who had no qualms about murdering anyone, including members of his family, who stood between himself and the English throne.

Shakespeare's play is highly entertaining political melodrama, a Punch and Judy show for adults, continually enlivened by the sly, supremely self-confident, and fast-talking villain who functions as its 'hero.' In his soliloquies and other asides to the audience, Richard lets us in on each of his nefarious schemes. We are flattered at being taken into his confidence—indeed, enlisted as virtual accomplices to his deeds—and, thus morally disarmed, share the thrill of his evil machinations until fairly late in the play. Since Richard dominates most of the play's action and repeatedly flaunts his skills as a master dissembler—alternately playing devoted brother, ardent lover, aggrieved brother-in-law, concerned uncle, and reluctant king—the role has always been considered a plum part for any actor.

It's not surprising that Ian McKellen, acclaimed since the late Sixties as one of England's leading Shakespearean actors as well as one with a passion for making the Bard 'relevant' for contemporary audiences, has produced what is perhaps the first film to historically transpose a Shakespeare play. His new film version of *Richard III,* an adaptation of Richard Eyre's 1990 Royal National Theatre production, updates the fifteenth-century War of the Roses between the York and Lancaster clans to a hypothetical history of Great Britain in the 1930s, a society likewise riven by civil war and ripe for a fascist coup d'etat. Although this time-shifting of Shakespeare is not always appropriate and often results in an awkward, forced topicality, in this case the cinematic updating, coscripted by McKellen and director Richard Loncraine, is both historically evocative and dramatically effective.

While modern-day Great Britain never underwent a dictatorship, Shakespeare's tale of this legendary tyrant provides the vehicle for a fanciful speculation of what a British fascist regime might have looked like. Actual British history of the period does offer some suggestive similarities. Widespread unemployment during the Depression years and an ineffectual coalition government of Labour and Conservative parties contributed to the rise of Oswald Mosley, for example, who proposed his British Union of Fascists as a political party of "doers, not talkers" who were prepared to resolve the national crisis. The fascist sympathies of King Edward VIII, who abdicated the throne in 1936, were well known (he even met with Hitler on a visit to Germany in 1937). Recently published intelligence reports suggest that if Hitler had won the war, he would likely have installed Edward on the throne as England's quisling king.

We shouldn't make too much of such real-life historical references, however, since the filmmakers are no more concerned with historical fidelity to the 1930s than Shakespeare was to the late fifteenth century. Shakespeare's historical sources were more hearsay than history, more legend than documented fact. The filmmakers have likewise characterized their adaptation of the play as an imagined, reinvented history of British politics in the Thirties. The historical transposition thus avoids the perpetuation of Shakespeare's flagrant distortions of the historical record, which always exercises the members of The Richard III Society, who contend that their boy is the victim of a vicious political smear campaign. More importantly, by shifting the narrative to a later but generically consistent, if fictional, historical setting, the film reinvigorates the play's social and political themes for contemporary viewers, and—aided by our familiarity with bloody dictators of more recent vintage, such as Hitler, Mussolini, Stalin, and Franco—transforms it into provocative political allegory.

McKellen and Loncraine's updating of the play nevertheless seems motivated more by esthetic than political reasons, more of an effort to make Shakespeare's play seem less old-fashioned and historically remote than a deliberate attempt to embody dramatically Kott's notion of the playwright's "Grand Mechanism" of history. (One also suspects McKellen was none too anxious to star in a traditional presentation which would set himself up for immediate comparisons with Laurence Olivier's landmark performance in his 1955 film of *Richard III*.) In fact, like most cinematic adaptations of Shakespeare, this *Richard III* is a highly condensed affair which eliminates or condenses many of the play's secondary characters, drops entire scenes, trims and rearranges much of the play's dialog, and understandably eliminates some of the more obvious anachronisms.

The cumulative effect of these cuts—including references to history recounted in earlier plays *(Richard III* is the concluding play in a tetralogy that follows the three parts of *Henry VI)*, a simplification of many of the characterizations (this is often done to heighten Richard's villainy), and a few brief but politically telling scenes involving common citizens and government functionaries—is to deny this cinematic adaptation its full potential as political commentary. While it may be desirable to keep the film to a commercial length (the film's running time is a fast-paced 104 minutes, while a full-length stage presentation runs to nearly four hours), Shakespeare aficionados are likely to be disappointed by the extensive textual cuts that reduce the film to a *Classics Comics* version of the original.

Compensating to some extent for the loss of so much of Shakespeare's verse and the play's historical background, this adaptation boasts a lavish period style and an imaginative, vibrant cinematic interpretation. Indeed, as an effort to popularize Shakespeare, the film has been shrewdly designed for a mass moviegoing audience that is more accustomed to looking than to listening. As a man of the theater, McKellen wisely engaged principal collaborators—including director Richard Loncraine *(Brimstone and Treacle, Bellman and True*, cinematographer Peter Biziou, and production designer Tony Burrough—who could help him present the play in a visually compelling manner. From the film's first images, in fact, it is clear that this is going to be decidedly cinematic Shakespeare. The film's pre-credits and main title treatment—involving a bit of historical exposition from *Henry VI, Part 3* in which Richard murders the rival Lancastrian King Henry VI and his son Edward at the Battle of Tewkesbury—is a knockout cinematic opening that would do any Hollywood action picture proud.

Loncraine has described his stylized approach as one that aims "to mesh the twentieth century imagery and sixteenth century dialog." Since the filmmakers were freely reinventing their own history, they sought out a series of real-life "eccentric spaces," as Loncraine describes them, that would become elements of the story in their own right. An abandoned Thames River power station dating from the Thirties, for example, becomes the dreaded Tower of London where Richard's brother, Clarence, and his nephew princes are murdered; the marble-lined, Reichstag-like expanse of London University's Senate House (site of Great Britain's Ministry of Information during WWII) becomes Richard's military headquarters; the ornate, Victorian Gothic-styled St. Pancras Chambers, the former Midland Grand Hotel, becomes the exterior of Edward's palace; and Steam Town, a train museum in Lancashire, featuring an authentic German locomotive, becomes Richard's military staging area for the Battle of Bosworth Field.

The character of each of these striking locations—some of them seen only briefly is accentuated by the filmmakers' dynamic widescreen compositions, striking camera angles, and wide-angle lenses that produce foreshortened perspectives, thereby lending an even more ominous quality to these already imposing edifices and vistas. Both Loncraine and director of cinematography Peter Biziou (whose previous credits include such visually offbeat films as Alan Parker's *Pink Floyd: The Wall* and Terry Gilliain's *Time Bandits)* have extensive backgrounds in TV commercials, and their ability to get the maximum visual pizzazz out of images glimpsed for only a split second is evident throughout.

At the center of this stylish and forceful production, McKellen portrays Richard of Gloucester as a professional soldier (presumably a graduate of the Sandhurst Royal Military Academy and WWI veteran). His battlefield exploits behind him, Richard now feels the itch of political ambitions, and, in order to realize them, he confides to us that he is "determined to prove a villain." He certainly looks and sounds the part, rarely appearing out of military uniform, with a perennially hangdog expression, a rakish, pencil-thin mustache, and clipped, upper-class diction, not to mention the character's trademark hunchback, withered left arm, contorted hand, and limping gait. But the clearest indication, in today's more health-conscious times, of Richard's truly evil and thoroughly decadent nature is that he is a chain smoker! In keeping with the production's overall tone of black comedy, McKellen brings a great deal of sly humor to the role, indulging in frequent winks and furtive glances at the camera, occasionally breaking into boisterous expressions of delight at the success of his schemes.

In a clearly commercial but dramatically apt casting ploy, the members of the Woodville family—Queen Elizabeth and her brother, Earl Rivers, who are regarded as ambitious outsiders seeking to exploit their position within the royal family—are portrayed, in the midst of an ensemble otherwise comprised of classically trained English stage and film actors, by American actors Annette Bening and Robert Downey, Jr. The most that can be said for Downey's role as the Queen's playboy brother is that it is thankfully brief (he is early on dispatched in *flagrante delicto* by one of Richard's henchmen). Blank verse has rarely been delivered more blankly. Although Annette Bening's American accent initially sounds jarring amidst all the Britspeak, she gives a spirited and often moving performance as the victimized but combative Queen Mother. She is one of the few who see through Richard's deceitfulness ("When he fawns," she notes, "he bites"), and who foils his final outrageous scheme to legitimize his dynastic claim.

Dressed, coifed, and jeweled in elegant Thirties' fashions, the Queen, her brother, and the other newly ensconced members of the royal court could be mistaken for the cast from a Noel Coward society comedy, except the goings-on here are far more grisly. Nigel Hawthorne portrays Clarence, Richard's elder but passive brother, as an amateur photography buff and a political naïf completely unaware of Richard's murderous treachery. Maggie Smith plays Richard's mother, the Duchess of York, as a crusty *grande dame* who spends most of her time in high dudgeon, condemning the behavior of her wicked son and prophesying his doom. Kristin Scott Thomas's Lady Anne, an exotic beauty too easily seduced by Richard's "honeyed words," soon realizes that she is merely a political pawn and takes to drugs to dull the pain of her loveless marriage. Jim Broadbent depicts the Duke of Buckingham, Richard's chief political ally, as the aspiring monarch's campaign manager, party propagandist, and media spin doctor, playing a crucial role in Richard's seizure of power before he, too, is discarded. Jim Carter's Lord Hastings, here the Prime Minister, is a principled government loyalist who, despite warnings, is doomed by his overweening self-confidence and obtuse inability to perceive Richard's tyrannical plans. Edward Hardwicke's Lord Stanley, on the other hand, survives because he is a seasoned political opportunist, able to play factions, publicly professing loyalty to Richard while privately biding his time (in a neat twist in this updated version, which acknowledges the decisiveness of modern, mechanized warfare, Stanley heads the Royal Air Force, so his last-minute battlefield defection to the rebel forces guarantees Richard's defeat).

The film's historical transposition of the play also inspires a series of novel, frequently amusing interpretations of classic scenes. Richard's famous opening soliloquy ("Now is the winter of our discontent/Made glorious summer by this son of York") begins at a coronation party as a public ode proclaimed for his newly enthroned brother Edward, continues as a self-pitying reflection in the palace *pissoir,* and concludes, after Richard spies us over his shoulder in the men's room mirror, as a conspiratorial aside.

Richard's notorious wooing of the newly widowed Lady Anne over the corpse of her husband, who has been murdered by Richard, is conducted in a military mortuary. Despite some heavy editing of the dialog, it still functions as a verbal tennis match, each 'player' sustaining volley after volley of brilliant repartee in blank verse, with Richard capping his verbal seduction with a respectful little military salute (which is about as romantic as this Richard ever gets).

The murders of Richard's numerous victims (all of which discreetly occurred offstage in Shakespeare's time) are gruesomely enacted in a series of Hammer horror film tableaux, sometimes with eerie political resonances. After hurling his trumped-up charges of treason against Hastings, who is quickly executed by hanging, Richard reclines on a sofa, blithely humming along with a jazz tune and gloating over photos of the Prime Minister's corpse, much as Hitler is reported to have privately viewed films of the excruciatingly slow hangings of the officers who tried to assassinate him in the July 1944 bomb plot.

Buckingham's clever manipulation of the Mayor and assembled government leaders into appealing to a Richard seemingly reluctant to assume the throne as the only legitimate successor to the late king is portrayed as a skillful piece of stage management (this medieval concern for the apparent legitimacy of dynastic claims echoes modern fascists' regard for the legal niceties which sanction their coups). Buckingham, having previously engineered a 'disinformation' campaign against the princes, continues to politically soften up the civic leaders while Richard is coyly sequestered in the green room with a couple of make-up girls. After these two political operators congratulate themselves on the success of their ruse, the scene segues to a Nuremberg-style mass rally, complete with, mammoth banners, where Richard, attired in jackboots and Mosleyesque black-shirt uniform, greets his chanting followers.

The film's concluding Battle of Bosworth Field, on the other hand, is a rather hasty affair and the import of Richard's demise and his successor's victory is somewhat muddled. Once his troops have been routed, Richard engages in a shootout with the young rebel Richmond (soon to be King Henry VII, who, in his own first visual 'aside' to the camera, flashes a conqueror's knowing smile). Then, perhaps by way of finally conceding that he *is* the devil incarnate, Richard seems to opt for self-immolation by tumbling into the flames (of hellfire?), a wicked smile on his face, as the soundtrack blares out Al Jolson's rendition of "I'm Sitting On Top of the World." It's a cleverly conceived, if surprisingly abrupt, fade-out for our villainous hero, but rather imprecise as any sort of political commentary.

Perhaps, Jan Kott's "Grand Mechanism" notwithstanding, we're asking too much of this stripped-down film version, not to mention Shakespeare's original play. *Richard III* has always been more effective as colorful and rousing melodrama, a concerto for lead actor, rather than a sober examination (like some of the later history plays) of the struggle for political power, of statecraft, the relationship of politics and morality, the role of religion and nationalist ideology in war, and the preconditions for social order and political unity. McKellen and his collaborators have nevertheless succeeded in revitalizing for contemporary audiences Shakespeare's fearsome bogeyman of English legend and, by putting him in more contemporary dress and surroundings, have also vividly demonstrated the continuing relevance of Shakespeare's social and political themes. Many moviegoers are also likely to be surprised that Shakespeare can be so ... well, entertaining.

The recent critical and box-office success of Kenneth Branagh's Henry V (1989) and *Much Ado About Nothing* (1993) clearly paved the way for this adaptation of *Richard III*, as well as Oliver Parker's *Othello*. These productions, as well as a spate of forthcoming Shakespeare films now in production including Branagh's full-length *Hamlet*, Royal Shakespeare productions of *Twelfth Night* and *A Midsummer Night's Dream*, and *Romeo and Juliet* with teen stars Leonard DiCaprio and Claire Danes—bode well for a renaissance of Shakespeare on the screen. The film industry may finally have realized, in fact, that the Bard is the ideal screenwriter. After all, the guy's got a helluva knack for plot-lines, his dialog is vivid and often quotable, he's adept in many different genres, and he doesn't mind having his material reworked by other writers.

LOS ANGELES TIMES, 12/29/95, Calendar/p. 1, Kenneth Turan

Richard of Gloucester is one of Shakespeare's most magnificent monsters and "Richard III" is a film audacious enough to match his astonishing villainy. Made with gusto, daring and visual brilliance, this stripped-down, jazzed-up "Richard" pulsates with bloody life, a triumph of both modernization and popularization.

Shakespeare's plays have been subjected to numerous interpretations, so many that when the Folger Shakespeare Filmography was published in 1979, it took 64 pages to list every one. There have been traditional versions, total updates like 1955's unlikely "Joe Macbeth," even films whose Shakespearean source was cleverly hidden, as was science-fiction classic "Forbidden Planet's" use of "The Tempest."

But while it's not uncommon on stage, what director Richard Loncraine and star Ian McKellen (who also collaborated on the screenplay) have done is rare on screen. They've kept to the spirit of Shakespeare's words (though the play is much-abridged here) but switched the setting from the 15th century to England of the 1930s. In the process they've liberated the same kind of energy that Akira Kurosawa did when he moved "Macbeth" to medieval Japan and came up with the magnificent "Throne of Blood."

McKellen toured extensively with the stage version of this production, but since film is a more realistic medium he and Loncraine (with splendid help from cinematographer Peter Biziou, production designer Tony Burrough and costume designer Shuna Harwood) have been able to create a convincing cinematic universe to house it in.

The setting is in effect an alternate England, what the country might have looked like in the 1930s if there'd been a civil war and motorcycle-riding black-shirted fascists (the followers of Sir Oswald Mosley, perhaps) had taken over the government and the monarchy. With inventive use of arresting locations and attention to period details like ticker tapes, cigarette holders and big-band music, "Richard" creates an unsettling crooked copy of those days, not a gimmick, but a breathing, functioning reality.

Employing this eye-catching look has also freed up the filmmakers creatively re-imagine every aspect of the play's plot line, like placing Richard's celebrated wooing of Lady Anne, the woman whose husband he's just killed, in a bloody and claustrophobic hospital morgue.

In addition to splitting Richard's initial "now is the winter of our discontent" speech into two parts, a public address and a private monologue delivered in a men's room, the film brazenly postpones it for 10 minutes, opening things instead with a literally smashing sequence of Richard at war that lets you know at once that this isn't going to be Shakespeare as usual.

While these pyrotechnics could compensate for a good deal of bad acting, in "Richard III" they don't have to. The title role has always attracted the best of actors (Sir Laurence Olivier did it on film, George C. Scott had his first major New York stage success with the part and Al Pacino will have a version at the Sundance Film Festival), but even in this group McKellen's delicious version is special.

Insinuator, instigator, a matchless deployer of nets and traps, McKellen's smirking Richard is master of oily dissimulation. With his awkward hump and withered arm, he is at once the scuttling apparition that dogs bark at and everyone's concerned false friend, "too childish, foolish for this world."

It's part of McKellen's gift to make it seem that Richard is taking the audience into his confidence via his monologues because his contemporaries are too dense to be appreciative and he has to share his consummate villainy with someone. Richard first describes and then shows how he'll woo Anne and coolly eliminate anyone who stands between him and the throne, including his two brothers, one of them Edward IV, the current monarch.

Supporting McKellen in this masterly performance are some of Britain's best actors, including Kristin Scott Thomas as the Lady Anne, Nigel Hawthorne and John Wood as Richard's brothers, Maggie Smith as their mother, the Duchess of York, and Jim Broadbent as the duplicitous Buckingham.

Not only are these players in exceptionally good form, they've made a conscious attempt to avoid declaiming, to speak Shakespeare's dialogue as if it were casual and conversational, which successfully makes the words sound as modern as possible.

The one place the casting has gone slightly astray is in using two Americans, Annette Bening and especially Robert Downey Jr., as Edward's Queen Elizabeth and her brother Earl Rivers. Though the filmmakers defend these seemingly commercial choices by saying the original two were outsiders at Edward's court (being members of the rival house of Lancaster), there is something unnecessarily jarring about hearing their domestic accents, though Bening, to her credit, does handle the role with assurance and authority.

But finally that is barely a blip as far as "Richard III's" overall impact is concerned. This is Shakespeare exciting enough for even the most dubious, which, after all, is no less than the man deserves.

NEW YORK, 1/15/96, p. 48, David Denby

I had a good time at *Richard III*, the mad, modern-dress production of Shakespeare's melodramatic potboiler. Is this a serious production of Shakespeare? Yes and no. Or rather, no and yes. The movie, based on Richard Eyre's London stage production, has been adapted for the screen by director Richard Loncraine and Ian McKellen, who plays King Richard; Loncraine and McKellen have cut and rearranged the text and moved the power struggle between the houses of Lancaster and York (you know, the Wars of the Roses) from the fifteenth century to the England of the mid-1930s. At times, we seem to be watching a decadent thirties fashion show in which the contentious royals, dressed to the teeth in oyster-white linens and long slinky gowns—the men meticulously shaved, the women laden with jewelry—ride about in Bentleys, smoking furiously and doing nasty things to one another. As always, Richard seduces the woman whose husband he has killed; he plants suspicion everywhere and murders every conceivable rival. The rudiments of Shakespeare's story remain intact. But we're very much aware of the production as a stunt, in which every line of poetry that doesn't fit the thirties setting has been excised. Richard is now a modern military man whose uniforms grow darker and darker—finally, they are black—and whose usurpation of the throne is a kind of Fascist putsch. Fraud and violence win out over enervated goodness.

At its most frivolous, the production appears to suggest that evil somehow emanates from high style. The cigarette dangling from McKellen's mouth, for instance, serves the same iconic function here as it did in those forties Hollywood movies in which the Nazi villains seemed to have wandered in from some campy party high above Hollywood Boulevard. (Is smoking really so wicked?)

Three things, however, save this *Richard III* from triviality: Shakespeare, whose unparalleled vigor, even in this rudely barber'd form, keeps things moving to a climax; Ian McKellen's performance; and the intense, blunt Englishness of the settings. The peculiar heavy luxury of the state rooms and the brutality of the modern industrial buildings give off a special modern dismay. No country as beautiful as this one has ever before produced such uncomfortable official spaces. In the end, I was half won over to the conceits of modern-dress Shakespeare. There is something in the play that illuminates the despair of between-the-wars Europe—the sense that affairs of state are slipping out of control, the nauseating realization that the most energetic and decisive person in the country is also the most evil. Richard takes over because the good people are too tired to stop him.

Any production of *Richard III* almost has to be a celebration of brazenness. After all, this is a very naughty play. Shakespeare made Richard ever so much brighter and more interesting than the virtuous characters, who come to life only when cursing Richard ("Blush, blush, thou lump of foul deformity," etc.). In his 1955 film version, Laurence Olivier used the intimacy of the camera to seduce us into complicity, starting right at the beginning with his reed-dry, cackling, slightly epicene reading of the great soliloquy "Now is the winter of our discontent." McKellen, a major actor and personality in Great Britain but far too little known here (he's had a negligible screen career), creates his own kind of excitement. In this version, the opening monologue begins as a very public speech delivered by Richard at a celebration of his brother's ascension to the throne; it continues, sotto voce, in a royal bathroom, where Richard, sighing as he sinks into a heavy piss, speaks of himself in quiet tones of disgust. He glances into a mirror and spots us looking at him; a gleam comes into McKellen's eye, and he turns, delighted (just like Olivier) to have a companion, taking us into his confidence as he explains his plans. From that point on, we know he is telling us, and only us, the truth. We are flattered, and, in turn, we repay his trust by withholding absolute judgment of his crimes.

Now in his mid-fifties, Ian McKellen is slender and starched, seemingly as bland as a mid-level Whitehall diplomat—a not quite handsome man, very tightly wrapped, very decisive but impersonal. Yet when he walks, you notice Richard's hump under the uniform, and the walk itself, tilted and unsteady, like a yacht with its sails askew, turns into an adventure of pure will. This is a mischievous, startlingly candid performance, almost a confession. McKellen is the most supremely conscious of Richards, an adventurer playing the cards that have been dealt him—physical deformity, intellectual superiority—without illusions. There are wonderful spurts of gaiety, including a great moment when McKellen dances up a narrow staircase in sheer jubilation. But there is little egotism and certainly no vanity. This Richard is onto everybody, especially himself. He does what he does because he can get away with it, playing the game to its final moments with a melancholy acceptance of his fate.

The battle scenes at the end are a shambles, but generally director Richard Loncraine works in a rapid-tableau style; that is, he uses realistic settings in a theatrical manner, pushing beyond realism, but not too far. The Americans (Annette Bening and Robert Downey Jr.) aren't very good, but Jim Broadbent, in a morning coat, is a plumply unctuous Buckingham, and Maggie Smith gets her blood up in a brief appearance as Richard's censorious mom. The movie has spirit, if not always sanity. One can feel the exhilaration of people doing something slightly experimental for a good-sized audience. *This Richard III* is not serious or essential, but it's thoroughly alive.

NEW YORK POST, 12/29/95, p. 39, Michael Medved

Why waste time with Oliver Stone's "Nixon' when Ian McKellen's "Richard III" can introduce you to the original Tricky Dick?

Actually, McKellen (as producer, screenwriter and star) takes the sort of liberties with the historical background of his project that even Stone wouldn't try—shifting scheming King Richard's brief, bloody reign from the 1480s to the 1930s.

In this audacious (and often outrageous) adaptation of Shakespeare's play, the embattled monarch delivers his famous line, "A horse! A horse! My kingdom for a horse!" when his jeep gets stuck in mud; as he finally plunges to a fiery death (from the girder of an uncompleted high rise!) the soundtrack blares with the sound of Al Jolsen crooning "I'm sittin' on top of the world!"

At the other end of the movie, Richard delivers part of his opening soliloquy (Now is the winter of our discontent ...") while relieving himself at a urinal, and his cruelly abused queen, Lady Anne (Kristin Scott Thomas) escapes her sorrows by injecting heroin into her shapely, silk-stockinged thigh. When Richard (with his Hitlerian moustache) seizes the throne, he and his supporters sport the menacing black uniforms, gleaming jackboots and bloody red banners of classical fascism.

In short, those who like their Shakespeare straight and respectful will despise this odd experiment, while those of more adventurous kidney should find it invigorating, original and electrifying—generally succeeding in its an aura of timelessness to its story.

Director Richard Loncraine ("The Wedding Gift," "Brimstone and Treacle") uses his swooping, circling, energetically artistic camera to capture a wealth of dazzling 1930s details—showing the sleek, gorgeous costumes and uniforms, elegant modern interiors, antique limousines and airplanes and trains and tanks, as stylishly as they've ever been captured before.

The visual storytelling is so superb, in fact, that Shakespeare's lines at times come as almost a distraction—which is a shame, because the splendidly virile McKellen and his co-stars have a magnificent feel for this musical, poetic language that is sorely lacking in other recent productions (like the Fishburne/ Branagh "Othello," for instance.)

The radical surgery to the text (cut down to much less than half its original length) also undermines the teeming richness of the play, reducing the remainder to one utterly fascinating, brilliantly played central character (McKellen) and a series of grisly, graphic murders—that plays like "Richard's Greatest Hits."

The supporting cast, even with trimmed parts, is impressive—especially Kristin Scott Thomas as Richard's doomed queen, Maggie Smith as his horrified mother, and Jim Broadbent as his co-conspirator Buckingham. Annette Bening is effective as the previous queen (married to Richard's brother) and Robert Downey Jr. plays Bening's brother, Rivers, as a callow playboy; both these characters are played here is Americans, to emphasize the fact that they're outsiders at court.

In sum, the move is a far cry from Olivier's faithful, authentic, magnificently colorful (and perhaps definitive) "Richard III" of 1955, but no one will be bored for a moment while watching it. This may not be good Shakespeare, but it is a riveting and wildly original work of cinema.

NEWSDAY, 12/29/95, Part II/p. 3, John Anderson

There are Shakespeare adaptations—the new "Othello" is one—that beg comparison to previous work. This isn't bad, necessarily, just inevitable. Conversely, there are Shakespeare adaptations that, for whatever reason, set their own standard. Richard Loncraine's "Richard III" is one of these.

Set in a not-so-fantastical '30s London, where power is taken at gunpoint and palaces are crawling with blackshirts, Loncraine's film is a pulp-fictional, post-nuclear take on Shakespeare's most malevolent monarch, who dispatches rivals with a bullet or a plot but arrives on the throne bloodsoaked and dissatisfied.

This is the gist of Richard's character, which is as malformed as his body. And whether or not one is the cause of the other, his thirst is never quenched.

Loncraine, whose previous films include "Brimstone and Treacle" and "The Wedding Gift," has never inspired awe, and doesn't here. The power of his "Richard III" lies in the stage adaptation by Richard Eyre (director of Broadway's current "Racing Demon"), which reworks the classic lines and scenes into quite palatable updates and innovations (Richard's "winter of our discontent" speech, for instance, is delivered as a public political address; later, he plots disorder at a urinal, noticing his audience only after he's glanced in the bathroom mirror.)

And then there is the performance by Ian McKellen, something devilish and delicious. His is an unctuous, squirming Richard, whose seduction of Lady Anne (the glorious Kristin Scott Thomas), the widow of his first victim, is as amazing a thing to watch as it's ever been, and whose sociopathic bloodlust is equally appalling. But he's an ingratiating villain regardless; such singleness of purpose demands at least some admiration.

The cast is something of a split personality. There is standup work by Jim Broadbent (Buckingham), Nigel Hawthorne (Clarence) and Maggie Smith (Richard's mother, the Duchess of York) as well as John Wood as Edward IV and Adrian Dunbar as Richard's hitman, James Tyrell. But while it may sound snobbish—or, God forbid, Anglophilic—I find that when American actors are cast among English in a Shakespeare production, the melody goes flat whenever the Americans open their mouths. Annette Bening, as the victimized Queen Elizabeth, fares better than most, giving a performance that lacks nothing in resolve, only in music. Robert Downey Jr., as her brother, Earl Rivers, fares less well. He's not bad, really. It's just that the film might have been flawless if those concerned had been less concerned with marketable American names.

"Richard" certainly overcomes these handicaps, which are more like hiccups in the great scheme of things. Loncraine adds nice flourishes—the gas mask whose wheeze ominously drowns out the gunfire, for example—and some moments that are delightfully over the top—such as the tank that bursts through a wall in the opening battle. It's McKellen, though, who commands the field, albeit with rotting nobility and a diseased soul. Like the swing version of Marlowe's "Come live with me and be my love ..." (which is heard at the film's early grand ballroom scene) his "Richard III" is a mischievous piece of work that winks as it blows us away.

NEWSWEEK, 1/29/96, p. 58, Jack Kroll

The great thing about "Richard III" is that unlike your usual Shakespearean film it's been completely reimagined as a movie. It's also fun, which is after all what those 16th-century groundlings were having at the Globe. Star Ian McKellen and director Richard Loncraine have set the story of the deformed, abominable Richard in 1930s England, with Richard's followers garbed in the black-shirted gear of Sir Oswald Mosley's Fascists. Loncraine gives you true movie visuals and rhythms as Richard rises to power, polishing off all the men, women and children in his way, in an England of art deco and prewar tensions. The modernizations are intelligently impudent: the opening speech ("Now is the winter of our discontent") is delivered by Richard (McKellen) at a posh hotel party, finishing the great soliloquy in the men's room. It works. The scene in which Richard persuades Anne, the widow of one of his victims, to marry him takes place in a morgue, with Anne (stunning Kristin Scott Thomas) lamenting over her husband's corpse. It works.

A great cast (Maggie Smith, Annette Bening, Robert Downey Jr., John Wood) delivers Shakespeare's words as both poetry and true conversation. The film reminds us that the Bard was the Oliver Stone of his day, creating a portrait of Richard that scholars have disputed ever since. You half expect McKellen to look into the camera and say, "Ages shall marvel at my devious ways/And none but I be known as Tricky Dick." Purists will cavil—or choke—and not everything works, but this film does more than rough justice to its source—including McKellen's portrait of a man who tries to redeem his deformed body by deforming his soul.

SIGHT AND SOUND, 5/96, p. 58, Lizzie Francke

England, the 1930s. With a bloody civil war over, Edward IV succeeds to the throne. His American wife Elizabeth and his three children are installed in the palace. Edward's younger brother, the military-minded Richard, however, plots to take over. First he seduces and marries Lady Anne, whose husband he killed in the war. Then, with the help of the Duke of Buckingham and aide James Tyrell, he orders the murder of his elder brother Clarence. Hearing the news of Clarence's death and believing himself responsible, Edward dies. As the two young princes are not yet old enough to succeed to the throne, Queen Elizabeth's brother Earl Rivers is put in power. But he too is soon despatched by Richard's henchmen.

Richard becomes Lord Protector, and orders that the young princes be locked up in the Tower. With the Prime Minister Lord Hastings dead also by Richard's hand—he secures the crown for himself. In order to strengthen his position, he has the young princes murdered, while also killing his wife Anne. Opposition to Richard grows with Henry Richmond, in exile in France, offering to lead the dissenting forces. The Queen Mother goes to join him, so disenchanted is she with her son. Richard tells Elizabeth that he wants to marry her daughter, the princess Elizabeth. This she refuses to agree to and swiftly arranges for her daughter to marry Richmond. Buckingham defects to Richmond's side as well. Richard goes to war with Richmond and is shot in battle.

As the current Shakespeare screen cycle moves into high gear, with the recent *Othello* plus imminent movies of *Hamlet* and *A Midsummer Night's Dream*, Richard Loncraine's reworking of Richard Eyre and Ian McKellen's stage production of *Richard III* proves to be the most dynamic seen in a while, easily demonstrating that film adaptations of Shakespeare can achieve a cinematic excellence. Even if it is a little obvious, the 1930s setting is welcome, giving the play's analysis of a power-broking despot some contemporary political resonances, with Richard rallying a disaffected proletariat to his cause (represented by the plain-speaking James Tyrell). At a trimmed-down 103 minutes, it makes for a chilling thriller, in which Richard's bottled spider's dream of totalitarian rule gradually comes true as he crushes those in his way. It is sure to delight many a school Shakespeare student dreading something more leaden.

Undoubtedly McKellen is the main attraction. He plays the gnarled wannabe King as a moustachioed, crooked-toothed spiv of a villain (with a touch of Dennis Hopper-style psychosis). He can beguile those around him, but not the audience, who are privy to his foul acts and his to-camera expostulations. But then again, even the viewer might be lulled by McKellen's solicitous delivery as he ensnares his victims with rhetoric. The performance is so successful that whenever Loncraine seeks to enhance it, it seems like too much. McKellen's slithering and snarling is disconcerting enough without, for example, the further emphasis on the bestial provided when he is imagined wearing a boar's head.

McKellen's robust physicality here takes him plausibly through a swashbuckling battle finale that wouldn't look out of place in some war-adventure. The "A horse! A horse! My kingdom for a horse!" speech delivered while riding a tank does jar—but its fame would hamper any interpretation. The cast's command of the text is mostly exemplary—words just slip out. In this respect *Richard III* shows how important it is that these Shakespearean cinema enterprises use actors from a classical theatre background, who are at ease with the complex phrasing. In the months of Kristin Scott Thomas, Maggie Smith, Jim Broadbent and Nigel Hawthorne, Shakespeare's language is at its vibrant best, giving conviction to the modern setting. This is not so much the case with Annette Bening, who spits out her iambic pentameters clumsily as Queen Elizabeth. One wonders why this co-production couldn't find an American star with more of an ear for Shakespeare's linguistic intricacies.

Richard III is a film to listen to as much as to watch (which sometimes makes Trevor Jones' crashing score in seem irritatingly superfluous), but it doesn't rely entirely on the measured pleasures of the text. Tony Burrough's design is perhaps the most imaginative and atmospheric use of locations in a British movie for a while. Cinematographer Peter Biziou's tight framing reinvents various bits of familiar architecture in a way that's arguably more aesthetically satisfying than the lavishly built sets or computer-generated scenery that a higher budget film might have demanded. With these strengths, *Richard III* turns the heritage theme-park version of Britain upside-down. The king's gothic and baroque old court is created with shots of St Pancras Station and the Royal Pavilion Brighton, while Richard's brave new fascistic world finds a home in the Shell Building. County Hall doubles for a grim new Tower of London, while the hollowed-out Battersea Power Station provides the battleground for the apocalyptic finale.

The damned state of Richard's nation—in which decadence and modernism go hand-in-hand—is measured by such details as Scott-Thomas' despairing Queen Anne smoking rolled up fivers, her alabaster arms covered with a junkie's bruises. Or King Edward listening to ragtime while inspecting photographs of an execution. Dominic West's clean-cut Richmond comes along like a heroic Kenneth Moore bent on liberating his country from the blackshirts. But the curl of the lip as he triumphantly smiles to camera suggests that corruption and privilege will continue. Shakespeare's critique of power does not wear thin.

TIME, 1/15/96, p. 67, Richard Corliss

Sex? Violence? We got em for you, and in the King's English. As every teacher knows, kids won't touch Shakespeare unless he is made all hot and gaudy and R-rated. So let's get with it, moviemakers! If the Bard writes about a Moor who loves a Venetian lady, show them naked in bed together, and have Iago woo Emilia from the rear. If the subject is villainy on a royal scale, as in *Richard III,* cram the screen with ingenious murders. Everyone says that if Shakespeare were alive today, he'd have been a screenwriter. But would he be Joe Eszterhas? Would he have shown one of his characters enjoying fellatio—then gasping in horror as a saber, thrust upward by an assassin hiding under the bed, suddenly emerges through the victim's stomach?

Actually, that murder, in the new film of *Richard III,* offers a cleverer twist on the orgasmic affinity of love and death than any devised by Eszterhas for *Basic Instinct.* It has the added jolt of literary blasphemy, like hearing a Tupac Shakur lyric sung in Westminster Abbey. Melodrama in Shakespeare? How awful, how scabrous, how very ... appropriate, since Will was a man of the theater who gloried in the trappings of stage sensation. And because Richard III and Iago are the two scurviest, most seductive villains in the canon, it is right for directors to find a movie equivalent, in images and action, for Shakespeare's pulsing poetry and Elizabethan bloodlust.

Oliver Parker's *Othello* is the more standard of the two, a solid reading that pulls out the stops on an easily played organ. This is, after all, a soap opera of the had-I-but-known variety. All the Moor has to do is ask his wife's servant, "Pray, did thee swipe fair Desdemona's hankie?" and the misunderstanding is resolved as smoothly as any episode of *Home Improvement.* But then there would be little allurement in the role for some of this century's most dominant actors.

That Orson Welles and Laurence Olivier both donned blackface in famous film versions doesn't mean no one else should try. Parker had the radical idea to cast a black man as Othello, and Laurence Fishburne brings an outsider's dignity to the role of Shakespeare's noblest chump. Irene Jacob is a lovely, sallow Desdemona, and Kenneth Branagh—looking bloated and rheumy, slithering snakelike on rooftops, whispering his venomous gossip as if it's his last confession—makes a fine Iago, a demi-devil working his cool wit to destroy those he might have loved.

Richard III, as conceived by actor Ian McKellen and director Richard Loncraine, is one bold customer. Here is Shakespeare's upper-class mass murderer reimagined as a clever fascist in the court of Edward VIII. The 1930s was a decade of ruthless strongmen, in both European politics and Hollywood movies. Gangsters, mesmerizing in their amoral ambition, were the men of the moment; they lent a sick thrill to the front page and entertainment section. This Richard is such a fellow, Hitler as Scarface. From the opening titles, which explode in a blast of artillery, to the closing image of Richard laughing on his way to a fiery hell, this is not just Shakespeare played on film. It is all movie—fully as cinematic as its clear antecedents in the killer-comedy genre, *Kind Hearts and Coronets* and *Dr. Strangelove.*

Not a word of the text is spoken until nearly 10 minutes into the film, when Richard delivers his "winter of our discontent" speech, in part to the triumphant house of York, in part to us in the audience as he urinates. Glamour and squalor, the blood of aristocrats and the mud of wild boars, are contrasted, then mixed as the corpses pile up in this Deco Armageddon. The movie, set in the Machine Age—tanks, motorcycles, machine guns—even finds a way to justify Richard's cry, "My kingdom for a horse!" A cast of British stage royalty (Maggie Smith, Nigel Hawthorne, John Wood) and Hollywood stars (Annette Bening and an overmatched Robert Downey Jr.) lend their eminence to the swank carnage. But it's all McKellen's show. He struts and purrs, swats underlings with his mummy's paw of a left hand, dies as uncontritely as he killed. Film and performance go withered hand in glove, with chutzpah to spare.

If Europe in the '30s seems too remote, consider Richard of Gloucester as the evil twin to Richard of Whittier. As a satanic conniver, McKellen combines the darkest dreams of the 37th U.S. President and his Secretary of State. He has the hunched posture of the cartoonist's Nixon, the brutal statecraft of the conspiracy theorist's Henry Kissinger. This movie is the fetid, enthralling goods, the Nixon that Oliver Stone didn't quite dare to make.

VILLAGE VOICE, 1/2/96, p. 52, Georgia Brown

Two tricky Dicks in one season. Two poisonous bunch-backed toads. In *Nixon*, Oliver Stone strives for Shakespearean heights and falls on his macduff, *Nixon* would've been better off as comedy, which it inadvertently is. Shakespeare's *Richard III* isn't strictly a comedy, but its demonic hero, blithely murdering his way to the top, is a macabre joker, a wacky monster whose exploits are so preposterous one ought to at least get some laughs. Stone's quaking Dick of Whittier could use some of Richard III's fire, his bullying, shameless nerve (if any trait defined Nixon, it was shameless nerve).

This isn't to say that I like Ian McKellen's performance as Richard III. Actually, I rather loathe it. The malignancy is too suave, too cool, and humorless despite the film's rollicking, put-on style. Olivier's crookback was much more fun. Springtime for Gloucester: that's the tone of this manic, stripped-down *Richard*. A jazzy jazz-age farce set in some vague prewar forever-England, it proposes to describe a 20th-century facist's rise and fall.

The whambang, nearly wordless opening has tour de force written all over it. It starts off at the King's battlefield headquarters at Tewksbury, as a ticket tape announces that Gloucester's forces are closing in. The old king, dressed as a 20th-century British officer, retires for the night; his son, an officer, too, prepares to tuck into his evening meal. Suddenly, rumbles, and a tank crashes through the wall. One lurching soldier in a gas mask—his labored breathing magnified like Darth Vader's—shoots the prince in the middle of his forehead, and then, point blank, his father. Peels off the mask. Guess who.

Flash forward to the York family's victory celebration in London—a luxurious ball. A big-band singer dips into a fetching "Come live with me and be my love and we will all those pleasures prove ..." Meanwhile, we're being visually introduced to the convivial Yorks: the new king, Edward IV (John Wood), his coolly beautiful queen, Elizabeth (Annette Bening), her foppish, late-arriving brother, Earl Rivers (Robert Downey Jr.), Edward's brother Clarence (Nigel Hawthorne), and the imposing mother of Edward, Clarence, and Richard, the Duchess of York (Maggie Smith). As one of the party's hosts, Richard suddenly strides to the bandstand, cuts off the music, takes the mike, taps it, and begins: "Now is the winter of our discontent ..."

Without missing a beat, he picks up the soliloquy as he ducks into the men's room, pisses into a urinal, peers into the mirror while washing his hand. Finally, spotting the camera behind, he whirls and winds up his monologue directly into our faces. Dazzling? Outrageous? Dumb?

Besides the hump on his back, the withered arm, and limp, McKellen has a Ronald Colman mustache and looks as if he takes a haircut every other day. He looks as if he reeks of cologne. After seeing the naive Clarence off to the tower, he woos the slinky, doped-up Anne (Kristin Scott Thomas) in the morgue, over her husband's corpse (he's the first man Richard killed above). The next time we see Anne she will be back on Richard's arm, wearing red, not black. After ordering the murders of her brother (Clarence, his brother-in-law Rivers, his two nephews (the famous princes in the tower), and an adviser, Hastings (Jim Carter), Richard will also get rid of Anne.

Everything about this *Richard III* is crisp, snappy, self-infatuated, and meticulously color-coded. (Several scenes feature conspicuous gashes of red.) McKellen and Richard Loncraine's screenplay is a radical abridgment (obviously), with several touches like making Elizabeth and her brother Americans, Anne a druggie, and Tyrell (Adrian Dunbar), Richard's trusted hit man, a smooth, nice-looking enlisted man (illustrating the banality of evil, no doubt). The most outrageous scene may be Rivers's impalement on a knife thrusting up through the mattress just as a whore in a pillbox hat sucks him off.

Sets are all lavish and meant to be startling: Edward's Victorian palaces, Richard's deco lair, marble Third-Reichian halls; the Tower is a faceless '30s-modern structure and the Battle of Bosworth takes place in sight of the Battersea Power Station. In one scene, Richard reclines on a divan perusing photos of the hanged Hastings (in the play there was Hastings's head to contemplate) while on a nearby coffee table sits a giant urn full of candied almonds. Known mainly for clever, overdesigned works—*Brimstone and Treacle* (from a Dennis Potter play) and *Bellman and True*—director Loncraine is listed in production notes as having directed 420 commercials. He's skillful. *Richard III* is designed to be *The Conformist*, part II.

Using first-rate actors, the movie succeeds in establishing, in a few amusing visual strokes, certain subsidiary characters like the sweetly oblivious Clarence or the opportunistic Buckingham (the wonderful Jim Broadbent would make a great Kissinger). When Richard's supporters start wearing Gestapo-type uniforms, Buckingham puts on the fanciest black-and-silver braid, whereas the modest, principled Lord Stanley remains in an old-fashioned dusty blue.

Comparisons to Hitler get more blatant (the boar's-head flag, resembles the Nazis') but don't really go anywhere. (Where can they go?) As the story of one warped man's ruthless rise, this is a simple tale of fear: Everyone's afraid of Richard, and Richard, like Stone's Nixon, is afraid of his mum. When the stern duchess curses him, his face momentarily falls. And when he goes down to Jolson belting, "I'm sitting on top of the world," we're meant to think of Cagney, Robinson, and Muni—all the little Caesars.

McKellen seems to be having a whale of a time. So why don't I have fun watching him? His Richard is such an aggressive, camera-hogging smoothie, I felt stifled, could hardly wait to make my getaway. Flashy and lurid, this *Richard*, like *Nixon*, is a wild bore.

Also reviewed in:
CHICAGO TRIBUNE, 1/19/96, Friday/p. H, Michael Wilmington
NEW REPUBLIC, 2/12/96, p. 30, Stanley Kauffmann
NEW YORK TIMES, 12/29/95, p. C3, Stephen Holden
NEW YORKER, 1/22/96, p. 86, Terrence Rafferty
VARIETY, 1/1-7/96, p. 81, Godfrey Cheshire

RIFT

A Curb Entertainment International release of an Off-Screen Productions production. *Executive Producer:* Edward S. Barkin and Gabriel J. Fischbarg. *Producer:* Gabriel J. Fischbarg, Edward S. Barkin and Tryan George. *Director:* Edward S. Barkin. *Screenplay:* Edward S. Barkin. *Director of Photography:* Lee Daniel. *Editor:* Tryan George. *Music:* Tryan George and Eric Masunaga. *Sound:* Felix Andrew. *Production Designer:* Mark C. Andrews. *Costumes:* Karin Bereson. *Running time:* 87 minutes. *MPAA Rating:* Not Rated.

CAST: William Sage (Tom); Timothy Cavanaugh (Bill); Jennifer Bransford (Lisa); Alan Davidson (Dr. Myron Messers).

NEW YORK POST, 6/2/95, p. 50, Bill Hoffmann

"Rift" is about the angst of being twentysomething in New York City and finding yourself hopelessly in love with your best friend's wife.

That's the predicament Tom (William Sage) is faced with as he pals around with his buddy Bill (Timothy Cavanaugh) by day and lusts after Bill's wife, Lisa (Jennifer Bransford), by night.

Tom is a fledgling writer of heavy-metal rock tunes, who, when he's not composing, lies around dropping acid and dreaming of Lisa.

Opportunity knocks when Bill and Lisa's marriage crumbles.

Should Tom act on his simmering lust? Does Lisa feel the same way about him? And what, if anything, should he tell Bill?

First-time director Edward Barkin explores these issues in this occasionally interesting, low-budget soap opera, which ultimately fails to click.

Too often, "Rift" falls into the category of ambitious but cliched student film.

The movie employs a psychobabblish narrative by lead character Tom that doesn't really work. And Tom's spooky dreams—repeated ad nauseam—smack of a student filmmaker desperately trying be artsy.

Barkin—who adapted the script from a play he wrote as a Yale student—knows how to let all three characters argue and brood. But we never really know enough about these people to see why they're friends in first place.

It's also difficult to imagine Tom's insatiable lust for Lisa, who comes off more or less as a self-absorbed, spoiled brat. And the shy and sensitive Tom's friendship with the loud and guttural Bill seems forced.

Midway through, Barkin adds a fourth character, a "Twilight Zone"ish psychiatrist who counsels—and confuses—Tom. The shrink only muddles the proceedings further—and pushes the film into a fast and unfulfilling conclusion.

I guess yuppie love isn't always easy, but it's got to be more compelling than "Rift" makes it out to be.

NEWSDAY, 6/2/95, Part II/p. B7, Gene Seymour

Ever wonder what boomers and slackers would do without the refrigerator? It's given just about every kid who was born after World War II something to stare at when television's too distracting. One of the characters in "Rift" has gone beyond just staring. He makes himself a sandwich inside, using all the available shelves. Even the formality of slicing the tomato is dispensed with. He just rips the sucker apart and tosses it on the bread.

That's one of the funnier bits in "Rift," which, like the fridge, is something chilly that you stare at for a while, surveying its interesting, if mostly lifeless, contents, wondering if there's a morsel worth savoring.

To be fair, there's more than a morsel. This first film by writer-director Edward S. Barkin, which premiered two years ago at the Sundance Film Festival, delivers some of the deadpan wit of Hal Hartley and Richard Linklater. Barkin also aspires to—and occasionally achieves—a funky surrealism that jumps and twitches to a pleasantly off-kilter rhythm. You hope that someday he'll use these gifts to tell stories about interesting people.

No such luck here. "Rift's" love triangle consists of a mope (William Sage from Hartley's "Simple Men"), a dope (Timothy Cavanaugh) and a simp (Jennifer Bransford). Tom (mope) is a rock musician who's imbibed so much acid that have nightmares. The big one is that his best buddy, Bill (dope), is going to kill him over his wife Lisa (simp), with whom Tom spends many of his waking hours in purely platonic bliss. The thing is, Tom really does carry a torch for Lisa. But he's too blocked to confide this to his shrink (Alan Davidson), who *also* seems to have a thing for Lisa.

It's a conventional story that Barkin strives too hard to tell unconventionally through a series of dream sequences, elliptical flashbacks and jump cuts. Such nervous pyrotechnics are usually part of the charm of rookie feature films. But one senses that Barkin is using his technical facility to cover up the lapses in his story instead of smoothing them out. He tries to create surprises that neither his plot nor his characters earn. Only the sinister therapist leaves a strong impression, both as a figment of Tom's imagination and as a suave tease.

VILLAGE VOICE, 6/6/95, p. 58, Abby McGanney Nolan

Tom (William Sage of *Simple Men)* is a blocked songwriter living off the dwindling royalties of a heavy metal tune called "Days of Pain." He's also the tortured third wheel to Bill (Timothy Cavanaugh), his oafish best friend, and Bill's pretty wife, Lisa (Jennifer Bransford). As he explains the third-wheel dynamic, "The other two people do something. You basically watch them do it ... Or watch Lisa."

Opening with a dark, dank dream sequence, *Rift* announces itself as an arty psychological portrait of a man consumed by guilt and longing. It follows through with more nightmares, slo-mo flashbacks, hallucinations, and even a menacing psychiatrist. Thankfully, first-time director Barkin also keeps dropping in humorous twists on the psychodrama formula. His cinematographer, rising indie star Lee Daniel *(Dazed and Confused)*, provides a fluid counterpoint to the shifting script.

Barkin gets good performances from his cast, especially Sage as the out-of-it introvert who spends much of his time lying in bed trying to separate his dream life from his real one. Cavanaugh, as the underachieving broker from Bayside, creates a memorable jerk you might actually end up feeling sorry for. Playing two extremes—a dream girl gliding through wordless flashbacks and a rather shrewish philanderer—Bransford doesn't get a whole lot to work with. It's not altogether clear why Tom would fall so hard for Lisa. *Rift* also suffers at times for its non-action orientation, but the spell is never completely broken.

Also reviewed in:
NEW YORK TIMES, 6/2/95, p. C14, Stephen Holden
VARIETY, 2/8/93, p. 75, Joe Leydon

RIVER OF GRASS

A Strand Releasing release of a Plan B Pictures presentation. *Producer:* Jesse Hartman. *Director:* Kelly Reichardt. *Screenplay:* Kelly Reichardt. *Story:* Kelly Reichardt and Jesse Hartman. *Director of Photography:* Jim Denault. *Editor:* Larry Fessenden. *Sound:* Matthew Sigal. *Production Designer:* David Doernberg. *Costumes:* Sara Slotnick. *Running time:* 80 minutes. *MPAA Rating:* Not Rated.

CAST: Lisa Bowman (Cozy); Larry Fessenden (Lee); Dick Russell (Jimmy Ryder).

LOS ANGELES TIMES, 10/13/95, Calendar/p. 16, Kevin Thomas

First-time writer-director Kelly Reichardt's "River of Grass," a winner about losers, evokes the tired lovers-on-the-run genre only to stand it on its head and shake out of it fresh meanings and humor.

At every turn, Reichardt confounds predictability, confronting us with the awful banality of many people's everyday lives rather than providing her characters with an escape from it. Yet Reichardt is so agile, ingenious and funny that she can make a lively, entertaining movie about how life isn't like the movies.

Lisa Bowman stars as Cozy, a 30ish mother of three who lives in a drab suburb of Florida's Broward County with her police detective father Jimmy (Dick Russell) and her dull husband. Cozy, who also narrates in a flat, affectless voice, becomes so overcome by her awareness of her loneliness, she dresses up one Friday night and heads for a local bar, where she meets Lee (Larry Fessenden). He's a man her age, an equally lonely layabout who also grew up in a broken home and who's at last been thrown out of the house he's shared his entire life with his grandmother and mother. Sheer chance has thrust a gun in Lee's hands.

Cozy and Lee could scarcely be more ordinary. Everything about them, starting with their appearance, is average. They lack the skills, financial security and opportunity to live anything but the bleakest existence.

But in crossing paths they ignite within each other the possibility of a life of freedom and adventure. Circumstances lead them to believe they could be killers on the lam, but they're essentially decent people capable of being thrown by the lack of a quarter at a toll gate. They haven't a clue as to how to be a Bonnie or Clyde.

The workings of fate, so crucial to the genre Reichardt is sending up, become for her a source of rueful humor, and she's blessed with a cameraman in Jim Denault able to help her immeasurably in sustaining the film's dry sense that life is always going to be off kilter for Cozy and Lee, played selflessly by Bowman and Fessenden.

In the film's other key role, Russell captures perfectly the sense of defeat experienced by Jimmy, a handsome man and onetime professional jazz drummer now in his paunchy, disillusioned 50s, Reichardt's own summing up of her movie couldn't be better: "A road movie without the road, a love story without the love and crime story without the crime."

NEW YORK POST, 8/4/95, p. 45, Bill Hoffmann

There are two Floridas in this country. There's the one of pristene, sun-swept beaches and perfectly tanned, beautiful people that the tourist boards like to promote.

Then there's the Florida of Kelly Reichardt's atmospheric new film, "River of Grass": a dismal state of down-and-out drifters, welfare moms, low-rent housing, fast-food strips and crime.

In other words: Poor White Trash Central.

In this depressing, but intriguing environment, lives 30-year-old Cozy, a bored and bothered mother of two, desperate to escape her dismal life in a tiny house on a barren stretch between Miami and the Florida Everglades.

She's sick to death of her husband who holds down a go-nowhere job at a local restaurant and her dad, an alcoholic cop who spends nights drinking gin and reliving his heyday as an after-hours jazz drummer.

Cozy (Lisa Bowman) gets her chance to bolt one night when she visits the local watering hole and meets Lee (Larry Fessenden), a thirtysomething slacker who lives uneasily with his mother and grandmother and desperately wants his own out.

When he and Cozy decide to go "pool hopping" around town, their bland lives are turned topsy-turvy when Lee takes a shot at a homeowner with a gun.

Believing they've killed the man, the pair go on the lam, shacking up in cheap motels and eating on the run.

Through a much-too-convenient plot twist, the smoking gun turns out to be the lost service revolver of Cozy's dad, who joins in a police manhunt for the broke pair as they try to get out of their impossible predicament.

As written and directed by New Yorker Reichardt, "River of Grass" has many faults. The script isn't all that believable and characters are too weakly drawn to be very compelling.

But the atmosphere she creates is real—sometimes a little too real for comfort.

Shooting on a shoestring budget, Reichardt—a Miami native who now lives in the East Village—portrays Florida as hell, a paradise long lost, a relocation spot for losers, a place, anybody with half-a-brain will avoid.

Her unflinching cameras show us the Sunshine State without filters, without makeup, without an MTV soundtrack and a glass of Tropicana.

It's this unnerving picture that gives "River of Grass" its strength, carrying it over its amateurish veneer.

It would be difficult to wholeheartedly recommend "River of Grass," but as a cinematic exercise in creating a moody, on-the-edge environment, it hits the bull's eye.

VILLAGE VOICE, 8/8/95, p. 48, Amy Taubin

"Cinema is a girl and a gun," quipped the youthful essentialist Jean-Luc Godard. Director-writer Kelly Reichardt may have had Godard on the brain when she made *River of Grass,* but I doubt that Cozy, her depressive protagonist, is the femme (fatale or otherwise) the master had in mind. Not even when she's nervously gripping her Dad's pistol with one hand and steering the car wheel with the other.

As played by Lisa Bowman, Cozy is a slightly pudgy 30-year-old with a discouraged face and thin little voice that's not quite up to the spoken narration the film has her carry. Haunted by a mother who abandoned her (and who she fantasizes ran off to join the circus) as well as by the previous owner of the house where she lives with her husband and their two children (said previous owner having murdered her husband and walled him up in the shower), Cozy practices pirouettes on the front lawn and preens like a tightrope walker about to make an ascent.

It's not a rope that Cozy has to walk but a line—the straight line that her police detective father describes as the law: "No man can stand with a foot on either side." And there's another line—between Florida's Broward and Dade counties—that Cozy crosses and recrosses without getting more than a couple of miles in either direction.

Reichardt has constructed a fragile but tough-minded, elliptically edited film with images and metaphors as condensed and over-determined as a dream. After impulsively walking out on her children, Kelly wonders whether her mother's life created her destiny or did one thing just lead to another? In its unassuming way, *River of Grass* is a meditation on free will versus determinism. Does a series of little things that get under a woman's skin turn her one day into a murderer? Maybe not.

Cozy dispiritedly bonds with Lee (Larry Fessenden), a 30-year-old slacker type who seems as tired as she does and looks a little like the young Jack Nicholson though minus a couple of front teeth. The two of them get into an accident with her father's gun. Convinced that they've killed someone, they try to take it on the lam but lack the energy, not to mention the loose change, to get past the first toll booth.

On the comedic level, *River of Grass* is about the failure of movie myths—it's an anti-*Bonnie and Clyde*. But more pressingly, it's about female subjectivity—about the rage that's born of loss. The women chafe against domesticity more than the men do.

Cozy's father gave up his career as a jazz drummer so he could make a regular salary and raise his kid. Cozy's husband works in a restaurant, and even Lee offers to settle down and get a job or two to make the rent. No matter how dreary those jobs are, they get you out of the house. It's being stuck at home with the kids that drives the women to cross the line.

Evocatively shot by Jim Denault, *River of Grass* is also a landscape movie. The "river of grass" is the Florida Everglades, pictured here as a thinly populated outpost of soggy fields, prefab ranch houses, tawdry bars, used record stores, and cheap motels. If the film has a flaw, it's that the landscape seems a little too real for the performances. And in turn, the performances seem a little too gentle for what we know about the territory. I kept wondering what Reichardt had done with the actual residents of Dade and Broward counties. *River of Grass* tries to be about a state of mind but sometimes the state of things gets in the way.

Also reviewed in:
CHICAGO TRIBUNE, 9/29/95, Friday/p. M, Michael Wilmington
NEW YORK TIMES, 8/4/95, p. C19, Stephen Holden
VARIETY, 2/7-13/94, p. 39, Todd McCarthy

ROB ROY

A United Artists release of a Talisman production. *Executive Producer:* Michael Caton-Jones. *Producer:* Peter Broughan and Richard Jackson. *Director:* Michael Caton-Jones. *Screenplay:* Alan Sharp. *Director of Photography:* Karl Walter Lindenlaub. *Editor:* Peter Honess. *Music:* Carter Burwell. *Music Editor:* Adam Smalley. *Choreographer:* Gillian Barton. *Sound:* David John. *Sound Editor:* Richard King. *Casting:* Susie Figgis. *Production Designer:* Assheton Gorton. *Art Director:* John Ralph and Alan Tomkins. *Set Designer:* Toad Tozer. *Set Decorator:* Ann Mollo. *Special Effects:* Ulrich Nefzer. *Costumes:* Sandy Powell. *Make-up:* Morag Ross. *Stunt Coordinator:* Vic Armstrong. *Running time:* 134 minutes. *MPAA Rating:* R.

CAST: Liam Neeson (Rob Roy); Jessica Lange (Mary); John Hurt (Montrose); Tim Roth (Archie Cunningham); Eric Stoltz (McDonald); Andrew Keir (Argyll); Brian Cox (Killearn); Brian McCardie (Alasdair); Gilbert Martin (Guthrie); Vicki Masson (Betty); Gilly Gilchrist (Iain); Jason Flemyng (Gregor); Ewan Stewart (Coll); David Hayman (Sibbald); Brian McArthur (Ranald); David Palmer (Duncan); Myra McFadyen (Tinker Woman); Karen Matheson (Ceilidh Singer); Shirley Henderson (Morag); John Murtagh (Referee); Bill Gardner (Tavern Lad); Valentine Nwanze (Servant Boy); Richard Bonehill (Gutherie's Opponent).

FILMS IN REVIEW, 7-8/95, p. 60, Andy Pawelczak

Rob Roy, a costume drama directed by Michael Caton-Jones, is a kind of Scoftish Western. Instead of Monument Valley it has the Highlands, dotted with menhir-like rocks that throw a prehistoric, mythical shadow across the action. It also has cattle thieves, a bushwacking, a showdown in a tavern, and an unambiguously noble hero played in fine, tight-lipped fashion by the statuesque Liam Neeson. If not as stirring as *The Last of the Mohicans,* of which it reminded me with its Redcoats and blood-drenched action scenes, it still has some rousing moments and the most sublimely nasty villain since *Mohicans'* Magwa.

Rob Roy (Neeson) is the head of a clan that lives in pastoral simplicity. The clansmen are like sixties communalists with their beards, long hair and tartans and their closeness to nature. When they hold a celebration, they dance the Highland fling, a beautiful young woman, an eighteenth century Joan Baez, sings a sweet, traditional folk melody, and the whole thing makes you nostalgic for the mythical days of the Be-in. Rob, the first among equals, is a legend among his own small band—when he thwarts a gang of cattle thieves, we see a young man recount the story to a group of star-struck children. His marriage to Mary (Jessica Lange) is idyllic—at one point he sprinkles daisy petals on her slumbering body, and their lovemaking is pre-lapsarian. As Mary, Lange is an appropriate bonny lass for Neeson— she's a strong, maturely beautiful woman.

This almost Edenic paradise is disrupted when Rob is hornswoggled by a pair of evil aristocrats. As the Marquis of Montrose, John Hurt is decadence personified, surpassed only by Tim Roth as his protege, Archie Cunningham. Bewigged and made-up, they're reminiscent of Kubrick's aristocrats in *Barry Lyndon,* a parallel that Caton-Jones emphasizes with a Kubrickian overhead shot of a formal garden and a big climactic duel at the end of the movie. In the picture's moral universe, artifice equals evil and the natural equals good, a simple moral arithmetic that lends itself to easy visual representation in juxtaposed shots of the rugged Neeson and the outrageously effete, perpetually sneering Roth. Roth, who last appeared as the stickup man in the diner episodes of *Pulp Fiction,* is an underrated actor who doesn't have the right looks for leading-man roles but is possessed of protean abilities. As the foppish, sadistic Cunningham, he amazingly avoids campiness, and all but steals the picture from Lange and Neeson.

Michael Caton-Jones' direction is workmanlike if uninspired. His cross cutting of a brutal murder in a spooky forest with a joyous clan celebration is obvious but somehow it works, helped not a little by the Chieftains' wailing pipes on the soundtrack. The shots of the Highlands are picturesque, and sometimes more than that, suggesting time's mysteries and sanctities. Lange and Neeson give adult, intelligent performances, and Hurt, and particularly Roth, are like a forbidden delight. In not asking to be taken too seriously, the film achieves its own level of dignity and resonance. It's good, unpretentious fun.

LOS ANGELES TIMES, 4/7/95, Calendar/p. 1, Kenneth Turan

"Rob Roy" is one of those familiar names that everyone's heard but no one can quite place. The nickname (roy means red in Gaelic) of an 18th-Century Scottish Robin Hood named Robert MacGregor whose story was embroidered by novelist Sir Walter Scott, it makes for a dashing and romantic film title as well. But if you wanted to name this particular movie for its most interesting, charismatic and fully realized character, you'd have to call it "Archie."

This is not to take away more than is necessary from non-redhead Liam Neeson, who as the tallest guy in the picture is appropriately commanding as Rob, and Celtic as well into the bargain. The kilt-wearing leader of his fierce clan, Rob is never flustered and in fact rarely so much as blinks. Madly in love with his fiery wife, Mary (Jessica Lange), Rob has an unbending sense of honor that leads him into the messy conflicts with authority that are the film's plot pivots.

But although Scottish director Michael Caton-Jones takes pains to show what an active sex life Rob and Mary have (must be those darn kilts), their bucolic interludes are blandly unconvincing and they push "Rob Roy" in a stately, decorous direction that is no more than moderately satisfying.

When Archie Cunningham is on screen, watch out. As played by the riveting Tim Roth, featured in "Reservoir Dogs" and "Pulp Fiction" he is an arresting combination of dandy and brute.

First introduced as a mincing, effete fop with a taste for elaborate clothes and willing servant girls, Archie is gradually revealed as an icy sociopath filled with a rage at his lack of position in the social order. The more frightening he becomes, the more we see into his inner life, the harder it is not to wish that this film were more about him and less about Mr. and Mrs. Roy. Perhaps director Caton-Jones, whose most successful films ("Scandal," "This Boy's Life") have had a dark edge, secretly wished this as well.

In fact, when Roth's character is on screen, everyone's acting goes up a notch. Neeson's scenes with him, including a classic sword fight, are the star's best, and even John Hurt, who has a tendency to coast through films, gets himself involved as the vicious Marquis of Montrose, Cunningham's patron and Rob Roy's most powerful enemy.

When the film begins, Rob is in the service of the Marquis, hunting down those who would steal the great man's cattle. But once he and best friend Alan McDonald (a surprisingly well-cast Eric Stoltz) step outside their station and borrow money from the Marquis to acquire some cattle of their own, assorted evil-doers take notice and soon Rob is in terrible trouble.

Screenwriter Alan Sharp, also a Scot, with considerable experience in Hollywood (having written everything from Robert Aldrich's "Ulzana's Raid" to Arthur Penn's "Night Moves"), has ignored the Walter Scott novel and based his story loosely on the real Rob's history. Aside from throwing in too many twists and assuming a familiarity with rivalry for the British throne that most Americans do not have, his script underlines the difficulties that can unseat modern historical dramas.

One problem is that much of what marks this film as of the 1990s, things like raunchy sex jokes and an unhealthy amount of violence, are distancing rather than inviting. At the opposite end of the spectrum, except for Cunningham's character, attempts to bring a period verisimilitude to the dialogue have the same effect by making the actors themselves uncomfortable.

Jessica Lange brings her usual presence and skill to the role of the doughy Mary, but having to handle dialogue like "You know I love the bones of you, Robert MacGregor" would daunt almost anyone. As for Neeson, the script so overloads his character with homiletic wisdom like "Honor is what no man can give you and none can take away … Honor is a man's gift to himself" that he almost seems to be speaking in italics.

Working with cinematographer Karl Walter Lindenlaub, director Caton-Jones has given "Rob Roy" a beautiful wide-screen look, filled with gorgeous vistas. But this film is like a color Xerox copy of the real thing: hard to tell from an original until you look closely at the details.

NEW STATESMAN & SOCIETY, 5/26/95, p. 23, Lizzie Francke

There is something very earthy about *Rob Roy*—and it is not just the vast and mottled Highland landscape. It is one of those films that seems fixated on bodily processes as the Trossachs' folkhero, played by Liam Neeson, and his band of kilted men all too frequently mark their ground—a sure signal that they are establishing their natural territorial rights. It is big on sex too, with ripples of raw energy flashing between Rob Roy and his fiery wife Mary (Jessica Lange in remarkable form), which seem particularly combustible when they are near the odd standing stone—they don't even need to touch each other and you know that they are going to conceive. Certainly, it's one of the more robust depictions of married life to reach the screens recently, with Mary very much the partner, rather than just being a symbol of wifely virtue. These two are the fecund people of the land indeed—human-standing stones that defiantly stand their ground.

As such, Michael Caton-Jones' film, from a script by Alan Sharp (who also wrote two key films of the 1970s, *Nightmoves* and *Ulzana's Raid),* is a hefty monument to the man who became a myth and one of the staples of the Scottish tourist industry. Rob Roy Macgregor was the most famous cattle-drover of them all, who roamed the hills in the late 17th and early 18th centuries and both worked for and fought against the wily English landowners. As a Scottish Robin Hood of sorts, but one who, instead of green tights, wears a plaid kilt as red and rust and blue as the lochs and hills, he is the perfect romantic figure—the noble if sometimes savage outlaw whom both William Wordsworth and Walter Scott immortalised. A more rigorous scrutiny of his history might reveal a less than perfect record; for instance he was nowhere to be seen in the 1715 Jacobite uprising, but for romance's sake that makes him even more perfect. The myth of Rob Roy is about the triumph of the individual spirit rather than the sweaty stuff of revolution. That it can be safely constructed so is born out by the publicity blurb for the film, which pitches it as a story about one hero and how his "love for one woman gave him honour, courage and, ultimately, his life".

Revealingly, Scott described Rob Roy as "blending the wild virtues, the subtle policy and unrestrained licence of an American Indian". It is easy to see why parallels are being drawn between Rob Roy and Michael Mann's adaptation of James Fenimore Cooper's *The Last of the Mohicans*. Both stories chart a struggle between those whose rights to the land are seen as natural and inalienable and the English invaders who want to "tame" the Highland wilderness for their own ends. They are westerns in reverse. Soon to follow is *Braveheart*, Mel Gibson's fling at the Highland tale, in which he plays the 13th-century rebel William Wallace complete with becoming blue woad make-up and shaggy mop-top. Certainly hair is important in these films. Rob Roy has flowing, unkempt locks signalling him as a wildman of the people (and of the long-haired cattle—at one point he even hides in a cow's carcass). It is the kind of masculine ease with nature that Robert Bly has been banging on his drum about. Playing Rob Roy up to the kilt, Neeson stalks across the frame with a sinewy grace. He is the kind of actor who was born to chew the cud with bovine-style contemplation. Or at least that expression of fretful concern on his face that he moulded for Schindler cannot be so easily tossed away. Indeed, with Neeson in the role, there is every evidence that there is as much brain in that head to match the brawn. It is necessary to *Rob Roy*'s credentials as an up-market action movie.

Compared to the strapping Rob Roy, the English aristocrats (John Hurt's Marquis of Montrose) for whom he tends cattle, and his silk-slippery sidekick, the aptly named Archibald Cunningham (Tim Roth) are porcelain brittle fops whose power is manifest in their income rather than their physical stature. The casting of Hurt and Roth, who last played together as a vicious assassin and his protegé in *The Hit* (1984), brings to bear all sorts of underhand meanings. They are cruel and treacherous, but there is also a powdered and coiffed effeminacy to their characters. One only has to think of Hurt's Quentin Crisp. Meanwhile Roth, who plays Cunningham with a ruthless precision, claims to have modelled the character on a cross between Basil Rathbone, the king of dastards, and sit-com queen John Inman. Rob Roy and his clan might get away with wearing skirts but, for the aristos, such cultivated feminisation is a blemish. Montrose and Co might have long curly locks too—but theirs are just wigs disguising whispy pates. Never has the rightful heir to a land that is still contested been made more apparent.

NEW YORK, 4/24/95, p. 69, David Denby

The highlands swashbuckler *Rob Roy* is long and repetitive, and at times obscurely plotted; but if you long for glens and mist, and have never witnessed Liam Neeson's epic knees, you should probably go see it. The movie features some nifty feats of physical heroism and a general atmosphere of excruciating exertion—even the horses have trouble moving on those spongy downs. Director Michael Caton-Jones, also working hard, alternates between utter squareness and an earthy, mock-Shakespearean vitality. The hero and heroine (Neeson and Jessica Lange) remain true to one another, whereas the villains who try to destroy them are ornate, fey, and witty. Needless to say, one longs for the villains, especially for Tim Roth as a bastard expelled from England and seeking to gain his way in Scotland by public acts of obsequious flattery and private acts of utmost viciousness. Roth's Archibald is a put-on, a ruffled *faux*-pansy who speaks with many flourishes of hands and elbows but wields a wicked saber in close combat. There is a clanging duel between him and Neeson in a great hall and enough malice and treachery to start two civil wars. *Rob Roy* has its longueurs, but basically it's fine. A few splashes of Johnny Walker Red or Laphroaig might have helped the audience through it—but no, it's just fine.

NEW YORK POST, 4/7/95, p. 45, Michael Medved

"Rob Roy" is an uneasy combination of the defiantly old-fashioned and the stylishly new-fangled—like "The Sea Hawk" blended with "Pulp Fiction."

On the one hand, it's a vintage Hollywood swashbuckler complete with larger-than-life hero, mincing villains, expertly staged sword play and windy speeches about honor ("It grows in you and speaks to you. Honor is man's gift to himself.")

At the same time, the movie tries to spice, its ancient story, with shock value. We witness two graphic urination scenes, three enthusiastic copulations and one vicious rape, together with countless wounds and mutilations.

At one key moment, our broad-shouldered hero (Liam Neeson) escapes the bad guys by cutting open the rotting carcass of a cow, pulling out the guts, and then hiding himself inside the stinking flesh. Perhaps it's not entirely a coincidence that two members of the "Pulp Fiction" cast (Tim Roth and Eric Stoltz) play important roles here.

There are even lines of dialogue that sound like whacked-out attempts at 18th-century Tarantino. "Do you know why Calvinists disapprove of f---ing standing up?" one kilted Scot asks another around a campfire.

In short, this odd version of the Rob Roy story has little in common with either the famous Walter Scott novel or the dull Disney film of 1954, though it does share their disregard for the historical reality. The real Robert Roy MacGregor (1671-1734) was a Scottish freebooter who burned, pillaged and otherwise annoyed the English authorities. This movie focuses on only one aspect of his complicated career—his feud with the effete Marquis of Montrose (John Hurt) over a disputed loan.

According to the movie, the gold is snatched by an amoral fop and expert swordsman (a wonderfully effective Tim Roth) who is a bastard in every sense of the word. To add insult to injury, Roth burns Rob Roy's home and sneeringly rapes his loving wife (Jessica Lange) who then strives mightily to keep the assault a secret; if her husband (clan leader of the fierce MacGregors) found out about the incidence, he might well sacrifice his life to avenge her honor.

With this dark, surprisingly downbeat plot, the movie lacks the one element you might reasonably expect in a cinematic tale of the "Scottish Robin Hood"; it is almost entirely devoid of fun. Director Michael Caton-Jones ("Scandal," "This Boy's Life") and writer Alan Sharp (both native Scots) don't even give us the expected rousing scene of the gathering of the clans.

Instead, there's more than two hours of dark and sadistic double-dealing incongrously featuring breathtaking highland scenery, a stirring musical score (by Carter Burwell) and some of the best actors in the business.

Neeson and Lange are both well-cast and their passionate performances help to create the sexiest, mmost romantic movie marriage we've seen in many a moon.

Their screen-filling star quality and the wild and glorious Scottish landscape will give moviegoers their money's worth, though no one would describe this earnest muddle as any man (or woman's) gift to himself.

NEWSDAY, 4/7/95, Part II/p. B3, Jack Mathews

When Liam Neeson first appears in a full body shot in Michael Caton-Jones' "Rob Roy," you know that the film has already leaped its biggest hurdle, which was how to approach an epic adventure story about a man who wore a skirt. Neeson, tall and strapping and with pretty good legs, has as powerful a physical presence on screen as Arnold Schwarzenegger, and he has the added advantage of being able to act!

Neeson plays Robert Roy MacGregor, a legendary 18th-Century Scottish outlaw who, like the mythical Robin Hood, has been idealized (in a novel by Sir Walter Scott, and in the poetry of Wordsworth) as a noble peasant fighting against corrupt authority and for personal honor.

In reality, MacGregor, who adopted the sobriquet Rob Roy, was a Highland pirate who, when he wasn't bounty hunting for cattle rustlers, was engaging in plunder and blackmail himself, playing the rival houses of Montrose and Argyll against each other, to the benefit of Clan MacGregor. Rob Roy was eventually entangled in a ruinous debt by the Duke of Montrose, and devoted years afterward to robbing the duke blind.

The movie, written and directed by Scots, takes that sketchy outline of Rob Roy's life and fills it out with some imaginative events, motivation and characters, and though it eliminates the darker shades of its hero's personality, delivers one of the most adult period adventure films to come along. Anchored by the powerful love story between MacGregor and his wife, Mary (Jessica Lange), "Rob Roy" is a closer cousin to "The Last of the Mohicans" than to "Robin Hood: Prince of Thieves."

In veteran screenwriter Alan Sharp's script, Rob Roy is set up not by the Duke of Montrose (John Hurt), but by the duke's bookkeeper (Brian Cox) and the opportunistic swordsman Archie

Cunningham (Tim Roth), who conspire to kill and rob a MacGregor clansman (Eric Stoltz) carrying the duke's loan to Rob Roy.

Archie is a pretty traditional swashbuckler villain, but Roth raises his sociopathic nature to new levels. An obsequious dandy around the duke, Archie is a sadistic killer, rapist and womanizer in his off-hours, and the dueling opponents amused by his foppish, limp-wristed affectations are soon terrorized by his lethal athletic grace.

The inevitable showdown swordfight between Archie and Rob Roy offers a spectacular contrast, not just in size—Neeson dwarfs the featherweight Roth—but in style and temperament. It's agility vs. strength, cool vs. passion, wrong vs. right. It's good and evil in the grand tradition of the Hollywood swashbuckler, but choreographed with blunt—and I have to say satisfying realism.

Take the R-rating seriously. There is a great deal of blunt realism, the most unsettling being a scene of violent rape, and the deaths, invariably from a loss of blood, are drawn out with clinical accuracy.

Still, "Rob Roy" is a stunning piece of romantic epic filmmaking. Its look is beyond spectacular. Shot on location in the rugged highlands of Scotland, with houses and an entire village built from 18th-Century blueprints, and using the interiors of centuries-old castles, "Rob Roy" gives history a literal pulse.

If that pulse is occasionally slowed by Rob Roy's solemn speeches, and by many murky night scenes, it races ahead whenever he and his earthy wife are together (their spontaneous lovemaking is the best case ever made for kilts), and in virtually every instance where Roth's archenemy, Archie, appears.

Try to tune your ear to Scottish burr before you go. The MacGregors' enemies speak a refined English, but the clansmen—and Neeson in particular—lay on the burr, and a few words are likely to escape unheard.

NEWSWEEK, 4/17/95, p. 66, Jack Kroll

When the Scots name a drink after a guy, you know he's a hero. I mean, just try to order a Robin Hood at your local saloon. *Rob Roy* was in fact the Scottish version of Robin. His square name was Robert MacGregor, an 18th-century drover (cattle driver) and outlaw who fought the feudal lords. Michael Caton-Jones's movie is a return to the romantic epics of yore, like Errol Flynn's "Captain Blood." Rob is played by Liam Neeson, the current paragon of Celtic virility. If Neeson lacks the sheer élan, the swash and chuckle of a Flynn, he has the absolute presence that gave such power to "Schindler's List." Neeson is romantic realism on the hoof, and that's what Caton-Jones was after.

Rob Roy is a freeholder in the feudal system of landowning nobles and their rent-squeezed tenants. Inevitably, the system screws him, in the persons of the Marquis of Montrose (John Hurt) and Cunningham (Tim Roth), a viciously evil young Englishman whose foppish exterior conceals his deadly swordsmanship. So it's war between the clan MacGregor and these Highland black hats, who burn, pillage and rape. Amid the carnage, the stubborn Rob Roy is determined to keep his honor, which, he instructs his young sons, means "You must never mistreat a woman or malign a man."

If honor is a word that comes all too often to Rob's lips, it's a better manifesto than "Hasta la vista, baby." But it bugs his more practical wife, Mary (Jessica Lange), whose own honor is sorely tried by the abominable Cunningham. Caton-Jones and screenwriter Alan Sharp (both Scottish) elevate the classic formulas of the epic romance to a level of literacy seldom seen in these Schwarzeneggerian days. The movie is like a beautiful visualization of those exciting novels by Robert Louis Stevenson and Walter Scott that boys used to read, only with sexier dialogue. "Do ye want to make a silk purse out of my sow's ear?" purrs Lange during a connubial, under-the-kilt encounter (although it's sex-object Neeson we glimpse in the nude). If the film has a somewhat stately pace, this is because Caton-Jones blessedly avoids the sight-bite editing and pace that's endemic today. The cast sinks its teeth into the juicy characters and juicier Scots accents. And the final sword fight between Neeson and Roth is the best since Flynn and Basil Rathbone were clanging away at each other. "Rob Roy" is a welcome paradox—an intelligent, rousing adventure for grown-up kids.

SIGHT AND SOUND, 6/95, p. 51, Kim Newman

Scotland, 1713. Robert Roy McGregor, leader of his highland clan, applies to the Marquis of Montrose for the loan of £1,000 to invest in cattle. Killearn, Montrose's factor schemes with Archibald Cunningham, the Marquis's English houseguest, to give the sum to Rob's friend McDonald in cash. Cunningham murders and robs McDonald, and Killearn spreads the story that McDonald has absconded to the Americas. Montrose offers to forget the loan, which is secured with the McGregor lands, if Rob testifies that the Duke of Argyll, the Marquis' rival, is a Jacobite.

Rob, a man of iron integrity, refuses and turns outlaw. While Rob is away, Cunningham raids his home and rapes his wife Mary. Rob and Alasdair kidnap Killearn, hoping the testimony of Betty, a maid impregnated by Cunningham who has overheard the scheme, will make him confess. But Betty hangs herself and Killearn taunts Mary, who is pregnant but does not know whether by Roy or Cunningham and has not told her husband about the rape, into stabbing him. Alasdair completes the murder and later shoots at redcoats raiding the McGregor lands, starting a skirmish in which he is fatally wounded by return fire.

As he dies, he tells Rob about the rape. Rob is captured by Cunningham and condemned to be hanged by Montrose, but escapes and seeks refuge with Argyll, who has been told by Mary of Montrose's plot against him and of Rob's refusal to bear false witness. Through Argyll, Rob petitions Montrose for a duel with Cunningham. Argyll forces a wager on Montrose whereby Rob's debt will be discharged it he bests Cunningham. The duel goes badly for Rob, but at last he kills Cunningham and is reunited with his clan.

Walter Scott has—a few versions of *Ivanhoe* apart—closer look at his action packed narratives reveals he was less interested in adventue than in tragedy, which has never played well in Peoria.

Rob Roy opens with a historical note about the breakdown of the clan system that has allowed for the benevolent influence of such men as Robert Roy McGregor, and some waffle about how it is possible to find honour in defeat, establishing that this is a tale of noble, bare-legged Indians displaced by corrupt colonists. It is a neat irony that the benchmark for such large scale historical adventures as this is Michael Mann's film of *The Last of the Mohicans,* which gives Scott the unsteady position of following a box office trail blazed by his imitator, James Fenimore Cooper.

There is a disjointedness about this largely entertaining and enjoyable picture. Michael Caton-Jones, who has been making half-way decent films from mostly promising material, stages astonishing moments, such as the appearance of two boatloads of rapacious redcoats out of the early morning mist or an escaping Rob's momentary concealment inside the rotten carcass of a dead cow. But he films the climactic duel as if it were a televised snooker match and all the confrontations between Liam Neeson's vigorous Rob and sundry hairier villains play like ninth-generation carbons of Sergio Leone stand-offs.

The Western element runs throughout the film: Eric Stoltz ponders emigration to the Americas, while Killearn compares the higlanders to Native Americans. This is the first notable credit in some years for the Scots writer, Alan Sharp, who wrote two of the great screenplays of the 70s, Robert Aldrich's *Ulzana's Raid* and Arthur Penn's *Night Moves,* both of which focused on less clear-cut heroic figures than Rob Roy and were tragedies rather than adventures. Neeson is so stiff a goodie that he can never follow the savage path of Ulzana, though the plot puts him in exactly the same position. Therefore, the script has to be cluttered with subplots, secondary baddies and circumstances to turn Rob into an outlaw. There is a briefly entertained suggestion that Rob's pride in his own integrity has brought his misfortunes upon him, but any action or motive that might make him flawed (or even interesting) is displaced onto stooges like the luckless Alasdair and the cheery McDonald.

Caton-Jones and Sharp are required to spend most of the time on Rob and Mary, affording Neeson a shot at being a genuine Hollywood hero and allowing Jessica Lange's presence to be asserted in scenes of domestic struggle and suffering. However, as with so many swashbucklers, all the interest is with the villians. *Rob Roy* constantly redeems itself by the quality of its perfidy: Tim Roth's Cunningham is a startling creation, pitched somewhere between Pee Wee Herman, Marius Goring in *A Matter of Life and Death* and Rupert of Hentzau, mincing through sword fights and making the most of acid lines and pained expressions; Brian Cox's Killearn is a masterful sniveller, piously hypocritical and the real brains of the villainy, and oddly one of the few authentically Scottish voices on the soundtrack; and John Hurt's Montrose, revealed to be the bastard Cunningham's probable father as he retrieves a cameo of the villian's mother from his dead body, is an effete and callous aristocratic swine, despairing of the untidiness of human contact as he tends his perfect garden.

Though their heroes never compete with their villains, Caton-Jones and Sharp offer enough pleasures between the history lessons and the Scott-scuttling to make this worthwhile. Few films in recent memory have dwelled to such an extent on the Scots pursuit of sheep-shagging, referred to in seemingly every exchange of insults between Englishman and Scot, lowlander and highlander. The most extraordinary moment, which even seems to appal Cunningham, comes after the raping and pillaging, as Mary washes herself and Alasdair, arriving too late, wades into the waters after the departing raiders, only for the redcoats to respond to his cries of 'English Bastards' with a mocking chorus of baaing.

VILLAGE VOICE, 4/11/95, p. 56, Amy Taubin

There are hooks aplenty in *Rob Roy*, but not enough to pull you through its 134 minutes. In the old days this kind of costume action adventure was shot efficiently on a studio back lot; directors back then knew they had to get you out of the theater before you realized you'd seen it all already. *Rob Roy* was shot on location in the Scottish Highlands, and I guess the powers that be figured if they paid for the landscape, they were going to get their money's worth—a calculation bound not to pay off at the box office. Or maybe big Liam Neeson, starring as Rob Roy, requires an extralong-sized movie. Or maybe director Michael Caton-Jones imagines he's David Lean. Still I don't understand why *Rob Roy* needed to be 40 minutes longer than *The Scarlet Pimpernel*.

Rob Roy is, after all, your basic western set in early-18th-century Scotland. There are the decent homesteaders (here the MacGregor clan led by courageous and compassionate Rob Roy and his beautiful, loyal wife Mary played by Jessica Lange); the rich, rapacious rancher (the English Marquis of Montrose played by John Hurt at his most despicably decadent); and the outlaw mercenary hired by the rancher to drive the homesteaders from their land by pillaging and plundering, murdering and raping (the sociopathic English bastard Cunningham played by Tim Roth, who steals every scene he's in).

Even while flashing its tony costumes and purple prose, *Rob Roy* makes a blatant play for the inner-city audience. The film is riddled with visceral violence (bodies, both human and animal, are skewered and disemboweled) and leavened with scatological and homophobic wordplay clever enough to earn a rapper's respect. The heavy-handed subtext suggests that conditions in a 'hood bled dry by corporate greed are still not half as barbaric as in 18th-century Scotland under the boot of the English nobility.

"I'm tired of seeing children hungry and old people cold," says Rob Roy, which doesn't necessarily make the movie a rallying cry for a Gingrich backlash. *Rob Roy* preaches nuclear family values and the boundless joy of monogamous marital sex. Rob is a "I could not love you, loved I not honor more" type of guy, which means that when he won't sell out to the Marquis, he's forced to hide in the hills, leaving Mary to be raped by Cunningham. Mary bears her shame in silence, not wanting to inflame Rob into reckless revenge, but he finds out anyway and many chase, battle, and escape scenes follow, culminating in a duel between Rob and Cunningham. Though I was a bit confused by the inscription at the opening of the picture that reads "this story symbolizes the attempt of the individual to ... even in defeat, retain respect and honor," in a film this formulaic, there's no doubt who's going to win.

I spent most of *Rob Roy* contemplating the mysteries of masculinity. What is it exactly that makes Liam Neeson seem so unadulteratedly male even when he's wearing a kilt and knee-high burlap boots to die for? (They may be authentic but they looked like Vivienne Westwood to me.) It's Neeson, not Lange, who gets the obligatory nude scene. He rises from an early morning swim like Ursula Andress in *Dr. No,* serene in the narcissistic knowledge of his own perfection. Neeson is, of course, sans bikini, although an artful shadow veils his reputedly impressive member. Alan Sharp's script falls somewhere between Sir Walter Scott and *The Bridges of Madison County.* Call me perverse, but I got sick of hearing Rob and Mary (who, try as they may, are always just Liam and Jessica) murmur "How fine you are to me" before, after, and even while they do the nasty. And they do it a lot. That Neeson and Lange survive with grace the dialogue, Caton-Jones's overblown direction, and a sappy orchestral score that heralds their every glance and touch is proof of their stellar abilities.

Still, the only reason to sit through *Rob Roy* is Roth's performance. A cursed, smiling, yellow-toothed villain, Roth's Cunningham has his antecedents in Olivier's Richard III (would that he'd had such a text to work with). Roth can switch in a millisecond from a tiptoeing, lisping fop to a steely sadist, punching a woman in the stomach or cutting a man's throat with such swift efficiency that it takes your breath away. Reveling in the give and take of hatred, he never panders or camps. At the WPLJ preview screening I attended, the audience was his.

Also reviewed in:
CHICAGO TRIBUNE, 4/7/95, Friday/p. C, Michael Wilmington
NEW YORK TIMES, 4/7/95, p. C1, Janet Maslin
NEW YORKER, 4/17/95, p. 109, Terrence Rafferty
VARIETY, 3/27-4/2/95, p. 75, Todd McCarthy
WASHINGTON POST, 4/7/95, p. D6, Rita Kempley
WASHINGTON POST, 4/7/95, Weekend/p. 44, Desson Howe

ROOMMATES

A Hollywood Pictures release of an Interscope Communications/Polygram Filmed Entertainment production. *Executive Producer:* Adam Leipzig and Ira Halberstadt. *Producer:* Ted Field, Scott Kroopf, and Robert W. Cort. *Director:* Peter Yates. *Screenplay:* Max Apple and Stephen Metcalfe. *Story:* Max Apple. *Director of Photography:* Mike Southon. *Editor:* John Tintori. *Music:* Elmer Bernstein. *Music Editor:* Kathy Durning. *Sound:* Douglas Axtell. *Sound Editor:* Bruce Fortune. *Casting:* Linda Lowy. *Production Designer:* Dan Bishop. *Art Director:* Jefferson Sage. *Set Decorator:* Dianna Freas. *Set Dresser:* Gregory Jones, John G. Morgan, Jr., David L. Wolfson, John Butler, Smith Hutchings, and Jamie Bishop. *Costumes:* Linda Donahue. *Make-up:* Barbie Palmer. *Make-up (Aging):* Bob Laden. *Make-up (Julianne Moore and Ellen Burstyn):* Leonard Engelman. *Stunt Coordinator:* John C. Meier. *Running time:* 100 minutes. *MPAA Rating:* PG.

CAST: Peter Falk (Rocky); D.B. Sweeney (Michael); Julianne Moore (Beth); Ellen Burstyn (Judith); Jan Rubes (Bolek Krupa); Joyce Reehling (Barbara); Ernie Sabella (Stash); John Cunningham (Burt Shook); PITTSBURGH 1963; Noah Fleiss (Michael, Age 5; Lisa Davis (Betty); Rohn Thomas (Kevin); Karl Mackey (Milan Postevic); Zygmund Szarnicki (Funeral Priest); Chance Marquez (Bully at Baseball Game); David Cutter (Peanut Vendor); PITTSBURGH 1973; David Tom (Michael, Age 15); Lillian Misko-Coury (Bakery Saleswoman); Kate Young (Nun); Noah Abrams (Stavinski); OHIO STATE UNIVERSITY & COLUMBUS 1983-85; Ilana Levine (E.R. Nurse); Scott Cohen (Attending Intern); Pattie Carlson (Second E.R. Nurse); Adrienne Wodenka (Third E.R. Nurse); Daniel Corbin Cox (Attending Physician); Joel de la Fuente (Toby); Raymond Wong (Deng); Wanqing Wu (Zhang); Zhe Sun (Liu); Mengze Shi (Fan); Ann Heekin (Cecilia); Scott Kloes (Cecilia's Son); Vicki Ross-Norris (Cecilia's Nurse); Frankie Faison (Professor Martin); Peter Klemens (Bartender); Donald R. Wilson (Reverend at Wedding); Ron Jaye (Good Morning Columbus Host); PITTSBURGH 1993; Courtney Chase (Lisa); Ryan Kelley (Mo); Katie Cardille-Rogal (Papergirl); Willard Scott (Himself); Bernard Canepari (Judith's Lawyer); Dorothy Silver (Housekeeper); Rosa Gamarra-Thomson (Cleaning Lady); THE PITTSBURGH MEDICAL CENTER; Gerry Becker (Dr. Minceberg); Jeffrey Howell (Surgeon); Nelle Stokes (Recovery Room Nurse); Mary Marini (O.R. Nurse); Robert Gardner (Assisting Surgeon); Robert Dyga (Profusionist).

LOS ANGELES TIMES, 3/3/95, Calendar/p. 6, Peter Rainer

"Roommates" is a lot better than it has any right to be. A generational family saga spanning 32 years, 1963-1995, it works the audience over with shameless vigor. But it has an ornery core. As Rocky Holeczek, the Polish immigrant grandfather who ages from 75 to 107, Peter Falk keeps the crankiness going full blast. He doesn't turn into a softy, he keeps his dignity, and that helps us keep our dignity too. If you have to endure a sudser, you could do a lot worse than "Roommates."

When Rocky's grandson Michael (D.B. Sweeney) is orphaned at age 5, the old baker takes the boy in. Thus begins an odd-couple confab that lasts for the rest of Rocky's long life. Little Michael becomes a physician, moves from Pittsburgh to Columbus, Ohio, to intern—and ended up rooming with his grandfather again. (A nice touch: Michael's insomnia is cured by the familiar comfort of Rocky's rattle-the-roof-beams snores.) Michael takes the couch, Rocky the water bed; upstairs a crew of Chinese students share the rent.

Does all this sound like a premise for a sitcom? But wait, there's more. Michael falls for a beautiful, wealthy social worker, Beth (Julianne Moore), and tries to get something going under Rocky's disapproving glare. But the disapproval is conditional: Marriage and kids are followed by the loud thud of family tragedy and reconciliation.

Director Peter Yates and screenwriters Stephen Metcalf and Max Apple (adapting his autobiographical book are too smart to play up the hearts and flowers. But their downplaying isn't necessarily the best solution either. Sometimes we enjoy a sudser most for its sheer outrageousness. "Roommates" is trying to be classy without really altering its basic wash cycle. It presumes a smart audience but only meets it halfway. If it had gone all the way, if it had dived deeper, it might have been a stunner—like Paul Mazursky's "Harry and Tonto," which it superficially resembles.

Still, "Roommates" is "square" in an appealing way. It stands up for family values, for true love, for the dignity of old age, for working-class ethics, for religion. It prides itself on how righteously unobjectionable it is. Rocky may be a handful but he's always right; he may dictate to people instead of talk to them, he may have a hard time telling his grandson he loves him, but his old immigrant's soul is meant to stand for everything we've lost sight of in this country. Grandfather Knows Best. His snoring is supposed to make us sleep better at night too.

The reason all this goes down easy is because Falk, underneath all his old-man makeup, comes through with the real McCoy. He's not doing ancient codger shtick here. There are moments in his performance, when he's playing with his grandchildren (who adore him) or dancing the polka at Michael's wedding, where we can see Rocky's entire life' in miniature. He's the kind of coot who is fixated on his own staying power: At 100 he procures a job for himself as a baker in a yuppie food emporium. Rocky sees no reason to slow down. Slowing down isn't how he got to be 100. And perhaps we can accept all this rah-rah righteousness in "Roommates" because we want to believe in people like Rocky—or at least in their myth.

D.B. Sweeney is personable but a little wan as Michael, but Julianne Moore is terrific. She often is: most recently in Robert Altman's "Short Cuts" and, last year, as Yelena in "Vanya on 42nd Street." (It was one of the three or four best performances of 1994.) Moore is poised for a great career, and it would be a major loss to movies if she loitered on screen playing conventional wifely roles.

Except that Moore doesn't do anything conventionally. In "Roommates " she creates a character, Beth, who insinuates herself sympathetically into everybody else's troubles. She has a way of being pouty yet sweet, and she's more than a match for Rocky. (It turns out that she plays poker even slower than he does.) When Beth is with her hoity-toity mother (well-played by Ellen Burstyn) you can see both what she is rebelling against and what she is embracing.

"Roommates" is a perplexing movie because the moments of phony-baloney emotion are mixed right in with the genuine. The sifting is sometimes a chore, but it's worth it.

NEW YORK POST, 3/3/95, p. 39, Michael Medved

Most American families include one or more immigrant relatives like Rocky Holeczek—colorful, crusty curmudgeons who stubbornly defend their old-world values of unwavering clan loyalty and ceaseless hard work.

Part of the genius of Peter Falk's performance in "Roommates"—easily the best work by any actor so far in '95—is the way he makes this character seem universal and familiar, at the same time that he is utterly, indelibly unique and specific.

We first meet Rocky in 1963 at the funeral of his daughter-in-law, where he startles the assembled guests by solemnly whistling "The Beer Barrel Polka" at graveside.

He's attempting to comfort his newly orphaned 5-year-old grandson, Michael; while other members of the family want to send the boy to an orphanage, the old man won't hear of it and insists that the kid must live with him.

"Conversation over!" he shouts to their objections, and in a series of exceptionally well-written scenes we watch the frightened child adjusting to his grandfather's world—his explosive snoring, his long hours of work at a bakery in the "Polish Hill" neighborhoods of Pittsburgh, and his intense passion for gin rummy.

The movie's superb, partially autobiographical script (by novelist Max Apple) follows the relationship between these two "roommates" over the course of 30 years, as Rocky ages from 77 to 107 while losing none of his edge or irritability.

The always capable young actor D.B. Sweeney plays Michael as an adult, and if he seems a bit overwhelmed by Falk's intensity it's because his quiet character is supposed to be similarly overwhelmed by his grandfather.

When Michael moves to Columbus, Ohio, for his medical residency, Rocky follows him there, taking over the house he shares with three Chinese exchange students (the old man calls them "the communists") and teaching them the finer points of poker.

He presents a more serious problem to Michael's budding relationship with an idealistic hospital social worker (the radiant Julianne Moore), interrupting their first starry-eyed attempts, at lovemaking with growling reminders that "nice girls" don't behave that way.

Somehow, their relationship survives this rocky start and the old man comes to play a major role in raising the great-grandchildren who arrive after Michael and his new love get married.

It's not, however, a simple situation of happily ever after, in fact, this family experiences so many painful setbacks that the movie's second half might have played like manipulative melodrama in the hands of a lesser director.

Fortunately, the veteran Peter Yates ("Breaking Away," "The Dresser" and many more) employs a light, sure touch, never puffing up the movie's big moments or trying to wring cheap tears from the audience. A lovely, lilting film score by the great Elmer Bernstein perfectly complements the mood nostalgic and emotional, but never schmaltzy.

To their immense credit, Yates and Falk steadfastly refuse to go soft on Rocky; he remains an impossible old geezer, an unrepentant tough guy who isn't for one moment sentimentalized. Like other immigrant patriarchs, he knows what he knows, and his indefatigable irascibility can teach a thing or two to all younger generations.

NEWSDAY, 3/3/95, Part II/p. B2, Jack Mathews

There is a professionalism about Peter Yates' "Roommates," and in the performance of its star, Peter Falk, that nearly lifts it above the artificial sentimentality and banal melodrama written into it. If that sounds like a backhanded compliment, quite the contrary. The hurdles set up by the story's creator, Max Apple, are humongous.

Apple, a writer whose forte is the short story, was inspired to write "Roommates" by his own grandfather, a man who remained alert and physically vital well past his 100th birthday, and continued to follow values and a work ethic established in him in the 19th Century.

That's a subject worth exploring. There's an old saying that you know you're getting old when people start treating you like a baby, and you can see that every morning on the "Today Show" when Willard Scott gives his googoo birthday greetings to centenarians across the country ("Look at that smile, is she a beauty?")

But how do you tell a story that is essentially a condition? Falk's Rocky Holeczek, the fictional incarnation of Apple's grandfather, is an ordinary man with extraordinary genes, living out an extended autumn with values planted way back in the early spring.

The device that Apple (and co-screenwriter Stephen Metcalfe) came up with—to explore Rocky's personality through his relationship with a grandson he raises—provides a general framework for a story, but it also sets some traps. There are only so many ways you can point up the differences between men raised 70 years apart, after which it becomes both trite and condescending.

Rocky, a baker who'd immigrated to the Polish Hill section of Pittsburgh as a child, was past 60 when the sexual revolution occurred, and still can't accept the idea of "decent people" sleeping together before they're married. There's a very funny scene where his grown grandson, Michael

(D.B. Sweeney), awakens the old man while trying to make love to his girlfriend on the couch, but Rocky's lingering Old World indignation and mistreatment of the woman seems to contradict the whole notion of his intellectual vitality.

Broken down to descriptive parts, "Roommates" is a roll call of geriatric stereotypes. A cantankerous old coot with a soft heart, his stubbornness barely concealing a wellspring of love, contrasted with the confounding new morality and conventions of the young. And, of course, his crotchetiness is there for comic relief, as he drives away housekeepers and gardeners, barks at his opponents at gin, sharply corrects a history professor about a labor incident in 1909 (Rocky was there!).

"Roommates" joins Rocky in his mid-70s when he insists on raising the 5-year-old Michael, after his parents have died. The story jumps ahead in 10-year increments, showing Michael growing up, becoming a medical student, and finally a married cardiologist with two children of his own. All the while, there is Rocky, either sharing living space with him, or lurking in the background. acting as the gatekeeper of his conscience.

The connecting thread is a literal one, the emotional bond between the two men. Rocky, we sense, is hanging on to his life for fear of leaving Michael unprepared for his. Michael, heavily coached in the merits of hard work, has to learn the hard way how to adjust emotionally to living in his own time.

You keep waiting for a dramatic event to hurtle the story toward a resolution of Michael's conflicts, and when it finally arrives it feels like a cheaply tragic convenience—God, or a screenwriter, saving, "You think you've got trouble, buddy, I'll show you trouble."

Despite it all, "Roommates" plants its hook, and those looking for a good cry will get it. Yates ("Breaking Away," "The Dresser") embraces the material without apology and got the performances he needed to make it work. Women are incidental to the central relationship, but Julianne Moore (the natural redhead in "Short Cuts") is very strong as the aggressive social worker whom Michael marries, and Ellen Burstyn is a nasty piece of business as the mother-in-law from hell.

But the movie belongs to Falk, who creates a level of personality for Rocky that goes well beyond the clichés. He's a joy to watch, and though his age range of 75-107 looks more like 65-87, he proves to be the grandfather of all our dreams.

Also reviewed in:
CHICAGO TRIBUNE, 3/3/95, Friday/p. C, Michael Wilmington
NEW YORK TIMES, 3/3/95, p. C10, Janet Maslin
VARIETY, 3/6-12/95, p. 63, Todd McCarthy
WASHINGTON POST, 3/3/95, p. D7, Rita Kempley
WASHINGTON POST, 3/3/95, Weekend/p. 38, Desson Howe

ROY COHN/JACK SMITH

A Strand Releasing release of a Good Machine/Pomodori Foundation/Laboratory for Icon & Idiom production. *Producer:* Ted Hope, James Schamus, and Marianne Weems. *Director:* Jill Godmilow. *Screenplay based on the play "Roy Cohn" by:* Gary Indiana. *Screenplay based on the play "What's Underground About Marshmallows" by:* Jack Smith. *Director of Photography:* Ellen Kuras. *Editor:* Merrill Stern. *Music:* Michael Sahl. *Sound:* Larry Lewinger. *Running time:* 91 minutes. *MPAA Rating:* Not Rated.

CAST: Ron Vawter (Roy Cohn/Jack Smith); Coco McPherson (Chica).

NEW YORK POST, 8/4/95, p. 44, Larry Worth

The most interesting part of "Roy Cohn/Jack Smith" is the credit sequence, noting that "Jonathan Demme presents" it, and that "the film could not have been made without the generous support of [director] Steven Soderbergh and [R.E.M.'s] Michael Stipe."

But judging from the end product, Demme, Soderbergh and Stipe had precious little control over quality. That burden fell to director Jill Godmilow, and she pretty much dropped the ball.

In a nutshell, Godmilow lensed a performance of the "Roy Cohn/Jack Smith" play during which Ron Vawter spent Act One impersonating infamous conservative lawyer Cohn, and Act Two playing controversial underground filmmaker Smith.

Of course, the disparate duo's common ground is that both were gay. But while Cohn hid behind the persona of a homophobic right-winger, Smith reveled in his campy, drag queen persona.

Apparently trying to find a message about mankind's Jekyll-Hyde nature, Godmilow intercuts lines from the two characters' monologues. So, as a nasal Cohn sanctimoniously addresses city council hearings on the gay rights bill, the fey Smith lies on a couch in harem getup, all glitter and goatee.

Part of the movie's problem rests with the late Vawter (who died of AIDS shortly after filming ended). His interpretation of Smith has him rambling incoherently in a Goofy voice. And while his Cohn is a more interesting mix of Jackie Mason-like shtick with a dash of Jerry Lewis, it can't compare to the Cohn interpretation of "Angels in America."

Granted, the content can certainly be intellectualized. But the presentation still seems amateurish and—worse—dull going.

Footage of audience members watching the play reflects many who seem less than entertained. Those catching the filmed "Roy Cohn/Jack Smith" will relate.

VILLAGE VOICE, 8/8/95, p. 48, Amy Taubin

Elegiac art is doomed to failure. It can't deliver what's wanted from it: nothing less than to raise its subject from the grave. *Roy Cohn/Jack Smith,* however, is an unusually dreadful piece of elegiac art. One reacts to it with anger, not because of the clumsy pretension of what's on the screen, but because of what's been missed and is lost forever—the opportunity to have, at the least, a straightforward record of a great performance by the incomparable actor Ron Vawter.

The communal effort that went into making the film was exemplary with a shooting schedule that was literally a matter of life and death (Vawter performed the two-part monologue *Roy Cohn/Jack Smith* for the last time in the fall of 1993; six months later he died of AIDS-related illnesses), coproducers Ted Hope and James Schamus put together a meager budget from the contributions of hundreds of people. Sadly, however, the producers were extraordinarily misguided in their choice of a director. The irony that's central to Vawter's performance, the tragicomic complications of drag as identity, the dialectics of the closet that shaped these two psyches in such radically different ways, were entirely lost on Jill Godmilow. Although the performance was shot documentary style with three cameras, Godmilow was not satisfied with the real-time continuity. Instead she decided to intercut fragments from both monologues as well as backstage and rehearsal footage, imposing banal comparisons and trivial relationships.

Unlike Vawter, whose power as an actor rested with his ability to make himself invisible in the interest of the characters he portrayed, Godmilow splatters her subjectivity across her film.

There is, however, a tiny gem embedded in the final credits—a home movie-style portrait of Vawter filmed by Ken Kobland. As elegiac art, nothing could be finer. My advice: loiter in the lobby till the film's almost over; those final minutes are worth the price of admission.

Also reviewed in:
NEW YORK TIMES, 8/4/95, p. C20, Stephen Holden
VARIETY, 9/26-10/2/94, p. 62, Emanuel Levy

RUN OF THE COUNTRY, THE

A Castle Rock Entertainment release of a One Two Nine production. *Executive Producer:* Nigel Wooll. *Producer:* Peter Yates and Ruth Boswell. *Director:* Peter Yates. *Screenplay based on his novel by:* Shane Connaughton. *Director of Photography:* Mike Southon. *Editor:* Paul

Hodgson. *Music:* Cynthia Millar. *Music Editor:* Andrew Glen. *Sound:* Ken Weston and (music) Brian Masterson. *Sound Editor:* Don Sharpe. *Casting:* Ros Hubbard, John Hubbard, Linda Lowy, and Mikie Heilbrum. *Production Designer:* Mark Geraghty. *Art Director:* David Wilson. *Set Decorator:* Mark Geraghty. *Special Effects:* Ian Wingrove. *Costumes:* Rosemary Burrows. *Make-up:* Alan Boyle. *Stunt Coordinator:* Eddie Stacey. *Running time:* 100 minutes. *MPAA Rating:* R.

CAST: Albert Finney (Father); Matt Keeslar (Danny); Victoria Smurfit (Annagh); Anthony Brophy (Prunty); David Kelly (Father Gaynor); Dearbhla Molloy (Mother); Carole Nimmons (Mrs. Prunty); Vinnie McCabe (Annagh's Uncle); Trevor Clark (Barman); Kevin Murphy (Big Man); Michael O'Reilly (Bouncer Patterson); P.J. Brady (Carolan); Miche Doherty (Dolan); Declan Mulholland (Farmer); Dawn Bradfield (Daphne); Paddy McGuinness (Lookout); Christy Mahon (Man); Pat Kinevane (McQuade); Joe Hanley (Monkey); Maureen Dow (Mrs. McKenna); Eileen Ward (Mrs. Lee); Thomas Lappin (Rennicks); Robin Hines (Soldier); Antoine Byrne (Wench); Seamus O'Rourke (Man at Annagh's); Joan Sheehy (Widdy McGinn); Noel Smith (Goblin Gilmour); Hugh B. O'Brien (Danny's Uncle); Aine Ni Mhuiri (Danny's Aunt); Sissy Connolly (Elderly Lady); Mary Reilly (Woman).

FILMS IN REVIEW, 11-12/95, p. 104, Eva H. Kissin

From time to time, some individuals and nations that have suffered a great deal are able to turn their problems into works of art. Ireland, bound by its repressive past and consumed by present difficulties, has exemplified this trend in literature, theater, and, more recently, in filmmaking.

The Run of the Country, starring the always brilliant Albert Finney, presents the Irish situation in microcosm. Finney, an aging malcontent police sergeant, has just lost his wife. He and his only son, Danny (played with great feeling by Matt Keeslar) are involved in a gripping oedipal situation over the dead wife and mother, whom both loved. Danny, a sensitive, intelligent 18-year-old, has nightmarish memories of his father breaking down his mother's door at night. His visions and filial jealousy and grief suggest his father had killed his mother with his sexual demands.

Danny is at loose ends in general, anchorless without his mother's supportive encouragement, always battling with his father, and uncertain of his own direction. In addition, his hormones are racing like the Irish Sweepstakes, and only his innate modesty and poetic nature tend to keep him on track.

Then he meets Annagh, a beautiful Irish Madonna who resembles his mother and matches his intelligence and sensibility. Annagh, with a Catholic father and Protestant mother, symbolizes the problem of the country itself. She is played with great freshness and deep feeling by Victoria Smurfit.

The couple fall in love and their absolute and total passion leads to its inevitable denouement. But this is Ireland, with a lingering theocracy bound by the laws of the church, and a divided nation in the middle of a civil war. The plight of the lovers who literally can't stay away from each other but are unable to live together because of their age, economic condition, and the state of their country, is the main focus of the film.

However, this is more than a story of star-crossed lovers. There is a strong sense of the green Irish countryside, and we see its poverty and how it copes with life's burdens. Cows, pigs, and bogs abound, and there is a great deal of warm local humor. When a disgusted Finney tries to eat his son's half cooked chicken, one can't help recall the younger Finney in *Tom Jones,* delectably consuming one of the most sexually exciting dinners ever served in a film. Another time, while searching for his runaway son in his friend Prunty's house, Prunty's mother, hoping to hide the boys, stuffs their steaming dinner plates into the drawer of the kitchen table. As the steam inevitably escapes, the sergeant remarks in deadpan style that he's "already eaten, thank you maam."

The Run of the Country is a splendid film about the problems of individuals set against the larger conundrums of their society. It is a moving, caring, and ancient story, Romeo and Juliet in Ireland. In addition, it puts some of our own very similar social problems in perspective. But at least we have the means to attempt more rational solutions than the cruel physical and emotional punishments inflicted on the young lovers in this film by their elders.

LOS ANGELES TIMES, 9/22/95, Calendar/p. 6, Kevin Thomas

Peter Yates' deeply affecting "The Run of the Country" is a poignant coming-of-age story set in a very idyllic-looking village in County Cavan, south of the northern Irish border.

Constantly lurking in the background are British troops, with the possibility of bloodshed. But what concerns 18-year-old Danny (Matt Keeslar) is the devastating loss of his beloved mother, which means that he and his strong, blunt father (Albert Finney), a police sergeant, are at last brought face-to-face without a buffer.

Dreamy, sensitive, a reader of contemporary Irish poetry, Danny has been all set to go to university, but now he's at loose ends and instantly clashes with his father, who already has his eye on another woman, much to the chagrin of his son. That the father really could love his wife deeply but still want to get on with his life is just the first of the many things that Danny needs to discover in a man he doesn't truly know. Self-made and constantly reminding his son of that fact, the father talks tough about life's hard realities but hasn't a clue as to how to express love for Danny—or even that he needs to do so.

This beautiful-looking film of much understanding—and no small measure of humor—marks an auspicious reunion of Yates and Finney, whose collaboration on "The Dresser" brought them both Oscar nominations and British Academy nominations and marked the beginning of an upward curve in the career of Finney as a star character actor that continues unbroken with this film. Shane Connaughton, himself an Oscar nominee for his script for "My Left Foot," adapted his own novel to the screen with much skill.

"The Run of the Country" unfolds gracefully on the screen while possessing the rich substance of a fine novel. It has a keen feeling of life being lived before our eyes—of our discovering what its people are all about at the same time they do so themselves. At its center is Danny, who is trying to make sense of his loss and of his life—and who is soon falling in love for the first time, with Annagh (Victoria Smurfit), poised and charming), an intelligent, ambitious auburn-haired beauty who also has an appreciation of poetry.

Events swirl around Danny, who in the words of a friend's mother has "the run of the country" as he moves through this period of limbo. Danny is a figure in a universal rite of passage, but all that he experiences is rooted firmly in the political realities of contemporary Ireland and in an Irish Catholicism that at once sustains and oppresses the people of Danny's world.

In his first starring role, Keeslar is rightly brooding and self-absorbed as Danny. Both Finney, whose emotional reserves are as rich as ever, as the blustery father, and Anthony Brophy as Danny's free-spirited, hell-raising best pal offer contrast and provide the film with its vitality. "The Run of the Country" is one of those worthy small films you can only hope will find the audience it deserves.

NEW YORK POST, 9/22/95, p. 45, Thelma Adams

The definition of cliche must be an Irish coming-of-age movie where the hero gets his girl pregnant.

Cutting a swath of green in "The Run of the Country," 18-year-old Danny (Matt Keeslar) is about to have one of those final, fateful summers. When his mother dies prematurely, Danny's apron strings are abruptly cut. The virginal youth runs wild on the border between the Republic of Ireland and its Northern brother, between school and university, between who he is and who he will become.

"The Run of the Country" reunites director Peter Yates and Albert Finney, who both earned Academy Award nominations for "The Dresser." As Danny's recently widowed father, Finney puts the "A" in authoritarian. It's a blustery role that Finney performs as easily as rolling over in his sleep, touching tender nerves with a dentist's precision.

Estranged from his loving-but-abusive father, Danny takes up with an unlikely character named Prunty (Anthony Brophy).

The character of Prunty—a latter-day leprechaun without the magical powers—is no slick advertisement for the Emerald Isle. Overplayed with squinty glee by Brophy, the greasy-haired, coarse, cursing, brawling blighter seems to have arrived from a different movie than the simple, slice-of-life, location-shot melodrama that prevails.

Annagh (Victoria Smurfit), a scrubbed and sassy colleen, is a fresh face (as fresh as the scent of Irish Spring). With humor and tenderness, the red-haired actress locks step with the girlfriend's "stations of the cross." She must meet someone cute, fall gently in love, burst into passion, fall back into remorse with the onset of pregnancy, and then struggle with "the most difficult decision of her young life."

Danny's part cries out for a vaguely spotty, awkward soul who hasn't quite grown into his body yet: a bandy-legged calf trying to blow like a bull. Instead, newcomer Keeslar looks like someone who has had girls circling him since his first birthday party, a John John Kennedy type. Danny's awkwardness with women seems as contrived and improbable as his friendship with Prunty.

It wouldn't be a by-the-numbers coming of age saga if, after requisite flow of tragedies, the movie didn't stop running wild and get down to the sentimental business at hand. Danny and his father reconcile with the natural force of magnets.

If we didn't write down the theme when Danny's da dictated it to us early in the film—"It's the living who have to resurrect themselves, not the dead"—Danny repeats for us now so that we won't go away empty-handed. Empty-headed is all right.

NEWSDAY, 9/22/95, Part II/p. B4, John Anderson

When he was a young man, Albert Finney made his bones playing characters who wore their appetites on their sleeves ("Tom Jones"). Now, as a far more mature and accomplished actor, he's taken to playing men who've buried their appetites within a walking tomb of softening flesh and hardening morality (the classics teacher in "The Browning Version"). And he has become a marvelous—and occasionally frightening—thing to watch.

"The Run of the Country" is not Finney's movie, precisely; he plays the father, and it is Matt Keeslar, who plays the post-adolescent son Danny, who has the putative hero's role. But Finney's character (referred to as Father or the Sergeant) exerts a muscular presence over the entire film, as a kind of warning of what Danny may become, and what Ireland may already be—and that, in short, is grievously unhappy.

The film, which reunites Finney and director Peter Yates for the first time since "The Dresser" in 1984, begins predictably enough, with a tourist's catalog of things Irish: lush, green vistas; spirited and melancholy music; a lone car traveling, a priest walking, and a wake. Here, Danny and his father are burying their mother and wife (played in flashbacks by Dearbhla Molloy) and getting ready to begin life with each other: Two single-minded men, neither of whom can cook, and neither of whom is comfortable with the other. It isn't long before Danny's moved in with his reprobate pal Prunty (Anthony Brophy) and the sergeant is disconcerted.

The predictability factor is a plague on "Run of the Country"—which refers to a post-adolescent's freedom and freedom to ruin his life—and it makes the film a bit less than it might have been. Danny's story is a litany of coming-of-age rituals: bar fights, drinking, a prank involving a pig and a priest, romance his—with the beautiful Annagh Lee (Victoria Smurfit)—and the occasional run-in with the sergeant, who is Danny's moral torment and penance. What is a surprise, however, is just how much Danny's going to go through before this unexpectedly tragic movie is through.

Shane Connaughton, who wrote both the novel and the screenplay, envisions Danny as an Irish Job, subjecting him to a trial by life experience. There is death, there is loss, there is education via brutal reality. Connaughton wants Danny to suffer all that Ireland has suffered, and as a result he becomes more symbolic than real.

But, of course, he's intended as a rather formless creature, one who needs to have life give him shape. The characters all live on the border with Northern Ireland; Annagh Lee is a Protestant from the north, installing in the film a Romeo-Juliet motif (or maybe "West Side, Story").

Danny's sexual initiation and casual rejection of his father's belief system places the men at odds, but also in a kind of parallel position: Danny's father has led a life of virtual chastity. Danny's birth was so difficult that his mother could have no more children and, given their strict Catholic beliefs, this meant sex was pretty much out. Danny remembers, however, watching his father break down his mother's bedroom door on occasions when devil lust had Da in his grip, and Danny's revulsion haunts him.

Keeslar is quite good in a thankless part; Danny is awkwardly unsympathetic, unlike Prunty, whom Anthony Brophy portrays as a craftily demented Irish sprite. As Annagh Lee, Victoria Smurfit seems too knowing and wise for the callow Danny, but she does light up the screen.

It is Finney, however, who is the real joy to behold—joy perhaps being the wrong word. The sergeant, for all his civility, is a seething mass of angry regret who wants Danny to go to America, not have sex, and not to do anything stupid or irreversible that will cut off his options. He's very human and we know him well—much like the story, a classic theme of innocence and experience into which Finney and Yates breathe some healthy new life.

SIGHT AND SOUND, 1/96, p. 47, Geoffrey Macnab

A small community on the Irish border. After the death of his mother, Danny, an 18-year-old boy, argues bitterly with his father, the local Garda sergeant, and decides to leave home. He moves in with his friend, Prunty, who lives on a nearby farm.

Danny is shy and naive, and Prunty resolves to teach him a few lessons about life. Their wild antics enrage the local priest and appall Danny's father. Danny spots a beautiful young woman first when their car breaks down, and later as he dangles from a crane after a bungee jump. She is Annagh Lee, who lives with her well-to-do family north of the border. He eventually meets her at an illegal cock fight and invites her to the cinema. They start an affair, but she becomes pregnant and Danny's father refuses to countenance paying for an abortion. Prunty offers to help the couple raise the money for the trip to England. When he, Danny and a friend are digging peat Prunty loses his footing, falls into a bog and is killed when a tractor topples over on him. At his funeral, Danny learns that he was in the IRA.

Annagh's family arrange for her to be sent away. She and Danny sneak away to spend time together before they're separated for good. During the night, she miscarries. He visits her home to declare his love for her, but is set upon by her relatives who beat him up, and tar and feather him. He's found the next morning in a shed by his father. The two are reconciled. The father is delighted that Danny has finally decided to leave the rural backwaters and start a new life elsewhere. He'd hoped Danny might go to America, but respects his son's decision to stay in Ireland and go to university in Dublin.

As its title suggests, *The Run of the Country* is as much preoccupied with landscape as with character. This is underlined both by the film's loving representation of the Irish countryside and by occasional bursts of self-conscious dialogue about the way the earth moulds and absorbs the people who dwell on it. This last telluric image is no mere metaphor: in a key scene, Prunty, the wild country boy, slips into the mud and drowns. Little wonder, then, that sometimes the movie is dragged under by the weight of its own symbolism.

Shane Connaughton's screenplay was adapted from his own novel. Although thematically complex, it is short on narrative incident. The interplay between the characters, their memories and sometimes inscrutable emotions matter more here than outside events. There are passing references to the 'troubles' and fitful attempts to capture the plight of youngsters in a rural backwater. However, although set in contemporary Ireland, and with a modern storyline the film has a curiously old-fashioned feel. The production design in particular helps keep the present at bay. The local Garda officer, played by Albert Finney, lives in a little house which seems to have been decorated in the 40s. There's no sign of a washing machine or a television. If he wants to relax, he listens to the wireless. Prunty's farm is similarly free of mod cons. Annagh cycles into view dressed like Phyllis Calvert in a wartime melodrama.

For all its scenic splendour, *The Run of the Country* lacks local flavor. It certainly has none of the abrasive energy of the recent Roddy Doyle adaptations. An English director who has spent most of his career in Hollywood (Peter Yates), a young American lead (Matt Keeslar) and a veteran English star (Albert Finney) aren't exactly the personnel to bring a quintessentially Irish story to the screen. The film is glossy and polished when it might have benefited from a rougher edge.

What it does offer is another fine performance from Albert Finney, who here collaborates with Peter Yates for the first time since *The Dresser*. He plays the Garda officer as a thickset, scowling, taciturn man who can only express his feelings through violence. Thus, when his son argues with him his response is simply to hurl crockery onto the floor. In flashbacks, he is depicted locked out of his wife's bedroom, bludgeoning the door with his pelvis, bullishly trying to break in. A frustrating marriage and a disappointing career have combined to numb his feelings. It's a thoroughly unsympathetic role, but Finney, without ever trying to soften the character, is able to suggest why he's such a brute. This makes it all the more affecting when he finally shows some compassion.

Not that Finney's is the major part. As in most rites-of-passage dramas, the emotions of the adolescent hero are foregrounded at the expense of everything else. Newcomer Matt Keeslar is largely left to carry the film. Clean-cut and looking suspiciously like fellow American Chris O'Donnell, he sometimes seems a little too smooth for a juvenile lead. Nevertheless, there's no faulting his intensity. Equally earnest is Victoria Smurfit as his girlfriend: the two establish a strong enough rapport to withstand the excruciating "who is your favourite poet?" dialogue.

While the love story at its core is handled delicately enough, there is much heavy-handed caricature along the way with comic turns from an eccentric country priest and a farmer who wants his pig blessed. Perhaps the most problematic figure is Prunty. Connaughton describes him as embodying Ireland itself: "outrageous, cunning, daring and loyal." He gambles, boozes, bets, lives off the land and even moonlights as a republican freedom fighter, but his sheer exuberance only shows up the lack of energy elsewhere. Despite neatly observed central performances and meticulously detailed *mise en scène*, this is simply too tame a piece to do justice to its own themes. Peter Yates (director of *Bullitt* and *Breaking Away)*, in pastoral mode, seems so intent on fetishising landscape, look and gesture that the narrative is never given a chance to crackle with life.

VILLAGE VOICE, 9/26/95, p. 86, Michael Atkinson

[*The Run of the Country* was reviewed jointly with *The Stars Fell on Henrietta*; see Atkinson's review of that film.]

Also reviewed in:
CHICAGO TRIBUNE, 9/22/95, Friday/p. L, Michael Wilmington
NEW REPUBLIC, 10/16/95, p. 36, Stanley Kauffmann
NEW YORK TIMES, 9/22/95, p. C3, Stephen Holden
VARIETY, 9/11-17/95, p. 105, Todd McCarthy
WASHINGTON POST, 9/29/95, p. F7, Hal Hinson
WASHINGTON POST, 9/29/95, Weekend/p. 44, Desson Howe

RUNAWAY BRAIN

A Walt Disney release. *Executive Producer:* Pam Coats. *Producer:* Ron Tippe. *Director:* Chris Bailey. *Story:* Tim Hauser. *Editor:* Nancy Frazen. *Music:* John Debney. *Music Editor:* Tom Carlson and Mark Green. *Sound:* Susan McLean and (music) John Richards. *Sound Editor:* Mark Mangini. *Art Director:* Ian Gooding. *Animation:* Andreas Deja. *Special Effects:* Dave Bossert and Jeff Topping. *Running time:* 7 minutes. *MPAA Rating:* G.

VOICES: Wayne Allwine (Mickey Mouse); Russi Taylor (Minnie Mouse); Kelsey Grammer (Dr. Frankenollie); Jim Cummings (Monster); Bill Farmer (Pluto).

LOS ANGELES TIMES, 8/11/95, Calendar/p. 4, Kevin Thomas

Playing with "A Kid in King Arthur's Court" is "Runaway Brain," the first Mickey Mouse cartoon in 42 years, an amusing vignette in which Mickey encounters a Frankenstein-like mad scientist who switches his brain with that of his monster creation. The tone of the cartoon is highly contemporary, but its handsome backgrounds have an appropriate retro '30s-'40s look. Directed by Chris Bailey and produced by Ron Tippe from Tim Hauser's story idea, "Runaway Brain" has Wayne Allwine and his wife, Russi Taylor, supplying the voices for Mickey and his girlfriend, Minnie, with Kelsey Grammer speaking for the mad scientist, named Dr. Frankenollie in homage of pioneering animators Frank Thomas and Ollie Johnston.

NEW YORK POST, 8/11/95, p. 42, Michael Medved

Is America really clamoring for a glimpse of Minnie Mouse in a bikini?

The animation department at Disney must think so, because that's one of the fleeting images they provide in "Runaway Brain," a frenetic seven-minute cartoon that's playing alongside "A Kid in King Arthur's Court" and that constitutes the first short-form appearance for Mickey and Minnie in 42 years.

The creators of this heavily-hyped new release proudly boast that it "brings Mickey into the present day with '90s settings and sensibilities." This is, perhaps, a polite way of saying that they've trashed the legacy of a noble mouse and blurred the image of the most beloved character in pop culture history.

The little story begins when Mickey forgets the anniversary of his first date with Minnie (since it occurred some 60 years ago, she really ought to forgive him) and agrees to take her on a Hawaiian vacation to make it up to her.

To get some quick cash to pay for the trip, he answers a newspaper ad offering generous payment for a "mindless day's work" and finds himself in the clutches of a mad scientist (the voice of TVs Kelsey Grammer) who switches his brain with that of a huge, hulking monster.

This leaves Mickey's mind inside of the lumbering giant, while the vicious brute's brain takes over the familiar body of the world's favorite rodent and proceeds to a nasty attack on Minnie.

For the record, I'll confess that part of my hostility to this technically accomplished piece of work stems from the fact that the intense scenes of Mickey Mouse suddenly behaving like a snarling demon were enough to provoke frightened tears and screams from my two youngest kids.

The animation, as you'd expect, is impressively three dimensional and frequently inventive but the colors, leaning generally toward blues and grays, only heighten the surprisingly dark, dreary atmosphere.

In place of the bright palette and lighthearted story lines employed in nearly all of Mickey's previous 118 cartoon shorts, this latest work is much closer to the violent, rock 'em/sock 'em style of Chuck Jones' classic work for Warner Brothers.

Of course, there's considerable artistry involved, but the whole approach seems misguided when it's applied to an international icon of sweetness and innocence. Whoever decided that Mickey Mouse (of all creatures) needed new "edge" in his much-heralded return to the screen, and elected to use the occasion to frighten little kids, might qualify as a real-life runaway brain.

NEWSDAY, 8/11/95, Part II/p. B5, Jonathan Mandell

[*Runaway Brain* was reviewed jointly with *A Kid in King Arthur's Court*; see Mandell's review of that film.]

RUNNING WILD

Producer: Phillippe Blot. *Running time:* 90 minutes. *MPAA Rating:* R.

CAST: Jennifer Barker (Carlotta); Mike Kirton (Vince); Dan Spector (Frankie); Daniel Dupont (Miller); Mitch Hara (Hitchhiker); John McConnell (Sheriff); Elliot Keener (Father Matthew).

NEW YORK POST, 5/19/95, p. 38, Bill Hoffmann

One of the goals of a road movie is to cover a lot of ground in a short period of time.

"Running Wild" is a glaring exception to this rule: it takes 90 long minutes to go absolutely nowhere.

The only trick this inept, crashingly dull feature has managed to pull off is grabbing a short theatrical release before hitting the shelves of your local video store. My advice: Save your eight bucks now and your $3.99 a few weeks from now.

Billed as a "charming and humorous story," the grab-bag plot begins with our young heroine, Carlotta, trying to commit suicide by swallowing pills and sticking a gun in her mouth.

It can't be too bad, though, because just a scene or two later she's recovered enough to go marry Vince, a car dealer twice her age. Her love isn't too strong, however, since in the wink of an eye she's making it with Vince's son, Frankie.

When they're caught in the act, Frankie, his best pal, Miller, and Carlotta dive into dad's classic Impala convertible and head south for Mexico.

That's where Carlotta meets a shady hitchhiker who dies while the two have sex in a cheesy motel—leaving his suitcase, containing a severed head, behind.

As the trio drift through the country trying to solve the mystery, they encounter crafty hookers, a swishy bartender, a wisecracking priest and a fat, bumbling cop.

Sound confusing? You bet.

The producers have sprinkled the soundtrack with some great old rock hits by performers like Steppenwolf, Blood, Sweat & Tears, Eddie Cochran and Billy Joe Royal, in a lame attempt to energize the proceedings. But none of the songs match the moods of the scenes they play over.

For best results, you might as well close your eyes and pretend you're listening to the radio.

NEWSDAY, 5/19/95, Part II/p. B7, John Anderson

When a movie's mantra is "life sucks" and the opening scene has your heroine attempting suicide, the message is something other than mirth. On the other hand, if you don't really have a message, or a point, you can toss everything into the mix and see what floats.

Things are fairly bobbing in "Running Wild," a kind of "Jules and Jim With a Vengeance" whose real purpose is Jennifer Barker—or, rather, the display of Jennifer Barker, who, as the wanton-but-repentant Carlotta, failed suicide and bride-to-be, is kept under as little wrap as possible for most of this movie. There's nothing wrong with this, necessarily. It would just be nice if something else was going on as well.

Oh yes, the story: The not-so-reformed Carlotta is set to marry Vince (Mike Kirton), a redneck California car dealer, until Vince's son Frankie (Dan Spector) and his near-idiot companion Miller (Daniel Dupont) arrive to cause disarray. Why Carlotta would find Frankie even vaguely attractive is the casting director's secret, but Vince finds Carlotta and Frankie *flagrante delicto* and gives murderous chase. The three amigos head for Mexico.

Along the way they pick up a hitchhiker (Mitch Hara) carrying a severed head in a bag; there's a bounty on the body part, and after the hitcher gives up the ghost while coupling with Carlotta, she heads off to claim the reward. Hilarity ensues.

You with me so far? Then for God's sake stop reading. If any of this sounds even vaguely intriguing, you've been grossly misled. The acting is awkward, the plot is a pastiche of borrowed story lines and the internal contradictions render logic useless, if not irrelevant. Barker shows some comedic promise, although the slow-mo T&A stuff is like bad "Baywatch" (a redundancy, I know), and it's touch to create a character when the script keeps changing your character's history.

John McConnell as the sheriff and Elliot Keener as Carlotta's brother, Father Matthew (uh huh), are the only really appealing ingredients on a rather tawdry combination platter of sexual and ethnic stereotypes that's a guided gastric missile.

S.F.W.

A Gramercy Pictures release of a Program Filmed Entertainment presentation of an A&M Films production in association with Propaganda Films. *Executive Producer:* Sigurjon Sighvatsson. *Producer:* Dale Pollock. *Director:* Jefery Levy. *Screenplay:* Danny Rubin and Jefery Levy. *Based on the novel by:* Andrew Wellman. *Director of Photography:* Peter Deming. *Editor:* Lauren Zuckerman. *Music:* Graeme Revell. *Music Editor:* Joshua Winget. *Sound:* David B. Chornow. *Sound Editor:* Douglas Murray. *Casting:* Owens Hill and Rachel Abroms. *Production Designer:* Eve Cauley. *Art Director:* Philip Messina. *Set Decorator:* Sandy Struth and Don G. Smith. *Special Effects:* Frank Ceglia. *Costumes:* Debra McGuire. *Make-up:* Cheryl Voss and Lisa Layman. *Stunt Coordinator:* Steve M. Davison. *Running time:* 92 minutes. *MPAA Rating:* R.

CAST: Stephen Dorff (Cliff Spab); Reese Witherspoon (Wendy Pfister); Jake Busey (Morrow Streeter); Joey Lauren Adams (Monica Dice); Pamela Gidley (Janet Streeter); David Barry Gray (Scott Spab); Jack Noseworthy (Joe Dice); Richard Portnow (Gerald Parsley); Edward Wiley (Mr. Spab); Lela Ivey (Mrs. Spab); Natasha Gregson Wagner (Kristen); Annie McEnroe (Dolly); Virgil Frye (Earl); Francesca P. Roberts (Kim Martin); Soon Teck Oh (Milt Morris); Blair Tefkin (Allison Ash); Steven Antin (Dick Zetterland); Melissa Lechner (Sandy Hooten); Lenny Wolpe (Phil Connors); Natalie Strauss (Rita Connors); Tobey Maguire (Al); Dana Allan Young (Johnny); John Roarke (Phil Donahue/Sam Donaldsone/Alan Dershowitz/Ted Koppel/Larry King Clones); Amber Benson (Barbara "Babs" Wyler); China Kantner (Female Pantyhose Gunman); Kathryn Atwood (Pebbles Goren); Caroline Barclay (Mindy Lawford); Sylvia Short (Doctor Travis); Sandra Phillips and Gary Grossman (Talent Agents); Michelle Seipp (Hotel Receptionist); Frank Collison (Stoner Witness); Stephanie Friedman (Dori Smelling); Adam Small (Burger Boy Manager); Ben Slack (Madison Heights Mayor); Carol Hankins (Nervous Woman on Talkshow); Kristen Ernst (Teenage Girl on Talkshow); Mil Nicholson (Woman at Homecoming); Charles Font and John Chaidez (Burger Boy Workers); Ada Gorn, Jon Gudmundsson, and Bernadette Elise (Photographers); Gary Coleman (Himself).

LOS ANGELES TIMES, 1/20/95, Calendar/p. 21, Peter Rainer

Ready for another movie about how the media are wrecking our lives? "S.F.W.," which was originally scheduled for release last year, is a low-grade, grunge companion piece to "Natural Born Killers." Based on the novel by Andrew Wellman, and directed and co-written by Jefery Levy, it wallops the audience with mega-heavy-metal boom-boom theatrics. There hasn't been this much attitude in a movie since—well, "Natural Born Killers." And, in its own small-scale way, it's just about as aggravating.

The film's conceit is that a small-town working-class teenager, Cliff Spab ("Backbeat's" Stephen Dorff) can rise to cult-hero by displaying his arrogant anomie in the face of danger. It all begins when Cliff and his buddy, Joe (Jack Noseworthy), along with three other shoppers including the well-off Wendy (Reese Witherspoon), are taken hostage in a convenience-store holdup.

The gang, armed not only with weapons but with video cameras, demand that their tapes of the crisis be aired on network TV (in retrospect a particularly poignant demand in light of all the new networks on the horizon). Spab incomes a hero by playing up to the camera and flaunting his nihilism. His slogan—So F---ing What—becomes his generation's motto. He becomes an anti-celebrity.

Why did the gang want the crisis aired? Is Spab genuinely bummed out or just scamming? Are his followers cretins or crusading renegades? "S.F.W." isn't big on answers, perhaps because it's not big on questions. As Spab becomes caught up in a media circus that encompasses T-shirts, coffee mugs, CDs, FBI agents, talk-show hosts, corrupt parents and even more corrupt politicians, his odyssey of redemption becomes more and more gratingly self-righteous.

Levy works in lots of ear-splitting rock and sound effects, and switches back and forth from film to video, but all his fancy footwork can't disguise the bug-eyed narcissism and soppy sentimentality at the core of this story. Spab affects Jesus-like poses but the film seems to be endorsing his own deification. And, despite trace elements of satire, Spab's approach-avoidance amorousness with Wendy is just as twinkly and bogus as anything in "Love Story." "S.F.W." is trying for the same thing Spab is: It wants to become a cult smash by mainlining the Zeitgeist.

It hits the wrong vein.

NEW YORK POST, 1/20/95, p. 43, Thelma Adams

Crank up that suburban angst and spit on all the easy targets!

Stephen Dorff ("Backbeat") plays Cliff Spab, a rebel without a cause in "S.F.W."

Spab ducks into the local Fun-Stop for a six-pack and—it could happen—a quartet of gun-and-video-camera toting terrorists take him hostage. The fiends turn the greasy-haired smart aleck into a national anti-hero by broadcasting his 36 days of terror on national TV.

Why ask why?

Like the charmless Spab himself, we're not supposed to give a damn. "S.F.W." stands for "So F--king What," a title which mirrors my attitude toward this Generation X groan-fest.

The romantic notion behind Jefery ("Inside Monkey Zetterland") Levy's fuzzy satire is that Spab doesn't give a damn because he cares too much. Dulled by the media, beer and reefer, zipless sex and a minimum wage job slinging burgers, Spab is too alienated and ineffectual—trapped in a tarmac jungle not of his own making—to take control of his life.

Captured on video, the irreverent hostage says: "So I'm bored as sh--. So f--king what? ... So I might die in here. So f--king what?"

And a nation cheers?

Later Wendy (Reese Witherspoon), the uptown girl and co-captive Spab adores, tells her grungy sweetheart: "You're message is that there is no message."

The problem for these children of Marshall "the medium is the message" McLuhan is that they might want to overthrow the global village, but they still feel entitled to 15 minutes of media fame. And then, when the limelight shines on them, they don't have anything new to say.

Levy's main target is the media circus surrounding the hostage crisis. The irony is that the young director would love for "S.F.W." to be his ticket to the center ring.

NEWSDAY, 1/20/95, Part II/p. B7, Jack Mathews

The title of Jefery Levy's "S.F.W." is an acronym for a phrase some people use when a simple "so what" doesn't quite express the level of their disdain. It's an attitude of aggressive indifference, a challenge more than a shrug, and no less than a philosophy of life in this misfired satire of Generation X, the media and the cult of celebrity.

Adapted from the Andrew Wellman novel by Levy and Danny Rubin, "S.F.W." focuses on some of the same issues flogged to a fare-thee-well in Oliver Stone's "Natural Born Killers" and Michael Lehmann's "Airheads," which came out about the same time last summer. "S.F.W." was also scheduled for release last year, but its distributor chose not to fight the competition.

Not that the issues were going to go away. With Susan Smith and O.J. Simpson vying for headlines and network news lead-ins this week, the media's crime-as-entertainment beat is as hot as ever, and beneath "S.F.W.'s" kaleidoscopic surface of MTV images and clumsy pop culture jokes rests some of the most intriguing notions of all.

It's the story of Chris Spab (Stephen Dorff), a 20 year-old, pot-smoking slacker who wins a bloody shootout with the terrorists who'd held him and others hostage in a convenience store for 36 days, only to emerge a prisoner of his unwanted fame. The media is hounding him, his family is trying to cash in on his heroism, and teenagers across America have turned his belligerent "so-what" attitude—seen in the nightly snippets of video provided by the terrorists to the networks—into a generational rallying cry.

Unwanted celebrity is a rare commodity these days, and trying to fathom its impact through the confusion and anxiety of someone upon whom it's been foisted is a worthy exercise. But Spab, a smart-mouthed cliché of nihilistic youth, is about as pleasant to be around as Tonya Harding, and though he is ultimately softened and wisened by his experience, his transformation gives us little to cheer.

Part of the problem is in the performance. Dorff, so good as the fifth Beatle in last year's "Backbeat," never gets beyond the Hollywood stereotype of alienated youth, a suspended adolescent whose life isn't nearly as empty as his head.

But Dorff and Reese Witherspoon, who plays Spab's equally underdeveloped fellow hostage, aren't given much of a chance. Levy made a conscious decision to subordinate story and character to a frenetic style, intended, like "Natural Born Killers," to create in the audience a sense of the chaos in our culture.

In the end, all we feel is irritated.

SIGHT AND SOUND, 3/95, p. 52, Louise Gray

Cliff Spab, a 20 year-old burger chef with a talent for the nihilistic one-liner, becomes an inadvertent media hero when he is taken hostage with four others and held for 36 days in a local Madison Heights supermarket, the 24-hour Funstop. The organisation of boiler-suited hostage takers named Split Image has no stated objective; they video their hostages and force television networks to broadcast the tapes. Nationwide America is soon captivated by Spab's ability to play to the camera.

His reaction to his situation is simple: "So fucking what?" Only a wounded Spab and his girlfriend Wendy survive the siege which leaves a local mother and Spab's friend Joe Dice dead.

On his release from hospital everyone wants a piece of Spab. While Wendy appears on every major chat show, he refuses all offers, yet his image is plastered across magazines and t-shirts. His catch phrase, abbreviated to the slogan "S.F.W.", has become a rallying cry for disaffected youth. Despite finding brief solace with his brother Scott and Joe's sister Monica, Spab's unwanted celebrity status becomes increasingly intrusive. FBI agent Parsley believes Spab was in league with Split Image. He has an arrest warrant issued on the spurious grounds that Spab assaulted a teenage boy. Meanwhile Spab's attempts to leave town fail. A flashback reveals that he and Joe shot and killed Split Image members before being shot themselves. Spab meets Wendy, they visit the Funstop and bed down at Spab's hotel. Next day, they appear on a school stage in front of hundreds of pupils who are chanting "S.F.W.". From their midst, pupil Babs Wyler shouts "everything matters" and guns down Wendy and Spab. Media attention now focuses on Babs and her acronym slogan "E.M.". The wounded couple lie in hospital together, repeating dialogue from the Funstop siege.

A gormless blond with a dead-end job visits a late night store to buy beer and junk food and is taken hostage by terrorists who look like refugees from the post-punk group "Devo". While being constantly televised, he witnesses three deaths and becomes the protector of fellow hostage Wendy. Split Image are more or less silent. Their cameras provide Spab with the chance to free-associate about his position as a dumb blond who is, furthermore, a 36-day hostage in a meaningless siege. "so fucking what?", a phrase provoked perhaps by the stress of the siege but one surely pertinent to his outside life, is taken and turned into something larger. Show hosts and anchormen speculate about his philosophy. Essentially a passive figure who exercises no control over his sense of alienation. His only touchstones with reality are an incoherent anger and a shell-shocked desire to find Wendy and relive their Funstop dialogue.

To say that *S.F.W.* is a deeply cynical film is an understatement. It is as much about the utter vacuity of the American media as it is about Spab's own emptiness. His derailed Forrest Gumpisms are, for the standard 15 minutes, thought to be fraught with existential meaning. The film switches continually between chat show transmissions, excerpts from TVM (an MTV pastiche) and Spab's own flashbacks. He, Wendy and Babs are all asked the same dumb questions by journalists. Such media cynicism is convenient. If all media is vapid and exploitative, then so too are any criticisms of it. With this logic, *S.F.W.* contains a strategy for its own critical immunity.

Since the film trades off the perennial adolescent search for meaning and purpose, this in-built critical pre-empting is perhaps academic. School playgrounds could soon find themselves dividing into camps: "S.F.W." versus "E.M.". Parallels might be sought linking Spab (a character created by Andrew Wellman for a 1989 novella) and the late rock star Kurt Cobain, who committed suicide last year. Since Wellman's book predates Cobain's death, the only link between Spab and the rock star is that they both were prisoners of their own mass-market image.

Spab's world is a suitably hopeless blue-collar community where a dignity in labour (burgers anyone?) is non-existent. For the most part, the characters are as vacant as late night parking lots, their values a down-market version of Bret Easton Ellis' modish nihilism. The only truly shocking moment occurs when hostage Kim Martin, a nursing mother, is killed. The packaging of Spab as a folk anti-hero is perhaps the most interesting aspect of the entire film. Here is a character completely constrained by junk culture, whose name has, for British audiences at least, an additional resonance: Spab being one letter different from Spam luncheon meat. Indeed, Spab returns from the siege to find his employer selling Spab-burgers. Individuality threatened by commodity status is not a new idea, but if many other films have provided a more trenchant analysis, in none has the protagonist's incoherence and fragility been as apparent as in *S.F.W.*

VILLAGE VOICE, 1/24/95, p. 60, James Hannaham

SFW (see also *Reality Sucks*), a film supposedly critical of the media that uses the techniques of the media to make it more attractive to people who are attracted to the media, and which stars the slightly-more-bearable-than-Ethan Hawke Stephen Dorff as Cliff Spab, pure white trash (Spab = Spam), yet photogenic and flippant enough to become a national and some other people—his best buddy Joe, a cute girl from the right side of the tracks for him to become romantically involved with, and some incidental Blacks and Koreans (later killed)—are taken hostage by a mysterious jumpsuit-clad terrorist organization called Split Image, who, armed with more cameras than guns, somehow sends videotapes of the hostages to the national news media, which Joe's sister feels did not pay enough attention to Joe, thereby causing his death, one of the scenes that our tortured hero mentally replays in glowing backlit flashbacks, only one of the film's snapply pretentious formal conceits, which also include plenty of TV parodies (usually starring the quite versatile John Roarke), gruesome closeups of ugly Americans like Spab's two-dimensional parents, and handheld camerawork of the kind made legit by MTV, a thinly veiled version of which Spab appears on in order to disprove the reports of his suicide, an act committed by Kurt Cobain, whose life bears some eerily calculated parallels with Spab, who like Cobain has become recognized for work for which he has postpartum depression, avoids the millions who mis-understand his non-credo (So Fucking What = Nevermind), and goes AWOL, but unlike Cobain doesn't think of himself as a loser but poses as one, reaping the benefits of the current loserocracy by declaring the world meaningless yet remaining completely smug and arrogant—"I'm not really a hostage, I just play one on TV"—renting luxury suites in fancy hotels with money that con-cerned citizens sent to his family during the crisis and being remarkably successful with women, a ploy seen through by young "activist" Babs Wyler, who provides the film's marvelously nihilistic but unearned payoff, turning our protagonists back into regular folk as we exit the theater thinking, "SFW."

Also reviewed in:
NEW YORK TIMES, 1/20/95, p. C8, Janet Maslin
VARIETY, 8/29-9/4/94, p. 43, Steven Gaydos

SABRINA

A Paramount Pictures release in association with Constellation Films of a Mirage/Scott Rudin/Sandollar production. *Executive Producer:* Ronald Schwary and Lindsay Doran. *Producer:* Scott Rudin and Sydney Pollack. *Director:* Sydney Pollack. *Screenplay:* Barbara Benedek and David Rayfiel. *Based on the film written by:* Billy Wilder, Samuel Taylor and Ernest Lehman. *Based on the play by:* Samuel Taylor. *Director of Photography:* Giuseppe Rotunno. *Editor:* Fredric Steinkamp. *Music:* John Williams. *Music Editor:* Ken Wannberg. *Sound:* Danny Michael and (music) Shawn Murphy. *Sound Editor:* J. Paul Huntsman. *Casting:* David Rubin. *Production Designer:* Brian Morris. *Art Director:* John Kasarda. *Set Decorator:* George De Titta, Jr. *Costumes:* Ann Roth. *Costumes (Harrison Ford):* Bernie Pollack. *Make-up:* Bernadette Mazur and Peter Robb-King. *Running time:* 127 minutes. *MPAA Rating:* PG.

CAST: Harrison Ford (Linus Larrabee); Julia Ormond (Sabrina Fairchild); Greg Kinnear (David Larrabee); Nancy Marchand (Maude Larrabee); John Wood (Fairchild); Richard Crenna (Patrick Tyson); Angie Dickinson (Ingrid Tyson); Lauren Holly (Elizabeth Tyson); Dana Ivey (Mack); Miram Colon (Rosa); Elizabeth Franz (Joanna); Fanny Ardant (Irene); Valeria Lemercier (Martine); Patrick Bruel (Louis); Becky Ann Baker (Linda); Paul Giamatti (Scott); John C. Vennema (Ron); Gregory Chase (Ron); Margo Martindale (Nurse); J. Smith-Cameron (Carol); Christine Lumeau-Lipton (Ticket Taker); Michael Dees (Singer at Larrabee Party); Denis Holmes (Butler); Jo-Jo Lowe (Red Head); Ira Wheeler (Bartender); Philippa Cooper (Kelly); Ayako (India); François Genty (Make-up Assistant); Guillaume Gallienne (Assistant); J.B. Benn (Magician); Peter McKernan (Helicopter Pilot); Ed Connelly (Gulf Stream Pilot); Ronald Schwary (Sheik); Kenneth A. MacDonald (Beggar); Alvin Lum (Tyson Butler); Siching Song (Mother in Hospital); Phil Nee (Father in Hospital); Randy Becker (Trainer); Susan Browning (Secretary); Saikat Mondal (Moroccan Waiter); Peter Parks (Senator).

LOS ANGELES TIMES, 12/15/95, Calendar/p. 1, Kenneth Turan

Though some of the choicest talent in Hollywood is involved, including stars Harrison Ford and Julia Ormond and director Sydney Pollack, "Sabrina" plays like a standard brand. A mild romantic comedy, undemanding and unobjectionable, it fits the definition of product, a film made not for love but because it was a package that could be sold.

That scenario rings true because anyone who truly cared about the 1954 Billy Wilder "Sabrina" (starring Audrey Hepburn, Humphrey Bogart and William Holden) would see that even though it's not an unapproachable classic, a successful remake was unlikely. While most audiences viewing this "Sabrina" won't know about the original, the vague sense of disappointment they're likely to feel stems from how unsuited it is to being made over.

Pollack and screenwriters Barbara Benedek and David Rayfiel stick reasonably close to what has come before, even reprising the "once upon a time on the North Shore of Long Island" voice-over opening that signals the fairy tale nature of the proceedings.

Doing the talking is church mouse Sabrina Fairchild (Ormond), a dowdy chauffeur's daughter whose favorite pastime is spying on the elaborate parties given by her father's employers, the wealthy Larrabee clan. That includes mother Maude (Nancy Marchand), all-business elder son Linus (Ford) and his younger scamp of a brother David (Greg Kinnear).

It's Mr. Wine, Women and Song that Sabrina has a special interest in. More delusional than Buzz Lightyear, she is completely obsessed with David, a man who barely acknowledges her existence and considers life out of his sight to be a "hopeless abyss of misery and despair."

It's thoughts like that that cause her wise father (John Wood) to ship Sabrina off to Paris for awhile. When she returns, loaded down with smashing clothes and continental savoir-faire, she finds that David, though engaged to wealthy heiress and doctor Elizabeth Tyson (Lauren Holly), is still too much of a rascal not to want to chase her around the backyard.

Irked by this new turn of affairs is stuffy Linus, who planned to use David's marriage to Elizabeth to make oodles of money for the family. Described as "the world's only living heart donor," Linus coldheartedly decides he is going to romance Sabrina to distract her from David. At least, that's the plan.

Though it has its amusing moments and some good comic turns from Dana Ivey as a starchy secretary and Miriam Colon as an emotional maid, "Sabrina" finds it difficult to attain a semblance of life. For a variety of reasons, the film's dynamic is simply not believable this time around.

One problem is that many of "Sabrina's" underpinnings feel dated. The original's emphasis on the horror of a chauffeur's daughter romancing a wealthy man's son has wisely been dispensed with, but still the whole notion of madcap playboys and gaga servant girls feels a trifle stale.

A more insurmountable difficulty is in the casting. For whatever success the original "Sabrina" had came from a particular chemistry between actors that would be almost impossible to duplicate today.

Audrey Hepburn was able, as no current actress would be, to look girlish one moment and devastating the next. To compensate, the filmmakers have had to load up Ormond early on with clunky glasses and so much unconvincing dowdy clothing that she looks as if she were dressed up for Halloween as one of the Beverly Hillbillies.

That situation is made worse by an understandable kind of miscasting in the male roles. In the original, Humphrey Bogart looked so dour and unhappy (he knew he was not the first choice for the role) and William Holden is so much of a hunk that Sabrina's fascination with the younger brother is perfectly understandable.

In the new "Sabrina," Kinnear is too much of a pipsqueak to be convincing as the mad Lothario every woman falls in love with. And even with glasses, a homburg and a worried look, Ford's Linus is so much handsomer than Kinnear's David that it seems only a matter of time until Ormond's Sabrina notices. And with that critical dynamic and others gone, "Sabrina" proves too flimsy a reed to be successfully replanted.

NEW YORK, 12/18/95, p. 51, David Denby

The new version of *Sabrina*, Directed by Sydney Pollack, is a big, slow, heavy valentine to old-fashioned Hollywood filmmaking. Once again, the chauffeur's daughter (Julia Ormond) has to choose between the playboy son (Greg Kinnear) of her father's employer and the playboy's stern older brother (Harrison Ford), who runs the family business. Why this young woman should serve as the fountain of youth for either of these two men is of course a question no one raises. *Sabrina* drips the patriarchal attitudes of yesteryear. It's an unconscious movie. Yet there's some wit in the screenplay and the chance to see Harrison Ford doing his peculiarly somber but effective version of a leading man.

NEW YORK POST, 12/15/95, p. 53, Michael Medved

Despite some halfhearted gestures toward updating the story for the 1990s, "Sabrina" maintains an inescapable 1950s fairy-tale flavor which will come as welcome news to all those who cherish the original Billy Wilder/Audrey Hepburn film.

This respectful remake, from versatile director Sydney Pollack (Tootsie," "Out of Africa," "The Firm"), projects the same sense of innocence and elegance, of wit and wonder, as the beloved 1954 version and thanks to spectacularly gorgeous production design, a lush score by John Williams, and an abundance of star power, the once-upon-a-time magic still works its durable charm.

Sabrina Fairchild (Julia Ormond) is the only child of the loyal chauffeur (the enormously amiable John Wood) to the powerful Larrabee family of Long Island's North Shore. Growing up in the apartment above the garage on a vast estate, she watches the Larrabees' glittering parties from a distance and develops a killer crush on the family's younger son, an irresponsible playboy portrayed by Greg Kennear (host of NBC's "Later" talk show) in an appropriately likable, lightweight movie debut.

He scarcely notices Sabrina, who is a plain, bookish girl hiding behind her wire-rims, until she goes away to Paris to work as a photographer's assistant for Vogue magazine, and then returns, utterly transformed, into a fashionable vision of loveliness.

By this time, Kinnear's gotten engaged to a doctor (Lauren Holly) who just happens to be the daughter of a tycoon (Richard Crenna), whose promising company is about to merge with the Larrabees' business interests.

Kinnear's workaholic older brother (Harrison Ford) is therefore horrified when his irresponsible sibling is instantly smitten with the new, improved Sabrina/Cinderella after just a few dances at a lavish garden party. This infatuation threatens not only an engagement, but a billion-dollar business deal, so Harrison Ford springs ruthlessly into action: he'll take it upon himself to steal Sabrina's attention to get her out of the way of his corporate plans.

Ford provides a far more convincing characterization than the miscast Humphrey Bogart did in the original film, giving a dignified, subtle new dimension to his driven, heartless character ("He thinks morals are paintings on walls and scruples are money in Russia") suddenly forced to confront the emptiness of his life. Ormond, meanwhile, isn't Audrey Hepburn (who is?), but her sense of down-to-earth decency and substance works nearly as well as her predecessors unforgettably girlish and ethereal sprite.

Above all, Ormond conveys a hugely appealing accessibility in a role that will go farther than her previous decorative work in "First Knight" and "Legends of the Fall" to making her a star of the first magnitude.

In the end, it's the whole make-believe world of this picture that seduces the audience as much as the cast. Despite a stately pace, no one will complain about spending two hours with such pretty and amusing people in such lovely costumes, flitting from gleaming office to posh mansion to adorable vacation home on Martha's Vineyard, while transported by sleek private jet or polished limousine.

Of course, the film's just a shallow fantasy when you stop to think about it, but with all this expertly rendered opulence, no wonder you come out of the theater feeling like a million dollars.

NEWSDAY, 12/15/95, Part II/p. B2, Jack Mathews

Somewhere in the middle of Sydney Pollack's remake of Billy Wilder's "Sabrina," Harrison Ford turns to costar Julia Ormond and, with a burst of irony that belies his character's own fogyism, says "It's the '90s, Sabrina."

The line was no doubt put there by Pollack and his writers as both a wink of acknowledgement to the audience and a nod of respect to the makers of the 1954 original. But its actual effect is to remind us just how hopelessly outdated the material is.

In fact, the material was outdated in 1954, and maybe misplaced, as well. The story, about a chauffeur's daughter who becomes the object of rivalry for wealthy and very dissimilar brothers on the estate where she grew up, bears a class consciousness that was of little relevance to most postwar Americans.

Nevertheless, with Audrey Hepburn cast in a role that was equal parts Eliza Doolittle and Cinderella, and with popular stars Humphrey Bogart and William Holden as her Professor Higgins and Prince Charming, "Sabrina" became one of the sentimental hits of Hollywood's most sentimental decade.

The first thought of people when the remake and its cast were announced was "poor Julia Ormond." Gorgeous as she is, the British actress is bound to be compared unfavorably to Hepburn, who played Sabrina at the peak of what is usually described as her "fawnlike beauty and gamine charm." Hepburn was 25 at the time, but she and Sabrina seemed to be blossoming from ingenue to sophisticated lady at the precise same time.

Ormond, Brad Pitt's heartsick lover in "Legends of the Fall," is long past the gamine stage, if she was ever in it. She is a little too full-bodied for a fawn and will be taken as gamine by no one, even in the opening scenes, when Sabrina appears in a frousy dress and wire-rimmed glasses, climbing her favorite tree to gawk, as she tells us she has all her life, at the elegant parties thrown by the super-rich Long Island Larrabees.

"Sabrina" strains for a contemporary feel, with private jets, helicopter hops to Martha's Vineyard, Concordes to Paris and hip references to the cyberspace race, it follows the original almost scene for scene, once again putting the pressure on the cast to elevate it above slight, romantic fantasy. Whether it's because heart-stopping romance is a harder sell these days or the chemistry isn't right, they don't pull it off.

But Ormond turns out to be the least of the film's problems. Like Hepburn, she has the ability to seem desperately, illogically, childishly in love with both of the brothers—Linus (Ford), the severe, overbearing head of the family business, and the hedonistic charmer David (talk show host Greg Kinnear)—to the exclusion of all other possibilities.

And when she reappears at the Larrabee's, after a year of grooming and growing up in Paris, she is a vision of poise and beauty. "You're dazzling," the suddenly alert David says, and so she is.

That moment identifies the hollowness at the center of the story. You can understand what the brothers see in her—her beauty for the superficial David, her simple passion for overly ambitious, self-denying Linus. But what does she see in them? This is not "How to Marry a Millionaire," and the brothers Larrabee, as played by Kinnear and Ford, are hardly worthy of her.

Kinnear, in his film debut, shows a nice screen presence, good-looking with an easy charm, but David is a wisp of a rich-kid stereotype. And Ford, despite some attempted whimsy, seems an ogre whether he's in his predatory business mood or being sentimental. When Linus discovers that after cruelly manipulating Sabrina's affections, he has fallen in love with her, you can't tell whether his feelings are coming from his heart or his ulcer.

Ford may be the closest star we have to Bogart, but rumpled, short and cranky as he seemed, Bogart really was a romantic, and Ford is not.

NEWSWEEK, 12/19/95, p. 69, Jeff Giles

If you've been pining for faithful remakes, you're going to love Sydney Pollack's *Sabrina*: it's every bit as dull as the original. Billy Wilder's 1954 movie concerned a chauffeur's daughter (Audrey Hepburn). Sabrina longed for the playboy David Larrabee (William Holden), but it was only after she had a Paris makeover that his eye roved her way. Alas, David was engaged to an heiress and his family was cooking up a business merger with hers. So David's joyless, workaholic brother, Linus (Humphrey Bogart), decided to dispose of Sabrina. He wooed her, planning to dump her. Then he fell in love and turned human.

How bad could a movie with that cast be? Pretty bad. It was muddled, and Bogart was miscast. (Wilder had wanted Cary Grant.) Pollack sticks to the plot, though he turns the Paris sequence into a weird homage to "Funny Face." Most of the ancient troubles return from the dead. Today, the Larrabees' black-tie life—the Lear-jet, the clamoring servants, the lawn parties with a swing band—sticks in your throat. But Pollack's three stars are more problematic. Let's look at the Bermuda Triangle and see why this cruise ship goes down.

Harrison Ford (Linus) thought too hard about his role. He should have dashed Linus off, playing up his wicked streak and oozing the charm he used in "Working Girl." But Linus is a grim, ashen man who knows he's wasted his life. He and Sabrina (Julia Ormond) have zero chemistry—they fall in love during a musical montage, a dead giveaway—and the message is pat. Make love, not paperwork. Come on, Harrison, you learned this stuff in "Regarding Henry."

Ormond is a promising actress, but even in a plunging party dress she's too remote to dazzle the way Sabrina should. She also seems too smart to let herself be jerked around by the Larrabee boys. (Nineties woman and all that.) A lesser actress might have played this Cinderella role better. Paging Sandra Bullock.

Greg Kinnear (David) is terrific. He's the only pure pleasure in "Sabrina," apart from great one-liners and snappy minor characters (Nancy Marchand as Mrs. Larrabee, Dana Ivey as Linus's secretary). Kinnear's a sweet and funny playboy in a camel-hair coat and tennis shorts. He deepens the cad role so much he hurts the climax: we're rooting for the wrong guy.

In struggling to make something better than a generic romantic comedy, Pollack has made something worse. "Sabrina" doesn't have nearly enough light or air. It's too bad the director cut Sabrina's French cooking classes, but then he seems to have forgotten how to make a soufflé.

SIGHT AND SOUND, 2/96, p. 53, Peter Matthews

Sabrina Fairchild is the chauffeur's daughter on the Long Island estate of the Larrabees. Gauche, and dreamy, she has developed a hopeless crush on David Larrabee, the handsome younger son. David's mother Maude has arranged for Sabrina to spend two years in Paris working for Vogue magazine. On the eve of her departure, Sabrina goes to David's room and admits her feelings; but she is mortified to discover she has been speaking to Linus—the frigid, businesslike elder brother.

In Paris, Sabrina blossoms into a young sophisticate under the maternal guidance of Irene, a *Vogue* executive. Back in Long Island, David has met Elizabeth Tyson, whose father Patrick owns an electronics company. Seeing the possibility of a profitable merger, Linus and Maude encourage the affair, and an engagement is announced. Sabrina returns from Paris, beautiful and self-assured. Not recognising her at first, David invites her to his mother's birthday bash. At the party, Sabrina dances with David, and he asks Sabrina to meet him later in the solarium, his favourite trysting-place, and ritually places two champagne glasses in his back pockets. Linus tells David to sit down—with catastrophic results. David is rushed to hospital.

Linus attempts to buy off Sabrina with a million dollars, but she refuses. Ordering his brother sedated, Linus invites Sabrina to fly with him to Martha's Vineyard, ostensibly to photograph a property. He proceeds to try and seduce her, only it's Linus who ends up succumbing to Sabrina's charms. After an intimate dinner, Linus declares his love and Sabrina falls nervously silent.

David recovers and proposes that he and Sabrina resume their drink in the solarium, but she declines. Meanwhile, the Tysons threaten to cancel the merger if Linus doesn't do something about Sabrina. Linus books two tickets to Paris for himself and Sabrina, intending to ditch her there with a comfortable settlement. Now in love with him, Sabrina accepts the invitation; but Linus grows conscience-stricken and confesses his cynical motives. Heartbroken, Sabrina leaves for Paris alone. Learning of Linus' callous plan, David charges into his office and slugs him. Then David deliberately insults Sabrina, and Linus slugs him back. David reveals that he and Elizabeth have eloped, the deal is signed and everyone urges Linus to join Sabrina in Paris. Leaping on the Concorde, he meets her as she arrives at her Paris apartment, and the pair embrace.

Sabrina can't be called a good movie but compared to such other recent examples of Gallic goat's cheese as *Forget Paris* and *French Kiss*, it's a fairly classy number. This is at least the third current Hollywood movie to pose its protagonists against the most crassly obvious of Parisian landmarks and so awaken their appetite for life and love. While this convention used to be charming in old romantic comedies such as *Ninotchka*, there seems little profit in reviving it now—unless one aspires to provide modern audiences with the embalmed old movie emotions of their grandparents.

The writers Barbara Benedek and David Rayfiel have preserved the story of the 'classic' 1954 film (directed by Billy Wilder and Scripted by Wilder, Samuel Taylor and Ernest Lehman) almost *virgo intacta:* the few contemporising touches—such as founding the Larrabee family fortune in fibre optics—are like paint on a cadaver. One might wish to argue that the timewarp in which the movie appears to exist is exactly how people like the Larrabees would choose to see themselves; and that the hermetic atmosphere—somewhere between a fairy tale and a mausoleum—has its barbed point.

Sydney Pollack manages to lend a surprising gravity to the feathery proceedings; and there are certain retro pleasures to be gained from his use of stately tableaux and slow dissolves to enshrine the glittering appurtenances of the super-rich. The original Sabrina had its own problems—mainly that Wilder's sour jeering at the Larrabees assorted badly with his desire to glorify Audrey Hepburn, as the ultimate *jeune fille.* Still, the combination of sentimentality and cheapjack cynicism gave the movie an undeniable edge; and Hepburn, just entering her Givenchy period, was never more beautiful.

The remake is less nastily ambiguous but also less interesting. One still sees how the quasi-feudal Larrabees arrange their marriages like their business deals; but Sabrina herself is far less troublesomely the *arriviste* who graduates from the leisure-class dream of David to the bedroom and boardroom of Linus. Where Wilder allowed a frisson of doubt to creep in, the new film-makers seem a more wholesome-minded lot: all they're after, basically, is that old-time gasp of collective admiration at the frumpy schoolgirl's metamorphosis into a bird of paradise. Julia Ormond isn't quite the ethereal heartbreaker Hepburn was, but she's certainly a dish in her own right; and she brings off some poignant moments of soul-searching before the script requires her to congeal into a tedious post-feminist truth-teller.

As the wastrel David, Greg Kinnear is too pleasantly flyweight to approximate William Holden's nauseated self-loathing in the role. But Harrison Ford is unexpectedly witty as Linus: he clearly enjoyed his chance to indicate banked fires beneath a poker face—an improvement on Humphrey Bogart who acted, in the 50s version, as if he hated his part above all else on earth. The new movie is actually a good deal more likeable than its predecessor, but a defanged class satire isn't necessarily what we want. Pollack and the writers have tried to humanise the plutocratic Larrabees, and they have made the servants into a jolly, freethinking crew. But these coy, democratising gestures only emphasise the obsolescence of the whole enterprise.

TIME, 12/19/95, p. 72, Richard Schickel

[*Sabrina* was reviewed with *Sense and Sensibility*; see Schickel's review of that film.]

VILLAGE VOICE, 12/19/95, p. 71, J. Hoberman

"Has there *ever* been a good remake?" the video store proprietor demanded, having instantly divined why I was renting the 1954 *Sabrina*. "Do any of them even make money?" As I ransacked my brain, he gave me his theory: Studios go for remakes because remakes are so easy to pitch. No one has to explain a treatment or imagine a scenario. Yes, and the titles are already presold.

Nicolas Cage's performance in *Leaving Las Vegas* and Terry Gilliam's upcoming *12 Monkeys* notwithstanding, the cine-centennial has been just about the dullest year for Hollywood movies that I can remember, and Sydney Pollack's *Sabrina* is symptomatic—a soporific, superfluous recycling of a dated picture that owed whatever charm it held 40 years ago to the wan sarcasm of its writer-director Billy Wilder and the strenuously doelike capering of its leading lady, Audrey Hepburn.

Wilder's *Sabrina* was the Cinderella story of a chauffeur's daughter (Hepburn) who grew up infatuated with her fathers megawealthy employer's wastrel son David (William Holden as a blond) and had to be strategically wooed by the playboy's sober older brother, the financial wizard Linus (Humphrey Bogart). Pollack's version is actually less naturalistic. Sabrina II (Julia Ormond) is more of an ugly duckling—she initially wears glasses. And where Sabrina I went to

Paris to study the culinary arts (her mother had been a cook), Sabrina II gets a glamour job as a gofer at Paris *Vogue,* even though she speaks no French. Her boss (Fanny Ardant) communicates with a wise, knowing twinkle.

An even more feeble romantic comedy than *The American President*—why don't we just declare a moratorium and spend the rest of the month at Film Forum's screwball retro?—Pollack's *Sabrina* is equally allergic to satire. The rich in this cozy scenario are like you and me—only nicer. Indeed, although the titles are the same, the star of the remake is actually Harrison Ford and his $20 million paycheck. In the original, Bogart takes his feckless kid brother out of commission by contriving to have him sit on a couple of champagne flutes. In the remake, the accident ... just kind of happens. Even onetime *Talk Soup* wiseguy Greg Kinnear has been de-smarmed for the cad role of David. Pollack is so wholesome he makes Wilder seem positively kinky by comparison—or maybe it's vice versa. Wilder will doubtless split a gut watching the effort Pollack expends in maintaining Sabrina's virginity.

Any way you parse it, *Sabrina* is a fantasy about dads and daughters. Better preserved and less dyspeptic than Bogart was at 54, Ford, who is just one year younger, hardly has to stretch to play a trimly attractive father figure. (Although Ford's ambiguous good-guy roles in the *Stars Wars* trilogy and *Blade Runner* made him something of a denatured, contemporary Bogart, he's long since been domesticated.) Ormond, unenviably cast in a no-win role, has a pert chipmunk smile but lacks anything approaching Hepburn's ferocious daddy's girl magic—Linus II will be educated rather than enchanted.

Thus, proceeding from one heart-warming lesson to another, the movie is drearily sentimental and ponderously slow. Despite the worst efforts of John Williams's trilling vibraphone, the lines are surrounded by a mighty cushion of dead air. Action? A fluffy little dog does run through it—not to mention the tediously wry Nancy Marchand as the boys' mother. Watching *Sabrina* is like leafing through the perfumed pages of a house, garden, and celebrity mag while under sedation. An afternoon on Martha's Vineyard provides the occasion for another fashion shoot. Take care you don't pass out, slack-jawed and drooling.

Incidentally, *Sabrina*'s prerelease puff pieces invariably refer to the original as a classic. Forget about it. Wilder's fairy tale is a lot closer to Disney than Lubitsch, while Bogart's morose wooing of the hyperactive Hepburn belies the universality of her appeal. Evidently Bogie detested the project, telling *Time* correspondent Ezra Goodman that Wilder was "the kind of Prussian German with a riding crop" while *Sabrina* itself was "a crock of crap." Only in Hollywood does that mean play it again, Sam.

Also reviewed in:
CHICAGO TRIBUNE, 12/15/95, Friday/p. C, Michael Wilmington
NEW YORK TIMES, 12/15/95, p. C25, Janet Maslin
NEW YORKER, 12/25/95-1/1/96, p. 146, Anthony Lane
VARIETY, 12/11-17/95, p. 82, Todd McCarthy
WASHINGTON POST, 12/15/95, p. F7, Desson Howe
WASHINGTON POST, 12/15/95, Weekend/p. 49, Desson Howe

SAFE

A Sony Pictures Classics release of an American Playhouse Theatrical Films presentation of a Chemical Films production in association with Good Machine/Kardana/Channel Four Films and Arnold Semler. *Executive Producer:* Lindsay Law, James Schamus, and Ted Hope. *Producer:* Christine Vachon and Lauren Zalaznick. *Director:* Todd Haynes. *Screenplay:* Todd Haynes. *Director of Photography:* Alex Nepomniaschy. *Editor:* James Lyons. *Music:* Ed Tomney. *Sound:* Neil Danziger. *Sound Editor:* Tim O'Shea. *Casting:* Jakki Fink. *Production Designer:* David Bomba. *Art Director:* Anthony Stabley. *Set Decorator:* Mary E. Gullickson. *Set Dresser:* Melanie Paizia and Yvonne Jean. *Costumes:* Nancy Steiner. *Make-up:* Deborah Larson and Chris Laurence. *Running time:* 119 minutes. *MPAA Rating:* R.

CAST: Julianne Moore (Carol White); Xander Berkeley (Greg White); Dean Norris (Mover); Julie Burgess (Aerobics Instructor); Ronnie Farer (Barbara); Jodie Markell (Anita); Susan Norman (Linda); Martha Velez-Johnson (Fulvia); Chauncy Leopardi (Rory); Saachiko (Dry Cleaners Manager); Tim Gardner (Department Store Dispatcher); Wendy Haynes (Waitress); Alan Wasserman (Client); Jean Pflieger (Client's Wife); Stephen Gilborn (Dr. Hubbard); Janel Moloney (Hairdresser); Brendan Dolan (Patrolman); John Apicella (Psychiatrist); Dana Anderson (Lynn); Wendy Gayle (Baby Shower Mother); Cassy Friel (Baby Shower Child); Frank Dent (Video Narrator); Peter Crombie (Dr. Reynolds); Sarah Davis (Sarah); Beth Grant (Becky, Auditorium Speaker); Jo Wilkinson (Listener No. 1); Gerrielani Miyazaki (Listener No. 2); Edith Meeks (Patient No. 1); Francesca Roberts (Patient No. 2); Elinor O. Caplan (Patient No. 3); Joe Comando (Exterminator); Lorna Scott (Marilyn); Peter Friedman (Peter Dunning); Kate McGregor Stewart (Claire); Tricia Dong (Wrenwood Patient); James Lyons (Cab Driver); Mary Carver (Nell); April Grace (Susan); Eleanor Graham (Singer); Mitch Greenhill (Accompanist); James LeGros (Chris); Rio Hackford (Lester); Jessica Harper (Joyce); Rravi Achar (Wrenwood Instructor); Brandon Cruz (Steve).

CHRISTIAN SCIENCE MONITOR, 7/25/95, p. 15, David Sterritt

"Safe," the new movie by Todd Haynes, has generated an unusual amount of debate among critics.

The main character is Carol White, a Los Angeles homemaker who develops health problems and concludes that chemicals in the environment are to blame. Told by her husband and friends that she's merely "stressed out," she turns to a cultlike self-help organization that leads her to increased isolation from the everyday world.

Is the movie promoting places like Wrenwood, the "wellness center" where Carol withdraws into a world of self-absorbed seclusion? Or is the film strongly critical of such "new age" silliness, seeing it as a trap no better than the mindless materialism she indulged before?

Perceptive moviegoers have no trouble detecting the picture's point of view on these questions—especially when the film reaches its chilling conclusion, carrying Carol's self-imposed exile to an extreme that Mr. Haynes obviously regards as profoundly regrettable.

Yet some reviewers have missed the movie's point, mistaking its subtlety and compassion for ambivalence, or even an endorsement of dubious contemporary fads. What confuses these critics is Haynes's bold refusal to hold his characters up for the easy ridicule that a more conventional film would shower upon them. Even the most misguided figures in his story are allowed a dignity and authenticity that make the movie's criticisms all the more persuasive.

Another stumbling block for some spectators is Haynes's insistence on avoiding the common cinematic cues that tell us how we're meant to think and feel. "Safe" doesn't coerce or manipulate its audience. Instead, it lets us discover its messages through our own thoughts, perceptions, and responses as we watch Carol's experiences.

In a recent interview, I asked Haynes how he arrived at his unusual approach to storytelling in "Safe," which is only his second feature-length film.

"As always, when I set out to make a film," he told me, "it was a challenge to myself. I wanted to overcome the obvious gaps between myself and a character like Carol, who's an easy target in obvious ways—her economic bracket, her lack of self-knowledge or identity—and people like the 'new age' characters. In both cases, I wanted to approach them by challenging my own innate criticisms or dismissals of aspects of their worlds ... I had no interest in condemning them or placing myself above them."

At the same time, Haynes didn't want Carol and the others to become "the attractive, larger-than-life, charming characters that most movies have a tendency to show." Instead he wanted Carol to evoke "the vulnerable aspects in all of us, the vulnerable sides of our identities that films rarely address. With the 'new age' stuff, I tried not to let my criticisms blind me, but I also wanted to explore aspects that I find really problematic. The film is more an indictment of 'new age' things than of the California life."

While he acknowledges that "Safe" breaks the Hollywood mold by avoiding emotional close-ups and other audience-controlling devices, Haynes notes that movie melodramas played a part in his planning.

"Melodrama inspired limits I decided to place on the film," he says. "Carol was going to be somebody completely enclosed in certain systems, whether it's L.A. social life or another system that replaces this. She never has an ability to completely break out. Although the film doesn't indulge in melodramatic style ... it's a 'woman's film' and comes out of that tradition."

Another key aspect of "Safe" is its interest in personal identity and how this is inflected by our social surroundings.

"Identity works when it's invisible," the filmmaker says. "As soon as you start thinking about who you are, and how much you're taking cues from the world and people around you, it suddenly seems artificial, fake, contrived ... L.A. and Wrenwood both have isolation built into them, but both are always telling you that you're not alone because there are other people just like you all around, and if you do these things, you'll be affirmed as part of the group.

"Carol is desperately alone, though, as are all the people around her ... Unlike most films, 'Safe' shows the cost that's entailed every time we join a group or give up the things in ourselves that can never really be harnessed."

Asked how he first became fascinated with movies, Haynes says it started early. "I began drawing obsessively at age 3," he recalls, "usually in relationship to films that had made a big impact on me. 'Mary Poppins' was the first. I got hooked on films like a lot of kids, but I probably took it a little further—in reenactments and re-creations and big after-dinner productions that my sister would star in."

After college, he left his native Los Angeles for New York and helped found Apparatus Productions, a nonprofit organization devoted to helping new filmmakers. He began developing his own movie ideas at the same time, based on his realization that "narrative film is ultimately the best medium to discuss social structures."

Although he doesn't paint a flattering portrait of family life in "Safe," the filmmaker is quick to credit his own family for helping him achieve his goals. "My parents were incredibly supportive," he says, "and always encouraged and celebrated my work. That gave me a sense of security and confidence. I knew I wanted to make films that were narrative but probably wouldn't be commercially viable."

It remains to be seen how commercially viable "Safe" will turn out to be, but it's already one of the year's most talked-about independent films, bearing out Haynes's theory about audiences.

"People are smarter than Hollywood gives them credit for," he says with enthusiasm. "There are people all over the country who want to see something different although they don't get a chance to very often."

LOS ANGELES TIMES, 6/30/95, Calendar/p. 12, Kenneth Turan

It starts with a sniffle. Then things get worse. And you think you know what's going to happen on screen. But you don't.

"Safe," the elegantly unnerving new film by Todd Haynes, is all about uncertainty. A strange illness descends on protagonist Carol White (Julianne Moore) and the insecurity and unease she feels spills over into the audience. Insidious and provocative, "Safe" refuses to lend a hand, avoids taking sides or pointing the way. Everything that happens in this beautifully controlled enigma is open to multiple interpretations, and that extends finally to the title's meaning as well.

A measure of "Safe's" subversiveness is that it mimics the forms of standard genres only to turn familiar conventions inside out. Its theme, for instance, is apparently the right-thinking one of the dangers of environmental pollution, but the deeper you get into the story, the more uncertain that becomes.

And while its "healthy woman gets sick and fights back" structure has a shrewd and superficial resemblance to numerous movies of the week, "Safe" finally encourages you to view all the stages of Carol's story as told in different ways, and even to think that perhaps her time of greatest illness is the closest she comes to a kind of life.

Set in the San Fernando Valley in 1987, "Safe" opens with a polished tracking shot (typical of the sharp, pristine quality of cinematographer Alex Nepomniaschy's images) that follows a Mercedes down a manicured street and behind the motorized gates of the luxury home where Carol lives with a bland husband (Xander Berkeley) and his son from a previous marriage.

With her tiny voice and passive character, uninvolved during sex and incapable of sweating in aerobics class, Carol has the doll-like existence of an up-to-date Stepford wife. A "total milkaholic" who wears pearls to lunch and spends her days gardening, exercising and worrying about furniture, Carol is a Nora who never even thinks of slamming the door, who looks around at her elite surroundings and is content.

Julianne Moore, who was a revelation in "Vanya on 42nd Street," continues to do remarkable work in a role she wanted so much she reportedly burst into tears when she got it. Ever so delicately, she animates this detached mouse, allowing us to feel for the kind of passive, emotionally disconnected character whose first thought when illness encroaches is to apologize for the inconvenience she's causing.

As sniffles are succeeded by unexpected tiredness, extended coughing, difficulty breathing and frightening fits, Carol's physical disintegration gets worse and worse. Her doctors are baffled, her husband frustrated, but it is Carol herself who thinks she's found the answer when she spots a flyer that asks the daunting question, "Do you smell fumes? Are you allergic to the 20th Century?"

What Carol is told she has is a disease you catch from your surroundings, something referred to as "an immune system breakdown based on environmental factors." Just living in the modern world, with its 60,000 chemical substances, is what has made her ill. Now she goes nowhere without a filter mask and an oxygen tank, and when she hears about the Wrenwood Center outside of Albuquerque, a place that offers a chemically free safe haven, she decides that this will be salvation.

Wrenwood is the final, ambiguous stage of Carol's journey, and what happens within its walls intensifies the questions that "Safe" encourages but refuses to answer conclusively. Is the regimen there truly a cure, and at what cost does it come? Is Carol's illness a reaction to her physical environment or could it be a psychological plea for release from the barren life of a good little girl? And in a world so rife with strange maladies and stranger remedies, how outmoded is the very concept of safeness?

Working with deliberation and controlled precision, writer- director Haynes, whose "Poison" took the Grand Jury Prize at Sundance and became a political *cause célèbre,* solidifies his reputation as one of the most intellectually challenging of current directors. Helped by composer Ed Tomney's ominous score, he has created not a simple cautionary tale about the air we breathe but a withering portrait of American society, an attack on the sterility and toxicity of modern life and the profound sense of malaise that can foster. Subtlety is the rarest quality in today's filmmakers and "Safe" demonstrates why it is valuable as well as scarce.

NEW STATESMAN & SOCIETY, 4/26/96, p. 26, Jonathan Romney

Early on in Todd Haynes' film *Safe*, the heroine reacts with horror when her new sofa arrives and turns out to be the wrong colour. "Black is not what we ordered," she protests, reacting in something little short of trauma. Here she is effectively stating the theme of the film: like all horror films (and *Safe*, though hardly a genre exercise, is a horror film nonetheless), this is a story about people getting something they did not order, and having to adjust their existences accordingly.

In *Safe*, that thing is "environmental illness", sometimes referred to as an allergy to the 20th century—an extreme sensitivity to those ambient toxins with which the immune system normally copes. Haynes' heroine is Carol White, who lives an antiseptically sedate domestic existence in the San Fernando Valley. Her undisturbed routine as a "house ... um, home-maker" breaks down through violent fits of fainting and coughing, and she embarks on a pilgrimage through hospitals, therapy and finally a secluded new age "safe haven".

This might sound very much like a case history sort of film, but it isn't. *Safe* alludes to and works off the medical-drama-of-the week genre of TV movie, but with none of the genre's cathartic pieties. For one thing, it's not that easy to pin down what Carol's problem is exactly, how we're supposed to feel about it, or what Haynes' point of interest in it is.

Julianne Moore, who gives a powerfully suggestive—because so blankly restrained— performance as Carol, says she was attracted to the project by the brilliance of the script. But it's hard to imagine *Safe* sparkling on paper, so finely tuned is its sardonic ambivalence. Nor does it entirely help to know about Todd Haynes's stance and his interests. A filmmaker very much informed by critical theory, he first became known with a bitterly ironic short about singer Karen Carpenter's anorexia, acted out by Barbie dolls. He then made the three-part feature *Poison* about social scapegoating, Aids and the erotic imagination of Jean Genet; it made him a leading light of what was being called "New Queer Cinema".

But it would be reductive to assume, as some critics have, that *Safe* is "really" about Aids; rather, it plugs into wider arguments around society, the body and identity that Aids politics has thrown up. *Safe* also confounds expectations of the knowing counter-cultural sarcasm that marks Haynes' other work; the irony here is so finely tuned that it resembles the ominous background hum that dominates Ed Tomney's score. Haynes' approach is constantly to distance us, to hold us back from making easy judgements about Carol, her ailment or those of the world she inhabits. He encourages us at different points to read the story literally as brooding science horror, or as a flat-out satire, first on the cocooning solipsism of late 1980s Californian Stepford suburbia, then on the no less-mendacious new-age ideology of holistic positivism. In the hands of another director, the same script might have ended up as literal melodrama or as farce, a sort of middle class middle-aged *Clueless*. There are such moments here: the aerobic class, where a friend complements Carol on not sweating, or muted one-liners, like the arrival on stage of Carol's safe haven guru: "Peter is a chemically sensitive Person With Aids, so he has an incredibly vast perspective."

But *Safe* resists easy answers through its rigorously impersonal stylisation. Haynes favours long shots, isolating Carol in dwarfing suburban architecture that is as monumentally chilly as Antonioni's 1960s settings. The soundtrack completes the sense of an antiseptic world: its ever present background hum is the palpable sound of Carol's own apparent absence. If Carol isn't safe here, where is she safe? But the "healthy" new world she enters is one that reduces sensation and tension ever further: a beatific TV programme heralds the prospect of "a period of learning to run warm and cool, not hot and cold".

At first, we are inclined to read Carol's illness as purely metaphoric, a reaction to the emotional repression she seems to collude with in her affectless suburbia. But, once she gets to her desert retreat of Wrenwood, that interpretation turns back on us. The charismatic guru coerces his residents to take responsibility for their illnesses, which he blames on their self hatred. We realise that to regard Carol's illness as metaphoric is no less punitive than to see it as psychosomatic. Either way, she takes the blame; yet, for most of the story, we are not really sure whether there's any Carol there to attache blame to—or even to attach an identity to.

The bitter irony of the story is that, where medical dramas conventionally result in an epiphany of self knowledge, Carol's leads to a dead end—she cuts herself both off from the world and, it seems, from a viable identity within it. *Safe* most directly addresses Aids culture in questioning the assumptions about identity that underlie a label like "Person With Aids"—for Carol, like the others at Wrenwood, finally finds an identity, as a person whose disease defines her entirely. It becomes the single hook she has to hang herself on. It leaves her safe, home alone in the deep freeze; meanwhile we're left feeling totally hit off-balance by *Safe*'s galvanising chilly discourse.

NEW YORK POST, 6/23/95, p. 38, Thelma Adams

Oh, alienation! The emptiness of driving a Mercedes at night between the mansionettes of the San Fernando Valley. The dark, sophomoric poetry of traffic and smog.

Bourgeois bashing is back and writer/director Todd Haynes is shooting tropical fish in a barrel in "Safe."

Haynes ("Poison") follows the opening tone poem with a scene of safe and unappealing sex. Carol (Julianne Moore) silently stares at the camera, patient and bored, while her husband, Greg (Xander Berkeley), rocks on top of her. Note his bald spot. Pity the poor, trapped heterosexuals for their coupling is short and nasty.

Oh, condescension! Haynes dissects his characters with a "you're vapid, I'm not" disdain. As it's meaningless sex within the bonds of marriage wasn't enough of a crack in the spiritual life of this winsome matron, the peach-wearing, porcelain-skinned Carol has begun to develop a mysterious illness.

With a bit of research, Carol becomes convinced that she has "20th Century Disease." The modern world of fumes and chemicals has become toxic to her. Despite a routine that consists largely of trips to the dry cleaners, hair dressers, aerobics palace, and chic restaurants, Carol is stressed out.

Even within the cocoon of material possessions, something is rotten in L.A. County.

In part, what is rotten is that it seems more like Houston than Los Angeles. Haynes seems to be writing about a milieu completely alien to him. When he sends Carol off to an afternoon baby shower, the women are overdressed and under-differentiated, Stepford Wives of the worst sort.

If Haynes doesn't believe in these people, why should we? How can we empathize with Carol when her environment is inhabited by biped extensions of the Brown University-educated Haynes' paranoia about the world of privilege in which he was raised? Of course this world is toxic—but that's how Haynes created it.

In its second hour, "Safe" brushes against satire. Carol travels to a touch-feely sleepaway camp in New Mexico to purge herself of toxins. The flat scenes cry out for a social satirist like Robert Altman to go in for the comic kill, or for Haynes to reveal some new emotional depth in the oft-lampooned New Age navel-gazing.

Haynes is a pretentious filmmaker, but he's not inept. The movie looks great and so does Moore—she rates the movie's single star. The "Short Cuts" actress is the radiant light at the movie's amber center. Even when she wanders across the screen, anemic, without makeup, with a silver-dollar-sized rash on her forehead, she projects an old-fashioned grace.

But Moore is no antidote for the most toxic movie I've seen this year.

NEWSDAY, 6/23/95, Part II/p. B4, Jack Mathews

The subject of Todd Haynes' "Safe" is an immune disorder known as "20th-Century Disease." It is a condition said to afflict people hypersensitive to the effluvium of an aerosol society—all that crap we breathe in from chemical sprays, exhausts, aromatics and decomposing landfills.

Though the condition has not been recognized as a disease by the medical community, its symptoms of exhaustion, nausea, nosebleeds, headaches, narcolepsy and disorientation are real enough to the people suffering from them, and it is a topic tailor-made for television talk shows and disease-of-the-week TV movies.

What it is not, at least in the coy hands of Haynes, is a very compelling subject for a motion picture. After a slow and very promising introduction to the illness, through an upscale Southern California housewife (Julianne Moore) who seems to be carrying the weight of the century on her back, "Safe" makes a sharp turn into the realm of New Age healing and hucksterism, and literally slogs through its final hour.

Haynes' first film, the 1991 "Poison," was a study in density and obfuscation—three separate stories dealing with deviant behavior—but it was not boring. "Safe" is not particularly dense, yet it moves with the pace of sap trying to get back into the tree.

I'm not sure what Haynes hoped to achieve with his deliberately anticlimactic structure. The first half of "Safe" makes a strong case for the reality of environmental disease; there is no question that Moore's Carol White is being progressively debilitated by airborne toxins. And the second half, set in a healing clinic in New Mexico, suggests that its advanced stage mimics depression to such an extreme that victims can only seek relief from their psychological symptoms.

Two hours is a long time to wait for that revelation, and though we certainly feel Carol's lethargy, the two hours fly by like four.

Moore, in a role I would liken to melting butter, makes "Safe" more compelling than it might be. We never know enough about who Carol White was before her illness to get a true sense of how far she has degenerated, but the transformation that we do see, from busy homemaker to psychological invalid, is amazing. Moore looks as if she weighs about 80 pounds by the end of the movie, and walks as if she weighs a ton.

Ultimately, "Safe" takes the form of a cautionary tale. If something isn't done about the poisoning of the environment, it tells us, the immobile face of Carol White and of the other walking wounded at the New Mexico clinic is the face of the future. With the medical community seemingly in cahoots with the pollution industry, we will slowly lose our war with the air.

That's a pretty dramatic ambition for a movie that has almost no drama of its own.

SIGHT AND SOUND, 5/96, p. 59, Tony Rayns

San Fernando Valley, 1987. Affluent home-maker Carol White finds her comfortable domestic and social routine disrupted by the delivery of a new couch in the wrong colour. Her husband

Greg (who has a 10-year-old son, Rory, by an earlier marriage) leaves her to deal with all household matters, and so she complains to the furniture store. Driving home she succumbs to a choking fit, apparently caused by the fumes from a truck on the freeway. A medical check-up reveals nothing, but she feels increasingly ill (she has a nosebleed after impulsively getting a perm at the but salon) and repeatedly cries off sex with Greg. She suspects that a fruit diet proposed by her friend Linda may have triggered the symptoms. Her doctor, attributing the problem to stress, refers her to a psychiatrist—who offers no help.

At her friend Barbara's birthday party, Carol suffers a major breakdown to her respiratory system. Utterly disoriented and distraught, she writes off for a videotape on environmental illness and then takes tests to determine which chemicals in everyday use have become noxious to her immune system. Greg accompanies her to a seminar, where a speaker stresses the need to provide 'safe havens' for chemically sensitive persons. Soon after, Carol has a life-threatening fit at the dry cleaner's and is rushed to hospital. Faced with more incomprehension from the medical establishment, she decides to retreat to Wrenwood, a safe haven for the chemically sensitive in the desert outside Albuquerque, New Mexico.

Welcomed to Wrenwood by its director Claire and her assistant Susan, Carol moves into a secluded cabin and tries to get used to the institution's rules and spirit. She initially recoils from the 'new age' rhetoric of the presiding guru Peter Dunning, a chemically sensitive person with Aids, who lives in a lavish mansion in the hills above Wrenwood and teaches the patients how correctly to blame themselves for their illnesses. Despite plentiful evidence of the shortcomings of Dunning's teachings (hypersensitive patient Harry dies, and his widow Nell succumbs to her rage against the world), Carol becomes convinced that Wrenwood will 'cure' her and develops a platonic friendship with fellow-patient Chris. She tells the visiting Greg and Rory that she has decided to take over Harry's 'safe house', a porcelain-lined dome. After giving a garbled speech of thanks to the other patients on her birthday, Carol (now with a mysterious lesion on her forehead) prepares for bed in the empty and sterile space of the safe house. Confronting her own image in the mirror, she tries to start working on her non-existent self-esteem.

For a film capable of arousing such strong responses—laughter, dread, amazement, anger—*Safe* has a studiously 'neutral' tone. So neutral, in for fact, that it leaves space for radically different audience responses. Most European viewers will come to the film with an ingrained cynicism about Californian middle-class lifestyles in general and 'new age' therapies in particular; they will tend to read the film as a satire from the very start. Todd Haynes' script has the odd throwaway line which certainly encourages this reading (at Barbara's birthday party: "Did you wrap that yourself?" "God, I wish I were that creative"), but such moments are outweighed by the emphasis on Carol's pain and distress, as 'real' as anything in *ER*, which makes it increasingly hard to see her as the butt of anyone's burnout. These emotional tensions beneath the film's glassily placid surface are of course deliberate, and disturbing in the most productive way.

The principles of restraint and subtlety which inform everything from Julianne Moore's heroic central performance to Ed Tomney's ambient-going-on-entropic score are in part Haynes' protest against Current fashions in filmmaking. No film could be further from the MTV-aesthetic than *Safe*. But the film's eerie stillness is also the flipside of the barrage of visual styles and syntaxes which Haynes offered in his previous feature *Poison*. Instead of requiring the viewer to see connections among three different narratives, each with its own distinct tone and visual idiom, *Safe* uses its carefully composed wide-angle shots to turn each viewer into a diagnostician, scanning the images for clues to an understanding of Carol's predicaments. The element of coercion on the part of the director is minimal in both cases, and the effect is curiously similar. Like Fassbinder before and after he immersed himself in melodrama, Haynes has found more than one way of engaging audiences without directly manipulating their responses.

So what are the roots of Carol's problems? Do they start with her name, Carol White, already so emblematic of her life of sweatless aerobics, pidgin Spanish (to instruct her Hispanic maids), synthetic gardening and passionless sex? Or with the delivery of the black sofa, as disruptive an element in a 'white' lifestyle as a virus in a healthy organism? Or with other incursions of 'dirt' like the oily fumes from a truck on the freeway (they distract her from the fundamentalist preacher on the car radio) or her step-son Rory's school essay on LA gangs ("Dad, how do you spell 'Uzi'?") or the crude dinner-table joke told by a friend of Greg's about a woman with a vibrator stuck inside her? The underlying question comes into focus even before Carol's attacks begin in earnest, when she watches a 'deep ecology' video which calls for "an understanding of the one-ness of all life". Carol takes the video as it was intended—as mildly consoling 'new age' balm but inevitably fails to ask herself how much of "all life" finds its way into her orderly, sanitised existence.

The second half of *Safe* centres on Carol's supposed cure at Wrenwood and implies, naturally enough, that the treatment proposed by Peter Dunning may be as noxious as the chemical toxins which sent her there in the first place. Dunning's line of argument is transparently clear: cut yourself off from the ills of the world, accentuate the positive in your view of the world ("environmentalism, multi-culturalism, a decline in drugs and promiscuity"), and your inner self will be transformed to healing effect. His watchword gives the film its title: "We are one with the power that created us. We are safe, and all is well in our world." We hear that Dunning is both chemically sensitive and HIV+, but cannot fail to notice that he betrays no symptom of any affliction; the well-being of his particular world is suggested with admirable economy by the single shot of his vast mansion, perched on the hill above Wrenwood. There are several other hints of the lies on which the 'safe haven' is founded—the proximity of a busy interstate freeway, the sight and sound of marauding coyotes in the ugly scrubland around the place—but the suggestion of satire is again kept in check by the emphasis on the mental and physical agonies of the inmates.

Neatly enclosed in square brackets, pulsing white and then turning red before fading from the screen, the main title of *Safe* expresses the mystery at the heart of the film. It's to do with the breaching of *cordons sanitaires*, with the way in which a placid and orderly life can suddenly be compromised by evidence of ineradicable dirt. In this respect, too, *Safe* is the flipside of *Poison*, the film in which Haynes celebrated the 'dirty' aspects of anti-social transgression. Taken together, the two features establish Todd Haynes as one of the few filmmakers in North America capable of asking provocative questions in ways which suggest that cinema has another century of creative development to look forward to. But *Safe* doesn't seriously try to explain how or why Carol's metabolism became contaminated; for Todd Haynes, environmental sickness is one more grisly fact of life, like Aids. What most concerns him is not the mystery of the disease itself—but the perplexing human responses to it: the apparent need to assign blame for it, the inability to accept that 'dirt', danger, chaos and all its works are an integral part of life.

TIME, 6/26/95, p. 79, Richard Corliss

In the San Fernando Valley in 1987, a man and a woman make love. Or rather, he does, plowing away at his passion. She studies the ceiling while holding him like a reluctant mother. Carol (Julianne Moore) and Greg (Xander Berkeley) live in suburban comfort, yet Carol is anything but comfortable. Ordinary fragrances and fumes make her ill. She hyperventilates in her car. She suffers from nosebleeds and vomiting. She can't ... she has trouble ... sentences are a problem for her. She has lost control of herself and her environment. "Where am I? Right now?" she asks her husband. "We're in our house," he says gently. "Greg and Carol's house."

Carol is "allergic to the 20th century," and *Safe* tells of her attempts to understand and conquer her condition at Wrenwood, a "chemical-free zone" in New Mexico. Writer-director Todd Haynes, who made the importantly weird short film *Superstar:The Karen Carpenter Story* and *Poison*, a minimalist epic of sex and longing in the age of AIDs, again has decay and estrangement in mind. This scarily confident, beautifully acted study is gnomic and anomic, like a TV disease movie made in an alternate universe. And in Moore's pretty, aggrieved face, Haynes finds the ideal vessel for his concerns.

Maybe suburbia is a genteel sham, or maybe not. Adherence to 12-step programs could be, as someone says here, "just another form of addiction." The Wrenwood patients could be searchers or fools, the staff fakers or dupes—or healers. The brazen majesty of Haynes' approach is that he spills no secrets, makes no obvious judgments. *Safe* is its own unique thing, as seductive as the sherbety decor of Carol's home, as mysterious as the illness that seizes her. It will also seize any viewer who dares to surrender to its spell. Feel free to laugh or scream.

VILLAGE VOICE, 6/27/95, p. 49, Georgia Brown

One of the strongest films in Cannes this year seemed barely there. Todd Haynes's lovely, spooky *Safe* flitted in and out like a firefly, a silent glimmer in the Mediterranean night. To catch the glow your eyes had to be glued to the spot.

Like all of Haynes's work, *Safe* doesn't make concessions to conventional expectations. It could be that people are put off by the ostensible subject, environmental illness—technically, Multiple Chemical Sensitivity—or, as the movie puts it, a flatout allergic reaction "to the 20th century." One still and luminous Calfornia evening, stepping out of the family Mercedes into the family garage, Carol White (Julianne Moore), sneezes. "Bless you," replies her husband, Greg (Xander Berkeley). God bless Carol White. By the end of *Safe,* the life of this San Fernando Valley housewife has been changed utterly.

When we meet Carol she's so pale and impeccable, she looks more like a doll than a living being. In her sterile mansion, she stands in the wings like a show room mannequin. Her tiny, babyish voice sounds robotic—as if the doll has batteries and a string to pull. Everything about Carol is self-denying. Having sex with her husband, she appears both bored and vaguely distressed. (Marital sex here looks patently ridiculous.) An aerobics class at the local health club provides a rare glimpse of messy color and movement. Unlike the other ladies, however, Carol is so cool she doesn't sweat (a detail that ties into Haynes's longstanding fascination with bodily secretions).

It's no wonder that Carol recoils at the delivery and installation of an ominous black couch. ("We ordered *teal,*" she insists.) At night she can't sleep and wanders her garden like a haunted maiden, or matron, out of Munch. In the daytime, she goes about her errands. At the hairdresser's, on a rare impulse, Carol decides to get a perm. Afterward, looking at herself in the mirror (even if he hadn't studied Lacan, Haynes would love mirrors), she squeals: From her nose flows a perfect rivulet of deep magenta.

Comedy or horror? Answer: Yes. Some viewers, critics among them, have a hard time catching Haynes's tone, much less his point of view. Some call him cold and academic. Jonathan Rosenbaum has used the word "heartless"—something I don't get at all. I find Haynes one of the most emotional and deeply compassionate of filmmakers—so emotional, intuitive, and empathic, that his movies, *Superstar: The Karen Carpenter Story, Poison,* and the short *Dottie Gets Spanked,* seem poised on the verge of breakdown. He seems unable not to deal with perilously fraught, intimate materials.

This said, the first time I saw *Safe,* I was smitten but mystified. Everything about the visual world grabbed me: the shimmering, hyperreal colors, the hilariously weird architecture and cold yet sensuous light, Carol's brooding nights in the garden of Evil—or is it Good? The ominous hyped sound: Carol gulping milk, and hovering copters, background voices like garbled transmissions from outer space. *Safe* makes you hold your breath. One reviewer from Sundance called it "suffocating." He didn't mean the word as a compliment, although it could be.

Like Freud's patients, Carol is just waiting to be diagnosed a hysteric. "Nervous disorder" is written all over her. On the other hand, she's suffering an objective illness, and so she'll get violated many times, in many ways, by those who treat her. Once she moves to Wrenwood, a New Age "healing" colony outside Albuquerque, she's at the mercy (odd word) of creepy, silky-toned gurus who preach that the ill are responsible for their illness, that right-thinking and a pure lifestyle can make them well. Quackery aside, illness, as it often is, is a blessing in that it forcibly removes her from an impoverished, unlived life.

In case you're unaware, Multiple Chemical Sensitivity is an authentic illness—"recognized as a legitimate disability by 10 United States Government agencies" and "protected by the Americans with Disabilities Act," so the film's production notes inform us. It's also an illness tailor-made for Haynes, whose ongoing subject is stigma. His films tend to focus on afflicted souls, too sensitive to live in this world. Aside from the fact that she has no song, Carol has much in common with the anorexic Karen Carpenter of Haynes's 1987 *Superstar*—the 43-minute underground moc-doc made with Barbie dolls (it was subsequently kept from distribution by Karen's brother, Richard). In the 1991 *Poison,* characters in each of the film's three "tales of transgression and punishment" die in escape attempts, last-ditch flights to far, far better worlds.

Eschewing an ending out of TV's "disease movies," Haynes leaves his heroine without wings to fly. *Safe* is less viscerally disturbing than *Poison*—which had toxic spittle and fatal facial fungus—and it's also less ecstatic. I miss Haynes's particular brand of transcendence. At the end, confronting menacing red splotches on her face (echoing similar "marks" in *Poison)*, Carol is so pathetic and deluded, I think Haynes means her to be more beautiful than ever.

Also reviewed in:
CHICAGO TRIBUNE, 7/28/95, Friday/p. J, Michael Wilmington
NATION, 8/14-21/95, p. 180, Stuart Klawans
NEW YORK TIMES, 6/23/95, p. C20, Janet Maslin
VARIETY, 1/30/95, p. 49, Todd McCarthy
WASHINGTON POST, 8/4/95, p. D2, Rita Kempley
WASHINGTON POST, 8/4/95, Weekend/p. 38, Desson Howe

SCARLET LETTER, THE

A Hollywood Pictures release of an Andrew G. Vajna presentation of a Lightmotive/Allied Stars/Cinergi/Moving Pictures production. *Executive Producer:* Dodi Fayed and Tova Laiter. *Producer:* Andrew G. Vajna and Roland Joffé. *Director:* Roland Joffé. *Screenplay:* Douglas Day Stewart. *Freely adapted from the novel by:* Nathaniel Hawthorne. *Director of Photography:* Alex Thomson. *Editor:* Thom Noble. *Music:* John Barry. *Music Editor:* Bob Badami and Clif Kohlweck. *Sound (music):* John Kurlander. *Sound Editor:* Dave McMoyler. *Casting:* Elisabeth Leustig and Priscilla John. *Production Designer:* Roy Walker. *Art Director:* Tony Wollard. *Set Designer:* Gordon White, Richard Harrison, and Rocco Matteo. *Set Decorator:* Rosalind Shingleton. *Set Dresser:* Gary Vandendor, Rex Fields, and Dan Owens. *Special Effects:* Martin Malivoire. *Costumes:* Gabriella Pescucci. *Make-up:* Fabrizio Sforza. *Make-up (Demi Moore):* Ronnie Specter. *Stunt Coordinator:* Brent Woolsey and Jeff Dashaw. *Running time:* 135 minutes. *MPAA Rating:* R.

CAST: Demi Moore (Hester Prynne); Gary Oldman (Arthur Dimmesdale); Robert Duvall (Roger Prynne/Chillingworth); Lisa Jolliff-Andoh (Mituba); Edward Hardwicke (John Bellingham); Robert Prosky (Horace Stonehall); Roy Dotrice (Thomas Cheever); Joan Plowright (Harriet Hibbons); Malcolm Storry (Major Dunsmuir); Jim Bearden (Goodman Mortimer); Larissa Lapchinski (Goody Mortimer); Amy Wright (Goody Gotwick); George Aguilar (Johnny Sassamon); Tim Woodward (Brewster Stonehall); Joan Gregson (Elizabeth Cheever); Dana Ivey (Meredith Stonehall); Diane Salinger (Margaret Bellingham); Jocelyn Cunningham (Mary Rollings); Francie Swift (Sally Short); Sheldon Peters Wolfchild (Moskeegee); Eric Schweig (Metacomet); Kristen Fairlie (Faith Stonehall); Sarah Campbell (Prudence Stonehall); Judd Jones (Mr. Bobbin); Anthony Paton (Town Beadle); Marguerite McNeil (Widow Wormser); Kennetch Charlette (Tarrantine Chief); Deborah Tennant (Quaker Lady); Kateri Walker (Female Sachem); Shaun R. Clarke (Militia Guardsman); Jay Carmichael (Militia Guardsman); Jason Parkhill (First Guardsman); Jeremy Keddy (Drummer Boy); Nicholas Rice (The Clerk); Len Doncheff (Trader); Ashley Nolan (Goody Hunter); Stephen Aderneck (Speaking Native); Evelyn Francis (Algonquin Native); Garry Joseph (Native Rider); Stephen Micalchunk (Passenger No. 1); Jeremy Akerman (Middle Aged Passenger); Jodhi May (Voice of Pearl).

LOS ANGELES TIMES, 10/13/95, Calendar/p. 1, Kenneth Turan

Nathaniel Hawthorne probably thought he knew something about writing, and through the years not a few people have agreed with him. But when the makers of "The Scarlet Letter" looked over his celebrated novel, it was more in pity than admiration.

True, the guy had come up with Hester Prynne, the adulterous young woman forced to wear a scarlet "A" on her clothing, usually considered a heroine to reckon with. But then Hawthorne, timid soul that he was, regrettably lost his nerve. He failed to turn Hester into the kind of fearless, take-charge, watch-my-dust individual strong enough to attract the attention of an actress like Demi Moore.

And, after placing his story in the Puritan-dominated Boston of the 17th Century, Hawthorne squandered numerous dramatic chances the setting was perfect for. Where was his clandestine sex scene, for pity's sake? Or his lyrical nude bathing interludes, one for each gender? Couldn't he have found room for rape, suicide and those nearby witch hunts? And weren't indigenous peoples hanging around the neighborhood? Where were his scalpings, his barebreasted maidens and his rampaging savages? The poor fool was wasting opportunities left and right. And when Hawthorne's downer of an ending is thrown in, it's amazing he sold any books at all.

Suffice it to say that while Hawthorne may have blown his chance, screenwriter Douglas Day Stewart and director Roland Joffe have seen theirs and taken it, adding all the above and more to their version of Hawthorne's undernourished story. When this film's opening titles read "freely adapted from," they are not being excessively modest.

Like the moral climate of the Massachusetts colony it depicts, this "Scarlet Letter" is equal parts piety and hysteria. In making a lusty bodice-ripper out of Hawthorne's carefully wrought chapters, the film is often an unintentionally amusing hoot. It takes itself so much in dead earnest, is so lugubrious a repository of lines like "How close they are, love and hate" and "Who is to say what is a sin in God's eyes?," that bemused laughter is often the only sane response.

From the moment she steps off the boat from England, sent ahead by her husband to set up house, Hester Prynne scandalizes every narrow-minded Puritan in the colony. Ms. Self-Reliance, she insists on wearing daring clothes, bathing in a tub, even buying her own indentured servants. "You are headstrong, Mistress Prynne," says one aghast local, and even the Rev. Arthur Dimmesdale (Gary Oldman) admiringly tells her, "Your tongue knows no rules."

Besides being a convincing speaker on the wages of sin, the Reverend is also a devotee of au natural bathing (as Hester happily discovers) and cares so much for the local Native Americans he spends his spare time translating the Bible into Algonquin. The only two admirers of Milton in town, he and Hester are soon making eyes at each other, but she is married and he is a Puritan, after all, so they agree to keep their distance.

To take her mind off of Dimmy, Hester befriends an eccentric local woman named Harriet Hibbons (Joan Plowright), who runs a combination multicultural commune and halfway house for wayward waifs. Soon Hester is heading up what looks like the first women's group in the New World, encouraging self-expression and shocking everyone with her brazen, free-spirited beliefs.

Then, one fateful day, word comes that Hester's husband, Roger, has supposedly fallen victim to those pesky savages. She and Dimmy can't keep their hands off each other any longer, and soon Hester is with child. Worse than that, resilient Roger (a misdirected Robert Duvall), an evil sort whose temperament has not been improved by months spent in captivity, secretly skulks into town and plots an awful revenge on Hester and whoever it is who seduced her.

"The Scarlet Letter" has been envisioned as an old-fashioned Joan Crawford-type star vehicle for Demi Moore, who—in addition to outraging public opinion—gets to be strong while suffering when those Puritan elders, noticeably lacking in a sense of humor, lock her up for refusing to name her baby's father. The only flaw in her presentation is a hairstyle featuring a presumably historically accurate pair of long, curly sidelocks that make her look, at least from the neck up, like a perky Hasidic teen-ager who can't stay out of trouble.

Giving a more restrained performance than one would've thought he had in him, Gary Oldman is as effective as director Joffe—who has made strained seriousness his trademark with films like "The Killing Fields," "The Mission" and "City of Joy"—allows anyone to be. Though it's unclear what the audience would be for a faithful rendition of the Hawthorne novel, the question of who would ever want to see this one is murkier still.

NEW YORK, 10/23/95, p. 57, David Denby

After about an hour of *The Scarlet Letter*, I asked myself for whom the bell tolls, and hearing "for thee," I left the theater immediately and escaped a certain doom in the cooling night air. In other words, life is not long enough to watch Demi Moore playing Hester Prynne. What I saw in that dismaying and languid hour was a big, swooning, 1955-style drama about repressed passion, nude bathing, and, finally, sex among the corn kernels (in the barn, you know). This version of *The Scarlet Letter* bizarrely features a scarlet *bird*, which flitters around during the dirty parts. Joan Plowright, as usual, was the only thing in the movie (sorry, first half of the movie) worth watching. As for Ms. Moore, she has to be the least expressive actress ever to achieve stardom, though that peculiar house of cards, her fame, may not remain standing forever. Those of you who think no one could make a good movie of Nathaniel Hawthorne's classic may want to take a look at the extraordinary silent version (from 1926) starring Lillian Gish and directed by Victor Sjöström.

NEW YORK POST, 10/13/95, p. 45, Michael Medved

The appalling new film version of "The Scarlet Letter" not only trashed Nathaniel Hawthorne's classic novel, but also wastes a surprisingly decent performance by Demi Moore.

She's actually well-cast as Hester Prynne, the strong, proud, Puritan heroine forced to wear the letter "A" as punishment for her adultery.

In the same spirit, screenwriter Douglas Day Stewart should be compelled to don the letter "S," in penance for his unspeakably Stupid, Sleazy, Screwy, and Shabby Script, which reduces a great story of sin and redemption to the level of Harlequin romance.

In fact, Stewart's gild-the-lily dialogue ("When your fist sliced through the air like a sword, and then struck your hand with such force, I wondered what pain lay behind such a gesture!"), bears a closer resemblance to the writer's previous efforts on "Blue Lagoon" than to anything in Hawthorne.

Thanks to Stewart's inane "improvements," idealistic young minister Arthur Dimmesdale (Gary Oldman, with an off-again-onagain Scotch accent) here is immediately identified as a good guy because he "struggles to keep alive the dream of building a bridge between the English and the Indians."

He's distracted, however, when Moore's character arrives from England ahead of her much-older husband to set up a home in Colonial Massachusetts.

Her affair with Oldman is dramatized in one of history's most laughably overdone sex scenes—while focusing on every pore and hair follicle of his two embracing stars, director Roland Joffe ("The Killing Fields," "The Mission") inexplicably but "artistically" inserts repeated glimpses of a red canary twittering on a window sill, and a smiling slave girl (Lisa Jolliff-Andoh) taking a bath.

The entire mess is then smeared and smothered with John Barry's schmaltzy music, a consistently intrusive presence offering banal echoes of other scores ("Out of Africa," "Dances With Wolves") by this distinguished composer.

Just when you think the movie can't possibly get any worse, Robert Duvall arrives on the scene. He plays Hester's elderly husband, presumed dead but now in Massachusetts under an assumed name to seek revenge against the as-yet unidentified party who has fathered a child with his wife.

It seems hard to believe that Oldman could ever appear in a film in which he's not the most intense over-actor, but here Duvall's mincing, snarling interpretation of his character as an ultra-violent psycho trumps the embarrassment of everyone else.

You also get to see more of Duvall's nude body than you do of Moore's—a prospect that will inspire enthusiasm in filmgoers of no known gender.

To add to the fun, Joffe and Stewart have "enriched" Hawthorne with a graphic rape scene, followed by a sadistic eye-gouging, a bloody scalping (perpetrated by a Puritan, not an Indian!) and a timely Indian surprise attack on the English settlement.

There's also insipid narration in the voice of the daughter of Dimmesdale and Hester. (My parents shared a love like no other ... Who is to say what is a sin in God's eyes?") spoken with a sodden solemnity by Jodhi May.

The film's incongruously handsome sets and well-chosen locations (mostly in Nova Scotia), can provide only fleeting distraction from the dramatic disaster that unfolds at center stage.

NEWSDAY, 10/13/95, Part II/p. B2, Jack Mathews

There is one moment of absolute ethical purity in Roland Joffe's "The Scarlet Letter," a film revisiting Nathaniel Hawthorne's classic tale of adultery and redemption in Puritan New England. And it comes at the very beginning, by way of a blunt disclaimer that the movie is "freely adapted" from the novel.

Well, it certainly is. Freely, ludicrously, badly, laughably. Our Thanksgiving turkey has arrived early this year, and let me tell you, pilgrims, it's plump!

It seems the further filmmakers get from the 1850 novel, the less confidence they have in it. The book has been adapted on film at least four times previously, and the best remains Victor Seastrom's 1926 silent version, with the deceptively demure Lillian Gish as the perfect Hester Prynne, a woman of passion and incipient free will whose obedience to her heart made her an outcast in her community.

Joffe's version stars the opposite-of-demure Demi Moore, Vanity Fair bodypaint cover girl and Hollywood hot tamale, who plays Hester less like a 17th Century victim than like the woman who discovered the G-spot. She doesn't merely give in to her passion for the Reverend Mr. Dimmesdale (Gary Oldman), but—in one of the movie's many hilarious missteps—to the sensual exploration of her own body. No wonder Hester doesn't resist wearing the scarlet "A" on her bosom; it's kind of a kick to put it on.

Oscar nominees Joffe ("The Killing Fields") and screenwriter Douglas Day Stewart ("An Officer and a Gentleman") have used Hawthorne's novel as a broad outline, borrowing its period, characters, and moral conflicts as a dramatic front for their own shallow musings on such late 20th Century issues as feminism, individualism, ecology, race, and religious dogmatism.

A quick refresher: "The Scarlet Letter" is the story of a married Englishwoman who, shortly after moving to her new home in Boston, bears an illegitimate child, and refuses to name her lover. Her defiance outrages the town's patriarchs, whose mantra is "order in all things," and her physician husband (Robert Duvall), who arrives after the fact and sets out with a devious scheme to find and destroy his rival.

The book does not end happily. While Hester remains defiant, she is beaten and scarred, left to live out her life alone and as a marked woman. The movie ends as cheerfully as a detergent commercial, with nary a stain nor a moral knot untied. In justifying their sweeping changes, the filmmakers say they merely did what Hawthorne was unable to do in his time, embrace Hester's passion and strength and reward her with a healthy male.

It's hooey of a particularly egregious nature. Joffe and Stewart have turned Hawthorne's profound examination of frontier morality into a bloated romantic adventure, complete with bloody action sequences, inane symbolism, and one of the silliest and least romantic sex scenes in the annals of the R rating.

Hawthorne didn't dare describe the heated moment that led to Hester's predicament; the deed was done and little Pearl born before his story opened. But Joffe, under no such restraint, decided to capture that unwritten literary event on film, and staged it as if it had the import of God's creation of Earth.

The lengthy scene begins when Dimmesdale shows up at Hester's cottage with the false information that her husband is dead, and that after only seven years of mourning, they'll be free to get it on. Hester can't wait seven minutes(!), and in a blink, she's wrestling the cumbersome togs off the good reverend on a bed of oats in the barn. It's an act of such raw animal passion that it sends her eavesdropping virgin slave scrambling back to the house to relieve herself in a tub of water while staring amorously at a red canary.

Hello?

Apart from its rank symbolism, "The Scarlet Letter" features a murky subplot about Dimmesdale's spiritual connection with a hostile tribe, and makes the madness of Hester's husband the direct cause of war. And the suspected witch Mrs. Hibbons (Joan Plowright) is developed into a woman of such 20th Century sensibilities she could be living a past life of Shirley MacLaine's.

With the exception of Duvall, who plays Roger Prynne/Chillingworth with what can only be described as regret, the actors are not at fault. Moore and Oldman, whose personas epitomize the freedom of their generation, are ridiculously miscast.

Moore doesn't suggest Hester's budding passion—she is in a full lather from the moment she first sees Dimmesdale swimming naked in a pool. And Oldman, at his best in roles calling for emotional abandon, is imprisoned behind Dimmesdale's pathetic silence, never revealing a hint of whatever causes Hester to lose her head.

When this is all over, Joffe and Stewart should be made to wear scarlet letters on their own chests. A "B"—for bomb—would be nice.

NEWSWEEK, 10/16/95, p. 87, David Ansen

You may be amazed, watching *The Scarlet Letter*, just how little you remember of that American classic they forced you to read in high school. How could you have forgotten that spicy scene—when Hester Prynne (Demi Moore) first glimpses the minister Arthur Dimmesdale (Gary Oldman) skinny-dipping in a Massachusetts pond, revealing a flash of his Pilgrim manhood? Not to mention the torrid consummation of their love atop a pile of grain, witnessed by Hester's mute black servant girl—who, deeply aroused, luxuriates autoerotically in a 17th-century hot tub. Funny how Hester's near rape by a lecherous colonist has slipped the mind, as well as Dimmesdale's valiant efforts to bring the Iroquois and the Puritans together. Or the surprising moment when nasty Chillingworth (Robert Duvall), Hester's vengeful husband, goes native and scalps the wrong man. Or the Robin Hood climax when the oppressed Indians charge to the rescue of the minister, about to be hanged. But surely you remember how, in the end, the Boston grinches come to their senses, forgive these hotblooded kids and vow to join a 12-step program for recovering Puritans?

OK, I'm making the last part up. As for the rest—none of which is found in Nathaniel Hawthorne—it's all up there on screen in Roland Joffé's stupefyingly wrong-headed movie. By turning Hester into a feisty feminist rebel and Dimmesdale into a hunky P.C. loverboy, it may sound as if Joffé and screenwriter Douglas Day Stewart have created a camp marvel. Be warned: you'll giggle only if you can stay awake.

Joffé is much too high-minded to merely give us a trashy bodice-ripper. (In an ideal world, he'd have cast Fabio and Suzanne Somers.) Determined to show up those Puritans for what they really were, he pillories his 17th-century villains on the rack of 1990s sexual politics. That's not just silly and smug; it's dramatic suicide. The real sin of this "Scarlet Letter" is that it doesn't respect the concept of sin. The story makes no sense if you rob it of guilt, remorse and redemption. Once you've "liberated" Hester, there's no reason she and the skinny-dipping minister don't immediately hop in their wagon and make haste to the nearest Club Med. The sooner the better.

SIGHT AND SOUND, 1/96, p.48, John Harkness

Massachusetts Colony, mid-17th Century. The governor and the reverend Arthur Dimmesdale attend the funeral of the local Indian chief. They speak with the new chief, Metacomet, who plainly does not like white people. Within a short while, a ship arrives from England carrying Hester Prynne, who arrives to prepare a home for herself and her husband. Her insistence on living alone and her fondness for scoopnecked tops scandalizes the locals. Prynne meets Dimmesdale, admires his preaching, and it is plain that they are attracted to one another. Word arrives that Prynne's husband has been killed by the Tarrantine Indians. Prynne and Dimmesdale have passionate sex on bags of grain in her barn. She gets pregnant, is accused of heresy and adultery, and is jailed by the Puritan elders. Hester refuses to divulge the name of her child's father.

After several months in prison, Prynne gives birth, is publicly shamed, and sentenced to forever wearing a scarlet letter "A" pinned to her bosom. It is revealed that Prynne's husband is alive. He's been living as a captive of the Indians, who let him go because they think he is crazy. He returns on the day of Hester's shame and joins the community under the name Chillingworth. He uses the entree provided by his medical skills to rail against heresy, witchcraft and the Indians. Three or four years pass and Hester is arrested for witchcraft with a couple of her friends. They are about to be hanged when Dimmesdale intervenes, announces that he fathered her child and offers to be hanged in her place. The Puritans are about to take him up on his offer when the Indians attack. After the battle, Prynne, Dimmesdale and their child leave for the Carolinas.

Think of an up-and-coming movie that features blood-spilling violence, sex, nudity, a rape scene, people dancing while wearing exotic headgear, and a female protagonist with a sneering contempt for her community. If you think *Showgirls*, you're right.

If you think *The Scarlet Letter*, you're also right. Anyone who's read Nathaniel Hawthorne's novel *The Scarlet Letter* may be confused by this, but the truth remains that Demi Moore looked at Hawthorne's dark meditation on the soul of Puritanism and conceived the potential bodice-ripper within. (The only point at which the novel and the film coincide occurs after more than an hour, when Prynne is sentenced to wear the scarlet "A", which is where the novel actually begins).

The last line of the film of *The Scarlet Letter* is a voice-over narration by Hester Prynne's daughter, Pearl, who asks "Who is to say what is a sin in the eyes of God'?" This is a legitimate question, but not in the context of *The Scarlet Letter*. Hawthorne's *The Scarlet Letter,* is a novel about the price of sin. Hester and Dimmesdale sin and are punished for it. Hawthorne was wrestling with his moral inheritance, with the dark anger that the Puritans brought to North America. Indians were not relevant save as set dressing. He was not concerned with establishing Hester Prynne as some sort of feminist heroine.

When the Americans talk about religious freedom in a modern context, they are not using the same arguments as the original colonists. The religious freedom sought in the American colonies was often the freedom to establish one's own theocratic community—the Puritans in Massachusetts, the Quakers in Pennsylvania, the Catholics in Maryland. A person does not arrive in the Massachusetts colony in the middle of the seventeenth-century looking for the freedom to worship as she chooses. The Puritans were in fact far more repressive than any of today's conservative Protestant denominations which makes one ask exactly what Demi Moore's Hester is expecting when she arrives.

The Puritan consciousness echoes down American history, and Moore, Roland Joffé and screenwriter Douglas Day Stewart are busy fighting echoes. From the point of view of hip Holly-wood liberalism, Dimmesdale's spiritrial *bona fides* are established not by his devotion to the Christian god, but because the Indians like him. I'm not sure why Hester's black female slave is around, except maybe to symbolise the silence that white patriarchy imposes on women. (Hester can't symbolise that, because she never shuts up.)

The slave may also be there to symbolise how Hester manages to run a working farm and yet maintain perfect nails. The makers of this film do not understand sin. They do not grasp the overall concept of hell and damnation, so central to the Puritan mindset which means that they are doomed from the outset. (Someone should have read Jonathan Edwards' sermon 'Sinners In The Hands Of An Angry God' before going into production, just to see what sort of people they were dealing with.)

If we leave aside the fact that this is an adaptation—the credits actually say *The Scarlet Letter* is freely adapted from the novel, which is true in the sense that apple sauce is freely adapted from apples—then we must figure out if it is a particularly good movie, and I don't think it is. *The Scarlet Letter* is actually worse than *Showgirls*. When we go to see *Showgirls* we expect Joe Eszterhas' trademark gynophobia and lap-dancers in Las Vegas. It is not based on a literary classic. It does not feature the highest paid female star in Hollywood. Its director had no responsibility for a film as good as *The Killing Fields*.

The Scarlet Letter's line of narrative causality makes no sense. Everyone keeps worrying about an Indian attack, but the Indians take years to descend upon the settlers in *deus ex machina* that would be rejected as too contrived by a manufacturer of Victorian melodrama. Why does Chillingworth commit suicide at the moment of his triumph? Why does Demi Moore's accent keep sliding around? Why on earth would a Puritan congregation have a minister with a Scots accent? Exactly what is the function of intercutting Prynne and Dimmesdale's sex scene with Prynne's slave masturbating in the tub? I have no answer for any of these questions, aside front the rampant human stupidity that seems to afflict Hollywood movies in direct proportion to the size of their budgets.

TIME, 10/23/95, p. 94, Richard Corliss

Among the top 20 paperbacks on *USA Today's* best-seller list is *The Scarlet Letter*—the Cliffs Notes version. Bibliophiles who purchase that slim volume in lieu of dozing over the original will get a much clearer view of Nathaniel Hawthorne's 1850 tale of heroism and hypocrisy than those visiting the new movie adaptation. It's a lugubrious, often ludicrous, wallow.

Even nonreaders know that Hester Prynne (Demi Moore in the movie) was the first woman in literature with her own rating: A, for adultery. She had an affair with the colony's preacher (Gary Oldman) and, while enduring her public shame, fought off the pernitions of her long-lost husband Roger (Robert Duvall). But this plot doesn't kick in until about the 11th or 12th hour of the film. Director Roland Joffé dwells instead on the nude bodies of Moore (caressing herself and Oldman (skinny-dipping) as Hester and the Rev fall in lust. And stay around for their epochally silly sex scene. It makes Hester's secret seem more like Victoria's.

Douglas Day Stewart's script has little use for the novel's other plot line: Hester's difficulty with her love child Pearl. But this Hester is readier to be martyr and lover than seamstress and mother. She is, you see, America's prototype feminist. (Caucasian feminist, that is—Pocahontas, in the Disney cartoon, beat Hester to the p.c. punch.) And the Rev, weak in the novel, is now a fiery film hero, deserving of the preposterous happy ending the filmmakers tack on.

The stars are actually pretty good—Moore holds the camera's gaze as securely as any actress—but they can't save this revisionist slog. The film blames the 17th century for not being the 20th and Hawthorne for not being Danielle Steel. If this Scarlet got a letter, it would be *F*.

VILLAGE VOICE, 10/24/95, p. 80, Amy Taubin

Even as unintended farce, Roland Joffé's feminist, as it were, reworking of an impacted 19th-century novel about the effect on the American soul of a religious fundamentalism as old as Plymouth Rock leaves much to be desired. Not even Gary Oldman as the confused Reverend Dimmesdale, his Cheshire cat smile all but obscured by straggly facial hair, could make this bodice-ripper bearable. I guess Oldman's given up on stardom—being the best and sexiest actor of his generation just isn't enough in Hollywood.

As for Demi Moore: who better suited to wear the scarlet *A*? It denotes not only Hester's sin of adultery but Moore's exalted standing in the Hollywood hierarchy. *A* also stands for the actor as auteur, which perhaps accounts for the shot in which Moore (or, more precisely, her body double) hikes up her skirts to reveal her pregnant belly—thus recalling the *Vanity Fair* cover that defined her stardom. Synthetic as Joffé's direction, Moore's Hester combines Jean Simmons's smile with a gait that, even under 20 pounds of petticoats, looks like Dietrich's in drag.

Despite the decorous dialogue, titillation is Joffé's game. In the erotic *pièce de résistance*, a dimly photographed Moore and Oldman roll around on a heap of rice, while a cheery red bird (the townfolk believe it's the devil but we know it's pure Disney, this being a Buena Vista release) and Hester's innocent but lascivious black servant girl (nowhere to be found in Hawthorne) look on. Overcome with secondhand emotion, the servant sinks into a tub of Hester's leftover bathwater clutching a candle to her bosom.

So why this sudden craze for costume romances? It's one way to get around the problem of safe sex.

Also reviewed in:
CHICAGO TRIBUNE, 10/13/95, Friday/p. C, John Petrakis
NEW REPUBLIC, 11/6/95, p. 28, Stanley Kauffmann
NEW YORKER, 10/30/95, p. 114, Anthony Lane
NEW YORK TIMES, 10/13/95, p. C16, Caryn James
VARIETY, 10/16-22/95, p. 94, Todd McCarthy
WASHINGTON POST, 10/13/95, p. F1, Rita Kempley
WASHINGTON POST, 10/13/95, Weekend/p. 44, Desson Howe

SEARCH AND DESTROY

An October Films release of a New Image production in association with October and Autumn Pictures. *Executive Producer:* Martin Scorsese, Avi Lerner, and Danny Dimbort. *Producer:* Ruth Charny, Dan Lupovitz, and Elie Cohen. *Director:* David Salle. *Screenplay:* Michael Almereyda. *Based on a play by:* Howard Korders. *Director of Photography:* Bobby Bukowski and Michael Spiller. *Editor:* Michelle Gorchow. *Music:* Elmer Bernstein. *Sound:* Pawel Wdowczak. *Casting:* Billy Hopkins, Suzanne Smith, and Kerry Barden. *Production Designer:* Robin Standefer. *Art Director:* Stephen Alesch. *Set Decorator:* Amy Tapper. *Costumes:* Donna Zakowska. *Running time:* 90 minutes. *MPAA Rating:* R.

CAST: Griffin Dunne (Martin Mirkheim); Illeana Douglas (Marie Davenport); Dennis Hopper (Dr. Waxling); Christopher Walken (Kim Ulander); John Turturro (Ron); Rosanna Arquette (Lauren Mirkheim); Ethan Hawke (Roger); Martin Scorsese (The Accountant).

CHRISTIAN SCIENCE MONITOR, 5/1/95, p. 13, David Sterritt

Painting and cinema are both visual arts, so one might think creative people would travel easily between them. Such crossovers are more the exception than the rule, however, and painter David Salle's first movie, "Search and Destroy," points up the pitfalls.

Salle's protagonist—Martin Mirkheim, played by Griffin Dunne—is himself an ambitious fellow who wants to make a debut film. Similarities between Mirkheim and Salle don't extend very far, since Salle is an established figure in the art world, while Mirkheim is a befuddled wheeler-dealer with a spotty business record, a failing marriage, and IRS agents hot on his trail.

But they appear to share a passion for accomplishment and a recognition that mass-audience filmmaking is less a matter of creative genius than of good fortune, connections, and money.

On some levels, "Search and Destroy" may be interpreted as Salle's account of how hard it is to enter an artistic field and how temptations may arise to compromise, cut corners, or abandon scruples.

Still, most of Mirkheim's adventures are too idiosyncratic to be mistaken for self-revelation on Salle's part. In the end, "Search and Destroy" tells us less about Mirkheim's artistic travails than about how Salle managed to weaken a promising story; he too eagerly struts his visual stuff instead of thinking his narrative through.

The screen is full of tantalizing characters, most notably a self-fulfillment guru whose novel Mirkheim wants to film and a shady entrepreneur whose cash Mirkheim wants to pocket. They're played by a marvelously eccentric cast, including Dennis Hopper and Christopher Walken as the two just mentioned, plus Illeana Douglas and John Turturro in other key roles. But instead of developing these figures coherently and convincingly, Salle catapults them from one offbeat episode to another as if they were two-dimensional bodies in a comic strip rather than complicated people in a movie.

Efforts to punctuate the plot with experimental touches—odd flashbacks, printed words super-imposed on the action, and so forth—reduce the movie's credibility quotient even more, staving off psychological involvement without adding much intellectual or aesthetic depth. Salle's eye for color and composition is evident in many individual shots, but this isn't enough to compensate for the movie's shortcomings.

All of which shows how hard it is to bridge the gap between painting and cinema, even for an artist as versatile as Salle, whose credits include "The Birth of a Poet," a performance-art collaboration with director Richard Foreman and author Kathy Acker. A lesson to be drawn from "Search and Destroy" is that film and painting call on such different sets of skills that the talents are rarely found in a single artist.

It's true that some major figures in painting and drawing—especially avant-gardists like Salvador Dali, Fernand Léger, and Jean Cocteau—have made noteworthy films. It's also true that some fine filmmakers, from Akira Kurosawa and Satyajit Ray to Andy Warhol and David Lynch, started their careers as painters or illustrators.

Leaving out distinctive cases like Cocteau and Warhol, though, painters usually end up making a definitive choice between the two art forms—treating film as a briefly indulged hobby, as Dali and Léger did, or leaving their canvases for the broader domain of the movie screen, as Kurosawa and Lynch have done. Indeed, when a filmmaker's work becomes too painterly the result can be static and lifeless.

This notwithstanding, a number of artists are lining up for a shot at cinematic success. Julian Schnabel, a much-respected painter, is said to be among them; so are the photographers Larry Clark and Cindy Sherman.

Now that the money-driven gallery boom of the '80s has faded, says one theory, artists need new territory to conquer. If history is a guide, however, moviemaking may hold more obstacles than opportunities for creators who are most at home with pictures that don't move.

LOS ANGELES TIMES, 5/5/95, Calendar/p. 2, Peter Rainer

Martin Mirkheim (Griffin Dunne) is the kind of hustling creep who just plows through the intense dislike people have for him. He's so transparently on the make that, in a way, his phoniness is his sincerity. He's an authentic phony.

"Search and Destroy," the directorial debut of the artist David Salle and adapted by Michael Almereyda from the Howard Korder play, begins with Martin trying to talk his way out of some IRS problems with the tax man (Martin Scorsese). It's a great comic set up: Martin is so unctuous that our sympathy shifts to the Feds. The whole movie is like that. Martin barges into the precincts of an "Iron John"-style TV guru, Dr. Luthor Waxling (Dennis Hopper), and, although he's restrained by security officers and tied to a chair, he makes a pitch for the movie rights to Waxling's self-realization novel "Daniel Strong."

Rebuffed for lack of cash, he gets involved with Waxling's secretary Marie (Illeana Douglas), a shady businessman (Christopher Walken) and his fright-wigged drug connection (John Turturro). Martin's odyssey to find financing plays like a nightmarish cabaret act with assorted goofs and creepos. It's probably also meant as a sly satire on how movies actually do get financed.

Smart and facetious, "Search and Destroy" is the kind of film that, like Martin, flaunts its pushiness. It may be a little cackle of a movie, but it's not like anything else out there right now. Salle, whose artwork often combines abstract doodling and lyric realism on the same canvas, attempts something similar here with his visual scheme and tonal shifts. The collision of gags and rhapsody is off-putting; as the film goes on, our laughter keeps getting undercut by small terrors. The mixture of moods keeps you off balance. "Search and Destroy," like Martin, not as easy to dismiss as you might wish it to be. It keeps outsmarting you.

Dunne played the role of Martin in the show's Broadway production, and he's perfected his gift for whiz-bang annoyingness. He's so obviously conniving that you can practically see the thought balloons above his head. When he gets close to Marie, and she pours out her script idea for a horror gore-fest, he's nonplussed but he's also charmed—he likes the fact that she's as weird as he is. (Dunne and Douglas work together with unabashed ease.)

Walken isn't playing anything here that he hasn't done to a T before, but that doesn't mean he doesn't do it surpassingly well. His character is like the reverse of Martin—calm and approachable on the outside, wacko at the core. Rounding out the cast of crazies, Turturro is alarmingly funny and Hopper serves up a definitive cameo of a huckster guru who swings his epiphanies like billy clubs.

Almereyda, the gifted writer-director of the neglected 1989 "Twister" and other films, has done a highly creditable job of adapting Korder's play, expanding Marie's role and tightening the horror. The dialogue has a glint to it, and so do the performers. The piece has its Mamet-y side—underneath it all is a drone about success and the American Dream and the fast buck and all that jazz. It comes across like one of Martin's cons. The only way to take this film seriously is to take it lightly.

NEW YORK, 5/15/95, p. 63, David Denby

The painter David Salle, in his first film as director, Search & Destroy, has a good time horsing around. The movie makes no particular sense, but then, it isn't supposed to; once you realize that, you can enjoy it. Search & Destroy is based on a play by Howard Korder, but as far as Salle is concerned, the play seems less a text than a pretext—a frame on which to hang the kind of hotspur acting riffs that light up a party. Griffin Dunne plays a showbiz cheapster, a failure who wants to make a movie from a ridiculous book, a didactic adventure story written by a self-help guru. As the would-be producer, Dunne who actually has produced movies reaches such levels of scummy desperation that he turns abjection into a new kind of vitality. Dennis Hopper, the guru, does the kind of exploding-forehead intimidation he's done before (Hopper literally browbeats the audience), but Christopher Walken, as a mysterious sinister businessman in dark suits worn like armor, gives his most alarmingly disembodied and nihilistic performance yet. And John Turturro, playing a speed freak, talks so much and so rapidly that he could populate a madhouse all by himself.

Explicitly, the movie is about cynicism and fakery, and parts of it may remind you of the more rancid passages in plays by David Mamet and David Rabe. Why was Salle attracted to this familiar stuff about con artists making preposterous movies? Perhaps showbiz desperation has some sort of power as a metaphor in the art world. Griffin Dunne's self-actualizing crumb-bum producer might be considered a kind of parody of the artist. He makes himself up, and for visual artists who operate without a strong dependence on tradition (David Salle has complained about New York artists' lack of a sense of tradition), that act of self-creation may seem nervy and cool. The movie itself is an art object, as opposed to a work of art, featuring backgrounds of solid color and sudden, arbitrary disruptions of context. Like most examples of hip filmmaking, *Search & Destroy* obeys no rules apart from its creators' whims. That it doesn't quite fall apart is a tribute to the perfervid intensity of its performers.

NEW YORK POST, 4/28/95, p. 43, V.A. Musetto

Memo to David Salle: Stick with painting!

The art-world fave makes his movie directorial debut today with "Search and Destroy." And, to put it kindly, the movie is a mess.

But let's start at the beginning. That's when "Search" features some wacky, over-the-top turns by Griffin Dunne, Illeana Douglas, Dennis Hopper, John Turturro and Christopher Walken (singing and dancing, no less).

There's even a cameo by Martin Scorsese (the movie's executive producer) as a Florida taxman. Plus appearances by Ethan Hawke and Rosanna Arquette.

Dunne plays a frantic, sleazy businessman whose marriage is on the rocks and who owes "$147,951, exclusive of interest and penalties" to the state of Florida. The way out of his woes, he thinks, is by making a movie—"the best f---ing movie since "Spartacus"—out of a book written by a late-night TV huckster (Hopper) who offers viewers—for the right price, of course—the secret to success.

Along the way, Dunne meets a ready-to-jump-into-the-sack secretary (played by Douglas, who in real life is Scorsese's girlfriend), a New York businessman of questionable ethics (Walken), and a psycho drug dealer (Turturro).

Their manic performances manage to keep "Search" moving along nicely despite the next-to-nothing plot and the overstylized, self-conscious direction.

But with about 30 minutes to go, the comedy (based on a play by Howard Korder, also featuring Dunne) turns unexpectedly and needlessly violent, and the movie unravels before our eyes. The final scenes make little sense.

Rumor has it that Scorsese took over post-production of Salle's efforts. Even he couldn't save "Search and Destroy."

NEWSDAY, 4/28/95, Part II/p. B7, Jack Mathews

Contemporary New York artist David Salle makes his debut as a motion picture director with the black comedy "Search and Destroy," and he should not throw away his brushes just yet. If this were a painting, it would be hung in the Gagosian Gallery's broom closet.

Salle doesn't show a great deal of aptitude for the film medium. The story, adapted by Michael Almereyda from Howard Korder's play about the troubles of an incompetent dreamer and hustler, lurches from one bad structural idea to another. It has no consistent tone, and when it comes time for farce and violence to merge, they do so with the wit of a mugging. Greatest sin of all, it isn't even particularly interesting to look at.

"Search and Destroy" stars Griffin Dunne as Martin Mirkheim, a failed Florida promoter whose attempt to get the movie rights to a self-help guru's philosophical adventure novel leads him to an increasingly bizarre series of events and characters. Though the movie opens in Florida, where Mirkheim's dissolved marriage and mounting tax debts are testing his unfounded confidence, and moves to Dallas, where he meets his idol Dr. Waxling (Dennis Hopper), it is essentially a New York movie.

It is there, on executive producer Martin Scorsese's turf, that Mirkheim ditches his last kernel of integrity and goes underworld with the weirdly sleazy drug dealer Kim Ulander (Christopher Walken) and a completely nuts small-time hood named Ron (John Turturro). Turturro, wearing a long black wig and a short fuse, plays Ron like Tiny Tim on PCP, and he's a sight to behold.

Scorsese's interest in the project (he also does a funny cameo as an unsympathetic IRS auditor) draws comparisons to his 1985 "After Hours," which also starred Dunne as a man drifting through a series of dark encounters in New York. But that character was likable; Mirkheim is an insufferable geek, the kind of get-rich-quick hustler and intellectual pretender who is often memorialized in self-flagellating satires about the film business.

The only pleasant figure in "Search and Destroy" is Illeana Douglas' Marie Davenport, the would-be horror film writer whom Mirkheim meets in Dallas and takes with him to New York. Douglas, the bar tart that Robert De Niro took a bite out of in "Cape Fear," has a wonderfully energetic and likable presence on film, and Marie's jovial innocence is welcome relief in the midst of this motley crew of hustlers and sadists.

The performances are all pretty good, though some of them were assured in the casting. All you have to do is say "Action!" to get weird and dangerous characterizations from Walken and Hopper. But there is nothing new or engaging about the story, and it would be a challenge for Scorsese himself to make an appealing story from one built entirely of desperation.

It was certainly out of reach of Salle, who might take a cue from Michael Jordan and be content with the sport he knows.

VILLAGE VOICE, 5/9/95, p. 67, J. Hoberman

Panther is brash and innocent [see Hoberman's review]. David Salle's *Search and Destroy* is brashly awful. There's a lot of wasted talent in this lugubrious maiden effort, including Rosanna Arquette, Ethan Hawke, Dennis Hopper, John Turturro, Christopher Walken, and Martin Scorsese (attached to the project as executive producer). Did art star Salle pay them off in paintings?

Adapted from Howard Korder's stage play, *Search and Destroy* is a sort of rancid *Candide,* with anticharismatic Griffin Dunne recreating his role as a Florida hustler who, not unlike Salle, feels like he's just gotta make a movie. To the degree that it is about anything, *Search and Destroy* concerns such irrational longings. Initially, Dunne has grandiose plans to adapt the didactic inspirational novel written by infomercial mogul Hopper. Then he hooks up with Hopper's assistant (Illeana Douglas), who has a more practical idea for a splatter sex flick. Then ... the deal falls apart and so does the movie.

Great '60s title notwithstanding, *Search and Destroy* is a film where almost nothing works. Scorsese reportedly felt compelled to take Salle's footage and edit it himself, giving particular piquance to the opening sequence where Dunne is audited by an IRS man played by Scorsese and found to owe $147,000 in taxes. Even so, the narrative never kicks in. Given its strident color-field compositions, stagy line readings, and gargoyle performances, *Search and Destroy* would actually play more powerfully as a slide show.

That the production stills are more compelling than anything in the movie is less a tribute to Salle's graphic skills than a factor of the cast's unbridled posturing. Characterizations shift from scene to scene and although Turturro is the chief frother, the goofiest lapse comes with Dunne and Douglas's genuine confusion as Walken, who at least has an evil sort of conviction, goes methodically out of control.

Also reviewed in:
CHICAGO TRIBUNE, 5/12/95, Friday/p. K, John Petrakis
NATION, 5/22/95, p. 735, Stuart Klawans
NEW REPUBLIC, 5/8/95, p. 26, Stanley Kauffmann
NEW YORK TIMES, 4/28/95, p. C16, Janet Maslin
VARIETY, 1/30-2/5/95, p. 49, Emanuel Levy
WASHINGTON POST, 5/12/95, p. B7, Hal Hinson

SECRET OF ROAN INISH, THE

A First Look Pictures and Jones Entertainment Group Ltd. release in association with Peter Newman Productions of a Skerry Movies production. *Executive Producer:* John Sloss, Glenn R.

Jones, and Peter Newman. *Producer:* Sarah Green and Maggie Renzi. *Director:* John Sayles. *Screenplay:* John Sayles. *Based on the novella "Secret of the Ron Mor Skerry" by:* Rosalie K. Fry. *Director of Photography:* Haskell Wexler. *Editor:* John Sayles. *Music:* Mason Daring. *Music Editor:* Nic Ratner. *Sound:* Clive Winter and (music) Mason Daring and Mark Tanzer. *Sound Editor:* Philip Stockton. *Casting:* Ros Hubbard and John Hubbard. *Production Designer:* Adrian Smith. *Art Director:* Henry Harris. *Set Decorator:* Tom Conroy. *Special Effects:* Trevor Neighbour. *Costumes:* Consolata Boyle. *Make-up:* Morna Ferguson. *Running time:* 102 minutes. *MPAA Rating:* PG.

CAST: Mick Lally (Hugh, Fiona's Grandfather); Eileen Colgan (Tess, Fiona's Grandmother); John Lynch (Tadhg Coneelly); Jeni Courtney (Fiona Coneelly); Richard Sheridan (Cousin Eamon); Cillian Byrne (Jamie); Pat Howey (Priest); Dave Duffy (Jim Coneelly); Declan Hannigan (Oldest Brother); Mairéad Ni Ghallchoir (Barmaid); Eugene McHugh and Tony Rubini (Bar Patrons); Micheal MacCarthaigh (Schoolmaster); Fergal McElherron (Sean Michael); Brendan Conroy (Flynn, Shopkeeper); Frankie McCafferty (Tim); Gerard Rooney (Liam Coneelly); Susan Lynch (Selkie); Suzanne Gallagher (Selkie's Daughter); Linda Greer (Brigid Coneelly); Eddie Erskine (Bar Patron).

CHRISTIAN SCIENCE MONITOR, 2/3/95, p. 13, David Sterritt

"The Secret of Roan Inish" reveals a side of John Sayles that we don't often see.

A fiercely independent filmmaker with a strong humanistic streak, Sayles is best known for pictures focusing on social issues. His works include "Matewan," about a labor dispute; "Eight Men Out," about corruption in baseball; "Lianna," about changing views of women and gay people; and his best movie, "The Brother From Another Planet," which views American race relations through the eyes of a man fleeing similar problems in a galaxy far, far away.

Fill out this list with pictures like "Return of the Secaucus Seven" and "City of Hope," and it's clear Sayles likes to fix his attention on pressing contemporary issues—which makes his new picture quite a surprise, since it trafficks in magic and myth from beginning to end. Its main characters are ordinary folks, to be sure, and Sayles takes care to detail the hard realities of their working-class lives. Still, the point of his story is that legends have a truth all their own, full of relevance and comfort to the people who believe in them.

The tale begins on Ireland's western coast, in a village where many residents have bittersweet memories of former homes they had to abandon because of changes in the local economy. Two such folks are Hugh and Tess, an aging couple who once lived on Roan Inish, an island that seems sadly distant even though it's visible from their seaside windows on a clear day.

Their lives undergo another change when they become the guardians of Fiona, their 10-year-old granddaughter. Much of the story is seen through her eyes, as she explores her new environment, hears lore and legends from the people who live there, and dreams of the day when she'll visit the offshore island that casts such a nostalgic spell over her family.

There's special power in two of the tales Fiona is told by new acquaintances—how her own baby brother was lost at sea in a floating cradle, and how her clan is descended from a "selkie," a mermaid-like creature that's part woman, part seal. We see these legends as the little girl envisions them, and we discover that they're not *merely* legends when we accompany her to Roan Inish, where the climax of the movie takes place.

In outline, "The Secret of Roan Inish" has all the ingredients for a sure-fire family entertainment, complete with magical fairy tales, wide-eyed adventures involving little violence or sexuality, and likable on-screen kinfolk to keep us company along the way.

As things turn out, the movie is less irresistible than it would like to be, mainly because Sayles is not a very graceful filmmaker. His heavy style is more suited to social realism than to the fanciful flights that Roan Inish inspires. He seems most involved with his Irish material when he's documenting the wishes, regrets, and day-to-day experiences of the most ordinary characters; the more-mythical aspects of the picture certainly interest him, but he doesn't manage to find the subtle resonances that would have made the story seem real as well as charming.

Still, there's much to enjoy in "The Secret of Roan Inish," including the spunky acting of Jeni Courtney as the young heroine and Eileen Colgan and Mick Lally as her grandparents. The vivid photography of northwestern Ireland is by Haskell Wexler, whose long credit list includes "Matewan," one of Sayles's best pictures. Mason Daring, a regular Sayles collaborator composed the effective music.

FILMS IN REVIEW, 3-4/95, p. 61, Eva H. Kissin

If you are vulnerable to Irish charm and can't resist a fairy tale, *The Secret Of Roan Inish* is for you. Although it takes place in 1946, it has the feeling of an earlier era because of its setting. Roan Inish, an isolated seal-dwelling island off the coast of Ireland, is caught in its own time warp. The eight-year-old heroine, Fiona Coneelly, is also something of an anachronism, a wide-eyed, long-haired blond out of *Alice In Wonderland* with some of the same curious, gutsy innocence of her famous predecessor.

Fiona is sent to stay on the mainland near Roan Inish with her grandparents because her mother is dead and her father can't care for her. Their home is close to Roan Inish where she once lived. The older generation had left the island after the apparent drowning of Jamie, Fiona's small brother, trapped in his cradle and rocked gently out to sea. You have to experience this to believe it!

Because Jamie's tragedy and the island are forbidden topics, they naturally intrigue young Fiona who can't accept their reality. She hears tales of the spirits on the island, of an ancestor who had mated with a seal woman and of the consequent protection by the seals of her family. She even hears rumors of their hereditary product, a black haired colleen who turns up among the fair-haired ones every generation. Her uncertain grandmother, caught between the present and the past, attempts to assure her that these are all superstitions.

Fiona's sentience, her own spirit, and the seals help her understand what might have been mere visions in another child.

And without giving away the end of this seal-fairy tale, there is hardly a scene richer in irony, since the piano on the Australian beach, than black-haired little Jamie "without a stitch," running between the protective seals and the familiar voice of his grandma calling him back. His bare little body running between his beached cradle and his beckoning human family create a delightful and totally unexpected suspense.

Jeri Courtnay does a good job as Fiona, and Eileen Colgan and Mick Lally are fine in their respective roles. The photography by Haskell Wexler and the music of Mason Daring are particularly satisfying in this Irish experience.

LOS ANGELES TIMES, 2/3/95, Calendar/p. 1, Kenneth Turan

The problem with most children's films is that they make older folk glad they're all grown up. Yes, we say, this sort of thing is fine for the kids, sweet and decent and good, but fortunately we can count on something a bit more substantial when it's our turn to watch.

"The Secret of Roan Inish" is not that kind of children's film. Though its protagonist is a 10-year-old girl, it is a crackling good tale with a sense of wonder and mystery strong enough to captivate any age group. A movie that believes in magic but knows enough not to be insistent about it, "Roan Inish" is just the kind of impressive independent work that has become habitual with writer-director John Sayles.

"Roan Inish's" story of young Fiona Coneelly's determination to penetrate to the secrets of her family's mysterious past, to understand the truth behind the legends she hears of curious appearances and disappearances, of animals with strange and disturbing powers, may not sound like ideal Sayles material, but in many ways it is.

For one thing, Sayles has always been interested in the human qualities of situations that cross the line into mythic: Both the "Black Sox" World Series scandal depicted in "Eight Men Out" and the West Virginia coal mine labor violence that was "Matewan's" backdrop fit that description as nicely as does "Roan Inish."

And Sayles' habitual straight-ahead filmmaking style turns out to be well-suited to transferring this kind of fable (based on a novella by Rosalie K. Fry) to the screen. Understanding that fantasy needs to be treated with respect but not fawned over, Sayles' matter-of-factness makes the magic seem all the more plausible and real.

Like many a young heroine, Fiona Coneelly (Jeni Courtney) is introduced with troubles to overcome. The time is just after World War II, her mother has died, and her father, a weary slave to his job in the city, has sent her to live with her grandparents Hugh (Mick Lally) and Tess (Eileen Colgan) on the isolated west coast of Ireland.

Though they now live on the mainland, the grandparents, in fact Fiona's entire family, used to have houses on the nearby small, mysterious island of Roan Inish, sharing the space with herds of seals. Economics and loneliness drove everyone from it, but life does not seem as sweet to the Coneellys away from their traditional home.

To make the loss painful, the family lingers over talks of the island and the past, shown in vivid voice-over flashbacks. Grandfather Hugh tells Fiona of the troubling disappearance of her brother, Jamie, an infant who floated out to sea in his cradle and was never seen again. And her cousin Tadhg (John Lynch) recounts the legend of ancestor Liam Coneelly who fell in love with a beautiful selkie, a creature half animal, half seal, who can be controlled only if her seal skin is stolen.

As Fiona hears these stories in bits and pieces, she comes to realize, in the best young heroine tradition, that she has a definite role to play. She believes that these are not just silly old rumors but indications of a critical contemporary situation that the adults are too dense to grasp, a situation that has been waiting for her help to resolve.

Though she gets some assistance from her older cousin Eamon (Richard Sheridan), Fiona is a splendidly self-reliant heroine. With the long golden hair of a fairy-tale princess and the feisty spirit of Nancy Drew, Fiona (perfectly played by non-professional Courtney) is a fearless creature, determined to do what needs to be done.

Helping to make Fiona's quest believable is the care that has been taken to make the film's setting authentic. Mason Daring's Celtic-themed original music creates an exquisite backdrop and Sayles' artful script has the feel of the land to it. Also, having actors of the caliber of Lally and Lynch, able to bring life to lines like "What the sea will take, the sea must have," is a considerable advantage.

If Sayles has a secret weapon, however, it is master cinematographer Haskell Wexler, who also shot "Matewan." A wizard with light, Wexler has captured the brooding, fog-bound romantic ambience that "Roan Inish" has to have to succeed, and he has done it in a casual way that refuses to call unnecessary attention to itself.

With its emphasis on what people owe to their physical surroundings, on the ancient kinship between man and the animal world that sometimes gets frayed around the edges, "The Secret of Roan Inish" manages to be both contemporary and timeless. Its enchantments are many, and they fall with happy equality on any age you can name.

NEW YORK POST, 2/3/95, p. 47, Thelma Adams

Many Irish stories are about leaving home, about being uprooted. In contrast, many American stories are about arriving, about coming to America.

American-born writer-director John Sayles' fable, "The Secret of Roan Inish" is about going and coming, about the Coneelly family and a rugged Irish paradise lost and remained.

With the advent of WWII, the Coneellies must evacuate their tiny, remote Roan Inish (Celtic for Seal Island) off Ireland's West coast. It takes the family's youngest girl—a pale, stubborn waif named Fiona (Jeni Courtney)—to learn the island's secret and return her family to their rightful place among the seals and sod.

Based on Rosalie Fry's 1957 novella, "Secret of Ron Mor Skerry," Sayles' magical movie is as much about storytelling as it is about a brave girl's journey. The narrative is composed of a series of interwoven stories, each one told in a different visual style, ranging from realistic to fantastic, from dark to light.

Like a beautiful tweed, the work of Academy Award-winning cinematographer Haskell Wexler ("Who's Afraid of Virginia Woolf?"), is marvelous without calling attention to itself.

The director of "City of Hope" and "Matewan" usually works in a realist vein, creating social commentary. In "Roan Inish,' Sayles uses his eye for detail, his ear for dialect and his commitment to grounding each scene emotionally in order to root even the most fantastical yarn in reality.

An exchange between Fiona and her 13-year-old cousin Eamon (Richard Sheridan), mirrors the give-and-take between truth and myth in "Roan Inish."

"That's just stories,' Fiona tells Eamon.

"Some stories are true," the 13-year-old responds.

Families—and cultures—are the stories that they tell. And the Coneellies are a family of fabulous storytellers. Fiona's grandfather, Hugh (Mick Lally), tells Fiona of the tragedy that befell the clan on evacuation day. The cradle of Fiona's baby brother, Jamie, was washed out to sea and the boy was lost, perhaps forever.

This dark day hangs over the Coneellies like a curse, but it's the tale of local fisherman, Tadhg (John Lynch), that glistens in memory. Considered "touched" by the locals, Tadhg tells Fiona the Celtic myth of the Selkie, a creature who is half-seal, half-woman.

Tadhg's story of a Selkie rising from the sea as a beautiful, wild-haired woman, marrying, and mothering a brood of children, and then returning to the waves is told with the minimum of special effects and a maximum of soul.

Could this seal woman have been the mother of all Coneellies?

The harsh reality of wartime dislocation and the enchantment of a fabulous creation myth are seamlessly welded into Sayles' most emotionally-satisfying film.

I laughed, I cried and, the most magical feeling of all, I glowed, while watching "The Secret of Roan Inish."

NEWSDAY, 2/3/95, Part II/p. B2, Jack Mathews

The sea and the creatures living above and below it are the spiritual masters of John Sayles' magical "The Secret of Roan Inish," a modern folk tale about the superstitions of the Irish fishing families living along the isolated, windswept coast of northwestern Ireland.

Sayles may be the most stubbornly independent of the new breed-of-independent filmmakers, and he is certainly the least predictable. His films have ranged from race relations ("The Brother From Another Planet") to big-city political corruption ("City of Hope") to the labor movement ("Matewan") to probing examinations of relationships between women ("Lianna," "Passion Fish"). The connecting thread through most of them is a passionate humanism; whatever the subject matter, his stories focus on the impact of events on their recognizable characters.

In "Roan Inish," Sayles' lightest and most fanciful film, events all spiral around the Coneelly family, and specifically around 10-year-old Fiona (Jeni Courtney), whose head is filled by her older kin with legends of the sea, with stories of the Coneelly clan's relationship with the seals and gulls at their old home on the island of Roan Inish.

"Roan Inish," adapted from a 1957 novella by Rosalie K. Fry, is a delicate blend of Celtic mythology and post-World War II Irish culture. The story is very tightly focused—there are barely a half-dozen speaking parts—but its setting makes it feel as big as the sea; and its series of legends, dramatized as they're being told to Fiona, give it the quality of an epic.

The central story is that of Fiona's determination to find her baby brother, Jamie, who, she has been assured, drowned when his cradle was swept into a stormy sea off Roan Inish the very day their parents were abandoning the island for a new life in the cities.

With her mother now dead and her father a maudlin drunk, Fiona is returned to the Irish coast several years later to live with her grandparents, just a short boat ride from Roan Inish. Soon, her sea-worshiping grandfather (Mick Lally) is regaling her with stories about the island. Among them, the one about a drowning Coneelly who was saved by a seal, after which the animals were revered icons of the sea. (Roan Inish obviously has nothing in common with Long Island, where some butcher continues to carve up seals along the coast.)

But the tallest tale is told to the blond, blue-eyed Fiona by her father's cousin (John Lynch), the rare "dark one" among the Coneellys, who attributes his looks to the marriage generations ago between an ancestor and a beautiful woman who emerged from the skin of a seal.

Sayles tells these stories without a hint of embarrassment. They are shot more like flashbacks than myths, and if you can share his passion for Irish folklore, you will be swept right along with Fiona, her cousin Eamon (Richard Sheridan), her romantic grandfather, and finally, her disbelieving grandmother (Eileen Colgan), as they return to Roan Inish to discover the secret of Jamie's disappearance.

The special effects could use a little more magic, but the lyrical nature of Sayles' dialogue and the marvelous performances of the angelic Jeni Courtney and the craggy Irish stage veteran Lally easily overcome the film's apparent budget restrictions. "The Secret of Roan Inish" gives the "Save the seals" slogan a whole new meaning.

SIGHT AND SOUND, 8/96, p. 63, Philip Kemp

Ireland, the 40s. Ten-year-old Fiona Coneelly's mother is dead and her father, who works in the city, can no longer cope with looking after her. He sends her to live with her grandparents, Hugh and Tess Coneelly, on the coast of Donegal. Hugh points out to Fiona the now-abandoned offshore island of Roan Inish, where all the Coneelly's used to live, and tells her how his great-grandfather, Sean Michael, was shipwrecked but saved by a seal, who bore him to the island. That night Fiona sees a light on Roan Inish.

Hugh reminds Fiona how, on the day of the evacuation, her baby brother Jamie was washed out to sea in his wooden cradle and lost, and warns her not to mention it to Tess. Fiona's young cousin Eamon, who intends to move back to Roan Inish when he grows up, tells her there are rumours of Jamie being sighted. Fiona persuades Hugh and Eamon to take her to the island when they go fishing. She finds warm ashes in a cottage, and small bare footprints on the beach. Later she meets another cousin, Tadhg, said to be "touched", who tells her that generations ago Liam Coneelly took as his bride a beautiful selkie (half-woman, half-seal) and had many children with her; but one day she found her sealskin that he had hidden, resume sealform and returned for ever to the sea.

Fiona talks Eamon into taking her to Roan Inish again. She catches sight of Jamie, but he runs away and escapes to sea in his cradle-boat. Returning home, she finds Hugh and Tess in despair; their landlord has given them notice to quit. On a foggy day Fiona finds herself mysteriously carried to Roan Inish in an oarless rowing-boat, seemingly propelled by the seals. Once again she sees Jamie and he flees, but she guesses that the seals want her family to move back to the island. Rescued by Hugh and Eamon, she broaches the idea; Hugh is tempted, but Tess remains scornful.

Secretly, Fiona and Eamon set about refurbishing the cottages on Roan Inish. One evening, with a storm brewing, Fiona blurts out to her grandparents that she has seen Jamie. To everyone's surprise, Tess believes her and calmly prepares for the whole family to sail to the island. Once there, they settle in and as the storm clears Jamie appears in his cradle. He tries to flee again, but three seals gently drive him up the beach to his family, and he is reunited with them.

At first sight, John Sayles' first non-American film looks like an odd choice for such a fiercely political film-maker: a gentle piece of Celtic myth-making whose message is the essentially conservative doctrine of getting back to your roots. But Sayles has never been doctrinaire, and running through much of his work has been a parallel but not necessarily contradictory strain, a concern with people trying to gain (or regain) control of their lives, often by coming to terms with who they are and where they started out from. Seen in this light, *The Secret of Roan Inish* takes up elements of *The Return of the Secaucus Seven, Baby It's You* and *Matewan* and follows on from *Passion Fish*, whose paraplegic heroine finds strength in returning to her native Louisiana bayous.

Sayles' films also display an acute sense of place and the Donegal coast is a gift to any visual artist. Haskell Wexler's photography captures the moist, shimmering light of the region, but we also get the texture of it: the drag of oars through seaweed clogged shallows, the fudgy chunkiness of dug peat. Sayles may be creating myth, but he's intent on rooting it in the fabric of actuality. Thus he avoids the windy portentousness of Mike Newell's exploration of mythical Irishry, *Into the West*.

The myth, too, works both on its own level—as an emanation of natural forces, of wind and water, seals and seagulls—and as a metaphor for social reality. The mixed ancestry of the Coneellys, half-human and half sea-creature, reflects their uneasy status on the western shoreline, in sight of their old home yet sundered from it. They may claim hopefully that, "The East is our future, the West is our past," but neither seems to offer refuge. To Tess, the city is, "Nothing but noise and dirt and people that's lost their senses," yet the island is, "nothing for us but sad memories." The dilemma's side-stepped rather than resolved by the film's ending: the cosy image of the family back in their old home, reunited around the recovered child, leaves out of account the pressures that drove them to quit the island in the first place. (To say nothing of the marginalised father, drunken and isolated in the big city.)

If *The Secret of Roan Inish* fails to come to grips with its own social implications, against that can be set an abundance of unforced charm and a sheer delight in story-telling. The film is a pleasure to look at and listen to, graced with a lilting, folk-based music score front Mason

Daring. Sayles, always known as an actors' director, draws strong, sinewy performances from his cast not least from the young discovery, Jeni Courtney, as the serious-eyed, unwinsome Fiona—and provides them with dialogue that's idiomatic without resorting to stage Irishry. There are quiet touches of sly humour: Tess, having heard Hugh recounting ancient legends, mutters, "Superstitious old man," before invoking the nocturnal protection of assorted saints and angels. In an age of overweening special effects, it's also refreshing to see a seal turn into a woman by nothing more intricate than slipping off an artificial sealskin.

VILLAGE VOICE, 2/7/95, p. 51, Georgia Brown

John Sayles Is a director I've wanted to like for a long time but his films have often felt awkwardly earnest and hortatory. Recently, without softening his social principles, Sayles has begun training his sights on people's longings for lost felicity, their sense of separation from essential things, particularly the natural world. First, there was the lovely, lucid drama of *Passion Fish;* now Sayles gives us *The Secret of Roan Inish,* a delicate romance that suggests that the kingdom under the sea and the one over it, like the way up and the way down, may be one and the same.

Ten-year-old Fiona Coneelly (Jeni Courtney) stands vigilant on the deck of a ship. Pinned to her drab woolen coat is a tag (the kind they affix to luggage), though the golden-haired Fiona, looking like a tiny Fra Angelico model, is anything but drab. Her father, slaving in some city sweatshop, has sent the child to live with grandparents by the sea. Until recent years, the whole Coneelly clan made its living as fishermen, but the younger generation has migrated to cities, leaving only the old couple (played by Eileen Colgan and Mick Lally), with a boy to help out, And even these three are displaced—stranded on the mainland in a rented cottage, directly across the water from their former home, Roan Inish, or island of the Seals.

As Fiona begins her new life, she learns the clan's secrets from a series of tales told by family members. In standing up for oral history, Sayles takes a risk in having so much of his narrative recited. As he employs it, the device demonstrates the power of a tale well told. The family stories have to do with a living link to the sea through a race of mythical creatures, the Selkies (half-human, half-seal).

In the past, Sayles has given us a good deal about the corruption of cities—and that's here in the background—but lately he's focused on roots and sources. In *Passion Fish,* Mary McDonnell's tough cookie New Yorker, victim of a traffic accident, returns to the Louisiana bayou house she'd grown up in. Both parents are dead, the family home is empty, but she's brought back to life by Alfre Woodard's no-nonsense nurse and David Strathairn's unsophisticated woodsman, a guide who, at one magical point, takes her into the swamps to meet the local wildlife.

Passion Fish was a comic romance for grown-ups; *Roan Inish* is a lyric romance for all ages. The movie immediately veers into the territory of classic fairy tales in that it's the story of a child on her own, who, by bravery, resourcefulness, and perseverance, rescues the realm. As in fairy tales, the animal world befriends the child and aids her quest. Some of the marvelous shots here are of seals, popping, up in the water to keep an eye on their charge.

One of *Roan Inish*'s first scenes briefly shows the burial of Fiona's mother. The stoic Fiona doesn't cry, but someone's baby does. This piercing cry simultaneously reflects Fiona's inner state and the cry of another lost child—her little brother, Jamie, who sailed off in his cradle when the family deserted Roan Inish. The death of the mother here becomes the signal event that sends the child out into the world to fulfill a task—specifically, to bring the brother home.

Like *The Secret Garden*'s Mary Lennox—an orphan shipped off to her uncle's mansion on the edge of the moors, a girl who also responds to cries in the night—Fiona seems singularly self-possessed, though, inside, she's mourning. In rescuing a child—a relative and surrogate—she'll heal herself. As Amy Taubin offered, *Roan Inish* also resembles *The Secret Garden* in that the children, Fiona and her 13-year-old cousin Eamon (Richard Sheridan), take it upon themselves, first, to find "the place," and then, since the place is abandoned and neglected, to renew it. Bringing the dead to life, they give hope to the adults who've been living in despair.

Another, probably coincidental, *Secret Garden* link: John Lynch, who played the warped uncle in Agnieszka Holland's film, turns up here as Tadhg, Fiona's "touched" cousin and "one o' of the dark ones," who recites a riveting story, holding his audience with his glittering pirate's eye.

Each time a story is told, Sayles illustrates, usually with a few carefully chosen strokes. (His cinematographer is the remarkable Haskell Wexler. When gulls attack, it comes like those shrill, ineffable moments out of *The Birds*. When the Selkie maiden, Nuala (played by Lynch's sister, Susan), slips out of her seal skin, the sight is at once immediately comprehensible yet utterly mysterious. With *The Secret of Roan Inish*, Sayles has achieved something modest, marvelous, and unforgettable.

Also reviewed in:
CHICAGO TRIBUNE, 3/3/95, Friday/p. C, Michael Wilmington
NEW YORK TIMES, 2/3/95, p. C12, Stephen Holden
VARIETY, 5/9-15/94, p. 76, Dennis Harvey
WASHINGTON POST, 3/17/95, p. B7, Rita Kempley
WASHINGTON POST, 3/17/95, Weekend/p. 38, Desson Howe

SENSE AND SENSIBILITY

A Columbia Pictures Release. *Executive Producer:* Sydney Pollack. *Producer:* Lindsay Doran. *Director:* Ang Lee. *Screenplay:* Emma Thompson. *Adapted from the novel by:* Jane Austen. *Director of Photography:* Michael Coulter. *Editor:* Tim Squyres. *Music:* Patrick Doyle. *Music Editor:* Roy Prendergast. *Choreographer:* Stuart Hopps. *Sound:* Tony Dawe. *Sound Editor:* Steve Hamilton. *Casting:* Suzy Catliff. *Production Designer:* Luciana Arrighi. *Art Director:* Andrew Sanders. *Set Decorator:* Ian Whittaker. *Special Effects:* Ricky Farns. *Costumes:* Jenny Beavan and John Bright. *Make-up:* Morag Ross. *Running time:* 135 minutes. *MPAA Rating:* PG.

CAST: James Fleet (John Dashwood); Tom Wilkinson (Mr. Dashwood); Harriet Walter (Fanny Dashwood); Kate Winslet (Marianne Dashwood); Emma Thompson (Elinor Dashwood); Gemma Jones (Mrs. Dashwood); Hugh Grant (Edward Ferrars); Emilie François (Margaret Dashwood); Elizabeth Spriggs (Mrs. Jennings); Robert Hardy (Sir John Middleton); Ian Brimble (Thomas); Isabelle Amyes (Betsy); Alan Rickman (Colonel Brandon); Greg Wise (John Willoughby); Alexander John (Curate); Imelda Staunton (Charlotte Palmer); Imogen Stubbs (Lucy Steele); Hugh Laurie (Mr. Palmer); Allan Mitchell (Pigeon); Josephine Gradwell (Maid to Mrs. Jennings); Richard Lumsden (Robert Ferrars); Lone Vidahl (Miss Grey); Oliver Ford Davies (Doctor Harris); Eleanor McCready (Mrs. Bunting).

FILMS IN REVIEW, 3-4/96, p. 65, Barbara Cramer

Return with us now to those thrilling days of yesteryear (circa the early 1800's) when passion and prose weren't purple (more like rose petal pink), and appetites of all kinds prevailed, even if not discussed in polite company. It's the mannered world of *Sense and Sensibility*, the latest of three critically acclaimed film romances adapted from the novels of Jane Austen, an English clergyman's spinster daughter who died a virgin at 41 in 1817.

Austen is finally getting her due after a 56-year hiatus from the big screen. (Her previous film, MGM's *Pride and Prejudice*, was released in 1940). Concurrently, she's represented by *Sense and Sensibility*—first published in 1811 when the author was 36—starring Emma Thompson (who also scripted), *Persuasion* (featuring Thompson's younger sister Sophie), and *Clueless* (a modern American updating of *Emma*). Also scheduled are a BBC miniseries of *Pride and Prejudice* due this year on television, and yet another *Emma*, this time, a classic period piece, once again to star Thompson and her mother, Phyllida Law, for the large screen.

What, one might wonder, could account for Austen's sudden almost across-the-board popularity?

But there's a *but*. Immediately after screening *S&S*, I proceeded to buy the paperback to see how Thompson's debut script gibed with the Austen original, and then to rent the video of *Pride and Prejudice* of a half-century ago—one of my all-time film favorites (its appeal remains untarnished by the years) to see how the two compared as motion picture entertainments.

My conclusions: Thompson is, indeed, a Renaissance woman. The Academy Award-winner, who recently displayed her remarkable talents in *Carrington,* did a skillful job adapting this classic period romance. And in an Oscar first, she was nominated simultaneously for both acting and scripting.

But juxtaposing the two films (*Pride* with *Sense*), her interpretation falls short. Though both films deal with similar subject matter, what's missing is the cinematic wit and sparkle of the 40's film (brilliantly adapted by author Aldous Huxley and Jane Murfin) which stars Laurence Olivier and Greer Garson, and which to date remains a cut above. Still, with some reservations, *S&S* is worth seeing, especially when one considers it was directed by Taiwanese Oscar-nominee Ang Lee (*The Wedding Banquet* and *Eat, Drink, Man, Woman*) who, remarkably, managed to bridge the synapse between his Asian sensibilities and Western culture, and still give us an engaging sense of what life was like in not quite so merrie olde England in the days of yore.

Though admittedly in film, authors seem to run in cycles. (The eighties found early twentieth century novelist E.M. Forster the writer of the moment, with five of his books, *A Passage to India, A Room with a View, Maurice, Where Angels Fear to Tread* and *Howards End,* translated for cinema.) Now in the mid-90's, it's fellow Brit Austen's turn.

In her domain, libidos exist only by genteel supposition. There's no sex of the Sharon Stone graphically splayed school of acting. (Austen had no such firsthand experiences; she wrote only about people and lifestyles she knew intimately.) Just lots of ladylike breastbeating angst and repressed passion in the 30's style of filmmaking or Barbara Cartland-type novels. Yet on film (and Hollywood take note), her stories are appealing, even without high-tech special effects. The absence of eroticism doesn't at all detract from the power of her characters' desires. They're eternal verities. *Sense and Sensibility* concerns the financial and emotional straits of two sisters of marriageable age, left without expectations of any kind after their father dies. Because of the law of the land (primogeniture), their half-brother inherits everything: their family estate and possessions. And what's worse, the ladies are left with no dowry to attract potential husbands. (Their youngest sister, deliciously played by Emilie François, is a tomboyish 12, so her yearnings aren't yet germane.)

Though slightly modified by Thompson's screenplay, the Cambridge-educated actor's adaptation does do justice to Austen's social satire of an era long past. (As Elinor, for example, the oldest of the three siblings, she's evolved from a 19-year-old to one in her later twenties. It's merely a minor adjustment.) Her Elinor is the *sense* of the title, stalwart, contained, and emotionally restrained. She falls hard for Hugh Grant, her step brother-in-law (replete with his usual tics and shticks), but grins and bears it stoically when he inexplicably withdraws from their relationship.

If she's the *Yin,* her impulsive younger sister Marianne (Kate Winslet of *Heavenly Creatures*) is the *Yang,* whose sensibilities are, shall we say, uncorseted. Her emotions hang out shamelessly—which doesn't sit well with the polite society of the time. She rejects the honorable overtures of her rich, sensible suitor Colonel Brandon (played too stolidly by Alan Rickman) when she's literally—understandably, but unwisely—swept off her feet by the dashing Willoughby (Greg Wise), a gorgeous no-goodnik who's every mother's nightmare.

To cut to the chase, the story ends happily for all, but it's a rough journey. It's also well-depicted, thanks to an unusually fine supporting cast of players: Gemma Jones as the mother, Harriet Jones as the sister-in-law from hell, Elizabeth Spriggs as the gossiping mother of Imelda Staunton (almost unrecognizable from her *Antonia and Jane* days), and especially Hugh Laurie as Staunton's acerbic husband, whose brief time on screen—with minimal dialogues worth his weight in box office receipts. The man does more with a raised eyebrow than most actors can with a long soliloquy.

LOS ANGELES TIMES, 12/13/95, Calendar/p. 1, Kenneth Turan

The movie business is nothing if not paradoxical, which is another way of saying that a year marked by careful attention paid to graphic and grotesque violence has also brought forth enough different approaches to the delicate novels of Jane Austen to inspire an academic symposium.

First came "Clueless," a sassy modernization of "Emma" that retained only the barest bones of Austen's plot. Then, courtesy of the BBC, came "Persuasion," the most authentically British version and the one closest to the spirit of the novels.

Finally, falling somewhere between those two poles, is "Sense and Sensibility," the audience-friendly Hollywood version of Austen, easygoing and aiming to please.

Like the two that came before it, "Sense and Sensibility," directed by Ang Lee ("The Wedding Banquet," "Eat Drink Man Woman") and starring Emma Thompson, who also wrote the script, is proof to any doubters of the resilience and continuing emotional power of an author who began writing 200 years ago.

The like-clockwork delight of "Sense's" plot, the shrewdness of Austen's characterizations plus excellent casting are enough to overcome whatever qualms, and there are some, viewers might have. The center always holds with Austen, enabling this film to turn out right even though some of it feels rather wrong.

For today's audiences, Austen's world is easy to lose yourself in. It was an age of extreme politeness and ritualized conversation, yet it was also a time when barriers to romance were everywhere. Love and money rarely traveled in the same circles, and questions of wealth and property were often the determining factor in who could marry and who could not.

The death of family patriarch Henry Dashwood sets "Sense's" plot in motion. The law forces him to leave the family estate of Norland in Sussex to John, his son from a previous marriage. And John's grasping wife, Fanny (a tart Harriet Walter), ensures that that means trouble to Mrs. Dashwood (Gemma Jones), the dead man's second wife, and the three daughters he left behind. There is the young Margaret (Emilie Francois) and the two older sisters who give the story its name, common-sensical Elinor (Thompson) and passionate, romantic Marianne (Kate Winslet).

Much more favorably inclined toward the Dashwoods, especially toward Elinor, is Fanny's brother Edward Ferrars (Hugh Grant). A man of disarming diffidence and charming humility, he and Elinor seem on the verge of forming "an attachment" when they are separated and the Dashwoods go to live in far-off Devonshire with the generous Sir John Middleton (Robert Hardy) and his mother-in-law, the comically vulgar Mrs. Jennings (Elizabeth Spriggs).

There the sensitive Marianne has to deal with a pair of suitors. First out of the blocks is the reserved, distant Colonel Brandon (Alan Rickman), a mournful gentleman with a secret tragedy in his past. Easily eclipsing him, however, is the dashing Willoughby, whose passion for poetry and wildflowers seems a perfect match for Marianne, who embraces his spirit with scandalous ardor. As for Elinor, complicating her measured regard for Edward Ferrars is an encounter with the smooth-tongued Lucy Steele (a wonderful part for Imogen Stubbs) who may or may not be on intimate terms with the gentleman.

The fun of "Sense and Sensibility," among other things, is wondering if anything will make Marianne more sensible and Elinor more emotional. In this the film is helped by some fine casting. Darkly handsome Greg Wise is an ideal Willoughby, Grant is approiately awkward and well-meaning as Mr. Ferrars, and Thompson is a clear-headed and careful Elinor. Best of the group is Winslet, just as impressive as the impulsive, unaffected, temperamental Marianne as she was as Juliet Hulme in the much applauded "Heavenly Creatures."

But if it hasn't tampered overmuch with essentials, this "Sense and Sensibility" is troublesome around the periphery. Part of the problem is that Taiwan-born Lee, though he does a more-than-credible job of directing, isn't sharp on the nuances of British behavior. Some of the performances, like Rickman's overly morose Colonel Brandon and the film's several comic eccentrics, are a beat or so off. And with a precise writer who was as acutely conscious of intangibles of character as Austen, that lack is noticeable.

Not helping as much as it might is Emma Thompson's script. Austen's original lines, for instance, "people always live forever when there is any annuity to be paid them," have an immediately recognizable bite, and Thompson, a first-time scriptwriter after all, is not up to matching them in her own work. More troublesome is her tendency to replace Austen's wit with a wisecrack tone. And periodic moments of raucous slapstick add a jarring note that broadens the proceedings, presumably to make them more palatable to a larger audience.

At day's end, however, it seems churlish to complain about a film that creates so much good feeling by its fail-safe close. The sensibility may be a bit off, but there is more than enough sense involved in this mid-Atlantic Austen to make up the difference.

NEW STATESMAN & SOCIETY, 2/23/96, p. 43, Lizzie Francke

When, about five years ago, Emma Thompson announced that she wanted to adapt *Sense and Sensibility*, I snorted at the thought. In some interview she explained that she was keen to do something for women, at least, that was the gist of her interest in the project. All very laudable, but I wondered why she couldn't invest in something a little more contemporary. So often the present seems to belong to men in films, the past to women—in the last couple of years this seems more so: to put it crudely, if one looks at the key cinematic flash-points there's *Pulp Fiction* and *Reservoir Dogs* for the boys, *The Piano* for the girls (it's no slip that jokes are being made about Jane Austen being the hottest thing next to Quentin Tarantino). So now, in retrospect, I think, thank god for the bonnet and laud Thompson's choice, for one wonders whether women would get a look-in on the screen at all without it.

One can chart the recent revival of interest in a variety of 19th-century heroines, *faux* or otherwise. First there was the mute Ada in Jane Campion's *The Piano*, who erupted into the cinema like a pale wraith from an Emily Brontë or Emily Dickinson text, while on the small screen one could find George Eliot's Dorothea Brooke in the exceptionally fine adaptation of *Middlemarch*. The extraordinary success of these projects fuelled the current mania for period pieces on both TV and cinema. Indeed, last year it was acknowledged that Gillian Armstrong and Robin Swicord's robust adaptation of Louisa May Alcott's classic girls' own story little *Women,* in which the exuberant Jo is the prototype heroine who rightfully wants to have it all, was only finally given the go-ahead after the box-office success of *The Piano* (while the rather insipid screen version of A S Byatt's *Angels and Insects* attempted to echo the Campion triumph—right down to using a very Nymanesque sounding score). Then there is Jane Austen's gallery of gallant girls with *Sense and Sensibility* joining the very jaunty, fizzy even, *Pride and Prejudice* and Roger Michell's austere, troubled *Persuasion,* which astutely tuned into the novel's more mournful mood. And with not just one but three versions of *Emma* to come.

The 19th century is revisited and played out over and over again. Not as a stale fixation, but with some of its expectations and frustrations aired now seeming, sadly, all too recognisable. With Jane Austen in particular, observations of a class-bound society, where interpersonal relations are governed by an exchange and mart, remain relevant even though the stakes may have changed. It is this that makes the trials of the Dashwood sisters, the spirited girls of slender means in *Sense and Sensibility* so oddly familiar. Emma Thompson and director Ang Lee read it as a tale of two young women hemmed in by so much, not least their own expectations and foibles, with Elinor's drywitted, stoic sense contrasted to Marianne's excessive, bubbling sensibility both needing balance. It follows them as they strain to break free to find fulfilment. All that defiant traipsing around in muddy fields is psychically, at least, something still to be identified with, as is the wilful Marianne learning that life might be about something more than meeting a man who knows his sonnets and can drive a fast barouche. It is this lush emotional texture that makes this, along with the other Austen adaptations, so compelling.

For Thompson and Lee's *Sense and Sensibility* is a very handsome and agreeable film. Lee, who directed such successes as The *Wedding Banquet* and *Eat Drink, Man Woman;* was an inspired choice. His films offer astute observations on cultures bound by stifling social conventions and etiquette. In particular *Eat Drink, Man Woman,* which was about a widowed father who could express his love for his four daughters only by cooking them elaborate meals that they could not eat, seems like a rehearsal for Austen, which is full of characters who either fill up their world with empty patter or cannot explain themselves at all.

Lee directs in a spare style. Cinematically, it is a film about absences. The lighting is naturalistic rather than "opulent period", and there is minimal use of music on the soundtrack. Meanwhile, the camera framing subtly infers the divisions between the public and private spaces that these characters inhabit and just how little space, indeed, there is for private contemplation. The bright screenplay is skilfully attuned to Austen's ironies, with Thompson laying a few extra of her own on top. One wonders in this respect if it was also her deliberate ploy to make the women in the film so exceptionally engaging and the men really rather dull. Thompson's Elinor and Kate Winslet's Marianne are quite delightful, while they are complimented by a jolly good display of English character acting from the likes of Harriet Walter as the spiteful Fanny Dashwood and Elizabeth Spriggs as the bustling Mrs Jennings. In comparison, Hugh Grant's

Edward Ferrars and Greg Wise's John Willoughby just seem to lend their good looks to the film. In the case of Wise, it is fitting, for Willoughby should be seen to be a rather bland, lost trophy, but to make booby prizes of them all is most telling.

NEW YORK, 12/18/95, p. 51, David Denby

The recent movies made from Jane Austin's novels possess one (and only one) advantage over the masterly originals: They ravish our senses with beauty and wealth, the splendor of early-nineteenth-century England. It's part of the achievement of both *Persuasion* and the new *Sense and Sensibility* that the luxury and amplitude onscreen never seem merely decorative. On the contrary, the emotional and erotic goings-on become intimately connected to the flowing lawns and great rooms, the servants and carriages and silver. Jane Austen wrote very candidly about money; the movies make her seem even more candid. We can now see, front and center, what remains in the background of the novels—the enormous prizes to be won in the marriage game. For women, it's a desperate situation. In the England of the early 1800s, property gets passed along through the male line, and women without a dowry enjoy very few options. Barred from the professions, or from earning a living except as a shopkeeper's wife or a governess, Jane Austen's impoverished gentlewomen must marry, and preferably marry well, or fall into penury or worse. The dishonorable among them turn into coolly calculating fortune-seekers; the honorable, who marry for love, look for signs of integrity and spiritual worth in the young men who remain their only gateway to comfort and dignity.

Sense and Sensibility is a successful and entertaining romantic comedy—a good but not great movie—that takes its special urgency from this background of social envy and fear. Two wealthy young men make advances to the Dashwood sisters, and then, caught in the money trap themselves (by wealthy, manipulative parents), they turn away, causing the women extreme anguish. Emma Thompson, who plays the elder of two disappointed sisters, Elinor Dashwood, adapted the book herself, and Thompson has brought the material as close to conventional romantic comedy as possible without betraying the anxieties lying behind the story. *Sense and Sensibility*, published in 1811, after much revision, is a fascinating work, but at times a bit prosy and overelaborate; it lacks the incomparable teasing brilliance of *Pride and Prejudice*. Perhaps inevitably, Thompson has dropped the long passages of reflection and debate while fleshing out the scenes of flirtation and courtship. She sticks to plot and emotion, the spurts of anticipation, pleasure, and heartbreak.

At first, Ang Lee may seem an odd choice for an English period movie. But the Taiwanese director of *The Wedding Banquet* and *Eat Drink Man Woman* understands the strains and stresses of social ritual extremely well. Lee stages the walks, dinners, teas, and balls very directly, without pomp; he has the characters jump right in, as if they were alive today. And he makes central use of the good-hearted but infuriating old vulgarian and gossip Mrs. Jennings (Elizabeth Spriggs), whose constant meddling and indiscreet joking drives all the young people crazy. The characters in Lee's earlier movies know the same double bind that Jane Austen's characters are caught in: Life in society can be excruciating, but there is no real alternative to it. The impetuous younger Dashwood sister, Marianne (Kate Winslet), loves scenery and storms, but when she walks off by herself, she sprains her ankle or catches pneumonia in the rain. Woman shall not live by romantic poetry alone.

Emma Thompson, whose high intelligence never spins into eccentricity—she has a grip on common emotions as well as common sense—anchors the movie just as Elinor anchors the book. But Elinor's love affair with the modest and self-deprecating Edward Ferrars (Hugh Grant), despite Thompson's writing fresh material for the two characters, remains a bit thin, and Grant is feeble, an actor relying on Hugh Grant shtick. Entering a room head down, shoulders hunched, Grant walks in so gingerly a fashion that he appears to be afraid of breaking the Wedgwood. He's too abashed, and when Edward pulls away from Elinor, we're so uncompelled by his presence that we're not sure what she's missing.

Much of our interest quickly passes to Marianne; the young actress who plays her, Kate Winslet, has the serious translucent glow of a girl in a period portrait—very pale skin, liquid eyes, and auburn curls bunched low on her forehead. At the same time, the full lips and penetrating stare suggest a passionate will bound for glory or trouble or both. Another good English actress! Marianne falls utterly for Willoughby, a tall and dark Byronic charmer played by the dashing young Greg Wise, whose sideburns turn sharply toward his cheeks like two daggers. Wise is as ripely sexual as the young Valentino. The rushed flirtation between these two, while owing little to Jane Austen, is a wonderful bit of comic-erotic theater.

Both Edward Ferrars and Willoughby disappear, and the two sisters, in their shock, are attended by the mournful and depressive Colonel Brandon, who, in the improbable person of Alan Rickman, is perhaps too saturnine and heavy-voiced to qualify as a lover. Rickman seems miscast. But Thompson and Lee get the relationship between the two suffering sisters right, the play of strength and weakness, candor and concealment—sense and sensibility merging in each sister, until both Marianne and Elinor become complete human beings. *Sense and Sensibility* concludes with a burst of joy that perhaps only the hard-hearted would not be touched by, and at the end, the viewer is brought back to the beauty and bounty of England. For me, the most striking moments in the movie are the most casual for instance, when the sunshine strikes a magnificent gray stone house as the darkgreen lawn glows like emerald on all sides. Of such things are the glory of the cinema made. Literature can do many of the other things better.

NEW YORK POST, 12/13/95, p. 43, Thelma Adams

Two Indians, Ismail Merchant and Ruth Prawer Jhabvala. An American, James Ivory. Now add Taiwan's Ang Lee to the list of non-Brits who are masters at making movies about the English.

Case in point, Lee's interpretation of Jane Austens "Sense and Sensibility."

Lee, who was nominated for Best Foreign Film Oscars for "The Wedding Banquet" and "Eat Drink Man Woman" may seem like an odd choice for this very Merchant Ivory production of a British classic. However, Lee's comedies about modern characters trying to balance the demands of family and societal traditions while remaining true to their own hearts are not so far afield from Austen's comedy of manners.

In her shrewd 1811 novel, Austen balanced intellect and emotion while parceling out her heroine between two sisters. The common-sensical Elinor Dashwood (Emma Thompson) suppresses the demands of her heart and retreats to her head. Her younger sister Marianne (Kate Winslet) lives every moment as if it were a Shakespeare sonnet, her head overwhelmed by the pounding of her heart.

Neither nature prepares the women for the romantic tussle ahead.

Elinor and Marianne find their fortunes drastically reduced when their aristocratic father dies. His estates are bequeathed to his son from a previous marriage, John (James Fleet). While John has been charged with taking care of his half-sisters, his greedy wife, Fanny (Harriet Walter), quashes that idea.

The cultured sisters discover that in matrimonial matters, the battle between head and heart can be secondary to the weight of a coin purse. Their lack of dowry frustrates their ability to marry the objects of their desire.

Fanny's brother Edward (Hugh Grant) has a shy, modest temperament perfectly suited to Elinor; the dashing Willoughby (Greg Wise) literally sweeps Marianne off her feet when she sprains her ankle during a rain-soaked walk that teeters on Bronte-like drama. Colonel Brandon (Alan Rickman) watches from the wings, in love with Marianne but burdened by a terrible (if romantic) secret.

At first sight, the 36-year-old Thompson makes for a long-in-the-tooth Elinor. (In the novel, the elder sister was a dewy 19.) The actress' winning performance quickly extinguishes this impression.

As Elinor is her family's backbone, so Thompson is the backbone of the cast. Her intelligent gaze and ironic sense mirror the author's narrative tone. When Elinor crosses from sense to sensibility, opening her heart to the audience, the Academy Award-winning actress takes the movie home in an emotional flood that levels the house.

Thompson, who also adapted the screenplay, could be angling for a rare double Oscar nomination. Balancing wit and emotional weight, her script guides its heroines over the obstacles that inhibit their progress toward the inevitable altar: the moment when both characters' lives snap into place and enter the happily-ever-after zone of matrimony.

Winslet, the vibrant young actress in the Anne Perry role in "Heavenly Creatures," holds her own with the formidable Thompson. The challenge here is not to play the emotional, flush-cheeked highs, but to register the quieter intimate moments between the two sisters, to make their rapport believable.

Grant contributes his patented stuttering charmer, his head perched on stiff shoulders as if it were an egg in a cup. One might complain about range, but the performance suits the role. The craggy-faced Rickman lends gravity as Marianne's bruised suitor, we want to continue watching him even as he hovers at the margin of the screen and story.

"Sense and Sensibility" is a near-perfect marriage of head and heart.

NEWSDAY, 12/13/95, Part II/p. B2, Jack Mathews

In a banner year of moviegoing for Jane Austen fans, the best was saved for last: Ang Lee's gorgeous, romantic, good-natured "Sense and Sensibility."

Those who raised their eyebrows when the production was announced, with a screenplay being written by the actress Emma Thompson and the directing assignment going to the Taiwanese Lee, may now lower them. Thompson's script was written with both a reverence for the novel's social and emotional detail and an abundance of her own good humor. And Lee, who showed plenty of sense and sensibility of his own with the art-house hits, "The Wedding Banquet" and "Eat Drink Man Woman," has made what is easily the season's most heartwarming picture.

The Austen revival, which began in midsummer with "Clueless," an "Emma"-inspired spoof of manners in "Beverly Hills 90210" country, and continued in September with the BBC's sober production of "Persuasion," offers something for all moods, while exploring the same social and romantic notions that occupied Austen right up to her death in 1817.

"Sense and Sensibility" was Austen's first major novel, written at a time when her own family was being uprooted and relocated, as are the Dashwoods a widow with three children—in her story. When we meet them, they are being indelicately evicted from their vast estate, which, by law, passes to a son from a previous marriage. The heir, John Dashwood (James Fleet), allows his avaricious wife, Fanny (Harriet Walter), to talk him out of a deathbed oath to provide for his step-family, forcing them to take up residence in a cousin's cottage and live on an annual pittance.

To most of us, Barton Cottage would be an upgrade, but it's a downscaled world for the humbled Dashwoods. For sensible Elinor (Thompson) and hopelessly romantic Marianne (Kate Winslet), the prospects of love, marriage and the future become linked with much greater urgency.

The bulk of "Sense and Sensibility" is devoted to the sisters' heartbreaking romantic experiences and the strain their contrasting temperaments place on them. Elinor is in love with Edward Ferrars (Hugh Grant)—a charming, if somewhat wimpy, cousin-in-law—and, while in a clear state of longing, cannot admit it even to herself. Marianne, on the other hand, wears her heart on her sleeve, ready to be claimed by the first Mr. Right who happens into the neighborhood.

Marianne's meeting with the gentleman hunk John Willoughby (Greg Wise) would be pretty ripe stuff if it weren't handled with such whimsical finesse. Thompson and Lee—rarely has the work of a writer and a director seemed more collaborative—turn the meeting into a romantic fantasy, with Willoughby literally sweeping Marianne up in his arms (to relieve her twisted ankle), and later, when she begins quoting Shakespeare, producing his own pocket volume of the Bard's sonnets. Wouldn't leave home without 'em.

The would-be romances are compounded by circumstances beyond the sisters' control. Elinor's Edward, it turns out, is in the fifth year of a secret engagement, and Willoughby, though he's equally smitten with Marianne, is compelled by his withering finances to court women of wealth, leaving the trail to her affections clear—or so he hopes—for the gentle, romantically haunted Col. Brandon (Alan Rickman).

There isn't a missed beat in any performance in the film. Thompson wrote herself the most complicated character, a woman of immense but stifled passion, and ought to pull off a unique career double—she could become the first woman nominated for Oscars in the same year for both acting and writing. Winslet, a revelation in "Heavenly Creatures," gives Marianne a heart that seems nearly twice her size.

But my favorite characters in the film are the Dashwoods' boisterous and giddily good-natured hosts Sir John Middleton (Robert Hardy) and his mother-in-law, Mrs. Jennings (Elizabeth Spriggs), who, whenever they show up, provide a lift.

NEWSWEEK, 12/19/95, p. 66, Jack Kroll

How about a Lifetime Achievement Oscar for Jane Austen at the next Academy Awards? Might as well, in view of the outpouring of films based on the work of the great 19th-century English novelist. After the superb "Persuasion" earlier this fall, we now have the brilliant and *Sense and Sensibility*, with Emma Thompson and Hugh Grant, to be followed in January by the BBC's delightful mini-series of "Pride and Prejudice" on the Arts & Entertainment network. Late 1996 will bring a movie version of "Emma" starring Gwyneth Paltrow, followed by a TV version of that novel from ITV. (And let's not forget this past summer's "Clueless," with Alicia Silverstone as a Beverly Hills reincarnation of Emma.) If all this strikes you as a hypermassive dose of Jane, think of it as an antidote to the fungus infection of Joe Eszterhas ("Showgirls," "Jade").

The popularity of Austen films in an age of marriage meltdown is fascinating, since most of her fictions are about the ordeal, both comic and dramatic, undergone by young women in the time of the Regency for whom marriage is an emotional, social and financial urgency. In "Sense and Sensibility," based on her first (1811) novel, the genteelly impoverished Dashwood sisters, Elinor (Emma Thompson) and Marianne (Kate Winslet) are opposites. Elinor is cool, rational "sense," Marianne is hot, romantic "sensibility." Thompson wrote the vigorous, faithful screenplay that vividly dramatizes Marianne's infatuation with the sexy cad Willoughby (Greg Wise), her rescue by the reserved, reliable Colonel Brandon (Alan Rickman) and Elinor's involvement with the mysteriously muffled Edward Ferrars (Hugh Grant).

As writer and actress, Thompson has all the right Austen rhythms. And, in a most unlikely directorial coup, Taiwan-born filmmaker Ang Lee ("Eat Drink Man Woman") orchestrates those rhythms with sensitivity and style. Twenty-year-old Winslet is wonderful as the passionate girl who almost dies when that passion is betrayed. The screen teems with superlative actors, brilliant costumes, gorgeous landscapes; it crackles with dialogue that turns English into verbal Mozart. Jane Austen, the spinster daughter of a village rector, who wrote her novels in the family sitting room on little sheets of paper that she could discreetly hide, is an enthralling artist.

That excitement is felt from another perspective in the six-hour BBC "Pride and Prejudice." Adapted by Andrew Davies and directed by Simon Langton, this is a TV production with cinematic impact. The relationship—part mating dance, part emotional kung fu—between the deliciously intelligent and independent Elizabeth Bennet (Jennifer Ehle) and the proud, snobbish aristocrat Darcy (Colin Firth) has a Shakespearean resonance. Watching their disaffection mutate into a complex kind of love is supremely civilized fun. And watching the six hours of interweaving plot lines, compelling characters and engaging actors (including the ravishing Susannah Harker as Elizabeth's sister Jane) makes you aware that Austen, perhaps the chief creator of the modern novel (Edmund Wilson compared her to James Joyce as a master of form) is also a progenitor of the soap opera, which is a diluted and debased form of her narrative of manners.

So, as the century comes to an end, Jane Austen, whose life and art crossed the line between the century of the Enlightenment and that of Romanticism, comes back into focus for a mass audience that would have blown her unblowable mind. The BBC telecast of "Pride and Prejudice" in England drew up to 11 million people for each weekly episode—the highest-rated costume drama ever in England. And as "Sense and Sensibility" goes into release, Penguin USA has a quarter of a million copies in print of their Signet tie-in. All this for a writer whose novels were published anonymously before her death at 41, who made about 800 pounds from her books, who described her method as "the little bit (two inches wide) of Ivory on which I work with so fine a Brush."

"Jane Austen is obviously the Quentin Tarantino of the middle classes," said Charles Denton, head of BBC drama. Well, they are probably the two best writers of dialogue in film today. Douglas McGrath (co-screenwriter of "Bullets Over Broadway") chose to adapt and direct the forthcoming "Emma" because "it's one of the funniest of all the great books. It's the social satire that makes it so delightful." Lindsay Doran, the producer of "Sense and Sensibility," thinks the Jane train was set in motion when Martin Scorsese made a film of Edith Wharton's "The Age of Innocence." "Everyone said, 'You can do that stuff and get away with it?' Executives and writers felt a lot braver about going back to their bookshelves."

Emma Thompson doesn't see the Austen films as period pieces. "You don't think people are still concerned with marriage, money, romance, finding a partner? Jane Austen is a genius who appeals to any generation." Although Thompson had never written a screenplay, Doran picked her to adapt the novel after seeing a PBS telecast of a series of comic skits that Emma had written, called "Thompson," some of which were in period, like a Robin Hood episode and one about a Victorian bride who was mystified by "the mouselike creature that had crawled out of her husband's trousers on their wedding night." Ang Lee came in when a colleague of Doran's saw his film "The Wedding Banquet." Doran says: "The idea of a foreign director was intellectually appealing even though it was very scary to have someone who didn't have English as his first language." Ang Lee says: "I thought they were crazy: I was brought up in Taiwan, what do I know about 19th-century England? About halfway through the script it started to make sense why they chose me. In my films I've been trying to mix social satire and family drama. I realized that all along I had been trying to do Jane Austen without knowing it. Jane Austen was my destiny. I just had to overcome the cultural barrier."

In "The Sense and Sensibility Screenplay and Diaries" *(Newmarket Press. $23.95)*, Thompson's fascinating journal of making the film, she talks about that cultural divide. Ang Lee practiced tai chi and had the actors meditate and "massage each other's pressure points. It's very painful. Loud screams ..." When Thompson and Grant made suggestions about scenes, Ang was shocked. In Taiwan, the director is the total boss. "He was deeply hurt and confused," writes Thompson. "It must have been terrifying—new actors, new crew, new country, and then us sticking our oars in."

That was smoothed over, and soon the real problems began: Winslet's phlebitis, Thompson's conjunctivitis and PMS, sheep collapsing from the heat. Meanwhile, the Jane Austen Society of North America had called to complain that Hugh Grant was too good looking to play Edward. The society, which has 2,646 members worldwide, is run by Garnet Bass out of Raleigh, N.C. For her, the Jane Austen revival has practical consequences. "Austen deals not only across classes, but person to person," she says. "I've learned to appreciate some of my relatives through reading Jane Austen." For Jane, whose family was her true universe, that might have pleased her the most.

SIGHT AND SOUND, 3/96, p. 50, Claire Monk

It is late eighteenth-century England. When their further dies, sisters Elinor and Marianne Dashwood, teenage Margaret and their mother lose their home and inheritance, Norland Park in Sussex, because it passes to John, Mr Dashwood's son by his first marriage. They are left £500 a year to live on between them. John's socially ambitious wife, Fanny, wastes no time in taking over at Norland, and when Mrs Dashwood's cousin Sir John Middleton offers the four women a cottage to live in on his Devon estate, they reluctantly accept—despite the unspoken attachment growing between the sensible Elinor and Fanny's shy brother Edward Ferrars.

Although Fanny claims that Edward's mother will never allow the match, Elinor is silently disappointed when he fails to visit Devon. Country life is made more of a trial by the crass matchmaking of Sir John and his mother-in-law Mrs Jennings, who try to pair up Marianne with Colonel Brandon, a sombre bachelor twice her age. Mrs Jennings tells Elinor of Brandon's "tragic past": barred from marrying the woman he loved, Eliza, he later learned she had fallen into prostitution and found her dying in a poorhouse.

Out walking, Marianne twists her ankle and is rescued by the handsome John Willoughby. Mesmerised by him, she rebuffs the smitten Brandon with cruel indifference, but Elinor grows suspicious about Willoughby when he shows an unexplained hostility to the Colonel. Willoughby suddenly departs for London with no plans to return, leaving Marianne distraught. Meanwhile, Elinor is forcibly befriended by a young woman, Lucy Steele, who confides that she has been secretly engaged to Edward for five years, against his mother's wishes.

Sent with Elinor to stay in London, Marianne becomes feverishly obsessed with trying to see Willoughby. Eventually she spots him at a ball, but his snub sends her into shock. A letter stating that his affections, "have long been engaged elsewhere," worsens her condition, and Elinor confides the situation to Brandon. Brandon reveals that Eliza left an illegitimate daughter, Beth, whom Brandon had promised to care for; a year ago, Willoughby made her pregnant. Cut off by his benefactor aunt in punishment, Willoughby abandoned Marianne in order to make a wealthy marriage.

Fanny explodes when Lucy reveals the secret engagement, and Edward who had been honoring it solely out of duty—is disinherited is a result. Brandon tells Elinor he plans to offer Edward the parish on his estate to make him financially able to marry Lucy, but that the offer must come from Elinor. Alone with Elinor, Edward finally expresses his feeling for her, but she insists he must stand by Lucy. Back in Devon, Marianne wanders in the rain until she collapses on the hill where she met Willoughby. Rescued by Brandon, she almost dies of a fever, but eventually pulls through. News arrives that Lucy and Mr Ferrars are married, but it turns out that when Edward was disinherited, Lucy married his younger brother instead. Edward proposes to Elinor and Marianne happily marries Brandon.

On the face of it, the Taiwanes-American director Ang Lee and England's most-adapted dead lady novelist might seem as perverse a pairing as *Sense and Sensibility*'s threatened union of Lucy Steele and Edward Ferrars—or indeed the marriage of convenience at the core of Lee's earlier film *The Wedding Banquet* in which a young, gay Taiwanese gets hitched to a Shanghaiese art student in order to deflect his parents' attention from his true sexuality. In practice, Lee's *Sense and Sensibility* is easily the most enjoyable and, more significantly, the least complacent—of the recent rash of Jane Austen adaptations.

While screenwriter-star Emma Thompson is already a likely Academy Award contender, the film's flavour owes as much to Lee's expertise as an observer of familial and social codes, constraints and conflict as it does to her droll feminist-revisionist script. Described by critic Tony Tanner as "a society which forced people to be at once very sociable and very private," the world of *Sense and Sensibility* has more than superficial affinities with the world of *The Wedding Banquet*—in which revellers invade the newlyweds' bedroom and refuse to leave until bride and groom are naked in bed together or the world of Lee's more recent *Eat Drink Man Woman*—in which three young Taipei career women sit down resentfully each night in obedience to the ritual of a meal cooked by their chef father. All three films focus on narrow social worlds in which private desires and emotions are subordinated to strict regulation by tradition, social mores and the law of the parent while at the same time being subjected to incessant public scrutiny.

Sense and Sensibility is about how two sisters of contrasting temperaments, Elinor (who has too much sense) and Marianne (who has too much romantic sensibility) deal—or fail to deal—with such contradictions. Where Elinor entirely conceals her feelings for Edward even as he haltingly tries to declare his love for her, Marianne cannot hide her emotions for five minutes even if this means being rude or cruel. To a modern audience, Marianne's spontaneous directness is more appealing than Elinor's self-repression, but in the society she inhabits, such openness is a transgression hence the mass shock which greets her reproach of Willoughby at the ball ("Good God, Willoughby! Will you not shake hands with me?"). As Marianne's subsequent psychosomatic illness hints, lone rebellion against such powerful social forces can be a route to madness.

A particular preoccupation in Thompson's script is the problem of female non-inheritance. Where in the novel the tortuous terms of which Elinor and Marianne's father inherited Norland Park from an uncle leave him powerless to pass it on to his wife and daughters, the film tells us that their inheritance is denied them by the law. ("Boys inherit, girls don't," Elinor bluntly tells Margaret.) The deathbed scene in which Mr Dashwood breaks the news to their half-brother John that his will contains barely any provision for the women gives us every reason to think this law is sanctioned by the father. This feminist sensibility extends to the reinvention of Elinor and Marianne's teen sister Margaret as a tomboy with a taste for tree houses and adventure—Eniile François, who plays her, is as impressive a find as Anna Paquin was in *The Piano*.

Where *Sense and Sensibility* really scores, though, is in a broad, self-mocking satirical energy, pleasingly at odds with both the politeness of older Austen adaptations and the sexed-up, patronising 'updating' of the BBC's recent *Pride and Prejudice*. The hunting-and-shooting Sir John Middleton is a figure of Dickensian boisterousness whose ribald prying into Elinor and Marianne's affairs of the heart is intrusive enough to make even the viewer squirm. Edward, on paper one of the dullest suitors in literary history, is here transformed in a miraculous departure from Hugh Grant's recent form—into a mumbling superhero muffled so deep in shyness that when he *does* speak his meaning stays runically opaque. (One hilarious scene has Thompson trying to coax a baffling sentence from him while his own horse snorts in disgust.)

On the down side, Grant's performance begs the question of what on earth Elinor sees in Edward—but then this *Sense and Sensibility*'s attitude to romance is tongue-in-check. The movie's prime amorous interest, Willoughby (played by Thompson's real-life lover Greg Wise), is unquestionably a sex god in waiting; but Wise's performance—from his entry on a white charger to his smarmy courtship of the breathless Marianne—is bracketed in such colossal ironic quote marks that it's impossible not to laugh even as you swoon. This subversive spirit even enables Lee to pull off the trick the novel never managed, namely persuading us that Marianne really *has* shifted her affections to Brandon but then, Austen's rheumaticky Colonel has been granted the dry wit of Alan Rickman. *Sense and Sensibility* might just be the heritage movie that girls who like boys who hate heritage movies will get away with taking those boys to see.

TIME, 12/18/95, p. 72, Richard Schickel

"Very moving. The heartbreak beneath the courtesies." So writes Emma Thompson in the production diary she has published, together with her screenplay for *Sense and Sensibility*. Clever girl. For writing this impeccable adaptation of the Jane Austen novel. For giving it a still, deep center with her delicately repressed (and then superbly released) performance in one of the title roles—she's "Sense," otherwise known as Elinor Dashwood. For defining in seven words the essence of romantic comedy. And for understanding that well over a century, before it became a movie genre, Austen had mastered its most basic conventions.

These include bringing handsome people—some of them silly, some of them wise, some of them rich, some of them poor—together in a variety of pleasing settings, arranging many misunderstandings and misalliances, equally productive of amusing conversations and embarrassing situations, then sorting everyone and everything out in the last chapter or act. It's a formula amply on display not only in *Sense and Sensibility* but also in Hollywood's major romantic offering of the Christmas season, *Sabrina*.

It's not as easy as it looks. The problem for the writer is to balance a wit that doesn't dry the piece out against sentiments that don't turn it soggy. For the actors it lies in playing highly stylized dialogue while remaining in touch with recognizable human nature. For the director, energy is the issue: too much of it and everyone goes bucketing off in the direction of farce; too little of it and the audience starts admiring the scenery. Or, to put the whole tricky business simply, everyone has to stay grounded in reality while at the same time subtly improving on it.

You can measure the accomplishment of *Sense and Sensibility* simply by observing that it meets all these contradictory standards. It does so while presenting us with a vast range of richly developed, gorgeously played characters ("Can everyone in England act?" Thompson reports director Ang Lee asking after one particularly fruitful casting session) and moving them gracefully through time and a lot of very pretty spaces without ever losing its conviction, its concentration or our bedazzled attention. Consider what dear Ms. Thompson's dear Miss Dashwood has to deal with. She is in unrequited love with Mr. Ferrars (Hugh Grant, marvelously blending probity and arrested development), who has foolishly promised himself to another. But of this misery she dare not speak, for other circumstances require that she be a brick: the death of her father and the loss of Norland, the stately digs where she and her all female family have been safe and content; the genteel but palpable anxiety of her mother (Gemma Jones), trying to be brave as poverty and spinsterhood loom for her girls; the hysterically misplaced passion of her sister Marianne (Kate Winslet)—the "Sensibility" of the title—nearly dying when that cad John Willoughby (Greg Wise) leaves her for a woman better endowed financially; the romantic occlusion that prevents Marianne from seeing what everyone else can see, that the good Colonel Brandon (Alan Rickman), despite a certain stiffness in his emotional joints, is her savior.

This is a lot of chaos for one provincial "control freak" (as Thompson describes her) to manage, and it's only natural that she submerge her interests while dealing with the muddle. Yet, by some patient alchemy, Thompson manages to hold our sympathetic concern despite her self-effacement. Precisely because of her witty, bold back playing, she finally achieves one of those privileged moments we are always hoping to find at the movies and so rarely do.

It occurs at the very last moment, when, suddenly, Mr. Ferrars appears at the remote cottage, located just this side of destitution, where the Dashwood ladies have taken refuge. Miraculously he is free of his entanglements, free at last to diffidently declare his love for Elinor. Whereupon she bursts into tears—not just tears but great, teacup-rattling sobs, a huge, whooshing release of long-suppressed emotions, both hers and ours. You feel like crying right along with her. You feel like laughing too. Mostly, though, you feel terrific, in touch with something authentic inside yourself.

This kind of joyous catharsis is what the old movie masters of romantic comedy—Frank Capra, Leo McCarey—sometimes delivered. You don't expect to find it in adaptations of classic literature. You don't expect to find it in modern movies. You certainly wonder how a Taiwan-born director like Lee (*The Wedding Banquet, Eat Drink Man Woman*) has managed to reach across time and cultures to deliver these delicate goods undamaged. Maybe some of that whoosh of delight one feels at the end of *Sense and Sensibility* is for him, and his emergence as a world-class director.

One has to wonder: Did Sydney Pollack feel a different kind of whoosh—something like the sound of wind being removed from sails—when he first beheld *Sense and Sensibility*? Pollack is its executive producer, without whose enthusiasm, it is said, the movie might never have been made. He is one of the few contemporary American directors blessed with a genuinely romantic spirit (*Out of Africa*) and no small gift for comedy *(Tootsie)*. He is also, by quirk of fate, Lee's chief competitor in the romantic-comedy market niche this season, as the producer-director of *Sabrina*.

This property also has a history: as a successful Broadway play, then as a Billy Wilder movie starring three beloved figures, Audrey Hepburn, Humphrey Bogart and William Holden. And, as you'll recall, it has a nice little story to tell too. It's the one about the chauffeur's daughter (Julia Ormond), living over the garage on a vast Long Island estate, in love since childhood with David (Greg Kinnear), the playboy living up the driveway. When she grows up and he notices her, that threatens his engagement, which in turn threatens the merger of two family firms that Linus (Harrison Ford), his older brother and a grumpy workaholic, has been nurturing. The latter sets out to seduce Sabrina for purely business purposes and ends up himself seduced by this wise child.

It ought to work as well now as it did in the '50s; Cinderella stories don't date any more than Jane Austen stories do. And the new acting team isn't half bad. Ford's muttering misanthropy may actually be funnier than Bogart's harder, more sardonic take on Linus. Ormond is no Audrey Hepburn, but Hepburn was sui generis, and Ormond does have a shy charm all her own. And there is a wastrely weakness about Kinnear's good looks that suits David more neatly than Holden's square-cut handsomeness did.

But in updating the script, Barbara Benedek and David Rayfiel have too often substituted topical one-liners (some of them quite funny) for well-joined badinage. This has a distancing effect. Even worse, someone made a disastrous decision to lengthen the early sequence in which Sabrina finds herself in Paris. Wilder got through her maturation at montage speed; Pollack lingers over it for 20 inconsequential minutes, a bring-down from which the movie never quite recovers.

And so it goes. Pollack and his team have cast good actors (John Wood, Nancy Marchand) in the supporting roles but have, at best, provided turns for them to do rather than parts for them to play. They have hired expensive locations, which are supposed to impart anthenticity to the film but which begin to look like over-considered stage sets. We remain outside the fourth wall looking in but are never drawn in; bemused perhaps, even agreeably complaisant, but never entirely amused.

In other words, they have fussed with *Sabrina*, but they have not really engaged it. They have not found the little twinges of pain, the awkward stumbles into vulnerability, that animate the best comedies, and the best love stories too. Wilder's film had a few of them—enough to ensure that the movie and its audience did not feel totally manipulated—but nothing on the grand scale of Thompson's great blowout.

VILLAGE VOICE, 12/19/95, p. 76, Georgia Brown

So, dear reader, let us resume our contemplation of human nature through the opposing temperaments of sisters: the eldest being a model of discipline, restraint, and composure (sense), the younger given to dangerous excess and spontaneous gusts of passion (sensibility). From last weeks *Georgia*, I mean, to an Anglo-American-Asian adaptation of Jane Austen's first novel, *Sense and Sensibility*.

The Austen adaptation served up by director Ang Lee, of *The Wedding Banquet* and *Eat Drink Man Woman*, is a fairly mild rendition of its source. (I prefer both *Clueless* and the spicier, messier *Persuasion.*) Lee's mise-en-scène, which some might liken to prose style, is tamely picturesque. Still, the basic story—of financially challenged women in love—makes for more exciting romantic comedy than Hollywood seems able to develop on its own.

Film and novel open with the death of the father—i.e., the loss of strong, just authority and financial security. On his deathbed, Henry Dashwood, owner of Norland, summons his heir, his son by a first marriage, Mr. John Dashwood (James Fleet), and extracts a promise to provide generously for his half sisters, Elinor (Emma Thompson), Marianne (Kate Winslet), and the much younger Margaret (Emilie Francois), as well as their mother (Gemma Jones).

Promises, promises. John's wife, Fanny, (Harriet Walker), whose sneer resembles the wicked queen's in *Snow White*, quickly demonstrates what a verbal promise is worth as she nags her husband into whittling down his support from 3000 pounds apiece to zero. John is pathetically weak, but so are most men in *Sense and Sensibility*; as the possessors of fortunes, they're in thrall to jealous mothers, grasping wives and devious fiancées.

It's a story that begins in grief, displacement, even barely controlled hysterics. Emma Thompson, who has written the screenplay, uses young Margaret's hiding in a tree house and under a table as an uninspired correlative. To show the posh serenity they're being ejected from, Lee tries to make Norland's interiors resemble Vermeers. When Fanny's sensible and sensitive brother, Edward Ferrars (Hugh Grant), pays a visit, he plays with Margaret, hems and haws but neatly sums up matters: "My dear Fanny, they've just lost their father. Their lives will never be the same!" (Stiffly hunched—with mortification, it seems—Grant looks like his head is jammed directly onto his ascot. His sense endears Edward to Elinor. In fact, the two seem to reach "an understanding." Horrified, Fanny informs her haughty mother—who wishes a lucrative alliance for her son—and he's sent away for the bulk of the movie. (It's the same in the book.)

The drafty, unkempt Devonshire cottage the four female Dashwoods repair to has those pseudo-distressed walls that one can find in every decorating mag today. (From Vermeer to *Elle Decor.*) Their new neighborhood isn't devoid of suitors. Marianne attracts both a rich old man of 35, Colonel Brandon (Alan Rickman, who's made to look truly, deeply stupid), and—her preference—the dashing young Willoughby (Greg Wise), who comes on like a soul mate but is in fact a cad. As Jane didn't say, Smart women, foolish choices—except that Marianne isn't the smart one.

Marianne is the passionate one. She may seem a far cry from *Georgia*'s Sadie Flood but she isn't really; she represents the danger of sliding off into the social abyss (like another Willoughby victim). Kate Winslet, who played one of the murdering girls in *Heavenly Creatures*, makes a blandly pretty but pretty bland Marianne. The scene in London where she's publicly rejected by Willoughby should tear the heart and it doesn't. When she lies feverish, nearly dying, it's so much clichéd tossing and turning.

The sisters' defining debates about taste, which take up a good bit of the novel, are abbreviated to a couple of poetry-reading scenes: basically, one likes it hot. (Rohmer's cinema of moral argument is actually quite close to Austen.) Restrained and secretive, Elinor is faced with the same fate as her sister, since Edward, like Willoughby, turns out to have a hidden attachment. Only by losing his fortune—and with it, the savage clutch of a penniless woman—does Edward gain his heart's desire.

My regard for Emma Thompson grows. Especially when I read Thompson bashing, like the one in the current *Vogue*. A British woman who sounds like one of those gossips in Austen's novels gushes over *Carrington* while reporting gleefully how Thompson is reviled and ridiculed in England. (Brits have a curious way of eating their own.) As she was the best thing in *Carrington*, Thompson is one of the few real pleasures in *Sense and Sensibility*. When the controlled Elinor finally bursts into tears and her face turns blotchy red, it's one sweet moment in a disappointing movie.

Also reviewed in:
CHICAGO TRIBUNE, 12/13/95, Tempo/p. 1, Michael Wilmington
NEW REPUBLIC, 1/8-15/95, p. 34, Stanley Kauffmann
NEW YORK TIMES, 12/13/95, p. C15, Janet Maslin
NEW YORKER, 12/18/95, p. 124, Terrence Rafferty

VARIETY, 12/4-10/95, p. 51, Todd McCarthy
WASHINGTON POST, 12/13/95, p. C1, Rita Kempley
WASHINGTON POST, 12/15/95, Weekend/p. 49, Desson Howe

SEVEN

A New Line Cinema release. *Executive Producer:* Gianni Nunnari, Dan Kolsrud, and Anne Kopelson. *Producer:* Arnold Kopelson and Phyllis Carlyle. *Director:* David Fincher. *Screenplay:* Andrew Kevin Walker. *Director of Photography:* Darius Khondji. *Editor:* Richard Francis-Bruce. *Music:* Howard Shore. *Music Editor:* Ellen Segal and Angie Rubin. *Sound:* Willie D. Burton and (music) John Kurlander. *Sound Editor:* Patrick Dodd and Willie D. Burton. *Casting:* Billy Hopkins, Suzanne Smith, and Kerry Borden. *Production Designer:* Arthur Max. *Art Director:* Gary Wissner. *Set Designer:* Elizabeth Lapp, Lori Rowbathom, and Hugo Santiago. *Set Decorator:* Clay A. Griffith. *Set Dresser:* John H. Maxwell. *Special Effects:* Peter Albiez. *Costumes:* Michael Kaplan. *Make-up:* Jean Black. *Make-up (Morgan Freeman):* Michael A. Hancock. *Special Make-up Effects:* Rob Bottin. *Stunt Coordinator:* Charles Picerni, Jr. *Running time:* 107 minutes. *MPAA Rating:* R.

CAST: Morgan Freeman (Somerset); Endre Hules (Cab Driver); Andy Walker (Dead Man at 1st Crime Scene); Daniel Zacapa (Detective Taylor at First Murder); Brad Pitt (Mills); Gwyneth Paltrow (Tracy); John Cassini (Officer Davis); Bob Mack (Gluttony Victim); Peter Crombie (Dr. O'Neill); Reg E. Cathey (Dr. Santiago); R. Lee Ermey (Police Captain); George Christy (Workman at Door of Somerset's Office); Hawthorne James (George the Night Guard at the Library); Roscoe Davidson (First Guard at the Library); Bob Collins (Second Guard at the Library); Jimmy Dale Hartsell (Library Janitor); Richard Roundtree (Talbot); Charline Su and Dominique Jennings (TV News Reporters); Allan Kolman (Forensic Man in the Law Office); Beverly Burke (TV Anchor Woman); Gene Borkan (Eli Gould, Sin of Greed); Julie Araskog (Mrs. Gould); Mario Di Donato (Fingerprint Forensic Man in Law Office); Alfonso Freeman (Fingerprint Technician); John C. McGinley (California); Harrison White and Robert Stephenson (Cops on SWAT Team); Michael Reid Mackay (Victor, Sin of Sloth); Kevin Spacey (John Doe); Richard Portnow (Dr. Beardsley); Tudor Sherrard (Coupon Man Outside Pizza Parlor); Mark Boone, Jr. (Greasy F.B.I. Man); Pamala Tyson (Thin Vagrant by John Doe's Apartment); Lennie Loftin (Policeman Who Takes Statement From Vagrant); Sarah Hale Reinhardt (Police Sketch Artist); Emily Wagner (Detective Sara at John Doe's Apartment); Martin Serene (Wild Bill); Michael Massee (Man in Booth at Massage Parlor); David Correia (First Cop at Massage Parlor); Ron Blair (Second Cop at Massage Parlor); Cat Mueller (Hooker, Sin of Lust); Leland Orser (Crazed Man in Massage Parlor); Lexie Bigam (Sweating Cop at Massage Parlor); Evan Miranda and Paul S. Eckstein (Paramedics at Massage Parlor); Heidi Schanz (Beautiful Woman, Sin of Pride); Brian Evers (Duty Sergeant); Shannon Wilcox (Woman Cop Behind Desk); Richard Schiff (Mark Swarr); Jim Deeth and John Santini (Helicopter Pilots); Charles Tamburro (SWAT Helicopter Pilot); Richmond Arquette (Delivery Man); Duffy Gaver (Marksman in Helicopter).

FILMS IN REVIEW, 1-2/96, p. 66, Edward Summer

One of the things that used to make movies scary was the movie theater itself. It was dark. When the mad doctor crept around the burial crypt during a good, old-fashioned black-and-white horror movie, it was nearly impossible to tell the difference between the shadows on the screen and the spooky space around you: the viewer was plunged into asphyxiating darkness. This blackness was like licorice, like varnished ebony, like squid ink. And it's this very blackness that has been lost in the evolution of film stocks, labs, theaters, and photographic aesthetics.

Classics like *Cat People* or *I Walked with a Zombie* don't make much atmospheric sense in modern movie theaters (not to mention on television) for many reasons, not the least of which is the physical density of the blacks in present day release prints. The amount of light reflected off the screen in the theater and, of course, modern safety regulations that require glaring "exit" lights every three inches don't help either. Black-and-white nitrate film had extraordinary black density as did both nitrate and safety film IB Technicolor. This was due in large part to the high light transmission of the nearly transparent nitrate base. In the case of nitrate black-and-white, the slower film speeds and low temperature developing resulted in black densities with high "gamma" or contrast. In the case of IB Tech, the overlay of all three imbibition matrices (cyan, yellow, magenta) resulted in a nearly opaque "black." But when nitrate stock and then IB Tech perished, so did this darkness.

In his first meeting with Beverly Wood, the Director of Technical Services at Deluxe Laboratories in Hollywood, David Fincher, director of *Seven,* explained that he didn't want the audience to be able to tell the difference between the darkness in the film and the screen masking. Obviously, Mr. Fincher and his director of photography Darius Khondji had seen the right movies.

A commercially successful thriller, *Seven* is a fairly conventional *noir* murder mystery distinguished by a "look" and a relatively "suggestive" sensibility absent from mainstream cinema for many years. Young filmmakers have grown up with the idea that "gruesome is scary." Certainly the box-office success some years back of *The Exorcist* did a lot to reinforce this idea, but anyone over 14 who isn't trying to impress their buddies with the ability to withstand stomach churning gore has long since tired of the lack of subtlety (to put it mildly) in the long parade of Freddies, Hellraisers, and Jasons with their endlessly elegant special effects entrails. Fincher wanted to do something different. With the help of Khondji and Rob Bottin's "animatronics," Fincher has succeeded remarkably well in recreating a strong echo of the genius of such teams as Jacques Tourneur and Nick Musaraca, who in the 1940's, collaborated on such masterpieces as *Out of the Past* and *I Walked with a Zombie,* films characterized by intelligent scripts, fine acting, and a distinctive black-and-white look. Tourneur and Musaraca along with Gregg Toland were certainly among the pioneers of what is now called "source" lighting (artificial light that appears to come from natural sources like windows or candles or light fixtures). When introduced, source lighting was a radical departure from the over lit, highly directional front lighting required by Technicolor. A brilliant modern example of interior and exterior source lighting is Vilmos Zsigmond's work in this year's *The Crossing Guard.* Tourneur was one of the first directors to insist on this look and Musaraca's cinematography realized it in a remarkable way: it is largely their work that defines what is now called film noir.

Fincher and Khondji set out to extend the realm of *color noir,* a look pioneered by John Alonzo in *Chinatown* and Jordan Cronenweth in *Blade Runner.* The difference here is their apparent search for inky blacks. This led them, ultimately, to Deluxe color laboratories in Los Angeles.

Normally, when Kodak color film is developed, it goes through a bleach that removes excess silver from the print. This is essential to produce the final image, but it also reduces the black contrast in the print. The gamma in a normal print might be about 3 which means that the blacks are somewhat transparent as compared to the white or clear parts of the film. Reportedly at the behest of Vittorio Storraro some years ago, Technicolor Rome developed a process that retained more of the silver in the print. According to Robert Harris (restorer of cinema's endangered masterpieces): "Silver retention, known at Technicolor as ENR, after Ernesto Novello of Technicolor Rome, is a process in which the print, rather than going through a final fix bath, is put through a special black and white developer, which 'develops' any live silver remaining after the color processing and gives the print a heightened black level." Since it isn't entirely a proprietary process, other labs have evolved their own versions of Silver Retention. Deluxe's is called CCE (Color Correction Enhancement) and CFI (Consolidated Film Industries) has given it the elegant appellation "No Bleach."

CCE at Deluxe involves what Ms. Wood termed a "secret sauce," so exactly what goes on is a mystery, but it is clearly some permutation of the manner in which the film is bleached: if more silver is preserved in the emulsion, the result is an extraordinarily dense, clean black and a contrast that in theory approaches infinity above what's called the "mid-scale" of contrast. Wood worked with both the director and cinematographer from day one to assure them that the film processing would meet their specifications. CCE is a fairly expensive process (about 50 percent higher than normal) because it involves a special developing machine which must be dedicated 24 hours a day to this single process and can't be used for any other developing work, so it's a process not undertaken frivolously.

But the look of *Seven* is not just in the lab work. It starts with the principal photography and the art direction. Unless everyone on the film team shares the same vision, the film won't look the way it's supposed to look. Filming involved use of the Panaflash (a way of exposing the film to a colored light before the actual scene is filmed), special filters (probably a light orange in color), control of the actual lighting on the set, and the color of the scenery and costumes.

Of the approximately 2500 release prints made for *Seven,* only about 200 are CCE prints. With unerring accuracy, this writer initially found the only theater in New York City that *wasn't* showing a CCE print, and so had to go back and see it again at another house. The differences are dramatic. The non-CCE print, made from a CCE internegative, is certainly moody, but ultimately looks a lot like any other film with de-saturated color. But with the CCE prints and proper projection (proper illumination in foot lamberts on the screen), the result is an image so inky that at times it is impossible to tell where the film image begins and the black velvet drapes around the screen end. If you enter the theater at the wrong time, you'd actually need help to find your seat. The flashlight exploration of the killer's house is a fine dramatic use of this technique.

Check with your local theater and see if they know which type of print they're showing. If they don't know, New Line Cinema's main office in New York City or Los Angeles can tell you. If *Seven* isn't playing anymore, wait for the laserdisc. A spokesman for New Line promises that the timing on the disc will be as close to the theatrical CCE as possible.

Within days of the release of *Seven,* Deluxe's phones were ringing off the hook with inquiries from high-profile directors who were seeking a "new" look. CCE is actually nothing new. *Seven* is just an extraordinary example of its proper use and, ironically, a reinvention of a long lost and, to some, sadly missed aesthetic.

LOS ANGELES TIMES, 9/22/95, Calendar/p. 1, Kenneth Turan

Noticeable skill has gone into the making of "Seven," but it's hard to take much pleasure in that. The story of two cops on the trail of a terrifying serial killer, "Seven" is most notable for how lovingly it lingers on the grotesque and repulsive details of the man's sadistic crimes. If movies were rated by how many showers are needed before viewers can feel human again, this picture would go off the chart.

The creative team behind "Seven"—specifically director David Fincher, screenwriter Andrew Kevin Walker and cinematographer Darius Khondji—would probably consider that last remark a compliment. Certainly they've expended great effort toward making "Seven" as creepy and distasteful an experience as they could. It's nice to have goals, fellas, but the truth is even sadism can be overdone.

The film's initial plot mechanism is a good one. Lurking in an unnamed major city is a brilliant but twisted individual determined to commit a series of murders based on the seven deadly sins, to turn the sin against the sinner in some kind of demented teaching tool to redeem humanity.

Want examples? You'll be sorry you asked. In murder one, a hugely fat individual is forced at gunpoint to eat more and more until his stomach bursts as a lesson against gluttony. In the second, a high-powered criminal attorney is required to cut a pound of flesh off his own body to illustrate the perils of greed. All of which is shown, via crime scene photos and caring close-ups of the victims, in unapologetically grotesque detail.

Thrown together to investigate this unholy mess are two detectives who are the inevitable polar opposites, partners with nothing in common except this increasingly lurid crime. Lt. William Somerset is a meticulous perfectionist, a veteran of 34 years on the force who has only one week left before retirement. As a soul-weary lone wolf who views police work as a cerebral exercise, Morgan Freeman is exceptional, giving a performance capable of holding this picture together during its periodic attempts at self-destruction.

Newly arrived in town is Detective David Mills (Brad Pitt), a cocky, motor-mouthed slob who'd rather kick down a door than knock on it. "Seven" does so poorly by this character, turning him into a fatuous, stereotypical dolt, that Pitt's usually effective presence is wasted.

Faring even worse is the talented Gwyneth Paltrow, who plays Mills' pure-of-heart wife, Tracy, a saintly personage whose presence in the picture is such a flimsy contrivance it's amazing any actress agreed to play it.

Feeble contrivance turns out to be one of "Seven's" deadly sins. Key plot points are not always believable, and a great many of the film's twists are visible a considerable way down the road.

When you add a level of pretension that indicates somebody believed this picture had profound things to say about the human condition, the results are regrettable.

What keeps "Seven" alive, aside from Morgan Freeman's performance, is the film's visual strength. A specialist in commercials and music videos who made his feature debut with "Alien³" director Fincher is someone who believes looks can kill. Working with cinematographer Khondji ("Delicatessen"), Fincher has used all manner of visual flourishes, including an unusual film developing process to ensure that no shot in the picture is an average one.

Regrettably, all this expertise, including an ability to create apartments so roach-ridden and rundown you can practically smell the decay, has been put in the service of what is basically a detailed viewing of the gruesome workings of a perverse mind. "Seven" does not seem like any-one's idea of entertainment, but public executions drew big crowds in their day and there is little reason to believe that human nature has gotten any more refined and elegant in the interim.

NEW STATESMAN & SOCIETY, 1/5/96, p. 35, Jonathan Romney

David Fincher's *Seven* is just what we needed to start the year—a high-concept thriller that is also mercilessly downbeat. It's calculated to leave you at once shattered—there's as much foreboding and nihilism as in the grimmest of Nordic art house *oeuvres* and exhilarated, from its visual panache and density of ideas. It uses surprise so effectively that I should say be warmed, by which I mean not only that you might prefer to see the film before you read this review, but also—are you sure you want to go into that dark room?

Seven is the consummate dark-room-horror story; it trusts in the power of thick, looming obscurity to chill the spine, something that has been rather discredited on screen since *The Shining* proved that wide, brightly lit corridors could do the trick just as well. It's set in an unnamed metropolis where it seems to rain three quarters of the time and be cloaked in purulent haze for the rest. The first thing its detective heroes do when they arrive at the scene of a crime is to narrow their eyes and peer into all-enveloping soupy murk, captured almost tangibly by Darius Khondji's remarkable claustrophobic photography. This is a film about "darkness visible"—darkness being a metaphor both for the moral miasma that seems to shroud the city, and for the hermeneutic obscurity the heroes face. (Fincher is an old hand at darkness, having previously negotiated the cloacal gloom of *Alien 3*.)

The high-concept hook is a series of murders on the Seven Deadly Sins; Gluttony is a man forced to eat himself to death; Pride a lawyer bled in his luxury apartment; and Sloth ... well, you really don't want to know about Sloth just yet. The shadows come as a mercy—what we see of the killer's horrific installation art, a mix of visual hints and ghastly textures is limited, but more than enough for delicate souls.

The seven sins premise sounds remarkably programmatic, a fail safe recipe for monotony; it takes the idea of serial killing to a reductively literal degree. The cleverness of Andrew Kevin Walker's script is that he manages to tweak things so that they don't follow the path you might expect. The other point of appeal is the relationship between the two cops. The older detective Somerset (Morgan Freeman) is a solitary man with a weight of experience on his back, who's about to retire with, you guessed, seven days to go. His young replacement Mills (Brad Pitt) sees himself as autonomous and street-smart, but is clearly out of his depth in this hell. He and his wife (Gwyneth Paltrow) have recently moved into a new flat; no one told them that the subway passes right by, plaguing them with Richter scale rumblings every few minutes. The two cops are stuck with each other, but the familiar Oedipal buddy setup is folded into a story about one man out to get experience, and one who simply has too much of it, who can read horror too well. It's a story of apprenticeship and of whatever apprenticeship's opposite is, of the downloading and uploading of knowledge.

Somerset, a contemplative man, is able to read the crimes as an art or literary critic might. He's the first to detect a pattern, which is obvious enough, but in the pattern he reads a narrative, which is less obvious. He gets into the criminal's head through what he's been reading, making his hypotheses from the killer's references to Milton, Chaucer, Thomas Aquinas, the Marquis de Sade.

The idea of a bookish detective has been with us from Oedipus to *The Name of the Rose*, although it tends not to be so popular with the traditionally anti-literary Hollywood. In its own way, *Seven* is deeply anti-literary too. It may suggest that literature makes Somerset more astute, but it also suggests that it makes monsters. These canonical texts, which Harold Bloom would approve of—even de Sade, the odd one out, has been legit since his endorsement of Breton, Barthes and Angela Carter—have served the killer as a primer in hatred and horror.

The film owes something to the topos common to many a country house mystery, that a text can reveal something about a crime. But *Seven* makes connections between crime and reading itself (Sade, of course, cultivated the notion of the "criminal text"). Another familiar idea is that by getting into the mind of your adversary, you risk being tainted by madness, a theme in common with the two films featuring an empathetic detective and that most dangerously literate (and European) of psychos, Hannibal Lecter. Here, it's suggested that to read what the killer reads is to delve into a hot pit of satanic repulsion. The contagion of the killer's books is partly, it seems, to do with the fact that they are European, as if the Old World were an unsavoury ghost haunting America, and these classics its grimoires. Presumably the killer would have ended up less warped if he'd read something wholesomely American, like Thomas Harris or Bret Easton Ellis.

The evil here turns out to be writing itself. Somerset tells Mills that in detective work he should never expect to find any clues. Then, in a breakthrough, they discover the killer's apartment, and once inside, they find *nothing but* clues: walls densely decorated with photos, shelf upon shelf of diaries filled with microscopic scribblings in which the graphomanic killer records everything that is in his head. It's the most terrifying moment in the film. There are no bodies, no visual horror, just the realisation of what is behind the slaughter—an artistically creative/destructive sensibility that is as overloaded and impenetrable as the city itself, and that manifests itself as an uncontrollable, excessive and excessively literary text. They're looking for a simple killer, a John Doe—it couldn't have been more horrifying if they'd walked in and found Umberto Eco himself.

NEW YORK, 11/13/95, p. 89, David Denby

Curious to see what could have made *Seven* such a big hit—and also an apparent favorite among young intellectuals—I found a movie of ghoulish chic. There isn't much violence in *Seven,* but there's a recurring scene in which two big-city cops (Morgan Freeman and Brad Pitt) walk into a dark, dank, dripping apartment and find the remnants of a human being who has been tortured and mutilated. The director, David Fincher, is demure about showing us the corpses—we get flashes, enough to titillate but not to nauseate. This is the kind of movie in which Morgan Freeman, a detective with a philosophical and literary bent, seeks the solution to the crimes in Chaucer and Dante. The intellectualism of *Seven* hides the true nature of the movie's hideous appeal from filmmakers and audience alike. Fincher, who comes out of commercials and music video, goes for a highly—and oppressively stylized—brownish silhouetting, as if the film stock had been dropped in tobacco juice and then pierced with lasers. *Seven* is gripping and intricate in a sordid way, and Freeman and Pitt, physical and spiritual opposites, become an oddly satisfying pair, but I was happy when the movie had played its last trick on me and could hold me no longer.

NEW YORK POST, 9/22/95, p. 39, Michael Medved

The title "Seven" refers to the seven deadly sins of Christian tradition—Gluttony, Greed, Sloth, Pride, Lust, Envy and Wrath. For filmmakers, an eighth deadly sin might be added: the crime of stylistic self-indulgence.

And when it comes to this transgression, then David Fincher, director of this intermittently impressive film, is utterly, unequivocally guilty.

As in his previous work on the dismally disappointing "Aliens³," Fincher infests every scene with his infernal fussing. The main characters are invariably drenched in picturesque rain and shot with cockeyed camera angles. Even a potentially thrilling chase scene is undermined by Fincher's penchant for sending pigeons fluttering toward the camera or viewing the principals from either high above or far below the action.

This inability to tell the story in direct and forceful fashion is a special shame with "Seven," since the script (written by Andrew Kevin Walker while working as a floor manager at New York's Tower Records) is diabolically clever, despite its reliance on stock characters and situations.

Morgan Freeman plays a world-weary cop on the verge of retirement, while Brad Pitt is a similarly standard-issue cocky young hotshot who turns up as his new partner. Both actors bring considerably more feeling to their characters than you might expect, as they try to solve a series of horrendously grisly murders.

An ingenious serial killer has been selecting victims—and savagely sadistic tortures—to illustrate each of the seven deadly sins.

For instance, the rich lawyer who represents "Greed" is forced to slice off a pound of his own flesh and then bleeds to death, while "Pride" is a top fashion model whose face is mutilated, then given a choice between death or survival as a disfigured freak.

To his credit, director Fincher re-creates these brutal attacks by showing the investigating officers discovering and discussing their gruesome aftermath, rather than staging the assaults themselves. The impact is only intensified by this cunning subtlety.

The killer is portrayed with chilling and unforgettable intensity by a versatile actor who has asked critics to avoid tipping audiences to his surprise appearance in this film. Unfortunately, the character he plays is yet another cliche—the same sort of Krazed Khristian Killer who has turned up in "Just Cause" and many other films.

By decorating his filthy lair with neon crosses and giving him pseudo-Biblical lines like, "I don't mourn those people any more than I mourn those who died in Sodom and Gomorrah," the filmmakers cast glancing aspersions on real-life believers who are, in actuality, hardly over-represented in the ranks of serial killers.

The film also lacks a convincing sense of place, as the location shifts—inexplicably from Manhattan (with apartments shaken by rumbling subways) to Los Angeles (with the cops traveling by freeway out to the desert).

The pretentious attempt to set this gritty tale in "Any City" USA (or "Rain City" USA) is only one more inane, artsy bit of interference for a director who seems to feel undisguised Envy for "The Silence of the Lambs" (he even uses a nerve-racking score by "Lambs" composer Howard Shore), but will end up inspiring Wrath though overblown Pride in his own intrusive touch.

NEWSDAY, 9/22/95, Part II/p. B2, Jack Mathews

"Because of Mr. Spacey's desire to keep the identity of the killer secret, members of the press are encouraged not to disclose his participation in the film."

That plea in the production notes for the wildly uneven thriller "Seven" has fallen on deaf ears here, as I assume it will with most other critics. Not to mention his participation would be to ignore the film's strongest performance and one of its few commendable elements.

Besides, identifying Spacey as the killer, a religious nut case committing a series of murders by way of doing God's work, gives nothing away. There are virtually no other suspects, and he doesn't even appear until detectives Morgan Freeman and Brad Pitt have figured out who he is.

By then, we've been subjected to so many numbing clichés about life in the trenches of an urban homicide department, and about the bonding process between a wily police veteran (Freeman) and his impulsive young partner (Pitt), that we might be heading for the exits if we didn't know the always interesting Spacey was yet to come.

"Seven," directed by David Fincher, who has worked mostly in TV commercials and music videos, is an exercise in atmospheric style. It's urban noir, all rain and shadows and odd angles, accompanied by a score that mixes electronic music with elements of classic jazz. The idea is to create a mood both familiar and foreboding, but it is, in fact, simply annoying.

The title refers to the Seven Deadly Sins of early Christian teachings—pride, greed, lust, envy, gluttony, anger and sloth, common human frailties regarded as deadly because they were believed to lead to greater sins. It only takes two mutilated bodies—those of an obese shut-in and a wealthy lawyer—and the words "Gluttony" and "Greed" left in grease and blood, for Lt. Somerset (Freeman) to realize there is a serial killer with a screw loose and a tight agenda somewhere in the city.

(Just which city is unclear. Most of the story seems to take place somewhere in New York, with yellow cabs and subways, but when the main characters drive out of town for the climactic scenes, they're in the parched desert of Southern California.)

What's a retiring burnout like Somerset to do? With only two of the deadly sins accounted for, it's clear there are five murders yet to come, and he is in his last week on the job. He doesn't know what he's going to do with his retirement—maybe start a farm or paint his house, he muses—but he sure can't leave a complicated case like this to a trigger-happy hothead like Pitt's Det. Mills.

So, with Mills' lonely bride (Gwyneth Paltrow) pushing them together, the dissimilar men begin to rest their hostilities and gradually come to like, trust and rely on each other, just as you would expect from having seen this setup played out a thousand times before.

At its best, "Seven" aims for something on the order of a "Silence of the Lambs," with a smart cop Somerset—trying to fathom the mind of a demented sadist. Spacey's John Doe is Hannibal Lecter with his own apartment, nutty but no dummy, and just as the two detectives think they've got him, it turns out he has them.

The Seven Deadly Sins angle is nothing more than a gimmick, an opportunity for one more spin on the crazy evangelist theme, and Spacey plays it to perfection. When Pitt tries to provoke him by asking him whether insane people actually know they're insane, you can see the killer turning the idea over and rejecting it behind his impassive eyes, then twisting it to his advantage.

Spacey gives a truly chilling performance, madness under glass, and without it "Seven" would be nothing.

NEWSWEEK, 10/2/95, p. 85, David Ansen

In the trail of a nut-case serial killer who's bumping off people who indulge in the seven deadly sins, cops Morgan Freeman and Brad Pitt get more use out of their flashlights than any sleuths since the Hardy Boys. Entering the dank rooms where the latest victims have been hideously tortured—the obese Gluttony victim, for example, has been force-fed until he bursts—it never occurs to these homicide pros to flick on the lights.

To do so would interfere with *Seven* director David Fincher's painterly notions of proper noir style—a style so chic, studied and murky it resembles a cross between a Nike commercial and a bad Polish art film. This is one mighty solemn thriller. Set in a rainy, portentously unnamed burg ('The City of Dread'?) where overhead lighting has yet to be invented, "Seven" seems to believe that if you drop enough references to Dante and Chaucer you have achieved seriousness, that depressive art direction amounts to a philosophical vision and that sheer unpleasantness will somehow elevate Andrew Kevin Walker's thin script into art. Wrong on all counts.

Underneath the dull barroom debates about the human condition, it's just another implausible thriller in which a weary but wise veteran cop on the brink of retirement (is there any other kind in Hollywood?) teams up with an impetuous rookie (yes, that's the other kind) to foil a brilliantly deranged psycho (see above). Freeman brings a calm, grave conviction to his part, and Pitt handles his first action role well. But the movie doesn't even offer the pleasure of a clever cat-and-mouse game. Stymied for half the story, our heroes finally come up with an unlikely scheme to identify their man, and bingo—get it right on the first try. Their prey, however, eludes them, giving us another hour's worth of mutilated corpses and a parting message to ponder: the world's not a nice place. Heavy.

SIGHT AND SOUND, 1/96, p. 49, John Wrathall

Homicide detective William Somerset is joined for his last seven days on the job by his replacement, David Mills, who has just moved to the city. When the discovery of a man who has apparently been forced to eat until he bursts (Gluttony) is followed by the bleeding to death of a rich lawyer, whose body is found with the word "GREED" written in blood on the carpet, Somerset suspects that the seven deadly sins may be providing the blueprint for a serial killer. Mills is hostile and skeptical, particularly when Somerset tells him to search for clues in Dante's *Divine Comedy,* but his wife Tracy asks Somerset to dinner in an attempt to reconcile the two detectives.

Following up fingerprints left at the scene of the Greed killing, Somerset and Mills find a third victim, Sloth, who has been tied to his bed for a year until he rots (and had his hand removed to plant the fingerprints). At the scene of the crime, Mills angrily chases away a photographer. Via a contact in the FBI, who operate a clandestine programme whereby they flag books in public libraries that might appeal to criminals and keep tabs on who takes them out, Somerset gets a list of suspects; during a routine visit to the home of one of them, John Doe, Somerset and Mills are shot at. Giving chase, Mills is knocked out by Doe, who spares his life.

Back at Doe's apartment, Somerset and Mills find photographs that prove he is the killer, including one of Mills taken at the Sloth crime scene. After the discovery of two more victims, Lust and Pride, John Doe gives himself up to Mills, saying he will only plead guilty if he is allowed to take Mills and Somerset to show them the last two victims. The two detectives drive Doe out into the desert where, at 7.00 on the seventh day, a courier delivers a package to Mills containing Tracy's head. Doe taunts Mills about how jealous he was of his happy marriage, until Mills shoots him, making Doe the sixth sin, Envy, and himself the seventh, Wrath.

"Long is the way/and hard that out of Hell leads up to light." To have a detective in a Hollywood thriller quoting *Paradise Lost* is perhaps extraordinary enough, but director David Fincher has gone further, deriving the whole look of his second feature from Milton's dictum. Working with cinematographer Darius Khondji, with whom he made commercials in the 80s before the Frenchman made his name internationally with *Delicatessen,* Fincher has created the most authentically hellish screen metropolis since Gotham City, a nameless warren of damp corridors, subterranean sex joints and dilapidated tenements, where it rains all the time. Long and hard indeed is the way to light: though the film progressively lightens, it's not until the final reel when Mills and Somerset drive Doe out into the desert that we see a scene shot in anything like daylight, and then it's an unforgiving glare which has you blinking in shock.

The irony, of course, is that when Mills, Somerset and Doe finally reach the light, they are still very definitely in Hell. *Seven* has an astoundingly bleak ending which brilliantly subverts the ingrained Hollywood cliché whereby the cop, who has had it up to here with the pressures of modern city life, shoots the psycho. Don Siegel may have given the climax of *Dirty Harry* a negative spin by having Eastwood toss his badge into the marsh, but audiences were surely cheering when he blew away Scorpio with a celebrated quip. It's hard to imagine even the most morally degraded audiences cheering when Mills shoots Doe, however, because *Seven* leaves us in no doubt that in doing so he has succumbed to Doe's power, and is now irredeemably damned.

Fincher, remember, is the man who in his first feature managed to terminate a big box-office franchise with a "happy" ending which consisted of the heroine committing suicide to prevent herself from giving birth. Though many of the images here recall *Alien³*—in particular the repeated shots of men tearing down dark corridors waving torches—Fincher seems more in control of his imagery in this film. *Seven* is packed with visual details which are plausible in terms of the plot, but carry a powerful abstract or symbolic charge. The hovel where the Gluttony victim has gorged himself to death on spaghetti has a Warholesque pile of cans of Clayton's Spaghetti Sauce; more creepily, the flat where Sloth is rotting away is festooned with hundreds of those Christmas-tree shaped air fresheners. And room after room reverberates eerily with strange, Lynchian rumbles and thumps which could be bad plumbing or noisy neighhours.

Many of these details, or course, may derive from Andrew Kevin Walker's inspired screenplay, which he reputedly wrote while working as a floor manager in a New York branch of Tower Records (where better to feel the city pushing you to breaking point?). Despite the sensationalist premise, which sounds a lot more formulaic in synopsis than it seems in the film, Walker's screenplay is impressively literate. It's tempting to speculate that the original seed of his idea was the FBI's book-flagging programme, which might have led him to wonder how a serial killer could be tracked down through what he read.

If some of the references—to Thomas Aquinas, *The Merchant Of Venice*—seem a little self-conscious, Walker is also capable of sending up his own name-dropping: Mills, instructed by Somerset to immerse himself in Dante and Chaucer, buys Cliff's Notes to the texts instead, and pronounces De Sade as if the Marquis were a cousin of the singer of 'Smooth Operator'. This is characteristic of the streak of morbid humour which runs through the whole film (asked about making the sharpened strap-on dildo with which Lust is fucked to death, an English leather goods merchant replies that he thought the customer, Doe, must be a performance artist). This droll and lugubrious tone is beautifully set by Morgan Freeman as the weary but enigmatic Somerset.

Seven's treatment of women, it has to be said, leaves something to be desired: the two touching early scenes in which the film seems to be going out of its way to make Mills' wife, Tracy, a real person, leave a nasty taste when it turns out she's just being set up as a victim. That apart, *Seven* has the scariest ending since George Sluizer's original *The Vanishing (Spoorloos,* 1988) with Mills only able to discover what the killer has done by becoming his victim—and stands as the most complex and disturbing entry in the serial killer genre since *Manhunter*.

TIME, 9/25/95, p. 68, Richard Schickel

They bicker and bond—a wise, weary detective (Morgan Freeman) in his last week before retirement and an eager kid (Brad Pitt) fresh from the country and ready to kick some big-city butt. Police partnerships don't come any lower concept than this. On the other hand, the serial killer they are pursuing, a creepy, brainy religious fanatic played by Kevin Spacey, is a high-concept kind of guy: he's trying to commit seven murders in seven days, each of them supposed to illustrate one of the seven deadly sins in some preposterously stomach-churning way.

Luckily, the setting for *Seven* (the title is the only understated thing about the picture) is an anonymous metropolis where it rains all the time and no one seems to have paid his light bill. The murk hides some (but not all) of the grisly details. Murk is also the auteurial hallmark of director David Fincher (*Alien 3*). Aiming to be a modern-day Bosch, he ends up doing MTV bosh.

His pretenses are curiously well matched to those of first-time screenwriter Andrew Kevin Walker, whose range of literary allusions runs from Dante to Chaucer but whose gift for low-genre necessities—suspense, jeopardy, snappy dialogue—is nonexistent. His big idea is that man is vile and that cities are catch basins for the worst of our fallen breed. He must be very young.

The actors, among them Gwyneth Paltrow as the young cop's wife (whom we immediately perceive as good, and therefore doomed), do their best to ground this twaddle in recognizable behavior. But it is very tiresome peering through the gloom trying to catch a glimpse of something interesting, then having to avert one's eyes when it turns out to be just another brutally tormented body.

VILLAGE VOICE, 10/3/95, p. 82, Amy Taubin

Despite corpses so grisly they turn the autopsy scene in *The Silence of the Lambs* into a pleasant memory, *Seven* is an overwhelmingly seductive movie. It's not easy to make a great film when you're working with a tacky serial killer script, but David Fincher comes close. And if *Seven* isn't a great film (the way *Touch of Evil* is, through and through), it is great film*making*, from the Nine Inch Nails opening credits to the Bowie/Eno cut at the close. Fincher honed his techno-Wagnerian aesthetic doing music videos—and fast cutting has nothing to do with it.

To get the plot out of the way while giving fair warning to squeamish viewers: Somerset (Morgan Freeman), a veteran homicide cop who's six days from retirement, and Mills, (Brad Pitt), his eager as a chipmunk replacement, are assigned to a particularly lurid murder investigation. A 300-pound man has been found naked and dead, his hands and feet bound, his face in a plate of spaghetti, a pail of vomit between his knees. He was force-fed until he burst. Before long, Somerset, the intellectual of the duo, realizes that they're up against a serial killer with a twisted biblical road map for murder. Each of his victims personifies one of the seven deadly sins: the first victim is gluttonous, the second greedy, and so forth.

If the screenplay sounds pat, it is. It's also pretentious, slipshod (you literally can see the denouement coming from miles away), and as right-wing as Newt's natterings about New York. In *Seven,* man is corrupt and cities are cesspools of contagion, spreading sin faster than TB. Forget the inequities of class or race, we're all just sinners and urban blight is the Lord's decor for the gates of hell. *Seven* may be the only movie of the year where all the cops are decent guys, trying to do the right thing in evil times. Somerset has never used his gun in 30 years, Mills has only fired his once, and both of them are completely color-blind. Mills has a wife (Gwyneth Paltrow) who's an angel of domesticity right out of John Ford. Though she hates and fears the city, she stands by her man.

What city is this? Every city (as opposed to *any* city), U.S.A. Fincher's concrete sense of place is the cornerstone of his directing talent. Working with production designer Arthur Max (who developed his apocalyptic style as a stage lighting designer for Pink Floyd and Genesis) and cinematographer Darius Khondji (who's currently lensing for Bertolucci), Fincher brings forth an acrid vision of post-industrial decay—all dank greens and glistening browns, the light filtered through smog so yellow you can taste it. The walls are peeling, the dust is thick, the clutter is out of control. Oh, city of entropy. If not for a couple of already obsolete computer terminals in the police station, you might think you were in a 1930s depression picture or a 1940s noir. In any event, it looks as if things have been spiraling downhill since just about the time motion pictures were invented.

Fincher favors setups so dark that Freeman's Somerset would become the invisible man if not for the hits of light off his cheekbones, and Pitt's face glows with the opalescence of the grave. There's an across-the-board revulsion for the body in this movie, not just for the marbled, putrefying flesh of the dead. Even in close-ups, Fincher keeps his distance (though it's low-angled shots he favors rather than eye-of-God overheads). Because the film is so chilly, my desire for Somerset to get out alive took me by surprise. My response had to do both with Freeman's enormously reserved acting style and Fincher's decision to give him a lot of reaction shots toward the end. (All the actors, including Pitt, are at the top of their game.)

Seven seems to be about the struggle to bring things to light. (With a script that had some reason for being other than titillation, this problem might have operated on a metaphoric as well as a material level.) As in his video for *Janie's Got a Gun,* Fincher loves the look of flashlights penetrating obscure and terrifying places. Fincher's first feature, *Alien³* (which was on my top 10 list for 1992 though not on many others), fell apart in the chase scenes through the bowels of the satellite penal colony. *Seven,* however, hits its stride with a chase that's so dark we see nothing but silhouettes hurtling through murky corridors, down a rain-drenched fire escape, and into a blind alley that's ominous as in a classic noir. Fincher manages the near impossible feat of suggesting spatial continuity even when we can't tell where we are or who is who.

Fincher and Khondji find new dimensions of expression in old-fashioned celluloid. The film was processed through a method known as silver retention, whereby the silver that's leeched out during conventional processing is rebonded. Silver retention produces more luminosity in the light tones and more detail in the darks. After I saw *Seven,* I telephoned a cinematographer I know and hyperbolically announced that on its 100th anniversary I had seen the future of film—silver retention. Some future, he replied. The process is so time consuming, not to mention expensive, that neither film labs nor producers want to get involved. Rumor has it that only a few hundred of the more than 2000 prints of *Seven* in distribution are produced by silver retention, which means you may have trouble seeing the film I'm reviewing.

While *Seven* is distinguished by its camerawork, Fincher also has stunning control over the rhythm and pace of individual scenes (his choice of angles is always surprising) and the overall shape of the film, which is very sexy in its rises and falls. This shapliness is much abetted by Howard Shore's score. Fincher thrills to aesthetic one-upmanship: *Seven* sounds like *The Silence of the Lambs* and looks something like Ulu Grosbard's underrated *True Confessions*—only more so. Fincher's desire to reinvent film technology, moreover, has him snapping at Kubrick's heels. Next time out, he should look for a script worthy of his enormous talent.

Also reviewed in:
CHICAGO TRIBUNE, 9/22/95, Friday/p. C, Michael Wilmington
NATION, 11/27/95, p. 683, Stuart Klawans
NEW YORK TIMES, 9/22/95, p. C18, Janet Maslin
VARIETY, 9/25-10/1/95, p. 91, Todd McCarthy
WASHINGTON POST, 9/22/95, p. D6, Rita Kempley
WASHINGTON POST, 9/22/95, Weekend/p. 43, Desson Howe

SEX, DRUGS AND DEMOCRACY

A Red Hat Productions release. *Producer:* Barclay Powers and Jonathan Blank. *Director:* Jonathan Blank. *Screenplay:* Jonathan Blank. *Director of Photography:* Jonathan Blank. *Editor:* Jonathan Blank. *Running time:* 87 minutes. *MPAA Rating:* Not Rated.

NEW YORK POST, 2/20/95, p. 29, Larry Worth

While "Sex, Drugs and Democracy" has plenty of the first two, it's woefully short on the latter, at least when it comes to equal rights.

Jonathan Blank's documentary is an embarrassingly one-sided look at Holland's relaxed attitudes toward prostitution, marijuana use and personal freedom.

Without doubt, an examination of the country's famous red-light district and its equally renowned "coffeeshops" makes for fascinating viewing. And some of Blank's subjects come up with great one-liners. (When asked about cops smoking pot, Amsterdam's police commissioner responds: "Off-duty or on?")

All that's well and fine. But Blank shoots himself in the foot when going on to say that virtually everyone in Holland supports the laidback rules, regs and attitudes.

He then starts throwing out endless statistics on low crime rates to solidify his arguments. But the figures—and accompanying talking heads—result in far more questions than answers.

Blank's shortage of style and organizational skills also becomes annoying. For instance, he explores the issue of legalized sex, then moves on to marijuana's benefits and Holland's lack of racial problems before returning for no discernible reason—to more interviews with prostitutes.

Blank later addresses abortion, homosexuality, environment and mercy-killing, defining the meaning of superficial along the way.

Add in grainy photography (which nixes any travelogue assets) along with an obtrusive rock score (courtesy of obscure American and Dutch bands) and the film could pass as the most amateurish of college productions.

Long before the anti-climax, moviegoers of all ages and political persuasions will be saying no to "Sex, Drugs and Democracy."

NEWSDAY, 2/17/95, Part II/p. B9, Jack Mathews

It sounds like a Utopian society dreamed up in a smoke-filled tent at Woodstock, '69. Legalized drugs, legalized prostitution, government-funded abortions, racial harmony, nationally mandated arts and leisure, nude beaches, early retirement, a pollution-free environment.

It is, in fact, modern Holland, which also comes with bucolic landscapes and scenic canals, and it is the subject of Jonathan Blank's unabashedly promotional documentary "Sex, Drugs & Democracy." This is an open invitation to free-spirited travelers throughout the world, and comes with everything but a pair of first-class tickets.

The truth is that the Dutch have evolved an efficiently open society, built on the principle of tolerance. Despite the easy accessibility of sex and drugs, Holland has some of the lowest drug addiction, venereal disease, teenage pregnancy and crime rates in the world, and through interviews with government officials, prostitutes, drug users and others, Blank has turned what would be the underbelly of most societies into a spic-and-span Disneyland of sin.

The Holland shown here is a vacation destination for the whole family. Mom and the kids can go out and look at windmills while dad visits the leash shop and takes in the live sex acts at the club, maybe goes to one of the bordellos and indulges some of those kinks his wife finds so revolting.

While the government officials quoted give rational explanations for the openness of their demonstrably successful social policies, much of the documentary is bluntly exploitative. It includes brief footage of those live sex acts, and totally extraneous clips of hardcore pornography.

Blank knows how to draw attention to himself (at Cannes, "Sex, Drugs" was promoted with a party promising a live sex act), but the film is so focused on the fringe beneficiaries of Holland's liberal democracy that you'd think victimless crime was its leading industry.

For people who believe tolerance is the key to a peaceful planet, Holland may be the closest any society has come to the Utopian ideal, and we all could learn from it. But in its joyful celebration of the most sensational activities operating within the law, the film will put off many of the people dreaming the dream.

Being tolerant is one thing, being forced to watch what you're tolerant of is another.

VILLAGE VOICE, 2/21/95, p. 56, Ben Greenman

When is a film about tolerance intolerable? When it's *Sex, Drugs & Democracy*, the fatuous whitewash of Dutch society directed and coproduced by Jonathan Blank.

Ostensibly a defense of Holland's decriminalization of prostitution and soft drugs, Blank's addle-headed polemic spends its entire 87 minutes staunchly refusing to make a single substantive point about one of the most conflicted societies in Europe. Blank would have you believe that this is a nation of potheads who wake up sometime around noon, stop by the red-light district for a quick stick (as prostitute or john), and then spend the afternoon soaking up rays on nude beaches, trancing out to the utopian vibe of the Dutch constitution. What's missing? The violent takeover of the Amsterdam prostitution and heroin industry by Slavic organized crime. The mid-'80s unrest over the government's tight control of the housing market. The growing incidence of AIDS among Amsterdam's streetwalkers. The archival footage of flooding that Blank keeps returning to seems incongruous in a film this shallow.

In this relentlessly superficial portrait—not Vermeer, but veneer—Blank occasionally moves into economics and religion, and one encounter with a lesbian cantor in an Amsterdam synagogue even threatens to become interesting. But the film always returns to the cheaply shot thrills of sex and drugs, not to mention the endless nattering about liberty. Dull as canal water—fittingly, the soundtrack includes a song titled "Wake Me When It's Over"—*Sex, Drugs & Democracy* stares blankly at its subject, proving that in the wrong hands, freedom's just another word for nothing left to say.

Also reviewed in:
CHICAGO TRIBUNE, 3/10/95, Friday/p. J, Michael Wilmington
NEW YORK TIMES, 2/17/95, p. C6, Stephen Holden
VARIETY, 6/27-7/3/94, p. 88, Ken Eisner
WASHINGTON POST, 4/1/95, p. C5, Rita Kempley

SHALLOW GRAVE

A Gramercy Pictures release of a Film Four International presentation in association with the Glasgow Film Fund of a Figment Film production. *Executive Producer:* Allan Scott. *Producer:* Andrew Macdonald. *Director:* Danny Boyle. *Screenplay:* John Hodge. *Director of Photography:* Brian Tufano. *Editor:* Masahiro Hirakubo. *Music:* Simon Boswell. *Sound:* Colin Nicholson. *Sound Editor:* Nigel Galt. *Casting:* Sarah Trevis. *Production Designer:* Kave Quinn. *Art Director:* Zoe MacLeod. *Special Visual Effects:* Tony Steers. *Costumes:* Kate Carin. *Make-up:* Graham Johnston. *Make-up (Special Effects):* Grant Mason. *Stunt Coordinator:* Clive Curtis. *Running time:* 93 minutes. *MPAA Rating:* R.

CAST: Kerry Fox (Juliet Miller); Christopher Eccleston (David Stephens); Ewan McGregor (Alex Law); Ken Stott (Detective Inspector McCall); Keith Allen (Hugo); Colin McCredie (Cameron); Victoria Nairn (Woman Visitor); Gary Lewis (Male Visitor); Jean Marie Coffey (Goth); Peter Mullan (Andy); Leonard O'Malley (Tim); David Scoular (Cash Machine Victim); Grant Glendinning (Bath Victim); Robert David MacDonald (Lumsden); Frances Low (Doctor); Bill Denistoun (Master of Ceremonies); John Bett (Brian McKinley); Tony Curren (Travel Agent); Elspeth Cameron (Elderly Woman); Paul Doonan (Newspaper Office Boy); Billy Riddoch (Newspaper Editor); Kenneth Bryans (Police Officer); John Hodge (D.C. Mitchell).

LOS ANGELES TIMES, 2/10/95, Calendar/p. 4, Peter Rainer

"Shallow Grave" confirms what many of us have long suspected. Living with roommates can make you murderous. The movie is a nasty little joke but, by the time it ends, you may feel like the joke is on you. It's a black comedy that gets progressively blacker—and redder.

David (Christopher Eccleston), Juliet (Kerry Fox) and Alex (Ewan McGregor), who share a cavernous apartment in central Scotland, are looking for a roommate. They grill prospective candidates inquisition style—they enjoy making them feel unworthy.

Perhaps this because, in their workaday lives, these three seem cowed and unformed—regular people. David, a gangly twit, works as a chartered accountant; Juliet works nights as a physician in a local hospital. Alex is a journalist. In their cocoon-like apartment they come into their own. Cut off from the outside world, they create their own romper room of knock-about neuroses. They take turns lording it over each other. It's a *folie à trois*.

In the course of their roomie search they end up with a fresh corpse in their flat. Their moral dilemma: Should they turn over to the police the valise bulging with cash belonging to the corpse? It doesn't take long for the shovels and hacksaws to come out, with body parts stuffed in the attic—and more parts to come.

What's shocking, and funny, about "Shallow Grave" is that the trio's transition from home-grown batty to butcher batty is accomplished without a hitch. Their sawing and stuffing is just an extension of their self-enclosed sniping. In a weirdly apt way, the bloodletting dovetails nicely into their careers: David is fanatical about accounting for body parts, Juliet spends a lot of time around corpses anyway, and Alex, in the film's tartest cackle, gets assigned by his newspaper to cover the murders.

Director Danny Boyle and screenwriter John Hodge (who is a physician!) keep the action spurting forward, but their approach is oblique. We seem to be catching the odds and ends of scenes; it's as if the filmmakers wanted to make a movie in which all the expected high points were skimped. (What we see, except for some garish torture flashbacks, is the bloody aftermath of the crimes.) The film is a modernist tease, but perhaps the modernism is there to distract from the basic pulp dreadfulness of the conception. "Shallow Grave" is a hermetically sealed shocker with a cast of characters who come across, like sporty zombies. Maybe this is why the film seems vaguely futuristic. It has a sci-fi sheen.

British black comedies about murder, like, say "The Ladykillers," used to specialize in tasteful grotesquerie. Cadavers were always good for a few chuckles. "Shallow Grave" is a nouveau version of those tasteful, garish chucklefests. It's much more bloody than its predecessors but, in a way, the too-hip smarty-pants badinage, askew camera angles and fractured storytelling are all attempts at spiffiness. They're attempts to pattern the gruesomeness into a style. Boyle and Hodge want us to know they're above the simple lowdown pleasure of the penny dreadfuls. They want to make a cut-'em-up with *class*.

Class has its place, but some of us prefer our cut-'em-ups a little more lowdown.

NEW YORK, 2/27/95, p. 110, David Denby

A thriller, I realize isn't necessarily the best place for a director to demonstrate sweetness of temperament. Nastiness, or at least coldness, is part of the specialized pleasure of the genre: If the audience is to be grabbed and held, if it is to enjoy danger, fear, and death, it has to be partly cut off from normal human response. But at the same time—and this is the hard part—the audience must believe what it sees. Particularly when a thriller is about ordinary people, we must be convinced that the characters are capable of doing what they are shown doing. In a director of thrillers, a feeling for reality—for ordinariness even—is strategically necessary. Despite his many perversities, Hitchcock had that feeling, which is one reason his films are so harrowing.

But I did not believe in the characters in *Shallow Grave*, a new thriller from Scotland written by John Hodge and directed by Danny Boyle. Three Edinburgh yuppies—a doctor (Kerry Fox), an accountant (Christopher Eccleston), and a tabloid journalist (Ewan McGregor)—behave in a way so utterly hostile that no one would possibly have anything to do with them. Infantile and sarcastic, like sophomores having a sugar fit, they dump on everyone. The three share a comfortable flat, and they advertise for an additional roommate, insulting every applicant who dares come to see them. When they finally accept someone—a rather diffident fellow—he promptly dies, leaving a suitcase filled with cash in his room. A bank robber or drug dealer, evidently. The three roommates take the swag and bury the body, first chopping it into pieces. Soon they are betraying one another.

From the beginning, the filmmakers go in for arch dialogue and off-center readings, in the creepily knowing manner of such Harold Pinter-Joseph Losey classics as *The Servant and Accident*. But a swinish manner is not the same thing as style. Clearly, the director wants to make it easier for us to relish the troubles of these monsters, but I was disengaged from the beginning—the show-off brutality just left me cold. And once the troubles begin, the filmmakers don't hold to even a minimal consistency. The characters behave in one way when the plot requires them to, and then in another when the plot requires *that*. It's a case of sheer directorial opportunism. What's at stake? Nothing. The characters are so flimsy as human beings, they don't even seem serious about greed, and greed is the only emotion that propels *Shallow Grave*.

I'm not happy to be writing this way. I'd rather respond to Danny Boyle's excitement. At last, a truly wicked Scottish movie! But Boyle may be too excited. He heads straight for camera pyrotechnics and shock cutting, and though his work is exceptionally menacing, it's also rather opaque. The camera rushes about wildly. There are mysterious torture episodes, and the violence is more bloody than convincing. I enjoyed Boyle's bold use of solid colors, and he does mean, clever things with a power drill. No doubt his talent will settle down next time. But until further notice, film is a matter of illusion, and Danny Boyle doesn't know how to trick us yet.

NEW YORK POST, 2/10/95, p. 47, Michael Medved

"Shallow Grave" is so diabolically disturbing it will make your skin crawl, which is exactly what it sets out to do. The secret of its impact is creating situations in which you can readily understand if not endorse the horrifying actions of the main characters.

Those three principals (played by superb but little-known actors named Kerry Fox, Christopher Eccleston and Ewan McGregor) are fashionable young flatmates in Edinburgh, Scotland, who get their sadistic jollies by tormenting the hapless strangers who've applied to rent the extra room in their spacious apartment.

Eventually, they settle on a mysterious older man named Hugo (Keith Allen) who seems just as smug and cool as they are. He turns out to be so cool, in fact, that the day after he moves in he's well below room temperature; they discover him lying dead naked in his room. Before they notify the police, however, they look under Hugo's bed and find a suitcase filled to overflowing with a fortune in cash.

They now face a formidable dilemma: They can either report the body to the authorities, or else dispose of it themselves and keep the loot. After all, Hugo has just moved in with them, and no one else even knows he's there. All they have to do is mutilate the corpse to obliterate its identifiable fingerprints, footprints and dental records.

Surely, that's a small price to pay for the wealth they stand to gain.

Director Danny Boyle and writer John Hodge (a Scottish physician, here making his movie debut) emphasize the lust for challenge and adventure that motivates the roommates more powerfully than simple greed. This inclination also unleashes some of the subtle sexual tension that had remained latent between the two men (Eccleston and McGregor) and one woman (Fox) who shared the flat and the conspiracy.

Director Boyle is a visual stylist of truly dazzling virtuosity: his film is so effectively edited and breathlessly paced that he easily seduces us into following the characters as they careen all too plausibly into mayhem—and madness.

Even the smallest scenes are inventively shot and brilliantly staged, often bathed in a blue light that ironically suggests the characters' cool, and gradually turns their world into a lurid neon hell.

The violence is profoundly unnerving, precisely because most of it, until the film's final, over-the-top confrontation, is presented in such a subtle style. As in Hitchcock (or Shakespeare, for that matter) the most chilling actions take place beyond our view; you hear, but never see, the most gruesome mutilations.

"Shallow Grave" has already drawn admiring attention at a number of European film festivals and Danny Boyle (a veteran of BBC productions) has been dubbed "the British Quentin Tarantino."

Actually, that title is unfair to Boyle: He's even more cinematically skilled and vastly more substantive than his American counterpart. This picture memorably evokes the chaotic dark side in urban life in each of us that bubbles and churns beneath our smug surface reality. "Shallow Grave", in other words, digs deeper than you'd expect.

NEWSDAY, 2/10/95, Part II/p. B5, Jack Mathews

"Pulp Fiction" fans, take note. Have I got a movie for you. It has funny bad guys, graphic violence, profanity, a hint of sexuality and some dark, dark humor.

The title is "Shallow Grave," and that's calling a spade a spade—or at least what stupid killers do with spades—dig until they have a hole deep enough to lay a body down and cover it with dirt, but not so deep a dog couldn't find the remains while trying to bury a bone of his own.

Like "Pulp Fiction," the bad guys in this story are also the good guys. They're three young British professionals sharing an expansive flat. The apartment is big enough to accommodate a fourth roommate, and the only applicant to meet the other three's high standards of hipness and professional cool is a novelist whom they find dead the morning after he moves in.

Among the man's belongings is a suitcase filled with money, creating an immediate moral dilemma for the roomies—Juliet (Kerry Fox), a rookie internist; David (Christopher Eccleston), an anal-retentive accountant, and Alex (Ewan McGregor), a hot-dog journalist. Do they call the police and remand the stiff to the custody of the coroner? Or, do they disassemble it and bury the pieces in the woods, as Alex proposes?

Their decision draws the attention of both the police, who are trying to find the dead man, and a pair of sadistic killers, who are trying to find the money, and it all escalates into serious mayhem.

Non-"Pulp Fiction" fans cannot blame this on Quentin Tarantino. It was written and produced before Pulp-mania arrived. The rest of us can thank English TV director Danny Boyle, screenwriter John Hodges, and that quirk in their otherwise punctilious nature that allows the British to wallow in black comedy.

There are scenes in "Shallow Grave" that, while not as gross as the infamous brain-splattering segment of "Pulp Fiction," are even more blunt. A man getting his shins walloped with a crowbar, another falling out of an attic and squashing his skull, another pinned to a hardwood floor by a knife plunged through his shoulder.

Yes, these events are played for laughs—gaspy, nervous laughs—and the filmmakers are able to get away with it because the victims all seem so deserving of their fate. Juliet, David and Alex are insufferable snobs, whom, when we first meet them, are grilling, rejecting and humiliating a parade of applicants for that fourth bedroom. Once the dirty money enters their lives, and liberates their really dark sides, the movie turns into a macabrely funny psychological thriller.

Describing the personality changes would be giving away too much, but the performances of the three principals particularly Fox, memorable as New Zealand novelist Janet Frame in Jane Campion's "An Angel at My Table" make the characters' transformations seem unerringly authentic.

"Shallow Grave" is ultimately a dark joke on the greedy nature of man, but its clever development provides a genuine sense of dread. Overall, director Boyle has struck a style closer to Hitchcock than Tarantino (think of "The Trouble With Harry" and "Frenzy"), but either comparison is meant as a compliment.

SIGHT AND SOUND, 1/95, p. 57, Philip Kemp

Three late-20ish friends—journalist Alex Law, accountant David Stephens and doctor Juliet Miller share a superb flat in Edinburgh and are looking for a fourth tenant. Prospective sharers are put through a tough interrogation. Only cool, poised Hugo meets their standards. He moves in—but soon afterwards is found dead in his room from a drug overdose. His suitcase contains a huge amount of money. The three decide to keep it and bury Hugo's body in the woods, mutilated to prevent identification. The task of mutilation falls to David.

With all traces of Hugo erased and the money stashed in the attic, Alex and Juliet relax, though David is still uneasy. Meanwhile two heavies, Goth and Andy, are on the trail of the loot. When Alex and Juliet go on a spending spree, and the flat below is broken into (resulting in a visit from the police), David's forebodings deepen; he moves into the attic and starts making preparations. Goth and Andy show up and attack Juliet and Alex, but David lures them into the attic and kills them. Their bodies are disposed of like Hugo's.

By drilling spy-holes in the attic floor, David keeps track of the others' movements. Having bought herself a ticket to Rio, Juliet becomes David's lover, arousing Alex's jealousy. The three bodies are unearthed, and Alex's editor sends him to cover the story. Alarmed by David's increasingly wayward behaviour, Alex starts to phone the police but is forestalled by David, who prepares to make off with the money. A savage three-way fight ends in the kitchen with Alex stabbed through the shoulder by David, and David stabbed to death by Juliet. Juliet hammers the knife deeper into Alex, pinning him to the floor, before leaving with the suitcase—but on reaching the airport finds only torn-up newspaper. As the police arrive at the flat, Alex lies in a pool of blood, which drips slowly through the floorboards on to the money he had hidden there.

Anyone who feared the British cinema was becoming mired in tasteful period adaptations and the twitteries of the idle rich should take heart from *Shallow Grave,* a black comedy as witty, stylish and cruel as anything from John Dahl or the Coen brothers. Right from the opening, as David's Sunset Boulevard-style posthumous voice-over gives way to a headlong skelter through the cobbled streets of Edinburgh New Town, the film fizzes with the exuberance of its own ruthless energy. This, you sense, is a movie that will take no hostages.

At this year's Dinard Festival, *Shallow Grave* picked up a brace of 'Hitchcock' awards (best film and best acting). It's an apt linkage—not for suspense, which the film scarcely deals in, but for the way it relishes the ghoulish details of death and dismemberment. The sound of a saw rasping on human wrist-bone comes over with scalp-crawling immediacy, and the unwieldiness of manoeuvring a dead body downstairs has rarely been more graphic. The mayhem is all the more telling—and all the funnier—for taking place in the Georgian elegance of the shared apartment. The set, based on a real flat, was constructed slightly larger than life-size, giving a pervasive sense of distortion—an impression aided by the subtly heightened lighting and colour scheme. When the trio discover Hugo's dead body, he lies naked and face upward, limbs asprawl, against a blood-red blanket on a royal-blue background—an opulent and disquietingly beautiful image.

Disquieting images, in fact, abound throughout the film. During Hugo's interrogation by the flatmates we get abrupt flashes (back? forward?) to a violent robbery at a cashpoint machine, all the more ominous for being shot from behind the machine's screen, as though being monitored by some cyborg crime-boss. And after David has drilled his multiple spyholes in the attic floor, the shafts of light streaming from below at various angles weirdly suggest a wartime city, blacked-out except for searchlights fingering the sky. Even in its quieter moments *Shallow Grave* never relaxes, maintaining with its quirky visual texture and taut editing a mood of steadily encroaching menace.

But the core of the action, the three-stroke motor that powers it on its inexorable route to catastrophe, is the relationship of the three main characters, the attractions, tensions and shifting emotional patterns between them. Within their luxurious, hermetically-sealed living-space (no visitors, no phone calls accepted), they play out their roles. At first Alex is the king, David the butt, with Juliet lazily aware of both men's unstated desire for her. As the crisis deepens, everything swivels: David discovers in himself a capacity for violence and takes up superego, god's-eye status, scuttling from spyhole to spyhole in his attic like a low-tech Dr Mabuse. Juliet gravitates to where the power is, and unexpectedly it's smartarse Alex who ends up with our sympathy. (Not least of the film's assets is demonstration-quality ensemble playing from Kerry Fox, Christopher Eccleston and Ewan McGregor.)

To claim *Shallow Grave* as a British film would be misleading. It's very much a Scottish film in its dry, razor-edged humour and its knack of cutting straight to the narrative quick: we never learn just how the heavies trace Hugo, and who cares anyway? True, occasional plot twists are strictly from stock (cash switched for newspaper), as are some of the characters, notably Ken Stott's quizzical police inspector. But as the first feature of its director, producer and writer it's an impressively assured achievement—hard, fast and wickedly enjoyable. If they continue in this vein, connoisseurs of black comedy should have cause to celebrate.

VILLAGE VOICE, 2/14/95, p. 52, Georgia Brown

The cynical *Shallow Grave* is an adrenaline movie, all flash and rush to denouement. A manic, relentlessly clever thriller set in Glasgow, it starts with speed, a car racing like mad down city streets. Turns out to be a prospective tenant traveling to apply for a flat for rent. A share, rather.

Perched nervously on the handsome curved sofa in a handsomely decorated space (who dreamed up the fancy paint job, we never learn), this nerd is interviewed—make that, teased—by three smarties: Juliet (Kerry Fox from *An Angel at My Table)*, David (Christopher Eccleston), and Alex (Ewan McGregor). Doctor, lawyer, and Indian chief. Uh, make that reporter.

It's hard to break into a close-knit family. The three flatmates are tight and mean. (By the end, you can't wait for them to get theirs.) Naturally, they don't want anyone who isn't up to their speed. Finally, Hugo qualifies. But Hugo's so cool that three days after he moves in they find him stone-cold dead on his bed, OD'd. Nearby is a suitcase stuffed with enough bills to make the three think twice about calling the police. Instead, they take the body to the woods, dismember it, and bury the torso. David, the meek, bespectacled lawyer, is elected to do the hacking and in the grisly process becomes a new man, a sort of crazed samurai. When Hugo's ruthless henchmen show up looking for the loot, David alone is alert and ready.

Directed with a surfeit of style by Britain's Danny Boyle, *Shallow Grave* has a charming message: Friendship flies when money beckons. Or, trust yuppies to turn killers. Or, we're all scum. (*Last Seduction* fans, this one's for you.) Coming on as it does as a psychological thriller, it's annoying to have psychology thrown to the winds. All in all, *Shallow Grave* is shallow but fun.

Also reviewed in:
CHICAGO TRIBUNE, 2/24/95, Friday/p. C, Michael Wilmington
NEW REPUBLIC, 3/13/95, p. 31, Stanley Kauffmann
NEW YORKER, 2/13/95, Anthony Lane, p. 93
NEW YORK TIMES, 2/10/95, p. C17, Janet Maslin
VARIETY, 5/30-6/5/94, p. 46, Derek Elley
WASHINGTON POST, 2/24/95, p.. C7, Hal Hinson
WASHINGTON POST, 2/24/95, Weekend/p. 36, Desson Howe

SHANGHAI TRIAD

A Sony Pictures Classics release of a Shanghai Film Studios/Alpha Films/UGC Images/La Sept Cinema production. *Executive Producer:* Wang Wei and Zhu Yongde. *Producer:* Jean Louis Piel. *Director:* Zhang Yimou. *Screenplay (Mandarin with English subtitles):* Bi Feiyu. *Based on the novel by:* Li Xiao. *Director of Photography:* Lu Yue. *Editor:* Du Yuan. *Music:* Zhang Guangtian. *Choreographer:* Wang Qing. *Sound:* Tao Jing. *Production Designer:* Cao Jiuping. *Art Director:* Huang Ximming and Ma Yongming. *Costumes:* Tong Huamiao. *Make-up:* Mi Zide and Yang Yu. *Running time:* 109 minutes. *MPAA Rating:* Not Rated.

CAST: Gong Li (Bijou [Xiao Jingbao]); Li Baotian (Mr. Tang, The Godfather); Li Xuejian (Liu Shu); Shun Chun (Number Two); Wang Xiao Xiao (Shuisheng, the Boy); Jiang Baoying (Widow); Fu Biao (Tang's No. 3); Chen Shu (Shi Ye); Liu Jiang (Fat Yu); Yang Qianquan (Ah Jiao).

FILMS IN REVIEW, 3-4/96, p. 66, Andy Pawelczak

In *Raise the Red Lantern*, Zhang Yimou told a story of women's oppression in pre-revolutionary China. The film was an extraordinary synthesis of almost operatic stylization and realism. With a camera that kept a discreet distance from its subjects, Yimou penetrated the rigid, ritualized surface of everyday Chinese life to unearth the inner lives of his characters. *Shanghai Triad* at first glance seems a long way from *Lantern* and Yimou's other tales of peasants, rich landlords, and functionaries, but this story of a gangster's concubine in thirties Shanghai is anything but a standard genre picture. The conventional trappings are all here—a smoky nightclub, a gang war, execution-style killings, a Godfather and consigliere—but in Yimou's hands they undergo a sea change into something rich and strange.

Bijou (Gong Li) is the mistress of Mr. Tang, a deceptively mild-mannered, even avuncular ganglord. Dressed in slinky red gowns that accentuate her suggestive walk, she's the Queen of Shanghai, an erotic icon who seems to dominate the besotted, indulgent Tang. The film is told from the point of view of Bijou's 14-year-old servant, Shuisheng (Wang Xiao Xiao), who is both dazzled by her and infuriated by her despotic, cruel behavior to underlings, and initially we share his perspective. Very soon, though, we begin to see how powerless she really is; she exists only to serve Tang, who at one point remarks that women's business is wind and men's business, no matter how small, is always important.

As Bijou, Gong Li is in a very different role than the one she usually plays for Yimou; her Bijou is sullen, childish, imperious, and corrupt. In the first half of the movie we see her in various dream-like settings: Tang's sumptuously overbearing mansion, her own large house, Tang's nightclub where she performs several torch songs, one á la Dietrich in tuxedo and top hat.

Gong Li is very good in these scenes: there's a stylized, marionette-like quality to her flaunted sexuality, together with a genuine eroticism that comes through in a scene with an extracurricular lover involving the aphrodisiac properties of a rose.

The film changes direction radically in the second half after an attempted assassination of Tang. The gang war is reminiscent of the bathhouse murder of Roderigo in Orson Welles' *Othello:* it's all shadow-play, bloodied men wandering through dark corridors, corpses piled up beside a pool of water. When Tang and his entourage retreat to a remote island, the movie opens up into the landscape of traditional Chinese painting with shots of water, reeds, a huge moon. In the new environment, Bijou begins to change too. As she talks to a peasant woman and her daughter, she remembers her own rural roots and something softer, more human seeps through her lacquered surface. In one of the film's best scenes, she tries to convince the peasant woman, whose lover has been murdered unbeknownst to her, to return to Shanghai with her. Yimou shoots the scene in the manner of Ozu with a stationary camera fixed on the symmetrically disposed women. As Bijou talks agitatedly and the peasant woman calmly weaves a basket, we see through an open door a bed of reeds blowing in an impending storm. It's an extraordinary image, conveying without melodrama all the latent horror of the scene and foreshadowing the film's ending in which Tang, very ably played by Li Baotian, emerges as much more cunning and insidious than we imagined.

The Chinese government prohibited Yimou from attending this year's showing of *Shanghai Triad* at the New York Film Festival, in retaliation for the Festival's screening of a movie about the Chinese democracy movement. There's nothing very political about *Shanghai* itself, unless you count as political its exposure of women's servitude in China 60 years ago. Perhaps the bureaucrats had a subtler agenda: there's something subversive about real art, and Yimou is an artist. *Shanghai Triad* is sui generis in its depiction of the brutal and the lyrical, and its ending is more wrenching than anything I've seen in recent films. The National Board of Review gave Yimou its Freedom of Expression award this year. It's an award richly deserved by this deeply humane artist.

LOS ANGELES TIMES, 12/20/95, Calendar/p. 1, Kevin Thomas

Zhang Yimou's "Shanghai Triad," a great gangster film, evokes the most exciting, glamorous, dangerous, cruel and corrupt city on Earth during the 1930s. What Chicago was to the United States in the '20s, Shanghai was to China the following decade.

The city was a magnet for European and U.S. exploitation and for Japanese aggression, a decadent society teetering on the abyss. Visually and structurally "Triad" is as striking as "Casino," but its characters are as involving as director Martin Scorsese's are not.

We view Shanghai's famous Bund, a shoreline row of vintage Western-style skyscrapers, through the eyes of a bright, tenacious 14-year-old boy, Shuisheng (capable, poised Wang Xiao Xiao), freshly arrived from the country. In the course of one week he will be introduced to cigarette lighters, telephones and ice cream and also the full range of human behavior, ranging from unspeakably savage ruthlessness to a selfless concern for others.

Shuisheng's uncle (Li Xuejian), a loyal soldier of the second tier to the city's leading underworld kingpin, Mr. Tang (Li Baotian), has summoned the boy to serve his boss' gorgeous mistress Xiao Jingbao (Gong Li), who also is the lead singer in an insipid revue at Tang's nightclub. The obsequious, bowing and scraping uncle assures Mr. Tang that the boy is "a third nephew of a close cousin," for the gang leader trusts only members of his own clan.

Shuisheng has been abruptly thrust into a world of overwhelming fury. Tang lives in an Art Deco palace with some interiors done in an overblown Beaux Arts style. He has given to Xiao Jingbao a darkly paneled English-style mansion done up in similar gangster-style elegance. Although his uncle demands that he be obediently grateful, Shuisheng simply wants to go home and with good reason: Xiao Jingbao is a veritable Dragon Lady, a hard, petty tyrant of limited singing talent and boundless arrogance and nastiness. It comes to us as no shock when Shuisheng discovers that she is two-timing her elderly protector with his handsome, ambitious young No. 2 man Song (Shun Chun).

On only his third day in Shanghai, Shuisheng's life is turned upside down by a St. Valentine's Day-like massacre, staged silhouette-style by Zhang behind the frosted doors of Tang's entrance foyer. Abruptly, Tang whisks his mistress, bejeweled and befurred, and her servant boy off to a remote island.

"Shanghai Triad" is one of the lushest-looking, most stunningly photographed (by Lu Yuc) films of the year, but its depiction of unabashed material splendor is instantly eclipsed by the natural beauty of this island retreat with its swaying pampas grass, magnificent skies and modest structures of simple beauty, (No less important is Zhang Guangtian's poignant, lyrical score, an effective counterpoint to an underworld saga.)

Left mainly to Shuisheng for company, Xiao Jingbao begins to reveal another self, a woman who has made others miserable out of her resentment toward her own misery as an ultimately helpless pawn to men, a onetime country girl who realizes that Shanghai is a snare that can become a hell on Earth.

She comes to treat Shuisheng kindly and to express tenderness to an adorable little girl, the daughter of a woman who lives on the island and is acting as her servant. In this deliberately stylized film—as stylized as his "Red Sorghum," "Ju Dou" and "Raise the Red Lantern"—Zhang has created a Garden of Eden in this earthly paradise. But how long will it prove to be a refuge for Xiao Jingbao?

Those who view movies in terms of politics first and art second can take the film as an indictment of the materialist West. But Zhang's vision is more universal, more profound, and his film is a cautionary tale on the dangers of materialism, regardless of cultural origin, as it affects the spiritual life of a contemporary China experiencing escalating economic expansion. (Curiously, Zhang did not point out the role of the underworld in the rise of Chiang Kai-shek—and vice versa.)

The impact of the violence in the seductive world Zhang has created is all the stronger for being presented with such discretion. Likewise, Li Baotian's Tang is a great deal scarier than Joe Pesci in "Casino," for his cruelty is combined with a refined wit and civility. As for Gong Li, it is the seventh performance for Zhang in a collaboration that is every bit as remarkable as that of Marlene Dietrich and Josef von Sternberg, who also made seven pictures together.

Now that Gong Li and Zhang Yimou have gone their separate ways in their personal lives we can only hope that "Shanghai Triad" is not their last film together. But if it is, it's a grand valedictory.

NEW STATESMAN & SOCIETY, 11/24/95, p. 33, Jonathan Romney

There are many promising threads in *Shanghai Triad,* the latest film by Chinese director Zhang Yimou, but too few to lead anywhere. You almost wish Zhang had gone for the epic length that Chen Kaige lavished on *Farewell My Concubine,* an ostensibly similar period piece about theatrical high and low life. But if he had, it may have ended up even more like the film it most resembles, visually at least—Bertolucci's opulent but hollow *The Last Emperor.*

You can see why Zhang is attracted to the film's topic, Shanghai gangland in the 1930s. He has had ongoing problems with the Chinese government, who objected to the pessimistic, torrid content of his *Ju Dou* though he won back favour with his rural, *vérite*-style *The Story of Qiu Ju,* he lost it again with *To Live.* It clearly made sense to make a film that would be inoffensive to the authorities, and *Shanghai Triad* fits the bill. It is set safely in the past, in an era whose distance is signal led by the ghostly echo of saxophones in the night club scenes.

It takes place in a world whose corruption could be seen as essentially western. Were it not for their long blackcoats, Zhang's villains could easily have walked out of *Once Upon a Time in America* or *Miller's Crossing,* and the plight of his heroine, club chanteuse Bijou (GongLi) could be attributed to her becoming over-westernised, forgetting her origins as a country girl. More than any of Zhang's films, the partly French-funded *Shanghai Triad* feels like a mainstream international product.

The first half-hour offers a tableau of gangland in a lawless boomtown; the story of one woman's uneasy situation in that world; and of a novice's introduction into a life of crime. It leads us to expect a costume version of Scorsese's *GoodFellas* and *Casino* rolled into one: in the event, it's a lavish sketch for a more complex film. The thread that takes us into the story, but ends up hanging loose, is the story of young country boy Shuisheng, who arrives in town to work for a powerful triad boss. He is assigned as servant to the boss' mistress Bijou, who acts like the queen of Shanghai, but whose fate is entirely dependent on her master's whim. The film covers

Shuisheng's first seven days in the Organisation, and some working week it is—violence, flight, betrayal and several song-and-dance numbers.

The film might have cohered better had Shuisheng remained its central figure, viewing things from a distance, even misreading them. But up until the climax he remains a passive witness, providing a largely reliable, if partial, view of an unfamiliar world. The film's real centre is Bijou, with whom Suisheng never fully interacts, if only because protocol forbids it (in Hollywood, they'd have wound up buddies).

Bijou herself is a petty tyrant and narcissist, but not a very interesting one. This Shanghai lily is the conventional fallen woman of gangster flicks, bad to the bone but with some goodness deep at the core. But her good soul only emerges at the end, in a striking but contrived image, a close-up of her weeping in the rain. All through the film, Gong Li is unrecognisable in her harsh make-up. Suddenly the mask is washed away, and Bijou's vulnerability is signified by the fact that her nose and cheeks are slightly raw. It's a lovely image, a celebration of Gong Li's iconic beauty and familiar, wholesome sexuality: but it's as close as we get to the character. The rest of Bijou is a repertoire of knowingly theatrical sulks.

There's a self-reflexive aspect to Bijou's character that plays on Li's own image—a sex symbol and national figure of scandal as the director's lover. Hence the irony of her playing a songbird at the beck and call of her Svengali-like boss ("I don't know what he sees in her," a henchman sneers). But the tenuousness of Bijou's empress-like position is so over-stressed that it merely reiterates the cliché of the spoilt but imprisoned mistress. If there is a Mandarin equivalent of the phrase "bird in a gilded cage", this is a very literal interpretation.

The world of the boss' empire is so enclosed that we don't get much of a sense of Shanghai, either. This complaint may seem tangential to Zhang's aims, but it matters to western audiences who are primarily aware of the city through the way it's been mythologised by film-makers like Sternberg or writers like André Malraux. You wouldn't know from the film just what a cosmopolitan city 1930s Shanghai was, and what contact, if any, westerners had with the Triad world. The absence of western culture makes this a very hermetic film, as if Zhang had simply translated *The Cotton Club* without incorporating the theme of clashing culturals that would make a Shanghai gang saga interesting in the first place.

The west here is purely an effect of style, visible in the club's tacky dance routines. But it's a borrowed westernism that undermines the film's credibility as a period piece. Something of a giveaway is Bijou's top-hat-and-tails routine. She seems to be doing a Dietrich, but look again at the presentation and the anachronistic poppy music, and you realise she's doing Madonna doing Dietrich. It makes her look too clumsy to be a vamp, and it makes the film look half-boiled. This is too much like second-hand Sternberg cut to the western model—Zhang's own *Shanghai Gesture*, but ultimately little more than a gesture.

NEW YORK POST, 12/21/95, p. 59, Thelma Adams

"If the boss dropped her, she'd be out in the streets. What a slut!"

So mobster Liu Shu (Li Xuejian) tells his country nephew Shuisheng (Wang Xiao Xiao) while teaching him the ropes of the Tang family business "Shanghai Triad,"—the vivid '30s-era gangster movie from Chinese director Zhang Yimou which opened the New York Film Festival.

On the boys first night in town, he and his uncle are sharing a table in a swanky Shanghai nightclub, watching Xiao Jingbao (Gong Li) perform. "Bijou" is the chanteuse mistress of their boss, the local godfather (Li Baotian).

The line, delivered with cheerful derision, has the lightness of a throwaway cliche about a gangster's moll. In fact it falls with the distant splash of a weighed anchor, presaging Bijou's tragedy. For all her material trappings and sexual power, the woman in the red-feathered headdress with lips to match leads a fragile existence entirely beyond her control—more fragile than she realizes.

Haughty and seductive, Bijou is a dominatrix on a diamond leash. In one of a string of overblown revue numbers, she performs her lover's favorite song, over-selling a bit of seductive piffle called "Pretending." It is only when Zhang repeats the tune later in the movie, that we can see the anger brimming beneath Bijou's painted mask.

Gong swaggers, sways and sneers, tearing into the role like a Hollywood glamour girl of the golden age. The actress has been Zhang's leading lady on-screen and off since his 1988 directorial debut, "Red Sorghum." During the filming of "Shanghai Triad," the couple's personal relationship disintegrated. The hostility is palpable. Zhang shoots Gong with a lens stripped of romanticism, but cannot mask a sensuality that has become almost frighteningly detached from love's emotion.

Working from a screenplay by Bi Feiyu, adapted from Li Xiao's novel, Zhang has used Bijou's story to reverse the gangster genre. (Triad is Chinese for gang.) Rather than subordinating the woman's story to the gang war plot, Zhang pushes the violence to the wings. It's the red of feathered costumes, not blood, that dominates. The power struggle between the godfather and his rival, Fat Yu, rages around Bijou, but it's Bijou who holds the center.

Zhang tells the saga of a country bumpkin raised to mafia princess from the point of view of the new arrival, Shuisheng. The 14-year-old is both goggled-eyed at Bijou's glamour and stung by her bitter treatment. Brought to Shanghai from the hinterlands to keep an eye on the godfather's mistress, the little man becomes the only person Bijou can trust. The near-silent Shuisheng becomes the instrument that puts Bijou back in touch with her country roots and her humanity.

Visually sumptuous, if slow to build, "Shanghai Triad" is a profound tragedy wrapped in red feathers. Gong steals the movie and our hearts.

NEWSDAY, 12/21/95, Part II/p. B7, Jack Mathews

Zhang Yimou, the former cameraman who has quickly become a master of Chinese film, and Martin Scorsese, who has long been a master of American film, grew up half a world apart, under systems light years apart, and as storytellers seem to have nothing in common.

So why is it when I saw Scorsese's "Casino," I was reminded of Zhang's "Shanghai Triad," and afterward thought, "There's the movie 'Casino' should have been"?

The answer is that "Shanghai Triad," which I saw in May at the Cannes Film Festival, is a better movie. About half as long, about twice as good. Less violent, more human. More poetic, less cynical.

There are obvious parallels between the films. Both deal with the underworld—1930s Shanghai, 1960s Las Vegas—where a hunger for power leads to betrayal among friends, and both have as their pivotal character a beautiful prostitute who becomes an unwitting wedge between two allied gangsters.

Where they differ most is in emphasis. Scorsese, perhaps bored with a story that was essentially a retelling of "GoodFellas" in Las Vegas, was so caught up in the mechanics of Las Vegas, the process of gambling and cheating and lying and stealing, that he allowed the documentary elements of his film to overwhelm the characters.

No such thing occurs in "Shanghai Triad." Although Zhang's films, from "Red Sorghum" to "Raise the Red Lantern," are known for their evocative visual composition, their greatest strength has been their focus on individuals, usually young women surviving with guile in a humbling patriarchal society. With all the dramatic trappings of decadent Shanghai, an Eastern version of Al Capone's Chicago, Zhang holds his focus steadily—through the eyes of a young boy—on Xiao Jingbao (Gong Li), a woman of humble roots who has risen through pluck, vanity, spectacular beauty, great ambition and a modicum of talent to become a popular nightclub singer and mistress of the city's most powerful gang lord.

The godfather (Li Baotian) has attained a level of royalty through his control of the opium and prostitution rings, and Xiao is merely the gem of a collection that includes ornate palaces, a fleet of luxury cars, nightclubs and restaurants, and enough politicians to keep him safely out of the reach of the law.

Xiao is the ultimate in high-maintenance molls. She has immense vanity, a huge need for attention, a child's temperament and the loyalty of a stray cat. And it is her straying with the godfather's first lieutenant (Shun Chun), a cunning young rebel with plans to take over the boss' operation, that kicks "Shanghai Triad" into high gear.

Zhang, showing a kind of restraint never seen in Hollywood, has made a very violent movie without rubbing our noses in the blood. There are a couple of classic mob executions, and a St. Valentine's Day massacre, but as with Greek tragedy, they occur off camera, suggested by lights and shadows and noise, or shown from a great distance. A scene where 14-year-old Shuisheng (an authentically wide-eyed Wang Xiao Xiao) discovers the bloody body of his uncle is far more powerful than all the blunt beatings of faceless thugs in "Casino."

"Shanghai Triad" is told in two distinct parts, with distinctly different visual styles. The first section, in deeply saturated reds and browns, takes place in Shanghai, at least in the shadowy dream of a Shanghai that once was. The second part, after a gang war prompts the injured godfather to collect his minions, as well as Xiao and Shuisheng, and go into seclusion on an isolated island, is shot in blues, greens and grays that are far more naturalistic and match the gloom that prevails there.

Zhang has said he intends the film as a cautionary tale against the materialism creeping back into Chinese life. Why not? Gangster movies have always been useful tools of political allegory. But the film works because it is so specifically human. Gong Li, in her most complex and daring performance, gives us the perfect tragic heroine, a woman whose vanity, ambition and self-importance have got her in far over her head. And the lessons she learns are lessons for us all.

SIGHT AND SOUND, 11/95, p. 50, Lizzie Francke

Shanghai, the 1930s. First day: country boy Shuisheng arrives in the city where his uncle Lui has arranged for him to work for a Triad Boss. Escorted to his new job, he witnesses a murder by the Boss' sidekick Song. At the Boss' mansion he is put to work for Bijou, the Boss' mistress, a showgirl. The Boss learns that Song shot one of his rival Fat Yu's men. He goes to Fat Yu to calm the situation. While he is away, Song visits Bijou.

Second day: at the club, Bijou is reprimanded for singing a number that the Boss particularly dislikes. That night, Shuisheng spies on her as she throws a tantrum. Third day: the Boss entertains Fat Yu at the club. Later, Shuisheng is woken by a noise. He finds many servants, including uncle Lui, dead. The Boss tells him this is Fat Yu's doing.

Fourth day: Shuisheng, Bijou and the Boss flee to a safe house on a remote island where the only inhabitants are the widow Cuihua and her daughter Ah Jiao. Anyone leaving or arriving on the island without the Boss' consent is to be killed. Fifth Day: Bijou goes to visit Cuihua and spies her secret lover. Sixth day: Bijou sees Cuihua's lover lying dead in the water. She lashes out at the Boss, who blames her for telling him what she saw. Later she and Cuihua talk till dawn. Then Bijou gives Shuisheng three coins for his future.

Seventh day: the Boss, comments that Ah Jiao looks like Bijou when she was a girl. He tells everyone that Song is arriving that afternoon. Shuisheng overhears men plotting to kill Bijou on behalf of Song. The boy rushes to tell the Boss and finds him with Bijou and Song. The Boss announces that he is aware of this plot, and that Song has been lured to the island. He and Bijou are to be executed. She pleads for Cuihua and Ah Jiao to be spared, but learns that Cuihua is already dead, and Ah Jiao is to be trained up as Bijou's replacement. The Boss believes that Bijou told Cuihua about what had been going on. Eighth day. The Boss returns to Shanghai with Ah Jiao and Shuisheng, who is hung up on the boat mast for trying to protect his mistress.

"Have you never seen blood?" asks Bijou of her *ingénue* servant Shuisheng, after he fails to find her red outfit. It's a resonant line in *Shanghai Triad*, a film about finding the horrific in an opulent world in which much is stained crimson. As he did with, *Ju Dou* and *Raise the Red Lantern*, Zhang Yimou here makes typical stylistic use of red hues in a gangster melodrama which has all the operatic grandeur of the best of '5th Generation' Chinese films. A parable about greed, *Shanghai Triad* follows a classic pattern: the city epitomises all that is corrupt while the country is a site of simple, honest values. Yimou explores this dichotomy through the three central characters, all of whom have their territory marked out for them. Shuisheng is the fresh innocent; the Boss—a sinister cockroach-like figure in his black mantle and dark glasses—is the festering city dweller, and Bijou is a former country girl now trapped in the Boss' tarnished (male) world.

Yimou structures the film mostly from Shuisheng's point of view, revealing, bit by bit, the full horror of the Boss' schemes. Exposition hinges on things only being briefly glimpsed or overheard—the full truth remaining obscured until the stark finale by which time Shuisheng's world has been turned literally upside-down (with the camera askew too), as he sails back to Shanghai hanging by his feet. The first killing is viewed from a distance. The massacre of the servants orchestrated by Fat Yu is seen as shadow play. Shuisheng overhears Bijou's death being plotted while crouching in the reeds. With so few dramatic events placed centre-frame, the violence that pervades *Shanghai Triad* is all the more unsettling. We don't witness these deaths but rather their consequences.

Zhang's exploration of betrayal and deception is astonishing for its elaborate visual schema—the blood reds and pallid blue-grays of the island scenes suggest a draining sickness. The film's strength derives from the character of Bijou. It is Gong Li's greatest role so far, surpassing her already sublime playing in *Ju Dou, Raise the Red Lantern* and *To Live*, playing to the hilt a spoilt strumpet commanding her little world in the most despotic of ways. With a disdainful click of her fingers, she can have a servant's tongue cut out. There is a certain vaudevillean style to Gong's characterisation. Head held disdainfully aloft, she sashays around in her satin frocks and high heels. But there is also a poignancy in such behaviour, as when Shuisheng spies her throwing a frenzied tantrum in her bedroom. In that moment, she seems to recognize that, in the Boss's world, she's no different from the baubles she is smashing.

The song 'Pretending' is her theme tune, although ultimately it is she who is duped by those around her. There is a delicate pathos in her brief friendship with Cuihua, her one moment in the company of another woman, and the instance on the dockside when she sings a nursery rhyme with the children—a sweet song which provides a desperate coda to the film. In these brief moments there erupts a full sense of what Bijou might be about. The moll with a heart: a familiar figure, her tragic status secured by the fact that she tries to play by the boy's rules but loses, discarded like a worn-out doll that can be easily replaced in the raw scheme of it all.

VILLAGE VOICE, 12/26/95, p. 70, J. Hoberman

A few years back, when Stone was floating the notion of a Mao Zedong biopic, he was interested in Chinese superstar Gong Li for the role of the Great Helmsman's wife, Jiang Qing. At the time, Gong was said to be unsure of herself, although Zhang Yimou's latest crowd pleaser, *Shanghai Triad*, featuring Gong as the showgirl mistress of an elderly gangster, suggests that this actress can play along.

Set in '30s Shanghai, *Shanghai Triad* is Zhang's most elaborate production to date. Filtering a tale of crime and betrayal through the eyes of a none-too-bright, 14-year-old bumpkin, it suggests something like a Bertoluccified version of *Billy Bathgate*. The movie is impeccably crafted and economically structured to end on a powerful image of evil triumphant. Still, it really is the Gong Li Show. While gangsters scheme, the Gongster saunters and shimmies, does a decorous soft-shoe and, appearing in red, amid a white-clad Rockette-style chorus line, sings a song about how she is the object of everyone's gaze: "On my body, I can feel your eyes roving up and down."

Gong's character starts out a vain star and winds up a poignantly unattainable woman; there's more than a taste of Dietrich and Sternberg here. As the most celebrated unmarried couple in world cinema, with a string of seven collaborations, Zhang and Gong broke up during the filming of *Shanghai Triad*. Celebrating her betrayal, her grace, and her mortality, the movie has the painful sense of a long goodbye.

Also reviewed in:
CHICAGO TRIBUNE, 2/16/96, Friday/p. C, Michael Wilmington
NEW YORK TIMES, 12/21/95, p. C12, Janet Maslin
VARIETY, 5/29-6/4/95, p. 52, Derek Elley
WASHINGTON POST, 12/20/95, p. C4, Rita Kempley

SHE LIVES TO RIDE

An Artistic License Films release of an Independent Television service presentation of a Filkela Films production. *Producer:* Alice Stone. *Director:* Alice Stone. *Screenplay (narration):* Diane Hendrix. *Director of Photography:* Maryse Alberti. *Editor:* Alice Stone. *Music:* Mason Daring. *Sound:* Scott Breindel. *Running time:* 76 minutes. *MPAA Rating:* Not Rated.

WITH: Wren Ross (Narrator) Jo Giovannoni; Amy Berry; Becky Brown; Jacqui Sturgess; Dot Robinson.

LOS ANGELES TIMES, 6/19/95, Calendar/p. 2, Kevin Thomas

Alice Stone's "She Lives to Ride" is a sheer delight, introducing us to several very different female motorcyclists as it casually shatters stereotypes right and left. This is feminism with such a good sense of humor that it suggests unlimited possibilities for women way beyond riding motorcycles. In turn, these female motorcyclists' sense of humor has gone a long way toward their winning acceptance by notoriously macho male bikers.

All of them are highly successful, highly articulate individuals who have lots more to say than simply to extol the pleasures of driving—rather than merely riding—motorcycles. Without a doubt, the film's star is 82-year-old Dot Robinson, a vibrant, attractive Florida great-grandmother with a pink Harley and lots of stories about her experiences as a pioneering female motorcyclist who fought for—and won—her right to compete with men in riding contests way back in the '30s.

Handsome, statuesque Jo Giovannoni founded a magazine, Harley Women, because motorcycle magazines are so male-oriented, only to have to fight to have it placed in racks with those very magazines because it was automatically assumed to be a cheesecake publication. She also tells us that female motorcyclists must learn to be their own mechanics: Nobody stops to help a woman stranded with a bike because everyone assumes that they're with a man who's gone for help.

Becky Brown admits she founded the Women in the Wind riding club because she didn't want to belong to an organization that might give her a "dykes on bikes" image. Then there's Jacqui Sturgess, a Manhattan advertising executive who belongs to the Sirens, a club that has led the New York City Gay and Lesbian Pride Parade since 1986, and says it's important for lesbians to have a higher profile than they do. Just as Giovannoni takes us to a South Dakota bikers' rally that attracts some 200,000 people, florist Amy Berry introduces us to a large convention of African American bikers.

Indeed, that a lone young black woman managed to motorcycle through the rigidly segregated pre-World War II South is just one of the fascinating nuggets of information that Stone, a filmmaker with a graceful, self-effacing style, unearths and presents in deft framing sequences crammed with archival images and clips.

NEW YORK POST, 7/28/95, p. 38, Bill Hoffmann

The term "biker chick" usually conjures up visions of a busty blonde bimbo holding on for dear life to her tattooed boyfriend as he zooms off into the desert on a souped-up Harley. Alice Stone's impressive documentary, "She Lives to Ride," quickly explodes that stereotype and gives women their due in the history and development of the male-dominated sport.

The film weaves the stories of five independent female bikers from all walks of life through a brief history of women in the sport dating back to the early 20th century.

It's a revelation to see footage of two fearless sisters, Adeline and Augusta Van Buren, as they bravely cycle cross-country on menacing and unpaved roads in 1916.

And the tale of a young black woman who biked solo through the segregated pre-World War II South is positively inspiring. But the stars of this show are the five very different women who not only embrace motorcycling but go out of their way to promote it.

Dot Robinson is the out-and-out scene stealer. This 82-year-old great-grandmother from Florida rides a pink Harley, which features a lipstick case built into the handlebars.

Dot, who has ridden for 70 years, tells how she really got hooked back in 1935 when she and her husband set the record for fastest time cross-country in a motorcycle with sidecar attached (89 hours).

While she may clock the most number of hours on the road, the other women certainly make up for that in spirit:

There's Jacqui Sturgess, a conservative Manhattan advertising exec in her professional life, who lets it all hang out as leader of the Sirens, a colorful lesbian bikers group.

And Amy Berry, a young black florist who dons a leather jacket, stuffs her pet Chihuahua inside it, and rides to meetings with her African-American cycle club.

There's also avid rider Jo Giovannoni, who founded "Harley Women" magazine after realizing that most other motorcycle publications featured little more than half-naked women suggestively perched across their bikes.

Much to her credit, director Stone presents her fascinating subjects in a straightforward, unhyped manner.

From the beginning, we care about these people as if they were our close friends—and pulling off that trick can be a documentary's toughest challenge.

Stone not only succeeds—but she manages to thoroughly entertain along the way. Even if you never plan to set foot on a motorcycle, "She Lives to Ride' will take you on a rewarding, one-of-a-kind trip.

VILLAGE VOICE, 8/1/95, p. 50, Stan Dauphin

First films about very different scenes, Alice Stone's *She Lives To Ride* and Wally White's *Lie Down With Dogs* have the good fortune of not having to speak for entire generations, allowing them to find voices a little more personal than the corporate-sponsored ones swirling around *Clueless.*

She Lives to Ride is a quiet documentary about five female motorcycle enthusiasts and the hogs they love. They are a disparate group but speak in similar tones about speed, freedom of movement, and power, their stories seconded by archival footage about women and motorcycles. There's Dot Robinson, a great-grandmother whose pink Harley and seeming sweetness disguise the fact that she's the Wilma Rudolph of women's competitive biking, holder of numerous records dating back to the '40s; there's laid-back Jo Giovannoni, founder and editor of *Harley Women* magazine; and then there's my fave, Amy Berry, a stout black woman from Queens who leads Stone into the demimonde of black biker clubs. Stone has access to interesting material here but hews so closely to the safe standards of public televison doc-making that *Ride* occasionally slips into folksy somnambulance. Stone is right not to crowd her subjects, but her touch is so soft that it often only barely gets their stories out of them.

Wally White doesn't have a soft touch, which will probably be his greatest strength as a director. *Lie Down With Dogs* takes its tide from the old joke about why dogs lick their own balls and literalizes it into 90 minutes of White (via a "character" he plays named Tommy) talking to the camera about a summer in Provincetown. It's a fun 90 minutes: jellybean Benitez supervised the consistently deep fried house mix that is *Lie Down's* soundtrack, while White the actor displays a definite gift for gab, endlessly spinning stories about the boys he beds down or wants to bed down. White the director gives himself plenty of room to play, shamelessly capturing every mug and ironic double take.

It's the kind of movie where the cast looks to be enjoying themselves more than seems called for by the script. *Lie Down* does occasionally slide into minor amateurishness with its intentionally cheesy rear projections and on-the-cheap editing. But just when things threaten to get a little too chaotic, White saves the day by uttering something pointedly and wickedly funny.

Also reviewed in:
NEW YORK TIMES, 7/28/95, p. C18, Stephen Holden
VARIETY, 5/9-15/94, p. 82, Daniel M. Kimmel

SHORT FILM ABOUT KILLING, A

A Film Polski release of a Film Unit "Tor" production. *Producer:* Rysard Chutkowski. *Director:* Krzysztof Kieslowski. *Screenplay (Polish with English subtitles):* Kryzysztof Piesiewicz. *Director of Photography:* Slawomir Idziak. *Editor:* Ewa Smal. *Music:* Zbigniew Preisner. *Art Director:* Halina Dobrowolska. *Set Decorator:* Grazyna Tkaczyk and Robert Czesak. *Sound:* Malgorzata Iaworska. *Costumes:* Malgorzata Obloza and Hanna Cwilko. *Make-up:* Dorotta Sewerynska. *Running time:* 84 minutes. *MPAA Rating:* Not Rated.

CAST: Miroslaw Baka (Jacek Lazar); Krzysztof Globisz (Piotr Balicki); Jan Tesarz (Waldemar Rekowski); Zbigniew Zapasiewicz (Bar Examiner); Barbara Ddziekan-Vajda (Girl in Cinema

Box-office); Aleksander Bednarz (Executioner); Jerzy Zass (Court Official); Zdzislaw Tobiasz (Judge); Artur Barcis (Young Man).

FILM QUARTERLY, Fall 1990, p. 50, Charles Eidsvik

When Krzysztof Kieślowski's *A Short Film About Killing* was named the recipient of the first European Film Prize, the "Felix," at the end of 1988, few filmgoers were familiar with Kieślowski's work. In a competition that included Wim Wenders's *Wings of Desire* and Louis Malle's *Au revoir les enfants*, the judges' choice of Kieślowski's strange and uncompromising film seemed to many European critics to be a deliberate provocation: both a European declaration of independence from the entertainment values of Hollywood and from the usual film festival adulation of big-name directors. Known primarily as a documentarist, Kieślowski had previously made important but minor features—in particular, *Camera Buff* (1975) and *No End* (1984)—and had won festival prizes for several other films, but was overshadowed by Poles such as Wajda, Zanussi, and Holland. Further, Kieślowski did not fit the usual "important director" mold: a one-time film professor whose recent work had been financed primarily by Polish television, his work is deliberately modest. (*A Short Film about Killing* and *A Short Film about Love* cost a fraction of even the absurdly low costs of most Polish features and both are, indeed, short by theatrical standards, at 85 and 90 minutes respectively—hence their titles.) The two films were produced as theatrical by-products of a Decalog on contemporary issues suggested by the Ten Commandments (and in which shorter, one-hour versions of the two "short films" also reside). But as his "short films" moved into European distribution, critical attention to Kieślowski did not abate. Though his work remained outside of any mainstream aesthetic, Kieślowski was invited to festival after festival, either as a participant or as a judge. Many European intellectuals now regard him as perhaps the most important, and certainly the most disturbing voice in Polish cinema. I will suggest why that is so and propose some terms in which Kieślowski's work might be understood.

What is special about Kieślowski's work? First, his starting point: a near-total despair about the everyday realities of housing-project Poland. For critics such as Munich's Peter Buchka*, Kieślowski's films are brilliant autopsies of a society where nothing works, not even everyday human connections between people; it is a land so moribund that (as Kieślowski has mumbled in interviews) no social movement, and certainly no work of art, can have much effect. Partly it is that the communal aspect of culture has broken down: lives are atomistic, with social structures keeping people apart rather than bringing them together. And partly the problem is ontological: Kieślowski sees the lives of individuals as ruled largely by chance rather than by fate or even probability. Like almost everyone in Poland's cities, Kieślowski's characters live in drab concrete silos, virtually caged, cut off from normal contact: their loneliness is nearly total, and their attempts to escape loneliness, whether by murder or love, form the spines of Kieślowski's stories. These characters fight not only the culture they live in but ever-present contingency: their hopes and plans have little more predictive value than a long-range weather forecast. As in his *No End,* in which he told three stories, each dependent on whether a character stepped on a train or not, Kieślowski has continued to be fascinated by the cavalier twists seemingly inconsequential events give to a life. His characters have little control over their lives and little chance of success even in small matters. Kieślowski's outlook may well be the gloomiest of any major director in Europe.

But what makes his work important is that he has invented a style that makes near-hopelessness exciting on a moment-by-moment-basis. Bringing to his fiction films the kind of tension found in nature documentaries depicting the moment-by-moment struggles of small animals or insects to survive, Kieślowski's films look and feel like no other film-maker's. He refuses the formulas of both the Eastern European art cinema and of Hollywood. His films are rhythmically rather like Ingmar Bergman's ascetic explorations in the period from *The Silence* through *The Passion of Anna,* but unlike Bergman's, they have little interest in reflexivity; his films are about people, not about movies.

---

* Peter Buchka, "Weitere Nachricht aus einem kaputten Land: Krzysztof Kieslowski's 'Kurzer Film ueber die Liebe", *Suddeutsche Zeitung*, 1 Juni, 1989.

Perhaps it is most accurate to describe Kieślowski's style as an antithesis to those classical fiction-film rhetorics in which each shot's job is to predict the next and in which the viewer is reassured by generic conventions that how the story is bound to end is predetermined. There is no clear way of predicting how a Kieślowski film (or even a Kieślowski scene or shot) will end; his camera follows, rather than leads, the actions of his often impulsive characters. In part Kieślowski's style derives from the documentary practice, born from necessity, of following rather than leading each "subject." But Kieślowski's shot structures and editing are not those of documentary, in which the cameraperson must stand back enough not to affect the subject, must frame loosely enough and with enough depth of field so that unexpected movement can be covered, and must use natural light. Rather, he has taken those elements of documentary that signal involvement with unpredictable, "live" people rather than with actors whose movements are blocked out in advance, and combined these elements with a rethought version of fiction film technique.

A Short Film about Killing looks the more radical of the two films. Certainly it is the more relentlessly pessimistic. Its structure is an intercutting of three stories: of a malicious young man who brutally murders a cabby; of the cabby; and of a law student facing exams, whose first case will be to defend that killer. The opening image announces the setting: a dead rat floats in a gutter in a grey concrete city under the dim yellow-brown light so common in an Eastern Europe fueled by high-sulfur coal. Then Kieślowski bluntly announces his theme: useless malice—a hanged cat dangles in a window. This theme will be played out several times: by a cabby, by a malicious killer, by the state. The presence of senseless malice ties the film together.

The story is low-mimetic and low-keyed. A cabby gets up in the morning, and begins to go about his day. A law student goes to take his final exam. And the "main" character, a young drifter, watches a beating in an alley, then goes about *his* day. He goes to a movie theater but is told the film is boring. He brings a snapshot to a photo shop to get it enlarged, and asks where he can get a cab. He walks to an overpass, and there, pushes a stone off a ledge. There is the sound of a car on the road below crashing, but he does not stop to watch. Malicious but with no goal for that malice, he goes to a square where cabs pick up fares. Frightened by the presence of cops, he goes to a cafe. There, he flirts through the window with a couple of little kids, wraps a cord around one hand, and leaves. He gets a cab, has the driver go into the countryside, strangles the driver with the cord, drags the body to a river, finds the driver still alive, smashes his head with a rock, and leaves. Following this senseless and brutal murder, the drifter drives around, lasting one night before he is caught. After that he has a trial, awaits execution, and is hanged. The drifter's story provides the spine of the narrative.

The second viewpoint is the victim's. The cabby washes his cab. A young couple want a ride; he takes off without them. He sees other potential customers: a woman with dogs; a homosexual, a drunk. He dodges them. He edgily avoids customers he does not want. But he is not simply mean: when he sees a stray dog, he gives the dog his sandwich. Eventually he picks up the young man. Once the young man begins to garrot him, the cabby struggles, as if forever, before he dies.

The third viewpoint, that of the law student, brings a humane perspective to the story. He takes his exam. The exam is one long confession of his problem with the law: the law is clear but circumstances are not; rules and reality conflict. Asked why he wants to be a lawyer, he replies that he wants to meet people he otherwise would never get to know. He passes his exam, and then he and his girlfriend go to a nearby cafe, where they talk about marriage. Later, the young lawyer's first case is to defend the killer. He loses. He visits the killer in death row. What bothers the lawyer most is that he remembers seeing the drifter in the cafe; that any diversion at that point could have changed the events that followed. The killer asks him to give the photo he had enlarged, a photo of a dead sister, to his mother, and explains that, but for an accident in which the sister was killed, after which he was kicked out of his family, his life could have been different. The lawyer observes the hanging, the carrying out of the state's malicious revenge, and leaves to grieve alone.

Of the three main characters, only the law student/lawyer would be in a movie by anyone but Kieślowski. The cabby is the jerk that city cabbies so often seem to be. He becomes truly sympathetic only when he struggles to breathe and pleads for his life. But that is part of Kieślowski's point: *anyone* finally at the point of dying is someone we identify with, and cannot stand to see die. Similarly with the murderer. As we watch him cause a car accident, and even more as we watch him first strangle, then bludgeon the cabby's head, he is utterly despicable: anyone in the audience would vote for the death penalty after watching these scenes. But he becomes oddly sympathetic sitting in a cell, doomed, and then fully sympathetic when, struggling against the guards, he is manhandled, shoved into the noose, and dies, his sphincter muscle letting go of the contents of his guts down his pants leg as he dies. Like the lawyer, we may feel no sympathy for what he has done, but want no part of the execution. That society decreed the death is no matter: murder can be nothing but malicious. What the execution makes of the executioners is beyond tolerance.

To get at the psychological ambience of his film, Kieślowski resorts to old tools: vignetting, bled-out color, high contrast. He films the killer's story expressionistically: cameraman Slawomir Idziak filtered the edges of the frame with a yellow-brown net or gel. Though the drifter's face, especially in close-up, looks relatively normal (though somewhat washed-out) the rest of the image goes yellow-brown: the young man lives in a mental chemical smog. The cabby's story is less filtered but grayed-out, with color-drained settings. The lawyer's story is more "human" in its tones; though Kieślowski desaturates color here too, faces and textures—a wooden desk, a landscape—seem almost normal. Yet overall the film is a document about the nearly unbearable.

In contrast, _A Short Film about Love_ is by turns comic and colorfully erotic; though nearly equally pessimistic about the setting of contemporary Poland, it is prettier to watch. The characters seem as lonely as those in _Killing,_ but basically harmless. The protagonist, Tomek, was raised in an orphanage; he works in a post office and lives with his best friend's mother. From the friend (who is now in Syria) Tomek acquired not only the room but the hobby of spying on Magda, a thirtyish artist with an active love life, who lives across the courtyard. The film begins with Tomek stealing a high-powered telescope so he can watch Magda more closely. Watching, he falls in love, not as adults tend to, but like a schoolboy crush—turned on, jealous, puerile, prankish, and frustrated. To see her more often, he invents ruses to get her to come to his post office window, and takes a second job delivering milk to her apartment building. Eventually he confesses he has been watching her. Furious, she has a boyfriend beat Tomek up. But when she sees his bruised face, she relents and agrees to a date. They have tea. Tomek confesses he also has stolen some of her mail. Outraged, she gets him to come to her place. There, unable to control himself, he ejaculates as soon as she has put his hand on her. She laughs at him and tells him that is love: a selfish urge that makes a mess. Tomek goes home and slits his wrists, but lives, because his landlady finds him and gets an ambulance. But the moment Tomek leaves, Magda, torn by guilt, tries to contact Tomek to get him to return. She begins to pursue him: she goes to the post office; she makes inquiries of his landlady. Finding what he has done, she becomes obsessed with getting in touch with him. In _A Short Film about Love_ eroticism is just one way in which the need to touch other people is expressed, but it is an inseparable part not only of Tomek's attraction to Magda (and later, perhaps, of her fascination with him) but also of the old landlady's attraction to Tomek. Made into spiritual shut-ins by the high-rise compartments in which they live and the bureaucracies in which they work, their attempts at love must necessarily be neurotic. But any attempt at love in Kieślowski's world is acceptable. Unlike films (such as _Peeping Tom_ or _Rear Window_) in which there is something perverse about voyeurism, in Kieślowski's world the urge to watch is at least a result of the desire to share another's life, and a potential preliminary to making closer contact.

Kieślowski's switched cameramen on _A Short Film about Love_, here working with Witold Adamek. Adamek lets color saturate; above all, he fills the film with bravura shot combinations, in which "fiction" setups are played against documentary techniques in order to create involvement. Adamek does not care about shadow detail: his key lights are hard, hitting in pools and often leaving a lot of the screen dark. Rather than model noses and cheekbones prettily with soft fill lighting, Adamek often uses harsh spotlights from above and the side, letting actors move into and out of pools of light. How we see the characters thus varies from moment to moment: one instant, for example, Magda looks astonishingly pretty; the next, completely ordinary. As a result, our perceptions even of a straightforward scene become complicated: we are not allowed the constancy effect, the stabilizing of our perceptions which prolonged contact with a person in everyday life (or conventional movie lighting) normally provides.

Adamek's camera stays glued to the characters, with continual correction of the framing as the actors move. The actors seem to move freely, impulsively, giving the impression of not having been blocked for ease of filming. (There also seems to be little or no "cheating" of their positions or movements to get them into frames and dolly shots neatly.) In some shots the camera seems shoulder mounted (but not shaky); the camera stays with the characters as if *it* were a character, fighting to be in the right place to see, but without the axle-grease smoothness and technical *savoir faire* of mainstream cinema's silky camera moves. Adamek enhances the effects of his edgy struggle to stay on top of the action by using relatively long lenses, tight compositions, and shallow depths of field. Often, as in documentaries, objects get in the way of what we want to see, and Adamek must move around them. The objects (as in documentary) do not seem planted for effect but just part of the clutter of reality. The camera continually reframes, refocuses, and then cuts to a new, better vantage point. As in a documentary, Adamek foregrounds the struggle with real locations, with the impulsiveness that makes real people so hard to document, with the contingencies that give documentary-like presence to a moment.

But the camera work still echoes and alludes to the standard conventions of fiction film. In interior scenes (such as one in which Tomek and Magda sit down for tea) Kieślowski and Adamek shoot from something close to the usual positions. But instead of the usual procedures for handling these positions, Kieślowski and Adamek invent their own. Conventional camera positions save set-up and lighting time by shooting such a scene from beginning to end from two positions; in the edit, segments from each position ping-pong back and forth. But *A Short Film about Love* rarely repeats camera setups precisely; as if they were shooting a documentary in sequence, Kieślowski and Adamek keep shifting, hunting for a fresh frame and perspective for each moment. Sometimes shots and cutting rhythms are unpredictable. For example, in the scene in which Magda runs from the post office, frustrated and humiliated by another prank summons to get mail, Tomek follows, and calls after her, confessing it is his fault. The camera sweeps with Tomek, stopping only after he does. Kieślowski comes in close for Magda's angry reaction as she tells Tomek to disappear, goes in a wide shot with Tomek as he tells her he saw her cry last night, then into a series of varied shots as she reacts and he confesses he has watched her and that he loves her. But none of these camera positions or the cuts between them gives the sense that the scene was rehearsed and repeated for each camera position; the impression is of a spontaneous event, caught by a chance perception.

The film's most conventional visual element is its use of saturated reds. Tomek covers his scope with red cloth, Magda's bedspread and telephone are red, and she has red stick-ons on her door; her weaving also has red motifs. Red is Magda's color, a gesture of rebellion against the greyness of the world in which she lives. Unlike the other characters, her response to other people, to objects, to life is openly tactile and, despite her bitterness and cynicism, passionate. Her tactility, her potential for touching other people, feels especially seductive in the context of Kieślowski's gray Poland.

In the film's final scene, Magda sees a light in Tomek's room. She runs to the apartment, and asks to see Tomek. He is asleep. Magda reaches to touch his bandaged wrists. The landlady stops her, trying to protect him. Magda then goes to the telescope, looks at her apartment, and imagines herself the night she cried, but now with Tomek with her as a friend to comfort her. When touch is impossible, the voyeuristic imagination takes over. But that at least gives the hope that there might be touch again, and with touch, a future.

Like Bergman's work in the 1960s, Kieślowski's is about loneliness and the search for human contact, for touch. Unlike Bergman's characters, however, Kieślowski's struggle against more than inner angst: their society gives them little chance that contingency will work for rather than against them. Peter Buchka many well be right that Kieślowski's films are an autopsy of Poland. But they are hardly a writing off of Polish people. One by one Kieślowski's characters struggle for contact. They are not all malicious killers. A young lawyer befriends a doomed man and weeps at his death. A landlady treats a young man as if he were her own son. A woman forgives a young man for spying on her. Each of these tries to reach out, to find something decent to do. And in this reaching out Kieślowski finds some small hope for, if not Poland, at least some of its people.

As Kieślowski's producer remarked to Kieślowski when he received the first European film prize, "So long as there are directors like you, Poland is not yet lost." That may or may not be true. But Kieślowski has found a form to make the struggle for spiritual survival in such a land exciting. That struggle can be filmed by treating stories as if they were real, by treating characters as if they were people, by treating film as if it were always a document. In Kieślowski's world most characters do not have much chance of success. But their struggle! Kieślowski has shown us an exciting way to film struggle. And in this showing, perhaps he has opened a new path for film-makers who do not want to forget their respect for reality when making fiction films.

MONTHLY FILM BULLETIN, 12/89, p. 371, John Pym

Warsaw. A drowned rat; a hanged cat. As dawn brakes, a misanthropic taxi driver, Waldemar Rekowski, readies his car, a dispirited young man, Jacek Lazar, wanders the city, and an apprehensive lawyer, Piotr Balicki, prepares for a qualifying oral examination. Jacek ignores an alleyway assault and drops a stone from a bridge, smashing a windscreen. Waldemar attempts to pick up Beata, a taunting young woman, then leaves a couple stranded, and later gives a piece of bread to a starved dog. At a photographic shop, Jacek orders a blow-up of a creased picture of a girl at her first communion. A man smiles at Jacek in a urinal and is pushed unceremoniously to the floor. Piotr, having passed his exam, weaves exultantly through the traffic on his moped, attracting a glower from the taxi driver. In a hotel bar, a handsome woman reads Piotr's palm and Jacek wraps a rope tightly round his hand. Jacek takes Waldemar's taxi and orders him to a desolate spot where he strangles and clubs him; when he refuses to die, Jacek crushes his skull with a rock. That evening, Jacek picks up Beata, his girlfriend: now they can go to the mountains ... The end of Jacek's trial: Piotr is distraught at the loss of his first case, but is told by a member of the bench that his closing speech attacking capital punishment was exemplary and that a more experienced advocate could not have saved Jacek. On the day of his execution, Jacek begs Piotr to intercede with his mother. He wishes to be buried beside his father in the place reserved for her. It transpires that the plot is also occupied by his sister Marysia, the girl in the communion photograph, who was killed five years ago by a tractor. The driver had been drinking with Jacek. The execution is falteringly carried out; Jacek's bowels open into a plastic tray. Later, beside a field, Piotr weeps bitterly.

Two stylistic features immediately distinguish *A Short Film About Killing*, the unremitting awfulness of its detail and the drained, filtered texture of its grainy photography, watery greens and yellows predominating, with the edges of the frame sometimes blurring into semi-obscurity. (In these two respects, and for the bleakness of its vision, this unforgettable moral tale may be compared with Tarkovsky's *Stalker*.) A third feature, a symbolic colour coding of desaturated reds and browns, later becomes apparent as the film's unifying motif. Krzysztof Kieslowski, a former documentarist, has a sharp eye for the commonplace detail which fixes a scene. In the hotel bar, for instance, Jacek's grimy hand extracts from a washing-up basket a knife coated with food. He wipes it on the edge of the receptacle and then with effort cuts the cord with which he will attempt to strangle the taxi driver: a blunt, inappropriate instrument to prepare for a botched, abominable deed.

Everything goes wrong with the killings: there is nothing short about either of them. The garrotte becomes entangled in the taxi driver's mouth, the wrench will not kill him, and where, Jacek wonders in desperation, is the rock which will deliver the *coup de grâce?* In the death cell, the curtain collapses, the rope is insufficiently taut, and no one seems sure just how much of his last cigarette the condemned man should be allowed to smoke. This is a biblical story—one in a series of the Ten Commandments made for television, of which two (this and a *Short Film About Love*) exist in feature form. During his oral examination, Piotr is asked to cite some learned authority for his views on capital punishment; the example of Cain, he suggests, has proved no deterrent to murder. His examiners smile at the neat, deflecting response. The acceptable coded criticism of a system which will never change, and which they, the compliant servants of the system, will never seek to change.

A Short Film About Killing was made in 1987: a period when the present wave of social changes breaking across Eastern Europe was unimaginable. Its tone might be summarised by the cynicism of those smiling faces and by the heartlessness of the old legal functionary who meets Piotr on the prison stairs on the day of the execution and makes a pleasantry about the young man's new family, as if neither of them were about to participate in a murder quite as terrible as the one committed by Jacek. What makes the film more than simply an unanswerable indictment of killing both criminal and judicial (there have been plenty of those from *I Want to Live* to *The Thin Blue Line*), and more than an infernal vision of Poland (in the last few years there has been no shortage of pessimistic Polish film-makers), is the great dramatic scene of Jacek's confession to Piotr, the lawyer/priest who has, we learn from the functionary on the stairs, married the woman who told his fortune in the bar and recently become a father. The poignancy of the new father hearing the fatherless boy's halting account of how, if his sister had not died, things might have been different, and the lawyer's—and our—realisation that the truth has come too late to save him, if indeed it ever could, lifts the story to a plane of tragic inevitability.

NEW YORK POST, 12/20/95, p. 38, Thelma Adams

"A Short Film About Killing" has a long murder scene.

No quick bullet to the head satisfies co-writer/director Krzysztof Kieslowski. The murderer is a burglar; his victim tenacious. The killer strangles, batters, bludgeons and finally shatters his victim's skull with a boulder—and all for the ownership of a car to please a girl who'll never want to ride in it.

Kieslowski has a thing for series. Think "Red," "White," and "Blue." Before the tricolor trilogy, he worked on the Dekalog with writing partner Krzysztof Piesiewicz, offering cinematic variations on the 10 Commandments.

Starting today, the Cinema Village will finally give "A Short Film About Killing" its New York theatrical premiere. Ultimately an anti-capital punishment diatribe, the 1987 riff on "thou shalt not kill" won the Cannes jury award in 1988.

With its bitter irony and bleak Polish setting, "Killing" shares a greater kinship to "White" than to its polished Western European siblings, "Red" and "Blue."

Jacek (Miroslaw Bika) orbits Warsaw and his victim in a series of scenes that flit with deceptive randomness between Jacek, a taxi driver (Jan Tesarz) and a green trial lawyer (Krzysztof Globisz) experiencing the happiest day of his life—he has just passed the bar exam.

A gangly, acne-faced young man with comic blond plumage, Jacek is chaos. He's as likely to toss a stone off a bridge and cause an accident on the road below as he is to flip chocolate pudding on a cafe window to the giggling delight of two little girls. Jacek is a mischievous hayseed grown into a twisted man-boy.

Kieslowski raises sympathy for the taxi driver ironically. His neighbors toss wet rags on his head. He hates cats. He leaves customers in the lurch—and gets his kicks out of it. He's such a complete curmudgeon that he's almost endearing.

Situated on the border of dark comedy and disaster, the fresh and twisted first hour climaxes in the murder. In the final third of "Killing," the trial lawyer comes forth, defending Jacek for his crime. The movie becomes flat. It loses its humanity and creative spark—in agitprop.

We enter the trial at the final judgment—hanging. The lawyer's anti-capital punishment speech occurs off-camera, although we are told it was brilliant. We are left with the lawyer's sentimental angst and a confession by Jacek of a tragic youthful incident that be credits for setting his feet on the path to unrighteousness.

Kieslowski undermines his own pat ending. He has made it impossible for us to share completely in the lawyer's sentimental tears at his failure to save Jacek from the noose. We have seen what the lawyer hasn't: Jacek's inept, brutal murder of an innocent, imperfect man.

SIGHT & SOUND, Winter 1988-89, p. 63, Paul Coates

Krzysztof Kieslowski's *A Short Film About Killing* is a work of visionary irony. The ironies set in with the very first images, as the titles roll: a dead rat in a puddle and a hanged cat dangling against the background of oppressively serried apartment blocks. Varsovians will recognise the irony that juxtaposes the dead creatures, emblems of an urban inferno, with blocks that in fact house many of Poland's best-known TV and film stars. The title itself secretes a lethal irony: this short film (it runs only 90 minutes) shows how lengthy and arduous is the process of doing a man to death. The time it takes will be marked excruciatingly by the slow progress of a bicycle across the yellow-lit horizon.

The ironies are not signs of authorial superiority, but the dissonances of tragedy. They strike in particular at a young lawyer, whose celebration of his graduation to the bar is pierced by a sudden premonition that his future will not be as straightforward as he hopes. The murderer he will be called on to defend is already drinking in the same café. It is in the scenes in which the young murderer wanders about Warsaw, his own future still open, that Kieslowski's film is most remarkable. The boy walks through a world drained to sepia by filters, with colour appearing only at the centre of each image. This partial desaturation echoes the effect of the tinted band across the windscreen of the taxi whose owner the boy will kill. With its realistic equivalent—perhaps even origin—Kieslowski's formal device is never ornamental: instead it suggests, quasi-expressionistically, the closing down of the world inhabited by Jacek, whose name we will not learn until he has completed the murder—as if the act gives him a name by attaching him to a fate.

At the centre of these sepia images there is virtually only one colour, red. During the film, Jacek pursues a series of unattainable girls dressed in red, the colour of life; and his pursuit leads naturally to the blossoming of another red, the blood that stains the taxidriver's head. Jacek covers the head with a brown checkered blanket that, as it were, completes the desaturation of the world's colours by obliterating even red. The only girl with whom the boy is associated before the murder is one seen in a crumpled photograph. She wears a white communion dress and even before the end, when we learn she is Jacek's dead younger sister, we suspect her fate: the boy asks a shop assistant, given the print for enlargement, whether it's true that one can tell from a photograph if a person is still alive.

Ironies proliferate. The taxi-driver feeds a stray dog, unaware that a human outlaw will shortly kill him. During the murder, Jacek makes frantic efforts to halt the nightmarishly prolonged blast of the car horn, yet only a horse in a field looks round; but then, no sooner has the horn fallen silent, a passing train picks up its note. The taxi-driver is congratulated on his good luck by a man selling lottery tickets; Jacek, meanwhile, refuses to let a gypsy read his fortune as he enters the café in which Piotr, the lawyer, is having his palm read by his girlfriend. This world of diabolic coincidence is clearly one of the circles of hell.

Jacek's crime may seem motiveless, its inevitability simply the effect of Kieslowski's expressionist style and the remorseless accumulation of such details as the severed head that is the taxi-driver's good-luck charm, which presages his strangulation, and the dead cat. With his fluffy punk hair and leather jacket, Jacek stalks Warsaw like an edgy, existential angel of doom. Yet it is not just the stylistic tour de force which persuades us to accept the experience of this appallingly protracted murder.

Kieslowski in fact offers several possible explanations: the boy's need to obtain a car; the search by means of a murder, for which one knows the penalty is hanging, for a form of suicide that will not preclude burial in consecrated ground alongside one's beloved sister (a motif first suggested by Jacek's visit to a cinema at which *Wetherby* is playing); the country boy's need to assert himself in the city; youth's revenge on age. If none of these explanations is privileged, it is partly because Kieslowski wishes to allow for the essential mysteriousness of human action. Equally significant, however, is his sombre insistence on the typicality of the crime in a contemporary Poland in the process of becoming hell.

The consequences of Poland's economic decline are seen to include a slide towards gratuitous viciousness in human relations. The taxi-driver deliberately leaves would-be passengers standing; Jacek informs others that his destination is the opposite of theirs: hostility is pervasive. In the midst of this darkness, Kieslowski locates hope in children and in the idealistic lawyer Piotr Balicki. Jacek flicks the dregs of coffee at a window through which two girls are watching him: their smiles transform his violence into play.

Piotr's defence of Jacek is useless: a daring cut excising everything between the recognition of the taxi and the judge's statement that the trial is closed. The lawyer's speech against the death penalty may be the best the judge has ever heard, but we are not shown it. This is partly because Piotr's role as a secular priest, hearing Jacek's last words in prison, is more important to Kieslowski. But it is also because the director has his own argument against capital punishment, framed purely filmically. Murder and execution are horrifyingly indistinguishable. As the militiamen bundle the condemned man into the death chamber, knocking down the curtain, and the man tightening the noose shrieks instructions to his assistant, the hysteria echoes Jacek's realisation of the difficulty of killing a man. Is the law, which has violence at its heart, partly responsible for Jacek's crime? This is the final and most deadly irony of Kieslowski's film.

VILLAGE VOICE, 12/26/95, p. 70, Amy Taubin

There are various schools of thought about the films of Krzysztof Kieslowski. My colleague Georgia Brown is a great admirer of his much acclaimed *Three Colors: Blue, White, Red* but has little interest in the *Decalogue*, the 10-part series based on the Ten Commandments that Kieslowski and his writing partner Krzysztof Piesiewicz made for Polish television in 1989. I find *Three Colors* irritatingly arch and nastily misogynistic, but I *am* interested in the *Decalogue* and think *A Short Film About Killing*, the feature that Kieslowski spun off from the fifth part of the series (based on the "Thou shalt not kill" commandment), to be one of the great films of all time.

Although *A Short Film About Killing* doesn't lack champions (among them Stanley Kubrick, who wrote a brief foreword to the British edition of the *Decalogue* screenplay, and Martin Scorsese), this is its first theatrical release in New York. Ed Arentz of the Cinema Village pried the film (and its companion piece *A Short Film About Love*) from its North American distributor just in time for the Christmas season.

To say that *A Short Film About Killing* is a profound indictment of capital punishment makes the film seem more polemical than it is. The questions of how and why people kill are posed not only in terms of the state but also on the individual level, and they're left open-ended, although, as far as the state is concerned, it's obvious which side Kieslowski and Piesiewicz (who is himself a lawyer) are on.

Elliptically structured, the film is basically a chamber piece for three characters: a young punk, the middle-aged taxi driver he murders, and the young lawyer who defends the punk. The kid has only the vaguest motive for the murder (he wants a car so he can run away with a girl he has a crush on), but he's been fogged out with rage and guilt ever since the sister he adored was run over accidentaly by one of his friends after they'd been out drinking. The taxi driver is no charmer—he's rude to his customers, brutish toward women—but he regularly shares his lunch with a stray dog. The lawyer knows the case is hopeless—that the kid will be hung no matter what he does—but he argues desperately against the death sentence ("the law should improve nature").

Both killings (the strangling and bludgeoning of the taxi driver by the kid and then the kid's execution) are as brutal as anything that's ever been put on film. Kieslowski lays bare just how hard it is to kill someone—especially when there are no guns involved. But what's most extraordinary about the film is its attention to behavior. It's through Kieslowski's minute observation of how people behave alone and in company that one learns something about what it is to be human. The killer is no demon; we might given a change in our own circumstances, do as he did. And are we not killers anyway if we passively assent to a system that pushes the death penalty? These are not esoteric questions in themselves, but there are few films that pose them in quite so complicated and nonjudgmental a manner.

Also reviewed in:
NEW YORK TIMES, 12/23/95, p. 21, Caryn James
VARIETY, 5/25/88, p. 18
WASHINGTON POST, 10/6/95, p. B7, Hal Hinson
WASHINGTON POST, 10/6/95, Weekend/p. 46, Desson Howe

SHORT FILM ABOUT LOVE, A

A Film Polski release of a Polish Film Producers' Corporation production. *Producer:* Ryszard Chutkowski. *Director:* Krzysztof Kieslowski. *Screenplay (Polish with English subtitles):* Krzysztof Piesiewicz and Krzysztof Kieslowski. *Director of Photography:* Withold Adamek. *Editor:* Ewa Smal. *Music:* Zbigniew Preisner. *Sound:* Nikodem Wold-Laniewski. *Art Director:* Halina Dobrowolska. *Set Decorator:* Grazyna Tkaczyk and Robert Czesak. *Set Dresser:* Magdalena Dipont. *Costumes:* Malgorzata Obloza and Hanna Cwiklo. *Make-up:* Dorrota Sewerynska. *Running time:* 85 minutes. *MPAA Rating:* Not Rated.

CAST: Grazyna Szapolowska (Magda);   Olaf Lubaszenko (Tomek);   Stefania Iwinska (Gospodyni); Piotr Machalica (Roman); Artur Barcis (Mlody Mezczyzna).

FILM QUARTERLY, Fall 1990, p. 50, Charles Eidsvik

[*A Short Film About Love* was reviewed jointly with *A Short Film About Kiling*; see Eidsvik's review.]

MONTHLY FILM BULLETIN, 5/90, p. 131, Tim Pulleine

Nineteen-year-old Tomek is an orphan, now lodging in a Warsaw high-rise flat with the mother of an absent friend, Marcin, and working as a post-office clerk. For a year, he has been spying, as Marcin did before him, on Magda, a thirtyish designer who quite frequently entertains lovers in her flat on the opposite side of the courtyard. He progresses from binoculars to a stolen telescope for this purpose, makes anonymous phone calls to Magda, and plays such tricks on her as notifying the gas board of a supposed leak in her flat while she is with a lover. He takes a supplementary job as a milkman to achieve contact of a sort with her, and also sends her phoney notices of money orders for collection at the post office in order to bring her into his presence. One of these, however, provokes a row between Magda and Tomek's superior, who accuses Magda of trying to get money by false pretences. In the upshot, Tomek follows Magda and confesses that he was responsible; she is furious and turns her back on him. However, she has become intrigued, and when a lover comes to her flat that evening, she arranges that their love-making be 'visible', then tells the man what is happening. He is outraged and after calling Tomek outside, knocks him down. But during Tomek's milk delivery next day, Magda engages him in conversation, and subsequently accepts his invitation to meet him at a café. There he tells her more about himself and his situation, and she suggests that he return to her flat. But this intimacy backfires on Tomek, and he flees in humiliation. He makes a suicide attempt, and while he is recovering in hospital Magda finds herself increasingly preoccupied by him, making enquiries of his landlady and other postal workers, and constantly looking out for his return home. Visiting his landlady's flat, she finds herself drawn to his telescope, and in her imagination undergoes the experience of 'watching' herself.

At the centre (both in terms of running time and otherwise) of Kieslowski's film is the sequence, framed and cut in an uncharacteristically academic fashion, in which Magda interrogates Tomek as to why he spies on her. "Because", he unhesitatingly replies, "I love you". But this notion of 'love' is one wholly bereft of correlatives: Tomek denies in response to further questions that he wants to make love to Magda or, say, to go away on a holiday with her. When she asks, "What do you want of me?", the answer is "Nothing". This scene is balanced a little later by that in which Magda takes Tomek back to her flat. Here, his assertion, "I love you", is met by her retort, "There's no such thing"; she then proceeds, in what seems to be an intentional way, to humiliate him by sexual arousal which causes him to ejaculate, whereupon she declares, "That's all there is to love".

The sado-masochistic—arguably even gloating—reductiveness of bodily function here might recall the comparable (and symbolically weighted) emphasis at the end of the execution sequence in *A Short Film About Killing*. And for all their ostensible dissimilarity, the two works do set up a pattern of correspondences. Both are constructed with deceptive formality: in *Killing,* two extended passages plus a brief coda; in *Love,* three 'acts'—Tomek's spying, his meetings with Magda, the aftermath of approximately equal duration. Where *Killing* is resolutely externalized, in playing off the action against the streets and public buildings of Warsaw, *Love* is no less resolutely interior: the occasional outdoor passages tend to be shot from disorientingly high angles, while the one sequence to involve a semblance of everyday life, the contretemps at the post office, seems oddly extraneous. And the expressionistically 'sicklied over' colour and wide-angle framing of *Killing* are countered here by a claustrally dark method of lighting and composition, with realism further qualified by incidentals like the recurring sight of a white-clad passerby toting a heavy suitcase (though this does not wholly dispense with literal-minded doubt as to why, even on a high storey, Magda seems never to close her curtains).

Like *Killing, Love* has a protagonist on the threshold of adulthood. Tomek is, of course, shown as a harmless rather than a malign figure, and the violence to which he is eventually driven is against himself; and there are some intimations of a rationale (his orphanage background) for his 'anti-social' demeanour. At the same time, where the hideously willed act of the murderer in the previous film seemed to proceed from a very lack of will (rendering him vulnerable simply because of the impossibility of feeling any sympathy for him), it is Tomek's incapacity for 'normal' feeling ("Have you ever cried?" his sympathetic landlady asks; "Once, a long time ago", he answers) which motivates the current film. His alienation is, in fact, lent a near-ritual quality by such details as his setting an alarm clock for the time of Magda's likely return home, or his stolidly drinking coffee and munching a roll while he peers through his telescope, and his 'blankness' is emphasised in the episode with the angry lover, in which Tomek makes no effort to defend himself.

What heightens the macabre effect is that Tomek's fraught breakthrough into 'real' feelings seems, if not to destroy, then to efface him: he significantly remains offscreen during the concluding passage, an effacement complemented by Magda's being moved at this point to enquire of the landlady what his name might be. In the culminating sequence, attention shifts to Magda herself, and to her entry into the imaginative world that Tomek's' deracination has led him to create (a movement visually anticipated in the credit sequence by the shot of a window being shattered, as if to admit entry into a hidden domain, and further intimated by the frequent use of reflections). But given the distinctively East European sinisterness which pervades Kieslowski's view of things, it is unsurprising that this concluding transference should feel less akin to a dream than to a nightmare.

NEW YORK POST, 12/29/95, p. 37, Larry Worth

Anyone who saw Krzysztof Kieslowski's romantically-skewed "Red," "White" and "Blue' would suspect that his "Short Film About Love" isn't your typical boy-meets-girl story. And within minutes of the opening credits, ample confirmation arrives.

The boy is Tomek, a 19-year-old postal clerk (enough said?), and the girl is Magda, a lovely 30ish blonde who lives in the apartment building across from his. Not so coincidentally, Tomek's telescope is pointed directly at her window.

Tomek's idea of doing dinner with Magda is to munch on a bagel while she nibbles a sandwich, as observed through his spyglass. But like any good stalker he yearns to get closer, so he starts delivering milk bottles to her doorstep and leaving notes that necessitate a post office visit.

And so it goes, until a few too many peeps at his dream woman cavorting with her lover. He can only sabotage their flings—as when calling to report a gas leak in Magda's apartment—so many times.

Finally, Tomek spills his guts to the object of desire. And that's when the story gets really interesting, as Kieslowski takes viewers for a wildly unpredictable, yet disturbingly credible, look at warring emotions.

Granted, the story could have come to an abrupt halt if Magda ever thought of pulling her shades, but that's a minor point in an otherwise inspired script.

Putting "Rear Window," "Passione D'Amore" and occasional dashes of humor in the blender, Kieslowski triumphs in this feature-length chapter of his "Decalogue" series (with each hour-long segment prompted by one of the Ten Commandments). By comparison, the powerful but flawed "Short Film About Killing" seems the work of a less-developed talent.

Instead of basic cross-cuts from confused murderer to well-meaning defense attorney, Kieslowski seesaws between the neighboring apartments, making viewers feel like conspirators in this unholy homage to voyeurism and obsession.

Superb casting completes the picture particularly with Olaf Lubaszenko's oddball protagonist. His average good looks play off shy, halting gestures, mixed with a perfect combination of giggles and violent outbursts. By steering clear of over-the-top cliches, he earns unexpected sympathy and understanding.

Looking like a young Lauren Hutton, Grazyna Szapolowska makes a fascinating amalgam of victim and victor. Her gradually realized metamorphoris is consistently arresting and duly provocative.

Along the way, "A Short Film About Love" cements Kieslowski's reputation as one of Poland's master filmmakers. meanwhile redefining the vagaries of l'amour.

SIGHT & SOUND, Spring 1990, p. 132, Jonathan Keates

After some two and a half millennia, art continues to relish the challenge presented by Aristotle's theory of the dramatic unities. If playwrights and story-tellers will not quite go the whole hog with Racine and Corneille, concentrating everything into a single intensely charged narrative episode, the appeal of the reductive principle, the action stripped to its ineluctable essentials, the work of art as bouillon cube or vitamin capsule, endures untarnished.

Krzysztof Kieslowski's *A Short Film About Love* is powerfully Aristotelian. Apart from three brief interventions by minor characters, the cast numbers only four and the action is exclusively located on a housing estate with its adjacent post office. The entire focus of the narrative is restricted to a single theme, and there are no concessions to decorative detail or attempts at creating a perspective for the protagonists beyond what we absolutely need to know in order to comprehend their motives, energies and illusions.

Tomek, desultorily studying Portuguese between stints as a postal worker, has become obsessed with thirty-year-old Magda who lives in the opposite apartment. Punctually at eight o'clock each night, when she returns home, he trains his telescope on her uncurtained windows, watching her dressing and undressing, the visits of her lovers and the sudden fluctuations in her mood.

At the post office he purloins her letters and at home he plagues her with heavy-breathing telephone calls. A yet bolder stratagem, calculated to interrupt the lovemaking caught in the frame of Tomek's jaundiced surveillance, brings in the gas man to repair the leak he has reported in Magda's kitchen. The chance for direct confrontation arrives when he gets himself a milk-round delivering bottles to her door.

When at length Tomek confesses all, in an ice-cream parlour where there is no ice-cream, and Magda takes him home, her response to his ardour is witheringly cynical. It is Tomek's attempted suicide which turns her into the watcher, scanning his window with a pair of opera glasses and pleading for scraps of news from his landlady, who herself has been observing the crucial meeting of the pair through the telescope.

Though Kieslowski has described himself as closest to the positions verging on realism, invoking the Italians, the Czechs and American cinema of the late 30s, the selective precision of this film effectively distances it from any such inspirations. The apartment block, one of those mournful East European concrete carcasses stained by rain and grime, is transfigured by Tomek's fantasy, as is Magda herself (the name has classic *femme fatale* overtones, handsomely emphasised by Grazyna Szapolowska's portrayal), whom the camera envisages as a slightly overblown Pre-Raphaelite siren, coddled within an affluence contrasted significantly with the drab interiors inhabited by the boy and his landlady.

Beautifully played by Stefania Iwinska, the latter becomes a figure of sibylline knowingness and resignation, her lopsided features lined with sardonic intelligence. Her counterpart in balancing the central couple is Magda's lover Roman (Piotr Machalica), seedy, dishevelled and ultimately incapable of seeing off his persistent rival.

As Tomek, Olaf Lubaszenko heightens our sense of the film as essentially an essay in romanticism. Thickset and puffy-faced, he projects a graceless ordinariness made vulnerable by innocence. His voyeurism is sad and hankering rather than gleefully lip-smacking, the half-comic, half-wretched passion of the swineherd for the princess. Only by rejecting it does Magda shed her sophistication and begin to understand.

Imaginative lighting does all, or nearly all. Kieslowski is clearly captivated by chiaroscuro tricks, flinging together veils of hostile, enveloping shadow and sudden, glaring fields of light, lamps in corridors, by bedsides, over doors and washbasins, the garish illumination of the apartment seen lurid and gleaming through the window, and the gloom of the poky little box from which Tomek peers inside it. Only daylight, muffled and discreet, seems radically out of touch with the prevailing mood.

Love-sickness is not something on which the late twentieth-century imagination chooses very often to dwell. In the cinema it has been either intolerably sentimentalised or else rendered absurd, so as to ward off embarrassment of an all too recognisable variety. Thus it requires a certain courage to direct the thrust of any narrative so entirely towards dignifying adolescent calf-love and humbling the beloved in the process. The cliché of older-woman-educates-younger-man is remorselessly stood on its head as Magda acknowledges the formulaic staleness at the heart of her scornful dismissal of Tomek's sincerity.

Like its predecessor, *A Short Film About Killing,* this is part of a sequence on the Ten Commandments. Which commandment is applicable here? Is it the one about covetousness or the prohibition of graven images? It doesn't matter that much. With or without its Biblical point of reference, Kieslowski's new film is a taut, sombre little masterpiece.

VILLAGE VOICE, 1/2/96, p. 52, Amy Taubin

Using a telephoto lens stolen from a film studio, a young man spies on a woman whose apartment windows face his. The man has the intense but slightly furtive manner of a badly socialized adolescent. He seems wrapped in a cocoon of sexual guilt. The woman is little more than a cliché of sexual liberation, her physical confidence edged with desperation. She's an artist of sorts, although the men who visit her are more interested in her body than her work.

The young man not only spies on the woman, he intercepts her mail (he works in the post office) and interrupts her lovemaking with anonymous phone calls. He even gets a second job as a milkman so he has an excuse to turn up on her doorstep. Eventually, he blurts out his feelings to her, whereupon, as a way of humoring him, she agrees to go out with him to a café. The consequences are radical and unexpected for both.

Like *A Short Film About Killing, A Short Film About Love* is expanded from a single section of *The Decologue,* a series based on the Ten Commandments that Kieslowski made for Polish television in 1989. Although *Love* lacks the intellectual complexity and gruesome power of *Killing,* it's still something of a tour de force. More minimalist than either *Rear Window* or *Peeping Tom,* the narrative is almost entirely distilled into the act of voyeurism. Kieslowski implicates us in his covetous gaze, allowing us to feel how the act of looking inspires erotically charged feelings of power and guilt. In his naiveté, the young man equates those feelings with love.

The woman knows better, and she rather callously disabuses the young man of his illusions. But for Kieslowski, the problem is not so much the young man's mistaking of voyeurism for love as the woman's cynical refusal of his adoration. The analysis of masculine desire is short-circuited by the cliché of the fallen woman's redemption through the male gaze. In that sense, *A Short Film About Love* previews the worst aspects of *Three Colors: Blue, White, Red.* Admirable though he is as a filmmaker, Kieslowski does not have my best interests at heart.

Also reviewed in:
NEW YORK TIMES, 12/29/95, p. C6, Stephen Holden
VARIETY, 10/5/88, p. 15
WASHINGTON POST, 10/13/95, p. F6, Rita Kempley

SHOW, THE

A Savoy Pictures release of a Rysher Entertainment presentation in association with Russell Simmons of a Tollin/Robbins film. *Executive Producer:* Stan Lathan and Rob Kenneally. *Producer:* Mike Tollin and Brian Robbins. *Director:* Brian Robbins. *Screenplay:* Jill Dove. *Sound:* Abdul Malik Abbot, Dwight Brown, Scott Evan, Evan Prettyman, Dave S. McJunkin, and Ben Moore. *Sound Editor:* Andrew DeCristofaro. *Production Designer:* Dave Lawson. *Art Director:* Tierien Steinbach. *Running time:* 90 minutes. *MPAA Rating:* R.

WITH: Craig Mack; Dr. Dre; Naughty by Nature; Run-DMC; Slick Rick; Tha Dogg Pound; The Notorious B.I.G.; Warren G; Wu-Tang Clan.

LOS ANGELES TIMES, 8/25/95, Calendar/p. 6, David Kronke

"The Show" is not much more than a glorified ad for its soundtrack album. As the filmmakers have clearly targeted this hip-hop documentary at the converted, they make no real effort to explore the music's sociocultural history in a thoughtful fashion. Assuming that fans will be content to see some behind-the-scenes movies of their heroes, there's not much effort to get the musicians to break out from behind their onstage facades.

Directed—if that's the word for it—by former TV sitcom actor Brian Robbins ("Head of the Class"), "The Show" is essentially an assemblage of footage of rappers discoursing—if *that's* the word for that—on whatever crosses their minds. Among those appearing are Dr. Dre, Naughty by Nature, Tha Dogg Pound, the Notorious B.I.G. and Warren C.

Robbins apparently didn't even try to coax insight from his subjects. Many just ramble along, words tumbling from their mouths in some of the same seductive cadences they use onstage. Nary a sentence passes without the use of one of three pet expletives or the phrase "Know what I'm sayin'?"

The film opens soberly, with brief footage of Snoop Doggy Dogg in court and rap impresario Russell Simmons—who calls success for some artists "a green light to hell"—visiting incarcerated rapper Stick Rick. The gangsta lifestyle is debated to a draw—more contempt is aimed at soft rhymers who ape the gangsta pose to sell records than those who actually pack heat and live on the edge.

A few entertaining moments are mined from this hodgepodge: Darryl McDaniel of Run-DMC recalls the horror he and his group felt when their handlers informed them of the moniker cooked up for the band; Warren G tries to negotiate business diplomatically while on tour, and a rap entourage to Japan turns up a number of cross-cultural laughs.

Other material is less newsworthy. We see a number of rappers inform the camera that their music tells us what's happening in the streets (based on several of the concert numbers, what's happening in the streets is that a few guys are trying to get crowds of people to put their arms in the air and wave them around). There's even a round-table discussion, much like the agents who gather to tell the story of "Broadway Danny Rose," reminiscing over the visionary who first coined the phrase "Yes, yes, y'all." At one point, Method Man blathers on about something or other and members of his entourage just tell him to shut up. Had the movie been made five or more years ago, when the music was just beginning to reach mainstream ears, this all might have seemed somewhat more revelatory.

Public Enemy—perhaps the most significant rap act in the music's history—appears only as a typed name on a page, an egregious oversight. And there's not much discussion of the numerous political attacks on the music.

The highlight is black-and-white concert footage of a special show staged for the film in Philadelphia. Unfortunately, the sound mix isn't great and songs aren't played out all the way through (at a recent screening, a group moan went up when the film interrupted a musical performance to return to its talking heads).

Ultimately, the unfocused windiness of the interview segments deplete the power of the music. Those interested should skip the middle man and go directly to the soundtrack. Know what I'm sayin'?

NEW YORK POST, 8/25/95, p. 49, Dan Aquilante

Most documentaries attempt to satisfy your curiosity; the best make you curious about the unknown. Somewhere in between lies "The Show."

Rather than continuing to allow "the establishment" to define rap as an obscene and violent black art, this film, by Brian Robbins, goes to the streets to document how rap became the hip-hop cultural revolution.

The picture is framed by The Show, a rap concert extravaganza held last December in Philadelphia which featured hip-hop heavyweights Notorious B.I.G., Wu-Tang Clan, Snoop Doggy Dog, Naughty by Nature, Warren G. and even old school's Run-DMC.

But don't think of this as a rap parallel to "The Last Waltz," Martin Scorsese's groundbreaking documentary/concert film about The Band. Though the black-and-white footage at the concert which expertly employs "300 cuts a minute" music video technique, The Show eventually becomes an aside to the interviews.

The color film used for the interviews with the leaders of the hip-hop nation is a startling contrast to the action inside the Armory, lending the B&W concert scenes an arty, yet unpretentious dream effect.

The two techniques separate what these men and women are on stage and what they are in life.

Hip-hop mogul Russell Simmons acts as a guide through this world. He, has street and business smarts, and is able to articulate the history, the philosophy and the direction the music is headed. The best interview segments are when Simmons speaks with the hip-hop elder statesmen like Kurtis Blow, Run DMC, Whodini and an incarcerated Slick Rick, who has most of the boast knocked out of him by the lengthy jail sentence he's serving.

These men all have a historical perspective and are able to break down the dynamics of the movement. Their accomplishments—good and bad—give their words a sense of credence absent from the many baby rapper interviews.

NEWSDAY, 8/28/95, Part II/p. B7, Jonathan Mandell

If now is the perfect time for a documentary about rap music—for rappers to explain their art, to answer their critics, to show their lives—"The Show" is not the perfect documentary.

Some in the big cast of big-time rappers do try to explain their art: "When we were out doing it," says Darryl McDaniels, DMC of Run-DMC, "it was just, fun."

Some do answer their critics, if only implicitly: "Hip-hop is the only way the rest of the country can learn what's going on in our neighborhoods," one says. "It's not like we're just going on a record and cursing."

Some do show, or at least tell, their lives: "If I wasn't in this studio," one says (minus the curses), "I'd be in your ... house ... slapping your kids around."

But "The Show" doesn't spend much time exploring or explaining, much less defending, the music's violent lyrics (and spends no time with its sexism). This is a concert film, a "That's Entertainment" for rap fans, who already know what they need to know about rap music, rap stars and hip-hop culture.

Unlike the old MGM cinematic medleys, there is a truncated, hodgepodge feel to "The Show"—a lot of rhyme but little apparent reason for the choice of rhymers. Why Craig Mack and Dr. Dre and Warren G, and not Queen Latifah, Ice-T, Ice Cube and Tupac Shakur? Of course, any good movie has to focus, but the selection seems random, arbitrary.

"The Show" is produced "in association with" Russell Simmons, the head of Def Jam Records, who could perhaps be taken as the focal point. He is certainly in the film a lot. We see him delivering words of supposed wisdom, and loyally visiting the prison where Slick Rick is serving time for attempted murder.

But Simmons disappears frequently, and we spend a long time with the 10-member Wu-Tang Clan from Staten Island as they tour Japan, where their Japanese fans dress, talk and even move like their hip-hop heroes. We also listen extensively to The Notorious B.I.G. and his mother, to Snoop Doggy Dogg and Tha Dogg Pound, and to Naughty by Nature.

A highlight of the film is a roundtable discussion (shown in too-short excerpts) about the origins of the music, featuring the grandfathers of rap, who are still pretty young themselves, including New York's own Afrika Bambaataa, Melle Mel and Kurtis Blow.

But the 20th or 30th time one younger rapper or another punctuates his rambling, repetitive comments with "You know what I'm saying?" the urge is great to reply, "Well, no."

VILLAGE VOICE, 8/29/95, p. 62, Gary Dauphin

The conventional wisdom about hip hop says that although there are countless essential cuts floating around in a good DJ's head one could carry a collection of consistently good *albums* in a small crate. *The Show* is feature-length proof of the thesis, a muddled documentary about a 1994 concert at the Philadelphia Armory that turns a high-profile lineup of acts and interviews into lengthy stretches of filler punctuated by flashes of what old-school rap legend Kid Creole calls the "buttah."

Buttah takes a little churning, but director Brian Robbins doesn't have a smooth or consistent stroke. *The Show* opens in conventional doc fashion—a series of talking heads dropping sound bites instead of science about hip hop-barely pausing before wandering into aimless bits, like Warren G.'s manager arguing on his cell phone, or a testy Russell Simmons (who coproduced *The Show)* paying a jailhouse visit to Slick Rick. The concert footage is reconstructed in a similarly haphazard manner, doled out in miserly samples that will only annoy audiences looking for beats and performances.

The faces that drop in and out of *The Show*'s overly unfocused frame belong to outsized celebrities, and the filmmakers don't do much except let the artists do their thing. Simmons's deadpan pronouncements never disappoint (his soliloquy about why he likes "tall, skinny bitches" is a convoluted marvel) and the extended sequence following Wu-Tang on tour in Japan sketches why artists go solo ("All you do is talk talk talk," says one of Wu-Tang's lesser lights to the Method Man). Unfortunately even with those patches of cream, *The Show* offers little info that isn't available in a BOXtalk interview segment. You may realize that Meth has a face that belongs on the big screen or wonder at the mysteries of Snoop Dogg's hair or Notorious Big's, well, bigness, but these are just errant blips, whose sudden movement crosses *The Show*'s static radar screen on their way somewhere else.

Also reviewed in:
CHICAGO TRIBUNE, 8/25/95, Tempo/p. 24, Rohan B. Preston
NEW YORK TIMES, 8/25/95, p. C5, Janet Maslin
VARIETY, 8/28-9/3/95, p. 66, Todd Everett
WASHINGTON POST, 8/25/95, p. D1, Richard Harrington

SHOWGIRLS

A United Artists release. *Executive Producer:* Mario Kassar. *Producer:* Alan Marshall and Charles Evans. *Director:* Paul Verhoeven. *Screenplay:* Joe Eszterhas. *Director of Photography:* Jost Vacano. *Editor:* Mark Goldblatt and Mark Helfrich. *Music:* David A. Stewart. *Music Editor:* Richard Whitfield. *Choreographer:* Marguerite Pomerhn-Derricks. *Sound:* Joseph Geisinger. *Casting:* Johanna Ray. *Production Designer:* Allan Cameron. *Art Director:* William F. O'Brien. *Set Designer:* Stan Tropp. *Set Decorator:* Richard C. Goddard. *Set Dresser:* Scott Kennedy, Michael S. Rutgard, and Sandra J. Renfroe. *Special Effects:* Burt Dalton. *Costumes:* Ellen Mirojnick. *Make-up:* David Craig Forrest. *Stunt Coordinator:* Gary Combs. *Running time:* 97 minutes. *MPAA Rating:* NC-17.

CAST: Elizabeth Berkley (Nomi Malone); Kyle MacLachlan (Zack Carey); Gina Gershon (Cristal Connors); Glenn Plummer (James Smith); Robert Davi (Al Torres); Alan Rachins (Tony Moss); Gina Ravera (Molly Abrams); Lin Tucci (Henrietta Bazoom); Greg Travis (Phil Newkirk); Al Ruscio (Mr. Karlman); Patrick Bristow (Marty Jacobsen); William Shockley (Andrew Carver); Michelle Johnston (Gay Carpenter); Dewey Weber (Jeff); Rena Riffel (Penny); Melinda Songer (Nicky); Melissa Williams (Julie); Lance Davis (Bell Captain); Jack McGee (Jack the Stagehand); Jim Ishida (Mr. Okida); Ungela Brockman (Annie); Bobbie Phillips (Dee); Dante McCarthy (Carmi); Caroline Key Johnson (Nadia); Joan Foley (Jail Matron); Terry Beeman (Felix); Kevin Stea (Daryl); Sebastian La Cause (Sal); Lisa Boyle (Sonny); Alexander Folk (Booking Sergeant); Matt Battaglia and Teo (Andrew Carver's Bodyguards); Elaine van Betten (Versace Salesperson); Alexander Zale (Doctor); Irene Olga Lopez (Personnel Woman); Julie Pop (Nurse); Jacob Witkin (Caesar); Jana Walker (Secretary); Christina Robinette (Receptionist); Jim Wise (Cheetah Loudmouth); Michael Shure and Geoff Calla (Cheetah Drunks); Rick Marotta (Long-Haired Drunk); Paul Bates (Cheetah Bouncer); Michael Cooke (Casino Lecher); Jean Barrett (Change Girl); Gary Devaney and Gene Ellison-Jone (Texans at Spago); Fernando Celis (Hector); Robert Dunn (Chimp Trainer); Ashley Nation (Julie's Daughter); Cory Melander (Julie's Son); Sean Breen and Katherine Manning (Reporters); Elizabeth Kennedy (Photographer); Warren Reno (Crave Club Bouncer); Ken Enomoto, Y. Hero Abe, and Odney Ueno (Cheetah Customers); Kathleen McTeague and Kristen Knittl (Al Torres' Girls); Sage Peart (Paramedic); Gregory R. Goliath (Cheetah Bouncer); Michael Washington (Crave Club Heckler).

LOS ANGELES TIMES, 9/22/95, Calendar/p. 1, Kenneth Turan

Small minds may say that "Showgirls," the first NC-17 film to get a wide studio release, is lacking in other accomplishments, but don't you believe it. Actually, it's hard to know which of this film's several attainments is the most surprising.

First off, this nominally risqué story of naked ambition among Las Vegas showgirls has somehow managed to make extensive nudity exquisitely boring. Then it has bested some stiff competition to set new low standards for demeaning treatment of women on film. And, perhaps most boggling of all, it has made it possible for viewers to look longingly back on "Basic Instinct" as the golden age of the director Paul Verhoeven/screenwriter Joe Eszterhas collaboration.

Everything you feared it might be and less, "Showgirls" is a movie made to be exploited, not seen. Both in print and in the TV teaser trailers, this picture manages to appear more involving and provocative than it actually is. No one is expecting "Thirty-Two Short Films About Glenn Gould," but even in the pulp trash genre certain minimal standards must be observed.

Instead, perhaps hypnotized into somnolence by all that nudity, Verhoeven and Eszterhas have neglected to provide the kind of passion and energy this kind of material cannot exist without. Lacking the combustible Sharon Stone and Michael Douglas in leading roles, "Showgirls" descends into incoherent tedium. Though the filmmakers' incessant talk about vision, artistry and honest self-expression lead one to expect a sexually explicit biopic about the Dalai Lama, what is in fact provided is depressing and disappointing as well as dehumanizing.

And though much has been made about how extensively researched "Showgirls" is, its entire dramatic shape is lifted from previous films, with great chunks of everything from Eszterhas' own "Flashdance" to "All About Eve" to the Busby Berkeley-choreographed "Forty-Second Street" periodically crashing down on the proceedings like boulders.

What plot there is revolves around a young woman named Nomi Malone (Elizabeth Berkley) who arrives in Las Vegas from parts unknown intent on making her mark as a dancer. Unable to find employment in the city's more rarefied boîtes, she catches on in a sleazy spot called Cheetah's Topless Lounge, where extra money can be made via provocative "you can touch them but they can't touch you" lap dancing in the back room.

To the unaided eye, the pouty, hot-tempered Nomi (shrilly played by Berkley) comes off as an irritating, self-absorbed twerp. So it is a double shock to discover that "Showgirls" expects us to identify with this infantile individual as a sensitive seeker after self-esteem and not be surprised when everyone else in the film takes an inexplicable interest in her well-being.

This group begins with Molly Abrams (Gina Ravera), who works as a costumer at the classy Stardust and introduces Nomi to Cristal Connors (Gina Gershon), the headliner in the hotel's "Goddess" stage show, who calls everyone "darlin'" and can either be ruthless or accommodating, depending on which page the script is on.

And don't the men show an interest as well. Though director Tony Moss (Alan Rachins doing "Forty-Second Street's" Warner Baxter) is strictly business, more personal attention comes from the Stardust's entertainment director Zack Carey (Kyle MacLachlan) and James Smith (Glenn Plummer), a dancer inexplicably AWOL from New York's Alvin Ailey troupe, who thinks Nomi's got too much raw talent to be hustling laps.

While there can be no doubt that Nomi lusts after Cristal's job, "Showgirls" is so incoherent from a character point of view that the nature of almost every other relationship in the film is baffling. As to the picture's deeper concerns about the effects of venal Vegas on this young woman's soul, Nomi is such a termagant one wonders if the city is not in more danger than she is.

Given the subject matter, it's inevitable that "Showgirls" indulges heavily in partial and complete female nudity, all of it to negligible erotic effect. In fact none of the film's sexual antics, including a surly lap dance by Nomi, is any kind of improvement over the nudie-cutie antics of skin flick auteurs of decades past like Russ Meyer and Radley Metzger, who must be wondering why no one ever gave them $35-million budgets to work with. And as if treating women as no more than interchangeable bodies wasn't enough "Showgirls" includes a sickening scene of violent rape that will disturb anyone still awake by the time it appears on screen.

Of all the opportunities "Showgirls" missed, the saddest one is the inability to make good use of its NC-17 rating by turning out a genuine piece of erotica or even good hearty trash. Instead Verhoeven and Eszterhas have combined to make a film of thunderous oafishness that gives adult subject matter the kind of bad name it does not need or deserve.

NEW YORK, 10/9/95, p. 78, David Denby

"Nimpulls," my little boy calls them. In the course of the new Paul Verhoeven movie, *Showgirls*—which fancies itself a deeply felt drama of the moral redemption of a Vegas lap dancer —the nimpulls get quite a workout. So does the rest of the female anatomy. But especially the nimpulls. Chomped and iced, kneaded and yanked, and everywhere exposed, the poor things couldn't have received worse treatment from malignant twins. If nothing else, Verhoeven has shown us what big-budget fetishism looks like: "I like nice tits," as one of the characters (a woman) delicately puts it, to which her companion (another woman) responds, "I like *having* nice tits." Verhoeven and screenwriter Joe Eszterhas have announced that the movie should be taken as a feminist statement. One way they "empower" women is to make them sound like cloddish men.

Verhoeven and Eszterhas are quite sure they know what men "like"—and women too. What they may not know, however, is that some of us hate failing into the hands of monomaniacs. While preaching integrity at us, the movie offers such nutty scenes as the one in which the heroine, Nomi (Elizabeth Berkley), having succeeded onstage as a dancer, gives a press conference—in a transparent glitter suit. Or the one in which a fat burlesque comic, performing at one of the lesser Vegas clubs, punctuates her jokes by flapping her arms, which causes the top of her dress to fall down. Over and over, the dress falls off the same talentless old bawd. Is Verhoeven insane? Is he fourteen? The entire movie keeps flashing the audience. *Showgirls* isn't very erotic, but it is most definitely lewd. The sole critical question is this: Will *Showgirls* reside with *Valley of the Dolls* and *The Other Side of Midnight* in the pantheon of great trash? Will it be revered and parodied in every gay bar from New York to Hong Kong? The answer, I think, is no. *Showgirls* is too coarsely stupid to become a camp classic.

This is a movie not so much mounted as strung out. Everything in it is overwrought, frenzied, empty. The Dutch-born Verhoeven once made interesting films like *Soldier of Orange* and *The Fourth Man*. But in the United States, the director quickly arrived at the lowest possible estimate of Hollywood and of himself, and instead of making interesting movies, Verhoeven has made *RoboCop* and *Basic Instinct*. The land of opportunity! Verhoeven is getting away with his cynical mock-showmanship. Preposterous as it is, *Showgirls* may even be a hit (the first weekend offered mixed evidence). Those who don't get off on the nudity and the sex—or what passes for sex—will get off on moral outrage. Verhoeven and Eszterhas win either way.

As filmmakers, both men seem to have lost touch with any kind of reality. In *Showgirls*, the simplest acts explode in our faces like homemade firecrackers. At the beginning, Nomi, dressed like a hooker with tons of eyeliner and some sort of evil purplish wax on her lips, hitches to Las Vegas. When the driver who picks her up, an Elvis type with an open shirt, comes on to her, she acts as if she's surprised and pulls a knife on him; he grabs at the wheel in panic and almost causes a huge truck to turn over. Later, in Vegas, after Elvis departs with her suitcase, Nomi pounds on a car parked nearby and gets drop-kicked in the belly by the owner of the car, Molly (Gina Ravera), a black seamstress. Nomi spits blood and nearly gets run over; then she falls into Molly's arms.

And that's the most believable part of the movie. Elizabeth Berkley is tall, with a long, long, slender body, eyes that pop out of her face, and an attitude of boundless enthusiasm. At least it looks like enthusiasm: Verhoeven may well have lined her clothes with electric wires, for Berkley flings herself wildly in and out of rooms, and dancing onstage, she whirls, thrusts, and kicks, her arms and legs jerking like pistons. To my eyes, she looks less like a dancer than a piece of gym equipment putting itself through an aerobic workout, yet everyone in the movie is bowled over by her talent. Berkley even *eats* violently, assaulting defenseless bags of chips. Like the ice-pick-wielding Sharon Stone character in *Basic Instinct*, Nomi is Eszterhas and Verhoeven's idea of a liberated woman: She spends the whole movie turning on her heel and walking out on people, even people who are trying to be nice, and when she's mad, she pulls a knife and kicks men in the balls. After 30 years of revolution in the life of women, Hollywood gives us these ludicrous caricatures of strength—female Rambos with stiletto nimpulls.

Nomi wants to get onto the stage of the Stardust, a hotel that puts on elaborate topless shows, and she's awed by the star, Cristal (Gina Gershon), who bursts out of a volcano and is surrounded by dancers grabbing at one another and removing whatever costume remains. There's another number, even better, featuring motorcycles and topless women in black leather. This, apparently, is the summit: show-business heaven. Verhoeven and choreographer Marguerite Pomerhn-Derricks stage these peculiar routines with grim determination and a stunning absence of irony. Didn't anyone notice that the numbers are a jerk's idea of erotic spectacle-kitsch monstrosities? Perhaps not. Insensitivity may have shaded into insensibility. A good part of the plot—an elaborate rivalry between Cristal and Nomi on the dance floor and in bed—has been lifted from one of the most familiar movies ever made, *All About Eve,* a bit of hijacking that suggests the filmmakers don't care what anybody thinks of them.

If made with even an ounce of affection, *Showgirls* could have worked. The tawdry, hustling milieu has a gamy fascination; the movie might have turned into a rowdy backstage musical. Working in the rear alleys of the sex trade, a director like Jonathan Demme or Robert Altman might have brought out the pathos and the humor in the tawdriness. Potentially, a long sequence in which girls are selected as dancers, trained on the spot, and then thrown into a stage show is a good one. But Verhoeven and Eszterhas treat everything with slick brutality, and one's enjoyment freezes. Most of the dramaturgy is at the level of the more flagrantly obvious soap operas, in which the characters are always denouncing or seducing one another. The snarling dialogue—"I'm erect, why aren't you?"—sounds like Jacqueline Susann rewritten by an idiot. If ever a movie needed a star and a few familiar faces, it's this one, but Verhoeven cast the whole movie with second-raters, which makes the material colder and more remote—more like pornography.

To make ends meet, Nomi works in the more relaxed atmosphere of the Cheetah Club, where the dancers wrap themselves around poles and occasionally, in the velvet back room, around individual customers. Cristal shows up with her lover, Zack (Kyle MacLachlin), the director of entertainment at the Stardust. In what is supposed to be a devastatingly perverse moment, Cristal, who has a decided interest in Nomi, pays for the young dancer to perform a lap dance upon Zack. (Lap dance *upon*? Or is it *with*? No copy editor can help me this time. In any case, she lap-dances him.) Elizabeth Berkley has the legs for lap-dancing, if not for dancing, and Kyle MacLachlan's helpless excitement as she snakes herself around him is amusing to watch—it's the one truly sexy moment in the movie. As for the rest, there's an immense amount of teasing and boasting, until at last we get a lovemaking scene between Nomi and Zack in his swimming pool, a very large, very gaudy pool indeed, surrounded by neon palm trees and fish mouths spraying water. As Nomi thrashes about, making waves, we get the funniest of the big Hollywood orgasms, a real lollapalooza.

We can laugh, but anyone who actually sits through the movie can't help feeling a voyeur. The crumminess may be intentional, a way of forcing complicity on the audience. *Listen, Buster, if it's so terrible, why don't you get up and leave? You're hooked, aren't you?* Okay, we admit it, we're hooked, but how about *them?* Judging by the filmmakers' remarks to the press, they have convinced themselves that *Showgirls* is a moral fable. They put on a $40 million burlesque show and announce, as Eszterhas said, that it contains "almost a deeply religious message." Why religious? Because Nomi, an ex-hooker, wins everything and then, turning her back yet again, walks away from her triumphs. She loses her job but gains "herself"' (whatever that might be). One senses the creation of a self-justifying myth: Eszterhas and Verhoeven may think that they can turn a trick and then walk away. But they can't. This is their second job of whoring together, and Eszterhas has also written the upcoming *Jade,* which is about a therapist by day and hooker by night who is suspected of murder. The pay is good, and the boys appear to enjoy the life. If the film's a hit, they'll be back on those illegal streets soon enough.

NEW YORK POST, 9/22/95, p. 45, Thelma Adams

My first impression of Paul Verhoeven's bit of NC-17 naughtiness, "Showgirls," was that it was about one thing: breasts. There was no story. Then I realized: breasts are the story. They just aren't news in my neighborhood.

This unintentionally funny, two-hour-plus, big-budget porn-fest lifts and separates breasts small, round, pointed, painted and spangled.

Welcome to screenwriter Joe "Flashdance" Eszterhas' locker room fantasy. Little is left to the imagination—nor is there much imagination to Joe E.'s multi-million-dollar script.

Call it "Fleshdance" or "Rocky" with a G-string, "Showgirls" is an American Dream retread about a talented nobody who moves to the metropolis to make it big and gets that once-in-a-lifetime shot at fame. The only twist here is that the city is Vegas, the dream is to be a legit dancer and the heroine's costumes tear away at the drop of a pastie.

Bare-assed bad-ass Nomi—sounds like "know-me"—thumbs into Glitter Gulch. She's a classic Eszterhas dreamgirl: blonde, blessed with much cleavage, fast with a knife and hostile as hell.

As Nomi, former TV teen star Elizabeth Berkley's prime asset is her ability to seem completely at ease with nothing but the sheen of sweat between her and the camera. When pressed into emotional service, she's a flounce-and-cry-and-pout-and-primp actress who emotes with her lip gloss.

Nomi starts off as a stripper—there are endless scenes of a naked Liz licking a metal pole and simulating sex with her stripper sisters—but aspires to art. Or a reasonable facsimile: dancing topless at a Stardust Hotel revue.

Enter Cristal (Gina Gershon), the reining topless star at the Stardust and her casino honcho/honey Zack (Kyle MacLachlan). Cue the "All About Eve" catfight, Nomi claws her way to the top, titillating her rival in the patented Eszterhas lesbian twist, before toppling Cristal off her dominatrix boots and onto her aging buttocks.

Decadent enough? "Showgirls" caters to the audience's most "Basic Instinct," the movie that first united Verhoeven and Eszterhas. Nomi's major moral conflict is keeping one step ahead of whoring—a struggle both director and writer seemed to have made peace with on their list collaboration.

"Showgirls" might have been produced by a studio, but it's only skin-flick deep.

NEWSDAY, 9/22/95, Part II/p. B3, Jack Mathews

Worst Movie of the Year is not a title to bestow lightly, not with a full three months remaining on the competition calendar. But some films are so spectacularly awful, so bereft of quality writing, directing and acting, there is simply no reason to wait.

Ladies and gentlemen, may I present, Mis Take, 1995 ... Paul Verhoeven's "Showgirls."

First things first. Yes, the much-anticipated first wide-release NC-17 movie is dirty. There are scenes of lap dancing, where a naked woman grinds her bottom on the lap of a paying customer until he yodels. There's a sex scene in a swimming pool conducted with such ferocious athleticism, it could become a medal event in the Olympics. (Nice finish. I give them a 9.8!) And the emcee at the topless Chi Chi Club, where much of the action takes place, is a 300-pound woman who flashes her breasts by flapping her arms, and tells jokes about her own wrinkled folds.

"Showgirls" is a con job, not a movie. Writer Joe Eszterhas, who has been getting $3 million-plus per script since "Basic Instinct," has cranked out something a high-school senior would be embarrassed to submit to Penthouse, and Verhoeven, who brought "Basic Instinct" to life, directed it with the horny enthusiasm of a sailor locked in a brothel.

The story, about a young woman (Elizabeth Berkley) who ascends from destitute drifter to Las Vegas lap dancer to Stardust Hotel chorine to "Goddess of The Strip," is a combination of "A Star Is Born," "All About Eve" and "Debbie Does Dallas." There is no plot, as such. She comes, she sees, she takes, she learns, she leaves.

There is a disgustingly violent rape scene, but it doesn't involve Berkley's Nomi Malone. There are no murders, no crooks and no mysteries, unless you actually care whether Nomi sleeps with the bisexual, coke-snorting diva (Gina Gershon) she is determined to replace, or if you share Stardust entertainment director Kyle MacLachlan's curiosity about Nomi's previous employment history. (Hint: Everytime someone suggests she's a hooker, she smacks 'em.)

Berkley, a willowy blonde with a glazed Little Annie Fannie look, dances with more abandon than talent, and cannot act at all. She goes through a range of emotions that includes anger, exhilaration, love, pain, tenderness and hostility. Unfortunately, she does them all at the same time, usually while nude, and often while licking a pole.

Not that anybody else is putting on an acting clinic. Eszterhas' dialogue is howlingly bad, and Verhoeven's mind seems to have been somewhere else when the actors were reading it. The movie looks great, with such elaborately tacky stage-show sets and costumes, you get the sickening feeling that you're actually there.

But Verhoeven, who made several sexually explicit Dutch movies before getting Sharon Stone to cross her legs in "Basic Instinct," was apparently more interested in seeing how much flesh he could pack into the movie than he was in telling a genuine story.

In any event, all hopes of "Showgirls" dashing the myth that there is no mainstream audience for adults-only movies are dashed themselves. If the movie has an audience at all, it will be men who already hang out at topless bars, or curious teenage boys who figure it will be easier to sneak past an usher than a bartender.

SIGHT AND SOUND, 1/96, p. 51, Claire Monk

A young woman, Nomi, hitches to Las Vegas, determined to succeed as a dancer. The driver who gives her a lift says he may be able to find her work, but vanishes with her suitcase. Losing all her cash in a gaming machine, she vandalises a car. Its owner, a young black woman, Molly, beats her up but, after hearing of Nomi's predicament, takes her into her home. They become best friends, and Nomi finds work stripping at the Cheetah Club, where lap-dancing is offered. Seeing Vegas' most extravagant erotic cabaret, *Goddess*—where Molly works as a dresser—fires Nomi's ambitions, and when Molly introduces her to the show's star, Cristal Connors, Nomi and Cristal instantly become keen rivals.

Nomi meets James, a black professional dancer, but when he admits to being aroused by her dancing, she deliberately provokes a fight between him and another man, and rejects his attempts to date her. Cristal comes to the Cheetah with her lover Zack, a senior member of *Goddess'* management. Nomi refuses when they offer her $100 for a private lap dance in the backroom, but the Cheetah's manager, Al, forces her to accept. Nomi is invited to audition for *Goddess,* but is humiliated to find Cristal watching. She storms out but still lands the job. She rushes to James to share her news, but he is in bed with another stripper. He repents, but she snubs him in favour of a lift from Zack. The jealous Cristal plies Nomi with champagne, makes sexual advances and humiliates her by feeling her breasts.

Sabotage causes Cristal's understudy to break her leg. Nomi invites herself to Zack's house and initiates frenzied sex in his pool. He gets her the job as the new understudy—but takes steps to investigate her past. Told that she will not be the understudy after all, Nomi covertly pushes Cristal downstairs, giving her a compound fracture—and gains the starring role in *Goddess.* Molly at first refuses to attend a lavish party for the new star, but relents when she hears that her idol, rock star Andrew Carver, will be there. At the party, Molly and Andrew seem mutually attracted, but then he and his two bodyguards viciously rape her. Preventing Nomi from calling the police, Zack reveals that he knows of her traumatised past and convictions for soliciting and possessing crack. Going to Carver in disguise as a whore, Nomi assaults him with a knife and hitches out of Las Vegas.

As is clear from the plot summary alone, director Paul Verhoeven and screenwriter Joe Eszterhas's first collaboration since *Basic Instinct* is driven by preoccupations other than psychological and narrative credibility. At the end of the screening I attended, the audience emerged in a half-derisive, half-dazed mood. Derisive because *Showgirls'* ludicrously crude dialogue, acting and sexual imagery invites the laughter of disbelief (Nomi has only to step naked into Zack's pool for stone dolphins to ejaculate water and champagne to overflow); dazed because after two hours the film's relentless tits-in-your-face display—intensified by Verhoeven's trademark high-impact visuals comes to feel like a never-ending nightmare. Coming at a moment when Verhoeven's reputation as an auteur is on a roll, *Showgirls'* failure to attract a big star cast—let alone US audiences—tells its own story.

Although the hype around *Showgirls'* status as the first major studio picture to be released with a US NC-17 certificate might lead you to think otherwise, it's not the subject matter itself that offends. Atom Egoyan's recent *Exotica*, which also has plenty of female nudity, is proof enough that the darker undercurrents of the psyche, which find their outlet in the buying and selling of sexual illusion, can generate a subtle, complex and humane cinema. What really repels here is the deep moral corruption of what the press notes refer to as Verhoeven and Eszterhas's "vision" and the perverse conception of sexuality and human relationships which their film naturalises.

Eszterhas plunders the *A Star Is Born* school of showbiz narrative not to satirise it but to abuse it. Through the doggedly persistent James, who functions as a token moral commentator on Nomi's values, the script dimly acknowledges the limitations of Nomi's career goal—to snarl her way through a pseudo-lesbian routine in a look-but-don't-touch upmarket show as opposed to snarling her way through a similar routine in a strip dive. Yet everything else about the film requires us to suspend this knowledge and identify with her 'progress'. The film presents James as sincerely believing in Nomi's natural talent as a dancer; but the message we gain from Nomi's rejection of him is that such a valuing of the authentic self over the commodified self and of erotic self-expression over commodified sexual display is to be despised. Indeed, it is by repeatedly exploiting herself as a sexual commodity that Nomi achieves domination and success, and when we finally see James dancing it turns out that he too works in a sex show.

Showgirls' would-be-Sadeian conception of female sexual 'power'—in which sex is fundamentally a weapon that women wield over men—is not only expediently self-justificatory in a film which ceaselessly exploits its female performers, but is itself milked for maximum voyeuristic potential by a set of visual codes culled straight from porn. Nomi twice pulls a knife on a man—once when the driver who gives her a lift to Vegas makes a very mild pass at her, and later in vengeance on the ludicrously-imagined rock star Carver. In both cases, Verhoeven ensures that she also exposes her breasts; thus the nominal message that Nomi is not to be messed with is subsumed beneath another message that her knife and her anger mean nothing because they are simply part of the sexual spectacle. If this sounds bad, *Showgirls'* voyeuristic exploitation of relations between women beggars belief: predictably, the snarling rival between Cristal and Nomi has clearly been conceived entirely to yield a series of butch-femme catfights, and even Nomi's friendship with Molly constantly teeters on the verge of lip-glossed pseudo-lesbianism.

It hardly needs stating that the one thing this endlessly prurient film never shows is female sexual pleasure. Like the spectacularly-staged numbers in *Goddess,* the fictional show which makes Nomi a star, the only fully consummated sex act in which we see her participate—with Zack in his pool—is a display of choreographed gymnastics from which any sense of inner sexuality is absent. Feature-film debutante Elizabeth Berkley, who plays Nomi, combines the non-personality and permanently gaping mouth of an inflatable doll with weird mood swings that are presumably meant to hint at Nomi's crack-addicted past—but then a director who sends her hitchhiking with her breasts hanging out and shopping in little more than a Wonderbra is clearly driven by considerations other than realism. "You'll love the music and the dance and the message will find an echo in your hearts," Eszterhas is quoted to have declared in a ludicrous defence of the movie. One wonders which of *Showgirls'* messages he had in mind.

TIME, 10/2/95, p. 74, Richard Corliss

What gets a movie the dread NC-17 rating these days? Normally the reasons children are forbidden to see films are explicit sex and spectacular spasm of violence. In the case of *Showgirls,* though, the list of no-nos might read, "Obscene level of incompetence, excessive inanity in the story line, gross negligence of the viewer's intelligence, a prurient interest in the quick buck."

Showgirls, a Las Vegas sex-and-dope opera from the *Basic Instinct* team of Joe Eszterhas (writer) and Paul Verhoeven (director), is one of those delirious, hilarious botches that could be taught in film schools as a How Not To. It tells the story of edgy, ambitious Nomi Malone (Elizabeth Berkley), a Vegas newcomer who gets a job as stripper at a seedy club, then screws her way to the star spot in a hotel revue, over the backs and other body parts of her rivals, notably headliner Cristal Connors (Gina Gershon).

The first NC-17 movie to be widely released since the rating was devised in 1990, *Showgirls* opened last week on 1,388 screens. Though many newspapers typically do not run ads for NC-17 films, only a few (including the major dailies in Oklahoma City and Fort Worth, Texas) refused to carry the *Showgirls* pitches. United Artists' high box-office hopes were stoked by avid interest in a teaser cassette in video stores, and by a million visitors a day to the *Showgirls* Website.

The risks are high. The $40 million film has no stars and has been critically drubbed. Its sole market value, beyond the Eszterhas-Verhoeven brand name, is its rating—the one most directors so fear that they will scissor their films (as Verhoeven did with *Basic Instinct)* to avoid getting it. *Showgirls* wears this stigma as a badge of honor and a sales pitch. "Leave your inhibitions at the door," the ads blare. Translation: Dirty movie ahead.

Would that it were. Hollywood films often wallow in bloodlust and sexual smirking—it's the Kingdom of Leer—but genuine eroticism is hard to find. Maybe Verhoeven is right when he says, "Americans have a problem accepting sexuality. American society is more impregnated with

Christian beliefs." And to those who find the very idea of sex unholy, it may be as pointless to prefer the erotic to the lurid as to choose a call girl over a hooker. But *Showgirls* is cold, antierotic. It just ain't sexy; it's only X-ie.

Verhoeven and Eszterhas may have needed the R rating after all. When they made *Basic Instinct*—a sexy R movie—they deployed atmosphere and innuendo to complement Sharon Stone's swank star turn. Here, with an NC-17 rating, the lads go slack; they let pubic hair and menstruation jokes do all the work. Since their leading lady can't act or dance or dazzle the camera, they've got problems they apparently didn't want to solve.

We don't blame Verhoeven, the director of two sleek, inventive Hollywood fantasies *(RoboCop, Total Recall)*, for making this movie—though we're surprised he can bear to watch it. The real culprit is Eszterhas, swami of the High Concept. He found Nazis in *The Music Box* and white supremacists in *Betrayed*, but cogent drama in neither. His favorite plot hook, sexual mutilation, bore rancid fruit in *Jagged Edge, Basic Instinct* and *Sliver*. At least those three had some sick kick to them. But if his women characters aren't psychos or sex-crime victims, the scripts get shrill and turgid. After an hour of naughty chat in *Showgirls*, you'll start hoping for somebody to kill somebody.

Eszterhas must be great at pitching stories, because the screenwriting craft eludes him. A mild gag here—the mispronouncing of Gianni Versace's name—is tortured into an endless motif. Nomi has a clouded past, but that doesn't explain why she is such a gratingly annoying creature. The giddiest moment in this *All About Evil* by way of *42nd Street* comes when a club owner is asked whether the revue should close down because the star is out sick. "Not a chance!" he actually says. "The show goes on!"

Eszterhas has urged teenagers to use fake IDs to get into his movie, to which Hollywood czar Jack Valenti declares, "Someone who would make that statement needs professional counsehng—it's so palpably stupid." The screenwriter also insists the film has a modern, even feminist moral: "The message is that you don't have to sell your soul to make it."

Which only proves he is as good at disinformation as he is at disentertainment. Nomi gets one job after having sex with the hotel's entertainment director (Kyle MacLachlan) and a better one after pushing the headliner down a flight of stairs. She has no soul to sell, no morals to corrupt. Kinda like the film. For 2 hrs. 11 min., *Showgirls* offers a slumming party inside the moviemakers' libidos. Ladies and gents, no matter how curious or horny you think you are, you don't want to be there.

VILLAGE VOICE, 10/10/95, p. 74, Georgia Brown

Your *Showgirls* review comes a week and a half late since distributors wouldn't screen their soft-core dud until the day before opening it. Crafty move. I had to go to a real theater where I discovered that admission is now eight dollars. Thirty or so single men also showed up, many in nifty suits fresh from the office. Three or four women joined us—perhaps the types screenwriter Joe Eszterhas says he was hoping to reach with his tale of a sex worker "who saves her own soul". Straightfaced, Eszterhas complained to Spike Lee (hosting *Larry King)* that MGM had "tawdryized my film." Jesus, this movie is depressing. They say *Kids* turns you off sex.

Elizabeth Berkley, who plays stripper Nomi Malone, looks to be either an android or a surgical wonder. Watching Paul Verhoeven's big ballooning closeups—*Showgirls* is shot in the style of a chintzy ($40 million) daytime soap—you keep searching for signs of life in the plastic universe of her visage. A hot-tempered bimbo out of nowhere, Nomi arrives in Vegas to make her way. One minute she's a shrewd, distrustful bitch pulling a knife on a guy who comes on to her; the next, she's a silly naïf falling for his con game.

I'm not one of those smitten with Verhoeven and Eszterhas's *Basic Instinct,* though I'm grateful for their bringing forth comedian Sharon Stone. This is by way of saying that, next to *Showgirls, Basic Instinct* is a kitsch masterpiece. If Russ Meyer had made it, *Showgirls* it might've been decent camp. If Joe Mankiewlcz had made it, it would've been *All About Eve.*

The best parts (I'm grasping at straws) feature Cristal (Gina Gershon, who looks a bit like Ruth Roman), the movie's Margo Channing and star stripper at the (relatively) high-class Stardust Hotel. Cristal has a foul mouth, a butch come-on, and a cute way of purring *darlin'.* She immediately picks out Nomi as her type (in a double sense) and begins toying with her. Cristal drags her club promoter-boyfriend Zack Carey (Kyle MacLachlan) to the sleazy Cheetah where Nomi strips, and offers the girl $500 to lap dance on Zack. (I found out what lap dancing is: about what it sounds like.) Given some steals from Adrian Lyne's opus as well as the level of Nomi's onstage and on-lap moves, the picture could be called *Thrashdancing*.

On *Larry King*, Jack Valenti "had to admit" that *Showgirls* was made with consummate Hollywood artistry and style—a giveaway that Valenti preaches values and ratings while flagrantly flacking the product. (The Valenti-Eszterhas roadshow, of course, is a setup.) I'd hoped *Showgirls* might at least be slummy fun, but it's shoddy and grim. Near the end there's a gang rape so ugly, so out of place in a camp comedy, that it can *only* be meant to stoke sick psyches.

Also reviewed in:
CHICAGO TRIBUNE, 9/22/95, Friday/p. C, Michael Wilmington
NEW REPUBLIC, 10/23/95, p. 29, Stanley Kauffmann
NEW YORK TIMES, 9/22/95, p. C1, Janet Maslin
VARIETY, 9/25-10/1/95, p. 91, Todd McCarthy
WASHINGTON POST, 9/22/95, p. D7, Rita Kempley
WASHINGTON POST, 9/22/95, Weekend/p. 43, Desson Howe

SISTER MY SISTER

A Seven Arts Releasing release of a Film Four International presentation in association with British Screen of an NFH production. *Producer:* Norma Heyman. *Director:* Nancy Meckler. *Screenplay (based on her play "My Sister in This House"):* Wendy Kesselman. *Director of Photography:* Ashley Rowe. *Editor:* David Stiven. *Music:* Stephen Warbeck. *Sound:* Chris Munro. *Sound Editor:* Glenn Freemantle. *Casting:* Sarah Bird. *Production Designer:* Caroline Amies. *Art Director:* Frank Walsh. *Set Dresser:* Luana Hanson. *Costumes:* Lindy Hemming. *Make-up:* Jenny Shircore. *Stunt Coordinator:* Jason White. *Running time:* 102 minutes. *MPAA Rating:* Not Rated.

CAST: Julie Walters (Madame Danzard); Joely Richardson (Christine); Jodhi May (Lea); Sophie Thursfield (Isabelle Danzard); Amelda Brown and Lucita Pope (Visitors); Kate Gartside (Sister Veronica); Aimee Schmidt (Young Lea); Gabriella Schmidt (Young Christine).

LOS ANGELES TIMES, 7/14/95, Calendar/p. 4, Kevin Thomas

"Sister My Sister" is a flawless film of astonishing power and impact created from a steadily increasing tension combined with acute observation of human behavior and attention to detail. Julie Walters, Joely Richardson, Jodhi May and Sophie Thursfield make up a superb ensemble cast in this chamber drama, set in 1932, in which dark humor underlines dire events.

Director Nancy Meckler and writer Wendy Kesselman are every bit as meticulous as the villain of their piece, a French provincial widow (Julie Walters) obsessed with perfection in the care of her Le Mans townhouse.

The rigorous, spare style of "Sister My Sister" reflects its claustrophobic tale of sexual repression and power plays, as did Zhang Yimou's strikingly similar, "Raise the Red Lantern."

Both films take us into the closed pre-World War II of women. Walters' Madame Danzard is an exceedingly proper widow of awe-inspiring smugness and complacency. Except for the occasional outing and social event, she spends most of her life in her parlor, dictating orders to her exceptionally obedient, near-mute servant (Richardson) and relentlessly crushing the spirit of her near-adult daughter (Thursfield), whom she dresses like a child. Danzard is so caught up in herself that she's oblivious to the sarcasm of her miserable daughter's retorts.

Richardson's Christine has sufficient insight into herself to realize that she responds well to Madame's iron hand but not enough to realize that bringing her pretty younger sister (May) into the household could prove disastrous.

Initially, the move seems ideal: Madame will be getting two servants for the price of one, and Christine will be getting the companionship she craves. What Christine surely couldn't have anticipated is that she would find herself falling madly in love with her sister, who would respond to her feelings in kind. How long can two young women, overwhelmed by a grand passion, behave like robots?

The women of "Sister My Love," like the nobleman's indolent, competing wives of "Raise the Red Lantern," are virtually without alternatives to directing their energies toward destroying themselves or each other or both. The narrowness and formality of the existence of the women in both films is truly suffocating, and Meckler and Kesselman capture this atmosphere every bit as forcefully as Zhang Yimou did.

A phonograph is one of the exceedingly few reminders that the Chinese film is set in the '20s; electricity is Danzard's only concession to the 20th Century in her gloomy residence.

If Kesselman wrote four wonderful parts, then Meckler got four equally fine portrayals. In a radical change of pace, Walters, an irresistibly showy actress, reveals tremendous restraint, creating an almost comically monstrous woman. Her Danzard dominates the household, but Richardson dominates the film as a woman whose emotions are increasingly at war with her circumstances.

May is a lovely innocent undeservedly caught up in madness, and Thursfield is admirable as a woman who has only her wit to protest her lot in life. It is a testament to Meckler and Kesselman's cinematic sense and that of their crew that it comes as a surprise that "Sister My Sister," based on the same incident that inspired Genet's "The Maids," was first a play.

NEW YORK POST, 6/23/95, p. 39, Thelma Adams

"Sister My Sister" is high-class trash.

Directed by Nancy Meckler from Wendy Kesselman's screenplay, this sexually charged melodrama ripped from French headlines of the 1930s is part "Masterpiece Theater," part true-crime recreation a la "America's Most Wanted."

Two attractive sisters, Christine (Joely Richardson) and Lea (Jodhi May), serve Madame Danzard (Julie Walters), a provincial bourgeois widow, and her daughter, Isabelle (Sophie Thursfield).

The maids start off as perfect help—discrete, dependable, subservient but something starts happening in their room at the top of the stairs. The balance between the Madame and the sisters, between mistress and servants, goes awry, with grisly results.

The fact that Jean Genet based "The Maids" on the same story adds to the project's pedigree; the fact that it's about incestuous lesbian killers, always titillating, adds torrid tabloid appeal. The resulting film is a hothouse "Upstairs, Downstairs."

The actresses are beyond reproach. Julie Walters ("Just Like a Woman") makes the underwritten Madame Danzard spring to life. Danzard represses the sisters. She is, in turn, repressed by the society at large: trapped in a big house, in a tight collar, with no freedom of mobility. In an unguarded moment, Walters dances by herself in the parlor, showing there's more under her corset than meets the eye. But Danzard's only power—and pleasure—is her control over her daughter and her maids. She wields this power with a white glove and an iron fist.

Richardson and May make strong sister/lovers. The actresses subtly shade the many-layered relationship. They are competing siblings: one is the mother's favorite, the other the more accomplished; one protects but is subject to a violent temper, the other nourishes but suffers from a fundamental weakness. Within the partnership, both filial and sexual, they engage in their own tug-of-war of dominance and submission.

The two tawny actresses create appealing tableaux. Shot in golden light in the most attractive garret in all of provincial France with the sisters wearing hand-sewn lingerie that would make a Victoria's Secret model swoon, these scenes are too soft-core slick, too honeyed, too buns undone. They are simultaneously tasteful and atwitter with an "aren't we naughty" feeling.

The look of the movie is relentlessly rich—even the blood that bookends the story is a carpet-matching burgundy. The camera occasionally returns to a faucet dripping in slow motion in case we forgot that tensions are silently building deep within the house. The trouble is that they build too quietly. When the final atrocity occurs it seems anti-climactic. We were all so busy looking at the perfect hats, the amber light illuminating the fine lace, the golden-purple upholstery, we got distracted from the dirty little tale at the drama's heart.

NEWSDAY, 6/23/95, Part II/p. B4, John Anderson

Turn lesbian, turn lethal. It's the cinema's sexual pathology du jour (as seen, or implied, in "Heavenly Creatures," "Fun," "Only the Brave," et al.). But, on the other hand, it certainly does provide strong roles for women in film.

In "Sister My Sister," it provides four: Christine (Joely Richardson) is the severe, high-strung and ultra-efficient maid to Madame Danzard (Julie Walters), an imperious and delusional gentlewoman living with her repressed and dowdy daughter Isabelle (Sophie Thursfield) in provincial France, circa 1932. Enter Christine's sister Lea (Jodhi May), girlish, shy, the object of Christine's obsessive love and the unwitting catalyst for mayhem.

We know from the start that butchery is going to occur, and we soon deduce to whom. After a brief sepia-toned introduction to the young sisters (Aimee and Gabrielia Schmidt), we are led, backwards, down a flight of attic stairs, until the walls become speckled, then streaked, then smeared in blood; we see a twisted foot in a leather pump. The inference is that the garret and the stairs and the landing are all of one house. And in a way they are.

Based on the same Le Mans murder case that inspired Jean Genet's "The Maids" in 1948—and that was reported, when it occurred, by Janet Flanner in The New Yorker—this debut film by veteran stage director Nancy Meckler (formerly of Great Neck) highlights the lesbian aspects of the story: Under soft-core lighting and with much unseen, the sisters move from protective siblings to fevered lovers. Their upbringing, presumably, has something to do with this aberrant behavior: They speak, often heatedly, of their mother, who shipped them out to work, or to convent school, and who even now demands all of Lea's wages during their Sunday afternoon visits; there is a flashback of Christine's unrequited love for a nun.

But it's not quite enough to convince us that there isn't simply something organically amiss in Christine's psychology or that we're being told the whole story. Or that nobody knows.

This lack of dramatic development is a shame, because the acting is first-rate: Richardson's Christine is a raw nerve, wracked by unvented sexual heat and unresolved anger at her mother; Lea is an innocent, which in the warped atmosphere of chez Danzards makes her both aberration and prey. Isabelle, in her childish haircut and clothing, is being stunted by Madame, who lives a life of the (disturbed) mind. Walters makes her hateful in her self-absorption.

But does she make us want to kill her? No. Should her dictatorial approach to housekeeping make the sisters want to kill her? I don't think so. The denouement of "Sister My Sister" is shocking, not just because it's brutal but because we've been so ill-prepared for anything so feral. Even with that pump at the bottom of the stairs.

SIGHT AND SOUND, 12/95, p. 51, Lizzie Francke

In 30s provincial France, Christine—a servant in the house of a Madame Danzard and her daughter, Isabelle—is joined by her younger sister, Lea. Danzard is happy with the new recruit, who proves to be as industrious as her sibling. The sisters dote on one another, but there is something strange about their closeness. One Sunday, their affection for each other turns into a sexual passion. This illicit relationship, conducted in the attic, is their only respite from servitude.

When Isabelle gives Lea a candy, Christine becomes jealous. Talk of Isabelle's impending marriage only exacerbates her concern that Lea will be sent away to work for the young mistress in her new home. The sisters argue, but end up in a passionate embrace. Danzard begins to notice their strange behaviour. Tensions come to a head as the young maids alter Isabelle's dress and argue with Danzard about the length of the hem. Danzard becomes increasingly weary of their impudent behaviour.

On a day when the Danzards are out, a fuse blows while Lea is ironing a satin blouse. The house goes dark and the blouse is burnt. Terrified, the sisters retreat into the attic. Madame and Isabelle return, and are enraged by what they find. Madame makes her way upstairs where she meets Christine. The confrontation comes to a violent climax as Lea joins her sister in attacking the Danzards, finally hacking them to death. The sisters are found guilty of murder. A postscript explains that Christine died in an asylum while Lea served 20 years, later working as a chambermaid after her release.

Sister My Sister completes the quartet of films released in the UK this year that deal with the murderous desires of young women (the others are *Heavenly Creatures, Fun* and *Butterfly Kiss*).

Like director Peter Jackson's and writer Frances Walsh's 50s New Zealand story *Heavenly Creatures, Sister My Sister* is also based on a real life *cause célèbre* killing: the famous Le Mans case of 1933, in which two sibling servants hacked their employers to death. Jean Genet based his play *The Maids* on the same event, using the incident to explore ritualistic games of domination and submission, dwelling on class as much as anything else. Played as a pantomime of perverse role-playing, productions of *The Maids* often make a virtue of and comment on their own staginess (the 1974 film version directed by Christopher Miles starring Glenda Jackson and Susannah York for example, was all overblown staginess).

Sister My Sister also started out as a theatre piece. Writer Wendy Kesselman became obsessed with the story after reading a contemporary newspaper account. Her retelling is very much a 'straight' one which attempts to invest the story with psychological realism through references to a cruelly neglectful mother who left the sisters in a convent where they experienced further abuse. Thus Lea and Christine's incestuous relationship is read as founded on their dysfunctional childhood. The sister's become emotional props for each other as one repressive environment is replaced by another, the second being the Danzard household, with Madame's fastidious routines—she wears white gloves to check the furniture for dust. The tone is set by Madame's own rather strangely domineering relationship with her frumpy, dullard daughter, Isabelle.

As a play, *Sister My Sister* might have drawn power from the stifling intensity of the characters' situation. These four women find themselves locked in roles that are going nowhere, those above and below stairs each in their own way are prisoners in this gloomy house. The over-stuffed drawing room terrain of Madame and Isabelle—is not much different from the bare attic where Lea and Christine find respite. Certainly, the film renders these places similarly dark and unprepossessing. But, under Nancy Meckler's direction (this is her feature film debut), *Sister My Sister* seems less claustrophobic than awkward. While storywise it is a distant relative of *The Maids,* thematically it is closer to *Les Enfants terribles* or *Les Parents terribles* with their imploding domestic situations that hinge on sexual transgression as characters attempt to grasp and own each other. Indeed, Meckler could learn from the cinema adaptations (by Melville and Cocteau respectively) of those plays, both more charged with a terrifyingly dark and erotic intensity than hers. Instead, this chamber of horrors piece palls under the trembling portentousness of it all.

The script and acting styles, which might have worked on stage, simply foreground the artificiality without making a virtue of it, or exploring it in depth. Thus, the potentially grotesque elements of the piece end up being embarrassing, such as when Julie Walter's vain, self-important Madame turns on the radio and starts to dance across the carpeted drawing room. Such a misjudged moment robs the film of any tension that might have been established. It also makes a fool of Walters, a gifted actress who in the past has proved herself capable of more than just snappy comedy but is confined here to ungainly caricature. Meanwhile, Lea and Christine's descent into madness is blown by the breathy hysteria of Jodhi May and Joely Richardson's too wayward performances. For a story which is about the way individuals seek to control and dominate each other, *Sister My Sister* lacks the directorial control required to draw one in.

VILLAGE VOICE, 7/4/95, p. 54, Amy Taubin

During the heady post-World War II period in which Simone de Beauvoir published *The Second Sex,* French male intellectuals from Lacan to Genet were having their say about the Papin sisters, the provincial housemaids who, early in the 1930s, murdered their mistress and her daughter in a notably grisly manner. Nancy Meckler's *Sister My Sister,* the latest entry in the flourishing women-who-kill-in-pairs genre, adds nothing to existing meditations on the Papins, and as movies go, compares unfavorably to Rafael Zelinsky's *Fun,* Nick Broomfield's doc on Aileen Wuornos, and even to *Heavenly Creatures.* It's claustrophobic, minimalist narrative is a bowdlerized version of Chantal Akerman's *Jeanne Dielman;* its diffused, softly colored cinematography is pointlessly reminiscent of fashion photography by Deborah Turbeville.

Sister My Sister is nicely decorative and totally insubstantial. Certainly, symbiotic attachments occasionally end in suicide or murder. In this film (and probably in the actual case history), there are multiple symbioses between the sisters, who were incestuously involved; between the maids and their employer; and between the employer and her daughter. Why these particular involvements culminated in murder is no clearer at the end of the film than it is at the beginning.

That said, Joely Richardson delivers a stunningly psychotic performance and Jodhi May manages to spend most of the film paralyzed with terror without ever going over the top. Which is more than can be said for Julie Walters, although I suspect her jarringly farcical manner was just what the director wanted. Meckler and her screenwriter Wendy Kesselman (whose script is adapted from her stage play *My Sister in This House*) make an issue of leaving men out of the picture (men are, on two occasions, heard but not seen). The inevitable conclusion is that when women are left to their own devices, bad things can happen. Sometimes that's true, but so what? Kesselman said in an interview that when she saw a newspaper photo of the sisters, she knew she had to write about them. That haunting photo (which I've also seen) is worth more than this 89-minute film.

Also reviewed in:
CHICAGO TRIBUNE, 9/22/95, Friday/p. Q, John Petrakis
NEW REPUBLIC, 7/17 & 24/95, p. 34, Stanley Kauffmann
NEW YORK TIMES, 6/23/95, p. C14, Caryn James
VARIETY, 11/7-13/94, p. 47, Emanuel Levy
WASHINGTON POST, 9/1/95, p. F1, Rita Kempley
WASHINGTON POST, 9/1/95, Weekend/p. 31, Desson Howe

SMOKE

A Miramax Films release of an NDF/Euro Space production in association with Peter Newman/Interal. *Executive Producer:* Bob Weinstein, Harvey Weinstein, and Satoru Iseki. *Producer:* Greg Johnson, Peter Newman, Hisami Kuroiwa, and Kenzo Horikoshi. *Director:* Wayne Wang. *Screenplay (based in his short story "Auggie Wren's Christmas Story"):* Paul Auster. *Director of Photography:* Adam Holender. *Editor:* Maysie Hoy. *Music:* Rachel Portman. *Music Editor:* James Flatto. *Sound:* Drew Kunins. *Sound Editor:* Robert Hein. *Casting:* Heidi Lovitt and Billy Hopkins. *Production Designer:* Kalina Ivanov. *Art Director:* Jeff McDonald. *Set Decorator:* Karen Wiesel. *Costumes:* Claudia Brown. *Make-up:* Patricia Regan. *Running time:* 112 minutes. MPAA Rating: R.

CAST: Giancarlo Esposito (1st OTB Man/Tommy); Jose Zuniga (2nd OTB Man/Jerry); Stephen Gevedon (3rd OTB Man/Dennis); Harvey Keitel (Auggie Wren); Jared Harris (Jimmy Rose); William Hurt (Paul Benjamin); Daniel Auster (Book Thief); Harold Perrineau (Rashid Cole); Deirdre O'Connell (Waitress); Victor Argo (Vinnie); Michelle Hurst (Aunt Em); Forest Whitaker (Cyrus Cole); Stockard Channing (Ruby McNutt); Vincenzo Amelia (Irate Customer); Erica Gimpel (Doreen Cole); Gilson Heglas (Cyrus, Jr.); Howie Rose (Baseball Announcer); Ashley Judd (Felicty); Mary Ward (April Lee); Mel Gorham (Violet); Baxter Harris (1st Lawyer); Paul Geier (2nd Lawyer); Malik Yoba (The Creeper); Walter T. Mead (Roger Goodwin); Murray Moston (Waiter); Clarice Taylor (Granny Ethel).

CINEASTE, VOL. XXI No. 4, 1995, Leonard Quart

Paul Auster writes cool, enigmatic novels *(City of Glass, The Music of Chance)* about the mysterious patterns underlying our daily lives. His first screenplay, *Smoke*, functionally directed by Wayne Wang *(Chan is Missing, The Joy Luck Club)* from an Auster screenplay, is a literate fable set in Brooklyn in 1990.

At the center of the film's slight, digressive narrative are the relationships between a tough, street-wise, and quick-witted cigar store manager, Auggie (played effortlessly and utterly convincingly by Harvey Keitel), a blocked, emotionally wounded novelist, Paul (William Hurt), who is a frequent customer, and a too-articulate and smooth runaway black teenager, Rashid (Harold Perrineau, Jr.). Rashid is befriended by both Auggie and Paul, who become his surrogate fathers.

All the main characters in the film—which include Auggie's brassy, vulnerable ex-girlfriend, Ruby (an over-the-top Stockard Channing reviving an old Susan Hayward role), her raging, drug-addicted, pregnant daughter, Felicity (Ashley Judd), and Rashid's long-missing, one-armed father, Cyrus (a moving performance by Forest Whitaker)—are living out a variety of violent and contrived Hollywood melodramas. Solitary, intelligent Rashid, on the run from some dangerous street criminals, is in search of his ex-alcoholic father, who is trying to create a new life running a down at the heels garage upstate. An eye-patch-wearing, tight-skirted Ruby has solicited Auggie's help (she claims he's the father) in an attempt to rescue her self-destructive daughter. Fortunately, however, the film cares less about how these tabloid stories evolve than about how art can give some order and radiance to fragmented lives. It's the film's stiller moments that are its most moving ones. The turbulent, tearful confrontation between Rashid and a guilt-ridden Cyrus, for example, is less affecting than the silent, unstated reconciliation they reach afterwards while smoking cigars around a supper table.

The various stories are either enacted or told primarily with minimal camera movement and in long takes, medium two-shots, and tight close-ups. Wang's straightforward direction does little more than ploddingly subordinate itself to Auster's gracefully written dialog and monologs. The vision of the film is carried by Auggie and Paul, who tell stories and provide epiphanies about daily existence. Rashid is also a storyteller—a boy who constantly needs to fabricate fictions about his own painful life.

It's the ungrammatical, colloquial Auggie who is the most eloquent and wise character in the film, and who has more of an instinct for observation than Paul, the professional writer. In *Smoke* the creation of art is within the grasp of everyone, not just professional artists. In a beautifully rendered scene, one which captures the essence of the film, Auggie shows Paul the collection of photos he's taken every day of the same view of the street corner outside his cigar store. When Paul rapidly and blindly flips through the photos, saying that they all look the same, Auggie tells him that if a person looks more closely at what's around him, he learns to see a great deal. He'll at least perceive the minute shifts in light, for example, and gain some insight into the people casually passing by on the street each day. What he sees may not be dramatic or epic, but it's sufficiently unpredictable and illuminating to be the material of art.

In *Smoke* these stories and perceptions provide a pattern to the mess of life. The squinting, hesitant, uneasy, Brooklyn-accented Paul, played competently, but with too much self-conscious straining for effect by Hurt, tells stories about fathers and sons to Rashid. They link neatly to Paul's becoming Rashid's mentor and substitute father, and Rashid's helping heal Paul's emotional and creative paralysis. The film generally skirts and sanitizes the film's racial component; it's much too facile, even patronizing, for Paul and Auggie to become Rashid's understanding, white substitute fathers, filling the void left by the black father who abandoned him. Of course, *Smoke* does not pretend to be a social realist film about Brooklyn or America's complex and unyielding racial tensions and divisions. The social gap between the projects and a Park Slope apartment is acknowledged, but left unexplored. Auster and Wang's aim is to construct a fable about the power of stories to create a semblance of order in our lives, and, in this particular fable, race provides no real obstacle to human connection.

Smoke is in the tradition of the European art film (the work of Eric Rohmer comes to mind) rather than either mainstream Hollywood or independents, like Quentin Tarantino, whose stylish, much-praised works are totally enmeshed in and inspired by traditional Hollywood genre films. The virtue of *Smoke* lies in the vitality of its language and conversation (a rarity in contemporary American film) and the subtly casual and incidental quality of its narrative. These qualities grant the film its unique appeal, despite the absence of Hollywood staples like a tightly shaped, action-filled plot, kinetic editing, or a painterly *mise-en-scène*. The film, however, has awkward moments where dialog and narrative either meander aimlessly or strike an artificial note. In these scenes, the film feels merely like a clever construct, and its talk seems without any real point or substance.

Smoke's final scenes, however, are exquisitely conceived. Paul has been asked to write a Christmas story for *The New York Times* and, blocked, asks Auggie if he has a story for him. Auggie fluently relates the story of chasing a thief out of his store, and of finding the wallet he has dropped and deciding to return it. The address is of an apartment in a Brooklyn public housing project, solely inhabited by the thief's old, blind, black grandmother, who mistakes

Auggie for her grandson. Auggie assumes the role, and celebrates Christmas with her. The story is then wordlessly reenacted, in black and white, under the credits, with Tom Waits raspingly singing the apt and poignant "Innocent When You Dream" on the soundtrack. This sequence is shot with a resonant, magical spareness that Wang's generally unimaginative direction rarely displays throughout the film. At its best, *Smoke,* like its final tale, pays homage to talk and stories that not only delight and beguile, but also lend shape to the bruised, incomplete lives that we lead and barely comprehend.

LOS ANGELES TIMES, 6/9/95, Calendar/p. 6, Peter Rainer

The Brooklyn cigar store run by Auggie Wren (Harvey Keitel) in "Smoke" is Schmooze Central for the neighborhood gabbers and ne'er-do-wells. Auggie presides over the fray like a particularly indulgent bartender. He massages the foibles of his regulars.

Pokey and episodic, "Smoke" is a stroll with a few of those regulars. The screenwriter, Paul Auster, embellishing a short-short story of his that originally appeared as a Christmas Day op-ed piece in the New York Times, employs the film medium as an extension of his literary art. With director Wayne Wang, he's worked out a series of set pieces that play like resonant enigmatic doodles.

Auster on film doesn't always work. The last attempt, "The Music of Chance," was a hollow/hip exercise. Auster is a sly storyteller, though, and in "Smoke" he makes the deflations part of the movie's texture. A lot of dramatic stuff impends but nothing builds to a crescendo; time and again we're gently brought back to a bemused anticlimax.

Auster and Wang divide the film into five distinct yet overlapping stories. The divisions aren't really necessary, but they impose a structure on what is essentially structureless. What ties everything together—at least as a visual motif—is smoking. The characters in this movie at one time or another are all seen smoking cigars or cigarettes, especially when they are letting off steam or celebrating some new twist in the cosmos.

The cosmos have not been kind. Paul Benjamin (William Hurt)lives alone in a ratty apartment after the death of his wife in an act of street violence. Unproductive, morose, he befriends a 17-year-old street kid who calls himself Rashid (Harold Perrineau), allowing him a few days in his home. Cast out into the street once more, Rashid, on the run from local toughs, follows up a tip on the whereabouts Upstate of his long-lost father (Forest Whitaker). Auggie is visited by an old flame, Ruby (Stockard Channing), who wears an eye patch and claims they had a daughter (Ashley Judd) 18 years ago who is now a pregnant crack addict.

All this may sound garish, but Wang who overdosed on suds with "The Joy Luck Club," doesn't force anything here. The miseries are gently displayed; they're accepted as a part of life, just as the occasional outbursts of delight are. "Smoke" doesn't go very deep, but it's pleasantly ruminative. Its characters are trying to make some sense out of the passing parade without being trampled by it.

A key scene comes when Auggie shows Paul his photo album collection—photos taken in front of his store at the same hour every day for 14 years. At first the albums seem like a great sick jest. But, from photo to photo, Wang allows us to savor the subtle changes in mood and composition. At first Paul quickly flips through the snapshots but Auggie cautions him by saying, "You'll never get it unless you slow down." This could also stand as the movie's motto. It needs to be savored.

The actors get into the slowness. They're uniformly wonderful in a minor key. In her brief, explosive cameo, Ashley Judd tears into the mellow mood with acetylene-torch force. (The film needs her boost of rage.) Keitel gives another of his superb, detailed character turns; we can see in the way Auggie moves about his store or drags on his cigarette a whole history of dreams deferred. Hurt plays Paul as closed off yet frighteningly open to upset. Paul is the official storyteller of the piece but it's really Auggie and Rashid and Ruby who are the cleverest and most upsetting tall-talers.

Wang brings us gradually closer to these people, moving from master shots to, finally, immense close-ups. It's a rather simplistic technique, but it works here. It respects our hesitancy in getting too close to these people too soon.

"Smoke" is as illusory as a smoke screen and just about as wispy. But, like Auggie's photo albums, it bears watching. It's a sweet, forlorn little snapshot.

NEW STATESMAN & SOCIETY, 4/19/96, p. 33, Lizzie Francke

Smoke is a film to mull over, to chew on. It reminds us that American cinema can still have a quiet, thoughtful and compassionate centre. It is also one of the most perfect examples of the literary and cinematic fusing together. The film evolved after the director Wayne Wang (whose credits range from the wild, free-wheeling *Chan is Missing* (1982) through to the more sedate and dependable adaptation of Amy Tan's *The Joy Luck Club* (1993)) read Paul Auster's "Auggie Wren's Christmas Story" in the *New York Times:* captivated, Wang asked the novelist to collaborate on a screenplay. Smoke is very much the product of that creative partnership. Even the opening credits—"a film by Wayne Wang and Paul Auster"—reject *auteurism*.

In the novelist's original piece, a writer, named Paul recounts the telling of a tale, which might or might not be of the tall variety, by his friend and fellow-Brooklynite Auggie Wren, who owns the neighborhood cigar stop. Somehow one can imagine Auster and Wang sitting over a snack in a local coffee shop, the yarn-spinning back and forth between them as they work on the screenplay and turn words into substantial images, with the characters of Auggie and Paul (played in the film by Harvey Keitel and William Hurt respectively) fleshed out with light. On one level one can read the film to be about the smokescreen of storytelling—it's ephemeral, diffused in the very air we breathe, but it's very necessary to life.

The opening shot, in which a train trundles along, a grey New York City looming in the background, marks out *Smoke*'s territory. This is Brooklyn, on the right side of the tracks with Manhattan a distant, and ultimately irrelevant, landmark. Wang and Auster's film is centred on a particularly vibrant community with Auggie's smoke shop the street corner hangout where the local men—the writer Paul included—meet for a cigar and a rap with the weathered-looking, voluble owner. It's the kind of set-up one finds at the heart of any "slice of life" soap opera and in a way *Smoke* is a soap in miniature, built upon the wisp-like but durable threads of various characters' stories which a serial would criss cross and spin out to infinite length. (But, going against the grain of the genre, it is a very male piece in which men's emotional responsibilities to those around them are dwelt upon fully.) There is even a soap-like quality to Auggie's hobby of taking a picture of his shop—"a record of my spot"—everyday, same place, same time. "Tomorrow and tomorrow and tomorrow, time creeps on its petty pace," mutters Auggie, as he opens up volumes of these pictures that stretch back over decades. Each is still like a little episode full of detail and life that needs to be pursued thoughtfully. As a collection it provides an astonishing sense of continuity.

As Paul flicks feverishly through Auggie's albums, he is instructed: "You'll never get it, if you don't slow down." In the same way, Smoke invites such contemplation, with the smallest details given at different moments all adding up to build a fuller picture. This way one gleans bits and pieces about those who inhabit the tale. One discovers that Paul is a widower—his pregnant wife Ellen was shot dead outside Auggie's shop during a robbery. Her smiling face appears in one of Auggie's pictures, prompting a moment that is weighed down by Paul's terrible grief as he broods on this fragment of his beloved wife.

In the recent Guardian Lecture at the National Film Theatre, Paul Auster showed three clips of films that have mattered to him. Small segments of Renoir's *La Regle du Jour,* Ozu's *Tokyo Story* and Ray's *The World of Apu* were screened, each clip pivoting on an intense emotional moment between two people, each done with a spare style that allowed for so much in the smallest of gestures. *Smoke* shares the same economical sensibility. One of the final shots in the film, in which the camera lingers exquisitely on Keitel's quizzical smile, demonstrates just how much can be packed into a single moment. It is all about the long drawl, the slowing down.

In another way, *Smoke* is a film in which timing is of the essence—it reflects Auster's preoccupation with chance, as apparent in his fiction. Auggie mentions his own regret that he had not kept Ellen in his shop longer. If only he had chatted with her, she might not have been hit by the bullet as she stepped outside. Meanwhile, Paul is saved from being knocked down by a car when a young man, Rashid (Harold Perrineau), grabs and hauls him back on to the kerb. Subsequently he becomes implicated in the life of this somewhat troubled boy from the Projects (whose mother it transpires, following a pattern, was killed in a car accident 12 years back), and party to his own line of fiction. In such a way the middle-class, white intellectual and young black kid's lives are intertwined—in this patch of Brooklyn racial and class integration is meshed out of coincidence. Playing paternal custodian of Rashid, Paul ends up learning from him and is born again as he is released from his mourning; the son becomes father of the man. Such is the mellow ebb and flow in *Smoke*. It's good, it's some cigar.

NEW YORK, 6/19/95, p. 74, David Denby

Somewhere in the middle of *Smoke*—A lovely movie written by New York novelist Paul Auster and directed by Wayne Wang—the great actor Forest Whitaker tells a story to a young man whom he barely knows. As he talks, Whitaker, a mechanic working in Peekskill, holds up his artificial arm: An unnecessary automobile accident killed his wife, and God punished his reckless driving by leaving him alive, with the artificial arm to remind him of his stupidity. The young man who listens (Harold Perrineau Jr.) is a glib, well-mannered poseur without an identity—that is, without a mother and father. He has come to Peekskill determined to work for the one-armed storyteller, and he pesters him with questions. Whitaker's acting is a tremendous piece of quicksilver volatility, shifting between rage and self-punishing submission to God's design. Wonderful and startling in itself, the scene is also a case of dramatic irony, since the audience knows what he does not know—that the boy who is listening is his son. We also know the tale won't end once it's told, that it will spill over into the movie. In *Smoke*, people tell stories, and the stories galvanize the lives of the listeners and comment on the lives of the storytellers.

Smoke starts slowly and becomes immensely pleasing, a deceptively quiet winner among the hollow big bangs of the summer season. The gentleness of this movie—gentleness without softness—is nearly revolutionary in American film at the moment. Largely set in the Park Slope section of Brooklyn (Auster's home turf), *Smoke* is a celebration of gratuitous acts of kindness. There are five major characters, and they all act benevolently for no particular reason—because it suits them, because they want to tell stories and storytelling and kindness seem linked to each other. In this movie, an unexpected act of kindness is always the beginning of a story. A few such gestures, a few such stories, the movie says, and you have a neighborhood. *Smoke* is about the persistence of neighborhood life, about people taking care of one another in the small stores and apartments and pubs of old Brooklyn.

Auster sets the movie in 1990, but the period feels more like 1950. Electronic culture hasn't taken everything over yet; the Dodgers might still be playing around the corner. In the beginning, as neighborhood characters gather at a corner cigar store, each person chimes in with his character tag line, and we think we might be listening to a radio play with pictures—an echo, perhaps, of something Auster heard in his youth. Auggie (Harvey Keitel), who runs the store, has no decent cigars to sell and has to save up to smuggle in cigars from Cuba. Which is highly characteristic of Auggie's life. An intellectual without portfolio, a great reader who never went to college (we find out why), Auggie has missed out on things, but he's self-sufficient and happy enough. Keitel lavishes his Brooklyn street smarts on this man; his rough, layered voice speaks of bad nights and black-coffee mornings. Auggie has a peculiar hobby: He takes pictures from the same street corner at precisely 8 A.M. every day. He shows the thousands of pictures to his friend Paul (William Hurt), a sad-sack novelist who hasn't written much since his wife died, and when Paul, leafing rapidly though the pictures, says, "They're all the same," Auggie advises him to slow down; he might learn something. The rest of the movie could be taken as evidence of what Paul learns.

Lost in thought, Paul wanders into the street and almost gets run over, but he's saved by a black teenager who calls himself Rashid—the same teenager who later goes in search of his father. Paul takes the boy in, and the two begin an unstable friendship. In his fogged and ruminative way, Hurt is quite charming: His Paul is a man who has lost the habit of effectiveness; ideas rattle around in his mind like odd shoes at the bottom of a closet. Attempting to play father to Rashid, Paul really needs a little fathering himself (Auggie provides it). There's a sweet-natured allure to all this tentativeness—the initial lack of obvious dramatic point, in its very oddity, captures our interest (the melodies are familiar but combined in new ways).

Auster provides a nominal plot: Rashid has a bag of cash that he leaves at Paul's apartment, and this cash, like the earrings in Max Ophuls's *The Earrings of Madame de...*, will pass from one character to another, picking up more meaning with each exchange. But mainly the movie proceeds through long, beautifully written and played two-character scenes. Material that at first seems loose and meandering is actually densely woven thematically; stories the characters tell one another begin to "rhyme" in complex ways with things the characters actually do. Hurt, a father figure, tells a story about fathers and sons to Rashid, who actually is looking for his father, and so on. In the most beautiful of the gratuitous gestures of kindness, Auggie finds a grandmother—not his actual grandmother but an elderly woman who needs his company on Christmas night.

Wayne Wang, who started very small years ago with the independent film *Chan Is Missing,* has grown in confidence. In his previous movie, *The Joy Luck Club,* he was working with conventionally winsome material, but at heart he's still an independent. He doesn't compete with Auster's chatty literariness; he uses a straightforward camera technique and no more cutting than is necessary. The camera generally starts well out, in master shot, and then moves in, as if the talk were bringing us closer. And Wang has become a great director of actors. Stockard Charming turns up as Auggie's old girlfriend, Ruby, a Brooklyn chippie in tight pants with a patch over her eye, and suddenly we realize why Auggie's life went off the rails. No one could resist Ruby, the kind of aggressive yet easily bruised woman who causes trouble. Channing is the most movieish presence in this generally realistic movie. She digs into this gutsy-vulnerable role in a way reminiscent of long-ago actresses like Ida Lupino and Susan Hayward.

The garrulous fluency of Auster's writing, combined with the simplicity of Wayne Wang's direction, makes for an enchanting urban-picaresque movie. Early on, William Hurt asks the question "What does smoke weigh?" and he recounts an experiment conducted by none less than Sir Walter Raleigh himself, who introduced tobacco into England. Raleigh weighed a cigar before and after smoking it (he weighed the ash too). The movie is just smoke—just talk—but of course, if there's soul in it, smoke weighs more than anything.

NEW YORK POST, 6/9/95, p. 38, Thelma Adams

Novelist turnned screenwriter Paul Auster blows "Smoke"—tells stories—in a funky, Brooklyn-set comedy directed by Wayne Wang ("Joy Luck Club").

Auster's alter ego, blocked novelist Paul Benjamin (William Hurt doing his round-shouldered, fallen yuppie shtick with a borough twang) is down on his luck. Both men inhabit Park Slope—but tragedy has hobbled Benjamin.

The married, prolific Auster has taken a true crime—the daylight armed robbery of a Seventh Avenue bank—and created a "what, if" scenario. What, if my wife had been there, what if she had taken a bullet, what if she had been pregnant? Paul Benjamin finds out and it nearly breaks him.

Benjamin turns for warmth to the owner of the corner cigar store, Auggie Wren (Harvey Keitel at ease playing a regular jamoke who keeps his clothes on and his nose clean). As in "Bullets Over Broadway," it's not the writing pro but the layman who excels as a storyteller.

Augie and Paul connect with other storytellers: a black student gives a different name to every one he meets (Harold Perrineau); a one armed mechanic delivers a self-scathing tale of woe (the tough and tender Forest Whitaker); and Augie's long-lost ex-girlfriend (the ever-surprising Stockard Channing) tells a shaggy dog-story about the daughter (Ashley Judd) he didn't know he sired.

One day, Augie shares his hobby with Paul. The cigar seller takes a photo of his store from the same angle at the same time of day, every day. Paul pages through Augie's photo album, amazed that all the pictures are identical. Keitel corrects him: Each one is different. Slow down. Life's in the details.

Careful, steady observation and the intrusion of chance mold Auster's writing. Characters whose only common link is their neighborhood, cross paths and alter each other's lives. The mundane and the profound mingle.

"Bulls -- t is a real talent, Augie," says Paul. Auster and Wang raise blowing smoke to the level of art.

NEWSDAY, 6/9/95, Part II/p. B5, Jack Mathews

The first dubious yarn, of many, in Wayne Wang's episodic "Smoke," told by novelist William Hurt to Brooklyn Cigar Store owner Harvey Keitel, is about the bet that Sir Walter Raleigh made with Queen Elizabeth I that he could weigh the smoke rising from burning tobacco.

What Sir Walter did to win his bet was weigh a fresh cigar, smoke it, weigh the ashes and the butt, then subtract the second number from the first. The difference was the weight of the smoke. No word on whether the Queen paid off.

I suspect that screenwriter Paul Auster opened "Smoke" with that apocryphal tale as a way of alerting us to the wafty nature of his own material. The movie, a series of overlapping vignettes about characters who at one time or another pass through Keitel's store, appears lighter than air, but you know it must weigh something.

What Auster, a successful New York novelist ("The Music of Chance") and director Wang ("The Joy Luck Club") have attempted with "Smoke" is to fashion a cinematic version of an anthology of literary short stories, slices of life whose values are measured in nuances rather than resolutions. They have succeeded at that—"Smoke" is a satisfying "read"—but there simply isn't enough going on to justify a feature film.

The connecting thread running through the stories, other than the smoldering cigars and cigarettes polluting each of them, is the role that chance has played in the lives of the five main characters, who are:

Paul (Hurt), a writer who's been blocked ever since his wife was killed by a stray bullet in a street shootout;

Rashid (Harold Perrineau Jr.), the teenager who saves Paul from an oncoming car, then moves in with him;

Rashid's father, Cyrus (Forest Whitaker), who's been missing from the boy's life ever since a drunken car accident left his wife dead 12 years earlier:

Auggie Wren (Keitel), the cigar store owner whose scheme to peddle smuggled Cuban cigars to New York lawyers and judges faces the most unlikely tragedy;

And Ruby (Stockard (Channing), the one-eyed ex-wife who shows up in Auggie's store, asking for money to help save a crack-addicted young woman who may or may not be his daughter (the odds are 50/50, mom figures).

The performances are good, particularly those of Hurt, even though his Brooklyn accent is a sometime thing; Keitel, who plays Auggie with uncharacteristic whimsy, and newcomer Perrineau. Ashley Judd appears for one scene, as Ruby's volatile daughter, and gives the movie a needed blast of energy.

Auster adapted the screenplay from a Christmas short story he wrote at the request of The New York Times, about a man who helps a lonely old blind lady enjoy her last Christmas while stealing from her. That story becomes the final set piece for "Smoke," related by Keitel to Hurt in lingering detail, then reenacted over the final credits.

I don't know what the Times editors told Auster when he turned it in, but it's a pretty lame Christmas story, and its message—good deeds, like train wrecks, occur without warning—is no reason to make a movie.

SIGHT AND SOUND, 4/96, p. 54, Chris Darke

Brooklyn, 1990. Auggie Wren owns the Brooklyn Cigar Co., a neighbourhood tobacconists. Among his regular customers is Paul Benjamin, a novelist in his thirties suffering from writer's block. Several years before, Paul's pregnant wife Ellen was gunned down outside the shop. Every morning, Auggie takes a photograph of the corner outside his store. One evening, as Auggie is closing, Paul calls by for some cigars. Auggie shows Paul the photographs. Paul sees a shot of Ellen and breaks down. A few days later Paul is almost run down by a bus, but is saved by a young teenager, Rashid Cole. To show his gratitude Paul buys Rashid lunch. Learning that he is on the run, Paul offers him a place to stay for a few days. Meanwhile, Auggie is visited by an ex-girlfriend of 18 years before, Ruby McNutt. She tells him he has a daughter, Felicity, living in Brooklyn, pregnant and addicted to crack. Auggie refuses to believe it.

Rashid's presence distracts Paul from writing, and he asks him to leave. Rashid's aunt comes looking for him. She tells Paul that Rashid's real name is Thomas Jefferson Cole and that his mother was killed and his father, Cyrus, injured in a car accident when he was a boy. Cyrus abandoned him and is now working in a gas station just outside the city. Rashid discovers that Cyrus has built a new family life for himself. Unaware of Rashid's true identity, Cyrus gives him a job. Ruby convinces Auggie to visit Felicity, who is violently rude and has had an abortion. Rashid returns to Brooklyn and tells Paul why he's on the run: he witnessed a heist by a local gangster, the Creeper, and picked up a bag containing $5,800. Rashid has hidden it in Paul's apartment. Paul begs him to return it but Rashid refuses.

Auggie offers Rashid a job but the young man accidentally ruins a shipment of Cuban cigars that cost $5,000. Paul orders Rashid to pay Auggie back with his own money. But the Creeper comes looking for him at Paul's apartment. Refusing to reveal anything, Paul gets badly beaten. Paul and Auggie trace Rashid to Cyrus' gas station where an emotionally explosive father/son encounter occurs. The Creeper is killed mid-heist. Auggie gives the $5,000 to Ruby for Felicity's welfare. Paul, his block overcome and now dating someone, tells Auggie that he has been commissioned to write a Christmas story, but is out of ideas. The two men go for lunch, where Auggie tells Paul the following story. Shortly after starting work at the store he chased a young boy who was stealing magazines. The boy escaped, dropping his wallet. At Christmas, Auggie found himself alone and decided to return the wallet. The young man's address was in the projects. Arriving there Auggie was welcomed by the boy's elderly, blind grandmother who mistook him for her kin. Auggie played along and the two ate Christmas dinner together. Later, Auggie departed, leaving the wallet but taking an obviously stolen camera with him. Some months later, and feeling guilty, Auggie decided to return the camera but the aunt was no longer at the address.

It's not often that one can argue for the screenwriter-as-auteur but *Smoke* demonstrates that a novelist's fictional world can make it to the screen without being compromised by approximation or a stolid fidelity to detail. Scripted by the novelist Paul Auster and directed with disarming selflessness by Wayne Wang, *Smoke* was initially conceived in 1990 when Wang read Auster's 'Auggie Wren's Christmas Story' in *The New York Times*. This story occurs at the end of the film, as told by Auggie to the novelist Paul Benjamin. *Smoke* expands on it by installing Auggie's "Brooklyn Cigar Company" at the film's core, while keeping the original story's ambiguous, fabulist tone. What is so pleasing about *Smoke* is that Auster's 'voice' as well as his preoccupations and motifs are recognisably intact and cinematically effective.

A fabulist is a liar by definition, one who concocts fictional ruses. While this aspect of Auster's fiction might put him in the company of other American fabulists like Don DeLillo, Robert Coover and Donald Barthelme, it's a tendency that has always existed alongside others in his work. From *The New York Trilogy* (metaphysical doubt sweated out in hard-boiled pulp idiom) to *The Invention of Solitude* (metafictional memoirs) to the grander historical scope of *Moon Palace,* Auster has increasingly placed his fascination with the self-as-fiction in specific settings and peopled these with regular guys in crisis. The crisis privileged above all in his work is fatherhood; so it is with *Smoke.* The place is the Brooklyn-in-microcosm of Auggie's store; the guys—Auggie, Paul, Cyrus and Rashid—are each depicted as men still being born, their identities forged by wrong turnings and everyday catastrophes, each unable to come to terms with his past without the help and friendship of the other. In the absence of trustworthy blood fathers, a surrogate counts.

If *Smoke* is predominantly male in focus, its men are shown to have been cut loose, often against their will, from family and intimate relationships. Paul, the blocked novelist whose pregnant wife Ellen was accidentally shot dead in a robbery outside Auggie's store, is a man disorientated by his own grief until he is delivered back to the world by Rashid's incursion. Auggie's friendship with Paul is also shadowed by the guilt Auggie feels at having served Paul's wife on the day of the robbery and not having kept her in the store for a few seconds longer. Rashid, the boy from the Projects (played by Harold Perrineau), conceals a fear and isolation that comes from his mother having died in a car driven by his drunken father, Cyrus, who he has not seen in 12 years. Cyrus—his grotesque cigar-shaped artificial arm a memento of his irresponsibility—is cultivating a new family life into which Rashid's arrival is a further unwelcome reminder of the past.

VILLAGE VOICE, 6/13/95, p. 54, Amy Taubin

At its heart, *Smoke* is a gentlemanly pissing contest between a fiction writer (Paul Benjamin, played by William Hurt) and a store manager (Auggie Wren, played by Harvey Keitel). In the end, Auggie beats Paul at his own game. He makes up a story that the bemused Paul admits is "right up there with the masters ... it pushes all the right buttons." And, as manager of the

Brooklyn Cigar Shop, the film's main location, he controls the film's central metaphor, sight gag, and atmospheric effect. There's hardly a scene in *Smoke* where somebody doesn't light up.

Though Paul is the obvious alter ego for *Smoke*'s screenwriter, novelist Paul Auster, Auggie, despite his obsession with taking snapshots, is also more of a surrogate for the writer of *Smoke* than for its director Wayne Wang. The story Auggie relates to Paul is in fact one Auster published under a separate title. But whether Auggie or Paul is the better storyteller matters less than the implication that *Smoke* is nothing if not a literary film. Wang's direction takes a back seat to Auster's text until the last five minutes, when something happens that transforms the relationship between word and image. It's the one interesting filmic moment, but it's too little, too late.

Adam Holender's exquisite cinematography notwithstanding, *Smoke* winds up seeming more like a play than a film (the theater being the medium where the writer usually emerges as top dog). Most of the action happens offscreen—or in the past. The actors deliver their lines in a stagy way, with frequent pauses to indicate thoughtfulness and spontaneity. The performances, across the board, are earnest without being convincing. (And, in fact, a feeling of frustration that so much had been left unexplored apparently led to a spinoff film, *Blue in the Face,* in which Keitel and several other actors from *Smoke* as well as some new cast members—Madonna, Lily Tomlin, Lou Reed, and as a committed smoker determined to quit, the uber-indie Jim Jarmusch himself—improvised on a series of situations suggested by Atister and Wang. *Blue in the Face* is still being tinkered with. No opening date is set.)

A typical Auster text, *Smoke* takes the kind of chance incident that reminds us that we are all always one breath away from death, and surrounds it with a multitude of oddball coincidences and synchronicities. The implication is that even the most seemingly senseless and disruptive event is part of a larger order to which fiction can provide a key or map.

Thus in *Smoke:* Paul is mourning the death of his pregnant wife, who walked out of the cigar store and into a shoot-out where she caught a fatal bullet. Auggie feels a little guilty about her death ("Sometimes I think ... if the store had been a little more crowded, it would have taken her a few more seconds to get out of here ..."), though not nearly so guilty as Paul. It's their guilt about a dead woman that forges the emotional bond between them and that motivates them to take responsibility for Rashid (Harold Perrineau Jr.), a 17-year-old runaway in search of his father. Said father (Forest Whitaker) is also still mourning his wife, killed 12 years earlier in a car accident, the result of his drunk driving. In *Smoke,* men come together over the bodies of dead women (there's even a dead granny—the ultimate button-pusher).

If this relegating of women to a purely catalytic position—the vehicle for male pain, guilt, and, such as it is, redemption—weren't irritating enough, the film is similarly paternalistic vis-a-vis race. Auster's Brooklyn isn't even on the same planet as Spike Lee's. In *Smoke,* black people need white people to prod them into doing the right thing (Auggie and Paul make Rashid come clean to his father) or to offer them a little TLC when their families leave them in the lurch.

Nevertheless, *Smoke* is more than the sum of its flaws. Given most of the movies out there, one can't altogether dismiss the film's literary ambition (however precious) or its belief in storytelling as a moral act, as a guide to living one's life. And if nothing else, who can resist a final credit sequence set to "Smoke Gets in Your Eyes"?

Also reviewed in:
CHICAGO TRIBUNE, 6/16/95, Friday/p. D, Michael Wilmington
NATION, 7/10/95, p. 68, Stuart Klawans
NEW REPUBLIC, 6/26/95, p. 28, Stanley Kauffmann
NEW YORK TIMES, 6/9/95, p. C19, Janet Maslin
VARIETY, 2/20-26/95, p. 76, David Stratton
WASHINGTON POST, 6/16/95, p. F7, Rita Kempley
WASHINGTON POST, 6/16/95, Weekend/p. 15, Desson Howe

SOMETHING TO TALK ABOUT

A Warner Bros. release of a Spring Creek production. *Executive Producer:* Goldie Hawn. *Producer:* Paula Weinstein and Anthea Sylbert. *Director:* Lasse Hallstrom. *Screenplay:* Callie Khouri. *Director of Photography:* Sven Kykvist. *Editor:* Mia Goldman. *Music:* Hans Zimmer and Graham Preskett. *Music Editor:* Laura Perlman. *Choreographer:* Toni Basil. *Sound:* Peter F. Kurland and (music) Jay Rifkin and Alan Meyerson. *Sound Editor:* Scott A. Hecker. *Casting:* Marion Dougherty. *Production Designer:* Mel Bourne. *Set Decorator:* Roberta Holinko. *Special Effects:* John D. Milinac. *Costumes:* Aggie Guerard Rodgers. *Make-up:* Sarah Mays. *Running time:* 105 minutes. *MPAA Rating:* R.

CAST: Julia Roberts (Grace King Bichon); Dennis Quaid (Eddie Bichon); Robert Duvall (Wyly King); Gena Rowlands (Georgia King); Kyrra Sedgwick (Emma Rae King); Brett Cullen (Jamie Johnson); Haley Aull (Caroline Bichon); Muse Watson (Hank Corrigan); Anne Shropshire (Aunt Rae); Ginnie Randall (Eula); Terence P. Currier (Dr. Frank Lewis); Rebecca Koon (Babaranelle); Rhonda Griffis (Edna); Lisa Roberts (Kitty); Deborah Hobart (Lorene Tuttle); Amy Parish (Lucy); Helen Baldwin (Mary Jane); Libby Whittemore (Nadine); Punky Leonard (Norma Leggett); Michael Flippo (Sonny); Beau Holden (Frank); Noreen Reardon (June); Bennie L. Jenkins (Dub); Rusty Hendrickson (Harry); J. Don Ferguson (Announcer); Mary Nell Santacroce (Mrs. Pinkerton); Shannon Eubanks (Jessie Gaines); Jamye Price (Annie); Brinley Arden Vickers (College Friend).

FILMS IN REVIEW, 11-12/95, p. 105, Andy Pawelczak

Just about everything in *Something to Talk About,* the new romantic comedy directed by Lasse Hallstrom *(What's Eating Gilbert Grape?),* is generic. There is the Southern patriarch, Wyly King (Robert Duvall), who owns a horse farm and lords it over everyone; his wife, Georgia (Gena Rowlands), the archetypal Southern wife who stays emphatically in the background; his daughter, Grace Bichon (Julia Roberts), who disrupts the family and the whole town with her very public separation from her husband, Eddie (Dennis Quaid), a charming skirtchaser; Grace's wise-cracking sister, Emma Rae (Kyra Sedgwick); and Grace and Eddie's precocious young daughter, Caroline (Haley Aull), who dreams of riding a full grown horse in the Grand Prix. But the screenplay writer, Callie Khouri, who won an Academy Award for *Thelma and Louise,* gives the familiar elements a contemporary, neo-feminist spin. The film never quite takes off, never quite communicates the giddy exhilaration of *Thelma and Louise,* though it does have some sharp, rapid-fire dialogue and finely nuanced performances by Roberts and Sedgwick.

Grace Bichon spends her days working for her father and attending meetings of the women's Charity League where the hot-button issue is the use of the women's own names (as opposed to Mrs. So-and-so) in the League's recipe book. There are signs early on that this rarefied life isn't very fulfilling for Grace—she has a habit of driving off and forgetting her daughter, and the spark in her marriage seems to have gone out long ago. When she sees her husband on the street kissing another woman, something repressed and manic breaks loose in her. Before long she's confronting him publicly in her nightgown and, in one of the film's notable comic scenes, exposing the sexual secrets of the women in the Charity League. The rest of the movie is about her coming into her own as a woman as she defies her father and ponders what to do about the now repentant, lovelorn Eddie.

Julia Roberts has a more substantial role here than in her last few films. Roberts, of course, was America's sweetheart in the late Eighties. With a smile that could disarm the most jaded, case-hardened cinephile, she combined working class menschiness and WASP glamor with chastity and a sweet sexiness. She was such an icon that the best bit in Robert Altman's *The Player* was a joke about Hollywood's use of her as Everyman's dream of the girl-next-door. As Grace, she has to use more of herself than usual as Grace moves from comic dishevelment to troubled soul searching to grown-up resolve, and her performance is good enough that never for a moment, at least while you're watching the picture, does it occur to you that the privileged Grace has been spoiled rotten.

Kyra Sedgwick as Grace's sister, Emma Rae, almost steals the picture. Her Emma Rae has a wry country-and-western twang in her speech and personality, and it that doesn't consort well with the character's upper middle class background, it's no matter—Sedgwick is funny, smart, and sexy. Dennis Quaid as Eddie Bichon is cast in a supporting role to the women; for most of the film he's somber and disturbed as Eddie pleading with Grace to take him back, and only at the end does Quaid get a chance to cut loose with his wall-to-wall smile. Robert Duvall as Grace's father struts around in high riding boots, and Gena Rowlands as his wife has a few good moments when she finally rebels against her husband's hegemony.

Callie Khouri's script is feminist without being strident—the only tendentious moment occurs when Roberts remarks that Southern women have been bred for centuries to have low expectations. Khouri excels at those private moments between women when they're not under the normative eye of Big Brother—the film's best scenes are those in which Roberts and Sedgwick joke and talk about life. Lasse Hallstrom's direction is intelligently non-intrusive, and Sven Nykvist's cinematography has the clarity and equanimity of his work with Bergman. In a period of elephantine thrillers and unfunny romantic comedies, *Something to Talk About* demonstrates that there might be life in Hollywood yet.

LOS ANGELES TIMES, 8/4/95, Calendar/p. 6, Kenneth Turan

"Something to Talk About" is like a slow-simmering stew, the kind that flavors familiar ingredients with special herbs and spices. Those spices surely accomplish wonders, but underneath it all you are left with the usual culinary suspects.

Making "Something" happen is an enviable creative team, starting with "Thelma & Louise" screenwriter Callie Khouri and Swedish director Lasse Hallstrom ("What's Eating Gilbert Grape?," "My Life as a Dog"). Each has a perfect understanding of the comically eccentric, and their collaboration gives the film a welcome off-center feeling, a human tempo and pacing that emphasize character whenever possible.

Attracted by that rare idiosyncratic quality is a fine cast, starting with star Julia Roberts and extending through Robert Duvall, Gena Rowlands, Kyra Sedgwick and Dennis Quaid. They work so well together that it takes a while to realize that underneath their success is a schematic story line that is weaker and more familiar than it should be.

Filmed largely in South Carolina, "Something" is set in unnamed Southern horse country, where tradition and the way things have always been done count for a great deal. They matter especially to Wyly King (Duvall), patriarch of King Farms, a willful, emotionally obtuse horse breeder who does what he wants and then tells his stable manager, "It's done, now roll with it."

Because that manager is his married daughter Grace King Bichon (Roberts), Wyly's belligerent tantrums are particularly troublesome, as is the fact that Grace's own strong-minded 10-year-old daughter Caroline (newcomer Haley Aull) wants to ride a potentially dangerous full-size horse in an upcoming Grand Prix equestrian event.

Harried as she thinks she is, Grace finds that things can get worse. While driving through town, she sees her husband, Eddie Bichon (Quaid), give a non-fraternal kiss to an attractive blonde. His adultery is soon confirmed, and how Grace responds to the world's oldest question—should, she forgive him and take him back?—is something for everyone to talk about.

Already stretched thin, irritated that "I don't have time for the nervous breakdown I deserve," Grace is turned by her crisis into a loose cannon with an unerring instinct for the wrong move. Soon both her shoot-from-the-hip sister Emma Rae (Sedgwick) and her patrician mother Georgia (Rowlands) find themselves having to deal with what the pressure does to Grace.

"Something to Talk About" is at its best when Khouri's juicy script is adroitly mixing comedy and pathos. Its other great strength is its collection of formidable and well-played female characters, live wires every one, and the adult way it treats a troubled marriage. Praise should also go to performers like Quaid, willing and able to humanize an unappealing character, and Duvall, a magician who can play anything, any time, anywhere.

Still, fine as its elements are, this film does not feel completely realized. Though its humor is largely telling, it can also descend into awkward farce. Plot points tend to be routine, situations do not always mesh with each other and the film can't seem to decide when and how it should end.

And, just as an aside, when is Julia Roberts going to allow herself to smile more than briefly in a major motion picture? Although it is heartening to see her involved with this kind of quality material, her long-ago sunniness remains a distant memory, like peace in Yugoslavia. Is it too much to hope that it might come back someday?

NEW YORK, 8/14/95, P. 42, David Denby

In such commercial projects as *Sleeping With the Enemy* and *The Pelican Brief*, Julia Roberts gave off so much uncertainty and even panic that one began to think of her unease as a signature tic, rather like Goldie Hawn's cocked head and self-infatuated giggle. Roberts seemed to be using fluster, dismay, even weakness to draw us closer to her. Why would a star need to use such transparently audience-flattering stratagems? We liked her well enough without them. Or was she really just *that* nervous? Either way, she seemed slightly out to lunch—a tall, skinny stalk trembling in the breeze. You thought: Calm *down,* honey. But in *Something to Talk About,* Roberts has taken control of what she wants to do. This time, she's playing a neurotic—a bright woman who can't figure out how to live her life—and she's in command of the role. Callie Khouri, of *Thelma & Louise* fame, wrote the screenplay (an original), and Khouri has a knack for creating pungent women. Roberts's character, Grace King Bichon, one of two grown daughters in a wealthy southern horse-breeding family, can't stop jabbing at people and then jabbing at herself. Grace works for her father, Wyly (Robert Duvall), an intelligent but ornery man, and loving the old bastard has worn her down. Her life is so dominated by him that she has grown indifferent to her husband, Eddie (Dennis Quaid), who has begun to fool around. The movie is about a few weeks in Grace's life in which everything falls apart and she tries to put it back together again.

Khouri, born in Texas and raised in Kentucky, may feel a natural closeness with a new generation of southern and southwestern women caught between traditionalism and independence. Raised to be subservient to fathers and husbands, they discover at a certain point that the old rules don't work anymore; personal dissatisfactions hit these women like flash storms. *Thelma & Louise* was a fantasy of escape so extreme in its commitment to personal liberation that it had no place to end but in death. Khouri wrote it as Isolde & Isolde on the road, and director Ridley Scott got carried away by the visual possibilities of two beautiful women riding a convertible across the mythic landscape of the West. Lasse Hallström, the Swedish director of *My Life As a Dog* and two erratic but interesting American productions, *Once Around* and *What's Eating Gilbert Grape?,* is a more domestic sort. In *Something to Talk About,* he has made a good movie about the way powerful families give you life and squeeze it out of you at the same time. Hallström takes hold of the southern milieu, and Khouri's material gives it depth with a network of relationships going back decades: From the tone of the hesitations and insults, we know we've walked right into the middle of something. Physically, the production, with its "plantation" house and outlying buildings and stables, suggests wealth without ostentation (the great Mel Bourne did the design). One can understand why the women haven't strayed very far: These people have something to hold on to.

They all enjoy the easy sense that they're allowed to get violent with one another. Grace's sister, the unmarried Emma Rae (Kyra Sedgwick), sits around making smart, nasty cracks like the heroine's friend in a thirties movie. The girls' mother, Georgia (Gena Rowlands), having long indulged her overbearing husband, winds up and fires, locking Wyly out of the house. Women telling off men, one realizes, is central to the movie. Emma Rae even administers a devastating knee to the groin of Grace's straying husband. It's a good bet that at least one man will be kneed in the nether regions in every movie written by Callie Khouri—it's her signature act of rebellion, a return to first principles. In Khouri's work, the male sex has been placed under suspicion. Men are seen as benevolent or vicious in their relations with women. They have no other significant qualities. The shoe is truly on the other foot: There are a lot of bad men out there, and a lot of women who need to punish them. Yet contrary to what some people wrote after *Thelma & Louise* came out, Callie Khouri is not a man-hater. In *Something to Talk About,* once she punishes men, she forgives them.

After skulking around holding his balls for a while, Dennis Quaid finally gets to open up his good-ol'-boy-husband-and-garden-variety-philanderer routine. Imploring and chagrined, Quaid suggests that the husband is more disappointed with himself than nasty. At the same time, his wife has become impossible. Grace makes scenes and forces intimacies on people; she's so self-absorbed that she rushes off and leaves her little daughter behind. This, at last, is the right kind of dithering comedy for Julia Roberts to play. She goes beyond ingratiation; she finally becomes an actress. Her Grace is at times so messed up she's unconsciously cruel. There's an integrity in split feelings, and Roberts finds it; her creator, Khouri, finds her own integrity by suggesting that a woman in the process of liberating herself can become one awful pain in the neck.

NEW YORK POST, 8/4/95, p. 45, Michael Medved

If you're burning with rage at some faithless spouse, I suppose you can get some vicarious satisfaction out of "Something to Talk About"—in which straying husband Dennis Quaid is savagely kneed in the groin by his sister-in-law, Kyra Sedgwick (falling to the ground and writhing in pain), then later eats poisoned fish prepared for him by his avenging wife (Julia Roberts), which places him in the hospital near death.

The problem is that these events are neither funny nor the least bit believable; like the rest of the movie, they exist only in some smug, airless, artificial world in which director (Lasse Hallstrom of "My Life as a Dog" and "What's Eating Gilbert Grape") and screenwriter (Callie Khouri of "Thelma & Louise") seem to be congratulating each other on their superiority to the pathetic characters that they torture on screen.

Roberts plays a hardworking wife in an unidentified Southern town who one day, while driving with her 10-year-old daughter, spots hubby Quaid lustily kissing an unidentified blonde on a street corner. This discovery not only explodes their marriage but throws the entire community into chaos, as Julia makes a scene at a local charity group, convincing the proper, prissy ladies that all their husbands have been similarly unfaithful.

She even persuades her mother (Gena Rowlands) that big daddy Robert Duvall, imperious ruler of a horse-breeding empire, has long had a roving eye. This strutting family tyrant (his name in the movie is "Wyly King") is then promptly locked out of his own house.

Duvall is well-cast in this role, but not even an actor of his stature can make us believe that this macho plantation patriarch would be instantly reduced to fumbling helplessness by his wife's first signs of assertiveness.

Similarly, the capable Quaid can do little with a role that is so poorly written. We learn nothing about the character or his affair—not even the name or marital status of the blonde babe he embraced—so when he determinedly tries to crawl back into Julia's good graces ("What ever happened to us, Grace?") it feels entirely phony.

There's no plot line or resolution to any of this, but the movie does contain a lot of scenes of pretty horses and equestrian competition. Perhaps it's symbolic when Julia's daughter rides to victory on a mount described by the announcer as a *gelding*—suggesting that women can work well with men if only they could find a way to get rid of all that pesky testosterone.

Julia Roberts became a star by projecting an achingly natural sense of vulnerability (just watch her work in "Mystic Pizza" or "Steel Magnolias"), but now she "does" vulnerability in almost a ritualistic way as part of her increasingly haughty and self-conscious star turns.

The direction here doesn't help, with Swedish filmmaker Hellstrom overdoing the local color (as he did before in "Gilbert Grape") which this time means plenty of Southern-fried cliches. Unfortunately, this annoyingly empty movie will leave people with little to talk about, but plenty to squawk about.

NEWSDAY, 8/4/95, Part II/p. B2, Jack Mathews

If you're going to make a movie on a subject as well-trod as marital infidelity, you'd best have a fresh point of view, and Lasse Hallstrom's "Something to Talk About," with a smart and frequently hilarious script by Oscar-winner Callie Khouri ("Thelma and Louise"), is as fresh as a 30 day injunction.

Actually, the film's marriage crisis, between Grace (Julia Roberts), the hardworking manager of a family-owned southern horse farm, and her philandering husband, Eddie (Dennis Quaid), is of secondary interest to Khouri. The writer, who has become one of the bright lights of feminism in Hollywood, uses Eddie's infidelity as a catalyst to start Grace working through her deeper conflicts about her career and her role in her family. Like many women of her generation, Grace's challenge is to stake out her own identity in a world still dominated by men.

When she went to college, Grace planned to become a veterinarian but was pushed off-course by the interests of two self-centered men: Eddie, a college boyfriend who'd gotten her pregnant and then impulsively proposed, and her autocratic father, Wyly (Robert Duvall), who wanted her in the family business. When we join her, Grace is fulfilling everybody's expectations but her own—she's Supermom to 10-year-old Caroline (Haley Aull), she's the cog in the community women's social club and she's the administrative workhorse on Dad's farm.

Then she catches Eddie swapping spit with a blond at high noon on Main Street, and her life, or the life she's leading for everyone else, begins to unravel.

"Something to Talk About" is not a well-plotted movie. There's some sub-text about a coming Grand Prix equestrian event in which Caroline may make her riding debut against her own grandfather, and it does work toward a resolution of Grace and Eddie's problems. None of this is very compelling, however, and the movie has no idea how or when to end.

But Khouri has written the year's best ensemble of characters, and Hallstrom ("What's Eating Gilbert Grape"), a director known for coaxing good work from his actors, has brought them bursting to life.

The something that most people will be talking about with this movie is Kyra Sedgwick, who, as Grace's feisty, foulmouthed sister Emma Rae, got most of Khouri's best lines, and works them like Michael Jordan going to the basket. She also got the best scene, delivering a knee to a sinner's groin so suddenly and forcefully it will have men in the audience doubled-over with sympathy pain.

Sedgwick does tend to steal the show, because Emma Rae is such a liberated member of this otherwise conforming family. But there isn't a weak spot in the cast. Roberts, setting aside her grating star mannerisms, gives her best performance in what is easily her most complex character. Grace not only has to rebuild her life, but she has to do it with a different set of specs, and Roberts takes her through an amazing amount of growth and change.

Duvall does wonders with Wyly, who in other hands might have been just another stubborn old man, quashing every attempt to erode his power. Duvall shows him to be a man who uses control over the three women in his life as a cover for his dependence on them. His helplessness in the face of their rebellion (the always brilliant Gena Rowlands is sensational as the dutiful wife giving vent to 30 years of frustration) becomes one of the film's greatest strengths.

"Something to Talk About" may not be a ground-breaker in sexual politics, but it's smart adult entertainment, and that's an unusual thing to find at movie theaters on a summer day.

NEWSWEEK, 8/7/95, p. 60, David Anson

Something to Talk About, the second movie written by Callie Khouri, probably won't ignite the op-ed passions that "Thelma and Louise" did, but you can't miss the Khouri touch—her sharp Southern tongue and her determination to tell tales from a fresh, female point of view. The women in this smart, highly entertaining comedy don't pack guns, but relations between the sexes are such that a well-placed knee in the groin can come in handy.

The knee belongs to Emma Rae King (Kyra Sedgwick), the groin is her brother-in-law Eddie's (Dennis Quaid) and the kick is an expression of solidarity with her sister Grace King Bichon (Julia Roberts), who's just discovered her husband's infidelity. Even before she uncovers the affair, Grace is frayed at the edges. Every time she drives off to an appointment, she forgets she's left her 10-year-old daughter behind.

Now, confronted with Eddie's philandering, something snaps in Grace, and she loses her tolerance for keeping up appearances. First she scandalizes her women's charity group. Then, moving back to the family manse, she troubles the waters with rude truths, setting off a chain reaction of pain and lunacy. Her rich, autocratic horsebreeding Daddy (Robert Duvall) fears that her marital woes will blow a real-estate deal with Eddie's father. Her mother (Gena Rowlands), oozing discreet Southern charm, urges her to forgive her husband and reconcile. Her dotty aunt recommends giving him a dose of poison—or "homeopathic aversion therapy," as she calls it.

The movie eventually boils down to one of the oldest romantic-comedy questions in the book: will husband and wife find a way to rekindle their lost love? This may disappoint some viewers expecting a more radical turn of events. But Khouri and director Lasse Hallstrom ("My Life as a Dog," "What's Eating Gilbert Grape") invigorate a conventional form with texture, warmth and a tangy feminist sensibility. Try to imagine a cross between Mary Chapin Carpenter and Philip

("The Philadelphia Story") Barry and you'll get an inkling of the movie's old bottle/new wine charm.

It may seem odd to entrust a Southern tale to the Swedish Hallstrom, but it was smart. Hallstrom hasn't acquired the bad Hollywood habit of hyping his material—he keeps the emotions honest, lets our sympathies ebb and flow between the characters in a scene. Grace is no saint, and Eddie more than a sinner. It's nice to see Roberts working with good material again, showing she can be both a star and a fine team player. From top to bottom, she's working with a thoroughbred ensemble. Sedgwick's blunt, ribald, Emma Rae is the crowd-pleasing part. Hers are the lines everyone will be quoting—raunchy enough to earn the movie an inappropriate R rating. What's refreshing, though, is that sooner or later every character, man or woman, gets his due. The humanity is spread around with a quirky, generous hand, reason enough to distinguish this quiet, low-tech comedy in a season of big-bang juvenilia.

SIGHT AND SOUND, 1/96, p. 52, Peter Matthews

Grace King Bichon manages the Southern horse ranch owned by her father, Wyly King, and she has a secure, if complacent, domestic routine with her husband, Eddie Bichon, and her young daughter, Caroline. But the cracks show in arguments with her domineering father, and in her genial negligence of Caroline. Yet Grace seems hardly aware of how stagnant her marriage has become.

She sees her husband kissing an unknown woman on the street during his lunch hour. That evening she angrily confronts Eddie, but he denies the affair. Grace turns to her parents for comfort, but Wyly—who is negotiating a land deal with Eddie's father merely tells her to quit making a spectacle of herself. Grace's mother, the sweetly compliant Georgia, advises her to forgive and forget. Only Grace's sister, the straight-talking Emma Rae, is unequivocally on her side—and forthrightly kicks Eddie in the groin.

At a charity meeting, an acquaintance informs Grace that she, too, had a fling with Eddie. In retaliation, Grace dishes the dirt about the husbands of her fellow volunteers. Now in fighting spirit, Grace visits irascible Aunt Rae, who advises her to prepare Eddie a special meal—with a little poison. At dinner, Grace and Eddie begin to thrash out their problem. Just when it appears they will be reconciled, Eddie falls ill and must be rushed to hospital.

Eddie now bitterly insists on a divorce. Annoyed by her mother's passivity, Grace tells her what everyone else knows—that Wyly, too, has philandered. Shocked, Georgia locks Wyly out of the house. After consulting a lawyer, Eddie decides that divorce is not what he wants after all. Grace, however, has begun to feel drawn to Buck, a horse trainer. Meeting him at a bar one night, she attempts a seduction, but can't go through with it.

Caroline's dream is to ride her beloved horse Possum at the upcoming Grand Prix, and Grace finally gives her permission. She blatantly defies her father's authority by allowing Hank, a ranch hand, to ride in competition against him. Hank and Caroline both win their events, Wyly gets embarrassingly trounced and Georgia takes back the chastened patriarch. At a party afterwards, Grace and Eddie dance together and begin to recapture some of their lost passion but Grace also dances with Buck. Some time later, Grace has followed her own dream of returning to veterinary college. She agrees to meet Eddie for a 'first date', but is clearly keeping her options open.

Something to Talk About is obviously—perhaps too obviously— intended to be a 90s riposte to such earlier consciousness-raising movies as Paul Mazursky's *An Unmarried Woman* (1977) and Martin Scorsese's *Alice Doesn't Live Here Anymore*, (1974). Like them, it charts a woman's halting progress from complacency to self-awareness following the breakdown of her marriage; and it has a similar sense of its own importance in defining the sexual and emotional *zeitgeist*. Those 70s films represented the first concerted mainstream effort to ask what a woman, newly liberated from domestic ties, could want *for herself*: the answer came with a characteristic mixture of evasion, confusion, rage and fumbling inarticulacy which, however, felt true to women's experience.

Lasse Hallström's new movie isn't entirely free of those semi-authentic, semi-maudlin passages in which the heroine gropes at tedious length to express her pent-up feelings. "I'm telling you this as me," the awakened Grace explains to her overbearing father—a line that ought to *become* legendary in the annals of redundant feminist psycho-babble. Yet even at its windiest, the movie retains the viewer's sympathy. For one thing, it's good to see a proper woman's picture again—one that takes its time weaving an undramatic texture of recognisable human behaviour—and whose low-key approach makes it almost unique among current Hollywood product. *Something to Talk About* admittedly lacks the urgency and primal excitement of its predecessors, but it's also far more collected in what it hopes to say; and the cosy pragmatism it ultimately settles for seems no less faithful to a period when utopianism about relationships his given way to *realpolitik*.

The screenplay is by Callie Khouri, who wrote *Thelma and Louise*; but anyone anticipating more nihilistic feminine revolt will be in for a shock. This time, Khouri has cannily situated her protagonist in the close-knit milieu of a Southern American small town, where Grace's bid for autonomy occurs within accepted limits where freedom must be carefully weighed against family and tradition. In the 70s archetype, the woman abandoned her old world to find herself—and in the rush of empowerment, the movies didn't dwell too much on the pain of those she left behind. Grace is hardly a household drudge like most of her forebears (She is shown as professionally successful if not wholly satisfied with the horse-breeding career she has inherited); so her capacity for self-determination is never in serious doubt. Khouri's script assumes that the primary battle has been won, and proceeds to peace negotiations with the old enemies: husbands and fathers.

It may be taken as emblematic that Gena Rowlands, who was formerly driven mad by patriarchy in John Cassavetes' 1974 *A Woman Under the Influence,* now appears as an addled matriarch with a bit of hidden gumption; and that Robert Duvall's bullying Wyly (similar to his role in *The Great Santini*) is revealed as toothless once he gets literally—knocked off his high horse. The movie aims at a general reconciliation where each party yields a little to the enrichment of both. Whether this is a reactionary or just a reasonable view it's difficult to say; but Khouri even has the temerity to indicate some blame on Grace's side. The 70s films nearly always drew the husband as an outright sleaze, so it was easy for the woman here to go off on her odyssey guilt-free. But Dennis Quaid's Eddie is merely your average, fallible guy, who strays because the marriage has lost its spark (which you can certainly believe from Julia Roberts's earnest, dishraggy performance). As no one ever questions the idea of marriage, the movie actually bypasses the 70s and harks back to such sophisticated 30s comedies as Leo McCarey's *The Awful Truth*, where fatigued couples engaged in childish pranks (like Grace's mock poisoning of Eddie) to revive that spark.

Not too sophisticated, however, since one must put up with such irritants as a freckled-faced moppet (who has the fully-formed feminist consciousness her mother lacks), a feisty and equally all-knowing sister and a mysterious black woman who hangs around for some shots of all-female solidarity, but whom the script seems reluctant to spell out as the maid. *Something To Talk About* is more interesting to talk about than to see maybe because its stress on post-feminist fine-tuning precludes the grand polemical gesture. Lasse Hallström's usual style of fey direction (seen at its best in *My Life as a Dog*) keeps Grace's trajectory well within the bounds of psychic tact, while Sven Nykvist's elegantly bleached-out cinematography has sapped her spirit from the start. The movie never scales any heights: on the other hand, it escapes the bathetic depths of its more radical ancestors (those cop-out endings where the dream man appeared to smooth over contradictions the filmmakers couldn't face). On its own pointedly reduced terms, it's an honest job.

TIME, 8/14/95, p. 67, Richard Schickel

Well, yes, Eddie (Dennis Quaid) is having an extramarital affair. And, yes, his wife Grace (Julia Roberts) finds out about it. And, for sure, there's hell to pay before they sort of sort it out.

But *Something to Talk About* is not your typical adultery comedy, all farcical fizz and frenzy. Written by Callie Khouri, it is another empowerment play, like her *Thelma and Louise*. That, however, was a high-concept piece, two girls enjoying the boyish pleasures of a crime-and-bonding spree. This film is harder to describe (almost the highest praise you can offer a movie these days), but it is equally good-natured and perhaps more intricately subversive in its assault on American patriarchy.

When Grace's marriage heads south, she packs up her daughter and heads home to the family horse farm and a confrontation with the past that made her what she is—a woman too emotionally guarded and self-denying for her own good. Dad (Robert Duvall) is the soft-drawling dictator of a prosperous domain. Mom (Gena Rowlands) is the perpetual placater, for whom niceness is a moral imperative. Big Sister (Kyra Sedgwick) has a tough but funny tongue and, one guesses, a damaged soul.

And Grace? Grace is simply beside herself. At her genteel woman's club she asks anyone else who has been sleeping with her husband to please identify herself. She also airs all the ladies' sexual secrets. The uproar is hilarious. Back at the ranch, she asserts herself—and the reality principle—more hesitantly.

She's always been everybody's good girl, sacrificing her dreams (she wanted to be a veterinarian) to others' expectations—marriage, motherhood, working in the family business. Her husband's philandering having broken this unwritten contract with convention, she is free to re-examine her options. In the process she undermines her father's authority, encourages her mother to join the revolution and, finally, goes back to school and, possibly, into a more realistic relationship with her now chastened mate.

Seems to you you've heard this song before? Yes. But it is very sweetly sung here. Khouri writes characters, not tracts; dialogue, not bumper stickers; and she has the good sense to let the men have their say—notably Eddie, who makes Grace understand that her distraction contributed to his wanderlust.

The director, Lasse Hallstrom (*My Life as a Dog*), is an unobtrusive craftsman who lets his actors breathe in an easy, unforced way, as if they were engaged not in a movie but in real lives. Roberts' willowy vulnerability and watchful intelligence have never been shown to better advantage. And Rowlands is simply great in a scene where she breaks the silence of the years in a richly emotional encounter with her husband. It is not, mostly, about anger; it is about self-astonishment—at all she had inside her; at her unexpected (and scary) bravado in letting it out. Her performance is emblematic of a movie that, a few sideslips into familiar sentiment aside (they usually involve Grace's child, played by Haley Aull), never lets its political correctness interfere with its delight in human incorrectness.

VILLAGE VOICE, 8/15/95, p. 46, Amy Taubin

There are various schools of thought on Julia Roberts. My friend Lisa, for example, is highly susceptible to her nervy, highstrung demeanor not to mention her fine-boned beauty and radiant yet vulnerable smile. "She moves me," says Lisa. I agree that Roberts possesses all the qualities Lisa ascribes to her, and yet she moves me less with each film. Maybe it's her choice of material that turns me off.

Something To Talk About is nothing if not a vehicle for Julia Roberts. If you're partial to her, you'll probably have a good time. If you're not, well, several of the sweaters worn by Roberts and by Kyra Sedgwick (who plays her sister) are worthy of serious contemplation. Not to mention the esoteric product tie-in—and if it wasn't for promotional purposes, then why was that bottle of Kiehl's lotion so prominently displayed?

In Something To Talk About, Roberts plays Grace King Bichon, a wealthy Southern woman with a philandering husband (Dennis Quaid) and a 10-year-old daughter (Haley Aull). Grace has given up her childhood dream of being a large-animal vet to manage her Daddy's thoroughbred horse farm. Now I can understand the logic of putting Julia Roberts—she of the "coltish" limbs and flaring nostrils—in a picture with a bunch of show horses. I also appreciate how Julia Roberts as a horsewoman evokes the memory of Elizabeth Taylor in *National Velvet*—two beauties following the same trail. (These are the kinds of desperately free associations that pass for creativity in Hollywood.) What I can't comprehend is why there's only one shot of Roberts on a horse (and in that shot, the person on the horse is so far from the camera that she could be a body double). Is Roberts scared of horses? Is she allergic?

In any case, this strange separation leads to some irreconcilable differences in the plot of *Something To Talk About*. On the one hand there's the story of Grace's floundering marriage; on the other, there are the endless machinations about who is going to ride which horse in the local Grand Prix. And since it's not going to be Grace, why would you care?

Especially since the other characters have no life outside of their relationship to Grace. Quaid, Sedgwick, Robert Duvall (who plays Grace's father) and Gena Rowlands (who plays her mother) are no more than Roberts's backup band. Although Quaid is supposedly screwing half the women in town, all he does onscreen is give an anonymous blond a quick nuzzle. Duvall and Rowlands play the stereotypical big daddy and big mama. Sedgwick comes on like the comic relief. With her tough-broad delivery and dialogue to match, she might have stolen the picture if only we'd been allowed to know a little more about her. Like what is such a savvy woman doing at the age of 30 still living with Mom and Dad?

Although Sven Nykvist's cinematography is pretty enough, the film lacks any specific sense of place. There's no evidence that director Lasse Hallström knows anything at all about the way wealthy Southerners live. But if one expected more from *Something To Talk About*, it's because the meandering script is by Callie Khouri, her first since *Thelma and Louise*. Maybe she should stick to cars instead of horses. In any event, star vehicles are not the way to go.

Also reviewed in:
CHICAGO TRIBUNE, 8/4/95, Friday/p. C, Michael Wilmington
NEW REPUBLIC, 9/11/95, p. 26, Stanley Kauffmann
NEW YORK TIMES, 8/4/95, p. C3, Janet Maslin
VARIETY, 7/31-8/6/95, p. 35, Todd McCarthy
WASHINGTON POST, 8/4/95, p. D6, Hal Hinson
WASHINGTON POST, 8/4/95, Weekend/p. 38, Desson Howe

SON OF THE SHARK

A Seven Arts Releasing Company release of a Gaumont/Compagnie des Images/France 3 Cinema/Premiere Heure/Saga Films/In Visible Films production. *Producer:* François Fries. *Director:* Agnès Merlet. *Screenplay (French with English subtitles):* Agnès Merlet. *Based on an original story by:* Agnès Merlet and Santiago Amigorena. *Director of Photography:* Gérard Simon. *Editor:* Guy Lecorne and Pierre Choukroun. *Music:* Bruno Coulais. *Sound:* Henry Morelle and Jean-Pierre Laforce. *Production Designer:* Laurent Allaire. *Running time:* 88 minutes. *MPAA Rating:* Not Rated.

CAST: Ludovic Vanendaele (Martin); Erick Da Silva (Simon); Sandrine Blancke (Marie); Maxime Leroux (The Father).

LOS ANGELES TIMES, 8/21/95, Calendar/p. 5, Kevin Thomas

Agnes Merlet's bleakly beautiful "Son of the Shark," inspired by a true story is at once less sensational and more powerful than "Kids" as it tracks unblinkingly yet compassionately a pair of rootless adolescent brothers, Martin (Ludovic Vandendaele) and Simon (Erick Da Silva), running wild in their wintry Belgian seaport town in the aftermath of their mother's abandonment of her family. Their surly, hard-drinking father (Maxime Leroux) seems neither to care for them nor to be able to control them; and in their very early teens, they are too young for prison.

These youths are reckless renegades they send a bus crashing over a cliff in the opening scene—yet Merlet allows us to care for them for they are clearly intelligent, reflective and nakedly starved for love and affection, which results in a close, intense bonding between them.

The film's title comes from Martin's remark that he sees himself as the son of a shark and dreams that he and his brother will somehow find respite in an undersea paradise. Merlet's ability to draw complex yet natural portrayals from her young actors is as amazing as her terse, authoritative style.

NEW YORK POST, 3/10/95, p. 46, Thelma Adams

Martin (Ludovic Vandendaele) and Simon (Erick Da Silva) are fish out of water. Abandoned by their mother, disowned by their father, too young to be imprisoned, too close to be separated for long by the impotent juvenile authorities, the junior vandals terrorize a tiny French town in Agnes Merlet's fact-based "Son of the Shark."

Martin, the eldest, struggles to comprehend his violent nature. He rereads a passage from a book on fish his mother gave him. His mantra becomes: "I am the son of a female shark." In the undersea world of hammerheads and great whites, his behavior wouldn't be considered abnormal.

Merlet goes overboard on the literary metaphor, punching the passage four times. Fortunately, Simon deflates it, teasing his brother: "I'm the son of a sardine and an anchovy."

The director uses stronger and subtler visual metaphors. When Martin returns home from reform school, his broken father barricades the door of their shabby apartment to confine his son. Martin slips out the window and balances on the roof ledge; above him are white cliffs and a neon cross, below a prostitute looks on.

Without faith in the future, without a sanctuary, Martin has nothing to lose. Violence is his only means of self-expression. There is only the ecstasy of risk. A shark dies standing still.

From the opening scene, Merlet captures the juvenile joy in delinquency. Martin and Simon, their Norman faces shining, steal a bus accompanied by a perky pop score. Only when they roll the bus over a cliff and it explodes on the shore below do we get a clue that these boys will up the ante of childish pranks.

Sooner or later in any story about sharks, we expect to see the finned creatures in a feeding frenzy. In "Son of the Shark," crimes against property escalate to attacks against people; violence feeds the narrative tension.

On one level, this searing character study is a high-class movie-of-the-week ripped from the French headlines.

But with the coiled energy of a first-time writer/director testing her wings, Merlet is able to find the poetry within the predatory pre-teens. She accomplishes this without sanctioning their amoral behavior or offering simple solutions.

NEWSDAY, 3/10/95, Part II/p. B5, John Anderson

Glass breaks, an engine starts and, as the opening credits dissolve, we watch the barely pubescent Vanderhoes brothers—Martin (Ludovic Vandendaele) and Simon (Erick Da Silva)—drive a stolen bus toward a cliff and the sea. We also hear a merry little ditty about a girl in pretty shoes:

Me and the Great Big Bunny
We will go and munch her kidneys
We will go and smash her head
We will go and munch her liver

Obviously, this isn't anyone's fairy tale, or even "The 400 Blows," which Agnes Merlet's "Son of the Shark" so strongly suggests. No, in telling her story about children with no future, Merlet has situated herself somewhere between Truffaut and "A Clockwork Orange," arranging her marriage of innocence and sin in much the same way the bus meets the shore after flying off the cliff.

Richly symbolic and profoundly sad, "Son of the Shark" introduces Martin and Simon in the midst of a not-uncommon crime spree: After destroying the bus, they leave a flaming bag of excrement on the doorstep of the local butcher (whom they will later rob) and then break into a movie house, which they trash. They are the scourge of their French village, and have turned its bourgeois morality against itself. Their father doesn't want them, no reformatory can hold them, and there is simply nothing to be done with two criminals when they've been judged too young for jail. In Rio de Janeiro, they'd be shot. In the north of France, they are afforded a much slower death.

Having based this, her first feature, on a real-life pair of prepubescent felons, Merlet is certainly not advocating harsher punishment. Martin and Simon, both of whom are played by first-time actors, are memorably grubby and deeply affecting. She is, however, probing the nature of what it is we call childhood, something society idealizes at the same time it allows children like Simon and Martin to live like stray dogs.

How did they get this way? "The less I think of it, the better off I am," says Martin, the older of the two, who is jaded enough to know the value of amnesia: When he tells Simon he's dreamt of being an angel, Simon asks what it takes to be one. "Forget everything," Martin says, "and disappear."

There is the occasional flash of innocence, but also apparently much to forget. In one reformatory, Martin's head is shaved, and the scars on his scalp indicate some brutality. This makes him look a little like a midget Hannibal Lecter, and, perhaps more meaningfully, a sawed-off Jean Genet: Martin is a sociopath with a poet's soul, which he pours out painfully to his young love, Marie (Sandrine Blancke), but which is certain to be corrupted by the malignant neglect of his life.

Martin's mantra—"I wish I were the son of a female shark ... I wouldn't be so mean"—is his plea for some power and release. But as a recurring motif, and the source of the film's title, it's a bit elusive in a story that takes an otherwise naked look at lost innocence. "I am the son of a sardine and an anchovy ..." Simon recites, mocking Martin. It's a chance to laugh, and you should take advantage of it. Because for all its style and its memorable boys, "Son of the Shark" is as grim as hunger.

VILLAGE VOICE, 3/14/95, p. 59, Gary Dauphin

Fourteen-ish Martin Vanderhoes (Ludovic Vandendaele) narrates *Son of the Shark* with the ghost-story whisper little boys will exchange in institutions after lights-out. Endlessly repeating his wish to have been born the son of a female shark (believing he'd be a big fish in a peaceful kingdom), Martin states early on that he doesn't want to talk about the vandalism, theft, and borderline sexual assault that are his and younger brother Simon's favorite forms of play. Reminiscent of *The 400 Blows* and loosely based on the real-life "Terrors of Ligon" (Ligon being the Vanderhoes' French seaside home), *Shark* is unflinching and understated at the same time, first-timer Agnes Merlet's fluid images showing what Martin can't or won't tell.

Abandoned by their mother and disowned by their father, Martin and Simon (Erick Da Silva) are misguided extremists of the boys-will-be-boys school of growing up, driven as much by boredom and native energies as by their material needs for food and shelter. Sending a city bus off a cliff here, stealing food and money there, they show their meanest streak in occasional fits of girl-abuse, only instead of dipping pigtails they force one victim to strip naked in a wintery field, having a good laugh while making off with her new coat and scarf.

Martin and Simon are either running away from the juvey homes set aside for boys too young for prison, or running towards each other, their dance a two-step wherein Simon runs towards Martin and Martin leads them both towards the sea he loves. Aside from the director, Martin is *Shark's* resident romantic, spending most of his downtime reading a book on the behavior of ocean goldfish, composing watery poetry to a crush about making love in the ocean ("once before drowning") while Merlet fills the screen with slowed-down underwater footage, flashes of dream sequences, and leisurely elegiac images of Ligon's stark beaches, docks, and railways.

Martin's crush Marie (Sandrine Blancke) is the only outsider who can intrude into the brothers' universe (*Shark's* adults are mostly brutes or dippy liberal enablers). Initially, Marie's sympathy for Martin is a sign of the boys' hidden goodness, but for her trouble she has to suffer Simon's jealousy and Martin's fits of slightly masturbatory delirium. In the end, Merlet's achievement is in eliciting a grudging respect for her pair of otherwise reprehensible subjects, so that when Martin (who earlier asserts that he always lies) ends *Son of the Shark* by explaining that he never knows what he'll do before he actually does it, you actually want to believe him.

Also reviewed in:
CHICAGO TRIBUNE, 6/2/95, Friday/p. L, Michael Wilmington
NEW YORK TIMES, 3/10/95, p. C14, Stephen Holden
VARIETY, 10/18/93, p. 52, David Stratton

SPECIES

A Metro-Goldwyn-Mayer Pictures release. *Executive Producer:* David Streit. *Producer:* Frank Mancuso, Jr. and Dennis Feldman. *Director:* Roger Donaldson. *Screenplay:* Dennis Feldman. *Director of Photography:* Andrzej Bartkowiak. *Editor:* Conrad Buff. *Music:* Christopher Young.

Music Editor: Thomas Milano. *Choreographer:* Holly Schiffer. *Sound:* Lee Orloff and (music) Robert Fernandez and Danny Wallin. *Sound Editor:* Jay Boekelheide. *Casting:* Amanda Mackey and Cathy Sandrich. *Production Designer:* John Muto. *Art Director:* Dan Webster. *Set Designer:* Mick Cukurs. *Set Decorator:* Jackie Carr. *Set Dresser:* Eric J. Bates, Robert Bleckman, Michael R. Driscoll, and William Kemper Wright. *Special Effects:* Jeff Jarvis. *Visual Effects:* Richard Edlund. *Costumes:* Joe I. Tompkins. *Make-up:* Kenny Myers. *Make-up ("Sil"):* H.R. Giger. *Special Make-up Effects:* Steve Johnson. *Stunt Coordinator:* Glenn Randall, Jr. and Max Kleven. *Running time:* 111 minutes. *MPAA Rating:* R.

CAST: Ben Kingsley (Xavier Fitch); Michael Madsen (Press Lennox); Alfred Molina (Stephen Arden); Forest Whitaker (Dan Smithson); Marg Helgenberger (Laura Baker); Natasha Henstridge (Sil); Michelle Williams (Young Sil); Jordan Lund and Don Fischer (Aides); Scott McKenna (Train Hobo); Virginia Morris (Mother); Jayne Luke (Snack Shop Clerk); David K. Schroeder (German Tourist); David Jensen (Conductor); Esther Scott (Female Conductor); Shirley Prestia (Dr. Roth); Willam Utay (Colleague); David Selburg (Government Man); Herta Ware (Mrs. Morris); Melissa Bickerton (Fitch's Secretary); Lucy Rodriguez (Wedding Dress Saleswoman); Scott Sproule (Team Driver); Stogie Kenyatta (Cop); Gary Bullock (Motel Clerk); Susan Hauser (Lab Worker); William Bumiller (Bouncer); Caroline Barclay (Drunken Girl); Matthew Ashford (Guy in Club); Anthony Guidera (Robbie); Sarah S. Leese (Screaming Woman); Whip Hubley (John Carey); Patricia Belcher (Admittance Clerk); Richard Fancy (Doctor); Leslie Ishii (Nurse); Marliese K. Schneider (Abducted Clerk); Robert Mendelson (Homeless Man); Pam Cook (Commercial Model); Lisa Liberati (Bathroom Bimbo); Ed Stone (Waiter); Dendrie Taylor (Marie); Kurtis Burow (Baby Boy); Dana Hee (Creature Performer); Frank Welker (Voice of Alien Sil).

FILMS IN REVIEW, 9-10/95, p. 59, Andy Pawelczak

The opening of *Species,* a derivative of the *Alien* movies directed by Roger Donaldson, has the matter-of-fact creepiness of a Cronenberg bio-thriller as a frightened young girl, imprisoned in a laboratory test chamber, is about to be gassed to death. The mood doesn't last long however—exhibiting superhuman strength, the girl smashes her way to freedom and ends up in LA where the movie turns into a peculiarly humorless and unsavory riff about life on the wild side in that city of the future where there are no taboos (as one character, who has probably overdosed on *Blade Runner,* puts it).

The girl is the product of an experiment in which a human egg was fertilized with extraterrestrial DNA. With her speeded-up metabolism, she turns overnight into a yummy blond (played by Natasha Henstridge) with a powerful reproductive instinct—she's genetically programmed to bear offspring through which her species will ultimately take over the earth. Naturally, she gravitates to a trendy rock club—it's actually called Club Id—where she prowls for a man. The movie's leering conceit has the girl continually frustrated in her attempts to have sex, and when this girl doesn't get what she wants, watch out: her creamy skin boils and erupts and the inner monster—the id itself, a slimy, frog-like creature—breaks out.

Not that she's all bad. She watches TV—it's how she learns about sex—with all the innocent wonderment of discovery, and at one point she plaintively says that she doesn't know who she is or what her mission is. At first glance, she's just another spacey LA chick with a model's high cheekbones and the perfect breasts (frequently exposed) of a sleek, marble Venus, though the only thing Venusian about her is her monstrous extra-terrestrial identity. It's no wonder the government puts together a crack team of specialists to destroy this sexually aggressive female.

As chief scientist Fitch, Ben Kingsley, in white sport jacket and black tee-shirt, isn't called on to do much more than look slightly deranged as he directs the hunt. Forest Whitaker turns in his patented twitchy performance as an "empath" who can sense people's feelings, and Alfred Molina does a poor imitation of an anthropology professor. Michael Madsen, a talented and often charming actor, is slumberous and dull as a government assassin who is romantically interested in the pretty molecular biologist indifferently played by Marg Helgenberger. The actors aren't helped by Dennis Feldman's wooden dialogue that has Madsen announcing that the alien must have been there when he discovers a dead body.

Species ends up in a sewer, appropriate enough given its take on sex, or at least on female sexuality. The extraterrestrial is the classic black widow spider woman, and sexual desire itself is figured as creepy-crawly insectoid lust. Even the film's normal sex is cold-hearted and slightly inhuman. It's a prudent anti-sex movie, and perhaps future cultural historians will view it as another symptom of the Age of AIDS. As a genre movie though, it's a dismal record of missed opportunities. Bio-thrillers have the capacity to make us deeply uneasy about the mysteries of the body—about sex and reproduction and those vestigially sacred fluids coursing and rippling through the organism—but *Species* never hit a nerve.

LOS ANGELES TIMES, 7/7/95, Calendar/p. 8, Peter Rainer

"Species" is a pretty good Boo! movie. It's not the kind of sci-fi film that's going to give Stanley Kubrick any sleepless nights, and it may not give the rest of us much sleeplessness either. Its primary purpose in life is to unleash a lot of gloppy morphing and mutating and make us go—all together now—*eeeuuuh*.

Which is not to say that "Species," directed by Roger Donaldson and scripted by Dennis Feldman, doesn't go in for the usual spate of "cautionary" warnings and thou-shall-not-play-God stuff. High-toned schlock is a standard ingredient in low-grade schlock, and "Species," despite an A-cast including Ben Kingsley, Forest Whitaker and Alfred Molina, is basically the same B-movie species as "Tarantula," "Them!" and "Attack of the Crab Monsters."

Or the "Alien" movies. The monster designer of "Species," as with those films, is H.R. Giger, and he does similar creepy-crawly work here. But the horror effects, by Richard Edlund and Steve Johnson, are quicker and blobbier. Donaldson goes in for quick surgical strikes where we see just enough of the creature to both repel us and make us want to see more.

Periodically, and less successfully, he works in a weirdo special effect where we apparently are supposed to be looking through the morph's eyes. It's hard to make out what is going on in these moments: It's as if we were peering into the lobster tank of a seafood restaurant through a pair of Blu-Blockers.

The high/low-toned gimmick in "Species" is that a creature—code-named Sil—has been secretly engineered in Utah by U.S. scientists after broadcasting our DNA code to the galaxies and receiving back a code from outer space. The resulting mutant, an intergalactic DNA cocktail, initially takes the form of an angelic-looking blond girl, but a girl with lethal powers who bursts out of a top-secret lab as she's about to be terminated. By the time she slips onto an Amtrak train, Sil has morphed into a leggy goddess (Natasha Henstridge). She's Species as Super-model.

At least those aliens have a sense of humor.

In pursuit of her destruction are project leader Xavier Fitch (Ben Kingsley); Press (Michael Madsen), a Marine-trained hit man; Dan (Forest Whitaker), an "empath" who can read feelings; Laura (Marg Helgenberger), a molecular biologist with a yen for Press; and Arden (Alfred Molina), a nebbishy Harvard anthropology professor. It's the kind of dream team you want in your corner when you're out hunting morphs.

Most of the hunt takes place in Los Angeles, where Sil disembarks in search of a hunk to mate with. The idea that a super-model mutant morph could sashay undetected in L.A. is a good joke. So is the way she learns the sex act from studying an adult channel in her hotel. Sil's predatory instinct and mating instinct are twinned. She hooks up with a smoothie who has the kind of gleaming condo that comes equipped with clap-on lights; showing unexpected taste, she moves on to a more giving guy with a back-yard jacuzzi.

The attempt to turn the pursuers into a slapstick wild bunch doesn't really come off. (Tonal shifts are not Donaldson's forte.) The cast can't seem to stay in the same movie together: Kingsley, complete with bald pate and sliced syllables, seems to be trying to morph into the late Donald Pleasence; Madsen affects a Mitchum-like sleepiness; Whitaker seems clueless about his role, maybe because the role itself is clueless. Dan's vaunted empathy—when, for instance, he walks in on a bloody murder scene—takes the form of saying things like "something horrible happened in here."

Duh.

"Species" is on equally specious grounds when it tries to work up radical feminist points, especially since the filmmakers specialize in gobs of appropriately gratuitous nudity. But it's fun to find in-your-face feminism rearing its Medusa head in this glop-a-thon. Sil, for example, was engineered as a female because women are supposedly "more docile." That gets a big laugh. So does the scene where Sil gets carried away and pokes her tongue clear through the skull of a paramour. Now *that's* deep kissing.

The filmmakers try to tantalize us with cosmic thoughts about which half of Sil—the human or the intergalactic—is truly the predatory half. It may not matter. It's not as if we're watching the Discovery Channel here. "Species" doesn't take you anywhere you haven't already visited in the sci-fi realm. But it's an amusingly scary recap of where we've been.

NEW YORK, 7/17/95, p. 49, David Denby

Species is a sci-fi horror movie with disgustingly damp, tentacled creatures right out of *Alien,* but it has its moments of amusement.

When the replicant, or whatever it is, wants to mate, it takes the form of a tall blonde beauty (model Natasha Henstridge) and heads for Los Angeles, where its habit of suddenly removing its clothes does not strike the predatory local males as anything unusual. Too bad for them. *Species* is sort of sleazy-sexy: Everyone in it, including most of a very strange team of scientists, is ready to rock. If you walk out before the long chase in the sewer at the end, you might have a fairly good time.

NEW YORK POST, 7/7/95, p. 35, Michael Medved

"Alien" meets "Attack of the Killer Bimbos" ...

That's the basic setup for "Species," a slick piece of work which offers an illogically alluring combination of sexual titillation and sci-fi horror.

The script (by Dennis Feldman) uses an ingenious premise to put the human race in jeopardy. For the last 20 years we've been sending messages about our planet into deepest space in hopes of getting some kind of response, and this story suggests that some unknown civilization finally answers back. These presumably friendly aliens send us the sequence of their DNA, along with the suggestion that we combine it with our own.

Ben Kingsley plays the cold-blooded head of a top secret lab who carries out this suggestion, injecting alien DNA into human ova and producing a superficially normal human female. When the child begins displaying some menacing characteristics, however, Kingsley decides to terminate her existence, only to see the child escape from the desert lab, hop a train, and head for L.A.

By the time she arrives, she has mutated into a staggeringly attractive adult with a phenomenally proportioned (and frequently displayed) body—played by 20-year-old model Natasha Henstridge. This superior creature begins searching California clubs for a male to father the new generation, while dispatching rejected suitors with gruesome gusto.

To put in end to her killing spree, Kingsley assembles a secret team to find the creature and destroy her. This odd squad includes a nerdy anthropologist (Alfred Molina), a sympathetic psychic (Forest Whitaker), a lonely molecular biologist (Marg Helgenberger) and a tough ex-Marine who's an expert in assassination (Michael Madsen).

Whenever the movie concentrates on these monster hunters, it sags badly; it's hard to accept that the authorities would entrust the survival of humanity to these four bickering bumblers.

When it follows the alien herself, however, the film is riveting—helped by spectacular special effects (designed by the creator of the original "Alien") that shows the translucent, horrifying (but still sexy) creature that inhabits its blond human shell.

Like many another monster movie there's an underlying message that sex is dangerous; this powerful female may be irresistible to all men who cross her path, but she manages to kill them in a variety of hideously unpleasant ways.

Director Roger Donaldson is a savvy pro who makes the most of his cast and the mechanical marvels at his disposal.

Although there are altogether too many scenes of unsuspecting humans creeping around dark corners—just waiting for something out there to *pounce*—and the movie as a whole runs at least 20 minutes too long, for those in the market for this sort of nightmarish film "Species" delivers the grisly goods.

NEWSDAY, 7/7/95, Part II/p. B2, Jack Mathews

Los Angeles just can't get a break. Fires, mud slides, earthquakes, riots, illegal aliens, celebrity murders.

And now this: Some horny alien is running around in the body of a high-fashion model trying to mate with every guy she meets in order to reproduce and bring down the ultimate insult on Angelenos—extinction!

Conjured up as a sort of earthbound version of the "Alien" series, Roger Donaldson's "Species" is a space-age horror fantasy about a catastrophic in-vitro fertilization experiment. Remember 20 years ago when we transmitted all that data about ourselves into the galaxy, in case there were other computer-literate civilizations on line out there? Well, according to the movie, we got some nice e-mail back from somebody, along with a genetic recipe for blending our DNA with theirs, and our scientists naturally decided to give it a whirl.

The result is a test-tube babe (Canadian model Natasha Henstridge) who is fast, loose and ovulating in L.A. All she needs is a healthy man with no common sense, and as Hugh Grant's friend Divine knows, you need only stand on a street corner in Hollywood and they will come to you.

"Species" is polished shlock, a grade Z horror movie with terrific production values, some nifty special effects, a story to rival "Plan 9 From Outer Space" and some of the worst, dialogue uttered in years.

"Something bad has happened here," says the psychic (Forest Whitaker), standing in a small train compartment with a murdered conductor and an empty cocoon large enough to have given birth to John Goodman.

Later, while chasing the alien through the L.A. sewer system, Michael Madsen's macho bounty hunter stumbles onto another fresh corpse and calls out to his companions, "She must have come through here."

I ask you, what chance do we have?

Besides the bounty hunter and the psychic, the team of alienbusters recruited by the taciturn scientist (Ben Kingley) includes a molecular biologist—and babe in her own right (Marg Helgenberger)—whose scientific curiosity is distracted by her own growing desire to mate with the bounty hunter, and a Harvard cultural behaviorist (Alfred Molina), who is determined to find a little action for himself during the junket.

Screenwriter Dennis Feldman, author of the equally thought-provoking "The Golden Child," must have had something in mind with his blend of lust and danger, and if you were to take it seriously, you might see the whole thing as an AIDS metaphor. I can't think of anything riskier than going to bed with a stranger who has spikes shoot out of her back when she's aroused.

You could also make the argument that "Species" is a rap on the new woman, the sex object cum predator. One of the film's few intended laughs comes when Kingsley explains that they made the test-tube baby a female so she would be "more docile and controllable."

"I guess you guys don't get around very much," says the well-traveled bounty hunter.

It's best not to think of "Species" as anything other than a scream-and-hug summer date movie. Things are popping out of dark corners constantly, some of the effects surrounding the alien's transformation from gorgeous—and frequently naked—human to shiny mechanical insect are fun, and the fatal sex scenes are a howl.

Look for my favorite; it *ends* with a French kiss.

SIGHT AND SOUND, 10/95, p. 60, Philip Kemp

In a remote government research lab in Utah, top scientist Xavier Fitch gives the order to have a young girl exterminated, but she escapes. Fitch assembles a team of experts to help track down the girl: biologist Laura Baker, anthropologist Stephen Arden, psychic Dan Smithson and ex-marine Preston Lennox. The girl, named Sil, was bred from alien DNA (beamed to earth by an unknown extraterrestrial race) injected into human ova. She grew to her present 13-year-old appearance in a few weeks. Alarmed by symptoms of her alien nature, Fitch decided to terminate the experiment.

On board a train bound for Los Angeles, Sil passes through a chrysalid stage and emerges as a beautiful young woman. Fitch and his team, tracing her through a stolen credit card, realise she plans to mate. At a night club, Sil is picked up by Robbie, a rich socialite. However, sensing he has diabetes, she rejects his advances and kills him. Evading Preston, Sil is injured in a car accident and taken to hospital by a passer-by, John Carey. She heals her own injuries and leaves with Carey. They are about to make love when Preston and Laura intrude; Sil kills Carey and once again escapes.

Sil lures her pursuers into a car chase culminating in a staged accident. Fitch declares the mission accomplished and leads his team back to the Biltmore Hotel to relax. Sil changes her appearance and makes for the Biltmore. There she seduces Stephen, becoming instantly pregnant. Sensing her presence, Dan alerts the others, but Sil kills Stephen and flees into the sewers. In the pursuit Fitch is killed by Sil; the others follow her into a tunnel leading to subterranean tar pits, where after metamorphosing into a totally alien shape she gives birth. Rescuing Dan from the newborn, Preston and Laura manage to kill both it and Sil, but a rat that has eaten a severed length of alien tentacle undergoes a strange mutation.

Walking cactuses, giant peapods, ambulatory dollops of raspberry jam—ever since the hyper-paranoid 50s, sci-fi cinema has been well supplied with malignant aliens come to devour humanity by subsuming our quivering substance into theirs. And the most deadly of these predators are always the ones (as in the various versions of *Invasion of the Body Snatchers*, or John Carpenter's *The Thing*) who look just like us. *Species* works a twist on this scenario by making its central entity semi-human to begin with, but then leaves the idea largely undeveloped. "Half us, half something else—I wonder which was the predatory half?" muses biologist Laura Baker, offering an intriguing re-take on the whole plot: that maybe the original extraterrestrial message really was well-intentioned, the alien race simply having no idea what a slimebucket species (namely us) they were merging their DNA with. But her remark comes only at the very end of the film, after the semi-alien has been—supposedly—destroyed.

There are earlier hints of the same submerged message—the venue where Sil does her sexual trawling is called The Id Club, suggesting she's tapping into unreconstructed areas of the human psyche—but it's never mined for its full potential. Instead *Species* mostly settles for the conventional alien-threat-to-humanity angle, following it through a series of well-orchestrated but routine situations and relying on atmosphere, design flair and emetic detail. Robbie, Sil's first pick-up, suffers the French kiss from hell (her tongue comes straight out the back of his head) and the chrysalid stage from which the full-grown Sil emerges looks like nothing so much as a giant, pulsating doner kebab.

Making her feature film debut, supermodel Natasha Henstridge not only looks drop-dead gorgeous but turns her inexperience to advantage: her air of slightly vacant puzzlement perfectly suits a six-week-old adult trying to make sense of an incomprehensible world. Her fellow lead actors, though, are left struggling with seriously underwritten roles, even if Michael Madsen does wonders with scant material. As the empath Dan, Forest Whitaker comes off worst, being limited to acting the human bloodhound ("She went that way") and coming out with startling insights like "She only kills when she feels threatened."

That *Species* borrows (from *Alien, Terminator II, Hellraiser III:* and *The Third Man*, to name but a few would hardly matter if its influences were assimilated, but instead they feel slung together, and the film doesn't always retain a grip on its own conventions. At one point, Sil seems either to have become telepathic or is speaking through Fitch's mouth—the latter option raising the possibility that Fitch too is an alien. But having served its plot purpose, the device vanishes. *Species* is pacy, stylish and consistently watchable, but as with so much Hollywood product (*Outbreak* was another recent example), an ingenious concept has been allowed to go for far less than it's worth. If given a little extra thought, a little less reliance on standard dramatic formulas, a much more interesting film could have been made here.

TIME, 7/17/95, p. 58, Richard Corliss

At Florida's Walt Disney World, the hot new "ride" is George Lucas' Alien Encounter. In this fond tribute to William Castle, sleaze showman extraordinaire of *13 Ghosts* and *The Tingler*, visitors enter a circular room, are strapped into seats and see a huge hideous monster writhing in a plastic tube. Then the alien escapes—and the lights go out. Heavy footsteps approach, and your seat gets a violent rattle. You feel the creature's breath and reptilian tongue on the back of your neck. An icky liquid drenches you; is it someone's exploding guts or your own fear-sweat? The experience is divinely cheesy: 3-D radio, aiming only to scare you nuts. And it works; the crowd happily screams along.

Until every mall theater seat can be juiced and goosed like the ones in Alien Encounter, movie directors will have to rely on mere sight and sound for their scare effects, and moviegoers will have to make do with spook shows like *Species*. Films, of course, can still do a thing or two that haunted houses can't: develop elaborate story lines, depict complex emotions, lift the audience by means other than hydraulics. *Species*, written by Dennis Feldman, does some of that, at least in its first hour. This sci-fi horror opus also has the summer's sexiest High Concept: *Alien* meets *The Fugitive*. The escaped monster is on the prowl for a mate in Los Angeles—and she's babe-a-licious!

The creature, hatched in the test-tube mating of an alien intelligence and a human ovum, is called Sil. As embodied by model Natasha Henstridge, Sil has a voluptuously thin form and a face—severe and curiously bland—that never reveals its secrets. That's perfect for *Species*, since the audience's sympathies are meant to shift uneasily between the determination of a crack search team to keep the creature from reproducing and the desire of Sil to increase and multiply, engulf and devour. So Sil goes cruising L.A. bars. A gorgeous blond who just wants sex shouldn't have trouble getting a date. But Sil is picky: no junkies, no diabetics. And no survivors. Her embrace is crushing; her French kiss is to die from.

For a while, director Roger Donaldson *(No Way Out)* keeps it all working smartly, like a serrated knife on the viewer's nerves. And the creature creators, H.R. Giger and Richard Edlund, make Sil in her alien mode look variously like evil pudding and a spiny octopus. The monster isn't the problem here; it's the humans, Sil's pursuers, who make *Species* turn specious. One of them (Forest Whitaker) is an "empath" who can intuit everything about Sil—her moods, motives and fears—everything except that she's standing right behind him. Alfred Molina, playing an expert in cross cultures (and Sil, when riled, is one very cross culture), doesn't get at all suspicious when a beautiful woman looking exactly like Sil shows up in his hotel bedroom and insists on having sex. Even Hugh Grant might decline that proposition.

Well, if smart people didn't do stupid things, there wouldn't be horror movies. And for those who indulge its inanities, this 2-D alien encounter has some final surprises, including its own baby boom. Watch out, folks. Sil has a baby. *Boom!*

VILLAGE VOICE, 7/4/95, p. 50, Amy Taubin

I went to a preview of *Species* with Ann, Georgia, and Georgia's friend Michael. Georgia chose the seats-way up front because she doesn't like anyone to come between her and the screen. I think if I had been sitting further back I wouldn't have jumped and screamed quite so much but, as it was, I left the theatre feeling like a pop tart, which, considering that *Species* is a horror movie, was exactly the way I was supposed to feel. Ann liked it the best. She thought it was a great summer movie (note to publicists: attribute this pull quote to Ann Powers, *Voice* music editor, and not to yours truly). Georgia and Michael were rather less enthusiastic (they were worn down by the last sequence which seems to take place in a sewer below the La Brea tar pits), and I was somewhere in between.

We all agreed with Ann that *Species* was like an expensive Troma movie. Expensive because it starred recognizable actors (Michael Madsen, Forrest Whitaker, Ben Kingsley), because it seemed from the alternately dumb-smart writing that half a dozen script doctors must have been called into service, and because in the chase scenes—most of the cuts matched up pretty well. And it was like a Troma movie in its essence because there was at least one easily recognizable quote from some other movie in every scene. I was impressed that director Roger Donaldson could do all that quoting without making you think *Species* was made by some brat who worked in a video all his life and who was out to prove how big his, well, his language vocabulary was. I'm also partial to movies that quote *Marnie* and have many scenes set in the girls' bathroom.

"It's about fear of Cindy Crawford," I said as we were leaving the theater, my eye having fallen on Richard Gere's rude *Esquire* cover line "Cindy Who?" "No, it's about fear of super models," said Ann who has an excellent ability to generalize from the specific.

To get to the specifics of *Species:* The premise is that our government has been in communication with an alien society galaxies away which has been so generous as to provide our scientists with the code for their DNA. The head scientist (Kingsley) mixes a batch of their DNA into a batch of our own and voila, within six months, he's got Sil, a nine-year-old girl straight out of *Children of the Corn.* ("We decided to make it female so it would be more docile and controllable.") However, when Kingsley notices some weird undulating bumps under her skin, he decides to terminate the experiment by pumping cyanide into her plastic bubble. Because this is just too close to Auschwitz for comfort, we're on her side when she breaks out and hops a train for L.A. (all within the first 10 minutes of the movie).

On the train, Sil eats a lot of junk food, whereupon big thick worms pop through her skin. The worms mass into a kind of cocoon from which emerges a perfectly formed five-foot, 10-inch blond (Natasha Henstridge). These particular alien effects were designed by H.R. Giger, which is why it feels like we've seen them somewhere before.

"L.A. is perfect for her. Nothing in this town is taboo or unacceptable," says one of the team Kingsley's assembled to track the alien. Natasha strides through Union Station and across Hollywood Boulevard as if the town were her runway. I don't know if she can act, but she manages to keep her eyes front all the time, which is what predators are supposed to do. Sil's biological clock is ticking. She needs to breed. For the rest of the movie, Sil searches L.A. for the perfect mate, ripping off her shirt at every opportunity. She's every guy's fantasy but her aggressive style—not to mention all those snakes and worms —turns dreams to nightmares.

Ann advises: "It's not a good dating movie." I'm afraid I agree.

Also reviewed in:
CHICAGO TRIBUNE, 7/7/95, Friday/p. D, Michael Wilmington
NATION, 8/28-9/4/95, p. 218, Stuart Klawans
NEW YORK TIMES, 7/7/95, p. C3, Caryn James
VARIETY, 7/10-16/95, p. 34, Godfrey Cheshire
WASHINGTON POST, 7/7/95, p. F6, Richard Harrington
WASHINGTON POST, 7/7/95, Weekend/p. 36, Joe Brown

SPIKE AND MIKE'S FESTIVAL OF ANIMATION '95

A Festival Films release of 13 animated shorts. *Director:* Tim Watts, David Stoten, Mo Willems, Bill Plympton, Mark Baker, Darren Butts, Joanna Quinn, Vanessa Schwartz, Dana Hanna, Erica Russell, Raman Hul, Michael Dudock de Wit, Alison Snowden, David Fine, and Nick Park. *Running time:* 96 minutes. *MPAA Rating:* Not Rated.

NEW YORK POST, 10/27/95, p. 42, Bill Hoffmann

Animation festivals tend to be hit-and-miss affairs, so I'm happy to report the latest collection of 13 shorts from the "Spike & Mike" folks hits the bull's-eye all around.

Seven either won or were nominated for Academy Awards, and the other six are just as good.

The program begins with "The Big Story"—a sidesplitting send-up of those great newspaper flicks like "Ace in the Hole"—with a clay-animated Kirk Douglas brilliantly voiced by master impressionist Frank Gorshin.

Next is the hysterical "Bob's Birthday," in which a 40-year-old dentist enters a mid-life crisis and wrecks his birthday surprise party in the process.

The historical ups and downs of Great Britain are wonderfully chronicled in "Britannia," which portrays the country as a vicious bulldog. I suspect the English government despised this one.

"Iddy Biddy Beat" is an affectionate tribute to the cheap, kitschy animation that ruled TV in the early '60s in shows like "Colonel Bleep."

While I'm not wild about computer animation, "Legacy" and "Sleepy Guy" are aces, the latter an on-target look at how exasperating it is to awaken from a dream too soon.

"Personal Hell" is an amusing glimpse at the pitfalls of placing personal ads.

You may be grossed out by "Nose Hair"—but you've got to admit it's different—quite different from the genteel "Triangle," which shows a pair of nude dancers in some impressive line-drawing animation.

"The Village" is the most odd of the lot, a weird tale of love and murder in a strange British village.

I've saved the best for last—Nick Park's Oscar-winning 1993 short, "The Wrong Trousers." This gem follows Wallace, an eccentric inventor, and his faithful dog, Gromit, and the amusing turn their lives take when a mysterious penguin rents a spare room in their home.

VILLAGE VOICE, 10/31/95, p. 80, Justine Elias

A 90-minute collection of 12 animated films, *Spike and Mike's '95* is a chance to catch the superb work of two-time Oscar winner Nick Park. *The Wrong Trousers* is a comic thriller featuring Park's clay animation duo of Wallace and his dog Gromit. Wallace, an impoverished English dweeb, rents Gromit's room to a sinister penguin. When the neglected Gromit runs away from home, he discovers the bird's scheme to use Wallace's invention, a pair of robotic pants, in a heist. The caper climaxes with a shoot-out atop a speeding toy train, with the intrepid Gromit frantically throwing down new track just in time.

As political commentary, Joanna Ouinn's *Britannia* rules. A rapacious English bulldog gnaws on a toy globe, sinking its jaws into Ireland, Africa, and India before a growing empire bites back. In an arresting final image, the fierce canine becomes a lap dog cowering amid Britain's newest citizens.

But it is Mark Baker's *The Village* that scores a palpable emotional hit. Using no dialogue, just the sound of marching feet, Baker brings to life a provincial, fortress-like society obsessed with sex, wealth, murder, and punishment. Sound familiar?

Also reviewed in:
NEW YORK TIMES, 10/27/95, p. C10, Janet Maslin
WASHINGTON POST, 9/8/95, p. F7, Richard Harrington
WASHINGTON POST, 9/8/95, Weekend/p. 44, Desson Howe

STALINGRAD

A Strand Releasing release of a Royal Film/Bavaria Film/B.A. Productions/Perathon production. *Executive Producer:* Mark Damon and Michael Krohne. *Producer:* Joseph Vilsmaier, Hanno Huth, and Günter Rohrbach. *Director:* Joseph Vilsmaier. *Screenplay (German with English subtitles):* Johannes Heide, Jürgen Büscher, and Joseph Vilsmaier. *Director of Photography:* Joseph Vilsmaier. *Editor:* Hannes Nikel. *Music:* Norbert J. Schneider. *Sound:* Günther Stadelman and (music) Malcolm Luker. *Sound Editor:* Friedrich M. Dosch and Thomas Knöpfel. *Production Designer:* Wolfgang Hundhammer and Jindrich Goetz. *Special Effects:* Karl Baumgartner, Daniel Braunschweig, Karl-Heinz Bochnig, Gerhard Neumeier, Uda Kötting, Helmut Hribernigg, and Lasse Sorsa. *Costumes:* Ute Hofinger. *Make-up:* Sylvia Leins, Alena Sedová, Paul Schmid, Zdenek Klika, Frantisek Havlicek, Frantisek Pilny, and Jiri Farkas. *Stunt Coordinator:* Jaroslav Tomsa and Peter Drozda. *Running time:* 138 minutes. *MPAA Rating:* Not Rated.

CAST: Dominique Horwitz (Fritz Reiser); Thomas Kretschmann (Hans von Witzland); Jochen Nickel (Manfred "Rollo" Rohleder); Sebastian Rudolph (Gege); Dana Vavrova (Irina); Martin Benrath (General Hentz); Sylvester Groth (Otto); Karel Hermanek (Captain Musk); Heinz Emigholz (Edgar); Oliver Broumis (MGM); Dieter Okras (Captain Haller); Zdenek Venci (Wölk); Mark Kuhn (Pflüger); Thorsten Bollloff (Feldman); Eckhardt A. Wachholz (Minister Renner); J. Alfred Mehnert (Lupo); Ulrike Arnold (Viola); Christian Knöpfle (Dieter); Filip Cap (Ludwig); Jaroslav Tomsa (Opa Erwin); Pavel Mang (Kolia); Oto Sevcik (Major Kock); Jophi Ries (Schröder); Svatoplunk (German Soldier); Otmar Dvorak (Von Lausitz); Karel Habl

(Adjutant); Thomas Lange and Karel Hlusicka (Doctors); Alexander Koller (Accordian Player); Petr Skarke, Hynek Cermak, and Cestmir Randa (Soldiers); Jan Preucil (Major/Pilot); Bohumil Svarc (Doctor/Pilot); Pirjo Leppanen (Crying Mother); Aale Mantila (Old Father).

LOS ANGELES TIMES, 4/26/96, Calendar/p. 4, Kenneth Turan

It's not even a name on the map anymore, having been called Volgograd since 1961, but a half century ago "Stalingrad" was a place no one could ignore.

Between September 1942 and February 1943, this city in the former Soviet Union was the site of a landmark in military history, a brutal battle between German and Russian troops that ended with a million dead and turned the tide of World War II against the Nazi war machine.

Made in Germany to commemorate the 50th anniversary of that action, "Stalingrad" is an expertly crafted epic war movie, a two-hour-and-15 minute immersion in the horrors of combat so grueling you can practically smell the stench of death.

In broad outline "Stalingrad" is very much a traditional battlefield saga, complete with its focus on a few men in a single platoon and the inclusion of such standard features as grousing about food and a "Dear John" letter from home.

But, coming from the producers of "Das Boot," "Stalingrad" also believes in being realistic to the point of becoming an antiwar war movie, one that emphasizes the complete futility of heroism and the stupidity of sacrificing endless human lives in pointless maneuvers.

And director Joseph Vilsmaier, working from a script he wrote with Johannes Heide and Jurgen Buscher, does not shy away from a sympathetic portrayal of the Russians or from showing Germans behaving with barbarism as well as heroism, both toward the enemy and each other.

The most impressive aspect of "Stalingrad" is its scope. Made for $20 million, a considerable budget by European standards, the film has spent most of its money carefully re-creating hellish scenes of battlefield destruction and displaying them on color film (also shot by Vilsmaier) muted to look like vintage footage.

The carnage takes place in two very different locales. At first the Germans and Russians engage in hand-to-hand and house-to-house fighting in a rabbit warren of sewers and bombed-out buildings. Then the scene shifts to the barren outskirts of the city, where burning tanks in the snow form an eerie backdrop to the continual slaughter.

"Stalingrad's" interest in reality means it does not stint on the graphic aspects of battle. Scenes of gaping wounds, of a man blown in half and rats feasting on corpses make this one epic the squeamish might want to stay away from.

Our companions on this tour of battlefield hell are three easily recognizable war movie types. In command is Lt. Hans Von Witzland (Thomas Kretschmann), an untested and idealistic young aristocrat. Just the opposite is his most experienced NCO, crusty Manfred "Rollo" Rohleder (Jochen Nickel). And rounding out the group is cheerful corporal Fritz Reiser (Dominique Horwitz), notable for his big ears and sensible attitude.

None of these actors is known to American audiences, and that unfamiliarity, plus the use of situations we rarely see—like German soldiers rioting to be on the last plane out of Stalingrad—add to this film's feeling of verisimilitude. Though the dialogue and situations are standard at times, the film's ability to re-create the complete disintegration of a formidable fighting machine is impressive.

NEW YORK POST, 5/24/95, p. 35, Larry Worth

Countless movies boil down to the old "war is hell" message, the latest of which is "Stalingrad." But what sets this one apart is the most indelible images of combat-induced horror since "The Deer Hunter."

Shots of Nazis using flame throwers to light their way through a maze of pitch-black sewer tunnels, only to illuminate rats gnawing on human corpses is the stuff of sheer nightmare. Ditto for scenes of the story's protagonists on a snow-encrusted wasteland, quivering in icy fissures as massive tanks role over their bodies.

And then there's the unending tableaus of bloody carnage, with a plethora of amputations and severed-but-still-twitching body parts underscoring all battles' devastation.

Making the fact-based narrative even more compelling is its multi-dimensional portrayal of German soldiers, pioneered by efforts like "All Quiet on the Western Front" and "Das Boot."

Instead of focusing on goose-stepping Aryans, the action centers on a bunch of confused and frightened young men. Sure, the senseless brutality inherent in most troopers' gung-ho mindset is front and center, but so's the ability to cry, question orders and ultimately find their humanity.

The story begins in the summer of '42, with a group of Nazi foot soldiers sunning themselves on the Italian Riviera, flush with pride from having pushed English forces back to the Nile in the African Campaign. Now, it's time to teach "Ivan" a lesson, with trains transporting the forces toward a "quick victory" in Stalingrad.

"Ivan" however, has other ideas, setting the stage for a shockingly strong show of force against those invading the Soviet borders. And while history books reveal that the Russians emerged victorious, Vilsmaier's effectively documents that "winner" is a relative term.

Unfortunately, Vilsmaier's writing abilities don't equal his talents behind the camera. The result is a choppy narrative structure, with character development sometimes seeming an afterthought.

Though no fault of the long-suffering, hard-working actors (all unknowns), it's often tough to tell the dirty half-dozen apart, particularly when they're on the tundra with faces obscured by wraparound headgear and icicles.

But even if the sum never equals its brilliantly bleak parts, "Stalingrad" forges its own paths of glory.

NEWSDAY, 5/24/95, Part II/p. B11, Jonathan Mandell

"Stalingrad," a well-made if predictable war movie by German director Joseph Vilsmaier about one of the most horrible battles of World War II, is told from the German point of view: Taking cover in a bombed-out factory, handsome Hans, a lieutenant who comes from a respected family of German officers, offers a piece of bread to a young Russian boy. The boy turns his head in refusal. "Yes, I know," the lieutenant replies in a tone of elegant sarcasm. "We're the beasts who invaded Russia."

This may not ring Bitburg bells of alarm for all American viewers, but it made this one rush to the history books.

Unlike the "conventional" war in Western Europe—where "the rules of war applied," a reference book explained—Hitler planned (in his own words) "a war of annihilation" against Russia. "The purpose of the campaign," historian Paul Johnson wrote in a book, was "extermination, expansion and settlement on a colonial basis."

"The *Wehrmacht,* the regular German army, was heavily involved in atrocities in Russia," Aaron Breitbart, senior researcher of the Simon Wiesenthal Center, told me. "They engaged in mass executions of Jews and Gypsies. It wasn't just the SS."

To be fair, "Stalingrad" does not glorify the war or the German army; quite the contrary. Some Germans are shown committing atrocities: one kicking a Russian prisoner of war to death in the mud, a firing squad shooting a group of Russian civilians (including that little Russian boy). This is a "war is hell" anti-war (and anti-officer) film in the tradition of "Paths of Glory" and "Platoon."

But we are clearly meant to identify with the four or five German soldiers whom we follow through the battle of Stalingrad, which resulted in more than a million deaths and marked the beginning of the end of the Third Reich.

The men are first seen in muscular health amid the Technicolor beauty of a beach in Italy, resting after a successful campaign in Africa. Over the more than two hours of this film, they move from the exhilarating expectation of conquest, through the skittishness of skirmish, through cruelty, disillusionment and despair, to the frozen whiteness of hunger, cold, insanity and death.

The cinematography is splendid, the acting superb, the intimate scenes compelling. But in the battle scenes, do they really expect us to root for the Germans? This is a film made for a German audience, with assumptions and distinctions (between types of Hitlerites, for example) that do not translate well (as perhaps our tortured Vietnam War films aren't fully understood abroad).

Yes, war destroys decency, forcing even some decent people to adopt a morality that is at best ambiguous. But it is hard to completely embrace such universal themes when they are plopped down in a specific place and time with a specific group that may come the closest of any this century to unambiguous evil.

SIGHT AND SOUND, 5/94, p. 55, Julian Graffy

Summer 1942. German troops recuperate in Italy after the North African campaign. Their wounded lieutenant is replaced by aristocratic Hans von Witzland, and as they are transported to the Eastern front to join the battle for Stalingrad, von Witzland and his NCO, Manfred "Rollo" Rohleder, bet over which of them will survive. In Stalingrad, Hans, Rollo and their men join in the bloody battle to capture a factory. Only 62 of their 400 men survive. Young Gege shoots one of their own men by mistake. A 13-year-old Russian, Kolia, is captured. They make a sortie down into the sewers, where a Russian woman, Irina, almost kills Hans, who is saved by another of his men, Fritz Reiser. A soldier is badly wounded. In an underground hospital they are arrested for trying to hasten his treatment.

December 1942. Hans and his men are in a penal battalion, sweeping mines in the snow with Russian POWs. They rehabilitate themselves in a bold mission to disable Russian tanks, but are then forced to act as an execution squad for saboteurs, including their earlier captive, Kolia. Hans attempts in vain to save the boy. By now the German army is in disorder. Hans, Fritz and Gege attempt to escape on one of the last flights out of the local airstrip. They do not get on the plane, and return past caravans of wounded and defeated men to Rollo and the others. The sadistic officer, Haller, shoots Gege and then, fearing for his life, promises them access to the officers' supplies. They kill him. They discover the cellar crammed with stores, and Irina, now a collaborator—the 'Germans' whore'. Hans saves her from Rollo's attentions and the group splits up again. Rollo joins the ranks of the surrendered, while Hans determines to escape with Irina. Now just Irina and two of the men are left. As they cross the steppe, she too is shot and the pitiless snows close in ...

The cruel struggle for Stalingrad was one of the great turning points of the Second World War, and the Russian victory was celebrated in Vladimir Petrov's epic 1949 film *The Battle of Stalingrad*, a companion piece to Chiaureli's *The Fall of Berlin*, both of which included many scenes of Stalin and his generals calmly plotting the rout of the foe. But the Russians are largely absent from Joseph Vilsmaier's *Stalingrad*, as are the High Command, whether German or Russian. Here, the soldiers' enemies are their own callous and incompetent superior officers and the unforgiving Russian winter.

War in this *Stalingrad* is the journey of ordinary men to disillusionment and despair. Vilsmaier takes pains from the start to establish the different backgrounds, characters and attitudes of his soldiers, but by the end bitter wisdom has made them indistinguishable. Their experience of fighting is not of strategy and heroics—not, indeed, of grand encounters on the field of battle—but a maelstrom of confusion, fear and unknowing, the experience so tellingly captured by Stendhal in *The Charterhouse of Parma* and Tolstoy in *War and Peace*. All of this is pretty conventional stuff in the modern anti-heroic mode familiar from movies about the Vietnam war, though the unflinching rendering of the ingloriousness of the humiliation may have been particularly eloquent for German audiences (the film was released in Germany to mark the fiftieth anniversary of the defeat). The treatment of the peripheral Russians—girl partisan, boy captive and assorted grieving family groups—is also perfunctory and overlarded with coincidence. The main achievement of Stalingrad lies elsewhere.

Vilsmaier worked as a cinematographer for years before turning to direction, and he is his own cinematographer here. He has a marvellous eye, whether for dense, crowded interiors or for landscape. The sequences of von Witzland and his men holed up for days in the destroyed factory they are fighting to capture, and later in the fetid underground hospital display an attention to detail reminiscent of Wolfgang Petersen's *Das Boot*, and Vilsmaier is equally good at making a whole landscape come alive with masses of people going about their business. A famous Russian film about the war, Grigorii Chukhrai's *The Ballad of a Soldier*, begins with its young hero disabling huge enemy tanks, and Vilsmaier offers a bravura hyperrealist version of this, shot from close up in the snow, sound and vision tensely magnified. Best of all, indeed, are the snowscapes, where his compositions in white and blue-black capture the legendary arduousness of the Russian winter in the tradition of nineteenth-century Russian painting. And the most effective of these is the inexorable, numbing white-out that freezes the life out of the last two survivors in the emptiness of the steppe as the film ends.

VILLAGE VOICE, 5/30/95, p. 47, J. Hoberman

Film Forum's idea of a summer action flick (complete with psychic air-conditioning), *Stalingrad* is a disaster film that similarly cries out for IMAX in demolishing scores of buildings and employing acres of extras.

Of course, *Stalingrad* has a more prosaic link to history than *Die Hard With a Vengeance.* This $14 million German superproduction, a compressed miniseries shot mainly in Czechoslovakia and Finland, masterminded by the producer of *Das Boot,* and directed by former cinematographer Joseph Vilsmaier, is the most spectacular of the various media productions commemorating the 50th anniversary of the military engagement, raging from September 1942 through January 1943, that marked the turning point—as well as the central German catastrophe—of World War II.

Stalingrad opens with German soldiers frolicking on the Italian Riviera before being shipped out to the Russian front ("we'll take that city in three days"), then jumps, as if to the final reel, to show the same battered men fighting through downtown Stalingrad building to building, engaging in hand-to-hand combat, shooting each other by mistake, getting blown up, and otherwise dying before they're even individuated. Survivors escape through rat-filled sewers to field hospitals piled up with screaming wounded. And this is before winter sets in, bringing starvation, gangrene, and death marches.

The Germans are told that they are defending "Christian values." Not only do their officers callously sacrifice individual men, but when an idealistic lieutenant intervenes to help a brutalized Russian POW, he gets knocked down himself and is laughingly told to protest to the Führer. The scene where battered combatants listen to Hitler's radio speech in praise of their "victory" inverts the deathless exchange in Vladimir Petrov's epic pseudo-documentary *Battle of Stalingrad* (1949): "If Comrade Stalin only knew what a difficult time we are having," one Soviet hero tells another. The solemn response: "He knows." Where the Soviet movie showed a mythological struggle, however, *Stalingrad* is hardly a Götterdammerung. (The most powerful sequence has a pair of once-stalwart stormtroopers lift identity papers from corpses and pass themselves off as wounded in an attempt to board a Berlin-bound airplane already under siege from hysterical German soldiers.)

Non-Nazis reproach other non-Nazis for going along with the program while German soldiers rebel against being forced to execute Russian civilians. The Nazi brass is personified by one sadistic captain—he shuttles from one atrocity to the next—and the, culpability of the officers is clinched when our guys discover a secret lair of goodies, complete with Russian woman tied to the bed. In short, the filmmakers have solved the problem of Stalingrad by staging it as an arctic Vietnam. The men are basically apolitical. Their greatest loyalty is to each other; their real enemy, as in *Platoon,* is ... themselves.

The old Soviet Union may have been the site of World War II's greatest bloodbaths but (perhaps because their losses during the battle have been estimated as four to eight times greater than the German casualties) there are relatively few Russians to be found in *Stalingrad.* The movie is an epic of German suffering that ends, not unaffectingly, with a "monument" of two German deserters frozen in the snow.

Also reviewed in:
CHICAGO TRIBUNE, 2/9/96, Friday/p. K, Michael Wilmington
NEW REPUBLIC, 6/5/95, p. 32, Stanley Kauffmann
NEW YORK TIMES, 5/24/95, p. C19, Stephen Holden
VARIETY, 1/4/93, p. 57, Eric Hansen
WASHINGTON POST, 3/29/96, p. B7, Hal Hinson
WASHINGTON POST, 3/29/96, Weekend/p. 46, Desson Howe

STARS FELL ON HENRIETTA, THE

A Warner Bros. release of a Malpaso production. *Producer:* Clint Eastwood and David Valdes. *Director:* James Keach. *Screenplay:* Philip Railsback. *Director of Photography:* Bruce Surtees. *Editor:* Joel Cox. *Music:* David Benoit. *Music Editor:* Stephen A. Hope. *Sound:* John Pritchett and (music) Bobby Fernandez. *Casting:* Phyllis Huffman. *Production Designer:* Henry Bumstead. *Art Director:* Jack G. Taylor, Jr. *Set Designer:* Stephen Myles Berger. *Set Decorator:* Alan Hicks. *Set Dresser:* Jenny Patrick. *Costumes:* Van Broughton Ramsey. *Special Effects:* John Frazier. *Make-up:* Manlio Rocchetti. *Stunt Coordinator:* Buddy Van Horn. *Running time:* 110 minutes. *MPAA Rating:* PG.

CAST: Robert Duvall (Mr. Cox); Aidan Quinn (Don Day); Frances Fisher (Cora Day); Brian Dennehy (Big Dave); Lexi Randall (Beatrice Day); Kaytlyn Knowles (Pauline Day); Francesca Ruth Eastwood (Mary Day); Joe Stevens (Big Dave's Driver); Billy Bob Thornton (Roy); Victor Wong (Henry Nakai); Paul Lazar (Seymour); Spencer Garrett (Delbert Tims); Park Overall (Shirl the Waitress); Zach Grenier (Larry Ligstow); Wayne DeHart (Robert); Woody Watson (Sterling); Rodger Boyce (P.G. Pratt); George Haynes (Stratmeyer); Robert Westenberg (Mr. Rumsfelk); Landon Peterson (Raymond Rumsfelk); Richard Lineback (Les Furrows); Dylan Baker (Alex Wilde); Cliff Stephens (Arnold Humphries); Rob Campbell (Kid); Tom Aldredge (Grizzzled Old Man); Jennifer Griffin (Brothel Madame); Laura Poe (Prostitute); Billy Streater (Poker Oilman); Danny Wantland (Hotel Clerk Cecil); Craig Erickson (Terry, Farmer #1); Jerry Haynes (George, Farmer #2); Robert A. Burns (Franklin, Farmer #3); Blue Deckert (Contractor); Stephen M. Berger (Roustabout); Monty Stuart (Gas Station Attendant); Lou Hancock (Old Tent Lady); Richard Reyes (Hotel Handyman); Richard L. Gray (Roughneck); Marietta Marich (Adult Pauline Narrator); David Sanders (Henchman).

LOS ANGELES TIMES, 9/15/95, Calendar/p. 2, Kenneth Turan

For a little picture like "The Stars Fell on Henrietta" to get made, powerful people have to fall in love with it. And although a good number did, including Robert Duvall, who gives the kind of deft performance that has become his trademark, it wasn't enough to raise this film out of the realm of the ordinary.

Both first-time screenwriter Philip Railsback and director James Keach had grandfathers who were Texas oil wildcatters during the 1930s, and they conceived "Henrietta" as homage to a class of men they felt deserved more appreciation.

Clint Eastwood shared their enthusiasm, and when he signed on as coproducer and agreed to make the film under his Malpaso banner, a lot of pieces fell into place. Among the Eastwood regulars on the production team are co-producer David Valdes, cinematographer Bruce Surtees, production designer Henry Bumstead and editor Joel Cox. And acting roles were given to Eastwood's former companion Frances Fisher (memorable in "Unforgiven") and their young daughter, Francesca Ruth Eastwood.

Although everyone involved does solid work, "Henrietta's" story does not finally seem worthy of so much attention. Slow and obvious, with a tendency to mistake unpleasantness for reality, it is worth seeing only for Duvall's memorable performance, yet another notch in his world championship belt, character acting division.

Duvall plays Mr. Cox, "not duke, not lord, just Mr. Cox," a veteran wildcatter who wanders through 1935 Texas accompanied by his cat, Matilda, and a dark cloud that signifies misfortune, not oil. Although Cox prefers to say, "I've had my ups and downs," no one else can remember any of the ups.

An eccentric hunchmeister who believes he can both hear and smell oil underground, Cox is a man of steely determination with the air of a devilish Mr. Scratch about him. With his bow tie, bowler hat and sparse goatee, he materializes like a cantankerous leprechaun on the farm Don Day (Aidan Quinn) owns with his wife, Cora (Fisher), just outside of Henrietta.

With three children and a dog to support and a hefty mortgage on his land, Day is not exactly in a supportive mood when Cox announces that he smells oil on the homestead and needs $5,000 to bring it to the surface.

Although the eventual outcome of this hunch is not much in doubt, time does have to be filled up, and Railsback's script splits the story line into two lackluster segments. Cox retreats to the metropolis of Big Stone, determined to get the drilling money any way he can, and Day, left to himself, finds that he's been so infected by the oil virus that he's willing to risk his marriage to get a well into the ground.

With the intention of giving "Henrietta" a bittersweet quality, both of these subplots have been peopled by noticeably sour-tempered individuals. But given the film's generally uninspired level of storytelling, all that accomplishes is to make the proceedings more unpleasant than they need to be.

Duvall's performance, however, is frankly on a different level than anything else in the film, so assured that even Matilda the cat can't steal a single scene. With his innate ability to create people whole, to make his familiar mannerisms and gestures work effectively in every situation, Duvall is an actor to wonder at. Although it is not within his power to save the picture, if you collect memorable performances "The Stars Fell on Henrietta" is worth a visit.

NEW YORK POST, 9/15/95, p. 42, Thelma Adams

Small pictures—character-driven, hard-scrabble, slice-of-life dramas about under-represented segments of the American experience—used to be the domain of American independent filmmakers. Now, while Young Turks Quentin ("Pulp Fiction") Tarantino and Bryan ("The Usual Suspects") Singer crank out genre movies, Warner Bros. carries on the "Heartland" tradition with "The Stars Fell on Henrietta."

It's 1935 and times are hard for farmers and oilmen alike. American eccentric Mr. Cox (Robert Duvall) cuts across the West Texas landscape in his battered Ford. As if his shabby brown bowler wasn't enough of a clue, we know he's a character by the cat riding shotgun.

The luckless oil wildcatter has never profited from a big strike. Cox still has a dream (even if his suit pockets hold nothing but lint) and, damn, if he doesn't smell oil on a dust-blown farm two spits from Henrietta, Texas. This could be the start of something big ...

Honest, hard-working cotton farmers Don and Cora Day (Aidan Quinn and Frances Fisher) own the property. They're just one payment away from bank foreclosure when Cox arrives with a risky proposition. Don, a dreamer himself, starts hoping for a lucky strike ...

Having set up the situation—a man, a cat and a dream pitch in to save the family farm—novice screenwriter Philip Railsback heaps on the adversity. Cora throws Don out, Cox gets tossed behind bars, the bank threatens, a terrible accident occurs. Cue the locusts and frogs and gas leaks.

In time worn root-for-the-underdog fashion, Railsback tosses in a string of evil authority figures: a mustached banker with a thing for Cora, a scornful teacher who spits on Don, and an oil fat cat played with villainous glee by Brian Dennehy.

James Keach (Jane Seymour's Husband) directs the script with an "American Playhouse" reverence. He achieves many beautiful images: an early shot of a star-filled sky dominating the land contrasts nicely with a later, nocturnal view of a dozen cars shooting across the black plane like a stellar daisy chain.

But Keach's vision remains as flat as a picture postcard. The director never achieves a rhythm or momentum to propel the movie through numerous dry patches, nor does he have the power to pull better performances out of weaker actors.

The skeletal-faced Duvall ("The Godfather") rises above the material. He gives his body a jerky grace as if every sore muscle and failed scheme still echoes in his shoulders, spine and knees. Playing off the cat and the Day's daughter Pauline, Duvall strikes up a flinty warmth that he keeps kindled in eyes that still dare to hope behind wrinkles that give a thousand reasons to abandon the dream.

However, Cox is a character part better suited to a major supporting role than carrying the blue-eyed Quinn, who hauls his body like a cotton sack, and a washed-out Fisher who keeps close to the faded wallpaper.

In the movie's coda, an aged Pauline Day recalls the last time she saw Cox. His parting words: "Hitch your wagon to a star, sweetheart."

Sometimes that just isn't enough. This creaky, well-intentioned Dust Bowl drama hitched itself to Duvall but, through no fault of the actors, "The Stars Fell on Henrietta" fails to strike oil.

NEWSDAY, 9/15/95, Part II/p. B3, Jack Mathews

I have no idea whether Philip Railsback intended his screenplay for "The Stars Fell on Henrietta" as a fairy tale, but that's how I saw it. Any story that depicts the Dust Bowl of the Great Depression with the kind of earnest hopefulness that runs through this movie is pure romance.

And as such, it's welcomed.

My parents, like the Joads in "The Grapes of Wrath," were driven from their Plains home by the double-whammy of the Depression and the drought in the mid-'30s, and sent down that same highway bound for glory in the dreamed-of Eden of California. (It was no such thing, of course, until the war put everyone to work.) "The Stars Fell on Henrietta" stays behind, in northern Texas, where farmers often gambled their last dimes drilling holes in their parched fields, hoping to strike oil before the banks called their loans.

That's the situation ultimately facing Don (Aidan Quinn) and Cora (Frances Fisher) Day in "The Stars Fell on Henrietta," after they rescue an apparent hobo (Robert Duvall) from a dust storm, and he begins to fill their and their two girls' heads with images of a sea of oil beneath their land. He can smell it, he says, and he can hear it, when he puts his ear to the ground. All he needs to bring it up is everything they've got.

Though the story pivots on the conflict between Don, who wants to drill, and Cora, who sees Mr. Cox as a snake oil salesman, the focus of "Stars" remains focused on Duvall's character, a self-proclaimed oilman who has sniffed out fortunes for some of Texas' richest men but never got a piece of the action.

With everything he owns in a suitcase, and his pet cat Matilda under his arm, Mr. Cox is about to give up and head for California himself, until he gets a whiff of the Days' farm. From then on, he is determined to poke a hole in their ground—right there where his nose, ears, divining rods and cat mark the spot—to call salvation up.

Mr. Cox is a wonderful character, his intentions pure from the moment we meet him, and Duvall was the perfect choice to play him. He's a man of immense dignity, confidence and stubbornness, willing to put up with any humiliation to follow his intuition. His failed attempts to promote money from insensitive investors are as painful to watch as his successful attempts to grab their money are pleasures to behold. A person down to his last hope can be pitiable or enviable, depending on whether he's a quitter or a dreamer, and Mr. Cox is no quitter.

"Stars" is a small, intelligent movie, one of the increasing number of such films we happily observe leaking through the commercial filters of Hollywood. The inevitable oil strike is a high dramatic moment, but don't go expecting a big scene every five minutes. Railsback has written the cinematic equivalent of a short story—rich on texture, thin on plot—and James Keach, making his debut as a feature-film director, handles it with the care of someone restoring a family album.

The movie, with the help of veteran production designer Henry Bumstead ("Vertigo," "The Sting") and cinematographer Bruce Surtees (a longtime collaborator of "Stars" producer Clint Eastwood), perfectly re-creates a place and time where gangly oil derricks served as beacons of light on the desperate landscape, and where the difference between the haves and the have-nots could be read by the shine on their shoes.

What happens to the people of Henrietta is as improbable as snow, but on behalf of those who lived through it, we can dream.

VILLAGE VOICE, 9/26/95, p. 86, Michael Atkinson

Smalltown, working-class bathos is one of Hollywood's favorite brands of malarkey—whetstone and treacle. The nobility of soil laborers, the beauty of impoverished landscapes, the warmth of families that have nothing but each other—moviemakers romantically fascinated, like Englishmen drawn to the desert. Never mind that poor, uneducated families I've known eat at themselves like cancer. Between long bouts of insufferable whimsy and predictable crisis, movies like *The Stars Fell on Henrietta* and *The Run of the Country* scan like a politician's fever dreams brought on by too much heartland sloganeering and top-shelf Scotch.

Henrietta, the first Malpaso film neither directed by not starring Clint Eastwood since *Ratboy*, follows Mr. Cox (Robert Duvall), a luckless and unpersuasive oil promoter trying to manifest his dreams and sniff out that Big Strike in the 1935 North Texas dust bowl. Cox is pure crackpot, but we're supposed to love him and have faith as he endures multiple humiliations, gets salt-of-the-earth clay farmers Aidan Quinn and Frances Fisher to splurge for a derrick, and talks to his cat. It's quite a lot to ask, especially since the muddled story-packed like a Tokyo subway with tragedy, mishap, and despair—is spoiling for a gusher from the first frame. Duvall has only his trademarked breathless chuckle to contribute. If you're ever in doubt that the movies being bittersweet, the single, plaintive piano chords will tap you on the shoulder. Hardly beset with renewed faith in the glories of idiotic whim, I wanted to shoot the piano player.

Peter Yates's *The Run of the Country* smarts even more, not the least reason being that it caricatures the Irish as flush-cheeked, beetle-browed Barbary apes. A coming-of-age tale set on the border of counties Cavan and Fermanagh, *Run* comes complete with an Oirish crony à la Barry Fitzgerald (Anthony Brophy), a few beer-sodden wakes, a bar brawl, a cockfight, and lots of peripheral blather about the Troubles. Our working-class-yet-university-bound hero Danny (the utterly opaque Matt Keeslar) has a saintly dead mother (for whom, apparently, a touch of unspoken oedipal ardor lingers), an old-fashioned bully of a dad (Albert Finney), and the aforementioned Fitzgeraldian buddy, whose black-toothed yowling might've made Robert Newton blush. Amid the potato digging and peat cutting, Danny is torn between going off like Apu or doing nothing a'tall, though he does decide to romance a freckled lass from the North. Yates drowns the movie in butterscotch, but little of it makes even sentimental sense, down to the unwanted pregnancy that miscarries after a convenient rat attack. (Don't ask.) *Henrietta*, with its oil-splitting phallus, and *Run*, with its Catholic pubertal confusion, are both struggles of self-justification, and can be read as essays on erection anxiety. We don't get a triumphant spurt of derrick-juice in Yates's movie, however, but a mean genital tar-and-feathering that teaches Danny a Life Lesson. Like, get out of Ireland.

Both movies are about poverty but manage to make it look swell and Martha Stewart-antiquey. *Henrietta* is several shampoos closer to *Little House on the Prairie* than to Walker Evans, or even *The Grapes of Wrath*. *The Run of the Country* has as much to do with Ireland as Killian's Irish Red. You won't feel guilty about squandering the $5 on popcorn and Sprite, especially if you go see *Crumb* again instead.

Also reviewed in:
CHICAGO TRIBUNE, 9/22/95, Friday/p. J, Michael Wilmington
NEW YORK TIMES, 9/15/95, p. C12, Stephen Holden
VARIETY, 4/24-30/95, p. 55, Todd McCarthy
WASHINGTON POST, 9/23/95, p. C4, Rita Kempley

STARTING PLACE

An Interama release of a Les Films d'Ici/La Sept/ Association of Vietnamese Film Makers/Channel Four/Centre National de la Cinematographie of France production. *Director:* Robert Kramer. *Screenplay (English, French and Vietnamese with English subtitles):* Robert Kramer. *Director of Photography:* Robert Kramer. *Editor:* Christine Benoit, Robert Kramer, and Marie-Hélène Mora. *Running time:* 80 minutes. *MPAA Rating:* Not Rated.

WITH: Robert Kramer; Linda Evans; Viet Tung.

NEW YORK POST, 4/26/95, p. 42, Larry Worth

With daily headlines turning Bosnia-Herzegovina, Chechnya and northern Iraq into the world's latest trouble zones, Vietnam's tragedies might seem long ago and far away. Unless, that is, you or a loved one had been there. Which is where director Robert Kramer comes in.

Having traveled to Saigon in 1969 to shoot "The People's War," he returned more than two decades later to document the fate of a battle-ravaged country and its inhabitants.

The result is "Starting Place," a colorful collage of faces, places, recollections and historic footage. But as in any collage, there's no focus for the images.

The desultory nature means audiences have to settle for fleeting glimpses of fascinating characters. For instance, a ballerina whose legs were crushed in a train accident is quickly introduced, and just as quickly dismissed for the next anecdote.

Kramer's questionable judgment extends to an interview with a middle-aged American woman who movingly recounts her experiences in Vietnam. But her testimony is denied its grim irony since Kramer withholds her true significance until the end credits.

Some of the more successful tableaus involve long patches with no dialogue, as when watching the peaceful flow of bicycle traffic across a bucolic bridge. The kicker is supplied by a passer-by: The spot is a reminder for residents of the artillery tire and bloodshed which defined it in the '60s.

What unites the segments is a collective determination to come to terms with the past, thereby getting on with the present.

The sentiment is voiced again and again in visits to a school for the blind, a gymnast's studio, a brick factory and beauty salon. But the talking heads prove an uneven lot, with tales of survival ranging from the riveting to rambling.

The bottom line: The assets are clear. But it's equally clear that Kramer didn't know where to begin, or end, "Starting Place."

VILLAGE VOICE, 5/2/95, p. 58, Ed Morales

Just in time to reinforce Robert McNamara's shocking revelation that the Vietnam War was a big mistake comes *Starting Place,* a two-year-old art doc by '60s radical newsreel pioneer Robert Kramer. The film marks Kramer's return to the subcontinent—in 1969 he and his film collaborative, The Newsreel, were invited to shoot a documentary in Hanoi, the aptly titled *People's War.* While you might expect *Starting Place* to be a sobering, sentimental old lefty's postmortem, it's actually a very impressionistic, somewhat unfocused, dialectical materialist collage that will frustrate those looking for the big picture.

Kramer's painterly excesses and romantic liberation logic can be traced to his 10-year stay in France, soaking up the residue of all that New Wave and Sartre. His Godardian camera pokes into the dusty memories of old Vietnamese comrades in the struggle, his understated offscreen voice obliquely getting the talking *têtes* to recount the way they shared the war with him, and where their lives have turned since then. One man proudly displays his translations of *Don Quixote,* and *The Last of the Mohicans,* another uncovers a cobwebbed movie camera he used with Kramer, a woman describes studying circus acrobatics in the Soviet Union, and an ex-dancer with shrapnel in his legs tells of how a ring from an American pilot became his talisman. But the stories are never quite complete, fading in and out like radio stations do as you drive cross-country.

Kramer mixes dark and grainy footage of the birth of his granddaughter, named for Ho Chi Minh, with quick-cutting bites of Vietnam being rebuilt—the sounds and shapes of steel and brick. Indulging in more quirky anti-narrative, Kramer employs claustrophobic closeups to introduce activist Linda Evans, who made the '69 trip with Kramer, and is now in a California prison for aiding a fugitive, but it's not explained who she is until the final credits. At one point she weeps over the war's effect on Vietnam's "gentle people," a notion that's soon contrasted with the testimony of the Vietnamese themselves. While one older man shows sympathy with the American pilots he shot at, a filmmaker laments how the younger generation is different: "Before people were willing to kill. Not anymore. That's the problem."

But it's clear that he's not pining away for a lost bloodthirstiness—it's the people's commitment to nationalism, a factor that McNamara admits he vastly underestimated, that seems to be wavering in '90s Vietnam. This idea imbues the film with an almost Cuban fatalism. "People don't feel they got what they hoped for," an older man sheepishly admits, and you can't help but think this is exactly how Kramer and the old New Left feels.

Also reviewed in:
NEW YORK TIMES, 4/26/95, p. C16, Stephen Holden
VARIETY, 10/11/93, p. 73, Deborah Young

STEAL BIG, STEAL LITTLE

A Savoy Pictures release of a Chicago Pacific Entertainment production. *Executive Producer:* Mel Pearl. *Producer:* Andrew Davis and Fred Caruso. *Director:* Andrew Davis. *Screenplay:* Andrew Davis, Lee Blessing, Jeanne Blake, and Terry Kahn. *Based on a story by:* Andrew Davis, Teresa Tucker-Davies, and Frank Ray Perilli. *Director of Photography:* Frank Tidy. *Editor:* Don Brochu and Tina Hirsch. *Music:* William Olvis. *Music Editor:* Michael T. Ryan. *Sound:* Scott D. Smith and (music) Doug Botnick. *Sound Editor:* Bruce Stambler and Jay Nierenberg. *Casting:* Amanda Mackey Johnson and Cathy Sandrich. *Production Designer:* Michael Haller. *Art Director:* Mark E. Zuelzke. *Set Decorator:* Gene Serdena. *Set Dresser:* Tighe Barry. *Special Effects:* Roy Arbogast. *Costumes:* Jodie Tillen. *Make-up:* Rick Sharp. *Stunt Coordinator:* Jery Hewitt. *Running time:* 130 minutes. *MPAA Rating:* PG-13.

CAST: Andy Garcia (Ruben Partida Martinez/Robert Martin); Alan Arkin (Lou Perilli); Rachel Ticotin (Laura Martinez); Joe Pantoliano (Eddie Agopian); Holland Taylor (Mona Rowland-Downey); Ally Walker (Bonnie Martin); David Ogden Stiers (Judge Winton Myers); Charles Rocket (Sheriff Otis); Richard Bradford (Nick Zingaro); Kevin McCarthy (Reed Tyler); Nathan Davis (Harry Lordly); Dominik Garcia-Lorido (Maria Martinez); Mike Nussbaum (Sam Barlow); Rita Taggart (Autumn McBride); Takaaki Ishibashi (Yoshi Takamura); Tom Wood (Dan McCann); Philip Arthur Ross (Tinker); Steven Robert Ross (Buzz); Natalija Nogulich (Alice); Joe Kosala (Sheriff Joe); Victor Rivers (Sheriff Vic); Sam Vlahos (Mauricio); Andy Romano (Clifford Downey); Ramon Gonzales (Julian); Salvatore Basile (Luis); Fred Asparagus (Angel); William Marquez (Rafael); Nelson Marquez (Emilio Campos); Richard Marquez (Eduardo); Leata Galloway (Agatha); Renee Victor (Rosa); Adam James (Tyler's Bodyguard); Drucilla A. Carlson (Tonya); Nina Beesley (Brandy); Candice Daly (Melissa); Cynthia Mace (Betty Myers); Karen Kondazian (Mrs. Agopian); Miguel Nino (Guardia Officer); Ron Dean and Jack Wallace (Nick's Boys); Robert Harris (Farley); Robert Langenbucher (Bailsman Aames); Time Winters (IRS Agent Cox); Tighe Barry (Glitch); Suzanne Goddard (Shakara); Joe Drago (Inmate); Duane Davis (Jailer); Roselynn Pilkington (Eddie's Secretary); Fred Lehto (Strange Man); Cody Glenn (INS Agent); Lee Debroux (INS Official); Robert Lesser (Agent Buchanan); Pamela Winslow (Melanie); Frank Ray Perilli (B.J.); Mick Pellegrino (Mission Father); Eddie Bo Smith (Bartender); Soren Hansen (Security Guard); Lizz Lang (Court Clerk).

LOS ANGELES TIMES, 9/29/95, Calendar/p. 8, Jack Mathews

[The following review by Jack Mathews appeared in a slightly different form in **NEWSDAY, 9/29/95, Part II/p. B4].**

The movie has not been made that would benefit from a laugh track, but given the obnoxiously loud music laid over Andrew Davis' "Steal Big, Steal Little" to achieve the same results, this might have been the time.

You speculate about filmmakers' choices at your own risk, but William Olvis' alternately saccharine and jaunty score feels like a post-production bailout, an attempt to make up in music what was missing in the script and on the set and only discovered in the editing.

Music is always there to assist the story, but here, it's a search-and-rescue mission. There is plenty to mask in "Steal Big," a fable about brotherhood, opportunity and American justice.

It's the story of immigrant Mexican twins Ruben and Robert Martinez (Andy Garcia, doubled) who are found abandoned in a ditch by wealthy Santa Barbara ranchers and raised, though by different parents, as heirs to the kingdom. It is essentially a good-twin/bad-twin story. Ruben is raised by the ranch's saintly matron, a boss woman who treats her illegal immigrants as family, and Robert by her greedy, mean-spirited ex-husband.

Their story is told, in confusing layers of flashbacks, as a news feature in progress, with Ruben, his wife Laura (Rachel Ticotin), and their animated pal Lou (Alan Arkin, in his best comic performance in a decade) telling an interviewer how Ruben inherited the ranch and then had to fight his brother and his circle of corrupt cops, judges and businessmen to keep it.

Garcia is a bit too viewer-friendly an actor to portray truly menacing figures, and he is never convincing as the evil twin. But he is a perfect fit for Ruben, whose big heart and blind allegiances make him easy prey for his brother, his opportunistic lawyer (Joe Pantoliano) and the various government agencies sent to harass him.

"Steal Big's" broad, little-people-vs-big-people setup aims for a sense of magic realism, and often succeeds. The depiction of immigrant ranch hands as a flock of hard-working angels under the protective wing of the soulful Ruben is more than a little patronizing. And the film's politics—Ruben preaches pure collectivism—will cause palpitations in affluent Montecito, which lent its lush landscapes and estates to the cause.

But it is a warm and fuzzy group following Ruben and the wily Lou into battle against the forces who would carve La Fortuna's 40,000 acres into housing tracts. Andrew Davis, who first worked as a cinematographer, has proved himself a fine stylist with a series of action movies (no small feat, he made both Chuck Norris and Steven Seagal look good) and with the superbly directed blockbuster in 1993, "The Fugitive."

"Steal Big" is his first major movie, however, in which he was intimately involved in the creation of the story, and in which character development is more important than events, and there's the problem. "Steal Big" stumbles all over the place, attempting to strike a tone that allows for great romantic highs, fraternal melodrama, whimsy and slapstick, and going over a shuddering speed bump with every transition.

The movie gets so silly at times, you feel like throwing a tomato at it. Olvis' score leaves no question as to how each scene is meant to play. But music, no more than a laugh track, can't make you feel it.

NEW YORK POST, 9/29/95, p. 42, Thelma Adams

Steel yourself for "Steal Big, Steal Little."

Andy Garcia plays his own evil twin. Andrew ("The Fugitive") Davis directs a classic Santa Barbara story: rich against poor, anglos against Hispanics, business interests versus the working man.

Corruption tips the scales of justice with dirty cops, sleazy lawyers and corrupt judges in the pocket of the highest bidder. Land grabs and tawdry family secrets cast shadows across the Spanish architecture, the mission and the fertile hills that roll down to the Pacific dotted with offshore oil refineries.

What's wrong with this picture?

Nothing—on paper.

It's simply that, from the moment the story begins in an awkward flashback, the elements fight each other like germs and antibodies.

Garcia plays Ruben Partida Martinez, the good bro, wearing a funky brown Borsalino, playing the harmonica and displaying a homegrown communal optimism on his sleeve along with his bleeding heart. The "we the people" guy drives a battered pick-up and lives off the land.

Ruben's evil twin, the assimilated Robert Martin, couldn't find his heart on his sleeve or in his chest cavity. He dresses slick, talks slicker, smokes cigars and bonds with the amoral movers and shakers at the upper echelons of Santa Barbara's closed society. Robert drives a red Porsche and speculates in real estate, capitalizing on the downfall of others.

When their adoptive mother dies, she leaves her huge estate to Ruben. He offers half to Robert, but the bad seed would rather swindle his twin out of the whole enchilada. It's Cain and Abel all over again.

The Martin(ez) twins are a part an ambitious actor can't resist—but should. For all the trick shots of the siblings standing in front of a half a dozen mirrors, Garcia, an actor who otherwise displays great charisma, never fully commits to either character. Both are gimmicks, not souls.

Director Davis, who co-wrote the convoluted script with a gang of three, can't quite commit to a style himself. At times romantic, antic, festive, muckraking and naively political, "Steal Big, Steal Little" switches from broadly comic to suddenly sentimental with hardly a beat in between.

The movie ends with one of those big action sequences that contributes to the tension in a thriller like "The Fugitive" but is farfetched here. When Garcia hangs from a hot air balloon by a thread while an evil white guy uses him for target practice and a pack of noble Chicanos rides over the range on horseback to save him, should we see him as Buster Keaton or Harrison Ford?

"The big steal big, so the little steal little," Ruben says, finally explaining the title. "when is it all going to stop?"

At well over two hours, not soon enough.

SIGHT AND SOUND, 7/96, p. 51, Liese Spencer

When orphaned twins are discovered in the grounds of Mona Rowland-Downey's estate, the millionaire dancer decides to adopt them. They look identical, but are moral opposites. When Mona splits with her greedy husband Clifford Downey, Ruben sides with Mona while his brother Robert takes after Downey.

Years later, Mona returns from a business trip to find that Robby, now the estate manager, has been siphoning off funds. She transfers control to the reluctant Ruben, with the proviso that he reconcile himself with his estranged wife Maria, who thought he was having an affair with their sister-in-law, Robby's ex-wife Bonnie. In Chicago, Ruben discovers Maria working for used car dealer Lou Pirelli. Returning with Maria and daughter Laura, Ruben finds Mona has died and left him the estate. Pursued by loan sharks, Lou turns up and moves into the ranch.

Robby refuses Ruben's offer of a half share in the estate and attempts to dispossess his brother and the ranch families who live and work on the estate using a corrupt local policeman and judge. Ruben and his allies survive green card raids and eviction notices but, under Robby's influence, Ruben's lawyer Eddie cons him into signing for a fraudulent bank loan that loses him the ranch. Robby tries to bribe Lou, letting slip that he had an affair with Bonnie in order to trick Maria. Lou phones Maria and Bonnie with this information and uses the bribe to pay off the Chicago hoods. He then goes to Mexico with Ruben, where they kidnap Eddie.

Dressing Eddie as a woman, they get him to record incriminating evidence on the judge, policeman and Robby's Corrupt partners. Having imprisoned Robby in his yacht, Ruben adopts his brother's personality and cancels the ranch development. Robby escapes but is jailed by officers who think he's Ruben. Knowing his real identity, Bonnie visits "Ruben" to tell him that she still loves his brother, Robby. Ruben is shot in an assassination attempt planned for Robby. Robby escapes and races to rescue his brother and the pair are finally reconciled. At a party that evening, everyone agrees to run the ranch as a commune.

In his last film, director Andrew Davis turned the long-running American television series *The Fugitive* into a relentlessly fast paced and visually exciting chase movie. At 135 minutes, *Steal Big, Steal Little* is more like a long-running movie that feels and looks like an American television series. With its slapstick morality and cartoon characterisations, what this vastly unentertaining dud resembles most is an interminable episode of *The Dukes of Hazard*, complete with the corpulent judges, their weak-minded sidekicks and golden-hearted crooks. Worst of all, in place of the Duke brothers, we have Andy Garcia trying to broaden his range by playing identical twins Ruben and Robby. Ruben is a decent millionaire who plays the harmonica and wears his hat back to front. He is supposed to be generous and unworldly, but in Garcia's hands (wide eyes and a strange, bobbing monkey walk) he just seems hopelessly dumb. Robby's nastiness, meanwhile, is signified by hanging out in the jacuzzi wearing nothing but a cowboy hat and chomping on a fat cigar.

Reworking the hackneyed good twin/bad twin mistaken identity scenario, Davis (who also co-wrote and produced this) aims for a colourful, carnivalesque style, marked especially by the procession which opens it. However, the film, with its unwieldy cast and escalating chain of ludicrous coincidences, seems to spin out of his directorial grasp almost from the start.

After the sentimental presentation of adoptive mother Mona (who signifies her bohemian status by running around her mansion with a scarf over her head) and her mercifully early death the film's tone eventual settles for broad comedy. But something terrible happened in the editing suite, so that although *Steal Big, Steal Little* lurches rapidly from one piece of family history to another and shuttles back and forth in time, it never seems to progress and instead becomes an indigestible, narrative mess. Where the complex plot of *The Fugitive* was enjoyable, this chopped-about story is just irritating. Essential pieces of the plot are frustratingly unclear. Characters perform inexplicable and unsatisfying personality changes (the most obvious being Robby's inevitable turnaround towards good). Tricky confrontations which require ingenious or subtle plotting to make them effective are simply despatched by a succession of *deux ex machina* resolutions. Threads are picked up, glanced at and dropped for ever. The worst and most unintentionally hilarious example is a plot-strand concerning a young Latino boy whom Ruben adopts at the start of the film but who never appears again. Perhaps Ruben throws him over when he hooks up with his old family. Who knows? After a while you stop trying to make sense of what is going on and let the nonsense wash over you.

Even then, this story of a Californian "Ruben Hood" still rankles. It might be Davis' neo-feudal vision that does it. While the basic premise of a millionaire landlord who keeps bundles of dollars under the mattress and fights with his ranch hands against corrupt big business merely stretches the film's plausibility to breaking point, the Latino caricatures on offer border on the offensive. A happy band of moustachioed men with large families, they are barely distinguished from one another and spend the majority of their time singing, dancing or shifting their possessions from shack to shack. To show his identification with these people of the land, Ruben (a modern *el patron*) jams with them in the barn and sets up for himself a simple, Californian home, tastefully covered with handmade Mexican tiles that references his Latino roots. They repay him with a rustic, wondering loyalty. They are little more than patronising cyphers of earthy goodness, but then again, all the other players are barely more than mere caricatures.

VILLAGE VOICE, 10/10/95, p. 82, Gary Dauphin

There's a glassy-eyed earnestness to the first half of *Steal Big, Steal Little,* an introductory milling about in the ways of folksy farmworkers on an idyllic California lemon ranch, that does little to get this movie going. That's a shame considering that *Steal Big* is a big-budget flick about a neglected subject (Mexican agri-labor), and although it turns out to be a slightly better product than recent fare from Hollywood, this happens only after the film sets its Latinness aside. *Steal Big* struggles mightily for an hour or so with the awkward weight of a distinctly PBS brand of multicultural gauziness (right down to raids by the INS and numerous dancing-singing farmworker sequences) before director Andrew Davis—whose résumé includes *The Fugitive,* a stint with PBS, and a cowriter credit on *Beat Street,* of all things—finally throws his hands up and rolls the surefire, chrome-plated action-comedy engine.

Sleepy-eyed Ruben Martinez (Andy Garcia) tells the sad-sack, voiceover tale of how his oily twin brother Robert Martin (also Andy Garcia) has broken up the commune-like tranquility of the ranch in order to slot another subdivision into LA.'s ever-expanding sprawl. The well-acted contrast between Ruben and Robert—one dreamily in touch with his heritage and the land, the other interested only in parceling both off to the highest bidder—is *Steal Big*'s main North-South dividing line. But the crisply paced events that eventually return the land to Ruben and his hard-working friends have more to do with con games and twin high jinks than ethnic identity. This isn't to say *Steal Big* isn't a well-made movie or a funny one (Alan Arkin is a hoot as a Chicago used-car dealer on the lam), is just that, except for the Mexican American window dressing, this is also a film you've seen many times before.

Also reviewed in:
CHICAGO TRIBUNE, 9/29/95, Friday/p. F, Michael Wilmington
NEW YORK TIMES, 9/29/95, p. C23, Caryn James
VARIETY, 9/18-24/95, p. 94, Leonard Klady
WASHINGTON POST, 9/29/95, p. F7, Hal Hinson

STRANGE DAYS

A Twentieth Century Fox release of a Lightstorm Entertainment production. *Executive Producer:* Rae Sanchini and Lawrence Kasanoff. *Producer:* James Cameron and Steven-Charles Jaffe. *Director:* Kathryn Bigelow. *Screenplay:* James Cameron and Jay Cocks. *Story (based on a story by):* James Cameron. *Director of Photography:* Matthew F. Leonetti. *Editor:* Howard Smith. *Music:* Graeme Revell. *Music Editor:* Josh Winget, Allan K. Rosen, and Patty Von Arx. *Sound:* Jeff Wexler and David Ronne. *Sound Editor:* Gloria S. Borders. *Casting:* Rick Pagano. *Production Designer:* Lilly Kilvert. *Art Director:* John Warnke. *Set Decorator:* Kara Lindstrom. *Set Dresser:* Roger Abel, A.T. Samona, Quent Schierenberg, Doug Sieck, Tristan Bourne, and

Jon Bush. *Special Effects:* Terry Frazee. *Costumes:* Ellen Mirojnick. *Make-up:* Mike Germain. *Make-up (Angela Bassett):* Marietta Carter-Narcisse. *Stunt Coordinator:* Doug Coleman. *Running time:* 145 minutes. *MPAA Rating:* R.

CAST: Ralph Fiennes (Lenny Nero); Angela Bassett (Lornette "Mace" Mason); Juliette Lewis (Faith Justin); Tom Sizemore (Max Peltier); Michael Wincott (Philo Gant); Vincent D'Onofrio (Burton Steckler); Glenn Plummer (Jeriko One); Brigitte Bako (Iris); Richard Edson (Tick); William Fichtner (Dwayne Engleman); Josef Sommer (Palmer Strickland); Joe Urla (Keith); Nicky Katt (Joey Corto); Michael Jace (Wade Beemer); Louise LeCavalier (Cindy "Vita" Minh); David Carrera (Duncan); Jim Ishida (Mr. Fumitsu); Todd Graff (Tex Arcana); Malcolm Norrington (Replay); Anais Munoz (Diamanda); Ted Haler (Tow Truck Driver); Rio Hackford (Bobby the Bartender); Brook Susan Parker (Cecile); Brandon Hammond (Zander); Donald Young and B.J. Crockett (Young Zander); Dex Elliott Sanders (Curtis); Ronnie Willis (Homeboy); David Packer (Lane); Paulo Tocha (Spaz Diaz); James Muro (Nervous POV); Ron Young (Nervous POV Voice); Art Chudabala (Thai Restaurant Owner); Erica Kelly (Restaurant Hostess); Marlana Young (Waitress); Ray Chang (Thai Restaurant Cook); Raul Reformina (Busboy); Chris Douridas (Talk Radio Host); Billy Worley (Dan from Silverlake); Amon Bourne (Dewayne); Lisa Picotte (Lori from Encino); Kylie Ireland (Stoned Looking Girl); Nicole Hilbig (Stoned Girl's Lover); Stefan Arngrim (Skinner); Agustin Rodriguez (Eduardo); Kelly Hu (Anchor Woman); Nynno Anderson (Angry Jeriko Fan); Liat Goodson (Retinal Fetish Bouncer); Honey Labrador (Beach Beauty); Delane Vaughn (Mace's Husband); Mark Arneson (Police Officer); James Acheson (Cop in Bathroom); John Francis (Death); Zoot (Mime); Royce Minor (Angry Black Kid); Milan Reynolds (National Guard Medic #1); Russell W. Smith (National Guard #2).

LOS ANGELES TIMES, 10/13/95, Calendar/p. 1, Kenneth Turan

What is it about Los Angeles that makes filmmakers think the world is going to end here first? Certainly the confluence of fire, earthquake and riot has not helped. Or is just getting stuck on the freeway on the way to the Valley enough to trigger apocalyptic thoughts?

"Strange Days," the latest epic of dystopia to come out of Hollywood, is a direct if feeble descendant of "Blade Runner," that venerable prophet of urban decay. Directed by Kathryn Bigelow from a script by James Cameron and Jay Cocks, "Days" is loaded with effective visual razzmatazz, but what the eyes giveth, the ears taketh away.

For whether it's the plot, the dialogue development or the acting itself, anything that stands apart from camera style is a thudding disappointment. "Strange Days" knows what it's about when it comes to creating a nightmare city of the near-future, but what is more frightening still is what's going on within its boundaries.

Set on the last two days of 1999, just before the start of the second millennium (known on the street as "2K"), "Strange Days" displays a provocatively sleazy, thoroughly corrupt City of the Angels. Production designer Lilly Kilvert (Oscar-nominated for the very different "Legends of the Fall") and her team persuasively create an ambience of free-floating anarchy where smoky riots are a year-round attraction and Santas have to run for their lives on Hollywood Boulevard.

Only one thing is completely different, and that is the availability, though only in bootleg form, of a new technology called SQUID, an acronym for Superconducting Quantum Interference Device. These wiry pieces of apparatus record memories and, more intriguing, allow other people to experience them exactly as they happened. In this voyeur's paradise, "a piece of someone's life, straight from the cerebral cortex," is available to those willing to pay for it.

Before explaining SQUID technology, "Strange Days," in a bravura sequence, allows us to experience it. Using lightweight and occasionally head-mounted steadicams plus quick panning and expert cutting, director of photography Matthew F. Leonetti and editor Howard Smith have come up with an extremely edgy point of view sequence that truly creates the feeling that the camera is inside another person's head.

But once "Strange Days" slows up enough to introduce its characters, all is lost. Protagonist Lenny Nero (Ralph Fiennes), an ex-cop and scuzzy dealer in these bootlegged memory discs, known as "clips," is so whiny he might as well be called Lenny Zero. The film, however, insists on presenting him as the last of the sensitive romantics, pining away for his lost girlfriend, an aspiring singer named Faith (Juliette Lewis).

Faith isn't really lost, she's simply taken up with Philo Gant (Michael Wincott), the nasty manager of hot rap singer Jeriko One (Glenn Plummer). Only two people unconvincingly stick by Lenny in his misery: fellow ex-cop Max Peltier (Tom Sizemore) and a tough limo driver and security expert named Lornette (Mace) Mason (Angela Bassett).

None of these characters is convincing and their dialogue is so tepid it's not even worth mocking. The same goes for the confusing plot, which involves the murder of Jeriko One and a prostitute named Iris (Brigitte Bako) who knows too much, though not enough to stay away from Lenny.

Through it all, "Strange Days" manages to be consistently loud, violent and sleazy, which is less of an accomplishment than it may sound. This tendency culminates in a particularly sadistic rape sequence, in which the victim, in a nod to Michael Powell's superior "Peeping Tom," is made to experience the rapist experiencing her fear. Swell stuff all around.

"Strange Days" does have a superior cast, but only Bassett manages to survive the numskull script, and that just barely. An underdressed Lewis is making a unfortunate habit of these tart-from-hell roles, and as for Ralph Fiennes, if this were his debut picture you would swear his future was all used up.

Though the creators of "Strange Days" may well be interested in its dramatic and thematic elements, they do not have the same touch for these moments as they do for camera pyrotechnics. No matter how much thought may have gone into "Strange Days," terribly little has come out the other end.

NEW YORK, 10/16/95, p. 60, David Denby

We're used to science-fiction movies set 25, 50, or 200 years in the future, but in *Strange Days*—a convulsively violent sci-fi thriller—the future is just a few nasty minutes away. Kathryn Bigelow's hyper-spaz movie begins on December 30, 1999, and ends two days later when a couple of survivors, a white man (Ralph Fiennes) and a black woman (Angela Bassett), stagger into the new millennium. Bigelow's former husband, director James Cameron, wrote the original story as well as the first version of the script (Jay Cocks collaborated on later versions), and Cameron has something unpleasant to tell us, something of particular moment for moviegoers: The greater and greater thrills we want out of the media are bound to destroy us. The setting of *Strange Days* is a Los Angeles jangled and coarsened by the Rodney King, Reginald Denny, and O.J. Simpson events, a city so media-ized in its relation to reality that the distinction between atrocity and vicarious thrill has been lost. Nearly everyone in the movie is jaded yet still unsatisfied, exhausted yet restless for more. The trouble is, the movie is all these things as well. The filmmakers have themselves lost the distinction between excitement and atrocity. They can't stop feasting on what they deplore.

Bigelow amplifies some familiar images into apocalypse. Riot and fire everywhere, police and tanks, the wealthy gliding by in bulletproof limos, the poor living in squalid nowheresvilles—much of this is familiar from news footage and from such earlier movies as Stephen Frears's *Sammy and Rosie Get Laid* and Ridley Scott's *Blade Runner*. In itself, the familiarity isn't damaging, but in *Strange Days* the lurid chaos floats through the background of shots, and after a while it seems merely decorative, with no greater moral interest than the sets on an opera stage. You can't be shocked by any of it because the director obviously isn't shocked. Nor does she make sense of any of it. In such films as *Near Dark* and *Blue Steel*, Bigelow fetishized violence. The hateful *Blue Steel*, for instance, was an example of formalist art pulp—all surfaces. *Strange Days* is bigger, wilder, and woollier than her previous movies, but the pulpiness still overwhelms the art. What's missing is humor, a sense of proportion and control. Bigelow is not fetishizing violence any more; she's riding in it. In *Strange Days,* she creates a holiday gaiety in the destruction. The people running rampant seem to be having a good time, and the movie inadvertently suggests that this is what life is like, so why not accept it? But that's not an undertone that links up well with the movie's explicit moralizing.

In the midst of the tawdry mess, the filmmakers establish their saint of darkness, their knight of good hope, a compromised man who is also an overwhelmingly good man—Lenny Nero (Fiennes), a former vice cop gone to seed, a man who suffers. At first, it seems that Lenny battens on the waste. Lenny peddles sensation. People who work for him put on "the wire"—a crown of electronic sensors that penetrate to the cerebral cortex—then commit real robbery and have sex. Everything these people do is digitally recorded. "Clips," the recordings are called, and when played back by one of Lenny's high-paying clients, the clips reveal the original experience with all its sensations and emotions intact, sight and sound, fear and delight, orgasm and, in one case, death. The voyeurs in *Strange Days* have gone way past the simple Peeping Tom-ism of movies and virtual reality. They taste the limits of human experience and live to be amazed by it. And once endured, the high is so great it has be repeated. The media have turned life itself into heroin.

Lenny is the candy man, a guilty fellow required by the moral scheme of the movie. to hit bottom and seek redemption. In the movie's *noir*-ishly paranoid story, some anonymous, nasty person is taking Lenny's game a step further and turning it against him. Lenny's friend Max (Tom Sizemore), another low-life ex-cop, sounds the *noir* theme when he says that you can't be paranoid *enough*. A prostitute working for Lenny has been raped and murdered, and the murderer leaves Lenny, as a taunt, a clip detailing the experience. And this murder, in some way, is also connected to the death under mysterious circumstances of a black political-rap singer. A clip of that exists as well, and people are killing for it. Poor Lenny! He's in terrible trouble, and he's miserable as a whipped dog. But the movie is in trouble, too. Bigelow shows us the clips, raising a depressing moral issue that she's not equipped to handle.

There's no doubt about it: The clips wrench a response out of us. The opening sequence puts us inside the head and body of some nameless thug holding up a Chinese restaurant. Unexplained, not yet anchored in the story, it's a heart-pounding bit of filmmaking—cinéma-vérité gone bananas. As the camera lunges around corners, the thug's arm thrusts out and pistol-whips a waiter; then the cops arrive, bringing more fear and excitement—the involvement is so great that in spite of our horror at what the robber does, we instinctively want him to get away, just as we do in our own lawless dreams. The sequence has a great surprise ending, which has the effect of punishing us for our eager curiosity. So far, so good. Voyeurism, which is essential to the movies, should be punished by the movies; we need to be reminded once in a while that we're a bunch of cowards sitting safely in the dark. There's an incredibly creepy scene in which Lenny sees a clip of someone stalking him, and he comes close to experiencing his own extinction. More punishment: Lenny is like the prurient young king in Euripides' *Bacchae*, who watches the Dionysian revelers from the safety of a tree but then gets pulled from the branches and devoured by the celebrants.

But the clip of the prostitute's death pushes us the wrong way. We see it from the point of view of the demented murderer-rapist, who increases the prostitute's terror by putting the crown on her head and making her experience the playback of his own excitement. The convolutions of the act go beyond creepiness. Conceptually, this is the sickest sequence in modern movies, and I came away from it feeling unclean. Lenny is shocked himself—he won't traffic in snuff clips—and we're supposed to appreciate his dismay. But wait a second: The clips aren't a real-world outrage. The filmmakers made it up; it's *their* metaphor. How can Cameron, Cocks, and Bigelow preach against snuff films and jaded sicko thrills after they've excited the audience with exactly those things? Bigelow is trapped in the contradictions of making a "moral" exploitation movie. What we're now getting in pictures like *Showgirls* and *Strange Days* is a new level of perfervid sensationalism in which moral awareness serves not as a frame of meaning or as a dash of common sense—but as still another sensational element. We're meant to be turned on by violence or sex and then turned on by our righteous disapproval of it.

Lenny suffers—for our sins, perhaps. He's a sleazebag Jesus. He loses his girl (Juliette Lewis) to a sinister rock promoter (Michael Wincott, of the gravel-pit voice), and as he rushes through the frenzied city trying to save people, he gets beaten up by his enemies again and again. A sweet loser, a romantic, he doesn't seem tough enough to have ever worked as a Los Angeles detective, and after a while a damp piteousness comes out in Ralph Fiennes that is most unpleasant. In what must be the mismatch of the decade, Angela Bassett—muscled, prim, and clean as a whistle—has been cast as Mace, a security expert who harbors a secret love for Lenny. Mace holds herself aloft from the carnival nihilism of the city. Lenny's guardian angel, protector of his better nature, she embodies all the virtues—and she kicks butt, another killer-woman karate expert. She's a black militant as well, and the movie, in a speechifying turn, suddenly takes a stand against police racism, which would seem a relatively minor issue in a city gone wildly out of control and burning to the ground. The filmmakers mix pop-apocalyptic cartooning and social outrage. The ending, in which one violent climax after another plays through nonstop street celebration of the new millennium, is a turbulent, overloaded mess. *Strange Days* has its provocative passages, but the picture is a degraded spectacle awash in sentiment.

NEW YORK POST, 10/6/95, p. 44, Thelma Adams

Imagine a worst-case scenario Los Angeles, December 1999, conceived by someone the day after the 1992 riots, someone who has just run out of Prozac and is convinced that the Big One is going to collapse Hollywood like last-year's sitcom pilots.

Muggers assault sidewalk Santas. Sunset Boulevard burns like Beirut. Rogue white cops perform summary executions on black rappers. This is an L.A. only singer Randy Newman could love. These are "Strange Days" as directed with millennarian fervor by Kathryn ("Point Break") Bigelow from a script written by ex-husband James ("The Terminator") Cameron and ex-critic Jay Cocks. With a combination of adrenalin rush and cold sweat, bad girl Bigelow cuts through the chaos to create a smart and flashy futuristic noir.

Cameron and Cocks have given the boot to the nerves-of-steel detective with the romantic heart sheltered behind a wall of thorns. Lenny Nero (Ralph Fiennes) is an ex-cop with a broken heart embroidered on his sleeve, a man with an excess of empathy and a shortage of cash, a vulnerable man.

Nero fiddles while L.A. burns. He's a used-memory hustler. Imagine porn available in sensurround on a Sony Walkman and you get the essence of "playback." Nero considers himself more dream weaver than pornographer, calling himself "the Santa Clause of the Subconscious. You say it, you even think it, you can have it."

Nero stops short at trading in "blackjacks"—futuristic snuff films. The ex-cop's world begins to constrict when he receives a hot playback direct from the censored "Cops" file, the memory of an event so incendiary it makes the Rodney King tapes and their aftermath seem like a backyard barbecue.

Bigelow shoots Fiennes ("Quiz Show") as sex-object, the fallen angel whom women love to save. His greasy hair halos soulful baby blues; his vanity insists that he always dresses well, even if he's trolling the savage streets after his car has been repossessed.

The faithless Faith (Juliette Lewis) has dumped the lovesick loser. The scrawny star of "Natural Born Killers" plays a rising singer who has traded up to an abusive music producer. While Nero wallows in the past, using playback to revisit happier days, the Faith of flesh and blood is no dreamgirl. Bigelow shoots Lewis as a sleazy sex kitten in peekaboo beaded numbers, her nipples more visible than her shifty eyes. The more this harlot with a heart of dust tramples on Nero, the more desperate he becomes to prove his love.

Mace (Angela Bassett), a single mom sporting a shoulder holster, reluctantly watches Nero's back. The woman with the name of a defensive weapon is torn between her desire to protect the man she loves and shield herself from heartache as she watches Nero make an ass out of himself with Faith. The Oscar-nominated star of "What's Love Got to Do With It" acts the hero's role with dignity, guts and great beauty.

Amid the fiery car chases, flying bullets, blood and broken glass of a souped-up thriller, Bigelow weaves a compelling adult love story with a modern twist. Born out of an apocalyptic vision of the future as we shed the second millennium, "Strange Days" concludes with a fleeting sense of rebirth: a feeling of elation, a hell-bent hope that justice will prevail, that love heals all wounds, even those made from weapons that have yet to be invented.

NEWSDAY, 10/13/95, Part II/p. B6, John Anderson

None dare call it synergy, but there's a lot of coincidence surrounding "Strange Days," which portrays Los Angeles as a spiritual septic tank and members of the LAPD as psychopaths, and arrives just as the Simpson verdict has already made America feel so good about itself.

But such are the vagaries of life, be it real or filmed—and the difference is at the heart of Kathryn Bigelow's millennial thriller. The film, with a story by James ("Terminator") Cameron and a screenplay by Cameron and Jay Cocks ("The Age of Innocence"), stars Ralph Fiennes as Lenny Nero, pusher of the future—but just barely. It's Dec. 30, 1999 and Lenny's stock in trade is "clips"—doses of human experience that are played back by people "on the wire." The experience is more than visual, and sex is a big part of it—"Real sex can kill you," Lenny says—although it's death that seems to be the overriding, unspoken thrill with which everyone is flirting.

Death—of cities, of spirit, of moral orientation—is everywhere. L.A., prepping for the biggest New Year's Eve party ever, is already on fire (one of the film's few unconvincing aspects is that whenever we hit the streets, it looks like the extras have just been cued to riot. You begin to wonder: Don't these people ever get tired?). As usual in pre-, post- and just plain apocalyptic nightmares, there's a hunger that needs to be filled. Enter SQUID Superconducting Quantum Interference Device—which was developed by the feds and has gone black market. Lenny, who tells himself he's on a mission of charity, is a high-tech entrepreneur filling the dream cavity.

He's done a little too much playback himself, though, even if he still won't deal in "blackjack"—death clips. "When they die, it just brings down your whole day," he sighs. Someone has delivered one anyway—in which a Lenny supplier named Iris (Brigitte Bako), who was being pursued by two very angry and lethal cops (Vincent D'Onofrio and William Fichtner), is raped and murdered. And we get to watch: The killer rapes Iris after plugging her brain waves into his—so she can feel what he feels (it's ugly and confusing). We're revulsed. And keep watching.

All this crime is distracting Lenny from trying to get to Faith (Juliette Lewis), the ex-girlfriend he revisits through his own album of clips, but who has taken up with a very unsavory record promoter named Philo Gant (Michael Wincott). Is Lenny strung out? He manages to summon up enough courage to get to the bottom of the murder conspiracy, but fuzzy judgment is the only possible explanation for his undying devotion to Faith. As portrayed by Lewis, she's like a partially anesthetized nerve ending, wagging about for stimuli.

It's unfortunate for Lewis that she's co-starring with Fiennes, who endows Lenny with a real conscience and an inner life. But it's even more unfortunate for her that Angela Bassett is in the film. As Mace, Lenny's best friend, guardian angel and why-aren't-they-in-love interest, Bassett is not just the story's spine but its entire central nervous system. She should be the leading actress of the next millennium. Lewis, on the other hand, appears to be waiting for the next space age.

"Strange Days" is a problematic film, not just because it starts out so convincingly and spirals downward so quickly, but because it seems oblivious to its own contradictions. It's obviously about film, but it's also about the end result of an accelerating appetite among mass audiences for harder, cheaper, faster thrills. Are the chips Lenny sells the end result of the kind of sensationalistic entertainment Hollywood is so fond of producing? Then perhaps the makers of "Strange Days," which is state-of-the-art action (albeit with a brain), might have acknowledged that their film is part of the very process it's condemning. The filmmakers are oblivious to their own complicity.

The violence in "Strange Days" is brutal and brief—real, in other words—except for two deeply flawed sequences, one of which is the finale. It's a scene that evokes Rodney King, "Robocop" and "Greed" in the kind of climax that Schwarzenegger usually crashes into. Prolonged and illogical, it also violates much of what's happened early on in the film. But this inconsistency is symptomatic of "Strange Days," which mixes the cerebral and the sleazy into a kind of cocktail one might drink to toast the end of the world.

NEWSWEEK, 10/16/95, p. 86, Jack Kroll

Strange Days doesn't just sit there on the screen and invite you to watch. It instantly yanks you into a dazzling opening sequence, a frenetic heist in which the careening camera makes you one of the heisters, breaking through doors, lurching down stairways, whacking people around. Director Kathryn Bigelow comes closer than any other filmmaker to turning movies into a virtual reality trip. In "Strange Days," virtual reality has become a digital drug, mainlined straight to your brain through a SQUID, a kind of electronic hairnet that records an individual's sensations onto discs. SQUID "playback" has become the ultimate vicarious experience: "Feel it, see it. This is a piece of someone's life," pitches Lenny Nero (Ralph Fiennes), an ex-cop who's become a SQUID pusher.

This Nero squiddles while Rome burns—or, in this case, Los Angeles. It's New Year's 1999, and L.A. is a millennial mess, streets seething with violence, gasoline at $50 a gallon. "It's the end of the world," says Lenny's pal Max (Tom Sizemore). "Everything's been done, every kind of music, every government, every breakfast food. We've used it all up." Lenny is pretty used up, a scruffy hustler who's hooked on his own discs, the ones showing his ex-girlfriend Faith (Juliette Lewis), a punk-rock singer who's left him for a vicious record mogul. When a killer starts sending Lenny horrifically violent discs of rape and murder, his vicarious life turns frighteningly real. To the rescue comes Mace (Angela Bassett), a security specialist who's trying to cure Lenny of the playback plague.

The script, by coproducer James Cameron and Jay Cocks, is a mixed grill of film noir, whodunit and cyberspace-out. But essentially the movie is a smart bomb detonated by the sensibility of Bigelow. The director has staked her turf in male preserves: Hell's Angelic bikers ("The Loveless," 1981), cowboy vampires ("Near Dark," 1987), tough cops ("Blue Steel," 1990). Originally a painter and conceptual artist, Bigelow, working with cinematographer Matthew F. Leonetti, galvanizes every inch of the screen with vibrant detail, capturing the images and rhythms of urban paranoia.

Despite her extravagant gifts, Bigelow has never made a major statement as a movie artist. "Strange Days" seems at first as though it's going to be the one. For about an hour the writing, acting and direction coalesce in a prismatic, hyperkinetic ode to end-of-century doom. And then the two-hours-plus film starts to subside into genre convention. As the New Century approaches in an eruption of racial conflict, murderous cops and battered heroes, the movie screeches into reverse and love conquers all. It's not that a happy ending is bad, it's that it comes from nowhere but a failure of nerve by ... whom? It's as if Orwell had ended "1984" by having Big Brother say, "Aw, heck, why am I such a mean creep? It's silly to keep torturing and killing these nice people. Let's have a ball!"

Among other things, this copout subverts Fiennes's performance as the most riveting sleazeball since Tony Curtis's maggoty press agent in "Sweet Smell of Success." Fiennes's eyes, like the dying embers of idealism, and his perverted salesman's smile, as he hawks his slices of other people's lives, carry the human message that the film compromises. Bassett is Bigelow's trademark figure of female power rising above male inanity. Stunning, rippling-muscled, Bassett turns a pulp persona into a heroic archetype. Bigelow needs a little heroism herself. She may take heart from her next project—Saint Joan, a woman in a man's world who didn't compromise her vision.

SIGHT AND SOUND, 1/96, p. 53, Philip Strick

Los Angeles, December 1999. As the city prepares to celebrate the millennium, ex-cop Lenny Nero hustles the latest illegal attraction recordings made directly from the brain by the Superconducting Quantum Interference Device (SQUID) which can be worn undetected. On playback, these 'clips' provide total involvement in the recorded experience. Intended for police use only, in Lenny's hands they supply access to any form of vicarious excitement. Lenny's private collection preserves vivid fragments of his past love affair with Faith, a rising pop-star now attached to ruthless promoter Philo Gant. Lenny keeps an eye on her through his friend Max Peltier, also an ex-cop, who works for Philo as a security guard. Lenny's only other friend is Mace, tough woman driver of an armoured limousine.

One of Lenny's contacts, Iris warns him that Faith is in danger, but has to run from the police before she can explain. At the enormous Retinal Fetish nightclub, Faith tells Lenny to leave her alone and Philo's thugs throw him out. Meanwhile, news that black activist and major pop star Jeriko One has been murdered by unknown killers, raises tensions in the city to a critical level. Viewing a clip sent to him anonymously, Lenny is horrified to find himself participating in the brutal rape and murder of Iris. Recalling that Iris mentioned a message left in his car, which has since been towed away, Lenny and Mace break into the compound and discover a clip in Lenny's vehicle. Two cops, Steckler and Engelman, seize the clip and then pursue Lenny and Mace, setting Mace's limousine on fire. They escape by driving it off a pier.

Having tricked the cops, Lenny plays the recovered clip; it reveals that Iris, wearing a SQUID, was witness to the murder of Jeriko One by Steckler and Engelman. As the massive New Year's Eve celebrations get under way, Faith tells Mace and Lenny that Philo sent Iris to 'tape' an encounter, with Jeriko One, Mace persuades Lenny to let her take the clip to the head of the police force, Palmer Strickland. Lenny tracks Philo down only to find him brain-damaged from a SQUID overload administered by Max, who killed Iris to satisfy his own cravings. In a ferocious struggle, Faith helps Lenny to defeat Max while Mace is pursued through the packed streets by the two cops. She manages to handcuff them, but armed soldiers knock her aside; the crowd rushes to her defence and a riot breaks out until Strickland, having checked the clip, orders the arrest of the two killers. Still attempting to destroy Mace, Engelman and Steckler are shot down. As the new century arrives, Lenny realises at last how much Mace really means to him.

While there can be little doubt that SQUID—a delicate electronic web fitting under the hairpiece so much more comfortably than other parasites we have known will be with us (by popular demand) by the year 2000, we may well question whether it will be more absorbing than *Strange Days* itself. The breathtaking Kathryn Bigelow style—racing visuals thunderously reinforced by sonic enclosure may not create reach the nose or tastebuds but it allows little other opportunity for detachment from the experience on show. Largely repeating with its opening number the chase sequence of *Point Break*, when bank-robber, cop, cameraman and audience negotiated an uncut succession of walls, doors, dogs and other obstacles with frantic immediacy, *Strange Days* re-educates us in the share-all process with a subjective burglary, complete with collapsing victims and untimely police arrival that leaves us plummeting from a rooftop.

Bigelow likes her audiences to plummet along with her protagonists (the least you could say about *Point Break,* example, is that it sweeps you off your feet), and this vertiginous preliminary flight, a disorientating topple towards impact with the unknown, readies us for the knife-edge of the century's final moments when the villain, too, hurtles to his fate. The same aerial vantage-point, high above the spangled city, that seduced (and, in her nightmares, overbalanced) the rookie cop in Bigelow's *Blue Steel* is again used to introduce the apocalyptic celebrations of *Strange Days,* an astonishing vista of seething crowds and spotlights that punch the sky. Grandeur on this scale is the stuff of instant addiction.

At ground level, the floating camera reverts to discreet third-party participation. While never pedestrian, the drama hustles like its central character, the floundering Lenny, from one beating to another, alternating crisis with shock, mystery with pursuit. The formula closely matches other James Cameron scripts such as *Aliens* or *Terminator 2: Judgement Day,* setting an urgent, escalating pace towards a decisive battle. Compounding the issue, Lenny's path is strewn with bad guys, a bewildering array by comparison with, say, *Blue Steel,* where they were all condensed into Ron Silver, or *Point Break* where—apart from one isolated cluster of gunmen—they weren't really bad anyway. Befitting an updated Chandleresque gumshoe thriller, *Strange Days* sprouts thugs from all sides, a colourful majority to impede Lenny's dogged progress towards some kind of truth.

Part of the fascination of the film's *noir*-ish allegiances is that the streets echo not with the occasional footstep but with warfare, a perpetual carnage of robberies, gunfights, and burning cars, observed as normal by Lenny but staged with an obvious glee by his directors who—in one particularly cheerful glimpse—even shows Santa Claus being mugged. That we can hardly take this lowlife inferno any more seriously than Brian De Palma's vision of an incandescent Bronx in *The Bonfire of the Vanities* is confirmed by the explanation stutteringly given by the rapist/killer when Lenny at last confronts him. Filmed from several disjointed angles (signs of indecision on Bigelow's part, or just the visual equivalent of his mental disintegration?), he is all charm and junkie incoherence, confessing to improvisations about death-squads and conspiracies that serve only to exaggerate the chaos. "Cheer up," he grins, "the world has only ten minutes to go."

Having shoved us to the brink with this vividly substantiated promise, having shown us a *fin-de-siècle* bedlam of intolerable dimensions in the form of the Retinal Fetish nightclub, having implicated us in the foulest uses (albeit necessarily and intriguingly self-censored) of the SQUID, and having finally—in the endless *Terminator*-style duel with killers who refuse to lie down and die—signalled the opening salvoes of a race war that was rehearsed in the Rodney King riots, Bigelow and Cameron stage a tantalising last-minute retreat. The new millennium arrives in a delirium of reconciliation and joy, of relief that the unsolvable can somehow, in this rare dawn, turn out to have been solved by the application of sheer unaccustomed goodwill. Lenny embraces, almost as an afterthought, the woman who has guarded him with muscle and loyalty throughout his erratic quest, and all else miraculously becomes irrelevant. It is the soft centre of the standard Cameron hard sell, a plot twist fashioned front opportunism which hints, as it did in *The Abyss*, at authentic loss and painful rediscovery. In this context, thanks to the impact of *Strange Days* as a whole, it is as welcome as it is unconvincing.

The Bigelow touch, growing surer with each film, imparts Cameron's hit-and-run tactics with an invaluable extra dimension. Her cast may have to tackle some abysmally trite dialogue, but under her guidance they come up with a lexicon of looks and gestures that makes it work. There is little complexity about Lenny (forget about SQUID, think of him as a petty drug-dealer and he becomes the *cliché* of innumerable straight-to-video qualities), but Ralph Fiennes renders him a clownish romantic—pathetic, stupid, but never dull. As his unnoticed bodyguard, Angela Bassett grabs her chance to play Schwarzenegger with a triumphant display of fistwork, maternalism, and glittering impatience while Juliette Lewis, not yet returned from the wastelands of *Natural Born Killers*, more isolated than ever in her private world of unfathomed sensuality, communicates superbly with barely a reference to normal speech. These may not necessarily be the company with which one would wish to greet a new beginning, but a better claim seems unlikely to be staked; as usual, Bigelow and Cameron, in their separate ways, are streets ahead of the competition.

VILLAGE VOICE, 10/17/95, p. 47, J. Hoberman

A flamboyant, gaseous, erratic comet, Kathryn Bigelow's *Strange Days* seeks and fails to secure its place—not so much in the firmament of the New York Film Festival as among the Reagan era's classic dystopias. *Videodrome*'s evocation of passive image-addiction is delivered with the muscular bombast of a *Terminator* or *RoboCop* for replay on *Blade Runner*'s apocalyptic Sunset Strip to wildly ambitious, disappointingly conventional effect.

Set on the last two days of 1999, *Strange Days* flirts with the idea of film as philosophical toy—the increasingly perfect simulation of a reality superior to our own. The movie is predicated on the notion of "clips"—half-hour chunks of digitally recorded subjective experience, another step toward the virtual reality André Bazin considered cinema's ultimate goal. Strange days to be sure: Addicted "wireheads" wear improved camcorders under their wigs and play back moments from somebody else's life. Thus, *Strange Days* opens with the jittery first-person camera in an automobile backseat en route to a heist and eventual swan dive off a skyscraper roof.

More cynical than *Lady in the Lake,* the 1946 noir in which the camera's point of view was identical to that of unseen detective Philip Marlowe, *Strange Days* essentially posits an anti-hero who traffics in the dubious kick of living through *him*. Lank, unshaven, and constantly on the make, Ralph Fiennes is smiling Lenny Nero, a disgraced vice cop turned super hustler, dealing illegal clips like a degenerate private eye peddling info: "I'm your priest, I'm your shrink ... I'm the Santa Claus of the subconscious." Lenny Nero fiddles while Los Angeles burns, auditioning lesbian porno clips or replaying his personal collection of dates with the lost love of his life, a glitter snarl chanteuse suggestively named Faith (Juliette Lewis).

Does the impending fin de siècle call for a new form of heroism? Introduced as the scuzzball of all time, Lenny is just one more tinsel-town romantic. He even has a moral code, refusing to handle snuff clips—no triple X, thank you. (Instead, he makes a G-rated wire of a walk on the beach for a paraplegic pal.) Nor does Lenny approve of Faith's new rock-manager boyfriend (the born-sinister Michael Wincott), a strung-out wirehead who may or may not be involved in the suspicious death of L.A.'s supposedly charismatic rap-messiah Jeriko One (Glenn Plummer). Mainly concerned with mooning after Faith and getting himself roughed up, Lenny naturally gravitates toward industrial-noise punk clubs with concentration-camp searchlights and chain-link fences. Still, he's basically a lovable slob—at least for his friends Mace (Angela Bassett) and Max (Tom Sizemore, who has a parallel role in the season's other Chandler revision, *Devil in a Blue Dress,* although not, as here, with a mop on his head).

So, down these mean streets ... Lenny cruises the famillar mega-tawdry neon-and-steam multiculti urban-sewer night-town landscape of Asian fast-food joints and tatooed skinheads, flaming cars and antiriot patrols. (A surprisingly upright police chief presides over the requisite rogue cops.) A longing for the Rapture mixes with a pervasive sense of impending race war although the characters spend more time insisting on their paranoia than the movie does constructing it. However high the concept and sensationalist the thrills, *Strange Days* offers surprisingly few futuristic details. Bigelow gooses up the basic L.A. private eye scenario with fast cuts, surging camera moves, and plentiful sexdeath clips, but the movie is long (nearly two-and-a-half hours) and repetitive—a wire where someone forgot to pull the plug.

Strange Days is a sincere action flick. Bigelow pledged her love to staged slugfests as long ago as her experimental short *Set-Up*. Her poetic vampire flick, *Near Dark*, and her gal cop *policier*, *Blue Steel*, demonstrated a willingness to reconsider genre conventions. But more a matter of mindless excitement and manufactured thrills, *Strange Days* mainly proves its own premise that sensory overload has atrophied the imagination. James Cameron coproduced and cowrote the project and his fingerprints are all over it—not the least in Bassett's character, a security driver with a fully armored limousine who (flexing the muscles developed to play Tina Turner) is the resident steroid toughie. Like Cameron's greatest star, *Strange Days* is pumped up and persistent—it just keeps on advancing towards the enforced hilarity of a grimly choreographed New Years Eve.

Stanley Kubrick's high modernist *2001*, the last studio movie to seriously address the millennium, prophesied cosmic transformation. *Strange Days* is more naturalistically corrupt and decadent—an exemplar of postmodernist "fun." It's a movie about the movie business—although not necessarily in the way the filmmakers would wish. In the midst of selling fantasy thrills, Lenny develops a conscience. He loses one Faith but gains another. Is it self-loathing or self-congratulation? The hero may eschew snuff clips but the storyline enables the filmmakers to revel in them—although, as one character suggests, movies are superior to playback because when the credits come up you know that it's over. In other words, narrative closure rules.

Strange Days conflates millenial madness with business as usual, combines big-budget determinism and chaos theory ("all this shit caused by a random traffic stop"), weds William Gibson to Raymond Chandler, invokes the Myth of Total Cinema and the absolute evidence of the Rodney King tape. But, the more things change ... Perhaps the strangest twist in this Big Statement wannabe is that, in the final analysis, the Great White Authority Figure prevails.

Also reviewed in:
CHICAGO TRIBUNE, 10/13/95, Friday/p. C, Michael Wilmington
NATION, 11/6/95, p. 551, Stuart Klawans
NEW REPUBLIC, 11/6/95, p. 28, Stanley Kauffmann
NEW YORK TIMES, 10/6/95, p. C20, Janet Maslin
VARIETY, 9/4-10/95, p. 71, Todd McCarthy
WASHINGTON POST, 10/13/95, p. F1, Hal Hinson
WASHINGTON POST, 10/13/95, Weekend/p. 44, Desson Howe

STUART SAVES HIS FAMILY

A Paramount Pictures release in association with Constellation Films. *Executive Producer:* C.O. Erickson and Dinah Minot. *Producer:* Lorne Michaels and Trevor Albert. *Director:* Harold Ramis. *Screenplay (based on his novel):* Al Franken. *Director of Photography:* Lauro Escorel. *Editor:* Pembroke Herring and Craig Herring. *Music:* Marc Shaiman. *Sound:* Willie Burton. *Casting:* Nancy Foy. *Production Designer:* Joseph T. Garrity. *Art Director:* Thomas P. Wilkins. *Set Designer:* Cosmas A. Demetriou and Thomas C. Reta. *Set Decorator:* Dena Roth. *Costumes:* Susie DeSanto. *Running time:* 100 minutes. *MPAA Rating:* PG-13.

CAST: Al Franken (Stuart Smalley); Laura San Giacomo (Julia); Vincent D'Onofrio (Donnie); Shirley Knight (Stuart's Mom); Harris Yulin (Stuart's Dad); Lesley Boone (Jodie); John Link Graney (Kyle); Julia Sweeney (Mea C.); Camille Saviola (Station Manager).

LOS ANGELES TIMES, 4/12/95, Calendar/p. 7, Peter Rainer

Al Franken is good enough, he's certainly smart enough. So, doggone it, why is "Stuart Saves His Family" so mediocre?

On "Saturday Night Live," Franken's Stuart Smalley is a hilarious concoction: a "caring nurturer" with his own public-access TV show "Daily Affirmation," a wardrobe of fuzzy pastel sweaters and an idiot grin. Stuart—not a licensed therapist—is every woozy balm dispenser we've ever seen on cable; he's so touchy-feely that he gives you the heebie-jeebies.

What makes Franken so funny on "Saturday Night Live"—and so touching—is his deep-down commitment to Stuart's dumpy self-love. Stuart has been through so many 12-step programs that he's groggy with uplift. (His sessions with Michael Jordan, or the "Bobbitts," were screwball classics.)

The problem with "Stuart Saves His Family" is that Franken, who wrote the screenplay based very loosely on his best-selling mock-self-help book—"I'm Good Enough, I'm Smart Enough, and Doggone It, People Like Me!"—is starting to take Stuart altogether too seriously. It's kind of creepy. He's made an *inspirational* goofball comedy. Stuart rescues his hyper-dysfunctional family in Minneapolis and triumphs over his compulsion to gorge Fig Newtons.

It was much funnier when we didn't see Stuart's family. And, if we have to see them, it would have been much funnier if they were strait-laced '50s sitcom types. But Franken, and his director Harold Ramis, want to demonstrate how our families screw us up—and they really *mean* it. So the Smalley family is a gaggle of horrors: His mom (Shirley Knight) seems lobotomized, his dad (Harris Yulin) is a ramrod nutcase, his sister Jodie is a chronic whiner/overeater, and his brother (Vincent D'Onofrio) lives at home and puffs marijuana. Stuart is the most normal in the bunch. He's a *victim*.

Franken also co-wrote the script for "When a Man Loves a Woman," which was a touchy-feely "Days of Wine and Roses" for the '90s. Some of that film's humidity seems to have dripped onto "Stuart Saves His Family." Doesn't Franken realize how funny he is when he's making fun of Victim Theology? He may be the only person in America who takes Stuart Smalley at his word.

NEW YORK POST, 4/12/95, p. 33, Michael Medved

It's good enough, it's smart enough, and, doggone it, some people are gonna like it!

As a matter of fact, anyone who's ever chuckled at the "daily affirmations" of Al Franken's popular Stuart Smalley character on "Saturday Night Live" will enjoy "Stuart Saves His Family"—a deft, witty and surprisingly touching piece of work.

Director Harold Ramis, who scored a major success with "Groundhog Day" two years ago, once again combines hilarious and poignant elements in a challenging and original comedy of ideas.

Most importantly, he never condescends to his main character. Yes, Stuart is a doofus, but he's a deeply endearing doofus, and the platitudes he's learned from his participation in innumerable 12-step programs all contain some kernel of truth.

Who can argue with him, for instance, when he declares: "The only person I can fix is me, because it is easier to put on slippers than to carpet the entire world!"

The movie's story begins when Stuart loses his embarrassingly "inspirational" cable access TV show after a dispute with his embittered alcoholic station manager (Camille Saviola).

As if this weren't enough to permanently shatter his painstakingly contrived optimism, he's called back home to Minneapolis to deal with a family crisis after the death of an elderly aunt.

As he confides to the audiences as part of the ironic narration that accompanies his story: "They say you can't go home again. In my case, it's more like you're crazy to go home again."

Stuart nonetheless leaves behind his best friend and Al-Anon sponsor (Laura San Giacomo) and decides to make the trip. He soon finds himself once more entangled with his alcoholic and growlingly abusive father (a perfectly understated Harris Yulin) and ditzy, fidgety, overweight mother (Shirley Knight) who, in Stuart's phrase, proves that "Denial isn't just a river in Egypt." His sister (Lesley Boone) is similarly troubled, addicted to food and exploitative ex-husbands, while big brother (Vincent D'Onofrio) is inert, angry, unemployed and perpetually stoned on grass or booze.

D'Onofrio, a consistently fine (and undervalued), actor, makes this familiar figure so compelling and believable that he very nearly steals the movie.

Stuart himself is also a thoroughly engaging creation—in fact, Franken brings such extraordinary vulnerability and conviction to the role that it's hard to escape the conclusion that the movie is his means of working through his own personal demons, and not just his fictional character's.

You end up feeling protective toward Stuart (and Franken), so that it's easy to forgive glaring flaws in both the man and the movie. Franken's screenplay (he previously cowrote the profitable melodrama, "When a Man Loves a Woman") here lacks any conventional dramatic arc, but it displays abundant sympathy and humor toward even its most troubled characters.

The movie, like Stuart himself, seems almost painfully eager to win our acceptance and affection, but it still has the dignity and good sense to avoid some gooey, sentimental resolution.

Like those goofy affirmations its protagonist proffers to the world, "Stuart Saves His Family" is odd, unfocused, terrible nervous, uncomfortably close to reality, and, ultimately, downright courageous.

NEWSDAY, 4/12/95, part II/p. B9, John Anderson

Family is about tradition, and "Stuart Saves His Family" is about tradition—the tradition of "Billy Madison," "Tommy Boy "Man of the House," "It's Pat," "Cabin Boy" and most other films even remotely related to "Saturday Night Live."

It seems that when one spends one's adult life on a TV show that's coasted on its own reputation for most of its existence, one loses one's appreciation for what's funny. Or appropriate. Or what might conceivably work as a motion picture. Or what might make you look even more ridiculous than the people you're ridiculing. It's understandable. When there's no standard of quality, it's like living in a bubble. At this point, a resounding pop would be music.

Lorne Michaels, who's managed to keep "SNL" on the air with what must be sleight of hand, is a producer of "Stuart Saves His Family," which figures. The very premise seems a blueprint for disaster: Take a character who's barely tolerable in five-minute segments—Al Franken's 12-step addict/New Age imbecile Stuart Smalley—and make him the centerpiece of a 90-odd minute, big-screen feature. Invest that feature with a quasi-serious treatment of domestic abuse, alcoholism and the various spiritual infirmities from which Stuart suffers. What you're left with is a film that mocks the concept of self-improvement, while relying on our sympathy for people who need it. It can't work, and doesn't.

Compounding the problem, the movie isn't very funny. Stuart loses his "Daily Affirmation" cable program right away, and spends most of the movie getting himself back on the air. Only when he steps out of his daffy posture of positive-thinking—"I'm a smart person, I'm an attractive person and, doggone it, people like me," he regularly tells himself—does he make contact with the audience, and suggest that maybe we're all in this together. Otherwise, the mix of social statement and stupid jokes is too incongruous to do anything but push us away.

"Stuart Saves His Family" is an odd animal, a depressing comedy. Is alcoholism funny? Is domestic abuse funny? How about a loveless familial existence? Sure, under the right circumstances. But those circumstances require the comic to establish a twisted sensibility, share it with the audience and maintain it. Franken, abetted by director Harold ("Ghostbusters") Ramis, segregates the humorous and nonhumorous elements of the story, and the seesaw effect only amplifies the pathetic state of Stuart's family, and their various crises.

When Aunt Paula dies, Stuart goes home and becomes involved in a family fracas over her gravesite, and a dispute over her will. "How's Dad?" Stuart asks his pothead brother Donnie (Vincent D'Onofrio) upon arriving. "What's he up to?" "Oh," Donnie answers, "about a quart a day." Badaboom. Their father (Harris Yulin) is a resolute alcoholic, as is Donnie. Their mother (Shirley Knight) and sister (Lesley Boone) console themselves with food, and the entire family makes Stuart their whipping boy. Anyone familiar with this kind of emotionally crippled household will sympathize, but, personally, if I want therapy I'll go to a professional.

VILLAGE VOICE, 4/25/95, p. 64, Laurie Stone

On *SNL*, Stuart Smalley's inventories of defeat tweak the age of confession, while copping to the pleasures of naval gazing. When he is nervous and unprepared on his public access show - which is always the case—he comforts himself with the bromide, "But that's ... okay." The line is funny, because nothing Stuart does is adequate. He is a complicated comic figure, because he is decent as well as a fuckup and part of him knows he is substituting psychobabble for reflection.

Unfortunately, *Stuart Saves His Family* is driven less by satirist Al Franken than by schmaltzmeister Smalley. A few winsomely mordant touches pierce the movie's New Age vapors—to soothe his sobbing, food junkie sister, Stuart applies the 13th step and counsels her over the phone, "I would never ordinarily say this, but is there any way you could get to a pound cake?" Mostly though, instead of skewering the culture of recovery, the movie—directed by the usually irreverent Harold Ramis—gets with the program. When Stuart's family surprises Dad with an intervention, the scene is played straight, hustling for lumps in the throat. When hard-edged Laura San Giacomo must, as one of Stuart's sponsors, sincerely spout such phrases as "shame spiral" and "don't beat yourself up," she can't help sounding like she's going to gag. Franken gleans a lot of mileage from his clown's mouth and Keaton-esque delivery, but in this movie, for which he wrote the script, he defangs one of *SNL*'s only surviving pointed characters and adds to the heap of dead balloons blown up from *SNL* sketches.

Also reviewed in:
CHICAGO TRIBUNE, 4/12/95, Tempo/p. 7, John Petrakis
NEW YORK TIMES, 4/12/95, p. C18, Janet Maslin
VARIETY, 4/17-23/95, p. 36, Joe Leydon
WASHINGTON POST, 4/12/95, p. C11, Hal Hinson
WASHINGTON POST, 4/14/95, Weekend/p. 36, Desson Howe

SUDDEN DEATH

A Universal Pictures release of a Signature/Baldwin/Cohen production in association with Imperial Entertainment. *Executive Producer:* Ash R. Shah, Sundip R. Shah, Anders P. Jensen, and Sunil R. Shah. *Producer:* Moshe Diamant and Howard Baldwin. *Director:* Peter Hyams. *Screenplay:* Gene Quintano. *Based on a story by:* Karen Baldwin. *Director of Photography:* Peter Hyams. *Editor:* Steven Kemper. *Music:* John Debney. *Music Editor:* Tom Carlson. *Sound:* Les Lazarowitz and (music) John Richards. *Sound Editor:* David Kneupper and Glenn T. Morgan. *Casting:* Penny Perry Davis and Deborah Brown. *Production Designer:* Philip Harrison. *Art Director:* William Barclay. *Set Designer:* Miguel Lopez-Castillo. *Set Decorator:* Caryl Heller. *Set Dresser:* Sarah Burt, Ralph Pivirotto, John N. Butler, and Gregory Jones. *Special Effects:* Garry Elmendorf. *Costumes:* Dan Lester. *Make-up:* Katalin Elek. *Stunt Coordinator:* Gary M. Hymes. *Running time:* 110 minutes. *MPAA Rating:* RR.

CAST: Jean-Claude Van Damme (Darren); Powers Boothe (Joshua Foss); Raymond J. Barry (Vice President); Whittni Wright (Emily); Ross Malinger (Tyler); Dorian Harewood (Hallmark); Kate McNeil (Kathi); Michael Gaston (Hickey); Audra Lindley (Mrs. Ferrara); Brian Delate (Blair); Steve Aronson (Dooley); Michael Aubele (Ace); Karen Baldwin (T.V. Director); Jennifer D. Bowser (Joan); Pat Brisson (Player #2); Glenda Morgan Brown (Mrs. Taylor); Jophrey Brown (Wooton); William Cameron (Secret Serviceman); Bernard Canepari (Jefferson); Jay Caufield (Tolliver); Alan Clement (Mr. Wirtz); Bill Clement (Pre-Game Announcer); Bill Dalzell III (Spota); Gil Combs (Secret Service #1); Jack Erdie (Scratch); Ed Evanko (Baldwin); David Flick (Spectator); Glenn Alan Gardner (Sugarman Driver); John Hall (Hallmark's Secret #2); Jeff Habbersted (Lewis); Mark Hager (Elevator SS Man); John Hateley (Briggs); Rosine "Ace" Hatem (Concessionaire); Jeff Hochendoner (Duckerman); Jeffrey Howell (Usborn); Brian Hutchison (Young Agent); Jeff Jimerson (Anthem Singer); Mark Kachowski (Beaumont); Callum Keith-King (Kitchen Assistant); Rick LeFevour (Ante Room SS Man); Tommy LaFitte (Sugarman Guard); Raymond Laine (Foss Man #1); Mike Lange (Play by Play Announcer); Butch Luick (Fat Man); Fred Mancuso (Pratt); Anthony Marino (Vendor); Larry John Meyers (Box Secret Service #2); Ken Milchick (Coach); Faith Minton (Carla); Paul Mochnick (Andre Ferrara); Brad Moniz (Toowey); Jean-Pierre Nutini (Employee #1); Daniel R. Pagath (Assistant Coach); Manny Perry (Brody); Allan Pinsker (Older Man); Douglas Rees (Spotter); Diane Robin (Mrs. Baldwin); Luc Robitaille (Himself); Thomas Saccio (Foss Helicopter Pilot); Vinnie Sciullo (Foss Man #2); Jack Skelly (Elderly Guard); Brian Smrz (Thug #2); Phil Spano (Player #1); Paul Steigerwald (Color Commentator); John Sterling (Kitchen Secret Service Agent); Harold Surratt (Hallmark's Secret Service #3); Rohn Thomas

(Mayor Taylor);   Milton Thompson, Jr. (Kurtz);   Dixie Tymitz (Mrs. Wirtz);   Fred Waugh (Bluto);   Rema D. Webb (Cindy);   Dean E. Wells (Kloner).

LOS ANGELES TIMES, 12/22/95, Calendar/p. 20, Kevin Thomas

"Sudden Death" is a treat for Jean-Claude Van Damme fans, a superior action thriller loaded with jaw-dropping stunts and special effects, and strong in production values. Expertly directed—and photographed—by Peter Hyams, it's Van Damme's biggest and best to date. It's also very violent, with a high body count, so parents need to think twice before allowing their children to see it.

Tailor-made for Van Damme, the sleek Universal release casts him as a firefighter traumatized by his failure to save a little girl in a house fire. Divorced and now working as a fire inspector, he draws marshal duty at Pittsburgh's Civic Arena, where the vice president of the United States (Raymond J. Barry), a hockey fan, will be attending the seventh game in the Stanley Cup Finals, in which the local Penguins are playing the Chicago Blackhawks.

Early in the game, to which Van Damme has taken his own youngsters (Whittni Wright and Ross Malinger), master criminal Powers Boothe, leading a large, professional team, has penetrated the owner's box and is holding the vice president hostage. His demands are simple: If $1.7 billion in frozen government funds are not transferred over to him—the scheme is intricate—he will not only assassinate Barry but also blow up the entire arena, filled with 17,000 fans.

"You'll be sorry," declares the spunky little Wright when she, too, falls into Boothe's clutches. We know that's true for sure, but Hyams and writer Gene Quintano, in adapting a story from associate producer Karen Baldwin, are consistently ingenious in generating and maintaining suspense as to how Van Damme is going to overcome so obviously formidable an adversary on such a tight deadline.

Van Damme's physical exploits are surely among his most audacious, and they are strongly motivated by his firefighter's absolute determination to succeed in his hair-raising mission. Van Damme's single-minded passion is nicely counterpointed by Boothe's sardonic mystery man, the suave, smirky type you love to hate. Wright and Malinger come across as real-life youngsters, and Dorian Harewood is solid as the lead Secret Service agent assigned to protect the vice president. "Sudden Death" provides an extra kick for hockey lovers, for it boasts considerable on-ice action and a cameo by Luc Robitaille.

NEW YORK POST, 12/22/95, p. 50, Michael Medved

It's the seventh game of the Stanley Cup finals and the TV announcers are offering the usual hype about the excitement of the moment: "You can feel the electricity in the air! THIS PLACE IS READY TO EXPLODE!"

In this particular instance, that declaration is more than mere hyperbole: a band of high-tech extortionists have rigged the Civic Arena in Pittsburgh with a series of bombs that will go off at the end of the hockey game unless outrageous monetary demands are met.

With 17,000 fans unaware of their peril, this would be a serious matter in any event, but the stakes are raised even higher by the presence of the vice president of the United States (Raymond J. Barry) in the owner's box high above the ice. Outside the besieged stadium, a dedicated Secret Service agent (Dorian Harewood) seems powerless to foil the plans of the bombers and their suave, sadistic leader, a rogue CIA agent nicely played by Powers Boothe.

In fact, the only hope to thwart the evil scheme is a former city fireman with a troubled past, who's now working as a fire inspector in the arena, but is forced into action when the terrorists grab his daughter (Whittni Wright of "I'll Do Anything") as one of their, hostages in the luxury box.

What chance could this lowly, lonely functionary stand against more than a dozen ruthless professional killers? Would it change your sense of the odds of the affair if you knew that Jean-Claude Van Damme played the fightin' fireman?

That's right, "The Muscles from Brussels" is back in his best role to date, but don't look to "Sudden Death" for any sudden explosions of originality. We're definitely in "Die Hard" territory, with screenwriter Gene Quintano ("Cop and a Half," "Police Academy 4") slavishly following the tired formula: he even calls the Van Damme character "McCord" to echo the Bruce Willis/"McClain" character in the original "Die Hard."

If Hollywood can make hay with Die Hard on a Boat ("Under Siege"), Die Hard on a Plane ("Passenger 57"), Die Hard on a Mountain ("Cliffhanger") and Die Hard on a Bus ("Speed"), then why not Die Hard at a Hockey Rink? It makes sense when the stunts are as spectacular as they are here, with director Peter Hyams ("Timecop," "2010") making imaginative use of helicopters and explosions and a scoreboard and a domed stadium that opens to, the sky at the flick of a switch.

The movie does go over the top when it shows Van Damme, who's supposed to be a French-Canadian hockey fanatic (hence the accent) enjoying a few Walter Mitty moments as he masquerades as a pro player to stand in for an injured goalie—not only saving the stadium but saving the game.

But even here, Hyams' game is slick and smart even concerning the gory excesses that seem to be written into the script. When bad guys get their hands french fried in a pot of boiling oil, or their heads severed on a kitchen conveyor belt, the director pulls back and lets you imagine the horrors rather than triumphantly displaying them. It's a strategy that leaves you thrilled, rather than ill, and works as smoothly as the rest of this above-average action film.

NEWSDAY, 12/22/95, Part II/p. B13, John Anderson

The original, "Die Hard" seems to have spawned more clones than "Stagecoach." But while being a clone means you're never alone, having a lot of company isn't necessarily a bad thing.

Take "Sudden Death," for example, which stars Claude Van Damme as a martial arts-adept arson inspector who finds himself caught up in a terrorist plot to hold the vice president of the United States (Raymond J. Barry) hostage at the Stanley Cup final. Van Damme's kids are at the game. His building's been invaded. His pride is on the line. And having once lost someone else's child during a big fire (seen amidst the opening credits), he's got a certain degree of post-traumatic plotline disorder.

If this stuff didn't work to some degree, it wouldn't be recycled so often. And since no one goes to a film called "Sudden Death" expecting Jean Renoir, what we're really interested in here is what they do with the basic formulas. Is it a kill-by-numbers exercise? Or is there a creative use of mayhem? In "Sudden Death," it's the latter, even though there's a distracting number of similarities to the mother film.

Like John McClane in "Die Hard," Darren McCord (yes, the Belgian-accented Van Damme, too, is of Irish descent) is a civil servant with an occupational attitude problem, a guy whose gifts for physical violence are unexplained but potent, and someone whose family members are among those being threatened by the bad guys. The implication is that the hero is not just some do-gooder willing to put his butt on the line for strangers, but also a dude whose loved ones need protecting. It gives the characters their character, in a manner of speaking.

What separates "Sudden Death" from the standard action/adventure clone—although not too far to separate it from a big take at the box office—is the mischief director/cinematographer Peter Hyams ("Outland," "2010") makes with his characters, as well as the way predictable setups don't end up so preditctably. During the initial seizure of the Pittsburgh Civic Arena (the Penguins are playing the Chicago Blackhawks), we meet people and see them doing things that in other films of this sort would be key plot points. And then Hyams blows them away in such cavalier fashion that you really begin to wonder where you are.

Some things, on the other hand, are exactly what they seem. Hallmark (Dorian Harewood), the ostensibly by-the-book FBI agent on the scene, tries to deter McCord from his lethal one-man rescue mission (in which he dispatches villains in every area of the building, utilizing whatever appliances or bludgeons are nearest at hand). They clash, they make up, they ... never mind. Likewise Joshua Foss, the gleefully homicidal hostage-taker and rogue fed who drips with such arrogance and malice that you can't wait for him to get his. These guys are basic, necessary and spectacularly ordinary.

The stunts are, of course, spectacularly excessive and make full use of the Civic Arena. "Sudden Death" has a lot of relatives (including John Frankenheimer's "Black Sunday," the blow-up-the-Super-Bowl film of 1977) but, as in man families, it's the eccentricities that make one stand out.

SIGHT AND SOUND, 5/96, p. 62, Tom Tunney

After planting a series of bombs in and around Pittsburgh's Civic Arena stadium, Joshua Foss's terrorist gang kidnap the US Vice President and assorted local dignitaries in the VIP lounge during an ice hockey game between the Pittsburgh Penguins and the Chicago Blackhawks. The gang hold the VIPs hostage and threaten to kill a number of them at the end of each period of play unless over $1 billion in frozen foreign government accounts is electronically transferred to them.

Stadium fire safety officer Darren McCord is also attending the game with his two young children, Emily and Tyler. Emily is kidnapped and taken hostage after she walks in on one of the terrorists. McCord goes after the terrorist and battles him successfully in the stadium kitchen. He then rushes to the nearest security guard who also turns out to be a terrorist. A further fight in the kitchen ends with McCord interrogating the villain using a hot plate before killing him. Aware now of the gang's plans, McCord starts defusing the bombs. Meanwhile the authorities' attempts to storm the stadium are thwarted. As the game continues, McCord is chased through the stadium, taking refuge on the rink, where he disguises himself as the goalkeeper and makes a crucial save. He then kills another villain in the dressing room.

Meanwhile as the Penguins score in the closing seconds, the game goes to a 'sudden death' play off—which delays Foss' final murders. With a home-made stun bomb McCord climbs up the outside of the stadium's huge dome roof. Killing the guard stationed there, he swings down into the stadium, throws his bomb through the VIP lounge window and then follows through himself, shooting as he goes. With all of his team dead, Foss grabs Emily and makes for the roof and his getaway helicopter. McCord follows, pushes Emily safely aside and shoots the chopper's pilot from below while hanging in mid-air from the chopper's rope ladder. He falls safely onto the domed part of the open roof and catches Foss's eye as the chopper slowly plunges tail first through it to explode in the centre of the now empty stadium.

Sudden Death sets itself the strictly limited task of accommodating Jean-Claude Van Damme within the modern lone warrior format first perfected in *Die Hard* and since much imitated by the likes of *Under Siege*, *On Deadly Ground* and *Cliffhanger*. The conventions of the sub-genre are now so obviously foregrounded that comedy has become as much a requirement as action. With a mature variant such as this movie, *Under Siege 2* or *Die Hard With a Vengeance*, one of the main sources of audience pleasure is to share in the filmmakers' gleeful sense of contrivance as they force their heroes through the same set of dangerous hoops as before. Contrivance thus becomes something to celebrate rather than to disguise.

Contrived convention number one is that a group of terrorists should attempt to take over a key location. Number two is that the ever-resourceful hero has to be isolated in some way from the authorities so that he can wage an increasingly spectacular (and ludicrous) one-man guerrilla war against them. Number three is that the terrorist leader should be witty, highly articulate, irredeemably cruel and driven by selfish rather than political goals. And number four is that this Manichean struggle should climax with a major stunt set piece in which the villain is killed. Narrative closure and the moral and physical superiority of the hero are thus asserted, typically with a huge explosion and/or the bad guy falling from a great height.

Sudden Death proficiently covers all four conventions and shows genuine panache in its handling of its many action set pieces. The use of the Pittsburgh Civic Arena (producer Howard Baldwin is the owner of the Penguins' team; his wife Karen Baldwin came up with the original story) makes for a suitably spectacular finale when McCord swings down through its distinctive opening roof like a latter day Tarzan. The stadium here almost becomes a character in its own right. That the ice hockey game goes on throughout the crisis allows the director Peter Hyams (*Narrow Margin*, *Stay Tuned*, *Timecop*) to exploit the hard knock physicality of that sport, both as an effective form of cross-cutting punctuation and as a rhythmic way of racking up the tension. Although the opening scenes, which set up the story's premise, are awkwardly presented, once the game starts, the plot shifts into a high gear which doesn't let up until the final big explosion.

Presenting the battle of wits between McCord and Foss as a game gives a tightly-knit sense of closure to the narrative: McCord has to defuse the bombs and save his daughter and the Vice President, whereas Foss has to secure the transfer of the funds, all by the end of the match. As a computer game format it's obviously ready made, but more importantly as a film narrative it has a directness and an economy which gain greatly from its unities of time and place. Asking for credibility is futile in this kind of scenario, where the aim is to offer the entertainingly incredible. So McCord bounds around the arena, dispatches sundry villains and defuses assorted bombs and then, in the comedy highlight, actually finds himself playing in goal for the home side. The screenplay's playful sense of humour is also much in evidence in the pivotal fight sequence which delivers the absurd spectacle of McCord kicking his way through a kitchen while dealing with an assassin dressed up as a giant penguin. This kind of crisply choreographed unarmed combat is what Van Damme does best and Hyams handles it with so much manic, fast-cutting relish that it almost thumps its way through the screen. In the acting rather than action stakes, Powers Boothe also delivers the goods with a smoothly sinuous performance which, again typically for the sub-genre, puts the accent on black comedy ("He needs a doctor!" "Not any more!").

Paradoxically it's Van Damme's very blank simplicity of his screen personality, which makes him so indispensable as an action hero. In the dullish *Nowhere to Run* his athletic style was cramped by a numbing relationship with Rosanna Arquette and in the disastrous *Street Fighter* he was too often sidelined by dull talk and ragged plot exposition. *Timecop,* which Peter Hyams also directed, was a much stronger vehicle and, here again, recognising that his star's acting limitations are also his strength, the director gives only the minimum of lip service to character while pushing the action for all its worth.

A less astute director would waste valuable time eliciting thoughtful reactions from his star to such clichéd plot points as the threat to his character McCord's child Emily. Hyams realises that, as an actor, Van Damme is a child's idea of what a grown up should be: brave, loyal, steadfast and true. Fundamentally, the heroes of this subgenre are no different at the end of their movies than they are at the start. The only difference is they've killed sundry bad guys and asserted, yet again, their moral and physical superiority to the world at large. The continuing voracious appetite for such warriors implies much about the real 90s worlds of work, the community and law enforcement.

It's also symbolically apt that this latest example of lone heroics should be set in a sports stadium. Violence as a ritualised spectator sport is the concept at the heart of the lone warrior subgenre. The insistence on violence as theatre strongly recalls the gladiatorial contests of Ancient Rome. The Romans had bread and circuses: the modern audience has Dolph Lundgren, Steven Seagal and Jean-Claude Van Damme. And, to invert the same analogy, the likes of Alan Rickman, Jeremy Irons and Powers Boothe will always get a big thumbs up so long as they amuse us on the way to their screen deaths. Not for nothing do the villains here smuggle their bombs into the stadium inside huge bags of popcorn.

VILLAGE VOICE, 12/26/95, p. 60, Gary Dauphin

Die Hard in a hockey arena (or is that 1977's Super Bowl nightmare *Black Sunday* in a hockey arena?), *Sudden Death* skates the slick surface of the formula action-movie pond, echoing enough familiar (and better) movies to keep an audience awake and not much more. Jean-Claude plays an ex-fireman here, to fire marshalling at the seventh game of the NHL finals after his failure to save a little girl during a movie-opening rescue scene. His kids are in the stands, as is the vice president, so when a group of high-tech terror-pros takes over the owners box and threatens to blow everyone to smithereens, its up to Jean-Claude, to you guessed it save the day. Doing a French-Canadian riff on Bruce Willis's public servant-cum-hero, Jean-Claude goes it alone inside the stadium, repelling up walls and disarming bombs (gee, being an ex-fireman sure is handy), while burly hockey fans root away unawares and the Secret Service bumbles it up in the stadium's sealed-off parking lot.

If it sounds as if *Sudden Death* references the bureaucratic milieu of *Die Hard* relentlessly, it does, right down to the black Secret Service agent holding the fort outside and a hyperintelligent terrorist-turned-kidnapper villain (Powers Boothe doing the Alan Rickman thing). Director Hyams (who has made a couple of mildly interesting sci-fi flicks: *Outland, 2010,* and *Timecop*) threatens throughout to make *Sudden Death* an effective and original thriller. Since the bad guys have linked their ransom schedule to the hockey game, the action on and off the ice runs in parallel, culminating with the niftily edited sequence when the game goes into sudden-death overtime. The moment is over in a puck's flash and there is unfortunately no instant replay, but for a brief moment *Sudden Death* is as exciting as its sources.

Also reviewed in:
CHICAGO TRIBUNE, 12/22/95, Friday/p. N, John Petrakis
NEW YORK TIMES, 12/22/95, p. C6, Stephen Holden
VARIETY, 12/11-17/95, p. 84, Derek Elley
WASHINGTON POST, 12/22/95, p. C7, Richard Harrington
WASHINGTON POST, 12/22/955, Weekend/p. 47, Desson Howe

SUM OF US, THE

A Samuel Goldwyn Company and Southern Star release in association with Australian Film Finance Corporation of a Hal McElroy-Southern Star production. *Executive Producer:* Errol Sullivan and Hal McElroy. *Producer:* Hal McElroy. *Director:* Kevin Dowling and Geoff Burton. *Screenplay based on his play by:* David Stevens. *Director of Photography:* Geoff Burton. *Editor:* Frans Vandenburg. *Music:* Dave Faulkner. *Sound:* Leo Sullivan and (music) Charles Fisher. *Casting:* Faith Martin. *Production Designer:* Graham (Grace) Walker. *Art Director:* Ian Gracie. *Set Decorator:* Kerrie Brown. *Set Dresser:* Faith Robinson. *Costumes:* Louise Spargo. *Make-up:* Lesley Rouvray. *Running time:* 95 minutes. *MPAA Rating:* Not Rated.

CAST: Jack Thompson (Harry Mitchell); Russell Crowe (Jeff Mitchell); John Polson (Greg); Deborah Kennedy (Joyce Johnson); Joss Moroney (Young Jeff); Mitch Mathews (Gran); Julie Herbert (Mary); Des James (Football Coach); Mick Campbell (Footballer); Donny Muntz (Ferry Captain); Jan Adele (Barmaid); Rebekah Elmaloglou (Jenny); Lola Nixon (Desiree); Sally Cahill (Greg's Mother); Bob Baines (Greg's Father); Paul Freeman (George); Walter Kennard (Barman); Stuart Campbell and Grahem Drake (Leather Men); Elaine Lee (Woman on Train); Ross Anderson (Gardener); Michael Burgess (Foreman); John Rhall (Dad's Brother); Helen Williams (Brother's Wife); Jan Merriman (Nurse).

LOS ANGELES TIMES, 3/8/95, Calendar/p. 8, Kevin Thomas

When we meet the father and son of the warm and deeply affecting "The Sum of Us," they strike us as typical Aussie blokes who have an especially close and affectionate relationship. They *are* in fact typical—the father is a robust, middle-aged Sydney ferry captain and the son is a plumber. They are both great-looking, masculine men. It's a kind of after-thought to mention that the son is gay.

Jack Thompson's Harry, however, is extroverted while Russell Crowe's Jeff, who is neither shy nor withdrawn, tends to seem understated in comparison to his life-force father.

Some time seems to have passed since Harry lost his wife, but her death has left its mark on both father and son. As it happens, Harry is now ready to apply to a dating service, just as Jeff has met a new man, Greg (John Polson).

In the first of a number of beautifully sustained sequences, Harry unwittingly overdoes the accepting father routine. In his eagerness to see Jeff find his supportiveness, he ends up making himself such a nuisance when Jeff brings Greg home for the first time that he succeeds only in driving Greg away.

Greg is overwhelmed by Harry, who is such a jarring contrast to his own profoundly homophobic father. Jeff finds himself retreating from romance while Harry meets Joyce (Deborah Kennedy), an attractive woman with whom he clicks instantly yet whom he hesitates to tell that his son is gay.

Then there's an effective development that transforms everything, with Harry becoming determined that his offspring leave his comfy nest and find his own love.

David Stevens, in adapting his own play, gives an old heart-tugging plot—in which a parent must get a devoted child to take care of himself—a fresh spin with the son's gayness. The film's Australian setting, furthermore, gives it a pungent particularity. In the land of Crocodile Dundee, gay men are often as macho as straight guys, and there's an open bluntness about both homosexuality and homophobia.

In making his directorial debut, Kevin Dowling made the shrewd move of sharing the directing credit with his veteran cinematographer, Geoff Burton. The result is an unusually self-effacing transposition of a play to the screen, one that has some acute visuals, none more so than a moment in which we see the TV glimpse of Greg in a gay parade that so horrifies his father.

NEW YORK POST, 3/8/95, p. 30, Michael Medved

Most recent films about gay characters display a grim, preachy tone as they focus on the horrors of the AIDS epidemic, or the pain of intolerance, or both.

The new Australian import "The Sum of Us" represents a welcome exception: It's a sunny, sentimental, supremely skillful film that wins big laughs while achieving an unexpected emotional impact.

It focuses on the relationship between the widower Harry Mitchell (Jack Thompson of "Breaker Morant"), a blue-collar bloke from Sydney, and his 24-year-old son, Jeff (Russell Crowe of "Proof" and "The Quick and the Dead"), a rugby-playing plumber who lives with his dad.

Harry is unequivocally proud of his boy and has learned to accept his sexual orientation. "He's ... 'cheerful.' I can't bear that other word," he declares in one of his regular confessions directly to the camera.

Unfortunately, Jeffs cheerfulness is undermined by his lonely status and his long-standing difficulty in finding "Mr. Right." When he comes home one night with a shy gardener, Greg (John Polson), Harry's enthusiastic encouragement of their relationship actually inhibits attempts at intimacy—especially since his attitude contrasts so sharply with Greg's parent's hostility to any hint of homosexuality.

Meanwhile, Harry's moving ahead with his own social life, hoping to find a replacement for the perfect love he once enjoyed with Jeff's mother. Through a video dating service he meets Joyce (Deborah Kennedy) a proper, ladylike middle-aged divorcee, but he hesitates to inform her about his son.

From that point forward, the surprises in the plot avoid all obvious excesses of either situation comedy or message melodrama. Even in its most painful moments, "The Sum of Us" maintains its cheeky, down-to-earth sense of humor.

Jack Thompson (a national icon in his native Australia) is attuned to all the nuances in his role as Harry. His character is fundamentally decent and well-meaning; but hardly perfect, he actually makes a nuisance of himself by trying much-too-hard to show support for a lifestyle which he can never fully understand.

As Jeff, Russell Crowe is similarly well-cast: He's a rising star who's so appealing and likable that we inevitably share Harry's affection for the lad.

The movie's major shortcoming involves the relationship between Jeff and Greg: The plot requires a powerful, life-changing passion, but despite intense moments of physical affection, nothing we see suggests a connection of that depth or durability.

Nevertheless, it's the father-son bond that occupies center stage in the story, and debuting director Kevin Dowling (who directed the off-Broadway stage version of "The Sum of Us") handles it masterfully.

Working with veteran cinematographer Geoff Burton (who's also credited as co-director), Dowling effortlessly opens up the play, providing a sweeping, affectionate view of daily life in Sydney that enriches the script by David Stevens, Oscar-nominated co-writer of "Breaker Morant."

"Ashamed of Jeff? Never!" Harry emphatically declares. "Our children are only the sum of us. And our parents. And our grandparents. And all the generations."

And like those children, this original and affecting film is even more than the sum of its parts.

NEWSDAY, 3/8/95, Part II/p. B9, John Anderson

Some men are born to alternative lifestyles, some have alternative lifestyles thrust upon them. Take Harry Mitchell (Jack Thompson), whose mother enjoyed a 40-year lesbian relationship after the death of his father. And whose son, Jeff (Russell Crowe), is also "cheerful" (Harry hates that other word). Harry's an enlightened guy. Of course, he's had to be.

"The Sum of Us," adapted by David Stevens from his award-winning play, is, as the advertising states, "not your typical father and son story." Harry is extraordinary, really: a solid, happy (not cheerful), middle-of-the-road sort of widower who likes a pint and would like a wife, he accepts Jeff's sexual orientation simply because it's his. And having come to terms with Jeff's nature, he wants his son to find Mr. Right. Jeff, not surprisingly, loves his father.

The problem for both Harry and Jeff, who talk, wink and mug at the camera when the other's not looking, is a common one—other people. Jeff, a plumber who plays rugby and knows how to wear a pair of shorts, is smitten with Greg (John Polson), a local gardener Harry thinks may be The One. When Jeff brings Greg home one night, Harry is his usual gregariously pesky, ultra-understanding self—making drinks, making chatter, bonding with Greg and giving him a little pep talk on safe sex. And Greg can't handle it; his own father could never be that open, and Harry's encouragement has the reverse of its intended effect.

It's largely the same thing with Joyce (Deborah Kennedy), the woman Harry wants to marry. When she inadvertently discovers Jeff is gay, she abandons Harry, ostensibly because he kept this "secret" from her. But what Joyce really is angry about is what she's learned—not just about Jeff, but about Harry, and certainly about herself.

Like Harry, "The Sum of Us" is simple and honest, a bit overbearing, and certainly naive. But Harry makes you feel good, because he is. Although they invest their film with tragedy, codirectors Kevin Dowling and Geoff Burton both making their feature debut—instinctively know when to back off. Nothing in the film not the acting, not the cinematography, not the directing—is as special as the story, but the filmmakers have the good sense not to get in its way.

Crowe, who was the vicious Nazi skinhead of "Romper Stomper" (and is also in the current "The Quick and the Dead"), certainly shows his range in "The Sum of Us." Although the movie is much concerned with Jeff's gayness, Jeff isn't—not the way Greg is, anyway—and it makes him real. This is thanks to Harry, of course, who turns out to be the one character who is hard to believe, because you see his sort in the movies about as often as you see it in life.

VILLAGE VOICE, 3/14/95, p. 61, Randy Gener

Within its small-scale borders, The Sum of Us pushes its wry portrait of a devoted father-son bond, each pulling actively for the other's happiness, to a tenderly ironic corner. Openly gay, 24-year-old plumber and rugby player Jeff Mitchell (Russell Crowe) gets along swimmingly with his straight dad, Harry (Jack Thompson), a widower in his late fifties, who's looking for romantic love, too. In fact, the two men so outpace the homophobic Aussie community that their love for each other actually gets in the way of their dealings with others. Overly solicitous, Harry looks burly like Archie Bunker, but his heart is pure Jewish mother by way of Tennessee Williams. Openness can be stifling, frankness claustrophobic. Their devotion represents at once a hopeful model and a terrifying ideal; being enlightened doesn't shield us from the costs of living.

Hokey stage devices mar this deeply resonant family drama, which belongs squarely in the Aussie wave of fish-out-of-water fables flavored with maddening quirkier-than-thou mannerisms and amiably exotic lingo. Yet The Sum of Us never wears out its radiant welcome. I like its lack of pretensions, the witty way it wears its heart (and ragged theatrical origins) on its sleeve. This small gem of a movie artfully freshens the muddy stream of paternal damage and deadbeats, lifting itself above the endless father-and-son debacles of pain, guilt, and love-unspoken-until-it's-too-late. The actors carve sneakily humorous performances, particularly Crowe. He fuses a vulnerable shyness, regular-joe maturity, and winsome self-mockery—several light-years away from his scummier roles in Romper Stomper and The Quick and the Dead. Move over, Mel Gibson. Make way for the new babe from Down Under.

Also reviewed in:
CHICAGO TRIBUNE, 4/21/95, Friday/p. I, John Petrakis
NEW YORK TIMES, 3/8/95, p. C19, Janet Maslin
VARIETY, 5/9-15/94, p. 80, David Stratton
WASHINGTON POST, 3/31/95, p. D7, Rita Kempley

SUPER 8 ½

A Strand Releasing release of a Jurgen Bruning production in association with Gaytown productions. *Executive Producer:* Jon Gerrans, Marcus Hu, and Mike Thomas. *Director:* Bruce LaBruce. *Screenplay:* Bruce LaBruce. *Director of Photography:* Donna Mobbs. *Editor:* Manse James and Robert Kennedy. *Sound:* Manse James. *Running time:* 99 minutes. *MPAA Rating:* Not Rated.

CAST: Bruce LaBruce (Bruce); Liza Lamonica (Googie); Mikey Mike (Johnny Eczema); Klaus Von Brucker (Pierce); Chris Teen (Wednesday Friday); Dirty Pillows (Jane Friday); WITH; Buddy Cole; Ben Weasel; Amy Nitrate; Vaginal Creme Davis; Richard Kern.

NEW YORK POST, 3/3/95, p. 45, Larry Worth

Fleeting scenes from Elizabeth Taylor's Academy Award-winning turn in "Butterfield 8" have little to do with the plot of "Super 8½." But they provide this hard-core gay film's only watchable moments.

The rest of star/writer/director Bruce LaBruce's follow-up to "No Skin Off My A--" is filled with the incoherent, disjointed ramblings of unlikable, multi-tattooed, body-pierced characters more suitable to a carny sideshow.

What passes for a storyline concerns a faded gay porn star (LaBruce) who believes he's making a comeback when a tough-talking lesbian director (Liza Lamonica) casts him in her new production.

But the leather-clad auteur has her own agenda, all of which leads to the has-been actor ending up in a straitjacket. But since viewers have already seen his fate in the opening shot, no surprises are in store.

That leaves audiences with the perfect opportunity for various mental exercises, like deciding whether LaBruce is less talented as A) alleged actor; B) alleged director; or C) alleged writer. Smart money's on door No. 3, since any trace of wit or creativity could have given some redemption to this claptrap.

LaBruce seems content to use his series of black-and-white films-within-a-film to lead from one sex scene to another. And on that aspect, cineastes should be warned: There's no shortage of needlessly explicit couplings, showing far more than some viewers may want—or be prepared—to see.

No saving graces are found in the cast. Aside from LaBruce's failures at camp humor, Liza Lamonica is astoundingly dull as both the heartless director and one half of an incestuous sister act. And a cameo from Scott "Kids in the Hall" Thompson will surely stand as the nadir of his career.

While the title refers to Fellini's ultimate treasure, it's ironic that "Super 8½" is the ultimate trash.

NEWSDAY, 3/3/95, Part II/p. B7, Gene Seymour

"Super 8½" calls itself a "cautionary" film. But it's hard to tell what this Canadian pseudo-documentary is cautioning its audience against. Could it be the wretched excesses of its subject, a hard-drinking, mentally collapsing star of gay porn films (writer-director Bruce LaBruce)? Or is it the rough, tough sex graphically depicted in clips from the star's films (such as "I Am a Fugitive From a Gang Bang")?

Since the film's buzzword is "exploitation," that's the most likely evil being attacked—though, as LaBruce emphasizes throughout, it's an evil that everyone here submits to, willingly and knowingly.

His protagonist, also named Bruce, allows himself to be filmed by an icy, imperiously ambitious documentarian named Googie (Liza Lamonica) who assures Bruce that the finished product will bring him back into the pantheon of cult icons. Both he and she know, however, that it's her own career that will ultimately benefit.

This transaction, as weirdly perverse as anything else in the film, is viewed from several different angles: Bruce's, Googie's, Bruce's professional rival's (Mikey Mike), his lover Pierce's (Klaus Von Brucker). Oh, yes. One also hears from the Friday "sisters" (Lamonica, Chris Teen), a pair of lesbian punkettes who become stars of Googie's own experiment in hard-core porn, "Submit to My Finger."

Such titles—and the funky film clips attached to them—make up the antic, scruffy humor that eases the film's sour, self-pitying tone, which becomes especially bothersome toward the film's muddled conclusion.

"Super 8½'s" grainy, black-and-white texture and jumpy, edgy nerviness may remind you (in a semi-wistful way) of the devil-may-care, self-conscious artiness of '60s underground films. But it's these very qualities that make it hard to keep track of Bruce's downfall. You're not entirely sure, at the end, how far—or exactly where—he's fallen. Or why you should care.

VILLAGE VOICE, 3/7/95, p. 60, James Hannaham

Filmed in the grittiest of sepia tones, queercore writer-director Bruce LaBruce's *Super 8½* presents a demimonde of has-been porn stars and directors—literal bottom feeders—fighting over crumbs of faux stardom and money that is so well-imagined and daring that it begins to resemble an actual demimonde reined in only by the camera's frame.

Mixing homage and parody, cinema vérité and mockumentary, this unruly and truly risky film sketches in the details of the career of a porn star-director identified only as "Bruce." He's the subject of a documentary by Googie, a lesbian art-porn filmmaker. This deconstructionist's wet dream switches mercilessly back and forth between Googie's interviews with Bruce, played by the director as a Warhol look- and act-alike, screen tests featuring the Friday sisters (the stars of "Submit to My Finger," the flick Googie intends to finance with proceeds from the documentary about Bruce), and the bizarre, poorly made blue oeuvre of both directors.

Multiple images of Warhol dominate. LaBruce as Bruce sits nonchalantly smoking a cigarette beneath a Warhol self-portrait, flinging barbs at the offscreen Googie while his naked hustler-breadwinner, Pierce, writhes under the clear plastic sheets behind him. "I know how exhausting exploiting people can be," he tells the camera. The exploitation extends in every possible direction: Googie to Bruce, Bruce to Pierce, LaBruce to Warhol, LaBruce to himself.

Not content to simply comment on the exploitative nature of film and celebrity, *Super 8½* contains its own ironic critique. Googie, watching and discussing Bruce's film *My Hustler, Myself*, states, "He was actually attempting to break down the traditional subject-camera relationship," while LaBruce as Bruce gives a blowjob onscreen. "He was an existentialist trapped in a porno star's body," Googie continues. "He was a maverick." Remember the old joke: Why does Benji the Dog lick his balls? Because he can.

Offensively funny, edgy, and sometimes even erotic in spite of itself, *Super 8½* out-Warhols Andy and company by demoralizing LaBruce as well as his supporting cast, a Factory-ful of characters from Vaginal Creme Davis to Scott Thompson's Buddy Cole character. Each performance has its own strange perfection, nailing that border between good acting and bad performing.

So appropriative he's innovative, LaBruce as Bruce answers the quintessential postmodern dilemma of originality by reasoning, "The critics would say it's ... a tribute, an update, a remake. Actually, I stole it. Why? Because I'm busy."

Also reviewed in:
NEW YORK TIMES, 3/3/95, p. C6, Stephen Holden
VARIETY, 6/20-26/94, p. 43, Dennis Harvey

SWIMMING WITH SHARKS

A Trimark Pictures release of a Cineville production in association with Neofight Film and Mama's Boy Entertainment. *Executive Producer:* Jay Cohen and Stephen Israel. *Producer:* Steve Alexander and Joanne Moore. *Director:* George Huang. *Screenplay:* George Huang. *Director of Photography:* Steven Finestone. *Editor:* Ed Marx. *Music:* Shaval Churchill. *Music Editor:*

Ed Marx. *Sound:* W. Philip Rogers and Giovanni Disimone. *Casting:* Andrea Stone Guttfreund and Laurel Smith. *Production Designer:* Veronika Merlin and Cecil Gentry. *Art Director:* Karen Haase. *Special Effects:* Dennis Dion. *Costumes:* Kristen Everberg. *Make-up:* Sarah Gaye Deal. *Make-up (Special Effects):* Martin Mercer. *Stunt Coordinator:* Mike Kirton. *Running time:* 93 minutes. *MPAA Rating:* R.

CAST: Kevin Spacey (Buddy Ackerman); Frank Whaley (Guy); Michelle Forbes (Dawn Lockard); Benicio del Toro (Rex); T.E. Russell (Foster Kane); Roy Dotrice (Cyrus Miles); Matthew Flynt (Manny); Patrick Fischler (Moe); Jerry Levine (Jack).

LOS ANGELES TIMES, 4/21/95, Calendar/p. 20, Peter Rainer

Hollywood movies about Hollywood are usually disparaged as ingrown, clubby affairs. And yet, from at least as far back as "Sunset Boulevard" to "The Player" and beyond, these movies are a surprisingly resilient breed. Vengeance is their lifeblood.

"Swimming With Sharks," the latest Tinseltown dig at Tinseltown, is being advertised as a jokey spoof, but it's something quite different: a dark slice of retribution that recalls Stephen King in his "Misery" mode. It's about a young naive Hollywood studio assistant Guy (Frank Whaley), who turn the tables on Buddy (Kevin Spacey), his imperially abusive boss. Writer-director George Huang, who has worked in various production capacities for films and Joel Silver's company and Universal and Paramount Pictures, is hunting big game. There's no affection or giddiness in his take on Hollywood. This movie has ashes in its month.

As fascinatingly repellent as it is, "Swimming With Sharks" takes out its Hollywood hatred in ways that seem absurdly overwrought. It's about how Hollywood shrink-wraps your soul and turns you into a monster like the monsters who have been gnawing on you.

To outsiders, all this rage and gnashing of teeth may seem silly and self-absorbed. Since when is it news that Hollywood corrupts? Huang doesn't really transcend the narcissism of the genre but Spacey provides one hell of a villain—and what would Hollywood-bashing be without a great chief meanie?

Spacey's Buddy—probably modeled on at least one of Huang's former bosses, though he bears a disconcerting resemblance to Gene Siskel—is a snarly power freak who snaps out his threats with chilly panache. He goes Robert Duvall in "Apocalypse Now" a few better: He loves the smell of napalm in the morning—and in the afternoon and the evening, too. Buddy isn't a lovable monster, he's a black hole of hate, and Spacey fries him to a crisp.

Guy's humiliation and vengeance might have had more weight if he had more weight. But Guy is a feather-light construction. Even when he's cuddling up with a development producer (Michelle Forbes) who wants to jump-start her career, he's minus an emotional force field. He lacks both guile and innocence. He's a peppy, frightened little cipher, so when his bile starts flowing you don't know how to take it.

"Swimming With Sharks" could turn into an in-joke wallow for disgruntled Hollywood types but the joke really isn't all that funny. Huang doesn't want it to be. In the grand scheme of things his target may be pint-sized but he's shooting with a bazooka.

NEW YORK POST, 4/21/95, p. 48, Larry Worth

Audiences haven't seen a movie with this much bite since "Jaws."

That's because the Great White has assumed human form in the body of Kevin Spacey, a longtime supporting actor who's made a specialty of cunning, witty, invective-spitting bastards. And in "Swimming With Sharks," he's in peak form as the quintessential man-eater.

Spacey literally commands the screen as Buddy Ackerman, a self-absorbed film studio executive who thrives on power, backstabbing and humiliating his underlings. Emphasis on the latter.

Enter Guy (Frank Whaley), a sweet-faced kid who's hoping to sell Buddy on his production assistant talents and his screenplay. If a p.a. job means withstanding Buddy's constant harangues—like a five-minute diatribe in front of co-workers over the difference between Sweet'n Low and Equal in Buddy's coffee—so be it. At least 'til the coffee cup is thrown at him.

Director/writer George Huang opens the film with Guy breaking into Buddy's palatial home and organizing a little "payback time" for his sadistic employer. Flashbacks then recall how the master-slave relationship evolved into Guy playing a '90s version of Baby Jane Hudson to Buddy's bound-up Blanche.

But no matter who's on top, Huang infuses the script with his scathing brand of acid-filled humor, a formula guaranteed to make viewers howl, right before wincing from recognition.

Ironically, the Hollywood setting is almost irrelevant; the film's universal appeal is its frighteningly accurate depiction of an egomaniacal boss and the dark side that victims must discover to survive.

That's, what keeps "Sharks" from falling into ground already trod by "The Player" and "Mistress." Indeed, Huang—making his strikingly assured debut—lets the cool sendup on L.A. and the wheeling/dealing filmmaking scene serve as icing on the cake. It also compensates for the plot's awkward romance between Guy and a lovely producer (Dawn Lockard), never mind a finale that's more clever than credible.

Speaking of credible: Frank Whaley, as the initially defenseless Guy. With his pompadoured boy-next-door looks, he projects naivete, frustration and untapped abilities, with just enough Neely O'Hara traces to hint at what's to come.

But Spacey still conquers all as the magnificent, magnetic martinet, a deliciously over-the-top mix of Gordon Gekko and J.J. Hunsecker. Here, he reduces his memorable turns in "The Ref," "Consenting Adults" and "Glengarry Glen Ross" to mere warm-ups.

Ultimately, Spacey not only bloodies the waters, he ensures that "Swimming with Sharks" goes for the jugular.

NEWSDAY, 4/21/95, Part II/p. B7, Jack Mathews

I take a back seat to no one in my appreciation for mean satires about Hollywood and the egomaniacs in power there. The town is swimming with sharks, which is the title of writer-director George Huang's first feature, and they deserve to be hooked, filleted and grilled at least once or twice a year.

But "Swimming With Sharks" goes beyond satire into violent revenge fantasy, and whatever points Huang was hoping to make are lost in the rank sourness of his story.

In fact, it may be the juice of sour grapes. Huang started his Hollywood career as a producer's assistant, and he has apparently created an alter ego for himself in Guy (Frank Whaley), a recent college grad and aspiring movie executive who takes his tyrannical studio boss (Kevin Spacey) hostage and tortures him.

"Swimming With Sharks" is told on parallel tracks: one in current time with Guy terrorizing the bound Buddy Ackerman, and the other a series of flashbacks explaining how Guy was driven to such extremes.

Ackerman, played with severe intensity by Spacey, is not a representative production executive, though the self-love and womanizing are about right. The humiliations he heaps on Guy, his full-time gofer, are not just the insensitive demands of an insecure ladder-climber; they are calculated to destroy the younger man's spirit and enthusiasm. He's a shark out of another tank.

"Swimming With Sharks" might have made for a better play. The psychological layers and revelations are achieved primarily through the dialogue between the captor and his hostage, and since the two are equally dehumanized by their encounters, it would seem enough to know that Guy *feels* justified. Certainly, Ackerman is as much of a monster tied up as he was back at the office.

The film, shot on a shoestring budget in three weeks, has only two major sets: the office and Ackerman's living room. And there are only three principle characters, the triangle being filled out by an ambitious producer (Michelle Forbes) who has had affairs with both men and is forced to take sides.

"Swimming With Sharks" has an even more cynical ending than the one that neatly concluded Robert Altman's "The Player," but the only moral we come away with is that to swim with sharks and survive, you've got to become one. Huang apparently has learned this lesson well, and the movie's viciousness may be his satirical way of declaring himself one of the boys.

For viewers who prefer satire with a little more subtlety than a shark fight, however, it's not a pretty sight.

SIGHT AND SOUND, 4/96, p. 55, Lizzie Francke

Guy is a young film school graduate who has just started to work for Buddy Ackerman, an senior executive at Keystone, a medium-sized Hollywood movie studio. Guy soon learns about Buddy's tyrannical behaviour. One morning, Buddy gives him a dressing down for some minor misdemeanour in front of Dawn, a development producer who is attempting to hustle up a project. Dawn seems to take pity on Guy and asks him out for a drink. Soon the two are dating. Dawn talks to Guy about her project, *Real Life*, a contemporary 'twentysomething' drama. Buddy is keen to be behind the next big hit at the studio and is on the lookout for a project for Foster Kane, a hot young director. Guy takes a chance to persuade Buddy that *Real Life* might be the project he is looking for. Buddy warms to this. Guy works on the script and Buddy takes it to the head of the studio, though Guy is not given much credit for his hard work. The project is given a green light.

Guy begins to feel as though his career is on the up. At the weekend Guy and Dawn work together on scripts. Guy gets a call from Buddy and jumps to find a telephone number for him in his address book at the studio. Dawn criticises Guy for running around after Buddy. They argue and she walks out. A couple of days later, Guy is eating out with other wannabe players. He is beeped by Buddy and goes to call him but, feeling dejected, he calls Dawn to see if she will see him that night. She says she's too busy and puts him off. Guy then calls Buddy who starts to fire him, but is interrupted by another call. By mistake, Buddy presses the conference button instead of call-waiting and Guy overhears Buddy arranging to see Dawn that night. Guy drives round to Buddy's, ties him up at gunpoint and beats and tortures him, repaying every indignity he has suffered. Buddy tries to convince Guy that he's had his own share of hard knocks. Dawn stumbles upon this confrontation and Guy is forced to choose between his mentor and his lover. A gunshot is heard. The following morning the police arrive and take away a body. A couple of days later, Guy is back in the office and has been promoted. Buddy congratulates him for saving his life.

Disaffection with Hollywood provides the inspiration for *Swimming With Sharks*, a black comedy about a young man's ruthless rise to the top. Hollywood has always been a murderous place—witness the pile of corpses heaped up by movies about the movie business, from *What Price Hollywood?*, George Cukor's 1931 film about the birth of a young star, to the three versions of *A Star is Born*, to *The Bad and the Beautiful*, *The Big Knife*, *Sunset Boulevard* and more recently *The Player*, and *The Big Picture*. In Hollywood, everyone has to watch out for the backstabber. Debut director George Huang here gives a knowing nod to *Sunset Boulevard* and *The Player* in particular, sharing with them a flashback structure which in this case alternates between the young executive Guy's showdown with his boss Buddy and the months of ritual humiliation leading up to it. Such is the vanity of movie folk that they love to see a reflection of themselves, even in a dark mirror. Certainly the industry is a canny subject to launch one's career on—the players, one images, will flock to see it, if only to guess which real Hollywood monster Buddy Ackerman is based on.

Huang, like his protagonist Guy, has the kind of resumé that belies his insider knowledge. He graduated front the University of Southern California's Producing Programm and went straight to Paramount where he worked as a reader for Howard Koch Jr. Subsequently, he worked as an executive assistant at Universal Pictures and then Silver Pictures where he observed at first hand a notorious figure who, like Ackerman, is keen on action movies. The press notes for the film, however, take pains to mention how supportive Huang's direct boss Barry Josephson was in helping him to set up *Swimming with Sharks*, so presumably Josephson is in the clear.

The key to the film's success is actor Kevin Spacey who not only makes his production debut, but also lifts the film's familiar conceit with his wonderfully poisonous performance as Buddy Ackerman. In the last year, after a varied career playing supporting roles, Spacey has established himself as a star Hollywood variant. With Buddy Ackerman, Spacey provides his most evil anti-hero yet messianic serial killing in *Se7en* seems small beer compared to Ackerman's all-too-plausible vindictiveness. It is a sly and exceptionally well executed assassination of a megalomaniac personality—from the way Ackerman doles out rules about how he likes his coffee with the right sort of sweetener (a choice which changes daily) to sending Guy scurrying off to find a telephone number because he is too lazy to look it up himself, to the grander crime of coldly claiming Guy's ideas for himself. Many assistants, not just those in the film business, will recognise the humiliations piled upon Guy and be able to laugh at them. Meanwhile, Frank Whaley plays the hapless young man as someone who feather by feather, has the stuffing slowly taken out of him. It makes painful viewing.

As such *Swimming with Sharks* is a succinct and hilarious character study with Michelle Forbes (last seen as the woman with the immaculate bob in *Kalifornia)* equally persuasive as the ambitious 'D-Girl' (Development Girl) who according to Buddy has used her body on her way to the top. In this respect one wishes that it could have avoided the somewhat clichéd showdown finale which is where the film stalls and palls (also, did we have to have a budding director called Foster Kane?). But that said, the rather nasty turn that the film takes gives it an edge on other satires—for most of all *Swimming with Sharks* proves that, in Hollywood, it is the boys who are more likely to get out alive.

VILLAGE VOICE, 5/2/95, p. 56, Jeff Salamon

Ever since Nathanael West sicced a plague of locusts on Kahn's Persian Palace Theatre, writers from the Coen brothers to James Ellroy have used Hollywood as the setting for secular Armageddons. Apparently, something in the American moral imagination bridles at the notion that our great westward trek culminates in a perpetual dream machine.

Tinseltown creative types, who are rarely more than bit players in the L.A. drama of earthquake, riot, and recession, nonetheless want a piece of that action. And since they are, by definition, trained to elevate the quotidian into the epic, they have no trouble hyping their own role, creating movies about moviedom in which Wolfgang Puck is the Fourth Horseman of what we might as well call the aSpagolypse. In *The Player* and *Barton Fink*, battles between studio heavies and artists result not in the familiar zero-sum executive shuffle, but in sexy, world-historical murder.

So the showbiz strivers in writer-director George Huang's debut, *Swimming With Sharks,* have a stake in simultaneously romanticizing and demonizing Hollywood: the stakes and madness are of an order those Wall Street pinstripers could never imagine, they tell each other—which is rather odd, seeing as how just a few years ago Hollywood considered high finance a perfectly loaded milieu. Swimming's protagonist, Guy (Frank Whaley), an idealistic young assistant on the make, is clearly a stand-in for Huang, who did time as a Lucasfilm intern and as an assistant to a top executive at Columbia Pictures. But despite the film's roman à clef nature, Huang is cagey enough that you can't tell what he thinks of Guy. Though not a straw man like Barton Fink—a self-righteous blowhard who couldn't punch or write his way out of a wrestling picture—Guy is something of a cipher; you're never sure if he's got the talent to warrant his idealism or if his desire to make small, "quality" movies is just a self-rationalization for his climb to the top.

Less ambiguous is Guy's megalomaniacal boss, Buddy Ackerman (Kevin Spacey). Though Buddy, with his rotating harem of bimbo starlets, ever-present car phone, and designer suits is a by-now-familiar type. Spacey gives a bravura performance that moves with perfect comic timing from a purr to a bark and back again.

In the film's nonlinear narrative, the story of Guy's humiliating education at Buddy's hands is constantly interrupted with the payback: scenes of Buddy's humiliating torture at Guy's hands. Though these scenes are shot with a gleeful, unflinching eye for violence that's almost Peckinpahesque, Huang doesn't set Buddy up as a straw dog just to knock him down. He gives Spacey all the best lines, including his constant taunt to Guy: "What is it you really want?" he asks over and over, and until the end the viewer is never really sure.

Though Huang makes a few missteps—Buddy gets to explain away his monstrousness with a Personal Tragedy, the denouement is too portentous by half, and Huang's idea of an inside joke is to name a hotshot young director Foster Kane—but his comic and directorial sense is unerring. And there's the rub: this nasty kiss-off to Hollywood is Huang's surefire entry into Hollywood's pantheon of hotshot young directors. In the film's genuinely stirring climax, Huang smashes the Oedipal subtext he's carefully built throughout, implying that for him success has replaced Freud's classic scenario as the primal drama.

Also reviewed in:
CHICAGO TRIBUNE, 5/12/95, Friday/p. H, John Petrakis

NEW YORK TIMES, 4/21/95, p. C16, Janet Maslin
VARIETY, 9/12-18/94, p. 40, Todd McCarthy
WASHINGTON POST, 5/12/95, p. B7, Hal Hinson

TALES FROM THE CRYPT PRESENTS DEMON KNIGHT

A Universal Pictures release. *Executive Producer:* Richard Donner, David Giles, Walter Hill, Joel Silver, and Robert Zemeckis. *Producer:* Gilbert Adler. *Director:* Ernest Dickerson. *Director, Crypt Keeper Sequences:* Gilbert Adler. *Screenplay:* Ethan Reiff, Cyrus Voris, and Mark Bishop. *"Tales from the Crypt" comic magazines originally published by:* William M. Gaines. *Director of Photography:* Rick Bota. *Editor:* Stepehn Lovejoy. *Music:* Ed Shearmur. *Music Editor:* Christopher Brooks. *Sound:* Tim Cooney and (music) Stephen McLaughlin. *Sound Editor:* Mark Cookson. *Casting:* Jaki Brown-Karman. *Production Designer:* Christiaan Wagener. *Art Director:* Colin Irwin. *Set Decorator:* George Toomer. *Set Dresser:* Beverly Sessums, Gara Morton, Jori Hudson, and Skip Davis. *Special Effects:* Thomas "Brooklyn" Bellisimo. *Visual Effects:* John T. Van Vliet. *Demon Effects:* Scott Patton. *Costumes:* Warden Neil. *Make-up:* Donna-Lou Henderson and Vonda K. Morris. *Stunt Coordinator:* Shane Dixon. *Running time:* 93 minutes. *MPAA Rating:* R.

CAST: John Kassir (Voice of the Crypt Keeper); Billy Zane (The Collector); William Sadler (Brayker); Jada Pinkett (Jeryline); Brenda Bakke (Cordelia); C.C.H. Pounder (Irene); Dick Miller (Uncle Willy); Thomas Haden Church (Roach); John Schuck (Sheriff Tupper); Gary Farmer (Deputy Bob Martel); Charles Fleischer (Wally Enfield); Tim deZarn (Homer); Sherrie Rose (Wanda); Ryan Sean O'Donohue (Danny); Tony Salome (Sirach); Ken Baldwin (Dickerson); Graham Galloway (Fred); Dale Swan (Bus Driver); Mark D. Kennerly (Other Collector); Peggy Trentini (Amanda); Kathy Barbour and Tina New (Crypt Keeper Starlets); Stephanie Sain (Radio Voice/Mavis); Tom Vincini (Crypt Keeper Body Double).

LOS ANGELES TIMES, 1/13/95, Calendar/p. 1, David Kronke

If ever there was a show-biz survivor, it's the Crypt Keeper. After being blacklisted in the '50s when "Tales From the Crypt," his horror comic book, was accused of polluting the minds of young readers, the Crypt Keeper re-emerged a few years back to host his own bloody HBO series, which also airs on Fox, presumably with the gore trimmed down—but you never know with Fox.

A tongue-in-cheek fright-fest, HBO's "Tales From the Crypt" has even won an award—just a CableACE, sure, but an award nonetheless. It seems that even though any number of unpleasant things happen in productions with which the Crypt Keeper is associated, he keeps finding work in this town.

Even though the Crypt Keeper appears in "Tales From the Crypt Presents Demon Knight" just long enough to pad it out to feature length with lame skits, he and the "Crypt" imprimatur are vital to the film. Based on the quality of the screenplay alone, "Demon Knight" is strictly a direct-to-video affair; with "Tales From the Crypt" tacked to the title, the budget expands exponentially to accommodate state-of-the-art special effects—most of them featuring dismemberment, naturally.

The story is fairly uninvolving nonsense concerning a satanic Collector (Billy Zane) battling a guy named Brayker (William Sadler) over a mystic key that will allow demons to overrun the planet. Their showdown takes place in a church converted into a hotel, where most of those in residence hang around just long enough to be killed in sundry grisly manners.

To aid him in recovering the key, the Collector conjures up a bunch of slime-dripping demons who can only be stopped by losing the use of their glow-in-the-dark lime-green eyes. Obviously, then, somebody's going to put an eye out.

There's not much effort to make anything about the story persuasive or compelling. In unnecessarily pretentious flashbacks, it's revealed that Christ himself had a hand, so to speak, in the key's history, and the filmmakers play fast and loose with the logic as to how the demons can enter the hotel after it's christened with blood from the key.

Director Ernest Dickerson, who abandoned an impressive career as Spike Lee's cinematographer to make movies such as this and "Surviving the Game," makes sure that the effects come frequently enough to rescue the faltering narrative. His work is competent, though he doesn't provide the kind of jolts a movie like this needs to keep audiences engaged.

Zane is wittily seductive as the malevolent Collector. As one of the hotel's denizens, Jada Pinkett, who has heretofore made good impressions in the otherwise forgettable "A Low Down Dirty Shame" and "Jason's Lyric," brings a depth to her role that the script never even hints at. A decent vehicle could make her a star.

Unfortunately, the rest of the cast is relegated to going through generic motions. "Tales From the Crypt Presents Demon Knight"—the title just tips off the tongue, doesn't it?—is the first of a projected three-feature package. Next time out, let's hope it involves a story that can stand on its own, without having to be propped up by the Crypt Keeper's silly patter.

NEW YORK POST, 1/13/95, p. 45, Thelma Adams

Gory Cooper. Robert Deadford. The Crypt Keeper brings his blend of deadly puns, gooey special effects, boobs and bones to the big screen in "Tales From the Crypt Presents Demon Knight." The movie is cable ready, ripped from the small screen where the humorous horror vignettes air after Garry Shandling on HBO.

The Crypt Keeper, a decomposing muppet-like thing, smugly introduces each story—an attitude that plagues the show.

Based on the '50s comic books developed by William Gaines of Mad magazine fame, the TV episodes promise more than they deliver. Technically slick, they're pat and punch-less—predictable moral tales.

The movie, shot on the cable show set, opens on Friday the 13th but lacks the gruesome single-mindedness of the Jason slasher flicks.

"Demon Knight" has the good looks and bland taste of pre-packaged food.

Executive produced by some Hollywood big foots, the crypt tales attract talent.

Ernest Dickerson, director of "Juice" and Spike Lee's cinematographer on "Do the Right Thing" and others, gives the movie the high-gloss treatment, but there's nothing Dickersonian in his direction of this genre parcel.

Billy Zane leads the cast as the Collector, a Beetlejuice-style baddie with underworld connections. Zane pulls off being scary and sexy with panache while trying to take an ancient key from the skeletal hero, Brayker (William Sadler).

As a put-upon ex-con, Jada Pinkett (the best thing about "A Low Down Dirty Shame") is a rising star.

From gruesome demons to oozy decapitations, the "Demon Knight" special effects are state-of-the-sticky-art—but the gags are so old they're covered with the dust of tombs.

NEWSDAY, 1/13/95, Part II/p. B7, John Anderson

"Fasten your drool cups and hold onto your vomit bags!" says the Crypt Keeper, and yeah, it's pretty good advice.

"Tales From the Crypt Presents Demon Knight" brings the popular HBO horror anthology to the big screen, although with a single story line and a bigger budget. Which translates into more splatter and hurtling body parts per frame and a rather impressive cast of character actors. What it never loses is its tongue-in-cheek attitude. "That's entertainment!" cackles the head of the recently guillotined Crypt. Keeper (who's a puppet, though he denies it) and whose savoir faire has the piquant bouquet of Catskills-in-formaldehyde.

CK's routines bookend the feature story line, which combines some rather hackneyed devices—road epic, pseudo-religious myth, satanic symbolism, Faustian deal-cutting—with an over-the-top sense of medical mayhem. It also toys with our expectations. We think Brayker (William Sadler), who has managed to escape a pursuit and fiery crash on a lonesome rural highway, is a lowlife; he immediately tries to steal a car, pulls a knife on a child, and holes up at a seedy roadhouse in a nervous sweat. But it's his pursuer, who we'll come to know as the

Collector (Billy Zane), who's the real vehicle of evil. Brayker, who carries a keyshaped vial that once held the blood of Christ, is singlehandedly keeping the world safe from Satan's new world order. The Collector wants the vial, and the souls of everyone at the roadhouse.

Sure it's absurd, and the violence is wholesale; it's "Night of the Living Dead" as directed by Sam Raimi. But the scenery chewing is gleeful. Sadler and Zane are insane. C.C.H. Pounder, as the crusty landlady Irene, has her arm torn off early and it hardly slows her down. Wally (Charles Fleischer), a disturbed postal employee in love with the resident hooker Cordelia (Brenda Bakke), becomes a ghoul almost right away, but his secret stash of hand grenades helps save the day. It may not be "Army of Darkness" but "Demon Knight" certainly has its charms.

Ernest Dickerson, the esteemed cinematographer and now director ("Juice"), may have seemed an unlikely choice to bring "Crypt"—based on the old E.C. horror comics—to the screen. But like his executive producers—Robert Zemeckis, Richard Donner, Walter Hill, Joel Silver and David Giles—he has a soft spot for the gross-out, and it shows.

SIGHT AND SOUND, 6/95, p. 54, Kim Newman

The Crypt Keeper, a monstrous film director, attends the premiere of his latest film Demon Knight ...

Wormwood, Texas. Frank Brayker, a 'Demon Knight', is pursued by the Collector, a servant of Hell, across country. Both survive a car crash, but the Collector convinces Sheriff Tupper and Deputy Martel that Brayker is getting away with stolen goods. Brayker takes refuge in a church converted into a motel, but the Collector, who reveals his evil by killing the Sheriff, besieges the place with demon hordes. Trapped with Brayker are Cordelia, a whore; Wally, a just-fired postal worker; Roach, one of Cordelia's customers; Jeryline, a woman convict on a work release scheme; Uncle Willy, a wino; Danny, a child and Irene, the motel manager.

Brayker is custodian of a key-shaped artefact originally filled with the sacred blood of Christ and passed down through the ages by a succession of Demon Knights, the last of whom replenished the artefact with his own blood and gave it to Brayker on a First World War battlefield. The Collector exerts his influence in an attempt to regain the key, which will give Evil dominion over the earth, and each of the motel inhabitants is tempted, possessed or killed until only Brayker and Jeryline remain. Brayker, mortally wounded, recharges the key with his own blood, and gives it to Jeryline, who resists the Collectors advances and destroys him by spitting blood in his face. Jeryline, now a Demon Knight, sets off to travel the world, and a new Collector arrives to pursue her ...

Having awarded the right of 'final cut' to the Crypt-Keeper, his producers decide to guillotine him. The severed head cackles.

The HBO television series Tales from the Crypt, based on the well-remembered EC horror comics of the 50s, has been running since 1988, with its distinguished producers Joel Silver, Walter Hill, Robert Zemeckis and Richard Donner luring a wide selection of big-name talents. Arnold Schwarzenegger, Michael J. Fox and Tom Hanks have all directed episodes, as have career directors such as John Frankenheimer, Russell Mulcahy, Steven E. de Souza and Rowdy Herrington, while Demi Moore and Patricia Arquette have taken lead roles. With a slightly slumming attitude, each of these stars has relished the chance for campy gore.

The current film which has, rather hopefully, a series title and a episode title, opens with a vignette in the typical Tales from the Crypt style as a voluptuous, blood-splattered starlet is menaced in the bath by the acid-rotted husband she has just brained with an axe. But this turns out to be an establishing gag that sets up the Crypt Keeper as a film-maker, abusing an unbilled John Larroquette's feeble zombie performance. There was an Amicus anthology called Tales from the Crypt in 1972, with Ralph Richardson as the Crypt Keeper, and even a sequel The Vault of Horror (1973), but Tales from the Crypt: Demon Knight opts not to go directly to the EC comics source material and instead comes up with a story not based on a comic book, or even (as in Creepshow) especially indebted to comics in theme and mood.

The Demon Knight script actually pre-existed the idea of making a Crypt spinoff film and was discovered and dusted off for the project which perhaps explains why it owes more to the post-George Romero world of Sam Raimi's The Evil Dead than to the comics that are its ostensible inspiration, although Tales from the Crypt was itself a key influence on the zombie-littered landscape of the modern American comedy-horror genre. The eternal opposition of the Demon

Knights and Collectors has to be taken on trust through speeches of explanation and tiny flashbacks to Golgotha and the battlefields of the First World War, but it is a servicable enough backdrop to the basic siege story, with the blood-filled key functioning both as the macguffin and as a weapon against the hordes of hell. There is a touch of Sam Raimi in the use of reanimated and possessed people against the survivors, and a trace of Romero in their specific weakness (here, the zombies can be killed if their glowing green eyes are burst); and the siege set-up owes a great deal to *Rio Bravo, The Birds, Night of the Living Dead, Assault on Precinct 13* and dozens of other scenarios of entrapment and being surrounded.

There is an attempt at an anthology feel as the Collector sets out to tempt or destroy each of the supporting characters: luring Uncle Willy into a world of bottomless bottles and topless girls, playing on Wally's crush on Cordelia, offering the sneaky Roach a straight bargain that he goes back on, finally attempting to seduce Jeryline to his side of the good/evil divide. This gives vignette-like scenes to each stooge and vaguely excuses the simple, comic-book characterisation whereby everybody is given one personality trait and embodies it to excess. Against this backdrop, William Sadler (who was in the *Tales from the Crypt* television pilot) and Billy Zane play nicely, with Sadler going for thin-lipped resolve and inner decency while Zane flamboyantly and aptly overplays, throwing in asides and jokes almost after the manner of the Crypt Keeper himself. There is no depth to these representatives of vast forces, and their cosmic see-sawing is pretty much a joke, but their struggle has a simplicity that is refreshing in an era of genre movies undone by muddy thinking.

The most pleasing aspect of *Demon Knight* is its old-fashioned adherence to horror principles like unity of space and time, the use of great old character actors (Roger Corman veteran Dick Miller) effective gross-outs (the Collector punching clear through Sherriff Tupper's head, Danny's especially ghastly possessed form), sly absurdity (a one-armed woman arming herself with a pump-action shotgun) and an eerily resonant ending (the new Collector waiting for the next bus to begin the cycle anew). The EC comics' morality, which is at least as distinctive as their fondness for repulsive physical detail, is hard to produce in a feature film, although such do-badders as Roach receive their merited comeuppances.

The film is limited by its refusal to probe deeply into its reference to theology, lifting a few bits of costume and imagery from Richard Stanley's *Dust Devil* but never even considering tackling its antagonists in the ambiguous, resonant style of Stanley. It doesn't even make much of its comic book stylisation beyond tilted camera angles and such speech balloon dialogue as "Who are you really?", but it aims for an unassuming, generally ingratiating popcorn picture with enough solid shocks to satisfy horror-starved fans in a dry period.

VILLAGE VOICE, 1/31/95, p. 54, Gary Dauphin

Set in a Southwest mission turned brothel, *Demon Knight*'s title tells you all you need to know about it. A celluloid enlargement of the popular HBO/Fox splatter series, it concerns the travails of a grizzled spiritual guardian (Brayker, played by William Sadler) and the key he's protecting. Once in a demon-knight-lifetime, seven stars and seven people align just so (demon night, get it?), and, well, all hell breaks loose, as hordes of slime-covered ghouls come after the relic and its caretaker. Liberally mixing *Night of the Living Dead* and countless passing-of-the-mystical-torch tales (with a dollop of Holy Grail myth thrown in for good measure), actual plot points only drop in once in a while like afterthoughts, taking second place to the random antics of sticky-wet monster puppets.

Populated mostly by demons and generic demon-bait, *Demon Knight* is more cable movie than EC Comics, a distinction that's sure to blur as the *Crypt* franchise expands. As head demon and lead innocent, Billy Zane and Jada Pinkett do decent turns, and Ernest Dickerson (Spike Lee's longtime camera jock and director of *Juice)* helms with the easy humor of someone who knows he's made for better things. From the looks of it, Dickerson likes the fit of the existing *Crypt*-format. *Demon Knight* neither chafes against its small-screen conventions nor loses its way in pursuit of the higher gore quotient allowed by the R-rating. It's a fun ride throughout, albeit one that won't linger past residual attacks of gooseflesh and popcorn nausea.

Also reviewed in:
CHICAGO TRIBUNE, 1/13/95, Arts Plus, John Petrakis
NEW YORK TIMES, 1/13/95, p. C20, Stephen Holden
VARIETY, 1/16-22/95, p. 95, Joe Leydon
WASHINGTON POST, 1/14/95, p. C5, Richard Harrington

TALES FROM THE HOOD

A Savoy Pictures release of a 40 Acres and a Mule Filmworks presentation. *Executive Producer:* Spike Lee. *Producer:* Darin Scott. *Director:* Rusty Cundieff. *Screenplay:* Rusty Cundieff and Darin Scott. *Director of Photography:* Anthony B. Richmond. *Editor:* Charles Bornstein. *Music:* Christopher Young. *Casting:* Robi Reed-Humes. *Production Designer:* Stuart Blatt. *Special Effects:* Kenneth Hall. *Running time:* 97 minutes. *MPAA Rating:* R.

CAST: WELCOME TO MY MORTUARY: Clarence Williams III (Mr. Simms); Joe Torry (Stack);   De'Aundre Bonds (Ball);   Samuel Monroe, Jr. (Bulldog);   ROGUE COP REVELATION: Wings Hauser (Strom); Tom Wright (Martin Moorehouse); Anthony Griffith (Clarence); Michael Massee (Newton); Duane Whitaker (Billy); BOYS DO GET BRUISED: David Alan Grier (Carl); Brandon Hammond (Walter); Rusty Cundieff (Richard); Paula Jai Parker (Sissy); KKK COMEUPPANCE: Corbin Bernsen (Duke Metger); Roger Smith (Rhodie); Art Evans (Eli); HARD CORE CONVERT: Rosalind Cash (Dr. Cushing); Lamont Bentley (Crazy K).

LOS ANGELES TIMES, 5/24/95, Calendar/p. 2, Kevin Thomas

With his high-energy, scabrously funny "Tales From the Hood," young African American writer-director Rusty Cundieff recharges the old horror anthology. He discovers in the thriller of the supernatural a means of attacking satirically such real-life evils as drugs, police brutality, abuse of children and women, racism and, gang killings that infect society at large as well as black communities.

A powerhouse of a movie, "Tales From the Hood" is operatic, great-looking, fast-moving, action-filled, tough-minded yet often hilarious, and bursting with imagination; this contemporary "Dante's Inferno" has wide crossover appeal.

In a witty turn as a Vincent Price-like mortician, Clarence Williams III serves as the film's key figure and narrator, when his elegant funeral parlor is invaded by three youthful drug dealers (Joe Torry, De'Aundre Bonds and Samuel Monroe Jr.) to whom he spins the "Hood's" four cautionary tales. The first tells of the predicament of a young black cop (Anthony Griffith) who witnesses the savage beating of a black activist (Tom Wright) by three white cops (Wings Hauser, Michael Massee and Duane Whitaker); Cundieff is as concerned with black solidarity as he is with Wright avenging his fate.

As for the second episode, it is hard to think of a film that communicates so unsparingly yet not exploitatively the full horror of a child (Brandon Hammond) and his mother (Paula Jai Parker) at the mercy of the mother's brutal lover (David Alan Grier); Cundieff casts himself as the concerned teacher of the boy who has learned to deal with Grier by envisioning him as a green monster.

Corbin Bernsen has never had such a splendid opportunity to pull out all the stops as a supposedly former member, of the KKK running for governor on an anti-affirmative action platform and living in an old plantation haunted by the restless souls, preserved in dolls made by an elderly black woman, of all the slaves whose master chose to slay them rather than set them free at the end of the Civil War. As with Griffith's cop, Cundieff has I no mercy for the slick young black man (Roger Smith) who's sold out to become the gleefully hateful racist's key campaign adviser. Also featured is the veteran Art Evans as the story's prophet figure.

With his final sequence, Cundieff brings together all of the mortician's tales as a scorchingly powerful prison deprogrammer (a majestically righteous Rosalind Cash) whose behavioral modification for a 20-year-convicted gangbanger (Lamont Bentley) encompasses a collage of archival photo images of white lynchings and tarring and feathering of blacks as a way of pointing up the sheer self-destructive folly and moral outrage of black-on-black killings.

Handsomely designed by Stuart Blatt, strikingly photographed by Anthony B. Richmond and boasting amusing special effects by Kenneth J. Hall, Cundieff's bold, raw yet uproarious allegory spills over with the language and the violence of the street, but his wit, vision, style and underlying seriousness sustain these elements. With the highly topical "Tales From the Hood," Cundieff more than fulfills the promise of his first film, "Fear of a Black Hat," his funny but uneven rap variation on "This Is Spinal Tap."

NEW YORK POST, 5/24/95, p. 35, Thelma Adams

Morticians. Vengeful dolls. Mad scientists. The undead. Voodoo powers. These are the bread and butter of stock horror.

In "Tales From the Hood," director Rusty Cundieff and his producer/writing partner Darin Scott (the team responsible for the largely overlooked rap satire "Fear of a Black Hat") have dipped into the files of "Night Gallery" "The Twilight Zone," and a thousand familiar scary TV movies and come up with a horror comedy that's startlingly fresh and satisfying. With its predominantly black cast and themes, these are vital tales from the dark side: funny, revealing and entertaining.

Our unholy host, mortician Mr. Simms (a dead-on Clarence Williams III, who carved his spot on Media Rushmore as a member of the "Mod Squad"), welcomes three gang-bangers into his funeral parlor. The trio plans to recover a drug cache and rip off the old man—but Simms has different ideas. Using corpses as points of departure, he tells the bad boys four scary stories.

The themes of these gory diversions are police brutality, child abuse and racism. In the first, three rogue cops led by Wings Hauser murder a black community activist, while a black rookie cop stands by. The director appears in the second as a teacher whose concern for the welfare of a battered young student leads him to a domestic drama with a wicked stepfather (played against type by a grim-faced David Alan Grier) and a supernatural solution. Corbin Bersen ("L.A. Law") makes a good heavy as a racial-slur spewing Southern politician who becomes a victim of the dark legacy of the plantation where he lives.

"Tales From the Hood" (Spike Lee is the executive producer) is the rare omnibus movie that builds from story to story, and travels from strength to strength. All the themes of the previous stories are tightly knotted in the fourth sobering tale about a murderous young gang-banger named Crazy K (Lamont Bentley) who's given a final chance at redemption by the archly named Dr. Cushing (Rosalind Cash).

Riffing on John Landis' "An American Werewolf in London," Crazy K's victims confront him. They appear as they died, wreathed in carnage, an ear failing at an odd angle, a limb ending in stringy guts, a child wearing a T-shirt with a blood rose over her heart.

The story stands as a powerful indictment of black-on-black violence. The dominant themes of personal responsibility and just rewards would make that old moralist Rod Serling proud.

"So you're going to blame all this s--t on me, Crazy K asks the doctor.

"You've got to take responsibility to break this chain," says Dr. Cushing, a scientist who's not so mad after all.

NEWSDAY, 5/24/95, Part II/p. B9, John Anderson

Horror's a funny thing. Usually. The heart-stopping face at the window, the pressurized fountain of blood, the manipulative quick cuts and kaleidoscopic disequilibrium—they make us gasp, but then they make us laugh; a physical jolt, followed by a giggle of embarrassment. Real horror? That's the province of Holocaust documentaries, CNN reports from Oklahoma City and the track of the Ebola virus.

Rusty Cundieff, who lanced the boil of gangsta rap last year with his docu-spoof "Fear of a Black Hat," knows all this, and aims to have it both ways. He does, too. In "Tales From the Hood"—four contemporary tales of fright that are well-paced, stylishly shot and as broadly acted as any "Nightmare"/"Night of"/"Prom Night" movie—he employs all the standard devices of the so-called horror film. But the abundant gore, the sadistically droll forces of evil, the human pond scum getting its comeuppance—they're all for comic relief. It's Cundieff's real world that's awful, and this is both his big joke and his smart innovation on a tired formula.

Like any scary story, "Tales" needs a narrator. It has the suitably sinister Mr. Simms (a wonderfully creepy Clarence William III), a demented mortician whose funeral home is visited by three gun-wielding boyz (Joe Torry, De'Aundre Bonds and Samuel Monroe Jr.) looking to cut a deal for a cache of drugs. (They are all stereotypical attitude and anger, but Cundieff is pan-racial in his use of cartoon characterizations.) Simms is in no hurry, though. Instead, he tells the increasingly nervous threesome the stories behind the four corpses he has lying about the place and pretty much scares them to death.

Cundieff would like to have a similar effect with his film, which was executive produced by Spike Lee and delivers heavy moral messages wrapped in blood-stained gauze. In the first tale, a political-activist minister (Tom Wright) is Rodney King-ed by three corrupt white cops (Wings Hauser, Anthony Griffith, Michael Massee) while a black rookie (Duane Whitaker) does nothing.

In the second tale, a young boy named Walter (Brandon Hammond) blames his recurrent injuries on the monster that lives in his house. His teacher (Cundieff) doesn't believe him, of course—but he learns there's some truth to the story.

The third tale centers on a David Duke-style southern politician named Duke Metger (Corbin Bernsen), whose gubernatorial campaign is pure race-baiting and buzzwords. His home once the scene of a post-Emancipation slave massacre—is said to be inhabited by dolls possessing the souls of those slaves. They come to get Duke, in a scene straight out of "Night Gallery."

The entire film recalls the "Twilight Zone"-"Outer Limits" style of anthology series, with surprise resolutions and moral messages, but the last tale takes the formula to its most ambitious end. In it, a hard-core hoodlum starts a gun battle that ends in wholesale slaughter, and is then sent to a "Clockwork Orange"-esque rehabilitation center. That he finally *can't* be saved from his own "I don't give a -" attitude amounts to Cundieff's strongest statement on black-on-black crime and moral responsibility. None of this detracts from the fun of "Tales From the Hood." In fact, this emphasis on contemporary horrors—drug-dealing police, child abuse, racist/political opportunism—makes the "horror" all the more palatable.

VILLAGE VOICE, 5/30/95, p. 60, Brian Parks

Bringing gangsta-Goth to the silver screen, Rusty Cundieff's *Tales From the Hood* is a hip-hop horror flick with a political will. Gruesome, garish, and goofy, it's successful despite itself.

Three dope dealers bust into a funeral home. They're after a hidden stash, but instead find the creepy funeral director (Clarence Williams III), a caped, B-movie castoff who stalls the robbers by leading them on a menacing tour through his mortuary. Ignoring their waved guns, he weaves among the caskets describing the lives of the dead people inside them. This is the framing device for *Tales's* four separate stories.

In the first, a black rookie cop unwittingly conspires with some white cops in the murder of a civil rights activist. The black cop's ensuing guilt leads him to help the ghost of the slain leader exact a very peculiar revenge. In the second tale, a kid who gets bullied at school and abused at home discovers a curiously Crayola superpower, which he adopts as a defense weapon. The third plot concerns a David Duke type (Corbin Bernsen) running for governor in a Southern state. He moves into a big plantation house, where, at the end of the Civil War, the white master murdered all of his slaves rather than set them free. Let's just say that the spirits of the house aren't too happy with their new tenant. And in the fourth story, a captured gang-banger faces a nauseating program of aversion therapy. It's a condensed *Clockwork Orange* that vividly equates gang violence with the rampages of the KKK.

Politically heavy-handed and not especially frightening, *Tales From the Hood* is nonetheless great agit-pop. Cundieff, whose last film was the inconsistent but amusing rap parody, *Fear of a Black Hat,* has fashioned a film whose true terror is racism. Normal horror movies hinge on an imaginative leap: that old hotels can be haunted, or that birds would indeed like to get together and peck your eyes out. But Cundieff's terrors start in a very real world: racist cops, child abuse, black-on-black violence. Cundieff and cowriter Darin Scott shift these issues into the supernatural to tell morality tales whose bottom line is the virtue of race solidarity.

Bigoted, murderous cops are scarier than ghosts, though, and that's something that Cundieff can't overcome. But the film—which no doubt had the working title *Tales From the Crips*—pleasurable because of its obvious dissonances. It's a volatile political tract, covered with lots of mass-cult butter.

Also reviewed in:
CHICAGO TRIBUNE, 5/24/95, Tempo/p. 7, John Petrakis
NEW YORK TIMES, 5/25/95, p. C18, Stephen Holden
VARIETY, 5/29-6/4/95, p. 54, Joe Leydon
WASHINGTON POST, 5/24/95, p. C1, Richard Harrington

TALK

A Filmopolis Pictures release of a Suitcase Films production in association with the Australian Film Commission. *Producer:* Megan McMurchy. *Director:* Susan Lambert. *Screenplay:* Jan Cornall. *Director of Photography:* Ron Hagen. *Editor:* Henry Dangar. *Music:* John Clifford White. *Sound:* John Dennison and Tony Vaccher. *Casting:* Liz Mullinar. *Production Designer:* Lissa Coote. *Costumes:* Clarrissa Patterson. *Running time:* 90 minutes. *MPAA Rating:* Not Rated.

CAST: Victoria Longley (Julia Strong); Angie Milliken (Stephanie Ness); Richard Roxburgh (Jack/Detective Harry); John Jarratt (Mac); Ella-Mei Wong, Tenzing Tsewang, and Kee Chan (Witnesses).

LOS ANGELES TIMES, 5/24/96, Calendar/p. 11, Kevin Thomas

Susan Lambert's ingenious and affecting "Talk" is a little gem of a movie, a witty and effervescent bittersweet comedy, shot through with humor and pain, that swiftly captures your attention and then involves your emotions as it gradually acquires depth.

It brings to mind in its jauntiness and vitality the comedies being made by women in Germany, most notably Dorris Dorrie.

Victoria Longley's Julia and Angie Milliken's Stephanie are old friends, thirtysomething collaborators on comic-book novels for adults. Stephanie arrives at Julia's sunny Sydney apartment to begin work but, as Julia is just back from a trip to Japan, they've got lots of catching up to do—more than either realizes.

What they discover in the course of the day is that neither woman fits the idealized picture each has of the other. Stephanie envies the breezy Julia's carefree single existence while Julia, all too aware of the ticking of her biological clock, craves what she believes is her friend's perfect life: a newly acquired house in the country with a man and their child. In different ways, however, both women are approaching a state of crisis.

In her feature debut, Lambert, a documentarian, and her writer, Jan Cornall, display a fine sense of proportion and balance: They know that their revelations are serious but not profound and that they're more effective played against humor; they also have the knack of keeping what in lesser hands could be a static basically two-character play consistently buoyant and cinematic.

They cleverly punctuate long stretches of dialogue with some live-action but cartoon-like fantasy sequences that emanate from Stephanie's tormented imagination and echo the graphic style of the women's novels.

Julia gets the film underway with an exuberant and clinical account of a near-tryst in Japan with an Englishman that has her hunky TV repairman (Richard Roxburgh) all but totally distracted from his work.

Indeed, a typically Australian candor in regard to sex characterizes the entire film, so capably carried by Longley and Milliken, both of whom manage to keep "Talk" from seeming too talky despite its reams of dialogue.

Roxburgh, in turn, more than upholds the Aussie tradition of good-humored virility.

NEW YORK POST, 10/20/95, p. 42, Larry Worth

No one can say the title is misleading. "Talk" is almost all its two heroines do.

And that's fine, if the banter's "Absolutely Fabulous." But wife/mother Julia and career woman Stephanie are like Patsy and Edina's dishrag dull cousins.

Following the pair on a day's worth of errands around Sydney, conversation runs the gamut from carping over electric bills to ill will for a stepmother. Not exactly enticing stuff.

In between work on the adult comic books that Julia illustrates and Stephanie writes, the gal pals move on to more intimate anecdotes, often in front of a hunky handyman. But when the dialogue gets to graphic details of ovulation, it's definitely more than one needs—or wants—to know.

To break up the action, or lack thereof, the two also indulge in elongated fantasies—sexual and otherwise. In a futuristic universe of neon colors and surreal imagery, they assume alter-egos capable of solving mysteries, exposing infidelity or murdering rivals.

Not surprisingly, the dream sequences emerge as the production's highlights. Though working within the confines of a small budget, first-time feature director Susan Lambert makes the most of imaginatively stylized sets, costumes and lighting.

But when the otherworldly drama switches back to the mundane, Lambert lets interest evaporate. She also tries too hard for a point-counterpoint sensibility; when one heroine indulges in a steamy afternoon delight, the other encounters heartbreak. Ah, the ying and yang of l'amour.

Not helping matters is a forgettable cast. Angie Milliken is irritatingly brittle as man-hungry Stephanie, while Victoria Longley's Julia proves less intriguing than the spit curl snaking down her Campbell's soup kid face. In addition, Richard Roxburgh's boy-toy does little more than display his pecs and leer on cue.

Regardless, "Talk" isn't cheap. Just dull.

VILLAGE VOICE, 10/24/95, p. 71, Leslie Camhi

Films are suddenly brimming over with feminine conversation. In *Talk,* the first feature by Australian documentary director Susan Lambert, a veritable river of conversation runs between Stephanie (Angie Milliken) and Julia (Victoria Longlay). These thirtysomethings collaborate in writing and illustrating comic book novels. One morning they meet for work at Stephanie's glamorous Sydney apartment, but she's returned from Japan and there's a lot to discuss: the affair she just missed having, the stage of her ovulatory cycle, the child she seems to want.

Meanwhile, the TV needs repairing, and new goldfish must be bought. On these essential errands and over endless cups of coffee, Julia (who lives in the country) slowly reveals the wreckage of her perfect nuclear family. At times, the film switches into comic-book mode; Julia, obsessed with her husband's affair, becomes Detective Julia, in search of the Missing Girl (Jacqueline McKenzie).

I must admit that the comic-book aesthetic is not one I embrace, I kept being put off by that red lightning bolt squiggle of hair on Detective Julia's forehead. But Langley and Milliken offer fine performances, mixing vibrancy with frustration and smoldering anger. The dialogue occasionally falls flat, but more often it's sharp and funny. I first wondered, why make women speak to each other, if all they're going to talk about is sex, mothers, and children? But then, I realized, that's a lot.

Also reviewed in:
NEW YORK TIMES, 10/30/95, p. C14, Caryn James
VARIETY, 6/6-12/94, p. 42, David Stratton

TALL TALE: THE UNBELIEVABLE ADVENTURES OF PECOS BILL

A Walt Disney Pictures release in association with Caravan Pictures. *Executive Producer:* Bill Badalato. *Producer:* Joe Roth and Roger Birnbaum. *Director:* Jeremiah Chechik. *Screenplay:* Steven L. Bloom and Robert Rodat. *Director of Photography.* Janusz Kaminski. *Editor:* Richard Chew. *Music:* Randy Edelman. *Music Editor:* John La Salandra and Michael T. Ryan. *Sound:* Robert Janiger. *Sound Editor:* Tim Chau and Rick Franklin. *Casting:* Jackie Burch. *Production Designer:* Eugenio Zanetti. *Art Director:* Jim R. Dultz. *Set Designer:* Greg Papalia, Daniel Maltese, and Jacques J. Valin. *Set Decorator:* Jerie Kelter. *Set Dresser:* G. Roger Abell, Douglas D. Sieck, Michael I. Holowach, Michael J. Vojvoda, Kai Blomberg, and Alan Baptiste.

Special Effects: Terry Frazee.   *Visual Effects:* Erik Henry.   *Costumes:* Wayne Finkelman.
Make-up: Ken Chase.   *Stunt Coordinator:* Ernie Orsatti.   *Running time:* 98 minutes.   *MPAA Rating:* PG.

CAST: Patrick Swayze (Pecos Bill);   Oliver Platt (Paul Bunyan);   Roger Aaron Brown (John Henry);   Nick Stahl (Daniel Hackett);   Scott Glenn (J.P. Stiles);   Stephen Lang (Jonas Hackett);   Jared Harris (Head Thug Pug);   Catherine O'Hara (Calamity Jane);   Moira Harris (Sarah Hackett);   Joseph Grifasi (Man in Top Hat);   John P. Ryan (Grub);   Scott Wilson (Zeb);   Bert Kramer (Bronson);   Eric Lawson (Sheriff);   Bill Rodgers (Captain of Industry);   Susan Barnes (Hag in Alley);   John Nance (Doctor);   Mike Moroff (Bar Room Bully);   Richard Zobel (Barkeep);   Michael J. Kosta (Farmer #1);   Timothy Glenn Riley (Farmer #2);   Darwyn Swalve (Lumberjack #1);   Jay S. York (Lumberjack #2);   Kevin Brown (Bettor #1);   E.B. Myers (Bettor #2);   James Oscar Lee (Spectator);   Sal Jenco (Big Jim).

LOS ANGELES TIMES, 3/24/95, Calendar/p. 8, Peter Rainer

If a good children's film is supposed to open the eyes of its young audience, then the somewhat misleadingly titled "Tall Tale: The Unbelievable Adventures of Pecos Bill" is mighty good. It's not made with any special feeling for childhood, the script is fairly hackneyed, and there are too many shots of amber waves of grain. But the film at least captures the mythic spaciousness of tall tales. It's a Disney kidfest re-imagined with a poet's eye.

Most of the poetry comes from the cinematographer, Janusz Kaminski, who shot "Schindler's List." Along with director Jeremiah Chechik and production designer Eugenio Zanetti, Kaminski brings out the rich colorations in the turn-of-the-century Old West. The imagery goes beyond Sierra Club poster art into a wilder, more rhapsodic realm. It's the Old West as dreamed by a particularly fervid boy. There's nothing decorative about this frontier.

Twelve-year-old Daniel Hackett (Nick Stahl) has an edgy relationship with his father Jonas (Stephen Lang), who can't understand why his son isn't enamored with the farm life. But when a villainous railroad baron (Scott Glenn) tries to murder Jonas and obtain the deed to his spread, the boy flies into action to rescue not only the family farm but his community's entire way of life.

Helped by three tall-tale heroes, Pecos Bill (Patrick Swayze), John Henry (Roger Aaron Brown) and Paul Bunyan (Oliver Platt), Daniel goes up against the baron and his minions. He becomes his own hero. Chechik and his screenwriters, Steven L. Bloom and Robert Rodat, are after big game, too. They want to make a father-son bonding epic, they want to contrast the meadowy pastoralism of Daniel's hometown with the encroaching industrial horrors.

They want to demonstrate that children—and not only children—need to believe in heroes as a way of believing in themselves. And they want to draw a parallel between turn-of-the-century America on the verge of the machine age and our own lost-innocence era. (How many times can we lose our innocence in the movies anyway?)

The filmmakers never really go beyond this hearty sampling of homilies—they seem content with a lot of fragranced cliches. But Nick Stahl is a welcome change of pace for this type of film. Instead of the scrubbed and bland youngsters who tend to turn up in these adventures, Stahl has a lived-in, ruminative look. You can certainly believe that he could dream up his three heroes and bring them to roaring life.

And the three actors who play his heroes are well cast, too: Swayze—who bears a striking resemblance to Kurt Russell in "Tombstone"—looks like a Remington cowboy but a little more cartoony; Platt's Paul Bunyan is a rumply, bitter butterball whose tree-chopping glories have been supplanted by machines; Brown's John Henry has a biceps-of-steel look that makes his legendary battle with a steel-driving contraption an even match.

The film would have been better if it played up the folkloric eccentricities of these three. They tend to devolve into platitudes; they're in the movie to make Daniel a man. And we could definitely use more of Catherine O'Hara's Calamity Jane, who only turns up in a brief cameo.

But "Tall Tale" also has some eye-popping set pieces, such as an infernally gray mining camp and a great steaming train that Daniel must stop. Buster Keaton, who loved trains in his movies, would have loved the big, seething chugger in "Tall Tale." Kids will love it, too, especially if it has been a long time since they've seen a real one up close.

NEW YORK POST, 3/24/95, p. 46, Thelma Adams

There's a sweet, sly little movie lodged in the belly of the bloated whale that is Disney's "Tall Tale: The Unbelievable Adventures of Pecos Bill."

Producer Joe Roth got the best that money could buy: "Schindler's List" cinematographer Janusz Kaminski and "Benny and Joon" director Jeremiah Chechik. Roth spoke and the FX guys delivered giant, special effects twisters.

They painted fields of butterflies onto the film in post-production when the critters wouldn't perform on command. The production schlepped to five states and 25 different locations from Monument Valley to Death Valley.

No less than dapper dancer Patrick Swayze holds the supporting role of Pecos Bill. Star-on-the-verge Oliver Platt plays Paul Bunyan. Scott Glenn is a cynical sidewinder of a villain, Stiles.

Catherine O'Hara graces a single stealing scene as Calamity Jane. Child star Nick Stahl, who went 10 rounds with Susan Sarandon in "Safe Passage," plays the lead. Even Burgess Meredith nods in for a crusty cameo.

So, Roth skimped on the script by writing partners Steven L. Bloom and Robert Rodat. Set in the American West in 1905, Bloom and Rodat ride the well-worn trail back to Oz.

Daniel Hackett (Stahl), enthralled by horseless carriages, wants to embrace Progress; his father (Stephen Lang) wants to keep him down on the farm. Railroad man Stiles wants to separate the Hacketts from their land and make Paradise Valley safe for strip mining and industrial waste.

After Stiles sidelines his father, Dan faces a dilemma: protect the farm or sell out. Dan does what any boy would do when faced with this adult challenge: He falls asleep in a rowboat.

When Dan awakens in the mythological West, he encounters Pecos Bill, Paul Bunyan and John Henry (Roger Aaron Brown). They wear chaps and spit, but they look and act a lot like the Tin Man, the Cowardly Lion and the Scarecrow.

After numerous adventures in which they firm up the boy's character and break Stile's little monkeys (including a suitably vile Jared Harris as Head Thug Pug), Bill, Bunyan and Henry teach Dan that classic lesson: "There's no place like home, there's no place like home."

Platt's Bunyan seems to have walked straight out of the first season of "Northern Exposure" and wrings comedy out of punchless lines. Swayze is perfectly cast as the heroic cowboy who can lasso a twister and ride it into the sky. Glenn does mean and nasty with a glee that would have made Margaret Hamilton envious.

But the actors and their shtick aren't given free rein in a movie that preaches when it should just kick back and entertain. "Maybe I'm just old-fashioned," crabs Bunyan, "but in my day we didn't take from the land, we just borrowed from it."

The biggest irony of all is that Profit, embodied by Stiles, turns out to be the movie's big bad guy. Is Disney telling tall tales or do they really not want to make money on this adventure? They should practice what they preach, then stop preaching and let us enjoy the movie.

NEWSDAY, 3/24/95, Part II/p. B7, John Anderson

There's no place like home, where they have to take you in, or Disney, where they *want* to take you in. Granted, that's the intent of a tall tale, but this one is a prime example of American hucksterism. And forgetfulness. And bald-faced gall. It's positively patriotic.

"Tall Tale: The Unbelievable Adventures of Pecos Bill" has plenty of exciting moments, some unexpectedly surreal cinematography by Janusz Kaminski ("Schindler's List") and boasts an enjoyable Patrick Swayze, which is no small boast. But it irritates as much as it entertains. And when the ads call the film "a 'Wizard of Oz' for the '90s," that's not necessarily a plug, it's just a description.

Appropriating not just folklore but film, "Tall Tales" sets up a trinity of previously unassociated legends—the hell-for-leather Pecos Bill (Swayze), the steel-drivin' John Henry (Roger Aaron Brown) and the tree-slaying Paul Bunyan (Oliver Platt)—in an "Oz" motif (Pecos as Scarecrow, John Henry as Tin Man and Paul Bunyan is the unCowardly Lion). The whole thing is then gussied up in an anti-capitalist, save-the-land message (anyone remember Disney's proposed Bull Run theme park?). All they need is a kid who wants to go home, and he arrives via Daniel Hackett (Nick Stahl, of "The Man Without a Face"), a child of fabled snottiness and mythic bad manners.

Have we mentioned "Shane"? Daniel's father, Jonas (Stephen Lang), is the Van Heflin-like holdout going head-to-head with railroad hitman J.P. Stiles (Scott Glenn), a Mephistophelian evildoer who rides a horse instead of a broom. The rest of the farmers, moral Munchkins, are frightened into selling Stiles their farms. Jonas resists, and gets shot.

What does Daniel do? Falls asleep in a boat, awakening in a yellow, dry-as-brick desert, where he's rescued from peril by Pecos Bill. Does he thank him? No, he gives him lip. And he gives Paul Bunyan lip. "He's just a kid," Pecos argues. "He's bad news, Bill," says Paul, whose dry wit and judge of character are the film's stronger points. John Henry doesn't say much, but I thought I saw him watching the kid and kneading the handle on his hammer.

All of which raises a question: Why are kids in movies aimed at kids so generally unlikable? Do moviemakers think that smart-ass children will appeal to other children? Are they simply unacquainted with any children but their own, who grow up in a kind of Oz underwritten by movies like "Tall Tale"? It's a puzzle, and an unfortunate one, because for all the good work by Swayze, Brown and Platt, and all the canyon rivers and moonscaped mesas that make it all so pretty, it's Nick Stahl's film, and his character's a brat. Frankly, I'd like to drop a house on him.

Also reviewed in:
CHICAGO TRIBUNE, 3/24/95, Friday/p. J, Michael Wilmington
NEW YORK TIMES, 3/24/95, p. C16, Janet Maslin
VARIETY, 3/20-26/95, p. 48, Joe Leydon
WASHINGTON POST, 3/24/95, p. C7, Rita Kempley

TANK GIRL

A United Artists Pictures release of a Trilogy Entertainment Group production. *Executive Producer:* Aron Warner and Tom Astor. *Producer:* Richard B. Lewis, Pen Densham and John Watson. *Director:* Rachel Talalay. *Screenplay:* Tedi Sarafian. *Based on the comic strip created by:* Alan Martin and Jamie Hewlett. *Director of Photography:* Gale Tattersall. *Editor:* James R. Symons. *Music:* Graeme Revell. *Music Editor:* Richard Bernstein. *Choreographer:* Adam Shankman. *Sound:* Mattheew Iadarola, Gary Gegan and (music) Armin Steiner. *Sound Editor:* Sandy Gendler and Val Kuklowsky. *Casting:* Pam Dixon Mickelson. *Production Designer:* Catherine Hardwicke. *Art Director:* Phillip Toolin, Charles D. Lee, Richard Yanez-Toyon, and Jim Dultz. *Set Decorator:* Cindy Carr. *Set Dresser:* Herb Morris, Paul E. Penley, and Glen Kennedy. *Special Effects:* Rochelle Gross. *Visual Effects:* Rochelle Gross. *Supervising Animator:* Andrew Knight and Steve Evangelatos. *Costumes:* Arianne Phillips. *Make-up:* Deborah Larsen. *Special Make-up Effects:* Stan Winston. *Stunt Coordinator:* Walter Scott. *Running time:* 103 minutes. *MPAA Rating:* R.

CAST: Lori Petty (Rebecca Buck/Tank Girl); Ice-T (T-Saint); Naomi Watts (Jet Girl); Don Harvey (Sergeant Small); Jeff Kober (Booga); Reg E. Cathey (DeeTee); Scott Coffey (Donner); Malcolm McDowell (Kesslee); Stacy Linn Ramsower (Sam); Ann Cusack (Sub Girl); Brian Wimmer (Richard); Iggy Pop (Rat Face); Dawn Robinson (Model); Billy L. Sullivan (Max); James Hong (Che'tsai); Charles Lucia (Captain Derouche); Roz Witt (Dr. Nikita); Brixton Karnes (Pilot); Will Nahkohe Strickland (Razor Ray); Charles Robert Harden (Zack); Tom Noga (Foreman); Bo Jesse Christopher (Town); John David Bland (Trooper Wayne); Jo Farkas (Sand Hermit); Stanton Davis (Father); Jillian Balch (Mother); Richard Schiff (Trooper in Trench); Kane Picoy (Trooper #1); Troy Startoni (Jet Pilot); Beth DePatie (Prostitute); Clayton Landey (Guard at Front Entrance); Roger Bohman (Technician); Frank Walton (Trooper in Basement); Richard Scott Sarafian (Flyer Trooper); Aaron Kuhr (Trooper at Pump Hanger); Kelly Cousineau (Young Rebecca); Chief Gordon and Kelly Kerby (Troopers); Jim Sullivan (Semi Driver); William A. Doyle (Dig Site Worker); Robert "Rock" Galotti (Long Hair); Peer Ebbighausen (Flyer Pilot).

LOS ANGELES TIMES, 3/31/95, Calendar/p. 6, Kenneth Turan

Watching "Tank Girl" is as disorienting as waking up in someone else's bad dream. You want to get out as fast as possible, but all the exits seem to be blocked.

Busy on the surface but numbing everywhere else, this largely live-action version of the cult comic book plays like an extended video for a group that is never going to make it. Heavy on attitude and posturing, it is the kind of production that tarnishes the word *cartoonish*.

"Tank Girl" is set in 2033, on a planet Earth turned into one enormous desert after a collision with a "humongous comet." It hasn't rained in 11 years, water is more precious than gold, and the dread Department of Water and Power "has got most of the water and all of the power."

Telling us all this, in typically annoying nasal tones, is Rebecca (Lori Petty), soon to be Tank Girl but first glimpsed riding a water buffalo outfitted with Day-Glo goggles. Rebecca herself is dressed in trademark psychedelic Salvation Army castoffs, just trying to get along in this devastated world.

Feisty, smart-mouthed, given to saying such irritating things as "It's been swell but the swelling's gone down," Rebecca theoretically exudes a kind of raffish charm but, as written by Tedi Sarafian, comes off instead as regrettably irrepressible.

Once she gets hold of her tank, and her new name, Tank Girl eventually squares off against Water and Power's villainous Kesslee, the umpteenth standard-issue power-mad psycho to be played by the tireless Malcolm McDowell. Kesslee is especially adept at wielding the film's key gizmo, a vacuum tube-shaped object that efficiently ends life by sucking all the water out of a person.

Helping Tank Girl fight the good fight is the imaginatively named Jet Girl (Naomi Watts) and a group of mutant beasts called Rippers, who combine the leaping ability of kangaroos with the *je ne sais quoi* of the human race. T-Saint, the leader of that group, is played by rapper Ice-T, who, like all the other Rippers, is close to unrecognizable under Stan Winston's "designed for the screen" makeup.

Distantly related to "Mad Max" but without any of the brilliance, let alone the madness, of that film, "Tank Girl" seems determined to win friends among the MTV generation. It throws lively animated footage into the mix whenever it can, and its soundtrack, coordinated by Courtney Love and featuring work by Hole and Portishead, is especially up to date.

NEW STATESMAN & SOCIETY, 6/23/95, p. 35, Jonathan Romney

The words "the movie" don't actually figure in the title of *Tank Girl*, but it's quite likely that people will find themselves referring to it nevertheless as *Tank Girl: the movie*. This is to distinguish it from the comic strip, but also from *Tank Girl* the trendy merchandising initiative (T shirts, boots, sticking plasters, for all I know, condoms) and *Tank Girl* the ready-made role model. There's been a glut of more or less successful comic adaptations in recent years, with more round the corner, and for the most part they create a wonderful opportunity to load cratefuls of shinny ephemera onto the market. Of course, who's to say that the doubtless forthcoming *Judge Dredd* helmets and *Casper The Friendly Ghost* phials of souvenir ectoplasm will prove any more successful than the *Dick Tracy* hats and radio watches?

What's slightly different about *Tank Girl* is that she's the only comic character I can remember that has been marketed not just as a trademark but as a lifestyle option. Punchy, libidinous and bald, the futuristic neo-punk soubrette has already been written about extensively as a blueprint, positive or negative, for a new academy of funky Bad Girls. She shoots, she farts, she bares her tits, she shags kangaroos—is this a good thing or a bad thing? Discuss. The film—or at least the idea behind it is pitched at a young, hip, irony literate audience, but you'd be forgiven for thinking its primary target was the swarm of think-piece writers out here in the media.

As is nearly always the case with think pieces, which have to leap into the dark to predict the next likely phenomenon, there's been a lot of jumping the gun. It's been assumed that *Tank Girl*, already culturally significant in a limited way, would become so on a major scale when the movie takes off. Well, there might have been plenty to say about the film, if it had lived up to the initial blueprint provided by Jamie Hewlett and Alan Martin's self-regarding but genuinely demented comic, *if* the original choice for the lead, Emily Lloyd, had kept the part and brought her own distinctive obnoxiousness to it, and if it had been any film but this drearily streamlined mess.

In the event, *Tank Girl* is too anaemically transatlantic to appeal to the British anarcho/hippie/student/clubber crowd who seem to make up its potential core audience, however small that might be; and too weird and slapdash to stand a chance of making sense to the American multiplex-goers, who gave it a prompt thumbs down.

The heroine, remember, is an anarchic semi-butch gun-slinging fashion plate with—just this once, OK?—attitude, who seems to have been transplanted straight from a Stoke Newington crustie commune to a war torn desert landscape, armed only with an array of Heath Robinson weapons, show-offy one-liners galore, and a range of subculturally signifying T-shirts (like an early and fondly remembered Stiff Records collectable). You can see why it only ran a week in Boise, Idaho.

Few films, literary adaptations or straight comic book lifts have struck me as being quite as inept an attempt to translate directly from the original. Director Rachel Talalay has tried to keep the look and the spirit of the comic, while grounding it in a recognisable film genre—the post apocalypse survival saga, after *Mad Max* and *Blade Runner*. It's a reasonable strategy; to stick too close to the original would have resulted in something very avant-garde indeed. The *Tank Girl* comic is an art-school slacker's incoherent babble masquerading as cartoon; spiked with digressions, gratuitous stylisation, graffiti as meaningless as the English inscriptions on Japanese-made leisurewear, it's what you'd get if you loaded Laurence Stern with acid and asked him to storyboard *Krazy Kat*.

Unfortunately, neither the spirit of the film nor its details make sense unless you have some knowledge of the original. If not, it's hard to understand why Tank Girl never actually has to replenish the limitless supply of T-shirts, why she expresses passion with the inscription "I snog you", why she dresses like a lesbian situationist performance artist but has a nice boyfriend who gets killed in the first five minutes (he was added just so that, heaven forbid, people wouldn't think she was a lesbian situationist performance artist).

Bearing that in mind, the film could have done without a proper narrative better still, without a proper character.

Everyone has their own idea of what Tank Girl looks like, and she does in any case look different from frame to frame, story to story one minute a fierce avenging slaphead, the next a parodically fleshy cheesecake fantasy for *Loaded* readers. So she might as well have been played by different actresses, just as the 1967 *Casino Royale* had several different James Bonds, including Woody Allen. Emily Lloyd for ten minutes, Patricia Arquette and Pauline Quirke for five each, Björk for at least 20—anyone but Lori Petty, who in the event we're actually stuck with, and who plays Tank Girl as an abrasive, hyperactive and mean-spirited Bronx brat.

The film throws everything and anything at the concept to make it catch fire: cod-Lichtenstein animation sequences, flashy SFX, an excruciating Cole Porter dance number, Courtney Love-Cobain (sic) as executive music co-ordinator. But *Tank Girl* is still a textbook example of Hollywood snapping up an interesting property and getting it wrong. Arch-villain Malcolm McDowell has one snappy gizmo here: a bottle that sucks the liquid from people's bodies and turns it into Evian water. The same gadget's obviously been used to extract from the movie the one thing it needs—Tank Girl herself.

NEW YORK POST, 3/31/95, p. 45, Thelma Adams

Lori Petty rocks as a gutsy, profane, next-age Calamity Jane in "Tank Girl." The big-eyed, bony-faced "Free Willy" star rides into the movie on yak-back. It's 2033 and she's having a bad hair day in the new millennium.

In this daffy, Mad Maxine Dystopia, water is power and the Water and Power company is monopolizing the liquid.

Malcolm McDowell ("Star Trek: Generations") plays the utility's CEO with mustache-twirling glee. He says of Petty, "My, my, she'll be fun to break."

With all the spirit and spite of two kids playing king of the mountain, McDowell and Petty square off in a battle of free will over fascism. The gonzo action-heroine, based on a British underground comic book, hits her stride when she gets a tank of her own.

"The sheer size of it," she marvels.

Rachel Talalay ("Freddy's Dead: The Final Nightmare") directs the movie as a glorious goof. Interspersed with animated sequences designed by Mike Smith ("Natural Born Killers") and "Tank Girl" comic creator Jamie Hewlett, the comedy sometimes stalls, undercut by a choppy episodic structure that mirrors the comics. Tedi Saraflan wrote the script.

But just when the movie seems to be grinding its gears and the zing is fading from Petty's one-liners, "Tank Girl" goes over-the-top. The cast breaks into an elaborate Busby Berkeley-inspired musical sequence set in a futuristic brothel, with Petty doing a dynamite version of a Cole Porter standard.

Even more unpredictable is the introduction of the wildly entertaining Rippers. A guerrilla band of genetically engineered animals, half-kangeroo, half-human, they huddle in an underground bowling alley, plotting the destruction of Water and Power.

The surprisingly good-hearted Rippers are one part Dartmouth frat boys frozen in the '60s (refugees from "Animal House"), one part government-issue sci-fi freaks. They dance wildly as a form of prayer, dine on crumpets and tea, revere Jack Kerouac—and are deadly killing machines.

Rapper Ice-T plays T-Saint, the fiercest brother among them, but it's the ditzy, boyish Booga (Jeff Kober) who turns Tank Girl on.

Girls just wanna have fun—and that goes double for "Tank Girl."

NEWSDAY, 3/31/95, Part II/p. B5, Jack Mathews

Three little words, that's all it takes to sum up the viewing experience of Rachel Talalay's comic book adventure "Tank Girl." And here they are: "Howard the Duck."

You remember Howard, the sarcastic, cigar-smoking, intergalactic poultry who leapt from the cult comic book shelf to the big screen and sent producer George Lucas running for cover? In making the same leap, the sarcastic, heavy-smoking heroine of "Tank Girl" may do the same for her producers, the team responsible for such box office hits as "Backdraft" and "Robin Hood: Prince of Thieves."

The movie that "Tank Girl" creators might like to have their film compared to is "Mad Max," whose barren, post-apocalyptic world it resembles, and which may well have inspired the Tank Girl comics, begun in 1988 by Jamie Hewlett and Alan Martin. The heroes of both are indefatigable forces of good fighting boarders on a devastated planet.

But there the parallel ends. "Tank Girl" is pure comic book stuff, with live-action intermixing with animation and panel drawings, a style choice that destroyed any chance of the film's working on the level of adventure. These interruptions jerk you in and out of the story, and are invariably done for no other purpose than to nudge you in the ribs.

Nudge *whom* is the big question. "Tank Girl" would seem to have no appeal to anyone other than the comic book's fans.

Set in the year 2033, after a comet has struck Earth and vaporized its surface water, "Tank Girl" pits sassy Rebecca Buck (Lori Petty) against the Water and Power Company that is greedily hoarding the planet's subterranean seas. Heading Water and Power is Kesslee (Malcolm McDowell), a psychotic despot given to ramming a spiked vacuum pump into subordinates and draining their private water reserves into an Evian bottle.

Rebecca, a tough chick who talks dirty and drives a mean tank, joins forces with the super-mechanic Jet Girl (Naomi Watts) and a band of mutant kangaroo men, and—armed with wisecracks—rushes into battle against Kesslee. If you've ever tried to beat a public utility with your attitude, you know the odds.

Some very good technical work was squandered on this mess, most notably the makeup designs for the kangaroo men done by Oscar winner Stan Winston ("Terminator 2"). There are some funny moments with these strange characters, who have the ears, paws, noses, tails and leaping ability of kangaroos, and the horny personalities of the Bowery Boys.

Front and center throughout, however, is Petty (the angry sister in "A League of Their Own"), in a performance that is less gutsy than it is flat-out irritating. I hate to attack one of the rare major studio movies featuring a dominant female character, especially one with the even rarer distinction of being directed by a woman. But if the genders are ever balanced in Hollywood, no one is going to look back on "Tank Girl" and its bawdy, beer-guzzling heroine as a landmark.

SIGHT AND SOUND, 7/95, p. 54, Leslie Felperin

2033. The Australian Outback. The world has become a vast desert and water a coveted commodity, one controlled by the Department of Water and Power (DWP), run by an evil genius named Kesslee. Rebecca Buck lives in an armed commune with her boyfriend, Richard, and his daughter, Sam. One night while Rebecca is on guard duty, the DWP raids the house and murders everyone for stealing water. Rebecca manages to kill several men, but is nevertheless captured and taken to Kesslee who tries to recruit her as a spy. She refuses and is sent to work in the mines.

Rebecca befriends Jet, a shy woman mechanic, and after a considerable struggle they escape together with a tank Rebecca has grown fond of (hence her nickname, Tank Girl). Wandering in the desert, they meet the reclusive Rain Lady who reveals that Sam is alive, but has been sold to a brothel in Silver City. Jet and Tank Girl find Sam held amidst the decadent hordes of the city. Everyone breaks into a dance routine, but they are interrupted by an invasion of the DWP's stormtroopers who kidnap Sam.

Tank Girl and Jet seek out the Rippers, a tribe of mutant creatures, half men, half kangaroo, who are awaiting the return of Johnny Prophet, their creator and leader. Booga, a dim but affectionate Ripper, becomes friendly with Tank Girl even though his colleague T-Saint mistrusts her. In order to prove her loyalty to their cause, Tank Girl almost single-handedly captures a shipment of weapons, only to find that the shipping cases contain the corpse of Johnny Prophet. She realises that Kesslee has planted a surveillance device on her and has been tracking her every move since she left the mines. The Rippers, Jet, and Tank Girl all join forces to invade the DWP's headquarters. While the others fight, Tank Girl battles Kesslee, eventually wins, and manages to save Sam at last.

Historically, older comic book heroes have fared better on the silver screen than their modern counterpoints. The old classic superheroes, Batman and Superman and their ilk, have found themselves rejuvenated in recent dramatisations, as if the modern 35mm camera were a life-refreshing gadget that might have appeared in the original strip's storylines. Thus, for a general audience, Tim Burton's version of *Batman*, an ambiguous and brooding creation, is more compelling character than the manly and irony-deficient figure of the original D.C. comics. On the other hand, today's comic book protagonists are far more interesting than their antecedents, being hip, relatively complex and dynamically drawn. Unfortunately, they end up getting cast in lousy movies.

Tank Girl is a superb example of this phenomenon. Fans of Jamie Hewlett and Alan Martin's original riot girl from dystopia, born in *Deadline* after the artists had grown weary of producing *Judge Dredd* for *2000 AD*, have probably prepared themselves to be disappointed, but may still be shocked at how shoddy the final product has turned out to be. Our heroine was once a vicious, nut-crunching, kangaroo-bonking baldy bitch. Hollywood has castrated our phallic mother of destruction, given her more hair, a child to protect and—the cruellest cut of all—plucked her eyebrows severely enough to make her look like Marlene Dietrich slumming it at Glastonbury festival. Once she had an aggressive polymorphously perverse sexuality and was an icon for lesbians worldwide; here she only kisses Jet to get her out of a spot of trouble, while her relationship with Booga, part kangaroo or not, is all fluffy love without the bestiality. If all that weren't bad enough, they've even put Björk on the soundtrack, the very personification of rehabilitated grunge-girliness for the masses. Lori Petty, too squeaky-voiced and Nautilus-conditioned to pull it off as TG, comes off as a valley girl rebelling against middle-class parents by shopping in thrift stores. As Moon Unit Zappa once said, gag me with a chainsaw.

Even if it's no surprise that the material would end up like this, smothered by a sanitary pad of wholesomeness, it still annoys because occasionally the film offers sly peeks at the better product it might have been. Asserting my feminine prerogative to ignore the evidence, I'd like to give director Rachel Talalay the benefit of the doubt and assume that the studio forced her to mangle this film. An excellent animation sequence and lots of rostrum shots of artwork by Hewlett disrupt the glossy texture from time to time to pleasing effect. One of the most interesting things about the best of the new comic book art is the way it plays with the frame and generally subverts conventions, and some of that playfulness survives in these 2-D interludes as it does in the joyfully superfluous Busby Berkeley-style song and dance sequence to Cole Porter's "Let's Do It". I can't help thinking that if Talalay had as much clout as an Oliver Stone she could have made *Tank Girl* as visually interesting and amoral as *Natural Born Killers*. Instead, as in the latter film, the computer generated predictability of script (written by a man, wouldn't you know) numbs the film. If Tank Girl were real she would have shot everyone rather than let this be released in her name.

VILLAGE VOICE, 4/11/95, p. 64, Gary Dauphin

The year is 2033, and though a comet may have robbed the Earth of its precious bodily fluids (i.e., fresh water), the pop-cult soup still has enough juice to keep a bright girl swimming in riffs from *Baywatch* to Cole Porter. Lifted from the pages of the well-regarded underground comic of the same name, Rebecca Buck—a/k/a Tank Girl—is the kind of character who'd rather quip than shoot her way through the postapocalypse. A water pirate in a *Mad Max*-ish desert wasteland that is the future, Rebecca begins the movie without a nickname, growing veggies with her way kewl b-friend and a multicultural clique of fellow techno-grungelets.

Rebecca and Co. joke away until their water theft runs them afoul of the public utility-cum--paramilitary organization known as Water and Power. After his men kill her beau, W&P CEO Kesslee (Malcolm McDowell playing his usually cultured sadist) wants to use our captured heroine to track down the Rippers—a deadly yet cuddly band of outlaw mutants. Lori Petty inhabits Tank Girl as a jangle of forehead, elbows, and one-liners—just like in the books—and when she gets her first look at an honest-to-god tank she cheerfully crawls across its cannon crotch first (the opening bars of Isaac Hayes's "Shaft" wafting through the background). The subsequent proof of Tank Girl's tubes (what x-chicks have in lieu of balls, I'm told) won't be a Stallone-style body count, though: It's the wreckage left behind by that mouth she's got on her. Hitting on all white-girl-with-attitude cylinders from the moment her voice skips and jerks across the desert, Tank Girl complains that the worst part of doing solitary in a straitjacket is that "it's really hard for me to play with myself." Later she one-ups Charlton Heston and the combined PBAs of America by basically telling Ice-T to go wash his mouth out (T is in a different kind of monster-drag here. His Ripper may be half-man, half-kangaroo, but the character's still as angry-black-man black as the day is long). Later, going Catwoman one better, she rescues her bud Jet Girl (Naomi Watts, whose accent is the only echo of the comix's Aussie roots) from a masher with a "don't mess with my girlfriend" ploy. Unsettling the initially grateful Jet Girl, she replies to her friend's. "Thanks for doing that" with a pouty, yet bug-eyed "Thanks for what?"

Besides the wit, the mouth, and the M5, the heavily alt-rock savvy soundtrack is *Tank Girl's* other big gun. The comix/zine scene that nurtured the *Tank Girl* comic has indie cred up the wazoo, so soundtrack executive producer Courtney Love (listed as Love-*Cobain* in the credits) supplies director Rachel Talalay with tunes from Bjork, Portishead, Hole, Bush, Belly, L7, and a Devo remix among others. Ice-T makes a game go of it acting wise, but too bad the use of his music was probably stipulated in his contract. Over-literalizing the hers-is-bigger motif with a plodding "she walks softly but she carries a big gun" refrain, his contribution is proof that even in the purportedly progressive indie rock/zine scene, blacks exist to authenticate white boys and girls' dick size (not to mention that his Rippers are basically a black frat in remote-control articulated latex).

Talalay uses the other songs to their best effect, aurally shoring up *Tank Girl*'s roller-coaster ride of visual look and mood. Her very current definition of movie fun is equal parts speed, volume, and a wicked directorial change-up: still-frame panels from the original comic, Lori Petty's near-Tourette's performance, vertiginous animated sequences drawn by Mike Smith (MTV's *Liquid Television* and the good parts of *Natural Born Killers)*, and the occasional musical production number (with dancing girls, even)—they all fit neatly into the mix. Future Tank and Jet girls will have to decide for themselves whether these two deserve a lasting place in the pantheon of alternative-chick cool, and comic purists will no doubt object that Kesslee is a composite villain. Either way, by the time his head disappears into a puff of electronic static with the words "This isn't over," I'm hoping he's right. Ideally to the tune of a sequel, a multipicture franchise, or Jumpin' Jehoshaphat, Tank Girl! a Saturday morning cartoon with requisite action figure.

Also reviewed in:
CHICAGO TRIBUNE, 3/31/95, Friday/p. H, Michael Wilmington
NEW YORK TIMES, 3/31/95, p. C10, Janet Maslin

VARIETY, 4/3-9/95, p. 142, Leonard Klady
WASHINGTON POST, 3/31/95, p. D7, Richard Harrington
WASHINGTON POST, 3/31/95, Weekend/p. 39, Desson Howe

THEREMIN: AN ELECTRONIC ODYSSEY

An Orion Picture Classics release of a Kaga Bay Productions film. *Producer:* Steven M. Martin. *Director:* Steven M. Martin. *Screenplay:* Steven M. Martin. *Director of Photography:* Frank De Marco. *Editor:* David Greenwald. *Music:* Hal Willner. *Sound:* Andy Green and Kim Aubry. *Running time:* 84 minutes. *MPAA Rating:* Not Rated.

WITH: Leon Theremin, Clara Rockmore, Robert Moog, Brian Wilson, Todd Rundgren, and Nicolas Slonimsky.

LOS ANGELES TIMES, 8/24/95, Calendar/p. 6, Kenneth Turan

Nothing on this Earth makes a sound quite like the theremin, a strange and wonderful musical instrument whose eccentric history has been turned into a whimsical, beguiling documentary called "Theremin: An Electronic Odyssey." No matter what your thresholds for pleasure and astonishment, this film, winner of the Filmmakers Trophy at Sundance, will cross them easily.

Making eerie, undulating tones that are difficult to describe but unmistakable once heard, the theremin—unknown to the general public—is a legend in several fields. It has made the soundtracks of numerous movies unforgettable, played a key part in the history of both electronic music and rock and earned a reputation for its inventor, Leon Theremin, as, says celebrated musicologist Nicolas Slonimsky, "the prophet of the future of music."

Invented by Theremin in his native Russia in 1920, the theremin is quite a bizarre piece of equipment. Its circuits are largely hidden by a wooden cabinet; all that's visible are a vertical antenna and a horizontal metal loop. What makes the theremin unusual is that it is played without being touched; merely moving your hands through the air over the cabinet varies loudness, pitch and timbre.

After demonstrating his invention to an approving Lenin, Theremin embarked on a world tour that eventually landed him in New York, where packed concerts at Carnegie Hall and a rapturous press reception followed. "Soviet Edison Takes Music From the Air," read one headline, while other stories were impressed by the instrument's "ethereal and heavenly sounds."

In New York, Theremin met the teen-age Clara Rockmore, who soon became a virtuoso on the instrument, capable of playing Bach for Leopold Stokowski, as well as the object of the inventor's attentions. One of the pleasures of Steven M. Martin's film is that we see Rockmore both then and now, in home movies as a glowing 18-year-old in an era when "we were always in evening clothes, it was very romantic," as well as in her current incarnation as the fierce priestess of the theremin cult, playing with delicacy, precision and beauty as her long red fingernails flash.

We also see Theremin himself in those home movies, a Gyro Gearloose elegantly turned out in white tie and tails with the kind of piercing eyes that unnerved people. A singular genius who speculated about raising the dead with electricity, Theremin went his own way in his private life as well, scandalizing his society friends by marrying not Rockmore but Lavina Williams, an African American ballerina.

If detailing all this was all "Theremin" had on its mind, it would suffice, but suddenly the movie and the man's life take an unexpected and riveting turn. In 1938, like a character in a science-fiction film, Theremin disappeared from New York without a trace. There were rumors of Soviet secret police involvement but, to his friends in Manhattan, he simply vanished, appropriately enough, into thin air. A sizable chunk of "Theremin" is concerned with the man's fate, and the film's investigation into exactly what happened has the pleasant and surprising air of a juicy mystery.

Theremin might be gone, but his influence if anything expanded, and another aspect of the movie details its extent. Robert Moog, for instance, the celebrated inventor of the Moog synthesizer, started out by building theremins at home when he was 14 and considers the instrument "the cornerstone of electronic music."

Most amusing are the clips and interviews that illustrate how the theremin was employed by Hollywood. Whether it was the DTs in "The Lost Weekend," amnesia in Miklos Rosza's Oscar-winning score for "Spellbound" or, most memorably, space aliens in "The Day the Earth Stood Still," whenever weird noises were called for, the theremin was ready.

And then came Brian Wilson of the Beach Boys, whose brief bout of nonstop eccentric enthusiasm for the theremin captures as much of his essence as the entire "I Wasn't Made for These Times" documentary. Frightened by the instrument when he heard it as a child, Wilson reconsidered while putting a particularly tricky song together, deciding "why not put a theremin in there," and the defining sound of "Good Vibrations" resulted.

Expertly orchestrating all these different strands is director Martin, also a theremin fan from childhood, who has a delicate appreciation of how simultaneously serious and silly this oddball story of a forgotten corner of musical history and popular culture is. By the time he brings everything together in a memorable climax played against the classic notes of "Good Vibrations," Martin's movie has made as vivid an impression as the music it celebrates with such charm.

NEW YORK POST, 9/8/95, p. 48, Michael Medved

Even though you may not know much about the electronic instrument called the Theremin, the chances are that you'd recognize its distinctively eerie sound. This pioneering contraption emits the otherworldly "oooo-weeeeoooo" warbling featured on the soundtrack of classic science fiction films ("The Day the Earth Stood Still," for example) as well as the Beach Boys hit "Good Vibrations."

Ingeniously designed to be played without contact—the performer expressively moves his bands in front of two antennae—the Theramin is the invention of a mad scientist whose story is every bit as haunting and bizarre as the tone produced by his instrument.

That story is now the basis for a spellbinding documentary, "Theremin: An Electronic Odyssey."

In the 1920s, Russian electronics professor Leon Theremin took the world by storm and single-handedly created the field of electronic music.

With his burning eyes and chiseled features, this "handsome devil" gave sold-out concerts throughout Europe and became a New York society favorite after establishing his studio on 54th Street. He fell in love with the glamorous Russian violin prodigy Clara Rockmore, who quickly became the world's leading virtuoso on the new instrument, but he scandalized his contemporaries by marrying an African-American ballerina named Lavina Williams.

Theremin remained an international celebrity and began developing other fascinating gadgets, including a musical electronic dance platform, light shows, and even a color television system, until he mysteriously disappeared in 1938.

He had been kidnapped from his Manhattan studio in front of his wife by agents of the dreaded Soviet NKVD (predecessor to the KGB), who dragged him back to Russia and threw him into a prison camp for "anti-Soviet" propaganda, while reports of his execution circulated widely in the West.

This disturbing tale is retold with captivating intensity by documentarian Steven M. Martin, who artfully blends archival footage, home movies, newspaper clippings, rare audio recordings and interviews with Theremin's surviving colleagues, including the still fascinating Clara Rockmore, who never gave up trying to learn the fate of her one-time mentor.

It turns out that Professor Theremin survived 25 brutal years in the Gulag, during which he invented the now-ubiquitous eavesdropping device known as the "bug," which proved such a boon to Soviet espionage that he won his release and a "prestigious" prize from Stalin himself. Later, he again ran into trouble with the authorities, who sternly disapproved of his continued interest in the "decadent" development of electronic music.

Amazingly, Theremin lived through these various ups and downs and in 1991, at age 95, he talked in Moscow with the makers of this film—who then brought him back to the United States for the first time in 53 years for a touching reunion with Clara Rockmore (duly captured on camera).

Director Martin wisely lets his story tell itself, with no omniscient narrator or shmaltzy underscoring of its most emotional elements. Comments from contemporary musicians like Robert Moog, inventor of the synthesizer, and a barely coherent Brian Wilson of the Beach Boys, emphasize the debt they all feel to Theremin.

But regardless of the ultimate historic significance of his invention, the professor himself remains such a compelling figure that this movie offers an unforgettable and richly satisfying cinematic experience.

NEWSDAY, 9/8/95, Part II/p. B4, John Anderson

The story that filmmaker Steven M. Martin set out to tell in 1991 was the history of Leon Theremin, who created the instrument that bears his name and thus created electronic music. What he ended up with was—like last year's "Hoop Dreams"—something that through a combination of perseverance and great good fortune took on a life of its own.

In giving us Theremin—a Russian electronics genius who came to New York in the '20s and was kidnapped back in the '30s—Martin sets us up. We hear from experts (including Robert Moog) about the importance of Theremin's work, how it inaugurated a new age in both music and electronics. We see remarkable archival footage and photographs of Theremin, his players, his Carnegie Hall performances. Astonishing home movies show Theremin with the 18-year-old Clara Rockmore, who was romanced by the professor and became the premier virtuoso on his instrument. We hear from friends and colleagues about his breakthrough work in television technology, his creation of a machine that would respond with sound to a dancer's movements, and his controversial marriage to a black dancer, Lavina Williams.

And we're told how he was kidnaped by Soviet agents in 1938, dragged back to the USSR and presumably executed for anti-Soviet propaganda.

Then, we meet Leon Theremin, who not only wasn't executed but, at age 94, is pretty spry. For more than 50 years, he was living in Russia where he spent time in a Soviet labor gang, was forced to work for the KGB (for whom he developed the "bug" or listening device), was rehabilitated, taught at the Moscow Conservatory of Music and was fired for continuing to work on electronic music.

Martin has too much to handle here. While the film is thorough and informative and offers a peek into just how byzantine and paranoid the Soviet system under Stalin was, it doesn't always proceed logically or clearly. But in large chunks, it's very entertaining.

Theremin's influence on the culture and country he had to leave so abruptly is traced through the use of the theremin—it looks like a desk wearing wands—in some classic movies: "Spellbound," "Lost Weekend," "The Day the Earth Stood Still." Most of these employ the theremin's sound to suggest eeriness: A clip from "The Mickey Mouse Club" is simply eerie.

Its use in rock is pursued mainly through the Beach Boys, who employed a theremin on "Good Vibrations." Martin includes a very amusing interview with a very unfocused Brian Wilson—he's much more together in the Don Was film "I Just Wasn't Made for These Times"—and allows him to ramble, which shifts the focus more than a bit off of his main subject.

And the real story, of course, is Theremin himself, who is reunited with Clara Rockmore in her New York apartment—her impatience with the camera is delightful—and provided some manner of closure for a life that was largely stolen from him. Although Theremin has died since the making of "An Electronic Odyssey," the fact that Martin was able to complete this film, and pay tribute to its subject, is at least a part of a happy ending.

VILLAGE VOICE, 9/12/95, p. 59, Amy Taubin

A graceful, evocative documentary about how historical events of great moment disrupt individual lives, *Theremin* tells the truth-is-stranger-than-fiction story of the Russian engineer, scientist, and musician Leon Theremin who invented the instrument that bears his name. The forerunner of the Moog synthesizer, the Theremin looked as uncanny as it sounded since it is played without being touched. Basically a wooden box with an antenna at either end, its internal circuitry creates a magnetic field that is manipulated through movements of the performer's hands. The Theremin has a range of several octaves and at its highest volume can overpower a full orchestra. Its quavery sound (timbre pitched between a squeaky door and chalk on a blackboard) became a staple of sci-fi and horror films in the '40s and '50s, but its boomer breakthrough came in the '60s when Brian Wilson used it in "Good Vibrations."

Theremin, who looked both in youth and old age much like Duchamp, emigrated to the U.S. in the '20s. Although his instrument embodied the meeting of art and science in 20th-century modernism (while also evoking the influence of the occult on the cultural avant-garde), its market-place debut unfortunately coincided with the 1929 stock market crash. Only 250 Theremins were sold. It was not the last of its inventor's ill-fated encounters with the forces of history.

In 1938, Theremin was kidnapped back to Russia by the secret police. His wife, the famed black dancer Lavina Williams, never saw him again. After years in labor camps, Theremin was rehabilitated so that the military could make use of his engineering brilliance. He invented a high-level surveillance device called "The Bug" for which he was awarded the Stalin Prize. Theremin's work for the KGB roughly coincided with the use of the Theremin in Hitchcock's spy thriller *Spellbound* and in such Cold War metaphor films as *The Day the Earth Stood Still*. Later, he was allowed to return to music but his instruments were destroyed after an article appeared about him in the *New York Times*. (The Soviets had reported him dead 20 years before.)

Theremin is all the more the affecting for having been made in the nick of time. Martin located the 95-year-old Theremin in Moscow in 1991, interviewed him on camera, then brought him back to the U.S. and filmed his reunion with the friends and colleagues who hadn't seen him in over 50 years. He died two years later. While maintaining a chronological thread, *Theremin* juxtaposes interview material, live performance documentation, Hollywood film clips, old newsreel and home-movie footage to foreground the surreal twists and absurd synchronicities of its subject's life. In Times Square, the wizard of electronics quizzically regards the cacophony of neon. Madame Blavatsky would have appreciated the film. So too might have Lenin, who once played Theremin's Theremin.

Also reviewed in:
CHICAGO TRIBUNE, 12/15/95, Friday/p. J., Michael Wilmington
NATION, 10/9/95, p. 399, Stuart Klawans
NEW YORK TIMES, 9/8/95, p. C8, Janet Maslin
VARIETY, 2/14-20/94, p. 39, Emanuel Levy
WASHINGTON POST, 1/26/96, p. F6, Hal Hinson
WASHINGTON POST, 1/26/96, Weekend/p. 38, Desson Howe

THINGS TO DO IN DENVER WHEN YOU'RE DEAD

A Miramax Films release of a Woods Entertainment production. *Executive Producer:* Marie Cantin, Bob Weinstein, and Harvey Weinstein. *Producer:* Cary Woods. *Director:* Gary Fleder. *Screenplay:* Scott Rosenberg. *Director of Photography:* Elliot Davis. *Editor:* Richard Marks. *Music:* Michael Convertino. *Music Editor:* Ken Wannberg. *Sound:* Jim Steube and (music) Shawn Murphy. *Sound Editor:* Richard L. Anderson and David Bartlett. *Casting:* Ronnie Yeskel. *Production Designer:* Nelson Coates. *Art Director:* Burton Rencher. *Set Decorator:* Anne D. McCulley. *Set Dresser:* Loren P. Lyons. *Costumes:* Abigail Murray. *Make-up:* Steve Artmont. *Make-up (Special Effects):* Todd Masters. *Stunt Coordinator:* John Branagan. *Running time:* 204 minutes. *MPAA Rating:* R.

CAST: Andy Garcia (Jimmy "The Saint" Tosnia); Christopher Lloyd (Pieces); William Forsythe (Franchise); Bill Nunn (Easy Wind); Treat Williams (Critical Bill); Jack Warden (Joe Heff); Steve Buscemi (Mister Shhh); Fairuza Balk (Lucinda); Josh Charles (Bruce); Gabrielle Anwar (Dagney); Christopher Walken (The Man with the Plan); Michael Nicolosi (Bernard); Bill Cobbs (Malt); Marshall Bell (Lt. Atwater); Glenn Plummer (Baby Sinister); Don Stark (Gus); Harris Laskawy (Ellie); William Garson (Cuffy); David Stratton (Alex); Deborah Strang (Dodie); Sarah Trigger (Meg); Jenny McCarthy (Blonde Nurse); Wiley Harker (Boris Carlotti); Joe Drago (Maitre D'); Chuck Bacino (Accordian Player); Don Cheadle (Rooster); Tiny Lister, Jr. (House); Bill Long ("The Dead Beat" Man); Cheree Jaeb (Little Girl); Sarah Levy Arbess (Girl #1); Larissa Michieli (Girl #2); Larry Raben (Young Man); Lynn Appelbaum (Young

Woman); Taylor Hale (Stevie); Archie Smith (Mr. Jergen); Harriet Medin (Old Woman); Bill Bolender (Stevie's Dad); Susan Merson (Woman with Cancer); Bill Erwin (70 Year Old Man); Nate Ingram and Jacob Berenger (Alley Hoods); Larry Curry, Jr. (Black Youth); Ruthay (Receptionist); Selina Mathews (Cynthia); Phil Boardman (Gym Teacher); William Denis (Businessman); Danny Romo (Montirez Brother).

LOS ANGELES TIMES, 12/1/95, Calendar/p. 1, Kenneth Turan

[The following review by Kenneth Turan appeared in a slightly different form in NEWSDAY, 12/1/95, Part II/p. B2.]

"Do they still have gangsters?" the beautiful Dagney asks Jimmy the Saint, trying to figure out who or what he is. "Say 'You dirty rat.'"

Jimmy can't handle the classic James Cagney line, but it's the only time that words fail him. A rhapsodic talker and sincere Lothario, Jimmy, like all the other characters in "Things to Do in Denver When You're Dead," is a wizard with language. Not exactly ordinary English either, but a wacky kind of pumped-up slang laced with mysterious, evocative phrases such as "buckwheats" and "boat drinks" and "give it a name."

More than its own language, "Denver's" tyro screenwriter Scott Rosenberg and first-time director Gary Fleder have created their own raucous and sentimental universe, a world that takes traditional gangster themes of loyalty and living by a code and twists them in dark and comic ways. Moviegoers who can make it past "Denver's" excessive violence—no small thing—and get on this film's off-center wavelength will find a grave *noir* comedy heavy with romantic regret, a cocky piece of work that flaunts its style and attitude and dares you not to be impressed.

Most impressed were the dozen or so excellent performers, from Andy Garcia and Gabrielle Anwar as Jimmy and Dagney to Jack Warden as the film's bluff narrator and Christopher Walken as the terrifying crime lord known simply as the Man With the Plan, none of whom could resist the heft and distinctiveness of the characters Rosenberg created.

Even in this impressive group Treat Williams stands out for the bravado of his performance as unstable hoodlum Critical Bill, so named because he leaves everyone he meets in critical condition. A mortuary driver introduced using a corpse as a punching bag ("I haven't touched a live person in years," he boasts), Critical Bill has a guileless, almost boyish quality that coats his psychopathic actions with an eerie calm. It is a tasty character and Williams makes just as much of it as John Travolta did in a similar career-reviving turn in "Pulp Fiction."

Denver's story revolves around Jimmy the Saint, a former seminarian who first soured on the church and then on crime. Now he hangs out in a malt shop called the Thick 'n Rich and runs a dubious video operation called Afterlife Advice ("Just Because They're Gone Doesn't Mean They Can't Guide") in which dying parents record timeless advice for their survivors.

But Jimmy's situation is about to change. He spots Dagney, a smiling ski instructor, across a crowded bar and pursues her with eccentric lines like "Girls who glide need guys who make them thump." When Jimmy's habitual secretiveness is added in, Dagney doesn't know whether to be baffled or impressed.

Jimmy is secretive because, much against his will, the all-powerful Man With the Plan has come back into his life. Turned into a paraplegic by an attempted rub-out, the Man is the devil in a wheelchair, bitter but still powerful. He dotes on his son Bernard, and he insists that Jimmy put a scare into the new boyfriend of Bernard's former girlfriend. "It's just an action, not a piece of work," he says, meaning no one is supposed to get hurt.

To do the job, Jimmy rounds up the usual gang of pals from the old days, except there is nothing usual about any of them. Aside from Critical Bill, there is Franchise (William Forsythe), a tattooed trailer park manager; the hot-tempered Easy Wind (Bill Nunn) and Pieces (Christopher Lloyd) whose obscure disease causes pieces of his extremities to drop off at slight provocation.

Not surprisingly, things go wrong with the action, as they tend to do in movies like this, and the sinister Mister Shhh (Steve Buscemi) puts in an appearance. All at once Jimmy finds himself frantically trying to manage his fragile relationship with Dagney, look after his crew, and even straighten out the life of a trouble-prone hooker named Lucinda (Fairuza Balk).

Though "Denver's" substance is familiar, it is flavored with the special piquant sauce Rosenberg's screenplay and Fleder's brisk direction provide. The actors, especially Garcia, also provide the charisma that helps propel the film over its occasional rough spots.

The hardest thing to take about "Things to Do in Denver When You're Dead" is its uncomfortable violence, its bloody shoot-outs and its horrific beatings. The shame of it is that, unlike films that have nothing but bloodshed going for them, "Denver" doesn't need the mayhem to attract a crowd. And that carnage may ultimately keep away the very moviegoers who could most appreciate its loopy, eccentric virtues.

NEW YORK POST, 12/1/95, p. 46, Thelma Adams

Andy, I love ya, but this hasn't been your year.

While John Travolta has been the comeback kid, Garcia has been stuck in second gear on the outskirts of stardom. The Cuban-born actor was sliced out of the box-office hit "Dangerous Minds" (he played Michelle Pfeiffer's boyfriend). Swept off the cutting-room floor, he bombed as his own evil twin in "Steal Big, Steal Little."

Garcia's the best thing going in "Things to Do in Denver When You're Dead." But the actor with the fall-into-my-spell soulful browns and the spitfire temper can't carry Gary Fleder's clever but clunky Reservoir Mutt.

The sons of Tarantino, college boys all, continue to spin glib, well-researched, hard-boiled tales packed with silver-tongued hoods and golden-hearted hookers. But, as true-love-interest Dagney (Gabrielle Anwar) asks Garcia's Jimmy the Saint: "You're doing the talking thing again ... Why?"

In Scott Rosenberg's screenplay, the characters talk so tough that even a little girl jumping rope withers a potential molester with: "What do you want, doofus?"

I'm a fan of stinging dialogue and snappy wiseguys, but there are more potholes in "Denver"'s plot than there are on the BQE.

Retired mobster and seminary dropout Jimmy is trying to go straight. He videotapes deathbed confessions of the terminally ill called Afterlife Advice. (If you didn't get wise from the title, this gangster comedy is, unfortunately, real about deep issues like dealing with death.)

Afterlife Advice is a terminally ill venture and debt-ridden Jimmy gets gulled back into the life by is former boss, the Man With the Plan (Christopher Walken). The Man offers Jimmy 50 grand to frighten the fiance of his son's ex-girlfriend. We have plunged into the quicksand of the unnecessarily convoluted.

Instead of pocketing the full fee for the simple action, Jimmy falls face down into the implausible. He rounds up his former crew, the gang that couldn't go straight. Treat Williams, Christopher Lloyd, William Forsythe and Bill Nunn flood their scenes with manic energy, manifesting outsized tics like Williams' habit of beating up corpses for sparring practice.

Why should smooth-talking smart-guy Jimmy hook up with these losers? If you think he's a saint, call it loyalty. If you think he's a dupe of a screenwriter desperate for a plot twist, join me in the hall for a smoke.

You know it's all over when Jimmy tells the boys: "[It's a] one-shot deal. We're in. We're out."

Me, too.

SIGHT AND SOUND, 5/96, p. 63, John Wrathall

Jimmy The Saint is a former gangster who now runs Afterlife Advice, a struggling Denver video company which records the thoughts of soon-to-be-deceased clients for their loved ones. He is summoned out of retirement by his wheelchair-bound ex-boss, The Man With A Plan. The Man's dim-witted son Bernard is brokenhearted because the love of his life, Meg, is about to marry someone else, and The Man wants Jimmy to frighten off the new boyfriend, Bruce. Needing the money to save his ailing business, Jimmy sets about recruiting his old team: Franchise, who now runs a trailer park; Pieces, a porn cinema projectionist; Critical Bill, a punch-drunk boxer who now works for a mortuary; and Easy Wind, who works in pest control. In the meantime, he meets the beautiful Dagney, falls instantly in love, and tries to straighten out a local prostitute, Lucinda, who wants to settle down with him and have a baby.

Posing as policemen, Pieces and Bill stop Bruce and Meg on the freeway outside Denver, but Bill blows a fuse and ends up killing them. Enraged, The Man hires hitman Mr Shhh to kill Jimmy's team, and tells Jimmy he will only spare him if he leaves town. Jimmy is unwilling to go. Mr Shhh works his way through Franchise, Pieces and Easy Wind, but is shot dead as he kills Bill. Meanwhile Jimmy kills Bernard to get back at The Man and having ensured Dagney's safety, impregnated Lucinda and recorded his own afterlife advice,—he surrenders himself to certain death at the hands of The Man's henchmen. In a bleached-out afterlife he shares drinks on board a yacht with the rest of his team.

New York, Chicago and Los Angeles are the traditional stamping grounds for movie gangsters, but Denver provides a surprisingly apt location for this elegiac debut from writer Scott Rosenberg and director Gary Fleder. The city's curious mixture of architecture—Old West streets next to glass skyscrapers (a product of the 70s oil boom), all against the backdrop of the Rocky Mountains—serves to illuminate the situation of Jimmy and his associates. They are anachronistic men of honour, stranded in a harsh modern world now that the metaphorical frontier has closed. There's a strong echo here of Peckinpah's *Pat Garrett And Billy The Kid*, as Jimmy bids farewell to his old colleagues, in the knowledge that he and they will soon be dead at the hands The Man With The Plan.

The presence of Christopher Walken and Steve Buscemi and the hip take on *film noir* and crime movie archetypes all make comparisons with Tarantino's films inevitable. Rosenberg's script conjures up a rich, poetic underworld slang and a gallery of vivid, exotically named characters; even the minor roles are fleshed out with funny, evocative details. The ex-boxer Critical Bill works out on the corpses in the mortuary. Pieces suffers from a strange condition that makes his fingers drop off. The Man With The Plan's two henchmen have cultivated extra-curricular interests in order to improve their conversation: one sports designer labels while the other, who reads the dictionary, peppers his speech with words like "specious" and "anon".

As with *Pulp Fiction*, the quality of the writing attracted a phenomenal line-up of actors for an $8 million independent, many of them cast cleverly against type. After years of studied eccentricity in three Back To The Futures and two Addams Families, Christopher Lloyd achieves a sleazy dignity as Pieces. Treat Williams, returning to the big screen after a six year layoff, transforms himself into the battered brute Critical Bill, and manages to make us feel for a man who beats up corpses and eats shit. As the fearsome mob boss The Man With The Plan, Christopher Walken may be revisiting former glories, but he has never had to do it paralysed from the neck down before. Andy Garcia, meanwhile, gets the role of a lifetime, revealing a new compassion alongside his customary cool as Jimmy The Saint.

Where Denver radically differs from the likes of Pulp *Fiction or The Usual Suspects,* however, is in its unaffected warmth of tone, enhanced by a wry running commentary delivered by Jack Warden's underworld old-timer, Joe Heff, from a booth at the local malt bar. With an additional chorus provided by the recurrent video clips recorded for Afterlife Advice—so that scenes of Jimmy's increasingly frantic efforts to put his life in order are juxtaposed with the deadpan philosophising of a bunch of crotchety senior citizens—this is also a rare American film, both humorous and serious about death.

VILLAGE VOICE, 12/5/95, p. 66, Georgia Brown

It's nice going to film festivals where a normally well-behaved critic can act up. When I saw *Things To Do in Denver When You're Dead* in Cannes, I booed it. I was the only one booing, which felt a bit strange but cathartic. (People to the left and right pretended not to know me.) I despise this movie even more than I despise *The Usual Suspects,* another pretentious, hokey, slick, hard-boiled, soft-shelled art-house gangster pic. Which is to say, there's a hungry audience out there.

The worst thing about *T.T.D.I.D.W.Y.D.* is not its cuteness but its smugness. If Andy Garcia delivers a terminally smug performance, he's only doing what writer Scott Rosenberg and director Gary Fleder tell him to do, namely act like he believes he's a saint. (Don't they know that saints don't advertise?) In reality, the character is a spectacularly careless sinner, a smooth-talking con man, a self-righteous schmuck. As if we need to be cued, however, Garcia's character is *called* Jimmy the Saint and practically everyone in the movie *tells* him what a noble fellow he is. And as they do, Jimmy the Saint from Flatbush (whole title) seems to get tears in his blank brown eyes.

Like youknowwhat and youknowwhatelse, *T.T.D.I.D.W.Y.D.* revolves around recruiting a team for an "action." Although J.T.S. rounds up the four thugs, the man who gives the order is The Man with the Plan (another creepy turn for Count Walken). Feeble and foul-mouthed, T.M.W.T.P. steers his wheelchair 'round his mansion-cum-museum while sucking on an oxygen pipe (*Blue Velvet* redux) and issuing cryptic orders. "Buckwheats!" he says (Buckwheats is *Denver*'s Keyser Soze) Pegged as the film's chorus, a crusty diner regular (played by Jack Warden) explains that the term means killing someone in a manner intended to be especially agonizing: "a bullet up the ass," for example. (Just as in youknowwhat and youknowwhatelse, homosexual longings are couched in jocular to and fro. "One day you're saving rain forests, next thing you know you're chugging cock," T.M.W.T.P. mockingly warns J.T.S. about associating with such kind. And when it comes to dying here, men can hardly do it without landing in one another's arms.)

As for the four ugly losers Jimmy comes up with, let's begin with Pieces (Christopher Lloyd), so named because his fingers and toes are dropping off from a circulatory disease—a hindrance to his projection of porno films. (We get to listen to someone's noisy climax while Pieces slurps Chinese food.) Then there's the honorable Franchise (William Forsythe)—actually, they're all honorable—tracked down in a trailer park where he lives with his sullen wife and their brood. Easy Wind (Bill Nunn), an exterminator of bugs, is the sweetest of the lot, just as Critical Bill (Treat Williams) is the sickest. Mortician's assistant and accused "fecal freak," Bill uses the corpses for punching bags. Although the movie deliberately milks the disgust factor, at least it only touches on what else Bill does.

The Man's Plan is idiotic to begin with: Fake cops are meant to scare off a boyfriend by stopping his van. Idiocy is compounded when Jimmy picks the two dumbest, Bill and Pieces, to pose as cops. Result: two dead bodies. It's at this point that the four recruits—for the time being, Jimmy is spared—are sentenced to execution by "the most lethal contract killer west of the Mississippi," Mr. Shhh (fearsome Steve Buscemi).

Meanwhile, the movie boasts a child molester (this is just to get the viewer's juices flowing), is well as a whole romantic subplot wherein Jimmy the Saint falls for Dagney the Dunce (Gabrielle Anwar photographed in a mist). "You glide," he informs her. And, "Girls who glide need men who make them thump." You'd think she'd glide away fast. But no, just a little tease—"I never kiss on the first date," he lies—and she's his slave. Given the movie's own premises, everything Jimmy does endangers this girl, even when he makes a slobbering show of returning her to her old boyfriend. (Haven't these guys seen *Casablanca?*)

I love how it's the fashion now for doomed, unsavory guys to maintain the masochistic devotion of wholesome and elegant young women. Every man wants his Dagney, as Jimmy puts it. In *The Usual Suspects*, there's Suzy Amis; in *Leavinq Las Vegas*, Elizabeth Shue (yes, she's supposed to be a hooker, but she's really a sorority girl). Its the same demand as in *Kids:* Not just a virgin, but the sweetest-faced pick of the freshest litter. You wish.

For added spice, Fairuza Balk bops down the walk as Lucinda, a child junkie-whore. She too worships Jimmy: "You're different, Jimmy. You got decency. And a nice ass." He beats the trick who roughed her up all over the boardroom table (gimme a break), and when Lucinda begs Jimmy to father her child—a baby is all this girl needs to clean up—he complies.

Okay, it's a dirty comedy it's supposed to be fun. And romantic. And touching. Tragic even. (The screenwriter reports that he drew on his father's death by cancer.) It's all infused with death and dying. Jimmy runs a video company, "Afterlife Advice," providing survivors with testaments from the deceased. (See Egoyan's *Speaking Parts* or *My Life.*) Taking a leaf from Scorsese, Fleder edits in Dean Martin's "Accentuate the positive" just as Jimmy undergoes a particularly brutal beating. Background locations like a carnival's ferris wheel and a natural-history museum for a tryst add nothing to these tried-and-true conventions.

Tarantino is ersatz, too, but his carny rides have kick and a lilt and, the first time around anyway, leave you giddy. When he tacks on grace and redemption, however, it's just talk—Quentin following formula. (Now, John Woo has an authentic Christian vision.) At this very moment, Mike Figgis's welcome *Leaving Las Vegas* is being lavishly praised despite—or because of—an unconvincing tastefulness. (Figgis's flashy *Stormy Monday* was 1987's *Denver.*) Kathryn Bigelow is suddenly getting huge press (and *Artforum* is the latest *Premiere*) just when she's morphed into James Cameron. In *Entertainment Weekly,* Singer announces that the keys to *The Usual Suspects's* success are "saturation" and "hipness." Next to all these movies' carefully studied hipness, *Casino's* terrible bloody-corpse coldness looks like so much self-defeating integrity.

Also reviewed in:
CHICAGO TRIBUNE, 2/16/96, Friday/p. H, Michael Wilmington
NEW YORK TIMES, 12/1/95, p. C10, Janet Maslin
VARIETY, 5/29-6/4/95, p. 55, Todd McCarthy
WASHINGTON POST, 2/16/96, p. F6, Rita Kempley
WASHINGTON POST, 2/16/96, Weekend/p. 48, Desson Howe

THREE WISHES

A Savoy Pictures release of a Rysher Entertainment presentation of a Gary Lucchesi/Clifford & Ellen Green production. *Executive Producer:* Larry Albucher. *Producer:* Gary Lucchesi, Clifford Green, and Ellen Green. *Director:* Martha Coolidge. *Screenplay:* Elizabeth Anderson. *Story:* Clifford Green and Ellen Green. *Director of Photography:* Johnny E. Jensen. *Editor:* Stephen Cohen. *Music:* Cynthia Millar. *Music Editor:* Kathy Durning. *Sound:* Lee Orloff and (music) Keith Grant. *Sound Editor:* Teresa Eckton. *Casting:* Aleta Chappelle. *Production Designer:* John Vallone. *Art Director:* Gae Buckley. *Set Designer:* Tom Reta. *Set Decorator:* Robert Gould. *Set Dresser:* Mara Massey. *Special Effects:* Phil Tippett. *Costumes:* Shelley Komarov. *Make-up:* John Elliot. *Make-up (Patrick Swayze):* Scott Eddo. *Stunt Coordinator:* Lisa Cain. *Running time:* 105 minutes. *MPAA Rating:* PG.

CAST: Patrick Swayze (Jack McCloud); Mary Elizabeth Mastrantonio (Jeanne Holman); Joseph Mazzello (Tom Holman); Seth Mumy (Gunny Holman); David Marshall Grant (Phil); Jay O. Sanders (Coach Schramka); Michael O'Keefe (Adult Tom); John Diehl (Leland's Dad); Diane Venora (Joyce); David Zahorsky (Little Leland); Brian Flannery (Brian); Brock Pierce (Scott); Davin Jacob Carey (Sackin); David Hart (Brian's Father); Scott Patterson (Scott's Father); Michael Laskin (Sackin's Father); Robert Starr (Hank); Simone Study (Brian's Mother); Lauren Sinclair (Scott's Mother); Annabelle Gurwitch (Leland's Mother); Moira Harris (Katherine Holman); Neil McDonough (Policeman); Brad Parker (Passerby); Philip Levien (Tool and Die Coach); Lawrence R. Baca (Colony Drive-In Coach); Bill Mumy (Neighbor); Colleen Camp (Neighbor's Wife); Brandon Lacroix (Little Magician); Jamie Cronin (Cindy); Alexander Roos (Hide and Seek Boy); Garette Ratliff Hensen (Neighborhood Teenager); Jay Gerber (Dr. Pavlick); William G. Schilling (Doctor); Tiffany Lubran and Kathryn Lubran (Holman Daughters); Marc Shelton (X-ray Technician); Vivien Strauss and Loanne Bishop (Bystanders); John Devoe and Ethan Jensen (Teenagers on Roof); Robb Turner (Man with Rake); Rosa (Betty Jane).

LOS ANGELES TIMES, 10/27/95, Calendar/p. 14, Kevin Thomas

"Three Wishes" is a wonderful film, full of warmth, humor and charm, a family drama with the possibility of the supernatural. It is an uncommonly accurate period piece, the kind that goes beneath the surface, and its stars, Mary Elizabeth Mastrantonio and Patrick Swayze, are in peak form.

It's the summer of 1955, and Jeanne (Mastrantonio), a young Korean War widow with two sons, Tom (Joseph Mazzello) and Gunny (Seth Mumy), are in their car when Jeanne swerves to avoid hitting a dog only to strike its owner, Jack (Swayze), breaking his leg. Jeanne ends up insisting that Jack, a drifter, stay with her family in their home in a pastel-hued Southern California tract—it brings to mind the one in "Edward Scissorhands."

While Jack is about as low-key and unobtrusive as a person could be, he cannot help but stand out in the neighborhood, rocking it with rumors of backyard sunbathing in the nude and acquiring the disparaging label "beatnik." Jack, handsomely bearded, and Jeanne, whose striking resemblance to Jackie Kennedy may be intended by the filmmakers, are highly attractive people, but Jack makes no move on her and she discourages him from the get-go. She in fact is just about to be courted seriously by an old beau, Phil (David Marshall Grant), a businessman who attributes his success to her inspiration.

What Jack radiates is a calm strength that awakens people to the potential within themselves. He's helpful in as self-effacing a way as possible but galvanizes the neighborhood when his Buddhist chant/yoga/meditation approach to coaching the youth baseball team propels it to unexpected triumphs. By then he's become for Tom the adored father he lost. Jeanne is falling in love with him, too, but is not prepared to acknowledge it.

Magical things do happen, mainly in relation to 5-year-old Gunny, but in such a way that if we so choose we can take them as an expression of the power of the imagination and perhaps faith, too. "Three Wishes" is a heart-tugger but one that pulls with genuine emotion. Inspired by European folklore, co-producers Clifford and Ellen Green wrote a 30-page outline for the film and hired Elizabeth Anderson, an unknown with a Sundance Writing Workshop fellowship, to develop it into a script.

They actually dare to suggest that if you do a good deed, as Jeanne did in giving Jack shelter, that you will be repaid in kind. Martha Coolidge, in turn, is just the right kind of straight-ahead yet sensitive director to keep this notion from seeming too sappy in these cynical times.

Even if 1955 happened to be a great year for you, the film constantly reminds us how pervasive conformity was back then. Jack tells Tom that "people aren't all alike, they just think they are," and his presence is crucial in reassuring Jeanne of her capability at a time when the pressure upon women to depend on a man was intense. This awareness undercuts the film's potential for gooey nostalgia yet acknowledges how much stronger a sense of community was 40 years ago, even though it was already disintegrating in most urban cities.

Production designer John Vallone brings to "Three Wishes" the same kind of authenticity he brought to Coolidge's film of Neil Simon's "Lost in Yonkers." Like "Devil in a Blue Dress," "Three Wishes" is accurate in its Atomic Age architecture and decor right down to the kitchen appliances. Similarly, costume designer Shelley Komarov's clothes are as period perfect for 1955 as they were for 1944 in "Yonkers." Cynthia Millar's score is emotional without being treacly, and this handsome, burnished film marks the seventh collaboration of Coolidge and cinematographer Johnny E. Jensen.

The hallmark of a Martha Coolidge picture is its performances, and under her direction Mastrantonio reveals many facets of the irresistible Jeanne, a conventional woman to all appearances but one capable of thinking for herself. It is a thoroughly endearing portrayal, as is that of Swayze as Jack. Having created a glamorous drag queen of dignity, strength and compassion in "To Wong Foo, Thanks for Everything, Julie Newmar," Swayze now shows us a man of strength held in reserve, a man with an aura of serenity rather than obvious mystery. Swayze holds the screen often, saying little and doing even less, through sheer presence. One of the most accomplished young actors in films, Mazzello, with "Jurassic Park," "Shadowlands" and "The River Wild" already behind him, is splendid as the bright, vulnerable yet tenacious 11-year-old Tom in a role that is arguably the film's most demanding and furthest-ranging. Mumy and Grant head the fine supporting cast. "Three Wishes" is the kind of film you wish they made more often.

NEW YORK POST, 10/27/95, p. 42, Michael Medved

"Three Wishes" does such an affectionate, uncannily accurate job of re-creating 1950's suburbia—complete with Davy Crockett T-shirts and freshly constructed tract homes for $13,000—that anyone who grew up in that environment will find it difficult to resist the movie's nostalgic and magical mood.

Mary Elizabeth Mastrantonio is radiantly effective as a middle-class mother who's been struggling to raise two boys since her pilot husband was shot down in the skies over Korea.

While running errands one afternoon in her small California town she swerves to avoid an unkempt mongrel dog, and ends up hitting the beast's master—a homeless wanderer named Jack McCloud (Patrick Swayze).

She feels so bad about breaking the leg of the soft-spoken, bearded figure that she defies disapproving friends and neighbors by inviting him to live in her spare room until his cast is removed and he can walk normally again.

Of course, the mysterious visitor ends up changing the lives of all three members of the family—especially the lonely older boy, yearning to feel accepted by his Little League teammates, flawlessly played by 11-year-old Joseph Mazello (Jurassic Park," "Shadowlands," "The Cure") who could be the most reliable child actor in Hollywood today.

His 5-year-old brother, meanwhile, is a sickly child haunted by vivid fears and fantasies, portrayed by an utterly natural, altogether adorable newcomer named Seth Mumy. This ailing little boy begins to see supernatural powers in the family's house guest and, most especially, in his all-knowing dog, identifying them with genies in stories who grant three wishes to strangers who do them a favor.

Director Martha Coolidge plays this material up the middle between realism and mysticism, keeping us guessing (right up to a moving and hugely satisfying surprise ending) about Jack's true identity.

As in her precious films (including "Rambling Rose" and the marvelous but overlooked "Angie") she gets sympathetic performances from her entire, cast and offers an array of handsome, lovingly composed images.

The movie's main weaknesses involve a complicated framing device set in the present day that doesn't really work, and a self-consciously sensitive characterization by Swayze that's a bit too introverted for a figure that just might be a magical messenger.

Nevertheless, for those who have been yearning for the magic of more intelligent, emotional family fare to engage parents along with their kids, this movie comes as one answered wish.

NEWSDAY, 10/27/95, part II/p. B9, John Anderson

I have to admit, I walked away from "Three Wishes" unclear about several things. Was Patrick Swayze's character, Jack McCloud, an angel? A reprise of "Ghost"? A figment? Was there any way this proto-hippie would have been allowed to sleep in a park in suburban 1955 without a few visitations of the nightstick and a one-way bus ticket elsewhere?

What *was* clear is how easy it is for a filmmaker to stake out a particular time period and project on it a sense of moral superiority. Much easier, say, than making the same kind of formulaic movie in contemporary time and having to deal with all the accompanying social issues you couldn't otherwise ignore. By looking back several decades, a director can re-create time to fit her outlook. Or make heroic a simple act of kindness.

Such an act is performed by Jeanne Holman (the delightful Mary Elizabeth Mastrantonio), a single mother whose serviceman husband's plane has been lost in Korea. She wants to start a business which, given the time, makes her quite adventurous. And she's equally decent: When she hits a homeless drifter with her car and breaks his leg, she decides the only thing to do is take him home (this is, again, 1955) until he mends.

The bum, Jack McCloud, is more than he appears, however. He's on what seems to be a spiritual quest. He meditates. He sunbathes nude in the backyard—throwing the neighborhood into apoplexy. And he's viewed as something of a threat by the male homeowners of the surrounding tract-housing development.

He's quickly perceived as a father figure by young Tom (Joseph Mazzello, of "Jurassic Park"), who sees himself as an outcast because he doesn't have a father. Although it makes Jack uncomfortable, he's adopted by Tom, who uses Jack as entrée to the local softball team. When Jack takes over managerial duties from Coach Schramka (the perpetually athletic Jay O. Sanders), he has them chanting "Om" and applying Zen principles to the art of outfielding.

Jack and Mom get close, and you know what's up, just as you know that Mom's putative boyfriend, Phil (David Marshall Grant), is a louse. The younger son, Gunny (Seth Mumy), who has even more problems than Tom, falls ill. He is then visited in his dreams—or are they?—by huge but apparently benevolent apparitions, who raise a question: If this kid is so timid, why isn't he screaming?

Martha Coolidge has made period pieces and genre films ("Ramblin' Rose," "Valley Girl") her forte, and in "Three Wishes" shows us that the '50s were repressed, women weren't liberated and conformity was godliness. To her, the past is not just prologue but a waiting canvas for her projections of self. This would be interesting, if it didn't feel so recycled.

SIGHT AND SOUND, 1/96, p. 55, Leslie Felperin

Edendale, California, the present. Tom is distraught at being on the edge of bankruptcy. While driving with his family one Memorial Day, he almost runs over a small yellow dog. He then sees and recognizes a shabby tramp walking into the cemetery, and has a flashback to his childhood. In 1955, Tom lives in Edendale with his widowed mother Jean and little brother Gunny. While driving to a Memorial Day picnic in the cemetery, Jean hits the same yellow dog that Tom avoids over 30 years later. When the family gets out of the car to look, the dog has become the shabby tramp whom the police chase off. We learn that Jean's husband was reported missing in action, presumed dead, in Korea. The dog later leads the family to the tramp, Jack, who's broken his leg in the accident. Jean insists he stay with them until his leg heals, despite the disapproval of her friends and neighbours. Jack becomes closer to all the members of the family. He helps Tom's baseball team improve by teaching them to win by not trying. Gunny develops cancer. After Gunny sees the dog transform into a cloud of magic fireworks, Jack explains that the dog is actually a genii who once granted him three wishes. He couldn't decide what he wanted so the genii had to wish for him, and he chose that Jack should be with him always. Gunny wishes for the ability to fly amongst fireworks. Jean wishes for Gunny to get better. Tom wishes for Jack to stay, but Jack cannot grant this wish. He says he now must make a wish for Tom and leaves, catching a lift on the highway. At the fairground, Gunny is granted his wish to fly and eventually, it is explained, recovers from his illness. To everyone's surprise, Tom's father returns from Korea where he'd been kept a prisoner of war.

Back in the present. A grown-up Tom meets Jack, unwithered by time, in the cemetery. Jack explains that his wish for Tom was not for Tom's father to return, as Tom had always thought, but for Tom to always be happy with his life as it was. Looking at his wife and family, Tom feels happiness despite his troubles. As he rejoins them, the camera reveals a gravestone with Jack's name on it, its dates implying that he died in the Second World War.

Three Wishes is a sentimental fable, one which cynical sophisticates will find is easy to sneer at. However, its relative success in the US this autumn cannot be so easily brushed aside. Although cunningly nostalgic, *Three Wishes* adroitly manipulates such currently fashionable themes as male angst about absent fathers and fear of commitment, belief in supernatural intervention and the more weathered problem of feminine independence—all solid blocks from which to build box-office success. And this is precisely the kind of film which you can take your kids to, especially when they are a bit too old for *Pocahontas* and too young to see *GoldenEye*.

A modest slice of suburban magic realism, *Three Wishes*' central narrative shows how a family's suffering (father's supposed death, brother's cancer) can be healed by wish fulfillment and the passive acceptance of ordinary tragedy—the supernatural vagabond Jack's final wish for the protagonist Tom is that he find happiness in whatever he gets in life. Semi-divine intervention by a wish-granting genii is a fantasy every child has, and here it's cleverly embedded in an idealised but authentically decorated 50s landscape of Little League games and pastel-paletted track housing. This tenuous attachment to realism makes the fantastic element all the more seductive. Consider the fact that a sizable quantity of Americans admits to believing in angels and it's easy to see how this film taps into the *geist* in *zeitgeist* (as in 'spirit of the age').

In the film's final account, everything tots up in favour of nuclear, traditional family values, but along the way director Martha Coolidge (who's directed such slightly grittier fare as *Angie, Crazy in Love* and *Rambling Rose*) manages to cook the books with surreal visual touches and sour snapshots of the all-American town. This 'edge community' of Edendale, a dense and entrapping terrain of ticky-tacky houses clinging tenuously to the dusty soil of the Southern Californian desert that starts just beyond its backyards, is shot in wide-angle panoramas. It looks identical to the suburban location used by Tim Burton for *Edward Scissorhands*—the resemblance adding a sinister edge. A trio of identically dressed blonde sisters that haunt the crowd at Tom's baseball games, belies the stringent conformity that the beatnik Jack supposedly violates. The road he travels may represent freedom on one level, but it's also a dangerous thoroughfare, teaming with speeding vintage vehicles. Given what we learn about Jack's nature by the film's conclusion, this route is also clearly the road to nowhere. No wonder when asked about the most amazing place he's been, Jack cites the gorgeously desolate salt flats of Utah, a "moonscape" where this ambivalent figure, not of this world, can be most at home in.

Playing an occult personality again, as he did in *Ghost*, Patrick Swayze here reconfirms his status as a star who acts surprisingly well (as opposed to an actor who has star-quality, such as Ralph Fiennes). Drawing on his athleticism and his gift for stillness, he scowls enigmatically while limping gracefully. This being a family film however, generic conventions dictate that he, Mary Elisabeth Mastrantonio and the cutesy kids must all be upstaged by Rosa, the dog who plays Betty Jane his sidekick, a shaggy blond mongrel well matched as Jack's alter ego, and the true genius of the piece.

Also reviewed in:
CHICAGO TRIBUNE, 10/27/95, Friday/p. G, Michael Wilmington
NEW YORK TIMES, 10/27/95, p. C12, Caryn James
VARIETY, 10/16-22/95, p. 95, Todd McCarthy
WASHINGTON POST, 10/27/95, p. D7, Hal Hinson

THROUGH THE OLIVE TREES

A Miramax Films release of a CIBY 2000 production. *Producer:* Abbas Kiarostami. *Director:* Abbas Kiarostami. *Screenplay (Farsi with English subtitles):* Abbas Kiarostami. *Director of Photography:* Hossein Djafarian and Farhad Saba. *Editor:* Abbas Kiarostami. *Sound:* Mahmoud Sanak Bashi. *Running time:* 108 minutes. *MPAA Rating:* Not Rated.

CAST: Hossein Rezai (Hossein); Mohamad Ali Keshavarz (Director); Farhad Kheradmand (Actor); Zarifeh Shiva (Mrs. Shiva); Tahereh Ladania (Tahereh); Hocine Redai (Hocine); Zarifeh Nourouzi (Kouly's Wife); Barastou Abbassi (Kouly's Daughter); Nasret Betri (Achiz); Azim Aziz Nia (Azim); Astadouli Babani (Teacher); N. Boursadiki (Tahra); Kheda Barech Defai (Teacher); Babek Ahmad Poor (Himself); A.li Ahmed Poor (Himself); Mahbanou Darabin; Kardouni Nouri.

LOS ANGELES TIMES, 2/10/95, Calendar/p. 6, Kevin Thomas

Iranian filmmaker Abbas Kiarostami's "Through the Olive Trees" couldn't be more understated or modest, yet in its indirect way it exerts a cumulative emotional tug. As funny as it is poignant, it was inspired by two young people involved in the making of an earlier Kiarostami film, "And Life Goes On," an account of a father and son traveling through earthquake-ravaged portions of Iran.

On the last day of shooting, Kiarostami realized that the young man playing a small role as a bridegroom was in real life in love with the young woman whom he had cast as the bride but who had spurned him repeatedly. This film envisions how a persistent suitor goes about trying to make real the role he is playing in the movie.

Kiarostami rounded up a cast of non-professionals, who in turn helped improvise their dialogue, with amazingly persuasive results. The setting is an earthquake-devastated village, where the newlyweds take over a damaged adobe house that the husband, a bricklayer, promises to restore to perfection.

Much of the humor—and sadness—occurs between takes of the film. For example, when its director (Mohamad Ali Keshavarz, the one professional actor in the cast and well-known in Iran) tells the bricklayer, Hossein (Hossein Rezai), to ask his bride, Tahereh (Tahereh Ladania), to look for his socks, he later reassures her that in real life he would never ask her to do such a thing.

Thankfully, "Through the Olive Trees" is not yet another solemn comment on art and reality, but rather a wry, compassionate observation on how events, whether they be a devastating earthquake or the making of a movie, affect people's dreams and destinies. In his sheer determination and innate decency Hossein recalls the little boy in Kiarostami's wonderful "Homework," in which a doughty 8-year-old, living in an ancient mountain village, embarks on a long trek by foot to return a notebook to a classmate who will be expelled if he doesn't have it with him at the beginning of school the following day.

NEW YORK POST, 2/17/95, p. 48, Thelma Adams

Abbas Kiarostami is a subtle filmmaker—perhaps too subtle for me.

"Through the Olive Trees," which I saw for the first time at last fall's New York Film Festival and watched again this week, is a film-within-a-film.

Set in remote, earthquake-devastated Iran, the movie follows a young Iranian couple, non-actors both, who are united during the making of "And Life Goes On ...," which is not a soap opera but Tehran-born Kiarostami's previous movie.

Kiarostami plants this simple romance behind-the-scenes in a low-budget production to chip away at way the reality of that nexus where life on the set meets life as it is lived in real time. Experiencing this noble effort is like watching paint peel—beautiful paint, but paint nonetheless.

The extended driver's-eye-view of rural, crumbling Iran as a truck speeds up and slows down en route to the rustic set, curving onto unpaved roads, halting to avoid livestock, is so realistic that I felt car sick. It's fascinating as a travelogue, but I've also seen this kind of you-are-there filmmaking years ago at Disneyland, where I traveled through a covered bridge and over a roller coaster without ever leaving my seat. It wasn't Iran, but I got the idea.

Kiarostami shows the demands of directing non-actors in difficult circumstances (all shots are exteriors, all amenities are limited by the quake damage, ominous clouds hover over every scene) with dry wit and affection.

Hossein Rezai and Tahereh Ladania, the amateurs, are a perfect match in their stubbornness. In take after take, they change their lines to fit their own lives or drop phrases altogether without apology.

Professional actor Mohamad Ali Keshavarz, standing in for Kiarostami in the role of the director, perseveres with a god-like patience.

Much has been made of the rhapsodic subtlety of the movie's conclusion, the lush final image set in windswept green fields beyond the olive trees. It left me largely untouched, like a beautiful vista that unfolds at the end of a long and winding truck ride through mountain roads seen through a nauseous haze.

In the past 12 months, my head has started to nod twice while screening movies—both times I was watching "Through the Olive Trees."

NEWSDAY, 2/17/95, Part II/p. B5, John Anderson

There's no end of movies about moviemaking, and no end in sight—Tom DiCillo's "Living in Oblivion" opens the New Directors/New Films series next month, and the "Day for Night" legacy will no doubt continue well beyond that. But Iranian director Abbas Kiarostami has added several twists to the reality pretzel with "Through the Olive Trees," which is also a trip through several layers of perception.

For a realist's movie, it's sentimental but ultimately moving, thanks mostly to the real-life Iranians who populate it. The film-within-the-film is called "And Life Goes on ..." (which was the title of another Kiarostami movie) and the director, played by Mohamad Ali Keshavarz, is casting locals, two of whom bring their own emotional drama to the film.

Hossein (Hossein Rezai), a former mason, is to play the husband of Tahereh (Tahereh Ladania). What no one knows ahead of time is that, off the set, Hossein has proposed to Tahereh, and been rejected by her family. As a result, she refuses to speak to him. And, already, the structure of Kiarostami's film is a teetering, multi-tiered house of artifice.

Adding to the weirdness is the locale: Shortly before filming, Iran was rocked with a devastating earthquake that has rendered the life of Kiarostami's real-life cast unreal: School is held in a tent, a woman gives her address as "behind those trees" and Hossein wakes up one morning in a bed in a field. The film is a minor eruption in a ruined world. It may be more tangible than most of their existence.

This entire structure would be an interesting, if self-absorbed, exercise if Kiarostami's "actors?" weren't so, well, real. In relating his romantic misfortune to the director, Hossein becomes the center of a touching modern parable: How he asked Tahereh's mother for her hand and was rejected on the ground that he had no house; how the earthquake then killed both Tahereh's parents and destroyed *their* house. How he audaciously re-proposed, citing their mutual lack of houses. And how he was rejected again by Tahereh's Maria Ouspenskaya-imitator grandmother. And when he walks away from her he finds himself in the middle of a scene, and gets chastised again. It's disorienting, to everyone.

Hossein's face is a monument to mournfulness and obstinance. His persistence in the face of total rejection makes us cheer him on as he uses the time between shots to tell Tahereh his thoughts on love, marriage and what their life could be. That he is met by total silence is painful. But he perseveres. And in the long walk through the olive trees that ends the film, the figures fade and fade, Hossein tailing Tahereh, until she finally stops, and speaks, and he runs back in what has to be ecstasy.

Kiarostami's final tease—in a film full of them—is not letting us hear the words that finally win her over.

SIGHT AND SOUND, 1/97, p. 52, Nick James

In the earthquake-ravaged Iranian village of Koker, in 1993, an actor, Mohammad Ali Keshavarz, announces to camera that he will be playing the part of a film director making a film. He is interrupted by a Mrs Shiva, his assistant, who tells him that a party of schoolgirls is now assembled for audition. He wanders through the black-robed teens, picking out certain girls. Later, Mrs Shiva arrives at the house of Tahereh, the chosen girl, to pick her up. Tahereh's grandmother tells her the girl has gone to borrow a dress. The girl arrives shortly with a 'modern' dress which Mrs. Shiva insists she can't wear.

The director is trying to shoot a scene in which Farhad Kheradmand (who is playing a film director) meets a young man carrying a sack up the steps of his house. The young man is supposed to answer a greeting from his young wife. However, he fails to answer her through several takes and it transpires that he stutters whenever he speaks to a young woman. The director lets him go and sends for Hossein, a helper at the crew's campsite. Hossein tries the scene but now it's the girl, Tahereh, who clams up. As the director drives Hossein back to the campsite, Hossein confesses that, before the 1990 earthquake, he was working opposite the girl's house and fell in love with her. He approached her mother about marrying Tahereh but was rebuffed. Tahereh's parents were then killed in the earthquake. He is still being denied by Tahereh's grandmother because he has no house and is illiterate.

The next day, Mrs Shiva gives a lift to a nomadic family. The director shows interest in casting a young woman among them, but is rebuffed. He asks Hossein if this girl could have replaced Tahereh and his affections. Hossein says no because she is illiterate. When the director accuses him of hypocrisy, he argues that like should never marry like or there would be no progress.

Hossein and Tahereh are performing another part of the scene they acted in before. The 'film director' character asks the young man if he's just been married. The young man describes how he and his wife lost so many family in the 1990 earthquake that they decided to marry immediately. In between takes Hossein pleads with Tahereh, asking her if her heart is with him. She ignores him. Tahereh, when speaking her lines, calls him Hossein and not Mr. Hossein as the script dictates (they are using their own names), but Hossein convinces the director that the script's formal address is now old-fashioned. When Tahereh is dismissed for the day, she elects to walk home. At the director's prompting, Hossein follows her across the fields, pleading his case all the way. Finally, in the far distance, we see her turn to him and he runs back, towards the camera, seemingly elated.

With this final segment, Abbas Kiarostami's trilogy of films set in the Northern Iranian village of Koker simultaneously reaches a point of maximum complexity and minimum drama. What started out in the first film, *Where Is My Friend's House?*, as a parable of childhood savvy—albeit one shot in a neo-realist style with certain self-reflexive trimmings—has become in this latest film a studious attempt to eradicate the old boundary between unmediated cinema verité and the shaping process of fiction film-making.

What *Through the Olive Trees* makes clear, despite its simple tale of two young lovers shrugging off the grief caused by an earthquake disaster, is that Kiarostami's mission is not simply to interrogate the film-making process. He wants to transend the unsettling dichotomy between showing real people retelling their real lives and fictionalising that retelling for a film. His aim is a representation that is simultaneously naturalistic and discreetly formal, in which film-making has demonstrably become as much a complicit part of Koker village life after the earth-quake as, say, living in a tent.

There is much irony to be derived from Kiarostami's success in achieving this balance, as he appears almost desperate to show us that the ordinary people he uses as actors can be just as difficult as Hollywood stars. The orphaned teenage girl, Tahereh, seems in need of proportionally as much pampering (in budget terms) as, say, Kim Basinger. Her ardent suitor, Hossein, although a willing factotum to the film crew, requires near-equal attention when acting. Even a teacher who appeared in *Friends' House* lobbies hard for a role in the film within the film. This is a tale of frail egos inflamed with survivors' pride. There's no room here for the sentimental impulses some reviewers detected in *Friends' House*.

While this is the first time in the trilogy that Kiarostami's subject is overtly the making of a film rather than the telling of a story, its complexity is compounded by the fact that the film being shot within it is *Olive Trees'* predecessor in the trilogy, *And Life Goes On ...* That latter film has its own self-reflexive element, but the motivation for it is that a 'director' tries to find out if two young boys from his film *Where Is My Friend's House?* have survived the earthquake. With *Olive Trees* Kiarostami has moved one step back from such an emotive pretext. Here it's simply the making of a film for its own sake that reveals the Koker locals to us.

There are several scenes, all presumably directed by Kiarostami, in which an actor playing a film director directs an actor playing a film director. This almost arrogant distancing process is perhaps self-mockingly lampooned when the director (played by Keshavarz) tells Kheradmand (who plays the 'director' in the inner film) about the ghosts of Poshteh, a ruined village near the crew's campsite, who will only return in echo the words "hello" and "goodbye". There are also several takes of scenes from the film within the film reproduced in all their professional monotony. In another scene, Hossein strays into a wood that looks familiar and disturbs the shooting of the crying baby scene from *And Life Goes On ...* It's a shock to realise that it is the trilogy viewer's memory of seeing that scene which makes the woods familiar in the first place. We get a glimpse of Babek Ahmed Poor, the lead amateur actor in *Friend's House,* looking increasingly like Eric Cantona as he nears his teens. All this familiarity with a people and a place that viewers of the entire trilogy have come to know well, softens the austerity of its analytical climax.

Nevertheless, there is some harshness left that is less easily dispelled. To a Westerner's perspective, Hossein's courtship method of wearing down Tahereh's resisitance might well be seen to rely too much on bullying and hectoring. It's a fierce, desperate and relentless tirade, ranging from reverent praise to wounded reproach. It comes from a tradition in which persistence in courtship is as much a virtue as it is in the medieval European Romance, and should be judged accordingly. What's harder to determine, though, is the way that this persistent form of loving also relates to Kiarostami's film-making process. There may be a sense in which the onscreen director's cajoling of his reluctant amateur artistes is mirrored in Hossein's passionate harangue or this may just be an over-investment of meaning on this reviewer's part. On the other hand, Kiarostami—seemingly happy playing Chinese Boxes with film form—ought not to presume that Hossein's stamina will be shared by his film's audience. For despite its conceptual success and fragile sense of intimacy, *Through the Olive Trees* is often a gruelling viewing experience.

VILLAGE VOICE, 2/21/95, p. 54, Gary Dauphin

A deceptively simple film set in the rolling hills of northern Iran, *Through the Olive Trees* takes the age-old tale of boy-pursues-girl and puts it through formal twists and paces as visually languid as they are demanding on the audience's powers of observation. Part improvisation, part romantic-vérité, *Olive Trees*'s plot is easy enough to follow onscreen but collapses in on itself during retelling, which I imagine was precisely Abbas Kiarostami's intention. Pay close attention and you'll discover that even when his camera settles into what seems like lethargy or his characters start one-tracking their obsessions, Kiarostami is really asking you to just look a little harder, outlining a personal filmic vocabulary whose Rosetta stone will, teasingly enough, remain a mystery until the film's closing moments.

A part of last year's New York Film Festival, as well as Iran's entry for this year's best foreign film slot at the Oscars, *Olive Trees* returns to the site and time of Kiarostami's *And Life Goes On* (1992). Retracing his earlier film, the dean of Iranian independent cinema tells the story of how one of *And Life Goes On*'s leads courted the other during shooting. *And Life Goes On* was already a film-within-a-film (it concerned a director making a film about village domesticities in the wake of a major earthquake), which in turn makes *Olive Trees* something of a plot-line mouthful. Hossein Rezai and Tahereh Ladania play themselves playing the characters from *And Life Goes On*.

A vérité gambit throughout (the actors are nonprofessionals improvising lines about their own lives), *Olive Trees* refers to itself as a film only in the first shot: Kiarostami's stand-in (Iranian commercial-cinema great Mohamad Ali Keshavarz) walks into the frame to announce, "My name is Mohamad Ali Keshavarz and I'll be playing the director." Kiarostami's three-level house of cards sways a bit before it's even fully in place, but a busybody assistant director appears to suture the gap in short order, telling Keshavarz/Kiarostami that it's time to cast the lead actress for *And Life Goes On*.

Since *Olive Trees* is basically about returning to a specific place for a second look, its characters' correct addresses (or lack thereof) will be one of its major concerns. The casting scene is a litany of names and addresses called out in-the-round, and the girl chosen to play the lead certainly knows the importance of her own place in the village. The first thing Tahereh does after being cast is delay a morning shoot by refusing to wear the peasant dress required for the scene, figuring that since she herself lives in a house and goes to school, there's no way her "character" would wear an illiterate's garb. Her male counterpart gets the same treatment as the dress. During their first scene playing the married couple from *And Life Goes On,* Tahereh refuses to speak and then puts up a wall of silence that is only broken by moody utterances from the *And Life Goes On* script. When Keshavarz asks Hossein what exactly he did to her to make her act that way, Hossein hedges and then confesses to the sin of courting outside his means—or as Tahereh's grandmother later spells out, "You're illiterate and you've got no home. You can't have her."

Hossein faces all this with a dogged persistence that will provide most of *Olive Trees*'s action and quiet comedy. Since *And Life Goes On* will be his best last chance to get close to Tahereh, he turns his every scene into an attempt to woo her. When he isn't apologizing to her that he would never, ever talk to her the way his *Life Goes On* character does, he's off telling her and Keshavarz why the literate should marry the illiterate (so every kid in Iran will have someone to help them with their homework, basically), his voice sliding into a desperate upper register as the rejections pile on. Kiarostami's camera is unflinching in its observation of all these details, and Keshavarz maintains a bemused distance throughout, at once worried that Tahereh's disdain for Hossein will delay shooting and yet at the same time obviously aware that Hossein's acting in *And Life Goes On* is feeding off the whole messy situation.

How Kiarostami weaves together these disparate threads is the film's closing gift to its audience. The last scene is less an ending about Hossein and Tahereh than it is a revelation of what Kiarostami has been doing throughout the film, the image comprising a cinematic gesture so in keeping with his always gentle intrusions that to even reveal its existence is to do Kiarostami something of a disservice. Let's just say that much like Hossein's final trip through the grove of the film's title, getting the point of *Olive Trees*'s ending requires a certain measure of faith, not so much in Hossein's blind love for Tahereh as in Kiarostami's love of all of them.

Also reviewed in:
CHICAGO TRIBUNE, 9/28/95, Tempo/p. 7, Michael Wilmington
NEW REPUBLIC, 3/20/95, p. 28, Stanley Kauffmann
NEW YORK TIMES, 2/17/95, p. C23, Stephen Holden
VARIETY, 5/23-29/94, p. 54, Deborah Young

TIE-DIED: ROCK 'N' ROLL'S MOST DEADICATED FANS

An ISA Releasing Limited release of a Cathay Sterling, Inc. & Padded Cell Pictures & Arrowood Productions presentation. *Executive Producer:* Joseph A. Kim, Sara Sackner, and Jennifer Fish. *Producer:* Marsha Oglesby and James Deutch. *Director:* Andrew Behar. *Director of Photography:* Hamid Shams. *Editor:* Andrew Behar and Sara Sackner. *Music:* Peter Fish. *Sound:* Tony Garrison and Dale Whitman. *Running time:* 88 minutes. *MPAA Rating:* R.

LOS ANGELES TIMES, 9/22/95, Calendar/p. 17, John Anderson

[The following review by John Anderson appeared in a slightly different form in **NEWSDAY, 9/22/95, Part II/p. B4.]**

That the Grateful Dead are neither seen nor heard in Andrew Behar's "Tie-Died: Rock 'n Roll's Most Deadicated Fans" should come as little surprise.

The band—which may have trucked its last after the recent death of guiding light Jerry Garcia—was always reluctant to acknowledge its camp followers, the Deadheads, and certainly never endorsed them. And for all their devotion, the Deadheads in the movie seem to get along perfectly well without the band.

But it's strange that the word *religion* is never uttered, because everything else Behar includes in this examination/celebration says exactly that.

The Deadheads—who'd go on the road with the group, turning parking lots into medieval fairs and doubling the size of small towns—have turned their lives over to what they perceive as a higher power.

In chronicling the Deadhead scene during the band's 1994 tour—and employing music made by the Deadheads themselves—Behar doesn't go far enough in examining just why certain people are drawn to the Dead's music.

He interviews enough of them—from grizzled ex-hippies who have been "on tour" since the '60s to young, love-soaked dilettantes who will soon be heeding the call of college and the corporate hive. He lets them generate their own auras of absurdity.

But while many of the Deadheads seem sincere about what their lives are about, Behar isn't actively skeptical of what he sees; he simply doesn't take enough of a jaundiced view of an often pathetic phenomenon. Or he's too nice a guy to burst anyone's bubble.

Or, he doesn't have the nerve to be critical of something he's become part of. There's a point in "Tie-Died" (preceded in theaters by "A Conversation with Ken Kesey" directed by Peter Shapiro) where he shifts gears and deals with the occasional ugliness of a Dead show, the sporadic violence, the way the attitudes in the lots have changed over the years, and the way mandatory minimum drug laws have been used to hassle and incarcerate people outside concerts. But it's just a perfunctory caesura in his hymn of praise to all things Dead.

In one of his better scenes, Behar follows a handful of Deadheads to a gallery show of Jerry Garcia art and records them informally reviewing a recent show. It is a startling example of inarticulateness, of yeahs and wows and far outs. And they all understand each other perfectly.

NEW YORK POST, 9/22/95, p. 44, Larry Worth

Being a Deadhead is more than a way of life. According to the documentary "Tie-Died: Rock 'n Roll's Most Deadicated Fans," being a Deadhead is a religion—with Jerry Garcia as its Jesus.

And in the Judas role? Director Andrew Behar, for having portrayed the Dead's devotees as a bunch of druggies, hustlers and losers.

After a few peace-and-love, we're-one-big-family testimonials, one Deadhead mom recalls amusement at her 13-year-old's dabbling with crack; a vendor then tells how he sleeps with a gun to ward off Deadhead robbers; and the next generation of Deadheads explains why they don't attend regular public schools.

The production will also prove unsettling for cineastes: Yes, it's entertaining in its own slapdash way, but Behar raises too many questions which remain unanswered.

Lensed a year before Garcia's death, Behar traveled from California parking lots to Boston's Sumner Tunnel to chat with Deadheads, most of whom look like leftover '60s hippies, with a few pierced eyebrows and shaved heads thrown in for '90s chic.

While the interviews are undeniably helter-skelter, there's a healthy range: tales of Deadheads in prison for drug sales segue to salesmen making big bucks from overpriced souvenirs (one guy estimates a $75,000 yearly income). Along the way, elderly general store clerks in Vermont relish a business boom from Deadheads; an 8-year-old heads to his 160th Dead show; and the son of legendary author and—Deadhead icon—Ken Kesey talks of his adopted "family."

Ironically, the son proves a more interesting subject than Dad, who's profiled in an accompanying 10-minute film, "A Conversation With Ken Kesey." Sadly, "Conversation" director Peter Shapiro specializes in static head shots and failing to put the writer's comments in perspective.

Relatively speaking, Behar proves more adept. But one can't help wishing he'd addressed some basics, such as how non-working Deadheads eat, or fill their gas tanks to get between concert venues.

More damning is the director's decision to never show Garcia or his band-mates, presumably to stress groupies over group. But how about putting a Grateful Dead song on the opening or closing credits?

Viewers need some connection with the subject of such undying adoration.

Equally frustrating is not having Garcia's death referenced in a preface or coda, bringing a dated feel to the production.

Clearly, the post-Garcia stories could justify a sequel. But if Behar opts to go behind, the camera again, a "Directing 101" refresher would be in order.

VILLAGE VOICE, 9/26/95, p. 75, Richard Gehr

Even tie-dye ain't what it used to be. Hippie nation's freak flag started out as the lovingly hand-tied and-dipped creations of someone's artistically inclined "old lady." Today's psychedelic sportswear is silk-screened for mass consumption. Sort of like post-"Touch of Grey" Deadhead culture itself.

Andrew Behar's sympathatic documentary about tour-culture, though, looks like the real thing. Beatific true believers, snaggle-toothed road gypsies, glassy-eyed cultists, adventurous nuclear families, spinning dervishes, fresh-faced daytrippers, visionary stoners, Ivy League stat-keepers, and greedy vendors all make their case for whatever it is they do at a Dead show. As a long-time Deadhead pal said when he saw this beautifully shot film, "There's road dust in every frame."

Strange attractors on America's cultural landscape for 30 years, the Grateful Dead provided the most subtly potent band-audience synergy in the history of rock. Which Is why the absence of their music in *Tie-Died*, presumably for economic reasons, seriously upends the film's reason for existence. Behar mainly makes do with the background pulse of parking-lot drum circles—hence the magnificent irony of the ersatz ethnicity running through this overwhelmingly white subculture.

In *A Conversion With Ken Kesey*, the Peter Shapiro short that precedes *Tie-Died*, the writer-dairy farmer's thumbnail appraisal of the Dead's appeal gracefully sets the stage for Behar's strange parade. Kesey's faith in the band's endurance, recorded before Jerry Garcia's death, of course, is a most Dead-worthy bitter-sweet reminder of death's merciless hand.

Also reviewed in:
CHICAGO TRIBUNE, 9/22/95, Friday/p. M, John Petrakis
NEW YORK TIMES, 9/22/95, p. C10, Janet Maslin
VARIETY, 2/20-26/95, p. 88, Emanuel Levy
WASHINGTON POST, 12/22/95, Weekend/p. 43, Kevin McManus
WASHINGTON POST, 12/25/95, p. D1, Richard Harrington

TIE THAT BINDS, THE

A Hollywood Pictures release of an Interscope Communications/PolyGram Filmed Entertainment production. *Executive Producer:* Ted Field, Jon Brown, and Robert W. Cort. *Producer:* David Madden, Patrick Markey, John Morrissey, and Susan Zachary. *Director:* Wesley Strick. *Screenplay:* Michael Auerbach. *Director of Photography:* Bobby Bukowski. *Editor:* Michael N. Knue. *Music:* Graeme Revell. *Music Editor:* Craig Pettigrew. *Sound:* Robert Eber and (music) Brian Masterson. *Sound Editor:* Steven D. Williams. *Casting:* Marci Liroff. *Production Designer:* Marcia Hinds-Johnson. *Art Director:* Bo Johnson. *Set Decorator:* Don Diers. *Set Dresser:* Jon P. Mooers. *Costumes:* Betsy Heimann. *Special Effects:* Richard Stutsman. *Make-up:* Jean A. Black. *Stunt Coordinator:* John Moio. *Running time:* 98 minutes. *MPAA Rating:* R.

CAST: Daryl Hannah (Leann Netherwood); Keith Carradine (John Netherwood); Moira Kelly (Dana Clifton); Vincent Spano (Russell Clifton); Julia Devin (Janie); Rray Reinhardt (Sam Bennett); Barbara Tarbuck (Jean Bennett); Ned Vaughn (Officer Carrey); Kerrie Cullen (Female Police Officer); Bob Minor (Male Police Officer); George Marshall Ruge (Detective 1); Tommy, Jr. Rosales (Detective 2); Laura Lee Kelly (Aide); Marquis Nunley (Boy Russell); Jenny Gago (Maggie); Carmen Argenziano (Phil Hawkes); Laurie Lathem (Alex); Willie Garson (Ray Tanton); Cynda Williams (Lisa-Marie Chandler); Bruce A. Young (Gil Chandler); Benjamin Mouton (Father in Restaurant); Jack Johnson (Boy in Restaurant); Melanie MacQueen (Waitress); Greg Collins (Bartender); Dana Gladstone (Dr. Brardford); Jesse Hays (Boy in School); Andrea Sandahl (Tina); Chris Ellis (Securtity Guard 1); Coleen Maloney (Security Guard 2); Shawn Rowe (Ogre's Wife); Melissa Hays (Princess); Steve Rosenbaum (The Ogre); Suzanne Krull (The Fox); Kevin Bourland (Man in Range Rover); Taylor Allbright (Girl in Schoolyard); Gene Lythgow (Detective Lorenz); Lynn Wanlass (Nurse); Kenny Alexander (Officer Wright).

LOS ANGELES TIMES, 9/9/95, Calendar/p. 4, Kevin Thomas

Sickeningly violent and relentlessly contrived, "The Tie That Binds," which opened Friday, may well be the most nauseating movie released by a major studio this year.

That's saying a lot, but keep in mind that this one centers on a 6-year-old child witnessing the most unspeakable acts of brutality for a good portion of its running time. No wonder Disney's Hollywood Pictures held off screening it long enough to prevent it from being reviewed on opening day.

Sleekly produced but blatantly obvious, it opens with a numbing double whammy. First, rampaging hippie-esque psychopaths John and Leann Netherwood (Keith Carradine, Daryl Hannah) rob and terrorize an older couple's in their home but are interrupted by the arrival of cops, who wind up with the crazed couple's little daughter Janie (Julia Devin)—and with the Netherwoods getting away. Second, at the police station the cops coldly snatch Janie's doll, provoking a way-over-the-top struggle on the child's part to get it back, involving some formidable stunt work.

When first-time director Wesley Strick (whose writing credits include "Wolf" and the "Cape Fear" remake) then cuts to Dana and Russell Clifton (Moira Kelly, Vincent Spano) driving and discussing adopting a child, writer Michael Auerbach telegraphs his entire plot. You know that the Cliftons are going to adopt Janie, and that after a terrific amount of violence and bloodshed, foreshadowed by that opening sequence, the Netherwoods will track down the Cliftons for a suitably savage standoff. The anticipation of all this does not generate Hitchcockian suspense but merely dread at its prospect.

What you don't anticipate, however, is just how full of holes the plot will be or how truly gory its unraveling or how stupid it will make the Cliftons look, despite the best efforts of Kelly and Spano, talented, personable and intelligent actors that they are.

The Cliftons opt for a public rather than private adoption because Russell, a contractor, is staving off bankruptcy. Questions about the couple's solvency aside, what right does any agency have in putting up for adoption the child of dangerous suspects who are on the loose—and not giving the prospective parents any inkling whatsoever that they and the child could be in very real danger?

If "The Tie That Binds" weren't such a numskull out-and-out exploitation picture it conceivably could have raised the issue of adoptive parents' right to know as much as possible about the child they intend to make their own, and also the special predicament of the endangered child ostensibly in official custody. In any event, the picture only gets progressively more protracted, dumber and bloodier. "The Tie That Binds" is one of those films that's so violent you have to wonder what the MPAA is saving its NC-17 rating for.

(To give credit where credit is due, it is stunningly photographed by Bobby Bukowski, who can count the notable Nancy Savoca films "Household Saints" and "Dogfight" among his worthier projects.)

Strick encourages Carradine and Hannah, both of whom have plenty of first-rate work to their credit, to pull out all the stops, creating a pair of monsters who would be laughable were not a child involved. Indeed, the film's one true note is the remarkable portrayal of little Julia Devin, who expresses convincingly and consistently the confusion, terror and conflicting emotions of all the terrible traumas that Janie has endured. You can only come away hoping that Devin herself has not been seriously affected by appearing in this sicko trash.

NEW YORK POST, 9/9/95, p. 17, Thelma Adams

In this corner are childless yuppie dream couple Russell and Dana Clifton (Vincent Spano and Moira Kelly). They're bright, they're emotionally connected and she's barren.

The Cliftons are too good to be true. "I can't seem to get in touch with my inner weasel," confesses Russ.

And in this corner are fertile felons from hell Leann and John Netherwood (Daryl Hannah and Keith Carradine). They're brazen, they're twisted and they have a darling little girl named Janie (Julia Devin) who has an unaccountable fear of the tooth fairy.

In Wesley Strick's "The Tie That Binds," the latest excusion in high-gloss yuppie horror, the real question is: Who are we supposed to root for, the yuppies or the yahoos?

Like "Pacific Heights" and "The Hand That Rocks the Cradle," this mildly entertaining thriller (which opened yesterday without advance screenings) plays on baby boomers' darkest fears. We've had Michael Keaton as the tenant from hell, and Rebecca De Mornay as the no-good nanny. Now, in the age of delayed parenthood, fertility clinics, and two-figure adoptions, along come the baddest possible birth parents.

John, the most demonic dad since Jack Nicholson started hearing voices in "The Shining," gives the prophetic advice: "[If] you take a kid from an orphanage, you make sure she's an orphan."

The Netherwoods leave their little precious parked in the back seat of their junker while terrorizing senior citizens in a late-night robbery. The police (forever inept in this genre) nab the 6-year-old, but her folks escape.

Flash forward to the Cliftons. Browsing the local orphanage, they fall for the fey but fearful Janie and take her back to their dream home. They should have known something was wrong when she was wearing prison-striped underwear.

The Netherwoods set out to get their little girl back. They're willing to shed a passel of plasma in order to get their flesh 'n' blood back. They might not set such a good example, but they're certainly devoted parents.

Spano and Kelly make attractive straight people, but the movie belongs to Hannah's spacy harridan and Carradine's carnivorous creep. Whether threatening the soft spot on a newborn's head to squeeze info out of his postpartum mom or toying with a cop who'd be better off dead, they take a joy in life for which the Cliftons can only pine.

NEWSDAY, 9/11/95, Part II/p. B7, Jack Mathews

In the unending quest for new twists to old thriller formulas, writer-director Wesley Strick has come up with one for "The Tie That Binds" that is stunning for its simplicity. It's a reverse "Bad Seed," the story of a perfectly wonderful child whose parents are meaner than a junkyard dog.

Of course, it doesn't make any sense, behavioral psychology-wise. What are the odds on a 6-year-old girl (Julia Devin) who's grown up in the backseat of stolen cars and whose parents are drifters, burglars and killers turning out so nice? She's like a feral child who emerges from a rabid wolf's hole and eats out of your hand.

"The Tie That Binds" pits psycho-parents Keith Carradine and Daryl Hannah against barren yuppies Vincent Spano and Moira Kelly, who become Janie's foster parents after her own are forced to make a hasty getaway from a robbery. Nothing complicated here; while the good parents bond with Janie, the bad parents are determined to track her down, leaving a trail of victims in their wake.

Carradine, usually cast as the low-keyed romantic, has unbridled fun playing a sadistic killer, and Hannah is genuinely creepy as a sociopath who sees herself as a contender for mother of the year. In fact, the performances are all fine. It is Strick's ludicrous script and his obvious direction (when architect Spano tells Janie to watch out for a hole in the floor of the upstairs bathroom, you can be sure someone will fall through it) that makes "The Tie That Binds" one of the year's must-skip movies.

Strick, making his debut as a director, has written several thrillers for seasoned directors—"Wolf" for Mike Nichols, "Cape Fear" for Martin Scorsese—but he saved his worst for himself.

SIGHT AND SOUND, 1/96, p. 56, Tom Tunney

Interrupted by the police during a violent break-in, itinerant criminals John and Leann Netherwood are forced to leave behind their six-year-old daughter Janie. She is subsequently adopted by Dana and Russell Clifton, a young middle-class couple who can't have any children of their own. Leann and John begin to track down Janie, murdering a policeman and an orphanage director along the way.

Though Janie starts to settle in with Dana and Russell, they are disturbed by the child's strange behaviour, which includes cutting her hands with a knife. They seek the help of their prosecutor friend Gil in tracing her biological parents. Russell matches Janie's pencil drawing of the "tooth fairy" with a computer mug shot of John. Leann makes an abortive attempt to abduct Janie from her school playground but is forced to flee alone when she's confronted at the gate by staff members. Realising that Janie's biological parents represent a real danger, Dana and Russell shift temporarily into Gil's home, while he and his wife, Lisa-Marie, go to hospital to await the birth of their child.

Ringing burglar alarms at Gil's house during the night are caused by a faulty window shutter, but the family move to another house which Russell is building. By threatening Lisa-Marie's newborn baby, John and Leann discover Janie's whereabouts and confront the other couple. John's plan to kill Dana and Russell and set fire to the building is frustrated when he puts a plastic bag on Dana's head that provokes Janie into attacking him. Russell breaks free but is subdued.

Leann keeps Janie and Dana at bay in a room downstairs, but when she sees the obvious devotion of Dana to the child, she realises that she's lost the battle for her affection. When she attempts to stop John entering the room he breaks her neck. Dana and Janie escape through a hole in the wall, pursued by John. However, when he catches up to them, the little girl stabs him in the stomach. He attempts to grab her but, just in time, Russell arrives to kill him with a blow to the head.

Wesley Strick scripted the 1991 version of *Cape Fear*, so it's surprising that his debut as a director should betray such a fundamental misunderstanding of all the rules of suspense. Suspense should be about manipulating the audience, teasing and deceiving and then finally satisfying our desire to be surprised. Unfortunately, apart from one tiny twist at the end, this film holds no surprises whatsoever.

Two of the movie's producers were responsible for *The Hand That Rocks the Cradle*. However, since that film was released in 1992, there's been many similarly-plotted psycho-killer movies involving the cop, the neighbor, the secretary and the kid from hell. One would expect a film made this late in the cycle to have something new to offer. Not so—this is a movie which sets up its crazy killer premise in its opening scene and then simply joins up all the dots.

Rather than attempting to disguise the obviousness of the script, Strick chooses to accentuate it. John's arrival in the orphanage director's office and Leann's sneaking into the hospital ward are utterly suspense-free. We half see them walk in and know who they are. And then they do the usual nasty things we've seen in all those other boring psycho-killer movies. There is a certain perverse satisfaction in guessing what will happen next and being proved right every time, but after about half an hour even that becomes tedious.

Strick racks up the sound level for John's brutal manhandling of his victims and in these scenes of crashing physical terror, the film could justly be accused of celebrating violence for its own sake. His over-use of abruptly cutting from these scenes (rather than seeing Officer Carrey's throat slit there's a cut to a blank screen, for instance) flashily draws attention to itself without imbuing the drama with any genuine shock value. His claim in the production notes to have told the story from the child's point of view is flatly contradicted by the consistently adult's eye-level objectivity of his camera.

One genuine point of interest however is the casting of Keith Carradine as Netherwood. Carradine's hippy unkempt appearance here, allied to his status as 70s icon (derived from his many high profile roles in the films of Robert Altman and Alan Rudolph) make it impossible not to think that his character is at least partly inspired by Charles Manson. John Netherwood is present as a purely elemental force of destruction. He descends swiftly on his suburban victims, shows no pity and has no sense of a larger social responsibility. He's a predator pure and simple and, importantly, Leann is presented less as his wife than as his willing disciple. His habit of taking snapshots of his victims is a grotesque parody of family values and if the film-makers hadn't weighed down their story with that dire adopting-couple hook, it could have spun off creatively into the same savagely satiric territory as *True Romance* or *Natural Born Killers*.

Rather than that kind of dangerous movie-making, Strick obviously just wants to replicate the success of *The Hand That Rocks the Cradle* and *Cape Fear*. So, there's the ideal middle-class couple in their ideal (but symbolically only half-built) middle-class house who defend their ideal middle-class values against an external (and lower-class) threat. The fact that the danger comes from the biological parents of the child is the film's one novel ingredient and should have been a fruitful area to explore. The orphanage director talks of "buyers' remorse", when Russell and Dana query the background of their child. A revealing contrast between two people who regard even children as a form of economic consumption and a poorer couple who believe in blood ties above all else is thus fleetingly suggested, but the idea isn't developed.

Instead, all that's on offer are the usual cosy platitudes: "We're all together and we're going to stay together," says Russell, while John is presented with a complete lack of social context. The issues of why he does what he does, why he stays with his wife and is so obsessed with his daughter are never explored. He's simply an all-purpose monster, the bogeyman who doesn't belong in the suburbs and has to be kept out at all costs.

Strick does falteringly attempt to present the tale as a modern day fairy story. A children's pantomime featured in the story is actually scarier than anything in the drama proper, while the final chase through the woods, complete with insert shots of wild life, seems to be a deliberate nod to *Night of the Hunter*. Of course, in that movie it was the greedy stepfather who was the evil force. Perhaps it's telling us something about modern consumerism that now it's the improvished natural father who's the villain and the upwardly mobile adoptive father who's the good guy. "I hate dream homes!" cries Netherwood in the film's most memorable line—perhaps he's seen too many predictable Hollywood thrillers.

Also reviewed in:
CHICAGO TRIBUNE, 9/11/95, Tempo/p.5, Mark Caro
NEW YORK TIMES, 9/9/95, p. 14, Stephen Holden
VARIETY, 9/11-17/95, p. 105, Todd McCarthy
WASHINGTON POST, 9/9/95, p. D2, Hal Hinson

TO DIE FOR

A Columbia Pictures release in association with Rank Film Distributors. *Executive Producer:* Jonathan Taplin and Joseph M. Caracciolo. *Producer:* Laura Ziskin. *Director:* Gus Van Sant. *Screenplay:* Buck Henry. *Based on the novel by:* Joyce Maynard. *Director of Photography:* Eric Alan Edwards. *Editor:* Curtiss Clayton. *Music:* Danny Elfman. *Music Editor:* Ellen Segal. *Sound:* Robert Fernandez and Bill Jackson. *Sound Editor:* Kelley Baker. *Casting:* Howard Feuer. *Production Designer:* Missy Stewart. *Art Director:* Vlasta Svoboda. *Set Decorator:* Carol A. Lavoie. *Special Effects:* Laird McMurray. *Costumes:* Beatrix Aruna Pasztor. *Make-up:* Patricia Green. *Running time:* 103 minutes. *MPAA Rating:* R.

CAST: Nicole Kidman (Suzanne Stone); Matt Dillon (Larry Maretto); Joaquin Phoenix (Jimmy Emmett); Casey Affleck (Russell Hines); Illeana Douglas (Janice Maretto); Alison Folland (Lydia Mertz); Dan Hedaya (Joe Maretto); Wayne Knight (Ed Grant); Kurtwood Smith (Earl Stone); Holland Taylor (Carol Stone); Susan Traylor (Faye Stone); Maria Tucci (Angela Maretto); Tim Hopper (Mike Warden); Michael Rispoli (Ben DeLuca); Buck Henry (Mr. Finlaysson); Gerry Quigley (George); Tom Forrester and Alan Edward Lewis (Fishermen); Nadine MacKinnon (Sexy Woman); Conrad Coates (Weaselly Guy); Ron Gabriel (Sal); Ian Heath, Graeme Millington, and Sean Ryan (Students); Nicholas Pasco (Detective); Joyce Maynard (Lawyer); David Collins, Eve Crawford, and Janet Lo (Reporters); David Cronenberg (Man at Lake); Tom Quinn (Skating Promoter); Peter Glenn (Priest); Amber-Lee Campbell (Suzanne, age 5); Colleen Williams (Valerie Mertz); Simon Richards (Chester); Philip Williams (Babe Hines); Susan Backs (June Hines); Kyra Harper (Mary Emmett); Adam Roth and Andrew Scott (Band Members); Tamara Gorski, Katie Griffin, and Carla Renee (Girls at Bar); Misha (Walter).

CHRISTIAN SCIENCE MONITOR, 9/26/95, p. 13, David Sterritt

Most satires of mass-media entertainment, like "Network" and "The Player," aim their humor at large-scale institutions with lots of money and clout. In real life, though, much of the media's noise can be traced to more marginal sources, from the drone of radio news stations to the low-budget oddities found on local cable shows.

"To Die For," directed by Gus Van Sant from a mischievous screenplay by Buck Henry, sets its sights on the most modest brand of media madness. The heroine is Suzanne, an aspiring TV personality who enters the job market armed with a junior-college degree and enough blind ambition to motivate an army of would-be stars.

Knowing that her inevitable success may be preceded by a tiny bit of time at the bottom of the ladder, she lands her first job at a New Hampshire cable station that needs a weatherperson for its evening newscast. Between her smiley-faced pronouncements about sun, clouds, and rain, she works on projects meant as springboards to higher things—which much amuses her boss, who respects her gumption but recognizes her limitations far better than she does.

Her career goes nowhere, and since the fault couldn't possibly lie in her own shortcomings, she starts looking for someone to blame. The likeliest prospect is her new husband, an easygoing guy whose laid-back manner is the opposite of her high-energy approach to life, love, and work. Already dissatisfied with him as a mate, Suzanne has used her latest news project—interviews with high-schoolers about their bored, aimless lives—to launch an extramarital affair with a boy who's even dimmer and duller than she is. Why not cajole him into eliminating her irksome spouse, whereupon her career will surely rocket to the lofty orbit for which it's destined?

Many of the funniest scenes in "To Die For" depict Suzanne's professional life, contrasting her optimistic dreams with the workaday reality of a low-glamour job on a no-glamour channel that cares less about setting the world on fire than just staying in business for the immediate future.

The movie ranges far beyond media satire, though, reserving its most cutting sarcasm for the middle-class milieu in which Suzanne and her family live. They're ordinary folks with ordinary homes, jobs, and problems, and they sincerely see themselves as decent citizens from head to toe.

What they don't perceive are the signs of greed, sexism, ethnic prejudice, and other ills that run subtly through the fabric of their lives—reaching a harrowing high point in Suzanne's murderous plot and the daunting deceptions that spring from it.

The filmmakers perceive these ills most clearly indeed, and explore them with blasts of withering humor. Nothing is spared, from the WASPish attitudes of the older generation to the lunk-headed foolishness of the high school crowd.

As in other Van Sant movies, such as "Drugstore Cowboy" and "My Own Private Idaho," the world of middle-class normality turns out to be less "normal" than it would like to believe, fostering urges and behaviors that are promptly wished away as too unpleasant or unsettling to contemplate. In such surroundings anything can happen.

This said, the sardonically titled "To Die For" is less biting in its views than Van Sant's previous pictures, which went further in probing the breadth and depth of contemporary American experience.

Making a commercial comedy like this is certainly a good career move for Van Sant, after the commercial and critical disaster of his recent "Even Cowgirls Get the Blues," but fans of his usually subversive cinematics should know he's on his best (i.e. most conventional) behavior this time around.

In keeping with this strategy, he puts less weight on visual style than on story and dialogue—which are charged with the darkly comic mood Henry has been cultivating since "The Graduate" almost 30 years ago. (Some critics have drawn comparisons with the Pamela Smart murder case of 1990.)

Nicole Kidman gives her most effective screen performance to date as Suzanne, making her irresistible and infuriating at the same time. Matt Dillon continues his long Van Sant collaboration with a smartly self-effacing portrayal of the ill-fated husband, and Illeana Douglas couldn't be better as his ever-suspicious sister. Special mention also goes to Joaquin Phoenix, who is poignantly good as the boyfriend with an itchy trigger finger.

The supporting cast was skillfully chosen, and Eric Alan Edwards's cinematography does an extraordinary job of bringing out the dangerous side of pastels—exactly the sort of touch Van Sant plans and executes with exquisite care, giving even his most lightweight movies an extra measure of sly significance.

LOS ANGELES TIMES, 9/27/95, Calendar/p. 1, Kenneth Turan

"To Die For" isn't afraid of the dark. A smart black comedy that skewers America's fatal fascination with television and celebrity, it employs an unerring nasty touch to parody our omnipresent culture of fame. And it uses a rather unlikely combination of talents to do the job.

Star Nicole Kidman, director Gus Van Sant and screenwriter Buck Henry have difficulty fitting into the same sentence, let alone the same film about a creature of the media whose mad passion for the limelight is as addictive as a drug. But, brought together by producer Laura Ziskin, they create the kind of unexpected synergy that Time Warner-Turner might copy.

Though he had an acting role in Van Sant's bloated "Even Cowgirls Get the Blues," screenwriter Buck Henry, whose credits date to "The Graduate," does not mimic the director's sensibility. His dialogue is clever and witty, he's at ease with parody and he knows how to skillfully adapt a novel, in this case pumping up the humor in Joyce Maynard's devilish book, which in turn was suggested by a real-life New England scandal of a few years back.

Working with a tight, classically structured script is definitely a departure for Van Sant, known for loopy, eccentric films like,"My Own Private Idaho." But the director was unexpectedly charged by the experience, adding his trademark absurdist sensibility to the mix as well as an empathy for inarticulate, inchoate teenagers that turns out to give this film a good deal of its impact.

Placing Nicole Kidman (who tends to be identified with films like "Days of Thunder" and "Far and Away," which she co-starred in with husband, Tom Cruise) in this company may seem like a stretch, but the opposite turns out to be true. Known as a more adventurous actress in her earlier career in Australia, Kidman's perfectly pitched comic performance, as fearless as it is poisonous, ends up being the kind of nervy knockout the film couldn't succeed without.

Using a dead-on American accent, Kidman plays Suzanne Maretto, formerly Suzanne Stone, who, "To Die For" immediately reveals, has brought an unlooked-for note of scandal to the town of Little Hope, N.H. Her husband, Larry, has been murdered, and America's tabloids, both print and TV, can't get enough of the possibility that Mrs. Maretto had a very particular hand in his death.

Suzanne is introduced doing what she loves best, talking to a camera and telling her version of the events leading up to what she demurely lowers her eyes and calls "my recent tragedy." But, she admits, brightening immediately, the situation is not without benefits for someone who believes, as Suzanne absolutely does, "You're not anybody in America if you're not on TV. What's the point of doing anything worthwhile if nobody's watching?"

Not necessarily agreeing are Suzanne's friends and relatives, whose on-camera reminiscences are intercut with conventional flashbacks and talk show appearances in "To Die For's" always involving structure. Through these multiple viewpoints we get a picture of a cold steel magnolia whose happy face passion for television celebrity flabbergasts everyone who comes into contact with her, a woman you say no to completely at your own risk.

Most taken with Suzanne, or "Sooze" as he calls her, is her husband, Larry (convincingly played by Matt Dillon), the kind of regular guy who is surprised to realize that artificial plants in the family Italian restaurant will eliminate the need for water. Though his suspicious sister Janice (a breakthrough role for Illeana Douglas) is dubious, Larry sees Suzanne as the kind of delicate golden girl he wants to take care of forever.

Seeing a more relentless side of Suzanne is Ed Grant (Wayne Knight), the station manager at WWEN, the local no-watt cable access channel that advertised for a gofer and ended up with a zealous self-described "on-air correspondent." Inevitably giving in to Suzanne's tireless pestering he lets her do the weather, which she treats with the gravity of the Normandy invasion, and then tentatively OKs a documentary on local high school kids called Teens Speak Out.

The teens in question, scuzzy pals Jimmy (Joaquin Phoenix), Lydia (Alison Folland) and Russell (Casey Affleck), are wistful losers who, as Ed Grant rightly comments, "would have a major struggle reciting the days of the week." But Suzanne, bless her, takes them seriously as career advancement fodder. Then, when husband Larry foolishly takes a stab at derailing her career plans, she realizes they might be useful in other ways as well.

The most accurate assault against the media age since "Network," "To Die For's" killer lines and wicked sensibility are given added poignancy by the off-center, sensitive performance of Joaquin Phoenix, River's younger brother, the only person more deluded about Suzanne than she is about herself. Told with a panache that extends from the opening credits to its closing frames, "To Die For" plays its themes for everything they're worth, and, regrettably, they seem to be worth more every day.

NEW YORK, 10/2/95, p. 81, David Denby

Suzanne Stone (Nicole Kidman), the New England beauty and weather girl who idolizes Jane Pauley, has reddish-blonde hair in a gossamer bob and a long, slender body sheathed in floral-print suits. Suzanne talks in a perky yet soft-breathing voice, crisp but never too insistent, the best voice for "maximizing" her abundant "career opportunities." Suzanne longs to be a "media professional." That's her only desire, though she is also a daughter, a wife (to Matt Dillon), and several other, more sinister things. Working at a local cable station in Little Hope, New Hampshire, Suzanne flirts her way through the weather report and then parades across the bedraggled town in an aura of spectacular grooming. She's clean and everything nice, the American girl and housewife with ambition in her brain and murder and greed in her heart.

At least that's the way we're meant to take her in Gus Van Sant's new movie To Die For, which turns out to be disappointingly cold and only distantly satirical. No one would argue that Van Sant and veteran screenwriter Buck Henry, adapting Joyce Maynard's journalistic novel, are not onto something real. At times, in recent years, it has seemed as if the media had eaten America whole. For millions of people, what happens on television, the "personalities" on TV, and, most of all, the opportunity to be on television are existence transfigured. "You aren't really anybody in America if you're not on TV," says Suzanne. "Because what's the point of doing anything worthwhile if nobody's watching?" Which is an extremely stupid remark but impossible to answer. To Die For is set in a dim, demoralized world—our world—in which exhibitionism has burned away shame, and Tonya and Nancy, Lyle and Erik, Amy and Joey reign supreme, not only to be enjoyed but to be emulated. No one around Suzanne has any culture, drives, or hopes.

According to the filmmakers, the box has sucked the vitality out of ordinary Americans. There is TV, and there is everything else—that is, nothing else.

But when filmmakers make their characters flat and affectless, then claim that television is doing it to them, you have the right to be suspicious. *To Die For* is clever but thin and redundant; the satire works intermittently and opportunistically, and some of the picture is just plain sour. Van Sant hits his peak right at the beginning of the movie. An apparent suspect in the murder of her husband, Suzanne passes through a brief and exuberant life as a tabloid superstar. She poses, she preens, she's "surprised" by the photographer. All through this scintillating episode, which is urged along by Danny Elfman's impish music and brilliantly edited by Curtiss Clayton, our heroine talks straight into the camera, narrating her life. Immediately, we see that this pastel-pink creature isn't going to make it as a star—she's too avid, too ignorant, a *Cosmo*-cover pea brain. But that's all we ever see in Suzanne. Tossing her hair and winking at us with her voice, Nicole Kidman appears to be spoofing Ann-Margret in her *Kitten With a Whip* period. She gives a knowing but monotonous performance. Van Sant just doesn't love Suzanne enough to make us care about her. She's an object, a symbol. She could be the stepdaughter of Faye Dunaway's Diana Christianson in *Network,* a powerful TV executive about whom it was said, "The only reality she knows comes to her over the TV set."

Buck Henry started out in satirical-slapstick TV in the early sixties and then wrote *The Graduate* and the screen adaptation of *Catch-22.* Van Sant has made sympathetic, fine-grained movies about addicts *(Drugstore Cowboy)* and sex hustlers *(My Own Private Idaho).* In other words, an old hipster has joined hands with a young hipster, and together they have vented their disgust at square America. Satire, which often depends on dropping a dimension or two, doesn't have to be fair, and this movie has some grotesquely funny moments. But Henry and Van Sant have hollowed Suzanne out, as if an ambitious, driven woman needed to be exposed as a jerk. Vaguely feminist emotions stir in my breast: Would they have done this to Matt Dillon if he were the ambitious one?

The hollowing-out leaves a huge dramatic hole. This bright-smiling zombie lives in a realistic world, and nothing she does makes any sense. Looking at Suzanne, we can't tell, for instance, why she marries Matt Dillon's ordinary-Joe restaurateur, a young man who, apart from his good looks, is patently too slow for her. Does she have any sexual feelings for him, or is she faking her way through that too? Recoiling from her husband, who wants children, Suzanne falls in with a trio of sad-sack, alienated, small-town white-trash teens. She seduces them and uses them. Lydia (Alison Folland), a heavy, depressed girl, develops a crush on Suzanne; so does Jimmy (Joaquin Phoenix, River's brother), who speaks out of a thick mental fog and has a harelip. Darkly, suddenly unhappy, these kids are deglamorized versions of the drifting, dreamy youths of Van Sant's earlier movies. He doesn't satirize them; they're too desperately vulnerable and needy. Instead, he treats them tenderly, and for a while, these characters become touching, especially Jimmy, whom no one has ever considered anything but stupid. When we first see him, he lives in an erotic daze: Masturbation may be the only thing holding him to life. Suzanne talks nice to him, and suddenly she's no longer a babe in his dreams but a woman right there in his bed. Poor Jimmy! He's not just a classic sap who falls for a bad girl; he's blissfully, almost disturbingly happy. His joy is the only sincere emotion in the movie, the only time the hollow derision stops.

But what are Suzanne's feelings for *him?* Does he represent some sort of sexual liberation for her? (If she only wants to use Jimmy, she sleeps with him more than she needs to.) Van Sant never shows us. And since we never feel any complicity with her overwhelming desire for success, we don't suffer when she steps over the line into criminality. Rather than challenge the audience, Van Sant has given us a condescending look at a self-deluded loser. For all its jokes, *To Die For,* a case of hipster malice, remains stonily superior to its subject.

NEW YORK POST, 9/27/95, p. 37, Michael Medved

Nicole Kidman has been nibbling at the edges of stardom for some six years, ever since her attention-getting turn in "Dead Calm." "To Die For" is the film that will place her, at age 27, squarely and irrevocably in the Hollywood big time. Never again can she be dismissed, in the supermarket tabloids or anywhere else, as "Mrs. Tom Cruise."

Her performance here is an Oscar-worthy marvel, creating an altogether absorbing character who is simultaneously chilling, vicious, vulnerable, irresistibly sexy and, in spite of herself, deeply, unforgettably funny.

Suzanne Stone lives in the dreary, symbolically-named town of Little Hope, N.H., but from earliest childhood she's convinced of her destiny as a top TV journalist.

"She's gonna be the next Barbara Walters," says Larry Maretto (Matt Dillon), who's so smitten with her drive and beauty that he defies his protective parents (Dan Hedaya and Maria Tucci) and worried sister (the excellent Illeana Douglas) to marry her.

Shortly after the wedding, Suzanne seems to justify her husband's high hopes by winning a job as the smiling weather-girl on a local cable channel, but she's soon embarrassed by his beer-guzzling, salt-of-the-earth habits and his job at his parents' prosperous Italian restaurant.

While shooting a TV documentary about the "Voices of Today's Teens" she forms an erotically charged connection with a pair of sullen high school losers (Joaquin Phoenix and Alison Folland), who are drawn into her schemes to escape to California and inevitable stardom.

Director Gus Van Sant ("Drug Store Cowboy," "My Own Private Idaho") tells this cruel tale (from the novel by Joyce Maynard, which was loosely based on the real-life case of a teacher who persuaded her teen-age lover to murder her husband) through a series of after-the-fact, tabloid TV-style interviews with all of the principals.

Suzanne in particular comes across with memorable tidbits of "media savvy" wisdom, like the observation that "Mr. Gorbachev would have still been in power today if he'd done what so many people suggested and gotten rid of that purple thing on his forehead" or the conclusion that "You're not anybody in America unless you're on TV. What's the point of doing anything worthwhile if nobody's watching?"

Certainly, the camera is watching Kidman as director Van Sant makes tireless, voyeuristic love to her remarkable face and form; Kidman's perfectly sculpted legs—clad in a dazzling and endless array of short, tightly clinging pastel outfits—may never have gotten more adoring exposure than they receive here.

However, Kidman's clothes—how could a character in her situation possibly have afforded them? point up one of the several lapses in logic that mar an otherwise marvelous movie.

More seriously, there's no explanation at all as to why a ruthlessly ambitious and pretentious femme fatale like Suzanne (whose little dog is named "Walter" after Mr. Cronkite) would ever have chosen the husband that she did.

In addition, in its ambition to be a piece of social commentary, the picture suffers from the same contradictions that characterized "Natural Born Killers": assaulting trashy TV obsessions at the same time that it inevitably celebrates (and exploits) them.

Nevertheless, it's difficult to resist even a flagrantly flawed film when it's electrified by a starring performance of such skillful subtlety and high-voltage magnetism.

As someone eyeing one of Kidman's pastel party frocks might say, it's to die for.

NEWSDAY, 9/27/95, Part II/p. B7, Jack Mathews

As America attends to the final arguments of the O.J. Simpson trial, the TV Show of the Century in which everyone from immigrant maids to limo drivers has had their promised 15 minutes of fame, it is fitting to find Gus Van Sant's devilish black comedy, "To Die For," arriving in theaters.

Written by Buck Henry, with pen and teeth equally sharpened, "To Die For" is the last word in doom-saying about the TV Age. It is a wicked and very, very funny satire about the effects of television on our culture, not because of the content that has Bob Dole doing impressions of Chicken Little, but because of the ludicrous amount of fame, wealth and power that is bestowed on those who carve out a place in it.

You've seen what the Simpson case has done for such bottom-feeders as Faye Resnick, Kato Kaelin and Mark Fuhrman ('Tis better to have shamed for fame, than never to have testified at all, Tennyson might have said). Imagine what the promise of TV fame can do to a natural blonde with the face of Deborah Norville and the ambition of Delilah.

That's just what Henry and Van Sant have done. "To Die For," featuring a breakout performance by Nicole Kidman, is the story of a TV monster, a woman raised and nurtured by the tube to ascend to that highest calling of news anchor, a role she will play if she has to kill someone.

Kidman's portrayal of the sociopathic Suzanne Stone is as cheeky as Henry's script. She's having a ton of fun walking in those shoes, strutting in those tight skirts, flirting with those comically bedroom eyes. Suzanne is an airhead, all right, but only in terms of her qualifications for the job she covets. She wouldn't know Bosnia from Banff, but she knows the ropes, and how to hang folks from them.

Told in a faux documentary style, "To Die For" opens with Suzanne enthusiastically speaking into the camera about things unspeakable. Her husband has been murdered, she stands accused, and it's pretty clear to the others interviewed on camera—particularly her disgusted sister-in-law (Illeana Douglas)—that she's guilty as charged.

The flashbacks between the interviews amount to something like an A&E biography of a notorious and, in this instance, proud criminal. Suzanne, we learn, is a woman whose need for adoration is a glass that's never filled. Larry Maretto (Matt Dillon), a decent working-class stiff who falls profoundly in love with her, does his best to massage her ego, but on the first night of their honeymoon she's sneaking out of the room to hustle some executives at a TV convention being held at the same hotel.

Nothing can deter her from her goal. She takes every humiliation as a valuable lesson, every rejection as a faint compliment. But when her husband becomes more of a nuisance than a fan, it's time for drastic action, and the three naive teenagers with whom she's making a video documentary are perfect pawns for a perfect crime.

Van Sant was clearly a gun for hire on this project. It's a major-studio movie, and after last year's disastrous "Even Cowgirls Get the Blues," he needed to prove that he could be trusted with an investor's money. Van Sant's faithful, who prize his scruffy looks at the victims of society's underbelly, may be disappointed by the slickness and commercial narrative of "To Die For."

But the film really belongs to Buck Henry, an elfin wit who has put his riotous touches on everything from political satire (the '60s TV show "That Was the Week That Was") to pop-culture commentary (he co-wrote "The Graduate"). "To Die For" deals with the same modern "crime pays" issues lanced in Oliver Stone's creepy "Natural Born Killers," but with enough detached perspective and humor to allow us to enjoy it without feeling like criminals ourselves.

NEWSWEEK, 10/2/95, p. 86, David Ansen

If you're looking for a warm and fuzzy movie, *To Die For* is not for you. The milk of human kindness does not flow from this very funny collaboration between director Gus Van Sant and writer Buck Henry, and that's one of the things that makes it refreshing. Satire has never been Hollywood's genre of choice, and it seems more endangered than ever in an era of talk-show confession, victimology (those poor Menendez boys!) and political correctness—an era inimical to the form's hanging-judge inclinations. The satirist looks down on his subjects, and this is not a nice thing to do if you think art's job is only to empower and ennoble. The trouble is we've left mean-spiritedness to the politicians, where it can do real damage. In the hands of an artist, a blast of nastiness can clear the mind of cant.

The target of "To Die For's" barbed wit is the American addiction to media celebrity. "What's the point of doing anything worthwhile if it's not on TV?" ponders Suzanne Stone (Nicole Kidman), the movie's fiercely ambitious anti-heroine. Suzanne wants to become the next Barbara Walters; she settles, for starters, as the weathergirl on the local cable station in her hometown, Little Hope, N.H. Suzanne, however, perceives an impediment to her aspirations—her adoring but less than brilliant husband, Larry Maretto (Matt Dillon), who wants her to bear his children and help him run his restaurant. Larry will have to go. To help her dispatch her hubby, this perky *femme fatale* enlists the support of three grungy high-school students who've signed up to star in her documentary about local teenagers. She unleashes her considerable sexual powers on these hapless low-rent kids—and they're putty in her hands.

Van Sant and Henry—taking off from a Joyce Maynard novel that was based on a real-life murder case—start their story after Suzanne's arrest, when everyone involved in the lurid affair is available for TV interviews. Thus the movie itself begins to take the form of a deranged episode of "Hard Copy." Everyone gets into the act: the parents of the victim and the accused rehash the tragedy on talk shows; Larry's sister Janice (the marvelously embittered Illeana

Douglas) dishes the despised Suzanne for the news crews; and the two dazed, out-of-it teens (Alison Folland and Joaquin Phoenix—River's younger brother) who fell in love with her awkwardly submit to the media's prying eye, eager to acquire their 15 minutes of fame. But it is Suzanne herself-putting on her best camera face to justify herself—who is the principal anchorwoman of her own story. Henry's script gleefully lets her hang herself with every media-savvy, self-improvement cliché in her arsenal.

Those who know Kidman only from her one-dimensional roles in "Far and Away" and "Batman Forever" are in for a treat: she's a smashing comedienne. The movie wouldn't work if Kidman overplayed her hand, condescending to the role. But she invests Suzanne with a deliciously self-deluded conviction, a cheerleader's witchy mixture of genuine naiveté, calculated sexuality and lethal cunning. She's a hoot.

It's a surprising movie from Van Sant too. Gone is the wiggy lyricism of "Drugstore Cowboy" and "My Own Private Idaho," replaced by a remarkably disciplined black-comic edge. The imprint of Henry's sardonic intelligence is obvious, but you can feel Van Sant's touch most strongly in the spooky pathos of Phoenix's odd and affecting performance (he's literally blurry with lust) and newcomer Folland's poignant portrayal of the abused Lydia. By the end, you realize the movie has slyly anatomized the class resentments of an entire community. In another director's hands, "To Die For's" satirical venom could have turned sour and obvious. Propelled by a steady stream of subtle jokes, Van Sant, Henry and their excellent company have conjured up a smart and wicked delight.

SIGHT AND SOUND, 11/95, p. 51, Philip Kemp

A worldwide media sensation erupts over a murder case concerning Suzanne Stone, glamorous weather presenter on the local cable TV station in Little Hope, New Hampshire. While Suzanne's relatives, in-laws and others involved in the case are interviewed on television, she herself narrates her story to an unseen listener ...

Ambitious and television-fixated from an early age, Suzanne is briefly diverted from her chosen career by falling for Larry Maretto, whose parents run the town's Italian restaurant. Despite the warnings of his sister Janice, a budding ice-skater, Larry marries Suzanne. On their honeymoon in Florida, while Larry goes deep-sea fishing, Suzanne ingratiates herself with a top television personality at a convention. Back in Little Hope, Suzanne bulldozes her way into the cable station WWEN, secures the job of weather presenter and bombards station head Ed Grant with ideas for programmes. He reluctantly approves a project involving high school kids, and she recruits three no-hopers: Jimmy, Russell and Lydia. Fascinated by her apparent interest in them, the three become devotedly attached to her.

Larry, urged on by his parents, is eager to start a family. Seeing her career threatened, Suzanne seduces Jimmy and tells him Larry mistreats her. Jimmy and Russell borrow a gun belonging to Lydia's father, break into the house and shoot Larry dead. With the aid of WWEN's taped footage, the police soon trace the teenagers and extract confessions from them, but Suzanne asserts her innocence, and is released on bail. In a television interview she claims that Larry was a junkie and that Jimmy and Russell were his suppliers. Completing her account of events to a camcorder, Suzanne takes the tape and drives to meet a man claiming to be a Hollywood producer. The man, a mafia operative, later phones Larry's father to report that Suzanne is safely under the ice of a frozen lake. While Lydia makes her first television appearance as a consultant on teenage dieting, Janice Maretto happily skates over the lake.

The message of *To Die For*—that the media, and television in particular, are threatening to usurp every alternative take on events—isn't so far from that of *Natural Born Killers*. But where Stone slammed his points relentlessly home, incurring the very faults he aimed to castigate, Van Sant's film skips playfully over the same territory, keeping its satire lightfooted and lethal. With Van Sant's idiosyncratic visual flair yoked to a sharp script from Buck Henry, it's easily his best work since *Drugstore Cowboy*, redeeming the chaotic waywardness of *Even Cowgirls Get the Blues*.

"I always knew who I was, and who I wanted to be," Suzanne confides to her unseen listener, adding later, "On TV is where we learn about who we really are." The contradiction is only apparent, since in her mind Suzanne has always been on television; for her, no other world exists. ("You aren't really anybody in America if you're not on TV," she tells Lydia.) Nicole Kidman plays her not merely as a bimbo, but as a woman who has concentrated down to one obsessively narrow focus, leaving herself brain-and-heart-dead outside it. At one point, as Larry talks to her about having kids, her subjective-angle shot of him shrinks to a tight circle around his head—expressive both of the gun she plans to have aimed at him, and of her tunnel-vision.

Kidman's exactly gauged—and very funny—performance is matched by those of her co-actors, none of whom is allowed to go over the top. Matt Dillon works a sympathetic variation on his preening grunge-rocker from *Singles*, genuinely touching in his starry-eyed inability to recognise the monster he's married to. There's a fine display of caustic disbelief from Illeana Douglas as his sister Janice, and an unbilled George Segal puts in a creepily avancular appearance as a predatory television star. As Lydia, the student least likely to, Alison Folland makes an impressive screen debut: graceless, lumpy, her mouth permanently adroop, she trots round after Suzanne in doggy devotion, seeing everything and understanding nothing.

Much of *To Die For*'s mordant wit derives from its fluent editing, deftly juxtaposing the various displaced narratives—voice-over, screen interview, reported speech—with the deglamourised reality. "It was the most exciting time of my life," Lydia's voice-over tells us, as we see her drearily minding Suzanne's lapdog while Suzanne and Jimmy are exercising the bedsprings. As Larry begs abjectly for his life before being blown away, the scene is intercut with Suzanne on television, concluding her usual weather report with a fulsome "special greeting to my husband", having chosen their first wedding anniversary for his death date.

These gags, glittering black comedy in themselves, are also intrinsic to the film's theme—that television, far from offering access to some inner truth, as Suzanne believes, distorts and devalues, sacrificing insight to facile celebrity. Even the most unpromising material can be turned to account. At the end of the film, with Suzanne dead, Lydia of all people is groomed for telestardom. As we watch, her image quadruples and finally fills the screen in multiple postage-stamp reproduction. Meanwhile Suzanne gazes sightlessly out through the ice—preserved, as she always wished, in frozen perfection behind a transparent screen.

VILLAGE VOICE, 10/3/95, p. 82, Amy Taubin

While *To Die For* is just the film Hollywood wanted Gus Van Sant to make, fans of his great *Mala Noche* and *My Own Private Idaho* or even that relative crowd pleaser *Drugstore Cowboy* may be more dubious about this basically conventional and extremely nasty bit of fluff. Screenwriter Buck Henry gooses up Joyce Maynard's fictionalized account of the Pamela Smart case (Smart, a New Hampshire schoolteacher, seduced her teenage lover into killing her husband) with dollops of *Disclosure* and *Natural Born Killers*. But for all *To Die For*'s cutely intimate asides to the camera and slightly elliptical editing, its parody of a TV-obsessed culture is tired, and its slagging off on Hollywood's favorite target—the ambitious woman—is misogyny at its lowest. Pamela Smart may have been a murderous, child abusing sociopath, and stupid to boot, but she deserved better than this. (I hated myself afterward for having laughed at all.)

Van Sant revels in making Smart—here named Suzanne Stone and played by Nicole Kidman, who will probably, parlay her tight-lipped cock-tease into an Academy Award nomination—grotesquely camped figure. He hates her and he envies her small seductive power. (The barely hidden message of the film: A boy who allows a woman to get her mouth on his cock will wind up doing life plus 30 years.) Kidman plays right into Van Sant's game by telegraphing her contempt for Suzanne at every opportunity. Didn't anyone ever teach her that the first rule of acting is to find compassion for your character?

To Die For only comes alive when the kids Suzanne ropes into her homicidal scheme are on screen. The kids are undoubtedly what drew Van Sant to the story and he should have kept his focus on them. Alison Folland and Casey Affleck are as affecting as any of the kids in *Kids* (Larry Clark shares Van Sant's fascination with the Pam Smart case), but Joaquin Phoenix as the adolescent who's so besotted with his teacher that he pulls the trigger on her husband (a touchingly mature Matt Dillon) is the film's object of desire. This Phoenix is not the chameleon his older brother River was. He's too startlingly exotic to disappear into a character's skin. But when his eyes light up with mixed emotion, he's truly to die for.

Also reviewed in:
CHICAGO TRIBUNE, 10/6/95, Friday/p. C, Michael Wilmington
NEW REPUBLIC, 10/23/95, p. 28, Stanley Kauffmann
NEW YORK TIMES, 9/27/95, p. C11, Janet Maslin
VARIETY, 5/29-6/4/95, p. 53, Todd McCarthy
WASHINGTON POST, 10/6/95, p. B1, Hal Hinson
WASHINGTON POST, 10/6/95, Weekend/p. 44, Desson Howe

TO WONG FOO, THANKS FOR EVERYTHING, JULIE NEWMAR

A Universal Pictures release of an Amblin Entertainment production. *Executive Producer:* Bruce Cohen. *Producer:* G. Mac Brown. *Director:* Beeban Kidron. *Screenplay:* Douglas Carter Beane. *Director of Photography:* Steve Mason. *Editor:* Andrew Mondshein. *Music:* Rachel Portman. *Music Editor:* Suzana Peric. *Choreographer:* Kenny Ortega. *Sound:* Harry Higgins, Ted Clark and (music) Keith Grant. *Sound Editor:* Michael Kirchberger, Maurice Schell, and Paul P. Soucek. *Casting:* Billy Hopkins, Suzanne Smith, Kerry Barden, and Pat DiStefano. *Production Designer:* Wynn Thomas. *Art Director:* Robert Guerra. *Set Decorator:* Ted Glass. *Set Dresser:* Wendell Bud Hill. *Costumes:* Marlene Stewart. *Make-up:* J. Roy Helland. *Running time:* 108 minutes. *MPAA Rating:* PG-13.

CAST: Wesley Snipes (Noxeema Jackson); Patrick Swayze (Vida Boheme); John Leguizamo (Chi Chi Rodriguez); Stockard Channing (Carol Ann); Blythe Danner (Beatrice); Arliss Howard (Virgil); Jason London (Bobby Ray); Chris Penn (Sheriff Dollard); Melinda Dillon (Merna); Beth Grant (Loretta); Alice Drummond (Clara); Marceline Hugot (Katina); Jennifer Milmore (Bobby Lee); Jamie Harrold (Billy Budd); Mike Hodge (Jimmy Joe); Michael Vartan (Tommy); RuPaul (Rachel Tensions); Julie Newmar (Herself); Joel Story (Little Earnest); Abie Hope Hyatt (Donna Lee); Jamie Leigh Wolbert (Sandra Lee); Shae Degan, Dean Houser, and Joe Grojean (State Troopers); Keith Reddin (Motel Manager); Naomi Campbell (Girl); William P. Hopkins (Small Guy); Dayton Callie (Crazy Elijah); Ron Carley (Old Man); Alexander Heimberg (Miss Understood); Joey Arias (Justine); Allen Hidalgo (Chita Riviera); Mishell Chandler (Miss Missy); Catiria Reyes (Herself); David Drumgold (Cappuccino Commotion); Clinton Leupp (Miss Coco Peru); Lionel Tiburcio (Laritza Dumont); Bernard A. Mosca (Olympia); Daniel T. "Sweetie" Boothe (Announcer); David Barton (Boy in Chains); Charles Ching (Coco LaChine); Mike Fulk (Victoria Weston); Niasse N. Mamadou (Lou); Brendan McDanniel (Candis Cayne); Shelton McDonald (Princess Diandra); Richard Ogden (Kabuki); James Palacio (Fiona James); Steven Polito (Hedda Lettuce); Philip Stoehr (Philomena); Martha Flynn (Vida's Mother); Billie J. Diekman (Florist); Shari Shell-True (Dance Teacher).

FILMS IN REVIEW, 11-12/95, p. 106, Barbara Cramer

Paradigms lost. This prosaic, obvious rip-off of last year's brilliant *Priscilla, Queen of the Desert,* a puckish, bittersweet road movie from Australia about three drag queens in the outback, clearly shows how Hollywood can make a sow's ear out of a silk purse.

And the bearers of those purses—crammed into panty girdles and stuffed into bras, dynel wigs, and more makeup than you can shake a lipstick at—are three straight actors (not that it matters) known more for their machismo than maternalism: Wesley Snipes, Patrick Swayze, and John Leguizamo.

Though the film's focus is more or less the same as *Priscilla* (i.e., the reaction to transvestites by an otherwise heterosexual world), much has been lost in the translation. The results couldn't be more different—or less convincing.

The scenario is simplistic. Three *gay caballeras,* en route from New York to Los Angeles for the drag queen equivalent of the Miss America contest, get stalled in a rural Midwestern Dogpatch when their vintage '67 Caddy convertible breaks down, and proceed to play (excuse the expression) fairy godmothers to the emotionally-needy local yokels.

Like Cinderella's benefactor, the sequined trio sprinkle generic solace and lifestyle solutions on the folks of Snydersville, Nebraska, a dreary wasteland of a town, and rain down goodness, mercy, and mascara on the sensually-deprived, lovelorn populace sorely in need of a boost—or, at least, a visit to the beauty parlor.

The first daub of color in an otherwise joyless, jejune horizon occurs when the Magi-mommas unearth a veritable storehouse of garish clothes from another era, replete with baubles, bangles, and boas. (Gee Toto, Nebraska was never like this.)

Off go the house dresses. Away go the townies' indifference toward feminine wiles. And when the drag queens drag the wishy-washy women to the local salon, what emerges, with wiggle and twist, are femme fatales unknown in those parts since days of Belle (or Brenda) Starr.

But the film doesn't work, Betty Friedan and Gloria Steinem would have a field day with these sisters from another planet. It's style over substance, distortion and kitsch over credibility.

Despite outrageous get-up and garb (fit for a Victoria's Secret or Frederick's of Hollywood catalogue), the three "heroines" seem cut-and-pasted burlesques of screen types from days of yore: Snipes, spawned out of Joan Crawford, is Noxeema Jackson, Swayze's Vida Boheme, the only one with a hint of a private life (he's the rejected scion of a Philadelphian Main Line family) bears an uncanny resemblance to Blanche DuBois, and Colombian-born Leguizamo's Chi Chi Rodriguez is a cross between Rosie Perez and Charo. (I'd love to see the film's English subtitles south of the border. According to a Cuban colleague, almost every Latin word he utters is a trashy Spanish obscenity.)

The film does have its share of broad one-liners and humor about broads, but unfortunately, this cross-country trip by cross-dressers lays an egg. The editing is choppy, and director Beeban Kidron (who helmed the wonderful *Antonia and Jane* and could have done better) adds little ingenuity to this lackluster fable which tries to prove that life *can* be beautiful if you go heavy on the eye-liner.

Most of the fine talent is wasted: Blythe Danner, Melinda Dillon, Stockard Channing as Arliss Howard's abused wife, and Chris Penn as a dumb local cop who doesn't realize at first that the gentlemen are no ladies—all get short shrift from Douglas Carter Beane's bromidic script. (Robin Williams has an unbilled cameo early on as a drag promoter, and his quip before the trio goes West, "Three sisters on their way to L.A. How Chekhov!" is about as funny as the dialogue gets.)

As for the film's unusual title, model-actress-dancer Julie Newmar—all 5' 11" of her—serves as the trio's eponymous mythic symbol of feminine pulchritude. Seems before they set off on their cross-country jaunt, Vida steals her signed cheesecake photo from the wall of a Chinese restaurant and brings it along for luck. The real Ms. Newmar, who, till now, was best known as the Catwoman on the original *Batman* TV series in the mid-Sixties, appears for a few brief seconds at the finale to crown one of the group "Drag Queen of the Year." It doesn't help much. The film's still a drag.

LOS ANGELES TIMES, 9/8/95, Calendar/p. 4, Kenneth Turan

If, as ads for "The Adventures of Priscilla, Queen of the Desert" insisted, drag is the drug, then "To Wong Foo, Thanks for Everything, Julie Newmar" is the overdose.

"Wong Foo's" drag queens on the road theme covers a great deal of the same plot territory as last year's Oscar winner (for best costume design, of course) from Australia but to considerably less effect. Unconvincing and annoying, a calculation on numerous fronts, is finally sugary enough to make the sentimental "Priscilla" play like a model of icy restraint.

What's different about "Wong Foo" touted by Universal as "the first mainstream Hollywood feature to deal with drag queens as drag queens," is its willingness to dress recognizable stars in full drag. Wesley Snipes, Patrick Swayze and John Leguizamo appear as Noxeema Jackson, Vida Boheme and Chi Chi Rodriguez, all of whom answer to the description of "gay men with way too much fashion sense for one gender."

"Wong Foo" opens with the street-smart Noxeema and the prim Vida primping for a mythical Manhattan event called the Drag Queen of the Year pageant. Good pals, they are happy to be declared the contests co-winners and recipients of a pair of round-trip airplane tickets to Hollywood.

Not so happy is poor Chi Chi, who barely has enough fashion sense for a single gender and is found by the two winners whining on a convenient staircase. In a fit of noblesse oblige, they take on the waif, initially referred to as "Little One," as a reclamation project.

They even decide to take Chi Chi to California with them, which means plane trips are out and the purchase of a barge-like 1967 Cadillac convertible is in. Using a pilfered photo of Julie Newmar autographed to the owner of a Chinese restaurant as a good luck charm, they gaudily hit the road. As one pal (Robin Williams, in an uncredited cameo) puts it, "how 'Three Sisters,' how Chekov."

Up to this point, "Wong Foo" is at least sporadically amusing. And while the lure of seeing macho types in drag may not be on a par with "Garbo Laughs" as an audience draw, the three actors have thrown themselves into the roles (and the clothes) without reservation. There is no opportunity for the kind of memorable performance Terence Stamp gave in "Priscilla," but, actors to the end, they are not shy about posing and preening.

Once the Cadillac gets out to Middle America, however, things get worse all around. The trio's flamboyance draws the lewd attentions of a crude county sheriff named Dollard (Chris Penn), who gets knocked out for his trouble and spends the rest of the picture in a tedious attempt to exact revenge.

And when that enormous Cadillac suffers the inevitable breakdown, the girls end up stranded in the hamlet of Snydersville, whose doltish inhabitants could be in a road show version of "Night of the Living Dead." All the women are lonely and depressed, none worse than Carol Ann (Stockard Channing), a victim of periodic beatings from sadistic husband Virgil (Arliss Howard). And most of the men are either brutes or fools or both.

Though they may totter on their heels, Noxy, Vida and Chi Chi know a thing or two about human nature, and, in the most trite way, they manage to solve everyone's problems, even their own, before the Cadillac rolls out of town. It's even more unconvincing than it sounds.

Screenwriter Douglas Carter Beane and director Beeban Kidron (who has wandered far from her witty "Antonia and Jane") don't seem to know any way to emphasize the humanity of their characters except by swaddling them in mushy clichés. The only real use "Wong Foo" has for drag is to disguise its banality, and those who remember not only "Priscilla" but the exceptional "Paris Is Burning" know what a waste that is.

NEW YORK POST, 9/8/95, p. 41, Michael Medved

"To Wong Foo, Thanks for Everything, Julie Newmar" tells the story of three glamorous New York drag queens who end up bringing joy, healing and outrageous hairstyles to a sleepy Mid-western town.

The only problem is that the three stars who play the principal roles don't look a bit like glamorous drag queens—let alone resembling *women* in any way—and the town they visit is filled with dumb caricatures and comes across as authentic as the plastic reconstructions of a tacky Wild West theme park.

As a result, the flimsy plot begins to—pardon the expression—drag. The action of the film is supposed to unfold over the course of a single weekend, but it seems like forever before this overblown idiocy crawls to its feeble finish.

The agony begins when Vida Boheme (Patrick Swayze) and Noxzeema Jackson (Wesley Snipes) share the honors as "Drag Queens of the Year" at a gala New York contest. They decide to use their prize money to make a trip to "fabulous" Hollywood, bringing along their frustrated friend Chi Chi Rodriguez (John Leguizamo) to give him/her spiritual lessons in what it takes to be a drag queen.

Meanwhile, their yellow Cadillac convertible breaks down near the dusty town of Snydersville (actually Loma, Neb.) and while waiting for repairs they manage to inspire battered wife Stockard Channing to stand up to her abusive husband (Arliss Howard), and bring new flash, color and choreography to the town's annual "Strawberry Social."

Macho stars Snipes and Swayze probably took these roles in order to "stretch" as actors, but unfortunately the stretch marks are visible all over their performances.

In other recent transvestite takes, from "The Crying Game" to "Wigstock" to "Priscilla, Queen of the Desert" (with a strikingly similar setup to this film but far richer characters), you can easily understand how people accept the protagonists as attractive females, but anyone here who thinks—for even a split second that Wesley Snipes is a woman must be either vision-impaired or terminally demented.

Leguizamo, on the other hand occasionally rises to the demands of his roll, spitting out silly lines ("I got more legs than a bucket of Kentucky Fried Chicken") with sexy, mambo-mouthed sass.

Unfortunately, the filmmaker's politically correct determination to avoid portraying the cross-dressing heroes as in any way pathetic leads to disastrous overcompensation, so that these people come across as unnaturally, one-dimensionally cheerful and sweet.

In her native Britain, director Beeban Kidron created a quirky comedy of female friendship ("Antonia and Jane), but like her previous Hollywood effort, "Used People," "Wong Foo," suffers from the absence of any convincing sense of place. The portrayal of the Nebraska location in so fuzzy that for the of the picture you're unsure whether the town's supposed to located in the Midwest or the South.

The film's title, by the way, refers to the inscription on a photo of Julie Newmar they've stolen from a restaurant to inspire them during their travels. The real Julie Newmar makes a brief appearance at the film's conclusion; unfortunately, she looks like a lifeless, waxworks version of herself—an appropriate comment on a film that tries for glitz and glamour but achieves only stupidity and shabbiness.

NEWSDAY, 9/8/95, Part II/p. B2, Jack Mathews

To the makers of "To Wong Foo, Thanks for Everything! Julie Newmar," thanks for nothing! Bad idea, bad title, bad execution. This story of three drag queens stranded in Red Neck, USA, is a royal drag.

It's been a while since a movie so unworthy of attention has received so much of it. When the early New York scenes were being filmed last year, the media and the curious rallied for a glimpse of hunks-in-heels Patrick Swayze and Wesley Snipes, and the observers seemed to marvel at their babeness.

Hardly. When Swayze, a sinewy athlete with muscles in his face, dons his gaudy makeup and costume for the annual New York drag queen beauty pageant and says, "Ready or not, here comes mama!," the image is more like "Papa's got a brand new bag." And the wide-shouldered Snipes, whose blond-wigged Noxeema Jackson will share the top prize with Swayze's Vida Boheme, is about as alluring in a strapless gown as Rush Limbaugh in a Republican frock.

"To Wong Foo" (the title is the inscription on a photograph worshipped by Vida) is a costume party with cool guys wearing feather boas and falsies. It is Hollywood exploiting the burgeoning drag culture while preaching tolerance of it.

We're supposed to love Vida, Noxeema and Chi Chi Rodriguez (John Leguizamo), the Hispanic queen wannabe who joins them on a cross-country jaunt to Hollywood for the national competition. To make sure we do, they are described—if not quite developed—as such vulnerable, winning characters, so gayly determined to bring style and humanity to the butt-scratchers of Snydersville, that there is no alternative.

Vida and Noxeema are about as threatening as Mother Teresa, whose altruism they share. Their rusty Cadillac convertible has no sooner been towed to town than they begin adopting wounded people. Vida takes on Carol Ann (Stockard Channing), the boarding house hostess with a dangerously abusive husband (Arliss Howard), while Noxeema, through her good-natured innocence and shared love for the movies of Dorothy Dandridge and Lena Horne, brings an old woman out of mute senility.

Meanwhile, they're making Snydersville as spiffy as a '60s psychedelic van.

With a cache of wacky fabric found in the attic of a general store, they redress the women of Snydersville to look like the reunion committee for Woodstock. They redecorate their own spare room as a den of softly lifted gaudiness. And they paint the town red, literally, to jazz up the annual Strawberry Social, where they will finally face the homophobic sheriff (an out-of-control Chris Penn) on their trail.

"To Wong Foo," directed by Beeban Kidron ("Antonia and Jane"), falls into a neverland of gender-bent comedy. Unlike the classics "Some Like It Hot" and "Tootsie," the men of "Foo" aren't out to fool anybody. Though Vida and Noxie can warm to battle when their hairy counterparts get tough, they are queens to their souls.

At the same time, they have no sexuality beneath their flashy outfits, and none of the psychological edge underpinning last year's sensational "The Adventures of Priscilla: Queen of the Desert." Chi Chi plays the slut at times, and Leguizamo, the only comedy actor in the film, steals the show in those scenes. But, as Bill Maher says of his irreverent TV show "Politically Incorrect," it has all been satirized for your protection. The filmmakers have taken great care to make sure audiences don't have to think for a second about the characters' actual sex lives.

Retired Los Angeles detective Mark Fuhrman may be the only person in the country mean enough to find the film disgusting, and the only one who might benefit from seeing it.

SIGHT AND SOUND, 12/95, p. 52, Nick James

Friends Noxeema Jackson and Vida Boheme are declared joint winners of the Drag Queen of New York competition. The prize is a free trip to LA as contestants for Drag Queen of America. Backstage, they meet a distraught contestant, Chi Chi Rodriguez. The maternal Vida asks her to celebrate with them. At a favourite bar, Vida cashes in the first class plane tickets so that Chi Chi can come with them to LA by car. Vida helps herself to the bar's framed photo of minor 60s starlet Julie Newmar.

They buy a run-down 1967 Cadillac and set off. Chi Chi is ordered not to refer to herself as a Drag Queen—she is merely a "boy in a dress". When she insists that they stop in a cheesy hotel, the others refuse. A policeman, Sheriff Dollard, stops them for speeding. He orders Vida out of the car and insists on a kiss. After a brief struggle he falls to the floor. Thinking him dead, the girls flee but the Cadillac soon breaks down. A young Midwestern boy, Bobby Ray, takes them to Snydersville, where they put up at a dismal rooming house run by Carol Ann, whose husband Virgil is the town mechanic. Meanwhile, Dollard, having found one of Vida's shoes, begins to track the girls down.

Virgil says the girls must wait a couple of days for a car part. The locals are agog at these richly-dressed sophisticates. Noxeema befriends an old lady, Beatrice, who turns out to be a movie buff, Vida bonds with battered wife Carol Ann and Chi Chi gets rescued by Bobby Ray from a gang rape. The discovery of a cache of 60s clothes in the store leads to a revamping of the female population. The local young men are brought into line and Virgil is given a pasting by Vida. However, Chi Chi has to be dissuaded from leading on Bobby Ray. Instead, she gives tips on how to win him over to his teen worshipper Bobby Lee. Dollard finally arrives on the day of the town's Strawberry festival, but his plan to arrest Vida is confounded when every woman claims that the missing shoe is hers. The festival is a roaring success. The next day, the girls leave and Vida gives her picture of Julie Newmar to Carol Ann who knew all along that Vida was really a man. In LA, it is Chi Chi who becomes Drag Queen of America, crowned by Julie Newmar herself.

Clearly conceived as a Hollywood attempt to follow up the success of the Australian director Stephan Elliot's *The Adventures of Priscilla, Queen of the Desert*, Beeban Kidron's *To Wong Foo* is a simpler film, one designed to make an acceptable alliance between major Hollywood stars and a bankable camp sensibility. Where Elliot's drag queen tour of the outback was something of an abrasive backstage bitchathon with music, here internecine strife between three cross-dressers stuck in the midwest is—after a few racial slurs at the beginning—soon reduced to a kind of Open University course in how to be a drag queen.

As *grandes dames* Vida Boheme and Noxeema Jackson, Patrick Swayze and Wesley Snipes are flamboyantly hysterical and little else, condescending beautifully to John Leguizamo's Chi Chi Rodriguez, who is merely, in their terms, a "boy in a dress". Chi Chi is required to learn charmingly anodyne maxims on the way to becoming a drag queen: "let good thoughts be your sword and shield," "ignore adversity" and "abide by the rules of love." Whether or not these are direct quotes from the works of Diana Vreeland, whose book is given by Noxeema to Snydersville's spotty store clerk to instant sartorial effect, they effectively sum up the genteel ethos of a film which appears to be walking on eggshells to avoid offending anyone. Nevertheless, while the gusto with which they otherwise enter into the spirit of things is to be commended, Swayze and Snipes are both given scenes in which they are allowed to physically humiliate men, as if to say no really, we're just acting—look how manly we are underneath.

Apart from a brief glimpse of Vida's mother, who is soon dismissed by her son as *nouveau riche*, *To Wong Foo* allows its frolicsome threesome to hit the road relatively unburdened by backstory. We learn that Vida is warm and maternal and that she works out a lot, that Noxeema takes no shit and is somewhat excitable and that Chi Chi knows every slut manouevre, but they otherwise remain as cardboard cut-out as their image of womanhood. Thus their instantaneous galvanising effect on the population of Snydersville is unconvincing, especially as the impact of their gaudiness and glamour is consistently undercut by the direction. The big musical production numbers here are shot in such a flat, head-on style they have little impact, and when there is a climactic crane shot that attempts an over-view of Snydersville's transformed community, it feels forced.

Of all of Beeban Kidron's past work it is perhaps her televised documentary *Hooker's, Hustlers, Pimps and Their 'Johns'* that makes her a likely candidate to direct this drag queen extravaganza, rather than her slight Hollywood melodrama *Used People* or her strong adaptation of Jeanette Winterson's *Oranges are Not the Only Fruit*. In that documentary, Kidron's sympathy with outsiders and her fascination with sexual role-play and dressing up in bland domestic settings led her to show several scenes of a potentially disturbing nature, while never once forgetting that she was dealing with real people. It's a pity that neither the risk-taking nor the sympathy is in evidence here.

TIME, 9/18/95, p. 108, Richard Corliss

Inside every gay man, the drag queen's fantasy credo goes, there's a beautiful woman just dying to accessorize. Take Vida Boheme (Patrick Swayze), the regal doyenne in *To Wong Foo Thanks for Everything Julie Newmar*. Vida is a Victoria among drag queens; she could be the perfect ad for sisterhood out of a 1947 *Good Housekeeping*. And Swayze, maintaining equipoise between camp and bathos, is every inch a lady.

Vida and her friend Noxeema Jackson (Wesley Snipes, another stud star who looks swell in Dynel) are on the road with a third dragster, Chi Chi Rodriguez (John Leguizamo, who is not so much a queen as a saucy serving wench). They stop for repairs in a nowhere town where all the men are brutes or louts, and all the women worn out trying to survive. That these Dust Bowl wallflowers are played by some of the most sophisticated actresses around (Stockard Charming, Blythe Danner and Melinda Dillon) suggests role playing weirder than any mere gender switching. It's as if a PBS cast of *The Three Sisters* got stranded in Oskaloosa.

To Wong Foo (whose unpunctuated title means ... oh, nothing very much) has its larkish side, when the male stars are doing their struts and their dish. But it soon goes sappily didactic. Director Beeban Kidron and scripter Douglas Carter Beane want you to believe that the drag queen, because he is at ease with his ersatz sexuality, is a true liberator: he can teach feminism to women and manners to men, in this awful place called Middle America. The movie has its own fantasy credo: that heterosexuals are the real objects of pity and scorn. And gay men? Poor them! In Hollywood films, they are either invisible or tortured—unless they dress for success.

VILLAGE VOICE, 9/12/95, p. 59, Amy Taubin

The *New York* magazine version of drag queen movies, *To Wong Foo, Thanks for Everything Julie Newmar* is slicked up, tamed down, with its fantasies safely attainable. It makes guys in dresses seem so wholesome that Bob Dole wouldn't have a problem accepting campaign contributions from them. Director Beeban Kidron even gets that dungeon Webster Hall to look as fit-up and loud as Vegas (not just faintly glowing the way it does when you've downed some ecstasy).

To Wong Foo leading trio (played by Wesley Snipes, Patrick Swayze, and John Leguizamo) wear dresses not to save their skins (Jack Lemmon and Tony Curtis in *Some Like It Hot),* nor to get a part on a soap (Dustin Hoffman in *Tootsie*), nor to spend more time with the kiddies (Robin Williams in *Mrs. Doubtfire*). They wear dresses because they are drag queens, plain and simple. And in fact there's a whole minute of dialogue explaining how a drag queen ("a gay man who has too much fashion sense to be trapped in one gender") is different from a transvestite ("a straight men who puts on a dress") or transsexual ("a man who decides he's a woman trapped in a man's body and does something to change that"). When Wesley Snipes, who plays the wiseass Noxeema Jackson, lays out this taxonomy of drag, he doesn't swallow the word *gay;* he says it loud and clear. But if you're expecting more than lip service, forget it. Whatever libido these girls have, it's all channeled into clothes. They aren't gay, they're neuters, queens from Amblin Entertainment.

A big, overlong, unsexy *Priscilla, Queen of the Desert, To Wong Foo* puts its three big girls in an ancient yellow Caddy convertible traveling cross country from New York to Hollywood to compete in a beauty pageant. They do not take the scenic route. The car breaks down and our heroines are stuck in the minuscule Midwestern town of Snydersville, population less than 100, where almost everyone takes them to their hearts. The multi-culti city mice give the white country mice some fashion tips and turn the annual Strawberry Social into the Red and Wild Festival. Red seems to be the only color on anyone's mind.

The performances are the pictures only selling point and two out of three just aren't good enough. Snipes, an effortless comedian, takes the obvious hip-slinging, nail-flicking route, spending most of his energy telegraphing the fact that he's still Wesley—all male and a really big star, no matter how much eyeliner he's wearing.

As Vida Boheme, Swayze is surprisingly convincing, though unnecessarily one-note. Swayze has the Terence Stamp dowager part and he plays it as Grace Kelly on the verge of morphing into Angela Lansbury. Portrait necklines and forearm gloves become him. The problem with Swayze is that he never gives Vida any downtime. I don't mean anything as obvious as letting his biologically determined characteristics slip out. But even as perfect a drag queen as Candy Darling had moments when she wasn't representing.

Snipes and Swayze are stars showing off how naughty they can be—not very. John Leguizamo is a skilled and talented actor giving a very good performance as a drag queen. He's so good he has us believing he's Chi Chi Rodriquez, ingenue and hustler whose passion is to win a beauty contest. The third wheel, Leguizamo is also the best thing in the picture. His exuberance is contagious. Sometimes when he and Snipes interact, Snipes stops condescending and just delivers.

Beeban Kidron's direction is bland and, well, draggy. The picture is oddly cut together. Scenes start and stop and then start up again out of nowhere. The townfolk for the most part are played by prominent New York actors (among them, Stockard Channing, Blythe Danner, Melinda Dillon). All of them seem confused about what sort of movie they're supposed to be in. Perhaps Kidron had some idea about how being a Midwesterner is as much of a masquerade as being a drag queen. In any case, when the faux drag queen and the faux battered white-bread wife got all kissy and declared themselves best friends for life, I didn't think how great it is that we can all get along. But rather, get real.

Also reviewed in:
CHICAGO TRIBUNE, 9/8/95, Friday/p. C, Michael Wilmington
NEW REPUBLIC, 10/9/95, p. 27, Stanley Kauffmann
NEW YORK TIMES, 9/8/95, p. C18, Janet Maslin
NEW YORKER, 9/18/95, p. 96, Anthony Lane
VARIETY, 9/4-10/95, p. 71, Todd McCarthy
WASHINGTON POST, 9/8/95, p. F1, Rita Kempley
WASHINGTON POST, 9/8/95, Weekend/p. 44, Joe Brown

TOM AND HUCK

A Walt Disney Pictures release of a Laurence Mark production. *Executive Producer:* Barry Bernardi and Stephen Sommers. *Producer:* Laurence Mark and John Baldecchi. *Director:* Peter Hewitt. *Screenplay:* Stephen Sommers and David Loughery. *Based on the novel "The Adventures of Tom Sawyer" by:* Mark Twain. *Director of Photography:* Bobby Bukowski. *Editor:* David Freeman. *Music:* Stephen Endelman. *Music Editor:* Todd Kasow and Joanie Diener. *Sound:* Walter P. Anderson. *Sound Editor:* Dane A. Davis. *Casting:* Gail Levin and Tricia Tomey. *Production Designer:* Gemma Jackson. *Art Director:* Michael Rizzo. *Set Decorator:* Ellen J. Brill. *Set Designer:* Daniel Bradford. *Set Dresser:* Gary Bannister, Drew Meyers, and Tommy Horn. *Special Effects:* Michael Nathan Arbogast. *Costumes:* Marie France. *Make-up:* Harriette Landau. *Stunt Coordinator:* Ben Scott. *Running time:* 93 minutes. *MPAA Rating:* PG.

CAST: Jonathan Taylor Thomas (Tom Sawyer); Brad Renfro (Huck Finn); Eric Schweig (Injun Joe); Charles Rocket (Judge Thatcher); Amy Wright (Aunt Polly); Michael McShane (Muff Potter); Marian Seldes (Widow Douglas); Rachael Leigh Cook (Becky Thatcher); Lanny Flaherty (Emmett); Courtland Mead (Sid); Peter Mackenzie (Mr. Sneed); Heath Lamberts (Schoolmaster Dobbins); William Newman (Doc Robinson); Joey Stinson (Joe Harper); Blake Heron (Ben Rodgers); Jim Aycock (Defense Lawyer); Andy Stahl (Sheriff); Andrian Roberts (Welshman); Tiffany Lynn Clark (Suzy Harper); Kellen Hathaway (Billy Newton); Mark Cabus (Farmer); Bronwen Murray (Mary); Paul Anthony Kropfl (Impatient Trial Spectator).

LOS ANGELES TIMES, 12/22/95, Calendar/p. 20, John Anderson

[The following review by John Anderson appeared in a slightly different form in **NEWSDAY, 12/22/95, Part II/p. B13.]**

Life on the Mississippi as told by Mark Twain would seem to be perfectly filmable, but almost never is. This is probably because those who have read the books have the real movies in their heads. And those who have read the books include the filmmakers.

In "Tom and Huck," the latest screen appearance by Twain's delinquent sons of Hannibal, Mo., the filmmakers whitewash the fence but not the story: This is a dark, violent and rather slow-moving adaptation (free but not loose) of "The Adventures of Tom Sawyer," the prequel to "Huckleberry Finn" and a story loaded with stories.

There's rafting, murder, courtroom drama, cave-ins, treasure and romance (sans ickiness); lethal knife-throwing, politically incorrect portraits of Native Americans (Injun Joe, played by Eric Schweig), town drunks (Muff Potter, played by Michael McShane), and the thickheaded/upstanding members of the community who are appalled by Tom and ostracize Huck. Although it's set in the 1840s, it has the timeless, Twainish and, above all, American themes of conformity, cynicism and hypocrisy.

That the film doesn't work so well is less the fault of the cast—Jonathan Taylor Thomas of TV's "Home Improvement" as Tom, and Brad Renfro ("The Client" "The Cure") as Huck than it is the director's and writers' failure to ignite all this dramatic ammunition. They're inconsistently faithful to Twain and inconsistently successful. But the young actors aren't faultless, either.

Certain young performers on the Hollywood fast track just seem fated to wind up in Mark Twain adaptations. In the '30s, Jackie Coogan and abbreviated grownup Mickey Rooney took their turns. In the '70s, it was Johnny Whitaker and auteur-to-be Ronny (Ron) Howard. Of late, the very talented Elijah Wood gave a perfectly acceptable, if pasteurized, portrayal of Huck ("The Adventures of Huck Finn").

"Tom and Huck" doesn't have quite the social conscience of "The Adventures of Huck Finn," but Tom Sawyer seems more natural a part for Thomas, hunk-idol of the prepubescent set and sitcom superstar (we'll say nothing about his costarring role with Chevy Chase in "Man of the House"). He has the right cockiness for Tom, who was always a bit too clever for his own good, and the intelligence to rise above, if not too far above, the intellectual sluggishness of his surroundings.

It's not quite the same love match between Huck and Brad Renfro, whose Finn is more dullard than naif, and more ignorant than innocent. Huck Finn is Twain's greatest creation, the portrait of native intelligence led astray by superstition and unchallenged racism. He was not, however, thuggish, which is what Renfro makes him.

The point is, Huck is Tom without the advantages of village life, family and education—even if it's faulty and riddled with its own brand of ignorance. Twain saw them as two sides of a dubious coin America in its primitive innocence, and enlightened corruption. Renfro and Thomas are considerably less than metaphorical, but they don't compensate by being particularly entertaining.

NEW YORK POST, 12/22/95, p. 50, Larry Worth

There's been no shortage of "Tom Sawyer" film adaptations since Jackie Coogan played Mark Twain's mischievous hero in 1930. But "Tom and Huck" is the first to have viewers rooting for murderous Injun Joe.

The chief reason can be summed up in three words: Jonathan Taylor Thomas. Granted, TVs "Home Improvement" kid star is now considered king of the child actors. But aside from making little girls' hearts beat faster, his success is harder to fathom than the muddy Mississippi.

As demonstrated in last year's dismal Chevy Chase vehicle, "Man of the House," Thomas applies one general-purpose smirk for all occasions. It's on view when he's sassing Aunt Polly, romancing Becky Thatcher, dodging Injun Joe's knife—or posing for Tiger Beat.

Relatively speaking, Brad Renfro's efforts as Huckleberry Finn make him seem the new Olivier. The lankier, infinitely more expressive teen star—who impressed in both "The Client" and "The Cure"—has a natural manner about him. So when the barefoot, pipe-smoking lad wanders off-screen, viewer interest follows.

Director Peter Hewitt tries to reclaim it in odd ways, like scare tactics. Perhaps taking a cue from the intensity of "Jumanji," the all-important graveyard scene (in which Injun Joe kills Doc Robinson while digging for buried treasure) is frighteneng and graphic. Equally sinister is a dream sequence when Injun Joe crashes into a child's bedroom with a bared dagger.

Perhaps to mollify the younger set, Disney has added a five-minute cartoon to the mix, "Timon and Pumbaa in Stand By Me." Unfortunate the comic sparring partners Tom "Lion King" simply sing the Lieber and Stoller tune as Pumbaa endures more catastrophes than Wile E. Coyote. Worse, the animation is uninspired.

But while too much attention in "Tom and Huck" went to thrills and chills, not enough went toward Hannibal's ambience. Although filmed in a small Alabama town, the setting has a manufactured feel not unlike a Disney World ride.

As for Stephen Sommers and David Loughery's script, it covers the tale's basics, but the contemporary-sounding dialogue leaves much to be desired.

At least the supporing cast is a mixed bag. Amy Wright's Aunt Polly and Marian Seldes' turn as the Widow Douglas are nicely forbidding. Yet, sullen Rachel Leigh Cook comes closer to Lolita than Becky Thatcher, despite those ungainly pantaloons. Meanwhile, Eric Schweig's Injun Joe is physically menacing, but emotively challenged.

The bottom line: "Tom and Huck" is best left to the legion members of Johnathan Taylor Thomas fan club.

Also reviewed in:
CHICAGO TRIBUNE, 12/22/95, Friday/p. C, John Petrakis
NEW YORK TIMES, 12/22/95, p. C16, Stephen Holden
VARIETY, 1/1-7/96, p. 83, Joe Leydon
WASHINGTON POST, 12/22/95, Weekend/p. 43, Kevin McManus
WASHINGTON POST, 12/23/95, p. B7, Han Hinson

TOMMY BOY

A Paramount Pictures release. *Executive Producer:* Robert K. Weiss. *Producer:* Lorne Michaels. *Director:* Peter Segal. *Screenplay:* Bonnie Turner and Terry Turner. *Director of Photography:* Victor J. Kemper. *Editor:* William Kerr. *Music:* David Newman, Michael Muhlfriedel, and J. Steven Soles. *Music Editor:* George A. Martin and Tom Villano. *Sound:* Hank Garfield and (music) Tim Boyle. *Sound Editor:* Terry Rodman. *Casting:* Pamela Basker, Ross Clydesdale, Barbara Harris, and Catherine Stroud. *Production Designer:* Stephen J. Lineweaver. *Art Director:* Alicia Keywan. *Set Designer:* Dennis Davenport. *Set Decorator:* Gordon Sim. *Special Effects:* Michael Kavanagh and Mike Vezna. *Costumes:* Patti Unger. *Make-up:* Irene Kent and Inge Klaudi. *Stunt Coordinator:* Branko Racki. *Running time:* 96 minutes. *MPAA Rating:* PG-13.

CAST: Chris Farley (Tommy Callahan); David Spade (Richard Hayden); Brian Dennehy (Big Tom); Bo Derek (Beverly); Rob Lowe (Paul); Dan Aykroyd (Zalinsky); Julie Warner (Michelle); Sean McCann (Rittenhauer); Zach Grenier (Reilly); James Blendick (Gilmore); Clinton Turnbull (Young Tommy); Ryder Britton (Young Richard); Paul Greenburg (Skittish Student); Philip Williams (Danny); David "Skippy" Malloy (Sammy); Roy Lewis (Louis); Austin Pool (Obnoxious Bus Kid); William Dunlop (R.T.); Jack Jessup (Priest); Michael Dunston (Singer at Wedding); David Hemblen (Archer); George Kinamis, Dov Tiefenbach and Mark Zador (Kids at Lake); Helen Hughes (Boardroom Woman); J.R. Zimmerman (Boardroom Man); Robert K. Weiss, Reg Dreger, and Lloyd White ('No' Managers); David Huband (Gas Attendant); Hayley Gibbins (Little Girl at Carnival); Julianne Gillies (Brady's Receptionist); Adison Bell (Mr. Brady); Cory Sevier (Boy in Commercial); Maria Vacratsis (Helen); Colin Fox (Nelson); Lorri Bagley (Woman at Pool); Lynn Cunningham (Pretty Hitchhiker); David Calderisi, Sven van de Ven, and Errol Sitahal ('Yes' Executives); Marc Strange (Toy Car Executive); Michael Ewing (Ticket Agent); Adrian Truss and Christopher John (Cops); Henry Gomez (Airport Cop); Lindsay Leese (Reservationist); Camilla Scott (Stewardess); Bunty Webb (Large Woman); Marilyn Boyle (Woman with Pen); Gino Marrocco (Cabbie); Gil Filar (Kid in Bank); Jonathan Wilson (Marty); Sandi Stahlbrand (News Reporter); Ron James and Brian Kaulback (Bank Guards); Mark Ingram and Jim Codrington (Security Guards); Pat Moffatt (Mrs. Nelson); Raymond Hunt, Robbie Rox, and Jerry Schaeffer (Restaurant Regulars); Taylor Segal (Flower Girl).

LOS ANGELES TIMES, 3/31/95, Calendar/p. 8, Kevin Thomas

From Fatty Arbuckle and Oliver Hardy to John Candy, hefty guys have always gotten big laughs on the screen, and when Hardy was teamed with spindly Stan Laurel, they became comedy legends. The rowdy, rambunctious, sweet-natured "Tommy Boy" suggests we may have a worthy successor to Candy in massive, jowly Chris Farley, who is especially funny when he's playing off David Spade, with first teamed on "Saturday Night Live." Farley reminds us just how liberating an agile, uninhibited, out-sized comedian can be in these times of caloric restraint.

Farley's happy-go-lucky Tommy Callahan has, after seven years, graduate from Marquette and head home for Sandusky, Ohio, to join the family auto-parts manufacturing firm run by his hearty dad, Big Tom (Brian Dennehy). Considerably less than thrilled to see him is Spade's Richard Hayden—an homage, perhaps, to the late, fastidious comedian of the same name. Richard is Big Tom's right-hand man, and keeping an eye on Tommy has now been added to his duties. Nevertheless, Tommy and Richard swiftly wind up on the road, having to sell half-a-million brake pads in order to save Callahan Auto Parts in the face of an unanticipated catastrophe.

Writers Bonnie and Terry Turner show plenty of skill in developing Tommy and Richard and their relationship. They indelibly identify Tommy as a guy who insists that the first name of the Hancock who signed the Declaration of Independence is Herbie. However, in Turners' smart writing and Segal's zesty, shrewd direction, and above all, in Spade's playing in the film's pivotal scene, Richard convinces us—and Tommy himself—that Tommy's not as really dumb as he seems but that, having been indulged all his life, he just has never bothered to grow up. Then it's up to Farley to convince us that, Tommy, like his late father, actually has the street smarts Richard insists he has. Tommy, in turn, has taken the starch out of Richard to the extent that we remember he's a young man after all.

One of the movie's many uproarious moments occurs when Tommy struggles to change clothes in a tiny airplane restroom. Farley and Spade take off like rockets, but they've got backing all the way from a terrific ensemble of actors, including Bo Derek as Tommy's not-so-nice new stepmother, Rob Lowe as the sarcastic "son," Dan Aykroyd as Big Tom's smarmy business rival and Julie Warner as the pretty, smart manager of Callahan's shipping department. "Tommy Boy" also knows when to get serious, and composer David Newman deftly keys the film's wide-ranging moods. "Tommy Boy" is a good belly laugh of a movie.

NEW YORK POST, 3/31/95, p. 45, Michael Medved

The hottest Hollywood formula of the moment involves slow-witted but likable heroes who are thrust into challenging or threatening situations, but emerge triumphant through the sheer force of their innocence and earthiness. This recipe not only helped "Forrest Gump" win its chocolate box full of Oscars but also enabled "Dumb and Dumber" to earn more than $100 million at the box office. Before that, the same basic setup worked for Bill and Ted or Wayne and Garth, celebrating the power of their invincible stupidity.

Now comes the latest entrant in the dumb-but-decent sweepstakes: Chris Farley of "Saturday Night Live," who plays the beefy, befuddled title character in the raucous new comedy "Tommy Boy."

The movie begins when he finally graduates from college after seven years of study with a D-plus average and returns home to Ohio to join the family auto parts business.

His wealthy widower father (Brian Dennehy) is temporarily distracted by his forthcoming marriage to Bo Derek who, emerging from a swimming pool in a tiny bikini, proves she's lost none of the unique talents that made her a star some 15 years ago.

She eventually brings her son(!) Rob Lowe into the Callahan family, and despite the fact that this surly loner appears to have attended the Jeffrey Dahmer charm school, Tommy Boy is determined to bond with his new "brother."

He also forms an unlikely friendship with David Spade, the snide efficiency expert in his father's company, when the two men hit the road together in a last-ditch effort to save the business.

Unless Tommy can magically transform himself into a super salesman, Callahan Auto Parts will close its doors, throwing hundreds out of work and crippling the hometown economy.

This do-or-die road trip offers the excuse for an endless succession of gross gags about urination, masturbation, toilet bowls, vomit, rotting deer carcasses, flatulence, and other joys of daily life.

As you might expect, the movie also delivers a lard bucket full of fat jokes nasty enough to make David Letterman's mean spirited Oscar night crack about Roger Ebert sound like a valentine.

If you happen to enjoy this sort of thing, you will probably laugh at parts of "Tommy Boy." Chris Farley, displays a flair for slapstick and a naturally lovable screen presence that forces you to smile each time he waddles into a scene, it's too bad that he often seems to be straining too hard to force laughs.

Teaming him with cynical straight man David Spade also seems like a questionable decision—as an updated version of Abbott and Costello they never generate real sparks or manage to decide who's on first.

The talent behind "Tommy Boy" brings together veterans of the hilarious "Naked Gun" series (director Peter Segal and producer Bob Weiss) with key players from Lorne Michaels' SNL stable (writers Bonnie and Terry Turner, and the two stars).

With this sort of comic pedigree you can be sure the result is no movie mutt, but despite the strenuous efforts of its lead player it's no purebred champion either.

NEWSDAY, 3/31/95, Part II/p. B2, John Anderson

Some comedians make you want to forget earthly concerns and abandon yourself to laughter. Chris Farley makes you want to go on a diet and get a haircut. So if you happen to be feeling generous, consider "Tommy Boy" a motivational exercise rather than a comedy.

Of course Farley, the "Saturday Night Live" regular, is less comedian than Fool, a role with an ancient tradition, and a specific purpose: While the comedian imposes a point of view on his or her audience, the Fool is a receptacle, enhancing the audience's self-image by being pathetic, ridiculous and a kind of whipping boy of the ego. If this explains in some way the marginal appeal of Chris Farley, bursting at his fleshy seams and struggling with space, it may also explain the disintegrating state of movie humor in general.

Farley may make people feel better, but his character, Tommy Callahan, just makes them nervous. Ever since he was a kid, the lumpish youth has been walking into glass doors and making a shambles of his life and furniture. Having graduated, barely, from Marquette University (which should sue) he enters the family business, Callahan Auto Parts, ushered by his father, Big

Tom (Brian Dennehy), into an office and a future. It's clear to everyone that Tommy is nothing like his powerhouse dad, nor is he the equal of Richard Hayden ("SNL's" David Spade), Big Tom's smarmier-than-thou right-hand man, who is, understandably, bent out of shape by the return of the heir presumptive.

Big Tom is inconsiderate enough to drop dead at his own wedding—to Beverly (Bo Derek)—during an unbelievable duet (and we don't mean that as a compliment) with Tommy of "What I Say?" Big Tom also leaves the town in the lurch: Callahan was in the midst of retooling, bank loans were pending, Zalinsky the Auto Parts King (Dan Aykroyd) now wants to buy them up and shut them down, the slinky Beverly and her "son," Paul (Rob Lowe, in the kind of role he does best), are circling like vultures, and the 300 plant employees are looking at a long stretch of daytime TV.

Which is better than late-night TV, at least on Saturdays, when "Tommy Boy" producer Lorne Michaels continues to perpetrate his brain-dead television program. There's little to separate the show from the film. In an effort to save the company, odd couple Tommy and Richard hit the road and experience a lackluster series of mishaps and episodes (I thought I was having one) that involve the gradual demolition of Richard's cherished convertible, a masturbation gag that isn't funny, insult gags that aren't funny, a tour of the Midwest that *really* isn't funny, plus Tommy making an ass of himself, Tommy saving the day, Tommy—yes, it true—getting the girl (Julie Warner) and Tommy saying "awesome."

All of which is perfectly in keeping with the "SNL" brand of comedy, which was once witty and is now infantile. If there's a bright spot in "Tommy Boy," it's David Spade, whose patently smug persona is based in self-doubt and insecurity. Then again, when self-doubt and insecurity seem refreshing, the situation is desperate.

SIGHT AND SOUND, 7/95, p. 56, Mike Atkinson

A perpetually tardy, ruinously stupid and grossly obese ne'er-do-well. Tommy Callahan graduates college by the skin of his teeth, achieving a D plus on a crucial exam. Proudly returning home to his father's troubled midwestern auto parts factory, he is greeted at the airport by Richard, a sarcastic, nerdy clerk at Callahan Auto Parts who Tommy has known since they were kids. Tommy's father surprises him with a white collar job and office at the plant, and announces that he is going to marry Beverly, a beautiful woman whose mean-spirited son Paul shows up in time for the wedding.

Tommy's father suffers a heart attack at the wedding and dies, sending the plant's refinancing plans into the wastebin. With losing the business the only alternative, Tommy resolves to put up his inheritance as collateral to the bank, which they accept providing he can sell his company's products on a cross-country sales run accompanied by know-all Richard. A born loser, Tommy spoils more sales than he makes, and he and Richard endure a hellish road trip. Eventually, they succeed in meeting the bank's quota, but return to find the orders tampered with (by Paul, really Beverly's bedmate), and the business doomed. In a last ditch effort, Richard and Tommy, who have now bonded as friends, masquerade as airline stewards to get to Chicago in time to stop Callahan auto parts from being bought. Beverly and Paul are revealed as con artists, and Tommy saves his family business—and the jobs of 300 employees.

Like a boot camp sending its recruits out into combat, *Saturday Night Live* has been schooling comic actors and embarking them on screen careers for over 17 years, ever since the dubiously talented Chevy Chase left the show after one season and made *Foul Play*. How this is managed business-wise remains something of a mystery since the show has been on the brink of financial and creative collapse for over a decade. With Eddie Murphy's first few glory days and the deathless, graceful film life of Bill Murray as exceptions, *SNL* alumni have never adapted very well to the movies, although the occasional cash cow (*The Blues Brothers*, *Wayne's World*) has grazed on our movie dollars. This would also seem to be the case with *Tommy Boy*, a small scale stage for the sociopathic flabbiness of Chris Farley and the crackling dryness of David Spade. Both began as standup comics before graduating to *SNL*, and both were much funnier outside the repetitive skit format of the show. Here, the two dig into their custom-fit roles like alehouse rats, and the surprise is that however slack, unoriginal and lowbrow-with-a-vengeance *Tommy Boy* may be, it's a masterwork of sharp comic timing compared to *Billy Madison*, *It's Pat*, *The Coneheads* or nearly any film starring Chase, Joe Piscopo or Jim Belushi.

The weight under which *Tommy Boy* must labour is its by-the-numbers, save-the-orphanage plot; why Hollywood decides to showcase performers like Farley and Spade and then saddle them with the dullest, most sanctimonious of feel-good storylines is a mystery for the ages. Better to simply dispense with the concept of plot altogether, as the intermittently amusing *Wayne's World* movies have done. Still, *Tommy Boy's* perhaps unwitting proximity to the pop socialism of *Roger and Me*—complete with evil magnates, desolated factory town, and the notion of jobs being kept irrespective of profit—may raise a few eyebrows, as will its view of ruthless salesmanship as a virtuous ideal. It's a film run through with unconscious revelations, even in its casting (Derek as a smarmy gold-digger, Aykroyd as a mendacious millionaire).

Given the unambitious nature of the material, Farley and Spade are very funny as, respectively, the world's crassest schmuck and the world's prickliest smartass. Farley approximates Lou Costello with his hellbent fat man schtick; he doesn't do much besides smack his head into things and blabber nonsense, but he's adept at it. Spade, on the other hand, need do no more than blink his eyes and put a little pepper on lines like "Did you eat a lot of paint chips when you were a kid?" to come off like a hilarious Generation X version of George Sanders. Truly, an appreciation of *Tommy Boy* is largely contingent on a fondness for crisply-timed and sometimes alarming physical gags. Like most comedy films, it is a matter of fancy, and the fancy in question may be directly proportional to the amount of lager consumed beforehand. Even so, if you were tickled by Hugh Grant's buffoonery in *Four Weddings and a Funeral*, check out Farley to see a master at work.

VILLAGE VOICE, 4/18/95, p. 63, Jeff Salamon

A funny thing happened to Chris Farley and David Spade on the way to their cinematic debut as a comedy team: everybody in America decided their TV show sucked. Nonetheless, from *Wayne's World 2* to *Billy Madison* to *Kevin Nealon, Queen of the Desert*, Hollywood keeps churning out those wacky *SNL* movies as fast as Lorne Michaels can take time off from tonight's Knicks game to sign the papers. *Tommy Boy* is the latest piece of sausage from the factory, and since it was mostly ground out of Chris Farley's hide, the fat-to-meat ratio is even higher than usual.

Tommy Boy's plot—such as it is—forces Tommy Callahan (Farley), the ne'er-do-well son of an auto parts tycoon, to get his act together when Dad (Brian Dennehy) dies of a heart attack at a crucial business juncture. For assistance, Tommy turns to Richard Hayden (Spade), the officious company man who resents the fact that Tommy has used his silver spoon to shovel all the ice cream he can find into his mouth. Fans of fourth-rate comedies will note a similarity to Adam Sandler's recent *Billy Madison*, which was also about a wealthy slob who had to prove he was worthy of his inheritance. (Is it possible that these heirs of the great *SNL* legacy are secretly ashamed of how badly they've pissed away a comedy empire? Dan Aykroyd and Chevy Chase may make lousy movies, but at least they knew how to sustain a three-minute skit.)

On the small screen Chris Farley's girth can reliably produce nervous laughter. But on the big screen he's just another special effect, no more impressive than Jabba the Hutt by mere virtue of being real. Director Peter Segal seems to disagree; at some point he decided that it would be funny enough just to film Farley hauling his bloated gut back and forth across the screen for two hours.

Costar Spade is virtually nonexistent amid this bulk (two words, David: *screen presence;* learn about it), and producer Michaels enforces the same rigorous standards of quality control that have distinguished his tenure on *SNL* the past few seasons. The sole standout here is Julie Warner. As Farley's improbably petite and brainy love interest, she provides viewers with a sympathetic figure—Warner looks as pained pretending to find Farley attractive as we do pretending to find him funny.

Also reviewed in:
CHICAGO TRIBUNE, 3/31/95, Friday/p. C, Michael Wilmington
NEW YORK TIMES, 3/31/95, p. C10, Caryn James
VARIETY, 4/3-9/95, p. 141, Brian Lowry
WASHINGTON POST, 3/31/95, Weekend/p. 39, Desson Howe

TOO OUTRAGEOUS ANIMATION

An Expanded Entertainment release of 27 animated short films. *Producer:* Terry Thoren. *Running time:* 88 minutes. *MPAA Rating:* Not Rated.

NEW YORK POST, 3/31/95, p. 44, Bill Hoffmann

Here's one animated series you'll never see on the Cartoon Network!

"Too Outrageous Animation," at the Quad, is a collection of lewd, crude and rude shorts that revel in their ability to shock.

These 27 cartoons wallow in a world of cartoon genitals, severed limbs, bizarre sex acts and third-grade bathroom humor.

And some of them are very, very funny.

But because all of these little films want to grab your sensibilities and turn them upside down, the collection soon becomes all too much. Shock, shock, shock turns quickly to boredom.

But there are moments of sheer brilliance.

Eric Fogel's "Expiration Date" explores cartoon violence, given that animated creatures like Road Runner and Bugs Bunny can perform relentlessly cruel acts on each other without coming away with so much as a scratch.

Here, a mean-spirited dog chases a terrified cat around the house until suddenly, both realize that the dog's "cartoon license" has expired. In the wink of an eye, the tables turn with the cat seeking a frenzied vengeance on his tormentor, hacking off his limbs, chopping off his head, etc.

Aleksander Sroczynski's "Vice Versa" from Poland should be held dear to the hearts of most New Yorkers. Here, a pedestrian takes exacting revenge on a bird who poops on him from the sky. It's hilarious.

In Keith Alcorn's "Who Calcutta the Cheese?" a little old lady and her pussycat get back at a pesky neighbor who passes a little too much wind during a visit one day. Its humor is infantile but satisfying.

Then there are shorts like Eric Pigors' "Let's Chop Soo-E!"—a mean-spirited, nasty little number about a game show in which the slaughter of a baby pig is the goal. Was animation invented for tripe like this?

All in all, "Too Outrageous Animation" should satisfy adventurous filmgoers looking for something different. For others, don't go expecting Walt Disney.

NEWSDAY, 3/31/95, Part II/p. B5, Gene Seymour

Producer Terry Thoren has tailored his "Too Outrageous Animation" as a made-for-midnight-showings version of his handsomely mounted "International Tournees of Animation." Nothing well-dressed about this Thoren 'toon fest, which spares little or nothing in its pursuit of the gross, the vulgar, the crude and scatological.

One thing "Too Outrageous ..." does have in common with the "Tournees" is the hit-and-miss quality of the shorts being served up. But the obvious compensation here is that they're *short* films, and if there's something you find mildly offensive, don't sweat it. The next one's bound to be *really* offensive.

The most conspicuous presence among the animators represented is a sick little Texas-based outfit called DNA Productions. (Guess there's just something about Texas, to which the world already owes so much for producing Mike ["Beavis and Butt-head"] Judge.) DNA's "Weird Beard" serial, in which a naive lad is given a truly painful lesson in how to be a pirate, pops up throughout the show like a blackhead. DNA's tabloid-TV parody, "Hard Edition," tells you everything you need know about toe-sucking in the South and why so many cross-dressers get run over by trains.

There's not just one, but *two* ribald variations on "Little Red Riding Hood." The title is the only thing Cassandra Einstein borrows intact for her own minimalist, Dionysian version. Mike Grimshaw, meanwhile, makes one of the world's best-known, best-loved dirty jokes the centerpiece of "Little Rude Riding Hood."

Other highlights: Caren Scarpulla's amazing "Liver, Lust or Louie" is a strong contender for best-in-show for its juicy, romance-comics design and its extravagantly decadent story of love-crazy kids who don't let a little thing like multiple-amputation ruin their fun.

Steven Fonti's "Yes, Timmy, There is a Santa Claus" was made at Cal Arts, where many of Disney's finest were schooled. Fonti's black-and-white holiday short starts out like caramel-sweet Disney but ends up like gimlet-sour Luis Buñuel.

Also reviewed in:
WASHINGTON POST, 2/3/95, p. D6, Richard Birmingham

TOP DOG

A Live Entertaiment release of a Tanglewood Entertainment Group production. *Executive Producer:* Tom Steinmetz and Seth Willenson. *Producer:* Andy Howard. *Director:* Aaron Norris. *Screenplay:* Ron Swanson. *Based on a story by:* Aaron Norris and Tim Grayem. *Director of Photography:* Joao Fernandes. *Editor:* Peter Schink. *Music:* Hummie Man. *Sound:* Jim Thornton. *Production Designer:* Norm Baron. *Set Decorator:* Bill Voland. *Costumes:* Vernika Flower-Crow. *Running time:* 87 minutes. *MPAA Rating:* PG-13.

CAST: Chuck Norris (Jake Wilder); Clyde Kusatsu (Capt. Callahan); Michele Lamar Richards (Savannah Boyette); Peter Savard Moore (Karl Koller); Erik von Detten (Matthew Swanson); Carmine Caridi (Lou Swanson); Reno (Himself); *WITH:* Herta Ware; Kai Wulff; Francesco Quinn; Timothy Bottoms.

LOS ANGELES TIMES, 4/29/95, Calendar/p.6, Kevin Thomas

If you have the feeling you've before, it may be because, in a sense, you may have. In 1989's "K-9" James Belushi played a headstrong San Diego cop reluctantly teamed with a German shepherd from the department's K-9 corps and in pursuit of drug kingpin.

In "Top Dog," Chuck Norris also plays a headstrong San Diego cop reluctantly teamed with a K-9 corpsman, a deceptively friendly looking purebred Briard, a French herding dog named Reno. They're out to nail a white supremacist gang intent on blowing up an international racial unity rally being held in San Diego's Balboa Park—along with a string of synagogues across the country.

Not nearly as effective as "K-9," "Top Dog" is essentially yet another standard Chuck Norris martial arts movie directed by his brother Aaron, with man-and-dog relationship thrown in for some comic relief. Reno really is a remarkable, appealing dog whose widely applauded abilities make a dent in the ego of Norris' surly loner.

Aaron Norris keeps things moving at a brisk clip, but "Top Dog" is determinedly elementary, not nearly as bright as its canine hero. Clyde Kusatsu nevertheless has a witty turn as Norris' captain, a man (improbably named Callahan) who's set his sights on the mayor's office. Michele Lamar Richards as a member of the K-9 cop squad gets to behave sensibly and to be brave, and Herta Ware manages a bit of whimsy as Norris' mother.

The film's production notes quote Aaron Norris as saying, wanted to make a film that I would be proud to take my kids to"—yet there is every reason to keep youngsters away from "Top Dog," which opens with an exploding building—a public housing project. A small boy's grandfather, a veteran cop, is slain within the film's first few minutes. Martial arts movies are inherently brutal, and when coupled with a terrorist theme, as is the case here, the result is totally unsuitable for youngsters—even if the Oklahoma bombing had never occurred.

NEW YORK POST, 4/28/95, p. 42, Thelma Adams

"Top Dog" walks the cop-and-pup beat in the grand tradition of "Turner & Hooch" and "K-9."

Jake (Chuck Norris) is a badge with a bad attitude. Reno is a shaggy mutt with a taste for jelly donuts and a nose for drugs. Together, they're partners with a bone to pick.

The rugged, bearded, boxer-wearing action hero performs the trademark face-kicking that has sealed Norris' reputation since Bruce Lee punched his ticket in "Return of the Dragon." Jake's opponents are white supremacists—mostly pasty guys with long, stringy hair and unplaceable accents—intent on launching an ethnic cleansing campaign on the streets of San Diego, "America's Finest City."

The stunts are satisfactory, particularly a night-time shootout with thugs in clown masks. The setup allows Norris to deliver the punch line ("You're under arrest, Bozo") with a genial, look-ma-I'm-telling-a-joke delivery.

Norris kicks butt, but his main function is to be the butt of the gags in this canine-knows-best comedy. Directed by Chuck's brother Aaron, "Top Dog" is a goofy-guy, shaggy-dog, we're-doing- this-for-fun (and worldwide video), don't-take-it-seriously, laid-back, low-wattage lark.

NEWSDAY, 4/29/95, Part II/p. B5, Jonathan Mandell

"Top Dog" could not be more tastelessly timed. It starts off with a group of right-wing white extremists blowing up a building. It ends with the heroes' thwarting of the plot by those same terrorists to blow up a racial unity rally in downtown San Diego on April 20, Hitler's birthday—which is one day after the date of the real-life terrorist explosion in Oklahoma City last week. The producers' insensitivity in not delaying the release of this movie is reason enough to stay away.

If not for the timing, "Top Dog" would merely be standard-issue Chuck Norris, martial artist on Dramamine, with what's meant to be a comic twist. Norris plays Jake, a San Diego police sergeant and loner who is made to work with a new partner, Sergeant Reno. The two have identical records—the same number of arrests and convictions, same number of gunshot wounds, same number of times suspended for insubordination—but Reno is a dog. His first partner was killed by the terrorists, and now Reno wants revenge.

Viewers attracted to a Norris kickfest are not expecting "The Taming of The Shrew," of course, but along with the predictable plot, the lifeless car chases and the simultaneously excessive and dull gunplay and fisticuffs, are jokes that might make a second grader groan. Reno eats Jake's chicken dinner instead of the beef glop in his dog dish, Reno tries on different silly hats and sunglasses at a dog fair, Reno holds the seatbelt in his mouth because of Jake's driving, Reno steals a bishop's red stole off his vestments.

Still, despite a strange repertoire of Method Acting swallows, coy pawplay and menacing growls, Reno is a far better comic actor than Norris, and he has better lines too.

The dopiness could perhaps be excused in a movie meant for the very young, but "Top Dog" isn't suitable for them, not with its scary music, its explicit mention of Nazism and the Ku Klux Klan, and the truly frightening parallels to current events.

Also reviewed in:
CHICAGO TRIBUNE, 4/30/95, Tempo/p. 7, John Petrakis
NEW YORK TIMES, 4/28/95, p. C16, Stephen Holden
VARIETY, 5/1-7/95, p. 37, Joe Leydon
WASHINGTON POST, 4/29/95, p. D3, Rita Kempley

TOTAL ECLIPSE

A Fine Line Features release of an FIT-Portman production with the participation of Capitol Films, produced with the participation of the European Coproduction Fund (U.K.) and Canal Plus and Le Studio Canal Plus. *Executive Producer:* Jean-Yves Asselin, Staffan Ahrenberg, and Pascale Faubert. *Producer:* Jean-Pierre Ramsay Levi. *Director:* Agnieszka Holland. *Screenplay:* Christopher Hampton. *Director of Photography:* Yorgos Arvanitis. *Editor:* Isabel Lorente. *Music:* Jan A.P. Kaczmarek. *Sound:* Michel Boulen and (music) Rafal Paczkowski. *Casting:* Margot Capelier. *Production Designer:* Dan Weil. *Art Director:* Nathalie Buck. *Set Decorator:*

Françoise Benoit-Fresco. *Costumes:* Pierre-Yves Gayraud. *Make-up:* Odile Fourquin. *Stunt Coordinator:* Patrick Cauderlier. *Running time:* 110 minutes. *MPAA Rating:* R.

CAST: Leonardo DiCaprio (Arthur Rimbaud); David Thewlis (Paul Verlaine); Romane Bohringer (Mathilde Verlaine); Dominique Blanc (Isabelle Rimbaud); Felicie Pasotti Cabarbaye (Isabelle, as a child); Nita Klein (Rimbaud's Mother); James Thierée (Frédéric); Emmanuelle Oppo (Vitalie); Denise Chalem (Mrs. Mauté de Fleurville); Andrzej Seweryn (Mr. Mauté de Fleurville); Christopher Thompson (Carjat); Bruce van Barthold (Aicard); Christopher Chaplin (Charles Cros); Christopher Hampton (The Judge); Mathias Jung (André); Kettly Noel (Somalian Woman); Cheb Han (Djami).

FILMS IN REVIEW, 1-2/96, p. 68, Kenneth Geist

In Los Angeles, in 1967, the 31-year-old show biz obscurity, Ken Geist, approached the famous, 63-year-old novelist Christopher Isherwood about expanding a Graham Greene short story I had optioned into a full length screenplay.

Though Isherwood rudely rejected the Greene story as "rubbish," I called back to propose his writing a script about the proto-hippie (hippies were in full flower in 1967)—16-year-old *wunderkind* poet Arthur Rimbaud. I thought Rimbaud's scandalous but artistically productive, runaway relationship with the married, established poet Paul Verlaine (who was 26 but whose baldness made him look considerably older) was a great subject for a film.

Isherwood was both familiar with the material and enthusiastic about the prospect. In the course of two meetings, he outlined dazzling scenes he envisioned. But he would not accept a commission to write a screenplay unless a name director was attached to the project. Isherwood designated his friend Tony Richardson, whom I had previously met, and for whom I had previously written three scripts, including *The Loved One.*

When I arrived in London in September, I met with Richardson's partner, who told me that Tony was on his way to Bali, but would stop to dine with Isherwood in L.A. to discuss the Rimbaud film. When I phoned Isherwood to learn whether Richardson was amendable, "Herr Issyvoo" said that, as Tony hadn't broached the topic, he had remained silent.

The following year, I read that a gifted 18-year-old English playwright, Christopher Hampton, had written a play about the Rimbaud-Verlaine affair, *Total Eclipse,* which was premiering in September at the Royal Court Theatre. I corresponded with Hampton, who was very keen to turn his play into a screenplay, and I made plans to attend the London opening.

The weekend before my departure, I received my acceptance from Columbia Law School, which my father insisted I attend. It proved to be the great second chance in life which I failed to take. I arranged with Columbia to phone them immediately after the opening to inform them whether I was going to pursue the film project or attend law school. (I had been forewarned that law school required a daunting study load for one ten years out of college, and that it would oblige me to compete with students ten years my junior. Graduating at the age of 35, I would be a complete novice.)

Hampton's first act—in which Rimbaud plays havoc with the staid Verlaine household and steals Paul from his wife and newborn—was brilliant comedy. The second act though, featuring scenes of the poets in bed and the dissolution of their relationship, was a big letdown. But I was thinking in terms of a film version which would expand rather than reproduce the play.

I should have waited, until after I had met with Hampton's noted agent, Margaret "Peggy" Ramsey, to phone Columbia. She wouldn't let her brilliant novice commit to writing a screenplay until an experienced director was attached to the project, and she would not provide me with introductions to these name English directors. Moreover, I only had one mimeographed script from the Royal Court to work with in those days before photocopiers were common.

In order to enlist John Schlesinger, I gave my only copy to Pablo Ferro, who had created the title sequence for *Midnight Cowboy.* Despite my warning him to keep the script in his office, Pablo left it in a cab. The cabdrivers' phone number left on my answering machine—an early, unreliable, cumbersome model—was partly obliterated, which meant getting all the addresses of drivers with his surname and sending them imploring telegrams. To find an English director for Hampton to work with meant hanging out in London for many months, and I had gone that route the year before with no success on the Graham Greene project.

Besides, I reasoned, American studios were looking to attract mass audiences and a film of a gay, down-and-out odyssey in Paris, London, and Brussels of the 1870's between two French poets had little mass audience appeal. Thus, I didn't pursue the film project or law school.

But now, 27 years later, a French producer, Jean-Pierre Ramsay Levi, has finally brought Hampton's *Total Eclipse* to the screen in the same month that another Hampton biographical film about the union of a homosexual writer and a hetero painter, *Carrington,* opened in New York.

While the all-English *Carrington* has enjoyed a major art house success, largely due to the acerbically witty dialogue Hampton has written for Lytton Strachey and the jeweled performance of Jonathan Pryce in the title role, the critically lambasted, polyglot *Total Eclipse* will quickly vanish.

Was *Eclipse* botched by the international, something-for-everyone alliance of California valley boy Leonardo DiCaprio as Rimbaud, working class Blackpool accented David Thewlis as a provincial Verlaine, French star Romane Bohringer as Mrs. Verlaine, and Polish director Agnieszka *(Europa, Europa)* Holland filming an Englishman's script? In part, yes.

The comedy of Hampton's play derives from the country bumpkin youth, Rimbaud, as the revolutionary who upsets the circumspect, bourgeois life and art of the sophisticated Parisian Verlaine. In the film, Verlaine is already an absinthe drinker as well as a man prone to punching his pregnant wife and, later, setting her hair on fire. That is, Rimbaud and Verlaine are two of a kind when it comes to outrage, violence, and debauchery. We don't understand that Verlaine's violence is caused by Rimbaud's example, nor that Verlaine's sexual conflict towards his wife is occasioned by the allure of Rimbaud's beauty. (Of course, DiCaprio, though he is made to resemble Rimbaud, is no beauty, while Romane Bohringer is! Fine Line has further emasculated the bedroom scenes by cropping out the male genitalia from the original print shown at the Toronto Film Festival in September.)

While the film has a wounding, stigmata-like symmetry—Rimbaud stabs Verlaine's palm early on and Verlaine shoots Rimbaud in the hand, ending the relationship—it lacks any real content. The outrageous acts are all on display here. Rimbaud breaking up a poet's gathering (Fantin Latour's well known painting of the poets, *Le Coin de Table,* is closely reproduced) by savaging the poet and urinating on his manuscript is emblematic. In addition to the aforementioned violence to his wife, Verlaine kicks his baby's bassinet into a wall. Only the outrage of Rimbaud wiping himself on a page he's torn from a valuable, illuminated manuscript is not depicted.

But except for the bathetic doggerel of "Absinthe," the poem Rimbaud mocks, we don't hear a single verse by Rimbaud or Verlaine in the entire picture. Holland or Hampton conceives of only one piece of poetic imagery. This is the obscure, repeated image of what appears to be a beating wing, which turns out to be a foreshadowing of a ripping cloth on the litter bearing Rimbaud toward an amputation of his tumorous leg. Other than "the wing" there is no cinematic imagery in the film to suggest that many of Rimbaud's symbolist poems were actually written in a state of deliberate derangement induced by drink and drugs. This would, evidently, be a poor object lesson for DiCaprio's young fans.

Only the French will bring a knowledge of the poets' work to the picture. For the rest of the world, Rimbaud and Verlaine appear to be merely a pair of degenerate hooligans.

It's one thing to throw in a gratuitous scene of the adult Rimbaud (DiCaprio with a funny little paste-on mustache and hair dye) as a trader in Africa, having sex with a black woman who squats on top of him—that's sexual maturity in a *Hamptoon*. However, the telescoped biography of Rimbaud post-Verlaine is all insignificant, anticlimactic filler in this film. What's significant is that Rimbaud, the greatest French poet of the late 19th century, stopped writing at the age of 19 and turned to such non-poetic, though adventurous pursuits as gun running. Rimbaud's creative life ends with his relationship to Verlaine, and that's where the film should have ended as well.

Of course, the film has a latter day parallel to Christopher Hampton's abortive career as a notable young playwright. But his current financial success in the cinematic arena overshadows his failure to become a significant writer for the theater.

Yes, Verlaine's abandonment of Rimbaud in London and the subsequent shooting in Brussels (when Rimbaud was about to leave Verlaine) contribute to Rimbaud's literary cessation. But we neither care about nor comprehend this twisted father and son relationship. Verlaine does mention Rimbaud's revitalizing his poetry, but we don't see any notable changes in the older poet.

Ms. Holland introduces some grating Polish chamber music, apparently to provide employment for her countrymen and elevate the tone of this tawdry enterprise. César Franck's chamber music would have been more lyrical and appropriate to the period. Then again, Franck was a French genius like Rimbaud and Verlaine. The only thing ingenious in *Total Eclipse* is DiCaprio's barking like a dog. It's a somewhat lesser gift.

LOS ANGELES TIMES, 11/3/95, Calendar/p. 4, Kenneth Turan

"Total Eclipse" is the art-house equivalent of "Casey at the Bat." Considerable ability has gone into a potential home run scenario, but the result is a big whiff all the way around.

Written by Christopher Hampton, responsible for "Dangerous Liaisons" and the upcoming "Carrington," directed by Agnieszka Holland, best known for "Europa, Europa" and "The Secret Garden," and starring Leonardo DiCaprio, David Thewlis and Romane Bohringer, "Total Eclipse" can't be accused of stinting on talent.

And its story of the tortured relationship between two of France's greatest 19th-Century poets, Paul Verlaine (Thewlis) and Arthur Rimbaud (DiCaprio), certainly has possibilities. The result, however, is a stagy and excessive mishmash that turns their wretched lives into a costumed version of Beavis and Butt-head.

Verlaine was already an established poet but not very happy when 16-year-old Rimbaud first wrote to and then visited him in Paris in 1871. Addicted to absinthe, married to a young woman (Bohringer) he doesn't care for and furious at the poverty that forces him to live with his stuffy in-laws, the older man considers both Rimbaud's new style of poetry and his rebellious lifestyle to be welcome changes.

Given that DiCaprio plays Rimbaud as a 19th-Century version of the Jim Carroll of "The Basketball Diaries," viewers may choose to think otherwise. Hampton's script and DiCaprio's acting create an obsessively self-obsessed Rimbaud whose every action exudes arrogance and prideful satisfaction.

Verlaine, however, finds him liberating both poetically and personally. He loves it when Rimbaud eats with his fingers, and when his young friend stands on a table and urinates on a lesser poet's work, the older man is beside himself with joy. This, Verlaine thinks, is how life should be lived. He leaves his wife, whom he has periodically abused, and embarks on a sexual relationship with his muse.

Made for each other, Verlaine and Rimbaud behave abominably to everyone in sight, much to their mutual amusement. Finally, having alienated all potential victims, they end up behaving abominably toward each other, kind of like an Oprah episode on "Poets Who Can't Get Along." Between Verlaine's whining and wheedling and Rimbaud's pouting snits, it's amazing either one ever has the time to write.

In fact, one of "Total Eclipse's" numerous difficulties is that it provides only a minimal idea of what each man's poetry is about, shedding neither heat nor light on their lives and offering no reason to care about their infantile antics. The film's entire team has so bought into the shopworn myth that geniuses must misbehave that no one has escaped unscathed. The script may insist that "the only unbearable thing is that nothing is unbearable," but those who wade through "Total Eclipse" will be able to cite at least one exception.

NEW YORK POST, 11/3/95, p. 40, Thelma Adams

In "Total Eclipse," precocious American actor Leonardo DiCaprio plays precocious 19th-century French poet Arthur Rimbaud. In the opening sequence, DiCaprio juts his chin toward the sun, devours an apple, chews on a pipe and contemplates suicide, overpunctuating every gesture.

Cut to a pristine, poetic image of a train slicing through the picturesque French countryside, a stanza of steam shooting above it. We are only five minutes into our artistic journey and I already feel like slapping brat packing poet DiCaprio/Rimbaud.

The situation does not improve when Rimbaud arrives on the doorstep of the established poet Paul Verlaine (David "Naked" Thewlis). It is 1871. Verlaine, having read a few of Rimbaud's poems, summons the 16-year-old bumpkin wunderkind to Paris. The 27-year-old Verlaine, homely inside and out, is married to the bourgeois Mathilde (Romane "The Accompanist" Bohringer). His poetry might be refined, but his treatment of his pregnant wife is coarse and boorish.

During a dispute about their abominable house guest, Verlaine slaps his wife. Later, he slings Mathilde from their bed to the floor, where she clutches her rounded belly in a motion that is both protective and pained.

When next seen, Mathilde has given birth: Are the two events linked? The script glosses over this possibility, giving us instead an opium-heated love scene between the poets followed by Verlaine shoving the newborn and cradle across the room and setting his wife's hair afire.

Six months pregnant myself, I could hardly watch the scenes of domestic violence. Followed by a bitter joke ("I haven't set fire to her since Thursday," Verlaine says to Rimbaud over absinthe) and the self-destructive antics of the poets' punk affair, I found myself devoid of sympathy for the pair. My heart had already left my throat when Mathilde bounced on the hardwood floor and could never find its way back to these two self-involved bruisers.

Screenwriter Christopher Hampton, whose "Carrington" opens here next Friday, has a great nose for a sexy literary love story. But "Carrington," set on the fringe of Britain's Bloomsbury Circle, eclipses this darker French tart.

"Carrington" is buoyed up by Lytton Strachey's stinging wit (and Jonathan Pryce's waspish performance); in "Eclipse," the grunge love story overshadows the poetics of Rimbaud and Verlaine. With their writings shoehorned into the text and their passion transformed into sweat and spite, the poetic spirit fades into a callow and pretentious middle-brow picture.

Both movies suffer because Hampton fumbles in framing the drama. Even more so in "Eclipse" than in "Carrington," which he also directed, Hampton lets the story stretch out agonizingly over the years once he has sounded his themes and the depths of the pivotal relationships.

Director Agnieszska Holland ("Europa Europa") assures that the film is pretty to watch—perhaps too pretty, given the nastiness of the principals. She draws heavily from the paintings of Verlaine contemporary Edouard Manet.

Holland cannot overcome the failings of an international cast: Thewlis has a British accent; Bohringer's is French; and DiCaprio speaks Americanese, adding vulgar anachronisms and an Arsenio Hall whoop.

"The only unbearable thing is that nothing is unbearable," says Rimbaud. He never had a chance to see "Total Eclipse."

SIGHT AND SOUND, 4/97, p. 52, Liese Spencer

France, 1892. The poet Verlaine meets with Arthur Rimbaud's sister Isabelle in a café. She asks him to give her the original copies of Rimbaud's early poetry, and he reminisces about his and the other poet's relationship.

1871. After sending some of his poetry to Verlaine, the 16-year-old Rimbaud arrives in Paris to stay with Verlaine at the apartment he shares with his young wife Mathilde and parents-in-law. Rimbaud's uncouth manners soon alienate Verlaine's relations so he finds Rimbaud an attic room. Rimbaud upsets the poetry salons of Paris by denouncing the work of established poets. Verlaine and Rimbaud begin an affair, Verlaine returning home only to beat his pregnant wife.

Verlaine and Rimbaud leave Paris and travel to Brussels. At a hotel there, Verlaine arranges a secret meeting with Mathilde. They sleep together and Mathilde suggests they emigrate to New Caledonia. Rimbaud appears at the hotel and argues tearfully with Verlaine. Eventually, Verlaine decides to embark for New Caledonia with Mathilde and her mother. While changing trains on the way, Verlaine spies Rimbaud and switches trains, abandoning Mathilde and her mother. Verlaine and Rimbaud take a boat to England where they fight and live in poverty. Verlaine receives a letter from Mathilde's lawyer asking for a divorce and a medical examination to prove the sexual relationship between the poets. Rimbaud struggles to write, venting his spleen on his adoring mentor.

After another fight Verlaine leaves for Brussels. Rimbaud follows. Rejected from the Spanish army and by his wife, Verlaine buys a pistol to commit suicide. Taunted by Rimbaud, he shoots him in the hand. Verlaine is imprisoned for two years. Rimbaud returns to the family farm to write. After Verlaine's release, the two meet, but Rimbaud rejects Verlaine's advances, leaving for Abyssinia to work as a trader.

Back in 1892, Isabelle supplies the rest of the story. After a fever, Rimbaud is brought back to France and his leg is amputated. He returns to Africa and dies there. After Isabelle leaves the café, Verlaine orders two absinths and hallucinates drinking with Rimbaud.

The intertitles that precede *Total Eclipse* sketch out the historical figures of Verlaine and Rimbaud, ending with the flourish that "what follows is their story, directly taken from their letters and poetry." Designed to assert the film's historical authenticity, this tag savours more of the disclaimers used to justify sensationalist dramas 'based on a true story'. However truthful, this is a turgid, vulgar study of these poets' relationship. It seems to take forever and still fails to understand it's protagonists, disguising a lack of psychological clarity with a barrage of melodrama.

Christopher Hampton's screenplay was probably too long to start with—it was adapted from one of his early plays, and feels thoroughly researched but all too inclusive. However, the film's failure owes more to the clumsy direction of Agnieszka Holland (*Europa, Europa, The Secret Garden*), who seems unable to think beyond the clichés of the tortured artist. In one early scene, Rimbaud is pictured as literally barking mad, woofing at a set of china dogs. The unequal relation between Rimbaud and his adoring but less talented mentor Verlaine, is repeatedly characterised by Rimbaud stomping or streaking off into the distance, with Verlaine struggling to catch up. After a number of such scenes it all begins to feel rather routine, as though the camera were pursuing and relentlessly detailing the domestic spats of two exceptionally dull queens.

Established early on, Holland's overwrought signalling of artistic and emotional tumult can't be sustained effectively for long, but instead of varying pace or tone, the director continues to crank up the melodrama until the film capsizes into ridiculous parody. After Rimbaud has stabbed Verlaine through the hand and Verlaine shot a hole through Rimbaud's palm, it's hard to feel particularly moved or even surprised by the long, dragged out sequence of a dying Rimbaud attempting to walk on crutches with an amputated leg. While Hampton's script blends biography with a meditation on the nature of poetry, scholarly nuances are lost in a welter of unintentionally bathetic detail. From showing Rimbaud violently fucking Verlaine to a close-up of Verlaine receiving an anal examination, no physical brutality is spared. It seems as if Holland wants to compensate for the cerebral, intangible nature of the poets' thoughts by battering home a crude physicality.

Given all this, it's not surprising that the relationship at the heart of the film fails to be compelling. As Verlaine, David Thewlis' rather lugubrious face looks unusually repulsive, a high waxy white forehead rising in a great dome above bulbous eyes and a long nose. At least Thewlis does a good job of inhabiting his unsympathetic character, whining and bullying in turns, and allowing his features to spread into a disingenuous, wide-eyed mask whenever he pronounces one of his self-aggrandising excuses.

The same cannot be said of Leonardo DiCaprio who's clearly out of his depth as Rimbaud. While suitably pert as an object of desire, his main technique for expressing the great soul of the poet is to offer a peculiar jerky walk. And while this European co-production features a number of different accents, it's DiCaprio's drawl that rankles the most. He delivers his observations on the human condition as if he were reading the label of a tin of soup. Worse still are the silent, supposedly epic sequences Rimbaud in Africa, where poor makeup and a pencil moustache make him look less aged than some kind of weird Valentino crossed with Ed Wood. Tellingly, David Thewlis' ageing Verlaine, dressed in a long, unconvincing beard and floppy hat looks uncannily like Jonathan Pryce, the star of Hampton's last film, *Carrington*.

VILLAGE VOICE, 11/7/95, p. 72, Georgia Brown

Given that *Total Eclipse*'s subject is two French poets, Rimbaud and Verlaine, one might expect at least a fraction of *The Kingdom*'s bountiful imagery or bouyant formal experimentation. [See Brown's review.] But no, this deadly literal drama, directed by Agnieszka Holland, hasn't a poetic boner in its body.

As biographers are keen to point out, poets are horrid human beings. I mean, they can be. Christopher Hampton, who seems to like rummaging in literary folks' garbage (next week, *Carrington*), here adapts an early play: Rimbaud and Verlaine go to pot. Basically, the narrative follows facts. The cocky teenaged provincial, Rimbaud (Leonardo DiCaprio), arrives in Paris and captures the heart of the established fruitcake, Verlaine (David Thewlis), who, besotted with passion and drunk on absinthe, proceeds to treat his pregnant, 18-year-old wife (Romane Bohringer) abominably. After tearing around Paris, offending colleagues and benefactors, the two men make off for the coast and to London, all the while continuing their furious lovers' quarrels.

When the insulted Verlaine (Rimbaud says he looks "like a cunt" carrying home a fish) retreats to Brussels, Rimbaud follows, whereupon Verlaine shoots Rimbaud in the hand and is sentenced to two years in prison. The sentence is for both aggravated assault and sodomy. (It's hard to see how the duo gets away with tearing up so many hotel rooms.)

Rimbaud, of course, was a marvelous boy (writing all his great poems between 16 and 19), and playing a raving genius can't be easy. (Repressed, inward types such as Eliot or Kafka are no doubt easier to represent.) Tom Hulce's goofy Mozart was just bearable, but then *Amadeus* had that old goat Salieri as narrator and antagonist. Salieri's nattering on about God's unfairness in not rewarding his own hard work, showering gifts on such a wastrel, was at least a distraction from Wolfie's antics.

Structured as a flashback—a bald, washed-up Verlaine reflects on the past, although there's only the vaguest sense that what we witness is his point of view—*Total Eclipse* provides no clever playwrightish conceits. We're expected merely to watch two creepy egotists lusting and raging and occasionally playing like puppies. Embarked on a course of acting out to end all actings-out, DiCaprio's bumpkin proclaims his superiority while putting his muddy boots on all the clean linen he can find. (Holland has DiCaprio biting an apple as if he's a boy genius biting an apple.) Thewlis's Verlaine is uglier and scarier—in one scene he sets fire to his wife's hair. Some aspects of the role may be reminiscent of the actor's tour de force in *Naked*, but *Naked* had a grim purpose and Johnny was never fey. Only in a few close-ups is Thewlis able to invest some nuance, some sly humor, into this loathsome figure.

Total Eclipse is a total waste. Go and you'll just have to try to get dopey images of these two loons out of your mind. Then again, the movie can be seen as someone's sinister attempt to make two men in love look ridiculous.

Also reviewed in:
CHICAGO TRIBUNE, 11/3/95, Friday/p. H, Michael Wilmington
NEW REPUBLIC, 12/4/95, p. 27, Stanley Kauffmann
NEW YORK TIMES, 11/3/95, p. C14, Janet Maslin
VARIETY, 9/11-17/95, p. 109, Todd McCarthy
WASHINGTON POST, 11/3/95, p. F6, Hal Hinson
WASHINGTON POST, 11/3/95, Weekend/p. 43, Desson Howe

TOY STORY

A Walt Disney Pictures release of a Pixar production. *Executive Producer:* Edwin Catmull and Steven Jobs. *Producer:* Ralph Guggenheim and Bonnie Arnold. *Director:* John Lasseter. *Technical Director:* William Reeves. *Screenplay:* Joss Whedon, Andrew Stanton, Joel Cohen, and Alec Sokolow. *Story:* John Lasseter, Andrew Stanton, Pete Docter, and Joe Ranft. *Editor:* Robert Gordon and Lee Unkrich. *Music:* Randy Newman. *Music Editor:* Jim Flamberg. *Sound:* Gary Rydstrom and (music) Frank Wolf. *Sound Editor:* Tim Holland. *Casting:* Ruth Lambert. *Animatiion Supervisor:* Pete Docter. *Art Director:* Ralph Eggleston. *Model & Shading Coordinator:* Deirdre Warin. *Shader & Visual Effects Supervisor:* Thomas Porter. *Running time:* 81 minutes. *MPAA Rating:* G.

VOICES: Tom Hanks (Woody); Tim Allen (Buzz Lightyear); Don Rickles (Mr. Potato Head); Jim Varney (Slinky Dog); Wallace Shawn (Rex); John Ratzenberger (Hamm); Annie Potts (Bo Peep); John Morris (Andy); Erik Von Detten (Sid); Laurie Metcalf (Mrs. Davis); R. Lee Ermey (Sergeant); Sarah Freeman (Hannah); Penn Jillette (TV Announcer).

FILMS IN REVIEW, 3-4/96, p. 67, Edward Summer

Surely no motion picture art is more pure than animation. Any normal motion picture involves pointing a camera at some real life object or human being and exposing a strip of film. Much of the art comes from the polished performances of flesh and blood actors, the sublime skill of cameramen, and the defining emphasis of carefully controlled lighting. In the animation of drawings, however, literally nothing exists until someone draws it. There is no motion until an artist renders it—one or more drawings for each frame of film, and there is no character until the animator imagines it and breathes life into otherwise inanimate pencil lines.

To break the rule, notable exceptions must exist—the stop-motion artists (Starevitch, O'Brien, Harryhausen, Danforth, Tippett, Vinton), the abstract object animators (Oskar Fischinger), the eclectic animators (Norman McClaren and the National Film Board of Canada)—but heretofore the primary exemplars of commercial animation involved drawings: the art of Walt Disney, Max Fleisher, the Warner Brothers Studio was the art of pen and ink and paint.

With the advent of the modern computer came, inevitably, computer animation. On the heels of multitudes of experimental shorts and commercials, *Tron* (1982) and *The Lost Starfighter* (1984) were breakthrough feature films. *Tron* involved the marriage of live-action and computer-animated images, while *The Last Starfighter* integrated computer-generated spaceships and physical objects that existed nowhere in real life. Over the past 15 years or so, we have been treated to other astonishing (and short) interludes, tidbits, and jewel boxes of animations created completely within the magnetic fields of computer chips. Many of these involved the translation of human drawings or scanned objects into images manipulated by computer software, but the results were like nothing seen before: sometimes crude, artificial, and unconvincing, at other times indistinguishable from film taken of real life. None of these gems of computer-generated movement were more astonishing and startling than the dinosaurs that stomped and scurried through *Jurassic Park* (1994).

In these films, pen, pencil, and paper—even light and sometimes celluloid film itself—are dispensed with entirely. So exquisite is the control of these systems, that the computer itself all but replaces traditional physical tools with monitors, digitizing systems, and track balls. The Disney Studio has used computer "ink and paint" to finish and color recent "animated" features like *The Lion King* (1994) and *Pocahontas* (1995), virtually eliminating real paint in the production of final screen images, though still relying upon the actual pencil drawings of human animators to draw the characters themselves.

Toy Story marks an historic moment in this on-going chronology of innovation. It is the first feature length motion picture produced entirely within computers. This feat is a triumph not only of technological scale, but equally of story and character. Had it been only a spurious outpouring of sparkling bits and bytes, there wouldn't be much to say: Pixar (the company that produced this delight) had done that before with *Tin Toy* (the 1989 Oscar-winning short). But the sense of life and the sheer entertainment value of what could easily be dismissed as a computer nerd's boondoggle tickles the cerebral cortex as much as it warms the heart.

A slim, but genuinely charming tale of the use and abuse of friendship, *Toy Story* pairs a cowboy doll, Woody (voiced by Tom Hanks), with a spaceman doll, Buzz Lightyear (voiced by Tim Allen), and chronicles their misadventures. *Toy Story* is a real audience pleaser full of silly jokes, chases, and suspense, along with a heavy dollop of heart-tugging character conflicts and reconciliations.

Just to stimulate your mathematical neurons for a moment, each frame of film has a resolution of approximately 1536 x 933 pixels (a tiny picture element dot somewhat equivalent to those little dots that you can see if you press your eyeballs up to your television set) so each frame of film has about 1,433,088 little dots in it. Multiply that by the Final Frame Count of the film which is about 110,064 frames and you get slightly more that 15.5 *billion* pixels. More than one trillion bytes of storage space was required for all the computer information, and it took 800,000 computer hours to compute these frames and nearly four years to complete the whole project. I'm impressed. Spun off from a company started originally by George Lucas, Pixar has been on the cutting edge of high-tech computer animation for more than a decade and will, in the future, do at least two more features under contract to Disney which, to say the least, has not been blind to the advantages of computer animation.

Oddly, despite the magnitude of this accomplishment, the technology is still in its infancy. The subject matter of the film lent itself well to the state-of-the-art: real toys have, for the most part, rather smooth surfaces which, in a relative sense, are easier to render. The scenes involving objects with highly textured surfaces (like roads, trees, or hair) required the greatest computer resources. On a frame-for-frame basis, the *Jurassic Park* dinosaurs were much more computer intensive to produce than the toys that star in this film, and really represent a far more detailed final image. What is to be applauded in *Toy Story* is the magical blend of fine storytelling with high-tech and the sheer persistence of the filmmakers in bringing it all to the screen.

LOS ANGELES TIMES, 11/22/95, Calendar/p. 1, Kenneth Turan

Guilt. Envy. Nervous breakdowns and rampant neuroses. If you've ever thought that toys had an easy life, "Toy Story" will set you straight.

Although its computer-generated imagery is impressive, the major surprise of this bright foray into a new kind of animation is how much cleverness has been invested in story and dialogue. Usually when a film credits seven writers, it's not a positive sign, but "Toy Story" turns out to be smart fun on a verbal as well as visual level.

Those writers (Joss Whedon, Andrew Stanton, Joel Cohen & Alec Sokolow, from a story by Stanton, director John Lasseter, Peter Docter and Joe Ranft) have kept "Toy Story" true to what has become one of Disney's most successful formulas, visible in everything from "Aladdin" to "The Nightmare Before Christmas": Supply enough on-screen pratfalls and visual dazzle to keep the kids occupied while luring the adults with feisty characterizations and wised-up jokes about "laser envy" and plastic corrosion awareness meetings.

What is special about "Toy Story" is that although "Tin Toy," a short co-directed by Lasseter, won an Oscar in 1988, this is the first time that computer-generated animation has been successfully stretched to feature length.

By giving its normally inanimate protagonists a magical three-dimensional quality, "Toy Story" creates the kind of gee-whiz enchantment that must have surrounded "Snow White" on its initial release. True, computer imagery still has trouble creating people that don't look like space aliens, but this film compensates by sensibly shoving the humans to the background and focusing on those darn toys.

Echoing a concept at least as old as Tchaikovsky's "The Nutcracker," "Toy Story" showcases toys springing to life when people aren't around. But rather than being idle playthings, these toys, the possessions of a small boy named Andy, turn out to be careworn adults, easily overwhelmed by worries and woes.

Rex, the toy dinosaur (Wallace Shawn), is in the grip of a crisis of confidence, worried that while he's "going for fearsome, it just comes off as annoying." Bo Peep (Annie Potts) fears her come-hither looks are being wasted, and gruff Mr. Potato Head (Don Rickles) alternates between grousing about mistreatment at the hands of Andy's infant sister ("ages 3 and up; it's on my box") to yearning for a Mrs. Potato Head to end his solitude.

Riding herd over these troubled folks is Woody (Tom Hanks), an old-fashioned floppy pull-string toy that has been Andy's favorite forever. So while the others worry that they'll turn into "next month's garage sale fodder" when new toys appear on the scene, Woody tries to calm them down with a pep talk about "being here for Andy when he needs us."

But the birthday party that opens the film turns out to be a serious shock to Woody. Andy is given a Buzz Lightyear space ranger action figure, complete with "more gadgets than a Swiss army knife," and it begins to look as if there's a new top toy in town.

Given to saying "to infinity, and beyond" at slight provocation, Buzz (Tim Allen) is one of "Toy Story's" pleasant surprises, because, unlike the rest of Andy's possessions, he doesn't realize that he really is a toy. Self-absorbed and delusional, given to fatuous pronouncements like "I come in peace," Buzz thinks he is a genuine space ranger, on a mission to save the universe from the menacing Emperor Zurg.

All this drives Woody crazy, as does the fact that Buzz's presence increasingly places his position as Andy's favorite toy in jeopardy. As "Toy Story" amusingly progresses, both Woody and Buzz confront these unpleasant realities and face the discomforting need to cooperate with each other to save themselves from a variety of troubles.

Starting with Tom Hanks, who brings an invaluable heft and believability to Woody, "Toy Story" is one of the best voiced animated features in memory, with all the actors (as well as Randy Newman, who contributed three songs and the score) making their presences strongly felt.

Continuously inventive, "Toy Story" has a number of cheerful set pieces that keep it lively. One of the cleverest is a visit to the fast-food Pizza Planet, where Buzz and Woody end up inside a kind of gum-ball machine whose inhabitants worship the claw that conveys them to the outside world. It's a deft, wacky sequence, complete with Woody shouting, "Stop it, you zealots," at the three-eyed figures, and it typifies why "Toy Story" is a captivating first step along animation's most promising new frontier.

NEW STATESMAN & SOCIETY, 5/29/96, p. 28, Lizzie Francke

They call it entoytainment. The toy and film/television industries have grown so enmeshed that *Variety*—the US movie trade's bible—is now just as likely to devote a special supplement to the American international Toy Fair as to the Cannes Film Festival. Indeed for studio executives, schmoozing the toy industry is as important as dining out on lamb's lettuce and Evian with "A" list stars. For a movie's spin-off merchandising is now not just a nice little side-earner, but a critical part of the revenue: Warner Bros has recently created its own toy division, while Dreamworks, the new outfit belonging to Steven Spielberg (the man who said that directing was like playing with a gigantic model train set) has struck a deal with the leading US manufacturer Hasbro to create its own original toy line. A medium-sized independent production company can now become a major player overnight if it has a toyable product. Such was the fortune of New Line, the company behind *The Mask* which saw Jim Carrey bounding into the big time along with a flotilla of cheap plastic durables.

For those proud owners of a battered pair of Mickey Mouse ears or a flashing Darth Vader sword (batteries not included), this might all seem very old news. The difference now is that the toy companies are calling the shots with film executives paying deference to the likes of Hasbro and other manufacturing giants like Mattel. Reputedly, Mattel execs advised Disney to include the hair plaiting scene in *Pocahontas* so that they could market the Braided Beauty Pocahontas doll. (Indeed, the press kits for the film contained a guide to all the merchandising opportunities.) It is also rumoured that last year's *Batman Forever* was rejigged to be more toyfriendly than its previous, darker incarnations.

That such toy-screen symbiosis has evolved should not surprise: their shared synthetic nature made it inevitable. Recent icons, such as Arnie Schwarzenegger or *Baywatch*'s *uber-frau* Pamela Anderson, look like they have been hatched out of plastic-injected moulds; indeed, dare I mention it, might even have been plastic-injected. Others are like fluffy munchkins—take Robin Williams, who, as if to prove a point, starred in *Toys*, the terrible Barry Levinson whimsy of a few years back, and has recently played in the board game extravaganza *Jumanji*.

Now, finally, with Disney's extraordinary break-through computer-generated animation extravaganza *Toy Story,* it's the turn for the toys to be the stars. It's all incredibly knowing piece which, while working as a rollicking adventure for children, has a polished, witty script (by a quartet of writers—Joss Whedon, Andrew Stanton, Joel Cohen and Alec Sokolow, who are all up for an Oscar) that points to whom its core audience might just as likely be. Hi-tech movie wizardry, as developed for Disney by the company Pixar, has evolved an animation style that is as 3-D as can be as it grafts images from a gamut of sources to give the film a hyper-real look. Such state-of-the-art stuff of the future, though, is used to recreate a very cosy and familiar set up. For the film is very much about the bits of plastic from the 1960s post baby boomers' childhood which, if they weren't owned, may at least be recollected from all those TV blipverts "From Mattel" that seeped into our kiddie brains. There is Slinky Dog (the one with the tubular wire tummy), Mr Potato head (the spud with the rearrangable face), Barrel of Monkeys (the fiddly bits that got scattered everywhere) and Raggedy Ann (just plain raggedy), who all play supporting roles in the film alongside its two newly hatched stars with a convincingly retro edge—Woody, the cowboy on a string, and Buzz Lightyear, a space ranger whose patter is as smooth as his gleaming surfaces. Not all the playbox contents made it into the movie. Barbie was reputed to have made an appearance, but apparently there was a little disagreement about her characterisation—something to do with her rescuing (or not) the film's hero.

Its neat little storyline is predicated on that old nursery myth that the toys have a life when the kids aren't looking—it's part of their uncanny nature (the more disturbing aspect of this is touched on briefly in the film). But be sure that here the toys all know their place that they are toys and nothing else. All except for Buzz, the new plaything in his owner Andy's life. He's convinced that he really is a spaceman sent to protect the universe from the Evil Emperor Zurg, which makes Woody, who until Buzz's landing had been ruling the range, feel rather superior. For the plastic cowboy knows that all things small and synthetic hail from Taiwan, while the most evil thing in their universe is plastic corrosion. Their combative stance, though, is soon dissipated when they both find themselves in the grubby hands of Sid, the sadistic boy next door—the kind who blows up his Action Men and delights in decapitating his sister's dolls.

The vivid animation makes you buy into Woody and Buzz's existential realm. So much so that *Toy Story* could be a plea for toy rights, or an indictment of kids' consumerist values as the old favorites quake in the fear of being rendered redundant by a wave of spanking new birthday presents—just as computer animation might be rendering the old pen-and-ink and "stop frame" style obsolete, along with all those trained to use them. But perhaps it's not just the animators who should worry. *Toy Story* is a celebration of the synthetic, with endless possibilities for Hollywood. Perhaps next time Arnie Schwarzenegger asks too much money for a film, producers will call on Pixar to knock up a lookalike. That thought should cut the stars down to size. But that's entoytainment.

NEW YORK, 12/4/95, p. 126, David Denby

In *Toy Story*, the new animated feature from Disney, a group of plastic toys—Mr. Potato Head, Slinky Dog, a piggy bank, and many others—gets battered and tossed by children. But the toys, picking themselves up when the children leave, are not hurt. What they do fear, it turns out, is that they will no longer be useful (their theme song ought be "As Long As He Needs Me"). Alone now, the toys tell jokes and complain like weary schoolteachers at a Friday-afternoon bitch session. Life as a plaything, it turns out, is not all play. Their master, Andy, a 6-year-old boy, is having a birthday party, and sure enough, disaster strikes: Woody, an old-fashioned pull-string cowboy, gets replaced as Andy's favorite by a smugly confident space action figure, Buzz Lightyear, who has a blinking laser beam and a computer-generated voice. Buzz is so stupid he doesn't even know he's a toy, but it doesn't matter: Woody's days may be numbered. Anguish and tumult tear apart the toy world.

Toy Story is a comedy that ends with a chase; it features the voices of Tom Hanks, Tim Allen, and Don Rickles, and much of it has a jokey, knockabout quality. But just as in many of the classic Disney animal cartoons *(Bambi, Dumbo,* etc.), there's an underlay of anxiety and fear—the fear of disrupted family relationships, the fear of abandonment. Those old Disney movies, with their mommies slaughtered and witches hovering nearby, hit children where they live. This time, however, we get a new and perverse twist: The "parent" figure is himself a child, Andy, who takes his toys for granted and throws them into a chest when he's no longer interested. And the villain is not a fox, a witch, or a pair of hunters but another child, Sid, of the shining braces, who lives next door and mutilates toys by sawing off their heads and then sewing the heads onto different bodies. Sid the Nazi. Since every toy has its own special identity, what Sid does is especially horrifying.

I have no idea how children will be affected by this portrait of them as thoughtless little beasts. As a parent and ex-child, however, I was highly gratified. *Toy Story* takes a number of surprising turns, and though I didn't fall in love with it—there's a lot of routine clobbering, scrambling, and zooming about—I remained interested and happy until the end (and children, I think, will adore it). The movie has some gravity, in both senses of the word. Disney and the specialists at a computer-animation company called Pixar have developed new techniques that give the figures a three-dimensional look, Woody, Mr. Potato Head, and the others don't appear "drawn" at all: They stand out from the backgrounds and seem to cast shadows, and when they run, they lift off the ground—and then land on it again. There really is *ground,* which is a fresh element in animated films. Yet something is lost amid the new realism—the fantasy and grandeur, the storms and monsters, of the old hand-drawn styles. There's nothing elemental or romantic about this movie, nothing to wonder over. The toys look like plastic figures that have moving limbs and features. And the humans look the same as the toys—which may well have been an intentional joke. All of them, toys and humans, share the same shiny plastic-figure molding, as if they were all part of a single consumerist universe in which everything is disposable.

The postmodernist jokes give the movie a spark. Buzz Lightyear joins the toy community, but he suffers from certain ontological confusions. He thinks he's an actual spaceman who needs to be heroic all the time. He and Woody fight, become enemies, and then, willy-nilly, friends, sticking together through thick and thin. When they're away from Andy's house, lost in the world, they wander into a "futuristic" pizza parlor that has been outfitted as a space station. Poor Buzz thinks he's in an actual space station. The joke made me wonder: Have the filmmakers (too many of them to list) been reading Guy Debord, Jean Baudrillard, or some of the other French theorists of illusion and representation? It's possible. It's also possible they just picked up an idea floating around everywhere: In our world, nature is dead, and everything is now a representation of one sort or another; we're all lost in the forest of simulacra. (The movie is filled with references to other movies, including, at one scary moment, an homage to Tod Browning's *Freaks.)*

In the same pizza parlor, Buzz and Woody fall into one of those primitive electromechanical games in which a claw comes down in a glass box and tries to pick up one of many little dolls with a round face and a tuft of hair. It's just a machine, but from the dolls' point of view, the claw is god. A creepy religious community of chanting believers, the dolls just long to ascend to the higher regions. *Toy Story* takes the comedy of scale, familiar from many animated films, and gives it a sorrowful twist: All the toys want is to play their role as toys—they want to get back to Andy. No doubt the politically correct will point out that the toys suffer from false consciousness, that they accept their subservience. Will there be a sequel in which the toys rise up in revolt?

NEW YORK POST, 11/22/95, p. 43, Michael Medved

The best news about "Toy Story" is that the film delivers a good story along with its great toys.

There's tenderness here together with technology, emotion as well as imagination, refreshing wit to accompany all the eye-popping wonders.

The picture may earn its place in cinema history as the first full-length feature animated entirely with computer graphics, but it will win the affection of its audience for the warmth, humor, and consistent intelligence of its well-crafted script (courtesy of six writers).

The story refreshes the old childhood fantasy about toys who only pretend to be inanimate in the presence of humans, but immediately spring to life when left alone in a boy's bedroom.

Woody, a string-pull talking cowboy (given voice by Tom Hanks), has enjoyed a long reign as the favorite of his 6-year-old owner, Andy. But his position as top toy is suddenly threatened by the arrival of a birthday gift named Buzz Lightyear (Tim Allen), a flashy space action figure with pop-out wings and flashing laser beam.

The other toys in the room—including Mr. Potato Head (Don Rickles), Slinky Dog (Jim Varney), Rex the dinosaur (Wallace Shawn) and many others also tilt toward Buzz, so that Woody thinks about getting rid of his rival.

Of course, everything goes wrong, leaving both toys lost in the outside world, forced to join forces (in the best tradition of mismatched buddy movies) to get back to Andy before the moving van arrives to take the family to a new home.

The biggest danger in their trek is the sadistic Sid, a neighborhood kid who blows up action figures with firecrackers or dismembers and reassembles "mutant" toys in his bedroom.

The desperate chase scenes that follow are at least as thrilling as anything in "Indiana Jones," thanks in large measure to the breathtakingly effective computer animation.

As developed by a pioneering company called Pixar (which has joined forces with Disney), the technology combines all the three-dimensional detail of stop-motion animation (like "The Nightmare Before Christmas) with the artful, free-flowing fluidity of traditionally drawn Disney classics.

Along the way "Toy Story" offers an utterly dazzling array of realistic settings and textures—from the waxy leaves of a house plant (used to hide a squad of intrepid toy soldiers), to the metal interior and long twisting passageways of a heating duct.

There's so much going on visually, in fact, that you scarcely notice the three Randy Newman songs on the soundtrack, which function more to heighten the mood and advance the story than as hummable, stand-alone entertainments.

In the end, adults may appreciate this cinematic achievement even more than their kids, since grownups can better savor its uniquely captivating look and a wealth of witty details (such as the "For Sale" sign on Andy's home from a company called "Virtual Realty").

It's hard to imagine moviegoers of any age who could remain indifferent to such vivid and richly realized characters, among the most entertaining to appear in any film (animated or live action) this year. After a long fall season comprised mostly of dreary disappointments, "Toy Story" manages to put some of the magic back into moviegoing.

NEWSDAY, 11/22/95, Part II/p. B4, Jack Mathews

As I tap the letters on my computer keyboard to make these words, I grow more and more amazed at what the digital animation team achieved in bringing the irrepressible, magical, 100 percent computer-animated "Toy Story" to the screen.

Word processing still strikes me as something of a miracle, and I haven't worked up the nerve yet to set foot on the Internet. To see cartoon characters created out of data bits interacting in a three-dimensional world and quickly lulling me into accepting them as individuals I care about ... well, it is great to be a kid again.

"Toy Story" might have been the "Toys 'R' Us Story" if Disney had included the toy store chain in this year's corporate expansion plans. Unlike so many Christmas movies aimed simultaneously at children's hearts and their parents' checkbooks, most of the toys on display here are off-the-shelf standards: Slinky Dog, Mr. Potato Head, Bo Peep, Etch-A-Sketch, Magic-8-Ball. There's a generic pink piggy bank, a big green tyrannosaurus rex, and a regiment of plastic cutout soldiers.

In other words, it is every kid's toy box, come to life, in a rousing fantasy-adventure about two very special toys: the old-fashioned, pull-string western sheriff Woody (voice of Tom Hanks), and the post "Star Wars" astronaut Buzz Lightyear (Tim Allen). They begin as rivals, become tentative allies and finally combat-buddies in a battle against a neighborhood bad seed named Sid and his vicious dog, Scud.

Take the word of someone who had hoped, computer animation would fall flat on its hard disc and leave the big screen canvas to the classicists: "Toy Story," made by Pixar Animation Studios for Disney, is simply great filmmaking! It is not that the computer draws better pictures. The creative work is done by artists who know how to work a keyboard and a paint brush mouse. But with its depth of field, and backdrops that verge on photorealism, it does create a heightened sense of urgency, and is easier, at least for adults, to become immersed in.

Still, it is the magic in the storytelling that determines the fate of any children's movie, and once the writers of "Toy Story" settled on the notion of a cast of characters made up largely of hand-me-down toys, they knew what to do with it.

The world we enter at first—the bedroom of 6-year-old human Andy—is a sanctuary where its plaything residents spend their off-hours fretting over their favored-toy status and the possibility of being replaced by incoming birthday and holiday gifts. Hope springs eternal for some; Mr. Potato Head dreams of the day a Miss Potato Head is added to the collection. But for Woody, Andy's take-everywhere best buddy, the arrival of flashy Buzz Lightyear—a battery-operated toy with an ego so large he thinks he's real—can only mean trouble.

In ways that are purely entertaining, Woody and Buzz find themselves on the road together, surviving a series of hair-raising adventures at truck stops and pizza palaces, and end up in the attic of next-door neighbor Sid, a pubescent monster with a penchant for mutilating toys. There, Buzz and Woody meet a legion of mutants, toys dismantled and horrifically reassembled by Sid, with a long-simmering score to settle.

Beyond the exhilarating action sequences, "Toy Story" is determinedly human and very, very funny. The sideline characters are marvelously developed, with fine voice performances from such real people as Don Rickles (Mr. Potato Head), John Ratzenberger of "Cheers" (Hamm, the piggy bank), Wallace Shawn (the gentle T-Rex), Jim Varney (Slinky Dog) and Annie Potts (Bo Peep).

Hanks, on a winning streak that obviously extends to disembodied voice work, gives Woody an awful lot of character for an insecure pull-string toy. And Allen turns Buzz' stubborn self-delusion into the most noble failing. Thanks to them, "Toy Story" is not only the best children's movie of 1995, it's the best buddy movie, too.

SIGHT AND SOUND, 3/96, p. 51, Leslie Felperin

The toys of a small boy, Andy, come to life as soon is he leaves the room and are led by Woody the cowboy, Andy's favourite. Woody is indignant when Andy is given a Buzz Lightyear astronaut for his birthday. Buzz refuses to believe he's a mere toy and insists that he's a real astronaut. Soon Buzz is the favorite toy. Determined that *he* will be the toy Andy takes to Pizza Planet one evening, Woody tries to push Buzz off the desk but accidentally knocks him out of the window. All the other toys accuse him of foul play. Buzz manages to stow away in the car, but both of them end up stranded at a gas station.

The two toys stow aboard a truck bound for Pizza Planet, but once there, Buzz can't resist crawling into a rocket shaped crane machine. Woody tries to get him out, but they are selected by Sid, the vicious boy who lives next door to Andy and who delights in blowing up and mutilating toys. At Sid's house they meet various "cannibal" toys Sid has made from mismatched toy parts. While trying to escape, Buzz sees a commercial on television advertising himself, realises that he really is a toy and slumps into a deep depression. When Sid recaptures them he straps Buzz to a rocket, planning to explode him the next day. Once alone, Woody encourages Buzz unsuccessfully to accept his toy nature, think of Andy and try to escape.

The next day, while Sid prepares Buzz for "blast-off", Woody hitches a plan with the abused toys. Scattering themselves around the garden, they come to life and menace Sid, terrifying him so much that he hides upstairs. However, their next task is to rejoin Andy and the other toys who are already on their way to Andy's new house. After several failed attempts at boarding the moving van, Buzz and Woody light the rocket still attached to Buzz which enables them to hurtle into the car Andy is travelling in. The next Christmas. Andy is given a puppy.

On paper, there's nothing very remarkable about *Toy Story*, an ordinary enough tale of rivalry (easily decoded as sibling rivalry) between two toys, an old-fashioned cowboy doll and spanking new spaceman, which is resolved by standard buddy-movie manoevres, bonding the protagonists through adversity. Peppered with pert gags and pop culture references, the film is not even uncharted territory for Disney, who have made tentative ventures into this terrain with the relelentlessly knowing *Aladdin*. Nor will it be remembered for its extraordinary box-office success (healthy, but not of *Batman Forever*-proportions). What has earned *Toy Story* its place in the film history books is the simple fact that it is the first full-length feature film to be entirely generated by computer.

Ever since J. Stuart Blackton and Albert E. Smith made what is arguably the first-ever stop-motion film in 1898, *The Humpty Dumpty Circus*, with Blackton's daughter's "wooden circus performers and animals" (sadly, no prints survive today), toys have been the favoured stars of animation. From the teleological perspective of so much animation history, it is befitting that this latest landmark should also star a toy cast, albeit of much more modern toys (which have seen their sales soar on the back of the film). Apparently it took director John Lasseter and the Pixar/Disney crew four years to make the film, and a few more years to develop the software and script. The photo-realistic quality of the rendering on the toys and surroundings is breathtakingly sharp and fine-grained. Computer animation excels at providing textures. and the film-makers use this strength to full effect here, almost luring you to reach out and touch the knobbly plastic texture of the dinosaur or the soft worn felt of Woody.

Ordinary cel animation cannot achieve the same density of colour, or the believeability of these lightning effects, and can rarely match the fluidity of 'camera' movement on display here. Providing a Woody-eye view of Andy's house as the boy runs downstairs and races around his living room, Lasseter shows off in the opening sequence. You can't really blame him he's been working up to such a moment throughout his whole career, perfecting the technology from *Luxor Jr.* to *Toy Story*'s most direct antecedent, *Tin Toy*. On a shelf in Andy's room the names of Pixar's major films are emblazoned on the spines of books, because those are indeed the tomes from which they learned their craft. Nonetheless, this bravura opening unfortunately highlights the technique's inadequacy in rendering human characters, such as Andy. Sid the baddie is rather better made, with his mouth full of metal braces, but Andy looks like a badly-made boy doll.

Yet technique is what the film is all about and it is so dazzling as to lull the viewer into ignoring a weak narrative, whose motivations and rules of existence are unclear. Indeed, the story itself is concerned with technophilia, having Andy prefer Buzz with his helmet that "does that whoosh thing" and his glow-in-the-dark decals (another great effect) over the merely talking string-pull Woody. One of the film's best jokes concerns some alien toys who live in a crane machine and have developed a cargo-cult worship of the crane which structures their lives. To rephrase Wittgenstein, for all the characters in *Toy Story*, technology is the limit of their world.

Despite these caveats, I still have to admit that I stifled a tear at the film's schmaltzy homage-to-*Dumbo* ending. Tom Hanks provides a fine voice characterisation for Woody, by turns strident and dinky-cute. Tim Allen is even better as Buzz, and the soundtrack's few songs, by Randy Newman, wisely avoid the clicléd slushiness of so many cartoon songs. There is a sweet-natured inventiveness throughout that makes *Toy Story* more than just a demo of the latest techniques, an imaginative facility of which J. Stuart Blackton would have been proud.

TIME, 11/27/95, p. 96, Richard Corliss

Characters in so many live-action movies these days are little more than cartoons. So where to turn for original characters with all-too-human weaknesses? Cartoons, of course. Consider the new Disney animated feature, John Lasseter's *Toy Story*, which is, incidentally, the first full-length film created wholly by computer and, not at all incidentally—by design, in fact—the year's most inventive comedy.

In Andy's bedroom the toys are alive. They are also working stiffs with the fear, every time a birthday approaches, that they will be replaced by more sophisticated gewgaws. Toy Town's leader, a cloth cowboy named Sheriff Woody (wonderfully voiced by Tom Hanks), talks to his charges as if he's a genial teacher and they are slow kids. Actually, they're finicky adults. Rex (Wallace Shawn), a sexually insecure dinosaur, dreams of being "the dominant predator." Mr. Potato Head (Don Rickles) grumbles about planned obsolescence while praying that Andy's new prized toy will be *Mrs.* Potato Head. It's not, though. It's an action figure called Buzz Lightyear (Tim Allen). Buzz's power is that—to Woody's chagrin—he seduces the old toys with his space-age gadgetry. His problem is that he thinks he's human.

So here, recognizably and delightfully, are two weird dudes: a political figure stripped of his moral authority and taking it with a lack of good grace, and a hero who is deeply delusional. Woody turns weak and spiteful; he contemplates criminal mischief to discredit his rival. ("I had power,/ I was respected,/ But not anymore," spits out Randy Newman in one of the film's three very grownup singalong tunes.) And Buzz is, in the blithest, most genial way, nuts. If you've never in your life seen a toy have a nervous breakdown, Buzz's will make it worth the wait.

Woody and Buzz become uneasy partners, *Defiant Ones*-style, when they are captured by Sid, the toy torturer next door. Sid must have spoken to a deep, dark streak in the animators, so lovingly do they detail the boy's atrocities. His bedroom, a playpen for Krafft-Ebing, is a place of ominous eccentric angles (his parents stuck him in the attic) and walls papered with posters for bands like Megadork. "The patient is prepped," he declares, revealing a doll with its head in a vise. This Sid is vicious.

Hiding beneath the bed are the results of Sid's experiments: mutant toys as bizarre as anything seen in a Hollywood film since the human oddities in Tod Browning's 1932 *Freaks*. Creepiest is Babyhead, a doll's head—its hair plucked, an eye missing—perched on Erector-set legs. The neat trick *Toy Story* pulls off is to make these creatures first repulsive, then poignant and finally heroic.

A kid's nightmare with a happy ending; a Rorschach drawing in fingerpaint—these are definitions of a Disney cartoon. *Toy Story*, though released by Disney, was not exactly generated by it. In the mid-'80s, Lasseter, a Disney alumnus, joined the Marin County computer lab Pixar and made three terrific shorts (*Luxo Jr.*, *Red's Dream* and *Tin Toy*) in which he invested metal objects such as lamps, unicycles and drummer-boy toys with life and heart. These films, forerunners to *Toy Story*, ingeniously show that things have wills and wits of their own and exist in intimate relation to their human masters. They're funnier too.

Like a Bosch painting or a *Mad* comic book, *Toy Story* creates a world bustling with strange creatures (check out the three-eyed alien-children toys in the Pizza Planet) and furtive, furry humor. When a genius like Lasseter sits at his computer, the machine becomes just a more supple paintbrush. Like the creatures in this wonderful zoo of a movie, *it's alive!*

VILLAGE VOICE, 11/28/95, p. 64, Georgia Brown

The grooviest character in John Lasseter's digitally animated boy story, *Toy Story*, is the vicious little metal-mouth kid-next-door, Sid, whose wall-to-wall braces put him in a line with *The Spy Who Loved Me*'s Jaws. Many things in Disney's first computer-generated universe are lifted from other movies. (Being a team project, story by committee, it makes it easier to openly acknowledge steals.) One simulated camera move, according to press notes, copies a Kenneth Branagh shot from *Frankenstein* (never mind *what* Branagh was copying), while another references Michael

Mann's *Miami Vice*. The hall carpet in Sid's house is out of *The Shining*, and a green plastic soldier is given the voice of *Full Metal Jacket*'s drill sergeant.

This is not to say that anyone should approach *Toy Story* with Kubrick in mind. Although Lasseter proudly cites buddy pictures *48 Hrs, Midnight Run*, and *The Defiant Ones* as influences, the ambience here is closer to *The Odd Couple*. The movie's buddies do get caught in some tight places, but essentially this is a domestic drama and the two "heroes" (voices by Tom Hanks and Tim Allen) are rather campy old fuddyduddies. Woody (Hanks) is a fussy cowboy with Gumby's rectangularity and a collapsible torso modeled on Ray Bolger's Scarecrow. His plastic antagonist-turned-ally is a pathetically puffed-up astronaut, Buzz Lightyear, with a chin the size of Leno's.

In the universe of Andy's toy bin, Woody is the old favorite, exploiting his stature and ever alert to the threat of changing times. When Andy's sixth birthday introduces Buzz, Woody's insecurity erupts (kids can identify this with the arrival of a new sibling) and he succeeds in getting Buzz flipped out the window. . The other toys—from the priggish Mr. Potato Head (Don Rickles) to token femme Bo Peep (Annie Potts)—blame Woody for Buzz's accident. Shunned and ashamed, Woody undertakes a rescue mission, which eventually involves a visit to Pizza Planet (nod to *Pulp Fiction?*), and incarceration in Sid's little shop of horrors.

Although *Toy Story* trumpets communal cooperation as essential for survival, the group's pervasive insecurity reminds me too much of boardrooms and newsrooms, not to mention Hollywood studios. Woody is like a CEO perpetuating his rule by subtle manipulation and suspect moralizing: "Being a toy is better than being a space ranger," says Woody as Buzz wakes to the fact that he's not on a mission to save the planet but just a made-in-Taiwan replicant. "What matters," says Woody, "is that we're there for Andy when he needs us." Substitute Michael Eisner?

Who is this Andy kid anyway? As far as we call tell, the focus of the toys' slavish devotion has done nothing to earn it. We couldn't even recognize Andy (usually represented by sneakers) if we met him at the mall with his equally faceless mom. This sort of computer imaging is better at representing sadistic Sid's operating chambers than it is at convincingly conveying warmth comfort, and refuge. No doubt the true test of *Toy Story*, however, is whether it markets the package, with Woody and Buzz toys under the tree. Old Spud-Head may be in for a second wind, too.

Also reviewed in:
CHICAGO TRIBUNE, 11/22/95, Tempo/p. 1, Mark Caro
NEW YORK TIMES, 11/22/95, p. C9, Janet Maslin
VARIETY, 11/20-26/95, p. 48, Leonard Klady
WASHINGTON POST, 11/22/95, p. B1, Rita Kempley
WASHINGTON POST, 11/24/95, Weekend/p. 54, Kevin McManus

TRAPS

A Filmopolis Pictures release of an Ayer Productions film in association with the Australian Film Finance Corporation and the assistance of the Australian Film Commission, Film Queensland. *Producer:* Jim McElroy. *Director:* Pauline Chan. *Screenplay:* Pauline Chan and Robert Carter. *Based on characters in the novel "Dreamhouse" by:* Kate Grenville. *Director of Photography:* Kevin Hayward. *Editor:* Nicolas Beauman. *Music:* Stephen Rae. *Sound:* John Shiefelbein. *Casting:* Alison Barrett. *Production Designer:* Michael Phillips. *Art Director:* Philip Drake and Trinh Quang Vu. *Costumes:* Davie Rowe. *Running time:* 97 minutes. *MPAA Rating:* R.

CAST: Saskia Reeves (Louise Duffield); Robert Reynolds (Michael Duffield); Sami Frey (Daniel Renouard); Jacqueline McKenzie (Viola Renouard); Kiet Lam (Tuan); Hoa To (Tatie-Chi); Thierry Marquet (Capt. Brochard).

LOS ANGELES TIMES, 12/1/95, Calendar/p. 10, Kevin Thomas

In Pauline Chan's awkward, painfully sincere "Traps," it's no wonder that Daniel Renouard (Sami Frey), the suave manager of a French Indochina rubber plantation, selected Michael Duffield (Robert Reynolds), a London-based Australian journalist working in tandem with his photographer-wife Louise (Saskia Reeves), to report glowingly of the order and control that the French have brought to Indochina.

For Duffield, who ludicrously believes that he and Louise are the best reporting team in Europe, is not only naive but obtuse. Having met Michael in Paris, Daniel realizes he's the right guy for Daniel's employer, the French Indo-Chinese Rubber Co., who wants to commission an important propaganda piece written presumably for the English-speaking media calling for an increased occupation force at a time (1950) when military control is eroding and civil war brewing. Just think, Michael could end up as editor in chief of all the company's publications if Daniel's bosses in Paris are pleased with his work.

Louise apparently wasn't along when Daniel and Michael met, for the second-generation French colonial might have thought twice about Michael's suitability had he had a chance to size her up. Louise is naive, too, but brighter and more open than her husband. Michael's promise to Louise of a terrific time in Southeast Asia evaporates as they discover the population sullen and fearful and guerrilla skirmishes far too close for comfort at Daniel's shabby but elegant palatial estate. Michael, as a result, immerses himself in self-denial all the more eagerly.

With her co-writer Robert Carter, Chan, a Vietnamese-born Australian in her feature debut, draws an all-too-literal parallel between the personal and the political as the disintegration of Louise and Michael's marriage is meant to echo the growing unrest in Indochina. Since Chan lacks the skill and subtlety to avoid the parallel from seeming arbitrary and schematic, she leaves the impression that there's a simple equation between being a lousy lover and a lousy journalist. But then "Traps" is an emphatically feminist work, with Louise's self-discovery and her forming a bond with Daniel's mercurial, miserable teen-aged daughter Viola (Jacqueline McKenzie) given equal—or more—weight than the oppressive plight of the Indochinese.

"Traps" is such a passionately committed film that it generates considerable raw emotion, and there's a great deal of honesty in the way Chan's four principals fumble around, sensing a need to connect with themselves and each other. But in delving into messy lives, entangled in politics and emotions, Chan has been unable to keep her film from seeming something of a mess itself.

NEW YORK POST, 12/1/95, p. 46, Larry Worth

A sense of enchantment and tragedy, conveyed through beautiful, bittersweet images, traditionally suffuse screen portraits of France's crumbling control over Vietnam. Most recently, "Indochine" and "The Lover" recreated those sad, tension-filled decades to near-perfection.

Though not, quite in their league, Pauline Chan's "Traps" provides a solid addition to the genre. It's a tale of intrigue set in the 50's, filled with complex characters battling private hells as a country teetered toward civil war.

The growing miasma is viewed through an Australian journalist and his and photographer/wife, sent to a remote Colonial plantation to do an "upbeat" article on France's role in Indochina. Not surprisingly, the handsome couple is hopelessly naive, about their own relationship as well as the sounds of gunfire and tortured screams on the night air.

Then there's the plantation's Old World owner, a walking enigma who needs to control all in his world. Accordingly, his biggest problem is a rebellious teenage daughter torn between European roots and the Vietnamese villagers she loves. The latter includes a young Asian man whose lure to the communist presence puts all their lives at risk.

Chan's screenplay, penned with Robert Carter, evolves into a fascinating tale of culture clashes, political turmoil and compromised beliefs. Much of the writing clearly reflects her upbringing in Vietnam, lending a heartfelt authenticity.

Chan's prowess also extends behind the camera, whether captureing the countryside's lush, dense, glades or some unexpectedly erotic love scenes.

But there's room for improvement: Chan occasionally drops narrative threads, ODs on symbolism, or picks up a catch phrase like "if you think about it, you'll never do it" and uses it as a labored framing device.

Thankfully, a fine cast proves distracting, nicely led by Saskia Reeves of "Antonia and Jane" fame and Robert Reynolds, a young Sam Neill lookalike. As the fresh-scrubbed hero and heroine, they beautifully spark Sami Frey's exotic, sexually ambiguous host.

Jacqueline McKenzie also shines as the sullen, ashen-faced daughter, coming off like the Addams Family's most manic member; meanwhile, Kiet Lam's turn as her conflicted servant and would-be beau fleshes out the theme of divided loyalties.

So despite a few rough edges, "Traps" ably captures a bygone era with the passion and elegance that defined it.

NEWSDAY, 12/1/95, Part II/p. B7, John Anderson

Louise Duffield (Saskia Reeves) is a photographer/wife—or is it wife/photographer?—who travels with her husband to Indochina in 1950 and gets Viet Conged (or Viet Minhed, given the year). She exists somewhere between Colonel Kurtz of "Apocalypse Now" and Tarzan's Jane, and her western facade will come tumbling down.

Based loosely on Kate Grenville's book, "Dreamhouse," "Traps" was the first English-speaking film shot in Vietnam since the diplomatic thaw of the 1980s (it was made in 1993), and is the first feature by Pauline Chan, a celebrated short-film maker. For all these firsts, it does walk familiar ground, with a familiar landmark: Louise is an Anglo in a strange land, appalled by the subjugation of the locals, orientalized and eroticized by the Asian heat, caught between cultures and struggling to find her moral compass.

Thwarting her is her own husband, Michael (Robert Reynolds), an Australian working for The Economist magazine in London who has come to do a story on the rubber plantation of Daniel Renouard (Sami Frey), but who falls under his influence. On the edges lurks Captain Brochard (Thierry Marquet), French muscle and sadistic keeper of the peace.

The struggle is between willful corruption and irresistible enlightenment, not a new theme, but as set in Vietnam of the '50s—when the French were taking their turn at controlling an uncontrollable "colony"—it carries deep echoes of the future. This is a Vietnam War prequel, with all the imminent disaster of a movie shot under a volcano.

The doom is communicated less by Chan's camera—although it possesses lush gestures and nervous tics—than by her cast. Reeves does a deft job casting Louise's growing nativism against her crumbling reserve. As Daniel, the Frenchman who knows he is part of a morally bankrupt political structure, Frey is, a model of rationalized decadence. Reynolds is a stuffy buffer, crumbling between their warring spirits.

But it's Jacqueline McKenzie, as Daniel's daughter Viola, who is the true herald of disequilibrium in "Traps." Having grown up in Vietnam but within the family/social construct of imperial France, she is truly a woman without a country, but certainly not without a personality. Belligerent to Louise and in love with Tuan (Kiet Lam), the houseboy/subversive, she is determined to be singular, and is singularly disturbed. She is also at the center of Chan's female-centric view, a victim from birth, and the lost side of Louise—who is an amorphous enough quantity as it is.

Don't leap to conclusions about this film based on the ethnicity of its director. Yes, Pauline Chan was born in Vietnam, but she is half Chinese as well, and has lived in Hong Kong, the United States and Australia. What "Traps" has is an unspecific nationality; its perspective is neither indigenous nor invasionary but simply there. Which makes its disconcerting nature all the weirder.

VILLAGE VOICE, 12/5/95, p. 61, Amy Taubin

The shadow of Marguerite Duras hangs over *Traps*, a somewhat heavy-handed, conventionally good-looking Australian film set in French colonial Indochina during the '50s. Even it director Pauline Chan didn't Intend it, *Traps* seems like a literalization of Duras's evocative memory pieces about power, desire, and madness among the French diplomatic set in Indochina between the two World Wars.

Like Duras, Chan focuses her narrative on a woman whose romantic crisis is exacerbated by the tensions between the Asian population and its French colonial rulers. Here a British photographer accompanies her sellout journalist husband to Vietnam and unwittingly stumbles into a revolution.

The film has some good performances, particularly from Sami Frey as a twisted Frenchman who prefers being the manager of an isolated rubber plantation to pushing papers in a Paris office and Saskia Reeves as the photographer whose marriage falls apart when she finds herself drawn into the Vietnamese struggle. Chan's exploration of the psychosexual dynamics between the photographer and her husband and between the plantation manager and his eccentric teenage daughter (Jacqueline McKenzie) oscillate from overly explicit to overly evasive. More compelling are scenes among the Vietnamese.

An ambitious first feature that doesn't quite hold together, *Traps* nevertheless suggests that Chan, who was born in Vietnam and acted in Hong Kong films, has a complicated perspective that will serve her well in the future.

Also reviewed in:
NEW YORK TIMES, 12/1/95, p. C14, Stephen Holden
VARIETY, 6/6-12/94, p. 36, David Stratton

TRUE BELIEVERS

A Dakin Films release. *Producer:* Robert Mugge. *Director:* Robert Mugge. *Editor:* Robert Mugge. *Director of Photography:* Bill Burke. *Music:* Scott Billington, Keith Case, and Peter Guralnick. *Running time:* 86 minutes. *MPAA Rating:* Not Rated.

WITH: Marian Levy; Bill Nowlin; Ken Irwin; Bill Morrissey; Marcia Ball; Little Jimmy King; Steve Riley; Irma Thomas; Beau Jocque; Alison Krauss.

LOS ANGELES TIMES, 6/5/95, Calendar/p. 4, Kevin Thomas

Ace music documentarian Robert Mugge's "True Believers," is a tribute to the 25th anniversary of the founding of Rounder Records, dedicated to recording American roots music.

Mugge includes such Rounder stars as Alison Krauss, Bill Morrisey, Irma Thomas and Marcia Ball in performance and interviews, as well as interviews with Rounders principals Marian Levy, Bill Nowlin and Ken Irwin. The gratifying result is an enjoyable film that shows that smart people of integrity can make a crucial cultural contribution and even prosper without giving in to greed. (But how come Mugge overlooked Rounder star—and Cinegrill stalwart—Charles Brown?)

NEW YORK POST, 5/I/95, p. 26, Chip DeFaa

If film Robert Mugge had done no more in his career than create "Sun Ra: A Joyful Noise" (1980) and "Saxophone Colossus" (1986)—still the best available films on jazz legends Sun Ra and Sonny Rollins—his reputation as a major producer/director of music documentaries would be secure.

One might assume that the combination of Mugge and blues, rhythm-and-blues, zydeco and folk would ensure another top film documentary. But "True Believers," Mugge's 17th film—though pleasant—falls a bit flat, compared to its best predecessors.

Mugge employs the same techniques that have always served him well. Happily, musical performances are presented intact; they are never cut short or obscured by voiceovers. Speakers tell their own stories at their own pace. The problem is that neither the musicians nor the speakers are as compelling as many Mugge has filmed in the past.

The film tells the history of Rounder Records, a highly respected independent label. Its founders, Bill Nowlin, Ken Irwin and Marian Levy, come across as painfully earnest, sincere, unpretentious and honest—but colorless compared to such larger-than-life past film subjects as Sonny Rollins and Sun Ra. And they are overly modest about their accomplishments.

Oddly, the inimitable Charles Brown, the most important R&B artist Rounder ever recorded, is not so much as mentioned (the film loses a half point just for that).

Rounder's Bullseye Blues division played a major role in Brown's great comeback. The fact that the records he made with them were more varied and interesting than most he made with others reflects well upon them and producer Ron Levy. It's a pity Mugge did not get a music expert to make the points that Rounders' founders fail to make.

Music shot on location in Louisiana, Texas and Kentucky gives the film some lift. Marcia Ball, a less important and original blues stylist than Brown (or than Irma Thomas, who is given lesser exposure later in the film) gets the honor of opening. Closing the film is wry, subtle folk singer Bill Morrisey.

In between, there's Cajun music (with wonderful shots of fans dancing), bluegrass (double Grammy winner Alison Krauss), and more. Audio quality is occasionally sub-par on the interview sequences, but never on the musical ones, which matter more.

NEWSDAY, 4/26/95, Part II/p. B7, Gene Seymour

Over the last 25 years, Rounder Records, a Cambridge, Mass., "indie" outfit, has assembled an eclectic inventory of folk, blues, zydeco and bluegrass artists. Which makes it a perfect subject for documentarian Robert Mugge, who himself has fashioned a varied body of work (including "Deep Blues," "The Kingdom of Zydeco," "The Gospel According to Al Green") celebrating America's rich musical heritage with maximum respect and minimal glitz.

"True Believers," however, turns out to be a less-than-perfect film, maybe because Mugge identifies too closely with Rounder's founders, Marian Leighton-Levy, Ken Irwin and Bill Nowlin. He's right to be paying tribute to these ex-hippies for establishing one of the few record companies where success and compromise are incompatible. He's wrong, however, in thinking they're as interesting as the artists they record.

As a consequence, one has to fight through moist thickets of platitudes such as, "We do all it for the love of the music," in order to get to the music itself. And even here, Mugge's touch isn't always as sure as it usually is. Rhythm-and-blues legend Irma Thomas comes across less magnetically than expected. The sequence with bluegrass star Alison Krauss at a Philadelphia radio station seems flat despite her dulcet reinvention of the Foundations' "Baby, Now That I've Found You."

The film's more striking visual moments happen almost by accident. One thinks of the high-energy recording session with Memphis blues guitarist Little Jimmy King and organist-producer Ron Levy (Marian's husband). The column of cigarette smoke rising between them is so thick and spectral it seems like a third member of the group. And there's something rapturous about the way Austin blues singer Marcia Ball deftly smooths her hair as she's laying down ferocious, double-clutching piano riffs.

It's nice to see such worthy, if underexposed artists like Ball, Krauss, Thomas, Tex Mex singer Tino Hinojosa and folksinger Bill Morrissey. But as far as the non-musicians in the film are concerned, the only one who needs more screen time is Gia, Rounder's harried, acerbic receptionist. If only she could have gotten away from the switchboard, what stories she could tell.

VILLAGE VOICE, 5/2/95, p. 59, Abby McGanney Nolan

Robert Mugge has made his name (and it's pronounced "muggy") making compelling documentaries about American music, including *Kingdom of Zydeco, Deep Blues*, and *Sun Ra: A Joyful Noise*. With his latest, about the Cambridge, Massachusetts-based Rounder Records, Mugge falters a bit. Instead of spending an extended period with a major eccentric (Mugge also did *Gospel According to Al Green)* or a lively subculture, *True Believers* tours around the country, giving quick, not always tantalizing, tastes of the Rounder artists.

The film, is half a portrait of this roots-music record company at work although we don't get much beyond introductions to most of the staff—and half a look at nine of the label's prize signings, including Irma Thomas, Bill Morrissey, and Alison Krauss. But except for a truly inspired song from a Beau Jocque zydeco dance concert and the opening number by Marcia Ball, *True Believers* seems to settle for less, i.e., a radio performance from Krauss, a seemingly impromptu tune from Bruce Daigrepont. Furthermore, the film doesn't seem edited with the usual Mugge care. Particularly expendable are the testimonials the Rounder founders give on behalf of their artists and the testimonials to Rounder the artists provide in turn. The music should be testimony enough.

Also reviewed in:
NEW YORK TIMES, 4/28/95, p. C18, Stephen Holden
VARIETY, 10/24-30/94, p. 69, Allen Young

TSAHAL

A New Yorker Films release of a Les Productions Dussart/Les Films Aleph/France 2 Cinema/Bavaria Films production. *Executive Producer:* Bertrand Dussart. *Director:* Claude Lanzmann. *Screenplay (English, Hebrew and French with English subtitles):* Claude Lanzmann. *Director of Photography:* Dominique Chapuis, Pierre-Laurent Chenieux, and Jean-Michel Humeau. *Editor:* Sabine Mamou. *Sound:* Bernard Aubouy. *Sound Editor:* Christian Dior. *Running time:* 300 minutes. *MPAA Rating:* Not Rated.

WITH: Avi Yaffe; Yuval Neria; Meir Weisel; Avigdor Kahalani; Yanush Ben-Gal; Zvika Greengold; Yossi Ben-Hanan; Adam Gen-Tolila; Ilan Leibovitch; Israel Tal; Arik Sharon; AT THE END OF A NIGHT OF AMBUSH: Ehud Barak Avihu Bin-Nun; Matan Vilnai; David Grossman; THE FIRST JUMP: Relik S. Adi Gan; Matan Vilnai; Arik Sharon; Muki Betzer; Schmuel Zuicker; Ariel Shifman; Avigdor Feldman; Schlomo Gazit; Amos Oz; Uri Ariel.

LOS ANGELES TIMES, 12/2/95, Calendar/p. 8, Kevin Thomas

The Nuart booked Claude Lanzmann's two-part, five-hour "Tsahal" long before the assassination of Israeli Prime Minister Yitzhak Rabin, but there's no question his death gives an edge and added meaning to this survey of the Israeli defense forces, which in Hebrew are called *Tsava Haganah LeIsraeli* hence, the acronym *Tsahal.*

Lanzmann, a veteran French journalist, has said this film grew out of "Shoah," his great, monumental documentary about the Holocaust, in that he was astonished to realize "that, between the mass deportation of the Jews of Warsaw to Treblinka in the summer of 1942 and the Six-Day War, hardly 25 years had elapsed." Consequently, "Tsahal" is essentially a celebration of a people discovering an identity, of a people who learned how to fight to establish and defend Israel through six major wars and to maintain a state of constant military preparedness.

Although this grueling documentary is largely in English, it is as parochial as "Shoah" is universal. Whereas in his 1985 film Lanzmann brought a chilling clarity to the operation of the Nazi extermination camps in Poland and illuminated their profound implications, he here assumes viewers' familiarity with all of Israel's wars and their circumstances. It doesn't seem too much to ask that in a 300-minute film at least a brief recap of those six conflicts be included.

The majority of the documentary is taken up with lengthy interviews with Israeli military leaders and men in the ranks. Everyone stresses the need for vigilance and dedication, and the veterans relate war stories that, in the absence of context, sound like the reminiscences of soldiers from any other country. Much of what they have to say is repetitive and is recited as the camera endlessly pans desert vistas.

If "Tsahal" is decidedly tedious, it nevertheless makes clear how a nation that has had to be prepared to fight simply to survive will inevitably possess a segment that, armed with religious belief, recoils from the pursuit of peace if it involves compromise. As vague as "Tsahal" is, it makes one realize the enormity of the challenge facing Rabin and the equal amount of courage he displayed. The film's most pertinent remarks are made by Lt. Gen. Ehud Barak, Tsahal chief of staff, who observes that his country's history is "a struggle between extremism and pragmatism ... we should find the middle ground."

"Tsahal" comes to life vividly only in the last half of its second part, when Lanzmann tackles the moral and strategic dilemmas created by policing the Gaza Strip and the West Bank and interviews Palestinians and Israelis who sympathize with their plight. For a climax, Lanzmann engages in a friendly but persistent debate with a young Israeli settling in a housing tract on the

West Bank. He says he ultimately has no fear of standing his ground, should government policy dictate his leaving sometime in the future, because "a Jew will never shoot another Jew."

NEW YORK POST, 1/27/95, p. 53, Larry Worth

Editing has never been Claude Lanzmann's strong point. But he's making progress.

His last project, the documentary "Shoah," contained some of the most moving Holocaust footage ever recorded. The bad news: It clocked in at an excessive 9½ hours. Accordingly, "TSAHAL," his follow-up film on the Israeli Defense Forces, seems like a breeze at only five hours.

Thankfully, the subject matter is fascinating. He opens with officers telling war tales as the camera pans over a desolate countryside, broken up only by the occasional tree.

Lanzmann makes the point that Israel's elongated struggle for independence has resulted in six major wars. But he errs in assuming audiences have a healthy knowledge of each conflict. Often, it's hard to determine which war a speaker is reflecting on.

Still, Lanzmann paints a diverse picture of TSAHAL (an acronym for Tsava Haganah LeIsraeli: Israeli Defense Forces) by segueing from tank factories to patrolling the Gaza Strip to interrogations of West Bank settlers. And that's for starters.

The strongest scenes involve TSAHAL's junior members, as when a grinning young soldier proudly reveals that his dust-covered tank has served as home for the last five years.

So what fuels their driving nationalism? One speaker explains: "We gave birth to ourselves from the ashes of the Shoah. So aggressiveness is a burning instinct."

One only wishes that Lanzmann who often shares the screen with his interview subjects—had spent more time with the army's female contingent (all Israeli citizens serve, with the exception of a few Orthodox Jews).

By concentrating on older male veterans, too many speakers blend together. The result: some slow patches which allow the mind to wander.

It's nothing that couldn't be remedied through editing. But Lanzmann fails to heed the age-old maxim that less is more.

NEWSDAY, 1/27/95, Part II/p. B7, Jack Mathews

There is an old joke inspired by the 1967 Six Day War between Israel and its Arab neighbors that goes something like this:

Having met stiff opposition from unseen Israelis up ahead, the invading Arabs send a scout out in the middle of the night to learn the size of the force they're up against. Soon, the scout returns in a panic, screaming, "Back! Back! It's an ambush. There are two of them."

No question, beginning in 1948, when they first fought to defend their new nation, the Israelis have had the reputation of being ferocious fighters. They had to be, given the centuries-old hostilities surrounding them, and the long knowledge, ghastly punctuated by the Holocaust, that their enemies not only wanted to defeat them, but to eradicate them from the face of the Earth.

How they developed such a powerful fighting spirit and such military superiority over the Arab states are the main subjects of "Tsahal" (Israeli Defense Forces), a two-part, five-hour documentary directed by Claude Lanzmann, whose-nine-hour "Shoah" provided the definitive moral postmortem on the Holocaust.

I wish I could say "Tsahal" ranks with that prodigious 1985 film, but it misses by a lot more than four hours. "Tsahal" is a tedious, unfocused and severely undisciplined work from so scrupulous a documentarian. It meanders over the near-five-decade history of Israel, intermixing talking-head interviews with combat veterans and fresh recruits, and using as visuals an endless string of unidentified landscapes of the arid, 8,000 square miles within and along the Israeli border.

You would think there would be a ton of information packed into a five-hour film, but there is not. You could learn as much about the military history of Israel in a magazine article that might take 20 minutes to read, and Lanzmann doesn't have enough meat or emotion for a documentary half its length. We spend long stretches with young soldiers in tank companies, with paratrooper and jet pilot trainees, and hear repeatedly why nearly every Israeli has to serve in the military (when you are surrounded by enemies, you are in a state of perpetual readiness for battle).

There are some interesting individual war stories, from veterans talking about their skirmishes, their wounds and their fears. But there is no conventional use of newsreel footage to illustrate the terror and circumstances, and worse, Lanzmann makes no effort to provide context for any of these tales.

We hear about the six individual wars fought since the foundation of the state of Israel in 1948, but the film never stands back and explains clearly who, what, where, when and why these events occurred. We don't even have the benefit of maps showing the location of such hot spots as the Gaza Strip and the Golan Heights, or how Israel is positioned in relation to Jordan, Syria, Lebanon and Egypt. We are literally kept in the dark.

Though Lanzmann interviews a couple of critics of modern Israeli policy—the use of torture against suspected terrorists, the sanctioned settling of the West Bank—he has made a film that could be used as inspiration for Israeli youth facing military service. And they may be the only people who find it interesting.

VILLAGE VOICE, 1/31/95, p. 45, J. Hoberman

Whatever might be said about Claude Lanzmann, it cannot be that he makes easy movies. *Shoah,* a nine-and-a-half hour immersion in the Holocaust that reduces *Schindler's List* to *Indiana Jones,* is difficult in one way; *Tsahal,* a follow-up documentary taking its name from the Hebrew acronym for the Israeli Defense Force, is difficult in another.

The subject matter is related, but the appeal couldn't be more different. Although *Tsahal* is only half as long as *Shoah* and rarely ever boring, it seems perversely inflated—the minutiae of genocide is bound to exert greater fascination than the logic of survival. Shot before the PLO accords, in 1991 and 1992, *Tsahal* is a movie that should please almost no one. Although a given to be attacked from the left, the group who set off tear gas at *Tsahal's* Paris premiere were right-wing extremists. And, while those indifferent to the Jewish state will scarcely be drawn to a meditation on its military force, the response within Israel (where Lanzmann's documentary is virtually ambient) should prove most contentious of all.

Those who recognized *Shoah's* profound originality aside, *Tsahal* has two basic constituencies: Palestinians and Diasporic Jews. And, as the former, conspicuous for most of the movie largely by their absence, will have scant sympathy for Lanzmann's lesson in the logic of Israeli hypervigilance and the psychology of Israeli aggression, so the latter may be exasperated by the filmmaker's distended exercise in the seemingly self-evident.

Nevertheless, *Tsahal* engages, particularly for those in the United States, the question of Jewish identity—like what is it? Beneath the relatively untroubled surface of American Jewish life is the anxiety that that very category has no meaning. "Authentic" Jews were either exterminated at Auschwitz or have settled on the West Bank of the Jordan. Hence the troubled identification with Israeli strength. As a leftish Israeli intellectual puts it in Philip Roth's novel *The Counterlife:* "American Jews get a big thrill from the guns. They see Jews walking around with guns and they think they're in paradise ... The beards to remind them of saintly Yiddish weakness and the guns to reassure them of heroic Hebrew force." But *Tsahal* is not that either; it succeeds as film to the degree it fails as propaganda.

Constructed almost entirely of interviews and reconstructed memories, *Tsahal* confirms the methodology that Lanzmann developed in order to make *Shoah:* the use of real time and mixed languages; the blunt, artless camera placement; the chronological spiraling around increasingly significant details; the deployment of seemingly raw chunks of footage to make specific, rationally worked out points; the emphasis on concrete recollection; the development of an existential present tense; and, here most problematically, the use of absence as a tangible element.

Tsahal begins with a black screen and the sound of combat. Soon, it becomes apparent that the taped transmission of a battlefield radio is being played back in a recording studio with an actual veteran of the engagement reliving his experience of nearly 20 years earlier. Lanzmann's response is to document his subject's response, both verbal and visual, to that document. This initial evocation of primal fear and its memory reverberate throughout. Recordings or voiceover recollections are juxtaposed with now-peaceful battlefields. Zionist triumphalism is conjoined with inherent vulnerability: More than one soldier appears to cry. The initial emphasis is on the 1973 war, which one officer compares to a burnt offering—"a massive execution for a whole generation." The cemeteries are filled with dead teenagers. The frequent aerial shots of Israel's gold and green landscape reinforce its geographical puniness.

Among the many criticisms Lanzmann made of *Schindler's List* was that, by postscripting the docudrama with a sequence shot in Israel at Schindler's grave, Spielberg redeemed Auschwitz to provide a theological rationale for the Holocaust. *Shoah* too ended in Israel. (Indeed, Art Spiegelman's *Maus* is among the few celebrated works dealing with the Holocaust from a Jewish perspective that does not imply a Zionist solution.) But Lanzmann is more materialist. As *Tsahal* defines the Holocaust as "what happened to the Jewish people when they were unarmed and they had no chance to defend themselves," so the film's consideration is that which Jews have become—the transformation of a people without means (some would say, will) to defend themselves.

The Nazi transport train provided *Shoah* with its most concrete metaphor for Jewish extermination, in *Tsahal* it is the Israel-made tank—"brainchild of the Jewish people" as one diminutive major general calls it—that stands for Jewish preservation. In depicting the armored Jew, *Tsahal* engages an ongoing theme in 20th-century Jewish life argued most famously by Viennese physician Max Nordau at the Second Zionist Congress in 1898. Suggesting that centuries of ghetto life had weakened the Jewish physiognomy, Nordau proposed a corrective regimen of physical culture. As newly forged Jewish hard bodies provided a suitable temple for rekindled Jewish nationalism, so these *Muskeljuden* (muscle Jews) would prefigure the political creation of a Jewish state.

Nordau's views on Jewish degeneration (derived in no small measure from the introjection of prevailing anti-Semitic stereotypes) were not only a Zionist tenet. The transformation of weak, "unproductive" peddlers and intellectuals into Tough Jews, to use Paul Breines's term, not only underscores the JDL credo but the Bundist (and later Communist) call for militant, armed, Jewish workers. In this sense, the Holocaust is the climax of Jewish victimization and the destruction of the traditional ghetto Jew; in its aftermath, *Muskeljuden* fought to establish a Jewish garrison state and thus the end of Jewish particularism. just as Jews would no longer be passive victims, so they could no longer serve as what Breines calls "the peace-loving conscience of a violent, non-Jewish world."

So it is in *Tsahal,* which devotes at least half of its length to conversations with Israeli generals. Some seem sensitive, others brusque, all appear complex. Not everyone Lanzmann interviews is as blunt as novelist David Grossman in observing, "we belong to the state." Through the selectivity of its emphasis, *Tsahal* presents the army as the source of Israeli social value. When Lanzmann dwells upon the unhappiness of a kid who does not do well enough to become an elite fighter pilot, he illustrates what one Israeli youth told *The New York Times* about army assignment: "This will determine how we are viewed for the rest of our lives."

Some years ago, a well-known critic of *Shoah* avidly confronted me in a screening room with the revelation that Lanzmann had received money from the Israeli government to help make the film the assumption being that this reduced the movie to Zionist propaganda. *Tsahal* suffers this problem in reverse.

Although the idea evidently came from Yitzhak Rabin (who suggested that Lanzmann follow *Shoah* with a movie about Israel's 1948 war of independence), the project was conspicuously not funded by Israel. Nevertheless, in palling around so uncritically with the Israeli military brass, Lanzmann gives the impression that, like the American Jew that Roth satirized in *The Counterlife,* he too thinks he's in paradise.

Because Lanzmann is a Diaspora Jew, *Tsahal* lacks both the confidence and the ambivalence an Israeli would have brought to the material. Lanzmann takes his title in the most literal sense—he is, in a word, defensive. *Tsahal's* first half is an almost completely unchallenged celebration of the Israeli Defense Force that must be read as much for what is missing as for what appears. For example, despite universal conscription, women are barely present. (There are only two who speak in the entire film.) Of course, this only makes evident the innate sexism of so mobilized a state. Similarly, a contradiction of Israeli civil society is apparent in *Tsahal's* failure to mention the paradox by which the ultraorthodox are exempt from military service.

While Lanzmann reproduces the Israeli army's greatest taboo in his refusal to speculate on Israel's nuclear arsenal, not until late in the movie does the 1982 invasion of Lebanon enter the equation. Only in the final hour do occupation and *intifada* even become issues, as Lanzmann shifts his attention to Gaza, documents border searches, and speaks to the question of illegal torture with such critics of the occupation as novelist Amos Oz and lawyer Avigdor Feldman (old-fashioned Jewish intellectuals both). That no Palestinian is interviewed to explicate "Zionism from the perspective of its victims" is part of Lanzmann's strategy. Throughout *Tsahal,* Israelis are individual figures of authority. The Palestinians who come increasingly to the foreground during the final movement are typically shown en masse and always as they are being "regulated."

Seen as a composition in negative as well as positive space, *Tsahal* does provide a portrait of Israel. But where is religious faith? Early on, Lanzmann seems pleased to document that several Tough Jewish generals are the (implicitly secular, certainly pragmatic) offspring of devout pre-*muskel* families. Later, in a creepy bit of comic relief, he playfully asks a middle-aged Palestinian who has fathered 10 children why his family is so large. The man answers that he had nothing to do with it: "God's will." This riposte continues to reverberate when Lanzmann soon after engages in a spirited, not unfriendly, exchange with a West Bank settler.

Attempting to establish the legal right by which the settler feels entitled to construct his house upon this land, then pointing out logical contradictions in the man's answers, Lanzmann is heir to a certain enlightened mode of discourse—let's call it "reason." Is his smile rueful or admiring or simply helpless when his various arguments are pulverized on the unyielding rock of the settler's zealotry? This triumph of the irrational (and a "muscle" worldview) is crucial to *Tsahal.* It illustrates a defeat more profound than Lanzmann may recognize.

Also reviewed in:
NATION, 2/6/95, p. 179, Stuart Klawans
NEW YORK TIMES, 1/27/95, p. C1, Janet Maslin
VARIETY, 10/3-9/94, p. 62, Emanuel Levy

12 MONKEYS

A Universal Pictures and Atlas/Classico release of an Atlas Entertainment production. *Executive Producer:* Robert Cavallo, Gary Levinson, and Robert Kosberg. *Producer:* Charles Rowen. *Director:* Terry Gilliam. *Screenplay:* David Peoples and Janet Peoples. *Inspired by the film "La Jetée"* by: Chris Marker. *Director of Photography:* Roger Pratt. *Editor:* Mick Audsley. *Music:* Paul Buckmaster. *Music Editor:* Robin Clarke. *Sound:* Jay Meagher. *Sound Editor:* Peter Joly. *Casting:* Margery Simkin and Mike Lemon. *Production Designer:* Jeffrey Beecroft. *Art Director:* William Ladd Skinner. *Set Decorator:* Crispian Sallis. *Special Effects:* Shirley Montefusco. *Costumes:* Julie Weiss. *Make-up:* Christina Beveridge. *Stunt Coordinator:* Phil Neilson. *Running time:* 130 minutes. *MPAA Rating:* R.

CAST: Bruce Willis (James Cole); Madeleine Stowe (Kathryn Railly); Brad Pitt (Jeffrey Goines); Christopher Plummer (Dr. Leland Goines); Joseph Melito (Young Cole); Jon Seda (Jose); Michael Chance (Scarface); Vernon Campbell (Tiny); H. Michael Walls (Botanist); Bob Adrian (Geologist); Simon Jones (Zoologist); Carol Florence (Astrophysicist); Bill Raymond (Microbiologist); Ernest Abuba (Engineer); Irma St. Paul (Poet); Joey Perillo (Detective Franki); Bruce Kirkpatrick and Wilfred Williams (Policemen); Rozwill Young (Billings); Nell Johnson (Ward Nurse); Fred Strother (L.J. Washington); Rick Warner (Dr. Casey); Frank Gorshin (Dr. Fletcher); Anthony "Chip" Brienza (Dr. Goodin); Joilet Harris (Harassed Mother); Drucie McDaniel (Waltzing Woman Patient); John Blaisse (Old Man Patient); Louis Lippa (Patient at Gate); Stan Kang (X-Ray Doctor); Pat Dias (WWI Captain); Aaron Michael Lacey (WWI Sergeant); David Morse (Dr. Peters); Charles Techman (Professor); Jann Ellis (Marilou); Johnnie Hobbs, Jr. (Officer No. 1); Janet L. Zappala (Anchorman); Thomas Roy (Evangelist); Harry O'Toole (Louie/Raspy Voice); Korchenko and Chuck Jeffreys (Thugs); Lisa Gay Hamilton (Teddy); Felix A. Pire (Fale); Matthew Ross (Bee); Barry Price, John Panzarella, and Larry Daly (Agents); Arthur Fennell (Anchorman); Karl Warren (Pompous Man); Christopher Meloni (Lt. Halperin); Paul Meshejian (Detective Dalva); Robert O'Neill (Wayne); Kevin Thigpen (Kweskin); Lee Golden (Hotel Clerk); Joseph McKenna (Wallace); Jeff Tanner (Plain Clothes Cop); Faith Potts (Store Clerk); Michael Ryan Segal (Weller); Annie Golden (Woman Cabbie); Lisa Talerico (Ticket Agent); Stephen Bridgewater (Airport

Detective); Franklin Huffman (Plump Businesswoman); JoAnn S. Dawson (Gift Store Clerk); Jack Dougherty, Lenny Daniels, and Herbert C. Hauls, Jr. (Airport Security); Charley Scalies (Impatient Traveler); Carolyn Walker (Terrified Traveler).

CHRISTIAN SCIENCE MONITORY 1/5/96, p. 12, David Sterritt

"Twelve Monkeys," the new extravaganza by Terry Gilliam, is a science-fiction epic with tentacles reaching toward the future and the past.

It's futuristic because it takes place in 2035, portraying a society that little resembles any we know today. It also uses the notion of time travel as a launching pad for its wild, sometimes violent plot.

Yet devoted science-fiction fans will find themselves remembering 1962, when French filmmaker Chris Marker completed "La Jetée," one of the genre's most celebrated movies. Although it's only about 30 minutes long and is told almost completely through still photographs, this gem of fantastic cinema has earned a near-legendary reputation for its innovative style and story.

"Twelve Monkeys" takes not only its time-twisting premise from Marker's masterpiece, but also much of its mood and some of its visual ideas. It's as if Gilliam were haunted by the earlier film and couldn't get it out of his mind until he'd somehow relived it in his own life.

This would give him much in common with the heroes of both "La Jetée" and his own movie—men chosen for a time-traveling mission because they have memories of a past that's as important to understand as it is hard to recapture.

The hero of "Twelve Monkeys" is named Cole, and as the story begins he's hardly a conventional good guy. He's a convict, in fact, held prisoner in an underground nation driven off the surface of the Earth by an epidemic that's wiped out 99 percent of humanity.

In this dystopian world, the only way out of jail is to volunteer for an assignment so dangerous it's probably impossible to pull off: journeying into the past, in search of the epidemic's cause and cure. Cole is eager to try it. Arriving in 1996, he meets two people: a psychiatrist who slowly realizes his time-travel chatter isn't as crazy as it sounds, an animal-rights activist who's driven less by ethical concerns than by hostility toward his father, an amoral scientist.

Braving many dangers, some of them etched on screen with creepy forcefulness, Cole tracks down a bizarre political group that may hold the key to the future. He also closes in on a long-held memory that drives him on.

"Twelve Monkeys" can't be called a remake of "La Jetée," even though it borrows directly from it. "La Jetée" is less a sci-fi adventure than a visual essay with a philosophical bent. By contrast, the new picture—written by David Peoples and Janet Peoples—is as rambunctious as the title suggests, spicing its plot with mind-bending action and Hollywood-style violence.

Its blend of provocative ideas and lightning-quick storytelling could strike box-office gold. Or it could prove too raffish and unrefined for art-film admirers, too complex and surrealistic for casual movie fans.

Then again, sheer star power could pull it through. Bruce Willis is bruisingly good as Cole, a character with more depth than he displays at first, and Brad Pitt is marvelously manic as the activist who keeps popping into his path. Madeleine Stowe does her most energetic acting to date as the skeptical psychiatrist. Christopher Plummer and David Morse contribute suitably weird touches as the famed scientist and his sinister assistant.

In the end, though, this is very much a Gilliam production, plunging the gifted director back into near-delirious terrain he's explored in film ranging from the hilarious "Time Bandits" through more problematic outings like "The Adventures of Baron Munchausen" and "The Fisher King," not to mention the brilliant "Brazil," still his finest achievement.

Almost every frame of "Twelve Monkeys" seems on the verge of either flying to pieces or collapsing under its own craziness—and while neither happens, the resulting sensation of utter precariousness is well-suited to the story and its themes. "Twelve Monkeys" is not for every taste, but it reconfirms Gilliam as a master imagemaker of our time.

FILMS IN REVIEW, 5-6/96, p. 64, Harry Pearson, Jr.

12 Monkeys has all the flaws of a good Terry Gilliam film and few of the virtues.

First off, there is an out-of-control Brad Pitt, incorporating almost a century's worth of cinematic clichés about the mentally ill in a caricature so bad that we come to see what a genuinely shallow talent his is. I mean right down to the glass eye he decided to use. (Is it still a secret that Gilliam is not an actor's director?) Pitt's character is so patently "crazy" in this film that you wonder why his father, an eminent virologist, and his animal rights activist friends don't see him as so nuts he couldn't lead a marching band, much less a guerrilla movement. Next there is a script from David and Janet Peoples (David being of *Blade Runner* scripting fame) that like the *Blade Runner* script, manages to confuse an audience because it relies too heavily upon source material that is, at best, a venture into the exotic, not part of the working vocabulary of a mainstream audience. In this case, the Peoples are paying homage to one of the most perfect science-fiction films ever made, *La Jetee*, which Director Gilliam readily says he's never seen, so its grammar isn't in his head either! (Unless you've read Philip K. Dick's *Do Androids Dream of Electric Sheep*, there is much in *Blade Runner* you simply won't get; for instance, the fact that virtually all of the planet's animals are extinct.)

La Jetee begins with images from a man's childhood. Of a woman on one of the long outdoor ramps at Orly Airport in the days before the nuclear apocalypse. Of the man rushing to meet her. Of the strange looking man who kills him. Of her horror. *(La Jetee*, which is 29 minutes long, is composed of still photographs, save for a brief moment near the film's conclusion.) This childhood memory is so central to the grown-up man, now a prisoner in a dank future underworld where mankind is dying out, that the future's scientists are able to successfully send him back to that time (and then, after he has successfully survived the trauma of time travel, into the further future to find the help that will allow humankind to survive). The prisoner finds his way back to the woman's time, and falls in love with her. Eventually, he outwits (with the help of his newfound friends in the far future) the scientists who want to kill him after the experiment's success and goes back to the past to be with the woman, there to be executed by one of the scientists he thought he had eluded. Thus, he foresaw, as a child, the moment of his own death. Classic and beautiful. And deserving of Criterion resurrection as a supplement to its laserdisc edition of *12 Monkeys*.

Gilliam's airport scene (unmemorably photographed inside a forgettable terminal) is first presented as a dream, one that changes in its details as the movie progresses. (Did someone decide at the last moment to make Pitt a goofy good guy to appease his teen fans? I wonder, because all of the early scenes point to him as the one who releases the virus.) This robs the scene of any of its obsessional power and leaves the audience wondering if the child who saw the shooting would indeed grow up to be Willis (clear enough if you know *La Jetee*). To accommodate our present-day perceptions of reality, the scourge that sends the remnants of mankind underground is a virus deliberately released in December of 1996 (giving this film a short shelf life). *La Jetee's* dreamy meditation upon the impossibility of living in the past has been yoked to the action adventure format, a forced conjugation that works neither as thriller nor dreamy meditation.

What is surprising, given Gilliam's artistic eye, is the caliber of the color film stock used, which is subpar. The digital surround sound, heard in several theatrical venues, is used with little or no imagination and no impact. There is a surprising technical sloppiness (rushed production?) of the kind we do not associate with this director. And the plot machinations become so convoluted that the ending not only contradicts what has come before but portends an unintended outcome. The idea behind Willis' time travels was for him to collect a sample of the pure virus, before it had mutated, so that the people of the future could develop a vaccine to it. But the lady scientist from the future arrives after the virus has been released (and thus it is infectious in the form that will kill five billion people) and is herself exposed to it, and so is the child Willis when it is released a few yards from where he is standing in the airport. In *12 Monkeys*, Willis' childhood memory becomes an omen, not an anchor to get him into the past. Indeed, it is one of the conceits of this film that the scientists of the future twice send him back to the wrong time and in one farfetched case, half a world away. (There is, can you believe it, an homage to *Vertigo* toward the end that makes this cinematic contraption more pot than pouri.) And while we're talking about ill-conceived, the movie comes to a virtual standstill in a madhouse sequence early on that seems to be there mostly to let Pitt grandstand as the craziest of the crazies.

In short, unlike the Chris Marker film to which it (supposedly) pays tribute, *12 Monkeys* is a messy melange. What it has going for it is a superb performance by Bruce Willis, whose growth as an actor has been a fascination to watch, a decent enough momentum once we get out of the madhouse and away from Pitt—but the tears, the deeply wrenching regrets, the longing in the original have all been ironed out by the Peoples and Gilliam, leaving us, in the end, not quite certain what all this ado has been about. (Was Gilliam making a commercial film for Universal just to show that he could in the wake of the *Brazil* controversy?)

LOS ANGELES TIMES, 12/27/95, Calendar/p. 1, Kenneth Turan

A man appears and announces he's a traveler from the future, from a world that has survived, but barely, a viral epidemic that slaughtered 5 billion people and caused those few left alive to abandon the surface of the Earth. He's immediately, thrown into a mental hospital, and no wonder. But what if, just possibly, he's telling the truth?

As set up by David Peoples (who had a hand in "Blade Runner" and wrote Clint Eastwood's "Unforgiven") and Janet Peoples, "12 Monkeys" has the sound of a conventional futuristic science-fiction thriller. But when Terry Gilliam, is the director, no project stays conventional for long.

A cheerful, eccentric visionary with a consistently irreverent point of view, Gilliam successfully joined an extravagant visual sense to a playful sensibility in "Time Bandits," the brilliant "Brazil" and "The Adventures of Baron Munchausen." Nothing he touches has a chance of remaining ordinary, and while that is usually a good thing, too much, of a good thing can become simply too much.

So on the one hand "12 Monkeys" is a magical Old Curiosity Shop, filled with strange and wonderful sights and happenings that capture the eye and intrigue the mind. But on the other, Gilliam gets so distracted by these diverting sideshows he loses his focus and forgets to pay attention to the mechanics of plot, allowing the film to wander into narrative cul-de-sacs it has difficulty finding its way out of.

A more conventional director would have made "12 Monkeys" more streamlined and easier to follow, perhaps even more exciting, but oh the things we would have missed out on along the way.

"12 Monkeys" is based on one of the classics of French avant-garde filmmaking, Chris Marker's unsettling 1962 short, "La Jetee," which tells its tale of a man so haunted by a childhood memory he pursues it into the past entirely with still photographs and voiceover narration.

James Cole (Bruce Willis) is similarly haunted by a chilling vision of a gun going off in an airport; it's the first sequence in "12 Monkeys" and it recurs periodically in the film, though Cole is certainly not in a dreamy situation.

The year is 2035 and, having abandoned the Earth's surface because of that extra-lethal virus, humanity has reconstructed a kind of civilization underground, from which coerced "volunteers" are periodically sent to the surface to bring back specimens for scientific evaluation.

Cole is one such volunteer, and the deserted city he finds when he surfaces, a skyscraper-filled automobile graveyard where tigers and bears roam at will, is only one of several strikingly imagined alien environments envisioned by Gilliam and his design collaborators.

Because of his success in this mission, Cole is dragooned into a more critical assignment. Even though what has been done cannot be undone, fuller knowledge of the past can help the ruling elite cope with the awful present, so Cole is shipped back to 1996 to attempt to determine exactly where and how the fatal virus outbreak begin. His only clue: the name of a shadowy group called 12 Monkeys.

But, in a touch Gilliam must have delighted in, the clunky time machine sends Cole back to 1990 instead. And as soon as he starts to talk, albeit monosyllabically, about what he is trying to do, the powers that be throw him into a mental institution where two very different people influence his life.

One is a motor-mouthed fellow inmate, psycho ward politician Jeffrey Goines (a surprisingly funny Brad Pitt), who has nonstop opinions on everything. The other is Dr. Kathryn Railly, a psychiatrist who specializes in the linkage of madness and prophecy and who, not surprisingly, thinks Cole is completely delusional.

Dr. Railly is played, in a shrewd bit of casting, by Madeleine Stowe, an excellent actress with a grounded, non-flighty persona. The sanity of her presence in a film where everyone else is either mad or might as well be is an essential audience surrogate, a welcome life raft as the plot of "12 Monkeys" gets crazier and crazier.

An unlikely love story combined with a visionary detective yarn, "12 Monkeys" is baffling and difficult to decipher at times, but it's never a standard brand. Mystifying, intriguing, even infuriating, it shows what happens when an unconventional talent meets straightforward material. Almost against his will, Gilliam finally succeeds in building some dramatic momentum, and when he does, "12 Monkeys" catches hold in a way an ordinary version probably wouldn't. Nobody, Gilliam would probably be happy to tell you, said this was going to be easy.

NEW YORK POST, 12/27/95, p. 34, Michael Medved

If 12 monkeys sat at 12 typewriters for 12 years, then it's entirely possible they'd come up with a screenplay that resembled "12 Monkeys."

As a matter of fact, it might have helped our simian scribes to first watch the French short "La Jetee" (1962), which allegedly inspired the "12 Monkeys" mess with its tale a bleak future world dispatching time travelers into the past to change history and save humanity.

Of course, the same concept turned up in the "Terminator" films (and even "Star Trek IV"), which managed to make their time traveling entertaining because they never took the material too seriously.

In "12 Monkeys," however, director Terry Gilliam ("Time Bandits," "Brazil," "The Fisher King") treats his flimsy plot with apocalyptic intensity—and without a trace of the humor or whimsy that's characterized his best work since his long-ago days with Monty Python.

Here Bruce Willis plays a brutalized prisoner in a grave new world in which the remnants of humanity live entirely underground, dreading a virus that has already killed more than 5 billion people. A panel of scientists sends Willis on repeated trips back to the 1980s and '90s to try to unravel the riddle of the "Army of the 12 Monkeys," a band of animal rights radicals suspected of releasing the deadly virus.

In his travels to the past, Willis winds up in a mental hospital beside Brad Pitt who embarrasses himself as a babbling twitching maniac. He also happens to be the son of a world famous virologist (Christopher Plummer), whose research may hold the key to a deadly plague awaiting the world.

Also assigned to the Willis Wacko Ward is a brilliant psychiatrist (Madeline Stowe) who, like most other shrinks in recent Hollywood films, is gorgeous, conveniently unattached, and partial to provocatively short skirts.

Much of the movie's dialogue concerns the main character's sanity, with endless speculation over whether he's actually an emissary from the future or just an obnoxious nutcase. With few lines worth delivering, Willis spews forth all sorts of non-verbal contributions—setting a world's record for slobber and drool, and later vomiting up an ocean of blood after he's used a knife to cut out two of his own teeth, which were suspected of transmitting his whereabouts to malevolent meanies.

To emphasize the idea that this is an adventurous, vulnerable performance, director Gilliam gives us three different scenes of Willis exposing his bare behind—plus a bonus shot of Brad Pitt similarly mooning the audience.

The fanciful production design that made even the lunatic excesses of "Brazil" and "Baron Munchausen" such fun to watch is nowhere in evidence here; scene after scene is dingy and dreary, with an obsessive emphasis on wretched and hyper-violent homeless encampments on the streets of Philadelphia.

"Maybe the human race deserves to be wiped out," muses Willis during one of his journeys through time, and after journeying for more than two hours though this malodorous madness one may begin to agree with him.

Promotional materials for the movie declare: "Between past and future, sanity and madness, and dreams and reality, lies the mystery of "12 Monkeys". The only real mystery concerning this wretched film is over how so many talented people could have wasted their time in making it.

NEWSDAY, 12/27/95, Part II/p. B2, Jack Mathews

Coming as it does at the tail-end of Hollywood's holiday rush, it seems more fitting than ever to introduce the latest Terry Gilliam film, a science-fiction thriller titled "Twelve Monkeys," with the old Monty Python tease, "And now for something completely different."

Gilliam, of course, has been doing things completely different throughout his career. As the lone American member of "Monty Python's Flying Circus," he stayed back in the studio while the others were out shooting skits and came up with those fabulous illustrations. And when he started making his own movies—the darkly funny 1977 "Jabberwocky" came first—few people knew quite what to make of him.

Since then, Gilliam has confused them further with the wildly imaginative children's fantasies "Time Bandits" and "The Adventures of Baron Munchausen," the brilliant social satire "Brazil," and the urban fable "The Fisher King."

And now for something ...

Inspired by "La Jette," a 1962 featurette by French avant-garde filmmaker Chris Marker, "Twelve Monkeys" is the story of a Baltimore mental patient (Bruce Willis) who claims to have been sent back from the future to collect information about a viral plague that will wipe out most of the world's population in 1996. Is he a delusional schizophrenic, or a true time traveler? And how would he know?

For Gilliam aficionados, a group to which I claim early membership, that brief plot description is a pass to fantasyland, the uniquely irreverent landscape of Gilliam's imagination, where time is relative, at best, and where the lines separating reality from fantasy, and madness from sanity, are often crossed.

Though "Twelve Monkeys" is told from the point-of-view of James Cole (Willis), a man so confused by his life, his memories, and his circumstances that he comes to believe the people assuring him he is nuts, the audience's guide through the dense thicket of plot is Dr. Kathryn Railly. Played with deceptive simplicity by the wonderful Madeleine Stowe, Dr. Railly becomes Cole's psychiatrist, his hostage, and ultimately, his ally in his frantic quest.

The story, by David Peoples ("Blade Runner"), and his wife, Janet Peoples, opens in the year 2035, in a post-viral apocalypse underground, where the survivors of the plague and their descendants are living in a makeshift totalitarian society. Somehow, with a Rube Goldberg technology cobbled together from debris brought down with them, they have managed to invent a time machine, and have decided to send Cole back to 1996 to search for something called the Army of 12 Monkeys and learn about the causes of the great plague.

In a twist that plays right into Gilliam's cynical view of man's arrogance, the machine misses the mark, and Cole arrives, naked and dazed, in 1990 Baltimore, ending up in a mental institution where he meets Dr. Railly and a hyperkinetic fellow inmate named Jeffrey Goines (Brad Pitt), the son of a Nobel prize-winning virologist. After escaping back to the future, and being returned a second time to 1996 Philadelphia, Cole meets the psychiatrist and Goines again, and finally discovers the truth about the plague, and his role in it.

"Twelve Monkeys" is a great marriage of talents. Willis and Pitt, in roles that fly in the face of their personas, do some of the best work of their careers. Pitt, in particular, will surprise people with his deftly funny characterization of a manic rebel, a fruitcake with a cause.

David Peoples, who also wrote Clint Eastwood's "Unforgiven," is one of Hollywood's best screenwriters, and as complicated as the plot may sound, he has crafted one of those narrative puzzles that ends with a rush of "Ah-hahs!"

The overlay of Gilliam's own obsessions—his bleak depiction of life in a dysfunctional 20th Century, where faith in technology has obliterated faith in magic will put off people trying to stay focused on the plot. Indeed, it was a gutsy move by Universal Pictures, the same studio Gilliam fought with over "Brazil," to trust such a seemingly mainstream project to him, and then to stand back while he filtered it through his own imagination and sent it back—like the metallic Samurai in "Brazil," or the scarlet knight in "The Fisher King"—to confound some viewers, and beguile others.

I have joked that "Twelve Monkeys" may only appeal to people who have written books about "Brazil." I think I am the only one. It definitely helps to have spent some time trying to fathom the mind of someone who can satirize the foibles of a century, which Gilliam did with "Brazil," reinvent the nature of time, as he did with "Time Bandits," or postulate lies as truths, as he did with "Baron Munchausen." All I know is that his visions are uniquely his, and film lovers in the mood for something completely different can always count on him.

SIGHT AND SOUND, 4/96, p. 56, Philip Strick

Philadelphia, 2035. Sheltering underground from a virus that has killed most of the world's population, a group of scientists sends randomly selected criminals to monitor conditions in the derelict city above. One such 'volunteer' is James Cole, a surly and violent convict haunted by the childhood memory of a man shot down in an airport corridor. Impressed by Cole's toughness and powers of observation, the scientists decide he is a suitable candidate for their desperate project to trace the virus to its source. Following clues assembled since the first outbreak in 1996, they send Cole back in time to identify those claiming responsibility, a group called The Army of the Twelve Monkeys. But the time-travel process delivers him to Baltimore in 1990, where he is diagnosed as schizophrenic by county psychiatrist Dr Kathryn Railly and detained in a mental institution. The phone number he has been given as a link with the future proves useless.

Befriended by one of the mental patients, Jeffrey Goines, who encourages him to attempt an escape, Cole finally shakes free by returning to 2035, explaining to his interrogators that they sent him to the wrong year. Their second attempt lands Cole in 1917 in the trenches of France. One of his fellow convicts, José, is carried by on a stretcher and Cole is shot in the leg before again finding himself in Baltimore in 1996. He traces Kathryn Railly to a lecture hall and demands to be driven to Philadelphia. Fascinated by his incoherent story, she submits to the journey which ends with the discovery of the Twelve Monkeys insignia sprayed on various walls. Cole follows the signs and drags Kathryn into the headquarters of the Freedom for Animals Association; terrified staff reveal that the Army of the Twelve Monkeys is headed by Jeffrey, crazed son of the virologist Dr Leland Goines.

Kathryn digs the bullet out of Coles's leg and he gate crashes a reception at the Goines' mansion. His arrival prompts Jeffrey to take fresh action on behalf of the animals that have suffered in his father's laboratory. Back in 2035, Cole's interrogators promise him a full pardon if he can now pinpoint the exact whereabouts of the virus. Although Cole has begun to suspect that these 'future' sessions are merely imaginary, Kathryn has the bullet analysed and realises that his story could be true. She warns Dr Goines who, as a precaution, allows only his assistant, Dr Peters, to know the access code to the deadly virus he has been working on. But Jeffrey's plan, as it turns out, is unrelated to the virus: the Army's grand gesture is to lock Dr Goines in a cage at the Philadelphia Zoo and release the zoo animals into the city. Crisis apparently averted, Kathryn and Cole plan a new future together and head for the airport, only to encounter, Dr Peters and realise that it is he who plans to scatter the virus worldwide. Phoning a warning message to 2035, Cole is handed a gun by José; he tries to stop Peters but is shot down by an airport security guard. As he dies, his younger self watches nearby. On the plane, Peters is unaware that the chatty fellow passenger beside him is a scientist from the future.

Although the standard response to remakes is to complain about their lack of originality and stature in comparison with their predecessors, a knee-jerk protest against all imitations of Chris Marker's time-traveling story *La Jetée* seems particularly unnecessary. For a start, Marker's story, told in frozen photographic instants except for one vital detail of movement, is a time capsule itself, representing a unique conjunction of missile-crisis anxiety, memory (as explored with Alain Resnais), *cinéma vérité*, and the influence of such friends as Jacques Ledoux and Ligia Borowczyk. At the same time, barely a film at all (Marker called it a *photo-roman)*, it hints at alternative ways of being told and of supplementary scenarios that might yet relate to it. Other time capsules still reach us from the same era but *La Jetée*, with almost pedantic formality and an audacious humour thoerising that time travel is all in the mind, is the one that leaves most to the imagination. Rising at last to the bait, Terry Gilliam's *12 Monkeys* sensibly admits to being 'inspired' by Marker, but makes no claim to reconstruction.

12 Monkeys' identity is elusive, a compilation of interests and notions in which an affection for Marker is swamped by other dramatic priorities. Jostling for space in an already challenging narrative are the familiar, Gilliam predilection for visual delirium and the gloomier concerns of the David and Janet Peoples' screenwriting team. As explored in *Blade Runner, Salute of the Jugger, Unforgiven* and *Hero,* the Peoples return to themes of tribalism, trials of strength and ruined futures. These elements are peripheral to the bright central core of *La Jetée*, but they become dominant and unbalancing forces in *12 Monkeys*. In part, this might also be blamed on the underwritten romance which, despite the simmering beauty of Madeline Stowe, refuses to raise much of a temperature. Although Gilliam's films previously have been well equipped with wonderfully resilient heroines, the mismatch here between time-travelling convict and Cassandra-Complex theorist seems to have defeated all concerned.

Most revealingly, the final close-up of the young Cole after witnessing the key death shows him staring not at the girl's face which may one day summon him across the years (as the parallel character in Marker's film does) but at the departing plane in which the virus is being carried off to infect the rest of the planet. This change of emphasis, resulting presumably from the need for a penultimate scene with virus-carrier and virus-hunter together on the same aircraft, drastically weakens the continuity and logic of Cole's obsessive dream, in which the airport death is constantly replayed. *12 Monkeys* turns the whole event into an inexplicable mystery, with unrecognisable people in confusing disarray, an incident which given the traumas of countless plague deaths to follow, the boy might have in fact quickly forgotten.

With Marker, the main mystery is the recurring paradox of time-travel fiction granted that the death of the traveller is essential so that he will be drawn back to the same moment in time, where (and when) does his assassin come from? In this version, the death of Cole is largely irrelevant to the tracing of the virus, except—perhaps—in that it acts as a magnet, pulling through the earlier hour for the (equally irrelevant?) Army of the Twelve Monkeys until the identity of the virus-carrier is at last clear. On the way, all of Cole's returns prove to be essential contributions to the 'final' event which is cynically engineered by the team in 2035. Left casually in abeyance is any explanation as to how Cole manages to return to the future under his own steam, or how he gets 'bounced' from 1917 to 1996. We might also wonder how the young Cole, alive during the first outbreak of the virus, managed to avoid infection.

The overriding question, of course, is why Cole's mission is not simply to destroy the virus and save civilisation, although in doing so he would wipe out the future that has invented time travel and would therefore be unable to destroy the virus, and so on. The solution to this one rests squarely in Gilliam territory, where death-defying fights against a malevolent bureaucracy have consistently been attempted since the days of *Jabberwocky*. In its nattering armies of ineffectual, self-important experts, *12 Monkeys* resurrects the cruel conspirators of *Brazil*, for whom personal survival is the only priority. Why save the world when they can settle for Philadelphia? "It's not about the virus at all," realises this new Munchausen, once again evading Death by confronting it, "it's about following orders." Fortunately, it is also about the kind of incongruities that bring out the best of Gilliam, zestfully at home in another derelict city, another garbage world, another labyrinth of cumbersome, cobbled-together machinery. It may be nothing more than an elaborate deception, if we read the allusions to *Vertigo* correctly, a wilderness of monkeys where Bruce Willis again indulges in masochism and Brad Pitt is a transcendent psychotic, but it would probably amuse Chris Marker no end.

TIME, 1/8/96, p. 69, Richard Corliss

In this ultimate retread decade, when movie people are so short on ideas that they remake old TV shows and bad French comedies, give Terry Gilliam points for trying something completely different. When the former Monty Python animator does a remake, it's of the moodiest, most elliptical sci-fi film ever: Chris Marker's 1963 *La Jetée*. Set in a toxic future, this French collage of photos chases time backward to a painful childhood image. Gilliam's *12 Monkeys* is an all-star, megamovie elaboration of this theme—just what you'd expect from the director of that brilliant dark-side retro-futuristic vision, *Brazil*.

The movie, written by David and Janet Peoples, begins in the year 2035. Most of the world has been killed by a virus that broke out in 1997. Cole (Bruce Willis) is sent back in time to find out what went wrong. Landing in a loony bin, he is aided by a nice doctor (Madeleine Stowe) and beset by a canny inmate (Brad Pitt, in a funny turn full of wild hand gestures, as if shaking off imaginary water). Can Cole fulfill his mission and save the planet?

Is it worth saving? Dour sci-fi satire always has this message: I have seen the future, and it sucks. In this teeming hell-hole (lots of clatter and clutter), madmen get the best lines, and a heroic time traveler hardly stands a chance. Intent on both dazzling and punishing the viewer, Gilliam gets lost in creepy spectacle and plenty of old film clips (notably *Vertigo*). But at the sight of three giraffes crossing a city bridge, you'll think of a more recent movie. A bad one. In its frantic mix of chaos, carnage and zoo animals, *12 Monkeys* is *Jumanji* for adults.

VILLAGE VOICE, 1/2/96, p. 45, J. Hoberman

The year has five days left and, suddenly, here is the best studio release of 1995—Terry Gilliam's *12 Monkeys*—running loose in Multiplex Nation. Can this big, baffling, soulful, even poetic action flick pass for some sort of weird Bruce Willis vehicle, unaccountably open-ended, and set in a funkier-than-usual futuristic dystopia?

The one-tenth of 1 per cent of American moviegoers who are now or have ever been cinema-studies majors might regard *12 Monkeys* as a desecration. The script, by Berkeley-based David and Janet Peoples, takes its premise from left Bank cine-metaphysician Chris Marker's quasi-canonical 1962 short, *La Jetée*. A melancholy meditation on *temps perdu,* presented almost entirely as a succession of freeze-frames, the Marker film is set in the aftermath of a nuclear war and concerns a prison-camp inmate chosen as the subject for an experiment in time travel.

Set some 40 years in the future, *12 Monkeys* is similarly postcataclysmic. A viral epidemic wiped out 99 per cent of humanity back in 1996; the survivors huddle in caverns beneath the surface of the earth. As in the Marker film, the imprisoned time traveler (Willis) has been selected for the vividness of his recutting, pre-apocalyptic dreams. Instructed to gather infonnation on the mysterious terrorist band known as the Army of the 12 Monkeys, who are suspected of unleashing the plague, Willis is repeatedly sent back in time.

As befits the movie's all-over sense of a decrepit, jerry-rigged civilization, Willis's temporal excursions have an additionally disorienting lack of exactitude. One trip lands him in the middle of a World War I battlefield, another results in his incarceration in a Philadelphia asylum-rocking, drooling, and watching Tex Avery cartoons on the dayroom TV. It is in this snake pit that he encounters his destined co-stars: a lovely hospital psychologist turned popular authority on millennial madness (the fine and focused Madeleine Stowe) and a flipped-out fellow patient (Brad Pitt) with an ecological obsession and a genetic scientist for a father.

No one in *12 Monkeys* is especially rational, but Pitt makes a bravura madman. Twitching and gesticulating, ranting and jabbering, rolling his eyes and lolling his tongue, he's a fugue in stereotypical behavior. Willis's character is unstable in another way—vanishing and rematerializing throughout the movie. Set deep in the granite of his shaved head, his liquid, beseeching eyes strain to comprehend what is happening—or, perhaps, to push evolution to its next stage. Only a professional brute like Willis could convey such visceral pathos. "I love the music of the 20th century," he howls, a simian brought to tears by the sound of Fats Domino's "Blueberry Hill" on the car radio.

La Jetée is a reverie on loss and memory, the paradox of motion, and the impossibility of representation. *12 Monkeys* is a comic celebration of doomsday rhetoric and mental disorder. (It's as though the Peoples caught a double bill of *La Jetée* and another early-'60s classic, Sam Fuller's *Shock Corridor,* and jumbled them up.) Less whimsical and baroque than Gilliam's previous fantasies, *12 Monkeys* is powerfully delusional; using bizarre angles and unexpected camera moves, the director manages to be both inside and outside the various characters' agitated mental states.

I was no particular fan of Gilliam's overwrought *Brazil,* and the futuristic sequences, which suggest the fussy *Brazil* misc-en-scène, are *12 Monkeys* least successful element. But, working here mainly with the crumbling civic architecture of Philadelphia's and Baltimore's downtowns, he creates a convincing world of skid-row signs and portents. The streets are filled with prophetic derelicts, some of them secret agents from the future with radio transmitters implanted in their teeth. Indeed, the overall consistency of the movie's musty dilapidation and medical clutter make for some of the most inspired production design since *Blade Runner* (to cite an earlier Peoples script).

Mainly a careening, stop-start chase, *12 Monkeys* achieves ultimate poignance with Willis's yearning to remain in doomed 1996: "I want *this* to be the present," he begs. But, as *La Jetée* had wondered, what is the movie-present exactly? In a final act of film-historical hubris, *12 Monkeys* turns itself into a mock Hitchcock movie. The last reel's introduction of *Vertigo*—another sacrilege for some—not only provides a further twist on the spiral of time but pays additional homage to Marker, who has himself quoted and written most eloquently on this masterpiece of lost, fetishistic love.

Disassociated characters disguise themselves as movie stars, zoo animals escape, dreams come true. A child watches its adult self die. All this and a Bruce Willis shoot-out too? You might even find yourself brushing away a tear as you go shuffling out of the 'plex and back into the mall.

Also reviewed in:
CHICAGO TRIBUNE, 1/5/96, Friday/p. C, Michael Wilmington
NEW YORK TIMES, 12/27/95, p. C11, Janet Maslin
NEW YORKER, 1/22/96, p. 84, Terrence Rafferty
VARIETY, 1/1-7/96, p. 81, Emanuel Levy
WASHINGTON POST, 1/5/96, p. F1, Rita Kempley
WASHINGTON POST, 1/5/96, Weekend/p. 32, Desson Howe

TWO BITS

A Miramax Films release of a Connexion Film presentation. *Executive Producer:* Joseph Stefano, Willi Baer, and David Korda. *Producer:* Arthur Cohn. *Director:* James Foley. *Screenplay:* Joseph Stefano. *Director of Photography:* Juan Ruiz-Anchia. *Editor:* Howard Smith. *Music:* Carter Burwell. *Music Editor:* Adam Smalley. *Sound:* Drew Kunin and (music) Michael Farrow. *Sound Editor:* John Howell Gibbens. *Casting:* Glenn Daniels. *Production Designer:* Jane Musky. *Art Director:* Tom Warren. *Set Decorator:* Robert J. Franco. *Set Dresser:* Chris Pascuzzo. *Special Effects:* Norman B. Dodge, Jr. and Bob Vazquez. *Costumes:* Claudia Brown. *Make-up:* Luigi Rocchetti. *Make-up (Al Pacino):* Manilio Rocchetti. *Running time:* 85 minutes. MPAA *Rating:* PG-13.

CAST: Jerry Barone (Gennaro); Mary Elizabeth Mastrantonio (Luisa); Al Pacino (Grandpa); Patrick Borriello (Tullio); Andy Romano (Dr. Bruna); Donna Mitchell (Mrs. Bruna); Mary Lou Rosato (Aunt Carmela); Joe Grifasi (Uncle Joe); Rosemary DeAngelis (Mrs. Conte); Ronald McLarty (Irish); Charles Scalies (Ballyhoo Driver); Joanna Merlin (Guendolina); Geoff Pierson (Dr. Wilson); Karen Shallo (Woman in Red); Nick Discenza (Father of Deceased); Rik Colitti (Vottima); Rose Arrick (Mother of Deceased); Joy Pinizotto (Bride); Louis Lippa (Father of the Bride); Johnny C. (Head Pallbearer); Gene D'Allesandro (Brother of Deceased); Anthony DeSando (Victor); Sheila Murphy (Mary Linguini); Jayne Haynes (Mrs. Rizzo); Joe Fersedi (Player #1); Mikey Viso (Petey); Rick Faugno (Player #2); Jon Napolitano (Player #3); Nicole Molina (Little Girl); Mario D'Elia (Petey's Dad); Mary Testa (Housewife); Ted Brunetti (Guendolina's Youngest Son); Tony Rosa (Guendolina's Eldest Son); Lynn Battaglia (Guendolina's Son's Wife); Joey Perillo (Ballyhoo Replacement Driver); Dominic Leporarti (Freddie); Skip Rose (Ball Player); Alec Baldwin (Narrator).

LOS ANGELES TIMES, 11/22/95, Calendar/p. 14, Jack Mathews

The following review by Jack Mathews appeared in a slightly different form in NEWSDAY, 11/22/95, Part II/p. B19.]

If we put our minds to it, most of us can isolate a moment from our childhood that stands out, above all others, for the lessons it taught us, for the changes it made in us, and for its power to transport us back. The question raised by "Two Bits," screenwriter Joseph Stefano's autobiographical reflections on the formative moment in his life, is how much these personal epiphanies have to say to anyone else.

The moment for Stefano, a child of the Depression, is Aug. 26, 1933, a day that begins with his alter ego, 12-year-old Genarro (Jerry Barone), determined to earn a quarter for the movies, and ends with his grandfather's death.

In this slight but earnestly told tale, the two events are inextricably linked. Gennaro is compelled to do odd jobs for the money because his ailing grandfather (Al Pacino) insists on dying before Gennaro can claim his promised 25-cent inheritance. Even though his grandfather assures him that his death is imminent, Gennaro cannot wait because ... well, because kids cannot wait.

The effectiveness of this kind of personal reminiscence, which invites us to relive experiences refracted through decades of subsequent living, depends completely upon the amount of empathy generated by and for the storyteller himself. At that, Stefano and director James Foley ("Glengarry Glen Ross"), with Alec Baldwin providing the voice-over narration, only partially succeed.

Barone, making his acting debut, has a natural presence, and it's easy enough to want to follow him along on a day that begins with his being unable to focus on anything other than his immediate goal—to be at the opening matinee of the new La Paloma movie palace—and ends with his having learned a good deal about values and the real world he is about to enter.

The major problem with the film is that the nickle-and-dime adventures themselves don't pack enough drama to underscore the urgency Gennaro is feeling. There are some terrific scenes between the boy and his grandfather, who is determined to impart some of his wisdom before he's gone, and Pacino—though you cannot look at him without seeing the dying Michael Corleone in the last scene of "The Godfather, Part III"—brings enormous sympathy to a man sizing up his life on what he is certain is the day it will end.

However, even at its brief hour-and-25-minute running time, "Two Bits" shows some stretch marks. We may end up with an appreciation for what the experience meant to its author, and, for those of us born before TV and "The Brady Bunch," even join him for a swim in movie nostalgia. We certainly can't deny the importance of Gennaro getting into the La Paloma at the earliest possible moment.

But unlike Steven Soderbergh's "King of the Hill," a superb adaptation of author A.E. Hotchner's memoirs about growing up in Depression-era St. Louis, "Two Bits" has little to say about its period or its setting. It remains strictly a slice of life, and as important as that slice is to Stefano, it's not quite enough for a fully realized movie.

VILLAGE VOICE, 11/28/95, p. 70, Leslie Camhi

One hot day in 1933, as puddles widen around the icebox, 12-year-old Gennaro wants a quarter for a ticket to La Paloma, South Philadelphia's newest "all air-cooled" movie palace. In the yard, his grandfather (Al Pacino) dispenses gnarly bits of wisdom as he lies dying; in the kitchen, his hard-working, long-suffering mother (Mary Elizabeth Mastrantonio) rails dough as she mutters about the "change of life." "There's a Depression going on," all his elders remind him. Still, Gennaro's boyish spirit is undaunted; his daylong epic quest for "two bits" will take him from the depths of human despair to the brink of ... Manhood.

The boy, newcomer Jerry Barone, benefits from an ingenue's disaffected grace, but he seems to have stepped directly from the streets of 1995 into this careful period setting; he moves like a modern boy and looks nourished on good food rather than depression potatoes. Mastrantanio may be a gifted actress, but here she's stiff as a wax mannequin in her authentic 1930s dresses. Wearing lots of makeup, Pacino sits alone in the front yard, a prisoner of his own magnificent character acting. The music is sappy, the hackneyed cinematography stoops to slow motion, and the light is unbearably golden. Director Foley (*Glengarry Glen Ross* and *After Dark, My Sweet*) is clearly in his element with the modern world of masculine alienation; the homespun warmth of yesteryear that he's so desperately reaching for in *Two Bits* just doesn't come through.

Also reviewed in:
CHICAGO TRIBUNE, 1/19/96, Friday/p. J, John Petrakis
NEW YORK TIMES, 11/22/95, p. C18, Stephen Holden
VARIETY, 10/16-22/95, p. 95, Todd McCarthy

UNDER SIEGE 2: DARK TERRITORY

A Warner Bros. release in association with Regency Enterprises of an Arnon Milchan-Seagal/ Nasso production. *Executive Producer:* Gary Goldstein. *Producer:* Steven Seagal, Steve Perry, and Arnon Milchan. *Director:* Geoff Murphy. *Screenplay:* Richard Hatem and Matt Reeves. *Based on characters created by:* J.F. Lawton. *Director of Photography:* Robbie Greenberg. *Editor:* Michael Tronick. *Music:* Basil Poledouris. *Music Editor:* Curtis Roush. *Sound:* Christopher Boyes and (music) Tim Boyle. *Sound Editor:* Alan Robert Murray and Walter Newman. *Casting:* Louis Di Giaimo and Emilie Talbot. *Production Designer:* Albert Brenner. *Art Director:* Carol Wood. *Set Decorator:* Kathe Klopp. *Special Effects:* Dale L. Martin. *Visual Effects:* Richard Yuricich. *Costumes:* Richard Bruno. *Make-up:* Jeff Simons. *Stunt Coordinator:* Dick Ziker. *Running time:* 100 minutes. *MPAA Rating:* R.

CAST: Steven Seagal (Casey Ryback); Eric Bogosian (Travis Dane); Everett McGill (Penn); Katheine Heigl (Sarah Ryback); Morris Chestnut (Bobby Zachs); Peter Greene, Patrick Kilpatrick, and Scott Sowers (Mercs); Afifi (Female Merc); Andy Romano (Admiral Bates); Brenda Bakke (Gilder); Sandra Taylor (Kelly); Jonathan Banks (Scotty); David Gianopoulos (David Trilling); Royce D. Applegate (Ryback's Cook); Nick Mancuso (Breaker); Christopher Darga and Don Blakely (Cooks); Dale Dye (Colonel Darza); Jim Clark and Stan Garner (Train Consultants); Silan Smith (Friendly Faced Engineer); Rick Wiles (Conductor); Kurtwood Smith (General Cooper); Denis L. Stewart (Holy-Merc); Jim Dirker and Ken Vieira (Helicopter Pilots); Todd O. Russell (Ryback's Driver); Warren Tabata (Bartender); Greg Collins (Huey Pilot); Wren T. Brown and Al Sapienza (Captains); D.C. Douglas and Thom Adcox Hernandez (Technicians); Catherine MacNeal (Assistant); Frank Roman (Aide); Jennifer Starr (ATAC Assistant); Ping Wu (SYSOS Officer).

LOS ANGELES TIMES, 7/17/95, Calendar/p. 2, Peter Rainer

In "Under Siege 2: Dark Territory" Steven Seagal is back as Casey Ryback, ex-Navy SEAL and current cook, and he's as snidely catatonic as ever. Ryback spends most of the movie cracking necks and clambering atop speeding trains, which is just as well, because whenever he slows down for a quiet scene with his estranged 17-year-old niece, Sarah (Katherine Heigl), he resembles one of those impassive cartoon characters whose only mobile feature is a movable mouth.

"Under Siege 2" isn't going to convince anyone that Seagal is Brando, though he often sounds a bit like him. But, taken strictly as an action sequel, the film is a lively show. It's a formula follow-up with formula dialogue and formula action but the director, Geoff Murphy, does extremely well within the sequel's narrow limits.

He doesn't deliver as an artist, and Murphy (the New Zealand director of the extraordinary "Utu," about a Maori uprising) is prodigiously an artist. But he delivers as a first-class hired hand, and that's not nothing. He plays out his improbable pyrotechnics for all they're worth.

If "Under Siege" was "Die Hard" on a ship, "Under Siege 2" is "Die Hard" on a train. (What's next? "Die Hard" on a Brentwood tour bus?) Ryback starts out the film on a Denver-to-Los Angeles luxury train with the niece he hasn't seen in five years. (Her father, Ryback's brother, died in a plane crash, and he's the only family she has.) En route, the great big choochoo gets hijacked by mercenaries headed by Travis Dane (Eric Bogosian), a curly-haired maniac fired by Washington after developing a deadly top-secret spy satellite.

Now, he and his band of lugs have commandeered the train Ryback, of course, just happens to be on it—and is using it as an untraceable computer command center to reclaim and deploy the satellite. His game: A billion-dollar payoff and the destruction, via satellite, of most of the Eastern seaboard.

The only reason to see a movie like this is for the quality of the action sequences and the nastiness of the villains. Murphy, who has had an uneven career in Hollywood—his best piece of direction was "Young Guns II"—does some amazing stuff with the train. He's so good at working it into the action that it upstages just about everybody—including Seagal and Bogosian. There's a flaming finale that looks as if it was as difficult to film as anything train-wise in "The Fugitive."

Villian-wise, the film is a bit of a letdown. Bogosian doesn't really get a chance to display his sporty venomousness; he's just a standard-issue meanie with nerdier hair and buggier eyes. The other actors, including Morris Chestnut as a porter who becomes Ryback's sidekick, are pretty standard-issue too, though Everett McGill, playing Dane's right-hand man, has a terrific moment when he's doused with pepper spray and inhales deeply—he says it's good for his sinuses.

This seems to be the guiding principle behind "Under Siege 2" as well. It's the kind of knockdown, dumb-down action picture that's supposed to clear the sinuses of its undemanding audience.

If that includes you, breathe deep.

NEW YORK POST, 7/15/95, p. 19, Thelma Adams

If the 1992 action hit "Under Siege" was "Die Hard" on a ship, then "Under Siege 2: Dark Territory" is "Die Hard" on a slow train to L.A.

Like its sleekly formulaic big brother, this Steven Seagal vehicle finds an embittered ex-federal employee holding the Free World hostage. But lost at sea is director Andrew Davis ("The Fugitive"), replaced by the decidedly earthbound Geoff Murphy ("Freejack").

Rogue zany Travis Dane (Eric Bogosian) hijacks a train and commandeers a deadly satellite in order to blackmail the feds for a billion bucks. Bogosian, sweating to inspire yucks without a single sure-fire laugh line, can't hold a Roman candle to the devilish tag team of Tommy Jones and Gary Busey who made "Under Siege" such addictive trash.

It's up to Casey Ryback (Seagal), chief cook and covert operative, to halt the evil Dane. After a setup as leisurely as train travel, Seagal bursts into a welcome 20 minutes of relentless bone cracking and a final knife fight so rote I longed for the face-off between Jones and Seagal in the original.

This scattershot sequel has one thing going for it: Steven Seagal. How the 6-foot-4 black belt with the beady eyes and whispery delivery ever become a star is one of the mysteries of Western Civ, but the man's man has presence.

After being the heir to the Chuck Norris minimal-acting, maximal-punch school of action heroes and starring in a string of B-movies with decent production values, the zen bone cruncher swam into the mainstream with "Under Siege."

Seagal promptly tossed away his new-found legitimacy by choosing to go auteur, directing himself in the 1993 bottom feeder, "On Deadly Ground."

"Dark Territory," which opened yesterday without Warner Bros. gracing critics with a screening, will do nothing to keep Seagal's reputation from sliding back to the B-movie basement.

NEWSDAY, 7/15/95, Part II/p. B5, Jonathan Mandell

When Steven Seagal emerged from the kitchen freezer of the battleship Missouri three years ago to doff his cook's hat and face down an entire army of colorfully demented terrorists, he did more than single-handedly save the world. He also made more money than usual. "Under Siege" was an action hit, distinguished from his usual neck-cracking, knuckle-headed gore-fests by the well-paced direction and the vivid villainy of Tommy Lee Jones and Gary Busey.

"Under Siege 2: Dark Territory," the inevitable sequel, begins promisingly enough, with a rocket launch, an expensive new satellite weapon in space, a war room full of men with medals and one beautiful and brainy babe.

How would they work Seagal into the action this time? A stowaway on the spaceship? A janitor on a nuclear-tracking submarine? Maybe a flight attendant on the Concorde?

Well, no. Former expert counterterrorist Casey Ryback now emerges from the kitchen freezer—on a train in the Southwest. In place of the rock and roller villains of the past, there's a sadistic Aryan with short blond hair, and a computer nerd. Gone is much of the pacing and the vivid acting. Even the babe is killed early on.

It's a rocky ride from there.

Ryback is traveling as a passenger with his teenage niece to visit the gravesite of his brother (one track in a whole railroad full of plot lines that are left unexplained and undeveloped). The train is hijacked by a new villain, Eric Bogosian, the computer nerd fired from his job with the government after developing the new satellite weapon. After setting up a little metal contraption on board and sticking a CD-ROM into a personal computer, he is able to take over the satellite weapon.

Though surely more costly to make, "Siege 2" somehow seems cheaper. The film ends with a spectacularly explosive train collision (which comes completely out of the blue), and dozens still lose their lives—actually thousands, if you include the site in China that Bogosian bombs (which is shown only as a bright spot on a computer screen and then a falling tower).

But the big suspense is supposed to be Bogosian's threat to destroy the Pentagon and Washington, D.C., unless he gets a billion dollars. In the original it was Honolulu and several billion dollars—proving that the filmmakers have set their sights lower. Logically, then, the villain in the next sequel should target Hollywood.

SIGHT AND SOUND, 11/95, p. 52, Peter Matthews

Brilliant but unstable expert Travis Dane, has been fired from a top secret government project making an orbiting super-weapon. Swearing revenge, he hijacks a luxury train, *The Grand Continental*, with the help of a band of mercenaries led by Penn. On board are Captains Gilder and Trilling, who work at the military intelligence agency. Dane threatens to blind them with a red-hot needle unless they reveal the digital code that unlocks the satellite's computer system. They give up the code and are summarily thrown from the train.

Dane can now control the Star Wars system from the train. He threatens to blow up the nuclear reactor under the Pentagon and lay waste to Washington, D.C., unless he is paid one billion dollars. To show he means business, Dane uses the satellite to destroy a chemical weapons plant in China.

Fortunately, also on board is former cook and ex-Navy SEAL Casey Ryback, travelling on vacation with his niece Sarah. When the commotion starts, Casey hides out and enlists the reluctant aid of a porter named Bobby Zachs. Casey faxes word to Washington of his presence on the train, and manages to kill a number of stray mercenaries before his identity is eventually uncovered by Dane and Penn. The villains take Sarah hostage.

The military officials decide to shoot down the satellite, but the resourceful Dane outfoxes them. Casey breaks into the control room where he obtains the CD controlling the weapons system. In a pitched battle, however, he apparently falls to his death, and Dane recovers the CD. But the unscathed Casey leaps from a pick-up truck back onto the moving train.

The Washington brass order the bombing of the train, but Dane thwarts them. He then switches tracks, and sets the train on a collision course with another train carrying 800,000 gallons of gasoline. Casey and Bobby save the other passengers. Penn threatens Sarah with a hand grenade, but Casey kills him. The armed forces explode the satellite in the nick of time, and a helicopter lifts all the good guys to safety as the two trains crash in a considerable pyrotechnic display.

Criticising *Under Siege 2* is about as superfluous an act as reviewing a tin of baked beans. Nothing one says can possibly affect the money-spinning capacity of so routine a corporate product, which does without style, characterisation or even basic coherence in order to give the undemanding audience worldwide what it presumably paid for: a spiralling body count and explosions.

Ten or 20 years ago, this kind of *reductio ad absurdum* film-making was thought to appeal to lonely urban men and pre-literate peoples; but now the big dumb action movie has become respectable, and post-literates are included as well. At the preview I attended, a row of young men behind me were happily quoting chapter and verse from *Timecop 2* and *Missing in Action 3*, eager to see how the latest Steven Seagal opus clocked stunts-wise and FX-wise against its competitors.

They probably weren't disappointed. *Under Siege 2* spends maybe 15 minutes setting up its threadbare computer-terrorist plot. In the remaining 85 or so, Seagal simply roams about dispatching mercenaries with the *blasé* air of a salesman fulfilling a quota. It seems beside the point to complain that the movie dehumanises death (a fair chunk of China gets reduced to cinders, and no one bats an eye) or that the director Geoff Murphy is incapable of building suspense. He too fulfils his quota for viewers who want serial jolts without the tedious armature of dramatic involvement. Structurally, *Under Siege 2* is just one damned thing after another, and kinaesthetically, it has no real payoff. Albeit, there's a gorgeous fireball at the end, but in the circumstances it functions less as the orgasmic release of accumulated tension than as a mechanical punctuation mark (! or perhaps !!!) telling customers they can—blessedly—go home.

Under Siege 2 qualifies as virtually a remake rather than a sequel, since about all the writers Richard Hatem and Matt Reeves have done is to introduce some slight variants on the paradigm (a train instead of a battleship, a jiving black sidekick for 'Miss July'), as if in some brazen display of neo-formalism. The movie practically comes out and says, 'Why tamper with a sure thing?'. Why indeed, unless you hope to send your audience out in something more than a mood of sodden acceptance? Jan de Bont's fantastically adroit and elating *Speed* put so dynamic a spin on its generic ingredients that it made them new. Even *Under Siege* (directed by Andrew Davis) chugged along efficiently if unmemorably, and managed to work up some minimal sense of peril. But *Under Siege 2* is a rather more abstract exercise in mayhem: for all the attention it pays to them, the terrorised passengers might as well be sacks of flour.

I'm far from being an enthusiast for this sort of affectless, rococo violence; but at least when John Woo does it, he choreographs like Busby Berkeley. Murphy stages the fight scenes so slackly and Michael Tronick edits so wham-bam fast that one loses the pleasure of lucidly articulated movement. The editing appears to cover a multitude of sins—not least the martial inadequacies of the star. As Casey Ryback, Seagal waggles his hands impressively from time to time, but otherwise scarcely exerts his portly bulk. His anomic indifference to the bone-crunching, neck-snapping natural justice he metes out might be satirical in another context; here, it just seems apt. A truly spirited action hero like Errol Flynn or Keanu Reeves makes you feel that no problem in the world can't be licked. The stolid, listless Seagal merely invites you to share in his own apathy.

Also reviewed in:
CHICAGO TRIBUNE, 7/17/95, Tempo/p. 2, Michael Wilmington
NEW YORK TIMES, 7/15/95, p. 16, Stephen Holden
VARIETY, 7/17-23/95, p. 51, Leonard Klady
WASHINGTON POST, 7/15/95, p. D1, Richard Harrington

UNDERNEATH, THE

A Gramercy Pictures release of a Populist Pictures production. *Executive Producer:* Joshua Donen, William Reid and Lionel Wigram. *Producer:* John Hardy. *Director:* Steven Soderbergh. *Screenplay:* Sam Lowry and Daniel Fuchs. *Director of Photography:* Elliot Davis. *Editor:* Stan Salfas. *Music:* Cliff Martinez. *Sound:* Paul Ledford. *Sound Editor:* Larry Blake. *Casting:* Ronnie Yeskel. *Production Designer:* Howard Cummings. *Art Director:* John Frick. *Set Designer:* Jeanette Scott. *Set Dresser:* Mike "Shelf" Malone. *Special Effects:* Jack Bennett. *Costumes:* Karyn Wagner and Kristen Anacker. *Make-up:* Lizbeth Williamson. *Stunt Coordinator:* Bobby Sargent. *Running time:* 99 minutes. *MPAA Rating:* R.

CAST: Peter Gallagher (Michael Chambers); Alison Elliott (Rachel); William Fichtner (Tommy Dundee); Adam Trese (David Chambers); Joe Don Baker (Clay Hinkle); Paul Dooley (Ed Dutton); Elisabeth Shue (Susan); Anjanette Comer (Mrs. Chambers); Dennis Hill (Guard, Tom); Harry Goaz (Guard, Casey); Mark Feltch (Guard, George); Jules Sharp (Hinkle's Assistant); Kenneth D. Harris (Mantrap Guard); Vincent Gaskins (Michael's Partner); Cliff Haby (Turret Operator); Tonie Perensky (Ember Waitress); Randall Brady (Ember Bartender); Richard Linklater (Ember Doorman); Helen Cates (Susan's Friend); Kevin Crutchfield (VIP

Room Flunky); Brad Leland (Man Delivering Money); John Martin (Justice of the Peace); Rick Perkins (TV Delivery Man #1); Paul Wright (TV Delivery Man #2); David Jensen (Satellite Dish Installer); Jordy Hultberg (TV Sports Reporter); Steve Shearer (Detective); Fred Ellis (Detective's Partner); Joe Chrest (Mr. Rodman).

LOS ANGELES TIMES, 4/28/95, Calendar/p. 2, Kenneth Turan

"The Underneath" doesn't add up. Made with polish and assurance, capably acted and intricately constructed, its overall impact is less than these parts would indicates it is good but, against all logic, it is not good enough.

That logic should not be a factor is appropriate because "The Underneath," as its title indicates, is yet another of those sinister film noirs, rife, with suspicion, double-crosses and misbehavior.

What the title doesn't tell you, and what the film's press material tiptoes around, is that the film is a fairly close remake of 1948's "Criss Cross," one of the most underrated of the classic noirs, written by Daniel Fuchs, directed by Robert Siodmak and starring a vibrant Burt Lancaster in one of his earliest roles.

Working from a script credited to Sam Lowry (apparently a pseudonym) and Fuchs, director Steven Soderbergh has used "The Underneath" as an excuse for some high-gloss filmmaking. Helped by cinematographer Elliot Davis, Soderbergh, still best known for his debut film, "sex, lies and videotape," has made this picture sparkle visually. He also makes the film's tricky plot structure, which mixes footage from several different time frames, work successfully.

"The Underneath" opens in the present (shot in grainy stock that almost seems to be tinted green) with security guard Michael Chambers (Peter Gallagher) riding in an armored car on a cash pickup run.

Almost immediately, the film goes into an extended flashback, showing Michael arriving back home in Austin for his mother's second marriage. Looking for a job, he goes to work for Clay Hinkle (Joe Don Baker) at the Perennial Armored Car company, where his new stepfather, Ed Dutton (Paul Dooley), is employed.

At loose ends emotionally, Michael soon seeks out his ex-wife Rachel (a tasty role for Alison Elliott), who is not exactly glad to see him. "How can you show your face without getting hurt?" she asks, and not in a concerned tone.

Clearly Rachel has not been waiting docilely for Michael's return. She is engaged to Tommy Dundee (William Fichtner), a local hard guy. There is still chemistry between these two, but Rachel is so peeved at Michael for how he acted in the past that she can barely talk to him.

Soon, in a flashback within a flashback (set apart by the fact that Michael wears a beard), their previous life is revealed. Michael was a gambling junkie while they were together, completely self-absorbed, the kind of feckless ne'er- do-well that women like Rachel find irresistible.

Back and forth and back ... "The Underneath" goes between these two flashbacks and the armored car present, which is also characterized by subtitles indicating the time of the action. It all plays more smoothly than it may sound, though a familiarity with the original film does help in figuring things out.

While all of this is effective, it doesn't go far enough. What "The Underneath" lacks is the kind of emotional connection that the best film noirs have. Instead of involving, this film is distancing, too given to admiring its own shiny surface. And at key points it is unable to make the more dicey aspects of the plot as convincing as they need to be.

Though he works hard and honorably at the role, part of the problem is that Peter Gallagher feets miscast as Michael Chambers, and it's not just that he lacks the coiled energy that made Burt Lancaster so memorable. After all, who doesn't?

Rather it's that though Gallagher can convey the moral weakness the character demands, he cannot make Michael into someone whose fate the audience cares about and willingly gets involved in. As his ex-wife says, Michael is someone who is not there, and once that becomes apparent, neither are we.

NEW YORK POST, 4/28/95, p. 41, Thelma Adams

There's too much tension in the life of the average New Yorker—and not enough in "The Underneath."

Steven Soderbergh, the wunderkind of "sex, lies, and videotape," has gotten on the John ("The Last Seduction") Dahl bandwagon and cranked out a neo-film noir. Soderbergh exhumes "Criss Cross," the 1949 cuckold classic where Yvonne DeCarlo toyed with ex-husband Burt Lancaster while carrying on with gangster Dan Duryea.

The script, credited to newcomer Sam Lowry and the late Daniel Fuchs of "Criss Cross" fame, tries to dent the surface of three skin-deep charmers: laid-back gambler Michael (Peter Gallagher); his ex-wife and would-be actress Rachel (Alison Elliott) and the new man in Rachel's life, club-owner-slash-kingpin Tommy (William Fichtner).

Even the new title has less pull than the original. "The Underneath" seems to refer less to the subterranean motivations off the three main characters, than to flash camera angles that catch the actors in turquoise, magenta, blue or yellow. Since this is film noir, don't forget that shot of the hero trapped in the shadow of the Venetian blinds!

Lovable loser Gallagher ("While You Were Sleeping) charms while looking out from under the dark canopy of his eyebrows, but it doesn't seem as if Lowry or Soderbergh are really interested in this blue-collar jamoke. During the gambler's riff on golf, I could feel the camera getting heavy, the director's attention wandering.

Newcomer Elliott masters slinky and seductive, but she's like a little girl in her mother's stilettos during the hard-boiled scenes the plot has in store for her. Veteran actors Joe Don Baker, Paul Dooley and Anjanette Comer lend interest m supporting roles without adding the weight this thriller so desperately needs.

"The Underneath" is crammed with stupid people making stupid decisions to take stupid actions. The artistry would come in if, despite this, the audience cared about the fates of Michael and Rachel. But I only felt something for Rachel when, referring to a robbery the trio plans, she says "I can't wait for this whole thing to be over." At that moment, I shared her pain.

NEWSDAY, 4/28/95, Part II/p. B3, Jack Mathews

When Steven Soderbergh's surprise art-house hit "sex, lies and videotape" made him the instant hero of American independent filmmakers six years ago, the unassuming director tried to spare himself the future label of turncoat by telling everyone within earshot that his true ambition was to make major studio movies.

Well, he has made three movies since "sex, lies and videotape," two of them within the studio system, and we're still waiting for him to sell out.

Soderbergh takes an intuitively intellectual approach to his subjects, whether it's the video camera's role in modern relationships ("sex, lies"), a 20th-Century literary enigma ("Kafka"), memories of growing up in Depression-era St. Louis ("King of the Hill") or, in the newly arrived "The Underneath," remake of a fairly routine '40s film noir.

"The Underneath," adapted by Sam Lowry and Daniel Fuchs from both the novel and screenplay behind Richard Siodmak's 1949 "Criss Cross," is a highly stylized potboiler in which Peter Gallagher takes on the role played in the original by Burt Lancaster. No, Gallagher can't hold a candle (or a match, or a firefly) to Lancaster, and the marquee gap is even greater between newcomers William Fichtner and Alison Elliott in roles first played by Dan Duryea, film noir's quintessential villain, and the exotic Yvonne De Carlo. But what "The Underneath" lacks in star power, it makes up in finesse and psychological depth.

I don't mean "The Underneath" is *real* deep. The simplistic plot, about a man with a past who returns to his hometown and gets into trouble trying to lure his ex-wife away from the local mob boss, doesn't give Soderbergh a lot to work with. The clichés of film noir are great for creating atmosphere, but hell on character development.

Soderbergh fragments his story into at least four time periods, using the past, the recent past, real time, and the near future to make us understand how his three characters got on their collision course with each other and destiny. "Criss Cross" drew its title from the betrayals that forced the deadly showdown; "The Underneath" takes it name from its concentration on motivation.

The movie starts in the future, with Michael Chambers (Gallagher) riding shotgun in an armored car with a man (Paul Dooley) we will learn is his new stepfather. Something is clearly up with Chambers, who's nervously watching other cars go by and registering landmarks as they pass. An armed robbery coming up? You bet, but who's involved and what's it all about?

Through the intricate, an sometimes confusing, intercutting of events from different periods, the picture of Chambers that emerges is one of a recklessly carefree spirit whose addiction to gambling cost him his marriage, alienated him from his police officer brother (Adam Trese) and forced him to run for his life.

Returning home for his widowed mother's wedding, he can't resist checking on his ex-wife Rachel, (Elliott). Realizing the passion still burns, he decides to take that armored car job, and, with the psychopathically jealous Tommy Dundee (Fichtner) lurking nearby, tries to win her back with the biggest gamble of his life. He offers to be the inside man for a robbery of his own truck by Dundee's gang, going against the odds he'll be double crossed.

Soderbergh gives the ending a different twist, but his interest is in examining the choices the characters make over years to get there. It adds at least the illusion of depth to a story that is pure pulp, and for film noir fans (hint: don't go if you aren't), that's the twist that makes it new.

SIGHT AND SOUND, 3/96, p. 54, Nick James

Michael Chambers, returns home to Austin, Texas, after some years for his widowed mother's remarriage. He is greeted by his loving mother and his brother David, a cop. That night he meets his prospective father-in-law, Ed Dutton, who suggests Michael can get a job with the security company he works for. Michael then goes to a local bar, and spots his former girlfriend Rachel dancing. They talk, but are interrupted by crook Tommy Dundee, Rachel's new lover, and Michael leaves.

Rachel calls and asks him why he came back. A flashback shows Michael's gambling days, when he would blow his winnings on extravagant presents for Rachel rather than pay his debts. Yet he was strangely inattentive to her. In the present, Michael takes a job at the security firm. He meets Rachel and they redeclare their love for one another. They decide to run away together. However, Rachel doesn't turn up to their pre-arranged meeting and when Michael inquires about her he learns she's gone away with Tommy. Michael finds brief solace with Susan, a bank teller he met on the bus back to Austin, but he is soon haunting Tommy's bar where he finds that Rachel and Tommy are married. He and Rachel rendezvous at the house where he used to live, and she complains that Tommy abuses her. They hear a noise downstairs which proves to be Tommy. Michael excuses their meeting by making up a story about a bank job he wants Tommy to do.

The robbery of the armoured cars is set up with an anonymous crew from out of town. They are to follow Michael's truck into the bank, in a white van supposedly delivering supplies using a code number that Michael acquires surreptitiously from Susan. Michael plans to double-cross Tommy with Rachel. On the day of the robbery though, he finds that it is Ed Dutton on the shift with him. At the bank, Susan walks out to where the robbery is about to happen. Dutton opens fire on the robbers as they throw gas canisters and is gunned down. Having ushered Susan back inside, Michael fires at them too, and is wounded.

Michael finds himself in hospital, a hero to some, but under suspicion from others. He is kidnapped and taken to meet Rachel and Tommy, who knows about the double-cross. He kills the kidnapper, but while he is loading the body in the car, Rachel gives Michael the gun. After he's shot Tommy and is wounded himself, Rachel relieves him of the gun and drives away with the money. But, the out of town crew turns out to have been led by the security firm chief himself, and they track her into the night.

There is a chill about the films of Steven Soderbergh that's hard to dispel. Like Atom Egoyan, he likes to needle his characters for their ordinariness, to tease the strangeness out of banal circumstances with unnerving pauses and edgy music. This approach was perfectly in keeping with the subject matter of his breakthrough film *sex, lies and videotape* with its pathological look at post-Aids suppressed-erotic love. It was less apt to his 30s period piece *The King of the Hill*, adulterating the child protagonist's wide-eyed, trusting point-of-view with anomie. With *The Underneath*, however—the second film version of the Daniel Fuchs novel *Criss Cross*, first filmed as a classic *film noir* starring Burt Lancaster, Dan Duryea and Yvonne De Carlo by Robert Siodmak in 1948—Soderbergh is trying to portray a character who is plausible, but hard to fathom, a man who has come back to his home town but doesn't appear to know why. An unease between people is therefore essential to the film's mood and structure.

The Underneath opens on the day of the climactic robbery. Using a complex flashback structure, it refers back to two periods of time—the chronological events since Michael Chambers' return building up to the robbery, and scene of Michael as he was before he left Austin: an obsessive gambler with Teflon-coated affability who, according to his psychotic cop brother David, "skated along on looks and charm just like a woman." These flashbacks are littered with portents of fate and references to gambling: Michael's stepfather-to-be Ed Dutton says at their first meeting, "when the planets don't line up there's nothing you can do about it"; Michael's former-lover Rachel practises announcing lottery numbers for an acting audition; his fellow security guards play cards constantly; and when he visits the club, he is stamped with the legend "SUCKER" ...

Luck and motivation are therefore the contrasted themes here, just as they are in the Robert Siodmak film, but Soderbergh calls the fatalism of *film noir* into question. Is Michael really the pawn of fate inscribed at the heart of the genre, or is he rather the inscrutable manipulator that his lovers keep telling him he is? Even his surname, Chambers, suggests more than one inner sanctum to his mind. Where Burt Lancaster in the original film is clearly lovesick, Peter Gallagher's Michael is just bewildered. He may have returned home for more than his ex-lover. Some way into the film, there is a key pairing of post-coital scenes that offers some clues. The first is in the past: "I feel like you're somewhere else, " says Rachel; "I feel like I'm in an ad for fine wine," is his reply. In the second, Susan, his casual fling, suggests he's hooked on someone else. "Sort of," he responds, and later adds, "There's what you want and what's good for you ... they never meet."

Rachel whom he wants and Susan who is good for him never do meet, but he seems to yearn as much for the thrill of his old gambling addiction as for the committed affections of either woman. Romancing Rachel again—despite her attachment to the murderous local hoodlum Tommy Dundee—offers the kind of risk that is the gambler's juice. Equally, Michael could be considering the robbery from the moment he gets the security job. In a film where all the supporting players know exactly who they are, and keep telling him ("you know me, I like money" says Rachel), it is Michael who is the random element. In other words, if the film has a dark heart, like all the great *noirs*, it may not be the clichéd Chandleresque rottenness of the world but the impossibility of Michael—or anybody else—knowing his own mind.

Michael's glassy inscrutability sits like a transparent mask on Gallagher's fulsome matinee-idol face. His huge pupils loom constantly into close-up without a trace of emotion. His is a perfectly listless performance, a still, bewildered centre around which several subtle marvels of character acting are achieved by others. Soderbergh's framing is so rigorous that the actors' freedom of movement often seems artificially constricted, yet Alison Elliot conveys all the ambiguity of the sleek, attention-seeking Rachel with a few half-cocked smiles and narrow-eyed appraisals. William Fichtner, too, seizes on small gestures to make Tommy Dundee an utterly convincing terror for Michael to behold.

But it seems that no Steven Soderbergh film can ever be performance-driven. The motor here is undoubtedly the rigorously constructed plot, a maze of crossing paths. However, the end of a maze is its centre and there's nothing there but Michael Chambers. Of course, the story has an ending, one as tacked-on and farcical as anything Chandler himself could have dreamed up, but it's this unknowable man that we're left with and it's a chilly feeling.

VILLAGE VOICE, 5/2/95, p. 45, J. Hoberman

As Hathaway and Siodmak represented the two poles of postwar noir, "neorealist" and "expressionist," so *The Underneath* is less site-specific and more overtly stylized than *Kiss of Death*. Where the latter is mildly schematic, *The Underneath* reworks the already intricate *Criss Cross* scenario into a stilted game of narrative tic-tac-toe, flashing forward and back amid three garishly color-coordinated time zones like a traffic light programmed for catastrophe.

In short, Steven Soderbergh has taken a better movie than did Schroeder and done far less with it. *The Underneath* combines an irritatingly placeless setting with the owlish superfluity of Soderbergh's ludicrous *Kafka*, his last exercise in noir stylistics. Not that there isn't a connection to the who's-kidding-whom? soap opera of *sex, lies, and videotape* in the script's close adherence to the shifting sexual loyalties of the Daniel Fuchs original. The protagonist (Peter Gallagher) returns to his hometown, finds a job driving an armored car, and immediately gets mixed up with his former spouse-equivalent (Alison Elliott). She tempts him—as Yvonne DeCarlo did hapless Burt Lancaster—then abruptly marries a local crime boss (William Fichtner), thus setting the stage for his participation as the inside man in a bank heist.

Lowry's update complicates the oedipal romance—not only is Gallagher's character trying to win back the gangster's girl, his colleague on the armored truck is his new stepfather—but the best bits of business, including the creepy hospital scene, are all derived from (and inferior to) the original. *The Underneath* is no less cerebral than *Criss Cross;* what it lacks is Siodmak's stylistic conviction. More than noir, the Soderbergh film suggests a gaggle of well-draped Hollywood types swarming around some imaginary Texas city (actually downtown Austin) in search of a perfume commercial. Smooth and superficial, it's an artier, not so amusing *Red Rock West.*

Svelter if no more engaging than he was as Andie MacDowell's faithless hubbie in *sex, lies, and videotape,* Gallagher resembles a comic-book Warren Beatty; Elliott, the ostensible object of his obsession, has the unformed blankness of a newborn pod from the original *Invasion of the Body Snatchers. The Underneath* features quite a few other bad perfs—or are they just fashionably affectless characterizations?

Also reviewed in:
CHICAGO TRIBUNE, 4/28/95, Friday/p. C, Michael Wilmington
NATION, 5/22/95, p. 736, Stuart Klawans
NEW REPUBLIC, 5/8/95, p. 26, Stanley Kauffmann
NEW YORK TIMES, 4/28/95, p. C12, Caryn James
VARIETY, 3/20-26/95, p. 47, Todd McCarthy
WASHINGTON POST, 4/28/95, p. D7, Rita Kempley
WASHINGTON POST, 4/28/95, Weekend/p. 44, Joe Brown

UNSTRUNG HEROES

A Hollywood Pictures release of a Roth/Arnold production. *Producer:* Susan Arnold, Donna Roth, and Bill Badalato. *Director:* Diane Keaton. *Screenplay:* Richard LaGravenese. *Based upon the book by:* Franz Lidz. *Director of Photography:* Phedon Papamichael. *Editor:* Lisa Churgin. *Music:* Thomas Newman. *Music Editor:* Bill Bernstein. *Sound:* Robert J. Anderson, Jr. and (music) Dennis Sands. *Sound Editor:* Anthony Mazzei. *Casting:* Gail Levin. *Production Designer:* Garreth Stover. *Art Director:* Chris Cornwell. *Set Decorator:* Larry Dias. *Set Dresser:* Roger Abell and Doug Sieck. *Costumes:* Jill Ohanneson. *Make-up:* Patricia A. Gerhardt. *Running time:* 93 minutes. *MPAA Rating:* PG.

CAST: Andie MacDowell (Selma Lidz); John Turturro (Sid Lidz); Michael Richards (Danny Lidz); Maury Chaykin (Arthur Lidz); Nathan Watt (Steven/Franz Lidz); Kendra Krull (Sandy Lidz); Joey Andrews (Ash); Celia Weston (Amelia); Jack McGee (Lindquist); Candice Azzara (Joanie); Anne DeSalvo (May); Lillian Adams (Aunt Estelle); Lou Cutell (Uncle Melvin); Sumer Stamper (Nancy Oppenheim); Sean P. Donahue (Ralph Crispi); Harold M. Schulweis (Rabbi Blaustein); Zoaunne LeRroy (Mrs. Kantruitz); Vince Melocchi (Inspector Marshall); Charles Patrick (In-Crowd Boy); Alison Chalmers (In-Crowd Girl); Chris Warfield (Mr. Clements); Wayne Duvall (Mr. Crispi); Andrew Craig (Man in Line); Becky Ann Baker (Mrs. Harris); Mary Mercier (Waitress); Len Costanza (Second Doctor); Peter Kaitlyn (Dr. Feldman); Julie Pinson (Nurse Franklin).

LOS ANGELES TIMES, 9/15/95, Calendar/p. 1, Kenneth Turan

"A hero" Selma Lidz tells her son Steven, "is anyone who finds his own way through this life." Only 12, Steven is on the verge of discovering how difficult that task can be. And how much help he can get from an unlooked-for source, his two fiercely eccentric uncles, the "Unstrung Heroes" of this lovely film's title.

Written by Richard LaGravenese and based on an autobiographical novel by Franz Lidz, "Unstrung Heroes" is a pivotal moment as well in the directing career of Oscar-winning actress Diane Keaton. Though she has directed TV movies, music videos and feature documentaries, this is Keaton's first drama for the large screen, and how much she and her team have accomplished is as impressive as how casually they seem to have done it.

For "Unstrung Heroes," while easy to absorb, is surprisingly rich in the feelings it conveys. It is at once a story of adolescent self-discovery in the face of terrible family crisis, a love note to motherhood and a passionate tribute to idiosyncratic behavior. And in its unexpected ability to mix slapstick with subtlety, sadness with mad farce, it touches an unusual and especially emotional chord.

Set, in Los Angeles in the early 1960s, "Heroes" seems at first to be focusing on Steven's father, Sid Lidz (sharply played by John Turturro). An oddball inventor whose not-ready-for-prime-time projects include a "perpetual-motion baby-jumper" and a "mild-monsoon sprinkler system," Sid talks as fast as a rocket, oblivious to the thoughts of his 12-year-old son (Nathan Watt) and the boy's younger sister, Sandy (Kendra Krull).

"Is Dad from another planet?" a troubled Steven asks his mother, who smiles with the reassuring knowledge that his father is just a bit different. As Selma Lidz, the warm, caring, human element in the Lidz equation, Andie MacDowell simply blossoms, giving an appealing and natural performance, one of her best ever, as the family's unflappable anchor.

Suddenly, that anchor threatens to give way. Selma collapses on the floor, stricken with an obviously serious but unnamed illness that both puzzles and frightens everyone, especially the children, who are told little about it. Sid, frantic for his own reasons and pleading Selma's need for rest, unthinkingly shuts their mother out of Steven's and Sandy's lives. Almost wild with the need for comfort of any kind, Steven takes off one night to visit his father's two brothers in their strange apartment in a rundown residence hotel.

Up to this point, the uncles have been shadowy figures to Steven, known largely through his father's scorn of them as cautionary examples of "what can happen to an undisciplined mind." Now, turning to them in desperation, he discovers a kinship with and a connection to their childlike comic idiosyncrasies.

Uncle Danny is the more assertive of the two, which is a polite way of saying he is a raging paranoid conspiracy theorist who thinks his pancakes might be bugged and is convinced "Idaho means Jew-hater in Cherokee."

"Seinfeld's" Michael Richards plays Danny with a daring, full-throttle brio, managing to make his character sympathetic as well as manic.

To say Uncle Arthur, exquisitely played by veteran actor Maury Chaykin is a collector does not hint at the scope of his ambition. Operating on the assumption that "people throw out a lot of things that are good," Arthur has made it his life's work to save all of them. And the brothers' apartment, jammed floor to ceiling with newspapers, rubber balls, wedding cake decorations and everything in between (all collected over a period of months by set decorator Larry Dias), is as vivid a presence as any of the film's actors.

Though "Unstrung Heroes"'thematic elements are uniformly strong, it is the film's treatment of Danny and Arthur that is especially impressive. The uncles are neither condescended to nor treated with gooey reverence, the way eccentrics usually are on film, but embraced, loved and respected as straight-ahead human beings.

Which, as Selma's illness worsens and Steven is allowed to spend the summer with the brothers, is how they treat their nephew. Positive that "our Steven has a rare gift," convincing him "you're the one to watch" and even deciding to change his name to the less ordinary Franz, they see possibilities in the young man neither his parents or even Steven himself imagined.

It was Diane Keaton's job to ride herd over this engaging menagerie, and she has done it with the kind of gentle but sure empathy toward all sorts of human behavior that has made all the difference. Moving in a way we are not accustomed to, "Unstrung Heroes" demonstrates that even the saddest stories can be wistful and joyous if the right people are involved in the telling.

NEW YORK POST, 9/15/95, p. 37, Michael Medved

In movies, insanity is far too often sentimentalized. From "Harvey" through "Don Juan De-Marco," delusions are portrayed as endearing and adorable in countless films that suggest that crazy people are actually more sane than the rest of us. In this context, first-time feature film director Diane Keaton deserves credit for keeping some rough edges on the "Unstrung Heroes" of her title. These two uncles are more than merely eccentric; they are so flagrantly psychotic that it's far easier to understand why most of their relatives hate their guts than it is to accept that their bright, sensitive 12-year-old nephew (Nathan Watt) would make them his guides to life.

The year is 1962, and the boy is desperate for warmth and support during the lingering illness of his adored mother (Andie MacDowell). His father is a hard-driving, unsmiling scientist and frustrated inventor (played with perfect pitch and fierce conviction by John Turturro) who is so passionately focused on trying to comfort his dying wife that he allows his boy to fall into the highly irregular orbit of his uncles.

These two bachelors share a downtown L.A. hotel apartment jammed from floor to ceiling with stacks of old newspapers going back 30 years, literally thousands of rubber balls retrieved from sewers, wedding cake figurines, old paper clips, souvenir Statues of Liberty and other colorful junk.

These items are collected by the gentle, childlike, unkempt and moon-faced Uncle Arthur (Maury Chaikin), while his brother Danny (a perfectly cast Michael Richards of TV's "Seinfeld") is an edgy paranoid who rages endlessly against dark fascist conspiracies. He disrupts one family gathering by insisting that Dwight Eisenhower is a Jew-hater ("I like Ike" is an obvious code for 'I Hate Kikes!'") and dreads the day when his all-powerful enemies will drag him away.

Their young nephew lives for a time with these two misfits ("Just pretend you're living with Dopey ... and Dopey," his ailing mother tells him) and quickly succumbs to their influence. At school, he disrupts the Pledge of Allegiance by singing the Internationale and screaming about the "crucified" Rosenbergs, while he horrifies his atheist father by suddenly insisting upon a bar mitzvah.

The film (based on a family memoir by Franz Lidz with a smart screenplay by Richard La Gravenese of "The Fisher King") never explains the contradiction of an unreconstructed Old Lefty free-thinker like Uncle Danny pushing his nephew toward conventional religion, and the Jewish rituals on screen lack any sense of depth or authenticity.

Director Keaton faces a bigger problem with her generally unsteady tone: She can't seem to decide whether to treat this story as a larger-than-life tall tale with magical-realist overtones, or whether to present the boy's recollections as part of a homey, understated memory film that relies (much too heavily) on snippets, of home movies.

Nevertheless, robust, remarkable performances, haunting and appropriately unhinged music by Thomas Newman, and the ongoing tribulations of this suffering family can hardly fail to move an audience. If nothing else, getting to know the young hero's impossible uncles will leave you feeling a bit better about your own outrageously eccentric relatives.

NEWSDAY, 9/15/95, Part II/p. B3, John Anderson

What defines an eccentric is relative. For proof, one need only look at any '30s screwball comedy, or even at Terry Zwigoff's documentary "Crumb," in which the subject is portrayed as a truly odd individual—until we meet his brothers. At that point, R. Crumb becomes just the tip of the iceberg.

Sid Lidz (John Turturro), around whom so much revolves in "Unstrung Heroes," is another tip off the old iceberg. Exhibiting all the sprung springs of the benignly mad scientist, he is a gifted inventor, frantic and addled and obsessed with his own creative process. At the same time, he is devoted to his wife Selma (Andie MacDowell), cares deeply for his children—Steven (Nathan Watt) and Sandy (Kendra Krull)—and maintains some reverence for social convention.

His brothers are another story—in another galaxy. Danny (played with abundant Kramer-isms by "Seinfeld's" Michael Richards) is a socialist paranoid who sees anti-Semitism behind every bush ("Idaho means 'Jew hater' in Cherokee," he tells Steven) and insults Sid's guests with virulent aplomb ("phony miserable bastids," "unmarried slave traders"). The gentle Arthur (Maury Chaykin) is Danny's antithesis, a gentle naif who finds fascination in life's detritus. Together, they live in a Los Angeles apartment/Neverland that the Collier brothers might have tidied up.

But the Lidzes are a family—the concept that not only keeps "Unstrung Heroes" strung, but makes it the utterly endearing movie it is. The film is, ostensibly, about Steven—who, when his mother becomes sick with cancer and his father cuts him off from her in misguided concern, runs off to live with Danny and Arthur; there the boy becomes reborn as Franz, dissenter from decorum, schoolroom singer of "L'Internationale." But the film is also about the forgiveness we afford our relations when no one else will, or can, and about the need for forgiveness, and about the need for individuality within that occasionally suffocating thing we call family.

"Unstrung Heroes" will never be called the most auspicious feature debut by a director (Orson Welles is always in the way), but that's partly because Diane Keaton has created such a small film—small meaning human in scale. Having practiced her directorial skills in several television productions and the documentary "Heaven," she seems perfectly adept at dramatic manipulation.

Keaton adopts the viewer into the Lidz family in various ways: The brothers' landlord—who, given the firetrap they live in, is probably right in wanting them evicted—is transformed into a Bob Barker-watching boor. When Danny disrupts a school political convention—in which the timid Steven is running for class president—it's to insult and harangue a smug junior achiever whom anyone could loathe. As observed by outsiders, Danny and Arthur are certifiable. But we've been made family members—so they're just a little peculiar.

With few exceptional moments (some of the kids' pranks after their mother gets sick feel a bit forced), "Heroes" hangs together marvelously, balancing the heartsick sentiment of a mother's slow death (the MacDowell-Watt scenes are quite touching) with the madcap behavior of Danny and Arthur. That the film is so funny is often due to Richards' accomplished mania, but also because Keaton nurses the tension between two kinds of absurdity—the personal and the cosmic.

As Sid, Turturro proves once again his status as one of our best actors and serves as fulcrum. Sid is a man of science—a secular Jew and humanist, he has rejected religious faith as superstition. But when he watches his own belief system fail him—as medicine allows Selma to slip away—he becomes a profoundly tragic figure, a victim of his own hubris, who needs nothing more at that point than a little simple faith.

Nathan Watt gives a thoroughly convincing performance as Steven/Franz, who is wracked by guilt when a stupid joke prompts Danny to have himself committed. But Danny, of course, forgives him. Whether audiences will forgive Keaton for imposing such emotional trauma upon them is a different question altogether.

NEWSWEEK, 9/25/95, p. 90, David Ansen

The Lidz family, whom we come to know intimately in director Diane Keaton's first feature film, *Unstrung Heroes*, would be considered eccentric in the best of times. In a still-provincial Los Angeles at the tail end of the Eisenhower era, they stand out like loony birds in a flock of pigeons. Dad Sid (John Turturro) is a wild-eyed inventor who pursues his profession with the single-minded faith that science can bring salvation. He turns his home into his workshop, where he preaches his religion of pure reason, prompting his 12-year-old son Steven (Nathan Watt) to wonder: "Is Dad from another planet?"

No, but perhaps his crazy uncles are. The dreamy, disheveled Uncle Arthur (Maury Chaykin) is an obsessive pack rat, filling the apartment he shares with his brother Danny with rubber balls, old newspapers, paper clips—objects he believes are invested with the soul of the city. Uncle Danny (Michael Richards) looks at the big picture—and sees conspiracies everywhere. A raving paranoid, he's convinced that Idaho is the Cherokee word for Jew-hater, and "I Like Ike" a code for "I hate kikes."

The rock at the center of Steven's life is his loving mother, Selma (Andie MacDowell). But suddenly her high spirit fades. Stricken with cancer, she withdraws to her bed. Unable to deal with the possibility of her death, Steven flees his suburban home to take refuge in the bizarre but, to him, utterly magical world of his two daft uncles.

The material, based on a memoir by author Franz Lidz, could easily have turned insufferably whimsical. But Keaton and her gifted screenwriter Richard LaGravenese ("The Bridges of Madison County," "A Little Princess") have fashioned a disarming gem, a movie as peculiarly funny as it is heartbreaking. It's one of those films in which everyone seems tuned to the same wavelength, producing fresh and buoyant work. Andie MacDowell as a Jewish mother? It sounds wrong, yet she's never been so touching. Watt is effortlessly endearing. Chaykin and Richards play off each other like a crackerjack—and cracked—vaudeville team. Only one scene strikes a false note: the pat resolution of Uncle Danny's delusions, set at a sanitarium so tastefully ap pointed you'd want to check in tomorrow.

Thanks to everyone involved, the movie radiates a hundred pleasures: from LaGravenese's perfect ear for the elocutions of a grammar-school election speech to the surprising orchestrations of Thomas Newman's score to the burnished glow of the cinematography. But the guiding spirit is clearly Keaton's, whose touch is both delicate and assured. You can detect her sensibility in every detail, from the California swap-meet style of interior decoration to her understanding of the outsider Steven's struggle to find his place in the world. He triumphs, as Keaton has in her varied career, not by blending in but by letting his true, eccentric soul blossom.

SIGHT AND SOUND, 12/95, p. 53, Geoffrey Macnab

In Los Angeles, inn the early 60s, 12-year-old Steven Lidz is unhappy. His inventor father, Sid, treats him without affection. His adored mother, Selma, is ailing. He is not popular at school and he doesn't get on with Amelia, the woman his father has hired to look after the family until Selma recovers.

Rather than stay at home and mope, Steven decides to move in for the summer with his two uncles, Danny and Arthur. The former is an arch conspiracy theorist, close to schizophrenia, who believes there are only eight honest people living in the world. The latter is an overweight dimwit who collects rubber balls. Although the uncles live in some disarray and are highly eccentric, they look after him and he enjoys his stay. Soon, he begins to behave as strangely as they do, sending his mother pancakes through the post. He follows their advice, changes his name to Franz, and prepares for his Bar Mitzvah. His anti-religious father is appalled.

As his mother grows more and more sickly, Steven returns home. His father still has little time for him, but Steven is more popular at school thanks to his new-found rebellious ways. He takes a friend to meet the uncles. The friend plays a cruel trick on Danny which so upsets him that he ends up institutionalised. His mother's condition is now terminal. One day, as he and his sister cook waffles, Selma dies. His grief-stricken father loses his temper at the wake, forbids Steven to use his home movie camera, and throws out all his old cans of film. Steven retrieves them from the garbage and disappears. His father is suddenly worried and drives around town with Arthur, looking for him. Eventually, they track him down to the church hall. Steven is watching the movies. Rather than upbraid him, his father sits down by his side. At last, the two manage to strike up a rapport.

Diane Keaton's first fully fledged feature as director (not counting her documentaries, television films and episodes of *Twin Peaks* and *China Beach*) begins in shudderingly banal fashion with a montage of home movie snippets, shot in best grainy black and white. It looks, at first, as if we're in the realm of *The Wonder Years*: inventor dad, John Turturro, shows off his latest con-traptions, happy young son dances to mom and pop's favourite Ray Charles record, and this threatens ominously to turn into yet another of those soggy, nostalgic, rites-of-passage dramas in which we're forced to endure a boy's growing pains back in the innocent, rose-tinted 60s.

Then, as the mother (Andie MacDowell) contracts a mystery ailment, it seems as if we're veering into terminal illness territory, generally the preserve of television movies. Fortunately, though, *Unstrung Heroes* turns out to be a much richer, more idiosyncratic affair than its opening might suggest. Keaton's direction, Richard LaGravenese's script and two fittingly odd per-formances by Maury Chaykin and Michael Richards as Arthur and Danny, the boy's unhinged uncles, all help undermine the homely naturalism of the early sequences.

As his tale of three brothers, it sometimes seems like a fictional counterpart to Terry Zwigoff's recent documentary, *Crumb*. Turturro's character, Sid, is a bastion of sanity compared to his sib-lings. Whereas he manages to keep himself sane through his inventions (as Robert Crumb himself did through his drawings), Arthur and Danny have nothing to anchor them to the everyday, and have taken off into realms of their own. One is fat and ingenuous, and spends most of his time collecting plastic balls from the city sewers. The other is a paranoid conspiracy-theorist, convinced that Eisenhower was a Nazi and with the bizarre conviction that there are only eight honest people in the USA. Among the film's funniest moments is the scene when the duo turn up to listen to Steven's school assembly to pick class president. Steven's own speech is a disaster. His main rival, a clean-cut all-American boy with a fetish for strong leadership, looks set to carry all before him until Danny starts haranguing him from the back of the hall, accusing him and his father of being fascists.

As in LaGravenese's most famous previous script, *The Fisher King*, the oddball, socially marginalised characters turn out to be both wiser and kinder than their ostensibly normal peers. Under their influence, Steven changes his name, and embraces religion and communism. He sings the 'Internationale' instead of the class anthem, and refuses to pledge his allegiance to a system that "fried the Rosenbergs". It can't be said there's anything especially original about the way Arthur and Danny are used as kindly idiot-savants: the mad but inspired relative is a leitmotif in many filmic evocations of childhood. At least the many eccentricities of the two uncles provide the story with its comic motor and enable the film-makers to escape from the dreary visual constraints entailed in depicting the typical 60s middle-class home. The oppressive atmosphere in Steven's own family is effectively contrasted with the imaginative release he finds at his uncles' place: it's is a magical lair, full of newspapers, plastic balls, toys, and bric-a-brac. Perhaps, the production design goes a little overboard to suggest as much. What looks like a small apartment is transformed under their touch into a virtual warehouse which seems to stretch forever.

The scenes involving Steven's parents are less successfully handled. John Turturro doesn't show much charm in what was probably a thankless role. "Mom, is Dad from another planet?" Steven asks about him. With his crazy inventions (contraptions such as his "perpetual motion baby jumper") and obsessive ways, he ought to come across as a mad professor-type. Instead, he's a stern, repressive sort, seemingly bereft of humour. Andie McDowell reprising her anguished mother routine from *Short Cuts*, is all simpers and sickly sighs. She's framed throughout as some sort of idealised Madonna figure.

At least, Keaton shoots in fluid fashion. A plethora of tracking shots, rapid editing and unusual camera angles ensure this is visually rather more dynamic than the average domestic drama. In its worst moments, it may suffer from over-familiarity and lapse into mawkishness. It's certainly uneven. But there's enough invention and imagination here to suggest that Diane Keaton is already an accomplished director. Her work is bound to get better.

TIME, 9/25/95, p. 68, Richard Schickel

Amid all the prim prattle about family values—a term definable only as a vague expression of nostalgia for a past that never was—the Lidz clan, dysfunctioning in Los Angeles in the 1960s, reminds us that the American home has been, often as not, a nuthouse. And that early, massive exposure to eccentricity can be the best possible preparation for the life that follows: what does not make us completely crazy makes us strong. Or at least tolerant and flexible, qualities that are largely absent from our book of virtues these days.

This lesson comes hard to 12-year-old Steven Lidz (Nathan Watt). His mother Selma (Andie MacDowell) is dying slowly, bravely, of cancer, and his father Sid (John Turturro) cannot offer him much consolation. In the best of times, Sid is a tense and cranky figure, obsessively working on impractical inventions. In these, the worst of times, he is mostly preoccupied with cursing God, fate and Selma's doctors. The kid badly needs a dose of chicken soup and diversion.

Which is where Sid's brothers—the *Unstrung Heroes* of this movie's title—come in. They live behind multilocked doors, surrounded by tons of old newspapers, in a downtown slum. Danny (Michael Richards of *Seinfeld*) is a wild-eyed, left-wing paranoid, certain that every knock on the door heralds the arrival of the FBI; Arthur (Maury Chaykin) is a soft-spoken collector of wedding-cake figures, snow domes and rubber balls that he teaches Steven to listen to, convinced the voices of the children who once bounced them still echo faintly inside.

Living on the margins of life and sanity, they have time for family history and sentiment, for religious tradition and, yes, for lost little boys.

They think a better name for Steven would be Franz Lidz, resonant as it is with romantic and artistic striving. They think a Bar Mitzvah is essential to his spiritual growth. And you never can tell when lessons in evading government functionaries (like a building inspector) will come in handy. Somehow they get Steven safely through his first encounters with mortality and onrushing manhood.

And somehow Diane Keaton, directing her first fictional feature, gets us safely through a movie that could have turned to mush at any moment. She knows how to touch on an emotion without squeezing every last tear out of it. She knows how to get a laugh without bringing down the whole fragile edifice of her film. She is helped a lot by a terrific cast, which understands that playing madness is very serious business, and by Richard LaGravenese's wonderfully modulated script. From *The Fisher King* through *A Little Princess* and *The Bridges of Madison County*, he has demonstrated a gift for conveying honest sentiment without permitting us to wallow in it, and he's at his craftsmanlike best here. The flaky charms of *Unstrung Heroes* will be lost on some hardened souls, and it does have its self-conscious, even slightly self-congratulatory moments. But don't listen to their braying. Listen instead for the minor-key melody of a very seductive movie.

VILLAGE VOICE, 9/26/95, p. 75, Georgia Brown

Both *Canadian Bacon* [see Brown's review] and Diane Keaton's *Unstrung Heroes* turned up last spring in Cannes's sidebar competition, Un Certain Regard, or, as we Americans pronounce it, Uncertain Regard. Cannes's notice probably helped Moore's movie finally win a release and it bestowed on *Unstrung Heroes* un certain small cachet, much of this gleefully undermined by an ugly story in the current *New York* magazine. (More on this below.)

Based on a family memoir by Franz Lidz, *Unstrung Heroes* is set in the early '60s and centers on 12-year-old Steven Lidz (Nathan Watt), a meek, frail-looking kid coming to terms with family *tsuris*. Steven's father, Sid (John Turturro), is an unworldly enthusiast with a thousand cracked schemes spinning in his brain, most of them to be executed at home. (I'm not clear what he does for a living.) "Is Dad from another planet?" Steven asks Mom (Andie MacDowell) in a bedtime colloquy. This is what the kids at school are saying. "Your dad" Mom lovingly confides, is *"a genius."*

It's hard at this point to know how *we* should take Dad, who seems merely comically preoccupied, his harmless schemes directed at cheering up this brooding child and his younger sister. It's when Sid's two brothers, the tubby, unkempt Arthur (Maury Chaykin) and the paranoid politico, Danny (Seinfeld's Michael Richards), upset a family gathering that the Lidzes gain some definition. (It also dawns around here that they're Jewish.) About the same time, Steven's mom shows signs of being mortally ill (cancer it is, giving the film the chance to develop a bathetic side). Whereas formerly the Milquetoast Steven was mortified when Dad acted weird, he now turns to these *really* weird uncles for solace. In fact, he runs off to live in their shabby hotel. (This is a stretch the same way that the boy's living alone in a hotel in Soderbergh's *King of the Hill* was.)

Anyway, focus shifts to Arthur and Danny and their kooky ways and living conditions. I've read of bachelor brothers who hoard newspapers, stacking them to the ceiling, but I've never envisioned those stacks as comprised of tidy, tied bundles. Likewise, Arthur's collections of wedding cake bride-and-grooms, Statue of Libertys, and lost rubber balls are displayed as immaculately as in any chichi Soho shop.

Eventually, however, I got the movie's very delicate, fragile point: that Sid was in fact holding to a precarious sanity and fighting for his own life and his family's. As Turturro's baffled grief over his wife suddenly translates into something latent and much larger, the film suddenly becomes rather moving.

New York attacks Keaton and Disney's Michael Eisner for moving the Lidzes' lefty Lower East Side to leafy L.A., down-playing the Jewishness, and losing an essential milieu. This is all true (when Steven visits Danny in a mental hospital I thought the uncle had come into an inheritance and bought a chateau), but what else is new? Jaded reviewer that I am, I was surprised so much Jewishness was retained—or even that the movie was made. What I'd like to comment on is how snide the piece is toward Keaton, convicting her of being a shiksa and of loony behavior and dress. The movie is about eccentrics, but, for goodness' sake, let's not put a certified eccentric in charge.

Here's one of the stories told on Keaton: "Lidz says that when he and his Uncle Arthur visited the set, Keaton turned on her heel and ran away from him until, cornered by the child actor Nathan Watt, she stage-whispered to the boy, 'I'm afraid of him'—meaning the man whose memoir she was filming. 'I think she's the only human being who's ever been intimidated by me in my entire life,' says the mild-mannered Lidz." No eccentric he!

No wonder Keaton was scared of Lidz, who's apparently a prime source for this holier-than-thou dump on her and her first feature. ("Cornered" by a child? Whose point of view is being taken?) I'd feel better about this breach of puff piece etiquette if it didn't pick on a fledgling director and a woman to boot. Perhaps *New York* will continue to spill embarrassing on-set tales featuring "eccentric" male hot shots and to put down their pictures before they're reviewed. Sure it will.

Also reviewed in:
CHICAGO TRIBUNE, 9/15/95, Friday/p. F, John Petrakis
NEW YORK TIMES, 9/15/95, p. C5, Janet Maslin
VARIETY, 5/22-28/95, p. 96, Todd McCarthy
WASHINGTON POST, 9/23/95, p. C4, Rita Kempley

UNZIPPED

A Miramax Films release of a Hachette Filipacchi Productions film. *Executive Producer:* David Pecker and Nina Santisi. *Producer:* Michael Alden. *Director:* Douglas Keeve. *Director of Photography:* Ellen Kuras. *Editor:* Paula Heredia. *Music:* Darren Solomon. *Sound:* Dominique Kerboeuf. *Running time:* 76 minutes. *MPAA Rating:* R.

WITH: Isaac Mizrahi, Sarah Mizrahi, Kate Moss, Cindy Crawford, Naomi Campbell, Christy Turlington, Linda Evangelista and Polly Allen Mellen.

FILMS IN REVIEW, 11-12/95, p. 107, Nicole Potter

The dirty winter streets of the city in pebbly black-and-white, maybe super-8? Isaac Mizrahi's very gay, very New York voice on one track, mournful piano on another, as we watch his grainy figure wander the sidewalks disconsolately. He's just read the review of his latest collection. Pronouncement? The glass is half empty, Isaac Mizrahi has lost his touch. This small tragedy is one of the probable "mornings after" familiar to anyone who has ever been the life of the party or given birth to a new work; restless and empty, with no place to go, after this terrific outpouring of ideas and energy. But by beginning with this post-climactic view of failure, director Douglas Keeve is playfully misleading the viewer. For Mizrahi may be in the doldrums, but there's always another bash, a new season. *Unzipped* documents the next collection, from the designer's initial inspiration (discovered while viewing *Nanook of the North),* to glitzy and colorful runway showing. And while the process of creation may be a nerve-racking experience, it's obviously a joyous one for Isaac Mizrahi.

Edited to include a melange of formats—16mm, 35mm, home movies, classic film clips, color, and black-and-white, *Unzipped's* form serves its content well. What better way to pay tribute to a designer who opines, "Between [Mary Tyler Moore] and Jackie Kennedy, they shaped this country." We're in the world of post-Modernism here, where appropriations from High Art and Junk culture are equally valid. Everything has to do with everything else, everything reflects on everything else. Back in the '80s, trendy magazine designers began to appropriate the associative, exploded form of music videos, fragmenting stories through the use of mixed and distorted typefaces, with unusual choice and placement of pictures. By way of justification, an editor I know stated that, "sometimes legibility has to be sacrificed in order to tell the whole story." We've come full circle now. Contemporary print design here seems to have influenced the pastiche-like quality of the screen layout.

Mizrahi is this chubby Jewish guy, dressed in sweatshirts and sneakers, smoking constantly, interacting with all these beautiful women, clothing their bodies—he pronounces Laws of Fashion, for God's sake. When I started to watch this movie I instantly thought of Ingrid Sischy, former editor-in-chief of *Artforum* magazine, who now holds that title at *Interview.* Ingrid once told me that the ratty coat she was wearing had been in her possession since the 11th grade. And it wasn't a nice coat either; babyshit yellow, dirty, wide lapels, and mid-calf length of the 70's. But I think she really delighted in mixing with the well dressed and the beautiful people while looking like that. She used to go to Very Important Art Openings in SoHo, and occasionally the sweet young thing sitting at the reception desk would mistake her for a bicycle messenger, which greatly amused Ingrid. Anyway, just as I was thinking this, who should appear on the screen, but Ingrid

Sischy. There's something intoxicating, if deceptive, about powerful people who present themselves as nonchalant schleps.

Mizrahi's key relationships are charmingly portrayed here. He happily admits to getting his passion for fashion from his doting mother, who wore her off-the-rack dresses back to front and appliquéd daisies onto her mules. It's heartwarming to watch her mingle unselfconsciously with Polly Mellen, Roseanne, Liza Minnelli, Naomi Campbell, Kate Moss, completely accepted in, and accepting of, Mizrahi's world of beautiful people. Mizrahi's work space appears to be fun and informal, even under the pressure of imminent presentation, and he says that his creative director Nina Santisi looks just "like Snow White" and is "like a sister."

It's to the credit of the filmmakers that I could leave a film filled with the likes of Christy Turlington, Naomi Campbell, Linda Evangelista, et al, and not feel the least bit covetous. These are not women like us; they are alien gazelles. The film made it clear to me that it was pointless to be a model-wannabe, and that was very freeing. It somehow made it okay to walk out into the lobby imitating them. Kind of how you feel when you see Fred and Ginger dance.

Throughout, *Unzipped* primes the viewer for the grande finale, the fashion show. And the engendered anticipation is satisfied. Whether or not one actually likes the clothes on display, the fast, colorful intercutting of back and forestage, exclusive paparazzi, movie star audience and famous models pays off. Mizrahi says, in response to the inevitable question, "It's always worth it."

"Yeah," one thinks, "It is."

I must say something about sense of occasion. I love that phrase, "sense of occasion." A friend of mine once said that in the theater you always want to give that to the audience. Now that we can watch movies in our living rooms any time we want to, our appreciation of movies as a special event has become deflated. This is nothing new; movie palaces have been dying a slow death since the advent of TV. I think that theaters like the Sony Lincoln Square (where I saw *Unzipped*) are attempting to bring back that sense of occasion. It actually does make sense. You really need to give people a compelling reason to go to a movie theater rather than waiting for the film to appear at the local video store six months later. One reason that people have continued to attend movies is because it gives them the illusion of being on the cutting edge, and the Sony theaters are trying to put that sense of anticipation back into the environment. Although I applaud the effort, I find the choice of environment emulated to be rather scary. Movie palaces today are evocative of airports and malls. I thought that old movie palaces were trying to give people a sense of elegance. Perhaps here, as in many contemporary film houses, the airport or the mall is emulated in order to stimulate people to feel as if they are embarking on a journey or else that they are about to buy something. I actually like the concept of readying myself for a journey, and of course every film watched is a journey of sorts. But I hate to fly, so emulating an airport is not the way to go for me. Evoking these vast spaces also brings with it their anonymity, and I can't understand why anyone would want to do that. Wouldn't we all prefer warmth and individuality in our surroundings?

LOS ANGELES TIMES, 8/11/95, Calendar/p. 16, Kenneth Turan

Is documentary filmmaking as easy as "Unzipped" makes it look? Is it simply a matter of finding a tart-tongued subject with a fascinating line of work, pointing the camera and coming up with a film clever enough to win the Audience Award at this year's Sundance Film Festival?

Though director Douglas Keeve no doubt has a full range of stories outlining in triplicate the troubles he's seen, the strength of "Unzipped" is how casual it seems, the way it creates the feeling that you're simply hanging out with its protagonist (and Keeve's former lover), celebrated New York fashion designer Isaac Mizrahi.

A sly monologuist and born entertainer, Mizrahi finds talking as natural as designing clothes and is on target at both. The kind of witty performer who holds the screen just doing a crossword puzzle, Mizrahi is enormous fun to be with and considerably more charismatic than the pop culture icons like Cindy Crawford and Naomi Campbell who make brief appearances to model his creations.

And, though Robert Altman seems to have perversely stepped on all the fashion jokes in "Ready to Wear," "Unzipped" benefits from the fact that there is something naturally funny about this industry. Here are all these nominal grown-ups getting into a series of tizzies about nothing more important than ... clothes. It's almost as ridiculous as the movie business itself.

"Unzipped" begins with Mizrahi making a lonely walk to his neighborhood newsstand to read the reviews of his Spring, 1994, collection. They are, in a word, dreadful—"the worst day in the world," he laments.

But Mizrahi, not the type to brood forever, soon finds inspiration for his Fall, '94, collection in an unlikely spot: Robert Flaherty's groundbreaking 1922 documentary on Eskimo life, "Nanook of the North," glimpsed on television. "All I want to do is fur pants," he enthuses to a friend on the phone. "But if I do them, I'll get stoned off 7th Avenue."

The Far North idea, however, won't go away, and soon a theme, variously referred to as "'50s cheesecake meets Eskimo fake fur" and "Giselle meets Fred Flintstone," begins to take shape. "Is it [an idea] worth doing?" Mizrahi asks rhetorically. "Yes, because it's the only one I have."

In-between getting peeks at Mizrahi preparing for the show, auditioning models and the like, "Unzipped" offers glimpses of what goes on in the rest of his life. We get to meet his proud mother and glib pals like Sandra Bernhard and watch him expertly orchestrate encounters with the eccentric but powerful fashion press.

Funniest of all, we get film-fan Mizrahi's impressions of some of his favorite movie moments, like the way Bette Davis says "yarnt" in "What Ever happened to Baby Jane?" or how impeccably groomed Loretta Young looks in 1935's "The Call of the Wild," though she's supposed to be nearly frozen to death. Aside from being great fun, these scenes illustrate the precise and unerring eye that contributes to Mizrahi's designing success.

After a few crises, like a rival French designer coming out with a similarly themed collection and Mizrahi's models initially resisting the idea of having to change behind a visible scrim, the show, "the most wonderful 20 minutes of a designer's life," takes place. Ellen Kuras, one of the best cinematographers in the independent world, smoothly switches to color footage here, and as the models stroll down the runway in Mizrahi's designs, audiences may feel a shared sense of accomplishment, as if we've worked on the show along with him.

This, of course, is sheer illusion. Though it is awfully entertaining, "Unzipped" doesn't give us much hard information about Mizrahi and its snapshot approach is too scattered to offer any sustained sense of what the process of designing a collection is really like. But asking for more is really asking for another movie, and though, like fashion itself, "Unzipped" exists only on the surface, it's too much fun to think about replacing with next year's model.

NEW YORK POST, 8/4/95, p. 44, Thelma Adams

Mrs. Mizrahi, I'm kvelling for you. Such a wonderful son you raised!

Mrs. Mizrahi's little boy, designer Isaac, has already ascended fashion's Mount Everest. Now, move over, Julia and Sandra—a star is born. A combination of gay exuberance and aesthetics and Brooklyn brass, Isaac conquers the screen in fashion photographer Douglas Keeve's effervescent peek under the skirts of the fashion industry.

"Unzipped" is the summer's funniest movie. But it's a documentary, how can that be? Stranger things have happened.

Keeve's well-structured, whirlwind tour of a season in the designer's life is bolstered by Ellen ("Swoon") Kuras' high-energy cinematography. Kuras changes formats like frocks: shifting from 16, super 16 and 35mm, from black-and-white to color.

The movie starts with the pans Mizrahi received for his spring 1994 collection. It continues through the creation of the 1994 fall line and closes with its triumphant unveiling before critics and celebrities at Manhattan's Bryant Park.

Mizrahi, with his pinchably plump body and shock-of-yarn coif, comes across as an adorable neurotic. Invested in American pop culture from "Nanook of the North" to Mary Tyler Moore, his influences are eclectic but familiar.

Why the Moore fetish? "Because I'm American and I'm not a stone," says Mizrahi. The TV star sits, ankles crossed, in his pantheon of inspirations: "Between her and Jackie Kennedy, they shaped this country."

But there's more to Mizrahi than fake fur and crinolines. He's also a driven perfectionist who would fly across the Atlantic to the Louvre to see 18th-century fake fur.

As the movie progresses, and tensions rise before the fall show, a serious, almost bluesy side of Mizrahi surfaces. Striking out at the invisible man behind the camera (Mizrahi's then-lover, now ex, Keeve), the designer denies that he's stressed out despite all evidence to the contrary.

The movie builds to a star-studded finale that drips with supermodels like sequins at a Long Island bar mitzvah. Naomi Campbell has class, Cindy Crawford has grit and Linda Evangelista has a high-pitched whine that could cripple a dog. One-name stars Liza and Roseanne and model groupies, Richard Gere and Kyle MacLachlan float past in cameos.

What's phenomenal about this final sequence, in addition to the theatrical genius of Mizrahi, is how emotionally moving it is. As the models glided down the runway in their gaily gaudy orange furs and were met with an explosion of on-screen applause, I was filled with a surge of joy. After all the laughter that had led up to that moment, my sudden tears were a complete surprise to me.

As Mizrahi's assistant tells his boss, "I am loving that."

NEWSDAY, 8/4/95, Part II/p. B9, Jack Mathews

Isaac Mizrahi, the fey wunderkind of New York's fashion world, has a personality to match the colorfully flamboyant clothes he designs.

The 30-year-old doughboy with the eraserhead hairdo has an original philosophy (Jackie Kennedy and Mary Tyler Moore shaped modern American life), deep spiritual values (he worships at a Ouija board) and a gift for critical detail (did you notice that after 13 days lost in the Arctic tundra in "Call of the Wild," Loretta Young still had on *perfect* eyeliner?).

All of which makes Mizrahi a wonderful subject for Douglas Keeve's "Unzipped," a lighter-than-air documentary that follows the designer from the morning after his disastrous spring '94 show to the morning after his triumph in the fall. You won't learn an awful lot about Mizrahi's true character (his personal life was clearly off-limits to the filmmaker), but this guy is sure fun to hang out with.

"Unzipped" plays as the flipside to "Ready to Wear," Robert Altman's rather mean-spirited parody of the Paris fashion scene. Keeves, a veteran fashion photographer, is dazzled by the passions and eccentricities of the characters inhabiting that world, and with Mizrahi functioning as a sort of manic-depressive cheerleader, his film compels the audience to join in the celebration.

There is obviously enormous pressure on designers to put on a good show twice a year. Their audiences are buyers and critics, both with the power to make or break their seasons, and they have to be won over as much with exuberance as with design. If you watch fashion show reports on CNN or VH-1 and wonder why there's so much excitement when the designer finally appears onstage with the models, "Unzipped" makes it all perfectly clear.

Fashion shows are huge productions, with models glide-walking down the runway, then scrambling backstage to get into their next outfit. In "Unzipped," we see some of the world's top models Naomi Campbell, Cindy Crawford, Kate Moss, Linda Evangelista—go through this mad drill, finding time to cheer each other on, and when it's all over, their relief and exhilaration is palpable.

For this particular show, Mizrahi made the daring decision to allow his live audience to watch the backstage madness while the show was in progress. Against his colleagues' better judgment, he ordered that the wall separating the dressing room from the stage be transparent, making the two activities—one all grace and dignity, the other frantically awkward—visible at the same time.

Rather than being a distraction, the gambit seemed to energize the show, enlist the audience as participants, and enhance the playful nature of the line of clothes being modeled. And it provided Keeve a happy ending he couldn't have imagined. Still, the real show here is Mizrahi, a man of wildly fluctuating moods, alternately giddy and depressed (particularly when he learns that another designer has chosen the same "Eskimo chic" concept), and invariably childlike. That last quality is underscored by the ubiquitous presence of Mizrahi's mother, standing by to praise her son's genius and regale others with his precocious sense of fashion. (At 4, she says with amazement, he was noticing daisies on women's shoes!)

Keeves' self-conscious blend of 8-mm. and 16-mm. film, his overuse of montage and quick cuts, is frustrating at times. Mizrahi's personality and passion for work are so compelling we don't need a lot of filmmaking tricks to hold our interest. Mizrahi is one of those subjects, like Niagara Falls, where all you need to do with a camera is aim and shoot.

SIGHT AND SOUND, 4/96, p. 57, Vicky Allan

The morning after his Spring 1994 show, fashion designer Isaac Mizrahi flicks through the newspapers to find unenthusiastic reviews. This is the story of how his next collection gets made. Beginning with Mizrahi's initial inspiration while watching Robert Flaherty's *Nanook of the North* on television, it documents the creation of film-inspired designs. Using a bizarre selection of aids, ranging from ouija boards through to his own mother, Sarah Mizrahi, to guide him, Mizrahi creates an Eskimo-based look involving brash and shaggy fake furs with boldly coloured evening dresses.

Mizrahi consults the fashion gurus, Candy Pratts of *Vogue* and Polly Mellen. He hangs out with the stars (Sandra Bernhard, Eartha Kitt and Mark Morris), swans about with supermodels (Naomi Campbell, Cindy Crawford) and talks movies with his design team. Minor hiccups beset his plans. Mizrahi's proposal that his show be staged with a transparent theatrical scrim behind which the models will be revealed changing, meets with a series of blank 'no's from the models. Worse still, his fabrics are proving difficult to obtain in time.

Mizrahi grows increasingly tense. The final blow is dealt when the newspapers reveal that Jean-Paul Gaultier has produced a similar Eskimo-inspired collection. But the show must go on. With scrim, half-naked models and costumes fully arranged, it hits the catwalk. The glamorously colourful collection is ecstatically received before an audience littered with stars. Mizrahi reads the reviews the following day. This time they are positive. He walks the New York streets with a smile.

Fashion designer Isaac Mizrahi says: "I'm happy where I am ... You can learn all you need to know about, say, Australia, from the Flintstones episode set there." Mizrahi sits at the heart of American culture, channel-hopping and thinking about Hollywood. He makes simple but opulent clothes which reflect American style and the movies of the 50s (seen through the filter of cable television and the 90s fashion world). Mizrahi revels in his starring role in *Unzipped*, fashion photographer Douglas Keeve's Warholian documentary (and directorial debut). With considerable comic charm, he explains his cinematic influences, paying tribute to the American entertainment industry and its host of icons—Snow White, Mary Tyler Moore, Bette Davis and others—the superstars who "shaped their country".

Unzipped is about how movies beget dresses and of how *cinema verité* has become chic. Keeve's filmic vision is mix-and-match *á la mode*, combining grainy black and white stock and colour home-movie footage with movie clips. An early viewing of *Nanook of the North* inspires the Eskimo motif in Mizrahi's final collection—a show of shaggy "weightless" furs and ecstatic colours, a "Giselle meets Fred Flintstone" or "50s cheesecake meets Eskimo". The Hollywood version of *The Call of the Wild* sets the tone—unruffled and dewy eyed even while freezing to death on the Tundra.

Not only does the cinema influence Mizrahi's designs, but it also permeates his whole way of thinking. Keeve uses a recurrent gag to underline the point: Mizrahi performs or describes a scene from a film and then gives you the real thing. Mizrahi is like a kid quoting his favourite adverts. His drawled "yarn't" comes from Bette Davis' "yarn't never going to leave this house" in *What Ever Happened to Baby Jane?*, his "there's only one star in this production" from *The Valley of the Dolls*.

Like any fashion collection *Unzipped* is a melding of genres and styles. Keeve's documentary is in the great putting-on-a-show tradition. Think of Judy Garland and Mickey Rooney shooting a video diary and you get the idea.

Where the rock world has a tradition of prying into the lives of celebrities, from D.A. Pennebaker's Dylan documentary *Don't Look Back* to Alex Keshishian's *In Bed with Madonna*, fashion has produced few such offerings (Wim Wender's *Notebook on Clothes and Cities* aside). With its host of big fashion names *Unzipped* hopes to cash in on the 90s cult of the supermodel.

Keeve proposes to unzip the lives of these silent queens of the catwalk, to reveal the personalities behind the star faces. Yet, his film is titillatingly cautious with them. Even Mizrahi's social circle has been edited down to the strictly professional—there's no mention of a personal life, except for the hints of a gay lifestyle in the music soundtrack. We get the pleasure of watching Linda Evangelista whining about her flat shoes, or Kate Moss attempting a monosyllabic coolness, but Keeve's zip stops short of indecency. He allows the models to do what they do well—be the Christy, Kate or Cindy from the magazines. The catwalk star system is clearly a parodic mirror of the Hollywood star system, as Robert Altman tirelessly revealed in his exhaustive caricatural and Tatiesque farce, *Prêt-à-Porter*. In *Unzipped*, Keeve follows suit. He attacks the fashion/Hollywood metaphor from all angles.

Whether as therapy for the disillusioned designer or an antidote for the fashion cynic, *Unzipped* is the perfect fashion movie. It presents us with a world which is all surface, a hectic buzz of bodies, cloth, shoots and shows—exactly what we always imagined it to be, and no more. The movie is a vehicle for the style industry, unzipping only another layer of style below the surface of a career. With grainy photography by Ellen Kuras (who shot *Swoon* and *Postcards from America*), it is satisfyingly chic throughout, with a burst of colour at the end, a visual 'up' to match the narrative climax. Having taken us through the trials and tribulations of preparations, Keeve ends on the high of Mizrahi's latest success. He delivers a feel-hip factor as much as a feelgood one. As a commodity that takes a subordinate place to Mizrahi's creations, *Unzipped* follows the cool-film equals cool-product equals cool-customer chain of logic, selling the world of *haute couture* as a Levis' advert sells jeans.

TIME, 8/14/95, p. 66, Martha Duffy

According to his doting mother, little Isaac Mizrahi delighted in the daisies on a pair of her mules when he was four. A few years later, he regularly pinched cash from his parents' dressing table while they slept and used it to buy fabric at a Brooklyn dry-goods emporium. At 17 he whipped up a special purple suit to wear on his first trip to Paris. No surprise, then, that young Isaac became a successful fashion designer whose business straddles youthful downtown chic and conservative uptown department stores.

Now 33, Mizrahi is the subject of *Unzipped*, one of the smartest and most entertaining documentaries to come along in years. *Unzipped* is everything that Robert Altman's fashion fizzle, *Ready to Wear*, should have been: funny, succinct and modestly instructive about a fairly recondite business.

The movie follows the designer as he prepares his fall 1994 collection. He is starting from behind. Critics trashed his previous collection, and he feels skinned by all the negative comment. Mizrahi is a witty, self-aware fellow, and his running commentary on his work life is often hilarious. He goes to see *Nanook of the North*, Robert Flaherty's classic 1922 documentary about Eskimos, and decides he wants to design only fur pants. He interviews hopeful models, although when his show finally opens, he seems to have hired only superstars like Naomi Campbell and Cindy Crawford. Working with Eartha Kitt, who wears his finery when she performs, he nuzzles her overwrought lapdog and remarks, "It's almost impossible to have any style at all without the right dogs."

It's all smart and glib and redolent of the kind of backchat—over the top or below the belt—that fuels the fashion biz. "It's so major!" gushes Polly Mellen, creative director of *Allure*. The result could be trivial if director Douglas Keeve were not also focusing on Mizrahi's gathering nerves. The low point comes when a staffer brings in a copy of *Women's Wear Daily* that headlines the latest from Jean-Paul Gaultier, the tallest tree in Mizrahi's particular sector of the fashion forest. Gaultier's revelation? Eskimo chic. Mizrahi throws the paper on the floor.

Mizrahi and Keeve were lovers during the filming, and the director has made wise use of their intimacy. Interspersed with the narrative are clips from home movies made during Mizrahi's boyhood, anecdotes from his mom and shots from favorite movies and TV shows. Mizrahi adores Mary Tyler Moore, and when the new collection is a hit, he throws his hat in the air just the way Mary Richards does in the MTM credits. This is the first time out for Keeve as director, and he does a poised job of presenting a warts-and-all portrait—Mizrahi the show-off, proud of every clever phrase he coins, and Mizrahi the serious craftsman, determined to build on his considerable gifts. Show-off and craftsman have one thing in common: they're both catnip to the camera. *Unzipped* could be the genesis of a second line for Mizrahi.

VILLAGE VOICE, 8/8/95, p. 43, Georgia Brown

The first time I saw *Unzipped* I was charmed, but then it was a charming evening. This was in Cannes and I saw Hugh Grant in person for the first time. Hugh and Elizabeth looked grand, which was more than I could say about many of the luminaries milling about at the Miramax AIDS benefit. Hostess Sharon Stone, who also looked great, auctioned off Naomi Campbell's navel ring. Since Campbell was wearing a long sheath, however, one couldn't see the ring. But Sharon patted Naomi's flat tummy and announced she could feel it: "It's there!" At this, an incredulous, accented voice piped up: "She swallow it?" (Did he think he'd have to dig in her doo-doo?)

But back to *Unzipped*. Douglas Keeve's documentary on his former boyfriend, designer Isaac Mizrahi, doesn't dabble in doo-doo. (You can also see Naomi's navel ring, close-up.) *Unzipped* is lighter than air, a bite of souffle, a swathe of chiffon, a boa of feathers. You get the idea. I liked it fine that night but wondered how it would hold up.

What I wouldn't have expected is that the second time was even better because I felt like one of the gang. Mizrahi was now a dear, dear friend. He's such a darling, a magnificent entertainer, a natural comic in the New York Jewish mode (he and his mom make a great team). All the cute things he says, the imitations he does, didn't grate or pall the second time around; they just became more adorable.

When Wenders did Yamamoto, he threw around a lot of theory, but I could tell he and Solveig were flying off to Tokyo for new wardrobes. Fashion docs are infomercials and there's no reason to think *Unzipped* proceeds from any purer motive. But *Unzipped* is great fun, and great looking, too. (It was shot by Ellen Kuras in color and black and white, and in a cool mix of formats.)

I'll mention some highlights: Isaac finding inspiration in *Nanook of the North*; finding himself in Paris without Sinutab; Isaac throwing his hat like Mary Tyler Moore; Isaac reporting the Ouija board's message, "Dominatrix shoes by day, flats by night"; Isaac doing Bette Davis in *Whatever Happened to Baby Jane?*, "Blanche, yern't ever gurrna leave that chair." You'd best hear this one yourself.

Also reviewed in:
CHICAGO TRIBUNE, 8/18/95, Friday/p. I, John Petrakis
NATION, 8/28-9/4/95, p. 216, Stuart Klawans
NEW REPUBLIC, 8/21 & 28/95, p. 30, Stanley Kauffmann
NEW YORK TIMES, 8/4/95, p. C1, Janet Maslin
VARIETY, 1/30-2/5/95, p. 47, Emanuel Levy
WASHINGTON POST, 8/18/95, p. G6, Rita Kempley
WASHINGTON POST, 8/18/95, Weekend/p. 42, Joe Brown

USUAL SUSPECTS, THE

A Gramercy Pictures release of a Polygram Filmed Entertainment and Spelling Films International presentation of a Blue Parrot/Bad Hat Harry production. *Executive Producer:* Robert Jones, Hans Brockman, François Duplat, and Art Horan. *Producer:* Bryan Singer and Michael McDonnell. *Director:* Bryan Singer. *Screenplay:* Christopher McQuarrie. *Director of Photography:* Newton Thomas Sigel. *Editor:* John Ottman. *Music:* John Ottman. *Music Editor:* Lia Vollack. *Sound:* Geoffrey Patterson. *Sound Editor:* Chuck Michael. *Casting:* Francine Maisler, Kathy Driscoll, and Lisa Miller. *Production Designer:* Howard Cummings. *Art Director:* David Lazan. *Set Decorator:* Sara Andrews. *Special Effects:* Roy Downey. *Costumes:* Louise Mingenbach. *Make-up:* Michelle Buhler. *Stunt Coordinator:* Gary Jensen. *Running time:* 105 minutes. *MPAA Rating:* R.

CAST: Stephen Baldwin (Michael McManus); Gabriel Byrne (Dean Keaton); Benicio Del Toro (Fred Fenster); Kevin Pollak (Todd Hockney); Kevin Spacey (Verbal Kint); Chazz Palminteri (Dave Kujan); Pete Postlethwaite (Kobayashi); Suzy Amis (Edie Finneran); Giancarlo Esposito (Jack Baer); Dan Hedaya (Jeff Rabin); Paul Bartel (Smuggler); Carl Bressler (Saul Berg); Phillip Simon (Fortier); Jack Shearer (Renault); Christine Estabrook (Dr. Plummer); Clark Gregg (Dr. Walters); Morgan Hunter (Arkosh Kovash); Ken Daly (Translator); Michelle Clunie (Sketch Artist); Louis Lombardi (Strausz); Frank Medrano (Rizzzi); Ron Gilbert (Daniel

Metzheiser);   Vito D'Ambrosio (Arresting Officer);   Gene Lythgow (Cop on Pier);   Smadar Hanson (Keyser's Wife);   Castula Guerra (Arturro Marquez);   Peter Rocca (Arturro's Bodyguard);   Bert Williams (Old Cop).

FILMS IN REVIEW, 11-12/95, p. 108, Andy Pawelczak

The Usual Suspects took me by surprise. The previews made it look like a hokey crime drama made up of loose odds and ends from other films and full of actors between bigger, more lucrative assignments. It turned out to be one of the summer's more successful pictures, and with good reason: this film by the Sundance-winning team of director Bryan Singer and writer Christopher McQuarrie *(Public Access)* almost succeeds in making the genre new. It's a literate, witty, stunningly photographed movie graced by excellent performances and a plot whose denouement forces you to rethink the whole film almost from the first frame.

A police lineup early in the film seems designed to announce the chutzpah of the whole enterprise. Five of the usual suspects (Gabriel Byrne, Stephen Baldwin, Kevin Pollak, Kevin Spacey, Benicio Del Toro) in a hijacking are told to step forward and repeat a line, and each does it with an individual, theatrical flair. Are these actors impersonating criminals—you can feel the actors' pleasure in this scene or criminals who enjoy acting, like Quentin Tarantino's thugs in *Reservoir Dogs* and *Pulp Fiction?* At any rate, the lineup suggests much of what is to follow: macho confrontations and posturing, and the possible treachery of one character who might in fact be acting.

In the film's convoluted narrative structure—here too it's under the saturnine influence of Tarantino—flashbacks recounted by one of the gang members alternate with a present-time police investigation. We know from the beginning, or at least we think we know, how things turn out—with the murder of a principal character and a shipboard explosion—so part of the narrative interest is in how we get there. The night I saw the movie the audience started out laughing at the movie's jokes and actorly shtick but soon settled down to a tense silence so as not to miss a single line of dialogue. The action scenes in this film—there are two beautifully staged heists and a murder in an elevator—actually afford a release from the wickedly dense unfolding of the plot.

The Usual Suspects depends on ensemble work more than most films do, and it's a measure of the actors' skills that they manage to individualize their characters. Gabriel Byrne is compelling as the putative gang leader looking to go straight but getting caught up in one criminal machination after another, and Baldwin, Pollak and Del Toro deftly fill out characters that aren't much more than sketches in the script. Dan Hedaya and Giancarlo Esposito, both excellent actors, have relatively small roles as cops, and Chazz Palminteri turns in a strong performance as a police interrogator. As Verbal, the character who narrates the flashbacks, Kevin Spacey almost steals the picture—he's an unlikely, soulful-eyed crook who doesn't seem to belong in this tough-guy company. One of the film's major characters never appears on screen; a master criminal called Keyser Sozé—his name is intoned with superstitious awe—he pulls the strings from behind the scene and plays an important role in the denouement.

Bryan Singer's direction has an appropriately dark, labyrinthine quality, and the film is full of energizing visual jokes that catch you off-guard. One example: a shot of a Japanese pavilion is accompanied by an off screen voice telling us about a meeting with a lawyer named Kobayashi. When we finally see this character, he's not Japanese at all; as played by Pete Postlethwaite (the father in *In the Name of the Father,* he's a sinister figure of indeterminate East European origin. Some critics have complained that *The Usual Suspects* is an empty exercise in gamesmanship; maybe so, but I wish that more films were as visually exciting and consistently entertaining. It's a notch or two above the usual thing.

LOS ANGELES TIMES, 8/16/95, Calendar/p. 1, Kenneth Turan

"The Usual Suspects" is a maze moviegoers will be happy to get lost in, a criminal roller coaster with twists so unsettling no choice exists but to hold on and go along for the ride. A fatalistic tale of power, betrayal, crime and punishment, spiced with just a whiff of romance, it is more than anything a polished exercise in pure virtuoso style.

The key stylist is director Bryan Singer, whose debut film, "Public Access," won the Grand Jury Prize at Sundance a few years back. "Suspects," with its fine control of the medium, shows

Singer to be an uncommon kind of natural filmmaker, disciplined rather than self-indulgent. Cinema is a game he enjoys, and as well as he plays it, he doesn't do it alone.

Helping him bridge the gap to bigger-budget films, Singer has brought most of his "Public Access" creative team with him, including co-producer Kenneth Kokin, editor-composer John Ottman and, most importantly, screenwriter Christopher McQuarrie, a friend since high school, whose plot sense and vigorous, profane dialogue jolt the film like a high-tension wire.

Singer also knows how to take advantage of the better class of actors now available. With nearly a dozen briskly performed key roles, and all but one of them male, "Suspects" is an accomplished ensemble piece, its characters, each with a distinctive line of mesmerizing chat, oozing macho attitude and hard-guy camaraderie.

The designated storyteller here, in a series of voice-over flashbacks that takes up most of the film, is Roger "Verbal" Kint (Kevin Spacey), a palsied con artist with a twisted foot and a weakness for talking too much.

Verbal is one of two survivors of an explosion in San Pedro harbor that opens the movie, a shipboard blast in which 27 men died over a reported $91 million in cocaine. But relentless U.S. Customs special agent David Kujan (Chazz Palminteri) thinks Verbal knows more than he admits, and his interrogation of the witness is the frame on which the plot unfolds.

Six months before the blast, Verbal relates, five hardened career criminals, himself included, were arrested after a truckload of gun parts was hijacked in Queens, "brought in on trumped-up charges to be leaned on by half-wits." The other four were the surly Todd Hockney (Kevin Pollak), cocky Michael McManus (Stephen Baldwin) and his partner Fred Fenster (Benicio Del Toro), and, most interesting of all, Dean Keaton (Gabriel Byrne).

An ex-cop who became a crook and who is now, with the help of criminal lawyer girlfriend Edie Finneran (Suzy Amis), trying to go straight again, Keaton is simultaneously admired by the others for his dark skills and taunted for abandoning them. But, as Verbal predicts, "you don't put guys like that in a room together, you never know what can happen." What goes down in this case is a plan for that classic one last job, which, of course, turns out to be anything but.

"Suspects'" other major strand deals with the second survivor of the explosion, an aged Hungarian gangster. Barely alive, he tells his interrogator that "he saw the devil and looked him in the eye." He saw, he tells the incredulous and astonished police, Keyser Soze.

Who is Keyser Soze? Only the greatest international criminal mastermind since Dr. Fu Manchu, and, a few people think, just as fictional. Is he, as someone says, "a spook story criminals tell their kids at night," or is his existence real, his nominally mythical status underlining the truism that "the greatest trick the devil ever pulled was convincing the world that he didn't exist." And Kobayashi (British actor Pete Postlethwaite), the hypnotic, unflappable attorney who mysteriously appears to speak for him, certainly is impressive enough. Soon everyone is wondering what is real, what is imaginary, and what exactly is going on?

Detailed as all this may sound, it is only a gloss on "The Usual Suspects'" narrative complexity. With cinematographer Newton Thomas Sigel's fluid camera-work leading the way, Singer and company employ several layers of flashbacks and an intricate way of breaking up scenes that make them seem even more elusive. Don't expect to completely follow the plot after the first viewing, or maybe even after the second. But like a tale from the "Arabian Nights," told for the sheer pleasure of storytelling, this elegant puzzle not only enjoys showing off, it also has something to show.

NEW STATESMAN & SOCIETY, 8/25/95, p. 29, Lizzie Francke

Dark. Dark. Dark. In the first few minutes of *The Usual Suspects* one is just peering into the gloom. A title goes up "San Pedro, California, Last Night". It's that mention of "last night". One already feels slightly off kilter but at the same time drawn into the immediacy of the tale. We, the audience, are already implicated. The picture becomes a little crisper. Mysterious figures in long coats mill about on an old cargo boat. Then there are the two shots in the inky night, quickly followed by a screen-filling blast as the boat goes up in billowing scarlet flames. The who, what, where and why of it are already set up—we don't have to be film buffs to know the formulaic questions that set a thriller in motion. The information that we glean in those oh so crucial opening minutes sets us back on our feet again—we know the genre, we know what to expect.

Round up the usual suspects ... Except in Bryan Singer's exceptional conundrum of a film it is swiftly made evident to us that we know nothing as the director and his screenwriter Christopher McQuarrie warp our expectations of everything that has gone before and let it blow up in our faces.

The trick is that ostensibly it all seems so "seen it all before" as the film flashes back to "six weeks ago". Following a robbery in Queens, five likely lads who make for an unlikely crew, are pulled in for questioning by the New York police and thrown into the cage together where, in turn, they use the occasion to devise a future heist of their own. They're a dishevelled bunch—hardly the sleeky suited posse of Quentin Tarantino's heist movie *Reservoir Dogs*. But then this film is not about such pop-art style. Keaton (Gabriel Byrne), McManus (Stephen Baldwin), Fenster (Benicio Del Toro), Hockney (Kevin Pollack) and Kint (Kevin Spacey) are the guys in the line-up, joking together as they are asked to repeat an incriminating line. It's like an audition as each stands forward, their characters delineated in an inflection of their voice. Keaton, the urbane ex-cop turned master-mind criminal; the slightly spaced out double act of partners McManus and Fenster; the wisecracking Hockney; and the hunched up but loquacious Kint—so loquacious that he is nicknamed "Verbal", his words running away with him as if he is making up for the fact that he is slowed down by a limp.

It is of course the gimpish Verbal who gets to tell the story. He's a petty con man somewhat bewildered by the fact that he's in the line-up for an armed hijack at all. Yet, for him it proves to be fun, "I got to feel notorious". That's Verbal for you. He's also called "Pretzel Man". And with a pretzel-like twist the film jumps back to the beginning—or is that six weeks forward to the aftermath of the incident at San Pedro? Out of the charred wreck 27 bodies are pulled while $91 million worth of dope is presumed to have gone up in the smoke. Only two survivors are caught—one festers in hospital where a circus' worth of doctors and policemen squabble by his bedside, the other is Verbal who winds up in the district attorney's office to find that there is a resolute special agent—David Kajun (Chazz Palminteri) on his case. Under the cop's incisive, pummelling interrogation, the criminal seems out of his league, out of his depth. But so by now are we.

As the plot's turns become too wily, with too many McGuffins littering the way, the film itself seems to metamorphose into something else more of an intense two-hander character study, a Mametesque face-off between Kajun and Verbal. Indeed, all the clues one needs are in the language and performance. Looking not dissimilar to Joe Mantegna, Palminteri, so brilliant in Woody Allen's *Bullets Over Broadway* as the dour humoured mobster who ends up feeding the playwright John Cusack with his best lines, knows how to rap. And Spacey can meet his rhythm—the tension between the two is deftly measured as they play each character so assured of their own version of the events. Kajun wants to nail the ring-leader Keaton, who he's convinced has got away. While, finally broken, Verbal insists that the real master-mind is one Kaiser Soze, a monstrous, blood-lusting figure on the criminal scene around whom the tallest tales have been spun, but whom most believe to be a myth.

But as Verbal reminds, "the greatest trick that the devil ever pulled was convincing the world that he didn't exist". As such it becomes a terrifically executed struggle between the two stories with the audience challenged as to whose they can trust, while the answer for those who look is evidently before their eyes. Such narrative minefields are the stuff of the grimmest *film noir* which is chock full of fallible story-tellers with tales as twisted as their hearts. But the flashback device which has been used over and over again—think of *Sunset Boulevard* told bleakly from the point of view of a dead man—is here used to particularly retina-scorching effect. See it once, see it ten times, you may still be left in the dark, but its the kind of disorientation that leaves you feeling deliriously giddy.

NEW YORK POST, 8/16/95, p. 33, Thelma Adams

There's nothing routine about "The Usual Suspects." Bryan Singer, working with his "Public Access" writing partner, Chris McQuarrie, has created a cinematic shell-game that seduces from the opening credits to the final twist. It's the summer's best thriller, bar none.

Twisted, funny, assured and completely joyful in its reinvention of the whodunit, "The Usual Suspects" has attracted a high octane cast for a low budget independent film that first drew raves at the Sundance Film Festival last winter.

Gabriel Byrne drops the cruise control of his recent performances ("Little Women" among them) to play Dean Keaton, an ex-cop-turned-thief. Is Keaton trying to go straight or is that just a cover for future violent schemes? Byrne uses his craggily-handsome-going-to-seed looks to keep us off balance: Are we being conned or is he?

The NYPD considers Keaton a pariah and arrests him as a heist suspect. The cops toss him into a holding cell with four pros with sticky fingers: McManus (Stephen Baldwin), Fenster (Benicio Del Toro), Hockney (Kevin Pollak) and Verbal Kint (Kevin Spacey). Is it a coincidence that McManus has a plan for a big emerald score and that it requires the help of this quintet behind bars, or is there Mr. Big pulling the strings?

What we know of the plot unravels in flashback. Six weeks later, Customs Agent David Kujan (Chazz Palminteri) interrogates the crippled Kint about a seemingly unrelated and particularly gruesome explosion on the San Pedro piers in Southern California. The lawman and the thief engage in a battle of wits, and the actors go head-to-head with Palminteri playing straight man to Spacey's freaky loser.

Spacey, who's been relegated by Hollywood to second-guess-never-gets-the-girl, dies-in-second-act roles in movies like "Outbreak," delivers another star-making performance. The actor does everything but tap dance and romance. At times, as motor-mouthed as a speed addict (hence "Verbal") or cowering beneath a pronounced widow's peak, cracking under pressure or incongruously steely, Spacey expresses an elastic range of emotions—often in the same sentence.

"There's a lot more to this story, believe me," agent Kujan tells Kint. With its ballistic dialogue, fast and furious editing, and an unbeatable ensemble cast unleashed by a young director who's both smart and committed, there's more entertainment value to this slick, serpentine thriller than in the line-up of big-budget usual suspects that have dominated the box office this season.

"The Usual Suspects" is the only movie this summer that demands a second look.

NEWSDAY, 8/16/95, Part II/p. B7, Jack Mathews

Cleverness can be its own reward in a movie. Consider the pleasures in such marvelous brain-twisters as "Sleuth," "Deathtrap" and "The Sting." It can also be kind of a pain in the aft when its sole purpose is to mislead and confound the audience, and that is the only feeling I had after the ultimate cleverness at the end of Bryan Singer's suspense noir "Usual Suspects."

Let me make my ambivalence clear. Singer, whose low-budget "Public Access" won a major award at the 1993 Sundance Film Festival, is a significant new talent. "Usual Suspects" is a superbly crafted movie, at every level, and the young filmmaker has gotten first-rate performances from an ensemble cast that includes such diverse talents as Kevin Spacey, Chazz Palminteri, Pete Postlethwaite and Gabriel Byrne.

But with a Rubik's Cube of a script from Christopher McQuarrie, the film is more work than pleasure. From the opening scene—of a boat exploding at a pier in San Pedro, Calif., and the image of charred bodies floating in the debris—"Usual Suspects" begins to weave a tale so dense that you watch in self-defense, afraid that if you miss a single strand of information, you won't get it when it's finished.

That effort proves unnecessary, because when the truth is finally revealed, the light bulb in our mind illuminates more baloney than truth. The ending is as unsatisfying as it is unpredictable, and ultimately a cheat.

You can give yourself a headache just describing the basic plot, but here goes. That opening explosion, which is survived by a mysterious Hungarian gangster and a gimpy New York hood named Verbal (Spacey), is the framing device for a series of intercut flashbacks. The gangster is pretty much toast, bandaged head to foot in a hospital bed, but Verbal is in good shape and reluctantly spilling the beans on a heist gone bad (one of many echoes of "Reservoir Dogs") to customs agent Dave Kujan (Palminteri).

Verbal, we learn from his story, is one of five felons rounded up for a police line-up six weeks before the boat explosion. None is guilty of the crime in question, but their long records for extortion, larceny and robbery make them the usual suspects. And while they're cooling their heels in the lockup, they discover a common link. They've all had experiences with a psycho/crime lord named Keyser Soze, and by the time they're released from jail, they've hatched a plan that will put them at direct odds with the fabled killer.

"Usual Suspects" shifts back and forth from the flashbacks leading up to the explosion to agent Kujan's frantic efforts afterward to find Keyser Soze, whom he suspects is one of America's most powerful drug traffickers. After all, the cargo on that ill-fated boat was said to be $91 million worth of cocaine.

If you don't mind being taken in, there is plenty to appreciate, particularly in the relationships between the five tempestuous felons. Spacey, whose work just gets better and better, is terrific as Verbal, a sleaze with a wise mouth and a penchant for tall tales; and Gabriel Byrne, as a tortured ex-cop, and Stephen Baldwin, as the gang's hot-tempered bruiser, provide plenty of emotional fireworks. And Postlethwaite is eerily menacing as Keyser Soze's eloquent and improbably named henchman Kobayashi.

"Usual Suspects" is one puzzle where the pieces are more enjoyable than the whole.

NEWSWEEK, 8/28/95, p. 58, Jack Kroll

In an age when all movie genres are being subverted, postmodernized, deconstructed, film noir is a tough genre to mess around with. For many true movie fiends, noir is the key American movie type, and the most fun when it's done right. *The Usual Suspects* is done right. Here's an intelligent movie, with no special effects, no infantile charades of violence, released during the summer splatter season.

You have to pay close attention to this film, to listen hard to its cross-fires of dialogue. Writer Christopher McQuarrie and director Bryan Singer are talented moviemakers who've made one previous film, "Public Access," which shared the Grand Jury Prize at the 1993 Sundance Festival. "Suspects" marks a big leap forward for this team. It's a tough movie about five tough guys who first meet in a jail cell where they've been brought as suspects in a heist. They are Keaton (Gabriel Byrne), who was a corrupt cop but is now trying to go straight (maybe); McManus (Stephen Baldwin), a short-fused break-in artist; Hockney (Kevin Pollak) a hardware specialist; Fenster (Benicio Del Toro), a weirdo who mumbles like a crook in a Dick Tracy comic, and "Verbal" Kint (Kevin Spacey), a crippled con man.

The collision of these five felons sets off a story line that's the most convoluted since Humphrey Bogart's classic "The Big Sleep." Out of jail, the fab five are conscripted by the sinister Kobayashi (Pete Postlethwaite). He's working for Keyser Söze, a Hungarian crime lord whose homicidal ferocity has made him a figure of terrifying legend. His mission for the five is to stop a rival crime boss's $91 million drug deal. The caper, masterminded by the invisible Söze, turns out to be booby-trapped by explosive bursts of deceit and death. The story is told in flashbacks, as it's dragged out of Verbal, the sole survivor (maybe) of the five, in a withering interrogation by Kujan (Chazz Palminteri), a federal agent obsessed by the elusive Söze.

"The Usual Suspects" has a surface resemblance to Quentin Tarantino's "Reservoir Dogs." But where Tarantino was out to deconstruct the film noir, to create the ultimate parody of the metaphysical gangster film, Bryan Singer wants to respect its classical form. He and McQuarrie do so, using fusillades of language that are as brutal as the movie's bullets and bombs. Newton Thomas Sigel's succulent photography and the double-duty gifts of John Ottman, who supplied both the trip-hammer editing and the mordant musical score, add to the seductive mood and narrative fascination. But what's most compelling is the brilliant acting by an irresistible ensemble: the urbane yet vicious Byrne, the baroque Postlethwaite, the relentless Palminteri and the creepily quiet Spacey. "The Usual Suspects" is the best, most stylish crime movie since Stephen Frears's 1990 "The Grifters." Movies still look great in basic noir.

SIGHT AND SOUND, 9/95, p. 61, Philip Kemp

In San Pedro harbour, California, a cargo ship explodes, leaving 27 dead. There are two survivors: a Hungarian named Arkosh Kovash, lying badly burnt in a hospital bed, and a crippled New York con-man, 'Verbal' Kint. Granted immunity from prosecution in return for his testimony, Kint is questioned by US Customs agent Dave Kujan. Kujan is convinced that Dean Keaton, a crooked ex-cop, masterminded the raid and survived. Meanwhile, Federal agent Jack Baer questions Kovash via an interpreter.

Kint recalls how he met Keaton six weeks earlier when they were pulled in on a police line-up, suspected of a truck hijack. Also in the line-up were entryman Michael McManus, his partner Fred Fenster, and explosives expert Todd Hockney. During their night in the holding cell,

McManus outlines a plan for holding up a 'taxi service' run for crooks by corrupt New York cops. Keaton, who is trying to go straight to please his girlfriend, attorney Edie Finneran, at first refuses to take part, but is persuaded by Kint.

The heist works perfectly, bringing down scandal on the NYPD, and McManus suggests they launder the loot through his regular LA fence, Redfoot. Mistrusting McManus, the others accompany him to California where Redfoot offers them another job robbing a Texan jeweller, Saul Berg. Berg, who proves to be a drug dealer, is killed in the shoot-out. The gang are later contacted by a lawyer, Kobayashi, claiming to represent the man who wanted Berg killed, the mysterious master criminal Keyzer Soze—a name also mentioned by the terrified Kovash.

Kobayashi explains that Soze engineered the original police line-up, because all five men have unwittingly trespassed on his territory. To make amends, they must now raid a drug-smuggling ship in San Pedro harbour run by Soze's rivals, an Argentinian gang. Initially the gang refuse and Fenster takes off, but he is traced and lulled by Soze's men. Keaton plans to kill Kobayashi until he learns the lawyer has Edie in his power. The four raid the ship—though Keaton leaves Kint on the pier to contact Edie if things go wrong—and find no drugs but an Argentinian, Marquez, who can identify Soze. While Kint watches from onshore, Hockney, McManus and Keaton are shot by Soze, who then blows up the ship.

Kujan furiously accuses Kint of lying, insisting that Keaton was really Soze and has faked his own death. But Kint sticks to his story and Kujan is obliged to let him go. Meanwhile Baer has had a police artist draw a picture of Soze from Kovash's description and faxes it through. As it arrives Kujan realises Soze's true identity.

When, in 1950, Hitchcock included a misleading flashback in *Stage Fright* it aroused great indignation: the director "Hadn't played fair" with his audience. It's perhaps symptomatic of a more cynical age, when the deconstructionist concept of the unreliable narrator has become a creative commonplace, that *The Usual Suspects* can be built around a long flashback narration that's a lie from start to finish. The final-reel revelation—that virtually nothing in the preceding 100 minutes can be taken as true—also, by way of bonus, neatly side-steps any critical objections to the massive holes in the plot. Implausible! Inconsistent! Well, of course it is.

Misdirecting the audience, in any case, is the stock-in-trade of any good thriller; *The Usual Suspects* just takes it a stage further. Even when not luring us into its maze of flashbacks the film deftly sets up tensions between perception and reality, playing off what's said about a given individual with the way that person seems to be: Kint's account of Keaton against Kujan's view against the Keaton that's shown to us. (The film's rich in K-names, maybe in homage to the great Czech maze-maker himself.) Singer draws from his cast (cops no less than crooks) edgy, sidelong performances that constantly hint at hidden motivations and past histories teetering on the brink of fantasy—a challenge to which his actors rise superbly. Pete Postlethwaite, faced with playing a non-Japanese lawyer with a Japanese name, displays admirable unfazability; making no attempt at a Mr Moto-style accent, he gives his performance a remote, fastidious spin with the faintest dash of oriental melancholy, like Gielgud playing Chang the Deputy Lama in *Lost Horizon*.

The Usual Suspects is Singer and McQuarrie's second film; their first, *Public Access* (which showed at the London Film Festival a couple of years ago), also played with deceptive appearances, if in less labyrinthine fashion. The protagonist of the earlier film is a clean-cut young man who infiltrates a sleepy burg's public cable station and sets the townsfolk at each other's throats. This disruption isn't his aim; though it amuses him; his secret agenda is yet more lethal. In the same way Kint's monologue conceals layers beneath layers, its ostensible purpose a verbal smokescreen for its true one. Or for what, after the final disclosure, we take to be its true one—since it may well be that Soze doesn't exist after all. Or that multiple Sozes exist, offering a mythic persona to be adopted by any underworld boss wanting to terrorise his rivals. "The greatest trick the Devil ever pulled," says Kint, "was convincing the world he didn't exist." An even greater one, he could have added, was convincing it that he did.

The theological allusion is apt. There's a near-religious intensity to much of the film: Gabriel Byrne's fallen-angel of a bent cop, the sacrificial myth of Soze's Hungarian origins and, at the heart of the film, the duel between Kujan and Kint, played out in a tiny, windowless office like a confessional where the Customs agent hounds his captive with all the fervour of a High Inquisitor. All the action scenes, tautly staged though they are, feed back into this claustrophobic space. Palminteri and Spacey play expertly off each other, the one circling and harrying, eyes narrowed and lip jutting, the other slumped in maudlin self-abasement or taking off on another meandering verbal riff. But with the exception of Suzy Amis, stuck with an underwritten token-female role, there's not a weak link in the cast, all responding with relish to Singer's tight direction and McQuarrie's sinewy writing. Dark, tortuous and richly atmospheric, *The Usual Suspects* is the most satisfyingly close-textured thriller for years; even once you know the twist in the tail, there's enough going on here on every level to make it equally rewarding viewing a second time around.

TIME, 8/28/95, p. 69, Richard Corliss

All right, now, have we had it with blockbusters? It's true, we paid only $6 or $8 to see the *Judge Dreddfuls* and the *Waterworlds Without End*, not the $80 million or $200 quillion the studios ponied up, but a lot of us still feel taken. All those tough-guy movies wore us down and knocked one another out. But now that the big boys have slunk away, adventurous viewers are seeking a late-summer tonic in independent cinema.

The films can be made for $7 million *(Desperado)* or less than a million *(Living in Oblivion)*. They may be based on plays *(Jeffrey*, from Paul Rudnick's comedy) or novels *(Nadja*, from Bram Stoker's *Dracula)*. The stars may be esteemed actors (Gabriel Byrne and Kevin Spacey in *The Usual Suspects)* or the director's girlfriend (Maxine Bahns in *The BrothersMcMullen)*. Some sing, the others don't. But all prove that films can be intimate as well as epic, that off-Hollywood is one destination for films of the next century.

In several of these miniature movies, familiar motifs recur. Even independent films can be dependent on trends.

1. **It's Tarantino time.** The popularity of Quentin Tarantino's *Pulp Fiction*—the first independent film to earn more than $100 million at the U.S. box office—will midwife plenty of melodramas with Tarantino's signature plot: men in groups and on a heist, talking until the dark night of the soul gives way to a red dawn.

A solid twist on Tarantino Cheek is *The Usual Suspects*, written by Christopher McQuarrie and directed by Bryan Singer. The film echoes Tarantino's *Reservoir Dogs*, but with less hysteria and a more intricate plot. For its quintet of thieves lusting for the big score, *The Usual Suspects* convenes five scarred souls, including a chatty gimp (Spacey) and an anguished antihero (Byrne). In California on a quick job, they run up against a vicious, unseen ganglord named Keyser Sozé—a name that has the smolder of Satan in it. One by one, the thieves ...

No, it's far too snarly a skein to unravel here. *The Usual Suspects* flatters you into thinking you're thinking, sorting out the dead ends and red herrings, when you are really being toyed with by an intelligence as devious as Sozé's. For those who don't care whodunit, the film has superior skulking by some wonderfully actory actors and brings high-wire wit to its high-gloss gamesmanship.

2. **It's only a movie, Ingmar.** Independent movies, like first novels, used to be autobiographical rites of passage. Now, too often, they are about making an independent movie, a format that quickly surrenders to ego and ennui. So Tom DiCillo's *Living in Oblivion* pleasantly surprises by its cunning. DiCillo's modesty is also his happy arrogance, for this is an indie movie about the filming of exactly three shots in an indie movie.

Director Nick Reve (Steve Buscemi) is trying to shoot a mother-daughter chat, a love scene and a dream sequence. Well, maybe they're all dream sequences: Reve? What's that French for? Or all nightmares, because everything goes hilariously wrong. The boom mike dips into the frame. The dwarf feels he's being exploited. Then there's movie star Chad Palomino (James Le Gros), an idiot hunk who unaccountably thinks he's a creative artist; imagine Kato Kaelin mistaking himself for Dustin Hoffman. The film is funny without pushing it and is acted with a deft, manic touch.

3. **Find a new ethnic group.** Half the stud heroes in action films have a surname beginning with Mc-, but there aren't many films about Irish Americans. Really Irish ones, with the guilt and the corned beef and the weekly Mass and the guilt. Edward Burns -writer, director and co-star of *The Brothers McMullen*—means to fill that gap with this frail fable of three Long Island siblings

(Burns, Jack Mulcahy, Mike McGlone) and their romantic angst. They talk, soulfully. They fret, winsomely. They annoy, a lot.

The Brothers McMullen might be the bad movie Nick Reve is trying not to make. The acting is mostly stodgy, especially by the family trio. Burns' dialogue reeks of the page; it's cluttered with more adjectives than a D+ student paper. And when the specter of clunky writing isn't hanging over the actors, the shadow of a boom mike is.

4. For Pete's sake, have fun! Paul Rudnick lives to be giddy. Court jester of the Plague Years, the gay playwright-essayist has brought his romantic comedy about AIDS (you'll have to take our word for it) pretty successfully to the screen. Jeffrey faces its antsy audience head on: when two men kiss, we see a shot of two movie-house couples, the guys gagging, the girls enthralled. Under Christopher Ashley's direction, Steven Weber is beguiling as a '90s Candide. He gets suave support from Patrick Stewart and a scene stolen from under him by Nathan Lane.

5. Everybody light up! In indie films every character, it seems, puffs on a cigarette—as a tribute to the tortured heroes of film noir, a gesture of offhand rebellion, a sacrament of elegance and fatalism. There's an entire movie—quite a bad one, full of unwontedly tortured acting and a wildly wrong camera style—called *Smoke*. That in turn spawned a companion film, the much better *Blue in the Face,* to be released in the fall. Both revel in the outlaw ecstasies of tobacco.

In Michael Almereyda's *Nadja*, smoking is one of the few pleasures a vampire can take without harm. The Dracula family has come to New York City, and Nadja (Elina Löwensohn) is a kind of Lydia Languish of the undead, striking fashionable poses as she plants her teeth in a few sweet necks. With her bleached face, impossibly high forehead and black hood, Löwensohn looks like Death in *The Seventh Seal,* only cuter.

Though this film's Van Helsing (lank, loopy Peter Fonda) sleeps inside a grand piano, *Nadja* is a fairly close reading of the Stoker tale. What distinguishes it is its serenely mannerist glamour. Almereyda shot parts in glorious "Pixelvision"—with a toy camera that gives the most garish images the patina of a dreamscape. *Nadja* is beyond a midnight movie; it's a late late show for the artistic couch potato.

6. When in doubt, do it again. A few years ago, Robert Rodriguez made the tamale western *El Mariachi* for an impossibly low $7,000. Now he has made a sequel for 1,000 times the budget, which is still nothing to Hollywood accountants. This time it's called *Desperado*. The avenging guitarist is played by actual movie star Antonio Banderas, but he's still a reluctant gunaholic. ("Bless me, Father," he confesses, "for I have killed quite a few men.") Salma Hayek, a Tex-Mex houri with soulful eyes and bosoms till Tuesday, is the sex interest. And *Living in Oblivion*'s Buscemi drops by to give *Desperado* the Indie Seal of Approval.

Rodriguez has gone from backyard to back lot in one jump, but he hasn't lost his pizazz as director and editor. The picture is great kinetic fun—an explosion of pop talent. As El Mariachi says, "It's easier to pull the trigger than to play a guitar—easier to destroy than to create." Rodriguez does both. Scaling the studio wall with this vigorous remake, he proves he can be both an artist and a hired gun. His future will be fun to watch.

There's nothing radical about most of these independent films; they're calling cards for directors with Hollywood dreams. They take old-fashioned genres and show the big boys how to do it in an even more old-fashioned way: small, smart and cheap. For these pictures are the soapbox racers that dare to compete against the sleek but bland big-studio vehicles. And who wouldn't prefer the Indie 500 to Hollywood's Formula One?

VILLAGE VOICE, 8/22/95, p. 45, Georgia Brown

Before too long, *Reservoir Dogs* is going to have a lot to answer for. The newest blame-it-on-Quentin is *The Usual Suspects,* a slick and cynical let's-all-get-together-for-a-heist thriller that turns at the end into a nasty shaggy-dog story.

Or maybe I'm just pissed that Gabriel Byrne gets bumped off. Don't panic, I'm not spilling any sacred beans; he takes a bullet in the movie's first scene—a sort of flash-forward in a maddeningly elaborate flash-backward. Byrne's Dean Keaton is the only guy in the lineup you'd pick for the movie's hero. Except that there's never anything beyond Byrne's sulky charisma to flesh out Keaton's crooked ex-cop turned debonair con man. (Suzy Amis plays Keaton's smart, respectable girlfriend, but this is one of the teensy-weensiest roles you're likely to see.)

Directed by Bryan Singer as if there was something to it, *The Usual Suspects* is told in flashback and the teller is Roger "Verbal" Kint (Kevin Spacey), whiny two-bit thief, a "cripple" or "gimp," as he calls himself. The sole survivor of the mighty dynamite blast that finishes off his pals (they were in the middle of a reported $91 million coke heist), Verbal slumps in the office of Special Agent Kujan (Chazz Palminteri) of the U.S. Customs Department and spins his yarn. Verbal's tale begins more or less when he and four other jokers are rounded up for a lineup. Besides Keaton, the others are hard-edged, hot-tempered McManus (Stephen Baldwin), efficient but nondescript Hockney (Kevin Pollack), and flaky, flamboyant Fenster (Benicio Del Toro)—crooks all, though it's hard to recall their specialties. Spacey's grating voice-over is filled with portentously enunciated lines like "It was all the cops' fault. You don't put guys like that alone in a room together.

Guys like what? Keaton alone seems to have brains—and about this we're only guessing. Working with these creeps, he seems to be slumming. Verbal explains how he got his moniker: "People say I talk too much." Believe me, he does. His monologue gets agonizingly repetitious (especially if you have to sit through it a second time, as I did). Poor Palminteri is cast as a sap of an investigator, a straight man who has to move to the side and allow this spiel to unspool. (Bad career move, Chazz.)

At some point talk turns to a mysterious mythical gangster from out of the old East bloc, a shape-shifting master criminal whose very name, Keyser Soze (pronounced Kaiser Sosay in hushed tones), strikes terror into the hearts of grown men. One of the movie's nicer touches is hiring Pete Postlethwaite (the father from *In the Name of the Father)* to play Soze's grave, dignified, quietly threatening emissary. Whenever Postlethwaite is on screen (not all that often) the movie takes a little bounce.

Kevin Spacey, this picture's hard lump of a heart, does his job, creating in Verbal an unlovable creep, though not one you'd credit with what the movie credits him with. The questions you find on the tip of your tongue at the end are, What? How? Who? This could be fun, I suppose, if anything here made sense or mattered. The second time around you expect a film to yield some layers, shed some secrets. But *The Usual Suspects* is not an onion; it's more of a tomato.

Also reviewed in:
CHICAGO TRIBUNE, 8/18/95, Friday/p. C, Michael Wilmington
NEW REPUBLIC, 8/21 & 28/95, p. 30, Stanley Kauffmann
NEW YORK TIMES, 8/16/95, P. C15, Janet Maslin
NEW YORKER, 8/14/95, p. 85, Anthony Lane
VARIETY, 1/30-2/5/95, p. 46, Todd McCarthy
WASHINGTON POST, 8/18/95, p. G1, Hal Hinson
WASHINGTON POST, 8/18/95, Weekend/p. 42, Desson Howe

VAMPIRE IN BROOKLYN

A Paramount Pictures release of an Eddie Murphy production. *Executive Producer:* Marianne Maddalena and Stuart M. Besser. *Producer:* Eddie Murphy and Mark Lipsky. *Director:* Wes Craven. *Screenplay:* Charles Murphy, Michael Lucker, and Christopher Parker. *Story:* Eddie Murphy, Vernon Lynch, Jr., and Charles Murphy. *Director of Photography:* Mark Irwin. *Editor:* Patrick Lussier. *Music:* J. Peter Robinson. *Music Editor:* Steve McCroskey. *Choreographer:* Eartha Robinson. *Sound:* Jim Stuebe and (music) Robert Fernandez. *Casting:* Eileen MacKnight. *Art Director:* Gary Diamond and Cynthia Charette. *Set Designer:* Philip Dargort and Henry Alberti. *Set Decorator:* Robert Kensinger. *Special Effects:* Peter M. Chesney. *Costumes:* Ha Nguyen. *Make-up:* Bernadine M. Anderson. *Stunt Coordinator:* Alan Oliney. *Running time:* 103 minutes. *MPAA Rating:* R.

CAST: Eddie Murphy (Maximillian/Preacher Pauley/Guido); Angela Bassett (Rita); Allen Payne (Justice); Kadeem Hardison (Julius); John Witherspoon (Silas); Zakes Mokae (Dr. Zeko);

Joanna Cassidy (Dewey);   Simbi Khali (Nikki);   Messiri Freeman (Eva);   Kelly Cinnante (Officer);   Nick Corri (Anthony);   W. Earl Brown (Thrasher);   Ayo Adeyemi (Bartender);   Troy Curvey, Jr. (Choir Leader);   Vicklyn Reynolds (Mrs. Brown);   William Blount (Deacon Brown);   Joe Costanza (Bear);   John La Motta (Lizzy);   Marcelo Tubert (Waiter);   Nick DeMauro (Caprisi);   Jerry Hall and Mark Haining (Couple in Park);   Wendy Robie (Zealot at Police Station);   Alyse Mandel (Cop);   Larry Paul Marshall (Greeter at Church);   Vince Micelli (Checker Player);   Ray Combs (Game Show Host).

LOS ANGELES TIMES, 10/27/95, Calendar/p. 1, Jack Mathews

[The following review by Jack Mathews appeared in a slightly different form in NEWSDAY, 10/27/95, Part II/p. B6.]

"I always wanted to make a comedy and Eddie Murphy always wanted to make a scary movie" is the way "Nightmare on Elm Street" creator Wes Craven describes the genesis of "Vampire in Brooklyn," a film that arrives with barely a snicker or a scare in it.

How can this be?

Craven is one of the masters of contemporary movie horror and a filmmaker who can be counted on, at the very least, to sucker-punch us with a cat or a killer bolting out of the dark now and then. And Murphy has built his entire career playing comically displaced characters; a streetwise Detroit cop in snooty Beverly Hills, a New York beggar passing himself off as a Wall Street maven, an African king who comes to America to find a wife.

The answer is that in merging their interests, Craven and Murphy subordinated their respective talents. Craven, who is used to working from his own scripts, was a hired gun on this project, which was conceived and tailored for Murphy by his brother Charles (he shares the final screenwriting credit with first-timers Michael Lucker and Chris Parker). And Murphy's maniacally hip comedy style is muzzled beneath the Prince of Darkness' gothic solemnity.

The film's two comic set pieces—one where the vampire turns into a fire-and-brimstone preacher, sermonizing about the goodness of evil, the other where he assumes the role of a gamey hoodlum—give Murphy a chance to do his thing, and his legion of fans, whose number is dwindling faster than a summer pond in the Kalihari, may appreciate the break. But these goofy sequences have nothing to do with the rest of the movie.

Murphy does strike a dashing figure as the black-clad, goateed, long-haired Maximillian, the last surviving vampire of the African branch of the Nosferatus, on location from his home in the Bermuda Triangle searching for the one woman on Earth with whom he can mate and perpetuate the bloodline of the Undead. Turns out she's a cop named Rita (Angela Bassett), who considers herself a night person but is otherwise oblivious to her genetic roots in Transylvania.

It's up to Max, with the help of his manservant Julius (Kadeem Hardison), to seduce the independent-minded cop and consummate a marriage made in hell.

It does sound more like "Love at First Bite" than "Dracula," but with Craven in charge of the illusions, and with a budget befitting a star vehicle, "Vampire in Brooklyn" has an ambitiously foreboding appearance. Art directors Gary Diamond and Cynthia Charette's sets—the New York scenes were all shot in Los Angeles—are darkly authentic. Cinematographer Mark Irwin, who did such great work a decade ago on David Cronenberg's "The Fly," has managed a lot of texture and detail for a story condemned to the night. And though the makeup for Murphy's preacher and mob characters is less convincing than a trick-or-treater in a Lance Ito mask, Max's transformation from insouciant charmer to yellow-eyed, white-fanged bloodsucker is pretty cool.

But it all occurs in a thrill-free zone. There isn't a moment of genuine suspense or tension in the film, and the paltry laughs are supplied not by Murphy but by Hardison, whose character, a low-life Brooklyn habitue forcefully turned into the vampire's bug-eating sidekick, spends the entire movie moaning about his decomposing body and embarrassing the boss with his earthy patter.

"Vampire's" tone fluctuates between the slapstick antics of Hardison and John Witherspoon, playing Julius' fatuous uncle, and the overwrought *danse macabre* with Murphy and Bassett. Trooper that she is, Bassett plays Rita as if she were a heroine, right out of Greek tragedy, or at least out of a better movie.

SIGHT AND SOUND, 6/96, p. 55, Kim Newman

Brooklyn, New York. Maximillian, a vampire, arrives from the Caribbean and enslaves wastrel Julius, turning him into a decaying ghoul, and declaring that he has come to America to search for a mate so that the undead race can continue. Maximillian's ship is full of drained corpses, which brings in homicide cop Rita Veder—who, unknown to herself, is the half-breed daughter of a vampire and an anthropologist—and her partner Justice. Maximillian realises that Rita is destined to be his bride.

Using his ability to metamorphose into a black preacher or a white gangster, he moves in on Rita's life, murdering her roommate Nikki and breaking up her potential relationship with Justice. When Rita is suspended for two days, Maximillian tells her who she is and tentatively bites her, hoping to kindle in her a bloodlust which will turn her into a full vampire. Justice realises that the supernatural is involved and consults Zeko, a wise old man who explains that Maximillian must be destroyed before Rita kills if she is to be saved. Justice and Zeko invade Julius' apartment. Maximillian bests Justice and encourages Rita to kill her partner, whereupon she turns on the vampire and drives a wooden knife into his heart, destroying him and lifting the curse from her. However, Maximillian's ring falls into Julius' possession; when the ghoul puts it on, he transforms into a vampire.

Vampire in Brooklyn opens with an eerie and apt rethinking of one of the strongest sequences in Bram Stoker's *Dracula:* a ship crewed by corpses arrives in a new world, and a vampire escapes from it in the form of a dog. The effect of the hulk crashing into the Brooklyn docks is one the current film's strongest visual moments, but it is undermined by the bickerings of a couple of comedy black characters out of *Sanford and Son,* who squelch the mood with laboured chatter. Unfortunately, this sets a tone for the whole film which oscillates between effective and inept comedy and horror, with all the wonkiness expected of a script originated by a superstar's brother.

Eddie Murphy's Maximillian (undead cousin to his Third World Prince of *Coming to America*) is allowed a measure of creepy dignity as he rips out hearts or makes golden eyes at the heroine. Early on, Kadeem Hardison's Julius complains about Maximillian's "Blacula shit", which may or may not be an acknowledgement that an almost identical streetwise dude-cum-vampire's minion was played by Richard Lawson in *Scream Blacula Scream* in 1973. Too much else here seems like a pillaging of earlier sources: the plot hinge that a semi-vampire can be saved if his/her master is destroyed before they have killed is from *The Lost Boys,* the infallible seductive power of dancing with a vampire comes from *Fright Night.*

Wes Craven, whose see-sawing between innovation and hackery continues to make his filmography sometimes pleasingly unpredictable, is an interesting choice for director, not least because of his underrated contributions to black-themed horror in *The Serpent and the Rainbow* and *The People Under the Stairs.* However, his background is in the modernist conventions of *Night of the Living Dead,* and has only the most tentative relationship with the Hammer horror this film wishes to play riffs on. Without the distracting need to dollop in tiresome comedy and an even more tiresome romantic triangle, Craven might have had something to add to the over-worked vampire sub-genre, especially in the light of his appropriations of the gothic for *The People Under the Stairs.* As it is, this is a collection of shallow, but entertaining skits and scares hung on a feeble plot thread about Maximillian's search for a mate that is no sooner resolved than it is contradicted by Julius' punchline transformation.

VILLAGE VOICE, 11/7/95, p. 67, Gary Dauphin

Vampire in Brooklyn, Eddie Murphy's latest stab at big-screen redemption, probably won't make anyone forgot his films, but it is a funny enough reminder of why anyone ever liked the guy in the first place. Maximillian, the Caribbean vampire (Murphy), comes to Brooklyn in search of a vampire halfling/lady cop (Angela Bassett), and from there suaves his way through three parts comedy and one part action-horror. Subplots abound (while Maximillian sleeps), and the most consistent laughs go to Kadeem Hardison (solidly hysterical as Max's decomposing servant); Allen Payne, as Bassett's love interest, plays the hero. Murphy does get two hilarious set pieces, in which he becomes a shady preacher and a low-rent mobster, but they're oddly retrospective riffs, effortless but ghostlike eruptions from Murphys comic past. He's groping for a way to integrate such shtick into the kind of multilayered attack that made his earlier work so successful.

Bassett and Craven are both missing in action here. Bassett reanimates Ola Ray from the *Thriller* video (right down to the wet-look wig), whereas Craven reproduces the look and feel not of actual Brooklyn but of an '80s Eddie Murphy movie. *Vampire*'s terror is existential, as when Hardison says of his unholy master's coif: "Who you think he is? Nick Ashford?" The audience's derisive snickers masked a kind of terror that mere mortals like us can only dimly understand but that must eat at a man like Murphy day and night. Given how well it evokes the walking dead thing that tends to happen to black superstars, *Vampire In Brooklyn* is, if nothing else, the product of a deep and abiding horror.

Also reviewed in:
CHICAGO TRIBUNE, 10/27/95, Friday/p. C, Michael Wilmington
NEW YORK TIMES, 10/27/95, p. C3, Caryn James
VARIETY, 10/30-11/5/95, p. 70, Brian Lowry
WASHINGTON POST, 10/27/95, p. D1, Hal Hinson
WASHINGTON POST, 10/27/95, Weekend/p. 48, Desson Howe

VILLAGE OF THE DAMNED

A Universal Pictures release of an Alphaville production. *Executive Producer:* Ted Vernon, Shep Gordon, and Andre Blay. *Producer:* Michael Preger and Sandy King. *Director:* John Carpenter. *Screenplay:* David Himmelstein. *Based on the book "The Midwich Cuckoos" by:* John Wyndham. *Based on the 1960 Screenplay by:* Stirling Silliphant. *Director of Photography:* Gary B. Kibbe. *Editor:* Edward A. Warschilka. *Music:* John Carpenter and Dave Davies. *Sound:* Thomas Causey. *Sound Editor:* John Dunn. *Casting:* Reuben Cannon. *Production Designer:* Rodger Maus. *Art Director:* Christa Munro. *Set Decorator:* Don De Fina and Rick Brown. *Set Dresser:* Don Watson and Jody Weisenfeld. *Visual Effects:* Bruce Nicholson. *Mechanical Effects:* Roy Arbogast and Bruno Van Zeebroeck. *Costumes:* Robin Michel Bush and Bob Bush. *Make-up:* Ken Chase. *Stunt Coordinator:* Jeff Imada. *Running time:* 95 minutes. *MPAA Rating:* R.

CAST: Christopher Reeve (Dr. Alan Chaffee); Kirstie Alley (Dr. Susan Verner); Linda Kozlowski (Jill McGowan); Michael Paré (Frank McGowan); Meredith Salenger (Melanie Roberts); Mark Hamill (Reverend George); Pippa Pearthree (Mrs. Sarah Miller); Peter Jason (Ben Blum); Constance Forslund (Callie Blum); Karen Kahn (Barbara Chaffee); Buck Flower (Carlton); Squire Fridell (The Sheriff); Darryl Jones (CHP); Ed Corbett (Older Deputy); Ross Martineau (Younger Deputy); Skip Richardson (Deputy); Tony Haney (Dr. Bush); Sharon Iwai (Eye Doctor); Robert L. Bush (Mr. Roberts); Montgomery Hom (Technician); Steve Chambers (Trooper #1); Ron Kaell (Trooper #2); Lane Nishikawa (Scientist); Michael Halton (Station Attendant Harold); Julie Eccles (Eileen Moore); Lois Saunders (Doctor at Clinic); Sidney Baldwin (Labor Room Physician); Wendolyn Lee (Nurse #5); Kathleen Turco-Lyon (Nurse #3); Abigail Van Alyn (Nurse #1); Roy Conrad (Oliver); Dan Belzer (Young Husband); Dena Martinez (Young Wife); Alice Barden (Woman at Town Hall); John Brebner (Man at Town Hall); Ralph Miller (Villager); Rip Haight (Man at Gas Station Phone). *THE CHILDREN:* Thomas Dekker (David); Lindsey Haun (Mara); Cody Dorkin (Robert); Trishalee Hardy (Julie); Jessye Quarry (Dorothy); Adam Robbins (Isaac); Chelsea DeRidder Simms (Matt); Renee Rene Simms (Casey); Danielle Wiener (Lily); Hillary Harvey (Mara at 1 year); Bradley Wilhelm (David at 9 Months/1 Year); Jennifer Wilhelm (Mara/David at 4 Months);

LOS ANGELES TIMES, 4/28/95, Calendar/p. 10, Kevin Thomas

With "Village of the Damned," a sleek and scary remake of the 1960 classic thriller of the supernatural, John Carpenter takes us back to a beautiful Northern California coastal community, the very same Marin County locale seen in his spooky 1980 film "The Fog."

With ease and dispatch, Carpenter acquaints us with key locals in the close-knit town: its doctor (Christopher Reeve), school principal (Linda Kozlowski) and clergyman (Mark Hamill), all of whom are likable, intelligent, unpretentious types. Just as we're beginning to envy the laid-back quality of life in this beautiful and picturesque village, we're stupefied to witness in an instant its every living creature losing consciousness, dropping in their tracks. After several hours in limbo during a sunny afternoon, everyone comes to, seemingly no worse for wear, although there have been some fatalities, the principal's husband (Michael Paré) among them. Soon after the funerals, 10 young women, including a virginal teen-ager (Meredith Salenger), find themselves pregnant.

Into an atmosphere charged with conflicting emotions—people are frightened but also thrilled with the mysteriously simultaneous pregnancies—arrives a federal government epidemiologist (Kirstie Alley), a tart-tongued, chain-smoking loner who suspects that the women have been impregnated via xenogenesis-i.e., by alien beings during that inexplicable blackout.

Drawing upon John Wyndham's 1957 novel "The Midwich Cuckoos" as well as the earlier film, writer David Himmelstein and Carpenter shrewdly treat Alley's opinion almost as a throwaway line, shifting our focus to the larger question of how to deal with the children after they're born—no one takes up Alley's no-pressure suggestion to think about abortion. The infants start demonstrating deadly telepathic powers, including the ability to read the minds of their elders. The youngsters, who tend to pack and seem to share a common mind, are like ultimate Hitler Youths; sober, single-minded, blue-eyed, blond Aryans.

Carpenter's stylish authority is crucial in keeping this lethal predicament and its fast-developing consequences from seeming too implausible to accept. As a result, the children, in their indifference to emotion and suffering, can emerge as symbolic of the effects of dehumanizing media images upon today's youngsters. The film also has subtle and various implications for women's rights and roles and also for the Darwinian theory of the survival of the fittest among competing species. "Village of the Damned" is the kind of supernatural allegory that invites you to find your own meanings in it as well as catching you up in its increasing tension, an effect underlined by the eerie, ominous score composed by Carpenter and Dave Davies.

"Village of the Damned" is a good-looking, well-wrought film with some knockout special effects, some dark humor and crisp portrayals. As fine as the stars are, amid a large and capable ensemble cast, the two standouts are Lindsey Haun as Reeve's icy, brilliant and implacable daughter and Thomas Dekker as Kozlowski's angelic-looking son, the one child among the towheads who suggests the possibility of possessing a capacity for human emotion and compassion.

NEW YORK POST, 4/28/95, p. 41, Bill Hoffmann

If you want a movie designed to give you the creeps, John Carpenter's "Village of the Damned" is a good choice.

A serviceable remake of the 1960 British thriller based on John Wyndham's sci-fi classic "The Midwich Cuckoos," this new production has plenty of eerie moments and enough shudders to provoke a nightmare or two.

The plot is simple. A dark cloud passes over the picturesque coastal town of Midwich, Calif., making its 2,000 residents pass out for several hours.

Soon many of the community's women mysteriously find themselves pregnant and nine months later they simultaneously give birth to babies who appear disturbingly similar.

As they grow, the white-haired youngsters develop unnatural bonds with each other and it's discovered they can read minds and will people to do their bidding.

Dr. Alan Chaffee (Christopher Reeve) finds this out the hard way when his own daughter (Lindsey Haun) wills mom (Karen Kahn) to stick her hand in a pot of boiling water.

Carpenter provides plenty of shock effects like this to jolt the viewer. One macabre scene shows the town after every body has passed out and, in particular, one poor fellow who had the misfortune to faint on top of his barbeque grill.

Shocks aside, the film is at its most chilling when the children, who dress alike and sport the same deadpan expressions, simply march around in pairs terrifying the hapless townsfolk. Their uniformity and evil stares send shivers up the spine.

It turns out the little devils are the products of an outer space germ and plan to take over the world.

With such an unsettling atmosphere, it's too bad Carpenter has to spoil it toward the end with a barrage of typical Hollywood pyrotechnics: ear-splittingly loud explosions, jarring gun play and the usual high-tech bloodletting.

I suppose that's the temptation and pitfall of having a sizeable budget to play with. But Carpenter, who chilled us thoroughly with the low-budgeted "Halloween," should've known better.

In an even more annoying touch, Businessman Carpenter upstages Director Carpenter at the finale, forsaking a satisfying ending to set up the possibility of endless sequels.

I also must make note of the very marginal performance of Kirstie Alley, who plays Dr. Susan Verner, the federal scientist brought in to probe the uncanny phenomenon. Best known as Sam Malone's feisty foil on "Cheers," Alley seems in sore need of a seat at her old bar.

In a thoroughly wooden performance, Alley drifts through her scenes chain smoking, looking bored and appearing as though she drifted into the wrong picture. Somebody get this woman a drink!

NEWSDAY, 4/28/95, Part II/p. B3, Jack Mathews

In 1957, when John Wyndham's novel "The Midwich Cuckoos" was published, and in 1960, when the film adaptation was released under the title "Village of the Damned," its simple story of alien children taking over a small town was made chilling by the fear of both creeping communism and extra-terrestrials.

Audiences brought these fears with them, and those were also reasons for the success of Don Siegel's classic 1956 "The Invasion of the Body Snatchers." Their absence in the space traveling, post-Cold War era renders John Carpenter's remake of "Village of the Damned" as pointless as Abel Ferrara's recent remake of "Body Snatchers."

Without the underlying paranoia, "Village" has barely enough of a story for an episode of "Twilight Zone." Nine months after a mysterious six-hour blackout in the small California coastal village of Midwich, a batch of platinum-haired children with glowing, iridescent eyes is born, and with the ability to both read and control human minds, sets off an epidemic of suicides.

They must be stopped before they mature and multiply, but how do Midwich's Dr. Chaffee (Christopher Reeve), government scientist Susan Verner (Kirstie Alley) and the host families cope with creatures who know what they're thinking?

The mind control in the original story was a clear allusion to the dreaded brainwashing myths of communism. Since we now know they didn't have enough know-how behind the Iron Curtain to wash their socks, it seems the most banal sort of sci-fi gimmick. And the children—nine in the Midwich brood, scores more reported in other hatcheries around the world—are more comic in their appearance and behavior than frightening.

The new "Village" plays as if it, too, were an allegory, but of what, Dennis the Menace? The filmmakers suggest some parallels to the issues of childhood violence in our society, but that's like trying to find something nutritious about a Twinkie after you've eaten it.

The updating done in David Himmelstein's script introduces the abortion debate to a story that necessarily danced around it 35 years ago. During the pregnancies of the Midwich moms, Dr. Verner offers them a choice—cost-free abortions, or $3,000-a-month stipends to go term and raise their possibly mutant babies under the medical care of federal researchers. Out of greed, maternalism or principle, they all opt for life and live to regret it, an analogy that won't be very poignant or useful to either side of the abortion issue.

Carpenter ("Starman," "Halloween") is an able science-fiction/horror film director, and he's made a very slick recreation of Wolf Rilla's 1960 version. But even with state-of-the-art optical effects spooking up the kids' eyes, and the freedom that comes with an R rating, he has duplicated none of the original's compelling eeriness.

Like Ferrara's "Body Snatchers" and a few of the film noir remakes pouring out of Hollywood, "Village of the Damned" is an exercise in self-gratification, an artist showing his love for an inspiring piece of work by reproducing it. The best movies of any genre are products of their time, and the time for this one has long passed.

VILLAGE VOICE, 5/9/95, p. 76, Richard Gehr

Even apart from the creepy, glowing eyes that caused British censors to ban that special effect, the modest 1960 Wolf Rilla science-fiction thriller that inspired John Carpenter's relatively expensive remake displayed an eerie elegance. Novelist John Wyndham's fable of alien children implanted in the wombs of village women during a mass fainting spell occasioned interesting psychic discomfort for at least a couple of reasons: the xenophobic suspicion that Communists were raising "superchildren," and the disquieting concept of women being impregnated by men other than their husbands. The disturbing *Village* happens to be the first movie I remember seeing. It also taught me a valuable lesson: that acting smarter than your parents might be punishable by death.

The new *Village*, on the other hand, hooks into the current baby boomlet. Only Carpenter's parents are suffering from either a cosmic version of the terrible twos, or the worst case of mass postpartum depression ever. David Himmelstein's script transcribes much of the original verbatim, but adds the possibility that one of the little Aryan-headed, fiery-eyed tots is salvageable, i.e., human. And, having manufactured the template for the modern cheap scare with *Halloween,* Carpenter naturally ups both body count and camp quotient. Christopher Reeve, Mark Hamill, and Kirstie Alley—a veritable fanboy walk of fame—all are offed in increasingly excruciating ways. *Village of the Damned*'s message? Kids still slay the darndest things.

Also reviewed in:
CHICAGO TRIBUNE, 4/28/95, Tempo/p. 24, Michael Wilmington
NEW YORK TIMES, 4/28/95, p. C8, Janet Maslin
VARIETY, 5/1-7/95, p. 36, Todd McCarthy
WASHINGTON POST, 4/28/95, p. D7, Richard Harrington

VIRTUOSITY

A Paramount Pictures release. *Executive Producer:* Howard W. Koch, Jr. *Producer:* Gary Lucchesi. *Director:* Brett Leonard. *Screenplay:* Eric Bernt. *Director of Photography:* Gale Tattersall. *Editor:* R.J. Sears and Rob Kobrin. *Music:* Christopher Young. *Sound:* Thomas D. Causey. *Production Designer:* Nilo Rodis. *Art Director:* Richard Yanez-Toyon. *Set Decorator:* Jay Hart. *Costumes:* Francine Jamison-Tanchuck. *Running time:* 120 minutes. *MPAA Rating:* R.

CAST: Denzel Washington (Parker Barnes); Kelly Lynch (Madison Carter); Russell Crowe (Sid 6.7); Stephen Spinella (Lindenmeyer); William Forsythe (William Cochran); Louise Fletcher (Elizabeth Deane); William Fichtner (Wallace); Costas Mandylor (John Donovan); Kevin J. O'Connor (Clyde Reilly).

LOS ANGELES TIMES, 8/4/95, Calendar/p.12, Kevin Thomas

"Virtuosity" is a sleek, brutal techno-thriller that generates nonstop action, but for at least some of us the fun is spoiled by its numbing body count and murky story line. On the other hand, it boasts the kind of elaborate special effects and spectacular production values that chat still come only from Hollywood.

For all its daunting technology and intricate visuals, the film is basically a simple struggle between good and evil and familiar cautionary tale about the dangers of the misuse of technology "Virtuosity" is set in 1999 Los Angeles, where racism, xenophobia and violence are worse than ever. This vision is expressed with confident panache by a vast team of filmmakers headed by producer Howard W. Koch Jr., director Brett Leonard and writer Eric Bernt.

Forget all the technical stuff, however, for the film's real inspiration is in casting Denzel Washington as its star. He brings a crucial humanity to the carnage—and, in turn, gets to muscle most effectively into Arnold and Sly superman territory, doubtless a shrewd career move for a prestige actor. Washington plays Parker Barnes, an LAPD officer serving a long sentence for killing a political terrorist who murdered Barnes' wife and daughter.

Now he's become a guinea pig at the government's Law Enforcement Technological Advancement Center, run by Louise Fletcher in her icy Nurse Ratched mode. He's subjected to its Virtual Reality Criminal Investigation Simulator, heralded as the ultimate police training device, in which he's pitted against the computer-generated Sid 6.7 (Russell Crowe), who embodies mankind's worst traits.

Indeed, when Sid inevitably escapes from cybrspace to become an android rampaging through the streets of L.A., we learn that a loose-cannon programmer had endowed Sid with the traits of some 200 of history's most evil individuals, including Charles Manson, Adolf Hitler and—you guessed it—Washington's nemesis, that deadly political terrorist. What's there to do but to spring Washington to try to catch this man-made monster?

This Paramount production belongs to a long line of movies that tend to distract the viewer with a barrage of technical jargon and impressive gadgetry from the fact that what's happening on the screen is really pretty elementary. What's more, one of the film's key points, raising the question of the role of the media in creating crazed outlaws, has been raised many times before. Yet there's no denying that cinematographer's Gale Tattersall's suitably harsh metallic images are superbly realized or that Nilo Rodis' production design—integrating intricate movie wizardry, a dark vision of the future and a gritty urban present—has remarkable and powerful aesthetic unity.

Washington has the kind of stature and star presence to hold together an often highly improbable chain of events, the most improbable of which is that Barnes' staunch clinical psychologist sidekick (a businesslike Kelly Lynch) would leave her 9-year-old daughter unguarded while she accompanies Washington in the pursuit of Sid.

Crowe's boyish looks set off Sid's maniacal glee effectively in a portrayal radically different from the actor's recent role as a diffident gay in the Australian film "The Sum of Us." "Virtuosity" doesn't always compute, but like last summer's "Speed," it is far more fully realized cinematically than many less commercial, more serious pictures.

NEW YORK POST, 8/4/95, p. 46, Michael Medved

Denzel Washington is such an accomplished performer, who generally picks his scripts so well, that his name above the title of a film usually guarantees a level of cinematic quality—or at least seriousness of purpose.

It therefore comes as something of a shock to find him associated with a piece of glitzy, high-tech junk like "Virtuosity," staggering through the sort of mindless, hyper-violent role more readily associated with the limited thespian resources of Steven Seagal.

Denzel first appears on screen laughably decked out in dread-locks and beard, which he's supposed to have grown in prison where he's serving a long sentence.

The year is 1999, and Washington plays a former L.A.P.D. hero who's been locked away for avenging himself on a terrorist mastermind who brutally killed his wife and daughter. As the film begins, he's hoping to reduce his time in prison by serving as guinea pig for a new virtual reality device that's been designed to train police officers.

This high-tech simulator, allows the users to pursue a computer-generated criminal named Sid 6.7 (Russell Crowe), who combines the personalities of 183 notorious killers—including the murderer of Denzel's family.

Naturally, this super-synthesized-serial killer isn't content to stay confined in his virtual box for long, and soon finds a way to escape into everyday reality. Quicker than you say "Terminator II," this unstoppable "nanotech android" launches into a deadly rampage.

Bullets can't stop him, and even dismemberment is nothing more than a temporary inconvenience, since he only briefly bleeds some glowing blue goop, before shattering glass to use its silicon to assemble a replacement limb.

In response, police take desperate measures: temporarily releasing Denzel so he can catch this force of all-powerful evil. His only assistance in this endeavor comes from a police-psychologist (Kelly Lynch) who, like all police psychologists in contemporary movies, is both beautiful and conveniently unattached.

The rest of the movie is just as formulaic and flimsy as this setup implies with big, bloody confrontations at a series of showy locales, including a trendy nightclub, a high-rise tower, a subway station, a crowded arena during a sporting event and (surprise! surprise!) a TV station during a live nation-wide broadcast.

Director Brett Leonard deploys some reasonably flashy special effects (just as he did in his two previous films "Lawnmower Man" and "The Hideaway"), but they're not enough to fill up all the empty space in the vacuous and predictable plot.

Denzel Washington looks thoroughly uncomfortable every moment on screen—or maybe that's just his attempt to act the part of an uneasy convict on temporary pass to catch a cyber-slaughterer.

As played by the fine Australian actor Russell Crowe (The Quick and the Dead," "The Sum of Us") that slaughterer emerges as a truly diabolical creation—smooth, sadistic and superhuman, with few hints of the indulgent overacting you usually get from such body-count bad guys. It's ironic that this supposedly computer-generated figure is the only vaguely lifelike element in a film that otherwise looks like it's been entirely created by the numbers.

NEWSDAY, 8/4/95, Part II/p. B2, Jack Mathews

Hollywood is entering the era of high-tech computers with a lot of old ideas. "The Net," which opened last week, uses the booming Internet as an excuse to repeat the most threadbare chase story. "Virtuosity," opening today, looks at the world of virtual reality with virtually nothing we haven't seen before.

Every scene in "Virtuosity," directed by "Lawnmower Man's" Brett Leonard, seems to leap out from another movie. "Westworld," "2001: A Space Odyssey," "Terminator," "Invasion of the Body Snatchers," "Batman" and "Last Action Hero" are some of the titles I jotted down while watching it, and I wasn't writing them down as reminders of things I liked.

Virtual reality, for those with computer-aversion syndrome, is a system allowing people to enter a three-dimensional computer world and, with the use of electronic masks and gloves, navigate their own course through it. VR is a breakthrough training system—you can program anything from the human body to an automobile engine and send a trainee inside—and it would seem to be a natural for sci-fi storytellers.

But so far, it's been used as a gimmick for unimaginative Hollywood hacks, a new tool for refitting old formulas, and "Virtuosity" is about as formulaic as it gets. There is a killer loose in 1997 Los Angeles, a character created as a fugitive in a virtual-reality police-training program who, having developed its own intelligence and sociopathic personality (echoes of HAL from "2001"), has found a way to escape into the real world.

Only convict and ex-cop Parker Barnes (a dour Denzel Washington), who had been tracking Sid 6.7 (Russell Crowe) as a guinea pig in VR experiments, can stop him. (That he is ill-prepared for the task is evident from the fact that he spends most of the movie pumping bullets into Sid, even though they don't hurt him.)

Sid—programed with the sadistic tastes of Hitler, Charles Manson, John Wayne Gacy and, by coincidence, the killer of Barnes' wife and daughter—is motivated by nothing more than a desire to murder on a mass scale before a live television audience. There's a hint of a "Natural Born Killers"-style satire on the media and America's passion for violence, but the movie is too silly to be taken seriously on any level.

"Virtuosity" treats its special effects as if they were a movie by themselves. Watch Sid morph back to his original shape whenever he is shot up or torn apart (á la the villain in "Terminator 2"). Watch him hatch in human form in a computer lab (like the pod people in "Invasion of the Body Snatchers"). Watch Barnes and Sid go one-on-one on a rooftop in both the real and fictional worlds (shades of "Last Action Hero").

The special effects are pretty amazing, and Crowe has fun playing Sid as a villain going about his misdeeds with the joy of a child discovering a room full of new toys. The humor Crowe brings to Sid, however, merely confirms my belief that the best way to exploit virtual reality in movies is through comedy. The system stimulates the imagination in ways that are great fun, not terrifying, and the breakthrough movie is likely to be closer in spirit to "E.T." than to "Alien."

VILLAGE VOICE, 8/15/95, p. 47, Gary Dauphin

Without having even seen it, my man Colson pegged *Virtuosity* perfectly by asking me if I liked it better than *Die Hard 3*. (I didn't.) A loud summer action flick in virtual drag, *Virtuosity* is directed by Brett Leonard (cf. *Lawnmower Man* and *Hideaway*) and concerns Parker Barnes (Denzel Washington), a trigger-happy cop-turned convict who faces off against a virtual villian named Sid 6.7 (played by an energetically hammy Russell Crowe). After Sid escapes from a VR police training simulation via that hopped-up next thing is known as nano-technology (a plausible future science explained in the same tone that Star Fleet engineers use to babble about anti-matter containment), Parker discovers that Sid's multiple-personality matrix not only includes iconic baddies like Hitler and Manson, but also the mad bomber who previously blew his wife and daughter to bits. Crowe makes a spirited go of it and Denzel is, as always, a pleasure, but *Virtuosity* is empty at the core, a retread of countless lunatic-on-the-loose scenarios. Director Leonard's skill at deploying effects is in ample evidence in side bits like a pornographic chess program, or the television newscasts with inset windows for foreign language simulcast and his taste in music is commendable (i.e., British trance-hoppers Tricky). But these moments are so subservient to Parker's blandly determined quest to Bring Sid Down that they're soon forgotten. As *Virtuosity*'s release means that the summer of the cyberpunk flick I was so looking forward to in May is over, let's hope things pick up in the fall with the upcoming *Hackers* and Kathryn Bigelow's *Strange Days*, since to date the movie trend of the future has been something of a dud: *Johnny Mnemonic* sank like the rectilinear stone that it was, and *The Net* is a nifty designer jeep (definitely a vehicle, but not very off-road), making *Virtuosity* at best an excuse to take in two hours of climate control.

Also reviewed in:
CHICAGO TRIBUNE, 8/4/95, Friday/p. I, Michael Wilmington
NEW YORK TIMES, 8/4/95, p. C14, Janet Maslin
VARIETY, 8/7-13/95, p. 33, Godfrey Cheshire
WASHINGTON POST, 8/4/95, p. D1, Hal Hinson

WAITING TO EXHALE

A Twentieth Century Fox release. *Executive Producer:* Terry McMillan and Ronald Bass. *Producer:* Ezra Swerdlow and Deborah Schindler. *Director:* Forest Whitaker. *Screenplay:* Terry McMillan and Ronald Bass. *Based upon the novel by:* Terry McMillan. *Director of Photography:* Toyomichi Kurita. *Editor:* Richard Chew. *Music:* Kenneth "Babyface" Edmonds. *Music Editor:* Carlton Kaller. *Sound:* Russell Williams II and (music) Dan Wallin. *Sound Editor:* Tim Chau. *Casting:* Jaki Brown-Karman. *Production Designer:* David Gropman. *Art Director:* Marc Fisichella. *Set Decorator:* Michael W. Foxworthy. *Set Dresser:* William Butler, Howard J. Clark, Tony Gibson, Bill Land, and Denise Ogawa. *Special Effects:* Thomas C. Ford. *Costumes:* Judy L. Ruskin. *Make-up:* Ellie Winslow. *Make-up (Whitney Houston):* Quietfire. *Make-up (Angela Bassett):* Roxanna Floyd. *Stunt Coordinator:* Rawn Hutchinson and Brandon Sebek. *Running time:* 120 minutes. *MPAA Rating:* R.

CAST: Whitney Houston (Savannah); Angela Bassett (Bernadine); Loretta Devine (Gloria); Lela Rochon (Robin); Gregory Hines (Marvin); Dennis Haysbert (Kenneth); Mykelti Williamson (Troy); Michael Beach (John Sr.); Leon (Russell); Wendell Pierce (Michael); Donald Adeosun Faison (Tarik); Jeffrey D. Sams (Lionel); Jazz Raycole (Onika); Brandon Hammond (John, Jr.); Kenya Moore (Denise); Lamont Johnson (Joseph); Wren T. Brown (Minister); Theo (On Air D.J.); Ken Love (D.J. at the Hermosa); Graham Galloway (Fireman); Starletta DuPois (Savannah's Mother); Shari L. Carpenter (Savannah's Assistant); Thomas R. Leander (Interviewer); Cordell Conway, Lee Wells, Jr., and Hope Brown (Group at Hermosa Table); Delaina Mitchell (Tarik's Girl Friend); Luis Sharpe (Herbert); Joseph S. Myers

(Security Guard at John's Office); Ezra Swerdlow (Wild Bill); Ellin La Var (Hairdresser); Patricia Anne Fox (Customer at Hair Salon); Wally Bujack (Judge).

LOS ANGELES TIMES, 12/22/95, Calendar/p. 1, Kenneth Turan

Gorgeous stars, drop-dead clothes, glamorous settings: "Waiting to Exhale" has all the trappings of a lush, old-fashioned romantic melodrama, the kind of classic "women's picture" that used to appears periodically in the 1950s, most likely directed by Douglas Sirk with titles like "Magnificent Obsession" and "All That Heaven Allows."

Some things, of course, have changed in the ensuing decades. Standards of sexual frankness are looser, a difference that "Exhale" takes gleeful advantage of, and, more to the point, Hollywood feels able to do something it never has before: build a glossy piece of commercial filmmaking around a quartet of African American actresses.

These changes help add life to "Exhale," a pleasant if undemanding piece of work that is diverting to sit through though it won't stand up to any kind of rigorous examination. In fact, the less seriously it takes itself, the more successful this film is.

"Exhale" is based on Terry McMillan's hugely successful novel (700,000 sold in hardback, more than 2 million in paper) that examined, with much-appreciated frankness, the life and loves of four close female friends living in contemporary Phoenix.

The film (written by McMillan and Ronald Bass) opens with Savannah (Whitney Houston) moving from Colorado to Arizona because "all the men in Denver are dead." Waiting for her in Phoenix, besides a challenging job, are three of her closest pals. They're all, in Savannah's phrase, "waiting to exhale," hoping to feel comfortable enough in a relationship to relax into the long haul.

Gloria (Loretta Devine), a beautician with a rambunctious teenage son, worries about having put on those extra pounds. Robin (Lela Rochon) is a beauty whose good sense in the business world never extends to the men in her life. And Bernadine, Bernie to her friends (Angela Bassett), is in the most trouble of all: Her wealthy husband lets her know on New Year's Eve that he's leaving her and their two children to move in with his white bookkeeper.

Sassy, independent, fiercely protective of one another, these women form a communal safety net, providing the support they all need as they navigate a world overrun by silver-tongued, untrustworthy men who are either married or liars or, more likely, both.

The best and funniest stuff in "Waiting to Exhale" is the women's acerbic outlook on the sexual predilections of the men they become entangled with. Directed with a light-fingered frankness by Forest Whitaker, the comic sex scenes between Robin and the oafish Michael (Wendell Pierce) and Savannah and the self-absorbed Lionel (Jeffrey D. Sams) are enormously funny, showing the kind of relaxed but ribald attitude toward sex few films can manage.

The only thing wrong with "Exhale's" sexual humor is that there isn't nearly enough of it. Because, except for an involving interlude between Bernie and a civil rights lawyer named Carl (an unbilled cameo by Wesley Snipes), the film's serious moments are stiff, standard and not nearly as affecting as what's accomplished with comedy.

This is only the second time behind the camera for actor Whitaker (the first was the much different "Strapped" for HBO), and sometimes his style is so laid-back, it feels as if no one is directing at all. "Exhale's" pace is so leisurely and undemanding that a beginning actress like Houston doesn't make that different an impression than a top-drawer professional like Angela Bassett.

Grounded in a smooth, wall-to-wall soundtrack written by Kenneth "Babyface" Edmonds and performed by numerous artists, "Waiting to Exhale" is easing listening for the eyes if you're in the mood and aren't too demanding. A good man may or may not be hard to find, but films about the search will always find an audience.

NEW YORK POST, 12/22/95, p. 45, Thelma Adams

"Waiting to Exhale" is a call-and-response movie:
• "Go, girl," the audience cries out when housewife Bernadine (Angela Bassett) torches her husband's BMW after he leaves her for another woman on New Year's Eve.

● "That's your mama," scolds the woman behind me when Savannah (Whitney Houston) raises her voice to her mother, and then hangs up the phone. And, wouldn't you know it, Savannah sets aside her struggle for independence and calls mom right back to apologize.

● "Shake it," cheers the woman across the aisle when pleasantly plump Gloria (Loretta Devine) turns her rump toward new neighbor Marvin (Gregory Hines) and walks away. This potential Mr. Right "likes his women with a little meat on their bones."

● "Don't *let* him in," warns a woman down in front when Robin (Lela Rochon)—career woman by day, bad girl by night—considers letting her good-looking, good-for-nothing married man of a boyfriend back into her apartment when he finally claims to have left his wife for real.

Bernadine, Savannah, Gloria and Robin are four Phoenix friends waiting for their lives to turn around, waiting for a real man to come along to make them gasp and abandon their anxieties. While they're "Waiting to Exhale," they're learning how to accept themselves. Sometimes, in an environment of cheating husbands, deadbeat dads and self-involved lovers, it takes a powerful dose of sisterhood to pull things together.

Terry McMillan, whose best seller inspired the movie, has joined with Ron Bass ("Joy Luck Club") to bring it to the screen. Framed between two New Year's Eve celebrations—one crammed with disappointment, the next filled with hope—this tart, funny story follows the quartet during one critical year.

The screenplay's chief flaw is that, although it works scene by scene, it keeps hitting the same notes. Bass and McMillan interweave the themes of the four women but never build a satisfying dramatic arc that's greater than the sum of the actresses.

That said, it's such a rare opportunity to see four attractive, articulate middle-class black women filling the big screen with their spirit, spunk, rage and honesty. It's enjoyable to sit and witness (or join in) on one long, glorious bitch session—fun enough to put up with some narrative wobble.

Forest Whitaker ("The Crying Game") makes his directorial debut and shows himself to be an able actor's director. The unstoppable Bassett ("Strange Days") leads the pack as the angry, upper-class wife who had it all and discovered it wasn't for keeps. Bassett always finds the key muscle in any character and flexes it beautifully.

Houston holds her own against stiff competition. Her star charisma shines through, but it's her naturalness that carries the performance. She knows the delicate call-and-response of girlfriends who step into the role of kin when traditional family fails. She also understands when it's time to step back into the chorus and when to let loose with a solo.

As the quartet stalks what McMillan presents as an endangered species—the real man—they rip into the guys they really meet with gusto. Despite a swoonable cameo by Wesley Snipes and a sympathetic performance by Hines, the men portrayed by Dennis Haysbert, Mykelti Williamson and Jeffrey Sams are tailor-made to complain to your girl-gang about.

"Waiting to Exhale" might stall as a date movie, but as an experience to be shared among girlfriends, sisters, mothers and daughters, I say "Go, girl."

NEWSDAY, 12/22/95, Part II/p. B2, Jack Mathews

Many men, it will come as no surprise to many women, are lousy lovers. But few could be any lousier than the self-gratifying, attention-deficit-disordered, slam-bam, thank you ma'am, "Was it as good for you as it was for me?" bozos who appeared in Terry McMillan's best-selling novel "Waiting to Exhale," and who are riotously reprised in Forest Whitaker's filmed adaptation.

The two scenes where these speed demons appear are nearly identical, but their insensitivity to the women they're with, and the priceless reactions of Whitney Houston's and Lela Rochon's characters, make it a point worth making and laughing about—twice.

In her novel, an assortment of experiences shared by four black single women living in Phoenix, McMillan takes a whip to black men, depicting most of them as liars, users, walkouts, layabouts and selfish cheats. It's tough stuff, and comes from the heart, but McMillan writes with such wit and sense of irony that the men are transformed from objects of scorn to comic monsters.

The film, co-written by McMillan and Oscar winner Ron Bass ("Rain Man"), lacks the energy and skillful characterizations of the novel and, in its obvious attempts to broaden its demographic appeal, much of the anger and colloquial language were softened. Also, where the novel was completely character-driven, the movie is carefully plotted, and its four individual stories of women and their relationships with men are resolved as glibly as a paint-by-numbers picture.

Nevertheless, "Waiting to Exhale" is a breath of fresh air, the first feature in my memory to focus totally on the feelings and views of black women and of the black middle class. Most films about African-Americans in the last few years have been set in urban ghettos, dealing with gangs, drugs and violence, and it's about time to break out.

The four women in "Waiting to Exhale" are best friends Savannah (Houston), a TV producer who's moved from Denver to Phoenix to get away from a dead-end relationship with a married man; Bernadine (Angela Bassett), a wife and mother whose husband has left her for a white assistant; Robin (Rochon), a successful businesswoman and romantic risk-taker who keeps waking up with Mr. Wrong, and Gloria (Loretta Devine), a hefty hairdresser dealing with the needs of a fatherless 17-year-old son, and a long bout of loneliness.

Into each life a new man or two will come, and they are mostly bad news. The exceptions are Gregory Hines' Marvin, a gentle widower who becomes Gloria's neighbor and love interest, and the sentimental businessman (Wesley Snipes) who falls instantly in love with Bernadine, but will not cheat on his dying wife.

Whitaker, an actor known best for his roles as Charlie Parker in Clint Eastwood's "Bird" and the captive American soldier in Neil Jordan's "The Crying Game," follows in the tradition of many actors-turned-directors, inspiring strong performances from everyone in his ensemble cast. He seems overly concerned with structure, and some scenes strain too hard for emotional payoffs. But he clearly has the right sensibilities for McMillan's material.

Bassett, the strongest of the four lead actresses, was given the meatiest dramatic role, and makes the most of it. We are introduced to Bernadine in a scene where her husband announces, as she's getting ready to go with him to a party, that he's decided to take his girlfriend instead, and that he, in fact, wants a divorce.

"Don't make this any harder on me than it is," he says, or words to that effect, and the audience is primed for a scene of sweet revenge when Bernadine loads his expensive wardrobe into his BMW and torches it.

Bernadine, the chief architect of his fabulously successful business, is hurting throughout the movie, but her healing parallels the dawning independence of her three friends. The women aren't giving up men by the time we leave them, but they've taken vows on whom they'll trust, and their newfound strength gives "Waiting to Exhale" a final kick that should make it one of the season's biggest hits.

NEWSWEEK, 1/8/96, p. 68, David Ansen

The crowds of women who made it the No. 1 movie in the country when it opened, *Waiting to Exhale* isn't just a holiday entertainment; it's an oasis in the middle of the desert. And when you're parched, the water doesn't have to be Evian. The success of this adaptation of Terry McMillan's best-selling novel—and the talk-back-to-the-screen relish it elicits from its target audience—is a measure of how neglected the black-middle-class female experience has been on film. Successful black women pop up primarily as window dressing in mainstream movies—think Anna Deavere Smith as a White House aide in "The American President." Small wonder that when Whitney Houston was cast as the object of desire in the amiably trashy "The Bodyguard," the box office exceeded all expectations. Black audiences, oversupplied with images of young, armed men in the 'hood, are hungry for glamorous self-reflections.

The mirror that actor turned director Forest Whitaker holds up in "Waiting to Exhale" is as glossy as those Technicolor women's movies turned out by producer Ross Hunter in the '50s ("Imitation of Life," "All That Heaven Allows"). Whitney Houston's Savannah, driving a silver Firebird, tools into Phoenix, Ariz., to start a new life. Angela Bassett's Bernadine lives in a sumptuous home with walk-in closets big enough in which to park that Pontiac. Lela Rochon's Robin is a dressed-for-success career woman. Loretta Devine's Gloria owns the hip beauty salon where her three friends come to prepare themselves for the quest that dominates this story—the search for Mr. Right.

"Waiting to Exhale" takes its old-fashioned soap-opera formula and refurbishes it for the age of Oprah. What that means is that while the script by McMillan and Ronald Bass serves up moonstruck romantic fantasies, it speaks in the language of self-empowerment and is fueled with an undercurrent of rage. The movie is torn: it wants to celebrate female self-sufficiency, but every woman in it defines herself in terms of men. With two glowingly idealized exceptions (played by Gregory Hines and an uncredited Wesley Snipes), the men these women pursue are woefully unworthy of their love. Boy-crazy Robin is the blindest, careering from crack-snorting Troy (Mykelti Willamson) to pudgy, clumsy Michael (Wendell Pierce) to old unreliable Russell (the actor named Leon). Sleek Savannah has no better luck with self-enamored Lionel (Jeffrey D. Sams) or married man Kenneth (Dennis Haysbert), who says he'll leave his wife.

Bernadine is in the most pain. She's just been dumped by her rich husband, who's trying to screw her out of the fortune she helped him build and has left her for his young blond bookkeeper. Her revenge begins with the burning of his car and clothes. Only the sweet, overweight single mom Gloria gets her knight in shining armor—the mellow widower (Hines) who moves in next door. The two good men in McMillan's tale have either dead or dying wives, and their goodness is revealed by their ability to keep their pants on.

The trouble with the movie's parade of cardboard men isn't just that they squelch any possibility of romantic interest; they make our heroines seem foolishly adolescent for pursuing them. Only when they are in each other's company do we get a glimpse of who these women are. The real juice in this broad, glitzy drama is its sisterly complaint, the heroines' sassy, sexually specific assessment of their romantic plight. But except for one drunken birthday celebration, these four actresses didn't convince me they were inseparable buddies—especially Houston, who seems adrift on her own private cloud. What saves "Waiting to Exhale" from terminal clunkiness is its ability to see the humor in all this misplaced yearning. At such moments, anyone who has ever found themselves furiously pursuing Mr. or Ms. Wrong will laugh with rueful self-awareness at this report from the sexual battlefront.

SIGHT AND SOUND, 2/96, p. 56, Amanda Lipman

Savannah arrives in Phoenix, Arizona on New Year's Eve to start a job as a television producer. She has been asked out to a party by Lionel, a man she knows only from phone calls. But when she meets the handsome Lionel, he turns out to have a girlfriend already. Bernadine is preparing to go out for the evening with her husband, John, when he tells her he is leaving her for another woman. Robin, knowing her married lover Russell will not turn up, settles in for an evening alone at home. Divorced Gloria is also staying in while her devoted son, Tarik, prepares to go out.

The next day, Bernadine sets fire to all of John's clothes and his car. Robin brings home Michael, and persuades herself she could be happy with him until he tries to show her up at work. Savannah is seeing Lionel but is fed up with his lack of drive. Bernadine storms into her husband's office and demands decent alimony. Gloria's ex husband, David, comes to visit and tells her he is gay. Robin starts seeing Troy but goes off him when she discovers he is a cocaine user. Bernie wins her legal battle for alimony. Sitting in a hotel bar, afterwards, she meets James, whose wife has cancer. They go up to her room but end up falling asleep together. Kenneth, Savannah's old flame, turns up. He is married with a child but wants to get back together with the delighted Savannah. Gloria strikes up a friendship with her new neighbour, Marvin.

On Savannah's birthday, the four women get together. Bernie drunkenly tries to phone John but is dissuaded. Gloria is preventing Tarik from going to Europe with the band he plays in. She argues with Marvin over it but relents. Robin reveals to Savannah that she once fell for a married man, became pregnant and ended up alone and having an abortion. As a result, Savannah brusquely finishes with Kenneth. Bernie receives a loving letter from James. Robin, who is now pregnant again, kicks out Russell. Gloria makes it up with Marvin. The following New Year's Eve, the four women celebrate together.

One of the most interesting aspects of Forest Whitaker's soapily-smooth directorial debut is that its characters inhabit an almost exclusively black, largely successful world. But that is not to say that the film is colour blind. For Bernadine's angriest accusations towards her husband, John, who runs off with a white woman, are that he is white inside and an Uncle Tom. And when Robin goes to a druggy party with Troy, her unease at finding herself in a room full of white people is palpable (in a striking visual metaphor not only is the room itself bleached white but Robin is wearing a white dress full of holes that show her black skin). The four women also have a few malicious remarks to make about white women who steal black men. All four are achievers:

Gloria has a beauty salon; Robin and Savannah are executives; Bernie has done a business Masters. And yet there is a distinct undercurrent of racial division. Then suddenly, as if to smooth out those nasty creases, we are presented with James, the black civil rights lawyer married to a white woman he loves. Tellingly, it is Bernie that he meets.

That encapsulates much of what happens in the film: it raises difficult, thorny issues, then strangles them with the velvet glove of liberalism. Take the friendship among the four women. Three of them patronise Gloria's salon, but it is never explained how well they know each other and what their friendship is about beyond the fact that they all get their hair done and are black. Instead of endorsing its idea that women can have great friendships without men, *Waiting to Exhale* leaves us with a picture of a bunch of isolated women thrown into a meaningless intimacy. Even more importantly, the way they interact seems extraordinary in the circumstances: while Bernie's husband has just left her for another woman, both Savannah and Robin are seeing married men. Yet not once does this create conflict among them. In fact, despite all sorts of areas just panting to be problematic, these women maintain a loving, positive—and deeply unconvincing—relationship.

The plot would have it that *Waiting To Exhale* is about women taking responsibility for their lives. But its avowedly feminist notions and stirring speeches are swamped by its insistence on what is essentially trouble-free glamour. The film's innate conservatism is highlighted visually in the fact that a closeup of Savannah putting on her make up at the start is lingered on with almost fetishistic adoration, while her boyfriend Lionel's session in front of the mirror is laughed off as vanity.

If the men are all foolish or devious, or both (with the exception of the eerily perfect James), at least they are consistently entertaining. As far as the women are concerned, it is only when they are allowed to be seen as less than iconic—that is, not in relationship to one another—that the film really gets going. Angela Bassett, who turns in quite a powerful performance as the grieving avenger Bernie, has one magnificent, manic scene, in which, without makeup and expensive clothes, she becomes a whirling dervish, throwing out her husband's extensive wardrobe and setting fire to it. The intensity of the situation is fired by sudden, thriller-style close ups. The first of two funny sex scenes, Robin's inwardly uncertain seduction of her colleague Mike, is a fine piece of tragi-comedy, filmed largely from her point of view as the fat man bobs up and down on top of her, shouting, while she desperately tries to pretend to herself that she really wants him.

Whitaker goes all out for giant closeup shots, giving an effect of intimacy that, unfortunately, is rarely matched by the substance of the film. When those close-ups move from head shots to hands, the film moves dangerously into the realm of the soft-focus advert. The notion of the title, that the foursome are holding their breaths, waiting for the moment when they find the right men and can exhale, gets lost before it goes anywhere—but perhaps that is just as well.

Because this is supposed to be a sassy, somewhat rebellious film about women really being themselves, Whitney Houston—far more lively here than she was in *The Bodyguard*—is often cutely raunchy. But just like the film itself, she can also be unbearably sanctimonious—tenderly chiding her friends for their lack of insight. And instead of full-on drama, we are left with too many gentle threats of a very unsatisfactory togetherness.

TIME, 1/8/96, p. 72, Richard Corliss

She has the scariest eyes in movies. They can radiate pain or anger with the immediacy of a lightning flash and the intensity of a witch's curse. Angela Bassett should be cast as Medusa or Medea, but because she is a movie star, she plays righteous cops and sanctified wives. She ought to be in terrific films; instead she appears in mediocre ones, where she stands out like Callas singing *Feelings* and shines like her own amazing, reproachful eyes.

Bassett does all the heavy emotional lifting in *Waiting to Exhale*, based on Terry McMillan's best seller. It's the old story—as old as *Four Daughters* in the '30s or *The Best of Everything* in the '50s or *Now and Then* last fall—about a quartet of young females looking for love and identity. Here the setting is Phoenix, Arizona, and the women are black, but everything else is familiar. Bernadine (Bassett) finds that her longtime husband is deserting her; Savannah (Whitney Houston) has a lover who won't leave his wife; Gloria (Loretta Devine) can't get her bisexual ex-husband into bed; and Robin (Lela Rochon) shacks up with a virtual Fiesta Bowl Parade of losers.

The men are all rotters except for two perfect guys (Gregory Hines and Wesley Snipes) who are ennobled by watching their good wives die.

Like most soap operas, this one wins hot tears from its audience by imagining the worst things that could happen to decent people. It ties its women to the railroad tracks of caprice and invites us to watch as a betraying beau comes chugging toward them. *Waiting to Exhale* doesn't have the idiot vigor to become a camp classic like the movie *Valley of the Dolls*. Forest Whitaker, a laid-back actor who directs this slow-fuse movie, lets his divas strut, smolder and tell off the skunks they once loved. This ain't art—it's more like tasty junk food. And Bassett provides the special sauce.

VILLAGE VOICE, 12/26/95, p. 66, Lisa Kennedy

The voice on the phone machine at the other end of the country was not that of the sister I was looking for. Still her message said it all. In the nicest, we-are-family voice, she said, I'm not home right now, but you can leave a message after the beep." Pause. In the background, Whitney shooped, shooped, shooped. "And sisters, remember to exhale." Beep.

Even more than her best-seller, the much anticipated screen adaptation of Terry McMillan's *Waiting To Exhale* balances its mini tales of romantic misadventure with a consistent vision of female friendship. Of sistahood. And for that we should all breathe a little easier. Phoenix gals Bernadine, Savannah, Gloria, and Robin may go through the few highs and frequent lows of hetero love African American style, yet it is their fondness for each other that anchors them and this often entertaining movie. Less biting as well as less complex than its namesake, *Waiting To Exhale* is a hoot (and only about 10 minutes too long).

Of course, there are many reasons why the movie must be playful, some of them cinematic (having to do with the telescoping of books to film) and some of them communal (as in, there is a place for no-holds-barred conversations about the goings-on between brothers and sisters, and then there is Hollywood). Scenes from the bedroom wars that in the book were at best bitterly funny have become the stuff of high comedy. The scamming, lying, cheating, arrogance of some of the brothers, particularly those who show up at immature Robin's door, is so transparent and the use of knowing voice-over to articulate female experience so apt that the brilliant absurdity of postmodern courting is undeniable.

Nearly all of *Exhale*'s versions of doggishness are an invitation for everyone to laugh. Nearly all but not quite; the fact that Bernadine's wealthy husband John has left her for a white woman carries a special weight in the film (one that existed prior to O.J. and will reverberate beyond that recent debacle). Angela Bassette's first scenes as this decimated spouse working up to a righteous, hysterical revenge are quasi-kabuki in their theatricality, and just as riveting.

That *Waiting to Exhale* asks the question "Where have all the good men gone?" in the same season half a million men tried to answer "to Washington, D.C." might strike a few as out of sync. But with its view of black middle-class aspirations, *Exhale* has more in common with Colin Powell than with Louis Farrakhan. After all, the former's obvious devotion to wife Alma places him squarely outside the dog pound so many *Exhale*'s men inhabit. As for the truth of the contention that there are no available black men, that those not married are druggies, are involved with white women, are gay, are ugly, and so on, I must defer to my straight sisters. But my own reflex is to accept this as the plight of these four characters rather than grant it some grand sociological vérité. Indeed, if there is a moment to *Exhale* belongs, let it be the moment of the reemerging "women's film"—an enjoyable to a year that saw *Boys on the Side, How To Make an American Quilt, Moonlight and Valentino*, to name a few.

There's something old Hollywood, something endearingly retro about *Exhale*, with its two-diva-strong ensemble. (Think of it as a more sisterly version of George Cukor's *The Women.*) While Whitney holds her own as TV producer Savannah in an understated way, hitting just the right note of exasperation and apology when she argues with her mother, it's Angela Bassett who once again commands, the screen in a fashion that doesn't strike one as acting so much as pure presence. Add to these two the divine Loretta Devine as Gloria and a fresh Lela Rochon as Robin and you have one of the most charming ensembles this year.

Needless to say, there is much more to mention about *Exhale*—such is the nature of African American cultural production in the late 20th century. One thing, however, is for certain. In the weeks following this film's opening, a number of talented African American directors with second features in the works—Julie Dash, Leslie Harris, and Darnell Martin among them—will be watching the box office receipts, waiting to exhale.

Also reviewed in:
CHICAGO TRIBUNE, 12/22/95, Friday/p. C, Michael Wilmington
NEW YORK TIMES, 12/22/95, p. C3, Stephen Holden
NEW YORKER, 1/15/96, p. 80, Anthony Lane
VARIETY, 12/18-31/95, p. 66, Godfrey Cheshire
WASHINGTON POST, 12/22/95, p. C1, Hal Hinson
WASHINGTON POST, 12/22/95, Weekend/p. 42, Desson Howe

WALK IN THE CLOUDS, A

A Twentieth Century Fox release of a Zucker Brothers production. *Executive Producer:* James D. Brubaker. *Producer:* Gil Netter, David Zucker, and Jerry Zucker. *Director:* Alfonso Arau. *Screenplay:* Robert Mark Kamen, Mark Miller, and Harvey Weitzman. *Based on the 1942 film "Quatro passi fra le nuvole," story and screenplay material by:* Piero Tellini, Cesare Zavattini and Vittorio de Benedetti. *Director of Photography:* Emmanuel Lubezki. *Editor:* Don Zimmerman. *Music:* Maurice Jarre. *Music Editor:* Dan Carlin, Sr. *Sound:* José Antonio Garcia and (music) Shawn Murphy. *Sound Editor:* Don Hall. *Casting:* John Lyons and Christine Sheaks. *Production Designer:* David Gropman. *Art Director:* Daniel Maltese. *Set Designer:* Robert Fechtman. *Set Decorator:* Denise Pizzini. *Set Dresser:* Mara Massey and Emilio Ricardo Aramendia. *Special Effects:* John McLeod and Bruno van Zeebroeck. *Costumes:* Judy L. Ruskin. *Make-up:* Julie Hewett. *Stunt Coordinator:* Jake Crawford. *Running time:* 100 minutes. *MPAA Rating:* PG-13.

CAST: Keanu Reeves (Paul Sutton); Aitana Sanchez-Gijon (Victoria Aragon); Anthony Quinn (Don Pedro Aragon); Giancarolo Giannini (Alberto Aragon); Angelica Aragon (Marie José Aragon); Evangelina Elizondo (Guadalupe Aragon); Freddy Rodriguez (Pedro Aragon Jr.); Debra Messing (Betty Sutton); Febronio Covarrubias (José Manuel); Roberto Huerta (José Luis); Juan Jimenez (José Marie); Ismael Gallegos (José's Musical Son); Alejandra Flores (Consuelo); Gema Sandoval (Maria); Don Amendolia (Father Coturri); Gregory Martin (Armistead Knox); Mary Pat Gleason (Bus Driver); John Dennis Johnston and Joseph Lindsey (Louts); Mark Matheisen (Soldier); Macon McCalman (Conductor); Ivory Ocean (Truck Driver); Fred Burri (Swiss Yodeller); Stephanie Maisler (USO Woman); Brad Rea (Soldier); Joe Troconis (Man at Gate); Loren Sitomer (Ten-year-old Boy).

LOS ANGELES TIMES, 8/11/95, Calendar/p. 1, Kevin Thomas

Alfonso Arau's romantic fable "A Walk in the Clouds", is so confounding a miscalculation that its every development causes your jaw to drop in sheer amazement.

Had this tempestuous love story been set in the immediate aftermath of World War I instead of World War II and been made then as a silent movie, it might have become a classic in a form and in an era more congenial to extravagant melodrama and patent make-believe. "A Walk in the Clouds" has an uncanny similarity to the equally misfired "A Time of Destiny," the largely forgotten '40s saga Gregory Nava made for Columbia release between "El Norte" and "My Family."

Considering the artificiality of "A Walk in the Clouds," it is astonishing to consider that it is based upon Alessandro Blasetti's 1942 more modest "Four Steps in the Clouds," which has been described by the late film historian Ephraim Katz as "a marvelously restrained tender romance which is widely acknowledged as an important forerunner of Italian neorealism." (Fernandel starred in a 1957, French remake, "The Virtuous Bigamist.")

"Restrained" is the last word that could describe "A Walk in the Clouds," the first English-language feature from Arau, whose wonderful "Like Water for Chocolate" became the top-grossing foreign film of all time. "Clouds'" sheer gorgeousness, full-bodied Maurice Jarre score and deliberately obvious use of sets and matte shots announce right off that we've entered a "magic realism" universe.

The film begins with returning Paul Sutton (Keanu Reeves) discovering the enormity of the mistake of his quickie wartime marriage to a floozy (Debra Messing)—shades of Dana Andrews and Virginia Mayo in "The Best Years of Our Lives."

Aboard a train bound for Sacramento from San Francisco, the fleeing Paul "meets cute"—an old Hollywood term for two young people colliding with each other, dropping stuff and discovering mutual attraction as they pick it up—a beautiful young woman, Victoria Aragon (Spanish actress Aitana Sanchez-Gijon).

She's heading for home in Napa Valley, where her aristocratic family, which can trace its ancestry back 400 years in Mexico, owns vineyards. Victoria is facing the unthinkable: telling her ultra-traditional father that she is pregnant but unmarried. Paul gallantly insists on passing himself off as her bridegroom, but there is that ticklish problem of his own marital status.

The Aragon holdings prove to be a virtual Shangri-La, as vast as the eye can see and dominated by an estate that could easily be mistaken for one of Father Serra's grandest missions. Presiding over this kingdom is no gentle High Lama but Victoria's bombastic father, Alberto (Italian actor Giancarlo Giannini), threatening to remain in a permanent state of apoplexy over his beloved daughter's surprise "marriage." Not even family patriarch Don Pedro (Anthony Quinn), given to endless dispensing of wisdom, can calm him down.

Even so, life *chez* Aragon seems a near-nonstop fiesta, as the family joyfully joins in picking grapes, with Victoria's grandmother (Evangelina Elizondo) even giving her ancestral Aztec blessing on the harvest. All this is so determinedly exuberant, so self-consciously folkloric, that it seems relentlessly contrived and not just a little silly. (Never mind that the family's accents don't match or that it's odd that any generation after Don Pedro should have an accent.)

Arau simply makes too many demands upon our capacity to suspend disbelief. That's too bad, because Reeves and the exquisite Sanchez-Gijon are themselves enchanting young lovers we're able to care about. The irony is that had "Like Water for Chocolate" been only half as successful and consequently Arau been given half as much money with which to indulge himself, "A Walk in the Clouds" just might have been twice as good.

NEW YORK POST, 8/11/95, p. 35, Michael Medved

"A Walk in the Clouds" may be the most maddening movie of the year, not because it's bad (it's actually elegant and intriguing for most of its running time) but because it's utterly ruined by an ending so atrocious, so insipid that it makes you question all the good work that's gone before.

Enduring the horrendous hokum of this finale is worse than watching some sore-armed relief pitcher come into a game in the ninth inning and blow a big lead.

Just imagine that the pitcher not only blows the game but proceeds to burn down the entire stadium.

That's actually an appropriate analogy, because this clunker of a climax involves an implausible and shabbily staged fire that consumes everything around it and leaves the entire picture in ashes.

Before the frustrating flames, Keanu Reeves is surprisingly effective as a soft-spoken, emotionally wounded GI who returns from World War II to a wife in San Francisco he scarcely knows (Debra Messing).

At her insistence, he resumes his pre-war job as a traveling chocolate salesman—a not-so-subtle reference to director Alfonso Arau's previous film, "Like Water for Chocolate," which sold like candy around the world.

In any event, on his first road trip Reeves meets a graduate student named Victoria (soulfully played by the ravishing Spanish actress Aitana Sanchez-Gijon) who's returning to her aristocratic Mexican-American family in their Napa Valley vineyard.

She confesses that she feels deathly afraid to admit to her father (Giancarlo Giannini) that she's pregnant, and that the father of the child, one of her professors, has no intention of marrying her.

Reeves nobly offers to rescue the stranger by coming home with her and posing for one night as her husband. Then the next morning he'll run off—having at least provided some explanation for the pregnancy and saving the family's honor. The problem is that Victoria's passionate clan makes it hard for him to leave—especially her earthy, eccentric grandfather (Anthony Quinn), who becomes Reeves' drinking buddy and romantic adviser.

Director Arau uses the "magical realism" style he popularized in "Chocolate" to portray the impossibly lush vineyard as a mystical Shangri-La, providing gorgeous sequences showing the protection of the vines against a midnight frost, ceremonial dancing on the grapes, and a drunken, moonlit serenade beneath Victoria's window.

At the same time, his hero is animated by a rare, old-fashioned code of honor—despite the slow, sensual seduction, Reeves won't have sex with Victoria while he's officially married to someone else.

It's easy to fall under the hypnotic spell of the film, feeling slightly tipsy from all the wine-drenched romanticism, but then the ending hits you with all the force of a cold shower the morning after.

Sobered up, you begin to spot faults you'd forgiven before—like the fact that nearly all Victoria's family members are mugging, overacting caricatures. By the end of the picture you even begin to expect Rod Steiger might walk in at any moment playing yet another "colorful" uncle—a sure sign that despite sweet beginnings, this movie brings in a bitter and disappointing harvest.

NEWSDAY, 8/11/95, Part II/p. B2, Jack Mathews

Alfonso Arau's directing career started in his native Mexico 28 years ago, but it wasn't until his sensual 1992 romantic fantasy "Like Water for Chocolate" that his name became internationally known.

"Like Water," adapted from his wife Laura Esquivel's best-selling novel about food, love and the connection between them, grossed more than $21 million in the United States alone, making it the most popular foreign-language film ever imported to this country. Its success also assured that his next film, whatever it turned out to be, would be one of the most anticipated movies of whichever year it arrived.

Well, it's arrived, its name is "A Walk in the Clouds," it's in English and, though it isn't quite as enchanting as "Like Water," it's terrific. Sentimental, sunny, romantic, magical and as improbable as a cow jumping over the moon, "A Walk in the Clouds" is an almost dream-like movie-going experience. If nothing else, its title should earn it some sort of award for truth in advertising.

The entire movie, about the romance between a World War II veteran (Keanu Reeves) and a pregnant woman (the beautiful Spanish actress Aitana Sanchez-Gijon) he meets on a train bound for northern California, is awash in storybook colors and images. The vineyard of Victoria Aragon's proud family of Mexican-Ameri-can wine-makers looks less like a vineyard than like a drawing you'd see on the label of a fine bottle of Bordeaux.

The Aragons' picturesque Mission-style home, and its surrounding vineyards, are nestled in an emerald-green valley under a sky whose color scheme rotates from powder blue to crimson red to moonlit sparkle. If you're looking for realism, Arau, seems to be saying, go pick a fight with your mate.

"A Walk in the Clouds" doesn't reach for any sort of authentic look; it merely evokes the postwar period, when veterans returned home with wildly exaggerated expectations and ended up going through adjustments almost as severe as going to war. For Reeves' Paul Sutton, who grew up an orphan, the thought that kept him going on the battlefield was the woman he'd met and married during one impetuous weekend, and who fails to meet his ship because she hasn't read any of his letters.

Betty Sutton (Betty Messing) is clearly a floozy, with a trunk full of unopened letters from GIs, but Paul's combination of loneliness and honor will keep him faithful, long after he has met the real woman of his dreams on that train.

The clever script, written by too many people to list, uses a sliver of an idea to open up a wealth of cultural experience. After learning of Victoria's plight—she's been made pregnant by a philandering professor at the college she's attending—Paul offers to go with her to her family's vineyard and pose as her husband, to save her from the wrath of her proud father (Giancarlo Giannini). The charade gradually grows into a commitment, as Paul warms to the charms of Victoria and her openly romantic and wise grandfather (a wonderful Anthony Quinn), and decides to force her petulant, emotionally aloof father to stop judging his daughter and learn to love her.

The elements of magical realism that made "Like Water" such a joyous surprise are here too. Arau knows how to use the tastes and textures of nature to heighten sensuality, and you don't know how horny squashing grapes with your bare feet can make you feel until you've been in the tub with Paul and Victoria.

Arau even manages to turn an exhausting rescue mission—the workers saving the grapes from an overnight frost—into a balletic courtship dance, with Victoria and Paul, inches apart, waving huge hand-held fans in slow, synchronous movements. I don't know how butterflies mate, but I hope it's like this.

The magical realism, the sometimes impossible blend of romantic fantasy and reality, overstretches itself occasionally. Arau has made Paul's wife such a dithering bimbo that his faithfulness to her seems less noble than silly, and the melodrama near the end seriously threatens the mood.

Still, "A Walk in the Clouds" is as fresh a love story as you'll see in a while, probably until Arau's next film.

SIGHT AND SOUND, 11/95, p. 53, Paul Burston

Northern California. The 1940s. When young GI Paul Sutton returns home from the war, he is a changed man. Haunted by nightmares of a bomb devastating an orphanage, by day he dreams of building a new life for himself and his young wife Betty.

She, on the other hand, is quite happy with the old one. Refusing to take his change of heart seriously, she pressures him into resuming his old job as a travelling chocolate salesman.

While he is on his travels, Paul runs into Victoria Aragon, the beautiful, pregnant and unmarried daughter of a vineyard owner. Traumatised at the thought of what her father will say, Victoria leans on Paul's shoulder and promptly throws up. Unperturbed, Paul offers to help her face her domineering father by posing as her husband. Flaunting matching fake wedding bands made from chocolate wrappers, the two arrive at the family vineyard and are warmly welcomed by everyone. Everyone, that is, except Victoria's father, who harbours suspicions that things are not quite as they seem, and resentment that his only daughter appears to have married a man without a respectable past (Paul is an orphan) or a promising future.

Befriended by the kindly family patriarch Don Pedro, who develops a taste for Paul's confectionery, Paul abandons his original plan of sneaking off and stays at the Aragon vineyard. As the harvest ritual begins, he and Victoria gradually fall in love. Paul, however, is torn by his sense of duty to his real wife Betty. When Victoria's father suddenly announces a big party to celebrate his daughter's wedding, it is time to come clean. Paul returns home, and Victoria is left to patch things up with her brooding papa.

Back home, Paul discovers Betty in bed with another man. Realising that Victoria is the girl for him after all, he hot-foots it back to the vineyard, where a sudden fire gives him the chance to prove his loyalty to the Aragon family. When the fire all but destroys the vineyard, it is Paul who salvages the one undamaged root, thereby securing the family's livelihood and the approval of Victoria's father.

A Walk in the Clouds, Alfonso Arau's follow-up to the acclaimed *Like Water for Chocolate* is like a chocolate box crammed full of strawberry creams—you know exactly what you're going to get, and there's always the danger that you'll be sick before you reach the end. Things begin promisingly enough, with a gorgeous title sequence reminiscent of 50s Hollywood at its most melodramatic—all sweeping strings and swollen, shining orbs, gradually revealed as grapes (symbol of fertility and, in the case of the man who grows them, of wrath). The scene is set for a tribute to the likes of Douglas Sirk, or at the very least a knowing pastiche of his work.

But that's about as knowing as this film gets. What follows is a plain old-fashioned movie without the charm of being old, or the sense to fashion itself as irony. And unlike Sirk, who had a natural understanding of good melodrama and always ensured that there was some dark psychological truth lurking behind the schmaltz, Arau is all sweetness and light. There is nothing to suggest that things might not work out in time for the final credits. Even the wrath of

Victoria's father is lightened by the love oozing from every other member of the family. It is romance without heartache, melodrama without drama. Confident that Paul and Victoria are going to end up in each other's arms, we hardly care whether they do or not.

That said, the film does have its attractions. Well, one anyway. Keanu Reeves was born to play the soppy Paul. Pretty but vacant, his airhead approach to acting makes him the natural choice for *A Walk in the Clouds*. Part of Reeves' appeal lies in his curious passivity. On screen he's the human equivalent of a black hole, helplessly absorbing everything projected his way. The audience's fascination with him is the fascination of waiting for the moment when he might finally implode.

A Walk in the Clouds is steeped in such moments. Here's Keanu reliving the horrors of war and life in the orphanage. Here's Keanu responding to the news that Victoria is pregnant ("It's a new life coming into the world. That's a miracle in itself.") Here's Keanu serenading his new lady-love whilst under the influence of too much wine. And here—at last!—is Keanu stripping down to his vest for some muscular heroics. At one point during the family conflict, Victoria's mama asks what the problem is. "This is the problem," says papa, gesturing to the dopey do-gooder. He's wrong, though: Reeves may be a disappointment in technical terms, but his star presence is what gives the film its centre.

What he can't do is lend it weight. Nor, despite their best efforts, can Aitana Sanchez-Gijon as Victoria, or Anthony Quinn as Don Pedro. Their roles are too small, their characters too under-developed to have any real impact. In an attempt to pin his flimsy confection of a film down, Arau lays on every hackneyed image of Hispanic love and pride known to man or Madonna. "We are very traditional people," says mama. "This modern world takes a bit of getting used to." But why get used to it at all, when the life you're living is so perfectly quaint?

Paul's motives for wanting to be a part of the Aragon family are obvious. Given the opportunity, who wouldn't swap a life on the road for the golden days and romantic nights, for treading grapes and getting sloshed while the cicadas chirp away merrily and some grinning idiot strums on a Spanish guitar? Unfortunately the viewer isn't so easily seduced. The growing sense of shameless manipulation reaches a natural peak at harvest time, when Paul gets a feel for the land and is rewarded with lingering reaction shots of sunny-faced, doe-eyed peasant women. The man from Del Monte, he say "No!"

TIME, 8/21/95, p. 69, Richard Schickel

It's the year's cutest meet: she throws up on him, and it's love at first hurl. Victoria (Aitana Sanchez-Gijon) has reason to feel queasy: she's pregnant but unmarried and is taking a bumpy train ride home to break the news to her very traditional family, proprietors of a vast Napa Valley vineyard. Paul (Keanu Reeves, whose blankness is used to good effect) has reason to be open to any romantic possibility: it's 1945, he's just been mustered out of the army and has discovered that his hasty wartime marriage was a mistake. Besides, *A Walk in the Clouds* being in the magic-realist vein, a playful fate seems to want them to get together.

After two more accidental meetings, he agrees to pretend to be her husband just for a night, to grant her respectability in the family's eyes, then to disappear. That, you know, is not going to be easy. She is beautiful (and meltingly portrayed by Sanchez-Gijon), her relatives are entertainingly fractious, and he, we discover, is an orphan with a lifelong need for the kind of noisy warmth they generate.

Magic realism dictates, moreover, that they be archetypes: Grandpa (Anthony Quinn) is a lusty old windbag; Dad (Giancarlo Giannini) is an uneasy martinet; Mom (Angelica Aragon) is full of soft romantic sentiment. They also, of course, have a fierce, primitive, mystical relationship with the land that nurtures them. The stranger must embrace the acreage before he can embrace their daughter.

This movie (written by Robert Mark Kamen, Mark Miller and Harvey Weitzman) is slicker and neater than director Alfonso Arau's widely beloved *Like Water for Chocolate*, but the calculated naiveté of its fabulism can be just as irritating. Yet if you're willing to be wowed, there's also a kind of romantic grandeur about the piece, something inspiriting in its sweeping statement of broad, basic emotions.

VILLAGE VOICE, 8/15/95, p. 46, Amy Taubin

Like Lasse Hallström, [The reference is to *Something To Talk About*; see Taubin's review.] Mexican director Alfonso Arau has some crucial gaps in his understanding of U.S. culture. Arau, who directed the vastly overrated *Like Water for Chocolate*, takes the storybook approach again in *A Walk in the Clouds*. Set in the Napa Valley just after World War II, it stars Keanu Reeves as a returning soldier who falls in love with the daughter (Aitana Sanchez-Gijon) of a Mexican wine-producing dynasty. Even with Hollywood's penchant for revisionist history, this is going too far. Not even under the guise of "magic realism" can Julio and Ernest Gallo be transformed into Hispanics and generations of abused migrant labor into members of the family.

In fact, *A Walk in the Clouds* is adapted from a 1942 Italian neorealist film *Four Steps in the Clouds*. Arau changed the family's identity from Italian to Mexican (claiming he felt more comfortable with Mexican culture). Maybe he doesn't realize he's trampling on the reality of California's ethnic hierarchy.

As Paul Sutton, a war hero who grew up in a Midwestern orphanage and craves nothing so much as the security of a properly patriarchal family, Reeves gives his standard young-prince performance. Although similar to Julia Roberts in his physical perfection, Reeves is less expressive an actor—he lacks Roberts's hysterical edge, her ability to rocket instantly from zero to 100 degrees. He moves better than Roberts does, but words do not fall trippingly from his tongue. His voice sounds caramel-coated and he couldn't time a laugh line if his career depended on it. Which it does not. Because for all his limitations, Reeves is more fascinating, as an icon, than Roberts. Maybe it's because he always seems like a stranger in a strange land, maybe it's because he makes masculinity into an act of social courtesy. It's his way of acting polite in public.

Wildly overblown (it's not just the grapes that are purple) and inconsistant in tone, *A Walk in the Clouds* plods though its romance-novel plot toward the inevitable love-conquers-all ending. As a storybook film, it could have taken some lessons from *Babe* (yes, the animatronic pig movie), which is easily the best Hollywood film of the summer. A children's film that adults can revel in, *Babe* is about mavericks and eccentrics, about breaking through stereotypes and received ideas. It has amazing sets that reconcile fantasy with the material world. And when Farmer Hoggett (James Cromwell) and the little pig gaze into each other's eyes, it's like seeing true love for the first time.

Also reviewed in:
CHICAGO TRIBUNE, 8/11/95, Friday/p. C, Michael Wilmington
NEW YORK TIMES, 8/11/95, p. C18, Janet Maslin
VARIETY, 7/31-8/6/95, p. 35, Godfrey Cheshire
WASHINGTON POST, 8/11/95, p. F1, Hal Hinson
WASHINGTON POST, 8/11/95, Weekend/p. 39, Joe Brown

WALKING DEAD, THE

A Savoy Pictures release of a Price Entertainment/Jackson-McHenry production. *Producer:* George Jackson, Douglas McHenry, and Frank Price. *Director:* Preston A. Whitmore II. *Screenplay:* Preston A. Whitmore II. *Director of Photography:* John L. Demps, Jr. *Editor:* Don Brochu and William C. Carruth. *Music:* Gary Chang. *Music Editor:* Sherry Whitfield. *Choreographer:* Aurorah Allain. *Sound:* Adam Joseph. *Sound Editor:* John Phillips. *Casting:* Jaki Brown-Karman. *Production Designer:* George Costello. *Art Director:* Joseph M. Altadonna. *Set Decorator:* Bill Cimino. *Set Dresser:* Charles Scaife. *Special Effects:* David H. Watkins. *Costumes:* Ileane Meltzer. *Make-up:* Stacye P. Branche. *Stunt Coordinator:* Randy "Fife". *Running time:* 90 minutes. *MPAA Rating:* R.

CAST: Allen Payne (Pfc. Cole Evans); Eddie Griffin (Pvt. Hoover Branche); Joe Morton (Sgt. Barkley); Vonte Sweet (Pfc. Joe Brooks); Roger Floyd (Cpl. Pippins); Ion Overman (Shirley Evans); Kyley Jackman (Sandra Evans); Bernie Mac (Ray); Jean Lamarre (Pvt. Earl Anderson);

Lena Sang (Barbara Jean);   Wendy Raquel Robinson (Celeste);   Dana Point (Edna);   Doil Williams (Harold);   Damon Jones (2nd Lt. Duffy);   Kevin Jackson (Deuce);   Viviene Sendaydiego (Vietnamese Woman);   Hank Stone (1st Sgt. Hall);   Velma Thompson (Brenda); Wilmer Calderon (Angelo);   Carlos Joshua Agrait (Carlos);   Frank Price (Mr. Dutkiewicz); Susan Ursitti (Ms. Glusac);   Sharon Parra (Zarla);   Frank Eugene Matthews, Jr. (Mr. Lake); Joshua Armstrong (Marine Recruiter);   Terrence King (Brenda's Lover);   Nicole Avant (Rhonda); Lisa Walker (Pippins' Girlfriend).

LOS ANGELES TIMES, 2/25/95, Calendar/p. 9, Kevin Thomas

"The Walking Dead" is a conventional war picture but with a key difference: It depicts the Vietnam experience from an African American point of view. Although at times awkward and unwieldy, it is marked by the passion and sincerity of writer-director Preston A. Whitmore II, who has created a small group of involving characters, acted persuasively by Allen Payne, Eddie Griffin, Joe Morton and Vonte Sweet, actors of considerable presence.

While on a dangerous mission—it is South Vietnam in 1972—evacuating whatever survivors there may be from an abandoned Viet Cong P.O.W. camp, Marine Sgt. Barkley (Morton), a strong, capable leader, and his men tell their stories via flashbacks. Most of them saw joining the Marines as way of bettering themselves, rising above racism, only to end up in a hell on Earth. There's not much of the familiar anti-war cant or extended commentary on the madness of their predicament; these young men are above all concentrating on simply staying alive.

Griffin is vibrant, funny, cynical and bitter as Pvt. Hoover Branche, who has survived two tours of duty and tries to resist becoming too attached to his fellow soldiers. Payne's Cpl. Cole Evans is a straightforward family man, decent and responsible. Sweet's Pvt. Joe Brooks is a naive 19-year-old who joined the Marines to impress his girlfriend. Griffin and Morton, whose sergeant lives with a terrible secret, are especially vibrant presences.

NEW YORK POST, 2/25/95, p. 15, Larry Worth

"The Walking Dead" is being advertised as the Vietnam version of "Glory"—i.e., the first film to deal with black soldiers in a "Platoon-like" scenario.

So much for truth in advertising. First-time writer-director Preston A. Whitmore II comes closer to the likes of "Superfly," making every white man into a worse enemy than any machine gun-toting Asian.

After all, doesn't an arrogant white commander almost get the whole squad killed in the first five minutes, despite the wise counsel of black Sergeant Barkley (Joe Morton)? And in flashbacks, viewers learn that a bitchy white female realtor refused housing to black Corporal Cole Evans (Allen Payne), his wife and young daughter in the States. Further, a Caucasian butcher arbitrarily fired black Private Hoover Branche (Eddie Griffin) for a minor offense in Detroit.

But wait. There's one honky in the squad: Corporal Pippens (Roger Floyd) is a gangster who joined the Marines to avoid a murder rap. But he turns firepower on his fellow soldiers and sticks a poker through a captive Vietnamese woman's eye, justifying his black cohorts to lead him around on a tether and refer to him as "crazy ass white boy."

Whitmore's lack of imagination and reliance on cliches proves no service to black men either, making them into "The Walking Cliches." Due to circumstances beyond their control, each takes drugs or kills for passion or suffers from too much machismo.

That's not even mentioning the idiotic storyline placing the heroes on a bogus mission to rescue POWs, Orlando locales that look more like Sherwood Forest than North Vietnamese jungles, and a reliance on '60s tunes for any sense of atmosphere.

Finally, amateurish acting from a largely unknown cast indicates that fame and fortune aren't in the immediate future for Allen Payne, Eddie Griffin, Joe Morton, Vonte Sweet and Roger Floyd.

Ironically, the best feature is the title. "The Walking Dead" sounds like a cheap scare flick; and sure enough, it's a bona-fide horror.

NEWSDAY, 2/25/95, Part II/p. B5, David Herndon

It's 1972. It's tough being a black man in America, and it's hell being a black man in Vietnam.

It's "The Walking Dead." It's about what it means to be a man, about what it means to kill and be killed, about watching out for your brother's back. It's about 90 minutes of angry-black-man-goes-to-war clichés, seasoned by about 30 minutes of fairly watchable acting.

Marine Sgt. Barkley (Joe Morton) isn't just a Sarge; he's Rev. The kind of man you'd want in your foxhole. Unless you were Pvt. Hoover Blanche (Eddie Griffin), a street dude with a bad attitude. ("I was broke and I needed a job and your favorite uncle wrote me a letter and I accepted.") He doesn't want to make friends with anybody, especially Lance Cpl. Cole Evans (Allen Payne), a family man who's disillusioned with being "imprisoned in black." Anyone who's ever seen a war movie knows that the likable youngster, Pvt. Joe Brooks (Vonte Sweet), is dead meat.

For a war movie, "The Walking Dead" has a relatively low kill-ratio. It's actually rather talky, and even though the dialogue is creaky, a couple of the actors make the most of their opportunities. Morton comes across as a solid pro, while Griffin steals the show with his foul-mouthed street characterization. He's a guy you hate to love.

If the charms of "The Walking Dead" are modest, so are its offenses. The film indulges in some simplistic racialist pandering to its target audience, but nothing too heinous. Implausibilities abound, but none more inexplicable than the happy face slapped on the ending. The dark tone that prevailed over the previous 89 minutes was another virtue of a film that doesn't have many to spare.

VILLAGE VOICE, 3/14/95, p. 59, Jason Vincz

When you think of films about The Nam—*Full Metal Jacket, Apocalypse Now*—you think bleak. Insanity. Depravity. Death. And you might think that a film about the African American experience in the Asian jungle—fighting a politician's war for an army that until very recently insisted on paleface heroes—would be unbearably bleak.

Well, after *Walking Dead*'s initial firefight leaves only five marines alive, things look pretty miserable. But the omnipresent specter of the VC can't keep our guys from sweet little reminiscences—eventually we get acquainted through cute flashbacks that re-abuse the Motown catalogue and explain in broad strokes how everyone ended up fighting for The Man.

Through all the guts and gunfire, only the cartoonishly high-strung whiteboy succumbs to paranoia, and while the bullets and shrapnel do seem to distress the other characters, none of them gets too hysterical. Where's the angst? Where's the madness? Where's the *Heart of Darkness*, you ask? Maybe that's the point—two tours in Nam is nothing after two decades in White America—but Preston Whitmore's story is so well-paced and so funny (thanks largely to Eddie Griffin) that you never get a chance to *brood* about it. Bodies are merely stepped over, and when the last comrade bites the rice paddy, you barely have time to lament his passing before the happy-ending music starts for the ones who make it out. That ending encapsulates *Walking Dead*'s inflappable make-it-home-for-Christmas optimism, and turns an otherwise brutal story into a good-natured buddy flick.

Also reviewed in:
CHICAGO TRIBUNE, 2/26/95, Tempo/p. 4, John Petrakis
NEW YORK TIMES, 2/25/95, p. 18, Stephen Holden
VARIETY, 2/27-3/5/95, p. 69, Emanuel Levy
WASHINGTON POST, 2/24/95, p. C1, Rita Kempley
WASHINGTON POST, 2/24/95, Weekend/p. 36, Desson Howe

WATERWORLD

A Universal Pictures and Lawrence Gordon release of a Gordon Company/Davis Entertainment Company/Licht/Mueller Film Corp. production. *Executive Producer:* Jeffrey Mueller, Andrew Licht, and Ilona Herzberg. *Producer:* Charles Gordon, John Davis, and Kevin Costner. *Director:* Kevin Reynolds. *Screenplay:* Peter Rader and David Twohy. *Director of Photography:* Dean Semler. *Underwater Photography:* Pete Romano. *Editor:* Peter Boyle. *Music:* James

Newton Howard. *Music Editor:* Jim Weidman.   *Sound:* Keith A. Wester and (music) Bruce Botnick.   *Sound Editor:* Lou Angelo, Simon Coke, Teri E. Dorman, Andy Kopetzky, Larry Mann, Nash Michael, Bob Newlan, Rodger Pardee, Gary Wright, David A. Arnold, Gordon Davidson, Michael Haight, Dave Kulczycki, Chuck Michael, Harry Miller III, Mark Pappas, and Karen Wilson. Casting: David Rubin.   *Production Designer:* Dennis Gassner.   *Art Director:* David Klassen. *Set Designer:* Gary Diamond, Marco Rubeo, Natalie Richards, John Dexter, Paul Sonski, and Darrell L. Wight.   *Set Decorator:* Nancy Haigh.   *Set Dresser:* Paige Augustine and Jimmy Meehan.   *Physical Effects:* Peter Chesney.   *Costumes:* John Bloomfield.   *Costumes (Kevin Costner):* Barbara Gordon.   *Make-up:* Fred Blau, Jr., Tania Kahale-Taylor, Jeanne Van Phue, Ellis Burman, Robert N. Norin, and Martie Scribner.   *Make-up (Body):* Carol Borden.   *Make-up (Special Effects):* The Burman Studio.   *Stunt Coordinator:* R.A. Rondell and Norman Howell. *Running time:* 120 minutes.   *MPAA Rating:* PG-13.

CAST: Kevin Costner (Mariner); Chaim Jeraffi (Drifter #1); Ric Aviles (Gatesman #1); R.D. Call (Enforcer); Zitto Kazann (Elder #3/Survivor #1); Leonardo Cimino (Elder #2); Zakes Mokae (Priam); Luke Ka'ili, Jr. (Boy #1); Anthony DeMasters (Boy #2); Willy Petrovic (Boy #3); Jack Kehler (Banker); Jeanne Tripplehorn (Helen); Lanny Flaherty (Trader #1); Robert Silverman (Hydroholic); Gerard Murphy (Nord); Tina Majorino (Enola); Sab Shimono (Elder #1); Rita Zohar (Atoller #1); Henry Kapono Ka'Aihue (Gatesman #2); Michael Jeter (Gregor); August Neves (Old Atoller); Tracy Anderson (Gatesman #3); Dennis Hopper (Deacon); Neil Giuntoli (Hellfire Gunner); Robert Joy (Ledger Guy); John Fleck (Doctor); David Finnegan (Toby); Gregory B. Goosen (Sawzall Smoker); William Preston (Depth Gauge Guy); Jack Black (Pilot); John Toles-Bey (Plane Gunner); Kim Coates (Drifter #2); Ari Barak (Atoll Man); Chris Douridas (Atoller #7); Alexa Jago (Atoll Woman); Sean Whalen (Bone); Robert LeSardo (Smitty); Lee Arenberg (Djeng); Doug Spinuzza (Truan).

FILMS IN REVIEW, 11-12/95, p. 109, Andy Pawelczak

The most depressing thing about *Waterworld*, a Kevin Costner production directed by Kevin Reynolds, is that it's not even a fiasco on the heroic scale of *Heaven's Gate* (which in retrospect doesn't look that bad)—it's just another mediocre action film with semi-literate pretensions. The hip young couple sitting next to me in the theater came primed to laugh at the picture, but it doesn't have enough faux pas and longueurs for even that ego-building, cheap pleasure. You just sit there tallying up the cost of the sets and special effects, wondering how they spent $170 million—its budget being the movie's main claim to distinction—on a few floating Rube Goldberg-like contraptions and some underwater cinematography.

Waterworld takes place in the not so distant future after the polar ice caps have melted (presumably because of the Greenhouse Effect) and the few remaining people have half-adapted to living on the surface of the ocean. Under such conditions, human society has regressed to a primitive, myth-haunted, tribal level—the movie's characters have names like Priam (Zekes Mokae) and Helen (Jeanne Tripplehorn) and the hero, an Odysseus-like figure played by Kevin Costner, is called simply, the Mariner. Reynolds and the screenplay writers, Peter Rader and David Twohy, have taken the Mad Max movies and transposed them to an aquatic wasteland. Where in *The Road Warrior* the survivors of the apocalypse long for the seashore, here the inhabitants of a vaguely medieval floating town dream of the never-seen, legendary Dry Land. The town is fortified to protect it from the depredations of a gang of barbarians called the Smokers, led by a character called The Deacon (Dennis Hopper), who conduct their nefarious business on hydrofoils—they're the equivalent of the brutish motorcycle gang in *The Road Warrior.*

Enter the Mariner, a kind of high seas drifter who sails into town to trade a handful of dirt, a valuable commodity in Waterworld, for provisions. He's promptly assaulted by a lynch mob for being a mutant (he's got discreet gills behind the ears and webbed feet), saved by the local sheriff, and then tried and sentenced to death by the town's elders. When the Smokers attack, he escapes along with the statuesque Helen and a young girl, Enola (Tina Majorino), with the Smokers in hot pursuit. Enola has a cryptic tattoo on her back that reputedly gives directions to Dry Land, and the rest of the movie involves the Mariner's protection of the child from the Smokers who covet that map.

Smokers and Enola—the very names hint at the picture's larger pretensions. Not satisfied with a simple action movie, Costner and company have given the film an unexceptionable ecological theme that wouldn't keep anyone away from the box office other than the most diehard right-wing fanatics. The Smokers are grungy polluters—their patron saint is Joe Hazelwood, the captain of the Exxon Valdez—and the young girl's name is probably meant to remind us of the Enola Gay, harbinger of the nuclear apocalypse. While the Smokers rampage on motorized vessels and fantasize about developing Dry Land once they appropriate it for themselves, the Mariner plies the seas on an ecologically correct sailing boat. None of this is surprising when you remember the half-baked, sentimental liberalism of Costner's *Dances with Wolves*.

As the Mariner, Costner plays it straight—he has the blanched, shell-shocked solemnity of a wallflower at an orgy. Even frequent acrobatic feats on the boat's rigging don't enliven his performance, and his scenes with Tripplehorn are romantically inert. As the Deacon, Hopper turns in his usual scenery-chewing performance, but at least he seems to be enjoying himself. Swigging Jack Daniels, lifting his arms in a gesture of mock papal blessing, all but winking at the audience, he's a cartoon predator reminiscent of the surreal comic villains in the Batman movies. His performance seems to come from a different film than the one Costner so ponderously inhabits.

Waterworld is the kind of movie in which you pay as much attention to the sets and costumes as you do to the storytelling and performances. For the record: the characters dress in rags that variously evoke medieval jesters, ancient oracles, Barbary pirates, and contemporary denizens of St. Mark's Place, and the sets have an ingenious jerry-built quality appropriate to the film's post-apocalyptic world. The director, Kevin Reynolds, stages the big battle scenes competently, but in between we're adrift in the doldrums. *Waterworld* is an aquatic Western, a mythopoeic epic, a big fish story, an ecological fable. What it's not is a satisfying movie.

LOS ANGELES TIMES, 7/28/95, Calendar/p. 1, Kenneth Turan

"Waterworld" doesn't come with instructions, but it should. Before entering the theater, take a breath and repeat three times, "It's only a movie. It's only a movie. It's only a movie."

Because after spending enough money to retire the national debt of a Third World country and generating more publicity than the fall of Rome, it is something of a reality check to discover that this Kevin Costner-starring epic is neither a fiasco nor anything that in a sane universe would have cost $175 million and counting.

Instead, it is a moderately successful guy's movie with both weak and strong elements where lots of things are brilliantly blown up and few things make any kind of sense. It's summer business as usual, the classic glass of (yes) water syndrome, either half full or half empty depending on your point of view.

One of "Waterworld's" cleverest moments is one of its first, when the camera moves in on the Universal Pictures globe logo as its land masses get slowly submerged, This is the future, a narrator tells us, "the polar ice caps have melted, covering the Earth with water. Those who survived have adapted to a new world."

It's a world whose people can be divided into strata that roughly correspond to the groups that populate traditional Westerns. Most vulnerable are the unadventurous average citizens, who dream of a perhaps mythical place called Dryland and whose towns are enormous man-made atolls (the one in the movie used 1,000 tons of steel) cobbled together out of random pieces of junk.

Making their lives miserable are the outlaws, here called smokers because they tool around on gas-powered Jet Skis, who live only to terrorize the decent. And then there are the lonely, enigmatic drifters whose relationship to pure good and evil is harder to pin down.

The Mariner, played by Costner, is the drifter's drifter, the kind of surly, seafaring curmudgeon who eats eyeballs without blinking and brings conviction to lines like "Killing is a hard thing to do well." He lives alone on his grungy, 60-foot trimaran and spends his life sailing farther, he says, "than most people have dreamed."

Given that the Mariner is introduced urinating into a jar and then drinking the recycled liquid, this character is not the kind of warm and cuddly hero audiences like best. But the biggest surprise of "Waterworld" has to be what an excellent job Costner does of making this hostile, cold-blooded character both believable and a convincing resident of this bizarre environment.

And, as visualized by production designer Dennis Gassner, with assists from art director David Klassen and physical effects director Peter Chesney, the world the Mariner inhabits ranks with Costner's performance as one of the film's most successful creations.

Gassner, an Oscar winner for "Bugsy," is equally admired for his exemplary work ("Barton Fink" and "The Hudsucker Proxy," among others) with the Coen brothers. He and his team have come up with what might, with equal justice, be called "Rustworld," a "Mad Max" on water society typified by that huge atoll, a fierce-looking amalgam of all kinds of scavenged material whose 30-foot walls and impressive gates are meant to keep the rest of the world at bay.

The action highlight of "Waterworld" comes early on, when those pesky smokers, Jet Skis and all, mount an all-out attack on the atoll. Expertly paced and edited, this sequence is alive and energetic, and holds out hope for the rest of the picture that it is not capable of fulfilling.

Given the tangled credit situation on "Waterworld," with two screenwriters (Peter Rader and David Twohy) named and others uncredited and the final editing coming under Costner's supervision after director Kevin Reynolds left the picture at the end of April, it is more difficult than usual to know who is responsible for what here. But whoever was at fault, the intensity and interest that "Waterworld" builds up during its first part gradually dissipates as the running time lengthens.

Finding themselves on the Mariner's trimaran are two characters so generic, it's amazing the script bothered to give them names. Helen (Jeanne Tripplehorn) is the inevitable woman, essential for looking attractive and saying things like "What's going on?" Enola (Tina Majorino) is a mouthy, little girl Helen has adopted who has the key to the plot tattooed on her back. a strange map that may or may not lead to the mythical Dryland.

While these characters are simply uninteresting, many of the others are downright irritating. Most upsetting of all is Dennis Hopper, inexcusably over the top as Deacon, the leader of the smokers who is painfully determined to get his hands on Enola and her map.

Though "Waterworld" has some haunting underwater visual moments, the film's impact is weakened by flat dialogue, an overemphasis on jokeyness and a plot that, despite all those screenwriters, does not satisfactorily hold together at any number of points.

Also not making sense is expending this much money on a film where, if the press reports are to be believed, considerable dollars had to be spent shooting simple conversation scenes that, as far as the audience cares, might as well have been done on a sound stage. Yes, verisimilitude is important, but even in Hollywood, shouldn't cost count for something?

NEW YORK, 8/7/95, p. 70, David Denby

Waterworld cost so much money (perhaps $200 million) that you really can't get indignant about the sum. An *$80 million* budget is an outrage: I'm shocked by anyone's spending that much money on a movie. But a budget of $200 million is beyond outrage; it's a joke, or perhaps a portent of something. The figure is meaningless, since it bears no relation to anyone's need or the audience's pleasure. Why not $300 million? Why not devote all of Hollywood's money to making just one movie each year? The entire industry could be employed in a single billion-dollar production, and critics, their lives made useful at last, could review first the trailer, then the product tie-ins, then the CD-Rom version ...

All right, everyone calm down. I would, however, like to know something from the people who made *Waterworld*—Kevin Costner and his partner in folly, Kevin Reynolds, and the various screenwriters and producers (I shall leave them nameless and spare their parents embarrassment). What is it about water? Did these fellows look at the ocean and offer the mountain climber's rationale for scaling a peak—because it's there? Water may be the most beautiful thing on the Earth (I'll take meadows, myself), but there's a good reason no one ever constructed an entire futuristic world on water before, and the reason isn't simply that it's difficult. People enjoy looking at calm expanses of water because the stuff is soothing, even boring—not as busy, you know, as downtown Tokyo. But what could make anyone think that a stage of shifting liquid without feature or variation, without storms or surf, would be a good setting for an entire movie?

Waterworld isn't a catastrophe. It isn't even bad. But it's not terribly interesting either. The plot has the fatalistic simplicity of an old B-movie. We're in the dreadful future, when the melting of the polar ice caps has covered the surface of the Earth with wet stuff. A few survivors, taunted by fantasies of dry land, hang on to the remnants of the earlier civilization, including the Mariner

(Kevin Costner), a sort of human amphibian, at home on land and on sea, where he breathes through gills behind his ears that bear an unfortunate resemblance to ... Anyway, many of the other survivors live in huge rust-colored "atolls," composed of the floating detritus of the old civilization—pipes, spars, girders, wheels, bits of plastic and rubbish, the pieces joined together in intricate Rube Goldberg machines. The people are mostly cracked, or at least desperate and cruel, and there are raunchy pirates led by Dennis Hopper called "smokers" (they do); they roar into view like demented bikers and attack anything that moves.

Pretty grim stuff. And pretty monotonous, too, since the human relations are rudimentary and the water stretches to the horizon completely. There's only so much you can do on water without beautiful ships or intricate relations of power and love. The filmmakers reach the limits of physical inventiveness after about an hour—Mariner's personal trimaran, made of oil-blackened stovepipes, does everything but fly—and then they are stuck repeating themselves. One senses a constant strain, the anxious labors of technicians setting themselves insuperable "problems" and then grimly "solving" them. Is this true heroism or an elaborate kind of idiocy made possible by money? The floating city that the set designers have so laboriously built doesn't even photograph well: All the intricate levels of it are colored the same rust brown, and one can hardly see what's there. The characters wear ugly fish-skin rags and talk in some nasty melted-ice-cap dialect, and everything is generally dank, wet, violent, and tawdry. (You would think that even if the people are fishy, they would at least be clean.) *Waterworld* has a certain rancid consistency to it, but I wouldn't describe it as fun. Costner runs, jumps, and leaps with earnest determination—there isn't a joke in this man anywhere—and the beautiful Jeanne Tripplehorn, who's stuck with him on the trimaran, nearly turns herself inside out trying to provoke *some* response. *Waterworld* offers adventure without the romance of adventure: Kevin Reynolds has made a grindingly "authentic" version of a world that doesn't exist. To top it off, the director and the screenwriters dare to preach at us: The ice-cap disaster was produced by human excess and greed. On their way to completing the most expensive movie ever made, Costner, Reynolds & Co. must have had plenty of time to absorb the lesson.

NEWSDAY, 7/28/95, Part II/p. B2, Jack Mathews

In the undetermined future depicted in "Waterworld," a time long after the polar ice caps have melted and left surviving humans floating on the debris of the 20th Century, there is good news and bad. There is no apparent land, which is very bad, especially for people with queasy stomachs. On the other hand, there seems to be an unlimited supply of filter cigarettes and Jack Daniels.

Party on, sailors!

With its estimated $180 million budget, "Waterworld," directed by Kevin Reynolds, is both the most expensive movie ever made and the most expensive cartoon. It is not a disaster on the order of "Howard the Duck," Universal's last overreaching humiliation. The floating sets are ingenious bits of tramp art. There are breathtaking stunts and stirring battle scenes. And the film's showcase sequence, an underwater tour of the remnants of a major city, is truly stunning.

But with its wisp of a story and its even greater wisp of an action star—a role that required a Mel Gibson got a Kevin Costner—"Waterworld" will be remembered more for its cost than for its achievement.

It certainly was an ambitious undertaking, shooting a movie almost entirely on the sea, with sets that range in size from a dinghy to a football field. God doesn't issue film permits, and weather problems indeed ran up the tab. But after you become accustomed to this floating society of collectivists, drifters and marauders, you're stuck looking at some of the bleakest people and sets imaginable.

"Waterworld" is a world that might have been designed by Rube Goldberg. People make do on the resources of a junkyard. The rusty hull of the Exxon Valdez is home to the marauders known as the Smokers, who are led by a bald, one-eyed megalomaniac known as the Deacon (played with delicious campiness by Dennis Hopper). The bulk of the other survivors have set up communities on grubby erector-set islands, from which they barter with drifters like the Mariner (Costner).

The Mariner, who has webbed toes and tiny gills behind his ears (both concealed so as not to spoil the star's image), is the requisite loner, using his cunning survival skills to fend off predators and keep himself and his hope—everybody's hope, to find mythical dry land—alive.

The story is comic-strip simple. The Mariner, with the storekeeper, Helen (Jeanne Tripplehorn), and her adopted daughter, Enola (Tina Majorino), in tow, sets out in his weathered trimaran to make sense of the map to dry land that has been mysteriously tattooed on the girl's back. Deacon, after learning of the map, sets out after them, and the chase is on.

Costner was well-prepared physically. He's buff and tough, and admirably athletic in what appear to be some pretty dangerous stunts. But there is that inevitable Costner problem—no core substance—and it becomes more noticeable as the Mariner's personality undergoes a massive change. He starts out as the classic outsider—brooding, stone-faced and emotionally aloof, downright cruel to Helen and Enola. But before you know it, he's turned into a big old lovable lunk—a man's man, a woman's man and an orphan's dream dad.

None of these characters are developed enough to support the intended sentiment. The romance growing between the Mariner and Helen is so dispassionate, especially at the crucial moment, that you have to wonder what his interest would have been if he hadn't been to sea for 30 years.

What made the "Mad Max" movies ("The Road Warrior" was the second of four) compelling was Max's history, the fact that he was a cop who became emotionally isolated after his wife and child were murdered by roving cyclists. The Mariner has no history; he seems to have merely appeared, like a barnacle attached to the hull of a ship.

"Waterworld" was a movie waiting to be stolen, and Hopper heartily obliged. He's been playing variations of this psychotic villain for years—as recently as last year's "Speed"—and he handles the role like a vaudevillian dancing around his hat. He's an old pro. "Waterworld" needed more of them.

NEWSWEEK, 7/31/95, p. 52, David Ansen

Waterworld is a pretty damn good summer movie.

There, I've said it.

The world, and Universal Pictures, can take a deep breath. The most expensive movie ever made—estimates range from $172 million to $200 million—is actually fun. And "fun," Lord knows, is the bottom line of that corporate invention known as the summer movie—a concept, like cyberspace, we didn't ask for, but which has become a permanent part of the American landscape.

"Waterworld," as you may have heard, has no landscape. It is set far in the post-apocalyptic future, after the polar caps have melted, burying the world as we know it under water and turning the horizon into an unending scape of sea. The survivors, floating on man-made atolls or navigating on boats, have become desperate scavengers, bartering and sometimes killing each other to obtain whatever meager detritus of the old world they can find. In *Waterworld*, pure dirt is as good as gold. This funky, rusty, dystopian vision will be instantly recognizable as a descendant of the junk-pile futurism of the "Mad Max" series.

But director Kevin Reynolds has found a jaunty, comic-book epic tone he can call his own, however derivative the elements. From our first glimpse of the hero (Kevin Costner), a strong, grouchy, silent type known as the Mariner, the movie lets us know it possesses some convention-tweaking wit. Shot from behind at a heroic low angle, the Mariner's first act is to piss in a plastic pot. He funnels the liquid through a Rube Goldbergish contraption, fills his mug with his purified urine and takes a swig. I'll take my hat off to any $200 million movie that gives me that for openers.

The Mariner sails his souped-up trimaran (a wonderful creation, this boat) into a floating city that is one of production designer Dennis Gassner's triumphs. (This fortresslike slag heap, built out of 1,000 tons of steel, alone cost a reported $5 million; it had to be rotated in the seas off Hawaii so that, from whatever angle a scene was shot, no glimpse of land appeared in the background.) Here Reynolds stages the first of "Waterworld's" several nifty action set pieces. The local Atollers are about to put Costner to death, thinking he's a spy, when they're attacked by the movie's piratical villains, the Smokers, led by the scurvy, bald-pated Dennis Hopper. Leaping over the city's parapets on water skis, the Smokers have a wild arsenal of makeshift weapons at their command. Rescued by Atoll dweller Helen (Jeanne Tripplehorn) and her adopted daughter

Enola (Tina Majorino), Costner must flee the besieged city with girl and woman in tow, while using his trusty harpoon gun to turn the attacking Smoker guns back on themselves.

It's a fiendishly complicated action sequence that Reynolds choreographs with real flair—unlike, say, the incoherent mayhem in "Batman Forever." That squalling summer cartoon quickly grew tedious—it was always in your face—but "Waterworld" doesn't wear out its welcome. It's well paced, and it never feels cluttered, no small thanks to the sea itself, which gives the story vast, gorgeous room to breathe.

The story is simple enough, really. Little Enola has a map tattooed on her back, which some believe can lead them to Dryland. But no one can decode it. The Smokers (who always have cigarettes dangling from their lips) want to get their hands on the girl—and get revenge on the Mariner. Will he, Helen, and Enola make it alive to Dryland—if it exists?

Now, "Waterworld" is not a tale one wants to examine too closely. Presumably it is set very far in the future, for the Mariner has had time to actually mutate into a new species—he's got webbed feet and little gills behind his ears. (Boy, can this guy swim!) But I kept thinking the Smokers' prediluvian cigarettes must be getting mighty stale by now. And what about those vintage airplanes that keep appearing? How are they still flying? But there's really no point in pursuing such questions: you'll have a much better time if you just play by the story's dotty rules.

Some weaknesses are not so easy to overlook. The screenwriters (Peter Rader and David Twohy get the credit, though other hands were involved) come up with some fairly hip satirical notions, but their heroine, Helen, is unaccountably lame, a throwback damsel who's semi-helpless in distress. Tripplehorn can't do a thing with the part, and the romantic spark between her and Costner is all wet. The more satisfying love story is the paternal one between Costner and Majorino, at 10 already a delightfully accomplished scene stealer. Though kids will probably love the comically scurrilous villains, who come on like a pack of over-the-hill bikers, this trope is getting pretty threadbare. And casting Hopper as a cracker Napoleon who rants about "manifest destiny" doesn't show much imagination. He could do wild-eyed megalomania in his sleep, and if he does it one more time, we'll all be dozing.

Costner has long since mastered the movie-star art of making a little go a long way. Beyond taciturn, his Mariner is a moody, uncivilized, selfish s.o.b., who tosses kids in shark-infested waters, thwacks his leading lady with an oar and barters her body to a popeyed, cuckoo scavenger for a few pieces of paper. The drollery of Costner's performance is his dare that we will fall for this brooding lout, which of course we do. His cool, collected charisma is always on the edge of clumsy, but it's real, and it works.

As does "Waterworld." It's not a great, edge-of-your seat action movie: for sheer kinetic excitement, Reynolds isn't in the same class as George ("The Road Warrior") Miller or James ("Terminator 2") Cameron. But it's a breezy, clever entertainment with stirring effects. The public, thanks to the media, knows just what hell it took to get this water-bedeviled adventure onto the screen: the 166-day shoot, a near-fatal accident, sinking sets, last-minute reshoots and the feud between director and star. The nice thing is that the movie itself doesn't show the signs of flop sweat and panic. It wants to give us a good time, and, by and large, it does just that.

Should we care that MCA/Universal was wacky enough to spend this kind of money (more, for what it's worth, than the entire budget of the National Endowment for the Arts)? The movie will practically have to break records just to break even. Sure, it's profligate, but it's not taxpayers' money. And the ramifications of the "Waterworld" affair are nothing compared with the fallout that accompanied the runaway budgets of "Heaven's Gate" and "Cleopatra." MCA, recently purchased by Seagram from Matsushita, is still sitting pretty, and its new owners have cleverly managed to unload the bulk of the movie's cost onto the Japanese. In contrast, Cimino's Western brought down United Artists, and the "Cleopatra" fiasco literally changed the face of Los Angeles. Right next to Beverly Hills sit the gleaming towers of Century City, built on what was once the back lot of 20th Century-Fox, and sold off by the studio to pay off its massive "Cleopatra" bills. Now those are consequences. There's only one sure lesson Hollywood will take from the money pit that was "Waterworld": only shoot movies when there's dirt under your feet.

SIGHT AND SOUND, 9/95, p. 62, José Arroyo

Sometime in the future, the polar ice caps have melted and the entire known world has been flooded. A lone Mariner goes into the Atoll (a floating settlement made out of scrap) to trade some handfuls of dirt, the most valuable commodity in Waterworld, for water and a tomato plant. When the Mariner refuses the offer of a woman so that he can add to the Atoll's gene pool, the settlers seize and examine him. Discovering him to be mutant with webbed feet and functioning gills, they cage him. When the Atoll is attacked by Smokers (piratical terrorists) led by Deacon, the dictator of a slave colony, the Mariner's cage falls into a quicksand recycler. Helen, the seller of supplies, and Enola, her adopted daughter, rescue the Mariner on condition he takes them with him on his boat. Enola is being pursued by Deacon because she has a map tattooed on her back which supposedly indicates the way to the mythic Dryland.

As the Mariner's supplies are low, he suggests to Helen that they throw the child overboard. Helen offers him her body if he'll let Enola stay; he declines her offer, but lets them both remain. Enola drives the Mariner to distraction by talking all the time but they eventually bond. When they are on the verge of starving, the Mariner uses himself as live bait and catch a monster fish. A passing trader wants to swap some paper for sex with Helen, and the Mariner agrees at first but then changes his mind. The Smokers spring a trap on them but they escape. To prove that there is no Dryland, the Mariner takes Helen in an ad hoc bathysphere to the ocean floor past the detritus of a submerged city.

They emerge to find Deacon and the Smokers aboard the trimaran and Enola in hiding. Enola gives herself away but the Mariner and Helen escape, he breathing for her underwater. The trimaran is left a wreck but the mariner finds a drawing that Enola has made showing a tree and flowers that match photos in a copy of *National Geographic* magazine that he has—therefore Dryland must exist. He and Helen are rescued by her Atoll friend, Gregor, an old inventor who takes them by balloon to a craft full of Atoll survivors. They refuse to help rescue Enola so the Mariner goes alone to the Slave Colony which inhabits the huge rusting hulk of an oil tanker. The Mariner destroys the Colony, rescues Enola and they are picked up by Helen and Gregor. They finally decipher Enola's tattoo and find Dryland. However, the Mariner decides that he does not belong on solid ground and heads out to sea alone.

Waterworld illustrates well why audiences generally prefer big-budget movies: if a film as banal and badly scripted as this one did not have expensive stars and production values, it would be unwatchable. In *Waterworld*, the gorgeous photography, the vast sets, the special effects and the presence of Kevin Costner and Dennis Hopper enable us to overlook, at least momentarily, the triteness of the whole enterprise. *Waterworld* is a very enjoyable entertainment, even, or perhaps especially, when one is laughing at it.

The film is a high concept one—*Mad Max* in the water instead of in the desert, with Kevin as Mel. It's not a bad concept, as far as these things go. The *Mad Max* films were funnier and had a sexual edge. But it has been so long since one last saw humour or edgy sexuality in a film starring the very earnest Mr. Costner (probably *Bull Durham*) that one has ceased to expect them. What is surprising is that Costner has no character to play. George Miller gave us enough information to know and understand why Max was mad, but the Mariner is a cipher. We know he has no kin and that he is a mutant. We don't know whether there are many others like him, who his family were and what happened to them, or what he longs for and desires. His love scene with Helen is passionless, perfunctory, and very brief. When he is not fighting someone, he generally stands erect at the top of trimaran looking mysteriously at the horizon while a wild wind blows his long hair. It is typical of this fuzzy-headed film to deal in such bankrupt archetypes. The Mariner is a mythic lone warrior à la Robert Bly.

The film's major fault seems to be the script. The story doesn't really work as sci-fi: it doesn't provide the necessary detail on character, situation or setting for us to be able to see a parallel between this imagined future and our own present. It is amazing that a radical change in a world doesn't create other ways of being: the film sees society as made up of 'responsible' citizens, gangsters and heroes; and gender as constituted by macho men and mothering women. The film could have made up for this shortcoming visually, but it doesn't. The design and photography, probably the best aspects of the film, brilliantly execute a shoddy notion but they do not transform it. The scene where we get to see the sunken city is a particular disappointment—however much it cost, it looks low-budget, perhaps because it is so brief. Surely the ruins of our present world could have been given a few more seconds of screen time. Aside from this, the film denies us story information that matters: how did Enola get to the Atoll colony. How did Deacon become so powerful? Where does everyone get the seemingly endless supply of cigarettes? And there are plot holes as well—what happens to the sharks we see when Helen and the Mariner are about to surface? Are they merely part of the Smokers who capture Enoia?

Despite all the water, *Waterworld* has no depth. It is hard to disagree with the film's pro-environment stance, but when it is articulated as 'irresponsibility and greed destroyed the world', it becomes too banal to be taken seriously. Where did the film-makers get that bit of wisdom? Crystals? Worse still, the film patronises its audience by clunkily spelling out its ever-so-important message—it is bad enough that the young girl is named after the *Enola Gay*, the plane which carried the Hiroshima atomic bomb, but when the Slave Colony sinks and a big close-up informs us that it is the remains of the *Exxon Valdez*, the disastrous Alaskan oil-tanker, I felt I'd been beamed into moronland.

The film is at its funniest when it is at its most serious. This is often when the film attempts to depict relationships (though not exclusively, as when we know they've discovered Dryland because we get a close-up of a pristine seagull aboard the balloon, descended from the misty heavens). I think this may be because the film goes to great lengths at the beginning to show Costner as unemotional. Perhaps it is also that the film-makers can only conceive of relationships as Hallmark slogans. That Helen tries to save Enola by taking her own clothes off and offering her body to the Mariner is an embarrassing cliche. But when the film-makers telegraph that the Mariner can now 'feel' by having him travel a great distance and single-handedly kill an army because "she's my friend", embarrassment is forsaken in favour of giggles.

Waterworld is a vanity production. Costner is at the centre of practically every shot, lovingly photographed to give the audience the best possible vantage-points from which to see Costner as courageous, as fair-minded, doing the right thing, and saving the world all by himself without expecting personal gain. This could have been as entertaining as reading the US Constitution. Contrary to expectation, however, watching Costner in *Waterworld* is a lot of fun. The role of the Mariner requires a lot of jumping, leaping and swinging from ropes at sea. The film has constructed these physical tests on Costner as little set-pieces in themselves and he passes them swimmingly. As demonstrated by fond memories of Douglas Fairbanks and other swashbucklers, (and as a possible explanation of stars' continued assertions that they perform their own stunts in spite of endless lists of stunt people in the final credits), watching agile, powerful bodies in motion is an audience-pleaser worth a bag of special effects. Here, Costner brings to mind Burt Lancaster in *The Crimson Pirate* minus the exuberance and teeth.

Costner, however, is only one of the film's pleasures. Dennis Hopper's been there and done something like the character of Deacon many times before, but it's hard to get enough of a good thing. The film's visuals have to be among the most beautiful in the cinema. And *Waterworld* contains several extremely entertaining set-pieces (the introduction with the Mariner drinking his own urine, the Mariner putting the trimaran in motion, the Mariner using himself as fish-bait) and action scenes (the water-skiing, the Mariner rescuing Enola by bungee-jumping from a balloon) that will long be remembered. All of this is perhaps not worth the film's budget (it definitely does not constitute Art), but I think it is well worth the price of admission.

VILLAGE VOICE, 8/8/95, p. 48, Amy Taubin

As everybody knows, *Waterworld* is the most expensive movie ever made though by no means the most inept. To put things in perspective, seven seconds of *Waterworld* cost more than *River of Grass* in its entirety. Which doesn't mean you'll get more bang for your eight bucks. Or, to be literal about it, you *will* get more banging and clanging—*Waterworld* is a noisily overbearing movie.

And yes, *Waterworld* is *Mad Max* gone aquatic. It's also haunted by *Apocalypse Now, The Searchers* (what isn't?), many Technicolor pirate movies of the '40s, and privileged moments from Kevin Costner's previous pictures (notably *Dances With Wolves* and *A Perfect World*). Such intertextuality doesn't make *Waterworld* postmodern, just schizophrenic in the manner of movies that try to be something to everyone in order to turn a profit.

Thus *Waterworld* embellishes the dark tale of a mutated mariner (Costner)—he's adapted to life after the polar ice caps have melted (some spin for a summer movie) by growing gills and webbed feet—with splashy battle scenes, comic book characters, and a ludicrously buoyant musical score. The culture of the future isn't merely all wet, it's also like a misbegotten Euro-pudding movie—

almost everyone speaks with a foreign accent, including Costner, who sometimes sounds more like down-under Mel than his SoCal self.

In any case, Costner's performance is more physical than verbal. He has the thankless task of trying to give momentum to action sequences totally lacking in narrative and spatial coherence. Indeed, it's the big action set pieces (literally the money shots) that sink the film, although whether the fault lies with director Kevin Reynolds's coverage or Costner's hack-job re-edit (after Reynolds's departure) is hard to say. And furthermore, who cares?

Though *Waterworld* relies on Costner's dour charisma, it gets what little humor it has from Dennis Hopper, who, as the villainous Deacon, leader of the Smokers (motorboat gangsters from hell), gives an unusually restrained though nonetheless eye-popping performance. An amalgam of the Brando and Duvall characters from *Apocalyse,* Deacon delivers the film's wittiest line when he toasts his hero, Captain Joe Hazelwood of the *Exxon Valdez.*

Also reviewed in:
CHICAGO TRIBUNE, 7/28/95, Friday/p. C, Michael Wilmington
NATION, 8/28-9/4/95, p. 216, Stuart Klawans
NEW YORK TIMES, 7/28/95, p. C1, Janet Maslin
NEW YORKER, 8/7/95, p. 83, Terrence Rafferty
VARIETY, 7/24-30/95, p. 69, Todd McCarthy
WASHINGTON POST, 7/28/95, p. B1, Rita Kempley
WASHINGTON POST, 7/28/95, Weekend/p. 38, Desson Howe

WHEN BILLY BROKE HIS HEAD ... AND OTHER TALES OF WONDER

An ITVS (Independent Television Service) film. *Producer:* Billy Golfus and David E. Simpson. *Director:* Billy Golfus and David E. Simpson. *Screenplay:* Billy Golfus. *Director of Photography:* Slawomir Grunberg. *Editor:* David E. Simpson. *Running time:* 58 minutes. *MPAA Rating:* Not Rated.

WITH: Billy Golfus (narrator and interviewer); Wade Blank; Kay Gaddis; Larry Kegan; Barb Knowlen; Paul Longmore; Joy Mincy-Powell; Ed Roberts; Robin Stephens; Lee Swenson.

NEW YORK POST, 11/29/95, p. 42, Larry Worth

Christopher Reeve's tragic horse-riding accident last May made many ponder the plight of the disabled. Some even wondered: Would the now-quadriplegic "Superman" be better off dead?

Billy Golfus' father would probably say yes. After all, he thinks the same thing about his 49-year-old brain-damaged son—even though that same son is not only ambulatory but earned a master's degree following the car accident that caused his condition.

Billy recorded his dad's sentiments—and much, much more—in a documentary that he directed, produced, wrote and narrated, "When Billy Broke His Head ... And Other Tales of Wonder."

First and foremost, Billy notes that he's tired of society's belief that the handicapped are anger-filled individuals deserving of the world's sympathy. Yet, that's where the film dishes up its biggest irony; Billy comes across as an extremely angry man and, yes, worthy of the utmost compassion.

As he travels cross-country visiting other disabled persons, Billy—to his credit—puts a humorous spin on the most dire situation. But how can one watch the likes of "Special Ed" Roberts who breathes through a respirator and sleeps in an iron lung without pity, no matter his accomplishments?

Integrated with such segments are clips from movies and TV shows which, according to Billy, send out the wrong message. He's insulted by Marilyn Hassett's "I'll never walk again" speech in "The Other Side of the Mountain," the antics of wheelchair-bound Peter Sellers in "Dr. Strangelove" and deformed curiosities in Tod Browning's "Freaks."

"Our worst barrier is people's attitude that we're defectives," says Billy, wearing a T-shirt with the Nietzsche quote, "Whatever doesn't kill me makes me stronger."

Clearly, this is a subject that raises no shortage of questions, and provides no easy answers. But at the very least, "Billy" is a thought-provoking, refreshingly acerbic took at America's largest minority.

On the same program is a completely different but equally effective effort, "Franz Kafka's It's a Wonderful Life."

Director/writer Peter Capaldi's inspired premise has the literary giant (perfectly played by Richard E. Grant) laboring over the writing of the first line of "Metamorphosis" in a dank, cockroach-ridden apartment. The angst-prone author is subsequently interrupted by neighbors—virginal dancing maidens who call him "Mr. K"—and other characters bearing a suspicious resemblance to those in Frank Capra's beloved classic.

The film, which richly earned an Oscar as 1994's best dramatic short, proves as hilarious as its title, offering the best bits of holiday cynicism since the grinch stole Christmas.

VILLAGE VOICE, 12/5/95, p. 68, Leslie Camhi

Billy Golfus had heard that disabled people were supposed to act "tragically brave" or "cute and inspirational." In his film, *When Billy Broke His Head,* they're articulate, direct, and often confrontational. Ten years ago, Golfus, a former disc jockey and radio producer, was thrown from his motor scooter and emerged from a coma partially paralyzed and brain-damaged. Now he's collaborated with filmmaker David Simpson on a documentary about the fight for civil rights among this country's 49 million people with disabilities.

In this loose road movie, Golfus travels to Chicago, where he witnesses a raucous group of disabled people using civil disobedience to mount a government protest. There he also visits a legally blind former violinist who every year must complete a 34-page form she can barely see to maintain the federal benefits that keep her in genteel poverty. In Berkeley, Golfus meets with "Special Ed" Roberts, a paraplegic who now directs the same state agency that, 14 years earlier, had denied him employment assistance. Roberts speaks positively of anger, and uses his wheelchair as a weapon while learning karate. Back home in Minneapolis, Golfus shows up for an appointment at a government office, where a member of the "helping professions" explains why his benefits will soon be reduced to provide him with less than a living wage. Finally, he interviews his 80-year-old father, who doesn't really believe that disability discrimination exists, though he hides his own deafness and age.

A quick montage of clips manages to suggest the remarkably addled images of the disabled promoted by popular culture; I wish it had been longer. I'd also have liked Golfus to have interviewed more people with disabilities who are neither artists nor activists, our modern heroes. Still, his relentless "bad attitude," honesty, and considerable charm carry this documentary to its striking conclusion: "Physical disabilities are not the problem," his pugnacious narration informs us, "it's the social attitudes we have to fight."

In an unusual double billing, *When Billy Broke His Head* is paired with *Franz Kafka's It's a Wonderful Life,* a short and hilarious film about a winter evening when the great Prague nihilist battled writer's block, killed a cockroach, and discovered that life was worth living. Kafka suffered from tuberculosis, but his primary disability was angst-ridden genius; we should all be so lucky.

Also reviewed in:
NEW YORK TIMES, 11/29/95, p. C17, Janet Maslin
VARIETY, 2/6-12/95, p. 75, Emanuel Levy

WHEN NIGHT IS FALLING

An October Films and Alliance Communications Corporation release of a Crucial Pictures Inc. production. *Producer:* Barbara Tranter. *Director:* Patricia Rozema. *Screenplay:* Patricia Rozema. *Director of Photography:* Douglas Koch. *Editor:* Susan Shipton. *Music:* Leslie Barber. *Casting:* Deidre Bowen. *Production Designer:* John Dondertman. *Set Decorator:* Megan Less. *Costumes:* Linda Muir. *Running time:* 96 minutes. *MPAA Rating:* Not Rated.

CAST: Pascale Bussières (Camille); Rachael Crawford (Petra); Henry Czerny (Martin); David Fox (Reverend DeBoer); Don McKellar (Timothy); Tracy Wright (Tory); Clare Coulter (Tillie); Karyne Steben (Trapeze Artist #1); Sarah Steben (Trapeze Artist #2); Jonathan Potts (Hang Glider #1); Tom Melissis (Hang Glider #2); Stuart Clow (Hang Glider #3); Richard Farrell (Board President); Fides Krucker (Roaring Woman); Thom Sokoloski (Man with Goatee); Jennifer Roblin (Waitress); Jacqueline Casey (Iron Swinger #1); Sigrid Johnson (Iron Swinger #2).

LOS ANGELES TIMES, 11/17/95, Calendar/p. 12, Jack Mathews

The following review by Jack Mathews appeared in a slightly different form in **NEWSDAY, 11/17/95, Part II/p. B6.]**

The artifice of Canadian director Patricia Rozema's lesbian love story "When Night Is Falling" is apparent long before her characters, the circus performer Petra (Rachael Crawford) and the religious college professor Camille (Pascale Bussieres), get down to business.

In fact, it's apparent in the opening image, a dreamlike fantasy of the naked Bussieres swimming underwater, symbolizing ... what? Moral claustrophobia? Repressed sexuality? A promo for a nudist Club Med? For a moment, you may think you're watching the opening to that new James Bond movie.

"When Night Is Falling," a phrase borrowed from Ingmar Bergman's "Fanny and Alexander," is one of the more blatantly wrong-headed entries in the current wave of independent gay and lesbian films. It is so focused on its own boldness, its dare-to-shock sensuality (the film got an NC-17 from the MPAA, but is being released unrated), that nothing else comes through.

What passes for a backdrop in Rozema's script strains so hard for contrast and moral conflict that it verges on audience insult.

What if an aggressively open lesbian were to develop a crush on a conservative college professor and the feeling, grudging as it may be, is mutual? Up the ante. Let's say the professor is in a long relationship with a minister and colleague, and that they are being considered for the co-chaplainship of their Protestant college. All they have to do is get married and pass a rigid board exam on devoutly homophobic Christian principle—the moral orals—and the job is theirs.

Wouldn't that be something?

It probably would, but Rozema, who made such a strong debut with her 1987 "I've Heard the Mermaids Singing," is so determined to make her primary point about the power of love that she overstates every incidental argument. Watching the movie is like reading a magazine article where every salient thought has been highlighted by somebody using a felt marker.

But beyond everything else, Rozema has simply failed to create plausible relationships between the two women, and between Camille and her tortured lover Martin (Henry Czerny).

On the surface, the women are fakes. Even for the surrealist avant-garde circus she belongs to, Petra is out of place. The role serves to show her as a grand eccentric and explain some of her outlandish behavior around Camille, but Crawford has no performance skills of her own. She may be prettier than the bearded lady but has less of an act.

Camille is an even larger contradiction. For someone immersed in mythology, which she teaches, and religion, which she lives, Camille shows no passion for either. And the crisis finally facing her is as old as pain. She has to choose between two lovers—one new and exciting, the other solid and dependable—and decide whether to run away with the circus or stay home and eat oatmeal.

The fact that all of this happens in about two days seriously undermines the drama. Rozema wants to have it both ways, to portray a romantic encounter as both pure lust and divined love, to build us up for some really hot sex, then cool us down with some soulful declarations of monogamous union. The whole thing makes for some pretty awkward eavesdropping on our part.

"I love your sex, I love your wisdom and the way you say, 'Switcheroo,'" Petra coos during a post-coital embrace with Camille. "I love that sadness that you get in your eyes some times ..."

Says Camille, moments later: "Listen, I love to look at you, I love to talk to you, I love your openness, I love what you do, I love you."

Ah, forget it.

NEW YORK POST, 11/17/95, p. 48, Larry Worth

Writer/Director Patricia Rozema sure paints a pretty picture. Her postcard-perfect landscapes and artistically-captured sunsets ensure that "When Night Is Falling" is a visual stunner.

Had she put half as much energy into the plot, this melodramatic, metaphor-laden mish-mash might have found a reason for being. Instead, it's the latest in lesbian chic, with yet another conservative heroine going for a walk on the wild side with a luscious libertine.

But what drives the film into near-parody are religious overtones. Camille (as in Paglia?) is a professor at a Protestant college and on the verge of sharing co-chaplain honors with her handsome fiance, Martin.

Then, unspeakable tragedy happens: Her pet puppy drops dead. Naturally, Camille does what any woman would do: stuffs the dog in the fridge and runs away to a Cirque du Soleil clone. There, she falls head over high-wire for Petra, the lovely trapeze artist.

Petra returns her dreamy gaze and the mating dance begins. She immediately tells Camille: "I'd love to see you in the moonlight with your head back and your body on fire." That's the level of subtlety—and stereotyped banter—that infects the production. In other words, when a verbal storm is brewing, thunder literally rumbles.

Rozema, who earlier showed a genuine sense of style and humor in "I've Heard the Mermaids Singing," manages restraint only in the lovemaking scenes (between Camille and Martin as well as with the gal pals). So, it's ironic that the film was denied an R rating, allegedly due to its strong sexual content.

Drooling deviants won't be the only ones to go home disappointed. Fans of Henry Czerny, who made such a disturbing impression as the priest-cum-pedophile in "The Boys of St. Vincent," is sadly wasted as Camille's all-consuming husband-to-be. And Pascale Bussieres' Camille and Rachael Crawford's Petra may be physically alluring, but their sparks couldn't light a match.

No matter. Half-baked debates over Christian ethics and repression, never mind sledgehammered symbols of birth and resurrection, ultimately take precedence. That's how "Night is Falling" goes from a misguided movie to sinfully stupid cinema.

VILLAGE VOICE, 11/21/95, Film Special/p. 24, Lisa Kennedy

It begins with a wet dream. A naked body plunges past, leaving a stream of lilting bubbles in its indigo wake. Another body appears reaching, touching. The images are explicit yet dreamy. Then there is that always primal vision of a force moving beneath a skin of ice. To break through or not?

The unconscious may write Camille's script in the early morning hours, but her wiry terrier Bob licks her to consciousness and the day. And what a day. In it, Camille and her lover Martin will be offered a shared chaplainship at the Calvinist college where they both teach (she: mythology, he: God's plan); Bob, a ball of fluff with profound metaphysical significance, will die mysteriously; and in a beautiful or at least spotless launderette, Camille will meet Petra—a lovely performer who comes to town with the Sirkus of Sorts.

Some directors are ham-fisted when they nod to their earlier work; Canadian Patricia Rozema is so subtle that it's unclear whether these opening images of *When Night is Falling* really hint at mermaids. No matter, the director of the sweet, intricately woven *I've Heard the Mermaids Singing* has returned with a gifted cast (leads Pascale Bussières, Rachael Crawford, and Henry Czerny in particular) and a beautiful film that plays (and playfulness is much in evidence here) with similar themes: triangulated desire, identification, and as Al Green sings, love and happiness—or more fittingly joy, with its claim on the lived sublime.

When Night Is Falling gives one more opportunity to those viewers who are not team players to find the romantic in its love affair. Not only is romance here for you, you'd have to close your mind to it, you'd have to willfully deny it, not to be moved. While it's not Rozema's primary project to throw down the gauntlet of spectatorship, *When Night Is Falling* is so good at telling its story of yearning, confusion, consummation, and, yes, confusion, that the call for viewer identification regardless of preference is irresistible. Unlike the wondrous *Wings of Desire*—which Rozema's film, with its use of the circus as the locale of love's human possibilities, is likely to be compared to—*When Night Is Falling* invites all of us to all of the party: After all the vision of Petra is an absurd, winning Cupid wreaking havoc with Camille's psyche is as boldly, mythically romantic as it is goofy.

Sure, there are a few ways to do critical violence to this romance: Why couldn't Martin be as diabolical as a Ralph Reed? Or why isn't more made of Petra's race? But what would be achieved by nailing this gem to our national crosses? (Didn't the MPAA in its pornographic\wisdom already err in precisely that way, giving the film an NC-17 rating?) Rozema's generosity demands to be treated in kind. When Martin finds out about Petra, his use of theologically tinged arguments are no more manipulative than any other lover's efforts to hold onto a beloved. They are desperate; they are human.

Early in the film, Petra and Camille speak of their first encounter "You touched me," Camille says, "I wanted to" Petra replies. *When Night is Falling* is like that. It is near impossible not to find it touching. And have no doubt that is it purpose.

Also reviewed in:
CHICAGO TRIBUNE, 11/24/95, Friday/p. C, Achy Obejas
NEW YORK TIMES, 11/17/95, p. C19, Stephen Holden
VARIETY, 2/20-26/95, p. 82, Derek Elley
WASHINGTON POST, 11/24/95, p. D8, Rita Kempley

WHILE YOU WERE SLEEPING

A Hollywood Pictures release in association with Caravan Pictures. *Executive Producer:* Arthur Sarkissian and Steve Barron. *Producer:* Joe Roth and Roger Birnbaum. *Director:* Jon Turteltaub. *Screenplay:* Daniel G. Sullivan and Fredric Lebow. *Director of Photography:* Phedon Papamichael. *Editor:* Bruce Green. *Music:* Randy Edelman. *Music Editor:* John La Salandra. *Sound:* Curt Frisk and (music) Dennis Sands. *Sound Editor:* J. Paul Huntsman. *Casting:* Amanda Mackey and Cathy Sandrich. *Production Designer:* Garreth Stover. *Art Director:* Chris Cornwell. *Set Designer:* Suzan Wexler. *Set Decorator:* Larry Dias. *Special Effects:* Guy Clayton, Jr. *Costumes:* Betsy Cox. *Make-up:* Pamela S. Westmore. *Stunt Coordinator:* Rick Le Fevour. *Running time:* 100 minutes. *MPAA Rating:* PG.

CAST: Sandra Bullock (Lucy); Bill Pullman (Jack); Peter Gallagher (Peter); Peter Boyle (Ox); Jack Warden (Saul); Glynis Johns (Elsie); Micole Mercurio (Midge); Jason Bernard (Jerry); Michael Rispoli (Joe Jr.); Ally Walker (Ashley Bacon); Monica Keena (Mary); Ruth Rudnick (Wanda); Marcia Wright (Celeste); Dick Cusack (Dr. Rubin); Thomas Q. Morris (Man in Peter's Room); Bernie Landis (Doorman); James Krag (Dalton Clarke); Rick Worthy (Orderly); Marc Grapey (Intern); Joel Hatch (Priest); Mike Bacarella (Mr. Fusco); Peter Siragusa (Hot Dog Vendor); Gene Janson (Man in Church); Krista Lally (Phyllis); Kevin Gudahl (Cop at ICU); Ann Whitney (Blood Donor Nurse); Margaret Travolta (Admitting Nurse); Shea Farrell (Ashely's Husband); Kate Reinders (Beth); Susan Messing (Celeste's Friend); Richard Pickren (Lucy's Father); Megan Schaiper (Young Lucy).

LOS ANGELES TIMES, 4/21/95, Calendar/p. 1, Peter Rainer

The amiable, methodically inoffensive "While You Were Sleeping" opens with a woman's honey-colored childhood memories of her deceased father but, even when the memories have faded into the present day, the honey continues to flow. It's a movie about the warm feeling you get when you belong to a family, and, throughout, the thermostat is turned up high.

Lucy (Sandra Bullock), who lives by herself, plus cat, has no family of her own. She works inside a token booth for the Chicago Transit Authority and moons over a handsome yuppieish exec, Peter Callaghan (Peter Gallagher), who shows up every day for the El. When he's rousted by muggers and left sprawling and unconscious on the tracks in the path of an oncoming train, Lucy rolls him to safety.

Through a set of farcical complications in the hospital room, Lucy is mistaken for the comatose Peter's fiancée by his sprawling extended family, including his aptly named father, Ox (Peter Boyle), mother Midge (Micole Mercurio), Midge's mother Elsie (Glynis Johns) and long-term family friend Saul (Jack Warden). Because she has a tremendous ache to be a part of a chummy, contentious clan like the Callaghans, Lucy goes along with the ruse.

She claims she doesn't want to shatter the Callaghans' illusions—she wants to bolster their fantasy that Peter, who broke away from the family, was ready to return to the fold with a caring cuddlebunny like her. But its clear she doesn't want to shatter her own fantasy either. The conflict comes when Lucy and Peter's brother, Jack (Bill Pullman) begin to take a mutually warming interest in each other. And what will happen when Peter snaps out of his coma?

The black comic possibilities in this material are sugared and softened. "While You Were Sleeping" is about as disturbing as a sitcom. It's a punchy and "heartfelt" and almost frighteningly in sync with its audience. It doesn't challenge, it coddles. Our oohs and aahs are elicited right down to the millisecond. Jon Turteltaub, who directed from a script by Daniel G. Sullivan and Frederic Lebow, was responsible for "3 Ninjas" and "Cool Runnings," the top-grossing, Disney live-action movies for 1992 an 1993, respectively, and he may make it three in a row here. He's become a real smoothie. In this movie about the vagaries of love, nothing is left to chance.

The people in "While You Were Sleeping" seem a bit too aware of how bumptiously cute they are. Right down to Lucy's lecherous neighbor Joe Jr. (Michael Rispoli), just about everybody in the movie has all the mettle of a Muppet. It's an adult comedy-romance with a kiddie core. Lucy's longing is desexualized; she's essentially the same child we saw in those honeyed flashbacks, except now she has an adult's sense of aloneness. She's the heart of the movie and heart is all she is allowed to display.

Bullock is a genuinely engaging performer, which at least gives the treacle some minty freshness. Her scenes with Pullman are amiable approach-avoidance duets that really convince you something is going on between them. Like Marisa Tomei, Bullock has a sky-high likability factor with audiences. She can draw us into her spunky loneliness—you want to see her smile. But she's been encouraged here to be a bit too floppy and winsome and touching—she and everybody else—and it's unnecessary. Bullock *already* is charming. She doesn't need to get all Chaplin-esque for us.

With a movie as sleek and self-satisfied as "While You Were Sleeping," with every audience-response button pushed with precision, even the clichés and tired routines may seem fresh for people who haven't seen many movies. There's a subplot involving "selective amnesia" that may be a subtle in-joke here: It helps in enjoying this film if you repress all the other times you've seen two women vying for the same man spin through revolving doors, or listened to comfy Capra-esque Christmas chats about the value of togetherness.

But perhaps the filmmakers are after the opposite effect, too—not selective amnesia but total recall. As they did with Lucy, they want audiences to evoke their own sugared memories—their own movie memories. They're true Hollywood alchemists. They turn pap into honey.

NEW STATESMAN & SOCIETY, 9/1/95, p. 29, Lizzie Francke

In Hollywood they call them date movies and this autumn there's a lot of dating going on. Opening this week, *While You Were Sleeping* is the first in the flurry of romantic comedies that are supposed to be enhancing the love-lives of boys and aids everywhere as they take the plunge, buy a large-size popcorn to share and sweat it out for an hour and a half in the local Odeon. Now, for my money, boy meets girl movies (and in Hollywood it is still very much boy meets girl) are not the kind of thing to go to if you are tentatively checking each other out. There is nothing more excruciating than sitting in the dark with someone you hardly know listening to such sweet nonsense as love at first sight.

No, films like *While You Were Sleeping* are meant for one to go to with a pack of ironically inclined friends who can easily brush aside the film's more fluffy sentiments. You see, these days it is so easy to be snide about romantic comedies. But deep down, the good ones ruffle even the most cynical audiences, while the best epitomise the complicated and sometimes treacherous process of forming emotional attachments. That said, contemporary romantic comedies rarely match the sublime anarchic spirit of the screwball romances of the 1930s and 1940s. Take the deliriously lunatic *Bringing Up Baby* in which Cary Grant and Katherine Hepburn found their path to true love strewn with two leopards, a ferocious little dog and the like—things that brought them together, but conversely also sent them flying in all directions before finally they had the wit to fall into each other's arms.

In *While You Were Sleeping* the obstacle between Lucy and Jack (Sandra Bullock and Bill Pullman) is a man in a coma. Set in Chicago, the film's kooky plot kicks off as Christmas looms. The lonely-heart Lucy, who sells subway tickets from a little glass booth, tries to avoid holiday-season hell by dreaming about one of her dark, dashing customers played by Peter Gallagher, most memorable as the preppy husband in *Sex, Lies and Videotape*—a man who hardly thanks her when she gives him his change. Fate intervenes, though, when Lucy rescues him after he has been pushed onto the railtrack and knocked out. Accompanying him to the hospital, she is presumed to be his fiancée—a misunderstanding too complicated to put right, especially when Peter Callaghan's (as she finds out he is called) large and jolly family turns up and embraces her as a new member of their fold. But then wholesome brother Jack turns up—his fleecy lumber-jacket shirts a soft contrast to Peter's Brooks Brothers couture—providing the film with its funny turn.

While You Were Sleeping did unexpectedly well in the US. Its success, one suspects, is mostly to do with the endearing performances from Bullock and Pullman. They are Hollywood's idea of a regular Josephine and Joe and they do it very well. Last seen in the driving seat in *Speed*, Bullock has a true feisty freshness. As Jack says, "You don't know whether to kiss her or arm-wrestle her." Meanwhile Pullman, who in the past has made a particular speciality of patsy roles—he was the lily-livered husband whom Linda Fiorentino ate for breakfast in *The Last Seduction*—finally gets the girl. But even here, he still has a slightly wary, bemused look about him as if he's scared that somewhere in Lucy's wardrobe of baggy, woolly things there lurks a little black number and a pair of sharp stilettos. But he need not be afraid. For this is not a film about dark machinations; these two are utterly decent, rather shy sorts who need a few fairy godmothers and godfathers to show them what's what—and in the extended Callaghan household there are plenty on hand. Produced by Disney subsidiary, Hollywood Pictures, *While You Were Sleeping* is very much the fairytale dressed down in everyday clothes. The trouble is that it casts a beguiling spell—for a moment you might just believe that romance is forever and that families are fun all the time.

NEW YORK, 5/8/95, p. 68, David Denby

Sandra Bullock, the rumpled heroine of the new screwball comedy *While You Were Sleeping*, doesn't have the perfect features of so many forgettable American actresses. She's more like one of those idiosyncratically beautiful Italian movie stars from the fifties, with a wide smile that takes over her face, dark eyes and hair, a puggish nose, and eyebrows that are down slightly in the middle. Her character, Lucy, living alone in Chicago, works in an El station as a token clerk. Loneliness has made Lucy rather distracted and awkward: A handsome passenger who buys a token every morning and whom she's been dreaming about, Peter (Peter Gallagher), falls onto the tracks; she saves his life, but when he slips into a coma, she can't bring herself to disappoint his family, all of whom think she has become Peter's fiancée. She wouldn't mind being his fiancée—she's projected all sorts of qualities onto him—and she revels in the attention, perhaps missing family love even more than romance. Lucy wears the coat of her dead father through the gray Chicago winter, and wraps up in sweaters and scarves. Pulled this way and that by longing and dismay, Bullock does a floppy-tailed star turn as this melancholy honeybunch.

While You Were Sleeping starts slowly. The early scenes of Lucy with Peter's family seem to go on forever, and I grew annoyed and rebellious because the first-time screenwriters, Daniel G. Sullivan and Fredric Lebow, use misunderstanding, coincidence, and accident to produce virtually every event in the story. Artifice always plays a large role in this kind of movie, but Sullivan and Lebow seemed to be cheating. They have a good romantic idea, however, and eventually develop it well. Peter's brother lack (Bill Pullman) shows up, and suddenly Lucy ignores her imaginary, comatose lover and has a wide-awake man to flirt with. "You're cheating on a vegetable," a friend tells her, but she goes on.

Peter Gallagher, who must have the ripest features since Victor Mature, is perfectly cast as Peter the sleeping beauty. Awake, Gallagher isn't much of an actor (he's a brooding sensual blank at the center of a new dud thriller, *The Underneath*). Bill Pullman is the male star here, and rightly so. Pullman was extremely funny as the masochistic, crooked saphead—a worm who deserved to be stepped on—in *The Last Seduction,* but I feared for his morale. How much punishment can a man take? In his own quiet way, Pullman has now had his revenge. As a regular guy who has never found the right girl, he matches Bullock in appeal. Pullman is more directly sexual than in the past, with a touch of angry smoke in his voice. He and Bullock connect the way lovers in screwball comedies always have, by sharing a sense of humor, which is how American movies always sublimate eroticism. The director, Jon Turteltaub *(Cool Runnings),* pulls the movie together. Peter's family seems more and more lovable, and Turteltaub keeps the screen populated with good minor characters. He turns standard foolish bits of business—Bullock and Pullman slipping and falling into each other's arms on the ice—into a prolonged aria of getting-to-know-you. The movie never explodes, but it doesn't have to. Quiet and sensitive will do just fine for a change.

NEW YORK POST, 4/21/95, p. 49, Thelma Adams

"While You Were Sleeping" is terminally cute.

Lucy (Sandra Bullock) and Peter (Peter Gallagher) meet cute. Lucy sells tokens on the Chicago El; Peter buys them. She falls for him and, then, her secret crush falls in front of her.

On Christmas Day, thugs push Peter onto the tracks. Lucy rescues him. Before he can thank her, Peter's comatose and in due to a hospital mix-up, everyone thinks Lucy is Peter's fiancée.

Peter's family is the cute and kooky team of Peter Boyle, Jack Warden and Glynis Johns.

Bill Pullman ("The Last Seduction") plays Peter's brother Jack. Pullman is not quite as cute as the deeply dimpled Gallagher ("The Player"), but Jack's cuddly, sincere—and conscious.

Named Lucy with shades of Ricardo, Bullock ("Speed") is chocolate cupcake cute. She dips Oreos in her cat's milk dish. She bonds with old men. She wears unfashionable knit caps (think Ali MacGraw in "Love Story").

She's perky in a smile-though-your-heart-is-breaking way. Jon Turteltaub ("Cool Runnings") sweetly directs this sleeping in Chicago script, but screenwriters Daniel Sullivan and Fredric Lebow's romantic comedy isn't funny enough to carry off this frothy confection.

There are no surprises. The set pieces around the dinner table or Peter's hospital bed are never hilarious enough to distract from the obvious progression that Lucy makes from coma boy to brother Jack. Don't let it be said that Bullock and Pullman can't do cute.

They make a game romantic pair, Sleeping Beauty and Prince Charming in jeans. Despite knowing that nothing can happen but their uniting before the final credits, we root for them.

Gallagher performs his gig lying down. When he finally awakens in the third act, we realize that the one Big, Bad Wolf who could possibly put some edge into the act has been wasted.

"While You Were Sleeping," with its soporific title, should have been called "The Unbearable Cuteness of Being."

NEWSDAY, 4/21/95, Part II/p. B2, Jack Mathews

Some occasionally inspired dialogue and a modicum of chemistry between costars Sandra Bullock and Bill Pullman rescue "While You Were Sleeping" from the muck of "Sleepless in Seattle" sentimentality. But it is a narrow escape.

Like "Sleepless in Seattle," this story is more about the longing for romance than romance itself. Idealized, sweet, pure, undiluted longing ... for that special someone out there who will set your heart pounding, curl your toes, ring bells in your head, and make you sing "Love Is a Many Splendored Thing" in the shower.

Bullock, the bus driver in "Speed," is in public transportation again, as Lucy, a lonely token taker on the Chicago train line who lives with her cat and two lifelong dreams, one of being swept off her feet by Mr. Right, another of being magically transported to romantic Florence to have her pristine passport stamped.

Lucy is convinced she's met the man of her dreams, a handsomely dressed commuter (Peter Gallagher) who drops a token into her cup every day but never seems to notice her. Then, on Christmas day, she receives a gift of fate wrapped in destiny. A pair of muggers toss her dream lover onto the tracks, and after risking her life to save him from an onrushing train, she suddenly finds herself part of his family.

Through a series of wildly unlikely events at the hospital, Lucy is mistaken for the injured man's fiancé, and as he lies in a coma, she spends the holidays bonding with her would-be in-laws, learning what an egotistical airhead she's been mooning over, and finally falling in love with his kind, sincere and soulful brother, Jack (Pullman). In her dreams, she had the right brood, just the wrong sibling.

First-time screenwriters Daniel Sullivan and Fredric Lebow dig deep into the molasses for some of their romantic notions, but not very deep into reality. Bullock and Pullman's characters are so obviously right for each other, in the Hollywood sense, that all the hurdles placed in their way—his loyalty to his brother, her guilt over the trumped-up engagement—seem ridiculous. All she'd have to do at any point in the story is fess up, explain the confusion, and start packing for Florence.

Still, the halting relationship between Lucy and Jack has just enough appeal to make you stick around for the big kiss. Bullock has a cute quotient to match that of Marisa Tomei, without the self-awareness, and Pullman, so often cast (as he was in "Sleepless in Seattle") as the odd man out, is genuinely appealing as a guy with his feet on the ground and his heart on his sleeve.

The film's liveliest scenes are those with the brothers' family, and their down-to-earth next door neighbor (Jack Warden). Sullivan and Lebow have a nice touch for scattershot repartee, and there are some good chuckles whenever they're all allowed to run on. Michael Rispoli also has some good moments as Lucy's harmlessly persistent suitor, even though the character has been played more than a Beatles album.

NEWSWEEK, 5/1/95, p. 70, Jeff Giles

Jon Turteltaub's *While You Were Sleeping* is a holiday movie through and through, though it's been marooned in this the cruelest month. Sandra Bullock, the enormously cool costar of "Speed," does her first star turn as Lucy, a lonely token-booth clerk for the Chicago Transit Authority. Lucy's in love with a callow Yuppie commuter named Peter Callaghan (Peter Gallagher), though he slips into a coma before she ever meets him. What the heck: it's a romantic comedy. At the hospital, Lucy tells Peter's family that she's his fiancée. They take her home for Christmas and cavort with remarkable spirit, considering they've got a son on life support. Peter's working-class brother, Jack (Bill Pullman), is suspicious of Lucy, but winds up falling for her. Plotwise, that about covers it. The first 45 minutes of the movie are too full of formula and forced cheer—and don't get us started on the smiley-faced soundtrack. Fortunately, Peter comes out of his deep sleep and wakes the whole movie up. His reaction to Lucy is wonderfully unexpected, and it sends a little jolt through everybody's performances. Turteltaub, who also directed the Jamaican bobsled comedy "Cool Runnings," gets some nice work out of Pullman (he of the unassuming charm and the squinty, quizzical smile) and a truly inspired turn from Gallagher (he of the eyebrows). It's hard to believe Bullock as a sad, grubby woman in fingerless gloves—a woman who dips Oreos in her cat's milk bowl. Still, she manages to strike the same chords as Julia Roberts and Meg Ryan, which is to say that she seems human and looks divine. In the end, "Sleeping" seems a sweet puff pastry. it delivers the warm fuzzies without apology, and you find yourself giving in. Sure, it's spring, but have yourself a merry little Christmas.

SIGHT AND SOUND, 9/95, p. 63, John Wrathall

Lucy Moderatz works in a ticket booth on Chicago's elevated railway run by the Chicago Transit Authority, where she fantasises about Peter Callaghan, a smart lawyer who buys a token from her every day. On Christmas Day, Peter is mugged on the platform, and Lucy saves him from being run over after he falls on the line. At the hospital where Peter lies in a coma, Lucy is mistaken for his fiancé by the Callaghan family, who insist that she come home to celebrate Christmas with them. There she meets Peter's brother, Jack. Jack grows suspicious of Lucy when he visits her apartment, where her slobbish Italian-American landlord, Joe Junior, pretends that he is Lucy's boyfriend. After being given Peter's effects at the hospital, Lucy lets herself into his apartment to feed his cat, and bumps into Jack, who tries in vain to catch her out.

Back at the hospital, Peter's godfather, Saul, tells Lucy he knows she isn't really Peter's fiancé; but since the family like her so much, he agrees to keep it a secret. Jack comes round to Lucy's again to deliver a sofa his parents want to give her; after his van is boxed in by parked cars, they spend the evening together. Giving Lucy a lift to the New Year's Eve party of one of her workmates, Jack is mistaken for her fiancé, whom they have heard about but of course never met. Meanwhile, Peter's ex-girlfriend Ashley has returned from Europe and is leaving messages on his answerphone. Back at the hospital, Peter wakes up; when he does not recognise Lucy, his family assume he is suffering from amnesia. Feeling he wants to start afresh after his narrow escape from death, he proposes to Lucy anyway. Before the wedding, Jack goes round to see Lucy, but they still can't bring themselves to declare their feelings for each other. At the registry office, Lucy interrupts the marriage ceremony, confessing all and running off when Ashley arrives to object to the wedding. With the whole family in tow, Jack finds Lucy working at the ticket booth and proposes. She accepts.

A plotline in which a protagonist passes herself off as the fiancé of a comatose accident victim is one more associated with film noir than comedy—last year's Spanish thriller *The Red Squirrel* and the wonderful 1949 Barbara Stanwyck vehicle *No Man of Her Own* are two that come to mind. But this resolutely good-natured romantic comedy avoids a single jarring note of darkness. It's Christmas. Peter's family, the Callaghans, live in a white clapboard house in the suburbs, complete with snow and fairy lights. There's kissing under the mistletoe, and 'Have Yourself A Merry Little Christmas' on the soundtrack. The synthetic feel of this modern fairy tale is only enhanced by the ethnic mix of the characters, which seems to have been worked out by an equal opportunities committee: the Callaghans are Irish-American; Peter's godfather, Saul, is Jewish; Lucy's landlord, Joe Junior, is Italian-American; and Jerry, her worldly-wise boss at the Chicago Transit Authority, is African-American.

Despite its slightly Benetton view of American society, however, *While You Were Sleeping* does not advocate class mobility. Lucy may think Peter is her "Prince Charming", but he is shown to be out of bounds, a rich, hotshot lawyer with an icy apartment decorated in chrome and black and white. In a bizarre detail, Peter also turns out to have only one testicle, as if a lawyer were only half a man. Lucy's landlord Joe Junior, by contrast, is too far downmarket: he wears his trousers at halfmast, builder-style, and wants to take Lucy to the Ice Capades. (In case that weren't enough, he also has a penchant for women's shoes.)

Lucy, after all, may work in a ticket booth, but she isn't really working class: as the film is at pains to point out, she had to leave college to work so that she could pay her late father's medical bills. Like a computer dating service, the plot fixes her up with her perfect social match, Jack Callaghan, who loves his family, but not to the point of devoting his whole life to the slightly distasteful family business (which is dealing in dead people's furniture). Instead he wants to go into business for himself, selling the chairs he makes with his own hands. Best of all, he reminds Lucy of her father. How perfect.

Produced by Disney offshoot Hollywood Pictures, *While You Were Sleeping* has a homogenised, family values feel that puts it firmly in the Disney tradition, as does the presence of Glynis Johns—the mother in Disney's *Mary Poppins*—as Peter and Jack's grandmother, Elsie. That it still manages to charm is thanks entirely to the perfect casting of Sandra Bullock and Bill Pullman, both getting a well-deserved shot at lead roles after years of support and both seizing the moment. With her tight little smile and a winning capacity for looking like she wants to disappear off the face of the earth in embarrassing situations, Bullock manages to make Lucy both plausibly ordinary and, as Jack puts it, "Really, really likeable". But it's something else Jack says about

Lucy that really pinpoints Bullock's brand of wholesome sexiness: "You don't know whether to kiss her or arm-wrestle her."

TIME, 5/1/95, p. 87, Richard Schickel

The center of the fairy tale a prince (Peter Gallagher), not the customary princess, lies sleeping. He's in a coma, having been saved from death by a pertly pining princess (Sandra Bullock) who, loving him from afar, is unaware that he's really a toad in disguise.

And that's just the beginning of the comic confusion. For his family, clustered around his bedside, get the impression that she's his fiancé and, being nice, warm people, take her into their circle. She doesn't have the heart to tell them the truth: that she's just a girl who works in a change booth on the Chicago El who never had the gumption to speak to him when he bought his tokens from her every morning. Luckily, the family harbors an authentic prince, Peter's brother Jack (Bill Pullman), whose initial suspicion of Lucy is, of course, the harbinger of true love.

So everything comes out all right in the end, which is not exactly startling. What is startling is how well *While You Were Sleeping* recaptures the true spirit of the best kind of modern fairy tale-classic romantic comedy. This is something Hollywood has been trying hard, and failing miserably, to revive in recent years. Though this kind of comedy occasionally skitters toward the screwball-mistaken identity, preposterous coincidence, even the odd pratfall are all judiciously permitted—it's really a grownup form. It needs smart dialogue and plausibly eccentric characters (Michael Rispoli contributes a beaut to this one, as an inappropriate suitor to Lucy, and such worthy veterans as Jack Warden and Glynis Johns give good comic weight too). Above all, it requires honorable sentiment—not to be confused with dishonest sentimentality.

All this *While You Were Sleeping* has. But its most attractive quality is its ease. The script by Daniel G. Sullivan and Fred Lebow wears its wit casually, and the director, Jon Turteltaub, is serenely confident of it, his actors and his audience. He lets scenes develop and characters—especially Bullock's alert and tender Lucy—merge at their own unforced pace. How nice it is to come out of a mainstream American movie feeling that you've been treated as an adult. And how rare.

Also reviewed in:
CHICAGO TRIBUNE, 4/21/95, Friday/p. H, Michael Wilmington
NEW REPUBLIC, 5/22/95, p. 28, Stanley Kauffmann
NEW YORK TIMES, 4/21/95, p. C16, Janet Maslin
NEW YORKER, 5/22/95, p. 96, Anthony Lane
VARIETY, 4/17-23/95, p. 36, Leonard Klady
WASHINGTON POST, 4/21/95, Weekend/p. 44, Kevin McManus
WASHINGTON POST, 4/24/95, p. D2, Hal Hinson

WHITE MAN'S BURDEN

A Savoy Pictures release of a UGC presentation in association with Rysher Entertainment of a Lawrence Bender/Band Apart production. *Producer:* Lawrence Bender. *Director:* Desmond Nakano. *Screenwriter:* Desmond Nakano. *Director of Photography:* Willy Kurant. *Editor:* Pietro Scalia. *Music:* Howard Shore. *Music Editor:* Ellen Segal. *Sound:* Ken King. *Sound Editor:* Victor Iorillo and Richard E. Yawn. *Production Designer:* Naomi Shohan. *Art Director:* John Ivo Gilles. *Set Designer:* Colin de Rou and Patrick M. Sullivan, Jr. *Set Decorator:* Evette F. Siegel. *Set Dresser:* Mike Malone, Brett V. Shirley, Jefferson Murff, John J. Grevera, Eric Kelly, Fred Haft, and Vartan "V.T." Tashjian. *Special Effects:* John E. Gray and Dale Newkirk. *Costumes:* Denise Martinez. *Make-up:* Judy Murdock. *Stunt Coordinator:* Ken Lesco. *Running time:* 96 minutes. *MPAA Rating:* R.

CAST: John Travolta (Louis Pinnock); Harry Belafonte (Thaddeus Thomas); Kelly Lynch (Marsha Pinnock); Margaret Avery (Megan Thomas); Tom Bower (Stanley); Andrew Lawrence

(Donnie Pinnock); Bumper Robinson (Martin); Tom Wright (Lionel); Sheryl Lee Ralph (Roberta); Judith Drake (Dorothy); Robert Gossett (John); Wesley Thompson (Williams); Tom Nolan (Johansson); Willie Carpenter (Marcus); Michael Beach (Policeman #1 Outside Bar); Lee Duncan (Policeman #2 Outside Bar); Wanda Lee Evans (Renee); Lawrence A. Mandley (Sheriff #1 at Eviction); William Hendry (Sheriff #2 at Eviction); Thom Barry (Landlord); Carrie Snodgress (Josine); Brian Brophy (Bank Teller); Chelsea Lagos (Cheryl); Duane R. Shephard, Sr.; (Maitre D' at Fashion Show); Bert Remsen (Hot Dog Vendor); Steve Wilcox (First Youth at Hot Dog Stand); Jason Kristopher and Seth Green (Youths at Hot Dog Stand); Alexis Arquette (Panhandler); Larry Nash (Policeman at Gas Station); Mae Elvis (Eleven Year Old Girl); Dean Hallo (Charles); Kerry Remsen (Pregnant Woman at Bus Stop); Googy Gress (Bystander at Bus Stop); Lisa Dinkins and Lawrence T. Wrentz (Shooting Policemen); Steve Larson (Bottle Thrower); Lawrence Bender (Bar Patron #1); Matt O'Toole (Bar Patron #2); Iain Jones (Bar Patron #3); Janet Hubert, Attallah Shabazz, and Willette Klausner (Dinner Guests); David C. Harvey (Factory Worker); *TV CLIPS:* Amy Powell (Newscaster); Keith Collier and Annamarie Simmons (Dancers); Rosie Tenison (Detective); Manny Jacobson (Himself); Dondre Whitfield (Terrence); Ingrid Rogers (Taylor).

LOS ANGELES TIMES, 12/1/95, Calendar/p. 1, Jack Mathews

[The following review by Jack Mathews appeared in a slightly different form in NEWSDAY, 12/1/95, Part II/p. B2.]

During the Los Angeles riots that followed the acquittal of the four police officers caught on video beating Rodney G. King, a woman from the all-white Simi Valley jury called a radio talk show and stunned by the reaction in the African American community, said it was clear to her and the other jurors that King had been in total charge of his destiny that night.

All he had to do to stop the beating, she said, was stop resisting.

It is for that woman, that jury and everyone who cannot imagine what it is to be routinely harassed and provoked by police that Desmond Nakano's "White Man's Burden" may do the most good. The movie, a "Twilight Zone"-style drama in which the class positions of black and white Americans are reversed, will—in regard to nearly everyone else—be preaching to the converted.

"White Man's Burden" works better as a conventional urban drama than as an essay on race relations, which is its resolute purpose. It is a mostly somber piece of work, the story of a struggling ghetto white man (John Travolta) who takes out his frustration over a lost job and his family's eviction from their home by kidnaping and demanding restitution from the company CEO who caused him to be fired.

The triggering incident occurs when Travolta's Lou Pinnock volunteers to deliver some material to the baronial home of CEO Thaddeus Thomas (Harry Belafonte), and while lost on the grounds, gets a glimpse through an upstairs window of the boss's wife (Margaret Avery) changing clothes. A lowly white man looking at the naked body of a powerful black man's woman? The distasteful thought prompts Thomas to drop a subconscious hint to one of his managers, and Pinnock is sacked.

After establishing the film's fantasy premise, and getting the outraged Lou alone for a weekend of running and hiding with his hostage, the film settles into a two-person allegory, with the lessons learned by each man about the other making an all-too-pat sermon about race relations in general.

Travolta and Belafonte play well off of each other, and the film is at its best exploring the prejudices and attitudes of their characters. But it's a familiar story, where only the colors have been changed.

Nakano, a Japanese American screenwriter ("Last Exit to Brooklyn") making his directing debut, hangs the success of his ambitious message on the assumption that by simply flopping the roles and stereotypes of blacks and whites, we will all be left equally disoriented.

It doesn't quite work that way. Black and white audiences may react differently to the film, as news stories about its segregated preview screenings suggest. There will certainly be more personal satisfaction, and a few good laughs, for blacks in the stream of altered cultural references: a white lawn jockey in a rich black neighborhood, TV commercials dominated by black actors, a poor white child's preference for a black super-hero doll over a white one.

But in Nakano's starkly contrasting world, where every scene occurs in the violent white ghetto or in a black Beverly Hills, and where racially mixed police patrols stand in for the paranoid middle class, there isn't much room for exploring the nuances of racism in the '90s.

In fact, Nakano's reversal has nothing to add and is nowhere near as eye-opening as "Black Like Me," a book and movie more than 30 years old about the experiences of white reporter John Howard Griffin, who darkened his skin and traveled as black man through the segregated South. The role-reversal gimmick there was real, and the white readers and viewers to whom, it was appealing, were compelled by their identification with Griffin to feel the hatred, indignity and humiliations routinely heaped on Southern blacks.

"White Man's Burden" hits the same buttons, and you begin to tick off a checklist of abuses that Lou and his wife (Kelly Lynch) and the other whites endure. But it does not have the same impact because beyond its superficial racial twists, it is a conventional drama so stacked against the power class that the racial issues become increasingly irrelevant.

It is always easier, if not emotionally inescapable, to sympathize with a common man wronged than the fat-cat responsible, and would be no matter what the color combination.

NEW YORK POST, 12/1/95, p. 39, Michael Medved

"White Man's Burden" offers a number of images so poignant and startling that they settle more or less permanently into the imagination and continue to echo for days after you've seen the picture.

I found it impossible, for instance, to shake the memory of the 5-year-old son of a desperate, unemployed factory worker (John Travolta), pathetically clutching the oversized plastic action figure he wants to buy.

The toy is a glitzy icon of a black super-hero; the child has stubbornly resisted his father's urging to get a doll who is white, like he is. After all, the people the boy sees on TV—cowboys, policemen, glamorous models, media evangelists, weathermen and comedians—are all black. The only white face appears on a newscast when the black anchorman inevitably identifies the murder suspect as a "male Caucasian."

This is the topsy-turvy world of "White Man's Burden" where, through an ingenious and well thought out reversal of fortune, the races have switched places. In this version of reality, America has always been dominated b a majority population of African descent, while those of European ancestry represent a dysfunctional, impoverished and violence-prone minority.

Attitudes in the majority community range from undisguised racism on the part of stylish business tycoon Harry Belafonte (who asserts that whites are genetically inferior), to compassion from his colleague's wife (Sheryl Lee Ralph), who praises the earthy vitality of white music and cites the adorable, hopeful faces of the "little white children" who benefit from one of her charities.

The story begins when Travolta, a dedicated worker and good family man, volunteers to run an after-hours errand for his black boss. He agrees to deliver a package to exclusive Bel Air ("I know that neighborhood. My ma used to clean house for a nice black family up there") and drives down the tree-shaded streets noting the occasional white hitching boys at the edge of manicured lawns.

At Belafonte's old-money estate, Travolta waits to complete his delivery, but the master of the house looks out his window and thinks that he sees the white staring lustfully at his gorgeous second wife (Margaret Avery). The wealthy executive later makes a passing comment to his associate about the delivery boy's impertinence, which results in Travolta losing a job.

When he can't pay the rent or support his harried wife (Kelly Lynch) and their two small children, the previously honest, respectful working stiff goes back to Bel Air to kidnap Belafonte and exact his revenge.

The best part of "White Man's Burden" is that it's so well-acted and sensitively directed that even without its fascinating central gimmick it would be an absorbing, thought-provoking melodrama.

First-time director Desmond Nakano previously wrote the Latino gang stories "Boulevard Nights" and "American Me." Nekano is, in fact, neither Hispanic, black nor white—he happens to be Japanese-American. As such, he demonstrates rich sympathy for all the characters in "White

Man's Burden," offering heartbreaking treatment of Travolta's desperation, but also showing that beneath the casual veneer of unthinking racism Belafonte is a fundamentally decent guy.

There's nothing electrifying or extraordinary about Nakano's filmmaking approach. He lets his story tell itself in an unadorned, matter-of-fact, fly-on-the-wall style—and the movie only gains force as a result.

In fact, Nakano will have to accept his own burden after "White Man's Burden' is released—since it will be hard for any young filmmaker to live up to such a powerful, provocative directing debut.

SIGHT AND SOUND, 2/97, p. 60, Kim Newman

An alternative America, where the positions of the white and black races are reversed. Factory hand Louis Pinnock, hoping to win a promotion, volunteers to deliver a package to the home of wealthy Thaddeus Thomas. At the Thomas mansion, Pinnock accidentally glimpses Mrs Thomas naked; Thomas mildly asks Lionel, Pinnock's boss, not to send Pinnock to the house again, whereupon Lionel dismisses Pinnock.

Already struggling to meet medical bills incurred by an ill baby and the promise of giving an expensive toy to his six-year-old son Donnie, Pinnock is unable to get a new job. He tries to talk with Thomas but is brushed off by the white maid, and suffers further when he is beaten up by racist cops and evicted by his landlord. Marsha, Pinnock's wife, is forced to move in with her mother, and Pinnock finds himself in a squat with a down-and-out named Stanley. Pinnock kidnaps Thomas and tries to extort the $3000 he reckons the rich man owes him, but is forced when the banks close to keep Thomas hostage over the weekend.

Spending time in the ghetto with the desperate Pinnock, Thomas develops a certain sympathy for the underdog, but makes an escape attempt when Pinnock tells him that he will probably have to kill him. Thomas breaks into a house and calls his wife, bringing the police to the ghetto, but is chased off by the residents and recaptured by Pinnock. When Thomas has a seizure, Pinnock tries to get him to hospital only to have his ailing truck die under him. Firing his gun to attract attention and staying with Thomas to explain that he needs medical attention, Pinnock is shot dead by the police. Later, Thomas tries to give Marsha money and is turned down.

The purpose of topsy-turvy fictions like *White Man's Burden*, which stretch back all the way to Swift's *Gulliver's Travels* where horses rule over men, is to force you to reassess the real world by depicting it through a distorting mirror in which familiar situations are turned inside-out. However, though it makes a few tentative stabs at creating African-flavoured Americana, this is too limited in its ambitions to prompt much in the way of racial analysis. Given that films like *Boomerang*, *Bad Boys* and *A Thin Line Between Love And Hate* already take place in an alternate world where blacks are conservatively-dressed, well-off and born winners, this story hardly needs to have a fantasy setting at all. The gradual unbending of Harry Belafonte's uppercrust financier comes from exposure to the gun of a growling and desperate John Travolta. It is a far less subtle, more achingly 'liberal' bit of cross-class kidnapping than that on display in the surprisingly similarly plotted *Kansas City*, so the film can't quite get itself to work as a character drama above and beyond its gimmick.

Japanese-American writer/director Desmond Nakano's script rifts on familiar sentiments (Thomas condemns whites for burning down their own neighbourhoods) or incidents (black cops administering the Rodney King-treatment to the innocent Pinnock). But it goes no further than the liberal Mrs Thomas's clucking over the cute white kids she stages a charity fashion pageant to support and her almost unnoticed doubletake when her son shows up with a white girlfriend. The ineffectuality of this approach can best be gauged by imagining how thin this film would seem if it was set in the real world with a rich white guy and a poor black one—the film would justifiably be condemned for cartoonish generalising about serious topics. Even the generally feeble TV show *Sliders*, which often visits worlds where women dominate men or scientists are valued above athletes, realises that it's not enough just to cast against type, by having cops and landlords and models be black and winos and drug dealers and maids white. To make it work, you have to unpick actual history and suggest how this situation came to be.

Shot on recognisable real world Los Angeles locations, this never evokes a history that has led to its version of the 90s. What if, say, a Moorish empire discovered America and imported Nordic slaves? Though this world has class divisions, it has no racially-charged religion (a few minor Islamic Symbols aside), slang (the script doesn't even come up with a term of racial abuse directed at whites), politics (there seems to be no white civil rights movement) or culture (where does popular music come from?). A channel-surfing montage shows a 'Whitebread' black sit-com, three black girls in an action show and a black Western hero in a Union Army uniform, and there's a neat bit when Stan the vagrant explains that blacks don't like to come to the ghetto because after dark white people look like ghosts. But this is too cartoonish a reversal to resonate; where, one asks, are the white versions of *The Cosby Show* and *Oprah*, and doesn't this world have its own Eddie Murphy, Louis Farrakhan, Spike Lee, Michael Jordan or Michael Jackson?

What *White Man's Burden* does have is Travolta, indulging his current clout with an offbeat project but also with a performance that really deserves a stronger film. Louis Pinnock is scripted as a cipher, a decent man forced out in the cold but passionately concerned with his family. Travolta plays him to the hilt, carting around a proletarian gut, and erupting into profane rages that distantly echo but don't imitate real-world black speech patterns, delivering a *Pulp Fiction*-ish tip to Thomas about pouring salt into ketchup so the right amount adheres to fries. But after all his work, he just ends up dead in the gutter so his wife, in a scene that rings amazingly false, can righteously turn down Thomas's offer of a money-stuffed envelope.

VILLAGE VOICE, 12/5/95, p. 68, Gary Dauphin

As the road to black-movie hell is often paved with nonblack good intentions, it's easy to imagine the amount of political earnestness and sincerity that went into the production of *White Man's Burden*. A film about a what-if America where white lawn jockeys decorate the yards of a black master class, *Burden*'s instructive possibilities are no doubt what attracted the likes of John Travolta, Harry Belafonte, and Lawrence Bender (producer of Tarantino films) the to the project. It will surprise some people, then given the above array of players and pedigrees, that *White Man's Burden* is such a truly awful film, its aggressively muddled politics contesting with its cliché ridden story line for your annoyance and occasional outrage.

Since *Burden* has the unobtrusive look of a TV movie (this is writer-director Desmond Nakano's first film, after adapting *American Me* and *Last Exit to Brooklyn*), the script and the overall concept are initially the most obvious of the film's flaws. Louis Pinnock (Travolta, beefy and with a bad dye job, sounding like a world-weary Vinnie Barbarino) is your average white guy in a black man's world, working a dead-end factory job in order to buy his son the pigmented action figure he's always wanted. When a misunderstanding with Thad (Belafonte as the racist plant owner) leaves Louis unemployed, Nakano delivers a series of blows to Louis's flagging manhood (eviction, a beating from racist black cops, Louis's woman entering the work force) until finally Louis explodes in a fit of white (or is that black?) rage, abducting Thad at gunpoint.

What ensues isn't the planned exchange of back pay but of redeeming looks at how the other half lives, Thad getting a lesson in the innate nobility of "those people," while Louis gets a chance to choose between his own safety and Thad's. Good-hearted Negro that he's intended to be beneath the skin, Louis of course chooses the latter.

The deprivations Louis suffers are all quite plausible in today's racial and economic climate, so plausible, in fact, that *Burden*'s claim that it's a courageous switcheroo starts to seem like a hustle. Most working-class white people in this country live like Louis, and Thad's tacky 'Ebony Fashion Fair' milieu is a black bourgie archetype unto itself. Moreover, despite the didactic good intentions of its script, *White Man's Burden*'s visual scheme has the insidious side effect off reproducing the worst of right-wing social fantasies: Hard working white man loses his job because of black man, gets to tie up black man and rough him up until black man sees the light. These are images you can trace back to Griffith's *Birth of a Nation*.

Also reviewed in:
CHICAGO TRIBUNE, 12/1/95, Friday/p. D, Michael Wilmington
NEW YORK TIMES, 12/1/95, p. C3, Stephen Holden
NEW YORKER, 12/11/95, p. 107, Anthony Lane
VARIETY, 9/25-10/1/95, p. 92, David Rooney
WASHINGTON POST, 12/1/95, p. F7, Rita Kempley
WASHINGTON POST, 12/1/95, Weekend/p. 48, Desson Howe

WIGSTOCK: THE MOVIE

A Samuel Goldwyn Company release. *Executive Producer:* Klaus Volkenborn, Susan Ripps, and Barry Shils. *Producer:* Dean Silver and Marlen Hecht. *Director:* Barry Shils. *Director of Photography:* Wolfgang Held. *Editor:* Wolfgang Held, Tod Scott Brody, and Barry Shills. *Music:* Peter Fish and Robert Reale. *Running time:* 85 minutes. *MPAA Rating:* Not Rated.

WITH: RuPaul; Alexis Arquette; Jackie Beat; Deee-lite; Lady Bunny; Lypsinka; Mistress Formika; Crystal Waters; Joey Arias.

LOS ANGELES TIMES, 6/9/95, Calendar/p. 6, Kevin Thomas

Part concert film, part documentary and totally fun, Barry Shils' "Wigstock: The Movie" captures the good cheer, outrageous humor and high energy of downtown Manhattan's annual Labor Day drag extravaganza, which surely must exhaust New York of its supply of sequins, feathers, Spring-o-laters—and, most of all, wigs. Wigs as tall as the Statue of Liberty—who remained wigless, but not because festival founder Lady Bunny didn't try.

Inclusiveness is the hallmark of the glittery occasion onstage and off. Performers may be transvestites, transsexuals—pre-ops included, of course—for that matter, they can even be straight or female. They can be obscure and not very good or they can be a true star, as is the glamorous, justly celebrated RuPaul or the wickedly satirical Lypsinka. And when the talented Joey Arias sings as Billie Holiday yet gets himself up like the last Empress of China, that seems perfectly OK with an audience that couldn't be more eclectic or enthusiastic: straight and gay, young and old, fat and thin, and crossing all racial lines.

Indeed, Wigstock, launched in 1984, outgrew its original Tompkins Square locale in the East Village and last year moved to the Christopher Street Piers, where it drew an audience of 20,000. Wigstock might not be able to happen anywhere else but New York, but there's something heartening in seeing that, of all things, a marathon drag revue could bring together so many people so joyously. Among the countless entertainers are the musical trio Dee-Lite, L.A.'s Jackie Beat, the formidable Mistress Formika and recording artist Crystal Waters.

Shils' laid-back, easygoing style suits the sunny summer holiday spirit of the occasion perfectly. "Wigstock" is not trying to be a sharp, incisive film like either "Paris Is Burning" or "The Queen," and its backstage banter is lighter, less bitchy; but then "Wigstock" is not a competition. There's no heavy probing of why men should want to dress up like women; these guys just want to because for them it's fun and it expresses how they feel about themselves.

A young African American man explains that when you have to deal with sexism, racism and homophobia every day of your life, Wigstock becomes a great escape. Shils, who combines footage from the 1993 and 1994 Wigstocks, never lets his film get too serious, yet it acknowledges, in touching fashion, the toll AIDS continues to exact in the drag community. "Wigstock" is a hoot, and, as an old man—possibly homeless—remarks, "It's not hurtin' nobody."

NEW YORK POST, 6/9/95, p. 39, Thelma Adams

Look ma, no mud! There are definite advantages to reinventing Woodstock in the asphalt jungle. "Wigstock: The Movie", celebrates the 10th anniversary of a kitschy Village event: a sybaritic sunfest created by and for drag queens but free and open to the public.

Barry Shils' buoyant documentary opens with transvestite Mistress Formika's fierce rendition of "The Age of Aquarius" from the musical "Hair." Sung through quivering purple lips, it becomes a passionate anthem to creativity, self-expression, and upside-down version of the American Way.

"Wigstock" concludes with John Kelly wearing the flat golden locks and earnest expression of Joni Mitchell (but a dress that's a tad glitzy for the lady of the canyon). Kelly croons an affected but affecting version of the '60s theme song "Woodstock." The words have been updated, but the refrain remains the same: "We are stardust, we are golden."

Sandwiched between these two songs is a good-natured, bawdy armchair tour of the 1994 musical revue mixed with scenes of the rowdy crowds at the Christopher Street piers, casual interviews and footage from past Wigstocks.

Self-proclaimed "Supermodel of the World" RuPaul, a stately and stunningly beautiful transvestite, comes as close to a headline act as this democratic concert contains. This home-town girl made good delivers the film's heartfelt message: "Hold onto your dream."

The creator of the music festival and emcee, Lady Bunny, stitches the day together. Dressed in a series of elaborate platinum wigs that would have made Marie Antoinette twitch, the large-framed Bunny prances the stage on shapely, shiny legs, the epitome of a Dame. As she says, this is a day we can "let our hair down."

"Wigstock" emerges as one of those rare New York excursions in street theater, at once outrageous and good-natured, where cops on the beat, bulldogs in wigs, grannies watching a free show and men in G-strings and Wonderbras can hang out and harmonize, in Lady Liberty's shadow.

NEWSDAY, 6/9/95, Part II/p. B5, John Anderson

No psychology, no tears, no weighty analyses of sociosexual shifting or Mom's role in the cosmos: "Wigstock: The Movie," Barry Shils' very affectionate—and virtually agitprop—documentary on drag's annual day in the sun, is strictly divas till dawn.

Besides providing latex-like support to cross-dressing and cross-dressers, director Shils lets the performers who populate Wigstock—including the statuesque RuPaul, the near-legendary Lypsinka (John Epperson), Dee-Lite and Crystal Waters—have free voice about lingerie, lipstick and the therapeutic qualities of cross-dressing. "Go out and get a wig and pair of high heels," RuPaul advises both gays and straights, "and strut your stuff."

"Mother Nature must be a drag queen'" squeals the weather approving Lady Bunny, a major fixture on the New York drag circuit and one of the festival's founders, who has hosted the all-day affair since its inception in 1984. Employing footage from both the 1993 festival in Tompkins Square Park and the '94 edition on the Christopher Street piers, the film provides snapshots of the revelers as well as full musical performances: Lypsinka's manic "But Alive" from "Applause" is a highlight, as Jackie Beat's "Kiss My ---," the quasi-rap "It's Natural" by Tabboo! and Water's "100% Pure Love." Other entertainments range from the " ----- You Symphony," directed by The Lady Bunny at "everyone who's ever held us back," to John Kelly's Joni Mitchell-impersonating rendition of "Wigstock" (sung to the tune of "Woodstock").

Self-celebratory and—considering the state of gay America—a bit Neroesque, "Wigstock" has much good-natured fun with the unsuspecting and unindoctrinated: tourists staring drop-jawed at some of the more outrageous participants; elderly park ladies unruffled by bench-sharing 6-foot-4 transvestites; actor-drag queen Alexis Arquette and colleague Jackie Beat vamping a couple of construction workers whose machismo is no match for high camp.

"Wigstock: The Movie" falls short of the emotional mark of a film such as "Paris Is Burning," which subjected the drag phenomenon to a far more sophisticated examination. But the movie's enthusiasm is infectious—even if, personally, there seemed to be a bit too much disco-mambo, and not enough show tunes and Lypsinka.

VILLAGE VOICE, 6/13/95, p. 58, James Hannaham

Wigstock is a joyous, colorful celebration of freedom of sexuality and identity that has a liberating and exhilarating effect on its attendees. *Wigstock: The Movie* takes that same East Village carnival of cross-dressing, chops it into a disorganized smattering of footage from 1993 and 1994 Wigstocks, splices in some careless interviews and dress-up shots, and its effect, for those who have attended, is like going through a scrapbook. You get some warm nostalgic waves, fond memories of specific people, not-so-fond memories of bitchy queens you hate, and you put it away feeling old.

Director Barry Shils dithers between documenting the performances, only one or two of which he presents in their entirety, and simplistic analysis, flimsier than chiffon, provided by the drag queens themselves. "Most men do drag because ... they like women's clothes," says *uber*-queen The"Lady" Bunny. Shils wants the film to explain something about the joy of genderfuck as performance, but he hasn't clued in that his subjects are a self-congratulatory, self-referential clique, and the feel-good propaganda and oversimplification get thicker than the makeup. Drag queens, after all, are big stars before they ever hit the stage, and the divas they idolize are prone to providing snappy sound bites rather than deep commentary. "It's a tribute to women," Bunny goes on, without ever being called on to acknowledge that (a) only a few "real" women participate, or (b) many women don't receive drag as a tribute.

Drag dresses up fluidity of gender identity, image, and performance, in a gorgeous, controversial sarong worthy of far more in-depth exploration than it gets here. The acts that exploit the transparent nature of drag arc the most interesting in this film—Crystal Waters pulling off her fake mustache; Floyd casting aside his falsies while singing, "What makes a man a man?"; and Joey Arias providing a demonstration of his Billie Holiday impersonation while dressed as a '50s greaser.

Wigstock, however, is drag in rag, a festival of artifice too far steeped in irony and stoned on its own endorphins to benefit from analysis. *Wigstock: The Movie*, trapped between documentary and concert film, loses its high because it's a celebration of showing forced to tell. What good is freedom if you don't set it free?

Also reviewed in:
NEW YORK TIMES, 6/9/95, p. C5, Caryn James
VARIETY, 2/13-19/95, p. 50, Emanuel Levy
WASHINGTON POST, 6/23/95, p. F7, Martha Sherrill
WASHINGTON POST, 6/23/95, Weekend/p. 38, Desson Howe

WILD BILL

A United Artists release of a Zanuck Company production. *Producer:* Richard D. Zanuck and Lili Fini Zanuck. *Director:* Walter Hill. *Screenplay:* Walter Hill. *Based on the play "Fathers and Sons" by:* Thomas Babe. *Based on the novel "Deadwood" by:* Pete Dexter. *Director of Photography:* Lloyd Ahern. *Editor:* Freeman Davies. *Music:* Van Dyke Parks. *Music Editor:* Bunny Andrews. *Sound:* Lee Orloff and (music) Murray McFadden. *Sound Editor:* Jay Wilkinson. *Casting:* Shari Rhodes and Joseph Middleton. *Production Designer:* Joseph Nemec III. *Art Director:* Daniel Olexiewicz. *Set Designer:* Steven Schwartz, William Law III, Carole L. Cole, and Daniel Ross. *Set Decorator:* Gary Fettis. *Set Dresser:* Eric J. Bates, Donald Kaeding, Jeffrey Kushon, Kurt Hulett, and Carl Cassara. *Special Effects:* Lawrence J. Cavanaugh. *Costumes:* Barry Kellogg. *Costumes (Ellen Barkin):* Dorie Halperin. *Make-up:* Gary D. Liddiard. *Make-up (Jeff Bridges):* Edouard Henriques III. *Make-up (Ellen Barkin):* Desne Holland. *Stunt Coordinator:* Allan Graf. *Running time:* 97 minutes. *MPAA Rating:* R.

CAST: Jeff Bridges (Wild Bill Hickok); Ellen Barkin (Calamity Jane); John Hurt (Charley Prince); Diane Lane (Susannah Moore); Keith Carradine (Buffalo Bill Cody); David Arquette (Jack McCall); Christina Applegate (Lurline); Bruce Dern (Will Plummer); James Gammon (California Joe); Marjoe Gortner (Preacher); James Remar (Donnie Lonigan); Karen Huie (Song Lew); Steve Reevis (Sioux Chief Whistler); Robert Knott (Dave Tutt); Pato Hoffmann (Cheyenne Leader); Patrick Gorman (Doctor); Lee deBroux (Carl Mann); Stoney Jackson (Jubal Pickett); Robert Peters (Mike Williams); Steve Chambers (Curly); Jimmy Medearis (Coke); Jason Ronard (Pink Buford); Dennis Hayden (Phil Coe); Teresa Gilmore (Jessie Hazlitt); John Dennis Johnston (Ed Plummer); Boots Southerland (Crook-Eye Clark); James Michael Taylor (Lew Scott); Loyd Catlett (Bob Rainwater); Janel Moloney (Earlene); Ted Markland (Tommy Drum); Monty Stuart and Merritt Yohnka (Soldiers); Dennis Deveaugh (Big Trooper); Jim Wilkey (Seth Beeber); Raleigh Wilson (Jack Slater); Charles Gunning (Frank Dowder); Chris Doyle (John Harkness); Virgil Frye (Buffalo Hunter); Lauren Abels (Singer at Funeral); Ritt Henn (Fiddle Player); Lise Hilboldt and Trisha Munford (Women in Church); Charlie Seybert (Citizen); Luana Anders (Sanitarium Woman); Roland Nip (Chinese Man); Mike Watson (Cowpoke); Thomas Wilson Brown (Drover); Robert Keith (Miner); Linda Harrison (Madam); Patricia M. Peters (Dancer); Anthony De Longis (Card Cheat); Bill

Bolender (Bartender at Way Station); Alisa Christensen and Patricia Pretzinger (Mann's No. 10 Saloon Bargirls); Peter Jason (Dave McCandless); Joseph Crozier (Old Timer); Mikey LeBeau (Young Jack); Jaime Elysse (Young Woman with Parasol); Jamie Marsh (Young Man); Burton Gilliam (Bartender); Del Roy and Steve Brasfield (Gamblers); Juddson Keith Linn (Cheyenne Rider).

CHRISTIAN SCIENCE MONITOR, 12/5/95, p. 13, David Sterritt

In a statement on his new western, "Wild Bill," filmmaker Walter Hill notes that in the past "much has been done to glamorize the frontier West," which in reality was "all too often a time of abysmal ignorance, rude poverty, and senseless violence." Hill then asks why we continuously celebrate this historical moment?"

That's a good question, but it was fresher when filmmakers started to ask it about 30 years ago. While it's true Hollywood celebrated the old West in countless simplistic pictures from the early, 1900s on, a wave of '60s and '70s films turned the old vision on its head. In revisionist hits like "A Fistful of Dollars" and "The Wild Bunch," directors like Sergio Leone and Sam Peckinpah eagerly splashed ignorance, poverty, and violence all over the screen. Critics still debate the usefulness of these exercises, but there's no questioning the power they exerted over moviegoers in the troubled era of Vietnam and Watergate.

"Wild Bill" follows this tradition so faithfully that western fans will find little in it they haven't seen before. The eponymous hero is Wild Bill Hickok, portrayed in a way that utterly rejects him as the romantic figure who strode through, say, Guy Madison's popular TV series in the '50s. Here he's dirty, dangerous, lecherous, and so ill-tempered that you wonder why a sane person would spend minutes in the same town with him.

His girlfriend, Calamity Jane, is somewhat more civilized but still nobody you'd want to mess with. Complicating their eventful lives and on-and-off love affair is their lurking awareness that Bill has more than his share of enemies, rivals, and thrill-seeking kids who'd kill him just for the dubious glory it would bring. Needless to say, one of them eventually guns him down, and it's as sorry an episode as one would expect at the end of a life and a movie so drenched in down-and-dirty sourness.

Hill knows his way around action-film territory, having racked up a long list of credits ranging from "The Warriors" and "The Driver" to "48 Hrs." and "The Long Riders," among many others. His filmmaking is often vigorous and stylish, but you'll rarely find much going on beneath the violent surfaces of his hard-hitting plots.

"Wild Bill" finds him at his most self-assured and least original. Devotees will enjoy his unabashed fondness for post-Peckinpah gore, grunge, and sleaze. Others will long for the days when Madison portrayed the same legendary character with a square jaw, a clean vest, and a moral code that made up in rectitude what it lacked in contact with the real world.

Jeff Bridges appears to have a great time wallowing in his wildly undignified role, and Ellen Barkin almost makes Calamity Jane seem like a character out of life rather than legend. The able supporting cast includes John Hurt as one of Bill's few friends, David Arquette as one of his many foes, Diane Lane as a woman he was once, involved with, and Marjoe Gortner as (appropriately) a local preacher. Don't blink or you'll miss Keith Carradine as Buffalo Bill Cody and Bruce Dern as an unlikely gunfighter. The production designer, Joseph Nemec III, has cooked up a convincing replica of Deadwood, S.D., and Lloyd Ahern has photographed it in suitably dark tones.

It's a job well done, but given the nastiness of the picture, not necessarily a job worth doing.

LOS ANGELES TIMES, 12/1/95, Calendar/p. 1, Jack Mathews

Walter Hill should have been born 25 or 30 years earlier and become a movie director when Westerns, those featuring the kind of romanticized, dime-novel tales debunked in Clint Eastwood's "Unforgiven," were appreciated.

Hill has a genuine passion for the Old West, Hollywood's Old West, made with a dash of history and a wagonload of legend, and he showed what he could do with that material in his crafty 1980 "The Long Riders." There, he replayed the exploits of Jesse James and his gang, using actor-brothers to portray the various outlaw siblings in the gang, and through the film's exuberance you could almost feel Hill behind the camera, maybe wearing a two-gun holster himself, cheering them on.

But that kind of unapologetic mythmaking is, sadly, gone from movies, and in his two latest passes at the genre—last year's "Geronimo" and "Wild Bill," opening today—Hill has had trouble finding a place for himself. With "Geronimo," an honorable effort to right some wrongs done the Apache' warrior in past movies, he seemed stifled by his commitment to history. And in "Wild Bill," which he wants us to see as a psychological profile of a legend's final days, he can't for the life of him let go of the legend.

Wild Bill is, of course, James Butler Hickok, the frontier lawman and gambler who packed a lot of life into his 39 years and went out in grand gunfighter fashion, assassinated by young Jack McCall while holding the since-famous "dead man's hand" (full house; aces over eights) in a poker game in Deadwood, S.D.

Hickok was the real deal among gunslingers, though he probably killed no more than 20 of the 200 men biographers of his day claimed for him. He was, by all accounts, a striking frontier figure, well-dressed and handsome, tall and menacing, and a man known throughout the West of the 1860s and '70s for his quick temper and sure aim.

Jeff Bridges fits the physical description to a T, right down to the flowing hair and bushy mustache; and over the course of the movie, gives us a marvelously rich and honest look at a simple man of legendary pluck trying, with his sight failing and his luck running out, to reconcile his fame with his own self-image. It's a remarkably full performance in a movie that simply cannot fill the space around him.

After an extended prologue, a series of time-compacted, unrelated action pieces that plays like a "Wild Bill's Best Kills" highlight film, the movie settles down in 1876 Deadwood, where Hickok is joined by old friends Calamity Jane (Ellen Barkin), California Joe (James Gammon) and Charley Prince (John Hurt), an effete Englishman who, for reasons of convenience (he narrates the story), has become Hickok's sidekick. Wild Bill will still draw and fire at the slightest provocation, but there's a tired soul inside that strapping frame, and a tug at his conscience that keeps drawing him to the pipe at Deadwood's Chinese opium den.

Hill adapted his script from a variety of sources that include Pete Dexter's novel "Deadwood," Thomas Babe's play "Fathers and Sons" and his own considerable research and imagination, and the seams are as visible as the stitches on the neck of Frankenstein's monster. The movie's tone is all over the place, from blustery shoot-outs, to moody introspection, to farce (Barkin's take on ripsnortin', lovesick Calamity Jane is a calamity in its own right), to a sort of wimpy Greek tragedy.

The film's wildest leap has Jack McCall (David Arquette) being the son of onetime Hickok girlfriend Susannah Moore (the lovely Diane Lane, giving her entire performance in a series of bleached-out black-and-white flashbacks) out to avenge a perceived offense. The device works to frame the story, and Hickok's cavalier dismissal and taunting of the young hothead underscores a frame of mind verging on suicidal. But the scenes between them are so disjointed in tone—it's legend; no, it's fact—that the tension is drained right out of them.

In the "Wild Bill" production notes, Hill refers, with an amen, to the line at the end of John Ford's "The Man Who Shot Liberty Valance": "When the legend becomes a fact, print the legend." Would that Hill had taken the advice. He's tried to print both the facts and legend, ending up with something that is alternately brilliant frustratingly self-conscious, in the end, pretty much a wash.

NEW YORK, 12/18/95, p. 51, David Denby

Why have so many intelligent critics lied about Walter Hill's *Wild Bill*? Apart from some of Jeff Bridges's line readings, this is a pretentious and laborious bore. Avoid.

NEW YORK POST, 12/1/95, p. 47, Michael Medved

James Butler (Wild Bill) Hickok (1837-1876) earned an international reputation as a marksman of uncanny precision and deadly accuracy, but his cinematic biographer Walter Hill ("Geronimo," "48 Hours") can't aim to save his life.

Wild Hill comes out with both guns blazing but fires everywhere at once, and his ambitious but fatally unfocused film fails to hit and of its targets.

Part of the problem stems from misguided attempts to stitch together disparate source material: "Wild Bill" is officially based on a colorful, elegiac historical novel ("Deadwood" by Pete Dexter) and an outrageous, tongue-in-cheek theater piece ("Fathers and Sons" by Thomas Babe), as well as Hill's own research on the real-life Hickok.

The result is an easy blend of ponderous, visually impressive historical revisionism in the style of Lawrence Kasdan's bloated "Wyatt Earp," and feeble, distracting stabs at quirky satire.

None of it works, especially since the already slow-moving picture feels as if it's been clumsily cut down from a much longer version.

The picture begins with Hickok's funeral as an English writer (John Hurt) offers flowery narration about his late friend's bloody career.

With Jeff Bridges in the title role, we catch quick, fleeting glimpses of Bill's work as a lawman in Kansas (where he shot one of his own deputies and feuded with members of Custer's 7th Calvary), and as a member of Buffalo Bill Cody's celebrated Wild West Show. All of this is based on history, but when the movie settles into the brawling gold rush town of Deadwood, S.D., the movie loses all credibility and narrative momentum.

Bill spends his days gambling and reconnecting with his lusty, tomboyish old flame Calamity Jane (Ellen Barkin), while confronting a twitchy punk named Jack McCall (David Arquette) who comes to town with the announced intention of murdering Hickok.

It turns out that Wild Bill had disgraced Jack's mother many years before, and in a series of flash-backs induced by visits to a Chinatown opium den we learn that this woman (Diane Lane) is actually Wild Bill's one true love.

These psychedelic flashbacks are the least effective moments in the movie, shot with wildly askew camera angles in high-contrast, overexposed black-and-white.

Meanwhile, back in the saloon, McCall inexplicably comes up with $1,000 in cash (a huge fortune in 1876!) to pay hired gunmen (James Remar, Stoney Jackson and others) to help dispatch Wild Bill. There's lots of conversation between the killers and their target that's meant to be funny but doesn't bring a single laugh.

Bridges, one of today's most consistently under-appreciated actors, gives his impossible role an aura of gruff heroism combined with the pathos of a lonely man trapped by his own legendary status. He bears an eerie resemblance to photographs of the actual Wild Bill and his appropriately dandified costumes (by Dan Moore) look splendid.

The production designer (Joseph Nemec) also went to great lengths to create perhaps the soggiest western street in movie history. As co-producer Lili Zanuck proudly boasts: "Our streets are full of mud and our bar girls have bruises," but it's the story that sinks in its own formless ooze and it's the audience's attention span that is badly bruised.

TIME, 12/4/95, p. 86, Richard Schickel

To some degree all gunfighter westerns are meditations on celebrity. As the hero proceeds along his increasingly corpse-strewn path, making one vivid assertion after another of his deadly prowess, he becomes a public figure, a source of rumor, legend and awe, just like a movie star. His reputation—always preceding him, simultaneously distancing and entrancing his public—becomes both a source of strength, making tremulous the hands of his enemies, and a source of danger, in that it encourages people who want a piece of his fame to form an entourage around him. Or challenge him to a deadly encounter.

Wild Bill, which is one of the dankest and most claustrophobic westerns ever made—a movie that deliberately shuts itself off from the clean, redeeming beauty of prairie, mountain and desert—takes the celebrity metaphor into new realms of darkness and hysteria. Written and directed by Walter Hill *(48 HRS.),* it presents Wild Bill Hickok (Jeff Bridges) as a moron with a fetish: if anyone touches his hat, he will shoot him. Not that he really requires an excuse to ven tilate any and all comers. It is just that this is what the man does when he's not repairing to an opium den and losing himself in bad pipe dreams. Or drinking too much. Or resisting the advances of Calamity Jane (Ellen Barkin).

The guy's on the kind of bad star trip tabloid journalism has made all too familiar to modern audiences. The trouble for him is that the founding of the Betty Ford Clinic is over a century in the future. The trouble for us is that *The Plainsman*, in which Gary Cooper and Jean Arthur played these figures in accordance with the conventions of their time—as protagonists in something pretty close to a screwball comedy—is 60 years in the past. In other words *Wild Bill* was born too soon for professional help, and we, it seems, were born too late for the more cheerful forms of mythologizing.

Hill's largest invention, one entirely in keeping with his apparent determination to make the most radically revisionist western ever, is a backstory shared by Wild Bill and Jack McCall (David Arquette), who history teaches us brought the gunman's career to an end by shooting him in the back. Seems that the former loved and rather crassly left a decent woman named Susannah Moore (the lovely Diane Lane). Seems McCall is her child by a previous liaison. Seems Hill has seen too many movies in which young Western gunmen are anachronistically portrayed as if they were modern juvenile delinquents with a large yellow streak running down the center of their, characters. Seems too that giving the punk something like a coherent motivation—the only one in the movie—goes, against the anarchic mood of the piece.

Or maybe not. Maybe Jack's implosive ambivalence—rage and cowardice are constantly, even comically, at war in him—can also be read as the bold and loopy signature of this crammed, darkly jostling movie, the almost saving gracelessness of which lies in the utter, doubtless misplaced, passion with which it is realized.

VILLAGE VOICE, 12/5/95, p. 61, J. Hoberman

The new Hollywood western, as embodied by movies like *Wyatt Earp* or *Maverick*, is your 1958 TV series writ large—mildly revisionist, generally streamlined, a few chunks of narrative revolving around the solar majesty of the iconic hero's recognizable brand name. It's corpses-go-walking time, but, up until a point, Walter Hill's *Wild Bill* manages to teach the zombie a few new tricks.

Brawny and sinewed, couched completely in flashback (and flashbacks within flashbacks), *Wild Bill* is a movie of big weather, thunderous fisticuffs, deafening shoot-outs. Wild Bill (Jeff Bridges) is introduced as a madman performing a bizarre William Tell maneuver, firing over his shoulder at the shot glass atop the head of the hound dog behind him. Hill wants to make sure you appreciate why (if not how) William Hickok got his nickname. The movie proceeds with a series of wonderfully discombobulated, white-out-punctuated vignettes. Wild Bill does ritual battle with a Sioux warrior in a blazing yellow field. Wild Bill decimates the most fetid little watering hole on the Great Plains because somebody dares to touch his hat.

The western is the most familiar of genres, but there are bits of business here I don't think I've ever seen before: Wild Bill, some sort of law officer, brawling with a saloon full of drunken soldiers and winding up shooting a few; Wild Bill, now a marshall in Abilene, getting so crazed in a shoot-out that he plugs his own deputy; Wild Bill appearing with Buffalo Bill (Keith Carradine) in a Bowery theater; Wild Bill facing off against a lunatic (Bruce Dern) in a wheelchair. Narrative per se only begins once Wild Bill lands in the muddy hellhole of Deadwood, South Dakota—a town where the whores are tougher than the cowboys and condemned men are kept in a giant birdcage on Main Street. "Every polecat in the territory is here and they ain't got a sheriff yet," some varmint tells him.

Wild Bill's Deadwood is rainier than *Blade Runner*'s Los Angeles and twice as violent. (Indeed, given Hill's sense of the West as a sagebrush South Central, it's remarkable that his revisionist view should not take into account the substantial number of black cowboys.) Still, this is the best of the icon westerns—including Hill's own *Geronimo,* a movie paralyzed by simultaneous desires to mythologize and demystify. Hill has no facility for characterization but, keeping his camera close to the actors, he's always willing to worship a star. Stoutly bewhiskered, Bridges glowers throughout from under his sombrero. It's an unapologetically opaque performance. Drained of all motivation, Bridges is a brooding, pure, solitary presence. "I'm just not in the mood" he sourly grouses while hot-tubbing with Calamity Jane (Ellen Barkin enjoying herself as a sort of bright-eyed, buckskin Peter Pan). Like more than one celeb before him, Wild Bill has acquired a taste for self-administered oblivion—especially since the town is being overrun by a loud-mouthed kid promising that he'll be the one to kill the great Wild Bill.

Hill's lighting gets more lurid each time Bill visits the opium den in Deadwood's mini-Chinatown. Despite the entertaining, bleached-out pipe dreams these excursions motivate, Wild

Bill's drug habit establishes an unflattering parallel to Robert Altman's truly poetic *McCabe and Mrs. Miller*, particularly once Bill begins recalibrating life as a failure. (Where the hell did things go wrong?" he asks the dope den's friendly, if uncomprehending, proprietress.) Indeed, once Bill's would-be assassin (David Arquette) is revealed to be something like the legendary gunslinger's rejected "son," the whole movie slips into a groggy stupor—even if the vacillating Hamlet does get to interrupt a version of the primal scene.

Waiting for the kid to contrive the famous poker game during which, as all students of the genre know, the 39-year-old hero will be shot in the back (I can still remember the illustration in my boyhood Landmark book), *Wild Bill* grinds to a halt. Bells toll, narrative swerves into ever more mawkish flashback. You might even feel like you're on drugs watching the movie inexorably slip out of the directors hands. Still, no less than its subject, *Wild Bill* has its past to live off—it's spooky enough, in any case, to justify Hill's final description of Deadwood as "a place of prophecy and visions."

Also reviewed in:
CHICAGO TRIBUNE, 12/1/95, Friday/p. C, Michael Wilmington
NEW YORK TIMES, 12/1/95, p. C3, Janet Maslin
NEW YORKER, 12/4/95, p. 115, Terrence Rafferty
VARIETY, 1/27-12/3/95, p. 80, Todd McCarthy
WASHINGTON POST, 12/1/95, p. F7, Hal Hinson
WASHINGTON POST, 12/1/95, Weekend/p. 48, Desson Howe

WILD BUNCH, THE (RESTORED VERSION)

Originally released by Warner Bros.-Seven Arts. *Director:* Sam Peckinhah. *Producer:* Phil Feldman. *Screenplay:* Walon Green and Sam Peckinpah. *Based on a story by:* Walon Green and Roy N. Sickner. *Director of Photography:* Lucien Ballard. *Editor:* Louis Lombardo. *Music:* Jerry Fielding. *Sound:* Robert J. Miller. *Art Director:* Edward Carrere. *Special Effects:* Bud Hubbard. *Costumes:* Gordon Dawson. *Make-up:* Al Greenway. *Running time:* 145 minutes. *MPAA Rating:* R.

CAST: William Holden (Pike Bishop); Robert Ryan (Deke Thornton); Ernest Borgnine (Dutch Engstron); Edmund O'Brien (Sykes); Warren Oates (Lyle Gorch); Ben Johnson (Tector Gorch); Jaime Sanchez (Angel); Strother Martin (Coffee); L.Q. Jones (T.C.); Emilio Fernandoz (Mapache); Albert Dekker (Pat Harrigan); Bo Hopkins (Crazy Lee); Dub Taylor (Wainscoat); Paul Harper (Ross); Jorge Russek (Zamorra); Alfonso Arau (Herrera); Chano Urueta (Don José); Bill Hart (Jess); Rayford Barnes (Buck); Steve Ferry (Sergeant McHale); Sonia Amelio (Teresa); Aurora Clavel (Aurora); Elsa Cardenas (Elsa); Elizabeth Dupeyron (Rocio); Yolanda Ponce (Yolis); Enrique Lucero (Ignacio); René Dupeyron (Juan); Ivan Scott (Paymaster); Señora Madero (Margaret); Pedro Galvan (Benson); Graciela Doring (Emma); Major Perez (Perez); Fernando Wagner (Mohr); Jorge Rado (Ernst); José Chavez (Juan José); Margarito Luna (Mapache's Assistant); Gonzalo Gonzalez (Telegraph Operator); Lilia Castillo (Lilia); Elizabeth Unda (Carmen); Julio Corona (Julio).

CHRISTIAN SCIENCE MONITOR, 3/10/95, p. 13, David Sterritt

A better-known rediscovery [the reference is to *I Am Cuba*] on the circuit is "The Wild Bunch," directed by Sam Peckinpah in 1969, and long notorious for escalating film violence to new levels at a time when Hollywood's long-honored censorship rules were breaking down. Peckinpah always insisted the movie's climactic shoot-out was meant to turn audiences away from violence by translating it into stylized slow motion, but his subsequent career—from the darkly brilliant "Straw Dogs" to the stupidly sanguinary "Convoy," among other pictures—revealed a fascination with bloodshed that many moviegoers were all too eager to share.

Warner Bros.' new reissue of "The Wild Bunch," restoring several minutes of footage that were trimmed over the director's protest, reconfirms my long-held opinion that it's neither a transgressive triumph on one hand nor an orgy of immorality on the other. It's just an unusually ambitious western with a rambling story, few well-developed characters, and a macho attitude that's more troubling for its misogyny than for its itchy trigger finger.

NEW YORK POST, 3/3/95, p. 49, Thelma Adams

Watching the late Sam Peckinpah's cut of "The Wild Bunch" (1969), there's a feeling of deja vu.

You've either seen the western before, or think you might have seen it, or you've seen scenes borrowed from it in hundreds of movies that followed. Milcho Manchevski's "Before the Rain," which premiered in New York last Friday, opens with Macedonian children circled around two turtles they torment and then set alight. The scene mirrors the opening of "The Wild Bunch": Frontier brats place red ants on sparring yellow scorpions and torch the lot. The difference (besides the 25 years between the movies) is that Peckinpah boldly holds the camera on the teaming tableau until the audience wants to look away—but can't. Despite close-ups of laughing, freckle-faced kids, Peckinpah robs the children's mirth of innocence.

"The Wild Bunch" begins and ends with laughter, but there's not a joyful chuckle in the entire 145 minutes. "Bunch" is a leather-hearted, paradise-lost, fin de siecle western set on the receding Texas frontier of 1913.

It was made when the '60s had come to a full boil and the world seemed, however falsely, to be radically split between the past and present.

A sneering, saddle-sore-faced William Holden stars as the aging leader of a group of desperadoes trying to pull off one final score. After an elaborate, ultra-violent ambush during an armed robbery, the railroad company chases Holden, Ernest Borgnine, and Warren Oates into Mexico.

Robert Ryan, Holden's former partner in crime, has been yanked out of prison by the railroaders and given a single choice: nail Holden or return to jail.

Loyalty, and how each character central to the drama defines it, is the movie's touchstone. The approximately 10 minutes of added footage in the director's cut enrich rather than alter the experience. They include dramatized flashbacks of incidents already explained in the dialogue, shedding light on Holden's romantic past and his relationship with Ryan.

The maverick director ("Straw Dogs," "The Getaway") made cinematic history for his breakthroughs in achieving a new "reality" in portraying violence.

Much is made—and rightly so—about the elaborate editing, the intercutting of multiple speeds of film in the same sequence, the hidden spurting gore pellets that include meat as well as stage blood, the inclusion of exit as well as entry bullet wounds during gun battles.

Gore is Peckinpah's genius, but "The Wild Bunch" succeeds because the story is firmly grounded in the granite of classic drama theme, plot and character. Seen 26 years later, the mayhem in "The Wild Bunch" is hard-core but no longer shocking.

Directors as diverse as Martin Scorsese, Oliver Stone, Kathryn Bigelow, Quentin Tarantino, John Woo and Manchevski have all heard Peckinpah's call. What seems the most '60s, and the most shocking, is the bimbo treatment of women.

The scene that haunted me over the years since my first viewing of "The Wild Bunch" was not the spaghetti-and-meatballs carnage of the final showdown but the California hot-tub cavorting of two outlaws with three plump Mexican women in a wine vat.

The silly, laughing, big-breasted whores are used and abused like washrags. I found the tub scene the most disturbing then and no movie since has desensitized me to the horrors of a world where men treat their horses better than their women, where loyalty is a credo among men and women need not apply.

NEWSWEEK, 3/13/95, p. 70, David Ansen

The reissue of the original cut of Sam Peckinpah's Western *The Wild Bunch* was supposed to commemorate its 25th anniversary. But the ratings board threw a wrench into Warner Brothers' birthday party when it slapped an NC-17 on the movie, rendering it unreleaseable. Was the director's cut that much more violent than the R-rated 1969 version? No, it was virtually the same two-hour, 25-minute movie. It took a year for Warners to prove to the board that more than eight of the 10 newly restored minutes were cuts made by the studio *after* the film's release. They were cuts made to speed up the movie, not to tone down the bloodshed: flashbacks that explained the betrayals that turned William Holden and his former partner Robert Ryan into enemies. Now, with the original R in place, "The Wild Bunch" is back in all its 70-mm glory.

In a quarter of a century, Peckinpah's bloody saga of a gang of outlaws fleeing to Mexico with bounty hunters on their trail has acquired the status of a classic. It wasn't always thus. David Weddle, in his recent biography of Peckinpah, "If They Move ... Kill 'Em!," describes the movie's first preview showing in Kansas City. Thirty people stormed out of the theater, some vomiting in the alley. "I want to get the hell out of this place," screamed one patron, horrified by the images of carnage. And though the film had many critical champions when it opened—both Pauline Kael and Richard Schickel voted for Peckinpah as best director in the National Society of Film Critics its opponents were rabid. "If you want to see 'The Wild Bunch'," warned Judith Crist, "be sure and take along a barf bag."

The violence in "The Wild Bunch" is still potent and unsettling, though it couldn't possibly cause the uproar it once did—a whole generation of Peckinpah-inspired directors have doubled the ante in shock tactics. But the arguments that rage about screen violence today are uncannily similar to the commotion raised in the Vietnam era—a debate ignited by Arthur Penn's "Bonnie and Clyde" in 1967 and fanned by one Peckinpah provocation after another ("Straw Dogs," "The Getaway"). The techniques that Peckinpah employed with such savage power in this Western—the startling use of slow motion, the machine-gun editing, the surgical but poetic realism of bullet-riddled flesh—have now been imitated and coarsened to the point of cliché. The moment of death had never been examined with such voluptuous spatial and temporal obsessiveness. Peckinpah shot his big, violent set pieces with six cameras running simultaneously at variable speeds, from 24 frames per second up to 120. Time is suspended, expanded and twisted into a hallucinatory explosion. "The Wild Bunch" contained more cuts—3,642—than any color film until then. But that was before MTV and "Natural Born Killers."

We may be more blasé about cinematic body counts now, but "The Wild Bunch" still retains its sorrowful, fatal power because of the complexity of Peckinpah's attitudes about violence. He forces us to confront our own voyeuristic ambivalence; we're alternately horrified by the butchery and exhilarated by the orgiastic energy his balletic spectacles stir up. Peckinpah took violence seriously—it was no postmodernist joyride—and he held to a primitive, fatalistic belief in man's innate thirst for blood. What was shocking was the destructive beauty Peckinpah's eye revealed—and forced us, squirming, to acknowledge.

From the opening scene, "The Wild Bunch" threw out the moral compass points we expected from a Western. We see Holden's Pike Bishop and his men riding into town wearing army uniforms (a disguise, we later learn). They attempt a robbery that turns into a bloodbath when the posse led by Ryan tries to ambush them. This set piece—in which the violence that claims innocent bystanders is played off the reactions of terrified but awestruck children—is doubly disorienting because the audience can't tell the good guys from the bad.

Here, there are only bad guys and worse—the difference lying in the code of loyalty that Pike and his men cling to. Peckinpah's cynicism goes hand in hand with his macho romanticism—by the end, he's transformed these reprobates into mythical figures. The one idealist in the group—Angel, the young Mexican—doesn't hesitate to shoot his former girlfriend when he discovers she's betrayed him. No one in the story blinks twice at this murder. Neither, I'm afraid, does Peckinpah.

It's not surprising that, with the notable exception of Kael, all of "The Wild Bunch's" most passionate partisans are men. Or that the directors who have most revered Peckinpah—Martin Scorsese, Walter Hill, John Milius, to name a few—are all makers of serious Guy Movies. Peckinpah's paranoia about women is on ample and lurid display. It's an unshapely classic, full of flaws: the gang's idyllic interlude in a Mexican village exudes gringo sentimentality, and Peckinpah, under the influence of "The Treasure of the Sierra Madre," overworks the stagy effect of hearty, ironic laughter. But what masterful, resonant images this movie hurls at you. There's an elaborately choreographed train robbery that's a marvel of precise action film-making—amazingly, we discover in Weddle's biography, Peckinpah worked out the intricate staging on the spot.

Underneath the movie, which is set on the eve of World War I, there's an elegiac plangency that stays with you long after the shocks have worn off. For the carnage that sets this Western apart is also internal. What haunts you is the world-weary, wind-bitten faces of the men who march into the final, apocalyptic conflagration with such eager, suicidal expectation; the ruined nobility of Ryan's face as he mourns his fallen foes. Neither heroes nor villains, they are men at the end of their rope and at the end of an era, men who have nothing left to give their hearts to but death. It's a tribute to Peckinpah's corrosive genius that, 26 years later, "The Wild Bunch" still won't go down easy.

SIGHT AND SOUND, 10/95, p. 62, Edward Buscombe

Southern Texas 1914. Pike Bishop and his gang have planned to rob a railroad office, but Deke Thornton, a former associate of Bishop, is lying in ambush. Bishop's gang shoot their way out, but in the battle many of the town's citizens are cut down. Thornton has been released from prison in order to catch Bishop, and is ordered by the railroad to pursue him. Bishop crosses the border into Mexico, where his gang meet Mapache, a vicious general fighting for Huerta against Pancho Villa. One of their number, a Mexican named Angel, kills the general's mistress, who had once been his lover. The gang extricate themselves from a tight spot by offering to rob a US army train carrying munitions.

Thornton has correctly guessed this next move, but the raw recruits and border riff-raff under his command are outwitted by Bishop's gang, who steal the weapons and then blow a bridge across the Rio Grande just as Thornton's men are crossing in pursuit. They successfully deliver the arms to Mapache and collect their reward. But Mapache deduces that Angel has diverted part of the arms shipment to his fellow villagers. He allows the Americans to go free but Angel is detained and brutally treated. Bishop and his men find they are unable to abandon Angel to his fate. They return to the village where Mapache's army is celebrating its new acquisitions. In a final confrontation Bishop and his three companions turn their guns on Mapache and his entire army, killing scores of them but perishing in the effort. Later Thornton arrives on the scene. His men loot the bodies and depart, and are then themselves killed by the villagers. Thornton decides not to return to the US; instead, he waits for old Sykes, the last surviving member of Bishop's gang.

Peckinpah's masterpiece, rereleased in the now fashionable form of a 'director's cut', eclipses all recent attempts to revive and update the Western, with the honourable exception of Eastwood's *Unforgiven*. 25 years ago Peckinpah decisively desanitised screen violence, with his slow-motion images of bullets ripping through flesh. Subsequent excesses have added nothing. *The Wild Bunch* is also one of the earliest and certainly one of the most moving expressions of the theme of the end of the West, which successive film-makers have turned into just another cliché. Peckinpah's heroes are victims of history, stranded by the ebbing away of the individualist values of the Old West, now replaced by realpolitik, faceless capitalist corporations and dehumanising technology. Peckinpah has a wonderful knack of making this come alive, contrasting past and present with a new twist to a traditional motif. Early in the film, during the bungled robbery which results in wholesale slaughter in a Texas border town, one of Pike Bishop's gang is shot off his horse and dragged down the main street, his foot caught in the stirrup. This image, familiar from a hundred other Westerns, is reprised in a new and ghastly form later. The Wild Bunch's Mexican member, Angel, is captured by General Mapache, tied to the back of his new motor car and dragged around the village square until his face is reduced to a bloody pulp. So much for progress. *The Wild Bunch* has much in common with Peckinpah's *Major Dundee* (1964). In each film a band of irregulars crosses the border into Mexico, where their leader, a man haunted by his past, tries desperately to keep together a disintegrating group. Each company recuperates in a Mexican village among the real people before being tested in a final confrontation with a force controlled by the European military tradition. In each, the leader is wounded in the thigh while making love with a woman. In each we hear 'Shall We Gather at the River', inescapably a reference to the Fordian Western.

This new version of *The Wild Bunch* is very welcome, but on examination appears to be something less than promised. The most detailed account of the film's production history is in David Weddle's recent biography *'If They Move ... Kill 'Em': The Life and Times of Sam Peckinpah*. According to Weddle, Peckinpah's initial rough cut ran to three hours, 45 minutes. His editor, Louis Lombardo, reduced this to two hours, 45 minutes. But Warner Bros wanted a two and a half hour movie. Accordingly, Lombardo and Peckinpah further trimmed the film to two hours 31 minutes. As a result of preview reactions and the need to avoid an X-rating in the USA for excessive violence, Peckinpah then took out another six minutes, reducing the total to two hours 25 minutes. This would appear to be the version now presented to us. Unfortunately, despite much enthusiastic critical response, box office was not good. Ken Hyman, Warners' head of production and a Peckinpah supporter, was replaced by a less sympathetic new regime, headed by Ted Ashley, who ordered producer Phil Feldman to cut another 10 minutes in order to placate exhibitors, who complained the film was too long. It is this version, two hours and 15 minutes, to which Peckinpah took violent exception, which has circulated the past 25 years, and it's the 10 minutes removed by Feldman from prints after the first release that have now been restored.

The extra minutes, comprising six scenes in all, are certainly worth having. Their most important function is to fill out the relationship between Bishop and Thornton, thus explaining Thornton's ambiguous feelings about his mission. Briefly, the scenes are: a flashback of Bishop and Thornton together in a brothel, in which Thornton is shot and captured, and Bishop escapes; a scene in which it becomes clear that Bishop has abandoned one of his gang during the ambush, who turns out to be the grandson of Sykes, an old man who looks after their horses; some extra footage in the Mexican villa where the gang rest up; a flashback showing Bishop getting shot in the leg by the husband of a woman he is in bed with; and a scene of Mapache's forces being attacked Villistas, in which Mapache makes this clear he intends to double-cross Bishop.

A print which has been seen several times on ITV since 1976 also two hours, 25 minutes (allowing for the approximately 4% speed-up on television), and all six scenes which the Warners press release now lists as 'restored' are in that ITV version. The only things missing are some frames removed by the TV censors; so for example when Mapache cuts Angel's throat, we don't actually see the blood spurt in the TV version, as we do big screen. Even this is included in the print held by the National Film and Television Archive, regularly screened at the Museum of the Moving Image, and which contains all that Warners have now restored. So don't get too excited you're about to witness footage never before seen in public. You have seen it already.

Peckinpah's films have sometimes been read as American versions of the Italian Spaghetti Westerns of the 1960s. Peckinpah, it is supposed, hammered the last nails into the coffin that Leone and his epigones built for the Hollywood Western. Both aestheticised violence. Bodies no longer simply fall over when shot, but spurt blood as they perform somersaults in slow motion. And the old Western values of honour and loyalty and justice appear irrelevant in a world ruled by greed and cynicism. But a quarter of a century later these similarities seem less important than the differences. Peckinpah (like Eastwood) has more in common with John Ford than with Sergio Leone. His roots in the West and the Western are deeper than Leone's, and where Leone sees only a sardonic nihilism, Peckinpah's tragic heroes are redeemed by a final gesture as romantic as it is doomed. Pike Bishop and his men finally rouse themselves to rescue comrade Angel. Four men cannot win against Mapache's army. They will lose their lives; but they will regain their honour. It's an extravagant gesture quite beyond the calculating Leone hero, but saved from vainglory by the laconic manner in which the action is justified. "Let's go," says Pike. "Why not?" says his sidekick Dutch.

VILLAGE VOICE, 3/7/95, p. 54, Georgia Brown

With customary bluntness Peckinpah once described *The Wild Bunch* as "what happens when men go to Mexico." You have to know what he meant by men: outlaws and peckerwoods, troublemakers, aging American adolescents and chronic losers. Once these jokers cross the border, they let fly. (Remember Marlowe's great lines: "Thou hast committed/Fornication—but that was in another country;/And besides, the wench is dead.") In another country we become ... ourselves.

In 1913, when the movie takes place, Mexico was in the throes of a civil war, with Pancho Villa arming the peasants. Undeterred, our gringos drink, brawl, bitch, laugh, whore, kick butt, and in the end, *almost* without meaning to, turn their talents to constructive killing and approach greatness.

The Wild Bunch, of course, is famous for its beautiful violence, but I should also like to invoke other key V-words: vanishing, vile, vultures, and—noting that the movie came out in 1969— Vietnam. You might substitute that country for Mexico in Peckinpah's sentence above.

Even when young, Peckinpah was making elegies, lamentations for the vanished West and the proverbial vanishing breed. His first feature of note and perhaps his gentlest, *Ride the High Country,* recruited two old gunslingers, Joel McCrea and Randolph Scott, and thus put death in the saddle. (Peckinpah himself was only 59 when he died, but he looked every bit of 90.) Likewise, Wild Bunch leader Pike Bishop (William Holden) and the man who hunts him, Deke Thornton (Robert Ryan), are grizzled warriors, tired guns; they've seen too much and, if you believe them, lived too long. The script is studded with lines like Pike's, "This was to have been my last," and "This is our last go-round, Dutch. This time we do it right." The film's final line, delivered by Edmond O'Brien's Sykes (Santa here is a foulmouthed coot) mocks the old-timers' eternal faith: "It ain't like it used to be, but it'll do." The laugh that greets this mighty load of irony echoes down the desert.

Indeed, what "used to be" is finished long before the movie begins. Hints of past deeds, none heroic, flutter by in flashbacks. Pike; we learn, is responsible for Deke's being put in prison. Now working for the corrupt railroad owner who got him out, Deke leads a couple of mangy bounty hunters, comic scum. Passing up a chance to kill Pike when he has him in his sights, Deke, with his band of vultures, keeps on his quarry's trail, as if to be around when the walls come tumbling down. Someone has called him the angel of death. More, he's the lost soul, man without men.

The point is that the old West—at least as represented by the old western with its values of rectitude, order, and gallantry—is already dead. In *The Wild Bunch's* opening sequence, Peckinpah takes John Ford's sweet hymn, "Shall We Gather at the River," gives it to a bunch of pinched, loony locals—the South Texas Temperance Union—and then blows a parade of these sorry, caricatured citizens to kingdom come. Immediately preceding this spectacular bloodbath, "Directed by Sam Peckinpah" appears on the stroke of Holden's muttered order, "If they move, kill 'em."

Peckinpah comes as close as any director to celebrating the vulgarity of the real West and eliminating gentility and sentimentality—except of course, where sentiments apply. Like all of Peckinpah's films, *The Wild Bunch* works at defining group and individual values. The group in this case includes Pike, Dutch (a subdued but monumental Ernest Borgnine), the volatile Gorch brothers (Ben Johnson and Warren Oates), and the decent, melancholy Angel Uaime Sanchez).

One value is the courage to defy odds. When the stolid Dutch warns Pike about the dangers of hijacking a train—"They'll be waiting for us"—Pike replies, "I wouldn't have it any other way," a line echoed later when odds are even starker. As many have pointed out, Peckinpah viewed movie making as revenge of the individual talent against the overwhelming forces of greed.

Then there's the value of sticking together. Coherence is tested right off when the bunch discovers that sacks of loot they just stole contain steel washers instead of gold. As the brothers Gorch peck at each other and turn on Angel, Pike ticks off the lesson: "When you side with a man, you stay with him. If you can't do that you're like some kind of animal. You're finished!"

What dawns on Pike slowly but inexorably is how often he's betrayed his own ethic. He abandons one cohort and coldly kills another who's wounded. The test comes as he watches Angel being tortured. The final decision to go up against the odds has often been criticized as unmotivated, a sudden, existential inspiration, but Peckinpah has documented Pike's changes. The moment where the movie lingers, pauses, letting the silence sink in as the bunch grasps their fate, is one of cinema's most sublime.

Meager virtues these may seem to some, but they set the outlaws apart from authorities like bankers and railroad barons, or General Mapache (Emilio Fernandez) and his German adviser. The truly virtuous in Peckinpah's scheme are generic "little people"—here docile Mexican villagers, people without complexity. The touching farewell-to-the-village scene—lines of peasants softly singing "La Golondrina" as the men ride out—Peckinpah says was unplanned and shot spontaneousiy. Treated like heroes, they go on to become heroes.

If Peckinpah's peasants are pure and childlike, his children are innocently vicious. The famous opening has a bunch of little monsters brewing a stew of scorpions and red ants. Like a refrain, Peckinpah shows kids relishing cruelty. A babe sucks a tit that pokes through mom's cartridge belt: They're brought up on it. You'd think that kids don't know fear. Two adorable blond tikes gleefully clutch each other as the world rains blood. No sense of trauma. Obviously the man didn't spend much time around his children.

So let's talk about *The Wild Bunch* and women. The range is from tight Texan biddies to Pike's lovely, soulful Mexican whore (who isn't really a whore) to the Indian Pike loved and who was killed for loving him to the bitch who shoots him. Par for the Peckinpah course. Peckinpah once cited a line he was forced to delete that he really wanted back: Ben Johnson's impromptu exclamation, "Look, nipples the size of my thumb!" When you watch the scene where this line undoubtedly came up, you could feel a bit nauseated, the poor woman looks so uncomfortable. I think we can take it as some kind of justice when Pike is fatally shot, first by a woman ("Bitch!" he explodes, wheeling on her and drilling her in the chest), and a second later, by a child.

Peckinpah always introduces bathing scenes where dirty men wash off blood, sweat, beers, or as in the case of *The Getaway,* the particular humiliation of confinement. Often in these golden rites, midst the guy-guy horseplay, they're joined by women, sometimes even women they love. Water, as *The Ballad of Cable Hogue* showed, is cherished in desert places and thus has a loaded meaning. Here the youngsters splash in a tub and the more sedate steam in a sauna, but the most memorable baptism comes to the opposition: When a dynamited bridge drops from under, Deke, his men, and their horses fall softly, slowly, shockingly, into the river. I love the way Peckinpah holds the water shot until we see the one guy swimming to retrieve some lost object.

A couple years ago, Warner's planned to rerelease *The Wild Bunch* but chickened out when the film got an NC-17 rating. Since the film is the same version that got an R in 1969 (though the version most Americans saw had been cut, without Peckinpah's approval, right after its initial release) and the same as on Warner's video release, the board eventually was prevailed upon to go along with the original R. As for the new print, Warner's in their usual lofty indifference declined to screen it in time for the *Voice* deadline. (Since cinematographer Lucien Ballard used the entire 70mm screen, the whole film literally can't be seen on video.) Nor have I previewed any of the prints in the Walter Reade's upcoming, most welcome retrospective, though I'm sure they haven't got back those 55 minutes chopped from *Major Dundee* back in 1964. Some things, like the West, are gone forever.

Also reviewed in:
CHICAGO TRIBUNE, 3/17/95, Friday/p. C, Michael Wilmington
NEW YORK TIMES, 6/26/69, p. 45, Vincent Canby
NEW YORK TIMES, 3/10/95, p. C17, Janet Maslin
NEW YORKER, 3/6/95, Terrence Rafferty, p. 127
VARIETY, 2/27-3/5/95, p. 70, Steven Gaydos
WASHINGTON POST, 3/31/95, Weekend/p. 39, Desson Howe
WASHINGTON POST, 4/1/95, p. C5, Hal Hinson

WILD REEDS

An IMA Films/Les Films Alain Sarde production with the participation of Canal Plus. *Executive Producer:* Jean-Jacques Albert. *Producer:* Alain Sarde and Georges Benayoun. *Director:* André Téchiné. *Screenplay (French with English subtitles):* André Téchiné, Gilles Taurand, and Olivier Massart. *Director of Photography:* Jeanne Lapoirie. *Editor:* Martine Giordano. *Sound:* François Groult. *Sound Editor:* Jean-Luc Marino. *Set Decorator:* Pierre Soula. *Costumes:* Brigitte Laleouse. *Make-up:* Youssef Ferhat. *Stunt Coordinator:* Alain Figlarz. *Running time:* 110 minutes. *MPAA Rating:* Not Rated.

CAST: Elodie Bouchez (Maïté); Gael Morel (François); Stéphane Rideau (Serge); Frédéric Gorny (Henri); Michele Moretti (Madame Alvarez); Nathalie Vignes (Young Bride); Jacques Nolot (Monsieur Morelli); Erik Kreikenmayer (Young Bridegroom); Michel Ruhl (Monsieur Cassagne); Fatia Maite (Aicha); Claudine Taulere (Nurse); Elodie Soulinhac (Girl at Party); Dominique Bovard and Monsieur Simonet (Guards); Chief Officer Carré (Officer); Paul Simonet (Bridegroom's Father); Charles Picot (Headmaster); Christophe Maitre (Gym Instructor); Bordes Fernand Raouly (Bridegroom's Mother); Michel Voisin (Priest); Denis Bergonhe (Pump Attendant).

LOS ANGELES TIMES, 5/10/95, Calendar/p. 12, Kenneth Turan

Though we are undeniably youth-obsessed as a culture, adolescence is an area not dealt with well on film, which is one of several reasons "Wild Reeds" is such an unexpectedly satisfying experience. Its cast of young French actors is completely unknown in this country, its focus on teen-age pain and confusion is hardly fresh territory, and its director, Andre Techine, has been working steadily for decades in his homeland without causing much of a stir over here.

But "Reeds" defies all preconceptions. Deserving winner of four Cesars (the French version of the Oscars) for best picture, best director, best screenplay and best new female discovery, the film's most impressive accomplishment is to remind us what sensitive filmmaking is realty all about.

For few terms in the critical lexicon have been abused as much as sensitivity, the label that tends to be placed on films that have the temerity to bludgeon tears out of an overmanipulated audience. "Wild Reeds," by contrast, treats the troublesome teen-age years with an almost surgical dispassion that turns out to be artful and moving.

Equally important, this is an intimate film that allows its confused, searching characters the space to be themselves, to discover what is in their hearts by the awkward but human process of trial and error. As a result, it is easier for viewers to become involved in their difficult process of determining who they are and where they fit in the indifferent larger world.

"Wild Reeds" is set in rural France in 1962, a time when society was torn by its own version of Vietnam, the Algerian conflict that pitted that country's desire for freedom against the refusal of Algerian-born French nationals to allow that to happen peacefully.

That trouble at first seems remote from the boarding school where Francois (Gael Morel) and Serge (Stephane Rideau) are classmates. While Serge is a farmer's son just trying to got by, Francois is an intellectual who enjoys art films and the company of Maite (Elodie Bouchez), the daughter of the boys' exacting teacher.

But what is happening in Algeria slowly makes itself felt, first in the wedding of Serge's brother, a soldier on leave from the war, and then in the arrival of Henri (Frederic Gorny). A refuge from Algeria and bitter opponent of independence who keeps his ear attached to a portable radio for news of the conflict, the older and more sophisticated Henri unmistakably exudes what Francois calls an "exiled to flicksville" hauteur.

Henri's implacable conservatism, which clashes with Maite's fervid Communism, is only one of any number of conflicts that surface as an intricate web of attraction, competition and irritation unexpectedly unites these four young people. All three boys are drawn to the naturally sensuous Maite (the part won actress Bouchez the best new female discovery Cesar), but Francois also finds himself sexually attracted to Serge, with results more complicated than anyone anticipates.

This lack of simplicity underscores what is best about "Wild Reeds," whose Techine, Gilles Taurand and Olivier Massart script knows enough not to attempt any kind of neat resolution of such emotionally turbulent material. The film perfectly understands the tentative experimentation and frequent self-loathing of adolescence, the difficulty of knowing whom to trust and how much to trust them, as well as how incendiary an age this can be, with uncertain psyches ready to explode at minimal provocation.

Director Techine has kept a firm but gentle hand on the proceedings, never letting the cast's uniformly fine actors stray from the truth. Dancing to vintage American rock 'n' roll tunes such as Del Shannon's "Runaway," these young people are the wild reeds of the film's title, buffeted but not broken by powerful winds while impatiently "waiting for life to begin."

NEW YORK POST, 6/30/95, p. 36, Thelma Adams

"Wild Reeds" begins with a scene so familiar in Gallic movies that it's nearly the French equivalent of a Hallmark Card. A country wedding stretches out in the sun: children spin on a hillside; the groom sings his young bride a bawdy song; the groomsmen get the pig drunk.

The groom, a young soldier, waltzes with his former teacher. It's 1962 at the tail end of the Algerian war and the groom surprises the Communist Madame Alvarez with a request: He wants to desert and needs her help. He confesses that he only married to escape Algeria. His bride was one of three girls he proposed to by mail—and the only one who consented.

The soldier's plea casts a pall over the proceedings. Director Andre Techine has upset our expectations. This is not an idyllic rite, but a poignant commentary about the strange bedfellows politics and love make.

The overture has revealed the theme and Techine shuttles the soldier and teacher into the background. The central players are three teens: Alvarez's politically committed daughter Maite (Elodie Bouchez); Maite's platonic beau Francois (Gael Morel); and Serge (Stephane Rideau), the soldier's younger brother.

The three are "wild reeds," resilient to the stresses of their time because of their youth. The trio reworks a Jules and Jim triangle with Francois at the center. While his relationship with Maite is emotionally intimate, one night he has sex with Serge.

Maite maturely handles the situation. She encourages Francois to come to terms with his sexuality, assuring him that they will remain friends in the most natural way: by dragging him onto a dance floor at a party and showing him a good time.

The arrival of Henri (Frederic Gorny), an anti-Communist Algerian-born Frenchman, challenges the trio. The film's weakness is that Henri doesn't make a convincing lightning rod.

Gorny's angry schoolboy act seems to cut the surrounding characters loose rather than galvanize them. His appeal to Maite satisfies a schematic in which each character comes to terms with their personal demons before they can achieve peace with each other—but their passion isn't convincing.

Also, "Wild Reeds" does little to sketch out a rocky patch of contemporary French history largely unfamiliar to American audiences. Because of this, Henri's role and the political dimension of the movie fail to register.

NEWSDAY, 6/30/95, Part II/p. B7, John Anderson

The illusion of carefree youth is, of course, just that. We all emerge molded in a cast of history, polished by other people's preconceptions, glazed by other people's deaths. There's nothing carefree about it, just naive and unprotected. But it makes us what we are.

The four "Wild Reeds" of Andre Techine's remarkable 1993 film, set in France circa 1962, are on the verge of becoming the people they'll be. Francois (Gael Morel) is a somewhat introverted boarding-school student with a literary bent; his best friend (not girlfriend), Maite, played by the wonderful and wonderfully young Elodie Bouchez, is a profoundly closed flower. Serge (Stephan Rideau), a loutish farm boy who knows much more than either of them, desires Maite but has a fling with Francois (confirming the latter's homosexuality to himself). Within the insular realm of pubescent longing, the three do a tribal dance of hopeless expectations and undefined desires.

Not so much landing in as hovering over their circle is Henri (Frederic Gorny)—a hard case—an Algerian-born French national who has come to France because of the war at home, and harbors deep resentments toward the French. He is turning 21, has little chance of graduating and little interest in anything but radio reports from home. His father was killed by a bomb in Algeria; Henri swears he saw him move in his coffin. Serge's brother, a soldier, has been killed there, too; Maite's mother, the teacher Mrs. Alvarez (Michele Moretti), might have hidden Serge's brother when he wanted to desert, but didn't and is literally sickened with guilt. Francois? He watches, orchestrates, longs for Serge. The war, like adolescence, takes no prisoners.

Techine portrays his characters as innocents, but does not equate innocence with stupidity. These are serious children, who speak thoughtfully to and about each other, about the world, about their lack of control over destiny. They might not always be right, but occasionally they are profound. And they are real, in a way young people on film so seldom are.

It may require some knowledge of the Algerian crisis to understand some of the dynamics—between Maite, for instance, who has been raised a communist, and Henri, who has lost so much to the war. It's indicative of youth, however, and of Techine's gift for capturing it, that politics cannot stop these two from finding each other, if only briefly. And hearing Maite say, "I love you, too, but that's no reason to live together," may be indicative of a too-wise filmmaker. But Maite is full of precocious comments on the adult world, which "Wild Reeds" makes all the more unwelcoming.

NEWSWEEK, 6/12/95, p. 65, David Ansen

The French are masters of the coming-of-age story, specialists in adolescent sexual awakening. The rites of passage that provoke Porky-like titters and guffaws in American movies are the occasion for a display of exquisite Gallic sensibilities. It's obviously a key moment in the national psyche, and it has been captured beautifully by André Téchiné in his moving, richly textured *Wild Reeds*. Téchiné's film stirred up deep passion in France, where it swept this year's César Awards (their Oscars) for best picture, director, screenplay and most promising female newcomer (Elodie Bouchez). It's set in 1962 in a boarding school in the southwest of France at a crucial moment in French consciousness—the Algerian war for independence, a traumatic event that divided the country much as the Vietnam War ripped apart the American social fabric.

Algeria means little to the bright, sensitive François (Gael Morel), who loves Ingmar Bergman films and Faulkner and is just beginning to discover that his sexual desires focus not on his pretty best friend Maité (Bouchez), but on the handsome peasant boy Serge (Stéphane Rideau), whose brother has just been sent to Algeria to fight. One brief schoolboy sexual encounter means everything to François, but it's just a one-time experiment to Serge, who's smitten with Maité. Complicating these sexual and class matters is the arrival of Henri (Frédéric Gorny), a right-wing *pied noir*—a French citizen born in Algeria and forced to leave North Africa because of the war. Sophisticated, self-destructive and seething with bitterness at his exile, Henri brings the volatile political passions of the outside world to this provincial enclave. He, too, is drawn to Maité, though everything in his fiercely nationalistic nature despises her communist sympathies, which she's inherited from her parents. In the sexual and political civil wars of these four teenagers, "Wild Reeds" discovers a microcosm of a society whose center no longer holds.

A major French director, Téchiné's films ("French Provincial") have rarely been seen in the United States. He's always been the master of a fluid cinematic style, but some of his films have seemed no more than chic surface. Not here. Working with semi-autobiographical material and from an honest, finely detailed screenplay (by Téchiné, Olivier Massart and Gilles Taurand), he reconstructs the passions of youth with clear-eyed, deeply engaged sympathy. Every character—not just the kids, but the teachers as well—comes alive with a complexity worthy of Jean Renoir. The lyricism of "Wild Reeds" doesn't cast a smoke screen of nostalgia, it brings us closer to the experience of adolescence. Though they dance to the Beach Boys and the Platters, and obsess about their crushes and confusions, François, Maité and Henri seem worlds apart from the 1962 teenagers in "American Graffiti." Their precocious self-awareness is specifically French, and it serves to protect them against the storms of childhood's end. Like the reed in the La Fontaine fable that gives the movie its title, these kids learn to bend without breaking.

SIGHT AND SOUND, 3/95, p. 50, Chris Darke

1962, Villeneuve-sur-Lot in southwest France. Pierre Bartolo, about to leave for service in Algeria, is getting married. He confides to a local schoolteacher, Madame Alvarez, that he wishes to desert and asks her, in her capacity as a Communist Party activist, to assist him. She declines.

At the boarding school where Alvarez teaches, the class includes local boys François and Serge (Pierre's brother), and new arrival Henri Mariani who is Algerian-born and unpopular with both classmates and teacher. François and Serge have an arrangement to help one another with their classwork which develops into a brief homosexual liaison. This leaves Serge unaffected but François is unhappily persuaded of his homosexuality. He confides his feelings to his closest friend, Madame Alvarez's daughter, Maité.

News arrives that Pierre has been killed in Algeria. Serge walks away from the funeral, disgusted by military rhetoric about his brother's heroism he knew that Pierre wanted to desert. François sends Maité after him. On hearing the news, Madame Alvarez suffers a nervous breakdown. Her replacement, Monsieur Morelli, offers Henri extra tuition to help him pass the baccalauréat. Henri's hostility subsides until he hears about OAS defeats in Algeria.

Raging, Henri leaves the boarding school at night, burning PCF posters as he goes. On the point of torching the local Communist HQ he spots Maité within. Hesitantly, she offers him coffee. Henri makes a nervous advance. She refuses him but reads him the letter from his mother that he has never dared open. After Henri reveals his original intention to incinerate the HQ Maïté orders him to leave.

On the eve of the baccalauréat results, François, Serge, Henri and Maïté go swimming together. Serge and François come to a reconciliation while Maïté and Henri make love before he leaves. Madame Alvarez, released from hospital, meets Monsieur Morelli for a meal where they discuss Henri. Morelli introduces his Algerian wife. Madame Alvarez watches as they drive away.

André Téchiné's most recent feature was originally commissioned by the Franco-German Television channel ATE as part of the series *Tons les garcons et les filles de leur âge* in which French directors, including Patricia Mazuy, Cedric Kahn and Olivier Assayas, were asked to contribute films based on their recollections of adolescence. *Le Roseaux sauvages* depicts that time when angst and euphoria go hand in hand, but Téchiné contains sentimental and familiar elements by addressing the wider political dimensions of his teenage years: 1962, the Evian Accords and the final actions of the Algerian War of Independence.

As context for the sentimental education of four adolescent characters, Téchiné's handling of this historical moment is delicate and telling. Henri, an Algerian-born French boy whose father died in the Algerian War, is the intercessor. As a self-proclaimed supporter of the neo-Fascist, anti-independence OAS, he brings the war firmly into the conciousness of the other teenagers. But as an unrepentant, antisocial, metropolitan dandy, dismissive of the provincialism of his peers, he takes an obdurate, adolescent pride in his pain, converting it into the badge of his difference from the others. François, in coming to terms with his homosexuality, is briefly smitten by Henri's darkness, whereas Serge, having lost his older brother in the War, regards Henri as the enemy, as does Maïté, the daughter of communist militant Madame Alvarez.

Just as Téchiné recruits the political to deepen his portrait of adolescent relationships, so period detail is accommodated with an unobtrusiveness that makes the film something other than the familiar parade of period pop nostalgia and fashion curiosity. As *Cahiers du cinema* has noted, Téchiné privileges "the tension of the moment above the recreation of the time, the dramatic detail over faithful historical reconstruction." Hit records of *lepoque yé-yé* (The Beach Boys, Chubby Checker, The Platters) and style details (Serge compliments Maïté on her hairstyle as being *"très Françoise Hardy"*) add density to characterisation and narrative development. With adolescence defined by the competing forces of sexual yearning and political intransigence, the setting in the south-west of France thus becomes an environment from which the young crave to escape—all except Serge who flatly states his intentions to marry and settle down in the region to lead the ancestral peasant life.

If Henri is the film's most enigmatic and disturbed character, François is the one with whom the film-maker seems to feel the greatest affinity, presenting his sexual confusion, self-loathing and intellectual excitement with great sympathy. François brings people together, encouraging Maïté to comfort Serge after his brother's funeral and, less intentionally, enabling the consummation of Maïté and Henri's furtive and impossible love. It is not that Téchiné gives François anything as straightforward as a preponderance of point-of-view shots, it is simply this trajectory that interests him most. In this sense, *Les Roseaux sauvages* gathers its force from the careful assembly of social moments and everyday locales—weddings, schoolrooms, cafés, funerals. The result is that by the close, when the four go swimming together while waiting for their baccalauréat results, a crucial threshold in their lives has been reached.

It is this sequence that best sums up the stylistic virtues of the film—unforced French naturalism that reaches an near-Renoirian lyricism on the banks of the river. Blessed with some finely judged, completely authentic performances, *Les Roseaux sauvages* is a film that avoids the potential wistfulness of its subject matter and that remains in the mind.

TIME, 6/12/95, p. 68, Richard Corliss

There's a beautiful scene between two intimate friends, Maïté (Elodie Bouchez) and François (Gaël Morel), in André Téchiné's *Wild Reeds*, set in the south of France in 1962. The two teens have kept company partly to defer any plunge into sexual commitment. Now François confesses he has had sex with someone else. Maïté is shocked. But with another boy—and she feels a kind of relief. As *Smoke Gets in Your Eyes* plays soulfully, she pulls François into a slow-dance clinch. Then, abruptly, the Beach Boys' *Barbara Ann* comes on. The two start jitterbugging, Maïté breaks into a giddy radiance, and with each twirl the two seem to lose years and cares—briefly recapturing a joyous, preadolescent innocence.

As the Algerian war stumbles blindly to a close, its fatal chaos is felt back home, where tragedy mixes with the melodrama that informs a teenager's every waking moment. Brains, groins, hearts—all work overtime in François, Maité and their friends; they face their glandular convulsions with a wonderful seriousness. Swathing them in the sunlight and streams of Provence, Téchiné treats all the kids (and their teachers) with affection and respect. He knows that for these handsome idealists, love is as important as sex. They are defining their blossoming identities by discovering the people they can't live without.

For French film in the coming years, one of those people will be Bouchez. Emotions play volcanically on her dark features; she illuminates Maité's moods with the flick of a pout or smile. *Wild Reeds* is a courtly ballad to intelligent passion, and Bouchez is its princess.

VILLAGE VOICE, 7/4/95, p. 54, Amy Taubin

I don't know what the fuss is about André Téchiné, a director whose visual style and sense of pace is so low-key that most of the time I can't figure out what he wants me to look at. *Wild Reeds,* which won four major Césars (the French Oscar) this year, is part of the French TV-funded *Boys and Girls of Their Time,* but compared to the inspired films in this series (Chantal Akerman's *Portrait of a Young Girl...*, Patricia Mazuy's *Travolta and Me,* and Claire Denis's *U.S. Go Home)* it's a bit of a washout. That it's also the only one to get commercial distribution is probably due to its obvious subcultural hook. *Wild Reeds* is a gay male coming of age film.

Set in 1962 toward the end of the Algerian War (a bloody conflict that polarized France, not to mention what it did to Algeria, in much the same way as the Vietnam War did the U.S.), *Wild Reeds* depicts the loosely knit connections of four teenagers, relationships made all the more bittersweet by the awareness that, once their bac exams are over, they probably will never see one another again. The strongest aspect of *Wild Reeds* is its intertwining of sex and politics, both of which are understood by the kids to be matters of life and death.

Wild Reeds is constructed as a round-robin of desire: middle-class François is attracted to farm boy Serge, who's attracted to François's best female friend Maite, a young communist who's attracted to the militant right-winger Henri. The film starts slowly but becomes more compelling as the relationships become more difficult. Téchiné's direction is best when he doesn't force things; when he needs to deliver heightened emotion, however, he falls back on Godardian lyricism (minus the crucial irony), as in the shot of François and Serge riding through the countryside on a motorbike, or worse, on the visual tropes of softcore as when Henri looms half naked at the water's edge over a trembling Maite, or when François and Serge swim in the sun-drenched river, their tender bottoms teasingly clad in white jockey shorts.

The relatively unknown cast is quite good, particularly Elodie Bouchez as Maite, who seems more like a real person, albeit a person of optional gravity, than any French movie actor I can think of. Téchiné knows how to direct actors. He also has empathy for adolescents. Too bad his filmmaking doesn't always measure up to what I suspect is in his mind.

Also reviewed in:
CHICAGO TRIBUNE, 7/21/95, Friday/p. F, Michael Wilmington
NATION, 7/31-8/7/95, p. 144, Stuart Klawans
NEW YORK TIMES, 6/30/95, p. C14, Caryn James
NEW YORKER, 7/31/95, p. 82, Terrence Rafferty
VARIETY, 6/13-19/94, p. 58, Emanuel Levy
WASHINGTON POST, 8/25/95, p. D5, Hal Hinson
WASHINGTON POST, 8/25/95, Weekend/p. 44, Desson Howe

WINDOW TO PARIS

A Sony Pictures Classics release of a Fontaine/Sodaperaga production in association iwth La Sept Cinema. *Producer:* Guy Seligmann. *Director:* Yuri Mamin. *Screenplay (French and Russian with English subtitles):* Yuri Mamin and Arkadi Tigai. *Director of Photography:* Sergei Nekrasov and Anatoli Lapchov. *Editor:* Olga Andrianova and Joele Van Effenterre. *Music:* Yuri Mamin and Aleksei Zalivalov. *Sound:* Leonide Gavritchenko. *Set Designer:* Vera Zelinskaia. *Costumes:* Natalya Zamakhina. *Running time:* 87 minutes. *MPAA Rating:* Not Rated.

CAST: Agnes Soral (Nicole); Serguei Dontsov (Nikolai); Viktor Michailov (Gorokhov); Nina Oussatova (Véra); Kira Kreylis-Petrova (Gorokhov's Mother-in-law); Natalja Ipatova (Gorokhov's Daughter); Viktor Gogolev (Kouzmitch); Tamara Timofeeva (Maria Olégovna); Andrej Ourgante (Gouliaiév); Jean Rupert (M. Prévost).

LOS ANGELES TIMES, 2/17/95, Calendar/p. 2, Kevin Thomas

Yuri Mamin's wacky, knockabout "Window to Paris," a sharp, no-holds-barred satire of the moral and fiscal bankruptcy of present-day Russia, risks being merely excruciating in order to be excruciatingly funny. It's the kind of calamitous, risk-taking comedy that you must lock into right at the start if it's not going to affect you like chalk scraping across a blackboard.

Spindly, weathered, straggly haired Serguei Dontsov stars as Nikolai, a music and aesthetics teacher in a St. Petersburg business high school, where he's regarded as obsolete. He, on the other hand, sees the school system, which has cut arts instruction, as turning out predators and ignoramuses, just as it did under communism. In any event, he's whipped his kids into a song-and-dance unit straight out of "Fame."

Nikolai, who has been sleeping in the school gym, at last lands a garret room in an apartment that is home to the Gorokhovs, a combative, overweight family given to a great deal of eating and drinking and singing. They are exuberant vulgarians, exasperating but capable of an embracing kindliness and generosity. They are clearly meant to be archetypal Russian survivors; they may get on your nerves, yet they're hearty enough to take life in stride.

After a night of revelry, Nikolai, Gorokhov (Viktor Mihailov) and some other boozy pals discover that there's a window behind the armoire in Nikolai's room. But the roof it goes onto is not in St. Petersburg but in Paris. It takes a while, understandably, for these guys to realize they're not in St. Petersburg anymore.

Paris has been a Mecca for Russians since before the Revolution, and here it represents Western prosperity and freedom. Architecturally, the two cities are similar, having been defined by 18th- and 19th-Century classical styles, but St. Petersburg, for all its own fabled beauty and grandeur, is shown to be run-down and ill-kempt in comparison to the City of Light.

An ancient chart discovered on the wall of Nikolai's room reveals that the Russians' "window of opportunity" will last only 20 days, with the wall closing up for another 20 years. In no time the Gorokhovs are hawking Russian souvenirs and even pianos in a Paris square, but their noisy ways draw the ire of Nicole (Agnes Soral).

While Nikolai finds himself attracted to Nicole, she and the Gorokhovs get into escalating donnybrooks, which culminate with Nicole finding herself wandering over a St. Petersburg at night that's something like the South Bronx—and wearing nothing but mules, a towel turban and a short satin dressing gown.

Dontsov is a warm, likable man who is the film's rueful, wise linchpin. For all his vaulting artistic spirit, Dontsov's Nikolai has his feet on the ground, he remains the realist while others get caught up in their self-absorbed flights of fancy. Each successive, frequently hilarious adventure experienced by Nikolai—and the others—allows Mamin further opportunity to skewer some aspect of current Russian society. Having ticked off a long list of ills, Mamin nevertheless is in fact making a plea for Russians to stay home and deal with them.

NEW YORK POST, 2/17/95, p. 48, Thelma Adams

"Window to Paris" drips with whimsy. It's the cinematic equivalent of porcelain Hummel figurines.

Nikolai (Serguei Dontsov) moves into a group flat in St. Petersburg. One drunken night, the lanky, frazzle-haired music teacher opens his armoire and finds a magical portal into Paris.

Cue the Eiffel Tower, cue the accordion.

Directing a script he cowrote with Arkadi Tigai, Russian Yuri Mamin conjures up children's classics such as C.S. Lewis' "The Lion, the Witch and the Wardrobe" and Lewis Carroll's "Through the Looking Glass." Mamin creates an adult fantasy that contrasts Russia and France, forcing East and West to meet.

The concept is promising; the implementation cloying.

From the vodka lines and obese women of St. Pete to the overflowing markets and sleek chic femmes of Paree, the view from "Window to Paris" is painted in broad strokes.

With the exception of the soulful Nikolai, the Russians are grotesque: greedy, drunken, coarse, sly, backward. Nicolai's neighbors use the window to plunder French goods and bilk Parisians.

The French fools the Russians encounter are spoiled and smug. Nicole (Agnes Soral), a Parisian taxidermist/artist, lives in luxury just beyond the window. It takes an unplanned trip to Russia, where she is mugged, beaten and jailed, before she can find her heart.

Whether traveling through the looking glass or the wardrobe or the window, into Neverland or across Oz, the moral remains the same: There's no place like home.

When Nikolai leads his waifish students on a field trip to France, they resist returning to Russia. In candy-colored Paris, the teacher lays it out to the kids in black and white: "You were born at the wrong time ... in a miserable country. But it's your country. Fix it up."

NEWSDAY, 2/17/95, Part II/p. B7, Jack Mathews

You know how thoroughly Western materialism has defeated Soviet communism when liberated Russian artists begin to acknowledge its superiority and its influence in their work. And in "Window to Paris," Russian filmmaker Yuri Mamin virtually hoists a flag of cultural surrender.

The movie itself is more Hollywood than Russian, a comic "Twilight Zone" episode that plays on the fantasies of abundance, the universal dream of magically transporting yourself into a different and better world. Mamin has a wonderful touch for this material, and has made a very funny movie. But much of the humor is at the expense of his own people, largely depicted here as fat, alcoholic peasants with the eating and social habits of slop hogs.

The exception among the Russians is Nikolai (Serguei Dontsov), a lean, shaggy-haired music teacher and piano tuner who remains apolitical in a country awkwardly trying to jettison its socialist past and convert to capitalism. We meet him as he is being dismissed from his teaching job—the school administrators are abandoning the arts to teach the principles of capitalism—and moving into a communal apartment in a rundown section of St. Petersburg.

There, after an evening of serious vodka quaffing, he and his boisterous companions discover a long-hidden window that leads onto a roof where a new world awaits, where the air is warmer, the buildings more colorful, and from where they have a view of the Eiffel Tower. On one side of that window is gray, militaristic Russia, with its food and housing shortages. On the other side is charming Paris, full of life and pride and fresh vegetables.

How that window functions, and for how long, are given some lame scientific explanations, but no matter. It's a terrific device for exploring the culture clash brought on by the collapse of the Soviet Union. The characters move back and forth between these two worlds with a single step, and each time reduce nearly 80 years of opposing social philosophies to a dizzy comic sketch.

There are a number of things going on at once. Some of the Russians get lost in Paris and can't find their way back to the window; some French follow Russians through the window and get lost in St. Petersburg. Nikolai, the most Franco-smitten of them all, lands a job as a pianist in Paris, only to show up for his first concert to learn that he's working for a nude orchestra. Welcome to naked decadence.

Meanwhile, Nikolai's roommates, the immediately corrupted Gorokhov (Viktor Michailov) and his family, are trying to find ways to latch on to some of the West's prosperity. They dress in

Russian folk costumes and try to peddle perestroika dolls on the streets. They dance, they play music, they haul rebuilt pianos out of their apartment and try to sell them on the Champs Elysée. Gorokhov even manages to make off with a motorcycle and a Citroën convertible.

The thread holding it all together is Nikolai's budding romance with Nicole (Agnes Soral), a French artist whose penthouse apartment is just outside the St. Petersburg window. Neither speaks the other's language, and it's a relationship built on massive conflicts. But Nikolai, played by Dontsov with a deft mix of warmth and whimsy, is such an engaging character, it's easy to accept the story's romantic twist.

What's hard to accept is the imbalance of the stereotyping done by Mamin. The French are full of life and charm and conviviality—no hint of their legendary disdain for foreigners—and the Russians are blustering fools. You can't help laughing when Gorokhov's rotund wife comes home wearing a French dress that fits her like a tourniquet, but the joke goes past jovial self-denigration to something sourly demeaning.

For the Russians, it seems, the Iron Curtain has been replaced with a looking glass, and it's going to take a while to adjust to the images on the other side.

VILLAGE VOICE, 2/21/95, p. 47, J. Hoberman

Will the 1990s be remembered as that period of relative tranquility preceding the chaotic aftermath of Russia's collapse? The post-Soviet story receives less attention on American TV than the least of Newt Gingrich's futuristic pronouncements, but it's a vision one gets in slow motion while enduring Yuri Mamin's purposefully loud, hectic comedy *Window to Paris*.

A self-reflexively French-Russian coproduction—part fizzless champagne, part sodden Molotov cocktail—*Window to Paris* may aspire to the classy but is far more interestingly hysterical. "There is such a thing as the aesthetics of the ugly," Mamin proclaimed of an earlier film. "Life is not all about beauty. Vulgarity, chaos, and paradox are all part of our social life, and they prompt the visual solution." Hence, *Window* opens its sash on a drab St. Petersburg plaza where a bedraggled band of street musicians befuddle an irate vodka queue by blasting the Internationale. (The vodka may have run out but there is no shortage of vodka jokes.)

Mamin's Russia is a land of followers, The idea of music as a form of social control is immediately picked up in the scene introducing the movie's hero, Nikolai Chizkov, an aesthetics teacher who tootles on a flute to lead his students dancing into class. Unkempt and dreamy, Chizhov is the requisite holy fool ("We prepare 'businessmen,' not musicians," his uptight administrator warn him) who becomes something of an international explorer after he obtains a room in a communal apartment that, as in one of C.S. Levis's Narnia novels, contains a magical passage into another world. That world, comrades, is ours.

As Chizhov and his new neighbors celebrate his arrival, the room's former occupant unexpectedly materializes through the window in search of her cat. The assembled sots naturally follow and drunkenly emerge into ... Paris! Noticing only a more temperate climate, they wander off into the enchanted night, naturally gravitating to the nearest café which they mistake, not altogether without reason, for a foreigners-only hard-currency bar.

Perhaps because of its own reliance on hard currency, *Window to Paris* tempers the grotesque exuberance associated with the most radical post-glasnost Petersburg productions. (Mamin, 48, is associated with Lenfilm's independent Troitsky Most studio, which produced the export hits *Taxi Blues* and *Freeze, Die, Come to Life,* as well as much Sokurov, and his own earlier satires, *Neptune's Holiday, The Fountain,* and *Sideburns*.) Since *Window to Paris* is predicated on allowing a gaggle of unattractive Russian bumpkins to run wild through the unimaginable consumer paradise of the, West ("so many churches and they don't even believe in God"), it makes a kind of sense that the movie's whimsy is so strenuous as to verge on the idiotic.

The beefy, manic Russians parade around town in traditional clothes, noisily hawking everything from perestroika dolls to grand pianos while pilfering anything that isn't nailed down. Paris is no match for this liberated, singleminded energy. Squatting on the Left Bank roof that mystically conjoins their dreary Petersburg flat, the Russians engage in a prolonged war of nerves with the dizzy sculptress Nicole; when she cuts their ladder to the street, they start marching through her studio.

The film's full horror is precipitated only when, chasing the Russians back to their lair, Nicole gets marooned, wearing only a nightgown, in St. Petersburg—a grim world of deprivation, insane violence, and bone-chilling darkness where she is brought home to be robbed by a vodka-swilling toilet attendant and subsequently arrested for vagrancy. (Mamin quoted *It's a Wonderful Life* in *Neptune's Holiday*; here he effectively plays out a version of the hellish last reel.) The Russians, who, back in Paris, are pleasantly engaged in hoisting an orange Citroen onto their roof to bring home through the window, riff that they sent her to Petersburg to be "reeducated."

Nicole's nightmare represents *Window*'s emotional peak. Increasingly raucous and decreasingly funny, the movie climaxes in a frenzy of audiovisual abuse. Chizhov rescues the traumatized Nicole, Nicole warms up to her wild and crazy new neighbors, then Chizhov's class arrives for a school trip. Immediately infected by the West, they become break-dancing panhandlers. To persuade his little hustlers to return, Chizhov has to invoke their "miserable bankrupt country" and launch into a patriotic plea for their help to make it a better place. (His speech doesn't even convince the scriptwriter who contrives a skyjacking to get the kids home.)

It's the aesthetics of ugliness to be sure. But *Window to Paris* is so unrelentingly crass it's almost likable—or do I mean poignant? This is a fantasy to bash your brain with. In his classic account of urban modernity, *All That Is Solid Melts Into Air,* Marshall Berman suggests that the streets of Baudelaire's Paris and those of Dostoyevsky's Petersburg represent modernism's two primal, polar-opposite scenes. The former is the modernism of advanced nations: Factories pump out commodities, confident multitudes pack the pulsating boulevards. The latter is the modernism of underdevelopment: Streets are designed for crowd control, store windows filled with expensive imports, the city a stage set populated by superfluous men.

The more things change ... Berman's description of Petersburg modernism precisely evokes the desperate mood of Mamin's film: "Forced to build on fantasies and dreams ... to be shrill, uncouth, and inchoate," Berman writes of this modernism, "it whips itself into frenzies of self-loathing, and preserves itself only through vast reserves of self-irony." *Window to Paris* is so painfully funny, you may forget to laugh.

Also reviewed in:
CHICAGO TRIBUNE, 3/17/95, Friday/p. H, Michael Wilmington
NEW REPUBLIC, 2/27/95, p. 27, Stanley Kauffmann
NEW YORK TIMES, 2/17/95, p. C6, Janet Maslin
VARIETY, 2/21-27/94, p. 36, Derek Elley
WASHINGTON POST, 4/7/95, p. D6, Rita Kempley

WINGS OF COURAGE

A Sony Pictures Classics release. *Executive Producer:* Antoine Compin and Charis Horton. *Producer:* Jean-Jacques Annaud. *Director:* Jean-Jacques Annaud. *Screenplay:* Alain Godard and Jean-Jacques Annaud. *Director of Photography:* Robert Fraisse. *Editor:* Louise Rubacky. *Casting:* Mary-Jo Slater and Stuart Aikins. *Production Designer:* Ian Thomas. *Costumes:* Aggie Rodgers. *Make-up:* Stephan Dupuis. *Running time:* 40 minutes. *MPAA Rating:* G.

CAST: Craig Sheffer (Henri Guillaumet); Elizabeth McGovern (Noëlle Guillaumet); Tom Hulce (St. Exupery); Val Kilmer (Jean Mermoz); Ken Pogue (Pierre Deley); Ron Sauve (Jean-Rene Lefebvre).

CHRISTIAN SCIENCE MONITOR, 4/21/95, p. 11, David Sterritt

You'll feel like you're in the picture! Movie advertisements have made that claim for years, but "Wings of Courage" makes good on the promise in a novel way. It's the first narrative movie presented in Imax 3-D, a new process combining the size of an Imax picture—10 times larger than 35mm film provides—with the depth of 3-D imagery.

All of which raises an important question: Do you *want* to be in this picture, which centers on an intrepid aviator making his way to safety after crashing his plane in the Andes?

Adventure fans may answer with a rousing yes, since it's unlikely that any previous film has served up so many bone-chilling landscapes and life-threatening situations with such an obsessive sense of realism. But if you prefer cozy firesides to frostbitten journeys, you may prefer to wait for some future Imax attraction offering milder, homier pleasures.

Be this as it may, Imax 3-D will probably be on the scene for some time to come, if only because it represents such a hefty investment on the part of producers and exhibitors who've decided to use it.

Large quantities of high-tech thingamabobs—from cameras as big as refrigerators to screens as high as eight-story buildings—are needed to provide the visual thrills available at the Sony Imax Theatre in Manhattan, where I checked out the new process, and similar facilities in other cities.

Such equipment doesn't come cheap, so Imax promoters will be doing their best to generate a steady stream of pictures designed to draw the largest possible audiences. The most recent move in this direction is a commitment from cable TV's popular Discovery Channel to produce films in the large format.

"Wings of Courage" takes Imax a significant step beyond the documentary fare that has been its main product until now. Craig Sheffer plays a French aviator who waves goodbye to his wife and employers—the great author Antoine de St. Exupery is among them—and takes his 1930 biplane on a mail run over the Andes Cordillera range. Savage weather forces him into a crash landing, whereupon he stashes the mail in a safe place and starts walking toward civilization, countless miles away.

"Feet of Courage" might be a more accurate title, since more of the movie focuses on Sheffer trudging through the snow than flying through the sky.

Other scenes show his faithful spouse (Elizabeth McGovern) and anxious comrades (Tom Hulce and Val Kilmer) waiting and fretting on the home front. A few musical and romantic interludes are also sandwiched into the scenario, showing Imax's entertainment versatility.

Kinks have not been completely eliminated from the Imax 3-D process, which is prone to "ghosts" and other visual imperfections. Nor is there much to crow about in the new PSE sound system, which delivers some of the soundtrack through tiny speakers in each moviegoer's liquid-crystal headset. This is the same headset you view the picture through, replacing the celluloid glasses that 3-D audiences had to put up with in the 1950s' when three-dimensional movies made their first bid for popularity.

More important than these technical shortcomings is the fundamental fact that "Wings of Courage" isn't much of a movie beyond its novelty value. Directed by Jean-Jacques Annaud, whose credits include such outdoorsy films as "Quest for Fire" and "The Bear," it's a perfunctory action yarn that cares more about the impact of its effects than the thoughtfulness of its drama.

Fortunately for audiences, the Imax 3-D headsets relaying from right eye to left eye and back, 48 times every second—create discomfort if used too long at a stretch, so "'Wings of Courage" has the great virtue of lasting a mere 40 minutes. That's enough time to showcase its technology without allowing its old-fangled narrative to become too tedious to bear. Less is more, even where gargantuan movie processes are concerned.

NEW YORK POST, 4/21/95, p. 50, Thelma Adams

It's a bird! It's a plane! No, it's Val Kilmer tangoing into my lap at the Sony IMAX Theater.

The screen is 8 stories tall. I'm wearing a state-o-the-art 3D helmet like a baseball cap on my head so it doesn't squash my nose. Daredevil pilot Craig Sheffer keeps whispering in my ear and my ear alone: "Don't think, Henri, just fly."

It took two cameras the size of refrigerators to film "Wings of Courage." Is it entertaining? You betcha. I loved it in the same way I enjoyed the squirming, impaled entrails wiggling over the audience in an Andy Warhol 3D extravaganza or the giant spurting hypodermic poking at the viewers in the Three Stooges' "Spooks."

But "Wings of Courage" isn't intended to take its place in history for its trick shots of tempting hors d'oeuvres on toothpicks within arms' reach. This manly tale of pilots Henri Guillaumet (Sheffer), Jean Mermoz (Kilmer) and Antoine de St. Exupery (Tom Hulce) flying mail over the Andes in the '30s is selling itself as the first 3D drama by an Academy Award-winning director, Jean-Jacques Annaud ("Black and White in Color").

"Wings of Courage" doesn't fly as a drama. It's a shadow, however big and imposing, of Howard Hawks' 1939 classic "Only Angels Have Wings." Hawks showed men and women battling each other and nature when showgirl Jean Arthur stumbled into a remote South American airfield and threw the boys' club into confusion by falling for ace pilot Cary Grant.

Annaud covers similar territory but turns it into second-rate Jack London. While Guillaumet's wife Noelle (Elizabeth McGovern) knits in a distant city, the pilot makes a mail run over the Andes in rough weather and crashes. The flight footage is as amazing as any to be found in "To Fly" or other non dramatic IMAX adventures. But there's no tension as this guy fumbles over the mountains with Kilmer's words ringing in his (and my) ears: "The Andes don't give men back—ever."

Novelist London knew enough to have his frostbitten characters forced to do the unthinkable, like crawl into the belly of a dead cow for warmth. I kept waiting for that fateful llama, but she never showed up.

Kilmer ("The Doors") almost manages to give Mermoz a larger-than-life panache before he disappears in the movie's early minutes. Hulce, the reliable star of "Amadeus," seems to be doing a muted Richard Milhaus Nixon imitation. Sheffer ("A River Runs Through It") makes no impression as the ostensible star, and the talented McGovern ("Ragtime") gives a treacly turn to lines that generally end in "dear."

What does this say for the great emotions Annaud intends to stir up with "Wings of Courage?" Thank goodness he failed because I wasn't sure how I would cope with tears fogging up my 3D helmet.

NEWSDAY, 4/21/95, Part II/p. B5, Jack Mathews

IMAX meets 3-D. Not since Godzilla met King Kong had filmmakers attempted a greater merger of big-screen novelties than "Transitions," the inaugural 3-D picture shown at Expo '86 in Vancouver. Now, nearly a decade and several successful IMAX 3-D nature films later, Sony Pictures Classics will see if it can stretch the merger to include dramatic features.

"Wings of Courage," opening today in the 6-month-old Sony IMAX 3-D Theater at Lincoln Square, is not exactly a full-length feature. It measures in at only 40 minutes. But it is long enough to answer what its director, Jean-Jacques Annaud, himself regards as the crucial question. Can 3-D be used to heighten the audience's emotional involvement in a story, just as it heightens our visceral response to images?

The answer, at least on this inaugural Sony venture, is the same as it has always been. No.

"Wings of Courage," based on the true story of pioneer French airmail pilot Henri Guillaumet's crash landing in the Argentine Andes in 1930, boasts a respectable Hollywood cast. Craig Sheffer, the older brother in "A River Runs Through It," is the stranded Guillaumet; Elizabeth McGovern is his fretting wife at home in Buenos Aires, and Tom Hulce is the mail-company boss leading the rescue effort. The Sony IMAX 3-D process, as this newspaper's Joe Gelmis wrote in his review of the new Lincoln Square theater last fall, is a sensation.

Equipped with $400 electronically controlled goggles, we take in the breathtaking aerial views of the snow-capped Andes as if we had our heads stuck out the window of an airplane. The eight-story-high by 100-foot-wide screen goes beyond our field of vision and, in moving our heads up, down, left and right to take in the rest of the image, we get none of the migraine-producing blur that has ended every previous run of 3-D features.

The problem with "Wings of Courage" is that it does not have enough inherent dramatic power for a conventional feature, let alone one that has to overcome the distractions of whizbang technology. As well as those goggles work, it's not exactly easy to forget they're strapped around your head, and though their crystal-clear built-in speakers do indeed add another dimension to the six-channel sound system (they're used here to let us listen in on the lost pilot's thoughts), they do more to push us out of the story than to draw us in.

Annaud, whose "Black and White in Color" won the foreign-language Oscar in 1977, is a great composer of images, and there are some exhilarating scenes in "Wings," particularly in the early moments when we see Guillaumet's biplane chugging through the thin air above and between the peaks of the Andes. The crash sequence, however, isn't as exciting as it should be (Annaud was limited by Sony's order for a G rating), and from then on, as Guillaumet climbs, crawls and claws his way through the mountains, both the story and the images become monotonous.

It seems an ill-fated ambition to make dramas for IMAX, in 3-D or otherwise. The whole idea of the format is to thrill the senses, and in doing that, the films blunt the intellect. "The Son of

Flubber" might be fun up there, but "Call of the Wild," which "Wings" sort of resembles, requires more dedicated reflection.

Also reviewed in:
CHICAGO TRIBUNE, 3/22/96, Friday/p. I, Michael Wilmington
NEW REPUBLIC, 5/29/95, p. 27, Stanley Kauffmann
NEW YORK TIMES, 4/21/95, p. C6, Caryn James
NEW YORKER, 4/24/95, p. 120, Anthony Lane
VARIETY, 4/24-30/95, p. 53, Godfrey Cheshire

WOODEN MAN'S BRIDE, THE

An Arrow Releasing release of a Long Shong Proudction Co., Ltd. film. *Executive Producer:* Yu Shu and Li Xudong. *Producer:* Wang Ying Hsiang. *Director:* Huang Jianxin. *Screenplay (Mandarin with English subtitles):* Yang Zhengguang. *Director of Photography:* Zhang Xiaoguang. *Editor:* Lei Qin. *Music:* Zhang Dalong. *Art Director:* Teng Jie. *Set Designer:* Yang Jianping. *Costumes:* Du Longxi. *Running time:* 114 minutes. *MPAA Rating:* Not Rated.

CAST: Chang Shih (Kui); Wang Lan (Young Mistress); Ku Paoming (Brother); Wang Yumei (Madame Liu); Wang Fuli (Sister Ma); Kao Mingjun (Chief Tang).

LOS ANGELES TIMES, 6/5/95, Calendar/p. 4, Kevin Thomas

Huang Jianxin's terse, stunning "The Wooden Man's Bride," shown in last year's Asian Pacific Film & Video Festival, is a folk tale in which a young woman (Wang Lan) is forced to marry her recently deceased fiancé in effigy, represented during the ceremony by a carved wooden bust held by her formidable mother-in-law's virile young retainer (Ku Paoming). The film is in the stark tradition of Asian cinema in which the utmost suffering and hardship are expressed in the most beautifully composed of images.

NEW YORK POST, 2/8/95, p. 39, Larry Worth

Chinese calendars proclaim this as the year of the pig. But when it comes to Chinese cinema, it's the year of the wooden man. As in "The Wooden Man's Bride," which China, and most countries, will be hard-pressed to top for some time.

Cineastes will justifiably compare director Huang Jianxin to Zhang Yimou, with specific references to Yimou gems like "Raise the Red Lantern" and "Ju Dou." There's even leading lady Wang Lan who can stand shoulder-to-shoulder with Yimou's stunning favorite, Gong Li.

But Jianxin also evokes sources as disparate as Kurosawa's "Yojimbo" and Stephen King's "Misery." And that's what imbues the tale of class, tradition and generational conflicts—never mind obsession, treachery, betrayal and murder—with exhilaration and amazement.

Set in Northern China of the 1920s, the drama unfolds as a young woman is carried by camel across the desert for her wedding in a neighboring hamlet. She errs only in tempting fate: defying a centuries-old custom by lifting the red veil from her face.

Big mistake. She's no sooner eyeballed a handsome servant (who's destined to become a central player in the scenario) than the group is beset by murderous bandits that abduct the virginal prize.

Meanwhile, back on the home front, more tragedy's in the wings. The bereaved groom accidentally kills himself while preparing to rescue his intended. But that doesn't mean he's completely out of the picture.

After being saved from the kidnappers, the heroine is forced by her iron-willed mother-in-law to pledge herself to a wooden icon of her late fiance, and treat it like a husband in every sense of the word.

Just your typical girl meets statue story? Screenwriter Yang Zhengguang is only warming up.

Thankfully, Jianxin proves the perfect complement for the hypnotic, metaphor-laden tale, injecting an epic Western sweep and a subtle sense of humor, like having the robbers double as a touring theatrical troupe.

Jianxin also emerges as a master of visual design. Here, a man doesn't simply ring the local church bell. He's framed underneath an arch, climbs a ladder in silhouette and then strikes the gong as a range of ice-capped mountains dwarf him from afar.

Equally arresting, and prophetic, is the depiction of the titular nuptials, with weathered white banners sailing defiantly against a gun-metal sky as heartbreakingly expressive Wang Lan tries to accept her fate.

Throughout, Lan is masterfully offset by Chang Shih's overly attentive servant, Wang Yumei's in-law from hell and Kao Mingjun's oddly alluring bandit chief.

The only drawback is a string of expletives which seem anachronistic to the time and place. Regardless, "The Wooden Man's Bride" is 1995's first must-see film.

NEWSDAY, 2/8/95, Part II/p. B11, John Anderson

Anyone familiar with the recent work of China's Fifth Generation of filmmakers will leave "The Wooden Man's Bride" with an indistinct feeling of deja vu—or whatever its Chinese equivalent is.

Evocative of Zhang Yimou's "Ju Dou" and "Raise the Red Lantern" in its storyline and faux classicism, of Chen Kaige's "Life on a String" in its mystical use of Mongolian landscapes, and of Tian Zhuangzhuang's "Blue Kite" in its allegory and irony, "Wooden Man" also possesses the sense of resigned loss that informs these post-Mao movies.

But director Huang Jianxin has his own rewards—including a quite westernized flair for the absurd and an easternized flair for the western: Mongolia may not be Monument Valley (although there are similarities), but for the first half of the film "Wooden Man's Bride" might be "The Searchers."

It's the '20s, China is still a feudal society, and a servant named Kui (Chang Shih) is dispatched to fetch the young woman (Wang Lan) who is betrothed to the son of the imperious Madame Liu (Wang Yumei). En route, their party is waylaid by members of the marauding Whirlwind Gang, who want the young bride for their chief. Rather than see Kui murdered, she surrenders herself to them.

Director Huang dwells in a tradition-rich milieu, but skews the traditions, reflecting them off real-world attitudes: When the bride's male servants want a glimpse of her face, for instance—good luck will result, they tell each other—she obliges them by casually stripping off her veil, and her informality deflates the ritual-bloated atmosphere. Likewise, the niceties of the wedding party are not just trampled by the rampaging bandits, they're made to look as pointless as they are. And so is Kui: Not only has he failed in his mission to fetch the bride, his life has been saved by a woman.

So back he goes in search of her, finding himself in a walled city run by Whirlwind gangsters and overseen by an Peking Opera-singing chief (Kao Mingjun). Subjected to a test, Kui impresses them with his bravery, is sent home with the bride, and is invited to return and be a bandit.

But the pair's ordeal has just begun. In their absence, Madame Lui's son, rushing to arm himself and rescue his bride, has shot himself to death. Grief unhinges Mom, who forces the girl to wed—and remain faithful to—a smirking wooden effigy of her dead son.

Although Kui and the young mistress will fall in love, and be found out, more important to Huang's ends are the uselessness of ritual and the cruelty of social mores—the bride's humiliation for having been abducted, for instance, or the class rift that separates the lovers.

While Mao may lurk behind every frame of the Fifth Generation films (is the wooden man the atrophied legacy of Chinese communism?), Huang's film manages to transcend cultural borders, with dramatic urgency and historical sweep. One distraction is the subtitling, which uses western vulgarities in some unlikely ways. In a film that already walks a fine line between formal and the flippant, the New World expletives push it too hard in the latter direction.

VILLAGE VOICE, 2/14/95, p. 49, J. Hoberman

Bandits attack a caravan of camels as they transport a beautiful bride across a boundless desert. Pursued by the Whirlwind Gang, a brawny servant named Kui carries the bride off on his back—until she surrenders to the bandits in order to save his life. When news of the abduction reaches the prospective bridegroom, he kills himself, perhaps accidentally. Kui, however, goes alone to the bandit lair and restores the girl to her mother-in-law, Madame Liu, who, in keeping with her rigid morality, determines the bride's intact maidenhead and compels her to marry a wooden replica of her dead son.

To anyone familiar with the development of China's Fifth Generation, Huang Jianxin's *The Wooden Man's Bride,* which opens the Film Forum's new calendar, is something like the generic Chinese art flick. The rugged, timeless landscape, bathed in golden light; the studied compositions of symmetrical courtyards, animated by fluttering silk banners; the cruel rural folkways consecrated in stately, chanting ceremonials; the repressed passions and unhurried pace; the feisty, innocent heroine victimized by a thousand years of institutionalized sexism—all were present in the original Fifth Generation feature, Chen Kaige's 1984 *Yellow Earth.* Since then, they've been massively popularized, in China and abroad, by Chen's erstwhile cinematographer, Zhang Yimou.

The Wooden Man's Bride recalls Zhang's first three Gong Li vehicles, *Red Sorghum, Ju Dou,* and *Raise the Red Lantern.* (Indeed, with her slim build and lush downturned mouth, Wang Lan, the actress in the Gong Li role, even resembles Gong Li, particularly in profile.) But is *The Wooden Man's Bride* a pastiche or a critique? Huang is the only member of the Fifth Generation to have dealt with the contradictions of Chinese socialism and contemporary urban life; *The Black Cannon Incident,* his 1985 debut feature in which a mild-mannered engineer is suspected of industrial espionage when a postal clerk misinterprets his propensity for playing chess by mail, was briefly banned for export. His science-fiction sequel, *Displacement* (1986), went even deeper into dark comedy, while *Transmigration* (1989) was one of the first Chinese movies to explore the issue of alienated urban youth.

Parody or not, *The Wooden Man's Bride* is like an allegory of an allegory. The movie was produced by a Taiwanese company using the resources of the Fifth Generation incubator, Xi'an Studio. But unlike other Xi'an films, Northern China is depicted less as a realm of documentary "realness" than as a dreamscape. Huang's taste for abstraction is everywhere apparent—most outrageously in a tableau of the bandit lair decorated with bloody corpses and carefully positioned minibonfires. The bandits even have a resident opera company, headed by their chief who is introduced singing the female lead. (That he is played by Taiwanese pop star Kao Mingjun adds another element of subtext.)

Compared to Zhang, Huang exhibits very little emotional pow. *The Wooden Man's Bride* has the feel of an exercise—which is what it is. The bride submits to a ritual examination and is thereafter charged with the care and feeding of her immobile husband—less than life-size but large enough to occupy a chair. Her wifely duties consist of moving him from the mantelpiece to the courtyard and then, each night, into her bed. It's typical of Huang's detached sense of humor that he and screenwriter Yang Zhengguang invented this custom (a charged metaphor for obeisance to the past), although not the crude virginity test during which the bride squats naked over a pile of ashes and is compelled to sneeze.

The long-widowed Madame Liu tells her unhappy daughter-in-law that "people should live for their reputation." Still, the bride understandably rebels against the regime of the wooden doll, which is unceremoniously kicked out of bed when she and Kui finally make love. Despite the deadpan absurdity of the bride's situation (and the brutality of her subsequent punishment), the film's real emphasis is on her deliverer. It's the burden of her injustice that transforms Kui into a bandit.

Although the Wooden Man is ultimately set aflame, the film's final image is of the monument erected to old Madame Liu's chastity. "Chinese history always condemns people like Kui and commends the action of Madame Liu," Huang told Taiwanese critic Peggy Chiao. Is it an additional irony that he fails to mention the bride who, albeit eponymous, is also anonymous?

Also reviewed in:
CHICAGO TRIBUNE, 11/10/95, Friday/p. L, Michael Wilmington
NEW YORK TIMES, 2/8/95, p. C15, Stephen Holden

VARIETY, 2/14-20/94, p. 41, David Rooney
WASHINGTON POST, 3/17/95, p. B7, Hal Hinson

WORLD AND TIME ENOUGH

A Strand Releasing release of a 1 in 10 production. *Producer:* Julie Hartley and Andrew Peterson. *Director:* Eric Mueller. *Screenplay:* Eric Mueller. *Director of Photography:* Kyle Bergersen. *Editor:* Laura Stokes. *Music:* Eugene Huddleston. *Production Designer:* Heather McElhatton. *Set Decorator:* Jennie Harris. *Costumes:* Elizabeth Wheat. *Running time:* 90 minutes. *MPAA Rating:* Not Rated.

WITH: Matt Guidry (Mark); Gregory G. Giles (Joey); Kraig Swartz (David); Peter Macon (Mike); Bernadette Sullivan (Marie).

LOS ANGELES TIMES, 10/6/95, Calendar/p. 10, Kevin Thomas

First-time Minneapolis writer-director Eric Mueller's "World and Time Enough" is a modest, tender, gay love story told with a keen sense of what it must be like to be homosexual in Middle America.

Mueller has written good parts for his lead actors and received from them focused, impassioned portrayals that sustain the film to a satisfying conclusion. "World and Time Enough" is a worthy example of unpretentious regional filmmaking, financed entirely by grants and fellowships.

Mark (Matt Guidry), whose HIV-positive status fires his work as an activist-artist, constantly putting up protest banners and temporary assemblages, and Joey (Gregory G. Giles) cope with Mark's diagnosis pretty well. What gets them down are their parental relations. As the film opens, Mark has gathered up the nerve to call his estranged, widowed father whereas Joey, suffering from a brutal and total rejection from his adoptive father, commences trying to find his birth parents.

The lovers live in a whimsically decorated loft, and Mark supports himself as a temp, never missing an opportunity to subvert the corporate culture. Joey is a garbage collector, spearing detritus in parks and along roads. The men balance each other in temperament: Mark is fiery while Joey is sweet-natured. You have to wonder why Joey doesn't set his sights higher professionally, but he does take a childlike joy in finding kitschy treasure amid the trash he collects.

Like many debut features, "World and Time Enough" gets better as it goes along, forsaking jauntiness for a more effective seriousness. You wish that Mueller had jettisoned his use of a narrator—a redundant, tedious device since the character is tiresomely gossipy and unfunny as well as a distraction, needlessly interrupting the ongoing momentum of the narrative. Mueller may have come to this opinion himself because he cuts to the narrator less and less as the film progresses. On the plus side is Joey's warm, mutually supportive relationship with his sister, well-played by Bernadette Sullivan.

NEW YORK POST, 9/1/95, p. 45, Bill Hoffmann

Can two gay young men with dead-end jobs, broken families and a mile-high list of other problems find love and happiness in Middle America?

That's the question posed by director Eric Mueller in his Minnesota-based, bittersweet comedy/drama, "World and Time Enough."

Mark (Matt Guidry) is an HIV-positive, avant-garde artist and office temp who sets phone books on fire and spits chewing gum on the sidewalk to tell an uncaring world it must wake up to the growing threat of AIDS.

"Leave a message and wear a condom," the angry Mark urges on his answering-machine tape.

His lover, Joey (Gregory Giles), is a laid-back garbage collector trying to come to grips with the fact that he is adopted and that his conservative foster dad has written off Mark and him as a pair of "fags."

"World and Time Enough" is less of a narrative story than a series of brief vignettes joined together by a wisecracking narrator, David (Kraig Swartz), who sits on a stool and addresses the camera with the bravado of a stand-up comic.

David is meant to be a self-depreciating nebbish who's one-liners complement the movie's often too-serious business.

But it's a risky technique that works far less than it ought to and makes "World and Time Enough" seem like more of an amateur production than its bright cast and spiffy production values deserve.

Mueller also weaves a heavy-handed undercurrent of anti-Catholicism into the picture that does little more than confuse the storyline.

The couple's sometimes rocky relationship is finally solidified when Mark gets injured while trying to build a cathedral (!) in his father's memory and Joey races into his wounded companion's arms—temporarily blocking out the ills of a cruel world.

The point is that despite the challenges of AIDS, prejudice, guilt, career and family these two face, love is the all-important key to peace and serenity.

It's a good message one wishes could have been presented with a bit more pizazz, a straighter (no pun intended) narrative and a little less preachiness.

Still, Mueller should be credited for taking a generally responsible and sobering look at gay life.

NEWSDAY, 9/1/95, Part II/p. B4, John Anderson

Eric Mueller claims to have financed his gay comedy/drama "World and Time Enough" entirely with state and federal grants. Is this the way we want our tax dollars spent? Absolutely. It's certainly a much better investment than, say, the B1 bomber.

And though "World and Time Enough" doesn't exactly soar either, it reaches for something, trying to compute the elusive integers of our age, gay life, the HIV quagmire and the intangibles of family. Does it succeed entirely? No. But it has a gentleness of purpose that's affecting.

The story is about two lovers who are happy with each other—a revolutionary concept in itself—but less happy with themselves. Mueller uses what is ordinarily a distracting device—a narrator, David (Kraig Swartz)—to introduce us to his subjects' story, and it works. Then he abandons it. But while David's there—crosslegged on a stool with a Tootsie Pop, making stylishly catty comments about his friends—he contrasts smartly with the more serious matter of the two lovers.

Mark (Matt Guidry) is an art student and political firebrand who creates temporary and sometimes incendiary sculptures that castigate government indifference to burning social issues ("Who has time for politics when you can get a facial?" David asks). Mark also happens to be HIV positive, and a control freak, so his understandable rage is kept pretty well bottled up.

Joey—who, according to David, is "a few tater tots short of a hot dish"—is a garbage picker in the city's parks, who collects the more interesting bits of detritus he finds—castoff toys, hardware, beauty accessories—and creates a kind of found-art himself. This pastime is treated by everyone as an unforgivable eccentricity, but there's little difference between his inadvertent art and Mark's very obvious attempts at profound social commentary. These unlikely characters meet, fall in love, and then try to find themselves.

Meeting these two is far more fun, and makes far more sense, than getting to know them. That Mueller tries to debunk particular concepts of society or culture—that families are strictly biological, for instance, or that art comes only from universities—is fine, and his heart is in the right place. But there are too many inexplicable and illogical details for us to swallow it all wholesale. Chew on it for a while, however, we certainly will.

VILLAGE VOICE, 9/5/95, p. 74, Gary Dauphin

There are hints of what the film *World Enough and Time* could have been under different circumstances (i.e., better performances and direction), but they come so late in the film that their not much use to a sympathetic reviewer. *World* is obviously a film full of bright ideas, but it could have used a good script doctor, laboring as it does under the weight of disparate narrative elements. The two principals (an HIV-positive artist and his garbage-collector boyfriend) are tendered clearly enough, but swirling around them are a haze of schematic subplots about adoption, cathedrals, art-with-a-capital-A, and of course, mortality. Exploring loss seems to be writer-director Eric Mueller's intention, but besides the fact that he seems unable to draw the necessary depth out of his characters, he's made the fatal mistake of inserting a thoroughly random narrator, a friend of the lovers who natters on about how he's going to shut up soon and let you "see for yourself," only to pop back on screen to shatter whatever Mueller is reaching for by nattering some more.

Also reviewed in:
CHICAGO TRIBUNE, 10/13/95, Friday, p. L, Michael Wilmington
NEW YORK TIMES, 9/1/95, p. C8, Stephen Holden
VARIETY, 6/27-7/3/94, p. 87, Dennis Harvey

ADDENDUM

The following reviews arrived too late to be included in this or previous issues of FILM REVIEW ANNUAL. The issue of FILM REVIEW ANNUAL in which the credits and film reviews appear are given in parenthesis after the name of the film.

ADVENTURES OF PRISCILLA, QUEEN OF THE DESERT, THE *(Film Review Annual, 1995)*

FILM QUARTERLY, Winter 1996-97, p. 41, Susan Barber

The Adventures of Priscilla, Queen of the Desert features the outback trek of two flamboyant drag queens, Tick and Adam (Hugo Weaving and Guy Pearce), and an aging transsexual, Bernadette (Terence Stamp). It represents a bold departure for a mainstream Australian film, particularly for a cinema that has made its reputation with macho swashbuckling heroes such as Breaker Morant, Mad Max, and Crocodile Dundee. Inspired by the gay male subculture in Sydney, *Priscilla* can be viewed within a group of films from the late 80s and 90s (frequently referred to as the New Australian Film Renaissance) which have broken new ground in exploring formerly taboo subjects: female sexuality in female-centered narratives (*Sweetie, The Piano, Muriel's Wedding*); homosexuality (*The Everlasting Secret Family and The Sum of Us*); and politically sensitive areas (white neo-Nazi Australians in *Romper Stomper*).

Set against a stunning backdrop of rainbow-colored sunsets and sweeping vistas—giving the Australian outback the allure that *Crocodile Dundee* gave the bush—*Priscilla* derives its name from the lavender-colored bus that transports the three to remote desert hotels to perform their dragshow cabaret. For Adam, the trip is a lark; for Tick, a means to rendezvous with his estranged wife and young son; for Bernadette, a chance to ease the pain of her husband's death. Their bitchy infighting and hilarious interactions with the locals are delicately balanced with dazzling show-stopping performances.

Significantly, *Priscilla*'s raucous characters—in addition to the film's crude and raunchy humor that primarily locuses, in graphic detail, on male and female bodies and genitalia—though typical of gay drag humor, provide a direct link to the "ocker" comedies from the early 1970s. The ocker was a highly popular and successful genre within Australia that kicked off the film renaissance and included films such as *Stork* (1971), *The Adventures of Barry McKenzie* (1972), and *Alvin Purple* (1973). These films feature vulgar and uncouth males (ockers) with a resolutely hedonistic outlook, and an obsession with bodily pleasures—sex, drinking, and women.[1]

The ockers were true Australian originals, part of a strong and spirited outburst of native cultural expression in defiance of "cultural cringe"; that is, the Australian sense of inferiority vis-á-vis "superior" dominant British and American cultures that had overshadowed Australia throughout much of its history. The ockers were also the first group of films from the Australian Film Development Corporation (A.F.D.C.), the initial government film funding agency (1971-1975) that proved to be quite successful in getting the fledgling industry on its feet with a deliberately commercial product.

The Adventures of Barry McKenzie, for example, features a colonial on holiday abroad, demonstrating his Australian uniqueness in comparison to the British. Barry's difference is played out in a variety of comical and crass scenes that enhance his Australian virility. For example, to impress a British woman whom he is wooing, Barry dumps curry down his drawers, because he has heard that "British women like it hot." Or to show his ingenuity during a studio fire, Barry and his mates chug a case of Foster Lager, urinating on the flames in order to put them out. Throughout the film, Barry's male potency is underscored by a stream of phallic references, such as "Percy the Python" or "My one-eyed trouser snake"—the latter is even put to song!

The ocker's crude bathroom and phallic-centered humor soon led to accusations that these films were "culturally debased" and too gauche for export. For a large Australian contingent—including industry activists, film-makers, critics, and even members of Parliament (many of whom had pushed for a government-subsidized industry)—the ockers were an embarrassment. This was a particularly sensitive issue for a country interested in making a bid for international recognition with a revived national cinema.

Subsequently, the new funding policy of the A.F.D.C. (soon to become the Australian Film Commission) shifted away from commercial concerns to a more serious-intentioned quality cinema of which the country could be proud. And the films that received its financial support, such as *Picnic at Hanging Rock* (1975), *The Chant of Jimmie Blacksmith* (1978), *My Brilliant Career* (1979), and *Breaker Morant* (1980), subsequently brought world attention to Australia as well as to the directors who helped to shape the 70s Renaissance: Peter Weir, Fred Schepisi, Gillian Armstrong, and Bruce Beresford. (Ironically, Bruce Beresford was the director of *The Adventures of Barry McKenzie,* as well as its sequel, *Barry McKenzie Holds His Own.)*

Twenty years later, *Priscilla* conjures up the ocker via its familiar drunk and rowdy scenes in bars on the road, as well as scenes done in deliberate bad taste: Adam, who is far more outlandish and crass than Barry, proudly shows off an "Abba turd" in a bottle to a startled Bernadette. This almost seems intended to one-up the scene where Barry McKenzie graphically vomits "chunder" on the hair of his unsuspecting psychiatrist. Tick also carries on the tradition of the ocker's phallic-centered humor through his tale of a friend "cracking the fat"—enlarging his penis.

Yet *Priscilla*'s world of gay dragsters and transsexuals is far from the blatantly heterosexual world of Barry McKenzie, Stork, and Alvin Purple. *Priscilla*'s milieu and characters would not have been possible as a mainstream film subject in the 70s, when Australian culture was more narrowly defined by a dependable and commercial genre that initially repressed a diverse culture and history in terms of gender, class, and race. *Priscilla* represents the evolution of the film industry in the last two decades, free of censorship and shaped by film-makers able to take advantage of more flexible financing structures and willing to take risks on otherwise marginalized aspects of Australian culture.

Unlike the maligned ocker, *Priscilla* has not been an embarrassment for the industry and country. The darling of the 1994 Cannes Film Festival, it quickly achieved worldwide popularity as the first of a wave of gay drag films, earning the coveted status of a crossover film that appealed to both gay and straight audiences with its cheeky camp style and audacious yet endearing characters. Duly praised for its sympathetic treatment of gay men, *Priscilla* was also voted the most popular film at the Los Angeles Gay and Lesbian Film Festival. This international validation boosted the film's reception at home in Australia, for *Priscilla* grossed $15 million (an outstanding response from a country with a population of 18 million).

However, *Priscilla*'s fame and high international profile have been at the expense of its three female characters, for the film lashes out at Ol' Shirl, the bar patron (June Marie Bennett), Cynthia the stripper (Julia Cortez), and Marion, Tick's estranged wife (Sarah Chadwick). This misogyny exceeds the frequent and irritating sexism exuded by the original ockers, which essentially reduced women to sex objects and/or nymphomaniacs.

Clearly ingrained in the ocker genre is a fear of female sexuality and women's power that can be directly linked to the larger social upheavals of the early 70s, when the women's movement gathered momentum and when feminists boldly challenged the traditional ideology and culture of sexism in Australia. Within a decade, women achieved equal status by law. Thus, the chauvinism of the ockers operated in the dual sense of the word—hyper-inflated masculinity as well as spirited and patriotic nationalism. The posturing and flaunting of Australian machismo served as a smoke screen for male fears over the loss of authority, power, and sexual prowess.

Priscilla is very telling about ongoing male anxieties over the increasing empowerment of women. What starts as a wild and rollicking ocker romp across the outback soon turns into a full-blown misogynistic and racist attack on the films's females that surpasses even the frequent misogyny of gay drag itself. (This point of view was not lost on the organizers of the Sydney Gay and Lesbian Mardi Gras, who refused to give the film or writer/director Stephan Elliott their support.) The film denigrates Ol' Shirl and Marion, who are lesbians, as well as Cynthia, an oversexed Filipino, all of whom present specific threats to white male patriarchal society. Coupled with this misogyny is a racism specifically directed at Asian women that reveals current white male alarm over shifting ethnicities of Australia, attitudes fueled since the 1970s, when the postwar white-only Australian attitudes fueled policy changed, opening up the country to non-Europeans, specifically Austrialia's Pacific Rim neighbors, and thus dramatically altering the ethnic mix.

Bernadette's scorching remarks to Ol' Shirl in the first town where she, Tick, and Adam perform makes the film's position toward lesbians quite clear. Ol' Shirl has an unbecoming slovenly and masculine appearance. With her unkempt short hair and her garb of undershirt and trousers, she is coded as butch or lesbian, which in Australian culture is linked to the unnatural, even the perverse. Further, Ol' Shirl's rough demeanor, as well as her broken English, suggests a low-class white trash, conjuring up a "bulldagger," which carries with it a grotesque and very real threat to masculinity. As if to "unsex" Ol' Shirl, Bernadette quickly bombards her with an openly hostile and vicious outburst which also implies a violent rape: "Why don't you just light your tampon and blow your box apart, because it's the only bang you're going to get!" Shocked and humiliated, Ol' Shirl hangs her head in shame as the men in the bar break into guffaws of laughter.

If Ol' Shirl is attacked as an awesome and offensive sexual deviant, Cynthia's raunchy and outlandish burlesque act codes her as obscenely sexual. Cynthia's main claim to fame is a trick with ping-pong balls: she seductively inserts them into her vagina and then pitches them at the bar's frenzied male audience. Poured into it provocative and tight-fitting black satin bustier and thong with electric black-and-white spiraled stockings, Cynthia conjures up the "damned whore," a historical male-defined Australian stereotype for women coined during the early days of the country's settlement in the late 18th century, when all female convicts were categorized as objects of sexual gratification whether, or not they became prostitutes. By deeming all women damned whores, men could relegate them to an inferior status, yet maintain the power dynamic, still reaping the benefits of using them for sexual gratification. This attitude clearly sums up the perspective of the ocker toward women. Like her ancestors, Cynthia must be controlled and punished for her aberrant sexuality. Indeed, she is roughly dragged off the stage by her husband Bob (Bill Hunter), and painfully held against her will.

Significantly, Cynthia's excessive sexuality and lewd behavior are linked to her Asian heritage. Thus she is a female incarnation of what is perceived as a very real threat to the purity of white Australian society. The growing number of Asian immigrants has been perceived by white Australians not only as competition for decreasing jobs, but also as a drain on the social system in the areas of welfare and unemployment benefits. In fact, within the past few years, anti-Asian sentiment has fueled tensions in urban areas, and spawned openly racist groups such as the neo-Nazi National Movement.

Adam's parody of a geisha girl (one of his drag outfits on the road) seeks to diminish the Asian "menace." His silly, cartoonlike costume, adorned with pastel-blue rubber hair, matching pink-and-blue fur, and satin bodice and G-string, blurs all diverse nationalities into one Asian-Pacific stereotype, just as the film reduces all Asians into a grotesque female type. Adam's outlandish appearance is non-threatening because his Asian-ness and feminine appearance are a masquerade, whereas Cynthia's is uncomfortably real. This *new* Australian is disruptive, inappropriate, and clearly out of place.

Accordingly, Bernadette and Adam banish "Cynthia" from the film altogether. The life-size inflatable plastic sex doll which they use to signal for help after their bus breaks down clearly alludes to her: "Cynthia" disappears into the sky over the outback, and after the film's conclusion and final credits, she lands in an unnamed Asian country, suggesting that this is where Asian women really belong—certainly *not* in Australia.

With Ol' Shirl and Cynthia ousted from the film, Bernadette takes center stage as the film's ideal woman, or "God's Police." Coined at the beginning of the 19th century, this other male-defined stereotype deemed women a civilizing role within family and society. As the young nation grew out from under convict status into social respectability, these "good and virtuous women" (usually wives and mothers, and clearly delineated from the damned whores) were expected to look after the moral interests of the nation under the paternal metaphor. Moreover, their duties frequently included the policing of other women, a job that Bernadette undertakes with great relish upon settling her sights on Ol' Shirl and Cynthia. It's as if Bernadette has realized her calling, transforming from a brooding widow and lackluster performer to a zealot, as she recivilizes this "intemperate social environment."[2]

If God's Police functioned in the 1840s amidst the dramatically changing male-dominated society where women were defined according to the needs of the nation as the foundation of the patriarchal family unit, then Bernadette is the 1990's rendition of God's Police, with an evangelical furor fueled by racist white male anxiety over deviant women-lesbians and oversexed foreigners—who have threatened the traditional social status quo.

By the time Bernadette, Adam, and Tick reach their final destination in Alice Springs, Bernadette has taken Cynthia's place as Bob's very chaste paramour, a role consistent with the puritanical aura associated with God's Police. We wonder how Marion, Tick's (estranged) lesbian wife will fare. Will she be a damned whore like Cynthia, or designated as perverse like Ol' Shirl? To our surprise, she typifies God's Police. Not only is she a model mother, having raised her son on her own (while developing a successful career as entertainment director in a large hotel), but a saintly and tolerant wife, open-minded about Tick's gay lifestyle and vocational choices.

However, in a dramatic shift, the film quickly demonstrates that Marion is completely fickle and unworthy of the title; she is not only a bad mother, but also a deceitful wife. (It's as if Elliott conceived of Marion only to chart her "regression.") Marion's most serious misstep is her sexual orientation, which has distracted her ability to mother, a fact not lost on her son, Benj, who strongly implies that he felt in competition with his mother's lover, and unfairly shunned. Further, Marion betrays Tick, causing him to be publicly humiliated in front of this son, as if she were threatened by Tick's presence. She deliberately lies to Tick, telling him that Benj will not be present at his drag performance, then she brings him anyway much to Tick's embarrassment. His distress is so great that he faints and ruins the show. Marion further undercuts Tick's attempts to be a good father by ostentatiously and inappropriately trying to pair him up with the hotel busboy, when an embarrassed Tick is clearly not interested in taking on any lovers. Marion's punishment for her aberrations is the loss of her job as entertainment director, replaced by none other than Bernadette. Marion is also ousted as mother, for Tick and Adam will serve as the new parents and heads of household back in Sydney, where they take Benj. With Marion, Ol' Shirl, and Cynthia out of the film, Bernadette stands as the new standard for Australian womanhood—the bastion of reactionary "family values" that privilege the male. There is no room for lesbians or Asians.

In speaking of *Priscilla,* Australian historian/sociologist Chris Berry has commented, "The misogyny of the [transsexual and] drag queens in *Priscilla* ... [allows] filmmakers and audiences (implied to be white, heterosexual and patriarachal) to hide behind someone else. "*We* didn't say that, ... it was the drag queens.'" Recall Adam's snide solution for the "Cynthia problem"—to "sell her off" before he and Bernadette send her off—as well as his contemptuous assessment of Marion—"She could sandbag the holes of old tankers with that tongue." Thus Bernadette and Adam are used as vehicles, suggesting a homophobic (and transsexual-phobic) strain in the film.

Priscilla dresses up the once embarrassing and gauche ocker genre for international consumption, rising the alluring and exotic flamboyance and spectacle of drag and transsexuality toward hostilities toward women who challenge traditional male ideals of womanhood and singling out Asian women in particular as scapegoats for all those Pacific Rim immigrants who "taint" white Australian society. Just as the ocker revealed male anxieties over women's empowerment in the early 70s, even as it celebrated (and countered with) aggressive male prowess as part of a wave of spirited Australian nationalism, *Priscilla* unveils current white male fears in Australia—fear of female sexual freedom, aberrant Asian women, single mothers, women in the business sector—as women continue to make critical strides in Australian society, and as the country becomes more ethnically heterogeneous.

Notes

1. Though frequently grouped with the ockers, Alvin himself is not an ocker at all, but a shy, repressed boy-man who does not resemble the more rambunctious Barry McKenzie or Stork.
2. Anne Summers, *Damned Whores and God's Police* (Sydney: Penguin Books, rev. ed., 1994), p. 347.

AUGUSTIN *(Film Review Annual, 1996)*

LOS ANGELES TIMES, 5/3/96, Calendar/p. 14, Kenneth Turan

"Augustin" is the sliest of films, an almost invisible comedy where the jokes are so deft they could sneak by unnoticed. Its aim is subtler than creating raucous roars of laughter but it's not any the less funny for that.

A character study of a truly eccentric character, "Augustin" explores the life of an oblivious individual who has no idea how amusing he is. In dead-earnest about all things he says and does, the invariably serene and self-satisfied epitome of comic dignity, Augustin is funnier and funnier the more serious he gets.

Only 61 minutes, "Augustin" was created by French writer-director Anne Fontaine for her Keatonesque actor brother, Jean-Chretien Silbertin-Blanc. Almost all his co-stars are nonprofessionals, but that only adds to the film's delights.

Introduced blithely pedaling through Paris as peppy Portuguese music plays on the soundtrack, Augustin Dos Santos is on his way to a casting agent, cheerfully unaware that he is a full day late for his appointment. No matter, he's brought publicity photos for her to consider. Yes, they are postage-stamp size. Is that a problem?

Though he's appeared as a Portuguese cod smuggler on TV and done features like "Better Off Deaf," Augustin is not a full-time actor. He also works for precisely 38 minutes a day as an obscure functionary in a Kafka-esque insurance company. Yes, someone else might consider it mind-numbing, but, Augustin carefully explains, "for someone with no skills it's a dream job."

Currently on tap in the acting department is a small part as a room-service waiter that Augustin prepares for as doggedly as if it were the lead in "Candide." He even manages to talk his way into a luxury hotel to get a day of on-the-job experience.

Here he chats with a guest about the weather in inane broken English and, in an thoroughly charming scene, helps a disbelieving chambermaid (Stephanie Zhang) make up a room, determinedly half-flirting with her while simultaneously taking serious notes on the kind of cleaning products she uses.

The climax of Augustin's unlikely acting ambitions is an audition he shares with Thierry Lhermitte, one of France's most popular actors who appears as himself. Writer-director Fontaine never rehearsed the actors together, and apparently didn't even show them each other's lines. So the look of nonplused astonishment that appears unbidden on Lhermitte's face is all the funnier for being completely genuine.

BLACK IS ... BLACK AIN'T *(Film Review Annual, 1996)*

CINEASTE, Vol. XXII No. 4, p. 55, Cliff Thompson

Toward the end of the documentary *Black Is ... Black Ain't,* after an interviewer asks the AIDS-stricken filmmaker and writer Marlon Riggs what he has dreamt about lately, Riggs replies that he has not experienced dreams so much as a series of flashing images that he likens to MTV. The same description could almost be applied to *Black Is ... Black Ain't,* which moves quickly, sometimes unannouncedly, from one subtopic to another in pursuit of its overarching theme: the validation of every form of black experience. Remarkably, the result is not a chaotic patchwork but a seamless whole, one that thoughtfully addresses many key issues involving blackness and is all the more impressive for doing so in a mere eighty-seven minutes.

Riggs's previous work includes the acclaimed documentaries *Tongues Untied* (1989), about the internal conflicts and ostracism he faced as a gay black man, and *Color Adjustment* (1992), an examination of images of blacks seen on television over the decades. Completed after his death in 1994, at the age of 37, *Black Is ... Black Ain't* merges many of the concerns of those two works. His final film also operates as a kind of last will and testament: he bequeaths the idea that rigid notions of what is or is not black behavior, of who is or isn't black, need to be abandoned for the sake of strengthening the sense of community within the race; he also passes on his faith that this will occur. At various points throughout the film, the emaciated Riggs is shown in a hospital, and should anyone question the relevance of this footage to his overall message, he explains that both being black and having AIDS entail "a struggle against the odds in the face of adversity, in the face of possible extinction." No black person, the film suggests, should be excluded from the effort to stave off such extinction.

Early on, *Black Is... Black Ain't* looks at the negative connotations that were attached for so long to the very word 'black.' It recalls how black people's transcendence of those associations and their embrace of the word, rather than of the white-imposed terms 'Negro' or 'colored,' amounted to an act of self-empowerment. The film goes on to demonstrate that black self-definition has the capacity to imprison as well as to liberate. On hand to help blast away counterproductive definitions of blackness are thinkers and activists such as Angela Davis, Cornel West, bell hooks, and Michele Wallace, as well as a number of less famous but thoughtful commentators.

This group reminds us that because slavery and its aftermath involved the emascula-tion—physical as well as psychological—of black men, the drive for black power was usually taken to mean a call for black male power, despite the needs of (and often with the complicity of) black women. That continues to result in the devaluing of black female contributions to the liberation struggle and in the subordination of black women in general. Michele Wallace observes that attacking black male sexism is the "job that no one wants to do" and that those, including her, who attempt to do so are punished for it, to the detriment of everyone involved. As bell hooks memorably puts it: "If the black thing is really a dick thing in disguise, we're in serious trouble."

Cornel West laments the fact that black masculinity is not associated with being emotionally demonstrative and that it is thus "difficult to be a black male and be in touch with your humanity." And narrow ideas about what constitutes male behavior are harmful in other ways, as well. The often-cited disdain for gay men in the black community, according to the film, exists because many see homosexuality as a concession to centuries of emasculation—as a "final break" with masculinity.

On a related note, *Black Is ... Black Ain't* pays homage to the key role of black churches in the liberation struggle, while pointing out those churches' rejection of homosexuality. Included in the film, however, are interviews with black lesbians who have found acceptance in a church that, contrary to common practice, opens its arms to homosexuals.

The film attacks rigid notions of blackness that concern appearance. "Why is there still so much commotion when we add a few salt-lookin' people to the stew?," one dark-skinned black woman wants to know. *"Black* folk been lookin' like *white* folk since the first traveler from Europe bred with the first African woman he encountered ... And since nobody is racially pure around here, what sense does it make for us to split hairs and genes trying to figure out *who's* got the true black blood?"

Counterbalanced with now-obligatory footage of the 1992 Los Angeles riots and their aftermath are interviews with forward-looking street kids. Although they still admit to running with gangs, these kids recognize the value of education—which they still hope to attain—and regret that they weren't set straight on this score earlier in life. Their words fly in the face of the notion that blackness equals a disdain for learning.

So, if blackness does not mean being male, sexist, and out of touch with one's emotions; if it doesn't mean being heterosexual; if it doesn't mean being an impoverished small-time criminal; if it doesn't even mean having dark skin and kinky hair, then what, in the view of this sometimes funny, often moving, always provocative documentary, does it mean? Angela Davis provides one answer: "You take some color, a dash or a big dollop, it don't matter, and you blend it with an assortment of physical features that reflect every face you might possibly encounter on this *great* earth, mix *that* up with a culture that just *loves* to improvise, signify, reclaim, renew, and read—and you've got, the recipe, for black folk." Works for me.

MADNESS OF KING GEORGE, THE *(Film Review Annual, 1994)*

FILM QUARTERLY, Spring 1996, p. 46, Craig Tepper

Huge, double antechamber doors bar our admittance. At a polite knuckle-rapping they open and, though the Royals are fully clothed, the dressers fall hushed, turning in shock at our intrusion. Greville, George III's new equerry, is revealed as the intruder, and we slip almost unnoticed into the Royal presence. But the odd reaction to our entrance into this curiously public/private zone suggests we have, in fact, crossed into another world.

A case history of a royal bout with a rare, chronic illness, *The Madness of King George* is undersized for a typical Brithistorical quality drama. Nicholas Hytner's brisk, attuned direction, the lush sets and costuming, and Nigel Hawthorne's superb performance can't quite conceal the film's loftier dreams. For Alan Bennett's screenplay (based on his play) might pass for a condensation of the works of the French philosopher Michel Foucault.

A member of the fabled British stage group Beyond the Fringe, Bennett's work for the stage, TV, and screen (*Habeas Corpus, Single Spies, Talking Heads*, and *A Private Function* among them) has already hinted at this kind of ambition. One comes away from this film with an exhilarated feeling not unlike what George III must feel at film's end: that one has been swung crazily around, had all one's frames of reference wildly shifted and then returned—but not quite to the same place. And this is where Foucault comes in.

It is Foucault's suggestion that the logical framework of an era is transparent (hence nearly invisible) to those in it, that such frameworks are neither fixed nor assimilable, and to glimpse this one must look to periods of dramatic change in worldview, like those that occurred some 200 years ago. Which, quite conveniently, is exactly the period of Bennett's film.

Much of Foucault's work, most relevantly *Madness & Civilization, The Order of Things, The Birth of the Clinic,* and *Discipline & Punish*, details an abrupt conceptual shift across a broad social and intellectual front at the end of 18th century which produced a new alignment—both of ideas and institutions—that changed not only what one thought about, but how one thought. Hardly unique, such epistemological ruptures, or paradigm changes, so reconfigure cognitive geography they create disjunctions. Eras, particularly in the history of ideas, are discontinuous.

This last shift in a brief period of time permitted the discovery of the human sciences—biology, linguistics, and economics—by revealing their subject: Man. Deposing God, King, and the Chain of Being as a model of the world, this new world view also necessarily reformed the social institutions of control, giving birth to the modern prison, school, hospital, and work place.

But while America and France were having the kind of social upheavals one might expect at such a time, what were the British up to? Bennett's answer is *The Madness of King George*. What we see as we enter the king's dressing rooms at Westminster with Greville in the year 1788 is George and family preparing for the opening of Parliament. The portrait Bennett and Hytner paint at the outset is of an irascible, energetic, and mercurial monarch whose abundant animal vitality has blessed him with 15 royal offspring by his German wife, Charlotte (Helen Mirren), and a greater love for pig farming than for affairs of state. But even here—fit, active, moving smartly along the back halls of Westminster, adjuring his dissolute son George, Prince of Wales, to be productive, and to marry—the monarch is subject to lapses. Addressing Parliament, he only belatedly inserts the word "former" in reference to the American colonies. This provokes Charles Fox, wily head of the "reformer" Whigs, to remark to George's prime minister, William Pitt the Younger, that the king has not written his own speech. Pitt replies, "The king will do as he's told." As George is about to board his carriage, his equerry reminds him of the throng of writ-bearing subjects who routinely wait outside. "Oh ... yes, right," George says, absent-mindedly stepping to receive petitions he will never read or pass judgment on.

Though he occasionally has to be reminded that his actual office is to keep up appearances, sunny George seems blithely unaware that his royal powers may have eroded. There is, however, little evidence of more than the usual royal eccentricity until one night, while climbing into bed with his queen, the king attempts a fart, and failing of it, is seized by intense intestinal pain. Learning of his father's indisposition, the prince (played with a wonderfully festering languor by

Rupert Everett) approaches Fox, who rapidly warms to the prince's suggestion that should the prince be installed as regent he, Fox, should become prime minister.

It is against these variously arrayed self-interested factions—Pitt, Fox, the prince, even his own lord chancellor—that the story of George's mysterious malady plays out. Though the king quickly recovers, what follows is a round of pre-dawn frenzies and randy assaults on the queen's sister, Lady Pembroke (Amanda Donohoe), that concludes in a nightmarish race up to the roof of Windsor Castle. Escaping imaginary floodwaters, King George desperately carries his youngest child to higher ground, with the queen in pursuit, calling fearfully after them. But the danger, as we see it, is foreshortened. Hytner shoots the delirious, spiraling climb up the narrow circular stairs from above; from our view, the deluded king is merely running in circles. It's a clever visual rhyme for the singularly personal revolution that has begun, and also for the Foucauldian idea that—given the utter discontinuity between epochs—progressive, linear time is an illusion. (At several points characters practically ejaculate, "There is no time!")

Despairing of his own sanity, George allows himself to be locked up and subjected to the authority of Baker, his physician, and Warren, physician to the Prince of Wales. Baffled by the king's infirmity, the two men enter a dim Royal College operating theatre to recruit yet a third doctor—the expert, Pepys. As they watch a grisly amputation, a Goyaesque scene of a whimpering patient being restrained by medical students in the dank pit below, Pepys cheerily explains that in the anfractuosities of the mind he finds "the stool most eloquent." What they will all ignore in the course of their investigations is the king's most vivid symptom, blue urine (though we'll learn in an epilogue it's a sign of porphyria, the disease he most likely suffered from). Shown the discolored urine, Pepys rolls his eyes away contemptuously and with a supercilious smile delivers a howler: "Medicine, sir, is a science of precise observation."

But the laugh here is set on a double-edge of anachronism. "For thousands of years, after all, doctors had tested patients' urine," Foucault observes in *The Birth of the Clinic,* his archaeology of medical perception.[1] But in undergoing an epistemological revolution at the end of the 18th century, the sign " ... no longer speaks the natural language of disease; it assumes shape and value only within the questions posed by medical investigation."[2] It's a temporary lapse, an oddity of the moment (an anachronism), that the king's urine is ignored. Indeed, it is Pepys's very modernity, his devotion to the system of an evolving "science" institutionalized in the authority of the Royal College, that makes him so airily dismissive of this antiquated sign. Urine, whose coloration could simply be read off a table, with its various shades corresponding to various distempers, is now no longer thought to have a *direct correspondence,* to be "eloquent" in expressing what is coming to be seen as an *underlying* disease process.

With the king showing no improvement and Fox and the Prince of Wales promoting a bill to install the prince as regent, Queen Charlotte and Lady Pembroke enlist Greville to call on one dour, humorless, and rather sadistic Dr. Willis, a man renowned for success with mental infirmities. Willis's favored treatment is the consistent application of restraint. At the least sign of rebellion, Willis (played with macabre intensity by Ian Holm) has George seized and set into a chair where he is bound hand and foot and gagged with leather straps. It is, not uncoincidentally, identical with a procedure found in the historical writings of Dr. Thomas Willis that forms a central part of Foucault's *Madness & Civilization.*

"The insane person, placed in a special house, will be treated, either by the doctor or by trained assistants, in such a way that he may be always maintained in his duty, in his appearance and habits, by warnings, by remonstrances, and by punishments immediately inflicted.[3]

The climactic center of the film occurs as George is forcibly strapped into the chair. Emphatically inscribed, the camera rises to ceiling height, accompanied by Handel's coronation music from *Zadok the Priest,* and slowly rotates counterclockwise, looking down on this harrowing scene. As George bellows, "I am the king of England, Doctor!" Willis growls with smug impunity, "You ... are *the patient*!!" It's a coronation in reverse. For George has become something even better than king: that newest of new things, the ever-improvable modern subjectivity—Man. This shift having made possible a view to the general underlying the specific (the man within the king), George, the man, now stands in for all of us. Terrified, gazing helplessly up at the ceiling, he mirrors our new-found reflexivity, to be poked, prodded, and relentlessly examined as the measure of all things. But from where did this new mutation in our seeing come?

A moment before, George, led forward and shown the chair, had murmured mournfully that while the implements of torture are shown to a felon to force a confession, they are shown to the king to secure his "silence"—a typically Foucauldian inversion. Precisely because of the king's special station, the technologies of torture—solely a sovereign's prerogative—are martialed, in his unique instance, to produce the opposite effect. But here Bennett turns mere philosophy into an other-worldly poetry, into that rarest of things, true soliloquy. By these logical rules it is the king alone who understands the truth of what he is saying. It is the blazing, brief insight of a man utterly isolated, a king who is mad, but mad north by northwest. In this signature scene, Bennett conflates torture with medical procedure, *Discipline & Punish* with *The Birth of the Clinic*, a conflation Foucault's work seems to invite:

> Something of the joust survived, between the judge who ordered the judicial torture and the suspect who was tortured; the "patient"—this is the term used to designate the victim—was subjected to a series of trials, graduated in severity, in which he succeeded if he "held out," or failed if he confessed. (The first degree of torture was the sight of the implements. In the case of children or of persons over the age of seventy one did not go beyond this stage.) ... In the practice of torture, pain, confrontation and truth were bound together, they worked together on the patient's body. ... In torture employed to extract a confession, there was an element of the investigation; there was also an element of the duel.[4]

What follows between Willis and George is as much a duel between doctor and patient as a medical investigation. Made to fear his stern captor, George eventually comes to obey Willis's merest glance. Even the Prince of Wales is shocked when Lady Pembroke repeats the whispered rumor that Willis's therapeutic successes are accomplished not so much by physical restraint as by means of his eyes: "You mean he looks at the king? Damned impudence."

Ian Holm's ferocious gaze, his snarling cry to the king's contumely that "I have you in my *eye*, sir," is a humiliation redoubled. Breaking, as it does, the classical taboo against looking directly at the king, his gaze also links the medical with the juridical subjection of George. But one suspects the Rasputin-like qualities of Bennett's Dr. Willis are a literary invention. George III was, in fact, attended by two Dr. Willis's (brothers). But Dr. Thomas Willis lived 100 years prior to King George's phorphyritic episodes. Foucault describes *The Birth of the Clinic* as "a book about space, about language, and about death; it is about the act of seeing, the gaze."[5] The gaze Foucault here examines, by which, "in a few years, the particular knowledge of the individual patient was structured,"[6] is his metaphor for our new way of seeing. That gaze, again deployed in *Discipline & Punish*, is there a metaphor for a corollary structuring—the panoptic organization of modern society—of an increasingly efficient surveillance, the arraying of individuals in a homogeneous space under the watchful eye of the warder, the teacher, and the factory foreman. It is with this disciplinary gaze, too, that Willis holds the king in check. Bennett's Willis, by his gaze, links the two works.

Under Willis's care at Kew, George asks his visiting lord chancellor and Pitt whether they are cold. Why? Because, George replies, he makes the weather "by mental powers." Thurlow berates Willis for promising to cure the king and failing. But it is because George is no longer a Shakespearean king, a Lear on the stormswept heath whose madness is personified by the weather, that his claim is now taken as a sign of madness. It's exactly this kind of idea Willis has been called upon to reform. Lear, in an Age of Kings, is author of his own sorrows. But not hapless George, who, caught in a whirlpool of history, flung into the Age of Man, is the sport of fate and subject to the as yet unperfected technologies of social control.

But the return of George's sanity is accomplished, Bennett tempts us to believe, not by Willis's gaze but by a deeply affecting performance of a scene from *King Lear*. As lucid and warm as the sunlight under which Nigel Hawthorne's George lovingly performs it, coaxing and correcting his actors who read the play seated on chairs in an idyllic field, the scene builds to a moment of wondrous realization and restoration. At first chary of accepting the change the lord chancellor now sees in him, George slowly perceives in this willingless to see him as recovered a difference. Since the difference is no difference, really, the king realizes it must consist in his having forgotten something. The light slowly dawning in his eyes, he pronounces his own cure as fondly as he has caressed Shakespeare's words. "I have always been myself, even when I was ill, only now I seem myself. And that's the important thing ... I have remembered how to seem."

However, lest we take too much consolation from the salutary effects of Shakespeare, this cure by the acting of plays was, Foucault points out (on the page opposite his quotation from Willis's *Opera Omnia*), another technique of the classical age, one applied hand in glove with the sterner medicines. Dubbed "The Cure by Theatrical Representation," it stands as the polar opposite to Willis's physical interventions. "Here, the therapeutic operation functions entirely in the space of the imagination."[7]

But if "seeming" to be king somehow got lost with George's madness, what is it George forgot? At his most agitated, George regressively insists on his divine right to take any female where and whenever he wishes, and furthermore maintains that his thoughts are the thoughts of God, and that—grabbing a maid's chamber-pot during a morning frenzy, crying as he strains to relieve himself, "Do it, England"—his body is coextensive with the whole of England. In short, George, like Lear, is confusing the past with the present. But where Lear yearns to be cared for by his daughters as he was by his mother, George's wish is for a return to the classical idea of himself as king.

What George is in danger of forgetting from the start is that he no longer is a king as conceived of in the classical age. His peculiar tragedy is that no one can explain the shift in perspective that requires his worldview be radically readjusted. Instead, these changes are inflicted on him—by the application of heated cups, of gags, restraints, and powerful purgatives—through a succession of painful humiliations to his flesh meant to lead his mind to the dawn of the light of truth. George, by his unique position, has to receive those changes alone until he is able to articulate them. Only the king could. It is his singular tragedy. But that this change in consciousness should be exacted through the king's body is no mere historical curiosity or unkind feature of a more primitive medical practice. A comprehensive system of control over human beings must begin with control over the body, from the smallest parts to the whole. The aim of disciplinary technology is to forge "a docile (body) that may be subjected, used, transformed and improved."[8] George's physical humiliations are the first awkward coercions of a new regimen soon to be extended across the whole of society.

Once George recognizes he is himself again, Thurlow races back to Westminster to forestall the vote on the Regency bill. Awaiting George's arrival, Hytner's camera, in a scene of self-reflexive parody, does a dizzying circuit about Thurlow as he giddily relates their performance to Pitt, suggesting that Lear's ending would be improved and the tragedy averted if the messenger were only to arrive on time. (It's a telling commentary on the action by virtue of its very anachronism; between 1681 and the early 19th century, Nahum Tate's bowdlerized *Lear* containing just this amendment was the only version extant in England, a version now often derided as being "Hollywood.") And so George pulls up in his carriage, the M.P.'s race out just as they're about to vote, and, having reassured them he is his old self once again, George turns to his supporters and remarks, "How's that, boys? Not bad, what, what."

Yet Bennett evokes a terrible poignancy as he at last reunites George with his devoted queen, having them share once again their loving jest of address: "Hello, Mr. King." "Hello, Mrs. King." What at first utterance was merely a sweet private joke has now become a formal declaration of their new state of affairs. For while America and France were having revolutions, the British, by setting the king on his head, were quietly reshaping their national psyche in his person; that is, specifically, exorcising from his mind and body, through the newly devolving authority vested in medicine and the law, the madness that therein resided God and England.

Notes

1.   Michel Foucault, *The Birth of the Clinic: An Archaeology of Medical Perception* (New York: Random House, 1973), p. 163.
2.   Ibid., p. 162.
3.   Thomas Willis, *Opera Omnia* (Lyons, 1681), Vol. II, p. 261.
4.   Michel Foucault, *Discipline & Punish: The Birth of the Prison* (New York: Vintage Books, 1979), p. 40.
5.   Op. cit., p. ix.

6. Ibid., p. 196.
7. Michel Foucault, *Madness & Civilization: A History of Insanity in the Age of Reason* (New York: Random House, 1965), p. 187.
8. *Discipline & Punish*, p. 139.

POSTCARDS FROM AMERICA *(Film Review Annual, 1995)*

LOS ANGELES TIMES, 7/21/95, Calendar/p. 6, Kevin Thomas

Steve McLean's scorching "Postcards From America" opens with a young man, David (James Lyons), hitchhiking across a desert. The vast wasteland he surveys mirrors the emptiness of his soul, and as the film moves forward with his experiences on the road it also begins flashing back to memories of his brutal life.

By the time we meet the adult David, he has been living on the edge virtually from the time he was born. During his childhood at the hands of a savage, gun-wielding alcoholic father (Michael Ringer, truly scary), remembered by his son as a man "who hated children, his wife, animals and obviously himself," he was in scarcely less danger than he was as a teen-age hustler working Times Square with his one good friend (Michael Imperioli).

Gritty, spare and dynamic, charged with emotion but free of sentimentality, "Postcards From America" is based on two collections of autobiographical writings by David Wojnarowicz, a controversial artist who had been at the center of a debate over government support of the arts when he died of AIDS at 37 in 1992.

This is rightly a primarily shadowy film, lit by virtuoso cinematographer Ellen Kuras much in the manner of Errol Morris' "The Thin Blue Line," and it captures the excitement as well as the desperation of surviving precariously.

The film is an odyssey, as David recalls his experiences, alternately comic, sad and dangerous, as a teen male hustler whose hard life so easily could have destroyed him but instead nurtures a reflective poetic sensibility and a capacity for love and tenderness. Personal tragedy, however, has propelled David on to the highway, rushing toward his destiny, embracing his fate.

The portrayals McLean gets from Olmo Tighe as the young David, Michael Tighe as the angelic-looking teen-age David and Lyons as the handsome adult David are remarkable—and remarkably well-matched.

"Postcards From America" captures the world of the street hustler and sexual outlaw—to borrow John Rechy's phrase—with raw authenticity as McLean explores interrelated aspects of family, sexuality and masculinity.

Working with Wojnarowicz, McLean initially conceived of the film as a documentary, and as it evolved into a narrative, he kept his promise to the artist not to make it a literal biography of his life.

Yet this tough, truthful yet compassionate film might have been even stronger had the film's David, like the actual Wojnarowicz, attended Manhattan's High School of Art and Music by day while hustling by night. As it is, we're left to puzzle how a man of no evident education or talent or even permanent address could narrate his own story with such eloquence.

VILLAGE VOICE, 7/25/95, p. 58, Georgia Brown

Like Larry Clark, David Wojnarowicz barely survived a difficult childhood and troubled adolescence and grew up to make art from it all. In *Postcards From America*, British director-writer Steve McLean makes a serious attempt to chart Wojnarowicz's autobiography on screen, though his protagonist tellingly never arrives at the artist part.

McLean adapts his script from Wojnarowicz's autobiographical *Close to the Knives* and *Memories That Smell Like Gasoline*, though the film looks as if it were conceived as a play—the kind made up of brief, charged scenes acted against black, unfurnished backdrops. On screen, these stylized sequences look uninventive and a bit tacky, even though the cinematographer is *Swoon*'s Ellen Kuras. The most compelling scenes tend to be ones from David's childhood (where he's played by Olmo Tighe). His glowering, underexpressed father (Michael Ringer) is the other central figure in these psychodramas. Once, while the father is watching Kennedy's funeral on TV he starts beating his son for insufficiently mourning the nation's president. His blows keep time to the drumbeats of the cortege.

In his late teens, David (Michael Tighe) and a friend (Michael Imperioli) make do as hustlers, robbing tricks, and crashing with drag queens. The film is intercut with lyric passages showing the adult David (Jim Lyons) hitchhiking out West, meditating on his romance with men in cars. Somehow Wojnarowicz's prose in the voiceovers manages to sound sappy, however, something his art never was.

PROFESSIONAL, THE *(Film Review Annual, 1995)*

FILMS IN REVIEW, 2/3/95, p. 36, Jonathan Romney

For the first 20 minutes or so, Luc Besson's *Leon* is a model of cut-throat efficiency as Jean Reno, as hitman Leon, disposes of scores of mob goons with piano-wire precision. The precision is Besson's too; these scenes are choreographed with staccato panache, as if, after the frenetic mess of his spy story *Nikita,* he had to prove he could do mayhem clean as well.

The last thing you expect *Leon* to become is a wry heartwarmer. But it does suddenly turn unapologetically feel-good, and Besson's greatest feat is to carry on juggling the excitement on one hand, while on the other keeping things just the right side of mawkish. Someone must have advised him never to work with kids and hitmen: and, after making two underwater movies, *The Big Blue* and *Atlantis*, he probably thought that was an easy dare.

The family down the corridor in Leon's New York brownstone get wasted by a bad guy—Gary Oldman with a pocketful of pills and a flamboyantly nasty crick in his neck. No one survives except for 12 year-old Mathilda (Natalie Portman), a streetwise gamine with a precociously no-nonsense attitude to survival. She begs a wary Leon to shelter her in his apartment, then persuades him to keep her on, using a blend of moral blackmail, appeal to sentiment, and what the film encourages us to read as outright seduction. Mathilda needs refuge, but she's also after revenge and wants him to teach her to be an assassin. Their relationship is chaste, yet unmistakeably sexual, even if the naive, bear-like Leon isn't aware of it; they check into a hotel as father and daughter, but she gets them thrown out by telling the manager they're lovers, and she's only half kidding.

Mathilda is most reminiscent of the brattish heroine of Raymond Queneau's *Zazie dans le Metro,* filmed by Louis Malle, who kept her uncle on a leash by denouncing him to all and sundry as an old pervert. Portman plays Mathilda as a cross between Catherine Demongeot in Malle's film and Besson's hellcat-from-UNCLE heroine Nikita: "Zazie dans le Subway". Her relationship with Leon is disconcerting and, it seems, unilaterally exploitative, as though Jodie Foster's child hooker in *Taxi Driver* had latched on to Travis Bickle for the free transport. But it's not entirely in the field of taboo: Besson seems to want to suggest an urban *Beauty and the Beast* tempered with only a frisson of louchness.

Nevertheless, *Leon* is presented very much as a seduction story. The film's most disturbing moment, precisely because it's presented as an innoctuous interlude, is when Mathilda tries to cheer her "daddy" up by impersonating Madonna doing her "Like a Virgin" routine. It's a strange double-layered masquerade, a child imitating an overtly sexual woman imitating a child. It's as if Besson planned it as a textbook variant on Graham Green's infamous review of Shirley Temple as a *de facto* porn performer: "Infancy with her is a disguise." But Mathilda's act only seems risque because it suggests that she isn't fully aware of her sexuality: it's what, in more innocent times, used to be called a joke for the dads—a wink of reassurance that girl's don't really know. Consider how much more perverse the scene would have been if instead Mathilda had done a chorus of "The Good Ship Lollipop".

In fact, Mathilda is presented as unimpeachably righteous, corrupted only insofar as she's been in premature contact with the hard truths of the city. She may dress like a hooker, but in reality she's an angel; this is the film's roundabout idealisation of childhood—the exterior is purely a foil for the good girl within, who finally flourishes with Mathilda's return to a secluded, convent-like school.

All Mathilda learns by the end is that she's effectively adult already. The child who really grows up here is Leon, who starts off as an embryonic creature waiting to be coaxed into the light of day. In his bare, dark flat, he's the existential hitman of French tradition, the minimal self of Melville's *Le Samourai*. A foundling in New York, tended by a surrogate father (Danny Aiello) who feeds him and assigns him errands, he has only one pleasure—going to see *Singin' in the Rain*. The shot of him beaming up at the screen is a little too pointed a reminder of his ambivalent nature—a shambling baby who terminates with Arnie-ish cold blood but is at heart is yearning for family ties. Mathilda teaches him to connect, and their relationship is less like father and daughter than older kid brother and younger big sister.

By identifying Leon as its centre, the film opts for innocuosness—soft-hearted parable rather than taboo-breaker. Its nexus of complexities dangles perverse sexuality in front of us, but defuses it through its fairytale structure—Leon is a good fairy guarding against Oldman's Big Bad Wolf, a villain with a talent for (literally) sniffing out trouble. And *Leon* is an effective indicator of Besson's own ultimately infantile appetites. This is a film that wants it all, the brash, cynical pleasures of Hollywood, but also Parisian romance and knowingness—to be *Terminator* and Tati, Peckinpah and Truffaut all at once. In this sense, it has it all. It has all the current hip toys, and makes them work stuningly well—Schwarzenegger jokiness, Tarantino frenzy, the glazier's nightmare of a John Woo action movie. But ultimately, in a traditional French way, it's saying thank heaven for little girls, for that's how grown men in movies get to stay little boys.

AWARDS

ACADEMY OF MOTION PICTURE ARTS AND SCIENCES
68th Annual Academy Awards — March 25, 1996

BEST PICTURE — *Braveheart*
Other Nominees: *Apollo 13; Babe; The Postman (Il Postino); Sense and Sensibility*

BEST ACTOR — Nicolas Cage in *Leaving Las Vegas*
Other Nominees: Richard Dreyfuss in *Mr. Holland's Opus*; Anthony Hopkins in *Nixon*; Sean Penn in *Dead Man Walking*; Massimo Troisi in *The Postman (Il Postino)*

BEST ACTRESS — Susan Sarandon in *Dead Man Walking*
Other Nominees: Elisabeth Shue in *Leaving Las Vegas*; Sharon Stone in *Casino*; Meryl Streep in *The Bridges of Madison County;* Emma Thompson in *Sense and Sensibility*

BEST SUPPORTING ACTOR — Kevin Spacey in *The Usual Suspects*
Other Nominees: James Cromwell in *Babe*; Ed Harris in *Apollo 13*; Brad Pitt in *12 Monkeys*; Tim Roth in *Rob Roy*

BEST SUPPORTING ACTRESS — Mira Sorvino in *Mighty Aphrodite*
Other Nominees: Joan Allen in *Nixon*; Kathleen Quinlan in *Apollo 13*; Mare Winningham in *Georgia*; Kate Winslet in *Sense and Sensibility*

BEST DIRECTOR — Mel Gibson for *Braveheart*
Other Nominees: Chris Noonan for *Babe*; Tim Robbins for *Dead Man Walking*; Mike Figgis for *Leaving Las Vegas*; Michael Radford for *The Postman (Il Postino)*

BEST FOREIGN-LANGUAGE FILM — *Antonia's Line* (Netherlands)
Other Nominees; *All Things Fair* (Sweden); *Dust of Life* (Algeria); *O Quatrilho* (Brazil); *The Star Maker* (Italy)

BEST ORIGINAL SCREENPLAY — Christopher McQuarrie for *The Usual Suspects*
Other Nominees: Randall Wallace for *Braveheart*: Woody Allen for *Mighty Aphrodite*: Stephen J. Rivele, Christopher Wilkinson, and Oliver Stone for *Nixon*; Joss Whedon, Andrew Stanton, Joel Cohen, and Alec Sokolow, story by John Lasseter, Peter Docter, Andrew Stanton, and Joe Ranft for *Toy Story*

BEST ADAPTED SCREENPLAY — Emma Thompson for *Sense and Sensibility*
Other Nominees: William Broyles Jr. and Al Reinert for *Apollo 13*; George Miller and Chris Noonan for *Babe*; Mike Figgis for *Leaving Las Vegas*; Anna Pavignano; Michael Radford, Furio Scarpelli, Giacomo Scarpelli, and Massimo Troisi for *The Postman (Il Postino)*

BEST CINEMATOGRAPHY — John Toll for *Braveheart*
Other Nominees: Stephen Goldblatt for *Batman Forever*; Emmanuel Lubezki for *A Little Princess*; Michael Coulter for *Sense and Sensibility*; Lu Yue for *Shanghai Triad*

BEST FILM EDITING — Mike Hill and Dan Hanley for *Apollo 13*
Other Nominees: Marcus D'Arcy and Jay Friedkin for *Babe*; Steven Rosenblum for *Braveheart*; Chris Lebenzon for *Crimson Tide*; Richard Francis-Bruce for *Seven*

BEST ART DIRECTION — Eugenio Zanetti for *Restoration*
Other Nominees: Michael Corenblith with set decoration by Merideth Boswell for *Apollo 13*; Roger Ford with set decoration by Kerrie Brown for *Babe*; Bo Welch with set decoration by Cheryl Carasik for *A Little Princess*; Tony Burrough for *Richard III*

BEST COSTUME DESIGN — James Acheson for *Restoration*
Other Nominees: Charles Knode for *Braveheart*; Shuna Harwood for *Richard III*; Jenny Beavan and John Bright for *Sense and Sensibility*; Julie Weiss for *12 Monkeys*

BEST MAKE-UP — Peter Frampton, Paul Pattison, and Lois Burwell for *Braveheart*
Other Nominees: Ken Diaz and Mark Sanchez for *My Family, Mi Familia*; Greg Cannom, Bob Laden, and Colleen Callaghan for *Roommates*

BEST ORIGINAL MUSICAL OR COMEDY SCORE — Alan Menken (music), Stephen Schwartz (lyric), and Alan Menken (orchestral score) for *Pocahontas*

Other Nominees: Marc Shaiman for *The American President*; John Williams for *Sabrina*; Randy Newman for *Toy Story*; Thomas Newman for *Unstrung Heroes*

BEST ORIGINAL DRAMATIC SCORE — Luis Bacalov for *The Postman (Il Postino)*
Other Nominees: James Horner for *Apollo 13*; James Horner for *Braveheart;* John Williams for *Nixon*; Patrick Doyle for *Sense and Sensibility*

BEST ORIGINAL SONG — "Colors of the Wind" from *Pocahontas*, music by Alan Menken and lyric by Stephen Schwartz
Other Nominees: "Dead Man Walking" from *Dead Man Walking*, music and lyric by Bruce Springsteen; "Have You Ever Really Loved a Woman" from *Don Juan DeMarco*, music and lyric by Michael Kamen, Bryan Adams, and Robert John Lange; "Moonlight" from *Sabrina*, music by John Williams and lyric by Marilyn Bergman; "You've Got a Friend" from *Toy Story*, music and lyric by Randy Newman

BEST SOUND — Rick Dior, Steve Pederson, Scott Millan, and David MacMillan for *Apollo 13*
Other Nominees: Donald O. Mitchell, Frank A. Montano, Michael Herbick, and Petur Hliddal for *Batman Forever*; Andy Nelson, Scott Millan, Anna Behlmer, and Brian Simmons for *Braveheart*; Kevin O'Connell, Rick Kline, Gregory H. Watkins, and William B. Kaplan for *Crimson Tide*; Steve Maslow, Gregg Landaker, and Keith A. Wester for *Waterworld*

BEST SOUND EFFECTS EDITING — Lon Bender and Per Hallberg for *Braveheart*
Other Nomines: John Leveque and Bruce Stambler for *Batman Forever*; George Watters II for *Crimson Tide*

BEST VISUAL EFFECTS — Scott E. Anderson, Charles Gibson, Neal Scanlan, and John Cox for *Babe*
Other Nominees: Robert Legato, Michael Kanfer, Leslie Ekker, and Matt Sweeney for *Apollo 13*

BEST DOCUMENTARY FEATURE — *Anne Frank Remembered*
Other Nominees: *The Battle Over Citizen Kane; Fiddlefest—Roberta Guaspari-Tzavara and Her East Harlem Violin Program; Hank Aaron: Chasing the Dream; Troublesome Creek: A Midwestern*

BEST DOCUMENTARY SHORT — *One Survivor Remembers*
Other Nominees: *Jim Dine: A Self-Portrait on the Walls; The Living Sea; Never Give Up: The 20th Century Odyssey of Herbert Zipper; The Shadow of Hate*

BEST ANIMATED SHORT — *A Close Shave*
Other Nominees: *The Chicken From Outerspace; The End; Gagarin; Runaway Brain*

BEST LIVE-ACTION SHORT — *Lieberman in Love*
Other Nominees: *Brooms; Duke of Groove; Little Surprises; Tuesday Morning Ride*

HONORARY AWARDS

Kirk Douglas for "50 years as a creative and moral force in the motion picture community."

Chuck Jones for "the creation of classic cartoons and cartoon characters whose animated lives have brought joy to our real ones for more than half a century."

SPECIAL ACHIEVEMENT AWARD

John Lasseter "for the development and application of techniques that made possible the first feature-length computer-animated film."

GORDON SAWYER AWARD

Donald C. Rogers to "recognize exceptional long-term accomplishments by an individual who has made substantial contributions toward the advancement of the science and technology of the motion picture."

SCIENTIFIC AND TECHNICAL AWARDS

Scientific and Engineering Awards (Plaque) to:

Arnold and Richter Cine Technik for "the development of the Arriflex 535 Series cameras."

Digital Theater Systems for "the design and development of the DTS digital sound system for motion picture exhibition."

Dolby Laboratories for "the design and development of the SR-D digital sound system for motion picture exhibition."

Sony Corp. for "the design and development of the SDDS digital sound system for motion picture exhibition."

Howard Flemming and Ronald Uhlig for "their pioneering work leading to motion picture digital sound."

Ronald Goodman, Attila Szalay, Stephen Sass and SpaceCam Systems Inc. for "the design of the SpaceCam gyroscopically stabilized camera system."

Colin Mossman, Joe Wary, Hans Leisinger, Gerry Painter and Deluxe Laboratories for "the design and development of the Deluxe Quad Format digital sound printing head."

David Gilmartin, Johannes Borggrebe, Jean-Pierre Gagnon, Frank Ricotta and Technicolor Inc. for "the design and development of the Technicolor Contact Printer sound head."

Iain Neil for "the optical design," Rick Gelbard for "the mechanical design", Eric Dubberke for "the engineering" and Panavision International L.P.," for the development of the Primo 3:1 zoom lens."

Martin Mueller for "the design and development of the MSM 9801 IMAX 65mm/15 per production motion picture camera."

Alvy Ray Smith, Ed Catmull, Thomas Porter and Tom Duff for "their pioneering inventions in digital image compositing."

Technical Achievement Awards (Certificate) to:

Pascal Chedeville for "the design of the L.C. Concept digital sound system for motion picture exhibition."

Jim Deas of the Warner Bros. Studio Facility for "the design and subsequent development of an automated patchbay and metering system for motion picture sound transfer and dubbing operations."

Clay Davis and John Carter of Todd AO for "their pioneering efforts in creating an automated patchbay system for motion picture sound transfer and dubbing operations."

Al Jensen, Chuck Headley, Jean Messner and Hazem Nabulsi of CEI Technology for "producing a self-contained, flicker-free color video-assist camera."

Peter Denz of Prazisions-Entwicklung Denz for "developing a flicker-free color video-assist camera."

David Pringle and Zhang Yan for "the design and development of Lightning Strikes, a flexible, high-performance electronic lightning effect system."

BHP Inc. for "their pioneering efforts developing digital sound printing heads for motion pictures."

Joe Finnegan for "his pioneering work in developing the Air Ram for motion picture stunt effects."

Gary Demos, David Ruhoff, Can Cameron and Michelle Feraud for "their pioneering efforts in the creation of the Digital Productions digital film compositing system."

Douglas Smythe, Lincoln Hu, Douglas S. Kay and Industrial Light and Magic for "their pioneering efforts in the creation of the ILM digital film compositing system."

Computer Film Co. for "their pioneering efforts in the creation of the CFC digital film compositing system."

Toulouse U Genie Des Systemes for "the concept"; Kodak Pathe CTP CINE for "the prototype"; and Eclair Laboratories for "the development and further implementation of the Toulouse Electrolytic Silver Recovery Cell."

NATIONAL SOCIETY OF FILM CRITICS
January 3, 1996

BEST PICTURE — *Babe*

BEST ACTOR — Nicolas Cage in *Leaving Las Vegas*

BEST ACTRESS — Elisabeth Shue in *Leaving Las Vegas*

BEST SUPPORTING ACTOR — Don Cheadle in *Devil in a Blue Dress*

BEST SUPPORTING ACTRESS — Joan Allen in *Nixon*

BEST DIRECTOR — Mike Figgis for *Leaving Las Vegas*

BEST SCREENPLAY — Amy Heckerling for *Clueless*

BEST FOREIGN FILM — *Wild Reeds* (France)

BEST DOCUMENTARY — *Crumb*

BEST CINEMATOGRAPHY — Tak Fujimoto for *Devil in a Blue Dress*

SPECIAL CITATION — *Latcho Drom* for experimental film

NEW YORK FILM CRITICS CIRCLE
January 7, 1996

BEST PICTURE — *Leaving Las Vegas*

BEST ACTOR — Nicolas Cage in *Leaving Las Vegas*

BEST ACTRESS — Jennifer Jason Leigh in *Georgia*

BEST SUPPORTING ACTOR — Kevin Spacey in *Swimming With Sharks, The Usual Suspects, Outbreak,* and *Seven*

BEST SUPPORTING ACTRESS — Mira Sorvino in *Mighty Aphrodite*

BEST DIRECTOR — Ang Lee for *Sense and Sensibility*

BEST SCREENPLAY — Emma Thompson for *Sense and Sensibility*

BEST CINEMATOGRAPHER — Lu Yue for *Shanghai Triad*

BEST FOREIGN-LANGUAGE FILM — *Wild Reeds* (France)

BEST DOCUMENTARY — *Crumb*

BEST NEW DIRECTOR — Chris Noonan for *Babe*

SPECIAL CITATION — Fabiano Canosa for his dedicated efforts as the longtime head of the former film program at the Papp Public Theater

GOLDEN GLOBE
53rd Annual Awards — January 21, 1996

BEST PICTURE (drama) — *Sense and Sensibility*

BEST PICTURE (comedy or musical) — *Babe*

BEST ACTOR (drama) — Nicolas Cage in *Leaving Las Vegas*

BEST ACTOR (comedy or musical) — John Travolta in *Get Shorty*

BEST ACTRESS (drama) — Sharon Stone in *Casino*

BEST ACTRESS (comedy or musical) — Nicole Kidman in *To Die For*

BEST SUPPORTING ACTOR — Brad Pitt in *12 Monkeys*

BEST SUPORTING ACTRESS — Mira Sorvino in *Mighty Aphrodite*

BEST DIRECTOR — Mel Gibson for *Braveheart*

BEST SCREENPLAY — Emma Thompson for *Sense and Sensibility*

BEST ORIGINAL SCORE —Maurice Jarre for *A Walk in the Clouds*

BEST ORIGINAL SONG — "Colors of the Wind" from *Pocahontas*, music by Alan Menken and lyric by Stephen Schwartz

BEST FOREIGN-LANGUAGE FILM — *Les Miserables* (France)

LOS ANGELES FILM CRITICS ASSOCIATION
December 16, 1995

BEST PICTURE — *Leaving Las Vegas*

BEST ANIMATED FILM — *Toy Story*

BEST ACTOR — Nicolas Cage in *Leaving Las Vegas*

BEST ACTRESS — Elisabeth Shue in *Leaving Las Vegas*

BEST SUPPORTING ACTOR — Don Cheadle in *Devil in a Blue Dress*

BEST SUPPORTING ACTRESS — Joan Allen in *Nixon*

BEST DIRECTOR — Mike Figgis for *Leaving Las Vegas*

BEST SCREENPLAY — Emma Thompson for *Sense and Sensibility*

BEST CINEMATOGRAPHY — Lu Yue for *Shanghai Triad*

BEST SCORE — Patrick Doyle for *A Little Princess*

BEST PRODUCTION DESIGN — Bo Welch for *A Little Princess*

BEST FOREIGN-LANGUAGE FILM — *Wild Reeds* (France)

BEST DOCUMENTARY FILM — *Crumb*

INDEPENDENT/EXPERIMENTAL FILM/VIDEO — *From the Journals of Jean Seberg*

CAREER ACHIEVEMENT AWARD — Andre de Toth

NEW GENERATION AWARD — Alfonso Cuaron

NATIONAL BOARD OF REVIEW
1995 NBR Awards — February 26, 1996

BEST PICTURE — *Sense and Sensibility*

BEST ACTOR — Nicolas Cage in *Leaving Las Vegas*

BEST ACTRESS — Emma Thompson in *Sense and Sensibility* and *Carrington*

BEST SUPPORTING ACTOR — Kevin Spacey in *Seven* and *The Usual Suspects*

BEST SUPPORTING ACTRESS — Mira Sorvino in *Mighty Aphrodite*

BEST DIRECTOR — Ang Lee for *Sense and Sensibility*

BEST FOREIGN-LANGUAGE FILM — *Shanghai Triad* (China)

BEST DOCUMENTARY — *Crumb*

FREEDOM OF EXPRESSION AWARD — Zhang Yimou for his battle against censorship in China

CAREER ACHIEVEMENT AWARD — James Earl Jones

ENSEMBLE ACTING AWARD — the cast of *The Usual Suspects*

SPECIAL AWARD — Betty Comden and Adolph Green for their screenwriting careers

BILLY WILDER AWARD — Stanley Donen

OUTSTANDING NEWCOMER AWARD — Alicia Silverstone

SPECIAL ACHIEVEMENT AWARD — Mel Gibson

CANNES FILM FESTIVAL
48th Annual Awards — May 28, 1995

BEST PICTURE (Golden Palm Award) — *Underground* (Yugoslavia)

BEST DIRECTOR — Mathieu Kassovitz for *La Haine*

BEST ACTOR — Jonathan Pryce in *Carrington*

BEST ACTRESS — Helen Mirren in *The Madness of King George*

GRAND JURY PRIZE — *Ulysses' Gaze* (Greece)

SPECIAL JURY PRIZE — *Carrington* (England)

TECHNICAL PRIZE — *Shanghai Triad* (China and France)

JURY PRIZE — *Don't Forget You're Going to Die* (France)

CAMERA D'OR (Best First Film) — *The White Balloon* (Iran)

PALME D'OR (Short Film) — *Gagarine* (Russia)

JURY PRIZE (Short Film) — *Swinger* (Australia)

INDEX

CAST

PRODUCERS

DIRECTORS

SCREENWRITERS

CINEMATOGRAPHERS

EDITORS

MUSIC

PRODUCTION CREW